*Reflexivity and Revolution
in the New Novel*

REFLEXIVITY
AND REVOLUTION
IN THE NEW NOVEL

Claude Ollier's
Fictional Cycle

CECILE LINDSAY

Ohio State University Press
Columbus

Library of Congress Cataloging-in-Publication Data

Lindsay, Cecile.
    Reflexivity and revolution in the New Novel : Claude Ollier's
fictional cycle / Cecile Lindsay
    p. cm.
    English and French
    Includes bibliographical references and index.
    ISBN 0-8142-0527-5
    1. Ollier, Claude—Criticism and interpretation.   I. Title
PQ2675.L398Z74   1990
843'.914—dc20   90-39016
                                                          CIP

The paper in this book meets the guidelines
for permanence and durability of the Committee
on Production Guidelines for Book Longevity
of the Council on Library Resources. ⊗

Printed in the U.S.A.

9 8 7 6 5 4 3 2 1

For my parents

Contents

ACKNOWLEDGMENTS   ix

LIST OF ABBREVIATIONS   x

INTRODUCTION   Reading *Le Jeu d'enfant:*
Readability and Reflexive Fiction   1

1 The Death of the Protagonist: Demystifying Fiction   25

2 Family Romance: The Origins of Fiction   62

3 Filiations: The Paternity of Fiction   88

4 Textual Intercourse: Allegories of Reading Fiction   124

5 The Science of the New Novel: Zero-Degree Fiction   154

CONCLUSION   Fictional Revolutions   173

NOTES   187

BIBLIOGRAPHY   203

INDEX   213

Acknowledgments

The introduction to this study is a revised version of "Child's Play: *Le Jeu d'enfant* and Beyond," *The Review of Contemporary Fiction* 8, no. 2 (Summer 1988). A small section of chapter 2 appeared as "The Topography of (Science) Fiction: Claude Ollier's *Life on Epsilon*," *Science-Fiction Studies*, no. 32 (March 1984). Chapter 4 is a substantially revised version of "Textual Intercourse: Reader Theory and the New Novel," *Structuralist Review* 2, no. 3 (Spring 1984). A slightly different version of chapter 5 appeared as "Le Degré zéro de la fiction: la science du Nouveau Roman," *Romanic Review* 74, no. 2 (March 1983).

I would like to thank the following people for their expert help in typing this manuscript: Pat Ariaz, Renée Curry, Karie Kozak, and Kim Grinsel. I would like to express my gratitude to Claude Ollier for the interest he has always taken in my work and for the patience and seriousness with which he has engaged it.

Abbreviations

E *Enigma*

Ei *Eté indien*

EN *L'Echec de Nolan*

FS *Fuzzy Sets*

Mo *Le Maintien de l'ordre*

Ms *La Mise en scène*

N *Navettes*

Our *Our ou Vingt ans après*

VE *La Vie sur Epsilon*

Introduction

Reading *Le Jeu d'enfant:*
Readability and Reflexive Fiction

> A man's maturity - consists in having found again the
> seriousness one had as a child, at play.
> —Nietzsche
> "Look! here is the world, which seems so dangerous!
> It is nothing but a game for children, just worth
> making a jest about."
> —Freud

In a scene from Claude Ollier's 1982 text *Mon Double à Malacca,* a father is watching his child at play. The five-year-old girl has selected a collection of pebbles from the shore and sets about arranging and rearranging them into various shapes and figures, thereby effecting a series of permutations whose guiding principle is not fully discernable by the father, observing from a distance. What he does recognize, however, is that despite her dissatisfaction with each of the successive configurations, the child does not seek to alter the primary elements of her game, the pebbles initially selected and disposed around herself: "D'où vient que le choix n'est remis en question? Ce serait 'un autre film,' disent les monteurs de pellicule. Qu'importe, s'il est plus satisfaisant? Mais non: elle est là dans le cercle et les unités qui bouclent la circonférence semblent dotées, du fait seul d'avoir été perçues et élues dans le premier temps, et ramassées, rapportées là, d'un prestige incomparable à celui de toute autre introduite ultérieurement dans la danse."[1] Like all games, the child's play is both arbitrary and rule-bound; while the initial choice of the component pieces is arbitrarily made, the subsequent moves are constrained by the very configura-

I

tion—size, number, shape—of that choice. And the pleasure of the game resides precisely in the exercise of the player's subsequent inventiveness in the face of those initial constraints:

> Il est donc un premier temps du jeu, sur lequel on ne revient pas, déterminant des classes et des prérogatives auxquelles on se tient quoi qu'il arrive. Une décision d'apparence primesautière, fonction du goût de l'instant et d'un sens précis de l'équilibre, a fondé sans retour une distinction, qualitative, une hiérarchie, et l'ordonnatrice se campe au centre d'une ostentatoire prédilection graphique. En fait, les manques ou défectuosités inhérents à la phase d'impulsivité initiale ont créé des contraintes, et l'intérêt tôt porté à l'exercice de ces contraintes a déjà fait son oeuvre: l'excitation soulevée par la difficulté en général s'est fixée tout entière sur cette difficulté-là, qui mobilise et accapare, tyrannise tout l'être vers sa résolution, au point que renoncer à cet effort, ou substituer une autre épreuve à celle-ci serait perçu comme une défaite, une régression. Voilà: elle s'est prise au jeu, à ce jeu qu'elle a monté sur rien ou presque, quelques cailloux sans qualités spécifiques prélevés sur la plage aux bons soins d'un désir soudain, dans l'instant surgi, révélé. (p. 34–35)

As in the epigraph from Nietzsche that prefaces this introduction, the seriousness of the child at play comes to reflect the preoccupations of the mature man; for the "prédilection graphique" of the child's game quickly becomes a model for the process of fictional creation:

> La voici à genoux sur le sable mouillé et apostrophant directement les fétiches, active, verbe vivace, délibéré—impératif et vocatif—, les mains en décalage fréquent avec les intimations de la voix, tâtonnant volontiers quand la parole vacille ou trébuche. Le grésillement du léger ressac ne permet pas d'entendre tout ce qu'elle dit. Des bribes d'énoncés passent entre deux lancers de vague, au terme d'un repli. Dans le trêve ou très brève suspension du flux, des mots se glissent en contrebande, des noms propres, des pronoms, beaucoup de négations, comme l'affirmation d'un pouvoir sans partage, d'une faculté innée de déplacer l'objet magique et de lui assigner un destin. (p. 35)

Like writing, this game is a process in flux, a tentative movement of hesitation and revision rather than an assured control of predetermined patterns. And in much the same way that the child's selection and manipulation of certain ordinary pebbles endow those pebbles with a magical force, so writing can be seen as a type of fetishization of language, one that elects and combines certain of its elements into a uniquely destined object. Finally, the child's game illustrates the profound physicality of writing, the insertion of the concrete writing subject within what Derrida has called the "general text" of the world.

In a 1971 essay entitled "Les Inscriptions conflictuelles," Ollier proposes his theory on what he calls the "engrenage sujet-société-langage," the mesh of a culturally situated subject using a socially conditioned language to create a text destined to translate that subject's personal reactions to the fictional elements elected. The play of these various conflictual inscriptions constitutes the very act, or process, of writing. For Ollier, the writer's body is the locus of these various currents; the body's relation to its immediate sensory environment (table and chair, light and sound) and to the materials used (paper, ink, erasers) makes the act of writing a profoundly corporal one: "C'est comme un mode de symbiose fuyant, dissimulé, observable entre la vie physiologique, singulièrement celle du système nerveux, et celle des articulations grammaticales mobilisées par la construction fictionnelle."[2] Thus the writing subject for Ollier is never abstracted from the social, cultural, discursive inscriptions that traverse the subject's activity. In this way, the economy of the child's created system is set against, and within, a general economy to whose vicissitudes it must submit:

> C'est qu'elle sait bien que l'économie de son système, pour retranchée précisément qu'elle l'ait voulue des contingences du dehors, reste sous le coup des lois de l'économie générale, dont elle dépend toujours, elle et ses cailloux, et tributaire par conséquent d'une certaine bienveillance, ou neutralité. . . . C'est ça l'"impact" de la réalité, elle le sent bien, et que le gain de jouissance qu'elle tire de sa combinatoire improvisée échappe au bilan des profits et pertes régissant le grand monde alentour; elle sait qu'elle le lui vole et inscrit le sien en marge, non pas ailleurs, en marge seulement, précairement, dans la fragilité d'une échappatoire superbe, revendiquée de tout son être, tremblotante, triomphante, assumée de tout son corps vibrant dans le creuset du jeu. (pp. 35–36)

The child's physical presence at the center of her game inscribes that game within the contingencies of the real but opposes its gratuitous economy of escapist pleasure *(jouissance)* to the balance sheet of profits and losses organizing the world at large. In "Les Inscriptions conflictuelles," too, Ollier describes the pleasure of writing as "cette stupéfiante volupté de l'inscription et de la rature" (p. 89). The terms of this opposition between the two economies recall Georges Bataille's enunciation of a general economy of *dépense* transcending, in certain sacred moments, the restricted economy of thrift governing everyday activity. The economy of the child's game is likewise one of pleasurable prodigality: "La loi de son marché vaut celle de l'autre, c'est une économie de gaspillage aussi, et elle sait qu'elle s'oppose aussi à la règle de rentabilité du marché adulte, et que profit ne s'y entend que de son propre fonctionnement, de la perfection propre du mouvement de ses mains, de sa langue, de ses yeux, et de l'équilibre merveilleux qu'elle leur imprime" (p. 36). Ollier's text reminds us that like the child's game, writing is played out on the margins of the real, and its fragile organization is always subject to the impact of the real; writing's functioning, while in one sense gratuitous, is yet never autonomous or inviolable; it never takes place somewhere else, *ailleurs.* However, a reversal of sorts, or at least a leveling, is operated in the hierarchy of the two economies with the notion of *gaspillage:* "La loi de son marché *vaut* celle de l'autre, c'est une économie de gaspillage *aussi*" (my emphasis). The law of *dépense* underlying the child's game works as a sort of *arché*-principle that would also ultimately characterize the economy of the "general text" of the world at large, whose structures, mechanisms, and institutions are finally, like writing and like a child's game, both arbitrary and rule-bound. In the same way, Freud's remark on the gamelike nature of the world, cited as an epigraph to this introduction, serves to illustrate the complex imbrication of gameplaying and the world.

The book containing this scene of a child at play follows by some seven years the final text of Ollier's eight-volume fictional cycle, *Le Jeu d'enfant,* which can be translated as "Child's Play" or "The Child's Game." Yet this scene nevertheless sheds much light on the nature of that serial venture: on its ground rules, its organization, its functioning, and its stakes. For in many ways the child's game replays the activity of the mature man. Initiated with the publication of *La Mise en scène* in 1958, the chain of eight fictions came to be consciously

linked, in the author's mind, after the conclusion of the second book
(*Le Maintien de l'ordre*) in 1961. From that point on, a collection of
fictional elements, scenes, situations, characters, and general concerns
were cast into a series of combinations that were reworked and rear-
ranged throughout the succeeding texts, until the publication of the
last volume, *Fuzzy Sets,* in 1975. In each of the fictions, a European
male protagonist undertakes an itinerary of investigation or exploration in an alien setting with whose language, laws, and terrain he is
unfamiliar. Each protagonist attempts to trace paths or roads in the
resistant, menacing space of his setting. Moreover, each protagonist
tries, with varying degrees of success, to account in writing for certain
mysterious events or phenomena encountered. The permutations of
these efforts at tracing a meaning, at tracking an elusive knowledge,
provide the foundation for a fictional elaboration that ranges from
colonial North Africa to New York, and from the modern site of
ancient Ur to a vaguely distant outer space. For a time, the projected
title of Ollier's fictional ensemble was "Itinéraire"; an even earlier
version was "Le Livre d'aventures." The initial choice of the elements
composing these eight texts derives from the writing subject's insertion
into a physical, cultural, historical, political Real, for example Ollier's
own experiences working in colonial North Africa and traveling in
North America. It is in the subsequent permutations upon those
chosen elements that the exercise of fictional elaboration resides. Like
the child's play on the beach, "monté sur rien ou presque," *Le Jeu
d'enfant* constitutes "l'affirmation d'un pouvoir sans partage, d'une
faculté innée de déplacer l'objet magique et de lui assigner un destin."

By its interplay of gratuitous and rule-bound behavior—its permutations on a chosen set of elements—*Le Jeu d'enfant* demonstrates
the gamelike nature of fictional elaboration. At the same time, it comprises an extended allegory of the act of writing as a play of various
forces. These forces are shown at work in the scene of the child's game
in *Mon Double à Malacca,* which presents an individual situated
within a given physical, cultural, historical reality, arranging and rearranging on the margins of that reality a set of elements chosen at the
prompting of impulses and desires arising from the individual's insertion within that greater economy. What results is at once an example
and an allegory of the play of fictional production. Thus *Le Jeu*

d'enfant exhibits from start to finish the self-referential, self-reflexive stance that many critics see as the common denominator of post-modern fiction.

To illuminate the nature of *Le Jeu d'enfant* by referring to a scene in a work that is both posterior and exterior to the cycle in no way breaks the rules of its game. For the principle of intertextuality provides one of the most important of those ground rules and paradoxically opens up the set of possible moves in the fictional game to include articulations with other texts. Ollier proposed his formulations of this principle in a talk delivered at the Nouveau Roman colloquium held at Cerisy in 1970:

> J'entends par fiction un système narratif provisoirement clos, dans lequel la narration elle-même fait intrigue et dispose le sens. C'est-à-dire, un système suffisant à fonder l'organisation totale du livre, et particulier à ce livre, mais toujours susceptible d'être repris, rouvert, pour introduire dans le système de ce livre un supplément de fiction, ou un développement fictionnel critique, ou donner naissance à un nouveau système fictionnel dérivé, articulé sur le premier, voire à plusieurs systèmes fictionnels articulés entre eux et sur le système originel. D'où la nécessité d'ajouter une nouvelle fonction au tableau: la fonction intertextuelle ou interfictionnelle, désignant cette virtualité de chaque texte à rouvrir son système pour une mise en branle nouveau de ses rouages.[3]

A given configuration of elements—a narrative system—is only provisionally closed and particular. Each system, be it one of the eight individual fictions of *Le Jeu d'enfant* or the entire chain, can be reopened, reorganized, and reread by the incorporation of new elements. These supplements defy chronology, for they can either predate or antedate the narrative system in question. They can derive from Ollier's own work or can be direct or modified seizures from the work of others; they can be either deliberate thefts or unplanned echoes of other works. Some of the authors whose works are woven into *Le Jeu d'enfant* are Lautréamont, Cervantes, Jules Verne, Flaubert, Borges, and Villiers de l'Isle-Adam. With this network of repetitions and borrowings, the intertextual narrative play of *Le Jeu d'enfant* adds a "nouvelle fonction," a new function to the ground rules of traditional narrative. Where fiction had conventionally dictated creative originality, logical chronology, and the closure of individual narratives, the brand of writing played out in *Le Jeu d'enfant* challenges these rules and proposes new variations on the old game of fiction.

The two epigraphs to this introduction also speak of children's games, and their authors, Nietzsche and Freud, can be seen as signal spirits for the kind of fiction exemplified by *Le Jeu d'enfant*. Nietzsche's project of a "revaluation of all values," along with his persistent questioning of grounding concepts and his commitment to experimentation with conventional philosophical discourse, all prefigure the revolutionary impulse behind the manifestos and innovations of much postmodern fiction. His critique of "depth" in *The Gay Science* prefigures Robbe-Grillet's attack on "le coeur romantique des choses" in *Pour un nouveau roman*.[4] Such a revolutionary project seeks to overturn unquestioned hierarchies and gives a new kind of seriousness to the play of thought and writing.

Freud, too, disrupted long-standing and fundamental metaphysical hierarchies with his formulations on the primacy of the unconscious: "It is essential to abandon the overvaluation of the property of being conscious, before it becomes possible to form any correct view of the origin of what is mental . . . the unconscious is the larger sphere, which includes within it the smaller sphere of the conscious."[5] This reversal of accepted hierarchies is reflected, as we have seen, in the scene from *Mon Double à Malacca,* in the paradoxical economies of writing and the real, where the gamelike nature of writing provides an *arché*-principle for the play of the general text of the world. What had conventionally been considered marginal or secondary is given a new status and value in Freud's revolutionary theories and in their fictional heirs. Freud's recognition of the primacy and force of the unconscious is translated, in postmodern fiction such as the New Novel, into a mistrust of old rules such as originality, authorial intention, and conscious control over all the ingredients and outcomes of artistic or fictional production. Here, the concept of intertextuality as a mode of fictional constitution allows for the recognition of just such unconscious reservoirs of elements and moves—on the side of the author and reader alike—comprising the play of fiction.

The revolutionary impact of Freud's work has fostered, in fiction, the creation of new ground rules and new game plans for narrative.

Still, it must be remembered that Freud's goal was not at all to elevate the unconscious to the status of prime determiner of human action; Freud sought, rather, to bring unconscious forces to the level of consciousness so that they might be understood and dealt with effectively. And this goal of greater self-consciousness, greater self-reflexivity is also an aim of postmodern texts like those of *Le Jeu d'enfant,* with their extended investigation into the nature and workings of fiction. Such a self-analysis on the part of fiction has often provoked charges of narcissism, of gratuitous autonomy, of being nothing, finally, but a solipsistic game. This kind of critique forgets, however, what Freud made clear: that any analysis, even a self-analysis, requires an analytical situation that includes an analyst as well as an analysand (though they may be different moments of the same individual subject). In fiction, it is the reader whose moves make the game possible, in the same way that any joke or jest requires a listener in order to be a joke at all, as Freud points out in his theory of *Witz.* And the reader, like the writer, is traversed by the conflictual inscriptions of society, language, and subjectivity. Thus the game of fiction is inescapably rooted in a concrete, complex network of cultural and historical relations, even as it provides a playful (but not frivolous) escape to the margins of the ordinary economy of the real. What both Nietzsche and Freud contribute to the revolutionary, reflexive goals of postmodern fiction like *Le Jeu d'enfant* is an appreciation of the seriousness and scope of play in the theater of human thought and activity.

Another postmodern writer whose work playfully proposes a reflexive and revolutionary assault on the rules of conventional fiction is Italo Calvino. His 1979 work *The Castle of Crossed Destinies* presents an extended game of tarot; in a chapter entitled "The Writer's Tale," Calvino proposes a vision of the author at work that resembles Ollier's image of the child at play: "Perhaps the moment has come to admit that only tarot number one honestly depicts what I have succeeded in being: a juggler, or conjurer, who arranges on a stand at a fair a certain number of objects and, shifting them, connecting them, interchanging them, achieves a certain number of effects."[6] The figure of the game and its play illuminates an important part of the intellectual heritage shared by Calvino and Ollier. It demonstrates how their radical brand of fiction deflates some of the seriousness of traditional and modernist mystification of writing and of literature, and it proposes a new brand of serious, or, as Calvino would put it, honest inquiry into the nature of fictional production. The implications of this new game necessarily extend beyond the activity of the writer to that of the reader of these fictions, and the question that must be raised is: have the rules of reading also changed? By its historical context, its innovative conceptualization and construction, and its impact on future discussion of the novelistic form, Ollier's *Le Jeu d'enfant* offers a unique perspective on this inquiry. But before the question about the rules of reading can be considered, a closer look at the wider context of Ollier's life and work, the history of the French New Novel, and the fate of its heirs will elucidate the singular importance of Ollier's fictional cycle for an understanding of the direction taken by modern fiction.

Claude Ollier was born on December 17, 1922, in Paris. After studies in law and commerce at the Ecole des Hautes Etudes Commerciales, he held various posts in industry, agriculture, banking, insurance, and in colonial administration in Morocco. He situates the birth of Ollier the author around 1930, in the encounter with a certain film, or perhaps a bit later, when he discovered jazz. Although he began writing as early as 1940, it was not until 1955, upon his return to France, that he was able to devote himself solely to writing. Ollier lived for eight years in Morocco and has traveled extensively in North and Central America, the Middle East, and the Far East. His writing testifies at every turn to the impact of other cultures and other landscapes, both urban and untamed. Since 1975 he has resided in a village near Paris with his daughter, Ariane, born in 1972.

With the publication of his prize-winning novel *(La Mise en scène)* in 1958, Claude Ollier was immediately associated with a group of French writers who came to be known as the New Novelists. The authors most often cited as practitioners of the New Novel were Alain Robbe-Grillet, Nathalie Sarraute, Claude Simon, Robert Pinget, Michel Butor, and later, Jean Ricardou. Although these writers differed significantly from each other, they nevertheless shared some important common denominators: a questioning and disrupting of conventional narrative form, of point of view, of temporality, and of representation in fiction. Like his contemporaries, Ollier was interested in fiction's capacity for problematizing its own conventions, while at the same time presenting innovations that would challenge the ways in which books are usually read, categorized, and evaluated.

During the decades of the fifties, sixties, and seventies, the New Novel became an increasingly self-reflexive form. Meditations on the act of writing and the nature of textuality were a recognizable signpost of the fictions of this loosely knit movement. Nor were these meditations limited to fictional writing; those writers who were dubbed New Novelists were as much theorists as artists; along with writers like Alain Robbe-Grillet, Claude Simon, Nathalie Sarraute, Jean Ricardou, and Michel Butor, Claude Ollier has published and lectured on the direction taken by his work as well as the critical questions it raises. Of course, the French writers grouped under the rubric of the New Novel have not been unique in their questioning of inherited fictional conventions or in their innovations in respect to the givens of traditional fiction; a similar challenge to standard generic codes and conventions has been mounted on many fronts by various European, North American, and Latin American writers. In her 1984 study entitled *Metafiction: The Theory and Practice of Self-Conscious Fiction,* Patricia Waugh proposes to examine what she sees as the dominant feature of postmodern fiction—its extreme self-consciousness:

> *Metafiction* is a term given to fictional writing which self-consciously and systematically draws attention to its status as an artefact in order to pose questions about the relationship between fiction and reality. In providing a critique of their own methods of construction, such writings not only examine the fundamental structures of narrative fiction, they also explore the possible fictionality of the world outside the literary fictional world.[7]

In both their fictions and their overtly theoretical works the New Novelists, like their counterparts, have been preoccupied with investigating how narratives have been and might be constructed, along with the implications of those constructions for traditional ways of thinking. This generalized commitment to theoretical concerns links the

New Novelists to each other and to their contemporaries in other countries.

Many critics of "metafictions" or "experimental" fictions rightly point out that these kinds of work are by no means absolutely new— that they have predecessors dating back as far as *Don Quixote, Le Berger extravagant,* and *Tristram Shandy* or as recently, in the French tradition, as the fabulations of Raymond Roussel. And yet the appearance of the first New Novels on the French literary scene in the fifties had the effect of a genuine scandal: polemics for and against Robbe-Grillet's early works were lively, and reactions such as Pierre de Boisdeffre's sarcastic *La Cafetière est sur la table: contre le "nouveau roman"* were characteristic of the shock wave generated in the literary world by those "new" novels. In the above-mentioned work, published in 1967, de Boisdeffre goes to considerable length, in chapters entitled "'L'antiroman' date de trois siècles" and "La 'Crise du roman' ne date pas d'hier," to prove that "Robbe-Grillet peut se réclamer d'une tradition aussi vieille que le genre romanesque lui-même!" Yet de Boisdeffre's comments on *La Jalousie* betray a rancor that the earlier works of that supposed tradition could never have inspired: "*La Jalousie* n'est pas l'histoire d'une conscience traquée, ce n'est même pas la description d'un *comportement,* c'est un exercice d'école—même pas drôle—où l'on prend le lecteur pour un sot. Bernard Frank dirait, en bon français, un *piège à cons.*"[8]

Despite the fact that novels like *La Jalousie* were not absolutely, but only relatively new, they hit a nerve back in the early fifties that has not stopped throbbing even today, as new works by this durable group of writers are met with the same kind of judgment and the same pronouncements of the movement's moribund state and imminent demise. Echoes of Pierre de Boisdeffre's sarcasm lingered on into the eighties, as exemplified in an article in *L'Express* reviewing new works by Robbe-Grillet, Butor, Pinget, Duras, and Beckett:

Vers les années 60, rappelez-vous, il fallait de l'audace pour oser soutenir que le Nouveau Roman était un gadget qui passerait comme le "hulla-hoop" ou les "scoubidous". Soutenu par un consortium hétéroclite d'académiciens bluffés et de thuriféraires en extase, Robbe-Grillet se

prenait alors pour Saint-Juste, et les écrivains n'avaient plus qu'à
marcher au pas. Très vite, heureusement, la tyrannie que faisaient
régner ce caporal et sa troupe s'est évanouie dans l'indifférence, et la
littérature a repris le rythme naturel de sa promenade. Les terroristes se
sont effacés peu à peu, comme des ombres, et 68 est passé par là pour
balayer ce qu'il en restait. Si les Simon, les Butor, les Pinget ont survécu à
l'oubli, ils doivent une fière chandelle au Lagarde et Michard, et à
quelques universités du Middle West qui n'ont pas encore épuisé leur
stock de "Gommes" et d'"Emploi du temps".[9]

For the ancien régime of consecrated literature, Robbe-Grillet and his
troops embodied the menace of revolution and terrorism; according to
this view, the improbable survival of their work is due only to the
gullibility and lack of common sense so typical of professors. The
unusual hostility aroused by these texts is symptomatic not only of the
enduring force of the ideology underpinning the traditional realistic-
psychological novel ("le rythme naturel de sa promenade") but also of
the strength of the challenge posed by these new fictions. For this
reason alone the phenomenon of the New Novel and its troubled
reception arguably merits close examination. A form that has so consistently raised hostility over the nature of its writing and reading must
surely yield insight into those activities both as they are conventionally
constructed and as they might be otherwise enacted.

A reason of a different order is the attribution of the 1985 Nobel
prize for literature to Claude Simon, which signals a recognition of the
contribution made by one of the New Novel's better-known exemplars
to the course taken by modern literature. Of course, it could be argued
that this official sanctification finally does spell the end of the New
Novel's radical impact, since its contestive force will be recuperated
and institutionalized by its new status. But I do not think this is or will
be the case. For it must be remembered that Claude Simon has always
been one of the most widely read and least attacked of the writers
associated with the New Novel label. His new status will not necessarily provoke a reevaulation of lesser known New Novelists, just as
Marguerite Duras's recent media popularity and official recognition
(in the form of the 1984 Prix Goncourt) has not necessarily signaled a
new openness to narrative innovations. The popular appeal of Duras's
L'Amant, which topped the best-seller lists in France for weeks on end,

probably lies elsewhere than in its contestation or blurring of generic forms or its lucid self-consciousness. The same critic who lambasts "ce pauvre Robbe-Grillet" for writing a novel that is also an extended grammar study (*Djinn, Un trou rouge entre les pavés,* 1981) and who castigates Robert Pinget for propagating a "brouillard artificiel" nevertheless praises what he sees in Duras's work as "un naturel, un talent au réalisme" and "une vérité quelque part."[10] For such readers, the contributions of these works to a radical questioning of received notions about fiction will always be obscured by a recuperative perspective that sees only the signposts of nineteenth-century verisimilitude: the clear, the natural, the real, the true.

Perhaps the most compelling reason for reexamining the New Novel now lies therefore in its complex, sustained relationship to other discourses that questioned, in the fertile decades of the sixties and seventies, received and ideologically grounded notions such as literary realism. Work done in the fields of phenomenology, structuralism, psychoanalysis, and what can loosely be called poststructuralism has provided fuel for the investigations and experiments operated by the novelistic form. The seminal contributions of thinkers like Lacan, Derrida, Deleuze, and Foucault find echoes in the New Novel's persistent questioning of the nature of the subject, of perception, of representation, and of discourse itself. And the inverse is also true: fictional interrogations of language codes and generic boundaries have fueled contemporary critical and philosophical inquiry. Recent studies such as David Carroll's *The Subject in Question: The Languages of Theory and the Strategies of Fiction,* Lynn Higgins's *Parables of Theory: Jean Ricardou's Metafiction,* and Dina Sherzer's *Representation in Contemporary French Fiction* have examined the imbrication of theory and fiction in the works of other French writers of Ollier's generation.[11] Among the works that have participated in this rich intellectual activity of the past thirty years, Claude Ollier's *Le Jeu d'enfant* occupies a singular position and it is in order to assess the nature and significance of that singularity that the present study has been written.

Initiated in the aftermath of the Second World War, *Le Jeu d'enfant* must be seen in the context of that historical event, which Ollier has called the "*catastrophe 'en amont',*" the catastrophe "upstream" of his works' elaboration. Indeed, long before there was talk of a New Novel,

Ollier had many discussions with Robbe-Grillet, whom he met in 1943. The two young men agreed on the impossibility of ever again writing in the same mode as did the nineteenth century. On the one hand, the writings of Sartre, Kafka, and Faulkner had already begun to question and alter the very foundations of narrative. On the other hand, and more fundamentally, "the events of the Second World War occurred in Europe in such a way as to provoke an upheaval in our consciences, our certitudes, and our vision of the world." The impact of the war on the European psyche meant, for Ollier, that writing also had to bear the mark of lost certitudes and an altered world vision. Yet the war is not an explicit subtext of *Le Jeu d'enfant;* it is, rather, an unspoken given upon which the cycle is elaborated as it seeks to examine experience in the new light of the postwar world. "As for the Second World War," Ollier says, "it lies behind every page of the eight books."[12] But the focus of *Le Jeu d'enfant* is the present and the future: the present that was colonial North Africa and the hypothetical future of encounters with other worlds. By making explicit the connection between a culture's production (its fiction) and its vision of the world (its ideology) *Le Jeu d'enfant* undertakes both to expose the bankruptcy of the old ethnocentric, Eurocentric vision and to investigate the alterity of unknown cultures and worlds. It does so by systematically challenging old narrative forms and improvising new ones.

Much of the innovative force of *Le Jeu d'enfant* derives from its architecture, which provides the format for the cycle's interrogation of the conventions of fiction and its projection of fictional alternatives. *Le Jeu d'enfant* is composed of eight fictions: *La Mise en scène* (1958); *Le Maintien de l'ordre* (1961); *Eté indien* (1963); *L'Echec de Nolan* (1967); *La Vie sur Epsilon* (1972); *Enigma* (1973); *Our ou Vingt ans après* (1974); *Fuzzy Sets* (1975). While each fiction can stand alone structurally and hermeneutically, the unity of the cycle is accomplished by the persistent and complex linking of its eight texts through the intertextual repetition of certain elements and passages. The novels form two discrete cycles consisting of four books each; however, these two cycles are linked to each other by numerical and geometrical relations as well as by textual and thematic echoes. Thus the concerns of the first and third works are replayed in the fourth; the fifth book takes up the problems of the first, transferred to a secondary level; elements of the first and seventh works are reorganized in the eighth. Within each text, numerical correspondences and geometrical patterns underlie the fictional elaboration, as in the fourth book, whose four parts correspond to four reports that take the perennial investigator to the four cardinal points of the globe.

In the first relay of the cycle, the fictions mix and mimic some of the consecrated genres of traditional literature: the colonial adventure, the police novel, the love story, the mystery. In so doing, they undermine the assumptions about mimesis that subtend those popular forms of realist fiction. By playing upon the consecrated codes of such types of fiction, Ollier both pays homage to the kinds of reading he enjoyed as a youth and at the same time subverts the vision of the world upon which they repose. For instance, where the traditional crime story ultimately closes with some kind of resolution or revelation, Ollier's version remains ambiguous to the end; it unmasks our ideological need to impress order on the chaos of events by frustrating our efforts to deduce a tidy explanation. In this respect, some of Ollier's books can be likened to early fictions by Robbe-Grillet, such as *Les Gommes* and *Le Voyeur,* which play on the *roman policier* genre, or *La Jalousie,* which provides an artful subversion of the colonial potboiler.

With the second relay, the fictions ascend abruptly to the realm of outer space to take up again the issues dealt with in the first books, but with the addition of a secondary, more self-referential level. Here, some of Ollier's texts put into play the codes of science fiction: space travel, unknown planets, global catastrophes, unheard-of phenomena. In these "science fictions," a magnified focus on the nature of reading and writing seems to propose an allegorical "science" of fiction in which the laws and principles of textuality are investigated from within. In his experimentation upon the givens of standard science fiction narrative and in the self-referentiality of his texts, Ollier can be compared to Samuel Delany, who is often pointed to as one of those science-fiction writers whose work blurs the distinction between science fiction and postmodern fiction (and theory—the work of writers like Lacan and Derrida also figures in Delany's novels). But while Delany also devotes considerable textual space to the construction of a viable, convincing vision of the science-fiction situation in question, Ollier's projected worlds tend to be less detailed and more abstractly allegorical of textuality.

While the eight novels of *Le Jeu d'enfant* form two discrete cycles consisting of four books each, the cycles are bound to each other by a network of intertextuality and by a satellite work, *Navettes,* whose short texts constitute a microcosm of and a commentary of sorts on the entire cycle's movement. Published with the conclusion of the first relay, *Navettes* counteracts the effect of tidy closure that might be imputed to the conclusion of a specific book or cycle. In much the same way, a series of radio plays written by Ollier during the same years, with titles such as "La Mort du personnage," "L'Attentat en direct," and "Réseau Ollier Navettes," opens up the cycle's itinerary to extraneous elaborations and alternate readings. The sustained investigation conducted by *Le Jeu d'enfant* and its theoretical satellites (including Ollier's own theorizings and comments in articles and interviews) irrevocably complicates notions of closure and organicism as it raises new questions about intentionality, originality, and authorial control. The singular interest and value of *Le Jeu d'enfant* thus reside in the scope, patience, and complexity of its inquiry into the nature of textuality and the acts of reading and writing, and, concomitantly, in its seismic questioning of the grounding world vision of Western culture.

By insisting on the singularity of *Le Jeu d'enfant,* I do not at all intend to assert that it is unique, unprecedented, or unparalleled. Indeed, Ollier's work intersects in significant ways with that of his contemporaries, especially the New Novelists. He shares with Robbe-Grillet many of the guiding principles of his fictional practice, and their early works, in particular, have much in common: a phenomenological interrogation of subjectivity, a disruption of plot, character, and chronology, and an insistence that the reader assume a more active role. Like Michel Butor, Ollier often takes a map, blueprint, floorplan, schedule, or itinerary as the point of fictional departure; both writers are concerned with demonstrating discontinuity in the form, chronology, and even typography of their works, and both make frequent use of borrowed intertexts. Claude Simon's obsession with time, history, memory, and the impossibility of narrating the past is also a concern of Ollier's later works. And many other common interests and practices link Ollier with postmodern writers in Europe and the Americas. Nor is the notion of a cycle of books unique to Ollier. Edmond Jabès's seven-volume poem entitled *Le Livre des questions* was finished in 1973, and his two-volume *Le Livre des ressemblances* in 1978; and Jean-Pierre Faye's six-volume *Hexagramme* spans the years 1958–70. Jabès's work provides a prolonged meditation on the process of writing and on the notion of the book. Faye, too, is a poet who seeks, in the novels of *Hexagramme,* to expand and amplify his poetic practice and experimentation on form. *Le Jeu d'enfant* shares some of the abiding concerns of these serial works, and its meticulously crafted language also calls for an analysis akin to poetics. But Ollier's cycle differs in many significant ways from those of Faye and Jabès, notably in its intricate architecture and intertextuality and in its focus on and questioning of the novelistic genre.

Ollier, of course, would be the first to object to the old notions of utter creative originality and uniqueness were they to be applied to *Le Jeu d'enfant.* And yet there is something of singular value to be gained from its study. As the fullest elaboration and examination of the questions raised by the New Novel and by the fertile theoretical issues that gave that movement its context, *Le Jeu d'enfant* provides a unique opportunity to assess a seminal moment in modern intellectual and creative activity.

Although (according to him) Ollier went several years after the completion of *Le Jeu d'enfant* without thinking about writing another book, he has continued to write and publish since the conclusion of the cycle in 1975. While many of the concerns that characterize *Le Jeu d'enfant* are also present in his more recent works, these books nevertheless differ significantly from the earlier fictions and are not treated in the present study. A brief survey of Ollier's later works will show both their divergence from and their relation to the earlier series. The first work published after *Fuzzy Sets* was *Marrakch medine* (1979), which was awarded the Prix France Culture. It is a work that defies generic classification and that seeks to approach the Islamic city in ways other than a perennial "orientalism" in the sense of the term denounced by Edward Saïd. *Marrakch medine* is composed of passages varying in length from several lines to several pages. Stories and dialogues accompany the observations and investigations of the Moroccan city and the area known as the medina by an unnamed narrator who is apparently a member of a small group of Western visitors. The reflective travel narrative is doubled by cryptic meditations on perception, memory, writing, and cultural opacity. This work further extends Ollier's examination of the Occidental spectator of an alien culture, language, religion, and landscape.

The 1982 work *Mon Double à Malacca* is the account of a summer vacation in Malaysia. Its protagonists are Chloé, five years old, and her father, Paul, fifty-five. This work continues the evolution toward the more openly autobiographical in its transmutations of Ollier's own travels. Similarly, *Une Histoire illisible* (1986) shows how the lived past becomes an unrecountable story, a mélange of fictional genres. In *Déconnection* (1988), Ollier explicitly treats what had been, in *Le Jeu d'enfant*, only an unspoken given: the experience of the Second World War, which shook all accepted values and left the European psyche permanently altered. In this fascinating and disturbing work, two narratives unfold simultaneously, in alternating passages of two or three pages in length. One narrative, recounted in the third person, is the story of Martin, an adolescent (probably French) conscripted to work in a German factory in the final years of the war. The other narrative takes place toward the end of our millenium. Certain unspecified "events" have caused a progressive decline in civilization; a mature man, a writer, lives alone in a small house on the outskirts of a village. His narrative is told in the first person. The population has dwindled, electricity and television are sporadic, there is no mail; the few remaining people exchange tobacco and alcohol for food. The historical catastrophe of the midcentury and the never-specified events of its conclusion are each seen through the eyes of one individual. At the conclusion of this enigmatic text, civilization as it has been is ending and the stage is set for something radically different to begin.

Thus Ollier's work after *Le Jeu d'enfant* links up with some of the concerns of the fictional cycle, while initiating new ones. Where *Le Jeu d'enfant* challenged the term *novel,* substituting for its ready-made baggage the less-loaded label of *fiction,* Ollier's most recent work makes it even more difficult to maintain distinctions between fiction, documentary, and autobiography.

A fascinating corollary to Ollier's thirty-year practice of writing is provided by his journal, whose three volumes, spanning the years 1950–80, were published in 1984, 1985, and 1989 at the suggestion of Ollier's friends Bernard Noël and Denis Roche. The works are entitled

Cahiers d'écolier, Fables sous rêve, and *Les Liens d'espace.* The entries in this journal include fragments of narrative, records of dreams, ideas for future books, comments on work in progress, travel notes, and daily observations. They provide a fascinating perspective on some of the sources and the gradual fabrication of *Le Jeu d'enfant.* But this "diary" again frustrates generic expectations, for it eschews the biographical details and sentiments typically associated with the form. Those readers seeking to learn about Ollier the citizen will have scant clues to follow apart from the psychoanalytic conclusions they are free to draw from the dream narratives recorded there. *Souvenirs écran* (1982) is a collection of Ollier's film criticism (on Godard, Fritz Lang, Hitchcock, and Buñuel, among others) originally published in the journals *Cahiers du Cinéma, Mercure de France,* and *Nouvelle Revue Française.* A group of short texts, some of which previously appeared in various journals, was published in 1981, entitled *Nébules.* These texts mix theory and literature in a reworking and elucidation of many of the issues investigated in *Le Jeu d'enfant.* Writing for Ollier not only provides a means of approach to the alterity of the non-Western, it also seeks to realign its own relations with what are conventionally seen as the "others" of written discourse itself: music, art, film, theory, philosophy. The bibliography included in the volume testifies to Ollier's long-standing interest in and involvement with radio, cinema, and artistic innovation. It is the rich diversity of Ollier's writing practice, coupled with the scope and rigor of his writing projects, that constitutes the enduring value of his work.

Clearly, many continuities with the concerns and procedures of Ollier's initial cycle can be discerned in his subsequent works, and a study of those connections would be a fruitful one that should be undertaken. But it is equally clear that a thorough analysis of *Le Jeu d'enfant* should precede any such study. It is for this reason that my study focuses solely upon the eight fictions of *Le Jeu d'enfant* and its major satellite, *Navettes.* Rooted in a seminal moment in recent French intellectual history and engaging many of the debates of that period, *Le Jeu d'enfant* provides the context—all the more now from more than a decade's distance—for a new look at that moment and those debates.

The first question raised upon approaching *Le Jeu d'enfant* is the one posed earlier in my discussion of the game as a new and radicalized image of fictional production: have the rules of reading also changed? How should self-conscious or reflexive fictions like these be read? How is the cycle's own metacommentary to be viewed, and what role are the author's extrafictional analyses to play? What critical moves are called for or preempted by a work that meditates on and allegorizes its own play? Far from resolving themselves at the beginning of my work on *Le Jeu d'enfant,* these questions become a dominant theme in my analysis. Indeed, the question of reading and of readability comprises one of the major problematics of postmodern fiction.[13] Michel Foucault evokes a similar problem in his study of the enigmatic Raymond Roussel, who is often cited as an early practitioner of some of the techniques that characterize contemporary fiction. The posthumous publication of *Comment j'ai écrit certains de mes livres,* Foucault claims, irremediably complicates the reading of Roussel's fiction. A work that explains itself, commenting on its own procedures and structures, multiplies the enigmas posed for the reader by the fact that some are supposedly revealed:

> Elle [la révélation] nous prescrit, pour lire l'oeuvre, une conscience inquiète; conscience en laquelle on ne peut se reposer, puisque le secret n'est pas à trouver comme dans ces devinettes ou charades que Roussel aimait tant; il est démontré et avec soin, pour un lecteur qui aurait donné, avant la fin du jeu, sa langue au chat. Mais c'est Roussel qui donne au chat la langue de ses lecteurs; il les contraint à connaître un secret qu'ils ne reconnaissaient pas, et à se sentir pris dans une sorte de secret flottant, donné et retiré, et jamais tout à fait démontrable. . . . L'impossibilité, ici, de décider lie tout discours sur Roussel non seulement au risque commun de se tromper, mais à celui, plus raffiné, de l'être.[14]

With *Le Jeu d'enfant,* the reader or critic runs many of the same risks: the possibility of falling into narrative traps; the impossibility of deciding conclusively on questions of meaning; the sense that one is playing into the hands of someone or something; perhaps even the painful (for a critic) silencing evoked by Foucault. This paranoia on the part of the reader faced with the enigmas of *Le Jeu d'enfant* is reflected in the works themselves, as a secret agency always seems to hover just out of reach behind the turns and twists of the intrigue in question. But this critical paranoia is perhaps a salutary one, for it prevents any reading from becoming too programmatic, too sure of its adequacy, and ultimately too restrictive of the texts' multiplicity.

My approach to the reading of *Le Jeu d'enfant* was not formulated at the outset of my investigations but was gradually enunciated during the constant rereading that constituted my analysis. In attempting to chart a safe but plausible course between the potential Scylla and Charybdis of "theory" and "fiction," I came to see the problem of that course as a central issue of my study, and indeed, of the type of metafiction that characterizes postmodern novels. In respect to definitively external theoretical statements made by the author in interviews or essays, the questions cannot be answered, manifestly, by giving him the last interpretive word. Nor can the problem be eliminated by simply censoring authorial commentary so that the fictions seem to speak for or about themselves. Each extreme poses artificial limits on both the reader and the texts. I have consequently attempted to deal with authorial commentary and theorizing in such a way as to let it participate in formulating questions, but not in providing conclusive answers. In respect to the cycle's own self-consciousness and its will to bring about change—its self-prescribed program of reflexivity and revolution—I have attempted to examine precisely that: what the cycle itself terms the *Projet*, the revolutionary project of interrogation of fiction (and all it entails) by and in fiction itself. While other general approaches to the study of Ollier's work are imaginable, I believe that mine engages the most significant aspects of *Le Jeu d'enfant* in its historical and intellectual context, while allowing for the interplay of a number of critical strategies that illuminate important issues in the field of contemporary fiction and theory.

The richness and complexity of *Le Jeu d'enfant* call for a multi-layered critical apparatus; what follows is an overview of my study's own game plan. It is well known by now that one of the principal aims of the early New Novels was to demystify the classical realist novel by unmasking its presuppositions (character, psychology, chronology, verisimilitude). But the major thrust of my study is not simply to show that *Le Jeu d'enfant* demystifies conventional fiction. While this is indeed an important part of the cycle's project, Ollier's texts also show, at certain conscious and unconscious levels, that the task is infinitely more complex and more difficult, and that ghosts (structures, patterns, features) of the traditional novel keep haunting the enterprise, never to be fully exorcised. This tension, then, provides the framing thesis of my study. My focus for analyzing both the conscious work of demystification and the unconscious resistance to it is what I call the triple subject of fiction: the protagonist, the writer, the reader. By focusing successively on these incarnations of O., the cycle's "hero," I am able to examine what was new about the New Novel when it was written, as well as what it is unable to throw off, what unconsciously remains of traditional fiction, or what is perhaps the very nature of narrative. This focus on the tripartite subject calls for an overarching critical perspective of Freudian and Lacanian psychoanalysis in order to shed light on the conscious and unconscious aspects of that subject and of the project constituted by the whole cycle. Such a perspective allows me to account for and explore the familial configurations and metaphors that dominate these fictions. Within the broad framework of psychoanalytic criticism, then, other critical approaches are used to examine the protagonist, writer, and reader of these postmodern fictions. Notably, Lukács's formulations on the novel are brought to bear on the anti-*Bildungsroman* of the protagonist operated by the first lap of the cycle. The issue of gender, filiation, and writing illuminates the contradictions inherent in the role of the writer. Reader-response theories are germane to my analysis of the place of the reader in Ollier's textual system as well as in metafiction in general. Linguistic criticism helps unmask the New Novel's (or more precisely, some of its theorists') "dream of scientificity." Through this multiple but interlinked critical approach, I aim to engage as much as is possible of the polyvalence of *Le Jeu d'enfant.*

In the first chapter of this study, I examine the textual processes of demystification undertaken in the first cycle of fictions. These books form a concerted effort to do away with the fictional protagonist as he has traditionally been conceived. What results, however, is not the death of the protagonist, as much that has been said for and against the New Novel proclaims, but rather his assumption to a higher, critical level of functioning. Despite the initial relay's interrogation of one of the cornerstones of the fictional genre—the hero—it has not fully succeeded in defining the positive nature of fiction. Thus the books of the second cycle suddenly ascend to outer space, to the realm of science fiction, and seem to propose themselves as a science of fiction that will analyze and correct the faulty trajectory of the first cycle. The self-conscious Project aims, in this way, at an enunciation of the fiction of the future, a fiction that will be disabused of its ideological illusions and purged, or at least made conscious of, its obsolete features.

It is evident that both relays of *Le Jeu d'enfant* are characterized by a persistent self-attention. Yet at the same time, the Project seems to unconsciously operate within fiction a schism between an ideal, self-conscious, demystifying fiction and an ideologically culpable "other," the realist novel of Western tradition. When Ollier's fictions seem to be casting a critical eye on themselves, they in fact run the risk of seeing only that "other." I therefore undertake, in chapters 2 and 3, an analysis aimed at discerning the relationship of the conscious Project to its unconscious or repressed "other." When the beleaguered fictional protagonist ascends to the realm of science fiction, he is split into a trinity of personages: the reading, writing, and fictional subjects. My investigation of their itineraries makes use of Freudian and Lacanian psychoanalytic terms and concepts; the status and relationships of the members of this trinity within the conscious Project, and in respect to fiction, are viewed in the sexual-political terms of a "family" metaphor. While the Project endorses the figurative death and expulsion of the conventional hero and the traditional father (or author) of fiction, the status of the reader is more ambiguous. Thus chapter 4 of this study examines the contradictory status attributed to the reader by reflexive fictions in general, and the New Novel in particular. The final chapter explicitly situates *Le Jeu d'enfant* in the context of one of the major issues of the structuralist era. It explores the relation of reflexivity in postmodern fiction to a generalized movement toward scientificity that characterizes that era and that, in literature, took the form of an effort at cultural, political, and ideological demystification (for example, the death of the subject). In this final chapter, an analysis of all the avatars of the perennial protagonist of *Le Jeu d'enfant* reveals the indissociable link between science and ideology and the tenacity of the subject as a principle of fictional construction, even in an era of reflexivity and demystification.

Much like a configuration of pebbles arranged on the beach by a child at play, the various incarnations of the subject of fiction (reader, writer, hero, father, son; male principle, female principle) form a shifting game plan throughout the cycle's eight volumes: "Je suis le voyageur, je suis le narrateur, l'exilé, l'intrus!" (*FS*, 56). An oscillation between the avatars of the subject dominates the *jeu* of *Le Jeu d'enfant* and provides the foundation for the cycle's reflexive, revolutionary project. The apparent spontaneity and gratuity of this play disguises, like the *fort-da* game of Freud's grandson, a complex structure of significant, unconscious family relations. Through an examination of the unconscious relations in *Le Jeu d'enfant,* this study proposes a critique of their self-conscious, reflexive Project, and hopes, thereby, to elaborate an approach to reading the reflexive, revolutionary works of contemporary literature.

I

The Death of the Protagonist: Demystifying Fiction

> Nous en a-t-on assez parlé du personnage! Et ça ne
> semble, hélas, pas près de finir. Cinquante années de
> maladie, le constat de son décès enregistré à maintes
> reprises par les plus sérieux essayistes, rien n'a encore
> réussi à le faire tomber du piédestal où l'avait placé le
> XIXᵉ siècle. C'est une momie à présent . . .
> —Robbe-Grillet

While disparate in setting, form, and narrative style, the first four novels of *Le Jeu d'enfant* have several common denominators: each presents an investigation conducted by a male protagonist in a foreign country whose language he does not speak and whose inhabitants confuse or threaten him. Each investigation eventually becomes a search for the protagonist's own identity and purpose in respect to the setting in which he finds himself. The protagonist's quest for self is grounded in the necessity to decipher his bewildering situation and is doubled by a secondary investigation, on the part of the reading and writing subjects, into the nature and function of the fictional protagonist. A wandering search provides the structure of these fictions, figuring as well the relationship of reader and writer to the unfolding narration. As these parallel investigations progress, however, a continual deterioration and disintegration of the protagonist takes place. An increasing degree of intertextual repetition contaminates the credibility of the story as it undermines the protagonist's individuality. Less and less the centering or focal point of a coherent narrative, the protagonist ultimately disappears and is presumed dead. The investigations into fictional structure and meaning are thus eroded at their apparent foundation—the protagonist of fiction.

It has been suggested that Hegel's *Phenomenology of Spirit* is a *Bildungsbiographie* with the "general spirit" as its protagonist, "the course of whose life is a painfully progressive self-education rendered in the plot-form of a circuitous journey from an initial self-division and departure, through diverse reconciliations and ever-renewing estrangements, conflicts, reversals, and crises of spiritual death and rebirth. This plot turns out to be the unwitting quest of the spirit to redeem itself by repossessing its own lost identity."[1] The notion of a pilgrimage of education—a questing journey coming back to itself with the achievement of greater self-consciousness—that forms the "plot" of Hegel's *Phenomenology* is taken up by George Lukács as the structure of the novelistic form. In *The Theory of the Novel* Lukács brings Hegel's historicization of aesthetic categories to bear upon his own formulation of the novel, which he considers the essential modern genre. Like Hegel, Lukács sees the Greek epic as the product of an integrated and organic civilization, one in which meaning is immanent within all of existence. Consciousness in an integrated civilization is immediate and undivided, so that the epic hero is internally homogeneous with his world:

> The epic hero is, strictly speaking, never an individual. It is traditionally thought that one of the essential characteristics of the epic is the fact that its theme is not a personal destiny but the destiny of a community. And rightly so, for the completeness, the roundness of the value system which determines the epic cosmos creates a whole which is too organic for any part of it to become so enclosed within itself, so dependent upon itself, as to find itself as an interiority—*i.e.,* to become a personality.[2]

For Lukács, the beginning of philosophy marks the end of this organic and immanent world, for philosophy is symptomatic of the rift between the individual and the world, between the inside and the outside, between the self and itself. Philosophy, for Lukács, thus inaugurates the play of exclusion and inclusion that marks Western thought.

The epic hero gives way to the epic individual living in estrangement from the external world, and therefore necessarily from his own essence. The epic cedes its place to the novel, whose fragmentation and heterogeneity make it representative of modern existence: "The novel is the epic of an age in which the extensive totality of life is no longer directly given, in which the immanence of meaning in life has become a problem, yet which still thinks in terms of a totality."[3] The structure of the novel now figures a search for the meaning that has become separated from and elevated above ordinary existence. The novel, for Lukács, is primarily biographical in form, structuring a fictional architecture in which unity and totality typically derive from the life story of a problematic individual seeking the meaning of his own existence. This individual has acquired a personality whose psychology is developed and analyzed in terms of its alienation.

The first four books of *Le Jeu d'enfant,* like many early New Novels, aim at a demystification—a *détournement*—of formulations of the novel such as that proposed by Lukács, which came to dominate Western fiction in the nineteenth century.[4] In the typology of the novel developed in *The Theory of the Novel,* Lukács gives a philosophical basis to certain recurrent trends in nineteenth-century narrative; the *roman d'apprentissage* depicting a young hero's journey toward mature knowledge also describes a stage in the novel's search for its own form. In adopting and subverting the structure of a self-interrogative journey, the fictions of Ollier's first cycle project an anti-*Bildungsroman* or *Unbildungsroman* whose development purports to undermine the traditional tenets and teachings of fiction, to unlearn an inherited tradition. Lukács's enunciation of the novel and the ideology in which it is rooted can be seen as the "other" from which and against which these fictions formulate themselves. The biography of an exemplary personality and his search for meaning is erected as the center of fiction only to be progressively marginalized and problematized. A bewildering doubling and subsequent multiplication of the protagonist's self duplicates the initial division in the Hegelian development of Spirit, but the notion of a progress toward unity on the part of the protagonist is subjected to a perpetual subversion and erosion.

The eight texts of *Le Jeu d'enfant* constitute a sustained inquiry into the nature of fiction. In taking the Lukácsian model of the novel as its "other," the first cycle of *Le Jeu d'enfant* seeks to define its own status through negation of what it is not.[5] It will undertake to accom-

plish this by means of a journey of reeducation aimed at the reading
and writing subjects of fiction as well as at the form itself. For the New
Novel sees itself above all as a *recherche,* as a narrative that investigates
and interrogates itself, questioning the ideological bases of novelistic
conventions. The risk run by this project resides in the Hegelian underpinnings of its questing structure: the definition of self through negation of the "other" threatens to result in a synthetic entity where the
desired distinctions tend to merge. It is in the light of this radical
project and its dangers that I will examine the strategies of demystification conducted throughout the first relay of *Le Jeu d'enfant* that are
aimed at the traditional hero of fiction.

I. *La Mise en scène:* Setting Up the Hero

Published in 1958, the first novel of *Le Jeu d'enfant* makes use of a
stereotypical narrative form drawn from popular French literature—
the colonial novel—in order to present two important Lukácsian bases
of a novel: a biographical hero, of sorts, or at any rate a fictional
subject, and that subject's search for identity and meaning. *La Mise en
scène* begins and ends with a sleepless night spent in Assameur, a
North African capital. No personal pronouns appear in the initial and
final segments, which seem to be filtered through the consciousness of
the unnamed and solitary protagonist. The middle section is a third-
person narration apparently centering on the same protagonist featured in the initial and final scenes, who now acquires a name and a
mission: Lassalle is an engineer whose task it is to establish a potential
road to a mine located in a wild, unmapped region of the North
African mountains. He is not without some guidelines, however, as a
colleague named Moritz has left preliminary sketches for a similar
investigation undertaken several years earlier. Some traces remain of an
even earlier effort under the direction of a Morel or a Moret, who has
since left the company. Armed with the maps, notes, and sketches of
his predecessors, Lassalle will attempt to impose a feasible route on the
uncharted blank space, the "tache blanche, une tache en forme d'ellipse" (*Ms,* 102) on the map he inherits.
    A member of the colonial elite and provided for in relative comfort

while at Assameur, Lassalle experiences increasing difficulties as he nears the unmapped ellipse. He is ill at ease with the change in climate, language, and customs; he suffers from the heat, the insects, and the nausea of riding in an automobile over winding roads. During the ascent on muleback into the mountain region, Lassalle is overtaken by Ba Iken, an Arab who has served in the colonial army and who can offer his services as translator and guide to the engineer en route to their common destination: the village of Ba Iken, situated near the center of the uncharted zone on Lassalle's map.

Lassalle interrogates Ba Iken on two subjects that have aroused his curiosity since his arrival: the fatal stabbing of a young girl whom he had glimpsed in the infirmary at Assameur, and the identity and fate of a geologist named Hessing or Gessing who had quite recently followed much the same itinerary as Lassalle himself. The information supplied by Ba Iken conflicts with what Lassalle has been led to believe by the colonial officials, displacing the time of the geologist's visit as well as the location of the stabbing, which may or may not have taken place in Ba Iken's own village. Lassalle's curiosity is stimulated by the apparent contradictions, and his initial search for a path to the mine is soon doubled by an investigation into the true circumstances of these mysterious events.

Pressed by Lassalle to clarify the confusing events, Ba Iken becomes the spokesman for the tribe, defusing the engineer's suspicions and displacing the respective time and place of the geologist's visit and the girl's murder. With his light hair and eyes, Ba Iken is a physical transition between the European and the Arabs, as well as a translator. All meetings with the local inhabitants are mediated through Ba Iken; his clarifications become a theatrical mise-en-scène, a scenario, where the events are staged or ordered into a version acceptable for viewing by the colonial intruder. Discerning certain flaws and evasions in Ba Iken's scenario, Lassalle becomes increasingly aware of the existence of an alternate, indigenous explanation for the mysterious circumstances. Lassalle gets glimpses of this variant version through a mute village boy who aids him in his daily explorations and eventually helps him discover a practicable path to the mine. With his blond hair, his penchant for guiding Lassalle's search, and his mimed responses to the engineer's questions, the boy becomes the theatrical son of Ba Iken.

His version of events takes its place alongside that of Ba Iken, which it nevertheless contradicts in several important areas. The multiple mise-en-scènes or theatrical settings with which Lassalle is faced place him in the position of the alienated Lukácsian hero, who similarly seeks the meaning that has fled from a degraded and heterogeneous world. But the settings offered to Lassalle also appear to be setups: traps laid by the colonized to detour the imperialist in his efforts to impose his own sense of order on a foreign terrain.

The engineer seeks out panoramic views in order to establish the most feasible approach to the mine: "Lassalle aime les vues d'ensemble: comme Moritz deux ans auparavant, il a tenu à monter dès le premier jour sur le djebel Addar, face à l'Angoun, de manière à se faire une idée générale du problème à rèsoudre, à embrasser d'un seul coup d'oeil toute l'étendue du versant sur lequel il va s'ingénier à tracer une piste" (*Ms,* 119). Lassalle finds that the oblique lighting of a rising or setting sun provides a more exact perspective of the scene than a noonday sun: "La lumière, verticale à cette heure du jour, écrase la montagne. Ce n'est plus la clarté oblique qui façonne au matin le juste modelé des formes, donnant la mesure des intervalles exacts, et qui la restitue le soir avant que la nuit s'installe" (*Ms,* 153). Just as he attempts to see the landscape clearly as a whole, Lassalle seeks a totalizing view of the situation he finds in the village. The noonday clarity of the various direct versions of these events does not seem to furnish an acceptable picture of the whole situation. Lassalle prefers to examine the events and claims in the oblique light of his own verifications, deductions, and reconstitutions. He therefore discredits most of Ba Iken's scenario, substituting for it a perspective glimpsed from various different angles. Just as he relies on Moritz's sketches and maps as well as on the boy's guidance in developing "un tracé cohérent" (*Ms,* 195) in the unmapped region, Lassalle relies on fragments of borrowed explanations to fill in the logical gaps in his understanding of the recent events and to reconstruct what he hopes will be a total and unique scenario.

Lassalle's progress in producing the scenario is slow. He lacks confidence in the reading he has made of the stories, pantomimes, conversations, and encounters he has seen or heard in his unfamiliar setting: "Mais la lassitude physique, l'inhabituelle contrainte de la chaleur et la transposition forcément infidèle des cheminements tortueux du dialecte parent faits et gestes d'une frange d'inconsistence derrière laquelle ils se retranchent, rebelles à toute interprétation, inaccessibles, insignifiants" (*Ms*, 226).

Lassalle's difficulty in working out an adequate picture of these mysteries is paralleled by his inability to write the journal where he intends to keep a record of his activities. From the beginning, he deliberates as to the content and scope of his daily notation. He finally opts for a skeletal outline of the day's activities that pertain strictly to the mining route and do not venture onto the improbable terrain of the mysterious scenarios. Although he has severely limited the scope of his daily entry, he cannot seem to keep it up to date with his activities, nor can he keep it entirely free from nonessential or speculative material. The simplified notation is never a satisfactory adequation to his daily actions, and it is precisely what he is trying not to write down—the mysterious events in the village—that comes to obsess him.

Lassalle gradually begins to suspect that the geologist and young girl had been involved in a triangular conflict whose outcome was fatal for both. The engineer's investigation of the ambiguous circumstances grows more urgent as he feels himself increasingly identified with the geologist who preceded him, and increasingly threatened with a similarly violent fate. Lassalle discovers an empty camera case with the inscription, Dr. H. Lessing.[6] The hostility he senses in the village and an ambiguous encounter with the dead girl's twin sister lead Lassalle to replace Lessing in an imagined or dreamed scenario; the protagonist of the scene is denoted only as *l'étranger,* and his adventure is that of Lassalle transposed to the location of Lessing's encampment. Lassalle now remembers the scene in the infirmary and reinterprets the dying girl's startled glance as a look of recognition. He begins to fear the man he assumes to be the dead girl's husband.

Despite his conscientious review and analysis of the various bits of information, Lassalle hesitates to formulate a definitive version linking motives and murders. He manages to create a coherent version of the troubling events only when he sees and copies a reputedly prehistoric rock carving, which finally stages the scenario whose elements he had already assembled:

L'homme vient d'être frappé, sa monture l'abandonne; le cavalier se tourne à présent vers l'enfant et s'apprête à lui faire subir le même sort. . . . Mais c'est postuler un double meurtre et déjà lui prêter toutes sortes de mobiles: rite, vengeance, trahison, jalousie. . . . Rien n'empêche évidemment de considérer les cinq figures comme un tableau unique. . . .
Entre l'enfant, le cavalier et l'âne, la relation est immédiate. Entre ces trois figures et les deux dernières, elle est plus discutable, plus ambiguë. La tentation est grande néanmoins de lier au premier groupe les trois figures de gauche et d'en induire une unité d'action propre à renouveler l'intérêt dramatique de la scène. Mais c'est postuler un double meurtre. (*Ms, 255*)

In spite of its lack of perspective and dubious unity, the carved scene provides for Lassalle a *mise en abyme* of precisely the mise-en-scène he has been imagining. Lassalle is never the primary author of his unwritten drama; just as he makes use of others' fragments of information to piece together a logical development of events, he relies on an anonymous representation of another possible crime to provide a totality for the scenario he envisions. Just as his mining route is "borrowed" from others, his reconstruction of the mystery by means of the rock carving is a retracing of an already dubious representation, a spurious setup for gullible tourists seeking exotic and prehistoric artifacts. The theatrical vocabulary points to the staged—selected, partial, interested— nature of fictional settings and puts into question the outcome of the protagonist's effort to find a meaning and an identity in relation to his world.

Once the prospective route (and the plausible motive for the murders) has been deduced, Lassalle prepares to leave. His uneasy feeling that he had somehow been in the same kind of danger as Lessing is dispelled as his own identity reasserts itself. Lassalle's name, which had not been mentioned for five chapters during which links with Lessing's fate had multiplied alarmingly, finally reappears as he prepares to return to the innocuous colonial sphere. Crossing a quickly rising river, Lassalle loses the camera case bearing Lessing's name. When he regains Assameur, however, a colonial official confuses him at first sight with Lessing, a confusion all the more unsettling since, as the official reports, Lessing was recently killed in an accident in the remote mountains. The information provided by the official confirms Lassalle's suspicions as to the itinerary and dates of Lessing's adventure. Lassalle is asked to provide a brief résumé of his mining project, to which he assents. But his résumé will reflect only the skeletal outline of his daily agenda; although the official's comments have supported the engineer's hypothesis on Lessing's fate, Lassalle can say nothing of the murders. He would be incapable of proving the truth of his claims, made up as they are of speculations on other people's assertions, contradictions, and admissions, and now lacking any corroborating physical evidence. The final, official version of the two deaths is a tribal mise-en-scène: open-ended, vague, deliberately inconclusive.

Despite the potential for character evolution in the circular narrative movement of *La Mise en scène,* which in a traditional novel would figure the acquisition of some essential insight on the part of the protagonist, no development or interior change is perceptible in Lassalle. His acquired knowledge is purely anecdotal and is never internalized as an enlightened awareness of, for example, his colonialist status or culpability. Lassalle remains a very partial character whose major traits are stubborn curiosity and a tendency toward physical malaise. Just as Lassalle cannot be seen as entirely unique and discrete from other characters, his unvoiced story is not his own. Lacking any other distinguishing traits, Lassalle is primarily a will to make sense of an original reality mediated by the borrowed texts he uses to explain it.

Lassalle's reconstruction of the murders is no more his own than the route he proposes to the colonial mining company; both impulses—that of building a road as well as of solving the mystery—stem from equally colonial instincts. Just as the West in its colonial era sought to profit from the natural resources of unknown regions, Lassalle attempts to elicit a definitive meaning from a multiplicity of possibilities, sensing that his safety and identity lie in that unique sense. In the same way that his agenda suppressed a multitude of facts and speculations, his story about the murders would be a colonization of previous versions. His account would be a single perspective, a straight, logical path suppressing the multiple and contradictory indigenous versions upon which it is based.

The coexistence of these two types of *récit* is figured in the novel by two literal paths, one tribal and the other colonial, descending from the mountains: "Dès lors les deux routes—la route moderne à voie unique et la route tribale aux multiples variantes—poursuivent de concert, parallèles sur les secteurs plans, sensiblement divergentes dès qu'un creux ou une bosse vient rompre la monotonie du relief, le sentier franchissant de front l'obstacle que la piste aborde de biais" (*Ms,* 248–49). Obstacles are met head-on by the modern, colonial route, whose univocal logic allows for only one right way to build a road or tell a story.[7] Discredited as he is in his own singularity, however, Lassalle is incapable of establishing a *voie unique* or a *voix unique,* a single path or voice, a coherent version of events that would occupy a privileged, singular status over the others. Although his deductions seem plausible, he cannot himself enunciate a story about them. The tribal versions have conducted a successful guerrilla-style campaign; colonialism is undercut on the level of Lassalle's unformulated *récit* as well as in the final, official version of the two deaths.

The white ellipse on Lassalle's map is the space of the fiction he should, as a colonialist, be able to enunciate. He should be able to trace in that lacunary space a unique path and a logical story. When he crosses the river during his descent, the map gets wet:

> Lassalle déploie la carte d'état-major sur les coussins. Le papier est tout à fait sec à présent, mais gondolé. La tache blanche, longue d'une quinzaine de centimètres, occupe le centre du pli inférieur de la feuille. Trois mots seulement la parcourent en guise d'explication: "Zone non cartographiée." Ce n'est évidemment pas une explication, mais c'est la seule mention qui figure dans toute la tache blanche, l'eau ayant délavé les quelques coups de crayon tracés l'autre jour dans l'intention de combler la lacune. (*Ms,* 275)

Although he seems to have developed a workable route and a plausible explanation, the tracings that Lassalle made of that route and that explanation are easily erased; the ellipse remains unmapped and the story unwritten, *inédit.* Only the material colonialism of the proposed route is enforced. Lassalle himself has barely managed to salvage a precarious identity.

In the Lukácsian vision of the novel, the meaningful search of a biographical hero creates a unity between the disparate elements of the
heterogeneous reality to be represented. Limits are posed on what is to
be narrated; the world is narrowed to the life story of the hero. The
remaining mass of heterogeneous phenomena is made to relate to the
hero or is suppressed. The extreme of this novelistic convention is the
Balzacian description, where every facet of setting mirrors the character, who reciprocally inflects decor with his or her personality. The
seeming totality is in fact highly selective: in *La Mise en scène,* it
becomes clear that any story or meaning offered is a colonial suppression of all that is left untold. When the assaults on Lassalle's identity
bring into question the notion of biographical closure, doubts are
equally cast upon the ultimate significance he would give to his colonial adventure. Narrative multiplicity and uncertainty, which would
be suppressed in a traditional novel, insinuate themselves in *La Mise en
scène* in a disruptive fashion, pointing to the subject's tenuous hold on
a meaning that, though plausible, is far from unique.

The final totality of meaning achieved at the outcome of this novel
seems somehow fragile, disjointed, and unvoiced in proportion to the
three-hundred-odd pages of textual space it fills. Something has happened in the space of the fiction to undermine the meaning organized
by its protagonist. *La Mise en scène* provides an apparently traditional
setting—a colonial adventure—for a subversive setup of certain novelistic conventions (a hero and a mystery to be solved) and of the expectations associated with those conventions. The demystification envisioned by this fictional staging aims to expose the repressed underpinnings of the colonialism of fiction and to point to something else
that fiction may become.

II. *Le Maintien de l'ordre:* The Fragility of Fictional Order

While the protagonist of *La Mise en scène* survived his adventure with
a precarious but intact identity, and while a completed story of murder
and revenge was reconstructed in that novel, the fictional subject and
his search assume alternate incarnations in the following books, and
with decreasing degrees of success. *Le Maintien de l'ordre* presents a

crime drama in which the protagonist has been followed and watched by two men. The title chosen for the English translation of this novel, *Law and Order*, points to the continued interrogation of a coercive Western sense of order faced with a non-Western ordering of perceptions and events. The setting is a North African city, a compendium of imported Western civilization and an older indigenous culture. A statue in *le parc Wilson* points eloquently to the interior of the country, apparently signaling a call to invasion: "Mais l'envolée martiale, sitôt franchi le premier rideau d'arbres, se heurte à un obstacle dérisoire: quelques baraques en bois, une salle de restaurant, une buvette, et, plus à droite, des terrains de jeu, huit rectangles de terre ocre séparés par de petites barrières de planches" (*Mo*, 31). The wilderness to be conquered is nothing but an inglorious extension of the banality of Western culture, whose games have been transferred to alien soil. In *Le Maintien de l'ordre*, colonialism is no longer as straightforward a case of political oppression and economic exploitation as it had appeared to be in *La Mise en scène*. Here the two civilizations have intertwined, feeding off each other in an uneasy but long-standing relationship of economic interaction, with Arabs and French working together in the colonial administration.

What had been the narrative code of the beginning and final sections of *La Mise en scène* is fairly consistent throughout *Le Maintien de l'ordre:* what is given to be read seems to be the unspoken observations and mental processes of an unnamed subject. Vague clues about the protagonist and his situation are gradually pieced together. He appears to be a French colonial administrator; in the course of his departmental investigations, he has witnessed some events that seem to point to criminal activities on the part of a band of individuals working in tacit accord with the police. The protagonist has seen some Arab youths who have apparently been abducted and tortured; their kidnappers, among whom figure some policemen, do not try to conceal their activities from the investigator: "Le gros homme appelé Ruiz est en bas des marches, les poings sur les hanches. Il fait un signe de tête désignant l'ensemble du hangar, l'ensemble des personnages, et avec un haussement de sourcils, un sourire large, cordial, sans retenue: 'Il faut bien s'entraider' (plus exactement: 'Il faut bien se donner un coup de main')" (*Mo*, 198). The protagonist's response must not have exhib-

ited the desired degree of helpfulness, for shortly afterwards he becomes aware of two men following him and waiting below his window.
He feels threatened but is not sure if the surveillance aims at actual
physical harm or simple intimidation to prevent him from voicing his
suspicions to authorities outside the corrupt police administration.

These events, observations, and hypotheses are presented in a narrative sequence whose progression is disrupted and unlinear. Although
some temporal indications are provided, the identity, significance, and
real sequence of many passages can only be hypothetically determined. A certain inexactitude in the subject's recollection of some
events or scenes, as in the passage cited above, further complicates any
effort to extract a coherent story line from the repetitive and disjointed
narrative.

The protagonist is himself impelled to make a coherent account of
the events he has witnessed and the hypotheses he has formed; he
seems to feel he should communicate what he has learned to L..., a
friend living outside the city. Thus the narration occasionally incorporates his attempts to compose a letter while hiding in his room. His
aim in writing the account recalls Lassalle's effort to limit his daily
journal to a strict inventory of the essential information concerning his
investigation: "La seule chose à présent, est de tout consigner le plus
clairement possible, sans détails oiseux, sans rien omettre d'essentiel"
(*Mo*, 106). But the protagonist of this crime drama does not achieve
even the engineer's minimal success in translating his experiences into
words. After writing the date, he is incapable of continuing: "La
première feuille du bloc-notes est toujours vierge, hormis la date
inscrite en haut, à gauche: *lundi treize août*. La lettre reste à écrire, à
rédiger le résumé intelligible de ces trois dernières journées" (*Mo*, 120).

Each time the protagonist sits at his desk to write the letter, he is
distracted by a map of the city fixed to the wall. Much of the narration
is given over to a contemplation of this map. The chaotic edifices and
streets of the old city form a network so complex and varied as to seem
completely unpatterned and irrational: "C'est comme si tout avait été
calculé au mieux pour gêner le passage, entraver la circulation,
empêcher les réflections et l'entretien, nuire à la surveillance, déjouer
les poursuites, favoriser le désordre et l'anarchie" (*Mo*, 110-11). When
contemplated for a time, however, the anarchic map can suddenly take

on a different configuration, as in a figure-ground illusion where two alternative objects can be discerned consecutively from a single image: "Mais il est une autre façon de voir les choses. . . . le plan de la vieille ville peut être regardé non plus comme le placage de striures citadines sur un fond uni de terrain vierge, mais comme la représentation minutieuse, sur le fond strié des édifices, d'un extraordinaire ensemble de voies de pénétration" (*Mo*, 112). In this second vision, the city map provides a figure for interpretive overdetermination, for a multiplicity of ways in and out that defies any single course.

Yet another reading of the map is the one provided by the administrator's symbols denoting the scene of various crimes occurring during the recent months. The multiplicity of the phenomena to be recounted underscores the inadequacy of the protagonist's attempted report: "Est-il exposé plus éloquent que ce canevas de croix multicolores se dessinant peu à peu sur le grand rectangle mauve, se développant en guirlandes à l'annonce des désordres et de leur répression?" (*Mo*, 121). The profusion of the city as schematized by its map and the multiplicity of its possible readings provides a figure of the protagonist's inability to put into words a single coherent reading of the recent events. An intelligible summary is impossible because the heterogeneous, displaced events defy the protagonist's efforts to distill and inscribe them in the logical, linear account of a letter. While Lassalle was able to make at least a marginal written account of some of his activities for each given date, the administrator can only write down the temporal specification. Since the protagonist is incapable of repressing the disordered events, his own account is censored. The "other" of the subject's story is a disorder that now refuses to be colonized, and that imposes itself by means of the map's hypnotic, paralyzing effect.

The protagonist of *Le Maintien de l'ordre* seems at once more aware and less materially effective than Lassalle. He has a detective's grasp of the events and of their import, is well informed about the criminal gang exerting its influence in the city, and even seems to predict the future course of events: "Un seul lien les unit: une même volonté d'humilier, de se prouver leur force à tout prix, non qu'ils ne sachent que leur ordre est condamné, et sa ruine imminente, mais ils veulent retarder le plus longtemps possible l'échéance" (*Mo*, 196). This protagonist knows how all the pieces of the mystery fit together except for his own role. His search centers on his own safety. He knows that he constitutes an obstacle to be overcome but is not sure of the nature of the pressure to be exerted on him. He feels he should make his conclusions known but is incapable of acting upon his conviction. His indecisiveness is characterized by a certain oscillation in his behavior, and by a marked inability to concentrate. His failure to sustain a focused attention prevents him from organizing a coherent account of his observations and deductions.

The protagonist's inability to write about the events is doubled by an ineffectual attempt to enunciate a spoken or conscious discourse. At several points in the course of the novel, the narrative code shifts suddenly from a narration where personal pronouns are suppressed into a first-person declaration. Each time the "je" of the speaking subject surfaces in the narration, it is to utter a single sentence describing a past action or reaction on the part of the protagonist. The declarative mode is never sustained, however; the narration always returns to an interiority in which the subject never speaks in his own voice. The protagonist's final attempt to produce a conscious discourse, his visit to the mysterious villa in the company of an Arab policeman, has a strange outcome. Several first-person statements evoke the approach to the villa, where two men silently and ominously await the pair. A certain apprehension accompanies the protagonist's final declaration, "J'étais là, marchant sur les graviers et Saïd derrière moi, tout près, presque à mes côtés. Les deux hommes, là-bas, ne bougeaient toujours pas. La voiture ne leur disait sans doute rien, son conducteur non plus . . . c'était plutôt l'uniforme de Saïd qui devait les intriguer, les retenir sur le moment d'une réaction immédiate ou d'une apostrophe brutale" (*Mo,* 188–89). The protagonist seems to feel his own identity cannot protect him (he is merely the driver of the car); his final effort to assert himself, by visiting the villa and by attempting to speak about the visit, gives way under the pressure of his apprehension as he approaches the two men:

> Dans le silence suspendu au franchissement de cet espace dérisoire, les jambes se mouvaient sur place sans progresser, les pieds allaient et venaient en cadence comme sur un tapis se déroulant en sens contraire,

les murs glissaient sans heurts comme un décor bien huilé, les deux
silhouettes s'approchaient doucement, irrésistiblement, immobiles et
indistinctes côte à côte en haut des marches, et brusquement se sont
trouvées là, tout près, à portée de la main. (*Mo, 189*)

This closeness at hand ("a portée de la main") to violence recalls the
ambiguous helping hand ("coup de main") of the earlier encounter
with the torturers. Inability to act—to raise a hand—neutralizes the
subject, who never again surfaces in a first-person declaration. He has
become a silhouette, a shooting-gallery target, an element in a mechanical scene or theatrical decor.

The protagonist has been unable to sustain either his will to act or
his will to enunciate a self-conscious discourse. The novel ends soon
after, with nothing resolved or written. The administrator's occasional
efforts to recount his actions or emotions, which ought to provide
essential psychological indices or clues to the mystery, point rather to
his failure as an effective center for the development of a conventional
roman policier. If the novelistic hero is supposed to seek his own
identity, eventually achieving the "mature virility" of greater self-
consciousness,[8] this protagonist in no way qualifies as a hero. Each
attempt at self-awareness relapses into unconsciousness, just as every
effort to make sense of events is overcome by the bewildering heterogeneity of the events in question.

Even given his failure to enunciate a conscious account of his experience, the protagonist's unvoiced observations might be taken as a
totalizing view of the situation if they were to develop coherently.
However, just as the protagonist is disturbed in his ability to make a
récit, he is equally inadequate as a vehicle for meaningful descriptive
observations. A considerable, even excessive, amount of the narration
is spent detailing the protagonist's perceptions from his seventh-floor
window; what is perceived is not reduced to a meaningful background
for the subject's progress, as it would be in a Lukácsian or realist novel,
but rather foregrounds itself so as to prevent any coherent progression.
Despite his panoramic elevation, the protagonist's perception is never
clear or stable, just as Lassalle's panoramic views were always, at
bottom, staged and illusory. From the opening lines of the novel, the

protagonist sees everything through a screen of smoke, dust, mist, or heat:

> Sur un grand écran uni, lisse, tendu d'un bout à l'autre de l'horizon, scintille une poussière pâle, ténue, une buée grisâtre voilant les vibrations de l'air et les remous de l'eau. Tout en haut, affluant du large, de gros nuages s'amoncellent, se disloquent, s'éloignent lentement vers le nord; en bas, de longues vagues déferlent, se brisent sur les hauts fonds, s'épandent sur les rochers plats qui bordent le rivage. Dans l'espace intermédiaire, la transition s'opère insensiblement: ciel et mer sont fondus en une matière indivise, translucide, couleur de plomb. Aucune ligne de partage ne s'interpose: en tout point filtre la même lumière tamisée, à l'éclat vif et aveuglant. (*Mo*, 9)

The horizon is never clearly distinguishable, nor can distances be fairly estimated. Many objects seem subject to a constant vibration that renders them unstable. A similar oscillation occurs on the level of the narration, both in a constant temporal switching and in the frequent repetition of passages, often unchanged, from earlier descriptions or from *La Mise en scène*.

Just as the illusion of progress is undermined on the level of the narration, the description of individual scenes, channeled through the subject's perceptions, seems fragmentary and sporadic rather than totalizing. The protagonist's inability to piece together a coherent story of recent events stems from a deeper disturbance in which his very perceptions are disjointed and partial. The protagonist's typical stance—looking out the window—is a figure of his mode of perception. Geometrical precisions abound in his observations, since he sees everything as framed by or inscribed within grills, windows, doorways, curtains, rearview mirrors, and so on: "Perez est toujours assis sur le banc, jambes écartées, bras allongés à hauteur d'épaule sur les lattes de bois. Sa tête s'inscrit juste dans le coin gauche de la fenêtre. . . . Le rideau, qui tombe légèrement de biais, découvre une partie du trottoir et de la chaussée. Des reflets se jouent sur la vitre, qui doivent permettre de voir sans être vu. Mais ce n'est pas une certitude" (*Mo*, 48). That the view is framed and partially masked by the window and

curtains underscores a theatricality in the protagonist's perceptions
not unlike that imposed on Lassalle: the administrator wants to create
a "tableau clair" (Mo, 121) of recent events; he feels part of a "décor
bien huilé" (Mo, 189). Even when he participates in an action, he is
fundamentally a spectator. His perceptions are never primary or total
but are always framed by various artificial stages and cut up into their
static component elements like the individual, successive frames of a
film.

A lighthouse on the coast provides one of the many spotlights in this
novel, illuminating the mise-en-scène that is presented as the subject's
perception, of either a landscape or an event. The light sources, both
natural and artificial, point to the theatrical, cinematic—that is,
selected—nature of what is given to be seen: "La nappe plus dense qui
couvrait le rivage s'était disloquée: des pans entiers de brume s'étaient
levés, démasquant d'étroits quartiers de ciel, d'où les rayons, plongeant
de biais comme les projectures d'une machinerie, étaient tombés au
hasard sur la ville, signalant des points précis à l'attention, très
éloignés les uns des autres, dans un ordre qui échappait à toute déf-
inition" (Mo, 64). The oblique lighting that for Lassalle seemed to give
a more accurate picture of a panoramic view in La Mise en scène now
underscores the partiality of the subject's vision; what he sees is a
collection of fragmentary tableaux whose order he neither controls
nor comprehends. The presence of all that is not given to be seen—all
that is suppressed by the limitations of the subject's biased perceptions—imposes itself through the manifest partiality of his vision.
This partiality can no longer be attributed to outside forces, as with
Lassalle, but becomes the protagonist's basic mode of perception.
Materially less effective than Lassalle, the colonial official is proportionately more cognizant of his own theatricality, his inclusion in some
narrative equivalent of a film noir.

The protagonist's efforts to assert himself as a presence and take
control of his experience never achieve the psychological validity of the
conventional hero. The interior monologue that constitutes the major
part of the narration is never interior in any psychological sense: we are
never the privileged spectators of intimate feelings or reflections. We
have only indirect, sparse indications of the physical or mental state of
the narrative's protagonist. We discover that, like Lassalle, the pro-

tagonist of *Le Maintien de l'ordre* exhibits a tendency towards physical malaise. He suffers from insomnia and from the heat and is particularly sensitive to the blinding daylight of the North African city. His curiosity is diminished by comparison to Lassalle's; this protagonist has lost some of the stubborn attentiveness that characterized the engineer. The subject's unreality as a psychological entity prevents him from conceiving of his own death as an absolute annihilation. It is envisioned instead as a scenario from a gangster movie:

> Deux voitures noires surgissent de l'ombre, tous feux éteints, roulant lentement à vingt mètres d'écart sur le boulevard désert. L'homme sort de chez lui, rabat la porte qui claque, fait quelques pas sur le trottoir. La première voiture approche, la rafale éclate, l'homme chancelle, tombe à genoux. La voiture passe, accélère, part à toute allure. Le blessé à genoux se tient le ventre, relève la tête, essaie de crier. Une fenêtre s'ouvre dans un immeuble voisin, une autre s'allume. La seconde voiture approche, la rafale éclate: le blessé s'écroule. (*Mo*, 94)

A borrowed excerpt from *La Mise en scène* follows, in which Lassalle imagines Lessing's murder. Thus the imagined death becomes fictional to the second degree: pictured by one fictional character about another and linked to a third. In the closing passage, the streetlights are slowly dimmed to mark the protagonist's death, while the neighboring windows light up one by one. The cinematic effects—the framing, the lighting, the scenario—are more vivid than any emotion attributable to the subject. It is too manifestly a borrowed, stereotypical event to be psychologically convincing. Its intertextual borrowings from film and fiction similarly challenge conventions of originality, realistic immediacy, and verisimilitude.

It is precisely for this lack of communicated emotion that one reviewer has reproached the novel: "From Robbe-Grillet's masterpiece we get a very good idea of what it is like to be jealous, but Ollier fails to convey to us the reality of fear, if that is what he is trying to do."[9] That the "reality of fear" is not conveyed in this novel is an exemplary truth for the demystification of the fictional subject. The failure of this particular subject to anchor a meaningful discourse, to communicate emotion, is designed to point to the peculiar status of the more "suc-

cessful" traditional heroes. Drained of its personality, the fictional
subject is seen here as a technical device for focusing and processing
verbal description.[10] The fictional narration is figured as a series of
selected tableaux projected through the (semi)consciousness of the
protagonist and animated by the machinations of a traditional reading, which sees a real personality in the protagonist and progress in a
static textuality. The hero has become one of many windows in the text
whose frames and hinges have suddenly imposed themselves on the
reader's field of vision.

There is no conclusion to this adventure; the protagonist never
leaves his room, never writes his letter, and is never attacked. Whatever
story can be reconstructed from the narration is even more partial and
less conclusive than the colonial adventure of the first novel, based as it
is on a biographical subject who is correspondingly less credible. The
hero as a well-oiled instrument for instilling meaning in the novel has
become a faulty tool requiring much more effort on the part of the
reader who manipulates it to produce a story from the text. While an
ironic order is being maintained in the corrupt colonial city, an order
of textual instability, fragmentation, and theatricality that began to
appear in *La Mise en scène* has increasingly asserted itself. The "other"
of traditional fiction grows stronger as the protagonist-hero is progressively minimized.

III. *Eté indien:* The Indian Summer of the Fictional Hero

Eté indien, the third fiction of *Le Jeu d'enfant,* returns to a named
protagonist: Morel's adventure is nominally that of a love story, perhaps a musical comedy. At any rate, it is permeated with cinematic
allusions. As in *La Mise en scène,* the first and final sections of the
novel present a narration in which any overt reference to the fictional
subject is suppressed. Both sections describe an aerial view of a wild,
marshy peninsula that might be located in Mexico. The initial descriptions of the two passages are nearly identical. While the first section
seems to indicate a hypothetical panorama, "On imaginerait un
monde chaotique, des terres bourbeuses, morcelées, la jungle, l'eau des
fleuves charriant des bêtes mortes. . . ." (*Ei, 7*), the last section, writ-

ten in the present tense, apparently describes a flight in progress: "C'est une terre chaotique qui surgit dans la trouée des nuages— bourbeuse, morcelée" (*Ei*, 213). Morel's vision directs the central portion of the narration. He has just landed in what appears to be New York City after a long and uncomfortable flight. It is late summer; he has been commissioned by his superiors, Moritz and Münch, to investigate the possibilities of producing a film in the primitive terrain glimpsed, remembered, or imagined in the initial segment. He will spend a weekend in the metropolis in order to interview an archaeologist, J.J. (pronounced Gigi in French), about potential locations for the filming.

While sight-seeing, Morel meets Cynthia. Their romantic interlude causes him to miss his flight and extend his stay through Monday. Although the densely populated island seems at times oddly familiar, as though he has visited it before, Morel nevertheless relies heavily on J.J. and Cynthia as guides and interpreters. The narration of Morel's encounters and excursions switches frequently from Mexico to New York, incorporating scenes apparently imagined by Morel and passages borrowed directly or in altered form from the first two novels of *Le Jeu d'enfant.*

Like Lassalle and the colonial administrator of the preceding novels, Morel seeks out elevated, panoramic views. He is disappointed to find that the scenes viewed from on high, like those seen by the protagonist of *Le Maintien de l'ordre,* are often obscured: either filtered through screens or masked by other objects. While the earlier protagonists do not seem to question the totality of their perceptions, Morel is always aware of the partiality of his vision. He doubts the validity of his observations, and his first impressions invariably turn out to be wrong, corrected by a plethora of statements in parentheses: "Par la porte fermée, il entrevoit le comptoir, les tabourets vissés au plancher (la salle est vide; était-elle donc si exiguë?), et à l'opposite, dans un lointain ensoleillé, mais se dégageant mal des édifices environnants, le gratte-ciel de verre qu'il avait un instant contemplé (il l'aurait cru plus neuf, plus élancé)" (*Ei*, 120). Morel is equally doubtful of his ability to carry out the investigation he has been assigned: "Moritz le fait bien rire, qui perd un temps considérable en parlotes oiseuses et tergiversations injustifiées, et subitement s'affole . . . l'envoie incontinent vers une destination lointain, exécuter dans un délai trop court un travail pour lequel il n'est assurément pas le plus qualifié" (*Ei,* 171). Morel does not, in effect, conduct his investigation or even his tourism with much competence: he gets lost, is nearly run over by a taxi, is consistently late, and even forgets the name of the archaeologist.

Morel's decreasing efficacy is accompanied by a growing passivity in comparison with the earlier protagonists. It is Cynthia who takes the initiative in their encounter and she who arranges a later flight when Morel has slept through his intended departure. They spend the extra day touring the countryside and beaches outside the city; Morel begins to drive but soon gives the wheel to Cynthia: "Par deux fois expulsé du circuit pour défaut d'attention, Morel renonce, s'arrête, cède la place à sa compagne" (*Ei,* 181). The engineer's will to make sense of events and the administrator's meticulous observations have degenerated, with the present protagonist, to a vague inattention, a uniform inability to concentrate on his current situation. A sexual episode with Cynthia is punctuated by descriptions of the panoramic view outside, as if Morel were continually distracted by the scene framed in the bay window of his Manhattan hotel room:

> Le fuselage là-bas scintille, argenté sous le projecteur de la tour. Un autre appareil déjà s'élance, décolle, prend de la hauteur, décrit un cercle, sort du champ.
> L'itinéraire de fuite tout en bas, lointain en contrebas de l'autre côté du fleuve, maintenant s'imprime sur les surfaces sombres et claires, sous la lumière mate, spectrale de la lune, dans le grand espace vide contigu à la façade de verre, à la paroi verticale contre laquelle bute le vent du nord, se divisent et glissent les rafales entre les croisillons d'acier, ici, devant la tablette et le bois du lit, dans la chaleur moite et la tension exaspérée sur le point de rompre, au centre de lignes se coupant en étoile sur le drap blanc, le dos nu et l'arrondi des hanches de part et d'autre de la taille étroite, flexible. (*Ei,* 164)

Morel exhibits a similar lack of attentiveness in respect to his investigations for the film to be produced in Mexico. When questioned as to the plot of the proposed film, he cannot remember a single detail. Some aspects come back to him suddenly at various points in the narration: of the three scenarios in question, one is a banal, sentimental intrigue of jealousy in a jungle setting; a second scenario would depict a crime drama, with two rival gangs pursuing each other in a labyrinthine city. The third proposal is even more vague in Morel's mind: "'Une histoire de conquête, je crois: de grandes batailles, un cataclysme, des milliers d'hommes en armes' . . ." (*Ei*, 123). Although his interest in the filming production is minimal and sporadic, he often seems to invent scenarios in which Cynthia or he himself figures. One such scene occurs when he is lost in the subway; he describes his own itinerary from a spectator's point of view and wonders if the film is to be a fiction or a documentary. Scenes involving the protagonist's movements would be fictional, while a technical description of an enormous bridge would fall into the realm of documentary.

Like the protagonist of the second novel, Morel often sees himself as an element in a cinematic staging, to the point where real scenes are difficult to distinguish from those imagined by the protagonist. He is not, however, the ideal spectator of either real or invented scenes: he is unable to pursue any fantasy at length, just as he cannot sustain an interest in J.J.'s conversation, in Cynthia's company, or even in his own investigations. The curiosity that characterized Lassalle and to a lesser extent the colonial administrator gives way with Morel to an almost constant physical malaise. A certain difficulty with light, elevation, and means of transport provokes in this protagonist a perpetual nausea, headache, and somnolence. The intense light of a late summer's sun reflected off the mirroring surfaces of skyscrapers disturbs Morel, much as the North African sunlight disturbed the protagonist of *Le Maintien de l'ordre*. A tendency toward dizziness in high places links Morel with the unnamed protagonist of the initial section of *Eté indien:* that protagonist's climb up a steep pyramid in Mexico recalls Morel's ascent in an elevator to New York's highest point, where he faints at his first glimpse of the panorama below him.

The lighting and elevation that should provide the fictional subject with a clear, privileged outlook on his surroundings instead provoke a discomfort so extreme that perception becomes impossible: he involuntarily closes his eyes, falls asleep, or loses consciousness. The spectator's position has become untenable. Light and elevation when combined with physical transport—cars, airplanes, subway—create a particularly disagreeable sensation for Morel: "la voiture penche, oscille, ses ressorts grincent, l'odeur âpre se répand, monte à la tête, une nouvelle ligne droite s'annonce, l'éclat de la lumière s'intensifie— lueur aveuglante, discontinue, fractionnée en vertiges minimes, en assoupissements brefs, lancinants . . ." (*Ei,* 12). Called upon to organize a coherent and total view of a situation while in transit, he can only drift into an uneasy and uncomfortable sleep. A traditional protagonist would form the moving center of meaning in his journey through a novel; his perceptions would organize what is given to be read. If metaphor is a form of transport of meaning from one level or object to another, then Morel with his malaises is (metaphorically) incapable of the meaningful, metaphorical motion required of him as a biographical subject. He finds perception painful and sustained attention virtually impossible; he is admittedly ill suited for his function as an investigator or as a vehicle of meaning in a fictional text. Morel has abandoned all pretense of a search; the stability and significance of the narration are put into question by the strange vertigo of the subject whose vision directs it.

This vertigo that cuts off perception, altering description and arresting the transfer of meaning, is of a specifically textual nature presaged by the experiences of the two earlier protagonists. For each protagonist, his status as a stranger and a spectator seems to underlie his inability to establish a singular identity and formulate a coherent, meaningful discourse about a certain reality. As Lassalle leaves the unmapped zone, he crosses a rising river whose swift currents, moving from left to right like a line of Western writing, hypnotize him and almost cause him to fall. It is at this point that he loses Lessing's camera case. He manages to regain his posture, just as he manages to rescue his identity from that of the murdered predecessor. What is lost is Lassalle's inscription of the trace for which he was responsible, the tracings he had made on the white ellipse of the unmapped region. Similarly, when the administrator of the second fiction contemplates the multiple readings inscribed in the map on his wall, he is mesmerized, incapable of action or enunciation. He has become a thoroughly passive spectator. Finally, Morel's very status as an elevated, privileged observer offers him textlike views of Manhattan that effectively extinguish him as a perceptive center: "la multitude des blocs d'habitation et d'artères quadrillées qui ont dû constituer l'essentiel des images qu'il ne peut se rappeler . . ." (*Ei, 32*).

While the early protagonists experience a milder vertigo than that of Morel, they share the textual nature of the latter's discomfort: each subject is disrupted precisely in his capacity to perform as a fictional protagonist and is menaced by a textual disorder in the space where he ought to be able, through his position as a subject, to anchor a meaningful story. By succumbing to a reading of alternate texts, the protagonists lose the ability to inscribe their own privileged texts, their own adventures. The blank ellipse is the zone where Lassalle, the colonialist, ought to be able to impose his interpretations, but it resists his tracings and destroys his evidence, retaining the unwritten profusion of the indigenous text. Similarly, the administrator's familiarity with the intricate, ancient city and its corrupt affairs ought to facilitate his efforts to create a written order or maintain a legal one; instead, the alternate orders fascinate and paralyze him. The lighting, elevation, and mobility that should give Morel a privileged view of the metropolis serve rather to suppress him as a directing presence by bringing the teeming city into a hallucinatory focus.

The protagonists' physical malaise has developed into a textual phenomenon recalling Blanchot's articulation of a hypnotic literary space that is never a textual adequation or expression of the real world, but rather a strangely vertiginous development of textuality itself, whose linear deployment suddenly becomes spatialized and multidimensional: ". . . où l'espace est le vertige de l'espacement. Alors règne la fascination."[11] The essential strangeness or malaise felt by these protagonists derives from their textual status, in which the linear placement, "l'espacement," of their experience produces a vertiginous sensation in relation to the chasm of all that is not said between the words of the text, between the singular, straightforward discourse they all attempt and its multiple, labyrinthine "other." Their position as textual subjects, as specific combinations of words destined to provide a meaningful center for the rest of the text, is dizzyingly precarious in its privileged elevation.

The ability of any textual element to distinguish itself from the literary space and impose a significance upon that space is thus brought into question, as the "vertige de l'espacement" in *Eté indien* results in the dissolution of its subject as a perceptive center. Morel is constantly blinded or put to sleep by the sun's reflection on mirrored skyscrapers; the fascination exerted on him by his status as a fictional subject whose vision should direct the text is similar to the spell cast on the reader or author who approaches a text, according to Blanchot: "Ce milieu de la facination, où ce que l'on voit saisit la vue et la rend interminable . . . c'est notre propre regard en miroir, ce milieu est, par excellence, attirant, fascinant: lumière qui est aussi l'abîme, une lumière où l'on s'abîme, effrayante et attrayante."[12] Morel's very position in the literary space creates the hypnotic malaise in which he is suppressed and drawn back into the uniformity of the text.

The increasing intertextuality of *Eté indien* also contributes to the reabsorption of its protagonist. The protagonists of the first three novels have all tended to merge with each other. Conventional notions of fictional progress are undermined by the sameness of their characters and their situations. The first two scenarios of Morel's proposed film recapitulate the plots of the first two novels on a banal, stereotypical level, while the first script, a tale of jealousy in an exotic setting, might even refer to someone else's novel, Robbe-Grillet's *La Jalousie.* An ironic *mise en abyme* of entertainment literature and cinema is accomplished by a profusion of films, scenarios, and novels within the novel itself. Like Morel, the reader feels that he or she has been here before. Morel himself is somehow familiar, as is his superior Moritz: Lassalle's immediate predecessor in the mining venture was named Moritz, but an earlier effort had been conducted by a Morel or a Moret.[13] And the protagonist of *Le Maintien de l'ordre* tries to contact a certain "L...". Like the engineer and the administrator, Morel is often designated simply as *l'étranger, le voyageur, le promeneur.* Before his departure, Cynthia gives Morel some photographs she took of him during their stay in New York. He has little to offer in return: "Morel, plus pauvre en souvenirs, ne trouve que deux images à lui donner: sur l'une, il chevauche seul à dos de mulet dans un cirque de pierraille; sur l'autre, il marche dans une ruelle déserte, ensoleillée, bordée de murs blancs aveugles. C'est tout ce qu'il possède; le reste n'est que papiers administratifs, nomenclatures anonymes, interchangeables, actes impersonnels" (*Ei,* 190–91). Morel's photographs evoke, by their images and the terms used to describe them, the textual past of the other two

protagonists, whose acts and names are as impersonal and interchangeable as his own. Incapable of sustaining a prolonged interest in
his situation, Morel has done nothing significant in the space of the
text; nor has his laconic itinerary led the reader to reconstruct a meaningful series of events. His name has become one of several interchangeable alphabetic pseudonyms. Even his impoverished past is not
uniquely his: Morel has been reabsorbed by the identities of the early
protagonists who were themselves only marginally able to perform as
fictional subjects. There is apparently nothing original or singular
about Morel or any other element of *Eté indien,* and the contagion of
repetition and reabsorption extends back to the earliest protagonists,
whose contradictory identities are again brought into question.

The only insights Morel seems to have or provoke in others are
ironic in nature: banal comments on the film to be produced can often
be viewed in light of Morel's own role as a fictional subject. When
discussing with J.J. the various possible scenarios, Morel first contradicts his host's assertion that setting might be the film's real concern:

—Beau décor, n'est-ce pas? . . . Perspectives sauvages . . . Arrière-plan
    de ruines . . . Peu importe l'histoire, finalement.
—Mais pas du tout, proteste Morel . . . C'est très important, l'histoire!
    (*Ei,* 58)

Later, however, after Morel sketches the third scenario of conquest and
cataclysm, he seems to have reversed his position. J.J. remarks:

—Il y a une crise du sujet.
—Le sujet n'est qu'un faux semblant. Ainsi, dans le premier cas, il y a la
    brousse, les ruines, les rencontres . . . (*Ei,* 124).

A crisis of the fictional subject—both the protagonist and his story—
underlies the evolution of the three fictions, while setting looms larger.
Morel seems to agree to the erasure of the fictional subject: "—mon
rôle est plus effacé" (*Ei,* 59). This dissolution of the fictional subject as
the perceptive center of the novel is accompanied by an ironic recognition, on Morel's part, of his own obsolescence. Finally, when he gives
Cynthia the photographs that discredit him as an original, unique

hero, Morel makes a strange declaration: "—La seule chose à faire, c'est un documentaire, prononce-t-il alors sans hésiter, tout uniment, comme pour répondre à une objection formulée de longue date" (*Ei,* 191). The long-standing objection would seem to be that of fiction versus documentary enunciated by Morel himself, of story versus setting, and possibly that of content versus form. The protagonist ironically proposes his own ouster, and with it the dismissal of a fiction that organizes itself around a protagonist who is no longer capable of maintaining a coherent hold on what is presented. He instead endorses a documentary approach in which a controlled presentation of a certain structure or setting would dominate. In so doing, Morel appears to endorse a structuralist vision of fiction in which traditional psychological realism and character development give way to a revolutionary textual play in which objects no longer circulate around protagonists like so many anthropomorphized props.

A theatrical or cinematographic metaphor underlies the paradoxical evolution in consciousness of the collective protagonist of the first three novels. Lassalle was never aware that he was an element in and a spectator of a mise-en-scène. The colonial administrator increasingly saw himself as a cinematic entity, while Morel began to invent his own films. As the protagonist grows less capable of the meaningful action he is supposed to perform, he becomes more aware of the filmic, staged nature of his existence. An ironic self-consciousness on Morel's part recalls the Lukácsian typology of the novel, in which the problematic individual's journey of education results in an increased awareness of his own situation. In this case, however, that self-consciousness turns against itself and against the novelistic form itself. Abandoning the pretense of a hero and a story, Morel rejects the banal, sentimental intrigues of the first film scenarios and the novels to which they correspond. The project of demystification has led the fictional protagonist to dismiss both his story and himself.

The third novel has presented the Indian summer of the fictional character and the adventure that derives its structure from him: during the final days of a prolonged summer in New York, a fragmentary, derisory love story has taken place. As Cynthia and Morel end their last day together at an outdoor film (a story of global destruction), snow begins to fall. The final section of the book appears to present

Morel's real flight to Mexico. The view from the porthole operates the usual suppression of the subject: "Cédant à l'éclat de la lumière—à la fatigue peut-être, à l'insomnie, la lassitude—, les yeux se ferment, la nuque fléchit . . ." (*Ei*, 210). Somnolence alternates with a vague uneasiness, and passages from the past(s) are dreamed or remembered, until an explosion wakens him:

> Et le réveil, brutal, vient dissocier ces éléments.
> Sous la violence du choc, l'avion a vacillé.
> C'est une terre chaotique qui surgit dans la trouée des nuages—
> bourbeuse, morcelée.
> Se rapproche, de plus en plus vite.
> Grandit, de la première à la dernière image . . . (*Ei*, 213)

The reference to a first and last image interjects a cinematic distance into what at first seems to be the brute experience of falling from the sky. It raises doubts about the status of this passage; is it a dream? an invented scenario? and if so, whose? And indeed, as the airplane slips beneath the water, the perspective no longer seems to be Morel's:

> L'eau stagnante, l'eau s'infiltrant sous les racines, les souches—
> glauques—, sous les tiges, les structures métalliques.
> La ligne de flottaison montant insensiblement le long de la paroi,
> irrépressiblement sous la lumière éparse, tamisée.
> Ciel blanc, nuages immobiles cachant les crêtes.
> Lianes torses reliant les rives, lobes tavelés, branches moussues d'où
> l'oiseau blanc s'envole.
> Battements d'ailes dans l'air moite, torpide.
> Palmes.
> Plumes.
> Fleurs rouges charriées par les méandres du fleuve, pivotant lentement
> sur elles-mêmes.
> Sans fin. Sous nul regard.
> A vau-l'eau. (*Ei*, 213-14)

Cataclysm has struck the fictional subject in the midst of his fragmentary, defective activity. His function as a perceptive center and a vehicle of meaning has pulled him into an abyss, submerging his adventure beneath the uniformity of a jungle marsh. The subject is carried away by the rising waters, ceding his place to a recurring motif: a primitive, untamed setting unhindered by the singular directing *regard* of any subject. The historical season of the fictional hero, with its emphasis on meaning, on content, on psychology, seems to have given way to the era of setting, of form. The expulsion of the fictional subject has been presaged since the beginning in a play on names: the itineraries of Lassal(Le)ssing both lead to Assameur *(à sa mort),* but Lassalle manages to recover enough identity to undo the textual trap. Subsequent developments weaken his hold, and, in the incarnation of Morel *(le mort),* the protagonist endorses his own trajectory toward destruction.

The first three novels have moved from an "uncivilized," primitive culture to a colonial city, and on to New York, the paradigm of the modern world, which is then transformed into the ancient ruins of another civilization, in a circular itinerary that hints at cataclysm and ruin not only for the European male protagonist, but for his civilization as well. The gradual emptying out and final (self-)dismissal of the hero points to the documentary as a possible alternative to the kind of fiction the protagonist has up to now embodied.

IV. *L'Echec de Nolan:* Fiction's Failures

The failure of the traditional narrative hero and the practicability of a documentary form of writing are explored in *L'Echec de Nolan.* The fourth book of Ollier's cycle is divided into four reports, in which an unnamed investigator from a mysterious intelligence agency attempts to explain the recent disappearance of another agent, Nolan. The first report presents the investigator's visit north to the border of two Scandinavian countries where he interviews Jurgensen, the sole survivor of a plane crash in which Nolan, along with two others, has disappeared; since no body was found, Nolan might yet be alive. Jurgensen speaks at length with the agent but can offer no real information, suggesting instead that the investigator delve further into Nolan's past. Thus the second report takes the investigator east to an Alpine country where Italian and German are spoken. The agent questions a certain Jäger, who, under a pseudonym, had known Nolan (who had also used a false name) ten years earlier in an ancient Arab city. The reader of *Le Maintien de l'ordre* recalls that its protagonist had a friend known only as L.... But Jäger has little help to offer and suggests, like his predecessor, that the search be extended to Nolan's very beginnings as an agent. A third report tells of the investigator's visit to the south to see a certain Jiminez, a blue-eyed Arab who had known Nolan some twenty years ago, who had at that time spoken French, and who has since come to live with his twin great-nieces in what appears to be Gibraltar.

Manifestly, "Nolan" was the real name of all the protagonists of the earlier novels. Their apparent adventures were only covers masking the real mission of a mysterious agent whose brilliant success in his first effort, twenty years ago, had brought him legendary fame: "les échos légendaires auréolaient Nolan d'une gloire désuète, quasiment romantique. Le personnage prenait stature de héros; ses gestes vrais, ou supposés, gagnaient valeur de référence. On le louangeait, le citait en exemple: efficace, effacé, opérant toujours seul" (*EN,* 146). Nolan's exemplary methods involved writing an account of his discoveries; the protagonists who had seemed incapable of written discourse are now revealed to be a man who wrote singularly captivating reports: "Alliance de la pérégrination pédestre et d'une écriture soumise à une stricte observance grammaticale: partant dès l'aube, arpentant tout le jour, rentrant à la nuit tombée, et cependant notant, consignant, relisant, rédigeant encore" (*EN,* 146–47). Nolan, as described here, was the very embodiment of the novelistic hero of the past, whose actions took on referential value, whose physical journey was translated into a meaningful *récit.*

Despite his legendary talent, Nolan gradually developed some difficulty in composing his reports: his later efforts began to be contaminated by reference to his cover, by extraneous descriptions and unrelated dialogues. The investigator feels that these problems in Nolan's reports might provide clues to his fate; the discussion of Nolan's disappearance thus becomes a critique of his written reports. Each witness is given a copy of Nolan's report pertaining to the mission in which that witness was involved. Jurgensen gives a spirited textual critique of the report corresponding to Morel's adventure, pointing out the gratuitous and disruptive nature of lengthy descriptive passages. Jäger notes a certain *alternance,* or oscillation, in the style of the "colonial administrator's" report: too many peripheral matters are pursued, leaving many issues in suspense. Nolan has been unable to keep to the essential theme in reporting on his missions; he has been unable to control the *détail fortuit,* the insistence of unrelated details into the body of the report.

The investigator is himself preparing a report, at least in the first two sections. Although the narration presents each interview as if it were in progress, the investigator makes occasional notations for the composition of the report: "Ici il conviendrait d'introduire une description élémentaire de Nolan" (*EN,* 26). Although the investigator works for an intelligence bureau, the reports that ought to give a factual, objective rendering of his findings soon give way to more personal observations and associations: "(ici, placer une évocation circonstanciée des deux changements de véhicule et des vicissitudes chaque fois aggravées du confort, des odeurs et des bruits)" (*EN,* 125–26). This protagonist suffers from a familiar malaise. Like the characters of the earlier novels, he is prey to physical discomforts that prevent him from carrying out his assigned observations and notations. His written reports grow increasingly subjective as they stray from the standard report format. In this way, he is progressively linked with the Nolan composite; digressions in his own report repeat adventures experienced by the previous protagonists. And like his alphabetical predecessors, Lassalle and Morel, the investigator begins to see himself as an element in a tableau: "Isa [Jäger's niece] désignes les sièges, invite les personnages à prendre place aux trois sommets du jeu, aux angles aigus des rôles et des permutations" (*EN,* 136). Here, the investigator sees himself and others as characters playing roles in a shifting game. Unable to dissociate himself from the report to be composed, this agent seems to be committing the same textual errors as Nolan. Neither author can organize a documentary text free from extraneous details, from personal observations, or from the staging of the situation by his own perspective.

Morel's cinematic dilemma is recalled: can portions of his imagined film be purely documentary? Even Morel's purportedly technical description of a bridge to be crossed is eventually nuanced by his anxiety:

> Une légère oscillation ébranle en permanence l'ensemble de l'édifice, résultante de nombreuses forces dont certaines, délicates à maîtriser,

procèdent elles-mêmes du jeu extrêmement irrégulier—en cette saison surtout—de plusieurs variables climatiques sujettes à des écarts imprévisibles. Mais sur les données moyennes calculées et retenues, des marges de sécurité si larges ont été adoptées qu'aucun risque de rupture ne menace, *du moins dans l'immédiat* (dans tout ce qui précède, en revanche, c'est plutôt le documentaire qui l'emporte). (*Ei*, 86; my emphasis)

Like the bridge, the film will be subject to unpredictable influences, to forces that are difficult to control. Slight variations could produce unforeseen divergences from the expected. What is presented as documentary is subtly contaminated by the subject in his dual role as spectator and protagonist. A hint of future danger completes a picture of uncertainty and unpredictability that inserts the documentarian into the vagaries of an uncontrollable plot.

The intelligence agent of *L'Echec de Nolan* similarly views two films during his investigations; while one is the purest of fictions, in which giant spiders attack a group of sailors, one is simply a series of snowy scenes: "C'est à peine s'il écoute l'explication sollicitée, lorgnant le petit écran où les images de neige, sobres et mates, purement documentaires *presque*" (*EN*, 169; my emphasis). The film is *almost* a documentary; even a field of snow or a blank page may be read and inflected to some extent by the perceiving subject. A perfectly neutral or controlled environment would seem to be impossible; divergence and digression must be the basis of documentary as well as fiction. Nolan's failure to stay on the main track has also become the present investigator's error and *errance*.

The interview with Jiminez shifts its focus from Nolan to the investigator himself, making explicit the progressive identification between the investigator and the previous protagonist(s): "'Tu lui ressemblerais sans doute, à la longue, peu à peu'" (*EN*, 206). While the others told him to *remonter plus loin*, to delve further into the past in his search for the germ of Nolan's failure, Jiminez tells the agent he may stay the night, or stay indefinitely, implying that his investigation has either concluded or failed. The Arab makes a second, more troubling revelation: another investigator visited him the day before, also asking questions about Nolan. He did not stay the night but moved on to tour the back country. The current investigator has now been doubled by someone who appears destined to make the same errors of digression as all his predecessors.

The fourth and final report further blurs the distinction between Nolan, the initial investigator, and his newly appeared double. The investigator has apparently disappeared: assuming that the agency doubted his efforts, he has decided to pursue the question of Nolan's failure on his own, going back west to an even earlier mission in what appears to be New York and the Caribbean. There he retraces Nolan's itineraries, revisiting his favorite sites. Finally he climbs to the top of a mountain that is supposed to offer a panoramic "beau point de vue" (*EN,* 228), recalling similar panoramas from the earlier books; the text ends with his ascension in progress:

> Progressant lentement dans le sable profond.
> Lentement—sur le sol souple et léger. (*EN,* 228)

The investigator has traced a circular itinerary, touching all four cardinal points, at least in reference to France. His inquiry has led him in a concentric motion around Western Europe. Each stop in his voyage brings him to a foreign frontier where languages and customs mingle and where he experiences, remembers, or dreams situations that are neither uniquely nor originally his own. Despite the scope of his investigations, he has resolved nothing. Instead of unveiling the mystery surrounding Nolan's failure and disappearance, the final protagonist merges with Nolan, commits the same errors, and eventually effects a similar disappearance. As one commentor has noted, with Nolan the protagonist is ultimately "non-là."[14]

In this fourth novel, the fictional protagonist has unwittingly operated an inquest into his own demise: he has found that his error lies precisely in his own *errance,* his inability to formulate or center a discourse that would correspond, without digressions or inflections, to the event or object to be recounted. Yet he is incapable of correcting his self-destructive trajectory. The mythical heroic subject, whose actions would take on a signifying "valeur de référence" and whose perception would relay a coherent vision of the world, has been progressively submerged beneath the rising tide of a rebellious textuality: with

Morel at the end of *Eté indien,* the hero apparently slipped beneath the surface of a deluge he could no longer resist.

But the death of the protagonist cannot yet be registered, nor can he be assigned a strict singularity: Morel metamorphoses into Nolan, whose body was never recovered from the sea, along with the bodies of two other men. The numerical coincidence reinstates the question of the unified identities of the first three protagonists: did all three drown? did any one escape? The final investigator, ostensibly a composite of the earlier heroes, disappears equivocally, leaving behind a double. While the series of names seems to be circular, with Moritz and Morel connecting the first adventure to the third, the alphabetic closure is reopened by the insertion of yet another series of superiors, Münch and Marshall. Morel's dramatic death has in no way inaugurated a fiction devoid of protagonists; in fact, phantoms of the same protagonist continue to haunt *L'Echec de Nolan.* Although the function and privilege of the mythical traditional hero have been shed, the possibility of a documentary—a subjectless rendering of a referent—has also been discounted. Something remains in a fiction to investigate and be investigated; something still manifests a will to know the nature of fiction, and something still inflects the fiction that contains it.

The failure illustrated in *L'Echec de Nolan* is also arguably the failure of an early, ambitious vision of the revolutionary potential of a structuralist practice of writing embodied in the New Novel. Robbe-Grillet's proclamation in *Pour un nouveau roman* of the demise of the protagonist (cited as an epigraph to this chapter) is complicated by the first relay of *Le Jeu d'enfant.* Although he may well be "une momie à présent," the dessicated novelistic convention that is the fictional hero is still capable of making a certain persistent kind of "acte de présence" (*Mo,* 134, 143, and *Le Jeu d'enfant,* passim). In this light, the first relay develops a self-critique, which culminates with the ultimate recognition of a certain failure: "Chacun le sait, pourtant, tous les livres l'indiquent. Cette voie est sans issue" (*EN,* 173).

Just as Nolan was revealed to have a cover project and a real mission, the fictional protagonist has pursued a dual track in the first four works of Ollier's cycle. The principal mission of the composite protagonist was to uncover and indict his own "other": the traditional

narrative hero. An ongoing project of demystification has thus subsumed the various covers in the first three novels of the first cycle and
has aimed at the reeducation of reader and writer through the progressive subversion of the *Bildungsroman* genre. But the figurative
death of the protagonist was followed by a swift resurrection, thus
complicating the revolutionary dismissal of the old regime's hero.
L'Echec de Nolan concludes with the protagonist of fiction irremediably multiple and ambiguous, but still in search of himself in the space
of the fiction.

The protagonist resurfaces in part to carry out a secondary mission:
the discrediting of documentary—pure description, pure objectivity—
as an alternative to conventional idealist fiction. The "other" of fiction
has thus been challenged and rejected in both its traditional ideological
form and in its impossible hypothetical alternative. The goal of the
fictional cycle's progressive auto-investigation is the increased self-
consciousness of the form itself. Fictional identity has been sought,
however, by means of negation: it is only through the indictment of
what it holds to be its "other" that the fictional *recherche* has examined
the nature of fiction. While these four novels have not revealed what
fiction precisely is, they do point, with Blanchot, to what it is not: "par
[l'oeuvre] arrive dans le temps un autre temps, et dans le monde des
êtres qui existent et des choses qui subsistent arrive, non pas un autre
monde, mais l'autre de tout monde, ce qui est toujours autre que le
monde."[15] Fiction defines itself through denunciation of its "other"
but is itself also essentially "otherness" in these fictions. If the first
cycle attempts to determine the nature of fiction, the negativity of its
demystifying approach threatens to reintegrate the essence of fictionality with its forbidden doubles. The demystifying protagonist should
undermine the notion of a subject who progressively achieves insight
into his relations with his fictional world. Yet Morel culminates an
evolution toward self-awareness when he states: "Le sujet n'est qu'un
faux semblant" (*Ei,* 124) and "mon rôle est plus effacé" (*Ei,* 59). While
the protagonist of these fictions never reassembles his fragmented self,
the ironic self-consciousness he achieves in the incarnation of Morel is
perilously close to the telos of the traditional novel or to the universal
histories of G. E. Lessing and Hegel, which have purportedly been set
up as the project's ideological "other."

The fictional subject's itinerary of investigation has not revealed the positive nature of fiction, has not answered the question, What is fiction? The *recherche* has not achieved the consciousness of positive identity that was the goal of the project of demystification. However, the form taken by the fictional subject's collective failure—a penchant for deviation, digression, and oscillation between self and "other"— may point toward a positive elucidation of fiction, for fiction's auto-interrogation appears to have fallen prey to the same inclinations. In the second cycle, an exploration into the sources of this *errance,* this *alternance,* seeks to uncover the germ of fiction itself. Such an exploration takes its point of departure in the failure to completely oust the fictional subject from the fictional scene. While the first relay of *Le Jeu d'enfant* rehearses structuralism's "death of the protagonist," it nevertheless ends up with a subject that is indeed altered and subverted, but still in need of analysis. Thus the second relay will engage the broader and more subtle critique of the subject undertaken in post-structuralist thought, notably in the work of Lacan, Derrida, and Foucault.

2

Family Romance:
The Origins of Fiction

> Le point central de l'oeuvre est l'oeuvre comme ori-
> gine, celui que l'on ne peut atteindre, le seul pourtant
> qu'il vaille la peine d'atteindre.
> —Blanchot
>
> Où et quand commencer? Question d'origine. Or qu'il
> n'y ait pas d'origine, c'est-à-dire, d'origine simple;
> que les questions d'origine transportent avec elles
> une métaphysique de la présence, c'est bien ce qu'une
> méditation de la trace devrait sans doute
> nous apprendre.
> —Derrida

In the final scene of *L'Echec de Nolan,* the protagonist, at once composite and doubled, climbs to the top of a mountain and disappears:

> En deux jours de marche soutenue, on atteint le sommet. . . .
> C'est un beau point de vue, dit-on, et l'occasion rêvée pour se recréer,
> entre deux éclipses . . .
> Au couchant du périple, avant le saut au point central—ou à son
> homologue sur un lointain système. (*EN,* 228)

While the protagonist has failed in all his cover missions as well as in
his generic project as a traditional fictional subject, his leap or
"assumption" to a "lointain système" does not appear to be a definitive
death; it soon becomes clear that the peregrinations of the pro-
tagonist(s) of the first four fictions are to be continued in the realm of
outer space, with the fifth work taking place on Epsilon, the fifth

planet of the distant *Système du Prisme.* Far from being eclipsed after the sun set on the journeys of the first cycle, the protagonist reaches a "beau point de vue" permitting some sort of re-creation at the central point of a distant yet homologous system.

In the first four novels, the investigations conducted by the pro-tagonists themselves into their own failure to form the center of an orderly, meaningful *récit* linked the source of that failure to an unavoidable deviation or digression. In the works of the second cycle, then, the fictional protagonist has not disappeared from the scene of Ollier's investigation into the nature of fiction but has rather continued his interrogative wanderings on another, higher level: literally, that of outer space, the domain of science fiction. With the fifth and sixth books, *La Vie sur Epsilon* and *Enigma,* the fictional sequence abruptly ascends to an alien sphere, which, though wildly unfamiliar, still retains something of the previous investigations, since a re-creation or reincarnation of the same protagonist seems to persevere. The higher level is thus dual: it is science fiction both as an established (popular) narrative genre stereotypically featuring unknown worlds and beings and also as a science of fiction, an investigation into the nature and functioning of fiction. Thus the leader of the expedition, known only by the initial O., conducts on the stellar landscape of Epsilon a quest that figures fiction's own search for its origins. The quest conducted in outer space is a homologue of the one conducted on earth in the first cycle: structurally similar in its investigative itinerary, the second quest doubles the first one on the higher level of autocriticism, of reflexivity, of a more sustained and subtle analysis of the fictional subject. With the leap into outer space, then, the fictional cycle resolutely enters a critical dimension aimed at correcting the *échec* of the first fictions through a systematic examination of and experimentation with fic-tionality. The "lointain système" to which O. ascends is that of the theoretical implications of his own activity.

Here the question of allegory arises, with the enunciation of dual levels, of parallel investigations, and of literal and critical hierarchies. As a rhetorical strategy, allegory says one thing and means another. It is thus, as Angus Fletcher points out, a modal concept: allegory encodes an enunciation, providing a message as to how the enuncia-tion is to be understood.[1] Derived from the Latin *allos* (other) and

agoreuein (to speak openly, in the assembly or market), allegory suggests both speaking other than openly and speaking openly but also
"otherly," that is, subversively. The political value of allegory is significant: an allegory can always be read or understood literally; in fact, the
dominant ideology or authority that is challenged will be blind to the
underlying allegory. Only those alerted to the presence of another level
of meaning will be able to construct a subversive reading. In the novels
of *Le Jeu d'enfant*'s second cycle, the mode of allegory is used to
demystify or subvert another modal concept, that of mimesis, which
encodes the message that what is read is an imitation of some reality.
While *La Vie sur Epsilon* could theoretically be read as a science fiction
tale that represents an imagined realm, it also offers a second,
coherent level of meaning in which mimetic assumptions are systematically disrupted. An allegory typically presents a progression on several levels: in *Gulliver's Travels,* in *Voyage to the Center of the Earth,*
and in *Pilgrim's Progress,* a voyage culminates in a new knowledge or a
greater awareness on the part of the protagonist. This new awareness
corresponds to a second level of allegorical progression perceived by
the reader. The protagonist of allegory is most often an abstraction or
personification rather than a psychologically rounded character. To an
extent, the composite protagonist of the first relay of *Le Jeu d'enfant*
fits such a description. In the second cycle, the protagonist grows even
more allegorical. In *Life on Epsilon* and the following novel, *Enigma,*
the protagonist O. is an embodiment of certain fictional qualities
rather than a coherent and unified individual character; his quests on
distant planets lead the reader to make certain conclusions about the
nature of fiction. In finding some other meaning within, behind, or
beyond the apparently open enunciation of a text, any literary commentary or criticism tends, as Northrop Frye has claimed, to make all
literature allegorical to some degree. In proposing an autocriticism as
well as in setting up coherently dual levels of progression, Ollier's
fiction places itself squarely within the allegorical model.[2]

In his pursuit of the source of his own *errance,* then, O. conducts a
quest that allegorizes fiction's own search for its origins, as the source
of the early protagonists' failure becomes, in *Epsilon* and *Enigma,* the
very germ of fiction.[3] On the planets of Epsilon and Iota, this allegorical search for origins is played out in terms of sexual difference

and in metaphors of family romance and conflict. In Freud's depiction of the family romance, the child entertains the fantasy of having been found by those who serve as his parents. The child then fantasizes or continually seeks a reunion with his real familial origins. This dual movement, of rejection of apparent origins on the one hand, and of persistent searching for a more genuine origin on the other hand, reflects O.'s situation in the model of fictional origin developed in *Epsilon* and *Enigma*. Ancient myths and symbols of the "feminine" join with the language and gestures of Freudian psychoanalysis to establish an opposition between the singular, "masculine" subject of fiction and a multiple, amorphous feminine matrix of fictionality. The evolution of this conflict eventually leads to the enunciation of a revolutionary model of fictional intertextuality that would explain fictional origins through the metaphorical relations between a generative, maternal matrix of textuality and a masculine "son," the individual fiction.

I. *La Vie sur Epsilon*

Epsilon is a planet of sand and snow. The four astronauts sent to explore it are inexplicably stranded by mechanical failure. To escape they must discover the laws governing the alien world. Their vessel has landed on a frontier that seems to divide the planet into equally virgin hemispheres. The astronauts follow this line of demarcation in hope of discovering some useful information about the planet. In their exploration of the planet's topography, they seem to be walking in a book magnified to delirious dimensions: pursuing the median line between sand and snow, they cross perpendicular furrows (*sillons,* a term in frequent use since the earliest novel) that are not unlike lines on a page. Their footprints, however, are always erased by a subterranean current: "aucun repère ne reste plus à lire, et 'revenir sur ses pas' acquiert ici valeur doublement figurée" (*VE,* 16). The booklike planet will not let the astronauts read their own traces. The protagonists' investigations are figurative to the second degree: the allegorical nature of their activity and of their relationship to Epsilon is established from the beginning, and the nature of the current that undermines their itinerary will need to be examined in that same doubly figurative light.

La Vie sur Epsilon is composed of five segments of decreasing length, lettered A through E, that repeat the fivefold configuration of this fifth book of *Le Jeu d'enfant*. The text is composed of discrete passages varying in length from one line to half a page to several pages. The primarily third-person, present-tense narration communicates the observations, thoughts, and actions of the leader, O., who first remains at the landing site and then ventures out to seek the erased traces of his three companions. The book opens with a passage that will be repeated in slightly altered form throughout the narration, calibrating through its modifications the anticipation and terror that form the atmosphere of this unearthly narration: "Au commencement, il n'attache pas une importance essentielle à ces métamorphoses: c'est une propriété de cette terre, se dit-il, de ce sable, de cette terre de neige et de sable, une qualité climatique, saisonnière peut-être, un état fluctueux des rapports entre lumière et ombre" (*VE,* 9). The metamorphoses that O. witnesses and experiences on Epsilon are paralleled by a narration that transforms the standard elements of the sci-fi thriller into an eerie encounter with the unknown that is textuality.

Soon after their arrival on Epsilon, the astronauts begin to encounter what they call "autochthonous" phenomena whose allegorical value sets the stage for an examination of fictionality. They first become aware of clouds of dancing blades *(lames)* or strips of cloth or paper *(lambeaux)* that resemble the turning pages of a book, specifically the kind whose pages must be cut before reading:

> elles prennent tournure de plaques oblongues, légèrement renflées, d'une texture fibreuse rêche, frangées d'escardes ou d'écailles. . . . De toute manière, l'articulation de ces plaques—chose remarquable—semble s'effectuer par l'entremise de charnières, ou coulisses, au demeurant indiscernables, et ces pièces délicates "joueraient," distendant les formes quadrangulaires, évanescentes, les ressoudant ici et là, les faisant pivoter, coincider ou se cliver. (*VE,* 22–23)

When physically penetrated, the blades produce a peculiar type of hallucination: inside the cloud, each astronaut relives as if it were his own an experience previously undergone by a companion on one of the other four planets of the system and subsequently recounted to the future hero of the episode; only the denouement of the scene differs from the original version. Each astronaut plays out another's scenario, rehearsing in a more oneiric, fantastic vein the persistent link between theatricality and fiction that was established in the first relay of the cycle. *Life on Epsilon* opens with one of these relived experiences; O. is irresistibly drawn to the turning blades and enters their shadowy corridors: "Il reconnut immédiatement les lieux. Qu'était-il venu faire ici la première fois? Déjà ces buissons d'acacias jalonnaient la piste, ces palmiers nains entrevus en marge, ces touffes d'alfa marquant le sillon médian entre les ornières de sable. La nuit tombait" (*VE,* 10). The protagonist of this brief passage has lost the jungle path on which he was driving; he is looking for a small village with red clay huts. The circumstances of his journey repeat those of the first time, and he eventually rejoins the road:

> Il se mit à rire et le remblai se dressa. Il fut sur la route. Plus tôt que prévu, les maisons apparurent, de hauts murs enduits d'ocre et de bleu. Personne en vue. Sur une plaque inconnue, des lettres effacées, à peu près illisibles. Un bruit de caquetage montait on ne sait d'où.
> Il considéra la plaque, interdit, rebroussant tout l'itinéraire: il n'avait jamais suivi cette piste, il ne s'était jamais ravitaillé ici.
> Ne s'était jamais arrêté devant ces arcades violines.
> N'avait jamais monté ces marches.
> Pénétré sous cette voûte. . . .
>
> N'avait jamais été—jamais si vite—entouré par les singes. (*VE,* 11-12)

On Epsilon, space, time, and perceptual identity have become floating and heterogeneous. The "subject" becomes simply a function to be filled by anyone who enters the story. The blades stage an illusion that allegorizes in a phenomenological sense the act of reading a fiction. In "Phenomenology of Reading," Georges Poulet proposes an intersubjective model of reading that would operate in much the same way:

> Such is the initial phenomenon produced whenever I take up a book, and begin to read it. At the precise moment that I see, surging out of the object I hold open before me, a quantity of significations which my mind grasps, I realize that what I hold in my hands is no longer just an

object, or even simply a living thing. I am aware of a rational being, of a consciousness; the consciousness of another, no different from the one I automatically assume in every human being I encounter, except that in this case the consciousness is open to me, welcomes me, lets me look deep inside itself, and even allows me, with unheard-of license, to think what it thinks and feel what it feels.[4]

In reading, one abandons one's own consciousness to a certain degree, acting out the recounted experience of another as if it were one's own memory, and yet unavoidably changing and personally inflecting that scenario. Life on Epsilon becomes a succession of these theatrical readings, and the narrative becomes a mix of stories from various places, planets, and times.

The déjà-vu quality of the borrowed experience points to the intertextuality of fiction, where any text can reevoke and recirculate previous readings. This passage also illustrates what, for Blanchot, is fundamental to the specific effect exercised by literature, that of the "règne fascinant de l'absence de temps":

> Plutôt qu'un mode purement négatif, c'est au contraire un temps sans négation, sans décision, quand ici est aussi bien nulle part, que chaque chose se retire en son image et que le "Je" que nous sommes se reconnaît en s'abîmant dans la neutralité d'un "Il" sans figure. Le temps de l'absence de temps est sans présent, sans présence. De ce qui est sans présent, de ce qui n'est même pas là comme ayant été, le caractère irrémédiable dit: cela n'a jamais eu lieu, jamais une première fois, et pourtant cela recommence, à nouveau, à nouveau, infiniment.[5]

The sense of an eternal return of the not-quite-the-same stems also from the splitting, replication, and yet persistence of a single protagonist in *Le Jeu d'enfant;* we learn that O. has undergone an apprenticeship on the other four planet-books of the Prism system. O.'s *roman d'apprentissage* perseveres into the futuristic textuality of the second relay.

While not physically harmful, the experience of the blades produces an indefinable uneasiness in O.: "il s'était évertué, sans grand succès, à rendre compte du phénomène nouveau: non plus oblitération simple de l'espace, et déambulation aveugle, mais fluctuances com-

binées de l'air et du sol . . . symptômes d'appréhension" (*VE*, 20–21).
On Epsilon, the fictional subject finds himself within the very space
and matter of textuality and of fiction: he wanders blindly among the
words, lines, and pages of a book that contains him, in which he leaves
no lasting mark, and over whose manifestations he has no apparent
control or privilege. The topography of Epsilon is thus a typography
that generates both O. and his story, or stories. The fictional protagonist is physically inside his own story—among words and lines—
and nowhere else. This situation, enormously magnified on Epsilon,
provokes in the leader of the expedition a specific and significant fear.
And the nature of this dread is sexual.

According to Freud, the sight of the female organ is frightening for
the masculine subject because it represents castration, indifference,
and loss of identity. In his 1922 essay "Medusa's Head," Freud inter-
prets the mythological decapitation of Medusa in terms of specularity
and castration: "The terror of Medusa is thus a terror of castration that
is linked to the sight of something. Numerous analyses have made us
familiar with the occasion for this: it occurs when a boy, who has
hitherto been unwilling to believe the threat of castration, catches sight
of the female genitals, probably those of an adult, surrounded by hair,
and essentially those of his mother."[6] Epsilon similarly disquiets O.
because it is immensely and stubbornly blank: just as footprints are
reabsorbed into the uniform smoothness of the planet's surface, the
long, conical spaceship is gradually subsiding into the sand. The virgin
planet refuses the adventurer's traces and threatens to swallow up his
only point of reference:

> un affaissement, et la plongée irrémédiable qui s'ensuivrait, l'absorption
> par le magma insondable, l'enfouissement irrépressible, ou (moins terri-
> ble?) la chute de côté, la rupture d'équilibre, l'un des piliers seulement
> s'enfonçant dans le vide créé, basculement total et bris de l'engin . . .
> appréhension formelle et imminence du danger, balancement, oscilla-
> tions sournoises, s'amplifiant à l'extrême . . . la chute ou l'enfouisse-
> ment? . . . Jusqu'où la nef s'enfoncerait-elle? (*VE*, 49)

The reabsorption or crashing detumescence of the phallic vessel represent castration on a global, catastrophic level. The vague apprehension

O. experiences on the alien planet is quickly revealed to be a patently, even parodically sexual anxiety. In its frightening superficial blankness and its even more terrifying promise of unfathomable depths, Epsilon is a figure of the mother, whose perceived lack carries the symbolic threat of annihilation.[7]

When other areas of the planet's surface are later discovered to be chaotic and disordered, lacking any governing principles, O. fears he will never be able to deduce the cause of the shipwreck or ever make sense of his borrowed experiences on the planet. With its blank, white expanses and its paths of chaotic rock and rubble, Epsilon is both virginal and pregnant with indecipherable meaning. Metaphorically female, the planet elicits two types of response from O. (the masculine subject and head of the expedition who fears already that his authority is questioned and his position of leadership unstable). Faced with a terrain that is now resolutely blank, now hopelessly overcoded, O. attempts to write and read on a global level. Epsilon's surface at first seems as invitingly blank as a sheet of ruled paper, with its countless empty furrows *(sillons)* like vaginas to be inscribed with the marks of a subject seeking to appropriate the virgin sphere, to sow his thoughts there.[8] But this uniformity cannot be dominated; what has seemed to be sheer blank surface becomes a bottomless pit—"magma insondable," the subject's fearful vision of the infinite space of the womb—that absorbs his writing, his would-be dissemination, without leaving a trace.[9]

Similarly, since any hope of escape lies in discovering the laws of Epsilon, O. attempts, in his explorations, to "read" the planet, to find an order behind the indecipherable topography that succeeds the earlier uniformity: "Un spectacle totalement *inédit* s'offre à sa vue, que les quatre ou cinq mètres d'élévation ne laissaient pas espérer. Au nord . . . un univers disparate, chaotique, s'érige, noir et blanc par moitiés divisés: pointements et surgissements comme un hérissement généralisé du roc à l'ouest et à l'est de la glace" (*VE*, 192; my emphasis). The planet's surface is *inédit*: not only unexpected but also unwritten. Epsilon's black and white topography cannot be read like words on a page. Although they maintain a communal logbook of their experiences on Epsilon, the astronauts realize that the planet is not coded and cannot be explained in the terms they are attempting to use; it is not governed by laws existing on Earth or on the other planets of the system. The only discernable temporal or spatial principles are negative ones: discontinuity, fragmentation, instability. Experiences on Epsilon seem to derive not from the decisions of the astronauts but from the autochthonous phenomena themselves. According to one astronaut's "Law of Symmetry," the phenomena seem to arrange encounters among the separated explorers by means of a complex correspondence of scenarios borrowed from the astronauts' experiences on other planets of the system. Any reading made of these strange phenomena is determined by past readings and is more a blind submission than a mastery. It is precisely by its traits that are perennially associated with femininity that the planet-book of Epsilon refuses domination or appropriation by the subject: through its indifference, its absence of order, and its unwillingness to provide a matrix against which the masculine subject can posit his identity, Epsilon threatens him with castration and loss.

O.'s anxiety escalates into terror with the final episode of *La Vie sur Epsilon*. Previously, the only climatic variations on the planet were subtle changes in the color of the light. But just as everything seems about to return to order, with lost astronauts retrieved and communications reestablished, O. notices a bright circle of red on the snow, then another and another. The spots of color spread, accompanied by a painful reddish light and an irritation of the skin: "c'est un fourmillement généralisé, comme si des milliers de corpuscules invisibles tourbillonnaient au ras de la peau, et provoquaient la démangeaison par le seul remuement de l'air" (*VE*, 263). The atmosphere swarms like corpuscles as the bright wave covers the planet's surface like a tide of blood: "Des noyaux de coagulation se développent à l'extrémité des veines, à leur intersection aussi, de loin en loin. En train de se raccorder, pour être plus précis—système capillaire en cours d'implantation et dont le stade ultime, ce soir . . . ou beaucoup plus tôt?" (*VE*, 264-65). By the time O. reaches the spaceship, the entire planet and surrounding sky have been inundated. His fears are confirmed and multiplied by a distressing discovery: an unknown sign—a star—has appeared on the newly refunctioning communication screen, supplanting the comforting rectangle that had for a time signified help was on its way.

The simultaneous appearance of the aggressive color and the unreadable sign provokes a crisis for O., with the bloodlike tide conveying a fearful complex of resonances. The color is first of all the mark of violence and struggle; when O. notices the red drops on the snow, he thinks he has been injured. The sight of blood is the reversal of natural order: that which is rightfully interior has suddenly, forcefully, become external; that which had appeared to be an empty, inviting matrix for the subject's inscription of himself has become an active, aggressive force that threatens him with extinction.

The fearful tide is also that of menstrual blood, evoking ancient fears of the mother, of eternal cycles, of an endless and bloody reproduction intimately connected with violence and death. The appearance of menstrual blood also evokes a periodicity, signaling that insemination has not occurred, but yet holding out the promise of future fertility for O.'s disseminating writing project. Thus, the book of Epsilon is also the body of some earth-mother whose autochthonous children are the rebellious and (for O.) uncontrollable elements and effects of fiction. If Epsilon is allegorically a text, then that text is profoundly feminine and maternal, representing all that is fearful to the masculine subject seeking identity, meaning, order, and closure.[10] The maternal capacity for infinite metamorphosis and reproduction presents a delirious regression into the textual past for the protagonist who would try to discover the source and explanation of his own condition:

> Au commencement, il n'attache pas une importance essentielle à ces métamorphoses. C'est une propriété de cette histoire, se dit-il, un état fluctueux des rapports entre espace et récit.
>
> Au commencement? Où serait l'origine? C'est un retour ici, une reconstitution. (*VE*, 78)

It is the feminine-maternal principle on Epsilon that terrifies the fictional subject, that threatens the foundations of his subjectivity, and that finally drives him mad: when rescued, O. is found sitting at his desk, writing in the air. His madness takes the form of a repetition compulsion, causing him to reiterate the form of his trauma. The unknown star that precipitates his insanity at the close of *La Vie sur*

Epsilon suggests in more ways than one the star of the seventeenth Enigma of the Tarot, beneath which a woman kneels by a pool of water.[11] In *Enigma,* the sixth fiction of Ollier's cycle, O. is sent to be cured of his madness to the planet Iota, whose inhabited surface is a six-pointed star; he is then sent to earth, where he convalesces in the presence of a woman he meets daily beside a spring. The sign of the feminine, both star and *source* (at once origin and wellspring), follows O. in his subsequent adventures and maintains its ascendancy over his interrogative itinerary.

II. *Enigma*

Enigma is divided into two parts corresponding to the phases of O.'s treatment. The narration of the first section, "Iota," is composed of several voices: that of a computer named Naïma; that of a ubiquitous third-person narrator; and that of O. himself in his notes, signaled by quotation marks but devoid of first-person pronouns. The passages are generally a page or two in length. Periodically, a separate single line referring to musical composition seems to provide a commentary on or counterpoint to the preceding passage. In the second section, "Ezzala," the narration is again distributed among several voices: that of a young woman named Nejma; that of an anonymous narrator; and that of what appears to be O.'s dreams, again signaled by quotation marks but never recounted in the first person. In contrast to the computer-style language of the first part, the prose here becomes highly poetic as it evokes O.'s pastoral convalescence. The single-line musical leitmotif of "Iota" has become in "Ezzala" one of cinematic terms like *traveling* and *flashes.* Many intertextual passages link the two parts of *Enigma* to each other and to the preceding fictions. Such is the heterogeneous, multilayered, and multi-toned narration from which the reader attempts to deduce a solution to the enigma posed by O.'s adventures.

The derangement brought about by the events on Epsilon manifests itself, in *Enigma,* through two primary symptoms; first, O. has forgotten his past. He recalls nothing of the crisis on Epsilon, nor does he remember any of his earlier missions, his apprenticeship on the other four planet-texts of the system. Secondly, in his capacity as leader of a pedestrian surveying team on Iota (*l'équipe F,* the letter after epsilon), he exhibits a familiar propensity for deviation and digression from the others: "La phase seconde est comme un aggravement de l'initiale, une réflexion outrée, mais qu'est-ce à dire, l'analyse tarde, l'écart se creuse, il le sent déjà, et la joie de se nuire, l'angle est inscrit, la divergence, il sait qu'il ne les va réduire et se donne pour relégué et rit sous cape et les autres là-bas s'éloignent" (*E,* 9). O.'s problem, like that of Nolan, seems to lie in his inability—willful or otherwise—to establish a coherent, continuous itinerary. Although O. has forgotten who he is, it is manifest that the link between Lassalle, Morel, Nolan, and O. is more than alphabetical and coincidental. In this second phase, O. is repeating the problematic patterns of his own past. With O., the protagonist has effected an assumption into the realm of science fiction but has not transcended the problems of his terrestrial incarnations. Just as the discussion of Nolan's disappearance became a critique of his written reports, with the cause of his failure residing in his textual *errance,* so the symptoms of O.'s madness are also the symptoms of fiction: O. must remember his past, just as a self-reflexive fiction continually seeks its own origin. And like O.'s deranged itinerary, fiction is composed of unpredictable deviations. If the source and elaboration of a fiction are thus linked to O.'s crisis, the allegorical enigma to be resolved is that of his insanity, first manifested in his senseless writing in the air and later confirmed by the ship's log, which was pronounced indecipherable.

On Iota, therefore, O. undergoes an experimental form of treatment aimed at understanding and curing his psychosis. This treatment resembles psychoanalysis in that it constitutes a rememoration or working-out of the past. It is O.'s daily task on Iota to lead a team of four mean (Juanos, Kline, Smernov, Toïshi) on a close inspection and mapping of a given triangular sector of the planet. In thus recreating his situation on Epsilon, O. is gradually led to reenact and remember the past he has forgotten. While the mapmaking recalls Lassalle's mission, the four colleagues repeat the number of protagonists in the first relay of *Le Jeu d'enfant,* or rather the four avatars of the same protagonist. O.'s medical treatment involves two females corresponding to the two sections of *Enigma.* In the first part, Naïma is an extremely advanced, apparently female computer whose task it is to derive, from all the available data concerning O., the explanation for and pattern of his abnormal conduct.

Naïma's analysis of O.'s actions provides the narrative voice for a considerable part of "Iota": "Ce qui le guide alors et le fait assumer l'acte de divergence—un voeu de destruction? Une séduction parfaite l'incline à modeler ses pas sur une empreinte qu'il se persuade de déceler dans la texture de la pierre et qu'il lit peut-être comme sienne, ailleurs inscrite, et négligée. Ancienne? . . . L'attente se prolonge, atermoiement muet" (*E*, 43–44). A recurrent vocabulary of textuality links O.'s aberrations to the acts of reading and writing; Naïma's analysis takes on the character of both literary criticism and dream interpretation. She recognizes that O.'s current behavior derives in some way from his past, and she postulates something like a Freudian death instinct as his motivation.

Freud links the notion of repetition to the death instinct in *Beyond the Pleasure Principle*. A compulsion to repeat traumatic or unpleasant memories or experiences overrides the pleasure principle in seeking to restore a state of the lowest possible excitation by releasing the cathexis associated with those memories. The universal quest of all life is thus the "return to the quiescence of the inorganic world."[12] On Iota, O. continually and unknowingly repeats the patterns of his former incarnations in an unconscious attempt to rejoin his origins: "La mécanique implacable de cette retraite quasiment instinctive au départ . . . le conduit tôt ou tard à revendiquer comme une prérogative la tâche de retrouver certain sillon premier, originel" (*E*, 66). If the *sillons*, as ubiquitous on Iota as on Epsilon, do have sexual meaning for O., then he is searching for his mother, his generatrix, his source. In his instinctive attempt to rejoin the originary maternal matrix, the earth-mother who represents for him lack and absence and who threatens him with extinction, O. is exhibiting a classic case of the death drive, the *Todestrieb* that Freud sees as the most primordial drive of all living substance.

Naïma advises her operator to delve further back into O.'s earliest years of apprenticeship for an explanation of his current illness, thus echoing the advice given to the investigator of Nolan's disappearance in the fourth novel. In this way, Naïma's goal parallels O.'s own unconscious motivations: both of them seek an origin that is multiple and obscure. Just as O.'s search is complicated by the multiplicity of *sillons* to follow, Naïma's interrogations are hampered by the variety of O.'s incarnations.

In the course of his daily expeditions on Iota, O. gradually repeats and remembers his experiences on Epsilon. The other members of his team participate in O.'s retracings: they know of his crisis on Epsilon and reenact with him scenes from that earlier expedition. This mimetic transfer, a *structurodrame* that recalls the techniques of psychodrama, finally leads O. to remember the episodes on Epsilon that culminated in the apparition of the unknown star, its disappearance, and his subsequent rescue. O. reestablishes contact with this part of his past when he finally recognizes one of his companions, Toïshi, as the man who rescued him on Epsilon:

> Et Toïshi s'avance au centre vrai du triangle devant la borne cernée de vert et parle et tout obstacle à la reconnaissance est levé.
>
> Et tout obstacle au renouement a été levé. (*E,* 115)

O.'s cure on Iota, effected by a process of remembering, is a simplification or even a parody of early psychoanalytic goals, in which conscious recall of repressed events was held to result in the diminution of neurosis. The psychoanalytic concepts and vocabulary evoked here and elsewhere in *Le Jeu d'enfant* serve as allegories of fictional elaboration rather than as serious principles of character development.

With O.'s reappropriation of his own past, his triangulation of Iota's surface is completed and Naïma conveys to her operator the conclusions of her research, which parallel that of her patient:

> Vois donc comme nos démarches convergent en cette phase ultime, comme nos procès se sont croisés: abstrait le mien . . . le sien, lié au contact des matières. La phase sixième est donc: de renouement. Avec un style je renouais; lui une écriture. En décalage incessamment, nos deux traques "jouaient." A leur principe était l'écart.
>
> Son "patron" de conduite? . . . "Creuser l'écart et trouver seul l'origine." (*E,* 109)

Naïma combines the role of interpretive analyst with that of textual critic in isolating the style or guiding principle behind O.'s aberrations.

The cause, the symptoms, and the treatment of O.'s madness have all been textual in nature: the fearful book of Epsilon finally drove O. to a delirious writing in the air, and an analytic critic was subsequently called on to interpret the style of his behavior. The sixth phase, or book, thus marks a *renouement,* a conscious reknotting of the threads binding previous protagonists and adventures. The progress of O.'s cure is marked in terms of a growing awareness of the intertextual ties that make every reading a rereading:

> Pour l'heure, il s'arrête, écoute, s'inquiète de repères . . .
> Lisant soudain la déraison marquée d'un épisode, une scène . . .
> Un texte . . .
> (Une discontinuité . . .) Le . . .
> Le relisant! (*E,* 67)

Although O. has remembered Epsilon as his most recent (textual) adventure, that maternal planet does not seem to constitute for him his absolute and earliest origins, his "sillon premier, originel," for he does not abandon his obsessional wanderings when sent to Earth to convalesce in the second part of *Enigma.*

In the Sudanese city of Ezzala, O. continues to reestablish contact with his own incarnations of the previous fictions. Here, his four Arab companions—Karim, Jamal, Taïbi, Saïd—repeat the initials of the *équipe F* on Iota. In the same way that Naïma was assigned to his case on Iota, Nejma is instructed to seduce O., to entertain him, and to aid in his recovery. Nejma is a familiar figure, linked in appearance and activity to the twin girls of *La Mise en scène,* to the twin great-nieces of the blue-eyed Arab in *L'Echec de Nolan,* and to a series of other women mysteriously glimpsed or encountered, often sexually, in the preceding fictions. Like the star Enigma of the Tarot, these women are almost always seen near a spring, filling an amphora. In *La Mise en scène,* the first of these apparitions surprises Lassalle asleep beside a spring: "Lassalle vient d'ouvrir les yeux. . . . Peut-être les avait-il entr'ouverts depuis quelques instants, car elle s'est enfuie. . . . Elle était devant lui, à trois ou quatre mètres de l'arbre, juste au milieu du champs, et maintenant elle se sauve, elle glisse à petits pas souples et coulés le long du sillon parallèle au mur. Des gouttes d'eau s'éclaboussant la chevelure, la robe, les jambes, les pieds nus" (*Ms,* 126–27). Nejma's point of view inaugurates "Ezzala," the second section of *Enigma,* with a similar scene: "Pour le second matin, je viens à la source, je me penche au-dessus des pierres, les oiseaux coupent en criant le cercle d'eau, hier il m'a regardée, l'amphore est remplie jusqu'au col, je peux fuir, la chaleur est sèche aujourd'hui, mes mains coupent le cercle d'eau" (*E,* 125). The women's connection with water, the water jar, and the *source* has mythic resonances of the "eternal feminine," the procreative element, and the origins of life.[13] The darker side of this fluid femininity, the menstrual taboo evoked by Epsilon's threatening tide, is equally connected with procreation. Like the ominous maternal planet, the ovum-shaped computer Naïma is bound up in O.'s self-destructive quest for his origins; Nejma, by contrast, incarnates for him all that is compelling, attractive, and pleasurable in the feminine principle.

Nejma is equally an embodiment of the feminine in a Nietzschean sense in that she is veiled, reticent, silent, and yet seductive. In aphorism 60 of *Joyful Wisdom,* Nietzsche compares woman to a silent ship sailing beyond the noisy breakers on the shore; for man, she represents the calm (truth, happiness, respite) he desires above all else. Her effect, however, is only an effect at a distance; the ghostly ship is in reality as bustling as the shore. Woman's deceptive distance is also that afforded by her veils, which permit her to seduce and retreat with the same gesture: "But perhaps this is the greatest charm of life: it puts a gold-embroidered veil of lovely potentialities over itself, promising, resisting, modest, mocking, sympathetic, seductive. Yes, life is a woman!"[14] While her clothing and scarves may be removed, Nejma's mouth is always covered by a veil; she rarely speaks but, rather, observes and listens to O.: "Le voile est bleu sur ma nuque, le mouchoir mauve à mes lèvres, sa main ne touchera pas le mouchoir mauve, il dit qu'il connaît tous les quartiers maintenant, j'écoute, tous les jardins jusqu'au désert" (*E,* 163). If Nejma, veiled, represents a hidden truth for O., she is also a silent and receptive analyst, eliciting from him revelations about that very truth, which is the fluid landscape of his own repressed past.

In Nejma's presence, then, O. recalls more and more of his earlier life. His real progress toward a cure is evident, however, in a series of dreams whose development is marked in terms of Freudian symbols.

What O. had forgotten about Epsilon was the feminine principle on that planet, a principle that threatened his very identity and subjectivity. It is with this feminine principle, and his repression of it, that O. must grapple in his dreams in Ezzala. Freud notes the analytical value of dream interpretation in neuroses deriving from a specific trauma: "The study of dreams may be considered the most trustworthy method of investigating deep mental processes. Now dreams occurring in traumatic neuroses have the characteristic of repeatedly bringing the patient back into the situation of his accident."[15] O.'s wandering search for the source of his own wandering is played out in the language of his dreams: "Cependant O. là-bas, endormi sous les arbres, renouait 'à mots couverts' une errance ancienne, et son sommeil, ce midi même, livrait la clef d'un champs inusité" (*E,* 127).

A psychoanalytic interpretation would thus uncover, in the initial dreams, a personal language of sexual fears reminiscent of O.'s experiences on Epsilon.[16] The first dream presents a vast red plain covered with *sillons* that suddenly becomes a moving sea of magma rising inexorably, threatening to absorb the subject. Although one dream opens and closes upon a peaceful swim in a deep, still lake, subsequent dreams generally present images of submersion and symbolic castration. One such dream (signaled as always by quotation marks) presents phallic towers and a distant sea: "'A flanc de colline neuf tours se dressent, ou phares très étroits, cylindriques, très hauts, dôtés de plateformes circulaires à mi-hauteur, qu'un parapet protège, en marbre gris, les tours ou minarets sont en marbre gris, de ce côté la vallée, de cet autre le ciel, là-bas, à droite, est-ce la mer?'" (*E,* 157). Cords attached to the columns begin to oscillate slowly, communicating at length their instability to the columns themselves: "'La course des pendules s'accélère, les tours ou minarets s'inclinent, se coupent de leur socle, neuf sifflements encore, et volent dans les airs, la mer à l'horizon bascule, les fûts démantelés tournoient, quel temps en fin de chute mesureront les pierres?'" (*E,* 158).

Eventually, the dreamed sea is masked and tamed by dikes, bridges, and fortifications, as the subject reasserts himself and fights off the impingement of the feminine fluidity that had first threatened him on Epsilon. O. is thus replaying in oneiric, symbolic terms the tensions that led to his crisis, thereby dredging fragments of his past lives from his unconscious. A description echoing that of Manhattan in *Eté indien* underlines the importance of the man-made grill imposed on the blank but potent presence of the sea: "Un tracé *audacieux* relie les îles entre elles, des voies aériennes se chevauchent, les chaussées bifurquent en courbes amples et compliquées, à grande hauteur le vent fait osciller le tablier des ponts, pour construire les arches on a détourné la mer, les piles s'ancrent dans le fond vide de la mer, quel dessein voilé, quelle urgence commandaient un si vaste labeur?" (*E*, 186; my emphasis). Against a ubiquitous matrix—the sea, the feminine—the subject insists on erecting his own audacious inventions or constructions, thereby affirming his (phallic) identity. This ground-figure situation recalls the urgency of O.'s effort to inscribe an identity on the recalcitrant surface of Epsilon. A conflictual oscillation in narrative focus is thus set up between the feminine matrix and the masculine subject whose quest forms the story being told. Although O. is lulled for a time by the prenatal dream of a return to the fluid matrix of the womb, his fears of that same fluidity reassert themselves and force him to insist on dominating what he fears.

Thus in a later dream, two giants follow a valley back to the source of the river that formed it:

> . . . de qui sont ces silhouettes sans rapport avec le paysage au loin, oblitérant les eaux du lac, progressant vers l'amont d'un pas démesuré?
> . . . quelle tâche les requiert? vers quel terme se hâtent ces géants?
> (*E*, 196)

The giants figure for O. his continual search "upstream" for an origin to his story, as well as his efforts to dominate the feminine water imagery that necessarily provides the place of origin. Despite his colossal efforts to finally get back to that originary point, his progress never seems to culminate in a discovery but rather continues indefinitely, always hastening toward its final term while never actually reaching it. In the same way, O.'s search for the source of his experience on Epsilon uncovered only a bizarre link with an ever-receding past accomplished by others (who are all, nonetheless, O.) on earlier and earlier missions, in earlier and earlier fictions.

The last dream presents a *paysage inconnu,* an unfamiliar and uncharted landscape. A chaotic compendium of the colors and forms of previous planets, the landscape is at once strange and familiar. It evokes the multiple elements of O.'s past adventures and demonstrates their vertiginous capacity for reorganization: "'. . . à quelle table de jeu se rapportent ces pièces, ce découpage aux tons perçants, insoutenables, ce monde vrillé, somptueux, qui capte l'oeil à brûle-pourpoint, où l'on entre de plain-pied, éberlué, sans voix?'" (*E*, 207). O.'s cure is classic: he finally remembers his repressed past not only as the planet-text that threatened him, but also as the feminine matrix, as a spiraling, labyrinthine set of variable, iterative elements that dazzle and amaze him. He is seduced by the permutations and combinations of these elements much as he was seduced by Nejma's enigmatic series of veils, but he takes his place in their world now, *de plain-pied,* as one element among many. O. is silent now, *sans voix* but also *sans voie:* with no further path of investigation to pursue. The metaphor of the game of inclusion and exclusion—of configuration and refiguration—now characterizes the nature of fiction, including that of the fictional hero. The resolution of O.'s insanity comes with the ironic recognition that the remembered past is still in some sense a *paysage inconnu,* susceptible to a continued mutation that captures the fictional subject and carries him along. Both the dark, threatening fluidity of Epsilon and the seductive aquatic imagery connected with Nejma seem to constitute the origin O. seeks and fears that he cannot localize as a fixed point.

In abandoning his earlier insistence on a privileged perspective ("Lutter pour ne pas lâcher pied, sauvegarder à tout prix une vue privilégiée" [*VE,* 78]), O. has stopped trying to dominate or colonize the *paysage inconnu,* electing rather to participate in the limited manner allowed him. He decides to remain in Ezzala, finally renouncing his *errance ancienne* in favor of domestic life as a laborer. His choice is emblematic of his situation; Ezzala is a mystical, labyrinthine city composed of concentric circles radiating from a central sanctuary established in honor of the "maître miséricordieux du Verbe": "Le centre est donc le sanctuaire qu'El Klam, dès la sixième heure, ordonna qu'on batît à l'endroit même où l'élan victorieux l'avait porté—ou bien la lassitude immobilisé le soir, ou la poussière, la soif, tel voile mauve sous tel oeil tiré" (*E,* 174). A holy book entitled *La Lecture* is placed on a mosaic table at the center of the sanctuary. The mosaic tiles trace a six-pointed star that forms, for the eyes of the Sages, the *figure essentielle* underlying the city's superficially circular structure. Thus both a star and a veiled woman are found at the center and origin of this city dedicated to the master of the *Verbe*. In the sixth hour, the sixth book of *Le Jeu d'enfant* seems to announce an end to the questing peregrinations of the fictional protagonist. All of O.'s searches have led him to this point, just as the progress of self-reflexive fiction returns unfailingly to the question of its own origin: "Nejma chantonne, il dit qu'il l'a cherchée longtemps" (*E*, 193).

The star is the emblem of the woman and of the enigma to be resolved. It was an unknown star with its accompanying feminine terrors that occasioned O.'s madness; it was by means of two females that his analysis and cure were effected, as well as by triangulation of the star Iota and perambulation of the star-shaped city, Ezzala. Flowers laid out in the shape of a star on Nejma's bed mark at once the place of the enigma and the means of its penetration. In becoming a citizen of Ezzala, in marrying Nejma, O. has been both enlightened and seduced. *Médusé,* he has been led by the twin females—Naïma and Nejma—to see what he searched for in the elusive, multiple, and ever-receding feminine itself. He is convinced by this feminine principle of his submission to her, of his identity within her. A series of stars leads O. to see the ancient city of Ezzala as an emblem of his situation: the city is only superficially circular, only *seemingly* centered around a figure like an *O;* the essential shape of the city is an occult, labyrinthine star, which reveals the emptiness of the circular structure—the zero—it underlies. Thus, a fiction, by allegorical extension, is only apparently centered around a subject like O.; a deeper principle of construction lies in the star, the very figure that demonstrates to the subject his subsumption within it. O.'s cure is effected when he renounces his claim to a privileged status and elects to live within the parameters of the figure that healed him.

III. Family Romance: An Intertextual Model

Like the *pharmakon,* that paradoxical drug in Plato's pharmacy that is both a poison and a remedy, the complex and emblematic feminine has operated a paradoxical effect on O., driving him mad and curing him with the same mechanisms, those of writing. And like the *pharmakon* of writing discussed by Derrida in "La Pharmacie de Platon," the feminine exerts its pharmaceutical effects by means of liquids, from the terrifying inundation of Epsilon to Nejma's healing presence beside the enigmatic *source.*[17]

The feminine is a fluidity to which O. is instinctively drawn but which he nevertheless comes to fear and reject. The primary drive to rejoin the womb is eventually supplanted, though never eradicated, by the later desire to suppress what is feared. If the feminine is a shifting and liquid matrix, then the masculine subject must try to form a solid, static figure against that amorphous ground; in Ezzala, the Freudian dreams that traced O.'s progress toward a cure took place in just these terms.[18] Yet O.'s cure has ostensibly made him accept his subsumption within that ground and his equality with other elements composing it. O. is supposedly part of that which is dissolved and suspended in the spiraling, fluid matrix, yet he is susceptible to the paradoxical effect of the whole—madness and cure—as if he were outside it. The resolution reached at the end of O.'s dreams in Ezzala is thus less simple than it first appeared, and his cure rests on a contradiction in the relationship of figure to ground, as O. is both dissolved within the feminine and also an integral solid in relation to its fluid effects.

If O. represents the interests of the masculine subject of fiction, the feminine too has been linked with textuality and writing since O.'s misadventures on Epsilon. The paradoxical relationship of O. to the feminine resides in the nature of writing itself and provides an allegorical answer to the question of fictional origins. In Plato's *Phaedrus,* Socrates recounts a myth explaining the origin of writing: the Egyptian demigod Theuth invented written characters and presented them to the king of gods as a device to aid the memories of men.[19] The king rejected the invention and condemned writing as a poison to memory, since it would induce men to forget spoken discourse. The feminine with which O. struggles operates just such a paradoxical effect, seeming to offer a cure for O.'s lost memory while in reality seducing him into an acceptance of an inferior status, into forgetting his original investigations. Significantly, O. no longer reads or writes on Ezzala. If knowledge, for Socrates, is a remembrance of the forms of the Real glimpsed in an earlier and purer state, then writing is no more than digression and forgetfulness in relation to the privileged state. Writing is a poison to the true memory of living, spoken discourse, which, Socrates claims, is the only way to recapture the perfect knowledge previously glimpsed. Writing is irrevocably cut off from its origin, which it nonetheless constantly attempts to repeat; its essential trait is an endless *errance:*

> You would imagine that they [speeches] had intelligence, but if you want to know anything and put a question to one of them, the speaker always gives one unvarying answer. And when they have been once written down they are tumbled about anywhere among those who may or may not understand them, and know not to whom they should reply, to whom not; and, if they are maltreated or abused, they have no parent to protect them; and they cannot protect or defend themselves.[20]

O. is just such a lost figure: wandering inside the space of textuality, he struggles through repetition to rejoin an impossible origin. His symptoms are those of fiction, a writing whose elaboration constitutes a search for an origin that retreats in infinite, intertextual regression into the magma of other texts.[21] If the feminine represents the amorphous infinity of writing, the Book of all texts, then O. embodies the finitude of an individual fiction claiming its own delimited status.

O.'s situation thus provides an allegory for the intertextual basis of fictional elaboration. The embodiment of a certain type of writing himself, O. can be dissolved in the intertextual matrix while submitting to its paradoxical effects. O. desires above all to locate and stabilize his own identity, to rejoin a fixed point of origin and enjoy the privileged view it affords him on the meaning of his life. Although he derives from and participates in the amorphous intertextual matrix, O. would like to freeze his own paradoxical identity into its solid, integral pole, relegating the fluid aspect to the (dominated) background. The individual fiction that O. embodies presents itself as a complete, integral figure, but it is nonetheless constantly open to manipulation by and interaction with the larger ground of Fiction that surrounds and permeates it. Suspended in this matrix, the individual fiction is at once, and/or consecutively, solid and fluid. Epsilon's strange "Law of Symmetry" by which earlier adventures/texts determine the present one is thus a principle of intertextual (re)production; it is the interplay and immixture of two poles of production, of feminine matrix and masculine subject (of Fiction and fiction). Permutations of the autochthonous phenomena on Epsilon produce the story relived by the subject, while individual variations still account for its denouement and still erect some kind of solid grill upon the medium, although this grill can at any moment be dissolved, reorganized, and reformed. Fictional elaboration derives from this conflictual oscillation and interplay between figure and ground, between son and mother, between individual fiction and Fiction, in which the figure is derived from the ground and yet not identical to it. An individual fiction replicates the fluid structure of the ground, while maintaining its own solidity as a specific if not permanent closure. The fiction that O. embodies can neither escape the structure of writing to rejoin an exterior, real origin, nor ever pinpoint its own unique source within that maternal structure of writing. The conflictual interplay of figure and ground must continue without resolution.

In the allegory of family strife developed here, O. represents the masculine subject of fiction. He is also a zero, a circle, and so embodies the tautological quest of a fiction that infinitely repeats itself to find its own starting point. But this circular investigation has always operated within the larger ground of the feminine, the labyrinth, and the star, and within the more general context of feminine fluidity and masculine solidity. In Ezzala, the star was the essential figure hidden beneath a larger set of circles. In the next fiction, *Our ou Vingt ans après,* the woman wears a star-shaped pendant in which a circle is inscribed. A symbolic reversal has accompanied O.'s cure: the circle is now subsumed within the star, and O.'s recognition is both matricial and maternal. The feminine labyrinth of the star is the ultimate enigma and emblem of O.'s madness and cure, presenting the final figurative model of intertextuality in which O.'s progress toward enlightenment allegorizes that of fiction itself. In Egyptian hieroglyphics a star signifies the rising up to an origin. The sign of the star is an element of the hieroglyphs for bringing up, educating, and teaching. O.'s guided wanderings have been part of a reeducation, an *Unbildungsroman* aimed at correcting his previous erroneous inclinations. O. has been initiated into the enigma of his source: the origin sought by a fiction is the labyrinthine structure of the writing by which it operates its research, of which it consists itself. Just as the star symbolically alludes to multiplicity, this origin is never a point, but rather a principle of instability and infinite regress.[22]

O.'s odyssey through *La Vie sur Epsilon* and *Enigma* has invariably pitted him, in a variety of figurations, against the feminine. In the enunciation of this allegorical opposition between mother and son, a model of intertextuality—a way of envisioning the genesis and elaboration of fiction—has been developed. With the fifth and sixth novels of the cycle, science fiction has become a science of fiction whose goal is to discover its own properties and principles. Of primary concern in this inquest is the origin and autonomy of individual texts; the method of investigation is the establishment of coherently allegorical progressions, conflicts, and personifications. A revolutionary genealogy has been proposed by the intertextual model developed here, a genealogy that subsumes the identity of individual fictions within a ubiquitous maternal womb.

The self-interrogative Project operated by *Le Jeu d'enfant* has effected a similar enlightenment. The psychoanalytic discourse of Freud and Lacan, the Tarot, and the network of myths and symbols permeating *La Vie sur Epsilon* and *Enigma* form, with those fictions, a relationship analogous to the mother-son model of intertextuality and can be seen as an exemplary case of that model. These symbols, metaphors, and languages are not simply allusions to various domains exterior to the text at hand; they are, rather, components of a system that contains the text at hand, inhabiting it in such a way as to evoke complex associations with a vast textual background. These associations guide the course of the reading by the weight of their resonances. Each intertext, or partial matrix, is thus both a textual, cultural past and part of a determining system. The Project has, in this manner, seen the question of fictional genesis as a question of intertextuality.

The language of psychoanalysis is nonetheless a privileged intertext for the Project's *recherche,* in that it constitutes the means by which the Project accomplishes its self-analysis. The special status of the psychoanalytic method as an instrument of self-examination—however parodically it may be used—raises questions of hierarchy and differentiation within the matrix as a unified, homogeneous entity. The Project's purportedly successful self-analysis has in some sense contradicted the revolutionary conclusion it arrived at: the privileged discourse of psychoanalysis has allowed the Project to affirm that no privileged closures can exist within the matrix of all texts. The Project achieves its conscious status by means of a theory that profoundly questions consciousness itself. In the same way, O.'s recognition of his position within a determining system paradoxically reaffirms him as a conscious subject who can take his critical distance from that system. And, far from reducing himself to a zero—an *homme nul*—O. continues his investigative journey in the next fiction. As the agent or embodiment of the Project in the outer space of Ollier's fifth and sixth fictions, the protagonist O. remains a paradoxical *point central,* the original question of origins to which the fiction continually returns. For in *Our ou Vingt ans après* the same question of genealogy, of origin, arises in a new light as O. conducts an investigation into the archaeological foundations of writing and the *paternity* of fiction.

3

Filiations:
The Paternity of Fiction

> The text of the encyclopedia said: for one of those
> gnostics, the visible universe was an illusion (or more
> precisely) a sophism. Mirrors and fatherhood
> are abominable because they multiply and
> disseminate that universe.
> —Borges

> Et il te dira que la Terre est une erreur, que les
> miroirs et la paternité sont choses abominables car
> ils la confirment et la multiplient.
> —Ollier

The seventh novel of *Le Jeu d'enfant* opens with a son witnessing his father's death. The group of Arab men whom O. has joined in Ezzala is gathered, seated in a circle, for a special ritual of passage effected by both son and father: "l'assemblée du soir reconduit le pacte, tient concile à bâtons rompus, *ça parle,* on pérore en tout lieu du local, une envolée de manches dénonce un grouillement dans les coins obscurs; une quinte déchire la poitrine du père, le gamin soudain muet relève d'un trait le pan de bleu entre ses cuisses, secoue sa verge entre deux doigts poissés, *le cercle des tanneurs hallucine l'absente*" (*Our,* 11; my emphasis). In the ceremony, the smoke of a golden herb accompanies the child's masturbation as well as many evocations of textuality, culminating in a passage reminiscent of *Enigma*'s allegorical outcome: "l'aiguille sur un sillon désaffecté, un texte sans nom d'auteur s'écrit une bonne fois pour toutes dans le quadrilatère étroit" (*Our,* 15). The father's death appears to follow upon the eviction of the author from the text: "on dirait que le gamin renonce, le pan de bleu s'abaisse sur le sexe pétri, cache les cuisses glabres, le capuchon recouvre le visage figé; la flamme vacille entre les tiges de métal, les postures guindées se défont, un peuple inconsistant observe l'agonie sourde" (*Our,* 15). At the end of this thirteen-page initial passage, the narration indicates that certain secrets have been revealed to the young *initié,* along with the names of seven lands he is to visit. A solitary line on the following page declares: "Le lendemain même, il arriva à Our" (*Our,* 20). The rest of the book presents the young man's visit to Ur, the greatest city of ancient Sumeria, where writing is said to have originated.

The reader surmises that it is O. who is dying, after an unspecified number of years in Ezzala as Nejma's husband and father of her son. The text of *Our ou Vingt ans après* is composed of short, enigmatic passages varying in length from a few lines to a few pages, and separated by several lines of blank space. In this way, the text visually exhibits the lacunae in its story-line. The passages comprising *Our* may be dialogue, poetry, song, incantation, or narrative; they derive from a number of sources and voices. Thus the narrative shifts among a variety of points of view both within and without the narration. Intertextual borrowings from many different sources, including the previous texts of *Le Jeu d'enfant,* complicate the already difficult task of reading and interpreting a text that has become even more heterogeneous and overdetermined than its predecessors.

What O. had come to see and accept by the end of *Enigma* was his inclusion in a structure wherein he had a certain identity, but over which he exercised no control. The inaugural passage of *Our ou Vingt ans après* suggests that this recognition can be seen in Lacanian terms as the resolution of the "mirror stage"—the mythic passage of the individual from an imaginary realm of false identifications into a socialized, symbolic order in which the individual is constituted as a subject. The prologue to the narrative proper of *Our* presents, in terms that are overtly and covertly those of psychoanalysis, both an initiation and a recognition. The phrase *ça parle* in the first passage cited makes explicit the recognition alluded to by at least seventeen other similarly elliptical statements, each of which is suspended between quotation marks and given an emphasis: "C'est bien *ça*"; "Maintenant *c'est* clair"; "*Il* faudrait être aveugle"; "*La Chose* parle d'elle-même"; "Il ne manquait plus que *ça*"; and finally "*Ça* n'arrive qu'à *moi*," at the apparent moment of the father's death. *Ça parle:* the id speaks; Freud's recognition of the primacy of the unconscious is seen by Lacan as a linguistic determination: "On se prenait à répéter après Freud le mot de sa découverte: *ça parle,* et là sans doute où l'on s'y attendait le moins."[1] For Lacan, the structure of language preexists the entry of any subject into that structure and conditions the possibilities of the subject's existence. The true subject of a given discourse is lodged in the unconscious. In the first section of *Our,* O. is dying, and his recognition is apparently that of the lesson learned in *Enigma:* that of the ascendancy of the maternal star, a vision of textuality where authorless texts are written once and for all, "une bonne fois pour toutes." O. abandons the imaginary realm in which he had tried to possess his origin by reuniting with it (her); now, he acknowledges that he is subsumed by his own (linguistic) nature within a textual system that determines him. For the fiction that O. embodies, the unconscious that determines him and speaks through him is the allegorically femi- nine intertextual matrix. The feminine functions here both as the structure of writing that inhabits and contains him and also as the mother, past, and origin he wants to identify with. O.'s cure—his recognition—is not the acquisition of an autonomous or privileged status, but rather an awareness of the truth about his position; that is, the impossibility of locating his origin or of establishing his autonomy.

The outcome of the struggle then seems to be that the circular quest of O., the individual son-fiction, necessarily inscribes itself within the maternal figure of the star. The fiction to be elaborated is thus one of triangulation, like O.'s laborious delineation of three-pointed sectors on the star-shaped surface of the Iotian settlement. Yet this triangular limit, reevoked in the prologue to *Our,* also evokes Oedipus and thereby raises again the question of the paternity of a fiction. If, in *La Vie sur Epsilon,* O. was Oedipus in desiring to possess the mother and bridge the gap between himself and his origin, in the seventh fiction he comes to occupy the position of the father in the Oedipal structure: his own son's initiation into a wandering search for the historical begin- nings of writing in *Our* is inaugurated by the masturbatory evocation of a woman ("le cercle des tanneurs hallucine l'absente") who can only be the Oedipal mother.

In Lacan's version of the Oedipal triangle, the son resolves the conflict when he takes on his father's name and enters into the symbolic order. In repressing his desire for the mother and her desire, the child substitutes a paternal metaphor for the earlier maternal identifications. *Our ou Vingt ans après* begins at the point where O.'s son is apparently resolving his own Oedipal crisis: the son takes on the father's name, and that name is, allegorically, that of fiction. In *L'Anti-Oedipe,* Gilles Deleuze and Félix Guattari point out that the resolution of one Oedipal situation marks the initiation of a second one.[2] But with O. and his son, the two resolutions seem illogically simultaneous. O.'s resolution (his recognition of matricial primacy and his marriage to Nejma) ostensibly took place years before the ritual in which his son accomplishes his own resolution of the Oedipal conflict and assumes his father's name. However, the opening ritual of *Our* is clearly one of recognition by O. as well as by his son. It now becomes clear that O.'s first resolution was partial or erroneous; he was mistaken in thinking he could abandon the fictional subject's quest as he sought to do at the end of *Enigma* by setting up a false scenario of his own disappearance. O.'s final recognition of his position and function comes only at his death, in *Our ou Vingt ans après.* O. now realizes that he will never be able to terminate the searching journey, that there is no exit from the system of fiction. For O. is reincarnated in his own son, just as all the earlier protagonists were revealed to be a single subject. As in the Alexandre Dumas novel echoed in the title, *Vingt ans après,* the cause will be taken up again in twenty years' time—that is, by the next generation. Like O., the son will conduct his investigation on the question of writing, on the corpus of the feminine. Like O. before him, the son looks backward toward an origin: he undertakes a journey to Ur, the legendary birthplace of writing. As *Our* progresses, the distinction between O. and his son is impossible to maintain. In the death ceremony of the opening passage, the absent woman is evoked by a circle of men, a masculine circle, an O; the mother's absence—that of the phallus—is indicated by the father, who comes to constitute in *Our* a challenge to the maternal metaphor of textuality. Thus the model of maternal or intertextual fictional production elaborated in the fifth and sixth novels of *Le Jeu d'enfant* comes to be challenged, in the seventh, by another model that focuses instead on the role of the father in the genealogy of fiction.

With the appearance of Oedipus, then, the writing subject of fiction becomes an issue, since the author is traditionally held to be the father of a text. The intertextual model enunciated in the previous chapter had seemed to minimize or even deny the role of the writing subject in the constitution of a fiction; a model that sees a text as the crossroad of multiple, heterogeneous elements from other texts has no need to posit a unified, controlling consciousness at the origin of that text. If the paternal model now emerges as a possible source of structure and direction, then the intertextual, matricial model is challenged. And *Our,* in effect, is replete with sets of fathers and sons, while the solitary woman who figures there is the object of controversy, struggle, violence, and betrayal.

In the archæology of writing conducted in *Our,* is the father now to be considered the temporal, historical beginning of a fiction? Is the figure of the father a more potent force than the intertextual model would indicate? What is the relationship of the writing subject to the text signed by that subject? If these are the questions to be explored in Ollier's seventh fiction, it is not insignificant that *Our ou Vingt ans après,* a novel about fathers and sons both biological and textual, should conjure up Alexandre Dumas *père,* who was himself much enmeshed in both types of filiation. Many of the questions that arise in *Our* as to the writing subject's status were raised in respect to Dumas's own work: plagiarism, authorial control or license, abuse of narrative coincidence. Dumas published prodigiously and was criticized for operating an *usine à romans* whose productions he signed, sometimes without even editing or revising them himself. He was further faulted for stretching the limits of credibility: for rearranging historical facts, and for too freely resorting to extravagant chance in matters of plot. While Dumas's critics judged him according to a vision of the author as one who accepts credit only for original material, and who respects the *vraisemblable* as well as the historical, their criteria of legitimacy reflect the problem of the status of the writing subject in *Our*—his originality, his control over the final product, his use of borrowed texts.

Just as traditional (historical, biographical) criticism has insisted on making Dumas a father responsible for his textual offspring (or on chastizing him for his irresponsibility), it has also maintained that

biological filiation and heredity have a specific bearing upon his novelistic production: "Il y a eu dans l'hérédité de Dumas, si l'on tient
compte des grands-parents, du père et de la mère, liberté désinvolte des
nobles, simplicité robuste du coeur plébéien, gentillesse et ostentation
des hommes de couleur. Tout cela a composé une originalité qui peu à
peu a passé de la personne dans l'oeuvre."[3] Here, originality and
inheritance are paradoxically juxtaposed and equated. Both are transmitted genetically from the parent to the author, and from the author
to his work. The author is both a father passing on his own genetic
makeup and a son who receives a certain inheritance necessary to and
constitutive of his own original brand of authorship. Eventually, in
traditional literary criticism, an author's inheritance was seen in the
way he was influenced by certain literary fathers whose themes, concerns, or style he perpetuated in his own work.

The traditional, biological vision of the author has been roundly
questioned in modern literature and commentary; the New Novel is no
exception to this interrogative trend. *Our* reopens the question of
textual genesis in order to challenge conventional views of the author.
In the seventh novel of *Le Jeu d'enfant* a pair of revolutions, one heir to
the other, purports to offer an alternative notion of the writing subject
through a radical upheaval in the political economy of classical and
romantic language. However, the notion of filiation as a constitutive
force in the production of a fiction is never abandoned. While textual
filiation is reinterpreted in terms of a radicalized writing subject, or
scriptor, the metaphor of biological filiation continues to weave a
troubling thread throughout the fiction. The family struggle that took
place on Epsilon was apparently not resolved in *Enigma*. In *Our,* the
ongoing investigation into the nature and origin of fiction has been
"Oedipalized": while the intertextual model of a maternal matrix of
fiction has not been left behind, a powerful paternal metaphor emerges
to challenge it, and with it many of the theoretical notions underlying
the New Novel. This paternal metaphor is not the straw man of tradition it initially seemed; its agent is once again O., who has demonstrated a remarkable tenacity in both cycles of Ollier's project: he has
incarnated the traditional fictional subject, has embodied a fiction's
search for its source, and now, in the incarnation of his own son,
investigates the archaeology of writing. The renewal of the Oedipal

quarrel now elucidates the problematic role of the writing subject in the formulation of a fiction. Throughout his modulations and evolutions, O. remains a pivotal point in the family romance of fiction.

I. Paternity and Fiction

> Paternity may be a legal fiction.
>
> —James Joyce

The traditional critic saw the novelist as the father of his fictions. In Western culture, a father insures the legitimacy of his heirs by giving them his name. No man wishes to claim the sons of other men as his own and would seem a fool were he to do so unwittingly; the pride of creation as well as material inheritance rest on the propriety of a man's son being strictly his own. Propriety and property are thus insured by laws governing the relationship of father to son. In order to receive the property rightfully due him, the son must first himself qualify as the nominal property and product of his father. Legitimacy in the realm of fiction is similarly linked, in the traditional vision, to property, patriarchy, and law; an author who claims another's words for his or her own is either careless or unscrupulous. Alexandre Dumas was more than once in trouble with the propriety of his day because of a certain nonchalance toward his progeny both biological and printed.

Later, Henry James came to be troubled by the parentage of a fiction to which he had given his name: "I profess a certain vagueness of remembrance in respect to the origin and growth of 'The Tragic Muse' . . . I can but look on the present fiction as a poor fatherless and motherless, a sort of unregistered and unacknowledged birth."[4] For James, the fiction is an heir who has been cut off from his parental heritage, and most particularly from his patrimony, since the birth has taken place neither registered in the father's name nor recognized by patriarchal law. A fiction whose paternal legitimacy is not strictly accounted for might well be the son of any man, or of many. The disjunction James felt between a unique father and his legitimate son is increasingly expressed in poetry, philosophy, fiction, and literary theory from the romantics to the poststructuralists. The early German romantic Novalis envisioned a syncretic Encyclopedia—a *Total-wissenschaft*—that would constitute the poetic unity of all books and all knowledge. For Novalis, the sciences have been divided into separate domains, just as human existence has been divided among individual humans; this division is accidental and unfortunate. It is therefore the task of poetry or literature to accomplish a synthesis among sciences, philosophies, religions, and individuals.[5] Such a synthesis already challenges the dyad of the singular author and his unique work.

The romantic poets saw poetry as the work of a transcendent, atemporal spirit. For Shelley, "a poet participates in the eternal, the infinite, and the one." Shelley further argues that in poetry, as in the plastic arts, the creator is never fully cognizant of the process in which he is involved: "the very mind which directs the hands in formation is incapable of accounting to itself for the origin, the gradations, or the media of the process."[6] While romantics like Shelley saw the individual author as the temporary embodiment of an atemporal spirit or muse, they felt the writer nevertheless produces texts both original and unique. For modern writers like Borges, on the contrary, no author can claim to be original. If all are incarnations of the Author, individual writers can only translate and annotate the work of previous incarnations. Writing, for Borges, is an *ars combinatoria* whose products are never the legitimate sons of the parent who signs them. The problem of fictional propriety that troubled Dumas's critics is no longer a problem for Borges: "Yes, everybody has his own trademark—or someone else's for that matter, since we seem to be plagiarizing all the time."[7]

Literary theory in the decades of the fifties, sixties, and seventies made much of this challenge to the vision of the author as a responsible father. Maurice Blanchot points to the tendency of a text to escape the restraint of legitimacy and filial propriety: "Il est toujours nécessaire de rappeler au romancier que ce n'est pas lui qui écrit son oeuvre, mais qu'elle se cherche à travers lui et que, aussi lucide qu'il désire être, il est livré à une expérience qui le dépasse si même elle ne le menace pas."[8] In "La Mort de l'auteur," Roland Barthes places Mallarmé, Valéry, Proust, and the surrealists among the precursors of the disappearance of the author. In the place of the traditional author, Barthes proposes a scriptor who comes into being simultaneously with the text and who has no being anterior to or exterior to the text:

> L'Auteur, lorsqu'on y croit, est toujours conçu comme le passé de son propre livre: le livre et l'auteur se placent d'eux-mêmes sur une même ligne, distribuée comme un *avant* et un *après*: l'Auteur est censé *nourrir* le livre, c'est-à-dire qu'il existe avant lui, pense, souffre, vit pour lui; il est avec son oeuvre dans le même rapport d'antécédence qu'un père entretient avec son enfant. Tout au contraire, le scripteur moderne naît en même temps que son texte.[9]

For Michel Foucault, authorship is a function built into discourse; the individual assumes this function upon taking up the writing task and relinquishes it upon leaving that work.[10] And in his interpretation of Socrates' condemnation of writing as a poison to memory, Derrida characterizes the written text as a nameless, fatherless outlaw:

> Il roule ça et là comme quelqu'un qui ne sait pas où il va, ayant perdu la voie droite, la bonne direction, la règle de rectitude, la norme; mais aussi comme quelqu'un qui a perdu ses droits, comme un hors-la-loi, un dévoyé, un mauvais garçon, un voyou ou un aventurier. Courant les rues, il ne sait même pas qui il est, quelle est son identité, s'il en a une, et un nom, celui de son père. Il répète la même chose lorsqu'on l'intérroge à tous les coins de rue, mais il ne sait plus répéter son origine.

Notions of legitimacy and property are abandoned or inverted, as when, in speaking of the writing subject's status in the New Novel, Jean Ricardou flatly declares, "Le scripteur est le produit de son produit."[11]

In structuralist and poststructuralist literary theory, then, the father has become child to the son. An alternative vision of what James called the "origin and growth" of a fiction is glimpsed by many contemporary theorists in the work of certain writers; this vision is especially accessible in the work of Borges. Himself preoccupied with literary filiation among writers of different periods, Borges asserts that he is "infested with literature." His thefts or intrusions from other texts, including his own, demonstrate his conviction that an individual text is the intersection of many texts, and that in combining and rearranging his literary heritage, an author paradoxically creates his own precursors.

Blanchot says of Borges: "Il se reconnaît en George Moor et en Joyce—
il pourrait dire en Lautréamont, en Rimbaud—capables d'incorporer à
leurs livres des pages et des figures qui ne leur appartenaient pas, car
l'essentiel, c'est la littérature, non les individus, et dans la littérature,
qu'elle soit impersonnellement, en chaque livre, l'unité inépuisable
d'un seul livre et la répétition lassée de tous les livres."[12]

The *ars combinatoria* of writing can be considered an intertextual
reweaving of previous literature, in which the fabrication of fiction
becomes a textile activity. The notion of a text as a *tissage* would
redefine literary filiation in such a way as to challenge the traditional
vision of the author as one who receives a certain inheritance from a
patriarchal line of influences and who then endows his son, the text,
with that same inheritance, which has paradoxically been transformed
into originality. Instead, the text is seen as a fabric of heterogeneous,
non-linear elements literally or figuratively borrowed from a great
many acknowledged and unacknowledged—or unacknowledgeable—
ancestors. The *fils* of literary filiation would no longer be son(s) but
rather threads that weave the writing subject fully as much as he or she
weaves them. For Barthes in *Le Plaisir du texte,* this view of textuality
goes far toward dissolving its subject: "*Texte* veut dire *Tissu;* mais
alors que jusqu'ici on a toujours pris ce tissu pour un produit, un voile
tout fait, derrière lequel se tient, plus ou moins caché, le sens (la
vérité), nous accentuons maintenant, dans le tissu, l'idée générative
que le texte se fait, se travaille à travers un entrelacs perpétuel; perdu
dans ce tissu—cette texture—le sujet s'y défait, telle une araignée qui
se dissoudrait elle-même dans les sécrétions constructives de sa toile."
That the metaphor of weaving became a privileged way of depicting
textuality in poststructuralist theory is remarked by Naomi Schor in
her 1976 essay, "Pour une thématique restreinte":

> Qu'il soit vertical, horizontal, ou transversal, le fil conducteur hante les
> textes de Barthes, de Derrida, et de Deleuze, non pas sous la forme
> typiquement structuraliste—c'est-à-dire métalinguistique—de l'isotopie
> gréimassienne, mais sous une forme poétique: le fil conducteur est de-
> venu métaphore filée et qui plus est, métaphore de la métaphore filée.
> Comme l'indiquent la "toile d'araignée" de Deleuze, la "tresse" de
> Barthes, et la "texture" de Derrida, le rapport entre le "textuel" et le

"textile" est en voie de devenir une des obsessions verbales, voire une des métaphores obsédantes de la critique actuelle.[13]

Textuality as *tissage* is also an acknowledged constitutive metaphor for Claude Ollier. In a theoretical essay, Ollier calls writing a "métier à navette"; fiction resembles a loom where the individual spins out a fabric from threads that already form a tangled knot, ready to be unrolled and reassembled.[14] In "Pulsion," a text by Ollier that appears in an issue of *L'Arc* dedicated to Jacques Derrida, the working space of the loom suggests a blank page:

> Examinons ce vide. Il est en forme de losange. Tirant à l'opposé, les lames ont ouvert quatre angles dans le réseau, ménageant ce couloir d'ombre où la petite embarcation imprime son sillage droit, charriant la trame des formules. Les duites à angle droit passent et repassent, à l'envers, à l'endroit, travaillant à la chaîne. Le peigne resserre les mailles, pour une plus stricte économie des termes et des moyens. Ça marche! Sur le rouleau blanc d'appel—la "vocation" des fils en chaîne?—un morceau de tissu s'engrange. Combien? Quelques mailles en ligne: s'y lit un dessin déjà, dans le tapis.[15]

The artisan who manipulates this loom is never entirely in control of the mechanism that produces the *tissu* of a text; just as the threads with which he works are not originally his own, the design produced is never fully the artisan's invention. It is, rather, the product of the individual's actions tempered by the presence of social forces, of literary heritage and conventions, of other artisans. These various components of the *tissu* are what Ollier calls "inscriptions conflictuelles": together they form a text that does not uniquely belong to the individual who signs it.[16] In fact, the mechanism of writing tends to appropriate the author ("A présent que tu as glissé le bras dans la mécanique et senti tout ton corps happé par les bobines"), tends to dissociate him from his product, his son: "Les figures sur le rouleau de départ . . . entrelacées aux trames rhétoriques logées de sa main même dans le creux de l'esquif pour le va-et-vient douteux: altérées sans délai, repérables encore par bribes dans la toile sous les coups du peigne niées dans leur ordonnance et leur reconnaissance paternelle."[17] Ollier's use of the weaving metaphor attests to his commitment to intertextuality, a concept that necessarily minimizes the paternal role of the writing subject in a text. Therefore, if filiation is to be conserved as a constitutive force in the production of texts, it must be conserved in the sense of an intertextual weaving of previous threads. In this sense, then, the *fils* must be threads that produce the position of the father rather than sons who owe their legitimate existence to him. The construction of *Our* can serve as the testing ground for this alternative notion of filiation, since the novel proposes, in introducing the Oedipal conflict into the question of fictional genesis, to explore the status of the writing subject. The *métaphore filée* of weaving forms a running network throughout *Our* as it does in the more clearly theoretical texts cited, and as it had already begun to do in *La Vie sur Epsilon,* where the textual phenomenon of the dancing blades/pages is described as "noir sur noir, des tresses de filaments ou noeuds de particules longiformes" (*VE,* 70). And yet *Our* also counts many real sets of fathers and sons among its protagonists. The question as to whether fictional filiation is textile or biological should be resolved or at least clarified by the vision of the author that emerges from *Our.*

An early passage in *Our,* already noted, sets the stage—in terms recalling at once the computer Naïma, the loom, and the blank page— for a repudiation of the traditional notion of the proprietary author: "l'aiguille sur un sillon désaffecté, un texte sans nom d'auteur s'écrit une bonne fois pour toutes dans le quadrilatère étroit" (*Our,* 15). The narration of *Our* is composed of fragments from various sources: dreams, telepathic thought-transfer, hieroglyphic tablets, an omniscient narrator, and accounts by individuals who inhabit the archaeological site at Ur, where the young visitor from Ezzala has been sent on a mission by his father's friends. The narration does not tell the story of the young man's visit but, rather, recounts how that visit was recorded on clay tablets and what became of those tablets. Just as the story told is displaced from the apparent narrative to a narrative about narrating, so the teller is multiplied and dispersed into various voices. The relationship between narrator and story in *Our* can be expanded to provide an allegorical figure of the writing subject in relation to the text written. A primary figure of this relationship develops from the transcription of the visitor's dreams; while the visitor sleeps, one of his hosts, also asleep, transcribes the dream as if it were a story: "Le texte passe, se faufile entre une présence muette dans le creuset du songe et l'absence sertie dans les échos tardifs d'un graphisme." (*Our,* 147). The host as a figure of the author is displaced from the origin of the text he is writing; not only is his text the transcription of a dream (and not the representation of some primary reality), it is not even his own dream. Nor is it the dreamer's original story; in Ur, the visitor's dreams are a network of memories, myths, and quotations. These elements are reworked, displaced, and condensed in a manner that suggests Freud's characterization of dream activity as well as Borges's notion of the text as a reworking of previous texts. Freud's formulation of the dream-work thus offers a model of fictional functioning.[18] If the text works like a dream, then the author is always secondary and displaced in respect to the text. Like the host Ea, the author does no more than transcribe and rearrange material that has no absolute origin.

In Ur, then, the figure of the author that emerges is both ancient and revolutionary: the scribe. Historically, the earliest writers were profes-sional Sumerian scribes whose function was to record economic and social transactions. Writing remained for centuries the domain of the scribes, who mastered hundreds of symbols as well as the technique of impressing them on tablets.[19] However, like Ea, these early writers generally did no more than record or copy, as the visitor notes upon examining the library of excavated tablets at Ur: "La tablette est signée du nom de l'auteur ou du copiste ou d'une filiation indéfinie de co-pistes" (*Our,* 119). The scribe, like Ea, is the agent of the transcription of texts that are secondary, multiple, and heterogeneous. The scribe is thus the antithetical predecessor of the traditional author whose text is held to be an original, personal expression. In *Our,* this author is revealed to be a copier, a scribe.

However, an element of paternity enters into this figure; the scribe is himself inscribed in a line of filiation from which he acquires his vocation: "Les traits d'emphase de ce morceau prennent ancre dans la *veine ancestrale* où puise, *par enseignement,* le scribe: symétrie des étapes, assomption des personnages, ménagement de l'effet. Rien d'é-tonnant, donc, qu'il ait modulé les accents du narrateur dans un ton où ce dernier n'aurait *songé* même à les *transcrire*" (*Our,* 38; my empha-sis). Ea's vocation is inherited, derived, and secondary like the dream-material he transcribes. However, this heredity does not imply the transmission of a unique or original genetic gift but rather the assumption, through education, of a position occupied by an infinite series of predecessors, so that the textile metaphor of filiation replaces what at first appears to be a biological model. While the scribe may exercise his prerogative to alter and modify as he transcribes, much of the new transcription is due rather to permutations of the dream-material itself: "Ces expressions ne naissent pas toujours de décisions manifestes: toutes sortes de tissus ironiques s'interposent entre le manifeste et le latent" (*Our*, 133). In his lack of conscious control over the *tissu* of the text, in his role as a transcriber and editor of previous texts, and in his refusal to claim any personal originality or expression, the ancient scribe resembles the modern *scripteur*. The figure of the author as an omniscient or self-expressive (self-productive) father would seem to be a historical construct whose era, as Barthes claims, coincides with the modern age and the rise of individualism and must end with the revolutionary advent of the *scripteur*.[20]

II. Conflictual Inscriptions

> Se considérer comme Dieu le père devant son
> monde, c'est un truc trop facile, et ça, on
> ne peut plus le faire.
> —Jean-Pierre Faye

In *Our*, the activity of the scribe is indeed connected with revolution. The passage where "un texte sans nom d'auteur s'écrit une bonne fois pour toutes" announces the beginning of a new era: "la ventilation neuve abolit le code policé des lectures, porte en queue de récit ce qui était en tête, la voix passive chevrote, les ombres issues des parois illustrent une action sans sujet réel" (*Our*, 15).

The upheaval in question is clearly a textual one, and the terms in which it is described also apply to the politics of the New Novel itself. The young visitor to Ur is told of not one revolution, however, but two; his arrival in Ur coincides with the anniversary of the first revolution, which apparently ended a period of colonial oppression—"le règne de l'astreinte franche" (*Our*, 75)—of the Middle Eastern land by a foreign

power. The anniversary is celebrated on July 14, the anniversary of
Iraq's independence from Britain as well as of the French Revolution.
A deeper connection must underlie the apparent *invraisemblance,* or at
least the coincidence, of this initial revolution in which the beginnings
of France's own revolution in the eighteenth century are collapsed into
the end of Western colonial activities in the twentieth century. The
significance of this paradoxical coincidence lies in the relationship
between the revolution and the scribe's vocation; one of the inhabitants tells of the days before the revolution, when interest in the
excavation of Ur grew rapidly, with more and more tablets coming
under scholarly scrutiny: "Les choses allaient bon train: des lettrés de
partout survenaient pour étude. On copiait, déchiffrait. . . . Plus on
déchiffrait, plus pâlissait l'éclat de la contrainte" (*Our,* 75).

Constraints were loosened by the scribal activities of copying,
deciphering, and studying. The secondary nature of the scribe's work
relates it to that of the literary critic. Both the struggle and the constraints of this early period are presented in terms evoking at once a
textual and a political activity. A dialogue between the visitor and
Enlil, the "maître des voies et des communications," establishes the
link between the political struggle and its textual consequences:

> —C'était l'hiver. Des flaques d'eau obstruent les chemins, on s'em-
> bourbe. . . . Il s'agissait d'établir un lien.
>
> —pour défaire ceux de la contrainte?
>
> —Ceux d'une certaine "économie," oui. Une première lutte nous a
> sauvés de bien des mots. . . . C'était l'anniversaire hier.
> Enlil s'arrête, fouille le sable du bout de sa sandale.
>
> —Nous y voyons bon augure: tu viens à point nommé!
> Et, un peu plus loin:
>
> —La seconde lutte sera plus dure encore. (*Our,* 60)

The revolution in Ur links the end of a certain political era, colonial
imperialism, with the end of a certain textual regime. But because the
anniversary is also that of France's own revolution, it links the end of
the ancien régime to the demise of that textual regime. While perhaps
incongruous in the context of the modern Middle East, this connec-

tion recalls what some, like Roland Barthes, have seen as a similar and significant juncture in French literary history. The end of the classical period of French literature is held to mark the disruption of a certain "economy" in which language was thought to function as tender, like paper money, transferring meaning from person to person without possessing a material value of its own. In an influential early work, *Le Degré zéro de l'écriture,* Barthes proposes this view of language in the classical period: "L'Art classique ne pouvait se sentir comme un langage, il *était* langage, c'est-à-dire transparence, circulation sans dépôt, concours idéal d'un Esprit universel et d'un signe décoratif sans épaisseur et sans responsabilité."[21] Literature, like language, was a means of exchanging sense between individuals. The constraints Enlil claims were loosened by the revolutionary closure of the classical age in Ur must have been those that naively fused language (and fiction) to the meanings they were intended to exchange.

In order to break the constraining ties of a classical economy of language, however, the early revolution in Ur had to forge new ties. If classical language was too tightly bound to what it represented in an exchange, the ties replacing that economy must be those of expression, linking the romantic author to the text that serves as a medium for his voice. While classical language was principally tied to an external referent of which it was the transparent conveyor, romantic language is now bound to the subjectivity of the author, which it is held to be capable of expressing. Literature becomes a means of conveying sentiment, and a second and more arduous revolution must now undo these ties.

The young visitor's arrival marks "le joint rêvé de l'articulation des deux luttes" (*Our,* 140). Just as he appears to be the descendant or the double of a first heroic visitor from Ezzala—"Quand vint le premier messager d'Ezzala, le souci d'une lutte était déjà dans nos têtes. Il le fortifia, l'orienta, nous dit à qui allier nos bras et nous aida à vaincre" (*Our,* 75–76)—so the second revolution is in some sense the son of the first: "Le decret d'aujourd'hui relance le destin de la première lutte et en parfait l'issue sans doute, la parachève. Par décalque de circuits et réseaux, et analogies de jointures, qui n'y voit les marques de la seconde aussi, logée tout en amont" (*Our,* 133). The source of the second struggle is to be found upstream, in the analogous junctions of the first revolution, since old constraints upon language were only superseded by new ones. Both classical and romantic regimes see language as an insubstantial conveyor of something else, object or sentiment, that exists outside and prior to its medium. Both regimes remain within the closure of a mimetic tradition.[22]

While the first revolution severed language's and fiction's arbitrary link with the external world, the second revolution must undo the more subtle and unquestioned ties that join a work to its author: "Les temps se répètent. . . . Les rets grossiers de l'astreinte cachaient les mailles plus fines auxquelles ils étaient noués, réseau armant toute parole, couvrant nos voix, tramant toute économie de ses fils" (*Our,* 76). The "économie de ses fils" is still a patriarchal, proprietary relationship. The terms of the oppression are both textile and mercantile: the "mailles" are at once stitches and coins, while the *trame* is equally a web and a plot to exploit or extort. The final revolution will be by far the more formidable because it must involve the disruption of an ideology enmeshed in the fabric of the language. A veritable apocalypse is called for: "Le bruit que fait *tout ce discours est devenu excessif,* ses voix se sont multipliées, le monde en est saturé comme d'une vermine et son tumulte rend le sommeil impossible. Que le ciel s'ouvre! Que les eaux noient ces bulles, ces canaux engorgés! . . ." (*Our,* 158; my emphasis). Although the first revolution "nous a sauvés de bien des mots," the remaining discourse is still deafeningly excessive. Both regimes are characterized by a surplus of language; since language is held to be a secondary entity applied to objects, sentiments, or concepts in such a way as to make them exchangeable, it must always be in excess of what it conveys. The multitude of voices claiming original authorship is always in excess of the single abstract Author or author-function of all literature. The apocalyptic struggle must therefore take place on the economic level of language and fiction.

In Ur, the first, classical period was an era of open political oppression whose economy was ostensibly based on exchange. Like property and paternity, language was regulated by patriarchal laws insuring correspondence between a son or a fiction and the name or referent given him or it by the father. Exchange of meaning or property was made possible by this common ground of accepted correspondence.

However, the scribal activities of copying and deciphering slowly undermined the monarchical regime where final authority for correspondence lay in the hands of one individual representing a divine law; in the allegorical history of Ur, that divine law is mimesis and the authority is that of authorship. The classical author is like a monarch, who holds his omniscient power from a divine source and whose mastery is unquestioned. The economy of the subsequent romantic regime carries on many of the constraints of the earlier period in a more subtle vein corresponding to a political regime of secret exploitation of natural resources rather than open colonial occupation. A textual regime linking language to the expression of internal, invisible referents obscures the fact that the excessive economy of the early period has not been corrected but has instead given rise to an even more exploitative regime.

Modern Ur is economically exploited in several ways: its liquid gold—oil—is systematically dredged up and conveyed to the exploiters by a complex network of canals and wells. The excavation of Ur's ruins for the purpose of exporting the ancient tablets to foreign museums is conducted with a similar organization, so that the terrain is literally riddled by a crisscrossing fabric of appropriation. The link between the *réseaux* of oil conduits and of ancient writings is exploitation:

> Cela, Mardouk, fils d'Ea, pourrait le dire . . . observant les écritures des chemins sur le sable rouge et les cailloux, les réseaux de percés et conquêtes, explorations et forages, invasions et narrations, enquêtes, imprimés sur et dans le sol par les envahisseurs et les copistes, tyrans, comptables et scribes officiels. Une contrainte se déchiffre en toute marque ou trace à la surface de la terre cuite au soleil ou à feu d'homme: conduites forcées en lignes droites ou courbes, brisant l'effet de sens et cloisonnant l'effort, drainant l'or jaune ou noir des marchands. (*Our,* 119)

The excavations, roads, and oil conduits are a kind of writing that exploits the earth by systematically cutting it and draining it of its riches. The exploitation is not simply the pillaging of ancient writings for museums and of the earth for oil; it is the disruption by writing of the integrity of the earth's surface. In sectioning and dividing the uniform surface, writing privileges a single sense while suppressing the remaining area; the terms of this exploitation recall Lassalle's colonial adventure in *La Mise en scène,* and the resistance of his map to his tracings of a mining route. The copiers and scribes of Ur are in league with avaricious merchants in impressing a web of "invasions et narrations" into the face of the earth. These *réseaux* recall the earlier net of open oppression—the *rets grossier* cast in a double language of weaving and economy.

The second revolution must therefore liberate the land itself. The inhabitants of Ur speak of the coming struggle in Marxist terms, as a change in social relations, as a reappropriation of the means of production: "Prédominante en ce jour est l'appropriation du réseau" (*Our,* 132). The second revolution, which is to end the mimetic closure of the classical-romantic era in modern Ur, must coincide with the end of capitalism and the ideology of the individual from which it derives.[23] The woven *réseaux* of writing cannot simply be abolished but must be won back by those who merit writing's wealth through their comprehension of its workings; not all scribes and copiers will participate in the revolution. A discussion among the seven inhabitants and their visitor establishes a differential notion of the *réseau* of writing in which meaning is not restricted to an ordinary, daily economy of exchange but is instead seen as a fabric of communicating, shifting signs not tied to external referents: "Les paroles que nous prononçons n'ont de sens que grâce au silence où elles baignent. Rien ne reste plus problématique que de savoir si chacune des mailles trouve sa raison d'être dans celle qui précède ou celle qui suit. Tous réseaux de cette force communiquent et les circuits branchés aux sources d'énergie se coupent, se compénètrent et prolifèrent en étoilement de signes et de systèmes" (*Our,* 132–33). This network of signification operates like the *trace* described by Derrida that determines the structure of the sign as nonpresence, as a relation of *espacement* to what has come before and what may follow.

The project of the second revolution in Ur must be a new conception of language fashioned along these lines: "Il faut capter d'abord cette matière, assimiler ses chiffres, ses formules, qu'un jour soit détourné son cours et inversé le sens du circuit, qu'un jour cet or sans masse, incolore, ductile, danse au bout de vos plumes et retourne le jeu" (*Our,* 133-34). Language must no longer be viewed as insubstantial tender; it must be seen as a material, liquid wealth to be reappropriated and radicalized. Similarly, the figure of the official scribe who does no more than record exchanges, who participates in the exploitative regime of language, must be abandoned in favor of a scribe who works on language as a material substance in its own right. Such is the scribe Ea, who, in transcribing the visitor's dreams, fashions language as a sculptor models clay or as a weaver composes his cloth: "Statuaire de graphes artificieux ou de fictions redoublées en leurs semblants de références, Ea recrée les personnages anciens et crois [sic] les fils de leurs légendes et tisse de ses doigts noueux la toile où toutes les fables devront se prendre. Trame inventée dans le matin, au jour le jour, pour le destin fictile du projet" (*Our,* 148).[24] The outcome of the projected revolution—a new vision of the writing subject—depends on the essential link between the fictional and the textile, the "fictile." The arrival of the visitor from Ezzala should mark a turning point in the realization of the radicalizing project.

In evoking the historical birthplace of writing and clarifying the nature of writing's initial link to economic activity, *Our* seeks to explode the myth of language as a medium of exchange. Language and fiction are unmasked as means of exploitation, which must be reappropriated by revolutionary forces possessing a new vision of the relationship between words and things, between texts and authors.[25] The individual who signs a text must be a scribe, a *scripteur,* a transcriber of dreams, whose work on language is both tactile and textile. In this revolutionary state, a fiction is placed at a remove from external referents and from the paternal figure who serves as the medium of its transcription. The traditional author as father to his work would thus be definitively replaced by the figure of the scribe. The development of the figure of the author as a scribe or artisan working on the materiality of language echoes Barthes's description of the evolution of literature from the "temps bourgeois" to the middle of the nineteenth century, when bourgeois consciousness lost its convictions as to its own universality: "L'Ecriture classique a donc éclaté et la Littérature entière, de Flaubert à nos jours, est devenue une problématique du langage. C'est à ce moment même que la Littérature a été consacrée

définitivement comme un objet."[26] In this way, the fictional developments of *Our* tend to affirm the antitraditional stance of much modern
literary theory.

Yet the final vision of the scribe in *Our* complicates the revolutionary schema by introducing a troubling biological filiation. As the plans
for the incipient rebellion accelerate, the inhabitants of Ur reveal that
they are all related to one of the others as father or son, just as the
visitor himself is either the son of O. or O. himself. Finally, the visitor
is led deep into the earth where the imprinted tablets are stored. A
labyrinth of passages eventually leads him to a mysterious figure
seated in the center of a room, engraving clay tablets with a stylus; the
tablets contain an exact transcription of what the visitor is thinking at
that very moment. The seated figure is Nabou, son of Mardouk; the
scribe Nabou becomes the final, dramatic vision of the author in and of
Our, since what he is transcribing is the text of *Our* itself. In Babylonian legend, Nabu is the patron of scribes, the creator of writing, and
the *dieu-scribe*.[27] Just as Mardouk supplanted his own father Ea as the
director of the system of excavations in Ur, so Nabou is destined to
revolt against Mardouk by allowing the secret tablets to be stolen.[28]
Control of the *réseaux* of tunnels in the earth and of writing on the
earth is passed from father to son, either voluntarily or through usurpation. Despite the apparent final ascendancy of the scribe, writing
and fiction are still somehow involved in a relationship of father to son
where filiation is undeniably biological. When Mardouk came to supplant his father, Ea, he assumed certain textual or literary functions as
if they were a genetic feature destined to appear at a specific age or
stage of development: "Sous le règne de l'astreinte franche, on me
confiait parfois le soin de ce domaine: j'y supplantai mon père vieillis-
sant. Son titre, de longue date, n'est plus qu'honorifique: 'Maître du
champs des fouilles,' tôt son fils le devient. J'y avais fait mes preuves,
certifiant les caractères latins d'un rapport dont j'eus comme malgré
moi connaissance" (*Our,* 75).

The scribe's revolutionary activity ought to be passed on as an
artisanal position filled through aptitude, training, or chance; it
should not be a genetic capacity transferred from father to son. However, in the final scenes of *Our,* the "veine ancestrale, où puise, par
enseignement, le scribe" (*Our,* 38) is patently the inherited blood of his

father, and not an entirely acquired skill. The paternal regime of textuality that was to have been definitively overthrown is suddenly reevoked with Nabou, Mardouk, and Ea. Authority and authorship are again linked and come to question any revolutionary role the scribe might have in the constitution of a text: "'Le scribe devrait couper là. . . .' Qui lui dicte où couper? . . . Qui rend visite à l'autre et lui souffle son dit?" (*Our*, 93). In this passage, someone else dictates to the scribe, whispering his lines to him from offstage. Admittedly, the revolutionary scribe was never thought to fashion his text according to his own autonomous will or intentions; as a *scripteur,* he should provide the medium by which are heard the various voices of many previous texts, which he then weaves into a heterogeneous, new narrative voice never integrally his own. The form and direction of the new text should derive from permutations of the previous textual matter itself. However, in *Our,* one voice dictates to the scribe, communicating to him not only his text but the form it will take and where it will be cut. If the scribe is not the master of the work he signs, someone else apparently is. The single master would then act as the text's father, dictating its shape with a solitary authoritative voice.

The figure of the *maître* in *Our* begins to form a systematic opposition to that of the scribe: in the school for scribes, the *maître* punishes a student scribe for not correctly copying a dictation; a distinction is made between "l'homme et ses maîtres" (*Our*, 122), where the maîtres are the seven major deities (Mardouk, Ea, and so on) whose names have been adopted by the present inhabitants of Ur. Each of the seven inhabitants is the *maître* of a particular domain—roads, excavations, the planetary system, communications. Just as Ea and Mardouk ruled the *réseaux* of roads and writings on the earth's surface, a *grand maître* regulated, in ancient Ur, the vital system of canals by which the desert was irrigated:

> —Là était le noeud du réseau pour l'adduction des eaux aux labours et
> aux prés. Grand maître était celui qui commandait aux débits et dispen-
> sait le flux selon le code écrit et tranchait souverainement des litiges.
> C'était à lui de calculer les pentes et l'ordre des dérivations, de marquer
> sur le livre les points de césure et de jonction. Il lui revenait aussi de
> décréter l'abandon des tracés que lézardaient trop de brèches. Toutes
> communications relevaient de son savoir, de son autorité toute

l'économie. Le creusement d'un canal valait bien l'érection d'un temple!
Tout le pouvoir allait au maître des canaux. (*Our,* 152–53)

The master of the canals is a divine or omnipotent authority who
establishes and controls a network spread over or carved into the
earth's integral surface. He controls the economy of this interwoven
réseau as if it were a text whose various traces, communications, and
caesuras he alone determines.

The *maître* has thus come to rival the scribe as a figure of the author;
while Ea and Mardouk at first seemed to belong to the weavers' guild,
traces of their royal and masterly lineage now complicate their revolutionary stance. The *code écrit,* according to which in many ways the
network of the text is constructed, resembles the patriarchal *code
patronymique* (*Our,* 91) that the scribe was to have discredited. Thus
the traditional biological metaphor of textuality has not been so readily left behind. While the scribe as author should manipulate certain
fils or threads from previous texts, he is now challenged by a *maître*
whose *fils* is a son, a woven text perhaps, but a text that the master
nevertheless fathers, and for which he alone is responsible. The *maître*
is a father whose son can revolt against him by escaping or exceeding
his design, but the son does so because the link between them is
biological.

The conflict between these two visions of the writing subject—one
revolutionary and demystified, one traditional and patriarchal—is evident also in certain theoretical remarks Ollier makes about the relationship between text and author: "Ce sont les INSCRIPTIONS CON-
FLICTUELLES dont nous nous sentons le plus communément
responsables, même si nous n'en assumons pas obligatoirement toute
la paternité."[29] While certain bastard elements enter into the construction of a fiction, a patriarchal core still persists, over which the author
takes some degree of responsiblity. At a Cerisy Colloquium, Ollier
proposed new approaches to the study of an individual author's relation to other writers: "Un premier type établirait, pour chacun, la
filiation littéraire particulière dont il apparaît, ou se sent *l'héritier,*
voire le continuateur."[30] In these theoretical remarks, the apparent
endorsement of a revolutionary scribal *tissage* is paradoxically couched
in a language of paternity and patrimony. The same contradiction is

evident in *Our;* if the vital second revolution does not succeed, must not the author emerge as the divine *Maître du verbe* first mentioned in *Enigma*, around whose sanctuary the holy city of Ezzala was constructed?

III. Oedipal Fictions

> Tout récit ne se ramène-t-il pas à l'Oedipe?
> —Barthes

At the conclusion of *Our,* an apocalyptic struggle does occur, but it is not the anticipated economic revolution destined to free textuality from the oppressive regime of the author. The figure of the scribe has been challenged by that of the *maître*; the nature of the second struggle must finally clarify the writing subject's relationship to his text. Just as a metaphor of biological filiation has proven unshakable from the foundation of the text, so the final struggle likewise involves a family: the primal family of Oedipus. What had appeared to be the resolution of an Oedipal situation in the opening passage of *Our* was in reality a prefiguration of the conflict to come over the role of the writing subject in the enunciation of a fiction.

Although O.'s son is often confused with O. himself in the narration of *Our,* many references are also made to his parents. The triangle consisting of O.–Nejma–their son is doubled by a triangle where Nejma is the object and means of interaction between two men: O. and the director of convalescents who sent Nejma to him. Similar triangles involve the twin girls of *La Mise en scène,* Cynthia in *Eté indien,* and all the daughters and nieces of *L'Echec de Nolan.* Every woman presented in the cycle occupies one point of a triangle whose other coordinates are masculine. In its general form, the Oedipal triangle becomes a potent metaphor for the rivalry of two individuals, generally men, for a desired object, typically a woman. René Girard's formulation of triangular mimetic desire makes of Oedipus a structural model for fiction.[31] Writing itself, which was shown to be triumphantly feminine in *La Vie sur Epsilon,* falls in *Our* into the domain of the triangular: the clay tablets are impressed with a stylus whose sharpened end makes triangular marks like those of ancient cuneiform. The global, amorphous textuality bears from the historical beginnings of writing the mark of a tripartite struggle, the stakes of which are credit for the creation of a fiction.

The Oedipal quarrel in *Our* takes place in terms of a creation myth from Mesopotamia, the birthplace of Western civilization and of its writing. The contested creation of a fiction is played out allegorically in the mythic struggle. Babylonian myth recounts that the destiny of men and gods and the right to mastery of the earth by the gods were recorded on secret tablets in the keeping of the great god Ea, later supplanted by a new divinity, Mardouk.[32] Similarly, in *Our*, Mardouk's son Nabou is responsible for certain secret tablets recounting the young visitor's stay in Ur; recounting, that is, how the story was told and by whom. The secret tablets must hold the final key to the origin of fiction. Nabou betrays his father and the others when he permits a young girl, Tiamât, to steal the tablets and subsequently escapes with her. Just as the young visitor tends to merge with his father (O.), Tiamât resembles Nejma, the visitor's mother. Tiamât is thus the third point in the Oedipal triangle, constituting the contested object of desire or exchange between two sets of fathers and sons. And like an object, she has been given to the young visitor just as Nejma was sent to his father: "Pour te servir, nous t'avons donné Tiamât" (*Our*, 41). Tiamât steals the tablets after she is raped by the young visitor; the terms and implications of this sexual violence will be discussed shortly. *Our* closes with Mardouk giving chase and the visitor preparing to depart in pursuit.

In Babylonian legend,Tiamât was a feminine presence, a primeval watery chaos. It is from her body that the world is created, according to two slightly different versions, each of which provides a significant allegory for the question of textual genesis in and of *Our*. One account maintains that Mardouk caught Tiamât in a net and then tore her body in two halves, forming heaven and earth. In a second version, Mardouk built land out of the liquid chaos (Tiamât) by constructing a grill of reeds upon the primeval water's surface.[33] This second mythical struggle recalls, term for term, the opposition established in *Enigma* between a fluid feminine totality and a solid masculine form, where the individual subject or fiction attempts to superpose a division or a grill upon the amorphous generative matrix of Fiction. In *Our,* this opposition forms a recurrent textile motif in which a woven network is projected upon the integral background of a feminine writing:

> Celui qui voit la substance de toute chose se révéler à *l'ombre du filet que la forme projette sur la surface ininterrompue du sens,* celui qui voit glisser cette ombre sur les cailloux et les limons disposés par le fleuve en son charriage millénaire de l'amont de rocailles au nord à l'aval amer des eaux du golfe, celui qui perçoit en toute enjambée la retenue progressive de ce flux dans le dessin infiniment repris des ondes d'alluvion sur la *terre fluide* qu'il arpente, celui-là concevra que le support consolidé de ses pas était voici quatre mille ans le rivage même de la mer. (*Our,* 154; my emphasis)

The fluid earth is the maternal matrix upon which determinate form is impressed. The *réseaux*—of writing, excavations, wells, canals—are so many *filets* that exploit the matrix through a systematic repression of its totality.

The terrestrial fluidity, whether it be oil or water or writing, comprises the country's entire wealth. The seven male inhabitants recognize this when they plan their second revolution: "une appropriation de l'or est décidée, dont le flux noir par les pompes des puits et les réseaux à fleur de sable constitue, hormis l'eau jaune et bleue des fleuves et l'ocre pâle des réliques étiquetées dans les musées, la seule richesse du pays" (*Our,* 123). The economic exploitation against which they revolt is in fact a sacrifice—a sectioning and dismemberment—of the integral feminine writing by a masculine writing of formal appropriation. Moreover, it is a sacrifice in which they themselves participate as masters and guardians of certain *réseaux.* Tiamât's legendary body is sacrificed so that the material world can be shaped; in *Our,* the young girl Tiamât is similarly presented as a ritual victim: "Victime au pied de l'autel, elle voyait tourner des cercles de feu. Un silence s'est fait dans son âme; elle se sentait mourir" (*Our,* 102).

Tiamât is twice raped by the visitor. Each time, the text is a pastiche, parody, or quotation of earlier literature, contrasting markedly with the surrounding passages. The following passage, for example, is by its tone and lexicon either a pastiche or a quotation of another text:

les belles chairs changent de couleur, la teinte de l'incarnat se mêle à
l'éclat du lys . . . elle veut fuir, il la poursuit, sa résistance enflamme le
scélérat, il ose montrer à quel point ses passions sont irritées . . . ses
contorsions et hurlement servent de risée à cet être perfide, rien ne
l'arrête, plus la fillette se plaint et plus éclate la sévérité de son bourreau.
(*Our*, 143)

This text is preceded by several borrowings taken virtually word for
word from the passage in Flaubert's *Salammbô* in which Mathô
approaches the sleeping princess:

Sa large tunique blanche se courbait en molles draperies, jusqu'à ses
pieds, suivant les inflexions de sa taille.[34]

In *Our*:

sa tunique violette se courbait en molles draperies, jusqu'à ses cuisses,
suivant les inflexions de sa taille. (*Our*, 100)

Ollier's text at once shortens the woman's robes and extends the erotic-
violent scenario. If Tiamât's virginal body is a figure of the intact
"surface ininterrompu du sens"—the fluid, feminine corpus of all fiction—then the visitor must embody the perennial masculine subject
and the individual fiction that seeks to inscribe himself or itself onto or
into that surface. The conflict of *La Vie sur Epsilon* was not resolved by
the psychoanalytic cure of *Enigma;* the terms of the struggle remain
unchanged in *Our*, revealing themselves even at the basis of the revolutionary struggle against classical and romantic mimesis. Tiamât's body
must be violated in order for a fiction to take place. The impression she
makes is already a literary one: "Un air d'intérêt et de sensibilité
répandu sur toute sa personne lui donnait l'air d'une héroïne de
roman" (*Our*, 101). Each time Tiamât is raped, the corpus of past
literature is pillaged to provide material for a present fiction; the
amorphous background is the means by which a solid grill is fore-
grounded. The feminine writing of a generalized Fiction provides the
fluid that permits the erection of a specific fiction.

    At once writing, oil, and water, this fluid is also, finally, the mater-
nal and virginal blood spilt for and by the individual (masculine)

fiction. After the visitor has raped Tiamât, he has an hallucinatory vision of her blood, of the star-shaped pendant she wore, and of his own parents, associated throughout *Our* with a blue and a black writing ("il cherchait en vain l'ombre des siens: étoile aux lettres noires et cercle bleu de la voyelle mâle") (*Our*, 156):

> le bleu des lettres, le noir des lettres brûle ses yeux, les branches de l'étoile, la chaîne brisée sur le drap, les six pointes aiguës brillent devant ses yeux, le cercle au centre de l'étoile, le bleu des lettres, le noir brûle ses yeux, la flamme sur le drap blanc, le sang, ce mot à son oreille, et sa terreur, ce mot suprême, le roi des mots. (*Our*, 144)

The rape of Tiamât reevokes the violence and transgression of the Oedipal family. The terrifying conjunction of blood and star recalls the final scene of *La Vie sur Epsilon*, while in *Enigma* the masculine-feminine opposition was likewise figured by a circle and a star. There, however, the intertextual model of fictional genesis had seemed to affirm the primacy of the maternal star; now, the visitor is told of a significant reversal when he asks about the pendant: "Chaque branche est phase de création. Le cercle au centre va grandir. Quand il atteindra les rais de l'étoile, l'oeuvre sera achevée" (*Our*, 161). The visitor's rape of Tiamât-Nejma completes the growth of the masculine circle, bringing about the accomplishment, or erection, of the fiction of *Our*. The emergence of the specific fiction is the triumphant and violent repression of the feminine that gave rise to it.

The allegorical opposition between masculine and feminine writings has created a fiction in which the feminine is both appropriated and repressed, yet continues to resist by provoking the Oedipal conflict between father and son: the rape that produces the fiction *Our* also provokes the woman's traitorous theft of the tablets that tell *Our*'s story. *Our* is born from the initiation of an Oedipal struggle rather than from any resolution of it; the specific fiction is erected only to be subsequently stolen back and reabsorbed into the body of all fiction. Its existence is a momentary and transitory act of figurative violence and exploitation. In that moment the two masculine poles of the Oedipal structure, having suppressed the maternal matrix, undertake a struggle for dominance and independence; just as Nabou usurps

Mardouk, the fiction now seeks autonomy from its father. And just as Socrates condemned writing as a traitorous son, according to the *Phaedrus,* the finished fiction from Henry James to the New Novelists has been depicted as a stranger to its author. The fiction eclipses or escapes the parent's plans and even his comprehension. Ollier endorses this attitude toward the completed fiction when, in "Pulsion," he characterizes it as a piece of fabric whose design spins out as if of its own accord, utilizing the author's vocabulary to its own ends: "Quelques mailles en ligne: s'y lit un dessin déjà, dans le tapis, Nabû enfant lance la barque alternative. . . . A très peu près, il a déjà tout dit de ce qu'il *voulait dire:* son lexique n'est pas loin d'être épuisé. Qu'il recommence donc."[35] Similarly, in *Our,* "l'étoffe excède le dessin" (*Our,* 12).

The struggle between father and son leaves neither the fictional subject nor the writing subject unthreatened by the other. Like Morel in *Eté indien,* the young visitor to Ur has a vertiginous hallucination when he climbs to the top of a tower. He sees himself with a human head in his hand, much like Hamlet; but like Count Ugolino in the ninth circle of Dante's *Inferno,* he is eating the grisly object ("une tête à la main, dont je rongeais le crâne" [*Our,* 126]).[36] Hamlet's ambivalent relationship with his father is juxtaposed with that of the imprisoned count who was forced by hunger to eat the bodies of his own dead sons. The subject's fear of castration and perdition at the hands of a father whom he has wronged, and the parallel guilt of a parent who has sacrificed his offspring for his own sake, are linked to fictional filiation in the terms of the hallucination. In his vision, the visitor recounts, he throws himself off the tower with the severed head; the following passage in *Our* is an almost verbatim "theft" from Lautréamont's *Les Chants de Maldoror:*[37]

> —Les hommes entendront le choc retentissant qui résultera de la rencontre du sol avec la tête de la conscience. On me verra descendre avec la lenteur de l'aigle, porté par une ruée invisible, et ramasser la tête, et je la forcerai à témoigner de la vengeance que je vais commettre pendant que la peau de mon front est immobile et calme encore. Je lâcherai le cordon du couperet avec l'expérience d'une vie entière, et le fer triangulaire tranchera sept têtes qui me regarderont avec douceur. (*Our,* 126–27)

If the "tête de la conscience" is the directing ego of the writing subject, then the son's revolt is the fiction's claim to autonomy. Castration is turned against the father, and the Oedipal *fer* is used to sever seven heads, separating seven autonomous fictions while beheading seven masterful deities. Yet these heads look on benevolently; a pact is formed even in the moment of apparent violence and betrayal between father and son. The fiction that emerges from the Oedipal moment of Nabou's betrayal of Mardouk is a paradoxical collusion between the two masculine terms of the triangle at the expense of the feminine pole they both desire. For in Lautréamont's text, "la conscience" is female, sent by the Creator to torture Maldoror, who beheads and vanquishes her: "Je chassai ensuite, hors de ma maison, cette femme, à coups de fouet, et je ne la revit plus."[38] Yet it must be remembered that *Les Chants de Maldoror* is itself notorious for its many thefts of passages from a variety of other sources. The ironic subtext of the allegorical struggle for textual autonomy and authorial paternity is the plagiarizing of one of the most infamous plagiarizers of French literature.

If the fictional subject has previously been proven masculine, now the writing subject is also shown to occupy one of the masculine positions on the Oedipal triangle. The writing subject and his offspring join forces to sacrifice the feminine so that the son can momentarily come into his own before being reintegrated into the primal textual chaos. The woven grill of writing is a masculine presence whose form, although temporary and borrowed, has annexed the productivity of the feminine ground. The maternal blood is usurped to serve as the "roi des mots" (*Our,* 144)—the king of words—so that a masculine hierarchy may be established: monarch, master, father, author. Although the individual fiction's existence is momentary, that moment is privileged in traditional literature beyond the scope of its temporal duration; its privilege rests on the specular weight of a visible form dredged up from and superposed upon a formless, and therefore imperceptible, depth. The specular prejudice of a phallocentric civilization privileges the visible moment of a much vaster system that, since it cannot be glimpsed in its totality, must be suppressed.

Specularity thus determines the Oedipal politics of fiction. Freud claimed that braiding or weaving constitutes perhaps woman's only original contribution to civilization; the braiding of pubic hair served the unconscious purposes of concealing the visible genital deficiency of the woman and fabricating a substitute phallus.[39] The scribal

tissage, which was to have overthrown the exploitative mimetic regime, would have been a feminine writing participating in the triumphantly feminine intertextual model of fictionality: a reweaving of
previous textuality divorced from parental ties of originality and purpose. As the medium through which various voices intertwine to
create a new, discontinuous, and heterogeneous narration, the scribe
would not participate in the traditional biological filiations of fiction.
But nepotism was nonetheless discovered even in the office of the
scribe: the fiction could not be a scribal writing, an autonomous feminine *tissage,* because it necessarily submitted to a masculine *maître*
who imposed a form, a *filet,* upon the amorphous scribal activity and
made of it a specific visible fiction.

A will to coopt masculinity underlies what Freud sees as the feminine
invention of braiding; with the Babylonian allegory in *Our,* the creation
of the world of a fiction conversely depends on a masterful and masculine usurpation of the supposedly feminine technique of weaving. In
"Pulsion," too, weaving becomes a masculine activity, the shuttle a phallus, and the fiction produced an ejaculation: "Le losange en tunnel où
piloter les mots joint les quatre coins de l'espace neuf où entailles ou
mailles ou lettres nomment ce qu'il advient au vide de se combler ainsi
par à-coups: la fiction—ou spasmes à navette, exacerbation du stile par
le désir d'immersion."[40] In endorsing the notion of writing as an intertextual *tissage*, "Pulsion" reinstates what a revolutionary theory of textual production had sought to dislodge: the masculine collusion of
father and son and their usurpation of a feminine intertextuality; in *Our,*
the apparent endorsement of scribal weaving is undermined by the contradictory but equally textile patrimony of the *maîtres* Ea and Mardouk. The *métier à navette* is a stubbornly masculine trade.

IV. Twenty Years After: The Persistence of the Writing Subject

> And I? And that amount, large or small, of myself,
> exquisitely personal, that I believed I was putting into it?
> —Italo Calvino

That the textual sons "Pulsion" and *Our* might escape their father's
design in no way contradicts the theoretical formulations enunciated

by Ollier; that the nature of their revolt consistently reaffirms the traditionally specular and colonialist basis of fiction is cause for greater concern. The birth of *Our* restates the biological metaphor from which fiction apparently cannot exit: any individual fiction that comes into being is the result of a violent, conflictual encounter between two types of writing, figuratively masculine and feminine; the fiction that emerges is a privileged moment produced out of the intertextual, scribal background by a solid and masterful specularity. The masculine-feminine opposition developed in *La Vie sur Epsilon* and *Enigma* adopts, in *Our,* an Oedipal structure in which the new-born fiction occupies the position of the son. The Oedipal situation is thus the very principle of fictional genesis. Fiction is propagated in terms of sexual reproduction; a fiction is an *être sexué.*

The implications of a sexual metaphor of fictional production are necessarily in conflict with some of the revolutionary aims allegorically proposed by *Le Jeu d'enfant* as well as in Ollier's more clearly theoretical texts. The *scripteur* proposed by Ollier and by much modern theory and fiction should have been able to sustain a purely feminine writing, an "other" writing challenging the standard, inherited forms of the traditional patrimony of fiction. The *scripteur* should have been able to sustain a *tissage* affirming intertextuality, discontinuity, and heterogeneity as the founding principles of a fiction as well as of Fiction. The feminine *tissage* was to supplant the traditional masculine regime of fictional filiation from author-father to fiction-son. Instead, the *scripteur* was unmasked as a participant in an Oedipal intrigue where both the textile and the filial came into play at the moment of fictional enunciation, with the feminine pole submitting to an exploitative suppression by the masculine positions. The sexual metaphor necessarily reinstates the division, conflict, and hierarchy that were traditionally part of the writing subject's relation to his text.

In recognition of this sexual impasse, *Our* offers an alternative vision of the genesis of fictional sense: an *asexual* process that would transcend the partial and therefore flawed sexuality of the feminine scribe and the masculine *maître.* If the textile cannot be separated from the biological, an alternative notion of textuality must be explored. This alternative vision must concentrate on the moment of enunciation, the specific fiction itself, while abandoning as immaterial any

productive forces anterior or exterior to that insular moment. The
return to an immanent perception of the text, like that of the formalist
or New Critical approaches, would dispense with the need to locate or
analyze the origin of fiction either in a revolutionary pan-textuality or
in a traditional filial relationship. Both the text and the textual considerations would thus be clearly delimited: "Le visiteur tire une bouffée
de sa pipe, ferme à demi les yeux comme pour rassembler ses esprits et
rejette lentement la fumée, tandis que les autres, regards baissés,
ménagent une sorte de vide à l'intérieur du cercle, où les paroles
sollicitées, aspirées, viendraient se prendre" (*Our*, 89). The visitor has
been asked to tell a story; the narration takes form inside the empty
circle, cut off from its source as well as from its receptors. It is a
material entity composed of dissociated words hooked together by a
chance or an accident or a design that need have no bearing on the
narration to be considered. The place of the narration—the *centre
vide*—appears throughout *Our*, as the room where Nabou writes, as
the space left when the sacred tablets are stolen, and as one of the
figures depicted on a fragment of ancient clay discovered by the visitor: "Une divinité, quelque ange ou démon, trois sinusoïdes parallèles,
un objet plat, un astre rayonnant, une sorte de stylet, des ailes de
dragon" (*Our*, 96). The visitor puzzles over the possible ways in which
the figures may be read, determining finally that the key must lie in the
circular form of its radiant star:

> saisissant tout à coup que, s'il est un sens à lire dans cette histoire en
> disposition consécutive et plane, il s'ordonne autour de la figure au
> centre, semant ses germes à tous les vents sur le pourtour, qui de si loin
> prend résolument l'allure d'un cercle, et comprenant, l'espace d'un
> éclair, que ce sens tourne, et indéfiniment dans tous les sens sans qu'il
> puisse le bloquer ou couper dans la chaîne et décider lui-même . . . et
> que s'il veut parler d'une globale appréhension toujours, c'est à ce tour-
> billon qu'il doit se référer, qui par instants là-bas apparaît immobile . . .
> et qu'en son centre, source du sens ou de son poudroiement, l'objet plat
> y est frappé comme une médaille dans l'argile et que ce qui est inscrit est
> illisible à l'oeil nu sous la lune. (*Our*, 98–99)

The *centre vide* here again figures the space of a narration. In the
moments when the whirling space appears immobile, a fiction forms.

This radiating center, both responsible for all meanings and ultimately destructive of any *sens unique,* recalls the symbol and standard of the *Dictionnaire Larousse; je sème à tout vent* might well be the fragment's unreadable inscription and the woman holding the flower its angelic or demonic deity. If fiction is a dictionary in virtual form, it is at once any meaning that momentarily takes shape and the space of dissolution of any specific sense. No separation can be made between a fiction and its source or sources. No process can be distinguished culminating in the birth of a fiction; nothing need exist outside or prior to the disseminating center that is at once the single fiction and all fictions. If the divinity figures a writing subject, that subject is then in no way the source of any meaning occurring inside the radiating center, according to the visitor's final illumination. Nothing need be considered except the center of the fragment: "Tout mobile qui se meut dans un cercle ou dans une ellipse ou dans une courbe quelconque se meut autour d'un centre auquel il tend" (*Our,* 136).

Yet the center is an *astre,* a heavenly body: a star that has resolutely taken on a circular form. The long-standing opposition between a masculine circle and a feminine star reappears at the moment when the sexual genesis of fiction seems to be definitely transcended. The empty yet potent circle is too burdened with past resonances to take up so easily its new incarnation as a neutral and self-contained fiction; the circle at the center must always be O. in his various avatars: at once the fictional subject, Oedipus, son, and father in the fiction and in the enunciation of the fiction; nor can the O. of *Ollier* be ignored. The disseminating center of a fiction cannot be attributed to only one of O.'s incarnations. A purely formal consideration of the fiction truncates and dismembers it. The writing subject cannot be dispelled from the center of Ollier's fictional cycle, which itself takes the form of a double spiral nearing its completion with the enunciation of the penultimate fiction, *Our:* "Un cercle a commencé de se refermer sur ce lieu qu'une navigation timorée a tôt circonscrit sans le dire, et désesténébré quelque peu de son blanc, si grande est la vertu de recul, une clarté prismatique qui, pour n'être issue que de trois pâles lunes, débusquait inexorablement de leurs terriers de neige les gnomes d'origine" (*Our,* 26). The hesitant and unspoken discoveries of the first cycle were confirmed by the self-critical stance of the second set of fictions. The clarity provided by the distant *Système du Prisme* illuminated, on Epsilon, the feminine matrix of writing, whose buried treasures would necessitate an archæology of the origin of fiction. The prism, according to the *Dictionnaire Larousse,* is literally a "solide triangulaire en verre blanc ou en cristal, qui sert à décomposer les rayons lumineux"; figuratively, the prism is yet another figure for the writing subject of fiction, who deflects and alters the language passing through him in such a way as to create a system of fiction. Yet this vision, too, is based on the tripartite configuration of three moons and three prismatic facets; the preceding passage is echoed near the end of *Our* in terms that make specific the familial metaphor: "La courbe a commencé de refermer sur le lieu qu'une pérégrination hésitante avait tôt circonscrit sans le dire, et désenténébré quelque peu de son blanc, par vertu de recul, un *faisceau prismatique* qui, pour n'être issu que de *trois pâles plumes,* délogeait sans merci de leurs fortins de papier les tropes d'origine" (*Our,* 109; my emphasis).

Again according to *Larousse,* a *faisceau* is composed of "gerbes de bouleaux liées autour d'une hâche, que portait le licteur romain devant certains magistrats comme signe de leur pouvoir." Symbol of the father's power, the prismatic *faisceau* is the sign of castration. Its source is equally phallic, yet also scriptural: three pale instruments of writing. It is the *faisceau* that uncovers the originary tropes at the basis of fiction and reveals the question of fictional origin to be always tropic, always figurative: always Oedipal. The center to which the fiction tends is thus a knot of filiation, a family struggle in which traditional patrimony is challenged but never completely ousted; and in which the son-fiction cannot transcend the sexual conflict from which he derives in order to achieve a transcendent, asexual status of his own. If O. is a *centre vide,* he is a centered void that still places the masculine writing subject at the heart of fictional enunciation. If O. is always Oedipus, he is also always Ollier; paternity still somehow lies at the core of fiction, comprising despite the design some unexpected thread in the final fabric of each fiction.

In *Our ou Vingt ans après,* the exemplary problems raised by Dumas's *Vingt ans après* have been reworked in light of a certain revolution in Western theories of literature, but the effect of that revolution has been to recirculate the problems rather than resolve them, and to illuminate certain of the contradictions inherent in literary revolutions. Just as O. in his incarnation as the fictional subject could not be definitively killed off by the demystifying Project, neither can the death of O. as author be confirmed: "Et ainsi se faisait qu'une première aventure se renouait, vingt ans après, avec ce qu'il lui plaisait de considérer ce soir-là comme sa dernière aventure" (*Our*, 186). Both hero and author obstinately maintain a central status in the fiction but refuse to be characterized as entities entirely generated by autonomous textual processes. The allegorical journey of the subject of fiction paradoxically preserves his position as a *point central;* not as the center of a stable, orderly individual fiction, but as the central, original question to which every fiction returns. The protagonist of traditional fiction disappeared at the end of the first cycle only to be resurrected in the second cycle as an immortal trinity that now includes the author and reader of fictions. In the following chapter we will see that in his final incarnation as the reading subject, O. will again investigate his own problematic insertion in the fictional text.

4

Textual Intercourse:
Allegories of Reading Fiction

> . . . le bonheur et l'innocence de la lecture, qui
> est peut-être en effet une danse avec un partenaire
> invisible dans un espace séparé, une danse joyeuse,
> éperdue, avec le "tombeau."
> —Blanchot

> Que ne puis-je regarder à travers ces pages
> séraphiques le visage de celui qui me lit.
> —Lautréamont

"Suis-je dans le livre?" With this password, O. seeks admittance to the ultramodern space vessel, the Octopus, where he believes Tiamât has taken refuge in her flight from Our with the stolen tablets recounting the origin of fiction. O.'s question inaugurates an allegory of reading in *Fuzzy Sets,* the last and most unconventional fiction of *Le Jeu d'enfant.* And the question of O.'s inclusion is indeed problematic from the outset, as the members of the space team hesitate to admit him on board the eight-armed vessel whose intertextual evocations embrace the seven previous fictions of the cycle. The astronauts rightly suspect that O.'s activity on board the vessel will be that of a spy: "combien sont-ils à tourner là en rond, conjecturant son inclusion dans l'ensemble ordonné des parenthèses où sont inclus les avatars du héros si vous le refoulez qui écrira la suite . . . l'intrus se donne à l'aléa des fables, *une fonction l'élit et l'investit d'intrigue.* . . ." (*FS,* 12; my emphasis). O. seeks in the branching structure of the vessel the secret space where the woman is hidden. The function he assumes is that of a reader faced with a text: lending himself to various peripeties and detours, he looks for the key to a meaning concealed within an ambiguous structure. The eight-armed spaceship of *Fuzzy Sets* becomes a figure not only of the entire fictional cycle of *Le Jeu d'enfant,* but of the structure of fiction itself. What the astronauts question is O.'s status as reader in respect to the vessel-book as a parenthetical arrangement already containing the other (now repressed) avatars of the hero: the protagonist and the author. The principal issue of *Fuzzy Sets* is enunciated from the first page as a question of inclusion: ". . . ceux qui sont 'dedans' et ceux qui sont 'dehors.'" (*FS*, 9). O.'s project as enacted in *Fuzzy Sets* is to determine the equivocal role and place of his current avatar, the reader of or in a fiction. His inaugural question, "Suis-je dans le livre?" echoes that posed by much contemporary literary theory and criticism. Titles such as the collection of essays *The Reader in the Text,* as well as Stanley Fish's "Literature in the Reader: An Affective Stylistics" and his book *Is There a Text in This Class?,* all attest to a growing interrogation of the spatial logistics of the audience-text relationship, an increasing concern with the place of the reader vis-à-vis the text being read.[1] The present chapter will examine this interrogation of the reader's place in Ollier's work and in that of contemporary theories of reading. The wandering search of O.'s third and last incarnation—the reader—takes place in terms of an opposition between "dedans" and "dehors," an opposition whose poles are already blurred by quotation marks, already the object of controversy in fictional practice and theoretical inquiry.

Thus begins the play of equivocal inclusion suggested by the book's title, *Fuzzy Sets,* and figured by its startling format, a sort of computer printout that makes liberal use of graphic gaps in the form of ellipses, parentheses, and pages on which the text is arranged into or around geometric shapes (stars, circles, keyholes, the figure eight) without respect to semantic continuity. Certain passages in this *roman à clef* mysteriously lack the beginning, middle, or end of every line; the text is traversed, semantically and syntactically, by the elliptical. The vessel itself becomes an ellipse to which O. is eventually, although provisionally, admitted:

à l'intérieur désormais de l'

ellipse ou "livre", une fois tranchée la question de l'appartenance sous le couvert chuchoté d'un mot de

passe. . . . (*FS*, 19–20)

The ellipse, which comes to figure the vessel-book and which is itself figured as a gap in the preceding passage, is a familiar lacuna, grown to interplanetary proportions from its modest beginnings as the uncharted zone on Lassalle's map in *La Mise en scène*. A metaphor of fictional structure, the ellipse is also the privileged lapse in a text where a truncated external element is inserted, a figure and a process basic to the intertextual functioning of the cycle.[2] With its intertextual splices and its secret chamber, the Octopus is the ellipse embodied. If the space-age configuration of *Fuzzy Sets* presents a vision of the future's fiction, then that fiction is a text in flux whose fuzzy borders and exaggerated lacunae point to the functional impossibility of a linear, integral reading. While the reader of a traditional novel may assume the text under consideration to be a coherent whole, the reader of *Fuzzy Sets* is forced to recognize its fragmentary nature. If the text of the future can no longer be apprehended as a totality unfolding itself in linear fashion, the position of the reader who approaches it can no longer be taken for granted; if the reader is no longer an outsider presented with an integral text, the question arises as to the reader's position in relation to its fragmented and heterogeneous structure. And in the same way that every author, as Borges says, creates his own precursors, no futuristic fiction can materialize without casting back the germ of its newness into the past. *Fuzzy Sets* makes manifest the elliptical nature of even the most apparently integral of traditional narratives and generalizes a mode of fictional structure out of its own hyperbolic format.[3]

As a figure of the reader, O. therefore attempts to determine what role he plays in respect to the ellipse-vessel-book, an investigation intimately connected with his search for the meaning he believes is hidden in that lacunary configuration: "Abrège! Coupe! Compare: c'est ici que la résolution s'esquisse. Entre deux mots, deux phrases— un trait, une virgule. . . . Hiatus entre les signes! Raisonne!" (*FS*, 98). O.'s dual quest—for identity and for meaning—is played out on board the Octopus in terms of his pursuit and capture of Tiamât: "Ressaisis-toi, passager nouveau! Reprends les fils, médite! Maudis ton sort et médis des tiens, mais garde ferme en ta main les rênes de l'intrigue—la Reine ailée qui perpétrait vengeance et que tu crois de tome en tome poursuivre et par tours de récit rattraper, de l'"exposition' coloniale au périple céleste où tu faillis t'égarer." (*FS*, 51). Tiamât is the textual secret O. investigates, the feminine enigma of written origins that he has pursued from the uncharted colonial zone of *La Mise en scène* to the stellar landscape of Epsilon, from the labyrinths of *Enigma* to the subterranean corridors of *Our*. In *Fuzzy Sets*, Tiamât comes to figure the elusive meaning contained in textual ellipses. Once on board the Octopus, O. observes and notes any clues that might reveal the space-ship's secret. His deductions finally permit him to locate the place of the enigma and penetrate the secret chamber, at once dissimulating structure and woman: "Un sentiment étrange le saisit . . . un senti-ment lié à la disposition des lieux: resserrées, coiffées en voûte par la chape supérieure de la nef, les parois latérales formant ogive en proue, c'est comme une salle souterraine, écartée, aveugle, une crypte" (*FS*, 159). O.'s success in discovering the womblike (and tomblike, recalling Freud's *Todestrieb*) hidden chamber will culminate in his rape of Tiamât:

> Elle était dans le livre, oui!—, la Tumultueuse, la Vengeresse . . . n'attend certes plus qu'on la délivre aujourd'hui; et celui qui a fait irruption agile dans la grotte en altitude, nanti de savoir neuf et d'illu-sions enfuies, sait bien que le pouvoir de délivrer ne lui sied plus. Mais foin de ces billevesées! Assume le bannissement du jour, partage le sort commun, approche sans arrière-pensée, sinon sans malice, ta
>
> partenaire
> vautrée sur le duvet cuivré du lieu d'exile, ou chambre de passe à qui monnaie d'élans lubriques sa qualité d'Elu! (*FS*, 159–60)

O.'s rape of Tiamât on board the Octopus repeats in terms of the reading subject a strategy that has already been seen at work, in *Our*, in the writing subject's activity. In the preceding chapter the individual text was posited as an *être sexué*, specifically masculine, and the *métier à navette* as a masculine and mastering vocation. If the subject—both fictional and writing—is a centered void around which revolves the fictional cycle, is the reader an equally masculine element in this con-figuration? If writing has a sex, what is the sex of reading? The terms of O.'s conquest on board the Octopus answer these questions by presenting reading as an allegorically sexual pursuit in which the reader defines *him*self in relation to his activity upon the feminine corpus of a textuality in flux.[4] If meaning was indeed hidden in the ambiguous vessel, then O. as a reader has triumphantly conquered a space for himself therein; he has made certain of his identity and (phallic) position by locating and invading the secret chamber: "Qu'il ait dû s'élever pour accéder à cette grotte l'étonne à peine: sa certitude ne vient-elle pas de plus profond encore? . . . la dame en noir était tout près de lui, il l'avait bien rejointe, la chaîne des déductions ne fait que recréer l'objet" (*FS,* 159). The logic O. employs is a patrimony that permits him to fix the elusive and feminine textuality of *Fuzzy Sets,* whose ellipses thematized the semantically elliptical and threatened him with noninclusion. He raises himself up—becomes erect—in order to attain the womb of the cavern. A penetration of fictional mysteries such as O. accomplishes appears to place the reader in a masterful position; the elliptical is filled in, the reader is in the book, like a key in a lock, precisely in the places where his logical faculties have permitted him to supply missing information. In its general structure, then, *Fuzzy Sets* proposes a sexualized allegory of reading that seeks to define the reader's status in terms of his activity within the text.

In reference to the reader figured in *Fuzzy Sets* and in the contemporary theories of reading discussed here, I deliberately use the masculine pronoun, for in both cases the reader is assigned a conventionally masculine role in the allegorically sexual economy of textuality. One question immediately comes to mind: what about the female reader? Clearly, these allegories of reading participate in a stereotypical kind of figuration that sometimes idealizes the feminine as the indeterminate, unknowable "other," and sometimes repeats distressingly time-worn images of the "eternal feminine." Such allegories do not address the question of the female reader, unless it be to make her an honorary man for the duration of her reading. While my conclusions in this chapter provide a critique of sexualized allegories of reading such as Ollier's, I do not undertake the much lengthier critique of the sexual-textual politics of *Le Jeu d'enfant.* While imminently valid, such an analysis exceeds the scope of the current discussion.

Both the sexual-textual model of reading at work in *Fuzzy Sets* and the conclusions about reading that it proposes are pertinent to the questions concerning reading posed by reflexive, revolutionary fiction and by the theories of reading developed in the latter half of this century. Before examining these models and theories of reading, however, it is important to look at their operative strategy: that of allegory. Chapter 2 posited the allegorical nature of Ollier's entire fictional interrogation, and Chapter 3 examined the first three books of the second cycle of texts in an allegorical light. The planets Epsilon and Iota as well as the ancient city of Ur were read as *paysages moralisés* carrying a second level of meaning whose aim was educational. The enigma is the oldest form of allegory, and riddling abounds not only in *Enigma* but in every fiction of the cycle, with Oedipus and the question of the Sphinx providing a pervasive figure of textuality in the fictions of the second cycle. Allegory is arguably the most important instrument of the fictional *recherche* proposed by *Le Jeu d'enfant,* as well as by many other New Novels, and by reflexive fictions in general.

After Goethe and the romantics, allegory was unfavorably compared to symbol and was criticized as artifical and didactic. New Criticism has often taken up the romantics' reservations about allegory.[5] André Breton similarly valorized metaphor over analogy, which he generally equated with the allegorism of Fourier. But recently, a number of critics claim, we have seen a critical rehabilitation of allegory after its depreciation by the romantics and New Critics. As Maureen Quilligan affirms, "we seem in the last quarter of a century to have reentered an allegorical age."[6] Theorists like Walter Benjamin, in his *Origin of the German Tragic Drama,* and Paul de Man, in his essay "The Rhetoric of Temporality," are seen as radically revising our ideas about allegory (although in very different ways).[7] And in *Postmodernist Fiction,* Brian McHale points to a resurgence in the practice of allegory in contemporary fiction, naming as examples works like Thomas Pynchon's *Gravity's Rainbow,* John Barth's *Giles Goat-Boy,* Jerzy Kosinski's *Being There,* Günter Grass's *The Flounder,* and Alain Robbe-Grillet's *Dans le labyrinthe.*[8] Claude Ollier is not alone in his use of sex to allegorize reading. The hero of Italo Calvino's 1979 novel *Se una notte d'inverno un viaggiatore* is its own reader, and the act of reading is ultimately revealed to parallel the act of love; and Robbe-Grillet's *Souvenirs du triangle d'or* links reading to a sadistic experimentation on female sexual fantasy. An examination of the final allegory of *Le Jeu d'enfant*—that of reading—will raise the question of the status of allegory itself in reflexive postmodern fiction, for allegory openly aims at readers and has to do with a certain type of reading.

In *Allegory, The Theory of a Symbolic Mode,* Angus Fletcher notes that the oldest notions of allegory see it as a divine will infusing the language of man with transcendent meaning: "it is a human reconstitution of divinely inspired messages, a revealed transcendental language which tries to preserve the remoteness of a properly veiled godhead."[9] Use of allegorical form must necessarily be a statement about revelation of meaning: the author of an allegory must believe the text can be framed in accordance with an external or transcendent scheme of reference. Such an openly didactic form, with a veiled but masterful will hovering above it and infusing it with meaning, seems at first to conflict categorically with the New Novel's stern dismissal of the intentionality or message of a writing subject, voiced here by Ollier but echoing statements made by most practitioners and theorists of the New Novel: "The book composes itself step by step, word after word, and it is given to be read word by word. The story that unfolds is the meaning of fiction. My 'procedure' consists in choosing and combining the words most likely to resound and to constitute the autonomous being composed of internal dependencies—which is fiction."[10]

Ollier's comment depicts the New Novel as an isolated being, seemingly cut off from either author or reader and functioning independently. According to this vision, there unfolds in the book a story whose meaning is that of fiction itself. In this autonomous being, fiction is no longer subject to any representative or expressive function but instead allegorizes its own construction. This notion of the work as an autonomous entity composed of internal dependencies takes its place within a tradition extending back through New Criticism to Kantian aesthetics. Northrop Frye suggests that any type of commentary necessarily makes an allegory of what it analyzes, as it attaches a secondary level of meaning to the existent structure of the work.[11] For a critical approach such as the one endorsed in Ollier's comment, that secondary level of meaning is self-generated and self-reflexive; the work is cut off from any external source or referent, generates its own laws, and provides for its own allegorical reading. In other words, the fiction is an allegory of writing.

The antimimetic potential of allegory lends itself aptly to the project of demystification that is so central to the New Novel.[12] The use of an allegorical mode permits the extravagant coincidences that have occurred throughout *Le Jeu d'enfant* and have effected its demystifying developments; for instance, the fact that O. is revealed to be the final (?) avatar of all the previous protagonists is at once *invraisemblable* and highly significant for the cycle's allegorical treatment of the fictional subject. As a political device, allegory can express the conflict between rival ideologies, valorizing one at the expense of the other. And yet the troubling issue (troubling at least for a revolutionary form) of a programmatic didacticism still hovers about the use of allegory. The contradiction evident here—didacticism and intentionality versus a politicized, autonomous demystification of fiction operated by fiction itself—is the question raised by the last and most revolutionary fiction of *Le Jeu d'enfant:* what exactly is the position and function of the reader in light of these two diametrically opposed visions of the controlling strategy of much modern and postmodern fiction? In proposing an allegory of reading, then, *Fuzzy Sets* opens up to questioning, in respect to the New Novel, not only the difficult and debated issue of the relationship between readers, writers, and texts, but also the very question of its guiding strategy, allegory. In casting its allegory in the sexual terms of masculine activity and feminine passivity, of conquest and seduction, *Fuzzy Sets* now situates the question of reading within the vexed and problematic framework of family romance that dominates the second cycle of *Le Jeu d'enfant.*

In the present chapter, the sexualized model of reading allegorized by *Fuzzy Sets* is compared to similar visions of reading proposed by contemporary reader-response theories. The contradictions that arise concerning the role of the reader in those theories are shown to parallel contradictions in the use of allegory in postmodern fiction. Finally, another model of reading is derived from *Fuzzy Sets*—one that, while still rooted in the allegory of family romance from which fiction does not exit, seems to provide a more satisfactory vision of the relations between the reader, the author, and textual meaning.

I. Reading Otherwise

> Parce que nous commençons à écrire, à écrire
> autrement, nous devons relire autrement.
>
> —Derrida

In "La Mort de l'auteur" Roland Barthes calls for a switch in critical attention away from the pole of writing to that of reading: "Nous savons que pour rendre à l'écriture son avenir, il faut en renverser le mythe: la naissance du lecteur doit se payer de la mort de l'Auteur." In "Pulsion," Ollier transfers responsibility for narrative direction from the author to the text itself: "La fiction filant de cache en cache se donne à suivre dans les friches entre les sillons." The empirical author is marginalized in the confrontation between reflexive fiction like the New Novel and its reader. In "Le Jeu du texte et du récit chez Claude Ollier," Léon Roudiez presents a vision of the textual phenomenon from which the author has in a sense evaporated: "l'histoire et le discours tendaient à s'évanouir pour ne plus laisser que le lecteur en présence du texte."[13]

This elision of the writing subject can be linked to the work of phenomenological theorists like Georges Poulet and Maurice Merleau-Ponty, whose concerns were shared by the early practitioners and proponents of the New Novel. For Poulet, the reader merges with the consciousness of a text; the borders between the work and the reader fall away, so that the reader begins to think "the thoughts of another." This other consciousness, however, is never that of the writer; the author falls from consideration in Poulet's vision of reading: "The subject who is revealed to me through my reading of it is not the author, either in the disordered totality of his outer experiences, or in the aggregate, better organized and concentrated totality, which is the one of his writings. Yet the subject which presides over the work can exist only in the work."[14] With the New Novel, the text has inherited some of the functions usually assigned to the writing subject and has taken the author's place, in respect to the reader, in a dual relationship rooted in both a phenomenological and a New Critical approach.[15] The allegory of reading proposed in *Fuzzy Sets* must be examined in light of this assumption of the writer's traditional position by the text.

The future of writing envisioned by much structuralist and post-structuralist thought is one where an enlightened practice of writing is necessarily accompanied by a new way of reading; thus Jean Ricardou's critical manifesto of the New Novel, *Le Nouveau Roman,* begins with the dedication: "Aux nouveaux lecteurs."[16] That the New Novel's readability has been, since its inception, the subject of controversy is demonstrated by titles such as J. A. G. Tans's *Romans lisibles et romans illisibles,* as well as by critical reactions ranging from the heated to the tepid:

> l'auteur exige la collaboration—il faudrait même dire la COMPLICITE intellectuelle—du lecteur qui préférera, longtemps encore, les séductions d'un art mieux accordé à la nature de la vie.
>
> Cette manière d'aborder l'oeuvre littéraire non comme un produit fini, mais comme une expérience où le lecteur finira par avoir plus de mal que l'auteur lui-même. . . .

Even a favorable review of *La Vie sur Epsilon* commiserates with and encourages the flagging reader: "L'ennui du lecteur est son épreuve à lui, et qui mérite d'être surmontée."[17]

The language of both defenders and detractors of the new practice of reading points to an increased participation on the part of the New Novel's reader, as well as an increased attention to that participation. The defenders claim that reading—particularly the reading of fiction—has traditionally been viewed as a passive role; the reader receives a message sent by the author, a message whose proper reception is encoded in its generic properties. Or the reader contemplates a text that provokes a subsequent affective or aesthetic reaction. The traditional position of the reader would thus be characterized by passivity, secondariness, and exteriority. The passivity of the novel's reader is equated with femininity by Ian Watt, who claims a sociohistorical context for the paradigm. In *The Rise of the Novel,* Watt ties the growth of the novel in the eighteenth century to the sedentary, leisurely lifestyle of its predominantly female public. Freed from many household activities by increased industrialization, he claims, women became the principal audience of much fiction, and the reading of fiction acquired connotations of passivity and frivolity. In *Fiction and the*

Unconscious, Simon Lesser discusses the rather dishonorable status
that the reading of fiction still holds, citing primarily the same reasons
as Watt offers in *The Rise of the Novel.*[18]

A certain shift in emphasis toward the activity and primacy of
reading is apparent in the work of Georges Poulet, whose theoretical
formulations influenced both the reading of New Novels and theories
of reading. Union with the consciousness of a literary work is initiated, according to Poulet, by the reader: "And so I ought not to hesitate
to recognize that so long as it is animated by this vital inbreathing
inspired by the act of reading, a work of literature becomes (at the
expense of the reader whose own life it suspends) a sort of human
being, that it is a mind conscious of its own objects."[19] Reading is an
act; the coming to life of the work's consciousness is only activated, in
Poulet's formulation, by the reader's initial approach to the text. The
reader animates the text but is subsequently suspended through his
union with the mind of the text. While Poulet speaks of the initial act
setting off the mechanisms of the text, explicators and practitioners of
the New Novel point to the process by which a reader progresses
through a text, "le rôle capital désormais dévolu au lecteur."[20] In an
essay entitled "Naissance d'une fiction," Ricardou stresses the productive relationship between the autogenerating text he posits and its
reader: "Tout livre qui . . . s'est produit en se lisant, exige de ses
lecteurs qu'ils continuent de le produire."[21]

The activity of the reader is increasingly important in the theoretical formulations that accompany the movement from New Novel
to New New Novel. In Sollers's *Logiques,* reading a text becomes a
generative activity whose production is not that of a text, but of the
reading subjects themselves; readers shatter the ideological structures
that inhabit them and create a new subjective identity by their new
relationship with the text: "Le lecteur . . . doit, non pas comme on le
dit trop souvent, fabriquer un livre par sa lecture, mais devenir à
chaque instant sa propre écriture—c'est-à-dire briser la parole qui en
lui est parlée par les préjugés afin de juger lui-même sur pièces,
d'accéder à sa propre génération."[22] The reader's activity as production or (auto)generation rejoins the sexualized allegory of reading
proposed by *Fuzzy Sets,* in which O. seeks his own identity in relation
to feminine textual mysteries. The productive process accomplished

by the reader as figured in *Fuzzy Sets* is one of finding the right keys, of discovering and filling in the logical and formal gaps in the text. O. produces and assures his phallic-logical identity through his position in the structure of the text. He has been performing this process, as protagonist, from *La Mise en scène* to *Our:* "Le visiteur, comme de coutume, a écouté avec un soin extrême, suppléant mentalement les lacunes, corrigeant les erreurs et les introversions" (*Our,* 183). In *Fuzzy Sets* this perennial activity becomes that of the reader.

II. The Sexual Politics of Reader Theory

> Much reading is, indeed, like girl-watching,
> a simple expense of spirit.
> —Geoffrey Hartman

In its emphasis on process and realization, and in its opposition between activity and passivity, the vision of the reader just enunciated resembles the formulations of several contemporary reader-response theories. Indeed, much literary criticism of the last three decades has found sex to be a tempting reservoir of metaphors for the act of reading as well as for writing and textuality in general. The epigraph to the present section of this chapter is a strikingly overt example of the sexualization of reading in recent criticism. The flippancy of Hartman's remark about the similarity of reading and girl-watching— both of which he sees as an infertile but innocuous activity—betrays the extent to which assumptions about sexuality and gender went unquestioned in the criticism of the sixties and seventies. In such criticism, a conventional view of sexuality seems as natural a metaphor for reading, writing, and textuality as the naturalness of those sexual conventions themselves (that is, male activity/female passivity; potency/fertility, and so on). While Hartman portrays the reader as a sort of harmless dirty old man (rather in the vein of "and those who can't, teach"), other theories of reader response propose a more vigorous version of the reader's activity. Both the New Novel and recent reading theory, then, developed in a critical climate in which sex and reading were regularly, almost routinely equated. Contemporary theories of reading share with the vision of the reader just enunciated in respect to *Fuzzy Sets* a highly (though not always consciously) sexualized vocabulary of reading. They also share the complications that, as I will show, arise from the paradigm provided by that sexual vocabulary.

Perhaps the most well known and most influential of the reader-response theories is that enunciated by the Constance School of *Rezeptionsästhetik*. In the decade of the seventies, the Constance School received an increasing attention from French theorists, and in some instances took the New Novel as the object of its research. The formulations of Wolfgang Iser, a principal figure in the Constance School, exhibit significant parallels with the question of the reader in *Fuzzy Sets*. Rooted in the phenomenological aesthetics of Roman Ingarten, Iser's theory of literary response proposes an "implied reader," a hybrid dialectical construct composed of two parts: a prestructuring of potential meaning by a text, and the reader's actualization of that potential through the active process of reading.[23] Iser's theory of literary effects is based on the novel, which he sees as rooted in a socio-historic context eliciting certain expectations and reactions. The implied reader's activity is one of concretization of the text, a movement of expectation and modification of expectations. The structuring of the text is thus a reader-included situation, where textual indeterminacies or discontinuities, in the form of "gaps" or "vacancies," trigger a process of visualization, of filling-in, on the part of the reader. Iser points to the New Novel as a form that thematizes the filling-in of these gaps. In France, Lucien Dällenbach proposes a theory of reading based in part on the formulations of Iser and the Constance School. Like Iser, Dällenbach claims that a reader's activity is occasioned by "the text's *Leerstellen* (a term translatable here as empty places, free places, or more succinctly, as gaps, blanks, or ellipses)."[24] Dällenbach differs from Iser, however, in his conception of the reader's treatment of those gaps in a narration: "On remarquera que la conception qu'Iser se fait des *Leerstellen* dans l'opération de lecture diffère, sur un point décisif, de celle que nous soutenons ci-dessous puisque, dans un cas, il s'agit essentiellement de remplir les trous, et, dans l'autre, de les percer." Dällenbach's analysis makes more explicit the sexual metaphor underlying both conceptions of what readers do with textual *trous;* he speaks of "textes pleins," of the "séduction exercée par le texte," and defends his "théorie des vides" against charges of critical "impuissance."[25] While Iser deals primarily with narratives, Michael Riffaterre proposes a semiotics of poetry in which the reader plays an important role "in" the text. Literariness, for Riffaterre, resides in intertextuality:

> In literary texts there are certain phrases or sentences that seem less acceptable than their context, a phenomenon linked to the intertext. As soon as the reader becomes aware of that intertext, the relative ungrammaticality is corrected or palliated. . . . Thus the correct, that is, the complete interpretation of the poem is made possible for the reader only by the intertext.[26]

The reader responsible for the potentially correct and complete palliation of ungrammaticalities has been called the Superreader, whose command of a particular sociolect permits him to recognize lacunae in the consistency of a text and to supply appropriate intertexts.

In *The Role of the Reader,* another semiotician, Umberto Eco, distinguishes between "open" and "closed" texts and stresses the "cooperative activity" of reading; the addressee is a constitutive element in the process of textual actualization and exists within the realm of the text: "To postulate the cooperation of the reader does not mean to pollute the structural analysis with extratextual elements. The reader as an active principle of interpretation is part of the picture of the generative process of the text."[27] The first chapter of *The Role of the Reader,* entitled "How to Produce Texts by Reading Them," demonstrates the potent, performative aspect of the reading activity in Eco's semiotics. And in respect to the uncharted areas of text semiotics, Eco invites his readers to perform such a process upon his own text: "Many of the present text theories are still heuristic networks full of components represented by mere 'black boxes.' In 'The Role of the Reader' I also deal with some black boxes. It goes without saying that the role of the reader of this book is to open and to overfill (by further research) all the boxes that my essays have necessarily left inviolate."[28]

While differing in particularities and in emphasis, these models all view reading as a forceful, productive activity, a process that invades or even violates a text by filling in or resolving its gaps, vacancies, black boxes, or lacunary ungrammaticalities. They point to a type of mastery that *Fuzzy Sets* seems to endorse or even take to shocking extremes in the terms of its allegory of reading as rape. *Fuzzy Sets* would then appear to make explicit the sexualization of reading that underlies, more or less unconsciously, the major thrust of contemporary reader theory. *Fuzzy Sets* joins these theories in reversing the poles of activity and passivity traditionally assigned to the reader and the author (more recently, the text). At the same time, however, it maintains the sexual identity conventionally assigned to those poles: O. is the active, mastering reader, Tiamât is the passive and feminine textual mystery whose elliptical nature must be made coherent. The New Novel thus appears to assign a privileged, virile role to its reader, and to readers in general by allegorical extension.[29] The outcome of O.'s adventure will have ramifications for any hermeneutics that places the reader, implicitly or openly, in a similar allegorical position. The following section traces that adventure and explores its ramifications.

III. The Reading Trap

> Lire souvent égale être leurré.
> —Roussel

The episode in which O. discovers and rapes Tiamât should be a parable of triumphant reading concluding O.'s figurative search for origin, meaning, and identity: the semantic and typographic gaps of *Fuzzy Sets* mark the interstitial place the reader occupies, the obscure location where he fills in the elliptical with his own essential contribution, thus making the text *plein* (both full and pregnant) with meaning. Yet a strange reversal complicates the analogy immediately after the rape; Tiamât has anticipated the attack, acquiescing instead of resisting as she did earlier in *Our:* "'Je ne t'ai pas résisté cette fois-ci; ce n'était plus *de mise*'" (*FS,* 164). Apparently, neither the earlier resistance nor the present acquiescence occurs spontaneously as an effect of or a response to O.'s imposed will, for the entire encounter is subsequently revealed to have been part of a mise-en-scène, another theatrical scenario: "Huit coups frappés à la cloison de gauche annoncent la fin de l'entracte. 'L'heure est venue, dit Tiamât, le temps de s'apprêter et d'entrer en scène'" (*FS*, 168). The hidden space O. discovers and appropriates is in reality a predetermined gap in a deliberate program, a setup. He has delivered himself up to a trap meant exclusively for him: "Et l'invité d'honneur—celui qui s'est invité de chic et a placé lui-même sa tête dans le piège . . ." (*FS*, 140). Instead of establishing his inclusion and identity in the book, O.'s active pursuit and possession of textual mysteries leave him a passive and dispossessed victim, dubious now of his status as the privileged reading subject: "'J'ai laissé le récit me voler mes actes. . . . Que les Sages aient misé sur le mauvais cheval est une autre affaire: un Elu plus éveillé aurait déjoué le piège—retourner les Textes sans s'y laisser "rouler"'" (*FS*, 176–77).

O.'s ordeal reflects in many respects that of the readers of the New Novel, who are led to form certain hypotheses as to the meaning of a text, only to see those notions turned against them in a perpetual subversion of their habitual, ideologically grounded ways of reading: "l'alternance précipitée, l'absence de support ou point d'appui à nos raisonnements et états d'âme déplacent tous repères en nos traditions et valeurs, irrémédiablement troublées par ces girations neuves ou révolutions culturelles" (*FS*, 37). O.'s vertigo is matched by that of the reader faced with *Fuzzy Sets'* textual gyrations. In Chapter 1, demystification was seen as a major goal in the New Novelist's project: much of the New Novel's narration is directed toward the undermining of reader expectations specifically aroused by the use of various novelistic conventions. Thus the New Novel may make use of stereotypical forms such as the police novel or the science fiction narrative in order to manipulate and dismantle their generic conventions. The New Novel's reader is not simply the dupe of a text that foresees and forestalls the reader's acts, but is also a pupil to be retrained and corrected of bad reading habits, a student to be introduced to a new method of writing, instructed in a new way of reading. Here, the *Unbildungsroman* becomes that of the reader. Jonathan Culler points out that the stories told by the various theories of reader response are also, invariably, idealized *Bildungsromane* of the reader's progress toward enlightenment.[30]

The reader of *Fuzzy Sets* is met with an exotic array of typographic gaps and an equally exotic assortment of intertextual references to other literary adventurers: Sinbad, Nemo, Cyrano. If the conventional reader attempts to rearrange the textual flux into a coherent linear narration, he must fill in its gaps and find a meaningful place for its external borrowings. The reader's recognition of logical gaps in the narration, the expectations aroused in him by literary or generic references, and his efforts to fill in or fill out the lacunary narration are the means by which he is led to question and correct his habitual way of reading fiction. The reader's generative input into the elliptical text transforms that text into a trap in which he has placed his own head, paradoxically bringing again into question his logic and the phallic identity it afforded him. The multiplication and exaggeration of narrative ellipses simultaneously arouse and undercut the reader's efforts to fill in or fill out the fiction's lacunary configuration; in this way, O.'s "projet/Eros" is always accompanied by a menacing "projet/Castrati"—with the term castration itself graphically amputated by the marginless edge of the page (*FS,* 85). The reader of *Fuzzy Sets* thus resembles the pupil in a Socratic dialogue: it is by means of his own responses—his own input, his logic—that he is trapped and taught.

In a speech delivered subsequent to his programmed act of rape, O. acknowledges the pedagogical outcome of his deductive activity on board the Octopus: "'Venu pour vous instruire, c'est vous qui m'instruisiez'" (*FS,* 177). With this inversion, a new and contradictory role for the reader appears, and one that the New Novel endorses as strongly as the other, masterful or active stance it assigned to the reader. Is the reader figured by O. now a rapist or a foil, a bold textual actualizer or a humbled pupil, "assiégeant" or "assiégé"? (*FS,* 31). This contradiction parallels the problem of allegory in *Le Jeu d'enfant* and in reflexive fiction in general: is this kind of allegory a politicized, antimimetic mode enlisted in the revolutionary struggle against realist ideology and convention, or is it a highly traditional form of didacticism disguising a stern intention behind futuristic textual innovations? The problem of intentionality and its relation to demystification is also evident in a remark made by Claude Ollier at the 1971 Cerisy Colloquium on the New Novel:

Dans la plupart des livres qu'on revêt du label Nouveau Roman on trouve des formes très traditionnelles d'écriture romanesque . . . le plus souvent elles sont utilisées avec une *intention* de contournement ou même de franc détournement. Le problème est intéressant en ceci que, parmi ces lecteurs bourgeois, la plupart ne lisent pas *correctement* la nouvelle fonction de ces formes, ne discernent pas *le but qu'elles poursuivent* dans le détournement du mécanisme de la fiction.[31]

A firm intention to instruct on the part of the writing subject is coupled with his recognition of the reading subject's ability to read incorrectly, and to ignore the political implications of the allegorical situation. Allegory is always endangered—or insured—by the fact that it can be taken literally, and that an orthodox view will most probably be blind to the narrative's revolutionary double. While the radical innovations of New New Novels such as *Fuzzy Sets* ought to preclude the recuperative reading that is possible in more subtly demystifying fictions, their instructive aspect is balanced by the possibility of a wrong or radically free reading.

In the *Symposium,* Plato shows that while Socrates claimed to be learning, he was in fact teaching his interlocutor. When he appeared to be the lover, he was in effect the beloved. The link between pedagogy and romance in the Socratic method is equally at the foundation of the reader's ambiguous adventures in *Fuzzy Sets;* is O. a sexual aggressor or merely seduced, active or passive? In *Enigma,* a giant "transcriptor" pylon marks the position from which every activity and process in the colony is organized, from which every message is captured, decoded, and disseminated: "De toutes les baies vitrées . . . on aperçoit le pylône transcripteur au point zéro de la planète, dressé vertical sur trente pieds de hauteur et perçant la coupole en son sommet, protégé au-delà par son manchon de plastique. C'est la cellule nerveuse de la vie de Iota: il capte les émissions . . . et les décode; il code et achemine en toutes ces directions les messages" (*E,* 25). If the pylon marks the reader's phallic and generative position in respect to textual meaning, it also demonstrates the extent to which that input is sterile and insulated by its plastic "manchon," so that any resultant offspring (message, recognition) appears to be the product of a form of planned parenthood. O.'s violent attack upon Tiamât and her part in that scenario suggest that the question of the reader's position in respect to the text be viewed in terms of a sadomasochistic pact, where the reader is actively and aggressively in the book, not as an external force spontaneously and willfully intruding, but rather as an anticipated and insulated, even welcomed incursion. Viewed in this light, the wrong reading Ollier fears is unlikely, since the activity of the reader would be strictly guided. An investigation of this pact should therefore resolve the contradictions that have up to now obscured our understanding of the reader's position in a sexualized model of reading and should clarify the ambiguous role of allegory in self-reflexive fictions like those proposed by the New Novel.

IV. The Place of the Reader

> One is pregnant only of one's own child.
> —Nietzsche

A suggestion of sadomasochism has accompanied O. from his initial apparition in *La Vie sur Epsilon,* since each "story of O." necessarily evokes for most readers Pauline Réage's popular classic of discipline and submission, *L'Histoire d'O.* Sadomasochism is conventionally considered a dialectical cooperation between two polarized positions. It is associated with a series of other binary oppositions: active/passive, masculine/feminine, master/pupil, master/slave. If these oppositions can be seen to cooperate in the allegory of O.'s relations with Tiamât, then the paradigm of sadomasochism will provide the definitive model of reading for the fiction of the future exemplified by *Fuzzy Sets;* it will locate the reader within certain highly specific parameters in the book and will clarify the power structure of the relationship between text and reader.

The sadomasochistic pact in *Fuzzy Sets* must be examined in light of the Oedipal situation, since no relationship between man and woman or between allegorically masculine and feminine entities in the entire cycle has escaped that primary structure. All the females in the various fictions are one woman, just as O. is every major protagonist.

Tiamât is in a sense O.'s wife and mother as well as his lover-victim. Incest and violence are linked to each other to a more or less explicit degree in every encounter. This sadomasochistic model finds certain parallels in Freudian psychoanalysis and in the literary criticism of René Girard, whose theory of the novel is based on a model of mediated, or metaphysical desire. For both Freud and Girard see sadomasochism not merely as an individual perversion or deviation, but, in more general terms, as the basis of human existence. In much the same way, the Oedipal affair in *Le Jeu d'enfant* can be seen to allegorize the tensions inherent in fictional structure itself; O.'s long-standing aggression-attraction toward Tiamât, far from being a narrative digression or diversion, forms part of the basis of fictional functioning.

Freud finds in sadism and masochism "excellent examples" of the fusional nature of all instincts, since a mixture of Eros and aggressiveness is recognizable in both sadism and masochism. Freud links the destructive tendency manifest in both drives to the death instinct that he posits as the basis of all organic life. In this light, masochism is the primary expression of the destructive impulse, and sadism a secondary and external application of that impulse.[32] In *Mensonge romantique, vérité romanesque*, René Girard similarly sees masochism as the existential basis of all metaphysical desire: "le masochiste désire exactement ce que nous désirons nous-mêmes; il désire l'autonomie et la maîtrise divine, sa propre estime et l'estime des *Autres* mais, par une intuition du désir métaphysique plus profonde que celle de tous ses médecins . . . il n'espère plus découvrir ces biens inestimables qu'auprès d'un maître dont il sera l'esclave humilié."[33] While the masochist plays out in his sexual life the existential role he assigns himself with a divine mediator, Girard asserts, the sadist is a masochist who comes to identify himself with the mediator, and assumes the master's omnipotent role. For both Freud and Girard, then, the sadomasochistic dialectic collapses into a primary existential masochism.

In O.'s allegorical confrontation with Tiamât the sadistic function similarly appears to fall away, and the opposition between the two poles becomes blurred. Neither O. nor Tiamât can be held fully responsible for the aggression that characterizes their encounter. As woman, enigma, and acquiescent victim, Tiamât should logically occupy a passive, masochistic position. Yet O. is placed on the same side of the binary polarization by his status as pupil; as a guided reader, his programmed virility is a paradoxically passive stance. We know that Freud cautioned against attributing to masculine and feminine psyches the activity and passivity that characterize the male and female sex cells, for "to achieve a passive aim may call for a large amount of activity."[34] Thus O.'s search for origin, meaning, and identity can only be an attempt to return to the maternal womb (tomb) and to the quiescence of unity with a lost or hidden plenitude, a passive aim that he has actively pursued throughout the fictional cycle as both protagonist and reader. O.'s rape of Tiamât immediately occasions the description of a primeval aquatic scene:

> il reste en elle, son ventre collé contre le sien, bouge en elle . . . écoute les battements, les frappements du coeur, sent couler le liquide encore, les contractions du muscle, le reste du corps inerte, relâché, absent, la reptation du muscle dans sa gaine, l'onde propagée par la dislocation ou béance, l'écart des lèvres dans la fissure moite ou déchirure, la chair qui se dérobe, s'effrite, pollue l'eau d'éboulis miniscules, mare ou marigot minime perdurant par renfort d'infiltrations renouvelées, averses, orages, s'enflant jusqu'au pourtour de l'affaissement, cuvette ou fosse, débordant, inondant l'étendue. (*FS*, 162–63)

Through sexual assault O. seeks the fluid femininity that affords him a return to a lost origin; he is slipping away, his minimal ejaculation absorbed by the inundation of the primal aquatic matrix. His reading thus aligns itself with the existential masochism underlying the Freudian death instinct. Neither O. as reader nor Tiamât as text can be said to occupy the sadistic position.

Viewed according to the paradigm of sadomasochism, the respective roles of O. and Tiamât coincide in a bewildering fashion, blurring the polarized oppositions that initially seemed to function allegorically in delimiting the reader's place. The paradigm does not form a coherent allegory; nor does it shed light on the nature of allegory itself, whose use in the New Novel is divided by similar contradictions. To cast Tiamât (or the text) as as masterful teacher plotting out the reader's every step runs counter to the ostensible terms of the paradigm, which seeks to turn the reader into a producer of meaning. Yet to envision O. as a free agent actively participating in the realization of a revolutionary textual meaning is equally untenable. There can be no complicitous pact between positions whose functions blur and shift in this manner.[35] At the end of *Fuzzy Sets,* Tiamât's hypnotic, masturbatory ritual culminates in her triumphant escape from the spaceship: "L'exilée du livre . . . Essor ultime!" (*FS,* 184). Both her onanism and her flight preclude the closure a cooperative union would have produced; original meaning is not "dans le livre." Whether the reader is in turn excluded from the book cannot be determined through analogy with sexual role, be it normal or perverted. Two central pages in *Fuzzy Sets* illustrate the failure of the sexual metaphor of reading to account for the phenomena of meaning. O. is close to deducing Tiamât's location. A page recounting a scene from the preceding novel *(Our)* in which O. rapes Tiamât is arranged around a phallus-shaped blank. The following page is printed around the shape of a keyhole, with, at center, the moment in *Fuzzy Sets* when O. deduces the location of the secret chamber: "le trou de la serrur ctionnelle, ou clef du sens . . . Sept chambre onge visitées . . . et la huitième? Le maillo te manquait! Le mot de la comptine*! Tu sais la trouver maintenant . . ." (*FS,* 151). Tiamât's flight from the book ultimately proves that O.'s phallic key neither unlocked the textual mysteries nor succeeded in filling in the "lapsus fictionis" (*FS,* 81–82).

In the familial structure of fiction as developed in Chapters 2 and 3, O. occupies the positions of both textual son (protagonist) and father (writing subject) in respect to the amorphous maternal matrix of textuality. The Oedipal situation was developed in the terms of Girard's triangular model: the feminine pole must at some point constitute the object of desire for the other two, who represent for each other the rival through whom desire is mediated. The problem inherent in the sadomasochism model as applied to the structure of fiction is precisely that it has only two terms. One element has been elided or repressed in the paradigm of reading it offers: the (paternal) position of the author. The problems posed by the allegory of *Fuzzy Sets,* and by allegory itself, stem from this omission. In developing a theoretical position on

---

*The *comptine* is a song sung in children's games, such as hide-and-seek, in order to determine which participant is "it," the seeker.

P a n s d'argile séchée
e n t r e les pierres,
une lampe brûle
dans le lointain
jaune sur les
illon entre l
et entourant
de ne pouvoir
ts sans la fair
incarnat le plus
rouge dans la lum
laine rèche et lan
le bas de la nuque
chaînette d'or heu
ant, halètera, elle
illes et la tensio
douleur quand le g
oudes arc-boutés s
la pression du musc
hambre sous la cla
s meurtrissant le c
fond quand le liqu
sses coulera dans
le cessera de se d

ou coulées de sable
senteurs exquises :
s u s p e n d u e
érectine en fond
boucle dans le s
bouche fraîche,
mains! Sur le v
duire deux doig
ton de rose et l'
endue sur le plaid
pâle, clouée sur la
tèbres saillant sur
dentif au bout de la
seins, les reins pli-
ongles contre les ma
ise la fera crier de
cera le seuil, les c
battre au moment o
ueur dans la petite c
lante, les deux main
te pétrie, humide au
ssant sous les secou
la jeune fille et el-
sera aller, inerte.

Fuzzy Sets, p. 150

reading, the New Novel has tended to replace the problematic and discredited author with an intentional entity called the *Texte*. The promotion of the *Texte* at first appears to smooth over some thorny aspects inherent in theories and allegories of reading: the *Texte* is now free to discipline and direct the reader without having to answer to charges of didacticism, without the theorist being accused of intentional fallacy, and without the author fearing charges of submission to doctrine. By transferring to the text the most troublesome attributes of the author, however, the elision of the writing subject only displaces the very pitfalls it was designed to avoid.

In light of the failure of the paradigm of sadomasochism to take into account the existence of the third term in fictional structure, an alternative vision of reading must be explored. Such a vision presents

les paupières closes, une lueur sous la tenture
cramoisie ponctuant les sursauts, un jour pâle
épelant les lignes : l'aube, glacis entre les lames
des rideaux... Quelle chambre ? Tresses répandues couvrant le plaid grenat d'un voile sombre... La
lumière proche les gaîne d'un brouillard d'argent.

Somnolence torpide e	quatre murs — clinique
à épopées. Que de	sautées dans les pa
ns du survol ! (L	mpossible dernier
chapitre). Inapt	boucler la boucle ?
Le gamin te relai	essuscité au siècle
proche ! Il remettr	ur le feuillet manquant,
le trou de la serrur	ctionnelle, ou clef du
s e n s... Sept chambre	onge visitées.. e t l a
huitième ? Le maillo	te manquait ! Le mot de
la comptine ! Tu sais	la trouver maintenant
au bout des tours d	au mauve. La couleur
vive effacera le ro	filtrant du corridor,
l'ombre de nuit ni	t'ont confiné en ce
tte fin de huitain	ek-end en altitude !
Vers l'exotisme or	Celle (Reine) qui t
ient depuis lundi	de l'intrigue et le

texte occulté. Enfance et paradis, catimini d'éveil. Il
n'est que de rejeter le plaid de sur ton corps et te glis-
ser à pas de loup. Soulever la tenture : sur la pointe des

Fuzzy Sets, p. 151

itself on board the Octopus and again takes an allegorical form. We
learn that O.'s own progress in earlier adventures has made possible
the invention of an amazing machine capable of transmitting, on
board the space vessel, living scenes in three dimensions. Colors,
sounds, tastes, and smells are fully experienced by the participants,
who are enveloped by a "sphère nébuleuse" at the outset of the transmission. As the figure of a utopian, immediate fiction, the *holoscope*
offers a phenomenological vision of reading, where an advanced technology eliminates the need for language: "L'avantage décisif d'un tel
mode de liaison, tu le saisis bien, est, par l'aménagement d'une confrontation intégrale directe, de situer tout problème en connaissance
juste de ses composantes matérielles affectives, c'est-à-dire perçues

coi bien sûr, et ne veut pas aller plus loin, il ne
peut pas, sent tout à coup qu'il ne peut passer outre,
une pellicule comme une voûte plastique le repousse, le
retient de participer totalement à l'action, il reste là

sur le pourtour, les main	tâtant la matière élas-
tique, spongieus	misole, s'efforçant
de lire les	chées, brouil-
lés en sui	vement des
lèvres, m	discontin
us, frag	instruct
ions ou	groupes
se trou	a plan
espaces	unifica-
tion com	la verte
et rousse	le bleu du
ciel, les ci	touchent pres-
que et le cactus	de l'arrière-plan,
mutilé là-bas inclus dans	le théâtre unique et le

vieillard chancelant au centre, sa bouche ouverte
aussi, doucement, sans plainte, aveugle ou résigné,
imaginant depuis longtemps la scène, mais il n'a pas
la parole, le dialogue par-dessus sa tête prend un

Fuzzy Sets, p. 69

sans intermédiaire aucun, sans déperdition aucune, sans 'bruit'" (*FS,* 77).

O. witnesses the transmission for the first time by accident; only the members of the space team (Sinbad, Noé, Cyrano, and so on) are fully integrated into the *holoscène,* participating as actors in the events taking place. O. cannot penetrate the fictional atmosphere created by the machine: "une pellicule comme une voûte plastique le repousse, le retient de participer totalement à l'action, il reste là sur le pourtour, les mains tâtant la matière élastique, spongieuse" (*FS,* 69). The rest of the page containing this passage (and ostensibly recounting the fiction that took place) is censored by a circular blank that renders most of the text fragmentary and discontinuous, thus unreadable in conventional terms. Two pages later a circular text of the same size recounts a ritual-like murder committed during the transmission; "Le meurtre s'est perpétué dans un cercle de paroles" (*FS,* 141). But the circular text does not fill in the original ellipse, does not semantically complete the fragmented passage. A portion of the text is irretrievably lost for the reader of *Fuzzy Sets,* just as O. cannot wholly penetrate the *holoscène.*

O. is disturbed by the scene he has witnessed, but the astronauts explain his malaise: "Une grande part de ton émoi, tu le sais bien, vient de ce que tu 'assistais' seulement, en position de chroniqueur ou voyeur" (*FS,* 75). The author and the reader, "chroniqueur" and "voyeur," are in the same position in respect to the *holoscène,* whose ellipse figures the gap where original meaning slips away in the same way that Tiamât escapes from the Octopus. But where Tiamât was opposed to and sought by the reader alone, the *holoscène* is equally unavailable to both *chroniqueur* and *voyeur.* All that can be perceived in this and all other transmissions is the renewed sacrifice of a certain "agent L." The victim's initial and the circumstances of one murder scene link him to Lessing, the originary protagonist of *La Mise en scène* whose murder set off Lassalle's alphabetical investigations, but who was himself never in the book. This death or figurative demystification of the fictional protagonist, while forming a significant part of the fictional cycle, is not *the* elliptical message of the *holoscène;* the demystification takes place only on the margins of the central ellipse. Nor is the ritual murder wholly explained as a didactic sacrifice of the expectations of the *Lecteur* by an omnipotent author. While these concerns approach the ellipse, they cannot fully account for it or fully occupy it.

The secret space of the ellipse is unknown to both the *chroniqueur* and the *voyeur* and is irrecoverable by either of them. It is the third point in a triangle of mediated desire, the textual battleground where author and reader make war on each other in parallel efforts to discover meaning. The ellipse is a telescoping figure of textual mystery: fictional cycle, spaceship, text, Tiamât, womb, origin, originary meaning. In this light, the *elliptical* is the foundation of textuality: "tu cherches le principe, il est écrit, en pointillé pour ainsi dire, c'est *toute l'affaire* d'interpoler . . ." (*FS,* 81; my emphasis). The ellipse is the place where the reader attempts to fill in what he thinks the author meant; and where the author tries to subvert what he supposes the reader will fill in. Interpolation is fundamental to the activity of both author and reader; meaning for each position is mediated through the other, just as, in the master-slave struggle posited by Hegel, each opponent desires the other's desire. But what is a battle to the death for recognition in the master-slave situation becomes, with author and reader, a paradoxical race to a figurative death: an original meaning each believes the other guards.

The nature of this struggle links it to Freud's formulation of a death instinct operating beyond the pleasure principle, and to the theory that Freud's colleague Sandor Ferenczi developed in conjunction with Freud's notion of the *Todestrieb* and repetition compulsion. Ferenczi posited at the basis of all human and animal life the existence of a "Thalassal regressive trend," a primary urge to rejoin the aquatic mode of existence abandoned in primitive times. The organism's desire to reestablish an interuterine situation is one of the "circuitous paths to death" whose ultimate aim is the quiescence of the inorganic world: "The Oedipus wish is precisely the psychological expression of an extremely general biological tendency which lures the organism to a return to the state of rest enjoyed before birth."[36] Ferenczi sees the sexual act as a "genital warfare" in which each partner attempts to penetrate the other, to rejoin the womb that the other is known or fantasized to possess. The reading and writing subjects struggle with each other in a similar way in their attempt to finally penetrate the original meaning the other purportedly possesses. Each seeks a stop to the confusion and perpetual movement of a textuality in flux; each attempts to freeze meaning by filling in fiction's ellipses. The stakes of this warfare preclude any treaty. Seen in this light, the Oedipal situation is an extremely general textual tendency that has characterized the fictional subject O. in all his incarnations. The place of the reader in a struggle of this nature can be neither stable nor predictable. The reader moves inside and outside the book as the shifting intersection of his or her real input with that imputed to him or her by the author. And the same must be said of the writing subject. The text is the space and the stakes of a variable confrontation: "En quel 'livre' sont-ils? . . . Celui dont le degré d'appartenance à l'ensemble ne cesse de varier au fil des pages, pris dans les lignes d'intersection ou d'exclusion totale" (*FS*,

ant que d'agrément taci-
le platonique objet de l
les écrans, arrache à poi-
hublots, que le bon air
de leur hypnotique pen-
tères. Le cercle au cen-
la pointe des étoi-
là pour communi-
« Je suis le le
jen-ai-

te. Ou mets les pieds dans
eur recensement : déchire
gnées les fils, enfonce les
des cimes tire ces gens
chant à percer les mys-
tre n'atteindra jamais
les, mais qui sera
quer la nouvelle ?
cteur, le   b
mé, l'en-

vié. »
p o u r la fon
que, l'émotive nou
frissons en ce survol
mer — à l'avenir ? au p
stricte pourtant de la fa-
Le jour perce et l'aveugla
valier d'antan ou d'adoube-
en vibration tragique, excé-
à mort. Regarde ! Ne dis mo

Tant pis
c t i o n p h a t i -
s comble : que de
qu'achoppe à arri-
assé ? — la conjonction
ble et de son favori !...
nte lueur au dehors. Che-
ment antique, te voici mué
dant le cadre ou comprimé
t ! Les cloisons se mettent

Fuzzy Sets, p. 60

90). The reader's activation of textual meaning can only be sporadic and fragmentary and cannot account for the totality of a fiction, since the reader, too, is an elliptical and partial entity that must be filled in or read: "'Je suis le le cteur, le b/ ien-ai- mé, l'en/ vié'" (*FS*, 60). The text cannot then be equated with the author's meaning, nor can it be seen to fully coincide with the reader's input. In their confrontation with each other and their desire to ascertain meaning, both author and reader constitute "fuzzy sets" shifting in and out of the fiction.

The question was posed earlier: does reading have a sex? The initial allegory of reading was a confrontation worked out in terms of sexual difference, but one in which the binary polarities of masculine and feminine, sadism and masochism, activity and passivity had to break down and admit of a disputed third term. The triangular model that follows it is a sexual struggle on the most primary and instinctual level: a battle to rejoin a state of interuterine certainty and union with meaning. The relationship of reading subject to writing subject cannot be a simple opposition between active virility and feminine passivity, or a pact between consenting partners.

In much the same way, a distinction between didacticism and demystification in the use of allegory cannot be maintained. The allegorical strategies that dominate reflexive fictions like the New Novel must be seen as a "fuzzy set" of both aims, with an equally unstable, undecidable outcome. As Brian McHale points out in his *Postmodernist Fiction,* postmodern allegories are much more elusive and slippery—fuzzier—than what we think of as the unequivocal traditional allegories.[37] The reader is paradoxically both bound and liberated by such an allegory: bound by didactic, manipulative strategies, but also liberated from unthought-out habits and assumptions. The oppositions and contradictions occasioned by the role of allegory in the New Novel cannot be resolved by positing the text as a new intentional subject. The *Texte* is necessarily dethroned from the transcendent position in which some reading theories have tended to place it. The text must be seen rather as the elliptical space of confrontation between the trinitary avatar(s) of the subject of fiction, figured in *Le Jeu d'enfant* by O. Far from operating a closure, the ellipse as fiction is the figure of an intertextual gap that can never be definitively filled, or even fixed as permanently empty.

In *Le Plaisir du texte,* Roland Barthes assumes the reader's position in order to characterize the persistent, and persistently erotic, triangle of reader-author-text in a critical age where the author has officially been declared missing in action:

> Comme institution, l'auteur est mort: sa personne civile, passionnelle, biographique, a disparu; dépossédée, elle n'exerce plus sur son oeuvre la formidable paternité dont l'histoire littéraire, l'enseignement, l'opinion avaient à charge d'établir et de renouveler le récit; mais dans le texte, d'une certaine façon, je *désire* l'auteur: j'ai besoin de sa figure (qui n'est ni sa représentation ni sa projection), comme il a besoin de la mienne.[38]

The allegory of reading worked out in *Fuzzy Sets* not only brings to light the assumptions and contradictions behind traditional reading aims but also points out those that subtend revolutionary textual practices and theories. A *holoscopic* vision of fictional functioning does not show the reader's place as either inside or outside the book. Rather, it replaces the traditional allegorical models of text-reader/passivity-activity/inside-outside with a no less allegorical, but less limiting vision of the reader-author-text relationship as a power play in flux, an uneasy ménage à trois where we must not lose sight of the desire to ascertain meaning as the third, albeit fuzzy element.

5

The Science of the New Novel:
Zero-Degree Fiction

Jadis le navigateur qui franchissait "la ligne," le parallèle
zéro, avait l'impression de se trouver à un moment
exceptionnel et à un point unique, zone sacrée dont le
passage symbolisait une initiation décisive. Ligne imag
inaire, point géographiquement nul, mais représentant
précisément par sa nullité ce degré zéro vers lequel on
dirait que l'homme tend, par le besoin d'atteindre un
repère idéal d'où, libre de lui-même, de ses préjugés,
de ses mythes et de ses dieux, il pourrait revenir avec
un regard changé et une affirmation nouvelle.

—Blanchot

The reflexivity of much postmodern fiction—its persistent, thematized
investigation of its own laws and mechanisms—situates it, for many, in
the general movement toward science that characterized the structuralist era. In his 1969 study, John Sturrock explicitly links the New
Novel's self-reflexive stance to the prestige of scientific endeavor:

> Other stimuli, too, have prompted the self-questioning that the New
> Novel displays, ones again that can be linked with the prodigious growth
> of science in this century, science in both its meanings: as a discipline and
> as a body of knowledge. This enormous and continually accelerating
> advance, in terms both of capacity and prestige, has brought with it a
> promotion in the epistemological virtues of the public or scientific fact.[1]

The "promotion in the epistemological virtues of the public or scientific fact" of which Sturrock speaks does not take the form, in critical

views on the New Novel, of a revival of the "novel as laboratory" hypothesis of Zola's *Le Roman Expérimental*. Rather, the scientific impetus of the New Novel is seen to lie in its potential for cultural, political, and ideological demystification. Since its earliest beginnings, the New Novel has sought to discover and demystify the ideological underpinnings of the conventions of the classic realist novel: mimesis, logocentrism, psychologism, humanism.

Roland Barthes's characterization of ideology points to the kind of demystification the New Novel would effect:

> Car l'idéologie, c'est quoi? C'est précisément l'idée *en tant qu'elle domine:* l'idéologie ne peut être que dominante. Autant il est juste de parler d'"idéologie de la classe dominante" parce qu'il existe bien une classe dominante, autant il est inconséquent de parler d'"idéologie dominante", parce qu'il n'y a pas d'idéologie dominée: du côté des "dominés" il n'y a rien, aucune idéologie, sinon précisément—et c'est le dernier degré de l'aliénation—l'idéologie qu'ils sont obligés (pour symboliser, donc pour vivre) d'emprunter à la classe qui domine. La lutte sociale ne peut se réduire à la lutte de deux idéologies rivales: c'est la subversion de toute idéologie qui est en cause.[2]

Transposing the terms of the sociopolitical struggle to the literary domain (a move advocated by many proponents of the New Novel), we see the New Novel as lacking an ideology of its own. Its force derives from its alienated perspective; its mission is the subversion of the reigning ideological formations. The "dernier degré de l'aliénation" would be the starting point of a movement aimed at a zero degree of ideology in fiction. The implications of such a stance point to a certain scientificity on the part of the New Novel: as an alienated, detached observer, the New Novel would be capable of a methodological vision where blind acceptance of ideological constructions of the novel would give way to a more rigorous appreciation of its workings. In its unmasking of the presuppositions of novelistic convention, and in its promotion of a formal, structural, or semiotic vision of narrative, the New Novel takes its place in a literary moment and in a literary movement that find corollaries in many of the "human sciences": psychoanalysis, linguistics, anthropology, and so on. Without attempting here to address the many issues raised by what Barthes[3] has elsewhere termed the "rêve (euphorique) de scientificité" of the conjectural sciences, I will examine in the present chapter the contribution made to those issues by one of the central exemplars of that dream of scientificity, the New Novel. In the science fictions of *Le Jeu d'enfant*, the protagonist O. presides at the encounter between the scientific and the ideological, figuring there a continual autointerrogation of the future of fiction. O.'s allegorical peregrinations in the second, critical cycle of *Le Jeu d'enfant* will provide a test case for the experiments in scientificity that characterize a major impetus in structuralist research.

The exemplary discoveries of linguists like Saussure, Jakobson, and Benveniste provided literary analysis with the bases of a "science naissante de l'écriture," according to Philippe Sollers,[4] who himself has been an important participant in the experiments of the literary avant-garde, notably through the journal and movement of *Tel Quel*. The foundations provided by structural linguistics were amplified and extended by subsequent literary criticism; the taxinomic formalism of Gérard Genette or of the early Tzvetan Todorov attests to a will to discern and codify textual laws on the part of structuralism and semiotics. Julia Kristeva's definition of the goals of a semiotic literary analysis provides one example of this will to develop a science of literature: "la science de la littérature est un discours toujours infini, une énonciation toujours ouverte de la recherche des lois de la pratique dite littéraire, et dans laquelle l'objectif consiste à *exposer l'opération* même qui produit cette 'science,' son 'objet,' et leur rapport, plutôt que d'appliquer empiriquement telle technique sur un objet indifférent."[5] In a previous essay entitled "La Sémiologie comme science critique," Kristeva had already established the nature of the relationship between, on the one hand, the discourse of this critical science, semiology, and, on the other hand, that of language: "Dans un mouvement décisif d'auto-analyse, le *discours* (scientifique) se retourne aujourd'hui sur les *langages* pour dégager leurs (ses) modèles."[6] Semiology is thus characterized by autoanalysis, autocriticism. As a method of literary analysis, its goal is equally that of provoking an autoanalysis on the part of the literary text itself: in turning back on language, such a science of literature would not describe or quantify its object accord-

ing to criteria or models that would be external to or independent of
that object, but would, rather, attempt to derive those models from the
object to which they will then be reapplied. In so doing, semiology
would at the same time discern and derive its own models. And yet the
priority of the (scientific) discourse remains intact: only after its
decisive, progressive movement of self-analysis does it turn back ("se
retourne") to operate upon individual cases ("les *langages*").

Kristeva nevertheless cautions against an idealization of science.
Although semiology "s'adresse au vocabulaire des sciences exactes,"[7] it
can still serve to demystify what Kristeva terms "le scientisme" and
"l'illusion techniciste"—that is, a naive belief in the exactitude, purity,
and neutrality of scientific discourse. Thus, in Kristeva's version of
semiology, a certain mistrust of science qualifies the effort to establish
a scientific way to approach literary texts. In a chapter of *Sémiotiké*
entitled "Le Texte et sa science," Kristeva again makes a distinction
between the language of the literary text and the discourse of the exact
sciences, while still retaining for literature a certain notion of scientificity:

> Sans s'opposer à l'acte scientifique . . . mais loin de s'égaler à lui et sans
> prétendre s'y substituer, le texte inscrit son domaine en dehors de la sci-
> ence et à travers l'idéologie, comme une mise-en-langage de la notation
> scientifique. Le texte transpose dans le langage, donc pour l'histoire so-
> ciale, les remaniements historiques de la signifiance rappelant ceux qu'on
> trouve marquées dans son domaine par la découverte scientifique.[8]

If semiology is a *"discours (scientifique)"* that turns back on *"les langages"* in order to analyze them and itself, then the literary text itself
transposes into language a scientific notation. This deference in respect to the priority and preeminence of the "acte scientifique" maintains that act as a privileged practice. Despite the distinctions made
between the discourse of hard science and the language of literature,
and despite the refusal of scientism, there nevertheless persists in
Kristeva's semiology a valorization of science. The scientificity of a
literary or semiotic discourse resides in its potential for autoanalysis;
therein lies its value as ideological contestation.

A similar distinction between scientific discourse and linguistic languages is apparent in the psychoanalytic theory of Jacques Lacan, who proposes to replace psychoanalytic discourse with a mathematical notion that would more closely figure the processes of the Symbolic in its complex relations with the Imaginary and the Real. Whereas Kristeva denounces scientism as part of a discredited idealism where science was held up as an extrasubjective, extraideological truth, Lacan sees in mathematics the hope of an exact knowledge. Toward the end of his career, Lacan's project was to transform the language of psychoanalysis into "mathèmes" that would communicate "sans équivocation" the scientific and universal foundations of psychoanalysis. Thus the matheme would permit the rigorous theorization of psychoanalysis as well as its precise transmission.[9]

The ideal of a mathematical precision and a purified form of communication becomes, in the domain of the novel, the search for a neutral, zero-degree fictional language, emptied of occulted traditional conventions, a language such as that described by Barthes in *Le Degré zéro de l'écriture:* "Si l'écriture est vraiment neutre, si le langage, au lieu d'être un acte encombrant et indomptable, parvient à l'état d'une équation pure, n'ayant plus d'épaisseur qu'une algèbre en face du creux de l'homme, alors la Littérature est vaincue."[10] Barthes immediately acknowledges that such an algebraic language is an impossibility, that it is always traversed by the ambiguities and unconscious reflexes inherent in a language that uses words rather than mathematical symbols. And yet this dream of a quasi-mathematical neutrality and purity characterizing the beginnings of the structuralist enterprise is not all that far from the language employed by Jean Ricardou (in 1973) in respect to Ollier's first novel: "Ainsi fonctionne la rigoureuse *machinerie* de *La Mise en scène:* les coïncidences s'y *multiplient innombrablement,* relevant le *calcul,* et exhibant ainsi, une fois encore, à tout instant, périlleusement, le récit comme tel."[11] In Ricardou's vision, Ollier's text is a sort of machine whose functioning reveals at its base, and as its base, a certain *calcul:* the specular equation of the narrative with itself. And, like any valid scientific or mathematical procedure, this equation can be repeated over and over again ("une fois encore") to exhibit, always, the same result. What the arithmetic of the text exhibits as a visible (empirical?) fact is the spectacle of the narrative that sees itself and presents itself to be seen as such: "le récit comme tel." The fiction becomes a sort of mathematical proof whose scientificity would derive, as in Kristeva's semiology, from its self-reflexive and self-analytical functioning. Ricardou's demonstration holds out the hope that, despite reservations such as those formulated by Barthes and Kristeva, a mathematical fiction can be conceived. And if such a fiction were ever to exist, it would surely be the New Novel, where complex numerical and geometric schemata form the basis of works by Ricardou, Ollier, Robbe-Grillet, and Butor. More fundamentally still, the New Novel consistently exhibits a determination to purify the form and language of fiction by unmasking and ousting the old automatisms of the traditional novel (of "Littérature," as in "Tout le reste est littérature"). The fictions of the second relay of *Le Jeu d'enfant* provide the context for an examination of the confrontation between an old fiction imprinted with an unconscious ideology and a new fiction whose scientific lucidity is directed at its own form and language.

It is worth recalling here that these later novels are science fictions: set in an unspecified future, their narratives (except for *Our* and the second half of *Enigma*) take place on the alien terrain of a distant star system. The protagonists' attempts to chart the planets' topography or to deduce the laws governing their strange phenomena are doubled by a second, allegorical research into the mechanisms and laws at work in language, writing, and fiction. Thus these science fictions become a *speculative fiction* in the sense given this term by a special issue of *La Quinzaine littéraire* devoted to science fiction: they become a fiction that analyzes itself, eliciting and making explicit its own laws.[12] This kind of fictional experimentation recalls the terms of Kristeva's definition of semiology as well as Ricardou's mathematical project of a calculated, self-demonstrating narrative. The science of fiction lies, manifestly, in its autospecularity. In the novels of Ollier's second cycle—*La Vie sur Epsilon, Enigma, Our,* and *Fuzzy Sets*—this science of fiction seems to question and redefine the nature of fiction itself. The enigma of the archaeological origins of writing is linked, here, to a visionary future replete with computers, advanced mathematics, and interplanetary technology.

O. is the protagonist who is reborn, in various guises, in each novel of *Le Jeu d'enfant*. At the cycle's center, at the point where the initial itinerary ascends to the second dimension of a critical science fiction, he receives for the first time the fragmentary name, O., that he will bear throughout the second cycle. The investigations of this multiplied protagonist figure the autointerrogation of Ollier's fictional cycle.

In *The Theory of the Novel,* Lukács argues that the protagonist plays a principal role in the structuration of a novel; the life of the protagonist gives the novel its form by furnishing a quest around which the fiction is elaborated. The novel's narrative is thus structured around the meaningful center constituted by its hero. In much the same way, O. occupies a special position at the literal center of *Le Jeu d'enfant:* between the two relays of the cycle. But he also resides at the figurative center of its reflexive, speculative project, in as much as he incarnates the triple subject of fiction (protagonist-author-reader). But where the traditional novel as described by Lukács would put the fictional subject squarely in his central place, O. puts into question all the privileges and attributes accorded him: meaning, psychology, verisimilitude, and even the very notion of centrality. On Epsilon, the alphabetical series of protagonists inaugurated with the first novel descends, with O., to a "zero degree" of the novelistic hero: allegorically stripped of his traditional qualities and attributes in the first fictions, the protagonist Lassalle-Morel-Nolan-O. is finally unmasked as a textual entity retaining no particular privilege over the text that contains it. Thus the protagonist's peregrinations on Epsilon take the metaphorical form of a blind quest, an excursion in a vast book. The life of the singular hero no longer constitutes the static center that gives the story its direction and meaning and about which the narrative is organized; for O. is quickly overtaken by an alphabetical élan consisting of his colleagues on Epsilon (Perros, Quilby, Rossen). And on the planet Iota, in *Enigma,* the same alphabetizing circles about O. with his companions Juanos, Kline, Smernov, and Toïshi, while Arab companions with the same initials populate Ezzala in the second part of the book. The alphabetization of the protagonist corresponds to an inventory of races and nationalities whose multiplication effectively complicates O.'s purported function as a singular center for the fiction in progress.

In addition to the death of the protagonist repeatedly demonstrated by the New Novel, similar obituaries have been written about the disappearance of the traditional author from the scene of fiction. Nor has the conventional reader been spared, as we have seen, in the New Novel's offensive against traditional novelistic practices. In *Fuzzy Sets,* the final volume of *Le Jeu d'enfant,* the spaceship Octopus is called a "crypte en vol" (*FS,* 123); it carries, in O., the remains of all these assassinated avatars of the retrograde subject of fiction:

> l'homme de l'équipe A continue de manger, de boire, ne fume pas encore, sobre de gestes, quasi immobile, mutant de satellite, avatar impossible du héros—n'échappant pas à la "récitation" sans doute, mais extérieure à sa violence, à l'épreuve des phrases; dans l'ensemble livresque, il se pourrait bien que son niveau d'appartenance soit voisin de zéro, tout bien pesé des effets de lecture, nuls en ce qui le concerne; l'entropie fictionnelle se nourrit de ce poids mort et de ceux de ses compagnons: non-Odyssée de l'"Octopus," égrénée, futile à l'once des légendes. (*FS,* 141)

A degradation and paring-down of fiction has been operated; while O. has not been eliminated from the machinations of fiction, he has been reduced to a virtual zero, to a dead weight dragging the cyclic itinerary to a halt. The "non-Odyssée" has in a sense been an entropic Odyssey, an epic journey in reverse gear, where the space-age hero nears a zero degree of inclusion within the totality ("l'ensemble livresque") of his world; the legends of epic adventures find no material in the Octopus's decaying orbit.

O. is the supplement (in Derrida's sense of the term) of the failed protagonists of the first relay; he both conserves and replaces them. He operates a sort of de-evolution in respect to his preceding avatars by gradually subtracting from them their conventional novelistic attributes. O. functions as the common denominator of the two relays, factoring fiction down to its foundations and canceling out its ideological multiplications. Precisely in the place where the traditional protagonist is centered in order to organize a narrative, O. operates as the plural, subversive center proper to the New Novel.

Such an O at the center would thus be a veritable zero as a novelistic hero—a cipher of a man, faceless, virtually without qualities or personality, who carries along his previous incarnations only in order to demonstrate their nullity. In his wanderings on Epsilon, O. is reduced to a point, to a mathematical coordinate in the space of the text. Could

such an entity serve as that *calcul,* identified by Ricardou, that sub-
tends fiction and makes it a specular equation of itself? Could an
analysis of O. as just such a mathematical zero provide, by factoring
out ideology, the equations and procedures by which a fiction elabo-
rates itself? For if the zero in mathematical theory is situated at the
midpoint between two numerical infinities, it is also the origin or the
point of departure for the very possibility of mathematics. The zero is
at once, and paradoxically, the origin and the center of an infinite and
infinitely variable system. O. would seem to hold an analogous position in respect to fiction: as the zero degree of fiction, O. is the central
point of departure and the very possibility of a self-reflexive, self-
critical narrative. With O., the fictional subject can be seen to function
as a zero, as a mathematical element at the base of the text and within
the graphic space of the text.

Ollier's O. is not a unique phenomenon among the New Novelists.
A protagonist named O. also figures in Claude Simon's 1969 novel, *La
Bataille de Pharsale.* Both male and female, Simon's O. also functions
as the errant and decentered center of fiction, and as a mechanism for
contesting the stability and integrality of the traditional protagonist.
And in Monique Wittig's *Les Guérillères,* also published in 1969, the
zero's form becomes a triumphant figure of the feminine in a science-
fiction future where a war of the sexes is waged and age-old myths are
exploded.

But if the zero can thus be seen to form the basis of a demystifying
mathematical textuality, it is also, undeniably, part of a vast and ancient reservoir of symbolic meanings among which figure the feminine, as in Simon's and Wittig's works. The zero as a circle (0) symbolic of the womb derives from the Buddhist tradition and is held to
represent the totality of creation. As a point (.), the zero figures for
Buddhist thought the germ of the phenomenological world.[13] Thus the
zero is both totality and embryo, at once already everything and nothing yet. These resonances circulating about the zero also echo in the
science fictions of *Le Jeu d'enfant:* in *Enigma,* the spherical computer
Naïma takes the form of an ovum containing all possible logical relations and thus allegorically all textual possibilities. Naïma's circuits
can therefore calculate, by induction, a typical pattern of behavior in
O.'s wanderings across the surface of Iota:

A l'intérieur de ce globe opaque, étanche, plusieurs milliers d'hélio-cadres composent le mécanisme cérébral de la machine . . . l'ensemble des cadres satisfait à l'intégralité du code universel des liaisons, que ces liaisons soient utilisées dans la pratique courante ou seulement déduite de la théorie. Il couvre donc virtuellement tout le champs des raisonne-ments possibles, du plus absurde au plus élaboré, du plus pauvre au plus démentiel. (*E, 20–21*)

It is not by chance that this machine is feminine, or that she is linked to Nejma, the flesh and blood female associated in the second half of *Engima* with sexuality and procreation. The metaphorical notion of the feminine as origin and source is tied, in O.'s story, to the mathe-matical form and concept of the zero.

The invention of the zero is thought to have taken place in the ancient Sumerian-Babylonian civilization, the reputed birthplace of writing and of Western civilization itself, and the setting for *Our.*[14] In *Our,* O. visits the Ur of the future (the site of an archaeological investi-gation) as a representative chosen to accomplish an equally archae-ological mission: the (allegorical) search for the origins of fiction. In going back to the source of Western civilization and its writing, O. exhumes layers of sedimentation in order to seek out an originary, founding principle; he seeks a zero degree. If, as was demonstrated earlier, O. forms the mathematical basis of fiction, then he is himself the impossible object of his own research. *Our* ends with Tiamât's theft of the secret tablets recounting the origin of *Our* as a text; the novel's circular structure derives from O.'s own tautological quest. The mathematical zero in these science fictions is thus also a meta-phorical nexus, a knot of metaphors: at once origin and goal, being and nothingness, infinite expansion and infinitesimal contraction. While a certain specularity is not absent from these metaphorical resonances, it is an autoanalysis that deflects and distorts its own image into a plurality of figures. If O. functions in these texts as a mathematical coordinate, as a zero, then that zero is neither purely mathematical, nor a simple specular equation. For while the concept of the zero forms the origin and basis of all mathematicity, it also presents itself as a metaphor for the mythical origin of all ficticity.

For the philosopher Jean-François Lyotard, in his *Economie libidi-*

nale, there is no zero that is not metaphorical; for Lyotard, the zero lies at the very foundation of Western metaphysics, which he describes as a political economy and against which he posits a libidinal economy.[15] In a libidinal economy, the human body is no longer conceived of as a volume possessing both an exteriority and an interiority; one would cease to filter all perception and thought through the theatricality of such a distinction between inside and outside, a distinction that has governed all of metaphysics and that derives from the zero:

> Aller de la pulsion à la représentation, mais sans se donner, pour décrire cette implantation, cette sédentarisation des influx, sans se donner la facilité suspecte du concept du manque, la facilité du truc d'une Altérité vide, d'un Zéro au silence duquel vient se heurter et briser la demande (demande, donc parole déjà? et adressée déjà, et à quelque chose? oui, à cet Autre; et par quelque chose, qui donc lui aussi déjà sait parler? . . .) si bien qu'avec ce truc de la demande et du silence du Zéro, eh bien en effet il ne reste plus qu'à inaugurer et faire marcher le théâtre et le pouvoir, le théâtre du pouvoir où vont se jouer les accomplissements du désir nés de ce prétendu manque même. (pp. 11–12)

> Ce qui s'engloutit dans la théologie théâtrique, pour nous qui venons bien après, qui avons des siècles, presque deux millénaires d'habitudes cicatrisantes entretenues par la religion, les religions, la métaphysique, le capital, c'est l'identité. Est-il possible que toute intensité ne soit souf-france que parce que nous sommes des religieux, des religieux du Zéro? (p. 20)

At the core of its mathematicity, the zero is a metaphysical, ideological concept. The ancient culture that gave birth to Western civilization gave it, in the same gesture and in the integrality of a circular symbol, both mathematicity and metaphoricity. An ideology that purports to distinguish identity from alterity has resided within scientificity since their simultaneous beginnings. Not only is the ideological distinction between the scientific and the fictitious undermined, but the same fate awaits any attempt to purify fiction of its ideological contagion by means of a scientific instrument (the zero, O.): the tool will have been contaminated from the very moment of its conception.

Even as a zero-degree hero, then, O. still returns the search for the nature and origin of fiction to the ideological closure that the New

Novel sought to undo. For Lyotard, the zero constitutes a would-be lack calling for language, an empty alterity facilitating the description of what is. Far from raising fiction to the level of a precise science, the zero plunges it into the interminable and approximate play of language. If O. is the numeral zero, he is also the letter O, situated near the center of the alphabet, and already in evidence in the serial initials of the protagonists. O. is the intersection of the infinite series of numbers and the (virtually) infinitely variable series of letters; to consider O. from a mathematical point of view leads his quest back to the metaphysical tradition which that research sought to question. The zero cannot be dissociated from metaphor, figure, and language.

O.'s other—linguistic—nature may thus provide an alternative approach to the problematics of Ollier's fictions, to the investigation into fiction's nature. Can an examination of the isolated vocable, the smallest linguistic unit—the letter and sound O—lead by another path to the zero degree of fiction, to its source and governing principles? Can O.'s participation in a linguistic system serve to shed light on the troubled calculus of the science fictions of *Le Jeu d'enfant*? To look now at the vocable O will be to hold out to the mathematical coordinate a linguistic mirror in which the relation between the scientific and the ideological in the New Novel project can be viewed from another angle.

The four fictions of the first cycle present, as I have argued, the allegorical death of the fictional character as he has been known up to now. Less and less capable of maintaining his privileged position in respect to his story, the protagonist is ultimately submerged by the rising tide of a rebellious, revolutionary textuality. In the third fiction, he disappears in a midocean airplane crash. An inquest is conducted in the fourth book, only to reveal the progressive identification of the investigator with the missing character(s). Finally, the investigator himself ascends a mountain and disappears:

> En deux jours de marche soutenue, on atteint le sommet—la terre rouge d'abord, puis les collines sableuses, les contreforts de grès et de schiste, la lave, jusqu'au plan de neige, sur le versant nord.
>
> C'est un beau point de vue, dit-on. Et l'occasion rêvée pour se recréer, entre deux éclipses. . . . Au couchant du périple, avant le saut

au point central—ou à son homologue sur un lointain système." (*EN,*
228)

This disappearance remains ambiguous; what is apparently a death is
somehow also transformed into a mystic assumption to a "lointain
système," to a new "point central" where the composite protagonist is
recreated in O. O. contains within himself at once a resurrection and a
transcendence of the hero(es) of the preceding fictions, and at several
points he assumes the pose of a Christ figure crucified on the double
surface of Epsilon: "Un pied sur chaque bord comme chevauchant la
ligne démarcative, l'homme vacille, se frotte les yeux, passe tout entier
côté sable, considérant avec étonnement la marque en croix de sa
silhouette sur l'une et l'autre matières meubles, déjà en cours d'efface-
ment" (*VE,* 30). O.'s quasi-theological assumption endows him with a
certain elevation—an *hauteur,* an *O-teur*—as well as with a privileged,
transcendent viewpoint that reaffirms the traditional hierarchy of the
hero in relation to the fiction. Far from being effaced or brought down
to the same level as every other textual entity, O. occupies a position
every bit as central as before, but which is now even more surely elevated by reason of O.'s trial of purification in which he drops his
former masks of humanism, psychology, and realism.

The function of this transcendent, centered O. can be divided into
an allegorical trinity in the narrative space of the science fictions of the
second cycle: O. figures at once the protagonist, the reader, and the
author. As a *zero*—an empty *hero*—O. sought the purified and emptied-
out zero degree of fiction; his quest formed an autospecularity where
the fiction plumbed its own structure. In his pilgrimage in search of
the nature of the planet-book Epsilon, O. as the transcendent protagonist has the same goal: he tries to get back to the very *source* or
wellspring of fiction, searching upstream (*en amont*) or even down-
stream (*en aval*) for the origin of his own meanderings. The repetition
of these aquatic terms throughout the cycle links the investigations
undertaken by O. to *eau,* to water, to the inevitable woman by the
spring, to the oval of the female genitals, to the sexual origin of life,
and to the traditionally feminine principles of the *Other*—*l'O-tre*—the
principles of difference, indeterminacy, and digression. In other words,
O. can also be linked to the very principle of writing itself. Thus the

structure of writing and of fiction as the continual search for an origin is repeated in the ambiguous and circular constitution of the fictional protagonist himself, who is at once, and paradoxically, the masculine subject seeking his origins, and the feminine principle of digression, infinite regress, and irretrievable origins. As the vocable *eau* and *O-tre,* O. intersects the quest of the mathematical zero in order to figure, in the protagonist himself, the structuration of fiction. In the unknown regions of (narrative) space, and by means of his linguistic nature, the protagonist O. is once again the agent of an autospecularity rooted in traditional hierarchies. For O.'s linguistic nature affirms the centrality of the protagonist, even in a fiction that contests any centralization.

In *Fuzzy Sets,* we saw, O.'s quest comes to figure the task of the reader who approaches an unconventional text with conventional ways of reading. O.'s pursuit of the woman who stole the tablets recounting the origins of fiction takes him to the Octopus, the eight-armed figure of *Le Jeu d'enfant.* His inaugural question "suis-je dans le livre?" is at once a password and an allegorical inquiry into the role of the reader who, like the protagonist, attempts to locate the woman-origin. *Fuzzy Sets* figures the text of the future: both the supplement and the culmination of all the preceding research. The elliptical, revolutionary configuration of *Fuzzy Sets* defies a totalizing, recuperative reading. Its exaggerated lapses point up the less apparent lacunae traversing all texts and emphasize the impossibility of a comprehensive, integral reading. The text of the future would thus be a coded, functional antitext, a cryptic computer printout continually subverting the expectations of the traditional reader. The reader's role vis-à-vis this textual geometry is a paradoxical one: it is the reader who provides the conventional assumptions necessary to any subversion, but who is also, by this very contribution, constantly thrown outside the text through its unreadable gaps. In a perpetual movement of equivocal inclusion, the reader is now inside, now outside the "fuzzy set" of the fiction.

But as we saw in the preceding chapter, this elliptical, geometrical, or mathematical scenario is not the only vision of the text of the future offered by *Fuzzy Sets.* Nor is it the only perspective on O. as the analogical reader on board the Octopus. The space-age technology of the *holoscope*—the *O-loscope*—offers an alternative way of viewing the reading process. Based now on the vocable O rather than the numeral zero, this vision comes to complicate the futuristic flux of *Fuzzy Sets*. Capable of transmitting on board the Octopus entire living scenes in three dimensions, the *holoscope*'s development is due to O.'s own theoretical progress in earlier adventures. The *holoscope* offers a utopic, total, and immediate fiction: an ultimate degree of mechanization has eliminated language as the instrument of fiction. In the *holoscènes,* or "sphères nébuleuses," the reader as figured by O. witnesses, without being able to intervene in, a ritual murder in which he is himself the disguised victim. The *holoscopic* fiction forms a sort of spheric solipcism, an O in which is staged the repeated sacrifice of the spectator. Thus O.'s password "suis-je dans le livre?" provokes the following qualification: "là n'est pas la question et ce n'en est pas une" (*FS,* 9). And indeed, the question is not there: the logistics of the reader-text relationship are inverted, for in a sense it is the book that resides within O., the analogical reader; for in a futuristic fiction like *Fuzzy Sets,* the reflexive function paradoxically depends on the traditional modes of reading expected of and furnished by the reader, modes without which any innovation would lose its impact and significance. All the text's blanks, all its lacunae, all its enigmas take place only within the confines of the reader's expected contribution. The *O-lofiction* is thus in one sense always a renewed sacrifice of the reader: the text of the future becomes, by its very ruptures and losses, a graphic allegory of the impossibility of a traditional linear reading. The reader surrounds the text, accomplishing through reading the unification of the fiction precisely in the places where the text is supposed to escape. This radically ciphered, coded, computerized text is located, by its ultimate technological invention—the *O-loscope*—within a new form of reading paradoxically more totalizing and more recuperative than the most dogmatic of conventional readings. With the allegory of reading, then, O.'s linguistic nature again provides a radical critique of the mathematical project of his numerical avatar, the zero.

When O. speaks in his own voice for the first time in the last pages of the final volume, it is in order to teach. "Holodidacte," like the new mechanism of projection, O. moves to the center of the circle formed by the astronauts of the Octopus. He speaks of the Project, and his lecture provides a commentary on the general movement of *Le Jeu d'enfant:* "Venu pour vous instruire, c'est vous qui m'instruisiez" (*FS,* 177). This reversal has to do not only with the would-be attack on the conventional reader, but also with the third avatar of the multiple hero of the cycle: the author. Evicted from the vessel immediately after his (filmed) speech, O. reappears, in the final scene of *Fuzzy Sets,* as the mysterious subject of a kind of report narrating his return to his birthplace, which appears to be Europe, specifically Paris. The concentric movement of the first cycle of fictions had circled about the place of origin to which the cycle now finally returns after its autocritical detour in outer space. For Europe figures here the origin of Western-style fiction, and Paris is the birthplace of Claude Ollier.

The reporter narrates O.'s return to the "vieux continent de prose" (*FS,* 188), which has meanwhile become a futuristic landscape: "Lieu substitué, en travesti: de scherzane, ajoliane, aimantelle, luciane. . . . Bleu, blanc, trop blanc, et mauve, ses yeux se ferment, il sait ce qui l'attend maintenant, à quoi bon scruter ces jeux d'ellipses, ces transparents niveaux, et questionner s'il fut construit une bibliothèque en ces banlieues planes?" (*FS,* 189). The airplane "Coda" reinserts O. into what very much appears to be modern Paris, with the space-age Centre Pompidou occupying center stage. A crowd is waiting but retreats in silence as the legendary O. descends and is wisked away. The report and the cycle end with an apostrophe to the reader: "'Sa main a pris la plume et tracé les spirales dans son corps. . . . Héros de bande, refoulé du texte. On n'attend de lui qu'une signature, le sait-il? . . . Lecteur, vois-tu? Ce reportage est une introduction, à sa manière. Didactique: je l'ai écrit dans le style ancien' (*Chroniques d'Ile-de-France.*)" (*FS,* 188–89). After O.'s speech, in which he acknowledges that it was he who was the pupil, but in which he nevertheless holds forth for ten pages concerning the construction and structure of the fictional cycle, O. is dismissed; all that is now required of him is a final signature. O. thus reassumes, at the end of the cycle, his final (repressed) avatar: that of the author, the *auteur,* the *O-teur*—an incarnation that he has never stopped bearing at the same time as the others, in an indissociable trinity.

Claude Ollier has noted in an interview that these ten pages comprise a metareflection on the various threads of *Le Jeu d'enfant,* and that "l'essentiel est indiqué là sur l'origine et les processus d'écriture des huit livres."[16] Do these pages then carry an intervention on the part of the author himself, through a spokesman who bears his own initial? In a work traversed by significant coincidences, this link between *hér-O* and *O-teur* cannot be dismissed, despite all that has been said and written about the death of the author in contemporary fiction, and particularly in the New Novel. In bringing the circle back to Paris, birthplace of Ollier himself, does the fictional cycle take the reflexive Project back to its geographical and historical source: the person of the author, ultimate authority, *O-torité*?

These final questions reopen the case of the role of the author in the New Novel, for this ultimate vision is of an author who is as central, as transcendent and as encompassing, as the protagonist and the reader. Already, on the plant Iota, a giant pylon marked the position of the "transcripteur" that organized all activity in that new world: "De toutes les baies vitrées . . . on aperçoit le pylône transcripteur *au point zéro* de la planète, dressé vertical sur trente pieds de hauteur . . . c'est la cellule nerveuse de la vie de Iota" (*E,* 25; my emphasis). At the zero degree of the fiction, the stylus of the *O-teur* occupies a phallic, generative position. Here, the vocable O and the number 0 unite to mark as ultimately hierarchical and metaphorical the calculus underlying the *O-llierian* New Novels: the intention to construct a fiction that will be self-critical, and thus also didactic in relation to the prescriptive tradition it inherits and opposes. Thus the science of the Project is inevitably wedded to the ideology it would oust, and the conclusion of these futuristic fictions reveals O.'s linguistic side to have been the more revolutionary, for it called into question, with each of O.'s avatars, both the absolute progress of technics and the telos of autocriticism.

Together the novels of *Le Jeu d'enfant* form a double spiral falling back upon its center ("les spirales dans son corps"), a process predicted in the penultimate book: "Tout mobile qui se meut dans un cercle ou dans une ellipse ou dans une courbe quelconque se meut autour d'un centre auquel il tend (*Our,* 136). The central point of the cycle is thus O., that unstable trinity divided in each of his avatars between a metaphorized cipher and a fragmented vocable capable of unmasking scientific or mechanistic illusions. Invested by ideology and reclaimed by a revolutionary science of the text, the triple subject of fiction remains, in the New Novel's research, fundamentally self-reflexive and yet simultaneously caught up in the hierarchies of the novelistic tradition. Although he is a multiple, wandering, and contestive center in *Le Jeu d'enfant,* O. nevertheless forms the center of a certain writing, and not the unconditional "other" of the novelistic tradition. O. thereby figures the tenacity of the subject as a principle of fictional construction.

While its high ambitions were generally brought down to earth by subsequent critical elaboration, structuralism's impulse to create a science of the text nevertheless resulted in a greater awareness of the interpenetration of the scientific and the literary, both in their goals and their operations. Indeed, one of poststructuralism's major accomplishments had been to radically question the categories and hierarchies defined and maintained by a tradition dating back at least to Plato's indictment of poetry: philosophy versus literature; scientific versus humanistic disciplines; history versus fiction, and so on. Science itself in the twentieth century has become increasingly critical of the traditional definition of what constitutes scientific inquiry: neutrality, objectivity, a telos of progress toward an eventually complete enlightenment concerning the mechanisms of natural law. The work of scientists like Werner Heisenberg and Albert Einstein introduced indeterminacy, relativity, and uncertainty into our vision of nature and of science's ability to explain it. Kurt Gödel's theorem of incompleteness holds that any mathematical system is necessarily incomplete because one must get outside the system in order to find the language necessary to prove it correct. The paradox arises when Gödel's theorem subjects the discourse of theoretical mathematics to its own discourse of validation. This self-referentiality of scientific procedures to science itelf has led, more recently, to the development of what some have called a "critical science": a science that examines its own position, its methods, and its unconscious assumptions. Works like *The Mismeasure of Man, Science and Gender, Not in Our Genes,* and *Biological Politics* investigate how science has traditionally been marshaled for far-ranging political and ideological ends, notably the oppression of women.[17] Here, as in O.'s science-fiction adventures, the self-referential impulse has revealed the link binding scientificity and ideology; and while the project of ever dissociating the two—of finding a zero-degree fiction or science—may now seem manifestly impossible, still it is clear that progress has been made toward elucidating the conditions of possibility and interrelations of science, fiction, and ideology.

Conclusion

Fictional Revolutions

> La pure répétition, ne changêat-elle ni une chose
> ni un signe, porte puissance illimitée de perversion
> et de subversion.
> —Derrida

In the introduction to this study of Claude Ollier's *Le Jeu d'enfant,* I quote a detractor of the New Novel who couches his criticism in an analogy with the French Revolution. The terms of his critique bear repeating now at the conclusion of my analysis, in 1989, the bicentennial of that momentous insurrection: "Robbe-Grillet se prenait alors pour Saint-Juste, et les écrivains n'avaient plus qu'à marcher au pas. Très vite, heureusement, la tyrannie que faisaient régner ce caporal et sa troupe s'est évanouie dans l'indifférence, et la littérature a repris le rythme naturel de sa promenade. Les terroristes se sont effacés peu à peu, comme des ombres, et 68 est passé par là pour balayer ce qu'il en restait."[1]

One of the aims of my study has been to show the superficiality and inaccuracy of this kind of judgment in respect to the writers of Ollier's generation and persuasion. None of the writers in question took orders from Robbe-Grillet or any other theoretician; nor have they faded away like shadows or been brushed aside by history. Indeed, a 1986 roundtable sponsored by *La Quinzaine littéraire* concluded that in the absence of a clearly definable literary avant-garde, the New Novel remains the last available reference point for experimentation in fiction. Still, the language of revolution—even terrorism—is echoed in Ollier's own discourse on the goals of his books; in respect to *Our ou Vingt ans après,* Ollier states: "Ce livre septième devait situer les sept

lieux d'une conspiration visant à retourner contre l'Occident sa Littérature inquiète—assez travestis pour semer discorde et panique, et
renverser le colonialisme de l'écrit."[2] According to these terms, *Le Jeu
d'enfant* would indeed have a seditious or insurrectionary mission to
accomplish; it constitutes a plot against an entire civilization. But the
specific target is the colonialism of that civilization's literature and the
ideological constructions that subtend it. The panic evoked here is also
the sense of disquietude and even terror that pervades all the fictions of
Le Jeu d'enfant; it is the terror of the standard European faced with the
cultural, psychological, or ideological "other," after the loss of solid
grounding effected by the catastrophe of the Second World War.

Just before the passage cited above, Ollier had outlined how intertextuality worked to both pillage and pay homage to the vast library of
all literature, be it high or low. In a later interview, Ollier evokes in
similarly insurgent terms the struggle at work on certain pages of
Fuzzy Sets, where columns of deliberately incomplete, semantically
discontinuous text vie for space: "Il s'agit d'une véritable lutte pour le
pouvoir d'imprimer la page, et, le texte de toujours—du 'siècle' si l'on
veut—en est finalement expulsé, banni."[3] Thus the professed goal of
Le Jeu d'enfant, as well as that of the New Novel and much postmodern fiction, is indeed to effect a kind of revolution through reflexivity, by pitting a subverted, travestied "Littérature" against itself.

Whether or not a revolution is actually accomplished by the two
relays of Ollier's cycle is another question, a question addressed now
at the conclusion of my study of the eight fictions. Or perhaps it would
be more accurate to ask what kind of revolution occurs, since as we
know the term has two distinct meanings. Dictionaries from before the
French Revolution cite only the term's primary meaning, that of a
rotation around an orbit, a recircling about a center or axis. Does *Le
Jeu d'enfant* effect a genuine overthrow of the old textual order, or
does it simply recirculate the same old elements? Evidence from the
preceding chapters' analysis supports both positions. I will approach
the question of revolution, then, by looking at another text by Ollier
which does and does not form part of the fictional cycle. This work,
Navettes, comprises a compendium of the cycle's movement and a
manifesto of its goals. It will serve to rehearse the major aims and
recapitulate the major accomplishments of *Le Jeu d'enfant,* thereby

allowing me to pose in succinct form the primary question it raises: that of the kind of revolution(s) effected by reflexive fiction.

The group of short works collected and published by Ollier under the title *Navettes* appeared in the same year (1967) as *L'Echec de Nolan*, the final novel of the first cycle of *Le Jeu d'enfant*. The texts in *Navettes* range chronologically from before *La Mise en scène* to the end of the initial cycle. Intertextual links with the first four fictions are abundant, and certain elements also anticipate the scientific fictions of the second set of novels. These short texts operate like shuttle-craft to *faire la navette* in weaving a net of connections between the two cycles. Ollier sees *Navettes* as a compendium of the general system of his major works: "*quelques satellites* accompagnent ces longs textes: ce sont d'une part les textes brefs rassemblés dans le recueil NAVETTES, et d'autres écrits depuis lors. . . . Ces textes participent aux révolutions du système, dont ils éclairent d'aventure certaines facettes."[4] The texts in *Navettes* provide a critical illumination of the integral cycle, yet participate in the system's revolutions through their intertextual insertion(s). These satellites paradoxically revolve *within* as well as *without* the fictional sphere of the major system; the notions of inside and outside as criteria of fictional closure are blurred by their intertextual movement.

That these corollary fictions can and should shed light on the major cycle's movement is one of the underlying principles of *Le Jeu d'enfant* and of the reflexive *recherche* that characterizes the New Novel: fiction should provide its own critique; analysis should take place within narration itself. Thus Ricardou admonishes that fiction must now constitute "l'aventure d'un récit" rather than "le récit d'une aventure."[5] It is this sternly self-conscious, self-questioning posture that Geoffrey Hartman has characterized as Cartesian: "The contemporary French novel has become Cartesian with a vengeance and turned on itself the philosopher's 'methodical doubt.' Where the insufficiency of a particular mode of realism (such as philosophy) merely spurs the American novel to new and starker realisms, the French novel attacks its own form, its apparent autonomy, the features that make it 'novelistic.' Yet it does so in the space of fiction itself."[6] If *Navettes* forms a compendium of the general system and participates in that system while illuminating it, then its short texts can be seen as theoretical satellites projecting information about the cycle from within the cycle. Specifically, these reflexive texts participate in, resume, and illuminate the professed revolutionary aims of the self-interrogative Project proposed by *Le Jeu d'enfant*. They can be considered as both a manifesto and an exemplary instance of the cycle's intertextual and self-critical doctrine.

The contestive, subversive movement of the eight novels of *Le Jeu d'enfant* has been toward an increasing textual disruption and graphic innovation. The fairly straightforward narrations of the early fictions give way to growing fragmentation and discontinuity as the cycle nears its conclusion, culminating in the radical form of *Fuzzy Sets*. Concomitantly, the novelistic protagonist is progressively drained of personality and stripped of distinguishing characteristics; he is eventually reduced to an almost abstract curiosity, a dogged will to investigate. An ongoing Project aimed at demystifying narrative conventions has turned the futuristic space vessel, the Octopus, into a "crypte en vol" (*FS*, 123), carrying, in O., the remains of a traditional hero and author purportedly laid to rest by an insurrectionary textuality. The death of the protagonist and the author was proclaimed by texts like Ollier's radio play "La Mort du protagonist" as well as by critical commentaries of the period like Barthes's "La Mort de l'auteur." Yet my analysis of the trinitary subject of fiction (protagonist-writer-reader) has tended to resurrect that subject as an abiding principle of fictional construction, thus calling into question the insurrection that was ostensibly mounting throughout the eight fictions. The status of a self-reflexive fiction that purports to purge itself is thus put into question in the course of an analysis that uncovers the perpetual reincarnation of certain exiled elements. And the question that must finally be asked at the end of *Le Jeu d'enfant* is, what is the nature and extent of the revolution that takes place here?

As a compendium of the whole cycle's impetus, *Navettes* can help provide answers to this final question. The first and last texts of *Navettes*, "Nocturne" and "Nocturne entre guillemets," together constitute a microcosm of the movement of *Le Jeu d'enfant* and can be read as a manifesto of its revolutionary direction. The relationship of *Navettes* to the cycle figures the autocritical stance of the Project: analysis must come from within fiction; theorizing is effected by interior satellites. If the initial and final texts of *Navettes* replicate and condense what I have claimed to be problematic in the movement of the major system, then the nature of the fictional revolution encountered in *Le Jeu d'enfant* can be illuminated by the orbits of those satellites, and the status of those Cartesian fictions can be clarified.

In "Nocturne" an unnamed protagonist recounts his attempt to climb a hill or a mountain. The ascent becomes increasingly dangerous as the protean terrain changes from gentle, forested hill to frightening crevices and sheer cliffs. Descent quickly becomes impracticable; a deep fissure opens at his feet and expands vertiginously. Moments of calm punctuate the protagonist's encounters with the surrealistic landscape: "Enfin, la chute se ralentit, s'achève. C'est le calme de nouveau. J'en profite pour gagner un rocher situé un peu plus haut, d'où je distingue la ligne du crête, toute proche. Juste comme je prends mon élan, la pierre se dresse et me frappe au front. . . . Toute la montagne se dresse" (*N,* 16). Each assault by the mountain and each plunge into the abyss is followed by a new effort. The text closes by repeating its own initial passage, whose last sentence also occurs at the end of *L'Echec de Nolan:* "Je monte au milieu des arbres. Mon pied glisse sur les aiguilles de pin, sur la terre ocre, la mousse qui s'agglomère en monticules. Lentement—meut—sur le sol souple et léger. . . ." (*N,* 17).

The perpetually renewed ascent of the protagonist of "Nocturne" (and of *L'Echec,* and so on) replicates on a magnified, simplified scale the searching journey of the Lukácsian hero that, as I argued in Chapter 1, *Le Jeu d'enfant* sets up as its ideological "other." The protagonist of "Nocturne," like the hero of a *Bildungsroman,* seeks the higher, transcendent meaning of his own life; he seeks an original, ideal unity with the world, a unity that is no longer possible in the heterogeneity and uncertainty of his present situation: "Le corps se porte instinctivement vers *l'amont,* les bras ballants *à la recherche d'une prise stable*" (*N,* 13; my emphasis). The alien, shifting setting threatens the protagonist with gaping crevices and sudden erections of mountains and trees, which together figure the sexuality of textual *espacement* and prefigure O.'s dilemma on the planet-book of Epsilon. Unable to integrate himself into his surroundings, the protagonist persists in seeking the transcendent, panoramic elevation he achieved in more conventional incarnations. The circular text whose ending is also its beginning shows the protagonist eternally repeating his impossible quest.

"Nocturne entre guillements," on the other hand, figures a descent. The scene is an alien planet, on which an astronaut lands in order to carry out a mission of investigation. He is a sort of Adam in the new world: "Toutes choses sont à nommer" (*N,* 185). But the objects he encounters are vaguely familiar, either pictured in his investigative manual or analogous to phenomena on his own planet, so that he tends to place every new noun in quotation marks: "Quel mot choisir? 'Amande'? 'Argane'? 'Pistache'? 'Olive'?" (*N,* 183). Objects are only provisionally named with labels borrowed from an analogous system. No inherent correspondence exists between approximative label and designated object. Analogies continue to multiply between Earth and the alien world. It becomes apparent that the planet is inhabited; the astronaut discovers the ruins of an outdoor theater and experiments with its acoustics: "Le jeu le captivant, il en vient à mimer, à déclamer, à se mettre lui-même en scène, à s'attribuer des rôles et à les répéter, se réprimandant, se distanciant de son émoi, se critiquant et se conspuant, s'applaudissant et se bissant" (*N,* 202). With daybreak, tourists enter the amphitheater. The alien astronaut mingles with them unnoticed. The reader is finally convinced that the planet is Earth when the astronaut checks into a motel.

While the protagonist of the first text attempts a perpetually renewed ascent toward a lost ideal, the astronaut of the final text effects a descent into the increasingly familiar, even the banal. The protagonist of "Nocturne" is at odds with his setting and can only attempt (and fail) to gain a panoramic stance in relation to it, to dominate it. The astronaut, by contrast, integrates quite easily into his new surroundings. What at first appears to be alien grows more and more familiar; everything he encounters can be given a name from other systems with which he is acquainted. The astronaut sees himself as an actor and can take a critical distance from the roles he gives himself. He can, in other words, see himself as the misguided protagonist of the first "Nocturne" and can critique his own performance. If "Nocturne" replicates the paradigm of the traditional protagonist seeking a transcendent meaning, "Nocturne entre guillemets" seems to correct the first text's ideological fallacy of progress and discovery from the futuristic perspective of science fiction. The two texts thus repeat the self-critical movement of *Le Jeu d'enfant,* which doubles its first, terrestrial cycle with a secondary relay of space-age critique, while conserving a single protagonist throughout.

The traditional novelistic hero sought to overcome his divorce from the world; he sought to reunite with the meaning that had become separate from and elevated above his life. In literature, this quest corresponds to a mimetic vision of narrative in which fiction is held to represent a primary, original reality through an adequation of language with things. A major goal of the New Novel is of course the subversion of this mimetic vision of fiction and the theory of language on which it is based. The nature that, in "Nocturne," threatened the protagonist with its vertiginous depths and heights is, in "Nocturne entre guillemets," eventually tamed through naming. When the astronaut assigns to the alien objects names borrowed from other systems, these names remain in quotation marks, stressing that the union of a signifier with a signified object is provisional and approximative. At the same time, the astronaut has bridged the gap between himself and his setting and has successfully defused the menace it conveyed. Every object and experience that posed a threat to the initial protagonist now becomes, for the second one, part of a homogeneous "fuzzy set" whose existence is solely textual and irrevocably secondary because it is quoted.

Quotation marks, whether implicit or explicit, are the basis of the intertextuality endorsed by these fictions. In putting everything described "entre guillemets," between quotes, the final text of *Navettes* dispels the illusion of a primary representation of objects, experiences, or meaning. Fictional description is only accomplished by recourse to other signifiers, which, divorced from any one-to-one correspondence with things, remain within a homogeneously secondary or textual sphere. Walter Benjamin recognized the subversive power of quotation, which is "not the strength to preserve, but to cleanse, to tear out of context, to destroy."[7] What is destroyed by quotation is the notion of the primary and the original; the primary adequation of language with reality is interrupted and complicated by the insertion of a previous text. The primary relationship of an author to his text—his originality—is similarly disrupted by the intercalation of external voices. If a text is a "mosaïque de citations,"[8] with both acknowledged and unacknowledged quotations, notions of the primary and the original become untenable. The subversive potential of quotation forms the foundation of the intertextual revolution proposed by *Le Jeu d'enfant*. A critical rejection of the traditional questing role of the protagonist thus occurs in the last text of *Navettes;* in place of that outmoded role, a new type of quest is substituted: a descent into a realm of homogeneous textuality, a realm characterized by secondariness.

In the final scene of "Nocturne entre guillemets" the protagonist seduces the girl who shows him to his motel room; the terms of the encounter either recall or prefigure all the women of the fictional cycle:

> "Vous n'avez pas de bagages?" dit-elle. Pour toute réponse, il lui montre le livre—l'ouvre sur une page blanche où coucher sa réplique.
>
> Elle rit. Jette un coup d'oeil au-dehors.
> S'attarde, hésitante.
>
> Comme il lui prend la main, repousse la porte derrière elle.
>
> Une aura bleutée baigne le site, scelle l'"écrit". (*N, 209*)

The menacing sexuality in the landscape of "Nocturne" was a figure of the unrecognized nature of textuality from which the protagonist continually sought to distinguish himself, which he sought to dominate. The astronaut, by contrast, perceives the link between the white sheets of a *livre* and a *lit* and is capable of consummating the *écrit*. He is comfortably at home in a homogeneously (inter)textual world. The astronaut has been cured of the "transcendental homelessness" suffered by the novelistic hero Lukács describes.[9]

The hero is thus afflicted, Lukács claims, because the novel is the art-form of a modern age in which the ideal organic unity of the epic Greek world has been lost but is constantly sought after. In an integrated civilization, such a transcendence would be impossible because no distinction between inside and outside can be made: "It is a homogeneous world, and even the separation between man and world, between 'I' and "you," cannot disturb its homogeneity." Forms lose their innate differences in an integrated world: "Totality of being is possible only where everything is already homogeneous before it has been contained by forms; where forms are not a constraint but only the becoming conscious, the coming to the surface of everything that had been lying dormant as a vague longing in the innermost depths of that which had to be given form."[10]

"Nocturne entre guillemets" proposes a very similar totality and homogeneity. In placing both "Nocturne" and the new, alien world "entre guillemets," it puts both anterior fiction and the supposed world or reality to be represented on a single, fictional plane. The result is a blurring of the distinction between anteriority and secondariness, between the real and the fictional. In its evolution from the first text of *Navettes* to the last, fiction presents itself as a singularly secondary entity, made up of other fictions and referring to other fictions or to other signifying systems rather than to a primary reality. Underneath the apparent forms delineated by quotation marks or by the provisional closure of individual books, a homogeneous, amorphous Book is suggested by the outcome of *Navettes*. While this conclusion sounds, by now, in the eighties, like a rather oft-played tape, it must be remembered that in the late sixties *Navettes* was a barometer of the critical issues of its time. The point it makes about language, representation, and fiction has remained one of the major insights of postmodern literature.

In *Navettes*, then, fiction's movement from "Nocturne" to "Nocturne entre guillemets" has achieved or relearned the kind of epic unity and homogeneity that, in Lukác's vision, the novelistic form saw as its irretrievable origin and ideal goal. The scientific, self-analytical future of fiction paradoxically returns to a kind of epic unity very much like the goal attributed to its professed "other," the bourgeois realist novel. In locating the nature of fiction in a unified totality—in the homogeneous secondarity of intertextuality—these texts extend and accomplish the unfinished project of their ideological "other."[11] And indeed, *Le Jeu d'enfant* possesses many epic qualities: its incorporation of many voices in the form of citations and pastiches evokes the collectivity of an oral, communal tradition; and the effort to excavate the origins of textuality—particularly in *Our*—gives an epic flavor to the protagonists' mission.

The demystifying Project of *Le Jeu d'enfant* does not characterize itself as an epic, however, but rather as a "clinique à épopées" (*FS,* 57) that will cure fiction of its grandiose illusions about its own origins and exploits. The Project is presented as a new, self-conscious kind of fable (*FS,* 104 and passim) that will correct the idealist mythology informing the ways in which traditional fiction is written and read. In the second, critical lap of *Le Jeu d'enfant,* the naturalistic myths of representation, expression, originality, and so on are countered and discredited by the allegorism of the fable, which typically conveys a moral message with its fictional content. The fable is at once more openly didactic and less subtly mimetic than the myths it replaces: it points to the correspondence of idea to fictional element but does not imply their essential identity. For instance, the spinning *lames* on Epsilon allegorized the turning pages of a book; they disrupted the fictional illusion, figuring instead the simultaneity of intertextual inclusion and exclusion: "Cloisonnement et déchirure à la fois, ruinant le mythe d'un présent stable, unique" (*VE,* 223). The protagonist O. becomes an allegorical element in the fable when, on board the Octopus, he assumes the function of the reading subject: "l'intrus se donne à l'aléa des fables, une fonction l'élit et l'investit d'intrigue . . ." (*FS,* 12). At the conclusion of *Fuzzy Sets,* the captain of the Octopus makes clear the pedagogical aspect of the progressive fable: "Vous voici devant nous en conjonction de fable, cités à témoignage et perpétuation de l'écrit. Tout se conclut selon nos voeux: le temps de nos révolutions s'achève; s'ouvre celui de l'Edit. Trace sera gardée de cette scène en nos mémoires, et ses images multipliées, publiées en tous lieux de mainmise et d'édification . . ." (*FS,* 175). The fable is a new epic, a cured novel, which has learned that the homogeneity of forms lies not in a primary, essential totality, but in the uniform secondariness of the written and the published.

The Project has thus achieved what its discredited "other" had always desired: a return to self-consciousness. In turning a critical eye upon itself, and in attempting to discern its own nature, however, the futuristic, revolutionary fiction has approached dangerously close to something it initially sought to purge: the notion of an evolution or progress toward meaning on the part of the fictional subject—the ethos of the *Bildungsroman.* The conventional hero could not achieve a valid understanding of his position, the Project proved, because he was locked into an ideological system that directed any *prise de conscience.*

What the Project would deny to the traditional protagonist—a Hegelian journey of self-education toward self-consciousness—it confers on the new fictional form itself.

O. is the *Elu,* the representative chosen to carry out the Project. The troubling proximity of his quest to that of the perennial novelistic hero is voiced in *Fuzzy Sets:* "Est-il héros de fable enfant ou de roman d'apprentissage?" (*FS,* 47). The emerging fable threatens to merge with the very form it has most sought to demystify. In attempting to differentiate itself from its "other," the cycle has in some sense rejoined that "other," like Girardian rivals/doubles whose efforts to underscore their differences bring them ever nearer to identity. While repetition of the "other's" desire has indeed subverted and altered it—for novelistic conventions have certainly been radically challenged in *Le Jeu d'enfant*—the idealist project is still fundamentally intact, even in its very act of posing the paranoid question cited above ("Est-il héros . . . ?"). The revolution effected has been in one sense a circular movement, an orbit around a subject who, despite all his radical adventures, remains in one important way the same. The common denominator between the warring doubles is their will to self-consciousness. The Cartesian impulse of the New Novel and of the "narcissistic" postmodern metafictions it exemplifies has not taken itelf as the object of its analysis so much as the rival from which it wants to distinguish itself.[12]

From its self-critical perspective, the fiction of *Le Jeu d'enfant* cannot fully see the repressed "other" residing within it. This is why my analysis of its autointerrogative stance took place not merely in terms of the project it seemed to propose for itself, but also in terms of its relationship to the "other" that forms the unconscious basis of that project. The problem of identity voiced by *Fuzzy Sets* ("Est-il héros de fable enfant ou de roman d'apprentissage?") is the problem of the fictional subject and is the issue that every chapter of this study has addressed in some form.

Chapter 1 showed that the self-conscious attempt on the part of the terrestrial cycle to kill off its protagonist resulted in his assumption, in a radically altered form, to the realm of science fiction. The "scientific" fictions of the second relay were to correct the errors of the first; however, the trinitary subject of fiction persisted as a principle of fictional construction and functioning, and the scientific fictions were in many ways as unconscious of their workings as their predecessors had been. The self-cure attempted in the novels of the second cycle still participated in the Cartesian, positivist project of the initial effort and carried over many of its blind spots. In Chapter 2, I examined how the genealogy of texts provided by this self-analysis was based on a revolutionary model of fictional origin and functioning, which set up origin as a simple duality, a struggle between a generative maternal matrix and an individual son-fiction. This dual origin was the triumphant corollary of another binary opposition, the Cartesian split of a fiction successfully doubting and examining itself. Chapter 3 showed how contradictions arising from this revolutionary formula pointed, in the seventh fiction, to a more complicated familial structure involving the paternal, authorial pole and raised doubts about the self-reflexive project. In Chapter 4 I discussed the sexualized allegory of reading and completed the psychoanalytic lap of my analysis, which viewed the composite, trinitary subject and its relationship to fiction in terms of an extended family romance: in terms of sexual difference, family politics, filiations accepted and repudiated, and Oedipal encounters. A psychoanalytic discourse aimed at interpreting the conscious language of these fictions sought to make manifest some of its unconscious structures, and to call into question its revolutionary status. Chapter 5 showed how the structuralist "rêve de scientificité," put to the test in *Le Jeu d'enfant,* reveals the tenacity of the subject as a principle of fictional construction, even in texts that seem to reach the zero degree of novelistic convention. O. haunts the center of the cycle and presides at its every revolution.

The last passage of *Fuzzy Sets* is a reporter's account of O.'s return to his *lieu natal,* to what appears to be Europe, and specifically Paris. The concentric movement of the first cycle of fictions (ending with *L'Echec de Nolan*) had closed in on its axis, the place of origin to which the system now returns after its autocritical detour in outer space. As we saw before, the "vieux continent de prose" to which O. returns has become a futuristic landscape: "Lieu substitué, en travesti: de scherzane, ajoliane, aimantelle, luciane. . . . Bleu, blanc, trop blanc, et mauve, ses yeux se ferment, il sait ce qui l'attend maintenant, à quoi bon scruter ces jeux d'ellipses, ces transparents niveaux, et questionner s'il fut construit une bibliothèque en ces banlieues planes?" The *lieu natal* has become a library; the landscape is a text: "repassant des doigts les lettres du paysage." As with "Nocturne entre guillemets," the outcome of the fictional movement is to create a universe of textuality where the line between reality and representation remains fuzzy. The report and the cycle end with an apostrophe to the reader: "'Lecteur, vois-tu? Ce reportage est une introduction: à sa manière. Didactique: je l'ai écrit dans le style ancien.' (*Chroniques d'Ile-de-France.*)" (*FS,* 188–89).

The conclusion of *Le Jeu d'enfant* suggests that while a cyclic revolution in the primary sense of the term has been accomplished, the nature of fiction has nevertheless been radically altered; it, too, is a "lieu substitué, travesti" by the changes it has undergone. Literature will never be the same again. The system returns to its point of departure, but the intervening developments have brought about the reeducation of all involved, and especially of the form itself, which now recognizes not only the style of the ancien régime but also the impossibility of fully changing that style or of fully overthrowing that regime.[13] Having subjected itself to its own scientific examination, the fiction of the future will be different from that of the past. But this reeducation, this revolution, has not aimed at purely scientific ends: an ideology is challenged by the guerilla tactics of espionage and subversion carried out by the Project; that ideology is never fully purged by the cycle's revolution but necessarily remains at the latent level of its subterranean organization. But perhaps this intermittent recognition is as close as we can get to an eviction of ideology in art—or would want to get, as Barthes affirms: "Certains veulent un texte (un art, une peinture) sans ombre, coupé de l''idéologie dominante'; mais c'est vouloir un texte sans fécondité, sans productivité, un texte stérile (voyez le mythe de la Femme sans Ombre). Le texte a besoin de son ombre: cette ombre, c'est *un peu* d'idéologie, *un peu* de représentation, *un peu* de sujet: fantômes, poches, traînées, nuages nécessaires: la subversion doit produire son propre *clair-obscur.*"[14] The value of Ollier's work lies not only in its meticulously crafted, sustained interrogation of the possibilities, potentialities, and limitations of fictional reflexivity and revolution, but in its clear-eyed recognition of the necessary, interminable pursuit of "(L mpossible dernier chapitre)" (*FS,* 151) on the subject of fiction.

Notes

INTRODUCTION

1. Claude Ollier, *Mon Double à Malacca* (Paris: Flammarion, 1982), p. 34. Subsequent citations will be noted in parentheses in the text.

2. Claude Ollier, "Les Inscriptions conflictuelles," *Pratiques* 10 (1971): 88.

3. Claude Ollier, "Vingt ans après," in *Nouveau Roman: hier, aujourd'hui* II (Paris: U.G.E., 1972), pp. 203-4.

4. Friedrich Nietzsche, *The Gay Science*. Translated by Walter Kaufmann. (New York: Random House, 1974); Alain Robbe-Grillet, *Pour un nouveau roman* (Paris: Editions de Minuit, 1963).

5. Sigmund Freud, *The Interpretation of Dreams,* vol. 5, *Complete Psychological Works,* ed. James Strachey (London: Hogarth, 1953-74), p. 612.

6. Italo Calvino, *The Castle of Crossed Destinies* (New York and London: Harcourt Brace Jovanovich, 1979), p. 105.

7. Patricia Waugh, *Metafiction: The Theory and Practice of Self-Conscious Fiction* (New York and London: Methuen, 1984), p. 2.

8. Pierre de Boisdeffre, *La Cafetière est sur la table: contre le "nouveau roman"* (Paris: Editions de la Table Ronde, 1967), pp. 19, 91-92.

9. Matthieu Galey, "Vingt ans après ou les survivants du Nouveau Roman," *L'Express* (April 4, 1981); 26-27.

10. Ibid.

11. David Carroll, *The Subject in Question: The Languages of Theory and the Strategies of Fiction* (Chicago and London: University of Chicago Press, 1982); Lynn Higgins, *Parables of Theory: Jean Ricardou's Metafiction* (Birmingham, Ala.: Summa Publications, 1984); Dina Sherzer, *Representation in Contemporary French Fiction* (Lincoln: University of Nebraska Press, 1986).

12. Cecile Lindsay, "Interview with Claude Ollier," *The Review of Contemporary Fiction* 8, no. 2 (Summer 1988); 18.

13. See Susan Suleiman, "The Question of Readability in Avant-Garde Fiction," *Studies in Contemporary Literature* 6, nos. 1 and 2 (Fall 1981-Spring 1982); 17-35.

14. Michel Foucault, *Raymond Roussel* (Paris: Gallimard, 1963), p. 10.

CHAPTER I

1. M. H. Abrams, *Natural Supernaturalism* (New York: Norton, 1971), p. 230. Abrams argues that the *Phenomenology*, with its allusive language, puns, irony, and narrative traps, resembles a fictional narrative of the *Bildungs-roman* genre.

2. Lukács differs from Hegel on this subject in one important aspect: Lukács claims the novelistic hero does not achieve total self-consciousness, as does the Hegelian Spirit at the end of its questing journey. Lukács nevertheless sets up a typology of the novel, which shows the form itself evolving toward greater self-consciousness. In its "virile," mature form the novel, like its (male) protagonist, achieves an ironic appreciation of the distance separating it or him from meaning in the world and from full self-consciousness. In its ultimate development, however, the novel as described by Lukács achieves a new epic unity through the organic wholeness of its use of temporality. Georg Lukács, *The Theory of the Novel* (Cambridge: MIT Press, 1971), p. 66.

3. Ibid., p. 56.

4. In "Vingt ans après," Ollier proposes this project: "C'est donc nécessité impérieuse que de reprendre . . . les formes fictionnelles en vigueur et, par un travail de perpétuel décentrage ne laissant aucun constituant hors-jeu, par un effet de *gauchissement, de détournement de leur visée idéologique,* de les tourner vers la lecture d'un sens autre" (p. 214).

5. Another famous "other" against which the early New Novel posited its own formulations was the persistence of a Balzacian-type realism well into the twentieth century. In *Pour un nouveau roman,* Alain Robbe-Grillet rejects the imperialistic anthropomorphism of Balzacian descriptions, where human meaning penetrates every object and setting, and where the narration takes the reader right to the "coeur romantique des choses" (p. 20).

6. Lessing as a protagonist is at once within and without the cycle of fictions, as he both precedes and to some extent replaces Lassalle. A second external connection links the philosopher-theologian G. E. Lessing to the questing structure of the fiction; like Hegel, Lessing conceived of the plot of history as the self-realization and self-education of humanity. In *Die Erziehung des Menschengeschlects* (1870), education takes on the metaphor of a laborious journey, and mankind's progress is translated into the maturational stages of an individual life. Thus, Lassalle's itinerary (in *Ms*) should be viewed in light of his predecessors and the significance with which they endow him.

7. This opposition between colonizers and colonized is also evident in Robbe-Grillet's *La Jalousie* (Paris: Editions de Minuit, 1957).

8. Lukács, *Theory of the Novel,* p. 71.

9. Vivian Mercier, review of *Le Maintien de l'ordre*, by Claude Ollier, *Nation* 213 (Sept. 13, 1971): 126.

10. This structuralist view of the demystified protagonist as a textual function rather than a psychologically realistic entity characterized many early New Novels as well as much critical writing on these novels. The novels and criticism of Jean Ricardou provide some of the most mechanical illustrations and demonstrations of what eventually became a *lieu commun* of the New Novel.

11. Maurice Blanchot, *L'Espace littéraire* (Paris: Gallimard, 1955), p. 24.

12. Ibid., p. 26.

13. Morel's name links his fate with that of his paronym in Bioy Casares's novel *The Invention of Morel* where, as Jean Ricardou points out, "l'inventif Morel n'est mort que pour mieux assurer les conditions de sa survie" (*Pour une théorie du Nouveau Roman* [Paris: Editions du Seuil, 1971], p. 197). The name also resonates as the amalgam of two precursors of the French *Un-bildungsroman,* Frédéric Moreau and Julien Sorel.

14. Philippe Boyer, "Topographies pour jeux de pistes," preface to Claude Ollier, *La Mise en scène* (Paris: Flammarion, 1982), p. 14.

15. Blanchot, *L'Espace littéraire,* p. 307.

CHAPTER 2

1. Angus Fletcher, *Allegory, The Theory of a Symbolic Mode* (Ithaca: Cornell University Press, 1964), p. 3.

2. Northrop Frye, *Anatomy of Criticism: Four Essays* (Princeton: Princeton University Press, 1957), p. 89. The use of allegory is central to the New Novel movement in general and indeed characterizes much postmodern fiction, whose self-referentiality turns on the establishment of dual levels of signification. Allegory as a rhetorical strategy of reflexive fiction will be addressed at greater length in Chapter 4.

3. That fiction inevitably narrates the scene of its own writing, or the search for its own origin, is a staple of New Novel criticism: "Par ces méta-phores du fonctionnement, la fiction opère en quelque façon, on le sait, la narration de sa narration" (Jean Ricardou, "Naissance d'une fiction," in *Nouveau Roman: hier, aujourd'hui* II, p. 385).

4. Georges Poulet, "Phenomenology of Reading," *New Literary History* 1 (1986): 54.

5. Blanchot, *L'Espace littéraire,* p. 22.

6. Sigmund Freud, "Medusa's Head," in *Sexuality and the Psychology of Love* (New York: Collier Books, 1963), p. 212.

7. In *The Fear of Women* (New York: Grune and Stratton, 1968), the psychiatrist Wolfgang Lederer links the fear of the mother to a paradoxical desire for a return to the womb. The terror occasioned by this desire resembles O.'s own apprehensions and similarly reflects a fear of the fluid—the current that erases the subject's marks: "The yearning for a return to the mother also has its dangers: in concrete terms, as pointed out by Horney, childhood attitudes, surviving in the adult man, may make him wonder whether his little penis . . . introduced into 'mother's' large vagina, may not be ridiculously inadequate. Horney attributes such phantasies to the boy, and it has been suggested that he may actually be afraid of falling into the maternal genital, of being submerged and drowned in it" (p. 233).

8. The term *sillon* (furrow), as in "le sillon courbe entre les fesses brunes" (*E*, 198), is increasingly employed in the novels of the second cycle as a figure of a sexualized textuality: "Sillons de grammaire irrigués dru par branle exceptionnel et divin élan" (*FS*, 183). The *sillon* aptly evokes the *dissémination* that characterizes the plurality and multiplicity of writing viewed as a metaphorically sexual act.

9. Ollier's use of contrasting masculine and feminine principles must be seen against the background of the deconstruction of "phallogocentrism" in the work of Jacques Derrida and the growing interest in Lacanian psychoanalysis in French critical thought since the sixties. As Alice Jardine points out in *Gynesis, Configurations of Woman and Modernity* (Ithaca: Cornell University Press, 1985), much modern thought entails a valorization of the feminine; the "woman-effect" that Jardine has called "*gynesis*" serves as a figure of the unrepresentable, the unsayable, the psychic "other" in modernity's critique of classical rationalism. By making the feminine the metaphorical "other" of traditional fiction, Ollier seeks to unmask the "metaphysics of presence" at work in conventional narratives. The cluster of attributes associated in *Le Jeu d'enfant* with the feminine—digression, fertility, castration, indeterminacy—are garnered from ancient myth, popular convention, and modern psychoanalysis; in valorizing them as figures of textuality or fictionality, Ollier is reversing the usual hierarchy in which they are fixed. Nevertheless, after much excellent work in feminist theory in the decades of the seventies and eighties, we have become more sensitive to the political implications of "essentializing" sexual difference, and of continuing to use sexual difference as a metaphor or figure of something else. In an essay on the place of woman in Derrida's work, Gayatri Spivak notes: "To see indeterminacy in the figure of women might be the effect of an ethicolegal narrative whose oppressive hegemony still remains largely unquestioned" ("Love me, love my ombre, elle," *Diacritics* [Winter, 1984]; 22). Thus, while Ollier's use of stereotypes of masculinity and feminin-

ity to explore the nature of fiction is justifiably open to criticism from a feminist-political perspective, this is not a critique I will undertake in the space of this study. Instead, I propose to view the question of the feminine in Ollier's work in the context of the critical issues and debates of its time—issues and debates where progress has since been made toward demythologizing sexual difference itself.

10. Throughout *La Vie sur Epsilon,* the feminine is conflated with the maternal. While some feminist theorists—most notably Hélène Cixous and Luce Irigaray—do link the two notions, many others, myself included, find such an identification highly problematic.

11. J. E. Cirlot, *A Dictionary of Symbols* (London: Routledge and Kegan Paul, 1966), p. 310.

12. Sigmund Freud, *Beyond the Pleasure Principle* (New York: Norton, 1961), p. 56.

13. Lederer points to the mythological connection between woman and water: "In Egyptian hieroglyphics, the water jar, symbol of the celestial goddess Nut, is also the symbol of femininity, 'female genital,' 'woman,' and the feminine principle. And in the mythological apperception of early man, breast and milk and rain; and woman and cow and earth and spring, belong together" (*Fear of Women,* p. 122). The conflict in *La Vie sur Epsilon* seems to polarize around these mythical associations.

14. Friedrich Nietzsche, *Joyful Wisdom,* trans. Thomas Common (New York: Russell and Russell, 1964), p. 269.

15. Freud, *Beyond the Pleasure Principle,* p. 7.

16. The allegorical interpretation suggested by these dreams is not a strictly Freudian approach as set forth in *The Interpretation of Dreams,* for Freud rejects what he calls the "symbolic" method of dream interpretation as unscientific. Rather, these dreams seem to present a stereotypical popularization of Freudian dream analysis that parallels Ollier's use of other stereotypical forms such as the colonial novel, the police mystery, or science fiction.

17. Jacques Derrida, "La Pharmacie de Platon," in *La Dissémination* (Paris: Editions du Seuil, 1972), pp. 71–197.

18. In "La 'Mécanique' des fluides," in *Ce Sexe qui n'en est pas un* (Paris: Editions de Minuit, 1977), Luce Irigaray proposes that the failure of science to elaborate a theory of the physical properties of fluids and its tendency to create an idealization or symbolization of fluids are symptomatic of a rationalism dominated by the masculine, by form, by solids. The feminine, or the fluid, becomes a backdrop, a *plan projectif,* upon which the solid subject is imposed and privileged: "Ce qui est en excès par rapport à la forme—ainsi, le sexe féminin—étant nécessairement rejeté en dessous ou au-dessus du système en

vigueur" (p. 109). In Ollier's text, the opposition between masculine subject and feminine fictional matrix is constructed in similar terms. While Irigaray sees this polarization as a philosophical, phallocentric model of repression of the feminine, Ollier's use of the terms indicates a greater degree of struggle between the fictional aspects embodied in the fluid and the solid; while the masculine subject attempts to relegate the amorphous matrix to a *plan projectif*, that fluidity is not readily repressed.

19. The mythical origins of writing reappear in the next fiction of the cycle, where O. encounters the modern incarnation of Nabu, the Sumarian *dieu-scribe*.

20. "The Phaedrus," in *The Works of Plato,* trans. Benjamin Jowett (New York: The Modern Library, 1928), p. 324.

21. Magma is a "thin, pasty suspension (as of a precipitate in water)," *Webster's New Collegiate Dictionary* (Springfield, Mass.: G. and C. Merriam Co., 1977). Again, a vocabulary of fluids and solids seems to characterize textuality's constant tension between a centering subject and a diffuse matricial background.

22. Cirlot, *Dictionary of Symbols,* p. 309. Cirlot claims that the figure of the star has for most cultures alluded to plurality.

CHAPTER 3

1. Jacques Lacan, *Ecrits* (Paris: Editions du Seuil, 1966), p. 222.

2. Gilles Deleuze and Félix Guattari, *L'Anti-Oedipe* (Paris: Editions de Minuit, 1972), p. 84.

3. Henri Clouard, *Alexandre Dumas* (Paris: Editions Albin Michel, 1955), p. 10.

4. Henry James, *The Art of the Novel* (New York: Charles Scribner's Sons, 1934), p. 79.

5. Michael Hamburger, *Reason and Energy* (London: Routledge and Kegan Paul, 1957), pp. 75–76.

6. Percy Bysshe Shelley, "A Defense of Poetry," in *Critical Theory Since Plato,* ed. Hazard Adams (New York: Harcourt Brace Jovanovich, Inc., 1971), p. 599.

7. Jorge Luis Borges, *Borges on Writing,* ed. Norman Thomas di Giovanni (New York: E. P. Dutton and Co., Inc., 1973), p. 26.

8. Blanchot, *L'Espace littéraire,* p. 306.

9. Roland Barthes, "La Mort de l'auteur," *Mantéia* 5 (1968); 13, 14–15. This text appears in translation in *Image-Music-Text,* trans. Stephen Heath (New York: Hill and Wang, 1977), pp. 142–48.

10. Michel Foucault, *L'Ordre du discours* (Paris: Gallimard, 1971), pp. 26–31.

11. Derrida, "La Pharmacie de Platon," p. 155. Jean Ricardou, "Terrorisme, théorie," in *Robbe-Grillet: Colloque de Cerisy* II (Paris: U.G.E., 1976), p. 11.

12. James, *The Art of the Novel*, p. 79; Borges, *Borges on Writing*, p. 6; Maurice Blanchot, *Le Livre à venir* (Paris: Gallimard, 1959), p. 142.

13. Roland Barthes, *Le Plaisir du texte* (Paris: Editions du Seuil, 1973), p. 100. Naomi Schor, "Pour une thématique restreinte," *Littérature* 22 (May 1976): 30–31.

14. Ollier, "Vingt ans après," p. 207.

15. Ollier's text "Pulsion" (*L'Arc* 54 [1975]; 53–58 [p. 53]) proposes a meditation on the process of writing in terms of the metaphor of weaving. The text clearly recalls the beginning of Jacques Derrida's "La Pharmacie de Platon," where texture and textuality are linked, and recalls as well the notion of the *pharmakon*, writing, as both poison and remedy. However, the relation of "Pulsion" to "La Pharmacie" is not one of allusion or reference but of intertextuality. Ollier not only extends and embroiders on the textile metaphor in Derrida's text but also incorporates and reworks certain passages from that text as well as from his own novels and other works. The text is thus a practical working-out of the theoretical notions it endorses.

16. Ollier, "Vingt ans après," p. 213.

17. Ollier, "Pulsion," p. 54.

18. Freud's enunciation of the dreamwork mechanisms in *The Interpretation of Dreams* was almost immediately taken up by the surrealists and likened to poetry. Modern theorists have continued to find Freud's terminology particularly apt in discussing literature. In "Ecriture et révolution," *Théorie d'ensemble* (Paris: Editions du Seuil, 1968), Philippe Sollers links the dreamwork mechanisms to all textuality and specifically to intertextuality: "Le concept *d'inter-textualité* (Kristeva) est ici essentiel: tout texte se situe à la jonction de plusieurs textes dont il est à la fois la relecture, l'accentuation, la condensation, le déplacement, et la profondeur" (p. 75). The intertextual reworking that comprises a text is accomplished on the dream level rather than on the level of conscious control by the author.

19. Thomas N. Greer, *A Brief History of Western Man* (New York: Harcourt Brace Jovanovich Inc., 1968), p. 16.

20. Barthes, "La Mort de l'auteur," pp. 12–14.

21. Roland Barthes, *Le Degré zéro de l'écriture* (Paris: Editions du Seuil, 1953), p. 8.

22. In *Le Degré zéro*, Barthes calls this closure "l'écriture bourgeoise" and maintains that romantic uses of literary language were fundamentally those of

the classical, monarchical era: "Aussi n'y a-t-il pas à s'étonner que la Révolution n'ait rien changé à l'écriture bourgeoise, et qu'il n'y ait qu'une différence forte mince entre l'écriture d'un Fénelon et celle d'un Mérimée. C'est que l'idéologie bourgeoise a duré, exempte de fissure, jusqu'en 1848 sans s'ébranler le moins du monde au passage d'une révolution qui donnait à la bourgeoisie le pouvoir politique et social, nullement le pouvoir intellectuel, qu'elle détenait depuis longtemps déjà. Et la révolution romantique, si nominalement attachée à troubler la forme, a sagement conservé l'écriture de son idéologie. Un peu de lest jeté mélangeant les genres et les mots lui a permis de préserver l'essentiel du langage classique, l'instrumentalité" (pp. 43–44).

23. In "La Mort de l'auteur," Barthes associates the notion of the author with the modern bourgeois era in Europe; he opposes to this modern notion a more ancient vision of the writing subject, one that resembles the scribe in *Our:* "dans les sociétés ethnographiques, le récit n'est jamais pris en charge par une personne, mais par un médiateur, shaman ou récitant, dont on peut à la rigueur admirer la 'performance' (c'est-à-dire la maîtrise du code narratif), mais jamais le 'génie.' *L'Auteur* est un personnage moderne, produit sans doute par notre société dans la mesure où, au sortir du moyen âge, avec l'empirisme anglais, le rationalisme français, et la foi personnelle de la Réforme, elle a découvert le prestige de l'individu" (p. 12). The ultramodern *scripteur* must then resemble the ancient scribe.

24. In *Télévision* (Paris: Editions du Seuil, 1974), Jacques Lacan insists on the materiality of the signifying chain's textile construction: "C'est le réel qui permet de dénouer effectivement ce dont le symptôme consiste, à savoir un noeud de signification. Nouer et dénouer n'étant pas ici des métaphores, mais bien à prendre comme ces noeuds qui se construisent réellement à faire chaîne de la matière signifiante" (p. 22). A language structured like the unconscious is a textual entity whose reading and fabrication constitute a literal process of weaving and unraveling.

25. One of the many motifs of Jacques Derrida's *La Carte postale: de Socrate à Freud et au-delà* (Paris: Flammarion, 1980) is the enormous potential for delays, detours, and dead letters within the "postal system" of messages sent and received that language is commonly assumed to comprise. And to further complicate the vision of language as communication, Derrida undermines the singularity of any given sender or addressee of messages. In their critique of structuralism, *Language and Materialism* (London: Routledge and Kegan Paul, 1977), Rosalind Coward and John Ellis propose a similar attack on the notion of language as a system of exchange or communication. While the early structuralism of Saussure and Lévi-Strauss provided a revolutionary, differential conception of language, they claim it still presupposed transcen-

dental subjects who exist outside language and who exchange meanings. They feel that the application of certain Marxist and psychoanalystic notions will correct this deficiency in the structuralist view of language: "With Marxism, the notion that economic relations are relations of exchange appears as a representation that is produced in a particular social practice, a representation which functions to provide a positionality for subjects within a system of contradictions. With psychoanalysis, the constitution of the human subject is shown to undercut any notion of language as a system of exchange between complete individuals. Its notion of the subjective moment and of the productive dissolution of structures is a theory of revolutionary practice" (pp. 23–24). The revolution in *Our* similarly participates in both the Marxist and the psychoanalytic critique of certain early structuralist assumptions about language and the subject, while still endorsing the structuralist notion of differentiality.

26. Barthes, *Le Degré zéro*, p. 8.

27. Edouard Dhorme, *Les Religions de Babylonie et d'Assyrie* (Paris: P.U.F., 1945), p. 152.

28. In "La Pharmacie de Platon," Derrida also notes the filiation and usurpation of the three generations of the Babylonian gods, Ea, Marduk, and Nabu, finding in the last one a figure very similar to the Egyptian demigod Thot, the inventor of writing mentioned in Plato's *Phaedrus* (p. 107).

29. Ollier, "Vingt ans après," p. 213; my emphasis.

30. Claude Ollier, in *Nouveau Roman: hier, aujourd'hui* II, p. 362; my emphasis.

31. While Girard does not directly discuss Oedipus in *Mensonge romantique, vérité romanesque* (Paris: Grasset, 1961), he ascribes a familial metaphor to the ubiquitous structural model consisting of desired object–mediator–desiring subject: if the desired object is a transfiguration or an illusion, then the hero's imagination is the mother of that child, while the mediator is its father (chap. 1; "Triangular Desire"). Girard deals explicitly with the Oedipal situation in *La Violence et le sacré* (Paris: Grasset, 1972).

32. Dhorme, *Les Religions*, p. 28.

33. Samuel Noah Kramer, *Mythologies of the Ancient World* (New York: Doubleday, 1961), p. 21, and Dhorme, *Les Religions*, p. 145.

34. Gustave Flaubert, *Salammbô* (Paris: Garnier-Flammarion, 1964), p. 101.

35. Ollier, "Pulsion," p. 53.

36. Dante, *The Inferno*, trans. John Ciardi (New York: New American Library, 1954), pp. 275–77. The sentence, however, is a direct borrowing from Lautréamont's *Les Chants de Maldoror*, in *Oeuvres complètes* (Paris: Garnier-Flammarion, 1969), p. 129–30.

37. Lautréamont, *Les Chants,* p. 130.
38. Ibid., p. 129.
39. Sigmund Freud, "Femininity," in *New Introductory Lectures on Psychoanalysis,* trans. James Strachey (New York: Norton, 1964), p. 117.
40. Ollier, "Pulsion," p. 54.

CHAPTER 4

1. *The Reader in the Text,* ed. Susan Suleiman and Inge Crosman (Princeton, N.J.: Princeton University Press, 1980). Stanley Fish, "Literature in the Reader: An Affective Stylistics," *New Literary History* 2, no. 1 (Autumn, 1970), pp. 21–67, and *Is There a Text in This Class?: The Authority of Interpretive Communities* (Cambridge, Mass.: Cambridge University Press, 1980).
2. The process is that of intertextuality. In "La Stratégie de la forme," *Poétique* 27 (1976): 257–81, Laurent Jenny defines intertextuality as the primary condition of literary *lisibilité* and transposes various rhetorical figures such as the ellipse or paronomasia into figures of intertextuality.
3. In *Animate Illusions* (Lincoln: University of Nebraska Press, 1974), Harold Toliver argues that literature necessarily calls for a nonlinear reading: "movement in a complex piece of verbal art is never straightforward—and like a point on a wheel, the pursuing mind of the reader, while going generally on, moves forward and down, starts backwards and up, and so on" (p. 227). The excessive movement often required by the New Novel's narration thematizes the impossibility of reading fiction in a linear fashion.
4. Roland Barthes associates reading with sexuality in *Le Plaisir du texte* "Il paraît qui les érudits arabes, en parlant du texte, emploient cette expression admirable: *le corps certain.* Le texte a une forme humaine, c'est une figure, un anagramme du corps? Oui, mais de notre corps érotique. Le plaisir du texte serait irréductible à son fonctionnement grammairien (phéno-textuel), comme le plaisir du corps est irréductible au besoin physiologique" (p. 29). Ollier sees writing in much the same terms; in "Les Inscriptions conflictuelles," he speaks of "cette stupéfiante volupté de l'inscription et de la rature" (p. 89).
5. See Cleanth Brooks and R. P. Warren, *Understanding Poetry* (New York: Harcourt Brace and World, 1950), pp. 274–78.
6. Maureen Quilligan, *The Language of Allegory: Defining the Genre* (Ithaca and London: Cornell University Press, 1979), p. 155.
7. See Christiane Von Buelow, "Vallejo's *Venus de Milo* and the Ruins of Language," *PMLA* 104, no. 1 (January 1989), pp. 41–52. In this article, Von Buelow finds in the revision of allegory proposed by Benjamin a model for analyzing an avant-garde poem.

8. Brian McHale, *Postmodernist Fiction* (New York and London: Methuen, 1987), pp. 140–41.

9. Fletcher, *Allegory*, p. 21.

10. Claude Ollier in an interview published in *French Novelists Speak Out*, ed. Bettina Knapp (New York: Whitson, 1976), p. 154.

11. Frye, *Anatomy of Criticism*, p. 89.

12. In "The Rhetoric of Temporality," published in *Interpretations: Theory and Practice* (Baltimore: Johns Hopkins University Press, 1969), Paul de Man links allegory to the trope of irony, finding in them the same rhetorical structure, one that points to distanciation as it systematically says one thing and means another. Allegory, like irony, consequently leads to a demystification of the organic symbolic world as well as the mimetic world and thus lends itself to the revolutionary intent of the New Novel's *recherche*.

13. Barthes, "La Mort de l'auteur," p. 17. Ollier, "Pulsion," p. 58. Léon Roudiez, "Le Jeu du texte et du récit chez Claude Ollier," in *Nouveau Roman: hier, aujourd'hui* II, p. 189.

14. Poulet, "Phenomenology of Reading," p. 58.

15. Any hermeneutics will tend to operate some type of elision of the author in favor of the text or the structure. In proposing to study the structure of poetic meaning, Michael Riffaterre takes as his point of departure a similar model in *Semiotics of Poetry* (Bloomington: Indiana University Press, 1978): "The literary phenomenon is a dialectic between text and reader" (p. 1).

16. Jean Ricardou, *Le Nouveau Roman* (Paris: Editions du Seuil, 1973).

17. Pierre de Boisdeffre, *La Cafetière est sur la table*, p. 14. R.-M. Albères, *Le Roman d'aujourd'hui* (Paris: Albin Michel, 1970), p. 225. Claude Mauriac, "Claude Ollier et la littérature-fiction," *Figaro Littéraire* 1377–III (Oct. 1972): 45.

18. Ian Watt, *The Rise of the Novel* (Berkeley: University of California Press, 1962); Simon Lesser, *Fiction and the Unconscious* (New York: Random House, 1962). As we see from these critical works of the sixties, the sexualization of fiction and of the reading of fiction has long been a critical commonplace. It is only with the recent emergence of feminist criticism that we have begun to analyze the discourse of criticism itself in terms of gender.

19. Poulet, "Phenomenology of Reading," p. 59.

20. Claude Ollier, "Lecture-écriture-lecture," *La Nouvelle Revue Française* 214 (Oct. 1970): 203.

21. Ricardou, "Naissance d'une fiction," p. 392.

22. Philippe Sollers, *Logiques* (Paris: Editions du Seuil, 1968), pp. 242–43.

23. Wolfgang Iser, *The Implied Reader* (Baltimore: Johns Hopkins University Press, 1974) and *The Act of Reading* (Baltimore: Johns Hopkins University Press, 1978).

24. Lucien Dällenbach, "Reflexivity and Reading," *New Literary History* II, no. 3 (Spring 1980): 437. An issue of *Poétique* entitled "Théorie de la réception en Allemagne" published essays from several representatives of the Constance School, noting the intersection of critical interests in France with those investigations of reader reception: "Si cette promotion du lecteur et des questions qu'elle implique est, en France, de date relativement récente, c'est qu'il aura fallu l'effraction de la clôture structurale et l'émergence d'un nouveau paradigme théorique . . . pour rendre possible une revalorisation qu'interdisait par principe un modèle du texte fondé sur la dichotomie saussurienne langue/parole" (Lucien Dällenbach, "Actualité de la recherche allemande," *Poétique* 39 [Sept. 1979]: 258).

25. Lucien Dällenbach, "Le Tout en morceaux," *Poétique* 42 (April 1980); 158–59n., 156 (and passim).

26. Michael Riffaterre, "Intertextual Scrambling," *Romanic Review* 68, no. 3 (May 1977) pp. 197–205 (p. 197).

27. Umberto Eco, *The Role of the Reader* (Bloomington, Indiana: Indiana University Press, 1979), p. 4.

28. Ibid., p. viii.

29. In "Le Roman est-il chose femelle?" (*Poétique* 25 [Dec. 1976]: 85–98), Michael Danahy argues that the novel as a genre has traditionally been treated as a feminine entity by the reading public and by literary criticism. In relation to historical works, to the epic, to poetry, and to drama, Danahy claims, the novel has been considered a frivolous, recreational genre or a bastardized form (woman necessarily being held responsible for illegitimate births). He points to the use of biological, sexual terms in elaborating the nature of literary genres in the work of Goldmann, Lukács, and Ian Watt and calls for an analysis of the novel that is free from sexual stereotypes.

30. Jonathan Culler, *On Deconstruction: Theory and Criticism after Structuralism* (Ithaca, N.Y.: Cornell University Press, 1982), p. 79.

31. Claude Ollier in *Nouveau Roman: hier, aujourd'hui* I, (Paris: U.G.E., 1972), p. 149; my emphasis.

32. Sigmund Freud, "Anxiety and Instinctual Life," in *New Introductory Lectures*, trans. James Strachey (New York: Norton, 1965), p. 93. First published in 1933, this essay represents a revision of Freud's earlier stance on the derivative status of masochism in respect to sadism ("Instincts and their Vicissitudes," published in 1915). In *Beyond the Pleasure Principle* (1920), Freud had already begun to see masochism as a regression linked to the death instinct, a position that he clarified in "The Economic Problem of Masochism," published in 1924.

33. René Girard, *Mensonge romantique*, p. 188.

34. Freud, "Femininity," p. 102.

35. In *Présentation de Sacher-Masoch* (Paris: Editions de Minuit, 1967), Gilles Deleuze argues that sadism and masochism are separate, integral entities that have been erroneously linked as complementary drives. While the language of the sadist is a performative related to the solitude and omnipotence of its author, the language of the masochist aims at education: "Le contrat masochiste n'exprime pas seulement la nécessité du consentement de la victime, mais le don de persuasion, l'effort pédagogique et juridique par lequel la victime dresse son bourreau" (p. 67). The impossibility of assigning traditional categories of activity and passivity to O. and Tiamât mirrors the contradictions Deleuze points out at the basis of the sadomasochistic construct.

36. Sandor Ferenczi, *Thalassa, a Theory of Genitality* (Albany: Psychoanalytic Quarterly, 1938), p. 19.

37. McHale, *Postmodernist Fiction,* p. 141.

38. Barthes, *Le Plaisir du Texte,* p. 46.

CHAPTER 5

1. John Sturrock, *The French New Novel* (London: Oxford University Press, 1969), p. 15.

2. Barthes, *Le Plaisir du texte,* pp. 53–54.

3. In his "Réponses," *Tel Quel* 47 (Fall 1971), Barthes talks about his own intellectual development: "Saussure m'ayant permis de définir (du moins je le croyais) l'idéologie, par le schéma sémantique de la connotation, j'ai cru alors avec ardeur à la possibilité de m'intégrer à une *science* sémiologique; j'ai traversé un rêve (euphorique) de scientificité" (p. 97).

4. Sollers, "Ecriture et révolution," p. 70.

5. Julia Kristeva, "Comment parler à la littérature?" *Tel Quel* 47 (Fall 1971), p. 29.

6. Julia Kristeva, "La Sémiologie: science critique et/ou critique de la science," *Théorie d'ensemble,* p. 80.

7. Ibid., p. 86.

8. Julia Kristeva, *Sémiotiké* (Paris: Editions du Seuil, 1969), p. 17.

9. Jacques Lacan, "Yale University, Kanzar Seminar," *Scilicet: tu peux savoir ce qu'en pense l'Ecole Freudienne de Paris* 6–7 (1976): 26. While a full discussion of this subject is impossible in this limited context, it is interesting to note a similar valorization or mystification of the exact sciences in the work of thinkers as dissimilar as Freud, Althusser, Bachelard, Northrop Frye, and I. A. Richards, and in the general reception of Foucault's "archaeological" method as a science. While for some, science is the ideal complement or

remedy for literature, philosophy, or literary criticism, for others science represents a threat to the integrity of those domains. For each one, however, science constitutes the definite and definable "other" of linguistic discourse.

10. Barthes, *Le Degré zéro* p. 57.

11. Ricardou, *Le Nouveau Roman*, p. 47; my emphasis. As the principal theoretician of the New Novel, Ricardou has exercised considerable influence not only on criticism of the novel, but also on the production of New Novels, which themselves participate actively in a theoretical elaboration. The terminology and techniques of science play a significant role in Ricardou's rigorous formalism, which makes extensive use of graphs, charts, mathematical formulas, and "technicist" vocabulary.

12. *La Quinzine littéraire* (Jan. 16, 1976).

13. Miriam and José Arguëlles, *The Feminine* (Boulder, Col.: Shambhala, 1977), pp. 138–140.

14. An analogous conception is thought to have developed independently in the Mayan civilization of central America.

15. Jean-François Lyotard, *L'Economie libidinale* (Paris: Editions de Minuit, 1974).

16. "Claude Ollier: Ce qui m'a fait écrire," interview with Jean-Marie Le Sidaner, *Europe* (Oct. 1978): 187.

17. See Richard Lewontin, Steven Rose, Leon J. Kamin, *Not in Our Genes* (New York: Pantheon Books, 1984); Janet Sayers, *Biological Politics* (London and New York: Tavistock, 1982); Ruth Bleier, *Science and Gender* (New York: Pergamon Press, 1984); Stephen Jay Gould, *The Mismeasure of Man* (New York: Norton, 1981).

CONCLUSION

1. Galey, "Vingt ans après" pp. 26–27.

2. Claude Ollier, "Comment j'ai écrit *Our*," *La Quinzaine littéraire* 200 (Dec. 16–31, 1974): 7.

3. Le Sidaner, "Claude Ollier: Ce qui m'a fait écrire," p. 182.

4. Ollier, "Vingt ans après," p. 211.

5. Ricardou, *Pour une théorie*, p. 32.

6. Geoffrey Hartman, "The Aesthetics of Complicity," *Georgia Review* 28, no. 3 (Fall 1974): 384.

7. Walter Benjamin cited by Hannah Arendt in her introduction to *Illuminations* (New York: Harcourt Brace Jovanovich, 1968), p. 4.

8. Kristeva, *Sémiotiké,* p. 85.

9. Lukács, *Theory of the Novel*, p. 41.

10. Ibid., pp. 32, 43.

11. If the novel is, for Lukács, the degraded epic of the modern age, it also seems to point, in *The Theory of the Novel,* toward a possible return to epic status. David Carroll argues in "Representation of the End(s) of History: Dialectics and Fiction" (*Yale French Studies* 59 [1980]; 201–29) that despite the surface pessimism of Lukács's formulations of the novel, the typology of the novel with which *The Theory of the Novel* ends points toward a new unity and totality. And in *Blindness and Insight* (New York: Oxford University Press, 1971), Paul de Man argues that Lukács sees in the novel's use of temporality a "recuperated organicism" (p. 57).

12. In *Narcissistic Narrative: The Metafictional Paradox* (Waterloo, Ontario: Wilfrid Laurier University Press, 1980), Linda Hutcheon discusses "narcissism"—the will to self-scrutiny—as the major defining impulse of postmodern fiction.

13. O.'s recognition of the "style ancien" coincides with the return of narrative and storytelling (albeit in quite different ways from the classic realist novel) in contemporary French literature. To name only one example: Philippe Sollers, who wrote unclassifiable works like *H* and *Nombres* in the seventies has now turned his prolific energies to narrative, with his novels *Les Femmes* (1983), *Portrait du joueur* (1984), and *Le Coeur absolu* (1987).

14. Barthes, *Le Plaisir du texte,* p. 53.

Bibliography

WORKS BY CLAUDE OLLIER

Literature

Le Jeu d'enfant

1. *La Mise en scène.* Paris: Editions de Minuit, 1958; Flammarion-G.F. 1982. *The Mise-en-Scène,* translated by Dominic Di Bernardi. Elmwood Park, Ill.: Dalkey Archive Press, 1988.
2. *Le Maintien de l'ordre.* Paris: Gallimard, 1961; Flammarion-Textes, 1988. *Law and Order,* translated by Ursule Molinaro. New York: Red Dust, 1971.
3. *Eté indien.* Paris: Editions de Minuit, 1963; Flammarion-Textes, 1981.
4. *L'Echec de Nolan.* Paris: Gallimard, 1967; Flammarion-Textes, 1985.
5. *La Vie sur Epsilon.* Paris: Gallimard, 1972; Flammarion-Textes, 1984.
6. *Enigma.* Paris: Gallimard, 1973.
7. *Our ou vingt ans après.* Paris: Gallimard, 1974.
8. *Fuzzy Sets.* Paris: U.G.E. 10–18, 1975.

Navettes. Paris: Gallimard, 1967.
Marrakch medine. Paris: Flammarion-Textes, 1979.
Nébules. Paris: Flammarion-Textes, 1981.
Souvenirs écran. Paris: Cahiers du Cinéma-Gallimard, 1981.
Mon Double à Malacca. Paris: Flammarion-Textes, 1982.
Une Histoire illisible. Paris: Flammarion-Textes, 1986.
Déconnection. Paris: Flammarion-Textes, 1988. *Disconnection,* translated by Domic Di Bernardi. Elmwood Park, Ill.: Dalkey Archive Press, 1989.
Feuilleton. Paris: Julliard, forthcoming.
Trucage en Amont. Paris: Flammarion-Textes, forthcoming.

Cahiers d'écolier (1950–60). Paris: Flammarion-Textes, 1984.
Fables sous rêves (1960–70). Paris: Flammarion-Textes, 1985.
Les Liens d'espace (1970–80). Paris: Flammarion-Textes, 1989.

Lubéron. With etchings by Claude Garanjoud. Stuttgart: Manus Presse, 1968.
La Relève. In *Insolations 2,* with drawings by Matta. Montpellier, France: Fata Morgana, 1968; U.G.E. 10–18, 1976.

Réseau de blets rhizomes. With etchings by Bernard Dufour. Montpellier, France: Fata Morgana, 1969.

Bon entendeur. In *Agraphes, Première donne*, 1980.

Les Preuves écrites. With engravings by René Bonargent. Châteauroux, France: Indifférences, 1984.

L'Ailleurs le soir. With woodcuts by Catherine Marchadour. Paris: Colorature, 1987.

Mesures de nuit. With impressions by Claude Garanjoud. Crest, France: La Sétérée, 1988.

Radio

"La Mort du personnage." 1964.
"L'Attentat en direct." 1965.
"Régression." 1965.
"Cinématographe" (with Jean-André Fieschi). 1965.
"Le Dit de ceux qui parlent." 1969.
"Pèlerinage." 1969.
"La Fugue" (with Jean-André Fieschi). 1969.
"Les Dires des années 30." 1970.
"L'Oreille au mur." 1971.
"Les Ailes." 1971.
"Une Bosse dans la neige." 1971.
"La Recyclade." 1971.
"Our-Musique" (music by Christian Rosset). 1975.
"Réseau-Ollier-Navettes." 1975.
"Opérettes entre guillemets" (music by Christian Rosset). 1977.
"Loi d'écoute." 1979.
"Computation." 1979.
"Détour." 1980.

Cinema

L'accompagnement. Screenplay by Claude Ollier and Jean-André Fieschi and directed by Jean-André Fieschi. 1966.

Ecoute voir. . . . Screenplay by Claude Ollier and Hugo Santiago and directed by Hugo Santiago. 1978.

La Mise en scène. Screenplay by Claude Ollier and Hamid Bensaïd. 1982.

Selected Articles

"*L'Herbe*" (on Claude Simon). *La Nouvelle Revue Française* 73 (Jan. 1959): 736–38.

"*Le Fiston* et *Lettre morte*" (on Robert Pinget). *La Nouvelle Revue Française* 81 (Sept. 1959): 532–34.

"Lecture-écriture-lecture." *La Nouvelle Revue Française* 214 (Oct. 1970): 202–4.

"Les Inscriptions conflictuelles." *Pratiques* 10 (1971): 81–90.

"Les Pulsions motrices dans l'acte d'écriture." *Marche Romane* 21, nos. 1–2 (1971): 33–35.

"Pulsion," *L'Arc* no. 54 (1975), pp. 53–58.

"Vingt ans après." In *Nouveau Roman: hier, aujourd'hui* II, pp. 199–214. Paris: U.G.E. 10–18, 1972.

"Comment j'ai écrit *Our*." *La Quinzaine littéraire* 200 (Dec. 16–31, 1974): 7.

"Vrai groupe ou faux." *Le Narraté libérateur* 3 (June 1980): 4.

"Relecture." *Le Figaro* (Sept. 4, 1981).

Preface to *Chroniques de la citadelle d'exil*, by Abdellatif Laâbi. Paris: Denoël, 1983.

"French Version." Translated by Cecile Lindsay. *The Review of Contemporary Fiction* 8, no. 2 (Summer, 1988): 30–37.

INTERVIEWS WITH CLAUDE OLLIER

"Le Roman est en train de réfléchir sur lui-même." *Les Lettres françaises* (March 12–18, 1959); 1, 4–5.

"Réponse à une enquête." *Premier Plan* 18 (Oct. 1961): 26.

Interview by Henri Ronse. *Les Lettres françaises* (Jan. 22, 1967): 13.

"Autoportrait." *Le Magazine littéraire* (Nov. 1967): 36–37.

Interview in *Le Soleil*, Quebec (Sept. 27, 1969): 34.

"Aventures du récit," by Jean-André Fieschi. *La Nouvelle Critique* (March 1973): 62–68.

Interview by Alain Coulange. *Gramma* 5 (1976): 134–44.

Interview by Bettina Knapp. In *French Novelists Speak Out,* pp. 148–64. New York: Whitson, 1976.

"Interview with Claude Ollier," by Jean-Max Tixier. *Sub-stance* 13 (1976): 38–44.

Interview by Jean-Marie Le Sidaner. *Impasses* 8 (Dec. 1977): 5–7.

"Ce qui m'a fait écrire." *Europe* (Oct. 1978): 182–89.

"Claude Ollier, Marrakech, l'Islam," by Alain Clairval. *La Quinzaine littéraire* (Feb. 16–29, 1980): 7–8.

"Deux villes, une mémoire," by Jacques Henric. *Art Press* (April 1980): 28–29.

Interview by Alain Poirson. *Révolution* (Nov. 10, 1980).

"Claude Ollier solitaire," by Jean-Maurice de Montrémy. *La Croix* (June 1, 1981): 10.

"Des Pratiques nouvelles," by Alain Poirson. *Révolution* (Aug. 7, 1981): 17–21.

Interview by Charles Haroche. *L'Humanité* (Oct. 5, 1981): 15.

"Les Jeux de Claude Ollier," by Bernard Noël. *Le Magazine littéraire* (Dec. 1984): 96–101.

Interview by André Curmi. *Médianes* (April–May, 1985): 5–7.

Interview by Cecile Lindsay. *The Review of Contemporary Fiction* 8, no. 2 (Summer 1988): 14–29.

STUDIES OF OLLIER'S WORK

Aas-Rouxparis, Nicole. "L'Espace fictionnel dans *La Mise en scène*." University Microfilms Int. 1984.

———. "Une Plongée orphique dans l'inconscient: *La Mise en scène* de Claude Ollier," *Degré Second:* Studies in French Literature 11 (September 1987): 45–49.

Alphant, Marianne. "Les Cahiers d'Ollier." *Libération* (Nov. 8, 1984).

———. "Ollier, la nuit chez Claude." *Libération* (Jan. 13, 1986).

Alter, J. V. "*La Vie sur Epsilon.*" *French Review* 47, no. 2 (Dec. 1973): 501–2.

Axman, Ingrid. "*Cahiers d'écolier* and Ollier's Fiction." *The Review of Contemporary Fiction* 8, no. 2 (Summer 1988): 126–30.

Bergala, Alain. "L'écran du doute." *Cahiers du cinéma* (Feb. 1982).

Bianciotti, Hector. "Une Démarche exemplaire." *La Quinzaine littéraire* 185 (Oct. 1972): 5–6.

Billaud, Jean. "Les Informateurs dans *Enigma*." *Sub-stance* 13 (1976): 80–90.

———. "*Marrakch medine* ou la puissance de l'Islam." *Encres vives* 93 (1980): 18–19.

Boyer, Philippe. "*Navettes, L'Echec de Nolan.*" *Les Lettres nouvelles* (March–April, 1968): 163–66.

———. "Sur la piste du sens." *La Quinzaine littéraire* 200 (Dec. 16, 1974): 4.

———. "Topographies pour jeux de piste." Preface to *La Mise en scène*, pp. 9–38. Paris: Flammarion, 1982.

———. "Topographies." *The Review of Contemporary Fiction* 8, no. 2 (Summer 1988): 101–6.

Brisac, Geneviève. "Claude Ollier ou l'enfance du regard." *Le Monde* (Nov. 16, 1984).

Calí, Andrea. *Pratiques de lecture et d'écriture: Ollier, Robbe-Grillet, Simon.* Paris: Editions Nizet, 1980.

———. *Testo e intertesto nelle "prima spirale" di Claude Ollier.* Lecce: Adriatica Editrice, 1978.

Calí, Andrea and Anna Maggi. "Descrizione et metafora nella *La Vie sur Epsilon.*" *Lettore di Provincia* 31–32: 53–75.

Calin, Françoise. "D'Alain Robbe-Grillet à Claude Ollier: Mise en scène d'un intertexte." *Stanford French Review* 5, no. 3 (1981): 363–79.

———. "Du perçu à l'imaginaire: lecture de *La Mise en scène.*" *Symposium* 31, 1–16.

———. "Au bord de l'écriture: étude des 'figures d'auteur' dans deux Nouveaux Romans." *French Forum* 2 (May 1982): 173–85.

Camproux, Charles. "*La Mise en scène.*" *Les Lettres françaises* (March 12, 1959): 3.

Cartano, Tony. "Claude Ollier." In *Dictionnaire de littérature française,* edited by Claude Bonnefoy, Tony Cartano, Daniel Oster, pp. 240–42. Paris: Jean-Pierre Delarge, 1977.

Chamboz, Bernard. "Claude Ollier: *Marrakch medine.*" *La Nouvelle Revue Française* 330–31 (July–Aug. 1980): 203–5.

Champagne, Roland. "*Marrakch medine.*" *French Review* 54, no. 2 (Dec. 1980): 368.

Cronel, Hervé. "*Our ou Vingt ans après.*" *La Nouvelle Revue Française* (Dec. 1974): 101–3.

Foucault, Michel. "Le Langage de l'espace." *Critique* (April 1964): 180–81.

Genardière, Philippe de la. "The Lesson of the Incipits." *The Review of Contemporary Fiction* 8, no. 2 (Summer 1988): 119–21.

Goebel-Schilling, Gerhard. "The Theater of Claude Ollier." *The Review of Contemporary Fiction* 8, no. 2 (Summer 1988): 139–46.

Goimard, Jacques. "Claude Ollier contre Claude Ollier." *Le Monde* (July 26, 1973).

Guibert, Jean-Jacques. "Affoler la boussole." *Révolution* (Dec. 10, 1982).

Guissard, Lucien. "Claude Ollier, une voix seule." *La Croix* (Nov. 17, 1984).

Houppermans, Sjef. "Quelques rails." In *Ecriture de la religion, écriture du roman,* edited by Charles Grivel, pp. 195–210. Groningue, Lille: Presses Universitaires de Lille, 1979.

———. "The Figure in *Le Jeu d'enfant.*" *The Review of Contemporary Fiction* 8, no. 2 (Summer 1988): 93–100.

———, ed. *Recherches sur l'oeuvre de Claude Ollier.* Groningen: Institut de Langues Romanes, Rijksuniversiteit, 1985.

Isaac, Marie-Odette. "Encarts de style." *Le Magazine littéraire* (Nov. 1974): 37–38.

Jean, Raymond. "Claude Ollier à l'orient des signes." *Le Monde* (Sept. 27, 1974).

———. "Claude Ollier at Times Square." *Sub-stance* 13 (1976): 52–56.

Jelloun, Tahar Ben. "*Marrakch medine: ce qui, dans la mémoire, 'dépose' d'une ville.*" *Actualités littéraires* 23 (Nov.–Dec. 1979): 5.

———. "*Marrakch medine.*" *Actualités littéraires* 21 (Sept. 1979): 5.

Khatibi, Abdelkebir. "*Marrakch medine.*" *Libération,* Casablanca (Jan. 18, 1980).

———. "Traces of a Trauma: on *Marrakch medine.*" *The Review of Contemporary Fiction* 8, no. 2 (Summer 1988): 107–13.

Knee, Robin. "*Le Jeu d'enfant:* An Intertextual Reading." *DAI* 44, no. 3 (Sept. 1983): 766A.

———. "Microstructural Intertextuality: Solving Claude Ollier's *Engima.*" *The Review of Contemporary Fiction* 8, no. 2 (Summer 1988): 73–79.

Laâbi, Abdellatif. "Claude Ollier and the Death of the Orient in *Marrakch medine.*" *The Review of Contemporary Fiction* 8, no. 2 (Summer 1988): 114–18.

Le Sidaner, Jean-Marie. "Claude Ollier voyageur au noir." *Le Magazine littéraire* (March 1980): 46–47.

———. "Le Mythe colonial dans *La Mise en scène.*" *Sub-stance* 13 (1976): 75–79.

Lindsay, Cecile. "Reflexivity and Revolution in the Novels of Claude Ollier." *DAI* 41, no. 10 (April 1981): 4414A.

———. "Textual Intercourse: Reader Theory and the New Novel." *Structuralist Review* 2, no. 3 (1984): 99–115.

———. "The Topography of (Science) Fiction: Claude Ollier's *Life on Epsilon.*" *Science-Fiction Studies* 2, pt. 1 (March 1984): 39–44.

———. "Le Degré zéro de la fiction: la science du Nouveau Roman." *Romanic Review* 74, no. 2 (March 1983): 221–32.

———. "Claude Ollier Today: An Introduction." *The Review of Contemporary Fiction* 8, no. 2 (Summer 1988): 7–10.

———. "Child's Play: *Le Jeu d'enfant* and Beyond." *The Review of Contemporary Fiction* 8, no. 2 (Summer 1988): 51–56.

Lorris, Robert. "*Enigma.*" *French Review* 48, no. 6 (May 1975): 1069–70.

Lovichi, Jacques. "Ollier in Wonderland." *Sub-stance* 13 (1976): 68–74.

Mauriac, Claude. "Claude Ollier et la littérature-fiction." *Le Figaro littéraire,* no. 1377–III (Oct. 1972): 45.

Meddeb, Abdelwahab. "Dans le quotidien d'une ville d'Islam." *Critique* (June, 1980): 661–64.

———. "An Unreadable Story (Une Histoire illisible): in the Name of the

Third Person." *The Review of Contemporary Fiction* 8, no. 2 (Summer 1988): 122–25.

Mellerski, Nancy. "Le Premier cycle de l'oeuvre de Claude Ollier." *DAI* 42, no. 3 (Sept. 1981): 1174A.

Montel, Jean-Claude. "*Enigma:* Or the Double Simulacrum." *The Review of Contemporary Fiction* 8, no. 2 (Summer 1988): 80–84.

Montrémy, Jean-Maurice de. "Sur la planète Ollier." *La Croix* (Nov. 23, 1985).

Noguez, Dominique. "*L'Echec de Nolan, Navettes.*" *La Nouvelle Revue Française* (Jan. 1968): 139–42.

Nuridsany, Michel. "Pleins feux sur Claude Ollier." *Le Figaro* (Nov. 5, 1982).

Otten, Anna. "*Nébules*" and "*Souvenirs écran.*" *World Literature Today* (Spring 1982): 304–5.

———. "*Mon Double à Malacca.*" *World Literature Today* (Fall 1983): 608.

———. "Claude Ollier's Heterogeneous Linguistic Topography of Polymorphic Experience." *The Review of Contemporary Fiction* 8, no. 2 (Summer 1988): 131–38.

Paire, Alain. "*Marrakch medine.*" *Esprit* IV, 2, no. 38 (Feb. 1980): 167–68.

Perros, Georges. "Claude Ollier: *La Mise en scène.*" In *Lectures: comptes rendus et articles critiques,* pp. 84–87. Cognac: Le Temps qu'il fait, 1981.

Poirot-Delpech, Bertrand. "Comme une ville sans pain: rééditions de Claude Ollier." Review of *La Vie sur Epsilon* and *Nébules. Le Monde* weekly 1703 (June 18–24, 1981): 12.

Ricardou, Jean. "Une description trahie." In *Problèmes du Nouveau Roman,* pp. 112–21. Paris: Editions du Seuil, 1967.

———. "*L'Echec de Nolan, Navettes.*" *La Quinzaine littéraire* 40 (Nov. 1967): 14.

———. "Le Prisme d'Epsilon." *Degrés.* (April 1973): 14.

———. "L'Enigme dérivée." In *Pour une théorie du nouveau roman,* pp. 159–99. Paris: Editions du Seuil, 1971.

Roche, Denis. "Pour saluer Claude Ollier." *Actualités littéraires* 32 (May 1981): 8–9.

Rosset, Christian. "'Our Music,' Ten Years After." *The Review of Contemporary Fiction* 8, no. 2 (Summer 1988): 85–92.

Roudiez, Léon. "Claude Ollier: *Law and Order.*" *Saturday Review* 54, no. 34 (Aug. 1971).

———. "Le Jeu du texte et du récit chez Claude Ollier." In *Nouveau Roman: hier, aujourd'hui* II, pp. 177–98. Paris: U.G.E. 10–18, 1972.

———. "Lecture ou peut-être minage d'*Enigma.*" *Sub-stance* 13 (1976): 56–67.

———. "Concealed Production in Ollier's First Novel." *The Review of Contemporary Fiction* 8, no. 2 (Summer 1988): 57–72.

Simon, Claude. "Le Retour du facteur humain: un nouvel épisode de l'oeuvre de Claude Ollier," *Pensée* 285 (1987): 77–88.

Steisel, Marie-Georgette. "Ollier ou l'Orient/Orient or Ollier." *Revue CEL-FAN Review* 2(1) (1982): 25–28.

Thibaudeau, Jean. "Avant-garde et science-fiction." *L'Humanité* (Nov. 21, 1975).

Times Literary Supplement. "Shuttle Service." Review of *L'Echec de Nolan* and *Navettes* (March 7, 1968): 233.

Times Literary Supplement. "Prismatic Perambulations." Review of *La Vie sur Epsilon* (March 19, 1972): 1387.

Times Literary Supplement. "Riddle of the Sands." Review of *Our ou Vingt ans après* (Oct. 11, 1974): 1138.

Tixier, Jean-Max. "The Fictional Development in *Le Maintien de l'ordre*." *Sub-stance* 13 (1976): 45–51.

——. "Un Avatar du Nouveau Roman." *Horizons du fantastique* 26: 8–9.

Villelaur, Anne. "Le Jeu de la diagonale." *La Quinzaine littéraire* (July 1–15, 1975): 8–9.

WORKS OF RELATED INTEREST

Carroll, David. *The Subject in Question: The Languages of Theory and the Strategies of Fiction.* Chicago and London: Univeristy of Chicago Press, 1982.

Faris, Wendy B. *Labyrinths of Language: Symbolic Landscape and Narrative Design in Modern Fiction.* Baltimore: Johns Hopkins University Press, 1988.

Gould, Karen. *Claude Simon's Mythic Muse.* Columbia, S.C.: French Literature Publication Co., 1979.

Henkels, Robert M. *Robert Pinget: The Novel as Quest.* Tuscaloosa: University of Alabama Press, 1979.

Hutcheon, Linda. *Narcissistic Narratives, the Metafictional Paradox.* Waterloo, Ont.: Wilfrid Laurier University Press, 1980.

——. *A Poetics of Postmodernism: History, Theory, Fiction.* New York: Routledge, 1988.

Jefferson, Ann. *The Nouveau Roman and the Poetics of Fiction.* Cambridge and New York: Cambridge University Press, 1988.

Lydon, Mary. *Perpetuum Mobile, a Study of the Novels and Aesthetics of Michel Butor.* Edmonton: University of Alberta Press, 1980.

McHale, Brian. *Postmodernist Fiction.* New York and London: Methuen, 1987.

Nash, Christopher. *World-Games: The Tradition of Anti-Realist Revolt.* New York and London: Methuen, 1987.

Newsom, Robert. *A Likely Story: Probability and Play in Fiction.* New Brunswick: Rutgers University Press, 1988.

Sherzer, Dina. *Representation in Contemporary French Fiction.* Lincoln: University of Nebraska Press, 1986.

Stoltzfus, Ben. *Alain Robbe-Grillet: The Body of the Text.* Rutherford, N.J.: Fairleigh Dickinson University Press, 1985.

Stonehill, Brian. *The Self-Conscious Novel: Artifice in Fiction from Joyce to Pynchon.* Philadelphia: University of Pennsylvania Press, 1988.

Waugh, Patricia. *Metafiction: The Theory and Practice of Self-Conscious Fiction.* New York and London: Methuen, 1984.

Index

Abrams, M. H., 188n. 1
Albères, R.-M., 197n. 17
Althusser, Louis, 199n. 9
Arguëlles, José, 200n. 13
Arguëlles, Miriam, 200n. 13

Bachelard, Gaston, 199n. 9
Barth, John, 129
Barthes, Roland, 95–96, 97–98, 101, 103, 107–8, 132, 152, 155–56, 158, 159, 176, 185, 192n. 9, 193nn. 13, 20, 21, 22, 194n. 23, 195n. 26, 196n. 4, 197n. 13, 199nn. 2, 38, 200n. 10, 201n. 14
Bataille, Georges, 4
Beckett, Samuel, 11
Benjamin, Walter, 129, 179, 196n. 7, 200n. 7
Benveniste, Emile, 156
Bioy Casares, Adolpho, 189n. 13
Blanchot, Maurice, 62, 68, 95, 97, 189nn. 5, 11, 12, 15, 192n. 8, 193n. 12
Bleier, Ruth, 200n. 17
Borges, Jorge, 6, 95, 96–97, 100, 126, 192n. 7, 193n. 12
Boyer, Philippe, 189n. 14
Breton, André, 129
Brooks, Cleanth, 196n. 5
Buñuel, Luís, 19
Butor, Michel, 9, 10, 11, 16, 159

Calvino, Italo, 8–9, 129, 187n. 6
Carroll, David, 13, 187n. 11, 201n. 11
Cervantes, Miguel de, 6
Cirlot, J. E., 191n. 11, 192n. 22
Cixous, Hélène, 191n. 10
Clouard, Henri, 192n. 3
Coward, Rosalind, 194n. 25
Culler, Jonathan, 139, 198n. 30

Dallenbach, Lucien, 136–37, 198nn. 24, 25
Danahy, Michael, 198n. 29
Dante Alighieri, 116, 195n. 36
De Boisdeffre, Pierre, 11, 187n. 8, 197n. 17
Delany, Samuel, 15
Deleuze, Gilles, 13, 91, 97–98, 192n. 2, 199n. 35
De Man, 129, 197n. 12, 201n. 11
Derrida, Jacques, 3, 13, 15, 61, 62, 83, 96, 97–98, 106, 161, 190n. 9, 191n. 17, 193nn. 11, 15, 194n. 25, 195n. 28
Dhorme, Edouard, 195n. 27
Dumas, Alexandre, 91, 92–93, 94, 95, 123
Duras, Marguerite, 11, 12–13

Eco, Umberto, 137, 198n. 27
Einstein, Albert, 171
Ellis, John, 194n. 25

Faulkner, William, 14
Faye, Jean-Pierre, 17
Ferenczi, Sandor, 150, 199n. 36
Fish, Stanley, 125, 196n. 1
Flaubert, Gustave, 6, 107, 114, 195n. 34
Fletcher, Angus, 63, 130, 189n. 1, 197n. 9
Foucault, Michel, 13, 20, 61, 96, 187n. 14, 193n. 10, 199n. 9
Fourier, François, 129
Freud, Sigmund, 1, 4, 7–8, 24, 65, 69, 75, 79, 86, 90, 100, 118, 127, 143, 144, 150, 187n. 5, 189n. 6, 191nn. 12, 15, 193n. 18, 196n. 39, 198n. 32, 199nn. 9, 34
Frye, Northrop, 64, 130, 189n. 2, 197n. 11, 199n. 9

Galey, Matthieu, 187n. 9, 200n. 1
Genette, Gérard, 156
Girard, René, 111, 143, 145, 195n. 31,
    198n. 33
Godard, Jean-Luc, 19
Gödel, Kurt, 171
Goethe, Johann Wolfgang von, 129
Goldmann, Lucien, 198n. 29
Gould, Stephen Jay, 200n. 17
Grass, Günter, 129
Greer, Thomas N., 193n. 19
Guattari, Félix, 91, 192n. 2

Hamburger, Michael, 192n. 5
Hartman, Geoffrey, 135, 175, 200n. 6
Hegel, Georg Wilhelm Freidrich, 26, 60,
    150, 188nn. 2, 6
Heisenberg, Werner, 171
Higgins, Lynn, 13, 187n. 11
Hitchcock, Alfred, 19
Horney, Karen, 190n. 7
Hutcheon, Linda, 201n. 12

Ingarten, Roman, 136
Irigaray, Luce, 191nn. 10, 18
Iser, Wolfgang, 136, 137, 197n. 23

Jabès, Edmond, 16–17
Jakobson, Roman, 156
James, Henry, 94, 96, 116, 192n. 4, 193n.
    12
Jardine, Alice, 190n. 9
Jenny, Laurent, 196n. 2
Joyce, James, 97

Kafka, Franz, 14
Kamin, Leon J., 200n. 17
Kosinski, Jerzy, 129
Kramer, Samuel Noah, 195n. 33
Kristeva, Julia, 156–57, 158, 159, 193n. 18,
    199nn. 5, 6, 7, 8, 200n. 8

Lacan, Jacques, 13, 15, 61, 86, 90, 91,
    158, 192n. 1, 194n. 24, 199n. 9
Lang, Fritz, 19
Lautréamont, Comte de (Isidore Du-
    casse), 6, 97, 116–17, 195n. 36, 196n. 37
Lederer, Wolfgang, 190n. 7, 191n. 13

Lesser, Simon, 134, 197n. 18
Lessing, G. E., 60, 188n. 6
Lévi-Strauss, Claude, 194n. 25
Lewontin, Richard, 200n. 17
Lindsay, Cecile, 187n. 12
Lukács, Georg, 22, 26–27, 35, 160, 180,
    188nn. 2, 8, 198n. 29, 200n. 9, 201n.
    11
Lyotard, Jean-François, 163–64, 165,
    200n. 15

McHale, Brian, 129, 152, 197n. 8, 199n.
    37
Mallarmé, Stéphane, 95
Mauriac, Claude, 197n. 17
Mercier, Vivian, 189n. 9
Merleau-Ponty, Maurice, 132
Moor, George, 97

Nietzsche, Friedrich, 1, 2, 7, 8, 78, 187n.
    4, 191n. 14
Noël, Bernard, 18
Novalis, 95

Ollier, Claude, 6, 9–10, 14, 15, 98–99,
    110, 116, 130, 140–41, 159, 169–70,
    173–74, 175, 187nn. 1, 2, 3, 188n. 4,
    190n. 9, 193nn. 14, 15, 16, 17, 195nn.
    29, 30, 35, 196n. 40, 197nn. 10, 20,
    198n. 31, 200nn. 2, 3, 4, 16; *Cahiers
    d'écolier*, 19; *Déconnection*, 18;
    l'Echec de Nolan, 14, 54–60, 62, 77,
    111; *Enigma*, 14, 63, 64, 73–82, 86, 88,
    89, 90, 91, 93, 112, 114, 115, 119, 127,
    159; *Eté indien*, 14, 44–54, 56–57,
    58–59, 80, 111, 116; *Fables sous rêve*,
    19; *Fuzzy Sets*, 4, 14, 124–31, 132,
    134–35, 136, 138–43, 159, 161, 167–69;
    Une Histoire illisible, 18; *Le Jeu
    d'enfant*, 4, 5–9, 13–17, 18, 19, 20–22,
    23, 24, 25, 27–28, 59, 61, 64–65, 68, 91,
    119, 124–25, 129–30, 140, 170–71,
    174–77, 181–85; *Les Liens d'espace*, 19;
    Le Maintien de l'ordre, 4, 14, 35–44,
    45, 47, 55; *Marrakch medine*, 17–18; *La
    Mise en scène*, 4, 9, 14, 28–35, 36, 41,
    42, 43, 44, 77–78, 106, 111, 126, 127,
    135, 149, 158; *Mon Double à Malacca*,

1, 5, 7, 18; *Navettes*, 16, 19, 174–81;
Nébules, 19; *Our ou Vingt ans après*,
14, 85, 87, 88–123, 127, 135, 138, 159,
173; *Souvenirs écran*, 19; *La Vie sur
Epsilon*, 14, 63, 64, 73, 86, 90, 99, 111,
114, 115, 119, 133, 159

Pinget, Robert, 9, 11, 13
Plato, 83–84, 141, 192n. 20, 195n. 28
Poulet, Georges, 67–68, 132, 134, 189n.
4, 197nn. 14, 19
Proust, Marcel, 95
Pynchon, Thomas, 129

Quilligan, Maureen, 129, 196n. 6

Réage, Pauline, 142
Ricardou, Jean, 9, 10, 13, 96, 133, 134,
158–59, 162, 175, 189nn. 3, 10, 13,
193n. 11, 197nn. 16, 21, 200nn. 5, 11
Richards, I. A., 199n. 9
Riffaterre, Michael, 137, 197n. 15, 198n.
26
Rimbaud, Arthur, 97
Robbe-Grillet, Alain, 7, 9, 11–12, 13, 14,
15, 16, 25, 43, 50, 59, 129, 159, 173,
187n. 4, 188n. 5
Roche, Denis, 18
Rose, Steven, 200n. 17
Roudiez, Léon, 132, 197n. 13
Roussel, Raymond, 11, 20

Saïd, Edward, 17
Sarraute, Nathalie, 9, 10
Sartre, Jean-Paul, 14
Saussure, Ferdinand de, 156, 194n. 25,
199n. 3
Sayers, Janet, 200n. 17
Schor, Naomi, 97–98, 193n. 13
Shelley, Percy Bysshe, 95, 192n. 6
Sherzer, Dina, 13, 187n. 11
Simon, Claude, 9, 10, 12, 16, 162
Sollers, Philippe, 134, 156, 193n. 18,
197n. 22, 199n. 4, 201n. 13
Spivak, Gayatri, 190n. 9
Sturrock, John, 154, 199n. 1
Suleiman, Susan, 187n. 13

Tans, J. A. G., 133
Todorov, Tzvetan, 156
Toliver, Harold, 196n. 3

Valéry, Paul, 95
Verne, Jules, 6
Villiers de l'Isle-Adam, Philippe
Auguste, 6
Von Buelow, Christiane, 196n. 7

Warren, R. P., 196n. 5
Watt, Ian, 133, 197n. 18, 198n. 29
Waugh, Patricia, 10, 187n. 7
Wittig, Monique, 162

Zola, Emile, 155

COLINVAUX'S
LAW
OF
INSURANCE

COLINVAUX'S
LAW
OF
INSURANCE

NINTH EDITION

ROBERT MERKIN

Professor of Commercial Law, University of Southampton
Consultant, Norton Rose Group

CONTRIBUTING EDITOR
JUDITH P. SUMMER
PhD. Solicitor (Non-practising)

SWEET & MAXWELL   THOMSON REUTERS

First Edition	1950
Second Edition	1961
Third Edition	1970
Fourth Edition	1979
Fifth Edition	1984
Sixth Edition	1990
Seventh Edition	1997
Eighth Edition	2006
Ninth Edition	2010

Published in 2010 by
Thomson Reuters (Legal) Limited
(Registered in England & Wales, Company No 1679046.
Registered Office and address for service:
100 Avenue Road, London, NW3 3PF)
Trading as Sweet & Maxwell
Typeset by Interactive Sciences Ltd, Gloucester
Printed and bound in the UK by CPI Antony Rowe, Wiltshire, SL14 6LH

For further information on our products and services, visit
www.sweetandmaxwell.co.uk

No natural forests were destroyed to make this product;
only farmed timber was used and replanted.

A CIP catalogue record for this book is available from the British Library.

ISBN 978-0-414-04233-9

Crown copyright material is reproduced with the permission of the Controller of
HMSO and the Queen's Printer for Scotland.

PREFACE

Colinvaux's Law of Insurance began life as *The Law of Insurance: Fire, Life, Accident and Guarantee* by William Porter, Henry Darrach and William Feilden Craies, first published in 1889 and consisting of an analysis of "Cases in the English, Scotch, Irish, American and Canadian courts." After eight editions, the last being published in 1933, the work was in 1948 revived and substantially expanded by Sidney Preston, who had recently retired from the insurance industry. Sadly, Mr Preston died before the book was published, and practising barrister Raoul Colinvaux, later to take over the editorship of *Carver's Carriage of Goods by Sea*, completed the manuscript. This was published in 1949 as a new work, *The Law of Insurance* by Preston and Colinvaux. The work appeared in future editions under Colinvaux's name, and was adapted and expanded to take account of the ever-increasing volume of decided cases and also the abolition of the workers' compensation scheme which had featured in the earlier editions. The final edition prepared by Raoul Colinvaux himself was the fifth, in 1984. The present author "inherited" the work for its sixth edition in 1990. Since that date, the number of decided cases just in England has grown incredibly, with much reinsurance litigation finding its way out of arbitration and into the courts, and this is so despite the virtual elimination of judicial decisions in consumer cases following the creation and expansion of the Ombudsman Scheme since 1981. The present edition is 300 pages longer than the last, and is a far cry from the author's first encounter with Colinvaux's *Law of Insurance*, the relatively slender third edition, as a student some 35 years ago. Most of the early "Scotch, Irish, American and Canadian" cases have disappeared over the years, although a smattering have been retained, cited on points on which there is no authority in England. A small number of leading cases from Hong Kong, Singapore, New Zealand and Australia have been added to the present edition. Citation of Australian authority is sparse, mainly because the Insurance Contracts Act 1984 (Cth) has marked a significant departure from common law authority on virtually all points.*

In the preface to the eighth edition it was predicted that the ninth edition would look very different, in the light of the review of insurance law undertaken by the English and Scottish Law Commissions in a five-year project starting at the beginning of 2006. The wisdom of Groucho Marx's dictum that it is unwise to make predictions, especially about the future,** has once again been proved. The Law Commissions have in that time produced a draft Bill on consumer insurance and eight issues papers, each of which is available on the Law Commissions' website and is a model of clarity and scholarship, but as yet there is little indication that any of their recommendations will find their way into law. However, somewhat unexpectedly, the Law Commissions' proposals for the reform of the Third Parties (Rights against Insurers) Act 1930 were, after eight years of dormancy, rushed through Parliament in just over three months and, at a date yet to be announced, the Third Parties (Rights against Insurers) Act 2010 will take effect. All of these matters are referred to at the appropriate points in the ninth edition.

The text is up to date as of the middle of July 2010. At the time of writing three major cases are awaiting resolution. First, the appeal to the Court of Appeal in *Durham v BAI (Run-Off)* [2009] Lloyd's Rep. I.R. 295, which will determine whether employers' liability policies written in the 1960s and 1970s respond to claims for exposure to asbestos, as was decided at first instance. The appeal was heard in November 2009, but as of July 2010 no judgment had been handed down. Whatever the outcome, the matter is unlikely to rest there. Secondly, in the last week of July 2010 the Supreme Court heard the appeal from the decision of the Court of Appeal in *Global Process Systems v Berhad* [2010] Lloyd's Rep. I.R. 221. This is one of the most significant cases on marine insurance for many decades, and potentially the Supreme Court could rewrite the law on causation, perils of the seas and inherent vice. Thirdly, the Court of Appeal is due to hear the appeal in *Masefield v Amlin* [2010] Lloyd's Rep. I.R. 345, the question being whether David Steel J. was right to hold that seizure of cargo by pirates does not constitute either an actual total loss or a constructive total loss by reason of the fact that the payment of a ransom and the release of the cargo are both all but inevitable.

In preparing this edition, my thanks are due to Dr Judith P. Summer, who wrote Chapter 12 on the role of the Financial Services Ombudsman, and Dr Ozlem Gurses, who read the manuscript and made a series of suggestions for change. As ever responsibility for errors and omissions is non-delegable. I am also grateful to Melanie and Lisa from the publishers, who respectively commissioned and saw the work through to publication.

Rob Merkin, July 2010.

* Prompting Michael Gill, who was elected President of the International Association of Insurance Law (AIDA) in May 2010, to comment that Australia has both the most unusual wildlife in the world and also the most unusual laws.
** Groucho's contributions to insurance law are much overlooked. In *A Night at the Opera*, his sales pitch for an accident policy that he was trying to sell to a hapless porter, was: "If you lose a leg, we'll help you look for it."

CONTENTS

	Page
Preface	v
Table of Cases	xiii
Table of Statutes	cxxxvii
Table of Statutory Instruments	cxlix
Table of Civil Procedure Rules	cliv
Table of European Legislation	clv
Table of Conventions and Treaties	clviii

PART I:
THE CONTRACT OF INSURANCE

	Para.
1. THE CONTRACT OF INSURANCE	
1. The Definition of Insurance	1–001
2. Formal Requirements for Insurance Contracts	1–012
3. Formation of Insurance Contracts	1–021
4. London Market Procedures	1–032
5. Renewal of Insurance Contracts	1–046
6. Temporary Cover	1–050
2. CONFLICT OF LAWS	
1. Jurisdiction of the English Courts	2–001
2. Determining the Law Applicable to Insurance Contracts	2–016
3. Significance of the Applicable Law	2–049
4. Non-Contractual Claims	2–061
3. CONSTRUCTION OF THE POLICY	
1. Principles of Construction	3–001
2. The Intentions of the Parties	3–004
3. Rules for Construing Words and Phrases	3–006
4. Custom	3–013
5. Incorporation	3–014
6. Judicial Control of Policy Terms	3–018
4. INSURABLE INTEREST	
1. The Significance of Insurable Interest	4–001
2. The Principle of Indemnity	4–004
3. Effect of Gambling Legislation	4–007
4. The Present Regulatory Structure	4–010
5. The Meaning of Insurable Interest	4–013
6. Insurance Effected by an Agent	4–019
7. Reform of the Law on Insurable Interest	4–025
5. THE RISK	
1. Commencement and Duration of Risk	5–001

  2. Increase of Risk 5–016
  3. Proximate Cause 5–029
  4. Illegality and Misconduct 5–035

6. UTMOST GOOD FAITH
  1. Non-Disclosure and Misrepresentation 6–001
  2. Materiality and Inducement 6–021
  3. Utmost Good Faith and Agency 6–035
  4. Material Facts 6–045
  5. Facts Which Need Not be Disclosed 6–063
  6. Remedies for Breach of Duty 6–075
  7. Duration of the Duty of Utmost Good Faith 6–101
  8. The Insurer's Duty of Utmost Good Faith 6–122
  9. Reform of the Law of Utmost Good Faith 6–132

7. TERMS OF INSURANCE CONTRACTS
  1. Terminology 7–001
  2. Insurance Conditions 7–002
  3. Insurance Warranties 7–020

8. THE PREMIUM
  1. Payment of the Premium 8–001
  2. The Amount of the Premium 8–008
  3. Renewal Premiums and Days of Grace 8–009
  4. Consequences of Non-Payment 8–011
  5. Return of Premium 8–019

9. CLAIMS
  1. Claims Conditions 9–001
  2. Co-operation and Proof of Loss 9–015
  3. Fraudulent Claims 9–020
  4. Limitation of Actions 9–037
  5. Claims Against Insurers by Third Parties 9–043
  6. Declaratory Relief 9–053

10. INDEMNITY
  1. Measure of Indemnity 10–001
  2. Limits on Recovery 10–029
  3. Reinstatement 10–040
  4. Settlements 10–053

11. THE RIGHTS OF INSURERS
  1. Subrogation 11–001
  2. Double Insurance and Contribution 11–044
  3. Abandonment and Salvage 11–066

12. STATUTORY CONTROL OF POLICIES
  1. The Financial Ombudsman Service 12–001
  2. Operation of the Ombudsman Scheme 12–014

PART II:
THE PARTIES

13. THE REGULATION OF INSURERS
1. Regulatory Structure 13–001
2. Insurance Business Regulated in the United Kingdom 13–007
3. The Single EEA Insurance Market 13–022
4. Conduct of Insurance Business in the United Kingdom 13–026
5. Transfers of Insurance Business 13–032
6. Lloyd's 13–038
7. Friendly Societies and Industrial Assurance 13–043
8. Competition Rules Affecting Insurers 13–044

14. THE ASSURED
1. Contractual Capacity 14–001
2. Co-Insurance 14–003
3. Unnamed Co-Assureds 14–019
4. Assignment 14–022

15. INSURANCE INTERMEDIARIES
1. General Agency Principles 15–001
2. Agents of Insurers 15–013
3. Underwriting Agents 15–020
4. Brokers 15–026

16. THE INSOLVENCY OF INSURANCE COMPANIES
1. Insolvency Proceedings Involving Insurers 16–001
2. The Protection of Policyholders 16–016

PART III:
SPECIAL TYPES OF INSURANCE CONTRACT

17. REINSURANCE
1. Definition of Reinsurance 17–001
2. Formation of Reinsurance Contracts 17–005
3. Terms of Reinsurance Contracts 17–011
4. Reinsurance Losses and Claims 17–016

18. LIFE AND ACCIDENT INSURANCE
1. Nature of Life and Accident Policies 18–001
2. Insurable Interest 18–004
3. Assignment of Life Policies 18–022
4. Utmost Good Faith 18–025
5. Coverage of Life Policies 18–032
6. Coverage of Personal Accident Policies 18–040

19. PROPERTY INSURANCE
1. Insurable Interest In Property 19–001
2. Utmost Good Faith 19–033
3. Coverage 19–034

20. LIABILITY INSURANCE
1. Principles Governing Liability Policies 20–001
2. Insurable Interest in Liability Insurance 20–062
3. Employer's Liability Insurance 20–063
4. Product Liability Policies 20–074
5. Directors' and Officers' Liability Insurance 20–078

21. THIRD PARTY RIGHTS UNDER LIABILITY POLICIES
1. Background 21–001
2. Third Parties (Rights Against Insurers) Act 1930 21–004
3. Third Parties (Rights Against Insurers) Act 2010 21–041

22. MOTOR VEHICLE INSURANCE
1. Compulsory Motor Insurance 22–001
2. Actions for the Proceeds of Compulsory Motor Policies 22–038
3. Uninsured and Untraced Drivers: The Motor Insurers Bureau .. 22–057
4. Compulsory Insurance: The International Dimension 22–080
5. Non-Compulsory Cover Under Motor Policies 22–086

23. FINANCIAL INSURANCE
1. Mortgagees' Interest Insurance 23–001
2. Legal Expenses Insurance 23–007
3. Guarantee Insurance 23–018
4. Fidelity Insurance 23–021
5. Insurance of Debts 23–029
6. After the Event Insurance 23–034
7. Business Interruption Insurance 23–042

24. MARINE INSURANCE
1. The Coverage of Marine Policies 24–001
2. Text of the Marine Insurance Act 1906 24–008
3. Insurable Interest 24–012
4. Insurable Value 24–033
5. Disclosure and Representations 24–034
6. The Policy 24–044
7. Double Insurance 24–054
8. Warranties, Etc 24–055
9. The Voyage 24–065
10. Assignment of Policy 24–074
11. The Premium 24–076
12. Loss and Abandonment 24–080
13. Partial Losses 24–098
14. Measure of Indemnity 24–101
15. Rights of Insurer on Payment 24–113
16. Return of Premium 24–116
17. Mutual Insurance 24–119
18. Supplemental 24–120
19. Form of Policy 24–127
20. Rules for Construction of Policy 24–128

25. WAR RISKS
1. The Insurability of War and Related Risks 25–001
2. Specific War Risks 25–003

Page
Index 1201

TABLE OF CASES

21st Century Logistic Solutions Ltd (In Liquidation) v Madysen Ltd [2004] EWHC 231; [2004] 2 Lloyd's Rep. 92; [2004] S.T.C. 1535; [2004] B.T.C. 5720; [2004] B.V.C. 779; [2004] S.T.I. 497; (2004) 101(12) L.S.G. 35; Times, February 27, 2004 QBD 5–037, 5–045

566935 BC Ltd (t/a West Coast Resorts) v Allianz Insurance Co of Canada [2006] B.C.C.A. 469 24–134

889457 Alberta Inc v Katanga Mining Ltd [2008] EWHC 2679 (Comm); [2009] 1 B.C.L.C. 189; [2009] I.L.Pr. 14 2–001

1013799 Ontario Ltd v Kent Line International Ltd (2000) 22 C.C.L.I. (3d) 312 (Ont SC) 15–034

A Cohen & Co Ltd v Plaistow Transport Ltd [1968] 2 Lloyd's Rep. 587 QBD 5–012

A Gagniere & Co Ltd v Eastern Co of Warehouses Insurance & Transport of Goods with Advances Ltd (1921) 8 Ll.L.R. 365 CA 1–018

AA Mutual Insurance Co Ltd v Bradstock Blunt & Crawley [1996] L.R.L.R. 161; Lloyd's List, November 22, 1995 (I.D.) QBD 15–001

AA Mutual International Insurance Co Ltd, Re [2004] EWHC 2430; [2005] 2 B.C.L.C. 8 Ch D (Companies Ct) 13–018, 16–013

AB Exportkredit v New Hampshire Insurance Unreported, 1988 .... 11–010, 23–030

AB v South West Water Services Ltd; Gibbons v South West Water Services Ltd [1993] Q.B. 507; [1993] 2 W.L.R. 507; [1993] 1 All E.R. 609; [1993] Env. L.R. 266; [1993] P.I.Q.R. P167; (1993) 143 N.L.J. 235; [1992] N.P.C. 146; Times, November 26, 1992; Independent, November 18, 1992 CA (Civ Div) 20–015

ABCI (formerly Arab Business Consortium International Finance & Investment Co) v Banque Franco-Tunisienne (Costs); sub nom. ABCI v BFT (Costs) [2003] EWCA Civ. 205; [2003] 2 Lloyd's Rep. 146 CA (Civ Div) 2–004

AC Harper & Co Ltd v Mackechnie & Co [1925] 2 K.B. 423; (1925) 22 Ll.L.R. 514 KBD 24–037, 24–037

AC Ward & Sons Ltd v Catlin (Five) Ltd [2009] EWCA Civ 1098 .... 7–037, 19–048

AC Ward & Sons Ltd v Catlin (Five) Ltd (No.2) [2009] EWHC 3122 (Comm) 5–050, 6–031, 6–106, 7–032, 7–034, 7–037, 19–048

Ace Capital Ltd v CMS Energy Corp [2008] EWHC 1843 (Comm); [2008] 2 C.L.C. 318; [2009] Lloyd's Rep. I.R. 414 2–006

ACE Insurance SA-NV (formerly Cigna Insurance Co of Europe SA NV) v Zurich Insurance Co [2001] EWCA Civ. 173; [2001] 1 All E.R. (Comm) 802; [2001] 1 Lloyd's Rep. 618; [2001] C.L.C. 526; [2001] I.L.Pr. 41; [2001] Lloyd's Rep. I.R. 504; (2001) 98(8) L.S.G. 46; Times, February 27, 2001 CA (Civ Div) 2–005, 17–014

AIG Europe (Ireland) Ltd v Faraday Capital Ltd [2006] EWHC 2707 (Comm); [2007] 1 All E.R. (Comm) 527; [2006] 2 C.L.C. 770; [2007] Lloyd's Rep. I.R. 267; reversed [2007] EWCA Civ 1208; [2008] 2 All E.R. (Comm) 362; [2007] 2 C.L.C. 844; [2008] Lloyd's Rep. I.R. 454 .... 3–005, 3–010, 7–016, 9–005, 9–008, 9–011, 20–089

AIG Europe (UK) Ltd v Ethniki; sub nom. AIG Europe (UK) Ltd v Anonymous Greek Co of General Insurances; Anonymous Greek Co of General Insurances v AIG Europe (UK) Ltd [2000] 2 All E.R. 566; [2000] 1 All E.R. (Comm) 65; [2000] C.L.C. 446; [2000] I.L.Pr. 426; [2000] Lloyd's Rep. I.R. 343 CA (Civ Div) 2–008, 2–029, 2–031, 2–043, 17–012, 17–014

AIG Europe (Ireland) Ltd v Faraday Capital Ltd [2007] EWCA Civ 1208; [2008] 2 All E.R. (Comm) 362; [2007] 2 C.L.C. 844; [2008] Lloyd's Rep. I.R. 454 17–025

AIG Europe SA v QBE International Insurance Ltd [2001] 2 All E.R. (Comm) 622; [2001] 2 Lloyd's Rep. 268; [2001] C.L.C. 1259; [2002] Lloyd's Rep. I.R. 22; Times, June 22, 2001 QBD (Comm) 2–008, 2–036, 17–012

AS Screenprinting Ltd v British Reserve Insurance Co Ltd [1996] C.L.C. 1470; [1999] Lloyd's Rep. I.R. 430 CA (Civ Div) 20–074, 20–075

A/S Tankexpress v Compagnie Financiere Belge des Petroles SA [1949] A.C. 76; [1948] 2 All E.R. 939; (1948–49) 82 Ll. L. Rep. 43; [1949] L.J.R. 170; (1949) 93 S.J. 26 HL 8–002

AW&E Palmer v Cornhill Insurance Co Ltd (1935) 52 Ll.L.R. 78 KBD 22–036, 22–100

AWB (Geneva) SA v North America Steamships Ltd [2007] EWCA Civ 739; [2007] 2 Lloyd's Rep. 315; [2007] 2 C.L.C. 117; [2007] B.P.I.R. 1023; (2007) 104(31) L.S.G. 27 2–006

AXA Re v Ace Global Markets Ltd [2006] EWHC 216; [2006] Lloyd's Rep. I.R. 683 QBD
    (Comm) 3–015, 17–012
AXA Equity & Law Life Assurance Society Plc (No.1), Re; AXA Sun Life Plc (No.1), Re
    [2001] 2 B.C.L.C. 447; (2001) 98(1) L.S.G. 23; Times, December 19, 2000 Ch D 13–033,
                                                                                            13–035
AXA Insurance UK Plc v Norwich Union Insurance Ltd [2007] EWHC 1046 (Comm);
    [2008] Lloyd's Rep. I.R. 122 .... 22–018, 22–036
AXA Reinsurance (UK) Ltd v Field [1996] 1 W.L.R. 1026; [1996] 3 All E.R. 517; [1996] 2
    Lloyd's Rep. 233; [1996] C.L.C. 1169; [1996] 5 Re. L.R. 184; (1996) 93(33) L.S.G. 24;
    (1996) 146 N.L.J. 1093; (1996) 140 S.J.L.B. 155; Times, July 2, 1996 HL 10–034, 10–034,
                                                                                            17–014
Abbey National Plc v Solicitors Indemnity Fund Ltd [1997] P.N.L.R. 306 QBD 23–023
Abel v Potts (1800) 3 Esp. 242 9–010
Abidin Daver, The. See Owners of the Las Mercedes v Owners of the Abidin Daver
Abrahams v Agricultural Mutual (1876) 40 U.C.Q.B. 175, 182 19–047
Abrahams v Mediterranean Insurance and Reinsurance Co [1991] 1 Lloyd's Rep. 216 CA
    (Civ Div) 1–033, 3–010, 15–035, 17–006
Absalom v TCRU Ltd (formerly Monument Insurance Brokers Ltd) [2005] EWCA Civ.
    1586; [2006] 1 All E.R. (Comm) 375; [2006] 1 C.L.C. 648 CA (Civ Div) 3–005, 3–012,
                                                                                            8–001, 15–033
Ace Insurance SA-NV v Seechurn. See Seechurn v Ace Insurance SA NV
Acey v Fernie (1840) 7 M. & W. 153 .... 7–048, 15–001, 15–013, 15–014, 15–015
Ackbar v CF Green & Co Ltd [1975] Q.B. 582; [1975] 2 W.L.R. 773; [1975] 2 All E.R. 65;
    [1975] 1 Lloyd's Rep. 673; 119 S.J. 219 QBD 15–034
Ackland v Lutley (1839) 9 Ad. & El. 879 5–004
Ackman and Scher v Policyholders Protection Board. See Scher v Policyholders Protection
    Board
Acme Wood Flooring Co v Marten (1904) 20 T.L.R. 229; (1904) 9 Com. Cas. 157 10–029
Adamastos Shipping Co Ltd v Anglo Saxon Petroleum Co Ltd; sub nom. Anglo Saxon
    Petroleum Co Ltd v Adamastos Shipping Co Ltd [1959] A.C. 133; [1958] 2 W.L.R. 688;
    [1958] 1 All E.R. 725; [1958] 1 Lloyd's Rep. 73; 102 S.J. 290 HL 3–011
Adams v Andrews [1964] 2 Lloyd's Rep. 347 QBD 22–073
Adams v Commissioner of Police of the Metropolis [1980] R.T.R. 289 DC 22–007
Adams v Dunne [1978] R.T.R. 281; [1978] Crim. L.R. 365 DC 22–011
Adams v Lindsell (1818) 1 B. & Ald. 681 6–0104
Adcock v Cooperative Insurance Society Ltd [2000] Lloyd's Rep. I.R. 657; Times, April 26,
    2000 CA (Civ Div) 10–026, 10–027
Addison v Brown [1954] 1 W.L.R. 779; [1954] 2 All E.R. 213; (1954) 98 S.J. 338 2–057
Adelaide Steamship Co Ltd v R. See Attorney General v Adelaide Steamship Co Ltd
Adelaide Steamship Co Ltd v R. (The Warilda) (1923) 14 Ll.L.R. 41 .... 25–004, 25–005
Adie & Sons v Insurances Corp (1898) 14 T.L.R. 544 .... 1–022, 1–025
Admiralty Commissioners v Brynawel SS Co Ltd (1923–24) 17 Ll.L.R. 89 KBD 25–005
Advance (NSW) Insurance Agencies Ply Ltd v Matthews (1989) 166 C.L.R. 606 14–012
Advent Capital Plc v GN Ellinas Imports-Exports Ltd [2005] EWHC 1242; [2006] 1 All E.R.
    (Comm) 81; [2005] 2 Lloyd's Rep. 607; [2005] 1 C.L.C. 1058; [2005] I.L.Pr. 57 QBD
    (Comm) 2–006
Aegis Electrical and Gas International Services Co Ltd v Continental Casualty Co [2007]
    EWHC 1762 (Comm); [2008] Lloyd's Rep. I.R. 17 ..... 3–005, 3–008, 17–014, 17–020, 17–021,
                                                                                            19–041, 20–058
Aeolian Shipping SA v ISS Machinery Services Ltd (The Aeolian); sub nom. ISS Machinery
    Services Ltd v Aeolian Shipping SA (The Aeolian) [2001] EWCA Civ. 1162; [2001] 2
    Lloyd's Rep. 641; [2001] C.L.C. 1708 CA (Civ Div) 2–033, 2–043
Aerospace Publishing Ltd v Thames Water Utilities Ltd [2005] EWHC 2987 QBD 10–015
Aetna Life v France, 94 U.S. 561 (1876) 18–029
Aetna Reinsurance Co (UK) Ltd v Central Reinsurance Corp Ltd [1996] L.R.L.R. 165;
    Lloyd's List, March 21, 1996 (I.D.) QBD 17–026
Afia Worldwide Insurance Co v Deutsche Ruck Versicherungs AG (1983) 133 N.L.J. 621 2–004,
                                                                                            2–040
Agapitos v Agnew (The Aegeon) (No.1) [2002] EWCA Civ. 247; [2003] Q.B. 556; [2002]
    3 W.L.R. 616; [2002] 1 All E.R. (Comm) 714; [2002] 2 Lloyd's Rep. 42; [2002] C.L.C.
    886; [2002] Lloyd's Rep. I.R. 573; (2002) 99(16) L.S.G. 38; (2002) 146 S.J.L.B. 66 CA
    (Civ Div); affirming [2002] Lloyd's Rep. I.R. 191 QBD (Comm) 6–110, 9–021, 9–024,
                                                                                 9–028, 9–029, 9–030, 9–031, 9–032, 9–033

Agapitos v Agnew (The Aegeon) (No.2); sub nom. Agapitos v Laiki Bank (Hellas) SA
[2002] EWHC 1558; [2003] Lloyd's Rep. I.R. 54 QBD (Comm) 7–032, 7–036, 7–045
Agheampong v Allied Manufacturing (London) Ltd [2009] Lloyd's Rep. I.R. 379 County
Court (London) 5–046, 22–026
Agip SpA v Navigazione Alta Italia SpA (The Nai Genova and The Nai Superba), Nai
Genova, The [1984] 1 Lloyd's Rep. 353 CA 1–018, 1–019
Agnew v Lansforsakringsbolagens AB [2001] 1 A.C. 223; [2000] 2 W.L.R. 497; [2000] 1 All
E.R. 737; [2000] 1 All E.R. (Comm) 321; [2000] C.L.C. 848; [2001] I.L.Pr. 25; [2000]
Lloyd's Rep. I.R. 317; (2000) 97(9) L.S.G. 39; (2000) 144 S.J.L.B. 109; Times,
February 23, 2000 HL 2–005, 2–008, 2–009, 13–017, 17–004
Agnew v Robertson, 1956 S.L.T. (Sh. Ct.) 90; (1956) 72 Sh. Ct. Rep. 255, Sh Ct
(Grampian) 22–096
Agra Foundations Ltd v Commonwealth Insurance Co (2001) 214 Sask. R. 255 20–047
Agra Trading Ltd v McAuslin; The Frio Chile [1995] 1 Lloyd's Rep. 182; Lloyd's List,
November 25, 1994 QBD (Comm) 10–003
Agresso Corp v Temple Insurance Co [2007] B.C.J. No.21 20–050
Aguilar v London Life Insurance Co, 70 D.L.R. (4th) 510 (1990) 18–046, 18–047
Aiden Shipping Co Ltd v Interbulk Ltd (The Vimeira) (No.2) [1986] A.C. 965; [1986] 2
W.L.R. 1051; [1986] 2 All E.R. 409; [1986] 2 Lloyd's Rep. 117; (1986) 130 S.J. 429
HL 20–055
Aiken v Harris (1999) 45 O.R. (3d) 266 20–049
Aiken v Stewart Wrightson Members Agency Ltd [1996] 2 Lloyd's Rep. 577; [1997] 6 Re.
L.R. 79CA (Civ Div); affirming [1995] 1 W.L.R. 1281; [1995] 3 All E.R. 449; [1995]
2 Lloyd's Rep. 618; [1995] C.L.C. 318; Times, March 8, 1995 QBD (Comm) 6–004, 6–073,
13–041, 15–030, 15–059, 17–007
Ainikolas I, The Lloyd's List, April 5, 1996 6–123
Aitchison v Lohre; sub nom. Lohre v Aitchison; Brandt v Lohre (1878–79) L.R. 4 App. Cas.
755 HL 24–112
Aitken v Financial Services Compensation Scheme Ltd 2003 S.L.T. 878; 2003 G.W.D.
19–591; Times, June 28, 2003 OH 16–024
Ajum Goolam Hossen & Co v Union Marine Insurance Co Ltd; Hajee Cassim Joosub v Ajum
Goolam Hossen & Co [1901] A.C. 362 PC (Mau) 7–038, 24–061
Akai Pty Ltd v People's Insurance Co Ltd [1998] 1 Lloyd's Rep. 90; [1997] C.L.C. 1508;
[1999] I.L.Pr. 24 QBD (Comm) 2–003, 2–005, 2–006
Akers v Motor Insurers Bureau [2003] EWCA Civ. 18; [2003] Lloyd's Rep. I.R. 427 CA (Civ
Div) 22–068
Aktor, The. See PT Berlian Laju Tanker TBK v Nuse Shipping Ltd (The Aktor), Aktor,
The
Al-Koronky v Time Life Entertainment Group Ltd [2006] EWCA Civ 1123; [2006] C.P. Rep.
47; [2007] 1 Costs L.R. 57; Times, August 28, 2006 23–042
Alba Life Ltd, Re [2006] EWHC 3507 (Ch) 13–035
Albeko Schuhmaschinen AG v Kamborian Shoe Machine Co (1961) 111 L.J. 519 2–051
Albert Life, Re (1871) L.R. 14 Eq. 72n 8–001
Albany Life Assurance Co v De Montfort Insurance Co Plc Unreported, 1995 .... 5–041, 9–016,
23–020
Albert v Motor Insurers Bureau [1972] A.C. 301; [1971] 3 W.L.R. 291; [1971] 2 All E.R.
1345; [1971] 2 Lloyd's Rep. 229; [1972] R.T.R. 230; 115 S.J. 588 HL 22–031, 22–097
Albion Fie v Mills (1828) 3 Wills. & S. 218 15–009
Albion Insurance Co Ltd v Body Corporate Strata Plan No.4303 [1983] 2 V.R. 339 5–049
Albion Insurance Co Ltd v Government Insurance Office of New South Wales (1969) 121
C.L.R. 342 11–044
Albion Mills Co v Hill (1922) 12 Ll.L.R. 96 OR 9–015, 9–025
Albon (t/a NA Carriage Co) v Naza Motor Trading Sdn Bhd [2007] EWHC 9 (Ch); [2007]
1 W.L.R. 2489; [2007] 2 All E.R. 719; [2007] 1 All E.R. (Comm) 795; [2007] 1 Lloyd's
Rep. 297; [2007] Bus. L.R. D87 2–004
Alchorne v Favill (1825) L.J.Ch. (O.S.) 47 .... 10–044, 10–052
Alcoa Minerals of Jamaica Inc v Broderick [2002] 1 A.C. 371; [2000] 3 W.L.R. 23; [2000]
B.L.R. 279; (2000) 2 T.C.L.R. 850; [2000] Env. L.R. 734; (2000) 144 S.J.L.B. 182;
Times, March 22, 2000 PC (Jamaica) 10–022
Alder v Moore [1961] 2 Q.B. 57; [1961] 2 W.L.R. 426; [1961] 1 All E.R. 1; [1960] 2 Lloyd's
Rep. 325; 105 S.J. 280 CA 3–010, 18–058
Aldrich v Norwich Union Life Insurance Co Ltd [1998] C.L.C. 1621; [1999] Lloyd's Rep.
I.R. 276 Ch D 13–026

Aldridge Estates Investments Co Ltd v McCarthy [1996] E.G.C.S. 167; Times, December 11,
    1996 QBD 6–029
Alexander Forbes Europe Ltd (formerly Nelson Hurst UK Ltd) v SBJ Ltd [2002] EWHC
    3121; [2003] Lloyd's Rep. I.R. 432; [2003] Lloyd's Rep. P.N. 137; [2003] P.N.L.R. 15
    QBD (Comm) 9–003, 9–010, 15–041, 15–055, 15–059, 20–042
Alexion Hope, The. *See* Schiffshypothekenbank Zu Luebeck AG v Norman Philip Comp-
    ton
Alfred James Dunbar v A&B Painters Ltd and Economic Insurance Co Ltd and Whitehouse
    & Co [1986] 2 Lloyd's Rep. 38 CA (Civ Div) 15–037, 15–056
Alfred McAlpine Plc v BAI (Run-Off) Ltd [2000] 1 All E.R. (Comm) 545; [2000] 1 Lloyd's
    Rep. 437; [2000] C.L.C. 812; (2001) 3 T.C.L.R. 5; 69 Con. L.R. 87; [2000] Lloyd's Rep.
    I.R. 352CA (Civ Div); affirming [1998] 2 Lloyd's Rep. 694; [1998] C.L.C. 1145; (1999)
    1 T.C.L.R. 92; 66 Con. L.R. 57 QBD (Comm) 6–107, 6–109, 6–114, 7–006, 7–007, 7–009,
                                                           7–015, 9–003, 9–004, 9–008, 9–024, 9–043, 21–023
Algemeene Bankvereeniging v Langton; sub nom. Algemeene Bankvereeniging v World
    Auxiliary Insurance Corp Ltd (1935) 51 Ll.L.R. 275; (1935) 40 Com.Cas. 247 CA 3–008,
                                                                                        15–04
Algoma Steel Corporation v Allendale Mutual Insurance Co, 68 D.L.R. (4th) 404 (1990) 19–034
Ali Reza-Delta Transport Co Ltd v United Arab Shipping Co SAG [2003] EWCA Civ. 684;
    [2003] 2 All E.R. (Comm) 269; [2003] 2 Lloyd's Rep. 450; Times, May 27, 2003 CA
    (Civ Div) 10–015
Alie v Bertrand & Frere Construction Co [2002] O.J. No.4697 20–049
Allagar Rubber Estates Ltd v National Benefit Assurance Co Ltd (1922) 12 Ll.L.R. 110 CA;
    affirming (1922) 10 Ll.L.R. 564 KBD 24–009, 24–066
Allden v Raven; The Kylie [1983] 2 Lloyd's Rep. 444 QBD 6–048
Allen v John [1955] 1 Lloyd's Rep. 27 DC 22–088
Allen v London Guarantee and Accident Co Ltd (1912) 28 T.L.R. 254 ... 10–033, 10–034, 20–047
Allen v Rescous Unreported, 1676 4–002
Allen v Robles [1969] 1 W.L.R. 1193; [1969] 3 All E.R. 154; [1969] 2 Lloyd's Rep. 61;
    (1969) 113 S.J. 484 CA (Civ Div) 7–019, 7–048, 9–003
Allen v Universal Automobile Insurance Co Ltd (1933) 45 Ll.L.R. 55 KBD 7–028, 7–038, 10–007
Allen Billposring v Drysdale [1939] 4 All E.R. 113 .... 5–041, 19–038
Allgemeine Versicherungs Gesellschaft Helvetia v Administrator of German Property [1931]
    1 K.B. 672; (1930) 38 Ll.L.R. 247; (1931) 144 L.T. 705 CA 24–096
Alliance Aeroplane Co Ltd v Union Insurance Society of Canton Ltd (1920) 5 Ll.L.R. 406
    KBD 1–019, 1–033
Allianz Insurance Co Egypt v Aigaion Insurance Co SA [2008] EWHC 1127 (Comm);
    [2008] 2 Lloyd's Rep. 595; [2008] 2 C.L.C. 211; [2009] Lloyd's Rep. I.R. 69 .... 1–024, 17–012,
                                                                                        24–078
Allianz Insurance Co Egypt v Aigaion Insurance Co SA, Ocean Dirk, The (No.2) [2008]
    EWCA Civ 1455; [2009] 2 All E.R. (Comm) 745; [2008] 2 C.L.C. 1013; [2009] Lloyd's
    Rep. I.R. 533; Times, January 20, 2009 .... 1–025, 1–034
Allianz Marine Aviation (France) v GE Frankona Reinsurance Ltd (The Treasure Bay) [2005]
    EWHC 101; [2005] Lloyd's Rep. I.R. 437 QBD (Comm) 3–005, 3–007, 3–009, 17–014
Allianz SpA (formerly Riunione Adriatica di Sicurta SpA) v West Tankers Inc (C–185/07)
    Front Comor, The (C–185/07) ; West Tankers Inc v Allianz SpA (formerly Riunione
    Adriatica di Sicurta SpA) (C–185/07) [2009] 1 A.C. 1138; [2009] 3 W.L.R. 696; [2009]
    All E.R. (EC) 491; [2009] 1 All E.R. (Comm) 435; [2009] 1 Lloyd's Rep. 413; [2009]
    E.C.R. I–663; [2009] 1 C.L.C. 96; [2009] C.E.C. 619; [2009] I.L.Pr. 20; 2009 A.M.C.
    2847; Times, February 13, 2009 ECJ 11–011
Allianz SpA (formerly Riunione Adriatica di Sicurta SpA) v West Tankers Inc (C–185/07)
    Front Comor, The (C–185/07) [2008] 2 Lloyd's Rep. 661; [2009] E.C.R. I–663 2–008,
                                                                                        11–011
Allianz Via Assurance v Marchant Unreported, 1997 .... 6–008, 17–001, 17–007
Allied Dunbar Assurance Plc, Re [2005] EWHC 28; [2005] 2 B.C.L.C. 220 Ch D
    (Companies Ct) 13–033, 13–035
Allison v Bristol Marine Insurance Co Ltd; sub nom. Allison v Bristol Marine Insurance Co
    (1875–76) L.R. 1 App. Cas. 209 HL 24–026, 24–031
Allis-Chalmers Co v Maryland Fidelity & Deposit (1916) 114 L.T. 433; (1916) 32 T.L.R.
    263 .... 1–022, 5–015, 6–0104, 23–021, 23–027
Allkins v Jupe (1875) L.R. 2 C.P.D. 375 18–009
Allobrogia Steamship Corp, Re [1978] 3 All E.R. 423; [1979] 1 Lloyd's Rep. 190 Ch D
    (Companies Ct) 21–006, 24–007
Alofs v Temple Insurance Co [2005] O.J. No.4372 20–083

Alluvials Mining Machinery Co v Stowe (1922) 10 Ll.L.R. 96 KBD 24–039
Alston v Campbell (1779) 4 Bro. P.C. 476 .... 19–025, 24–029
Aluminium Wire and Cable Co Ltd v Allstate Insurance Co Ltd [1985] 2 Lloyd's Rep. 280
    QBD 5–048, 5–049, 21–027
Amalgamated Investment & Property Co Ltd (In Liquidation) v Texas Commerce Inter-
    national Bank Ltd [1982] Q.B. 84; [1981] 3 W.L.R. 565; [1981] 3 All E.R. 577; [1982]
    1 Lloyd's Rep. 27; [1981] Com. L.R. 236; 125 S.J. 623 CA (Civ Div) 6–098
Ambatielos v Anton Jurgens Margarine Works [1923] A.C. 175; (1922) 13 Ll.L.R. 357HL 3–017
Ambler v Graves-Togo (1930) 36 Ll. L. Rep. 145 19–007
American Airlines Inc v Hope; sub nom. Banque Sabbag SAL v Hope [1974] 2 Lloyd's Rep.
    301 HL 1–033, 1–034
American Assurance Co v Temple Insurance Co 94 O.R. (3d) 534 (2007) 20–050
American Casualty Co v Rahn 854 F. Supp. 494 (WD Mich, 1994) 20–047
American Centennial Insurance Co v Insco Ltd [1996] L.R.L.R. 407; [1997] 6 Re. L.R. 138
    QBD (Comm) 10–034, 10–036
American Express Services Europe Ltd v Tuvyahu Unreported, 2000 CA (Civ Div) 8–002
American International Marine Agency of New York Inc v Dandridge [2005] EWHC 829;
    [2005] 2 All E.R. (Comm) 496; [2005] 1 C.L.C. 1102; [2005] Lloyd's Rep. I.R. 643
    QBD (Comm) 1–040, 5–017, 7–048, 17–012
American International Specialty Lines Insurance Co v Abbott Laboratories [2002] EWHC
    2714; [2003] 1 Lloyd's Rep. 267; [2004] Lloyd's Rep. I.R. 815 QBD (Comm) 2–006, 3–015,
                                                                                                17–012
American Motorists Insurance Co (AMICO) v Cellstar Corp [2002] EWHC 421 (Comm);
    [2002] 2 Lloyd's Rep. 216; [2002] C.L.C. 925 .... 2–022, 2–043
American Motorists Insurance Co (AMICO) v Cellstar Corp [2003] EWCA Civ 206; [2003]
    2 C.L.C. 599; [2003] I.L.Pr. 22; [2003] Lloyd's Rep. I.R. 295; (2003) 100(18) L.S.G. 35;
    Times, April 1, 2003 CA (Civ Div) 2–007, 2–022, 2–030, 2–036, 2–048
American Surety Co v Wrightson (1910) 27 T.L.R. 91; (1910) 103 L.T. 663; (1910) 16 Com.
    Cas. 37 .... 11–052, 11–056, 11–063, 23–023
American Tobacco Co v Guardian Assurance Co; Societe Anonyme Des Tabacs D'orient et
    D'outre Mer v Alliance Assurance Co (1925) 22 Ll.L.R. 37 CA 5–031, 25–003
Amey Properties Ltd v Cornhill Insurance Plc [1996] L.R.L.R. 259; [1996] C.L.C. 401;
    Independent, December 18, 1995 (C.S.); Lloyd's List, March 19, 1996 (I.D.) QBD
    (Comm) 5–051, 22–036, 22–093
Amicable Insurance Society v Bolland (1830) 4 Bligh (N.S.) 194 .... 5–045, 18–035
Amin Rasheed Shipping Corp v Kuwait Insurance Co; The Al Wahab [1984] A.C. 50; [1983]
    3 W.L.R. 241; [1983] 2 All E.R. 884; [1983] 2 Lloyd's Rep. 365; (1983) 127 S.J. 492
    HL 2–005, 2–032, 2–033, 2–040, 2–049, 24–127
Anbest Electronic Ltd v CGU International Insurance Plc [2008] H.K.E.C. 562 24–066
Anchor Assurance, Re (1870) L.R. 5 Ch. 632 1–048
Anctil v Manufacturers Life Insurance Co [1899] A.C. 604 PC (Can) 4–011, 18–015, 18–038
Anders & Kern UK Ltd (t/a Anders & Kern Presentation Systems) v CGU Insurance Plc (t/a
    Norwich Union Insurance) [2007] EWHC 377 (Comm); [2007] 2 All E.R. (Comm)
    1160; [2007] Lloyd's Rep. I.R. 555; affirmed on other grounds [2007] EWCA Civ 1481;
    [2008] 2 All E.R. (Comm) 1185; [2008] Lloyd's Rep. I.R. 460 .... 1–022, 19–046
Andersen v Marten [1908] A.C. 334 HL 5–015
Anderson v Commercial Union Assurance Co (1885) 55 L.J.Q.B. 146 .... 10–040, 10–047, 19–033
Anderson v Edie (1795) 2 Park 14 18–020
Anderson v Equitable Assurance Society of the United States [1926] All E.R. Rep 93 2–030
Anderson v Fitzgerald (1853) 4 H.L Cas. 484 ..... 6–016, 6–031, 6–075, 7–022, 7–029, 7–030, 8–022,
                                                                                                8–025
HLAnderson v Morice (1876) L.R. 1 App. Cas. 713; affirming (1874–75) L.R. 10 C.P. 609
    Ex Chamber 4–005, 4–009, 4–014, 4–016, 4–017, 19–007, 20–062, 24–020
Anderson v Norwich Union Fire Insurance Society [1977] 1 Lloyd's Rep. 253 CA (Civ
    Div) 19–035
Anderson v Pacific Fire & Marine Insurance Co (1871–72) L.R. 7 C.P. 65 CCP 6–013, 6–014
Anderson v Pitcher (1800) 2 Bos. & Pul. 164 7–022
Anderson v Thornton (1853) 8 Exch. 425 .... 8–025, 24–039
Andreas Lemos, The. See Athens Maritime Enterprises Corp v Hellenic Mutual War Risks
    Association (Bermuda)
Andree v Fletcher (1789) 3 T.R. 266 .... 8–022, 18–009
Andrews v HE Kershaw Ltd [1952] 1 K.B. 70; [1951] 2 All E.R. 764; [1951] 2 T.L.R. 867;
    115 J.P. 568; 49 L.G.R. 827; 95 S.J. 698 KBD 22–009
Andrews v Herne (1662) 1 Lev. 33 4–002

Andrews v Patriotic Assurance (No.2) (1886) 18 L.R.Ir. 355 .... 10–017, 11–014, 11–054, 19–017, 19–022
Aneco Reinsurance Underwriting Ltd (In Liquidation) v Johnson & Higgins Ltd; sub nom.
    Aneco Reinsurance Underwriting Ltd v Johnson & Higgs Ltd [2001] UKHL 51; [2001]
    2 All E.R. (Comm) 929; [2002] 1 Lloyd's Rep. 157; [2002] C.L.C. 181; [2002] Lloyd's
    Rep. I.R. 91; [2002] P.N.L.R. 8 HL; affirming [2000] 1 All E.R. (Comm) 129; [1999]
    C.L.C. 1918; [2000] Lloyd's Rep. I.R. 12; [2000] Lloyd's Rep. P.N. 1; [2000] P.N.L.R.
    152 CA (Civ Div); affirming in part [1998] 1 Lloyd's Rep. 565; Times, November 14,
    1997 QBD (Comm) .. 6–043, 6–054, 6–116, 15–028, 15–036, 15–045, 15–047, 17–001, 17–007
Angel v Merchants' Marine Insurance Co [1903] 1 K.B. 811 CA 24–086
Anghelatos v Northern Assurance Co Ltd (The Olympia); London Joint City & Midland
    Bank v Northern Assurance Co Ltd (1924) 19 Ll.L.R. 255 HL 9–025
Anglo African Merchants Ltd v Bayley; Exmouth Clothing Co Ltd v Bayley [1970] 1 Q.B.
    311; [1969] 2 W.L.R. 686; [1969] 2 All E.R. 421; [1969] 1 Lloyd's Rep. 268; 113 S.J.
    281 QBD (Comm) 3–013, 6–005, 6–073, 15–041, 15–043
Anglo-Californian Bank v London and Provincial Marine and General Insurance Co Ltd
    (1904) 20 T.L.R. 665; (1904) 10 Com. Cas. 1 .... 7–024, 10–029, 23–021, 23–030
Anglo-International Bank Ltd v General Accident Fire & Life Assurance Corp Ltd (1934) 48
    Ll.L.R. 151 HL 3–007, 3–011
Annear & Co v Attenborough. See JC Annear & Co Ltd v Attenborough
Annen v Woodman (1810) 3 Taunt. 299 .... 8–021, 8–027, 24–061, 24–062
Ansari v New India Assurance Ltd [2008] EWHC 243 (Ch); [2008] Lloyd's Rep. I.R. 586 ...... 5–050, 19–034
Ansari v New India Assurance Ltd [2009] EWCA Civ 93; [2009] 2 All E.R. (Comm) 926;
    [2009] Lloyd's Rep. I.R. 562 .... 5–019, 5–026, 5–027, 7–032, 19–048
Ansoleaga y Cia v Indemnity Mutual Marine Insurance Co Ltd (1922) 13 Ll.L.R. 231 CA 9–025
Anstey v British National Premium Life Association Ltd (1908) 24 T.L.R. 871; (1908) 99
    L.T. 765 .... 6–083, 18–038
Antec International Ltd v Biosafety USA Inc [2006] EWHC 47 (Comm) 2–005
Anton Durbeck GmbH v Den Norske Bank ASA [2002] EWHC 1173 (Comm) 2–064
Appel v Aetna Life, 86 App. Div. Rep. S.C.N.Y. 83 (1903) 18–042
Appleby v Myers; sub nom. Appleby v Meyers (1866–67) L.R. 2 C.P. 651 Ex Chamber ... 10–047
Appledore Ferguson Shipbuilders Ltd v Stone Vickers Ltd. See Stone Vickers Ltd v
    Appledore Ferguson Shipbuilders Ltd
Arab Bank Plc v John D Wood (Commercial) Ltd; Arab Bank Plc v Browne [2000] 1 W.L.R.
    857; [2000] Lloyd's Rep. I.R. 471; [2000] Lloyd's Rep. P.N. 173; [1999] E.G.C.S. 133;
    (1999) 96(47) L.S.G. 30; (2000) 144 S.J.L.B. 6; [1999] N.P.C. 134; Times, November
    25, 1999 CA (Civ Div) 11–001, 11–002, 23–020
Arab Bank Plc v Zurich Insurance Co; Banque Bruxelles Lambert SA v Zurich Insurance Co
    [1999] 1 Lloyd's Rep. 262; [1998] C.L.C. 1351 QBD (Comm) 6–038, 6–039, 6–043, 7–033,
        7–039, 7–041, 14–003, 14–012, 14–014, 15–004, 15–023, 20–081
Arab Monetary Fund v Hashim (No.9) [1993] 1 Lloyd's Rep. 543 2–056
Arbitration between Barr-Brown and N.I.M.U. Insurance Company, Re [1942] N.Z.L.R.
    444 6–018
Arbory Group Ltd v West Craven Insurance Services [2007] Lloyd's Rep. I.R. 491; [2007]
    P.N.L.R. 23 .... 15–034, 15–036, 15–047, 15–051, 15–056
Arbuthnot Pensions & Investments Ltd v Padden. See Padden v Arbuthnot Pensions &
    Investments Ltd
Arbuthnott v Fagan; Deeny v Gooda Walker Ltd (Agency Agreement: Construction) [1996]
    L.R.L.R. 135; [1995] C.L.C. 1396; Independent, October 1, 1993CA (Civ Div) 13–041, 13–040
Arbuthnott v Feltrim Unreported, 1995 13–041
Arbuthnott v Feltrim (No.2) Unreported, 1996 13–041
Ard Coasters v Attorney General. See Attorney General v Ard Coasters Ltd
Argonaut Marine Insurance Co Ltd (In Liquidation), Re [1932] 2 Ch. 34; (1932) 42 Ll.L.R.
    171 Ch D 24–009
Argy Trading Development Co v Lapid Developments [1977] 1 W.L.R. 444; [1977] 3 All
    E.R. 785; [1977] 1 Lloyd's Rep. 67 QBD 15–026, 19–015
Arig Insurance Co Ltd v SASA Assicurazione Riassicurazione SPA Unreported, 1998 QBD
    (Comm) 17–012
Arlet v Lancashire & General Assurance Co Ltd (1927) 27 Ll.L.R. 454 KBD 6–047
Armadora Occidental SA v Horace Mann Insurance Co [1977] 1 W.L.R. 1098; [1978] 1 All
    E.R. 407; [1977] 2 Lloyd's Rep. 406; 121 S.J. 406 CA (Civ Div) 2–033, 2–037, 2–039

Armagas Ltd v Mundogas SA (The Ocean Frost) [1986] A.C. 717; [1986] 2 W.L.R. 1063;
  [1986] 2 All E.R. 385; [1986] 2 Lloyd's Rep. 109; (1986) 83 L.S.G. 2002; (1986) 130
  S.J. 430 HL 15–001
Armar Shipping Co v Caisse Algerienne d'Assurance et de Reassurance (The Armar) Armar,
  The [1981] 1 W.L.R. 207; [1981] 1 All E.R. 498; [1980] 2 Lloyd's Rep. 450 .... 2–032, 2–033
Armitage v Winterbottom (1840) 1 Man. & G. 130 .... 4–020, 19–013
Armstrong International Ltd v Deutsche Bank Securities Inc Unreported July 11, 2003
  QBD 2–043
Armstrong v Turquand (1858) 9 I.C.L.R. 32 .... 6–002, 7–020
Aron & Co v Miall. See J Aron & Co Inc v Miall
Arterial Caravans v Yorkshire Insurance Co [1973] 1 Lloyd's Rep. 169 QBD ... 6–052, 6–070, 6–072,
                                                                                                      6–073, 15–019
Arthur Average Association for British, Foreign and Colonial Ships, Re (1874–75) L.R. 10
  Ch. App. 542 24–007
Arthur Average, De Winton's Case (1876) 34 L.T. 942 8–023
Arthur Carr & Co v Matthews Wrightson & Co Ltd (1924) 18 Ll.L.R. 170 KBD 15–032
Ascott v Cornhill Insurance Co Ltd (1937) 58 Ll.L.R. 41 KBD 6–053
Asfar & Co v Blundell [1896] 1 Q.B. 123 CA 6–073
Ashby v Bates (1846) 15 M. & W. 589 18–029
Ashley v Ashley (1829) 3 Sim. 149 .... 14–026, 18–022
Ashmore v Society of Lloyds (No.2), Times, July 30, 1992 13–039
Ashmore Benson Pease & Co Ltd v AV Dawson Ltd [1973] 1 W.L.R. 828; [1973] 2 All E.R.
  856; [1973] 2 Lloyd's Rep. 21; [1973] R.T.R. 473; 117 S.J. 203 CA (Civ Div) 5–037
Ashton Investments Ltd v OJSC Russian Aluminium (Rusal) [2006] EWHC 2545 (Comm);
  [2007] 1 All E.R. (Comm) 857; [2007] 1 Lloyd's Rep. 311; [2006] 2 C.L.C. 739; [2006]
  Info. T.L.R. 269; Times, October 31, 2006 2–004
Ashton v Turner [1981] Q.B. 137; [1980] 3 W.L.R. 736; [1980] 3 All E.R. 870; [1981] R.T.R.
  54; 124 S.J. 792 QBD 22–034
Ashworth v Builders' Mutual (1873) 17 Am.Rep. 117 19–047
Ashworth v Peterborough United Football Club Unreported, 2002 .... 23–037, 23–039
Aspen Insurance UK Ltd v Pectel Ltd [2008] EWHC 2804 (Comm); [2009] 2 All E.R.
  (Comm) 873; [2009] Lloyd's Rep. I.R. 440 ...... 7–003, 7–004, 7–014, 9–004, 9–006, 20–040
Assicurazioni Generali de Trieste v Empress Assurance Corp Ltd [1907] 2 K.B. 814 KBD 11–023,
                                                                                                      11–035
Assicurazioni Generali SpA v Arab Insurance Group (BSC) [2002] EWCA Civ. 1642; [2003]
  1 W.L.R. 577; [2003] 1 All E.R. (Comm) 140; [2003] 2 C.L.C. 242; [2003] Lloyd's Rep.
  I.R. 131; (2003) 100(3) L.S.G. 34; Times, November 29, 2002 CA (Civ Div); affirming
  [2002] C.L.C. 164; [2002] Lloyd's Rep. I.R. 633 QBD (Comm) ... 1–034, 6–011, 6–015, 6–028,
                                                                                    6–102, 7–022, 7–032, 17–007, 20–022
Assicurazioni Generali SpA v CGU International Insurance Plc [2004] EWCA Civ. 429;
  [2004] 2 All E.R. (Comm) 114; [2004] 2 C.L.C. 122; [2004] Lloyd's Rep. I.R. 457;
  (2004) 148 S.J.L.B. 475 CA (Civ Div) 17–019, 17–020, 20–058
Assicurazioni Generali SpA v Ege Sigorta AS [2002] Lloyd's Rep. I.R. 480 QBD (Comm) 1–033,
                                                                                                      2–005, 2–036, 2–043
Assitalia le Assicurazioni d'Italia SpA v Overseas Union Assurance Ltd [1995] L.R.L.R. 76
  QBD (Comm) 2–056
Associated Japanese Bank (International) Ltd v Credit du Nord SA [1989] 1 W.L.R. 255;
  [1988] 3 All E.R. 902; [1989] Fin. L.R. 117; (1989) 86(8) L.S.G. 43; (1988) 138 N.L.J.
  Rep. 109; (1989) 133 S.J. 81 QBD 10–057
Associated Oil Carriers Ltd v Union Insurance Society of Canton Ltd [1917] 2 K.B. 184
  KBD 6–022, 6–051
Assunzione, The (No.1) [1954] P. 150; [1954] 2 W.L.R. 234; [1954] 1 All E.R. 278; [1953]
  2 Lloyd's Rep. 716; (1954) 98 S.J. 107; Times, December 18, 1953 CA 2–040
Assurances Generales de France IART v Chiyoda Fire and Marine Co (UK) Ltd; sub nom.
  AGF v Chiyoda Fire and Marine Co (UK) Ltd; Unat SA v Rhone Mediterranee
  Compagnie Francese di Assicurazione Riassicurazoni [1992] 1 Lloyd's Rep. 325 QBD
  (Comm) 2–008
Astrovlanis Compania Naviera SA v Linard; The Gold Sky [1972] 2 Lloyd's Rep. 187 QBD
  (Comm) 9–025, 24–112
Athel Line Ltd v Liverpool & London War Risks Assocoiation Ltd (No.2) [1946] K.B. 117;
  (1946) 79 Ll.L.R. 18 CA 25–005
Athenian Tankers Management SA v Pyrena Shipping; The Arianna [1987] 2 Lloyd's Rep.
  376 QBD (Comm) 24–062

Athens Maritime Enterprises Corp v Hellenic Mutual War Risks Association (Bermuda) (The
    Andreas Lemos) [1983] Q.B. 647; [1983] 2 W.L.R. 425; [1983] 1 All E.R. 590; [1982]
    2 Lloyd's Rep. 483; [1982] Com. L.R. 188; (1982) 79 L.S.G. 1257; 126 S.J. 577 QBD
    (Comm) 24–0135, 25–010
Atherfold v Beard (1788) 2 T.R. 610 .... 4–002, 4–003
Atkinson v Abbott (1809) 11 East 135 .... 5–036, 24–064
Atlantic Metal Co Ltd v Hepburn [1960] 2 Lloyd's Rep. 42 QBD (Comm) 9–017
HLAtlantic Transport Co v R. (The Maryland and The Pacuare) (1921) 9 Ll.L.R. 208 25–005
Atlantic Underwriting Agencies Ltd and David Gale (Underwriting) Ltd v Compania di
    Assicurazione di Milano SpA [1979] 2 Lloyd's Rep. 240 QBD (Comm) 2–004, 2–040
Attaleia Marine Co Ltd v Bimeh Iran (Iran Insurance Co) (The Zeus) [1993] 2 Lloyd's Rep.
    497 QBD (Comm) 10–059
Attorney GeneralAttorney General v Adelaide Steamship Co Ltd (No.1); sub nom. Adelaide
    Steamship Co Ltd v Crown, The [1923] A.C. 292; (1923) 14 Ll.L.R. 549 HL 25–005
Attorney General v Ard Coasters Ltd; sub nom. Ard Coasters Ltd v Crown, The; Liverpool
    and London War Risks Insurance Association Ltd v Marine Underwriters of SS Richard
    de Larrinaga [1921] 2 A.C. 141; (1921) 7 Ll.L.R. 150 HL 25–005
Attorney General v Blake [2001] 1 A.C. 268; [2000] 3 W.L.R. 625; [2000] 4 All E.R. 385;
    [2000] 2 All E.R. (Comm) 487; [2001] I.R.L.R. 36; [2001] Emp. L.R. 329; [2000]
    E.M.L.R. 949; (2000) 23(12) I.P.D. 23098; (2000) 97(32) L.S.G. 37; (2000) 150 N.L.J.
    1230; (2000) 144 S.J.L.B. 242; Times, August 3, 2000; Independent, November 6, 2000
    (C.S) HL 20–015
Attorney General v Forsikringsaktieselskabet National; sub nom. Forsikringsaktieselskabet
    National v Attorney General [1925] A.C. 639; (1925) 22 Ll.L.R. 4 HL ... 1–012, 2–040, 13–017,
                                                                                                              17–003, 17–004
Attorney General v Murray [1904] 1 K.B. 165 CA 4–011, 18–015
Attorney General v Glen Line (1930) 37 Ll. L.R. 55 11–035
Attorney General v Imperial Tobacco. See Imperial Tobacco Ltd v Attorney General
Auditor, The (1924) 18 Ll.L.R. 403 11–041
Audsley v Leeds City Council, Times, June 2, 1988 QBD 19–038
Austin v Drewe (1815) 4 Camp. 360 5–048
Austin v Drewe (1816) 6 Taunt. 436 .... 9–015, 19–039
Austin v Zurich General Accident & Liability Insurance Co Ltd [1945] K.B. 250; (1945) 78
    Ll.L.R. 185 CA; affirming [1944] 2 All E.R. 243; (1944) 77 Ll.L.R. 409 KBD 11–001,
                                    11–034, 11–049, 11–051, 11–052, 11–058, 11–062, 22–027,
                                                                                                              22–088
Australia & New Zealand Bank Ltd v Colonial & Eagle Wharves Ltd [1960] 2 Lloyd's Rep.
    241QBD (Comm) 6–037, 6–055, 10–036
Australian Agricultural Co v Saunders (1874–75) L.R. 10 C.P. 668 CCP 3–013, 11–056
Australian Insurance Co v Jackson (1875) 33 L.T. 286 .... 24–064, 24–138
Australian Widows Fund Life Assurance Society Ltd v National Mutual Life Association of
    Australasia Ltd [1914] A.C. 634 PC (Aus) 3–015, 17–001, 17–005
Avandero (UK) Ltd v National Transit Insurance Co Ltd [1984] 2 Lloyd's Rep. 613 QBD
    (Comm) 21–019, 21–031
Avon CC v Howlett [1983] 1 W.L.R. 605; [1983] 1 All E.R. 1073; [1983] I.R.L.R. 171; 81
    L.G.R. 555; (1983) 133 N.L.J. 377; (1983) 127 S.J. 173 CA (Civ Div) 10–062
Avon Insurance Plc v Swire Fraser Ltd [2000] 1 All E.R. (Comm) 573; [2000] C.L.C. 665;
    [2000] Lloyd's Rep. I.R. 535 QBD (Comm) 6–015
Avonale Blouse Co Ltd v Williamson & Geo. Town (1947–48) 81 Ll.L.R. 492 KBD 15–037
Axa General Insurance Ltd v Gottlieb; sub nom. Gottleib v Axa General Insurance Ltd [2005]
    EWCA Civ. 112; [2005] 1 All E.R. (Comm) 445; [2005] 1 C.L.C. 62; [2005] Lloyd's
    Rep. I.R. 369; [2005] N.P.C. 20; Times, March 3, 2005 CA (Civ Div) 9–003, 9–024, 9–026,
                                                                                                              9–032
Axa Insurance Ltd (formerly Winterthur Swiss Insurance Co) v Akther & Darby Solicitors
    [2009] EWCA Civ 1166; [2009] 2 C.L.C. 793; 127 Con. L.R. 50; [2010] P.N.L.R. 10;
    (2009) 106(45) L.S.G. 16; (2009) 159 N.L.J. 1629; [2009] N.P.C. 129; Times, December
    15, 2009 23–035
Axa Pacific Insurance Co v Guildford Marquis Towers Ltd [2000] B.C.T.C. 37 20–050
Ayrey v British Legal & United Provident Assurance Co Ltd [1918] 1 K.B. 136 KBD 6–073,
                                                                                   7–020, 15–002, 15–017
B (A Minor) v Knight [1981] R.T.R. 136 QBD 22–009
B v B July 29, 2008 Preston District Registry B (A Minor) v Knight [1981] R.T.R. 136
    QBD 2–064

BAS Capital Funding Corp v Medfinco Ltd [2003] EWHC 1798 (Ch); [2004] 1 Lloyd's Rep.
652; [2004] I.L.Pr. 16 2–004
BC Enterprise SDN BHD v Bank of China Group Insurance Co Ltd [2003] H.K.B.C. 712 1–023,
6–0117
BP (Libya) Ltd v Hunt. *See* BP Exploration Co (Libya) Ltd v Hunt (No.2)
BP Exploration Co (Libya) Ltd v Hunt (No.2) [1983] 2 A.C. 352; [1982] 2 W.L.R. 253;
[1982] 1 All E.R. 925; Times, February 5, 1981 HL; affirming [1981] 1 W.L.R. 232; 125
S.J. 165 CA (Civ Div); affirming [1979] 1 W.L.R. 783; 123 S.J. 455 QBD .. 10–027, 10–062
BP Exploration Operating Co Ltd v Kvaerner Oilfield Products Ltd [2004] EWHC 999;
[2004] 2 All E.R. (Comm) 266; [2005] 1 Lloyd's Rep. 307 QBD (Comm) ... 3–005, 11–028,
14–003
BP Plc v AON Ltd (No.1) [2005] EWHC 2554; [2006] 1 Lloyd's Rep. 549 QBD (Comm 2–005,
2–056
BP Plc v AON Ltd (No.2) [2006] EWHC 424 (Comm); [2006] 1 All E.R. (Comm) 789;
[2006] 1 C.L.C. 881; [2006] Lloyd's Rep. I.R. 577; (2006) 103(14) L.S.G. 31 ...... 6–120, 9–012,
15–031, 15–034, 15–039, 15–050, 20–039
BP Plc v GE Frankona Reinsurance Ltd [2003] EWHC 344; [2003] 1 Lloyd's Rep. 537 QBD
(Comm) 1–023, 1–031, 1–040, 6–0120
BP Plc v National Union Fire Insurance Co [2004] EWHC 1132 (Comm) 2–005
BTR Plc (Leave to Appeal), Re [2000] 1 B.C.L.C. 740 CA (Civ Div) 16–005
Babatsikos v Car Owners Mutual Insurance Co [1970] 2 Lloyd's Rep. 314; (1970) V.R. 297
CA (Vic) 6–031
Back v National Insurance Co of New Zealand Ltd [1996] 3 N.Z.L.R. 363 .... 6–005, 6–011, 6–092
Bacon v McBride (1984) 5 C.C.L.I. 146 20–049
Baghbadrani v Commercial Union Assurance Co Plc [2000] Lloyd's Rep. I.R. 94 QBD ... 6–094,
6–098, 6–0107, 6–0115, 9–021, 9–026, 10–055
Bah Lias Tobacco and Rubber Estates Ltd v Volga Insurance Co Ltd (1920) 3 Ll.L.R. 155 24–065
Bailey v Gould (1840) 4 Y. & C. 221 19–031
Bain Clarkson v Owners of the Sea Friends; The Sea Friends [1991] 2 Lloyd's Rep. 322;
Times, April 18, 1991CA (Civ Div) 24–078
Bain v Case (1829) 3 C. & P. 496 24–072
Baines v Ewing (1865–66) L.R. 1 Ex. 320 Ex Ct 15–001, 15–013, 15–015
Baines v Holland (1855) 10 Exch. 802 7–036
Baker v Adam (1910) 102 L.T. 248 .... 14–027, 24–074
Baker v Black Sea & Baltic General Insurance Co Ltd; sub nom. Black Sea & Baltic General
Insurance Co Ltd v Baker [1998] 1 W.L.R. 974; [1998] 2 All E.R. 833; [1998] C.L.C.
820; [1998] Lloyd's Rep. I.R. 327; (1998) 95(23) L.S.G. 26; (1998) 148 N.L.J. 782;
(1998) 142 S.J.L.B. 171; Times, May 21, 1998 HL; reversing in part [1996] L.R.L.R.
353; [1996] 5 Re. L.R. 202CA (Civ Div); affirming [1995] L.R.L.R. 261 QBD
(Comm) 6–117, 17–013, 17–015, 17–021, 17–024, 17–027
Baker v Courage [1989] 9 C.L. 297 CC (Andover) 22–023
Baker v Lombard Continental Insurance Plc Unreported, 1996 CA (Civ Div) 6–041
Baker v Provident Accident & White Cross Insurance Co Ltd [1939] 2 All E.R. 690; (1939)
64 Ll.L.R. 14 KBD 22–017
Baker v TE Hopkins & Son Ltd; Ward v TE Hopkins & Son Ltd [1959] 1 W.L.R. 966; [1959]
3 All E.R. 225; 103 S.J. 812 CA; affirming [1958] 1 W.L.R. 993; [1958] 3 All E.R. 147;
102 S.J. 636 QBD 18–049
Baker v Yorkshire Fire and Life Assurance Co [1892] 1 Q.B. 144 QBD 10–044
Ballance v Brown [1955] Crim. L.R. 384 22–088
Ballantyne v MacKinnon [1896] 2 Q.B. 455 CA 24–112, 24–134
Ballast Plc, Re; St Paul Travelers Insurance Co Ltd v Dargan [2006] EWHC 3189 (Ch);
[2007] B.C.C. 620; [2007] B.P.I.R. 117; [2007] Lloyd's Rep. I.R. 742 .... 11–002, 11–011,
11–013, 11–043, 15–038
Balmoral Steamship Co Ltd v Marten; sub nom. Steamship Balmoral Co v Marten [1902]
A.C. 511 HL 10–009
Bamburi, The. *See* Owners of the Bamburi v Compton
Banco Atlantico SA v British Bank of the Middle East [1990] 2 Lloyd's Rep. 504; Financial
Times, June 5, 1990 CA 2–027, 2–030
Banco de Barcelona v Union Marine Insurance Co Ltd (1925) 22 Ll.L.R. 209 9–025
Bancroft v Heath (1901) 17 T.L.R. 425 .... 15–033, 17–012
Bandar Property Holdings Ltd v JS Darwen (Successors) Ltd [1968] 2 All E.R. 305; (1968)
19 P. & C.R. 785 QBD 19–018
Bangor & North Wales Mutual Marine Protection Association, Re Baird's Case [1899] 2 Ch.
593 24–007

Bank Leumi le Israel BM v British National Insurance Co Ltd [1988] 1 Lloyd's Rep. 79
    (Note) CA (Civ Div) [1988] 1 Lloyd's Rep. 71 QBD (Comm) 6–116
Bank of America National Trust and Savings Association v Chrismas; The Kyriaki [1994] 1
    All E.R. 401; [1993] 1 Lloyd's Rep. 137; Times, August 26, 1992 QBD (Comm) 9–038,
                                                                              10–022, 24–088
Bank of America National Trust and Savings Association v Taylor; The Kyriaki [1992] 1
    Lloyd's Rep. 484; Financial Times, May 24, 1991 QBD (Comm) 2–004
Bank of Athens SA v Royal Exchange Assurance; The Eftychia (No.2) (1937) 59 Ll.L.R. 67
    CA 9–025
Bank of Baroda v Vysya Bank Ltd [1994] 2 Lloyd's Rep. 87; [1994] 3 Bank. L.R. 216; [1994]
    C.L.C. 41 QBD (Comm) 2–043
Bank of British North America v Western (1884) 7 Ont. App. 166 11–044
Bank of Credit and Commerce International SA (In Liquidation) v Ali (No.1) [2001] UKHL
    8; [2002] 1 A.C. 251; [2001] 2 W.L.R. 735; [2001] 1 All E.R. 961; [2001] I.C.R. 337;
    [2001] I.R.L.R. 292; [2001] Emp. L.R. 359; (2001) 98(15) L.S.G. 32; (2001) 151 N.L.J.
    351; (2001) 145 S.J.L.B. 67; (2001) 145 S.J.L.B. 70; Times, March 6, 2001 HL 10–055,
                                                                                    10–058
Bank of New South Wales v Royal Insurance (1880) 2 N.Z.L.R. 337 10–044
Bank of New South Wales v South British Insurance Co Ltd (1920) 4 Ll.L.R. 266 14–027
Bank of New York Mellon v GV Films Ltd [2009] EWHC 2338 (Comm); [2010] 1 Lloyd's
    Rep. 365 2–006
Bank of Nova Scotia v Hellenic Mutual War Risk Association (Bermuda) Ltd (The Good
    Luck) [1992] 1 A.C. 233; [1991] 2 W.L.R. 1279; [1991] 3 All E.R. 1; [1991] 2 Lloyd's
    Rep. 191; (1991) 141 N.L.J. 779; Times, May 17, 1991; Independent, May 31, 1991;
    Financial Times, May 21, 1991 HL; reversing [1990] 1 Q.B. 818; [1990] 2 W.L.R. 547;
    [1989] 3 All E.R. 628; [1989] 2 Lloyd's Rep. 238; (1990) 87(10) L.S.G. 34; Times,
    April 20, 1989 CA (Civ Div); reversing [1988] 1 Lloyd's Rep. 514 QBD (Comm) 5–005,
                           6–103, 6–107, 6–127, 6–128, 6–131, 7–018, 7–039, 7–040, 7–047,
                                            8–016, 11–001, 11–013, 14–029, 23–001
Bank of Scotland v Euclidian (No.1) Ltd [2007] EWHC 1732 (Comm); [2008] Lloyd's Rep.
    I.R. 182; (2007) 157 N.L.J. 1083 23–030
Bankers & General Insurance Co v E Brockdorff & Co (1922) 10 Ll.L.R. 22 KBD 24–077
Bankers Insurance Co Ltd v South [2003] EWHC 380; [2004] Lloyd's Rep. I.R. 1; [2003]
    P.I.Q.R. P28 QBD 3–018, 7–004, 7–009, 8–029, 9–003, 9–004
Banque Financière de la Cite SA (formerly Banque Keyser Ullmann SA) v Westgate
    Insurance Co (formerly Hodge General & Mercantile Co Ltd); sub nom. Banque Keyser
    Ullmann SA v Skandia (UK) Insurance Co; Skandia (UK) Insurance Co v Chemical
    Bank; Skandia (UK) Insurance Co v Credit Lyonnais Bank Nederland NV [1991] 2 A.C.
    249; [1990] 3 W.L.R. 364; [1990] 2 All E.R. 947; [1990] 2 Lloyd's Rep. 377; (1990)
    87(35) L.S.G. 36; (1990) 140 N.L.J. 1074; (1990) 134 S.J. 1265 HL; affirming [1990]
    1 Q.B. 665; [1989] 3 W.L.R. 25; [1989] 2 All E.R. 952; [1988] 2 Lloyd's Rep. 513;
    [1989] Fin. L.R. 1; (1989) 133 S.J. 817; Times, August 24, 1988; Independent, August
    19, 1988; Financial Times, August 12, 1988 CA (Civ Div); reversing [1987] 2 W.L.R.
    1300; [1987] 2 All E.R. 923; [1987] 1 Lloyd's Rep. 69; [1987] Fin. L.R. 134; (1987) 84
    L.S.G. 1965; (1987) 131 S.J. 775 .... 6–001, 6–079, 6–100, 6–107, 6–112, 6–122, 6–123, 6–124,
                                       6–125, 6–126, 6–130, 6–131, 10–022, 15–036
Banque Financière de la Cite SA v Parc (Battersea) Ltd [1999] 1 A.C. 221; [1998] 2 W.L.R.
    475; [1998] 1 All E.R. 737; [1998] C.L.C. 520; [1998] E.G.C.S. 36; (1998) 95(15)
    L.S.G. 31; (1998) 148 N.L.J. 365; (1998) 142 S.J.L.B. 101; Times, March 2, 1998 HL ... 11–002
Banque Monetaca & Carystuiaki v Motor Union Insurance Co Ltd (1923) 14 Ll.L.R. 48
    KBD 24–135
Banque Paribas (Suisse) SA v Stolidi Shipping Co Ltd Unreported, 1995 QBD ... 15–045, 15–062
Bansalou v Royal Insurance, 15 Lt. Cam. Rep. 1 19–033
Barber v Fleming (1869–70) L.R. 5 Q.B. 59 QB 24–026
Barber v Fletcher (1779) 1 Doug K.B. 305 .... 6–014, 6–116
Barber v Imperio Reinsurance Co (UK) Ltd Unreported, 1993 .... 6–092, 6–093
Barber v Morris (1831) 1 Mood. & R. 62 18–004
Barclay v Cousins (1802) 2 East 544 .... 4–017, 10–019, 10–020
Barclay v Stirling (1816) 5 M. & S. 56 24–095
Barclays Bank Ltd v WJ Simms Son & Cooke (Southern) Ltd [1980] Q.B. 677; [1980] 2
    W.L.R. 218; [1979] 3 All E.R. 522; [1980] 1 Lloyd's Rep. 225; 123 S.J. 785 QBD
    (Comm) 10–060, 10–061

Barclays Bank Plc v Fairclough Building Ltd (No.1) [1995] Q.B. 214; [1994] 3 W.L.R. 1057; [1995] 1 All E.R. 289; [1994] C.L.C. 529; 68 B.L.R. 1; 38 Con. L.R. 86; (1995) 11 Const. L.J. 35; [1995] E.G.C.S. 10; (1994) 91(25) L.S.G. 30; (1994) 138 S.J.L.B. 118; Times, May 11, 1994 CA (Civ Div) 15–051
Baring v Christie (1804) 5 East 398 24–058
Baring v Claggett (1802) 3 B. & P 201 24–058
Baring v Stanton (1876) L.R. 3 Ch. D. 502 CA 15–033
Barker v Corus UK Plc. *See* Barker v Saint Gobain Pipelines Plc
Barker v Janson (1868) L.R. 3 C.P. 303 .... 1–009, 10–006, 10–007, 10–009
Barker v Saint Gobain Pipelines Plc; sub nom. Barker v Corus (UK) Plc; Murray (Deceased) v British Shipbuilders (Hydrodynamics) Ltd; Patterson (Deceased) v Smiths Dock Ltd [2006] UKHL 20; [2006] 2 W.L.R. 1027; [2006] I.C.R. 809; (2006) 89 B.M.L.R. 1; (2006) 103(20) L.S.G. 27; (2006) 156 N.L.J. 796; (2006) 150 S.J.L.B. 606; [2006] N.P.C. 50; Times, May 4, 2006 HL 5–015, 11–050, 11–055
Barker v Walters (1844) 8 Beav. 92 8–022
Barking and Dagenham LBC v Stamford Asphalt Co Ltd, 82 B.L.R. 25; 54 Con. L.R. 1; Times, April 10, 1997 CA (Civ Div) 11–026
Barlee Marine Corp v Trevor Rex Mountain (The Leegas) [1987] 1 Lloyd's Rep. 471 QBD (Comm) 1–040
Barnard v Faber [1893] 1 Q.B. 340 CA 7–026, 7–028, 17–012
Barnes v London, Edinburgh and Glasgow Life Insurance Co [1892] 1 Q.B. 864 QBD 18–008, 18–015
Barnet Group Hospital Management Committee v Eagle Star Insurance Co [1960] 1 Q.B. 107; [1959] 3 W.L.R. 610; [1959] 3 All E.R. 210; [1959] 2 Lloyd's Rep. 335; 123 J.P. 521; 103 S.J. 619 QBD 22–017, 22–022, 22–031
Barnett & Block v National Parcels Insurance Co Ltd (1942) 73 Ll.L.R. 17 CA 5–011, 6–015
Barr v Biffa Waste Services Ltd [2009] EWHC 1033 (TCC); [2010] 3 Costs L.R. 291; (2009) 25 Const. L.J. 547 23–041
Barraclough v Brown [1897] A.C. 615 HL 24–096
Barras v Hamilton, 1994 S.C. 544; 1994 S.L.T. 949; 1994 S.C.L.R. 700; Times, June 10, 1994 IH (2 Div) 11–032, 14–019
Barrett Bros (Taxis) Ltd v Davies; sub nom. Lickiss v Milestone Motor Policies at Lloyds [1966] 1 W.L.R. 1334; [1966] 2 All E.R. 972; [1966] 2 Lloyd's Rep. 1; 110 S.J. 600 CA 7–019, 9–003, 9–009, 9–010
Barrett v DPP [2009] EWHC 423 (Admin); [2010] R.T.R. 2 22–007
Barrett v Jermy (1849) 3 Ex. 535; 154 E.R. 957 5–019
Barrett v London General Insurance Co Ltd [1935] 1 K.B. 238; (1934) 50 Ll.L.R. 99 KBD 7–023, 22–036, 22–092
Bartlett & Partners Ltd v Meller [1961] 1 Lloyd's Rep. 487 QBD (Comm) 5–009, 5–014
Bartoline Ltd v Royal & Sun Alliance Insurance Plc [2006] EWHC 3598 (QB); [2007] 1 All E.R. (Comm) 1043; [2008] Env. L.R. 1; [2007] Lloyd's Rep. I.R. 423 .... 10–038, 20–010
Barwick v English Joint Stock Bank (1867) L.R. 2 Ex. 259 15–004
Barzillai v Lewis (1782) 3 Doug. K.B. 126 24–058
Bates v Hewitt (1866–67) L.R. 2 Q.B. 595 QB 5–023, 6–021, 6–064, 6–065, 24–035
Bates v Robert Barrow Ltd; Ansell v Robert Barrow Ltd [1995] 1 Lloyd's Rep. 680; [1995] C.L.C. 207; Times, February 9, 1995 QBD (Comm) 13–020, 15–034
Batey v Jewson Ltd [2008] EWCA Civ 18 14–029
Baugh v Crago [1976] 1 Lloyd's Rep. 563; [1975] R.T.R. 453; [1976] Crim. L.R. 72DC 22–010
Bawden v London, Edinburgh and Glasgow Assurance Co [1892] 2 Q.B. 534 CA 15–019, 18–056
Baxendale v Fane (The Lapwing) [1940] 66 Ll.L.R. 174; [1940] P. 112 PDAD ... 24–003, 24–134
Baxendale v Harvey (1859) 4 H. & N. 445 .... 5–019, 5–022, 6–103
Baybut v Eccle Riggs Country Park Ltd Times, November 13, 2006 3–018
Baycorp Advantage Ltd v Royal and Sun Alliance Insurance Australia Ltd [2003] N.S.W.S.C. 941 20–052
Baynham v Philips Electronic (UK) Ltd [1995] O.P.L.R. 253; Times, July 19, 1995 QBD 1–021
Byswater Carriers Pte Ltd v QBE Insurance (International) Pte Ltd [2005] 1 S.L.R. 69 24–136
Baytur SA v Finagro Holdings SA [1992] Q.B. 610; [1991] 3 W.L.R. 866; [1991] 4 All E.R. 129; [1992] 1 Lloyd's Rep. 134; (1991) 135 S.J.L.B. 52; Times, June 21, 1991; Independent, June 19, 1991; Financial Times, June 26, 1991 CA 21–062
Bayview Motors Ltd v Mitsui Marine & Fire Insurance Co Ltd; sub nom. Mitsui Marine & Fire Insurance Co Ltd v Bayview Motors Ltd [2002] EWCA Civ. 1605; [2002] 2 All E.R. (Comm) 1095; [2003] 1 Lloyd's Rep. 131; [2003] Lloyd's Rep. I.R. 117; (2003) 100(1) L.S.G. 23; Times, November 25, 2002 CA (Civ Div) 24–066, 24–086, 24–088, 24–112, 25–012

Beacon Carpets v Kirby [1985] Q.B. 755; [1984] 3 W.L.R. 489; [1984] 2 All E.R. 726; (1984) 48 P. & C.R. 445; (1984) 81 L.S.G. 1603; (1984) 128 S.J. 549 CA (Civ Div) 10–048, 19–017
Beacon Insurance Co Ltd v Langdale [1939] 4 All E.R. 204; (1939) 65 Ll.L.R. 57 CA 20–045
Beacon Life & Fire v Gibb (1862) 1 Moo. P.C.C. (N.S.) 73 .... 1–017, 3–011, 19–039
Beals v Home Insurance (1867) 36 N.Y. 522 10–044
Bean v Stupart (1778) 1 Doug K.B. 11 .... 7–022, 7–024, 7–026
Beatson v Haworth (1796) 6 T.R. 531 24–071
Beauchamp v Faber (1898) 3 Com. Cas. 308 .... 9–026, 17–012
Beauchamp v National Mutual Indemnity Insurance Co Ltd (1937) 57 Ll.L.R. 272; [1937] 3 All E.R. 19 KBD 5–020, 6–021, 7–029, 7–032
Beazley v Horizon Offshore Contractors Inc (The Gulf Horizon) [2004] EWHC 2555; [2005] I.L.Pr. 11; [2005] Lloyd's Rep. I.R. 231 QBD (Comm) 2–003, 2–008
Becker v Marshall (1922) 12 Ll.L.R. 413 CA 6–021, 6–051, 6–052, 6–073
Becker Gray & Co v London Assurance Corp [1918] A.C. 101 HL 5–029, 5–030
Beckett v West of England Marine Insurance Co (1871) 25 L.T. 739 24–130
Beckwaite v Nalgrove (1810) 3 Taunt 41 24–035
Bedford Insurance Co Ltd v Instituto de Resseguros do Brasil [1985] Q.B. 966; [1984] 3 W.L.R. 726; [1984] 3 All E.R. 766; [1984] 1 Lloyd's Rep. 210; [1985] Fin. L.R. 49; (1985) 82 L.S.G. 37; (1984) 134 N.L.J. 34; (1984) 128 S.J. 701 QBD (Comm) 13–018, 13–019, 13–020
Bedfordshire Police Authority v Constable [2008] EWHC 1375 (Comm); [2009] Lloyd's Rep. I.R. 39 .... 3–005, 20–010, 25–010
Bedfordshire Police Authority v Constable [2009] EWCA Civ 64; [2009] 2 All E.R. (Comm) 200; [2009] Lloyd's Rep. I.R. 607 20–028
Bedham v United Guarantee Co (1852) 7 Ex. 744 23–026
Bedouin, The [1894] P. 1 CA 6–045, 6–065
Bee v Jenson (No.1) [2006] EWHC 2534 (Comm); [2007] R.T.R. 9; [2007] Lloyd's Rep. I.R. 451 22–025
Bee v Jenson (No.2) [2007] EWCA Civ 923; [2007] 4 All E.R. 791; [2007] 2 All E.R. (Comm) 1172; [2008] R.T.R. 7; [2008] Lloyd's Rep. I.R. 221; (2007) 104(37) L.S.G. 34; (2007) 151 S.J.L.B. 1228; Times, October 17, 2007 .... 11–002, 11–011, 22–025
Bekhor (AJ) & Co Ltd v Bilton [1981] Q.B. 923; [1981] 2 W.L.R. 601; [1981] 2 All E.R. 565; [1981] 1 Lloyd's Rep. 491; [1981] Com. L.R. 50; (1981) 125 S.J. 203 CA 23–040
Belco Trading Co v Kondo [2008] EWCA Civ 205 23–041
Belfour v Weston (1786) 1 T.R. 310 .... 19–017, 19–020
Bell v Bell (1810) 2 Camp 475 24–065
Bell v Carstairs (1810) 2 Camp. 543 6–0116
Bell v Carstairs (1811) 14 East 374 .... 24–003, 24–058
Bell v Gibson (1798) 1 Bos. & P. 345 24–045
Bell v Lever Brothers Ltd; sub nom. Lever Bros Ltd v Bell [1932] A.C. 161 HL 1–001, 10–055, 10–057
Bell v Lothiansure Ltd (Preliminary Procedure), 1990 S.L.T. 58; Times, February 2, 1990 OH 15–034
Bell Taverns (Scotland) Ltd v v National Insurance and Guarantee Corp [2009] CSOH 69; 2009 G.W.D. 18–295 OH 10–029, 10–044
Bellamy v Brickenden (1861) 2 John. & H. 137 19–027
Bellhouse v Mellow (1859) 4 H. & N. 116 5–004
Benatti v WPP Holdings Italy Srl aig [2007] EWCA Civ 263; [2007] 1 W.L.R. 2316; [2007] 2 All E.R. (Comm) 525; [2008] 1 Lloyd's Rep. 396; [2007] 1 C.L.C. 324; [2007] I.L.Pr. 33; (2007) 104(15) L.S.G. 21; Times, April 16, 2007 2–008
Benham v United Guarantee and Life Assurance Co (1852) 7 Ex. 744 .... 6–102, 7–032
Benjamin v State Insurance Ltd (1998) 10 ANZ Insurance Cases 74,645 6–028
Bennett v Richardson [1980] R.T.R. 358 DC 22–009
Bennett v Yorkshire Insurance Co Ltd [1962] 2 Lloyd's Rep. 270 QBD 7–013
Bennett (t/a Soho Pizzeria) v Axa Insurance Plc [2003] EWHC 86; [2004] Lloyd's Rep. I.R. 615 QBD (Comm) 7–024, 19–039
Bennett Steamship Co Ltd v Hull Mutual Steamship Protecting Society Ltd [1914] 3 K.B. 57 CA 24–006
Bensaude & Co v Thames and Mersey Marine Insurance Co Ltd [1897] A.C. 609 HL 7–024
Benson v Chapman (1849) 2 H.L.C. 496 24–0112
Bent v Highways & Utilities Construction Ltd [2010] EWCA Civ 292 22–025
Beresford v Royal Insurance Co Ltd [1938] A.C. 586 HL .. 5–037, 5–041, 5–043, 5–044, 18–033, 18–034, 18–035

Berger and Light Diffusers Pty Ltd v Pollock [1973] 2 Lloyd's Rep. 442 QBD (Comm) 6–027,
            6–056, 6–0120, 14–008, 24–035
Berisford v New Hampshire Insurance Co. *See* S&W Berisford Plc v New Hampshire
    Insurance Co Ltd
Berk v Style [1956] 1 Q.B. 180; [1955] 3 W.L.R. 935; [1955] 3 All E.R. 625; [1955] 2
    Lloyd's Rep. 382; 99 S.J. 889 QBD 24–081
Berliner Motor Corp v Sun Alliance and London Insurance Ltd [1983] 1 Lloyd's Rep. 320;
    [1983] Com. L.R. 9 QBD (Comm) 21–023
Bermon v Woodbridge (1781) 2 Doug K.B. 781 .... 8–020, 8–021, 24–061
Bernadone v Pall Mall Services. *See* Martin v Lancashire CC
Bernaldez Case (C–129/94). *See* Criminal Proceedings against Bernaldez
Berndtson v Strang (1867–68) L.R. 3 Ch. App. 588, Lord Chancellor 19–007
Berriman v Rose Thomson Young (Underwriting) Ltd [1996] L.R.L.R. 426; [1996] C.L.C.
    1283; [1996] 5 Re. L.R. 121; Lloyd's List, August 1, 1996 (I.D.) QBD (Comm) 13–041
Berrycroft Management Co Ltd v Sinclair Gardens Investments (Kensington) Ltd (1997) 29
    H.L.R. 444; (1998) 75 P. & C.R. 210; [1997] 1 E.G.L.R. 47; [1997] 22 E.G. 141; [1996]
    E.G.C.S. 143; [1996] N.P.C. 127; Times, September 30, 1996 CA (Civ Div) 19–019, 19–022
Berthon v Loughman (1817) 2 Stark. 258 6–024
Bestquest Ltd v Regency Care Group [2003] Lloyd's Rep. I.R. 392 CC (London) 14–010
Beswick v Beswick [1968] A.C. 58; [1967] 3 W.L.R. 932; [1967] 2 All E.R. 1197; 111 S.J.
    540 HL 18–024
Betty, Re; sub nom. Betty v Attorney General [1899] 1 Ch. 821 Ch D 19–031
Beurgsgracht, The. *See* Glencore International AG v Ryan
Bevan v Gartside Marine Engines Ltd [2000] B.C.J. No.528 24–006
Bhopal v Sphere Drake Insurance Plc [2002] Lloyd's Rep. I.R. 413 CA (Civ Div) 7–048, 15–035,
            15–054
Bhugwandass v Netherlands India Sea and Fire Insurance Co of Batavia (1889) L.R. 14 App.
    Cas. 83 PC (UK) 1–012, 1–023
Biccard v Shepherd (1861) 4 Moo. P.C.C. 471 .... 24–061, 24–062
Biddle v Johnston [1965] 2 Lloyd's Rep. 121; 109 S.J. 395 DC 22–010, 22–015, 22–088
Biddle, Sawyer & Co Ltd v Peters (Walter) (t/a Burose & Peters) [1957] 2 Lloyd's Rep. 339
    QBD (Comm) 24–080
Bier v Mines de Potasse d'Alsace. *See* Handelswekerij GJ Bier BV v Mines de Potasse
    d'Alsace SA (C–21/76)
Biggar v Rock Life Assurance Co [1902] 1 K.B. 516 KBD ... 6–075, 8–025, 15–013, 15–019, 18–031
Biggin & Co Ltd v Permanite Ltd [1951] 2 K.B. 314; [1951] 2 All E.R. 191; [1951] 2 T.L.R.
    159; (1951) 95 S.J. 414 CA 15–059
Bilbie v Lumley (1802) 2 East 269 .... 6–095, 10–060
Binks v Department of the Environment [1975] R.T.R. 318; [1975] Crim. L.R. 244; (1975)
    119 S.J. 304 QBD 22–006
Bird v Appleton (1800) 8 T.R. 562 5–038
Bird v Brown (1850) 4 Exch. 786 15–003
Bird's Cigarette Manufacturing Co Ltd v Rouse (1924) 19 Ll.L.R. 301 KBD 24–035, 24–080
Birrell v Dryer; sub nom. Birell v Dryer (1883–84) L.R. 9 App. Cas. 345 HL 7–024, 24–070
Birse Construction Ltd v Haiste Ltd [1996] 1 W.L.R. 675; [1996] 2 All E.R. 1; [1996] C.L.C.
    577; 76 B.L.R. 31; 47 Con. L.R. 162; [1996] P.N.L.R. 8; (1996) 93(2) L.S.G. 29; (1996)
    140 S.J.L.B. 25; Times, December 12, 1995 CA 15–032
Biscard v Shepherd (1861) 14 Moo. P.C.C. 471 24–062
Bishop v Pentland (1827) 7 B. & C. 219 24–080
Bisset v Royal Exchange Assurance (1821) 1 Sh. (Ct. of Sess) 174 10–044
Bisset v Wilkinson [1927] A.C. 177 PC (NZ) 6–013
Blaaupot v Da Costa (1758) 1 Eden 130 .... 11–001, 11–002, 11–036
Black King Shipping Corp v Massie; The Litsion Pride [1985] 1 Lloyd's Rep. 437; (1984)
    134 N.L.J. 887 QBD (Comm) 6–107, 6–108, 6–112, 6–113, 6–115, 9–004, 9–021, 9–032,
            14–029, 23–001, 24–078
Blackburn v Liverpool Brazil and River Plate Steam Navigation Co [1902] 1 K.B. 290
    KBD 24–080, 24–134
Blackburn Low & Co v Haslam (1888) L.R. 21 Q.B.D. 144 QBD 6–037, 6–041
Blackburn Low & Co v Vigors (1887) L.R. 12 App. Cas. 531 HL 6–036, 6–037, 6–042
Blackburn Rovers Football & Athletic Club Plc v Avon Insurance Plc (Preliminary Issues)
    [2005] EWCA Civ. 423; [2005] 1 C.L.C. 554; [2005] Lloyd's Rep. I.R. 447 CA (Civ
    Div); reversing [2004] EWHC 2625; [2005] Lloyd's Rep. I.R. 239 QBD (Comm) 3–009,
            5–031, 18–044, 22–090

Blackburn Rovers Football & Athletic Club Plc v Avon Insurance Plc [2006] EWHC 840;
(2006) 150 S.J.L.B. 574 QBD 18–044
Blackenhagen v London Assurance Co (1808) 1 Camp. 454 24–073
Blackett Magalhaes & Colombie v National Benefit Assurance Co (1921) 8 Ll.l.R.
293CA 24–039, 24–063
Blackett v Royal Exchange Assurance Co (1832) 2 Cr. & J. 244 3–013
Blackhurst v Cockell (1789) 3 T.R. 360 .... 7–022, 24–060
Blackley v National Mutual Life Association of Australasia Ltd [1970] N.Z.L.R. 919 6–004
Bladon, Re; sub nom. Dando v Porter [1912] 1 Ch. 45 CA; affirming [1911] 2 Ch. 350 Ch
D 19–030
Blascheck v Bussell (1916) 33 T.L.R. 74 .... 1–009, 3–011, 10–006, 18–002
Blower v Great Western Railway; sub nom. Blower v Great Western Railway Co (1871–72)
L.R. 7 C.P. 655 CCP 24–080
Boag v Economic Insurance Co Ltd [1954] 2 Lloyd's Rep. 581 QBD 11–056, 19–044
Boag v Standard Marine Insurance Co Ltd [1937] 2 K.B. 113; (1937) 57 Ll.L.R. 83 CA 11–008,
11–041, 11–053, 11–054, 24–097
Board of Management of Trim Joint District School v Kelly; sub nom. Trim Joint District
School Board of Management v Kelly [1914] A.C. 667 HL (UK-Irl) 18–052
Board of Trade v Hain Steamship Co Ltd; sub nom. Hain Steamship Co Ltd v Board of Trade
[1929] A.C. 534; (1929) 34 Ll.L.R. 197 HL 25–004, 25–005
Boardman v Phipps [1967] 2 A.C. 46; [1966] 3 W.L.R. 1009; [1966] 3 All E.R. 721; (1966)
110 S.J. 853 HL 20–086
Boddington v Castelli (1853) 1 E. & B. 879 9–038
Boden v Hussey [1988] 1 Lloyd's Rep. 423; [1988] 1 F.T.L.R. 372 CA (Civ Div) 10–059
Bodine v Exchange Fire (1872) 51 N.Y. App. 117 8–004
Boehm v Bell (1799) 8 T.R. 154 19–014
Boggan v Motor Union Insurance Co Ltd (1923) 16 Ll.L.R. 64 HL (UK-Irl) 25–009, 25–010
Boiler Inspection and Insurance Co of Canada v Sherwin Williams Co of Canada Ltd [1951]
A.C. 319; [1951] 1 Lloyd's Rep. 91; [1951] 1 T.L.R. 497; 95 S.J. 187 PC (Can) 5–031
Boissevain v Weil [1950] A.C. 327; [1950] 1 All E.R. 728; 66 T.L.R. (Pt. 1) 771; 94 S.J. 319
HL 2–057
Bolands Ltd v London & Lancashire Fire Insurance Co Ltd; sub nom. London and Lancashire
Fire Insurance Co Ltd v Bolands Ltd [1924] A.C. 836; (1924) 19 Ll.L.R. 1 HL
(UK-Irl) 3–006, 3–007, 3–008, 25–010
Bolivia v Indemnity Mutual Marine Assurance Co Ltd [1909] 1 K.B. 785 CA 6–040, 6–065,
24–135, 25–009, 25–010
Bollom & Co Ltd v Byas Moseley & Co Ltd. See JW Bollom & Co Ltd v Byas Mosley &
Co Ltd
Bols Distilleries BV (t/a Bols Royal Distilleries) v Superior Yacht Services Ltd [2006] UKPC
45; [2007] 1 W.L.R. 12; [2007] 1 All E.R. (Comm) 461; [2007] 1 Lloyd's Rep. 683;
[2007] 1 C.L.C. 308; [2007] I.L.Pr. 46 PC (Gibraltar) 2–008
Bolton MBC v Municipal Mutual Insurance Ltd [2006] EWCA Civ. 50; [2006] 1 W.L.R.
1492; [2006] 1 C.L.C. 242; [2007] Lloyd's Rep. I.R. 173; (2006) 103(9) L.S.G. 31;
(2006) 150 S.J.L.B. 226; Times, February 9, 2006; Independent, February 9, 2006 CA
(Civ Div); affirming in part [2006] Lloyd's Rep. I.R. 15 QBD 3–003, 3–012, 5–015, 6–092,
7–018, 7–020, 11–059, 18–059, 20–007
Bolton v Gladstone (1809) 2 Taunt. 85 24–058
Bolton v New Zealand Insurance Co [1995] 1 N.Z.L.R. 224 .... 6–106, 7–037
Bond v Commercial Union Assurance Co Ltd (1930) 35 Com.Cas. 171 6–070
Bond v Commercial Union Assurance Co Ltd (1930) 36 Ll.L.R. 107 KBD 6–048, 19–033, 22–087
Bond v Nutt (1777) 2 Cowp. 601 7–038
Bond Air Services v Hill [1955] 2 Q.B. 417; [1955] 2 W.L.R. 1194; [1955] 2 All E.R. 476;
[1955] 1 Lloyd's Rep. 498; 99 S.J. 370 QBD 6–031, 7–044
Bondrett v Hentigg (1816) Holt N.P. 149 5–030
Bonham v Zurich General Accident & Liability Insurance Co Ltd [1945] K.B. 292; (1945)
78 Ll.L.R. 245 CA 22–031, 22–097
Bonner v Cox; sub nom. Bonner v Cox Dedicated Corporate Member Ltd [2005] EWCA Civ.
1512; [2006] Lloyd's Rep. I.R. 385; [2006] 1 All E.R. (Comm) 565; [2006] 1 C.L.C.
126 CA (Civ Div) ... 1–023, 1–024, 1–034, 6–030, 6–104, 6–111, 6–112, 7–003, 7–007, 14–008,
15–028, 15–042, 17–005, 17–013, 17–015
Bonner-Williams v Peter Lindsay Leisure Ltd [2001] 1 All E.R. (Comm) 1140 QBD (TCC) ... 6–038,
7–014, 7–015, 19–039
Bonney v Cornhill Insurance Co Ltd (1931) 40 Ll.L.R. 39 KBD 22–088
Boral Resources Ltd v Pyke (1990) 93 A.L.R. 89 11–032

Borders v Swift [1957] Crim. L.R. 194 DC 22–015
Boreal Insurance Inc v Lafarge Canada Inc (2004) 70 C.R. (3d) 502 20–048
Borradaile v Hunter (1843) 5 M. & G. 639 .... 18–033, 18–034
Boss v Kingston [1963] 1 W.L.R. 99; [1963] 1 All E.R. 177; [1962] 2 Lloyd's Rep. 431; 61
    L.G.R. 109; 106 S.J. 1053 DC 14–022, 22–027
Boston Corp v France Fenwick & Co Ltd (1923) 15 Ll.L.R. 85; (1923) 28 Com. Cas. 367
    KBD 24–096
Boston Fruit Co v British & Foreign Marine Insurance Co Ltd [1906] A.C. 336 HL; affirming
    [1905] 1 K.B. 637 CA 4–022, 4–023, 14–008, 24–045
Bottomley v Bovill (1826) 5 B. & C. 210 .... 24–069, 24–138
Bouillon v Lupton (1863) 33 L.J.C.P. 37 24–073
Bouillon v Lupton (1863) 5 C.B.N.S. 113 .... 24–061, 24–068
Boulton v Houlder Bros & Co [1904] 1 K.B. 784 CA 6–107
Bousfield v Barnes (1815) 4 Camp. 228 11–044
Bousfield v Cresswell (1810) 2 Camp 545 15–041
Bovis Construction Ltd v Commercial Union Assurance Co Plc [2001] 1 Lloyd's Rep. 416;
    [2002] T.C.L.R. 11; [2001] Lloyd's Rep. I.R. 321; [2000] N.P.C. 133 QBD (Comm) 5–033,
                                                            11–001, 11–013, 11–052, 11–060, 20–076
Bowden v Vaughan (1809) 10 East 415 6–014
Bowmakers Ltd v Barnet Instruments Ltd [1945] K.B. 65 CA 5–038, 5–045
Bowman v DPP (1990) 154 J.P. 524; [1991] R.T.R. 263; [1990] Crim. L.R. 600; (1990) 154
    J.P.N. 441 DC 22–008
Bowring v Amsterdam London Insurance. See CT Bowring & Co Ltd v Amsterdam London
    Insurance Co Ltd
Bowring v Elmslie (1790) 7 T.R. 216n 9–025
Bowskill v Dawson (No.2) [1955] 1 Q.B. 13; [1954] 3 W.L.R. 275; [1954] 2 All E.R. 649;
    98 S.J. 523 CA 18–024
Boyd v Colonial Mutual Life Assurance Society (1910) 29 N.Z.L.R. 41 6–012
Boyd & Forrest (A Firm) v Glasgow & South Western Railway Co (No.3) [1915] A.C. 526;
    1915 S.C. (H.L.) 20; 1915 1 S.L.T. 114 HL 6–082
Boyd v Dubois (1811) 3 Camp. 133 24–080
Boynton v Monarch Life Insurance Company of New Zealand Ltd [1973] 1 N.Z.L.R. 606 8–016
Bracegirdle v Apter (1951) 49 L.G.R. 790 22–002
Bradburn v Great Western Railway (1874) L.R. 10 Ex. 1 .... 11–001, 11–013, 18–002
Bradford v Symondson (1880–81) L.R. 7 Q.B.D. 456 CA 8–029, 24–020
Bradley v Eagle Star Insurance Co Ltd [1989] A.C. 957; [1989] 2 W.L.R. 568; [1989] 1 All
    E.R. 961; [1989] 1 Lloyd's Rep. 465; [1989] B.C.L.C. 469; [1989] I.C.R. 301; [1989]
    Fin. L.R. 253; (1989) 86(17) L.S.G. 38; (1989) 86(3) L.S.G. 43; (1989) 139 N.L.J. 330;
    (1989) 133 S.J. 359; Times, March 3, 1989; Independent, March 3, 1989; Guardian,
    March 7, 1989; Daily Telegraph, March 10, 1989 HL 20–034, 21–014
Bradley & Essex & Suffolk Accident Indemnity Society, Re [1912] 1 K.B. 415 CA 3–018, 7–013,
                                                                    7–014, 9–004, 20–068
Brain v Yorkshire Rider Ltd [2007] Lloyd's Rep. I.R. 564 County Court (Leeds) 22–025
Braithwaite v Employers Liability Assurance Corp (James D Day, Third Party) [1964] 1
    Lloyd's Rep. 94; Times, December 18, 1963 QBD 10–044
Braithwaite v Thomas Cook Travellers Cheques [1989] Q.B. 553; [1989] 3 W.L.R. 212;
    [1989] 1 All E.R. 235; [1988] Fin. L.R. 362; (1989) 86(16) L.S.G. 35; (1988) 138 N.L.J.
    Rep. 233; (1989) 133 S.J. 359; Independent, July 22, 1988 QBD 5–050
Bramhill v Edwards [2004] EWCA Civ. 403; [2004] 2 Lloyd's Rep. 653 CA (Civ Div) 22–087
Brandon v Curling (1803) 4 East 410 19–058
Brandt's v Dunlop. See William Brandt's Sons & Co v Dunlop Rubber Co Ltd
Branfoot v Sounders (1877) 25 W.R. 650 18–020
Braunstein v Accidental Death (1861) 1 B. & S. 782 .... 3–004, 9–019
Brennan v Bolt Burdon; sub nom. Brennan v Bolt Burden; Brennan v Islington LBC [2004]
    EWCA Civ. 1017; [2005] Q.B. 303; [2004] 3 W.L.R. 1321; [2004] C.P. Rep. 43; (2004)
    101(34) L.S.G. 31; (2004) 148 S.J.L.B. 972; [2004] N.P.C. 133; Times, August 27, 2004
    CA (Civ Div) 10–057, 10–058
Bretton v Hancock [2005] EWCA Civ. 404; [2005] R.T.R. 22; [2005] Lloyd's Rep. I.R. 454;
    [2006] P.I.Q.R. P1; Independent, April 20, 2005 CA (Civ Div) 22–009, 22–012
Brewer v DPP [2004] EWHC 355 (Admin); [2005] R.T.R. 5; Times, March 5, 2004 22–007
Brewster v Blackmore (1925) 21 Ll.L.R. 258 KBD 10–006
Brewster v National Life Insurance Society (1892) 8 T.L.R. 648 .... 15–019, 18–005, 18–022
Brewtnall v Cornhill Insurance Co Ltd (1931) 40 Ll.L.R. 166 KBD 6–018

Bridges & Salmon Ltd v Owner of The Swan (The Swan); Marine Diesel Service (Grimsby)
    Ltd v Owner of The Swan [1968] 1 Lloyd's Rep. 5; (1968) 118 N.L.J. 182 PDAD 4–024
Bridges v Hunter (1813) 1 M. & S. 15 .... 24–036, 24–037
Briggs v Gibson's Bakery [1948] N.I. 165 HC (NI) 22–088
Briggs v Merchant Traders' Association (1849) L.R. 13 Q.B. 167 .... 18–020, 24–022
Bright & Co (Insurance) Ltd v Wright (1946) 79 Ll.L.R. 207 MCLC 15–033
Bright v Ashfold [1932] 2 K.B. 153; (1932) 43 Ll.L.R. 25 KBD 22–036, 22–037
Brine v Featherstone (1813) 4 Taunt. 869 6–014
Brinkibon v Stahag Stahl und Stahlwarenhandels GmbH; sub nom. Brinkibon Ltd v Stahag
    Stahl und Stahlwarenhandelsgesellschaft mbH [1983] 2 A.C. 34; [1982] 2 W.L.R. 264;
    [1982] 1 All E.R. 293; [1982] 1 Lloyd's Rep. 217; [1982] Com. L.R. 72; [1982] E.C.C.
    322; 126 S.J. 116 HL 2–004
Brintons Ltd v Turvey; sub nom. Turvey v Brintons Ltd; Higgins v Campbell & Harrison Ltd
    [1905] A.C. 230 HL 18–040
Brisette v Crown Life Insurance Co, 72 D.L.R. (4th) 138 (1990) 5–041
Bristol & West Plc v Bhadresa; Bristol and West Plc v Mascarenhas [1999] C.P.L.R. 209;
    [1999] 1 Lloyd's Rep. I.R. 138; [1999] Lloyd's Rep. P.N. 11; (1999) 96(1) L.S.G. 23;
    Times, November 23, 1998 Ch D 20–055, 20–056
Bristow v Sequeville 155 E.R. 118; (1850) 5 Ex. 275 2–025
Bristow Helicopters Ltd v Sikorsky Aircraft Corp [2004] EWHC 401 (Comm); [2004] 2
    Lloyd's Rep. 150; [2005] 2 C.L.C. 856 2–065
Brit Syndicates Ltd v Italaudit SpA (In Liquidation) (formerly Grant Thornton SpA) [2008]
    UKHL 18; [2008] 2 All E.R. 1140; [2008] 2 All E.R. (Comm) 1; [2008] 1 C.L.C. 385;
    [2008] Lloyd's Rep. I.R. 601; (2008) 152(12) S.J.L.B. 30 ...... 6–075, 7–040, 14–003, 14–012
Britain Steamship Co Ltd v King, The; sub nom. Petersham, The; Green v British India
    Steam Navigation Co Ltd; British India Steam Navigation Co Ltd v Liverpool &
    London War Risks Insurance Association Ltd [1921] 1 A.C. 99; (1920) 4 Ll.L.R. 245
    HL 5–030, 25–004, 25–005
Britannia Steamship Insurance Association v Ausonia Assicurazioni SpA [1984] 2 Lloyd's
    Rep. 98 CA (Civ Div) 2–004, 2–040, 2–051
British & Foreign Insurance Co Ltd v Wilson Shipping Co Ltd; sub nom. Wilson Shipping
    Co Ltd v British & Foreign Marine Insurance Co Ltd [1921] 1 A.C. 188; (1920) 4
    Ll.L.R. 371 HL 24–111
British & Foreign Marine Insurance Co Ltd v Gaunt; sub nom. Gaunt v British & Foreign
    Marine Insurance Co Ltd (No.3) [1921] 2 A.C. 41; (1921) 7 Ll.L.R. 62 HL ... 5–041, 6–065,
                                        9–015, 19–034, 19–055, 24–006, 24–112
British & Foreign Marine Insurance Co v Samuel Sanday & Co; sub nom. Sanday & Co v
    British & Foreign Marine Insurance Co [1916] 1 A.C. 650 HL 6–051, 24–069, 24–086
British and Foreign Marine Insurance Co Ltd v Sturge (1897) 2 Com.Cas. 24 17–008
British American v Joseph (1857) 9 Lr.Can.Rep. 448 19–044
British Aviation Insurance Co, Re [2005] EWHC 1621 Ch D (Companies Ct) 16–005
British Bank of the Middle East v Sun Life Assurance Co of Canada (UK) [1983] 2 Lloyd's
    Rep. 9; [1983] Com. L.R. 187; (1983) 133 N.L.J. 575 HL 15–001
British Cash & Parcel Conveyors Ltd v Lamson Store Service Co Ltd [1908] 1 K.B. 1006
    CA 20–006, 20–055
British Citizens Assurance Co v L Woolland & Co (1921) 8 Ll.L.R. 89 KBD 15–051, 24–038
British Credit Trust Holdings v UK Insurance Ltd [2003] EWHC 2404; [2004] 1 All E.R.
    (Comm) 444; [2004] C.P. Rep. 25 QBD (Comm) 7–014, 9–004, 9–040, 9–053, 23–029
British Dominions General Insurance Co Ltd v Duder [1915] 2 K.B. 394 CA 17–004, 17–024
British Eagle International Airlines Ltd v Compagnie Nationale Air France [1975] 1 W.L.R.
    758; [1975] 2 All E.R. 390; [1975] 2 Lloyd's Rep. 43; 119 S.J. 368 HL 17–002
British Equitable Assurance Co Ltd v Baily; sub nom. Baily v British Equitable Assurance
    Co [1906] A.C. 35 HL 1–017
British Equitable Insurance Co v Great Western Railway (1869) 38 L.J.Ch. 314; (1869) 20
    L.T. 422 .... 6–102, 14–027, 18–029
British Equitable Insurance Co v Musgrave (1887) 3 T.L.R. 630 .... 18–028, 18–029
British Fishing Boat Insurance Co v Starr. See North British Fishing Boat Insurance Co Ltd
    v Starr
British General Insurance Co Ltd v Mountain (1919) 1 Ll.L.R. 605; (1919) 36 T.L.R. 171
    HL 17–024, 20–047
British School of Motoring Ltd v Simms [1971] 1 All E.R. 317; [1971] R.T.R. 190 Assizes
    (Winchester) 15–026
British Traders Insurance Co v Monson 111 C.L.R. 86; (1964) 38 A.L.J.R. 20 HC (Aus) 10–006

British Westinghouse Electric & Manufacturing Co Ltd v Underground Electric Railways Co
of London Ltd (No.2) [1912] A.C. 673 HL 11–016
British Workman's Assurance Society v Cunliffe (1902) 18 T.L.R. 425, affirmed (1902) 18
T.L.R. 502 .... 8–022, 18–012, 18–017
British-American Tobacco Co Ltd v Poland (1921) 7 Ll.L.R. 108 CA 24–072
Briton Medical and General Life Assurance Co Ltd (1887) 3 T.L.R. 670 16–006
Britton v Royal Insurance Co (1866) 4 F. & F. 905 .... 6–046, 6–056, 9–020, 9–025, 9–033
Broad v Waland (1942) 73 Ll.L.R. 263 KBD 19–033, 22–087
Broad & Montague Ltd v South East Lancashire Insurance Co Ltd (1931) 40 Ll.L.R. 328
KBD 6–053, 6–075
Broadhurst & Ball v American Home Insurance (1990) 40 O.A.C. 261 20–050
Bromley LBC v A Ellis (Luff & Sons, Third Party) [1971] 1 Lloyd's Rep. 97; (1970) 114 S.J.
906 CA (Civ Div) 15–027, 15–034, 15–062
Brook v Trafalgar Insurance Co Ltd (1946) 79 Ll.L.R. 365 CA 7–020, 9–013, 9–014, 15–017
Brooks v McDonnnell (1836) 1 Y. & C. Ex. 502 24–092
Brotherton v Aseguradora Colseguros SA (No.1) [2002] Lloyd's Rep. I.R. 848 QBD
(Comm) 1–032, 2–005
Brotherton v Aseguradora Colseguros SA (No.2); sub nom. Brotherton v La Previsora SA
Compania de Seguros [2003] EWCA Civ. 705; [2003] 2 All E.R. (Comm) 298; [2003]
2 C.L.C. 629; [2003] Lloyd's Rep. I.R. 746; (2003) 147 S.J.L.B. 658 CA (Civ Div 6–033,
6–034, 6–045, 6–050, 6–062, 6–077, 6–116, 6–130
Brotherton v Aseguradora Colseguros SA (No.3) [2003] EWHC 1741; [2003] Lloyd's
I.R. 762; [2003] Lloyd's Rep I.R. 876 QBD (Comm) ... 6–044, 6–062, 6–065, 6–066, 6–069,
17–007, 17–008, 19–033
Brough v Whitmore (1791) 4 T.R. 208 24–127
Broughton Park Textiles (Salford) Ltd v Commercial Union Assurance Co Ltd [1987] 1
Lloyd's Rep. 194 QBD 9–025
Browlie v Campbell (1880) L.R. 5 App. Cas. 295, 359 6–021
Brown v Abbott (1965) 109 S.J. 437 DC 22–006
Brown v GIO Insurance Ltd [1998] C.L.C. 650; [1998] Lloyd's Rep. I.R. 201; (1998) 95(9)
L.S.G. 29; Times, February 18, 1998 CA (Civ Div) 1–021, 10–032
Brown v Guardian Royal Exchange Assurance Plc Unreported, 1992 20–043
Brown v KMR Services Ltd (formerly HG Poland (Agencies) Ltd); Sword Daniels v Pitel
[1994] 4 All E.R. 385; [1994] C.L.C. 492; Independent, April 19, 1994; Guardian, April
22, 1994 13–041
Brown v KMR Services Ltd (formerly HG Poland (Agencies) Ltd); Sword Daniels v Pitel
[1995] 4 All E.R. 598; [1995] 2 Lloyd's Rep. 513; [1995] C.L.C. 1418; [1995] 4 Re.
L.R. 241; Times, July 26, 1995; Independent, September 13, 1995; Lloyd's List,
October 3, 1995 (I.D.) CA (Civ Div); affirming [1994] 4 All E.R. 385; [1994] C.L.C.
492; Independent, April 19, 1994; Guardian, April 22, 1994 QBD 13–041
Brown v Leeson (1792) 2 H. Bl. 43 4–002
Brown v Roberts [1965] 1 Q.B. 1; [1963] 3 W.L.R. 75; [1963] 2 All E.R. 263; [1963] 1
Lloyd's Rep. 314; 107 S.J. 666 QBD 22–009
Brown v Royal Insurance Co (1859) 1 E. & E. 853 .... 10–044, 10–047
Brown v Smith (1813) 1 Dow. 349 .... 24–135, 24–138
Brown v Tayleur (1835) 4 A. & E. 241 24–070
Brown v Zurich General Accident and Liability Insurance Co Ltd [1954] 2 Lloyd's Rep. 243
QBD 22–091, 22–093
Brown & Davis Ltd v Galbraith [1972] 1 W.L.R. 997; [1972] 3 All E.R. 31; [1972] 2 Lloyd's
Rep. 1; [1972] R.T.R. 523; 116 S.J. 545 CA (Civ Div) 10–044
Brown and Brown v Albany Construction Co [1995] N.P.C. 100 CA (Civ Div) ... 11–001, 11–006
Browne v Vigne (1810) 12 East 283 24–066
Browne's Policy, Re; sub nom. Browne v. Browne [1903] 1 Ch. 188 Ch D 18–014
Browning v JWH Watson (Rochester) Ltd [1953] 1 W.L.R. 1172; [1953] 2 All E.R. 775; 117
J.P. 479; 51 L.G.R. 597; 97 S.J. 591 QBD 22–010
Browning v Phoenix Assurance Co Ltd [1960] 2 Lloyd's Rep. 360 QBD 22–088, 22–096, 22–098
Browning v Provincial Insurance Co of Canada (1873–74) L.R. 5 P.C. 263 PC (Can) 4–024
Brownsville Holdings Ltd v Adamjee Insurance Co Ltd (The Milasan) [2000] 2 All E.R.
(Comm) 803; [2000] 2 Lloyd's Rep. 458 QBD (Comm) 7–037, 7–048, 9–025, 19–034,
24–001, 24–134
Brownton Ltd v Edward Moore Inbucom Ltd [1985] 3 All E.R. 499; (1985) 82 L.S.G. 1165
CA (Civ Div) 11–004
Bruce v Jones (1863) 1 H. & C. 769 .... 1–009, 10–007, 11–044
Brunton v Marshall (1922) 10 Ll.L.R. 689 KBD 1–009, 10–006

Bryan v Forrow; sub nom. Forrow v Bryan [1950] 1 All E.R. 294; 114 J.P. 158; 48 L.G.R.
    347; [1950] W.N. 91; 94 S.J. 194 DC 22–088
Bryant v Primary Industries Insurance Co Ltd [1990] 2 N.Z.L.R. 142 10–051
Buchanan v Motor Insurers Bureau [1955] 1 W.L.R. 488; [1955] 1 All E.R. 607; [1954] 2
    Lloyd's Rep. 519; 119 J.P. 227; 99 S.J. 319 QBD 22–007
Buchanan & Co v Faber (1899) 4 Com.Cas. 223 .... 4–009, 24–017, 24–061
Buckland v Palmer [1984] 1 W.L.R. 1109; [1984] 3 All E.R. 554; [1985] R.T.R. 5; (1984) 81
    L.S.G. 2300; (1984) 128 S.J. 565 CA (Civ Div) 11–015
Bucks Printing Press Ltd v Prudential Assurance Co Unreported, 1991 QBD (Comm) 6–107,
                                                                                                    9–024, 9–029
Bufe v Turner (1815) 6 Taunt. 338 19–033
Bugge v Taylor (1940) 104 J.P. 467 22–007
Bugge v Taylor [1941] 1 K.B. 198 KBD 22–007
Buller v Harrison (1775) 2 Cowp. 565 10–063
Bulling v Frost (1794) 1 Esp. 235 4–002
Bullock v Domitt (1796) 6 T.R. 650 19–021
Bumper Development Corp v Commissioner of Police of the Metropolis [1991] 1 W.L.R.
    1362; [1991] 4 All E.R. 638; (1991) 135 S.J. 382; Times, February 14, 1991; Guardian,
    March 5, 1991 CA 2–025
Burgess v Wickham (1863) 3 B. & S. 669 .... 3–005, 24–062
Burgess's Policy (1915) 85 L.JCh. 273 18–024
Burlinson v Hall (1883–84) L.R. 12 Q.B.D. 347 QBD 14–026
Burn v Taylor (1823) R. & M. 28 4–002
Burnand v Rodocanachi Sons & Co (1881–82) L.R. 7 App. Cas. 333 HL 11–001, 11–036
Burns v Cotton Unreported, 1988 11–015
Burns v Currell [1963] 2 Q.B. 435 22–006
Burns v Shuttlehurst Ltd; sub nom. Burns v General Accident Fire and Life Assurance Corp
    Plc [1999] 1 W.L.R. 1449; [1999] 2 All E.R. 27; [1999] P.I.Q.R. P229; (1999) 96(6)
    L.S.G. 35; Times, January 12, 1999 CA (Civ Div) 21–010, 21–018, 21–040
Burridge v Haines (1918) 87 L.J.K.B. 641 9–018
Burridge & Son v Hames & Sons Ltd (1918) 118 L.T. 681 7–047
Burrows v Jamaica Private Power Co Ltd [2002] 1 All E.R. (Comm) 374; [2002] C.L.C. 255;
    [2002] Lloyd's Rep. I.R. 466 QBD (Comm) 1–033, 1–049, 2–003, 2–005, 2–007
Burt v British Transport Commission (1955) 166 E.G. 4 19–018
Burton v Road Transport & General Insurance Co Ltd (1939) 63 Ll.L.R. 253 KBD 22–088
Burts & Harvey Ltd v Vulcan Boiler and General Insurance Co Ltd (No.2); Alchemy Ltd v
    Vulcan Boiler and General Insurance Co Ltd (No.2) [1966] 1 Lloyd's Rep. 354 QBD 10–022,
                                                                                                    10–027
Burts & Harvey Ltd v Vulcan Boiler and General Insurance Co Ltd (No.1); Alchemy Ltd v
    Vulcan Boiler and General Insurance Co Ltd (No.1) [1966] 1 Lloyd's Rep. 161; 116
    N.L.J. 639 QBD 10–003, 19–055
Bushell v General Accident [1992] 12 C.L. 314 CC (Andover) 5–050
Busk v Royal Exchange Assurance Co (1818) 2 B. & Ald. 73; 06 E.R. 294 .. 5–048, 19–039, 24–062,
                                                                                                    24–080
Busk v Walsh (1812) 4 Taunt. 290, 292 8–022
Butcher v Dowlen [1981] 1 Lloyd's Rep. 310; [1981] R.T.R. 24; 124 S.J. 883 CA (Civ
    Div) 6–031
Butler v Standard Fire (1879) 4 Ont.App. 391 19–044
Butler v Wildman (1820) 3 B. & Ald. 398 .... 24–002, 24–139
Byas v Miller (1897) 3 Com.Cas. 79 4–023
Byrne v Motor Insurers' Bureau [2007] EWHC 1268 (QB); [2008] 2 W.L.R. 234; [2007] 3
    All E.R. 499; [2008] R.T.R. 1; [2007] 3 C.M.L.R. 15; [2007] Eu. L.R. 739; [2008]
    Lloyd's Rep. I.R. 61; [2007] P.I.Q.R. P25; (2007) 104(25) L.S.G. 38; (2007) 157 N.L.J.
    858; (2007) 151 S.J.L.B. 811; Times, June 15, 2007; affirmed [2008] EWCA Civ 574;
    [2009] Q.B. 66; [2008] 3 W.L.R. 1421; [2008] 4 All E.R. 476; [2008] R.T.R. 26; [2008]
    3 C.M.L.R. 4; [2008] Eu. L.R. 732; [2008] Lloyd's Rep. I.R. 705; [2008] P.I.Q.R. P14;
    (2008) 158 N.L.J. 860; (2008) 152(22) S.J.L.B. 31; Times, July 2, 2008 ...... 22–059, 22–077
Blackwell (Contractors) Ltd v Gerling Allegemeine Verischerungs-AG [2007] EWHC 94
    (Comm); [2007] Lloyd's Rep. I.R. 511; on appeal [2007] EWCA Civ 1450; [2008] 1 All
    E.R. (Comm) 885; [2008] Lloyd's Rep. I.R. 529 .... 5–050, 19–034, 19–059, 24–134
CCM Policies Ltd v Amin Unreported, 2001 QBD 14–023
CCR Fishing v Tomenson Inc; The La Pointe [1991] 1 Lloyd's Rep. 89; 1990 A.M.C. 1443;
    69 D.L.R. (4th) 112 (1990) Sup Ct (Can); reversing [1989] 2 Lloyd's Rep. 536 CA (BC);
    affirming [1986] 2 Lloyd's Rep. 513 Sup Ct (BC) 6–120, 24–080

CGU Insurance Ltd v AMP Financial Planning Pty Ltd [2007] H.C.A. 36 .. 15–059, 20–038, 20–044,
 20–085
CGU Insurance Ltd v Corrections Corp of Australia Staff Superannuation Pty Ltd [2008]
 F.C.A.F.C. 173 20–040
CGU Insurance Ltd v Porthouse [2008] H.C.A. 30 20–024
CGU International Insurance Plc v AstraZeneca Insurance Co Ltd [2005] EWHC 2755
 (Comm); [2006] 1 C.L.C. 162; [2006] Lloyd's Rep. I.R. 409 ...... 2–030, 2–033, 17–004, 17–019
CGU International Insurance Plc v Szabo [2002] 1 All E.R. (Comm) 83; [2002] C.L.C. 265;
 [2002] Lloyd's Rep. I.R. 196 QBD (Comm) 2–007, 2–032, 2–033, 2–036, 2–043
CNA Insurance Co Ltd v Office Depot International (UK) Ltd [2005] EWHC 456; [2005]
 Lloyd's Rep. I.R. 658 QBD (Comm) 2–006
CNA International Reinsurance Co Ltd v Companhia de Seguros Tranquilidade SA [1999]
 C.L.C. 140; [1999] Lloyd's Rep. I.R. 289 QBD 1–022, 3–016, 17–004, 17–012
CSE Aviation Ltd v Cardale Doors Ltd Unreported, 2002 QBD (Comm) 11–012
CT Bowring & Co Ltd v Amsterdam London Insurance Co Ltd (1930) 36 Ll.L.R. 309
 KBD 24–080
CTI v Oceanus Mutual. See Container Transport International Inc v Oceanus Mutual
 Underwriting Association (Bermuda) Ltd (No.1)
CTN Cash and Carry Ltd v General Accident Fire and Life Assurance Corp [1989] 1 Lloyd's
 Rep. 299 QBD 7–034, 7–039
CVG Siderurgicia del Orinoco SA v London Steamship Owners Mutual Insurance Associa-
 tion Ltd (The Vainqueur Jose) [1979] 1 Lloyd's Rep. 557 QBD (Comm) 9–003, 21–020,
 21–057
Cadre SA v Astra Asigurari SA [2005] EWHC 2626; [2006] 1 Lloyd's Rep. 560 QBD
 (Comm) 2–006
Cahill v Cahill; sub nom. Cahill v Martin (1882–83) L.R. 8 App. Cas. 420 HL (UK-Irl) ... 18–014
Caisse Populaire v Societe d'Assurances, 19 D.L.R. (4th) 411 (1984) 14–010
Caledonia North Sea Ltd v London Bridge Engineering Ltd; sub nom. Caledonia North Sea
 Ltd v British Telecommunications Plc; Caledonia North Sea Ltd v BT Plc; Caledonia
 North Sea Ltd v Norton (No.2) Ltd (In Liquidation); EE Caledonia Ltd v London Bridge
 Engineering Ltd [2002] UKHL 4; [2002] 1 All E.R. (Comm) 321; [2002] 1 Lloyd's Rep.
 553; 2002 S.C. (H.L.) 117; 2002 S.L.T. 278; 2002 S.C.L.R. 346; [2002] C.L.C. 741;
 [2002] B.L.R. 139; [2002] Lloyd's Rep. I.R. 261; 2002 G.W.D. 6–178; Times, February
 13, 2002 HL 11–032, 11–034, 11–056
Caledonia Subsea Ltd v Micoperi 2003 S.C. 70; 2002 S.L.T. 1022; 2003 S.C.L.R. 20; 2002
 G.W.D. 25–842; Times, September 6, 2002 CS (IH) 2–043
Calf v Sun Insurance Office; sub nom. Calf and Sun Insurance Office's Arbitration, Re [1920]
 2 K.B. 366; (1920) 2 Ll.L.R. 304 CA 3–003, 19–046
Callaghan v Dominion Insurance Co Ltd [1997] 2 Lloyd's Rep. 541; Times, July 14, 1997
 QBD 1–002, 9–037, 9–038, 9–041, 17–027
Callaghan (t/a Stage 3 Discotheque) v Thompson [2000] C.L.C. 360; [2000] Lloyd's Rep.
 I.R. 125 QBD (Comm) 6–048, 6–093, 6–094, 6–095, 6–098, 15–041
Callendar v Oelrichs (1838) 5 Bing. N.C. 58 15–034
Callery v Gray (No.1); sub nom. Callery v Gray (No.2); Callery v Gray (Nos.1 and 2);
 Russell v Pal Pak Corrugated Ltd (No.1) [2002] UKHL 28; [2002] 1 W.L.R. 2000 HL;
 affirming [2001] EWCA Civ. 1117; [2001] 1 W.L.R. 2112; [2001] 3 All E.R. 833;
 [2001] 2 Costs L.R. 163; [2001] Lloyd's Rep. I.R. 743; [2001] P.I.Q.R. P32; (2001) 151
 N.L.J. 1129; Times, July 18, 2001; Independent, July 24, 2001; Daily Telegraph, July
 24, 2001 CA (Civ Div) 23–035, 23–036, 23–038, 23–039
Callery v Gray (No.2); Russell v Pal Pak Corrugated Ltd (No.2) [2001] EWCA Civ. 1246;
 [2001] 1 W.L.R. 2142; [2001] 4 All E.R. 1; [2001] C.P.L.R. 501; [2001] 2 Costs L.R.
 205; [2002] R.T.R. 11; [2001] Lloyd's Rep. I.R. 765; (2001) 98(35) L.S.G. 33; (2001)
 145 S.J.L.B. 204; Times, October 24, 2001 CA (Civ Div) 23–035, 23–037, 23–038, 23–039
Callisher v Bischoffsheim (1869–70) L.R. 5 Q.B. 449 QB 10–055
Callwood v Callwood [1960] A.C. 659; [1960] 2 W.L.R. 705; [1960] 2 All E.R. 1; (1960) 104
 S.J. 327 PC (West Indies) 2–025
Cambridge v Motor Insurers Bureau; sub nom. Cambridge v Callaghan [1998] R.T.R. 365;
 Times, March 21, 1997 CA (Civ Div) 22–069
Camden v Andersen (1794) 5 T.R. 709 19–030
Camden v Anderson (1798) 1 Bos. & P. 272 5–036
Camelo v Britten (1820) 4 B. & Ald. 184 24–064
Campbell v Innes (1821) 4 B. & Ald. 423 6–051
Campbell v Richards (1833) 5 B & Ad. 840 .... 6–024, 6–031, 15–036
Campbell and Phillips v Denman (1915) 21 Com.Cas. 357 10–001

Campbell Discount Co Ltd v Gall [1961] 1 Q.B. 431; [1961] 2 W.L.R. 514; [1961] 2 All E.R.
104; 105 S.J. 232 CA 3–005
Canada Landed Credit Co v Canada Agricultural Insurance (1870) 17 Grant (U.C.) 418 19–047
Canada Rice Mills Ltd v Union Marine & General Insurance Co Ltd [1941] A.C. 55; [1940]
4 All E.R. 169; (1940) 67 Ll.L.R. 549 PC (Can) 24–134
Canada Trust Co v Stolzenberg (No.2) [2002] 1 A.C. 1; [2000] 3 W.L.R. 1376HL; affirming
[1998] 1 W.L.R. 547; [1998] 1 All E.R. 318; [1998] C.L.C. 23; [1998] I.L.Pr. 290;
Times, November 10, 1997 CA (Civ Div) 2–001
Canadian Imperial Bank of Commerce v Dominion of Canada General Insurance Co, 46
D.L.R. (4th) 77 (1987) 14–003, 14–010, 14–012
Canadian Imperial Bank of Commerce v Insurance Company of Ireland, 75 D.L.R. (4th) 482
(1991) 23–004
Canadian Indemnity Co v Andrews & George Co [1952] 4 D.L.R. 690 Sup Ct (Can) 20–009
Canadian Indemnity Co v Canadian Johns-Manville Co, 72 D.L.R. (4th) 478 (1990) 6–065
Canadian Indemnity Co v Walkem Machinery Ltd, 53 D.L.R. (3d) 1 (1976) 5–042
Canadian Pacific Ltd v Base Fort Security Services (BC) Ltd, 77 D.L.R.(4th) 178 (1991) 14–007,
14–008
Canadian Superior Oil Ltd v Concord insurance Co Ltd Unreported, 1990 21–024
Canadian Transport Co Ltd v Court Line Ltd. See Court Line Ltd v Canadian Transport Co
Ltd
Candolin v Vahinkovakuutusosakeyhtio Pohjola (C–537/03) [2005] E.C.R. I–5745; [2006]
R.T.R. 1; [2005] 3 C.M.L.R. 17; [2006] Lloyd's Rep. I.R. 209 ECJ 22–032, 22–035
Canelhas Comercio Importacao e Exportacao Ltd v Wooldridge; sub nom. Wooldridge v
Canelhas Comercio Importacao e Exportacao Ltda [2004] EWCA Civ. 984; [2005] 1 All
E.R. (Comm) 43; [2004] 2 C.L.C. 469; [2004] Lloyd's Rep. I.R. 915; (2004) 148
S.J.L.B. 943 CA (Civ Div) 3–008, 19–052
Canning v Farquhar (1885–86) L.R. 16 Q.B.D. 727 CA 1–024, 1–027, 1–029, 1–031, 6–102
Canning v Maritime Insurance Co Ltd (1936) 56 Ll.L.R. 91 KBD 9–025
Cannon Screen Entertainment Ltd v Handmade Films (Distributors) Ltd (1989) 5 B.C.C. 207;
[1989] B.C.L.C. 660 2–006
Cantiere Meccanico Brindisino v Janson [1912] 3 K.B. 452CA; affirming [1912] 2 K.B. 112
KBD 6–027, 6–062, 6–065, 6–070, 6–073, 24–062
Cantieri Navali Riuniti SpA v Omne Justitia NV; The Stolt Marmaro [1985] 2 Lloyd's Rep.
428 CA (Civ Div) 2–004, 2–037, 2–040
Cape & Dalgleish v Fitzgerald [2002] UKHL 16; [2002] C.P. Rep. 51; [2002] C.P.L.R. 509;
[2003] 1 C.L.C. 65 HL 10–056
Cape Plc v Iron Trades Employers Insurance Association Ltd [2004] Lloyd's Rep. I.R. 75;
[1999] P.I.Q.R. Q212 QBD (Comm) 1–019, 1–020, 3–005, 6–028, 6–065, 6–071, 6–092
Capel-Cure Myers Capital Management Co Ltd v McCarthy [1995] L.R.L.R. 498; Lloyd's
List, August 9, 1995 (I.D.) QBD 5–029, 20–025, 20–047
Capemel v Roger H Lister [1989] I.R. 319 9–004
Capital Annuities Ltd, Re [1979] 1 W.L.R. 170; [1978] 3 All E.R. 704; 122 S.J. 315 Ch D 16–006
Caple v Sewell [2001] EWCA Civ. 1848; [2002] Lloyd's Rep. I.R. 627 CA (Civ Div) 18–043,
20–027, 22–098
Capt JA Cates Tug & Wharfage Co Ltd v Franklin Fire Insurance Co; sub nom. Captain JA
Cates Tug & Wharfage Co Ltd v Franklin Insurance Co [1927] A.C. 698; (1927) 28
Ll.L.R. 161 PC (Can) 24–088
Captain JA Cates Tug and Wharfage Co Ltd v Franklin Insurance. See Capt JA Cates Tug &
Wharfage Co Ltd v Franklin Fire Insurance Co
Captain Panagos, The. See Continental Illinois National Bank & Trust Co of Chicago v
Bathurst
Captain Panagos, The. See Continental Illinois National Bank & Trust Co of Chicago v
Alliance Assurance Co Ltd
Car & Universal Finance Co Ltd v Caldwell [1965] 1 Q.B. 525; [1964] 2 W.L.R. 600; [1964]
1 All E.R. 290; 108 S.J. 15 CA 21–032
Card Protection Plan Ltd v Customs and Excise Commissioners (C–0349/96) [1999] 2 A.C.
601; [1999] 3 W.L.R. 203; [1999] All E.R. (E.C.) 339; [1999] S.T.C. 270; [1999] E.C.R.
I–973; [1999] 2 C.M.L.R. 743; [1999] C.E.C. 133; [1999] B.T.C. 5121; [1999] B.V.C.
155; Times, March 18, 1999 ECJ 1–010
Carden v CE health Casualty and General Insurance Ltd; CE Health Casualty and General
Insurance v Grey 1993 NSW LEXIS 8082 20–081
Carlingford Australia General Insurance Ltd v EZ Industries Ltd [1988] V.R. 349 3–010
Carlton v R&J Park Ltd (1922) 12 Ll.L.R. 246CA; affirming (1922) 10 Ll.L.R. 818 KBD 5–050,
6–052

Carmichael & Sons (Worcester) v Cottle [1971] R.T.R. 11; 114 S.J. 867; Times, November
    4, 1970 DC 22–009
Carmichael's Case. *See* English & Scottish Law Life Assurance Association v Carmichael
Carnill v Rowland [1953] 1 W.L.R. 380; [1953] 1 All E.R. 486; [1953] 1 Lloyd's Rep. 99;
    117 J.P. 127; 51 L.G.R. 180; 97 S.J. 134 DC 22–011
Caroline, The v War Risk Underwriters (1921) 7 Ll.L.R. 56 KBD 25–005
Carpenter v Ebblewhite [1939] 1 K.B. 347; (1938) 62 Ll.L.R. 1 CA 22–058
Carr & Co v Matthews Wrightson & Co. *See* Arthur Carr & Co v Matthews Wrightson & Co
    Ltd
Carr and Sun Fire Insurance Co, Re (1897) 13 T.L.R. 186 .... 9–017, 9–018, 14–029
Carreras Ltd v Cunard Steamship Co Ltd [1918] 1 K.B. 118 KBD 10–029, 19–022
Carruthers v Gray (1811) 3 Camp. 142 24–058
Carruthers v Sheddon (1815) 6 Taunt 14 .... 4–012, 6–047, 24–030, 24–048
Carruthers v Sydebotham (1815) 4 M. & S. 577 24–134
Carstairs v Allnutt (1813) 3 Camp. 497 24–064
Carstairs v Hamilton Unreported, 1998 22–006
Carter v Boehm (1766) 3 Burr. 1706 .... 6–073, 6–077
Carter v Boehm (1766) 3 Burr. 1905 .... 6–002, 6–024, 6–031, 6–063, 6–065, 6–073, 6–122, 6–123,
    6–130, 8–026
Cartwright v MacCormack [1963] 1 W.L.R. 18; [1963] 1 All E.R. 11; [1962] 2 Lloyd's Rep.
    328; 106 S.J. 957 CA 1–052, 5–004
Carvill America Inc v Camperdown UK Ltd; Carvill America Inc v XL Speciality Insurance
    Co Ltd [2005] EWCA Civ. 645; [2005] 2 Lloyd's Rep. 457; [2005] 1 C.L.C. 845; [2006]
    Lloyd's Rep. I.R. 1 CA (Civ Div); affirming [2004] EWHC 2221; [2005] Lloyd's Rep.
    I.R. 55 QBD (Comm) 2–004, 3–013, 8–023, 15–033
Case v Davidson (1816) 5 M. & S. 79 24–095
Cassel v Lancashire & Yorkshire Accident insurance Co Ltd (1885) 1 T.L.R. 495 ... 9–003, 9–007
Castellain v Preston (1882–83) L.R. 11 Q.B.D. 380 CA 1–009, 4–019, 11–001, 11–036, 19–006,
    19–009, 19–020, 19–025, 19–030
Castle Insurance Co v Hong Kong Islands Shipping Co (The Potoi Chau) [1984] A.C. 226;
    [1983] 3 W.L.R. 524; [1983] 3 All E.R. 706; [1983] 2 Lloyd's Rep. 376; (1983) 127 S.J.
    616 PC (HK) 9–038, 10–022, 10–059
Caterpillar Financial Services Corp v SNC Passion [2004] EWHC 569; [2004] 2 Lloyd's
    Rep. 99 QBD (Comm) 2–030
Caterpillar Inc v Great American Insurance, 62 F. 3d 1995 (7th Circuit, 1995) 20–052
Cathay Pacific Airways Ltd v Nation Life & General Assurance Co Ltd [1966] 2 Lloyd's
    Rep. 179; 110 S.J. 583; Times, June 29, 1966 QBD (Comm) 18–055
Catlin Syndicate Ltd v Adams Land & Cattle Co [2006] EWHC 2065 (Comm); [2006] 2
    C.L.C. 425; [2007] Lloyd's Rep. I.R. 96 .... 2–005, 2–006
Cator v Great Western Insurance Co of New York (1872–73) L.R. 8 C.P. 552 CCP 10–021
Caudle v Sharp; Grove v Sharp [1995] L.R.L.R. 433; [1995] C.L.C. 642; [1995] 4 Re. L.R.
    389; Lloyd's List, August 3, 1995 (I.D.) CA (Civ Div) 10–034
Cavalier Insurance Co Ltd, Re [1989] 2 Lloyd's Rep. 430; Times, May 31, 1989 Ch D 8–022,
    13–020, 18–010
Cavaliere v Legal Services Commission [2003] EWHC 323; [2003] 3 Costs L.R. 350QBD 21–018
Cave v Cave (1880) L.R. 15 Ch. D. 639 Ch D 6–042
Cavell USA Inc v Seaton Insurance Co [2009] EWCA Civ 1363; [2009] 2 C.L.C. 991; [2010]
    Lloyd's Rep. F.C. 197; Times, January 12, 2010 2–003
Cawley v National Employers, Accident & General Assurance Association Ltd (1855) Cab.
    & El. 597 9–003
Cawley v National Employers' Accident & General Insurance Association Ltd (1885) 1
    T.L.R. 255 .... 5–030, 9–007
Cazenove v British Equitable Assurance Co (1859) 29 L.J.C.P. 160 6–010
Cazenove v British Equitable Assurance Co (1859) 6 C.B.(N.S.) 437 7–037
Cee Bee Marine v Lombard Insurance Co [1990] 2 N.Z.L.R. 1 15–057
Cehave NV v Bremer Handels GmbH; The Hansa Nord; sub nom. Cehave NV v Bremer
    Handelgesellschaft mbH; The Hansa Nord [1976] Q.B. 44; [1975] 3 W.L.R. 447; [1975]
    3 All E.R. 739; [1975] 2 Lloyd's Rep. 445; 119 S.J. 678 CA (Civ Div) 1–001, 3–007
Cementation Piling and Foundations Ltd v Commercial Union Insurance Co Plc; Cementa-
    tion Piling and Foundations Ltd v Aegon Insurance Ltd [1995] 1 Lloyd's Rep. 97; 74
    B.L.R. 98; 47 Con. L.R. 14 CA (Civ Div) 10–003
Centennial Insurance Co v INSCO Ltd. *See* American Centennial Insurance Co v Insco
    Ltd
Central Bank of India Ltd v Guardian Assurance Co Ltd (1936) 54 Ll.L.R. 247 PC (Ind) 9–026

Central Insurance Co Ltd v Seacalf Shipping Corp (The Aiolos) [1983] 2 Lloyd's Rep. 25 CA
(Civ Div) 11–001, 11–004
Centre Reinsurance International Co v Freakley [2005] Lloyd's Rep I.R. 284, affirming
[2005] Lloyd's Rep I.R. 22 .... 21–010, 21–018, 21–019, 21–028, 21–033, 21–034, 21–036,
21–063
Century Bank v Young (1914) 84 L.J.K.B. 385 .... 9–015, 23–022
Century Insurance Co of Canada v Case Existological Laboratories Ltd (The Bamcell II)
[1984] 1 W.W.R. 97 7–034
Century Surety Co v Dewey Bellows Operating Co Ltd 2009 B.L. 187750 (SD Tex Septmber
2, 2009) 20–050
Cepheus Shipping Corp v Guardian Royal Exchange Assurance Plc; The Capricorn [1995] 1
Lloyd's Rep. 622 QBD 4–017, 24–019, 24–026
Ceylon Motor Insurance Association v Thambugala [1953] A.C. 584; [1953] 3 W.L.R. 486;
[1953] 2 All E.R. 870; [1953] 2 Lloyd's Rep. 289; 97 S.J. 555 PC (Cey) 22–045
Chalgray v Aspley (1965) 109 S.J. 394 DC 22–006
Chalmers v Bell (1804) 3 B. & P. 604 24–064
Champion Investments Ltd v Ahmed [2004] EWHC 1956 QBD 10–057
Chan King Wan v Honest Scaffold General Contractor Ltd [1998] 2 H.K.C. 358 11–008
Chan Yiu Sun v Yip Kim Cheung [1990] 1 H.K.C. 524 .... 7–014, 9–008
Chandler v Poland (1932) 44 Ll.L.R. 349 KBD 10–055
Chandris v Argo Insurance Co Ltd [1963] 2 Lloyd's Rep. 65; 107 S.J. 575 QBD (Comm) 9–038,
10–022
Chaplin v Boys [1971] A.C. 356; [1969] 3 W.L.R. 322; [1969] 2 All E.R. 1085; [1969] 2
Lloyd's Rep. 487; (1969) 113 S.J. 608 HL 2–061
Chaplin v Reid (1858) 1 F. & F. 315 19–018
Chapman v Chapman (1851) 13 Beav. 599 14–026
Chapman v Fraser (1793) 1 Park (8th ed.) 456 8–022
Chapman v Parlby, 62 L.G.R. 150; [1964] Crim. L.R. 230; 108 S.J. 35 DC 22–007
Chapman v Pole (1870) 22 L.T. 306, 307 .... 8–001, 9–026, 10–015
Chapman & Co Ltd v Kadirga Denizcilik Ve Ticaret AS. See JA Chapman & Co Ltd (In
Liquidation) v Kadirga Denizcilik ve Ticaret AS
Chapman Ltd v Christopher. See TGA Chapman Ltd v Christopher
Charente Steamship Co v Director of Transports (1922) 10 Ll.L.R. 514 CA 25–005
Charles v Altin (1854) 15 C.B. 461; 39 E.R. 335 15–045
Charles Griffin & Co Ltd v De-La-Haye [1968] 2 Lloyd's Rep. 253 QBD 10–015, 10–022
Charlesworth v Faber (1900) 5 Com.Cas. 408 .... 17–007, 17–012
Charlton v Fisher; sub nom. Churchill Insurance v Charlton [2001] EWCA Civ. 112; [2002]
Q.B. 578; [2001] 3 W.L.R. 1435; [2001] 1 All E.R. (Comm) 769; [2001] R.T.R. 33;
[2001] Lloyd's Rep. I.R. 387; [2001] P.I.Q.R. P23; (2001) 98(10) L.S.G. 45; Times,
February 21, 2001; Independent, March 12, 2001 (C.S); Daily Telegraph, February 20,
2001 CA (Civ Div) .. 3–006, 5–042, 5–046, 20–031, 21–022, 22–007, 22–027, 22–028, 22–029,
22–034, 22–036, 22–038, 22–039, 22–040, 22–054, 22–056, 22–060,
22–086
Charman v Gordian Run-Off Ltd. See Charman v New Cap Reinsurance Corp Ltd
Charman v Guardian Royal Exchange Assurance [1992] 2 Lloyd's Rep. 607 QBD
(Comm) 17–019, 17–020
Charman v New Cap Reinsurance Corp Ltd; Charman v Gordian Runoff Ltd; Gordian Runoff
Ltd (fomerly GIO Insurance Ltd) v HIH Casualty & General Insurance Ltd; New Cap
Reinsurance Corp Ltd v HIH Casualty & General Insurance Ltd [2003] EWCA Civ.
1372; [2004] 1 All E.R. (Comm) 114; [2004] Lloyd's Rep. I.R. 373 CA (Civ Div);
reversing [2002] EWHC 2290; [2003] Lloyd's Rep. I.R. 337 QBD (Comm) ... 1–047, 3–009,
15–035, 17–010
Charman v WOC Offshore BV [1993] 2 Lloyd's Rep. 551 CA (Civ Div) 2–015
Charnock v Liverpool Corp [1968] 1 W.L.R. 1498; [1968] 3 All E.R. 473; [1968] 2 Lloyd's
Rep. 113; 112 S.J. 781 CA (Civ Div) 10–044
Chartbrook Ltd v Persimmon Homes Ltd [2009] UKHL 38; [2009] 1 A.C. 1101; [2009] 3
W.L.R. 267; [2009] Bus. L.R. 1200; [2009] 4 All E.R. 677; [2010] 1 All E.R. (Comm)
365; [2009] B.L.R. 551; 125 Con. L.R. 1; [2010] 1 P. & C.R. 9; [2009] C.I.L.L. 2729;
[2009] 27 E.G. 91 (C.S.); (2009) 153(26) S.J.L.B. 27; [2009] N.P.C. 86; [2009] N.P.C.
87; Times, July 2, 2009 .... 1–018, 3–005
Charter Reinsurance Co Ltd (In Liquidation) v Fagan [1997] A.C. 313; [1996] 2 W.L.R. 726;
[1996] 3 All E.R. 46; [1996] 2 Lloyd's Rep. 113; [1996] C.L.C. 977; [1996] 5 Re. L.R.
411; (1996) 140 S.J.L.B. 148; Times, May 24, 1996; Independent, June 21, 1996 HL 3–006,
3–007, 7–015, 9–041, 17–004, 17–017, 20–035, 21–024

Chartered Trust & Executor Co v London Scottish Assurance Corporation Ltd (1923) 39
    T.L.R. 608 24–030
Charterhouse Development (France) Ltd v Sharp; Charterhouse Development (France) Ltd v
    Financial Instututions Insurance Brokers Ltd; Charterhouse Development (France) Ltd
    v Royal Bank Insurance Services Ltd [1998] Lloyd's Rep. I.R. 266 QBD (Comm) ... 20–010,
                                                                                      20–015, 20–025
Chase v Ram Technical Services Ltd [2000] 2 Lloyd's Rep. 418 QBD (Comm) 2–004, 2–005,
                                                                                                2–007
Chattock v Shawe (1835) 1 M. & R. 498 18–029
Chaurand v Angerstein (1791) Peake 43 6–015
Chemetics International Ltd v Commercial Union Assurance Co of Canada (1984) 11 D.L.R.
    (4th) 754 .... 20–028, 20–083
Cherney v Deripaska [2007] EWHC 965 (Comm); [2007] 2 All E.R. (Comm) 785; [2007]
    I.L.Pr. 49 2–001
Cherney v Deripaska (No.2) [2009] EWCA Civ 849; [2009] C.P. Rep. 48; [2009] 2 C.L.C.
    408; (2009) 159 N.L.J. 1138; Times, October 13, 2009 2–004
Cherry Ltd v Allied Insurance Brokers Ltd [1978] 1 Lloyd's Rep. 274 QBD 15–040
Cheshire v Thompson (1918) 29 Com.Cas. 114 6–065
Cheshire & Co v Vaughan Bros & Co. See Thomas Cheshire & Co v Vaughan Bros & Co
Chicago St Louis & New Orleans Railroad Co v Pullman Southern Car Co, 139 U.S. 79
    (1891) 11–034
Chief Constable of Avon and Somerset v Fleming [1987] 1 All E.R. 318; (1987) 84 Cr. App.
    R. 345; [1987] R.T.R. 378; [1987] Crim. L.R. 277; Times, November 3, 1986 DC 22–006
Childs v Coghlan [1968] Crim. L.R. 225; 118 N.L.J. 182; 112 S.J. 175 DC 22–006
China Traders Insurance Co Ltd v Royal Exchange Assurance Corp [1898] 2 Q.B. 187 CA 6–107,
                                                                                                17–001
China-Pacific SA v Food Corp of India (The Winson) [1982] A.C. 939; [1981] 3 W.L.R. 860;
    [1981] 3 All E.R. 688; [1982] 1 Lloyd's Rep. 117; 125 S.J. 808 HL 24–112
Chippendale v Holt (1895) 65 L.J.Q.B. 104 17–019
Chitty v Selwyn & Martyn (1742) 2 Atk. 359 24–095
Choko Star, The. See Industrie Chimiche Italia Centrale and Cerealfin SA v Alexander G
    Tsavliris & Sons Maritime Co
Chowne v Baylis (1862) 31 Beav. 351 14–026
Chrismas v Taylor Woodrow Civil Engineering Ltd; Chrismas v Sir Robert McAlpine Ltd
    [1997] 1 Lloyd's Rep. 407 QBD (Comm) 3–011, 20–028, 20–083
Christie v Secretan (1799) 8 T.R. 192 24–061
Chubb Insurance Co of Europe SA v Davies [2004] EWHC 2138; [2004] 2 All E.R. (Comm)
    827; [2005] Lloyd's Rep. I.R. 1 QBD (Comm) 21–019, 21–055
Chui Man Kwan v Bank of China Group Insurance Co Ltd [2008] H.K.B.C. 1190 ... 11–046, 11–047,
                                                                                                11–051
Churchill v Norris (1938) 138 L.T. 255 22–010
Cia de Seguros Imperio v Heath (REBX) Ltd (formerly CE Heath & Co (America) Ltd); sub
    nom. Companhia de Seguros Imperio v Heath (REBX) Ltd [2001] 1 W.L.R. 112; [2000]
    2 All E.R. (Comm) 787 CA (Civ Div); affirming [1999] 1 All E.R. (Comm) 750; [1999]
    C.L.C. 997; [1999] Lloyd's Rep. I.R. 571; [1999] Lloyd's Rep. P.N. 571; Independent,
    May 3, 1999 (C.S.) QBD (Comm) 15–022, 15–061
Cigna Insurance Co v Gulf United States Corp 1997 W.L. 1878757 (D Idaho 1997) 20–087
Cigna Life Insurance Co of Europe SA NV v Intercaser SA de Seguros y Reaseguros [2002]
    1 All E.R. (Comm) 235; [2001] C.L.C. 1356; [2001] Lloyd's Rep. I.R. 821 QBD
    (Comm) 3–015, 17–012
Cildero v Scottish Accident (1892) 19 R. (Ct. of Sess.) 355 18–051
Circle Freight International Ltd v Medeast Gulf Exports Ltd [1988] 2 Lloyd's Rep. 427 CA
    (Civ Div) 3–017
Citadel Insurance Co v Atlantic Union Insurance Co SA [1982] 2 Lloyd's Rep. 543; [1982]
    Com. L.R. 213; [1984] E.C.C. 191 CA (Civ Div) 2–004, 2–040, 6–120
Citibank NA v Brown Shipley & Co Ltd; Midland Bank Plc v Brown Shipley & Co Ltd
    [1991] 2 All E.R. 690; [1991] 1 Lloyd's Rep. 576; (1990) 140 N.L.J. 1753; Independent,
    December 3, 1990 (C.S.); Financial Times, November 20, 1990 QBD (Comm) 10–060
Citibank NA v Excess Insurance Co Ltd (t/a ITT London and Edinburgh) [1999] C.L.C. 120;
    [1999] Lloyd's Rep. I.R. 122QBD 20–025, 20–055, 20–056
Citizens Insurance Co of Canada v Parsons; Queen Insurance Co v Parsons (1881–82) L.R.
    7 App. Cas. 96 PC (Can) 1–055
City and Westminster Properties (1934) Ltd v Mudd [1959] Ch. 129; [1958] 3 W.L.R. 312;
    [1958] 2 All E.R. 733; 102 S.J. 582 Ch D 3–017

City Polytechnic of Hong Kong v Blue Cross (Asia Pacific) Insurance Ltd [1995] 2 H.K.L.R.
  103 1–023
City Tailors v Evans (1921) 126 L.T. 439 10–021
City Tailors v Evans (1921) 38 T.L.R. 230 .... 1–009, 3–011, 5–041, 10–006, 10–007
City Tailors v Evans (1921) 9 Ll.L.R. 394; (1921) 91. L.J. K.B. 379 CA; reversing (1921) 7
  Ll.L.R. 195 KBD 4–017, 10–018, 10–038
Claim by Helbert Wagg & Co Ltd, Re; Prudential Assurance Co Ltd, Re [1956] Ch. 323;
  [1956] 2 W.L.R. 183; [1956] 1 All E.R. 129; (1956) 100 S.J. 53 2–030
Claims Direct Test Cases, Re [2003] EWCA Civ. 136; [2003] 4 All E.R. 508; [2003] 2 All
  E.R. (Comm) 788; [2003] 2 Costs L.R. 254; [2003] Lloyd's Rep. I.R. 677; [2003]
  P.I.Q.R. P31; (2003) 100(13) L.S.G. 26; (2003) 147 S.J.L.B. 236; Times, February 18,
  2003 CA (Civ Div); affirming [2003] Lloyd's Rep. I.R. 69 Sup Ct Costs Office 8–001,
                                                                    23–036, 23–037, 23–038
Clan Line Steamers Ltd v Board of Trade; The Clan Matheson [1929] A.C. 514; (1929) 34
  Ll.L.R. 1 HL 25–004, 25–005
Clapham v Cologan (1813) 3 Camp. 382 .... 6–008, 24–059
Clapham v Langton (1864) 10 L.T. 875 24–062
Clark v Ardington Electrical Services. See Lagden v O'Connor
Clark v Blything (1823) 2 B. & C. 254 11–001
Clark v Tull (trading as Ardington Electrical Services). See Lagden v O'Connor
Clark & Sons Ltd v Finnamore, 32 D.L.R. (3d) 236 (1972) 11–038
Clarke v Kato; sub nom. Clarke v General Accident Fire & Life Assurance Corp Plc; Cutter
  v Eagle Star Insurance Co Ltd [1998] 1 W.L.R. 1647; [1998] 4 All E.R. 417; (1999) 163
  J.P. 502; [1999] R.T.R. 153; [1999] P.I.Q.R. P1; (1998) 95(43) L.S.G. 31; (1998) 148
  N.L.J. 1640; (1998) 142 S.J.L.B. 278; [1998] N.P.C. 142; Times, October 23, 1998;
  Independent, October 27, 1998 HL 22–007, 22–030
Clarke v National Insurance and Guarantee Corp [1964] 1 Q.B. 199; [1963] 3 W.L.R. 710;
  [1963] 3 All E.R. 375; [1963] 2 Lloyd's Rep. 35; 107 S.J. 573 CA 7–023, 22–036, 22–092,
                                                                               22–099
Clarke v Vedel [1974] R.T.R. 26 .... 22–057, 22–060
Clarkson v Young (1870) 22 L.T. 41 24–039
Clason v Simmons (1741) 6 T.R. 533n 24–073
Clay, Re [1937] 2 All E.R. 548 18–014
Clay, Re; sub nom. Clay v Booth; Deed of Indemnity, Re [1919] 1 Ch. 66 CA 9–053
Clay v Harrison (1829) 10 B. & C. 99 19–007
Cleaver v Delta American Reinsurance Co (In Liquidation) [2001] UKPC 6; [2001] 2 A.C.
  328; [2001] 2 W.L.R. 1202; [2001] 1 B.C.L.C. 482; [2001] B.P.I.R. 438; [2002] Lloyd's
  Rep. I.R. 167; (2001) 145 S.J.L.B. 85 PC (CI) 17–017
Cleaver v Mutual Reserve Fund Life Association [1892] 1 Q.B. 147 CA 18–014, 18–035
Cleland v London General Insurance Co Ltd (1935) 51 Ll.L.R. 156 CA 6–018, 6–048, 21–021,
                                                                           21–057, 22–087
Clements v London & North Western Railway Co [1894] 2 Q.B. 482 CA 14–002
Clements v National General Insurance Co, Times, June 11, 1910 19–047
Clifford v Hunter (1827) 3 C. & P. 16 24–062
Clift v Long [1961] Crim. L.R. 121 DC 22–008
Clift v Schwabe (1846) 3 C.B. 437 .... 3–008, 18–034
Clinton v Windsor Life Assurance Co Ltd Unreported, 2001 CA (Civ Div) 10–062
Close Invoice Finance Ltd v Watts [2009] EWCA Civ 1182 23–030
Club Estates Ltd v Woodside Estates Co (Amersham) Ltd. See Cottage Club Estates Ltd v
  Woodside Estates Co (Amersham) Ltd
Clugas v Penaluna (1791) 4 Term Rep. 466; 100 E.R. 1122 2–057
Clunis v Camden and Islington HA [1998] Q.B. 978; [1998] 2 W.L.R. 902; [1998] 3 All E.R.
  180; (1997–98) 1 C.C.L. Rep. 215; (1998) 40 B.M.L.R. 181; [1998] P.N.L.R. 262;
  (1998) 95(2) L.S.G. 23; (1998) 142 S.J.L.B. 38; Times, December 10, 1997; Independ-
  ent, December 9, 1997 CA 5–046
Clydebank & District Water Trustees v Fidelity & Deposit Co of Maryland, 1916 S.C. (H.L.)
  69; 1915 2 S.L.T. 357HL; affirming 1915 S.C. 362; 1915 1 S.L.T. 129 IH (1 Div) 23–026,
                                                                                          23–031
Clydesdale Financial Services Ltd v Smailes [2009] EWHC 3190 (Ch) 8–004, 8–020, 23–034
Coast Ferries Ltd v Century Insurance Co of Canada [1974] N.R. 436 24–003
Coast Lines v Hudig & Veder Chartering NV [1972] 2 Q.B. 34; [1972] 2 W.L.R. 280; [1972]
  1 All E.R. 451; [1972] 1 Lloyd's Rep. 53; (1971) 116 S.J. 119; Times, December 8,
  1971 CA 2–040
Cobb v Whorton [1971] R.T.R. 392 DC 22–006

Cobb v Williams [1973] R.T.R. 113; [1973] Crim. L.R. 243 DC 22–009
Cobb & Jenkins v Volga Insurance Co Ltd (1920) 4 Ll.L.R. 178 KBD 24–134
Cochran v Leckie's Trustee (1906) 8 F. (Ct of Sess.) 975 19–013
Cock Russell & Co v Bray Gibb & Co (1920) 3 Ll.L.R. 71 KBD (Comm Ct) 15–034
Cockrane v Fisher (1835) 1 C. M. & R. 809 24–068
Coggs v Bernard (1703) 1 Smith's Leading Cases (13th ed.) 175 19–010
Cohen Sons & Co v National Benefit Assurance Co Ltd (1924) 18 Ll.L.R. 199; (1840) 40
    T.L.R. 347 KBD 24–003, 24–080, 24–134
Cohen Sons & Co v Standard Marine Insurance Co Ltd. See George Cohen Sons & Co v
    Standard Marine Insurance Co Ltd
Cohen v Plaistow' Transport. See A Cohen & Co Ltd v Plaistow Transport Ltd
Coker v Bolton [1912] 3 K.B. 315 KBD 3–008, 24–097
Colby v Hunter (1827) 3 C. & P. 7 7–022
Cole v Accident Insurance Co Ltd (1899) 5 T.L.R. 736 .... 3–010, 5–048
Cole v Accident Insurance Co Ltd (1889) 61 L.T. 227 .... 18–041, 18–051
Coleman's Depositories Ltd and Life & Health Assurance Association's Arbitration, Re
    [1907] 2 K.B. 798 CA 1–055, 3–003, 3–009, 5–001, 9–002, 9–004, 9–006, 9–018
Colledge v Harty (1851) 6 Exch. 205 7–022
College Credit Ltd v National Guarantee Corp Ltd [2004] EWHC 978; [2004] 2 All E.R.
    (Comm) 409; [2005] Lloyd's Rep. I.R. 5 QBD (Comm) 23–030
Collen v Wright (1857) 8 El. & Bl. 647 15–009
Collett v Morrison (1851) 9 Hare 162 7–031
Collingridge v Royal Exchange Assurance Corp (1877–78) L.R. 3 Q.B.D. 173 QBD 11–001,
                                                14–022, 19–008, 19–009, 19–016
Colonia Versicherung AG v Amoco Oil Co (The Wind Star) [1997] 1 Lloyd's Rep. 261;
    [1997] C.L.C. 454; [1997] 6 Re. L.R. 86 CA (Civ Div); affirming [1995] 1 Lloyd's Rep.
    570; [1995] C.L.C. 51 QBD (Comm) 11–036, 14–007, 14–029
Colonial Fire & General Insurance Co Ltd v Chung Unreported, 2002 7–015
Colonial Fire & General Insurance Co Ltd v Harry [2006] UKPC 53; [2008] Lloyd's Rep.
    I.R. 382 PC (Trinidad and Tobago) 22–048
Colonial Insurance Co of New Zealand v Adelaide Marine Insurance Co (1886) L.R. 12 App.
    Cas. 128 PC (Trin) 4–016, 19–007
Colonial Mutual General Insurance Co Ltd v ANZ Banking Group (New Zealand) Ltd [1995]
    1 W.L.R. 1140; [1995] 3 All E.R. 987; [1995] 2 Lloyd's Rep. 433; [1995] C.L.C. 1047;
    [1995] 4 Re. L.R. 275; (1995) 92(28) L.S.G. 39; (1995) 139 S.J.L.B. 152; [1995] N.P.C.
    111; Lloyd's List, July 11, 1995 (I.D.) PC (NZ) 14–010, 14–026
Colouras v British General Insurance Co Ltd (1922) 12 Ll.L.R. 220 9–025
Comber v Anderson (1808) 1 Camp. 523 .... 15–034, 15–041
Comeau v Roy (1999) N.B.R. (2d) 242 20–049
Comerford v Britannic Assurance Co Ltd (1908) 24 T.L.R. 593 ..... 15–001, 15–013, 15–015, 15–018
Commercial Marine Piling Ltd v Pierse Contracting Ltd [2009] EWHC 2241 (TCC); [2010]
    1 All E.R. (Comm) 1087; [2009] 2 Lloyd's Rep. 659; [2009] 2 C.L.C. 433; [2009]
    I.L.Pr. 54; [2009] N.P.C. 107 .... 2–004, 2–043
Commercial Union Assurance Co Ltd v Niger Co Ltd; Niger Co Ltd v Guardian Assurance
    Co Ltd (1922) 13 Ll.L.R. 75 HL 6–103, 24–072
Commercial Union Assurance Co Plc v NRG Victory Reinsurance Ltd; Skandia International
    Insurance Corp v NRG Victory Reinsurance Ltd [1998] 2 All E.R. 434; [1998] 2 Lloyd's
    Rep. 600; [1998] C.L.C. 920; [1998] Lloyd's Rep. I.R. 439; Times, March 19, 1998 CA
    (Civ Div) 17–018, 17–020, 20–034, 20–057, 20–061, 20–085
Commercial Union Assurance Co Plc v Simat Helliesen & Eichner Inc [2000] I.L.Pr. 239;
    [2001] Lloyd's Rep. I.R. 172 QBD (Comm) 2–005, 2–006, 2–043
Commercial Union Assurance Co Plc v Sun Alliance Insurance Group Plc; Commercial
    Union Assurance Co Plc v Guardian Royal Exchange Plc [1992] 1 Lloyd's Rep. 475
    QBD (Comm) 1–047, 3–011, 5–008, 17–014
Commercial Union Assurance Co v Gamman (1908) 10 G.L.R. 672 8–003
Commercial Union Assurance Co v Hayden [1977] Q.B. 804; [1977] 2 W.L.R. 272; [1977]
    1 All E.R. 441; [1977] 1 Lloyd's Rep. 1; (1976) 120 S.J. 855; Times, October 26, 1976
    CA (Civ Div) 11–062
Commercial Union Assurance Co v Lister (1873–74) L.R. 9 Ch. App. 483CA in Chancery ... 11–006,
                                                11–009, 11–013, 11–017, 11–042, 19–025
Commercial Union Assurance Co Plc v Sun Alliance Insurance Group Plc [1992] 1 Lloyd's
    Rep. 475 1–033
Commercial Union Life Assurance Co Ltd, Re [2009] EWHC 2521 (Ch) 13–035

Commission of the European Communities v Denmark (252/83) [1986] E.C.R. 3713; [1987]
    2 C.M.L.R. 169 ECJ 13–003
Commission of the European Communities v France; sub nom. Co-Insurance Services, Re
    (C–220/83) [1986] E.C.R. 3663; [1987] 2 C.M.L.R. 113 ECJ 13–003
Commission of the European Communities v Germany; sub nom. Insurance Services, Re
    (C–205/84) [1986] E.C.R. 3755; [1987] 2 C.M.L.R. 69; Times, January 13, 1987 ECJ 13–003
Commission of the European Communities v Ireland (C–211/07) [2008] E.C.R. I–33; [2008]
    Lloyd's Rep. I.R. 526 ECJ 22–067
Commission of the European Communities v Ireland; sub nom. Co-Insurance Services, Re
    (C–206/84) [1986] E.C.R. 3817; [1987] 2 C.M.L.R. 150 ECJ 13–003
Commission of the European Communities v Italy (C–518/06) [2009] E.C.R. I–3491; [2009]
    3 C.M.L.R. 22 ECJ 22–009
Commissioners of Customs and Excise v Barclays Bank. See Customs and Excise
    Commissioners v Barclays Bank Plc
Commissioners of Customs and Excise v Pools Finance (1937) Ltd. See Customs and Excise
    Commissioners v Pools Finance
Commonwealth, The [1907] P. 216 CA 11–017, 11–018
Commonwealth Construction Co v Imperial Oil, 69 D.L.R. (3d) 558 (1976) 14–004
Commonwealth Insurance Co v Groupe Sprinks SA [1983] 1 Lloyd's Rep. 67 QBD
    (Comm) 15–034, 15–036
Commonwealth Shipping Representative v Peninsular and Oriental Branch Service; sub nom.
    Peninsular & Oriental Branch Service v Commonwealth Shipping Representative
    [1923] A.C. 191; (1922) 13 Ll.L.R. 455HL; affirming [1922] 1 K.B. 706; (1922) 10
    Ll.L.R. 465CA 25–005
Commonwealth Smelting Ltd v Guardian Royal Exchange Assurance Ltd [1986] 1 Lloyd's
    Rep. 121 CA (Civ Div); affirming [1984] 2 Lloyd's Rep. 608; (1984) 134 N.L.J. 1018;
    Times, August 7, 1984 QBD (Comm) 3–007, 3–008, 19–041
Compagnia Tirrena Di Assicurazioni SpA v Grand Union Insurance Co Ltd [1991] 2 Lloyd's
    Rep. 143 QBD (Comm) 7–048
Compagnie Tunisienne de Navigation SA v Compagnie d'Armement Maritime SA; sub nom.
    Compagnie d'Armement Maritime SA v Compagnie Tunisienne de Navigation SA
    [1971] A.C. 572; [1970] 3 W.L.R. 389; [1970] 3 All E.R. 71; [1970] 2 Lloyd's Rep. 99;
    (1970) 114 S.J. 618 HL 2–030, 2–035, 2–037, 2–038, 2–052
Companhia de Seguros Imperio v Heath (REBX) Ltd. See Cia de Seguros Imperio v Heath
    (REBX) Ltd (formerly CE Heath & Co (America) Ltd)
Compania Colombiana de Seguros v Pacific Steam Navigation Co (The Colombiana);
    Empressa de Telefona de Bogota v Pacific Steam Navigation Co; The Colombiana
    [1965] 1 Q.B. 101; [1964] 2 W.L.R. 484; [1964] 1 All E.R. 216; [1963] 2 Lloyd's Rep.
    479; 108 S.J. 75 QBD (Comm) 11–004, 11–016
Compania Maritima San Basilio SA v Oceanus Mutual Underwriting Association (Bermuda)
    Ltd [1977] Q.B. 49; [1976] 3 W.L.R. 265; [1976] 3 All E.R. 243; [1976] 2 Lloyd's Rep.
    171; 120 S.J. 486 CA (Civ Div) 24–007, 24–047, 24–062
Compania Martiartu v Royal Exchange Assurance Corp; sub nom. Compania Naviera
    Martiartu v Royal Exchange Assurance Corp [1924] A.C. 850; (1924) 19 Ll.L.R. 95
    HL 9–025
Compania Merabello San Nicholas SA, Re [1973] Ch. 75; [1972] 3 W.L.R. 471; [1972] 3 All
    E.R. 448; [1972] 2 Lloyd's Rep. 268; 116 S.J. 631 Ch D 21–006
Compania Naviera Bachi v Henry Hosegood & Son Ltd (1938) 60 Ll.L.R. 236; [1938] 2 All
    E.R. 189 KBD 24–138
Compania Naviera Micro SA v Shipley International Inc (The Parouth) [1982] 2 Lloyd's
    Rep. 351 CA (Civ Div) 2–052
Compania Naviera Santi SA v Indemnity Marine Assurance Co Ltd (The Tropaioforos)
    [1960] 2 Lloyd's Rep. 469 QBD (Comm) 9–025
Compania Naviera Vascongada v British & Foreign Marine Insurance Co Ltd (The Gloria)
    (1936) 54 Ll.L.R. 35 KBD 9–025
Company, Ex p. ND Pritchard, Re; sub nom. Company (No.008725 of 1991 and No.008727
    of 1991), Re [1992] B.C.L.C. 633; Financial Times, November 22, 1991 Ch D 16–004,
                                                                                        17–015, 17–026
Company (No.000359 of 1987), Re; sub nom. International Westminster Bank v Okeanos
    Maritime Corp [1988] Ch. 210; [1987] 3 W.L.R. 339; [1987] 3 All E.R. 137; [1987]
    B.C.L.C. 450; [1988] P.C.C. 64; (1987) 84 L.S.G. 1811; (1987) 131 S.J. 938 Ch D ... 21–006
Company (No.008725 of 1991), Re, Ex p. Pritchard. See Company, Ex p. ND Pritchard,
    Re
Company (No.012209 of 1991), Re [1992] 1 W.L.R. 351; [1992] 2 All E.R. 797 Ch D 16–004

Company (No.013734 of 1991), Re [1992] 2 Lloyd's Rep. 415; [1993] B.C.L.C. 59; Times,
    May 8, 1992; Financial Times, June 3, 1992 Ch D 16–004, 17–017, 20–035
Company (No.007923 of 1994), Re Unreported, 1995 15–021
Company of African Merchants v British Insurance Co (1873) L.R. 8 Ex. 154 .... 24–072, 24–073
Computer & Systems Engineering Plc v John Lelliott (Ilford), 54 B.L.R. 1; Times, February
    21, 1991 CA (Civ Div) 19–037, 19–042
Commerzbank AG v Price-Jones. *See* Jones v Commerzbank AG
Comunidad Naviera Baracaldo v Norwich Union Fire Insurance Society Ltd (1923) 16
    Ll.L.R. 156 KBD 9–025
Comyn Ching & Co (London) Ltd v Oriental Tube Co Ltd [1981] Com. L.R. 67; 17 B.L.R.
    47 CA 15–059
Concordato Italiano Incendio [1990] O.J. L15/25 13–045
Concrete Ltd v Attenborough (1939) 65 Ll.L.R. 174 KBD 5–049
Condogianis v Guardian Assurance Co Ltd [1921] 2 A.C. 125; (1921) 7 Ll.L.R. 155 PC
    (Aus) 6–010, 6–018, 6–052, 7–024, 7–031, 7–037, 18–029
Congentra AG v Sixteen Thirteen Marine SA (The Nicholas M) Nicholas M, The [2008]
    EWHC 1615 (Comm); [2009] 1 All E.R. (Comm) 479; [2008] 2 Lloyd's Rep. 602;
    [2008] 2 C.L.C. 51 2–063
Conklin Co Inc v National Union Fire Insurance Co 1987 W.L. 108957 (D Minn. 1987) ... 20–087
Conn v Westminster Motor Insurance Association [1966] 1 Lloyd's Rep. 407; 116 N.L.J.
    894CA; reversing [1966] 1 Lloyd's Rep. 123; 116 N.L.J. 554 QBD 7–015, 22–036, 22–093
Connecticut Fire Insurance Co v Kavanagh [1892] A.C. 473 PC (Can) 1–053
Connecticut Mutual Life Insurance Co of Hertford v Moore (1880–81) L.R. 6 App. Cas. 644
    PC (Can) 6–019, 7–037, 18–029
Connecticut Mutual v Akens, 150 U.S. 468 (1893) 18–029
Connecticut Mutual v Union Trust Co, 112 U.S. 250 (1884) 18–029
Connecticut Mutual Life Insurance Co of Hertford v Moore (1880–81) L.R. 6 App. Cas. 644
    PC (Canada) 18–029
Connell v Motor Insurers Bureau [1969] 2 Q.B. 494; [1969] 3 W.L.R. 231; [1969] 3 All E.R.
    572; [1969] 2 Lloyd's Rep. 1; 113 S.J. 489 CA (Civ Div) 22–031, 22–097
Connelly v New Hampshire Insurance Co Ltd, 1997 S.L.T. 1341; 1997 S.C.L.R. 459; [1997]
    6 Re. L.R. 367; 1997 G.W.D. 18–840 OH 18–049, 18–059
Consolidated Freightways Inc v Moore, 229 P. 2d 882 (1951) 11–034
Consolidated Life Assurance Co Ltd, Re Unreported, 1996 Ch D 13–036
Con-Stan Industries of Australia Pty Ltd v Norwich Winterthur Insurance (Australia) Ltd
    (1986) 64 A.L.R. 481 8–003
Conservation Council of New Brunswick Inc v Encon Group Inc [2005] N.B.J. No.109 20–050
Conservation Council of New Brunswick Inc v Encon Group Inc [2006] N.B.C.A. 51 20–049
Conservation Council of New Brunswick Inc v Encon Group Inc [2006] N.B.J. No.190 20–049
Constantinou v Aegon Insurance Co (UK) Ltd Unreported, 1996 CA 6–048
Container Transport International Inc v Oceanus Mutual Underwriting Association (Ber-
    muda) Ltd (No.1) [1984] 1 Lloyd's Rep. 476 CA (Civ Div) 6–021, 6–024, 6–027, 6–054,
                                                       6–073, 6–090, 6–107, 6–116, 24–007
Continental Assurance Co of London Plc (In Liquidation) (No.3), Re; sub nom. Hughes v
    Hogg Insurance Brokers Ltd [2000] B.C.C. 65; [1999] 1 B.C.L.C. 751; (1999) 96(6)
    L.S.G. 32; Times, January 14, 1999 Ch D 16–008, 16–011
Continental Bank NA v Aeakos Compania Naviera SA [1994] 1 W.L.R. 588; [1994] 2 All
    E.R. 540; [1994] 1 Lloyd's Rep. 505; [1994] I.L.Pr. 413; Times, November 26, 1993 CA
    (Civ Div) 2–003
Continental Illinois National Bank & Trust Co of Chicago v Alliance Assurance Co Ltd; The
    Captain Panagos DP [1989] 1 Lloyd's Rep. 33 CA (Civ Div); affirming [1986] 2 Lloyd's
    Rep. 470 QBD (Comm) 6–107, 9–025, 9–032, 24–138
Continental Illinois National Bank & Trust Co of Chicago v Bathurst; The Captain Panagos
    DP [1985] 1 Lloyd's Rep. 625; [1985] Fin. L.R. 224 QBD (Comm) 10–006, 23–004, 24–011,
                                                                                                          24–033
Continental Insurance Co v Dia Met Minerals Ltd (1996) 20 B.C.L.R. (3d) 331 20–050
Contingency Insurance Co Ltd v Lyons (1939) 65 Ll.L.R. 53 CA 22–048
Cook v Field (1850) L.R. 15 Q.B.D. 460 4–017
Cook v Financial Insurance Co Ltd [1998] 1 W.L.R. 1765; [1999] Lloyd's Rep. I.R. 1; (1999)
    46 B.M.L.R. 1; (1999) 96(3) L.S.G. 31; (1999) 143 S.J.L.B. 52; Times, December 4,
    1998 HL 18–044, 18–060
Cooke & Arkwright v Haydon [1987] 2 Lloyd's Rep. 579; (1987) 283 E.G. 1068 CA (Civ
    Div) 20–011
Coolee Ltd v Wing Heath & Co (1930) 38 Ll.L.R. 157 KBD 15–031

Coolee v Wing Heath & Co (1930) 47 T.L.R. 78 15–037
Cooper Henderson Finance Ltd v Colonial Mutual General Insurance Co [1990] 1 N.Z.L.R.
    1 14–020
Cooper v Farmers' Mutual Insurance Society [2001] C.T.C. 652 20–048
Cooper v General Accident Fire & Life Assurance Corp; sub nom. RW Cooper v General
    Accident, &C., Corp Ltd (1922) 13 Ll.L.R. 219 HL (UK-Irl) 25–009
Cooper v Knight (1901) 17 T.L.R. 299 2–004
Cooper v Motor Insurers Bureau [1985] Q.B. 575; [1985] 2 W.L.R. 248; [1985] 1 All E.R.
    449; [1985] R.T.R. 273; (1985) 82 L.S.G. 202; (1985) 129 S.J. 32 CA (Civ Div) 22–017,
                                                                                      22–018
Cooper v Pacific Mutual (1871) 8 Am.Rep. 705 8–004
Cooper v Toronto Casualty Insurance [1928] 2 D.L.R. 1007 19–047
Co-operative Fire v Saindon, 56 D.L.R. (3d) 556 (1975) 5–042
Cooperative Retail Services Ltd v Taylor Young Partnership Ltd; Cooperative Retail Services
    Ltd v Hoare Lea & Partners; Cooperative Retail Services Ltd v Carillion Construction
    Ltd (formerly Tarmac Construction (Contracts) Ltd); Cooperative Retail Services Ltd v
    East Midlands Electricity Electrical Installations Services Ltd (t/a Hall Electrical) (In
    Liquidation) [2002] UKHL 17; [2002] 1 W.L.R. 1419; [2002] 1 All E.R. (Comm) 918;
    [2003] 1 C.L.C. 75; [2002] B.L.R. 272; [2002] T.C.L.R. 9; 82 Con. L.R. 1; [2002]
    Lloyd's Rep. I.R. 555 HL; affirming [2000] 2 All E.R. 865; [2000] B.L.R. 461; (2001)
    3 T.C.L.R. 4; 74 Con. L.R. 12; [2001] Lloyd's Rep. I.R. 122; (2000) 16 Const. L.J. 347;
    Independent, October 2, 2000 (C.S); Independent, July 14, 2000 CA (Civ Div) 11–026,
                                                                                      11–027, 14–018
Co-operator's Insurance Co v Ross [2003] 65 O.R. (3d) 135 20–049
Cooter & Green v Tyrrell [1962] 2 Lloyd's Rep. 377 CA 10–044
Copley v Lawn; Maden v Haller [2009] EWCA Civ 580; [2010] Bus. L.R. 83; [2010] 1 All
    E.R. (Comm) 890; [2009] R.T.R. 24; [2009] Lloyd's Rep. I.R. 496; [2009] P.I.Q.R. P21;
    Times, July 15, 2009 22–026
Corbin v Payne, Times, October 11, 1990 CA (Civ Div) 20–012, 20–087
Corcos v De Rougemont (1925) 23 Ll.L.R. 164 KBD 6–018, 22–087
Corfield v Buchanan (1913) 29 T.L.R. 258 24–007
Corfield v Groves [1950] 1 All E.R. 488; 66 T.L.R. (Pt. 1) 627; [1950] W.N. 116; 94 S.J. 225
    KBD 22–012, 22–013
Cork v Rawlins; sub nom. Rawlins, Re [2001] EWCA Civ. 202; [2001] Ch. 792; [2001] 3
    W.L.R. 300; [2001] 4 All E.R. 50; [2001] B.P.I.R. 222; [2001] Lloyd's Rep. I.R. 587;
    (2001) 98(18) L.S.G. 44; Times, March 15, 2001; Independent, March 19, 2001 (C.S)
    CA (Civ Div) 18–061
Cormack v Gladstone (1809) 11 East 347 24–070
Cormack v Washbourne (formerly t/a Washbourne & Co); sub nom. Cormack v Excess
    Insurance Co Ltd [2000] C.P.L.R. 358; [2000] C.L.C. 1039; [2002] Lloyd's Rep. I.R.
    398; [2000] Lloyd's Rep. P.N. 459; (2000) 97(15) L.S.G. 39; Times, March 30, 2000;
    Independent, March 31, 2000 CA (Civ Div) 20–055
Cornfoot v Royal Exchange Assurance Corp [1904] 1 K.B. 40 CA 5–004, 24–065
Cornhill Insurance Co Ltd v L&B Assenheim (1937) 58 Ll.L.R. 27 KBD 6–053, 10–060
Cornhill Insurance Plc v DE Stamp Felt Roofing Contractors Ltd [2002] EWCA Civ. 395;
    [2002] Lloyd's Rep. I.R. 648 CA (Civ Div) 7–016, 7–036
Cornish v Accident Insurance Co Ltd (1889) L.R. 23 Q.B.D. 453 CA ... 3–009, 3–010, 5–048, 5–050,
                                                                               18–041, 18–050, 18–051
Cornish v Lynch (1910) 3 B.W.C.C. 343 20–047
Coromin Ltd v AXA Re [2007] EWHC 2818 (Comm); [2008] Lloyd's Rep. I.R. 467 23–042
Coronation Insurance Co v Clearly Canadian Beverage Corp (1999) 117 B.C.A.C. 22 20–052
Coronation Insurance Co v Taku Air Transport Ltd, 85 D.L.R. (4th) 609 (1992) 6–067
Cory v Burr. See John Cory & Sons v Burr
Cory v Patton (1873–74) L.R. 9 Q.B. 577 QB 6–040, 6–103, 15–003
Cory & Sons v Friedlander. See Wm Cory & Sons v Friedlander
Cosford Union v Poor Law & Local Government Officers' Mutual Guarantee Association
    Ltd (1910) 103 L.T. 463 .... 5–026, 23–024
Costain-Blankevoort (UK) Dredging Co Ltd v Davenport (Inspector of Taxes) (The Nassau
    Bay) [1979] 1 Lloyd's Rep. 395; [1979] S.T.C. 320; 51 T.C. 349; [1978] T.R. 369; 123
    S.J. 35; Times, November 17, 1978 Ch D 5–031
Cottage Club Estates Ltd v Woodside Estates Co (Amersham) Ltd [1928] 2 K.B. 463 KBD 21–029
Cotten v Fidelity & Casualty Co (1890) 41 Fed. Rep. 506 18–029

Countrywide Assured Group Plc v Marshall [2002] EWHC 2082; [2003] 1 All E.R. (Comm)
    237; [2003] Lloyd's Rep. I.R. 195; [2003] Lloyd's Rep. P.N. 1; [2002] Pens. L.R. 537;
    (2002) 99(44) L.S.G. 32 QBD (Comm) 10–032, 10–034, 10–036
County Homesearch Co (Thames & Chilterns) Ltd v Cowham [2008] EWCA Civ 26; [2008]
    1 W.L.R. 909; [2008] 1 E.G.L.R. 24; [2008] 15 E.G. 178; [2008] N.P.C. 10 3–018
Coupar Transport (London) Ltd v Smith's (Acton) Ltd [1959] 1 Lloyd's Rep. 369 QBD ... 11–031
Court v Martineau (1782) 2 Doug K.B. 161 .... 6–070, 6–073
Court Line Ltd v Canadian Transport Co Ltd; sub nom. Canadian Transport Co Ltd v Court
    Line Ltd [1940] A.C. 934; (1940) 67 Ll.L.R. 161 HL 11–031
Courtney & Fairbairn Ltd v Tolaini Brothers (Hotels) Ltd; sub nom. Courtney & Fairburn v
    Tolaini Bros (Hotels) [1975] 1 W.L.R. 297; [1975] 1 All E.R. 716; 2 B.L.R. 97; (1974)
    119 S.J. 134; Times, November 29, 1974 CA (Civ Div) 1–021
Cousins v D&C Carriers Ltd [1971] 2 Lloyd's Rep 230 24–009
Cousins v Sun Life Assurance Co [1933] Ch. 126 CA 18–014
Coven SpA v Hong Kong Chinese Insurance Co [1999] C.L.C. 223; [1999] Lloyd's Rep. I.R.
    565 CA (Civ Div) 10–003, 24–066
Coward v Motor Insurers Bureau [1963] 1 Q.B. 259; [1962] 2 W.L.R. 663; [1962] 1 All E.R.
    531; [1962] 1 Lloyd's Rep. 1; 106 S.J. 34 CA 22–031, 22–097
Cowell v Yorkshire Provident Life Assurance Co (1901) 17 T.L.R. 452 9–004
Cowie v Barber (1814) 4 Cowp. 100 24–064
Cox v Bankside Members Agency Ltd [1995] 2 Lloyd's Rep. 437; [1995] C.L.C. 671; Times,
    May 16, 1995; Independent, June 9, 1995; Lloyd's List, August 29, 1995 (I.D.) CA (Civ
    Div) 7–015, 9–004, 10–036, 20–030, 20–036, 20–045, 21–010, 21–016, 21–019, 21–023,
                21–025, 21–026, 21–028, 21–031, 21–060, 21–064, 23–040
Cox v Deeny [1996] L.R.L.R. 288 QBD (Comm) 20–030
Cox v Orion Insurance Co Ltd [1982] R.T.R. 1 CA (Civ Div) 9–029
Cox v White [1976] R.T.R. 248; [1976] Crim. L.R. 263 DC 22–007
Coxe v Employers Liability Association Corp Ltd [1916] 2 K.B. 629 KBD 5–031
Coxe v PhillipsCA. Temp. Hardw. 237 4–002
Coxwold, The [1942] A.C. 691 5–030
Crabb v Crabb (1834) 1 My. & K. 511 18–006
Craft Enterprises (International) Ltd v AXA Insurance Co [2004] EWCA Civ. 171; [2004] 2
    All E.R. (Comm) 123; [2004] 2 C.L.C. 427; [2005] Lloyd's Rep. I.R. 14 CA (Civ
    Div) 2–033
Craig v Penn (1841) Car. & M. 43 18–030
Craig's Executor, Re (1870) L.R. 9 Eq. 706 16–011
Crane v Hannover Ruckversicherungs AG [2008] EWHC 3165 (Comm); [2010] Lloyd's
    Rep. I.R. 93 .... 1–023, 1–034, 6–004, 6–008, 6–013, 6–015, 6–102, 6–103
Craufurd v Hunter (1798) 8 T.R. 13 4–002
Crawford v Haughton; sub nom. Crawford v Houghton [1972] 1 W.L.R. 572; [1972] 1 All
    E.R. 535; [1972] R.T.R. 125; [1972] Crim. L.R. 788; (1971) 116 S.J. 125 DC 22–009
Credit Agricole Indosuez v Unicof Ltd (No.1) [2003] EWHC 77 (Comm) 2–004
Credit Lyonnais v New Hampshire Insurance Co Ltd [1997] 2 Lloyd's Rep. 1; [1997] 2
    C.M.L.R. 610 CA (Civ Div) 2–048
Credit Suisse First Boston (Europe) Ltd v MLC (Bermuda) Ltd [1999] 1 All E.R. (Comm.)
    237; [1999] 1 Lloyd's Rep. 767; [1999] C.L.C. 579 2–006
Crema v Cenkos Securities Plc [2010] EWHC 461 (Comm) 15–032
Cricklewood Property & Investment Trust Ltd v Leighton's Investment Trust Ltd; sub nom.
    Leighton's Investment Trust Ltd v Cricklewood Property & Investment Trust Ltd [1945]
    A.C. 221; [1945] 1 All E.R. 252 HL 19–020
Criminal Proceedings against Bernaldez (C–129/94) [1996] All E.R. (EC) 741; [1996] E.C.R.
    I–1829; [1996] 2 C.M.L.R. 889; Times, May 6, 1996 ECJ 22–029, 22–036, 22–044
Crisp v Marshall [1997] C.L.Y. 1761 22–063
Crocker v General Insurance Co Ltd (1897) 3 Com. Cas. 22 24–066
Crocker v Sturge [1897] 1 Q.B. 330QBD (Comm) 24–066
Croft v Lyndsey (1676) Freeman Ch. 1 19–031
Crofts v Marshall (1836) 7 C. & P. 597 .... 3–013, 24–080, 24–134
Cross v British Oak Insurance Co Ltd [1938] 2 K.B. 167; (1938) 60 Ll.L.R. 46 KBD 22–045
Cross v Kirby Unreported February 18, 2000 5–046
Crossley v City of Glasgow Life Assurance Co (1876–77) L.R. 4 Ch. D. 421 Ch D 14–026
Crossley v Road Transport & General Insurance Co (1925) 21 Ll.L.R. 219 KBD 22–093
Crowley v Cohen (1832) 3 B. & A. 478 .... 4–012, 6–047, 17–008, 19–007, 19–010, 19–012, 19–044,
                                                                                24–029, 24–048

Crows Transport v Phoenix Assurance Co [1965] 1 W.L.R. 383; [1965] 1 All E.R. 596;
    [1965] 1 Lloyd's Rep. 139; 109 S.J. 70 CA 5–010
Crowson v HSBC Insurance Brokers Ltd Unreported January 26, 2010 .... 9–044, 15–062, 20–081
Croxford v Universal Insurance Co Ltd; Norman v Gresham Fire and Accident Insurance
    Society Ltd [1936] 2 K.B. 253; (1936) 54 Ll.L.R. 171 CA 22–037, 22–048
Crozier v Phoenix (1870) 13 New.Br. (2 Han.) 200 19–044
Crozier v Thompson (1922) 12 Ll.L.R. 291 KBD 25–009
Cruickshank v Northern Accident Assurance Co (1895) 3 S.L.T. 167 IH (2 Div) 15–019
Cruikshank v Northern Accident (1895) 23 R. 147 18–029
Cullen v Butler (1816) 5 M. & S. 461 .... 11–001, 24–139
Cunard Steamship Co Ltd v Marten [1903] 2 K.B. 511 CA 10–029, 24–112
Cunard v Hyde (1859) 29 L.J.Q.B. 6 24–064
Cunard v Hyde (No.1) (1858) E.B. & E. 670 24–064
Cunard v Hyde (No.2) (1859) 2 E. & E. 1 24–064
Cuppitman v Marshall (1924) 18 Ll.L.R. 277 KBD 9–025
Currie v Bombay Native Insurance Co. See MR Currie & Co v Bombay Native Insurance
    Co
Curtis v Chemical Cleaning & Dyeing Co [1951] 1 K.B. 805; [1951] 1 All E.R. 631; [1951]
    1 T.L.R. 452; 95 S.J. 253 CA 15–018
Curtis & Harvey (Canada) Ltd (In Liquidation) v North British & Mercantile Insurance Co
    Ltd [1921] 1 A.C. 303; (1920) 5 Ll.L.R. 8 PC (Can) 5–030
Curtis & Sons v Mathews [1919] 1 K.B. 425CA; affirming [1918] 2 K.B. 825 KBD 3–011,
                                                                           25–003, 25–004, 25–006
Customs and Excise Commissioners v Barclays Bank Plc [2006] UKHL 28; [2006] 3 W.L.R.
    1; (2006) 103(27) L.S.G. 33; (2006) 156 N.L.J. 1060; (2006) 150 S.J.L.B. 859; Times,
    June 22, 2006 HL 15–009, 15–031, 15–062
Customs and Excise Commissioners v Pools Finance [1952] 1 All E.R. 775; [1952] 1 T.L.R.
    792; [1952] W.N. 165; 96 S.J. 229 CA 15–002
Cutter v Eagle Star Insurance Co Ltd. See Clarke v Kato; sub nom. Clarke v General
    Accident Fire & Life Assurance Corp Plc; Cutter v Eagle Star Insurance Co Ltd
DG Finance Ltd v Scott and Eagle Star Insurance Co Ltd [1999] Lloyd's Rep. I.R. 387 CA
    (Civ Div) 19–006, 19–013, 19–030
DP Mann v Coutts & Co 2003. See Mann v Coutts & Co
DR Insurance Co v Central National Insurance Co of Omaha (In Rehabilitation) [1996] 1
    Lloyd's Rep. 74; [1996] 5 Re. L.R. 482; Lloyd's List, November 2, 1995 (I.D.) QBD
    (Comm) 2–004
DR Insurance Co v Seguros America Banamex; DR Insurance Co v Imperio Compahnia de
    Seguros [1993] 1 Lloyd's Rep. 120 QBD (Comm) ... 13–017, 13–019, 13–020, 15–021, 17–003,
                                                                                                17–004
DSG Retail Ltd v QBE International Insurance Ltd; DSG Retail Ltd v Royal London General
    Insurance Co Ltd; DSG Retail Ltd v Reliance National Insurance Co; DSG Retail Ltd
    v Lexington Insurance Co; DSG Retail Ltd v Sirius (UK) Insurance Plc [1999] Lloyd's
    Rep. I.R. 283 QBD (Comm) 7–031
D&F Estates Ltd v Church Commissioners for England [1989] A.C. 177; [1988] 3 W.L.R.
    368; [1988] 2 All E.R. 992; 41 B.L.R. 1; 15 Con. L.R. 35; [1988] 2 E.G.L.R. 213; (1988)
    4 Const. L.J. 100; [1988] E.G.C.S. 113; (1988) 85(33) L.S.G. 46; (1988) 138 N.L.J. Rep.
    210; (1988) 132 S.J. 1092 HL 20–076
D&J Koskas v Standard Marine Insurance Co Ltd (1927) 27 Ll.L.R. 59; [1927] 137 L.T. 165
    CA 3–004, 3–011, 3–018
Da Costa v Edmonds (1815) 4 Camp. 142 6–065
Da Costa v Firth (1766) 4 Burr. 1966 11–067
Da Costa v Jones (1778) 2 Cowp. 37 4–002
Daher v Economical Mutual Insurance Co (1996) 31 O.R. (3d) 472 20–050
Dakin v Oxley (1864) 15 C.B. N.S. 646 24–026
Dalby v India and London Life Assurance Co (1854) 15 C.B. 365 ..... 4–004, 4–009, 11–005, 18–004,
                                                                                     18–008, 18–022
Daley v Hargreaves [1961] 1 W.L.R. 487; [1961] 1 All E.R. 552; (1961) 125 J.P. 193; 59
    L.G.R. 136; 105 S.J. 111 DC 22–006
Dalgleish v Brooke (1812) 5 East 295 7–022
Dalgleish v Buchanan (1854) 16 Ct of Sess. (2nd Series) 322 .... 19–007, 19–013
Dalglish v Jarvie (1850) 2 H. & Tw. 437; 42 E.R. 89; (1850) 14 Jur. 945; (1850) 2 Mac. &
    G. 231; (1850) 20 L.J. Ch. 475; (1850) 15 L.T. O.S. 341 .... 6–005, 6–021, 6–037
Daly v Lime Street Underwriting Agencies [1987] 2 F.T.L.R. 277; [1987] Fin. L.R. 331;
    Times, June 8, 1987 QBD 1–032

Dane v Mortgage Insurance Corp Ltd [1894] 1 Q.B. 54 CA 11–066, 23–019, 23–029, 23–030
Danepoint Ltd v Allied Underwriting Insurance Ltd [2005] EWHC 2318 QBD (TCC) 9–026,
9–026, 9–029, 9–030
Daniels v Harris (1874–75) L.R. 10 C.P. 1 CCP 24–062, 24–063
Daniels v Vaux [1938] 2 K.B. 203 KBD 22–010, 22–012
Dann v Hamilton [1939] 1 K.B. 509 KBD 22–033
Danvers v Thistlewaite (1669) 1 Lev. 44 4–002
Darrell v Tibbitts (1879–80) L.R. 5 Q.B.D. 560 CA 11–054, 19–016, 19–021, 19–025
Datec Electronic Holdings Ltd v United Parcels Service Ltd [2007] UKHL 23; [2007] Bus.
L.R. 1291; [2007] 1 W.L.R. 1325; [2007] 4 All E.R. 765; [2007] 2 All E.R. (Comm)
1067; [2007] 2 Lloyd's Rep. 114; [2007] 1 C.L.C. 720; [2007] R.T.R. 40; (2007) 151
S.J.L.B. 670; Times, May 18, 2007 24–134
Davey v Towle [1973] R.T.R. 328; [1973] Crim. L.R. 360 DC 22–002
Davian v Canadian Order of Foresters (1923) 61 C.S. 492 18–029
Davidson v Guardian Royal Exchange Assurance [1979] 1 Lloyd's Rep. 406; 1979 S.C. 192;
1981 S.L.T. 81 IH (2 Div) 10–044, 10–052
Davies v Hosken (1937) 58 Ll.L.R. 183; (1937) 53 T.L.R. 798;[1937] 3 All E.R. 192 KBD ... 20–009,
20–031, 23–021
Davies v National Fire & Marine Insurance Co of New Zealand [1891] A.C. 485 PC (Aus) 6–010,
6–018, 6–031
Davies and Cranton v Royal Insurance Plc Unreported, 1998 9–025
Davies' Policy Trusts, Re [1892] 1 Ch. 90 Ch D 18–014
Davis v Garrett (1830) 6 Bing. 716 24–070
Davitt v Titcumb [1990] Ch. 110; [1990] 2 W.L.R. 168; [1989] 3 All E.R. 417 Ch D 14–013,
14–027, 18–020, 18–035
Dawson v Atty (1806) 7 East 367 24–058
Dawsons Bank Ltd v Vulcan Insurance Co Ltd (1934) 50 Ll.L.R. 129 PC (Ind) 19–033
Dawsons Ltd v Bonnin [1922] 2 A.C. 413; (1922) 12 Ll.L.R. 237; 1922 S.C. (H.L.) 156; 1922
S.L.T. 444 HL 3–007, 6–023, 6–031, 7–021, 7–022, 7–026, 7–029, 7–030, 7–031, 7–032,
19–033, 22–086, 22–087
De Bussche v Alt (1878) L.R. 8 Ch. D. 286 CA 24–078
De Costa v Scandret (1723) 2 P.Wms. 170 .... 8–022, 24–035, 24–036
De Costa v Scandrett (1823) 2 Eq. Ca. Ab. 636 6–062
De Hahn v Hartley (1786) 1 T.R. 343 .... 7–022, 7–038, 7–043
De Marco v Scottish Metropolitan Assurance Co Ltd; Barclay's Bank Ltd v Scottish
Metropolitan Assurance Co Ltd; Gazan v Scottish Metropolitan Assurance Co Ltd
(1923) 14 Ll.L.R. 220 KBD 9–025
De Mattos v North (1867–68) L.R. 3 Ex. 185 Ex Ct 24–015
De Maurier (Jewels) Ltd v Bastion Insurance Co and Coronet Insurance Co Ltd [1967] 2
Lloyd's Rep. 550; (1967) 117 N.L.J. 1112 QBD (Comm) 3–010, 7–025, 7–034, 22–091,
22–094
De Meza & Stuart v Apple van Straten Shena & Stone [1975] 1 Lloyd's Rep. 498 CA (Civ
Div) 15–026
De Monchy v Phoenix Insurance Co of Hartford. See Phoenix Insurance Co v De Monchy;
sub nom. De Monchy v Phoenix Insurance Co of Hartford
De Souza v Home & Overseas Insurance Co Ltd [1995] L.R.L.R. 453; Times, September 19,
1990; Independent, July 30, 1990; Guardian, October 5, 1990 CA (Civ Div) 18–040, 18–041,
18–042, 18–045, 18–046, 18–047, 18–049, 18–059
De Vaux v J'Anson (1839) 7 Scott 507 20–062
De Vaux v J'Anson (1839) 5 Bing. N.C. 519 .... 24–026, 24–134
De Vaux v Salvador (1836) 4 Ad. & El. 420; 111 E.R. 845 24–007
De Wolf v Archangel Maritime Bank & Insurance Co Ltd (1873–74) L.R. 9 Q.B. 451 QB 24–065
Deacon v AT (A Minor) [1976] R.T.R. 244; [1976] Crim. L.R. 135 DC 22–007
Dean v Hornby (1854) 3 El. & Bl. 180; 118 E.R. 1108 .... 24–086, 24–135
Dearle v Hall (1828) 3 Russ. 1 .... 14–026, 14–028
Debs v Sibec Developments [1990] R.T.R. 91; Times, May 19, 1989 QBD 10–001
Debtors (Nos.4449 and 4450 of 1998), Re; sub nom. McAllister v Society of Lloyd's [1999]
1 All E.R. (Comm) 149; [1999] B.P.I.R. 548; [1999] Lloyd's Rep. I.R. 487 Ch D 13–042
Decorum Investments Ltd v Atkin (The Elena G) [2001] 2 Lloyd's Rep. 378; [2002] Lloyd's
Rep. I.R. 450 QBD (Comm) 6–004, 6–062, 6–063, 6–065, 24–038
Dee Conservancy Board v McConnell [1928] 2 K.B. 159; (1928) 30 Ll.L.R. 200 CA 24–096
Deeny v Gooda Walker Ltd (No.1) [1996] L.R.L.R. 183; [1994] C.L.C. 1224; Times, October
7, 1994; Independent, October 5, 1994 QBD 13–041, 13–042

Deeny v Gooda Walker Ltd (No.3) [1995] 1 W.L.R. 1206; [1995] 4 All E.R. 289; [1996]
    L.R.L.R. 176; [1995] C.L.C. 623; [1995] 4 Re. L.R. 117; Times, May 5, 1995 QBD
    (Comm) 13–041
Deeny v Gooda Walker Ltd (No.4) [1996] L.R.L.R. 168; [1995] S.T.C. 696; Times, June 29,
    1995; Lloyd's List, September 28, 1995 (I.D.) QBD 13–041
Deeny v Stewart Wrightson Ltd Unreported, 1995 13–041
Deep Vein Thrombosis and Air Travel Group Litigation, Re [2005] UKHL 72; [2006] 1 A.C.
    495; [2005] 3 W.L.R. 1320; [2006] 1 All E.R. 786; [2006] 1 All E.R. (Comm) 313;
    [2006] 1 Lloyd's Rep. 231; [2005] 2 C.L.C. 1083; [2006] P.I.Q.R. P14; (2006) 87
    B.M.L.R. 1; (2006) 103(3) L.S.G. 26; (2005) 155 N.L.J. 1925; (2006) 150 S.J.L.B. 29;
    Times, December 12, 2005; Independent, December 13, 2005 HL 10–033, 18–042
Deepak Fertilisers & Petrochemicals Corp Ltd v Davy McKee (London) Ltd; sub nom.
    Deepak Fertilisers & Petrochemicals Corp Ltd v ICI Chemicals & Polymers Ltd;
    Deepak Fertilisers & Petrochemical Corp Ltd v Davy McKee (UK) London Ltd [1999]
    1 All E.R. (Comm.) 69; [1999] 1 Lloyd's Rep. 387; [1999] B.L.R. 41; (1999) 1 T.C.L.R.
    200; 62 Con. L.R. 86 CA (Civ Div) 4–013, 11–028, 14–007, 14–018, 19–032
Deepak Fertilisers v ICI Chemicals. See Deepak Fertilisers & Petrochemicals Corp Ltd v
    Davy McKee (London) Ltd
Definitely Maybe (Touring) Ltd v Marek Lieberberg Konzertagentur GmbH (No.2); sub nom.
    Definitely Maybe (Touring) Ltd v Marck Lieberberg Konzertagentur GmbH (No.2)
    [2001] 1 W.L.R. 1745; [2001] 4 All E.R. 283; [2001] 2 All E.R. (Comm) 1; [2001] 2
    Lloyd's Rep. 455; [2002] C.L.C. 360; [2002] I.L.Pr. 9; Daily Telegraph, April 10, 2001
    QBD (Comm) 2–043
Delahaye v British Empire Mutual Life (1897) 13 T.L.R. 245 .... 6–013, 18–028
Delany v Stoddart (1785) 1 T.R. 22 24–073
Delver v Barnes (1807) 1 Taunt 48 .... 17–001, 17–004
Demetriades & Co v Northern Assurance Co Ltd (The Spathari); sub nom. Demetriades & Co
    v Northern Assurance Co Ltd; S.S Spathari Demetriades & Co v Northern Insurance Co
    Ltd; Borthwick v British General Assurance Co; Cambitsis v Norwich Union Fire
    Insurance Society (1925) 21 Ll.l.R. 265; 1925 S.C. (H.L.) 6; 1925 S.L.T. 322 HL 6–051
Den Dankse Bank A/S v Skipton Building Society Unreported, 1997 .... 7–015, 10–061, 15–062
Denby v English & Scottish Maritime Insurance Co Ltd; sub nom. Denby v MJ Marchant;
    Yasuda Fire & Marine Insurance Co of Europe Ltd v Lloyd's Underwriting Syndicate
    No.229 [1998] C.L.C. 870; [1998] Lloyd's Rep. I.R. 343; Times, March 16, 1998 CA
    (Civ Div) 1–034, 3–010, 10–032
Dennard v Plant. See Lagden v O'Connor
Dennehy v Bellamy [1938] 2 All E.R. 262; (1938) 60 Ll.L.R. 269 CA 21–029
Dennistoun v Lillie (1821) 3 Bli. 202 .... 6–014, 6–016
Dent v Blackmore (1927) 29 Ll.L.R. 9 .... 6–052, 22–087
Dent v Smith (1868–69) L.R. 4 Q.B. 414 QB 24–059
Department of Trade and Industry v St Christopher Motorists Association Ltd [1974] 1
    W.L.R. 99; [1974] 1 All E.R. 395; [1974] 1 Lloyd's Rep. 17; (1973) 117 S.J. 873 Ch
    D 1–006
Desouza v Waterlow [1999] R.T.R. 71; [1998] P.I.Q.R. P87; Independent, October 27, 1997
    (C.S.) CA (Civ Div) 22–045
Deutsche Bank AG v Highland Crusader Offshore Partners LP [2009] EWHC 730 (Comm);
    [2009] 2 Lloyd's Rep. 61; [2009] 1 C.L.C. 535 .... 2–003, 2–005
Deutsche Bank AG v Sebastian Holdings Inc [2009] EWHC 3069 (Comm); [2010] 1 All E.R.
    (Comm) 808; [2009] 2 C.L.C. 949 2–005
Deutsche Genossenschaftsbank v Burnhope [1995] 1 W.L.R. 1580; [1995] 4 All E.R. 717HL;
    reversing [1995] B.C.C. 488CA (Civ Div); reversing [1993] 2 Lloyd's Rep. 518 QBD
    (Comm) 19–049
Deutsche Ruck AG v Zion insurance Co Ltd. See Deutsche Ruckversicherung v Zion
    Insurance Co Ltd
Deutsche Ruck Akt v Group Josi Re Co SA v Walbrook Insurance Co Ltd; sub nom. Group
    Josi Re (formerly Group Josi Reassurance SA) v Walbrook Insurance Co Ltd; Deutsche
    Ruckversicherung AG v Walbrook Insurance Co Ltd [1996] 1 W.L.R. 1152; [1996] 1 All
    E.R. 791CA (Civ Div); affirming [1995] 1 W.L.R. 1017; [1994] 4 All E.R. 181; [1995]
    1 Lloyd's Rep. 153; [1994] C.L.C. 415; (1994) 91(25) L.S.G. 30; (1994) 138 S.J.L.B.
    111; Times, May 6, 1994 QBD (Comm) 6–036, 6–055, 15–023, 17–007
Deutsche Ruck Akt v Walbrook Insurance Co Ltd. See Deutsche Ruck Akt v Group Josi Re
    Co SA v Walbrook Insurance Co Ltd

Deutsche Ruckversicherung AG v La Fondaria Assicurazioni SpA (formerly Societa Italia di Assicurazioni SpA) [2001] 2 Lloyd's Rep. 621; [2002] Lloyd's Rep. I.R. 475 QBD (Comm) 2–004, 15–022
Deutsche Ruckversicherung v Zion Insurance Co Ltd Unreported, 2001 QBD (Comm) 15–022
Deutsche Ruckversicherungs AG v La Fondaria Assicurazioni SpA. *See* Deutsche Ruckversicherung AG v La Fondaria Assicurazioni SpA
Deutsche Schachtbau– und Tiefbohrgesellschaft mbH v Ras Al-Khaimah National Oil Co; sub nom. DST v Rakoil; Deutsche Schachtbau– und Tiefbohrgesellschaft mbH v Ras Al-Khaimah National Oil Co (Garnishee Proceedings); Deutsche Schachtbau– und Tiefbohrgesellschaft mbH v Shell International Petroleum Co Ltd (Nos.1 and 2) [1990] 1 A.C. 295; [1988] 3 W.L.R. 230 HL; reversing [1987] 3 W.L.R. 1023; [1987] 2 All E.R. 769; [1987] 2 Lloyd's Rep. 246; [1987] 1 F.T.L.R. 17; (1987) 131 S.J. 1486 CA (Civ Div) 2–034
Devaux v Steele (1840) 6 Bing. N.C. 358 24–017
Devco Holder and Burrows & Paine v Legal & General Assurance Society [1993] 2 Lloyd's Rep. 567 CA (Civ Div) 5–050, 22–094
Dever, Ex p. *See* Suse & Sibeth, Ex p. Dever, Re
Dhak v Insurance Co of North America (UK) Ltd [1996] 1 W.L.R. 936; [1996] 2 All E.R. 609; [1996] 1 Lloyd's Rep. 632; [1996] 5 Re. L.R. 83; [1997] P.I.Q.R. P101; (1996) 146 N.L.J. 247; Times, February 8, 1996; Independent, February 20, 1996; Lloyd's List, May 9, 1996 (I.D.) CA (Civ Div) 18–041, 18–049, 18–059
Diab v Regent Insurance Co Ltd [2006] UKPC 29; [2007] Bus. L.R. 915; [2007] 1 W.L.R. 797; [2006] 2 All E.R. (Comm) 704; [2006] 1 C.L.C. 1084; [2006] Lloyd's Rep. I.R. 779 PC (Belize) 6–0129, 7–013, 7–018, 9–003, 9–007, 9–018, 9–034
Dickenson v Jardine (1867–68) L.R. 3 C.P. 639 CCP 11–001
Dickinson v Del Solar [1930] 1 K.B. 376; (1929) 34 Ll.L.R. 445 KBD 20–012
Dickinson v Motor Vehicle Insurance Trust (1987) 163 C.L.R. 500 22–030
Dickson v Devitt (1916) 21 Com. Cas. 291 .... 15–034, 15–035, 15–051
Dickson Watch & Jewellery Co Ltd v Mow Tai Insurance & Reinsurance Co Ltd [1985] 1 H.K.C. 505 11–054
Diffori v Adams (1884) 53 L.J.Q.B. 437 24–070
Digby v Atkinson (1815) 4 Camp. 275 19–021
Digby v General Accident Fire and Life Assurance Corp Ltd [1943] A.C. 121; [1942] 2 All E.R. 319; (1942) 73 Ll.L.R. 175 HL 3–009, 22–027, 22–032
Diggens v Sun Alliance and London Insurance Plc [1994] C.L.C. 1146; Independent, August 22, 1994 (C.S) CA (Civ Div) 6–0107
Dimond v Lovell [2002] 1 A.C. 384; [2000] 2 W.L.R. 1121; [2000] 2 All E.R. 897; [2000] R.T.R. 243; [2000] C.C.L.R. 57; 2000 Rep. L.R. 62; (2000) 97(22) L.S.G. 47; (2000) 150 N.L.J. 740; Times, May 12, 2000; Independent, May 17, 2000 HL; affirming [2000] Q.B. 216; [1999] 3 W.L.R. 561; [1999] 3 All E.R. 1; [1999] R.T.R. 297; [1999] C.C.L.R. 46; (1999) 96(21) L.S.G. 40; (1999) 149 N.L.J. 681; (1999) 143 S.J.L.B. 181; Times, May 3, 1999 CA (Civ Div) 11–016, 22–024, 22–025, 22–026
Dimskal Shipping Co SA v International Transport Workers Federation; The Evia Luck (No.2) [1992] 2 A.C. 152; [1991] 3 W.L.R. 875; [1991] 4 All E.R. 871; [1992] 1 Lloyd's Rep. 115; [1992] I.C.R. 37; [1992] I.R.L.R. 78; Times, November 8, 1991; Independent, January 15, 1992; Financial Times, November 12, 1991 HL 2–055
Direct Line Insurance Plc v Fox [2009] EWHC 386 (QB); [2009] 1 All E.R. (Comm) 1017 ..... 9–031, 9–033
Direct Line Insurance Plc v Khan [2001] EWCA Civ. 1794; [2002] Lloyd's Rep. I.R. 364 CA (Civ Div) 5–035, 9–021, 9–024, 9–026, 11–029, 14–003, 14–013, 14–014
Ditchburn v Goldsmith (1815) 4 Camp. 152 4–002
Dixon v Hovill (1828) 4 Bing. 665 15–034
Dixon v Reid (1822) 5 B. & Ald. 597 24–138
Dixon v Sadler (1839) 5 M. & W. 405 .... 24–061, 24–080
Dixon v Sadler (1841) 8 M. & W. 895 24–061
Dixon v Whitworth (1879) 4 C.P.D. 371 24–112
Dobson v General Accident Fire and Life Assurance Corp [1990] 1 Q.B. 274; [1989] 3 W.L.R. 1066; [1989] 3 All E.R. 927; [1989] 2 Lloyd's Rep. 549; [1990] Crim. L.R. 271; (1989) 86(40) L.S.G. 43; (1989) 133 S.J. 1445 CA (Civ Div) 3–008, 10–002, 19–049
Dobson v Land (1850) 8 Hare 216 19–027
Dobson v Sotheby (1827) Mood. & M. 90; 173 E.R. 1091 .... 5–020, 5–022, 7–038

Dodson v Peter H Dodson Insurance Services [2001] 1 W.L.R. 1012; [2001] 3 All E.R. 75;
    [2001] 1 All E.R. (Comm) 300; [2001] 1 Lloyd's Rep. 520; [2001] R.T.R. 13; [2001]
    Lloyd's Rep. I.R. 278; (2001) 98(4) L.S.G. 49; Times, January 24, 2001; Independent,
    January 26, 2001 CA (Civ Div) 14–022, 22–027
Dodwell & Co Ltd v British Dominions General Insurance Co Ltd [1955] 2 Lloyd's Rep. 391
    KBD 24–081
Doe d. Darlington v Ulph (1849) 18 L.J.Q.B. 106 19–022
Doe d. Muston v Gladwin (1845) L.R. 6 Q.B. 953 19–021
Doe d. Pitt v Lanning (1814) 4 Camp. 73 6–015
Doe d. Pitt v Shewin (1811) 3 Camp. 134 19–022
Doe d. Pittman v Sutton (1841) 9 Car. & P. 706 .... 19–021, 19–022
Doheny v New India Assurance Co Ltd [2004] EWCA Civ. 1705; [2005] 1 All E.R. (Comm)
    382; [2005] Lloyd's Rep. I.R. 251 CA (Civ Div) 3–008, 3–010, 6–018, 6–059, 6–071, 6–072
Doll-Steinberg v Society of Lloyds [2002] EWCA Civ. 996 QBD (Admin) 13–039
Dolphin Maritime & Aviation Services Ltd v Sveriges Angfartygs Assurans Forening [2009]
    EWHC 716 (Comm); [2010] 1 All E.R. (Comm) 473; [2009] 2 Lloyd's Rep. 123; [2009]
    1 C.L.C. 460; [2009] I.L.Pr. 52 9–044
Dome Mining Corp Ltd v Drysdale (1931) 41 Ll.L.R. 109 KBD 9–026
Domicrest Ltd v Swiss Bank Corp [1999] Q.B. 548; [1999] 2 W.L.R. 364; [1998] 3 All E.R.
    577; [1999] 1 Lloyd's Rep. 80; [1998] C.L.C. 1451; [1999] I.L.Pr. 146; Times, July 16,
    1998; Independent, July 20, 1998 (C.S.) QBD 2–004
Domingo Mumbru Sociedad Anonima v Laurie (1924) 20 Ll.L.R. 189 KBD 9–025
Dominion Bridge Co Ltd v Toronto General Insurance Co Ltd [1964] 1 Lloyd's Rep. 194;
    (1963) 40 D.L.R. (2d) 840 Sup Ct (Can) 20–009
Dominion Mosaics & Tile Co v Trafalgar Trucking Co [1990] 2 All E.R. 246; 26 Con. L.R.
    1; [1989] 16 E.G. 101; (1989) 139 N.L.J. 364; Times, March 31, 1989; Independent,
    March 8, 1989 CA (Civ Div) 10–012, 10–015, 10–016, 10–031
Domsalla (t/a Domsalla Building Services) v Dyason [2007] EWHC 1174 (TCC); [2007]
    B.L.R. 348; [2007] T.C.L.R. 5; 112 Con. L.R. 95; [2007] C.I.L.L. 2501 .... 10–044, 15–009
Donaldson v Manchester Insurance (1836) 14 S. 601 .... 6–058, 19–013
Donohue v Armco Inc [2001] UKHL 64; [2002] 1 All E.R. 749; [2002] 1 All E.R. (Comm)
    97; [2002] 1 Lloyd's Rep. 425; [2002] C.L.C. 440HL 2–006
Dora, The. See Inversiones Manria SA v Sphere Drake Insurance Co, Malvern Insurance Co
    and Niagara Fire Insurance Co
Dora Foster, The [1900] P. 241 24–111
Dorigo y Sanudo v Royal Exchange Assurance Corporation (1922) 12 Ll.L.R. 126 9–025
Dornoch Ltd v Mauritius Union Assurance Co Ltd [2005] EWHC 1887 (Comm); [2006]
    Lloyd's Rep. I.R. 127; (2005) 102(35) L.S.G. 42; affirmed [2006] EWCA Civ 389;
    [2006] 2 All E.R. (Comm) 385; [2006] 2 Lloyd's Rep. 475; [2006] 1 C.L.C. 714; [2006]
    Lloyd's Rep. I.R. 786 .... 2–005, 2–036, 2–037, 2–043, 2–052, 2–063, 2–064, 3–015
Dornoch Ltd v Mauritius Union Assurance Co Ltd (No.2) [2007] EWHC 155 (Comm);
    [2007] Lloyd's Rep. I.R. 350 .... 10–034, 19–045, 23–025, 23–027
Dornoch Ltd v Westminster International BV (No.3) [2009] EWHC 1782 (Admlty); [2009]
    2 Lloyd's Rep. 420; [2009] 2 C.L.C. 226; [2010] Lloyd's Rep. I.R. 1 .... 1–040, 11–003, 24–094,
                                                                        24–096
Dornoch Ltd v Westminster International BV WD Fairway, The (No.2) [2009] EWHC 889
    (Admlty); [2009] 2 All E.R. (Comm) 399; [2009] 2 Lloyd's Rep. 191; [2009] 1 C.L.C.
    645; [2009] Lloyd's Rep. I.R. 573 .... 24–088, 24–089, 24–092, 24–093, 24–094, 24–096
Dorset CC v Southern Felt Roofing Co, 48 B.L.R. 96; (1990) 10 Tr. L.R. 96; (1990) 6 Const.
    L.J. 37 CA (Civ Div) 11–026, 14–007
Douglas v Scougall (1816) 4 Dow. 269 24–061
Douglas (A&D) Pty Ltd v Lawyers Private Mortgages Pty Ltd [2006] F.C.A. 691 20–047
Downs v Green (1844) 12 M. & W. 481 .... 18–005, 18–007
Doyle v Olby (Ironmongers) Ltd [1969] 2 Q.B. 158; [1969] 2 W.L.R. 673; [1969] 2 All E.R.
    119; 113 S.J. 128 CA (Civ Div) 6–080
Doyle v Powell (1832) 4 B. & Ad. 267 24–072
DPP v Fisher; sub nom. Chief Constable of Norfolk v Fisher (1992) 156 J.P. 93; [1992]
    R.T.R. 93; [1991] Crim. L.R. 787; (1992) 156 J.P.N. 28 DC 22–010
DPP v Gomez (Edwin) [1993] A.C. 442; [1992] 3 W.L.R. 1067; [1993] 1 All E.R. 1; (1993)
    96 Cr. App. R. 359; (1993) 157 J.P. 1; [1993] Crim. L.R. 304; (1993) 157 J.P.N. 15;
    (1993) 137 S.J.L.B. 36; Times, December 8, 1992; Independent, December 4, 1992
    HL 19–049
DPP v Heritage; sub nom. R. v Heritage [2002] EWHC 2139; (2002) 166 J.P. 772; (2002) 146
    S.J.L.B. 223 QBD (Admin) 22–009

DPP v Kavaz [1999] R.T.R. 40QBD 22–002
DPP v Neville (Francis John) (1996) 160 J.P. 758; [1996] C.O.D. 229; (1996) 160 J.P.N.
   1078; *Independent,* January 8, 1996 (C.S.) QBD 22–008
DPP v Saddington; sub nom. Chief Constable of North Yorkshire v Saddington (2001) 165
   J.P. 122; [2001] R.T.R. 15; [2001] Crim. L.R. 41; Times, November 1, 2000;
   Independent, November 3, 2000 DC 22–006
DPP v Vivier [1991] 4 All E.R. 18; (1991) 155 J.P. 970; [1991] R.T.R. 205; [1991] Crim. L.R.
   637; (1991) 155 L.G. Rev. 588 DC 22–007, 22–008
Drake Insurance Plc (In Provisional Liquidation) v Provident Insurance Plc [2003] EWCA
   Civ. 1834; [2004] Q.B. 601; [2004] 2 W.L.R. 530; [2004] 2 All E.R. (Comm) 65; [2004]
   1 Lloyd's Rep. 268; [2004] 1 C.L.C. 574; [2004] R.T.R. 19; [2004] Lloyd's Rep. I.R.
   277 CA (Civ Div); reversing [2003] EWHC 109; [2003] 1 All E.R. (Comm) 759; [2004]
   R.T.R. 11; [2003] Lloyd's Rep. I.R. 781; Independent, March 31, 2003 (C.S) QBD
   (Comm) 6–025, 6–026, 6–030, 6–033, 6–034, 6–062, 6–077, 6–092, 6–099, 6–130, 11–016,
                                                                          11–046, 11–058, 11–060, 15–028, 22–043
Drake Insurance Plc, Re [2001] Lloyd's Rep. I.R. 643 Ch D (Companies Ct) ... 3–010, 8–019, 8–020,
                                                                          16–011, 22–047
Dream Maker Game Shop v China Merchants Insurance Co Ltd Unreported, 2003 11–066
Drinkwater v Corp of London Assurance (1767) 2Wils. 363 .... 3–010, 25–006
Driscol v Passmore (1798) 1 Bos. & P. 200 24–068
Driscoll v Bovil (1798) 1 Bos. & P. 313 24–073
Drummond v Deey (1794) 1 Esp. 151 8–022
Du Pont de Nemours v Agnew. *See* EI Du Pont de Nemours & Co v Agnew (No.2)
Duckett v Williams (1834) 2 C. & M. 348 .... 7–022, 7–029, 7–030, 17–012
Duckworth v Scottish Widows Fund (1917) 33 T.L.R. 430 18–037
Dudgeon v Pembroke (1876–77) L.R. 2 App. Cas. 284 HL; reversing (1875–76) L.R. 1
   Q.B.D. 96, Ex Chamber; reversing (1873–74) L.R. 9 Q.B. 581 QB 3–011, 24–062, 24–064,
                                                                          24–134
Dufaur v Professional Life (1858) 25 Beav. 599 .... 3–009, 18–034
Duff v Gant (1852) 20 L.T.O.S. 71 18–029
Duffell v Wilson (1808) 1 Camp. 40 8–026
Dufour v Professional Life (1855) 25 Beav. 599 14–026
Dunbar v A&B Painters Ltd. *See* Alfred James Dunbar v A&B Painters Ltd and Economic
   Insurance Co Ltd and Whitehouse & Co
Dunbar v Plant [1998] Ch. 412; [1997] 3 W.L.R. 1261; [1997] 4 All E.R. 289; [1998] 1 F.L.R.
   157; [1997] 3 F.C.R. 669; [1998] Fam. Law 139; (1997) 94(36) L.S.G. 44; (1997) 141
   S.J.L.B. 191; Times, August 13, 1997 CA (Civ Div) 18–020, 18–035, 20–031
Dunbeth, The [1897] P. 133 PDAD 24–071
Duncanson v Continental Insurance Co, 69 D.L.R. (4th) 198 (1990) 19–039
Dunlop Bros & Co v Townend [1919] 2 K.B. 127 KBD 24–048, 24–051
Dunlop Haywards (DHL) Ltd (formerly Dunlop Heywood Lorenz Ltd) (In Liquidation) v
   Barbon Insurance Group Ltd (formerly Erinaceous Insurance Services Ltd (formerly
   Hanover Park Commercial Ltd)) [2009] EWHC 2900 (Comm); [2010] Lloyd's Rep. I.R.
   149 .... 1–019, 1–033, 3–005, 15–026, 15–030, 15–031, 15–032, 15–034, 15–035, 15–037,
                                                                          15–051
Dunlop Haywards (DHL) Ltd (formerly Dunlop Heywood Lorenz Ltd) v Erinaceous
   Insurance Services Ltd (formerly Hanover Park Commercial Ltd) [2008] EWHC 520
   (Comm); [2008] Lloyd's Rep. I.R. 676; [2008] N.P.C. 40 .... 15–031, 15–032
Dunlop Haywards (DHL) Ltd (formerly Dunlop Heywood Lorenz Ltd) v Erinaceous
   Insurance Services Ltd (formerly Hanover Park Commercial Ltd) [2009] EWCA Civ
   354; [2009] Lloyd's Rep. I.R. 464 .... 1–018, 1–019, 1–033, 1–034, 15–031, 15–032
Dunlop Pneumatic Tyre Co Ltd v Selfridge & Co Ltd [1915] A.C. 847 HL 11–038
Dunmill v DPP [2004] EWHC 1700 (Admin) 22–007
Dunn v Campbell (1920) 4 Ll.L.R. 36 CA 1–022, 3–010, 19–033
Dunn v Ocean Accident & Guarantee Corp Ltd (1933) 47 Ll.L.R. 129CA; affirming (1933)
   45 Ll.L.R. 276 KBD 6–048, 7–037
Dunn v Ocean Accident & Guarantee Corp Ltd (1933) 50 T.L.R. 32 15–019
Dunthorne v Bentley [1996] R.T.R. 428; [1996] P.I.Q.R. P323; [1999] Lloyd's Rep I.R. 560;
   Times, March 11, 1996 CA (Civ Div) 22–030
Durham v BAI (Run Off) Ltd [2008] EWHC 2692 (QB); [2009] 2 All E.R. 26; [2009] 1 All
   E.R. (Comm) 805; [2009] Lloyd's Rep. I.R. 295 .. 2–063, 3–005, 3–010, 3–013, 5–015, 11–050,
                                                                          18–059, 20–007, 20–008, 20–034, 20–069
Durham Bros v Robertson [1898] 1 Q.B. 765 CA 14–026
Durrant v MacLaren [1956] 2 Lloyd's Rep. 70 QBD 22–011

Durrell v Bedereley (1816) Holt N.P. 283 .... 6–021, 6–024, 6–031, 6–062
Duus Brown & Co v Binning (1906) 11 Com. Cas. 190 11–023
Dwyer v Edie (1788) 2 Park on Ins. 914 4–016
Dynamics Corp of America (In Liquidation) (No.2), Re [1976] 1 W.L.R. 757; [1976] 2 All
    E.R. 669; 120 S.J. 450 Ch D 16–009
Dynamit AG (Vormals Alfred Nobel Co) v Rio Tinto Co Ltd [1918] A.C. 260 HL 2–057
E Dibbens & Sons (In Liquidation), Re [1990] B.C.L.C. 577; Times, December 18, 1989 Ch
    D 14–021, 19–005, 19–013
ERC Frankona Reinsurance v American National Insurance Co [2005] EWHC 1381; [2006]
    Lloyd's Rep. I.R. 157 QBD (Comm) 1–034, 6–004, 6–008, 6–011, 6–037, 6–039, 6–041,
                                        6–055, 6–105, 7–024, 15–023, 20–022
EW Berk & Co Ltd v Style [1956] 1 Q.B. 180; [1955] 3 W.L.R. 935; [1955] 3 All E.R. 625;
    [1955] 2 Lloyd's Rep. 382; 99 S.J. 889 QBD 24–080
Eagle Oil Transport Co Ltd v Board of Trade; Anglo-Mexican Petroleum Products Co Ltd v
    Board of Trade (1925) 23 Ll.L.R. 301 KBD 25–005
Eagle Recovery Services v Parr [1998] C.L. 405 CC (St Helens) 22–023
Eagle Star & British Dominions Insurance Co Ltd v Cayzer Irvine & Co Ltd (1928) 30
    Ll.L.R. 19 KBD 11–016
Eagle Star & British Dominions Insurance Co Ltd v Rainer (1927) 27 Ll.L.R. 173 KBD 1–033
Eagle Star Insurance Co Ltd, Re [2006] EWHC 1850 Ch D (Companies Ct) 13–033, 13–035
Eagle Star Insurance Co Ltd v Cresswell; sub nom. Eagle Star Insurance Co Ltd v JN
    Cresswell [2004] EWCA Civ. 602; [2004] 2 All E.R. (Comm) 244; [2004] 1 C.L.C. 926;
    [2004] Lloyd's Rep. I.R. 537; (2004) 148 S.J.L.B. 632 CA (Civ Div); reversing [2003]
    EWHC 2224; [2004] 1 All E.R. (Comm) 508 QBD (Comm) 3–011, 3–017, 6–129, 7–015,
                                    9–003, 9–004, 17–025, 20–045, 20–051, 20–058
Eagle Star Insurance Co Ltd v Games Video Co (GVC) SA (The Game Boy) [2004] EWHC
    15; [2004] 1 All E.R. (Comm) 560; [2004] 1 Lloyd's Rep. 238; [2004] Lloyd's Rep. I.R.
    867 QBD (Comm) 6–013, 6–056, 7–032, 9–029
Eagle Star Insurance Co Ltd v Provincial Insurance [1994] 1 A.C. 130; [1993] 3 W.L.R. 257;
    [1993] 3 All E.R. 1; [1993] 2 Lloyd's Rep. 143; [1993] R.T.R. 328; (1993) 143 N.L.J.
    920; (1993) 137 S.J.L.B. 143; Times, June 9, 1993 PC (Bah) 11–059
Eagle Star Insurance Co Ltd v Spratt [1971] 2 Lloyd's Rep. 116 CA (Civ Div) 1–032, 1–033,
                                                                1–034, 15–041
Eagle Star Life Assurance Co Ltd v Griggs and Miles [1998] 1 Lloyd's Rep. 256;
    Independent, October 20, 1997 (C.S.) CA (Civ Div) 15–008, 15–013
Earle v Harris (1780) 1 Doug. K.B. 357 .... 7–038, 24–068
Earle v Rowcroft (1806) 18 East 126 24–138
East Midland Area Traffic Commissioners v Tyler [1938] 3 All E.R. 39 22–097
Eastwood v Kenyon (1840) 11 Ad. & E. 438 23–018
Ebsworth v Alliance Marine Insurance Co (1872–73) L.R. 8 C.P. 596 CCP 4–013, 4–019, 19–025,
                                                                24–030
Ecclesiastical Commissioners v Royal Exchange (1895) 11 T.L.R. 476 ... 14–022, 19–008, 19–009
Ecclesiastical Insurance Office Plc v Axa Insurance Plc [2006] EWHC 634 QBD 5–051
Economic v Le Assicurazioni d'Italia Unreported, 1996 17–013
Economic Fire Office Ltd, Re (1896) 12 T.L.R. 142 15–014
Economides v Commercial Union Assurance Co Plc [1998] Q.B. 587; [1997] 3 W.L.R. 1066;
    [1997] 3 All E.R. 636; [1997] C.L.C. 1169; [1998] Lloyd's Rep. I.R. 9; Times, June 27,
    1997 CA (Civ Div) 6–004, 6–013, 6–057, 6–072
Eddystone Marine Insurance Co Ex p. Western Insurance Co, Re [1892] 2 Ch. 423 Ch D 17–017,
                                                                20–035
Eden v Mitchell [1975] R.T.R. 425; [1975] Crim. L.R. 467; (1975) 119 S.J. 645 DC 22–009
Eden v Parkinson (1781) 2 Doug. K.B. 732 .... 24–058, 24–059
Edmunds v Lloyds Italico & l'Ancora Compagnia di Assicurazioni & Riassicurazione SpA
    [1986] 1 W.L.R. 492; [1986] 2 All E.R. 249; [1986] 1 Lloyd's Rep. 326; (1986) 83
    L.S.G. 876; (1986) 130 S.J. 242 CA (Civ Div) 10–022, 10–024, 14–029
Edmunds v Simmonds [2001] 1 W.L.R. 1003; [2001] R.T.R. 24; [2001] P.I.Q.R. P21; Times,
    November 21, 2000; Independent, November 13, 2000 2–064
Edney v De Rougemont (1927) 28 Ll.L.R. 215 OR 10–015
Edward Owen Engineering Ltd v Barclays Bank International Ltd [1978] Q.B. 159; [1977]
    3 W.L.R. 764; [1978] 1 All E.R. 976; [1978] 1 Lloyd's Rep. 166; 6 B.L.R. 1; 121 S.J.
    617 CA (Civ Div) 23–031
Edwards v AA Mutual Insurance Co (1985) 3 ANZ Insurance Cases 60,668 ..... 6–004, 6–023, 6–071
Edwards v Aberayron Mutual Ship Insurance Society Ltd (1875–76) L.R. 1 Q.B.D. 563 Ex
    Chamber 3–015

Edwards v Footner (1808) 1 Camp. 530 .... 6–101, 24–039
QBDEdwards v Minster Insurance Co Ltd Unreported, 1994 21–023
Edwards v Motor Union Insurance. *See* John Edwards & Co v Motor Union Insurance Co
  Ltd
Edwards v West (1877–78) L.R. 7 Ch. D. 858 Ch D 19–017
Edwards & Co v Commercial Union Motor Union Insurance Co. *See* John Edwards & Co v
  Motor Union Insurance Co Ltd
Egan Lawson Ltd v Standard Life Assurance Co; sub nom. Standard Life Assurance Co v
  Egan Lawson Ltd [2001] 1 E.G.L.R. 27; [2001] 08 E.G. 168; [2000] N.P.C. 128 CA (Civ
  Div) 15–033
Egan v Bower (1939) 63 Ll.L.R. 266 KBD 22–011
Egerton v Brownlow (1853) 4 H.L. Cas. 1 5–037
Egerton v Furzeman (1825) 1 C. & P. 613 4–002
Egmont's (Earl of) Trusts, Re; sub nom. Lefroy v Earl of Egmont [1908] 1 Ch. 821 Ch D 10–015,
                                                                                        19–030
Egon Oldendorff v Libera Corp (No.1) [1995] 2 Lloyd's Rep. 64; [1996] C.L.C. 482 QBD
  (Comm) 2–038, 2–052, 2–053
Egon Oldendorff v Libera Corp (No.2) [1996] 1 Lloyd's Rep. 380; [1996] C.L.C. 482;
  Independent, December 18, 1995 .... 2–038, 2–052
EI Du Pont de Nemours & Co v Agnew (No.1) [1987] 2 Lloyd's Rep. 585; [1987] F.L.R. 376;
  [1987] 2 F.T.L.R. 487 CA (Civ Div) 2–005, 2–033, 2–037, 2–039, 2–040
EI Du Pont de Nemours & Co v Agnew (No.2) [1988] 2 Lloyd's Rep. 240; [1990] E.C.C. 9;
  [1988] 2 F.T.L.R. 39 CA (Civ Div 2–006
Eide UK Ltd v Lowndes Lambert Group Ltd (The Sun Tender) [1999] Q.B. 199; [1998] 3
  W.L.R. 643; [1998] 1 All E.R. 946; [1998] 1 Lloyd's Rep. 389; [1998] C.L.C. 266;
  (1998) 95(4) L.S.G. 34; (1998) 148 N.L.J. 86; Times, December 29, 1997 CA (Civ
  Div) 1–033, 8–005, 14–003, 14–016, 24–044, 24–078
Eider, The [1893] P. 119 PDAD 2–004
Eisinger v General Accident, Fire and Life Assurance Corp [1955] 1 W.L.R. 869; [1955] 2
  All E.R. 897; [1955] 2 Lloyd's Rep. 95; 99 S.J. 511 QBD 10–002
El Ajou v Dollar Land Holdings Plc (No.1) [1994] 2 All E.R. 685; [1994] B.C.C. 143; [1994]
  1 B.C.L.C. 464; [1993] N.P.C. 165; Times, January 3, 1994 CA (Civ Div) 5–046, 6–036,
                                                                                        6–042
Elaz International Co v Hong Kong & Shanghai Insurance Co Ltd [2006] H.K.E.C. 825 24–064,
                                                                                        24–066
Elcock v Thomson [1949] 2 K.B. 755; [1949] 2 All E.R. 381; (1948–49) 82 Ll.L.R. 892; 65
  T.L.R. 566; 93 S.J. 562 KBD 1–009, 1–011, 4–004, 10–010
Electro Motion Ltd v Maritime Insurance Co Ltd and Bonner [1956] 1 Lloyd's Rep. 420
  QBD 19–34
Eleftheria, The. *See* Owners of Cargo Lately Laden on Board the Eleftheria v Owners of the
  Eleftheria
Eleison v Parker (1917) 81 J.P. 265 22–006
Elf Enterprise (Caledonia) Ltd v London Bridge Engineering Ltd [2000] Lloyd's Rep. I.R.
  249 .... 11–034, 11–056
Elfie A Issaias v Marine Insurance Co. *See* Elias Issaias, The
Elgood v Harris [1896] 2 Q.B. 491 QBD 11–020
Elias Issaias, The; sub nom. Issaias (Elfie A) v Marine Insurance Co, Ltd; Issaias, The v
  Marine Insurance Co Ltd (1923) 15 Ll.L.R. 186 CA 9–025, 24–0138
Elizabeth v Motor Insurers Bureau [1981] R.T.R. 405 CA (Civ Div) 22–074
Elkhorn Developments Ltd v Sovereign General Insurance Co [2001] B.C.J. No.630 7–034
Elkins v Cartlidge [1947] 1 All E.R. 829; 177 L.T. 519; 91 S.J. 573 KBD 22–008
Ellerbeck Collieries Ltd v Cornhill Insurance Co Ltd [1932] 1 K.B. 401; (1931) 41 Ll.L.R.
  57 CA 5–015
Ellerman Lines Ltd v Lancaster Maritime Co Ltd; The Lancaster [1980] 2 Lloyd's Rep. 497
  QBD (Comm) 24–022
Ellinger & Co v Mutual Life Insurance Co of New York [1905] 1 K.B. 31 CA 7–028, 18–034
Elliott v Grey [1960] 1 Q.B. 367; [1959] 3 W.L.R. 956; [1959] 3 All E.R. 733; 124 J.P. 58;
  57 L.G.R. 357; 103 S.J. 921 QBD 22–009
Elliott v Royal Exchange Assurance Co (1866–67) L.R. 2 Ex. 237 Ex Ct 9–017
Elliott v Wilson (1776) 4 Bro. P.C. 470 24–070
Ellis v Hinds. *See* John T Ellis Ltd v Hinds
Eloc Electro-Optieck and Communicatie BV, Re [1982] Ch. 43; [1981] 3 W.L.R. 176; [1981]
  2 All E.R. 1111; [1981] I.C.R. 732; 125 S.J. 412 Ch D 21–006
Elson v Crooks (1912) 106 L.T. 462 .... 18–010, 18–015, 18–017

Eltham vKingsman (1818) 1 B. & Ald. 683 4–002
Elton v Brogden (1747) 2 Str. 1264 24–073
Elton v Larkins (1832) 8 Bing. 198 6–065
Emanuel & Co v Andrew Weir & Co (1914) 30 T.L.R. 518 .... 5–017, 17–012
Emperor Goldmining Co Ltd v Switzerland General Insurance Co Ltd [1964] 1 Lloyd's Rep.
    348 Sup Ct (NSW) 10–039, 24–112
Empire SS Co Inc v Threadneedle Insurance Co (1925) 22 Ll.L.R. 534 KBD 9–025
Employers' Liability Trigger Litigation. See Durham v BAI (Run Off) Ltd
Empress Assurance Corporation Ltd v Bowring & Co Ltd (1905) 11 Com. Cas. 107 15–028
Encia Remediation Ltd v Canopius Managing Agents Ltd [2007] EWHC 916 (Comm);
    [2007] 2 All E.R. (Comm) 947; [2007] 1 C.L.C. 818; [2008] Lloyd's Rep. I.R. 79;
    [2007] Env. L.R. D17 .... 3–005, 20–009, 20–028, 20–083
Engel v Lancashire & General Assurance Co Ltd (1925) 21 Ll.L.R. 327 KBD 4–005, 19–011
Engel v Lancashire & General Assurance Co Ltd (1925) 41 T.L.R. 408 19–010
Engelbach's Estate, Re; sub nom. Tibbetts v Englebach [1924] 2 Ch. 348 Ch D 18–024, 19–030
England v Guardian Insurance Ltd [1999] 2 All E.R. (Comm) 481; [2000] Lloyd's Rep. I.R.
    404 QBD (TCC) 10–022, 11–002, 11–007, 11–023, 11–037
English v Western [1940] 2 K.B. 156; (1940) 67 Ll.L.R. 45 CA 3–010
English & American Insurance Co Ltd v Axa Re SA [2006] EWHC 3323 (Comm); [2007]
    1 C.L.C. 1; [2007] Lloyd's Rep. I.R. 359 .... 17–019, 20–058
English & Scottish Law Life Assurance Association v Carmichael; sub nom. Carmichael v
    Carmichael's Executrix, 1920 S.C. (H.L.) 195; 1920 2 S.L.T. 285 HL 4–011
English Insurance v National Benefit Insurance. See National Benefit Assurance Co Ltd, Ex
    p. English Insurance Co Ltd, Re
Enlayde Ltd v Roberts [1917] 1 Ch. 109 Ch D 15–026, 19–018, 19–022
Ennstone Building Products Ltd v Stanger Ltd; sub nom. Ennstone Building Products Ltd
    (formerly Natural Stone Products Ltd) v Stanger Ltd (formerly TBV Stanger Ltd) (No.2)
    [2002] EWCA Civ. 916; [2002] 1 W.L.R. 3059; [2002] 2 All E.R. (Comm) 479; [2003]
    1 C.L.C. 265; [2002] B.L.R. 347; [2002] T.C.L.R. 23; [2002] P.N.L.R. 42; (2002) 99(35)
    L.S.G. 34; (2002) 146 S.J.L.B. 200; Independent, July 4, 2002 CA (Civ Div) 2–043
Enterprise Oil Ltd v Strand Insurance Co Ltd [2006] EWHC 58; [2006] 1 Lloyd's Rep. 500;
    [2006] 1 C.L.C. 33 QBD (Comm) ... 3–001, 15–027, 17–004, 17–018, 17–019, 20–009, 20–025,
                                               20–031, 20–047, 20–057, 20–060
Equitable Fire and Accident Office Ltd v Ching Wo Hong [1907] A.C. 96 PC (Sing) ... 8–004, 8–016,
                                                  11–046, 11–058
Equitable Life Assurance of the United States v Mitchell (1911) 27 T.L.R. 213 18–014
Equitable Life Assurance Society, Re Canada Life Ltd Unreported February 14, 2007 13–035
Equitable Life Assurance Society of the United States v Bertie (1890) 8 N.Z.L.R. 579 6–012
Equitable Life Assurance Society v General Accident Assurance Corp Ltd (1904) 12 S.L.T.
    348 OH 17–005
Equitable Trust Co v Whittaker (1923–24) 17 Ll.L.R. 153 KBD 10–034, 23–027
Equitable Trust Co of New York v Henderson (1930) 38 Ll.L.R. 187; (1930) 47 T.L.R. 90
    KBD 3–008, 23–021, 23–022
Equitable Trust Co of New York v Whittaker. See Equitable Trust Co v Whittaker
Equitas Insurance Ltd (formerly Speyford Ltd), Re [2009] EWHC 1595 (Ch); [2010] Lloyd's
    Rep. I.R. 69 .... 13–035, 13–042, 17–001
Equitas Ltd, Re [2008] EWHC 2960 (Ch); [2009] Bus. L.R. 509; [2009] Lloyd's Rep. I.R.
    642; Times, December 22, 2008 13–033
Equitas Ltd v Allstate Insurance Co [2008] EWHC 1671 (Comm); [2009] 1 All E.R. (Comm)
    1137; [2009] Lloyd's Rep. I.R. 227 2–005
Equitas Ltd v Horace Holman & Co Ltd [2007] EWHC 903 (Comm); [2007] Lloyd's Rep.
    I.R. 567 15–043
Equitas Ltd v R&Q Reinsurance Co (UK) Ltd [2009] EWHC 2787 (Comm); [2009] 2 C.L.C.
    706 .... 13–042, 17–001, 17–020, 20–058, 20–060
Equitas Ltd v Wave City Shipping Co Ltd [2005] EWHC 923; [2005] 2 All E.R. (Comm) 301
    QBD (Comm) 17–002
Equity & Provident Ltd, Re [2002] EWHC 186; [2002] 2 B.C.L.C. 78; Daily Telegraph, June
    13, 2002 Ch D 16–004
Erich Gasser GmbH v MISAT Srl (C–116/02) [2005] Q.B. 1; [2004] 3 W.L.R. 1070; [2005]
    All E.R. (EC) 517; [2005] 1 All E.R. (Comm) 538; [2004] 1 Lloyd's Rep. 222; [2004]
    1 Lloyd's Rep. 445; [2003] E.C.R. I–14693; [2004] I.L.Pr. 7; Times, December 12, 2003
    ECJ 2–008
Eridania SpA (formerly Cereol Italia Srl) v Oetker; The Fjord Wind [2000] 2 All E.R.
    (Comm) 108; [2000] 2 Lloyd's Rep. 191; [2000] C.L.C. 1376 CA (Civ Div) 24–062

Eschig v UNIQA Sachversicherung AG (C–199/08) [2010] 1 All E.R. (Comm) 576; [2010] 1 C.M.L.R. 5; [2010] C.E.C. 533 ECJ 23–012
Espin v Pemberton (1859) 3 De. G. & J. 547 6–042
Esso Petroleum Co Ltd v Hall Russell & Co Ltd; The Esso Bernicia [1989] A.C. 643; [1988] 3 W.L.R. 730; [1989] 1 All E.R. 37; [1989] 1 Lloyd's Rep. 8; 1988 S.L.T. 874; (1988) 85(42) L.S.G. 48; (1988) 132 S.J. 1459; Times, October 7, 1988 HL 11–011
Esso Petroleum Co Ltd v Mardon [1976] Q.B. 801; [1976] 2 W.L.R. 583; [1976] 2 All E.R. 5; [1976] 2 Lloyd's Rep. 305; 2 B.L.R. 82; 120 S.J. 131 CA (Civ Div) 3–005
Etchells v Eagle Star (1928) 72 S.J. 242 20–044
Etherington and Lancashire & Yorkshire Accident Insurance Co's Arbitration, Re [1909] 1 K.B. 591 CA 3–010, 5–030, 5–031, 6–018, 18–041
Euler Hermes UK Plc v Apple Computer BV [2006] EWCA Civ. 375, [2006] Lloyd's Rep. I.R. 691 CA (Civ Div) 10–059
Euro Cellular (Distribution) Plc v Danzas Ltd (t/a Danzas AEI Intercontinental) [2003] EWHC 3161; [2004] 1 Lloyd's Rep. 521 QBD (Comm) 15–026
Eurocross Sales Ltd v Cornhill Insurance Plc [1995] 1 W.L.R. 1517; [1995] 4 All E.R. 950; [1996] L.R.L.R. 1; [1995] B.C.C. 991; [1995] 2 B.C.L.C. 384; Times, September 5, 1995; Lloyd's List, November 15, 1995 (I.D.) CA (Civ Div) 14–029
Eurodale Manufacturing Ltd (t/a Connekt Cellular Communications) v Ecclesiastical Insurance Office Plc [2003] EWCA Civ. 203; [2003] Lloyd's Rep. I.R. 444; (2003) 100(13) L.S.G. 26; Times, February 28, 2003 CA (Civ Div) 3–010, 3–011, 3–017, 5–004, 5–011, 24–066
Euro-Diam Ltd v Bathurst [1987] 2 W.L.R. 1368; [1987] 2 All E.R. 113; [1987] 1 Lloyd's Rep. 178; [1987] Fin. L.R. 247; (1987) 84 L.S.G. 1732; (1987) 131 S.J. 775; affirmed [1990] 1 Q.B. 1; [1988] 2 W.L.R. 517; [1988] 2 All E.R. 23; [1988] 1 Lloyd's Rep. 228; [1988] F.T.L.R. 242; [1988] Fin. L.R. 27; (1988) 85(9) L.S.G. 45; (1988) 132 S.J. 372 CA (Civ Div) 1–011, 2–058, 5–038, 5–039, 5–045, 7–023, 24–064
Europ Assistance Insurance Ltd v Temple Legal Protection Ltd [2007] EWHC 1785 (Comm); [2008] Lloyd's Rep. I.R. 216 15–020
Europe Mortgage Co v Halifax Estate Agencies [1996] E.G.C.S. 84; [1996] N.P.C. 68; Times, May 3, 1996 QBD 11–033
European Assurance Society v Bank of Toronto (1875) 7 Rev. Leg. 57 23–022
European International Reinsurance Co Ltd v Curzon Insurance Ltd [2003] EWCA Civ. 1074; [2003] Lloyd's Rep. I.R. 793; (2003) 100(36) L.S.G. 43; (2003) 147 S.J.L.B. 906; Times, August 21, 2003 CA (Civ Div) 15–031
HLEvans v Bignold (1868–69) L.R. 4 Q.B. 622 QB 18–007
Evans v Clarke [2007] Lloyd's Rep. I.R. 16 .... 7–009, 22–007
Evans v Dell [1937] 1 All E.R. 349 22–010
Evans v Employers Mutual Insurance Association Ltd [1936] 1 K.B. 505; (1935) 52 Ll.L.R. 51 CA 7–020, 7–048, 15–017, 20–044
Evans v Lewis [1964] 1 Lloyd's Rep. 258; [1964] Crim. L.R. 472; 108 S.J. 259 DC 22–011
Evans v Maritime Medical Care Inc, 87 D.L.R. (4th) 173 (1992) 11–047
Evans v Motor Insurers Bureau. See White (Brian) v White (Shane).
Evans v Secretary of State for the Environment, Transport and the Regions (C–63/01) [2005] All E.R. (EC) 763; [2003] E.C.R. I–14447; [2004] R.T.R. 32; [2004] 1 C.M.L.R. 47; [2004] Lloyd's Rep. I.R. 391; Times, December 9, 2003 ECJ 22–059, 22–073
Evans v Secretary of State for the Environment, Transport and the Regions [2001] EWCA Civ. 32; [2001] 2 C.M.L.R. 10; [2002] Lloyd's Rep. I.R. 1 CA (Civ Div) 22–059
Evans v Secretary of State for the Environment, Transport and the Regions (No.3) [2006] EWHC 322 QBD 22–073
Evans v TNT Logistics Ltd [2007] Lloyd's Rep. I.R. 708 County Court (Pontypridd) 22–025
Evans v Walkden [1956] 1 W.L.R. 1019; [1956] 3 All E.R. 64; 120 J.P. 495; 54 L.G.R. 467; 100 S.J. 587 DC 22–089
Evans v Ward (1930) 37 Ll.L.R. 177 KBD 15–027
Evanson v Crooks (1912) 106 L.T. 264 18–017
Everett v Desborough (1829) 5 Bing. 503 18–029
Everett v Hogg, Robinson & Gardner Mountain (Insurance) [1973] 2 Lloyd's Rep. 217 QBD (Comm) 15–056
Everett v London Assurance (1865) 19 C.B.N.S. 126 .... 5–030, 9–015, 19–041
Everson v Flurry [1999] 8 C.L. 406 CC (Slough) 1–006, 1–007, 22–025
Evialis SA v SIAT [2003] EWHC 863; [2003] 2 Lloyd's Rep. 377; [2003] 2 C.L.C. 802; [2003] I.L.Pr. 43; [2004] Lloyd's Rep. I.R. 187 QBD (Comm) 2–015, 2–022, 2–047, 2–048
Ewer v National Employers Mutual General Insurance Association Ltd (1937) 57 Ll.L.R. 172; [1937] 2 All E.R. 193 KBD 6–018, 6–052, 6–053, 9–026

Ewing v Sicklemore (1918) 35 T.L.R. 55 .... 5–014, 19–007

Excelsior Group Productions Ltd v Yorkshire Television Ltd [2009] EWHC 1751 (Comm) 3–005

Excess Insurance Co Ltd v Allendale Mutual Insurance Co [2001] Lloyd's Rep. I.R. 524 CA
(Civ Div) 2–005

Excess Insurance Co Ltd v Mander [1997] 2 Lloyd's Rep. 119; [1995] L.R.L.R. 358; [1995]
C.L.C. 838; Lloyd's List, May 18, 1995 (I.D.) QBD (Comm) 3–015, 17–012

Excess Liability Insurance Co Ltd v Mathews (1925) 31 Com.Cas. 43 17–019

Excess Life Insurance Co Ltd v Fireman's Insurance Co of Newark New Jersey [1982] 2
Lloyd's Rep. 599 QBD (Comm) 1–017, 15–028

Exchange Theatre Ltd v Iron Trades Mutual Insurance Co Ltd [1984] 1 Lloyd's Rep. 149 CA
(Civ Div); affirming [1983] 1 Lloyd's Rep. 674 QBD 5–022, 6–103, 9–025, 10–014

Exposito v Bowden (1857) 7 E. & B. 763 7–045

Eyre v Glover (1812) 16 East 218 .... 4–009, 4–017, 10–021

F Gliksten & Son Ltd v State Assurance Co (1922) 10 Ll.L.R. 604 KBD 1–021, 15–015, 25–010

FBTO Schadeverzekeringen NV v Odenbreit (C–463/06) [2008] 2 All E.R. (Comm) 733;
[2007] E.C.R. I–11321; [2008] I.L.Pr. 12; [2008] Lloyd's Rep. I.R. 354 2–014

FH Vahlsing Inc v Hartford Fire Insurance Co, 108 S.W. 2d 947 (1937) 11–034

FNCB Ltd (formerly First National Commercial Bank Plc) v Barnet Devanney (Harrow) Ltd
(formerly Barnet Devanney & Co Ltd); sub nom. FNCB Ltd v Barnet Devanney & Co
Ltd [1999] 2 All E.R. (Comm) 233; [1999] Lloyd's Rep. I.R. 459; [1999] Lloyd's Rep.
P.N. 908; [2000] P.N.L.R. 248; (1999) 96(28) L.S.G. 28; Times, September 28, 1999;
Independent, July 19,1999 (C.S.) CA (Civ Div); reversing [1999] C.L.C. 11; [1999]
Lloyd's Rep. I.R. 43 QBD 5–023, 14–003, 14–010, 14–012, 15–034, 15–035, 15–055,
15–059

FR Lurssen Werft GmbH & Co KG v Halle [2009] EWHC 2607 (Comm); [2010] C.P. Rep.
11; [2010] Bus. L.R. D55 2–005

FW Berk & Co v Style [1956] 1 Q.B. 180; [1955] 3 W.L.R. 935; [1955] 3 All E.R. 625;
[1955] 2 Lloyd's Rep. 382; 99 S.J. 889 QBD 24–112

F&K Jabbour v Custodian of Israeli Absentee Property [1954] 1 W.L.R. 139; [1954] 1 All
E.R. 145; [1953] 2 Lloyd's Rep. 760; 98 S.J. 45 QBD 9–038, 14–029

FR Lurssen Werft GmbH & Co KG v Halle [2009] EWHC 2607 (Comm); [2010] C.P. Rep.
11; [2010] Bus. L.R. D55 2–036

Fabriques de Pmduites Chiminiques v Large. See La Fabrique de Produits Chimiques Societe
Anonyme v Large

Facer v Vehicle & General Insurance Co Ltd [1965] 1 Lloyd's Rep. 113; Times, December
9, 1964 QBD 15–003, 15–019

Factories Insurance Co Ltd v Anglo-Scottish General Commercial Insurance Co (1913) 29
T.L.R. 312 2–003

Factortame Ltd v Secretary of State for the Environment, Transport and the Regions (Costs)
(No.2); sub nom. R. (on the application of Factortame Ltd) v Secretary of State for
Transport, Local Government and the Regions (Costs: Champertous Agreement) [2002]
EWCA Civ. 932; [2003] Q.B. 381; [2002] 3 W.L.R. 1104; [2002] 4 All E.R. 97; [2003]
B.L.R. 1; [2002] 3 Costs L.R. 467; (2002) 99(35) L.S.G. 34; (2002) 152 N.L.J. 1313;
(2002) 146 S.J.L.B. 178; Times, July 9, 2002; Independent, July 10, 2002; Daily
Telegraph, July 11, 2002 CA (Civ Div) 23–034

Fairchild v Glenhaven Funeral Services Ltd (t/a GH Dovener & Son); Babcock International
Ltd v National Grid Co Plc; Fox v Spousal (Midlands) Ltd; Matthews v Associated
Portland Cement Manufacturers (1978) Ltd; Dyson v Leeds City Council (No.2);
Pendleton v Stone & Webster Engineering Ltd; Matthews v British Uralite Plc [2002]
UKHL 22; [2003] 1 A.C. 32; [2002] 3 W.L.R. 89; [2002] 3 All E.R. 305; [2002] I.C.R.
798; [2002] I.R.L.R. 533; [2002] P.I.Q.R. P28; [2002] Lloyd's Rep. Med. 361; (2002)
67 B.M.L.R. 90; (2002) 152 N.L.J. 998; Times, June 21, 2002; Independent, June 25,
2002; Daily Telegraph, June 27, 2002 HL 5–015, 11–050

Fairfield Shipbuilding & Engineering Co Ltd v Gardner Mountain & Co Ltd (1912) 104 L.T.
288 24–078

Falcon Insurance Co (HK) Ltd v Cheshire Cat Restaurant & Pub Co Ltd [2007] H.K.E.C.
2084 .... 11–001, 11–006, 11–013, 11–035

Falkner v Ritchie (1814) 2 M & S. 290 24–138

Family Insurance Corp v Lombard Canada Ltd (2000) B.C.T.C. 273 20–050

Fanning v London Guarantee & Accident Co (1884) 10 Vict.L.R. 8 23–025

Fanti, The. See Firma C-Trade SA v Newcastle Protection and Indemnity Association

Fanti, The and the Padre Island, The. See Firma C-Trade SA v Newcastle Protection and
Indemnity Association

Faraday Capital Ltd v Copenhagen Reinsurance Co Ltd [2006] EWHC 1474 (Comm); [2007]
    Lloyd's Rep. I.R. 23 .... 17–019, 17–025, 20–058, 20–060
Farmer v Legg (1797) 7 T.R. 186 24–064
Farmers Co-op, Ltd v National Benefit Assurance Co, Ltd (1922) 13 Ll.L.R. 530 CA 3–011
Farnham v Royal Insurance Co Ltd [1976] 2 Lloyd's Rep. 437 QBD 5–020, 5–022
Farnum v Phoenix (1890) 17 Am. St. Rep. 233 8–004
Farr v Motor Traders Mutual Insurance Society Ltd [1920] 3 K.B. 669 CA 5–021, 7–034, 22–086,
                                                                                                                          22–100
Farra v Hetherington (1931) 40 Ll.L.R. 132 KBD 6–052, 22–087
Farrandoc, The. *See* Robin Hood Flour Mills Ltd v NM Paterson & Sons Ltd
Farrell v Federated Employers Insurance Association Ltd [1970] 1 W.L.R. 1400; [1970] 3 All
    E.R. 632; [1970] 2 Lloyd's Rep. 170; 114 S.J. 719 CA (Civ Div) 9–003, 9–006, 9–043,
                                                                                                                          21–023
Farrell Estates Ltd v Canadian Indemnity Co, 69 D.L.R. (4th) 735 (1990) 11–006
Farrell v Whitty (C–356/05) [2007] E.C.R. I–3067; [2007] 2 C.M.L.R. 46; [2007] C.E.C.
    718; [2007] Lloyd's Rep. I.R. 525 ECJ 22–031
Fawcus v Sarsfield (1856) 6 E. & B. 192 .... 24–062, 24–134
Feasey v Sun Life Assurance Co of Canada; Steamship Mutual Underwriting Association
    (Bermuda) Ltd v Feasey [2003] EWCA Civ. 885; [2003] 2 All E.R. (Comm) 587; [2004]
    1 C.L.C. 237; [2003] Lloyd's Rep. I.R. 637; (2003) 100(34) L.S.G. 30; (2003) 147
    S.J.L.B. 813; Times, July 12, 2003 CA (Civ Div); affirming [2002] EWHC 868; [2002]
    2 All E.R. (Comm) 492; [2003] 2 C.L.C. 936; [2002] Lloyd's Rep. I.R. 807; (2002)
    99(28) L.S.G. 30; Times, June 17, 2002 QBD (Comm) 1–009, 4–001, 4–002, 4–009, 4–011,
                                                                      4–013, 4–015, 6–008, 11–028, 14–004, 14–018, 15–022, 17–004,
                                                                      17–007, 18–004, 18–007, 18–008, 18–021, 19–032, 20–022,
                                                                                                                          20–062
Federal Business Development Bank v Commonwealth Insurance (1983) 2 C.C.L.I. 200 ... 7–034
Federation General Insurance Co v Knott Becker Scott [1990] 1 Lloyd's Rep 98 15–062
Federation Insurance Ltd v Wasson (1987) 163 C.L.R. 303 .... 14–003, 14–017
Feise v Aquilar (1811) 3 Taunt. 506 10–007
Feise v Parkinson (1812) 4 Taunt. 640 .... 8–025, 24–039
Felicie, The. *See* London Steamship Owners Mutual Insurance Association Ltd v Bombay
    Trading Co Ltd
Felthouse v Bindley (1862) 11 C.B.N.S. 869 1–025
Fender v St John Mildmay; sub nom. Fender v Mildmay [1938] A.C. 1 HL 5–037
Fenton v J Thorley & Co Ltd [1903] A.C. 443 HL 18–040
Fenton Insurance Co v Gothaer Versicherungsbank VVaG [1991] 1 Lloyd's Rep. 172; Times,
    July 4, 1990 QBD (Comm) 7–006, 8–017, 17–011
Ferguson v Aberdeen Parish Council, 1916 S.C. 715; 1916 1 S.L.T. 393 IH (2 Div) 19–013
Fermes Dionne Ltee/Dionne Farms Ltd v Fermes Gervais Ltee (20020 255 N.B.R. (2d) 6 20–049
Ferrarini SpA v Magnol Shipping Co Ltd (The Sky One) [1988] 1 Lloyd's Rep. 238 2–004
Ferreira v Companhia de Seguros Mundial Confianca SA (C–348/98) [2000] E.C.R. I–6711
    ECJ 22–001
Ferruzzi France SA and Ferruzzi SpA v Oceania Maritime; The Palmea [1988] 2 Lloyd's
    Rep. 261 QBD (Comm) 10–044
Ferrymasters Ltd v Adams [1980] R.T.R. 139; [1980] Crim. L.R. 187 DC 22–010
Ferryways NV v Associated British Ports (The Humber Way) Humber Way, The [2008]
    EWHC 225 (Comm); [2008] 2 All E.R. (Comm) 504; [2008] 1 Lloyd's Rep. 639; [2008]
    1 C.L.C. 117 4–021
Fidelity & Casualty Co of New York v Mitchell [1917] A.C. 592 PC (Can) 5–030, 5–031, 5–032,
                                                                                                                          22–090
Fidelity Life Assurance Co Ltd, Re Unreported, 1976 16–006
Field v Metropolitan Police Receiver [1907] 2 K.B. 853 KBD 25–010
Field Steamship Co Ltd v Burr [1899] 1 Q.B. 579 CA 24–112
Fifth Liverpool Starr Building Society v Travellers' Accident insurance Co (1893) 9 T.L.R.
    221 10–029
Figre Ltd v Mander [1999] Lloyd's Rep. I.R. 193 QBD (Comm 7–006, 8–016, 8–017, 17–011
Fillis v Bruton (1782) I Park's Marine Insurances 414 24–037
Financial Services Authority v Fradley (t/a Top Bet Placement Services); sub nom. Financial
    Services Authority v Woodward [2005] EWCA Civ. 1183; Times, December 1, 2005
    CA (Civ Div) 13–019
Financial Services Authority v Martin [2005] EWCA Civ. 1422; [2006] P.N.L.R. 11; Times,
    December 7, 2005 CA (Civ Div) 13–031

Financial Services Authority v Rourke (t/a JE Rourke & Co) [2002] C.P. Rep. 14; (2001) 98(46) L.S.G. 36; Times, November 12, 2001 Ch D 9–053

Financial Services Compensation Scheme Ltd v Larnell (Insurances) Ltd (In Creditors Voluntary Liquidation); sub nom. Financial Services Compensation Scheme v Larnell Insurance [2005] EWCA Civ. 1408; [2006] 2 W.L.R. 751; [2006] C.P. Rep. 14; [2006] P.N.L.R. 13 CA (Civ Div) 21–015, 21–017

Fines Flowers v General Accident Insurance, 81 D.L.R. (3d) 139 (1978) 15–034

Finlay v Mexican Investment Corp [1897] 1 Q.B. 517 QBD 23–030

Financial Ombudsman Service Ltd v Heather Moor & Edgecomb Ltd [2008] EWCA Civ 643; [2009] 1 All E.R. 328; (2008) 105(29) L.S.G. 35; (2008) 158 N.L.J. 896 ... 12–004, 12–008

Finnish Marine Insurance Co Ltd v Protective National Insurance Co [1990] 1 Q.B. 1078; [1990] 2 W.L.R. 914; [1989] 2 All E.R. 929; [1989] 2 Lloyd's Rep. 99 QBD (Comm) 2–003, 2–004

Fiona Trust & Holding Corp v Privalov [2007] UKHL 40; [2007] Bus. L.R. 1719; [2007] 4 All E.R. 951; [2007] 2 All E.R. (Comm) 1053; [2008] 1 Lloyd's Rep. 254; [2007] 2 C.L.C. 553; 114 Con. L.R. 69; [2007] C.I.L.L. 2528; (2007) 104(42) L.S.G. 34; (2007) 151 S.J.L.B. 1364; Times, October 25, 2007 .... 2–003, 3–015, 5–015

Fire & All Risks Insurance Co Ltd v Powell [1966] V.R. 513 5–046

Fire Insurance [1982] O.J. L80/76 13–045

Firebrase v Brett (1688) 1 Vern. 469 4–002

Fireman's Fund Insurance Co Ltd v Western Australian Insurance Co Ltd (1927) 28 Ll.L.R. 243; (1927) 138 L.T. 108 KBD 17–017

Firma C-Trade SA v Newcastle Protection and Indemnity Association (The Fanti); Socony Mobil Oil Co Inc v West of England Shipowners Mutual Insurance Association (London) Ltd; The Padre Island (No.2) [1991] 2 A.C. 1; [1990] 3 W.L.R. 78; [1990] 2 All E.R. 705; [1990] 2 Lloyd's Rep. 191; [1990] B.C.L.C. 625; (1990) 134 S.J. 833 HL; reversing [1989] 1 Lloyd's Rep. 239; Times, December 27, 1988 CA (Civ Div); reversing in part [1987] 2 Lloyd's Rep. 299 QBD (Comm) ... 9–037, 9–041, 20–035, 21–007, 21–024, 21–034, 21–037, 21–059, 21–063

Firmin & Collins v Allied Shippers [1967] 1 Lloyd's Rep. 633; 117 N.L.J. 836; 111 S.J. 313 QBD 5–011

First Alternative Insurance Co Ltd, Re Esure Insurance Ltd Unreported March, 2007 13–035

First Energy (UK) v Hungarian International Bank [1993] 2 Lloyd's Rep. 194; [1993] B.C.C. 533; [1993] B.C.L.C. 1409; [1993] N.P.C. 34; Times, March 4, 1993 CA (Civ Div) 15–001

First National City Bank of Chicago v West of England Shipowners Mutual Protection and Indemnity Association (Luxembourg); The Evelpidis Era [1981] 1 Lloyd's Rep. 54 QBD (Comm) 14–026, 24–074

First National Commercial Bank Plc v Barnet Devanney (Harrow) Ltd. See FNCB Ltd (formerly First National Commercial Bank Plc) v Barnet Devanney (Harrow) Ltd (formerly Barnet Devanney & Co Ltd)

First Russian Insurance Co Ltd (In Liquidation) v London and Lancashire Insurance Co Ltd [1928] Ch. 922; (1928) 31 Ll. L. Rep. 151 2–040

Fischmel Vertriebs-Gesellschaft mbH v Yorkshire Insurance Co Ltd. See Neue Fischmehl Vertriebsgesellschaft Haselhorst mbH v Yorkshire Insurance Co Ltd

Fisher v Liverpool Marine Insurance Co (1873–74) L.R. 9 Q.B. 418, Ex Chamber 24–044

Fisher v Smith (1878–79) L.R. 4 App. Cas. 1 HL 24–078

Fisher v Unione Italiana de Riassicurazione SPA [1999] Lloyd's Rep I.R. 215; [1998] C.L.C. 682 QBD 2–008

Fisk v Brian Thornhill & Son (A Firm) [2007] EWCA Civ 152; [2007] Lloyd's Rep. I.R. 699; [2007] P.N.L.R. 21; (2007) 151 S.J.L.B. 334 15–032

Fisk v Masterman (1841) 8 M. & W. 165 .... 8–032, 11–045

Fitton v Accidental Death Insurance (1864) 17 C.B.N.S. 122 .... 3–010, 5–030, 18–041, 18–059

Fitzherbert v Mather (1785) 1 Term Rep. 12; 99 E.R. 944 .... 6–036, 6–040, 15–004, 24–036

Fitzpatrick v Robert Norman Job and Wendy Barbara Job t/as Jobs Engineering [2007] W.A.S.C.A. 63 .... 20–028, 20–083

Fjord Wind, The. See Eridania SpA (formerly Cereol Italia Srl) v Oetker

Fleetwood's Policy, Re [1926] Ch. 48 Ch D 18–014

Fleming v Hislop (1886) L.R. 11 App. Cas. 686 HL 19–039

Fletcher v Inglis (1819) 2 B. & Ald. 315 24–134

Flexsys America LP v XL Insurance Co Ltd [2009] EWHC 1115 (Comm); [2009] 1 C.L.C. 754; [2010] Lloyd's Rep. I.R. 132 20–032

Flint v Flemyng (1830) 1 B. & Ad. 45 .... 20–062, 24–026

Flood v Irish Provident Assurance Co Ltd [1912] 2 Ch. 597 (Note); (1912) 46 Ir. L.T. 214 CA (UK-Irl) 8–024

Floods of Queensferry Ltd v Shand Construction Ltd (Costs) [2002] EWCA Civ. 918; [2003]
Lloyd's Rep. I.R. 181 CA (Civ Div) 14–029, 18–022
Floyd v Bush [1953] 1 W.L.R. 242; [1953] 1 All E.R. 265; [1953] 1 Lloyd's Rep. 64; (1953)
117 J.P. 88; 51 L.G.R. 162; 97 S.J. 80 DC 22–006
Flying Colours Film Co v Assicurazioni Generali SpA [1993] 2 Lloyd's Rep. 184 CA (Civ
Div); reversing [1991] 2 Lloyd's Rep. 536 QBD (Comm) 3–009, 3–010, 4–017, 10–021
Foley v Classique Coaches Ltd [1934] 2 K.B. 1 CA 8–008
Foley v Moline (1814) 5 Taunt. 430 24–037
Foley v Tabor (1861) 2 F. & F. 663 .... 6–064, 6–065, 7–043, 24–062
Foley v United Fire and Marine Insurance Co (1869–70) L.R. 5 C.P. 155 Ex Chamber 24–130
Fomin v Oswell (1813) 3 Camp. 357 15–034
Fong Wing Shing Construction Co Ltd v Allianz Insurance (Hong Kong) Ltd [2003] 3
H.K.C. 561 20–037
Fong Wing Shing Construction Co Ltd v Assurances Generales De France (HK) Ltd [2003]
H.K.E.C. 653 9–008
Fontana v Skandia Life Assurance Ltd Unreported 2002 CA (Civ Div) 1–025, 1–048, 8–010,
10–055
Fooks v Smith [1924] 2 K.B. 508; (1924) 19 Ll.L.R. 414 KBD 24–111
Forbes v Aspinall (1811) 13 East 323 .... 8–029, 10–008
Forbes v Edinburgh Life (1830) 10 S. (Ct. of Sess.) 451 6–073
Ford v Bradford & Bingley Building Society Unreported, 1997 .... 6–107, 14–003
Forfar Weavers Ltd v MSF Pritchard Syndicate, 2006 S.L.T. (Sh Ct) 19; 2006 G.W.D. 6–111,
Sh Ct (Glasgow) 7–032
Forgan v Pearl Life Assurance Co (1907) 51 S.J. 230 18–007
Forney v Dominion Insurance Co [1969] 1 W.L.R. 928; [1969] 3 All E.R. 831; [1969] 1
Lloyd's Rep. 502; 113 S.J. 326 QBD (Comm) 10–034, 20–047
Forrest v Glasser [2006] EWCA Civ 1086 .... 9–003, 9–009, 20–038
Forrest & Sons Ltd v CGU Insurance Plc [2006] Lloyd's Rep. I.R. 113 QBD (Merc) ... 5–018, 5–019,
6–054, 7–018, 9–014, 19–034
Forrester v Pigou (1813) 1 M. & S. 9 6–116
Forsakringsaktiebolaget Skandia (Publ), Re; sub nom. Proceedings brought by Forsakring-
saktiebolaget Skandia (C–240/99) [2001] 1 W.L.R. 1617; [2001] All E.R. (EC) 822;
[2001] S.T.C. 754; [2001] E.C.R. I–1951; [2001] 2 C.M.L.R. 34; [2001] B.T.C. 5213;
[2001] B.V.C. 281; [2001] S.T.I. 501; Times, March 20, 2001 ECJ 1–010
Forsakringsaktielskapet National of Copenhagen v Attorney General. See Attorney General
v Forsikringsaktieselskabet National
Forshaw v Chabert (1821) 3 Brod. & Bing. 158 .... 7–043, 24–062
Forsikringsaktieselskapet Vesta v Butcher [1989] A.C. 852; [1989] 2 W.L.R. 290; [1989] 1
All E.R. 402; [1989] 1 Lloyd's Rep. 331; [1989] Fin. L.R. 223; (1989) 133 S.J. 184 HL;
affirming [1988] 3 W.L.R. 565; [1988] 2 All E.R. 43; [1988] 1 Lloyd's Rep. 19; [1988]
1 F.T.L.R. 78; [1988] Fin. L.R. 67; (1988) 4 Const. L.J. 75; (1988) 85(31) L.S.G. 33;
(1988) 132 S.J. 1181 CA (Civ Div); affirming [1986] 2 All E.R. 488; [1986] 2 Lloyd's
Rep. 179 QBD (Comm) 2–030, 2–036, 2–044, 2–050, 3–011, 3–015, 15–028, 15–034,
15–051, 17–012, 17–014
Fort v Lee (1811) 3 Taunt. 381 24–037
Fortisbank SA v Trenwick International Ltd [2005] EWHC 399; [2005] Lloyd's Rep. I.R.
464 QBD (Comm) 9–040, 9–042, 23–025, 23–029
Foskett v McKeown [2001] 1 A.C. 102; [2000] 2 W.L.R. 1299; [2000] 3 All E.R. 97; [2000]
Lloyd's Rep. I.R. 627; [2000] W.T.L.R. 667; (1999–2000) 2 I.T.E.L.R. 711; (2000)
97(23) L.S.G. 44; Times, May 24, 2000; Independent, July 3, 2000 (C.S) HL 15–003
Fosse Motor Engineers Ltd v Conde Nast & National Magazine Distributors Ltd [2008]
EWHC 2037 TCC 24–134
Foster v Mentor Life (1854) 3 E. & B. 48 17–005
Foster v Mutual Life (1904) 20 T.L.R. 15 8–026
Foster v Standard Insurance Co of New Zealand Ltd [1924] N.Z.L.R. 1093 6–047
Foster v Thackeray (1781) 1 T.R. 57 4–002
Foster v Wilmer (1746) 2 Str. 1249 24–070
Foster's Policy, Re; sub nom. Menneer v Foster [1966] 1 W.L.R. 222; [1966] 1 All E.R. 432;
110 S.J. 151 Ch D 18–024
Fournier v Valentine (1930) 38 Ll.L.R. 19 KBD 6–56
Fowkes v Manchester & London Life Insurance Co (1862) 3 F. & F. 440 .... 6–047, 8–022
Fowkes v Manchester & London Life Insurance Co (1863) 3 B. & S. 917 ..... 3–010, 18–028, 18–028,
18–029
Fowler v Scottish Equitable Life (1858) 28 L.J. Ch. 225 .... 1–019, 8–024

France Fenwick & Co v North of England Protection and Indemnity Association. *See* William
    France Fenwick & Co Ltd v North of England Protecting and Indemnity Association
Francovich v Italy (C–6/90); Bonifacti v Italy (C–9/90) [1991] E.C.R. I–5357; [1993] 2
    C.M.L.R. 66; [1995] I.C.R. 722; [1992] I.R.L.R. 84; Times, November 20, 1991 ECJ 22–059,
                                                                        22–073
Frangos v Sun Insurance Office Ltd (1934) 49 Ll.L.R. 354 KBD 24–134
Frans Maas (UK) Ltd v Sun Alliance and London Insurance Plc [2003] EWHC 1803; [2004]
    1 Lloyd's Rep. 484; [2004] Lloyd's Rep. I.R. 649 QBD (Comm) 5–050
Fraser v BN Furman (Productions) Ltd [1967] 1 W.L.R. 898; [1967] 3 All E.R. 57; [1967]
    2 Lloyd's Rep. 1; 2 K.I.R. 483; (1967) 111 S.J. 471 CA (Civ Div) 5–049, 15–037, 15–056,
                                                                15–058, 20–031
Fraser River Pile & Dredge Ltd v Can-Drive Services Ltd (1997) 98 B.C.A.C. 138 11–038
Fraser Shipping Ltd v Colton [1997] 1 Lloyd's Rep. 586 QBD (Comm) 6–0106, 24–037, 24–039,
                                                                24–053, 24–083, 24–086
Freakley v Centre Reinsurance International Co [2004] EWHC 2740; [2005] 2 B.C.L.C. 530;
    [2005] Lloyd's Rep. I.R. 264 Ch D 18–022, 21–028
Freakley v Centre Reinsurance International Co [2006] UKHL 45; [2007] Bus. L.R. 284;
    [2006] 1 W.L.R. 2863; [2006] 4 All E.R. 1153; [2006] 2 All E.R. (Comm) 943; [2006]
    B.C.C. 971; [2007] 1 B.C.L.C. 85; [2006] B.P.I.R. 1405; [2007] Lloyd's Rep. I.R. 32;
    (2006) 103(41) L.S.G. 35; (2006) 156 N.L.J. 1613; (2006) 150 S.J.L.B. 1395; Times,
    October 16, 2006 21–028
Freeland v Glover (1806) 7 East 457 .... 6–070, 6–073
Freesman and Royal Insurance Co of Canada (1986) 29 D.L.R. (4th) 621 10–006
Frenkel v MacAndrews & Co Ltd [1929] A.C. 545; (1929) 33 Ll.L.R. 191 HL 24–070
Freshwater v Western Australian Assurance Co Ltd [1933] 1 K.B. 515; (1932) 44 Ll.L.R. 282
    CA 21–029, 21–054, 22–027
Frewin v Poland [1968] 1 Lloyd's Rep. 100; (1968) 118 N.L.J. 156 QBD (Comm) 10–012
Friedlander v London Assurance (1832) 1 Moo. & R. 171 6–015
Friends Provident Life & Pensions Ltd v Sirius International Insurance Corp [2005] EWCA
    Civ. 601; [2005] 2 All E.R. (Comm) 145; [2005] 2 Lloyd's Rep. 517; [2005] 1 C.L.C.
    794; [2006] Lloyd's Rep. I.R. 45; Times, June 8, 2005 CA (Civ Div); reversing in part
    [2004] EWHC 1799; [2004] 2 All E.R. (Comm) 707; [2005] Lloyd's Rep. I.R. 135 QBD
    (Comm) ... 1–001, 3–005, 3–015, 3–018, 6–109, 7–006, 7–007, 7–008, 7–009, 7–015, 9–003,
                                            9–004, 9–011, 9–013, 15–027, 15–041, 20–039
Friends Provident Life Office, Re [1999] 1 All E.R. (Comm.) 28; [1999] Lloyd's Rep. I.R.
    547; [1999] 1 B.C.L.C. 192; (1999) 96(4) L.S.G. 38; (1999) 143 S.J.L.B. 27; Times,
    January 4, 1999; Independent, December 14, 1998 .... 13–017, 17–003
Friere v Woodhouse (1817) Holt N.P. 572 6–065
Froom v Butcher [1976] Q.B. 286; [1975] 3 W.L.R. 379; [1975] 3 All E.R. 520; [1975] 2
    Lloyd's Rep. 478; [1975] R.T.R. 518; 119 S.J. 613 CA (Civ Div) 22–035
Frost v James Finlay Bank Ltd [2002] EWCA Civ. 667; [2002] Lloyd's Rep. I.R. 503; [2002]
    Lloyd's Rep. P.N. 473; [2002] 25 E.G.C.S. 150 CA (Civ Div); reversing [2001] Lloyd's
    Rep. Bank. 302; [2002] Lloyd's Rep. I.R. 429; [2001] Lloyd's Rep. P.N. 629; [2001]
    N.P.C. 101 Ch D 15–026, 15–037, 15–059
Fry v Fry (1859) 27 Beav. 144 19–031
Fryer v Morland (1876) L.R. 3 Ch. D. 675 Ch D 1–048, 18–022
Fuerst Day Lawson Ltd v Orion Insurance Co Ltd [1980] 1 Lloyd's Rep. 656 QBD (Comm) ... 9–015,
                                                10–003, 19–007, 19–034, 24–009
Fuji Finance v Aetna Insurance [1994] 4 All E.R. 1015, affirmed [1996] 4 All E.R. 608 1–003,
                                               1–008, 13–011, 18–001, 18–019
Furey v Eagle Star [1922] W.C. & Ins.Rep. 149, 225 7–037
Furness Withy & Co Ltd v Duder [1936] 2 K.B. 461; (1936) 55 Ll.L.R. 52 KBD 20–009, 24–005
Furness Withy (Australia) Ltd v Metal Distributors (UK) Ltd (The Amazonia) Amazonia,
    The [1990] 1 Lloyd's Rep. 236; Independent, December 4, 1989; Financial Times,
    November 15, 1989 CA 2–058
GD Construction (St Albans) Ltd v Scottish & Newcastle Plc [2003] EWCA Civ 16; [2003]
    B.L.R. 131; 86 Con. L.R. 1; [2003] Lloyd's Rep. I.R. 809; [2003] 6 E.G. 144 (C.S.);
    (2003) 100(11) L.S.G. 31; [2003] N.P.C. 8; Times, January 28, 2003 11–031
GE Frankona Reinsurance Ltd v CMM Trust No.1400; The Newfoundland Explorer [2006]
    EWHC 429; [2006] 1 All E.R. (Comm) 665; [2006] Lloyd's Rep. I.R. 704; Times, May
    2, 2006 QBD (Admlty) 3–007, 3–010, 7–037
GE Reinsurance Corp (formerly Kemper Reinsurance Co) v New Hampshire Insurance Co;
    GE Reinsurance Corp v Willis Ltd [2003] EWHC 302; [2004] Lloyd's Rep. I.R. 404
    QBD (Comm) 7–026, 15–051, 17–007, 17–013, 17–014

GFP Units v Monksfield [1972] 2 Lloyd's Rep. 79 QBD 22–088
GH Renton & Co Ltd v Black Sea and Baltic General Insurance Co Ltd [1941] 1 K.B. 206;
    (1940) 68 Ll.L.R. 71 KBD 24–066
GIE Reunion Europeenne v Zurich Espana (C–77/04) [2006] 1 All E.R. (Comm) 488; [2005]
    E.C.R. I–4509; [2005] I.L.Pr. 33; [2006] Lloyd's Rep. I.R. 215 2–009
GIO Insurance v Leighton Contractors Unreported, 1995 NSW 6–107
GMA v Unistorebrand International Insurance AS. *See* L'Alsacienne Premiere Societe
    Alsacienne et Lorraine d'Assurances Contre L'Incendie les Accidents et les Risques
    Divers v Unistorebrand International Insurance AS
GRE Assurance of New Zealand Ltd v Roberts [1991] 2 N.Z.L.R. 106 19–012
GRE Insurance Ltd v QBE Insurance Ltd [1985] V.R. 83 11–060
Gabay v Lloyd (1825) 3 B. & C. 793 .... 5–030, 24–134
Gadd v Houghton (1876) L.R. 1 Ex.D. 357 4–024
Gairdner Stenhouse (1810) 3 Taunt. 16 24–071
Gale v Lewis (1846) 9 Q.B. 730 .... 3–003, 15–015, 15–017
Gale v Mitchell (1785) Park on Insurance 797 8–021
Gale v Motor Union Insurance Co Ltd; Loyst v General Accident Fire & Life Assurance Co
    Ltd [1928] 1 K.B. 359; (1926) 26 Ll.L.R. 65 KBD 11–048
Galle Gowns Ltd v Licenses & General Insurance Co Ltd (1933) 47 Ll.L.R. 186 KBD 6–046
Galliford (UK) Ltd (t/a Galliford Northern) v Markel Capital Ltd [2003] EWHC 1216 QBD
    (Merc) 21–011
Galloway v Guardian Royal Exchange (UK) Ltd [1999] Lloyd's Rep. I.R. 209 CA (Civ
    Div) 6–018, 6–107, 9–026
Gambles v Ocean Insurance Co (1876) 1 Ex. D. 141 24–047
Gan Insurance Co Ltd v Tai Ping Insurance Co Ltd (No.1); Royal Reinsurance Co Ltd v
    Central Insurance Co Ltd [1998] C.L.C. 1072; [1999] Lloyd's Rep. I.R. 229 .. 2–029, 2–031,
                                                                                                                    2–036, 2–043
Gan Insurance Co Ltd v Tai Ping Insurance Co Ltd (No.1); Royal Reinsurance Co Ltd v
    Central Insurance Co Ltd [1999] 2 All E.R. (Comm) 54; [1999] C.L.C. 1270; [1999]
    I.L.Pr. 729; [1999] Lloyd's Rep. I.R. 472; Independent, June 30, 1999 CA (Civ Div) 2–005,
                                                                                                    2–007, 17–012, 17–014
Gan Insurance Co Ltd v Tai Ping Insurance Co Ltd (No.2) [2001] Lloyd's Rep. I.R. 291;
    reversed on other grounds [2001] EWCA Civ. 1047; [2001] 2 All E.R. (Comm) 299;
    [2001] C.L.C. 1103; [2001] Lloyd's Rep. I.R. 667 CA (Civ Div) ... 3–010, 6–014, 6–074, 6–109,
                                                    6–129, 9–003, 9–004, 10–022, 17–025, 20–045, 20–051, 20–058,
                                                                                                                    20–061
Gan Insurance Co Ltd v Tai Ping Insurance Co Ltd (No.3) [2002] EWCA Civ. 248; [2002]
    C.L.C. 870; [2002] Lloyd's Rep. I.R. 612 CA (Civ Div) 7–013, 17–019, 17–025, 20–037
Gan Insurance Co Ltd v Tai Ping Insurance Co Ltd (Preliminary Issues) [2001] C.L.C. 776;
    [2001] Lloyd's Rep. I.R. 291 3–009
Gandy v Adelaide Marine Insurance Co (1870–71) L.R. 6 Q.B. 746 QB 6–065, 6–074
Gard Marine & Energy Ltd v Tunnicliffe [2009] EWHC 2388 (Comm); [2010] Lloyd's Rep.
    I.R. 62 .... 2–004, 2–008, 2–036
Garden v Ingram (1852) 23 L.J. Ch. 478 .... 18–022, 19–017, 19–021, 19–025
Gardner v Moore [1984] A.C. 548; [1984] 2 W.L.R. 714; [1984] 1 All E.R. 1100; [1984] 2
    Lloyd's Rep. 135; [1984] R.T.R. 209; (1984) 81 L.S.G. 1444; (1984) 128 S.J. 282 HL 5–046,
                                                                                                    21–022, 22–029, 22–060
Garfield Container Transport Inc v Chubb Insurance Co of Canada (2002) 114 A.C.W.S. (3d)
    110 24–066
Garner v Moore (1855) 3 Drew. 277 .... 18–004, 19–031
Garrels v Kensington (1799) 8 T.R. 230 24–058
Garrett v Hooper [1973] R.T.R. 1; [1973] Crim. L.R. 61 DC 22–009
Garthwaite v Rowland (1947–48) 81 Ll.L.R. 417 MCLC 15–027
Gas Float Whitton No.2, The. *See* Wells v Owners of the Gas Float Whitton No.2 Gas Float
    Whitton No.2, The
Gate v Sun Alliance Assurance Unreported, 1993 HC (NZ) 6–047, 6–049, 6–054, 6–107, 14–003,
                                                                                                                    14–013
Gater Assets Ltd v Nak Naftogaz Ukrainiy [2008] EWHC 237 (Comm); [2008] 1 Lloyd's
    Rep. 479; [2008] 1 C.L.C. 141 17–001
Gatoil International Inc v Arkwright-Boston Manufacturers Mutual Insurance Co; The
    Sandrina [1985] A.C. 255; [1985] 2 W.L.R. 74; [1985] 1 All E.R. 129; [1985] 1 Lloyd's
    Rep. 181; 1985 S.C. (H.L.) 1; 1985 S.L.T. 68; (1985) 82 L.S.G. 524; (1984) 120 S.J. 870
    HL 24–078

Gaughan v Tony McDonagh & Co Ltd [2005] EWHC 739; [2006] Lloyd's Rep. I.R. 230;
    [2005] P.N.L.R. 36 QBD (Comm) 6–106, 15–037, 15–061
Gaunt v Gold Star Insurance Co Ltd [1991] 2 N.Z.L.R. 341 15–033
Gawler v Raettig [2007] EWHC 373 (QB) 22–035
Geach v Ingall (1845) 14 M. & W. 95 18–029
Gedge v Royal Exchange Assurance Corp [1900] 2 Q.B. 214 QBD (Comm) 24–013
Gee & Garnham Ltd v Whittall [1955] 2 Lloyd's Rep. 562 QBD 19–034, 24–080
Geismar v Sun Alliance and London Insurance Ltd [1978] Q.B. 383; [1978] 2 W.L.R. 38;
    [1977] 3 All E.R. 570; [1977] 2 Lloyd's Rep. 62; [1977] Crim. L.R. 475; 121 S.J. 201
    QBD 2–058, 5–038, 19–014
General Accident Fire & Life Assurance Corp v Hunter; sub nom. Hunter v General Accident
    Fire & Life Assurance Corp Ltd; Hunter v General Accident Corp [1909] A.C. 404;
    1909 S.C. (H.L.) 30; 1909 2 S.L.T. 99 HL 1–023
General Accident Fire & Life Assurance Corp Ltd v Campbell (1925) 21 Ll.l.R. 151 KBD 6–052,
    17–007
General Accident Fire & Life Assurance Corp Ltd v JH Minet & Co Ltd (1942) 74 Ll.L.R.
    1 CA 15–051
General Accident Fire & Life Assurance Corp Ltd v Midland Bank Ltd [1940] 2 K.B. 388;
    (1940) 67 Ll.l.R. 218 CA 10–063, 11–029, 14–003, 14–015, 19–025
General Accident Fire & Life Assurance Corp Ltd v Shuttleworth (1938) 60 Ll.L.R. 301
    KBD 22–048
General Accident Fire & Life Assurance Corp Ltd v Tanter; The Zephyr [1985] 2 Lloyd's
    Rep. 529; Financial Times, July 30, 1985CA (Civ Div); reversing in part [1984] 1
    W.L.R. 100; [1984] 1 All E.R. 35; [1984] 1 Lloyd's Rep. 58; (1984) 134 N.L.J. 35;
    (1983) 127 S.J. 733 QBD (Comm) 1–023, 1–038, 6–116, 14–008, 15–028, 17–005
General Accident Insurance Co of Canada v Ontario Provincial Police Force (1988) 30
    C.C.L.I. 178 20–050
General Accident Insurance Corp v Cronk (1901) 17 T.L.R. 233 .... 1–022, 1–025, 8–012, 8–024
General Feeds Inc Panama v Slobodna Plovidba Yugoslavia (The Krapan J) Krapan J, The
    [1999] 1 Lloyd's Rep. 688 15–059
General Insurance Co of Trieste Ltd (Assicurazioni Generali) v Cory [1897] 1 Q.B. 335 QBD
    (Comm) 7–022
General Insurance Co of Trieste Ltd v Corporation of the Royal Exchange (1897) 2
    Com.Case. 144 17–012
General Insurance Corp of New Brunswick v Fulton, 75 D.L.R. (4th) 382 (1991) 5–023
General Insurance of Trieste v Miller (1896) 12 T.L.R. 395 17–002
General Motors Corp v Royal & Sun Alliance Insurance Plc [2007] EWHC 2206 (Comm);
    [2007] 2 C.L.C. 507; [2008] Lloyd's Rep. I.R. 311; (2007) 104(40) L.S.G. 28 .... 2–003, 2–006
General Motors Ltd v Crowder (1931) 40 Ll.L.R. 87 KBD 9–003, 9–008
General Omnibus Co v London General Insurance (1932) 66 Ir. L.T. 96 20–043
General Provincial, Re, Ex p. Daintree (1870) 18 W.R. 396 .... 6–053, 18–038
General Reinsurance Corp v Forsakringsaktiebolaget Fennia Patria [1983] Q.B. 856; [1983]
    3 W.L.R. 318; [1983] 2 Lloyd's Rep. 287; (1983) 127 S.J. 389 CA (Civ Div); reversing
    [1982] Q.B. 1022; [1982] 2 W.L.R. 518; [1982] 1 Lloyd's Rep. 87; [1981] Com. L.R.
    280; 126 S.J. 32; Times, November 4, 1981 QBD (Comm) 1–033, 1–034, 1–036, 1–037,
    1–038, 6–116
General Rolling Stock Co, Re; sub nom. Joint Stock Discount Co's Claim (1871–72) L.R. 7
    Ch. App. 646 CA in Chancery 21–017
General Shipping & Forwarding Co v British General Insurance Co Ltd (1923) 15 Ll.L.R.
    175 KBD 7–022, 10–006, 10–009
General Star International Indemnity Ltd v Stirling Cooke Brown Reinsurance Brokers Ltd
    [2003] EWHC 3; [2003] I.L.Pr. 19; [2003] Lloyd's Rep. I.R. 719 QBD (Comm) ... 2–005, 2–006
Genforsikrings Aktieselskabet (Skandinavia Reinsurance Co of Copenhagen) v Da Costa
    [1911] 1 K.B. 137 KBD 24–044
George and Goldsmiths & General Burglary Insurance Association Ltd's Arbitration, Re
    [1899] 1 Q.B. 595 CA 3–004, 3–010, 8–001, 19–046
George Cohen Sons & Co v Standard Marine Insurance Co Ltd (1925) 21 Ll.L.R. 30 KBD 6–065,
    6–073, 24–062, 24–083, 24–086
George Hunt Cranes Ltd v Scottish Boiler & General Insurance Co Ltd [2001] EWCA Civ.
    1964; [2002] 1 All E.R. (Comm) 366; [2003] 1 C.L.C. 1; [2002] Lloyd's Rep. I.R. 178;
    (2003) 147 S.J.L.B. 60 CA (Civ Div) 3–003, 7–013, 7–014, 21–023
George Kallis (Manufacturers) Ltd v Success Insurance Ltd [1985] 2 Lloyd's Rep. 8 PC
    (HK) 24–068

Gerling General Insurance Co v Canary Wharf Group Plc [2005] EWHC 2234; [2006] 1
Lloyd's Rep. 68 QBD (Comm) 10–003, 10–039
Gerling Konzern General Insurance Co v Polygram Holdings Inc; Copenhagen Reinsurance
Co (UK) Ltd v Polygram Holdings Inc [1998] 2 Lloyd's Rep. 544 QBD (Comm) 7–032,
15–027
Gibson v Service (1814) 5 Taunt. 433 24–064
Gibson v Small (1843) 4 H.L. Cas. 353 .... 24–020, 24–061, 24–062
Gilbert v Sykes (1812) 16 East 150 4–002
Giles v Thompson; Devlin v Baslington; Sanders v Templar [1994] 1 A.C. 142; [1993] 2
W.L.R. 908; [1993] 3 All E.R. 321; [1993] R.T.R. 289; (1993) 143 N.L.J. 884; (1993)
137 S.J.L.B. 151; Times, June 1, 1993 HL 11–004, 14–029, 20–043, 22–024
Gilheaney v McGovern [2009] N.I.Q.B. 38 22–026
Gill v Insurance Corporation of British Columbia, 50 D.L.R. (4th) 148 (1988) 14–012
Girdlestone v North British Mercantile Insurance Co (1870–71) L.R. 11 Eq. 197 Ct of
Chancery 6–031, 7–044
Gladitz, Re; sub nom. Guaranty Executor & Trustee Co Ltd v Gladitz [1937] Ch. 588 Ch D ... 18–014
Gladstone v King (1813) 1 M. &S. 35 6–040
Glafki Shipping Co SA v Pinios Shipping Co (The Maria) (No.2) [1986] 2 Lloyd's Rep. 12
HL; affirming [1985] 1 Lloyd's Rep. 300CA (Civ Div); reversing [1984] 1 Lloyd's Rep.
660 QBD (Comm) 1–009, 4–009, 10–007, 24–013
Glaser v Cowie (1813) I M. & S. 52 15–034
HLGlasgow Assurance Corporation Ltd v William Symondson & Co (1911) 104 L.T. 254 6–027,
6–031, 6–053
Glasgow Assurance Corporation Ltd v William Symondson & Co (1911) 16 Com. Cas.
109 15–028
Glasgow Assurance Corporation Ltd v William Symondson & Co (1911) 27 T.L.R. 245 ... 6–118
Glasgow Assurance Corporation v Welsh Insurance Corp. See Liquidators of Glasgow
Assurance Corp Ltd v Welsh Insurance Corp Ltd
Glasgow Training Group (Motor Trade) Ltd v Lombard Continental Plc, 1989 S.C. 30; 1989
S.L.T. 375; Times, November 21, 1988 OH 19–035
Gledstanes v Royal Exchange Assurance Corp (1864) 34 L.J.Q.B. 30 .... 24–020, 24–051
Gledstanes v Royal Exchange Assurance Corp (1864) 5 B. & S. 797 24–051
Glen v Lewis (1853) 8 Ex. 607 .... 5–019, 5–022, 6–103, 7–027, 19–039
Glen Line v AttorneyGeneral (1930) 6 Com. Cas. 1 .... 11–017, 24–095
Glen's Trustees Lancashire & Yorkshire Accident (1906) 8 F. (Ct. of Sess.) 915 3–011
Glencore International AG v Alpina Insurance Co Ltd [2003] EWHC 2792; [2004] 1 All E.R.
(Comm) 766; [2004] 1 Lloyd's Rep. 111 QBD (Comm) 1–008, 1–023, 1–031, 5–029, 6–011,
6–023, 6–029, 6–030, 6–065, 6–087, 6–117, 6–120, 10–002, 10–037,
17–001
Glencore International AG v Alpina Insurance Co Ltd (Further Quantum Issues) (No.2)
[2004] EWHC 66; [2004] 1 All E.R. (Comm) 858; [2004] 1 Lloyd's Rep. 567 QBD
(Comm) 10–001, 24–051
Glencore International AG v Portman. See Marc Rich & Co AG v Portman
Glencore International AG v Ryan; The Beursgracht (No.1); Glencore International AG v
Ryan; The Beursgracht (No.2) [2001] EWCA Civ. 2051; [2002] 1 Lloyd's Rep. 574;
[2002] C.L.C. 547; [2002] Lloyd's Rep. I.R. 335 CA (Civ Div); affirming [2001] 2
Lloyd's Rep. 602 CC (Central London) 1–031, 3–008, 7–006, 7–009, 17–001, 17–011
Glencore International AG v Ryan; The Beursgracht (No.2) [2001] 2 Lloyd's Rep. 608 CC
(Central London) 8–017, 20–047, 20–051
Glengate-KG Properties Ltd v Norwich Union Fire Insurance Society Ltd [1996] 2 All E.R.
487; [1996] 1 Lloyd's Rep. 614; [1996] C.L.C. 676; 49 Con. L.R. 78; [1996] 5 Re. L.R.
50; (1996) 12 Const. L.J. 266; Times, January 12, 1996; Independent, January 22, 1996
CA (Civ Div); affirming [1995] 1 Lloyd's Rep. 278; (1995) 11 Const. L.J. 233; [1994]
N.P.C. 103 QBD (Comm) 4–013, 4–017, 10–019, 10–021, 19–007
Gleniffer Finance Corp Ltd v Bamar Wood & Products Ltd [1978] 2 Lloyd's Rep. 49; (1979)
37 P. & C.R. 208; 122 S.J. 110 QBD 19–022
Glenmuir Ltd v Norwich Union Fire insurance Society Ltd Unreported, 1995 ...... 5–050, 22–094
Glicksman v Lancashire & General Assurance Co Ltd [1927] A.C. 139; (1926) 26 Ll.L.R. 69
HL; affirming [1925] 2 K.B. 593; (1925) 22 Ll.L.R. 179 CA 6–018, 6–031, 6–053, 6–070,
Gliksten & Son Ltd v State Assurance Co. See F Gliksten & Son Ltd v State Assurance
Co
Global Multimedia International Ltd v ARA Media Services [2006] EWHC 3107 (Ch);
[2007] 1 All E.R. (Comm) 1160; Times, August 1, 2006 2–025

Global Process Systems Inc v Syarikat Takaful Malaysia Bhd (The Cendor Mopu) Cendor
    Mopu, The [2009] EWCA Civ 1398; [2010] 1 Lloyd's Rep. 243; [2009] 2 C.L.C. 1056;
    [2010] Lloyd's Rep. I.R. 221; Times, March 2, 2010 .. 5–034, 24–080, 24–081, 24–134, 24–135
Global Process Systems Inc v Syarikat Takaful Malaysia Bhd (The Cendor Mopu) [2009]
    EWHC 637 (Comm); [2009] 2 All E.R. (Comm) 795; [2009] 2 Lloyd's Rep. 72; [2009]
    Lloyd's Rep. I.R. 511 24–003
Globe & Rutgers Fire Insurance Co v Truedell [1927] 2 D.L.R. 659 .... 11–006, 11–042
Gloucestershire HA v MA Torpy & Partners Ltd (t/a Torpy & Partners) (No.2) [1999]
    Lloyd's Rep. I.R. 203 QBD (OR) 20–055
Glover v Black (1763) 1 Wm. Bl. 396 19–027
Glover v Black (1763) 3 Burr. 1394 10–021
Glynn v Margetson & Co; sub nom. Margetson v Glynn [1893] A.C. 351 HL 3–011
Goddard & Smith v Frew (1939) 65 Ll.L.R. 83; [1939] 4 All E.R. 358 CA 20–006, 20–009,
                                                                          20–031, 23–021, 23–029
Goddard v Garrett (1692) 2 Vern. 269 4–002
Godfrey Davis Ltd v Culling [1962] 2 Lloyd's Rep. 349; (1962) 106 S.J. 918 CA 10–044
Godfrey v Britannic Assurance Co Ltd [1963] 2 Lloyd's Rep. 515; (1963) 107 S.J. 536
    QBD 18–028, 18–029
Godin v London Assurance Co (1758) 1 Burr. 489 .... 11–044, 24–078
Godonoaga v Khatambakhsh (2000) 132 O.A. 391 20–049
Godsal v Webb (1838) 2 Keen 99 14–026
Godsall v Boldero (1807) 9 East 72 18–004
Goit v National Protection (1844) 25 Barb. (N.Y.) 189 8–004
Golden Ocean Assurance and World Mariner Shipping SA v Martin (The Goldean Mariner)
    [1990] 2 Lloyd's Rep. 215; Times, June 20, 1990 CA (Civ Div); reversing [1989] 2
    Lloyd's Rep. 390 QBD (Comm) 2–004
Golding v Royal London Auxiliary Insurance (1914) 30 T.L.R. 350 .... 6–102, 7–037, 15–019
Goldmid v Gillies (1813) 4 Taunt. 803 24–092
Goldschmidt v Marryat (1809) 1 Camp. 559 6–107
Goldschmidt v Whitmore (1811) 3 Taunt. 508 24–138
Goldsmith Williams (A Firm) v Travelers Insurance Co Ltd [2010] EWHC 26 (QB) ... 5–047, 14–013
Goldstein v Salvation Army Assurance Society [1917] 2 K.B. 291 KBD 18–010, 18–015
Gomer & Co v Pitt & Scott Ltd (1922) 12 Ll.L.R. 115 CA 15–034
Good v Elliott (1790) 3 T.R. 693 .... 4–002, 4–003
Good Luck, The. See Bank of Nova Scotia v Hellenic Mutual War Risk Association
    (Bermuda) Ltd
Goodbarne v Buck [1940] 1 K.B. 771; [1940] 1 All E.R. 613; (1940) 66 Ll.L.R. 129 22–010,
                                                                                                          22–011
Gooding v White (1913) 29 T.L.R. 312 6–056
Goole and Hull Steam Towing Co Ltd v Ocean Marine Insurance Co Ltd [1928] 1 K.B. 589;
    (1927–28) 29 Ll.L.R. 242 KBD 1–009, 10–006, 11–018, 11–034
Gordon v Rimmington (1807) 1 Camp. 123 .... 5–041, 19–040
Gordon, Re; Lloyds Bank and Parratt v Lloyd and Gordon [1940] Ch. 851 Ch D 18–024
Gorely, Ex p. (1864) 4 De G. J. & S. 477 10–051
Gorham v British Telecommunications Plc [2000] 1 W.L.R. 2129; [2000] 4 All E.R. 867;
    [2001] Lloyd's Rep. I.R. 531; [2000] Lloyd's Rep. P.N. 897; [2001] P.N.L.R. 2; [2000]
    Pens. L.R. 293; (2000) 97(38) L.S.G. 44; (2000) 144 S.J.L.B. 251; Times, August 16,
    2000 CA (Civ Div) 6–131
Gorman v Hand–0in–Hand (1877) Ir.R. 11 C.L. 224 19–044
Goshawk Dedicated Ltd v Rop Inc [2006] EWHC 1730 (Comm); [2006] Lloyd's Rep. I.R.
    711 2–006
Goshawk Dedicated Ltd v Tyser & Co Ltd [2006] EWCA Civ. 54; [2006] 1 All E.R. (Comm)
    501; [2006] 1 Lloyd's Rep. 566; [2006] 1 C.L.C. 198; Times, April 4, 2006; Independent
    February 16, 2006 CA (Civ Div); reversing [2005] EWHC 461; [2005] 2 All E.R.
    (Comm) 115; [2005] Lloyd's Rep. I.R. 379 QBD (Comm) 3–013, 6–111, 8–007, 15–027,
                                                                              15–028, 15–042, 18–005
Goshawk Syndicate Management Ltd v XL Speciality Insurance Co [2004] EWHC 1086;
    [2004] 2 All E.R. (Comm) 512; [2004] 2 C.L.C. 783; [2004] Lloyd's Rep. I.R. 683 QBD
    (Comm) 17–014
Gosling v Howard [1975] R.T.R. 429 DC 22–009
Gould v Curtis (Surveyor of Taxes) [1913] 3 K.B. 84 CA 1–009, 18–001
Goulstone v Royal Insurance (1858) 1 F. & F. 276 .... 4–017, 9–020, 9–026, 9–033, 19–014

Governors of the Peabody Trust v Michael Reeve [2008] EWHC 1432 (Ch); [2009] L. & T.R. 6; [2008] 3 E.G.L.R. 61; [2008] 43 E.G. 196; [2008] 23 E.G. 116 (C.S.); [2008] 2 P. & C.R. DG12; Times, June 9, 2008 3–018
Grace v Leslie & Godwin Financial Services Ltd [1995] L.R.L.R. 472; [1995] C.L.C. 801; Times, May 16, 1995; Independent, June 12, 1995 (C.S.); Lloyd's List, June 13, 1995 (I.D.) QBD (Comm) 15–033, 15–041, 15–051, 15–061
Graham v Barras (1834) 5 B. & Ad. 1011 24–068
Graham v Entec Europe Ltd (t/a Exploration Associates) [2003] EWCA Civ. 1177; [2003] 4 All E.R. 1345; [2003] 2 All E.R. (Comm) 811; 92 Con. L.R. 35; [2004] Lloyd's Rep. I.R. 660; Times, September 10, 2003 CA (Civ Div) 11–011
Graham v Western Australian Insurance Co Ltd (1931) 40 Ll.L.R. 64 KBD 6–016
Graham Joint Stock Shipping Co Ltd v Merchants Marine Insurance Co Ltd; The Ioanna (No.1); sub nom. Graham Joint Stock Shipping Co v Motor Union Insurance Co [1924] A.C. 294; (1923–24) 17 Ll.L.R. 241 HL 14–007, 14–008, 14–029
Graham Joint Stock Shipping Co Ltd v Motor Union Insurance Co Ltd [1922] 1 K.B. 563; (1921) 9 Ll.L.R. 381 CA 6–0107
Gran Gelato Ltd v Richcliff (Group) Ltd [1992] Ch. 560; [1992] 2 W.L.R. 867; [1992] 1 All E.R. 865; [1992] 1 E.G.L.R. 297; [1991] E.G.C.S. 136; (1992) 142 N.L.J. 51; Times, December 19, 1991; Independent, December 18, 1991 Ch D 15–036
Granada UK Rental & Retail v SPN Fareway and Motor Insurers Bureau [1995] C.L.Y. 3238 CC (Wigan) 22–057
Grand Union v Evans-Lombe Ashton Unreported, 1989 3–013
Grant Smith & Co v Seattle Construction & Dry Dock Co; McDonnell Ltd v Seattle Construction & Dry Dock Co [1920] A.C. 162 PC (Can) 24–134
Grant v Aetna Assurance (1862) 15 Moo. P.C.C. 516 .... 5–020, 6–014, 7–032, 18–037
Grant v Hill (1812) 4 Taunt. 380 4–023
Grant v King (1802) 4 Esp. 175 .... 24–065, 24–072
Grauds v Dearsley (1935) 51 Ll.L.R. 203 KBD 9–025
Gray v Barr [1971] 2 Q.B. 554; [1971] 2 W.L.R. 1334; [1971] 2 All E.R. 949; [1971] 2 Lloyd's Rep. 1; 115 S.J. 364 CA (Civ Div) 5–030, 5–042, 5–046, 20–031, 22–029
Gray v Blackmore [1934] 1 K.B. 95; (1933) 47 Ll.L.R. 69 KBD 22–036, 22–037, 22–096
Gray v Lloyd (1812) 4 Taunt. 136 24–064
Gray v Thames Trains Ltd [2009] UKHL 33; [2009] 1 A.C. 1339; [2009] 3 W.L.R. 167; [2009] 4 All E.R. 81; [2009] P.I.Q.R. P22; [2009] LS Law Medical 409; (2009) 108 B.M.L.R. 205; (2009) 159 N.L.J. 925; (2009) 153(24) S.J.L.B. 33; Times, June 19, 2009 .... 5–044, 20–083
Great Atlantic Insurance Co v Home Insurance Co; sub nom. Great Atlantic Insurance Co v American Foreign Insurance Association; Great Atlantic Insurance Co v CE Heath & Co (International); Great Atlantic Insurance Co v Frank Elger & Co [1981] 2 Lloyd's Rep. 219; affirmed [1981] 1 W.L.R. 529; [1981] 2 All E.R. 485; [1981] 2 Lloyd's Rep. 138; 125 S.J. 203 CA (Civ Div) 15–050
Great Britain 100 A1 Steamship Insurance Association v Wyllie (1889) L.R. 22 Q.B.D. 710 CA 8–006
Great Britain Mutual Life Assurance Society (No.2), Re (1881–82) L.R. 20 Ch. D. 351 CA 16–006
Great Hill Equity Partners II LP v Novator One LP [2007] EWHC 1210 (Comm) 3–005
Great North Eastern Railway Ltd v Avon Insurance Plc; sub nom. Great Northern Eastern Railway Ltd v Avon Insurance Plc; GNER v Avon Insurance Plc [2001] EWCA Civ. 780; [2001] 2 All E.R. (Comm) 526; [2001] 2 Lloyd's Rep. 649; [2001] Lloyd's Rep. I.R. 793 CA (Civ Div) 1–033, 1–039, 1–049
Great North Eastern Railway Ltd v JLT Corporate Risks Ltd [2006] EWHC 1478 (Comm); [2007] Lloyd's Rep. I.R. 38; [2006] P.N.L.R. 34 .... 15–034, 15–038, 15–061
Great Peace Shipping Ltd v Tsavliris Salvage (International) Ltd [2002] EWCA Civ. 1407; [2003] Q.B. 679; [2002] 3 W.L.R. 1617; [2002] 4 All E.R. 689; [2002] 2 All E.R. (Comm) 999; [2002] 2 Lloyd's Rep. 653; [2003] 2 C.L.C. 16; (2002) 99(43) L.S.G. 34; (2002) 152 N.L.J. 1616; [2002] N.P.C. 127; Times, October 17, 2002; Independent, October 22, 2002 CA (Civ Div) 1–021, 10–057
Great West Development Marine Corp v Canadian Surety Co [2000] B.C.T.C. 339 20–050
Great Western Insurance Co, Re. See Secretary of State for Trade and Industry v Great Western Assurance Co SA
Great Western Insurance Co of New York v Cunliffe (1873–74) L.R. 9 Ch. App. 525CA in Chancery 15–033, 15–034
Greater Britain Insurance Corp Ltd v CT Bowring & Co (Insurance) Ltd (1926) 24 Ll.L.R. 7 CA 24–078

Greaves v Drysdale [1936] 2 All E.R. 470; (1936) 55 Ll.L.R. 95CA; reversing (1935) 53
  Ll.L.R. 16 KBD 9–015
Grecoair Inc v Tilling [2004] EWHC 2851; [2005] Lloyd's Rep. I.R. 151QBD (Comm) ... 17–002,
                                                                                          20–008
Green v British India Steam Navigation Co . See Britain Steamship Co Ltd v King, The
Green v Elmslie (1792) 1 Peake N.P. 212 5–030
Green v Ingham (1867) L.R. 2 C.P. 525 14–026
Green v Russell, McCarthy (Third Party) [1959] 2 Q.B. 226; [1959] 3 W.L.R. 17; [1959] 2
  All E.R. 525; 103 S.J. 489 CA 18–002, 18–024
Green v Young (1702) 2 Ld. Raym. 840 24–070
Green & Son Ltd v Tunghan & Co (1913) 30 T.L.R. 64 15–033
Greene Wood & McClean LLP v Templeton Insurance Ltd [2008] EWHC 1593 (Comm);
  [2009] Lloyd's Rep. I.R. 61 .... 2–004, 23–034
Greenfield, Re, Jackson v Greenfield. See Jackson v Greenfield
Greenhill v Federal Insurance Co Ltd [1927] 1 K.B. 65; (1926) 24 Ll.L.R. 383 CA 6–073, 24–039
Greenleaf Associates v Monksfield [1972] R.T.R. 451 .... 19–050, 22–088
Greenock Steamship Co v Maritime Insurance Co Ltd [1903] 1 K.B. 367 ..... 8–008, 24–053, 24–061,
                                                                                          24–062
QBDGregoriades v Imperial Ottoman Bank (1926) 26 Ll.L.R. 92CA; affirming (1926) 25
  Ll.L.R. 68 KBD 15–026
Gregory v Christie (1784) 3 Doug. 419 24–070
Gregson v Gilbert (1783) 3 Doug. 232 .... 5–048, 24–080
Grell-Taurel Ltd v Caribbean Home Insurance Co Ltd [2002] Lloyd's Rep. I.R. 655 CA
  (Trin) 25–009
Griffin v Squires [1958] 1 W.L.R. 1106; [1958] 3 All E.R. 468; 123 J.P. 40; 56 L.G.R. 442;
  103 S.J. 5; 102 S.J. 828 DC 22–007
Griffin v UHY Hacker Young & Partners (A Firm) [2010] EWHC 146 (Ch) 5–046, 20–086
Griffiths v Bramley-Moore (1878–79) L.R. 4 Q.B.D. 70 CA 4–016, 24–031
Griffiths v Fleming [1909] 1 K.B. 805 CA 4–014, 4–017, 18–014, 18–015, 18–018, 18–019
Griffiths Policy, Re [1903] 1 Ch. 739 Ch D 18–014
Grimaldi Ltd v Sullivan [1997] C.L.C. 64 CA (Civ Div) 10–001, 10–018, 15–027, 19–054
Grist v Bailey [1967] Ch. 532; [1966] 3 W.L.R. 618; [1966] 2 All E.R. 875; 110 S.J. 791 Ch
  D 10–057
Grogan v London and Manchester Industrial Assurance (1855) 2 T.L.R. 75 18–027
Groom v Crocker [1939] 1 K.B. 194; (1938) 60 Ll.L.R. 393 CA 20–045
Group Josi Re Co SA v Walbrook Insurance Co Ltd; sub nom. Group Josi Re (formerly
  Group Josi Reassurance SA) v Walbrook Insurance Co Ltd; Deutsche Ruckversicherung
  AG v Walbrook Insurance Co Ltd [1996] 1 W.L.R. 1152; [1996] 1 All E.R. 791; [1996]
  1 Lloyd's Rep. 345; [1995] C.L.C. 1532; [1996] 5 Re. L.R. 91 CA (Civ Div) 6–004, 6–036,
                                            6–037, 6–039, 6–041, 6–042, 6–043, 13–020, 15–023
Group Josi Reinsurance Co SA v Universal General Insurance Co Ltd (C–412/98). See
  Universal General Insurance Co (UGIC) v Group Josi Reinsurance Co SA; sub nom.
  Group Josi Reinsurance Co SA v Compagnie d'Assurances Universal General Insurance
  Co (UGIC) (C–412/98)
Groupama Insurance Co Ltd v Channel Islands Securities Ltd [2002] Lloyd's Rep. I.R. 843 2–003,
                                                                                          2–005
Groupama Insurance Co Ltd v Overseas Partners Re Ltd [2003] EWCA Civ 1846; [2004] 1
  All E.R. (Comm) 893; [2004] C.P. Rep. 18; [2004] 1 C.L.C. 779; (2004) 148 S.J.L.B.
  28 .... 6–004, 6–015, 6–106, 7–033, 17–007
Groupama Navigation et Transports v Catatumbo CA Seguros [2000] 2 All E.R. (Comm)
  193; [2000] 2 Lloyd's Rep. 350; [2000] C.L.C. 1534; [2001] Lloyd's Rep. I.R. 141 CA
  (Civ Div) 3–016, 17–014
ECJGrover & Grover Ltd v Mathews [1910] 2 K.B. 401 KBD 1–033, 4–023, 14–008, 15–003
Groves v Amp Fire and General Insurance (NZ) [1990] 2 N.Z.L.R. 408 CA (NZ) 18–041
Grundy (Teddington) Ltd v Fulton [1983] 1 Lloyd's Rep. 16 CA (Civ Div) 3–008, 19–049
Grunther Industrial Developments Ltd v Federated Employers Insurance Association Ltd
  (No.2); sub nom. Federated Employers Insurance Association Ltd v Grunther Industrial
  Developments Ltd [1976] 2 Lloyd's Rep. 259 CA (Civ Div) 9–025
Guardian Assurance Co Ltd v Sutherland (1939) 63 Ll.L.R. 220; [1939] 2 All E.R. 246
  KBD 6–047, 22–027, 22–048, 22–088
Guepratte v Young (1851) 4 De G. & Sm. 217; 64 E.R. 804 2–054
Guibert v Readshaw (1781) 2 Park on Insurance 637 24–073
Gullett v Evans (No.2) (1929) 35 Ll.L.R. 239 KBD 1–019

Gunns v Par Insurance Brokers [1997] 1 Lloyd's Rep. 173 QBD ... 5–050, 6–028, 6–065, 15–036, 15–057
Gurnell v Gardner (1863) 4 Giff. 626 14–026
Gurney v Grimmer (1932) 44 Ll.L.R. 189 CA 17–019
Gurtner v Circuit [1968] 2 Q.B. 587; [1968] 2 W.L.R. 668; [1968] 1 All E.R. 328; [1968] 1 Lloyd's Rep. 171; 112 S.J. 63; 112 S.J. 73 CA (Civ Div) 22–057, 22–058, 22–060
H (Deceased), Re [1990] 1 F.L.R. 441; [1990] Fam. Law 175 18–035
H Cousins & Co v D&C Carriers [1971] 2 Q.B. 230; [1971] 2 W.L.R. 85; [1971] 1 All E.R. 55; [1970] 2 Lloyd's Rep. 397; (1970) 114 S.J. 882 CA (Civ Div) 11–022
HIB Ltd v Guardian Insurance Co Inc. See Hogg Insurance Brokers Ltd v Guardian Insurance Co Inc
HIH Casualty & General Insurance Co Ltd v Waterwell Shipping Inc Unreported, 1998 NSWCA 24–004, 24–081
HIH Casualty & General Insurance Ltd v Axa Corporate Solutions (formerly Axa Reassurance SA); HIH Casualty & General Insurance Ltd v New Hampshire Insurance Co [2002] EWCA Civ. 1253; [2002] 2 All E.R. (Comm) 1053; [2003] Lloyd's Rep. I.R. 1 CA (Civ Div); affirming [2002] Lloyd's Rep. I.R. 325 QBD 6–089, 7–018, 7–048
HIH Casualty & General Insurance Ltd v Chase Manhattan Bank; Chase Manhattan Bank v HIH Casualty & General Insurance Ltd [2003] UKHL 6; [2003] 1 All E.R. (Comm) 349; [2003] 2 Lloyd's Rep. 61; [2003] 1 C.L.C. 358; [2003] Lloyd's Rep. I.R. 230; (2003) 147 S.J.L.B. 264 HL; reversing in part [2001] EWCA Civ. 1250; [2001] 2 Lloyd's Rep. 483; [2001] C.L.C. 1853; [2001] Lloyd's Rep. I.R. 703 CA (Civ Div); reversing in part [2001] 1 All E.R. (Comm) 719; [2001] 1 Lloyd's Rep. 30; [2001] C.L.C. 48; [2001] Lloyd's Rep. I.R. 191; Times, September 19, 2000 QBD (Comm) 1–023, 6–001, 6–010, 6–017, 6–036, 6–040, 6–044, 6–069, 6–074, 6–079, 6–081, 6–082, 6–083, 6–084, 6–086, 6–088, 6–100, 6–118, 6–131, 15–001, 15–036, 17–006, 23–033
HIH Casualty & General Insurance Ltd v JLT Risk Solutions Ltd (formerly Lloyd Thompson Ltd) [2006] EWHC 485; [2006] Lloyd's Rep. I.R. 493; [2006] 1 C.L.C. 499; (2006) 103 L.S.G. 32 QBD (Comm) 15–028, 15–038, 15–051
HIH Casualty & General Insurance Ltd v JLT Risk Solutions Ltd (formerly Lloyd Thompson Ltd) [2007] EWCA Civ 710; [2008] Bus. L.R. 180; [2007] 2 All E.R. (Comm) 1106; [2007] 2 Lloyd's Rep. 278; [2007] 2 C.L.C. 62; [2007] Lloyd's Rep. I.R. 717; [2008] P.N.L.R. 3; (2007) 104(30) L.S.G. 35 .... 15–051, 15–054
HIH Casualty & General Insurance Ltd v New Hampshire Insurance Co [2001] EWCA Civ. 735; [2001] 2 All E.R. (Comm) 39; [2001] 2 Lloyd's Rep. 161; [2001] C.L.C. 1480; [2001] Lloyd's Rep. I.R. 596 CA (Civ Div); affirming [2001] 1 Lloyd's Rep. 378; [2001] Lloyd's Rep. I.R. 234; [2001] C.L.C. 481 QBD (Comm) ... 1–010, 1–011, 1–022, 1–033, 3–005, 3–015, 3–016, 5–017, 6–082, 6–084, 7–026, 7–039, 7–047, 17–012, 17–014
HIT Entertainment Ltd v Gaffney International Licensing Pty Ltd [2007] EWHC 1282 (Ch) 2–005
HLB Kidsons (A Firm) v Lloyd's Underwriters [2007] EWHC 1951 (Comm); [2008] 1 All E.R. (Comm) 769; [2008] Lloyd's Rep. I.R. 237; [2008] Bus. L.R. D28; reversed in part [2008] EWCA Civ 1206; [2009] Bus. L.R. 759; [2009] 2 All E.R. (Comm) 81; [2009] 1 Lloyd's Rep. 8; [2008] 2 C.L.C. 617; [2009] Lloyd's Rep. I.R. 178 .... 6–038, 6–112, 9–009, 9–010, 9–011, 9–012, 9–013, 14–003, 14–014, 20–037, 20–039, 20–040, 20–041, 20–042, 20–089
HSBC Rail (UK) Ltd v Network Rail Infrastructure Ltd (formerly Railtrack Plc) [2005] EWCA Civ. 1437; [2006] 1 W.L.R. 643; [2006] 1 All E.R. 343; [2006] 1 All E.R. (Comm) 345; [2006] 1 Lloyd's Rep. 358; (2006) 103(1) L.S.G. 17; Times, December 23, 2005 CA (Civ Div) 11–012
HTV v Lintner (JFK) [1984] 2 Lloyd's Rep. 125 QBD 5–050
Haas v Atlas Assurance Co Ltd [1913] 2 K.B. 209 KBD 18–022
Haase v Evans (1934) 48 Ll.L.R. 131 KBD 1–033, 6–053, 6–056
Habas Sinai Ve Tibbi Gazlar Isthisal Endustri AS v Sometal Sal [2010] EWHC 29 (Comm); (2010) 160 N.L.J. 145 3–015
Habib Bank Ltd v Central Bank of Sudan [2006] EWHC 1767 (Comm) 2–004
Hadden v Bryden (1899) 1 F. (Ct. of Sess.) 710 4–011
Hadenfayre v British National Insurance Society; Trident General Insurance Co v Lombard Elizabethan Insurance Co [1984] 2 Lloyd's Rep. 393; (1984) 134 N.L.J. 1017 QBD (Comm) 5–026, 6–0103, 9–004
Hadfield v Knowles Unreported, 1993 22–068
Hadley v Baxendale 156 E.R. 145; (1854) 9 Ex. 341 .... 10–023, 10–025

Hagedorn v Oliverson (1814) 2 M. & S. 485; 105 E.R. 461 .... 4–023, 15–003
Hagedorn v Whitmore (1816) 1 Stark. 157 .... 5–032, 24–0134
Haghiran v Allied Dunbar Insurance [2001] 1 All E.R. (Comm) 97 CA (Civ Div) 18–055
Hahn v Corbett (1824) 2 Bing 205 .... 5–030, 24–111
Haigh v Brooks (1839)10 A. & E. 309 10–055
Haigh v de Ia Cour (1812) 3 Camp. 319 10–007
Haigh v Lawford (1964) 114 L.J. 208 CC 11–042
Hain Steamship Co v Board of Trade. See Board of Trade v Hain Steamship Co Ltd
Hain Steamship Co v Tate & Lyle. See Tate & Lyle Ltd v Hain Steamship Co Ltd
Hair v Prudential Assurance Co Ltd [1980] 1 Lloyd's Rep. 52 7–038
Hair v Prudential Assurance Co [1983] 2 Lloyd's Rep. 667; (1983) 133 N.L.J. 282 QBD 5–020,
                                                                                    6–072, 7–032
Hales v Reliance Fire and Accident Insurance Corp Ltd [1960] 2 Lloyd's Rep. 391; Times,
    November 30, 1960 QBD 5–020, 6–064, 7–032, 19–033
Halford v Kymer (1830) 10 B. & C. 724 .... 4–014, 18–015
Halhead v Young (1856) 6 E. & B. 312 .... 5–009, 19–007
Halifax Building Society v Keighley [1931] 2 K.B. 248 KBD 19–026
Halifax Building Society/Standard Life Assurance Co [1992] O.J. C131/2 13–045
Hall v Hayman [1912] 2 K.B. 5 KBD 24–086
Hall v Janson (1855) 4 B. & B. 500 3–013
Hall v Newall Heating Ltd and AGF Insurance Ltd Unreported April 14, 2010 21–040
Hall & Long v The Railroad Companies, 80 U.S. 367 (1871) 11–034
Hall Bros Steamship Co Ltd v Young [1939] 1 K.B. 748; (1939) 63 Ll.L.R. 143 CA 20–009,
                                                                                20–010, 24–005
Hall D'Ath v British Provident Association (1932) 48 T.L.R. 240 ...... 1–004, 1–005, 13–011, 13–018
Halley, The. See Liverpool, Brazil and River Plate Steam Navigation Co Ltd v Benham (The
    Halley) Halley, The
Halpern v Halpern [2007] EWCA Civ 291; [2008] Q.B. 195; [2007] 3 W.L.R. 849; [2007]
    3 All E.R. 478; [2007] 2 All E.R. (Comm) 330; [2007] 2 Lloyd's Rep. 56; [2007] 1
    C.L.C. 527; Times, May 14, 2007 2–028
QBDHalvanon Insurance Co Ltd v Companhia de Seguros do Estado de Sao Paulo [1995]
    L.R.L.R. 303 CA 9–039, 17–027
Hambro v Burnand [1904] 2 K.B. 10 23–029
Hamill v Hamill Unreported July 24, 2001 2–064
Hamilton v Al-Fayed (Costs); sub nom. Hamilton v Fayed (Costs); Al-Fayed v Hamilton
    (Costs) [2002] EWCA Civ. 665; [2003] Q.B. 1175; [2003] 2 W.L.R. 128; [2002] 3 All
    E.R. 641; [2002] C.P. Rep. 48; [2002] 3 Costs L.R. 389; [2002] E.M.L.R. 42; (2002)
    99(25) L.S.G. 34; (2002) 146 S.J.L.B. 143; Times, June 17, 2002; Independent, July 1,
    2002 (C.S) CA (Civ Div) 20–055
Hamilton v Mendes (1761) 2 Burr. 1199 24–086
Hamilton v Sheddon (1837) 3 M. & W. 49 24–072
Hamilton & Co v Eagle Star & British Dominions Insurance Co Ltd (1924) 19 Ll.L.R. 242
    KBD 6–016, 6–031, 6–053
Hamilton Fraser & Co v Pandorf & Co; sub nom. Pandorf & Co v Hamilton Fraser & Co
    (1887) L.R. 12 App. Cas. 518 HL 5–030, 19–055, 24–134
Hamilton's (Duke of) Trustees v Fleming (1870) 9 M. 329 IH (1 Div) 19–024
Hamishmar Insurance Agency Ltd v FirstCity Partnership Ltd [2009] EWHC 256 (Comm);
    [2010] Lloyd's Rep. I.R. 215 3–005
Hamlyn v Crown Accidental Insurance Co Ltd [1893] 1 Q.B. 750; (1893) 68 L.T. 701 CA 18–041,
                                                                                18–046, 18–047
Hammill v Gerling Global Life Insurance Co, 71 D.L.R. (4th) 566 (1990) 18–030
Hammond v Reid (1820) 4 B. & Ald. 72 24–073
Hampshire Land, Re [1896] 2 Ch. 300 6–039
Hampshire Land Co (No.2), Re [1896] 2 Ch. 743 Ch D 5–046, 6–043, 6–055
Hampton v Toxteth Cooperative Provident Society Ltd [1915] 1 Ch. 721 CA ... 1–003, 1–004, 1–007,
                                                                                        13–011
Hamptons Residential Ltd v Field [1998] 2 Lloyd's Rep. 248; (1998) 95(23) L.S.G. 28 CA
    (Civ Div) 20–037, 20–042
Handelsbanken ASA v Dandridge; The Aliza Glacial; sub nom. Svenska Handelsbanken AB
    v Dandridge [2002] EWCA Civ. 577; [2002] 2 All E.R. (Comm) 39; [2002] 2 Lloyd's
    Rep. 421; [2002] C.L.C. 1227; [2003] Lloyd's Rep. I.R. 10 CA (Civ Div) 5–032, 25–013
TimesECJHandler v Mutual Reserve Fund Life Association (1904) 90 L.T. 192 .... 1–048, 7–048
Hanis v University of Western Ontario (2003) 67 O.R. (3d) 539 20–050
Hansen v Marco Engineering [1948] V.L.R. 198 20–044

Hansen v Norske Lloyd Insurance Co Ltd (1919) 1 Ll.L.R. 185 HL 4–023, 15–003
Harbourfield Engineering Co Ltd v Falcon Insurance Co (Hong Kong) Ltd [2003] H.K.E.C.
    959 .... 20–033, 20–040, 20–048
Harbutt's Plasticine Ltd v Wayne Tank & Pump Co Ltd; sub nom. Harbutts Plasticine v
    Wayne Tank & Pump Co Ltd [1970] 1 Q.B. 447; [1970] 2 W.L.R. 198; [1970] 1 All E.R.
    225; [1970] 1 Lloyd's Rep. 15; (1969) 119 N.L.J. 1164; 114 S.J. 29; Times, December
    9, 1969 CA (Civ Div) 5–034, 11–022
Harcourt v FEF Griffin [2007] EWHC 1500 (QB); [2008] Lloyd's Rep. I.R. 386; [2007]
    P.I.Q.R. Q9 .... 21–040, 21–066, 23–040
Harding v Wealands [2006] UKHL 32; [2007] 2 A.C. 1; [2006] 3 W.L.R. 83; [2006] 4 All
    E.R. 1; [2006] 2 C.L.C. 193; [2006] R.T.R. 35; (2006) 156 N.L.J. 1136; (2006) 150
    S.J.L.B. 917; Times, July 6, 2006 .... 2–063, 2–064, 2–065
Harding Maughan Hambly Ltd v Compagnie Europeenne de Courtage d'Assurances et de
    Reassurances SA [2000] 1 All E.R. (Comm) 225; [2000] 1 Lloyd's Rep. 316; [2000]
    C.L.C. 524; [2000] Lloyd's Rep. I.R. 293 QBD (Comm) 15–033
Harding v Victoria Insurance Co Ltd [1924] N.Z.L.R. 267 6–010
Hardy v Motor Insurers Bureau [1964] 2 Q.B. 745; [1964] 3 W.L.R. 433; [1964] 2 All E.R.
    742; [1964] 1 Lloyd's Rep. 397; 108 S.J. 422 CA 5–046, 21–022, 22–028, 22–029, 22–034,
                   22–060
Hare v Barstow (1844) 8 Jur. 928 3–010
Hare v Gocher [1962] 2 Q.B. 641; [1962] 3 W.L.R. 339; [1962] 2 All E.R. 763; 126 J.P. 395;
    60 L.G.R. 278; (1962) 13 P. & C.R. 298; 106 S.J. 531 DC 5–004
Hare v Groves (1796) 3 Anstr. 687 19–017
Hare v Travis (1827) 7 B. & C. 14 .... 24–068, 24–070
Hare v Whitmore (1778) 2 Cowp. 784 7–038
Harford v Maynard (1785) 1 Park on Marine Insurance 36 24–136
Hargreaves v Parsons (1844) 13 M. & W. 561 23–018
Harley v Smith [2010] EWCA Civ 78 2–056
Harman v Kingston (1811) 3 Camp. 150 24–051
Harmer v Armstrong [1934] Ch. 65 CA 19–030
Harocopos v Mountain (1934) 49 Ll.L.R. 267 KBD 24–062
Harper v Interchange Group Ltd [2007] EWHC 1834 (Comm); (2007) 104(36) L.S.G. 28 1–018,
                    3–005
Harper v Mackechnie. See AC Harper & Co Ltd v Mackechnie & Co
Harrington Motor Co Ltd, Ex p. Chaplin, Re; sub nom. Chaplin v Harrington Motor Co Ltd
    (in Liquidation) [1928] Ch. 105; (1927–028) 29 Ll.L.R. 102; 59 A.L.R. 1111 CA 17–002,
                    21–001
Harrington v Halkeld (1778) 2 Park's Marine Insurance 639 24–073
Harrington v Link Motor Policies at Lloyd's; sub nom. Harrington v Pinkey [1989] 2 Lloyd's
    Rep. 310; [1989] R.T.R. 345; Times, May 12, 1989 CA (Civ Div) 22–045
Harrington v Pearl Life Assurance Co (1914) 30 T.L.R. 613 .... 1–027, 1–028, 1–031, 6–104
Harris & Dixon (Insurance Brokers) Ltd v SF Graham (Run-Off) Ltd Unreported, 1989 24–078
Harris v Poland [1941] 1 K.B. 462; (1941) 69 Ll.L.R. 35 KBD 5–048, 19–039
Harris v Society of Lloyd's [2008] EWHC 1433 (Comm); [2009] Lloyd's Rep. I.R. 119 13–042,
                    17–001
Harris v Sturge; Harris v Eagle Star & British Dominions Insurance Co Ltd (1923) 14 Ll.L.R.
    20 KBD 9–025
Harrison v Alliance Assurance Co Ltd [1903] 1 K.B. 184 CA 18–024
Harrison v Cooperative Insurance Co (1968) 118 N.L.J. 910 22–007
Harrison v Ellis (1857) 7 E. & 8. 465 19–044
Harrison & Dixon (Insurance Brokers) Ltd v SF Graham (Run-Off) Ltd Unreported, 1989 15–032
Harrison & Ingram Ex p. Whinney, Re [1900] 2 Q.B. 710 CA 1–048, 18–022
Harrison (David) v Hill, 1932 J.C. 13; 1931 S.L.T. 598 HCJ 22–007
Harrisons Ltd v Shipping Controller; sub nom. T&J Harrisons Ltd v Shipping Controller
    [1921] 1 K.B. 122; (1920) 4 Ll.L.R. 429 KBD 25–004, 25–005
Harristown Development Corp v International Insurance Co 1988 M.D. Pa 20–047
Harrower v Hutchinson (1869–70) L.R. 5 Q.B. 584 Ex Chamber 6–065, 6–073, 24–039
Harse v Pearl Life Assurance Co [1904] 1 K.B. 558CA; reversing [1903] 2 K.B. 92 KBD 4–009,
                6–012, 8–022, 18–009, 18–010, 18–015
Hart v Standard Marine Insurance Co Ltd (1889) L.R. 22 Q.B.D. 499 CA 7–038
Hartley v Buggin (1781) 3 Doug. K.B. 39 24–070

Hartley v Rice (1808) 10 East 22 4–002

Harvest Trucking Co Ltd v Davis (t/a PB Davis Insurance Services) [1991] 2 Lloyd's Rep.
638; (1991) 135 S.J.L.B. 443; Times, March 20, 1991 QBD 15–037

Harvey v Ventilatoren-Fabrik Oelde GmbH (1989) 8 Tr. L.R. 138; Financial Times,
November 11, 1988 CA (Civ Div) 3–011

Haseldine v Hosken [1933] 1 K.B. 822; (1933) 45 Ll.L.R. 59 CA 5–046, 20–031

Hassett v Legal & General Assurance Society Ltd (1939) 63 Ll.L.R. 278 KBD 21–023

Hatch, Mansfield & Co v Weingott (1906) 22 T.L.R. 366 23–028

Hatley v Liverpool Victoria Friendly Society (1918) 88 L.J.K.B. 237 .... 4–011, 18–016

Hatton v Hall [1997] R.T.R. 212; [1999] Lloyd's Rep. I.R. 313; Times, May 15, 1996 CA
(Civ Div) 22–009, 22–067

Havelock v Hancill (1789) 3 T.R. 277 24–138

Havens v Middleton (1853) 10 Hare 641 19–022

Haward v Fawcetts (A Firm) [2006] UKHL 9; [2006] 1 W.L.R. 682; [2006] P.N.L.R. 25;
[2006] 10 E.G.C.S. 154; [2006] N.P.C. 25; Times, March 3, 2006 HL 15–061

Hawk Insurance Co Ltd, Re [2001] EWCA Civ. 241; [2002] B.C.C. 300; [2001] 2 B.C.L.C.
480 CA (Civ Div) 16–005

Hawley v Luminar Leisure Ltd; sub nom. Hawley v Luminar Leisure Plc [2006] EWCA Civ.
18; [2006] Lloyd's Rep. I.R. 307; [2006] P.I.Q.R. P17; (2006) 150 S.J.L.B. 163 CA (Civ
Div) 5–041, 5–042, 5–046, 5–047, 18–052, 20–031

Haworth v Dawson (1947) 80 Ll.L.R. 19 KBD 22–041, 22–089

Haworth v Sickness & Accident Assurance (1891) 28 S.L.R. 394 23–026

Haycock's Policy, Re (1875–76) L.R. 1 Ch. D. 611 Ch D 9–038, 18–023

Haydon v Lo & Lo [1997] 1 W.L.R. 198; [1997] 1 Lloyd's Rep. 336; [1997] C.L.C. 626;
(1997) 147 N.L.J. 125; (1997) 141 S.J.L.B. 35; Times, January 23, 1997 PC (HK) 20–084

Hayler v Chapman [1989] 1 Lloyd's Rep. 490; Times, November 11, 1988CA (Civ Div) 11–015

Hayward v Norwich Union Insurance Ltd [2001] EWCA Civ. 243; [2001] 1 All E.R. (Comm)
545; [2001] R.T.R. 35; [2001] Lloyd's Rep. I.R. 410; Times, March 8, 2001;
Independent, March 2, 2001; Daily Telegraph, March 6, 2001CA (Civ Div); reversing
[2000] Lloyd's Rep. I.R. 382; Independent, December 20, 1999 (C.S.) QBD .. 3–005, 5–012,
5–050, 22–094

Hazel (for Lloyd's Syndicate 260) v Whitlam; sub nom. Whitlam v Lloyds Syndicate 260 (t/a
KGM Motor Policies at Lloyds) [2004] EWCA Civ. 1600; [2005] Lloyd's Rep. I.R. 168
CA (Civ Div) 15–027, 15–036, 22–087

Heap-Hammond v TNT UK Unreported June 15, 2007 Yeovil County Court 22–025

Hearts of Oak Permanent Building Society v Law Union & Rock Insurance Co Ltd (1936)
55 Ll.L.R. 153; [1936] 2 All E.R. 619 KBD 6–004, 7–021, 7–032, 7–037, 23–026

Heath Lambert Ltd v Sociedad de Corretaje de Seguros [2004] EWCA Civ. 792; [2004] 1
W.L.R. 2820; [2005] 1 All E.R. 225; [2004] 2 All E.R. (Comm) 656; [2005] 1 Lloyd's
Rep. 597; [2005] 2 C.L.C. 366; [2004] Lloyd's Rep. I.R. 905; (2004) 101(28) L.S.G. 34;
(2004) 148 S.J.L.B. 793; Times, July 2, 2004 CA (Civ Div); affirming [2003] EWHC
2269; [2004] 1 Lloyd's Rep. 495 QBD (Comm) 2–033, 8–004, 8–018, 15–028, 15–031,
15–032, 24–077, 24–078

QBDHeather v Webb (1876) 2 C.P.D. 1 4–018

Heaton v Axa Equity & Law Life Assurance Society Plc [2002] UKHL 15; [2002] 2 A.C.
329; [2002] 2 W.L.R. 1081; [2002] 2 All E.R. 961; [2002] C.P. Rep. 52; [2002] C.P.L.R.
475; [2003] 1 C.L.C. 37; Times, May 15, 2002 HL 10–056

Hebdon v West (1863) 3 B. & S. 579 .... 4–018, 18–001, 18–004, 18–008, 18–019, 18–020

Heckman v Isaac (1861) 4 L.T. 825; (1862) 6 L.T. 383 .... 19–022, 19–024

Hector Hunter Furs v Independent Insurance Ltd Unreported, 1998 QBD 9–026

Heesens Yacht Builders BV v Cox Syndicate Management Ltd; The Lady Halima; The Red
Sapphire [2006] EWCA Civ. 384; [2006] 2 Lloyd's Rep. 35 CA (Civ Div); reversing
[2006] Lloyd's Rep. I.R. 103 QBD (Comm) 5–001, 24–009

Helfand v National Union Fire Insurance Co 13 Cal. Rptr. 2d 295 (Cal CA, 1992) 20–047

Hellenic Industrial Development Bank SA v Atkin; The Julia [2002] EWHC 1405; [2003]
Lloyd's Rep. I.R. 365 QBD (Comm) 10–027

Hellenic Steel Co v Svolamar Shipping Co Ltd (The Komninos S) Komninos S, The [1991]
1 Lloyd's Rep. 370; Financial Times, January 16, 1991 CA 2–037, 2–056

Hemmings v Sceptre Life Association Ltd [1905] 1 Ch. 365; (1905) 92 L.T. 221 Ch D 7–020,
7–031, 18–026

Henchman v Offley (1782) 3 Doug. K.B. 135 24–051

Henderson v Merrett Syndicates Ltd (No.1); sub nom. McLarnon Deeney v Gooda Walker
    Ltd; Gooda Walker Ltd v Deeny; Arbuthnott v Fagan; Hallam-Eames v Merrett
    Syndicates Ltd; Hughes v Merrett Syndicates Ltd; Feltrim Underwriting Agencies Ltd
    v Arbuthnott; Deeny v Gooda Walker Ltd (Duty of Care) [1995] 2 A.C. 145; [1994] 3
    W.L.R. 761; [1994] 3 All E.R. 506; [1994] 2 Lloyd's Rep. 468; [1994] C.L.C. 918;
    (1994) 144 N.L.J. 1204; Times, July 26, 1994; Independent, August 3, 1994 HL 13–041,
                                                                                15–009, 15–044
Henderson v Robson (1949) 113 J.P. 313; 47 L.G.R. 512; 93 S.J. 424 DC 22–096
Henderson v Underwriting and Agency Association Ltd [1891] 1 Q.B. 557 QBD 6–107
Henkle v Royal Exchange (1749) 1 Ves. Sen. 317 1–020
Henrich Hirdes GmbH v Edmund; Henrich Hirdes GmbH v Peek Puckle (International) Ltd;
    The Kiel [1991] 2 Lloyd's Rep. 546; Financial Times, March 8, 1991; Lloyd's List, July
    5, 1991 QBD (Comm) 5–004
Henry & M'Gregor Ltd v Martin (1918) 34 T.L.R. 504 25–005
Henson v Blackwell (1845) 4 Hare 434 18–020
Hentig v Staniforth (1816) 5 M. & S. 122, 123–125 .... 8–022, 18–012
Hepburn v A Tomlinson (Hauliers) Ltd; sub nom. A Tomlinson (Hauliers) Ltd v Hepburn
    [1966] A.C. 451; [1966] 2 W.L.R. 453; [1966] 1 All E.R. 418; [1966] 1 Lloyd's Rep.
    309; 110 S.J. 86 HL ... 4–005, 4–020, 5–009, 5–014, 19–005, 19–012, 19–013, 19–032, 20–006,
                                                                                            24–029
Herbert v Carter (1787) 1 T.R. 745 24–031
Herbert v Champion (1807) 1 Camp. 134 10–057
Herbert v Poland (1932) 44 Ll.L.R. 139 KBD 9–025
Herbert v Railway Passengers Assurance Co (1938) 60 Ll.L.R. 143; [1938] 1 All E.R. 650
    KBD 22–045, 22–088
Hercules Insurance v Hunter (1836) 14 Sh. (Ct. of Sess.) 1137 10–015
Herley Industries Inc v Federal Insurance Co Inc 2009 B.L. 179695 (ED Pa, August 21,
    2009) 20–087
Herman v Phoenix Assurance Co Ltd (1924) 18 Ll.L.R. 371 CA 6–031, 9–025, 9–026
Herring v Janson (1895) 1 Com.Cas. 177 .... 1–009, 6–056, 10–007
Heselton v Allnutt (1813) 1 M. & S. 46 24–070
Heskell v Continental Express Ltd [1950] 1 All E.R. 1033; (1949–50) 83 Ll.L.R. 438; [1950]
    W.N. 210; 94 S.J. 339 KBD 5–032
Hewden Tower Cranes Ltd v Wolffkran GmbH [2007] EWHC 857 (TCC); [2007] 2 Lloyd's
    Rep. 138; [2007] B.L.R. 273; [2007] I.L.Pr. 43; [2008] Bus. L.R. D9 2–008
Hewer v Cutler [1974] R.T.R. 155; [1973] Crim. L.R. 762 DC 22–009
Hewison v Meridian Shipping Services Pte Ltd [2002] EWCA Civ 1821; [2003] I.C.R. 766;
    [2003] P.I.Q.R. P17; (2003) 147 S.J.L.B. 24; Times, December 28, 2002; Independent,
    February 10, 2003 5–046
Hewitt v London General Insurance Co Ltd (1925) 23 Ll.L.R. 243 KBD 8–008, 17–004, 24–053,
                                                                                24–068, 24–070
Hey v Wyche (1842) 12 L.J.Q.B. 83 19–018
Heyman v Darwins Ltd [1942] A.C. 356; [1942] 1 All E.R. 337; (1942) 72 Ll.L.R. 65 HL 7–005
Heyman v Parrish (1809) 2 Camp. 149 24–138
Heyward v Rodgers (1804) 4 East 590 6–074
Hibbert v Marten (1808) 1 Camp. 538 24–138
Hibbert v Martin (1808) Park on Marine Insurance 473 24–062
Hibbert v Pigou (1783) 3 Doug. K.B. 224 7–022
Hibernia Foods Plc v McAuslin; The Joint Frost [1998] 1 Lloyd's Rep. 310 QBD (Comm) ... 24–009,
                                                                                            24–066
Hickie and Borman v Rodocanachi (1859) 4 H. & N. 455 24–095
Hicks v Newport, Abergavenny & Hereford Railway (1857) 4 B. & S. 403n 18–002
Hicks v Shield (1857) 7 El. & Bl. 633 24–026
Hiddle v National Fire and Marine Insurance Co of New Zealand [1896] A.C. 372 PC (Aus) ... 9–003,
                                                                                            9–017
Hide v Bruce (1783) 3 Doug. K.B. 213 7–038
Highland Crusader Offshore Partners LP v Deutsche Bank AG [2009] EWCA Civ 725;
    [2010] 1 W.L.R. 1023; [2010] Bus. L.R. 515; [2009] 2 All E.R. (Comm) 987; [2009] 2
    Lloyd's Rep. 617; [2009] C.P. Rep. 45; [2009] 2 C.L.C. 45; Times, October 15, 2009 2–006
Highlands Insurance Co v Continental Insurance Co [1987] 1 Lloyd's Rep. 109 (Note);
    Times, May 6, 1986 QBD (Comm) 6–004, 6–013, 6–014, 6–081, 6–087, 17–005
Hill v Citadel Insurance Co Ltd [1997] L.R.L.R. 167; [1997] C.L.C. 579 CA (Civ Div);
    affirming [1995] L.R.L.R. 218; [1995] C.L.C. 69QBD (Comm) 6–008, 6–061, 6–073, 6–105,
                                                                                17–007, 17–009

Hill v Mercantile & General Reinsurance Co Plc; Berry v Mercantile & General Reinsurance
   Co Plc [1996] 1 W.L.R. 1239; [1996] 3 All E.R. 865; [1996] L.R.L.R. 341; [1996]
   C.L.C. 1247; [1996] 5 Re. L.R. 461; (1996) 93(35) L.S.G. 32; (1996) 146 N.L.J. 1313;
   (1996) 140 S.J.L.B. 192; Times, August 15, 1996 HL; reversing [1995] L.R.L.R. 160;
   [1994] C.L.C. 828; [1995] 4 Re. L.R. 1; Times, July 25, 1994 CA (Civ Div) 17–018, 17–019,
                                                                                    17–020, 17–021, 20–058
Hill v Secretan (1798) 1 Bos. & P. 315 4–016
Hill Samuel Life Assurance, Re Unreported, 1995 13–036
Hillas v Arcos. *See* WN Hillas & Co Ltd v Arcos Ltd
Hindustan Steam Shipping Co v Admiralty Commissioners (1921) 8 Ll.L.R. 230 KBD 25–005
Hine Bros v Steamship Insurance Syndicate Ltd (1895) 72 L.T. 79 15–041
Hironaka v Co-operators' General Insurance Co [2005] A.J. No.1313 20–049
Hiscox v Outhwaite (No.3) [1991] 2 Lloyd's Rep. 524 QBD (Comm) 17–020, 17–021
Hitchins (Hatfield) Ltd v Prudential Assurance Co Ltd [1991] 2 Lloyd's Rep. 580; 60 B.L.R.
   51; Financial Times, April 17, 1991CA (Civ Div) 19–034
Hobbs v Hannam (1811) 3 Camp. 93 24–031
Hobbs v Marlowe [1978] A.C. 16; [1977] 2 W.L.R. 777; [1977] 2 All E.R. 241; [1977] R.T.R.
   253; 121 S.J. 272 HL 11–001, 11–002, 11–013, 11–017, 11–018
Hodge v Security Insurance (1884) 33 Hun. N.Y. 583 8–004
Hodgkins v Wrightson, Times, March 24, 1910 9–026
Hoff v De Rougemont (1929) 34 Com.Cas. 291 .... 6–031, 6–056
Hoff v Union Insurance of Canton. *See* Trading Co L&J Hoff v Union Insurance Society of
   Canton Ltd
Hoffmann (C) & Co v British General Insurance Co (1922) 10 Ll.L.R. 434 KBD 24–062
Hogg v Horner (1797) 2 Park on Insurance 782 8–027
Hogg v Nicholson (George), 1968 S.L.T. 265 HCJ Appea 22–007
Hogg Insurance Brokers Ltd v Guardian Insurance Co Inc [1997] 1 Lloyd's Rep. 412 QBD
   (Comm) 2–004, 2–041
Holdsworth v Lancashire and Yorkshire Insurance Co (1907) 23 T.L.R. 521 .... 7–048, 15–019
Holdsworth v Wise (1828) 7 B. & C. 794 .... 24–061, 24–062
Holland v Bennett [1902] 1 K.B. 867 CA 2–004
Holland v Russell (1863) 4 B. & S. 14 10–063
Holliday v Western Australian Insurance Co Ltd (1936) 54 Ll.L.R. 373 KBD 8–002
Hollingsworth v Brodrick (1837) 7 Ad. & E. 40 24–061
Holman & Sons Ltd (Owner of the SS Nefeli) v Merchants Marine Insurance Co Ltd [1919]
   1 K.B. 383 KBD 10–029
Holmes v Cornhill Insurance Co Ltd (1948–49) 82 Ll.L.R. 575 KBD 22–087
Holmes v Payne [1930] 2 K.B. 301; (1930) 37 Ll.L.R. 41 KBD 3–007, 10–001, 10–064, 11–067,
                                                                                                              24–089
Holmes v Scottish Legal Life Assurance Society (1932) 48 T.L.R. 306 .... 7–031, 18–029
Holnan v Johnson (1775) 1 Cowp. 341 5–035
Holt Motors v South East Lancashire Insurance Co Ltd (1930) 37 Ll.L.R. 1 .... 6–018, 6–053, 22–087
Holt's Motors v South-East Lancashire Insurance (1930) 35 Com.Cas. 281 .... 6–053, 6–070, 7–037
Homburg Houtimport BV v Agrosin Private Ltd (The Starsin); sub nom. Owners of Cargo
   Lately Laden on Board the Starsin v Owners of the Starsin; Hunter Timber Ltd v
   Agrosin Private Ltd [2003] UKHL 12; [2004] 1 A.C. 715; [2003] 2 W.L.R. 711; [2003]
   2 All E.R. 785; [2003] 1 All E.R. (Comm) 625; [2003] 1 Lloyd's Rep. 571; [2003] 1
   C.L.C. 921; 2003 A.M.C. 913; (2003) 100(19) L.S.G. 31; Times, March 17, 2003 HL 3–005
Home & Colonial Insurance Co Ltd v London Guarantee & Accident Co Ltd (1928) 32
   Ll.L.R. 267 KBD 10–058
Home & Overseas Insurance Co v Mentor Insurance Co (UK) [1990] 1 W.L.R. 153; [1989]
   3 All E.R. 74; [1989] 1 Lloyd's Rep. 473; (1989) 86(7) L.S.G. 36; (1989) 133 S.J. 44
   CA (Civ Div) 17–016, 17–017, 20–035
Home District Mutual insurance Co v Thompson (1847) 1 E. & A. 247 10–044
Home Insurance Co of New York v Gavel (1928) 30 Ll.L.R. 139 PC (Can) 11–047, 11–058
Home Insurance Co of New York v Victoria Montreal Fire Insurance Co [1907] A.C. 59 PC
   (Can) 3–011, 3–015, 17–012
Home Insurance Co, Re [2005] EWHC 2485Ch D (Companies Ct) 16–005
Home Mutual Fire Insurance v Garfield (1871) 14 Am.Rep. 27 10–044
Home Office v Lownds. *See* Lownds v Home Office; sub nom. Home Office v Lownds;
   Lownds v Secretary of State for the Home Department
Homeserve Membership Ltd (formerly Homeserve GB Ltd) v Revenue and Customs
   Commissioners [2009] EWHC 1311 (Ch); [2009] S.T.C. 2366; [2010] Lloyd's Rep. I.R.
   47; [2009] B.T.C. 8088; [2009] S.T.I. 1964 15–033

Hong Kong Borneo Services Co v Pilcher [1992] 2 Lloyd's Rep. 593 QBD (Comm) 3–015,
10–022, 10–056, 17–019
Hongkong Fir Shipping Co Ltd v Kawasaki Kisen Kaisha Ltd (The Hongkong Fir) [1962] 2
Q.B. 26; [1962] 2 W.L.R. 474; [1962] 1 All E.R. 474; [1961] 2 Lloyd's Rep. 478; (1961)
106 S.J. 35 CA 7–001, 7–007, 24–062
Hong Kong Nylon Enterprises Ltd v QBE Insurance (Hong Kong) Ltd [2003] H.K.E.C. 199 ... 6–074,
24–066
HLHood v West End Motor Car Packing Co [1917] 2 K.B. 38CA 24–039
Hood's Trustees v Southern Union General Insurance Co of Australasia Ltd [1928] Ch. 793;
(1928) 31 Ll.L.R. 237 CA 7–004, 21–001
Hooley Hill Rubber & Chemical Co Ltd and Royal Insurance Co Ltd's Arbitration, Re; sub
nom. Hooley Hill Rubber & Chemical Co Ltd v Royal Insurance Co Ltd [1920] 1 K.B.
257; (1919) 1 Ll.L.R. 25 CA 3–007, 5–030, 6–012, 6–0123, 7–033, 15–018, 19–041
Hooper v Accidental Death Insurance Co (1860) 3 H. & N. 546 18–054
Hope v Dominion of Canada General Insurance Co [2000] O.T.C. 426 20–049
Hopewell Project Management Ltd v Ewbank Preece Ltd [1998] 1 Lloyd's Rep. 448 QBD 4–013,
11–027, 14–004, 14–007, 14–008, 19–032
Horbury Building Systems Ltd v Hampden Insurance NV [2004] EWCA Civ. 418; [2004] 2
C.L.C. 453; [2004] B.L.R. 431; (2004) 148 S.J.L.B. 477 CA (Civ Div) 9–053, 20–075,
20–076
Hordern v Commercial Union (1887) 56 L.J.P.C. 78 3–010
Hore v Whitmore (1778) 2 Cowp. 784 .... 7–045, 24–068
Horn v Anglo-Australian Life (1861) 30 L.J.Ch. 511 .... 18–033, 18–034
Horn Linie GmbH & Co v Panamericana Formas e Impresos SA (The Hornbay) Hornbay,
The [2006] EWHC 373 (Comm); [2006] 2 All E.R. (Comm) 924; [2006] 2 Lloyd's Rep.
44 2–053
Hornal v Neuberger Products [1957] 1 Q.B. 247; [1956] 3 W.L.R. 1034; [1956] 3 All E.R.
970; 100 S.J. 915 CA 9–025
Horncastle v Equitable Life Assurance Society of the United States (1906) 22 T.L.R. 735 15–001,
15–013, 15–018
Horne v Norwich Union Insurance LtdUnreported, July 2005 9–026
Horne v Poland [1922] 2 K.B. 364; (1922) 10 Ll.L.R. 275KBD 6–046, 6–051
Horneyer v Lushington (1812) 15 East 46 24–065
Horry v Tate & Lyle Refineries [1982] 2 Lloyd's Rep. 416 QBD 6–0122, 10–055
HorseCArriage and General Insurance Co v Petch (1916) 33 T.L.R. 131 .... 11–035, 11–042
Horsfall v Thomas (1862) 1 H. & C. 90 6–017
Horwood v Land of Leather Ltd [2010] EWHC 546 (Comm) 7–014, 9–016, 11–006, 11–042,
20–033, 21–023
Hough v Guardian Fire and Life Assurance Co Ltd (1902) 18 T.L.R. 273 15–019
Hough v Head (1855) 55 L.J.Q.B. 43 .... 5–004, 5–015
Houghton, Ex p. (1810) 17 Ves. 251 19–030
Houghton v Scholfield; sub nom. Houghton v Schofield [1973] R.T.R. 239; [1973] Crim. L.R.
126 DC 22–007
Houghton v Trafalgar Insurance Co Ltd [1954] 1 Q.B. 247; [1953] 3 W.L.R. 985; [1953] 2
All E.R. 1409; [1953] 2 Lloyd's Rep. 503; 97 S.J. 831 CA; affirming [1953] 2 Lloyd's
Rep. 18 QBD 1–055, 3–010, 22–036, 22–099
Houghton (RA) and Mancon Ltd v Sunderland Marine Mutual Insurance Co Ltd (The
Ny-Eeasteyr) [1988] 1 Lloyd's Rep. 60 QBD (Comm) 24–134
Houldsworth v Glasgow City Bank (1879–80) L.R. 5 App. Cas. 317 HL 15–004
Household Fire & Carriage Accident Insurance Co Ltd v Grant (1878–79) L.R. 4 Ex. D. 216
CA 2–051
Howard Farrow Ltd v Ocean Accident & Guarantee Corp Ltd (1940) 67 Ll.L.R. 27 KBD 5–049
Howard v GT Jones & Co [1975] R.T.R. 150; [1974] Crim. L.R. 606 DC 22–009
Howard v Refuge Friendly Society (1886) 54 L.T. 644 .... 8–022, 18–011, 18–015, 18–017
Howard Marine & Dredging Co Ltd v A Ogden & Sons (Excavations) Ltd [1978] Q.B. 574;
[1978] 2 W.L.R. 515; [1978] 2 All E.R. 1134; [1978] 1 Lloyd's Rep. 334; 9 B.L.R. 34;
122 S.J. 48 CA (Civ Div) 3–005
Howarth v Pioneer Life (1912) 107 L.T. 155 .... 8–022, 18–010
Howell v Kightley (1856) 21 Beav. 331 19–022
Howells v Dominion Insurance Co Ltd Unreported, 1999 ..... 6–037, 6–039, 6–048, 6–062, 6–105,
8–004
Howes v Prudential (1883) 49 L.T. 133 14–026
Hubbard v Glover (1812) 3 Camp. 313 6–014
Huckman v Fernie (1838) 3 M. & W. 505 18–029

Hucks v Thornton (1815) Holt N.P. 30 24–138
Hudson v Bilton (1856) 2 Jur.(N.S.) 784 24–068
Hudson v Harrison (1821) 3 Brod. & Bing. 97; 129 E.R. 1219 24–088
Hughes v Liverpool Victoria Legal Friendly Society [1916] 2 K.B. 482 CA 8–022, 8–026, 18–010
Hughes v Pump House Hotel Co Ltd (No.1) [1902] 2 K.B. 190 CA 14–026
Huguenin v Rayley (1815) 6 Taunt. 186 .... 6–070, 18–027
Hull v Cooper (1811) 4 East 479 24–065
Hulse v Chambers [2001] 1 W.L.R. 2386; [2002] 1 All E.R. (Comm) 812; [2002] R.T.R. 24;
    Times, July 13, 2001; Independent, June 25, 2001 2–064
Hulton (E) & Co v Mountain (1921) 8 Ll.L.R. 249 CA 3–009, 20–050
Hume v AA Mutual International Insurance Co Ltd [1996] L.R.L.R. 19QBD 1–032
Hunt v Severs; sub nom. Severs v Hunt [1994] 2 A.C. 350; [1994] 2 W.L.R. 602; [1994] 2
    All E.R. 385; [1994] 2 Lloyd's Rep. 129; [1994] P.I.Q.R. Q60; (1994) 144 N.L.J. 603;
    (1994) 138 S.J.L.B. 104; Times, May 2, 1994; Independent, May 5, 1994 HL ... 11–016, 22–024
Hunt Cranes Ltd v Scottish Boiler and General Insurance Co. See George Hunt Cranes Ltd
    v Scottish Boiler & General Insurance Co Ltd
Hunter v Potts (1815) 4 Camp. 203 19–055
Hunting & Son v Boulton (1895) 1 Com.Cas. 120 24–129
Hurrell v Bullard (1863) 3 F. & F. 445 15–034
Hurst Stores & Interiors Ltd v ML Europe Property Ltd [2004] EWCA Civ. 490; [2004]
    B.L.R. 249; 94 Con. L.R. 66; (2004) 148 S.J.L.B. 421 CA (Civ Div) 10–057
Hurstanger Ltd v Wilson [2007] EWCA Civ 299; [2007] 1 W.L.R. 2351; [2008] Bus. L.R.
    216; [2007] 4 All E.R. 1118; [2007] 2 All E.R. (Comm) 1037; (2007) 104(16) L.S.G.
    23; (2007) 157 N.L.J. 555; (2007) 151 S.J.L.B. 467; [2007] N.P.C. 41; Times, May 11,
    2007 15–033
Hurstwood Developments Ltd v Motor & General & Andersley & Co Insurance Services Ltd;
    sub nom. Hurstwood Developments Ltd v Motor & General & Aldersley & Co
    Insurance Services Ltd [2001] EWCA Civ. 1785; [2002] Lloyd's Rep. I.R. 185; [2002]
    Lloyd's Rep. P.N. 195; [2002] P.N.L.R. 10 CA (Civ Div) 15–060
Hussain v Brown [1996] 1 Lloyd's Rep. 627; Times, December 15, 1995; Lloyd's List,
    February 13, 1996 CA (Civ Div) 7–032
Hussain v Brown (No.2) [1996] 1 Lloyd's Rep. 627 .... 5–019, 5–023, 6–107, 6–109, 6–112, 6–113,
                                                6–114, 7–008, 9–024, 19–047
Hussain v GAN Assurance Co [2007] H.K.E.C. 361 .... 7–014, 9–006, 20–037
Hutchins Bros v Royal Exchange Insurance Corp [1911] 2 K.B. 398 CA 24–003
Hutchinson v Wright (1858) 25 Beav. 444 19–025
Hutchison v National Loan Fund Life (1845) 7 D. (C of Sess.) 467, 476 7–038
Hutton v Waterloo Life (1859) 1 F. & F. 735 .... 18–028, 18–030
Hvalfangerselskapet Polaris A/S v Unilever Ltd; Hvalfangerselskapet Globus A/S v Unilever
    Ltd (1933) 46 Ll.L.R. 29HL; reversing (1932) 42 Ll.L.R. 215 CA 1–018, 1–019
Hyams v Paragon Insurance Co Ltd (1927) 27 Ll.L.R. 448 KBD 8–026
Hydarnes Steamship Co v Indemnity Mutual Marine Assurance Co [1895] 1 Q.B. 500 CA 3–005,
                                                3–011, 24–130
Hyderabad (Deccan) Co v Willoughby [1899] 2 Q.B. 530 QBD (Comm) 24–009, 24–072
ING Insurance Co v SREIT (Park West Centre) Ltd [2009] N.S.J. No.158 20–050
IP Metal Ltd v Ruote Oz SpA (No.1) [1993] 2 Lloyd's Rep. 60 QBD (Comm) 2–003
IRB Brasil Resseguros SA v CX Reinsurance Co Ltd [2010] EWHC 974 (Comm) ... 10–034, 17–020,
                                                17–023, 20–058
Icarom (formerly Insurance Corp of Ireland) v Peek Puckle International [1992] 2 Lloyd's
    Rep. 600 QBD (Comm) 15–034
Ide and Christie v Chalmers and White (1900) 5 Com.Cas. 212 24–009
Ide v ATB Sales Ltd [2008] EWCA Civ 424; [2009] R.T.R. 8; [2008] P.I.Q.R. P13; (2008)
    152(18) S.J.L.B. 32 24–134
If P&C Insurance Ltd (Publ) v Silversea Cruises Ltd [2004] EWCA Civ. 769; [2004] Lloyd's
    Rep. I.R. 696; Times, August 13, 2004 CA (Civ Div); reversing in part [2003] EWHC
    473; [2004] Lloyd's Rep. I.R. 217 QBD (Comm); reversing in part [2003] EWHC 473;
    [2004] Lloyd's Rep. I.R. 217 QBD (Comm) 5–033, 6–043, 10–034, 23–042, 25–004, 25–014
Ikarian Reefer, The. See National Justice Compania Naviera SA v Prudential Assurance Co
    Ltd (The Ikarian Reefer) (No.1)
Ikerigi Compania Naviera SA v Palmer; The Wondrous; Global Transeas Corp v Palmer
    [1992] 2 Lloyd's Rep. 566; Financial Times, July 9, 1992 CA (Civ Div) 24–112
Imageview Management Ltd v Jack [2009] EWCA Civ 63; [2009] Bus. L.R. 1034; [2009] 2
    All E.R. 666; [2009] 1 All E.R. (Comm) 921; [2009] 1 Lloyd's Rep. 436; [2009] 1
    B.C.L.C. 724; Times, March 24, 2009 15–007

Immerzeel v Santam Ltd Unreported December, 2005 Supreme Court of Appeal of South
Africa 20–038
Imperial Marine Insurance Co v Fire Insurance Corporation Ltd (1879) 4 C.P.D. 166 17–008,
24–051
Imperial Tobacco Ltd v Attorney General [1981] A.C. 718; [1980] 2 W.L.R. 466; [1980] 1
All E.R. 866; 124 S.J. 271 HL 1–003
Imperio Reinsurance Co (UK) Ltd v Iron Trades Mutual [1993] Re L.R. 213 6–092
Incerto v Landry (2000) 47 O.R. (2d) 622 20–050
Independent Air Travel Ltd, Re [1961] 1 Lloyd's Rep. 604 Ch D 18–024
Indian Oil Corp Ltd v Vanol Inc [1991] 2 Lloyd's Rep. 634 3–015
Industrie Chimiche Italia Centrale and Cerealfin SA v Alexander G Tsavliris & Sons
Maritime Co (The Choko Star) (1990); Industrie Chimiche Italia Centrale v Pancristo
Shipping Co SA; Industrie Chimiche Italia Centrale v Bula Shipping Corp [1990] 1
Lloyd's Rep. 516; Independent, March 21, 1990 CA (Civ Div); reversing [1989] 2
Lloyd's Rep. 42 QBD (Admlty) 24–112
Ing Re (UK) Ltd v R & V Versicherung AG [2006] EWHC 1544 QBD (Comm) 15–001, 15–003,
15–022
Ing Insurance Co of Canada v Federated Insurance Co of Canada 75 O.R. (3d) 457 92005) 20–052
Ingham v Agnew (1812) 15 East 517 24–064
Ingleton of Ilford v General Accident Fire and Life Assurance Corp [1967] 2 Lloyd's Rep.
179 QBD 5–012
Inglis v Stock; sub nom. Stock v Inglis (1884–85) L.R. 10 App. Cas. 263 HL; affirming
(1883–84) L.R. 12 Q.B.D. 564 CA 4–011, 11–042, 19–007, 20–062, 24–022, 24–031
Ingram v Caledonian Insurance Co (1932) 42 Ll.L.R. 129 KBD 8–002
Ingram-Johnston v Century Insurance Co Ltd, 1909 S.C. 1032; 1909 2 S.L.T. 10 IH (1 Div) ... 1–029
Inland Kenworthy Ltd v Insurance Corporation of British Columbia, 66 D.L.R. (4th) 374
(1990) 14–013
Inland Waterways Insurers EC Bull 5, 1969 13–045
Inman Steamship Co Ltd v Bischoff (1881–82) L.R. 7 App. Cas. 670; [1881–85] All E.R.
Rep. 440 HL 6–070, 24–080
Insurance Co of Africa v Scor (UK) Reinsurance Co Ltd [1985] 1 Lloyd's Rep. 312 CA (Civ
Div) 9–004, 17–019, 17–021, 17–024, 17–025, 20–058
Insurance Co of the State of Pennsylvania v Grand Union Insurance Co [1990] 1 Lloyd's
Rep. 208CA (HK) 17–014, 17–019
Insurance Company of Pennsylvania Ltd v IBM UK Ltd, October 12, 1989 Chartered
Surveyor Weekly 11–011
Insurance Corp of Ireland v Strombus International Insurance Co Ltd [1985] 2 Lloyd's Rep.
138 CA (Civ Div) 2–005
Insurance Corp of the Channel Islands Ltd v McHugh [1997] L.R.L.R. 94 QBD (Comm) 6–129,
9–012, 9–021, 9–026, 9–032, 10–022, 10–027
Insurance Corp of the Channel Islands v Royal Hotel Ltd [1998] Lloyd's Rep. I.R. 151 QBD
(Comm) ... 6–017, 6–028, 6–045, 6–048, 6–049, 6–050, 6–054, 6–090, 6–094, 6–095, 6–097,
6–098, 6–107, 6–114, 6–116
Insurance of North America v Hope (1871) 11 Am.Rep. 48, 49 10–044
InsuranceWide.com Services Ltd v Revenue and Customs Commissioners [2010] EWCA Civ
422; [2010] B.V.C. 606; [2010] S.T.I. 1474 15–026
Integrated Container Service v British Traders Insurance Co [1984] 1 Lloyd's Rep. 154;
(1984) 81 L.S.G. 353 CA (Civ Div); affirming [1981] 2 Lloyd's Rep. 460; [1981] Com.
L.R. 212 QBD (Comm) 24–112
Interfoto Picture Library Ltd v Stiletto Visual Programmes Ltd [1989] Q.B. 433; [1988] 2
W.L.R. 615; [1988] 1 All E.R. 348; (1988) 7 Tr. L.R. 187; (1988) 85(9) L.S.G. 45;
(1987) 137 N.L.J. 1159; (1988) 132 S.J. 460 CA (Civ Div) 1–022, 3–017, 3–018
Intergraph Best (Vic) Pty Ltd v QBE Insurance Ltd [2005] V.S.C.A. 180 20–080
Intermunicipal realty & Development Corp v Gore Mutual Insurance Co [1981] 1 F.C. 151 6–075,
8–020, 15–033
International Lottery Management Ltd v Dumas [2002] Lloyd's Rep. I.R. 237 QBD 6–006, 6–009,
6–013, 6–028, 6–043, 6–054, 6–072, 6–074, 6–116
International Management Group (UK) Ltd v Simmonds; sub nom. International Manage-
ment Group (UK) Ltd v Simmons [2003] EWHC 177; [2004] Lloyd's Rep. I.R. 247
QBD (Comm) 5–033, 6–043, 6–062, 6–074, 6–116, 7–036, 7–037, 7–042, 23–042
Interpart Comerciao e Gestao SA v Lexington Insurance Co [2004] Lloyd's Rep. I.R. 690
QBD (Comm) 9–029, 9–030

Inversiones Manria SA v Sphere Drake Insurance Co, Malvern Insurance Co and Niagara
    Fire Insurance Co; The Dora [1989] 1 Lloyd's Rep. 69 QBD (Comm) 1–040, 6–031, 6–045,
                        6–048, 6–049, 6–050, 6–055, 6–056, 6–063, 6–074, 6–121, 24–037,
                                                                                24–038
Investors Compensation Scheme Ltd v West Bromwich Building Society (No.1); Investors
    Compensation Scheme Ltd v Hopkin & Sons; Alford v West Bromwich Building
    Society; Armitage v West Bromwich Building Society [1998] 1 W.L.R. 896; [1998] 1
    All E.R. 98; [1998] 1 B.C.L.C. 531; [1997] C.L.C. 1243; [1997] P.N.L.R. 541; (1997)
    147 N.L.J. 989; Times, June 24, 1997 HL 3–005
Ioakimidis Policy Trusts, Re; sub nom. Ioakimidis v Hartcup [1925] Ch. 403 Ch D 18–014
Ionides v Pacific Fire & Marine Insurance Co (1871–72) L.R. 7 Q.B. 517 Ex Chamber;
    affirming (1870–71) L.R. 6 Q.B. 674 QB 1–033, 6–103, 6–120, 24–035, 24–039, 24–051
Ionides v Pender (1873–74) L.R. 9 Q.B. 531 QB 6–022, 6–024, 6–031, 6–056
Ionides v Pender (1872) 27 L.T. 244 24–138
Ionides v Universal Marine Insurance Association (1863) 14 C.B.N.S. 259 ...... 3–007, 5–029, 5–030,
                                                                                5–031
Iran Continental Shelf Oil Co v IRI International Corp [2002] EWCA Civ 1024; [2004] 2
    C.L.C. 696 2–043
Irish Insurance Federation[1987] OJ C120/5 13–045
Irish National Insurance Co and Sedgwick v Oman Insurance Co [1983] 2 Lloyd's Rep. 453
    QBD (Comm) 6–031
Irish Shipping Ltd v Commercial Union Assurance Co Plc (The Irish Rowan) [1991] 2 Q.B.
    206; [1990] 2 W.L.R. 117; [1989] 3 All E.R. 853; [1989] 2 Lloyd's Rep. 144; (1990)
    87(5) L.S.G. 39; (1990) 134 S.J. 426; Times, May 5, 1989 CA (Civ Div) 2–004, 2–005,
                                                                        21–006, 21–009, 21–046
Iron Trades Mutual Insurance Co Ltd v Companhia De Seguros Imperio [1992] Re L.R.
    213 .... 6–073, 6–103, 6–106, 17–009, 17–026
Iron Trades Mutual Insurance Co Ltd v JK Buckenham Ltd [1990] 1 All E.R. 808; [1989] 2
    Lloyd's Rep. 85 QBD (Comm) 15–061
Ironfield v Eastern Gas Board [1964] 1 W.L.R. 1125; [1964] 1 All E.R. 544; 108 S.J. 691,
    Assizes (Bury St Edmunds) 22–023
Irvin v Hine [1950] 1 K.B. 555; [1949] 2 All E.R. 1089; (1949–50) 83 Ll.L.R. 162; 65 T.L.R.
    768 KBD 24–086, 24–103, 24–112
Irving v Manning (1847) 1 H.L.C. 287 .... 1–009, 10–007
Irving v Richardson (1831) 2 B. & Ad. 193 .... 4–019, 6–047, 24–029
Irving v Richardson (1831) 1 Mo. & R. 153 24–048
Isaacs v Royal Insurance Co (1870) L.R. 5 Ex. 296 5–004
Isitt v Railway Passengers Assurance (1889) L.R. 22 Q.B.D. 504 QBD 5–030, 18–041, 18–059
Islamic Arab Insurance Co v Saudi Egyptian American Reinsurance Co [1987] 1 Lloyd's
    Rep. 315; [1987] E.C.C. 434 CA (Civ Div) 2–005, 2–040
Islamic Republic of Iran Shipping Lines v Zannis Compania Naviera SA (The Tzelepi)
    [1991] 2 Lloyd's Rep. 265 QBD (Comm) 15–008, 15–033
Islander Trucking Ltd (In Liquidation) Ltd v Robinson & Gardner Mountain (Marine) Ltd
    [1990] 1 All E.R. 826 QBD (Comm) 15–061
Italia Express (No.2), The. See Ventouris v Mountain
Izzard v Universal Insurance Co Ltd [1937] A.C. 773; (1937) 58 Ll.L.R. 121 HL 22–017
J Aron & Co Inc v Miall (1928) 31 Ll.L.R. 242 CA 24–074
JC Annear & Co Ltd v Attenborough (1940) 68 Ll.L.R. 147 KBD 5–015
J Lowenstein (J) & Co v Poplar Motor Transport (Lymm) [1968] 2 Lloyd's Rep. 233 QBD 5–011,
                                                                                5–012
JA Chapman & Co Ltd (In Liquidation) v Kadirga Denizcilik ve Ticaret AS [1998] C.L.C.
    860; [1998] Lloyd's Rep. I.R. 377; Times, March 19, 1998 CA (Civ Div) 7–040, 8–016,
                                                            8–018, 8–027, 15–028, 24–077, 24–078
JAS v Gross (1998) 231 A.R. 228 20–050
JJ Lloyd Instruments v Northern Star Insurance Co; The Miss Jay Jay [1987] 1 Lloyd's Rep.
    32; [1987] F.T.L.R. 14; [1987] Fin. L.R. 120 CA (Civ Div); affirming [1985] 1 Lloyd's
    Rep. 264 QBD (Comm) 5–033, 7–023, 24–134
JRM (Plant) v Hodgson [1960] 1 Lloyd's Rep. 538 DC 22–011, 22–091
JW Bollom & Co Ltd v Byas Mosley & Co Ltd [2000] Lloyd's Rep. I.R. 136; [1999] Lloyd's
    Rep. P.N. 598 QBD (Comm) 15–035, 15–045
Jabbour v Custodian of Israeli Absentee Property. See F&K Jabbour v Custodian of Israeli
    Absentee Property
Jackson v Greenfield [1998] B.P.I.R. 699 Ch D 21–005, 21–013
Jackson v London Motor Sports Ltd (1940) 66 Ll.L.R. 16 KBD 15–026

Jackson v Mumford (1902) 8 Com.Cas. 61 24–003

Jackson v Turquand (1869) L.R. 4 H.L. 305 8–024

Jacobs v Batavia & General Plantations Trust Ltd [1924] 2 Ch. 329CA; affirming [1924] 1
 Ch. 287 Ch D 3–005

Jacobs v Coster (t/a Newington Commercials Service Station) [2000] Lloyd's Rep. I.R. 506
 CA (Civ Div) 20–041

Jacobs v Motor Insurers Bureau [2010] EWHC 231 (QB); [2010] 1 All E.R. (Comm) 1128;
 [2010] Lloyd's Rep. I.R. 244 22–081

Jacobson v Yorkshire Insurance Co Ltd (1933) 45 Ll.L.R. 281 KBD 7–015

Jaffray v Society of Lloyd's; sub nom. Society of Lloyd's v Jaffray [2002] EWCA Civ. 1101;
 (2002) 146 S.J.L.B. 214 CA (Civ Div) 13–042

Jaglom v Excess Insurance Co Ltd [1972] 2 Q.B. 250; [1971] 3 W.L.R. 594; [1972] 1 All
 E.R. 267; [1971] 2 Lloyd's Rep. 171; 115 S.J. 639 QBD (Comm) 1–034, 1–037

James v British General Insurance Co Ltd [1927] 2 K.B. 311; (1927) 27 Ll.L.R. 328 KBD 5–046,
 20–031, 22–028, 22–029, 22–034

James v CGU Insurance Plc [2002] Lloyd's Rep. I.R. 206 QBD (Comm) ... 3–004, 6–005, 6–028,
 6–045, 6–049, 6–052, 6–059, 6–072, 6–076, 6–105, 9–025, 10–038,
 19–033

James v Lawyers' Professional Indemnity Co [2006] O.J. No.46 20–050

James & Son v Smee; Green v Burnett [1955] 1 Q.B. 78; [1954] 3 W.L.R. 631; [1954] 3 All
 E.R. 273; (1954) 118 J.P. 536; 52 L.G.R. 545; 98 S.J. 771 QBD 22–009, 22–010

James Archdale & Co Ltd v Comservices Ltd [1954] 1 W.L.R. 459; [1954] 1 All E.R. 210;
 98 S.J. 143 CA 11–031

James Budgett Sugars Ltd v Norwich Union Insurance Ltd [2002] EWHC 968; [2003]
 Lloyd's Rep. I.R. 110 QBD (Comm) 10–034, 20–075, 20–076

James Miller & Partners v Whitworth Street Estates (Manchester) Ltd. See Whitworth Street
 Estates (Manchester) Ltd v James Miller & Partners Ltd

James Nelson & Sons Ltd v Nelson Line (Liverpool) Ltd (No.1) [1906] 2 K.B. 217 CA ... 11–011

James Vale & Co v Van Oppen & Co Ltd (1921) 6 Ll.L.R. 167 KBD 15–034

James W Elwell, The [1921] P. 351; (1921) 8 Ll.L.R. 115 PDAD 24–024

James Yachts v Thames & Mersey Marine Insurance Co [1977] 1 Lloyd's Rep. 206 Sup Ct
 (BC) 24–064

Jan De Nul (UK) Ltd v Axa Royale Belge SA (formerly NV Royale Belge); sub nom. Jan De
 Nul (UK) Ltd v Royale Belge SA [2002] EWCA Civ. 209; [2002] 1 All E.R. (Comm)
 767; [2002] 1 Lloyd's Rep. 583; [2002] Lloyd's Rep. I.R. 589 CA (Civ Div); affirming
 [2000] 2 Lloyd's Rep. 700; [2001] Lloyd's Rep. I.R. 327 QBD (Comm) 3–016, 10–003,
 10–018, 20–014, 20–031, 20–075

Jani-King (GB) Ltd v Pula Enterprises Ltd [2007] EWHC 2433 (QB); [2008] 1 All E.R.
 (Comm) 451 3–005

Janson v Driefontein Consolidated Mines Ltd; sub nom. Driefontein Consolidated Gold
 Mines Ltd v Janson; West Rand Central Gold Mines Co Ltd v De Rougemont [1902]
 A.C. 484 HL 5–036, 19–058

Janson v Poole (1912) 18 Com.Cas. 9 24–048

Jascon 5, The. See Talbot Underwriting Ltd v Nausch Hogan & Murray Inc

Jason v Batten (1930), Ltd; sub nom. Jason v British Traders Insurance Co [1969] 1 Lloyd's
 Rep. 281; (1969) 119 N.L.J. 697 QBD 5–030, 5–031, 22–090

Jenkins v Deane (1933) 103 L.J.K.B. 250 .... 11–059, 14–022

Jenkins v Deane (1933) 47 Ll.L.R. 342 KBD 15–001, 15–013, 15–017, 22–099

Jenkins v Deane [1933] 3 All E.R. 699 22–092

Jester-Barnes v Licenses & General Insurance Co Ltd (1934) 49 Ll.L.R. 231 KBD 6–048, 22–087

Jeston v Key (1870–71) L.R. 6 Ch. App. 610 CA in Chancery 14–026

Joachin v Abel [2001] O.T.C. 299 20–049

Joel v Harvey (1857) 29 L.T.O.S. 75 3–006

Joel v Law Union & Crown Insurance Co [1908] 2 K.B. 863 CA 6–004, 6–005, 6–016, 6–018,
 6–021, 6–031, 6–064, 6–070, 6–071, 7–021, 7–029, 18–028,
 18–029

John A Pike (Butchers) Ltd v Independent Insurance Co Ltd [1998] Lloyd's Rep. I.R. 410 CA
 (Civ Div) 3–010, 19–046

John Cory & Sons v Burr; sub nom. Cory & Sons v Burr (1882–83) L.R. 8 App. Cas. 393
 HL 3–007, 5–029, 5–030, 25–012

John Edwards & Co v Motor Union Insurance Co Ltd; sub nom. Edwards v Motor Union
 Insurance Co Ltd; The White Rose [1922] 2 K.B. 249; (1922) 11 Ll.L.R. 170 KBD ... 4–009,
 11–001, 11–006, 11–016

John F Hunt Demolition Ltd v ASME Engineering Ltd [2007] EWHC 1507 (TCC); [2008]
      Bus. L.R. 558; [2008] 1 All E.R. 180; [2008] 1 All E.R. (Comm) 473; [2008] B.L.R.
      115; [2007] T.C.L.R. 6; 114 Con. L.R. 105; [2007] C.I.L.L. 2496 .... 11–028, 15–059
Jones (James) v DPP (1999) 163 J.P. 121; [1999] R.T.R. 1; Times, April 23, 1998 22–009
John Martin of London Ltd v Russell [1960] 1 Lloyd's Rep. 554 QBD (Comm) 24–066
John Meacock v Bryant & Co (1942) 74 Ll.L.R. 53 KBD 11–005, 23–029, 23–033
John Rigby (Haulage) v Reliance Marine Insurance Co [1956] 2 Q.B. 468; [1956] 3 W.L.R.
      407; [1956] 3 All E.R. 1; [1956] 2 Lloyd's Rep. 10; 100 S.J. 528 CA 5–010
John T Ellis Ltd v Hinds [1947] K.B. 475; [1947] 1 All E.R. 337; (1947) 80 Ll.L.R. 231; 63
      T.L.R. 181; [1947] L.J.R. 488; 176 L.T. 424; 91 S.J. 68 KBD 22–009, 22–010, 22–011,
                                                                              22–088, 22–089
John Wyeth & Bros Ltd v Cigna Insurance Co of Europe SA NV (No.1) [2001] EWCA Civ.
      175; [2001] C.L.C. 970; [2001] Lloyd's Rep. I.R. 420 CA (Civ Div) ... 20–047, 20–049, 20–052,
                                                                              20–054, 20–076
HLJohnson v Ball (1851) 5 De G. & Sm. 85 18–024
Johnson v Coventry Churchill International Ltd [1992] 3 All E.R. 14 2–061
Johnson v IGI Insurance Co Ltd [1997] 6 Re. L.R. 283 CA (Civ Div) 6–072, 18–054
Johnson v Mutual of Omaha Insurance Co, 139 D.L.R. (3rd) 358 (1982) 18–059
Johnson & Co v Bryant (1896) 1 Com. Cas. 363 5–004
Johnson & Perrott Ltd v Holmes (1925) 21 Ll.L.R. 330 KBD 25–009
Johnston v Salvage Association (1887) L.R. 19 Q.B.D. 458 CA 20–034
Johnston v Sutton (1779) 1 Doug. 254 24–064
QBDJones Construction Co v Alliance Assurance Co Ltd [1961] 1 Lloyd's Rep. 121 CA 1–047,
                                                                              5–005
Jones v Birch Bros Ltd (Licenses & General Insurance Co) [1933] 2 K.B. 597; (1933) 46
      Ll.L.R. 277 CA 20–062, 22–027, 22–037
Jones v Chief Constable of Bedfordshire [1987] R.T.R. 332; [1987] Crim. L.R. 502 DC ... 22–003
Jones v Commerzbank AG; sub nom. Commerzbank AG v Jones; Commerzbank AG v Price-
      Jones; Price-Jones v Commerzbank AG [2003] EWCA Civ. 1663; (2003) 147 S.J.L.B.
      1397; [2004] 1 P. & C.R. DG15; Times, November 26, 2003; Independent, December 4,
      2003 CA (Civ Div) 10–062
Jones v Environcom Ltd [2010] EWHC 759 (Comm) 6–053, 9–053, 15–036, 15–054, 15–056,
                                                                              15–057, 19–034
Jones v Neptune Marine Insurance Co (1871–72) L.R. 7 Q.B. 702 QB 24–130
Jones v Provincial Insurance Co Ltd (1929) 35 Ll.L.R. 135 KBD 7–013, 22–093
Jones v Randall (1774) 1 Cowp. 37 4–002
Times
Jones v Trollope Colls Cementation Overseas Times, January 26, 1990 CA 2–056
Jones v Welsh Insurance Corp Ltd (1937) 59 Ll.L.R. 13; (1937) 54 T.L.R. 22 KBD 22–096
Jones & James v Provincial (1929) 46 T.L.R. 71 .... 7–015, 7–028
TimesJordan Grand Prix Ltd v Baltic Insurance Group; sub nom. Baltic Insurance Group v
      Jordan Grand Prix Ltd; Baltic Insurance Group v Quay Financial Software [1999] 2
      A.C. 127; [1999] 1 W.L.R. 134; [1999] 1 All E.R. 289; [1999] C.L.C. 527; [1999] 1
      Lloyd's Rep. I.R. 93; Times, December 17, 1998 HL 2–009, 2–010
Jordan Nicolov, The. See Montedipe SpA v JTP-RO Jugotanker
Joscelyne v Nissen [1970] 2 Q.B. 86; [1970] 2 W.L.R. 509; [1970] 1 All E.R. 1213; (1969)
      114 S.J. 55 CA (Civ Div) 1–019
Joseph v Law Integrity Insurance Co Ltd [1912] 2 Ch. 581 CA 1–008, 18–001
Joyce v Kennard (1871–72) L.R. 7 Q.B. 78 QBD 10–029, 19–007, 19–044, 24–029
Joyce v Realm Marine Insurance Co (1871–72) L.R. 7 Q.B. 580 QB 17–012
Joyce v Swann (1864) 17 C.B. N.S. 84 19–007
Judd v Merrett [1997] L.R.L.R. 21; Lloyd's List, June 13, 1996 (I.D.) CA (Civ Div) 13–041
Julian Praet et Cie S/A v HG Poland Ltd (Injunction) [1960] 1 Lloyd's Rep. 416 CA 8–007
Jureidini v National British & Irish Millers Insurance Co Ltd [1915] A.C. 499 HL 9–034
KR v Royal & Sun Alliance Plc [2006] EWHC 48; [2006] Lloyd's Rep. I.R. 327 QBD ... 20–025,
                                                                              20–031, 20–086
K/S Lincoln v CB Richard Ellis Hotels Ltd [2009] EWHC 2344 (TCC); [2009] B.L.R. 591;
      127 Con. L.R. 188; [2010] P.N.L.R. 5 5–045
K/S Merc-Skandia XXXXII v Certain Lloyd's Underwriters (The Mercandian Continent)
      [2000] Lloyd's Rep. I.R. 694, affirmed [2001] Lloyd's Rep. I.R. 802 ... 5–017, 6–017, 6–054,
                                6–075, 6–105, 6–106, 6–107, 6–109, 6–110, 6–112, 6–114, 6–115,
                                6–129, 7–007, 7–009, 9–003, 9–017, 9–022, 9–032, 10–022,
                                                          17–025, 20–045, 20–047, 21–023
Kacianoff v China Traders Insurance Co Ltd [1914] 3 K.B. 1121 CA 5–030

Kahler v Midland Bank Ltd [1950] A.C. 24; [1949] 2 All E.R. 621; 65 T.L.R. 663; [1949]
    L.J.R. 1687 HL 2–057
Kahn v Corbett (1824) 2 Bing. 205 24–080
Kaines v Knightly (1681) Skinner 54 1–012
Kajima UK Engineering Ltd v Underwriter Insurance Co Ltd [2008] EWHC 83 (TCC);
    [2008] 1 All E.R. (Comm) 855; 122 Con. L.R. 123; [2008] Lloyd's Rep. I.R. 391;
    [2008] C.I.L.L. 2567 .... 9–009, 20–042
Kaltenbach v Mackenzie (1873) 3 C.P.D. 467 .... 11–067, 24–091
Kamidian v Wareham Holt [2008] EWHC 1483 (Comm); [2009] Lloyd's Rep. I.R. 242 6–013,
    6–056, 19–007
Kammins Ballrooms Co Ltd v Zenith Investments (Torquay) Ltd (No.1) [1971] A.C. 850;
    [1970] 3 W.L.R. 287; [1970] 2 All E.R. 871; (1971) 22 P. & C.R. 74; (1970) 114 S.J.
    590 HL 6–090, 6–098, 7–018, 9–014
Kansa General Insurance Co (1991) 2 O.R. (2d) 269 20–050
Kansa Insurance Co v Elbow Skiing Ltd (1991) 6 C.C.L.I. (2d) 299 20–047
Kanson Crane Service Co Ltd v Bank of China Group Insurance Co Ltd [2003] H.K.E.C.
    1139 9–040
Kapur v JW Francis & Co (No.2) [2000] Lloyd's Rep. I.R. 361; [1999] Lloyd's Rep. P.N. 834
    CA (Civ Div) 15–036
Kastor Navigation Co Ltd v AGF MAT; The Kastor Too; sub nom. Kastor Navigation Co Ltd
    v Axa Global Risks (UK) Ltd; The Kastor Too [2004] EWCA Civ. 277; [2005] 2 All
    E.R. (Comm) 720; [2004] 2 Lloyd's Rep. 119; [2004] 2 C.L.C. 68; [2004] 4 Costs L.R.
    569; [2004] Lloyd's Rep. I.R. 481; Times, April 29, 2004 CA (Civ Div); reversing in
    part [2002] EWHC 2601; [2003] 1 All E.R. (Comm) 277; [2003] 1 Lloyd's Rep. 296;
    [2003] 2 C.L.C. 489; [2003] Lloyd's Rep. I.R. 262 QBD (Comm) ... 5–032, 24–088, 24–092,
    24–096, 24–097, 24–111, 24–134
Kaufmann v British Surety Insurance Co Ltd (1929) 33 Ll.L.R. 315; (1929) 45 T.L.R. 399
    KBD 15–019, 22–097
Kausar v Eagle Star Insurance Co Ltd; sub nom. Eagle Star Insurance Co Ltd v Kausar [1997]
    C.L.C. 129; [2000] Lloyd's Rep. I.R. 154; [1996] 5 Re. L.R. 191; (1996) 140 S.J.L.B.
    150; Times, July 15, 1996 CA (Civ Div) 5–019, 5–023, 5–027, 6–005, 6–103
Kawasaki Kisen Kabushiki Kaisha of Kobe v Bantham Steamship Co Ltd (No.2) [1939] 2
    K.B. 544; (1939) 63 Ll.L.R. 155 CA 25–004
Kazakstan Wool Processors (Europe) Ltd v Nederlandsche Credietverzekering Maatschappij
    NV [2000] 1 All E.R. (Comm) 708; [2000] C.L.C. 822; [2000] Lloyd's Rep. I.R. 371
    CA (Civ Div) 7–004, 23–030
Keeley v Pashen [2004] EWCA Civ. 1491; [2005] 1 W.L.R. 1226; [2005] R.T.R. 10; [2005]
    Lloyd's Rep. I.R. 289; (2004) 101(45) L.S.G. 32; Times, November 17, 2004 CA (Civ
    Div) 22–029, 22–086, 22–096, 22–097, 22–098
Keeling v Pearl Assurance Co (1923) 129 L.T. 573 .... 15–019, 18–026
Keen, Re; sub nom. Evershed v Griffiths [1937] Ch. 236 CA 18–024
Keevil & Keevil Ltd v Boag (1940) 67 Ll.L.R. 263 CA 6–107
Keighley Maxsted & Co v Durant (t/a Bryan Durant & Co); sub nom. Durant & Co v Roberts
    [1901] A.C. 240 HL 4–021, 14–008, 15–003
Kelly v Cornhill Insurance Co Ltd [1964] 1 W.L.R. 158; [1964] 1 All E.R. 321; [1964] 1
    Lloyd's Rep. 1; 1964 S.C. (H.L.) 46; 1964 S.L.T. 81; 108 S.J. 94 HL 22–027, 22–088
Kelly v London & Staffordshire Fire Insurance Co (1833) Cab. & El. 47 15–014
Kelly v Mackle [2009] N.I.Q.B. 39 22–025
Kelly v National Insurance Co of New Zealand Unreported, 1994 14–003
Kelly v Norwich Union Fire Insurance Ltd [1990] 1 W.L.R. 139; [1989] 2 All E.R. 888;
    [1989] 2 Lloyd's Rep. 333; [1989] Fin. L.R. 331; (1989) 5 Const. L.J. 215; [1989]
    E.G.C.S. 52; (1990) 87(1) L.S.G. 32; (1990) 134 S.J. 49 CA (Civ Div) ... 5–015, 9–037, 10–034,
    19–038
Kelly v Solari (1841) 9 M. & W. 54 .... 8–022, 10–058, 10–060, 10–061
Kelsall v Allstate Insurance Co, Times, March 20, 1987 CA (Civ Div) 6–013, 6–021, 7–033
Kenai Corp v National Union Fire Insurance Co 136 B.R. 59 (S.D.N.Y., 1992) 20–047
Kenburn Waste Management v Bergman [2006] C.L.C. 644 2–043
Kennecott Utah Copper Corp v Cornhill Insurance Plc (t/a Allianz Cornhill International)
    [1999] 2 All E.R. (Comm) 801; [2000] C.L.C. 273; [2000] Lloyd's Rep. I.R. 179QBD
    (Comm) 1–039
Kennecott Utah Copper Corp v Minet Ltd [2003] EWCA Civ. 905; [2004] 1 All E.R. (Comm)
    60 CA (Civ Div); reversing [2002] EWHC 1622; [2003] Lloyd's Rep. I.R. 37; [2003]
    P.N.L.R. 18 QBD (Comm) 15–056

Kennedy v Gad (1828) 3 C. & P. 376 4–002
Kennedy v Green (1834) 3 My. & K. 699 6–039
Kennedy v Smith; sub nom. Kennedy v Ansvar Insurance Co Ltd, 1975 S.C. 266; 1976 S.L.T.
    110 IH (1 Div) 7–032
Kensington, Ex p. (1813) 2 E. & B. 79 14–026
Kent v Bird (1777) 2 Cowp. 583 .... 4–009, 24–013, 24–014
Kenyon v Berthon (1778) 1 Doug. 12n 7–022
Kern Corporation Ltd v Walter Reid Trading Pty Ltd [1987] C.L.R. 164 10–051
Kerr v Lawyers' Professional Indemnity Co (1995) 25 O.R. (3d) 804 20–049
Kerridge v Rush [1952] 2 Lloyd's Rep. 305 QBD 22–011, 22–099
Kettlewell v Refuge Assurance. *See* Refuge Assurance Co Ltd v Kettlewell
Kewley v Ryan (1794) 2 H. Bl. 343 .... 24–051, 24–070
Kidston v Empire Marine Insurance Co (1866) L.R. 1 C.P. 535 24–112
Kidston v Empire Marine Insurance Co (1867) L.R. 2 C.P. 357 24–099
Kier Construction v Royal Insurance (UK), 30 Con. L.R. 45 QBD (OR) 5–049, 9–003
Killick v Rendall; Nugent v Rendall [2000] 2 All E.R. (Comm) 57; [2000] C.L.C. 1217;
    [2000] Lloyd's Rep. I.R. 581; Independent, April 19, 2000 CA (Civ Div) 18–043
King v Brandywine Reinsurance Co (UK) Ltd (formerly Cigna RE Co (UK) Ltd) [2005]
    EWCA Civ. 235; [2005] 2 All E.R. (Comm) 1; [2005] 1 Lloyd's Rep. 655; [2005] 1
    C.L.C. 283; [2005] Env. L.R. 33; [2005] Lloyd's Rep. I.R. 509 CA (Civ Div); affirming
    [2004] EWHC 1033; [2004] 2 All E.R. (Comm) 443; [2004] 2 Lloyd's Rep. 670; [2004]
    2 C.L.C. 981; [2004] Lloyd's Rep. I.R. 554 QBD (Comm) 2–033, 2–037, 2–038, 2–050,
                       3–003, 3–011, 7–007, 7–009, 7–015, 9–038, 10–039, 14–014,
                                17–018, 17–020, 20–042
*Times*HLKing v Crown Energy Trading AG [2003] EWHC 163; [2003] 2 C.L.C. 540; [2003]
    I.L.Pr. 28; Times, March 14, 2003 QBD (Comm) 2–001
King v Glover (1806) 2 Bos. & P.N.R. 206 20–062
King v Travellers Insurance Association Ltd (1931) 41 Ll.L.R. 13; (1931) 48 T.L.R. 53
    KBD 3–006, 19–053
King v Victoria Insurance Co Ltd [1896] A.C. 250 PC (Aus) 11–001, 11–016
King (Deceased), Re; sub nom. Robinson v Gray; King, Re [1963] Ch. 459; [1963] 2 W.L.R.
    629; [1963] 1 All E.R. 781; [1963] R.V.R. 245; 107 S.J. 134CA 1–014, 10–048, 19–002,
                                             19–017
King (Or Fiehl) v Chambers & Newman (Insurance Brokers) [1963] 2 Lloyd's Rep. 130
    QBD 15–035
Kingscroft Insurance Co Ltd v Nissan Fire & Marine Insurance Co Ltd (No.1) [1999] Lloyd's
    Rep. I.R. 371CA (Civ Div); affirming Lloyd's List, May 16, 1996 (I.D.) QBD (Comm) ... 6–036,
                                  6–037, 6–039, 15–023
Kingscroft Insurance Co Ltd v Nissan Fire & Marine Insurance Co Ltd (No.2) [2000] 1 All
    E.R. (Comm) 272; [1999] C.L.C. 1875; [1999] Lloyd's Rep. I.R. 603 QBD (Comm) 1–023,
                    1–047, 3–004, 3–005, 5–008, 6–008, 6–065, 6–095, 7–006, 14–008,
                            15–028, 17–005, 17–007, 17–008
Kingscroft Insurance Co v HS Weavers (Underwriting) Agencies [1993] 1 Lloyd's Rep. 187;
    Times, August 21, 1992 Ch D 15–020
Kingston v Knibbs (1808) 1 Camp. 508 24–037
Kingston v Phelps (1793) 1 Peake 299 .... 24–070, 24–073
Kirby v Cosindit Societa Per Azioni [1969] 1 Lloyd's Rep. 75 QBD (Comm) 1–047, 8–008
Kirby v Smith (1818) 1 B. & Ald. 672 .... 24–035, 24–036
Kiriacoulis Lines SA v Compagnie d'Assurances Maritimes Aeriennes et Terrestres
    (CAMAT) (The Demetra K) [2002] EWCA Civ. 1070; [2002] 2 Lloyd's Rep. 581;
    [2003] 1 C.L.C. 579; [2002] Lloyd's Rep. I.R. 795 CA (Civ Div) 1–020, 3–017, 5–033,
                                            19–039
Kiriri Cotton Co Ltd v Dewani; sub nom. Kiriri Cotton Ct v Dewani [1960] A.C. 192; [1960]
    2 W.L.R. 127; [1960] 1 All E.R. 177; 104 S.J. 49 PC (EA) 18–010
Kirkaldy & Sons Ltd v Walker [1999] 1 All E.R. (Comm.) 334; [1999] C.L.C. 722; [1999]
    Lloyd's Rep. I.R. 410 QBD (Comm) 6–070, 6–074, 7–048, 24–038
Kirkbride v Donner [1974] 1 Lloyd's Rep. 549 MCLC 7–032, 22–089
Kirkpatrick v South Australian Insurance Co Ltd (1886) L.R. 11 App. Cas. 177 PC (Aus) 8–002
Kitchen Design & Advice Ltd v Lea Valley Water Co [1989] 2 Lloyd's Rep. 221; Times,
    March 14, 1989 QBD 10–055, 11–039
Kleinwort v Shepherd (1859) 1 E. & E. 447 25–012

Kleinwort Benson Ltd v Lincoln City Council; Kleinwort Benson Ltd v Birmingham City
    Council; Kleinwort Benson Ltd v Southwark LBC; Kleinwort Benson Ltd v Kensington
    and Chelsea RLBC [1999] 2 A.C. 349; [1998] 3 W.L.R. 1095; [1998] 4 All E.R. 513;
    [1998] Lloyd's Rep. Bank. 387; [1999] C.L.C. 332; (1999) 1 L.G.L.R. 148; (1999) 11
    Admin. L.R. 130; [1998] R.V.R. 315; (1998) 148 N.L.J. 1674; (1998) 142 S.J.L.B. 279;
    [1998] N.P.C. 145; Times, October 30, 1998; Independent, November 4, 1998 HL 6–012,
                                                                    10–058, 10–060, 18–012
Kleinwort, Sons & Co v Dunlop Rubber Co (1907) 97 L.T. 263 10–063
Kleovoulous of Rhodes, The. See Sunport Shipping Ltd v Tryg Baltica International (UK)
    Ltd
Kler Knitwear Ltd v Lombard General Insurance Co Ltd [2000] Lloyd's Rep. I.R. 47 QBD ... 7–034
Knaggs v Elson (1965) 109 S.J. 596 DC 22–007
Knapp v Ecclesiastical Insurance Group Plc [1998] Lloyd's Rep. I.R. 390; [1998] P.N.L.R.
    172; Times, November 17, 1997 CA (Civ Div) 15–061
Knauf UK GmbH v British Gypsum Ltd (No.1) [2001] EWCA Civ 1570; [2002] 1 W.L.R.
    907; [2002] 2 All E.R. 525; [2001] 2 All E.R. 2–04(Comm) 960; [2002] 1 Lloyd's Rep.
    199; [2002] C.L.C. 239; [2002] I.L.Pr. 30; (2001) 145 S.J.L.B. 259; Times, November
    15, 2001; Independent, November 7, 2001 2–004
Knight v Axa Assurances [2009] EWHC 1900 (QB); [2009] Lloyd's Rep. I.R. 667 ...... 2–014, 2–062,
                                                                                   22–085
Knight v Cambridge (1724) 1 Str. 581 24–138
Knight v Faith (1850) 15 Q.B. 649 5–015
Knight v Hosken (1943) 75 Ll.L.R. 74 CA 20–052
Knoller v Evans (1936) 55 Ll.L.R. 40 KBD 10–027
Knox v Wood (1808) 1 Camp. 543 .... 4–009, 20–062
Koebel v Saunders (1864) 33 L.J.C.P. 310 24–063
Kohanski v St Paul Guarantee Insurance Co 78 O.R. (3d) 684 (2006) 20–087
Kolden Holdings Ltd v Rodette Commerce Ltd [2007] EWHC 1597 (Comm); [2007] 4 All
    E.R. 62; [2007] 2 All E.R. (Comm) 737; [2008] 1 Lloyd's Rep. 197; [2007] 2 C.L.C.
    355; [2007] I.L.Pr. 50; (2007) 157 N.L.J. 1010 2–008
Komninos S, The. See Hellenic Steel Co v Svolamar Shipping Co Ltd (The Komninos S)
    Komninos S, The
Konkola Copper Mines Plc v Coromin Ltd [2006] EWCA Civ. 5; [2006] 1 All E.R. (Comm)
    437; [2006] 1 Lloyd's Rep. 410; [2006] 1 C.L.C. 1; (2006) 103(6) L.S.G. 34 CA (Civ
    Div); affirming [2005] EWHC 898; [2005] 2 All E.R. (Comm) 637; [2005] 2 Lloyd's
    Rep. 555; [2005] 1 C.L.C. 1021; [2005] I.L.Pr. 39; [2006] Lloyd's Rep. I.R. 71 QBD
    (Comm) 2–003, 2–004, 2–005, 2–008
Korea Foreign Insurance Company v Omne Re SA [1999] Lloyd's Rep. I.R. 509 CA 10–055,
                                                                                   17–022
Korea National Insurance Co v Allianz Global Corporate & Specialty AG [2008] EWCA Civ
    1355; [2008] 2 C.L.C. 837; [2009] Lloyd's Rep. I.R. 480; [2009] Bus. L.R. D59; Times,
    December 22, 2008 9–036
Korea National Insurance Corp v Allianz Global Corporate & Specialty AG (formerly
    Allianz Marine & Aviation Versicherungs AG) [2007] EWCA Civ 1066; [2007] 2
    C.L.C. 748; [2008] Lloyd's Rep. I.R. 413 20–058
Koskas v Standard Marine. See D&J Koskas v Standard Marine Insurance Co Ltd
Kosmar Villa Holidays Plc v Trustees of Syndicate 1243 [2007] EWHC 458 (Comm); [2007]
    2 All E.R. (Comm) 217; [2007] 1 C.L.C. 642; [2008] Lloyd's Rep. I.R. 43; reversed
    [2008] EWCA Civ 147; [2008] Bus. L.R. 931; [2008] 2 All E.R. (Comm) 14; [2008] 1
    C.L.C. 307; [2008] Lloyd's Rep. I.R. 489; (2008) 105(11) L.S.G. 24; Times, March 11,
    2008 ...... 6–090, 6–098, 7–018, 7–019, 7–020, 7–047, 7–048, 9–014, 9–018, 10–054, 20–044
Krall v Burnet (1877) 2 W.R. 305 3–013
Krantz v Allen & Faber (1921) 9 Ll.L.R. 15 6–052
Kreet v Rawcliffe Unreported, 1984 22–007
Kumar v AGF Insurance Ltd [1999] 1 W.L.R. 1747; [1998] 4 All E.R. 788; [1999] Lloyd's
    Rep. I.R. 147; [1999] P.N.L.R. 269 QBD (Comm) 6–085, 6–100, 7–031, 7–037, 7–039,
                                                              7–047, 7–048, 20–023, 20–024
Kumar v Life Assurance Co of India [1974] 1 Lloyd's Rep. 147; (1973) 117 S.J. 833 QBD 7–037,
                                                                                   18–029
Kusel v Atkin; The Catariba [1997] 2 Lloyd's Rep. 749; [1997] C.L.C. 554 QBD (Comm) 24–103,
                                                                                   24–111
Kuwait Airways Corp v Kuwait Insurance Co (No.3) [2000] 1 All E.R. (Comm) 972; [2001]
    C.P. Rep. 60; [2000] Lloyd's Rep. I.R. 678 QBD (Comm) 10–026, 10–027

Kuwait Airways Corp v Kuwait Insurance Co SAK (No.1) [1999] 1 All E.R. (Comm.) 481;
    [1999] 1 Lloyd's Rep. 803; [1999] C.L.C. 934 HL; affirming in part [1997] 2 Lloyd's
    Rep. 687 CA (Civ Div); affirming in part [1996] 1 Lloyd's Rep. 664 QBD (Comm) ... 5–034,
                                                        10–032, 10–034, 25–012
Kuwait Airways Corp v Kuwait Insurance Co SAK (No.2) [2000] 1 All E.R. (Comm) 182;
    [2000] 1 Lloyd's Rep. 252; [2000] C.L.C. 498; [2000] Lloyd's Rep. I.R. 439 QBD
    (Comm) 11–021
Kuwait Oil Tanker Co SAK v Al-Bader (No.3) Unreported December 17, 1998 2–059
Kuwait Oil Tanker Co SAK v Al-Bader (No.3) [2000] 2 All E.R. (Comm) 271; (2000) 97(23)
    L.S.G. 44; Times, May 30, 2000; Independent, June 26, 2000 CA 2–059
Kyle Bay Ltd (t/a Astons Nightclub) v Underwriters Subscribing under Policy No.
    019057/08/01 [2006] EWHC 607; [2006] Lloyd's Rep. I.R. 718; Times, May 29,
    2006QBD (Comm); affirmed [2007] EWCA Civ 57; [2007] 1 C.L.C. 164; [2007]
    Lloyd's Rep. I.R. 460 .... 1–019, 10–055, 10–057, 23–042
Kynance Sailing Ship Co Ltd v Young (1911) 16 Com. Cas. 123 .... 24–066, 24–071
Kyzuna Investments Ltd v Ocean Marine Mutual Insurance (Europe) (The Solveig) [2002]
    Lloyd's Rep I.R. 292 10–006
Kyzuna Investments Ltd v Ocean Marine Mutual Insurance Association (Europe) [2000] 1
    All E.R. (Comm) 557; [2000] 1 Lloyd's Rep. 505; [2000] C.L.C. 925; [2000] Lloyd's
    Rep. I.R. 513; (2000) 97(12) L.S.G. 44; (2000) 144 S.J.L.B. 142; Times, March 31, 2000
    QBD (Comm) 1–009, 1–033
LEC (Liverpool) Ltd v Glover (t/a Rainhill Forge) [2002] T.C.L.R. 17; [2001] Lloyd's Rep.
    I.R. 315 CA (Civ Div) 3–010, 19–039
La Banque Financière de Ia Cite v Westgate Insurance Co Ltd. See Banque Financiere de la
    Cite SA (formerly Banque Keyser Ullmann SA) v Westgate Insurance Co
La Fabrique de Produits Chimiques Societe Anonyme v Large [1923] 1 K.B. 203; (1922) 13
    Ll.L.R. 269 KBD 19–046, 24–136
La Positiva Seguros v Reaseguros SA v Jessel Unreported, 2000 .... 3–016, 5–015, 23–025
Ladbroke v Lee (1850) 4 De G. & Sm. 106 24–029
Ladd v Marshall [1954] 1 W.L.R. 1489; [1954] 3 All E.R. 745; (1954) 98 S.J. 870 CA 9–035
Laemthong International Lines Co Ltd v Abdullah Mohammed Fahem & Co [2005] EWCA
    Civ 519; [2005] 2 All E.R. (Comm) 167; [2005] 1 Lloyd's Rep. 688; [2005] 1 C.L.C.
    739 9–044
Lagden v O'Connor; sub nom. Clark v Tull (t/a Ardington Electrical Services); Burdis v
    Livsey; Clark v Ardington Electrical Services; Dennard v Plant; Sen v Steelform
    Engineering Co Ltd [2003] UKHL 64; [2004] 1 A.C. 1067; [2003] 3 W.L.R. 1571;
    [2004] 1 All E.R. 277; [2004] R.T.R. 24; [2004] Lloyd's Rep. I.R. 315; (2003) 153
    N.L.J. 1869; (2003) 147 S.J.L.B. 1430; Times, December 5, 2003 HL; affirming [2002]
    EWCA Civ. 510; [2003] Q.B. 36; [2002] 3 W.L.R. 762; [2003] R.T.R. 3; [2002] Lloyd's
    Rep. I.R. 524 CA (Civ Div) 1–021, 10–022, 15–047, 22–025, 22–026
Laing v Boreal Pacific [2000] F.C.J. No.1665 24–062
Laing v Commercial Marine Insurance Co Ltd (1895) 1 Com.Cas. 1; (1895) 1 T.L.R. 358 24–039
Laing v Commercial Union Assurance Co Ltd (1922) 11 Ll.L.R. 54 Ch D (Irl) 8–011
Laing v Union Marine Insurance Co Ltd (1895) 1 Com.Cas. 11; (1895) 1 T.L.R. 358 .... 6–070, 6–095
Laing v Glover (1813) 5 Taunt. 49 7–038
Laird v Securities Insurance (1895) 22 R. (Ct. of Sess.) 452 23–030
Lake v Commercial Union Assurance Co of Canada, 72 D.L.R. (4th) 239 (1990) 5–034
Lake v Reinsurance Corporation Ltd, 1967 (3) S.A. 124 (W.) 8–013
Lake v Simmons [1927] A.C. 487; (1927) 27 Ll.L.R. 377 HL 3–010
Laker Vent Engineering Ltd v Templeton Insurance Co Ltd [2009] EWCA Civ 62; [2009] 2
    All E.R. (Comm) 755; [2009] Lloyd's Rep. I.R. 704 .... 6–028, 20–040, 20–041, 23–014
L'Alsacienne Premiere Societe Alsacienne et Lorraine d'Assurances Contre L'Incendie les
    Accidents et les Risques Divers v Unistorebrand International Insurance AS [1995]
    L.R.L.R. 333 QBD (Comm) 1–001, 1–003, 1–010, 6–001, 6–041, 6–072, 6–118, 15–021
Lam v Federation of Small Businesses [2002] EWCA Civ. 1457 CA (Civ Div) 14–003
Lam Charn Yung v AXA China Region Insurance Co (Bermuda) Ltd [2007] 1 H.K.L.R.D.
    770 18–029
Lamb Head Shipping Co Ltd v Jennings; The Marel [1994] 1 Lloyd's Rep. 624 CA (Civ
    Div) 24–134
Lamb v Cotogno (1988) 164 C.L.R. 1 22–023
Lambert v Cooperative Insurance Society Ltd [1975] 2 Lloyd's Rep. 485 CA (Civ Div) 6–021,
                                                                                 6–048, 6–105
Lambert v Keymood Ltd [1999] Lloyd's Rep. I.R. 80; [1997] 2 E.G.L.R. 70; [1997] 43 E.G.
    131; [1996] N.P.C. 58 QBD 5–050, 11–032, 19–017

Lancashire CC v Municipal Mutual Insurance Ltd [1997] Q.B. 897; [1996] 3 W.L.R. 493; [1996] 3 All E.R. 545; [1996] C.L.C. 1459; (1996) 160 L.G. Rev. 612; (1996) 93(21) L.S.G. 27; (1996) 140 S.J.L.B. 108; Times, April 8, 1996 CA (Civ Div); affirming [1995] L.R.L.R. 293; Times, July 9, 1994 QBD 5–041, 5–046, 20–015, 20–087

Lancashire Insurance Co v Inland Revenue Commissioners; Vulcan Boiler and General Insurance Co Ltd v Inland Revenue Commissioners [1899] 1 Q.B. 353 QBD 18–001, 20–034

Lane v Nixon (1866) L.R. 1 C.P. 412 24–061

Lang v Anderton (1824) 3 B. & C. 495 24–068

Langdale v Mason (1780) 2 Park on Insurance 965 25–006

Langford v Legal & General Assurance Society [1986] 2 Lloyd's Rep. 103 QBD 5–012

Langhorn v Allnutt (1812) 4 Taunt. 511 24–072

Langman v Valentine [1952] 2 All E.R. 803; [1952] 2 T.L.R. 713; 116 J.P. 576; 50 L.G.R. 685; [1952] W.N. 475; 96 S.J. 712 DC 22–009, 22–010, 22–089

Larchgrove (Owners) v R. See Owners of the SS Larchgrove v King, The

Larizza v Commercial Union Assurance Co, 68 D.L.R. (4th) 460 (1990) 5–006

Lark v Outhwaite [1991] 2 Lloyd's Rep. 132 QBD (Comm) 20–057

Laroche v Spirit of Adventure (UK) Ltd [2008] EWHC 788 (QB); [2008] 4 All E.R. 494; [2008] 2 All E.R. (Comm) 1076; [2008] 2 Lloyd's Rep. 34; (2008) 158 N.L.J. 593; Times, April 23, 2008 21–014

Larrinaga v Societe Franco-Americaine (1923) 29 Com.Cas. 1 1–031

Laughlin v Sharon High Voltage Inc (1993) 12 O.R. (3d) 101 20–050

Laurence v Davies [1972] 2 Lloyd's Rep. 231 CC (Exeter) 22–091

Lavabre v Wilson (1779) 1 Doug. 284 24–073

Law v London Indisputable Life Insurance Policy Co (1855) 1 K. & J. 223 .. 4–017, 18–015, 18–020, 18–022

Law v Thomas (1964) 62 L.G.R. 195 22–006

Law Car and General Insurance Corp (No.2), Re; sub nom. JJ King & Sons (Ltd) Case (No.2), Re; Old Silkstone Collieries (Ltd) Case (No.2), Re [1913] 2 Ch. 103 CA 16–011

Law Fire Assurance Co v Oakley (1888) 4 T.L.R. 309 .... 11–035, 11–042

Law Guarantee Trust & Accident Society (Godsons Claim), Re [1915] 1 Ch. 340 Ch D 17–002

Law Guarantee Trust & Accident Society Ltd, Re; sub nom. Liverpool Mortgage Insurance Co's Case [1914] 2 Ch. 617 CA 17–017, 23–019, 23–029

Law Guarantee Trust & Accident Society v Munich Reinsurance Co [1912] 1 Ch. 138 Ch D ... 5–023, 5–026, 23–030

Law Guarantee Trust & Accident Society Ltd v Munich Reinsurance Co (1915) 31 T.L.R. 572 6–120

Law Society v Shah [2007] EWHC 2841 (Ch); [2009] Ch. 223; [2008] 3 W.L.R. 1401; [2008] Bus. L.R. 1742; [2007] B.P.I.R. 1595; [2008] Lloyd's Rep. I.R. 442; Times, December 20, 2007 .... 21–015, 21–043

Law Society v Sephton & Co [2006] UKHL 22; [2006] 2 W.L.R. 1091; (2006) 156 N.L.J. 844; (2006) 150 S.J.L.B. 669; [2006] N.P.C. 56; Times, May 11, 2006 HL 15–061

Law Union & Rock Insurance Co Ltd v Moore's Taxi Ltd, 22 D.L.R. (2d) 254 (1959) 22–030

Lawrence v Aberdein (1821) 5 B. & Ald. 107 .... 5–030, 24–134

Lawrence v Accidental Insurance Co Ltd (1880–81) L.R. 7 Q.B.D. 216; (1881) 45 L.T. 29 QBD 5–029, 5–030, 18–041, 18–060, 22–090

Lawrence v Commissioner of Police of the Metropolis; sub nom. R. v Lawrence (Alan) [1972] A.C. 626; [1971] 3 W.L.R. 225; [1971] 2 All E.R. 1253; (1971) 55 Cr. App. R. 471; 115 S.J. 565 HL 19–049

Lawrence v Howlett [1952] 2 All E.R. 74; [1952] 1 Lloyd's Rep. 483; [1952] 1 T.L.R. 1476; (1952) 116 J.P. 391; 50 L.G.R. 531; [1952] W.N. 308; 96 S.J. 397 QBD 22–006

Lawrence v Sydebotham (1805) 6 East 45 24–073

Laycock v Road Transport & General Insurance Co Ltd (1940) 67 Ll.L.R. 250 KBD 22–091

Layher Ltd v Lowe, 58 Con. L.R. 42; [2000] Lloyd's Rep. I.R. 510; (1997) 73 P. & C.R. D37; Times, January 8, 1997 CA (Civ Div) 20–041

Lazard Bros. v Brooks (1932) 38 Com. Cas. 46 23–021

Le Cheminant v Pearson (1812) 4 Taunt. 367 .... 24–058, 24–111

Le Feuvre v John Sullivan and Anne Sullivan, otherwise Anne Le Sueur. See William James Le Feuvre v John Sullivan and Anne Sullivan, otherwise Anne Le Sueur

Le Pypre v Farr (1716) 2 Vern. 516 4–002

Lea v Hinton (1854) 4 De G.M. & G. 823 18–020

Leaders Shoes (Australia) Pty Ltd v Liverpool & London 7 Globe Insurance Co Ltd [1968] 1 N.S.W.R. 279 24–066

Leathem v Terry (1803) 3 B. & P. 479 24–099

Leathley v Drummond; Leathley v Irving [1972] R.T.R. 293; [1972] Crim. L.R. 227 DC 22–002,
                                                                                          22–015
Leathley v Tatton [1980] R.T.R. 21 DC 22–009
Lebon & Co v Straits Insurance Co (1894) 10 T.L.R. 517 6–053
Ledingham v Ontario Hospital Serv'ices Commission, 46 D.L.R. (3d) 699 (1974) 11–017
Lee On Realty v Kwok Lai Cheong [1985] 2 H.K.C. 592 22–093
Lee v Abdy (1886) L.R. 17 Q.B.D. 309 14–030
Lee v Beach (1762) Park on Insurance 468 24–061
Lee v British Law Insurance Co [1972] 2 Lloyd's Rep. 49 CA (Civ Div) 18–029
Lee v Poole [1954] Crim. L.R. 942 DC 22–096
Lee v Southern Insurance Co (1870) L.R. 5 C.P. 397 24–112
Leeds v Cheetham (1827) 1 Sim. 146 .... 10–049, 14–021, 19–017, 19–020, 19–021
Leen v Hall (1923) 16 Ll.L.R. 100 KBD 6–065
Lees v Motor Insurers Bureau [1952] 2 All E.R. 511; [1952] 2 Lloyd's Rep. 210; [1952] 2
    T.L.R. 356; [1952] W.N. 409; 96 S.J. 548 QBD 22–009, 22–012, 22–017, 22–018
Lees v Whiteley (1866) L.R. 2 Eq. 143 .... 14–021, 19–021, 19–025, 19–026
Leete v Wallace (1888) 58 L.T. 577 15–033
Lefevre v Boyle (1832) 3 B. & Ad. 877 14–027
Lefevre v White [1990] 1 Lloyd's Rep. 569; Times, November 1, 1989 QBD 9–039, 10–022,
                                                        21–029, 21–030, 22–036, 22–093
Legal & General Assurance Society Ltd v Drake Insurance Co (t/a Drake Motor Policies at
    Lloyd's) [1992] Q.B. 887; [1992] 2 W.L.R. 157; [1992] 1 All E.R. 283; [1991] 2 Lloyd's
    Rep. 36; [1992] R.T.R. 162; (1992) 89(2) L.S.G. 30; Times, January 15, 1991; Financial
    Times, January 15, 1991CA (Civ Div); reversing [1989] 3 All E.R. 923 QBD 11–052,
                                                        11–059, 11–060, 22–036, 22–043
Legge v Byas, Mosely & Co (1901) 7 Com. Cas. 16 15–041
Leigh v Adams (1871) 25 L.T. 566 24–039
Lek v Mathews (1927–28) 29 Ll.L.R. 141 HL 9–026
Lemos v British & Foreign Marine Insurance Co Ltd (1931) 39 Ll.L.R. 275 KBD 9–025
Lennard's Carrying Co Ltd v Asiatic Petroleum Co Ltd [1915] A.C. 705 HL 5–046
Lens v Excess Insurance Co Ltd (1916) 32 T.L.R. 361 15–027
Leo Rapp Ltd v McClure [1955] 1 Lloyd's Rep. 292 QBD 3–008, 5–011, 19–044
Leo Steamship v Corderoy (1896) 1 Com.Cas. 300 17–002
Leon v Casey [1932] 2 K.B. 576; (1932) 43 Ll.L.R. 69 CA 6–107, 24–009
Leppard v Excess Insurance Co Ltd [1979] 1 W.L.R. 512; [1979] 2 All E.R. 668; [1979] 2
    Lloyd's Rep. 91; (1979) 250 E.G. 751; 122 S.J. 182 CA (Civ Div) 10–014, 10–041
Leroux v Brown (1852) 12 C.B. 801; 138 E.R. 1119 2–054
Les Affreteurs Reunis SA v Leopold Walford (London) Ltd; sub nom. Leopold Walford
    (LONDON) Ltd v Les Affreteurs Reunis SA [1919] A.C. 801 HL 14–006
Lester Bros (Coal Merchants) Ltd v Avon Insurance Co Ltd (1942) 72 Ll.L.R. 109 KBD 22–088,
                                                                                          22–089
Lester v Garland (1808) 15 Ves. 248 5–004
Letts v Excess Insurance (1916) 32 T.L.R. 361 1–018
Levinger v Licenses & General Insurance Co Ltd (1936) 54 Ll.L.R. 68 Ch D 4–017, 22–096
Levy v Assicurazione Generali [1940] A.C. 791; (1940) 67 Ll. L. Rep. 174 PC (Palestine) 25–009
Levy v Baillie (1831) 7 Bing. 349 9–026
Levy v Scottish Employers (1901) 17 T.L.R. 229 .... 1–052, 15–013
Levy & Co v Merchants Marine Insurance Co (1885) Cab. & Ell. 474 24–030
Lewis v Rucker (1761) 2 Burr. 1167 .... 1–009, 10–007
Lewis Emanuel & Son Ltd v Hepburn [1960] 1 Lloyd's Rep. 304 QBD (Comm) 10–019, 10–021,
                                                                                          25–016
Lewis v Norwich Union Healthcare Ltd [2010] Lloyd's Rep. I.R. 198 County Court (Central
    London) 6–028, 12–013, 15–036, 18–029
Lewis Ltd v Norwich Union Fire Insurance Co [1916] A.C. 509 8–001
Lexington Insurance Co v Multinacional de Seguros SA [2008] EWHC 1170 (Comm);
    [2009] 1 All E.R. (Comm) 35; [2009] Lloyd's Rep. I.R. 1 .... 6–090, 6–098, 7–018, 9–016,
                                                        9–018, 17–025, 20–044
Leyland Shipping Co Ltd v Norwich Union Fire Insurance Society Ltd [1918] A.C. 350 HL ... 5–029,
                                                        5–030, 5–032, 19–055
Liberian Insurance Agency Inc v Mosse [1977] 2 Lloyd's Rep. 560 QBD ... 6–090, 6–106, 6–107,
                                                        20–043, 24–035, 24–053
Liberty National Bank of New York v Bolton (1925) 21 Ll.L.R. 3 CA 23–022

Libyan Arab Foreign Bank v Bankers Trust Co [1989] Q.B. 728; [1989] 3 W.L.R. 314; [1989] 3 All E.R. 252; [1988] 1 Lloyd's Rep. 259; [1987] 2 F.T.L.R. 509; (1989) 133 S.J. 568 .... 2–044, 2–057, 2–058
Libyan Arab Foreign Bank v Manufacturers Hanover Trust (No.2) [1989] 1 Lloyd's Rep. 608 2–044
Lickiss v Milestone Motor Policies at Lloyd's. *See* Barrett Bros (Taxis) Ltd v Davies
Lidgett v Secretan (1869–70) L.R. 5 C.P. 190 CCP 5–015, 24–065
Lidgett v Secretan (No.2) (1870–71) L.R. 6 C.P. 616 CCP 24–111
Liesbosch, The; sub nom. Owner of the Liesbosch v Owners of the Edison; Liesbosch Dredger v SS Edison [1933] A.C. 449; [1933] All E.R. Rep. 144; (1933) 45 Ll.L.R. 123 HL 10–022, 15–047, 22–026
Life and Casualty Insurance Co of Tennessee v Brown, 95 Ga. App. 354 (1957) 18–059
Life Association of Scotland v Forster (1873) 11 M. (Ct. of Sess.) 351 ..... 6–013, 6–021, 17–012, 18–028, 18–029
Lim Trading Co v Haydon [1968] 1 Lloyd's Rep. 159; (1968) 118 N.L.J. 230 HC (Sing) 3–008, 19–049
Limbrick v French [1993] P.I.Q.R. P121 QBD 22–017, 22–032
Limit (No.3) Ltd v ACE Insurance Ltd [2009] N.S.W.S.C. 514 .... 11–057, 11–059, 11–060
Limit (No.2) Ltd v Axa Versicherung AG (formerly Albingia Versicherung AG) [2007] EWHC 2321 (Comm); [2007] 2 C.L.C. 610; [2008] Lloyd's Rep. I.R. 330; affirmed [2008] EWCA Civ 1231; [2008] 2 C.L.C. 673; [2009] Lloyd's Rep. I.R. 396; [2009] Bus. L.R. D41 ...... 6–008, 6–011, 6–105, 6–106, 6–117, 6–118, 7–003, 7–006, 7–009, 7–020, 8–017, 9–003, 15–036, 17–006, 17–007
Limit (No.3) Ltd v PDV Insurance Co Ltd [2005] EWCA Civ. 383; [2005] 2 All E.R. (Comm) 347; [2005] 1 C.L.C. 515; [2005] Lloyd's Rep. I.R. 552; Times, April 14, 2005 CA (Civ Div) 2–005, 2–007, 9–053
Lincoln Assurance Ltd, Re Unreported, 1996 .... 13–033, 13–036
Lincoln National Life Insurance Co v Employers Reinsurance Corp; Manufacturers Life Insurance Co v Employers Reinsurance Corp; American United Life Insurance Co v Employers Reinsurance Corp [2002] EWHC 28; [2002] Lloyd's Rep. I.R. 853 QBD (Comm) 2–004, 2–007, 2–043
Lincoln National Life Insurance Co v Sun Life Assurance Co of Canada; sub nom. Sun Life Assurance Co of Canada v Lincoln National Life Insurance Co [2004] EWCA Civ. 1660; [2006] 1 All E.R. (Comm) 675; [2005] 1 Lloyd's Rep. 606; [2005] 2 C.L.C. 664 CA (Civ Div) 17–018, 20–034
Lind v Mitchell (1928) 32 Ll.L.R. 70 CA 24–086, 24–112, 24–134
Lind v Mitchell (1928) 45 T.L.R. 54 24–003
Lind v Mitchell [1928] All E.R. 447 24–080
Linden Alimak v British Engine Insurance [1984] 1 Lloyd's Rep. 416; (1984) 134 N.L.J. 204 QBD 5–043, 5–049, 20–031
Lindenau v Deshorough (1828) 8 B. & C. 586 ..... 6–021, 6–031, 6–037, 18–020, 18–029, 18–031
Lindsay v Jamson (1859) 4 H. & N. 699 24–065
Lindsay & Pirie v General Accident Fire and Life Assurance Corporation Ltd (1914) S.A.R. (App. D.) 574 25–009
Lindsay Blee Depots Ltd v Motor Union Insurance Co Ltd; Motor Union Insurance Co Ltd v Provincial Insurance Co Ltd (1930) 37 Ll.L.R. 220 KBD 24–066
Linelevel Ltd v Powszechny Zaklad Ubezpieczen SA; The Nore Challenger [2005] EWHC 421; [2005] 2 Lloyd's Rep. 534 QBD (Comm) 19–014, 24–017, 24–112
Linford v Provincial Horse and Cattle Insurance Co (1864) 34 Beav. 291 ...... 1–051, 15–014, 15–015
Lion Mutual Marine Insurance Association v Tucker; sub nom. Lion Mutual Marine Insurance Association Ltd v Tucker (1883–84) L.R. 12 Q.B.D. 176; (1883) 32 W.R. 546CA 8–006, 24–007
Lipkin Gorman v Karpnale Ltd [1991] 2 A.C. 548; [1991] 3 W.L.R. 10; [1992] 4 All E.R. 512; (1991) 88(26) L.S.G. 31; (1991) 141 N.L.J. 815; (1991) 135 S.J.L.B. 36; Times, June 7, 1991; Independent, June 18, 1991; Financial Times, June 11, 1991; Guardian, June 13, 1991 HL 10–062
Liquidators of Glasgow Assurance Corp Ltd v Welsh Insurance Corp Ltd, 1914 S.C. 320; 1914 1 S.L.T. 139 IH (2 Div) 13–017, 17–002
Lishman v Northern Maritime Insurance Co (1875) L.R. 30 P. 179 .... 6–103, 6–106, 7–022
Lister v Romford Ice and Cold Storage Co Ltd; sub nom. Romford Ice & Cold Storage Co v Lister [1957] A.C. 555; [1957] 2 W.L.R. 158; [1957] 1 All E.R. 125; [1956] 2 Lloyd's Rep. 505; 121 J.P. 98; 101 S.J. 106 HL ... 11–013, 11–032, 20–001, 22–007, 22–030, 23–028
Litsion Pride, The. *See* Black King Shipping Corp v Massie

Liverpool & London War Risk v Ocean SS Co. *See* Ocean Steamship Co Ltd v Liverpool and
    London War Risks Association Ltd
Liverpool & London War Risks Insurance Association v Marine Underwriters of SS Richard
    de Larringa [1921] 2 A.C. 144 25–005
Liverpool, Brazil and River Plate Steam Navigation Co Ltd v Benham (The Halley) Halley,
    The (1867–69) L.R. 2 P.C. 193 PC (United Kingdom) 2–061
Liverpool Corp v Roberts (T and HR) (Garthwaite, Third Party) [1965] 1 W.L.R. 938; [1964]
    3 All E.R. 56; [1964] 2 Lloyd's Rep. 219; 109 S.J. 510, Assizes (Liverpool) 22–036, 22–093
Liverpool Starr-Bowkett Building Society v Travellers' Accident Insurance (1893) 9 T.L.R.
    221 23–028
Livie v Janson (1810) 12 East 648 24–111
Lloyd Instruments Ltd v Northern Star Insurance Co Ltd; The Miss Jay Jay. *See* JJ Lloyd
    Instruments v Northern Star Insurance Co
Lloyd v Fleming (1872) L.R. 7 Q.B. 299 14–025
Lloyd v Grace Smith & Co [1912] A.C. 716 HL 15–004, 23–023
Lloyd v Singleton [1953] 1 Q.B. 357; [1953] 2 W.L.R. 278; [1953] 1 All E.R. 291; (1953)
    117 J.P. 97; 51 L.G.R. 165; 97 S.J. 98; 97 S.J. 396 DC 22–010
Lloyd's Underwriters Association/Institute of London Underwriters [1993] O.J. L4/26 13–045
Lloyds Bank Ltd v Eagle Star Insurance Co Ltd [1951] 1 All E.R. 914; [1951] 1 Lloyd's Rep.
    385; [1951] 1 T.L.R. 803 KBD 18–036, 22–089, 22–090
Lloyds TSB General Insurance Holdings Ltd v Lloyds Bank Group Insurance Co Ltd [2001]
    Lloyd's Rep I.R. 237 5–029
Lloyds TSB General Insurance Holdings Ltd v Lloyds Bank Group Insurance Co Ltd [2001]
    EWCA Civ 1643; [2002] 1 All E.R. (Comm) 42; [2002] C.L.C. 287; [2002] Lloyd's
    Rep. I.R. 113; [2002] Lloyd's Rep. P.N. 211; [2001] Pens. L.R. 325 5–031
Lloyds TSB General Insurance Holdings Ltd v Lloyds Bank Group Insurance Co Ltd; Abbey
    National Plc v Lee [2003] UKHL 48; [2003] 4 All E.R. 43; [2003] 2 All E.R. (Comm)
    665; [2004] 1 C.L.C. 116; [2003] Lloyd's Rep. I.R. 623; [2003] Pens. L.R. 315; (2003)
    153 N.L.J. 1270; (2003) 147 S.J.L.B. 935 HL 10–036
Lloyd's v Harper (1880–81) L.R. 16 Ch. D. 290 CA 19–030
Lloyd-Wolper v Moore [2004] EWCA Civ. 766; [2004] 1 W.L.R. 2350; [2004] 3 All E.R.
    741; [2004] R.T.R. 30; [2004] Lloyd's Rep. I.R. 730; (2004) 148 S.J.L.B. 791; Times,
    August 6, 2004; Independent, June 24, 2004 CA (Civ Div) 22–010, 22–043
Lock v Leatherdale [1979] R.T.R. 201; [1979] Crim. L.R. 188 DC 22–007
Locker & Woolf Ltd v Western Australian Insurance Co Ltd (1935) 153 L.T. 334 6–053
Locker & Woolf Ltd v Western Australian Insurance Co Ltd [1936] 1 K.B. 408; (1936) 54
    Ll.L.R. 211 CA 6–045, 22–087
Lockwood v Moreira Unreported, 1998 Ontario CA 10–044
Lockyer v Offley (1786) 1 T.R. 252 .... 24–065, 24–138
Lofft v Dennis (1859) 28 L.J.Q.B. 168 19–017
Lo-Line Electric Motors Ltd, Re [1988] Ch. 477; [1988] 3 W.L.R. 26; [1988] 2 All E.R. 692;
    (1988) 4 B.C.C. 415; [1988] B.C.L.C. 698; [1988] P.C.C. 236; [1988] 2 F.T.L.R. 107;
    (1988) 138 N.L.J. Rep. 119; (1988) 132 S.J. 851; Times, April 7, 1988; Independent,
    April 20, 1988; Financial Times, April 27, 1988 Ch D 20–082
Lombard Australia v NRMA Insurance [1969] 1 Lloyd's Rep. 575 CA (NSW) .. 11–029, 14–003,
                                                                                  14–013, 23–001
Lombard Insurance Co Ltd v Kin Yuen Co Pte Ltd; The Pab, Lloyd's List, July 25, 1995
    (I.D.) CA (Sing) 24–047
London & Lancashire Fire v Bolands. *See* Bolands Ltd v London & Lancashire Fire
    Insurance Co Ltd
London & Lancaster v Graves (1883) 43 Am. Rep. 35 19–044
London & North West Railway Co v Glyn (1859) 1 El. & El. 652 ..... 4–005, 4–020, 19–011, 19–012,
                                                                         19–013, 19–030
London & Provincial Leather Processes Ltd v Hudson [1939] 2 K.B. 724; (1939) 64 Ll.L.R.
    352 KBD 10–001, 19–034
London & Scottish Assurance Corp Ltd v Ridd (1939) 65 Ll.L.R. 46 KBD 22–015
London and Lancashire Life Assurance Co v Fleming [1897] A.C. 499 PC (Can) 8–002, 15–014,
                                                                                    15–015
London and Manchester Plate Glass Co Ltd v Heath [1913] 3 K.B. 411 CA 7–020, 7–047, 9–015,
                                                                          10–054, 25–009, 25–010
London Assurance v Clare (1937) 57 Ll. L. Rep. 254 9–026
London Assurance Co v Johnson (1737) West t. Hard. 266; 25 E.R. 930 11–011
London Assurance Co v Mansel; sub nom. London Assurance v Mansel (1879) L.R. 11 Ch.
    D. 363 Ch D 1–011, 6–010, 6–021, 6–031, 6–053, 6–058, 8–022

London Assurance Co v Sainsbury (1783) 3 Doug. 245 11–011
London Chatham & Dover Railway Co v South Eastern Railway Co [1893] A.C. 429 HL 10–024
London County Commercial Reinsurance Office Ltd, Re [1922] 2 Ch. 67; (1922) 10 Ll.L.R.
    370 Ch D 1–019, 4–009, 8–031, 17–001, 17–004, 17–008, 24–009, 24–015
London Crystal Window Cleaning Co Ltd v National Indemnity Insurance Co Ltd [1952] 2
    Lloyd's Rep. 360 QBD 5–049
London General Insurance Co Ltd v General Marine Underwriters Association Ltd [1921] 1
    K.B. 104; (1920) 4 Ll.L.R. 382 CA 6–004, 6–065, 17–008
London Guarantie Co v Fearnley (1879–80) L.R. 5 App. Cas. 911 HL (UK-Irl) 7–013, 9–016,
                                                                                                             23–026
London Helicopters Ltd v Heliportugal LDA-INAC [2006] EWHC 108 (QB); [2006] 1 All
    E.R. (Comm) 595; [2006] 1 C.L.C. 297; [2006] I.L.Pr. 28 2–004
London Leather Processes v Hudson. See London & Provincial Leather Processes Ltd v
    Hudson
London Life Association, Re, Independent, February 27, 1989 (C.S.) Ch D 13–035
London Marine Insurance Association, Re (1869) L.R. 8 Eq. 176 24–007
London Steamship Owners Mutual Insurance Association Ltd v Bombay Trading Co Ltd;
    The Felicie [1990] 2 Lloyd's Rep. 21 (Note) QBD (Comm) 9–039, 11–004, 21–029, 21–030,
                                                                                                             21–062
London Tobacco Co (Overseas) Ltd v DFDS Transport Ltd; sub nom. London Tobacco Co
    (Overseas) v PBC [1994] 1 Lloyd's Rep. 394 CA (Civ Div) 5–010
Lonrho Exports Ltd v Export Credits Guarantee Department [1999] Ch. 158; [1998] 3 W.L.R.
    394; [1996] 4 All E.R. 673; [1996] 2 Lloyd's Rep. 649; [1997] C.L.C. 259 Ch D 11–022,
                                                                                                             23–032
Lonsdale & Thompson Ltd v Black Arrow Group Plc; sub nom. Lonsdale & Thompson Ltd
    v Black Arrow Group Plc and American International Underwriters UK Ltd [1993] Ch.
    361; [1993] 2 W.L.R. 815; [1993] 3 All E.R. 648; [1993] 2 Lloyd's Rep. 428; (1993) 65
    P. & C.R. 392; [1993] 25 E.G. 145; [1992] E.G.C.S. 154; Times, December 11, 1992 Ch
    D 4–016, 10–004, 10–051, 14–021
Looker v Law Union & Rock Insurance Co Ltd [1928] 1 K.B. 554 KBD 1–027, 1–028, 1–029,
                                                                                                             6–104, 8–004
Loraine v Thomlinson (1781) 2 Dougl. 585 3–005
Lothian v Henderson (1803) 3 B. & P. 499 24–058
Louden v British Merchants Insurance Co [1961] 1 W.L.R. 798; [1961] 1 All E.R. 705;
    [1961] 1 Lloyd's Rep. 154; 105 S.J. 209 QBD 18–030, 18–053, 22–036, 22–089
Louis Dreyfus & Cie v Parnaso Cia Naviera SA (The Dominator) [1960] 2 Q.B. 49; [1960]
    2 W.L.R. 637 CA; reversing [1959] 1 Q.B. 498; [1959] 2 W.L.R. 405; [1959] 1 All E.R.
    502; [1959] 1 Lloyd's Rep. 125; 103 S.J. 221 QBD (Comm) 3–017
Lovell v Accident Insurance (1875) 39 J.P.J. 293 18–050
Lovett v Worldwide (NZ) Ltd Unreported October 29, 2004 HC (NZ) 6–123
Lower Rhine and Wurtemberg Insurance Association v Sedgwick [1899] 1 Q.B. 179 CA ... 5–017,
                                                                                                             8–024, 17–012
Lowlands Steam Shipping Co Ltd v North of England Protecting and Indemnity Association
    (1921) 6 Ll.L.R. 230 KBD 1–019
Lownds v Home Office; sub nom. Home Office v Lownds; Lownds v Secretary of State for
    the Home Department [2002] EWCA Civ. 365; [2002] 1 W.L.R. 2450; [2002] 4 All E.R.
    775; [2002] C.P. Rep. 43; [2002] C.P.L.R. 328; [2002] 2 Costs L.R. 279; (2002) 99(19)
    L.S.G. 28; (2002) 146 S.J.L.B. 86; Times, April 5, 2002 CA (Civ Div) 23–035
Lowry v Bordieu (1780) 2 Doug K.B. 468 .... 4–009, 8–022, 18–011, 24–014
Loyaltrend Ltd v Creechurch Dedicated Ltd [2010] EWHC 425 (Comm) 5–015, 7–014, 9–006,
                                                                                                             9–011, 23–042
Lozano v Janson (1859) 2 E. & E. 160 25–012
Lubbe v Cape Plc (No.2); Afrika v Cape Plc (Stay of Proceedings) [2000] 1 W.L.R. 1545;
    [2000] 4 All E.R. 268; [2000] 2 Lloyd's Rep. 383; [2003] 1 C.L.C. 655; [2001] I.L.Pr.
    12; (2000) 144 S.J.L.B. 250 HL; reversing [2000] 1 Lloyd's Rep. 139; [2000] C.L.C. 45;
    [2000] I.L.Pr. 438; (1999) 96(48) L.S.G. 39; (2000) 144 S.J.L.B. 25; Times, December
    3, 1999 CA (Civ Div) 2–005
Lubbock v Potts (1806) 7 East 449 .... 8–022, 18–009, 24–064
Lucas (L) v Export Credits Guarantee Department [1974] 1 W.L.R. 909; [1974] 2 All E.R.
    889; [1974] 2 Lloyd's Rep. 69; 118 S.J. 461 HL 11–004, 23–032
Lucasfilm Ltd v Ainsworth [2009] EWCA Civ 1328; [2010] E.C.D.R. 6; [2010] E.M.L.R. 12;
    [2010] F.S.R. 10; (2010) 33(4) I.P.D. 33021; Times, January 4, 2010 2–008
Lucena v Craufurd (1806) 1 Taunt. 325 .... 4–023, 15–003, 24–017, 24–021

Lucena v Craufurd (1806) 2 Bos & P. 269 ...... 4–002, 4–013, 4–016, 4–017, 8–001, 10–007, 10–019,
10–021, 18–015, 23–021
Luckie v Bushby (1853) 13 C.B. 864 .... 9–038, 10–022
Luke v Lyde (1759) 2 Burr. 882 24–095
Lumbermans Mutual Casualty Co v Bovis Lend Lease Ltd (Preliminary Issues); sub nom.
    Lumbermens Mutual Casualty Co v Bovis Lend Lease Ltd (Preliminary Issues) [2004]
    EWHC 2197; [2005] 2 All E.R. (Comm) 669; [2005] 1 Lloyd's Rep. 494; [2005] 2
    C.L.C. 617; [2005] B.L.R. 47; 98 Con. L.R. 21; [2005] Lloyd's Rep. I.R. 74; [2004] 42
    E.G.C.S. 160 QBD (Comm) 17–019, 20–034, 20–059, 20–060, 20–077
Lynch v Dalzell (1729) 4 Bro. P.C. 431 .... 6–046, 8–020, 14–022, 14–024
Lynch v Dunsford (1811) 14 East 494 .... 6–036, 6–062, 24–035, 24–036
Lynch v Hamilton (1810) 3 Taunt. 15 6–062
Lynch v Hamilton (1810) 3 Taunt. 37 .... 6–032, 24–038
Lynne v Gordon Doctors & Walton (1991) 135 S.J.L.B. 29; Times, June 17, 1991 QBD ... 18–013
Lyons v JW Bentley Ltd (1944) 77 Ll.L.R. 335 KBD 6–051, 6–052, 15–036
Lyons v May [1948] 2 All E.R. 1062 KBD 22–010, 22–088
Lyons v Providence (1881) 43 Am.Rep. 32, 33 19–044
MCA Records Inc v Charly Records Ltd (No.5) [2001] EWCA Civ 1441; [2002] B.C.C. 650;
    [2003] 1 B.C.L.C. 93; [2002] E.C.D.R. 37; [2002] E.M.L.R. 1; [2002] F.S.R. 26;
    Independent, November 26, 2001 20–078
MDIS Ltd v Swinbank [1999] Lloyd's Rep. I.R. 516 20–025
MH Smith (Plant Hire) v DL Mainwaring (t/a Inshore) [1986] 2 Lloyd's Rep. 244; Times,
    June 10, 1986 CA (Civ Div) 11–011
MJ Harrington Syndicate 2000 v Axa Oyak Sigorta AS [2006] EWHC 112 QBD (Comm) 7–003,
7–029, 7–048, 17–006
MR Currie & Co v Bombay Native Insurance Co (1869–71) L.R. 3 P.C. 72 PC (Burma) 24–112
M/S Aswan Engineering Establishment Co Ltd v Iron Trades Mutual Insurance Co Ltd
    [1989] 1 Lloyd's Rep 289 .... 5–049, 20–009, 20–031
MW Wilson (Lace) Ltd v Eagle Star Insurance Co Ltd 1993 S.L.T. 938 IH (Div 2) 19–042
MWH International Inc v Lumbermens Mutual Casualty Co [2007] B.C.J. No.559 20–047
M'Farlane v Royal London Friendly Society (1886) 2 T.L.R. 755 .... 4–004, 18–005, 18–022
M'Millan v Accident Insurance Co. See McMillan v Accident Insurance Co Ltd
Mabey & Johnson Ltd v Ecclesiastical Insurance Office Plc [2000] C.L.C. 1570; [2001]
    Lloyd's Rep. I.R. 369 QBD (Comm) 10–032
Mabey & Johnson Ltd v Ecclesiastical Insurance Office Plc (No.2) [2003] Lloyd's Rep I.R.
    10 10–036
Mac, The (1882) L.R. 7 P.D. 126 CA 24–006
M'Allester v Haden (1810) 1 Samp. 438 4–002
McAll v Brooks [1984] R.T.R. 99 CA (Civ Div) 11–016, 22–024
McAllister v Society of Lloyd's. See Debtors (Nos.4449 and 4450 of 1998), Re
McAndrew v Bell (1795) 1 Esp. 373 24–037
Macaura v Northern Assurance Co Ltd [1925] A.C. 619 HL 4–014, 18–020, 19–014, 19–029
Macbeth & Co Ltd v Maritime Insurance Co Ltd [1908] A.C. 144 HL 24–086
McBlain v Dolan, 1998 S.L.T. 512; [2001] Lloyd's Rep. I.R. 309 OH 22–045
McCall v Poulton [2008] EWCA Civ 1313; [2009] C.P. Rep. 15; [2009] R.T.R. 11; [2009]
    1 C.M.L.R. 45; [2009] Eu. L.R. 383; [2009] Lloyd's Rep. I.R. 454; [2009] P.I.Q.R.
    P8 .... 22–024, 22–059, 22–062, 22–064
M'Carthy v Abel (1804) 5 East 388 .... 24–095, 24–097
McCarthy v British Oak Insurance Co Ltd (1938) 61 Ll.L.R. 194; [1938] 3 All E.R. 1 KBD ... 22–097
McCarthy v FF Dixon & Co (London) Ltd (1924) 19 Ll.L.R. 58 KBD 15–041
McCarthy v St Paul International Insurance Co Ltd [2007] F.C.A.F.C. 28 20–052
McClure v Girard Fire (1876) 22 Am.Rep. 249 19–044
McClure v Lancashire Insurance (1860) 13 Ir.Jur. 63 19–044
Maccoll & Pollock Ltd v Indemnity Mutual Marine Assurance Co Ltd (1930) 38 Ll.L.R. 79
    KBD 24–003
McCormick v National Motor & Accident Insurance Union (1934) 40 Com.Cas. 76 .... 6–048, 6–070,
6–093, 7–019, 20–044, 20–062, 21–021, 22–015
M'Culloch v Royal Exchange (1813) 3 Camp. 406 8–031
MacDonald v Carmichael (Alister McPherson) 8963; sub nom. McDonald v Carmichael
    (Alister McPherson); Orr v Carmichael (Alister McPherson), 1941 J.C. 27; 1940 S.N.
    83; 1941 S.L.T. 81 HCJ Appeal 22–006
MacDonald v Howdle, 1995 S.L.T. 779; 1995 S.C.C.R. 216 HCJ Appeal 22–010
Macdonald v Law Union Fire & Life Insurance Co (1873–74) L.R. 9 Q.B. 328 QB 18–028

Macdonald v National Mutual Life Association of Australasia Ltd (1906) 14 S.L.T. 173
OH 18–005
McDonnell v Beacon Fire (1857) 7 U.C.C.P. 308 6–058
Macdowall v Fraser (1779) 1 Doug K.B. 260 .... 7–022, 24–037
McEacham, Re (1911) 103 L.T. 900 19–031
McEwan v Guthridge (1860) 13 Moo. P.C.C. 304 19–039
McGeown v Direct Travel Insurance; sub nom. Direct Travel Insurance v McGeown [2003]
EWCA Civ. 1606; [2004] 1 All E.R. (Comm) 609; [2004] Lloyd's Rep. I.R. 599; (2003)
147 S.J.L.B. 1365; Times, November 27, 2003 CA (Civ Div) 3–006, 3–010, 18–054
McGinn v Insurance Corporation of Ireland, 73 D.L.R. (4th) 193 (1991) CA (Alberta) 6–053
McGoona v Motor Insurers Bureau [1969] 2 Lloyd's Rep. 34 QBD 22–045, 22–097, 22–098
McGowan & Co v Dyer (1872–73) L.R. 8 Q.B. 141 QBD 15–004
McGowin Lumber & Export Co Inc v Pacific Marine Insurance Co (1922) 12 Ll.L.R. 496
KBD 15–041
McGrath v Riddell [2008] UKHL 21; [2008] 1 W.L.R. 852; [2008] Bus. L.R. 905; [2008] 3
All E.R. 869; [2008] B.C.C. 349; [2008] B.P.I.R. 581; [2008] Lloyd's Rep. I.R. 756;
(2008) 105(16) L.S.G. 26; (2008) 152(16) S.J.L.B. 30; Times, April 11, 2008 16–001
McGregor v Prudential Insurance Co Ltd [1998] 1 Lloyd's Rep. 112 QBD 9–025
McGurk & Dale v Coster [1995] 10 C.L. 521 CC (Southport) 22–007
McInnes v National Motor and Accident Insurance, Ltd; sub nom. Victor McInnes v National
Motor and Accident Insurance Union Ltd [1963] 2 Lloyd's Rep. 415; 1963 S.L.T. (Sh.
Ct.) 52; (1963) 79 Sh. Ct. Rep. 148, Sh Ct (Glasgow) 22–093
McIntosh v Royal & Sun Alliance 2007 F.C. 23 7–034
McKay v Eagle Star & British Dominions Insurance Co (1879) 18 M.C.R. (N.Z.) 83 14–022
Mackay v London General Insurance Co Ltd (1935) 51 Ll.L.R. 201KBD ... 6–048, 6–053, 22–087
Mackender v Feldia AG; sub nom. Mackenda v Feldia [1967] 2 Q.B. 590; [1967] 2 W.L.R.
119; [1966] 3 All E.R. 847; [1966] 2 Lloyd's Rep. 449; (1966) 110 S.J. 811; Times,
October 19, 1966 CA 2–005, 2–051, 2–057
Mckenna v City Life Assurance Co [1919] 2 K.B. 491 KBD 8–009
Mackenzie v Coulson (1869) L.R. 8 Eq. 368 .... 1–018, 6–001
Mackenzie v Whitworth (1875) 1 Ex. D. 36 .... 6–047, 10–021, 17–004, 24–048
Mackie v European Assurance (1869) 21 L.T. 102 .... 1–052, 1–054, 15–001, 15–004, 15–015
Mackintosh v Marshall (1843) 11 M. & W. 116 6–065
McKnight v Davies [1974] R.T.R. 4; [1974] Crim. L.R. 62; (1973) 117 S.J. 940 DC 19–050,
                                                                                                22–041
MaClay, Re, Independent, October 14, 1991 (C.S) QBD 22–015
McLean Enterprises v Ecclesiastical Insurance Office [1986] 2 Lloyd's Rep. 416 QBD 10–014,
                                                                                        10–027, 10–049
Maclean v McCabe (Patrick John), 1964 S.L.T. (Sh. Ct.) 39; [1965] Crim. L.R. 241, Sh Ct
(Tayside) 22–006
McLellan v Fletcher (1987) 137 N.L.J. 593; (1987) 3 P.N. 202; Times, June 3, 1987 18–013
Maclenan v Segar [1917] 2 K.B. 325 KBD 18–049
McLennan v Segar. See Maclenan v Segar
MacLeod Ross & Co v Compagnie d'Assurances Generales l'Helvetia of St Gall [1952] 1 All
E.R. 331; [1952] 1 Lloyd's Rep. 12; [1952] 1 T.L.R. 314; [1952] W.N. 56; 96 S.J. 90
CA 19–007
McLeod v Buchanan [1940] 2 All E.R. 179 .... 22–010, 22–012
McLoughlin v O'Brian [1983] 1 A.C. 410; [1982] 2 W.L.R. 982; [1982] 2 All E.R. 298;
[1982] R.T.R. 209; (1982) 79 L.S.G. 922; 126 S.J. 347 HL 18–059
McMahon v AGF Holdings (UK) Ltd; National Employers Mutual General Insurance
Association Ltd v AGF Holdings (UK) Ltd [1997] L.R.L.R. 159; [1997] 2 B.C.L.C. 191
Ch D (Companies Ct) 17–002
McMaster v New York, 183 U.S. 25, 35 (1901) 1–048
MacMillan Bloedel Ltd v Youell (1993) 95 B.C.L.C. (2d) 130 10–038
McMillan v Accident Insurance Co Ltd, 1907 S.C. 484; (1907) 14 S.L.T. 710 IH (2 Div) 15–001,
                                                                                                    15–013, 15–019
McMinn v McMinn [2006] EWHC 827; [2006] 3 All E.R. 87; Times, May 2, 2006 QBD 19–050,
                                                                                                    22–041
McNaghten's Case (1843) 10 Cl. & F. 200; 8 E.R. 718 HL 5–041
McNealy v Pennine Insurance Co [1978] 2 Lloyd's Rep. 18; [1978] R.T.R. 285; 122 S.J. 229
CA (Civ Div) 15–034, 18–031, 22–087
McNeil v Law Union & Rock Insurance Co Ltd (1925) 23 Ll.L.R. 314KBD 15–033
McNiel Riley & Coulson v Steamship Mutual Underwriting Association Ltd (1940) 67
Ll.L.R. 142 KBD 15–033

MacRobbie v Accident Assurance (1886) 23 S.L.R. 391 18–053
MacShannon v Rockware Glass Ltd; Fyfe v Redpath Dorman Long Ltd; Jardine v British
    Steel Corp; Paterson v Stone Manganese Marine Ltd [1978] A.C. 795; [1978] 2 W.L.R.
    362; [1978] 1 All E.R. 625; 122 S.J. 81 HL 2–005
Madby v Gresham Life (1861) 29 Beav. 439 8–019
Magee v Pennine Insurance Co [1969] 2 Q.B. 507; [1969] 2 W.L.R. 1278; [1969] 2 All E.R.
    891; [1969] 2 Lloyd's Rep. 378; 113 S.J. 303 CA (Civ Div) 10–057
Magellan Pirates, The (1853) 1 Ecc. & Ad. 81, 84 24–135
Magnus v Buttemer (1852) 11 C.B. 876 24–134
Maharanee Seethadevi Gaekwar of Baroda v Wildenstein [1972] 2 Q.B. 283; [1972] 2 W.L.R.
    1077; [1972] 2 All E.R. 689; 116 S.J. 221 CA (Civ Div) 2–003
Maher v Groupama Grand Est [2009] EWCA Civ 1191; [2010] 2 All E.R. 455; [2009] 2
    C.L.C. 852; [2010] R.T.R. 10 .. 2–014, 2–026, 2–054, 2–059, 2–062, 2–065, 21–047, 22–085
Mahli v Abbey Life Assurance Co Ltd; sub nom. Malhi v Abbey Life Assurance Co [1996]
    L.R.L.R. 237; [1994] C.L.C. 615; [1995] 4 Re. L.R. 305; Times, June 2, 1994;
    Independent, July 4, 1994 (C.S.) CA (Civ Div) 6–065, 6–095, 15–017
Mahonia Ltd v JP Morgan Chase Bank (No.1) [2003] EWHC 1927; [2003] 2 Lloyd's Rep.
    911 QBD (Comm) 2–057
Maignen & Co v National Benefit Assurance Co (1922) 10 Ll.L.R. 30 KBD 1–019, 24–081
Mailet v Halifax Insurance ING Canada [2003] N.B.J. No.5 20–050
Main, The [1894] P. 320 PDAD 10–009
Mair v Railway Passengers Assurance (1877) 37 L.T. 356 .... 3–006, 18–030, 18–053, 22–089
Makedonia, The. See Owners of Cargo Lately Laden on Board the Makedonia v Owners of
    the Makedonia
Malik v Moneywise Investments Plc [2009] Lloyd's Rep. I.R. 141 15–036
Mallough v Barber (1815) 4 Cowp. 150 15–034
Mamidoil-Jetoil Greek Petroleum Co SA v Okta Crude Oil Refinery AD (No.1) [2001]
    EWCA Civ. 406; [2001] 2 All E.R. (Comm) 193; [2001] 2 Lloyd's Rep. 76 CA (Civ
    Div) 8–008
Man v Shiffner & Ellis (1802) 2 East 523 14–027
Manby v Gresham Life Assurance Co (1861) 4 L.T. 347 9–019
Manchester Liners Ltd v British and Foreign Marine Insurance Co (1901) 7 Com.Cas. 26 24–080
Mander v Commercial Union Assurance Co Plc; Mander v Prudential Assurance Co Ltd;
    Mander v Gyngell Dobinson Gregory Co Ltd [1998] Lloyd's Rep. I.R. 93 QBD
    (Comm) 1–040, 6–101, 6–118, 6–120, 15–059, 17–006, 17–007
Mander v Equitas Ltd [2000] C.L.C. 901; [2000] Lloyd's Rep. I.R. 520 QBD (Comm) 3–013
Mandrake Holdings Ltd v Countrywide Assured Group Plc [2005] EWCA Civ. 840 CA (Civ
    Div); affirming [2005] EWHC 311 Ch D 10–022
Manfield v Maitland (1821) 4 B. & Ald. 582 .... 24–017, 24–026
Manfredi v Lloyd Adriatico Assicurazioni SpA (C–295/04) [2007] Bus. L.R. 188; [2007] All
    E.R. (EC) 27; [2006] E.C.R. I–6619; [2007] R.T.R. 7; [2006] 5 C.M.L.R. 17 ECJ 13–045
Manifest Shipping Co Ltd v Uni-Polaris Insurance Co Ltd (The Star Sea); sub nom. Manifest
    Shipping Co Ltd v Uni-Polaris Shipping Co Ltd; The Star Sea [2001] UKHL 1; [2003]
    1 A.C. 469; [2001] 2 W.L.R. 170; [2001] 1 All E.R. 743; [2001] 1 All E.R. (Comm) 193;
    [2001] 1 Lloyd's Rep. 389; [2001] C.L.C. 608; [2001] Lloyd's Rep. I.R. 247; Times,
    January 23, 2001 HL 6–001, 6–079, 6–106, 6–107, 6–108, 6–109, 6–110, 6–112, 6–114,
                                    6–115, 6–125, 6–130, 9–021, 9–024, 9–032, 9–033, 23–001, 24–062,
                                    24–078
Mann Macneal & Steeves Ltd v Capital & Counties Insurance Co Ltd; Mann Macneal &
    Steeves Ltd v General Marine Underwriters Association Ltd [1921] 2 K.B. 300; (1920)
    5 Ll.L.R. 424 CA 6–073
Mann v Coutts & Co [2003] EWHC 2138; [2004] 1 All E.R. (Comm) 1; [2004] 1 C.L.C.
    301QBD (Comm) 15–020
Mann v Forester (1814) 4 Camp 60 24–078
Mann v Lexington Insurance Co [2001] 1 All E.R. (Comm) 28; [2001] 1 Lloyd's Rep. 1;
    [2000] C.L.C. 1409; [2001] Lloyd's Rep. I.R. 179; Times, November 29, 2000; Daily
    Telegraph, October 24, 2000 CA (Civ Div) 10–034, 17–014
Manning v Society of Lloyd's; sub nom. Society of Lloyd's v Colfox; Philips v Society of
    Lloyd's [1997] C.L.C. 1411; [1998] Lloyd's Rep. I.R. 186 QBD (Comm) 13–042
Mans v London Assurance (1935) 52 Ll. L.R. 211 9–025
Maple Leaf Macro Volatility Master Fund v Rouvroy [2009] EWHC 257 (Comm); [2009] 2
    All E.R. (Comm) 287; [2009] 1 Lloyd's Rep. 475 2–003

Marc Rich & Co AG v Portman; sub nom. Glencore International AG v Portman [1997] 1
    Lloyd's Rep. 225 CA (Civ Div); affirming [1996] 1 Lloyd's Rep. 430; Lloyd's List,
    February 21, 1996 (I.D.) QBD (Comm) 6–028, 6–029, 6–045, 6–052, 6–065, 6–072, 6–073,
                                                                            11–041, 24–037
Marc Rich & Co AG v Societa Italiana Impianti pA (The Atlantic Emperor) (No.1) [1989]
    1 Lloyd's Rep. 548; [1991] I.L.Pr. 562 CA (Civ Div) 2–052
Marc Rich Agriculture Trading SA v Fortis Corporate Insurance NV [2004] EWHC 2632;
    [2005] Lloyd's Rep. I.R. 396 QBD (Comm) 9–029, 9–032, 24–112
Marcel Beller Ltd v Hayden [1978] Q.B. 694; [1978] 2 W.L.R. 845; [1978] 3 All E.R. 111;
    [1978] 1 Lloyd's Rep. 472; [1978] R.T.R. 344; 122 S.J. 279 QBD 5–042, 5–043, 18–035,
                                                                18–049, 20–031, 22–090
March (Earl of) v Pigot (1771) 5 Burr. 2802 4–002
March Cabaret Club & Casino v London Assurance; March Cabaret Club & Casino v
    Thompson & Bryan [1975] 1 Lloyd's Rep. 169 QBD 6–001, 6–021, 6–048, 6–049, 6–050
Marconi Communications International Ltd v PT Pan Indonesia Bank TBK [2004] EWHC
    129 (Comm); [2004] 1 Lloyd's Rep. 594; [2004] 2 C.L.C. 570 .... 2–043, 2–051
Mardorf v Accident Insurance Co [1903] 1 K.B. 584 KBD ... 5–030, 5–031, 18–041, 18–046, 18–059
Margate Theatre Royal Trust Ltd v White (t/a A1 Moleing Services) [2005] EWHC 2171;
    [2006] Lloyd's Rep. I.R. 93 QBD (TCC) 3–005, 8–001, 12–013
Margetts and Ocean Accident & Guarantee Corp Ltd's Arbitration, Re [1901] 2 K.B. 792
    KBD 24–006
Marina Offshore Pte Ltd v China Insurance Co (Singapore) Pte Ltd [2006] S.G.C.A. 28;
    [2007] 1 Lloyd's Rep. 66; [2007] Lloyd's Rep. I.R. 383 CA (Singapore) 7–025, 24–134
Marine Insurance Co Ltd v Grimmer [1944] 2 All E.R. 197 .... 1–031, 24–020
Maritime Insurance Co v Alianza Insurance Co of Santander (1907) 13 Com.Cas. 46 24–047
Maritime Insurance Co v Stearns [1901] 2 K.B. 912 KBD 17–012, 24–065
Mark Rowlands Ltd v Berni Inns Ltd [1986] Q.B. 211; [1985] 3 W.L.R. 964; [1985] 3 All
    E.R. 473; [1985] 2 Lloyd's Rep. 437; [1985] 2 E.G.L.R. 92; (1985) 276 E.G. 191 CA
    (Civ Div) ... 1–014, 4–003, 11–032, 14–010, 18–007, 19–002, 19–005, 19–017, 20–062, 22–027
Mark v West Yorkshire Insurance Co [1989] 10 C.L. 224 6–005
Markel Capital Ltd v Gothaer Allgemeine Versicherung AG [2008] EWHC 2517 (Comm);
    [2009] Lloyd's Rep. I.R. 433 15–024
Markel International Co Ltd v Craft (The Norseman) Norseman, The [2006] EWHC 3150
    (Comm); [2007] Lloyd's Rep. I.R. 403 2–006
Markel International Insurance Co Ltd v La Republica Compania Argentina de Seguros
    Generales SA [2004] EWHC 1826; [2005] Lloyd's Rep. I.R. 90 QBD (Comm) 2–005, 6–055,
                                                                6–060, 17–007
Markel International Insurance Co Ltd v Surety Guarantee Consultants Ltd [2008] EWHC
    1135 (Comm); [2009] Lloyd's Rep. I.R. 77 15–022
Markel International Insurance Co Ltd v Surety Guarantee Consultants Ltd [2009] EWCA
    Civ 790 15–022
Markham General Insurance Co v Bennett 81 O.R. (3d) 389 (2006) 20–087
Markovitch v Liverpool Victoria Friend Society (1912) 28 T.L.R. 188 6–073
Marles v Philip Trant & Sons Ltd (No.2) [1954] 1 Q.B. 29; [1953] 2 W.L.R. 564; [1953] 1
    All E.R. 651; 97 S.J. 189 CA 5–039
Marmion v Johnston (1928) 31 Ll.L.R. 78 Assizes (Liverpool) 24–134
Marryat v Wilson (1799) 1 Bos. & P. 430 24–064
Marsden v City & County Assurance Co (1865) L.R. 1 C.P. 232 ..... 5–029, 5–030, 9–013, 9–015,
                                                                15–017
Marsden v Reid (1803) 3 East 572 .... 3–004, 6–116, 24–071
Marsh v Moores [1949] 2 K.B. 208; [1949] 2 All E.R. 27; 65 T.L.R. 318; 113 J.P. 346; 47
    L.G.R. 418; [1949] L.J.R. 1313; 93 S.J. 450 KBD 22–009, 22–010, 22–088
Marshall and Scottish Employers Liability Co (1901) 85 L.T. 757 .... 6–011, 6–023, 6–058, 6–105,
                                                                18–002
Marshall Bros v Furness, Withy & Co (1924) 18 Ll.L.R. 514 25–005
Marshall v Emperor Life Assurance Society (1865–66) L.R. 1 Q.B. 35 QB 7–044
Marstrand Fishing Co Ltd v Beer (The Girl Pat) (1936) 56 Ll.L.R. 163 KBD 24–083, 24–086,
                                                                24–138
Marten v Nippon Sea and Land Insurance Co Ltd (1898) 3 Com.Cas. 164 17–012
Marten v Vestey Bros Ltd [1920] A.C. 307; (1920) 2 Ll.L.R. 113 HL 24–065, 24–066, 24–071
Martin v Dean [1971] 2 Q.B. 208; [1971] 2 W.L.R. 1159; [1971] 3 All E.R. 279; [1971]
    R.T.R. 280; 115 S.J. 369 QBD 22–012

Martin v Lancashire CC; Bernadone v Pall Mall Services Group Ltd; Haringey Healthcare
    NHS Trust v Independent Insurance Ltd [2000] 3 All E.R. 544; [2001] I.C.R. 197;
    [2000] I.R.L.R. 487; [2000] Lloyd's Rep. I.R. 665; (2000) 2 L.G.L.R. 1026; (2000)
    97(24) L.S.G. 39; Times, May 26, 2000 CA (Civ Div) 20–073
Martin v Redshaw, 65 D.L.R. (4th) 476 (1990) 22–006
Martin v Sitwell (1691) 1 Show. 156 .... 4–002, 8–029
Martin v Stanborough (1924) 41 T.L.R. 1 22–095
Martin v Travellers' Insurance Co (1859) 1 F. & F. 505 18–041
Martin Maritime Ltd v Provident Capital Indemnity Fund Ltd; The Lydia Flag [1998] 2
    Lloyd's Rep. 652 QBD (Comm) 24–003, 24–062
Martineau v Kitching (1862) L.R. 7 Q.B. 436 .... 19–007, 19–013
Martini Investments v McGuin; sub nom. Martini Investments v McGinn [2000] 2 Lloyd's
    Rep. 313; [2001] Lloyd's Rep. I.R. 374 QBD (Comm) 5–015, 5–030, 5–033, 19–041
Marubeni Hong Kong and South China Ltd v Mongolia (Jurisdiction) [2002] 2 All E.R.
    (Comm) 873; Independent, November 25, 2002 .... 2–036, 2–052
Maryland, The (1921) 9 Ll.L.R. 208 25–005
Marzouca v Atlantic and British Commercial Insurance Co [1971] 1 Lloyd's Rep. 449 PC
    (Jam) 19–047
Masefield AG v Amlin Corporate Member Ltd Bunga Melari Dua, The [2010] EWHC 280
    (Comm); [2010] 2 All E.R. 593; [2010] 1 All E.R. (Comm) 1067; [2010] 1 Lloyd's Rep.
    509; (2010) 160 N.L.J. 312 .... 5–015, 10–001, 24–063, 24–083, 24–086, 24–112, 24–135,
                                                                                24–136
Mason v Harvey (1853) 8 East 819 .... 9–003, 9–017
Mason v Sainsbury (1782) 3 Doug. 61 .... 11–001, 11–067
Masri v Consolidated Contractors International (UK) Ltd; sub nom. Masri v Consolidated
    Contractors Group SAL [2005] EWCA Civ. 1436; [2006] 1 W.L.R. 830 CA (Civ Div);
    affirming [2005] EWHC 944; [2005] 1 C.L.C. 1125 QBD (Comm) 2–004
Massmutual Asia Ltd v Leung Kwok Key [2004] H.K.E.C. 517 15–008
Mastin v Blanchard [1995] 9 CL. 355; [1995] C.L.Y. 3727 CC (Mold) 22–057, 22–062
Matadeen v Caribbean Insurance Co Ltd [2002] UKPC 69; [2003] 1 W.L.R. 670; Times,
    January 20, 2003 PC (Trin) 21–030
Matalan Discount Club (Cash & Carry) Ltd v Tokenspire Properties (North Western) Ltd;
    Richmond Cladding Systems Ltd v Parmenter Unreported May 18, 2001 QBD (TCC) 5–049,
                                                          5–050, 11–028, 11–030, 20–011
Mathie v Argonaut Marine Insurance Co Ltd (1925) 21 Ll.L.R. 145 HL 6–058, 11–044
Matthey v Curling; sub nom. Curling v Matthey [1922] 2 A.C. 180 HL 19–009, 19–020
Mattocks v Mann [1993] R.T.R. 13; Times, June 19, 1992 CA (Civ Div) 22–024
Matvieff v Crossfield (1903) 8 Com. Cas. 120 15–041
Maulder v National Insurance Co of New Zealand [1993] 2 N.Z.L.R. 351 14–013
Maurice v Goldsborough Mort & Co Ltd [1939] A.C. 452; (1939) 64 Ll.L.R. 1 PC (Aus) 4–005,
                                                      10–009, 10–019, 10–021, 19–010
Mauritius Oil Refineries Ltd v Stolt-Nielsen Nederlands BV (The Stolt Sydness) Stolt
    Sydness, The [1997] 1 Lloyd's Rep. 273; [1997] C.L.C. 417 2–035
Maxwell v Price [1960] 2 Lloyd's Rep. 155 HC (Aus) 14–022
May v DPP [2005] EWHC 1280 QBD (Admin) 22–007
May & Butcher Ltd v King, The [1934] 2 K.B. 17; [1929] All E.R. Rep. 679 HL 8–008
Mayall v Mitford (1837) 6 Ad. & El. 670 7–038
Mayban General Assurance BHD v Alstom Power Plants Ltd [2004] EWHC 1038; [2004] 2
    Lloyd's Rep. 609; [2004] 2 C.L.C. 682; [2005] Lloyd's Rep. I.R. 18QBD (Comm) 24–080,
                                                                                24–134
Maydew v Forrester (1815) Holt. 80 15–036
Maydhew v Scott (1811) 3 Camp. 205 7–022
Maynard v Rhode (1824) 1 C. & P. 360 18–029
Mayne v Walter (1787) 3 Dougl. 79 6–004
Mayne Nickless v Pegler [1974] 1 N.S.W.L.R. 228 .... 1–051, 1–053
Mazarakis Bros v Furness Withy & Co (1924) 18 Ll.L.R. 152CA; affirming (1923–24) 17
    Ll.L.R. 113 KBD 25–004, 25–005
Mead v Davidson (1835) 3 Ad. & El. 303 24–020
Meadows Indemnity Co Ltd v Insurance Corp of Ireland Plc; sub nom. Meadows Indemnity
    Co Ltd v International Commercial Bank Plc [1989] 2 Lloyd's Rep. 298; Times, May
    23, 1989 CA (Civ Div) 2–005, 2–007, 9–053
Medical Defence Union Ltd v Department of Trade [1980] Ch. 82; [1979] 2 W.L.R. 686;
    [1979] 2 All E.R. 421; [1979] 1 Lloyd's Rep. 499; [1979] E.C.C. 101; 123 S.J. 338Ch
    D 1–006, 1–007, 13–011, 21–020, 24–007

Medical Mutual Insurance Co of Maine v Indian Harbor Insurance Co 2009 B.L. 219379 (1st
　　Cir, October 8, 2009) 20–080
Mehnaz v Sabre Insurance Co Ltd [2007] EWCA Civ 1525 10–028
Melik (Victor) & Co v Norwich Union Fire Insurance Society and Kemp [1980] 1 Lloyd's
　　Rep. 523 QBD 7–032, 7–048, 19–048
Mentz Decker & Co v Maritime Insurance Co [1910] 1 K.B. 132 KBD 24–053, 24–073, 24–138
Menzies v North British (1847) 9 D. (Ct. of Sess.) 694 10–021
The Mercandian Continent, The. See K/S Merc-Skandia XXXXII v Certain Lloyd's
　　Underwriters (The Mercandian Continent)
Mercantile and General Reinsurance Co Plc v London Assurance Unreported, 1989 11–011
Mercantile Marine Insurance Co v Titherington (1864) 5 B. & S. 765 .... 3–011, 24–065
Mercantile Mutual Holdings Ltd v Territory Insurance Office [1989] 5 A.N.Z. Cases
　　60.939 15–020
Mercantile Steamship Co Ltd v Tyser (1880–81) L.R. 7 Q.B.D. 73 QBD 6–045, 24–080
Mercers of the City of London v New Hampshire Insurance Co. See Wardens and
　　Commonalty of the Mystery of Mercers of the City of London v New Hampshire
　　Insurance Co Ltd
Merchants & Manufacturers Insurance Co Ltd v Davies [1938] 1 K.B. 196; (1937) 58 Ll.L.R.
　　61CA 22–048
Merchants & Manufacturers Insurance Co Ltd v Hunt (Charles & John (An Infant)) [1941]
　　1 K.B. 295; (1940) 68 Ll.L.R. 117CA 6–001, 6–013, 6–074, 22–048
Merchants Marine Insurance Co Ltd v Liverpool Marine & General Insurance Co Ltd (1928)
　　31 Ll.L.R. 45 CA 5–031, 17–019
Merchants Marine Insurance Co Ltd v North of England Protecting and Indemnity
　　Association (1926) 26 Ll.L.R. 201CA 24–006
Mercury Communications Ltd v Communication Telesystems International [1999] 2 All E.R.
　　(Comm) 33; [1999] Masons C.L.R. 358 QBD (Comm) 2–005
Meridian Global Funds Management Asia Ltd v Securities Commission [1995] 2 A.C. 500;
　　[1995] 3 W.L.R. 413; [1995] 3 All E.R. 918; [1995] B.C.C. 942; [1995] 2 B.C.L.C. 116;
　　(1995) 92(28) L.S.G. 39; (1995) 139 S.J.L.B. 152; Times, June 29, 1995 PC (NZ) 5–046,
　　　　　　　　　　　　　　　　　　　　　　　　　　　　　　　　　　6–038, 20–040
Merino v Mutual Life (1904) 21 T.L.R. 167 8–026
Merrett v Capitol Indemnity Corp [1991] 1 Lloyd's Rep. 169 QBD (Comm) 11–036, 15–041
Merrill Lynch International Bank Ltd (formerly Merrill Lynch Capital Markets Bank Ltd) v
　　Winterthur Swiss Insurance Co [2007] EWHC 893 (Comm); [2007] 2 All E.R. (Comm)
　　846; [2007] 1 C.L.C. 671; [2008] B.P.I.R. 129; [2007] Lloyd's Rep. I.R. 532 ..... 9–009, 10–027,
　　　　　　　　　　　　　　　　　　　　　　　　　　　　　　　　　　　　23–029
Metal Box Ltd v Currys Ltd [1988] 1 W.L.R. 175; [1988] 1 All E.R. 341; (1987) 84 L.S.G.
　　3657; (1988) 132 S.J. 52 QBD 11–022
Metal Scrap & By Products Ltd v Federated Conveyors Ltd, and Tribble (Third Party) [1953]
　　1 Lloyd's Rep. 221 QBD 5–011
Metcalfe v Perry (1814) 4 Camp. 123 24–071
Metropolitan Life v Madden (1941) 117 Fed.Rep. 446 18–029
Meyer v Gregson (1784) 3 Doug. 402 8–021
Meyer v Ralli (1876) 1 C.P.D. 358 24–112
Meyer Koulish Co v Cannon, 28 Cal. Rptr. 757 (1963) 11–034
Miceli v Union Marine & General Insurance Co Ltd (1938) 60 Ll.L.R. 275 CA 24–134
Michael Phillips Architects Ltd v Riklin [2010] EWHC 834 (TCC) 23–041
Michaels v Valentine (1923) 16 Ll.L.R. 244 MCLC 15–037
Michelham's Will Trusts, Re [1964] Ch. 550; [1963] 2 W.L.R. 1238; [1968] 2 All E.R. 188;
　　107 S.J. 254 Ch D 5–037
Micklefield v Hepgin (1794) 1 Anst. 133 4–002
Micro Design Group Ltd v Norwich Union Insurance Ltd [2005] EWHC 3093; [2006]
　　Lloyd's Rep. I.R. 235 QBD (TCC) 1–021, 6–059, 9–026
Middle Eastern Oil v National Bank of Abu Dhabi [2008] EWHC 2895 (Comm); [2009] 1
　　Lloyd's Rep. 251; [2008] 2 C.L.C. 1026 .... 2–003, 2–005, 2–064
Middlesbrough BC v Safeer [2001] EWHC Admin 525; [2001] 4 All E.R. 630; [2002] 1 Cr.
　　App. R. 23; (2002) 166 J.P. 48; [2002] R.T.R. 3; [2001] Crim. L.R. 922; (2002) 166
　　J.P.N. 72; (2001) 98(30) L.S.G. 37; Times, August 16, 2001 DC 22–002
Middleton v Wiggin [1996] L.R.L.R. 129; [1996] Env. L.R. 17; Independent, August 31,
　　1995; Lloyd's List, February 7, 1996 (I.D.) CA (Civ Div) 3–010
Middlewood v Blakes (1797) 7 T.R. 162 .... 24–039, 24–039, 24–070
Midland Bank Plc v Brown Shipley & Co Ltd. See Citibank NA v Brown Shipley & Co
　　Ltd

Midland Bank Plc v Laker Airways Ltd; sub nom. Midland Bank Plc and Clydesdale Bank
Plc v Laker Airways Ltd, Morris and Laker Airways (International) Ltd [1986] Q.B.
689; [1986] 2 W.L.R. 707; [1986] 1 All E.R. 526; [1986] E.C.C. 329; (1985) 129 S.J.
670; Financial Times, June 14, 1985 CA (Civ Div) 9–053
Midland Insurance Co v Smith and Wife (1880–81) L.R. 6 Q.B.D. 561 QBD 5–041, 11–024
Midland International Trade Services v Sudairy Financial Times, May 2, 1990 2–059
Midland Mainline Ltd v Eagle Star Insurance Co Ltd; sub nom. Midland Mainline Ltd v
Commercial Union Assurance Co Ltd; WAGN Railway Ltd v St Paul International
Insurance Co Ltd [2004] EWCA Civ. 1042; [2004] 2 Lloyd's Rep. 604; [2004] 2 C.L.C.
480; [2004] Lloyd's Rep. I.R. 739; (2004) 148 S.J.L.B. 1062 CA (Civ Div); reversing
[2003] EWHC 1771; [2004] Lloyd's Rep. I.R. 22 QBD (Comm) 5–034, 10–032, 10–034,
19–055
Mighell v Reading. *See* White (Brian) v White (Shane)
Mildred v Maspons; sub nom. Maspons y Hermano v Mildred Goyeneche & Co (1882–83)
L.R. 8 App. Cas. 874 HL 24–078
Miliangos v George Frank (Textiles) Ltd [1976] A.C. 443; [1975] 3 W.L.R. 758; [1975] 3 All
E.R. 801; [1976] 1 Lloyd's Rep. 201; [1975] 2 C.M.L.R. 585; (1975) 119 S.J. 774 HL ... 2–059
Miller, Gibb & Co, Re [1957] 1 W.L.R. 703; [1957] 2 All E.R. 266; [1957] 1 Lloyd's Rep.
258; 101 S.J. 392 Ch D 11–020
Miller v Hales [2006] EWHC 1529 QB 22–018, 22–041
Miller v Law Accident Insurance Co [1903] 1 K.B. 712 CA 25–012
Miller v Warre (1824) 1 Car. & P. 237 .... 20–062, 24–026
Miller v Woodfall (1857) 8 E. & B. 493 24–095
Milles v Fletcher (1779) 1 Doug. K.B. 231 11–066
Millichap v Pontrilas Timber & Builders' Merchants LtdUnreported, 1992 .... 7–015, 9–003
Mills v Toner [1995] C.L.Y. 3726 CC (Liverpool) 22–057
Mills (John) v Smith (Robert) [1964] 1 Q.B. 30; [1963] 3 W.L.R. 367; [1963] 2 All E.R.
1078; [1963] 1 Lloyd's Rep. 168; 107 S.J. 175; Times, February 12, 1963 QBD 19–055
Minett v Anderson (1794) Peake 277 24–065
Ministry of Defence and Support of the Armed Forces for Iran v Faz Aviation (formerly FN
Aviation Ltd) [2007] EWHC 1042 (Comm); [2008] 1 All E.R. (Comm) 372; [2008] 1
B.C.L.C. 599; [2007] I.L.Pr. 42 2–001
Mint Security v Blair, Miller (Thomas R) & Son (Home) and Darwin Clayton (E C) and Co
[1982] 1 Lloyd's Rep. 188 QBD 1–019, 5–022, 6–092, 6–103, 7–038, 7–039, 7–040, 7–048,
15–031, 15–037
Miruvaor Ltd v National Insurance Co Ltd [2003] H.K.E.C. 237 24–066
Misirlakis v The New Zealand Insurance Co Ltd (1985) 3 A.N.Z. Insurance Cases 60–633 6–070
Mitchell v Edie (1787) 1 T.R. 608 11–001
Mitchell Conveyor & Transporter Co Ltd v Pulbrook (1933) 45 Ll.L.R. 239 KBD .. 5–017, 6–103
Mitchell-Henry v Norwich Union Life Insurance Society Ltd [1918] 2 K.B. 67; 2 A.L.R.
1644 CA 8–002
Mitsubishi Corp v Castletown Navigation (The Castle Alpha) Castle Alpha, The [1989] 2
Lloyd's Rep. 383 2–038
Mitsubishi Electric UK Ltd v Royal London Insurance (UK) Ltd [1994] 2 Lloyd's Rep. 249;
[1994] C.L.C. 367; 74 B.L.R. 87 CA (Civ Div) 10–037
Mitsui v Mumford [1915] 2 K.B. 27 KBD 10–001
Moate v Moate [1948] 2 All E.R. 486; 92 S.J. 484 Ch D 18–006
Moens v Heyworth (1842) 10 M. & W. 147 6–001
Moir v Royal Exchange Assurance Co (1815) 3 M. & S. 461 24–068
Molinos de Arroz v Mumford (1900) 6 T.L.R. 469 10–001
Molloy v Mutual Life (1905) 22 T.L.R. 59 8–026
Monenco Ltd v Commonwealth Insurance Co [2001] S.C.J. No.50 20–049
Monetaca v Motor Union Insurance Co Ltd. *See* Banque Monetaca & Carystuiaki v Motor
Union Insurance Co Ltd
Monk v Warbey [1935] 1 K.B. 75; (1934) 50 Ll.L.R. 33 CA 22–010, 22–012, 22–013, 22–070
Monksfield v Vehicle and General Insurance Co [1971] 1 Lloyd's Rep. 139 MCLC ... 9–008, 11–059,
21–023
Monkton Court Ltd (t/a CATS) v Perry Prowse (Insurance Services) Ltd [2000] 1 All E.R.
(Comm) 566; [2002] Lloyd's Rep. I.R. 408 QBD (Merc) 20–055
Montedipe SpA v JTP-RO Jugotanker; The Jordan Nicolov [1990] 2 Lloyd's Rep. 11 QBD
(Comm) 11–004, 21–029
Montoya v London Assurance Co (1851) 6 Ex. 451 .... 5–030, 24–134
Montreal Assurance v McGillivray (1859) 13 Moo. P.C.C. 87 8–002

Moody (DHR) (Chemists) v Iron Trades Mutual Insurance Co [1971] 1 Lloyd's Rep. 386;
  [1971] R.T.R. 120; 69 L.G.R. 232; (1970) 115 S.J. 16 QBD 22–096
Moon Fung Hong Co Ltd v Hong Kong International terminals Ltd [2007] H.K.E.C. 929 11–011
Moon King, The [1895] 2 Q.B. 550 24–063
Moonacre, The. *See* Sharp v Sphere Drake Insurance
Moor Line Ltd v King (1920) 4 Ll.L.R. 286 KBD (Comm Ct) 5–030, 25–004, 25–005
Moore, Ex p. Ibbetson, Re (1878) L.R. 8 Ch. D. 519 CA 14–026, 18–022
Moore Large & Co Ltd v Hermes Credit & Guarantee Plc (sued as Credit & Guarantee
  Insurance Co Plc) [2003] EWHC 26; [2003] 1 Lloyd's Rep. 163; [2003] Lloyd's Rep.
  I.R. 315 QBD (Comm) ... 6–010, 6–070, 6–072, 6–092, 6–095, 6–097, 6–105, 7–020, 23–030
Moore v Evans [1918] A.C. 185 HL; affirming [1917] 1 K.B. 458 CA 5–015, 5–030, 10–001,
                                                                                         11–067
Moore v Lunn; Munson Steamship Line v Lunn (1923) 15 Ll.L.R. 155 CA 24–062
Moore v Mourgue (1776) 2 Cowp. 479 15–034
Moore v Secretary of State for Transport [2007] EWHC 879 (QB); [2007] Eu. L.R. 645;
  [2007] Lloyd's Rep. I.R. 469; [2007] P.I.Q.R. P24 22–073
Moore v Woolsey (1854) 8 E. & B. 243 9–019
Moore Stephens (A Firm). *See* Stone & Rolls Ltd (In Liquidation) v Moore Stephens (A
  Firm)
Moorgate Estates Ltd, Re; Moorgate Estates Ltd v Trower [1942] Ch. 321 Ch D 19–027
Mopani Copper Mines Plc v Millennium Underwriting Ltd [2008] EWHC 1331 (Comm);
  [2008] 2 All E.R. (Comm) 976; [2008] 1 C.L.C. 992; [2009] Lloyd's Rep. I.R. 158;
  [2008] Bus. L.R. D121 .... 1–033, 3–017
Moran, Galloway & Co v Uzielli [1905] 2 K.B. 555 ...... 4–009, 4–013, 18–020, 19–014, 19–029,
                                                                                         24–017
Morck v Abel (1802) 3 Bos. & P. 35 .... 8–022, 18–009
Morgan v Price (1849) 4 Exch. 615 11–044
Morgan v Pryor (1823) 2 B. & C. 14 6–062
Morin v Bonhams & Brooks Ltd [2003] EWCA Civ 1802; [2004] 1 All E.R. (Comm) 880;
  [2004] 1 Lloyd's Rep. 702; [2004] 1 C.L.C. 632; [2004] I.L.Pr. 24 2–063
Morison v Universal Marine Insurance Co (1873) L.R. 8 Exch. 197 .... 6–002, 6–062
Morley v Moore [1936] 2 K.B. 359; (1936) 55 Ll.L.R. 10 CA 11–013
Morley & Morley v United Friendly Insurance [1993] 1 W.L.R. 996; [1993] 2 All E.R. 47;
  [1993] 1 Lloyd's Rep. 490; (1993) 137 S.J.L.B. 222; Times, February 8, 1993 CA (Civ
  Div) 3–009, 18–049, 18–050, 22–090
Morrell v Irving Fire (1865) 33 N.Y. 429 10–044
Morris v Britannic Assurance Co Ltd [1931] 2 K.B. 125 KBD 18–015
Morris v Ford Motor Co [1973] Q.B. 792; [1973] 2 W.L.R. 843; [1973] 2 All E.R. 1084;
  [1973] 2 Lloyd's Rep. 27; 117 S.J. 393 CA (Civ Div) 11–002, 11–013, 11–032
Morrison v Co-operators' General Insurance Co [2004] N.B.J. No.290 20–049
Morrison v Muspratt (1827) 4 Bing. 60 .... 6–102, 18–029
Morrison v Universal Marine Insurance Co (1872–73) L.R. 8 Ex. 197, Ex Chamber;
  reversing (1872–73) L.R. 8 Ex. 40 Ex Ct 1–033, 1–034, 6–065, 6–092, 7–020
Morrison Steamship Co Ltd v Owners of Cargo Lately Laden on Board the Greystoke Castle;
  sub nom. Owners of Cargo Lately Laden on Board The Greystoke Castle v Owners of
  The Cheldale [1947] A.C. 265; [1946] 2 All E.R. 696; (1947) 80 Ll.L.R. 55; 63 T.L.R.
  11; [1947] L.J.R. 297; 176 L.T. 66 HL 9–038
Morser v Eagle Star & British Dominions Insurance Co Ltd (1931) 40 Ll.L.R. 254 KBD 6–052
Mortgage Insurance Corp Ltd v Inland Revenue Commissioners (1887) 57 L.J.Q.B. 174 ... 23–029
Morton Insurance Brokers Ltd v Sidhu [2008] EWHC 417 (QB) 15–028
Moses v Pratt (1814) 4 Camp. 297 8–021
Moss v Byrom (1795) 6 T.R. 379 24–138
Mostcash Plc (formerly UK Paper Plc) v Fluor Ltd (No.1) [2002] EWCA Civ 975; [2002]
  B.L.R. 411; 83 Con. L.R. 1; (2003) 19 Const. L.J. 200 CA (Civ Div) 10–058
Motor & General Insurance Co v Cox [1990] 1 W.L.R. 1443; [1991] R.T.R. 67; (1990) 134
  S.J. 1190 PC (Bar) 5–001, 22–015, 22–039
Motor and General Insurance Co v Pavey [1994] 1 W.L.R. 462; [1994] 1 Lloyd's Rep. 607
  PC (Trin) 9–003
Motor Co of Canada Ltd v Prudential Assurance Co Ltd, 15 D.L.R. (2d) 273 (1959) 5–034
Motor Insurers Bureau v Meanen; sub nom. Meanen v Motor Insurers Bureau; Meanen v
  MIB [1971] 2 All E.R. 1372 (Note); [1971] 2 Lloyd's Rep. 251; 1971 S.C. (H.L.) 148;
  1971 S.L.T. 264 HL 22–031, 22–097
Motor Oil Hellas (Corinth) Refineries SA v Shipping Corp of India (The Kanchenjunga)
  [1990] 1 Lloyd's Rep. 391; Times, February 19, 1990 HL .. 6–090, 6–098, 7–018, 7–048, 9–014

Motor Union Insurance Co Ltd v Mannheimer Versicherungs Gesellschaft [1933] 1 K.B. 812;
(1932) 43 Ll.L.R. 241 KBD 17–002
Motteux v London Assurance (1739) 1 Atk. 545 .... 1–018, 24–073
Mottram Consultants Ltd v Bernard Sunley & Sons Ltd [1975] 2 Lloyd's Rep. 197; 2 B.L.R.
28; 118 S.J. 808 HL 3–017
Moulder v National Insurance Co of New Zealand [1993] 2 N.Z.L.R. 351 .... 14–003, 14–013
Mount v Larkins (1831) 8 Bing. 108 .... 24–065, 24–072
Mountain v Whittle; sub nom. Whittle v Mountain [1921] 1 A.C. 615; (1921) 6 Ll.L.R. 378
HL 3–011, 24–003, 24–070, 24–0134
Moussa H Issa NV v Grand Union Insurance Co Ltd [1984] H.K.L.R. 137 11–009
Moxon v Atkins (1812) 3 Camp. 200 .... 6–065, 24–065
M'Swiney v Royal Exchange Assurance Co (1849) L.R. 14 Q.B.D. 634 19–007
Muirhead v Forth and North Sea Steamboat Mutual Insurance Association; sub nom.
Muirhead v Forth and North Sea Steamboat Mutual Assurance Association [1894] A.C.
72; (1893) 1 S.L.T. 325 HL 1–009, 7–022, 10–007
Mulchrone v Swiss Life (UK) Plc [2005] EWHC 1808; [2006] Lloyd's Rep. I.R. 339 QBD
(Comm) 1–022, 1–024, 7–003, 9–038, 9–041, 18–003
Muller v Thomson (1811) 2 Camp. 610 7–038
Mulvey v Gore District Mutual Fire (1866) 25 U.C.Q.B. 424 8–025
Mumford v Hardy [1956] 1 W.L.R. 163; [1956] 1 All E.R. 337; [1956] 1 Lloyd's Rep. 173;
54 L.G.R. 150; 100 S.J. 132 QBD 22–010, 22–011, 22–089
Mumford Hotels Ltd v Wheeler [1964] Ch. 117; [1963] 3 W.L.R. 735; [1963] 3 All E.R. 250;
107 S.J. 810 Ch D 1–014, 11–032, 14–021, 19–017, 19–026
Munchener Ruckversicherungs-Gesellschaft AG (t/a Munich Reinsurance Co) v Com-
monwealth Insurance Co [2004] EWHC 914; [2004] 2 C.L.C. 665; [2005] Lloyd's Rep.
I.R. 99 QBD (Comm) 2–005
Mundi v Lincoln Assurance Ltd [2005] EWHC 2678; [2006] Lloyd's Rep. I.R. 353 Ch D 1–048,
6–030, 6–031, 6–105, 18–003, 18–029, 18–030
Mundy's Trustee v Blackmore. See Trustee of GH Mundy (A Bankrupt) v Blackmore
Municipal Mutual Insurance Ltd v Sea Insurance Co Ltd [1998] C.L.C. 957; [1998] Lloyd's
Rep. I.R. 421 CA (Civ Div); reversing in part [1996] L.R.L.R. 265; [1996] C.L.C. 151,;
Lloyd's List, June 11, 1996 (I.D.) QBD (Comm) 3–003, 5–015, 7–015, 10–036, 17–012,
17–014, 17–019, 17–023
Municipal Mutual Insurance v Pontefract Corp (1917) 116 L.T. 671 8–012
Munro Brice & Co v War Risks Association; Munro Brice & Co v Marten; Munro Brice &
Co v King, The [1920] 3 K.B. 94; (1920) 2 Ll.L.R. 2CA; reversing [1918] 2 K.B. 78
KBD 9–015
Murdock v Heath (1899) 80 L.T. 50 .... 23–029, 23–030
Murfin v Ashbridge [1941] 1 All E.R. 231 CA 20–044
Murfitt v Royal Insurance (1922) 38 T.L.R. 334 .... 1–012, 1–054, 15–015
Murphy v Brentwood DC [1991] 1 A.C. 398; [1990] 3 W.L.R. 414; [1990] 2 All E.R. 908;
[1990] 2 Lloyd's Rep. 467; 50 B.L.R. 1; 21 Con. L.R. 1; (1990) 22 H.L.R. 502; 89
L.G.R. 24; (1991) 3 Admin. L.R. 37; (1990) 6 Const. L.J. 304; (1990) 154 L.G. Rev.
1010; [1990] E.G.C.S. 105; (1990) 87(30) L.S.G. 15; (1990) 134 S.J. 1076; Times, July
27, 1990; Independent, July 27, 1990 HL 20–076
Murphy v Murphy; sub nom. L v M (A Child); Murphy (A Child) v Holland [2003] EWCA
Civ 1862; [2004] 1 F.C.R. 1; [2004] Lloyd's Rep. I.R. 744; [2004] W.T.L.R. 239 CA
(Civ Div) 14–003, 14–015, 18–014
Murphy v Young & Co's Brewery Plc; Murphy v Sun Alliance and London Insurance Plc
[1997] 1 W.L.R. 1591; [1997] 1 All E.R. 518; [1997] 1 Lloyd's Rep. 236; [1997] C.L.C.
469; [1998] 1 Costs L.R. 94; [1997] 6 Re. L.R. 113; Times, January 8, 1997;
Independent, December 6, 1996 CA (Civ Div) 23–016
Murray v Kelly Unreported 4–002
Murray v Legal & General Assurance Society [1970] 2 Q.B. 495; [1970] 2 W.L.R. 465;
[1969] 3 All E.R. 794; [1969] 2 Lloyd's Rep. 405; 113 S.J. 720 QBD 21–025
Murray v Scottish Automobile & General Insurance Co Ltd, 1929 S.C. 48; 1929 S.L.T. 114
IH (1 Div) 22–097
Musawi v RE International (UK) Ltd [2007] EWHC 2981 (Ch); [2008] 1 All E.R. (Comm)
607; [2008] 1 Lloyd's Rep. 326; [2007] N.P.C. 137 2–028
Mutual Life Assurance Society v Langley (1886) L.R. 32 Ch. D. 460 CA 14–028
Mutual Life Insurance Co v Ontario Metal Products Co Ltd [1925] A.C. 344 PC (Can) 6–021,
6–023

Mutual Reinsurance Co Ltd v Peat Marwick Mitchell & Co; sub nom. Mutual Reinsurance
Co Ltd v KPMG Peat Marwick [1997] 1 Lloyd's Rep. 253; [1996] B.C.C. 1010; [1997]
1 B.C.L.C. 1; [1997] P.N.L.R. 75; Times, October 15, 1996 CA (Civ Div) 20–082
Mutual Reserve v Foster (1904) 20 T.L.R. 715 1–018
Mutzenbecher v La Aseguradora Espanola [1906] 1 K.B. 254 CA 2–004
Myers v Dortex International Ltd [2000] Lloyd's Rep. I.R. 529; Times, March 18, 1999 CA
(Civ Div) 20–044
Mylius v Royal Insurance Co Ltd [1928] V.L.R. 126 10–052
N Michalos (N) & Sons Maritime SA v Prudential Assurance Co (The Zinovia); Public Corp
for Sugar Trade v N Michalos & Sons Co [1984] 2 Lloyd's Rep. 264 QBD (Comm) 9–025
NM Rothschild & Sons (CI) Ltd v Equitable Life Assurance Society [2003] Lloyd's Rep. I.R.
371 QBD 18–022
NM Superannuation Pty Ltd v Young [1993] 113 A.L.R. 39 18–001
NRG Victory Reinsurance Ltd Unreported, March 2006 16–005
NRG Victory Reinsurance Ltd, Re [1995] 1 W.L.R. 239; [1995] 1 All E.R. 533; [1995] 4 Re.
L.R. 214; Times, November 8, 1994 Ch D 13–017, 17–003
NSW Medical Defence Union Ltd v Transport industries Insurance Co Ltd (1984)
N.S.W.L.R. 107 6–107
NV Rotterdamse Assurantiekas v Golding Stewart Wrightson Ltd Unreported, 1989 15–033
Nai Genova, The. See Agip SpA v Navigazione Alta Italia SpA (The Nai Genova and The
Nai Superba), Nai Genova, The
Nairn v South East Lancashire Insurance Co Ltd, 1930 S.C. 606; 1930 S.L.T. 458 IH (2
Div) 20–055
Nam Kwong Medicines & Health Products Co Ltd v China Insurance Co Ltd [2002]
H.K.C.U. 792 .... 6–029, 6–037
Napier v UNUM Ltd (formerly NEL Permanent Health Insurance Ltd) [1996] 2 Lloyd's Rep.
550; [1996] 7 Med. L.R. 349 QBD 9–019, 10–057, 17–015, 18–057
Napier (Lord) and Ettrick v RF Kershaw Ltd (No.1); Lord Napier and Ettrick v Hunter [1993]
A.C. 713; [1993] 2 W.L.R. 42; [1993] 1 All E.R. 385; [1993] 1 Lloyd's Rep. 197; (1993)
137 S.J.L.B. 44; Times, December 16, 1992; Independent, December 11, 1992 HL;
reversing [1993] 1 Lloyd's Rep. 10; Times, July 17, 1992; Financial Times, July 22,
1992 CA (Civ Div) 10–030, 11–002, 11–006, 11–008, 11–010, 11–011, 11–013, 11–014,
11–017, 11–018, 11–019, 11–020, 11–042, 11–043
Napthen v Place [1970] R.T.R. 248 DC 22–010
Nash (t/a Dino Services Ltd) v Prudential Assurance Co Ltd; sub nom. Dino Services Ltd v
Prudential Assurance Co Ltd [1989] 1 All E.R. 422; [1989] 1 Lloyd's Rep. 379; [1989]
Fin. L.R. 316 CA (Civ Div) 19–046
Nash v R (1995) 27 O.R. (3d) 1 20–049
Nassau Bay, The. See Costain-Blankevoort (UK) Dredging Co Ltd v Davenport (Inspector of
Taxes)
Nasser v United Bank of Kuwait (Security for Costs) [2001] EWCA Civ 556; [2002] 1
W.L.R. 1868; [2002] 1 All E.R. 401; [2001] C.P. Rep. 105 23–041
Natal Land & Colonization Co Ltd v Pauline Colliery and Development Syndicate Ltd [1904]
A.C. 120 PC (Natal) 14–008
National Bank of Greece SA v Outhwaite; sub nom. National Bank of Greece SA v RM
Outhwaite 317 Syndicate at Lloyds [2001] C.P. Rep. 69; [2001] C.L.C. 591; [2001]
Lloyd's Rep. I.R. 652 QBD (Comm) 2–004
National Benefit Assurance Co Ltd, Ex p. English Insurance Co Ltd, Re; sub nom. National
Benefit Assurance Co Ltd, Re [1929] A.C. 114; (1928) 31 Ll.L.R. 321 HL 17–002
National Benefit Assurance Co Ltd, Re (1933) 45 Ll.L.R. 147 Ch D 19–007
National Benefit Assurance Co Ltd, Re (No.2); sub nom. National Benefit Assurance Co Ltd,
Re [1931] 1 Ch. 46; (1930) 37 Ll.L.R. 153 Ch D 24–044
National Carriers v Panalpina [1981] A.C. 675 19–020
National Company for Co-operative Insurance v St Paul Reinsurance Co Ltd Unreported,
1997 .... 10–056, 15–004, 17–019
National Employers Mutual General Insurance Association v Haydon [1980] 2 Lloyd's Rep.
149CA (Civ Div); reversing [1979] 2 Lloyd's Rep. 235 QBD 11–048
National Employers Mutual General Insurance Association v Jones; sub nom. NEMG
Insurance Association v Jones [1990] 1 A.C. 24; [1988] 2 W.L.R. 952; [1988] 2 All E.R.
425; [1988] R.T.R. 289; (1989) 8 Tr. L.R. 43; (1988) 138 N.L.J. Rep. 118; (1988) 132
S.J. 658 HL 10–001
National Farmers' Union Mutual Insurance Society Ltd v Dawson [1941] 2 K.B. 424; (1941)
70 Ll.L.R. 167 KBD 22–036

National Farmers Union Mutual Insurance Society Ltd v HSBC Insurance (UK) Ltd [2010] EWHC 773 (Comm) 11–051
National Farmers' Union Mutual Insurance Society Ltd v Tully, 1935 S.L.T. 574 OH 22–048
National Filtering Oil Co v Citizen's Insurance of Missouri (1887) 13 N.E. 337 4–013
National Insurance & Guarantee Corp v Imperio Reinsurance Co (UK) Ltd [1999] Lloyd's Rep. I.R. 249 QBD (Comm) 15–003, 15–034, 15–037, 15–051, 15–052, 15–053
National Justice Compania Naviera SA v Prudential Assurance Co Ltd (The Ikarian Reefer) (No.1) [1995] 1 Lloyd's Rep. 455 CA (Civ Div); reversing [1993] 2 Lloyd's Rep. 68; [1993] F.S.R. 563; [1993] 37 E.G. 158; Times, March 5, 1993 QBD (Comm) 9–025, 24–135
National Justice Compania Naviera SA v Prudential Assurance Co Ltd (The Ikarian Reefer) (No.2); sub nom. Comninos v Prudential Assurance Co Ltd [2000] 1 W.L.R. 603; [2000] 1 All E.R. 37; [1999] 2 All E.R. (Comm) 673; [2000] 1 Lloyd's Rep. 129; [2000] C.P. Rep. 13; [2000] C.L.C. 22; [2000] 1 Costs L.R. 37; [2000] I.L.Pr. 490; [2000] Lloyd's Rep. I.R. 230; (1999) 96(41) L.S.G. 35; (1999) 96(42) L.S.G. 40; (1999) 149 N.L.J. 1561; (1999) 143 S.J.L.B. 255; Times, October 15, 1999; Independent, October 20, 1999; Independent, November 22, 1999 (C.S.) CA (Civ Div) 9 2–008, 20–037
National Mutual of Australasia v Smallfield [1922] N.Z.L.R. 1074 .. 2–009, 18–028, 18–029, 20–056
National Navigation Co v Endesa Generacion SA (The Wadi Sudr) Wadi Sudr, The [2009] EWCA Civ 1397; [2010] 1 Lloyd's Rep. 193; [2009] 2 C.L.C. 1004; [2010] I.L.Pr. 10; Times, February 8, 2010 2–008
National Oil Co of Zimbabwe (Private) v Sturge [1991] 2 Lloyd's Rep. 281; Financial Times, March 12, 1991 QBD (Comm) 25–008
National Oilwell (UK) Ltd v Davy Offshore Ltd [1993] 2 Lloyd's Rep. 582 QBD (Comm) 1–011, 4–013, 4–020, 4–021, 4–022, 4–023, 5–041, 6–046, 11–027, 11–028, 11–029, 11–032, 11–038, 14–003, 14–004, 14–007, 14–008, 14–013, 14–018, 14–019, 15–003, 15–006, 19–015, 19–032, 20–081, 24–009, 24–045, 24–048, 24–080, 24–112
National Standard Life Assurance Corp (No.2), Re [1918] 1 Ch. 427 Ch D 1–008
National Trust for Places of Historic Interest or Natural Beauty v Haden Young Ltd, 72 B.L.R. 1; Times, August 11, 1994; Independent, August 31, 1994 CA (Civ Div) 11–031, 14–007
National Westminster Bank Plc v Somer International (UK) Ltd [2001] EWCA Civ. 970; [2002] Q.B. 1286; [2002] 3 W.L.R. 64; [2002] 1 All E.R. 198; [2001] Lloyd's Rep. Bank. 263; [2001] C.L.C. 1579; Independent, June 26, 2001 CA (Civ Div) 10–062
Nationwide Building Society v Dunlop Haywards (DHL) Ltd (t/a Dunlop Heywood Lorenz) [2009] EWHC 254 (Comm); [2010] 1 W.L.R. 258; [2009] 2 All E.R. (Comm) 715; [2009] 1 Lloyd's Rep. 447; [2010] Lloyd's Rep. P.N. 68; [2009] P.N.L.R. 20 15–032
Naumann v Ford [1985] 2 E.G.L.R. 70; (1985) 275 E.G. 542; (1985) 82 L.S.G. 1858 Ch D ... 11–016, 19–018
Nautilus Insurance Co v Country Oaks Apartments Ltd 566 F. 3d 452 at 454 (5th Cir 2009) ... 20–050
Naviera de Canarias SA v Nacional Hispanica Aseguradora SA (The Playa de las Nieves) [1978] A.C. 853; [1977] 2 W.L.R. 442; [1977] 1 All E.R. 625; [1977] 1 Lloyd's Rep. 457; 121 S.J. 186 HL 24–080
Navigators Insurance Co v Atlantic Methanol Production Co LLC [2003] EWHC 1706; [2004] Lloyd's Rep. I.R. 418 QBD (Comm) 2–005
Nawaz v Crowe Insurance Group [2003] EWCA Civ. 316; [2003] C.P. Rep. 41; [2003] R.T.R. 29; [2003] Lloyd's Rep. I.R. 471; [2003] P.I.Q.R. P27; Times, March 11, 2003; Independent, March 7, 2003 CA (Civ Div) 22–045
Nayyar v Denton Wilde Sapte [2009] EWHC 3218 (QB); [2010] P.N.L.R. 15 .... 5–046, 20–086
Nelson Marketing International Inc v Royal & Sun Alliance Insurance Company of Canada 2006 B.C.C.A. 327 24–080
Nelson v Board of Trade (1901) 84 L.T. 565 1–003
Nelson v Salvador (1829) Mood. & M. 309 24–068
Nelson & Co, Re [1905] 1 Ch. 551 Ch D 16–006
Nepean v Marten (1895) 11 T.L.R. 256 17–017
Nesbitt v Lushington (1792) 4 T.R. 783 24–135
Neter (NE) & Co Ltd v Licenses & General Insurance Co Ltd (1944) 77 Ll.L.R. 202 KBD 24–134
Netherlands v Youell; Netherlands v Hayward [1998] 1 Lloyd's Rep. 236; [1998] C.L.C. 44 CA (Civ Div); affirming [1997] 2 Lloyd's Rep. 440 QBD (Comm) 11–029, 11–032, 14–003, 14–004, 14–013, 14–018, 24–003, 24–112
Netherlands Insurance Co Est 1845 Ltd v Karl Ljungberg & Co AB; The Mammoth Pine [1986] 3 All E.R. 767; [1986] 2 Lloyd's Rep. 19 PC (Sing) 24–112
Nettleship v Weston [1971] 2 Q.B. 691; [1971] 3 W.L.R. 370; [1971] 3 All E.R. 581; [1971] R.T.R. 425; 115 S.J. 624 CA (Civ Div) 22–033

Neue Fischmehl Vertriebsgesellschaft Haselhorst mbH v Yorkshire Insurance Co Ltd (1934)
50 Ll.L.R. 151 KBD 24–038, 24–062
New Hampshire Insurance Co v Grand Union Insurance Co Ltd [1995] 2 H.K.C. 1 17–013
New Hampshire Insurance Co Ltd v MGN Ltd [1997] L.R.L.R. 24; [1996] C.L.C. 1728
CA 20–081
New Hampshire Insurance Co v Oil Refineries Ltd (Avoidance for Non Disclosure) [2002]
2 Lloyd's Rep. 462; [2003] Lloyd's Rep. I.R. 386; Daily Telegraph, April 18, 2002 QBD
(Comm) 6–073, 20–022
New Hampshire Insurance Co v Whiteley [2003] EWHC 1613 QBD (Comm) 15–020
New Hampshire Insurance Co Ltd v MGN Ltd; Maxwell Communication Corp Plc (In
Administration) v New Hampshire Insurance Co Ltd [1997] L.R.L.R. 24; [1996] C.L.C.
1728 CA (Civ Div) 1–023, 1–024, 1–025, 1–033, 6–103, 6–107, 6–109, 6–112, 6–113,
14–003, 14–012, 14–013, 14–014, 20–060
New Hampshire Insurance Co Ltd v Philips Electronics North America Corp (No.1) [1998]
C.L.C. 1062; [1998] I.L.Pr. 256; [1999] Lloyd's Rep. I.R. 58 CA (Civ Div) 2–007, 23–021,
23–022, 23–023
New Hampshire Insurance Co Ltd v Strabag Bau AG [1992] 1 Lloyd's Rep. 361; [1992]
I.L.Pr. 478; Times, November 26, 1991; Financial Times, November 26, 1991 CA (Civ
Div) 2–009
New India Assurance Co v Yeo Beng Chow [1972] 1 W.L.R. 786; [1972] 3 All E.R. 293;
[1972] 1 Lloyd's Rep. 479; [1972] R.T.R. 356; 116 S.J. 373 PC (Mal) 22–093
New South Wales Leather Co Pty Ltd v Vanguard Insurance Co Ltd (1991) 25 N.S.W.L.R.
699 24–020
New York v Statham (1876) 93 U.S. 24 1–048
New York Life Insurance Co v Chittenden, 112 N.W. 96 (1907) 10–064
New Zealand Forest Products Ltd v New Zealand Insurance Co Ltd [1996] 2 N.Z.L.R. 20 20–052
PCNewberry v Simmonds [1961] 2 Q.B. 345; [1961] 2 W.L.R. 675; [1961] 2 All E.R. 318;
125 J.P. 409; 59 L.G.R. 309; 105 S.J. 324 QBD 22–006
Newbon v City Mutual Life Assurance Society Ltd (1935) 52 C.L.R. 723 8–016
Newbury International Ltd v Reliance National Insurance Co (UK) and Tyser Special Risks
[1994] 1 Lloyd's Rep. 83 QBD (Comm) 4–010, 6–004, 6–073, 15–058, 20–062
Newbury v Davis [1974] R.T.R. 367; [1974] Crim. L.R. 262; (1974) 118 S.J. 222 QBD ... 22–010
Newby v Reed (1763) 1 Wm. Bl. 416 .... 11–044, 11–052
Newcastle Corp v Walton [1957] Crim. L.R. 479 22–007
Newcastle Fire Insurance Co v Macmorran & Co (1815) 3 Dow. 255 ..... 5–002, 5–025, 7–038, 7–040
Newcastle Protection and Indemnity Association v Ships (USA) Inc [1996] 2 Lloyd's Rep.
515 QBD (Comm) 14–003
Newfoundland Explorer, The. See GE Frankona Reinsurance Ltd v CMM Trust No.1400
Newis v General Accident (1910) 11 C.L.R. 620 8–004
Newman v Newman (1885) L.R. 28 Ch. D. 674 Ch D 14–026, 14–028
Newsholme Bros v Road Transport & General Insurance Co Ltd [1929] 2 K.B. 356; (1929)
34 Ll.L.R. 247 CA 1–017, 3–005, 6–070, 15–004, 15–019
Ngo Chew Edible Oil Pte v Knight [1988] 1 S.L.R. 414 24–088
Nichol v Leach [1972] R.T.R. 416; [1972] Crim. L.R. 571 DC 22–006
Nicholas v New Zealand Insurance Co [1930] N.Z.L.R. 699 6–018
Nichols v American Home Assurance Co 68 D.L.R. (4th) 321 (1990) 20–043
Nichols v American Home Assurance Co [1990] 1 S.C.R. 801 20–049
Nichols v Scottish Union and National Insurance Co (1885) 2 T.L.R. 190 .... 11–054, 19–025
Nichols & Co v Scottish Union and National Insurance Co (1885) 2 T.L.R. 190 4–020
Nicholson v Power (1869) 20 L.T. 580 6–093
Nigel Upchurch Associates v Aldridge Estates Investment Co [1993] 1 Lloyd's Rep. 535
QBD 21–010, 21–039
Niger Co Ltd v Guardian Assurance Co Ltd. See Commercial Union Assurance Co Ltd v
Niger Co Ltd
Nima Sarl v Deves Insurance Public Co Ltd (The Prestrioka) [2002] EWCA Civ. 1132;
[2002] 2 All E.R. (Comm) 449; [2003] 2 Lloyd's Rep. 327; [2003] 1 C.L.C. 600; [2002]
Lloyd's Rep. I.R. 752; (2002) 99(38) L.S.G. 34; Times, October 17, 2002 CA (Civ
Div) 24–068, 24–073
PCNiru Battery Manufacturing Co v Milestone Trading Ltd (No.1) [2003] EWCA Civ. 1446;
[2004] Q.B. 985 CA (Civ Div); affirming [2002] EWHC 1425; [2002] 2 All E.R.
(Comm) 705 QBD (Comm) 10–062

Nishina Trading Co Ltd v Chiyoda Fire & Marine Insurance Co Ltd; The Mandarin Star [1969] 2 Q.B. 449; [1969] 2 W.L.R. 1094; [1969] 2 All E.R. 776; [1969] 1 Lloyd's Rep. 293; 113 S.J. 222 CA (Civ Div); affirming [1968] 1 W.L.R. 1325; [1968] 3 All E.R. 712; [1968] 2 Lloyd's Rep. 47; 112 S.J. 417 QBD (Comm) 3–008, 24–112, 24–136

Nisshin Shipping Co Ltd v Cleaves & Co Ltd [2003] EWHC 2602; [2004] 1 All E.R. (Comm) 481; [2004] 1 Lloyd's Rep. 38; [2003] 2 C.L.C. 1097; (2003) 153 N.L.J. 1705 QBD (Comm) 9–052

*Times*CANoble Assurance Co v Gerling-Konzern General Insurance Co [2007] EWHC 253 (Comm); [2007] 1 C.L.C. 85; [2008] Lloyd's Rep. I.R. 1 2–006

Noble Resources and Unirise Development v George Albert Greenwood; The Vasso [1993] 2 Lloyd's Rep. 309 QBD (Comm) 24–112

Noble v Kennaway (1780) 2 Doug K.B. 510 6–065

Noblebright Ltd v Sirius International Corp [2007] Lloyd's Rep. I.R. 584 .... 6–052, 6–070, 6–071

Noel v Poland [2001] 2 B.C.L.C. 645; [2002] Lloyd's Rep. I.R. 30 QBD (Comm) 13–042, 20–059

Non-Marine Underwriters, Lloyd's of London v Scalera [2000] 1 S.C.R. 551 ...... 20–049, 20–050

Nonnen v Kettlewell (1812) 16 East 176 6–015

Norglen Ltd (In Liquidation) v Reeds Rains Prudential Ltd; Mayhew-Lewis v Westminster Scaffolding Group Plc; Levy v ABN AMRO Bank NV; Circuit Systems Ltd (In Liquidation) v Zuken-Redac (UK) Ltd [1999] 2 A.C. 1; [1997] 3 W.L.R. 1177; [1998] 1 All E.R. 218; [1998] B.C.C. 44; [1998] 1 B.C.L.C. 176; 87 B.L.R. 1; (1997) 94(48) L.S.G. 29; (1997) 147 N.L.J. 1773; (1998) 142 S.J.L.B. 26; (1998) 75 P. & C.R. D21; Times, December 1, 1997 HL 14–029

Norman v Ali (Limitation Period) [2000] R.T.R. 107; [2000] Lloyd's Rep. I.R. 395; [2000] P.I.Q.R. P72; (2000) 97(2) L.S.G. 30; (2000) 144 S.J.L.B. 18; Times, February 25, 2000; Independent, February 7, 2000 .... 22–013, 22–070

Norman v Aziz [2000] Lloyd's Rep. I.R. 52 QBD 22–012, 22–013, 22–059, 22–070

Norman v Gresham Fire & Accident Insurance Society Ltd (1935) 52 Ll.L.R. 292 KBD ... 22–087

Norman v Ricketts (1886) 3 T.L.R. 182 8–002

Normhurst Ltd v Dornoch Ltd [2004] EWHC 567; [2005] Lloyd's Rep. I.R. 27 QBD (Comm) 10–022, 23–042

Normid Housing Association Ltd v Ralphs & Mansell (Third Party Rights: Mareva Injunction); sub nom. Normid Housing Association Ltd v R John Ralphs; Normid Housing Association Ltd v John S Mansell; Normid Housing Association Ltd v Assicurazioni Generali SpA [1989] 1 Lloyd's Rep. 265; 21 Con. L.R. 98; [1988] E.G.C.S. 108; Times, November 15, 1988 CA (Civ Div) 21–038, 21–063

Norreys v Hodgson (1897) 3 T.L.R. 421 15–033

Norstrom Inc v Chubb & Sons, 54 F. 3d (9th circuit, 1995) 20–052

North, Ex p. Hasluck, Re [1895] 2 Q.B. 264 CA 5–004

North & South Trust Co v Berkeley; sub nom. Berkeley v North & South Trust Co [1971] 1 W.L.R. 470; [1971] 1 All E.R. 980; [1970] 2 Lloyd's Rep. 467; (1970) 115 S.J. 244 QBD (Comm) 15–041, 15–043

North Atlantic Insurance Co Ltd v Bishopsgate Insurance Ltd [1998] 1 Lloyd's Rep. 459 QBD (Comm) 17–027

North Atlantic Insurance Co Ltd v Nationwide General Insurance Co Ltd [2004] EWCA Civ. 423; [2004] 2 All E.R. (Comm) 351; [2004] 1 C.L.C. 1131; [2004] Lloyd's Rep. I.R. 466; (2004) 148 S.J.L.B. 508 CA (Civ Div) 15–020, 15–022, 15–023, 15–024, 15–025

North Britain, The [1894] P. 77 CA 20–010

North British & Mercantile Insurance Co v London Liverpool & Globe Insurance Co (1877) L.R. 5 Ch. D. 569CA ... 11–001, 11–044, 11–052, 11–054, 11–062, 19–010, 19–012, 19–025

North British & Mercantile Insurance Co v Moffatt (1871–72) L.R. 7 C.P. 25 CCP 4–005, 4–019, 4–020, 19–007, 19–011, 19–012, 24–030

North British Fishing Boat Insurance Co Ltd v Starr (1922) 13 Ll.L.R. 206 KBD .. 6–053, 6–065, 17–008

North British Rubber Co Ltd v Cheetham (1938) 61 Ll.L.R. 337 CA 6–107

North Central Airlines Inc v City of Aberdeen, South Dakota, 370 F. 2d 129 (1966) 11–034

North Coast Sea products Ltd v ING Insurance Company of Canada 2004 B.C.C.A. 95 24–112

North of England Pure Oil Cake Co v Archangel Maritime Insurance Co (1874–75) L.R. 10 Q.B. 249 QBD 14–022, 24–032

North of England Steamship Insurance Asc v Armstrong (1869–70) L.R. 5 Q.B. 244, QB 11–017

North Star Shipping Ltd v Sphere Drake Insurance Plc [2006] EWCA Civ. 378; [2006] 1 C.L.C. 606 CA (Civ Div); affirming [2005] EWHC 665; [2005] 2 Lloyd's Rep. 76; [2005] 2 C.L.C. 238 QBD (Comm) 6–030, 6–031, 6–034, 6–045, 6–045, 6–050, 6–059, 10–007

Northern Counties of England Fire Insurance Co (1885) 1 T.L.R. 629 16–011

Northern Counties of England Fire Insurance Co, Re; sub nom. Macfarlane's Claim, Re
(1881) L.R. 17 Ch. D. 337 Ch D 16–011
Northern Suburban Property & Real Estates Co Ltd v British Law Fire Insurance Co Ltd
(1919) 1 Ll.L.R. 403 KBD (Comm Ct) 9–017
Northwestern Mutual Life Insurance Co v Adams 144 N.W. 1108 (1914) 14–030
Norton v Royal life Assurance Co (1885) 1 T.L.R. 460 .... 9–020, 9–026
Norwich City Council v Harvey (Paul Clarke) [1989] 1 W.L.R. 828; [1989] 1 All E.R. 1180;
45 B.L.R. 14; (1989) 5 Const. L.J. 154; (1989) 86(25) L.S.G. 45; (1989) 139 N.L.J. 40;
(1989) 133 S.J. 694; Times, January 11, 1989; Independent, January 16, 1989 (C.S.);
Independent, January 6, 1989 CA (Civ Div) 11–031
Norwich Equitable Fire, Re (1887) 57 L.T. 241 .... 1–012, 17–002
Norwich Provident Insurance Society, Re; sub nom. Bath's Case (1878) L.R. 8 Ch. D. 334
CA 23–021
Norwich Union Fire Insurance Co v Colonial Mutual Fire Insurance Co Ltd; sub nom.
Norwich Union Fire Insurance Society Ltd v Colonial Mutual Fire Insurance Co Ltd
[1922] 2 K.B. 461; (1922) 12 Ll.L.R. 215 KBD 5–017, 17–012
Norwich Union Fire Insurance Society Ltd v Traynor [1972] N.Z.L.R. 504 6–010
Norwich Union Fire Insurance Society Ltd v WMH Price Ltd; sub nom. Norwich Union Fire
Insurance Society Ltd v William Price Ltd [1934] A.C. 455; (1934) 49 Ll.L.R. 55 PC
(Aus) 10–057, 2488, 24–089
Norwich Union Insurance Ltd v Meisels [2006] EWHC 2811 (QB); [2007] 1 All E.R.
(Comm) 1138; [2007] Lloyd's Rep. I.R. 69 .... 6–004, 6–030, 6–046, 6–048, 6–050, 6–054,
6–059, 6–071
Norwich Union Life Insurance Co Ltd v Qureshi; Aldrich v Norwich Union Life Insurance
Co Ltd [1999] 2 All E.R. (Comm) 707; [1999] C.L.C. 1963; [2000] Lloyd's Rep. I.R.
1; Times, August 13, 1999CA (Civ Div); affirming [1998] C.L.C. 1605; [1999] Lloyd's
Rep. I.R. 263 QBD (Comm) 6–123, 6–125, 6–132, 13–026
Norwich Union Linked Life Assurance Ltd, Re [2004] EWHC 2802; [2005] B.C.C. 586 Ch
D (Companies Ct) 13–033, 13–036
Notara v Henderson (1871–72) L.R. 7 Q.B. 225 Ex Chamber 24–112
Noten v Harding. See TM Noten BV v Harding
Notman v Anchor Assurance (1854) 4 C.B.N.S. 476 .... 3–010, 5–018
Nottingham v Aldridge [1971] 2 Q.B. 739; [1971] 3 W.L.R. 1; [1971] 2 All E.R. 751; [1971]
1 Lloyd's Rep. 424; [1971] R.T.R. 242; (1971) 10 K.I.R. 252; 115 S.J. 328 QBD 22–017
Novus Aviation Ltd v Onur Air Tasimacilik AS [2009] EWCA Civ 122; [2009] 1 Lloyd's
Rep. 576; [2009] 1 C.L.C. 850 2–005
Noyes v North-Western (1885) 54 Am.Rep. 641 19–044
Nsubuga v Commercial Union Assurance Co Plc [1998] 2 Lloyd's Rep. 682 QBD (Comm) 1–022,
9–026
Nukila, The. See Promet Engineering (Singapore) Pte Ltd v Sturge
Nuovo Consorzio Centrale Guasti Alle Macchine, Re (Nuovo Cegam) [1984] 2 C.M.L.R. 484
CEC 13–045
Nurdin & Peacock Plc v DB Ramsden & Co Ltd [1999] 1 W.L.R. 1249; [1999] 1 All E.R.
941; [1999] 1 E.G.L.R. 15; [1999] 10 E.G. 183; [1999] 09 E.G. 175; [1999] E.G.C.S.
19; (1999) 96(8) L.S.G. 29; (1999) 149 N.L.J. 251; [1999] N.P.C. 17; Times, February
18, 1999 Ch D 10–060, 10–061
Nuvo Electronics Inc v London Assurance (2000) 49 O.R. (3d) 5–006, 6–052
O&R Jewellers Ltd v Terry [1999] Lloyd's Rep. I.R. 436 QBD 15–034, 15–036, 15–057
OT Africa Line Ltd v Magic Sportswear Corp [2004] EWHC 2441 (Comm); [2005] 1
Lloyd's Rep. 252 2–063
OT Computers Ltd (In Administration), Re; sub nom. First National Tricity Finance Ltd v
Ellis; First National Tricity Finance Ltd v OT Computers Ltd (In Administration); Nagra
v OT Computers Ltd [2004] EWCA Civ. 653; [2004] Ch. 317; [2004] 3 W.L.R. 886;
[2004] 2 All E.R. (Comm) 331; [2004] 2 B.C.L.C. 682; [2004] 2 C.L.C. 863; [2004]
B.P.I.R. 932; [2004] Lloyd's Rep. I.R. 669; Times, May 31, 2004 CA (Civ Div) 13–013,
21–007, 21–008, 21–039, 21–045, 21–065, 23–017
O'Brien v Anderton [1979] R.T.R. 388 22–006
O'Brien v Hughes-Gibb & Co (No.2) [1995] L.R.L.R. 90; Independent, May 13, 1994 Ch
D 15–030, 15–034, 15–048, 15–051
O'Brien v Trafalgar Insurance Co Ltd (1945) 78 Ll.L.R. 223; 43 L.G.R. 107; (1945) 109 J.P.
107 CA 22–007
Oake v Cowley Unreported, 1988 22–008
Oakley v Ultra Vehicle Design Ltd (In Liquidation) [2005] EWHC 872 (Ch); [2006] B.C.C.
57; [2005] I.L.Pr. 55; [2006] B.P.I.R. 115 2–029

Ocean Accident & Guarantee Corp Ltd v Cole [1932] 2 K.B. 100; (1932) 43 Ll.L.R. 26 KBD 8–004, 22–015
Ocean Accident and Guarantee Corporation v Williams (1915) 34 N.Z.L.R. 924 6–047
Ocean Masters Inc v Allianz AGF MAT Ltd 2007 N.L.C.A. 35 24–064
Ocean Steamship Co Ltd v Liverpool and London War Risks Association Ltd (The Priam); sub nom. Liverpool and London War Risks Association Ltd v Ocean Steamship Co Ltd [1948] A.C. 243; [1947] 2 All E.R. 586; (1947–48) 81 Ll.L.R. 1; 63 T.L.R. 594; [1948] L.J.R. 304; 177 L.T. 623; 92 S.J. 25 HL; affirming in part [1946] K.B. 561; (1946) 79 Ll.L.R. 467 CA; reversing [1946] 1 All E.R. 123; (1946) 79 Ll.L.R. 58 KBD 5–030, 5–031, 5–032, 25–005
Oceanic Steamship Co v Faber (1907) 13 Com.Cas. 28; (1907) 23 T.L.R. 673 .... 1–031, 5–015, 24–003
O'Connor v BDB Kirby & Co; sub nom. O'Connor v DBD Kirby & Co [1972] 1 Q.B. 90; [1971] 2 W.L.R. 1233; [1971] 2 All E.R. 1415; [1971] 1 Lloyd's Rep. 454; [1971] R.T.R. 440; 115 S.J. 267 CA (Civ Div) 15–036
O'Connor v Bullirnore Underwriting Agency Ltd, Times, 10 March, 2004 6–018
O'Connor v Royal Insurance [1996] C.L.Y. 5142 CC (Central London) 22–007
Oddy v Phoenix Assurance Co [1966] 1 Lloyd's Rep. 134; (1966) 116 N.L.J. 554 Assizes (Cornwall) 19–035, 19–036
Odenbreit v FBTO Schadeverzekeringen NV (C–463/06) [2008] 2 All E.R. (Comm) 733; [2007] E.C.R. I–11321; [2008] I.L.Pr. 12; [2008] Lloyd's Rep. I.R. 354 ECJ 21–047, 22–085
Odyssey Re (London) Ltd v OIC Run-Off Ltd [2001] Lloyd's Rep I.R. 1 .... 1–021, 6–038
Oei v Foster (formerly Crawford) and Eagle Star Insurance Co Ltd [1982] 2 Lloyd's Rep. 170 QBD 20–028, 20–083
Office Appliance Trades Association of Great Britain & Ireland v Roylance (1940) 67 Ll.L.R. 86 KBD 25–003
O'Kane v Jones; The Martin P [2003] EWHC 3470; [2004] 1 Lloyd's Rep. 389; [2005] Lloyd's Rep. I.R. 174 QBD (Comm) 1–021, 4–020, 6–047, 6–059, 6–071, 6–074, 6–092, 6–106, 10–057, 11–046, 11–054, 11–058, 11–059, 11–062, 14–007, 14–008, 19–014, 24–017, 24–030
Olafsson v Gissurarson [2006] EWHC 3162 (QB); [2007] 2 All E.R. 88; [2007] 1 All E.R. (Comm) 776; [2007] 1 Lloyd's Rep. 182; (2007) 157 N.L.J. 30; Times, December 22, 2006 2–004
Oldfield v Price (1860) 2 F. & F. 80 11–067
Oldman v Bewicke (1786) 2 Hy. Bl. 577n 9–003
O'Leary v AXA Pacific Insurance Co 95 O.R. (3d) 315 (2009) 20–049
O'Mahoney v Joliffe; O'Mahoney v Motor Insurers Bureau (1999) 163 J.P. 800; [1999] R.T.R. 245; [1999] Lloyd's Rep. I.R. 321; [1999] P.I.Q.R. P149; Times, February 24, 1999 CA (Civ Div) 22–009, 22–067
Omega Group Holdings Ltd v Kozeny [2002] C.L.C. 132 2–026
Omega Inn Ltd v Continental Insurance Co, 55 D.L.R. (4th) 766 (1988) 23–042
Oom v Bruce (1810) 10 East 225 .... 8–022, 18–012
Ophthalmic Innovations International (UK) Ltd v Ophthalmic Innovations International Inc [2004] EWHC 2948; [2005] I.L.Pr. 10 Ch D 2–043
Opossum Exports Ltd v Aviation and General (Underwriting Agents) Pty Ltd (1984) 3 A.N.Z. Insurance Cases 78,829, 78,837 6–090
Orakpo v Barclays Insurance Services Co Ltd [1995] L.R.L.R. 443; [1994] C.L.C. 373; Lloyd's List, August 22, 1995 (I.D.) CA (Civ Div) 6–018, 6–072, 6–093, 6–107, 6–114, 9–026, 9–032, 15–013
Orakpo v Manson Investments Ltd [1978] A.C. 95; [1977] 3 W.L.R. 229; (1978) 35 P. & C.R. 1; 121 S.J. 632 HL 11–002
O'Reilly v Gonne (1815) 4 Camp. 249 24–073
Orica Ltd v CGU Insurance Ltd [2003] N.S.W.C.A. 331 20–007
Oriental Steamship Co Ltd v Tylor [1893] 2 Q.B. 518 CA 24–026
Orion Insurance Co Plc v Sphere Drake Insurance Plc [1992] 1 Lloyd's Rep. 239 CA (Civ Div); affirming [1990] 1 Lloyd's Rep. 46; Independent, February 1, 1990 QBD (Comm) 1–021
Orr v Trafalgar Insurance Co Ltd (1948–49) 82 Ll.L.R. 1 CA 22–096, 22–097
Osiris Insurance Ltd, Re [1999] 1 B.C.L.C. 182 Ch D (Companies Ct) 16–005
Osman v Moss (J Ralph) [1970] 1 Lloyd's Rep. 313 CA (Civ Div) 5–046, 15–034
Oswell v Vigne (1812) 15 East 70 24–058
Ougier v Jennings (1800) 1 Camp. 505n 24–070
Outokumpu Stainless Ltd v AXA Global Risks (UK) Ltd [2007] EWHC 2555 (Comm); [2008] Lloyd's Rep. I.R. 147 .... 3–005, 3–006, 10–003, 10–019

Overbrooke Estates Ltd v Glencombe Properties Ltd [1974] 1 W.L.R. 1335; [1974] 3 All E.R. 511; 118 S.J. 775 Ch D 6–088, 15–001
Overseas Commodities Ltd v Style [1958] 1 Lloyd's Rep. 546 QBD (Comm) 6–106, 6–107, 7–038, 24–081
Overseas Marine Insurance Co Ltd, Re (1930) 36 Ll.L.R. 183 CA 4–009, 17–004, 24–015
Overseas Medical Supplies Ltd v Orient Transport Services Ltd [1999] 1 All E.R. (Comm) 981; [1999] 2 Lloyd's Rep. 273; [1999] C.L.C. 1243 CA (Civ Div) 15–026
Overseas Union Insurance Ltd v New Hampshire Insurance Co (C–351/89) [1992] Q.B. 434; [1992] 2 W.L.R. 586; [1992] 2 All E.R. 138; [1992] 1 Lloyd's Rep. 204; [1991] E.C.R. I–3317; [1991] I.L.Pr. 495; Times, August 20, 1991; Financial Times, July 19, 1991ECJ 2–008
Overseas Union Insurance Ltd v Turegum Insurance Co [2001] 3 S.L.R. 330 .... 1–032, 1–040
Overseas Union Insurance v Incorporated General Insurance [1992] 1 Lloyd's Rep. 439; Times, December 11, 1991; Financial Times, December 4, 1991 CA (Civ Div) 2–004, 2–005, 2–040
Owens v Brimmell [1977] Q.B. 859; [1977] 2 W.L.R. 943; [1976] 3 All E.R. 765; [1977] R.T.R. 82 QBD 18–050, 22–033
Owners of the Bamburi v Compton (The Bamburi) [1982] 1 Lloyd's Rep. 312; [1982] Com. L.R. 31, Arbitration 24–086
Owners of the Las Mercedes v Owners of the Abidin Daver [1984] A.C. 398; [1984] 2 W.L.R. 196; [1984] 1 All E.R. 470; [1984] 1 Lloyd's Rep. 339; (1984) 134 N.L.J. 235; (1984) 128 S.J. 99 HL 2–005
Owners of the SS Larchgrove v King, The (1919) 1 Ll.L.R. 498 KBD (Comm Ct) 25–005
Owusu v Jackson (t/a Villa Holidays Bal Inn Villas) (C–281/02) [2005] Q.B. 801; [2005] 2 W.L.R. 942; [2005] 2 All E.R. (Comm) 577; [2005] 1 Lloyd's Rep. 452; [2005] E.C.R. I–1383; [2005] 1 C.L.C. 246; [2005] I.L.Pr. 25; Times, March 9, 2005 ECJ 2–005, 2–008
Oxford v Austin [1981] R.T.R. 416 DC 22–007
Oxford Aviation Services Ltd v Godolphin Management Co Ltd [2004] EWHC 232 QBD 15–026
P Samuel & Co Ltd v Dumas; sub nom. P Samuel & Co Ltd v Motor Union Insurance Co Ltd [1924] A.C. 431; (1924) 18 Ll.L.R. 211 HL; affirming [1923] 1 K.B. 592; (1922) 13 Ll.L.R. 503CA 4–016, 5–030, 5–032, 5–041, 5–047, 7–022, 7–047, 11–029, 14–003, 14–012, 14–013, 19–025, 23–001, 24–134
P&B (Run-Off) Ltd v Woolley [2002] EWCA Civ. 65; [2002] 1 All E.R. (Comm) 577; [2002] C.L.C. 717; [2002] Lloyd's Rep. I.R. 344; Times, February 18, 2002 CA (Civ Div) 13–041
P&I Clubs Pooling Agreement, Re [1999] C.M.L.R. 646 13–045
P&I Clubs, Re [1985] O.J. L276/2 13–045
P&O Developments Ltd v Guy's & St Thomas NHS Trust [1999] B.L.R. 3; 62 Con. L.R. 38; (1999) 15 Const. L.J. 374 15–059
P&O Steam Navigation Co v Youell [1997] 2 Lloyd's Rep. 136; Times, April 1, 1997 CA (Civ Div) 20–025, 20–040, 20–036, 20–059
PCW Syndicates v PCW Reinsurers [1996] 1 W.L.R. 1136; [1996] 1 All E.R. 774; [1996] 1 Lloyd's Rep. 241; [1995] C.L.C. 1517; [1995] 4 Re. L.R. 373; Times, October 10, 1995; Independent, September 8, 1995; Lloyd's List, December 7, 1995 (I.D.) CA (Civ Div) 6–004, 6–036, 6–041, 6–042, 6–043, 15–023
PWS Holdings Plc v Edmondson Unreported, 1996 15–054
PT Berlian Laju Tanker TBK v Nuse Shipping Ltd (The Aktor), Aktor, The [2008] EWHC 1330 (Comm); [2008] 2 All E.R. (Comm) 784; [2008] 2 Lloyd's Rep. 246; [2008] 1 C.L.C. 967 .... 1–018, 3–005
PT Karumin Granite v Insurance Company of North America [1993] 1 S.L.R. 650 24–003
Pacific & General Insurance Co Ltd v Hazell; Pacific & General Insurance Co Ltd v Home & Overseas Insurance Co Ltd [1997] L.R.L.R. 65; [1997] B.C.C. 400; [1997] 6 Re. L.R. 157 QBD (Comm) 7–006, 8–007, 8–017, 17–011
Pacific & General Insurance Co Ltd (In Liquidation) v Baltica Insurance Co (UK) Ltd [1996] L.R.L.R. 8; Lloyd's List, January 16, 1996 (I.D.) QBD (Comm) 17–026
Pacific Employers Insurance Co v Non-Marine Underwriters, 71 D.L.R. (4th) 731 (1990) 11–054
Padden v Arbuthnot Pensions & Investments Ltd; sub nom. Arbuthnot Pensions & Investments Ltd v Padden [2004] EWCA Civ. 582; [2004] C.P. Rep. 36; (2004) 101(24) L.S.G. 32; (2004) 148 S.J.L.B. 631 CA (Civ Div) 9–053, 21–010
Padre Island (No.1), The. See Socony Mobil Oil Co Inc v West of England Ship Owners Mutual Insurance Association (London) Ltd
Padre Island (No.2), The. See Socony Mobil Oil Co Inc v West of England Shipowners Mutual Insurance Association (London) Ltd
Padstow Total Loss & Collision Assurance Association, Re (1881–82) L.R. 20 Ch. D. 137 24–007
Page v Fry (1800) 2 Bos. & P. 240 .... 4–016, 4–019, 24–031

Page v Scottish Insurance Corporation (1928) I.J.K.B. 308 11–006
Page v Smith [1996] A.C. 155; [1995] 2 W.L.R. 644; [1995] 2 All E.R. 736; [1995] 2 Lloyd's
  Rep. 95; [1995] R.T.R. 210, [1995] P.I.Q.R. P329; (1995) 92(23) L.S.G. 33; (1995) 145
  N.L.J. 723; (1995) 139 S.J.L.B. 173; Times, May 12, 1995; Independent, May 12, 1995;
  Lloyd's List, May 25, 1995 (I.D.) HL 18–059
Paget v Poland (1947) 80 Ll.L.R. 283 KBD 22–088
Pailor v Cooperative Insurance Society Ltd (1930) 38 Ll.L.R. 237 CA 22–088, 22–096
Paine v Catlins [2004] EWHC 3054; 98 Con. L.R. 107; [2005] Lloyd's Rep. I.R. 665 QBD
  (TCC) 3–009, 5–050, 5–051, 19–039
Paine v Meller (1801) 6 Ves. 349 19–008
Palatine Insurance Co Ltd v Gregory; sub nom. Gregory v Palatine Insurance Co Ltd [1926]
  A.C. 90; (1925) 23 Ll.L.R. 12 PC (Can) 7–028
Palmer v Cornhill Insurance Co Ltd. See AW&E Palmer v Cornhill Insurance Co Ltd
Palmer v Fenning (1833) 9 Bing. 460 24–065
Palmer v Hawes (1841) Ellis. Ins. 131 18–029
Palmer v Marshall (1832) 8 Bing. 317 24–065
Palmer v Naylor (1854) 10 Exch. 382 24–135
Palmer v Palmer [2008] EWCA Civ 46; [2008] C.P. Rep. 21; [2008] 4 Costs L.R. 513; [2008]
  Lloyd's Rep. I.R. 535 20–055
Palmieri v Misir [2003] O.J. No.3518 20–049
Palyart v Leckie (1817) 6 M. & S. 290 8–022
Pan American World Airways Inc v Aetna Casualty and Surety Co, The [1975] 1 Lloyd's
  Rep. 77; [1974] 1 Lloyd's Rep. 207 US Ct 25–003, 25–004, 25–008
Pan Atlantic Insurance Co Ltd v Pine Top Insurance Co Ltd [1989] 1 Lloyd's Rep. 568 CA
  (Civ Div); affirming [1988] 2 Lloyd's Rep. 505; Times, May 23, 1988; Independent,
  May 9, 1988 .... 4–024, 15–023, 15–024, 22–048
Pan Atlantic Insurance Co Ltd v Pine Top Insurance Co Ltd [1995] 1 A.C. 501; [1994] 3
  W.L.R. 677; [1994] 3 All E.R. 581; [1994] 2 Lloyd's Rep. 427; [1994] C.L.C. 868;
  (1994) 91(36) L.S.G. 36; (1994) 144 N.L.J. 1203; (1994) 138 S.J.L.B. 182; Times, July
  27, 1994; Independent, August 4, 1994 HL; affirming [1993] 1 Lloyd's Rep. 496; Times,
  March 8, 1993 CA (Civ Div); affirming [1992] 1 Lloyd's Rep. 101 QBD (Comm) 1–011,
                          6–001, 6–002, 6–003, 6–005, 6–017, 6–020, 6–021, 6–024, 6–027,
                          6–028, 6–073, 6–079, 6–081, 6–084, 6–087, 6–095, 6–100, 6–107,
                          6–114, 6–116, 6–125, 6–130, 17–008, 24–030
Pan-United Shipyard Pte Ltd v India [2000] 4 S.L.R. 303 20–028
Panamanian Oriental Steamship Corp v Wright (The Anita) [1971] 1 W.L.R. 882; [1971] 2
  All E.R. 1028; [1971] 1 Lloyd's Rep. 487; 115 S.J. 345 CA (Civ Div); reversing [1970]
  2 Lloyd's Rep. 365 QBD (Comm) 24–083, 24–086, 24–088
Pang Wai Chung v Hoi Tat Rubber Factory [1992] 2 H.K.C. 447 11–042
Pangood Ltd v Barclay Brown & Co Ltd [1999] 1 All E.R. (Comm.) 460; [1999] Lloyd's
  Rep. I.R. 405; [1999] Lloyd's Rep. P.N. 237; [1999] P.N.L.R. 678 CA (Civ Div) 15–031,
                                                          15–032, 15–035
Papademitriou v Henderson [1939] 3 All E.R. 908 24–080
Papera Traders Co Ltd v Hyundai Merchant Marine Co Ltd (The Eurasian Dream) (No.1)
  [2002] EWHC 118; [2002] 1 Lloyd's Rep. 719 QBD (Comm) 24–062
Paradine v Jane (1647) Aleyn. 26 19–020
Parfitt v Thompson (1844) 13 M. & W. 392 24–062
Paris v Gilham (1813) Coop. G. 56 10–051
Parker v Potts (1815) 3 Dow. 23 24–061
Parker & Heard Ltd v Generali Asscicurazioni SpA Unreported, 1988 .... 6–056, 6–107, 9–024
Parkin v Dick (1809) 11 East 502 .... 5–036, 24–064
Parklane Floral & Balloons Design v Allianz Insurance (Hong Kong) Ltd [2006] H.K.E.C.
  109 7–015
Parmeter v Cousins (1809) 2 Camp. 235; 170 E.R. 1141 .... 24–061, 24–065
Parouth, The. See Compania Naviera Micro SA v Shipley International Inc
Parr's Bank v Albert Mines (1900) 5 Com.Cas 116 .... 8–019, 23–029
Parry v Ashley (1829) 3 Sim. 97 19–031
Partenreederei M/S Heidberg v Grosvenor Grain & Feed Co Ltd (The Heidberg) (No.2)
  Heidberg, The [1994] 2 Lloyd's Rep. 287 2–052
Pasquali & Co v Traders & General Insurance Association (1921) 9 Ll.L.R. 514 KBD 1–019
Passmoor v Gibbons [1979] R.T.R. 53; [1978] Crim. L.R. 498 DC 22–009
Passmore v Vulcan Boiler & General Insurance Co Ltd (1936) 54 Ll.L.R. 92; (1936) 154 L.T.
  258 KBD 3–010, 18–043, 20–027, 22–098
Patel v London Transport Executive [1981] R.T.R. 29 CA (Civ Div) 22–023

Patel v Windsor Life Assurance Co Ltd [2008] EWHC 76 (Comm); [2008] Lloyd's Rep. I.R.
359 .... 6–047, 9–025, 14–027, 18–005
Pateras v Royal Exchange Assurance (1934) 49 Ll.L.R. 400 KBD 9–025
Paterson v Harris (1861) 1 B. & S. 336 .... 10–030, 24–134
Paterson v Powell (1832) 9 Bing. 320 8–022
Patrick v Eames (1813) 3 Camp. 441 24–026
Patrick v Royal London Mutual Insurance Society Ltd. *See* Ronson International Ltd v
Patrick
Patteson v Northern Accident [1901] 2 Ir. R. 262 20–045
Paul Smith Ltd v H&S International Holding Inc [1991] 2 Lloyd's Rep. 127 3–015
Pawson v Watson (1778) 1 Doug. K.B. 12n 7–024
Pawson v Watson (1778) 2 Cowp. 785 .... 6–015, 6–116, 18–028
Paxman v Union Assurance Society Ltd (1923) 15 Ll.L.R. 206; (1923) 39 T.L.R. 424 KBD ... 15–019
Payton v Brooks [1974] 1 Lloyd's Rep. 241; [1974] R.T.R. 169 CA (Civ Div) 10–017
Peabody v Eagle Star insurance Co Ltd Unreported, December 1998 CC (Worksop) 3–010, 5–050,
19–049
Pearl Assurance Plc v Kavanagh [2001] C.L.Y. 3832 CC (Milton Keynes) 3–018, 22–043
Pearl Assurance (Unit Linked Pensions) Ltd, Re [2006] EWHC 2291 (Ch); (2006) 103(38)
L.S.G. 33; (2006) 150 S.J.L.B. 1250; [2007] Bus. L.R. D10 13–035
Pearl Life Assurance Co v Johnson; Pearl Life Assurance Co v Greenhalgh [1909] 2 K.B. 288
KBD 1–022
Pearson Plc v Excess Insurance Co Ltd Unreported, 1988 .... 3–010, 6–018, 15–035
Pearson v Amicable Assurance (1859) 27 Beav. 229 14–026
Pearson v Commercial Union Assurance Co (1875–76) L.R. 1 App. Cas. 498 HL 3–007, 19–044,
24–070, 24–072
Pedder v Mosley (1862) 31 Beav. 159 18–024
Pedley v Avon Insurance [2003] EWHC 2007 QBD 6–006, 6–052, 6–059
Peekay Intermark Ltd v Australia & New Zealand Banking Group Ltd [2006] EWCA Civ.
386; [2006] 1 C.L.C. 582 CA (Civ Div) 6–011
Pellas (E) & Co v Neptune Marine Insurance Co (1879–80) L.R. 5 C.P.D. 34 CA 9–038, 14–026
Pendennis Shipyard Ltd v Magrathea (Pendennis) Ltd; sub nom. Pendennis Shipyard Ltd v
Margrathea (Pendennis) Ltd (In Liquidation) [1998] 1 Lloyd's Rep. 315; (1997) 94(35)
L.S.G. 35; (1997) 141 S.J.L.B. 185; Times, August 27, 1997 QBD (Merc) 20–055
Pender v Commercial Bank of Scotland Ltd 1940 S.L.T. 306 OH 14–030
Peninsular and Oriental Branch Service v Commonwealth Shipping Representative (The
Geelong). *See* Commonwealth Shipping Representative v Peninsular and Oriental
Branch Service
Penniall v Harborne (1848) 11 Q.B. 368 .... 19–022, 19–025
Pennington v Crossley & Son (1897) 77 L.T. 43 8–002
Pennsylvania Co for Insurances on Lives and Granting Annuities v Mumford [1920] 2 K.B.
537; (1920) 2 Ll.L.R. 444 CA 5–015, 10–034, 10–037, 23–027
People's Department Stores Ltd Inc, Re (1998) 23 C.B.R. (4th) 200 20–087
Percy v West Bay Boat Builders and Shipyards Ltd Unreported, 1997 15–037
Perks v Clark (Inspector of Taxes) [2001] EWCA Civ 1228; [2001] 2 Lloyd's Rep. 431;
[2001] S.T.C. 1254; [2002] I.C.R. 302; 74 T.C. 187; [2001] B.T.C. 336; [2001] S.T.I.
1086; (2001) 98(33) L.S.G. 32; (2001) 145 S.J.L.B. 214; Times, October 2, 2001 24–006
Perrins v Marine & General Travellers' Insurance Society (1859) 2 El. & El. 317 .... 6–073, 7–037,
18–031
Perry v Equitable Life Assurance Society of the United States of America (1929) 45 T.L.R.
468 2–030
Perry v Tendring DC; Thurbon v Tendring DC, 30 B.L.R. 118; 3 Con. L.R. 74; [1985] 1
E.G.L.R. 260; (1984) 1 Const. L.J. 152; [1985] C.I.L.L. 145 QBD 19–038
Persson v London Country Buses [1974] 1 W.L.R. 569; [1974] 1 All E.R. 1251; [1974] 1
Lloyd's Rep. 415; [1974] R.T.R. 346; 118 S.J. 134; Times, December 24, 1973 CA (Civ
Div) 22–073
Pesquerias y Secaderos de Bacalao de Espana SA v Beer [1949] 1 All E.R. 845 (Note);
(1948–49) 82 Ll.L.R. 501; [1949] W.N. 189; 93 S.J. 371 HL; affirming (1947) 80
Ll.L.R. 318 CA; reversing (1946) 79 Ll.L.R. 417; (1946) 175 L.T. 495 KBD ... 24–088, 24–111,
25–004
Peters v General Accident Fire & Life Assurance Corp Ltd (1938) 60 Ll.L.R. 311; [1938] 2
All E.R. 267 CA 14–022, 14–024, 22–010, 22–027, 22–088

Petrofina (UK) Ltd v Magnaload Ltd [1984] Q.B. 127; [1983] 3 W.L.R. 805; [1983] 3 All
   E.R. 35; [1983] 2 Lloyd's Rep. 91; 25 B.L.R. 37; (1983) 80 L.S.G. 2677; (1983) 127 S.J.
   729 QBD (Comm) 4–005, 11–027, 11–028, 14–003, 14–004, 14–018, 19–010, 19–012,
                                                                                            19–032
Petroleo Brasileiro SA v Petromec Inc; Petromec Inc v Petroleo Brasileiro SA [2005] EWHC
   2430 QBD (Comm) 8–008
Pettitt v Pettitt; sub nom. P v P [1970] A.C. 777; [1969] 2 W.L.R. 966; [1969] 2 All E.R. 385;
   (1969) 20 P. & C.R. 991; 113 S.J. 344 HL 18–006
Petty v Wilson (1869) L.R. 4 Ch. 574 18–022
Peyman v Lanjani [1985] Ch. 457; [1985] 2 W.L.R. 154; [1984] 3 All E.R. 703; (1984) 48
   P. & C.R. 398; (1985) 82 L.S.G. 43; (1984) 128 S.J. 853 CA (Civ Div) 6–095
Phelps v Auldjo (1809) 2 Camp. 350 .... 24–069, 24–073
Philadelphia National Bank v Poole [1938] 2 All E.R. 199 .... 10–034, 23–027
Philadelphia National Bank v Price (1938) 60 Ll.L.R. 257 CA; affirming (1937) 58 Ll.L.R.
   238KBD 23–021
Philip Powis Ltd, Re [1998] B.C.C. 756; [1998] 1 B.C.L.C. 440; (1998) 95(11) L.S.G. 36;
   Times, March 6, 1998 CA (Civ Div) 21–014
Phillips v Baillie (1784) 3 Doug K.B. 374 7–038
Phillips v Barber (1821) 5 B. & Ald. 161 .... 24–134, 24–139
Phillips v Chapman (1921) 8 Ll.L.R. 356 CA; affirming (1921) 7 Ll.L.R. 139 KBD 9–025
Phillips v Eyre (1870–71) L.R. 6 Q.B. 1 2–061
Phillips v Headlam (1831) 2 B. & Ad. 383 24–062
Phillips v Irving (1884) 7 Man. & G. 325 24–072
Phillips v Nairne (1847) 4 C.B. 343 .... 24–062, 24–086
Phillips v Rafiq [2006] EWHC 1461 QBD 22–067
Phillips v Royal London Mutual (1911) 105 L.T. 136 .... 8–022, 18–010, 18–012
Phillips v Symes (A Bankrupt) [2008] UKHL 1; [2008] 1 W.L.R. 180; [2008] 2 All E.R. 537;
   [2008] 1 All E.R. (Comm) 918; [2008] 1 Lloyd's Rep. 344; [2008] 1 C.L.C. 29; [2008]
   I.L.Pr. 21; (2008) 152(4) S.J.L.B. 28; Times, January 28, 2008 2–008
Phillips v Syndicate 992 Gunner [2003] EWHC 1084; [2003] 2 C.L.C. 152; [2004] Lloyd's
   Rep. I.R. 426 QBD 11–050, 11–055, 21–024
Phillips & Co v Whatley [2007] UKPC 28; [2008] Lloyd's Rep. I.R. 111; [2007] P.N.L.R. 27;
   (2007) 104(20) L.S.G. 28; (2007) 151 S.J.L.B. 612 PC (Gibraltar) 7–048, 15–056
Phillips (ABW) and Stratton (Albert) v Dorintal Insurance Ltd [1987] 1 Lloyd's Rep. 482
   QBD (Comm) 17–014
Phoenix Assurance Co v Spooner [1905] 2 K.B. 753KBD 11–042, 19–009
Phoenix Dynamo Manufacturing Co Ltd v Mountain (1921) 6 Ll.L.R. 369 KBD 5–005, 5–014
Phoenix General Insurance Co of Greece SA v Halvanon Insurance Co Ltd; sub nom.
   Phoenix General Insurance Co of Greece SA v Administratia Asigurarilor de Stat [1988]
   Q.B. 216; [1987] 2 W.L.R. 512; [1987] 2 All E.R. 152; [1986] 2 Lloyd's Rep. 552;
   [1987] Fin. L.R. 48; (1987) 84 L.S.G. 1055; (1987) 131 S.J. 257; Financial Times,
   October 15, 1986 CA (Civ Div) 6–111, 7–007, 9–003, 13–020, 15–042, 17–007, 17–013,
                                                                                            17–015
Phoenix Insurance Co v De Monchy; sub nom. De Monchy v Phoenix Insurance Co of
   Hartford (1929) 34 Ll.L.R. 201; (1929) 35 Com. Cas. 67 HL; affirming (1928) 30
   Ll.L.R. 194 CA 3–018, 19–007, 24–080
Phoenix Life, Re (1862) 2 J. & H. 441 .... 8–024, 15–003
Phoenix Life Assurance Co v Sheridan (1860) 6 H.L. Cas. 745 .... 1–048, 8–004
Phyn v Royal Exchange Assurance Co (1798) 7 T.R. 505 .... 24–070, 24–073, 24–138
Picken v Guardian Assurance Co of Canada (1993) 66 O.A.C. 39 20–050
Pickering v Buck (1812) 15 East 38 15–001
Pickersgill & Sons Ltd v London and Marine Provincial Insurance Co Ltd (1912) 107 L.T.
   305 14–027
Pickett v Roberts; sub nom. Pickett v Motor Insurers Bureau [2004] EWCA Civ. 6; [2004]
   1 W.L.R. 2450; [2004] 2 All E.R. 685; [2004] R.T.R. 28; [2004] Lloyd's Rep. I.R. 513;
   [2004] P.I.Q.R. P24; (2004) 148 S.J.L.B. 117 CA (Civ Div) 22–068
Pickup v Thames and Mersey Marine Insurance Co Ltd (1878) 3 K.B. 594 24–061
Pictorial Machinery Ltd v Nichols (1940) 45 Com.Cas. 334 23–026
Pictorial Machinery Ltd v Nicolls (1940) 67 Ll.L.R. 461 KBD 5–049
Pictorial Machinery Ltd v Nicolls (Costs) (1940) 67 Ll.L.R. 524 KBD 20–047
Piddington v Co-operative Insurance Society Ltd [1934] 2 K.B. 236 .... 22–036, 22–096
Piermay Shipping Co SA v Chester; The Michael [1979] 2 Lloyd's Rep. 1 CA (Civ Div) 9–025,
                                                                                            24–138

Pike (Butchers) Ltd v Independent insurance Co. *See* John A Pike (Butchers) Ltd v Independent Insurance Co Ltd

Pilkington UK Ltd v CGU Insurance Plc [2004] EWCA Civ. 23; [2005] 1 All E.R. (Comm) 283; [2004] 1 C.L.C. 1059; [2004] B.L.R. 97; [2004] T.C.L.R. 5; [2004] Lloyd's Rep. I.R. 891; [2004] N.P.C. 10 CA (Civ Div) 3–003, 7–009, 7–014, 10–034, 10–039, 20–076, 21–010

Pim v Reid (1843) 6 Man. & G. 1 .... 5–017, 6–103

Pimm v Lewis (1862) 2 F. & F. 778 6–064

Pindos Shipping Corp v Frederick Charles Raven (The Mata Hari) [1983] 2 Lloyd's Rep. 449 QBD (Comm) 1–019, 1–034

Pine Top Insurance Co v Unione Italiana Anglo Saxon Reinsurance Co [1987] 1 Lloyd's Rep. 476 QBD (Comm) 3–015, 17–012

Pink v Fleming (1890) L.R. 25 Q.B.D. 396 CA 5–032, 24–080

Pioneer Concrete (UK) Ltd v National Employers Mutual General Insurance Association Ltd [1985] 2 All E.R. 395; [1985] 1 Lloyd's Rep. 274; [1985] Fin. L.R. 251 QBD (Comm) ... 7–013, 9–003, 9–004, 9–006, 9–043, 21–023

Piper v Royal Exchange Assurance (1932) 44 Ll.L.R. 103 KBD 6–056, 9–025, 10–057, 19–007, 24–031

Pipon v Cope (1808) 1 Camp. 434 .... 24–064, 24–138

Piracy Jure Gentium, Re; Reference under the Judicial Committee Act 1833, Re [1934] A.C. 586; (1934) 49 Ll.L.R. 411 PC (UK) 24–135

Pirelli General Cable Works Ltd v Oscar Faber & Partners [1983] 2 A.C. 1; [1983] 2 W.L.R. 6; [1983] 1 All E.R. 65; (1983) 265 E.G. 979; Times, December 11, 1982 HL 5–015, 15–061

Pitman v Universal Marine Insurance Co (1881–82) L.R. 9 Q.B.D. 192 CA 24–103

Pittegrew v Pringle (1832) 3 B. & Ad. 514 .... 24–068, 24–129

Pitts v Hunt [1991] 1 Q.B. 24; [1990] 3 W.L.R. 542; [1990] 3 All E.R. 344; [1990] R.T.R. 290; (1990) 134 S.J. 834; Times, April 13, 1990; Independent, May 11, 1990 CA (Civ Div) 22–033, 22–034, 22–035, 22–060

Plaistow Transport v Graham [1966] 1 Lloyd's Rep. 639; 116 N.L.J. 1033 QBD 5–012

Planche v Fletcher (1779) 1 Doug. 251 .... 6–065, 24–064

Planton v DPP. *See* R. (on the application of Planton) v DPP

Plaza Fibreglass Manufacturing Ltd v Cardinal Insurance Co 68 D.L.R. (4th) 586 (1990) 10–022

Pleasurama v Sun Alliance and London Insurance [1979] 1 Lloyd's Rep. 389 QBD 10–014

Plymouth and South West Co-operative Society Ltd v Architecture, Structure & Management Ltd [2006] EWHC 3252 (TCC); 111 Con. L.R. 189; [2007] Lloyd's Rep. I.R. 596 20–055

Pocock v Century Insurance Co Ltd [1960] 2 Lloyd's Rep. 150 Assizes (Leeds) 18–054

Poland v Julien Praet et Cie SA [1961] 1 Lloyd's Rep. 187 CA 1–047

Pole v Fitzgerald (1754) Amb. 214 24–138

Pole v Rogers (1840) 2 Mood. & R. 287 18–030

Police v Bishop [1956] Crim. L.R. 569 22–091

Policy No.6402 of the Scottish Equitable Life Assurance Society, Re [1902] 1 Ch. 282 Ch D 18–024

Policyholders Protection Board v Official Receiver [1976] 1 W.L.R. 447; [1976] 2 All E.R. 58; 120 S.J. 130 Ch D 16–023

Polivitte Ltd v Commercial Union Assurance Co Plc [1987] 1 Lloyd's Rep. 379 QBD 9–025

Pollard Ashby & Co (France) Ltd v Franco-British Marine Insurance Co Ltd (1920) 5 Ll.L.R. 286 KBD 15–041

Polpen Shipping Co Ltd v Commercial Union Assurance Co Ltd [1943] K.B. 161; (1942) 74 Ll.L.R. 157 KBD 24–006

Polurrian Steamship Co Ltd v Young [1915] 1 K.B. 922 CA 24–086

Poole v Adams (1864) 10 L.T. 287 19–009

Poole v HM Treasury [2007] EWCA Civ 1021; [2008] 1 All E.R. (Comm) 1132; [2007] 2 C.L.C. 727; [2008] Eu. L.R. 309; [2008] Lloyd's Rep. I.R. 134; (2007) 104(43) L.S.G. 32; Times, December 24, 2007 13–042

Poole Harbour Yacht Club Marina Ltd v Excess Marine Insurance Ltd [2001] Lloyd's Rep. I.R. 580 QBD (Comm) 20–048, 20–051

Pope v St. Leger (1693) 1 Salk. 344; 91 E.R. 301 4–002

Popi M, The. *See* Rhesa Shipping Co SA v Edmunds

Port Glasgow & Newark Sailcloth Co v Caledonian Ry (1892) 29 S.L.R. 577 18–002

Port-Rose v Phoenix Assurance (1986) 136 N.L.J. 333 QBD 5–050

Portage La Prairie Mutual Insurance Co v Commission du District d'amenagement du Madawaska [2006] N.B.J. No.454 20–049

Portavon Cinema Co Ltd v Price (1939) 161 L.T. 417 .... 10–051, 11–054

Portavon Cinema Co Ltd v Price [1939] 4 All E.R. 601 .... 4–023, 10–051

Porter v Addo; sub nom. Porter v Motor Insurers Bureau [1978] 2 Lloyd's Rep. 463; [1978]
R.T.R. 503; 122 S.J. 592; Times, May 18, 1978 QBD 22–067
Porter v GIO [2002] N.S.W.S.C. 20–047, 20–080
Porter v NEL Unreported, 1992 18–057
Porter v Zurich Insurance Co [2009] EWHC 376 (QB); [2009] 2 All E.R. (Comm) 658;
[2009] N.P.C. 38 .... 5–041, 5–042, 7–008, 9–003
Portvale Steamship Co Ltd v Royal Exchange Assurance Corp (1932) 43 Ll. L. Rep. 161 24–066
Post Office v Norwich Union Fire Insurance Society Ltd [1967] 2 Q.B. 363; [1967] 2 W.L.R.
709; [1967] 1 All E.R. 577; [1967] 1 Lloyd's Rep. 216; 111 S.J. 71 CA (Civ Div) ... 20–034,
21–010, 21–014, 21–018, 21–023, 21–049
Potter v Rankin (1873) L.R. 6 H.L. 83 HL 11–066, 11–067, 24–088, 24–091, 24–111
Poullorizos (N) & Co v E Capelcure & Co Ltd (1926) 26 Ll.l.L.R. 19 KBD 15–041
Powell v Brodhurst [1901] 2 Ch. 160 Ch D 14–015
Powell v Hyde (1855) 2 E. & E. 160 25–012
Power v Butcher (1829) 10 B. & C. 329 .... 15–033, 24–077
Powles v Innes (1843) 11 M. & W. 10 14–022
Powney v Coxage, TimesTimes, March 8, 1988 QBD 22–063
Pozzolanic Lytag Ltd v Bryan Hobson Associates [1999] B.L.R. 267; (1999) 1 T.C.L.R. 233;
63 Con. L.R. 81; [1999] Lloyd's Rep. P.N. 125; (1999) 15 Const. L.J. 135; (1999) 143
S.J.L.B. 30; Times, December 3, 1998 QBD (TCC) 15–026
Practice Statement (Ch D: Schemes of Arrangements with Creditors) [2002] 1 W.L.R. 1345;
[2002] 3 All E.R. 96; [2002] B.C.C. 355; (2002) 146 S.J.L.B. 99 16–005
Pratt v Aigaion Insurance Co SA (The Resolute) [2008] EWCA Civ 1314; [2009] 2 All E.R.
(Comm) 387; [2009] 1 Lloyd's Rep. 225; [2008] 2 C.L.C. 756; [2009] Lloyd's Rep. I.R.
149; Times, December 3, 2008 .... 3–005, 3–007, 3–010, 7–032, 7–034, 7–037
Pratt v Patrick [1924] 1 K.B. 488 KBD 22–009
Prenn v Simmonds [1971] 1 W.L.R. 1381; [1971] 3 All E.R. 237; (1971) 115 S.J. 654 HL 3–005
Prentice v Hereward Housing Association [2001] EWCA Civ. 437; [2001] 2 All E.R.
(Comm) 900; Times, March 30, 2001 CA (Civ Div) 9–035
Prentis Donegan & Partners Ltd v Leeds & Leeds Co Inc [1998] 2 Lloyd's Rep. 326; [1998]
C.L.C. 1132 QBD (Comm) 8–018, 15–031, 15–032, 24–078
Presentaciones Musicales SA v Secunda [1994] Ch. 271; [1994] 2 W.L.R. 660; [1994] 2 All
E.R. 737; (1994) 138 S.J.L.B. 4; Times, November 29, 1993 CA (Civ Div) 15–003
President of India v Lips Maritime Corp (The Lips); sub nom. Lips Maritime Corp v
President of India [1988] A.C. 395; [1987] 3 W.L.R. 572; [1987] 3 All E.R. 110; [1987]
2 Lloyd's Rep. 311; [1987] 2 F.T.L.R. 477; [1987] Fin. L.R. 313; (1987) 84 L.S.G. 2765;
(1987) 137 N.L.J. 734; (1987) 131 S.J. 1085 HL 10–022, 10–023, 10–025
Priam, The. See Ocean Steamship Co Ltd v Liverpool and London War Risks Association
Ltd
Price v Livingstone (1881–82) L.R. 9 Q.B.D. 679 CA 24–068
Price v Maritime Insurance Co Ltd [1901] 2 K.B. 412 CA 24–017
Price v Society of Lloyd's [2000] Lloyd's Rep. I.R. 453 QBD (Comm) 13–042
Pride Valley Foods Ltd v Independent Insurance Co Ltd [1999] 1 Lloyd's Rep. I.R. 120 CA
(Civ Div) 10–022
Price & Co v A1 Ships Small Damage Insurance Association Ltd (1889) L.R. 22 Q.B.D. 580
CA 3–007
Prifti v Musini Sociedad Anonima de Seguros y Reaseguros [2003] EWHC 2796; [2004] 1
C.L.C. 517; [2004] Lloyd's Rep. I.R. 528 QBD (Admin) 2–008, 6–062, 17–007, 17–012
Prince of Wales Assurance Society v Athenaeum Assurance Society; sub nom. Prince of
Wales Assurance Co v Harding (1858) 3 C.B.N.S. 756n; EB. & E. 183; 27 L.J.Q.B. 297;
4 Jur.N.S. 851; 31 L.T.O.S. 149 8–002
Prince of Wales Assurance v Palmer (1858) 25 Beav. 605 .... 5–041, 8–022
Prince of Wales Life v Harding. See Prince of Wales Assurance Society v Athenaeum
Assurance Society
Princette Models Ltd v Reliance Fire and Accident Insurance Corp Ltd [1960] 1 Lloyd's Rep.
49 QBD 5–012
Pringle v Hartley (1774) 3 Atk. 195 11–066
Printpak v AGF Insurance Ltd [1999] 1 All E.R. (Comm.) 466; [1999] Lloyd's Rep. I.R. 542;
Times, February 3, 1999 CA (Civ Div) 6–076, 7–039
Pritchard v Merchants' and Tradesmen's Mutual Life Assurance Society (1858) 3 C.B.N.S.
622 .... 1–021, 1–031, 1–048, 8–009, 8–024, 10–057
Probatina Shipping Co Ltd v Sun Insurance Office Ltd (The Sageorge) [1974] Q.B. 635;
[1974] 2 W.L.R. 666; [1974] 2 All E.R. 478; [1974] 1 Lloyd's Rep. 369; 118 S.J. 331
CA (Civ Div) 6–107

Proforce Recruit Ltd v Rugby Group Ltd [2007] EWHC 1621 (QB); [2008] 1 All E.R.
    (Comm) 569 3–005
Project Asia Line Inc v Shone; The Pride of Donegal [2002] EWHC 24; [2002] 1 Lloyd's
    Rep. 659 QBD (Comm) 24–062
Promet Engineering (Singapore) Pte Ltd v Sturge (The Nukila) [1997] 2 Lloyd's Rep. 146;
    [1997] C.L.C. 966; Times, April 10, 1997CA (Civ Div); reversing [1996] 1 Lloyd's Rep.
    85; [1996] C.L.C. 294; Independent, December 4, 1995 (C.S.); Lloyd's List, November
    15, 1995 (I.D.) QBD (Comm) 5–015, 10–003, 24–003, 24–112
Property Insurance Co Ltd v National Protector Insurance Co Ltd (1913) 12 Asp. M.L.C.
    287; 18 Com.Cas. 119; 57 S.J. 284; 108 L.T. 104 .... 6–069, 6–118, 17–007
Protapapa v Dominion Insurance Co Ltd [1954] 1 Lloyd's Rep. 402 QBD 8–007
Protea Leasing Ltd v Royal Air Cambodge Co Ltd [2002] EWHC 2731 (Comm); Times,
    January 13, 2003 .... ??–???
Proudfoot Plc v Federal Insurance Co [1997] I.R.L.R. 659 QBD (Comm) 23–022, 23–024
Proudfoot v Montefiore (1866–67) L.R. 2 Q.B. 511 QB 6–036, 6–037, 15–017
Provincial Insurance Co Ltd v Crowder (1927) 27 Ll.L.R. 28 KBD 15–041
Provincial Insurance Co Ltd v Morgan & Foxon; sub nom. Morgan and Provincial Insurance
    Co Ltd, Re; Morgan & Foxon v Provincial Insurance Co Ltd [1933] A.C. 240; (1932)
    44 Ll.L.R. 275 HL 3–010, 5–021, 5–022, 7–021, 7–029, 7–034, 7–037, 22–086
Provincial Insurance Co of Canada v Leduc (1874–75) L.R. 6 P.C. 224 PC (Can) 4–024, 19–025,
                                                                        24–030, 24–031, 24–088, 24–089
Prudent Tankers SA v Dominion Insurance Co; The Caribbean Sea [1980] 1 Lloyd's Rep.
    338 QBD (Comm) 24–003
Prudential Insurance Co v Inland Revenue Commissioners [1904] 2 K.B. 658; 73 L.J.K.B.
    734; 53 W.R. 108; 48 S.J. 605; 91 L.T. 520; 20 T.L.R. 621 KBD ... 1–002, 1–003, 1–006, 1–009,
                                                                                        1–010, 18–001
Prudential Life Insurance Co Ltd v Manitoba Public Insurance Corp (1976) 67 D.L.R. (3d)
    521 20–050
Prudential Staff Union v Hall [1947] K.B. 685; (1947) 80 Ll.L.R. 410; 63 T.L.R. 392; [1948]
    L.J.R. 619 KBD 4–018, 4–019, 18–007, 19–030, 20–006
Pryke v Gibbs Hartley Cooper Ltd; Excess Insurance Co Ltd v Gibbs Hartley Cooper Ltd
    [1991] 1 Lloyd's Rep. 602 QBD (Comm) 1–001, 1–010, 6–001, 6–118, 15–020, 15–028,
                                                                                                15–043
Pugh v Knipe [1972] R.T.R. 286; [1972] Crim. L.R. 247 DC 22–008
Pugh v Leeds (1777) 2 Cowp. 714 5–004
Pugh v London Brighton & South Coast Railway Co [1896] 2 Q.B. 248 CA 18–043, 18–049,
                                                                                                18–059
Puller v Glover (1810) 12 East 124 10–019
Puller v Staniforth (1809) 11 East 232 10–019
Pumbien v Vines [1996] R.T.R. 37 22–009
Punjab National Bank v De Boinville [1992] 1 W.L.R. 1138; [1992] 3 All E.R. 104; [1992]
    1 Lloyd's Rep. 7; [1992] E.C.C. 348; (1991) 141 N.L.J. 85; Times, June 4, 1991;
    Financial Times, June 5, 1991 CA (Civ Div) 1–033, 3–017, 14–027, 15–044, 15–062
Qualifying Insurers Subscribing to the ARP v Ross & Co [2004] EWHC 1181; [2004]
    U.K.C.L.R. 1483; [2006] E.C.C. 5; [2004] Eu. L.R. 879 Ch D 13–044
Quantum Processing Services Co v Axa Insurance UK Plc [2008] EWCA Civ 1640 12–031
Quebec Fire v Louis (1851) 7 Moo. P.C. 286 11–001
Quebec Marine Insurance Co v Commercial Bank of Canada (1869–71) L.R. 3 P.C. 234 PC
    (Can) 7–043, 24–061, 24–062
Queen Insurance Co v Vey (1867) 16 L.T. 239 10–049
Queen Insurance v Parsons. See Citizens Insurance Co of Canada v Parsons
Queen of Spain v Parr (1869) 39 L.J. Ch. 73 15–033
Queensland Government Railways and Electric Power Transmission v Manufacturers Mutual
    Insurance [1969] 1 Lloyd's Rep. 214 HC (Aus) 19–034
Queensland Mines Ltd v Hudson [1978] 1 A.J.L.R. 379 20–086
Quicke's Trusts, Re; sub nom. Poltimore v Quicke [1908] 1 Ch. 887 Ch D 10–051
Quin v National Assurance (1839) Jones & Carey 316 Ex Ch 1–017, 3–010
Quinby Enterprises Ltd (In Liquidation) v General Accident Fire and Life Assurance
    Corporation Public Ltd Co [1995] 1 N.Z.L.R. 736 6–049
Quinn Direct Insurance Ltd v Law Society of England and Wales [2009] EWHC 2588 (Ch);
    (2009) 153(42) S.J.L.B. 29 .... 9–129, 20–037
Quinta Communications SA v Warrington [1999] 2 All E.R. (Comm) 123; [2000] Lloyd's
    Rep. I.R. 81 CA (Civ Div) 1–032

Quorum A/S v Schramm (Costs) [2002] 2 All E.R. (Comm) 179; [2002] 2 Lloyd's Rep. 72; [2002] C.L.C. 77; [2002] Lloyd's Rep. I.R. 315; (2003) 19 Const. L.J. 224 QBD (Comm) 10–027, 10–028
Quorum A/S v Schramm (Damage) [2002] 2 All E.R. (Comm) 147; [2002] 1 Lloyd's Rep. 249; [2002] C.L.C. 77; [2002] Lloyd's Rep. I.R. 292 QBD (Comm) ... 10–003, 10–006, 10–013, 10–017
Quorum AS v Schramm (No.1) [2002] Lloyd's Rep I.R. 292 1–009
R. v Carr-Briant [1943] K.B. 607; [1943] 2 All E.R. 156 CCA 22–009
R. v Chairman of the Regulatory Board of Lloyd's, Ex p. Macmillan; sub nom. R. v Regulatory Board of Lloyd's of London, Ex p. MacMillan [1995] L.R.L.R. 485; [1995] 4 Re. L.R. 42; Times, December 14, 1994; Lloyd's List, May 3, 1995 QBD 13–039
R. v Deputy Insurance Ombudsman Ex p Francis Unreported May 20, 1998 12–013
R. v Flannagan and Higgins (1884) 15 Cox C.C. 403 4–001
R. v Gomez. See DPP v Gomez (Edwin)
R. v Gordon (1781) St. Tr. 485 6–006
R. v Insurance Ombudsman Bureau Ex p. Aegon Life Assurance Ltd [1995] L.R.L.R. 101; [1994] C.L.C. 88; [1994] C.O.D. 426; Times, January 7, 1994; Independent, January 11, 1994 12–013
TimesQBDR. v Morris (David Alan); sub nom. Anderton v Burnside [1984] A.C. 320; [1983] 3 W.L.R. 697; [1983] 3 All E.R. 288; (1983) 77 Cr. App. R. 309; (1984) 148 J.P. 1; [1983] Crim. L.R. 813 HL 19–049
R. v Panel of the Federation of Communication Services Ltd Ex p. Kubis Unreported September 3, 1997 12–013
R. v Personal Investment Authority Ombudsman Bureau Ltd, Ex p. Royal & Sun Alliance Life & Pensions Ltd [2002] Lloyd's Rep. I.R. 41 QBD 1–003, 3–010, 8–001
R. v Phipps (Owen Roger); R. v McGill (John Peter) (1970) 54 Cr. App. R. 300; (1970) 54 Cr. App. R. 301; [1970] R.T.R. 209; [1970] Crim. L.R. 290 CA (Crim Div) 19–050, 22–041
R. v Preddy (John Crawfor; R. v Slade (Mark); R. v Dhillon (Rajpaul Singh) [1996] A.C. 815; [1996] 3 W.L.R. 255; [1996] 3 All E.R. 481; [1996] 2 Cr. App. R. 524; (1996) 160 J.P. 677; [1996] Crim. L.R. 726; (1996) 160 J.P.N. 936; (1996) 93(31) L.S.G. 29; (1996) 146 N.L.J. 1057; (1996) 140 S.J.L.B. 184; Times, July 11, 1996; Independent, July 17, 1996 HL 23–022
R. v Secretary of State for Transport, Ex p. National Insurance Guarantee Corp Plc [1996] C.O.D. 425; Times, June 3, 1996 QBD 22–017, 22–018
R. v Shaw [1974] R.T.R. 225; [1974] Crim. L.R. 672 CA (Crim Div) 22–007
R. v Stewart (1840) 12 Ad. & El. 773 18–016
R. v Wilson (Rupert) [1997] 1 W.L.R. 1247; [1997] 1 All E.R. 119; (1996) 93(35) L.S.G. 33; (1996) 140 S.J.L.B. 202; Times, August 14, 1996 CA 13–018

R. (on the application of Bridges) v Society of Lloyd's, Times July 30, 1992 13–039
R. (on the application of Cook) v Financial Ombudsman Service [2009] EWHC 426 (Admin) 12–012
R. (on the application of Factortame) v Secretary of State for Transport. See Factortame Ltd v Secretary of State for the Environment, Transport and the Regions (Costs) (No.2)
R. (on the application of Fogg) v Secretary of State for Defence; sub nom. Fogg v Secretary of State for Defence [2005] EWHC 2888; [2006] 1 Lloyd's Rep. 579; (2006) 156 N.L.J. 23; Times, January 13, 2006 QBD (Admin) 25–005
R. (on the application of Garrison Investment Analysis) v Financial Ombudsman Service [2006] EWHC 2466 (Admin) 12–013
R. (on the application of Geologistics Ltd) v Financial Services Compensation Scheme [2003] EWCA Civ. 1905; [2004] 1 W.L.R. 1719; [2004] 3 All E.R. 39; [2004] 1 All E.R. (Comm) 943; [2004] Lloyd's Rep. I.R. 336; Times, January 15, 2004 CA (Civ Div) 16–024
R. (on the application of Heather Moor & Edgecomb Ltd) v Financial Ombudsman Service [2008] EWCA Civ 642; [2008] Bus. L.R. 1486; (2008) 158 N.L.J. 897 .... 12–009, 12–010, 12–013
R. (on the application of Heather Moor & Edgecomb Ltd) v Financial Ombudsman Service [2009] EWHC 2701 (Admin) 12–009, 12–010
R. (on the application of IFG Financial Services Ltd) v Financial Ombudsman Service Ltd [2005] EWHC 1153 (Admin); [2006] 1 B.C.L.C. 534 12–013
R. (on the application of Johnson) v Council of Society of Lloyd's Unreported, 1996 13–039
R. (on the application of Lorimer) v Corporation of Lloyd's Unreported, 1992 13–039
R. (on the application of Mooyer) v Personal Investment Authority Ombudsman Bureau Ltd [2001] EWHC Admin 247; [2002] Lloyd's Rep. I.R. 45 12–013

R. (on the application of Sunspell Ltd (t/a Superlative Travel)) v Association of British Travel
Agents [2001] A.C.D. 16; Independent, November 27, 2000 12–013
R. (on the application of Thompson) v Law Society [2004] EWCA Civ 167; [2004] 1 W.L.R.
2522; [2004] 2 All E.R. 113; (2004) 101(13) L.S.G. 35; (2004) 154 N.L.J. 307; (2004)
148 S.J.L.B. 265; Times, April 1, 2004; Independent, March 29, 2004 12–010
R. (on the application of West) v Lloyd's of London [2004] EWCA Civ. 506; [2004] 3 All
E.R. 251; [2004] 2 All E.R. (Comm) 1; [2004] 2 C.L.C. 649; [2004] H.R.L.R. 27; [2004]
Lloyd's Rep. I.R. 755; (2004) 148 S.J.L.B. 537 CA (Civ Div) 13–039
RB Policies at Lloyd's v Butler [1950] 1 K.B. 76; [1949] 2 All E.R. 226; (1948–49) 82
Ll.L.R. 841; 65 T.L.R. 436; 93 S.J. 553 KBD 11–011
RSA Pursuit Test Cases, Re Unreported May 27, 2005 .... 8–001, 8–008, 22–033, 23–038, 23–039
R&H Hall Ltd v WH Pim Junr & Co Ltd; sub nom. Arbitration Between R&H Hall Ltd and
WH Pim Junior & Co Ltd, Re (1928) 30 Ll.L.R. 159; [1928] All E.R. Rep 763 HL 10–016
R&R Developments Ltd v AXA Insurance UK Plc [2009] EWHC 2429 (Ch) 6–018, 6–059, 6–071
R+V Versicherung AG v Risk Insurance & Reinsurance Solutions SA (No.1) [2004] EWHC
2682; [2006] Lloyd's Rep. I.R. 253 QBD (Comm) 15–022
R+V Versicherung AG v Risk Insurance & Reinsurance Solutions SA (No.2) [2006] EWHC
42 QBD (Comm) 15–022
QBDRaiffeisen Zentralbank Osterreich AG v Five Star General Trading LLC (The Mount I);
sub nom. Raiffeisen Zentral Bank Osterreich AG v An Feng Steel Co Ltd; Raffeisen
Zentralbank Osterreich AG v Five Star General Trading LLC; The Mount I [2001]
EWCA Civ. 68; [2001] Q.B. 825; [2001] 2 W.L.R. 1344; [2001] 3 All E.R. 257; [2001]
1 All E.R. (Comm) 961; [2001] 1 Lloyd's Rep. 597; [2001] C.L.C. 843; [2001] Lloyd's
Rep. I.R. 460; (2001) 98(9) L.S.G. 38; (2001) 145 S.J.L.B. 45; Times, February 21, 2001
CA (Civ Div) 14–023, 14–026, 14–029, 14–030, 24–074
Rainbow Technicoloured Wood Veneer Ltd v The Canmar Conquest [2000] F.C.J. No.1032 ... 24–080
Raine v Bell (1808) 9 East 195 24–073
Ralli Bros v Compania Naviera Sota y Aznar; sub nom. Compania Naviera Sota Y Aznar v
Ralli Bros [1920] 1 K.B. 614; (1919) 1 Ll. L. Rep. 649 2–030
Ralli Bros v Compania Naviera Sota y Aznar; sub nom. Compania Naviera Sota Y Aznar v
Ralli Bros [1920] 2 K.B. 287; (1920) 2 Ll.L.R. 550 CA 2–057
Ralston v Bignold (1853) 21 L.T. 106 .... 9–003, 9–007
Ramco Ltd v Weller Russell & Laws Insurance Brokers Ltd [2008] EWHC 2202 (QB);
[2009] Lloyd's Rep. I.R. 27; [2009] P.N.L.R. 14 ...... 15–034, 15–035, 15–045, 15–046, 19–011,
19–012
Ramco (UK) Ltd v International Insurance Co of Hanover; sub nom. Ramco (UK) Ltd v
International Insurance Co of Hannover Ltd [2004] EWCA Civ. 675; [2004] 2 All E.R.
(Comm) 866; [2004] 2 Lloyd's Rep. 595; [2004] 1 C.L.C. 1013; [2004] Lloyd's Rep.
I.R. 606; (2004) 148 S.J.L.B. 69 5CA (Civ Div); affirming [2003] EWHC 2360 QBD
(Comm) 3–003, 4–005, 4–020, 19–011, 19–012
Ramwade Ltd v WJ Emson & Co Ltd [1987] R.T.R. 72; (1986) 83 L.S.G. 2996; (1986) 130
S.J. 804 CA 15–047
Randal v Cockran (1748) 1 Ves. Sen. 98 .... 11–001, 11–002, 11–034, 11–036, 11–066, 24–091
Randall v Lithgow (1883–84) L.R. 12 Q.B.D. 525 QBD 18–022
Randall v Motor Insurers Bureau [1968] 1 W.L.R. 1900; [1969] 1 All E.R. 21; [1968] 2
Lloyd's Rep. 553; 112 S.J. 883 QBD 22–008, 22–060
Randhawa v Da Rosa [2000] O.T.C. 738 20–049
Rasnoimport V/O v Guthrie & Co Ltd [1966] 1 Lloyd's Rep. 1 QBD (Comm) 15–009
Ravenscroft v Provident Clerks' Assurance (1885) 5 T.L.R. 3 23–022
Rayner v Preston (1880–81) L.R. 18 Ch. D. 1 CA 4–020, 10–049, 10–051, 14–021, 14–022,
19–006, 19–009, 19–021
Reader v Bunyard (1987) 85 Cr. App. R. 185; [1987] R.T.R. 406; [1987] Crim. L.R. 274
DC 22–006
HLCAReardon Smith Line Ltd v Hansen-Tangen (The Diana Prosperity); Hansen-Tangen v
Sanko Steamship Co Ltd [1976] 1 W.L.R. 989; [1976] 3 All E.R. 570; [1976] 2 Lloyd's
Rep. 621; 120 S.J. 719 HL 3–005, 3–007
Red Sea, The [1896] P. 20 CA 24–026, 24–095
Red Sea Insurance Co Ltd v Bouygues SA [1995] 1 A.C. 190; [1994] 3 W.L.R. 926; [1994]
3 All E.R. 749; [1995] L.R.L.R. 107; [1994] C.L.C. 855; 44 Con. L.R. 116; [1995] 4 Re.
L.R. 231; (1994) 91(41) L.S.G. 42; (1994) 138 S.J.L.B. 174; Times, July 21, 1994;
Independent, September 26, 1994; Lloyd's List, September 30, 1994 PC (Hong Kong) ... 2–061
Redbridge LBC v Municipal Mutual Insurance Ltd [2001] Lloyd's Rep. I.R. 545; [2001]
O.P.L.R. 101 QBD (Comm) 5–031, 5–041, 20–025
Redman v Wilson, Re (1845) 14 M. & W. 476 .... 24–080, 24–134

Redmond v Smith (1844) 7 Man. & G. 457 .... 5–036, 5–037, 24–064
Reed v Royal Exchange Assurance Co (1975) Peake Add. Cas. 70 18–014
Rees v Mabco (102) Ltd (1999) 96(4) L.S.G. 40; (1999) 143 S.J.L.B. 22; Times, December
    16, 1998 CA (Civ Div) 21–012
Refuge Assurance, Re Unreported, 2001 13–033
Refuge Assurance Co Ltd v Kettlewell; sub nom. Kettlewell v Refuge Assurance Co Ltd
    [1909] A.C. 243HL; affirming [1908] 1 K.B. 545CA; affirming [1907] 2 K.B.
    242KBD 8–026, 15–004
Regina Fur Co v Bossom [1958] 2 Lloyd's Rep. 425 CA; affirming [1957] 2 Lloyd's Rep.
    466 QBD 6–048, 6–055
Rego v Connecticut Insurance Placement Facility (1991) 593 A. 2d 491 6–114
Reichhold Norway ASA v Goldman Sachs International [2000] 1 W.L.R. 173; [2000] 2 All
    E.R. 679; [1999] 2 All E.R. (Comm) 174; [1999] 2 Lloyd's Rep. 567; [2000] C.L.C. 11;
    Times, July 20, 1999 CA 2–005
Reid v Employers' Accident (1899) 1 F. (Ct. of Sess.) 1031 3–016
Reid v Rush & Tompkins Group [1990] 1 W.L.R. 212; [1989] 3 All E.R. 228; [1989] 2
    Lloyd's Rep. 167; 27 Con. L.R. 4; [1990] R.T.R. 144; [1990] I.C.R. 61; [1989] I.R.L.R.
    265; (1989) 139 N.L.J. 680 CA (Civ Div) 15–026, 20–001, 20–066
Reischer v Borwick [1894] 2 Q.B. 548CA 5–029, 5–030, 5–032, 5–033
Reliance Marine Insurance Co v Duder [1913] 1 K.B. 265 CA 14–008, 17–006, 24–048
Reilly v National Insurance & Guarantee Corp Ltd [2008] EWHC 722 (Comm); [2008] 2 All
    E.R. (Comm) 612; [2008] Lloyd's Rep. I.R. 695 .... 3–005, 20–076
Rendall v Combined Insurance Co of America [2005] EWHC 678; [2006] Lloyd's Rep. I.R.
    732; [2005] 1 C.L.C. 565 QBD (Comm) 6–003, 6–013, 6–073
Rendlesham v Dunne [1964] 1 Lloyd's Rep. 192; 114 L.J. 208, CC (Westminster) 22–089, 22–095
Republic of Bolivia v Indemnity Mutual Marine Assurance Co Ltd. See Bolivia v Indemnity
    Mutual Marine Assurance Co Ltd
Re-Source America International Ltd v Platt Site Services Ltd (2005) 106 Con. L.R. 15 ... 10–016
Revell v London General Insurance Co Ltd (1934) 50 Ll.L.R. 114; (1935) 152 L.T. 258
    KBD 6–018, 6–048, 6–071, 22–037
Rexodan International Ltd v Commercial Union Assurance Co Plc; sub nom. Rodan
    International Ltd v Commercial Union Assurance Co Plc [1999] Lloyd's Rep. I.R. 495
    CA (Civ Div) 20–075, 20–076
Reynard v Arnold (1874–75) L.R. 10 Ch. App. 386CA in Chancery 19–017, 19–022
Reynolds v Accidental Insurance Co (1870) 22 L.T. 820 18–041
Reynolds v GH Austin & Sons Ltd [1951] 2 K.B. 135; [1951] 1 All E.R. 606; [1951] 1 T.L.R.
    614; (1951) 115 J.P. 192; 49 L.G.R. 377; 95 S.J. 173 KBD 22–010
Reynolds v Phoenix Assurance Co Ltd [1978] 2 Lloyd's Rep. 440 QBD 6–031, 6–048, 6–049,
                                                6–050, 10–014, 10–031, 10–051, 23–001
Rhesa Shipping Co SA v Edmunds (The Popi M); Rhesa Shipping Co SA v Fenton Insurance
    Co Ltd [1985] 1 W.L.R. 948; [1985] 2 All E.R. 712; [1985] 2 Lloyd's Rep. 1; (1985)
    82 L.S.G. 2995; (1985) 129 S.J. 503 HL; reversing [1984] 2 Lloyd's Rep. 555 CA (Civ
    Div) 10–027, 24–003, 24–061, 24–134
Ricci Burns Ltd v Toole [1989] 1 W.L.R. 993; [1989] 3 All E.R. 478; (1988) 138 N.L.J. Rep.
    312; Times, October 12, 1988 CA (Civ Div) 10–053, 15–049
Rice v Baxendale (1861) 7 H. & N. 96 10–015
Rich v Parker (1798) 7 T.R. 705 24–058
Richard Aubrey Film Productions Ltd v Graham [1960] 2 Lloyd's Rep. 101 QBD 10–016
Richards v Murdoch (1830) 10 B. & C. 527 .... 6–024, 6–031
Richards v Port of Manchester Insurance Co Ltd; sub nom. Richards v Port of Manchester
    Insurance Co Ltd, and Brain (1934) 50 Ll.L.R. 132; (1934) 152 L.T. 413 CA 22–010, 22–012
Richardson v Pitt-Stanley [1995] Q.B. 123; [1995] 2 W.L.R. 26; [1995] 1 All E.R. 460;
    [1995] I.C.R. 303; [1994] P.I.Q.R. P496; Times, August 11, 1994; Independent,
    September 6, 1994 CA (Civ Div) 20–051
Richardson v Roylance (1933) 47 Ll.L.R. 173 KBD 7–015
Richfine Development Ltd v Rivington [2008] H.K.E.C. 1113 7–037
Rickards v Forestal Land Timber & Railways Co Ltd (The Minden); sub nom. Middows Ltd
    v Robertson; The Wangoni; WW Howard Bros & Co Ltd v Kahn; The Halle; Forestal
    Land Timber & Railways Co Ltd v Rickards; The Minden; Robertson v Middows Ltd;
    The Wangoni; Kahn v WW Howard Bros & Co Ltd; The Halle [1942] A.C. 50; (1941)
    70 Ll.L.R. 173 HL 5–041, 24–069, 24–073, 24–086
Rickman v Carstairs (1833) 5 B. & Ad. 651 .... 8–029, 10–008
Ridley v Bradford Insurance Co [1971] R.T.R. 61 18–030
Ridsdale v Newnham (1815) 3 M. & S. 456 24–068

Rigby v Sun Alliance and London Insurance Ltd [1980] 1 Lloyd's Rep. 359; (1979) 252 E.G.
    491 QBD (Comm) 20–028, 20–083
Rimpacific Navigation Inc v Daehan Shipbuilding Co Ltd [2009] EWHC 2941 (Comm);
    [2010] Bus. L.R. D61 .... 2–005, 2–006
Rio Tinto Co Ltd v Seed Shipping Co Ltd (1926) 24 Ll.L.R. 316 KBD 24–062
Ritchie v Salvation Army Assurance [1930] 1 A.C. Rep. 31 14–002
Rivaz v Gerussi Bros & Co; Rivaz v Gerussi (1880–81) L.R. 6 Q.B.D. 222 CA 6–022, 6–027,
                                                                                                            19–007, 24–051
Roadworks (1952) Ltd v Charman [1994] 2 Lloyd's Rep. 99 QBD (Comm) 1–040
Roar Marine Ltd v Bimeh Iran Insurance Co (The Daylam) [1998] 1 Lloyd's Rep. 423 QBD
    (Comm) 1–040, 10–056
Robb v Gow Bros (1905) 8 F. (Ct. of Sess.) 90. 107 8–002
Robert Irving & Burns v Stone [1997] C.L.C. 1593; [1998] Lloyd's Rep. I.R. 258; [2003]
    Lloyd's Rep. P.N. 46; (1997) 94(41) L.S.G. 28; Times, October 30, 1997 CA (Civ
    Div) 10–036, 20–038
Roberts v Anglo-Saxon Insurance Association Ltd (1927) 96 L.J.K.B. 590; 137 L.T. 243; 43
    T.L.R. 359; 27 Ll. L. Rep 313 CA 3–011, 7–034, 22–086
Roberts v Avon Insurance Co Ltd [1956] 2 Lloyd's Rep. 240 QBD 6–010, 6–073
Roberts v Eagle Star Insurance Co Ltd [1960] 1 Lloyd's Rep. 615 QBD 7–013, 19–048
Roberts v Plaisted [1989] 2 Lloyd's Rep. 341; Times, July 19, 1989 CA (Civ Div) 6–010, 6–018,
                                                                       6–019, 6–031, 6–070, 6–072, 6–073, 15–036
Roberts v Security Co Ltd [1897] 1 Q.B. 111 CA 1–025, 1–030, 8–004, 8–016
Roberts v State Insurance General Manager [1974] 2 N.Z.L.R. 312 .... 5–051, 22–093
Robertson v Ewer (1786) 1 T.R. 127 24–138
Robertson v Hamilton (1811) 154 East 522 .... 4–016, 4–019, 24–029, 24–031
Robertson v London Guarantee & Accident Co Ltd, 1915 1 S.L.T. 195 OH 22–088
Robertson v Marjoribanks (1819) 2 Stark. 573 6–116
Robin Hood Flour Mills Ltd v NM Paterson & Sons Ltd (The Farrandoc) [1967] 2 Lloyd's
    Rep. 276 Ex Ct (Can) 24–062
Robinson Gold Mining Co v Alliance Insurance Co [1904] A.C. 359 HL 25–012
Robinson v Touray (1811) 3 Camp. 158 24–051
Robson v Marriott Unreported, 1997 CA (Civ Div) 22–045
Roche v Roberts (1921) 9 Ll.L.R. 59 KBD 9–013, 15–027, 15–036, 15–041
Rodan International Ltd v Commercial Union. See Rexodan International Ltd v Commercial
    Union Assurance Co Plc
Roddick v Indemnity Mutual Marine Insurance Co Ltd [1895] 2 Q.B. 380 CA 7–022
Rodocanachi v Elliott (1874) L.R. 9 C.P. 518; 43 L.J.C.P. 255; 2 Asp. M.L.C. 399; [1874–80]
    All E.R. Rep. 618; 31 L.T. 239 .... 10–001, 24–009
Roe v RA Naylor Ltd; sub nom. Roe v Naylor [1917] 1 K.B. 712; (1918) 87 L.J. K.B. 958
    KBD 3–005

Roerig v Valiant Trawlers Ltd [2002] EWCA Civ 21; [2002] 1 W.L.R. 2304; [2002] 1 All
    E.R. 961; [2002] 1 Lloyd's Rep. 681; [2002] C.L.C. 629; [2002] P.I.Q.R. Q8; (2002) 152
    N.L.J. 171 .... 2–064, 2–065
Rogers v Davis (1777) 2 Park (8th ed.) 601 11–044
Rogers v Grazebrooke (1842) 12 Sim. 557 19–025
Rogers v Merthyr Tydfil CBC [2006] EWCA Civ 1134; [2007] 1 W.L.R. 808; [2007] 1 All
    E.R. 354; [2007] 1 Costs L.R. 77; [2006] Lloyd's Rep. I.R. 759; (2006) 150 S.J.L.B.
    1053 .... 23–037, 23–038
Rogers v Whittaker [1917] 1 K.B. 942 KBD 25–006, 25–008, 25–009, 25–010
Rogerson v Scottish Automobile & General Insurance Co Ltd (1931) 41 Ll.L.R. 1; [1931] 1
    All E.R. Rep. 606HL; affirming (1930) 38 Ll.L.R. 142 CA 14–022, 22–027
Rohan Investments Ltd v Cunningham [1999] Lloyd's Rep. I.R. 190; [1998] N.P.C. 14 CA
    (Civ Div) 19–037
Rombach v Piedmont Life (1883) 48 Am.Rep. 239 18–014
Ronson International Ltd v Patrick; sub nom. Patrick v Royal London Mutual Insurance
    Society Ltd [2006] EWCA Civ. 421; [2006] 1 C.L.C. 576; Times, May 8, 2006CA (Civ
    Div); affirming [2005] EWHC 1767; [2005] 2 All E.R. (Comm) 453; [2006] Lloyd's
    Rep. I.R. 194 QBD 5–041, 5–042, 5–043, 7–009, 7–010, 9–004
Rookes v Barnard (No.1) [1964] A.C. 1129; [1964] 2 W.L.R. 269; [1964] 1 All E.R. 367;
    [1964] 1 Lloyd's Rep. 28; 108 S.J. 93 HL 20–015
Roper v Lendon (1859) 1. E. & E. 825 .... 9–003, 9–007, 9–017
Roscow v Corson (1819) 1 Taunt. 684 24–138

Roselodge Ltd (formerly Rose Diamond Products Ltd) v Castle [1966] 2 Lloyd's Rep. 113;
116 N.L.J. 1378 QBD (Comm) 6–031, 6–048, 6–055
Ross v American Home Assurance Co (1999) O.T.C. 360 .... 20–050, 20–083
Ross v Bradshaw (1761) 1 Wm. Bl. 312 7–033
Ross v Hunter (1790) 4 T.R. 33 .... 24–073, 24–138
Ross Hillman Ltd v Bond [1974] Q.B. 435; [1974] 2 W.L.R. 436; [1974] 2 All E.R. 287;
(1974) 59 Cr. App. R. 42; [1974] R.T.R. 279; 118 S.J. 243 DC 22–010
Rossano v Manufacturers Life Insurance Co [1963] 2 Q.B. 352; [1962] 3 W.L.R. 157; [1962]
2 All E.R. 214; [1962] 1 Lloyd's Rep. 187; 106 S.J. 452 QBD (Comm) 2–025, 2–057
Rossiter v Trafalgar Life Assurance Association (1859) 27 Beav. 377 .... 1–052, 15–014
Rotating Equipment Services Inc v Continental Insurance Co [2004] A.J. No.1340 20–049
Rothschild (J) Assurance Plc v Collyear [1998] C.L.C. 1697; [1999] Lloyd's Rep. I.R. 6;
[1999] Pens. L.R. 77; Times, October 15, 1998 QBD (Comm) 6–086, 20–023, 20–024,
20–038, 20–041, 20–058
Rothwell v Chemical & Insulating Co Ltd [2007] UKHL 39; [2008] 1 A.C. 281; [2007] 3
W.L.R. 876; [2007] 4 All E.R. 1047; [2007] I.C.R. 1745; [2008] P.I.Q.R. P6; [2008] LS
Law Medical 1; (2008) 99 B.M.L.R. 139; (2007) 104(42) L.S.G. 34; (2007) 157 N.L.J.
1542; (2007) 151 S.J.L.B. 1366; Times, October 24, 2007 .... 18–059, 20–007, 20–008
Routh v Thompson (1809) 11 East 428 .... 4–017, 4–018
Routh v Thompson (1811) 13 East 247 4–023
Row v Dawson (1749) 1 Ves.Sen. 331 14–026
Rowan v Universal Insurance Co Ltd (1939) 64 Ll.L.R. 288 CA 22–091
Rowcroft v Dunmore Unreported, 1801 24–134
Rowe v Kenway; Rowe v United Friendly Insurance Co Ltd (1921) 8 Ll.L.R. 225 KBD 21–037,
21–063
Rowett Leakey & Co v Scottish Provident Institution [1927] 1 Ch. 55 CA 2–050, 3–008, 18–034
Rowlinson Construction v Insurance Co of North America (UK) [1981] 1 Lloyd's Rep. 332
QBD 3–007
Royal and Sun Alliance Insurance Co of Canada v Fibreglass Canada Inc (1999) O.T.C.
196 20–050
Royal & Sun Alliance Insurance Plc v Dornoch Ltd; sub nom. Dornoch Ltd v Royal & Sun
Alliance Insurance Plc [2005] EWCA Civ. 238; [2005] 1 All E.R. (Comm) 590; [2005]
1 C.L.C. 466; [2005] Lloyd's Rep. I.R. 544 CA (Civ Div); affirming [2004] EWHC 803;
[2004] 2 C.L.C. 133; [2004] Lloyd's Rep. I.R. 826 QBD (Comm) 3–005, 3–010, 7–016,
9–004, 9–011, 17–025
Royal & Sun Alliance Insurance Plc v Hume [2009] CSIH 24; 2009 G.W.D. 13–206 22–037
Royal & Sun Alliance Insurance Plc v MK Digital FZE (Cyprus) Ltd [2006] EWCA Civ.
629 2–008
Royal & Sun Alliance Insurance Plc v Retail Brand Alliance Inc [2004] EWHC 2139; [2005]
Lloyd's Rep. I.R. 110 QBD (Comm) 2–007
Royal & Sun Alliance Insurance (Singapore) Ltd v Metico Marine Pte [2006] 3 S.L.R. 333 7–025
Royal Bank of Canada v Cooperatieve Centrale Raiffeisen-Boerenleenbank BA [2004]
EWCA Civ 7; [2004] 2 All E.R. (Comm) 847; [2004] 1 Lloyd's Rep. 471; [2004] 1
C.L.C. 170; (2004) 148 S.J.L.B. 147 .... 2–005, 2–006
Royal Boskalis Westminster NV v Mountain [1999] Q.B. 674; [1998] 2 W.L.R. 538; [1997]
2 All E.R. 929; [1997] L.R.L.R. 523 CA (Civ Div) 2–025, 2–057, 6–107, 6–114, 9–024,
24–063, 24–064, 24–088, 24–112
Royal Boskalis Westminster NV v Mountain Unreported December 18, 1995Ch D 24–096
Royal Brompton Hospital NHS Trust v Hammond (No.3) [2002] UKHL 14; [2002] 1 W.L.R.
1397; [2002] 2 All E.R. 801; [2002] 1 All E.R. (Comm) 897; [2003] 1 C.L.C. 11; [2002]
B.L.R. 255; [2002] T.C.L.R. 14; 81 Con. L.R. 1; [2002] P.N.L.R. 37; Times, April 26,
2002 HL 15–060
Royal Exchange Assurance Corp v Sjoforsakrings AB Vega; sub nom. Royal Exchange
Assurance Corp v Sjorforsakrings Aktiebolaget Vega [1902] 2 K.B. 384 CA .. 2–037, 2–040,
2–057, 24–047
Royal Exchange v M'Swiney (1850) 14 Q.B. 646 4–017
Royal Insurance Company v Coleman (1906) 26 N.Z.L.R. 526 6–018
Royal Insurance Company v Coronation Insurance (1993) 17 C.C.L.I. (2d) 13 20–050
Royal London Mutual Insurance Society Ltd v Barrett (Inspector of Taxes) [2003] EWCA
Civ. 789 13–017
Rozanes v Bowen (1928) 32 Ll.L.R. 98CA 6–001, 6–052, 15–027, 15–036
Ruben v Great Fingall Consolidated [1906] A.C. 439 HL 15–004
Ruby Steamship Corp Ltd v Commercial Union Assurance Co Ltd (1933) 46 Ll. L. Rep. 265
CA 24–078

Rugg v Minett (1809) 11 East 210 19–007
Rummens v Hare (1876) 1 Ex. D. 169 18–022
Rushton v Martin [1952] W.N. 258 22–010
Russell v Canadian Insurance Co (1999) 11 C.C.L.I. (3d) 284 .... 24–080, 24–081
Russell v Provincial Insurance Co Ltd [1959] 2 Lloyd's Rep. 275 QBD (Comm) 24–062
Russell v Thornton (1860) 6 H. & N. 140 .... 6–040, 24–035, 24–036
Russell v Wilson, Times, May 26, 1989; Independent, June 2, 1989 CA (Civ Div) 11–011
Russel Metals Inc v Ball Construction Inc [2007] O.J. No.4673 20–049
Rust v Abbey Life Insurance Co Ltd [1979] 2 Lloyd's Rep. 334 CA (Civ Div) 1–025, 1–026
Ruys v Royal Exchange Assurance Corp [1897] 2 Q.B. 135 QBD 11–067
Ryoden Engineering Co Ltd v New India Assurance Co Ltd [2008] H.K.E.C. 135 21–029
S (Deceased) (Forfeiture Rule), Re [1996] 1 W.L.R. 235; [1996] 1 F.L.R. 910; [1996] 3
     F.C.R. 357; [1996] Fam. Law 352 Ch D 18–014, 18–035
S Pearson & Son Ltd v Dublin Corp [1907] A.C. 351 HL (UK-Irl) 6–082
S v Gross (2002) 100 Alta. L.R. (3d) 310 20–049
SA d'Intermediaries Luxembourgeios v Farex Gie. *See* Societe Anonyme d'Intermediaries
     Luxembourgeois (SAIL) v Farex Gie
SAIL v Farex Gie. *See* Societe Anonyme d'Intermediaries Luxembourgeois (SAIL) v Farex
     Gie
SCA (Freight) Ltd v Gibson [1974] 2 Lloyd's Rep. 533 QBD (Comm) 5–010, 5–013
SCOR v ERAS (International) Ltd. *See* Societe Commerciale de Reassurance v Eras
     International Ltd (No.2)
SCOR v ERAS (International) Ltd. *See* Societe Commerciale de Reassurance v Eras
     International Ltd (formerly Eras (UK))
S&M Carpets (London) Ltd v Cornhill Insurance Co Ltd [1982] 1 Lloyd's Rep. 423CA (Civ
     Div); affirming [1981] 1 Lloyd's Rep. 667 QBD 9–025
S&M Hotels Ltd v Legal and General Assurance Society Ltd [1972] 1 Lloyd's Rep. 157; 115
     S.J. 888; Times, November 19, 1971 QBD 19–035
S&W Berisford Plc v New Hampshire Insurance Co Ltd; sub nom. NGI International
     Precious Metals v New Hampshire Insurance Co [1990] 2 Q.B. 631; [1990] 3 W.L.R.
     688; [1990] 2 All E.R. 321; [1990] 1 Lloyd's Rep. 454; [1990] I.L.Pr. 118 QBD
     (Comm) 2–003, 2–005, 2–011
S-B (Children) (Care Proceedings: Standard of Proof), Re [2009] UKSC 17; [2010] 2 W.L.R.
     238; [2010] P.T.S.R. 456; [2010] 1 All E.R. 705; [2010] 1 F.L.R. 1161; [2010] 1 F.C.R.
     321; [2010] Fam. Law 231; (2009) 153(48) S.J.L.B. 33; Times, December 18, 2009 9–025
Sabah Shipyard (Pakistan) Ltd v Pakistan [2002] EWCA Civ 1643; [2003] 2 Lloyd's Rep.
     571; [2004] 1 C.L.C. 149; Times, November 27, 2002 2–006
Sadler Bros Co v Meredith [1963] 2 Lloyd's Rep. 293 QBD 5–009, 5–010, 5–011
Sadlers Co v Badcock (1743) 2 Atk. 554 .... 8–020, 10–040, 14–024, 19–002
Safadi v Western Assurance (1933) 46 Ll.L.R. 140 KBD 24–066, 24–074
Safeway Stores Inc v National Union Fire Insurance Co, 64 F. 3d 1282 (9th Circuit, 1995) 20–047,
     20–052
Safeway Stores Ltd v Twigger [2010] EWHC 11 (Comm); (2010) 160 N.L.J. 144 .... 5–046, 20–086
Sailing Ship Blairmore Co Ltd v Macredie; sub nom. Blairmore Co Ltd v Macredie; Blaimore
     Co Ltd v Macredie; Blaimore, The [1898] A.C. 593; (1898) 6 S.L.T. 91 HL 24–086
Salem, The. *See* Shell International Petroleum Co Ltd v Gibbs
Salmon (AP) Contractors v Monksfield [1970] 1 Lloyd's Rep. 387 MCLC 22–092, 22–099
Salt v Helley [2009] N.I.Q.B. 69 22–026
Salvador v Hopkins (1765) 3 Burr. 1707 .... 6–065, 24–070
Salvin v James (1805) 6 East 571 8–009
Samcrete Egypt Engineers & Contractors SAE v Land Rover Exports Ltd [2001] EWCA Civ.
     2019; [2002] C.L.C. 533 CA (Civ Div) 2–043, 3–017
Samengo-Turner v J&H Marsh & McLennan (Services) Ltd [2007] EWCA Civ 723; [2007]
     2 All E.R. (Comm) 813; [2007] C.P. Rep. 45; [2007] 2 C.L.C. 104; [2007] I.L.Pr. 52;
     [2008] I.C.R. 18; [2008] I.R.L.R. 237 2–006
Samuel v Royal Exchange Assurance (1828) 8 B. & C. 119; 108 E.R. 987 ... 24–066, 24–072, 24–073
Samuelson v National Insurance and Guarantee Corp Ltd [1986] 3 All E.R. 417; [1985] 2
     Lloyd's Rep. 541; [1987] R.T.R. 94 CA (Civ Div) 22–036, 22–096
Sanderson v Busher (1814) 4 Camp. 54n 7–022, 7–038
Sanderson v Cunningham [1919] 2 I.R. 234 1–025
Sands v O'Connell [1981] R.T.R. 42 DC 22–010
Sanger (t/a SA Jewels) v Beazley [1999] Lloyd's Rep. I.R. 424 QBD (Comm) 5–012
Sangster v General Accident (1896) 24 R. 56 18–050
Santer v Poland (1924) 19 Ll.L.R. 29 KBD 19–033, 22–087

Sargasso, The. *See* Stargas SpA v Petredec (The Sargasso) Sargasso, The
Sargent v GRE (UK) Ltd [2000] Lloyd's Rep. I.R. 77; [1997] 6 Re. L.R. 281; [1997] P.I.Q.R.
    Q128; Times, April 25, 1997 CA (Civ Div) 3–006, 3–010, 18–054
Sarginson Brothers v Keith Moulton & Co Ltd (1942) 73 Ll.L.R. 104 Assizes
    (Birmingham) 15–034, 15–035
Sarwar v Alam; sub nom. Sawar v Alam [2001] EWCA Civ. 1401; [2002] 1 W.L.R. 125;
    [2001] 4 All E.R. 541; [2002] 1 Costs L.R. 37; [2002] R.T.R. 12; [2002] Lloyd's Rep.
    I.R. 126; [2002] P.I.Q.R. P15; (2001) 151 N.L.J. 1492; Times, October 11, 2001; Daily
    Telegraph, September 25, 2001 CA (Civ Div) 23–036
Saskatchewan Wheat Pool v Royal insurance Co of Canada, 64 D.L.R. (4th) 135 (1990) ... 5–033
Sassoon (ED) & Co v Western Assurance Co [1912] A.C. 561 PC (Shanghai) 24–134
Sassoon (ED) & Co Ltd v Yorkshire Insurance Co (1923) 16 Ll.L.R. 129CA; affirming
    (1923) 14 Ll.L.R. 237 KBD 24–080
Sassoon (MA) & Sons Ltd v International Banking Corp [1927] A.C. 711PC (Ind) 3–017
Satyam Computer Services Ltd v Upaid Systems Ltd [2008] EWCA Civ 487; [2008] 2 All
    E.R. (Comm) 465; [2008] 2 C.L.C. 864; [2008] Bus. L.R. D131; Times, May 27, 2008 ... 2–003
Saunders v Edwards [1987] 1 W.L.R. 1116; [1987] 2 All E.R. 651; (1987) 137 N.L.J. 389;
    (1987) 131 S.J. 1039 CA (Civ Div) 5–045
Saunders v Ford Motor Co [1970] 1 Lloyd's Rep. 379 QBD 10–055
Sawtell v London (1814) 5 Taunt. 359 24–039
Scanlan v Sceales (1849) 13 Ir. L.R. 71 .... 18–028, 18–029
Scaramanga v Stamp (1880) 5 C.P.D. 295 24–073
Scarr (Kate) & General Accident Assurance Corp Ltd's Arbitration, Re [1905] 1 K.B. 387
    KBD 5–030, 18–041, 18–042, 18–046, 18–049, 22–090
Sceales v Scanlan (1843) 6 L.R.Ir. 367 .... 7–026, 7–027
Schebsman (Deceased), Ex p. Official Receiver, Re; sub nom. Trustee v Cargo Super-
    tintendents (London) Ltd [1944] Ch. 83; [1943] 2 All E.R. 768 CA 18–024
Scher v Policyholders Protection Board (No.1); Ackman v Policyholders Protection Board
    (No.1); Royal Insurance (UK) Ltd v Scher; Royal Insurance (UK) Ltd v Ackman [1993]
    3 W.L.R. 357; [1993] 3 All E.R. 384; [1993] 2 Lloyd's Rep. 533; (1993) 143 N.L.J.
    1064; (1993) 137 S.J.L.B. 179; Times, July 16, 1993; Independent, July 16, 1993 HL;
    affirming [1993] 2 W.L.R. 479; [1992] 2 Lloyd's Rep. 321; Times, August 18, 1992 CA
    (Civ Div) 13–018, 16–011, 16–020, 16–024
Schiffahrtsgesellschaft Detlev Von Appen GmbH v Voest Alpine Intertrading GmbH;
    Schiffahrtsgesellschaft Detlev Von Appen GmbH v Weiner Allianz Versicherungs AG
    [1997] 2 Lloyd's Rep. 279 CA (Civ Div) 11–004, 11–011
Schiffshypothekenbank Zu Luebeck AG v Norman Philip Compton (The Alexion Hope)
    [1988] 1 Lloyd's Rep. 311; [1988] F.T.L.R. 270; [1988] Fin. L.R. 131; Times, January
    5, 1988; Independent, January 20, 1988; Financial Times, January 13, 1988 CA (Civ
    Div); affirming [1987] 1 Lloyd's Rep. 60; Financial Times, October 29, 1986 QBD
    (Comm) 5–041, 9–015, 14–013, 19–039, 23–001, 24–135
Schloss Bros v Stevens [1906] 2 K.B. 665 KBD 6–065, 24–009
Schneiderman v Metropolitan Casualty Co, 220 N.Y.S. 947 (1961) 25–004
Schoolman v Hall [1951] 1 Lloyd's Rep. 139 CA 6–031, 6–048, 6–070
Schroder v Thompson (1817) 7 Taunt. 462 .... 24–072, 24–073
Schuler (L) AG v Wickman Machine Tool Sales Ltd; sub nom. Wickman Machine Tool Sales
    Ltd v L Schuler AG [1974] A.C. 235; [1973] 2 W.L.R. 683; [1973] 2 All E.R. 39; [1973]
    2 Lloyd's Rep. 53; 117 S.J. 340 HL 7–001
Scindia Steamships (London) Ltd v London Assurance [1937] 1 K.B. 639; (1936) 56 Ll.L.R.
    136 KBD 24–003
Scott v Avery (1856) 5 H.L. Cas. 811 HL 22–037
Scott v Copenhagen Reinsurance Co (UK) Ltd [2003] EWCA Civ. 688; [2003] 2 All E.R.
    (Comm) 190; [2003] 2 C.L.C. 431; [2003] Lloyd's Rep. I.R. 696; (2003) 147 S.J.L.B.
    697 CA (Civ Div) 1–011, 5–030, 10–001, 10–034, 17–020
Scott v Coulson [1903] 2 Ch. 249CA 1–021, 8–029
Scott v Globe Marine Insurance Co Ltd (1896) 1 Com.Cas. 370 .... 24–029, 24–048
Scott v Irving (1830) 1 B. & Ad. 605 15–041
Scott v Optimum Frontier Insurance Ltd [2006] O.J. No.4204 20–049
Scott v Thompson (1805) 1 B. & P. 181 24–073
Scottish & Newcastle Plc v GD Construction (St Albans) Ltd; sub nom. GD Construction (St
    Albans) Ltd v Scottish & Newcastle Plc [2003] EWCA Civ. 16; [2003] B.L.R. 131; 86
    Con. L.R. 1; [2003] Lloyd's Rep. I.R. 809; [2003] 6 E.G.C.S. 144; (2003) 100(11)
    L.S.G. 31; [2003] N.P.C. 8; Times, January 28, 2003 CA (Civ Div) 11–026, 19–039

Scottish Amicable v Northern Assurance (1883) 11 R. (Ct. of Sess) 287 ..... 10–017, 10–043, 10–046,
    11–054
Scottish Coal Co Ltd v Royal and Sun Alliance Insurance Plc [2008] EWHC 880 (Comm);
    [2008] Lloyd's Rep. I.R. 718 ...... 1–047, 5–008, 5–019, 5–027, 5–050, 6–028, 6–073, 6–092,
    7–007, 7–015, 10–016, 23–042
Scottish Equitable Life Policy 6402, Re. See Policy No.6402 of the Scottish Equitable Life
    Assurance Society, Re
Scottish Equitable Life v Buist (1877) 4 R. (Ct. of Sess.) 1076; (1878) 5 R. (Ct. of Sess.) 64 6–092,
    8–016, 18–030
Scottish Equitable Plc v Derby; sub nom. Derby v Scottish Equitable Plc [2001] EWCA Civ.
    369; [2001] 3 All E.R. 818; [2001] 2 All E.R. (Comm) 274; [2001] O.P.L.R. 181; [2001]
    Pens. L.R. 163; (2001) 151 N.L.J. 418; Independent, May 7, 2001 (C.S); Daily
    Telegraph, March 27, 2001 CA (Civ Div) 10–062
Scottish Lion Insurance Co Ltd, Petitioner [2010] CSIH 6; 2010 S.L.T. 459; 2010 S.C.L.R.
    167; 2010 G.W.D. 7–117 IH (1 Div) 16–005
Scottish Marine Insurance Co v Turner (1853) 1 Macq. H.L. Cas. 334 24–095
Scottish Metropolitan Assurance Co Ltd v Groom (1924) 20 Ll.L.R. 44; (1923) 39 T.L.R. 407
    CA 17–024
Scottish Metropolitan Assurance Co Ltd v P Samuel & Co Ltd [1923] 1 K.B. 348; (1922) 12
    Ll.L.R. 395 KBD 10–063
Scottish Metropolitan Assurance Co Ltd v Stewart (1923) 15 Ll.L.R. 55 KBD 1–033, 5–004
Scottish National Insurance Co Ltd v Poole (1912) 107 L.T. 687 .... 5–017, 17–012
Scottish Provident v Boddam (1893) 9 T.L.R. 385 6–016
Scottish Shire Line Ltd v London & Provincial Marine & General Insurance Co Ltd [1912]
    3 K.B. 51; (1912) 107 L.T. 46 KBD 6–045, 24–026, 24–037, 24–039
Scottish Special Housing Association v Wimpey Construction (UK) Ltd [1986] 1 W.L.R.
    995; [1986] 2 All E.R. 957; 1986 S.C. (H.L.) 57; 1986 S.L.T. 559; 34 B.L.R. 1; 9 Con.
    L.R. 19; (1986) 2 Const. L.J. 149; (1986) 83 L.S.G. 2652; 130 S.J. 592 HL 11–031
Scottish Union & National Insurance Co v Davis [1970] 1 Lloyd's Rep. 1 CA (Civ Div) ... 11–006
Scragg v United Kingdom Temperance & General Provident Institution [1976] 2 Lloyd's
    Rep. 227 QBD (Comm) 3–008, 18–037
Screen Partners London Ltd v VIF Filmproduktion GmbH & Co Erste KG; sub nom. Screen
    Partners London Ltd v VIF Film Production GmbH & Co; Screen Partners London Ltd
    v VIF Filmproducktion GmbH & Co Erste KG [2001] EWCA Civ. 2096; [2002] Lloyd's
    Rep. I.R. 283 CA (Civ Div) 23–033
Sea Emerald SA v Prominvestbank - Joint Stockpoint Commercial Industrial & Investment
    Bank [2008] EWHC 1979 (Comm) 15–003
Sea Insurance Co v Blogg [1898] 2 Q.B. 398 CA 24–068, 24–129
Sea Insurance Co v Hadden & Wainwright (1883–84) L.R. 13 Q.B.D. 706 CA 11–035, 24–095
Sea Voyager Maritime Inc v Bielecki (t/a Hughes Hooker & Co); sub nom. Bielecki, Re
    [1999] 1 All E.R. 628; [1999] B.C.C. 924; [1999] 1 B.C.L.C. 133; [1998] B.P.I.R. 655;
    [1999] Lloyd's Rep. I.R. 356; Times, October 23, 1998 Ch D 21–013
Sea Trade Maritime Corp v Hellenic Mutual War Risks Association (Bermuda) Ltd (The
    Athena) Athena, The [2006] EWHC 2530 (Comm); [2007] 1 All E.R. (Comm) 183;
    [2007] 1 Lloyd's Rep. 280; [2006] 2 C.L.C. 710; [2007] Bus. L.R. D5 .... 2–003, 3–015
Seaconsar (Far East) Ltd v Bank Markazi Jomhouri Islami Iran (Service Outside Jurisdiction)
    [1994] 1 A.C. 438; [1993] 3 W.L.R. 756; [1993] 4 All E.R. 456; [1994] 1 Lloyd's Rep.
    1; [1994] I.L.Pr. 678; (1993) 143 N.L.J. 1479; (1993) 137 S.J.L.B. 239; Times, October
    15, 1993; Independent, October 20, 1993 HL 2–004
Seagate Shipping Ltd v Glencore International AG (The Silver Constellation) [2008] EWHC
    1904 (Comm); [2009] 1 All E.R. (Comm) 148; [2008] 2 Lloyd's Rep. 440; [2008] 2
    C.L.C. 350 3–005
Seagrave v Union Marine Insurance Co (1865–66) L.R. 1 C.P. 305 CCP 24–030
Seaman v Fonnereau (1734) 2 Str. 1183 .... 6–032, 6–062, 24–035
Searle v AR Hales & Co Ltd; Hand v AR Hales & Co Ltd [1996] L.R.L.R. 68; [1995] C.L.C.
    738 QBD 6–125, 6–131, 15–028, 15–033
Seashell Shipping Corp v Mutualidad de Seguros del Instituto Nacional de Industria [1989]
    1 Lloyd's Rep. 47; Times, August 11, 1988; Independent, August 25, 1988 CA (Civ
    Div) 2–005
Seashore Marine SA v Phoenix Assurance Plc (The Vergina) (No.2) [2002] 1 All E.R.
    (Comm) 152; [2001] 2 Lloyd's Rep. 698; [2001] C.L.C. 1441; [2002] Lloyd's Rep. I.R.
    51 QBD (Comm) 5–033, 24–112, 24–134
Seaton v Burnand; sub nom. Seaton v Heath [1900] A.C. 135 HL 6–032, 23–020, 23–029
Seaton v London General Insurance Co Ltd (1932) 43 Ll.L.R. 398 KBD 22–091

Seavision Investment SA v Evennett (The Tiburon) [1992] 2 Lloyd's Rep. 26; Times, January 29, 1992; Independent, February 4, 1992 CA (Civ Div); affirming [1990] 2 Lloyd's Rep. 418 QBD (Comm) 1–040, 6–121, 15–034, 15–046, 15–056, 24–059

Sebel Products v Customs and Excise Commissioners [1949] Ch. 409; [1949] All E.R. 729; 65 T.L.R. 107; 65 T.L.R. 207; [1949] L.J.R. 925; 93 S.J. 198 Ch D 10–059

Secretary of State for Trade and Industry v Great Western Assurance Co SA; Secretary of State for Trade and Industry v Loxley House (London) Ltd; D&L Underwriting Agencies Ltd; Company (No.007816 of 1994), Re; Company (No.007818 of 1994), Re; Company (No.007819 of 1994), Re; Company (No.007820 of 1994), Re; Company (No.007821 of 1994), Re; Company (No.007822 of 1994), Re [1997] 2 B.C.L.C. 685; [1999] Lloyd's Rep. I.R. 377; [1997] 6 Re. L.R. 197 CA (Civ Div) 13–019, 15–021, 15–028, 15–041

Secunda Marine Services Ltd v Liberty Mutual Insurance Co 2006 N.S.C.A. 82 24–003

Seddon v Binions; Stork v Binions [1978] 1 Lloyd's Rep. 381; [1978] R.T.R. 163; 122 S.J. 34 CA (Civ Div) 20–027, 22–098

Sedgwick Tomenson Inc v PT Reasuransi Uman Indonesia [1990] 2 Lloyd's Rep. 334 QBD (Comm) 6–120

Seechurn v Ace Insurance SA NV; sub nom. Ace Insurance SA NV v Seechurn [2002] EWCA Civ. 67; [2002] 2 Lloyd's Rep. 390; [2002] Lloyd's Rep. I.R. 489 CA (Civ Div) 9–041, 9–042

Seele Austria GmbH & Co KG v Tokio Marine Europe Insurance Ltd [2008] EWCA Civ 441; [2009] 1 All E.R. (Comm) 171; [2008] B.L.R. 337; [2008] Lloyd's Rep. I.R. 739 ... 19–059

Seele Austria GmbH & Co KG v Tokio Marine Europe Insurance Ltd [2009] EWHC 2066 (TCC); [2009] B.L.R. 481; 126 Con. L.R. 69 .... 9–037, 9–038, 10–019, 10–034

Seele Austria GmbH Co KG v Tokio Marine Europe Insurance Ltd (No.2) [2009] EWHC 255 (TCC); [2009] B.L.R. 261 10–034

Seismik Sukrurtig AG v Sphere Drake Insurance Co Plc [1997] 8 C.L. 351 QBD ... 1–034, 6–014

Seligman v Eagle Insurance Co [1917] 1 Ch. 519 Ch D 1–048, 18–039

Sellar v McVicar (1804) 1 B. & P. 23 24–068

Seller v Work (1801) 1 Marshall on Insurance 305 15–036

Sempra Metals Ltd (formerly Metallgesellschaft Ltd) v Inland Revenue Commissioners [2007] UKHL 34; [2008] 1 A.C. 561; [2007] 3 W.L.R. 354; [2008] Bus. L.R. 49; [2007] 4 All E.R. 657; [2007] S.T.C. 1559; [2008] Eu. L.R. 1; [2007] B.T.C. 509; [2007] S.T.I. 1865; (2007) 104(31) L.S.G. 25; (2007) 157 N.L.J. 1082; (2007) 151 S.J.L.B. 985; Times, July 25, 2007 .... 10–022, 10–023, 10–025

Sentinel Securities Plc, Re [1996] 1 W.L.R. 316 Ch D 1–006

Service Motor Policies at Lloyd's v City Recovery Ltd [1997] 10 C.L. 423 CA (Civ Div) 22–023

Severn Trent Water v Williams [1995] 10 C.L 638; [1995] C.L.Y. 3724 CC (Watford) 22–007, 22–057, 22–060

Sexton v Mountain (1919) 1 Ll.L.R. 507 KBD (Comm Ct) 5–015

Shackleton v Sun Fire (1884) 54 Am.Rep. 379 19–047

Shakur v Pilot Insurance Co, 73 D.L.R. (4th) 337 (1991) 9–015

Shamil Bank of Bahrain EC v Beximco Pharmaceuticals Ltd (No.1); sub nom. Beximco Pharmaceuticals Ltd v Shamil Bank of Bahrain EC [2004] EWCA Civ. 19; [2004] 1 W.L.R. 1784 CA (Civ Div); affirming [2003] EWHC 2118; [2003] 2 All E.R. (Comm) 849 QBD (Comm) 2–028

Shanly v Allied Traders Insurance Co Ltd (1925) 21 Ll.L.R. 195 KBD 5–019, 6–103

Sharab v Prince Al-Waleed Bin Tala Bin Abdal-Aziz-Al-Saud [2009] EWCA Civ 353; [2009] 2 Lloyd's Rep. 160 2–004

Sharp v Gladstone (1806) 7 East 24 24–095

Sharp v Pereira; sub nom. Sharp v Pereria; Sharp v Motor Insurers Bureau [1999] 1 W.L.R. 195; [1998] 4 All E.R. 145; [1999] R.T.R. 125; [1999] Lloyd's Rep. I.R. 242; [1998] P.I.Q.R. Q129; Times, July 25, 1998; Independent, June 29, 1998 (C.S.) CA (Civ Div) 10–053, 22–063

Sharp v Sphere Drake Insurance; The Moonacre [1992] 2 Lloyd's Rep. 501 QBD (Comm) 4–013, 4–015, 4–024, 6–045, 6–046, 6–052, 6–065, 6–105, 15–034, 15–051, 19–014, 19–029, 24–017

Sharpe v Williamson [1990] 3 CL, para.243 9–008

Sharratt v London Central Bus Co Ltd (No.2) [2004] EWCA Civ. 575; [2004] 3 All E.R. 325; [2004] 3 Costs L.R. 422; (2004) 101(23) L.S.G. 32; (2004) 154 N.L.J. 891; (2004) 148 S.J.L.B. 662 CA (Civ Div) 23–038

Shave v Rosner [1954] 2 Q.B. 113; [1954] 2 W.L.R. 1057; [1954] 2 All E.R. 280; 118 J.P. 364; 52 L.G.R. 337; 98 S.J. 355 QBD 22–010

Shaw v Foster (1872) L.R. 5 H.L. 321 14–026

Shaw v Globe Indemnity [1921] 1 W.W.R. 332 CA (BC) 18–056
Shaw v Robberds (1837) 6 A. & E. 75 .. 5–017, 5–019, 5–022, 5–048, 6–103, 7–032, 7–038, 18–049,
                                                                                          19–039
Shaw v Royce Ltd [1911] 1 Ch. 138 Ch D 23–030
Shawe v Felton (1801) 2 East 109 24–065
Shearwater Marine Ltd v Guardian Insurance Co (1997) 29 B.C.L.R. (3d) 13 7–034
Sheldon Deliveries v Willis [1972] R.T.R. 217; [1972] Crim. L.R. 241 DC 22–010
Sheldon v RHM Outhwaite (Underwriting Agencies) Ltd [1996] A.C. 102; [1995] 2 W.L.R.
     570; [1995] 2 All E.R. 558; [1995] 2 Lloyd's Rep. 197; [1995] C.L.C. 655; [1995] 4 Re.
     L.R. 168; (1995) 92(22) L.S.G. 41; (1995) 145 N.L.J. 687; (1995) 139 S.J.L.B. 119;
     Times, May 5, 1995; Independent, May 9, 1995; Lloyd's List, May 24, 1995 (I.D.) HL ... 15–061
Shell International Petroleum Co Ltd v Coral Oil Co Ltd (No.1) [1999] 1 Lloyd's Rep. 72 3–015
Shell International Petroleum Co Ltd v Gibbs (The Salem) [1983] 2 A.C. 375; [1983] 2
     W.L.R. 371; [1983] 1 All E.R. 745; [1983] 1 Lloyd's Rep. 342; [1983] Com. L.R. 96;
     (1983) 133 N.L.J. 400; (1983) 127 S.J. 154; Times, February 18, 1983 HL; affirming
     [1982] Q.B. 946; [1982] 2 W.L.R. 745; [1982] 1 All E.R. 1057; [1982] 1 Lloyd's Rep.
     369; [1982] Com. L.R. 58; 126 S.J. 205 CA (Civ Div); reversing [1982] 1 All E.R. 225;
     [1981] 2 Lloyd's Rep. 316; [1981] Com. L.R. 221 QBD (Comm) 24–135, 24–138, 25–12
Shell UK Ltd (t/a Shell (UK) Exploration & Production) v CLM Engineering Ltd (formerly
     Land & Marine Engineering Ltd) [2000] 1 All E.R. (Comm) 940; [2000] 1 Lloyd's Rep.
     612; [2000] C.L.C. 1005 QBD (Comm) 10–003
Shephard v Cartwright; sub nom. Shephard, Re [1955] A.C. 431; [1954] 3 W.L.R. 967;
     [1954] 3 All E.R. 649; 98 S.J. 868 HL 18–006
Shilling v Accidental Death (1857) 2 H. & N. 42 .... 18–002, 18–005, 18–007, 18–015, 18–029
Shilling v Accidental Death (1858) 1 E. & F. 116 .... 4–003, 4–010
Shinedean Ltd v Alldown Demolition (London) Ltd (In Liquidation) [2006] EWCA Civ. 939
     CA (Civ Div); reversing [2005] EWHC 2319; [2006] 1 All E.R. (Comm) 224; [2005]
     2 C.L.C. 1159 QBD (TCC) 7–014, 9–016, 9–017, 17–025
Shirley v Sankey (1800) 2 Bos. & P. 130 4–002
Shirley v Wilkinson (1781) 3 Doug. 41 24–037
Shoot v Hill (1936) 55 Ll.L.R. 29 KBD 7–013, 9–025, 9–026, 9–029, 19–048
Shore v Bentall (1828) 7 B. & C. 798n 24–080
Shulton (Great Britain) v Slough BC [1967] 2 Q.B. 471; [1967] 2 W.L.R. 1289; [1967] 2 All
     E.R. 137; 131 J.P. 355; 65 L.G.R. 326; 111 S.J. 232 DC 22–010
Sibbald v Hill (1814) 2 Dow. 263 .... 6–017, 6–045, 6–058
Sickness & Accident Assurance Association v General Accident Assurance Corp Ltd (1892)
     29 S.L.R. 836; 19 R. 977 .... 1–031, 5–004, 11–001, 11–046, 11–052, 11–058
Sidaways v Todd (1818) 2 Stark. 400 .... 19–010, 19–013, 19–030
Sienkiewicz v Greif (UK) Ltd [2009] EWCA Civ 1159; [2010] 2 W.L.R. 951; (2009) 106(45)
     L.S.G. 17; (2009) 153(44) S.J.L.B. 34; Times, November 13, 2009 11–050
Sigma Finance Corp (In Administration), Re [2009] UKSC 2; [2010] 1 All E.R. 571; [2010]
     B.C.C. 40; (2009) 159 N.L.J. 1550; (2009) 153(42) S.J.L.B. 29 3–005
Silbermann v CGU Insurance [2003] N.S.W.C.A. 203; [2005] H.C.A. 16 ... 20–048, 20–050, 20–051,
                                                                                          20–087
Silcock & Sons Ltd v Maritime Lighterage Co (JR Francis & Co) Ltd (1937) 57 Ll.L.R. 78
     CA 24–062
Sillem v Thornton (1854) 3 E. & B. 868 .... 5–020, 5–025, 10–029
Silverton v Goodall [1997] P.I.Q.R. P451 CA (Civ Div) 22–069
Simcock v Scottish Imperial Insurance Co (1902) 10 S.L.T. 286 OH 4–014, 18–004, 18–019
Simmonds v Cockell [1920] 1 K.B. 843; (1920) 2 Ll.L.R. 230 KBD (Comm Ct) 3–010, 7–037
Simner v New India Assurance Co Ltd [1995] L.R.L.R. 240; Times, July 21, 1994 QBD ... 6–004,
                                                6–036, 6–037, 6–092, 6–093, 6–036
Simon Brooks Ltd v Hepburn [1961] 2 Lloyd's Rep. 43QBD (Comm) 19–044
Simon Container Machinery Ltd v Emba Machinery AB [1998] 2 Lloyd's Rep. 429 QBD
     (Comm) 4–019, 19–006
Simon Haynes Barlas & Ireland v Beer (1945) 78 Ll.L.R. 337 KBD 6–052, 6–093
Simon Israel & Co v Sedgwick [1893] 1 Q.B. 303 CA 24–009, 24–068, 24–069
Simon Warrender Pty Ltd v Swain [1960] 2 Lloyd's Rep. 111; (1959) 18 D.L.R. (2d) 598 Sup
     Ct (NSW) 20–031
Simonds v Hodgson (1832) 3 B. & Ad. 50 24–024
Simons (t/a Acme Credit Services) v Gale (The Cap Tarifa) [1958] 1 W.L.R. 678; [1958] 2
     All E.R. 504; [1958] 2 Lloyd's Rep. 1; 102 S.J. 452 PC (Aus) 7–038
Simpson v Accidental Death Ins. Co (1857) 26 L.J.C.P. 289 18–003
Simpson v Accidental Death Insurance Co (1857) 2 C.B.N.S. 257 .... 5–005, 8–009

Simpson v Scottish Union Insurance Co (1863) 1 Hem. & M. 618; (1863) 32 L.J. Ch. 329 10–051,
    10–052, 19–020, 19–026
Simpson & Co v Thomson; Simpson & Co v Burrell (1877–78) L.R. 3 App. Cas. 279; (1877)
    5 R. (H.L.) 40 HL 11–011, 11–024, 11–027
Simpson Steamship Co v Premier Underwriting Association (1905) 10 Com.Cas. 198; (1905)
    92 L.T. 730 .... 6–058, 7–036, 7–040, 24–070
Sinclair v Maritime Passengers' Assurance Co (1861) 3 E. & E. 478 ..... 18–041, 18–042, 18–046,
    18–060
Sinclair Harder O'Malley Ltd v National Insurance Co of New Zealand [1992] 2 N.Z.L.R.
    706 20–041
Sinclair's Life Policy, Re [1938] Ch. 799 Ch D 18–024
Sindall (William) Plc v Cambridgeshire CC. See William Sindall Plc v Cambridgeshire
    CC
Singh v Rathour [1988] 1 W.L.R. 422; Times, October 20, 1987 CA (Civ Div) ... 22–027, 22–088
Singh v Solihull MBC [2007] EWHC 552 (Admin); [2007] 2 C.M.L.R. 47 22–036
Sinnott v Bowden [1912] 2 Ch. 414 Ch D 10–051, 19–026
Sinnott v Municipal General Insurance [1989] C.L. 297, CC (Liverpool) 5–050
Sirius International Insurance Co (Publ) v FAI General Insurance Ltd; sub nom. Sirius
    International Insurance Corp Ltd v FAI General Insurance Co Ltd [2004] UKHL 54;
    [2004] 1 W.L.R. 3251; [2005] 1 All E.R. 191; [2005] 1 All E.R. (Comm) 117; [2005]
    1 Lloyd's Rep. 461; [2005] 1 C.L.C. 451; [2005] Lloyd's Rep. I.R. 294; (2004) 101(48)
    L.S.G. 25; (2004) 148 S.J.L.B. 1435; Times, December 3, 2004 HL 3–005, 17–001
Sirius International Insurance Corp v Oriental Assurance Corp [1999] 1 All E.R. (Comm.)
    699; [1999] Lloyd's Rep. I.R. 343 QBD (Comm) 6–013, 6–015, 6–103, 6–116, 17–006
Sitra Wood Products Pte Ltd v Royal & Sun Alliance (Singapore) Pte Ltd [2001] 4 S.L.R.
    121 24–112
Siu Yin Kwan v Eastern Insurance Co Ltd [1994] 2 A.C. 199; [1994] 2 W.L.R. 370; [1994]
    1 All E.R. 213; [1994] 1 Lloyd's Rep. 616; [1994] C.L.C. 31; (1994) 144 N.L.J. 87;
    (1994) 138 S.J.L.B. 26; Times, December 16, 1993 PC (HK) ... 1–014, 4–003, 4–021, 6–046,
    14–007, 14–010, 15–006, 19–002, 20–062, 22–027
Skey v The Mutual Life Association of Australasia (1895) 13 N.Z.L.R. 321 CA (NZ) 8–002
Skipper v Grant (1861) 10 C.B.N.S. 237 11–067
Sky One, The. See Ferrarini SpA v Magnol Shipping Co Ltd, (The Sky One)
Skyline Gold Corp v American Home Insurance [1997] B.C.T.C. G22 20–050
Skype Technologies SA v Joltid Ltd [2009] EWHC 2783 (Ch); [2009] Info. T.L.R. 104 2–005
Slater v Buckinghamshire CC; Slater v Stigwood (t/a as Stigwoods) [2004] EWCA Civ.
    1478; (2004) 148 S.J.L.B. 1368 CA (Civ Div); affirming [2004] EWHC 77; [2004]
    Lloyd's Rep. I.R. 432 QBD 7–014, 22–030
Slattery v Mance [1962] 1 Q.B. 676; [1962] 2 W.L.R. 569; [1962] 1 All E.R. 525; [1962] 1
    Lloyd's Rep. 60; 106 S.J. 113 QBD 6–056, 9–015
Sleigh v Tyser [1900] 2 Q.B. 333 QBD 7–047, 24–062, 24–063
Slough Estates Canada Ltd v Federal Pioneer Ltd (1994) 20 O.R. (3d) 329 20–050
Smaill v Buller District Council [1998] 1 N.Z.L.R. 190 6–009
Small v United Kingdom Marine Mutual Insurance Association [1897] 2 Q.B. 311 CA 24–138
Smart v Allen; sub nom. Smart v Allan [1963] 1 Q.B. 291; [1962] 3 W.L.R. 1325; [1962] 3
    All E.R. 893; 127 J.P. 35; 126 J.P. 35; 60 L.G.R. 548; 106 S.J. 881 QBD 22–006
Smit Tak Offshore Services Ltd v Youell [1992] 1 Lloyd's Rep. 154; (1992) 89(2) L.S.G. 31;
    Times, November 11, 1991; Financial Times, November 5, 1991 CA (Civ Div) 3–009,
    20–012, 20–026
Smith, and Others (Underwriters) v Robertson, and Others (Merchants) (1814) 2 Dow 474;
    3 E.R. 936 HL 24–089
Smith v Accident Insurance Co (1870) L.R. 5 Ex. 302 .... 3–010, 5–030
Smith v Alexander and Alexander [1965] 1 Lloyd's Rep. 283 DC 5–004
Smith v Associated Dominions Assurance Society Pty Ltd (1956) 95 C.L.R. 381 8–016
Smith v Cologan (1788) 2 T.R. 188n 15–034
Smith v Colonial Mutual Fire Insurance Co Ltd (1880) 6 V.L.R. 200 10–047
Smith v Cornhill Insurance [1938] 3 All E.R. 145; (1938) 54 T.L.R. 869 5–030
Smith v Hughes (1870–71) L.R. 6 Q.B. 597; [1861–73] All E.R. Rep. 632; (1871) 19 W.R.
    1059 QB 3–004
Smith v Lascelles (1788) 2 T.R. 187 .... 4–016, 15–026, 15–034, 19–025, 19–030
Smith v Merchants' Fire of New York [1925] 3 W.W.R. 91 1–025
Smith v Pearl Assurance Co Ltd [1939] 1 All E.R. 95; (1939) 63 Ll.L.R. 1 CA 21–029
Smith v Price (1862) 2 F. & F. 748 .... 15–034, 15–045
Smith v Ralph [1963] 2 Lloyd's Rep. 439 DC 14–022, 22–010

Smith v Reynolds (1856) 1 H. & N. 221 10–020
Smith v Surridge (1801) 4 Esp. 25 .... 24–065, 24–072, 24–073
Smith v White Knight Laundry Ltd [2001] EWCA Civ. 660; [2002] 1 W.L.R. 616; [2001] 3
    All E.R. 862; [2001] C.P. Rep. 88; [2003] B.C.C. 319; [2001] 2 B.C.L.C. 206; [2001]
    P.I.Q.R. P30; Independent, July 2, 2001 (C.S) CA (Civ Div) 21–014
Smith (Plant Hire) Ltd v Mainwaring (t/a Inshore). *See* MH Smith (Plant Hire) v DL
    Mainwaring (t/a Inshore)
Smith's Estate, Re; sub nom. Bilham v Smith [1937] Ch. 636 Ch D 19–031
Snowden v Davis (1808) 1 Taunt. 359 10–063
Soares v Thornton (1817) 7 Taunt 627 24–138
Societa Esplosivi Industriali SpA v Ordnance Technologies (UK) Ltd (formerly SEI (UK)
    Ltd) [2007] EWHC 2875 (Ch); [2008] 2 All E.R. 622; [2008] 2 B.C.L.C. 428; [2008]
    R.P.C. 12; [2008] Bus. L.R. D37 20–078
Societe Anonyme d'Intermediaries Luxembourgeois (SAIL) v Farex Gie [1995] L.R.L.R.
    116; [1994] C.L.C. 1094 CA (Civ Div) 6–036, 6–037, 6–039, 6–042, 6–055, 6–061, 6–117,
                             6–118, 6–120, 15–028, 15–036, 17–005, 17–007, 17–015
Societe Anonyme Maritime et Commerciale de Geneva v Anglo-Iranian Oil Co Ltd [1954]
    1 W.L.R. 492; [1954] 1 All E.R. 529; [1954] 1 Lloyd's Rep. 1; 98 S.J. 178 CA 3–011
Societe Commerciale de Reassurance v Eras International Ltd (formerly Eras (UK)); sub
    nom. Eras EIL Actions, Re [1992] 2 All E.R. 82 (Note); [1992] 1 Lloyd's Rep. 570;
    Times, November 28, 1991; Independent, January 27, 1992 (C.S.); Financial Times,
    November 29, 1991 CA (Civ Div) 15–061
Societe Commerciale de Reassurance v Eras International Ltd (No.2); sub nom. Eras EIL
    Actions (No.2), Re [1995] 2 All E.R. 278; [1995] 1 Lloyd's Rep. 64 QBD (Comm) 2–006
Societe d'Avances Commerciales v Merchants Marine Insurance Co; The Palitana (1924) 20
    Ll.L.R. 140 CA 9–025
Societe Financiere et Industrielle du Peloux v Axa Belgium (C–112/03) [2006] Q.B. 251;
    [2006] 2 W.L.R. 228; [2005] 2 All E.R. (Comm) 419; [2005] E.C.R. I–3707; [2005]
    I.L.Pr. 32 ECJ 2–013, 2–015
Societe Nationale Industrielle Aerospatiale (SNIA) v Lee Kui Jak [1987] A.C. 871; [1987]
    3 W.L.R. 59; [1987] 3 All E.R. 510; (1987) 84 L.S.G. 2048 PC (Bru) 2–006
*Times*QBD*Times*CASociety of Lloyd's v Fraser [1998] C.L.C. 1630; [1999] Lloyd's Rep.
    I.R. 156 CA (Civ Div) 13–042
Society of Lloyd's v Henderson; sub nom. Society of Lloyd's v Lowe; Society of Lloyd's v
    Stockwell; Society of Lloyd's v Richardson; Society of Lloyd's v Buckley [2005]
    EWHC 850 QBD (Comm) 13–039, 13–042
Society of Lloyd's v Jaffray. *See* Jaffray v Society of Lloyd's; sub nom. Society of Lloyd's
    v Jaffray
Society of Lloyd's v Levy; sub nom. Society of Lloyds v Levy; Society of Lloyd's v Johnson
    [2004] EWHC 1860; [2004] 3 C.M.L.R. 56; [2004] 3 C.M.L.R. 1233 QBD (Comm) 13–042
Society of Lloyd's v Lyons, Leighs and Wilkinson Unreported, 1997 13–042
Society of Lloyd's v Morris [1993] 2 Re. L.R. 217; Independent, June 21, 1993 17–001
Society of Lloyd's v Noel [2001] EWCA Civ. 521 CA (Civ Div) 13–042
Society of Lloyd's v Robinson. *See* Napier (Lord) and Ettrick v RF Kershaw Ltd (No.2)
Society of Lloyd's v Surman [2004] EWHC 2967; [2005] 2 C.L.C. 1119 Ch D 13–042
Society of Lloyd's v Twinn (Geoffrey George); Society of Lloyd's v Twinn (Gail Sally)
    (2000) 97(15) L.S.G. 40; Times, April 4, 2000 CA (Civ Div) 13–042
Society of Lloyd's v White [2000] C.L.C. 961; [2002] I.L.Pr. 10; (2000) 144 S.J.L.B. 190;
    Times, April 14, 2000 QBD (Comm) 13–042
Socony Mobil Oil Co Inc v West of England Ship Owners Mutual Insurance Association
    (London) Ltd (The Padre Island) (No.1); Mobil Oil Co Inc v West of England Ship
    Owners Mutual Insurance Association (London) Ltd [1984] 2 Lloyd's Rep. 408 QBD
    (Comm) 21–007, 21–029
Socony Mobil Oil Co Inc v West of England Shipowners Mutual Insurance Association
    (London) Ltd (The Padre Island) (No.2) [1987] 2 Lloyd's Rep. 529; [1988] Fin. L.R. 44
    QBD (Comm) 8–016, 21–007, 21–024
Soden v British & Commonwealth Holdings Plc (In Administration) [1998] A.C. 298; [1997]
    3 W.L.R. 840; [1997] 4 All E.R. 353; [1997] B.C.C. 952; [1997] 2 B.C.L.C. 501; (1997)
    94(41) L.S.G. 28; (1997) 147 N.L.J. 1546; Times, October 22, 1997; Independent,
    October 21, 1997 HL 20–080
Sofi v Prudential Assurance Co Ltd [1993] 2 Lloyd's Rep. 559 CA (Civ Div) 5–050, 7–017,
                                                                         22–094
Sohio Supply Co v Gatoil (USA) Inc [1989] 1 Lloyd's Rep. 588 CA (Civ Div) 2–003
Solicitors' and General Life Assurance Society v Lamb (1864) 1 De G. J. & Sm. 251 11–005

Solle v Butcher [1950] 1 K.B. 671; [1949] 2 All E.R. 1107; 66 T.L.R. (Pt. 1) 448 CA 10–057
Solvency Mutual Guarantee Co v Freeman (1861) 7 H. & N. 17; 31 L.J. Ex. 197 23–025
Solvency Mutual Guarantee Co v Froane (1861) 7 H. & N. 5; 31 L.J. Ex. 193 ...... 1–047, 23–025
Solvency Mutual Guarantee Co v York (1858) 3 H. & N. 588; 27 L.J. Ex. 487 .... 8–012, 23–025
Solvency Mutual Guarantee Society, Re; Hawthorne's Case (1862) 31 L.J. Ch. 625; 8
     Jur.N.S. 934 15–017
Sommerfield v Lombard Insurance Group (2005) 74 O.R. (3d) 571 20–050
Sonatrach Petroleum Corp (BVI) v Ferrell International Ltd [2002] 1 All E.R. (Comm) 627
     QBD (Comm) 2–032
Sons of Gwalia Ltd v Margaretic [2007] H.C.A. 1 20–080
Sookun v HardoyalUnreported, 2001 Ch D 1–048
Soole v Royal Insurance Co [1971] 2 Lloyd's Rep. 332 QBD 7–019, 20–044
Sousa v Waltham Forest LBC Unreported January 12, 2010 County Court (Leeds) 11–011
South Australia Asset Management Corp v York Montague Ltd [1997] A.C. 191; [1996] 3
     W.L.R. 87; [1996] 3 All E.R. 365; [1996] 5 Bank. L.R. 211; [1996] C.L.C. 1179; 80
     B.L.R. 1; 50 Con. L.R. 153; [1996] P.N.L.R. 455; [1996] 2 E.G.L.R. 93; [1996] 27 E.G.
     125; [1996] E.G. 107 (C.S.); (1996) 93(32) L.S.G. 33; (1996) 146 N.L.J. 956; (1996)
     140 S.J.L.B. 156; [1996] N.P.C. 100; Times, June 24, 1996; Independent, July 2, 1996 ... 15–047
South Australian Insurance Co v Randell (1869–71) L.R. 3 P.C. 101 PC (Aus) 19–011
South Carolina Insurance Co v Assurantie Maatshappij De Zeven Provincien NV; South
     Carolina Insurance Co v Al Ahlia Insurance Co; South Carolina Insurance Co v Arabian
     Seas Insurance Co; South Carolina Insurance Co v Cambridge Reinsurance Co Ltd
     [1987] A.C. 24; [1986] 3 W.L.R. 398; [1986] 3 All E.R. 487; [1986] 2 Lloyd's Rep. 317;
     [1987] E.C.C. 1; (1986) 83 L.S.G. 2659; (1986) 136 N.L.J. 751; (1986) 130 S.J. 634
     HL 2–026
South Pacific Manufacturing v New Zealand Consultants [1992] 2 N.Z.L.R. 282 15–013
South Staffordshire Tramways Co Ltd v Sickness & Accident Assurance Association Ltd
     [1891] 1 Q.B. 402 CA 5–004, 10–033
Southampton Container Terminals Ltd v Hansa Schiffahrts GmbH (The Maersk Colombo);
     sub nom. Southampton Container Terminals Ltd v Schiffahrtsgesellschaft "Hansa
     Australia" MGH & Co [2001] EWCA Civ. 717; [2001] 2 Lloyd's Rep. 275; (2001)
     98(24) L.S.G. 43; (2001) 145 S.J.L.B. 149; Times, June 13, 2001 CA (Civ Div) 10–015
Southampton Leisure Holdings Plc v Avon Insurance Plc [2004] EWHC 571 QBD 5–031, 18–044
Southcombe v Merriman (1842) Car. & M. 286 .... 7–033, 18–030
South-East Lancashire Insurance Co Ltd v Croisdale (1931) 40 Ll.L.R. 22 KBD 1–019, 1–023,
                                                    1–024, 8–019
Southwest Georgia Financial Corp v Colonial American Casualty & Surety Co 2009 B.L.
     201259 (MD Ga, September 21, 2009) 20–085
Sovereign Life Assurance Co (In Liquidation) v Dodd [1892] 2 Q.B. 573 CA 16–005
Sovereign Marine & General Insurance Co Ltd, Re [2006] EWHC 1335 Ch D (Companies
     Ct) 16–005
Soya GmbH Mainz KG v White [1983] 1 Lloyd's Rep. 122; [1983] Com. L.R. 46; (1983) 133
     N.L.J. 64 HL 24–080, 24–081, 24–134
Spalding v Crocker (1897) 2 Com.Cas. 189 1–033
Sparenborg v Edinburgh Life Assurance Co [1912] 1 K.B. 195 KBD 8–027
Sparks v St Paul Insurance Co 100 N.J. 325 (1985) 20–089
Sparkes v Marshall (1836) 2 Bing. N.C. 761 .... 4–016, 11–042, 19–007
Spencer v Clarke (1878) L.R. 9 Ch. D. 137 Ch D 14–026, 14–028
Speno Rail Maintenance Australia Pty Ltd v Metals & Minerals Insurance Pte Ltd (2009) 253
     A.L.R. 364 .... 11–006, 11–065
Sphere Drake Insurance Ltd v Euro International Underwriting Ltd [2003] EWHC 1636;
     [2003] Lloyd's Rep. I.R. 525; Times, August 11, 2003 QBD (Comm) 15–022, 15–028,
                                                      17–013
Sphere Drake Insurance Plc v Basler Versicherungs Gesellschaft; Orion Insurance Co Plc v
     Basler Versicherungs Gesellschaft [1998] Lloyd's Rep. I.R. 35 QBD (Comm) .. 1–021, 15–020,
                                                       17–027
Sphere Drake Insurance v Gunes Sigorta Anonim Sirketi [1988] 1 Lloyd's Rep. 139 CA (Civ
     Div) 2–003
Spiliada Maritime Corp v Cansulex Ltd; The Spiliada [1987] A.C. 460; [1986] 3 W.L.R. 972;
     [1986] 3 All E.R. 843; [1987] 1 Lloyd's Rep. 1; [1987] E.C.C. 168; [1987] 1 F.T.L.R.
     103; (1987) 84 L.S.G. 113; (1986) 136 N.L.J. 1137; (1986) 130 S.J. 925; Financial
     Times, November 25, 1986 HL 2–005
Spinney's (1948) Ltd v Royal Insurance Co Ltd [1980] 1 Lloyd's Rep. 406 QBD (Comm) 5–031,
                        25–004, 25–006, 25–007, 25–008, 25–009, 25–011

Splents v Lefevre (1863) 11 L.T. 114 15–004

Spooner-Kenyon v Yorkshire-General Life Assurance Co Ltd (1982) 2 A.N.Z. Insurance
     Cases 60–476 8–016

Spraggon v Dominion Insurance Co Ltd; Dominion Insurance Co Ltd v Tomrley (Trundle)
     (1941) 69 Ll.L.R. 1 CA 22–089

Spriggs v Wessington Court School Ltd [2004] EWHC 1432; [2005] Lloyd's Rep. I.R. 474
     QBD 6–089, 6–091, 6–094, 6–096, 20–008, 21–019, 21–032

Springer v NEM Insurance Co Ltd. *See* Thornton Springer v NEM Insurance Co Ltd

Sprung v Royal Insurance (UK) Ltd [1997] C.L.C. 70; [1999] 1 Lloyd's Rep. I.R. 111CA
     (Civ Div) 10–014, 10–022, 15–047

Spurrier v La Cloche [1902] A.C. 446 PC (Jersey) 2–035, 2–036

Squires v Whisken (1811) 3 Samp 140 4–002

St Ivel Ltd v Wincanton Group Ltd [2007] EWHC 2906 (Comm) 3–005

St John Shipping Corp v Joseph Rank Ltd [1957] 1 Q.B. 267; [1956] 3 W.L.R. 870; [1956]
     3 All E.R. 683; [1956] 2 Lloyd's Rep. 413; 100 S.J. 841 QBD 2–058, 5–036, 5–037, 5–046

St Margaret's Trust Ltd v Navigators and General Insurance Co Ltd (1948–49) 82 Ll.L.R.
     752, KB 6–037, 24–080, 24–112

St Mary's Cement Company Inc v ACE INA Insurance [2008] O.J. No.2622 20–050

St Paul Fire & Marine Insurance Co (UK) Ltd v McConnell Dowell Constructors Ltd; sub
     nom. St Paul Fire & Marine Insurance Co (UK) Ltd v McDonnell Dowell Constructors
     Ltd [1996] 1 All E.R. 96; [1995] 2 Lloyd's Rep. 116; [1995] C.L.C. 818; 74 B.L.R. 112;
     45 Con. L.R. 89; [1995] 4 Re. L.R. 293; Lloyd's List, June 8, 1995 (I.D.) CA (Civ Div);
     affirming [1993] 2 Lloyd's Rep. 503; 67 B.L.R. 72; 37 Con. L.R. 96 QBD (Comm) ... 1–033,
                                                    6–024, 6–028, 6–073, 6–102

St Paul Fire & Mrine Insurance Co v Durabla Canada Ltd (1996) 29 O.R. (3d) 737 20–050

St Paul Fire & Marine Insurance Co v Guardian Insurance Co of Canada [1983] 1 D.L.R.
     342 20–038

St Paul Fire & Marine Insurance Co v Morice (1906) 22 T.L.R. 449 .... 2–050, 17–014

Staatssecretaris van Financien v Arthur Andersen & Co Accountants CS (C–472/03) [2005]
     S.T.C. 508; [2005] E.C.R. I–1719; [2005] 2 C.M.L.R. 51; [2006] B.T.C. 5159; [2006]
     B.V.C. 228; [2005] S.T.I. 363 ECJ 15–013, 15–026

Stace & Francis Ltd v Ashby [2001] EWCA Civ. 1655 CA (Civ Div) 11–007

Stainbank v Fenning (1851) 11 C.B. 51; 138 E.R. 389 .... 4–018, 18–020, 24–024

Stainbank v Shepard (1853) 13 C.B. 418 4–018

Stamma v Brown (1743) 2 Str. 1173 24–138

Standard Bank Plc v Agrinvest International Inc [2007] EWHC 2595 (Comm); [2008] 1
     Lloyd's Rep. 532 .... 2–003, 2–006

Standard Life Assurance Co v Egan Lawson Ltd. *See* Egan Lawson Ltd v Standard Life
     Assurance Co; sub nom. Standard Life Assurance Co v Egan Lawson Ltd

Standard Life Assurance Ltd v Oak Dedicated Ltd [2008] EWHC 222 (Comm); [2008] 2 All
     E.R. (Comm) 916; [2008] 1 C.L.C. 59; [2008] Lloyd's Rep. I.R. 552; [2008] P.N.L.R.
     26 .... 1–033, 10–036, 13–037, 15–034, 15–035, 15–051, 15–057, 15–059

Standard Oil Co of New York v Clan Line Steamers Ltd; sub nom. Standard Oil Co of New
     York v Owners of the Clan Gordon [1924] A.C. 100; (1923–24) 17 Ll.L.R. 120; 1924
     S.C. (H.L.) 1; 1924 S.L.T. 20 HL 24–062

Standard Steamship Owners Protection & Indemnity Association (Bermuda) Ltd v GIE
     Vision Bail [2004] EWHC 2919; [2005] 1 All E.R. (Comm) 618; [2005] 2 C.L.C. 1135;
     [2005] Lloyd's Rep. I.R. 407 QBD (Comm) 2–008, 2–015

Standard Steamship Owners Protection and Indemnity Association Ltd v Gann [1992] 2
     Lloyd's Rep. 528; Financial Times, June 19, 1992 QBD (Comm) 2–003, 2–005

Standard Steamship Owners Protection & Indemnity Association (Bermuda) Ltd v Oceanfast
     Shipping (The Ainikolas I) (1996) Lloyd's List, April 5 .... 8–006, 9–021

Stanley v Western Insurance Co (1868) L.R. 3 Ex. 71 .... 5–030, 19–041

Stanton & Stanton Ltd v Starr (1920) 3 Ll.L.R. 259 KBD (Comm Ct) 1–019, 15–035

Stanton v Collinson [2010] EWCA Civ 81; [2010] R.T.R. 26; (2010) 154(8) S.J.L.B. 29 ... 22–035

Star Sea, The. *See* Manifest Shipping Co Ltd v Uni-Polaris Insurance Co Ltd

Starfire Diamond Rings Ltd v Angel [1962] 2 Lloyd's Rep. 217; 106 S.J. 854 CA 5–012

Stargas SpA v Petredec (The Sargasso) Sargasso, The [1994] 1 Lloyd's Rep. 412 15–059

Starkey v Hall (1936) 55 Ll.L.R. 24 KBD 22–015

Starlight Shipping Co v Tai Ping Insurance Co Ltd (Hubei Branch) Alexandros T, The [2007]
     EWHC 1893 (Comm); [2008] 1 All E.R. (Comm) 593; [2008] 1 Lloyd's Rep. 230;
     [2007] 2 C.L.C. 440 11–011

Starr (E) & Co Ltd v Clifford & Sons (1918) Ltd (1922) 10 Ll.L.R. 649 KBD 15–032

Starsin, The. *See* Homburg Houtimport BV v Agrosin Private Ltd

State Fire Insurance v Liverpool & London Globe Insurance [1952] N.Z.L.R. 5 11–051
State Government Insurance Office (Qld) v Brisbane Stevedoring Pty Ltd (1969) 123 C.L.R.
    228 11–041
State Insurance General Manager v Bettany [1992] 2 N.Z.L.R. 275 10–015
State Insurance General Manager v Hanham (1990) 6 A.N.Z. Insurance Cases 60–990 6–071
State Insurance General Manager v McHale [1992] 2 N.Z.L.R. 399 6–005
State Insurance General Manager v Peake [1991] 2 N.Z.L.R. 287 .... 6–019, 6–071
State Insurance v Fry (1991) 6 A.N.Z. Insurance Cases 77,237 .... 6–006, 6–069
Statoil ASA v Louis Dreyfus Energy Services LP (The Harriette N) Harriette N, The [2008]
    EWHC 2257 (Comm); [2009] 1 All E.R. (Comm) 1035; [2008] 2 Lloyd's Rep. 685;
    (2008) 158 N.L.J. 1377 10–057
Stavers v Curling (1836) 3 Bing.N.C. 355 3–004
Stavers v Mountain, Times, July 27, 1912 10–021
Steamship Balmoral v Marten. See Balmoral Steamship Co Ltd v Marten
Stearns v Village Main Reef Gold Mining Co (1905) 21 T.L.R. 236 11–036
Stebbing v Liverpool & London & Globe Insurance Co [1917] 2 K.B. 433 KBD 7–044
Steel v Lacy (1810) 3 Taunt. 285 .... 6–051, 24–058
Steel v State Line Steamship Co (1877–78) L.R. 3 App. Cas. 72 HL 24–062
Steelclad v Iron Trades Mutual Insurance Co, 1984 S.C. 71; 1984 S.L.T. 304 IH (2 Div) 11–054
Steinberg v Scala (Leeds) Ltd [1923] 2 Ch. 452 CA 14–002
Stemson v AMP General Insurance (NZ) Ltd [2006] UKPC 30 PC (NZ) 9–029, 9–030, 9–031
Stephen (AP) v Scottish Boatowners Mutual Insurance Association; The Talisman; sub nom.
    Stephen v Scottish Boatowners Mutual Insurance Association; The Talisman; Stephen v
    Scottish Boatowners Mutual Insurance Association [1989] 1 Lloyd's Rep. 535; 1989
    S.C. (H.L.) 24; 1989 S.L.T. 283 HL 24–112
Stephens v Australasian Insurance Co (1872–73) L.R. 8 C.P. 18 CCP 24–029, 24–031, 24–048,
                                                                                                        24–051
Stern v Norwich Union Fire Insurance Society Unreported, 1996 CA (Civ Div) 5–012, 5–051
Stevenson v Snow (1761) 3 Burr 1237. 1240 8–020
Stevenson v Snow (1777) 3 Cowp. 666 8–021
Stewart v Aberdein (1834) 4 M. & W. 211 15–041
Stewart v Bell (1821) 5 B. & Ald. 238 .... 6–065, 24–037
Stewart v Greenock Marine Insurance Co (1848) 2 H.L. Cas. 159 24–095
Stewart v Oriental Fire & Marine Insurance Co Ltd [1985] Q.B. 988; [1984] 3 W.L.R. 741;
    [1984] 3 All E.R. 777; [1984] 2 Lloyd's Rep. 109; [1984] E.C.C. 564; [1985] Fin. L.R.
    64; (1984) 81 L.S.G. 1915; (1984) 134 N.L.J. 584; (1984) 128 S.J. 645 QBD (Comm) 13–020
Stewart v Wilson (1843) 2 M. & W. 11 24–062
Stewart & Co v Merchants Marine Insurance Co Ltd (1885–86) L.R. 16 Q.B.D. 619 CA 10–030
Stinton v Stinton; sub nom. Stinton v Motor Insurers Bureau [1995] R.T.R. 167; [1999]
    Lloyd's Rep. I.R. 305; (1995) 92(1) L.S.G. 37; Times, November 23, 1994 CA (Crim
    Div) 22–009, 22–045, 22–067
Stirling v Vaughan (1809) 11 East 619 .... 4–016, 15–003, 19–031
Stock v Inglis. See Inglis v Stock
Stockdale v Dunlop (1840) 6 M. & W. 224 .... 4–017, 4–018, 10–021
Stockton v Mason [1978] 2 Lloyd's Rep. 430; [1979] R.T.R. 130 CA (Civ Div) ... 1–054, 15–028
Stocznia Gdanska SA v Latreefers Inc; sub nom. Latreefers Inc, Re; Stocznia Gdanska SA
    v Latvian Shipping Co (Abuse of Process) [2000] C.P.L.R. 65; [2001] B.C.C. 174;
    [2001] 2 B.C.L.C. 116; [2001] C.L.C. 1267; Times, March 15, 2000; Independent,
    February 15, 2000 CA (Civ Div) 16–001, 21–006
Stokell v Heywood [1897] 1 Ch. 459 Ch D 18–003
Stokes v Cox (1856) 1 H. & N. 533 .... 5–020, 5–022, 19–039
Stokoe v Cowan (1861) 4 L.T. 675 18–022
Stolos Compania SA v Ajax Insurance Co (The Admiral C) [1981] 1 Lloyd's Rep. 9; [1980]
    Com. L.R. 4 CA (Civ Div) 15–041
Stolt Marmaro, The. See Cantieri Navali Riuniti SpA v Omne Justitia NV; The Stolt Mar-
    maro
Stone v Licenses & General Insurance Co Ltd (1941) 71 Ll.L.R. 256 KBD 22–096
Stone v Marine Insurance Co Ocean Ltd of Gothenburg (1875–76) L.R. 1 Ex. D. 81,
    Exchequer Div 24–066
Stone v Reliance Mutual Insurance Society [1972] 1 Lloyd's Rep. 469 CA (Civ Div) 6–065,
                                                                                            6–067, 15–002, 15–019

Stone & Rolls Ltd (In Liquidation) v Moore Stephens (A Firm) [2008] EWCA Civ 644;
[2008] 3 W.L.R. 1146; [2008] Bus. L.R. 1579; [2008] 2 Lloyd's Rep. 319; [2008] 2
B.C.L.C. 461; [2008] Lloyd's Rep. F.C. 426; [2008] P.N.L.R. 36; (2008) 105(25) L.S.G.
26 15–005
Stone & Rolls Ltd (In Liquidation) v Moore Stephens (A Firm) [2009] UKHL 39; [2009] 1
A.C. 1391; [2009] 3 W.L.R. 455; [2009] Bus. L.R. 1356; [2009] 4 All E.R. 431; [2010]
1 All E.R. (Comm) 125; [2009] 2 Lloyd's Rep. 537; [2009] 2 B.C.L.C. 563; [2009] 2
C.L.C. 121; [2009] Lloyd's Rep. F.C. 557; [2009] B.P.I.R. 1191; [2009] P.N.L.R. 36;
(2009) 159 N.L.J. 1218; (2009) 153(31) S.J.L.B. 28; Times, August 11, 2009 ...... 2–058, 5–044,
                                                        5–046, 5–047, 6–039, 6–043,15–005, 20–086, 20–087
Stone Vickers Ltd v Appledore Ferguson Shipbuilders Ltd [1992] 2 Lloyd's Rep. 578CA
(Civ Div); reversing [1991] 2 Lloyd's Rep. 288; Times, January 30, 1991QBD
(Comm) 11–027, 11–028, 14–003, 14–007, 19–032
Stoneham v Ocean, Railway and General Accident Insurance Co (1887) L.R. 19 Q.B.D. 237
QBD 7–013, 9–004
Storebrand Skadeforsikring AS v Finanger (E1/99) [1999] 3 C.M.L.R. 863; [2000] Lloyd's
Rep. I.R. 462 EFTA 22–035, 22–036
Stormont v Waterloo Life (1858) 1 F. & F. 22 18–034
Stott (Baltic) Steamers Ltd v Marten [1916] 1 A.C. 304 HL 24–002, 24–134
Stowers v GA Bonus Plc [2003] Lloyd's Rep. I.R. 402 CC (London) 6–052, 6–073, 15–036,
                                                                        15–054, 15–057
Strachan v Universal Stock Exchange Ltd (No.1); sub nom. Universal Stock Exchange Ltd
v Strachan (No.1) [1896] A.C. 166 HL 4–009
Stribley v Imperial Marine Insurance Co (1875–76) L.R. 1 Q.B.D. 507 QBD 24–036, 24–037
Strickland v Turner (1852) 7 Ex. 208 .... 8–029, 10–057
Stringer v English and Scottish Marine Insurance Co Ltd (1868–69) L.R. 4 Q.B. 676 24–083
Strive Shipping Corp v Hellenic Mutual War Risks Association (Bermuda) Ltd (The Grecia
Express) [2002] EWHC 203; [2002] 2 All E.R. (Comm) 213; [2002] 2 Lloyd's Rep. 88;
[2003] 1 C.L.C. 401; [2002] Lloyd's Rep. I.R. 669 QBD (Comm) 6–031, 6–032, 6–050,
                                6–052, 6–056, 6–062, 6–065, 6–077, 6–092, 6–130, 17–009, 17–026,
                                                                24–040, 24–112, 25–015
Strong & Pearl v S Allison & Co Ltd; Strong v British General Insurance Co Ltd (1926) 25
Ll.L.R. 504 KBD 15–034, 15–035
Strong v Harvey (1825) 3 Bing. 304; 130 E.R. 530 24–007
Stroude v Beazer Homes Ltd [2005] EWCA Civ 265; [2005] N.P.C. 45; Times, April 28,
2005 3–005
Structural Polymer Systems Ltd v Brown; The Baltic Universal [1999] C.L.C. 268; [2000]
Lloyd's Rep. I.R. 64 QBD (Comm) 11–048, 20–052, 20–052, 20–059
Stuart v Freeman [1903] 1 K.B. 47 CA 1–048, 5–005, 8–009
Sturge v Hackett; sub nom. Cunningham v Hackett [1962] 1 W.L.R. 1257; [1962] 3 All E.R.
166; [1962] 1 Lloyd's Rep. 626; 106 S.J. 568 CA 20–028, 20–083
Sulphite Pulp v Faber (1895) 111 T.L.R. 547 17–012
Sumitomo Bank Ltd v Banque Bruxelles Lambert SA [1997] 1 Lloyd's Rep. 487; [1996]
E.G.C.S. 150; Independent, November 11, 1996 (C.S.) QBD (Comm) 6–069, 6–118, 14–007,
                                                                        15–026
Sumitomo Marine & Fire Insurance Co Ltd v Cologne Reinsurance Co of America, 552
N.Y.S. 2d 891 (1990) 6–092
Summers v Congreve Horner & Co [1992] 40 E.G. 144; [1992] E.G.C.S. 101; [1992] N.P.C.
91; Times, August 24, 1992 CA (Civ Div) 20–031
Sumpiles Investments Pte Ltd v Axa Insurance Singapore Pte Ltd [2006] 3 S.L.R. 12 7–037,
                                                                        9–024, 24–003, 24–004
Sun Alliance & London Insurance Plc v PT Asuransri Dayan Mitra TBK (The No 1 Dae Bu)
[2006] EWHC 812 (Comm) 2–007, 24–047, 24–129
Sun Alliance Pensions Life & Investments Services Ltd v RJL; Sun Alliance Pensions Life
& Investments Services Ltd v Anthony Webster [1991] 2 Lloyd's Rep. 410 QBD 15–008
Sun Fire and Wright (1834) 3 N. & M. 819 4–017
Sun Fire Office v Hart (1889) L.R. 14 App. Cas. 98 PC (Wind) .. 1–047, 3–006, 3–007, 5–007, 8–019
Sun Life Assurance Co v Jervis [1943] 2 All E.R. 425 CA 1–022
Sun Life Assurance Co of Canada v CX Reinsurance Co Ltd (formerly CNA Reinsurance Co
Ltd) [2003] EWCA Civ. 283; [2004] Lloyd's Rep. I.R. 58 CA (Civ Div) 1–034
Sun Life Assurance Co of Canada v Jervis [1944] A.C. 111; (1943) 113 L.J.K.B. 174 HL 1–017,
                                                                        1–018
Sun Life Assurance Co of Canada v Lincoln National Life Insurance Co. See Lincoln
National Life Insurance Co v Sun Life Assurance Co of Canada

Sun Life of Canada Assurance Co, Re Unreported, 1999 CA 13–036
Suncorp Insurance and Finance v Milano Assicurazioni SpA [1993] 2 Lloyd's Rep. 225 QBD
    (Comm) 15–003, 15–022, 15–053
Sunderland Marine Mutual Insurance Co Ltd v Wiseman (The Seaward Quest) Seaward
    Quest, The [2007] EWHC 1460 (Comm); [2007] 2 All E.R. (Comm) 937; [2007] 2
    Lloyd's Rep. 308; [2007] 1 C.L.C. 989 2–004
Sunport Shipping Ltd v Atkin; The Kelovoulos of Rhodes. See Sunport Shipping Ltd v Tryg
    Baltica International (UK) Ltd
Sunport Shipping Ltd v Tryg Baltica International (UK) Ltd (The Kleovoulos of Rhodes); sub
    nom. Sunport Shipping Ltd v Atkin; The Kleovoulos of Rhodes [2003] EWCA Civ. 12;
    [2003] 1 All E.R. (Comm) 586; [2003] 1 Lloyd's Rep. 138; [2003] 1 C.L.C. 772; [2003]
    Lloyd's Rep. I.R. 349; (2003) 100(11) L.S.G. 33; Times, February 3, 2003 CA (Civ
    Div) 3–003, 25–013
Super Chem Products Ltd v American Life & General Insurance Co Ltd [2004] UKPC 2;
    [2004] 2 All E.R. 358; [2004] 1 All E.R. (Comm) 713; [2004] 1 C.L.C. 1041; [2004]
    Lloyd's Rep. I.R. 446; (2004) 148 S.J.L.B. 113; Times, January 28, 2004 PC (Trin) ... 1–022,
                                                                                9–018, 9–034, 9–042
Supershield Ltd v Siemens Building Technologies FE Ltd [2010] EWCA Civ 7; [2010] 1
    Lloyd's Rep. 349; [2010] B.L.R. 145; 129 Con. L.R. 52; [2010] N.P.C. 5 15–059
Supple v Cann (1858) 9 Ir. C.L. 1 8–004
Surf City, The [1995] 2 Lloyd's Rep. 242; Lloyd's List, July 17, 1995 (I.D.) QBD (Admlty) ... 11–038
Surrey CC and Mole DC v Bredero Homes Ltd [1993] 1 W.L.R. 1361; [1993] 3 All E.R. 705;
    [1993] 25 E.G. 141; [1993] E.G.C.S. 77; 137 S.J.L.B. 135; [1993] N.P.C. 63; Times,
    April 16, 1993 CA (Civ Div) 20–015
Surrey Heath BC v Lovell Construction Ltd, 48 B.L.R. 108; 24 Con. L.R. 1; (1990) 6 Const.
    L.J. 179 CA (Civ Div) 11–026, 11–031
Survey Research Co Ltd v Sentry Insurance Co Ltd Unreported December 9, 1985; [1986]
    H.K.E.C. 11 1–051
Suse & Sibeth, Ex p. Dever, Re (1887) L.R. 18 Q.B.D. 660 CA 2–035
Sutch v Burns (1943) 60 T.L.R. 1 22–027
Sutherland v Pratt (1843) 13 L.J. Ex. 246; 12 M. & W. 16 .... 24–020, 24–045
Sutherland v Pratt (1843) 2 Dowl. N.S. 813; 12 L.J. Ex. 235; 7 Jur. 261; 11 M. & W. 296 4–005,
                                                                                19–008, 24–022
Sutherland v Sun Fire Office (1852) 14 D. 775 10–043
Sutherland Marine v Kearney and Noonan (1851) 16 Q.B. 925 .... 3–008, 3–009
Svenska Handelsbanken AB v Dandridge (The Alicia Glacial). See Handelsbanken ASA v
    Dandridge
Svenska Handelsbanken v Sun Alliance and London Insurance Plc (No.2) [1996] 1 Lloyd's
    Rep. 519; [1996] C.L.C. 833 QBD (Comm) 6–015, 6–069, 6–092, 6–118, 7–006, 7–026,
                                                                                23–030
Swain v Law Society [1983] 1 A.C. 598; [1982] 3 W.L.R. 261; [1982] 2 All E.R. 827; (1982)
    79 L.S.G. 887; 126 S.J. 464 HL 8–001, 14–003
Swainbank and Co-operative Insurance, Re [1953] 1 A.C. 29 18–015
Swainland Builders Ltd v Freehold Properties Ltd [2002] EWCA Civ 560; [2002] 2 E.G.L.R.
    71; [2002] 23 E.G. 123; [2002] 17 E.G. 154 (C.S.) 1–018
Swan v Maritime Insurance Co [1907] 1 K.B. 116 KBD 1–033, 8–005, 13–011, 24–044
Swan, The. See Bridges & Salmon Ltd v Owner of The Swan
Sweeney v Kennedy (1948–49) 82 Ll.L.R. 294 HC (Irl) 7–021, 7–032, 22–089
Sweeting v Pearce (1859) 9 C.B.N.S. 534 15–041
Swete v Fairlie (1833) 6 Car. & P. 1 18–028
Swiss Reinsurance Co v United India Insurance Co Ltd [2005] EWHC 237; [2005] 2 All E.R.
    (Comm) 367; [2005] 1 C.L.C. 203; [2005] Lloyd's Rep. I.R. 341 QBD (Comm) 5–026,
                                                                                5–028, 8–020, 8–021, 17–012
Sword Daniels v Pitel. See Brown v KMR Services Ltd (formerly HG Poland (Agencies)
    Ltd); Sword Daniels v Pitel
Symington & Co v Union Insurance Society of Canton Ltd; sub nom. Symington & Co v
    Union Insurance Society of Canton Ltd (1928) 97 L.J.K.B. 646; 18 Asp. M.L.C. 19; 34
    Com.Cas. 23; [1928] All E.R. Rep. 346; 139 L.T. 386; 44 T.L.R. 635; 31 Ll.L.R. 179
    CA 24–002
Symington & Co v Union Insurance Society of Canton Ltd; sub nom. Symington & Co v
    Union Insurance Society of Canton Ltd (No.2) (1928) 141 L.T. 48 1–055
QBDT O'Donoghue (T) Ltd v Harding [1988] 2 Lloyd's Rep. 281; Financial Times, July 27,
    1988 QBD 5–012

TFW Printers Ltd v Interserve Project Services Ltd [2006] EWCA Civ. 875; (2006) 103(28)
L.S.G. 27 CA (Civ Div) 11–028, 14–018
TGA Chapman Ltd v Christopher [1998] 1 W.L.R. 12; [1998] 2 All E.R. 873; [1997] C.L.C.
1306; [1998] Lloyd's Rep. I.R. 1; Times, July 21, 1997 CA (Civ Div) 20–055, 23–016
TH Adamson & Sons v Liverpool and London and Globe Insurance Co Ltd [1953] 2 Lloyd's
Rep. 355 QBD 9–007
TM Noten BV v Harding [1990] 2 Lloyd's Rep. 283 CA (Civ Div); reversing [1989] 2
Lloyd's Rep. 527 QBD (Comm) 24–080, 24–081
TSB Bank Plc v Robert Irving & Burns [2000] 2 All E.R. 826; [1999] Lloyd's Rep. P.N. 956;
[1999] Lloyd's Rep. I.R. 528; [2000] P.N.L.R. 384 CA (Civ Div) 20–045
T&N Ltd, Re [2005] EWHC 2990 (Ch); [2006] 1 W.L.R. 1792; [2006] 3 All E.R. 755 2–061
T&N Ltd, Re [2006] EWHC 1447 Ch D (Companies Ct) 20–066, 20–069, 21–019, 21–033,
21–038, 21–063
T&N Ltd (Breach of Agreement), Re; sub nom. Curzon Insurance Ltd v Centre Reinsurance
International Co [2005] EWHC 2991; [2006] Lloyd's Rep. I.R. 370 Ch D (Companies
Ct) 9–016, 13–018, 17–025
T&N Ltd (In Administration) v Royal & Sun Alliance Plc [2003] EWHC 1016; [2003] 2 All
E.R. (Comm) 939; [2004] Lloyd's Rep. I.R. 106; (2003) 153 N.L.J. 750 Ch D 1–019, 3–005,
11–035, 20–068, 21–007
T&N Ltd v Royal & Sun Alliance Plc [2002] EWHC 2420 (Ch); [2002] C.L.C. 1342; [2004]
Lloyd's Rep. I.R. 102 20–068
T&N Ltd (No.3), Re. See T&N Ltd (Breach of Agreement), Re
T&N Ltd (No.4), Re. See T&N Ltd, Re
Tabbs v Bendelack (1801) 3 Bos. & P. 207n 24–058
Tai Ping Insurance Co v Tugu Insurance Co Ltd [2001] H.K.E.C. 506 11–063
Tait v Levi (1811) 14 East 481 .... 24–070, 24–073
Talbot Underwriting Ltd v Nausch Hogan & Murray Inc (The Jascon 5) [2006] EWCA Civ.
889 CA (Civ Div); [2006] 2 Lloyd's Rep. 195 affirming [2005] EWHC 2359; [2005] 2
C.L.C. 868 QBD (Comm) 4–020, 4–021, 6–028, 6–046, 6–091, 6–092, 10–004, 11–036,
14–006, 14–007, 15–006, 15–035, 15–059, 24–080
Tamil Nadu Electricity Board v ST-CMS Electric Co Private Ltd [2007] EWHC 1713
(Comm); [2007] 2 All E.R. (Comm) 701; [2008] 1 Lloyd's Rep. 93; 1 A.L.R. Int'l
795 2–025
Tan Keng Hong v New India Assurance Co [1978] 1 W.L.R. 297; [1978] 2 All E.R. 380;
[1978] 1 Lloyd's Rep. 233; [1978] R.T.R. 253; 122 S.J. 82 PC (Mal) 22–017
Tankexpress v Compagnie Financiere. See A/S Tankexpress v Compagnie Financiere Belge
des Petroles SA
Tanner v Bennett (1825) Ry. & M. 182 24–003
Tapa v Attorney-General [1977] 2 N.Z.L.R 35 8–004
Tappoo Holdings Ltd v Stuchbery [2006] F.J.S.C. 1 .... 5–031, 25–008
Tarbuck v Avon Insurance Plc [2002] Q.B. 571; [2001] 3 W.L.R. 1502; [2001] 2 All E.R.
503; [2001] 1 All E.R. (Comm) 422; [2001] B.P.I.R. 1142; [2002] Lloyd's Rep. I.R.
393; (2001) 151 N.L.J. 18 QBD (Comm) 21–007, 21–045, 23–017
Tarleton v Staniforth (1794) 5 T.R. 695 .... 3–004, 3–010, 8–009
Tasker v Cunningham (1819) 1 Bligh. 87 24–069
Tate & Lyle Ltd v Hain Steamship Co Ltd; sub nom. Hain Steamship Co v Tate & Lyle Ltd
[1936] 2 All E.R. 597; (1936) 55 Ll.L.R. 159; 52 T.L.R. 617; 41 Com. Cas. 350; [1936]
W.N. 210 HL; reversing (1934) 49 Ll.L.R. 123; 50 T.L.R. 415; 39 Com. Cas. 259; 151
L.T. 249 CA 7–005, 9–038
Tate & Sons v Hyslop (1884–85) L.R. 15 Q.B.D. 368 CA 6–022, 6–024, 6–045, 11–041
Tate Gallery Board of Trustees v Duffy Construction Ltd [2007] EWHC 361 (TCC); [2007]
1 All E.R. (Comm) 1004; [2007] B.L.R. 216; [2007] Lloyd's Rep. I.R. 758 .... 3–002, 11–030,
14–003, 14–014, 19–037, 19–042
Tate Gallery Board of Trustees v Duffy Construction Ltd (No.2) [2007] EWHC 912 (TCC);
[2008] Lloyd's Rep. I.R. 159 .... 5–050, 14–014
Tatham v Hodgson (1796) 6 T.R. 656 24–080
Tatham Bromage & Co v Burr (The Engineer) Engineer, The [1898] A.C. 382 HL 20–010
Tattersall v Drysdale [1935] 2 K.B. 174; (1935) 52 Ll.L.R. 21 KBD 14–022, 20–062, 22–027,
22–088
Taussik v DPP Unreported, 2001 22–008
Taylor v Allon [1966] 1 Q.B. 304; [1965] 2 W.L.R. 598; [1965] 1 All E.R. 557; [1965] 1
Lloyd's Rep. 155; 109 S.J. 78 DC 1–023, 1–026, 1–051, 8–009
Taylor v Builders Accident Insurance Ltd (1997) M.C.L.C. 247 .... 7–006, 7–015, 9–003
Taylor v Caldwell (1863) 3 B. & S. 826 10–047

Taylor v Dunbar (1868–69) L.R. 4 C.P. 206 CCP 24–002, 24–080
Taylor v Eagle Star Insurance Co Ltd (1940) 67 Ll.L.R. 136 KBD 6–018, 6–048, 22–087
Taylor v Liverpool and Great Western Steam Co (1873–74) L.R. 9 Q.B. 546 QB 24–136
Taylor v Mead [1961] 1 W.L.R. 435; [1961] 1 All E.R. 626; 125 J.P. 286; 59 L.G.R. 202; 105
    S.J. 159DC 22–006
Taylor v National Insurance & Guarantee Corp [1989] 6 C.L. 248 CC (Norwich) 3–010, 22–036
Taylor v O'Wray & Co [1971] 1 Lloyd's Rep. 497 CA (Civ Div) 11–015
QBDTaylor v Yorkshire Insurance [1913] 2 I.R. 1 .... 6–053, 15–019
Tektrol Ltd (formerly Atto Power Controls Ltd) v International Insurance Co of Hanover Ltd
    [2005] EWCA Civ. 845; [2006] 1 All E.R. (Comm) 780; [2005] 2 Lloyd's Rep. 701;
    [2005] 2 C.L.C. 339; [2006] Lloyd's Rep. I.R. 38 CA (Civ Div); reversing [2004]
    EWHC 2473; [2005] 1 All E.R. (Comm) 132; [2005] Info. T.L.R. 130; [2005] Lloyd's
    Rep. I.R. 358 QBD (Comm) ... 3–006, 3–009, 3–010, 5–031, 5–032, 5–034, 19–034, 19–051,
                                                                                                                         25–015
Telewest Communications Plc (No.1), Re [2004] EWCA Civ. 728; [2005] B.C.C. 29; [2005]
    1 B.C.L.C. 752 CA (Civ Div); affirming [2004] EWHC 924; [2004] B.C.C. 342; Times,
    May 27, 2004 Ch D (Companies Ct) 16–005
Telford and Wrekin BC v Ahmed [2006] EWHC 1748 DC 22–011
Temple Legal Protection Ltd v QBE Insurance (Europe) Ltd [2009] EWCA Civ 453; [2010]
    1 All E.R. (Comm) 703; [2009] 1 C.L.C. 553; [2009] Lloyd's Rep. I.R. 544; (2009)
    153(14) S.J.L.B. 27 15–020
Tempus Shipping Co Ltd v Louis Dreyfus & Co; sub nom. Louis Dreyfus & Co v Tempus
    Shipping Co Ltd [1931] A.C. 726; (1931) 40 Ll.L.R. 217 HL; affirming [1931] 1 K.B.
    195; (1930) 37 Ll.L.R. 273CA; reversing in part [1930] 1 K.B. 699; (1930) 36 Ll.L.R.
    159 KBD 19–039
Tennant v Henderson (1813) 1 Dow. 324 6–065
Tesco Stores Ltd v Constable [2008] EWCA Civ 362; [2008] 1 C.L.C. 727; [2008] Lloyd's
    Rep. I.R. 636; [2008] C.I.L.L. 2593; (2008) 105(17) L.S.G. 28 .... 20–009, 20–075, 20–086
Tesco Supermarkets Ltd v Nattrass [1972] A.C. 153; [1971] 2 W.L.R. 1166; [1971] 2 All E.R.
    127; 69 L.G.R. 403; (1971) 115 S.J. 285 HL 5–046
Thames & Mersey Marine Insurance Co Ltd v Gunford Ship Co Ltd; sub nom. Gunford
    Steamship Co Ltd (in Liquidation) v Thames & Mersey Marine Insurance Co Ltd,;
    Gunford Ship Co Ltd (in Liquidation) and Liquidator v Thames & Mersey Marine
    Insurance Co Ltd; Gunford Steamship Co Ltd and Liquidator v Thames & Mersey
    Marine Insurance Co; Southern Marine Mutual Insurance Association Ltd v Gunford
    Ship Co Ltd [1911] A.C. 529; 1911 S.C. (H.L.) 84; 1911 2 S.L.T. 185 HL ... 6–056, 10–007,
                                                                                                                         24–039
Thames & Mersey Marine Insurance Co Ltd v Hamilton Fraser & Co; sub nom. Hamilton,
    Fraser & Co v Thames & Mersey Marine Insurance Co Ltd (1887) L.R. 12 App. Cas.
    484 HL 3–004, 3–006, 24–003, 24–134, 24–139
Thames & Mersey Marine Insurance Co v British & Chilian Steamship Co [1916] 1 K.B. 30
    CA 11–018
Thames & Mersey Marine Insurance Co v Gunford Ship Co (1981) 105 L.T. 312 6–058
Thames & Mersey Marine Insurance Co Ltd v HT Van Laun & Co [1917] 2 K.B. 48 HL 24–069,
                                                                                                              24–070, 24–072
Thames Fire Co v Hawks (1858) 1 F. & F. 406 10–044
Thames Steel Construction Ltd and Northern Assurance Co, 55 D.L.R. (4th) 639 (1988) ... 5–015
Thellusson v Ferguson (1780) 1 Doug K.B. 360 24–070
Theobald v Railway Passengers' Assurance Co (1854) 10 Ex. 45 .... 4–004, 10–019, 10–021, 11–005,
                                                                                                    18–001, 18–002, 18–041, 18–043
Theodorou v Chester [1951] 1 Lloyd's Rep. 204 KBD 19–034
Thiselton v Commercial Union Assurance Co Ltd [1926] Ch. 888; (1926) 25 Ll.L.R. 321 Ch
    D 1–017
Thomas v Commissioner of Police of the Metropolis [1997] Q.B. 813; [1997] 2 W.L.R. 593;
    [1997] 1 All E.R. 747; Times, December 12, 1996; Independent, December 19, 1996 CA
    (Civ Div) 6–048
Thomas v Dando [1951] 2 K.B. 620; [1951] 1 All E.R. 1010; [1951] 1 T.L.R. 1067; 115 J.P.
    344; 49 L.G.R. 793 DC 22–007
Thomas v Hooper; Thomas v Cooper (1986) 150 J.P. 53; [1986] R.T.R. 1; [1986] Crim. L.R.
    191 DC 22–009
Thomas v National Farmers Union Mutual Insurance Society [1961] 1 W.L.R. 386; [1961] 1
    All E.R. 363; [1960] 2 Lloyd's Rep. 444; 105 S.J. 233 QBD 4–005, 19–003
Thomas v Tyne & Wear Steamship Freight Insurance Association (1917) 117 L.T. 55 24–062
Thomas v Tyne & Wear Steamship Freight Insurance Association [1917] 1 K.B. 938 KBD 24–062

Thomas & Co v Brown (1891) 4 Com.Cas. 186 11–031
Thomas (M) & Son Shipping Co v London & Provincial Marine & General Insurance Co
(1914) 30 T.L.R. 595 24–062
Thomas Cheshire & Co v Vaughan Bros & Co [1920] 3 K.B. 240; (1920) 3 Ll.L.R. 213 CA 4–009,
15–036, 15–058, 24–015
Thomas Wilson Sons & Co v Owners of Cargo of the Xantho; The Xantho (1887) L.R. 12
App.Cas. 503 HL 19–055, 24–134
Thompson v Adams (1889) L.R. 23 Q.B.D. 361 QBD 1–033
Thompson v Calvin (1830) Ll. & Wels. 140 24–086
Thompson v Equity Fire Insurance Co [1910] A.C. 592 PC (Can) 5–022
Thompson v Gillespy (1855) 5 E. & B. 209 24–068
Thompson v Hopper (1856) 6 E.B. & E. 172 .... 5–017, 6–103, 9–029, 24–070, 24–080
Thompson v Hopper (1858) E.B. & E. 1038 .... 5–041, 24–062
Thompson v Lodwick [1983] R.T.R. 76 CA (Civ Div) 22–010
Thompson v Rowcroft (1803) 4 East 34 24–095
Thompson v Taylor (1795) 6 T.R. 478 20–062
Thompson v Whitmore (1810) 3 Taunt. 227 .... 24–134, 24–139
Thomson v Buchanan (1782) 4 Bro. Parl. Cas. 482 6–037
Thomson v Weems (1883–84) L.R. 9 App. Cas. 671 HL 1–011, 3–010, 6–013, 7–022, 7–026,
7–027, 7–030, 7–033, 7–037, 8–001, 8–027, 18–028, 18–030
Thor Navigation Inc v Ingosstrakh Insurance Co Ltd [2005] EWHC 19; [2005] 1 Lloyd's
Rep. 547; [2005] 1 C.L.C. 12; [2005] Lloyd's Rep. I.R. 490 QBD (Comm) 1–009, 1–019,
3–013, 10–006, 23–034
Thorman v New Hampshire Insurance Co (UK) Ltd; sub nom. Home Insurance Co v New
Hampshire Insurance Co (UK) Ltd [1988] 1 Lloyd's Rep. 7; 39 B.L.R. 41; [1988] 1
F.T.L.R. 30; [1988] Fin. L.R. 5; Times, October 12, 1987 CA (Civ Div) 10–036, 20–038
Thornton Springer v NEM Insurance Co Ltd [2000] 2 All E.R. 489; [2000] 1 All E.R.
(Comm) 486; [2000] C.L.C. 975; [2000] Lloyd's Rep. I.R. 590; (2000) 97(13) L.S.G.
42; (2000) 144 S.J.L.B. 147 QBD (Comm) 20–025, 20–048, 20–049, 20–051, 20–052
Thornton-Smith v Motor Union Insurance Co Ltd (1913) 30 T.L.R. 139 15–019
Through Transport Mutual Insurance Association (Eurasia) Ltd v New India Assurance Co
Ltd; The Hari Bhum (No.1) [2004] EWCA Civ. 1598; [2005] 1 All E.R. (Comm) 715;
[2005] 1 Lloyd's Rep. 67; [2004] 2 C.L.C. 1189; [2005] I.L.Pr. 30; (2004) 148 S.J.L.B.
1435 CA (Civ Div) 2–006, 2–008
Thurtell v Beaumont (1824) 1 Bing. 339 5–041
Thwaites v Aviva Assurances Unreported February, 2010 .... 2–014, 21–047
Tiburon, The. See Seavision Investment SA v Evennett
Tickel v Short (1750) 2 Ves. Sen. 239 .... 15–034, 15–045
Tidswell v Ankerstein (1792) Peake 204 19–031
Tiernan v Magen Insurance Unreported, 1998 .... 2–005, 2–007, 2–036
Tilley & Noad v Dominion Insurance Co (1987) 2 E.G.L.R. 34; (1987) 284 E.G. 1056 20–024
Timber Shipping Co SA v London and Overseas Freighters; sub nom. London & Overseas
Freighters Ltdv Timber Shipping Co SA [1972] A.C. 1; [1971] 2 W.L.R. 1360; [1971]
2 All E.R. 599; [1971] 1 Lloyd's Rep. 523; 115 S.J. 404 HL 3–017
Timberwest Forest Corp v Pacific Link Ocean Services Corp 2008 F.C. 801 11–038
Times Fire v Hawke (1858) 1 F. & F 406 10–043
Tinline v White Cross Insurance Association Ltd [1921] 3 K.B. 327 KBD 5–046, 20–031, 22–028,
22–029, 22–034
Tinsley v Milligan [1994] 1 A.C. 340; [1993] 3 W.L.R. 126; [1993] 3 All E.R. 65; [1993] 2
F.L.R. 963; (1994) 68 P. & C.R. 412; [1993] E.G.C.S. 118; [1993] N.P.C. 97; Times,
June 28, 1993; Independent, July 6, 1993 HL 5–038, 5–046, 6–132, 20–086
Tioxide Europe Ltd v CGU International Insurance Plc [2005] EWCA Civ. 928; [2005] 2
C.L.C. 329; [2006] Lloyd's Rep. I.R. 31CA (Civ Div); affirming [2004] EWHC 2116;
[2005] Lloyd's Rep. I.R. 114 QBD (Comm) 5–050, 7–019, 9–010, 9–013, 10–033, 10–037,
15–027, 15–041, 20–076
Tobin v Harford (1862) 34 L.J.C.P. 37 10–008
Tobin v Harford (1864) 17 C.B.N.S. 528 8–029
Todd v Ritchie (1816) 1 Stark. 240 24–138
Tofts v Pearl Life Assurance Co Ltd [1915] 1 K.B. 189 CA 18–016
Tolhurst v Associated Portland Cement Manufacturers (1900) Ltd; Associated Portland
Cement Manufacturers (1900) Ltd v Tolhurst [1903] A.C. 414HL; affirming [1902] 2
K.B. 660 CA 14–024
Tomlinson (Hauliers) Ltd v Hepbum. See Hepburn v A Tomlinson (Hauliers) Ltd

Tonicstar Ltd (t/a Lloyds Syndicate 1861) v American Home Assurance Co [2004] EWHC
    1234; [2005] Lloyd's Rep. I.R. 32 QBD (Comm) 2–005, 2–036
Tonkin v UK Insurance Ltd [2006] EWHC 1120; [2006] All E.R. (D) 310 (May) .. 9–024, 9–026,
                                            10–012, 10–014, 10–022, 10–027
Toomey v Banco Vitalicio de Espana SA de Seguros y Reaseguros [2004] EWCA Civ. 622;
    [2004] 1 C.L.C. 965; [2005] Lloyd's Rep. I.R. 423; (2004) 148 S.J.L.B. 633 CA (Civ
    Div); affirming [2003] EWHC 1102; [2004] Lloyd's Rep. I.R. 354 QBD (Comm) 6–028,
                                6–116, 7–026, 17–007, 17–012, 20–022
Toomey v Eagle Star Insurance Co Ltd (No.1) [1994] 1 Lloyd's Rep. 516 CA (Civ Div) 17–004
Toomey v Eagle Star Insurance Co Ltd (No.2) [1995] 2 Lloyd's Rep. 88; [1995] 4 Re. L.R.
    314 QBD (Comm) 6–080, 6–084
Torni, The [1932] P. 78; (1932) 43 Ll. L. Rep. 78; 48 T.L.R. 471; 101 L.J. P. 44; 147 L.T. 208
    CA 2–057
Toropdar v D [2009] EWHC 567 (QB) 9–053
Tosich v Tasman Investment Management Ltd [2008] F.C.A. 377 20–083
Total Graphics Ltd v AGF Insurance Ltd [1997] 1 Lloyd's Rep. 599 QBD (Comm) 5–017, 5–039,
                        6–107, 6–112, 9–003, 9–028, 15–036, 20–009, 21–022, 21–023,
                                                                21–060
Touche Ross & Co v Baker (Colin) [1992] 2 Lloyd's Rep. 207; (1992) 89(28) L.S.G. 31;
    (1992) 136 S.J.L.B. 190; Times, June 22, 1992; Independent, June 24, 1992; Financial
    Times, June 24, 1992 HL 1–035
Toulmin v Anderson (1808) 1 Taunt. 227 24–138
Toulmin v Inglis (1808) 1 Camp. 421 .... 5–017, 6–103
Towle v National Guardian Insurance Society (1861) 30 L.J. Ch. 900 .... 15–014, 23–026
Township of Center v First Mercury Syndicate Inc 117 F. 3d 115 (3rd Cir. 1997) 20–087
Tracy-Gould v Maritime Life Assurance Co, 89 D.L.R. (4th) 726 (1992) 18–041, 18–049
Trade Indemnity Co Ltd v Workington Harbour and Dock Board (No.1); sub nom.
    Workington Harbour and Dock Board v Trade Indemnity Co Ltd [1937] A.C. 1; (1936)
    54 Ll.L.R. 103 HL 13–009, 23–031
Trade Indemnity Plc v Forsakringsaktiebolaget Njord [1995] 1 All E.R. 796; [1995] L.R.L.R.
    367; Times, August 4, 1994 QBD (Comm 2–005
Traders & General Insurance Association v Bankers & General Insurance Co (1921) 9
    Ll.L.R. 223 KBD 24–081
Traders and General Insurance v Bankers & General Insurance (1921) 38 T.L.R. 94 17–019
Tradigrain SA v SIAT SpA; sub nom. Traidigrain SA v SIAT SpA [2002] EWHC 106; [2002]
    2 Lloyd's Rep. 553; [2002] C.L.C. 574 QBD (Comm) 6–118
Trading Co L&J Hoff v Union Insurance Society of Canton Ltd (1929) 34 Ll.L.R. 81 CA 6–056
Trafalgar Insurance Co of Canada v Imperial Oil Ltd (2001) 57 O.R. (3d) 425 20–049
Trafigura Beheer BV v Kookmin Bank Co (Preliminary Issue) [2006] EWHC 1450 (Comm);
    [2006] 2 All E.R. (Comm) 1008; [2006] 2 Lloyd's Rep. 455; [2006] 1 C.L.C. 1049 2–063
Traill v Baring (1864) De G. J. & S.M. 318 .... 6–011, 17–007
Trans Trust SPRL v Danubian Trading Co Ltd [1952] 2 Q.B. 297; [1952] 1 All E.R. 970;
    [1952] 1 Lloyd's Rep. 348; [1952] 1 T.L.R. 1066; (1952) 96 S.J. 312 CA 10–025
Transcontinental Underwriting Agency v Grand Union Insurance Co [1987] 2 Lloyd's Rep.
    409; [1987] 1 F.T.L.R. 35 QBD (Comm) 4–024, 15–024, 24–030
Transit Casualty Co (In receivership) v Policyholders Protection Board [1992] 2 Lloyd's Rep.
    358 (Note); Times, May 24, 1991 Ch D 16–011, 16–024
Trans-Pacific Insurance Co (Australia) Ltd v Grand Union Insurance Co Ltd (1990) 6 A.N.Z.
    Insurance Cases 60–949 Sup Ct (NSW) 6–107, 7–006, 7–009, 9–003, 9–018
Transport & Trading Co Ltd (In Liquidation) v Olivier & Co Ltd (1925) 21 Ll.L.R. 379
    KBD 15–034, 15–045
Transthene Packaging Co Ltd v Royal Insurance (UK) Ltd [1996] L.R.L.R. 32; Lloyd's List,
    June 21, 1995 (I.D.) QBD 6–002, 6–075, 6–107, 6–115, 7–032, 9–021, 9–026, 9–037, 9–038,
                                            9–039, 9–041, 10–023, 19–039
Travel & General Insurance Co Plc v Baron; sub nom. Travel & General Insurance Co Plc
    v Barron (1989) 133 S.J. 1109; Times, November 25, 1988 QBD 13–009, 23–019
Travelers Casualty & Surety Co of Canada v Sun Life Assurance Co of Canada (UK) Ltd
    [2006] EWHC 2716 (Comm); [2007] Lloyd's Rep. I.R. 619 ..... 2–036, 2–043, 2–048, 7–037,
                                                            9–003, 9–008
Travelers Casualty & Surety Co of Europe Ltd v Sun Life Assurance Co of Canada (UK) Ltd
    [2004] EWHC 1704; [2004] I.L.Pr. 50; [2004] Lloyd's Rep. I.R. 846 QBD (Comm) ... 2–005,
                                                    2–022, 2–030, 2–037, 2–048
Travellers Casualty & Surety Co of Europe Ltd v Commissioners of Customs and Excise
    [2006] Lloyd's Rep. I.R. 63; [2006] V. & D.R. 230 VAT Tribunal ... 13–009, 17–001, 23–018

Tredegar (Lord) v Harwood; sub nom. Viscount Tredegar v Harwood [1929] A.C. 72 HL 19–018, 19–022

Tredway v Machin (1904) 91 L.T. 310 19–015

Tremelling v Martin [1971] R.T.R. 196 DC 22–015

Trendtex Trading Corp v Credit Suisse [1982] A.C. 679; [1981] 3 W.L.R. 766; [1981] 3 All E.R. 520; [1981] Com. L.R. 262; 125 S.J. 761 HL 11–004

Trenton Cold Storage Ltd v St Paul Fire & Marine Insurance Co (1999) 11 C.C.L.I. (3d) 127 11–048

Trew v Railway Passengers Assurance Co (1861) 6 H. & N. 839 .... 18–041, 18–046, 18–059

Tribe v Tribe [1996] Ch. 107; [1995] 3 W.L.R. 913; [1995] 4 All E.R. 236; [1995] C.L.C. 1474; [1995] 2 F.L.R. 966; [1996] 1 F.C.R. 338; [1996] 71 P. & C.R. 503; [1996] Fam. Law 29; (1995) 92(28) L.S.G. 30; (1995) 145 N.L.J. 1445; (1995) 139 S.J.L.B. 203; [1995] N.P.C. 151; (1995) 70 P. & C.R. D38; Times, August 14, 1995 CA (Civ Div) 8–022, 18–011

Trickett v Queensland Insurance Co Ltd [1936] A.C. 159; (1935) 53 Ll.L.R. 225 PC (NZ) 7–023, 7–038, 22–036, 22–092

Trident General Insurance Co Ltd v McNeice Bros Pty Ltd (1988) 165 C.L.R. 107 HC (AUS) 14–009

Trim v Kelly. *See* Board of Management of Trim Joint District School v Kelly

Trinder Anderson & Co v Thames and Mersey Marine Insurance Co; Trinder Anderson & Co v North Queensland Insurance Co; Trinder Anderson & Co v Weston Crocker & Co [1898] 2 Q.B. 114 CA 5–041, 5–048, 24–080, 24–134

Trinity Insurance Co Ltd v Overseas Union Insurance Ltd [1996] L.R.L.R. 156QBD 17–026

Trow v Ind Coope (West Midlands) Ltd [1967] 2 Q.B. 899; [1967] 3 W.L.R. 633; [1967] 2 All E.R. 900; 111 S.J. 375 CA (Civ Div) 5–004

Trustee of GH Mundy (A Bankrupt) v Blackmore (1928) 32 Ll.L.R. 150Ch D 6–052, 6–053, 22–087

Tryg Baltica International (UK) Ltd v Boston Compania de Seguros SA [2004] EWHC 1186; [2005] Lloyd's Rep. I.R. 40 QBD (Comm) 2–004, 2–005, 2–007, 2–036, 2–043, 9–053, 14–008, 15–028, 15–031, 17–005

Trygg Hansa Insurance Co Ltd v Equitas Ltd; sub nom. Equitas Ltd v Trygg Hansa Insurance Co Ltd [1998] 2 Lloyd's Rep. 439; [1998] C.L.C. 979 QBD (Comm) 3–015, 17–012

Tudor Jones v Crowley Colosso Ltd [1996] 2 Lloyd's Rep. 619; Lloyd's List, August 1, 1996 (I.D.) QBD (Comm) 15–030, 15–031, 15–032, 15–034, 15–051

Tumbull & Co v Scottish Provident Institution (1896) 34 S.L.R. 146 18–019

Tunno v Edwards (1810) 12 East 488 24–092

Turcan, Re (1889) L.R. 40 Ch. D. 5 CA 14–029, 18–022

Turnbull v Garden (1869) 38 L.J. Ch. 331 15–033

Turnbull v Janson (1877) 3 L.T. 635 24–062

Turner (CF) v Manx Line Ltd [1990] 1 Lloyd's Rep. 137; Financial Times, November 3, 1989 CA (Civ Div) 20–028, 20–083

Turner v Grovit; sub nom. Turner, Re (C–159/02) [2005] 1 A.C. 101; [2004] 3 W.L.R. 1193; [2004] All E.R. (EC) 485; [2004] 2 All E.R. (Comm) 381; [2004] 2 Lloyd's Rep. 169; [2004] E.C.R. I–3565; [2004] 1 C.L.C. 864; [2004] I.L.Pr. 25; [2005] I.C.R. 23; [2004] I.R.L.R. 899; Times, April 29, 2004 ECJ 2–008

Turner v Metropolitan Life Assurance Company of New Zealand (1988) 5 A.N.Z. Insurance Cases 60–861 8–016

Turpin v Bilton (1843) 5 Man. & G. 455 15–034

Tweddle v Atkinson (1861) 1 B. & S. 395 11–038

Twizell v Allen (1839) 5 M. & W. 337 6–107

Tyco Fire & Integrated Solutions (UK) Ltd (formerly Wormald Ansul (UK) Ltd) v Rolls Royce Motor Cars Ltd (formerly Hireus Ltd) [2007] EWHC 3159 (TCC); [2007] B.L.R. 419; (2008) 24 Const. L.J. 60; reversed [2008] EWCA Civ 286; [2008] 2 All E.R. (Comm) 584; [2008] 1 C.L.C. 625; [2008] B.L.R. 285; 118 Con. L.R. 25; [2008] Lloyd's Rep. I.R. 617; [2008] 2 E.G.L.R. 113; [2008] 14 E.G. 100 (C.S.); (2008) 105(15) L.S.G. 25; (2008) 152(14) S.J.L.B. 31 .... 3–002, 11–026, 11–027, 19–037, 19–042

Tyler v Whatmore [1976] R.T.R. 83; [1976] Crim. L.R. 315 DC 22–089

Tyrie v Fletcher (1761) 3 Burr. 1237 8–021

Tyrie v Fletcher (1774) 2 Cowp. 666 .... 8–020, 11–045, 16–008

Tyson v Gurney (1789) 3 T.R. 477 .... 24–058, 24–059

UBS AG v HSH Nordbank AG [2009] EWCA Civ 585; [2010] 1 All E.R. (Comm) 727; [2009] 2 Lloyd's Rep. 272; [2009] 1 C.L.C. 934 .... 2–003, 2–005

UCB Corporate Services Ltd v Thomason [2005] EWCA Civ. 225; [2005] 1 All E.R. (Comm) 601CA (Civ Div); affirming [2004] EWHC 1164; [2004] 2 All E.R. (Comm) 774 Ch D 10–055

US Trading Ltd v AXA Insurance Co Ltd Unreported March 17, 2008 .. 1–022, 7–028, 7–036, 9–024

Underwriting v Nausch Hogan & Murray (The Jascon 5). See Talbot Underwriting Ltd v Nausch Hogan & Murray Inc

Underwriting Members of Lloyd's Syndicate 980 for 1999, 2000, 2001, 2002, 2003, 2004 and 2005 v Sinco SA [2008] EWHC 1842 (Comm); [2009] 1 All E.R. (Comm) 272; [2008] 2 C.L.C. 187; [2008] I.L.Pr. 49; [2009] Lloyd's Rep. I.R. 365 2–003

Union Camp Chemicals Ltd (t/a Arizona Chemical) v ACE Insurance SA NV (formerly Cigna Insurance Co of Europe SA NV) [2001] C.L.C. 1609; [2003] Lloyd's Rep. I.R. 487 QBD (TCC) 3–005, 3–015

Union Insurance Society of Canton Ltd v George Wills & Co [1916] 1 A.C. 281 PC (Aus) 7–026, 7–038, 24–051

Union International Insurance Co Ltd v Jubilee Insurance Co Ltd [1991] 1 W.L.R. 415; [1991] 1 All E.R. 740; [1991] 2 Lloyd's Rep. 89; [1994] I.L.Pr. 188; Times, December 7, 1990 QBD (Comm) 2–004

Union Marine Insurance Co Ltd v Martin (1866) 35 L.J.C.P. 181 11–055

Unipac (Scotland) Ltd v Aegon Insurance Co (UK) Ltd, 1996 S.L.T. 1197; [1996] C.L.C. 918 IH (2 Div) 7–031

Unitarian congregation of Toronto v Western (1866) 26 U.C.Q.B. 175 11–062

United Africa Co Ltd v Owners of the Tolten (1946) 79 Ll.L.R. 349; [1946] P. 135 CA 24–135

United General Commercial Insurance Corp Ltd, Re; sub nom. United General Commercial Insurance Corp, Re; United General Commercial Insurance Corp Ltd [1927] 2 Ch. 51; (1927) 27 Ll.L.R. 63 CA 13–018, 13–019

United India Insurance Co Ltd v Hyundai Engineering Construction Co Ltd [2005] H.K.E.C. 811 .... 8–019, 8–023

United Insurance Co of Libya v Aon Ltd [2007] EWHC 1583 (Comm); [2008] Lloyd's Rep. I.R. 166 .... 15–033, 15–037

United Kingdom Mutual Steamship Assurance Association v Boulton (1898) 3 Com.Cas. 330 24–095

United London & Scottish Insurance Co Ltd, Re; sub nom. Brown's Claim [1915] 2 Ch. 167 CA 3–007, 18–041, 18–045, 18–046, 18–050, 18–051, 18–059

United Marketing Co v Kara [1963] 1 W.L.R. 523; [1963] 2 All E.R. 553; [1963] 1 Lloyd's Rep. 331; 107 S.J. 312 PC (Ken) 15–037

United Mills Agencies Ltd v Harvey Bray & Co [1952] 1 All E.R. 225 (Note); [1951] 2 Lloyd's Rep. 631; [1952] 1 T.L.R. 149; 96 S.J. 121 KBD 15–034

United Project Consultants Pte Ltd v Leong Kwok Onn [2005] 4 S.L.R. 214 5–046

United Scottish Insurance Co Ltd v British Fishing Vessels Mutual War Risks Association Ltd; The Braconbush (1945) 78 Ll.L.R. 70 KBD 25–005

United States Shipping Co v Empress Assurance Corp [1908] 1 K.B. 115CA; affirming [1907] 1 K.B. 259 KBD 24–027

Unity Insurance Brokers Pty Ltd v Rocco Pezzano Pty Ltd (1998) 192 C.L.R. 603 15–059

Universal General Insurance Co (UGIC) v Group Josi Reinsurance Co SA; sub nom. Group Josi Reinsurance Co SA v Compagnie d'Assurances Universal General Insurance Co (UGIC) (C–412/98) [2001] Q.B. 68; [2000] 3 W.L.R. 1625; [2000] All E.R. (EC) 653; [2000] 2 All E.R. (Comm) 467; [2000] E.C.R. I–5925; [2001] C.L.C. 893; [2000] C.E.C. 462; [2000] I.L.Pr. 549; [2001] Lloyd's Rep. I.R. 483; Times, August 9, 2000 ECJ 2–009, 13–017

Universal Steam Navigation Co Ltd v James McKelvie & Co; sub nom. Ariadne Steamship Co Ltd v James McKelvie & Co [1923] A.C. 492; (1923) 15 Ll.L.R. 99 HL 4–024

Universal Stock Exchange v Strachan. See Strachan v Universal Stock Exchange Ltd (No.1)

Universities Superannuation Scheme Ltd v Royal Insurance (UK) Ltd [2000] 1 All E.R. (Comm) 266; [2000] Lloyd's Rep. I.R. 524 QBD (Comm) 9–037, 23–025

University of Western Ontario v Yanush, 56 D.L.R. (4th) 552 (1988) 5–042, 11–032

Universo Insurance Co of Milan v Merchants Marine Insurance Co Ltd [1897] 2 Q.B. 93 CA 24–077

Unrau v Canadian Northern Shield Insurance Co [2004] B.C.J. No.33 20–049

Unum Life Insurance Co of America v Israel Phoenix Assurance Co Ltd [2002] Lloyd's Rep. I.R. 374 CA (Civ Div) 1–040

Upjohn v Hitchens; Upjohn v Ford [1918] 2 K.B. 48 .... 5–041, 19–022

Usher v Noble (1810) 12 East 639 .... 10–016, 24–027

Uzielli v Commercial Union insurance Co (1865) 12 L.T. 399 24–037

Uzielli & Co v Boston Marine Insurance Co (1884–85) L.R. 15 Q.B.D. 11 CA ... 17–004, 24–112
Vale v Van Oppen. *See* James Vale & Co v Van Oppen & Co Ltd
Vallance v Dewar (1808) 1 Camp. 503 .... 6–065, 24–070
Vallejo v Wheeler (1774) 1 Cowp. 143 24–138
Van Grutten v Digby (1862) 31 Beav. 561; 54 E.R. 1256 2–054
Van Oppen v Bedford Charity Trustees; sub nom. Van Oppen v Clerk to the Trustees of the
    Bedford Charity; Van Oppen v Bedford School Trustees [1990] 1 W.L.R. 235; [1989] 3
    All E.R. 389; (1989) 139 N.L.J. 900CA (Civ Div); affirming [1989] 1 All E.R. 273;
    (1988) 138 N.L.J. Rep. 221 QBD 15–026, 20–001
Vance v Forster (1841) lr. Circ. Rep. 47 .... 10–015, 10–031, 10–040
Vandepitte v Preferred Accident Insurance Corp of New York; sub nom. Vandepitte v
    Preferred Accident Insurance Co of New York [1933] A.C. 70; (1932) 44 Ll.l.L.R. 41 PC
    (Can) 4–018, 19–030, 20–055, 22–027, 22–088
Vandyck v Hewitt (1800) 1 East 96 8–022
Varnak, The (1869) L.R. 2 P.C. 505 24–026
Vasso, The. *See* Noble Resources and Unirise Development v George Albert Greenwood
Vastgrand Industrial Ltd v Hong Kong and Shanghai Insurance Co Ltd [2002] H.K.C.U
    475 5–031
Vaughan Motors and Sheldon Motor Services Ltd v Scottish General Insurance Co Ltd
    [1960] 1 Lloyd's Rep. 479 QBD 7–032
Vavasseur v Vavasseur (1909) 25 T.L.R. 250 14–026
Vehicle & General Insurance Co v Elmbridge Insurances [1973] 1 Lloyd's Rep. 325
    MCLC 8–003
Vellino v Chief Constable of Greater Manchester [2001] EWCA Civ 1249; [2002] 1 W.L.R.
    218; [2002] 3 All E.R. 78; [2002] P.I.Q.R. P10; [2001] Po. L.R. 295; (2001) 151 N.L.J.
    1441; Times, August 9, 2001 .... 5–045, 5–046
Velos Group Ltd v Harbour Insurance Services Ltd [1997] 2 Lloyd's Rep. 461 CC (Central
    London) 8–023, 15–031, 15–033, 24–078
Vemon v Smith (1821) 5 B. & Ald. 1 19–021
Ventouris v Mountain; The Italia Express (No.2) [1992] 1 W.L.R. 887; [1992] 3 All E.R. 414;
    [1992] 2 Lloyd's Rep. 216; Financial Times, January 14, 1992 CA (Civ Div) 9–038
Ventouris v Mountain; The Italia Express (No.3) [1992] 2 Lloyd's Rep. 281; Financial Times,
    February 12, 1992 QBD (Comm) 10–022, 11–023
Verband der Sachversicherer eV v Commission of the European Communities (45/85) [1987]
    E.C.R. 405; [1988] 4 C.M.L.R. 264; [1988] F.S.R. 383; Times, February 7, 1987 ECJ 13–045
Verderame v Commercial Union Assurance Co Plc [1992] B.C.L.C. 793; [2000] Lloyd's Rep.
    P.N. 557; [1955–95] P.N.L.R. 612; Times, April 2, 1992; Independent, May 25, 1992
    (C.S) CA (Civ Div) 15–047, 15–062
Verelst's Administratrix v Motor Union Insurance Co Ltd; sub nom. Administratrix of Mary
    Madge Verelst v Motor Union Insurance Co Ltd [1925] 2 K.B. 137; (1925) 21 Ll.l.L.R.
    227 KBD 9–008, 9–043
Verna Trading Pty Ltd v New India Assurance Co Ltd [1991] 1 V.R. 129 24–066
Vernon v Smith (1821) 5 B. & Ald. 1 10–051
Vero Insurance Ltd v Baycorp Advantage Ltd [2004] N.S.W.C.A. 390 .... 20–052, 20–080
Vero Insurance Ltd v Power Technologies Pty Ltd [2007] N.S.W.C.A. 226 ..... 5–049, 5–051, 20–007,
    20–028, 20–083
Vesta v Butcher. *See* Forsikringsaktieselskapet Vesta v Butcher
Vestey Bros Ltd v Motor Union Insurance Co Ltd (1922) 10 Ll.l.L.R. 270 KBD 9–002
Vezey v United General Commercial Insurance Corp Ltd (1923) 15 Ll.l.L.R. 63, MCLC 9–003
Victor Melik & Co v Norwich Union Fire Insurance Society and Kemp [1980] 1 Lloyd's Rep.
    523 QBD 5–019, 15–035
Village Main Reef Gold Mining Co Ltd v Stearns (1900) 5 Com.Cas. 246 6–107
Vincentelli v John Rowlett & Co (1911) 1O S L.T. 411, 414 19–034
Viney v Bignold (1888) L.R. 20 Q.B.D. 172 QBD 9–003
Virk v Gan Life Holdings Plc [2000] Lloyd's Rep. I.R. 159; (2000) 52 B.M.L.R. 207 CA (Civ
    Div 9–041
Visscherrij Maatschappij Nieuwe Onderneming v Scottish Metropolitan Assurance Co
    (1922) 10 Ll.l.L.R. 579; (1922) 27 Com.Cas. 198 CA 6–056, 9–025, 24–138
Vita Food Products Inc v Unus Shipping Co Ltd (In Liquidation) [1939] A.C. 277; (1939) 63
    Ll.l.L.R. 21 PC (Can) 2–030, 2–057
Vitol SA v Arcturus Merchant Trust Ltd [2009] EWHC 800 (Comm) 2–005
Voaden v Champion (The Baltic Surveyor and the Timbuktu) [2002] EWCA Civ. 89; [2002]
    1 Lloyd's Rep. 623; [2002] C.L.C. 666 CA (Civ Div) 10–031
Voison v Royal Insurance Co of Canada, 53 D.L.R. (4th) 299 (1989) 18–041

Vokins Holdings Ltd v Robin Moors Allnutt & Partners; sub nom. Vokins Holdings Ltd v
    Vokins Construction Ltd [1996] C.L.C. 584; [1996] P.N.L.R. 354 CA (Civ Div) 9–053

Vorarlberger Gebietskrankenkasse v WGV-Schwabische Allgemeine Versicherungs AG
    (C–347/08) [2010] 1 All E.R. (Comm) 603; [2010] C.E.C. 377; [2010] I.L.Pr. 2; [2010]
    Lloyd's Rep. I.R. 77 ECJ 2–014
Vortigern, The [1899] P. 140 CA 24–061, 24–062
Vural v Security Archives Ltd [1989] E.G.L.S. 2 .... 10–049, 10–051, 14–021, 19–017, 19–019
WASA International (UK) Insurance Co Ltd v WASA International Insurance Co Ltd
    (Sweden) [2002] EWHC 2698; [2003] 1 All E.R. (Comm) 696; [2003] 1 B.C.L.C. 668;
    (2003) 100(9) L.S.G. 27; Times, December 31, 2002 Ch D 13–035, 13–037, 17–003
WH Smith & Son v Clinton (1908) 25 T.L.R. 34 5–037
WISE Underwriting Agency Ltd v Grupo Nacional Provincial SA [2004] EWHC 1706
    (Comm) 6–003, 6–004, 6–090
WISE Underwriting Agency Ltd v Grupo Nacional Provincial SA [2004] EWCA Civ. 962;
    [2004] 2 All E.R. (Comm) 613; [2004] 2 Lloyd's Rep. 483; [2004] 2 C.L.C. 1098;
    [2004] Lloyd's Rep. I.R. 764; (2004) 148 S.J.L.B. 913 CA (Civ Div); reversing [2003]
    EWHC 3038; [2004] 1 All E.R. (Comm) 495 QBD (Comm) 6–003, 6–004, 6–005, 6–072,
                                            6–073, 6–090, 6–092, 6–129, 17–007, 17–008, 19–034
HLWade v Simeon (1846) 2 C.B. 548 10–055
Wadsworth Lighterage and Coaling Co Ltd v Sea Insurance Co Ltd (1929) 34 Ll.L.R. 285 24–081
Wailes v Stapleton Construction and Commercial Services Ltd; Wailes v Unum Ltd [1997]
    2 Lloyd's Rep. 112 QBD 10–028
Wainewright v Bland (1835) 1 Mood. & R. 481; 174 E.R. 165 ..... 5–037, 6–058, 18–006, 18–007,
                                                                         18–013, 18–035
Wainwright v Bland (1836) 1 M. & W. 32 .... 4–001, 6–070
Waldwiese Sftung v Lewis Unreported July 21, 2004 2–043
Walford v Miles [1992] 2 A.C. 128; [1992] 2 W.L.R. 174; [1992] 1 All E.R. 453; (1992) 64
    P. & C.R. 166; [1992] 1 E.G.L.R. 207; [1992] 11 E.G. 115; [1992] N.P.C. 4; Times,
    January 27, 1992; Independent, January 29, 1992 HL 1–021, 6–001
Walker v Bradford Old Bank Ltd (1883–84) L.R. 12 Q.B.D. 511 QBD 14–026
Walker v British Guarantee Association (1852) 21 L.J.Q.B. 257 23–021
Walker v Derwent Unreported, 1747 4–002
Walker v Maitland (1821) 5 B. & Ald. 171 24–080
Walker v Pennine Insurance Co [1980] 2 Lloyd's Rep. 156 CA (Civ Div) 9–022, 9–040
Walker v Railway Passengers' Assurance (1910) 129 L.T. 64 18–050
Walker & Sons v Uzielli (1896) 1 Com.Cas. 492 17–012
Wallace v Telfair (1788) 2 T.R. 188n 15–026
Walton v Airtours Plc [2002] EWCA Civ. 1659; [2003] I.R.L.R. 161; [2004] Lloyd's Rep.
    I.R. 69CA (Civ Div) 18–054
Walton v Newcastle-on-Tyne Corp [1957] 1 Lloyd's Rep. 412 QBD 22–007
Waples v Eames (1746) 2 Str. 1243 24–065
Ward v Beck (1863) 13 C.B. N.S. 668 24–029
Ward v Law Property Assurance and Trust Society (1856) 27 L.T. 155; (1856) 4 W.R. 605 5–015,
                                                                         9–007, 23–026
Wardens and Commonalty of the Mystery of Mercers of the City of London v New
    Hampshire Insurance Co Ltd; sub nom. Mercers Co v New Hampshire Insurance Co Ltd
    [1992] 1 W.L.R. 792; [1992] 3 All E.R. 57; [1992] 2 Lloyd's Rep. 365; 60 B.L.R. 26;
    29 Con. L.R. 30; (1993) 9 Const. L.J. 66; Financial Times, June 4, 1992 CA (Civ
    Div) 13–009, 23–019
Waring & Gillow v Doughty, Times, February 21, 1922 10–047
Warre v Miller (1825) 4 B. & C. 538 24–071
Warren v Henry Sutton & Co [1976] 2 Lloyd's Rep. 276 CA (Civ Div) 15–036
Warrender v Swain. See Simon Warrender Pty Ltd v Swain
Warwick v Scott (1814) 4 Camp. 62 7–022
Warwicker v Bretnall (1883) L.R. 23 Ch. D. 188 Ch D 14–002
Wasa International Insurance Co Ltd v Lexington Insurance Co [2008] EWCA Civ 150;
    [2008] Bus. L.R. 1029; [2008] 1 All E.R. (Comm) 1085; [2008] 1 C.L.C. 340; [2008]
    Env. L.R. 39; [2008] Lloyd's Rep. I.R. 510 CA; reversed [2009] UKHL 40; [2010] 1
    A.C. 180; [2009] 3 W.L.R. 575; [2009] Bus. L.R. 1452; [2009] 4 All E.R. 909; [2009]
    2 Lloyd's Rep. 508; [2009] 2 C.L.C. 320; [2009] Lloyd's Rep. I.R. 675; [2010] Env.
    L.R. D1; Times, August 14, 2009 .... 2–032, 2–033, 2–036, 2–040, 2–050, 5–015, 6–047,
                              10–032, 17–001, 17–004, 17–008, 17–012, 17–014, 17–018,
                                                                         20–057

Wasserman v Blackburn (1926) 43 T.L.R. 95 .... 23–021, 23–022
Watchorn v Langford (1813) 3 Camp. 422 3–006
Waterkeyn, The v Eagle Star & British Dominions Insurance Co Ltd (1920) 5 Ll.L.R. 42
    KBD (Comm Ct) 15–034, 18–020, 23–029
Waters v Eddison Steam Rolling Co (1914) 78 J.P. 327 22–006
Waters v Monarch Fire & Life Assurance Co (1856) 5 El .& Bl. 870 ... 4–005, 4–019, 4–020, 19–010,
                                                        19–011, 19–012, 19–013, 19–030, 19–032
Watkins v O'Shaughnessy [1939] 1 All E.R. 385 22–010
Watkins v Rymill (1882–83) L.R. 10 Q.B.D. 178 QBD 1–022
Watkins & Davis Ltd v Legal & General Assurance Co Ltd [1981] 1 Lloyd's Rep. 674
    QBD 9–025
Watkinson (AF) & Co Ltd v Hullett (1938) 61 Ll.L.R. 145 KBD 5–025
Watson Norie v Shaw [1967] 1 Lloyd's Rep. 515; 117 N.L.J. 157; (1967) 111 S.J. 117 22–025
Watson v Clark (1813) 1 Dow. 336 24–061
Watson v Mainwaring (1813) 4 Taunt. 763 18–029
Watson v Pears (1809) 2 Camp. 294 5–004
Watson v Swann (1862) 11 C.B. N.S. 756 .... 4–023, 14–008
Watt v Southern Cross Assurance Co Ltd [1927] N.Z.L.R. 106 .... 6–011, 6–102
Watts v Simmons (1924) 18 Ll.L.R. 177 KBD 9–015
Waugh v Morris (1872–73) L.R. 8 Q.B. 202 QBD 24–064
Way v Modigliani (1787) 2 T.R. 30 .... 24–047, 24–068, 24–069, 24–070
Wayne Tank & Pump Co Ltd v Employers Liability Assurance Corp Ltd [1974] Q.B. 57;
    [1973] 3 W.L.R. 483; [1973] 3 All E.R. 825; [1973] 2 Lloyd's Rep. 237; 117 S.J. 564
    CA (Civ Div) 5–029, 5–034
Wayne Wilkinson Insurance Ltd v Kaiaua Downs Ltd (1995) 8 A.N.Z. Insurance Cases
    75,782 6–070
Webb, Re [1941] Ch. 225 Ch D 18–024
Webb v Bracey; sub nom. Webb and Hughes (t/a Wright & Webb) v Bracey [1964] 1 Lloyd's
    Rep. 465; (1964) 108 S.J. 445 QBD 1–047
Webb v Fairmaner (1838) 3 M. & W. 473 5–004
Webb and Hughes (t/a Wright & Webb) v Bracey. See Webb v Bracey
Weber v Employers Liability Assurance Corp (1926) 24 Ll.L.R. 321 KBD 7–032
Webster v General Accident, Fire and Life Assurance Corp [1953] 1 Q.B. 520; [1953] 2
    W.L.R. 491; [1953] 1 All E.R. 663; [1953] 1 Lloyd's Rep. 123; 97 S.J. 155 QBD 7–020,
                                                                       9–013, 9–014, 10–001
Weddell v Road Transport & General Insurance Co Ltd [1932] 2 K.B. 563; (1931) 41 Ll.L.R.
    69 KBD 11–048, 11–062
Wedderburn v Bell (1807) 1 Camp. 1 24–062
Weigall v Waters (1795) 6 T.R. 488 19–021
Weir & Co v Girvin & Co [1900] 1 Q.B. 45CA; affirming [1899] 1 Q.B. 193 QBD 24–026
Weir v Aberdeen (1819) 2 B. & Ald. 320 .... 6–070, 7–048, 24–062, 24–073
Weir v Wyper, 1992 S.L.T. 579; 1992 S.C.L.R. 483; Times, May 4, 1992 OH 22–034
Weissberg v Lamb (1950) 84 Ll.L.R. 509; 101 L.J. 51, MCLC 24–112
Welch v Royal Exchange Assurance [1939] 1 K.B. 294; (1938) 62 Ll.L.R. 83 CA 7–013, 7–015,
                                                                       9–003, 9–019, 17–015
Weldon v GRE Linked Life Assurance Ltd [2000] 2 All E.R. (Comm) 914 .... 8–002, 14–029
Weldrick v Essex & Suffolk Equitable Insurance Society Ltd (1949–50) 83 Ll.L.R. 91
    KBD 22–017, 22–045
Welex AG v Rosa Maritime Ltd; The Epsilon Rosa (No.2) [2003] EWCA Civ. 938; [2003]
    2 Lloyd's Rep. 509; [2003] 2 C.L.C. 207 CA (Civ Div) 2–053
Wells v Owners of the Gas Float Whitton No.2 Gas Float Whitton No.2, The [1897] A.C. 337
    HL 24–006
Welts v Mutual Life Insurance Co, 48 N.Y. 34 (1871) 25–004
Wembley Urban District Council v Poor Law Mutual (1901) 17 T.L.R. 516 .... 23–024, 23–026
Wenigers Policy, Re [1910] 2 Ch. 291 Ch D 14–028
West v National Motor and Accident Insurance Union [1955] 1 W.L.R. 343; [1955] 1 All E.R.
    800; [1955] 1 Lloyd's Rep. 207; 99 S.J. 235 CA 6–075, 6–092, 7–005, 7–039, 7–040, 7–048
West London Pipeline & Storage Ltd v Total UK Ltd [2008] EWHC 1296 (Comm); [2008]
    C.P. Rep. 35; [2008] 1 C.L.C. 935; [2008] Lloyd's Rep. I.R. 688 .... 21–040, 21–066, 23–040
West of England Fire Insurance Co v Isaacs [1897] 1 Q.B. 226 CA 11–042
West of England v Batchelor (1882) 51 L.J.Ch. 199 14–028
West Tankers Inc v RAS Riunione Adriatica di Sicurta SpA (The Front Comor) [2005]
    EWHC 454; [2005] 2 All E.R. (Comm) 240; [2005] 2 Lloyd's Rep. 257; [2005] 1 C.L.C.
    347 QBD (Comm) 2–006, 11–011

West Wake Price & Co v Ching [1957] 1 W.L.R. 45; [1956] 3 All E.R. 821; [1956] 2 Lloyd's
  Rep. 618; 101 S.J. 64 QBD 1–009, 5–032, 10–036, 20–009, 20–025, 20–031, 20–034,
                                                              20–038, 20–046, 20–084
West Yorkshire Trading Standards Service v Lex Vehicle Leasing Ltd [1996] R.T.R. 70
  QBD 22–009
Westacott v Centaur Overland Travel [1981] R.T.R. 182 DC 22–006
Westbury v Aberdein (1837) 2 M. & W. 267 .... 24–035, 24–036, 24–039
Westenhope, The Unreported, 1870 24–007
Western Assurance Co of Toronto v Poole [1903] 1 K.B. 376 KBD 17–019
Westminster Fire Office v Glasgow Provident Investment Society (1888) L.R. 13 App. Cas.
  699 HL 10–017, 10–021, 10–046, 10–051, 11–054, 18–020, 19–025
Westminster Fire Office v Reliance Mutual insurance Co (1903) 19 T.L.R. 668 24–066
Weston v Emes (1808) 1 Taunt. 115 3–005
Westridge Construction Ltd v Zurich Insurance Co [2004] S.J. No.43 20–050
Westwood v Bell (1815) 4 Camp. 349 24–078
Wetherell v Jones (1832) 3 B. & Ad. 221 5–037
Weyerhaeuser v Evans (1932) 43 Ll.L.R. 62 KBD 18–042
Whaley v Cartusiano, 68 D.L.R. (4th) 58 (1990) 5–042
Wharton (J) (Shipping) Ltd v Mortleman [1941] 2 K.B. 283; (1941) 70 Ll.L.R. 56 CA 25–005
Wheelton v Hardisty (1857) 8 E. & B .232 .... 6–004, 6–013, 6–070, 6–073, 7–026, 7–029, 7–031,
                                                              18–028, 18–029, 18–038
White v British Empire Mutual Life (1868) L.R.7 Eq. 394 18–034
White v Dobinson (1844) 14 Sim. 273 .... 11–002, 11–020
White v Jones [1995] 2 A.C. 207; [1995] 2 W.L.R. 187; [1995] 1 All E.R. 691; [1995] 3
  F.C.R. 51; (1995) 145 N.L.J. 251; (1995) 139 S.J.L.B. 83; [1995] N.P.C. 31; Times,
  February 17, 1995; Independent, February 17, 1995 HL 15–009
White v London Transport Executive [1971] 2 Q.B. 721; [1971] 3 W.L.R. 169; [1971] 3 All
  E.R. 1; [1971] 2 Lloyd's Rep. 256; [1971] R.T.R. 326; 115 S.J. 368 CA (Civ Div) 22–076
White (Brian) v White (Shane); Mighell v Reading; Evans v Motor Insurers Bureau [2001]
  UKHL 9; [2001] 1 W.L.R. 481; [2001] 2 All E.R. 43; [2001] 1 All E.R. (Comm) 1105;
  [2001] 1 Lloyd's Rep. 679; [2001] R.T.R. 25; [2001] 2 C.M.L.R. 1; [2001] Lloyd's Rep.
  I.R. 493; [2001] P.I.Q.R. P20; (2001) 98(15) L.S.G. 33; (2001) 151 N.L.J. 350; (2001)
  145 S.J.L.B. 67; Times, March 6, 2001; Independent, April 30, 2001 (C.S) HL;
  reversing [1999] 1 C.M.L.R. 1251; [1999] Eu. L.R. 389; [1999] Lloyd's Rep. I.R. 30;
  [1999] P.I.Q.R. P101; Times, October 12, 1998CA (Civ Div); affirming [1997] 3
  C.M.L.R. 1218; Times, November 10, 1997 QBD (Comm) 3–006, 22–041, 22–058, 22–059,
                                                              22–066, 22–067, 22–068, 22–073, 22–076
White Child & Beney v Simmons; White Child & Beney v Eagle Star & British Dominions
  Insurance (1922) 11 Ll.L.R. 7; (1922) 38 T.L.R. 616 CA 25–006
Whitehead v Price (1835) 2 Cr.M. & R. 447 .... 5–020, 7–038
Whitehead v Unwins (Yorks) [1962] Crim. L.R. 323 DC 22–096
Whiteley Insurance Consultants (A Firm), Re [2008] EWHC 1782 (Ch); [2009] Bus. L.R.
  418; [2009] Lloyd's Rep. I.R. 212 .... 13–018, 13–020, 15–021, 16–011
Whitesea Shipping & Trading Corp v El Paso Rio Clara Ltda, Marielle Bolten, The [2009]
  EWHC 2552 (Comm); [2010] 1 Lloyd's Rep. 648; [2009] 2 C.L.C. 596 .... 2–006, 11–011
Whiting v New Zealand Insurance Co Ltd (1932) 44 Ll.L.R. 179 KBD 24–080
Whittam v WJ Daniel & Co (Amendment to Writ) [1962] 1 Q.B. 271; [1961] 3 W.L.R. 1123;
  [1961] 3 All E.R. 796; (1961) 105 S.J. 886 CA 1–019
Whittingham v Thornburgh (1690) 2 Vern. 206 .... 4–002, 8–022
Whitwell v Autocar Fire & Accident Insurance Co Ltd (1927) 27 Ll.L.R. 418 Ch D 1–028, 6–004,
                                                              6–103
Whitworth Street Estates (Manchester) Ltd v James Miller & Partners Ltd; sub nom. James
  Miller & Partners Ltd v Whitworth Street Estates (Manchester) Ltd [1970] A.C. 583;
  [1970] 2 W.L.R. 728; [1970] 1 All E.R. 796; [1970] 1 Lloyd's Rep. 269; 114 S.J. 225
  HL 3–012
Wi-Lan v St Paul Guarantee Insurance Co [2005] A.J. No.1416 20–049
Wickham van Eyck (A Firm) v Norwich Union Insurance Ltd [2009] EWHC 2625
  (Comm) 23–015
Widefree Ltd (t/a Abrahams & Ballard) v Brit Insurance Ltd [2009] EWHC 3671 (QB) 9–019,
                                                              19–058
Wiggins Teape Australia Pty Ltd v Baltica Insurance Co Ltd [1970] 2 N.S.W.R. 77 24–066
Wilkie v Geddes (1815) 3 Dow. 57 24–062
Wilkie v Gordian Run-Off Ltd [2003] N.S.W.S.C. 1059 .... 20–048, 20–051, 20–087
Wilkinson v Car & General insurance Co Ltd (1913) 110 L.T. 468 9–019

Wilkinson v Coverdale (1793) 1 Esp. 75 15–026
Wilkinson v Downton [1897] 2 Q.B. 57 QBD 18–043
Wilkinson v Fitzgerald [2009] EWHC 1297 (QB); [2010] 1 All E.R. 198; [2010] 1 All E.R.
    (Comm) 278; [2009] 3 C.M.L.R. 33; [2010] Lloyd's Rep. I.R. 278; [2009] P.I.Q.R.
    P20 .... 22–032, 22–043
Wilkinson v General Accident Fire and Life Assurance Corp [1967] 2 Lloyd's Rep. 182
    Assizes (Manchester) 14–022, 15–001, 15–013, 15–015, 22–027
Willcocks v New Zealand Insurance Co [1926] N.Z.L.R. 805 .... 6–018, 6–064
Willesden BC v Municipal Mutual Insurance Ltd (1945) 78 Ll.L.R. 256; (1945) 172 L.T. 245
    CA 19–044, 22–096
William Brandt's Sons & Co v Dunlop Rubber Co Ltd [1905] A.C. 454 HL 14–026
William France Fenwick & Co Ltd v North of England Protecting and Indemnity Association
    [1917] 2 K.B. 522 KBD 25–004
William Jackson & Sons Ltd v Oughtred & Harrison (Insurance) Ltd [2002] Lloyd's Rep.
    I.R. 230 QBD (Comm) 15–034
William James Le Feuvre v John Sullivan and Anne Sullivan, otherwise Anne Le Sueur
    (1855) 10 Moo. P.C. 1; 14 E.R. 389 PC 14–030
William Pickersgill & Sons Ltd v London and Provincial Marine & General Insurance Co Ltd
    [1912] 3 K.B. 614 KBD 6–056, 9–038
William Sindall Plc v Cambridgeshire CC [1994] 1 W.L.R. 1016; [1994] 3 All E.R. 932; 92
    L.G.R. 121; [1993] E.G.C.S. 105; [1993] N.P.C. 82; Times, June 8, 1993 CA (Civ
    Div) 6–081
Williams v Atlantic Assurance Co Ltd [1933] 1 K.B. 81; (1932) 43 Ll.L.R. 177CA ... 6–056, 10–020,
                                                                                        24–030, 24–074
Williams v Baltic Insurance Association of London Ltd [1924] 2 K.B. 282; (1924) 19 Ll.L.R.
    126 KBD 1–015, 4–002, 4–019, 20–006, 20–062, 22–027, 22–088
Williams v Jones [1975] R.T.R. 433 DC 22–009
Williams v Natural Life Health Foods Ltd [1998] 1 W.L.R. 830; [1998] 2 All E.R. 577;
    [1998] B.C.C. 428; [1998] 1 B.C.L.C. 689; (1998) 17 Tr. L.R. 152; (1998) 95(21) L.S.G.
    37; (1998) 148 N.L.J. 657; (1998) 142 S.J.L.B. 166; Times, May 1, 1998 HL ... 15–036, 20–078,
                                                                                        20–083
Williams v North China Insurance Co (1875–76) L.R. 1 C.P.D. 757 CA ... 4–023, 10–007, 15–003
Williams v Russell (1933) 149 L.T. 190 22–002
Williams v Thorp (1828) 2 Sim. 257 18–022
Williams and Thomas and Lancashire and Yorkshire Insurance Co (1902) 19 T.L.R. 82 9–006,
                                                                                        9–013
Williams Bros v Ed T Agius Ltd [1914] A.C. 510 HL 3–011
Williamson v O'Keeffe [1947] 1 All E.R. 307; 63 T.L.R. 152; 111 J.P. 175; 176 L.T. 274
    KBD 22–010
Willis v Glover (1804) 1 Bos. & P. 14 24–037
Willis v Poole (1780) 2 Park on Insurance 935 18–029
Willis Faber & Co v Joyce (1911) 27 T.L.R. 388 .... 15–001, 15–015
Willis Management (Isle of Man) Ltd v Cable & Wireless Plc; sub nom. Cable & Wireless
    Plc v Valentine [2005] EWCA Civ. 806; [2005] 2 Lloyd's Rep. 597 CA (Civ Div) 8–008
Willis SS Co v United Kingdom Mutual War Risks Association (1947) 80 Ll.L.R. 398
    KBD 25–005
Willmott v General Accident Fire & Life Assurance Corp Ltd (1935) 53 Ll.L.R. 156 KBD 24–062
Wills (CJ) & Sons v World Marine Insurance Co Ltd (The Mermaid) [1980] 1 Lloyd's Rep.
    350 KBD 24–003
Willumsen v Royal Exchange Insurance Co Ltd, 63 D.L.R. (3d) 112 (1975) 11–006, 11–042
Wilson v Avec Audio-Visual Equipment [1974] 1 Lloyd's Rep. 81 CA (Civ Div) 8–007
Wilson v Hurstanger. See Hurstanger Ltd v Wilson
Wilson v Jones (1867) L.R. 2 Ex. 139 4–017
Wilson v Martin (1856) 1) Ex. 684 24–026
Wilson v Nelson (1864) 33 L.J.Q.B. 220 .... 1–009, 10–006
Wilson v Rankin (1865–66) L.R. 1 Q.B. 162 Ex Chamber 24–064
Wilson v Salamandra Assurance Co of St Petersburg (1903) 88 L.T. 96 6–037
Wilson v Wilson (1854) 14 C.B. 616 19–022
Wilson and Scottish Insurance Corp Ltd, Re [1920] 2 Ch. 28 Ch D 1–011, 10–014, 10–015
Wilson Bros Bobbin Co Ltd v Green [1917] 1 K.B. 860 KBD 24–112
Wilson, Holgate & Co Ltd v Lancashire & Cheshire Insurance Corp Ltd (1922) 13 Ll.L.R.
    486 KBD 1–033, 6–058, 24–080
Wimbledon Park Golf Club v Imperial Insurance Co (1902) 18 T.L.R. 815 .... 10–051, 10–052

Wimpcy Construction (UK) Ltd v Poole (DV) [1984] 2 Lloyd's Rep. 499; 27 B.L.R. 58;
(1984) 128 S.J. 969; Times, May 3, 1984 QBD (Comm) 20–009
Windle v Dunning & Son Ltd [1968] 1 W.L.R. 552; [1968] 2 All E.R. 46; 132 J.P. 284; 66
L.G.R. 516; (1968) 112 S.J. 196 DC 22–009
Windsor v Chalcraft [1939] 1 K.B. 279; [1983] 2 All E.R. 751; (1938) 61 Ll.L.R. 69 CA 22–044
Windus v Tredegar (1866) 15 L.T. 108 8–009
Wing v Harvey (1854) 5 De G.M. & G. 265 .... 6–091, 7–020, 8–016, 15–016, 15–017, 18–037
Wing Lung Insurance Co Ltd v Lo Wai Fai [2008] H.K.E.C. 305 22–048
Wing Lung Insurance Co Ltd v Kong Yau Choi [2008] H.K.E.C. 1363 22–048
Wingate Birrell & Co v Foster (1877–78) L.R. 3 Q.B.D. 582 CA 24–070
Winicofsky v Army & Navy General Assurance (1919) 88 L.J.K.B. 1111; (1919) 35 T.L.R.
283 .... 5–030, 7–037, 19–047
Winnetka Trading Corp v Julius Baer International Ltd [2008] EWHC 3146 (Ch); [2009]
Bus. L.R. 1006; [2009] 2 All E.R. (Comm) 735 2–005
Winnick v Dick, 1984 S.L.T. 185 22–033
Winspear v Accident Insurance Co Ltd (1880–81) L.R. 6 Q.B.D. 42; (1880) 43 L.T. 459 CA ... 5–030,
18–060, 22–090
Winter v DPP [2002] EWHC 1524; [2003] R.T.R. 14 QBD (Admin) 22–006
Winter v Irish Life Assurance Plc [1995] 2 Lloyd's Rep. 274; [1995] C.L.C. 722; Lloyd's
List, May 18, 1995 (I.D.) QBD 6–040, 15–028, 15–036, 18–028, 18–029
Winterthur Swiss Insurance Co v AG (Manchester) Ltd (In Liquidation) [2006] EWHC 839
QBD (Comm) 23–034
With v O'Flanagan [1936] Ch. 575 CA 6–011
Withers v Delaney (C–158/01) [2002] E.C.R. I–8301 ECJ 22–031
Wolemberg v Royal Co-operative Collecting Society (1915) 84 L.J.K.B. 1316 8–033
Wolff v Horncastle (1798) 1 Bos & P. 316 .... 4–011, 18–020, 24–022, 24–030
Wolf & Korkhaus v Tyser & Co (1921) 8 Ll.L.R. 340 KBD 15–041
Wong Wing Fai Co SA v Netherlands Insurance Co (1945) [1989–1981] 1 S.L.R. 242 24–138
Wood v Dwarris (1856) 11 Exch. 493 .... 7–031, 18–038
Wood v General Accident Fire & Life Assurance Corp (1948–49) 82 Ll.L.R. 77; 65 T.L.R.
53; [1948] W.N. 430; 92 S.J. 720 KBD 22–098
Wood v Perfection Travel Ltd [1996] L.R.L.R. 233; [1996] C.L.C. 1121; Lloyd's List, April
23, 1996 (I.D.) CA (Civ Div) 6–089, 20–044, 21–012, 21–032
Wooding v Monmouthshire and South Wales Mutual indemnity Society Ltd [1939] 4 All ER.
570 .... 21–007, 24–007
Woods v Cooperative Insurance Society Ltd, 1924 S.C. 692; 1924 S.L.T. 529 IH (1 Div) 11–046,
11–058
Woodside v Globe Marine Insurance Co Ltd [1896] 1 Q.B. 105 QBD 10–008, 10–009, 24–111
Woodward v James Young (Contractors) Ltd, 1958 J.C. 28; 1958 S.L.T. 289; [1959] Crim.
L.R. 131 HCJ 22–006
Woolcott v Excess Insurance Co Ltd and Miles, Smith Anderson & Game Ltd (No.2) [1979]
2 Lloyd's Rep. 210 QBD 15–027
Woolcott v Sun Alliance and London Insurance Ltd [1978] 1 W.L.R. 493; [1978] 1 All E.R.
1253; [1978] 1 Lloyd's Rep. 629; 121 S.J. 744 QBD 6–048, 6–072, 11–029, 14–003, 14–012,
15–013
Woolf v Claggett (1800) 3 Esp. 257 24–062
Woolfall & Rimmer Ltd v Moyle [1942] 1 K.B. 66; (1941) 71 Ll.L.R. 15 CA 5–049, 7–032,
20–031
Woolmer v Mailman (1763) 2 Burr. 1419 7–040
Woolridge v Boydell (1778) 1 Doug K.B. 16 .... 24–068, 24–070
Woolwich Building Society (formerly Woolwich Equitable Building Society) v Inland
Revenue Commissioners [1993] A.C. 70; [1992] 3 W.L.R. 366; [1992] 3 All E.R. 737;
[1992] S.T.C. 657; (1993) 5 Admin. L.R. 265; 65 T.C. 265; (1992) 142 N.L.J. 1196;
(1992) 136 S.J.L.B. 230; Times, July 22, 1992; Independent, August 13, 1992;
Guardian, August 19, 1992 HL 10–061
Woolwich Building Society v Brown [1996] C.L.C. 625; Independent, January 22, 1996
(C.S.) QBD (Comm) 11–033
Woolwich Building Society v Daisystar Ltd Unreported March 16, 2000 11–007
Woolwich Building Society v Taylor [1995] 1 B.C.L.C. 132; [1994] C.L.C. 516; Times, May
17, 1994 Ch D 21–039
Workman & Army & Navy Co-operative Supply Ltd v London & Lancashire Fire Insurance
Co (1903) 19 T.L.R. 360 15–033

Workvale Ltd (No.2), Re; sub nom. Workvale Ltd (In Dissolution), Re [1992] 1 W.L.R. 416; [1992] 2 All E.R. 627; [1992] B.C.C. 349; [1992] B.C.L.C. 544; (1992) 89(14) L.S.G. 28 CA (Civ Div) 21–014
Worsley v Tambrands Ltd (Costs) [2002] Lloyd's Rep. I.R. 382 QBD (Comm) 23–017
Worsley v Wood (1776) 6 T.R. 710 .... 7–038, 9–003, 9–020
Worthington v Curtis (1875–76) L.R. 1 Ch. D. 419 CA 4–011, 18–015
Wright and Pole, Re (1834) 1 Al. & El. 621 .... 4–017, 10–016, 10–019, 10–021
Wulfson v Switzerland General Insurance Co Ltd (1940) 67 Ll.L.R. 190; (1940) 56 T.L.R. 701 KBD 5–011, 6–015, 19–044
Wunsche Handelsgesellschaft International mbH v Tai Ping Insurance Co Ltd [1998] 2 Lloyd's Rep. 8; [1998] C.L.C. 851 CA (Civ Div) 19–007, 24–009, 24–031, 24–080
Wurttembergische AG Versicherungs Beteiligungsgesellschaft v Home Insurance Co (No.2) [1999] 1 All E.R. (Comm.) 535; [1999] Lloyd's Rep. I.R. 397; Independent, March 22, 1999 (C.S.) CA (Civ Div) 15–023
Württembergische AG Versicherungs Beteiligungsgesellschaft v Home Insurance Co Unreported, 1994 .... 15–020, 17–019
Wurttembergische AG Versicherungs Beteiligungsgesellschaft v Home Insurance Co (No.1) [1997] L.R.L.R. 86; [1996] 5 Re. L.R. 192 CA 15–020
Wyatt v Guildhall Insurance Co Ltd [1937] 1 K.B. 653; (1937) 57 Ll.L.R. 90KBD ... 22–031, 22–097
Wylie v Wake Unreported, 2000 22–045
Wyndham Rather Ltd v Eagle Star & British Dominions Insurance Co Ltd (1925) 21 Ll.L.R. 214 CA 1–022, 1–055
Wynniatt-Husey v RJ Bromley (Underwriting Agencies) Plc [1996] L.R.L.R. 310 QBD (Comm) 13–041
Wynnstay Steamship Co Ltd v Board of Trade; WI Radcliffe Steamship Co Ltd v Board of Trade (1925) 23 Ll.L.R. 278 KBD 25–005
XL Insurance Ltd v Owens Corning [2001] 1 All E.R. (Comm) 530; [2000] 2 Lloyd's Rep. 500; [2001] C.P. Rep. 22; [2001] C.L.C. 914 QBD (Comm) 2–006
Xantho, The. See Thomas Wilson Sons & Co v Owners of Cargo of the Xantho
Xenos v Fox (1868–69) L.R. 4 C.P. 665 Ex Chamber 24–112
Xenos v Wickham (1867) L.R. 2 H.L. 296 HL 1–033, 15–001, 15–040
Yager and Guardian Assurance Co, Re [1912] 29 T.L.R. 53; (1912) 108 L.T. 38 .... 1–028, 6–021, 6–053, 6–102, 8–004
Yallop, Ex p. (1808) 15 Ves. 60 .... 4–016, 19–030
Yangtsze Insurance Association Ltd v Lukmanjee [1918] A.C. 585 PC (Cey) 4–020
Yarl's Wood Immigration Ltd v Bedfordshire Police Authority [2009] EWCA Civ 1110; [2010] 2 W.L.R. 1322; [2010] 2 All E.R. 221 .... 20–010, 25–010
Yasin, The [1979] 2 Lloyd's Rep. 45 QBD (Comm) 11–027
Yasuda Fire & Marine Insurance Co of Europe Ltd v Orion Marine Insurance Underwriting Agency Ltd [1995] Q.B. 174; [1995] 2 W.L.R. 49; [1995] 3 All E.R. 211; [1995] 1 Lloyd's Rep. 525; [1994] C.L.C. 1212; [1995] 4 Re. L.R. 217; Times, October 27, 1994 QBD (Comm) 15–020
Yates v White (1838) 4 Bing. N.C. 272 11–001
Yechiel v Kerry London Ltd [2010] EWHC 215 (Comm); [2010] Lloyd's Rep. I.R. 295 ... 15–037
Yona International Ltd v La Reunion Francaise SA D'Assurances et de Reassurances [1996] 2 Lloyd's Rep. 84 QBD (Comm) 1–025, 15–022
Yonge v Toynbee [1910] 1 K.B. 215 CA 15–009
Yorke v Yorkshire Insurance Co Ltd [1918] 1 K.B. 662 KBD 6–018, 6–031, 7–033, 7–037, 18–029, 18–030
Yorkshire Dale Steamship Co Ltd v Minister of War Transport [1942] A.C. 691; (1942) 73 Ll.L.R. 1 HL 5–030, 5–041, 25–005
Yorkshire Insurance Co Ltd v Campbell [1917] A.C. 218PC (Aus) 3–005, 3–010, 3–011, 7–022, 7–030, 7–040
Yorkshire Insurance Co Ltd v Craine [1922] 2 A.C. 541; (1922) 12 Ll.L.R. 399 PC (Aus) 7–019, 7–048
Yorkshire Insurance Co Ltd v Nisbet Shipping Co Ltd [1962] 2 Q.B. 330; [1961] 2 W.L.R. 1043; [1961] 2 All E.R. 487; [1961] 1 Lloyd's Rep. 479; 105 S.J. 367 QBD (Comm) 11–002, 11–004, 11–017, 11–018
Yorkshire Water Services Ltd v Sun Alliance and London Insurance Plc (No.1) [1997] 2 Lloyd's Rep. 21; [1997] C.L.C. 213; (1996) 93(34) L.S.G. 34; (1996) 140 S.J.L.B. 193; [1997] Env. L.R. D4; Times, August 20, 1996 CA (Civ Div) 1–011, 3–003, 9–025, 10–038, 10–039, 20–010, 20–013, 20–057
Youell v Bland Welch & Co Ltd (No.1) [1992] 2 Lloyd's Rep. 127 CA (Civ Div) 1–033, 3–010, 15–035, 17–014

Youell v Bland Welch & Co Ltd (No.2) [1990] 2 Lloyd's Rep. 431QBD (Comm) 1–023, 15–028,
                              15–030, 15–031, 15–032, 15–034, 15–037, 15–047, 15–051,
                              17–005
Youell v Kara Mara Shipping Co Ltd [2000] 2 Lloyd's Rep. 102; [2000] C.L.C. 1058; [2001]
     I.L.Pr. 34; [2001] Lloyd's Rep. I.R. 553; Times, April 10, 2000 QBD (Comm) 2–004, 2–005,
                              2–006
Youell v La Reunion Aerienne [2008] EWHC 2493 (Comm); [2009] 1 All E.R. (Comm) 301;
     [2009] I.L.Pr. 23; [2009] Lloyd's Rep. I.R. 405 .... 2–008, 2–009, 2–014
Young v Merchants Marine Insurance Co Ltd [1932] 2 K.B. 705; (1932) 43 Ll.L.R. 277
     CA 11–035
Young v Sun Alliance and London Insurance Ltd [1977] 1 W.L.R. 104; [1976] 3 All E.R.
     561; [1976] 2 Lloyd's Rep. 189; 120 S.J. 469 CA (Civ Div) 3–002, 3–006, 3–010, 19–035,
                              19–036, 19–037
Young v Turing (1841) 2 M. & G. 593 24–086
Yuill & Co v Robson [1908] 1 K.B. 270CA; affirming [1907] 1 K.B. 685 KBD (Comm Ct) ... 15–026,
                              15–034
Yule v Life and Health Assurance Association, 1904 6 R. 347 15–019
Yung Hong Wai v Ng Shing Unreported, 1994 11–015
Zeller v British Caymanian Insurance Co Ltd [2008] UKPC 4; [2008] Lloyd's Rep. I.R. 545
     PC (Cayman Islands) 6–013
Zephyr, The. See General Accident Fire & Life Assurance Corp Ltd v Tanter
Zeus Tradition Marine Ltd v Bell (The Zeus) V [2000] 2 All E.R. (Comm) 769; [2000] 2
     Lloyd's Rep. 587; [2000] C.L.C. 1705CA (Civ Div); reversing [1999] 1 Lloyd's Rep.
     703; [1999] C.L.C. 391 QBD (Comm) 3–005, 3–010, 6–063, 7–003, 24–038
Ziel Nominees Pty Ltd v Accident Insurance Co (1975) 7 A.L.R. 667 10–051
Zincroft Civil Engineering Ltd v Sphere Drake Insurance Plc (1996) Lloyd's List, December
     23 9–035
Zivnostenska Banka National Corp v Frankman [1950] A.C. 57; [1949] 2 All E.R. 671 HL 2–057
Zuhal K, The and Selin, The [1987] 1 Lloyd's Rep. 151; [1987] 1 F.T.L.R. 76; Financial
     Times, November 11, 1986 QBD (Admlty) 13–009, 23–019
Zurich General Accident & Liability Insurance Co Ltd v Buck (1939) 64 Ll.L.R. 115 KBD ... 15–015
Zurich General Accident & Liability Insurance Co Ltd v Livingston (No.2), 1940 S.C. 406;
     1940 S.L.T. 350 IH (1 Div) 6–013, 6–048
Zurich General Accident & Liability Insurance Co Ltd v Morrison [1942] 2 K.B. 53; [1942]
     1 All E.R. 529; (1942) 72 Ll.L.R. 167 CA 6–021, 6–027, 22–036, 22–048, 22–087
Zurich General Accident and Liability Insurance Co v Rowberry [1954] 2 Lloyd's Rep. 55
     CA 15–001, 15–027, 15–034
Zurich Insurance Co v Metals and Minerals Insurance Pte (2009) 261 A.L.R. 468 11–065
Zurich Insurance Co v Shield Insurance Co [1988] I.R. 174 Sup Ct (Irl) 11–056
Zurich Professional Ltd v Karim [2006] EWHC 3355 (QB) 5–047, 14–013

TABLE OF STATUTES

1677 Statute of Frauds (29 Car. 2
c.3)—
s.4 23–018
1719 Royal Exchange and London As-
surance Corporation Act (6
Geo. 1 c.18) ("the Bubble
Act")
1745 Marine Insurance Act (19 Geo. 2
c.37) 4–003, 18–009, 24–012,
24–014, 24–097
1774 Life Assurance Act (14 Geo. 3
c.48) 1–014, 1–015, 4–003,
4–005, 4–009, 4–010,
4–011, 4–015, 4–021,
4–026, 8–022, 8–031,
14–010, 18–001, 18–002,
18–004, 18–005, 18–007,
18–011, 18–015, 18–019,
19–002, 19–005, 20–006,
20–062, 22–027
s.1 .... 4–003, 4–021, 5–036, 18–004,
18–005, 18–007, 18–008, 18–009,
18–022, 19–002, 19–017, 19–022,
19–026, 20–062
s.2 .... 1–013, 1–014, 1–016, 4–003,
4–021, 4–022, 4–026, 14–010,
18–007, 18–009, 19–002, 20–062,
22–027
s.3 .... 4–004, 4–005, 9–048, 18–004,
18–008, 19–002, 19–005, 20–062
s.4 .... 1–014, 1–016, 19–001, 19–002
Fire Prevention (Metropolis) Act
(14 Geo. 3 c.78) 9–044
s.83 .... 10–050, 10–051, 10–052,
14–010, 14–020, 19–006, 19–009,
19–020
1785 Insurances on Ships (25 Geo.3
c.44) 4–003
1788 Marine Insurance Act (28 Geo. 3
c.56) 1–016, 4–003, 4–021,
4–022, 19–002, 19–005
1838 Judgments Act (1 & 2 Vict.
c.110)—
s.17 10–024
1845 Gaming Act (8 & 9 Vict.
c.109) 4–007, 18–011
s.18 .... 4–002, 4–003, 4–009, 4–010,
4–021, 19–001
1846 Fatal Accidents Act (9 & 10
Vict. c.93) 24–007
s.2 18–002
1847 Harbours, Docks and Piers
Clauses Act (10 & 11 Vict.
c.27) 24–007
1851 Evidence Act (14 & 15 Vict.
c.99) 6–024

1854 Merchant Shipping (Repeal) Act
(17 & 18 Vict. c.120) 24–007
s.183 24–025
1861 Malicious Damage Act (24 & 25
Vict. c.97)—
s.58 25–015
1862 Companies Act (25 & 26 Vict.
c.89) 24–007
1867 Policies of Assurance Act (30 &
31 Vict. c.144) ... 14–026, 14–029,
18–001, 18–023
s.3 .... 18–023, 18–024
s.4 18–023
s.5 .... 18–023, 18–024
s.6 18–023
Sch. 18–023
1868 Policies of Marine Assurance
Act (c.86) 14–026
1870 Life Assurance Companies Act
(33 & 34 Vict. c.61) 1–001,
13–002, 16–011
1871 Lloyd's Act (34 & 35 Vict.
c.xxi) 13–039
1873 Judicature Act (36 & 37 Vict.
c.66) 18–023
s.25(6) 14–026
1874 Infants' Relief Act (37 & 38
Vict. c.62) 14–002
1875 Friendly Societies Act (38 & 39
Vict. c.60) 13–015
1882 Married Women's Property Act
(45 & 46 Vict. c.75) 9–044,
18–014
s.11 .... 18–014, 18–024, 18–035
1886 Riot (Damages) Act (49 & 50
Vict. c.38) 20–010, 20–028
s.2(2) 25–010
s.4 25–010
1891 Stamp Act (54 & 55 Vict. c.39)
.... 2–037
s.93 10–058
s.98 1–002
1893 Sale of Goods Act (56 & 57 Vict.
c.71)—
s.4 4–018
1896 Life Assurance Companies (Pay-
ment into Court) Act (59 &
60 Vict. c.8) 18–001, 18–024
Friendly Societies Act (59 & 60
Vict. c.25)—
s.1 18–016
1906 Marine Insurance Act (6 Edw. 7
c.41) 1–011, 4–010, 4–016,
6–045, 19–001, 19–007,
24–008
s.2(1) 24–009, 24–011

(2) 1–011
s.3 24–011
(2) 24–011
s.4 .... 1–009, 4–010, 4–021, 24–016,
24–019, 24–097
(1) 4–009, 24–012
(2) 4–009, 24–012, 24–097
(a) 4–009
(b) 4–009, 24–012, 24–015
s.5 24–017
(1) 24–017
(2) 4–013, 24–017
s.6 24–014
(1) 24–018, 24–019, 24–020
proviso 4–005, 24–018
(2) 24–018, 24–020
s.7 24–021
(1) 4–016, 24–021
(2) 4–016, 19–007, 24–021
s.8 4–016
(3) 6–066
s.9 24–023
(1) 17–004
s.10 24–024
s.11 24–025
s.12 24–026
s.13 24–027
s.14 .... 24–022, 24–028
(1) 24–028, 24–029
(2) 24–028, 24–029
(3) 24–028, 24–031
s.15 .... 14–022, 24–032
s.16 ..... 1–011, 4–001, 10–011, 10–015,
24–033, 24–0101
(3) 10–016
ss.17–20 6–135
s.17 .... 6–001, 6–077, 6–0107, 6–108,
6–109, 6–110, 6–115, 6–122,
6–123, 6–136, 6–142, 24–034
ss.18–20 .... 6–107, 6–136
s.18 .... 6–036, 6–107, 6–123, 17–008,
24–034
(1) 6–002, 6–004, 6–101
(2) 1–028, 6–001, 6–004, 6–021,
6–027, 6–037, 6–045, 6–059,
6–103, 6–120
(c) 6–129
(3) 6–065
(a) 6–063
(b) ... 6–064, 6–065, 6–066, 11–041
(c) 6–068
(d) 6–074
s.19 .... 6–036, 6–037, 6–040, 6–041,
6–042, 6–043, 6–055, 6–069,
6–116, 15–036, 24–041
(a) 6–035, 6–041, 6–042, 6–043
(b) 6–040
s.20 .... 6–107, 6–123, 24–042
(1) 6–007
(2) 1–028, 6–001, 6–021, 6–027,
6–103, 6–120
(3) 6–013, 6–014
(4) 6–015
(5) 6–013, 6–014

(6) 6–101
s.21 .... 1–033, 24–043
s.22 ...... 1–004, 1–011, 1–033, 8–005,
13–011, 24–044
s.23 .... 4–021, 4–022, 24–045
s.24 24–046
s.25 .... 5–003, 24–047
(1) 24–047
s.26 24–048
(1) 1–021
(2) 24–048
(3) 24–048
s.27 .... 1–009, 24–049
(1)–(2) 6–056
(2) 10–006
(3) 4–004, 6–056, 10–007, 11–017
(4) 24–086
s.28 .... 10–006, 24–050
s.29 24–051
(3) 24–051
(4) 24–051
s.30 24–052
s.31 24–053
(1) 8–008
(2) 5–018, 8–008, 8–032, 24–053
s.32 .... 6–058, 24–054
(1) 11–044
(2) 11–044
(b) 11–044
ss.33–41 6–074
s.33 .... 1–011, 7–038, 7–039, 24–055
(1) 7–021
(2) 7–023
(3) 7–041
s.34 24–056
(1) 7–045
(2) 7–038, 7–043
(3) 7–046, 24–064
s.35 .... 7–022, 24–057
(1) 7–026
(2) 1–011, 7–024
ss.36–41 7–023
s.36 24–058
(1) 24–058
(2) 24–058
s.37 24–059
s.38 24–060
s.39 .... 7–023, 24–047, 24–061
(1) 5–017, 7–023, 22–036
(2) 24–061
(3) 24–061, 24–073
(5) 24–062
s.40 24–063
(1) 24–061
(2) 24–061
s.41 .... 5–037, 5–039, 24–064
ss.42–49 7–022
s.42 .... 1–030, 24–065, 24–072
s.43 ...... 1–030, 5–025, 24–047, 24–067
ss.43–49 1–011
s.44 .... 24–068, 24–073
ss.45–49 .... 5–028, 6–103
s.45 .... 7–036, 24–068, 24–069, 24–073
(2) 24–069

s.46 .... 5–013, 24–070
  (1) 24–070
  (2)(a) 24–070
  (3) 24–070
s.47 24–071
s.48 24–072
s.49 .... 24–070, 24–072, 24–073
  (1) 24–073
    (b) 24–069
    (d) 24–070
  (2)(g) 24–073
s.50 ... 1–011, 14–026, 14–029, 24–032,
                     24–074
  (1) 24–074
  (2) 24–074
  (3) 24–074
s.51 .... 1–011, 24–075
s.52 .... 8–005, 24–076
s.53 .... 1–011, 8–003, 24–077
  (1) 8–023, 15–028, 15–032,
                 24–077, 24–078
  (2) 14–016, 15–033, 24–078
s.54 .... 1–025, 1–030, 24–079
s.55 .... 24–006, 24–080
  (1) 5–029
  (2)(a) 5–041, 9–025, 24–001,
    24–003, 24–073, 24–081, 24–112
    (b) 24–072, 24–080
    (c) 19–055, 19–056
s.56 24–082
  (1) 10–001
s.57 .... 10–001, 24–083
  (1) 24–092
s.58 24–084
s.59 .... 5–002, 24–073, 24–085
s.60 .... 10–001, 24–086
  (1) 24–086, 24–092
ss 61–62 10–001
s.61 .... 24–087, 24–092
s.62 .... 24–086, 24–088, 24–093
  (1) 24–092
  (2) 24–093
  (4) 24–088
  (5) 24–088
  (6) 24–089, 24–093
  (7) 24–111
s.63 .... 24–089, 24–090, 24–093
  (1) 11–066, 24–088, 24–089,
    24–091, 24–092, 24–093, 24–094,
                 24–095, 24–096
  (2) 24–095, 24–097
s.64 24–098
s.65 .... 24–098, 24–112
s.66 24–100
s.67 24–101
  (1) 10–009, 24–101
  (2) 24–101
s.68 .... 23–003, 24–102
  (1) 10–009
s.69 .... 10–010, 10–031, 24–103
  (1) 1–011
s.70 .... 10–010, 24–104

s.71 24–105
  (1) 10–010
  (3) 10–010
s.72 .... 10–011, 24–106
s.73 24–107
s.74 24–108
s.75 25–109
  (2) 10–007, 10–008
s.76 24–110
s.77 .... 10–005, 24–111
  (1) 24–111
  (2) 24–111
s.78 .... 1–011, 10–039, 24–112
  (1) 24–112
  (2) 24–099
  (4) 24–112
s.79 ... 11–001, 11–017, 24–093, 24–113
  (1) 11–066, 24–089, 24–092,
          24–093, 24–094, 24–096
s.80 .... 11–061, 24–113
  (1) 11–059, 11–062
s.81 ... 1–011, 10–029, 11–068, 24–101,
                     24–115
ss.82–84 11–045
s.82 24–116
  (a) 8–023
  (b) 8–023
s.83 .... 8–019, 24–117
s.84 .... 6–075, 6–088, 6–124, 7–040,
                 24–019, 24–118
  (1) 6–075, 7–003, 7–040, 8–020,
         8–022, 18–009, 19–004
  (2) 8–021, 8–022
  (3)(a) .. 7–003, 7–040, 8–025, 19–004
    (b) 8–029
    (c) 8–031, 18–009
    (d) 8–030
    (e) 8–033
    (f) 8–032, 8–034, 11–045
s.85 .... 8–006, 25–119
  (1) 24–007
  (2) 1–003, 13–014, 24–007
s.86 .... 1–011, 14–008, 15–003, 24–120
s.87 24–121
s.88 .... 24–072, 24–122
s.89 .... 1–033, 24–065, 24–123
s.90 24–124
s.91 24–125
s.92 24–125
s.93 24–125
s.94 24–126
Sch.1 ... 2–040, 24–065, 24–127, 25–001
  r.1 24–128
  r.2 .... 1–027, 24–129
  r.3 .... 1–027, 24–129, 24–130
  r.4 24–131
  r.5 24–132
  r.6 .... 24–073, 24–133
  r.7 .... 14–013, 24–002, 24–134

r.8 .... 24–002, 24–135
r.9 .... 24–002, 24–136
r.10 24–137
r.11 .... 24–003, 24–138
r.12 24–139
r.13 24–140
r.14 24–141
r.15 .... 24–033, 24–142
r.16 .... 24–026, 24–143
r.17 24–144

1909 Marine Insurance (Gambling
        Policies) Act (9 Edw. 7
        c.12) 4–005, 4–010, 4–027,
                                                  24–016
    s.1(1) 24–016
        (a) 24–016
        (b) 24–016
        (2) 24–016
    Assurance Companies Act (9
        Edw.7 c.49) 1–001, 13–011,
                                                  16–011
    s.30 1–004

1911 Lloyd's Act (1 & 2 Geo. 5
        c.lxii) 13–039
    s.10 13–039

1914 Deeds of Arrangement Act (4 &
        5 Geo.5 c.47) 21–043

1923 Industrial Assurance Act (13 &
        14 Geo. 5 c.8) 13–016, 13–043
    s.3 18–016

1925 Lloyd's Act (15 & 16 Geo. 5
        c.xxvi) 13–039
    Settled Land Act (15 & 16 Geo.
        5 c.18)—
    s.102 19–030
    Trustee Act (15 & 16 Geo. 5
        c.19)—
    s.19 19–030
    s.20 19–030
    Law of Property Act (15 & 16
        Geo. 5 c.20) 14–029
    s.40 2–054
    s.47 .... 19–006, 19–007, 19–009
        (1) 19–009
        (2) 19–009
        (3) 19–009
    s.53(1)(c) 14–026
    s.61(a) 5–004
    s.101 21–044
        (1) 19–028
        (ii) 19–026, 19–027
    s.108(3) 19–026, 19–028
        (4) 19–026, 19–028
    s.136 .... 11–004, 14–026, 14–029,
                                                  18–023

1927 Landlord and Tenant Act (17 &
        18 Geo.5 c.36)—
    s.16 19–024
    Statute Law Revision Act (17 &
        18 Geo.5 c.42) 24–125

1930 Third Parties (Rights against In-
        surers) Act (20 & 21 Geo. 5
        c.25) 2–014, 9–043, 15–062,
                          20–035, 21–002, 21–003,
                          21–004, 21–006, 21–009,
                          21–013, 21–015, 21–017,
                          21–019, 21–020, 21–022,
                          21–023, 21–025, 21–028,
                          21–029, 21–030, 21–041,
                          21–042, 21–044, 21–045,
                          21–046, 21–049, 21–053,
                          21–054, 21–056, 21–057,
                          21–058, 21–059, 21–060,
                          21–061, 21–062, 21–063,
                          21–064, 21–065, 22–038,
                                                  23–017
    s.1(1) 21–005, 21–007, 21–010,
              21–018, 21–024, 21–030, 21–036
        (2) 21–005
        (3) 21–034, 21–035, 21–036,
                                                  21–037
        (4) 21–033
        (a) 21–033
        (b) 21–031
        (5) 21–008
        (6) 21–005
    s.2 .... 21–023, 21–039, 21–040
        (1)–(1A) 21–039
        (1) 21–039
        (2) 21–039
        (3) 21–039
    s.3 21–038
    s.3A 21–005
    Road Traffic Act (20 & 21 Geo.
        5 c.43) 21–002, 22–001, 22–012,
                          22–036, 22–038
    s.30(4) 20–062
    s.36(1)(b) 22–017, 22–031
        (ii) 22–017

1934 Road Traffic Act (24 & 25 Geo.
        5 c.50) 21–002, 22–001, 22–036,
                                                  22–038

1939 Trading with the Enemy (2 & 3
        Geo. 6 c.89) 5–036

1941 Landlord and Tenant (War Dam-
        age) Act (2 & 3 Geo. 6
        c.72)—
    s.11 19–018

1943 Law Reform (Frustrated Con-
        tracts) Act (6 & 7 Geo. 6
        c.40) 10–047
    s.1(3) 10–047
    s.2(5)(b) 10–047

1945 Law Reform (Contributory Neg-
        ligence) Act (8 & 9 Geo. 6
        c.28) 15–051, 22–035
    s.1(1) 15–051
    s.4 15–051

1948 Industrial Assurance and Friend-
        ly Societies Act (11 & 12
        Geo. 6 c.39)—
    s.1 18–016
    s.6(1) 18–016

Agricultural Holdings Act (11 &
12 Geo. 6 c.63) 19–003
1951 Lloyd's Act (14 & 15 Geo. 6
c.viii) 13–039
1952 Marine and Aviation (War Risks)
Insurance Act (15 & 16
Geo. 6 & 1 Eliz. 2 c.57) ... 25–002
s.1 24–044
s.2 24–044
s.7 24–044
Defamation Act (15 & 16 Geo. 6
& 1 Eliz. 2 c.66)—
s.11 20–009
1954 Law Reform (Enforcement of
Contracts) Act (2 & 3 Eliz.
2 c.34) 23–018
1955 Army Act (3 & 4 Eliz. 2
c.18)—
s.166(2)(b) 22–003
Air Force Act (3 & 4 Eliz. 2
c.19) 22–003
1958 Children Act (6 & 7 Eliz. 2
c.65)—
s.9 18–015
Insurance Companies Act (6 & 7
Eliz. 2 c.72)—
Sch.3 16–011
1959 Finance Act (7 & 8 Eliz. 2
c.58) 24–045
Sch.8 .... 24–043, 24–047
1960 Road Traffic Act (8 & 9 Eliz. 2
c.16)—
s.203(4) 22–017
(a) 22–031
1961 Factories Act (9 & 10 Eliz. 2
c.34) 20–063
Suicide Act (9 & 10 Eliz. 2
c.60) 5–044, 18–033
s.2 18–034
1965 Carriage of Goods by Road Act
(c.37) 5–010
Nuclear Installations Act
(c.57) 20–002
1967 Misrepresentation Act (c.7) 6–114
s.2(1) 6–044, 6–080, 6–081, 6–088,
6–119, 15–036
(2) 6–081
Companies Act (c.81) 1–001
1968 Theft Act (c.60) 19–049, 22–041
s.1 .... 10–002, 19–049, 19–050
s.8 19–052
s.9 19–051
s.12 19–050
(1) 19–050
(6) 19–050
1969 Employers' Liability (Defective
Equipment) Act (c.37) 20–001,
20–063
Family Law Reform Act
(c.46) 14–001
s.19 18–014

Employers' Liability (Compulsory Insurance) Act (c.57) ... 1–015,
16–024, 20–063, 20–069,
20–069, 21–023, 21–040,
22–017, 22–018
s.1(1) 20–064, 20–068, 20–070
(3)(b) 20–063
(c) 20–064
(d) 20–064
(3A) 20–063
s.2(1) 20–066
(a) 20–068
(b) 20–068
(c) 20–068
(d) 20–068
(2)(a) 20–066
(b) 20–066
s.3 20–065
s.4(1) 20–071
(2) 20–071
(3) 20–071
s.5 20–070
s.5A 20–070
s.5B 20–070
1970 Administration of Justice Act
(c.31)—
s.44 10–024
s.44A 2–059, 10–024
1971 Motor Vehicle (Passenger Insur-
ance) Act (c.36) 22–031
Criminal Damage Act (c.48) 5–041
1972 Road Traffic Act (c.20) 22–001,
22–041
Civil Evidence Act (c.30) 2–025
Local Government Act (c.70)—
s.140 .... 4–003, 13–009, 18–002
s.140A 13–009
s.140B 13–009
s.222 22–002
1973 Insurance Companies Amend-
ment Act (c.58)—
s.50 18–007
Local Government (Scotland)
Act (c.65)—
s.86(1) 13–009
1974 Consumer Credit Act (c.39) 22–024,
22–025, 23–029
s.8 22–024
s.15 22–024
s.65 22–024
s.127 22–024
Friendly Societies Act (c.46) 1–005,
13–015, 13–042
Solicitors Act (c.47)—
s.37 20–003
Insurance Companies Act
(c.49) 1–001, 13–032
Rehabilitation of Offenders Act
(c.53) 6–048, 12–019
s.4 6–048
s.6 6–048
s.7(3) 6–048
1975 Sex Discrimination Act (c.65) 6–051

Policyholders Protection Act
(c.75) 16–016, 16–017, 16–019,
16–020, 16–025
1976 Fatal Accidents Act (c.30) 22–067
s.4 18–002
Adoption Act (c.36) 18–015
Race Relations Act (c.74) 6–051
1977 Insurance Brokers (Registration)
Act (c.46) 15–010
National Health Service Act
(c.49)—
s.16A 22–003
s.16BA 22–003
s.23 22–003
s.26 22–003
Unfair Contract Terms Act
(c.50) 1–001, 3–018, 10–045,
11–031, 12–001, 20–059
s.2 1–001
s.3 1–001
s.4 1–001
Sch.1
para.1 10–042
(a) 3–018
1978 Export Guarantees and Overseas
Investment Act (c.18) 23–032
National Health Service (Scotland) Act (c.29) .. 20–065, 22–003
s.15 22–003
s.16 22–003
Civil Liability (Contribution)
Act (c.47) 2–004, 11–026,
11–052, 15–032, 23–034
s.1(1) 15–060
1979 Vaccine Damage Payments Act
(c.17) 20–017
Estate Agents Act (c.38)—
s.16 20–003
Sale of Goods Act (c.54) 4–018,
19–007, 20–009
s.3 14–002
s.8 8–008
s.11 7–005
(3) 4–016
s.16(3) 10–016
s.18
r.1 19–007
rr.2–5 19–007
s.20 19–007
(2) 4–016, 19–007
(3) 19–007
s.20A 4–016, 19–007
s.20B 19–007
s.41 19–007
s.47 19–007
s.48(1) 19–007
(2) 19–007
s.51 10–016
(3) 10–016
1980 Limitation Act (c.58) ... 6–078, 15–061,
16–027, 21–017, 22–059,
22–077
s.2 15–061

s.5 .... 6–078, 9–037, 15–061, 17–027,
21–030
s.8 9–037
s.11 .... 22–013, 22–077
s.12 20–078
s.14A 11–011, 15–061
(5) 11–011
s.28 22–077
s.32 .... 6–078, 10–058, 15–061
s.33 21–014
s.36 .... 6–078, 15–061
1981 Insurance Companies Act
(c.31) 1–001
ss 49–52 13–032
s.52B 13–032
Sch.2C 13–032
Sch.2E 13–032
Senior Courts Act (c.54) 20–089
s.18(1)(j) 15–046
s.20(2)(p) 24–078
s.33 21–040
s.35 20–044
s.35A 2–059, 10–024, 11–022,
21–026
(1) 10–024
(6) 10–024
s.51 .... 2–009, 20–055, 20–056, 23–016
1982 Lloyd's Act (c.xiv) 13–001, 13–039
s.3 13–039
s.4 13–039
s.5 13–039
s.6 13–038
s.7 13–039
s.8 13–039
s.9 13–039
ss 10–12 13–039
s.14 13–039
Civil Jurisdiction and Judgments
Act (c.27) 2–001
s.41 2–001
Sch.4 2–001
Forfeiture Act (c.34) 18–035
s.1 18–014
(1) 5–041, 18–035
(2) 18–035
s.2 18–014
(1) 18–035
(2) 18–035
(4) 18–035
s.5 18–035
Insurance Companies Act
(c.50) 1–001, 13–002, 13–043
s.94B(1A) 2–017
s.96A 2–017
Sch.3A 2–017
1984 Foreign Limitation Periods Act
(c.16) 2–056, 2–065
s.1 2–056
s.2 2–056
Road Traffic Regulation Act
(c.27) 22–076
s.101 22–023
County Court Act (c.28)—
Pt 6 21–043

Pt 6A 21–043
s.69 12–042
Friendly Societies Act (c.62) ... 13–043,
16–016
1985 Companies Act (c.6)
s.651 21–014
Local Government Act (c.51)—
Pt IV 20–065, 22–003
Landlord and Tenant Act
(c.70) 14–020, 19–018
Sch.1 19–019
para.2 19–019
para.3 19–019
para.4 19–019
para.5 19–019
para.6 19–019
1986 Latent Damage Act (c.37) 15–061
s.3 19–038
Insolvency Act (c.45) 16–015,
20–086, 21–013
Pt I 21–005, 21–039, 21–044
Pt II 16–013, 21–044
Pt III 21–044
Pt IV, Ch 2 21–044
Pt IV, Ch 6 21–044
Pt V 21–044
Pt VIIA 21–043
Pt VIII 21–039, 21–043
Pt IX 21–043
ss.1–7 16–014
ss.8–27 16–013
s.8(4) 16–013
s.19(5) 21–028
ss.28–49 16–015
s.72A 16–015
ss.73–251 16–002
s.122 16–004
s.123 16–004
s.135 21–044
s.155 21–040
s.176A 16–010
s.214 .... 16–013, 20–086
s.221 21–006
s.262 21–013
s.426 16–001
Sch.2B 16–013
Financial Services Act (c.60) ... 13–002,
15–010
s.47 .... 6–132, 13–026
s.132 13–020
Public Order Act (c.64)—
s.1 25–010
(1) 25–010
s.10 25–010
1987 Minors' Contracts Act (c.13) 14–002
s.1 14–002
Landlord and Tenant Act
(c.31) 19–019
Sch.3
para.7 19–019
para.8 19–019
Consumer Protection Act
(c.43) 21–014

1988 Access to Medical Reports Act
(c.29) 18–029
Road Traffic Act (c.52) 1–015, 3–018,
5–042, 9–044, 11–059,
16–024, 20–001, 20–068,
20–070, 21–023, 22–001,
22–015, 22–054, 22–062,
22–076, 22–084
Pt VI ... 1–015, 22–001, 22–064, 22–065
s.43 22–017
s.95 18–029
s.143 .... 22–008, 22–029, 22–033,
22–043, 22–060
(1) 22–002, 22–009, 22–012
(b) 22–012
(2) 22–002
(3) 22–003, 22–009
(4) 22–006
s.144 .... 22–003, 22–060, 22–064,
22–082
(1A)–(1B) 22–003
(2) 22–003
s.145 .... 20–017, 22–014, 22–023,
22–027, 22–029, 22–031, 22–033,
22–053
(2) 22–016
(3) 22–008, 22–027, 22–028,
22–032
(a) 22–019, 22–020
(aa) 22–020, 22–021
(b) 22–021
(c) 22–022
(4)(a) 22–017, 22–019
(b) 22–019
(c) 22–019
(d) 22–019
(e) 22–019
(f) 22–019
(4A) 22–017, 22–018
(a), (b) 22–018
(5)–(6) 22–016
s.146 22–004
s.147 22–015
(1) 22–015, 22–039
(1A)–(1E) 22–015
(4)(a), (b) 22–015
(4A) 22–015
(4B) 22–015
(4D) 22–015
(5) 22–015
s.148 .... 11–060, 22–029, 22–036,
22–039, 22–096
(1)–(4) 22–036
(2) 22–086
(4) 22–036
(5)–(6) 22–037
(5) 5–049
(7) 20–062, 22–009, 22–027,
22–033, 22–038, 22–088
s.149 22–017
(4)(b) 22–033
s.150 22–036

s.151 .... 11–060, 21–002, 22–012,
    22–015, 22–029, 22–034, 22–038,
    22–039, 22–040, 22–041, 22–042,
    22–043, 22–044, 22–047, 22–056,
                 22–072, 22–098
(1) 22–039
  (a)–(b) 22–048
(2) 22–088
  (a) 22–039
  (b) 22–041
(3) 22–039, 22–040, 22–041,
                      22–043
(4) 11–060, 22–041
(5) 22–040, 22–043
  (a) 22–042
  (b) 22–042
  (c) 22–042
(6)(a) 22–042
  (b) 22–042
(7) 11–060
  (a) 22–043
  (b) 22–039, 22–043
(8) 3–018, 22–033, 22–043
s.152 .... 6–136, 22–015, 22–038,
                  22–044, 22–056
(1)(a) 22–044, 22–045
  (b) 22–044, 22–046
  (c) 22–044, 22–047
(2)–(4) 22–048
(2) 22–044
(3) 22–048
(4) 22–048
s.153 22–038
s.154 .... 22–015, 22–069
s.156 22–015
ss.157–159 22–062
ss.157–161 22–022
s.157 .... 20–017, 22–022
s.158 20–017
  (3) 21–022
s.159(1) 22–022
s.161 22–022
  (1) 22–014
  (3) 22–019
s.165(1)–(2) 22–015
s.165(3)–(4) 22–015
s.170(1)–(6) 22–015
s.171 22–015
s.173 22–015
s.174 22–015
  (5) 22–015
s.185 22–055
  (1) 22–006
s.189 22–006
  (2) 22–006
s.192(1) 22–007
Road Traffic Offenders Act
  (c.53) 22–076
1989 Law of Property (Miscellaneous
      Provisions) Act (c.34) 23–018
Companies Act (c.40)
s.141 21–014
Children Act (c.41)
Sch.8, para.11A 18–015

1990 National Health Service and
      Community Care Act
      (c.19)—
Pt I 22–003
s.60(7) 20–065, 22–003
Contracts (Applicable Law) Act
  (c.36) 2–018
s.2(2) 2–030, 2–050
  (3) 2–018
s.3(1), (2) 2–018
  (3)(a), (h) 2–018
s.4A 2–019
1991 Water Resources Act (c.57) 20–010
Land Drainage Act (c.59)
Sch.2, para.1 4–003
Export and Investment Guaran-
  tees Act (c.67) 23–032
1992 Friendly Societies Act (c.40) 1–005,
          13–001, 13–015, 13–016,
          13–032, 13–042, 13–043
s.5 13–015
s.93 13–015
s.99 .... 18–015, 18–016
1993 Reinsurance (Acts of Terrorism)
      Act (c.18) 25–002
s.1 25–014
s.2(2), (3) 25–014
Osteopaths Act (c.21) 20–003
1994 Vehicle Excise and Registration
      Act (c.22) 22–015, 22–036,
                22–082, 22–086
Local Government etc. (Scotland) Act (c.39)—
s.2 .... 20–065, 22–003
1995 Merchant Shipping Act (c.21) ... 20–004
Pt IX 22–003
s.192A 20–004
Sale of Goods (Amendment) Act
  (c.28) 19–007
Landlord and Tenant (Cove-
  nants) Act (c.30) 19–021
Private International Law (Miscellaneous Provisions) Act
  (c.42) 2–061
ss 1–4 2–059
s.1 10–024
ss 9–15 2–062
s.9 2–062
  (1), (2) 2–062
  (4), (5) 2–062
s.10 2–062
s.11 2–064
  (1) 2–063
  (2)(c) 2–063
s.12 2–064
s.14 2–061
s.15A 2–061
Disability Discrimination Act
  (c.50) 6–050, 18–029
s.3 18–029
s.19 18–029
Criminal Injuries Compensation
  Act (c.53) 20–017

1996 Employment Rights Act (c.18)—
  s.235 25–016
  Arbitration Act (c.23) .. 2–001, 13–014, 22–073
  s.2 .... 2–001, 2–038
  s.3 .... 2–001, 2–038
  s.9 .... 2–001, 2–005
  s.46 .... 2–034, 17–016
  s.49 .... 2–059, 10–024
  ss.67–69 2–001
  s.69 .... 2–034, 21–054
  Housing Grants Construction and Regeneration Act (c.53)—
  s.108 21–011
1997 Policyholders Protection (c.18) 16–016
  Social Security (Recovery of Benefits) Act (c.27) 20–016, 20–020, 20–021, 22–022
  s.1 20–021
  ss.4–5 20–021
  s.6 20–021
  s.7 20–021
  ss.8–9 20–021
  s.10 20–021
  ss.11–14 20–021
  s.22 20–021
  Sch.1 20–021
  Sch.2 20–021
  Merchant Shipping and Maritime Security Act (c.28) 20–004
1998 Competition Act (c.41) 13–002, 13–044, 15–010
  Ch I 13–044, 22–026
  Ch II 13–044
  s.9 13–044
  s.50 13–044
1999 Road Traffic (NHS Charges) Act (c.3) 20–016, 22–022, 22–062, 22–075
  s.15 22–022
  s.18 22–022
  Access to Justice Act (c.22) 21–040
  s.29 .... 23–035, 23–038
  Contracts (Rights of Third Parties) Act (c.31) 4–006, 6–083, 9–044, 9–049, 9–050, 9–051, 9–052, 10–048, 10–051, 11–038, 14–006, 14–009, 14–010, 14–019, 14–020, 15–031, 15–062, 17–002, 18–007, 18–008, 18–014, 18–024, 19–006, 19–011, 19–013, 19–017, 19–021, 20–008, 20–081, 21–002, 21–003, 22–027, 22–048, 22–058, 22–088, 23–001
  s.1(1) 9–044
  (a) 11–038, 14–009
  (b) 11–038, 14–009
  (2) 9–044, 11–038, 14–009, 19–017, 20–008
  (b) 14–009
  (3) 9–044, 10–048, 11–038, 14–009, 20–008
  (4) 9–045, 9–052
  (5) 9–048
  s.2(1) 9–046
  (3) 9–046
  (4) 9–046
  (5) 9–046
  (6) 9–046
  s.3 9–047
  (2) 9–047
  (3) 9–047
  (4) 4–006, 9–047, 18–008
  (5) 9–047
  s.4 .... 9–047, 9–050, 9–051
  s.5 9–051
  s.7(3) 9–052
  s.8(1) 9–052
2000 Financial Services and Markets Act (c.8) 1–001, 1–003, 1–004, 1–005, 6–139, 12–001, 13–001, 13–002, 13–013, 13–014, 13–015, 13–016, 13–019, 13–022, 13–032, 13–041, 13–042, 15–010, 15–011, 15–018, 16–001, 16–003, 16–013, 16–016, 17–003, 18–001, 20–063, 20–086, 22–016, 23–009, 23–018, 23–021, 24–007
  Pt VII 13–040
  ss.2–6 13–004
  ss.7–11 13–004
  ss.15–18 13–005
  s.19 ..... 1–001, 5–036, 13–007, 13–018, 15–021, 15–023
  s.20 .... 1–001, 13–007, 13–009
  (2) 13–007, 13–020
  (a) 13–020
  (b) 13–020
  (c) 13–020
  (3) 13–007, 13–020
  s.21 .... 13–026, 15–021
  s.22 .... 4–008, 13–007
  s.23 .... 1–001, 13–007, 13–020
  s.25 13–026
  s.26 .... 1–001, 13–020, 13–025
  (1) 13–020
  (2) 13–020
  s.28 13–020
  (2) 13–020
  (3) 13–020
  (4) 13–020
  (5) 13–020
  (7) 13–020
  (9) 13–020
  s.31 13–025
  s.34 13–025
  s.38 13–007
  s.39 .... 13–007, 15–013, 15–018
  (3) 13–026

ss.40–54 13–021
s.41 13–021
ss.45 47 13–031
s.47 13–025
ss.56–58 .... 13–027, 13–031
ss.59–63 13–027
s.61 13–027
s.64 13–027
s.71 6–132
s.104 13–032
s.105(1)–(2) 13–032
   (4) 13–032
s.107 13–033
s.108 13–033
s.109 13–033
s.110 13–033
s.111 13–034
s.112 13–037
   (1)–(7) 13–036
   (2)(b) 13–037
   (2A)–(2C) 13–037
   (3)(d) 13–036
   (8) 13–036
s.112A 13–037
s.114 13–037
s.114A 13–037
s.116 13–037
s.132 13–005
ss.138–157 13–004
s.142 13–005
s.150 13–004
s.152 13–005
s.158 13–005
ss.165–177 13–030
s.169 13–025
ss.178–192 13–027
ss.193–202 13–025
s.205 13–031
ss.206–211 13–031
ss.207–211 13–031
s.212 16–018
s.213 16–017
   (3)–(6) 16–018
s.214 16–017
s.215 .... 16–013, 16–017, 16–029
   (3)–(4) 16–018
s.216 .... 16–017, 16–026
s.217 16–028
s.218 16–018
s.219 16–018
s.220 16–018
s.221 16–018
s.222 16–018
s.223 16–018
s.224 16–018
s.228(2) 12–002, 12–003
   (5) 12–010
   (6) 12–010
s.229(2)(a) 12–036
   (b) 12–041
   (3)(a) 12–036
   (b) 12–036
   (5) 12–036
   (8) 12–010

   (a) 12–042
   (b) 12–043
   (9) 12–043
s.230(3) 12–004
   (4) 12–004
s.231 12–011
s.232 12–011
s.316 13–040
s.318 13–040
s.323 13–040
s.324 .... 13–032, 13–040
s.334 13–043
s.335 13–043
s.338 13–043
ss.340–346 13–028
s.356 16–014
s.360 16–013
ss.363–364 16–015
s.365 16–003
s.366 16–003
s.367 .... 16–003, 16–015
s.368 16–004
s.369(1) 16–004
   (2) 16–004
s.370 16–004
s.371 16–004
s.376 16–007
   (2)–(3) 16–007
   (4)–(7) 16–007
   (8)–(9) 16–007
   (10)–(11) 16–007
s.377 16–006
s.378 16–012
s.380 13–031
s.382 13–031
s.397 ... 6–132, 13–026, 15–018, 18–010
ss.404–408 13–005
s.418 13–019
Sch.1 13–004
Sch.2, para.20 13–007
Sch.3, Pt II, para.16 13–025
Sch.6 21–016
Sch.12 13–034
Sch.13 13–005
Sch.17, para.16 .... 12–010, 12–043
Terrorism Act (c.11)—
s.1 ....25–014y8
Limited   Liability   Partnerships
     Act (c.12) 21–005
Insolvency Act (c.39)—
s.4(5) 16–014
Sch.1, para.2 16–014
Sch.2 16–014
2002 Commonhold and Leasehold Re-
         form Act (c.15) 19–019
s.164 19–017
Enterprise Act (c.40) ... 13–044, 16–010,
                           16–013, 16–015
s.251 16–010
s.252 16–010
s.359 16–013
ss.361–362A 16–013

2003 Health and Social Care (Community Health and Stan-
dards) Act (c.43) ... 22–062, 22–075
Pt 3 ... 20–016, 20–020, 20–021, 22–022
s.150(1) 20–017
(2) 20–017
(3) 20–017
(4) 20–017
(5)–(6) 20–017
(7) 20–017
(9) 20–018
(11) 20–017
(14) 20–017
s.151(1)–(3) 20–018
(4)–(6) 20–018
(7)–(8) 20–018
(9) 20–018
(10) 20–018
s.153(1)–(2), (4) 20–018
(3) 20–018
(11)–(12) 20–018
s.154(2) 20–018
(9)–(10) 20–018
s.155(1)–(2) 20–018
(7) 20–018
s.156(1) 20–019
(4) 20–019
(7) 20–019
s.157(1) 20–019
(2) 20–019
(3) 20–019
(4)–(5) 20–019
(6) 20–019
s.158(1) 20–019
(3) 20–019
(4) 20–019
(6) 20–019
s.159(1)–(3) 20–019
s.160(1), (2) 20–020
s.161 20–020
s.164(1)–(4) 20–017
s.169 20–016
Sch.10 20–017
Para.4 20–017
2004 Civil Partnership Act (c.33) 18–014
s.1 18–014
s.70 18–014
s.253 18–014
2005 Gambling Act (c.19) 4–001, 4–002,
4–007, 4–009, 4–010,
4–027, 19–001, 20–062
s.3 4–008
s.9 4–008
(b) 4–008
s.10 4–008
s.334 4–002
s.335 ..... 1–009, 4–008, 4–010, 19–001,
24–012
(1) 4–002, 4–008, 4–009, 4–010
(2) 4–002, 4–008, 4–009, 4–010
2006 Consumer Credit Act (c.14) 12–014
Compensation Act (c.29) 12–015
s.3 11–050
Fraud Act (c.35) 9–023

s.2 9–024
(1)–(5) 9–023
s.3 9–024
(1) 9–023
s.4 .... 9–023, 9–024
s.5 9–023
National Health Service Act
(c.41)—
s.18 20–065
s.25 20–065
National Health Service (Wales)
Act (c.42)—
s.18 20–065
Companies Act (c.46) ... 20–078, 20–086
ss.39, 40 .... 2–029, 14–001
s.170(3)–(4) 20–078
s.171 20–078
s.172 20–078
s.173 20–078
s.174 20–078
s.176 20–078
s.177 20–078
s.178 20–078
s.205 20–079
s.232(1) 20–079
(2) 20–079
(b), (c) 20–079
(3) 20–079
s.233 20–079
s.234 20–079
(1)–(6) 20–079
s.235 20–079
s.236 20–079
s.237 20–079
s.238 20–079
s.250 20–082
s.251 20–082
s.661 20–079
s.860 17–002
ss.895–901 16–005
s.896 .... 16–028, 21–013
(1) 16–005
s.899 21–044
s.1000 21–044
s.1001 21–044
s.1003 21–044
ss.1029–1031 21–014
s.1030 21–014
(2) 21–014
(4) 21–014
s.1031(3) 21–014
s.1139 2–003
s.1157 20–079
s.1173(1) 20–082
2010 Third Parties (Rights against Insurers) Act (c.10) ... 1–001, 2–014,
6–089, 9–043, 16–019,
20–008, 20–035, 20–072,
21–003, 21–041, 21–045,
21–055, 21–057, 21–064,
22–038, 23–016
s.1(1) 21–049
(2) 21–049, 21–062
(3) 21–049

(4) 21–049
(5) 21–045
s.2 .... 21–049, 21–051, 21–052
(1) 21–051
(2) 21–051
    (a) 21–051, 21–052, 21–054
    (b) 21–051, 21–053
(4) 21–052
(5) 21–052
(6) 21–051
(7) 21–054
(8) 21–051
(9) 21–053, 21–054
(10) 21–053
(11) 21–051
s.3 21–051
ss.4–7 21–042
s.4 21–063
(2), (3) 21–043
s.5(1)–(3) 21–043
s.6(1)–(2) 21–044
(1) 21–043
(3) 21–044
(4) 21–044
(6) 21–044
(9) 21–044
(10) 21–053
s.7 21–044
s.8 21–050
s.9 21–058
(1)–(4) 9–043
(2) 21–058
(3) 21–058
(4) 21–058
(5)–(6) 20–035, 21–059
s.10 21–060
s.11 21–065
s.12 21–052
s.13 21–047

s.14(1)–(3) 21–056
(6)(b) 21–056
(7) 21–056
s.15 21–045
s.16 .... 21–045, 23–017
s.17 21–063
s.18 21–046
s.21 21–003
Sch.1 21–065
    para.1(1) 21–066
    para.1(2) 21–067
    para.1(3) 21–066, 21–067
    para.1(4) 21–066
    para.1(4)(a) 21–066
    para.1(6) 21–066, 21–067
    para.2 21–067
    para.2(1) 21–068
    para.2(2) 21–068
    para.2(3) 21–066, 21–068
    para.2(4) 21–068
    para.3 .... 21–067, 21–069
    para.4 .... 21–067, 21–069
    para.5 21–065
    para.6 21–065
    para.7 21–068
Sch.3 21–003
Equality Act (c.15) 6–051
s.2 6–051
s.13 6–051
s.15 17–002
s.19 6–051
s.29 6–051
Sch.3, Pt 5 (paras 20–32) 6–051
    para.20 6–051
    para.21 6–051
    para.22(1), (3) 6–051
    para.23 6–051
2010 Bribery Act (c.23)
    s.2 15–007

TABLE OF STATUTORY INSTRUMENTS

1965 Rules of the Supreme Court (SI
    1965/1776)—
    Ord.29
    rr.9–11 22–063
    r.11 22–063
    Ord.72, r.10 6–107
1971 Motor Vehicles (International
    Motor Insurance Card)
    Regulations (SI
    1971/792) 22–083
1972 Motor Vehicles (Third Party
    Risks) Regulations (SI
    1972/1217) 22–04, 22–15
    reg.6 22–015
    reg.7 22–015
    reg.9(1)(a) 22–015
    reg.12(1) 22–015
    (2) 22–015
    (3) 22–015
    reg.13 22–015
1973 Motor Vehicles (Third Party
    Risks) Regulations (SI
    1972/1283) 22–015
    Motor Vehicles (Compulsory In-
    surance) (No.2) Regulations
    (SI 1973/2143) 22–001, 22–083
1983 Electrically Assisted Pedal Cycle
    Regulations (SI 1983/
    1168) 22–006
    Consumer Credit (Agreements)
    Regulations (SI 1983/
    1553) 22–024
1985 Insurance Companies (Winding-
    Up) Rules (SI 1985/95) 16–011
1986 Insolvency Rules (SI
    1986/1925) 16–002, 16–009
    r.4.91 16–009
    r.4.181 16–010
1987 Motor Vehicles (Compulsory In-
    surance) Regulations (SI
    1987/2171) 22–001
1989 Consumer Credit (Exempt
    Agreements) Order (SI
    1989/869) 22–025
1990 Insurance Companies (Legal Ex-
    penses) Regulations (SI
    1990/1159) 23–009
    reg.3 23–009
    reg.4 23–011
    reg.5 23–012
    reg.6 23–012
    reg.7 23–012
    reg.8 23–013
    reg.9 23–013

Insurance Companies (Legal Ex-
    penses Insurance) (Applica-
    tion for Authorisation) Reg-
    ulations (SI 1990/1160) 23–009
Insurance Companies (Amend-
    ment) Regulations (SI
    1990/1333)—
    reg.6 2–017
1992 Motor Vehicles (Third-Party
    Risk Deposit) Regulations
    (SI 1992/1284) 22–003, 22–004
Insurance Companies (Amend-
    ment) Regulations (SI
    1992/2890) 22–001
Motor Vehicles (Compulsory In-
    surance) Regulations (SI
    1992/3036) 22–001, 22–017
1993 Insurance Companies (Amend-
    ment) Regulations (SI
    1993/174)—
    reg.5 2–017
Road Traffic Accidents (Pay-
    ment for Treatment) Order
    (SI 1993/2474) 22–022
1994 Insurance Companies Regula-
    tions (SI 1994/1516) 23–009
Insurance Companies (Third In-
    surance Directives) Regula-
    tions (SI 1994/1696) 22–016
Unfair Terms in Consumer Con-
    tracts Regulations (SI
    1994/3159) 22–043
1995 Offshore Installations and Pipe-
    line Works (Management
    and Administration) Regu-
    lations (SI 1995/738)—
    reg.2 20–070
    reg.3 20–063
    reg.21 20–064
    (3) 20–066
Offshore Installations (Preven-
    tion of Fire and Explosion,
    and Emergency Response)
    Regulations (SI 1995/
    743) 20–063
1996 Disability Discrimination
    (Meaning of Disability)
    Regulations (SI 1996/
    1455) 18–029
1997 Insurance (Lloyd's) Regulations
    (SI 1997/686) 13–040
Social Security (Recovery of
    Benefits) Regulations (SI
    1997/2205) 20–021

Social Security (Recovery of
  Benefits) (Appeals) Regulations (SI 1997/2237) 20–021
1998 General Osteopathic Council
  (Professional Indemnity Insurance Rules) Order in
  Council (SI 1998/1329) 20–003
  Employers Liability (Compulsory Insurance) Regulations
  (SI 1998/2573) 5–049, 20–063,
                20–068, 20–071, 21–0040
  reg.1 20–066
  reg.2 20–068
  (2) 20–068
  reg.3(1) 20–067
  (a) 20–067
  (2) 20–067
  reg.4(2) 20–071
  (4) 20–072, 21–040
  (5) 20–072
  reg.5(2) 20–071
  reg.6 20–071
  reg.7 20–071
  reg.8 20–071
  reg.9 20–065
  reg.10 20–072
  Sch.1 20–071
  Sch.2 20–065
  para.14 22–018
1999 Road Traffic (NHS Charges)
  Regulations (SI 1999/
  785) 22–022
  Road Traffic (NHS Charges)
  (Reviews and Appeals)
  Regulations (SI 1999/
  786) 22–022
  Road Traffic (NHS Charges)
  (Commencement No.1)
  Order (SI 1999/1075) 22–022
  Unfair Terms in Consumer Contracts Regulations (SI
  1999/2083) 1–022, 3–018,
              5–007, 7–004, 7–053,
              8–020, 9–04, 9–33, 9–052,
              12–034
  reg.3(1) 3–018
  (2) 3–018
  (4) 3–018
  (5) 3–018
  reg.4(1) 3–018
  reg.6 3–018
  Sch.2 3–018
  para.(c) 3–018
  para.(d) 3–018
  para.(f) 3–018
  para.(i) 3–018
  para.(n) 3–018
1999 Unfair Arbitration Agreements
  (Specified Amount) Order
  (SI 1999/2167) 9–052
  Motor Vehicles (Third Party
  Risks) (Amendment) Reg-
  ulations (SI 1999/2392) 22–015

2000 Motor Vehicles (Compulsory Insurance) Regulations (SI
  2000/726) 22–008
  Limited Liability Partnership
  Regulations (SI
  2000/3316) 21–005
2001 Financial Services and Markets
  Act 2000 (Regulated Activities) Order (SI 2001/
  544) 1–001, 13–007, 15–010
  art.2 .... 13–008, 13–011
  art.3 1–001
  art.10 ... 1–001, 4–008, 13–007, 13–018
  (1), (2) 13–010
  art.11 .... 4–008, 13–007
  art.12 .... 13–007, 13–012
  art.56 13–041
  art.57 13–041
  art.58 4–008
  art.59 13–010
  art.60 13–010
  Sch.1 1–001
  Pt I 13–009
  Financial Services and Markets
  Act 2000 (Carrying on Reg-
  ulated Activities by Way of
  Business) Order (SI
  2001/1177) 13–018
  Financial Services and Markets
  Act 2000 (Exemption)
  Order (SI 2001/1201) 13–007
  Financial Services and Markets
  Act 2000 (Designated Pro-
  fessional Bodies) Order (SI
  2001/1226) 13–007
  Financial Services and Markets
  Act 2000 (Financial Promo-
  tion) Order (SI
  2001/1335) 13–026
  Financial Services and Markets
  Act 2000 (Rights of Action)
  Regulations (SI 2001/
  2256) 13–004, 13–020
  Motor Vehicles (Third Party
  Risks) (Amendment) Reg-
  ulations (SI 2001/2266) 22–015
  Financial Services and Markets
  Act 2000 (Meaning of
  "Policy" and "Policyhold-
  er") Order (SI 2001/
  2361)—
  art.2 16–020
  art.3 16–019
  Financial Services and Markets
  Act 2000 (EEA Passport
  Rights) Regulations (SI
  2001/2511) 13–023, 15–010
  Financial Services and Markets
  Act 2000 (Mutual Socie-
  ties) Order (SI 2001/
  2617) 13–043

Financial Services and Markets Act 2000 (Insolvency) (Definition of "Insurer") Order (SI 2001/2634) 16–001
Financial Services and Markets Act 2000 (Law Applicable to Contracts of Insurance) Regulations (SI 2001/2635) 2–017, 2–020, 2–046
reg.2(1) 2–048
reg.3(1) 2–020
  (1A) 2–019
reg.4 2–048
  (2) 2–048
  (3) 2–048
  (4) 2–048
  (6) 2–048
  (7) 2–016
  (8) 2–048
  (9) 2–048
reg.5 2–048
reg.6 2–023
reg.7 2–048
reg.8 (2) 2–048
  (3) 2–048
reg.9 2–048
Financial Services and Markets Act 2000 (Controllers) (Exemption) Order (SI 2001/2638) 13–043
Financial Services and Markets Act 2000 (Transitional Provisions, Repeals and Savings) Financial Services (Compensation Scheme) Order (SI 2001/2967) 16–017
Financial Services and Markets Act 2000 (Treatment of Assets of Insurers on Winding Up) Regulations (SI 2001/2968) 16–012
reg.3 16–012
reg.4 16–012
Financial Services and Markets (Control of Business Transfers) (Requirements on Applicants) Regulations (SI 2001/3625) 13–032, 13–033, 13–037
reg.4 13–033
Insurers (Winding-Up) Rules (SI 2001/3635) 16–07, 16–008, 16–011, 16–012
r.2 16–007
r.5 16–012
r.6 16–011
r.7 16–011
r.8 16–011
r.9 16–012
r.10 16–012
r.11 16–012
r.12 .... 16–007, 16–011, 16–012
r.13 16–012
r.16 16–007

r.17 16–007
r.18 16–007
r.20 16–009
r.21 16–007
r.23 16–007
r.24 16–012
r.25 16–007
r.26 16–012
Sch.1 16–011
  para.1 16–011
Sch.2 16–011
Sch.3 16–011
Sch.4 16–011
Sch.5 16–011
2002 Financial Services and Markets Act 2000 (Administration Orders Relating to Insurers) Order (SI 2002/1242) 16–013
art.5 16–013
Financial Services and Markets Act 2000 (Variation of Threshold Conditions) Order (SI 2002/2707) 13–021, 22–016, 22–080
European Communities (Rights against Insurers) Regulations (SI 2002/3061) 2–014, 21–002, 22–001, 22–038, 22–050, 22–056, 22–085
reg.2(1) 22–051, 22–052, 22–053, 22–054, 22–055
  (3) 22–053, 22–056
reg.3(1) 22–051
2003 Motor Vehicles (Compulsory Insurance) (Information Centre and Compensation Body) Regulations (SI 2003/37) 22–001, 22–081, 22–083, 22–085
reg.3 22–082
reg.4 22–082
reg.5 22–082
reg.6 22–082
reg.10 22–081
reg.11 22–081
reg.12 22–081
reg.13 22–081
  (2)(b) 22–081
reg.14 22–081
reg.15 22–081
Sch., Pt I 22–082
Pt II 22–082
Insurance Mediation Directive (Miscellaneous Amendments) Regulations (SI 2003/1473) 15–010
Markets Act 2000 (Regulated Activities) (Amendment No.2) Order (SI 2003/1476) 15–010

Financial Services and Markets
Act 2000 (Administration
Orders Relating to Insurers)
(Amendment) Order (SI
2003/2134) 16–013
2004 Insurers (Reorganisation and
Winding Up) Regulations
(SI 2004/353) 16–001, 16–010
Financial Services and Markets
Act 2000 (Transitional Pro-
visions, Repeals and Sav-
ings) (Financial Services
Compensation Scheme)
(Amendment) Order (SI
2004/952) 16–017
Financial Conglomerates and
Other Financial Groups
Regulations (SI 2004/
1862) 13–028
Financial Services and Markets
Tribunal Rules (SI
2004/2474) 13–005
Employers' Liability (Compul-
sory Insurance) (Amend-
ment) Regulations (SI
2004/2882) 20–065
Leasehold Houses (Notice of In-
surance Cover) (England)
Regulations (SI
2004/3097) 19–017
Contracts (Applicable Law) Act
1990 (Commencement No
2) Order (SI 2004/3448) 2–018
2005 Leasehold Houses (Notice of Insurance Cover) (England)
(Amendment) Regulations
(SI 2005/177) 19–017
Disclosure of Vehicle Information Regulations (SI
2005/2833) 22–081
Disability Discrimination (Service Providers and Public
Authorities Carrying Out
Functions) Regulations (SI
2005/2901) 18–029
2006 Transfer of Undertakings (Protection of Employment)
Regulations (SI 2006/
246) 20–073
Cross-Border Insolvency Regu-
lations (SI 2006/1030) 21–009
Compensation Act 2006 (Contribution for Mesothelioma
Claims) Regulations (SI
2006/3259) 11–050
Gambling Act 2005 (Com-
mencement No. 6 and Tran-
sitional Provisions) Order
(SI 2006/3272) 4–002
Personal Injuries (NHS Charges)
(General) and Road Traffic
(NHS Charges) (Amend-
ment) Regulations (SI
2006/3388) 20–016, 22–022

reg.2(1) 20–018
    (2) 20–018
    (3) 20–018
reg.3 20–018
reg.3A 20–018
reg.5 20–020
regs 6–8 20–019
reg.6 20–018
regs 7–10 20–019
reg.7 20–017
reg.8 20–019
reg.9 20–017
reg.10 20–017
Health and Social Care (Com-
munity Health and Stan-
dards) Act 2003 (Com-
mencement) (No. 11) Order
(SI 2006/3397) 20–016, 22–022
Personal Injuries (NHS Charges)
(Reviews and Appeals) and
Road Traffic (NHS
Charges) (Reviews and
Appeals) (Amendment)
Regulations (SI
2006/3398) 20–016, 22–022
reg.2 20–019
reg.3 20–019
reg.4 20–019
reg.5 20–019
2007 Personal Injuries (NHS Charges)
(Amounts) Regulations (SI
2007/115) 20–016
reg.5 20–019
Motor Vehicles (Compulsory
Insurance) Regulations (SI
2007/1426) 22–019, 22–042
Financial Services and Markets
Act 2000 (Motor Insurance)
Regulations (SI 2007/
2403) 22–001, 22–020
Motor Vehicles (Compulsory
Insurance) (Information
Centre and Compensation
Body) (Amendment) Reg-
ulations (SI 2007/2982) 22–081
Reinsurance Directive Regula-
tions (SI 2007/3253) 13–032
Financial Services and Markets
Act 2000 (Reinsurance Di-
rective) Regulations (SI
2007/3255) 13–032
2008 Personal Injuries (NHS Charges)
(Amounts) Amendment
Regulations (SI 2008/
252) 20–016
Consumer Protection from Un-
fair Trading Regulations (SI
2008/1277) 9–019
Financial Services and Markets
Act 2000 (Control of Busi-
ness Transfers) (Require-
ments on Applicants)
(Amendment) Regulations
(SI 2008/1467) 13–037

Financial Services and Markets
Act 2000 (Amendments
to Part 7) Regulations
(SI2008/1468) 13–037
Financial Services and Markets
Act 2000 (Amendment of
section 323) Regulations
(SI 2008/1469) 13–032, 13–040
Employers' Liability (Compul-
sory Insurance) (Amend-
ment) Regulations (SI
2008/1765) 20–071
Insurance Accounts Directive
(Lloyd's Syndicate and Ag-
gregate Accounts) Regula-
tions (SI 2008/1950) 13–040
Law Applicable to Non-Contrac-
tual Obligations (England
and Wales and Northern Ire-
land) Regulations (SI
2008/2986) 2–061, 2–065
Legislative Reform (Lloyd's)
Order (SI 2008/3001) 13–039
2009 Personal Injuries (NHS Charges)
Amendment Regulations
(SI 2009/316) 20–016
Personal Injuries (NHS Charges)
Amendment (No. 2) Reg-
ulations (SI 2009/834) 20–016

Law Applicable to Contractual
Obligations (England and
Wales and Northern Ire-
land) Regulations (SI 2009/
3064) 2–065
reg.2 2–019
reg.3 2–056
reg.5 2–019
Financial Services and Markets
Act 2000 (Law Applicable
to Contracts of Insurance)
Regulations (SI 2009/
3075)—
reg.2 2–019
reg.3 2–019
reg.4 2–047
reg.5 2–031
Civil Jurisdiction and Judgments
Regulations (SI 2009/
3131) 2–001
2010 Motor Vehicles (Third Party
Risks) (Amendment) Reg-
ulations (SI 2010/1115) 22–015
Motor Vehicles (Electronic
Communication of Certifi-
cates of Insurance) Order
(SI 2010/1117) 22–015

TABLE OF CIVIL PROCEDURES RULES

1998 Civil Procedure Rules (SI 1998/3132) 2–008, 21–046, 22–061, 22–069
r.3.10 2–004
Pt 6 .... 2–001, 2–003
r.6.3 2–003
r.6.5 2–003
r.6.7 .... 2–003, 2–004
r.6.12 2–003
r.6.24 2–004
    (2) 2–004
PD6A 2–003
PD6B 2–003, 2–004, 9–054, 21–047
    para.3.1(1)–(3) 2–004
    (3) 21–047
    (6)-(9) 2–004
    (6) 21–047
    (6)(c) 2–039
    para.18 20–056
r.7.2 20–038
    (1) 22–045
PD8B 22–001
r.18.1 .... 21–066, 23–040
    (1)(b) 21–040
Pt 19 .... 9–051, 21–030
r.19.1 21–030
r.19.4 .... 21–030, 21–062
    (2) 21–030
    (3) 21–030
r.19.6 2–004
Pt 23 .... 21–016, 21–049
Pt 25 .... 10–053, 15–049, 20–036
r.25.7(1) 22–063
    (a) 22–063 (2), 22–063
r.25.13 .... 9–053, 23–041
Pt 31 21–066
r.31.6 21–069
r.31.14 23–040
r.31.16 21–040
Pt 36 22–001
r.40.20 21–010
r.43.2(1)(m) 23–038
Pt 44 10–028
r.44.12A 23–035
r.44.15 23–040
PD44, para.19(4) 23–040
Pt 45 22–001
Pt 52 9–035
Pt 58, r.58.14 6–107
CPR Costs Direction—
s.11, para.10 23–038

TABLE OF EUROPEAN LEGISLATION

Directives

1964 Dir.64/225 Council Directive on the abolition of restrictions on freedom of establishment and freedom to provide services in respect of reinsurance and retrocession [1963–1964] O.J. 131 17–003

1972 Dir.72/166 First Motor Insurance Directive [1972] O.J. L103/1 ... 22–001, 22–008, 22–036, 22–083

art.1 22–020

art.3 22–020

Dir.72/430 Council Directive amending Council Directive 72/166 [1972] O.J. L291/162 22–001

1973 Dir.73/239 First Non-Life Directive [1973] O.J. L228/3 .... 13–003, 13–008, 13–042

art.5(d) 2–023

1977 Dir.77/187 Acquired Rights Directive 20–073

1978 Dir.78/343 Community co-insurance Directive 2–031

Dir.78/473 Co-Insurance Directive [1978] O.J. L151/25 ... 13–003

1979 Dir.79/267 First Life Directive [1979] O.J. L63/1 .... 13–003, 13–008

art.1(2)(e) 13–010

(3) 13–010

1985 Dir.84/5 Second Motor Insurance Directive [1984] O.J. L8/17 .... 22–001, 22–005, 22–041, 22–073, 22–077

art.1(4) 22–067

art.2 22–041

1988 Dir.88/357 Second Non-Life Directive [1988] O.J. L172/1 ...... 2–017, 2–020, 13–003, 22–001

art.2(d) 2–022

1987 Dir.87/344 Legal Expenses Insurance Directive 23–009

1990 Dir.90/232 Third Motor Insurance Directive [1990] O.J. L12/33 .... 22–001, 22–017

art.1 .... 22–017, 22–031

art.2 .... 22–008, 22–018, 22–020

Dir.90/619 Second Life Directive [1990]O.J. L330/50 ..... 2–017, 13–003

1991 Dir.91/674 on the annual accounts and consolidated accounts of insurance undertakings [1991] O.J. L374/7 13–028

1992 Dir.92/49 Third Non-Life Insurance Directive [1992] O.J. L228/1 13–003

Dir.92/96 Third Life Insurance Directive [1992] O.J. L360/1 .... 13–003, 22–016

1993 Dir.93/113 Council Directive concerning the use and marketing of enzymes, microorganisms and their preparations in animal nutrition [1993] O.J L95/29 3–019

1998 Dir.98/18 Council Directive on safety rules and standards for passenger ships 20–005

Dir.98/29 on the harmonisation of the law relating to the provision of export credit insurance 23–032

2000 Dir.2000/26 Fourth Motor Insurance Directive [2000] O.J. L181/65 .... 22–001, 22–016, 22–049, 22–080, 22–085

Dir.2000/31 E-Commerce Directive 13–026

2001 Dir.2001/17 Directive of the European Parliament and of the Council of on the reorganisation and winding-up of insurance undertakings [2001] O.J. L110/28 ... 16–001, 16–010, 16–013

2002 Dir.2002/65 Directive of the European Parliament and of the Council of concerning the distance marketing of consumer financial services 13–026

Dir.2002/78 Commission Directive adapting to technical progress [2002] O.J. L34/17 13–028

Dir.2002/ Directive 2002/83/EC of the European Parliament and of the Council concerning life assurance [2002] O.J. 345/1 13–003

art.(1) 2–022

Dir.2002/92 Mediation Directive [2003] O.J. L9/3 ... 13–003, 15–010

2003 Dir.2003/51 Modernisation
     Directive 13–040
2005 Dir.2005/14 Fifth Motor Insur-
     ance Directive [2005] O.J.
     L149/14 .... 2–014, 2–022, 22–001,
                 22–005, 22–017, 22–019,
                 22–020, 22–074, 22–083
     Dir.2005/29 Directive of the Eu-
     ropean Parliament and of
     the Council concerning
     unfair business-consumer
     commercial practices in the
     internal markets [2005] O.J.
     L149/22 9–019
     Dir.2005/68 Reinsurance Direc-
     tive [2005] O.J. L323/1 13–032,
                                    17–003
2006 Dir.2006/46 European Parlia-
     ment and Council
     Directive 13–028
2007 Dir.2007/44 European Parlia-
     ment and Council
     Directive 13–003, 13–032
     Dir.2007/64 Payment Services
     Directive 12–016
2008 Dir.2008/19 European Parlia-
     ment and Council
     Directive 13–003
     Dir.2008/36 European Parlia-
     ment and Council
     Directive 13–003
     Dir.2008/37 European Parlia-
     ment and Council
     Directive 13–003
2009 Dir.2009/20 First European and
     Council Directive 20–004
     Dir.2009/103 Consolidated
     Motor Insurance Direc-
     tive 22–001, 22–003, 22–020,
                22–024, 22–049, 22–059,
                22–077, 22–080, 22–085
     art.1(1) 22–055
       (4) 22–020
     art.3 .... 22–021, 22–084
       (1) 22–020
     art.4 22–083
     art.7 22–084
     art.8 .... 22–049, 22–084
     art.9 .... 22–017, 22–019
     art.10 .... 22–059, 22–073
       (2) 22–067
       (3) 22–074
     art.11 22–072
     art.12(1) 22–017, 22–018, 22–031,
                                          22–032
       (3) 22–017
     art.13 22–036
       (1) 22–039, 22–041
       (2)–(3) 22–041
       (3) 22–035
     art.14 22–020
       (1) 22–008
     art.15 22–020
     art.16 .... 22–005, 22–018

art.17 22–042
art.21 .... 22–016, 22–080
art.22 .... 22–081, 22–084
art.23 22–080
art.26 22–082
Dir.2009/138 Solvency II
     Directive 13–003, 13–032,
                           16–001, 17–003

Regulations

1991 Reg.1534/91 Council Regulation
     on the application of Article
     85 (3) of the Treaty to cer-
     tain categories of agree-
     ments, decisions and con-
     certed practices in the
     insurance sector [1991] O.J.
     L143/1 13–046
1992 Reg.3932/92 Commission Reg-
     ulation on the application of
     Article 85 (3) of the Treaty
     to certain categories of
     agreements, decisions and
     concerted practices in the
     insurance sector [1992] O.J.
     L398/7 13–046
2001 Reg.44/2001 Council Regulation
     on jurisdiction and the rec-
     ognition and enforcement
     of judgments in civil and
     commercial matters (Brus-
     sels Regulation) [2001] O.J.
     L12/1 .... 2–001, 2–014, 2–048,
                   9–054, 20–056, 21–046
art.1(3) 2–008
art.2 2–008
art.5 2–008
  (1) 2–008
  (5) 2–010, 2–011
art.6 .... 2–008, 2–010
  (1) 2–008
arts 8–14 .... 2–009, 2–010
art.8 .... 2–011, 2–014
art.9 .... 2–011, 2–014, 21–047
  (1)(b) 2–014, 22–085
art.10 .... 2–012, 2–013, 2–014
art.11 21–047
  (1) 2–013, 22–085
  (2) 2–014, 21–047, 22–085
  (3) 2–010, 2–014, 22–085
art.12(1) 2–009
  (2) 2–010
art.13 2–015
art.14 .... 2–013, 2–015
art.23 2–008
art.27 2–008
art.28 2–008
art.30 2–008
art.60 2–001

2004 Reg.139/2004 Council Regulation on the control of concentrations between undertakings (the EC Merger Regulation) [2004] O.J. L24/1 13–045

2005 Reg.358/2005 concerning the authorisations without a time limit of certain additives and the authorisation of new uses of additives already authorised in feedingstuffs [2005] OJ L57/3 13–046

2007 Reg.864/2007 Council regulation on the law applicable to non-contractual obligations (the Rome II Regulation) ... 2–061, 2–065, 22–081
    art.2 2–065
    art.3 2–065
    art.4(1)–(3) 2–065
        (1) 22–081
        (3) 22–081
    art.5 2–065
    art.6 2–065
    art.7 2–065
    art.8 2–065
    art.9 2–065
    arts 10–12 2–065
    art.13 2–065
    art.14 .... 2–065, 14–030
        (2) 14–030
    art.15 2–065
    art.16 2–065
    art.18 2–065
    art.19 2–065
    art.20 2–065
    art.23 2–065
    art.24 2–065
    art.26 2–065
    arts 27, 28 2–065
    art.31 2–065

2008 Reg.593/2008 Council Regulation on the law applicable to contractual obligations (the Rome I Regulation) 2–008, 2–017, 2–019, 2–022, 2–023, 2–029, 2–030, 2–033, 2–034, 2–038, 2–040, 2–042, 2–048, 2–052, 21–046, 21–048
    Recital 12 2–037
    Recital 13 2–028

    arts 3, 4 .... 2–021, 2–023, 2–045
    art.3(1) 2–030, 2–036
        (2) 2–033
        (5) 2–029
    art.4 2–042
        (1) 2–044
    art.6 .... 2–021, 2–023, 2–045, 2–048
        (1) 2–045
        (2) 2–045
        (3) 2–045
        (4) 2–045
    art.7 .... 2–023, 2–048
        (1) 2–021
        (3) 2–047
        (4) 2–047
        (5) 2–022, 2–047
        (6) 2–023
    art.9(2) 2–057
        (3) 2–058
    art.10 2–051
        (1) 2–029, 2–053
        (2) 2–029, 2–053
    art.11 .... 2–029, 2–054
        (1) 2–054
        (4) 2–054
    art.12 2–050
        (1) 2–050
        (d) 2–056
        (2) 2–050
    art.13 2–029
    art.14 14–030
        (1) 14–030
    art.15 11–011
    art.20 .... 2–049, 2–050
    art.22 2–019
    art.25 2–019

2009 Reg.392/2009 on the liability of carriers of passengers by sea of April 23, 2009 20–005

2010 Reg.267/2010 on the application of Article 101(3) of the Treaty on the Functioning of the European Union to certain categories of agreements, decisions and concerted practices in the insurance sector [2010] OJ L83/1 13–046
    art.2 13–046
        (a), (b) 13–046
    art.3 13–046
    art.5 13–046
    art.6 13–046
    art.7 13–046

TABLE OF CONVENTIONS AND TREATIES

1950 European Convention on Human
    Rights 12–009
1956 Convention on the Contract for
    the International Carnage of
    Goods by Road (CMR) 5–010
    art.1(1) 5–010
1957 Treaty on the Functioning of the
    European Union (Cmnd.
    4864) 13–003, 13–045
    art.101 13–045
    (1) 13–045, 13–046
    (3) 13–046
    art.102 13–045
    art.234 .... 2–018, 22–059
1968 European Community Conven-
    tion on Jurisdiction and En-
    forcement of Judgments in
    Civil and Commercial
    Matters—Brussels
    Convention 2–001
1969 International Convention on
    Civil Liability for Oil Pollu-
    tion Damage—
    art.VII 20–004
1974 Athens Convention relating to
    the Carriage of Passengers
    and their Luggage by Sea as
    amended by the Protocol of
    2002 20–005
    York Antwerp Rules, revised
    1994 and 2004 24–0100
1980 Rome Convention on the Law
    Applicable to Contractual
    Obligations 2–018, 2–019,
                    2–020, 2–029, 2–038,
                    2–040, 2–052
    art.1(1), (2) 2–021
    art.3 .... 2–018, 2–021, 2–022, 2–024,
                    2–027, 2–041
    (1) 2–028

    (3) 2–030
    (4) 2–029, 2–030
    art.4 .... 2–021, 2–022, 2–024, 2–027,
                    2–041, 2–043
    (1) 2–041, 2–042, 2–044
    (b) 2–042
    (2) 2–041, 2–042, 2–043
    (3) 2–041, 2–042, 2–043
    (4) 2–041, 2–042
    (5) 2–041, 2–043
    art.5 .... 2–021, 2–045
    art.6 .... 2–021, 2–022, 2–024
    (1) 2–024
    art.7 2–021
    (1) 2–024, 2–030
    (2) 2–030
    art.8 2–021
    (1) 2–029, 2–051
    (2) 2–029, 2–053
    art.9 .... 2–029, 2–054
    (2), (3) 2–030
    art.10 .... 2–050, 2–051
    (1), (2) 2–029
    art.11 2–029
    art.12 .... 2–060, 14–030
    (1) 14–030
    art.13 .... 2–060, 11–011
    art.14 2–050
    (1), (2) 2–060
    art.15 .... 2–049, 2–060
    art.16 .... 2–057, 2–060
    art.17 2–060
    art.18 2–018
    art.21 2–030
1989 Lugano Convention 9–054
2007 Nairobi International Conven-
    tion on the Removal of
    Wrecks 20–005
2009 Lisbon Treaty 13–045
    Lugano Convention 9–054

PART I:
THE CONTRACT
OF
INSURANCE

CHAPTER 1

THE CONTRACT OF INSURANCE

1. THE DEFINITION OF INSURANCE

Need for a general definition. In the early days of the development of the law **1–001** of insurance it was occasionally found that insurers who had taken premiums from assureds would either disappear or prove financially unable to meet legitimate claims against them. Consequently, since 1870 the conduct of insurance business in the United Kingdom has been regulated by statute. At first the regulation took the form of requiring those wishing to act as insurers to deposit a fixed sum of money with the Secretary of State in earnest of their good faith and financial probity,[1] but in later years governments have taken wider powers to control the activities of insurers,[2] most recently to comply with the harmonisation requirements of the EU single market for insurance. The current governing legislation is the Financial Services and Markets Act 2000, which regulates all forms of insurance business consisting of "effecting and carrying out contracts of insurance",[3] a term which is extensively but not exhaustively defined in the Financial Services and Markets Act 2000 (Regulated Activities) Order 2001,[4] the predecessors of which the courts have been called upon to construe on a number of occasions. The main significance of the definition of insurance business in the context of the 2000 Act concerns authorisation, for a person who carries on a regulated activity in the form of insurance business without the authorisation of the Financial Services Authority faces criminal penalties[5] and the further possibility of being unable to enforce contracts entered into without the necessary authorisation.[6] The 2000 Act further regulates all aspects of the conduct of insurance business.[7]

The law relating to contracts of insurance is part of the general law of contract.[8] It rarely occurs, in cases determinable on common law principles, that any question as to the exact meaning of insurance is really material, for, other than the doctrine of utmost good faith which applies only to insurance contracts,[9] the law of insurance has few significant principles of its own. The other

[1] Life Assurance Companies Act 1870; Assurance Companies Act 1909.

[2] Companies Act 1967; Insurance Companies Act 1974; Insurance Companies Act 1981; Insurance Companies Act 1982, which consolidated earlier legislation.

[3] Financial Services and Markets Act 2000 (Regulated Activities) Order 2001, SI 2001/544 art.10.

[4] Financial Services and Markets Act (Regulated Activities) Order 2001 art.3 and Sch.1.

[5] Financial Services and Markets Act 2000 ss.19 and 23.

[6] Financial Services and Markets Act 2000 ss.20 and 26.

[7] See Ch.14, below.

[8] *Cehave v Bremer* [1976] Q.B. 44 at 71. See also *Friends Provident Life and Pensions Ltd v Sirius International Insurance Corp* [2006] Lloyd's Rep. I.R. 45.

[9] See Ch.6, below. No such duty applies outside the insurance context: *Bell v Lever Brothers Ltd* [1932] A.C. 161; *Pryke v Gibbs Hartley Cooper* [1991] 1 Lloyd's Rep. 602; *GMA v Unistorebrand International Insurance AS* [1995] L.R.L.R 333.

important differences between insurance contracts and the general run of contracts are the status of warranties and the principle of indemnity. Statutes under which the meaning of "insurance" might arise are the Unfair Contract Terms Act 1977, which imposes general controls over contractual exclusion clauses[10] but excludes from its ambit contracts of insurance, and the Third Parties (Rights against Insurers) Act 2010, which transfers the benefits and burdens of a contract of insurance against liability to the claimant victim of an insolvent assured.

1–002   **The meaning of "insurance".** Insurance has been defined in broad terms as "an agreement to confer upon the insured a contractual right which, prima facie, comes into existence immediately when loss is suffered by the happening of an event insured against, to be put by the insurer into the same position in which the insured would have been had the event not occurred, but in no better position."[11] In *Prudential Insurance v IRC*,[12] a case which concerned stamp duty and in which the court was required to determine whether a particular contract amounted to "a policy of insurance depending on a life".[13] Channell J. said that insurance was a contract which bore a number of characteristics:

> "When you insure a ship or a house you cannot insure that the ship shall not be lost or the house burnt, but what you do insure is that a sum of money shall be paid upon the happening of a certain event. That I think is the first requirement in a contract of insurance. It must be a contact whereby for some consideration, usually but not necessarily in periodical payments called premiums, you secure to yourself some benefit, usually but not necessarily the payment of a sum of money, upon the happening of some event. Then the next thing that is necessary is that the event should be one which involves some amount of uncertainty. There must be either uncertainty whether the event will ever happen or not, or if the event is one which must happen at some time there must be uncertainty as to the time at which it will happen. The remaining essential is . . . that the insurance must be against something. A contract which would otherwise be a mere wager may become an insurance by reason of the assured having an interest in the subject matter—that is to say, the uncertain event which is necessary to make the contract amount to an insurance must be an event which is prima facie adverse to the interest of the assured."

As this definition was set out for the purposes of identifying insurance business for statutory purposes, it may be that its terms refer to the practical indicia of insurance as well as to the substantive matters which go to make an insurance contract.

In practice the most difficult issues arise in distinguishing insurance from various other forms of financial product which operate to similar effect. Detailed guidance is provided by the FSA Handbook.[14]

1–003   *Premium as assessment of risk.* Most forms of insurance entail money payments by the assured to the insurer.[15] In *Prudential Insurance* Channell J. referred to the payment by the assured "of some consideration, usually but not necessarily . . .

---

[10] Unfair Contract Terms Act 1977 ss.2, 3 and 4.

[11] *Callaghan v Dominion Insurance Co* [1997] 2 Lloyd's Rep. 541, per Sir Peter Webster.

[12] *Prudential Insurance v IRC* [1904] 2 K.B. 658.

[13] Stamp Act 1891 s.98.

[14] The link is *http://fsahandbook.info/FSA/html/handbook/PERG/6* [Accessed June 16, 2010].

[15] But not always: "after the event" policies used for the funding of litigation only require payment of a premium if the assured is successful in the litigation and the premium is recoverable by way of costs from the other defendant.

periodical payments called premiums". However, there is no mention of this requirement in the 2000 Act.[16] In the ordinary insurance case the assumption that the assured will pay periodic sums described as premiums will be justified. However, the underlying purpose of regulatory legislation—to prevent insurance insolvencies—demands that the statutory controls cannot be sidestepped by attaching some label other than "premium" to the payments made by the assured. The reference to "periodical payments" was presumably intended to refer to the fact that a premium is paid for a period of cover[17]: by their nature, premiums are indivisible for the relevant period, and although they may be paid in instalments this is normally under some form of credit arrangement.

Where apportionable money payments are made, they will not always be referred to as premiums: in the case of mutual insurance, consideration for the insurer's obligations takes the form of "calls" by the mutual insurer on its members to ensure that there are sufficient funds available to meet losses in any one period.[18]

Difficulty has been encountered where insurance forms a part of some wider arrangement, so that sums payable by the assured have been in consideration of a non-insurance benefit with insurance being provided incidentally and free. There is conflicting authority on whether an apportionment of an amount representing premium has to be paid in order to give rise to insurance,[19] although the modern view would doubtless be that in the world of commerce there is no such thing as a free gift, and that some part of the assured's payment would be subjected to a notional apportionment as consideration for insurance benefits.[20]

Assuming that a premium is payable, one of the fundamental indicia of insurance is that the premium is calculated by reference to the risk. If the sum payable by the policyholder is not linked to actuarial or risk considerations, that fact may of itself indicate that the contract is not one of insurance, although if there is sufficient link between risk and premium then a finding of insurance may be made, as in *Fuji Finance v Aetna Insurance*,[21] where a policy was held to be one of life insurance even though the assured was entitled during the currency of the policy to switch the investments paid for by his lump sum premium of £50,000 and was entitled to the same benefits either on voluntary surrender or on death. By contrast, the sale of an insurance business from one insurer to another is not itself a contract of insurance, as the purchase price cannot be regarded as a "premium" in the sense in which that word is generally understood.[22]

The need for a policy document. There is no general requirement under the 2000 **1–004** Act for insurers to issue a policy document, although earlier legislation referred specifically to "the carrying on of insurance *under policies of insurance*"[23] and it was held in cases decided under that legislation that a contract not contained

---

[16] However, in the extended definition of "insurance business" drawn up for the purposes of the Financial Services and Markets Act 2000, various forms of contract analogous to insurance, e.g. fidelity bonds, performance bonds and other financing or security instruments, are treated as insurance contracts if one or more premiums are paid.

[17] The duration of which may be in dispute: see *R. v Personal Invstment Authority Ombudsman Bureau Ex p. Royal & Sun Alliance Life & Pensions Ltd* [2001] Lloyd's Rep. I.R. 41.

[18] Section 85(2) of the Marine Insurance Act 1906 recognises that mutual insurance does not fit the accepted pattern in this regard.

[19] *Nelson v Board of Trade* (1901) 84 L.T. 565 (insurance); *Hampton v Toxteth Co-operative Society* [1915] 1 Ch. 721 (not insurance).

[20] Cf. *Attorney-General v Imperial Tobacco* [1980] 1 All E.R. 866.

[21] *Fuji Finance v Aetna Insurance* [1996] 4 All E.R. 608.

[22] Cf. *GMA v Unistorebrand* [1995] L.R.L.R. 333.

[23] Assurance Companies Act 1909 s.30.

in a policy was not a contract of insurance.[24] Having regard to the evident aim of the legislation to control the activities of those carrying on what is in essence insurance, it is clear that under the present law the absence of a policy does not establish that insurance business is not being carried on,[25] though clearly the existence of a policy will almost inevitably lead to a finding that insurance business is being carried on.

1–005 *The need for a profit motive.* There is early authority for the proposition that a non-profit-seeking society which provides benefits for its members does not carry on insurance business,[26] although this can scarcely represent the law. The purpose of regulatory legislation is to control those who for the purposes of insurance take the policyholder's money at the inception of the contract, so leaving the policyholder to rely on their financial probity in paying out should a loss occur. Today the activities of friendly societies are regulated by the provisions of the Friendly Societies Acts 1974 and 1992, as modified by the Financial Services and Markets Act 2000, so that the precise point could not now arise in quite the same way. It might be noted that the Financial Services Authority's Handbook issued under the authority of the Financial Services and Markets Act 2000 requires insurance companies to prepare a profit and loss account in respect of each year of trading, and go on to substitute a requirement for an income and expenditure account in the case of a company not trading for profit. From this it is apparent that the draftsman contemplated that such a company falls within the statutory controls.

1–006 *Money or corresponding benefit.* The usual form of consideration to be provided by an insurer is money, although property policies may well confer upon the insurer an option to reinstate or replace damaged or lost property: the latter is probably what Channell J. had in mind in *Prudential Assurance* when referring to "some benefit, usually but not necessarily the payment of a sum of money." Other forms of consideration will, however, suffice, and it has been held that the provision of a chauffeur for a disqualified driver,[27] a hire car for a driver whose own car is undergoing repair following an accident[28] and a television set pending repairs to the owner's own set,[29] are insurance benefits forming part of an insurance business in that no proper distinction could be drawn between cash benefits and the provision of money's worth. It has nevertheless been doubted whether a contract which provided defence services for claims made against the beneficiary is one of insurance,[30] although this is arguably an unduly restrictive approach and it should suffice that some form of benefit is conferred.

1–007 *The insurer's obligation.* A contract of insurance taken at its narrowest is one under which the insurer is under some obligation to provide indemnity to the

---

[24] *Hampton v Toxteth Co-operative Society* [1915] 1 Ch. 721; *Hall D'Ath v British Provident Association* (1932) 48 T.L.R. 240.

[25] At one time policies were not always issued in respect of London Market placements, and the Marine Insurance Act 1906 s.22, recognises that a contract of insurance is perfectly valid even though no policy has been issued, although there may be enforcement difficulties in such a case. Since 2001 it has become market practice for policies to be issued in all cases.

[26] *Hall D'Ath v British Provident Association* (1932) 48 T.L.R. 240 (medical expenses).

[27] *Department of Trade and Industry v St Christopher's Motorists Association* [1974] 1 All E.R. 395.

[28] *Everson v Flurry* [1999] 8 C.L. para.406.

[29] *Re Sentinel Securities* [1996] 1 W.L.R. 316.

[30] *Medical Defence Union v Department of Trade* [1979] 2 All E.R. 421.

assured. There is authority for the proposition that there is no insurance where the benefit contemplated by the contract lies in the discretion of the insurer, e.g. where a friendly society has the right to discontinue its insurance fund[31] and where a society whose benefits included the provision of a defence for members facing claims was not required to fund a defence but merely to give full and fair consideration to the question of whether it should do so[32]:

> "One is in a different world from the world of insurance when the only contractual right is a right to have a claim fairly considered . . when a person insures I think that he is contracting for the certainty of proper consideration being given to his claim . . . ".[33]

This reasoning has little to recommend it, particularly where the member genuinely believes that his claim will be accepted and has not insured elsewhere accordingly, and more recently it has been held that benefits which are subject to an objective precondition—as opposed to a subjective discretion—are insurance benefits.[34]

Uncertain event. The sums must be payable on the occurrence of an event which **1–008** is uncertain in terms either of if it will happen (indemnity insurance) or when it will happen (life insurance). If the assured can control the event, there is no insurance, although this statement requires modification in the case of endowment insurance which pays out either on the death of the assured or on the happening of an earlier event, i.e. the expiry of a given period of time, or, once the policy has run for a sufficiently lengthy period, the decision of the assured to surrender the policy for its accrued surrender value. The existence of the right to surrender does not convert the contract from one of insurance into something else, even in the exceptional contractual situation when the surrender value becomes equal to the amount payable under the policy in the event of death, as death remains the basis of the contract and it is irrelevant that the predominant purpose of the policy was investment[35] and that other events could trigger payment.[36]

The need for an uncertain event precludes the possibility of insurance being placed after a loss has, to the knowledge of the assured, occurred. On this basis a declaration to a non-obligatory open cover cannot validly be made after the assured has become aware of a loss to the subject matter.[37]

Loss and indemnity. *Prudential Insurance* was a life assurance case in which the **1–009** assured was to receive a certain sum if he lived to the age of 65. Channell J. nevertheless regarded loss as an essential element of insurance and was of the view that the assured would indeed suffer a loss by reaching 65, in that he would, by that age, be less able to provide for himself by earning his own living. This artificial analysis was rejected by the Court of Appeal in *Gould v Curtis*,[38] where

---

[31] *Hampton v Toxteth Co-operative Society* [1915] 1 Ch. 721.

[32] *Medical Defence Union v Department of Trade* [1979] 2 All E.R. 421.

[33] *Medical Defence Union v Department of Trade* [1979] 2 All E.R. 421, per Megarry V-C.

[34] *Everson v Flurry* [1999] 8 C.L. para.406 (provision of temporary vehicle as long as the accident was not the fault of the assured and the assured's own vehicle was, immediately prior to the accident, roadworthy).

[35] *Fuji Finance Ltd v Aetna Insurance Co Ltd* [1996] 4 All E.R. 608, where the full sum became payable after five years.

[36] Cf. *Joseph v Law Integrity Insurance Co* [1912] 2 Ch. 581; *Re National Standard Life Assurance Corp* [1918] 1 Ch. 427.

[37] *Glencore International AG v Alpina Insurance Co Ltd* [2004] 1 Lloyd's Rep. 111.

[38] *Gould v Curtis* [1913] 3 K.B. 84.

Buckley L.J. drew a distinction between contingency and indemnity insurance.[39] In the former class, contingency insurance loss is not required, and instead the contract is to be construed simply as an agreement to pay a specified sum of money on the happening of a particular event, whether or not that event is adverse to the assured. Life and, usually, accident insurance is of this nature,[40] but there are other cases, as where in a liability policy the insurer agrees to pay any claim (though it may be a bad one) unless leading counsel advises that it can be successfully contested.[41] The second class, indemnity insurance, encompasses all forms of policies on property, profits and, in the marine context, adventures, and loss forms an essential element of indemnity insurance so that the assured's recovery is quantified by reference to the amount of his loss.

The assured will not, however, always receive a perfect indemnity. There is nothing to prevent the parties agreeing in the policy on the value of the thing insured.[42] If they do so, the valuation is conclusive[43] unless it is so gross as to be fraudulent[44] and the assured will be entitled to recover the agreed value in the event of a total loss or, if the loss is partial, a proportion (the depreciation in its actual value) of the agreed value.[45] There is nothing illegal about a valued policy,[46] and despite dicta in *Castellain v Preston*[47] it is clear that a contract of insurance that gives the assured more than an indemnity may be enforceable, provided it is not invalid on other grounds.[48] Rates of premium are generally computed in proportion to the sum insured. Insurers therefore generally accept the assured's valuation for the purpose of fixing the sum insured. By over-insurance they will earn a higher premium, and yet remain liable for the actual loss only. They are more likely, in fact, to object to under-insurance, on the ground that in the event of a partial loss, and subject to any average conditions, they may be liable to the full extent of the loss notwithstanding the lowness of the premium in proportion to the value of the thing insured. A contract is prima facie one of pure indemnity, but it may be framed otherwise,[49] and whether or not a policy is intended to be a valued policy is mainly a matter of construing the policy itself.[50] Convenience alone is a sufficient reason why valued policies should be allowed by law.[51] The contract contained in them has been described

[39] *Gould v Curtis* [1913] 3 K.B. 84 at 95.

[40] See also *Feasey v Sun Life Assurance Co of Canada* [2003] Lloyd's Rep. I.R. 637.

[41] Devlin J. in *West Wake Price v Ching* [1957] 1 W.L.R. 45 at 51.

[42] See s.27 of the Marine Insurance Act 1906, which codifies the principles in the text.

[43] *Bruce v Jones* (1863) 1 H. & C. 769; *Barker v Janson* (1868) L.R. 3 C.P. 303; *Herring v Janson* (1895) 1 Com. Cas. 177; *Muirhead v Forth & North Sea Steamboat Insurance* [1894] 2 A.C. 72.

[44] In which case the policy may be avoided for breach of the duty of utmost good faith: see Ch.6, below.

[45] *Elcock v Thomson* [1949] 2 K.B. 755.

[46] At one time a gross overvaluation would have led to the contract being struck down as a wager, but that possibility has been removed by s.335 of the Gambling Act 2005. See, for the earlier position: *Lewis v Rucker* (1761) 2 Burr. 1167; *Irving v Manning* (1847) 1 H.L.C. 287 at 308; *City Tailors v Evans* (1922) 38 T.L.R. 230. In *Glafki Shipping v Pinios Shipping (The Maria) (No.2)* [1984] 1 Lloyd's Rep. 660 Hobhouse J. held that the proper construction of the Marine Insurance Act 1906 s.4 was that a marine policy made on interest could not become a wager merely because of over-valuation of the subject-matter.

[47] *Castellain v Preston* (1883) 11 QBD 380.

[48] *Irving v Manning*, above, per Patteson J. at 307.

[49] *City Tailors v Evans* (1922) 38 T.L.R. 230 at 234.

[50] *Wilson v Nelson* (1864) 33 L.J.Q.B. 220; *Blascheck v Bussell* (1916) 33 T.L.R. 74; *Brunton v Marshall* (1922) 10 Ll. L.R. 689; *Kyzuna Investments Ltd v Ocean Marine Mutual Insurance Association (Europe)* [2000]1 Lloyd's Rep. 505; *Quorum AS v Schramm (No.1)* [2002] Lloyd's Rep. I.R. 292; *Quorum AS v Schramm (No.1)* [2002] Lloyd's Rep. I.R. 292; *Thor Navigation Inc v Ingosstrak Insurance* [2005] 1 Lloyd's Rep. 547.

[51] *Barker v Janson* (1868) L.R. 3 C.P. 303.

as "not an ideal contract of indemnity, but of indemnity according to the conventional terms of the bargain."[52] Valued policies, though common in the case of insurance on ships and profits, are rare in the case of goods and buildings on land, other than in respect of unique items, such as works of art.[53]

If the policy is not valued, it will specify a maximum sum recoverable—the sum insured—and where the value of the thing lost exceeds that sum, then the insurers are only bound to pay the value of the thing lost even though that is less than the sum insured. Here the principle of indemnity comes into operation to limit their liability to the loss actually suffered by the assured, for their undertaking is to pay that loss only. The words "Sum insured" have been held to mean no more than a cap on the limit of indemnity, and do not convert a policy into a valued policy even if the subject matter would normally be insured under a valued policy.[54]

Transfer of risk. Although this point is not developed in the *Prudential* **1–010** *Assurance* definition, it is clear that one of the determining factors is whether a risk is being transferred by the assured to the insurer. If no risk is transferred, then there can be no insurance. Thus, a contract under which a broker is empowered to accept risks on behalf of an insurer by means of a binding authority is not a contract of insurance in its own right, as the contract of itself does not operate to transfer risks but merely provides a mechanism for transfer under individual contracts to be made at a later date.[55] The same analysis applies to reinsurance treaties.[56] Again, if the parent company of an insurer agrees to provide administrative services for the insurer, while not taking an assignment of rights and liabilities under the insurer's contracts with its policyholders, that agreement is not one for the provision of insurance services.[57] It was held in *GMA v Unistorebrand*[58] that a contract for the transfer of the liabilities of an insolvent insurer to another insurer is not one of insurance.

Marine and non-marine insurance. Insurance law may be divided into marine **1–011** and non-marine insurance law. A lack of reported case law has, until relatively recently, hampered the development of insurance law throughout its history, and it is only since Lord Mansfield became Chief Justice in 1756 that even marine decisions have provided a satisfactory body of insurance law. Before that date no more than 60 insurance decisions in all had been reported,[59] and since at that time the whole case was left to a jury of merchants without any minute statement from the Bench of the principles of law on which insurances were established, those cases were of little value. Lord Mansfield, however, instituted the radical innovation of instructing the jury in full upon the rules of insurance law in each case and it is his judgments, principally in marine cases, which now form the

---

[52] Per MacKinnon J. in *Goole Steam Towing Co v Ocean Marine* [1928] 1 K.B. 589 at 594.

[53] However, valued policies are not always used for works of art: see *Quorum AS v Schramm (No.1)* [2002] Lloyd's Rep. I.R. 292.

[54] *Kyzuna Investments Ltd v Ocean Maine Insurance Association (Europe)* [2000] 1 Lloyd's Rep. 505 (unique yacht); *Quorum AS v Schramm (No.1)* [2002] Lloyd's Rep. I.R. 202 ("La Danse Grecque" by Degas); *Thor Navigation Inc v Ingosstrak Insurance* [2005] 1 Lloyd's Rep. 547 (vessel).

[55] *Pryke v Gibbs Hartley Cooper* [1991] 1 Lloyd's Rep. 602.

[56] *HIH Casualty and General Insurance v New Hampshire Insurance* [2001] Lloyd's Rep. I.R. 224.

[57] *Re Forsakringsaktiebolaget Skandia* (C-240/99) [2001] E.C.R. I-1951, distinguishing *Card Protection Plan v Commission* (C-349/96) [1999] ECR I-973.

[58] *GMA v Unistorebrand* [1995] L.R.L.R. 333.

[59] See Park, *Marine Insurance*, Introduction.

backbone of English, American and Commonwealth insurance law. Marine principles were codified by the Marine Insurance Act 1906.

The 1906 Act contains a code of the law governing marine insurance, although it must necessarily be read subject to the many cases construing its words. There is no equivalent code relating to non-marine insurance of any description. Marine insurance law has, owing to its long and peculiar history, been more influenced by continental jurisprudence than other branches of the common law. Lord Mansfield, for instance, did not hesitate to cite foreign sources, such as the great Ordonnance de la Marine of 1681, as authorities for propositions of marine law. It is not therefore always safe to rely on marine decisions as sources of non-marine insurance law unless it is clear, from judicial dicta or otherwise, that the same principles are applicable. Thus it has been laid down that the principle of utmost good faith and the rights of subrogation and contribution apply to both types of insurance.[60] In the case of insurable interest, on the other hand, while marine decisions are of great assistance in determining non-marine questions, the statutes relating to interest differ widely in the case of marine and non-marine insurance. And even where the principles are identical, their application may vary. Thus, while in the case of both types of insurance the assured is bound to disclose material facts, previous refusals to insure by other insurers will generally be held to be material in non-marine but not in marine cases.[61]

It may nevertheless be assumed that the rules of law are identical,[62] subject to the differences set out in the paragraphs. This table takes no account of rules obviously applicable only to one or other branch of the law, such as rules relating to the implied warranty of seaworthiness[63] or constructive total loss in marine insurance law or the rules of reinstatement which belong peculiarly to the law of fire insurance. Doctrines peculiar to maritime law, such as the liability of participants in a maritime adventure to general average contribution in the event of an extraordinary sacrifice to avert a common peril, and the concept of the warranty of legality[64] likewise have no application in the field of non-marine insurance law.

The differences between marine insurance law and non-marine insurance law may be summarised as follows[65]:

(a) A contract of marine insurance cannot be enforced unless it is embodied in a formal policy.[66] A contract of non-marine insurance is required to be in no special form, and is enforceable even if it is only oral.

(b) Owing to the special form of a Lloyd's policy, which is made in the assured's own name and in the name of every other person to whom the same may appertain, the assured may assign the benefit of a marine policy on parting with the subject-matter.[67] With the exception of life insurance

---

[60] *Pan Atlantic Insurance v Pine Top Insurance* [1994] 3 All E.R. 581.

[61] See *London Assurance v Mansel* (1879) 11 Ch. D. 363 at 368.

[62] *Thomson v Weems* (1884) 9 App. Cas. 671 at 684; *Elcock v Thomson* [1949] 2 K.B. 755. Section 2(2) of the Marine Insurance Act 1906 states generally that nothing in the Act "shall alter or affect any rules of law applicable to any contract of insurance other than a contract of marine insurance." This rule has not always prevailed when non-marine insurance questions have been considered in the courts.

[63] But roadworthiness is relevant to motor vehicle and transport insurance law and "seaworthiness" may be pertinent accordingly to non-marine problems by way of analogy or to secure consistency in insurance law.

[64] *Euro-Diam Ltd v Bathurst* [1987] 1 Lloyd's Rep. 178, affirmed [1988] 2 All E.R. 23.

[65] Marine insurance is discussed in detail in Ch.24, below.

[66] Marine Insurance Act 1906 s.22.

[67] Marine Insurance Act 1906 ss.50 and 51.

policies, non-marine policies cannot be effectively assigned without the consent of the insurers, even if the policy is issued by Lloyd's.

(c) Policies of marine insurance are "subject to average", in that if the assured is underinsured he is deemed to be his own insurer for the uninsured proportion.[68] Other insurances are only "subject to average" in that sense, if expressly made so.

(d) The amount recoverable under a marine policy is measured by the value at the commencement of the risk and not by the value at the time of the loss.[69] In non-marine insurance it is the value at the time of the loss that supplies the measure of indemnity.[70]

(e) Adjustments "new for old" are regulated by custom in marine insurance.[71] Elsewhere, adjustments "new for old" are not so regulated, and depend upon the terms of the contract.

(f) A contract of marine insurance may be ratified after the assured has become aware of the loss.[72] It is uncertain whether or not a contract of non-marine insurance may be ratified after the assured has become aware of the loss.[73]

(g) In marine insurance, statement of fact bearing upon the risk introduced into the policy is to be construed as a warranty.[74] In other contexts the ordinary rules of construction apply in determining whether such statements are warranties.[75]

(h) Express marine warranties must be set out or incorporated by reference in the policy.[76] Non-marine warranties need not be incorporated in the policy itself.

(i) Any increase in the risk in the form of delay, deviation or change of voyage discharges a marine insurer automatically in the case of a voyage policy.[77] In other forms of insurance, increase of risk does not affect the insurer's obligations under the policy.

(j) The broker is personally liable to the insurer for payment of the premium under a marine policy.[78] The same principle has not been extended to other forms of insurance, and the broker is not personally liable to the insurer for payment of the premium.

(k) There is a statutory obligation on the assured under a marine policy to prevent or mitigate the loss.[79] There is no equivalent duty on the assured under any other form of policy to seek to prevent or mitigate the loss.[80]

(l) Marine insurance recognises the concept of "constructive total loss", which allows the assured to recover for a total loss where the insured subject matter is not entirely destroyed or otherwise lost to him. There is no such doctrine in non-marine insurance law.[81]

---

[68] Marine Insurance Act 1906 s.81.
[69] Marine Insurance Act 1906 s.16.
[70] *Re Wilson and Scottish Insurance* [1920] 2 Ch. 28.
[71] Marine Insurance Act 1906 s.69(1).
[72] Marine Insurance Act 1906 s.86.
[73] *National Oilwell (UK) v Davy Offshore* [1993] 2 Lloyd's Rep. 582.
[74] See the terms of s.33 (nature of warranty) of the Marine Insurance Act 1906.
[75] *Thomson v Weems* (1884) 9 App. Cas. 671 at 684. See also *HIH Casualty v New Hampshire Insurance* [2001] Lloyd's Rep. I.R. 224, affirmed on this point [2001] Lloyd's Rep. I.R. 596.
[76] Marine Insurance Act 1906 s.35(2).
[77] Marine Insurance Act 1906 ss.43–49.
[78] Marine Insurance Act 1906 s.53.
[79] Marine Insurance Act 1906 s.78.
[80] *Yorkshire Water v Sun Alliance* [1997] 2 Lloyd's Rep. 21.
[81] See, e.g. *Scott v Copenhagen Reinsurance Co (UK) Ltd* [2003] Lloyd's Rep. I.R. 696.

2. Formal Requirements for Insurance Contracts

1–012 **Background.** A contract of insurance is generally embodied in a formal document called a policy, a term borrowed from the Italian merchants who introduced the practice of insurance into this country.[82] While the word is generally used to describe a formal document, it may be used to describe any contract of insurance however informal.[83] At common law there was no requirement for insurance agreements to be in any particular form, and it remains the case that at common law an oral agreement for insurance is legally binding.[84] However, the principle has gradually been eroded by legislation and practice. The position may now be summarised as follows.[85]

1–013 **Life policies.** Section 2 of the Life Assurance Act 1774 provides that it is not lawful to make any policy or policies on the life or lives of any person or persons, or other event or events, without inserting in such policy or policies the person or persons' name or names interested therein, or for whose use, benefit, or on whose account such policy is so made or underwritten. This provision is discussed in Ch.19, below. The Act does not require a life insurance contract to be in the form of a policy, although the Act presumes that this will be the case.

As a measure of consumer protection, Pt 6 of the Financial Services Authority's Conduct of Business Rules confer upon the policyholder under a long-term policy a cooling-off period within which there is a right to withdraw from the policy or to cancel it within 30 days of its formation or within the period specified by insurers—a minimum of 14 days—running from the date on which the assured received a post-sales notification from the insurers.

1–014 **Policies on real property.** The only potential formal requirement relating to policies on real property is that contained in s.2 of the Life Assurance Act 1774, concerning the insertion of the names of all persons interested. It has long been assumed that the 1774 Act is applicable to real property covers. Such a conclusion follows from the wording of ss.1 and 2 of the 1774 Act, which makes it clear that its provisions apply to policies on "events" as well as lives, and from the express exclusions from the Act in s.4, which takes only policies on "ships, goods and merchandises" outside its operation. Despite dicta which have extended the 1774 Act beyond the life context,[86] the most recent English judicial authority on the point has favoured practicality over strict wording, and has held that the 1774 Act is confined to life and other non-indemnity policies.[87]

1–015 **Liability policies.** The Employers' Liability (Compulsory Insurance) Act 1969 and Pt VI of Road Traffic Act 1988 require, respectively, employers and the

---

[82] The Italian "polizza" is derived from "polyptych", a tablet of several folds (as distinguished from diptych, etc.), used in late Latin for an account or memorandum book.

[83] *Re Norwich Equitable Fire* (1887) 57 L.T. 241; *Forsikringsaktieselskabet National v Attorney General* [1925] A.C. 639 at 642.

[84] *Murfitt v Royal Insurance* (1922) 38 T.L.R. 334; *Kaines v Knightly* (1681) Skinner 54; *Bhugwandass v Netherlands India Sea & Fire* (1888) 14 App. Cas. 83.

[85] For marine policies, see Ch.24, below.

[86] *Re King* [1963] Ch. 459, 485. Contrast the silence of the court on the issue in *Mumford Hotels Ltd v Wheeler* [1964] 1 Ch. 117.

[87] *Mark Rowlands Ltd v Berni Inns Ltd* [1985] 3 All E.R. 473; *Siu v Eastern Insurance Co Ltd* [1994] 1 All E.R. 213.

drivers of motor vehicles to maintain insurance in respect of third party risks. Other forms of compulsory insurance are also found under UK law.[88] Neither the 1969 nor the 1988 Act specifies in terms that such insurance must be in writing, but both talk in terms of insurance "policies" as opposed to "cover". Moreover, each Act requires a certificate of insurance to be sent to the assured to confirm that cover exists. It is to be assumed that the 1774 Act has no application to liability insurance.[89]

Policies on goods. Section 4 of the Life Assurance Act 1774 exempts from the ambit of the Act policies on "ships, goods and merchandises". Goods policies are nevertheless regulated by the Marine Insurance Act 1788 which remains in force other than in respect of marine policies. The 1788 Act is in the following terms: **1–016**

> "It shall not be lawful for any person or persons to make or effect, or cause to be made or effected, any policy or policies of assurance upon any goods, merchandises, effects or other property whatsoever, without first inserting or causing to be inserted in such policy or policies of assurance the name or names or the usual style and form of dealing of one or more of the persons interested in such assurance . . . or the name or names, or the usual style and form of dealing of the person or persons residing in Great Britain, who shall receive the order for and effect such policy or policies of assurance, or of the person or persons who shall give the order or direction to the agent or agents immediately employed to negotiate or effect such policy or policies of assurance."

There are significant differences between this wording and that of s.2 of the Life Assurance Act 1774. Most importantly, the Marine Insurance Act 1788 is satisfied if the name of any one of the persons interested in the policy is inserted. Given that this requirement will generally be fulfilled as a matter of course, the 1788 Act would appear to be of limited, if any, effect.

Content of policy. The general rule of contract that, where the terms of a contract are reduced into writing, oral evidence is not admissible to vary or contradict them and the writing alone can be looked at as containing the terms of the contract, is applicable to policies of insurance.[90] However, this does not mean that the whole of the contract between the parties will necessarily be embodied in the policy: non-marine warranties frequently appear in the proposal alone. Moreover, statements of a promissory nature in a prospectus delivered by the insurers to the assured may form part of a collateral agreement between them and bind the insurers, although no mention is made of them in the policy,[91] but such statements cannot be called in aid to construe the terms of the policy itself.[92] But a statement in a prospectus that loans would be made at the rate of 4 per cent on an assurance company's policies was held not to amount to a collateral agreement to charge no higher rate[93] and the publication in a prospectus of a company's practice in the distribution of profits was held not to affect its right to   **1–017**

---

[88] Including oil pollution and riding schools.

[89] See *Williams v Baltic Insurance Association of London*, discussed in Ch.20, below.

[90] *Quin v National Assurance* (1839) Jones & Carey 316 (Ire.); *Beacon Life v Gibb* (1862) 1 Moo. P.C.C.(N.S.) 73 at 97; Greer L.J. in *Newsholme Brothers v Road Transport Insurance* [1919] 2 K.B. 356.

[91] *Thiselton v Commercial Union Assurance Co* [1926] 1 Ch. 888. See also *Sun Life of Canada v Jervis* (1943) 113 L.J.K.B. 174; [1944] A.C. 111; *Excess Life v Firemen's Ins of Newark, New Jersey* [1982] 2 Lloyd's Rep. 599.

[92] *British Equitable Assurance Co v Baily* [1906] A.C. 35 at 41, per Lord Lindley.

[93] *Thiselton v Commercial Union Assurance Co* [1926] 1 Ch. 888.

vary that practice by altering its byelaws, where the policy was issued subject to the deed of settlement of the company (by which they could be altered) and its byelaws.[94] In *Sun Life of Canada v Jervis*[95] it was held that an illustration setting out the benefits the assured would receive formed part of the contract between him and the company, since the proposal form was incomprehensible unless read in conjunction with it.

1–018   Rectification of policy. Should the contract of insurance contain terms contradictory to or inconsistent with a prior understanding between the parties, either of them may seek the rectification of that agreement, either as a separate action or—more commonly—in the course of a claim on the policy.[96] Rectification often involves an error between the slip and the policy. However, given that the slip is a binding contract in its own right, the issue may arise where there is a variation between the documents leading up to the slip and the slip itself.[97] The position was lucidly summarised by Bankes L.J. in *A. Gagniere & Co Ltd v The Eastern Company of Warehouses Insurance*[98]:

> "If you prove the parties have come to a definite parol agreement, and you then afterwards find in the document which is intended to carry out that definite agreement something other than that definite agreement has been inserted, then it is right to rectify the document in order that it may carry out the real agreement between the parties. But in order to bring that doctrine into play it is necessary to establish beyond doubt that the real agreement between these parties was that which it is sought to insert in the document in place of the agreement which appears there."

More recently, the requirements for rectification have been restated as being convincing proof that: (i) there was a previous common intention as to what was intended to be in the policy, together with some outward expression of the accord; (ii) the common intention had to continue up to the date that the parties entered into a binding contract; (iii) there had be clear evidence that the instrument as executed did not accurately represent the true agreement of the parties at the time of its execution; and (iv) the instrument would, if rectified, have to accurately represent the true agreement of the parties at that time.[99]

It is unlikely that this doctrine will be of any importance in consumer insurance, since this class of business normally consists of the issue of a standard form policy, and it will be impossible to show that the insurer ever intended to issue anything else. However, rectification is in theory available upon proof of the necessary facts. Thus, for example where, as a result of clerical error, the assured is given incorrect information as to premium rates, the policy may be rectified. Again, where the proposal was made by reference to an illustration setting out the scale of the policyholder's benefits, and a policy was subsequently executed on less advantageous terms after acceptance of the proposal by the company, it was held that the assured was entitled to rectification of the policy in

---

[94] *British Equitable Assurance Co v Baily* [1906] A.C. 35.
[95] *Sun Life of Canada v Jervis* (1943) 113 L.J.K.B.174.
[96] *Motteux v London Assurance* (1739) 1 Atk. 545; *Mutual Reserve v Foster* (1904) 20 T.L.R. 715: *Letts v Excess Insurance Co Ltd* (1916) 32 T.L.R. 361.
[97] *Dunlop Heywards (DHL) Ltd v Erinaceous Insurance Services Ltd* [2009] EWCA Civ. 354.
[98] *A. Gagniere & Co Ltd v The Eastern Company of Warehouses Insurance* (1921) 8 Ll. L.R. 365, 366–367. Cf. *Harper v Interchange Group* [2007] EWCA Civ 1834 (Comm).
[99] *The Nai Genova* [1984] 1 Lloyd's Rep. 353; *Swainland Builders Ltd v Freehold Properties Ltd* [2002] 2 E.G.L.R. 71; *Dunlop Haywards (DHL) Ltd v Erinaceous Insurance Services Ltd* [2009] Lloyd's Rep. I.R. 464; *Chartbrook Ltd v Persimmon Homes Ltd* [2009] UKHL 38.

order to give effect to the contract contained in the illustration and the proposal.[100]

The right to rectification arises in its simplest case where there has been a prior **1–019** contract binding on the parties.[101] Normally, however, the question will be whether the parties had a common understanding short of agreement which they intended to be manifested in the final contract.

The initial question is the existence of a previous common intention which has been manifested in some way.[102] In *Chartbrook Ltd v Persimmon Homes Ltd*[103] the House of Lords decided that the test of previous common intention is objective and not subjective. If it appears that the assured intended one thing and the insurers intended something else, the assured has no right to insist on a policy of the kind he wants,[104] as the governing principle is that if only one of the parties is under some misapprehension, no rectification is possible.[105] Thus in *Cape Plc v Iron Trades Employers Insurance Association*[106] it was held that there was no common understanding as to scope of pneumoconiosis exclusion in employers' liability policy. The assured may, however, be able to recover any premiums he may have already paid as money paid to the insurers under a mistake of fact.[107] Mere clerical errors may be rectified on this principle. In *Nittan (UK) Ltd v Solent Steel Fabrication Ltd*[108] the policy named the insured as "Sargrove Electronic Controls Ltd". This was the name of a dormant company controlled by the claimants, who were trading under the name "Sargrove Automation". The Court of Appeal held that the error could be ignored, and treated the policy as referring to the claimants.

The common intention must continue up to the date on which the parties entered into the binding contract, which in a London market placement may be the slip rather than the policy itself.[109] The fact that there has been a later contract plainly cannot of itself be determinative of what was intended, as if that was the

---

[100] *Sun Life Assurance Co v Jervis* (1943) 113 L.J.K.B. 174.

[101] *Hvalfangerskapet v Unilever* (1932) 42 Ll. L.R. 215 at 220; *Mackenzie v Coulson* (1869) L.R. 8 Eq. 368 at 375; *PT Berlian Laju Tanker TBK v Nurse Shipping Ltd (The Aktor)* [2008] 2 Lloyd's Rep. 246; *Dunlop Haywards (DHL) Ltd v Erinaceous Insurance Services Ltd* [2009] Lloyd's Rep. I.R. 464.

[102] *Alliance Aeroplane Co v Union Insurance Society of Canton* (1920) 5 Ll. L.R. 406; *Maignen & Co v National Benefit Insurance Co* (1922) 10 Ll. L.R. 30; *Joscelyn v Nissen* [1970] 2 Q.B. 86; *Mint Security v Blair* [1982] 1 Lloyd's Rep. 188; *Pindos Shipping Corporation v Raven* [1983] 2 Lloyd's Rep. 449.

[103] *Chartbrook Ltd v Persimmon Homes Ltd* [2009] UKHL 38.

[104] *Fowler v Scottish Equitable Life* (1858) 28 L.J. Ch.225; *South-East Lancashire v Croisdale* (1931) 40 Ll. L.R. 22; *Hvalfangerskapet v Unilever* (1932) 42 Ll. L.R. 215.

[105] *Lowlands Steam Shipping Co Ltd v North of England P & I Association* (1921) 6 Ll. L.R. 230; *Pasquali v Traders & General Insurance Association* (1921) 9 Ll. L.R. 514; *Stanton & Stanton v Starr* (1920) 3 Ll. L.R. 259; *Re London County Commercial Reinsurance Office Ltd* [1922] 2 Ch. 67; *Gullett v Evans* (1929) 35 Ll. L.R. 239; *Pindos Shipping Corp v Raven (The Mata Hari)* [1983] 2 Lloyd's Rep. 449; *Agip SpA v Navigation Alta Italia, SpA (The Nai Genova)* [1984] 1 Lloyd's Rep. 353; *Thor Navigation Inc v Ingosstrak Insurance (The Thor II)* [2005] 1 Lloyd's Rep. 547; *Kyle Bay Ltd (t/a Astons Nightclub) v Certain Lloyd's Underwriters* [2006] Lloyd's Rep. I.R. 718, affirmed [2007] Lloyd's Rep. I.R. 460 without reference to this point.

[106] *Cape Plc v Iron Trades Employers Insurance Association* [2004] Lloyd's Rep. I.R. 75, followed on the same point in *T&N Ltd v Royal & Sun Alliance Plc* [2004] Lloyd's Rep. I.R. 134, where a further argument based on estoppel by convention was similarly rejected on the ground that consensus between the parties had not been demonstrated.

[107] *Fowler v Scottish Equitable Life* (1858) 28 L.J. Ch. 225.

[108] *Nittan (UK) Ltd v Solent Steel Fabrication Ltd* [1981] 1 Lloyd's Rep. 633. See also: *Whittam v David* [1962] 1 Q.B. 271; *Riverlate Properties v Paul* [1975] Ch.133.

[109] *Dunlop Heywards (DHL) Ltd v Erinaceous Insurance Services Ltd* [2009] Lloyd's Rep. I.R. 464; *Dunlop Haywards (DHL) Ltd v Barbon Insurance Group Ltd* [2010] Lloyd's Rep. I.R. 149 (Comm).

case then rectification would never be possible. In ascertaining whether there was an intention which continued up to the date of the executed instrument, an important indication may be whether there have been a number of changes at the stage between provisional and final agreement: if there have been many alterations to the wording then it may be difficult to prove a continuing common intention to maintain any particular term, but if only that term has not been recorded accurately or at all in the executed instrument then the applicant for rectification may have a somewhat easier task in showing that a mistake had been made.[110]

1–020   As to the third stage, there is a strong presumption that the policy embodies the real contract between the parties, and a strong case is required to rebut that presumption and to support a claim for rectification, especially after the loss.[111] Thus, in *Kiriacoulis Lines SA v Compagnie d'Assurance Maritime (The Demetra K)*[112] a marine policy on a vessel was originally drafted in September 1995 on the terms of the Institute Hull Clauses, containing the usual coverage for fire (whether or not deliberately set) and excluding loss caused by war risks and malicious acts relating to the detonation of weapons of war. The underwriter agreed by endorsement in October 1995 to extend cover to these excluded perils. On renewal in September 1996 the broker presented a slip which referred to war risks being insured perils, but the underwriter was by this time unwilling to provide such cover and deleted the references to war risks on the slip. The vessel was subsequently destroyed by fire set by an unknown person, and the underwriter asserted that it had been the common intention of the parties on renewal to delete cover for malicious acts. The Court of Appeal rejected the rectification argument. The Court of Appeal noted that the 1995 policy in its original format would not have precluded recovery, as the original exclusion for malicious acts was operative only in relation to war risks. The 1995 endorsement had not, therefore, affected the claim. The renewal merely deleted the 1995 endorsement, restoring the policy to its original form, and there was no evidence of any common intention to go further and to remove cover for all malicious acts. On the facts, the parties had not considered the total exclusion of loss caused by malicious acts but had confined their attention to the slip itself, and none of the requirements for rectification had been satisfied.

A court can refuse rectification on the ground of laches if insurers claiming rectification have for a period of years not raised any objection to the operation of the policy in unamended form.[113]

3. FORMATION OF INSURANCE CONTRACTS

1–021   **Ordinary contractual principles.** There will be a binding contract only if the terms are agreed with reasonable certainty, although the law does accept that a binding contract can exist if there is a mechanism for agreeing unresolved terms

---

[110] *Dunlop Heywards (DHL) Ltd v Erinaceous Insurance Services Ltd* [2009] Lloyd's Rep. I.R. 464.

[111] *Henkle v Royal Exchange* (1749) 1 Ves. Sen. 317.

[112] *Kiriacoulis Lines SA v Compagnie d'Assurance Maritime (The Demetra K)* [2002] Lloyd's Rep. I.R. 795.

[113] *Cape Plc v Iron Trades Employers Insurance Association* [2004] Lloyd's Rep. I.R. 75.

at a later stage.[114] A policy made on the basis that the premium is to be agreed is perfectly valid.[115] The rule in s.26(1) of the Marine Insurance Act 1906 that the subject-matter must be specified with reasonable certainty is an application of the general rule that a contract is void for uncertainty if there is a fundamental gap in the agreement between the parties which makes it impossible for the court to determine the obligations of either of them. The fact that the terms of a policy may be varied by one party or the other, does not bring the uncertainty rule into play.[116] Equally, the fact that one party has a discretion as to how the contract is to operate, is not enough to make an insurance contract void for uncertainty.[117]

It is also necessary for the parties to have an intention to create legal relations. There will rarely be a dispute about this as regards the creation of a contract of insurance as the matter is to be determined objectively rather than by the understandings or intentions of the parties,[118] although the position may be complicated in the event of an apparent agreement for the settlement of claims under a policy.[119] An apparent insurance agreement may also fail on ordinary contractual principles for want of consideration, although it has been held that a notional insurance premium of £1 was sufficient consideration where the insurance formed a part of a wider arrangement under which the assured was to be provided with a hire car following damage to his own.[120] Finally, the contract must not be vitiated by fundamental mistake, as where the subject matter has been lost[121] before the contract was entered into or never existed.[122] A mistake is, however, operative only if the agreement is incapable of performance[123]: thus a policy is not vitiated by mistake simply because the parties wrongly believed that an earlier policy had been cancelled.[124]

Offer

Offer by the assured. The first step in the making of a contract of insurance is the proposal or application by means of which the assured gives to the insurers particulars of the risk which he wishes them to undertake. This will generally be the offer, which the insurer is free to accept or reject. Before that the assured will probably have found out from the insurers, either directly or through an agent, the terms on which they are usually willing to grant insurances of the kind he wants,   **1–022**

---

[114] There is no such thing as a contract to negotiate. Lord Wright said obiter that there could be in *Hillas v Arcos* [1932] All E.R. 494 "if there is good consideration . . . though in the event of repudiation by one party the damages may be nominal . . . " Lord Denning M.R. in *Courtney v Tolani* [1975] 1 All E.R. 716 rejected that dictum as bad law, because no court could estimate the damages, and that view was subsequently upheld by the House of Lords in *Walford v Miles* [1992] 1 All E.R. 453 on the basis that a contract to negotiate is too uncertain to be enforced.

[115] *Gliksten v State Insurance* (1922) 10 Ll. L.R. 604.

[116] *Baynham v Philips Electronics Ltd, The Times*, July 19, 1995.

[117] *Brown v GIO Insurance* [1998] Lloyd's Rep. I.R. 201.

[118] *Clark v Tull (trading as Ardington Electrical Services)* [2002] Lloyd's Rep. I.R.524.

[119] See: *Orion Insurance Co Plc v Sphere Drake Insurance Plc* [1990] 1 Lloyd's Rep. 465; *Sphere Drake Insurance Plc v Basler Versicherungsgesellschaft* [1998] Lloyd's Rep. I.R. 35; *Re Odyssey (London) Ltd* [2001] Lloyd's Rep. I.R. 1 (all cases arising out of the same facts, with different conclusions being reached).

[120] *Dennard v Plant* [2002] Lloyd's Rep. I.R. 524.

[121] *Pritchard v Merchants' Life* (1858) 3 C.B. (N.S.) 622; *Scott v Coulson* [1903] 2 Ch. 249. Note that marine policies may be made on a lost or not lost basis.

[122] *Micro Design Group Ltd v Norwich Union Insurance Ltd* [2006] Lloyd's Rep. I.R. 235.

[123] *Great Peace Shipping Ltd v Tsavliris Salvage (International) Ltd (The Great Peace)* [2002] 4 All E.R. 689.

[124] *O'Kane v Jones* [2005] Lloyd's Rep. I.R. 174.

but, where the contract is subsequently reduced into writing, its terms will not be affected by anything which is said or done at this stage.[125] In accordance with general principle, there is a binding contract as soon as the insurer has unconditionally accepted the offer on terms which do not differ from those proposed by the assured and there are no major terms to be agreed.[126] There is a serious conceptual problem here, in that a proposer for insurance is unlikely to be aware of the insurer's usual terms, and there is indeed some authority for the proposition that for this reason any offer must come from the insurer and not the assured, who merely makes an invitation to treat.[127] However, this approach would seem to rest on the old theory of subjective consensus in contract, and the better, and generally accepted, view is that of objective consensus: the proposer applies for insurance on what are understood to be the insurer's general terms. If the insurer has accepted the offer on those terms, they form the terms of the cover and it is thus not open to the assured to seek to reject the policy on the basis that it contains terms not mentioned in the proposal form issued by the insurer on the basis that the insurer has responded with a counter-offer,[128] nor may the assured successfully argue that certain terms of the policy are not binding for want of having been brought to his attention in the pre-contractual period.[129] The now accepted position is that the insurer's terms are binding on the assured even if they have not been brought to the assured's attention prior to the making of the contract, at least provided that the terms are incorporated by some form of express wording on the proposal form,[130] and it is irrelevant that the assured has not read them.[131] That said, the common law recognises an exception in relation to terms which are particularly harsh or unusual, as these must be drawn specifically to the attention of the other party if they are to be treated as binding.[132] Moreover, in the case of consumer insurance it may be that the assured's express attention has to be drawn to obligations imposed upon him by the insurer's usual terms.[133] The assured is for his part entitled to the benefit of terms offered by the insurer.[134] If there have been previous dealings between the insurer and the assured, the argument that the contract is made on previously agreed terms is plainly overwhelming.[135]

---

[125] *Dunn v Campbell* (1920) 4 Ll.L.R. 36. In *Pearl Life v Johnson* [1909] 2 K.B. 288 the recitals to a life policy by deed stated that it was made on the basis of a proposal the proposal had not in fact been signed by the policy holder or her authority, and premiums had been paid. Held, that the insurers were estopped from contending that there was no contract.

[126] *Mulchrone v Swiss Life (UK) Plc* [2006] Lloyd's Rep. I.R. 339.

[127] *Alliss-Chalmers Co v Fidelity & Deposit Co of Maryland* (1916) 114 L.T. 433.

[128] *General Accident Insurance Corp v Cronk* (1901) 17 T.L.R. 233.

[129] *Super Chem Products Ltd v American Life and General Insurance Co* [2004] Lloyd's Rep. I.R. 446.

[130] *Wyndham Rather Ltd v Eagle Star & British Dominions Insurance Co Ltd* (1925) 21 Ll. L.R. 214; *Nsubuga v Commercial Union Assurance Co Plc* [1998] 2 Lloyd's Rep. 682; *Anders & Kern Ltd v CGU Insurance Plc* [2007] Lloyd's Rep. I.R. 555, affirmed on other grounds [2008] Lloyd's Rep. I.R. 460; *US Trading Ltd v Axa Insurance Co Ltd* [2010] Lloyd's Rep. I.R. 505.

[131] *Watkins v Rymill* (1883) 10 QBD 178.

[132] *Interfoto Picture Library Ltd v Stiletto Visual Programmes* [1989] 1 Q.B. 433; *US Trading Ltd v Axa Insurance Co Ltd*, March 17, 2008.

[133] This was the view of Thomas J. in *Nsubuga v Commercial Union Assurance Co Plc* [1998] 2 Lloyd's Rep. 682, basing his view on the effect of the now replaced Statements of Insurance Practice 1986. However, it may be that the same result follows from the Unfair Terms in Consumer Contracts Regulations 1999, SI 1999/2083: failure by the insurer to make terms available prior to the making of the contract may prevent reliance on them.

[134] *Sun Life Assurance Co v Jervis* [1943] 2 All E.R. 425.

[135] *Adie & Sons v Insurances Corp* (1898) 14 T.L.R. 544.

It is often the case that an insurance contract incorporates, by reference, the terms and conditions of some other document, including another insurance policy. In such a case, the court must try to give effect to express terms and incorporated terms, and this may mean adapting the incorporated terms to make sense of them in the context of the policy into which they have been incorporated. This is typically a reinsurance problem, as it is standard practice for the terms of the direct policy to be incorporated into the facultative reinsurance, giving rise to a variety of inconsistencies and irrelevancies, although the same problem may be encountered at the direct level. The court will do its best to make sense of the composite contract, but exactly what has and has not been incorporated—and in what form—remains a matter of uncertainty until resolved by a court.[136]

Offer by the insurer. There are a number of situations in which the offer to insure may come from the insurer. The following lists some of the possibilities: **1–023**

(1) The insurer has introduced new terms or conditions while purporting to accept the assured's offer, or has spelt out issues left open in the original offer by the assured (such as the level of premium): in such cases the insurer is making a counter-offer, which takes effect in law as an offer in its own right.[137]

(2) On the renewal of a policy it is common for insurers to send to assureds a renewal notice. The wording of such a document might well be construed as an offer to grant a further policy on the same risk.[137a] However, the assured's duty of utmost good faith is owed on every renewal of an indemnity policy, so that a renewal notice could equally well be construed as either a conditional offer to renew, or as an invitation to treat requesting the assured to make a fresh offer.[138]

(3) Open covers, binding authorities and reinsurance treaties—indeed, all contracts *for* insurance under which contracts *of* insurance are subsequently to be made[139]—may amount to standing offers by the insurers or reinsurers to provide cover for any risk falling within the contractual description which may subsequently be accepted by the assured or reinsured. Accordingly, each individual declaration to the insurers or reinsurers is probably an acceptance of the standing offer.[140]

---

[136] *CNA International Reinsurance Co Ltd v Companhia de Seguros Tranquilidade SA* [1999] Lloyd's Rep. I.R. 289; *HIH Casualty & General v New Hampshire Insurance* [2001] Lloyd's Rep. I.R. 596.

[137] *South East Lancashire Insurance v Croisdale* (1931) 40 Ll. L.R. 22; *New Hampshire Insurance Co v MGN Ltd* [1997] L.R.L.R. 24.

[137a] *Axa Corporate Solutions SA v National Westminster Bank Plc* [2010] EWHC 1915 (Comm).

[138] The former view of matters appears to have been taken in *Taylor v Allon* [1966] 1 Q.B. 304.

[139] See the distinction drawn by Aikens J. in *HIH Casualty & General v Chase Manhattan Bank* [2001] Lloyd's Rep. I.R. 191.

[140] *Bhugwandass v Netherlands India Sea and Fire Insurance Company of Batavia* (1888) 14 App. Cas. 83; *General Accident v Tanter (The Zephyr)* [1985] 2 Lloyd's Rep. 529; *Youell v Bland Welch (No.2)* [1990] 2 Lloyd's Rep. 431; *Kingscroft Insurance v Nissan Fire & Marine (No.2)* [1999] Lloyd's Rep. I.R. 603; *Glencore International AG v Alpina Insurance Co Ltd* [2004] 1 Lloyd's Rep. 111; *BP Plc v Frankona Reinsurance Ltd* [2003] 1 Lloyd's Rep. 537; *Bonner v Cox* [2006] Lloyd's Rep. I.R. 385; *Crane v Hannover Ruckversicherungs-Aktiengesellschaft* [2008] EWHC 3165 Comm (the point did not arise on appeal [2010] Lloyd's Rep. I.R. 93); *BC Enterprise SDN BHD v Bank of China Group Insurance Co Ltd* [2003] H.K.E.C. 712.

(4) The insurer may have made a direct approach to the assured stating that insurance is available at given rates. More generally, insurance might be offered to any person fulfilling specific conditions, such as the possession of a particular newspaper or some other form of certificate.[141]

(5) An unconditional response by an insurer to a tender for cover will amount to an offer by the insurer. It has been held in Hong Kong that if an insurer submits a tender in request for bids for an insurance scheme, there is an implied contract that the tender will not be withdrawn within the deadline for acceptance set out in the document requesting tenders.[142]

Acceptance

1–024 *Acceptance or counter offer by insurers.* Where the assured has made an offer to the insurer, there may be circumstances in which the insurer's positive response cannot be construed as an acceptance and instead is to be regarded as a counter offer. One illustration of this possibility is where a condition is imposed by the insurer on binding acceptance, for example that the premium be paid or that a policy be issued. A condition may not be imposed by the insurers once the contract has been made.[143] If the condition is one which is to be found in the insurer's standard terms, it may be assumed that the assured's offer was made on the basis of the condition and that there is a binding contract subject to the fulfilment of a condition subsequent. If, on the other hand, the condition is an unusual one, it is better to regard the insurer as having made a counter offer which the assured is free to accept or to reject. There is nevertheless a clear distinction between a suspensory provision which operates to prevent any agreement between the parties, and a suspensory provision which does not affect the binding nature of any agreement but merely provides for the suspension of cover under the policy until the necessary conditions have been fulfilled. This distinction, which rests solely upon the words used, is of particular significance where the risk has in some way altered between the date of the apparent agreement and the date on which the risk begins to run, and is discussed further below.

A further possibility is that, at the date of the assured's offer to the insurer, major terms of the subsequent insurance required to be settled, for example the level of premium to be paid. The insurer's response, detailing the missing term,[144] is, in the absence of clear wording, best construed as a counter-offer which the assured is free to accept or reject either by communication or by tender of the proper premium. In rare cases the proper construction might be that the insurer is setting out an invitation to treat, requesting the assured to make an offer for insurance on the stated terms, but in general the insurer's response ought to be regarded in a more serious light and as an offer capable of acceptance.[145] Finally, the insurers may simply issue a policy which does not conform to the

---

[141] *General Accident Fire and Life Assurance Corp v Robertson* [1909] A.C. 404.

[142] *City Polytechnic of Hong Kong v Blue Cross (Asia Pacific) Insurance Ltd* [1995] 2 H.K.L.R. 103.

[143] *Mulchrone v Swiss Life (UK) Plc* [2006] Lloyd's Rep. I.R. 339; *Bonner v Cox* [2006] Lloyd's Rep. I.R. 385; *Allianz Insurance Co Egypt v Aigaion Insurance Co SA* [2009] Lloyd's Rep. I.R. 69 Comm.

[144] There can be a perfectly good contract if the matter is held over.

[145] *Canning v Farquahar* (1866) 16 QBD 727.

cover requested by the assured. Such conduct amounts to a counter offer which the assured is free to accept or reject.[146]

Acceptance by the insurer. Assuming that all material terms have been agreed **1–025** between insurer and assured, and that the insurer has not determined to insert into the policy terms other than those generally applicable, at least without the assured's consent, a binding contract will arise as soon as the insurer has performed an unqualified act of acceptance. This may occur in a number of ways: the assured may be notified by the insurer of his acceptance[147]; or a policy may have been issued[148]; or the assured may have tendered, and the insurer accepted, the premium.[149] It is to be noted, however, that the mere fact that the insurers have banked a cheque tendered by the assured does not of itself amount to acceptance, as there may be other conditions to be met by the assured.[150] The ordinary rule that the fact of acceptance must be notified will be fulfilled in most of the cases where there has been acceptance in fact by the insurer. However, where an insurer signs a policy in the form of a deed without delivering it to the assured, a binding contract apparently comes into being even in the absence of any notification.[151]

The vexed question whether silence can constitute acceptance is of particular significance in the insurance context, for there may be cases in which the insurer, having received a proposal, either fails to act on it or neglects to notify the assured of a decision to accept it. General contractual principle dictates that mere silence by the insurer cannot amount to acceptance.[152] Moreover, it is unlikely that an insurer who sits upon a proposal for an inordinate length of time will be estopped from denying the existence of an agreement.[153] In particular, if the insurer is insisting upon a particular term which is unacceptable to the assured, the fact that there is prolonged silence from the insurer does not mean that he has agreed to waive the term.[154] Nevertheless, it may be that silence will amount to acceptance where the insurer has imposed upon himself an obligation to notify the assured within a given period in the event of the proposal being rejected: in such a case, silence as a method of acceptance is not imposed but is freely proffered.[155]

---

[146] *South East Lancashire Insurance v Croisdale* (1931) 40 Ll. L.R. 22; *New Hampshire Insurance Co v MGN Ltd* [1997] L.R.L.R. 24.

[147] *Adie v The Insurance Corp* (1898) 14 T.L.R. 544, which makes the point that subsequent correspondence between the parties seemingly denying agreement cannot affect the earlier binding agreement. See also *Allianz Insurance Company-Egypt v Aigaion Insurance Co SA (No.2)* [2009] Lloyd's Rep. I.R. 533, where notification of acceptance was held to create a binding contract even though the offer made by the assured omitted an important warranty that the parties had previously agreed should be included: in such circumstances there is a binding contract, and the missing term is to be resolved by rectification and not by a denial of overall consensus.

[148] *General Accident Insurance v Cronk* (1901) 17 T.L.R. 233; *Rust v Abbey Life Assurance Co* [1979] 2 Lloyd's Rep. 334. In accordance with the postal acceptance rule, the posting of the policy may be enough to complete the contract: *Sanderson v Cunningham* [1919] 2 Ir. 234.

[149] See s.54 of the Marine Insurance Act 1906, which provides that, in the case of a marine policy effected by the broker which acknowledges the receipt of an unpaid premium, the acknowledgment is binding as between insurer and assured although not as between insurer and broker.

[150] *Fontana v Skandia Life Assurance Ltd* Unreported, 2002.

[151] *Roberts v Security Co Ltd* [1897] 1 Q.B. 111 (a contract under seal).

[152] *Felthouse v Bindley* (1862) 11 C.B.N.S. 869.

[153] *Rust v Abbey Life Assurance* [1979] 2 Lloyd's Rep. 334.

[154] *Yona International Ltd v La Reunion Francaise SA dAssurances et de Reassurances* [1996] 2 Lloyd's Rep. 84.

[155] *New Hampshire Insurance Co v MGN Ltd* [1997] L.R.L.R. 24. See also *Smith v Merchants' Fire of New York* [1925] 3 W.W.R. 91.

1–026 *Acceptance by the assured.* Where the offer emanates from the insurer, there will be a binding contract as soon as the assured has notified his unconditional acceptance and has fulfilled any conditions imposed upon him by the insurer.[155a] The question which gives rise to the most difficulty is the extent to which notification is required for acceptance to be complete. Assuming that there is nothing in the insurer's offer which requires notification of acceptance, reliance by the assured upon the policy—or at least a failure to object to its terms—is generally all that is required.[156] There is no reliance if the assured, having received an offer of cover, seeks insurance elsewhere.[157]

Formation and increase of risk

1–027 *Significance and construction of suspensory provisions.* The insurer may impose some condition which must be satisfied before the insurance becomes operative. Typical conditions are: payment of the premium; the inspection of the insured subject matter; the issue of a policy; or the subject matter of the insurance being in a given place or condition. Such a clause may be interpreted either as a provision preventing the conclusion of any agreement between the parties, or as a term of the concluded agreement which stipulates the starting point of the running of cover. The proper construction may be important for two purposes: in determining the date at which the assured's duty of utmost good faith comes to an end; and in ascertaining whether the insurer is under any liability for a loss occurring before the condition has been fulfilled.

It is a matter of construction as to whether a clause is suspensory of agreement or suspensory of risk. In many cases, the matter will be clear: thus, a provision in a marine policy which states that cover is provided "from" or "at and from" a given port refers to the date at which the risk commences and not to the existence of an agreement.[158] However, clauses such as "no insurance can take place" are inherently ambiguous. The practice of the courts has been to hold that such phrases go to the very existence of the agreement itself.[159]

1–028 *Duration of the duty of utmost good faith.* Where the contract has been finally concluded, but cover is suspended until a given condition has been fulfilled, it is necessarily the case that the assured's duty of utmost good faith lapses on the conclusion of the agreement. This is the case because the insurer cannot at this stage vary the premium or refuse to accept the risk once agreement has been reached, so that any such facts cannot be material within the definition of that term.[160] Consequently, facts of which the assured ought to have been aware and which arise between agreement and commencement of cover need not be disclosed and, in the same way, false representations made between those dates must be regarded as immaterial.

The position is otherwise where the agreement itself has yet to come into being, for the rule remains that the assured is under a duty of utmost good faith until the contract has been concluded. Thus, any deterioration in the health of the

[155a] *Axa Corporate Solutions SA v National Westminster Bank Plc* [2010] EWHC 1915 (Comm).

[156] *Rust v Abbey Life Assurance Co* [1979] 2 Lloyd's Rep. 334.

[157] *Taylor v Allon* [1966] 1 Q.B. 304.

[158] Marine Insurance Act 1906 Sch rr.2 and 3.

[159] *Canning v Farquhar* (1886) 16 QBD 727; *Harrington v Pearl Life Assurance Co* (1914) 30 T.L.R. 613; *Looker v Law Union and Rock Insurance Co Ltd* [1928] 1 K.B. 554.

[160] See Marine Insurance Act 1906 ss.18(2) and 20(2).

prospective assured under a life policy must be disclosed to the insurer, failing which the policy is voidable for concealment.[161]

Commencement of the insurer's liability

Clauses preventing the existence of an agreement. There is consistent authority **1–029** for the proposition that an insurer is not liable for a loss which has occurred prior to the inception of the policy and pending the fulfilment of a condition which will bring the policy into effect. Three distinct factors produce this result. First, in many cases the assured warrants by express provision the condition of the subject matter at the date of the policy. Consequently, if the subject matter has ceased to comply with the description before the condition imposed in the policy has been fulfilled, the assured will be in breach of warranty and the insurer will correspondingly be entitled to determine the policy.[162] Secondly, an offer is not to be construed as open indefinitely, and must be accepted within a reasonable time.[163] If the assured has waited until circumstances to change before acceptance, the offer may be treated as having lapsed.[164] Finally, and more generally, the insurer cannot be liable in these circumstances simply because at the date of the loss an unconditional offer and an unconditional acceptance of that offer are not in existence, so that there is no agreement.[165]

Clauses suspending the commencement of the risk. If a loss occurs after the **1–030** parties have reached a binding agreement for insurance but before a condition bringing the insurer on risk has been satisfied, the ability of the assured to recover depends, in the absence of any warranty as to the state of the subject matter when the risk commences, on the nature of the condition. A number of possible cases may be considered:

(1) The risk is to commence on a specified day, and the subject matter is lost or damaged beforehand. In this situation the assured undoubtedly cannot recover.

(2) The risk is to attach at a specified place, as is frequently the case with marine policies. Here the risk does not attach unless the insured subject matter arrives at the stated place and the adventure commences within a reasonable time, and the risk will never attach where the adventure commences from some other place.[166]

(3) The risk is to commence on the payment of the premium. The question here is whether the assured is entitled to tender the premium after a loss has occurred. There will be no difficulty where the policy specifies that the premium has been received despite the fact that it has yet to be paid, as the insurer will be estopped from denying his statement of fact.[167] In other cases it may be that the position depends upon whether or not a

---

[161] *Re Yager and Guardian Assurance Co* [1912] 29 T.L.R. 53; *Whitwell v Autocar Fire and Accident Insurance Co* (1927) 27 Ll. L.R. 418; *Harrington v Pearl Life Assurance Co* (1914) 30 T.L.R. 613; *Looker v Low Union and Rock Insurance Co Ltd* [1928] 1 K.B. 554.

[162] *Looker v Low Union and Rock Insurance Co Ltd* [1928] 1 K.B. 554.

[163] *Canning v Farquhar* (1886) 16 QBD 727, 733.

[164] It is, however, possible for insurers to leave open an offer indefinitely: *Ingram-Johnson v Century Insurance* 1909 S.C. 1032. In a modern setting, standard offers may be found in, e.g. reinsurance treaties or offers by reinsurers to reinsure such underwriters as may accept specific forms of direct risk.

[165] *Canning v Farquhar* (1886) 16 QBD 727.

[166] Marine Insurance Act 1906 ss.42 and 43.

[167] *Roberts v Security Co Ltd* [1897] 1 Q.B. 111; Marine Insurance Act 1906 s.54.

policy has been issued: where a policy has been issued, the insurer may be unable to deny that a binding agreement has come into existence and the payment of the premium has been waived, whereas if the policy has not been issued the insurer cannot be bound as he was not on risk when the loss occurred. These propositions have yet to be tested in the English courts.

(4) The risk is to commence on the issue of a policy by the insurer, and at the date of the loss the premium has been tendered and accepted but a policy has yet to be issued. It is probable that in this situation the insurer's acceptance of the premium raises an estoppel against the denial of a binding contract, and specific performance is obtainable by the assured for the issue of a policy. On that basis, the insurer would be obliged to meet the claim.

1–031 *Loss before issue of policy.* Cases where the loss occurs before the issue of a policy require special care.

(a) Where no binding contract has been formed, an offer to insure cannot be accepted after the loss so as to bind the insurers.[168]

(b) Where there is provisional cover the assured will be able to recover.

(c) Where the insurer is not on risk, but there is a binding contract to issue a policy, the doctrine of frustration applies. Thus if the assured becomes mortally ill before the policy is issued and the risk begins to run,[169] the contract is automatically dissolved: "An agreement to undertake to relieve against risks necessarily assumes that when it comes to be fulfilled by issuing the policy the events are still risks, and does not apply if before fulfilment, and there being no delay for which the insurer is alone responsible, the events have been converted into certainties."[170] This does not mean that a mere change in the risk dissolves the contract, however commercially disastrous to the insurer[171]: the peril insured against must virtually have become a certainty.

(d) Where the loss occurs, unknown to the insurers but known to the assured, and they afterwards issue a policy which they were not bound to issue, they will be entitled to avoid it on the ground of the failure of the assured to disclose the loss.[172]

Thus, in no case can the assured recover where the loss occurs before the beginning of the term covered by the policy,[173] nor, it will be seen from the above propositions, will a policy normally have retrospective effect unless it is made "lost or not lost". Voyage policies and policies of reinsurance may, however, have retrospective effect without those words.[174] But even a life policy may be retrospective provided the intention of the parties is made clear.[175]

---

[168] *Canning v Farquhar* (1886) 16 QBD 727.
[169] *Harrington v Pearl Life* (1914) 30 T.L.R. 613.
[170] *Sickness & Accident Assurance Association v General Accident Assurance Corp* (1892) 29 S.L.R. 836 at 840, per the Lord President.
[171] Cf. Lord Sumner in *Larrinaga v Societe Franco-Americaine* (1923) 29 Com. Cas. 1 at 18, 19.
[172] *Canning v Farquhar* (1886) 16 QBD 727.
[173] *Oceanic Steamship Co v Faber* (1907) 23 T.L.R. 673.
[174] *Marine Insurance v Grimmer* [1944] 2 All E.R. 197.
[175] Byles J. in *Pritchard v Merchants' Life* (1858) 3 C.B. (N.S.) 622 at 644, 645.

Open covers require special consideration. An open cover may be: (a) obligatory on both sides, in that the assured is required to declare risks and the underwriters are bound to accept them; (b) facultative on both sides, in that the assured has a discretion whether to declare and the underwriters have a discretion whether to accept any declarations; or (c) facultative/obligatory, in that either the assured is not required to make declarations but the underwriters are required to accept them, or that the assured is required to make declarations but the underwriters are not required to accept them. In situation (1), the risk will normally attach automatically to the policy as soon as the assured has accepted the risk in question so that no declaration of it to the insurers is required in order to fix the cover.[176] In situation (3), by contrast, the assured cannot validly make a declaration to the policy once he has become aware that a loss affecting the risk has occurred,[177] and the open cover may itself provide that risks may be declared only during its currency.[178]

4. LONDON MARKET PROCEDURES

The procedure in outline. The formation of insurance agreements at Lloyd's   **1–032** and in the London market[179] typically takes the following course. A potential applicant may not approach Lloyd's underwriters directly but must act through the medium of a broker recognised by Lloyd's.[180] The Lloyd's broker prepares a brief document containing all the particulars of the proposal necessary to allow underwriters to make a decision whether or not the risk is acceptable and at what premium; this document is known as the "slip". The broker determines which underwriters are most likely to wish to subscribe to the risk, and submits the slip to them in turn; each underwriter receiving the slip will be the representative of a Lloyd's syndicate, and will be authorised to bind the members of his syndicate in relation to specified risks.[181] The broker's search will generally begin with an underwriter who is well regarded in the market and whose judgment is trusted (the "leading underwriter"), as it is then a simpler task for the broker to obtain further subscriptions from other underwriters representing other syndicates (the "following market"). If the leading underwriter is willing to provide cover, he will stamp the name of his syndicate on the slip and sign the slip, a process known as "scratching", and will further state on the slip the amount of liability that is to be undertaken, either in percentage terms or in absolute financial terms.

[176] *Glencore International AG v Ryan (The Beursgracht)* [2002] Lloyd's Rep. I.R. 335, affirming the first instance decisions of Judge Hallgarten QC, [2001] 2 Lloyd's Rep. 602 and [2001] 2 Lloyd's Rep. 608.

[177] *Glencore International AG v Alpina Insurance Co Ltd* [2004] 1 Lloyd's Rep. 111.

[178] *BP Plc v Frankona Reinsurance Ltd* [2003] 1 Lloyd's Rep. 537.

[179] In the following paragraphs, reference will be made just to the Lloyd's market. However, risks placed in London involving a combination of Lloyd's underwriters and insurance companies operate in the same way.

[180] The requirements for the recognition of Lloyd's brokers were relaxed at the beginning of 2001 amd were further relaxed in 2008.

[181] The question of the authority of an underwriter to scratch a slip and thereby to bind the syndicate arose in *Eagle Star Insurance Co Ltd v Spratt* [1971] 2 Lloyd's Rep. 116. Here the slip had been scratched by a deputy underwriter who had not been a party to the preliminary negotiations. The Court of Appeal nevertheless held that the head underwriter had by his conduct conferred apparent authority upon the deputy underwriter to scratch the slip, and was thus estopped from denying that authority. See also *Daly v Lime Street Underwriting Agencies Ltd, The Times,* June 8, 1987.

The slip will be presented to underwriters in the following market by the broker until the requisite level of subscription has been obtained.

During the course of the negotiation, documents shown to the underwriters will normally be scratched by them so that there can be no dispute thereafter as to whether or not they have been seen. If there is no scratch and no copy in the underwriter's files, proving that the document has been seen will be difficult. Once a slip has been scratched, earlier draft wordings are inadmissible as evidence as to the meaning of the slip itself.[182]

On full subscription, the broker will prepare policy wording which will be submitted to the assured for his approval, and to the leading underwriter for approval on behalf of the following market (assuming, as is generally the case, that the following market has delegated such authority to the leading underwriter by a "leading underwriter" clause: see below). The wording is then presented to Lloyd's Policy Signing Office, renamed "In-Sure" in 2001, which issues a single policy on behalf of all the contributing underwriters, representing the terms and conditions set out in the slip. The policy is a composite one, binding each subscribing syndicate. Moreover, each underwriting member of the subscribing syndicates—a "Name"—is a party to a contract with the assured[183]: accordingly the resulting contracts are multi-party as far as the members of Lloyd's are concerned, and each name is jointly and severally liable for the full sum insured. On occasion, and particularly at the reinsurance level, the parties may agree that no formal policy is to be issued, in which case the slip is referred to as a "slip policy".[184]

Pending the issue of final wording, the broker may issue to the assured a "cover note". This is not used in the sense of temporary cover, but rather is a statement by the broker to the assured of the cover obtained and of those subscribing to it. As the document is not issued by underwriters themselves, it does not form any part of the contract between the assured and the underwriters and thus has no legal status, as at best it indicates the cover which the broker intended to secure.[185] A cover note may, therefore, be relevant in the event that the assured brings proceedings against the broker for failure to obtain appropriate cover.

Slip and policy

1–033   *Status of slip where policy is issued.* A slip, once scratched by an underwriter, constitutes a legally binding contract providing for insurance cover in its own right.[186] Thus, where a loss occurs between the date at which the slip has become fully subscribed and the date at which the policy is issued, the assured may

---

[182] *Brotherton v Aseguradora Colseguros SA* [2002] Lloyd's Rep. I.R. 848.

[183] *Hume v AA Mutual International Insurance* [1996] L.R.L.R. 19.

[184] See *Quinta Communications SA v Warringron* [2000] 1 Lloyd's Rep. I.R. 81.

[185] *Overseas Union Insurance Ltd v Turegum Insurance Co* [2001] 3 S.L.R. 330.

[186] In some nineteenth-century cases, the view was taken that a slip was no more than an application for insurance (*Xenos v Wickham* (1867) L.R. 2 H.L. 296; *Ionides v Pacific Fire & Marine* (1871) L.R. 6 Q.B. 674; (1872) L.R. 7 Q.B. 517), while in others it was regarded as a temporary contract to be replaced by a formal policy (*Morrison v Universal Marine Insurance Co* (1873) L.R. 8 Ex. 197; *Thompson v Adams* (1889) 23 QBD 361; *Grover & Grover v Matthews* [1910] 2 K.B. 401; *Haase v Evans* (1934) 48 Ll. L.R. 131. As late as *American Airlines Inc v Hope* [1974] 2 Lloyd's Rep. 301 Lord Diplock expressed the view that the slip was merely temporary. The contractual effect of a slip was confirmed by the Court of Appeal in *General Reinsurance Corp v Fenna Patria* [1983] 2 Lloyd's Rep. 287. The earlier authorities were disapproved by Rix L.J. in *HIH Casualty v New Hampshire Insurance* [2001] Lloyd's Rep. I.R. 596: see below.

recover. Indeed, a duty of utmost good faith attaches to the slip itself.[187] There is no need as such for the issue of a policy thereafter.[188] In principle the policy, if issued, is merely a formal representation of the agreement of the parties. On this basis, ss.21 and 89 of the Marine Insurance Act 1906 provides that reference may be made to the slip in any legal proceedings involving a marine policy. These statutory rules do not mean, however, that the policy is devoid of legal effect, for s.22 of the Marine Insurance Act 1906 states that a contract of marine insurance is inadmissible in evidence unless embodied in a marine policy. A slip is probably not a *policy* of insurance,[189] so that a policy must be issued before any action may be brought by the assured[190]; for this reason there is no objection to a policy being issued after a loss has taken place if it has not been issued at an earlier stage.

The status of the policy once the slip has been issued is not completely free from doubt. It has long been established that, in the event of any conflict between the wording of the slip and the wording of the policy, the policy may be rectified following an application by the assured so that the policy accords with the original agreement in the slip.[191] It is less certain whether an insurer can apply for rectification, as the view was expressed in *Eagle Star v Spratt*[192] that Lloyd's is expressly authorised by subscribing underwriters to issue a policy on their behalves, so that they are not in a position to dispute its terms. However, a body of authority had developed by virtue of which the status of the slip as an autonomous contract was placed in doubt. While it was accepted that a slip could be used as the basis for rectifying errors in the policy, it came to be questioned whether a slip could be used as an aid to the construction of the policy itself. The rationale of that principle was that the policy itself was the contract between the parties in succession to the slip, and that the parties intended from the outset that the slip would be replaced by the policy,[193] with the result that the slip could not be used as an aid to the construction of the policy.[194] In *HIH Casualty and General Insurance Ltd v New Hampshire Insurance Co*[195] Rix L.J. analysed the earlier authorities and concluded that there was no rule of law which rendered the slip immaterial once the policy had been issued: even if the policy did replace the slip, it would nevertheless always be permissible to look at the slip "as part of the

---

[187] Thus, a slip is not binding if the underwriter is induced to sign it on the strength of a representation that the document is a declaration to an existing open cover rather than an entirely fresh risk: *Abrahams v Mediterranean Insurance and Reinsurance* Co [1991] 1 Lloyd's Rep. 216.

[188] *Burrows v Jamaica Private Power Co Ltd* [2002] Lloyd's Rep. I.R. 466.

[189] See *Ionides v Pacific Fire & Marine Insurance Co* (1871) L.R. 6 Q.B. 674; (1873) L.R. 7 Q.B. 517. This issue has ceased to be of practical importance since the repeal of the stamp duty legislation which required the affixing of a stamp to marine policies.

[190] But see *Swan v Maritime Insurance* Co [1907] 1 K.B. 116, followed by the Court of Appeal in *Eide v Lowndes Lambert (The Sun Tender)* [1998] 1 Lloyd's Rep. 389.

[191] *Spalding v Crocker* (1897) 2 Com. Cas. 189; *Wilson Holgate & Co Ltd v Lancashire and Cheshire Insurance Corporation Ltd* (1922) 13 Ll. L.R. 486; *Alliance Aeroplane Co v Union Insurance Society of Canton* (1920) 5 Ll. L.R. 406; *Scottish Metropolitan Association v Stewart* (1923) 15 Ll. L.R. 55; *Eagle Star & British Dominion Insurance Co Ltd v Rainer* (1927) 27 Ll. L.R. 173; *Commercial Union Assurance Co Plc v Sun Alliance Insurance Group Plc* [1992] 1 Lloyd's Rep. 475.

[192] *Eagle Star v Spratt* [1971] 2 Lloyd's Rep. 116.

[193] *New Hampshire Insurance Co v MGN Ltd* [1997] L.R.L.R. 24 (Potter J.—the point did not arise in the Court of Appeal).

[194] *Youell v Bland Welch & Co Ltd (No.1)* [1992] 2 Lloyd's Rep. 127. See also: *Punjab National Bank v De Boinville* [1992] 1 Lloyd's Rep. 7; *St Paul Fire & Marine Insurance Co (UK) Ltd v McConnell Dowell Constructors Ltd* [1993] 2 Lloyd's Rep. 503.

[195] *HIH Casualty and General Insurance Ltd v New Hampshire Insurance Co* [2001] Lloyd's Rep. I.R. 596.

matrix or surrounding circumstances of a later contract"; and it could not be said that the parties had intended that the policy should supersede the slip without examining the slip. Rix L.J.'s conclusion was that, where it was not common ground that the slip had not been superseded by the policy, both documents had to be construed by the court. These comments were obiter and the point remains unresolved, some cases giving priority to the policy[196] while others regarding the issue of the policy as a mere ministerial act.[197] In *Standard Life Assurance Ltd v Oak Dedicated Ltd*[198] weight was given to the slip as an aid to the construction of the policy. In that case a prohibition on the assured's ability to aggregate small losses for the purposes of a deductible was contained only in the schedule to the policy and not its main body, but Tomlinson J. was satisfied that the fact that the same restriction appeared in the slip showed that the parties had intended the schedule to the policy to be of the same weight as the wording of the policy itself so that the restriction on aggregation prevailed. Tomlinson J. also commented that the result of the *HIH* case was that the slip would generally be superseded by the policy. In *Mopani Copper Mines Plc v Millennium Underwriting Ltd*,[199] the slip was held to be admissible evidence as part of the factual matrix to ascertain the meaning of the policy itself. By contrast, in *Dunlop Heywards (DHL) Ltd v Erinaceous Insurance Services Ltd*[200] the binding contract was held to have been embodied in the slip, and the drafting of the subsequent policy was regarded as no more than an administrative act. However, in that case there was no tension between the slip and the policy.

Potential difficulties arising from the Lloyd's procedure

1–034   *When is the contract made?* It now settled law that a contract of insurance is entered into when the slip is scratched by an underwriter,[201] and not at the later date when the slip is fully subscribed.[202] It is possible for the parties to have entered into a binding contract prior to scratching. Thus, in *Allianz Insurance Company-Egypt v Aigaion Insurance Co SA (No.2)*,[203] a binding contract was held to have been created by reinsurers not scratching the slip but signifying their acceptance of it by stating, in response to a slip, "Cover is bound with effect from 31.03.05 as we had quoted . . . Our documents to follow." The absence of a key term in the slip, previously agreed between the parties, was held not to prevent a binding contract from having been made on the terms set out in the slip. It is to be noted that the reinsurers did not seek rectification in the proceedings, but relied upon the argument that there was no contract at all. Similarly, in *Crane v Hannover Ruckversicherungs-Aktiengesellschaft*[204] a binding contract of reinsurance was held to have been made in circumstances where the reinsurers issued a

---

[196] *Great North Eastern Railway v Avon Insurance Plc* [2001] Lloyd's Rep. I.R. 793; *Unum Insurance Co of America v Israel Phoenix Assurance Co* [2002] Lloyd's Rep. I.R. 374.

[197] *Assicurazioni Generali SpA v Ege Sigorta AS* [2002] Lloyd's Rep. I.R. 480, per Colman J. See also *Kyzuna Investments Ltd v Ocean Marine Mutual Association* [2000] 1 Lloyd's Rep. 505.

[198] *Standard Life Assurance Ltd v Oak Dedicated Ltd* [2008] Lloyd's Rep. I.R. 552.

[199] *Mopani Copper Mines Plc v Millenium Underwriting Ltd* [2009] Lloyd's Rep. I.R. 158.

[200] *Dunlop Haywards (DHL) Ltd v Erinaceous Insurance Services Ltd* [2009] Lloyd's Rep. I.R. 464.

[201] *Morrison v Universal Marine Insurance Co* (1873) L.R. 8 Ex. 197; *Eagle Star Insurance Co Ltd v Spratt* [1971] 2 Lloyd's Rep. 116; *American Airlines Inc v Hope* [1974] 2 Lloyd's Rep. 301; *General Reinsurance Corp v Forsikringsaktiebolaget Fennia Patria* [1982] 1 Lloyd's Rep. 87, affirmed [1983] 2 Lloyd's Rep. 287.

[202] As suggested by Donaldson J. in *Jaglom v Excess Insurance Co* [1972] 2 Q.B. 250.

[203] *Allianz Insurance Company–Egypt v Aigaion Insurance Co SA (No.2)* [2009] Lloyd's Rep. I.R. 533.

[204] *Crane v Hannover Ruckversicherungs-Aktiengesellschaft* [2010] Lloyd's Rep. I.R. 93.

standing offer to potential reinsureds and the reinsured notified the reinsurers of their acceptance of direct risks: slips were subsequently scratched by the reinsurers, but these were held to be no more than formal confirmation of the earlier binding agreements. Again, in *Dunlop Haywards (DHL) Ltd v Barbon Insurance Group Ltd*,[205] an agreement was found to be in existence prior to the scratching of the slip, albeit only a provisional one. Brokers had prepared a Firm Order Notification (FON) sheet, which was presented to underwriters at the end of April 2005, and the risk incepted with effect from May 1, 2005. The FON was, however, subject to slips, and thereafter slips were scratched and policies were issued. It was common ground that the FON created a binding obligation between the parties, although it was unnecessary for the court to decide on the precise nature of the FON contract other than that it was intended to be superseded when slips were scratched.[206] In general, however, the slip is the predominant method by which the contract will be made.[207] It follows that an underwriter who intends to scratch a slip but who has failed to do so will not be treated as contractually bound[208] unless there is some other manifestation of acceptance.

A scratch on a slip is, however, only the case where the slip is a firm offer and not a request for a quotation, and the underwriters have scratched it unconditionally. Whether or not the slip has been scratched unconditionally has to be determined objectively and not by reference to the underwriter's actual beliefs: it has been held that a scratch which has been underlined,[209] made subject to the qualification "TBE" (to be entered)[210] or made in pencil[211] is unconditional. The underwriter may specifically impose conditions which have to be satisfied before the scratch on the slip becomes binding on him, in which case there is no binding agreement until the condition is satisfied, although any such condition must be imposed before the scratching is complete.[212] A scratched slip is not deprived of its binding effect simply because one of the parties is under a mistaken belief as to its meaning.[213]

The rights and obligations of individual underwriters. Each subscribing under-   **1–035**
writer, on scratching the slip, accepts individual, rather than collective, obligations to the assured. This rule carries over to the policy itself which is generally
expressed as binding the underwriters "each for his own part and not one for
another", making it clear that the liability of each is several and not joint or joint

---

[205] *Dunlop Haywards (DHL) Ltd v Barbon Insurance Group Ltd* [2010] Lloyd's Rep. I.R. 149.

[206] In earlier proceedings, *Dunlop Haywards (DHL) Ltd v Erinaceous Insurance Services Ltd* [2009] Lloyd's Rep. I.R. 464, the Court of Appeal had accepted that the FON created an agreement between the parties, but that had in any event been common ground between the parties.

[207] *Pindos Shipping Corp v Raven (The Mata Hari)* [1983] 2 Lloyd's Rep. 449; *Denby v English and Scottish Maritime Insurance Co Ltd* [1999] L.R.L.R. 343; *Assicurazioni Generali SpA v Arab Insurance Group (BSC)* [2003] Lloyd's Rep. I.R. 131; *Sun Life Assurance Co of Canada v CX Reinsurance Co Ltd* [2004] Lloyd's Rep. I.R. 86; *Dunlop Heywards (DHL) Ltd v Erinaceous Insurance Services Ltd* [2009] Lloyd's Rep. I.R. 464.

[208] *Seismik Sukrurtig AG v Sphere Drake Insurance Co Plc* [1997] 8 C.L. 351; *Assicurazioni Generali SpA v Arab Insurance Group (BSC)* [2002] Lloyd's Rep. I.R. 633, affirmed [2003] Lloyd's Rep. I.R. 131.

[209] *Eagle Star Insurance v Spratt* [1971] 2 Lloyd's Rep. 116.

[210] *ERC Frankona Reinsurance v American National Insurance Co* [2006] Lloyd's Rep. I.R. 157.

[211] *Bonner v Cox Dedicated Corporate Member Ltd* [2005] Lloyd's Rep. I.R. 569. The point did not arise on appeal, [2006] Lloyd's Rep. I.R. 385.

[212] *Bonner v Cox Dedicated Corporate Member Ltd* [2006] Lloyd's Rep. I.R. 385, where the condition was imposed after scratching.

[213] *Bonner v Cox Dedicated Corporate Member Ltd* [2006] Lloyd's Rep. I.R. 385.

and several.[214] Given that each subscription creates a separate contract, the assured owes a duty of good faith to each subscribing underwriter individually, although there remains a some conflict in the cases on the question whether a false statement made to one underwriter is deemed to have been made to others who rely upon that underwriter's scratching.[215]

1–036 *The position prior to full subscription.* The principle that an underwriter is bound by his scratching of a slip necessarily means that he is liable for his stated proportion of the total amount for which insurance has been obtained once the risk has incepted, even though the loss has occurred prior to the broker having obtained full subscription to the slip. There is no implied condition or custom that the slip must be fully subscribed before a contract is entered into, and neither the assured nor the underwriter can unilaterally treat themselves as discharged from a partially-subscribed slip.[216]

1–037 *Modifications to a partly subscribed slip.* Once a slip has been scratched by an underwriter, he is bound by the terms of the slip which were current at that time. If the wording of the slip has been modified at a later stage at the insistence of another underwriter, earlier scratchings cannot unilaterally be treated as having been varied to meet the new terms, and the assured will simply have different contracts with different terms.[217]

1–038 *Oversubscription.* There is only one recognised exception to the rule that a slip, once scratched, is binding and cannot be varied unilaterally. It is common practice on the Lloyd's market for brokers to obtain more than 100 per cent subscription on a slip, and indeed in reported cases the level of subscription has reached as high as 300 per cent. This practice satisfies the immediate needs of the broker's client, as the attainment of 100 per cent subscription may be more rapid,[218] but it doubtless serves rather longer-term purposes, including allowing the broker both to deal with more syndicates than would otherwise be possible and to demonstrate to the client the range of his market contacts and skills. Whatever the justifications for oversubscription, the legal difficulty posed stems from the fact that, life assurance apart, the principle of indemnity renders any insurance in excess of 100 per cent superfluous and a waste of premium, so that it is necessary for the broker to reduce proportionately the subscription of each underwriter until the amount insured equals 100 per cent. However, given that there is a binding contract between the assured and each underwriter, such reduction, or "signing down", is technically a series of breaches of contract. Thus, prima facie, a strict legal analysis of the position is that signing down is not permissible and that the assured is obliged to pay a premium representing insurance far in excess of the amount recoverable by the assured even in the

---

[214] *Touche Ross v Baker* [1992] 2 Lloyd's Rep. 207.

[215] See Ch.4, below.

[216] *General Reinsurance Corp v Forsikringsaktiebolaget Fennia Patria* [1982] 1 Lloyd's Rep. 87, reversed on this point [1983] 2 Lloyd's Rep. 287.

[217] *General Reinsurance Corp v Forsikringsaktiebolaget Fennia Patria* [1983] 2 Lloyd's Rep. 287. It was this precise problem which led Donaldson J. to suggest in *Jaglom v Excess Insurance Co Ltd* [1972] 2 Q.B. 250 that the slip was not binding until fully subscribed.

[218] If underwriters are aware that the slip is going lobe oversubscribed and that liabilities will ultimately be reduced, each may be more willing to subscribe for a larger part of the risk. See below.

event of a total loss: it is of course arguable that the broker whose negligence produced the oversubscription would ultimately have to meet the excess premium payments. However, the Court of Appeal in *Fennia*[219] accepted that it was the customary right of a Lloyd's broker to reduce the liabilities of the subscribing underwriters to "write down" the liabilities of each subscribing underwriter proportionately, so that the coverage is reduced to 100 per cent. The customary right may be excluded where the scratch is annotated "to stand" or by equivalent wording.

The possibility that the subscription of each underwriter may be reduced to an uncertain extent makes it difficult for any underwriter to assess at the outset the amount for which the slip is to be initialled to produce, after reduction, the desired proportion of the risk. Consequently, the broker will generally be asked to provide a "signing indication", that is, his assessment of the likely subscription level to be obtained for the slip. However, a signing indication which proves to be erroneous will cause some loss to the underwriter: if the degree of oversubscription is greater than indicated, the underwriter will receive proportionately less of the risk than he had hoped for; if, on the other hand, the degree of oversubscription is less than indicated by the broker, the underwriter may face a greater proportion of the risk than he may have judged prudent. It was held in *General Accident Fire and Life Assurance Corp v Tanter (The Zephyr)*[220] that a signing indication given by a broker is a promise by the broker to use his best endeavours to achieve the level of subscription promised, so that a failure to exercise best endeavours may lead to an action against the broker for breach of contract. It was further held in *The Zephyr* that the action is open only to an underwriter to whom a signing indication has been given, and not to an underwriter who assumes that such an indication has been given to others at an earlier stage in the placement.

Policy endorsements. At various stages during the currency of the policy, the **1–039** assured may seek a revision of the cover provided to him. This is generally achieved by an endorsement to the policy, in the form of an amendment slip which is scratched by the underwriters or, more commonly, by the leading underwriter on behalf of the rest of the market. Not every negotiation between the broker and the leading underwriter during the currency of the policy will take effect as an endorsement, as such communications may simply be a restatement of the position as understood by the parties[221] or possibly a book-keeping exercise intended to ensure that the policy is operating properly.[222]

Placement arrangements used in the London market

Leading underwriter clauses. The most important device used in the Lloyd's **1–040** market to ensure that the obligations of all subscribing underwriters are concurrent is the "leading underwriter" clause. There is no standard wording for this type of clause but the general purpose is to permit the leading underwriter to

[219] *General Reinsurance Corp v Forsikringsaktiebolaget Fennia Patria* [1983] 2 Lloyd's Rep. 287.

[220] *General Accident Fire and Life Assurance Corp v Tanter (The Zephyr)* [1984] 1 Lloyd's Rep. 75, reversed in part [1985] 2 Lloyd's Rep. 529.

[221] *Great North Eastern Railway v Avon Insurance* [2001] Lloyd's Rep. I.R. 793.

[222] *Kennecott Utah Copper Corp v Cornhill Insurance Plc* [2000] Lloyd's Rep. I.R. 179.

agree the terms of the policy,[223] to agree amendments to the slip,[224] to waive conditions[225] or to agree that any disputes shall be resolved by arbitration[226] and thereby to bind all subscribers to the slip. The clause may also extend to the acceptance of declarations under an open cover or other facility,[227] and to settlements,[228] although even if there is an express mention of settlements the clause may nevertheless not cover the exercise of subrogation rights or any decision by an underwriter whether or not to assert his right of salvage over subject matter which has been paid for on a total loss basis.[229] A leading underwriter clause is of no assistance unless the terms have been agreed on behalf of the following market by the leading underwriter. In particular, it cannot operate during the placement process should the following market insist upon alterations to the slip which had not been demanded by the leading underwriter, as here the leading underwriter is bound by the terms originally agreed by him even though they may be less favourable than those imposed by the following market. A broker who has resubmitted the slip to the leading underwriter for changes to be made by him in such circumstances would arguably be in breach of his duty to the assured.

The leading underwriter is often the first subscribing underwriter, and it is irrelevant that that underwriter has taken only a small part of the risk in comparison to underwriters in the following market.[230]

It has been suggested that the leading underwriter is the agent of the following market and accordingly faces liability to those underwriters in the event that his agreement with the assured prejudices their interests.[231] An alternative explanation of the mechanism is that a leading underwriter is not the agent of the following market but that his actions are simply the "trigger" by which the following market becomes bound. On this analysis, an action beyond the leading underwriter's mandate may be effective to bind him, but does not bind the following market as there is no triggering event which causes the underwriters in

---

[223] *Unum Life Insurance Co of America v Israel Phoenix Assurance Co Ltd* [2002] Lloyd's Rep. I.R. 374.

[224] *Barlee Marine Corp v Mountain (The Leegas)* [1987] 1 Lloyd's Rep. 471. Contrast *Inversiones Manria SA v Sphere Drake Insurance Co Plc (The Dora)* [1989] 1 Lloyd's Rep. 69.

[225] *Roadworks (1952) Ltd v Charman* [1994] 2 Lloyd's Rep. 99.

[226] *Overseas Union Insurance Ltd v Turegum Insurance Co* [2001] 3 S.L.R. 330. But contrast *Unum Insurance Co of America v Israel Phoenix Assurance Co Ltd* [2002] Lloyd's Rep. I.R. 374, where the arbitration clause was entered into by the leading underwriter after the policy had been avoided, and accordingly the following market was not bound by the agreement.

[227] *BP Plc v GE Frankona Reinsurance* [2003] 1 Lloyd's Rep. 537 (leading underwriter clause did not bind following market to declarations made to leading underwriter—individual declarations were required).

[228] *Roar Marine Ltd v Bimeh Iran insurance Co* [1998] 1 Lloyd's Rep. 423. Where a leading underwriter clause does contain a statement that the leading underwriter's decisions on settlements of claims are to be followed by other underwriters, such provision is binding on them, and there is no basis for implying any provision that the leading underwriter's settlement decisions are to be taken in a bona fide and businesslike fashion, as would be the case with a reinsurance agreement. The difference is that the reinsured and the reinsurers may have different interests, whereas co-insurers may be presumed to have the same interest. Thus, as far as the assured is concerned, the market is obliged to follow the leading underwriter's settlements despite the usual rule that contracts at Lloyd's are distinct.

[229] See *Dornoch Ltd v Westminster International BV (No.3)* [2009] EWHC 1782 (Admlty), where the phrase "Claims to be agreed by the slip leader hereon and X-changing Claims Services and such agreement to be binding on all underwriters" was held not to give the leading underwriter authority to waive the right of salvage on behalf of the entire market.

[230] *Unum Insurance Co of America v Israel Phoenix Assurance Co Ltd* [2002] Lloyd's Rep. I.R. 374.

[231] *Roadworks (1952) Ltd v Charman* [1994] 2 Lloyd's Rep. 99.

the following market to be bound; in the same way, the leading underwriter cannot be in breach of any warranty of authority, as he has not held himself out as having the authority to bind the following market.[232] It is unclear which of these approaches is correct.[233]

A leading underwriter clause is a contract between the assured and the underwriters, and is thus generally irrevocable, and in particular will not lapse simply because the leading underwriter has not exercised his powers. If the insurance is avoided ab initio for non-disclosure or misrepresentation, the leading underwriter clause is itself null and void,[234] and it has also been held that the leading underwriter cannot waive a breach of warranty which has the effect of terminating the risk automatically[235] although it is difficult to see why this should be the case given that the policy itself remains in existence.

Line slips. The cumbersome contract formation procedure at Lloyd's is also commonly streamlined by the use of line slips. A line slip is an authority conferred upon one syndicate by a number of other syndicates, authorising that syndicate to accept risks of a specified description and up to a specified amount on their behalves. Accordingly, by approaching a single syndicate, a broker may be able to obtain a substantial proportion of the necessary placement without the need to approach individual subscribing underwriters. The placing of the risk is done by means of an "off slip" issued by the underwriter.[236] The underwriters who have subscribed to the line slip are not bound until the off slip has been issued.[237] Whether there is a binding agreement between underwriters is a question of fact.[238]

1–041

As a line slip is an independent agency agreement between underwriters, the assured is not a party to it and it follows that the terms of the line slip, unlike those of a placing slip, cannot be relied upon by the assured to contradict the terms of the policy itself.[239]

Fronting arrangements. It is common practice for insurer A to act as a "front" for insurer B, with the effect that the policy itself is issued by A but acting on behalf of B. The usual reason for this is to allow B to offer insurance in a country in which it has no authorisation.[240] The relationship between A and B in these

1–042

---

[232] *Mander v Commercial Union Assurance Co Plc* [1998] Lloyd's Rep. I.R. 9, adopting the dicta of Steyn J. in *The Tiburon* [1990] 2 Lloyd's Rep. 418 at 422.

[233] The point was recognised but left open in *Unum life Insurance Co of America v Israel Phoenix Assurance Co Ltd* [2002] Lloyd's Rep. I.R. 374 and *American International Marine Agency of New York v Dandridge* [2005] Lloyd's Rep. I.R. 643.

[234] *Unum Life Insurance Co of America v Israel Phoenix Assurance Co Ltd* [2002] Lloyd's Rep. I.R. 374.

[235] *American International Marine Agency of New York v Dandridge* [2005] Lloyd's Rep. I.R. 643.

[236] The operation of line slips is described in *Balfour v Beaumont* [1984] 1 Lloyd's Rep. 272, where the issue was whether risks accepted under a line slip had been validly reinsured.

[237] *Denby v English and Scottish Maritime Insurance Co Ltd* [1999] Lloyd's Rep. I.R. 343. See also *Limit No.2 Ltd v Axa Versicherung* AG [2008] Lloyd's Rep. I.R. 330, reversed in part on other grounds [2009] Lloyd's Rep. I.R. 396.

[238] *Syndicate 1242 at Lloyd's v Morgan Read & Sharman* [2003] Lloyd's Rep. I.R. 412.

[239] *Touche Ross & Co v Baker* [1992] 2 Lloyd's Rep. 207.

[240] Although note that under the EC's Single Market programme for insurance, policies may be sold across EC national boundaries as long as the insurer is authorised by the relevant regulatory authorities of its home state.

circumstances may vary: in some cases Λ will be the agent or trustee of B;[241] in others Λ may pass on the risks to B by way of reinsurance.

1–043 **Placement principles and contract certainty.** At the end of 2000 Lloyd's initiated a thorough review of its procedures, and in 2001 published the document London Market Principles 2001. LMP 2001 contained protocols and standards for the placing of risks and for the handling of claims in the London market. The essential principles were: (a) a standardised structure for the slip to ensure clarity and completeness at the outset, removing the need for terms subsequently to be agreed with the leading underwriter on behalf of the following market; (b) a single leading underwriter to manage the underwriting and administrative process and to have significantly greater powers to act on behalf of the following market; (c) greater use of pre-defined policy wordings; (d) greater use of leading underwriter clauses which empower the leader to agree changes on behalf of the London market; (e) the leading underwriter to be responsible for ensuring that sufficient policy details are maintained on behalf of the market to simplify subsequent claims processing; (f) ensuring that documentation is in a single document produced by the broker nominated by the leading underwriter; (g) de-linking of procedures so that each individual stage can be speeded up, e.g. the separation of the provision of closing information and the settlement of the premium; (h) a central slip/policy registration service for the whole market; (i) the leading underwriter is to be responsible for risk registration; (j) the introduction of a market-wide risk coding system; (k) the progressive introduction of the production of all documents in electronic format; (l) the removal of expired wordings.

Compliance with LMP 2001 became compulsory in the Lloyd's market on January 2, 2004 and the vast majority of slips duly conformed with LMP 2001 from that date. However, LMP 2001 proved to be short-lived. In December 2004, the Financial Services Authority challenged the London Market to find a solution to the problem of inadequate documentation which has long bedevilled the creation and confirmation of insurance and reinsurance contracts, a practice referred to by the FSA as "deal now detail later". The reversal of the traditional haphazard approach was regarded by the FSA as essential to the creation of an efficient, orderly and fair market which operated in a transparent fashion and which was competitive. The deadline for a market solution was given as December 2006.

Taking up this challenge, two working groups were established by the market, the Subscription Market Reform Group (which was concerned with the "slip" market) and the Non-Subscription Market Reform Group (which was concerned with all other insurance transactions). These Groups issued Codes of Practice. On January 4, 2007 the Financial Services Authority announced that the UK insurance industry had met the challenge laid down by it to achieve a solution to contract certainty in the United Kingdom, in that 90 per cent of contracts in the subscription market and 88 per cent of the contracts in the non-subscription market had achieved contract certainty. In the light of that, there would be no administrative intervention.

In June 2007 the Contract Certainty Steering Committee published a consolidated Code of Practice, the Contract Certainty Code of Practice (CCCP) which consolidated and replaced all previous contract certainty guidance. The consolidated Code of Practice applies to both the Subscription and Non-Subscription

---

[241] *Sedgwick Tomenson Inc v PT Reasuransi Umum Indonesia* [1990] 2 Lloyd's Rep. 334.

Markets but is concerned only with general insurance issued by companies authorised and regulated by the FSA; it also applies to reinsurance. The Code is not legally binding and has the status of industry guidance. It is published on the internet. Accompanying the Code is a new Market Reform Contract (MRC), whose use became mandatory in November 2007. A data dictionary setting out in detail the data to be included in the MRC is also published on the internet.

The Contract Certainty Code of Practice. The principles set out in the CCCP are **1–044** as follows:

"(A) When entering into the contract, the insurer and broker (where applicable) must ensure that all terms are clear and unambiguous by the time the offer is made to enter into the contract or the offer is accepted. All terms must be clearly expressed, including any conditions or subjectivities.

(B) After entering into the contract, contract documentation must be provided to the insured promptly.

(C) Demonstration of performance: insurers and brokers must be able to demonstrate their achievement of principles (A) and (B).

(D) In respect of contract changes: contract changes need to be certain and documented promptly.

(E) Where there is more than one participating insurer, when entering into the contract, the contract must include an agreed basis on which each insurer's final participation will be determined. The practice of post-inception over-placing compromises Contract Certainty and must be avoided.

(F) After entering into the contract, the final participation must be provided to each insurer promptly.

(G) Where the contract has not met the principles, the insurer and broker (where applicable) have a responsibility to resolve exceptions to any of the above principles as soon as practicable and without undue delay."

The Market Reform Contract. A MRC must contain the details set out in the **1–045** published guidance. The MRC consists of a series of sections:

(1) Risk details, consisting of: unique market reference; type of policy; name and address of assured; period; the interest insured; monetary limits; geographical scope; conditions; choice of law and jurisdiction; amount of premium and premium payment terms; any taxes payable by the assured and administered by the insurers; storage of information; documentation including a copy of the contract document or policy.

(2) Information, consisting of any information provided to insurers to support the assessment of the risk at the time of placement, either in full or, if inappropriate, clearly referenced and made available to all subscribing insurers.

(3) Security Details, consisting of: the subscriptions of subscribing insurers in percentage terms of the financial limits; terms of signing down (so that if a line is written "to stand" it may not be signed down). It is not permitted to include a line condition "wording to be agreed": all wording must be agreed before the insurer commits to the contract.

(4) Subscription Agreement: this establishes the rules to be followed for processing and administration of post-placement amendments and transactions. The name of the slip leader must be clearly identified, any leading underwriter agreement must be specified and the claims agreement procedure is to be specified.

(5) Fiscal and Regulatory issues specific to the insurers involved in the risk must be shown, in particular taxes which are deducted from the premium retained by the insurer.

(6) Broker Remuneration & Deductions—information relating to brokerage, fees and deductions from premium.

5. RENEWAL OF INSURANCE CONTRACTS

1–046   **Significance of renewal.** The effect of the renewal of a contract of insurance depends upon the nature of the policy. In general a life policy is regarded as a single continuing contract, and the present practice is for premiums to be paid on a regular basis without reference to policy years. By contrast, other forms of insurance are for a fixed period—a year in most cases, but longer for certain commercial risks, e.g. construction—so that renewal creates a fresh contract. The most important implication of the creation of a new contract of non-life insurance is the reattachment of the duty of utmost good faith on each renewal.

1–047   **Agreement as to renewal.** Policies of insurance are not renewable beyond their original term unless they are expressed to be so, and where there is no provision for renewal they can only therefore be renewed by a new agreement between the parties. Where there is a provision for renewal it may give the assured an unconditional right to renew or, as is generally the case, renewal may be conditional on the assent of both parties.[242] The latter class includes policies which may be renewed by tender of a further premium by the assured and by the acceptance of that premium by the insurers,[243] and also those policies, known as "self-renewing", which provide that they shall be automatically renewed unless either of the parties shall give notice of an intention not to renew.[244] It is a matter of construction whether a policy is self-extending, although most policies are not of this type.[245] A policy which provides "Extension held covered at a premium to be arranged" provides cover until agreement has been reached.[246] The effect of the letters "NCAD" (notice of cancellation at anniversary date) is uncertain: the phrase has been held that the policy is to be regarded as renewed automatically unless 120 days notice of cancellation has been given,[247] although it has also been decided that the phrase operates as a provisional notice of cancellation so that the policy comes to an end unless renewed following the risk being presented prior to the anniversary date.[248] The phrase has now fallen into

[242] As to apparent hybrid, see *Re Commercial Travellers and Duck* [1951] 1 D.L.R. 576.

[243] *Sun Fire v Hart* (1889) 14 App. Cas. 98.

[244] *Solvency Mutual v Froane* (1861) 7 H. & N. 5. Thus in Belgium motor insurance policies are "self-renewing" and go on from year to year unless one side or the other gives notice cancelling them: per Devlin L.J. in *Poland v Julien Praet* [1961] 1 Lloyd's Rep. 187 at 190. As to notice of cancellation of builder's risk policy see *Kirby v Cosindit* [1969] 1 Lloyd's Rep. 75.

[245] *Jones Construction Co v Alliance Assurance Co* [1961] 1 Lloyd's Rep. 121 (contractor's all risks policy); *Webb and Hughes v Bracey* [1964] 1 Lloyd's Rep. 465 (professional indemnity policy).

[246] *Kirby v Cosindit* [1969] 1 Lloyd's Rep. 75.

[247] *Commercial Union v Sun Alliance* [1992] 1 Lloyd's Rep. 475.

[248] *Kingscroft Insurance Co v Nissan Fire & Marine Insurance Co Ltd (No.2)* [1999] Lloyd's Rep. I.R. 603.

disuse.[249] In *Scottish Coal Co Ltd v Royal and Sun Alliance Plc*[250] it was held that the phrase "It is noted and agreed by underwriters hereon that provisional notice of cancellation is given as at April 1, 2000 to the Insured" meant that the policy would terminate automatically on April 1, 2000 if the insurers were not satisfied with the risk as presented to them so that there was a duty of disclosure attaching to the April 1, 2000 renewal; the court rejected the suggestion that "NCAD" meant that the risk was renewed automatically on April 1, 2000 and that if the risk proved unsatisfactory the insurers had merely given notice of cancellation as of April 1, 2001.

There are other forms of wording relating to renewals which are used on the London market, particularly in relation to reinsurance contracts, but which have no fixed or even obvious legal meaning. Thus, some policies framed as indefinite or for a fixed period of years are stated to be "subject to annual re-signing"; it would seem that the additional words are inconsistent with the primary statement as to duration and have procedural rather than substantive meaning. Nevertheless, where the underwriter does have the right to cancel a contract early by notice of cancellation, and a presentation is made to the underwriter to persuade him not to exercise that right, it is far from clear whether a duty of utmost good faith applies to that presentation given that the policy is not renewed but continued: it may be that there is no duty of disclosure in such a case, but that any misrepresentation by the broker or assured gives the underwriter the right to claim damages insofar as loss has been suffered by reliance on the misrepresentation.

Renewal of life policies. A life policy may be expressed to be either: (a) an annual contract, which the assured has the right to renew,[251] by payment of a further premium, or (b) an entire contract for life, subject to forfeiture on the failure of the assured to pay any of the annual premiums.[252] The distinction is important where the death occurs during the days of grace, the period allowed for the payment of the premium after the termination of the policy period. English policies generally fall into the first category, but they may fall into the second, as where a debtor insures his life in favour of his creditor and covenants to pay the premiums, for there the assured has not only an option but a duty to renew.[253] If the assured fails to renew by the appointed day a policy renewable by payment of a further premium, his right to do so can only be revived by the assent of the insurers, and if they give this assent subject to conditions a new contract will be formed thereby.[254] **1–048**

Some life covers confer upon the assured the right to apply for further cover on the expiry of the term of the original policy. In such a case it is a matter of the proper construction of the policy as to whether the exercise of the option creates a fresh contract or simply an extension of the original contract.[255]

[249] Such a clause was included in the contract in *Charman v Gordian Run-Off Ltd* [2004] Lloyd's Rep. I.R. 373, but was not relied upon.

[250] *Scottish Coal Co Ltd v Royal and Sun Alliance Plc* [2008] Lloyd's Rep. I.R. 718.

[251] *Pritchard v The Merchants' Life* (1858) 3 C.B.(N.S.) 622 at 643, per Willes J.; *Phoenix Life v Sheridan* (1860) 8 H.L.C. 745 at 750; *Stuart v Freeman* [1903] 1 K.B. 47.

[252] *New York v Statham* (1876) 93 U.S. 24 at 30; *McMaster v New York*, 183 U.S. 25 at 35 (1901). See also: Jessel M.R. in *Fryer v Morland* (1876) 3 Ch. D. 675 at 685; *Re Anchor Assurance* (1870) L.R. 5 Ch. 632 at 638; *Re Harrison and Ingram Ex p. Whinney* [1900] 2 Q.B. 710 at 718; *Fontana v Skandia Life Assurance Ltd* Unreported, 2000.

[253] See *Seligman v Eagle Insurance* [1917] 1 Ch. 519 at 524, per Neville J.

[254] *Handler v Mutual Reserve* (1904) 90 L.T. 192; *Mundi v Lincoln Assurance Ltd* [2006] Lloyd's Rep. I.R. 353 Ch (fresh duty of utmost good faith on reinstatement).

[255] *Sookun v Hardoyal* Unreported, 2001 (fresh contract).

1–049   Terms of renewal. A renewal is presumed to be on the terms of the earlier cover unless there is express agreement to the contrary. If there are renewal negotiations, and there is no evidence of agreement to varied terms, the terms of the earlier policy will remain in place for the renewed policy.[256]

6. TEMPORARY COVER

1–050   The significance of temporary cover. Although the time between an application for insurance and its subsequent grant will not generally be lengthy, the potential assured will frequently desire some form of temporary cover pending the commencement of the full policy. In the case of motor insurance, for which insurance is compulsory, temporary cover takes on a particular significance. Temporary insurance is common in many classes of insurance, although the form in which it is effected may range from oral agreement to formal documentation; the term "cover note" is the widely accepted generic term for these various agreements, and will be adopted in what follows.[257] A cover note must be distinguished from an arrangement under which an insurer agrees to provide insurance from the date of the completion, or receipt by the insurer, of an application by the assured. In this situation there is no independent preliminary agreement for insurance, but simply one agreement with retroactive effect. This distinction is important in determining the terms on which temporary cover has been granted.

The creation of temporary cover

1–051   *Formalities.* It is normally obvious whether or not the insurer is offering to provide temporary cover, although borderline cases of construction may arise where the assured is given a receipt or other similar document on his completion of the proposal form and tender of the first premium.[258] Similarly, it will normally be plain whether or not the assured has accepted the offer of temporary cover. Some difficulty is posed by the decision of the Divisional Court in *Taylor v Allon*,[259] in which the defendant was convicted of driving without insurance even though the defendant's policy, which had expired, provided temporary cover pending renewal. The Court reached this conclusion on the basis that the defendant had not accepted the insurer's offer of temporary cover but had manifested an intention to reject it by seeing alternative insurance. This decision can be explained only on the basis that the assured had decided to reject the offer, although it may be that an assured under a cover note who does not appreciate that temporary insurance has been granted, or an assured who despite having been given a cover note continues to obtain quotes from other insurers, will be regarded as not having accepted the offer of temporary cover.[260]

---

[256] *Great North Eastern Ry v Avon Insurance Plc* [2001] Lloyd's Rep. I.R. 793; *Burows v Jamaica Private Power Co Ltd* [2002] Lloyd's Rep. I.R. 466.

[257] Contrast the cover note issued by a broker to the assured in the course of a London market placement, which is not a contractual document but merely a statement by the broker as to the terms on which he has placed cover. See above.

[258] *Linford v Provincial Horse and Cattle Insurance Co* (1864) 34 Beav. 291.

[259] *Taylor v Allon* [1966] 1 Q.B. 304.

[260] But see *Survey Research Co Ltd v Sentry Insurance Co Ltd* [1986] H.K.E.C. 11, in which an offer of temporary cover pending agreement on renewal premium was held to subsist beyond the renewal date even though the assured had sought better terms from the insurers in that period.

An offer for the provision of temporary cover may be subject to a condition, for example that the insurer is not to be bound until a satisfactory proposal or other application has been received by the insurer.[261] In this type of case it will be a matter of construction whether the temporary cover commences when the proposal is received or whether the agreement is retroactive and operates from the date at which the proposal was completed.

There is, at least some doubt as to whether a cover note is a binding contract, as there may be difficulty in identifying consideration moving from the assured. This issue cannot arise where the temporary cover is conferred by the retroactive operation of the full insurance, but in other cases it might be necessary to resort to the rather artificial analysis that the assured's consideration for the cover note is his making of the offer for full insurance.

Duration of temporary cover. Temporary cover will run from its stated com- **1–052** mencement date and may come to an end on the occurrence of a stated event. This event may be: the expiry of a fixed period, although the date at which the period expires may require careful construction of the precise wording of the agreement[262]; the date at which the policy itself is issued or at which cover is refused[263]; or revocation of the cover note by the insurer—a cover note construed in this way is one of those exceptional contracts terminable at will by one of the parties. General contractual principle indicates that, subject to contrary provision, notice of revocation must be received by the assured before it can become effective.[264] On this basis a revocation given to the assured's agent which is not communicated to the assured is inoperative.[265]

Where no termination date or other provision for termination has been incorporated, it is probably the case that temporary cover expires within a reasonable time of its grant.

Temporary cover and the duty of utmost good faith. There is no English authority **1–053** on the question whether the assured owes a duty of utmost good faith prior to entering into an agreement of temporary cover. This question will not frequently be of significance, as it is the general practice for temporary cover to be granted on the assured's completion of the proposal, and it may be anticipated that any breach of duty in relation to the subsequent main insurance contract would be regarded as a breach of duty in relation to the temporary cover.[266] This is undoubtedly the case at least where the cover note is in reality a retrospective grant of insurance under the main policy. There is Australian authority for the proposition that there is an independent duty of utmost good faith applying to the

---

[261] See *Mayne Nickless v Pegler* [1974] 1 N.S.W.L.R. 228. The word "satisfactory" was here held to mean that the proposal did not contain any false statements.

[262] *Cartwright v MacCormack* [1963] 1 All E.R. 11, in which the Court of Appeal ruled that the wording provided temporary cover until midnight on the fifteenth day following the issue of the cover note, as opposed to the same time on the fifteenth day as that at which the cover note had been issued.

[263] *Mackie v European Assurance* (1869) 21 L.T. 102; *Levy v Scottish Employers' Insurance* (1901) 17 T.L.R. 229.

[264] *Rossiter v Trafalgar Life Assurance Association* (1859) 27 Beav. 377.

[265] *Connecticut Fire Insurance Co v Kavanagh* [1892] A.C. 473 appears, it might be thought incorrectly, to indicate to the contrary.

[266] There might nevertheless be severe analytical problems with this result. Thus, if the temporary cover is in the form of a separate contract for which no premium is payable and which is granted automatically on the completion of a proposal form without any scrutiny of the form by the insurer, it is difficult to see how the definition of materiality—i.e. facts which may affect the amount of premium to be charged—can ever be satisfied.

cover note even though there has not been at that stage a request by the insurer for any information whatsoever.[267] This reasoning is not entirely satisfactory,[268] as it disregards the eminently practical point that there may be little opportunity for the assured to make full disclosure pending his receipt of a proposal form and of warnings from the insurer as to what is required. Certainly, imposing a full duty of utmost good faith upon an assured who arranges insurance by telephone is unrealistic. It is suggested that, unless there is fraud on the assured's behalf, it might be possible for a court to find that an insurer who is willing to grant temporary cover in this way has waived the disclosure of any further information, at least until a formal proposal has been completed.

1–054   **The issue of temporary cover by agents.** A broker appointed by the assured will for most purposes be the agent of the assured. However, the law permits an agent to act for both parties to a transaction as long as this is done with the assent of the main principal or if there is no possible conflict created by the agent between the interests of the main principal and those of the third party. Consequently, there is no objection in law to a broker being authorised by one or more insurers to grant temporary cover to any applicant for insurance, and in *Stockton v Mason*[269] the Court of Appeal went further and held that commercial usage has conferred upon brokers the authority to issue cover notes binding upon those insurers with whose policies the broker in question is permitted to act as intermediary.

Where an agent appointed by an insurer purports to issue temporary cover, the validity of that cover will depend upon the authority of the agent. If the agent has actual authority to issue temporary cover, whether express or necessarily implied, no problem arises. Again, where the agent is of a class of agents who would normally have the power to issue binding cover notes, the insurer will be bound unless there is some unusual limitation on the particular agent's power which has been communicated to the assured. The most difficulty arises where the agent is a mere commissioning agent or of some other class which would not generally have the power to issue binding temporary insurances. Here, the issue is whether the insurer has, by its conduct, held the agent out as having the power, as where the agent has been issued with blank cover notes[270] or where the agent has for a considerable period and with the knowledge of the assured issued cover notes which have been treated as binding by the insurer.[271]

1–055   **The content of temporary cover.** There will frequently be difficulty in determining the precise terms of temporary cover, simply because a cover note which evidences such cover is by its nature a far less complex document than a full policy. Moreover, it should not be forgotten that certain forms of temporary cover may not be evidenced by a document at all, as where an insurer by

---

[267] *Mayne Nickless v Pegler* [1974] 1 N.S.W.L.R. 228.

[268] Nor indeed is the analysis of the need for a satisfactory proposal. It has been pointed out that there was probably a binding agreement for a cover note made by telephone, so that the subsequent written cover note containing a condition that a satisfactory proposal was to be submitted to preserve the temporary cover could not be effective: see Birds, (1977) 40 M.L.R. 79. However, it might be countered that the oral cover note was probably terminable at will by the insurer (see above), so that the presentation of the written cover note was a fresh agreement with which the assured had to comply.

[269] *Stockton v Mason* [1978] 2 Lloyd's Rep. 430.

[270] *Mackie v European Assurance Society* (1869) 21 L.T. 102.

[271] *Murfitt v Royal Insurance Co* (1922) 38 T.L.R. 334.

telephone agrees to hold the assured covered until a policy is issued. Consequently there is room for argument as to both the scope of the protection provided and the obligations of the assured under the temporary cover in the event of a loss within the period of the cover note. Such cases as there have been have involved the latter issue, and in particular whether the assured has complied with the formalities of the claims procedure set out in the policy.

As a matter of practice temporary cover may be in any one of four forms: (1) a proper document specifying the actual rights and duties of the parties; (2) a full insurance policy which is made retroactive to the date at which the assured applied for insurance; (3) an agreement which specifically incorporates the terms of any subsequent policy to be issued by the insurer, in which case the policy terms are binding on the assured[272]; or (4) an agreement which simply agrees to provide temporary cover without referring to its scope or to the terms of the policy, although the policy terms are to be regarded as binding by reason of the general proposition that an assured is deemed to apply for insurance on the standard terms contained in the insurer's usual form of policy[273] if this is correct, the insurer probably cannot plead fresh limitations or additional conditions imposed in the policy as issued by the insurer.

The difficulty faced by an assured who suffers a loss within the period of temporary cover is that, other than in case (1), he may not be aware of the policy conditions which govern the formalities of his claim. This problem is probably not acute in first-party claims, as the assured is in the circumstances likely to notify the insurer immediately a loss has occurred: where this is done orally but the policy requires written notification, the insurer's acceptance of the oral notice would probably be regarded by the courts as raising an estoppel against it. Liability policies potentially raise rather more difficult issues, as these frequently require immediate notification of the occurrence of an event likely to give rise to a claim in the future, as opposed to the claim itself; it is readily conceivable that notification conditions are less likely to be met here. Whatever the context, where the assured fails to comply with notification conditions in a policy which has yet to be issued to him, any sympathy demonstrated towards the assured by the courts is readily understandable. It has indeed been held by a majority of the Court of Appeal that the assured is not bound by the uncommunicated terms of the policy itself, irrespective of the general rule that an assured applies for cover on the insurers' usual terms.[274]

---

[272] *Wydham Rather Ltd v Eagle Star & British Dominions Insurance Co Ltd* (1925) 21 Ll. L.R. 214; *Houghton v Trafalgar Insurance Co Ltd* [1953] 2 Lloyd's Rep. 218, affirmed on another point [1954] 1 Q.B. 247.

[273] See above.

[274] *Re Coleman's Depositories Ltd and Life and Health Assurance Association* [1907] 2 K.B. 798. See also: *Symington v Union Insurance of Canton (No.2)* (1928) 141 L.T. 48; *Queen Insurance v Parsons* (1881) 7 App. Cas. 96.

CHAPTER 2

CONFLICT OF LAWS

1. Jurisdiction of the English Courts

2–001 **Legal structure.** The English courts may hear an insurance or reinsurance dispute with an international element if they possess the jurisdiction to do so. Two classes of case have to be considered. First, where the defendant is domiciled in one of the 27 countries of the European Union (EU) or one of the three members of the European Free Trade Association (EFTA) which is party to the European Economic Area Agreement (EEA)[1] with the EU, jurisdictional rules are laid down which govern the allocation of disputes between the courts of those countries; those rules make special provision for insurance disputes. Jurisdictional disputes between EU states are governed by the Brussels Regulation, European Council Regulation 44/2001,[2] replacing the Brussels Convention 1968, and jurisdictional disputes between EU and EFTA states are governed by the Lugano Conventions. The first Lugano Convention of 1989 remains in force as between the EU and Switzerland and Iceland, and is based on the Brussels Convention 1968. The second Lugano Convention of 2008,[3] which follows the Brussels Regulation, came into force as between the EU and Norway on January 1, 2010, but has yet to be ratified by Switzerland and Iceland. Jurisdiction between the constituent parts of the United Kingdom is governed by Sch.4 to the Civil Jurisdiction and Judgments Act 1982, which applies principles similar to those in the Brussels Regulation.

In all other cases, where the defendant is not domiciled in the EEA, the English courts operate their own jurisdictional rules set out in the Civil Procedure Rules, Pt 6. The domicile of the defendant at the date of the issue of the proceeding determines whether the European or domestic jurisdictional rules are applicable to a dispute.[4] For this purpose, a company is domiciled where it has any of[5] its registered office, its place of incorporation, its central administration or its principal place of business.[6] An individual is domiciled in the United Kingdom

---

[1] Iceland and Norway. Switzerland is a member of EFTA but is not a party to the EEA.

[2] Which came into force on March 1, 2002. The Brussels Convention was implemented in England by the Civil Jurisdiction and Judgments Act 1982, subsequently modified to take account of the adoption by the EU of the Brussels Regulation.

[3] The new version was implemented in England by the Civil Jurisdiction and Judgments Regulations 2009 (SI 2009/3131).

[4] *Canada Trust Co v Stozenberg (No.2)* [1998] 1 All E.R. 318; *Cherney v Deripaska* [2007] EWHC 965 (Comm); *Ministry of Defence and Support for the Armed Forces for the Islamic Republic of Iran v Faz Aviation Ltd* [2007] EWHC 1042 (Comm).

[5] Brussels Regulation art.60. A company may, therefore, be domiciled in more than one place.

[6] The two latter concepts overlap substantially, although central administration refers to administrative or secretarial functions whereas principal place of business is concerned with substantive decisions: *King v Crown Energy Trading AG* [2003] EWHC 163 (Comm); *889457 Alberta Inc v Katanga Mining Ltd* [2008] EWHC 2679 (Comm).

if he is a UK resident and the nature and circumstances of his residence indicate that he has a substantial connection with the United Kingdom.[7]

The parties may agree to have their dispute resolved by arbitration rather than by a court. The English courts are required to decline jurisdiction where proceedings are brought in breach of an arbitration clause unless the clause is null and void, inoperative or incapable of being performed,[8] although if the seat of the arbitration[9] is in England, Wales or Northern Ireland the English courts will under the Arbitration Act 1996 have the power to provide assistance to the parties in matters such as the appointment of arbitrators and also to hear appeals against arbitral awards where there is a want of jurisdiction, serious irregularity or (exceptionally only) error of law.[10]

Jurisdiction: cases not involving the EEA. There are two stages to an assertion of jurisdiction by the English courts. At the first stage the claimant must establish a right to serve an English claim form on the defendant, either in England or with the permission of the court in some other jurisdiction. At the second stage the English court must be satisfied it is appropriate for the case to be heard in England.   **2–002**

Service of claim form in England.[11] A claim form may be served on any individual who is in England, even only temporarily.[12] A claim form may also be served on a partnership by serving any partner or person who has control of the partnership's business,[13] on a company registered in England[14] at its registered office[15] and on an overseas company conducting business within the jurisdiction at its address in Great Britain as notified to the Registrar of Companies for that purpose.[16] Service can in addition be effected on a person who has submitted to the jurisdiction of the English courts, e.g. by nominating a solicitor or agent in England who is authorised to receive service,[17] or who enters into an agreement which either confers jurisdiction only on the English courts (an exclusive jurisdiction clause[18]) or under which the defendant agrees to submit to the jurisdiction of the English courts if the claimant opts to commence proceedings   **2–003**

[7] Civil Jurisdiction and Judgments Act 1982 s.41.
[8] Arbitration Act 1996 s.9.
[9] As defined in ss.2 and 3 of the 1996 Act.
[10] Arbitration Act 1996 ss.67–69.
[11] See CPR Pt 6 and Practice Directions 6A and 6B.
[12] *Maharanee of Baroda v Wildenstein* [1972] 2 Q.B. 283.
[13] CPR r.6.3.
[14] Which is thus deemed to be present in England: Companies Act 2006 s.1139.
[15] CPR r.6.5.
[16] Companies Act 2006 s.1139.
[17] CPR rr.6.7 and 6.12. See: *Sphere Drake Insurance Plc v Sigorta Anomim Sirketi* [1988] 1 Lloyd's Rep. 139; *Burrows v Jamaica Private Power Co Ltd* [2002] Lloyd's Rep. I.R. 472.
[18] There is a presumption in favour of exclusivity. For illustrations of the wording required to create an exclusive jurisdiction clause, see: *Sohio v Gatoil* [1989] 1 Lloyd's Rep. 588; *IP Metal Ltd v Ruote OZ SpA* [1993] 2 Lloyd's Rep. 60; *Continental Bank NA v Aeakos Cia Naviera SA* [1994] 2 All E.R. 540; *Beazley v Horizon Offshore Contractors Inc* [2005] Lloyd's Rep. I.R. 231; *Konkola Copper Mines Plc v Coromin* [2006] 1 Lloyd's Rep. 410; *Sea Trade Maritime Corp v Hellenic Mutual War Risks Association (Bermuda) Ltd (The Athena) (No.2)* [2006] EWHC 2530 (Comm); *Standard Bank Plc v Agrinvest International Inc* [2007] EWHC 2595 (Comm); *Underwriting Members of Lloyd's Syndicate 980 v Sinco SA* [2009] Lloyd's Rep. I.R. 365; *Middle Eastern Oil LLC v National Bank of Abu Dhabi* [2008] EWHC 2895 (Comm); *Cavell USA Inc v Seaton Insurance* [2009] EWCA Civ 1363; *Maple Leaf Macro Volatility Master Fund v Rouvroy* [2009] EWHC 257 (Comm); *Deutsche Bank AG v Highland Crusader Offshore Partners LP* [2009] EWHC 730 (Comm). In *General Motors Corp v Royal and Sun Alliance Plc* [2008] Lloyd's Rep. I.R. 311 it was held that a consent order under which the parties agreed not to challenge the jurisdiction of the English courts amounted to an exclusive jurisdiction agreement.

in England (a permissive jurisdiction clause[19]), in each case as long as the matter in issue falls within the scope of the clause. A jurisdiction clause may be unilateral, in that one party but not the other is required to bring an action in the English courts.[20] England is frequently selected as a neutral jurisdiction for the resolution of a dispute between parties who have no connection with England, and there is no public policy basis for the English courts refusing to assert jurisdiction in such a case.[21] Jurisdiction clauses are construed widely, in accordance with the one-stop-shop principle, in order to prevent fragmentation of proceedings.[22]

A defendant who has been sued in England and who appears in the proceedings in order to raise substantive issues and not merely to contest jurisdiction[23] is to be taken to have submitted to the jurisdiction in respect of the dispute between the parties.[24]

2–004   *Service of claim form outside the jurisdiction.* A claim form may also be served abroad on a person not physically in England, although the permission of the court is required for such service.[25] Permission may be obtained if three requirements are satisfied: the claimant has shown a good arguable case that one of the grounds of jurisdiction set out in CPR, PD 6B exists; the claimant has shown that there is a serious issue to be tried; and the claimant has shown that England is the forum in which the case should properly be tried.[26] The grounds of "exorbitant" jurisdiction most relevant to insurance and reinsurance cases set are as follows.

[19] *Berisford v New Hampshire Insurance Co* [1990] 1 Lloyd's Rep. 544; *Standard Steamship Owners Protection and Indemnity Association (Bermuda) v Gann* [1992] 2 Lloyd's Rep. 528.

[20] *Groupama Insurance Co Ltd v Channel Islands Securities Ltd* [2002] Lloyd's Rep. I.R. 843. If the clause is non-exclusive but confers upon one party the right to bring proceedings in a given jurisdiction while the other agrees to submit to the courts of that jurisdiction if the option is exercised, then the exercise of the option has the effect of converting the clause into an exclusive jurisdiction clause.

[21] *Akai Pty v People's Insurance Co* [1998] 1 Lloyd's Rep. 90.

[22] *Fiona Trust & Holding Corp v Privalov* [2007] UKHL 40; *Satyam Computer Services Ltd v Upaid Systems Ltd* [2008] EWCA Civ 487; *UBS AG v HSH Nordbank AG* [2009] EWCA Civ 585.

[23] *Finnish Marine Insurance Co Ltd v Protective National Insurance Co* [1989] 2 All E.R. 929.

[24] But not in respect of some ancillary dispute: *Factories Insurance Co Ltd v Anglo-Scottish General Commercial Insurance Co* (1913) 29 T.L.R. 312.

[25] Service has to be effected within the time limits laid down by the CPR, namely four months for a domestic claim form and six months where permission for service abroad has been granted: CPR r.6.7. The form and manner of service are a matter for the place where service is to be effected. The English court cannot, by use of its general power in CPR r.3.10, excuse a breach of foreign procedure: *Olafsson v Gissurarson* [2006] EWHC 3162 (QB). If it is not possible to serve the claim form under the relevant local procedure either at all or within a reasonable time, then the English court has a broad discretion under CPR r.6.24 to permit an alternative form of service abroad. It is not necessary for the form of service to be expressly permitted under local law, as long as it is not contrary to that law (*Habib Bank Ltd v Central Bank of Sudan* [2006] EWHC 1767 (Comm)). CPR r.6.24(2) provides that an English court may not authorise or require any act which is contrary to the law of the country in which the claim form is to be served (as applied in *The Sky One* [1988] 1 Lloyd's Rep. 238; *Knauf UK GmbH v British Gypsum Ltd* [2002] 1 W.L.R. 907; and *BAS Capital Funding Corp v Medfinco* [2004] 1 Lloyd's Rep. 677) and any judgment obtained in England in contravention of this provision must be set aside without any possibility of a discretion being exercised to waive or correct the error (*Credit Agricole Indosuez v Unicof Ltd* [2003] EWHC 77 (Comm)).

[26] *Seaconsar Far East Ltd v Bank Marzaki Jamhouri Islami Iran* [1994] 4 All E.R. 456. In ascertaining whether the claimant has a good arguable case, it must be shown by the claimant that he has the better of the argument on the material available: *Konkola Copper Mines v Coromin Ltd* [2006] 1 Lloyd's Rep. 410; *Ashton Investments Ltd v OJSC Russian Aluminium* [2006] EWHC 2545 (Comm); *Cherney v Deripaska (No.2)* [2009] EWCA Civ 849 ; *Sharab v Al-Saud* [2009] EWCA Civ 353.

(1) *A claim is made for a remedy against a person domiciled within the jurisdiction.*[27] This ground covers a person domiciled in England who is not physically present at the relevant time.

(2) *A claim is made for an injunction ordering the defendant to do or refrain from doing an act within the jurisdiction.*[28] This ground forms the basis for the grant of an anti-suit injunction against a person who, in breach of an arbitration or exclusive jurisdiction clause, commences proceedings in some other forum or jurisdiction.[29]

(3) *A claim is made against someone on whom the claim form has been or will be served (otherwise than in reliance on this paragraph) and—(a) there is between the claimant and that person a real issue which it is reasonable for the court to try; and (b) the claimant wishes to serve the claim form on another person who is a necessary or proper party to that claim.*[30] This head may be used where the assured has commenced proceedings against insurers and wishes to join brokers to the proceedings so that in the event the claim against the insurers fails there is a default claim against the brokers.[31] In the case of a policy which is subscribed to by a number of insurers, it will be appropriate to join all of them to the same action.[32] A co-assured who has not made a claim against the insurers cannot be said to be a necessary or proper party to an action by the claimant assured.[33] It is also possible to use the procedure in CPR r.19.6 under which the court may order that one or more persons having the same interest in the claim may be joined to the proceedings: by this means it is possible to join to an English action against an insurer any co-insurers even though they are domiciled outside the jurisdiction and whether[34] or not[35] the insurer against whom the action has been commenced had been designated as the leading underwriter.

(4) *A claim is made in respect of a contract where the contract—(a) was made within the jurisdiction; (b) was made by or through an agent trading or residing within the jurisdiction; (c) is governed by English law; or (d) contains a term to the effect that the court shall have jurisdiction to determine any claim in respect of the contract.*[36] There are four separate grounds under this head, and in each case the claim must be "in respect of a contract",[37] a phrase which applies equally where the claim is for breach of contract or for a declaration that no contract exists.[38]

---

[27] CPR PD 6B para.3.1(1).

[28] CPR PD 6B para.3.1(2).

[29] *Youell v Kara Mara Shipping Co* [2000] 2 Lloyd's Rep. 102.

[30] CPR PD 6B, para.3.1(3).

[31] Cf. *Carvill America v Camperdown UK Ltd* [2006] Lloyd's Rep. I.R. 1.

[32] *Golden Ocean Assurance Co v Martin (The Goldean Mariner)* [1989] 2 Lloyd's Rep. 390.

[33] *Chase v Ram Technical Services* [2000] 2 Lloyd's Rep. 418.

[34] *Irish Shipping Ltd v Commercial Union Assurance Pie (The Irish Rowan)* [1989] 2 Lloyd's Rep. 144.

[35] *Bank of America National Trust and Savings Association v Taylor* [1992] 1 Lloyd's Rep. 484; *National Bank of Greece v Outhwaite* [2001] Lloyd's Rep. I.R. 652.

[36] CPR PD 6B para.3.1(6).

[37] A claim for contribution under the Civil Liability (Contribution) Act 1978 falls within this head even though the party seeking contribution is not a party to the contract in question: *Greene Wood & McLean v Templeton Insurance Ltd* [2008] EWHC 1593 (Comm). However, a restitutionary claim based on the argument that there is no contract falls outside this head: *Albon v Naza Motor Trading* [2007] 1 W.L.R. 2489; *Sharab v Al-Saud* [2009] EWCA Civ 353.

[38] *DR Insurance Co v Central National Insurance Co of Omaha* [1996] 1 Lloyd's Rep. 74; *HIB Ltd v Guardian Insurance Co Inc* [1997] 1 Lloyd's Rep. 412. The earlier view that this ground applied

For the purposes of ground (a) the English court will apply English law to determine where the contract was made,[39] and in the case of a contract initiated by slip that place will normally be the place where the slip was scratched.[40] The ground cannot be used by a third party to determine whether there is a contract between two other persons.[41]

Ground (b) is concerned with the agent of the defendant and not the agent of the claimant,[42] and for most purposes the broker is the agent of the assured so that a broker's activities within the jurisdiction are relevant only to a claim against the assured unless the broker has been specifically authorised by insurers to carry out some function on their behalf.[43] Ground (b) will, however, confer jurisdiction on the English court where the insurers have acted through an underwriting agent trading or domiciled in England.[44] It is not necessary that the contracts in dispute were made within the jurisdiction: the focus is on where the agent resides or trades.[45]

Ground (c), applicable law, is discussed below: this head may be used where there is a dispute as to the existence of the contract and the court concludes that the contract, if it exists, would be governed by English law.[46]

As to ground (d), any dispute as to the validity of an exclusive jurisdiction clause is to be determined by the law which, assuming validity, would apply to it.[47]

(5) *A claim is made in respect of a breach of contract committed within the jurisdiction.*[48] This head requires the court to ascertain the law applicable to the policy and then to apply that law to decide where the alleged breach of contract occurred. As far as English law is concerned, a repudiatory breach whereby notice is given by one party to another that the contract will not be performed takes effect when and where the repudiation is received,[49] and an actual breach in the form of a failure to pay a sum due takes place where the claimant or his agent was due to be

---

only to claims under valid contracts, expressed in *Finnish Marine Insurance Co Ltd v Protective National Insurance Co* [1989] 2 All E.R. 929, no longer holds good.

[39] *Brinkibon v Stahag Stahl* [1982] 1 All E.R. 293.

[40] *Citadel Insurance Co v Atlantic Union Insurance Co SA* [1982] 2 Lloyd's Rep. 543.

[41] *HIB Ltd v Guardian Insurance Co Inc* [1997] 1 Lloyd's Rep. 412 (broker seeking declaration as to validity of insurance contract).

[42] *Union International Insurance Co Ltd v Jubilee Insurance* [1991] 1 All E.R. 740.

[43] *Tryg Baltica International (UK) Ltd v Boston Compania de Seguros SA* [2005] Lloyd's Rep. I.R. 40. See also *Sharab v Al-Saud* [2009] EWCA Civ 353, where there was no evidence that the defendant's agent traded or resided in the jurisdiction.

[44] *Afia Worldwide Insurance Co v Deutsche Ruck Versicherungs AG* (1983) 133 N.L.J. 621.

[45] *Lincoln National Life Insurance Co v Employers Reinsurance Corp* [2002] Lloyd's Rep. I.R. 853.

[46] *Britannia Steamship Insurance Association v Ausonia Assicurazioni SA* [1984] 2 Lloyd's Rep. 98.

[47] *Youell v Kara Mara Shipping Co* [2000] 2 Lloyd's Rep. 102.

[48] CPR PD 6B para.3.1(7).

[49] *Cooper v Knight* (1901) 17 T.L.R. 299, although contrast *Holland v Bennett* [1902] 1 K.B. 867 which focused on the place at which the notice was sent. It has also been suggested that the relevant place is that at which the innocent party decides to accept the repudiation (*Atlantic Underwriting Agencies v Compania di Assicurazioni di Milano SpA* [1979] 2 Lloyd's Rep. 240), although it is difficult to see why this affects the question of whether or not there is a breach. See also *Mutzenbecher v La Aseguradora Espanola* [1906] 1 K.B. 254, where all of the relevant events occurred in England.

paid[50] as the principle is that the debtor must seek out his creditor[51] unless the policy otherwise provides. There is no implied term in a contract of insurance that the place where the broker carries on business is the place where sums due under the policy are to be paid: unless the arrangements between the parties have established that position, the general rule remains that sums due to the reinsured are payable in the place of the reinsured's domicile or place of business.[52]

(6) *A claim is made for a declaration that no contract exists.*[53] This head applied only where, if a contract was found to exist, it would have been made within the jurisdiction, or by or through an agent trading within the jurisdiction, or governed by English law, or providing for English jurisdiction. The head permits the court to assert jurisdiction over a claim for negative declaratory relief where it is alleged that there is no contract between the parties, resolving any doubts as to whether such jurisdiction exists under other heads.

(7) *A claim is made in tort where—(a) damage was sustained within the jurisdiction; or (b) the damage sustained resulted from an act committed within the jurisdiction.*[54] This head is of particular importance for claims against brokers for breach of duty or misrepresentation, and it is now settled that ground (a) is concerned with the place where direct, as opposed to indirect, loss is actually felt,[55] and that ground (b) looks to the place where the tort was committed or the false statement was made.[56]

Discretion. Once a head of jurisdiction has been established, the court has a discretion to decide whether or not to assert jurisdiction over the dispute. Jurisdiction will be asserted if England is the most appropriate place for the action to be heard. A number of considerations will be relevant to this question. **2–005**

First, if the parties have agreed that the dispute is subject to the exclusive jurisdiction of the English courts, then jurisdiction will almost inevitably be asserted,[57] even if the clause imposes obligations on one party only,[58] and it is irrelevant that the result is the fragmentation of proceedings between different

---

[50] *Citadel Insurance Co v Atlantic Union Insurance Co SA* [1982] 2 Lloyd's Rep. 543; *Overseas Union Insurance Ltd v Incorporated General Insurance* [1992] 1 Lloyd's Rep. 439; *Deutsche Ruckversicherungs AG v La Fondaria Assicurazioni SpA* [2001] 2 Lloyd's Rep. 621; *Sharab v Al-Saud* [2009] EWCA Civ 353.

[51] *The Eider* [1893] P 119 at 137; *Masri v Consolidated Contractors International (UK) Ltd* [2005] EWHC 944 (Comm); *Commercial Marine Piling Ltd v Pierse Contracting Ltd* [2009] EWHC 2241 (TCC); *Gard Marine & Energy Ltd v Lloyd Tunnicliffe* [2009] EWHC 2388 (Comm).

[52] *Gard Marine & Energy Ltd v Lloyd Tunnicliffe* [2009] EWHC 2388 (Comm), in which Hamblen J. ruled that sums due under a reinsurance agreement were payable in Switzerland, the place of the reinsured's business, rather than in London, the place of the reinsured's broker's business. As had been held in *The Stolt Marmaro* [1985] 2 Lloyd's Rep. 428, the fact that such payments are made did not elevate market practice into an implied term.

[53] CPD PD 6B para.3.1(8).

[54] CPD PD 6B para.3.1(9).

[55] *ABCI v Banque Franco Tunisienne* [2003] EWCA Civ 205.

[56] *Domicrest Ltd v Swiss Bank Corp* [1999] 1 Lloyd's Rep. 80; *ABCI v Banque Franco Tunisienne* [2003] EWCA Civ 205; *London Helicopters Ltd v Heliportugal Lda-Inac* [2006] EWHC 108 (QB); *Sunderland Marine Mutual Insurance Co Ltd v Wiseman (The Seaward Quest)* [2007] EWHC 1460 (Comm).

[57] *Youell v Kara Mara Shipping Co* [2000] 2 Lloyd's Rep. 102; *Ace Insurance SA-NV v Zurich Insurance Co* [2001] Lloyd's Rep. I.R. 504; *Middle Eastern Oil LLC v National Bank of Abu Dhabi* [2008] EWHC 2895 (Comm); *UBS AG v HSH Nordbank AG* [2009] EWCA Civ 585; *Vitol SA v Arcturus Merchant Trust Ltd* [2009] EWHC 800 (Comm); *UBS AG v HSH Nordbank AG* [2009] EWCA Civ 585; *Skype Technologies SA v Kasesalu* [2009] EWHC 2783 (Ch); *Deutsche Bank AG v Sebastian Holdings Inc* [2009] EWHC 3069 (Comm); *Rimpacific Navigation Inc v Daehan Shipbuilding Co Ltd* [2009] EWHC 2941 (Comm).

[58] *Groupama Insurance Co v Channel Islands Securities Ltd* [2002] Lloyd's Rep. I.R. 843.

jurisdictions. Equally, if the jurisdiction clause is not mandatory but merely confers upon the claimant the right to sue in England, a decision by him to exercise that right will similarly result in a decision to assert jurisdiction; the parties are to be held to their bargain[59] and it can scarcely lie in the defendant's mouth to argue that England is not the most convenient forum.[60]

Secondly, if the parties have chosen to go to arbitration, the English action must be stayed,[61] and if the parties have opted for the exclusive jurisdiction or non-exclusive of the courts of some other place then that choice will normally be honoured by the English courts staying their proceedings.[62] However, there is a discretion to refuse a stay even in the face of a jurisdiction clause if the outcome would be unnecessary fragmentation of proceedings[63] or if matters such as the location of evidence, the ability of the foreign court to apply English law, the connection of the parties with the chosen jurisdiction and any possible prejudice to the claimant in respect of security, enforcement and procedural time bars render the foreign jurisdiction inappropriate.[64] A service of suit clause, by contrast, is not one which confers jurisdiction and is to be given little or no weight.[65]

Thirdly, in the absence of any choice of jurisdiction, the fact that the contract is governed by English law may be an important, albeit not conclusive,[66] indication in favour of English jurisdiction.[67] This is particularly the case where the dispute is one relating to the meaning of the contract or the legal rights of the

[59] *Standard Steamship Owners Protection and Indemnity Society (Bermuda) Ltd v Gann* [1992] 2 Lloyd's Rep. 528; *Mercury Communications Ltd v Communication Telesystems International* [1999] 2 All E.R. (Comm) 33; *Royal Bank of Canada v Cooperative Centrale Raiffeisen-Boerenleenbank BA* [2004] 1 Lloyd's Rep. 471; *BP Plc v National Union Fire Insurance Co* [2004] EWHC 1132 (Comm); *Antec International Ltd v Biosafety USA Inc* [2006] EWHC 47 (Comm); *HIT Entertainment Ltd v Gaffney International Licensing Pty Ltd* [2007] EWHC 1282; *Winnetka Trading Corp v Julius Baer International Ltd* [2008] EWHC 3146 (Ch); *Deutsche Bank AG v Highland Crusader Offshore Partners LP* [2009] EWHC 730 (Comm).

[60] *S & W Berisford & Co v New Hampshire Insurance* [1990] 1 Lloyd's Rep. 454; *Excess Insurance v Allendale Mutual Insurance Co* [2001] Lloyd's Rep. I.R. 524; *Munchener Ruckversicherungs Gesellschaft v Commonwealth Insurance Co* [2005] Lloyd's Rep. I.R. 99; *BP Plc v Aon Ltd* [2006] 1 Lloyd's Rep. 549.

[61] Arbitration Act 1996 s.9.

[62] *Ace Insurance SA-NV v Zurich Insurance Co* [2001] 1 Lloyd's Rep. 618; *Burrows v Jamaica Private Power Co Ltd* [2002] Lloyd's Rep. I.R. 466; *Groupama Insurance Co v Channel Islands Securities Ltd* [2002] Lloyd's Rep. I.R. 843; *Konkola Copper Mines Plc SA v Coromin Ltd (No.2)* [2006] EWHC 1093 (Comm); *AWB (Geneva) SA v North America Steamships Ltd* [2007] EWCA Civ 739.

[63] *Donohue v Armco Inc* [2002] 1 Lloyd's Rep. 425; *Carvill America Inc v Camperdown UK Ltd* [2006] Lloyd's Rep. I.R. 1.

[64] *The Eleftheria* [1970] P. 94; *Atrata Potato Co Ltd v Egyptian Navigation Co (The El Amria)* [1981] 2 Lloyd's Rep. 19; *Konkola Copper Mines Plc v Coromin* [2006] 1 Lloyd's Rep. 410.

[65] *Excess Insurance v Allendale Mutual Insurance Co* [2001] Lloyd's Rep. I.R. 524; *Ace Insurance SA-NV v Zurich Insurance Co* [2001] Lloyd's Rep. I.R. 504; *Munchener Ruckversicherungs Gesellschaft v Commonwealth Insurance Co* [2005] Lloyd's Rep. I.R. 99; *Travelers Casualty & Surety Co of Europe Ltd v Sun Life Assurance Co of Canada Ltd* [2004] Lloyd's Rep. I.R. 846. However, once a party with an option to sue in some other jurisdiction has exercised that option, and the clause requires the other party to submit to the jurisdiction of the court in question, then the clause is to be treated in the same way as an exclusive jurisdiction clause and the English courts will accordingly intervene in exceptional circumstances only: it is not enough that the substantive agreement is governed by English law: *Catlin Syndicate Ltd v Adams Land & Cattle Co* [2007] Lloyd's Rep. I.R. 96.

[66] *Amin Rasheed Shipping Corp v Kuwait Insurance Co* [1983] 2 All E.R. 884; *Novus Aviation Ltd v Onur Air Tasimacilk AS* [2009] EWCA Civ 122.

[67] *Mackender v Feldia AG* [1967] 2 Q.B. 590; *Islamic Arab Insurance Co v Saudi Egyptian American Reinsurance Co* [1987] 1 Lloyd's Rep. 315; *El Du Pont de Nemours v Agnew* [1987] 2 Lloyd's Rep. 585; *Seashell Shipping Corp of Panama v Mutalidad de Seguros del Istituto Nacional*

parties on placement.[68] If the issue between the parties is one of fact rather than one of law, e.g. whether a loss occurred at all or in what circumstances, or whether a fact stated or withheld was true, then the need to apply English law is less compelling.[69] The fact that the contract is governed by a foreign law is not regarded by the English courts as a compelling reason for refusing jurisdiction, given that the expert factual evidence of the content of foreign law can be given, although a stay will be granted if there is no good reason for the English courts to assert jurisdiction.[70]

Fourthly, if there are proceedings in existence or pending in some other jurisdiction, it may be appropriate for the English court to stay its own proceedings[71] so as to avoid the prospect of conflicting judgments.[72] However, the principle of *lis alibis pendens* will not deter an English court from asserting jurisdiction where the foreign proceedings have been brought in blatant disregard of an exclusive jurisdiction or arbitration clause.[73]

Finally, the court will weigh up all other surrounding relevant factors to determine whether England is the most convenient forum for the hearing of the action or whether there is some more convenient forum.[74] If the latter is shown, the English proceedings will be stayed. Relevant factors include[75]: the domicile

---

de Industria [1989] 1 Lloyd's Rep. 47; *Overseas Union Insurance Ltd v Incorporated General Insurance* [1992] 1 Lloyd's Rep. 439; *Commercial Union Assurance v Simat Helleisen & Eichner Inc* [2001] Lloyd's Rep. I.R. 172; *Brotherton v Aseguradora Colseguros SA* [2002] Lloyd's Rep. I.R. 848; *General Star International Indemnity Ltd v Stirling Cooke Brown Reinsurance Brokers Ltd* [2003] Lloyd's Rep. I.R. 719; *Markel International Insurance Co Ltd v La Republica Compania Argentina de Seguros Generales SA* [2005] Lloyd's Rep. I.R. 90; *Tonicstar Ltd v American Home Assurance Co* [2005] Lloyd's Rep. I.R. 40; *Tryg Baltica International (UK) Ltd v Boston Compania de Seguros SA* [2005] Lloyd's Rep. I.R. 32; *FR Lurseen Werft GmbH & Co KG v Halle* [2009] EWHC 2607 (Comm); *Royal & Sun Alliance Insurance Plc v Rolls-Royce Plc* [2010] EWHC 1869 (Comm).

[68] For illustrations, see *Meadows Insurance Co Ltd v Insurance Corp of Ireland* [1989] 2 Lloyd's Rep. 298; *Berisford v New Hampshire Insurance Co* [1990] 1 Lloyd's Rep. 454; *Gan Insurance Co v Tai Ping Insurance Co* [1999] Lloyd's Rep. I.R. 472; *Agnew v Lansforsakrings* [2001] 1 A.C. 223; *Assicuriayoni Generali v Ege Sigorta* [2002] Lloyd's Rep. I.R. 480; *Travelers Casualty and Surety Co of Europe Ltd v Sun Life Assurance Co of Canada (UK) Ltd* [2005] Lloyd's Rep. I.R. 846; *Markel International Insurance Company Ltd v La Republica Compania Argentina de Seguros Generales SA* [2005] Lloyd's Rep. I.R. 90.

[69] *Insurance Co of Ireland v Strombus International Insurance Co* [1985] 2 Lloyd's Rep. 138; *Trade Indemnity Insurance v Forsakrings Njord* [1995] L.R.L.R. 367; *Chase v Ram Technical Services* [2000] 2 Lloyd's Rep. 418; *Navigators Insurance Co Ltd v Atlantic Methanol Production LLC* [2004] Lloyd's Rep. I.R. 418.

[70] *BP Plc v Aon Ltd* [2006] 1 Lloyd's Rep. 549.

[71] This is not possible where the defendant is domiciled in England, the power to stay being lost under the Brussels Regulation in that situation: *Owusu v Jackson* [2005] 1 Lloyd's Rep. 452. It is still an open question whether the power to stay is lost if other proceedings are actually in existence: the conflicting authorities were discussed by Blair J. in *Royal & Sun Alliance Insurance Plc v Rolls-Royce Plc* [2010] EWHC 1869 (Comm). One established restriction on the *Owusu* principle arises where the contract contains an exclusive jurisdiction clause nominating a country outside the European Union: *Konkola Copper Mines v Coromin* [2006] Lloyd's Rep. I.R. 71, affirmed on the grounds [2006] 1 Lloyd's Rep. 410.

[72] *El Du Pont de Nemours v Agnew* [1987] 2 Lloyd's Rep. 585; *Dornoch Ltd v Mauritius Union Assurance Co Ltd* [2006] Lloyd's Rep. I.R. 127, affirmed [2006] Lloyd's Rep. I.R. 786.

[73] *Akai v People's Insurance Co* [1998] 1 Lloyd's Rep. 90.

[74] The doctrine of forum non conveniens was adopted and then perfected by the House of Lords in *MacShannon v Rockware Glass Ltd* [1978] A.C. 795, *The Abidin Daver* [1984] A.C. 398 and *Spiliada Maritime Corp v Cansulex Ltd* [1986] 3 All E.R. 843.

[75] See, by way of illustration: *Irish Shipping Ltd v Commercial Union Assurance Plc (The Irish Rowan)* [1989] 2 Lloyd's Rep. 144; *Tiernan v Magen Insurance* Unreported, 1998; *Navigators Insurance Co Ltd v Atlantic Methanol Production LLC* [2004] Lloyd's Rep. I.R. 418; *Limit (No.3) v PDV Insurance Co Ltd* [2005] Lloyd's Rep. I.R. 552; *Dornoch Ltd v Mauritius Union Assurance Co Ltd* [2006] Lloyd's Rep. I.R. 127, affirmed [2006] Lloyd's Rep. I.R. 786.

of the parties; the existence of related proceedings capable of giving rise to conflicting judgments; the location and availability of witnesses; the place where documents are kept; the availability of legal aid; the ability to enforce any judgment; and the possible need to join third parties. The only relevant issues relate to the litigation itself: there are no wider public policy matters to be taken into consideration.[76]

The English court may, in a case where there is overlapping jurisdiction with the courts of another country, order a stay of English proceedings on case management grounds, so that the relevant issues can be dealt with in the proper order in the respective courts. The power is to be exercised in exceptional circumstances only.[77]

2–006 *Anti-suit injunctions.* Where the English court regards foreign proceedings as vexatious or oppressive, which is almost inevitably the case if the action is in breach of an arbitration or jurisdiction clause,[78] it may grant an anti-suit injunction against the claimant in those proceedings preventing him from continuing his action.[79] Relief may be refused in the discretion of the court, as where the applicant has delayed in seeking relief or where the conduct of the defendant does not justify restraint.[80] In *Through Transport Mutual Assurance Association (Eurasia) Ltd v New India Assurance Co Ltd*[81] the Court of Appeal refused an anti-suit injunction on the ground that the claimant in the foreign proceedings brought against the insurers was not in breach of the arbitration clause in the insurance agreement because he was not the assured but merely a person exercising statutory rights to sue the insurers following the insolvency of

[76] *Lubbe v Cape Industries Plc* [2000] 1 Lloyd's Rep. 139.

[77] *Reichhold Norway ASA v Goldman Sachs International* [1999] 2 Lloyd's Rep. 567; *Konkola Copper Mines Plc v Coromin Ltd* [2006] 1 Lloyd's Rep. 410; *Equitas Ltd v Allstate Insurance Company* [2009] Lloyd's Rep. I.R. 227; *Deutsche Bank AG v Sebastian Holdings Inc* [2009] EWHC 3069 (Comm).

[78] The test being whether the court is satisfied that there is a good arguable case that the parties have agreed upon exclusive jurisdiction or arbitration: *Rimpacific Navigation Inc v Daehan Shipbuilding Co Ltd* [2009] EWHC 2941 (Comm) which holds that the claimant has to show that there is a good arguable case that there is a binding contract between the parties which contains the relevant clause and that it is not enough for the claimant to show that, if a contract existed, it would arguably contain the relevant claims.

[79] *Société Nationale Industrielle v Le Kul Jak* [1987] 3 All E.R. 510; *Donohue v Armco Inc* [2002] 2 Lloyd's Rep. 425; *Akai v People's Insurance Co* [1998] 1 Lloyd's Rep. 90; *Youell v Kara Mara Shipping Co* [2000] 2 Lloyd's Rep. 102; *XL Insurance v Owens Corning* [2000] 2 Lloyd's Rep. 500; *Commercial Union Assurance Co v Simat Helliesen & Eichner* [2001] Lloyd's Rep. I.R. 172; *General Star International Indemnity Ltd v Stirling Cooke Brown Reinsurance Brokers Ltd* [2003] Lloyd's Rep. I.R. 719; *West Tankers Inc v Ras Riunione Adriatica di Sicurta SpA (The Front Comor)* [2005] EWHC 454 (Comm); *CNA Insurance Co Ltd v Office Depot International (UK) Ltd* [2005] EWHC 456; *Advent Capital Plc v G N Ellinas Imports-Exports Ltd* [2005] EWHC 1242 (Comm); *Cadre SA v Astra Asigurari SA* [2005] EWHC 2626 (Comm); *Samengo-Turner v J & H Marsh & McLennan (Services (Ltd)* [2007] EWCA Civ 723; *Standard Bank Plc v Agrinvest International Inc* [2007] EWHC 2595 (Comm); *Goshawk Dedicated Ltd v Rop Inc* [2006] Lloyd's Rep. I.R. 711; *Noble Assurance Co v Gerling-Konzern General Insurance Co (UK)* [2008] Lloyd's Rep. I.R. 1; *General Motors Corp v Royal and Sun Alliance Plc* [2008] Lloyd's Rep. I.R. 311; *Ace Capital Ltd v CMS Energy Corp* [2009] Lloyd's Rep. I.R. 414.

[80] See, e.g. *El Du Pont de Nemours v Agnew* [1988] 2 Lloyd's Rep. 240; *SCOR v Eras International Ltd* [1995] 2 All E.R. 278; *American Specialty Lines Insurance Co v Abbott Laboratories* [2003] 1 Lloyd's Rep. 267; *Goshawk Dedicated Ltd v Rop Inc* [2006] Lloyd's Rep. I.R. 711; *Catlin Syndicate Ltd v Adams Land & Cattle Co* [2007] Lloyd's Rep. I.R. 96; *Whitesea Shipping and Trading Corp v El Paso Rio Clara Ltda (The Marielle Bolten)* [2009] EWHC 2552 (Comm); *Bank of New York Mellon v GV Films* [2009] EWHC 2338 (Comm).

[81] [2005] 1 Lloyd's Rep. 67. Cf. *Markel International Co Ltd v Craft* [2007] Lloyd's Rep. I.R. 403; *AWB (Geneva) SA v North America Steamships Ltd* [2007] EWCA Civ 739.

the assured. Declaratory relief was thought to be adequate. Equally, where the jurisdiction clause is non-exclusive, and merely permits a party to bring proceedings in England, an action brought by the other party in some other court of competent jurisdiction cannot without more be regarded as vexatious or oppressive.[82]

Negative declaratory relief. Underwriters frequently seek from the English **2–007** courts, in advance of any proceedings by the assured, a declaration that they are entitled to avoid, or otherwise are not liable to meet a claim under, a policy. At one time this procedure was regarded as forum shopping, in an attempt to pre-empt the assured from commencing an action in his home jurisdiction. However, more recently it has been recognised that this type of action should be treated in precisely the same way as any other, and that the court should exercise its discretion to hear a claim for negative declaratory relief as long as there is some useful purpose to be served by the proceedings. An issue as to the validity or scope of a policy governed by English law is thus appropriately dealt with by negative declaratory relief,[83] although the courts will exercise caution to ensure that the purpose is not purely forum shopping, that the issue is not hypothetical in that there is no actual or potential claim against the underwriters[84] and that any concurrent proceedings in another jurisdiction are not undermined.[85]

Jurisdiction: EEA cases

Ordinary jurisdictional rules. The Brussels Regulation lays down a series of **2–008** general rules for determining jurisdiction within the EU, although these are modified in certain cases, including insurance. The Brussels Regulation does not apply to arbitration (art.1(3)).[86] The ordinary rules nevertheless remain applicable to reinsurance, and may be outlined as follows. The starting point is that the defendant has to be sued in the place of his domicile (art.2). However, the claimant may, in the alternative, bring proceedings in other places in any of the situations listed in art.5. In establishing a head of jurisdiction, the claimant is required to show that he had a much better argument than the defendants, on the material available before the court, the test used for determining jurisdiction

[82] *Highland Crusader Offshore Partners LP v Deutsche Bank AG* [2009] EWCA Civ 725, distinguishing earlier cases in which anti-suit injunctions had been granted in these circumstances: *Cannon Screen Entertainment Ltd v Handmade Films (Distributors) Ltd* (1989) 5 B.C.C. 207; [1989] B.C.L.C. 660; *Credit Suisse First Boston (Europe) Ltd v MLC (Bermuda) Ltd* [1999] 1 Lloyd's Rep. 767; *Sabah Shipyard (Pakistan) Ltd v Islamic Republic of Pakistan* [2003] 2 Lloyd's Rep. 571; *Royal Bank of Canada v Centrale Raiffeisen-Boerenleenbank* [2004] 1 Lloyd's Rep. 471.
[83] *New Hampshire Insurance Co v Philips Electronics North America Corp* [1999] Lloyd's Rep. I.R. 58; *Gan Insurance Co v Tai Ping Insurance Co* [1999] Lloyd's Rep. I.R. 472; *Lincoln National Life Insurance Co v Employers Reinsurance Corp* [2002] Lloyd's Rep. I.R. 881; *CGU International Insurance v Szabo* [2002] Lloyd's Rep. I.R. 196; *Tiernan v Magen Life* Unreported, 1998; *Tryg Baltica International (UK) Ltd v Boston Compania De Seguros SA* [2005] Lloyd's Rep. I.R. 40; *Sun Alliance & London Insurance Plc v PT Asuransri Dayan Mitra TBK, The No.1 Dae Bu* [2006] Lloyd's Rep. I.R. 860.
[84] *Meadows Insurance Co v Insurance Co of Ireland* [1989] 2 Lloyd's Rep. 298; *Limit (No.3) Ltd v PDV Insurance Co Ltd* [2005] Lloyd's Rep. I.R. 552; *Royal & Sun Alliance Insurance Plc v Retail Brand Alliance Inc* [2005] Lloyd's Rep. I.R. 110.
[85] *American Motorists Insurance v Cellstar Corp* [2003] Lloyd's Rep. I.R. 295; *Chase v Ram Technical Services* [2000] 2 Lloyd's Rep. 418; *Burrows v Jamaica Private Power Co Ltd* [2002] Lloyd's Rep. I.R. 466.
[86] See *Youell v La Reunion Aerienne* [2009] Lloyd's Rep. I.R. 405, where it was noted by Tomlinson J. that a legal relationship was not taken outside the Brussels Regulation simply because the agreement between the parties contained an arbitration clause. The dispute had to relate to the arbitration clause itself for the exclusion to operate.

under the CPR in cases not involving the Brussels Regulation.[87] The most important is art.5(l), under which in "matters relating to a contract", the defendant may be sued "in the place of the performance[88] of the obligation in question". The obligation in question is that which is the main focus of the proceedings,[89] and includes the obligation of the reinsured to comply with the duty of good faith in presenting the risk so that reinsurers can seek negative declaratory relief in the jurisdiction in which the risk was placed.[90] The place of performance of the obligation in question is to be judged by reference to the law applicable to the contract, as determined by the court of the forum in accordance with its conflict of laws rules[91]; in England, these are the rules set out in the Rome I Regulation, discussed below.

Article 6(1) of the Brussels Regulation permits a court to join a third party to proceedings over which it has jurisdiction, even though the third party is not domiciled in the Member State of the proceedings. However, there must be a clear link between the primary claim and the claim against the third party which renders it expedient to hear the two claims together in order to avoid conflicting judgments, and also the provision may not be used to secure joinder in circumstances in which the third party is really the primary defendant. The issue of expediency arose in *Gard Marine & Energy Ltd v Lloyd Tunnicliffe.*[92] The reinsured, a Bermudan company, obtained reinsurance under two slips, one placed in the London Market and one placed in the Swiss Market. Proceedings were commenced in England against both sets of reinsurers, and the Swiss reinsurers asserted a want of jurisdiction. Hamblen J. held that it was appropriate in the circumstances for the reinsured to be able to rely upon art.6(1). The wordings of the two contracts were the same, English law governed each of them and there were no factual differences between the claims against the two sets of reinsurers. Given the risk of conflicting judgments, and given also that the placing brokers faced a fallback action from the reinsured depending upon the outcome of the actions against the reinsurers, Hamblen J. felt that it was expedient for the Swiss reinsurers to be joined to the action against the English reinsurers.

The parties may also agree that the courts of a place are to have exclusive or permissive jurisdiction (art.23). The agreement must be in writing or evidenced in writing, or in a form which accords with the parties' practices, or in a form which accords with the usage of the market.[93] The certainty principle precludes the incorporation of a jurisdiction clause from an insurance contract into a reinsurance contract simply by the latter being declared to be "as original",[94]

---

[87] *Gard Marine & Energy Ltd v Lloyd Tunnicliffe* [2009] EWHC 2388 (Comm).

[88] Which may be agreed. In the absence of any agreement, assuming the contract is governed by English law, the place in which money is to be paid is that of the creditor: see above.

[89] *Fisher v Unione Italiana di Riassicurazioni SpA* [1999] Lloyd's Rep. I.R. 215; *AIG Group v The Ethniki* [2000] Lloyd's Rep. I.R. 343; *Royal & Sun Alliance Insurance Plc v MK Digital Fze (Cyprus) Ltd* [2006] EWCA Civ 629.

[90] *Agnew v Lansforsakringsbolagens AB* [2000] Lloyd's Rep. I.R. 317; *Youell v La Reunion Aerienne* [2009] Lloyd's Rep. I.R. 405.

[91] *Gard Marine & Energy Ltd v Lloyd Tunnicliffe* [2009] EWHC 2388 (Comm).

[92] *Gard Marine & Energy Ltd v Lloyd Tunnicliffe* [2009] EWHC 2388 (Comm).

[93] See: *Beazley v Horizon Offshore Contractors Inc (The Gulf Horizon)* [2005] Lloyd's Rep. I.R.231; *Hewden Tower Cranes Ltd v Wolfkran GmbH* [2007] EWHC 857 (TCC); *Bols Distilleries BV v Superior Yacht Services Ltd* [2007] 1 W.L.R. 12; *Benatti v WPP Holdings Italy SRL* [2007] EWCA Civ 263.

[94] *AIG Group v The Ethniki* [2000] Lloyd's Rep. I.R. 343; *AIG Europe v QBE International Insurance* [2002] Lloyd's Rep. I.R. 22.

although incorporation of a jurisdiction clause is in principle possible if the contract contemplates such incorporation.[95]

In the event that the courts of two or more countries possess jurisdiction over the same dispute[96] under the Brussels Regulation, any conflict is resolved by a strict "first seised" rule in art.27 which gives exclusive jurisdiction to the court first seised.[97] That court has no discretion to stay its proceedings and must hear the action, and this is the case whenever the court obtains jurisdiction by virtue of the defendant's domicile even if the potential competing court is outside the EEA.[98] Any challenge to the jurisdiction of the court first seised must be resolved by that court,[99] so that it is not possible to obtain an anti-suit injunction in England even to restrain a person from commencing an action elsewhere in the EEA in breach of an exclusive jurisdiction clause nominating England,[100] or in breach of an arbitration clause[101] or in circumstances where the action is plainly oppressive.[102]

Jurisdiction over matters relating to insurance. The ordinary rules of the   **2–009**
Brussels Regulation are displaced by arts 8–14 in respect of "matters relating to insurance". A "matter" is any dispute under a policy, including one as to its validity,[103] and a matter "relating to insurance" excludes a dispute which is merely incidental to the policy or a claim.[104] The insurance rules are designed to give a measure of protection to the perceived weaker party to an insurance contract, although it has been held that the words encompass all forms of

---

[95] *Standard Steamship Owners' Protection and Indemnity Association (Bermuda) Ltd v GIE Vision Bail* [2005] Lloyd's Rep. I.R. 407.

[96] If the actions are merely related, in that they involve different parties or some different issues, art.28 confers a discretion on the court not first seised to assert jurisdiction to the extent that there is no possibility of conflicting judgments: *Assurances Generales de France IART v Chiyoda Fire & Marine Co* [1992] 1 Lloyd's Rep. 325; *Prifti v Musini Sociedad Anonima de Seguros y Reaseguros* [2004] Lloyd's Rep. I.R. 528.

[97] Under art.30 seisin occurs when the document instituting the proceedings is first lodged with the court. In English law this refers to the issue rather than to the service of the claim form: *Royal & Sun Alliance Insurance Plc v MK Digital FZE (Cyprus) Ltd* [2006] EWCA Civ 629; *Kolden Holdings Ltd v Rodette Commerce Ltd* [2007] EWHC 1597 (Comm). The position before the adoption of the Civil Procedure Rules in April 1988 was assumed to be that an English court was seised on service rather than on issue, but even that has since been doubted by Lord Mance and Lady Hale in *Phillips v Symes* [2008] UKHL 1.

[98] *Owusu v Jackson* [2005] 1 Lloyd's Rep. 452, subject to the possibility that the power to stay is restored where there are actual competing proceedings (*Royal & Sun Alliance Insurance Plc v Rolls-Royce Plc* [2010] EWHC 1869 (Comm)) and to the exception in *Konkola Copper Mines v Coromin* [2006] Lloyd's Rep. I.R. 71 where a stay is permitted if the contract contains an exclusive jurisdiction clause in favour of a non-EEA jurisdiction. See also *Lucasfilm Ltd v Ainsworth* [2009] EWCA Civ 1328.

[99] *Overseas Union Insurance Ltd v New Hampshire Insurance Co* [1992] 1 Lloyd's Rep. 204.

[100] *Erich Gasser GmbH v MISAT Srl* [2004] 1 Lloyd's Rep. 445.

[101] The exclusion of arbitration from the Brussels Regulation, by art.1.3, was held by the English courts not to preclude anti-suit injunctions to support arbitration clauses (*Through Transport Mutual Insurance Association (Eurasia) Ltd v New India Assurance Co Ltd* [2005] 1 Lloyd's Rep. 67), but the European Court of Justice in *Allianz SpA (formerly Riunione Adriatica di Sicurta SpA) v West Tankers Inc* (C-185/07) [2009] 1 All E.R. Comm 435 has precluded that possibility. The extent to which declaratory relief can be granted, at least in advance of a judgment in foreign proceedings, remains uncertain: see *National Navigation Co v Endesa Generacion SA* [2009] EWCA Civ 1397.

[102] *Turner v Grovit* [2005] 2 Lloyd's Rep. 169.

[103] *Jordan Grand Prix Ltd v Baltic Insurance Group* [1999] Lloyd's Rep. I.R. 93.

[104] See *National Justice Compania Naviera SA v Prudential Assurance Co Ltd (The Ikarian Reefer) (No.2)* [2000] 1 Lloyd's Rep. 129 (claim for costs against a third party under s.51 of the Senior Courts Act 1981 is not a matter relating to insurance).

consumer and commercial insurance,[105] excluding only disputes between insurers, such as reinsurance[106] and contribution claims.[107] In *Youell v La Reunion Aerienne*[108] the dispute was one between French leading underwriters and English co-insurers, the latter having refused—in alleged breach of an alleged leading underwriter clause—to follow a settlement. The assured's full claim had been paid by the French insurers, and they had obtained an assignment of the assured's rights against the English co-insurers. Tomlinson J. held that the action was one between insurers and was thus not a matter relating to insurance for the special jurisdictional rules in Regulation 44/2001. The learned judge distinguished the present case from one involving subrogation rights. In subrogation proceedings brought in England the action is in the name of the assured rather than the assured. Accordingly, the *Youell* ruling would not apply in a subrogation action.

2–010   *Claims by the insurers.* Any action by insurers (whether or not domiciled in the EU)[109] against the policyholder, the assured or the beneficiary of a policy[110] must be brought in the Member State of the assured's domicile (art.12(1)), although there is an exception if the claim arises out of the operations of the assured's agent, in which case the action may in the alternative be brought in the Member State where the agent carries on its operations (art.5(5)). A further exception arises in relation to liability insurance: where an action is brought against an insurer under a liability policy by the third party victim, and the relevant national law requires or permits the joinder of the assured, the court has jurisdiction over the assured irrespective of his domicile (art.11(3)).

Article 12(2) of Regulation 44/2001, having provided that the assured may be sued only in the place of his domicile, goes on to state that "[t]he provisions of this Section shall not affect the right to bring a counterclaim in the court in which, in accordance with this Section, the original claim is pending". An insurer may, therefore, raise a counterclaim against the assured in the courts of the place in which the assured has chosen to commence his action if that place is a contracting state other than that of the assured's domicile. However, it was decided by the House of Lords in *Jordan Grand Prix Ltd v Baltic Insurance Group*[111] that a counterclaim can be made only against a person who has commenced the proceedings, and that it is not possible to join any third party to the action as co-defendant. In this case, insurers sought to join as co-defendants, to proceedings commenced in England against them, three Irish defendants who had not participated in the action as claimants. Their Lordships ruled that the counterclaim could not be pursued against them in England. First, given that the basic rule under the Brussels Regulation was that a defendant was to be sued in the place of his domicile, any exception to that rule was to be construed narrowly. This pointed to the conclusion that a person not domiciled in England or who had not been a claimant could not be made the defendant to a counterclaim in

---

[105] *New Hampshire Insurance Co v Strabag Bau AG* [1992] 1 Lloyd's Rep. 454.

[106] *Agnew v Lansforsakringsbolagens AB* [2000] Lloyd's Rep. I.R. 317; *Group Josi Reinsurance Co SA v Universal General Insurance Co* [2001] Lloyd's Rep. I.R. 483.

[107] *GIE v Zurich Espana and Soptrans* (C-77/04) [2005] E.C.R. I-4509.

[108] *Youell v La Reunion Aerienne* [2009] Lloyd's Rep. I.R. 405,

[109] *Jordan Grand Prix Ltd v Baltic Insurance Group* [1999] Lloyd's Rep. I.R. 93.

[110] The meaning of these three separate terms is unclear, and was left open in *Jordan Grand Prix Ltd v Baltic Insurance Group* [1999] Lloyd's Rep. I.R. 93. It would seem to encompass any third party with an interest in the policy even though he is not a party to it. The term "assured" will be used as shorthand for these concepts in what follows.

[111] *Jordan Grand Prix Ltd v Baltic Insurance Group* [1999] Lloyd's Rep. I.R. 93.

England. Secondly, art.12(2) was, for the purposes of the insurance rules, silent on the joinder of third parties to a counterclaim, in direct contrast to the general rules in the Brussels Regulation which, under art.6, permit such joinder. Thirdly, the purpose of arts 8–14 was to protect assureds, and this would be weakened if joinder of the type asserted was permissible.

Claim against insurers. Any action by an assured against the insurers is not so 	**2–011**
restricted. If the assured is domiciled within the European Union, the assured may bring the action in the Member State of his own domicile (art.9). Alternatively, and whether or not[112] the assured is domiciled within the EU, he may bring an action in the place of the insurers' domicile (art.8). Finally, if the insurers are not domiciled within the EU, the assured (irrespective of his own domicile) may bring his action in the courts of the Member State in which the insurers' agent carried on its operations (art.5(5)).

Property insurance. In the case of insurance on real property, the assured may 	**2–012**
sue in the place where the harmful event affecting the property occurred (art.10).

Liability insurance: actions by the assured. Special provision is made for 	**2–013**
liability insurance. A liability insurer may be sued, as an alternative to any of the places set out in the insurance rules, in the courts of the place where the harmful act occurred (art.10). In the event that the injured party has brought proceedings against the assured, the insurer may be joined to those proceedings wherever they take place as long as the law of the jurisdiction in question permits joinder (art.11(1)).[113]

Liability insurance: actions by the victim. The Brussels Regulation also makes 	**2–014**
provision for the case in which a third party brings proceedings directly against a liability insurer. Article 11(2) provides that "Articles 8, 9 and 10 shall apply to actions brought by the injured party directly against the insurer, where such direct actions are permitted." This means that the special insurance rules and the liability insurance rules are all applicable to the third party's action. There are nevertheless two important matters not resolved by art.11(2).

The first, is that it is not clear from the wording whether the third party is treated as the assured so that, for example, he has a right to sue in the place of his own domicile, or whether he simply acquires the assured's rights and may thus be unable to bring proceedings in the courts of his own domicile unless the assured is domiciled there, the insurer is domiciled there or the harmful event took place there. The point was resolved in favour of the former, wider, approach, by the European Court of Justice in *FBTO Schadeverzekeringen NV v Oden-breit*,[114] in which a victim domiciled in Germany but injured in The Netherlands by an assured domiciled in that jurisdiction and with liability insurers also domiciled in that jurisdiction, was held to be entitled to pursue the insurers in

---

[112] *Berisford v New Hampshire Insurance* [1990] 1 Lloyd's Rep. 454.

[113] Brussels Regulation, art.11(1). See *Societe Financiere et Industrielle du Peloux v Axa Belgium* (112/03) [2006] Lloyd's Rep. I.R. 676, in which the Belgian group liability insurers of the French assured's Belgian parent company were joined to proceedings brought against the assured in France. The European Court of Justice held that art.14 of the Brussels Regulation, which allows an insurer and an assured domiciled in the same Member State to agree that the courts of that Member State are to have exclusive jurisdiction, did not allow that clause to be enforced as between the insurer and an insured subsidiary domiciled in another Member State.

[114] *FBTO Schadeverzekeringen NV v Odenbreit* (C-463/06) [2008] Lloyd's Rep. I.R. 354.

Germany. Article 9(1)(b) permitted an action to be brought in the domicile of the assured, beneficiary or policyholder, and art.11(2) extended art.9(l)(b) so as to permit an action by the victim in his own domicile.

The second is the meaning of the proviso "where such direct actions are permitted". This phrase does not identify the system of law under which the direct action must be permitted. There are at least three possibilities: the law governing the tort action between the third party and the assured; the law governing the insurance policy; and the law of the forum, the place in which the action is brought. The first can be dismissed, because the action against the insurers is plainly not one in tort: the insurers have not committed any tort.[114a] The choice is thus between the law of the policy and the law of the forum. It will not matter if the claim is one arising out of a motor accident, because the Fifth Motor Insurance Directive, European Parliament and Council Directive 2005/14 requires Member States to provide direct actions against motor insurers.[115] Accordingly, in *Maher v Groupama Grand Est*[116] claimants domiciled in England and injured in a road accident in France caused by the negligence of a French-domiciled driver were entitled to bring a direct action in England against the assured's motor liability insurers: that was so even though it would not have been possible under the tort jurisdiction rules in Regulation 44/2001 to have proceeded in England against the driver himself (other than, possibly, by joining him to the proceedings against his insurers). That requirement is not necessarily satisfied in other forms of liability insurance. In England, for example, a direct action is permitted only if the assured has become insolvent: Third Parties (Rights against Insurers) Acts 1930 and 2010. In *Thwaites v Aviva Assurances*[117] the court opted for the law governing the policy. In *Thwaites* the claimant was injured in France by the alleged negligence of the assured, and commenced an action against the assured's liability insurers in England. The policy was governed by French law, which permitted a direct action in those circumstances; by contrast, English law, the law of the forum, did not permit a direct action. The court ruled that the relevant law was the law applicable to the policy and not the law of the forum, so that the action could go ahead.

In the event that a direct action may be brought by the victim of a negligent assured against the assured's insurers in the Member State in which the assured is domiciled, a further question arises as to whether a person who has acquired the victim's rights can rely upon them to bring an action against the insurers in the Member State of the victim's domicile. A subrogated claim, or a claim by an equitable assignee, at least where English law is applicable, does not give rise to a problem, because the claim is to be brought in the name of the victim so that the position is unaffected. The difficult case is that in which the claim has to be brought in the name of the person who has acquired the victim's rights. Where the assignee is an insurer, the claim is to be treated as brought by one insurer against another and the matter is accordingly not one relating to insurance within the special jurisdictional rules for insurance in the Brussels Regulation.[118] The

---

[114a] *Through Transport Mutual Insurance Association (Eurasia) Ltd v New India Assurance Co Ltd* [2005] 1 Lloyd's Rep 67; *Youell v Kara Mara Shipping Co Ltd* [2000] 2 Lloyd's Rep 102. This analysis has been rejected in New Zealand, the court holding that a direct claim against insurers is tortious in nature.

[115] In England, see the European Communities (Rights against Insurers) Regulations 2002 (SI 2002/3061).

[116] *Maher v Groupama Grand Est* [2009] EWCA Civ 1191. See also *Knight v Axa Assurance* [2009] Lloyd's Rep. I.R. 667.

[117] *Thwaites v Aviva Insurance* Unreported, February 2010 Mayors and City of London Court.

[118] *Youell v La Reunion Aerienne* [2009] Lloyd's Rep. I.R. 405.

position of other assignees was discussed by the European Court of Justice in *Voralberger Gebietskrankenkasse v WGV-Schwäbische Allgemeine Versicherungs AG*.[119] The victim, who was domiciled in Austria, was injured in a road traffic accident in Germany. She received payment from the Austrian social insurance fund, which commenced proceedings against the negligent driver's insurers in Austria. The European Court of Justice ruled that a social security body was not a weaker party, and thus was unable to rely upon the insurance rules. This ruling is uncertain in its scope. It seems to follow that an assignee who is not an economically powerful party, e.g. the family of a deceased victim, have the same right as the victim to bring proceedings in the Member State of the victim's domicile. However, it is possible to imagine circumstances in which the deceased victim's executor is a bank or other financial institution. It is uncertain whether the *Voralberger* decision should be regarded as distinguishing between assignees on the basis of their economic strength, thereby giving rise potentially arbitrary outcomes depending upon the identity of the assignee, or whether the true basis is that a social security institution is akin to an insurer and thus precluded from reliance on the special jurisdiction rules on that basis.

Where the law under which the third party action is permitted so allows (i.e. the law governing the policy), the assured himself may be joined to the proceedings and the court has jurisdiction over him even if the assured is not domiciled in that jurisdiction (art.11(3)). In *Maher*, the Court of Appeal was sceptical of the suggestion that art.11(3) could be triggered only where the insurers wished to join the assured.

Jurisdiction agreements in insurance matters. Articles 13 and 14 of the **2–015** Brussels Regulation restrict the ability of the insurers to remove by contract the protections conferred by the insurance rules. An exclusive jurisdiction agreement is valid only if it falls into one of the following categories:

(a) it is made after the dispute has arisen or the assured has voluntarily submitted to the jurisdiction of the court in question;

(b) the policy gives the assured the additional right to sue in a country other than those permitted by the insurance jurisdiction rules extends the rights of the assured;

(c) the parties are both domiciled or habitually resident in the same Member State and the agreement confers exclusive jurisdiction on the courts of that Member State—this provision cannot affect the ordinary rights of a co-assured who is domiciled in a different Member State[120];

(d) the assured is not domiciled within a Member State, unless the policy is a compulsory liability policy or relates to real property in the EU;

(e) it covers commercial risks in respect of loss or damage to sea-going ships, offshore installations or aircraft;

(f) it covers goods in transit[121] by ships or aircraft, other than passengers' baggage;

(g) it covers, in respect of the use or operation of ships, aircraft or offshore installations: (1) liability for loss of or damage to goods in transit, other

---

[119] *Voralberger Gebietskrankenkasse v WGV-Schwäbische Allgemeine Versicherungs AG* (C-347/08) [2009] EUECJ.

[120] *Société Financière et Industrielle du Peloux v Axa Belgium* (C-112/03) [2006] Q.B. 251.

[121] See *Evialis v SIAT* [2003] 2 Lloyd's Rep. 600.

than in respect of passengers or their baggage; (2) financial loss,[122] in
particular loss of freight; and (3) and ancillary risks and interests.[123]

(h) it covers large commercial risks, including: (1) risks relating to railway
rolling stock, aircraft and ships; (2) credit and suretyship risks; and (3)
risks relating to land vehicles, fire and natural forces, and liability, as long
as the assured has any two of a balance sheet total of €6.2 million, a net
turnover of €12.8 million and an average of 250 employees during the
relevant financial year.

2–015A   **Submission to jurisdiction.** Article 24 of the Brussels Regulation provides
that:

> "Apart from jurisdiction derived from other provisions of this Regulation, a court of a
> Member State before which a defendant enters an appearance shall have jurisdiction.
> This rule shall not apply where appearance was entered to contest the jurisdiction."

It has been held that a submission to jurisdiction overrides an exclusive
jurisdiction clause entered into by the submitting party,[123a] and in *Vienna
Insurance Group v Bilas*[123b] the European Court of Justice ruled that an assured
who submits to the jurisdiction of a court thereby loses his protection under the
insurance rules. A submission thus has the same effect as a post-dispute
agreement on jurisdiction. It was also held that the court in question is not under
any duty to ensure that the assured is fully appraised of the consequences of such
submission, although the European Court of Justice indicated that it was open to
a court to point those consequences out to the assured.

2. DETERMINING THE LAW APPLICABLE TO INSURANCE CONTRACTS

History of the legal structure

2–016   *The common law.* On the basis that the English court has jurisdiction over an
insurance dispute, it remains for the court to determine whether English law or
some other law is to be applied to the agreement. That law was at common law
referred to as the "proper" or "governing" law but, in the light of European
harmonisation measures since the latter part of the twentieth century, has become
known as the "applicable" law. The common law evolved a series of rules for
determining the law governing contractual obligations, but these have been
superseded by European measures: the common law remains relevant only to
those matters excluded from the European legislation, most importantly, arbitration agreements. The common law was swept away in 1991 in two separate steps:
by rules affecting insurance contracts where the risk was situated in the EU; and
by rules for all other contracts including insurance contracts whose risk was not
situated in the EU and reinsurance contracts.

2–017   *The Insurance Directives.* The Insurance Directives, which created a Single
European Market for insurance by allowing an insurer authorised in the Member

---

[122] Including employers' liability: *Standard Steamship Owners' Protection and Indemnity Association (Bermuda) Ltd v GIE Vision Bail* [2005] Lloyd's Rep. I.R. 407.
[123] A provision to be construed narrowly: *Charman v WOC Offshore BV* [1993] 2 Lloyd's Rep.
551.
[123a] Case 150/80 *Elefanten Schuh v Jacqmain* [1981] E.C.R. 1671.
[123b] Case C-111/09, [2010] EUECJ.

State of its head office to establish branches in other EU States and to sell directly into other EU countries from any EU branch, without interference from the regulatory authorities of the host, were accompanied by rules for determining the law applicable to insurance contracts affecting risks located within the EU. These rules were designed as an alternative to an approach which proved to be politically impossible to achieve, namely the harmonisation of substantive insurance law, and their purpose was to allow each Member State to maintain or adopt measures which allowed its residents the protection of local insurance law rather than be subject to the vagaries of some other insurance law chosen by the insurers. This was achieved in two Directives. The Second Non-Life Directive of June 1988[124] set out choice of law rules for "general business" (i.e. all types of non-life policy) where the policy insured a risk situated in the EU. These rules became effective in the United Kingdom on July 1, 1990 under the Insurance Companies (Amendment) Regulations 1990[125]; the effect of the Regulations was to insert a new definition section, s.96A, and a new Sch.3A containing the detail of the rules, into the Insurance Companies Act 1982. Those Regulations were repealed and replaced in a modified form by the Financial Services and Markets Act 2000 (Law Applicable to Contracts of Insurance) Regulations 2001,[126] with effect from the end of November 2001. The second relevant Directive was the Second Life Directive, adopted by the EU in November 1990 and transposed into English law with effect from May 20, 1993.[127] The 1993 Regulations added to the ICA 1982 a definition of when a risk was situated in the EU[128] and added a new part to ICA 1982 Sch.3A, selling out choice of law rules. Those provisions were also replaced at the end of November 2001 by the Financial Services and Markets Act 2000 (Law Applicable to Contracts of Insurance) Regulations 2001. The 2001 Regulations continue to apply to insurance contracts entered into before December 17, 2009, but ceased to have effect to contracts made on or after that date: such contracts are now regulated by the Rome I Regulation, discussed below.

The Rome Convention 1980. On April 1, 1991 the United Kingdom brought into **2–018** force the Contracts (Applicable Law) Act 1990, which implemented into domestic law the Rome Convention on the Law Applicable to Contractual Obligations 1980.[129] The Rome Convention was an agreement between EU Member States, although was not mandatory and each Member State was free to adopt or decline it. The Convention laid down applicable law rules for most forms of commercial contract and, following implementation by the 1990 Act, was to be applied by the UK courts to conflict of laws disputes arising before them. As far as insurance was concerned, the Rome Convention excluded any insurance policy whose risk was situated in any EU Member State, as such the applicable law rules for such contracts were provided by the EU Insurance Directives. However, reinsurance agreements were outside the Directives and thus, irrespective of the situation of the risk, fell within the Rome Convention. There was nothing in the Rome Convention to limit its application to contracts made in, or between nationals of, Contracting States, so that it was perfectly

---

[124] Council Directive 88/357/EEC.

[125] SI 1990/1811 reg.6.

[126] SI 2001/2635.

[127] Insurance Companies (Amendment) Regulations 1993 (SI 1993/174) reg.5.

[128] ICA 1982 s.94B(1A).

[129] The Rome Convention was republished in consolidated form in [2005] OJ C334/1, following amendments made on the accession to the Convention of the 10 new EU Member States on April 14, 2005.

possible for a dispute between nationals of two non-contracting states, which was brought before the English courts, to be subjected to Convention choice of law rules.

The choice of law rules set out in the Rome Convention were to be applied by the courts of Contracting States whether or not the system of law specified was the law of a Contracting State.[130] Contracting states were under an obligation to ensure uniform application of the rules of the Convention,[131] and questions of construction may be referred to the European Court of Justice by the national court hearing the case in which the point arose.[132] The English courts could, in dealing with an issue arising under the Convention, take note of the authoritative report by Professors Giuliano and Lagarde.[133] The rules of the Rome Convention applied as between the constituent parts of the United Kingdom.[134]

2–019 *The Rome I Regulation.* In December 2005 the European Commission proposed to replace the Rome Convention with an EU Regulation binding on all Member States, although there were no significant substantive changes to the Rome Convention put forward. A wider-ranging proposal was tabled in December 2006 by the EU Presidency, and was published on March 2, 2007. Under the proposal, the applicable law rules in the Insurance Directives were to be repealed, and insurance was to be brought within the scope of the Rome Convention. After opposition from the UK was dropped, the proposals were ultimately adopted on June 17, 2008, by European Parliament and Council Regulation 593/2008/EC "on the law applicable to contractual obligations", the Rome I Regulation. This Regulation came into force on June 17, 2009, and applies to contracts entered into on or after December 17, 2009.[135] The Rome I Regulation thus superseded the Insurance Directives and the Rome Convention 1980 and the rules for determining the law applicable to insurance contracts as set in the Insurance Directives with effect from that date. The Financial Services and Markets Act 2000 (Law Applicable to Contracts of Insurance) Regulations 2009[136] reg.2, adds new 3(1A) into the Financial Services and Markets Act 2000 (Law Applicable to Contracts of Insurance) Regulations 2001, making it clear that they do not apply to contracts of insurance entered into on or after December 17, 2009. The Law Applicable to Contractual Obligations (England and Wales and Northern Ireland) Regulations 2009[137] reg.2, similarly disapplies the Rome Convention from contracts governed by the Rome I Regulation by adding a new s.4A to the Contracts (Applicable Law) Act 1990, to that effect.

The Rome I Regulation has effected some substantive changes to the Rome Convention, and there are also useful clarifications. There are two aspects of particular significance. The first is that the conflict of laws rules applicable to the vast majority of contracts, including insurance contracts, are now contained in a

---

[130] art.3.

[131] art.18.

[132] Contracts (Applicable Law) Act 1990 s.3(1)–(2). The procedure is set out in the Brussels Protocol to the Convention, and is analogous to the procedure under art.234 of the EU Treaty. The protocol came into force on March 1, 2005: Contracts (Applicable Law) Act 1990 (Commencement No.21 Order 2004, SI 2004/3448. The report of Professor Tizzano on the Rome Convention, published in [1990] OJ C219/1 was authoritative and could be taken into account by the English Courts: Contracts (Applicable Law) Act 1990 s.3(3)(h).

[133] Contracts (Applicable Law) Act 1990 s.3(3)(a). The report is published in [1980] OJ C282/1.

[134] Contracts (Applicable Law) Act 1990 s.2(3).

[135] Rome I Regulation art.25.

[136] SI 2009/3075.

[137] SI 2009/3064.

single instrument rather than to be gleaned from a combination of Directives, implementing legislation and statutory instruments and a Convention. The second is that, because Rome I is an EU measure, disputes as to its meaning can be referred to the European Court of Justice for preliminary rulings.

The United Kingdom has extended the Rome I rules to conflict of laws disputes between the constituent parts of the United Kingdom, although there are modifications to this principle in respect of insurance contracts.[138]

Summary of the legal structure

Contracts entered into before December 17, 2009.[139] The law applicable to a   **2–020** contract coming before the English courts will be determined in accordance with the following structure.

(1) A non-life policy insuring a risk situated within the EU is governed by the rules in the Financial Services and Markets Act 2000 (Law Applicable to Contracts of Insurance) Regulations 2001, implementing the Second Non-Life Directive. Such policies are excluded from the Rome Convention 1980.

(2) A non-life policy insuring a risk situated outside the EU is governed by the Rome Convention.

(3) A life policy insuring a risk situated within the EU is governed by the choice of law rules in the Financial Services and Markets Act 2000 (Law Applicable to Contracts of Insurance) Regulations 2001, implementing the Second Life Directive. The Rome Convention is inapplicable.

(4) A life policy insuring a risk situated outside a Member State is governed by the Rome Convention.

(5) Reinsurance agreements are governed by the Rome Convention, as they are excluded from the Financial Services and Markets Act 2000 (Law Applicable to Contracts of Insurance) Regulations 2001 by reg.3(1).

A problem arises where the risk is situated inside the EU but the insurer is outside the EU, as it appears that neither set of rules applies.

Contracts entered into on or after December 17, 2009. The general rules for   **2–021** determining the applicable law are set out in arts 3 and 4. The Regulation lays down choice of law rules in civil and commercial matters other than revenue and administrative matters (art.1.1). It excludes, under art.1.2[140]:

(a) questions involving the status or legal capacity of natural persons other than whether the issue is whether a valid contract has been made;

(b) obligations arising out of family relationships;

(c) obligations arising out of matrimonial property regimes;

(d) obligations arising under bills of exchange, cheques and promissory notes and other negotiable instruments to the extent that the obligations under such other negotiable instruments arise out of their negotiable character;

---

[138] SI 2009/3075 reg.3; SI 2009/3064 reg.5. Provision for multi-jurisdiction Member States is laid down by art.22 of the Rome I Regulation.

[139] The common law continues to apply to contracts entered into before the Rome Convention and the Insurance Directives came into force.

[140] The list is more or less the same as that in the Rome Convention.

(e) arbitration agreements and agreements on the choice of court[141];

(f) questions governed by the law of companies and other bodies, relating to their constitutions;

(g) the question whether an agent is able to bind a principal, or an organ to bind a company or other body corporate or unincorporated, in relation to a third party;

(h) the constitution of trusts and the relationship between trustees and beneficiaries;

(i) obligations arising out of dealings prior to the conclusion of a contract, which are governed by the Rome II Regulation on non-contractual obligations;

(j) life and sickness insurance contracts issued by bodies other than insurance companies and which provide benefits for employees or self-employed persons.

The general rules are modified in four cases: contracts of carriage (art.5); consumer contracts (art.6); insurance contracts (art.7); and employment contracts (art.8). As far as insurance contracts are concerned, the structure established by the Insurance Directives and the Rome Convention is retained by the Regulation, although the documents are merged and therefore the lacuna as to insurers domiciled outside the EU has been filled. The special choice of rules for insurance contracts set out in art.7 apply to: insurance contracts covering risks situated within the EU; and large risks whether situated inside or outside the EU. It follows that if the risk is a large one there is no need to determine where it is situated. The general applicable law rules in Rome I govern: reinsurance agreements; and risks which are not large risks and which are situated outside the EU. Accordingly, it is necessary to determine the situation of a non-large risk in the latter case. The position may be summarised as follows.

1. Reinsurance contracts irrespective of the situation of the risk are governed by the general rules in arts 3 and 4 of the Rome I Regulation. The parties are free to choose the applicable law (art.3), failing which there is a default presumption which points towards the law of the place where the reinsurer has its head office (art.4).

2. Insurance risks situated outside the EU which are not large risks and which do not involve consumers are governed by the general rules in arts 3 and 4 of the Rome I Regulation. The parties are free to choose the applicable law (art.3), failing which there is a default presumption which points towards the law of the place where the insurer has its head office (art.4).

3. Insurance risks situated outside the EU which are not large risks but which do involve consumers are governed by art.6 of the Rome I Regulation. The applicable law is law of the place where the consumer has his habitual residence, subject to the right of the parties to choose another law insofar as is permitted by local law. However, if the insurer does not pursue activities in the consumer's home state and has not targeted the consumer (i.e. a case in which the consumer has taken the initiative in seeking insurance outside his home state), then the general rules in arts 3 and 4 apply.

---

[141] The most likely interpretation of this exclusion is that only the independent arbitration or jurisdiction obligation is outside the Rome I Regulation, so that the mere fact that an insurance contract contains an arbitration clause does not exclude it from the Rome I Regulation.

4. If the risk is a large one, whether it is situated inside or outside the EU, the case is governed by art.7.1 of the Rome I Regulation, which applies arts 3 and 4. Thus the parties are free to choose the applicable law, but if they have not done so then there is a default presumption in favour of the insurer's head office.

5. If the risk is not a large risk, and is situated within the EU, then art.7 applies. In general terms the applicable law is that of the situation of the risk (normally the assured's habitual residence), but the parties are free to choose some other law if the local law so permits.

Situation of the risk in insurance cases. The situation of an insurance risk is **2–022** relevant under both the pre-December 2009 regime and the Rome I Regulation. As regards the former, the situation of the risk determines whether the applicable law rules are those found in the Rome Convention or in the Insurance Directives. As regards the Rome I Regulation, the situation of the risk is relevant where the risk is not a large risk, in which case risks situated outside the EU are governed by arts 3, 4 and 6, whereas risks situated inside the EU are governed by art.7.

The place in which a risk is situated is defined by art.2(d) of Council Directive 88/357/EEC (the Second Non-Life Directive) and art.1(1) of European Parliament and Council Directive 2002/83/EC (the Consolidated Life Directive). Under art.2(d): (i) a property risk is situated where the property itself is situated; (ii) in the case of a vehicle, the risk is situated in the place of registration, although in the case of a motor vehicle dispatched from one EEA state to another, for the period of 30 days beginning with the day on which the purchaser accepts delivery, the risk is to be treated as situated in the state of destination and not the state of registration[142]; (iii) in the case of a travel policy for less than four months, the risk is situated where the policy was taken out; and (iv) in all other cases the risk is situated where the policyholder has his habitual residence (natural person) or where the establishment to which the contract relates is situated (legal person).[143] A life risk is situated in the place where the policyholder has his habitual residence.

It is not always easy to define the place where a non-large risk is situated, e.g. where the policy covers risks both inside and outside the EU. In particular, an assured can have more than one habitual residence, as where the assured divides his time more or less equally between two places. In such a case, a policy on, say, personal effects may be difficult to classify where those effects are carried by the assured, or—equally difficult—where some effects are kept within the EU but some are kept outside the EU. Before the adoption of the Rome I Regulation the English courts regarded it as artificial and unduly problematic to regard such policies as divisible as regards applicable law rules. The point arose in a commercial context in *American Motorists Insurance Co v Cellstar Corp*.[144] The assured was a company incorporated in Delaware with its principal place of business in Texas, although it carried on the business of supplying wireless communication equipment throughout the world. The policy was described as a "Global Transportation Policy", which covered the assured and its subsidiaries

---

[142] The purpose of this provision is to allow a vehicle to be purchased in one EEA State for export to another, with the result that the risk is situated in the destination state rather than the original registration state. This was introduced by the Fifth Motor Insurance Directive, European Parliament and Council Regulation 2005/14/EC.

[143] This will generally be the place from which the business is carried on: *Evialis SA v SIAT* [2003] 2 Lloyd's Rep. 377.

[144] *American Motorists Insurance Co v Cellstar Corp* [2003] Lloyd's Rep. I.R. 359.

worldwide. David Steel J. held that the risk was situated outside the EU. The learned judge was strongly of the view that the contract should be governed by a single legal regime, as the application of different laws could lead to startlingly different results in different jurisdictions. The appropriate test was whether the risks were predominantly inside or outside the EU, and as the policy encompassed many risks in a variety of countries only three of which were within the EU, the relevant choice of law rules were those in the Rome Convention. The Court of Appeal, on appeal,[145] adopted a different approach. It noted that the choice of law rules for insurance contracts made no provision for the possibility that risks covered by a single policy might be situated both inside and outside the EU and that those rules only dealt with a policy covering one or more risks situated within the EU. The Court of Appeal's construction of the Insurance Directives was that they were not designed to apply to non-EU insurers who happened to write risks situated within the EU, but nevertheless left open the question whether the United Kingdom's implementation of the Directives gave rise to the situation that the choice of law rules in the Directives applied to all policies covering risks situated in the United Kingdom irrespective of the identity of the insurers. The Court of Appeal also addressed the issue of who the "policyholder" was in the case of a contract of this type and identified three possible approaches:

(a) the parent company alone was the policyholder, with the subsidiaries simply being insured persons;
(b) the parent company and each of the subsidiaries was independently a policyholder; and
(c) the parent and the subsidiaries constituted a single policyholder.

Possibility (b) was unattractive on the basis that it gave rise to the possibility of dividing up the policy with different applicable laws being relevant to each policyholder. The Court of Appeal thus favoured (a), with a fallback of (c) in the event that (a) was wrong. On either analysis the policyholder's central administration was in Texas. The Court of Appeal chose not to decide whether the choice of law rules in the Directive applied where the policy covered risks both inside and outside the EEA and was content to assume that it did. However, as the Court of Appeal pointed out, if that was the correct interpretation then the choice of law rules themselves were not fully applicable as some of them referred to the law of the EU Member State where the risk is situated as determining whether the parties can choose some other law: if policy holder was not established in the EU then that test, where it was relevant, could never apply.

These problems have been addressed by the Rome I Regulation, Recital 33 of the Rome I Regulation clarifies the position by adopting a divisibility approach previously rejected by the English courts:

"Where an insurance contract not covering a large risk covers more than one risk, at least one of which is situated in a Member State and at least one of which is situated

---

[145] *American Motorists Insurance Co v Cellstar Corp* [2003] Lloyd's Rep. I.R. 359. See also *Travelers Casualty & Surety Co of Europe Ltd v Sun Life Assurance Co of Canada (UK) Ltd* [2004] Lloyd's Rep. I.R. 846, where the point was similarly left open. In the trial of this action, *Travelers Casualty and Surety Co of Canada v Sun Life Assurance Co of Canada (UK) Ltd (No.1)* [2007] Lloyd's Rep. I.R. 619. The court found it unnecessary to decide whether a global policy covering a group of companies located in different jurisdictions was subject to the EU rules or the Rome Convention rules and was satisfied that in either case the outcome was the same and that the applicable law was that of Ontario, the place of the parent company's head office.

in a third country, the special rules on insurance contracts in this Regulation should apply only to the risk or risks situated in the relevant Member State or Member States."

Where the contract covers risks situated in more than one Member State, the contract is to be considered as constituting several contracts each relating to only one Member State: Rome I Regulation, art.7.5.

Large risks and mass risks. The distinction between large risks and other risks   2–023
is relevant under both the pre-December 2009 regime and the Rome I Regulation. As regards the former, if the risk is situated in the EU and it is not a large risk, restrictions are imposed upon the right of the parties to choose an applicable law other than the law of the place where the risk is situated, whereas there are no such restrictions as regards large risks.[146] As regards the Rome I Regulation, a large risk wherever situated is governed by the rules in art.7 (which applies arts 3 and 4), whereas a non-large risk situated outside the EU is governed by arts 3, 4 and 6, and a non-large risk situated inside the EU is governed by art.7.

A large risk is one determined by subject matter, turnover and employment numbers. Article 5(d) of the First Non-Life Directive, Council Directive 73/239/EEC,[147] defines a large risk as a commercial risk falling into any of the following categories:

  (i) all risks relating to railway rolling stock, aircraft, ships, liability for aircraft and liability for ships;
 (ii) risks relating to credit and suretyship as long as the policyholder is engaged in an industrial or commercial activity in one of the liberal professions;
(iii) risks relating to land vehicles, fire and natural forces, motor vehicle liability, general liability and miscellaneous financial loss, as long as the policy holder has any two of a balance sheet total of €6.2 million, a net turnover of €12.8 million or an average of 250 employees during the financial year.

Consumer insurances. If a risk is a large risk, then by definition the assured   2–024
will not be a consumer, and art.7.1 of the Rome I Regulation adopts arts 3 and 4 of the Rome I Regulation as the rules governing the determination of the applicable law. If the risk is not a large risk, then the rules for determining the applicable law vary: (a) if the risk is situated outside the EU and the assured is not a consumer, the relevant rules are those in arts 3 and 4; (b) if the risk is situated outside the EU and the assured is a consumer, the relevant rules are those in art.6; and (c) if the risk is situated inside the EU then whether or not the assured is a consumer the relevant rules are contained in art.7. For the purposes of distinguishing (a) and (b), it is therefore necessary to define the term "consumer". The relevant definition is found in art.6.1 of the Rome I Regulation, which defines a consumer as a natural person who has concluded a contract for a purpose which can be regarded as being outside his trade or profession with another person acting in the exercise of his trade or profession.

---

[146] The Financial Services and Markets Act 2000 (Law Applicable to Contracts of Insurance) Regulations 2001 reg.6.
[147] Applied to the Rome I Regulation by art.7.6.

2–025   **Proof of foreign law.** Where an English court reaches the conclusion that the applicable law is English law, that law will be applied in the usual way and no further problem arises. However, where the applicable law is found to be that of some other country, an English judge will be faced with the problem of having to decide the case on what may be unfamiliar principles. The general rule here is that the content of foreign law is a matter of fact, to be proved by the evidence of expert witnesses; merely laying the text of a foreign law before the court will not necessarily be adequate for this purpose.[148] Before the passing of the Civil Evidence Act 1972, there had been some conflict of judicial opinion as to the requisite qualifications of potential witnesses on the content of foreign law, and, in particular, whether evidence from persons without professional legal qualifications or qualified but no longer practising, was admissible.[149] However, the matter was resolved by s.4(1) of the Civil Evidence Act 1972, which states that:

> " . . . [I]n civil proceedings a person who is suitably qualified to do so on account of his knowledge or experience is competent to give expert evidence, irrespective of whether he has acted or is entitled to act as a legal practitioner".

If the law applicable to a contract is not English law, but the person seeking to rely upon the foreign law in question refuses or fails to prove its content, there is no presumption that English law is the governing law. The true principle here is that if foreign law is neither pleaded nor proved, the court will presume that the parties are content to proceed on the basis that there is no difference between English law and the applicable law.[150] However, if the evidence of foreign experts is not conflicting, the English court cannot reject the evidence and undertake its own researches.[151]

2–026   **Substance and procedure.** While an English court will honour the applicable law of an agreement whenever it has jurisdiction to hear an action on that agreement, the applicable law is relevant only to substantive issues of law arising under the agreement: all matters of procedure are to be determined in accordance with English law and practice. Moreover, the classification of issues into those of substance and those of procedure is a matter primarily for English domestic law.[152] The distinction between substance and procedure is not always clear-cut, but it is nevertheless established that where the issue is procedural in English law then English law will prevail irrespective of the applicable law.[153]

2–027   **Determining the applicable law.** The following paragraphs examine the general rules in arts 3 and 4 of the Rome I Regulation for determining the law

---

[148] *Callwood v Callwood* [1960] A.C. 659.

[149] Compare *Bristow v Sequeville* (1850) 5 Ex. 275 with *Rossano v Manufacturers' Life Insurance Co* [1963] 2 Q.B. 352.

[150] *Royal Boskalis Westminster NV v Mountain* [1999] Q.B. 674; *Tamil Nadu Electricity Board v ST-CMS Electric Co Pte Ltd* [2007] EWHC 1713 (Comm); *Global Multimedia International Ltd v Ara Media Services* [2007] 1 All E.R. (Comm) 1160.

[151] *Bumper Development Corp Ltd v Commissioner of Police of the Metropolis* [1991] 4 All E.R. 638.

[152] *Maher v Groupama Grand Est* [2009] EWCA Civ 1191. One exception is the formal validity of a contract, classified as a matter of procedure by the common law but of substance by the Rome Convention and the Rome I Regulation.

[153] *South Carolina Insurance Co v Assurantie Maatschappij "de Zeven Provincien" NV and Al Ahli Insurance Co* [1987] 1 A.C. 24, applied in *Omega Group Holdings Ltd v Kozeny* [2002] C.L.C. 132.

applicable to a contract of insurance. The contracts are: reinsurance agreements irrespective of the situation of the risk; large risks[154]; and non-large risks where the risk is situated outside the EU and the assured is not a consumer. The same rules apply under the Rome Convention, to reinsurance agreements irrespective of the situation of the risk, and to risks situated outside the EU.

The ascertainment of the applicable law of an insurance contract is, at common law, a three-stage process. First, the agreement may contain an express choice of law clause; in the overwhelming majority of cases, the choice will be regarded as conclusive. Secondly, in the absence of a choice of law clause, the courts will examine the agreement for evidence of an implicit choice of applicable law. Thirdly, if the applicable law cannot be ascertained from the terms of the contract, the court must itself decide which system of law is applicable to the agreement; that choice will rest upon the determination of the system of law with which the agreement has its closest connection. This approach is, with some modification, retained by the Rome Convention and the Rome I Regulation in respect of large risks, but a different approach is adopted in the case of other insurances. Where the application of these rules indicates a foreign applicable law, it is not open to the English courts to refuse to apply that law on the basis that it might yield "an unsatisfactory if not unjust result".[155] This, however, is subject to the exceptions on freedom of choice of law discussed below.

Express choice of law agreements

Choice of law agreements and the applicable law. The traditional view of the English courts has been that an express agreement as to the law governing a contract is to be honoured. The principle of party autonomy was retained by the Rome Convention, the basic principle being set out in art.3.1:   **2–028**

> "A contract shall be governed by the law chosen by the parties. The choice must be expressed or demonstrated with reasonable certainty by the terms of the contract or the circumstances of the case. By their choice the parties can select the law applicable to the whole or a part only of the contract."

The cornerstone of the Rome I Regulation is also party autonomy. Article 3.1 of the Regulation has reformulated the test as follows:

> "A contract shall be governed by the law chosen by the parties. The choice shall be made expressly or clearly demonstrated by the terms of the contract or the circumstances of the case. By their choice the parties can select the law applicable to the whole or to part only of the contract."

At common law it is permissible for the parties to choose only the law of a country, and not a general system of law such as *lex mercatoria* or religious principles.[156] That approach was retained by the Rome Convention.[157] The position has been modified by the Rome I Regulation, recital 13 of which states

---

[154] Rome I Regulation art.7.2.
[155] *Banco Atlantico SA v British Bank of the Middle East, Financial Times*, June 5, 1990.
[156] *Musawi v RE International (UK) Ltd* [2007] EWHC 2981 (Ch).
[157] *Shamil Bank of Bahrain v Beximco Pharmaceuticals Ltd* [2003] 2 All E.R. Comm 849; *Musawi v R E International (UK) Ltd* [2007] EWHC 2981 (Ch); *Halpern v Halpern* [2007] EWCA Civ 291, which also held that an express choice of a system of law other than that of a country does not render the contract void for uncertainty because in such a case the court would then be obliged to apply the relevant default choice of law rules under the Rome Convention.

that the parties are not precluded from incorporating by reference into their contract a non-State body of law or an international convention. It may be that recital 13 does not authorise a complete abandonment of the law of a country, but simply says that other principles can be "incorporated by reference".

It is to be noted that the Rome Convention referred to a choice of law "expressed with reasonable certainty", whereas the Rome I Regulation is concerned with a choice of law "expressly or clearly demonstrated by the terms of the contract" and it would appear from the wording that the Rome I test for express agreement is somewhat stricter than was the case under the Rome Convention.

2–029 *Form of agreement.* There is nothing in the Rome I Regulation that specifies the form of an express choice of law agreement. All that is required is a clear demonstration of intention. It would seem from cases decided under the Rome Convention that such an agreement may be oral as long as its existence can be established.[158] The validity or otherwise of a choice of law agreement is to be tested under the putative applicable law, that is, the law which would have applied to the contract had the choice been clearly valid.[159] Where a contract is alleged to be invalid for failure to comply with the formal requirements of the putative applicable law, it will be saved if it was valid under the law of the country where the agreement was concluded or under the law of a country in which one of the parties was present when the contract was concluded.[160] If the objection to validity is the incapacity of one of the parties,[161] such incapacity may be pleaded only by the party under the incapacity and the plea will succeed only if the other party was or ought to have been aware of the incapacity.[162]

For a choice of law clause to be effective, it has to be agreed between the parties: a general incorporation of the terms of another contract containing a choice of law clause is not regarded by the English courts as effective to incorporate a choice of law clause.[163]

2–030 *Policy restrictions on express choice of law.* In many cases the choice of a system of law as the applicable law will conflict with what would on objective grounds be regarded as the proper law, by reason of the connection of the contract with a given legal system. As far as the common law is concerned, and this principle is retained by the Rome Convention and the Rome I Regulation with some minor modifications, the courts have nevertheless regarded intention as the overriding factor in determining the applicable law, rather than simply as one

---

[158] *Oakley v Ultra Vehicle Design Ltd* [2005] EWHC 872 (Ch).

[159] Rome I Regulation, arts 3.5 and 10.1, re-enacting Rome Convention, arts 3.4 and 8.1. This is, however, subject to the exception in the Rome I Regulation art.10.2 (Rome Convention art.8.2) that a party can rely upon the law of his habitual residence to demonstrate that he did not consent to the agreement if in the circumstances it would not be reasonable to apply the putative applicable law to his conduct. Thus if silence is not consent under the domestic law of one party but amounts to consent under the putative applicable law, that party's silence may be treated by the court as absence of consent.

[160] Rome I Regulation art.11; Rome Convention art.9.

[161] This refers only to the incapacity of a natural person, e.g. minority or mental illness. Legal persons are deemed to be of full capacity under EU law; Companies Act 2006 ss.39 and 40.

[162] Rome I Regulation art.13; Rome Convention art.11.

[163] *Gan Insurance Co Ltd v Tai Ping Insurance Co Ltd* [1999] Lloyd's Rep. I.R. 229; *AIG Group (UK) Ltd v The Ethniki* [1998] 4 All E.R. 301.

factor which has to be taken into account in some broader enquiry. This proposition, taken to its logical conclusion, amounts to a statement that it is not necessary for there to be any connection between the contract and the chosen law other than the choice of law clause itself. A useful illustration is *Anderson v Equitable Assurance Society of the United States*,[164] in which the court did not question the binding effect of a choice of law clause nominating English law as the governing law, contained in a contract of insurance negotiated in Russia and which provided for payment in German currency. All doubts on this point were settled by the decision of the Privy Council in *Vita Food Products Inc v Unus Shipping Co Ltd*,[165] where the Privy Council was of the opinion, obiter, that a contract between a Nova Scotian shipping company and an American company under which the shipper was to carry a cargo from Newfoundland to New York in a Nova Scotia-registered ship, and which contained a clause nominating English law as the governing law, was indeed governed by English law. Lord Wright went so far as to state that "connection with English law is not as a matter of principle essential".[166] Despite occasional judicial dicta asserting that there is a need for some objective connection between the contract and the chosen system of law before an English court will give effect to that law,[167] there is no English case in which an express choice of law clause has been disregarded for want of connection alone. Certainly the English courts have no power to disregard a choice of law clause simply because it produces inconvenient results.[168] There may nevertheless be exceptional cases in which the English courts might refuse to apply an express choice of law clause. Four possibilities are suggested by the authorities.

First, Lord Wright qualified his broad statement in the *Vita Food Products* case by adding that the expressed intention had to be "bona fide and legal", and that there had not to be any reason "for avoiding the choice on the ground of public policy".[169] Although these dicta have yet to be applied in an English court, it may be assumed that they cover attempts by the parties to evade prohibitions imposed by law on the contract in the place in which it was made or was to be performed, and also attempts by one party in a position of superior bargaining strength to deprive the other of the benefit of protective legislation to which he would otherwise have been entitled. The Rome I Regulation embodies the public policy rule in a series of provisions; the chosen law cannot oust the mandatory rules of the country in which all elements relevant to the situation are located if that country's law has not been chosen (art.3.3)[170]; the parties cannot oust the mandatory principles of EU law if there is a choice of the law of a country outside the EU and all the elements relevant to the situation are located in one more EU states (art.3.4); the mandatory laws of the forum are not to be deprived of effect even if another law is validly chosen (arts 9.2 and 21)[171]; and the court may give effect to overriding mandatory rules of law in the country of the place of performance insofar as those mandatory rules render performance illegal

---

[164] *Anderson v Equitable Assurance Society of the United States* [1926] All E.R. Rep. 93.
[165] *Vita Food Products Inc v Unus Shipping Co Ltd* [1939] A.C. 277.
[166] *Vita Food Products Inc v Unus Shipping Co Ltd* [1939] A.C. 277 at 290.
[167] See *Re Helbert Wagg & Co Ltd* [1956] Ch. 323 at 341.
[168] *Banco Atlantico SA v British Bank of the Middle East*, Financial Times, June 5, 1990.
[169] *Vita Food Products Inc v Unus Shipping Co Ltd* [1939] A.C. 277 at 291.
[170] Cf. art.3.3 of the Rome Convention.
[171] Cf. art.7.2 of the Rome Convention.

(art.9.3).[172] The effect of art.3.3 is to prevent the parties from sidestepping the mandatory rules of the natural applicable law by the simple device of opting for a different applicable law. It has been held in England, in *Caterpillar Financial Services Corp v SNC Passion*,[173] that the correct approach to this provision is to consider whether, at the date of the agreement to choose a particular law, all other elements relevant to the situation were connected with some other country, disregarding any matters laid down by the mandatory rules of the law which would have been applicable but for the express choice of law.

The second exception is where the choice of law clause is either meaningless or incapable of application. In *Compagnie D'Armement Maritime SA v Compagnie Tunisienne de Navigation SA*[174] the Court of Appeal felt able to disregard a clause in a contract of carriage of oil by sea, stating that: "This contract shall be governed by the law of the flag of the vessel carrying the goods", when the goods were carried in a number of vessels bearing different flags. On appeal, the House of Lords preferred to interpret the clause as meaning that the contracts were to be governed by the law of the flag of the ship primarily used by the carrier, and on this basis held French law to be the applicable law. This decision would appear to hold good under the Rome I Regulation as the choice would seem to fail for want of being clearly demonstrated as required by art.3.1.

The third exception, suggested by the facts of *Perry v Equitable Life Assurance Society of the United States of America*,[175] is that an objectively ascertained proper law will be applied by the English courts if the intention of the parties, to have their contract governed by a named law, has been frustrated. In *Perry*, an American insurer had issued life policies on Russian subjects through its Russian office. The proper law of the agreements was stated to be the law of Russia. Legislation subsequently passed in Russia terminated the right of the insurer to carry on business in Russia, and the assureds argued that, as Russian law could no longer be applied to the agreements, their proper law was American law. Branson J. rejected this contention as, on the facts, the circumstances which had arisen appeared to have been contemplated by the agreement, which stipulated that in the event of discontinuance of business, accounts were to be made in the manner authorised by the Russian government. It is nevertheless clear that, had this clause not been present, the claimants' argument might well

---

[172] Under art.7.1 of the Rome Convention, the courts may give effect to the mandatory laws of a third country, other than the forum and the country providing the applicable law, with which the contract has a close connection. This provision is less specific than the version which appears in the Rome I Regulation, which focuses on the mandatory rules of the place of performance, and the UK opted out of it: Contracts (Applicable Law) Act 1990 s.2(2). There is no possible opt-out from the Rome I Regulation. The principle would seem to be recognised at common law: in *Ralli Bros v Compania Naviera Sola y Aznar* [1920] 1 K.B. 614 the court held that a contract governed by English law but to be performed in Spain could not be enforced in England as Spanish law rendered such performance illegal. It is not clear, however, whether the court was applying a rule of English law that a contract governed by English law will not be enforced if its performance would be illegal in the place of performance, or whether it was adopting the wider principle that the English courts will not enforce a contract—whatever its applicable law—if it requires a performance which is illegal in some other jurisdiction.

[173] *Caterpillar Financial Services Corp v SNC Passion* [2004] EWHC 569 (Comm), decided under the Rome Convention.

[174] *Compagnie D'Armement Maritime SA v Compagnie Tunisienne de Navigation SA* [1971] A.C. 572.

[175] *Perry v Equitable Life Assurance Society of the United States of America* (1929) 45 T.L.R. 468.

have had some force. It is unclear how this problem will be dealt with under the Rome I Regulation.

Fourthly, it is conceivable that a contract, while governed as a whole by the chosen law, is divisible, and that parts of it may be governed by another more appropriate law. This was held to be possible by Hobhouse J. in *Forsikringsaktielskapet Vesta v Butcher*[176] in order to overcome problems of non-matching cover which had arisen where the identical terms of an insurance and a reinsurance agreement were found to have different consequences under their respective applicable laws. The Court of Appeal and House of Lords,[177] however, preferred a less dramatic solution: the contracts were both governed in their entirety by their natural proper laws, but the words used in the reinsurance agreement were to be given the meaning that would have been afforded to them if construed in accordance with the proper law of the insurance agreement. Despite the reticence of the Court of Appeal and House of Lords in *Vesta*, it is now confirmed by art.3.1 of the Rome I Regulation, echoing art.3.1 of the Rome Convention, that the parties are free to select the law applicable to the whole or a part only of their contract. In the event that the chosen laws for the different parts of a contract are irreconcilable, it would seem that the court is required to disregard the choices and to deal with the matter as if no choice had been made. In *American Motorists Insurance Co v Cellstar Corp*[178] the Court of Appeal, faced with a composite policy involving a number of policyholders in various countries, held that the parties could not conceivably have intended to choose a different applicable law for each policyholder.[179]

Co-insurers. Where there are a number of subscribing underwriters to a single   **2–031**
risk, English law treats each of them as having a separate contract with the assured. It is thus possible for each subscription to be governed by a different applicable law. In practice this problem is avoided by a single choice of law clause in the slip signed by all subscribing underwriters, so that all are bound on the same terms. There may be cases in which the choice of law clause is agreed only with the leading underwriter, and a question can then arise as to whether the following market are bound by it. The English courts are unlikely to regard a choice of law clause as having been validly incorporated by general reference from one contract into another.[180] The separability point is confirmed by reg.5 of the the Financial Services and Markets Act 2000 (Law Applicable to Contracts of Insurance) Regulations 2009,[181] which provides that where the risk to which the contract relates is covered by Community co-insurance,[182] co-insurers are not to be treated as parties to the contract. The courts would almost certainly reach the same result.

---

[176] *Forsikringsaktielskapet Vesta v Butcher* [1986] 2 All E.R. 588.

[177] *Forsikringsaktielskapet Vesta v Butcher* [1988] 1 F.T.L.R. 78; [1989] 1 All E.R. 402.

[178] *American Motorists Insurance Co v Cellstar Corp* [2003] Lloyd's Rep. I.R. 395.

[179] This approach was followed in *Travelers Casualty and Surety Co of Europe Ltd v Sun Life Assurance Co of Canada (UK) Ltd* [2004] Lloyd's Rep. I.R. 846 and *CGU International Insurance Plc v AstraZenica Insurance Co Ltd* [2006] Lloyd's Rep. I.R. 409.

[180] See *Gan Insurance Co Ltd v Tai Ping Insurance Co Ltd* [1999] Lloyd's Rep. I.R. 229; *AIG Group (UK) Ltd v The Ethniki* [1998] 4 All E.R. 301, affirmed on other grounds [2000] Lloyd's Rep. I.R. 343.

[181] SI 2009/3075.

[182] As defined by Council Directive 78/343/EC, which applies to co-insurance operations where the risk is a large one and is situated in the EU.

2–032   *Floating choice of law.* The common law does not permit a floating choice of law whereby the applicable law varies depending upon future events.[183] The view taken by the English courts is that the parties must know from the outset which law governs their relationship. In *CGU International Insurance Plc v Szabo*[184] the policy was a global policy covering risks in a variety of different jurisdictions. It was argued unsuccessfully that there was no single applicable law and that the law applicable to any one claim was that of the place in which the claim arose. Toulson J., while accepting that the parties were entitled to choose different laws for different parts of their contract, held that that situation was quite different from that in which a different law might apply to a particular obligation depending upon the place in which the obligation arose. A similar decision, albeit not one in the insurance context, is *Sonatrach Petroleum Corporation v Ferrell International*,[185] in which Colman J. refused to enforce a contract term under which the law applicable to the dispute depended upon the forum in which the dispute was resolved, on the basis that the parties were entitled to know the applicable law from the outset.

2–033   *Variation in the applicable law.* A distinction should be drawn between a pure floating choice of law clause which, from the outset, fails to identify an applicable law and provides that the law is to be ascertained at some later date, and a clause which permits the applicable law to be altered at a later date at the option of one or other of the parties. The common law recognises that any choice of law initially agreed by the parties or recognised by the law may be varied by the agreement of the parties, a point assumed by Toulson J. in *Szabo* and confirmed by art.3.2 of the Rome I Regulation, which provides that the parties are free to alter the applicable law at any time without prejudice to the formal validity of the contract.[186] The question of which law governs the validity of the agreement to change the applicable law is not specifically referred to, although it would seem that the validity of the change is to be governed by the original applicable law. It is unclear from art.3.2 whether an alteration of the applicable law has retrospective as well as prospective effect.

The common law has also recognised the validity of a clause which confers upon one or other of the parties the right to exercise an option under which the applicable law is to be changed. This form of option is commonly conferred by a service of suit clause under which the policyholder is given the right to bring proceedings in the courts of a specified place and the underwriter agrees to submit to the jurisdiction of the courts of that place, the clause also providing that the dispute is to be determined by the law of that place. This form of clause is taken to mean that the contract has an initial applicable law, determined either by agreement or by the application of the ordinary principles of the Rome I Regulation, but that exercise of the option by the bringing of proceedings in the named courts operates as the execution of an agreement to change the law applicable to the dispute. The notion is a curious one, as it effectively means that the parties are changing the applicable law retroactively and not simply

---

[183] *Armor Shipping Co Ltd v Caisse Algerienne* [1981] 1 W.L.R. 207. The principle that the applicable law cannot float was confirmed by the House of Lords in *Amin Rasheed Shipping Corporation v Kuwait Insurance Co* [1984] A.C. 50 and *Wasa International Insurance Co Ltd v Lexington Insurance Co* [2009] Lloyd's Rep. I.R. 675.

[184] *CGU International Insurance Plc v Szabo* [2002] Lloyd's Rep. I.R. 196.

[185] *Sonatrach Petroleum Corp v Ferrell International* [2002] 1 All E.R. (Comm) 627.

[186] Echoing art.3.2 of the Rome Convention. See *Aeolian Shipping SA v ISS Machinery Services Ltd* [2001] EWCA Civ 1162, where the Court of Appeal found that the parties had not entered into an express agreement to that effect.

prospectively. This could have the consequence that conduct which at the time it was carried out was recognised as lawful by the initial applicable law could retrospectively be regarded as impermissible by a change of the applicable law as effected by the exercise of an option to sue in an agreed jurisdiction. The reverse is also true. If, for example, a risk is placed in the London market under English applicable law, and material facts are not disclosed, an action by the policyholder in some other jurisdiction under a clause of this type will lead to the application of the law of that jurisdiction to the placement, potentially leaving the underwriters with inferior or indeed no rights in relation to the placement. That said, the inclusion of this type of clause does not affect the initial validity of the contract. Even if there is no other provision relating to the initial applicable law, that applicable law can be determined in accordance with the conflict of laws rules relevant to the policy. Accordingly, the initial process is exactly the same as if there had been no variation clause at all.

As curious as this possibility may appear to be, it is apparently recognised by English law. The issue first arose indirectly before the Court of Appeal in *Armadora Occidental SA v Horace Mann Insurance Co*,[187] where the contract provided that an action could be brought in New York at the option of the assured. In fact proceedings were brought in England and it was argued that New York law nevertheless governed the agreement. The Court of Appeal refused to give any weight to the unexercised option and did not comment on what effect an exercise of the option would have had. The point was specifically considered by the Court of Appeal in *El Du Pont de Nemours & Co v Agnew*,[188] another case in which a discretion given to the policy holder had not been exercised. Here, Bingham L.J. commented as follows:

> "[T]he drafting of this clause appears to contemplate that the proper law of the contract may float until exercise of an option by the insured. But this is not a concept to which an English Court could give effect, since the rights and obligations of contracting parties crystallize when a contract is made (subject to consensual variation thereafter), and contracts can only crystallize with reference to an existing proper law since they cannot exist in a legal vacuum: *Amin Rasheed* at pp 370 and 65C; *Armor Shipping Co Ltd v Caisse Algerienne d'Assurance et de Reassurance* [1980] 2 Lloyd's Rep. 450; [1981] 1 WLR 207. It may, I suppose, be theoretically possible for a proper law to be retrospectively varied on exercise of a contractual option, but that does not dispense with the need for a pre-existing proper law, and since the option has not been exercised it is not in any event this case."

In *Heath Lambert Ltd v Sociedad de Corretaje de Seguros*[189] a reinsurance agreement made in London between a Venezuelan reinsured and London market reinsurers was stated to be governed by Venezuelan law and subject to Venezuelan jurisdiction "if so required". Deputy High Court Judge Jonathan Hirst QC construed this provision as a floating choice of law clause so that the reinsured had the right to opt for both Venezuelan jurisdiction and choice of law. It does not appear to have been argued that the clause was invalid to the extent that it applied to choice of law, and the court's view was that the contract was governed by English law but that the reinsurers had the right to opt for Venezuelan law. However, as the option had not been exercised by the time that English proceedings had been commenced, it was too late for the option to be

---

[187] *Armadora Occidental SA v Horace Mann Insurance Co* [1977] 2 Lloyd's Rep. 406.
[188] *El Du Pont de Nemours & Co v Agnew* [1987] 2 Lloyd's Rep. 585.
[189] *Heath Lambert Ltd v Sociedad de Corretaje de Seguros* [2004] 1 Lloyd's Rep. 495. The point did not arise on appeal, [2004] Lloyd's Rep. I.R. 905.

exercised. What is assumed by this decision is that there is no objection in principle to a clause of this type, as long as the option is exercised right from the outset so that the rights of the parties are fixed immediately. The court indeed appears to have had this very point in mind, the judge commenting that it could not be the case that rights under the contract could vary from time to time.

Colman J.'s approach in *King v Brandywine Reinsurance Co (UK) Ltd*[190] was somewhat different. The learned judge specifically stated that the effect of a "New York suable" clause was:

"[T]o confer on the assured an option to select the jurisdiction of the New York courts. If that option is exercised by the assured, the insurers are obliged to comply with all procedural requirements necessary to give the New York court, and all matters arising are to be determined in accordance with New York law and practice. This clearly provides for an express choice of law, but it is contingent on the assured being entitled to exercise the option as to jurisdiction and on the assured having exercised it."

A clause to similar effect was considered by the Court of Appeal in *Craft Enterprises (International) Ltd v Axa Insurance Co.*[191] This case concerned an open cover issued by Swiss insurers to the assured, a trader. The policy contemplated that certificates of insurance would be issued by the assured to third party purchasers of goods on CIF terms, and that those third parties would be able to sue the insurers. The policy stated that it was subject to Swiss law and practice, and that disputes would be submitted to the Swiss courts, but that a party who had title to the goods had the right to require that claims would be settled in accordance with English law and practice as if the policy or certificate had been signed in London. The assured sought to rely upon this clause to justify the bringing of an action by it in England with respect to goods to which the assured had retained title. The Court of Appeal, rejecting this argument, held that the clause had nothing to do with jurisdiction but was instead concerned only with choice of law, and conferred upon the purchaser of goods who had been issued with a certificate the right to demand the application of English law. Waller L.J., having noted that there had been no attempt to argue that the clause was to that extent invalid and that the point would not be decided as it did not arise, nevertheless indicated that it had perhaps been sensible for this point not to have been taken. It may be, therefore, that the dicta in both *King v Brandywine* and *Craft Enterprises* support the proposition that it is perfectly valid for the insurers to agree that they will be bound by the exercise of an option by the assured to nominate a different applicable law. However, the comments in both cases were purely obiter and it may be thought that the conceptual problem of retroactivity is sufficiently weighty to regard this type of clause as an attempt to adopt a floating choice of law clause and is to that extent invalid.

The inclusion of a service of suit clause nominating a particular jurisdiction is not of itself enough to overturn an express choice of law clause. In *CGU International Insurance Plc v AstraZeneca Insurance Co Ltd*[192] a policy of insurance was expressly stated to be governed by English law, although the policy conferred upon the assured the right to commence proceedings in any court of competent jurisdiction in the US and the insurers agreed to submit to the jurisdiction of that court. It was argued by the assured that the policy was

---

[190] *King v Brandywine Reinsurance Co (UK) Ltd* [2004] Lloyd's Rep. I.R. 554 affirmed on other grounds [2005] Lloyd's Rep. I.R. 509.

[191] *Craft Enterprises (International) Ltd v Axa Insurance Co* [2005] Lloyd's Rep. I.R. 14.

[192] *CGU International Insurance Plc v AstraZeneca Insurance Co Ltd* [2005] Lloyd's Rep. I.R. 409.

governed by the law of Iowa, on the basis that if the assured had commenced proceedings in that jurisdiction the local court would have applied the conflict of laws rules of Iowa and would have concluded that the policy was governed by the law of Iowa. Cresswell J. rejected this argument, holding that the policy was governed by English law from the outset and the mere possibility that the assured might have commenced proceedings in Iowa, and that the Iowa court might have disregarded the English choice of law clause, did not amount to an intention by the parties to override their express choice of English law and to subject their policy to the law of Iowa. This conclusion does not touch on the possibility that the parties could have agreed that, in the event that proceedings were commenced in Iowa, the applicable law would be that of Iowa. The issue in *CGU* was in determining the initial governing law. However, as noted above, that would appear to have been a legitimate option. It was subsequently held by the House of Lords in *Wasa International Insurance Co Ltd v Lexington Insurance Co*[193] that if a contract of reinsurance is by implication governed by English law, and the underlying insurance is subject to a service of suit clause which allows the applicable law to be determined by any US court of competent jurisdiction, the law ultimately chosen in the United States will not supersede the English law interpretation of coverage clauses in the reinsurance policy.

Choice of law by arbitrators. Commercial insurance agreements commonly contain arbitration clauses, and where such clauses incorporate the arbitration rules of institutions such as the International Chamber of Commerce or UNCITRAL the arbitrators are empowered to choose the applicable law where the parties themselves have not done so. Such clauses were recognised by the common law, and the Arbitration Act 1996 s.46, now provides that, in the absence of any express choice of law agreement, the arbitrators are themselves to determine the law which they regard as appropriate to provide the relevant choice of law rules. The discretion in the 1996 Act is framed in the widest possible discretionary terms, and it is difficult to see how any decision by the arbitrators on the selection of the appropriate choice of law rules could be challenged, given that the matter is one of discretion rather than of law.[194] The Act on this point codifies the common law. In *Deutsche Schachtbau-und Tiefbohrgesellschaft mbH v R'As Al Khaimah National Oil Co*[195] a contract between a German company and a R'As Al Khaimah company was to be performed in R'As Al Khaimah and any disputes were to be arbitrated in Geneva under ICC Rules. In the absence of an express choice of law clause, the arbitrators chose to apply "internationally accepted principles of law governing contractual relations". The Court of Appeal ruled that the delegation to the arbitrators was lawful, and also that the system of law chosen by them was sufficiently well recognised to constitute a valid choice of law. It is unclear how the Rome I Regulation applies to delegated choice of law, as it is far from easy

2–034

---

[193] *Wasa International Insurance Co Ltd v Lexington Insurance Co* [2009] Lloyd's Rep. I.R. 675.

[194] It might be possible to challenge their application of the selected choice of law rules to the determination of the applicable law on the ground of error of law, under the Arbitration Act 1996 s.69. However, this would be possible in the English courts only where English conflict of laws rules are adopted, as the court's jurisdiction over errors of law under the 1996 Act is confined to errors of English law. Accordingly, if the arbitrators decide that some foreign law should provide the choice of law rules, and they then erroneously apply the choice of law rules of that foreign law in their selection of the applicable law, the matter is outside the jurisdiction of the English courts.

[195] *Deutsche Schachtbau-und Tiefbohrgesellschaft mbH v R'As Al Khaimah National Oil Co* [1987] 2 All E.R. 769.

to reconcile the terms of the Arbitration Act 1996 s.46, with the Regulation, but it is improbable that the English courts would refuse to give effect to such a clause.

2–035 *Choice of law and incorporation of foreign law.* It is necessary to distinguish between an express clause which actually nominates a system of law as the applicable law, and a clause which merely incorporates into the contract specific provisions of a prescribed law. It is perfectly legitimate for the parties to agree that a specific part of their contract is to be governed by a stated system of law without them going so far as agreeing that the entire contract is to be governed by that law.[196] This device is indeed a useful one, as it eliminates the need for the parties to spell out in their contract the individual provisions of the law by which they wish that part of their contract to be governed. Perhaps the most important consequence which stems from the distinction between a choice of law clause and an incorporation clause is that, in the event of a change in the law of the country whose law has been adopted, in the former case the agreement is to be governed by the law as altered, whereas in the latter case the parties remain unaffected by the change in the law, on the basis that their intention was merely to adopt particular rules to govern one part of their relationship. The normal effect of an incorporation clause, then, is to modify the applicable law to the extent agreed. However, in the absence of an express choice of law clause or any other obvious connection with a system of law, it may be that an incorporation clause will be given the broader interpretation of a general indication as to the proper law intended by the parties to govern the entire contract. In *Spurrier v La Cloche*,[197] the assured, who was resident in Jersey, insured his stamp collection with an English company, Sun Fire Office, under a standard form English policy. The policy was negotiated and executed in Jersey by agents of Sun Fire, and both premiums and losses were payable in Jersey. Incorporated into the agreement was a clause by virtue of which there was to be arbitration in accordance with the English arbitration legislation. It will be noted that the express clause was not a choice of law clause or an agreement that any arbitration proceedings were to be held in London, but was merely an incorporation provision affecting the conduct of the arbitration. The House of Lords held, attaching much weight to the arbitration provision, that the applicable law of the agreement was English law. The decision is perhaps open to some doubt, for it is clear that the courts today give less weight to arbitration clauses and, a fortiori, to clauses incorporating the arbitration rules of some other country, than was once the case,[198] but it is nevertheless a useful illustration of the potential importance of an incorporation clause in the absence of an express choice of law provision.

An incorporation clause, unlike a choice of law clause, is subordinate to the objective intentions of the parties where that clause is inconsistent with that intention. In *Ex p. Dever, Re Suse and Sibeth*,[199] the assured, who was domiciled in England, effected in 1876 a life policy on his own life for the sum of £6,000 with the London branch of the Equitable Life Assurance Society of New York, through its London office, the premium being payable in England. The proceeds

---

[196] If the contract incorporates a foreign law which of itself implements an international convention on which there is English authority, the parties are assumed to have adopted the English rather than the foreign interpretation: *Mauritius Oil Refineries v Stall Neilsen* [1997] 1 Lloyd's Rep. 273.

[197] *Spurrier v La Cloche* [1902] A.C. 446.

[198] See *Compagnie Tunisienne de Navigation SA v Compagnie D'Armement Maritime SA* [1971] A.C. 572.

[199] *Ex p. Dever, Re Suse and Sibeth* (1887) 18 Q.B.D. 660.

were payable to the assured's wife "for her sole use, if living, in conformity with the statute". The Court of Appeal proceeded on the assumption that the agreement was governed by English law. The statute to which reference had been made was a New York statute of 1870 which permitted a married woman to insure the life of her husband for her own benefit, although the statute also required a proportion of the proceeds to be applied to satisfy the husband's creditors in the event of his insolvency. In July 1883 the assured became bankrupt, and thereafter his wife took over responsibility for paying the premium. When she subsequently cashed in the policy, the husband's trustee in bankruptcy claimed that the reference to the New York statute entitled him (the trustee) to a proportion of the proceeds in line with New York law. Despite the apparent incorporation of New York law, the Court of Appeal unanimously held that the true object of the parties had not been to incorporate the provisions of the New York statute into the agreement, but merely to make it clear that the proceeds of the policy were payable to the wife. Bowen L.J. put the matter thus[200]:

> "It seems to me impossible to suppose that it was intended to incorporate into the contract provisions of American law which apply only to American creditors. That would be to incorporate into the contract something which had nothing to do with its fulfilment, and would be inoperative and insensible."

Implied choice of law

General principles. At common law, even where the parties to an agreement had   **2–036**
not expressly nominated the system of law which was to govern their agreement, the courts would take account of other clauses in the agreement in determining whether an implied choice had been made. Relevant provisions would be jurisdiction and arbitration clauses, which were a good, but not necessarily conclusive, indication that the proper law was intended to be the law of the place of the nominated jurisdiction or arbitral seat. Similarly, as was the case in *Spurrier v La Cloche*,[201] a clause incorporating specific provisions from a system of law would at common law, in the absence of any other clear applicable law, point towards a choice of the incorporated law as the law applicable to the entire agreement.

The Rome I Regulation, like the Rome Convention before it, seemingly adopts the same principle. Article.3.1 of the Rome I Regulation provides that the parties are free to choose the applicable law if the choice is "expressly or clearly demonstrated by the terms of the contract or the circumstances of the case." Although the Convention applies a more rigid test than that in the Rome Convention, choice "with reasonable certainty by the terms of the contract or the circumstances of the case", the two formulations are unlikely in practice to reach different results.

There are alternative possibilities here[202]: a choice of law must be clearly demonstrated, based either on "the terms of the contract"; or "the circumstances of the case". The latter possibility focuses on the negotiations that have taken place between the parties in order to determine what their intention might have

---

[200] *Ex p. Dever, Re Suse and Sibeth* (1887) 18 Q.B.D. 660 at 667.
[201] *Spurrier v La Cloche* [1902] A.C. 446.
[202] *Marubeni Hong Kong and South China Ltd v Mongolian Government* [2002] 1 All E.R. (Comm) 873; *Dornoch Ltd v Mauritius Union Assurance Co Ltd* [1986] Lloyd's Rep. I.R. 786.

been independently of the terms of the policy itself.[203] The former possibility focuses on the terms of the contract to see whether it is possible to glean from both the documents used and their provisions a clear association with a particular country. That view appears in the Giuliano and Lagarde Report, albeit that the comments were directed to the formulation in the Rome Convention[204]:

"The choice of law by the parties will often be express but the Convention recognises the possibility that the court may, in the light of all the facts, find that the parties have made a real choice of law although this is not expressly stated in the contract. For example, the contract may be in a standard form which is known to be governed by a particular system of law even though there is no express statement to this effect, such as a Lloyd's policy of marine insurance. In other cases a previous course of dealing between the parties under contracts containing an express choice of law may leave the court in no doubt that the contract in question is to be governed by the law previously chosen where the choice of law clause has been omitted in circumstances which do not indicate a deliberate change of policy by the parties. In some cases the choice of a particular forum may show in no uncertain manner that the parties intend the contract to be governed by the law of that forum, but this must always be subject to the other terms of the contract and all the circumstances of the case. Similarly, references in a contract to specific Articles of the French Civil Code may leave the court in no doubt that the parties have deliberately chosen French law, although there is no expressly stated choice of law. Other matters that may impel the court to the conclusion that a real choice of law has been made might include an express choice of law in related transactions between the same parties, or the choice of a place where disputes are to be settled by arbitration in circumstances indicating that the arbitrator should apply the law of that place."

This would seem to be an admirable summary of the position under English law, as subsequent decisions demonstrate. In *AIG Europe SA v QBE International Insurance*[205] the court thought that a reinsurance placed between two French concerns by Luxembourg brokers was likely to be governed by French law. In *Assicurazioni Generali SpA v Ege Sigorta AS*[206] it was again assumed that contracts placed on the London market by London brokers with London reinsurers using local forms of wording were by necessary implication intended to be governed by English law. In *Tieman v Magen Insurance Co Ltd*[207] and *Gan Insurance Co Ltd v Tai Ping Insurance Co Ltd*,[208] both of which had much the same facts, the same conclusion was reached. In *CGU International Insurance Plc v Szabo*[209] it was held that there was a good arguable case a policy was governed by English law in that it had been negotiated, concluded and issued in England; the insurers had their headquarters and registered office in England; the registered office of the assured was in London; the premium was in sterling; and

---

[203] See *Dornoch Ltd v Mauritius Union Assurance Co Ltd* [2006] Lloyd's Rep. I.R. 127, affirmed [2006] Lloyd's Rep. I.R. 786, where Aikens J.—whose judgment was upheld on appeal—concluded that there was a "stalemate" on this matter in the absence of detailed evidence from the parties. That case, as are many applicable law cases, raised a jurisdictional issue in which an attempt to establish jurisdiction was based on the applicable law being that of England. The nature of proceedings of this type is such that there is unlikely to be detailed evidence of what transpired.

[204] [1980] OJ C282/1 at para.17. See also *FR Lurseen Werft GmbH & Co KG v Halle* [2009] EWHC 2607 (Comm).

[205] *AIG Europe SA v QBE International Insurance* [2002] Lloyd's Rep. I.R. 22.

[206] *Assicurazioni Generali SpA v Ege Sigorta SA* [2002] Lloyd's Rep. I.R. 480.

[207] *Tieman v Magen Insurance Co Ltd* Unreported, 1998.

[208] *Gan Insurance Co Ltd v Tai Ping Insurance Co Ltd* [1999] Lloyd's Rep. I.R. 229. See also *Tonicstar Ltd v American Home Assurance Co* [2005] Lloyd's Rep. I.R. 32 and *Tryg Baltica International (UK) Ltd v Boston Compania De Seguros SA* [2005] Lloyd's Rep. I.R. 40.

[209] *CGU International Insurance Plc v Szabo* [2002] Lloyd's Rep. I.R. 196.

various terms of the policy, e.g. the claims conditions, contained provisions consistent with English law. The use of a Lloyd's policy and London market wordings were held in *Gard Marine & Energy Ltd v Lloyd Tunnicliffe*[210] to amount to an implied choice of English law. The reinsurance in this case had been placed by means of two slips, one in the London Market and one in the Swiss Market, although Hamblen J. took the view that the use of London brokers and London documents led to the conclusion that "In reality . . . this was not a Swiss Market placement. It was a case of a Swiss reinsurer being invited to participate in a London market placement". The court did not, therefore, reach a conclusion on the question of whether the fact that the placement was on an overseas market overrode any finding that the use of London Market documents pointed by implication towards English law.

In *American Motorists Insurance Co v Cellstar Corp*[211] the policy was negotiated and issued in Texas to an assured with its principal place of business in Texas by an insurance company incorporated in Illinois and authorised to carry on insurance business in Texas. The negotiations were conducted by a Texas broker. David Steel J. and the Court of Appeal held that the circumstances were such that they were consistent only with an implicit choice of Texas law, a position reinforced by the fact that the policy included a Time for Suit clause which referred to the limitation periods of "the laws of the State within which this policy is issued". The same conclusion was reached on not dissimilar facts in *Travelers Casualty & Surety Co of Canada v Sun Life Assurance Co of Canada (UK) Ltd (No.2)*,[212] in which the named assured under a global excess liability policy was the Ontario parent of a group with subsidiaries in a number of different countries, including England. The policy was subscribed to by underwriters in Toronto, New York and London, with the largest share of 60 per cent having been accepted in London albeit not on standard London market terms. Christopher Clarke J., having rejected the suggestion—in line with *American Motorists*—that the cover for each subsidiary was governed by a different applicable law, held that there had been an implied choice of the law of Ontario. This was because: the named assured was the Canadian parent company; the risk was placed by Canadian brokers; the Policy Period was defined by reference to Standard Time in Toronto; payment of losses in any currency other that US dollars was to be at the exchange rate published in Toronto; claims were to be notified based on the knowledge of the assured's Assistant Vice-President, who was based in Toronto; the language and spelling of the policy was North American; the policy was an excess layer policy, with the primary layer covers being by implication governed by the law of Ontario; the policy was negotiated in Toronto and New York; 40 per cent of the subscribing market participated through Ontario enterprises, and although London market subscribers had taken a 60 per cent share they had not done so on standard London market terms; and premium payment and claims management was conducted in Toronto.

In reinsurance cases a London placement using London market documentation will not necessarily be conclusive of an implicit choice of English law, particularly where the direct policy being reinsured is governed by some other law. In such a case the terms of the direct policy may have been incorporated into the reinsurance, and independently of incorporation a proportional reinsurance contract is presumed to have been made on the basis that it provides "back to

---

[210] *Gard Marine & Energy Ltd v Lloyd Tunnicliffe* [2009] EWHC 2388 (Comm).

[211] *American Motorists Insurance Co v Cellstar Corp* [2003] Lloyd's Rep. I.R. 359.

[212] *Travelers Casualty & Surety Co of Canada v Sun Life Assurance Co of Canada (UK) Ltd (No.2)* [2007] Lloyd's Rep. I.R. 619.

back" coverage with the direct policy so that—if necessary—its terms are to be construed in accordance with the law governing the direct policy whatever the law applicable to the reinsurance may happen to be.[213] In this type of situation, it may be that the conflicting features are self-cancelling and that art.3.1 of the Rome I Regulation cannot be relied upon.[214] Nevertheless, it is clear from the authorities that in most cases the implication to be drawn from a London market placement is that the parties have with reasonable certainty chosen English law as the governing law.[215] Even if that implication cannot be made, for example, by reason of conflicting indicia, the courts are almost certain to come to the conclusion that the contract has its closest connection with England and thus is governed by English law under the default presumption in art.4 of the Rome I Regulation.

2–037   *Jurisdiction clauses.* Recital 12 to the Rome I Regulation, which did not appear in the Rome Convention, states that an agreement between the parties to confer on one or more courts or tribunals of a Member State exclusive jurisdiction to determine disputes under the contract should be one of the factors to be taken into account in determining whether a choice of law has been clearly demonstrated. The English cases are consistent with this approach. In *Royal Exchange Assurance Corp v Sjoforsakrings Aktiebolaget Vega*,[216] a reinsurance agreement on marine risks was entered into by an English reinsured and a reinsurer with its head office in Sweden. The policy itself was executed in Sweden, and expressly stated that: "In case of any dispute under the policy, the Vega Company agree to be bound in all things by the jurisdiction and decision of the English law courts." On the strength of this clause, the reinsurer argued that the reinsurance agreement was governed by English law and was thus unenforceable under the Stamp Act 1891, whereas the reinsured claimed the contract was more closely connected with Sweden and should be governed by Swedish law, under which the contract would have been valid. Collins M.R. and Mathew L.J. in the Court of Appeal effectively held that the jurisdiction clause was conclusive evidence of the intention of the parties to nominate English law as the governing law. Cozens-Hardy L.J., who considered the matter more fully, agreed with the ultimate conclusion of his brethren that English law was the proper law, but did so on the rather broader basis that a jurisdiction clause is weighty, but not conclusive, evidence that the law of the chosen forum is to be the proper law. However, the reasoning of the majority of the Court of Appeal, while possibly limited to some extent by the decision of the House of Lords in *Compagnie Tunisienne de Navigation SA v Compagnie d'Armement Maritime SA*,[217] that arbitration clauses are not conclusive evidence of intent, has never been disapproved, and *Vega* remains an important authority on this matter.[218] The general rule thus remains that an exclusive jurisdiction clause is a powerful pointer towards an implied

---

[213] *Forsakrings Vesta v Butcher* [1989] 1 Lloyd's Rep. 331, although note the limits on this principle set out in *Wasa v Lexington* [2009] Lloyd's Rep. I.R. 675.

[214] So held in relation to the Rome Convention: *Dornoch Ltd v Mauritius Union Assurance Co Ltd* [2006] Lloyd's Rep. I.R. 127.

[215] *Wasa v Lexington* [2009] Lloyd's Rep. I.R. 675.

[216] *Royal Exchange Assurance Corp v Sjoforsakrings Aktiebolaget Vega* [1902] 2 K.B. 384.

[217] *Compagnie Tunisienne de Navigation SA v Compagnie d'Armement Maritime SA* [1971] A.C. 572.

[218] See *The Komninos S, Financial Times*, January 16, 1991, in which the Court of Appeal held that a bill of lading which provided that the "British courts" were to have jurisdiction over any dispute was a strong indication of the choice of English law as the proper law of the contract.

choice as the governing law of the substantive law of the nominated jurisdiction.[219]

There is an important legal difference between a mandatory jurisdiction clause of the type used in the *Vega* case, which requires any dispute to be put before the courts of a stated jurisdiction, and a merely permissive jurisdiction clause. An example of the latter was considered by the Court of Appeal in *Armadora Occidental SA v Horace Mann Insurance Co.*[220] The clause was in the following terms: "Any suit hereunder may be brought against these insurers in any court of competent jurisdiction within the United States of America." The court noted that the use of the word "may" was inconsistent with any obligation upon the assured to pursue his claim before the American courts only, but merely provided the assured with an option to do so. Thus interpreted, the clause could not have any impact upon the determination of the proper law of the agreement, and, consequently, it was disregarded by the Court of Appeal in its decision as to the proper law.[221] As discussed above, if this type of clause is to have any effect at all it operates to vary the applicable law where the option conferred by it is exercised. However, as Colman J. pointed out in *King v Brandywine Reinsurance Co (UK) Ltd*[222] the clause is not of any real weight in determining the initial law applicable to the contract. In the learned judge's words:

> "[A]n unexercised option to select a body of law could not normally give rise to more than the most minimal implication that the contract was to be governed by that law. There would have to be some other weightier features of the contract which gave rise to that implication to the effect that it arose as at the moment when the contract was made regardless of whether the option was exercised in the future."

Arbitration clauses. It has long been the law that the choice of a forum for   **2–038**
arbitration carries with it an implied choice of the law of that forum, in that there is little merit in appointing English arbitrators if they are to be required to apply some other law. The leading authority is *Compagnie Tunisienne de Navigation SA v Compagnie d'Annement Maritime SA*,[223] which decided that there is a strong, albeit not conclusive, presumption in favour of the law of the seat[224] of the arbitration. That said, there are few cases in which the presumption has been rebutted: perhaps the leading modern example is *Mitsubishi Corp v Castletown Navigation Ltd (The Castle Alpha)*,[225] where virtually every factor other than the London arbitration clause pointed towards Japanese law. The presumption in favour of the seat of the arbitration has been held by the English courts to have been preserved by the Rome Convention,[226] and this undoubtedly holds good under the Rome I Regulation.

---

[219] *Dornoch Ltd v Mauritius Union Assurance Co Ltd* [2006] Lloyd's Rep. I.R. 786.

[220] *Armadora Occidental SA v Horace Mann Insurance Co* [1977] 2 Lloyd's Rep. 406. See below.

[221] Cf. *Cantieri Navali Riuniti SpA v NV Omne Justitia* [1985] 2 Lloyd's Rep. 428 and *El Du Pont de Nemours & Co v Agnew* [1987] 2 Lloyd's Rep. 585.

[222] *King v Brandywine Reinsurance Co (UK) Ltd* [2004] Lloyd's Rep. I.R. 846. See also *El Du Pont de Nemours & Co v Agnew* [1987] 2 Lloyd's Rep. 585. These cases were followed on this point in *Travelers Casualty & Surety Co of Europe Ltd v Sun Life Assurance Co of Canada (UK) Ltd* [2004] Lloyd's Rep. I.R. 846.

[223] *Compagnie Tunisienne de Navigation SA v Compagnie d'Armement Maritime SA* [1971] A.C. 572.

[224] Terminology formalised by the Arbitration Act 1996 ss.2 and 3.

[225] *Mitsubishi Corp v Castletown Navigation Ltd (The Castle Alpha)* [1989] 2 Lloyd's Rep. 383. Cf. *King v Brandywine Reinsurance Co (UK) Ltd* [2005] Lloyd's Rep. I.R. 509.

[226] By Mance J. in *Egon Oldendorff v Libera Corp (No.1)* [1995] 2 Lloyd's Rep. 64 and by Clarke J. in its sequel, *Egon Oldendorff v Libera Corp (No.2)* [1996] 1 Lloyd's Rep. 380.

2–039   *"Follow London" clauses.* The "follow London" clause was given judicial
consideration for the first time in *Armadora Occidental SA v Horace Mann
Insurance Co.*[227] The case concerned policies of insurance on 29 ships owned by
Panamanian and Liberian companies, and effected in the United States by
brokers in San Francisco. All the policies were negotiated and executed in San
Francisco, and were placed with insurers in various parts of the world: 39 per
cent of the risk was placed in the US market; 30 per cent in the United Kingdom
(one-third of which was at Lloyd's); 17 per cent in Japan; 8 per cent in Belgium;
and 5 per cent in Greece. An attempt was made by one of the Panamanian
shipowners to sue in the English courts an American insurer, HM, which had its
place of business in Florida and did not have representation in England: an
application was made for service on HM out of the jurisdiction under what is now
CPR PD 6B para.3.1(6)(c), on the basis that the insurances were governed by
English law. Kerr J. and the Court of Appeal were of the opinion that, prima
facie, the insurances placed in the US market were governed by American law,
as those agreements were most closely connected with that law. However, Kerr
J., whose judgment was approved by the Court of Appeal, went on to hold that
the position had been altered by the inclusion in the agreement of what was
termed a "follow London" clause in the following form:

> "Assurers herein shall follow Lloyd's underwriters and/or British insurance companies
> in regard to accounts, terms, conditions, alterations, extension endorsements, cancella-
> tions, surveys and settlement of claims hereunder and all matters pertaining to this
> insurance with or without prior notice. Notice to Lloyd's underwriters and/or British
> insurance companies of any matter requiring notice shall be deemed notice to American
> underwriters and/or American insurance companies interested in these insurances."

Kerr J. and the Court of Appeal held that the inescapable intention of the
parties was to nominate English law as the law governing the agreements, on the
strength of the fact that American insurers had agreed to be bound by the conduct
of English insurers operating under English law.

No express or implied choice of law: the intention of the parties

2–040   *The common law.* Before the provisions of the Rome Convention and the Rome
I Regulation are discussed, it may be helpful to indicate the general principles
which were adopted at common law immediately before the implementation of
the European measures. There are a number of insurance and reinsurance cases
on the point, and they may still provide useful guidance. The common law
principles are as follows.

Where an English court does not possess any express or implied guidance from
the parties as to the law they wish to govern their agreement, it must ascertain the
applicable law in accordance with the presumed intentions of the parties. The
common law in place immediately before the implementation of the Rome
Convention examined the question purely objectively; by weighing the relevant
factors and determining, on balance, with which system of law the contract is
most closely connected. Relevant factors which were taken into account
included: the place of residence of the parties to the agreement; the place at
which the contract was made; the place of performance; and the currency of the

---

[227] *Armadora Occidental SA v Horace Mann Insurance Co* [1977] 2 Lloyd's Rep. 406. Cf. *El Du
Pont de Nemours & Co v Agnew* [1987] 2 Lloyd's Rep. 585.

transaction.[228] In the relatively few cases where the courts have had to determine the proper law of an insurance agreement, the location of the head office of the insurer initially tended to be the most important factor. There may well be sound policy grounds for such a conclusion, as it is in the interests of an insurer to have all its agreements governed by the same system of law, for placement to be regulated by the law of the country in which the risk was underwritten, for its standard form wordings will then receive a consistent interpretation, and meaning will not depend upon arbitrary factors such as the place in which the contract was to be performed or the assured's place of residence. This principle was, moreover, particularly consistent with the practice of life insurance, as most risks of this nature will normally be considered at head office only and authority to issue policies will generally not be conferred upon branches.

The early cases on life insurance regarded the place of the insurer's head office as the most important—albeit not conclusive—indication of the applicable law, overriding the place of performance.[229] Early marine cases displayed a similar tendency towards the head office of the insurer.[230] It has been suggested[231] that the head office principle was never applied in reinsurance cases, and that the key feature was the head office of the reinsured. However, the three authorities cited for that proposition do not support it. *First Russian Insurance Co v London and Lancashire Insurance Co*[232] decided only that, for Russian regulatory purposes, a Russian reinsurer was not carrying on business in England. In *Forsikringsaktie-selskapet National of Copenhagen v Attorney General*[233] the question was not applicable law but rather whether a reinsurer operating a branch office in England was within the English regulatory structure. Of more significance was *Royal Exchange Assurance Corp v Sjoforsakrings Aktiebolaget Vega*,[234] in which the Court of Appeal held that a marine reinsurance agreement between a Swedish reinsurer and an English ceding company, and executed in Sweden was governed by English law, although in that case the parties had agreed on English exclusive jurisdiction and virtually every other factor—the policy form, placement, payment of losses—pointed to England.

However, by the time that the common law was superseded by the Rome Convention, there had been a shift away from a focus on the insurers' head office and towards a balancing process whereby all relevant factors were taken into account. The issue has arose most commonly in the context of reinsurance, and it was clear from the cases that great weight would be given to the means by which the policy came into being and to the manner in which it was administered thereafter. *Amin Rasheed Shipping Corp v Kuwait Insurance Co (The Al Wahab)*[235] concerned a marine policy, issued by a Kuwaiti insurance company to

[228] *The Assunzione* [1954] P. 150; *Coast Lines Ltd v Hudig and Veder Chartering NV* [1972] 2 Q.B. 34; *Atlantic Underwriting Agencies and David Gale (Underwriting) Ltd v Compagnia di Assicurazioni di Milano SpA* [1979] 2 Lloyd's Rep. 240.

[229] *Pick v Manufacturers' Life Insurance Co* [1958] 2 Lloyd's Rep. 93; *Rossano v Manufacturers Life Insurance Co* [1963] 2 Q.B. 352. But contrast *Buerger v New York Life Assurance Co* [1927] All E.R. Rep. 342.

[230] *Greer v Poole* (1880) 5 QBD 272; *Armadora Occidental SA v Horace Mann Insurance Co* [1977] 2 Lloyd's Rep. 406 in which, but for a "follow London" clause, the place of the insurer's residence would have prevailed; *Atlantic Underwriting Agents and David Gale (Underwriting) Ltd v Compagnia di Assicurazioni di Milano SpA* [1979] 2 Lloyd's Rep. 240.

[231] Monachos [1972] J.B.L. 206.

[232] *First Russian Insurance Co v London and Lancashire Insurance Co* [1928] 1 Ch. 922.

[233] *Forsikringsaktieselskapet National of Copenhagen v Attorney General* [1925] A.C. 639.

[234] *Royal Exchange Assurance Corp v Sjoforsakrings Aktiebolaget Vega* [1902] 2 K.B. 384.

[235] *Amin Rasheed Shipping Corp v Kuwait Insurance Co (The Al Wahab)* [1983] 1 All E.R. 873, affirmed [1983] 2 All E.R. 884.

a Liberian company resident in Dubai. The policy was in the old standard Lloyd's form contained in MIA 1906 Sch.1, and losses were payable in Kuwait but in sterling. The Court of Appeal, by a majority, held that the applicable law of the agreement was English law despite the considerations that the insurer was resident in Kuwait and that the place of the making and performance of the contract was Kuwait; the majority of the Court[236] reasoned that at the time the contract had been made Kuwait had not possessed an insurance code of its own, and that the policy provisions were unintelligible without reference to the English MIA 1906, so that the form of the policy was the decisive factor. Robert Goff L.J., approving the views of Bingham J. at first instance, dissented from this conclusion, and held that Kuwaiti insurance law was adequately developed to be able to deal with problems arising from a policy in Lloyd's form. In the view of Robert Goff L.J., what mattered was that "the policy was issued in Kuwait, by a Kuwaiti insurance company carrying on business in Kuwait, and . . . it provided for performance in Kuwait".[237] The House of Lords preferred the majority view expressed in the Court of Appeal, although Lord Wilberforce expressed his approval in principle of the reasoning of Robert Goff L.J. and Bingham J.in the courts below.[238] Perhaps the most important decision was *Citadel Insurance Co v Atlantic Union Insurance Co SA*.[239] In this case, reinsurance had been arranged in London and by London brokers between a Greek reinsurer and a Canadian reinsured. Bingham J. held that the fact that the mechanical process of formation had taken place in England was immaterial, England merely being a "convenient facility for an international transaction". The Court of Appeal, however, rejected this approach entirely. Its view was best expressed by Kerr L.J.[240]:

"In all of these circumstances it seems to me that there is no candidate other than London and English law as the centres of gravity with which this business had its closest connection. [The claimants' brokers] could have stipulated for the law of New York, but they did not do so. Like the defendants they wished to operate on the London market and left the governing law open. The whole of the business, both from the point of view of the defendants as reinsurers and the reinsured [claimants], was run by [brokers] in London. All the documents are here, and it is only by an examination of those documents that it is possible to determine the rights and wrongs of the dispute . . . [What Bingham J.] calls the 'mechanisms' were in fact, the substance of the whole business; and London is in effect the only place where these transactions between the [claimants] and the defendants can be said to be located."

This approach is illustrated by *Cantieri Navali Riunita SpA v NV Omne Justitia*,[241] in which insurance had been placed through London brokers with some 44 insurers located throughout the world, although the first-named underwriters were all English. The policies in question in the proceedings had been underwritten by Italian insurers under contracts executed in Italy, although it was apparently conceded that the proper law of the contracts made with the

---

[236] Donaldson M.R. and May L.J.

[237] *Amin Rasheed Shipping Corp v Kuwait Insurance Co (The Al Wahab)* [1983] 1 All E.R. 873 at 887.

[238] *Amin Rasheed Shipping Corp v Kuwait Insurance Co (The Al Wahab)* [1983] 2 All E.R. 884 at 896.

[239] *Citadel Insurance Co v Atlantic Union Insurance Co SA* [1982] 2 Lloyd's Rep. 543.

[240] *Citadel Insurance Co v Atlantic Union Insurance Co SA* [1982] 2 Lloyd's Rep. 543 at 549–550.

[241] *Cantieri Navali Riunita SpA v NV Omne Justitia* [1985] 2 Lloyd's Rep. 428, followed in *El Du Pont de Nemours & Co v Agnew* [1987] 2 Lloyd's Rep. 585. Cf. also *Royal Exchange Assurance Corp v Vega* [1902] 2 K.B. 384.

English underwriters would determine the proper law of the Italian policies; for this reason, the argument centred on the policies issued by the English underwriters. Those policies were in the Lloyd's SG form and had been broked in London by English brokers, although the policies incorporated the American Institute hull clauses and conferred upon the assured the option to sue in the New York courts. The Court of Appeal held that the "centre of gravity" of the contracts was England rather than the United States, so that English law was the applicable law. In reaching this decision the court felt able to disregard the "New York suable" clause as it was merely permissive and not mandatory, a point referred to earlier in this chapter, and it also ruled that the incorporation of the American Institute Hull Clauses did not necessarily override the inference from the use of a Lloyd's standard policy that English law was the proper law, as the English courts were perfectly competent to apply the American clauses. The additional significant factor pointing towards English law was held to be that the policies had been arranged by English brokers on the London market using standard English broking slips. The fact that the head offices of the insurers were located in England was not regarded as material in itself, and it may be that this decision witnesses a move away from that approach towards stress on the form of the policy and the process of its formation.

The "centre of gravity" approach, which focuses attention on the role of those involved in the formation and administration of the agreement, found favour in the courts on a number of subsequent occasions,[242] and the head office of the insurers was largely irrelevant if all other indications were in favour of some other jurisdiction.[243] As is seen below, this is much the position reached under the Rome Convention and the Rome I Regulation.

The Rome Convention: general principles. Article 4 of the Rome Convention, **2–041** omitting art.4.3 which is concerned with immovable property and art.4.4 which is confined to contracts for the carriage of goods, sets out the following principles for determining the law applicable to a contract in the absence of any express or implicit choice.

> "4.1 To the extent that the law applicable to the contract has not been chosen in accordance with Art.3, the contract shall be governed by the law of the country with which it is most closely connected. Nevertheless, a severable part of the contract which has a closer connection with another country may by way of exception be governed by the law of that other country.
>
> 4.2 Subject to the provisions of paragraph 5 of this article, it shall be presumed that the contract is most closely connected with the country where the party who is to effect the performance which is characteristic of the contract has, at the time of conclusion of the contract, his habitual residence, or in the case of a body

---

[242] *Afia Worldwide Insurance Co v Deulsche Ruck Verischerungs AG* (1983) 133 N.L.J. 621 (weight given to the facts that the agreements were negotiated in London, executed in London and on forms commonly used on the London market); *Britannia Steamship Insurance Association v Ausonia Assicurazioni SpA* [1984] 2 Lloyd's Rep. 98 (the parties conceding that the proper law was English law, given that the agreement was made and administered by London brokers); *Islamic Arab Insurance Co v Saudi Egyptian American Reinsurance Co* [1987] 1 Lloyd's Rep. 315 (acceptance by the Court of Appeal that it was arguable that English law was the proper law, given that matters had been arranged in London by London brokers). See, most importantly, *Wasa International Insurance Co Ltd v Lexington Insurance Co* [2009] UKHL 40, a case which discussed insurance and reinsurance policies placed in 1977. The House of Lords had no doubt that both contracts were, in accordance with English conflict of laws rules, governed by the law of the state in which they had been placed.

[243] *Overseas Union Insurance Ltd v Incorporated General Insurance* [1992] 1 Lloyd's Rep. 439.

corporate or unincorporated, its central administration. However, if the contract is entered into in the course of that party's trade or profession, that country will be the country in which the principal place of business is situated or, where under the terms of the contract the performance is to be effected through a place of business other than the principal place of business, the country in which that other place of business is situated.

4.5 Paragraph 2 shall not apply if the characteristic performance cannot be determined, and the presumptions in paragraph 2 . . . will be disregarded if it appears from the circumstances as a whole that the contract is more closely connected with another country."

Article 4.1 thus lays down the basic principle that in the absence of any express or implicit choice of law the applicable law will be the law of the place with which the contract has its closest connection. Article 4.2 then provides presumptions as to what that place will be. There are no less than four separate presumptions here, all of which focus on the party who is to effect the performance which is characteristic of the contract. The view taken by the English courts is that the characteristic performance of an insurance or reinsurance contract is that of the insurer or reinsurer, as the relevant performance is the provision of cover. As is explained by the Giuliano and Lagarde Report,[244] the mere payment of money for a service is not a characterising performance:

"[I]n bilateral (reciprocal) contracts whereby the parties undertake mutual reciprocal performance, the counter-performance by one of the parties in a modem economy usually takes the form of money. This is not, of course, the characteristic performance of the contract. It is the performance for which the payment is due, i.e. depending on the type of contract, the delivery of goods, the granting of the right to make use of an item of property, the provision of a service, transport, insurance, banking operations, security, etc. Which usually constitutes the centre of gravity and the socio-economic function of the contractual transaction."

On this basis, it would seem to be correct to put forward the proposition that the performance which is characteristic of a contract of (re)insurance is payment by the underwriters in the event that a valid claim is made.[245] Where the contract is one for the supply of services, e.g. broking services, the presumptive applicable law is that of the place of the broker's place of business.[246] On the assumption that the (re)insurer is the person whose performance characterises the performance, there are no less than four possible presumptions intertwined in art.4.2 of the Rome Convention:

(a) the contract is most closely connected with the country where that person is an individual and has, at the time of conclusion of the contract, his habitual residence;

(b) the contract is most closely connected with the country where that person is an incorporated or unincorporated body and has, at the time of conclusion of the contract, its central administration;

(c) if the contract is entered into in the course of that person's trade or profession, the contract is most closely connected with the country in which his principal place of business is situated; and

(d) where under the terms of the contract the performance is to be effected through a place of business other than that person's principal place of

[244] [1980] OJ C282/11, para.20.
[245] *Dornoch Ltd v Mauritius Union Assurance Co Ltd* [2006] Lloyd's Rep. I.R. 786.
[246] *HIB Ltd v Guardian Insurance Co Inc* [1997] 1 Lloyd's Rep. 412.

business, the contract is most closely connected with the country in which that other place of business is situated.

These presumptions are, however, ousted if the contract is more closely connected with some other country.

The Rome I Regulation: general principles. Article 4 of the Rome I Regulation **2–042** operates on a quite different basis. Instead of a basic presumption in favour of the law of the country which has the closest connection with the contract, art.4.1 sets out a list of presumptive rules for different forms of contract, namely: (a) sale of goods (the law of the country of the seller's habitual residence); (b) provision of services (the law of the country where the service provider has his habitual residence; (c) a right in immovable property (the law of the country where the property is situated); (d) a tenancy of immovable property for private use and for not more than six months (the law of the country where the landlord has his habitual residence); (e) a franchise contract (the law of the country where the franchisee has his habitual residence); (f) a distribution contract (the law of the country where the distributor has his habitual residence); (g) a contract for the sale of goods by auction (the law of the country where the auction takes place); (h) a contract concluded within a multilateral system which brings together or facilitates the bringing together of multiple third-party buying and selling interests in financial instruments and governed by a single law (that law).

In the case of a contract which falls outside these presumptive rules, or where the elements of a single contract are covered by two or more presumptive rules, a general presumptive rule is provided by art.4.2:

> "4.2 [T]he contract shall be governed by the law of the country where the party required to effect the characteristic performance of the contract has his habitual residence."

"Habitual residence" is defined by art.19:

> "1. For the purposes of this Regulation, the habitual residence of companies and other bodies, corporate or unincorporated, shall be the place of central administration. The habitual residence of a natural person acting in the course of his business activity shall be his principal place of business.
> 2. Where the contract is concluded in the course of the operations of a branch, agency or any other establishment, or if, under the contract, performance is the responsibility of such a branch, agency or establishment, the place where the branch, agency or any other establishment is located shall be treated as the place of habitual residence.
> 3. For the purposes of determining the habitual residence, the relevant point in time shall be the time of the conclusion of the contract."

The specific and general presumptive rules are ousted in the two situations set out in arts 4.3 and 4.4:

> "4.3 Where it is clear from all the circumstances of the case that the contract is manifestly more closely connected with a country other than that indicated in paragraphs 1 or 2, the law of that other country shall apply.
> 4.4 Where the law applicable cannot be determined pursuant to paragraphs 1 or 2, the contract shall be governed by the law of the country with which it is most closely connected."

The only potentially significant provision for present purpose is art.4.1(b), which states that "a contract for the provision of services shall be governed by the law of the country where the service provider has his habitual residence". There is some dispute as to whether this provision applies to contracts of insurance and reinsurance. If it does, the default presumption is that the applicable law is that of the country where the (re)insurer has his habitual residence. However, if (re)insurance is not covered by art.4.1(b), then the next step is to turn to the default provision in art.4.2, namely that the contract is governed by the law of the country where the party required to effect the characteristic performance of the contract has his habitual residence. The characteristic performance of a contract of insurance or reinsurance is that of the insurer or reinsurer, so the test points to its habitual residence. Recital 21 adds that "In order to determine that country, account should be taken, inter alia, of whether the contract in question has a very close relationship with another contract or contracts." Thus, in either case, the applicable law is determined by the (re)insurer's habitual residence.

The Rome I Regulation, echoing the Rome Convention, provides for two exceptions. First, under art.4.3, where it is clear from all the circumstances of the case that the contract is manifestly more closely connected with some other country, the law of that other country shall apply. Secondly, under art.4.4, where the applicable law cannot be determined by the default rules, the contract shall be governed by the law of the country with which it is most closely connected.

2–043   *Application to (re)insurance cases.* Article 4 of the Rome Convention, stripped to its basics, provides that there is a presumption in favour of the country where the (re)insurer's principal place of business is situated. However, if the policy is issued by an autonomous branch or agency, the presumption is replaced by one in favour of the law of the country in which the issuing branch or agency has its principal place of business.[247] That presumption is ousted if the contract is more closely connected with some other country. The Rome I Regulation operates in much the same way. Whether or not (re)insurance is regarded as a "service", there is a presumption in favour of the reinsurer's principal place of business, although where the contract is concluded in the course of the operations of an autonomous branch or agency the presumption is in favour of the law of the place where the branch or agency has its principal place of business. In each case, if the performance which characterises the contract cannot be identified then the applicable law is the law of country with which the contract is most closely connected, although this provision cannot have a part to play in (re)insurance cases because the relevant performance can readily be identified as that of the underwriter.[248] Again in both cases the presumption may be ousted: in the case of the Rome Convention that occurs if the contract is more closely connected with some other country (art.4.5); under the Rome I Regulation the contract must be *manifestly* more connected with some other country. The difference in wording is designed to strengthen the presumption under the Rome I Regulation (art.4.3).

The addition of the word "manifestly" as a precondition of ousting the presumption in favour of the (re)insurer's principal place of business is unlikely

---

[247] The width of this presumption is unclear, although the view which prevails in England is that the contract must by its terms contemplate that it will be issued by the branch or agency for the presumption to apply: *Iran Continental Shelf Oil Co & Ors v IRI International Corp* [2002] EWCA Civ 1024; *Ennstone Building Products Ltd v Stanger Ltd* [2002] EWCA Civ 916.

[248] In *Dornoch Ltd v Mauritius Union Assurance Co Ltd* [2006] Lloyd's Rep. I.R. 127 Aikens J. was dismissive of the notion that the characterising performance of a reinsurance contract could not be readily ascertained.

to have affected the law. The Rome Convention was silent on the strength of the presumption, and early cases found that it was ousted relatively easily,[249] but in later cases the English courts adopted the approach that the operation of the presumption is not to be lightly disregarded and that it will be relevant unless there are compelling features which point towards some other jurisdiction.[250] Such compelling features are unlikely to be found in the vast majority of (re)insurance cases, because the features of the contract which provide the closest connection to a country are likely to be those found in the place of the underwriter's principal place of business. London market insurers and reinsurers, particularly in the Lloyd's market, accept risks in London from London brokers, and indeed in most of the cases decided under the Rome Convention the courts have held it to be unnecessary to rely upon art.4 at all, and have treated the situation as giving rise to an implied choice of law under art.3. Colman J., in *AIG Group (UK) Ltd v The Ethniki*,[251] was content to apply the presumption in the Rome Convention to a reinsurance agreement made in London with London reinsurers, as there was no indication that the law of any other place was more closely connected with the contract. In *Gan Insurance Co v Tai Ping Insurance Co Ltd*[252] (reinsurance) and *Commercial Union Assurance Co Plc v Simat Helliesen & Eichner Inc*[253] (insurance), Cresswell J. held that contracts negotiated and made in London with London market insurers, in London market language, were governed by English law. In *Gan*, Cresswell J. further held that, in the event that it had been necessary to rely upon the presumption in art.4.2 of the Rome Convention, the agreement was most closely connected with England and there was nothing which pointed towards the ousting of that presumption as there was no other country with which the contract had a greater connection. In *Assicurazioni Generali SpA v Ege Sigorta AS*[254] and *Dornoch Ltd v Mauritius Union Assurance Co Ltd*[255] London market contracts were again held to be governed by English law, and in *American Motorists Insurance Co v Cellstar*

---

[249] *Bank of Baroda v Vvsya Bank Ltd* [1994] 2 Lloyd's Rep. 87; *Definitely Maybe v Konzertagentur* [2001] 4 All E.R. 223; *Kenburn Waste Management v Bergman* [2002] F.S.R. 44: *Aeolian Shipping SA v ISS Machinery Services Ltd* [2001] EWCA Civ 1162; *Marconi Communications International v Pt Pan Indonesia Bank Ltd TBK* [2004] 1 Lloyd's Rep. 594.

[250] *Samcrete Egypt Engineers Ltd v Land Rover Export Ltd* [2001] EWCA Civ 2019; *Iran Continental Shelf Oil Co & Ors v IRI International Corp* [2002] EWCA Civ 1024; *Ennstone Building Products Ltd v Stanger Ltd* [2002] EWCA Civ 916: *Armstrong International Ltd v Deutsche Bank Securities Inc* Unreported, July 11, 2003 QBD; *Waldwiese Sftung v Lewis* Unreported, July 2004; *Ophthalmic Innovations International (United Kingdom) Ltd v Ophthalmic Innovations International Inc* [2004] EWHC 2948; *Pablo Star Ltd v Emirates Integrated Telecommunications Co PJSC* [2009] EWCA Civ 1044. The Scottish courts have adopted the same approach: *Caledonia Subsea v Micoperi SRL* Unreported 2002. There will of course be cases where the supplier's principal place of business has little or nothing to do with the contract, so that the presumption can be rebutted: *Commercial Marine Piling Ltd v Pierse Contracting Ltd* [2009] EWHC 2241 (TCC).

[251] *AIG Group (UK) Ltd v The Ethniki* [1998] 4 All E.R. 301, affirmed on other grounds [2000] Lloyd's Rep. IR 343.

[252] *Gan Insurance Co v Tai Ping Insurance Co Ltd* [1999] Lloyd's Rep. I.R. 229. See also *Tonicstar Ltd v American Home Assurance Co* [2005] Lloyd's Rep. I.R. 32 and *Tryg Baltica International (UK) Ltd v Boston Compania De Seguros SA* [2005] Lloyd's Rep. I.R. 40. In each case it was held that English law was the governing law in the situation discussed in the text, either by reason of implied choice of law or, in the alternative, by reason of the presumption in favour of the reinsurers' place of business.

[253] *Commercial Union Assurance Co Plc v Simat Helliesen & Eichner Inc* [2001] Lloyd's Rep. I.R. 172.

[254] *Assicurazioni Generali SpA v Ege Sigorta AS* [2002] Lloyd's Rep. I.R. 480.

[255] *Dornoch Ltd v Mauritius Union Assurance Co Ltd* [2006] Lloyd's Rep. I.R. 786.

Corp[256] a contract made in Texas between parties situated in Texas was held to be the subject of an implicit choice of the law of Texas.

Where there are a number of insurers each with its head office in a different jurisdiction, a strict application of art.4 of the Rome Convention could, on a strict application of the presumption, lead to the situation where the law applicable to each subscription will vary. This possibility faced Moore-Bick J. in *Lincoln National Life Insurance Co v Employers Reinsurance Corp*[257] and the learned judge's solution was hold that the presumption was rebutted and that it was necessary to find a single country with which the contracts were most closely connected: that country was held to be England on the basis that the placements had all been negotiated in England by London market brokers using London market documentation. The opposite situation prevailed in *American Motorists Insurance Co v Cellstar Corp*,[258] in which the policy was taken out by a corporation with its head office in Texas but carrying on its business in all parts of the world, the policy covering worldwide activities. David Steel J. and the Court of Appeal held that the performance characteristic of a contract of insurance was the provision of insurance cover, and given that the cover was provided all over the world it was appropriate to look to the law of Texas, the place in which both parties were situated and in which the contract had been made. Again, in *CGU International Insurance Plc v Szabo*[259] a global policy was held to be governed by English law on the grounds that: the policy was negotiated, concluded and issued in England; the insurer had its headquarters and registered office in England; the premium was in sterling; and various terms of the policy, e.g. the claims conditions, contained provisions consistent with the application of English law principles. Toulson J. was not prepared to accept that there was no single applicable law, and that the law varied according to the place in which a claim was made. In *Travelers Casualty and Surety Co of Canada v Sun Life Assurance Co of Canada (UK) Ltd (No.2)*,[260] the policy was issued to a Canadian parent company and covered subsidiaries of the assured worldwide, and was subscribed to by underwriters in Canada, New York and London. Accordingly, both the insured parties and the underwriters were spread amongst different jurisdictions. Plainly, in such a case, the presumption in favour of the insurers' head office cannot operate and Christopher Clarke J. held that any presumption was rebutted in favour of the place with which the contract had its closest connections, which was Ontario.[261]

2–044   *"Hybrid" policies: differing applicable laws for a single agreement.* The discussion thus far has proceeded on the assumption that a contract can be governed only by a single proper law. There is no logical reason precluding different aspects or parts of a contract from being governed by different proper

---

[256] *American Motorists Insurance Co v Cellstar Corp* [2002] EWHC 421 (Comm), affirmed [2003] Lloyd's Rep. I.R. 359.

[257] *Lincoln National Life Insurance Co v Employers Reinsurance Corp* [2002] Lloyd's Rep. I.R. 853.

[258] *American Motorists Insurance Co v Cellstar Corp* [2002] EWHC 421 (Comm), affirmed [2003] Lloyd's Rep. I.R. 359.

[259] *CGU International* [2002] Lloyd's Rep. I.R. 196.

[260] *Travelers Casualty & Surety Co of Canada v Sun Life Assurance Co of Canada (UK) Ltd (No.2)* [2007] Lloyd's Rep. I.R. 619.

[261] The court had in any event concluded that there had been an implied choice of the law of Ontario, so the presumption was never called into play.

laws, and in *Forsikringsaktieselskapet Vesta v Butcher*[262] Hobhouse J. applied this reasoning to a reinsurance agreement. The particular problem in that case was that the underlying insurance agreement was governed by the Norwegian law, whereas the reinsurance agreement was, on the "centre of gravity" test discussed above, clearly governed by English law. As a result of differences between the Norwegian and English law of warranties, the reinsurance agreement was not as wide in scope as the insurance agreement. Hobhouse J. held that this difficulty could be overcome, and that effect could be given to the intentions of the parties to enter into back-to-back agreements, by the approach that, while the reinsurance agreement was governed by English law, the construction and meaning of the warranty in it was to be in accordance with Norwegian law. Hobhouse J.'s description of the contract as "hybrid" was disapproved by the Court of Appeal[263] as giving rise to unnecessary confusion, but the Court of Appeal nevertheless upheld Hobhouse J.'s ultimate decision. O'Connor and Neill L.JJ. accepted that Norwegian construction and meanings were applicable to the warranty in the English contract, while Sir Roger Ormrod took the view that business efficacy demanded the implication of a term that the warranty in the English contract would be given effect to in accordance with Norwegian law. The House of Lords agreed with the majority reasoning of the Court of Appeal that the reinsurance agreement was governed in its entirety by English law, although its wording was to be construed in accordance with Norwegian law meanings.[264] The principle that different parts of a contract can be governed by different applicable laws is now expressly recognised by art.4.1 of the Rome I Regulation, re-enacting the equivalent wording in art.4.1 of the Rome Convention.

Consumer risks situated outside the EU. The following paragraphs examine   **2–045** the rules in the Rome I Regulation and the Rome Convention relating to the determination of the law applicable to a consumer risk which is situated outside the EU.

Article 6 of the Rome I Regulation applies to any contract by a natural person for a purpose which can be regarded as being outside his trade or profession with another person acting in the exercise of his trade or profession. This definition causes borderline difficulties in the case of mixed policies, but it would seem that the classification of the policy as commercial or consumer depends upon the assured's primary intention.[265] In this situation, the basic rule laid down by art.6.1 is that the law applicable to the contract is the law of the country where the consumer has his habitual residence, a term which is not defined by the Rome I Regulation for the purposes of a natural person who is a consumer. That general rule is, however, applicable only where the supplier:

(a) pursues his commercial or professional activities in the country where the consumer has his habitual residence, or

(b) by any means, directs such activities to that country or to several countries including that country, and the contract falls within the scope of such activities.

---

[262] *Forsikringsaktieselskapet Vesta v Butcher* [1986] 3 All E.R. 588. The principle is now well established in other contexts: see *Liberian Arab Foreign Bank v Manufacturers Hanover Trust Co (No.1)* [1988] 1 Lloyd's Rep. 259; *Liberian Arab Foreign Bank v Manufacturers Hanover Trust Co (No.2)* [1989] 1 Lloyd's Rep. 608.

[263] [1988] 1 F.T.L.R. 78.

[264] [1989] 1 All E.R. 402.

[265] Giuliano and Lagarde Report, at p.23.

In these situations, art.6.3 provides that choice of law rules are the general rules set out in arts 3 and 4. In either of these cases, it is apparent that the insurance company has advertised to the consumer in one or other fashion. It follows that a consumer assured who has insured with an insurer who does not carry business in the country of the assured's habitual residence and who has not advertised or approached the assured in that country, must himself have taken the initiative in approach the insurer. In such circumstances, special consumer protection rules are assumed to be unnecessary.

The default position can be ousted by agreement, in accordance with the general principles set out in art.3, but choice is subject to an important restriction in art.6.2:

> "Such a choice may not, however, have the result of depriving the consumer of the protection afforded to him by provisions that cannot be derogated from by agreement by virtue of the law which, in the absence of choice, would have been applicable on the basis of paragraph 1."

In other words, if the parties have chosen another law, the mandatory provisions of the assured's own law remain in place by way of a measure of consumer protection.

Article 6.4 also states that art.6 does not apply to, inter alia, "a contract for the supply of services where the services are to be supplied to the consumer exclusively in a country other than that in which he has his habitual residence." It is unclear whether an insurance contract is one for services, but on the assumption that it is, in the situation governed by art.6.4 the ordinary rules in arts 3 and 4 are applicable.

The provisions of art.5 of the Rome Convention are to much the same effect.

2–046 **Non-large risks situated within the EU.** The following paragraphs examine the rules in the Rome I Regulation relating to the determination of the law applicable to a risk which is not a large risk but which is situated within the EU. The rules are based upon the principles established in the Insurance Directives, as implemented in England by the Financial Services and Markets Act 2000 (Law Applicable to Contracts of Insurance) Regulations 2001, for risks of all types (other than reinsurance) situated in the EU. It is necessary to consider the two regimes separately.

2–047 *The Rome I Regulation.* In the absence of any express choice of applicable, the contract is to be governed by the law of the Member State in which the risk is situated at the time of conclusion of the contract (art.7.3). This is a mandatory provision rather than a presumption, so proof that the contract is more closely connected with some other country is not material. Where the contract covers risks situated in more than one Member State, the contract is to be considered as constituting several contracts each relating to only one Member State (art.7.5).

Article 7.3 of the Rome I Regulation permits an express choice of law, but with strict limitations. The parties may choose any of the following.

(a) The law of any Member State where the risk is situated at the time of conclusion of the contract, although if that law permits greater freedom of choice then the parties may take advantage of that freedom. If that law is a law of any part of the United Kingdom, the parties to that contract may also choose as the law applicable to the contract: (i) the law of another country; or (ii) the law of another part of the United Kingdom.[266]

(b) The law of the country where the policy holder has his habitual residence although if that law permits greater freedom of choice then the parties may take advantage of that freedom. If that law is a law of any part of the United Kingdom, the parties to that contract may also choose as the law applicable to the contract: (i) the law of another country; or (ii) the law of another part of the United Kingdom.[267]

(c) In the case of life assurance, the law of the Member State of which the policyholder is a national.

(d) For insurance contracts covering risks limited to events occurring in one Member State other than the Member State where the risk is situated, the law of that Member State.

(e) Where the policyholder of a contract falling under this paragraph pursues a commercial or industrial activity or a liberal profession and the insurance contract covers two or more risks which relate to those activities and are situated in different Member States, the law of any of the Member States concerned or the law of the country of habitual residence of the policy holder, although if that law permits greater freedom of choice then the parties may take advantage of that freedom. If that law or any of those laws is a law of any part of the United Kingdom, the parties to that contract may also choose as the law applicable to the contract (i) the law of another country; or (ii) the law of another part of the United Kingdom.[268]

One distinction is made between consumer cases and other cases. Where the assured is a consumer, art.6 of the Rome I Regulation applies, and the effect is that the mandatory rules of the place of the assured's habitual residence will operate irrespective of the choice of some other law.

There is minor modification for compulsory insurance. Article 7.4 states that a policy must comply with the requirements of the relevant domestic law imposing the requirement, and any contradictory rule in the law applicable to the policy is to be disregarded. Further, it is open to a Member State to require that a compulsory policy is to be governed by the law of that Member State. Where the contract covers risks situated in more than one Member State, the contract is to be considered as constituting several contracts each relating to only one Member State (art.7.5).

If there is a dispute as to whether there has been a choice of law, the question is to be answered by applying the law of the place where the risk was situated. In *Evialis SA v SIAT*[269] the assured entered into a contract for the carriage of goods, the risk under which was situated in Italy. The goods were insured under a certificate of insurance issued in accordance with an open cover: the open cover was expressly governed by Italian law, whereas the certificate of insurance was governed by English law. The issue was the law applicable to determining which of these documents prevailed. Andrew Smith J. held that Italian law, being the place of the situation of the risk, was presumptively the governing law unless the

---

[266] The Financial Services and Markets Act 2000 (Law Applicable to Contracts of Insurance) Regulations 2009 (SI 2009/3075) reg.4.

[267] The Financial Services and Markets Act 2000 (Law Applicable to Contracts of Insurance) Regulations 2009 (SI 2009/3075) reg.4.

[268] The Financial Services and Markets Act 2000 (Law Applicable to Contracts of Insurance) Regulations 2009 (SI 2009/3075) reg.4.

[269] *Evialis SA v SIAT* [2003] 2 Lloyd's Rep. 377.

parties had chosen some other law. In answering that question Italian law had to be applied as that was the default law, and the court was satisfied that the evidence of Italian law showed that an Italian court would have regarded the open cover as the overriding provision. Accordingly, as a matter of Italian law there had been no choice of English law, and the contract was thus governed by Italian law. Andrew Smith J. noted that, had English law been applied to the question, priority would have been given to the certificate of insurance and that would have led to the conclusion that there had been an agreement to oust Italian law.

2–048   *The Insurance Directives.* Article 7 of the Rome I Regulation re-enacts, in much simpler form, the provisions of the Insurance Directives and the 2001 Regulations. The 2001 Regulations draw a distinction between general (non-life) insurance and life insurance.

As far as general insurance is concerned, reg.4 of the 2001 Regulations allows the assured the benefit of his own domestic law, although it is permissible for him to agree to the application of some other law in accordance with the choice of law rules of domestic law. There are, however, overriding public policy considerations set out in reg.5 of the 2001 Regulations, namely that: (a) the mandatory provisions of English law continue to apply despite the fact that another applicable law has been validly chosen; and (b) if all the other elements relevant to the situation at the time when the parties make their choice are connected with one EU state only, the application of the mandatory rules of that State is not prejudiced. The effect of reg.5 is reproduced by art.6 of the Rome I Regulation. Regulation 4(2) of the 2001 Regulations lays down the same default rule as is found in the Rome I Regulation. If the policyholder resides in an EU state in which the risk is situated, the applicable law is the law of that EU state unless, if such a choice is permitted under the law of that EU state, the parties to the contract choose the law of another country.[270] English law does not impose any restrictions on choice. Regulation 4(3) deals with the situation in which the policyholder does not have his habitual residence within the territory of the EU state where the risk is situated: here the parties may choose either the law of the State where the risk is situated the law of the country in which the policyholder has his habitual residence. There is no presumption as to the applicable law in this situation. Regulation 4(4) governs business risks situated in two or more EU states, and allows the parties to choose the law of any of those states and of the country in which the policyholder resides. If the risks covered by the contract are limited to events occurring in one EU state other than the EU state in which the risk is situated, the parties may choose the law of the former EU State as the applicable law: reg.4(6). These rules are relaxed in the case of large risks, reg.6 permitting the parties to choose the applicable law.

If no law has been chosen, the default rule in reg.4(8) is that the applicable law is that of the country which is most closely connected with the contract. Regulation 4(9) then states that the contract is rebuttably presumed to be most closely connected with the EU state in which the risk is situated[271]: under the

---

[270] See *Evialis SA v SIAT* [2003] 2 Lloyd's Rep. 377, discussed above.

[271] See *Credit Lyonnais v New Hampshire Insurance Co* [1997] 2 Lloyd's Rep. 1, where the Court of Appeal held that the relevant presumption was that in Regulation 44/2001, namely, the law of the place of habitual residence of the party who was to effect the characterising performance. The 2001 Regulations reg.7, modified the position by making it clear that the Rome Convention determined the applicable law. See also: *American Motorists Insurance Co v Cellstar Corp* [2003] Lloyd's Rep. I.R. 395; *Travelers Casualty & Surety Co of Europe Ltd v Sun Life Assurance Co of Canada (UK) Ltd* [2004] Lloyd's Rep. I.R. 846; *Travelers Casualty and Surety Co of Canada v Sun Life Assurance Co of Canada (UK) Ltd (No.2)* [2007] Lloyd's Rep. I.R. 619.

Rome I Regulation, if the risk is not a large risk, this is a strict rule and not a presumption.

As regards life insurance, the Rome I Regulation requires the law applicable to a life policy to be the law of the place of the assured's nationality. The earlier law was more flexible. The basic presumption is that the applicable law is the law of the EU "state of the commitment".[272] This phrase is defined as meaning: (a) in the case of a policyholder who is an individual, the EU state in which he resided on the date of the policy; (b) in any other case, the EEA state in which the establishment of the policyholder to which the policy relates was situated when the policy was entered into.[273] The basic principle is, therefore, that the assured gets the benefit of his domestic law.

If the law of the Member State identified in (1) so permits, the parties may choose the law of another country.[274] Where the United Kingdom is the Member State of the commitment, free choice will be permitted. If the assured is an individual and resides in one EU state other than that of which he is a national or citizen, the parties are free to choose the law of either Member State.[275] As is the case with the non-life choice of law rules: (a) the mandatory rules of any part of the United Kingdom remain in place irrespective of the applicable law of the contract.[276]

3. SIGNIFICANCE OF THE APPLICABLE LAW

Renvoi. Renvoi, or remission, arises where an English court determines the law applicable to a contract and then has to apply the law of that country to the contract. The question becomes whether the English court will then apply the substantive law of the country or whether the English court will apply that country's conflict of laws rules. An application of the latter may mean that a different applicable law might be produced. It was settled at common law that, if the commercial intentions of the parties were to be furthered, any express or implied choice of a system of law was to be held to be limited to the domestic provisions of that law, and that renvoi for this reason ought to have no place so far as contracts are concerned.[277] The non-recognition of renvoi has been confirmed by art.20 of the Rome I Regulation.[278]   2–049

Construction of the contract. The applicable law governs all matters of substance arising under a contract; matters of procedure are governed by the law of the forum of the proceedings. A useful, if non-exhaustive, aide-memoire, is provided by art.12 of the Rome I Regulation.[279] As is the case with the Rome Convention, the applicable law governs (art.12.1):   2–050

(a) interpretation;
(b) performance;

---

[272] SI 2001/2635 reg.8(2).
[273] SI 2001/2635 reg.2(1).
[274] SI 2001/2635 reg.8(2).
[275] SI 2001/2635 reg.8(3).
[276] SI 2001/2635 reg.9.
[277] *Amin Rasheed Shipping Corp v Kuwait Insurance Co* [1983] 2 All E.R. 884.
[278] Re-enacting art.15 of the Rome Convention.
[279] Re-enacting art.10 of the Rome Convention.

(c) within the limits of the powers conferred on the court by its procedural law, the consequences of a total or partial breach of obligations, including the assessment of damages in so far as it is governed by rules of law;

(d) the various ways of extinguishing obligations, and prescription and limitation of actions; and

(e) the consequences of nullity of the contract.[280]

Article 12.2 also states that, "in relation to the manner of performance and the steps to be taken in the event of defective performance, regard shall be had to the law of the country in which performance takes place".

Article 20 of the Rome I Regulation[281] goes on to provide that the contract rules of the applicable law provide the burden of proof and presumptions of law.

The law applicable to a contract, once it has been determined by an English court, governs the obligations of the parties to the contract. In an insurance context, the applicable law will be looked to for the meaning of the words used by the parties in granting coverage and excluding liability, the circumstances in which the insurer will become liable to the assured, and whether or not the conduct of either party amounts to a breach of contract.[282] One problem which arises from these principles is that, as the meaning of words is a matter for the applicable law, the assured may not in fact have the degree of cover assumed by him to be the case. The point is illustrated by *St Paul Fire & Marine Insurance Co v Morice*,[283] in which Kennedy J. held that the use of the word "mortality" in a marine reinsurance on a bull did not in English law cover its slaughter by reason of an outbreak of foot-and-mouth disease despite the fact that the reinsured had been liable to the original assured on the same wording under a policy governed by New York law.[284] Again, in *Rowatt Leaky & Co v Scottish Provident Institution*,[285] a Scottish company issued a life policy in England to an English company on the life of a debtor, the law applicable to the contract being English law. The policy excluded liability, by means of a warranty, for suicide within six months from the date of the policy, although the warranty was stated "not to affect the interests of bona fide onerous holders", a term which had a technical meaning in Scots law but which was unknown as such in English law. The Court of Appeal, having determined that English law was the applicable law, had to construe the phrase in accordance with English meanings and rules of construction, and on that basis held evidence as to the use of the phrase in Scots law to be inadmissible; the Court of Appeal did concede that evidence of Scots law might have been admissible had it not been possible to give any meaning whatsoever to the phrase in English law, although it is scarcely conceivable that those circumstances could ever arise. The law of the place of performance, then,

---

[280] The equivalent provision of the Rome Convention was disapplied in England, by the Contracts (Applicable Law) Act 1990 s.2(2), because the common law classified the issues arising from nullity as restitutionary rather than contractual. That exclusion no longer applies.

[281] Re-enacting art.14 of the Rome Convention.

[282] *Wasa International Insurance Co Ltd v Lexington Insurance Co* [2009] Lloyd's Rep. I.R. 675.

[283] *St Paul Fire & Marine Insurance Co v Morice* (1906) 22 T.L.R. 449.

[284] But note that in *Wasa International Insurance Co Ltd v Lexington Insurance Co* [2009] Lloyd's Rep. I.R. 675 Lord Collins expressed the view that *St Paul* was wrongly decided. That reasoning relates, however, to the reinsurance context and does not affect the basic proposition that the interpretation of a contract is a matter for its applicable law.

[285] *Rowatt Leaky & Co v Scottish Provident Institution* [1927] 1 Ch. 55.

is to be disregarded, even though it may be the best indication of what the parties did actually intend.

However, the reasoning adopted by the House of Lords in the *Vesta*[286] case may be of assistance. It was there held that it is possible for the wording of a reinsurance agreement to be construed in accordance with the meaning of that wording under the applicable law of the original insurance agreement, as this is presumed to be the intention of the parties unless there is clear wording to the contrary. In this way, inconsistency between insurance and reinsurance may be prevented, even though different laws are applicable to each agreement.

There is nevertheless unwillingness in the English courts to reach the position that entirely different conclusions as to the proper construction of a policy may be reached by different legal systems unless—as in cases such as *Vesta*—this is clearly the position under the respective laws. In *King v Brandywine Reinsurance Co (UK) Ltd*[287] the assured—Exxon—had taken out a property and liability policy that extended to clean-up costs in respect of "debris". The policy contained various arbitration provisions that pointed to New York law as the applicable law, although Colman J., at first instance, held that those provisions were insufficiently certain and that English law was the governing law. The learned judge then proceeded to find that, as a matter of English law, the clean-up costs incurred by the assured following the grounding of the *Exxon Valdez* were not in relation to "debris" on the basis that spilt oil was not "debris". The learned judge went on to find that, had he been wrong on the application of English law. New York law would have reached the opposite conclusion and, as such, there would have been cover. The Court of Appeal upheld the outcome of Colman J.'s judgment, but rejected his reasoning. The Court of Appeal found that the arbitration provisions in the policy pointed strongly to the application of New York law, but that New York law would have reached exactly the same conclusion as English law on the meaning of "debris" and that there was no cover, particularly given the position under English law. The Court of Appeal, the judgment of which was delivered by Waller L.J., expressed the following view on interpretation[288]:

> "[W]e find it difficult to accept that a New York court and [an] English court would reach a different conclusion on the construction of a policy negotiated as this one was between organisations well-versed in what they were seeking to cover and well-versed in the risks that were likely to materialise from the business being carried on by the various assureds. Both systems of law are seeking to identify what the parties agreed, and both systems of law use similar pointers to ascertain that intention The judge erred in not bringing in at this point of his judgment the compelling points which he had already accepted when considering what the parties intended as a matter of the construction of the policy on the basis that English law was the proper law."

Formation

The "putative applicable law" principle. Article 10 of the Rome I Regulation[289]   **2–051** provides that "The existence and validity of a contract, or of any term of a contract, shall be determined by the law which would govern it under this Regulation if the contract or term were valid." In other words, the court must first

---

[286] *Forsakrings Vesta v Butcher* [1989] 1 All ER 402. But see *Wasa International Insurance Co Ltd v Lexington Insurance Co* [2009] Lloyd's Rep. I.R. 675 for the limits of the *Vesta* principle.
[287] *King v Brandywine Reinsurance Co (UK) Ltd* [2005] Lloyd's Rep. I.R. 509.
[288] At [116].
[289] Re-enacting art.8.1 of the Rome Convention.

assume that there is a contract, it must then decide which law would apply to it, and finally it must use the rules of that law to decide whether or not a contract exists. This approach can with some justification be described as circular, but it is nevertheless generally recognised as the appropriate solution to the problem, and reflects the pre-existing common law "putative proper law" doctrine which had regularly been applied by the English courts. An illustration may be of assistance. Let it be supposed that an English assured submits a proposal for insurance to an insurer resident in Switzerland, the Swiss company affirming its acceptance of the risk by a letter sent to England but which fails to arrive. In English law the contract has been validly concluded, for posting amounts to acceptance,[290] but under Swiss law a posted acceptance becomes binding only when it is received. An English court faced with this dispute would have to assume the validity of the contract to determine whether its proper law would be that of England or Switzerland, and would then decide the issue in accordance with art.10 of the of the Rome I Regulation.[291] In *Britannia Steamship Insurance Association Ltd v Ausonia Assicurazioni SpA*[292] the question was whether or not the reinsurance agreement had been signed on behalf of the reinsurer by a person with the ostensible authority to bind the reinsurer or, in the alternative, whether a reinsurer had acquiesced to the contract by its conduct. The Court of Appeal held that it was correct to apply English law as the putative applicable law to determine the agency and estoppel issues.

In *Mackender v Feldia AG*,[293] Lloyd's underwriters insured the stock in trade of three diamond merchants, incorporated respectively in Belgium, Italy and Switzerland, under a policy which had been drafted, signed and issued in England, but which contained a clause selecting Belgian law as the applicable law and requiring all actions to be brought exclusively before the Belgian courts. Following a claim on the policy, the underwriters alleged that the assureds had been involved in diamond smuggling; the underwriters commenced proceedings in England seeking a declaration that the policy was voidable and had been set aside, and sought permission from the English courts to serve those proceedings on the assured outside the jurisdiction. The Court of Appeal held that the question of non-disclosure raised here did not go to the validity of the contract but only to the rights of the insurers under the policy; it thus followed that the agreed law governed the dispute and that permission for service outside the jurisdiction had to be refused. However, both Lord Denning and Diplock L.J. indicated in their judgments that, had the question been one not of voidability but of existence—for example, whether the parties had reached any agreement at all—the issue would have to be decided by reference to English law as the putative applicable law, the agreement having the closest connection with England, disregarding the terms of the agreement. The approach of the courts is, therefore, to determine initial validity in accordance with English law as the law of the forum.

2–052   *The impact of express provisions.* The existence of an exclusive jurisdiction, arbitration or choice of law clause will be a valuable, and in the latter case all but

---

[290] *Household Fire Insurance Co v Grant* (1879) 4 Ex. D. 216.

[291] Facts suggested by *Albeko Schumaschinen v Kamborian Shoe Machine Co* (1961) 111 S.J. 519. See also *Marconi Communications International v Pt Pan Indonesia Bank Ltd TBK* [2004] 1 Lloyd's Rep. 594.

[292] *Britannia Steamship Insurance Association Ltd v Ausonia Assicurazioni SpA* [1984] 2 Lloyd's Rep. 98.

[293] *Mackender v Feldia AG* [1967] 2 Q.B. 590.

decisive, indicator of the law applicable to an agreement. As far as a jurisdiction or arbitration clause is concerned, the general assumption is that the judicial or arbitral forum selected by the parties indicates a choice of the substantive law of that forum with reasonable certainty, as required by art.3 of the Rome I Regulation: this point was discussed in the previous chapter. The difficulty that may arise is that the validity of the clause itself may itself be in issue, and it will be necessary as a preliminary point to decide whether there is a valid clause in existence so that its significance (or otherwise) in ascertaining the applicable law can be determined. The approach adopted by the English courts is to apply English law to that question, on the basis that the English forum must apply its own law, and if those rules point towards the existence of the clause, then the clause may itself be used in determining law applicable to the agreement. This approach is one that was adopted before the implementation of the Rome Convention and the Rome I Regulation,[294] and has been applied in subsequent decisions.[295] In *Marc Rich & Co AG v Societa Italians Impianti PA (The Atlantic Emperor)*,[296] where the dispute concerned the validity of a London arbitration clause in a sale agreement, English principles of offer and acceptance were applied to determine whether or not there was an agreement to arbitrate. In *Dornoch Ltd v Mauritius Union Assurance Co Ltd*[297] a reinsurance agreement was entered into between an insurance company in Mauritius and London Market reinsurers. It was alleged by the reinsured that the reinsurance agreement incorporated an exclusive jurisdiction clause in favour of the courts of Mauritius and accordingly that there had been an implied choice of the law of Mauritius to govern the reinsurance agreement. The Court of Appeal held that the question of incorporation had to be resolved in accordance with English law as the law of the forum, and that the allegedly incorporated jurisdiction clause had to be disregarded: where the question to be resolved was the existence of a particular term, the law of the forum had to be applied, and the putative applicable law was only relevant where the dispute was as to the existence of the agreement itself.

There may in many cases be a challenge not just to the arbitration, jurisdiction or choice of law clause but to the very existence of the agreement itself. In this situation the putative applicable law principle discussed in the preceding paragraph is relevant, and the English court will assume the validity of the agreement in order to determine which law is to be applied to the validity question. This will also involve assuming the validity of the relevant clause. In *The Parouth*[298] an agreement, the validity of which was disputed, contained an arbitration clause specifying London as the forum for arbitration. The Court of Appeal held that, on the assumption that the agreement and the arbitration clause were valid, the contract would have been governed by English law on the basis of the presumption that the applicable law follows the forum for arbitration, and that English law ought to be applied to determine the existence or otherwise of the agreement. Again, in *Egon Oldendorff v Libera Corp (No.1)*,[299] Mance J. ruled that the validity of a contract between German and Japanese concerns was

---

[294] *Compagnie Tunisienne de Navigation SA v Compagnie d'Amement Maritime SA* [1971] A.C. 572.

[295] *Egon Oldendorff v Libera Corp* [1906] 1 Lloyd's Rep. 380; *Marubeni Corp v Government of Mongolia* [2002] 2 All E.R. (Comm) 873.

[296] *Marc Rich & Co AG v Societa Italiens Impianti PA (The Atlantic Emperor)* [1989] 1 Lloyd's Rep. 548.

[297] *Dornoch Ltd v Mauritius Union Assurance Co Ltd* [2006] Lloyd's Rep. I.R. 786.

[298] *The Parouth* [1982] 2 Lloyd's Rep. 351.

[299] *Egon Oldendorff v Libera Corp (No.1)* [1995] 2 Lloyd's Rep. 64.

to be determined in accordance with English law on the basis of an arbitration clause that would have been regarded as incorporated by English law had the contract been valid.

These principles necessarily cannot apply where there is more than one arbitration clause allegedly in existence, each pointing towards a different applicable law. That situation arose in *Partenreederei M/S Heidberg v Grosvenor Grain & Food Co Ltd (The Heidberg)*,[300] in which Judge Diamond broke the deadlock by applying English law to determine which, if either, of the two clauses was incorporated into the agreement, on the basis that the English courts are to apply English law to any dispute before them unless there is a clear obligation in the contract to do otherwise.

2–053 *The Article 10(2) exception.* Article 10.2 of the Rome I Regulation[301] provides, by way of exception to the putative applicable law in art.10(1), that that law may be disregarded in one specific situation. Under art.10(2):

> "[A] party, in order to establish that he did not consent, may rely upon the law of the country in which he has his habitual residence if it appears from the circumstances that it would not be reasonable to determine the effect of his conduct in accordance with the law specified in [art.10.1, ie, the putative applicable law]."

The purpose of this exception is to save a party from being found to have entered into an agreement under the rules of the applicable law by virtue of conduct which, under his home law, would not have regarded him as being bound. The most cited illustration is the situation where a party fails to respond to an offer, in accordance with his domestic law which provides that his silence is not taken to be assent, whereas under the putative applicable law, silence is assent: in such circumstances it is assumed that art.10.2 would allow him to rely upon his domestic law to deny the existence of a contract. In *Egon Oldendorff v Libera Corp (No.2)*[302] a dispute arose as to the existence of a chaterparty under which the claimant allegedly agreed to charter two vessels from the defendant, a contract which the defendant denied having assented to. The claimant asserted that the contract contained a London arbitration clause, thereby rendering English law the putative applicable law: it was common ground that, if this was right, on the application of English law principles to the agreement itself the arbitration clause would have been incorporated. The defendant asserted that the arbitration clause would not have been incorporated under Japanese law, and in accordance with art.10.2 the arbitration clause had to be disregarded with the effect that the putative applicable law was Japanese law, under which there would have been no contract. Mance J. rejected this use of art.10.2, and held that, if there was a contract, the defendant's conduct indicated that he was aware that it contained an arbitration clause. On the basis of assumed incorporation, the putative applicable law was English law, and under that law the arbitration clause was clearly binding. This decision was followed in *Welex AG v Rosa Maritime (The Epsilon Rosa)*.[303] Here, the claimant, the holder of bills of lading governed by English law, asserted that it was not bound by an arbitration clause contained in a charterparty which had been incorporated into the bills of lading, on the

---

[300] *Partenreederei M/S Heidberg v Grosvenor Grain & Food Co Ltd (The Heidberg)* [1994] 2 Lloyd's Rep. 28.

[301] Re-enacting art.8.2 of the Rome Convention.

[302] *Egon Oldendorff* [1995] 2 Lloyd's Rep. 64.

[303] *Welex AG v Rosa Maritime (The Epsilon Rosa)* [2002] EWHC 2033 (Comm). See also *Horne Linie GmbH v Panamericana Formas e Impresos SA* [2006] EWHC 373 (Comm).

ground that law applicable to incorporation should not be English law but rather the law of Switzerland, the place of the claimant's habitual residence, and that under Swiss law the arbitration clause would have been void. David Steel J. rejected this analysis, and held that it was reasonable for English law to be applied to the question of formation as the claimant had not raised any other objection to the incorporation of the charterparty and the entire transaction was entirely conventional.

Formalities. It is rare in most jurisdictions for commercial contracts to be **2–054** subjected to formal legal requirements in order to achieve validity or enforceability, although such requirements are frequently encountered in the case of consumer contracts to provide some protection for the apparently weaker party. English law has few formal requirements for the creation of insurance agreements. How, then, does the common law regard a contract of insurance which does not comply with the formalities of any legal system with which the agreement has a close connection? Two propositions may be put forward. First, and as a consequence of the rule that English procedural rules apply to any action brought before an English court whatever the proper law of the contract in question, if an English formal requirement is classified by the court under English law[304] as procedural rather than substantive, then the English formal rule must be complied with. Unfortunately, the English courts have tended to classify most English formal requirements as procedural rather than substantive and have, as a result, refused to hear actions on contracts entirely valid by their applicable law. The leading authority is *Leroux v Brown*,[305] in which a contract for the sale of land, governed by French law, was held to be unenforceable in England for want of compliance with the now repealed Law of Property Act 1925 s.40, which required contracts for the sale or other disposition of land to be evidenced in writing. If the spirit of this decision were to be generally adopted by the English courts, and all formal matters were held to raise issues of procedure rather than substance, it would follow that many insurance agreements valid by their foreign applicable law could not be sued upon in England.

The second proposition, which is relevant where no difficulty is caused by English formal requirements, is that the contract will be regarded as valid if the formalities either of the law of the place at which the contract was made[306] or of the applicable law[307] have been complied with. The alternative permitted by English law is in accordance with commercial sense: it is clearly appropriate that where a contract is made in a certain place based on advice by lawyers versed in the law of that place, compliance with the legal formalities required there should be regarded as adequate; conversely, the presence of the parties in a particular place when their contract was concluded may have been entirely fortuitous, and it is therefore sensible to ignore the formal requirements for contracting in that place if the applicable law has been complied with.

All of this is now subject to art.11 of the Rome I Regulation.[308] The rules under the Regulation, insofar as relevant to the present discussion, are as follows:

---

[304] *Maher v Groupama Grand Est* [2009] EWCA Civ 1191.
[305] *Leroux v Brown* (1852) 12 C.B. 801.
[306] *Gueprafte v Young* (1851) 4 De G. & Sm. 217.
[307] *Van Grutten v Rigby* (1862) 31 Beav. 561.
[308] Re-enacting art.9 of the Rome Convention.

"1. A contract concluded between persons who, or whose agents, are in the same country at the time of its conclusion is formally valid if it satisfies the formal requirements of the law which governs it in substance under this Regulation or of the law of the country where it is concluded.
2. A contract concluded between persons who, or whose agents, are in different countries at the time of its conclusion is formally valid if it satisfies the formal requirements of the law which governs it in substance under this Regulation, or of the law of either of the countries where either of the parties or their agent is present at the time of conclusion, or of the law of the country where either of the parties had his habitual residence at that time.
3. A unilateral act intended to have legal effect relating to an existing or contemplated contract is formally valid if it satisfies the formal requirements of the law which governs or would govern the contract in substance under this Regulation, or of the law of the country where the act was done, or of the law of the country where the person by whom it was done had his habitual residence at that time."

These rules are disapplied in the case of consumer contracts, in which case the form is to be governed by the law of the place where the consumer has his habitual residence.[309]

It appears to follow from art.11.1 that the formal requirements of the law of the forum as such no longer provide the exclusive test for formal validity, and that *Leroux v Brown*, for so long a blot on English jurisprudence, no longer represents English law.

2–055   Duress. The House of Lords established in *Dimskal Shipping Co SA v International Transport Workers' Federation (The Evia Luck)*[310] that the question whether a contract is voidable for duress is to be determined according to its applicable law. That case was particularly strong, as the pressure complained of took place in Sweden, a jurisdiction in which the pressure was of a type not contrary to the law. However, their Lordships ruled that the legality of the pressure was governed by English law as the law applicable to the contract, and that on this basis the contract was voidable for duress.

2–056   Limitation periods. At common law, limitation periods laid down by statute were classified as procedural rules, with the consequence that an action for breach of contract which was time-barred by English law could not be brought in England whether or not the action was time-barred under its applicable law. However, the Foreign Limitation Periods Act 1984 s.1, swept away the common law rule, and in its place the position now is that limitation periods are to be treated as matters of substance rather than matters of procedure. Consequently, in the case of a contract, the English court will disregard domestic limitation periods and concern itself only with those time-bars imposed by the applicable law.[311] However, s.2 of the 1984 Act does permit the English courts to disregard a foreign limitation period if applying it would cause "undue hardship" to the claimant.[312]

---

[309] Rome I Regulation, art.11.4

[310] *Dimskal Shipping Co SA v International Transport Workers' Federation (The Evia Luck)* [1991] 4 All E.R. 871.

[311] See, e.g. *Assitalia-Le Assicurazione d'Italia SpA v Overseas Union Insurance Ltd* [1995] L.R.L.R. 76; *BP Plc v Aon Ltd* [2006] Lloyd's Rep. I.R. 577.

[312] See *The Komninos S, Financial Times*, January 16, 1990 (reversed [1991] 1 Lloyd's Rep. 371 on the ground that English law was the proper law, so that the FLPA 1984 was not relevant); *Jones v Trollope & Colls Cementation Overseas Ltd, The Times*, January 26, 1990; *Arab Monetary Fund v Hashim* [1993] 1 Lloyd's Rep. 543; *Harley v Smith* [2010] EWCA Civ 78.

As seen above, art.12.1(d) of the Rome I Regulation states that the applicable law governs limitation periods. The right of the English court to disregard a limitation period set out in the applicable law is, therefore, inconsistent with the Rome I Regulation. For that reason, reg.3 of the Law Applicable to Contractual Obligations (England and Wales and Northern Ireland) Regulations 2009[313] disapplies the Foreign Limitation Periods Act 1984 where the Rome I Regulation is applicable.

Illegality

Contracts illegal in their formation. Difficulties will arise under this head where **2–057** a contract of insurance which is connected with various legal systems, for example where the place of the performance of the contract or the domicile of the parties is not the same as the place providing the applicable law, is perfectly lawful under one of the legal systems but unlawful under one or more of the others. The guiding principle adopted by the English courts is that a contract which is illegal under its applicable law may not be sued upon in the English courts despite the fact that it would have been lawful had English law been its proper law, or that it was valid in the place where it was made.[314] Moreover, it is clear from the decisions such as *Royal Exchange Assurance Co v Vega*[315] that the courts will not take legality into account when determining the applicable law, on the basis that there is no presumption that the parties intended to make a lawful contract. The position where the applicable law renders a contract unlawful is, therefore, clear. However, difficulties arise where a contract is lawful under its applicable law but unlawful under some other system of law with which it is connected. Three particular difficulties may be contemplated:

First, the contract is unlawful under the law of the forum, English law. As stated above, this will not be fatal per se to a claim in the English courts unless English law is also the applicable law, although the contract will nevertheless be unenforceable if it in some way offends against domestic public policy. This rule is seemingly preserved by art.9.2 of the Rome I Regulation,[316] which states that "Nothing in this Regulation shall restrict the application of the overriding mandatory provisions of the law of the forum." An English statute which prohibits contracts is unlikely to be regarded as requiring unenforceability on public policy grounds unless it is clear that the statute extends to non-domestic contracts.[317] This point apart, there are few authorities on the impact of domestic public policy, although it appears to be the case that its scope is narrower in this context than is the case in purely domestic contracts.[318] A clear example of an agreement that would not be enforced in England is one which involves trading with the enemy.[319] The public policy principle is supplemented by the rule that an express choice of law which is clearly intended to evade the law of England, or of any other country for that matter, is to be disregarded.

Secondly, the contract is unlawful by the law of the place in which it was made. There would be little point in an English court refusing to enforce a contract on this ground alone as, in the modern world, the *lex loci contractus* may

---

[313] SI 2009/3064.

[314] *Kahler v Midland Bank* [1950] A.C. 24; *Libyan Arab Foreign Bank v Bankers Trust Co* [1989] 3 All E.R. 252. See also *Mahonia Ltd v JP Morgan Chase Bank* [2003] EWHC 1927 (Comm).

[315] *Royal Exchange Assurance Co v Vega* [1902] 2 K.B. 384.

[316] See also art.16 of the Rome Convention.

[317] *Boissevain v Weil* [1950] A.C. 327.

[318] *Addison v Brown* [1954] 2 All E.R. 213.

[319] *Dynamit A/G v Rio Tinto Co Ltd* [1918] A.C. 292.

be fortuitous and have little or no connection with the contract.[320] Similarly, illegality under the law of the domicile of either of the parties is not, per se, fatal to the enforcement of a contract in England.[321]

Thirdly, the contract is unlawful by the law of the place in which it is to be performed. It is settled that the English courts will not enforce a contract, the law applicable to which is English law, if the law of the place where it is to be performed renders the contract unlawful,[322] for English domestic contract law does not permit the enforcement of agreements to perform unlawful acts. Similarly, although there is no modern authority on the point, a contract governed by a foreign law which is lawful under that law but which is to be performed in England where it is unlawful, will not be enforced by the English courts.[323] This rule is inconsistent with the general primacy of the applicable law, and seems to operate as an exception to that principle, for the rule applies whether or not the contract is one which offends English public policy. What has yet to be clearly decided is whether the English courts would enforce a contract valid by its foreign applicable law but illegal in some other foreign place of performance. In principle, illegality by the *lex loci solutionis* should not be a bar to enforcement in the English courts, which are concerned only with the applicable law if England is unaffected by the contract, but there are dicta which indicate unenforceability.[324] Nevertheless, the better view appears to be to the contrary. In *Royal Boskalis Westminster NV v Mountain*[325] the Court of Appeal provided an inconclusive discussion of the point. Phillips L.J. held that such a contract would not be enforced in England, but its validity would be recognised. Pill L.J. held that English public policy precluded both recognition and enforcement. Stuart-Smith L.J. held that the contract was simply illegal under English law.

2–058   *Contracts involving illegality in performance.* As far as English domestic law is concerned, where two parties have entered into a lawful contract but one of them commits an unlawful act while performing his side of the bargain, the contract itself will not be rendered illegal[326] but the guilty party might, in appropriate circumstances, be precluded from bringing proceedings for enforcement; in general, the contract will be unenforceable where the guilty party is required to plead his unlawful act in order to establish his claim, or where the benefit sought by him is a direct consequence of his own wrongdoing.[327]

The effect of the application of these rules to domestic insurance agreements is that unlawful conduct on the part of the assured will, if forming a part of the assured's cause of action or if designed to allow the assured to profit from his own wrong, debar recovery.[328] Where an agreement sued upon in the English courts has an international element, the matter becomes more complex, for the act in question may be illegal under any one of a number of legal systems: the

---

[320] *Vita Food Products Inc v Unus Shipping Co* [1939] A.C. 277 at 296–300. disapproving dicta to the contrary in *The Torni* [1932] P.78 at 88.

[321] *Rossano v Manufacturers' Life Insurance Co* [1963] 2 Q.B. 352.

[322] *Ralli Brothers v Compania Naviera Sota y Aznar* [1920] 2 K.B. 287: *Mackender v Feldia AG* [1967] 2 Q.B. 590 at 601, per Diplock L.J.

[323] For an old illustration, involving smuggling, see *Clugas v Penaluna* (1791) 4 T.R. 466.

[324] See, e.g. the *Ralli Brothers* decision, [1920] 2 K.B. 287 at 323, per Scrutton L.J.; *Zivnostenska Banka v Frankman* [1950] A.C. 57 at 79, per Lord Reid.

[325] *Royal Boskalis Westminster NV v Mountain* [1997] 2 All E.R. 929.

[326] *St John Shipping Corp v Joseph Rank Ltd* [1957] 1 Q.B. 267.

[327] *Stone & Rolls Ltd v Moore Stephens* [2009] UKHL 39.

[328] *Geismur v Sun Alliance and London Insurance Ltd* [1978] Q.B. 383; *Euro-Diam Ltd v Bathurst* [1986] 2 F.T.L.R. 639.

applicable law; the law of the place in which the contract was made; the law of the place in which the contract was performed; and English law as the law of the forum. In this type of case, the courts must undertake a three-stage enquiry: first, to which systems of law is the contract connected in any of the above senses; secondly, is illegal performance under any one or more of those legal systems material to enforcement in England; and thirdly, is there sufficient connection between the illegal conduct and the claim under the policy?

The leading authority on these matters is the decision of Staughton J. in *Euro-Diam Ltd v Bathurst*.[329] The assured in this case had supplied diamonds to a purchaser in Germany under an invoice which, at the purchaser's request, understated the purchase price; it was assumed by Staughton J. that the purpose of this was to deceive the German customs authorities. Following the loss of the diamonds in a manner entirely unconnected with the fraud, the underwriter refused to indemnify the assured, pleading the assured's complicity in a design unlawful under German law. Staughton J. held that the underwriter's defence failed on the basis that German law had no connection with the insurance agreement and that English law alone fell to be considered: the contract had been made, performed and sued upon in England, and was governed by English law. Consequently, illegality under German law was not material to the claim and, as nothing illegal had been done in England, the underwriter had no defence. It was not necessary, therefore, for Staughton J. to consider the further questions of whether, had the contract been connected in any way with German law, it would have been unenforceable, and whether the illegality was sufficiently proximate to the loss to debar recovery. As to the former question, Staughton J. appears to have been of the view that conduct unlawful under the applicable law or under the law of the forum would prima facie have provided a good defence to the insurer, and that illegality under the law of the place of performance alone might have done so[330]; this accords with the principles established by the courts for the enforcement of contracts unlawful in their inception, discussed above. As to the latter question, Staughton J. was of the view that the conduct of the assured was in any event immaterial, as illegality did not have to be pleaded by him to establish his claim, nor would permitting the claim further or assist any unlawful design.

The principles espoused in *Euro-Diam* are now to be read in the light of art.9.3 of the Rome I Regulation. This is in the following terms:

> "Effect may be given to the overriding mandatory provisions of the law of the country where the obligations arising out of the contract have to be or have been performed, in so far as those overriding mandatory provisions render the performance of the contract unlawful. In considering whether to give effect to those provisions, regard shall be had to their nature and purpose and to the consequences of their application or non-application."

Thus, if the overriding mandatory provisions of the law of the country in which the contract is to be performed renders the performance illegal, the English courts are to give effect to those mandatory rules and to apply them to the contract. It is doubtful, however, whether revenue laws qualify as overriding mandatory

---

[329] *Euro-Diam Ltd v Bathurst* [1986] 2 F.T.L.R. 639, affirmed on other grounds [1988] 2 All E.R. 23. See also *Furness Withy Aluminium Pty Ltd v Metal Distributors (UK) Ltd (The Amazonia)* [1990] 1 Lloyd's Rep. 236.

[330] As to this, see *Libyan Arab Foreign Bank v Bankers Trust Co* [1989] 3 All E.R. 252, where Staughton J. held that the English courts will not enforce a contract which is intended to result in, or necessarily requires, illegality in the place of performance.

provisions for this purpose, so that there would have been no basis for the English court to apply German law to the agreement.

2–059 **Interest.** The power of the English High Court to award interest on a sum due is contained in the Senior Courts Act 1981, s.35A. It was held by Hobhouse J. in *Midland International Trade Services Ltd v Sudairy*[331] that this is a procedural rather than a substantive statute. That was so because English law did not recognise a right to interest by way of damages for late payment of money, and s.35A had been enacted to fill that gap; the power in s.35A arose only in connection with legal proceedings; and an award of interest was discretionary. The correct application of s.35A to a claim governed by a foreign law was considered by the Court of Appeal in *Maher v Groupama Grand Est.*[332] In this case the claimant sought interest on damages awarded by the English court in respect of a tort committed in France. The Court of Appeal, following *Midland*, held that s.35A was a procedural rather than substantive provision. That meant that if there was a substantive right to interest under French law as the law applicable to the tort, then the amount of that interest was governed by s.35A, although the English court would have regard to the amount that would have been awarded by a French court in fixing the sum to be awarded under s.35A.

The English courts are empowered to award damages in a currency other than sterling,[333] and if this is done the rate of interest on a judgment debt may be varied from the statutory figure laid down by the Judgments Act 1838 s.17, which is presently 8 per cent, to reflect the strength of the currency in question.[334] Arbitrators, unless the parties have agreed otherwise, may award simple or compound interest at any rate they regard as just.[335]

2–060 **Assignment, subrogation, contribution and set-off.** As under the Rome Convention, art.12, the relationship between an assignor and an assignee is governed by the contract of assignment (art.14.1), although the law governing the claim itself determines assignability and the relationship between the assignee and the debtor (art.14.2).

The Rome I Regulation deals for the first time with contractual subrogation, and treats it in the same way as assignment: the relationship between the creditor and the third party indemnifier is governed by the law applicable to the contract between them (art.14.1) whereas the relationship between the third party and the debtor, including the circumstances in which subrogation can be invoked, is governed by the law applicable to the claim (art.14.2). As regards subrogation arising as a matter of law, art.15 replicates art.13 of the Rome Convention by providing that the law governing the third party's obligation to indemnify the creditor (e.g. the policy of insurance) determines whether and to what extent subrogation rights exist.

The Rome I Regulation, unlike the Rome Convention lays down the rule as regards contribution claims that the law governing contribution is the law governing the obligation of the person seeking contribution to make payment

---

[331] *Financial Times*, May 2, 1990. See also Moore-Bick J. in *Kuwait Oil Tanker SAK v Al Bader* Unreported, December 17, 1998, although the point was left open on appeal, [2000] 2 All E.R. (Comm) 271.

[332] *Maher v Groupama Grand Est* [2009] EWCA Civ 1191.

[333] *Miliangos v George Frank (Textiles) Ltd* [1976] A.C. 443.

[334] Private International Law (Miscellaneous Provisions) Act 1995 ss.1–4, inserting the Administration of Justice Act 1970 s.44A.

[335] Arbitration Act 1996 s.49.

although those from whom contribution is sought can rely upon any defences in the law governing their own obligation to the creditor (art.16).

Finally, in respect of set-off, art.17 of the Rome I Regulation states that where the right to set-off is not agreed by the parties, set-off shall be governed by the law applicable to the claim against which the right to set-off is asserted.

4. NON-CONTRACTUAL CLAIMS

The common law and its displacement. The rules discussed earlier in this **2–061** chapter apply only to contract claims. Claims in tort as between insurer and assured are unlikely, but tortious claims by the assured against his broker remain a possibility. In what follows, it is assumed that this is the appropriate scenario. Further, there may be restitutionary actions, e.g. to recover sums wrongly paid. The common law rules which governed the right of a claimant to bring proceedings in England in respect of a wrong done to him abroad ultimately became, prior to their abolition by the Private International Law (Miscellaneous Provisions) Act 1995, impossibly complex and reflected little credit upon English law. The root decision was *Phillips v Eyre*,[336] which developed the principle known as the "double actionability" rule. Under this principle, an action could be brought in the English courts only if the act was:

(a) actionable in England, as the *lex fori*; and
(b) actionable in the place where the act took place, the *lex loci delicti*.

The double actionability principle was confirmed by the House of Lords in *Chaplin v Boys*,[337] a decision of labyrinthine complexity and which did not admit of a clear ratio. It was nevertheless possible to say after *Chaplin v Boys* that the predominant law was the *lex fori* and that, once actionability under the local law and English law had been established, the scope of liability would be determined by English law. *Chaplin v Boys* did, however, recognise that the double-actionability rule was not absolute, and that in appropriate circumstances the fact that the act was not actionable under the *lex loci delicti* might be disregarded. This exception was applied in *Johnson v Coventry Churchill International Ltd*.[338] In that case, an employee working abroad temporarily, and injured abroad in the course of his employment, was held to be entitled to sue his employers in England for failing to provide a safe system of work, despite the fact that no equivalent action was available in Germany: Kay QC ruled that, as the action was substantially connected with England, the double-actionability requirement could be waived.

The foundations of *Phillips v Eyre* were further undermined by the Privy Council's decision in *Red Sea Insurance Co v Bouygues SA*.[339] There, an action was commenced by contractors against their construction insurers in Hong Kong, in relation to losses incurred in Saudi Arabia. The insurers contested liability, and raised a subrogation counterclaim against the suppliers of concrete to the contractors. The suppliers sought to have the subrogation counterclaim struck out on the basis that, even though under Saudi law a subrogation action was possible

---

[336] *Phillips v Eyre* (1870) L.R. 6 Q.B. 1, following *The Halley* (1868) L.R. 2 P.C. 193.
[337] *Chaplin v Boys* [1971] A.C. 356.
[338] *Johnson v Coventry Churchill International Ltd* [1992] 3 All E.R. 14.
[339] *Red Sea Insurance Co v Bouygues SA* [1994] 3 All E.R. 749.

in the circumstances, under English law (which operated in Hong Kong), subrogation proceedings cannot be brought until the insurer has indemnified its assured, which had not occurred here. The double actionability principle had not, therefore, been satisfied. The Privy Council, making inroads into the second limb of *Phillips v Eyre*, ruled that double-actionability did not apply where it would cause injustice, and that in appropriate circumstances any particular issue could be resolved solely by reference to the law of the place in which the act occurred. As the matter was almost exclusively connected with Saudi Arabia, the fact that there was no available action in Hong Kong was no bar to proceedings in Hong Kong.

The result of these cases was that, while the double-actionability rule continued to exist, it could be disregarded in the interests of justice where the claim was most closely connected with either the place in which the act occurred or England was the forum. In *Johnson*, the court disregarded the law of the place in which the act occurred and focused on English law as the law of the forum, whereas in *Red Sea* the court disregarded the law of the forum and held that the matter was governed solely by the law of the place in which the act occurred. It was apparent after these cases that the law had become uncertain and accordingly had lost its credibility. Moreover, an investigation by the Law Commission revealed that in most jurisdictions the actionability of a tort committed abroad is based solely on the question whether the act was actionable where it took place and not whether it was actionable in the place where the action was heard.

The common law principles set out in the above paragraphs are now of historical interest only. The Private International Law (Miscellaneous Provisions) Act 1995, which came into force on May 1, 1996,[340] swept away the old law and replaced it with the concept of the law applicable to a tort. The 1995 Act was, however, destined to be short-lived. European Parliament and Council Regulation 864/2007/EC of July 11, 2007, on "The Law Applicable to Non-Contractual Obligations" (the Rome II Regulation), which came into force with respect to acts or omissions on or after January 11, 2009, has superseded the 1995 Act where the claim falls within the Rome II Regulation.[341] The 1995 Act will nevertheless remain relevant for some years, at least until the limitation period for tort claims has expired, and accordingly in the following paragraphs both regimes are discussed.

Part III of the Private International Law (Miscellaneous Provisions) Act 1995

2–062   *The concept of the applicable law.* Sections 9 to 15 of the 1995 Act repealed the common law principles and replace them with a new framework, giving primacy to the *lex loci delicti*. Under s.9 of the 1995 Act, when a claim in respect of an act committed abroad comes before an English court, that court is required to ascertain the "applicable law". The applicable law has two roles. First, the substantive rules of the applicable law are to be applied by the English courts in determining whether the action is one which can properly be classified as in tort,

---

[340] The 1995 Act applies to acts or omissions giving rise to a claim on or after that date: s.14. This wording was construed in *Re T&N Ltd (No.2)* [2005] EWHC 2990 (Ch) as referring to negligent acts occurring on or after that date, so that the law applicable to a claim by a person who has been exposed to a harmful substance before May 1, 1996 but who suffers injury thereafter is to be determined by common law rules and not by the rules in the legislation.

[341] Law Applicable to Non-Contractual Obligations (England and Wales and Northern Ireland) Regulations 2008 (SI 2008/2986) inserting, to this effect, s.15A into the 1995 Act.

and thus within the 1995 Act.[342] This may mean that a cause of action not recognised in England as tortious, or indeed at all, is nevertheless to be treated as a tort action if it would be so classified under the applicable law. Secondly, the substantive rules of the applicable law alone are to be used in determining whether the claimant has a cause of action against the defendant,[343] a point emphasised by the express repeal by s.10 of the common law principle of double actionability. Thus, in the situation in which an assured brings proceedings against his broker, the only law which is relevant to the assured's claim is the applicable law. For each of these purposes the domestic, as opposed to the conflict of laws, rules of the applicable law are relevant. The possibility that the applicable law might, under its conflicts rules, refer the question to some other law is, therefore, to be disregarded,[344] and renvoi is thereby excluded. The law of the forum continues to govern procedural issues, including—most importantly—the measure of damages for breach of a tortious duty.[345]

The meaning of "applicable law". The key issue is the meaning of the phrase **2–063** "applicable law". Section 11(1) of the 1995 Act provides that, as a general rule, the applicable law is "the law of the country in which the events constituting the tort in question occur". Section 11(1) is at its easiest to apply if all of the elements of the tort occur in one place, as that place will fix the applicable law.[346] In many situations, however, the negligent act and the consequences of the negligent act—each of which constitutes an element of the tort—may take place in different countries. Here, s.11(1) cannot apply and s.11(2) sets out three fallback rules:

(1) In a death or personal injury case, the applicable law is provided by "the law of the country where the individual was when he sustained the injury". This provision gives rise to complex and unresolved issues. Consider, for example, a claimant who is exposed to a harmful substance in country A, and who suffers ill-health later in country B. Section 11(2)(a) does not indicate where the injury was sustained, although it might be argued that the place of exposure, country A, would constitute the relevant country as it is the exposure which gives rise to the subsequent injuries.[347]

(2) In a property damage case the applicable law is provided by "the law of the country where the property was when it was damaged". This provision appears to be relatively straightforward.

(3) In any other case, the applicable law is provided by the law of the place in which "the most significant element or elements of those events occurred".[348] This provision is that most relevant to a professional

---

[342] 1995 Act s.9(1)–(2).

[343] 1995 Act s.9(4).

[344] 1995 Act s.9(5).

[345] *Harding v Wealands* [2006] UKHL 32. In *Maher v Groupama Grand Est* [2009] EWCA Civ 1191 a direct action in England against motor insurers in respect of an accident occurring in France was held to be tortious in nature, so that the measure of damages for injury was governed by English law in accordance with *Harding v Wealands*. The Court of Appeal further held that the award of interest was substantive and thus governed by the law of France, although the amount of interest was a procedural matter and thus for English law See also *Knight v Axa Assurance* [2009] Lloyd's Rep. I.R. 667.

[346] *Protea Leasing Ltd v Royal Air Camboge Co Ltd* [2002] EWHC 2731 Comm.

[347] The meaning of "sustained" in relation to injuries caused by exposure is of some complexity. See *Durham v BAI (Run-Off) Ltd* [2009] Lloyd's Rep. I.R. 295.

[348] See *OT Africa Line Ltd v Magic Sportswear Corp* [2004] EWHC 2441 (Comm).

negligence claim, including a claim against a broker, and is also the most problematic. Let it be supposed that the broker, who is located in London, has transmitted advice to a US client to insure with a Ruritanian insurer, advice which is accepted by the US client instructing the broker to place insurance in Ruritania. Suppose further that the Ruritanian insurer proves to be insolvent. There are at least three candidates for the applicable law in a negligence suit: English law, as the law of the country in which advice was given, U.S. law, as the law of the place in which the advice was received and acted upon, and Ruritanian law as the law of the place in which the loss was suffered. Equally, it may be that there are two claims, one in respect of the advice and one in respect of the placing of the cover, each of which is governed by a different applicable law.

In *Morin v Bonhams & Brooks Ltd*[349] the Court of Appeal held, in a case involving misrepresentation in England which was relied upon in Monaco, reliance taking the form of the purchase of a vehicle, the applicable law under s.11(2)(c) was that of Monaco on the ground that the most significant elements of the tort had taken place in Monaco. The Court of Appeal recognised that the making of a misrepresentation was an essential element in the tort, but that the most significant aspect of the tort was reliance. There is thus at least an indication that in the example given above the governing law would be either the law of the United States or the law of Ruritania. This approach was followed by Aikens J. in *Dornoch Ltd v Mauritius Union Assurance Co Ltd*.[350] In this case, reinsurance was placed in the London market by brokers who used as a part of the presentation a proposal form completed by the assured, a bank in Mauritius. The reinsurers sought to avoid the reinsurance for misrepresentation and joined the assured to the proceedings so that damages could be obtained against the assured in the tort of deceit in the event that the reinsurers were found to be liable to the reinsured. The alleged deceit related to the manner in which the assured had conducted its business. Aikens J. held that there were six elements that went to make up the tort: (i) the manner in which the assured had conducted its business; (ii) the completion of the proposal form by the assured; the transmission of the proposal form to brokers in England; (iv) the presentation of the proposal form to the reinsurers; (v) reliance by the reinsurers; and (vi) loss suffered by the reinsurers. Elements (i) and (ii), and part of (iii), all occurred in Mauritius, but Aikens J. held that the critical factor in a misrepresentation case was reliance, and as that—along with the other elements—had occurred in England, the tort was governed by English law. This reasoning was approved in its entirety by the Court of Appeal.[351]

2–064 *Exceptions: displacement of the general rule.* Section 12 is in the following terms:

"(1) If it appears, in all the circumstances, from a comparison of—
   (a) the significance of the factors which connect a tort or delict with the country whose law would be the applicable law under the general rule; and
   (b) the significance of any factors connecting the tort or delict with another country, that it is substantially more appropriate for the applicable law for

---

[349] *Morin v Bonhams & Brooks Ltd* [2004] 1 Lloyd's Rep. 782.

[350] *Dornoch Ltd v Mauritius Union Assurance Co Ltd* [2006] Lloyd's Rep. I.R. 127.

[351] *Dornoch Ltd v Mauritius Union Assurance Co Ltd* [2006] Lloyd's Rep. I.R. 127. See also: *Trafigura Beheer BV v Kookmin Bank Co* [2006] EWHC 1450 (Comm); *Congentra AC v Sixteen Thirteen Marine SA* [2008] EWHC 1615 (Comm).

determining the issues arising in the case, or any of those issues, to be the law of the other country, the general rule is displaced and the applicable law for determining those issues or that issue (as the case may be) is the law of that other country.

(2) The factors that may be taken into account as connecting a tort or delict with a country for the purposes of this section include, in particular, factors relating to the parties, to any of the events which constitute the tort or delict in question or to any of the circumstances or consequences of those events."

The cases demonstrate that the general rule in s.11 is not to be displaced lightly.[352] Further, as noted by Aikens J. in *Dornoch Ltd v Mauritius Union Assurance Co Ltd*[353] in the situation where the applicable law has been determined under s.11 as that of the place where the most significant elements of the tort occurred, s.12 requires the court to consider precisely the same factors again and thus cannot be of any significance. The most commonly litigated issue to come before the English courts is that of an accident taking place abroad but involving English parties temporarily in that place, and the cases are for the most part of the view that the effect of s.11 is that the cause of action is to be determined by the law of the place in which the accident occurred.[354] Until the decision of the House of Lords in *Harding v Wealands*[355] there was an assumption that the assessment of damages was a matter of substance to be assessed in accordance with the applicable law under s.11, and the English courts were divided on the question whether s.12 was to be used to disapply the foreign law measure of damages in respect of a tort committed abroad.[356] In *Harding* their Lordships ruled that damages are a matter of procedure rather than substance, and accordingly are to be assessed under English law as the law of the forum, thereby rendering this debate redundant.[357]

The Rome II Regulation. European Parliament and Council Regulation **2–065** 864/2007/EC of July 11, 2007, on "The Law Applicable to Non-Contractual Obligations" (the Rome II Regulation) came into force with respect to events giving rise to damage on and after January 11, 2009 (art.31, although there is some doubt on this point[357a]) and harmonises the rules of the EU Member States on the law applicable to tort, restitutionary and related claims in civil and

---

[352] *Anton Durbeck GmbH v Den Norske Bank ASA* [2002] EWHC 1326 (QB); *Middle Eastern Oil v National Bank of Abu Dhabi* [2008] EWHC 2895 (Comm).

[353] *Dornoch Ltd v Mauritius Union Assurance Co Ltd* [2006] Lloyd's Rep. I.R. 127, affirmed [2006] Lloyd's Rep. I.R. 786.

[354] *Hulse v Chambers* [2002] 1 All E.R. Comm 802; *Harding v Wealands* [2004] EWCA Civ 1735; but contrast *B v B* Preston District Registry, July 29, 2008.

[355] *Harding v Wealands* [2006] UKHL 32.

[356] In *Edmunds v Simmonds* [2001] 1 W.L.R. 1003, following *Hamill v Hamill* Unreported, July 24, 2001, the English measure of damages was held to be more appropriate where the case was heard in England, and s.12 was used to disapply the applicable law, an approach approved by Waller L.J. in the Court of Appeal in *Roerig v Valiant Trawlers Ltd* [2002] 1 W.L.R. 2304 in respect of a person from overseas injured in England and suing in England. That conclusion was nevertheless thrown into doubt by the Court of Appeal in *Harding v Wealands* [2005] 1 All E.R. 415, where the use of s.12 was rejected.

[357] In the event that a person from overseas is injured in England, and brings an action in England, then under the Harding principle English law will govern the measure of damages. Independently of that principle, earlier cases had decided that if English law governed the cause of action then English law ought to provide the measure of damages: *Roerig v Valiant Trawlers Ltd* [2002] 1 W.L.R. 2304; *Bristow Helicopters Ltd v Sikorsky* [2004] 2 Lloyd's Rep. 150. The alternative reasoning is no longer relevant.

[357a] The point has been referred to the European Court of Justice in *Homawoo v GMF Assurance SA* [2010] EWHC 1941 (QB).

commercial disputes. There are significant changes to the structure laid down by the 1995 Act. Because there is no common definition of "non-contractual obligations" within the European Union, the Regulation creates its own autonomous concept, namely, damage arising out of "tort/delict, unjust enrichment, *negotiorum gestio* or *culpa in contrahendo*" (art.2). There are exclusions for public authority disputes, family matters, negotiable instruments, trusts, invasion of privacy rights (including defamation) and claims affecting the constitutions of companies (art.1). The Regulation is also without prejudice to other EU rules and to international conventions providing for applicable law (arts 27 and 28).

The general rule in art.4.1 is that the law applicable to a non-contractual obligation arising out of a tort is the law of the country (whether inside or outside the European Union: art.3) in which the damage occurs irrespective of the country in which the event giving rise to the damage occurred and irrespective of the country or countries in which the indirect consequences of that event occur. That general rule is modified in two respects. First, where the parties both have their habitual residence in the same country at the time when the damage occurs, the law of that country shall apply (art.4.2). "Habitual residence" for this purpose means: (a) in respect of company its place of central administration or of the relevant branch or agency; and (b) in respect of an individual in business means his or her principal place of business (art.23). Secondly, where it is clear from all the circumstances of the case that the tort is manifestly more closely connected with a country other than either of those, the law of that other country shall apply (art.4.3). A manifestly closer connection is for this purpose not defined, but "might be based in particular on a pre-existing relationship between the parties, such as a contract, that is closely connected with the tort/delict in question". The effect of this is that there are two default rules, one based on the place of the tort and other based on the place of the parties common habitual residence, but either of those can be modified in the event that the tort is manifestly more closely connected with another country.

The Regulation then goes on to lay down specific rules for: product liability claims (art.5); unfair competition claims (art.6); environmental damage claims (art.7); infringement of intellectual property rights (arts 8 and 13); claims arising out of industrial action (art.9); and restitutionary claims (arts 10–12). Contribution claims are governed by the law applicable to the tort (art.20).

It is also permitted by art.14 for the parties to enter into an agreement, after the event giving rise to the damage has taken place, as to the law to be applied. If the parties are both commercial concerns, such agreement is permissible in advance of the event. Any choice of law must be demonstrated with reasonable certainty, must not affect the rights of third parties and must be without prejudice to the mandatory rules of the country in which the damage occurs where the law of some other country has been chosen. It is also without prejudice to the mandatory and public policy rules of the forum (arts 16 and 26).

The applicable law, once ascertained, governs: (a) the basis and extent of liability, including the determination of persons who may be held liable for acts performed by them; (b) the grounds for exemption from liability, any limitation of liability and any division of liability; (c) the existence, the nature and the assessment of damage or the remedy claimed[358]; (d) within the limits of powers conferred on the court by its procedural law, the measures which a court may take

---

[358] Thereby reversing the rule in *Harding v Wealands* [2006] UKHL 32. See *Maher v Groupama Grand Est* [2009] EWCA Civ 1191.

to prevent or terminate injury or damage or to ensure the provision of compensation; (e) the question whether a right to claim damages or a remedy may be transferred, including by inheritance; (f) persons entitled to compensation for damage sustained personally; (g) liability for the acts of another person; (h) the manner in which an obligation may be extinguished and rules of prescription and limitation, including rules relating to the commencement, interruption and suspension of a period of prescription or limitation (art.15).[359] Renvoi is excluded, so the law to be applied is the substantive internal law of the country in question and not its conflict of laws rules (art.24).

Insurers are directly affected in two respects. First, if the applicable law of the tort or the law applicable to the policy of insurance so permits, the claimant may bring the claim directly against the defendant's insurers (art.18). Secondly, if the victim is insured, the law applicable to the contract of insurance determines whether and to what extent his insurers have subrogation rights against the defendant in accordance with the law applicable to the tort (art.19).

---

[359] Law Applicable to Non-Contractual Obligations (England and Wales and Northern Ireland) Regulations 2008 (SI 2008/2986) disapply the Foreign Limitation Periods Act 1984 in this context.

CHAPTER 3

CONSTRUCTION OF THE POLICY

1. PRINCIPLES OF CONSTRUCTION

3–001   **The context of construction.** A policy of insurance is a contract between insurer and assured. As such, it is subject to the rules of construction which apply to any contract in English law, although there are also certain rules which have been evolved to deal with the particular problems of insurance law. The rules of construction have been developed gradually since the time of Lord Mansfield in the second half of the eighteenth century. Rules of construction are necessary, partly because in many cases the parties fail to make their intentions clear in the wording which they adopt (often because they have simply not anticipated the problem which later arises), and partly because the inherent ambiguities of language may make it impossible to state the parties' intentions in such a way that no misinterpretation is possible. Consequently, the courts have tried to lay down consistent principles by which ambiguities and apparent contradictions may be resolved. The disputes which are likely to arise in the construction of policies of insurance may be identified as falling into a number of categories. First, there may be disputes as to the meaning of specific words relating to the cover provided. Secondly, there may be disputes as to whether a particular clause was intended to apply in the events which have happened. Thirdly, there may be an apparent contradiction between different clauses in the same policy. This sometimes arises where special clauses have been inserted which depart from the standard form wording of the policy. The parties are of course free to lay down their own rules of construction.[1]

3–002   **Significance of rules of construction.** There are countless judicial pronounce-ments on the correct approach to construction, and numerous rules or principles of construction have been developed by the courts over the years. Laying down rules of construction for policy documents is fraught with difficulty. Many different "rules" have been identified but all are subject to exceptions and, depending on the exact construction given to each, there may be conflicts between them which require the court to apply one at the expense of another. For example, the word "flood" in the insuring phrase "storm, tempest or flood" may plausibly be given its natural meaning as an aggregation of water, its contextual meaning of a violent event or a meaning most favourable to the assured on the basis that the wording is that of the insurers: in *Young v Sun Alliance and London*

---

[1] See, e.g. the clause in *Enterprise Oil Ltd v Strand Insurance Co Ltd* [2007] Lloyd's Rep. I.R. 186: "In the event of any conflict of interpretation between the various clauses and conditions contained in this Policy, the broadest and least restrictive wording to the benefit of the Insured shall always prevail."

Insurance Ltd[2] the Court of Appeal preferred the contextual meaning and thus deprived the assured of an indemnity for loss caused by a gradual seepage of water. The Court did not articulate why it preferred that rule over the others.

Significance of precedent. Certainty is naturally considered to be of great **3–003** importance in dealing with commercial documents such as insurance policies. Consequently, as a matter of principle, when once the meaning of a word has been established by judicial decision, later courts will follow that interpretation, even when not strictly bound to do so under the doctrine of precedent.[3] In *Ramco (UK) Ltd v International Insurance Co of Hannover Ltd*[4] Waller L.J., speaking of scope of a property policy secured by a bailee, held that it would be inappropriate for the Court of Appeal to overrule earlier cases which had held that the phrase "goods held in trust or commission or for which he is responsible" allowed the bailee to recover only for goods for which he faced liability, in that:

> "If a form of words has been in use for 80 years which describes one sort of insurance rather than the other, it would be meddlesome for this court to decide that the selected form of words do not achieve their intended purpose, unless there were some real reason for supposing that the form of words is unsatisfactory in practice. The fact that the form of words is the subject-matter of a previous decision of this court is a compelling reason why the courts should not depart from that settled meaning . . . "

There are two dangers here, however. First, where the wording differs in important respects from that used in earlier formulations, it is dangerous to construe it by analogy with the earlier provisions, since it may well be that the wording has deliberately been altered for the purpose of overcoming the original decision. Secondly, the original decision is binding only as to the use of a particular word in a particular context—it should not be assumed that a word must mean the same in every insurance policy in which it appears if the surrounding circumstances are different. Over-strict application of the doctrine of precedent to the construction of policies is thus to be avoided.[5]

The English courts are reluctant to rely upon US authorities in the determination of the meaning of words used in a contract governed by English law,[6] on the grounds both of the sheer number of US authorities and the consumer-friendly attitude of certain US courts, and the Court of Appeal has also held that, in applying New York rules of construction to a policy written in the English market

---

[2] *Young v Sun Alliance and London Insurance Ltd* [1976] 3 All E.R. 561. But see now *Tate Gallery (Trustees) v Duffy Construction Ltd* [2007] Lloyd's Rep. I.R. 758; *Tyco Fire & Integrated Solutions (UK) Ltd v Rolls-Royce Motor Cars Ltd* [2007] EWHC 137 (TCC) (the point did not arise on appeal, [2008] Lloyd's Rep. I.R. 617).

[3] *Gale v Lewis* (1846) 9 Q.B. 730; *George Hunt Cranes Ltd v Scottish Boiler and General Insurance Co Ltd* [2002] Lloyd's Rep. I.R. 178; *The Kleovoulous of Rhodes* [2003] 1 Lloyd's Rep. 138.

[4] *Ramco (UK) Ltd v International Insurance Co of Hannover Ltd* [2004] Lloyd's Rep. I.R. 606. This decision was applied in a sequel action against brokers, *Ramco Ltd v Weller Russell & Laws Insurance Brokers Ltd* [2009] Lloyd's Rep. I.R. 27.

[5] *Re Calf and Sun Insurance Office* [1920] 2 K.B. 366 at 382; *Re Coleman's Depositories Ltd and Life and Health Assurance Association* [1907] 2 K.B. 798 at 801.

[6] *Municipal Mutual Insurance Ltd v Sea Insurance Co Ltd* [1998] Lloyd's Rep. I.R. 421; *Yorkshire Water Services Ltd v Sun Alliance & London Insurance Plc* [1997] 2 Lloyd's Rep. 21; *Pilkington United Kingdom Ltd v CGU Insurance Plc* [2004] Lloyd's Rep. I.R. 891; *Bolton Metropolitan Borough Council v Municipal Mutual Insurance* [2006] Lloyd's Rep. I.R. 15, affirmed [2007] Lloyd's Rep. I.R. 173.

and with international effect, it was to be presumed that the New York courts would come to the same conclusion as the English courts.[7]

2. THE INTENTIONS OF THE PARTIES

3–004   **The principle of objectivity.** The essence of contract is agreement between the parties, and it is often said that the function of a court, in interpreting a contractual document, is to give effect to the intentions of the parties. It is only the intention of the parties as declared by the words of the policy which may be taken into account.[8] The task of the court is to reach the meaning of the parties through the words they have used,[9] assuming that they mean what they say, and looking only at the policy. The aim can be achieved fairly readily where it appears that both parties had the same intentions. Unfortunately, the nub of many contractual disputes is that the parties have different views as to what was intended and as to the meaning of the contractual provisions. English law's approach to this problem is clear[10]:

> "If, whatever a man's real intention may be, he so conducts himself that a reasonable man would believe that he was assenting to the terms proposed by the other party, and that other party upon that belief enters into a contract with him, the man thus conducting himself would be equally bound as if he had intended to agree to the other party's terms."

This passage sets out the objective principle of construction. The test is objective, and relates to what a reasonable person in the position of the parties would have believed. It is irrelevant that one party to the contract secretly intended that they should bear a different meaning. Specialist knowledge, in the possession of a party, is also to be disregarded as an aid to construction. The latter point is of particular significance in the insurance or reinsurance context, as commercial transactions, and in particular reinsurance agreements, often involve numerous parties on each side and, while it is the case that an insurance policy is, as a matter of law, to be construed as constituting a bundle of separate agreements between the insurers and the assureds, any specialist knowledge by one party should not be permitted to colour the interpretation of the overall transaction.[11]

---

[7] *King v Brandywine Reinsurance Co (UK) Ltd* [2005] Lloyd's Rep. I.R. 509.

[8] Lord Kenyon C.J. in *Tarleton v Staniforth* (1794) 5 T.R. 695 at 699; Lawrence J. in *Marsden v Reid* (1803) 3 East 572 at 579; Tindal C.J. in *Stavers v Curling* (1836) 3 Bing. N.C. 355 at 370; Crompton J. in *Braunstein v Accidental Death* (1861) 1 B. & S. 782 at 797; Collins L.J. in *Re George and Goldsmiths Insurance* [1899] 1 Q.B. 595 at 610; Bankes L.J. in *Koskas v Standard Marine* (1927) 27 Ll. L.R. 59.

[9] Lord Halsbury L.C. in *Thames & Mersey Marine v Hamilton, Fraser* (1887) 12 App.Cas. 484 at 490.

[10] *Smith v Hughes* (1871) L.R. 6 Q.B. 597 at, 607, per Blackburn J.

[11] See the comments of Moore-Bick J. in *Kinigscroft Insurance Co Ltd v Nissan Fire & Marine Insurance Co Ltd (No.2)* [1999] Lloyd's Rep. I.R. 603 and again in *James v CGU Insurance* [2002] Lloyd's Rep. I.R. 206, in each of which the learned judge stated that the actual knowledge of one underwriter should not be allowed to colour the interpretation of subsequent contracts involving other underwriters and made on the same terms.

The factual matrix. The principles which govern the construction of commer- **3–005**
cial contracts were restated by Lord Hoffmann in his seminal speech in *Investors
Compensation Scheme v West Bromwich Building Society.*[12] The guiding principles place considerable weight upon the factual matrix surrounding the contract
as well as the actual words used by the parties. The principles may be
summarised as follows.

(1) Interpretation is the ascertainment of the meaning which the document
would convey to a reasonable person having all the background
knowledge which would reasonably have been available to the parties in
the situation in which they were at the time of the contract, i.e. the factual
matrix.[13]

(2) The factual matrix should include absolutely anything which would have
affected the way in which the language of the document would have been
understood by a reasonable man. This means that expert evidence of
market understandings at the time are material.[14]

(3) The law excludes from the admissible background the previous negotiations of the parties[15] and their declarations of subjective intent.[16] On this
basis the premium calculations used by the underwriters are inadmissible, as they are simply the underwriters' subjective view as to the
scope of the policy.[17] Such evidence may nevertheless be relevant to the

---

[12] *Investors Compensation Scheme v West Bromwich Building Society* [1998] 1 All E.R. 98. Cf. *The Starsin* [2003] 1 All E.R. (Comm) 625.

[13] See: *Friends Provident Life & Pensions Ltd v Sirius International Insurance Corp* [2005] Lloyd's Rep. I.R. 535, affirmed [2006] Lloyd's Rep. I.R. 45; *Durham v BAI (Run-off) Ltd* [2009] Lloyd's Rep. I.R. 295; *Pratt v Aigaion Insurance Co SA* [2009] Lloyd's Rep. I.R. 149. Thus, if the contract forms part of a series between the parties, it is generally appropriate to construe each of the contracts in the same way: *Allianz Marine Aviation (France) v GE Frankona Reinsurance Ltd London* [2005] Lloyd's Rep. I.R. 437; *Bedfordshire Police Authority v Constable* [2009] Lloyd's Rep. I.R. 607.

[14] *Zeus Tradition Marine Ltd v Bell* [1999] 1 Lloyd's Rep. 703, reversed on other grounds [2000] 2 Lloyd's Rep. 387; *Outokumpu Stainless Ltd v Axa Global Risks (UK) Ltd* [2008] Lloyd's Rep. I.R. 147.

[15] Lord Mansfield in *Loraine v Thomlinson* (1781) 2 Dougl. 585 at 587; *Jacobs v Batavia & General Plantation Trust Ltd* [1924] 1 Ch. 287; *Aegis Electrical and Gas International Services Co Ltd v Continental Casualty Co* [2008] Lloyd's Rep. I.R. 17; *Proforce Recruit Ltd v The Rugby Group* [2007] EWHC 1621 (QB); *Great Hill Equity Partners II LP v Novator One LP* [2007] EWHC 1210 (Comm); *Seagate Shipping Ltd v Glencore International AG* [2008] EWHC 1904 (Comm); *Hamishmar Insurance Agency Ltd v First City Partnership Ltd* [2009] EWHC 256 (Comm). Presentations made to the insurers on placement are admissible: *Encia Remediation Ltd v Canopius Managing Agents Ltd* [2008] Lloyd's Rep. I.R. 79.

[16] *Weston v Emes* (1808) 1 Taunt 115 117; *Burges v Wickham* (1863) 3 B. & S. 669 at 696: *Yorkshire Insurance v Campbell* [1917] A.C. 218 at 225; *Hydarnes Steamship Co v Indemnity Mutual Marine* [1895] 1 Q.B. 500 at 504; *Newsholme Brothers v Road Transport and General Insurance* [1929] 2 K.B. 35; *Hayward v Norwich Union* [2001] Lloyd's Rep. I.R. 410; *Prenn v Simmonds* [1971] 1 W.L.R. 1381; *Reardon Smith Line v Yngvar Hansen-Tangen* [1976] 1 W.L.R. 989; *Hayward v Norwich Union* [2001] Lloyd's Rep. I.R. 410; *Beazer Homes Ltd v Peter Stroude* [2005] EWCA Civ 265; *Royal & Sun Alliance Plc v Dornoch* [2005] Lloyd's Rep. I.R. 544; *AIG Europe (Ireland) Ltd v Faraday Capital Ltd* [2007] Lloyd's Rep. I.R. 267, reversed on other grounds [2009] Lloyd's Rep. I.R. 454; *Reilly v National Insurance and Guarantee Corp Ltd* [2009] Lloyd's Rep. I.R. 483; *Durham v BAI (Run-Off)* [2009] Lloyd's Rep. I.R. 295; *Dunlop Haywards (DHL) Ltd v Barbon Insurance Group Ltd* [2010] Lloyd's Rep. I.R. 295.

[17] *Absalom v TCRU Ltd* [2005] EWCA Civ 1586; *Margate Theatre Royal Trust Ltd v White* [2006] Lloyd's Rep. I.R. 93, a particularly strong case because insurers were able to show that they rated plumbing work higher than pipe moleing work, but a policy taken out by a pipe moleing company was nevertheless held by its terms to cover plumbing work.

question whether there was misrepresentation or mistake vitiating the contract.[18] Evidence of negotiations is exceptionally admissible where the parties have agreed that a form of words is to have a specific meaning, but the "private dictionary" exception cannot oust an express contrary definition in the agreement itself.[19] Evidence as to the content of earlier contracts between the parties is, however, freely admissible.[20]

(4) The meaning which a document would convey to a reasonable man is not the same thing as the meaning of its words. The meaning of words is a matter of dictionaries and grammar: the meaning of the document is what the parties using those words against the relevant background would reasonably have been understood to mean.

(5) The "rule" that words should be given their "ordinary and natural meaning" reflects the commonsense proposition that we do not easily accept that people have made linguistic mistakes, particularly in formal documents. On the other hand, if one would nevertheless conclude from the background that some thing must have gone wrong with the language, the law does not require judges to attribute to the parties an intention which they plainly could not have had.[21]

The position reached by the English courts[22] is that the court's role is to ascertain the intention of the parties from the words they have used, taking into account the factual matrix in appropriate cases and not simply in cases of ambiguity. In general, it is to be assumed that the parties have not made linguistic errors in their contract and intend that their words are to be given their ordinary and natural meaning. The clearer the language used by the parties the less easy it is for a court to depart from its ordinary and natural meaning and, while it is legitimate in some cases for the courts to "manipulate" the language used by the parties, this should not be done simply to repair what the court might regard as a bad bargain. That said, if it is clear that something has gone wrong in the drafting, the court may take account of other documents and of market evidence to ascertain what was really intended. Lord Steyn in *Sirius International Insurance Co (Publ) v FAI General Insurance Ltd*[23] sought to establish a wider approach to construction, incorporating a "tendency against literalism" and a commercial approach to interpretation in "one-off" contracts. However, insofar

---

[18] *Roe v RA Naylor Ltd* (1918) 87 L.J.K.B. 956; *Campbell Discount Co v Gall* [1961] 1 Q.B. 431; *Esso Petroleum v Mardon* [1976] Q.B. 801; *Howard Marine v Ogden* [1978] Q.B. 574.

[19] *Harper v Interchange Group* [2007] EWCA 1834 (Comm); *St Ivel Ltd v Wincanton Group Ltd* [2007] EWHC 2906 (Comm). Rectification may nevertheless be possible in such a situation. In *Chartbrook Ltd v Persimmon Homes Ltd* [2009] UKHL 38, applied in *Excelsior Group Productions Ltd v Yorkshire Television Ltd* [2009] EWHC (Comm) 1751, the House of Lords confirmed the exclusionary rule and doubted the existence of suggested exceptions to it.

[20] *HIH Casualty and General Insurance Ltd v New Hampshire Insurance Co* [2001] Lloyd's Rep. I.R. 596, which decides that a slip is admissible evidence to construe the policy, a matter discussed at p.27 et seq, above. See also: *Jani-King (GB) Ltd v Pula Enterprises Ltd* [2007] EWHC 2433 (QBD); *PT Berlian Laju Tanker TBK v Nurse Shipping Ltd (The Aktor)* [2008] EWHC 1330 (Comm).

[21] As in: *Union Camp Chemicals Ltd v Ace Insurance SA-NV* [2003] Lloyd's Rep. I.R. 484; *BP Exploration Operating Co Ltd v Kvaerner Oilfield Products Ltd* [2005] 1 Lloyd's Rep. 307.

[22] See *Kingscroft Insurance Co Ltd v Nissan Fire & Marine Insurance Co Ltd (No.2)* [1999] Lloyd's Rep. I.R. 603.

[23] *Sirius International Insurance Co (Publ) v FAI General Insurance Ltd* [2005] 1 Lloyd's Rep. 461.

as these comments go beyond the *West Bromwich* guidelines, they have been treated with some caution.[24]

Expert evidence as to the parties' mutual intentions and expectations is admissible in insurance cases to demonstrate the market meaning of particular words or phrases.[25]

A policy must be construed in accordance with the state of knowledge at the time the wording was prepared, as it is to be assumed that their intention was to insure on that basis. Thus, in *Cape Plc v Iron Trades Employers Insurance Association Ltd*[26] Rix J. held that a policy exclusion for pneumoconiosis did not apply also to mesothelioma, as at the date of the policy the two were recognised as separate prescribed diseases even though at one time they had generally been grouped together.

3. Rules for Construing Words and Phrases

Contractual context. It is dangerous to rely upon a word without taking account of the context in which it appears. It will generally be necessary to consider the contract as a whole, to determine the role of any particular word or phrase within it.[27] Again, a policy which is issued in a particular statutory context, e.g. a motor policy, is to be construed in accordance with that context.[28] Thus the word "accident" is to be given a broad meaning, and encompasses any incident involving the insured car, even if that incident was deliberately caused. Again, the phrase "knew or ought to have known" is to be construed as requiring either actual knowledge or blind-eye knowledge, to accord with EC requirements as to the scope of the liability of the Motor Insurers Bureau to the passengers of uninsured drivers.

The most important specific application of the context principle is the *ejusdem generis* rule of construction, which provides that where general words are linked with particular words they must be construed as limited to the same genus as the

3–006

---

[24] See the comments of Longmore L.J. in *Royal & Sun Alliance v Dornoch* [2005] Lloyd's Rep. I.R. 544, emphasising that it is not the function of the courts to rewrite the contract where the parties, by the use of wholly inappropriate wording, have not said what they must have meant. But contrast the more expansive approach in *Pratt v Aigaion Insurance Co SA* [2009] Lloyd's Rep. I.R. 149. Lord Steyn's approach appears to have been embraced by Lord Collins in *Re Sigma Finance Corp* [2009] UKSC 2, in his comment that "An over-literal interpretation of one provision without regard to the whole may distort or frustrate the commercial purpose. This is one of those too frequent cases where a document has been subjected to the type of textual analysis more appropriate to the interpretation of tax legislation which has been the subject of detailed scrutiny at all committee stages than to an instrument securing commercial obligations."

[25] *Zeus Tradition Marine Ltd v Bell* [1999] 1 Lloyd's Rep. 703, reversed on other grounds [2000] 2 Lloyd's Rep. 587.

[26] *Cape Plc v Iron Trades Employers Insurance Association Ltd* [2004] Lloyd's Rep. I.R. 103, applied in *T&N Ltd v Royal and Sun Alliance Plc* [2004] Lloyd's Rep. I.R. 134.

[27] *Charter Reinsurance Co v Fagan* [1966] 3 All E.R. 46, where their Lordships ruled that the phrase "actually paid" in an excess of loss reinsurance ultimate net loss clause referred not to physical payment by the reinsured, but rather by the reinsured incurring a liability to pay: the prima facie clear meaning of "actually paid" was held to be ousted by the context of the contract itself; *Sargent v GRE (UK) Ltd* [2000] Lloyd's Rep. I.R. 77 (policy designed for armed forces and to be construed accordingly; *McGeown v Direct Travel Insurance* [2004] Lloyd's Rep. I.R. 599 (meaning of permanent disability clause to be given a consistent meaning for both employed and unemployed persons).

[28] *Charlton v Fisher* [2001] Lloyd's Rep. I.R. 387 (meaning of "accident"); *White v White* [2001] Lloyd's Rep. I.R. 493 (meaning of "ought to have known").

particular words, applies to policies of insurance.[29] Thus an insurance of a vessel against the perils of the seas, men-of-war, fire, etc. and "all other perils", has been held not to cover the explosion of a donkey boiler.[30] Again "household furniture, linen, wearing apparel and plate" has been held to include household linen but not linen drapery goods bought on speculation.[31] Where general words follow a list of specific matters, those matters dictate the ambit of the general words.[32] Equally, where general words are followed by a list of specific illustrations, the general words are limited accordingly.[33] The parties to a policy may however make it clear that the rule is not to apply.[34] Such a case is *London and Lancashire Fire Assurance Co v Bolands*.[35] Here, the House of Lords chose to give the "riot" its technical legal meaning, which included armed robbery, even though it appeared in an exclusion primarily concerned with war and associated risks.

The need to take into account the policy as a whole may also mean that the underlying purpose of the policy is not to be undermined or sidestepped by clauses which are on their face capable of having that effect. In *Outokumpu Stainless Ltd v Axa Global Risks (UK) Ltd*[36] a property policy taken out by a steelworks covered "accidental loss or destruction of or damage to the Property insured". There was an express exclusion for loss caused by radiation, although the policy went on to provide that "the insurance . . . is extended to include loss destruction or damage due to contamination caused by the use of radioactive scrap materials utilised in the manufacturing process". The assured by accident contaminated waste material which but for the contamination could have been disposed of free of charge but as contaminated had to be disposed of at a cost of some £6.8 million, that sum being claimed from the insurers under the extension clause. The court ruled that the loss was not covered. The policy itself was a property cover, and although the extension was not by its terms restricted to property and appeared to extend to consequential loss its correct interpretation was merely as a modification to the exception for radiation losses. Accordingly, as the claim was not for property damage, there was no recovery. The point made by the court is that a policy is not to be treated as a whole, so that a minor term was not to be construed as providing for an entirely separate and additional basis of cover outside the terms of the insuring clause itself.

3–007 **Ordinary and natural meaning.** The basic rule for the construction of any contractual document, including a contract of insurance,[37] is said to be that words must be given their natural and ordinary meanings, a point which has been

---

[29] Lord Coleridge C.J. in *Mair v Railway Passengers Assurance* (1877) 37 L.T. 356 at 358, but see Denman J. at 359.

[30] *Thames & Mersey Marine v Hamilton Fraser (The Inchmaree)* (1887) 12 App. Cas. 484. The standard marine clauses do now, however, cover such perils.

[31] *Watchorn v Langford* (1813) 3 Camp. 422. See also: *Mair v Railway Passengers Assurance* (1877) 37 L.T. 356; *King v Travellers' Insurance Association* (1931) 48 T.L.R. 53; *Young v Sun Alliance* [19761 2 Lloyd's Rep. 189; *Tektrol Ltd v International Insurance Co of Hannover Ltd* [2006] Lloyd's Rep. I.R. 38.

[32] *King v Travellers' Insurance Association* (1931) 48 T.L.R. 53.

[33] *Joel v Harvey* (1857) 29 L.T.O.S. 75.

[34] *Sun Fire v Hart* (1889) 14 App. Cas. 98.

[35] *London and Lancashire Fire Assurance Co v Bolands* [1924] A.C. 836.

[36] *Outokumpu Stainless Ltd v Axa Global Risks (UK) Ltd* [2008] Lloyd's Rep. I.R. 147.

[37] "It is desirable that the same legal principles should apply to the law of contract as a whole and that different legal principles should not apply to different branches of that law": per Roskill L.J. in *Cehave v Bremer* [1976] Q.B. 44 at 71, approved by Lord Wilberforce in *Reardon Smith v Hansen-Tangen* [1976] 1 W.L.R. 989 at 998.

restated in a variety of forms over the years. The starting point is that the terms and conditions of a policy must be construed literally[38] and according to their natural and ordinary meaning,[39] even though the result is harsh and technical.[40] Thus it has been held that "gas" in an insurance policy is to be given its ordinary or popular sense and not a philosophical or scientific meaning,[41] and "fire" does not include explosion,' although explosion, scientifically speaking, might involve ignition.[42] In construing policies the ordinary rules of grammar must be observed.[43] The ordinary and natural meaning approach has to some extent been superseded by the factual matrix analysis, discussed above.[44]

Technical terms. Insurance policies are likely to contain a number of technical terms. If the term does not have any ordinary and popular sense, the technical meaning will be appropriate.[45] More problematic is a term that has a general meaning and a different technical meaning. In some cases the ordinary and natural meaning test has been applied to those terms used in the policy which do have an everyday meaning.[46] However, the weight of authority is in favour of the proposition that general rule is that a technical term must be construed in accordance with its technical meaning in the relevant trade[47] unless there is some contextual or other reason for a different approach.[48] In *Commonwealth Smelting v Guardian Royal Exchange*,[49] the Court of Appeal ruled that there was no "explosion" where a piece of metal caused the outer casing of a motor to shatter: some physical or chemical reaction was required before there could be said to

3–008

[38] Lord Fitzgerald in *Cory v Burr* (1883) 8 App. Cas. 393 at 405; Lord Watson in *Sun Fire v Hart* (1889) 14 App. Cas. 98 at 104; Warrington L.J. in *Re United London and Scottish, Browne's Claim* [1915] 2 Ch. 167 at 172.

[39] Lord O'Hagan in *Pearson v Commercial Union* (1876) 1 App. Cas. 498 at 510; *GE Frankona Reinsurance Ltd v CMM Trust No 1400 (The Newfoundland Explorer)* [2006] EWHC 429 (Adm); *Pratt v Aigaion Insurance Co SA* [2009] Lloyd's Rep. I.R. 149.

[40] Viscount Haldane in *Dawsons v Bonnin* [1922] 2 A.C. 413 at 424. See *Rowlinson Construction Ltd v Insurance Company of North America (UK) Ltd* [1981] 1 Lloyd's Rep. 332, where the interpretation rendered the policy of little use to the assured.

[41] *Re Hooley Hill Rubber & Chemical Co Ltd* [1970] 1 K.B. 257.

[42] *Commonwealth Smelling v Guardian Royal Exchange* [1984] 2 Lloyd's Rep. 608.

[43] Willes J. in *Ionides v Universal Marine* (1863) 14 C.B.N.S. 259 at 289; Lord Esher M.R. in *Price v AI Ships' Small Damage Insurance* (1889) 22 Q.B.D. 580 at 584; Lord Sumner in *London & Lancashire Fire v Bolands* [1924] A.C. 836 at 848; Roche J. in *Holmes v Payne* [1930] 2 K.B. 301; Lord Russell in *Anglo International Bank v General Accident* (1934) 48 Ll. L.R. 151 at 155.

[44] In *Charter Reinsurance Co Ltd v Fagan* [1996] 3 All E.R. 46 at 57, Lord Hoffmann noted that "in some cases the notion of words having a natural meaning is not a very helpful one. Because the meaning of words is so sensitive to syntax and context, the natural meaning of words in one sentence may be quite unnatural in another. Thus a statement that words have a particular natural meaning may mean no more than that in many contexts they will have that meaning. In other con texts their meaning will be different but no less natural."

[45] *Sutherland Marine v Kearney and Noonan* (1851) 16 Q.B. 925; *Coker v Bolton* [1912] 3 K.B. 315.

[46] *Leo Rapp Ltd v McClure* [1955] 1 Lloyd's Rep. 292 (enclosed yard not a "warehouse").

[47] Or sports. Thus where a life policy excluded from full benefit death as a result of "motor racing, motor speed hill climbs, motor trials or rallies", it was held that the words were used in a technical sense, and that evidence was admissible as to their meaning in the sport: *Scragg v UK Temperance* [1976] 2 Lloyd's Rep. 227.

[48] *Clift v Schwabe* (1846) 3 C.B. 437; *Glencore AG v Ryan (The Beursgracht)* [2002] Lloyd's Rep. I.R. 335; *Doheny v New India Assurance Co Ltd* [2005] Lloyd's Rep. I.R. 251.

[49] *Commonwealth Smelting v Guardian Royal Exchange* [1984] 2 Lloyd's Rep. 608, followed in *Aegis Electrical and Gas International Services Co Ltd v Continental Casualty Co* [2008] Lloyd's Rep. I.R. 17.

have been an explosion in the technical sense of the word. Again, words such as "riot"[50] and "theft"[51] have been given their meaning in law.

The technical meaning of a term may not be appropriate if the assured is situated outside the jurisdiction,[52] and in such a case the appropriate test is how the term would have been viewed by reasonable businessmen. It has accordingly been held that words such as theft, robbery and forgery do not necessarily bear their English law meaning where the policy is on a foreign risk.[53]

3–009   **Reasonable construction.** The guidelines in the *West Bromwich* case contemplate that, although words are to be given their usual or technical meanings, there is an assumption that the parties do not intend to achieve unreasonable results. This does not mean that the court must disregard all other considerations to produce what might be regarded as an unreasonable result,[54] but rather that the more unreasonable result the less likely it is that the parties could have intended it. English law does not recognise the concept that the policy must be construed in accordance with the reasonable expectations of the assured,[55] although it has been said that a policy should be construed other than in a way which would "unwarrantably diminish the indemnity which it was the purpose of the policy to afford".[56] In some cases, however, the wording may be so clear that the court is constrained to construe them as they stand even though the result might not be commercially sensible, as is the case where inappropriate words have been used for the type of policy in question.[57]

The courts will strive to construe the policy so as to make it an effective legal document. Thus where it is ambiguous it will be presumed to be made with the person who had an interest in the subject-matter and not void for wagering,[58] and it is to be presumed that a motor-vehicle policy affords the cover required by statute.[59] The courts will also strive to give sense to a contract term even though its meaning is obscure, as the alternative is to treat the clause as void for uncertainty.[60]

---

[50] *London & Lancashire Fire Assurance Co v Bolands* [1924] A.C. 836.

[51] *Grundy (Teddington) Ltd v Fulton* [1983] 1 Lloyd's Rep. 16; *Lim Trading Co v Haydon* [1968] 1 Lloyd's Rep. 159; *Dobson v General Accident Fire and Life Assurance Corp* [1989] 3 All E.R. 927.

[52] Although see *Rowatt Leaky & Co v Scottish Provident Institution* [1927] 1 Ch. 55.

[53] *Algemeene Bankvereeniging v Langton* (1935) 40 Com. Cas. 247; *Nishna Trading Co v Chiyoda Fire & Marine Insurance Co Ltd* [1969] 2 Q.B. 449; *Equitable Trust Co of New York v Henderson* (1930) 47 T.L.R. 90; *Canelhas Comercio Importacao e Exportacao Ltd v Wooldridge* [2004] Lloyd's Rep. I.R. 905; *Rowatt, Leakey & Co v Scottish Provident Institution* [1927] 1 Ch. 55.

[54] There are cases which have veered towards this approach. Of the many examples, see: *Re Coleman's Depositories Ltd and Life and Health Assurance Association* [1907] 2 K.B. 798; *Hulton & Co Ltd v Mountain* (1921) 8 Ll. L.R. 249.

[55] *Smit Tak Offshore Services Ltd v Youell (The Mare)* [1992] 1 Lloyd's Rep. 154.

[56] *Morley v United Friendly Insurance Plc* [1993] 1 Lloyd's Rep. 490 at 505, per Beldam L.J. See also: *Cornish v Accident Insurance Co* (1889) 23 Q.B.D. 453; *Flying Colour Film Co Ltd v Assicurazioni Generali SpA* [1993] 2 Lloyd's Rep. I.R. 184; *Blackburn Rovers Football & Athletic Club Plc v Avon Insurance Plc* [2005] Lloyd's Rep. I.R. 239, reversed on other grounds [2005] Lloyd's Rep. I.R. 447; *Paine v Catlins* [2004] EWHC 3054 (TCC): *Allianz Marine Aviation (France) v GE Frankona Reinsurance Ltd London* [2005] Lloyd's Rep. I.R. 437; *Tektrol Ltd v International Insurance Co of Hanover Ltd* [2006] Lloyd's Rep. I.R. 38.

[57] *Gan Insurance Co Ltd v Tai Ping Insurance Co Ltd (No.2)* [2001] Lloyd's Rep. I.R. 291.

[58] *Sutherland Marine v Kearney and Noonan* (1851) 16 Q.B. 925; *Coker v Bolton* [1912] 3 K.B. 315.

[59] Lord Wright in *Digby v General Accident* [1943] A.C. 121 at 141. Cf. *Dufaur v Professional Life* (1858) 25 Beav. 599.

[60] *Charman v Gordian Run-Off Ltd* [2003] Lloyd's Rep. I.R. 337, affirmed with less difficulty as to the meaning of the words used [2004] Lloyd's Rep. I.R. 373.

Contra proferentem. Ambiguities are common in policies and it is often very **3–010** uncertain what the parties to them mean.[61] It is said that where a policy is ambiguous, it must be construed against the party who has drafted it[62] for his own protection.[63] In a doubtful case the turn of the scale ought to be given against the speaker, because he has not clearly and fully expressed himself,[64] as nothing is easier than for the insurers to express themselves in plain terms.[65] This rule of construction applies equally to questions on applications for insurance,[66] any list of insured risks,[67] any list of exclusions[68] and any provision which confers rights[69] or imposes obligations on the assured.[70]

The rule is an aid to the construction of ambiguous documents: it does not permit the artificial creation of an ambiguity in order to reach a particular result.[71] The English courts have not accepted that a clause is ambiguous if a literal construction of it would "produce a both unexpected and irrational result".[72] Even where a clause is ambiguous taken alone, the *contra proferentem* rule does not apply if its meaning becomes clear in the context of the overall policy[73] or if there is extraneous evidence relating to the risk to show what the parties intended.[74] The fact that clearer wording might have been used is no basis for

---

[61] Wilmot C.J. in *Drinkwater v London Assurance* (1767) 2 Wils 363 at 364.

[62] Lord Kenyon in *Tarleton v Staniforth* (1794) 5 T.R. 695 at 699; Blackburn J. in *Fowkes v Manchester & London Life* (1863) 3 B. & S. 917 at 929–930; Willis J. in *Fitton v Accidental Death* (1864) 17 C.B.N.S. 122 at 135; Kelly C.B. in *Smith v Accident Insurance* (1870) L.R. 5 Ex. 302; *Re Etherington and Lancashire & Yorkshire Accident* [1909] 1 K.B. 591 at 596; Blackburn J. in *Thomson v Weems* (1884) 9 App. Cas. 671 at 682; Viscount Sumner in *Lake v Simmons* [1927] A.C. 487, 508–511; *Taylor v National Insurance Corp* [1989] 6 C.L. 248; *Sargent v GRE (UK) Ltd* [2000] Lloyd's Rep. I.R. 77.

[63] *Simmonds v Cockell* [1920] 1 K.B. 843 at 845, per Cockburn C.J.

[64] Wilmot C.J. in *Drinkwater v London Assurance* (1767) 2 Wils. 363 at 364; *Houghton v Trafalgar* [1954] 1 Q.B. 247.

[65] *Notman v Anchor* (1858) 4 C.B.N.S. 476 at 481; *Provincial Insurance v Morgan* [1933] A.C. 240 at 250; *Tektrol Ltd v International Insurance Co of Hanover Ltd* [2006] Lloyd's Rep. I.R. 38, per Buxton L.J.

[66] Bankes L.J. in *Dunn v Campbell* (1920) 4 Ll. L.R. 36 at 39; *de Maurier (Jewels) v Bastion Insurance Co* [1967] 2 Lloyd's Rep. 550 at 559–560.

[67] *Peabody v Eagle Star Insurance Co Ltd* Unreported December 1998; *Durham v BAI (Run Off) Ltd* [2009] Lloyd's Rep. I.R. 295.

[68] *Houghton v Trafalgar Insurance Co Ltd* [1954] 1 Q.B. 247; *English v Western* [1940] 2 K.B. 156; *Flying Colours Film Co Ltd v Assicurazioni Generali SpA* [1991] 2 Lloyd's Rep. 536; *Zeus Tradition Marine Ltd v Bell (The Zeus V)* [2000] 2 Lloyd's Rep. 587; *Pike (Butchers) Ltd v Independent Insurance Co* [1998] Lloyd's Rep. I.R. 410.

[69] *Re Drake Insurance Plc* [2001] Lloyd's Rep. I.R. 643.

[70] *Royal & Sun Alliance v Dornoch* [2005] Lloyd's Rep. I.R. 544; *Taylor v National Insurance & Guarantee Corp* [1989] 6 C.L. 248; *Pratt v Aigaion Insurance Co SA* [2009] Lloyd's Rep. I.R. 149.

[71] Lord Denman C.J. in *Hare v Barstow* (1844) 8 Jur. 928 at 929; *Cornish v Accident Insurance* (1889) 23 Q.B.D. 453 at 456; *Cole v Accident Insurance* (1889) 5 T.L.R. 736 at 737; *Re George and Goldsmiths' & General Burglary Insurance Association* [1895] 1 Q.B. 595 at 600; *Alder v Moore* [1960] 2 Lloyd's Rep. 325; *Middleton v Wiggins* [1996] L.R.L.R. 129; *LEC (Liverpool) Ltd v Glover* [2001] Lloyd's Rep. I.R. 315; *R. v Personal Investment Authority Ombudsman Bureau Ex p. Royal & Sun Alliance* [2002] Lloyd's Rep. I.R. 41; *McGeown v Direct Travel Insurance* [2004] Lloyd's Rep. I.R. 599; *GE Frankona Reinsurance Ltd v CMM Trust No.1400 (The Newfoundland Explorer)* [2006] Lloyd's Rep. I.R. 704.

[72] *Carlingford Australia General Insurance Ltd v EZ Industries Ltd* [1988] V.R. 349.

[73] du Parcq J. in *Passmore v Vulcan Boiler & General Insurance* (1936) 154 L.T. 258 at 259; Lord Sumner in *Yorkshire Insurance v Campbell* [1917] A.C. 218 at 223; *Young v Sun Alliance* [1976] 2 Lloyd's Rep. 189; *Doheny v New India Assurance Co Ltd* [2005] Lloyd's Rep. I.R. 251.

[74] *Hare v Barstow* (1844) 8 Jur. 928; *Hordern v Commercial Union* (1887) 56 L.J.P.C. 78.

regarding the actual wording as ambiguous: that approach would entail an unjustifiable degree of hindsight.[75]

While it is the case that the *contra proferentem* principle normally works in the assured's favour, in many situations, particularly contracts placed at Lloyd's the wording may have been prepared by the broker. Evidence is admissible to show who in fact was responsible.[76] As the broker is the agent of the assured, the *contra proferentem* principle is not applicable in the usual way and any ambiguity will in those circumstances be construed against the assured and in favour of the insurer.[77] However, the Court of Appeal noted in *Youell v Bland Welch (No.1)*[78] that the rule consists of two quite distinct limbs: that words are to be construed against the person who put them forward; and that words of exclusion are to be construed narrowly. Accordingly, if an insurance policy prepared by a broker contains an exclusion clause, the *contra proferentem* principle may be negatived entirely and the court must seek other means to construe the wording. The courts, when faced with standard market wordings, will give them a fixed meaning irrespective of which side proposed the terms.[79]

3–011   **Policy to be looked at as a whole.** Effect must, if possible, be given to every word in the policy,[80] and a reasonable construction must therefore be given to each clause in order to give effect to the plain and obvious intention of the parties as collected from the whole instrument. It is no objection to a clause that it is redundant[81] or inserted out of an excess of caution.[82] Sometimes it is plain that a particular provision cannot apply to the facts of a particular contract,[83] although effort must be made to construe a policy so as to give each provision in it some meaning.[84] Individual words may nevertheless be ignored where they have plainly been added in error.[85]

Modern forms of drafting—which often consist of cutting and pasting precedents without due regard to how the various provisions in them can be

[75] *GE Frankona Reinsurance Ltd v CMM Trust No.1400 (The Newfoundland Explorer)* [2006] Lloyd's Rep. I.R. 704.

[76] *Quin v National Assurance* (1839) Jones & Carey 316 (Ire); *Abrahams Mediterranean Re* [1991] 1 Lloyd's Rep. 216: *Denby v English & Scottish Maritime Insurance Co* [1998] Lloyd's Rep. I.R. 343.

[77] *Abrahams v Mediterranean Insurance & Reinsurance Co Ltd* [1991] 1 Lloyd's Rep. 216; *Eurodale Manufacturing Ltd v Ecclesiastical Insurance Office Plc* [2003] Lloyd's Rep. I.R. 444. The same principle will apply to the construction of the broker's proposal form: *Pearson Plc v Excess Insurance Co Ltd* Unreported 1988. Cf. also *Denby v English & Scottish Maritime Insurance Co* [1998] Lloyd's Rep. I.R. 34.

[78] *Youell v Bland Welch (No.1)* [1992] 2 Lloyd's Rep. 127. Cf. *Zeus Traditional Marine Ltd v Bell* [1999]1 Lloyd's Rep. 703.

[79] *Gan Insurance Co v Tai Ping Insurance Co (Nos 2 and 3)* [2001] Lloyd's Rep. I.R. 667; *Royal and Sun Alliance v Dornoch* [2004] Lloyd's Rep. I.R. 826, distinguished in *AIG Europe (Ireland) Ltd v Faraday Capital Ltd* [2008] Lloyd's Rep. I.R. 454.

[80] Lord Sumner in *Yorkshire Insurance v Campbell* [1917] A.C. 218 at 224; Atkin L.J. in *City Tailors v Evans* (1927) 38 T.L.R. 230 at 234; Scrutton L.J. in *Roberts v Anglo-Saxon Insurance* (1927) 96 L.J.K.B. 590 at 594; *Commercial Union v Sun Alliance* [1992] 1 Lloyd's Rep. 475.

[81] *Curtis v Mathews* [1918] 2 K.B. 825, affirmed [1919] 1 K.B. 425.

[82] *SA Maritime v Anglo-Iranian* [1954] 1 W.L.R. 492.

[83] *City Tailors v Evans* (1927) 38 T.L.R. 230; Lord Penzance in *Dudgeon v Pembroke* (1877) 2 App. Cas. 284 at 293; Rigby L.J. in *Hydarnes SS Co v Indemnity Mutual Marine* [1895] 1 Q.B. 500 at 509; *Home Insurance of New York v Victoria-Montreal Fire* [1907] A.C. 59; *Forsakringsaktiesel-skapet Vesta v Butcher* [1989] 1 All E.R. 402.

[84] *Beacon Life v Gibb* (1862) 1 Moo. P.C.C. (N.S.) 73.

[85] *Glen's Trustees Lancashire & Yorkshire Accident* (1906) 8 F. (Ct of Sess) 915 at 917–918, per Lord Dunedin.

reconciled—may give rise to directly conflicting[86] or redundant[87] clauses, and the court may have no option but to recognise that one or other of those clauses is superfluous and that it is necessary to consider which should be given priority. In such a case, words specifically added are to be given priority over the standard terms,[88] and if a contract is contained in more than one document greater weight should be given to the later in date on the basis that where the later instrument conflicts with the earlier it is presumed to be the intention of the parties so to vary it.[89] There is no rule that large print is to be preferred to small print, and a clause must not be ignored simply because it is difficult to read,[90] although this reasoning may now have been superseded by the principle that unusual or onerous terms must be brought to the express attention of the other party.[91]

Where the policy contains recitals recourse may be had to them in construing an ambiguous clause in the policy,[92] but where the operative words are unambiguous the recitals cannot be resorted to in order to vary their grammatical meaning.[93]

Subsequent conduct. The conduct of the parties after the making of the contract cannot be admitted as an aid to construction. The meaning of the contract must be determined at the time when it is made. Were it otherwise the result could be that "a contract meant one thing the day it was signed but, by reason of subsequent events, meant something different a month or a year later."[94] An underwriter may not, therefore, introduce as evidence of the meaning of the policy documents and figures which were prepared after the contract was made.[95] Further, an endorsement to the policy is not relevant to the construction of its original wording.[96]   3–012

4. CUSTOM

The general custom of the market in which the parties are operating is admissible evidence[97] in two respects: it may be the basis for implying a term into the   3–013

---

[86] See Lord Birkenhead in *Mountain v Whittle* [1921] A.C. 615 at 621.

[87] *King v Brandywine Reinsurance Co (UK) Ltd* [2005] Lloyd's Rep. I.R. 509, where it was commented that policies often contained redundant terms.

[88] *Mercantile Marine Insurance Co v Titherington* (1864) 5 B. & S. 765; *Glynn v Margetson* [1893] A.C. 351; *Dudgeon Pembroke* (1877) 2 App. Cas. 284; *Mountain v Whittle* [1921] A.C. 615; *Farmers Co-op Ltd v National Benefit Assurance Co* (1922) 13 Ll. L.R. 530; *Admastos Shipping Co v Anglo-Saxon Petroleum Co* [1959] A.C. 133; *Commercial Union Assurance Co Plc v Sun Alliance Insurance Group Plc* [1992] 1 Lloyd's Rep. 475; *Christmas v Taylor Woodrow* [1997] 1 Lloyd's Rep. 407; *Eurodale Manufacturing Ltd v Ecclesiastical Insurance Office Plc* [2003] Lloyd's Rep. I.R. 444; *Eagle Star Insurance Co Ltd v Cresswell* [2004] Lloyd's Rep. I.R. 437.

[89] *Williams v Agius* [1914] A.C. 510; *Kaufmann v British Surety Insurance* (1929) 45 T.L.R. 399.

[90] *Koskas v Standard Marine* [1927] 137 L.T. 165. See, however, *Harvey v Ventilatorenfabrik Velde Financial Times*, November 11, 1988.

[91] See below.

[92] Swinfen Eady L.J. in *Blascheck v Russell* (1916) 33 T.L.R. 74, 75.

[93] Lord Russell of Killowen in *Anglo-American International Bank v General Accident* (1934) 48 Ll. L.R. 151 at 155.

[94] *James Miller & Partners v Whitworth Street Estates (Manchester) Ltd* [1970] A.C. 583, 603.

[95] *Absalom v TCRU Ltd* [2005] EWCA Civ 1586.

[96] *Bolton Metropolitan Borough Council v Municipal Mutual Insurance Ltd* [2007] Lloyd's Rep. I.R. 173.

[97] Lord Lyndhurst C.R. in *Blackett v Royal Exchange* (1832) 2 G. & J. 244: *Crofts v Marshall* (1836) 7 C. & P. 597.

policy; or it may be an aid to the construction of the policy.[98] Alleged custom cannot be used to create an entire contract where there was none before: the courts have accordingly rejected the argument that there is some form of customary implied agreement, based on market practice, between a broker and an underwriter under which the underwriter is entitled to view or take copies of documents in the broker's placing and claims files,[99] although such a contract has been held to exist on the grounds of business efficacy.[100] A custom will be made out only if it is notorious, universally followed[101] and reasonable,[102] and it will not be permitted to contradict the express words of the agreement[103] although it may explain them and give rise to a less obvious meaning.[104]

5. INCORPORATION

3–014   It is perfectly permissible for the terms of a contract to be found in some other document which has been incorporated by reference into the contract. Two questions here arise: how may incorporation be effected; and what weight is to be given to the incorporated terms.

3–015   **Achieving incorporation.** Policy provisions may be incorporated by express or implied[105] reference to other documents or contracts. Facultative reinsurance contracts written in the London market have traditionally incorporated the terms of the direct policy by means of various formulations, the current version being the "full reinsurance clause" which provides that the terms of the reinsurance are "as original". This has generated a good deal of litigation, the general outcome of which is that terms relating to coverage may be incorporated,[106] terms imposing obligations or benefits on the assured will not be incorporated so as to

---

[98] See *Durham v BAI (Run Off) Ltd* [2009] Lloyd's Rep. I.R. 295, where it was not shown that there was an established market custom that employers' liability policies were to be construed as covering the date of exposure rather than the onset of injury, but market practice was an important consideration in construing ambiguous wording in the former fashion.

[99] *Goshawk Dedicated Ltd v Tyser & Co Ltd* [2005] Lloyd's Rep. I.R. 379.

[100] *Goshawk Dedicated Ltd v Tyser & Co Ltd* [2005] Lloyd's Rep. I.R. 379: on appeal, [2007] Lloyd's Rep. I.R. 224, the argument based on custom was not pursued.

[101] *Grand Union v Evans-Lombe Ashton* Unreported, 1989; *Thor Navigation Inc v Ingosstrak Insurance (The Thor II)* [2006] Lloyd's Rep. I.R. 1, in which Gloster J. rejected the suggestion that it was customary in the London marine market for the words "sum insured" to be regarded as creating a valued policy: the evidence pointed to the opposite conclusion.

[102] *Anglo African Merchants Ltd v Bayley* [1970] 1 Q.B. 311; *Carvill America Inc v Camperdown UK Ltd* [2005] Lloyd's Rep. I.R. 55, where the suggestion that there was a custom whereby brokerage earned by reinsurance brokers that were paid by reinsurers was regarded as unreasonable. The Court of Appeal, [2006] Lloyd's Rep. I.R. 1, did not comment on this point and held that the existence or otherwise of the custom should go to trial.

[103] Lord Campbell C.J. in *Hall v Janson* (1855) 4 B. & B. 500 at 509–510; *Krall v Burnet* (1877) 2 W.R. 305; *Australian Agricultural Co v Saunders* (1875) L.R. 10 C.P. 668 at 677.

[104] *Mander v Equitas Ltd* [2000] Lloyd's Rep. I.R. 520.

[105] *Edwards v Aberayron Insurance Society Ltd* (1876) 1 QBD 563 (rules of mutual insurance society).

[106] If there is no inconsistent wording then coverage clauses may be incorporated, although if the two contracts are governed by different applicable laws there may be an issue as to whether the law governing the direct policy will be applied to the interpretation of the clause as incorporated into the reinsurance: *Wasa International Insurance Co Ltd v Lexington Insurance Co* [2009] Lloyd's Rep. I.R. 675, where the majority view was that there would almost invariably be a common construction giving rise to matching cover, although *WASA* itself was held to be an exceptional case in that the clause in question related to the fundamental question of duration.

impose corresponding obligations or benefits on the reinsured[107] and dispute resolution provisions—arbitration,[108] jurisdiction[109] and choice of law[110] clauses—will not be incorporated at all unless there is express reference to them in the reinsurance agreement.

The criteria for incorporation were laid down by David Steel J. in *HIH Casualty and General Insurance Ltd v New Hampshire Insurance Co.*[111] A term may be incorporated if: (1) it is germane; (2) it makes sense, subject to permissible "manipulation", altering the names of the parties to match those in the main agreement; (3) it is consistent with its new context; and (4) it is apposite for inclusion. To this list may be added the further requirement that the clause to be incorporated must be in existence before the contract into which it is to be incorporated comes into being. Thus, in the context of reinsurance, a term which is added to a direct policy at a later date, and after the making of the reinsurance, will not by virtue of such inclusion be carried across into the reinsurance unless the reinsurance agreement makes express provision for its unilateral modification following amendment to the direct policy.[112] Incorporation is used in a number of contexts in insurance. It is common for the proposal form to be incorporated into the policy by means of a "basis of the contract clause", so that the assured's answers on it form express warranties.

The most important commercial context in which terms are incorporated from one contract into another arises where insurance is arranged in layers, in that the terms of the primary layer policy may be incorporated into the excess layer policies so as to ensure that the coverage is consistent across the layers. *Hong Kong Borneo Services Co Ltd v Pilcher*[113] raised the question whether a clause prohibiting the recovery of interest by the assured contained in the first-layer policy, had been incorporated into the second-layer policy by the words "as per primary insurance". Evans J. held that no special principles applied to this type of case, and that the incorporation took effect according to its terms. In *Friends*

---

[107] *Home Insurance Co of New York v Victoria-Montreal Fire Insurance Co* [1907] A.C. 59; *Australian Widows Fund Life Assurance Society Ltd v National Mutual Life Association of Australia Ltd* [1914] A.C. 634; *Forsikringsaktieselskapet Vesta v Butcher* [1989] 1 All E.R. 402; *HIH Casualty and General Insurance Ltd v New Hampshire Insurance Co* [2001] Lloyd's Rep. I.R. 595. See, generally, Butler and Merkin, *Reinsurance Law*, Part B.

[108] *Pine Top Insurance Co v Unione Italiana Anglo-Saxon Reinsurance Co Ltd* [1987] 1 Lloyd's Rep. 476; *Excess Insurance Co Ltd v Mander* [1995] L.R.L.R. 358; *Trygg Hansa Insurance Co Ltd v Equitas* [1998] 2 Lloyd's Rep. 439; *Cigna Life Insurance Co of Europe SA-NV v Intercaser SA De Seguros y Reaseguros* [2001] Lloyd's Rep. I.R. 821; *American International Special Lines Insurance Co v Abbott Laboratories* [2004] Lloyd's Rep. I.R. 825. These above rules relate to the purported arbitration of an arbitration clause from one contract (insurance) into another (reinsurance) or from an earlier contract into a later contract between the same parties: *Habas Sinai Ve Tibbi Gazlar Isthisal Endustri AS v Sometal SAL* [2010] EWHC 29 (Comm). Where a contract incorporates a document or set of rules which contain an arbitration clause, ordinary rules of interpretation apply and arbitration clauses are not treated differently to any other clauses. See: *Axa Re v Ace Global Markets Ltd* [2006] Lloyd's Rep. I.R. 683; *Sea Trade Maritime Corp v Hellenic Mutual War Risks Association (Bermuda) Ltd (The Athena (No.2))* [2006] EWHC 2530 (Comm).

[109] *Arig Insurance Company Ltd v Sasa Assicurazione Riassicurazione SPA* Unreported, 1998; *AIG Group (UK) Ltd v The Ethniki* [2000] Lloyd's Rep. I.R. 343; *AIG Europe SA v QBE International Insurance Ltd* [2002] Lloyd's Rep. I.R. 22; *Dornoch Ltd v Mauritius Union Assurance Co Ltd* [2006] Lloyd's Rep. I.R. 786.

[110] *Gan Insurance Co Ltd v Tai Ping Insurance Co Ltd* [1999] Lloyd's Rep. I.R. 229.

[111] *HIH Casualty and General Insurance Ltd v New Hampshire Insurance Co* [2001] Lloyd's Rep. I.R. 234, affirmed [2001] Lloyd's Rep. I.R. 596.

[112] *Excess Insurance Co Ltd v Mander* [1995] L.R.L.R. 359; *Cigna Life Insurance Co of Europe SA-NV & Ors v Intercaser SA de Seguros y Reaseguros* [2001] Lloyd's Rep. I.R. 821; *American International Speciality Lines Insurance Co v Abbott Laboratories* [2002] EWHC 2714 (Comm).

[113] *Hong Kong Borneo Services Co Ltd v Pilcher* [1992] 2 Lloyd's Rep. 593.

Provident Life & Pensions Ltd v Sirius International Insurance Corp[114] liability cover was arranged in layers. The primary layer policy was written on a claims made basis, so that notification to the insurers of events which could give rise to a claim were insured, even though the claims themselves did not arise until after the policy had expired. The excess layer policy incorporated the terms of the primary layer policy. Colman J. had little difficulty in holding that these provisions had been incorporated into the excess layer policy, as it was invariable practice for claims made policies to be extended to liabilities arising in later years. The incorporation of the terms of the primary layer into the excess layer will, however, depend upon the relevance of those terms to excess layer cover. In *Union Camp Chemicals Ltd v Ace Insurance SA-NV*[115] it was held that a condition precedent contained in a primary layer public liability policy had been incorporated into an excess of loss policy covering public liability, by virtue of the fact that the excess layer policy had been expressed to be on the same terms and conditions as original and there was an intention for the two contracts to be back to back. However, provisions in the primary layer policy which related to employers' liability, which was not covered by the excess of loss policy, were held not to have been incorporated as they had no relevance to the excess layer cover. In *Dornoch Ltd v Mauritius Union Assurance Co Ltd*[116] the primary layer reinsurance policy contained an exclusive jurisdiction clause. The excess layer reinsurance incorporated the terms of the primary layer reinsurance by general words of incorporation and also referred to a "jurisdiction clause" although no wording was ever agreed. Aikens J. held that the jurisdiction clause in the primary layer policy had not been incorporated into the excess layer policy: general words of incorporation were not of themselves sufficient to effect incorporation of dispute resolution provisions,[117] and the reference to "jurisdiction clause" in the excess layer policy indicated that the parties had intended to treat jurisdiction separately from other provisions even though they had not actually got round to producing appropriate wording.[118] The Court of Appeal, dismissing an appeal against Aikens J.'s decision,[119] ruled that the parties had plainly intended to incorporate some jurisdiction clause but, given that there were two possible candidates and that no choice had been made between them, the words "jurisdiction clause" were meaningless.

One issue which has arisen in a number of cases is the incorporation of a standard form arbitration clause into an agreement which contains an exclusive jurisdiction clause: the approach which has come to be accepted in this situation is that the arbitration clause prevails, and the exclusive jurisdiction clause is taken to mean that the English courts have exclusive curial jurisdiction over the arbitration.[120]

---

[114] *Friends Provident Life & Pensions Ltd v Sirius International Insurance Corp* [2005] Lloyd's Rep. I.R. 45, affirmed on other grounds [2005] EWCA Civ 601.

[115] *Union Camp Chemicals Ltd v Ace Insurance SA-NV* [2003] Lloyd's Rep. I.R. 484.

[116] *Dornoch Ltd v Mauritius Union Assurance Co Ltd* [2006] Lloyd's Rep. I.R. 127, affirmed [2006] EWCA Civ 389.

[117] See the authorities cited above.

[118] See also *American International Speciality Lines Insurance Co v Abbott Laboratories* [2004] Lloyd's Rep. I.R. 815: no incorporation of arbitration clause.

[119] *Dornoch Ltd v Mauritius Union Assurance Co Ltd* [2006] Lloyd's Rep. I.R. 786.

[120] *Paul Smith v H&S International Holding Inc* [1991] 2 Lloyd's Rep. 127; *Shell International Petroleum Co Ltd v Coral Oil Co Ltd* [1999] 1 Lloyd's Rep. 72; *Axa Re v Ace Global Markets Ltd* [2006] EWHC 216 (Comm). The decision in *Indian Oil Corp v Vanol Inc* [1991] 2 Lloyd's Rep. 634, giving priority to the exclusive jurisdiction clause, is probably no longer reliable. This view is confirmed by *Sea Trade Maritime Corp v Hellenic Mutual War Risks Association (Bermuda) Ltd (The Athena (No.2))* [2006] EWHC 2530 (Comm).

Effects of incorporation. As to the weight to be given to incorporated terms, **3–016** assuming that there is no inconsistency or overlap, the incorporated terms are to be treated as if they were written into the contract itself and are to be given effect accordingly.[121] The difficult case is that in which there has been held to be incorporation even though the incorporated terms cannot easily be reconciled with those in the main agreement.[122] It was commented by H.H. Judge Jack QC in *La Positiva Seguros y Reaseguros SA v Jessel*[123] that insurance policies are often built up over a period of time, incorporating words from different sources. It is thus to be expected that there will be overlaps, and for that reason there is no need to give independent effect to every word in the policy: the same point may well be dealt with in two separate clauses and in two different ways.

In such cases it may be necessary to disregard inappropriate or conflicting terms and to "manipulate" wording so that references appropriate to the original contract can be replaced with references to the contract into which the wording has been incorporated. Thus, in reinsurance cases where a direct policy is incorporated into the reinsurance, the use of words such as "insurer" in the direct policy will have to be altered to "reinsurer".[124] Other manipulation may also be required to ensure that, e.g. notice provisions, make sense in their incorporated context. In some circumstances a term incorporated from a direct policy into a reinsurance agreement may even override a term of the reinsurance where it is clear that the purpose of the incorporation was to achieve back to back cover. Manipulation is not, however, an inevitable process, and the court will refuse to manipulate incorporated wording if it would create quite different rights and liabilities in the new contract. Such a case was *HIH Casualty and General Insurance Ltd v New Hampshire Insurance Co.*[125] Here, the direct policy contained a clause which excluded the right of the insurers to avoid the policy for non-disclosure or misrepresentation. The terms of the original policy were incorporated into the reinsurance, and the insurers asserted that the exclusion provision—with the appropriate manipulation of its wording—operated at the reinsurance level so that reinsurers had no right to avoid the reinsurance for non-disclosure or misrepresentation by the insurers. The Court of Appeal held that the words should be incorporated in their unmanipulated form, so that the clause did no more than define the circumstances in which the reinsurers were obliged to indemnify the insurers, i.e. that the reinsurers remained on risk under the reinsurance even though the insurers had to make payment to their assured in circumstances in which the insurers would otherwise have had a defence. As Rix L.J. pointed out, to give the exclusion full effect in the reinsurance would have created new rights and obligations at the reinsurance level.

Deletions. There is a good deal of authority for the proposition that it is **3–017** permissible for the courts to have regard to deletions from contracts in order to

---

[121] Lord Treyner in *Reid v Employers' Accident* (1899) 1 F. (Ct of Sess) 1031 at 1036.

[122] For the problems of trying to ascertain the meaning of a contract from a series of incorporated clauses. See *Jan de Nul (UK) Ltd v NV Royal Belge* [2001] Lloyd's Rep. I.R. 327.

[123] *La Positiva Seguros y Reaseguros SA v Jessel* Unreported, September 6, 2000. Cf. *Groupama v Catatumbo* [2001] Lloyd's Rep. I.R. 141.

[124] *CNA International Reinsurance Co Ltd v Companhia de Seguros Tranquilidade SA* [1999] Lloyd's Rep. I.R. 289.

[125] *HIH Casualty and General Insurance Ltd v New Hampshire Insurance Co* [2001] Lloyd's Rep. I.R. 596.

determine that which the parties intended to avoid,[126] although some cases have taken the view that a deletion is to be disregarded because the parties never intended it to form a part of the contract.[127] The Court of Appeal was faced with the inconsistencies in the case law in *Punjab National Bank v de Boinville*,[128] where one of the questions was the ascertainment of who was the assured under contracts of insurance against, inter alia, political risks. The assured was described as "Punjab National Bank a/c Esal Commodities Ltd". The relationship between the parties was that Esal was an exporter, and the Bank had agreed to finance Esal's operations. Esal had placed the relevant policies. It was unclear from this wording which of the parties was the assured, and the Court of Appeal, relying upon various deletions which substituted the word "Esal" for "the assured", held that the intention of the amendments was to make it clear that some person other than Esal was the assured. On this reasoning, the Bank was to be regarded as the assured under the policies.[129] Words deleted may on either view of the law, be admissible for the limited purposes of resolving ambiguities and showing what the parties had not resolved in their agreement.[130]

6. JUDICIAL CONTROL OF POLICY TERMS

3–018   Contract terms are subject to three forms of judicial scrutiny. First, under the general provisions of the Unfair Contract Terms Act 1977, standard form contracts are subject to a reasonableness requirement. Secondly, under the Unfair Terms in Consumer Contracts Regulations 1999,[131] the terms of consumer contracts are subjected to a fairness requirement. Thirdly, the common law, as expressed by the Court of Appeal in *Interfoto Picture Library Ltd v Stiletto Visual Programs Ltd*,[132] will not give effect to particularly onerous or unusual contract terms unless these are expressly brought to the attention of the other party. The 1977 Act does not apply to insurance contracts[133]: the justification for this exclusion is that many policy conditions are concerned with the risk run by the insurer, so that any attempt to regulate those terms would be to rewrite the basis on which the premium had been set by the insurer. *Interfoto*, by contrast, does apply, and may be illustrated by cases such as *Re Bradley and Essex and Suffolk Accident Indemnity Society*[134] where the Court of Appeal noted that the insurer could not convert a mere condition into a condition precedent without bringing

---

[126] *City and Westminster Properties v Mudd* [1959] 1 Ch. 129 at 140–141; *Louis Dreyfus & Cie v Parnaso Compania Naviera SA* [1959] 1 Q.B. 498: *Timber Shipping Co SA v London and Overseas Freighters Ltd (The London Explorer)* [1972] A.C. 1 at 15–16; *Mottram v Sunley* [1972] 2 Lloyd's Rep. 197. Contrary comments (see *Sassoon v International Banking Corp* [1927] A.C. 711 at 721, *Ambatielos v Anton Jurgens* [1923] A.C. 175 at 185) are in practice ignored.

[127] *Sassoon & Sons v Interational Banking Corp* [1927] A.C. 711; *Samcrete Egypt Engineers Ltd v Land Rover Export Ltd* [2001] EWCA Civ 2019; *Eurodale Manufacturing v Ecclesiastical Insurance Office Plc* [2003] Lloyd's Rep. I.R. 444.

[128] *Punjab National Bank v de Boinville* [1992] 3 All E.R. 104.

[129] See also: *Kiriacoulis Lines SA v Compagnie d'Assurance Maritime Aerieenes et Terrestres (The Demetra K)* [2002] Lloyd's Rep. I.R. 823; *Eagle Star Insurance Co Ltd v Cresswell* [2003] EWHC 2224 (Comm), reversed on other grounds [2004] Lloyd's Rep. I.R. 437.

[130] *Mopani Copper Mines Plc v Millennium Underwriting Ltd* [2009] Lloyd's Rep. I.R. 158.

[131] SI 1999/2083 implementing Council Directive 93/113/EC.

[132] *Interfoto Picture Library Ltd v Stiletto Visual Programs Ltd* [1989] Q.B. 433. See also *Circle Freight v Medeast Gulf Exports* [1988] 2 Lloyds Rep. 427.

[133] 1977 Act Sch.1 para.1(a).

[134] *Re Bradley and Essex and Suffolk Accident Indemnity Society* [1912] 1 K.B. 415.

this to the assured's attention. The *Interfoto* case has also disposed of cases such as *Koskas v Standard Marine Insurance Co*,[135] in which the Court of Appeal allowed an insurer to rely upon an onerous notice of loss clause despite its illegibility. In the same way, the decision of the House of Lords in *De Monchy v Phoenix Insurance Co of Hartford*[136] to the effect that a policy may be enforced even if the assured has not received notice of the terms and it is a combination of microscopic type, blurred printing and crabbed handwriting, is unlikely to be given much weight in the modern context.

The 1999 Regulations, by contrast, apply to most forms of consumer contracts and include insurance contracts. A term which is caught by the Regulations is void. Under the Regulations, as applied to insurance, a term is deemed to be unfair if:

(a) it has not been individually negotiated, i.e. it has been drafted in advance and the assured has not been able to influence its substance,[137] the burden of proof being on the insurer if the assured alleges lack of individual negotiation[138]; and

(b) it is contrary to the requirement of good faith[139]; and

(c) it creates a significant imbalance in the parties' rights and obligations.[140]

In every case, under reg.6, the unfairness of a contractual term is to be assessed by "taking into account the nature of the goods or services for which the contract was concluded and by referring, at the time of the conclusion of the contract, to all the circumstances attending the conclusion of the contract and to all the other terms of the contract or of another contract on which it is dependent".

Schedule 2 to the Regulations sets out an illustrative list of terms which may fall foul of the fairness requirement. Transposing that list to the insurance context, terms which might be thought at least potentially to be at risk might include:

(a) a term conferring on the insurer the right to terminate the policy at any time (Sch.2, paras (c) and (f));

(b) a term under which the assured forfeits the premium in the event that the policy is avoided (Sch.2, para.(d));

(c) any term which is not reasonably accessible to the assured prior to the making of the contract (Sch.2, para.(i))—it may suffice, however, if the insurer informs the applicant for insurance that the policy wording is available for inspection;

(d) any term which provides that the insurer's agent is the agent of the assured for the purposes of the completion of the proposal (Sch.2, para.(n));

(e) any term which restricts the assured's access to judicial remedy, e.g. a term which shortens the limitation period by requiring judicial proceedings to be brought within a fixed period.

---

[135] *Koskas v Standard Marine Insurance Co* (1927) 27 Ll. L.R. 59.

[136] *De Monchy v Phoenix Insurance Co of Hartford* (1929) 34 Ll. L.R. 194.

[137] SI 1999/2083 reg.3(1). The presence in the contract of terms which have been individually negotiated does not prevent the Regulations applying to the remaining terms: reg.3(4).

[138] SI 1999/2083 reg.3(5).

[139] SI 1999/2083 reg.4(1).

[140] SI 1999/2083 reg.4(1).

Regulation 3(2) imposes a fundamental restriction on the operation of the Regulations. It excludes from judicial scrutiny "core provisions", i.e. any term which either defines the subject matter of the contract or concerns the adequacy of the price or remuneration as against the services supplied, provided that the term is expressed in "plain, intelligible language". This provision effectively means that the assured cannot challenge the fairness of an insuring clause or of an exceptions clause by asserting that the premium charged is too high when set against the actual cover provided, unless the wording is couched in complexities. Similarly, the amount of a deductible would seem to fall within the core provision. It is uncertain whether the core provision excludes from scrutiny wording which is on its face plain and intelligible, but which bears a hidden meaning, e.g. "riot", "theft" or "event". In addition, reg.7 requires that any term in a consumer contract which has not been individually negotiated has to be given the interpretation most favourable to the assured.[141] This provision applies to unclear written terms, not implied terms,[142] and is in effect a codified version of the *contra proferentem* rule as it usually applies against insurers.

In applying the 1999 Regulations the starting point is to determine whether the term under consideration is one that defines the subject matter or the adequacy of the price or remuneration. It is apparent that the premium itself, the insuring clause and the exceptions clause will fall within this category, and that in these circumstances the question is whether the term is one that has been expressed in plain, intelligible language, failing which it is to be construed against the insurers and its fairness falls to be considered. In *Bankers Insurance Co Ltd v South*[143] a travel policy taken out by a friend of the assured, and under which the assured was one of a number of insured persons, excluded cover for the assured's liability incurred "involving your ownership or possession of any . . . motorised water-borne craft". The assured injured a third party in jet-ski collision. One was whether the exclusion encompassed what had occurred. Buckley J. held that the exclusion was a "core" provision so that it was not subject to the fairness test, and instead the only question was whether it had been expressed in plain, intelligible language. Buckley J.'s view was that a jet-ski was in ordinary parlance a motorised waterborne craft and that there was no ambiguity involved. However, even if that were wrong, the term was not unfair as the assured had been given the opportunity to read the policy and the policy was a cheap one.

If the term is not a "core" term, but is ancillary to the main obligations of the insurer under the policy, then it is to be judged by the fairness test. It would seem from the limited authority under the Regulations that a clause is automatically void only to the extent that it is incapable of operating fairly, and thus remains valid but merely unenforceable where giving effect to the clause would act unfairly in the circumstances. In *South* the further issue was the binding effect of conditions precedent to the insurers' liability in the form of an obligation to notify as soon as reasonably possible all incidents that may result in a claim and an obligation to forward all relevant communications to the insurer. The assured was in serious breach of each of these provisions. Buckley J. held that conditions precedent were by their nature unfair as they precluded recovery irrespective of the seriousness of the assured's breach. The learned judge went on to hold that the Regulations did not strike down the clauses in their entirety, but instead prevented the insurers from treating them as conditions precedent to liability

---

[141] *Governors of The Peabody Trust v Michael Reeve* [2008] EWHC 1432 (Ch).
[142] *County Homesearch Co (Thames & Chilterns) Ltd v David Cowham* [2008] EWCA Civ 26; *Baybut v Eccle Riggs Country Park Ltd*, *The Times*, November 13, 2006.
[143] *Bankers Insurance Co Ltd v South* [2004] Lloyd's Rep. I.R. 1.

unless the breach was one that caused serious prejudice to the insurers. In so deciding Buckley J. rejected the alternative suggestion that the condition precedent element of a clause was automatically wiped out leaving the clause as a bare condition. Buckley J. held that on the facts before him the breach by the assured was a serious one, so that the assured was unable to recover.[144] This aspect of the decision can no longer stand following the decision of the Court of Appeal in *Friends Provident v Sirius*, which holds that a claim is lost for breach of condition only where the breach operated as a repudiation of the policy as a whole. The effect of the Regulations would thus be to allow full recovery despite breach of a condition precedent.

The Regulations were also considered by District Judge Hickman in *Pearl Assurance Plc v Kavanagh*.[145] The clause in this case was contained in a motor policy, and sought to impose upon the assured an absolute obligation to repay to the insurers sums that they were required by the Road Traffic Act 1988 to pay to a third-party victim in circumstances where there was no liability under the policy itself. In *Kavanagh* the insurers became liable under s.151, to a third party for liability incurred by an unauthorised driver of the assured's vehicle. Under s.151(8) the assured is liable to indemnify the insurer only where the assured had caused or permitted the use of the vehicle so the effect of the clause was to remove the protection granted by the statutory provision. The court ruled that the clause was to be construed *contra proferentem* so that it arguably replicated s.151(8), but if that was wrong then the clause was unfair as it had not been individually negotiated or drawn to the assured's attention but sought to remove statutory protection from her.

---

[144] *Bankers Insurance Co Ltd v South* [2006] Lloyd's Rep. I.R. 45.
[145] *Pearl Assurance Plc v Kavanagh* [2001] C.L.Y. 3832.

CHAPTER 4

INSURABLE INTEREST

1. THE SIGNIFICANCE OF INSURABLE INTEREST

4–001   **Need for insurable interest.** Experience on both sides of the Atlantic has demonstrated that permitting a person to insure a subject matter which he has no interest in preserving, and in which he has no interest other than the policy itself, gives rise to two dangers. First, there is the possibility that the assured is doing no more than wagering with the insurer on the continued safety of the insured subject matter. Wagering has long been frowned upon in England, although admittedly not always on moral grounds: thus in the sixteenth century wagering was thought to be a significant distraction from the far more important task of archery practice, and in that century and the early part of the seventeenth century private gambling was justifiably regarded as resulting in a diversion of potential funds away from the great state lotteries, the proceeds of which financed English involvement in wars. The eighteenth century witnessed a greater moral impetus to attempts to ban gambling, based on the notions that gambling promoted idleness amongst the lower classes and dishonour and suicide amongst the aristocracy.[1] Strong objection was also taken to the practice which developed in the eighteenth century of the publication by newspapers of the odds on the survival of ailing personalities to allow wagering to take place; it was widely believed that the mere publication of pessimistic forecasts on the likely longevity of specified individuals precipitated the demise of many of them.[2] The gambling objections to insurance without interest may appear to be somewhat quaint to the modern eye, particularly since the characteristics of wagering which are most damaging—its addictiveness, and the danger that those indulging in it are not aware of the relevant odds—are hardly likely to apply in the sophisticated world of insurance, and this particular objection to gambling by insurance must remain one of personal morality. Further, the Gambling Act 2005 has liberalised the laws on gambling and has removed historical prohibitions on the enforcement of gambling contracts.

A second, and probably more fundamental, objection to insurance without interest is that an assured who stands to benefit from the early destruction of what has been insured will be tempted to take steps to bring about such early destruction. The Marine Insurance Act 1745, the earliest English statute governing insurable interest, recognised the issue in its preamble:

> "It hath been found by experience, that the making of insurances, interest or no interest, or without further proof of interest than the policy, hath been productive of many pernicious practices, whereby great numbers of ships, with their cargoes, have . . . been fraudulently lost or destroyed."

---

[1] See Blackstone, *Commentaries on the Laws of England* (1765/69) Vol.IV at p.171.
[2] Welford, *Insurance Guide and Handbook* 4th edn (1901), pp.27 and 28.

The danger of fraudulent destruction ought not perhaps to be overstated. Even where insurable interest does exist there is a similar danger, particularly in life cases,[3] in situations in which insured property has been overvalued, and in the context of marine insurance where the value of the insured subject matter is taken at the date of the policy and not at the time immediately prior to the loss.[4] Moreover, if insured subject matter is lost in suspicious circumstances, the existence of a policy in the hands of a person without interest might provide a strong indication as to the cause of the loss. The risk of detection has not, however, proved to be a sufficient deterrent against this type of conduct.[5]

It was suggested by Langley J. in *Feasey v Sun Life Assurance Co of Canada*[6] that gambling by means of insurance undermines the security of the insurer, and that this may have been a motivating factor underlying the eighteenth-century legislation prohibiting insurance without interest.

History of insurable interest

The attitude of the courts. Wagering agreements in the seventeenth century were enforceable in much the same way as other forms of contract.[7] The common law courts had little opportunity to rule on the validity of wagers dressed up as insurance, although there are early cases in which wagers in the form of marine policies were held to be unenforceable by the courts of equity, apparently on the ground that the intention of the parties had been not to gamble but to insure.[8] MacGillivray and Parkington[9] are of the view that had the parties made clear their intention to gamble the policies would have been enforced, and this is certainly consistent with the generous approach of the courts to gambling before the middle of the eighteenth century. These early cases were in any event overcome by the parties specifying that interest was not required: the phrases "policy proof of interest" ("ppi") or "interest or no interest" were pressed into use for this purpose. However, something of a change of attitude towards wagering agreements occurred in the course of the eighteenth century, and while wager policies were generally enforceable[10] the courts began to refuse to enforce wagers on a number of independent grounds, most importantly that: proceedings on a wager were frivolous and a waste of judicial time[11]; the wager might lead to corruption in public affairs[12]; the wager might result in physical violence or

4–002

---

[3] See *R. v Flannagan and Higgins* (1884) 15 Cox C.C. 403.

[4] Marine Insurance Act 1906 s.16.

[5] As is shown by *Wainwright v Bland* (1836) 1 M. & W. 32.

[6] *Feasey v Sun Life Assurance Co of Canada* [2002] Lloyd's Rep. I.R. 835.

[7] *Andrews v Herne* (1662) 1 Lev. 33: *Danvers v Thistlewaite* (1669) 1 Lev. 44; *Firebrase v Brett* (1688) 1 Vern. 469.

[8] MacGillivray and Parkington cite in favour of this proposition the following cases: *Whittingham v Thornburgh* (1690) 2 Vern. 206; *Martin v Sitwell* (1691) 1 Show. 156; *Goddard v Garrett* (1692) 2 Vern. 269; *Le Pypre v Farr* (1716) 2 Vern. 516.

[9] MacGillivray and Parkington at para.15. See also the comments of Langley J. in *Feasey v Sun Life Assurance Co of Canada* [2002] Lloyd's Rep. I.R. 835. at para.162.

[10] See Lord Kenyon in *Craufurd v Hunter* (1798) 8 T.R. 13, 23; Roche J. in *Williams v Baltic Assurance* [1924] 2 K.B. 282 at 289. Contrast Lord Eldon in *Lucena v Craufurd* (1806) 2 Bos. & P. 269. 321.

[11] *Brown v Leeson* (1792) 2 H. Bl. 43; *Squires v Whisken* (1811) 3 Samp. 140; *Egerton v Furzeman* (1825) 1 C. & P. 613; *Kennedy v Gad* (1828) 3 C. & P. 376. The cases were not consistent, for the courts were at other times prepared to enforce wagers as to the rules of unlawful games: *Pope v St Leger* (1693) 1 Salk 344; *Bulling v Frost* (1794) 1 Esp. 235; *M'Allester v Haden* (1810) 1 Samp. 438.

[12] *Foster v Thackeray* (1781) 1 T.R. 57; *Atherfold v Beard* (1788) 2 T.R. 610. An earlier unreported decision of Lord Mansfield, in *Murray v Kelly* is to the same effect. Earlier cases did not recognise the distinction between public and private wagers: see *Andrews v Herne* (1662) 1 Lev. 33 (wager on whether Charles II would be restored to the throne).

immorality[13]; the wager might adversely affect the interests of a third party[14]; and hearing the dispute might result in the production of improper evidence.[15] These situations represented exceptions to the general rule that wagers were enforceable at common law, but there was no doubt that they demonstrated a shifting judicial attitude that could easily have led to recognition that wagers were void at common law had legislation—in the form of s.18 of the Gaming Act 1845—not intervened and rendered wagers null and void. The common law attitude to wagers has once again become of significance, in that on September 1, 2007 the Gambling Act 2005 came fully into effect: Gambling Act (Commencement No.6 and Transitional Provisions) Order (SI 2006/3272). As outlined below, the 2005 Act has repealed s.18 of the Gaming Act 1845 (Gambling Act 2005 s.334) and in its place has substituted a general principle that wagers are enforceable (Gambling Act 2005 s.335(1)), but without prejudice to any rule of law (other than a rule of law relating specifically to gambling) which makes wagers unlawful (Gambling Act 2005 s.335(2)). If the common law rule is indeed that some wagers are unlawful at common law for reasons other than pure gambling, then s.335(1) could be deprived of much of its effect.

4–003   *The legislative response.* Parliament's first attempt to control the growth of insurance without interest was the Marine Insurance Act 1745: this Act rendered void marine policies made without interest, or which provided that the policy itself was to be conclusive proof of interest ("ppi" policies) or was made "interest or no interest", phrases which had developed following the decisions cancelling insurances made without interest, referred to earlier. The prohibition in the 1745 Act was extended to other forms of insurance by the Life Assurance Act 1774, otherwise known as the Gambling Act 1774. The 1774 Act is still in force today and, despite its title, was at least arguably intended to apply to all forms of insurance other than those expressly excluded in s.4, namely those on ships, goods and merchandises. Recent authority has nevertheless decided that the 1774 Act was concerned purely with life and other non-indemnity policies,[16] including accident policies.[17] The Life Assurance Act 1774, where it applies, requires the assured to possess insurable interest at the inception of the policy (s.1), demands the insertion into the policy of the names of all persons interested

---

[13] *Allen v Rescous* 83 E.R. 505; *Walker v Derwent* Unreported, 1747; *Jones v Randall* (1774) I Cowp. 37; *Hartley v Rice* (1808) 10 East 22; *Gilbert v Sykes* (1812) 16 East 150 (which recognised that wagering on the life of another—Napoleon—might produce undesirable consequences); *Burn v Taylor* (1823) R. & M. 28.

[14] The notorious decision in *Earl of March v Pigot* (1771) 5 Burr 2802 indicates that the wager would be illegal only if physical violence involving the third party might follow, although later decisions deprecated that limitation: *Da Costa v Jones* (1778) 2 Cowp. 37; *Good v Elliott* (1790) 3 T.R. 693; *Micklefield v Hepgin* (1794) I Anst. 133; *Ditchburn v Goldsmith* (1815) 4 Camp. 152; *Eltham v Kingsman* (1818) 1 B. & Ald. 683.

[15] *Coxe v Phillips* Ca. Temp. Hardw. 237; *Da Costa v Jones* (1778) 2 Cowp. 37; *Atherfold v Beard* (1788) 2 T.R. 610; *Shirley v Sankey* (1800) 2 Bos. & P. 130.

[16] *Mark Rowlands Ltd v Berni Inns Ltd* [1985] 3 All E.R. 473; *Siu v Eastern Insurance Co Ltd* [1994] 1 All E.R. 213.

[17] *Shilling v Accidental Death* (1858) 1 E. & F. 116, although Life Assurance Act 1774 does not apply to an accident or policy taken out by a local authority for the benefit of its employees injured on authority business: Local Government Act 1972 s.140. See also the Land Drainage Act 1991 Sch.2 para.1, which disapplies the 1774 Act where a drainage board insures the life of any member of the board, although the proceeds must—after expenses—be paid to the deceased's personal representatives. It is of interest to note that in the aftermath of the 1774 Act, Buller J. took the view that it applied to all wagers and not simply to insurances without interest: *Good v Elliott* (1790) 3 T.R. 693: *Atherfold v Beard* (1788) 2 T.R. 610.

in it (s.2), and restricts the assured's recovery to an amount not exceeding his interest (s.3).

These Acts were followed by an Act in 1785, passed "for regulating insurances, on ships and on goods, merchandises or effects" with the object of putting an end to the practice of issuing policies in blank, without inserting in them the name of the assured. This Act led however to "great mischiefs and inconveniences" and was repealed by the Marine Insurance Act 1788 which applied to marine policies and policies on goods, and required the insertion into the policy of the names of any one person interested in it. Much of the 1788 Act remains in force.

Subsequently Parliament passed the Gaming Act 1845 s.18, the effect of which was to render null and void all contracts made by way of gaming or wagering, whether in the form of insurance or otherwise. The final stages in the legislative history are the Marine Insurance Act 1906, which repealed Marine Insurance Act 1745 in full and the Marine Insurance Act 1788 in so far as it applies to marine insurance, and introduced new provisions to much the same effect, the Marine Insurance (Gambling Policies) Act 1909, which imposes criminal liability for certain forms of gambling in the form of marine insurance and, most recently, the repeal of s.18 of the 1845 Act with effect from September 1, 2007 and its replacement with a general right to enforce wagering contracts.

2. THE PRINCIPLE OF INDEMNITY

The principle and its exceptions

The essence of insurance is that the assured may recover only what he has lost, **4–004** i.e. that it provides no more than indemnity. The indemnity principle is nevertheless subject to two important modifications. First, because it is impossible to measure the value of a life, policies on lives are for the most part not indemnity agreements and the assured under a life policy is entitled to insure for an unlimited amount.[18] Life policies are, therefore, agreements under which the insurer agrees to pay a given sum on the death of the life assured or, in the case of endowment insurance, on the earlier of either a specified date or the death of the life assured. It will be appreciated, however, that certain forms of life policy are actually intended to cover measurable loss, as in the case where a creditor insures his debtor for the amount of the debt, so that the assured is in fact seeking indemnity; in these cases s.3 of the 1774 Act will operate to hold the assured to the amount of his interest, irrespective of the amount for which the policy has been taken out. It might be noted that personal accident policies are also to be regarded as non-indemnity insurance, even though the indemnity element is strong in most cases.[19]

The second modification concerns valued policies. Under a valued policy the value of the insured subject matter is agreed between the parties at the outset and, on the happening of an insured event, the agreed sum is payable without the need for the assured to quantify his actual loss. The conclusiveness of the agreed valuation is confirmed by s.27(3) of the Marine Insurance Act 1906. Where there is a valued policy on a subject matter within the Life Assurance Act 1774, such

---

[18] *Dalby v India & London Life Assurance Co* (1854) 15 C.B. 365; *M'Farlane v The Royal London Friendly Society* (1886) 2 T.L.R. 755.

[19] *Theobald v Railway Passengers' Assurance Co* (1854) 10 Ex. 45.

as a "keyman" policy by an employer on his employee it would appear that s.3 of the 1774 Act is overridden by the valuation. This assumption clearly underlies *Elcock v Thomson*,[20] where the assured was able to recover a sum calculated on the agreed value of the insured building even though there had been a clear overvaluation and the assured was claiming far more than a true indemnity. The point is probably now largely academic, as the 1774 Act has now been confined to non-indemnity policies so that the issue is likely to arise only in the case of a life policy made on limited interest.

4–005 **Indemnity and insurable interest.** The principle that an assured may not recover more than he has lost and the principle that most insurances must be supported by insurable interest will often lead to the same conclusion. However, the principles are distinct, as the following points demonstrate.

1. Life and accident policies are not contracts of indemnity, but they are nevertheless required to be supported by insurable interest under the terms of the Life Assurance Act 1774.
2. The question of indemnity becomes important only where a loss has occurred, for indemnity is concerned with the quantification of loss. By contrast, the rules of insurable interest are mainly concerned with ensuring that a person who has no prospect of suffering a loss is prevented from insuring in the first place.
3. Where an assured is unable to satisfy the indemnity requirement by proving any loss, the position is quite simply that he cannot recover under the policy. Thus, in the case of contractual interest, subject to the express terms of the contract, it is the time of the loss that is all-important, for unless the assured can prove interest at that time he cannot recover, for he has suffered no loss for which an indemnity is payable.[21] Failure to demonstrate insurable interest is potentially more serious: where a marine policy without interest amounts to a gambling policy the Marine Insurance (Gambling Policies) Act 1909 imposes criminal sanctions; and where the policy is governed by Life Assurance Act 1774 the agreement between the parties is illegal, thereby preventing either party from suing on it or claiming restitution of payments made under it.
4. The principle of indemnity takes effect as an implied term in the agreement between the parties, whereas the rules of insurable interest are statutory and may not be waived by agreement. Two consequences flow from this difference. First, if the policy is a valued one the assured is discharged from demonstrating the amount of his loss, although it remains open to the insurer to challenge the claim on the basis that the assured possessed no insurable interest. Secondly, the parties may simply agree that the policy is not to be one of indemnity. Thus, assuming that the assured can demonstrate insurable interest, and that s.3 of the Life Assurance Act 1774 is not applicable, he is permitted to recover an

---

[20] *Elcock v Thomson* (1948) 82 Ll. L. Rep. 892.

[21] *Andersen v Morice* (1876) L.R. 1; App. Cas. 713. The only exception to this principle exists in the marine context, where the assured insures "lost or not lost" and acquires an interest after the loss: *Sutherland v Pratt* (1843) 11 M. & W. 296, a rule now codified in the Marine Insurance Act 1906, proviso to s.6(1).

amount in excess of his actual loss whether for his own benefit or for the benefit of other interested persons.[22]

Third party claimants. Under the Contracts (Rights of Third Parties) Act 1999,   **4–006** a non-contracting person who is either given enforcement rights under a contract of insurance, or is at least named or identified as beneficiary, has the power to enforce the contract for his own benefit. A third-party beneficiary may, therefore, have a direct claim under the policy. An issue of some complexity is the amount recoverable by him. It would seem that the third party is restricted to recovering an amount representing his own insurable interest: this is the effect of s.3(4) of the 1999 Act, which provides that the insurers have as against the third party any defence which they could have raised against him had he been a party to the contract. It follows that the third party can recover only in respect of his own loss, unless he has a pervasive insurable interest which permits him to recover the losses of persons insured under the policy and other third parties, in which case the third party must account to those other persons for the sums obtained by him.

3. Effect of Gambling Legislation

Gaming Act 1845. The Gaming Act 1845 brought an end to the great   **4–007** uncertainty relating to the validity of wagers at common law, and brought the general law into line with the statutory provisions relating to marine and life insurance contracts. Section 18 provided as follows:

> "All contracts or agreements, whether by parole or in writing, by way of gaming or wagering, shall be null and void; and no suit shall be brought or maintained in any court of law or equity for recovering any sum of money or valuable thing alleged to be won upon any wager."

This section has now been repealed by the Gambling Act 2005.

Gambling Act 2005: application to insurance. Section 335 of the Gambling   **4–008** Act 2005 provides as follows:

> "(1) The fact that a contract relates to gambling shall not prevent its enforcement.
> (2) Subsection (1) is without prejudice to any rule of law preventing the enforcement of a contract on the grounds of unlawfulness (other than a rule relating specifically to gambling)."

Section 335 sets out in subs.(1) the general proposition that the fact that a contract relates to gambling is not to prevent its enforcement. There is a saving in subs.(2) for any rule of law "preventing the enforcement of a contract on the grounds of unlawfulness" unless the unlawfulness emanates from a rule relating

---

[22] *Waters v Monarch Fire & Life Assurance Co* (1856) 5 E. & B. 870; *London & North-Western Ry v Glyn* (1859) 1 E. & E. 652; *North British & Mercantile Insurance Co v Moffatt* (1871) L.R. 7 C.P. 25; *Engel v Lancashire & General Assurance Co Ltd* (1925) 21 Ll. L.R. 327; *Maurice v Goldsborough Mart & Co* [1939] A.C. 452; *Thomas v National Farmers' Union Mutual Insurance Society* [1961] 1 All E.R. 363; *Tomlinson (Hauliers) v Hepburn* [1966] A.C. 451; *Petrofina (UK) Ltd v Magnaload* [1984] 1 Q.B. 127; *Ramco (UK) Ltd v International Insurance Co of Hannover Ltd* [2004] Lloyd's Rep. I.R. 606; *Ramco Ltd v Weller Russell & Laws Insurance Brokers Ltd* [2009] Lloyd's Rep. I.R. 27.

specifically to gambling. The result, therefore, is that: (a) gambling contracts are valid; (b) any rule of law that does not relate specifically to gambling and that renders the contract unlawful remains operative; and (c), by way of exception to (b), any rule of law that relates specifically to gambling and that renders the contract unlawful ceases to have effect.

It is uncertain whether the Gambling Act 2005 applies to insurance at all. The definition of gambling in s.3 of the 2005 Act is gaming, betting or participating in a lottery. The definitions of gaming and lotteries are irrelevant to insurance, but in principle the definition of "betting" may catch insurance. Betting, as defined by s.9, is making or accepting a bet on—

(a) the outcome of a race, competition or other event or process,
(b) the likelihood of anything occurring or not occurring, or
(c) whether anything is or is not true.

It is irrelevant under s.9 of the 2005 Act that the event has occurred and that one party knows the outcome. If insurance without interest is betting, then it can only fall within s.9(b), although it is far from obvious that insurance is a bet on the *likelihood* of an event occurring, but rather it is a bet on the *possibility* of an event occurring. It follows that insurance without interest may not be a "bet" at all and so does not qualify as gambling: if that is right then it is not caught by s.335(1) at all. An alternative route to the same conclusion is that s.10 of the Gambling Act 2005 excludes from the definition of gambling any regulated activity within s.22 of the Financial Services and Markets Act 2000, and effecting and carrying on insurance business is a regulated activity by art.10 of the Financial Services and Markets Act 2000 (Regulated Activities) Order 2001, SI 2001/544—under art.58 arranging insurance at Lloyd's is also a regulated activity—although art.11 excludes insurance effected by an EEA firm from a branch outside the United Kingdom and under a co-insurance arrangement where the firm is not the leading insurer. Thus, if the insurance is issued by an insurer required to be authorised in the United Kingdom, then again it will not be saved by s.335.

4–009   **Gambling Act 2005: specific forms of insurance.** On the assumption that the 2005 Act is potentially applicable to insurance, at least in some situations, applying this section to insurable interest is a matter of some difficulty. It is necessary to consider each class of insurable interest.

Turning first to life assurance, the Life Assurance Act 1774 requires the assured to have insurable interest at the date of the policy,[23] failing which the insurance is unlawful.[24] A life policy not supported by insurable interest is not necessarily a gambling contract, and indeed in *Feasey v Sun Life Assurance Co of Canada*[25] Waller L.J. specifically noted that the gambling was not the antithesis of insurable interest. A contract struck down by the 1774 Act is not, therefore, a gambling contract, but simply one that is not supported by insurable interest. It might be thought on this basis that s.335(1) has no effect on the statutory insurable interest requirement for life assurance. Even if that is wrong, then the Life Assurance Act 1774 is preserved by s.335(2) because it sets out a rule of law that provides for unlawfulness and it is not a statute that relates specifically to gambling.[26]

---

[23] *Dalby v India & London Life Assurance Co* (1854) 15 C.B. 365.
[24] *Harse v Pearl Life Assurance Co* [1904] 1 K.B. 558.
[25] *Feasey v Sun Life Assurance Co of Canada* [2003] Lloyd's Rep. I.R. 637.
[26] The problem here is the 1774 Act's alternative "Gambling Act" title, although there are reasons other than pure gambling that led to the passing of the legislation.

Marine insurance is somewhat more problematic, The Marine Insurance Act 1906 s.4(1) avoids every contract of marine insurance "by way of gaming or wagering". General definitions of this phrase outside the insurance context have indicated that a contract can only be a wager when both parties intend it to be so.[27] Perhaps too much ought not to be read into this as, insurance aside, it is difficult to think of many situations in which one party is wagering while the other is not. Section 4(2) of the Marine Insurance Act 1906 provides that a policy is deemed to be "by way of gaming or wagering" in two situations:

(a) where the assured has not an insurable interest as defined by this Act, and the contract is entered into with no expectation of acquiring such an interest,[28] or

(b) where the policy is made "interest or no interest", or "without further proof of interest other than the policy itself", or "without benefit of salvage to the insurer", or subject to any other like term.

The proviso to the Marine Insurance Act 1906 s.4(2) states that a policy made without benefit of salvage to the insurer is not by way of gaming or wagering if there is no possibility of salvage. The Marine Insurance Act 1906 s.4(2)(b) has no relevance outside the marine context; such phrases are confined to marine insurance. Where terms such as those contained in the Marine Insurance Act 1906 s.4(2)(b) do appear in the policy, it is obvious that the insurer is prepared to wager, although it is worth remembering that the Marine Insurance Act 1906 s.4(2)(b) operates to avoid a "ppi" or equivalent policy, whether or not the assured has an interest.[29] The Marine Insurance Act 1906 s.4(2)(a), by contrast, implies that a policy may be a wager even though the insurer has no intention of wagering, although it should be said that the few cases on the meaning of this provision have made it clear that there has to be a mutual intention to wager.[30] If the assured has an insurable interest, and overvalues that interest, the contract is not made by way of wagering under s.4(2)(a).[31]

There is no legislation that requires insurable interest for any other form of insurance.[32] Prior to the passing of the Gaming Act 1845 the common law position was that policies without interest were valid, although there were a number of exceptions that could render such policies unenforceable and, in some cases involving public policy, unlawful. The common law was overtaken by the 1845 Act. The repeal of s.18 of the 1845 Act has left the position that policies without interest are unaffected by any prohibition on gambling unless there is some rule of law (necessarily the common law, in the absence of any applicable legislation) that renders such policies unenforceable by reason of their unlawfulness. It would be unfortunate in the extreme if the validity of the insurance policies taken out without interest should depend upon a series of cases decided in the hundred years preceding 1845. It is submitted that the effect of the

[27] See, e.g. *Universal Stock Exchange v Strachan* [1896] A.C. 166 at 167 and 168, per Cave J.

[28] *Kent v Bird* (1777) 2 Cowp. 583; *Lowry v Bordieu* (1780) 2 Doug. K.B. 468.

[29] *Cheshire & Co v Vaughan Bros & Co* [1920] 3 K.B. 240; *Edwards & Co v Commercial Union Motor Union Insurance Co* [1922] 2 K.B. 249; *Re London County Commercial Reinsurance Office* [1922] 2 Ch. 67; *Re Overseas Marine Insurance Co Ltd* (1930) 36 Ll. L. Rep. 183.

[30] *Knox v Wood* (1808) 1 Camp. 543; *Eyre v Glover* (1812) 16 East. 218; *Andersen v Morice* (1879) L.R. 1 App. Cas. 713; *Buchanan & Co v Faber* (1899) 4 Com. Cas. 223; *Moran, Galloway & Co v Uzielli* [1905] 2 K.B. 55.

[31] *Glafki Shipping Co SA v Pinios Shipping Co (The Maria (No.2))* [1984] 1 Lloyd's Rep. 660.

[32] As already commented, the Life Assurance Act 1774 is confined to life and personal accident insurance and does not extend to other types of cover.

Gambling Act 2005 is to remove the need for insurable interest at the outset of a policy, although this is likely to be of little significance given that the indemnity principle is untouched by the 2005 Act, and it remains the case that the assured must prove his loss when the peril occurs. There is little point, therefore, in the assured taking out a policy without interest given that he can never recover under it, assuming, of course, that there is no move to write policies on a "ppi" basis, a practice that was permitted by the common law in the marine context before 1745, when it was outlawed as regards marine policies.

4. The Present Regulatory Structure

4–010   **Application of legislative and common law principles.** The application of the rules relating to insurable interest, indemnity and wagering to specific classes of insurance may be outlined as follows.

(1) Life policies are required by Life Assurance Act 1774 to be supported by insurable interest at their inception, failing which they are illegal. The position is not affected once the Gambling Act 2005, because the 1774 Act is either outside s.335(1) of the Act or at least is preserved by s.335(2) of that Act. As life policies are not contracts of indemnity, it is not necessary for the assured to demonstrate insurable interest at the date of the death of the person on whose life the policy was procured. An accident policy, whether or not it is construed as a pure indemnity policy, is regarded as a life policy for the purposes of Life Assurance Act 1774 and is subject to the rules laid down in that Act.[33]

(2) Marine policies are governed exclusively by Marine Insurance Act 1906 and the Marine Insurance (Gambling Policies) Act 1909, the combined effect of which is that the assured must possess an insurable interest at the outset, and must suffer a loss in order to mount a claim on the occurrence of an insured peril. The insurable interest rules are unlikely to be affected by s.335 of the Gambling Act 2005. If they are then the insurable interest requirement in s.4 may be regarded as having been superseded, although the indemnity principle is left intact so that the assured will still have to prove his loss on the happening of the insured peril.

(3) Polices on non-marine goods are unaffected by the Life Assurance Act 1774 and the Marine Insurance Act 1906. The position at the inception of insurance is, following the repeal of s.18 of the Gaming Act 1845, governed by the Gambling Act 2005, which removes the prohibition on gambling. It would seem, therefore, that there is no statute or common law principle which requires insurable interest at inception. The position following a loss is governed by the indemnity principle, so that the assured must prove his loss. This rule is unaffected by the Gambling Act 2005.

(4) Policies on land and buildings at one time gave rise to difficulties, for the assumption had been that they were within Life Assurance Act 1774, with the results that insurable interest was be required at the outset, while the indemnity principle demanded loss on the occurrence of an insured

[33] *Shilling v Accidental Death* (1857) 2 F. & F. 116.

peril. The modern view is that the 1774 does not apply to policies on land and buildings, and the position is the same as that appertaining to goods, set out in (3) above.

(5) Liability policies are subject to the same principles as those on land and buildings, as such contracts are of indemnity and thus outside Life Assurance Act 1774.

(6) Other policies which do not have specific statutory requirements for insurable interest are valid under the Gambling Act 2005 even if made without interest. Thus a contract for the payment of a sum based on the outcome of a sporting event where the assured's intention is not to protect himself against a possible liability (such as the obligation to award a prize for a particular achievement, e.g. a hole in one at a golf tournament) but rather to raise investment capital was held to be unenforceable under the Gaming Act 1845 s.18 (*Newbury v Reliance International Insurance*[34]) but the repeal of that section renders such a policy valid from the outset. The assured must of course prove a loss if he is to recover.

Effects of payment on policy made without interest. Insurance companies and   **4–011** underwriters do sometimes seek to evade their just obligations on the ground of want of interest, and it is the duty of the court always to lean in favour of an insurable interest, if possible, for after the underwriters or company have received the premium the objection that there was no insurable interest is often a technical objection and one which has no real merit as between the assured and the insurer.[35] "Time was," said Buller J. in 1798,[36] "when no underwriter would have dreamed of making such an objection if his solicitor had suggested a loophole by which he might escape he would have spurned at the idea." There is nothing illegal about the insurers paying on a policy other than a life policy without interest, because a policy within the Life Assurance Act 1774 which is made without interest is unlawful,[37] although even in the case of a life policy the policyholder will be entitled to retain the insurance moneys as against the personal representatives of the deceased, as the illegality does not affect the rights of rival claimants between themselves.[38] Except in the case of marine policies,[39] a policy will not be invalid simply because it contains a provision that the insurers will pay, interest or no interest.[40]

Interest need not be stated. It is not necessary to state in a policy of insurance   **4–012** the precise nature of the assured's insurable interest. A person who has different kinds of interest in property may cover them all by one insurance without stating in the policy the number or nature of the interests.[41] Only the subject-matter of the insurance and the identity of the assured need be correctly described.

[34] *Newbury v Reliance International Insurance* [1994] 1 Lloyd's Rep. 83.
[35] Brett M.R. in *Stock v Inglis* (1884) 12 Q.B.D. 564, affirmed (1885) L.R. 10; App. Cas. 263; *Feasey v Sun Life Assurance Co of Canada* [2003] Lloyd's Rep. I.R. 637.
[36] In *Wolff v Homcastle* (1798) 1 Bos. & P. 316 at 320–321.
[37] *Worthington v Curtis* (1875) L.R. 1 Ch. D. 419; *Attorney-General v Murray* [1904] 1 K.B. 165; Shearman J. in *Hatley v Liverpool Victoria Friendly Society* (1918) 88 L.J.K.B. 237; *Carmichael's Case* 1920 S.C. (HL) 195.
[38] *Worthington v Curtis* (1875) L.R. 1 Ch. D. 419: *Hadden v Bryden* (1899) 1 F. (Ct of Sess) 710; *Attorney-General v Murray* [1904] 1 K.B. 165.
[39] Marine Insurance Act 1906 s.4(2)(b).
[40] *Anctil v Manufacturers' Life* [1899] A.C. 604.
[41] *Carruthers v Sheddon* (1815) 6 Taunt. 14; *Crowley v Cohen* (1832) 3 B. & Ad. 478.

5. The Meaning of Insurable Interest[42]

4–013   **General definition.** The root decision is that in *Lucena v Craufurd*.[43] In that case the Commissioners of Admiralty had taken possession of a Dutch ship during the Napoleonic Wars, and wished to insure it for its voyage home from St Helena to England, and the House of Lords was ultimately required to decide whether the Commissioners had sufficient insurable interest to support such a policy. The House of Lords was prepared to hold that an interest did exist on these facts, and was largely influenced by the advice of Lawrence J.[44]:

> "A man is interested in a thing to whom advantage may arise or prejudice happen from the circumstances which may attend it; and whom it importeth that its condition as to safety or other quality should continue. Interest does not necessarily imply a right to the whole or a part of the thing, nor necessarily and exclusively that which may be the subject of privation, but the having some relation to, or concern in, the subject of the insurance; which relation or concern, by the happening of the perils insured against, may be so affected as to produce a damage, detriment or prejudice to the person insuring. And where a man is so circumstanced with respect to advantage or benefit but for those risks or dangers, he may be said to be interested in the safety of the thing. To be interested in the preservation of a thing is to be so circumstanced with respect to it as to have the benefit from its existence, prejudice from its destruction. The property of a thing and the interest derivable from it may be very different. Of the first the price is generally the measure; but by interest in a thing, every benefit and advantage arising out of or depending on such a thing may be considered as being comprehended."

It will be appreciated that the formulation of Lawrence J. is an extremely wide one. The learned judge carefully distinguished interest from a right of ownership, and suggested that the proper test is that of possible prejudice following loss of the insured subject matter. Significantly, the right of the assured to possess the property was not referred to by Lawrence J. Not all the members of the House of Lords were prepared to view the matter so widely. Lord Eldon indeed appears to have contemplated a much narrower conception of interest[45]:

> "[Insurable interest is] a right in the property, or a right derivable out of some contract about the property, which in either case may be lost upon some contingency affecting the possession or enjoyment of the property."

Lord Eldon's definition thus rests upon the assured's ownership of, or right to possess, the insured subject matter. There are a number of situations in which the difference between the views of Lord Eldon and Lawrence J. become of importance, typified by the fact that the assured is reliant upon a particular subject matter for certain purposes but without having any legal or equitable ownership of it or any right to possess it. Thus a street vendor who pitches his

---

[42] Insurable interest as it applies to life, marine, property and liability policies is discussed in the relevant chapters of this work, below.

[43] *Lucena v Craufurd* (1806) 2 Bos. & P.N.R. 269.

[44] *Lucena v Craufurd* (1806) 2 Bos. & P.N.R. 269 at 302. To similar effect are the words of Finch J. in *National Filtering Oil Co v Citizen's Insurance of Missouri* (1887) 13 N.E. 337, that "if there be a right in or against the property which some court will enforce . . . a right so closely connected with it and so much dependent for value upon the continued existence of it alone, as that a loss of the property will cause pecuniary damage to the holder of the right against it, he has an insurable interest".

[45] (1806) 2 Bos. & P.N.R. 269 at 321. Cf. *Ebsworth v Alliance Marine Insurance Co* (1873) L.R. 8 C.P. 596.

stall outside a building housing a public attraction has no interest in the building as far as Lord Eldon is concerned, but may well be able to insure that building if the formulation of Lawrence J. is correct. As a matter of practicality the courts have yet to be called on to resolve a question of this nature, as a street vendor can validly insure against business interruption rather than against the loss of the building, and it is probably the case that most insurers would refuse to issue a buildings policy in these circumstances, but it is worthy of note that the precise width of the concept of insurable interest awaits modern determination. As far as marine insurance is concerned, an approach somewhere between the two views has been adopted by s.5(2) of the Marine Insurance Act 1906, which refers to:

> "[A]ny legal or equitable relation to . . . any insurable property at risk . . . in consequence of which [the assured] may benefit by the safety or due arrival of the insurable property, or may be prejudiced by its loss, or by damage thereto, or by the detention thereof, or may incur liability in respect thereof."

The only limitation is imposed by the words "legal or equitable relation". It is likely that this formulation represents the traditionally accepted position in non-marine insurance. The most recent authorities on the definition of insurable interest nevertheless indicate that traditional narrow concepts do not match current commercial practices,[46] and that a somewhat wider definition may be required. In *Sharp v Sphere Drake Insurance (The Moonacre)*[47] the court rejected the view that insurable interest had to be based upon the assured being the equitable or legal owner of the property in question, and held that an insurable interest in property might arise merely because the assured owed a duty to exercise reasonable care in respect of the property. Subsequently, in *National Oilwell (UK) Ltd v Davy Offshore Ltd*[48] Colman J. extended this principle to a case in which the assured was not in possession of property but in a close physical relation to it: using this approach, it was held that a subcontractor involved in a construction project had insurable interest in the entire contract works even though his responsibility was confined to supplying goods constituting a part of the overall works. The basis of insurable interest in such a case is that if the works are destroyed or damaged, the subcontractor's own contract will be brought to an end.[49] In the light of these cases, it might be said that an insurable interest exists if: the assured has legal or equitable title to the subject matter; or if the assured is in possession of the subject matter; or if the assured is not in possession of the subject matter but may be either responsible for, or suffer loss in the event of, any damage to the subject matter.[50]

Pecuniary interest. It has been said that insurable interest must be a pecuniary interest.[51] "It must be in a reasonable sense capable of valuation in money".[52]   **4–014**

---

[46] It was indeed said by Walton J. in *Moran, Galloway & Co v Uzielli* [1905] 2 K.B. 555 at 563 that "The definition of insurable interest has been continuously expanding, and dicta in some of the older cases, which would tend to narrow it, must be accepted with caution".

[47] *Sharp v Sphere Drake Insurance (The Moonacre)* [1992] 2 Lloyd's Rep. 501.

[48] *National Oilwell (UK) Ltd v Davy Offshore Ltd* [1993] 2 Lloyd's Rep. 582.

[49] *Deepak Fertilisers v ICI Chemicals* [1999] 1 Lloyd's Rep. 387.

[50] *Glengate-KG Properties Ltd v Norwich Union Fire Insurance Society Ltd* [1996] 2 All E.R. 487; *Hopewell Project Management Ltd v Ewbank Preece Ltd* [1998] 1 Lloyd's Rep. 448; *Feasey v Sun Life Assurance Corp of Canada* [2003] Lloyd's Rep. I.R. 637, Waller L.J. noting that it "difficult to define insurable interest in words which will apply in all situations", at para.66.

[51] Lord Tenterden in *Halford v Kymer* (1830) 10 B. & C. 728 at 728; *Macuara v Northern Assurance* [1925] A.C. 619.

[52] *Simcock v Scottish Imperial Insurance Co* (1902) 10 S.L.T. 286.

However, the difficulty of such valuation is no bar to a finding of insurable interest. Thus profits which might be exceedingly difficult to calculate are commonly insured by valued policies, as are works of art incapable of being afforded a certain fixed value. Legal obligations, such as the obligation of a wife towards her husband, may give an insurable interest in the life of another, although they cannot be strictly described as "pecuniary". Nor can the unlimited interest of a man in his own life be so described.[53] Again, it has been said that it is not necessary that a pecuniary loss must follow from the event insured against: it is sufficient that such loss might follow.[54] In short, pecuniary loss affords a most unsatisfactory test as to the existence of an insurable interest.

4–015 **Absence of any intention to gamble.** It is apparent that the function of requiring insurable interest to support a policy is to preclude the possibility of gambling by the assured. It would seem to follow that, as long as the assured is not gambling, there is every reason to uphold the contract even though the interest possessed by the assured does not fit into any established category. It has been said that as long as the assured is not gambling the policy should be enforceable,[55] and although in *Feasey*[56] the Court of Appeal rejected the suggestion that a policy which is not a wagering policy automatically satisfies common law and statutory insurable interest requirements, in particular those under the Life Assurance Act 1774, that Court's view was that the absence of any intention to gamble was an important consideration in determining whether insurable interest existed, and that it was unattractive to hold that a carefully crafted commercial agreement should fall for want of insurable interest. *Feasey* itself involved what would otherwise have been a simple and straightforward reinsurance agreement. The reinsured, Steamship Mutual, a P & I club, had agreed to indemnify its shipowner members against liability claims brought by employees and other persons injured on board the members' vessels. Up to 1994 Steamship Mutual had reinsured its liabilities at Lloyd's under ordinary reinsurance agreements which indemnified it for payments made to members. However, Lloyd's announced in 1994 that with effect from 1995 its risk codes would be amended so that bodily injury and related elements of liability policies were, for reinsurance purposes, to be classified as long-tail liability unless payments were on a fixed benefit basis varying only with the degree of injury or illness incurred, with the result that additional reserves for long-tail cover were required to be maintained by reinsuring syndicates. To overcome this change, the reinsuring underwriter in conjunction with a broker developed a new form of reinsurance for Steamship Mutual. The Club was no longer to be reinsured on the basis of its liability. Instead, the reinsurance policy was expressed to be one based on injuries suffered by employees and persons on board vessels: in the event of any injury suffered, the syndicates would make payment to Steamship Mutual based on a fixed-scale which related to the injury itself and to its likely duration. The amounts payable to Steamship Mutual for various forms of injury and duration did not correspond with the individual sums actually paid by Steamship Mutual to members, although in the aggregate Steamship Mutual did not make any profit. In short, the totality of the sums paid was much as would have been the case had the reinsurance been based on Steamship Mutual's liability, but for regulatory

---

[53] Kennedy L.J. in *Griffiths v Fleming* [1909] 1 K.B. 805 at 820–823.
[54] Lord O'Hagan in *Andersen v Morice* (1876) L.R. 1 App. Cas. 713 at 742.
[55] *The Moonacre* [1992] 2 Lloyd's Rep. 501; *Feasey v Sun Life Assurance Corp of Canada* [2002] Lloyd's Rep. I.R. 835.
[56] *Feasey v Sun Life Assurance Co of Canada* [2003] Lloyd's Rep. I.R. 637.

reasons the reinsurance was framed as personal accident rather than liability. The insurable interest issue raised by this arrangement was the need for Steamship Mutual to prove that it had insurable interest in the lives of its members' employees. The Court of Appeal held by a majority that the contract was supported by insurable interest. The reasoning did not focus on the absence of any intention to gamble. Waller L.J. laid down a three-step test for the validity of a policy under insurable interest rules:

(1) What is the subject matter of the policy? This is to be ascertained from the terms of the policy.

(2) What is the interest of the assured in the insured subject matter?

(3) Does the policy cover the assured's interest? This is also a matter of policy construction, and it was perfectly possible for a policy on a specific subject matter also to cover a wider interest possessed by the assured, e.g. liability to a third party for the loss of the insured subject matter or loss of profits.

This approach is concerned not with the absence of any intention to gamble as such, and gives greater attention to the terms of the policy itself. Applying these tests to the facts, Waller and Dyson L.JJ. held that the subject matter of the policy was the lives of employees, that Steamship had an insurable interest in its own liability, and that the policy on its proper construction covered Steamship's insurable interest in its liability even though it was framed as life policy. Ward L.J.'s dissenting judgment was based on the propositions that the only insurable interest possessed by Steamship was in its own liability but that such an interest was not within the scope of what was framed as a life policy only.

Limited interests. A limited legal or equitable interest, e.g. a bare legal estate **4–016** held by a trustee, is insurable.[57] The Marine Insurance Act 1906, which in the present context represents the general law, gives three examples of the insurability of limited interests.

(1) A defeasible interest, i.e. an interest which is liable to be determined by subsequent events, is insurable (Marine Insurance Act 1906 s.7(1)).[58] A specific example of this is provided by s.7(2)[59]: a purchaser of goods has an insurable interest in them even though he has the right to reject them for breach of condition[60] or the right to treat them as at the seller's risk due to delay in delivery.[61] The fact that the interest of the assured is liable to be defeated by a third person or is voidable does not invalidate a policy under the Life Assurance Act 1774.[62]

(2) A contingent interest, i.e. an interest depending upon the fulfilment of certain conditions, is insurable (Marine Insurance Act 1906 s.7(1)). On this basis insurance may be taken out on anticipated future profits and, in the marine insurance context, on freight.

---

[57] Marine Insurance Act 1906 s.8.

[58] *Lucena v Craufurd* (1806) 2 Bos. & P.N.R. 269; *Stirling v Vaughan* (1809) 11 East 619; *Colonial Insurance Co of New Zealand v Adelaide Marine Insurance Co* (1886) L.R. 12 App. Cas. 128.

[59] Based on *Sparkes v Marshall* (1836) 2 Bing. N.C. 761 and *Anderson v Morice* (1876) L.R. 1 App. Cas. 713.

[60] Under the Sale of Goods Act 1979 s.11(3).

[61] Sale of Goods Act 1979 s.20(2).

[62] *Hill v Secretan* (1798) 1 Bos. & P. 315; *Dwyer v Edie* (1788) 2 Park on Ins. 914.

(3) A partial interest of any nature is insurable (Marine Insurance Act 1906 s.8[63]). Thus, in the context of land and buildings, a tenant can insure premises to the value of his tenancy and a mortgagee can insure premises to the amount of the mortgage debt.

A strict legal interest in property is not necessary to create an insurable interest, an equitable interest is sufficient.[64] Lord Eldon could say in 1808 that it had always been held that a *cestui que trust* had an insurable interest in respect of his equitable interest.[65] Where insurance is effected by a person with a limited interest, the amount recoverable by him under the policy can be no more than an indemnity. This will constitute the value of the assured's own interest plus the amount of any liability of the assured to apply the proceeds in favour of a third party.[66] The question whether the assured with a limited interest has insured on his own behalf alone or on behalf of some third party with a separate limited interest, as agent for that third party, is considered below.

4–017   **Expectancies.** It has been said that a party has an interest in an event if he will gain an advantage if it happens and suffer a loss if it does not.[67] However, it is important to distinguish between interests which are contingent upon the happening of one or more given events, and mere expectancies. The rule here is that an expectation of acquiring an interest in a subject matter is not the same thing as possessing an actual interest, albeit contingent, and that an expectation is not insurable. Thus, while the assignee of an interest in stock due to vest in the assignor on the assignor reaching the age of 30 has an insurable interest in the life of the assignor,[68] the purported buyer of property under a void or unenforceable contract has only the expectation that he will ultimately become the owner of the property.[69] A thing may not be insured merely because there is a chance that some collateral benefit may arise should it not be lost.[70] On this basis, a contingent buyer of goods, who has not obtained property, risk or possession, has no insurable interest in the goods themselves even though he expects at a future date to acquire them,[71] although he does have sufficient interest to maintain a policy against anticipated loss of profits, and a shareholder has no interest in his company's liability for wrongful acts.[72] But there is nothing to prevent a shareholder from insuring his own shares, in which he has an insurable interest, against loss suffered owing to the failure of an adventure in which the company is engaged, however difficult the calculation of the loss, and in *Wilson v Jones*[73]

[63] e.g. joint ownership (*Page v Fry* (1800) 2 Bos. & P. 240; *Robertson v Hamilton* (1811) 154 East 522; *Griffiths v Bramley-Moore* (1878) L.R. 4 Q.B.D. 70) or ownership of part of an undivided bulk in accordance with s.20A of the Sale of Goods Act 1979.

[64] Ashhurst J. in *Smith v Lascelles* (1788) 2 T.R. 187 at 188; *Hill v Secretan* (1798) 1 Bos. & P. 315; Lord Eldon in *Lucena v Craufurd* (1806) 3 Bos. & P. 75 at 103; *Samuel & Co Ltd v Dumas* [1924] A.C. 431 at 443, 444, 450, 460.

[65] *Ex p. Yallop* (1808) 15 Ves. 60 at 67, 68.

[66] *Lonsdale & Thompson Ltd v Black Arrow Group Plc* [1993] 3 All E.R. 648.

[67] Blackburn J. in *Wilson v Jones* (1867) L.R. 2 Ex. 139, citing Lawrence J. in *Barclay v Cousins* (1802) 2 East 544 at 546–561 and in *Lucena v Craufurd* (1806) 3 Bos. & P. 75; *Cepheus Shipping v Guardian Royal Exchange (The Capricorn)* [1995] 1 Lloyd's Rep. 622.

[68] *Law v London Indisputable Life Insurance Policy Co* (1855) 1 Kay & J. 223.

[69] *Stockdale v Dunlop* (1840) 6 M. & W. 22. Cf. *Cook v Field* (1850) L.R. 15 Q.B.D. 460.

[70] Lord Ellenborough in *Routh v Thompson* (1809) 11 East 428.

[71] Lord Eldon in *Lucena v Craufurd* (1806) 2 Bos. & P.N.R. 269 at 325; *Anderson v Morice* (1875) L.R. 10 C.P. 606; *Glengate v Norwich Union* [1995] 1 Lloyd's Rep. 278.

[72] *Levinger v Licences & General* (1936) 56 Ll. L. Rep. 68.

[73] *Wilson v Jones* (1867) L.R. 2 Ex. 139.

the adventure of laying down a submarine cable was insured by a shareholder in that way. On the same principle, a husband who is living with his wife has an insurable interest in her property, for he is by law entitled to share her enjoyment in it,[74] and she, no doubt, has a similar insurable interest in his property as their rights and duties are largely reciprocal.[75]

The only exception to the rule that an expectancy cannot found an insurable interest concerns anticipated profits; the law has always treated insurance against loss of profits as insurance against a contingency rather than against an expectancy, although it remains the case that profits, being a form of consequential loss, are irrecoverable under an insurance policy unless specifically insured.[76] Thus where one has an insurable interest in premises, one can insure against loss of profits due to their destruction[77] provided one does so in express terms.[78]

Moral obligations. A moral, as opposed to a strictly legal, claim either on the assured or possessed by the assured is in the same way a mere expectancy,[79] and an engagement binding in honour only is not enough to support an insurable interest.[80] Thus a father has no insurable interest in the possible personal liability of his child in tort "since natural love and affection does not give such an interest in law",[81] nor does the general concern of a trade union in the welfare of its members give it an insurable interest in their losses or liabilities.[82] There are many other examples of the point in the older cases. **4–018**

A purchaser of goods under a contract which was enforceable under s.4 of the Sale of Goods Act 1893 (now 1979) had no insurable interest in them.[83] Where a bank manager promised, without consideration, not to call in a loan within his lifetime, it was held that the borrower had no insurable interest in his life.[84] The expectation of an ex gratia payment by the Crown will not support an insurance.[85] A discharge in bankruptcy extinguishes the debt for all purposes[86] and the insurable interest of the creditor ceases thereby even if the debtor subsequently promises to pay and is therefore under a moral obligation to do so.

6. Insurance Effected by an Agent

The issues raised. The rules relating to insurable interest give rise to particular difficulties where insurance is effected by an agent (generally a broker) on behalf **4–019**

---

[74] *Goulstone v Royal Insurance Co* (1858) 1 F. & R. 276.

[75] See Vaughan Williams L.J. in *Griffiths v Fleming* [1909] 1 K.B. 805 at 815.

[76] *Barclay v Cousins* (1802) 2 East 544; *Eyre v Glover* (1812) 16 East 218; *Royal Exchange v M'Swiney* (1850) 14 Q.B. 646; *Stockdale v Dunlop* (1840) 6 M. & W. 224.

[77] *City Tailors v Evans* (1921) 91 L.J.K.B. 379.

[78] *Re Sun Fire and Wright* (1834) 3 N. & M. 819; *Re Wright and Pole* (1834) 1 Al. & El. 621; *Flying Colours Film v Assicurazioni Generali SpA* [1993] 2 Lloyd's Rep. 184.

[79] See generally *Hebdon v West* (1863) 3 B. & S. 579.

[80] *Stockdale v Dunlop* (1840) 6 M. & W. 224; *Stainbank v Penning* (1851) 11 C.B. 51; *Stainbank v Shepard* (1853) 13 C.B. 418.

[81] Lord Wright in *Vandepitte v Preferred Accident Insurance Corp of New York* [1933] A.C. 70 at 80.

[82] *Prudential Staff Union v Hall* [1947] K.B. 685.

[83] *Stockdale v Dunlop* (1840) 6 M. & W. 224.

[84] *Hebdon v West* (1863) 3 B. & S. 579.

[85] *Routh v Thompson* (1809) 11 East 428 at 432, 433, per Lord Ellenborough.

[86] *Heather v Webb* (1876) 2 C.P.D. 1.

of the assured where it is the agent's intention that his principal is to be a party to the contract. The basic rule here is that a person with an insurable interest may insure his own interest, or he may insure the interests as others as well as his own.[87] Thus a joint tenant or tenant in common has such an interest in the entirety as will enable him to insure the whole, including the interests of other joint tenants or tenants in common.[88] Equally, a person with no interest in the subject matter may insure on behalf of another, as agent or trustee. Further, in appropriate circumstances a person may insure the interests of others even though he has no insurable interest and is not acting as their agent or trustee. Thus: an employer or association may insure the lives and property of employees and members for their benefit[89]; a bailee of goods liable only for negligence may insure the goods bailed to their full value against any loss[90]; the owner of a motor vehicle may insure against third party liability incurred in its use by himself or others[91]; and where the assured has possession, even though he has no interest at all, he can make an insurance also covering the interest of the owner of the subject matter insured.[92]

4–020 **Policy for assured or for assured and third party.** The question whether an assured with a limited interest intends to protect the interests of others as well as his own is one of construction, and the answer to it depends upon the circumstances of each individual case.[93]

The wording of the policy may at the very least provide valuable evidence in this respect,[94] and it cannot be contradicted by the assured's subjective and uncommunicated intention.[95] If the assured was under no duty to insure on behalf of anyone else and if there is nothing to show that he intended to do so, the presumption will be that he intended to cover his own interest and nothing more.[96] By contrast, if the assured is under an obligation to insure the interests of another person, then it must be assumed that any policy taken out by him was intended to cover both his own interest and that of the other person.[97] In one case where the rules of a building society entitled the mortgagees to insure property mortgaged at the mortgagor's expense, the insurance moneys being applicable "to the payment of the amount secured", it was held that an insurance by them

---

[87] *North British Insurance Co v Moffatt* (1871) L.R. 7 C.P. 25; *Simon Container Machinery Ltd v Emba Machinery AB* [1998] 2 Lloyd's Rep. 429. A dictum of Brett J. in *Ebsworth v Alliance Marine* (1873) L.R. 8 C.P. 596 at 637, 638, implying that the assured's interest must be legal and not merely equitable, appears to be wrong: see Bovill C.J. in *Ebworh*, at 608, 609 and also the many cases cited in that case, especially *Robertson v Hamilton* (1811) 14 East 522 and *Irving v Richardson* (1831) 2 B. & Ad. 193. See also Bowen L.J. in *Castellain v Preston* (1883) L.R. 11 Q.B.D. 380, 398.
[88] *Page v Fry* (1800) 2 Bos. & P. 240.
[89] *Prudential Staff Union v Hall* [1947] K.B. 685.
[90] *Waters v Monarch Fire & Life Assurance Co* (1856) 5 El. & Bl. 870.
[91] *Williams v Baltic Insurance Association of London Ltd* [1924] 2 K.B. 282.
[92] Keating J. in *North British Insurance Co v Moffatt* (1871) L.R. 7 C.P. 25 at 30, 31.
[93] See: *Rayner v Preston* (1881) L.R. 18 Ch. D. 1 at 10; *Yangtse Insurance v Lukmanjee* [1918] A.C. 585.
[94] *Waters v Monarch Fire & Life Assurance Co* (1856) 5 El. & Bl. 870; *London & North West Railway Co v Glyn* (1859) 1 El. & El. 652; *North British Insurance Co v Moffatt* (1871) L.R. 7 C.P. 25; *Ramco (UK) Ltd v International Insurance Co of Hannover Ltd* [2004] Lloyd's Rep. I.R. 606; *Talbot Underwriting v Nausch Hogan & Murray (The Jascon 5)* [2005] EWHC 2359 (Comm), affirmed [2006] Lloyd's Rep. I.R. 531; *Ramco Ltd v Weller Russell & Laws Insurance Brokers Ltd* [2009] Lloyd's Rep. I.R. 27.
[95] *Tomlinson (Hauliers) v Hepburn* [1966] A.C. 451.
[96] *Armitage v Winterbottom* (1840) 1 Man. & G. 130.
[97] *National Oilwell v Davy Offshore* [993] 2 Lloyd's Rep. 582: *O'Kane v Jones* [2005] Lloyd's Rep. I.R. 174.

covered the mortgagor's interest.[98] If an insurer wishes to insure a person such as a carrier with a limited interest to confine their liability to his interest, it should be careful to employ precise words to that effect in the body of the policy.[99]

Undisclosed agency. English law recognises the admittedly anomalous rule that, **4–021** where an agent purports to contract on his own behalf but is in reality acting on behalf of a principal, that principal may at any time during the currency of the agreement assert that he is a party to it and thereafter may sue or be sued under it.[100] The agent himself remains a party to the agreement. The main limitation on this doctrine is that it is not open to an undisclosed principal to claim to be a party to an agreement which the agent had no authority to make.[101]

The application of the undisclosed principal rule to insurance contracts is, nevertheless, subject to three doubts. First, the identity of the assured is of itself a material fact unless it is clear that the named assured is acting as agent for an unidentified third party and the insurers choose not to inquire who the true principal is intended to be, in which case disclosure of the identity of the true assured may be treated as having been waived.[102] Even if the doctrine of undisclosed principal does apply to insurance contracts, the wording of the policy must be such as not to preclude any person other than those named or identified in the policy from deriving benefit under it.[103] A second difficulty is that the statutory rules laying down the insurable interest requirement additionally require the insertion into the policy of the name of the true assured, failing which the insurance is void. The third problem is that where insurable interest is required by law at the inception of the policy, it is arguable that the agent must possess some insurable interest in his own right in order to preserve its initial validity. A contrary argument is that the doctrine of undisclosed agency operates to vest the contract in the principal not from the date at which he asserts his right to be a party to it but from the date at which the agreement was entered into; consequently, the assured/principal's own insurable interest retroactively validates the policy. Which of these approaches is correct largely depends upon ascertaining the proper basis for the doctrine of undisclosed agency, which is still a matter of some debate, but if the latter view is correct it leads to the conclusion that the legality of the policy depends upon whether the undisclosed principal chooses to assert his rights.

---

[98] *Nichols & Co v Scottish Union and National Insurance Co* (1885) 2 T.L.R. 190.

[99] Erle C.J. in *Waters v Monarch Fire & Life Assurance Co* (1856) 5 El. & Bl. 870.

[100] *Keighley Maxsted & Co v Durant* [1901] A.C. 240. See generally *Bowstead on Agency*, pp.312–325.

[101] *Keighley Maxsted & Co v Durant* [1901] A.C. 240.

[102] In *National Oilwell (UK) Ltd v Davy Offshore Ltd* [1993] 2 Lloyd's Rep. 582 Colman J. held that the doctrine of undisclosed principal was applicable to marine insurance, although the contrary appears not to have been argued. The same assumption was made by the Privy Council in *Siu v Eastern Insurance Co Ltd* [1994] 1 All E.R. 213, although that case is explicable by the waiver principle set out in the text. In *Talbot Underwriting v Nausch Hogan & Murray (The Jascon 5)* [2005] EWHC 2359 (Comm) Cooke J. had strong reservations as to the applicability of the undisclosed principal doctrine to insurance contracts by reason of the materiality of the assured's identity. The Court of Appeal on Appeal in *The Jascon 5* [2006] Lloyd's Rep. I.R. 531 did not rule on the point.

[103] This was the ground for the ruling in *The Jascon 5* [2006] Lloyd's Rep. I.R. 531. See also the statement of principle of Lord Lloyd in *Siu v Eastern Insurance Co Ltd* [1994] 1 All E.R. 213: "The terms of the contract may, expressly or by implication, exclude the principal's right to sue, and his liability to be sued. The contract itself, or the circumstances surrounding the contract, may show that the agent is the true and only principal." Cf. *Ferryways NV v Associated British Ports* [2008] EWHC 225 (Comm).

The application of the above principles to the various classes of insurance is thus as follows.

(1) Marine insurance. The Marine Insurance Act 1906 s.23, requires the insertion into a marine policy of the name of the assured "or of some person who effects the insurance on his behalf". This provision clearly permits an agent to insure as agent, but it is uncertain whether it permits him to insure as principal in the course of an undisclosed agency.[104] There is, however, no difficulty with the insurable interest requirement, as an agent insuring on behalf of an undisclosed principal is not wagering contrary to the terms of s.4 of the 1906 Act.

(2) Life insurance. Life policies are governed by Life Assurance Act 1774 s.2 of which renders an insurance unlawful if the names of the persons interested in the policy do not appear on it. Consequently, there is no room for the application of the undisclosed principal rule in this class of insurance, irrespective of the question whether the prohibition on the making of insurance without interest in s.1 of the 1774 Act prohibits an agent without interest entering into an agreement on behalf of an undisclosed principal.

(3) Policies on goods. Assuming that the assured's identity is not a material fact, it would seem that the doctrine of undisclosed principal will operate here. An agent insuring on behalf of the assured is not a gambler within the prohibition in the Gaming Act 1845 s.18, and the Marine Insurance Act 1788, which requires the insertion into a policy of the names of all interested parties, is seemingly satisfied where the name of the agent alone is inserted, although again there is a doubt as to whether this is satisfied where the agent insures as principal and not as agent.

(4) Policies on land and buildings. Such policies fall outside the Life Assurance Act 1774. The Marine Insurance Act 1788 does not apply to policies other than those on goods.

Ratification

4–022 *The availability of ratification.* A principal whose existence has been disclosed may ratify an insurance agreement made on his behalf, but without his authority, by his agent. It is sufficient in marine insurance and in relation to policies on goods and real property that the agent has indicated that he is acting for a principal, and it is not necessary for the agent to go further and name the principal: this is confirmed by the Marine Insurance Act 1906 s.23[105] and by the Marine Insurance Act 1788. Where the 1774 Act is applicable, it would appear that s.2 requires the name of the assured to be inserted, and not just the fact that an assured with interest is the principal.

4–023 *The timing of ratification.* In the general law of agency ratification of a contract by the principal may take place at any time, even after a breach of contract by the

[104] In *National Oilwell (UK) Ltd v Davy Offshore Ltd* [1993] 2 Lloyd's Rep. 582 the court applied the doctrine to a marine policy without considering this point.

[105] The only person who can ratify is, however, the agent's intended principal. See *Boston Fruit Co v British & Foreign Marine Insurance Co Ltd* [1906] A.C. 336, where brokers acting on behalf of owners procured a policy covering all interests in the insured subject matter. It was held by the House of Lords that charterers were not entitled to the benefit of the policy by way of ratification, even though their interest was covered by the wording, as the brokers had not intended to insure on behalf of the charterers. See also *National Oilwell (UK) Ltd v Davy Offshore Ltd* [1993] 2 Lloyd's Rep. 582.

third party, subject to the overriding rule that ratification cannot unfairly prejudice the third party and in particular cannot remove his vested rights. An issue which has arisen in the insurance context is whether ratification is available after a loss has occurred and the assured has become aware of that loss. In marine insurance it is settled that ratification after loss is permissible,[106] a principle which makes perfect sense when it is remembered that the insurer agrees to insure from the date of the policy and not from the date of its ratification. Moreover, the rule is not in principle anomalous, for a claim under a policy is in law equivalent to a cause of action for breach of contract, so that if ratification is available for the latter it ought equally to be available for the former. However, non-marine authority is clear that the marine rule as to ratification is an anomaly and is not to be extended to other classes of insurance[107]; consequently, a non-marine policy made by an agent without his principal's authority cannot be ratified by the principal once he has become aware that a loss has occurred, and possibly after a loss has occurred whether or not he is aware of it. The commercial logic of the non-marine rule has nevertheless been doubted, and it may be that the first instance decisions and obiter statements upon which it is founded would not today be followed.[108]

The rights and liabilities of the agent. Plainly if the agent is authorised by the assured or the assured has ratified the policy, the assured may bring an action upon the policy.[109] Equally, it is an accepted rule of law that an agent may make himself personally liable on a contract and, by the same token, obtain a right to sue under it. There are a number of clear situations where this may occur, for example where the contract is by deed and where the principal is undisclosed. An agent may, perhaps most importantly, become a party to a contract where that situation is to be inferred from the proper construction of the contract. Indeed, the rule would appear to be that the agent will be a party in his own right unless there are clear words indicating that he is contracting merely "as agent" or "for and on behalf of" a principal.[110] This rule applies equally in the insurance context: thus an underwriting agent acting on behalf of a reinsurance pool which enters into retrocession agreements[111] with retrocessionaires on behalf of the pool, and is described in the retrocession agreement as the retrocedant, is a party to the retrocession and may sue under it.[112]

4–024

[106] Marine Insurance Act 1906 s.86, based on *Lucena v Craufurd* (1806) 1 Taunt. 325; *Routh v Thompson* (1811) 3 East 274; *Grant v Hill* (1812) 4 Taunt. 380; *Hagedom v Oliverson* (1814) 2 M. & F. 485; *Watson v Swann* (1862) 11 C.B.N.S. 756; *Williams v North China Insurance Co* (1876) L.R. 1 C.P.D. 757; *Byas v Miller* (1897) 3 Com. Cas. 79; *Boston Fruit Co v British & Foreign Marine Insurance Co* [1906] A.C. 336: *Hansen v Norske Lloyd Insurance Co* (1919) 1 Ll. L. Rep. 66.

[107] *Williams v North China Insurance Co* (1876) L.R. 1 C.P.D. 757: *Grover & Grover Ltd v Matthews* [1910] 2 K.B. 401; *Portavon Cinema Co Ltd v Price* [1939] 4 All E.R. 601.

[108] See the comments of Colman J. in *National Oilwell (UK) Ltd v Davy Offshore Ltd* [1993] 2 Lloyd's Rep. 582.

[109] *Browning v Provincial Insurance* (1873) L.R. 5 P.C. 263 at 272, 273.

[110] *The Swan* [1968] 1 Lloyd's Rep. 5 (where there was some ambiguity); *Gadd v Houghton* (1876) L.R. 1 Ex. D. 357; *Universal Steam Navigation Co v McKelvie* [1923] A.C. 492.

[111] i.e. reinsurance of reinsurance.

[112] *Transcontinental Undewriting Agency v Grand Union Insurance Co Ltd* [1987] 2 Lloyd's Rep. 409. There are, however, severe difficulties with this decision: (a) the use of the word "retrocedant" in respect of the underwriting agent is not conclusive, as it is consistent both with the capacity of the agent and a description of the fact that he was acting as agent for the retrocedant; (b) given that an underwriting agent cannot incur any personal liability under a reinsurance agreement, as it is not an insurer, it is difficult to see exactly what liability it was seeking to retrocede; in short, it had no insurable interest. Moreover, practice does not support the decision. Usually retrocessionaires are regarded as parties to the retrocession for the purpose of suing or being sued under it.

In addition, a rule peculiar to insurance brokers permits a broker to sue for the full amount of the assured's loss irrespective of whether or not the contract is capable of being construed as making the broker a party to it, subject to the broker having to account for the proceeds of the policy to the assured. This rule has its origins in marine insurance[113] but Hirst J. has confirmed that it is applicable to all classes of insurance.[114] It should nevertheless be said that the precise scope of the principle is uncertain, and in *The Moonacre*[115] the High Court refused to allow the shareholder of a one-man company to sue on a policy taken out in his own name on the company's property. The court ruled that the *Transcontinental* principle could not operate as a substitute for insurable interest.

7. Reform of the Law on Insurable Interest

4–025   **The reform process.** As a part of the English and Scottish Law Commissions' reform programme launched in January 2006, the Law Commissions published an issues paper on the future of insurable interest in January 2008. The issues paper makes modest proposals to modify the law.

The Law Commissions recognise two functions of insurable interest: to distinguish insurance from other contracts; and to prevent gambling. On the former point the Law Commissions are of the view that it is possible to develop a definition of insurance which does not refer to insurable interest, and that more significant characteristics include assumption of risk, payment of a premium for risk transfer and the obligations of the parties. On the latter point the Law Commissions felt that it remained necessary to retain insurable interest in life insurance, so as to separate insurance from gambling, but saw no need for insurable interest for non-life insurance.

It should be stressed that the Law Commissions have only at this stage identified the problem areas and put forward provisional suggestions. The consultation process may well produce different final conclusions.

4–026   **Life insurance.** The law relating to life assurance was regarded by the Law Commissions as suffering from three weaknesses: a narrow and restrictive definition of insurable interest; technical requirements affecting the Life Assurance Act 1774; and the rule under the 1774 Act that interest is not required at the date of the death of the life assured. The Law Commissions refused to take the step of abolishing the insurable interest requirement entirely, because: there is an instinctive objection to the possibility that a stranger might hold a life policy; and life insurance should be permitted only where there is a legitimate need to insure. In the light of those considerations the Law Commissions have recommended the following changes in the law:

(1) The definition of insurable interest should be extended so as to recognise natural love and affection, so that insurance should be permitted on the lives of cohabitees, adult children by parents and parents or guardians by

---

[113] *Provincial Insurance Co of Canada v Leduc* (1874) L.R. 6 P.C. 22.
[114] *Transcontinental Underwriting Agency v Grand Union Insurance Co Ltd* [1987] 2 Lloyd's Rep. 409; *Pan Atlantic Insurance Co Ltd v Pine Top Insurance Co Ltd* [1988] 2 Lloyd's Rep. 505.
[115] *Sharp v Sphere Drake Insurance (The Moonacre)* [1992] 2 Lloyd's Rep. 501.

dependants. Less remote relationships—such as parents on infant children, siblings, grandparents/grandchildren—should also be regarded automatically as being supported by insurable interest. Where such interest exists, insurance should be permitted up to an unlimited amount.

(2) The range of pecuniary interests presently recognised by the law as valid insurable interests for the purposes of life policies should be extended to expectation interests, so that the amount of insurance taken out by the assured is not confined to the amount of insurable interest at inception.

(3) Even in the absence of love and affection and pecuniary interest, a life policy should be permitted if the life assured has consented to the taking out of the policy. Consent is not required where insurable interest otherwise exists, but it may be the basis for a policy where there is no insurable interest.

(4) The sanction for taking out a policy without interest should not be illegality, but instead the policy should simply be void.

(5) The requirement in Life Assurance Act 1774 s.2 that the name or names of persons interested in the policy must be inserted into it, should be repealed.

Various issues have yet to be resolved. These include whether life insurers should be under a duty to check whether the proposer has insurable interest and whether a life policy should lapse on the termination of the policyholder's insurable interest, as where the assured debtor repays his debt or where the assured employee resigns.

Indemnity insurance. The Law Commissions have been somewhat bolder in this context. Following the Australian example, the Law Commissions have concluded that there is no reason to demand insurable interest at the date the policy is taken out and that there is sufficient protection against gambling and potential deliberate destruction by requiring the assured to prove its loss at the date of the occurrence of the insured peril, i.e. the common law indemnity principle. It may be that this recommendation simply reflects the position reached—possibly unintentionally—by the passing of the Gambling Act 2005. The Law Commissions are consulting on the further question of whether insurers should be under a duty to check whether a proposer does in fact possess an insurable interest. **4–027**

Two further recommendations relating to marine insurance are: (a) the abolition of the redundant Marine Insurance (Gambling Policies) Act 1909 and thereby the sanction of criminality; and (b) the requirement for the names of all interested parties to be inserted into the policy.

CHAPTER 5

THE RISK

1. COMMENCEMENT AND DURATION OF RISK

Commencement of cover

5–001 *Date of contract and inception of risk.* There is a distinction between the date at which a contract of insurance comes into being and the date at which the risk attaches, for these will frequently not coincide. It is perfectly possible for the insurer to agree that the risk is to commence from the date of agreement, and indeed policies which are not issued until some time after the date of the agreement may be backdated—possibly subject to the payment of the premium—to that date. In the absence of any contrary policy provision, it would seem to be the case that the completion of the offer and acceptance fixes the date of the contract and, therefore, the commencement of the risk. More usually, however, the insurer will come on risk at some time after a binding agreement for insurance has been entered into by the parties. The inception of the risk may be postponed in a number of ways by policy provisions, the most important of which are these:

(1) The insurer is not to be liable until the premium has been paid, or paid and accepted. In this type of case it must be determined whether, once the premium has been paid, the insurer's liability commences from the date of payment or is backdated to the date of the agreement.

(2) The insurer is not to be liable until a policy has been issued. Once again, the policy must be construed to determine whether the insurer's liability commences from the date of the issue of the policy or whether it is deemed to have started when the agreement to insure was originally made.

(3) The insurer is not to be liable until both the premium has been paid and the policy issued.

(4) The insurer's liability is to commence on a specified day or at a specified time. This may be a date before the issue of a policy or even before the date of the agreement, e.g. the date of the commencement of earlier temporary cover.[1]

(5) In the case of a policy on goods in transit, or a marine voyage policy, the risk may commence as soon as the goods are in transit or the voyage has commenced.

(6) The risk may run from the date of a particular triggering event during the currency of the policy, e.g. in the case of insurance of the risk under a

---

[1] *Motor and General Insurance Co v Cox* [1990] 1 W.L.R. 1443.

guarantee of work performed, the date on which the guarantee took effect by the completion of the work during the currency of the policy.[2]

Where the insurer's liability is backdated to a period prior to the issue of a policy, it is a nice question whether the terms of the policy subsequently issued bind the assured in the event of a loss in that period. Authority for the proposition that the assured is not bound by, for example, notification provisions of which he was not aware, is to be found in the decision of the Court of Appeal in *Re Coleman's Depositories Ltd and Life and Health Assurance Association*,[3] although it would seem that this case is out of line with ordinary principles of incorporation by reference.

Conditions preventing the attachment of the risk. The policy itself or the general law may impose additional limits on the attachment of the risk. The most important conditions which have this effect are as follows: **5–002**

(1) The assured has warranted that particular circumstances relating to the insured subject matter are or are not in operation when the policy is to come into being. If the assured's statement is untrue, he is in breach of warranty and the risk will not attach.
(2) The assured may have described the subject matter to be insured. If the subject matter does not meet that description in a manner which renders the liability to be faced by the insurer different from that which was originally agreed, the risk will not attach.[4]
(3) The policy may provide that the risk is not to attach if the assured has taken out any similar policy on the same subject matter with any other insurer.
(4) In the case of marine voyage policies, failure by the assured to ensure that the voyage starts from the right place or at the right time will prevent the risk from attaching.[5]

Time and voyage policies. Most policies are stated to run between given dates, although others may last for the duration of a particular project. The latter class is typified by marine voyage policies which last for period of a named voyage, although "transit" policies are now often issued against accidents to persons whilst they are travelling from one place to another, or on goods whilst they are being sent from one place to another by land, sea or air. Goods in transit policies and marine policies may be expressed in terms of the voyage itself rather than any fixed time period.[6] **5–003**

Duration of time policies. Disregarding for present purposes the special cases of marine voyage policies and goods in transit policies, most insurance policies are **5–004**

---

[2] See *Heesens Yacht Builders BV v Cox Syndicate Management Ltd (The Red Sapphire)* [2006] Lloyd's Rep. I.R. 103, reversed on appeal, [2006] Lloyd's Rep. I.R. 476 on the ground that the guarantee risk was an endorsement to a policy covering construction risks on vessels work on which had commenced during the currency of the policy and the endorsement similarly was triggered by the commencement of work and not by the date of delivery.

[3] *Re Coleman's Depositories Ltd and Life and Health Assurance Association* [1907] 2 K.B. 798.

[4] *Newcastle Fire Insurance Co v Macmorran & Co* (1815) 3 Dow. 255 is a representative authority.

[5] Under s.59 of the Marine Insurance Act 1906 a transhipment does not operate to discharge the liability of the insurer,

[6] See s.25 of the Marine Insurance Act 1906, discussed in Ch.24, below.

stated to commence at or on a given day, date or time, and are stated to expire at the end of a fixed period or at a given day, date or time. The precise commencement and termination dates are thus a matter of contract,[7] although the courts have laid down a number of presumptions to deal with the use of ambiguous language.

The main issue which has fallen to be resolved is whether a policy which runs between stated dates is inclusive or exclusive of those dates. On occasion this is made clear by the parties, by stating that the risk runs from date A to date B, both dates inclusive,[8] but it is more common to find a policy expressed as running "from date A to date B". The presumption adopted by the courts in this situation is that date B,[9] but not date A,[10] is covered, as the use of the word "from" implies an exclusion of the earlier date.[11] The rule may produce surprising results where a policy is expressed to run from a particular time, as is generally the case with motor policies. In *Cartwright v McCormack*[12] a motor cover note was expressed to commence at 11.45am on December 2, and was to be effective for 15 days "from the commencement of the risk". An accident occurred at 5.45pm on December 17, and it was held by the Court of Appeal that the cover note had remained in force on that day. In accordance with the presumption that the first stated day is excluded, the first day calculating the running of the 15 days was December 3, so that the accident occurred on the 15th day. A policy which commences "after" a named day clearly excludes that day,[13] and a policy which is taken out and which commences on the same day will not—unless otherwise stated—start before the actual time at which it was issued.[14]

Different considerations will apply where other wording is used. Thus, in the case of a policy the cover under which is expressed to last for a period "beginning with" a given day, the first day will be included.[15] Again, where a policy is stated to run from one day to another,[16] or from the occurrence of a specified event, that event marks the commencement of the cover. This was held to be the case in *Cornfoot v Royal Exchange Assurance Co*,[17] in which marine cover was to run for 30 days from the arrival of the vessel in port; the wording was construed as meaning that the insurer was on risk for 30 consecutive periods of 24 hours commencing from 11.30am, the precise time at which the vessel arrived in port, so that a loss at 5.30pm on the 30th day was not covered. In *Heinrich Hirdes GmbH v Edmunds (The Kiel)*.[18] A vessel was insured under a time policy "at and from 16 June 1980 to 15 June 1981, both days inclusive". The cover was then renewed for "12 months at June 16 1981", and a further

---

[7] A. L. Smith L.J. in *Re North* [1895] 2 Q.B. 264 at 272.

[8] As in *Hough v Head* (1855) 55 L.J.Q.B. 43.

[9] Terms of years are generally construed as including the last day: *Pugh v Leeds* (1777) 2 Cowp. 714; *Ackland v Lutley* (1839) 9 Ad. & El. 879.

[10] *Watson v Pears* (1809) 2 Camp. 294; *Webb v Fairmaner* (1838) 3 M. & W. 473; *Bellhouse v Mellow* (1859) 4 H. & N. 116.

[11] *Isaacs v Royal Insurance Co* (1870) L.R. 5 Ex. 296; *Johnson & Co v Bryant* (1896) 1 Com. Cas. 363; *South Staffordshire Tramway Co v Sickness and Accident Assurance Association* (1891) 1 Q.B. 402. Contrast *Scottish Metropolitan Assurance Co v Stewart* (1923) 15 Ll. L.R. 55, where the word "from" was held to be inclusive.

[12] *Cartwright v McCormack* [1963] 1 All E.R. 11.

[13] *Lester v Garland* (1808) 15 Ves. 248.

[14] *Smith v Alexander* [1965] 1 Lloyd's Rep. 283.

[15] For analogies see: *Hare v Gocher* [1962] 2 Q.B. 641 (commencement of statute); *Trow v Ind Coope* [1967] 2 Q.B. 899 (validity of claim form).

[16] Rowlatt J. in *Scottish Metropolitan Assurance v Stewart* (1923) 39 T.L.R. 407 at 409.

[17] *Cornfoot v Royal Exchange Assurance Co* [1904] 1 K.B. 40.

[18] *Heinrich Hirdes GmbH v Edmunds (The Kiel)* [1991] 2 Lloyd's Rep. 546.

extension was granted "for a period of one month . . . until 16 July 1982". Underwriters were held liable for a loss which had occurred on July 16, 1982. On the face of things that day was included, in accordance with general principle, and the fact that it was arguable that the second annual policy had terminated at midnight on June 15, 1982, giving a final period of insurance for a month and a day, was not sufficient to oust the general rule that the last mentioned days is covered. This case indicates that the *contra proferentem* principle works strongly in the assured's favour in questions of duration and that the court will strive wherever possible to construe a policy as providing continuous coverage,[19] although it cannot be said there is a presumption to this effect.[20]

Unless a contrary intention appears "month" means calendar month.[21]

Termination of the risk

General rules as to duration. Where non-life insurance is concerned, the policy will come to an end at the time stated in it or on the occurrence of a stated event.[22] The assured will rarely be entitled to renew a non-life policy, although he will have the right to submit an offer for renewal by a tender of the renewal premium; where the insurer has sent a renewal notice to the assured,[23] it is at least arguable that the notice is an offer capable of acceptance by the submission of the premium, but there is no case which holds that the insurer must send a renewal notice to the assured. It is of course open to an insurer to frame a non-life policy in such terms that it is to last for a fixed period, subject to the assured paying premiums in accordance with the intervals demanded by the policy. This type of arrangement is in common use in the construction industry. In the absence of clear wording, however, the insurer is not obliged to offer or to accept renewal even where the consequences of failure to renew place the assured in severe difficulties, as in the case of a construction policy where the building work overruns but the insurers refuse to extend cover beyond the originally agreed period.[24] The assured must, therefore, either obtain a policy which confers upon him a right of renewal or ensure that the duration agreed is suitable for his purposes.

By contrast, in the case of life assurance the policy is regarded as perpetual subject to the assured tendering the premium when it falls due: thus an insurer cannot refuse to renew a life policy, as the assured's tender of the premium is not the offer of a new contract but is rather the exercise of a contractual right to keep the policy on foot.[25] For this reason, a loss occurring in the "days of grace",

5–005

---

[19] *Eurodale Manufacturing Ltd v Ecclesiastical Insurance Office Plc* [2003] Lloyd's Rep. I.R. 440.

[20] In *The Kiel* the underwriters, in support of their contention that the one-month endorsement commenced on June 16, 1982, argued that there was a presumption of continuity of cover. Thus, if the second annual policy lasted for a year and terminated on June 15, 1992, it had to be supposed that the parties intended the extension to begin immediately on the termination of the second annual policy, i.e. on June 16, 1982. Hirst J. refused to accept the existence of any such presumption. Cf. *Sickness & Accident v General Accident* (1892) 19 R. (Ct of Sess) 977.

[21] Law of Property Act 1925 s.61(a).

[22] e.g. in a goods policy, when the goods are delivered to the purchaser: *Phoenix Dynamo Manufacturing Co v Mountain* (1925) 6 Ll. L.R. 369.

[23] He is not obliged to do so, however: *Simpson v Accidental Death Insurance Co* (1857) 2 C.B.N.S. 257. Quaere whether this rule has been sidestepped by the notion that the insurer owes a continuing duty of utmost good faith, as adopted in *The Good Luck* [1989] 2 Lloyd's Rep. 238. It is now at least arguable that the insurer is under a duty to disclose to the assured that the policy is about to come to an end.

[24] *Jones Construction Co v Alliance Assurance Co* [1961] 1 Lloyd's Rep. 121.

[25] *Stuart v Freeman* [1903] 1 K.B. 47.

pending payment of the premium, will be covered under a life policy but not under any other policy.

5–006   *The effect of giving notice to terminate.* The date from which a notice to terminate takes effect will depend upon the wording of the policy and the construction of the words used in the notice of cancellation. The general principle is that a notice of termination cannot take effect until it has been received, so that a loss which occurs between the sending of a notice of cancellation and its receipt will be covered. It has also been held that a cancellation, once received, is only effective at the end of that day, so that the insurers remain on risk until the end of the day on which they receive notice of cancellation.[26] In *Nuvo Electronics Inc v London Assurance*[27] the assured obtained an open cover which was terminable on 30 days written notice to be sent by post to the broker, and without prejudice to risks which had attached at the date of the notice. On July 10, 1996 the insurers faxed a notice to the broker giving 30 days' notice of cancellation effective on August 10, 1996. The assured sent a cargo of goods by air from San Francisco to Toronto on August 10, 1996, and it was subsequently lost. The court held that the loss was covered: the notice of cancellation had not been sent by post; and it had not identified the time of day at which the notice was to take effect. The court's view was that, in the absence of clear words to the contrary, the notice only came into effect at the end of the day which it had identified, so that it had remained in force throughout August 10, 1996 and terminated only at midnight on that day

5–007   *The validity of early termination clauses.* Many forms of policy confer upon the insurer an absolute right—exercisable for any or no reason—to terminate the policy on notice. Such clauses are valid at common law even though they may defeat the assured's expectations, as where insurers purport to cancel where there has been an increased risk of loss to the assured.[28] These clauses are widely used, although they may in consumer contracts, fall foul of the Unfair Terms in Consumer Contracts Regulations 1999.[29]

5–008   *Automatic contractual extension or renewal.* Some policies make provision for automatic extension of the cover where the risk insured against continues to run beyond the duration of the policy, subject to the payment by the assured of an agreed or pro rata premium. The marine insurance "held covered" clause is the clearest illustration of automatic extension. Provisions for the automatic renewal of cover are perhaps less common. In this situation, the insurer normally reserves some right to cancel, and states that the assured is entitled to automatic renewal unless a positive decision to cancel is taken. In *Commercial Union Assurance Co Plc v Sun Alliance Insurance Group Plc*,[30] reinsurance cover was expressed to be for 12 months "with 120 days NCAD". Evidence demonstrated that "NCAD" is an abbreviation for "notice of cancellation at anniversary date". Steyn J., rejecting the reinsurer's contention that the phrase was meaningless, upheld the reinsured's argument that "NCAD" meant that the reinsurance agreement was to

---

[26] *Larizza v Commercial Union Assurance Co* 68 D.L.R. (4th) 460 (1990).

[27] *Nuvo Electronics Inc v London Assurance* (2000) 49 OR (3d).

[28] *Sun Fire Office v Hart* (1889) 14 App. Cas. 98 (fire policy cancelled following threats of arson).

[29] SI 1999/2083.

[30] *Commercial Union Assurance Co Plc v Sun Alliance Insurance Group Plc* [1992] 1 Lloyd's Rep. 475.

be treated as automatically renewed unless 120 days" notice of termination had been given by the reinsurer. However, later authorities have taken the view that NCAD does operate as notice of termination at the next renewal date,[31] so that if the assured makes disclosure to the insurers in the NCAD period and the risk is found to be unsatisfactory, the insurers, the clause does not have the effect of requiring the insurers to renew and to maintain cover until the period of insurance has come to an end: instead, the agreement is treated as cancelled if agreement cannot be reached.[32]

Goods in transit policies

Problems raised by goods in transit policies. Transit policies are used in respect of the overland carriage of goods. Transit policies may be taken out by the owner of goods or by a carrier as bailee.[33] In these cases the risk begins when the journey or the transit begins[34] and it ends when the destination is reached, unless the policy otherwise provides. Transit risks may also be covered by floating[35] or declaration[36] time policies on goods, but the same principles apply to any particular transit of any particular goods, so far as the extent of transit risks is in issue. Ascertaining the duration of such policies is not, however, free from difficulty, and three questions arise in their interpretation: (1) when does the transit commence; (2) what are the duties of the assured during the course of transit; and (3) how long does transit last?

5–009

Commencement of transit. There is some uncertainty as to whether goods are "in transit" before they have been loaded. It has been held that goods awaiting loading are in transit, on the principle that "When you take a parcel to the post office or to a railway station and you hand it over and get a receipt, the goods are in transit from the moment the post office or the railway takes them",[37] although it has also been said that "Transit has in its nature the element of carriage and the carriage starts . . . when the goods are placed on the vehicle".[38] The Lloyd's standard form for this class of insurance provides indemnity against the assured's "legal liability as a carrier under the [Geneva Convention of 1956] for loss of or damage to goods whilst in transit per insured's vehicle". The Carriage of Goods by Road Act 1965, which was passed to bring English law into line with the Convention, provides that the carrier is liable "between the time when he takes over the goods" and delivery. Thus, in those cases to which the Carriage of Goods by Road Act 1965 applies,[39] it is clear that the transit must be considered to begin when the carrier takes over the goods. This will happen when the carrier receives the goods against a consignment note.[40]

5–010

---

[31] *Kingscroft Insurance Co v Nissan Fire and Marine Insurance Co Ltd (No.2)* [1999] Lloyd's Rep. I.R. 603; *Scottish Coal Co Ltd v Royal and Sun Alliance Plc* [2008] EWHC 880 (Comm).

[32] *Scottish Coal Co Ltd v Royal and Sun Alliance Plc* [2008] EWHC 880 (Comm).

[33] See Ch.4, above.

[34] *Halhead v Young* (1856) 6 E. & B. 312, per Lord Campbell C.J. at 324.

[35] See, e.g. *Tomlinson v Hepburn* [1966] A.C. 451 HL; *Sadler Bros Co v Meredith* [1963] 2 Lloyd's Rep. 293.

[36] See, e.g. *Bartlett & Partners v Meller* [1961] 1 Lloyd's Rep. 487.

[37] *Crow's Transport v Phoenix Assurance Co* [1965] 1 W.L.R. 383 at 388.

[38] *Sadler Bros & Co v Meredith* [1963] 2 Lloyd's Rep. 293 at 307. Ackner J. noted the conflict of views, in *SCA (Freight) v Gibson* [1974] 2 Lloyd's Rep. 533, but did not need to decide between them as the goods in question had already been loaded.

[39] The Convention on the Contract for the International Carriage of Goods by Road (CMR) applies where the place for the taking over of the goods and the place designated for delivery are in two different countries of which at least one is a contracting state: art.1(1).

[40] Carriage of Goods by Road Act 1965.

Other forms of policy may cover the goods as soon as they are held "in trust" by the assured. This phrase does not bear its technical meaning and refers simply to the fact that the assured has taken possession of the goods.[41]

The assured is deemed to take possession of goods as soon as they are received by a person authorised by the assured in this regard. It is irrelevant that the agent has a fraudulent intention at that date: this was held to be the case in *John Rigby (Haulage) Ltd v Reliance Marine Insurance Co Ltd*,[42] where the insurer was on risk following receipt by an agent. Some policies may seek to overcome this rule by requiring that the transit commences only when the goods are received by a genuine agent. In *London Tobacco (Overseas) Ltd v DFDS Transport Ltd and Sun Alliance and London Insurance Plc*[43] a goods in transit policy excluded "theft by bogus subcontractor". The goods were delivered to an authorised subcontractor who had the intention from the outset of absconding with the goods, which indeed occurred. The Court of Appeal ruled that the subcontractor may have been dishonest, but he was not "bogus" in that he was a genuine subcontractor. On this reasoning the exclusion did not apply and the insurers were liable.

5–011 *What is "transit"?* Once the transit has commenced, the usual form of cover protects the goods during 'the normal course of transit'. The transit referred to here is the moving of goods from one place to another, although the general rule is that transit is deemed to continue while the vehicle in which the goods are being carried is parked. In *Sadler v Meredith*[44] Roskill J. held that, in the policy concerned, "transit" meant the passage or carriage of goods from one place to another goods were still "in transit" when a van (which was stolen) was temporarily parked. The only relevant words in the policy were "in transit": this, therefore, is a key decision. The policy will also cover the goods during temporary storage in the course of transit,[45] although there are likely to be stated minimum security requirements. The policy may require the goods to be garaged,[46] in a warehouse[47] or in storage,[48] although a clause of this type is ineffective if it requires the assured to drive the vehicle at times or for periods not permitted by the general law.[49]

The policy may also require the goods to be carried in lorries hired by the assured or contractors or subcontractors, in which case the policy will nevertheless apply even though the goods misappropriated by a subcontractor who had obtained possession of the lorries under a hiring agreement voidable for fraud.[50]

---

[41] *John Rigby (Haulage) Ltd v Reliance Marine Insurance Co Ltd* [1956] 2 Q.B. 468.

[42] *John Rigby (Haulage) Ltd v Reliance Marine Insurance Co Ltd* [1956] 2 Q.B. 468.

[43] *London Tobacco (Overseas) Ltd v DFDS Transport Ltd and Sun Alliance and London Insurance Plc* [1994] 1 Lloyd's Rep. 394.

[44] *Sadler v Meredith* [1963] 2 Lloyd's Rep. 293.

[45] *Eurodale Manufacturing Ltd v Ecclesiastical Insurance Office Plc* [2003] Lloyd's Rep. I.R. 440.

[46] *Barnett & Block v National Parcels Insurance Co Ltd* (1942) 73 Ll. L.R. 17 (enclosed yard with high walls but no roof is not a garage).

[47] *Leo Rapp Ltd v McClure* [1955] 1 K.B. 292 (enclosed yard not a warehouse); *Firmin & Collins Ltd v Allied Shippers Ltd* [1967] Lloyd's Rep. 633 (railway arch not a public warehouse).

[48] *Wulfson v Switzerland General Insurance Co* (1940) 67 Ll. L.R. 190 (goods in yard and covered with tarpaulins are in store).

[49] *Lowenstein & Co Ltd v Poplar Motor Transport (Lymm) Ltd* [1968] 2 Lloyd's Rep. 233.

[50] *Metal Scrap & By-Products Ltd v Federated Conveyors Ltd* [1953] 1 Lloyds Rep. 221.

Goods "left unattended". It is common for policies to require the assured to take **5-012** care of the subject matter during the course of transit, and the assured may be required to warrant that there are adequate security measures in operation.[51] Perhaps the most important provision contained in goods in transit policies is the exception for loss while the goods are "left unattended". This phrase has resulted in a number of borderline decisions. In *Starfire Diamond Rings v Angel*[52] the driver positioned himself 37 yards away from his vehicle, with his back to it, in order to answer a call of nature. The Court of Appeal held on these facts that the vehicle had been left unattended, as it could not be said to have been attended during the driver's absence. All three judges of the Court of Appeal were in agreement that the expression "left unattended" was not "susceptible of any prolonged exegesis".[53] This case was followed in *Ingleton Ltd v General Accident Fire and Life Assurance Corp*,[54] in which the driver left his vehicle outside a customer's premises for 15 minutes while he made a delivery: the fact that he could see the vehicle, but was unable to prevent any rapid theft from it, led Phillimore J. to conclude that it had been left unattended.

By contrast, in *Plaistow Transport Ltd v Graham*[55] the relevant clause in the policy read: "Warranted Vehicles garaged in locked garage at night except when employed in night journeys but then never unattended". The driver was asleep in his lorry in a lay-by on a night journey when, during the journey, goods were stolen from the vehicle. Nield J. held that the lorry was not unattended. Again, in *Langford v Legal and General Assurance Society*,[56] the assured left her car outside her house for a few seconds, in a position where it was not visible from the house; the car was here held not to have been left unattended. The same conclusion was reached in *O'Donoghue v Harding*.[57] Here the assured's salesman had left a case containing jewellery locked in his car for a few moments while he was paying for petrol: he had parked at the petrol pump closest to the garage, and most of the car was visible to him except for a few seconds during which he was signing a credit card slip. Otton J. held that the theft from the car had been carefully planned, and it could not be said that the car had been left unattended. *O'Donoghue* was distinguished by Longmore J. in *Sanger v Beazley*,[58] in which the assured's car was similarly broken into at a service station while he was in the lavatory. The assured in *Sanger* had not been able to see his car and thus to observe any attempt to interfere with it, and there was in any event another car which obscured his line of vision. The effect of this decision is that if a driver does leave his car for any reason, any failure to maintain reasonable observation of it will result in it being regarded as "left unattended".

A related security clause removes the insurer's liability where the vehicle is stolen at a time at which the keys have "been left" in or on the vehicle. If keys

---

[51] See, e.g. *Princette Models Ltd v Reliance Fire and Accident Insurance Corp* [1960] 1 Lloyd's Rep. 49 (duty not breached where driver's cab left unlocked, as there was no access to the back of the vehicle through the cab).

[52] *Starfire Diamond Rings v Angel* [1962] 2 Lloyd's Rep. 217.

[53] *Starfire Diamond Rings v Angel* [1962] 2 Lloyd's Rep. 217 at 220, per Diplock L.J.

[54] *Ingleton Ltd v General Accident Fire and Life Assurance Corp* [1967] 2 Lloyd's Rep. 179. See also: *Lowenstein v Poplar Motor Transport* [1968] 2 Lloyd's Rep. 233; *Cohen v Plaistow Transport* [1968] 2 Lloyd's Rep. 587.

[55] *Plaistow Transport Ltd v Graham* [1966] 1 Lloyd's Rep. 639.

[56] *Langford v Legal and General Assurance Society* [1986] 2 Lloyd's Rep. 103.

[57] [1988] 2 Lloyd's Rep. 281. See also *Stern v Norwich Union Fire Insurance Society* Unreported, 1996 (ring treated as being worn if not physically on the assured's finger but within the assured's sight and reach).

[58] *Sanger v Beazley* [1999] Lloyd's Rep. I.R. 424.

are left in the vehicle, it is irrelevant that the vehicle has not been left unattended: the question is whether the assured has moved away from the keys.[59]

5–013 *Deviation.* Unless there is a stated route for the transit, it is open to the assured to take any reasonable route, including legitimate stops along the way. What is not permitted, however, is deviation from the agreed risk, as where the vehicle carrying the goods is taken on a joy ride.[60] The use of the word "deviation", suggesting as it does an analogy with s.46 of the Marine Insurance Act 1906[61] is, however, dangerous in this context, since any marine deviation wholly discharges the insurers from liability as from the time of deviation. There is no obvious basis, for importing this doctrine into the law of transit insurance generally. A departure from the route on a frolic is not part of the transit, but that does not mean that the assured cannot resume the transit and remain insured, in the absence of an express provision in the policy to that effect.

5–014 *Termination of transit.* The date at which the transit comes to an end is a matter for the policy itself. In general, the risk under a transit policy determines contemporaneously with the termination of the transit. However, there are a number of possible points at which a transit may determine; the duration of the risk will depend upon which is selected by the parties. When the transit ends is, theoretically, a difficult problem. Suppose the insurance were to cover "goods in transit" and nothing more: there is no authority to determine, for instance, whether transit would end on the arrival of a land vehicle at the *terminus ad quem* or on the completion of unloading of the goods. This problem has arisen for centuries in the context of marine voyage policies, although the matter is now governed by express wording, typically the "warehouse to warehouse".[62] Terrestrial policies usually give a similar guide and may extend to the time at which unloading is complete.[63] Lloyd's Goods in Transit Policy and Lloyd's Goods in Transit (CMR) Policy both by different drafting methods afford transit cover "to any address" (within a territorial limit) and "in transit" is provided to include "unloading . . . and unpacking". Some policies may require the goods to be deposited at their final destination, whereas others talk of the goods being "finally disposed of" by the assured. In the latter case, safe delivery to the warehouse of destination will terminate the transit.[64] In *Phoenix Dynamo Manufacturing Co v Mountain*[65] a policy covered a flying boat in transit by road until the point at which it was handed over to the Air Ministry. It was held that the transit had not terminated even though it had been examined and passed by the Air Ministry and then dismantled for transportation, as there had been no final delivery.

A policy covering risks during conveyance by land does not cover risks arising after goods have been put in barges for conveyance by inland waterways.[66]

5–015 **Time of loss.** In determining whether the a claim for a loss falls within the time limits specified by the policy, it is necessary to define exactly what the policy covers. The guiding principle is that the insured event must occur during the

---

[59] *Hayward v Norwich Union Insurance Ltd* [2001] Lloyd's Rep. I.R. 410.
[60] *SCA Freight v Gibson* [1974] 2 Lloyd's Rep. 533.
[61] See Ch.24, below.
[62] See Ch.24, below.
[63] *Tomlinson v Hepburn* [1966] A.C. 451.
[64] *Bartlett & Partners v Meller* [1961] 1 Lloyd's Rep. 487.
[65] *Phoenix Dynamo Manufacturing Co v Mountain* (1921) 6 Ll. L.R. 369.
[66] *Ewing v Sicklemore* (1918) 35 T.L.R. 55.

currency of the policy, even though it is not possible to quantify the loss until some later date and even though the fact that the peril has occurred is not apparent at the time. The key issue, therefore, is identifying the insured peril.

In the case of liability insurance, the policy may provide an indemnity on a "claims made" basis, an events basis or on an injury basis. In the first case the insurer is liable only for those claims made by or against the assured during the currency of the policy, so that if the assured has been negligent in year 1 and a claim has been made against him in year 2, the insurer in year 1 is not liable whereas the insurer in year 2 will be required to provide an indemnity.[67] In the case of an events-based liability policy, the assured's negligence in year 1 will be regarded as the event giving rise to the insurer's liability, so that the insurer in year 1 will be required to indemnify the assured irrespective of the fact that no claim is made on the assured until year 2.[68] In the case of an injury liability policy, the year in which the injury is suffered is the relevant policy year, even though the incident giving rise to injury (e.g. exposure to a harmful substance) may have occurred in an earlier year.[69] There may be other triggers of liability under a liability policy. Thus in the case of insurance against liability under the Workmen's Compensation Acts where it was the time of the certified disablement that fixed the employer's liability, it was that date that had to fall within the period covered if the insurers were to be liable.[70]

In fidelity insurance it is the date of the misappropriation, not its discovery that must fall within the term of the policy,[71] unless the policy otherwise provides.[72]

So far as property policies are concerned, the normal presumption is that the trigger of the insurer's liability is the occurrence of an insured peril even though it is not apparent at the time that the assured has suffered a loss.[73] Thus, where the owner of a vessel insures against loss from latent defect, he is not covered where an old defect is merely discovered during the term of the policy.[74] Again, where a vessel is seized during the currency of a policy the underwriters are not relieved from liability because it has not been condemned by a Prize Court during that period, although the loss cannot be assessed until it is so condemned.[75] The loss must actually have occurred, a point illustrated by cases such as *Moore v Evans*,[76] in which jewels were in enemy territory but not yet seized during the

---

[67] Although year 1 insurers may be liable if the policy confers upon the assured the right to notify circumstances which may give rise to a claim, and if he does so the claim is deemed to have been made in the year of notification.

[68] *Durham v BAI (Run Off)* [2009] Lloyd's Rep. I.R. 295.

[69] *Bolton Metropolitan Borough Council v Municipal Mutual Insurance* [2006] EWCA Civ 50.

[70] *Ellerbeck Collieries v Cornhill Insurance* [1932] 1 K.B. 401.

[71] *Allis Chalmers v Fidelity Deposit* (1916) 32 T.L.R. 263; *Ward v Law Property* (1856) 4 W.R. 605; *Pennsylvania Insurance v Mumford* [1920] 2 K.B. 537.

[72] *La Positiva v Jessel* Unreported, September 6, 2001.

[73] *Knight v Faith* (1850) 15 Q.B. 649; *Lidgett v Secretan* (1870) L.R. 5 C.P 190; *Anderson v Martin* [1908] A.C. 334; *Wasa International Insurance Co Ltd v Lexington Insurance Co* [2009] Lloyd's Rep. I.R. 675. See also *Hough v Head* (1885) 55 L.J.Q.B. 43, in which an insurance of freight, in which the ship met with an accident during the period of the insurance but this was not discovered until after its termination: it was held that the loss was not covered by the policy. However, that was because freight had been paid throughout the policy term, and there had, therefore, been no loss of freight during that time.

[74] *Oceanic v Faber* (1907) 23 T.L.R. 673. There is generally no cover under a marine policy merely because a latent defect has become patent, as some independent damage is required: *Promet Engineering v Sturge (The Nukila)* [1997] 2 Lloyd's Rep. 146.

[75] Lord Loreburn in *Andersen v Marten* [1908] A.C. 334 at 339.

[76] *Moore v Evans* [1918] A.C. 185. See also *Masefield AG v Amlin Corporate Member Ltd* [2010] EWHC 280 (Comm).

currency of the policy. Even if such goods are taken into enemy territory under pressure of the enemy's government, there will be no loss during the currency of the policy unless the goods are actually requisitioned during that period.[77]

The general principle, that the insurer's liability under a property policy is based on the time of the occurrence of the peril and not on the time at which damage becomes apparent, can be altered by express wording, although the modern tendency of the courts is to construe policies in accordance with this principle. In *Kelly v Norwich Union Fire and Life Insurance Ltd*[78] the assured's householders' policy covered him for loss arising from any "events" occurring between October 1977 and October 1981." Prior to October 1977 the assured's premises had suffered a burst pipe and a further burst occurred in 1980. Cracks appeared in the house early in 1981 and these were attributed to water damage. It was not clear, however, which of the bursts had led to the cracking. The assured argued that the insured "event" was the cracking, which had occurred during the currency of the policy. The insurer's counter-argument was that the "event" was the accident giving rise to the loss, i.e. the bursting of pipes, and that the assured could not recover as he had not proved that the burst giving rise to the loss had occurred during the currency of the policy. The Court of Appeal preferred the insurer's construction of the word "event". The policy may, however, specifically look to damage and not to the event. In *Martini Investments v McGinn*[79] it was held that the obligation on the insurers to cover the assured against "loss or damage sustained" during the currency of the policy meant precisely what it said, and that it was necessary to look at the date of damage. If the policy covers damage sustained, and damage to property has occurred over a lengthy period, it is necessary to allocate the damage as between the insurers on risk over that period.[80]

It may not always be possible to determine the date on which a loss has occurred. In *Municipal Mutual Insurance Ltd v Sea Insurance Ltd*[81] a liability policy was in force for a period of three years, and in that period there were numerous instances of pilferage for which the assured was liable but which could not be dated. The Court of Appeal held that it was appropriate to allocate the losses proportionately across the period covered by the policy. The allocation was significant for reinsurance purposes, as the reinsurance was in force for the latter half of the first year, the full second year, and earlier half of the third year.

Although it is now established that the trigger of an insurer's liability under a property policy insuring against events is not the manifestation of physical damage but rather the occurrence of the peril which gave rise to that physical damage,[82] the actual result in *Kelly v Norwich Union* turned upon the fact that the peril which had given rise to the loss could not be ascertained. It may be queried whether the decisions of the House of Lords in *Fairchild v Glenhaven Funeral*

---

[77] *Fooks v Smith* [1924] 2 K.B. 508.

[78] *Kelly v Norwich Union Fire and Life Insurance Ltd* [1989] 2 All E.R. 888. Cf. *Sexton v Mountain* (1919) 1 Ll. L.R. 507 and *Re Thames Steel Construction Ltd and Northern Assurance Co* 55 D.L.R. (4th) 639 (1988); but contrast *Annear & Co v Attenborough* (1940) 68 Ll. L.R. 147.

[79] *Martini Investments v McGinn* [2001] Lloyd's Rep. I.R. 374.

[80] This principle, established by *Knight v Faith*, was confirmed by the House of Lords in *WASA International Insurance Co Ltd v Lexington Insurance Co*, in which the House of Lords held that a property policy covered loss caused during the period of cover and not damage which was discovered during the period of cover resulting from earlier perils, and cf. *Loyaltrend Ltd v Creechurch Dedicated Ltd* [2010] EWHC 425 (Comm).

[81] *Municipal Mutual Insurance Ltd v Sea Insurance Ltd* [1998] Lloyd's Rep. I.R. 421.

[82] This is consistent with tort law generally: *Pirelli General Cable Works Ltd v Oscar Faber & Partners* [1983] 2 A.C. 1.

Services Ltd[83] and *Barker v Corus UK Plc*[84] have any impact on this outcome. *Fairchild* establishes that where an employee has been exposed to asbestos or some other harmful substance by two or more employers, and has been struck down with a disease resulting from exposure, each of the employers is liable for the loss all loss, although this is modified by *Barker* so that the liability is proportionate, resting on time on risk or other relevant factors. The analogy with these cases is immediately apparent. If insurer A is on risk in year 1, and insurer B is on risk in year 2, then each has accepted a duty to hold the assured harmless, the assured has suffered a loss against which he should have been protected, and science cannot determine whether the loss was more likely to have been caused in year 1 or in year 2. Accordingly, each insurer should take its own proportionate share of the loss based on a time on risk basis, so that the loss should be divided equally between them. Indeed, as a matter of practice, insurers consecutively on risk apportion liability between themselves in subsidence and heave cases where the exact date of the insured peril—as opposed to the manifestation of damage—cannot be ascertained. A more problematic arises where the assured had in year 1 chosen not to take out property cover and had done so only in year 2. Here, only one insurer is involved, and imposing liability on that insurer by reference to *Fairchild* goes somewhat further than the principle underlying *Fairchild* that if there are two tortfeasors whose responsibilities cannot be separated each should be liable. That said, in *Barker* the majority held that as long as the loss arose from two or more exposures to the same causative agent, then there could be recovery even though only one involved a breach of duty, and it follows that *Fairchild* would remain applicable to a case such as *Kelly*.

2. INCREASE OF RISK

Increase of risk and change of risk. There is a distinction at common law 5–016
between cases in which the danger of loss increases during the currency of the policy, and cases in which the very nature of the subject matter insured has altered: the former has no adverse effects on the policy, whereas the latter operates automatically to discharge the insurer on the basis that what was agreed between the parties has ceased to exist. The distinction between an alteration of the risk and an alteration in the subject matter may at the margins be fine, but it is nevertheless crucial. The common law rules may be modified by express agreement, and it is common for policies of all classes to contain various restrictions on increase of risk by the assured.

Increase of risk

Common law principles. The principle that increase of risk during the currency 5–017
of the policy is permitted at common law is demonstrated by the leading case of *Pim v Reid*.[85] Pim carried on the business of a papermaker, and effected an insurance on the premises in which the business was carried on. Subsequently, a large quantity of cotton waste was cleaned and dyed there. A fire occurred when some of it was in the mill and, although insurers generally declined to insure premises where cotton waste was kept or used, the company was held liable. It

---

[83] *Fairchild v Glenhaven Funeral Services Ltd* [2002] 3 All E.R. 305.
[84] *Barker v Corus UK Plc* [2006] UKHL 20.
[85] *Pim v Reid* (1843) 6 Man. & G. 1.

will be noted that the assured had altered his trade without informing the company, but it was nevertheless held that the assured had not been under any duty to disclose this fact: the policy contained an express clause requiring disclosure of hazardous conduct, but the court ruled that this was confined in its operation to pre-contractual negotiations. A similar conclusion was reached in *Shaw v Robberds*,[86] where a fire policy was effected in respect of a kiln, which was to be used only for drying corn; the insurers were held not to be entitled to treat the policy as terminated following the use of the kiln to dry bark for, in the absence of any warranty to the effect that the kiln was to be used only for drying corn, there was nothing in the common law to prevent a more hazardous use being undertaken.

Marine insurance authorities demonstrate the same point. In *Toulmin v Inglis*[87] the assured received on board his vessel a number of Spanish prisoners of war, who were not kept under restraint. The vessel was lost following a mutiny in which the prisoners had played a prominent part, but the underwriters were nevertheless held liable as there had been nothing in the policy to prevent the assured from rendering the voyage more hazardous. The principle that the implied warranty of seaworthiness in voyage policies does not extend beyond the date of the commencement of the voyage[88] has the same basis.[89] The principle applies even to fraud on the part of the assured. If the assured has engaged on a course of conduct which is fraudulent, and this has the effect of increasing the risk, the insurers have no right to treat themselves as off risk.[90]

The rule which permits a variation of risk applies also in the context of reinsurance, although the position there is complicated by the use of words which purport to incorporate into the reinsurance the coverage terms found in the direct policy. The general effect of the cases is that, in the absence of incorporation, reinsurers are not bound by fundamental alterations to the direct risk brought about by the issue of new insurance cover,[91] although the use of words such as "subject to the same terms and conditions as original" appear to operate as a waiver of the right to deny coverage for new risks.[92]

It follows from these cases that, subject to contract, the assured is not precluded from recovering under his policy where the risk has increased, even if the assured himself deliberately increased the risk. There is no implied condition precluding an increase of risk, and any continuing duty of good faith owed by the assured can operate only where there is some policy term upon which it can bite.[93]

---

[86] *Shaw v Robberds* (1837) 6 Ad. & El. 75. See also: *Mitchell Conveyor and Transport Co Ltd v Pulbrook* (1933) 45 Ll. L.R. 239.

[87] *Toulmin v Inglis* (1808) 1 Camp. 421.

[88] See, e.g. *Thompson v Hopper* (1856) 6 E.B. & E. 172.

[89] Marine Insurance Act 1906 s.39(1).

[90] *Total Graphics Ltd v AGF Insurance Ltd* [1997] 1 Lloyd's Rep. 599 at 606, per Mance J.

[91] *Lower Rhine and Wurtemberg Insurance Association v Sedgwick* [1899] 1 Q.B. 179; *Norwich Union Fire Insurance Society Ltd v Colonial Mutual Fire Insurance Co Ltd* [1922] 1 K.B. 461; *HIH Casualty and General Insurance Ltd v New Hampshire Insurance Co* [2001] Lloyd's Rep. I.R. 224; *American International Marine Agency of New York Inc v Dandridge* [2005] Lloyd's Rep. I.R. 643.

[92] This was the view of A.L. Smith L.J. in *Lower Rhine and Wurtemberg*, although Collins L.J. disagreed on the point. Subsequently, in *Scottish National Insurance Co Ltd v Poole* (1912) 107 L.T. 687 the former view was adopted, although the point did not arise on the facts as the original policy was found not to have been cancelled and replaced. See also *Emanuel & Co v Andrew Weir & Co* (1914) 30 T.L.R. 518.

[93] *K/S Merc Skandia XXXXII v Certain Lloyd's Underwriters* [2001] Lloyd's Rep. I.R. 802.

Contractual provisions against increase of risk. The common law tolerance of **5–018**
post-contractual increases of risk is normally modified by express provision.
Typical clauses may operate in any of the following ways.

(1) The assured may be required to warrant that in general the risk will not
be increased or, more specifically, that a particular course of action will
or will not be taken. Thus, in fire insurance on premises the assured may
warrant that particular substances will not be brought on to the premises
or that particular activities will not be carried on; in life assurance the
assured may warrant that he will not take part in dangerous sports; and
in marine insurance the assured may warrant that the vessel will not enter
into a war zone. The term may not be expressed as a warranty as such but
may have the same effect, as where a policy provides that the risk is to
terminate automatically on an increase of risk.[94]

(2) The insurer may insist upon being informed if the risk alters either
generally or in a specified manner. This may be coupled with the right of
the insurer to alter the terms of the insurance and to increase the premium.[95]

(3) The policy may permit an increase of risk subject to the insurer being
informed of any anticipated or actual increase of risk and its granting
permission.[96]

(4) The policy may provide that the cover shall be suspended for any period
in which the risk is increased in a particular manner. This type of
provision is often referred to as either suspensory or a delimitation of the
risk.

A number of issues of construction arise in considering terms of the above
types. In particular, the consequences of the assured's conduct will vary with the
nature of the clause and what is permitted or proscribed by it. The issues are
discussed in the following paragraphs.

The meaning of increase of risk. Before the assured can be said to have increased   **5–019**
the risk it is necessary to examine the cover provided by the policy to ascertain
whether what has been done by the assured was contemplated from the outset;
conduct anticipated by the policy clearly cannot be said to have increased the risk
as defined by the policy.[97] Further, even where the conduct in question is not
contemplated by the policy, it is incumbent upon the insurer to prove that the risk
was increased. These points are demonstrated by *Baxendale v Harvey,*[98] where a
policy was effected under which the assured could not erect new machinery
which increased the risk of fire. The claimants disclosed to the insurer, prior to
the inception of the risk, the presence on the premises of a steam engine which
was used for hoisting goods. During the currency of the policy the steam engine
began to be used for grinding provender for the assured's horses, and for this
purpose grinding machines were erected. The court held that neither of these acts
amounted to a breach of warranty: the steam engine had been specified in the

---

[94] As in *Forrest & Sons Ltd v CGU Insurance Plc* [2006] Lloyd's Rep. I.R. 113.

[95] If no method of calculating the amount of any increased premium has been agreed, the assured
must pay a reasonable sum: Marine Insurance Act 1906 s.31(2).

[96] If permission is granted, the assured has a reasonable time in which to increase the risk in the
manner permitted: *Notman v Anchor Assurance* (1854) 4 C.B.N.S. 476.

[97] Thus, in *Shaw v Robberds* (1837) 6 Ad. & El. 75 the assured was held not to have warranted that
a kiln used by him for drying corn would not be used for any other purpose.

[98] *Baxendale v Harvey* (1859) 4 H. & N. 445.

policy so that its use in this manner had been contemplated, while the erection of grinding machines did not have the effect of increasing the risk.[99] The decision suggests that an increase of risk clause is not to be read literally, but rather is to be treated as reflecting the common law distinction between increase of risk (which does not trigger the clause) and change of risk (which does). Indeed, in *Kausar v Eagle Star Insurance Co Ltd*[100] it was held, in the case of a clause which required notification to the insurers in the event of an increase of risk, that the clause was to be construed as doing no more than codifying the common law distinction between increase of risk and change of risk, and that it applied only to the latter situation. The notion underlying these cases is that the assured should not be under onerous continuing duties in the absence of clear wording. That approach was adopted by David Steel J. in *Scottish Coal Co Ltd v Royal and Sun Alliance Plc*,[101] where the increase of risk clause stated that in the event of "material change in the original risk . . . the policy shall be avoided unless the continuance be agreed by endorsement signed by the company." David Steel J held that the *Kausar* principle applied, and that there was only a material change in the risk if there was a fundamental change to its nature and not simply an increase in risk: a change in working practices was, applying that approach, held not to amount to a material change.

It is nevertheless the case that everything turns upon the precise wording of the increase of risk clause. Where the assured has warranted that the risk will not be increased, the mere installation of potentially hazardous equipment is not a breach of the warranty, but any use of it which has the effect of increasing the risk will amount to a breach.[102] In *Barret v Jeremy*[103] the claimants, varnish makers, insured their stock in trade under a policy which provided that any alteration to the claimants' buildings which increased the risk of fire had to be notified immediately to the insurers, failing which the policy would become void. During the currency of the policy the claimants fitted boilers and used them to boil varnish. The insurers sought to set the policy aside for breach of warranty. The trial judge directed the jury to consider whether the risk had in fact been increased by the boiling of varnish, but on appeal this direction was held to be erroneous; the true question, in the view of the court, was whether the use of boilers for any purpose increased the risk. In *Forrest & Sons Ltd v CGU Insurance Plc*[104] it was held that the assured had increased the risk, and had thereby triggered the operation of a condition removing cover, by re-commissioning dangerous frying equipment which insurers had believed was no longer in use following the introduction of boiling equipment.

The leading authority on the matter is now *Ansari v New India Assurance Ltd*.[105] The policy stated that:

> "This insurance shall cease to be in force if there is any material alteration to the Premises or Business or any material change in the facts stated in the Proposal Form or other facts supplied to the Insurer unless the Insurer agrees in writing to continue the insurance."

---

[99] See also *Shanly v Allied Traders Insurance Co Ltd* (1925) 21 Ll. L.R. 195, in which a change in the use of a building from a theatre to a cinema was held not to have increased the risk.

[100] *Kausar v Eagle Star Insurance Co Ltd* [2000] Lloyd's Rep. I.R. 154. See below.

[101] *Scottish Coal Co Ltd v Royal and Sun Alliance Plc* [2008] Lloyd's Rep. I.R. 718.

[102] *Glen v Lewis* (1853) 8 Ex. 607.

[103] *Barret v Jeremy* (1849) 3 Ex. 535.

[104] *Forrest & Sons Ltd v CGU Insurance Plc* [2006] Lloyd's Rep. I.R. 113.

[105] *Ansari v New India Assurance Ltd* [2009] Lloyd's Rep. I.R. 562.

The proposal form stated the business carried on at the premises by the assured's tenant was the wholesaling of kitchens and that the premises were protected by an automatic sprinkler installation. It was alleged by the insurers that at the time of the loss by fire the assured's tenant was carrying on the rather different business of selling motor cycles and that the sprinkler system had been disabled. The Court of Appeal held that the insurers were discharged from liability, although attention was confined to the position as it related to the sprinkler system.[106] The Court of Appeal was satisfied that the assured had represented that the premises were protected by a properly functioning sprinkler system and not simply that a system had been installed[107] and that the disabling of the system amounted to a "material change". In so deciding, the Court of Appeal held that the term "material" did not import the test for the duty of utmost good faith, as materiality in that context meant no more than that a prudent underwriter would have been interested in the changed circumstances, a "relatively undemanding" threshold. Instead, the Court of Appeal felt that the question should be whether the changed circumstances had had a significant bearing on the risk, a test which the Court of Appeal felt was easily satisfied on the facts. The difficulty with *Ansari* is reconciling the outcome with that in *Kausar*, and indeed it was forcefully argued that the clause could have been construed in the same way, discharging the insurers only where the risk had actually altered in nature. The Court of Appeal chose to distinguish *Kausar* by focusing on the terms of the clause in *Ansari*, but it might be thought that the distinction between the two cases is not obvious and that future interpretation of this type of wording is open to doubt.

Present and continuing warranties. Where the insurer does insist upon a **5–020** warranty, it is a matter of construction whether that warranty relates to the future conduct of the assured or whether it is enough that at the inception of the risk the assured has complied with the terms of the warranty. Clear words will be necessary where the insurer wishes to procure a continuing, as opposed to a present, warranty. In general, if the warranty relates to the future, failure by the assured to comply with its terms brings the risk to an end.[108] A number of cases may be contrasted. In *Hales v Reliance Fire Assurance*[109] the assured's warranty that his premises were not used for storing inflammable material other than lighter fuel was held to be continuing, so that temporary storage of fire works allowed the insurer to terminate the policy. A continuing obligation was, in *Beauchamp v National Mutual Indemnity Insurance Co*,[110] similarly held to be imposed where the assured warranted that it did not use explosives. In *Farnham v Royal Insurance*[111] the condition was in usual form against "any alteration after the commencement of this insurance . . . whereby the (fire) risk of destruction or

---

[106] By reason of a non-invalidation clause in the policy, the assured was affected only by a breach of the policy by the tenant if the assured was aware of it. The evidence showed that the assured was aware of the inoperability of the sprinkler system, so there was no need to consider whether he had been aware of the unauthorised business. The trial judge had found that the assured had knowledge of that as well, but there was no real reliance on the change of business on appeal.

[107] Distinguishing *Victor Melik & Co Ltd v Norwich Union Fire Insurance Society Ltd* [1980] 1 Lloyd's Rep. 523 (promise confined to initial installation) and *Hussain v Brown (No.2)* [1996] 1 Lloyd's Rep. 627 (no breach if operative alarm not actually set).

[108] Cf. *Sillem v Thornton* (1854) 3 E. & B. 868; *Whitehead v Price* (1835) 2 Cr.M. & R. 447; *Dobson v Sotherby* (1827) 1 M. & M. 90, 92 at 93; *Grant v Aetna Insurance* (1862) 15 Moo. P.C.C. 516.

[109] *Hales v Reliance Fire Assurance* [1960] 2 Lloyd's Rep. 391.

[110] *Beauchamp v National Mutual Indemnity Insurance Co* [1937] 3 All E.R. 19.

[111] *Farnham v Royal Insurance* [1976] 2 Lloyd's Rep. 437.

damage is increased". Farm buildings were insured against the fire risk of carriers and transit warehousing. The assured allowed a third party to arrange for repairs on the premises to cargo containers stored there, and a fire occurred. Ackner J. held that the insurers were entitled to avoid the policy for breach of condition. To the knowledge of the assured, repair work involving the use of welding equipment took place within the barn, and that, the judge found, increased the risk.

By contrast, in *Stokes v Cox*,[112] a warranty to the effect that the assured did not employ a steam engine on his premises was held not to be continuing. In *Hair v Prudential Assurance Co Ltd*[113] the assured completed in September 1977 a "Hearth and Home" proposal form stating (1) that the buildings were kept in a good state of repair, (2) that the premises were inhabited by the proposer's son, and (3) that they were regularly left unattended. The value was given as £8,000. In November 1978 a serious fire gutted the property: the Prudential denied liability on the grounds that the premises were not in a good state of repair, were not occupied, were uninhabitable, and that the assured had paid £230 for the property because there was a closing order in existence. Woolf J., giving judgment for the assured held that: (1) when the form was signed the evidence on a balance of probability showed that the property was in a good state of repair (and did not materially change thereafter); (2) although the property did become uninhabited for long periods, the questions in the proposal form were directed towards the state of affairs when the form was signed, there was no warranty by the proposer that the position would not change thereafter; and (3) the closing order was not a material fact.

5–021   *Warranties and clauses delimiting the risk.* There is a series of cases in which promises by the assured as to the use of premises or goods have been construed not as warranties but as suspensory provisions. In this type of case, therefore, the assured can recover as long as the premises or goods are being used for a purpose contemplated by the policy at the time of the loss.[114] The distinction between a warranty and a clause delimiting the risk is based on the construction of the policy in which the term appears, so that any attempt to rationalise the cases is perhaps futile.

5–022   *Isolated breaches of warranty.* The general principle which operates where the assured has broken a warranty is that the risk terminates automatically as from the date of the breach: it is immaterial that the breach was temporary, that it did not have the effect of increasing the risk, and that it had been remedied by the assured prior to any loss. It follows that an isolated breach of warranty permits the insurer to terminate the policy.[115] The wording of the warranty may, however, admit of the construction that a temporary or isolated increase of risk does not amount to a breach. This will be the case in particular where the prohibition is against alteration of the use of premises, as isolated instances will not amount to alteration of use.[116] The principle is that, as in the construction of other conditions, if the insurers wish to make it a condition precedent to the validity of

---

[112] *Stokes v Cox* (1856) I H. & N. 533.
[113] *Hair v Prudential Assurance Co Ltd* [1983] 2 Lloyd's Rep. 667.
[114] See in particular *Farr v Motor Traders Mutual Assurance Society* [1920] 3 K.B. 699; *Provincial Insurance Co v Morgan* [1933] A.C. 240.
[115] *Glen v Lewis* (1853) 8 Ex. 607.
[116] Lord Denman C.J. in *Shaw v Robberds* (1837) 6 Ad. & El. 75. This case was disapproved by Parke B. in *Glen v Lewis* (1853) 8 Ex. 607 at 619, but was cited with apparent approval by Lord Wright in *Provincial Insurance Co v Morgan* [1933] A.C. 240 at 255.

the policy that there shall be no alteration in the risk, they must do so in distinct terms.[117] In *Shaw v Robberds*[118] the assured warranted that the trade specified in his fire policy—that of drying corn by the use of a kiln—was the only trade for which the insured premises would be used without the consent of the insurer. During the currency of the policy a vessel laden with bark sank near to the assured's premises, and the assured gratuitously allowed the kiln to be used to dry the bark. This conduct was held not to amount to a change in the business carried on by the assured on the insured premises and that, while it was a more hazardous enterprise than drying corn, nothing in the policy ousted the common law rule that increases of risk do not affect the validity of the policy. In *Mint Security Ltd v Blair*,[119] occasional lapses by the assured security company in adhering to its stated procedures were held not to be a breach of its warranty that its procedures would not be "varied".

The distinction between temporary increases of risk and changes of use may, however, be a fine one. In *Farnham v Royal Insurance Co Ltd*,[120] the assured warranted that there would not be any alteration whereby the risk of destruction of or damage to the premises was increased: Ackner J. held that this warranty had been infringed when the assured had allowed the premises to be used for welding operations. By contrast, in *Exchange Theatre Ltd v Iron Trades Mutual Insurance Co Ltd*,[121] the Court of Appeal held that an almost identical warranty had not been broken where the assured had introduced onto the premises a petrol generator and petrol.

Notification clauses. Where the policy requires the assured to notify the insurer **5–023** in the event that the risk is increased, it is apparent that the duty has to be subject to some limitations to prevent it from becoming unduly onerous. A series of old cases concluded that a condition requiring notification of any increase in the risk does not apply to increases which might be taken to be within the contemplation of the parties at the time of taking out the insurance.[122] Where the assured states the trade for which premises are to be used, the insurers may be taken to know all facts relating to the general course of such trade.[123]

The most recent authorities have made it clear that notification provisions are to be construed in a manner which does not impose day-to-day obligations upon the assured. The point is clearly illustrated by the decision of the Court of Appeal in *Kausar v Eagle Star Insurance Co Ltd*.[124] In this case, a policy on commercial premises stated that the assured was obliged to tell the insurers "of any change of circumstances after the start of the policy which increases the risk of injury or damage". After inception, the assured received threats of damage from a tenant against whom repossession proceedings had commenced, and a window (not covered by the policy) had been broken. These events were not notified to the insurers, and the Court of Appeal held that the clause did not require such

---

[117] Martin B. in *Baxendale v Harvey* (1859) 4 H. & N. 445 at 450, citing *Stokes v Cox* (1856) 1 H. & N. 533.

[118] *Shaw v Robberds* (1837) 6 Ad. & El. 75. See also: *Dobson v Sotheby* (1827) Mood. & M. 90; *Thompson v Equity Fire* [1910] A.C. 592.

[119] *Mint Security Ltd v Blair* [1982] 1 Lloyd's Rep. 188.

[120] *Farnham v Royal Insurance Co Ltd* [1976] 2 Lloyd's Rep. 437.

[121] *Exchange Theatre Ltd v Iron Trades Mutual Insurance Co Ltd* [1983] I Lloyd's Rep. 674.

[122] *Law Guarantee Trust v Munich Reinsurance* [1912] 1 Ch. 138 at 154.

[123] Shee J. in *Bates v Hewitt* (1867) L.R. 2 Q.B. 595 at 610.

[124] *Kausar v Eagle Star Insurance Co Ltd* [2000] Lloyd's Rep. I.R. 154 (decided in 1996), followed in *First National Commercial Bank Plc v Barnet Devanney (Harrow) Ltd* [1999] Lloyd's Rep. I.R. 43, reversed on other grounds [1999] Lloyd's Rep. I.R. 479.

notification. The Court's view was that the clause did no more than restate the general common law distinction between increase of risk and change of risk, and that the clause applied only to change of risk: giving the clause the wide meaning contended for by the insurers would, in the Court's view, have rendered the policy unworkable, as the assured would have been under a continual duty to inform the insurers of changing circumstances. The ruling that the clause did no more than reproduce the common law was given additional force by the consideration that the policy was in "user-friendly" language, and that it was only to be expected that such a policy would set out the assured's general rights. An increase of risk clause in any event refers only to that part of the risk which has been taken into account by the insurer when fixing the premium and other terms.[125]

In the limited cases in which a notification clause has been broken, the consequences of breach depend upon the nature of the condition. If the clause amounts to a condition precedent to the insurer's liability, the insurer is simply not liable. If, by contrast, the clause is a bare condition, the insurer is not discharged from liability, but will be able to recover damages—by way of set-off or counterclaim against the policy monies—for any loss occasioned by the breach. In *Hussain v Brown (No.2)*[126] the assured failed to inform the insurers that his business premises had been left unoccupied, a factor which was held to have increased the risk and which thus amounted to a breach of the condition.[127] The evidence to the court demonstrated that, had the information been given to the insurers, they may have insisted upon an inspection of the premises, and may then have insisted upon the installation of additional security devices. The court assessed the prospect that these events would have occurred, and would have prevented a fire, was 50:50, and reduced the assured's accordingly.

Change of risk

5–024 *The rights of the insurer at common law.* Where the change occurring is not merely an increase in the risk faced by the insurer, but amounts to a substantive change in the insured subject matter itself, the common law discharges the insurer from all liability for loss to the subject matter. This consequence follows even though the alteration in the subject matter does not necessarily increase the risk of loss, and even though the alteration was beyond the control of the assured. To determine whether or not there has been a change in the subject matter, it is necessary to construe the policy to determine exactly what subject matter was contemplated by the parties as falling within its coverage. To this end, an express warranty describing the subject matter will be conclusive evidence of the scope of the policy; the use of a warranty will have the further advantage, so far as the insurer is concerned, that the deviation from the policy description need not be material for the policy to be set aside, whereas if a warranty is not used it is incumbent on the insurer to demonstrate that the change was in some way material in that it had the effect of removing the subject matter insured from the scope of the policy. It is convenient to examine the cases under two headings: those in which the subject matter fails to comply with the policy description from the outset, and those in which the alteration takes place during the currency of the policy.

---

[125] *General Insurance Corp of New Brunswick v Fulton* 75 D.L.R. (4th) 382 (1991).

[126] *Hussain v Brown (No.2)* Unreported, 1996.

[127] Quaere whether this result can stand with the more generous approach of the Court of Appeal in *Kausar*.

Failure to meet description from the outset. Where a policy is stated to cover   **5–025**
subject matter of a particular description, and the subject matter has never met
that description, the risk simply fails to attach and the policy is void. Thus in
Newcastle Fire Insurance Co v Macmorran & Co[128] the assured warranted that
the insured building did not possess more than two feet of stoving; the fact that
the building had more than that amount prevented the risk from attaching, and
any dispute as to the significance of the deviation was rendered unnecessary by
the fact that the description had been warranted. The further example is where the
assured under a marine policy specifies the port of the vessel's departure but the
vessel commences its voyage from another port: under s.43 of the Marine
Insurance Act 1906, the risk simply does not attach.

Subsequent alteration in the subject matter insured. The same principles apply.   **5–026**
If the assured has warranted that the subject matter will continue to meet its
description throughout the currency of the policy, any immaterial alteration in
that description will deprive the assured of his rights: by contrast, if there is no
continuing warranty, the insurer must demonstrate that the change rendered the
subject matter different from that which was originally insured. The question of
exactly what degree of change has this effect is more likely to arise in cases of
this type than in cases of failure to meet description from the outset, as warranties
will not be construed as continuing unless expressly stated to be so. Once again,
all will turn upon the construction of the policy. The leading modern authority is
Swiss Reinsurance Co v United India Insurance Co Ltd.[129] Here, insurers issued
a construction all risks policy in respect of the construction of a power plant. The
contractors did not receive payment and walked off site. Morison J. held that this
had the effect of bringing the policy to an end at common law: the policy was
against building risks, such as bad weather, fire and the like, and not against the
very different risks associated with loss of property left unattended on a disused
building site. In *Ansari v New India Assurance Ltd*[130] it was seemingly held at
first instance that the absence of an operative sprinkler system, contrary to what
had been stated in the proposal form, crossed the line between increase of risk
and alteration of risk. The case is perhaps better explained by the presence of an
express clause which brought the risk to an end if there was a material alteration
to what had been said in the proposal form and the actual position, as was held
on appeal by the Court of Appeal.[131]

A contrasting decision is *Law Guarantee Trust & Accident Society v Munich
Reinsurance Co,*[132] in which the claimants had provided contingency insurance
against the risk of non-payment of the interest on certain debentures issued at 4.5
per cent. The claimants reinsured their liability with the defendants. Subsequently, a court order reduced the interest to 3 per cent and, following the
liquidation of the issuing company, claims were made against the claimants who
in turn claimed against the defendants. It was argued by the defendants that the
reduction in the rate of interest was a material variation in the insured subject
matter, so that their liability was discharged. This argument was rejected by

---

[128] *Newcastle Fire Insurance Co v Macmorran & Co* (1815) 3 Dow. 255. See also: *Sillem v
Thornton* (1854) 3 E. & B. 868; *Wilkinson & Co v Hullett* (1938) 61 Ll. L.R. 145.
[129] *Swiss Reinsurance Co v United India Insurance Co Ltd* [2005] Lloyd's Rep. I.R. 341. See also:
Cosford Union v Poor Law & Local Government Officers' Mutual Guarantee Association Ltd (1910)
103 L.T. 463; *Hadenfayre Ltd v British National Insurance Ltd* [1984] 2 Lloyd's Rep. 393.
[130] *Ansari v New India Assurance Ltd* [2008] Lloyd's Rep. I.R. 58.
[131] *Ansari v New India Assurance Ltd* [2009] Lloyd's Rep. I.R. 582.
[132] *Law Guarantee Trust & Accident Society v Munich Reinsurance Co* [1912] 1 Ch. 138.

Warrington J. who pointed out that the alteration was not outside the range of the risk that the defendants had agreed to run.[133]

5–027   *Express provisions dealing with alteration of the subject matter.* There may well be a continuing warranty to the effect that the assured will not alter the subject matter insured, and that any alteration will terminate the policy from that point. Policy terms may not, however, be so wide-ranging, and the policy may, for example, permit alterations in the subject matter subject to notification to the insurer, the permission of the insurer or the right of the insurer to charge a higher premium and to alter the terms of the policy. The only question where a clause of any of these types is used is whether the insurer thereby waives his superior common law right to terminate the policy for alteration. There is little doubt that, in the majority of cases, the courts would hold the policy provisions to be exhaustive of the insurer's rights on alteration of the subject matter. In *Ansari v New India Assurance Ltd*[134] the policy provided that the risk would automatically terminate in the event of a material increase of risk. Patten J. held that the distinction drawn by the common law and in *Kausar v Eagle Star Insurance Co Ltd*[135] between change of risk and alteration of risk was not applicable, and that the clause was triggered by a change in risk which did not amount to a change in the nature of the risk insured. However, on the facts Patten J. found such a change in any event. On appeal to the Court of Appeal,[136] the learned judge's decision was upheld, but on the ground that the disabling of the sprinkler system amounted to a material change in the facts stated by the assured in the proposal form, and that the clause itself was concerned not with the distinction between increase and change of risk but rather with the different question of whether there had been a material change in what had been stated. In *Scottish Coal Co Ltd v Royal and Sun Alliance Plc*[137] the increase of risk clause stated that in the event of "material change in the original risk . . . the policy shall be avoided unless the continuance be agreed by endorsement signed by the company." David Steel J. held that this clause was to be interpreted in accordance with the principle in *Kausar* and that there was only a material change in the risk if there was a fundamental change to its nature and not simply an increase in risk: a change in working practices was, applying that approach, held not to amount to a material change.

5–028   *Suspension of the risk.* It is assumed by the authorities that, in the absence of any express wording to the contrary, the effect of an alteration in the subject matter insured that takes it outside the scope of the agreed cover is to bring an automatic end to the cover. It clearly cannot be the case, in the absence of some express provision, that the policy is avoided ab initio and the risk is regarded as never having attached. By analogy with the continuing warranty cases, the position is that the policy is terminated as from the date of the alteration, thereby leaving the assured's rights in respect of pre-alteration losses intact. There is, nevertheless, a further possibility, namely that an alteration of the subject matter merely suspends the operation of the policy and that the risk is potentially capable of reattaching in the event that the subject matter is again altered but to meet its

---

[133] The reinsurance was in the form of an obligatory treaty under which the reinsurers were required to accept any risk declared to them by the reinsureds.
[134] *Ansari v New India Assurance Ltd* [2008] Lloyd's Rep. I.R. 586.
[135] *Kausar v Eagle Star Insurance Co Ltd* [2000] Lloyd's Rep. I.R. 154.
[136] *Kausar v Eagle Star Insurance Co Ltd* [2009] Lloyd's Rep. I.R. 562.
[137] *Scottish Coal Co Ltd v Royal and Sun Alliance Plc* [2008] Lloyd's Rep. I.R. 718.

original description. There is ample analogous authority for the adoption of the suspension approach in the form of the description of the risk cases,[138] although could not be applied to cases in which the alteration was irrevocable. Moreover, the suspensory argument could not easily be pressed in marine voyage insurances where the assured has altered the subject matter insured by delay, deviation or change of voyage, as ss.45 to 49 of the Marine Insurance Act 1906 make it clear that the policy terminates on the alteration and that it does not become reinstated should the alteration come to an end.

Some policies may provide for suspension of termination in specified circumstances. In *Swiss Reinsurance Co v United India Insurance Co Ltd*[139] condition 12 of a 44-month Construction All Risks policy provided that:

> "Should the Work insured or any part thereof be entirely stopped by any cause whatsoever and the Insured give notice thereof, the cover under the Policy shall continue without interruption up to a maximum period of six months without additional premium with any further extension of this period to be agreed by the Insurer, provided that the Insured shall take reasonable precautions to protect the Work from physical loss or damage during the period of cessation."

During the currency of the policy, on June 17, 2001, construction work came to an end by reason of failure to pay the contractors. Condition 12 was invoked and the policy remained in existence. The position had not altered by December 17, 2001, the date on which the six-month indulgence granted by condition 12 came to an end, and the reinsurers treated the policy as at an end. The insurers, in seeking damages from the reinsurers for breach of contract, argued that the effect of condition 12 was to grant six months' cover from the date upon which the work stopped, and at the end of that period the risk continued for the balance of the unexpired 44-month period. The reinsurers successfully argued that the effect of condition 12 was merely suspensory, in that, but for condition 12, the risk would have at common law terminated automatically on June 17, 2001 by reason of alteration of risk and the effect of condition 12 was to maintain the policy in existence for an additional period of six months at the end of which the parties would revert to their common law position. Accordingly, unless work had recommenced by December 17, 2001, the risk would automatically terminate, as was the case.

3. PROXIMATE CAUSE

The nature of the doctrine. It is necessarily the position that an insurer is to be **5–029** liable only for those losses which occur as the result of the fortuitous[140] operation of insured perils, although if there is only one cause of loss the assured is free to classify that cause as he thinks fit so as to bring it within the terms of the policy.[141] It is frequently the case, however, that loss arises from a series of events, some of which are insured perils and some of which are either uninsured or excluded perils, and here it is the task of the court to deter mine which of those perils was the actual proximate cause of the loss. The principle is codified in s.55(1) of the Marine Insurance Act 1906:

---

[138] See Ch.7, below.
[139] *Swiss Reinsurance Co v United India Insurance Co Ltd* [2005] Lloyd's Rep. I.R. 341.
[140] *Glencore International AG v Alpina Insurance Co Ltd* [2004] 1 Lloyd's Rep. 111.
[141] *Capel-Cure Myers Capital Management Ltd v McCarthy* [1995] L.R.L.R. 498.

"[U]nless the policy otherwise provides, the insurer is liable for any loss proximately caused by a peril insured against, but . . . he is not liable for any loss which is not proximately caused by a peril insured against."

There is no difference in the application of the law of proximity, between marine and non-marine insurance law,[142] and the test for causation is the same in insurance as in general tort law.[143] The proximity rule is based on the presumed intention of the parties,[144] and means that if the insured cause is within the risks covered, the insurers are liable in respect of the loss but if it is within the perils excepted the insurers are not liable.[145] While it is relatively simple to state the doctrine of proximate cause, ascertaining the proximate cause of a loss in any particular case may be a matter of some difficulty. The vast number of authorities on the matter may be of little assistance for, as has been said by Chalmers[146]:

"[T]hough the rule is universally admitted, lawyers have never attempted to work out any philosophical theory of cause and effect, and it is probably as well for commerce that they have never made the attempt. The numerous decisions on the rule are rough and ready applications of it to particular facts. As might be expected, many of the decisions are difficult to reconcile. But the apparent inconsistencies may be regarded as depending rather on inferences of fact than on matters of law."

5–030   **Ascertaining the proximate cause of a loss.**   The leading authority is *Leyland Shipping Co Ltd v Norwich Union Fire Insurance Society Ltd*,[147] in which the House of Lords laid to rest the view that the proximate cause was the last event to occur. The vessel Ikara was insured under a policy covering perils of the sea but excluding war perils, and was torpedoed by an enemy submarine off Le Havre. The Ikara managed to reach Le Havre but she was ordered out and was subsequently lost in a gale while moored in the unprotected outer harbour. The House of Lords held that the proximate cause of the loss was a war peril, and that on the facts the chain of causation between the firing of the torpedo and the loss of the vessel in a gale had not been broken. A variety of formulations of the proximate cause test were as put forward by their Lordships, including: the direct cause; the immediate cause from which the loss arose as a natural consequence; the dominant cause; an event from which the subsequent loss was a reasonable possibility or an obvious or necessary result; and the cause which possessed the qualities of reality, predominance and efficiency.[148] Ultimately the test rests upon common sense.[149]

Although it is impossible to lay down clear rules for the application of the proximate cause doctrine, it is possible to identify three broad classes of case.

The first class consists of "inevitability" cases, where the occurrence of peril A renders inevitable the occurrence of peril B. Here, peril A, as the death blow,

---

[142] *Becker Gray v London Assurance* [1918] A.C. 101.

[143] *Lloyds TSB General Insurance Holdings Ltd v Lloyds Bank Group Insurance Co Ltd* [2001] Lloyd's Rep. I.R. 224.

[144] *Reischer v Borwick* [1894] 2 Q.B. 548 at 550; *Becker Gray v London Assurance* [1918] A.C. 101 at 112; *Leyland v Norwich Union* [1918] A.C. 350 at 362, 370.

[145] *Ionides v Universal Marine* (1863) 14 C.B.N.S. 259; *Marsden v City & County Insurance* (1865) L.R. 1 C.P. 232; *Cory v Burr* (1883) 8 App. Cas. 393; *Lawrence v Accidental Insurance* (1881) 7 Q.B.D. 216; *Wayne Tank Co v Employers Liability Assurance Corp* [1974] Q.B. 57.

[146] *Chalmers Marine Insurance Act 1906* 9th edn (1983), p.78.

[147] *Leyland Shipping Co Ltd v Norwich Union Fire Insurance Society Ltd* [1918] A.C. 350.

[148] See [1918] A.C. 350 at 358, 362, 363, 370,

[149] *Gray v Barr* [1971] 2 Q.B. 554 at 557, per Lord Denning M.R.

would appear to be the proximate cause of the loss. This is illustrated by the facts of *Leyland Shipping* itself.[150]

The second class consists of "weakening" cases, where the occurrence of peril A, whether or not it causes damage to the insured subject matter, puts that subject matter at greater risk from peril B or makes the occurrence of peril B more likely. Isolating the proximate cause of the loss is at its most contentious in this type of case. The issue is often expressed in terms of *novus actus interveniens*: is peril B a new operative cause in its own right, or is it the consequence of peril A?[151] By way of example, in marine insurance, it has been held that where a sea peril endangers the vessel and loss results as a direct but not inevitable consequence of that peril, the loss is caused by perils of the seas, as where animals on board a vessel injure themselves through fear in the course of a storm at sea[152] and where the penetration of sea water rotted a cargo of hides the fumes from which ruined an accompanying cargo of tobacco.[153] Similar issues are raised by the situation in which a vessel has been stranded by reason of a war peril and the vessel or cargo has been seized by third parties: the loss has generally been put down to perils of the seas rather than theft or seizure.[154] A further illustration of the difficulty is the case in which the assured under an accident policy is the victim of an accident which leads to his death from natural causes. The courts have been inconsistent in their approach here. It has generally been held that an accident which has prompted death from natural causes is the proximate cause of the loss and that the natural causes do not break the chain of causation.[155] Conversely, if the assured has a pre-existing natural weakness, which has led to him suffering an accident, the accident has normally been held to be the proximate cause of the assured's death, as where the assured has had a fit and has fallen into a river[156] or in front of a train,[157] although if the assured's latent condition is worsened by an accident then the latent condition is to be regarded as the proximate cause of illness or death.[158] The most that can be said of these conflicting authorities is that the courts have tended to adopt a sympathetic approach to the beneficiaries of accident policies. In the context of property insurance it has been held that where an air-raid facilitates the stealing of goods from a building, stealing and not the air-raid is the proximate cause of their

---

[150] See also: *Reischer v Borwick* [1894] 2 Q.B. 548; *Samuel & Co Ltd v Dumas* [1924] A.C. 431. Contrast *Hamilton, Fraser & Co v Pandorf & Co* (1887) 12 App. Cas. 518.

[151] Atkinson J. in *Smith v Cornhill Insurance* (1938) 54 T.L.R. 869 at 872.

[152] *Lawrence Aberdein* (1821) 5 B. & Ald. 107; *Gabay v Lloyd* (1825) 3 B. & C. 793.

[153] *Montoya v London Assurance Co* (1851) 6 Ex. 451.

[154] *Bondrett v Hentigg* (1816) Holt N.P. 149; *Hahn v Corbett* (1824) 2 Bing. 205. But contrast: *Green v Elmslie* (1792) 1 Peake N.P. 212; *Ionides v Universal Marine Insurance Association* (1863) 14 C.B.N.S. 259; *Cory v Burr* (1883) 8 App. Cas. 393.

[155] *Fitton v Accidental Insurance Co* (1864) 17 C.B.N.S. 122 (accident resulting in a hernia); *Isitt v Passengers Assurance Co* (1889) 22 Q.B.D. 504 (assured confined to bed following an accident and developed pneumonia); *Mardorf v Accident Insurance Co* [1903] 1 K.B. 584 (scratch leading to death from septicaemia); *Re Etheringron and Lancashire and Yorkshire Accident Insurance Co* [1909] 1 K.B. 591 (accidental soaking on fall from a horse resulting in pneumonia); *Smith v Cornhill Insurance* [1938] 3 All E.R. 145 (assured suffering from the shock of a motor accident wandered into a river and drowned). But contrast: *Smith v Accident Insurance Co* (1870) L.R. 5 Ex. 302 (onset of erysipalis following an accident to the assured held to be the proximate cause); *Cawley v National Employers' Accident* (1885) 1 T.L.R. 255 (death by dislodgment of a gallstone consequent upon a fall held not to be within an accident policy).

[156] *Winspear v Accident Insurance* (1880) 6 Q.B.D. 42. Cf. *Reynolds v Accidental Insurance Co* (1870) 22 L.T. 820.

[157] *Lawrence v Accidental Insurance Co* (1882) 7 QBD 216.

[158] *Re Scarr and General Accident Assurance Corp* [1905] 1 K.B. 307; *Fidelity and Casualty Co of New York v Mitchell* [1917] A.C. 592; *Jason v Batten (1930) Ltd* [1969] 1 Lloyd's Rep. 281.

loss,[159] where a fire encourages a mob to plunder, and a plate glass is broken as a result, it is the lawlessness of the mob and not the fire which is the proximate cause[160]; an explosion which led to the deposit of corrosive ash on a house was the proximate cause of the damage to the house, as the corrosion was the natural and probable cause of the explosion itself[161]; and where a building is damaged by a fire which leads to an explosion, the explosion is the proximate cause of the loss.[162]

The third class consists of "state of affairs" cases, the situation in which peril A occurs and, while it does not cause any loss or weakening by itself, induces the assured to alter his conduct and peril B occurs in the course of the new state of affairs which has been brought about. Although there is some inconsistency in the cases, peril B will normally be regarded as the proximate cause of the loss in this situation because peril A has simply not operated.[163] Thus, if a vessel is aware of enemy submarines or some other peril in its vicinity, and changes its course to avoid them, the loss of the vessel in a storm on its new route is proximately caused by the perils of the sea and not by war risks.[164] In the same way the abandonment of a voyage through fear of capture is not loss by capture[165] and the danger of losing goods by seizure is not loss by seizure.[166] Where an airport was seized by invading troops and an aircraft on the ground at the time was simply left there, the destruction of the aircraft by subsequent bombing in a liberation operation was not proximately caused by the original seizure of the airport as there was no inevitable causal connection between the initial occupation and the subsequent physical loss of the aircraft.[167]

5–031   Effect of express wording. The insurer may, by appropriate wording, exclude the doctrine of proximate cause. This may be done in one of two ways. First, the scope of a peril may be widened, so that that the peril becomes operative if it has played any part in the loss. Thus if the policy excludes a loss which is directly or indirectly caused by a specific peril, there can be no recovery even if the peril played only an indirect part in the loss. An example is *Coxe v Employers' Liability Insurance Corp*[168] where a life policy which excluded death directly or indirectly caused by war risks did not respond where the assured was killed by

---

[159] *Winicofsky v Army & Navy Insurance* (1919) 35 T.L.R. 283.

[160] *Marsden v City & County Insurance* (1865) L.R. 1 C.P. 232.

[161] *Martini Investments v McGinn* [2001] Lloyd's Rep. I.R. 374.

[162] *Everett v London Assurance* (1865) 19 C.B.N.S. 126; *Stanley v Western Insurance Co* (1868) L.R. 3 Ex. 71; *Re Hooley Hill Rubber & Chemical Co Ltd* [1920] 1 K.B. 257; *Curtis & Harvey (Canada) Ltd v North British & Mercantile Insurance Co* [1921] 1 A.C. 303.

[163] *Kacianoff v China Traders* [1914] 3 K.B. 1121.

[164] *The Coxwold* [1942] A.C. 691; *Moor Line v King and United Kingdom War Risks Association* (1920) 4 Ll. L.R. 286; *British Steamship Co v R.* [1921] 1 A.C. 99; *Green v British Indian Steam Navigation Co* [1921] 1 A.C. 99. See also: *Yorkshire Dale SS Co v Minister of War Transport* [1942] A.C. 691; *Liverpool & London War Risk v Ocean SS Co* [1948] A.C. 243.

[165] *Becker, Gray v London Assurance* [1918] A.C. 101.

[166] *Moore v Evans* [1918] A.C. 185.

[167] *Scott v Copenhagen Reinsurance Co (UK) Ltd* [2003] Lloyd's Rep. I.R. 696.

[168] *Coxe v Employers' Liability Insurance Corp* [1916] 2 K.B. 629. See also: *Oei v Foster* [1982] 2 Lloyd's Rep. 170; *American Tobacco Co v Guardian Assurance Co* (1925) 22 Ll. L.R. 37. In *Spinneys (1948) Ltd v Royal Insurance Co Ltd* [1980] 1 Lloyd's Rep. 406 Mustill J. warned that this and similar wording does not extend to causes which are a "part of history". See also *Tektrol Ltd v International Insurance Co of Hanover Ltd* [2005] EWHC 2473 (Comm), in which Langley J. ruled that defining an "indirect cause" was, in the words of Mustill J. in *Spinney's*, a matter of instinct. Langley J. also applied the alternative test of whether there was an increased risk of loss. In *Tappoo Holdings Ltd v Stuchbery* [2008] Lloyd's Rep. I.R. 34 looting following an attempted coup in Fiji was held to be the indirect cause of the coup.

a train during a wartime blackout. Again, in *Blackburn Rovers Football & Athletic Club Plc v Avon Insurance Plc*[169] a policy exclusion in an accident policy on a footballer for injury "attributable either directly or indirectly to arthritic or other degenerative conditions in joints, bones, muscles, tendons or ligaments" prevented recovery where the player suffered a training ground injury which exacerbated a pre-existing degenerative condition of the lower spine.

Secondly, the doctrine may be restricted by a policy term which stipulates that a loss is covered only if it results solely, exclusively or directly from a stated insured peril.[170] In *Orient-Express Hotels Ltd v Assicurazioni General SpA*[170a] the assured's hotel, situated in New Orleans, was insured against material damage, and also against business interruption losses "directly arising from Damage". The floods in New Orleans in 2005 caused physical damage to the hotel, but led also to the closure of New Orleans for a short period. Both of these matters led to business interruption losses. Hamblen J. held that the policy required business interruption losses to be caused "directly" by physical damage to the hotel, and that the assured could recover only to the extent that the losses would not have arisen had the damage to the hotel not occurred.

It is unclear exactly which forms of words are necessary to oust the doctrine of proximate cause. Phrases such as "due to", "arising from"[171] and "resulting from"[172] seem to add nothing to the general proximate cause rule. The term "consequences of" is equally problematic, although the weight of authority supports the view that ordinary proximity principles apply.[173]

Losses arising from concurrent causes

Meaning of concurrent cause. In the majority of cases it will be possible to isolate a proximate cause from the chain of circumstances leading up to the loss, and where there are two or more causes the court will strive to identify the proximate cause.[174] However, if it is not possible to identify which of two or more causes is the proximate cause, they will be regarded as concurrent   **5–032**

---

[169] *Blackburn Rovers Football & Athletic Club Plc v Avon Insurance Plc* [2005] Lloyd's Rep. I.R. 447.

[170] *Merchants' Marine Insurance Co Ltd v Liverpool Marine & General Insurance Co Ltd* (1928) 31 Ll. L.R. 45; *Jason v Batten (1930) Ltd* [1969] 1 Lloyd's Rep. 281; *Fidelity & Casualty Co of New York v Mitchell* [1917] A.C. 592; *Re Etherington* [1909] 1 K.B. 591; *Southampton Leisure Holdings Plc v Avon Insurance Plc* [2004] EWHC 571 (QB). Contrast: *Mardorf v Accident Insurance Co* [1903] 1 K.B. 584; *Boiler Inspection Co v Sherwin-Williams* [1951] 1 A.C. 319; *Vastgrand Industrial Ltd v Hong Kong and Shanghai Insurance Co Ltd* [2002] H.K.C.U. 475. In the latter case the policy covered loss "directly caused by . . . typhoon and windstorm". The claimant's factory flooded following heavy storms which led to the swelling of the Pearl River, but the insurers denied liability on the basis that the storms had subsided some days before the flooding. The Court's view was nevertheless of the view that the loss was covered, and that the term "direct cause" need not be the most important cause but had to be a substantive cause.

[170a] *Orient-Express Hotels Ltd v Assicurazioni General SpA* [2010] EWHC 1186 (Comm).

[171] *London Borough of Redbridge v Municipal Mutual Insurance Ltd* [2001] Lloyd's Rep. I.R. 545.

[172] *Lloyds TSB General Insurance Holdings Ltd v Lloyds Bank Group Insurance Co Ltd* [2002] Lloyd's Rep. I.R. 113.

[173] *Ionides v Universal Marine Insurance Association* (1863) 14 C.B.N.S. 259; *Liverpool & London War Risks v Ocean SS Co* [1948] A.C. 243; *The Nassau Bay* [1979] 1 Lloyd's Rep. 395.

[174] This was the majority view in *Reischer v Borwick* [1894] 2 Q.B. 548. In *Leyland Shipping v Norwich Union* [1918] A.C. 350 Lord Dunedin stated that, if there are two causes, one or other of them must be chosen as the proximate one. See also *Fidelity & Casualty Co of New York v Mitchell* [1917] A.C. 592 at 596; *Samuel v Dumas* [1923] 1 K.B. 592 at 619, on appeal [1924] A.C. 431 at 467; *Pink v Fleming* (1890) 25 Q.B.D. 396 at 397.

proximate causes.[175] There can, however be concurrent causes only where the two causes are of equal efficiency and each of them operating alone is capable of causing the loss.[176] There can only be recovery if one of the concurrent proximate perils is an insured peril and the other is an uninsured peril: if one of the proximate causes is excluded, the assured may not recover.

5–033   *Concurrent peril uninsured.* In the situation in which the loss is caused concurrently by insured peril and an uninsured peril, the assured is permitted to recover, on the basis that the loss was the result of the operation of an insured peril. The leading modern authority is *Lloyd Instruments Ltd v Northern Star Insurance Co Ltd (The Miss Jay Jay).*[177] The vessel here had been poorly designed, with defects rendering her unseaworthy, and she sank in rough but not unexceptional conditions on a short voyage. The policy was a time policy and thus did not contain a seaworthiness warranty and it was simply the case that loss by reason of unseaworthiness was not an insured peril. The Court of Appeal held that it was impossible to determine which of the two causes was dominant, and that both were to be regarded as proximate causes of the loss: on that basis the assured was able to recover. The principle has been applied in a series of subsequent cases involving insured and uninsured perils.[178]

5–034   *Insured peril and excluded peril.* However, where the loss results from an excepted peril and from an insured peril, operating as concurrent proximate causes, the position is different. The point was considered in *Wayne Tank and Pump Co Ltd v Employers Liability Assurance Corp.*[179] In earlier proceedings[180] the assured had been found liable for a factory fire caused by its installation of equipment for storing and conveying liquid wax. Evidence in the earlier proceedings demonstrated that the assured been negligent in two respects: by using unsuitable and dangerous plastic material in conjunction with a defective thermometer when installing the equipment; and by leaving the equipment switched on and left unattended to operate in the factory before being properly tested. The assured's liability policy covered the latter but there was an express exclusion for "damage caused by the nature or condition of any goods . . . sold or supplied by or on behalf of the assured." The Court of Appeal held on the facts that the proximate cause of the fire was the supply of defective equipment, a loss which fell within the exception to the assured's policy. However, all three judges

---

[175] Lindley L.J. in *Reischer v Borwick* 1894] 2 Q.B. 548 at 550–551; *Hagedorn v Whitmore* (1816) 1 Stark. 157; *Ocean SS Co v Liverpool & London War Risks Association* [1946] K.B. 561 at 575; *West, Wake, Price & Co v Ching* [1956] 3 All E.R. 821; *Heskell v Continental Express* [1950] 1 All E.R. 1033.

[176] *Kastor Navigation Co Ltd v Axa Global Risks (UK) Ltd* [2003] Lloyd's Rep. I.R. 262, on appeal, [2004] Lloyd's Rep. I.R. 481; *Svenska Handelsbanken v Dandridge* [2003] Lloyd's Rep. I.R. 10; *Tektrol Ltd v International Insurance Co of Hanover Ltd* [2006] Lloyd's Rep. I.R. 38.

[177] *Lloyd Instruments Ltd v Northern Star Insurance Co Ltd (The Miss Jay Jay)* [1987] 1 Lloyd's Rep. 32. Cf. *Saskatchewan Wheat Pool v Royal Insurance Co of Canada* 64 D.L.R. (4th) 135 (1990); *Reischer v Borwick* [1894] 2 Q.B. 584.

[178] *Seashore Marine SA v Phoenix Assurance* [2002] Lloyd's Rep. I.R. 51; *Bovis Construction Ltd v Commercial Union Assurance* [2001] Lloyd's Rep. I.R. 321; *Martini Investments v McGinn* [2001] Lloyd's Rep. I.R. 374; *If P & C Insurance Ltd v Silversea Cruises Ltd* [2004] Lloyd's Rep. I.R. 217; *International Management Group (UK) Ltd v Simmonds* [2004] Lloyd's Rep. I.R. 247; *Kiriacoulis Lines SA v Compagnie D'Assurance Maritime, Aériennes E.R. Terrestres (The Demtrra K)* [2002] Lloyd's Rep. I.R. 823.

[179] *Wayne Tank and Pump Co Ltd v Employers Liability Assurance Corp* [1974] Q.B. 57. Cf. *Lake v Commercial Union Assurance Co of Canada* 72 D.L.R. (4th) 239 (1990); *Motor Co of Canada Ltd v Prudential Assurance Co Ltd* 15 D.L.R. (2d) 273 (1959).

[180] *Harbutt's "Plasticine" Ltd v Wayne Tank and Pump Co Ltd* [1970] 1 Q.B. 447.

expressed the further view that it was unnecessary to "strive to find a dominant cause if, as here, there are two causes both of which can properly be described as effective causes of the loss", and that in the event that the assured has suffered a loss which is proximately caused by an insured event and by an excepted peril, the exception is to prevail.[181] The justification for this approach is not entirely clear, although the rationalisation contained in the judgment of Lord Denning that the general words of coverage must bow to the particular words of exclusion is probably the most commonly accepted basis of the rule.

There is a logical fallacy in the reasoning. Let it be supposed that the assured had procured parallel cover for loss caused by defective goods but excluding liability arising from defective installation. Had the Court of Appeal based its decision on a finding of concurrent proximate causes, the assured would have been precluded from recovering under each of the policies. The decision has nevertheless been applied in later cases.[182]

4. ILLEGALITY AND MISCONDUCT

Significance of illegality. There are six situations in which illegality and misconduct on the part of the assured may defeat a claim even though the loss is proximately caused by an insured peril: **5–035**

    (1) where the policy is illegal in its formation as the result of an express or implied statutory prohibition on a policy of that description;

    (2) where the insurance contemplates conduct by the assured which is prohibited by law;

    (3) where the insured subject matter is tainted by illegality;

    (4) where the conduct of the assured following the commencement of the risk has the effect of vitiating the entire contract of insurance on public policy grounds;

    (5) where the assured has, by his wilful misconduct, caused or contributed to the circumstances of his loss, or where his unlawful conduct justifies the rejection of his claim;

    (6) where the assured has, by his negligence, caused or contributed to the circumstances of his own loss.

Although the result may be in each of these situations that the assured cannot recover under his policy, the reasons for this will vary as between them. In cases (1), (2) and (4) the entire contract of insurance is treated by the law as illegal and void, with the consequences that no claim may be submitted under it and the assured forfeits his premium on the principle in *pari delicto potior est conditio defendentis*. If a policy is illegal, the fact that the insurers do not wish to take the point will not necessarily assist the assured, for the court is required to take the point itself if it comes to the court's notice, and to refuse to give judgment on

---

[181] There may be an exception in respect of marine insurance where the insured peril is a peril of the sea and the excluded peril is inherent vice. In that situation, it would appear that the inherent vice exception will not operate if there is a peril of the sea. See *Global Process Systems Inc v Berhad* [2010] Lloyd's Rep. I.R. 221.

[182] *Kuwait Airways Corp SAK v Kuwait Insurance Co SA* [1999] Lloyd's Rep. I.R. 803; *Midland Mainline Ltd v Commercial Union Assurance Co Ltd* [2004] Lloyd's Rep. I.R. 239; *Tektrol Ltd v International Insurance Co of Hanover Ltd* [2006] Lloyd's Rep. I.R. 38.

the policy.[183] In cases (3), (5) and (6), however, the policy itself is unaffected by the illegality or misconduct, and the assured is simply prevented from recovering for loss in so far as it has occurred to the tainted subject matter or results from misconduct, as the case may be.

Illegal conduct on the part of a co-assured under a composite policy will not affect the rights of the innocent assured[184] unless the guilty co-assured was at the time acting as the agent of the other.[185]

5–036   **Insurance policies prohibited by statute.** It is frequently a matter of some difficulty to determine whether a statute which imposes a prohibition on a particular class of conduct also has the intention of rendering illegal as formed any contracts which involve the performance of that conduct. The simplest case is that in which the act of contracting is itself prohibited by statute; here there can be no doubt that contracts are rendered unlawful. A clear example is the statutory bar on trading with the enemy in time of war; any insurance procured by an enemy alien from an English insurer is unlawful on this ground, and becomes so in the event of war breaking out,[186] although a loss incurred before the outbreak of war is recoverable after peace has been declared.[187] Insurance made without interest, contrary to s.1 of the Life Assurance Act 1774 is a further illustration of illegality in the formation of a contract. A more modern example of express prohibition is to be found in s.19 of the Financial Services and Markets Act 2000, which provides that a person may not carry on any regulated business in the United Kingdom, including insurance business, unless authorised to do so by the Financial Services, although the legislation goes on to allow enforcement of the policy by the assured and, in some circumstances, by the insurer.[188]

The more difficult case is that in which there is no express prohibition on contracting in the statute, but the conduct to be performed under a contract is precisely that prohibited by the statute. In every case it is a matter of construing the statute to determine whether the intention of Parliament was to ban contracts or merely to impose fines upon those transgressing its terms, a process which will rarely be straightforward.[189] A series of marine cases decided in the Napoleonic era demonstrates the fine distinctions that may be drawn: statutes which conferred exclusive trading rights on the East India Company[190] and which prohibited the export of naval provisions[191] were held to outlaw insurances covering the subject matter in question, whereas statutes which prevented trading in particular ports[192] and which required the crew to be given written contracts[193] were held merely to be intended to impose penalties.

5–037   **Unlawful conduct contemplated by the policy.** A distinction has to be drawn between cases in which conduct by the assured which is either illegal or contrary

---

[183] *Holnan v Johnson* (1775) 1 Cowp. 341; *Gedge Royal Exchange* [1900] 2 Q.B. 214.
[184] See Ch.15, below.
[185] *Direct Line Insurance v Khan* [2002] Lloyd's Rep. I.R. 364.
[186] Trading with the Enemy Act 1939.
[187] *Janson v Driefontein Mines* [1902] A.C. 484, which also decides that a policy taken out by a person who subsequently becomes an enemy alien is thereupon frustrated.
[188] See Ch.1 of this work.
[189] The leading analysis remains that of Devlin J. in *St John Shipping Corp v Joseph Rank Ltd* [1957] 1 Q.B. 267.
[190] *Camden v Anderson* (1798) 1 Bos. & P. 272.
[191] *Parkin v Dick* (1809) 11 East 502.
[192] *Atkinson v Abbott* (1809) 11 East 135.
[193] *Redmond v Smith* (1844) 7 Man. & G. 457.

to public policy is inevitable and inherent in the nature of the risk,[194] and cases in which illegal conduct by the assured might possibly occur, for it has long been the law that no policy is void simply because it might lead to crime.[195] In the former class of case it would appear that the entire policy is to be regarded as unlawful, on the ordinary common law principle that an agreement to facilitate an illegal act or to provide indemnity for the consequences of an unlawful act is itself void for illegality.[196] As was said by Tindal C.J. in *Redmond v Smith*,[197] a marine case:

"A policy on an illegal voyage cannot be enforced; for it would be singular if, the original contract being invalid and therefore incapable to be enforced, a collateral contract founded on it could be enforced."

This principle would appear to rationalise a series of earlier marine cases in which assureds had been unable to enforce policies on voyages rendered unlawful for contravention of statutory provisions. These cases have been codified by s.41 of the Marine Insurance Act 1906.[198]

By contrast, a contract of insurance which is not from the outset on an illegal adventure, or which does not necessarily contemplate conduct by the assured which is unlawful, is not itself an illegal contract. Thus it has been held that an insurance is valid even though it might operate as a restraint on marriage.[199] The real issue where the assured initially intends or has chosen at some later stage, to break the law during the currency of a policy, is whether he is thereby disentitled from recovering under the policy in respect of a loss, for his subsequent illegality cannot affect the validity of the policy at the date of its formation. The leading general authority on this matter is *St John Shipping Corp v Joseph Rank Ltd*,[200] in which the question was whether freight was recoverable by a carrier who had deliberately overloaded the vessel in contravention of the merchant shipping laws. Devlin J. rejected the contention that the carrier's unilateral conduct rendered the contract illegal in its inception, and adopted the reasoning of Tenterden C.J. in *Wetherell v Jones*[201]:

"[T]he consideration and the matter to be performed are both legal, we are not aware that a plaintiff has ever been precluded from recovering by an infringement of the law, not contemplated by the contract, and in the performance of something to be done on his part."

By way of example, the notion that a motor policy is unlawful as formed because it raises the possibility that the assured may break the road traffic laws but nevertheless recover from the insurer in respect of any loss or injury thereby suffered or caused, is untenable. Indeed, the only situation in which a contract

---

[194] *Egerton v Brownlow* (1853) 4 H.L. Cas. I. It was on that basis that the law at one time prohibited seamen from insuring their wages as this would induce them to relax their efforts to bring a ship to port: *Fender v St John Mildmay* [1938] A.C. 1 at 13, per Lord Atkin. See now s.11 of the Marine Insurance Act 1906, which permits such insurances.

[195] *Wainewright v Bland* (1835) I Moo. & R. 481; *Beresford v Royal Exchange* [1938] A.C. 586.

[196] *WH Smith & Son v Clinton* (1908) 25 T.L.R. 34.

[197] *Redmond v Smith* (1844) 7 Man. & G. 457 at 474.

[198] See Ch.24, below.

[199] *Re Michelham's Will Trusts* [1964] 1 Ch. 550.

[200] *St John Shipping Corp v Joseph Rank Ltd* [1957] 1 Q.B. 267.

[201] *Wetherell v Jones* (1832) 3 B. & Ad. 221 at 225. See also *21st Century Logistic Solutions Ltd v Madysen* [2004] EWHC 231 (QB) (contract of sale valid despite intention of seller to use contract to defraud the VAT authorities).

will be unlawful as formed when it is capable of legal performance is that in which at the outset both parties share the intention or understanding that its performance is to be unlawful: in that case, the common law strikes down the agreement as one to perform an unlawful act.[202]

5–038   **Insurance of tainted subject matter.** The issue in this category of case is whether the assured can recover in respect of the loss of a subject matter which had, prior to the inception of the policy, been put to some unlawful use or had otherwise been tainted by illegality. Two principles emerge from the limited number of authorities on this issue. First, an insurance policy on a subject matter of this kind is not in itself unlawful, although the insurer may have other grounds for denying liability. Accordingly, if the subject matter insured has been stolen by the assured, his action may fail for want of insurable interest or for inability to prove loss; again, default by the assured in informing the insurer of previous illegality may, in the appropriate circumstances, amount to non-disclosure of a material fact. The second principle is the need either for some connection between the prior illegality and the circumstances of the loss or for an attempt by the assured to derive benefit from his unlawful conduct. This stems from the common law notion that a claimant is to be precluded from recovering only where the illegal conduct forms an essential part of his case. Thus, the bailor of goods under an illegal hire-purchase agreement is permitted to recover his goods on default by the bailee, but only by virtue of the bailor's ownership of the goods and not under a contractual provision, because to plead the contract is also to raise the spectre of its illegality.[203]

The insurance cases are not fully consistent. In *Bird v Appleton*[204] the insurer of a cargo was held to be bound to pay for its loss even though it had been purchased using sums illegally obtained by the assured: the court held it to be inappropriate to enquire as to the origins of the insured subject matter in this way. A different result was, however, reached in *Geismar v Sun Alliance and London Assurance Ltd*,[205] where the assured was held to be unable to recover under a household contents policy for items of jewellery which had been stolen from him, the insurers having established that these had been purchased abroad by the assured and smuggled into the country without the payment of excise duties. Talbot J., having held that the assured had an insurable interest in the smuggled jewellery, went on to decide that to allow him to recover for its loss was against public policy, as he ought not to profit from his own wrong. This decision was approved by the Court of Appeal in *Euro-Diam Ltd v Bathurst*,[206] although that case turned on quite different facts. The *Geismar* decision is doubtful: it necessarily cannot be the case that every illegality involving insured subject matter prior to its coverage by a policy of insurance permits the insurer to deny liability, and it can scarcely be said that the assured either needed to plead his own illegality or was seeking to profit from criminality. The case may nevertheless be supportable on the basis that the goods were liable to seizure and were "potentially without value", in which case the assured had suffered no loss.

---

[202] *Ashmore, Benson, Pease & Co Ltd v Dawson Ltd* [1973] 2 All E.R. 856.
[203] *Bowmakers Ltd v Barnet Instruments Ltd* [1945] K.B. 65.
[204] *Bird v Appleton* (1800) 8 T.R. 562.
[205] *Geismar v Sun Alliance and London Assurance Ltd* [1978] 1 Q.B. 383.
[206] *Euro-Diam Ltd v Bathurst* [1988] 2 All E.R. 23.

It would seem, in the light of the decision of the House of Lords in *Tinsley v Milligan*[207] that *Bird v Appleton* remains good law and that *Geismar* cannot be supported. In *Tinsley* the House of Lords held that recovery was precluded on public policy grounds only where the claimant was forced to rely upon or plead his own illegality, and that the fact that the title on which he relied was acquired in the course of carrying through an illegal transaction did not meet that test.

Post-contract illegality vitiating the policy. English law does not recognise the possibility that a contract, which is lawful in its inception and which is capable of lawful performance, can become illegal as formed simply because one of the parties to it breaks the law in the course of his performance. The most that can happen in such circumstances is that the guilty party is precluded from enforcing the agreement,[208] and even this will only be the case where the illegality was closely connected to the loss and was sufficiently serious in nature to bring notions of public policy into play or where the assured sought indirect benefit from his illegal conduct. Thus, the mere fact that the assured has been guilty of fraud during the currency of the policy is of no consequence unless it is directed against the insurers themselves.[209]   **5–039**

Marine policies are a special case, as there is a warranty of legality in s.41 of the 1906 Act which, if broker, terminates the risk as of the date of the illegal conduct.[210] As far as non-marine insurance is concerned, there is no equivalent warranty and post-contract illegality does not affect the legality of the policy as a whole. These points were decided in *Euro-Diam Ltd v Bathurst*,[211] in which insurers refused to indemnify the assured for loss of jewels following a burglary, on the ground that a number of offences under German law had been committed in connection with the diamonds, facilitated by the assured's conduct, and in particular that there had been a series of frauds on the German tax authorities. At first instance[212] Staughton J., whose analysis was approved by the Court of Appeal, held that there was no implied warranty of legality or equivalent implied term, and even if that was wrong it did not extend to breach of foreign laws. More fundamentally:

> "Suppose that a motor car is insured for a calendar year, and is driven in January in excess of the speed limit. Would that be an answer to a claim for loss by theft or fire or a road accident in June? If a publican insured his stock of glasses and they were stolen in June, would it matter that they had been used for drinking after permitted hours in January?"

Loss following the assured's misconduct. Given that an illegal act following the inception of the policy does not render the entire policy illegal, the further question is whether the assured is entitled to recover despite his unlawful act. There are at least four independent grounds on which loss by an insured peril may operate to deprive the assured of the right to recover.   **5–040**

Wilful misconduct. If the loss has resulted from deliberate destruction of the insured subject matter by the assured, he will be denied recovery on the strength of the fundamental principle that insurance is against contingencies and not   **5–041**

[207] *Tinsley v Milligan* [1993] 3 All E.R. 65.
[208] *Marles v Philip Trant & Sons Ltd* [1954] 1 Q.B. 29.
[209] *Total Graphics Ltd v AGF Insurance Ltd* [1997] 1 Lloyd's Rep. 599.
[210] See Ch.24, below.
[211] *Euro-Diam Ltd v Bathurst* [1988] 2 All E.R. 23.
[212] *Euro-Diam Ltd v Bathurst* [1987] 1 Lloyd's Rep. 178.

against certain events, and in such a case the assured has not merely exposed the insured subject matter to injury, he has actually injured it himself.[213] This rule has no necessary connection with illegality, and is concerned simply with the fact that the assured has brought about his own loss either deliberately or at the very least recklessly[214]; mere negligence does not suffice.[215] Thus if the assured sets fire to his property[216] or scuttles his ship,[217] he cannot recover, and any attempt to do so would amount to a fraudulent claim.[218] Deliberate destruction is not necessarily illegal, although cases of illegality may fall within this principle, as, for example, where the beneficiary of a life policy murders the life assured.[219] The wilful misconduct rule has been codified by s.55(2)(a) of the Marine Insurance Act 1906, the opening words of which are that "The insurer is not liable for any loss attributable to the wilful misconduct of the assured." It will be noted that the phrase used is "attributable to" as opposed to "proximately caused by". This wording makes it clear that the term "wilful misconduct" is an abstract concept and cannot be a causative peril in its own right; it will merely be the reason for the occurrence of an insured peril. Thus, if the assured deliberately sets fire to his property, his loss is proximately caused by fire, and wilful misconduct operates as an implied exception to the coverage granted by the policy rather than as an uninsured proximate cause in its own right.[220]

In exceptional circumstances the assured's state of mind may excuse deliberate destruction of the insured subject matter by him. A claim may be made following deliberate destruction only if the assured can bring himself within the test for insanity laid down in *M'Naghten's Case*,[221] namely that the assured was so insane that he was not legally responsible for his actions. That test was applied in *Porter v Zurich Insurance Co*,[222] a case in which the assured deliberately set fire to his own house with the intention of committing suicide, but changed his mind and escaped from the house. The court ruled that the assured had failed to meet the high standard of proving insanity and thus was unable to recover for fire damage to the house. Wilful misconduct on the part of the assured's agents for

---

[213] *Thurtell v Beaumont* (1824) 1 Bing 339; *British Marine v Gaunt* [1921] 2 A.C. 41 at 57; *Beresford v Royal Insurance* [1938] A.C. 586 at 595; *Yorkshire Dale SS Co v Minister of War Transport* [1942] A.C. 691 at 704.

[214] *National Oilwell (UK) Ltd v Davy Offshore Ltd* [1993] 2 Lloyd's Rep. 582; *Ronson International Ltd v Patrick* [2006] EWCA Civ 421; *Porter v Zurich Insurance Co* [2009] EWHC 376 (QB).

[215] *Albany Life Assurance Co v De Montfort Insurance Co Plc* Unreported, 1995 (negligent selection of borrowers by bank under guarantee policy).

[216] *Upjohn v Hitchens* [1918] 2 K.B. 48 at 58; *City Tailors v Evans* (1921) 38 T.L.R. 230 at 233–234.

[217] *Samuel v Dumas* [1924] A.C. 431.

[218] Deliberate destruction of the assured's own property is not of itself unlawful under the Criminal Damage Act 1972. It would appear to be the case that any claim made on an insurance policy following such destruction would involve an offence under the Theft Acts, although if such an intention was not present at the date of the destruction but was obtained by the date of the claim, the insurer would be discharged not on grounds of illegality but on the twin grounds of wilful misconduct and fraudulent claim.

[219] *Prince of Wales Assurance v Palmer* (1858) 25 Beav. 605; *Brisette v Crown Life Insurance Co* 72 D.L.R. (4th) 138 (1990) (joint life policy; proceeds payable to survivor). This principle has now been confirmed by the Forfeiture Act 1982 s.1(1), which prohibits recovery by an assured of a benefit accruing to him in consequence of his unlawful act.

[220] *The Alexion Hope* [1987] 1 Lloyd's Rep. 60, affirmed [1988] 1 Lloyd's Rep. 31.

[221] *M'Naghten's Case* (1843) 10 Cl & Fin 200.

[222] *Porter v Zurich Insurance Co* [2009] EWHC 376 (QB).

which the assured is vicariously liable does not preclude recovery,[223] and in any event vicarious liability can arise with or without criminality on the part of employees or agents so that it cannot be said that criminality has given rise to the liability.[224] Wilful misconduct by the assured's agents with his privity will nevertheless preclude recovery.[225]

The rule is directed against misconduct only, and does not cover cases where the assured, properly and without any fraud on his part, causes the loss in question,[226] as where he causes the loss in the performance of a duty to the State under whose law the policy was made. Thus, where the captain of a British vessel set fire to it to prevent it falling into the hands of French privateers, it was held that the loss fell within the fire cover provided by the policy and that recovery was not precluded.[227]

Some risks, from their nature, exclude any wilful human agency. Thus "collapse" of a building has been held not to include demolition in obedience to an order of a local authority or other intentional destruction.[228]

Cover restricted to "accidents". It is settled that an accident, for the purposes of an insurance policy, is an act which has unintended consequences. However, if the consequences were intended, or if the consequences while unintended were inevitable so that the assured can be regarded as having acted with reckless disregard for them, then it is clear from the authorities that there is no accident and the assured is precluded from recovery by the terms of the policy itself as well as on the grounds of public policy.[229] It follows that whether or not something is an accident has to be looked at from the point of view of the assured, so that if the assured did not intend the consequences then what has occurred is accidental. In *Hawley v Luminar Leisure Plc*[230] the assured's employee, a doorkeeper, committed a criminal assault on a third party for which the assured was held to be vicariously liable. The assured's policy provided indemnity in respect of liability arising from "accidental bodily injury to any person". It was held by the Court of Appeal that the phrase had to be judged from the point of view of the assured itself, and not from the point of view of the victim or the perpetrator, and from the assured's point of view the third party's injuries were plainly accidental as the employee's conduct had not been sanctioned by the assured. The same principle will apply to a first party cover which excluded accidental loss: an assured who is killed while driving under the influence of alcohol may be said to have been the victim of an accident for the purposes of a life policy.[231]

It may be a nice question whether the assured intended the consequences of his act or acted in reckless disregard of them so as to prevent the consequences of his

5–042

---

[223] *Hawley v Luminar Leisure Plc* [2006] EWCA Civ 18. On this basis an assured may recover under a liability policy for an award of punitive damages against him based on the conduct of his employees, provided that the policy is consistent with such recovery: *Lancashire County Council v Municipal Mutual Insurance Ltd* [1995] L.R.L.R. 393.

[224] *London Borough of Redbridge v Municipal Mutual Insurance Ltd* [2001] Lloyd's Rep. I.R. 545.

[225] *Midland Insurance v Smith* (1881) 6 Q.B.D. 561; *Samuel v Dumas* [1924] A.C. 431.

[226] *Thompson v Hopper* (1858) E. B. & E. 1038; *Trinder v Thames & Mersey Marine* [1898] 2 Q.B. 114.

[227] *Gordon v Rimmington* (1807) 1 Camp. 123. See also *Rickards v Forestal Land* [1942] A.C. 50.

[228] *Allen Billposring v Drysdale* [1939] 4 All E.R. 113.

[229] *Ronson International Ltd v Patrick* [2006] Lloyd's Rep. I.R. 194.

[230] *Hawley v Luminar Leisure Plc* [2006] Lloyd's Rep. I.R. 307.

[231] *Marcel Beller Ltd v Hayden* [1978] Q.B. 694.

act from being an accident. In the difficult case of *Gray v Barr*,[232] where the death of a third party resulting from a struggle with the assured while the assured was holding a loaded shotgun was determined by the majority of the Court of Appeal not to be an "accident", as there was nothing accidental about the assured's possession of a loaded shotgun even though the assured's evidence was that he did not intend to use the shotgun and had been acquitted of murder in earlier criminal proceedings.[233] *Gray v Barr* was distinguished by the Court of Appeal in *Charlton v Fisher*,[234] in which the assured deliberately used his car to ram another vehicle and in so doing inflicted injury on a person who, unknown to the assured, was in that other vehicle. The majority of the Court of Appeal, Kennedy and Laws L.JJ., held that the claimant's injuries were an "accident", although their reasoning turned on the consideration that insurance of third party risks was compulsory under the Road Traffic Act 1988, so that the word "accident" in the policy should derive its meaning from the statutory back-ground: the intention of the policy was that any injury suffered by a third party should be regarded as accidental. Rix L.J., dissenting on the point, preferred the view that an assured should be taken to have intended the inevitable conse-quences of his intentional act of causing damage, and accordingly that the claimant's injuries had not been inflicted accidentally. The ruling in *Charlton v Fisher* effectively confirms the *Gray v Barr* approach, although prevents its operation in the special context of compulsory motor insurance.

5–043   **Policy excluding criminal conduct.** The policy may contain an express exclusion for loss arising from unlawful conduct, whether or not the assured intends to break the law. Such a clause is, therefore, potentially wider than the common law exclusion of wilful misconduct.[235] In *Marcel Belier Ltd v Hayden*[236] the policy excluded "death which resulted directly or indirectly . . . from the assured's own criminal act": it was held that the clause was not limited to crimes of moral turpitude, and that the assured, by driving under the influence of alcohol and speeding, had broken the law and, because there was the stipulated causative link between the crimes and the loss, the insurer was able to deny liability.

Other forms of wording may simply replicate the common law. Thus a clause which requires the assured to take all reasonable precautions to adhere to safety regulations is not broken unless the assured has deliberately or recklessly infringed those regulations,[237] and a clause which excludes the insurers' liability for "any wilful, malicious or criminal acts" will not apply where the assured has not committed any offence but has nevertheless negligently caused a loss by a deliberate act whose consequences were both unintended and not reckless.[238]

[232] *Gray v Barr* [1971] 2 Q.B. 554. See also *Whaley v Cartusiano* 68 D.L.R. (4th) 58 (1990).

[233] For similar Canadian authority, see: *Co-operative Fire v Saindon* 56 D.L.R. (3d) 556 (1975)—injuries caused by brandishing a lawnmower in the course of an argument were accidental; *University of Western Ontario v Yanush* 56 D.L.R. (4th) 552 (1988)—setting a fire which got out of control was an accident; *Canadian Indemnity Co v Walkem Machinery Ltd* 53 D.L.R. (3d) 1 (1976)—collapse of crane accidental even though resulting from deliberate failure to maintain the crane.

[234] *Charlton v Fisher* [2001] Lloyd's Rep. I.R. 387.

[235] Although if it is confined to wilful or malicious acts then it reflects the common law: *Porter v Zurich Insurance Co* [2009] EWHC 376 (QB).

[236] *Marcel Belier Ltd v Hayden* [1984] 1 Lloyd's Rep. 416.

[237] *Linden Alimak Ltd v British Engine Insurance Ltd* [1984] 1 Lloyd's Rep. 416.

[238] *Patrick v Ronson International Ltd* [2006] Lloyd's Rep. I.R. 194.

Public policy

The scope of public policy. The common law public policy principle states that **5–044** an assured whose wrongdoing results in a loss should not be able to recover an indemnity for that loss. The true basis of the public policy doctrine is far from clear, and it has been variously suggested that it rests upon notions of deterrence, of punishment and of preventing the wrongdoer from making a profit from his acts. Whatever the proper explanation of public policy may be, there are relatively few cases in which it will operate independently to deprive the assured of the right to recover, because, leaving aside the possibility of express policy provisions, public policy and deliberate infliction of loss will often apply to the same facts. For example, in *Beresford v Royal Insurance Co*[239] the estate of an assured under a life policy was held not to be able to recover following the assured's sane suicide, both because the assured had deliberately caused his own loss and because the assured had committed a crime and thus had offended public policy rules. The latter ground of the decision was removed by the Suicide Act 1961, but the public policy exception would even today produce the same result were the facts of *Beresford* to recur, at least where the policy did not contain a clause including sane suicide as an insured peril.

The relevant principles have been restated in a series of cases involving tort claims. In *Moore Stephens v Stone & Rolls Ltd*[240] the House of Lords denied recovery in tort to a company whose allegation was that its auditors had been negligent in failing to identify the fraud of an individual who was the company's controlling mind and thus whose fraud was imputed to the company itself. In so deciding the House of Lords held that a claim was barred by the principle *ex turpi causa non oritur actio* if the claimant was forced to plead or rely on his own illegality where the illegality was inextricably linked with the claim. Earlier, in *Gray v Thames Trains Ltd*,[241] the House of Lords dismissed a tort action by a claimant who had committed murder, the claim being his character had been affected by an accident which had been the fault of the defendants. Lord Hoffmann stated the rule as follows:

"In its wider form, it is that you cannot recover compensation for loss which you have suffered in consequence of your own criminal act. In its narrower and more specific form, it is that you cannot recover for damage which flows from loss of liberty, a fine or other punishment lawfully imposed upon you in consequence of your own unlawful act. In such a case it is the law which, as a matter of penal policy, causes the damage and it would be inconsistent for the law to require you to be compensated for that damage."

It would thus appear that the public policy doctrine is of independent significance only where the unlawful act was not designed to cause the loss, because if there was a desire to cause the loss then the claim is debarred by reason of the assured's conduct, illegal or not. The operation of the independent public policy doctrine has, therefore, two aspects: the relationship between the illegality and the loss, for it is clear that illegality which is too remote from the loss cannot bar the assured, and a question of proximity arises; and nature of the assured's conduct, for it is clear that not every breach of the law which has given rise to the loss is either sufficiently serious or would produce sufficiently harmful

---

[239] *Beresford v Royal Insurance Co* [1938] A.C. 586.
[240] *Moore Stephens v Stone & Rolls Ltd* [2009] UKHL 39.
[241] *Gray v Thames Trains Ltd* [2009] UKHL 33.

consequences to justify the insurer in refusing to meet its obligations to the assured on public policy grounds.

5–045   *Proximity.* As far as proximity is concerned, unless a causative line is somewhere drawn the assured would in many cases, by denying him recovery under his policy, be punished for his general bad character or conduct. As was said by Sir Murray Stuart-Smith in *Vellino v Chief Constable of the Greater Manchester Police*[242]:

> "The operation of the principle arises where the claimant's claim is founded upon his own criminal or immoral act. The facts which give rise to the claim must be inextricably linked with the criminal activity. It is not sufficient if the criminal activity merely gives the occasion for the tortious conduct of the defendant."

The principle was set out in an insurance context in *Euro-Diam Ltd v Bathurst*,[243] in which the assured suffered loss from burglary of diamonds which had earlier during the currency of the policy been used to assist a third party to contravene German revenue laws. There was no suggested connection between the circumstances of the burglary and the previous unlawful conduct, but the insurer argued that the assured could not recover under a contract of insurance which had become "tainted with illegality". Staughton J., applying the general common law doctrine that a claimant is entitled to succeed if he can establish a legal right without having to plead his own unlawful act,[244] held that the insurer was liable:

> " ... [I]n my judgment a claim may be said to be tainted with illegality in English law ... if the plaintiff needs to plead or prove illegal conduct in order to establish his claim; or by virtue of ... if the claim is so closely connected with the proceeds of crime as to offend the conscience of the court."

The Court of Appeal, expanding upon this reasoning, held that the illegality principle operated to defeat a claimant if:

(1) he is forced to found his claim upon an illegal act, as in the old case of *Amicable Insurance Society v Bolland*[245] (no recovery under life policy following execution of life assured for a capital crime);

(2) granting relief would enable him to benefit from his unlawful act[246]; or

(3) the case falls within a residual class in which public policy demands that no remedy should be granted.

There is, then, a distinction in principle between the assured under a motor policy whose untaxed car is stolen (no proximity) and the assured under a motor policy

---

[242] *Vellino v Chief Constable of the Greater Manchester Police* [2002] 1 W.L.R. 218, at para.70.

[243] *Euro-Diam Ltd v Bathurst* [1987] 1 Lloyds Rep. 178, affirmed [1988] 2 All E.R. 23. See also: *21st Century Logistics Solutions Ltd v Madysen* [2004] EWHC 231 (QB); *K/S Lincoln v CB Richard Ellis Hotels Ltd* [2009] EWHC 2344 (TCC).

[244] *Bowmakers Ltd v Barnet Instruments Ltd* [1945] K.B. 65; *Saunders v Edwards* [1987] 2 All E.R. 651.

[245] *Amicable Insurance Society v Bolland* (1830) 4 Bligh N.S. 194.

[246] It was noted in *K/S Lincoln v CB Richard Ellis Hotels Ltd* [2009] EWHC 2344 (TCC) that the court will not generally assist a claimant to recover the benefit of his own wrongdoing, whether or not the claimant has pleaded or expressly relied on the illegality on making the claim.

whose car is involved in an accident while exceeding the speed limit (proximity).

Culpability. Even where the relevant nexus between the assured's unlawful **5–046**
action and the loss can be established by the insurer, it does not follow that the
assured should automatically be deprived of the benefit of his policy. In the first
place, the illegality may be causative of the loss, but may be trifling: an example
is that of an assured under a motor policy whose car is stolen while illegally
parked. Secondly, the assured's loss may have resulted from a crime of
negligence rather than from any positive intention to do damage. At one time it
was thought that there was no automatic public policy rule which precluded
recovery in these cases, in that there was no justification in public policy for a
finding of illegality: denying insurance recovery is a far greater sanction than that
imposed by the criminal law; the deterrence value of such a rule is doubtful; and
the assured can hardly be said to be seeking to recover the fruits of his unlawful
activity in these circumstances. The issue here is common to all forms of
contract, and the solution originally adopted by English law was to deny that a
wrongdoer is without more to be stripped of contractual rights, and to examine
in every case the nature of the illegality and the consequences of a finding for or
against the guilty party.[247] As was said by Diplock L.J. in *Hardy v Motor Insurers
Bureau*[248]:

> "The court's refusal to assert a right even against the person who has committed the
> anti-social act, will depend not only on the nature of the anti-social act but also on the
> nature of the right asserted. The court has to weigh the gravity of the anti-social act and
> the extent to which it will be encouraged by enforcing the right sought to be asserted
> against the social harm which will be caused if the right is not enforced".

It was thus held that an assured who deliberately overloaded his vehicle and who
incurred liability when the vehicle became wedged under a low bridge, was able
to recover from his insurers because the nature of the criminality was thought not
to be such as to require the imposition of a civil penalty.[249] In the same way,
intoxicated[250] or speeding[251] drivers have been held to be entitled to indemnification for liability in respect of injuries inflicted on third parties, although assureds
who have deliberately[252] or recklessly[253] inflicted injury on a third party have
been barred from indemnification by public policy.[254]

The principles on culpability set out above were apparently overturned by the
House of Lords in *Tinsley v Milligan*[255] in favour of the more stringent principle
that if there is a sufficient connection between the assured's criminality and the

[247] See *St John Shipping Corp v Joseph Rank Ltd* [1957] 1 Q.B. 267, where Devlin J. upheld the
right of a carrier to sue for freight, despite a deliberate breach by him of the merchant shipping
legislation in conducting the voyage.

[248] *Hardy v Motor Insurers Bureau* [1964] 2 Q.B. 745 at 767–768, approved by the House of Lords
in *Gardner v Moore* [1984] 1 All E.R. 1100.

[249] *Fire & All Risks Insurance Co Ltd v Powell* [1966] V.R. 513.

[250] *James v British General Insurance Co* [1927] 2 K.B. 311.

[251] *Tinline v White Cross Insurance Association Ltd* [1921] 3 K.B. 327.

[252] *Hardy v Motor Insurers Bureau* [1964] 2 Q.B. 745; *Gardner v Moore* [1984] 1 All E.R.
1100.

[253] *Gray v Barr* [1971] 2 Q.B. 554; *Charlton v Fisher* [2001] Lloyd's Rep. I.R. 387.

[254] On this basis the decisions in both *Tinline* and *James* were doubted by the Court of Appeal in
Haseldine v Hosken [1933] 2 K.B. 822. For the right of the victim of a motor accident to recover
directly from the assured's insurers or from the Motor Insurers Bureau irrespective of the nature of
the assured's conduct, see Ch.22.

[255] *Tinsley v Milligan* [1993] 3 All E.R. 65.

loss then there can be no recovery. Their Lordships held in *Tinsley* that a contract which was illegal in its formation was unenforceable whether or not the illegality was of a type which offended the "public conscience". It was initially unclear whether this reasoning was confined to contracts illegal as formed, so that it did not apply to the situation in which the assured had been guilty of a trivial illegality which was causative of his loss, and although the "public conscience" test in its earlier form is no longer good law, this does not mean that proximity is the sole basis upon which the *ex turpi causa* principle is triggered. In effect the courts have replicated the "public conscience" test by insisting that an illegal act debars recovery only where there is conduct on the part of the assured which is in some way "reprehensible or grossly immoral"[256]: "there must be an element of moral turpitude or moral reprehensibility involved in the relevant conduct."[257] There is an absence of moral culpability in three situations.

First, the illegality is that of an agent of the assured for which the assured is merely vicariously liable. There is a clear distinction between vicarious liability which is imposed upon the assured under general principle that he is responsible for the acts of his employees and authorised agents, and primary liability which is imposed upon the assured by reason of his participation in, or condonation of, the acts of his agents. It is only the latter which triggers the *ex turpi causa* rule precluding recovery by the assured.[258] Where the assured is a company, it is necessary to determine whether the agents who have perpetrated the wrongdoing controlled the company so that their acts can be imputed to the company in a manner which renders the company primarily liable.[259] The fact that the agents of a company have defrauded the company would seem not to prevent imputation, although the point awaits final determination.[260]

Secondly, where the assured has committed a criminal offence, the assured has appropriate mens rea. This may give rise to an issue where the offence is one of strict liability, because an offence may be committed by an assured who was unaware of any wrongdoing just as it may be committed by an assured who was aware of wrongdoing. In this type of case it would seem that the correct analysis is that the mere commission of the offence is insufficient, and that *mens rea* is necessary in order to defeat the claim. An analogy is *Osman v Ralph Moss Ltd*,[261] in which a person driving without insurance as the result of being informed by his brokers that he was covered and was able to recover from them the fine imposed upon him for committing a strict liability offence. This principle was

---

[256] *United Project Consultants Pte Ltd v Leong Kwok Onn* [2005] 4 S.L.R. 214; *Moore Stephens v Stone & Rolls Ltd* [2009] UKHL 39, the formulation of Lord Phillips at paras 24–27.

[257] *Safeway Stores Ltd v Twigger* [2010] EWHC 11 (Comm), per Flaux J. at para.26.

[258] *Hawley v Luminar Leisure Plc* [2006] Lloyd's Rep. I.R. 307: *Lancashire County Council v Municipal Mutual Insurance Ltd* [1995] L.R.L.R. 393; *Safeway Stores Ltd v Twigger* [2010] EWHC 11 (Comm).

[259] *Lennard's Carrying Co v Asiatic Petroleum* [1915] A.C. 705; *Tesco Supermarkets v Nattrass* [1972] A.C. 153; *El Ajou v Dollar Land Holdings Plc* [1994] 2 All E.R. 685; *Meridian Global Funds Management Asia Ltd v Securities Commission* [1995] UKPC 5; *Moore Stephens v Stone & Rolls Ltd* [2009] UKHL 39.

[260] In *Re Hampshire Land Co* [1896] 2 Ch. 743 it was held that the knowledge of an agent or employee seeking to defraud a company was not imputed to his company. The better view of this decision is that it is confined to knowledge, and that was so held by Lords Phillips and Brown, two of the three majority judges in *Moore Stephens v Stone & Rolls Ltd* [2009] UKHL 39. Lord Walker assumed that *Re Hampshire Land* did preclude imputation of conduct where the company itself was the victim of fraud. The point was left open by Flaux J. in *Safeway Stores Ltd v Twigger* [2010] EWHC 11 (Comm).

[261] *Osman v Ralph Moss Ltd* [1970] 1 Lloyd's Rep. 313. See also *Griffin v Uhy Hacker Young & Partners* [2010] EWHC 16 (Ch).

confirmed in *Clunis v Camden and Islington Health Authority*[262] in which Beldam L.J. commented[263] that:

"In the present case the plaintiff has been convicted of a serious criminal offence. In such a case public policy would in our judgment preclude the court from entertaining the plaintiff's claim unless it could be said that he did not know the nature and quality of his act or that what he was doing was wrong."

Thirdly, independently of the specific issue of strict liability offences:

"In the case of criminal conduct this has to be sufficiently serious to merit the application of the principle. Generally speaking a crime punishable with imprisonment could be expected to qualify. If the offence is criminal but relatively trivial, it is in any event difficult to see how it could be integral to the claim."[264]

Determining whether conduct is trivial or culpable is to be determined on a case by case basis.

Wilful misconduct by a third party. The general rule is that an assured is not precluded from recovering by reason of the wilful misconduct of a third party. However, this will not be the case if the assured has condoned the wilful misconduct of that other party[265] or where the conduct of the third party is attributed to the assured under the rules of agency.[266]   **5–047**

Under a composite policy the rights of each co-assured are quite distinct, so that conduct by one co-assured which precludes recovery by him will not preclude recovery by others who are not implicated in that conduct. However, the conduct of a co-assured may give rise to a loss which is not an insured peril, so that the innocent co-assured will not be able to recover for that reason.[267]

Loss following the assured's negligence

The common law position. It is well established that the assured's negligence is to be disregarded in determining the liability of the insurer. The principle that that casualties brought about by negligence are insured is an old one,[268] and it does not matter whether the negligence is that of the assured or his servants. This stems from the notion that negligence itself is not by its nature a "peril" but is, rather, one possible reason why a peril has occurred. It is, consequently, misleading to speak of negligence as a proximate cause of loss and the only question in law is whether the peril which has caused the loss (whether or not   **5–048**

---

[262] *Clunis v Camden and Islington Health Authority* [1998] Q.B. 978. Cf. *Cross v Kirby* Unreported, February 18, 2000 CA; *Hewison v Meridian Shipping Pte* [2002] EWCA Civ 1821; *Agheampong v Allied Manufacturing (London) Ltd* [2009] Lloyd's Rep. I.R. 379; *Nayar v Denton Wilde Sapte* [2009] EWHC 3218 (QB).

[263] *Clunis* [1998] Q.B. 978 at 989.

[264] *Vellino v Chief Constable of the Greater Manchester Police* [2007] 1 W.L.R. 218, per Sir Murray Stuart-Smith at para.70.

[265] *Hawley v Luminar Leisure Ltd* [2006] Lloyd's Rep. I.R. 307. See also *Zurich Professional Ltd v Karim* [2006] EWHC 3355 (QB) and *Goldsmith Williams (A Firm) v Travelers Insurance Company Ltd* [2010] EWHC 26 (QB): the effect of these cases is all that is required is condonation of a fraudulent course of conduct rather than the specific acts which have given rise to the claims.

[266] *Stone & Rolls v Moore Stephens* [2009] UKHL 39.

[267] See *Samuel & Co v Dumas* [1924] A.C. 431 (deliberate scuttling of vessel not a peril of the sea).

[268] *Austin v Drewe* (1815) 4 Camp. 360 at 362; *Shaw v Robberds* (1837) 6 Ad. & El. 75 at 84.

occasioned by the assured's negligence) is inside or outside the scope of the policy.

Thus, in the context of marine insurance: insurance on a vessel against fire is enforceable if the fire is negligently started by the crew,[269] and insurance on freight is not lost if the vessel suffers a stranding (a peril of the sea) following negligent navigation by the crew[270]; but the perishing of a cargo following delay due to the negligence of the crew is not recoverable under a cargo policy which does not cover loss by delay.[271] The position is the same in the case of non-marine insurance: the assured may recover under a fire policy on his premises even if the fire has been started following his own negligence[272]; the liability insurer of an assured subcontractor cannot deny liability where the works are damaged by a fire negligently started by the assured[273]; and an assured who hides her insured jewellery in a fire grate for safety, but later forgets this fact and lights a fire in the grate, may still recover.[274] There are also numerous illustrations from accident policies, e.g. where the assured has crossed a railway line and is knocked down,[275] or carelessly drinks a dose of poison instead of medicine.[276]

5–049   *Reasonable care clauses in liability policies.* A common feature of liability policies is the requirement on the assured to take reasonable precautions to avoid any loss. Taken literally, such clauses, insofar as they are drafted as conditions precedent to liability, would appear to deprive liability policies of much of their meaning, for if the assured can recover only when he has not been negligent, most of the situations in which he might face liability are excluded from coverage. To overcome this difficulty, the courts have construed clauses of this nature as meaning that the assured must not act in reckless disregard of ordinary standards of reasonableness, but that he can recover if he has merely been negligent. The assured is thus debarred only when, in the words of Diplock L.J.[277] it can be "shown affirmatively that the failure to take precautions . . . was done recklessly, that is to say with actual recognition of the danger and not caring whether or not that danger was averted". This principle has been applied in all classes of liability insurance and the assured has been able to recover despite contravening a reasonable care clause [278] unless recklessness can be shown,[279] although it should be noted that in both motor and employers liability insurance—where liability cover is compulsory—insurers cannot rely upon a

[269] *Busk v Royal Exchange Assurance Co* (1818) 2 B. & Ald. 73.
[270] *Trinder Anderson & Co v Thames and Mersey Insurance Co* [1898] 2 Q.B. 114.
[271] *Gregson v Gilbert* (1783) 3 Doug. 232.
[272] *Shaw v Robberds* (1837) 6 Ad. & El. 75.
[273] *Aluminium Wire and Cable Co Ltd v Allstate Insurance Co Ltd* [1985] 2 Lloyd's Rep. 280.
[274] *Harris v Poland* [1941] 1 K.B. 462.
[275] *Cornish v Accident Insurance* (1889) 23 Q.B.D. 453.
[276] *Cole v Accident Insurance* (1899) 5 T.L.R. 736.
[277] *Fraser v Furman* [1967] 3 All E.R. 57 at 62.
[278] *Aluminium Wire and Cable Co Ltd v Allstate Insurance Co Ltd* [1985] 2 Lloyd's Rep. 280; *Howard Farrow v Ocean Accident & Guarantee Corp* (1940) 67 Ll. L.R. 27; *Woolfall & Rimmer Ltd v Moyle* [1942] 1 K.B. 66; *Concrete Ltd v Attenborough* (1939) 65 Ll. L.R. 174; *London Crystal Window Cleaning Co Ltd v National Mutual Indemnity Insurance Co Ltd* [1952] 2 Lloyd's Rep. 360; *Pictorial Machinery v Nicholls* (1940) 67 Ll. L.R. 461; *Linden Alimak Ltd v British Engine Insurance Ltd* [1984] 1 Lloyd's Rep. 416; *Kier Construction v Royal Insurance (UK)* 30 Con. L.R. 45; *Matalan Discount Club (Cash & Carry) Ltd v Tokenspire Properties (North Western) Ltd* Unreported, 2001. The position is the same in Australia: *Albion Insurance Co Ltd v Body Corporate Strata Plan No.4303* [1983] 2 V.R. 339; *Vero Insurance Ltd v Power Technologies Pty Ltd* 2007 NSWCA 226.
[279] *M/S Aswan Engineering Establishment Co Ltd v Iron Trades Mutual Insurance Co Ltd* [1989] 1 Lloyd's Rep. 289.

reasonable care clause to defeat a claim made against the assured by a third party.[280]

Reasonable care clauses in first party policies. The reluctance of the courts to **5–050** permit insurers to reject claims under liability policies on the ground of the assured's negligence is readily understandable, given that the true effect is to deprive the injured third party of any realistic chance of obtaining a meaningful remedy against the assured. There is, however, less of a case for judicial generosity where the policy covers only the assured or his property rather than his liability, as the interests of third parties are not necessarily at stake. Early cases indeed indicated that the assured under a first party would fare less well under a reasonable care provision,[281] assuming of course that the clause was a condition precedent to the insurers' liability.[282] Nevertheless, the Insurance Ombudsman felt that it was appropriate to apply the recklessness test to reasonable care clauses in first-party policies, and in 1985 set out the questions which he then asked himself when presented with a lack of reasonable care defence in a theft case:

(1) What was the value of the goods at risk?
(2) What was the reason for having them in the place from which they were stolen?
(3) What precautions were actually taken to safeguard them?
(4) Were there any alternatives open to the policyholder?

This analysis gradually came to be accepted by the courts,[283] and was confirmed in two landmark Court of Appeal decisions. In *Devco Holder v Legal and General Insurance Society*[284] the assured had insured his car, a Ferrari, under a motor policy covering both first and third party losses and containing a reasonable care clause. The car was stolen while parked in a station car park with its keys in the ignition: the driver had intended to leave the car for only a few minutes while collecting some papers from his office, but had been detained. The Court of Appeal accepted that the driver had been reckless in knowingly accepting the risk of loss, and that on any test he had failed to take reasonable care. However, the Court saw some force in the argument put for the assured that the standard of care for the purposes of the clause was recklessness and not mere negligence: given that the clause applied equally to both the first party and liability sections of the policy, and that the liability test had been established as being no higher than recklessness, the Court was sympathetic to the view that the restricted meaning of reasonable care clauses should extend to both parts of the policy. This analysis was confirmed in *Soft v Prudential Assurance*,[285] a case

---

[280] Road Traffic Act 1988 s.148(5); Employers Liability (Compulsory Insurance) Regulations 1998 (SI 1998/2573).

[281] *Cornish v Accident Insurance Co* (1889) 23 Q.B.D. 453; *Carlton v R & J Park* (1922) 22 Ll. L.R. 246.

[282] If it is not, the only possible remedy is damages: *HTV v JFK Lintner* [1994] 2 Lloyd's Rep. 125.

[283] *Port-Rose v Phoenix Assurance* (1986) 136 N.L.J. 333 (handbag stolen from airport trolley); *Sinnott v Municipal General Insurance* [1989] C.L., para.297 (goods left locked out of sight in car boot). Contrast *Braithwaite v Thomas Cook Travellers' Cheques Ltd* [1989] 1 All E.R. 235 (assured falling into intoxicated sleep on a London tube train while carrying travellers' cheques in a transparent plastic bag).

[284] *Devco Holder v Legal and General Insurance Society* [1993] 2 Lloyd's Rep. 567.

[285] *Soft v Prudential Assurance* [1993] 2 Lloyd's Rep. 559.

which involved theft from a car. The assured and members of his family, having a few minutes to spare, visited Dover Castle. The car was left unattended for some seven minutes, during which time various items of jewellery left locked in the glove compartment were stolen. The policy covered both first and third party losses and required the assured to take "all reasonable steps to safeguard any property insured". The Court of Appeal held that it was appropriate to apply the liability test of recklessness to the clause, to avoid the possibility of the clause bearing two different meanings depending upon whether the claim was for loss or liability; on that test, the Court of Appeal held that S had not been reckless in that the jewellery had not been in the public view and the risk—while appreciated by S—was regarded by him as minimal. Lloyd L.J. commented that no distinction should be drawn between first and third party policies. The Ombudsman's four principles, set out above, were expressly adopted. These and subsequent cases have given rise to the following propositions.

First, where a reasonable care clause is applicable both to first party loss and to third party liability, the liability test of recklessness is applicable in determining whether the assured's obligation has been broken.[286]

Secondly, where the clause is applicable only to first party loss, dicta in *Soft* indicate that the position is the same, and that mere negligence by the assured will not defeat his claim, and that has been confirmed by later cases.[287] Thus, where a co-assured contractor has been accused of breach of a reasonable care clause, he has been entitled to the benefit of the policy as the allegations amount to no more than negligent performance of obligations under the construction contract.[288]

Thirdly, as a reasonable care clause is an exclusionary provision, the burden of proof is on the insurer to demonstrate that the assured has acted recklessly.

Fourthly, if the assured has inadvertently put his property in danger, e.g. if he has accidentally left property exposed in his car or keys in the ignition, it would seem that he has not been reckless, as there must be some appreciation of the risk.[289] This is so even if there is some reason for leaving keys in the ignition, e.g. because it is difficult to remove them[290] or because the assured believed that the car could not be taken as it was protected by an immobiliser.[291] The test of whether the assured appreciated that he was running a risk is wholly subjective, so that if the assured is deprived of his property by a trick then he has not acted recklessly even though a reasonable person would not have been deceived.[292]

---

[286] *Matalan Discount Club (Cash & Carry) Ltd v Tokenspire Properties (North Western Ltd)* Unreported, May 18, 2001.

[287] e.g. *A C Ward & Sons Ltd v Catlin (Five) (No.2)* [2009] EWHC 3122 (Comm).

[288] *CA Blackwell (Contracts) Ltd v Gerling General Insurance Co* [2007] Lloyd's Rep. I.R. 511 (the point did not arise on appeal, [2008] Lloyd's Rep. I.R. 529); *Tate Gallery (Trustees) v Duffy Construction Ltd (No.2)* [2008] Lloyd's Rep. I.R. 159.

[289] Cf. *Tioxide Europe Ltd v CGU International Insurance Plc* [2005] Lloyd's Rep. I.R. 114, affirmed on other grounds [2006] Lloyd's Rep. I.R. 31 (products liability policy—no reason to believe that additive might cause loss); *Paine v Catlins* [2004] EWHC 3054 (TCC) (fire policy). In *Ansari v New India Assurance Ltd* [2008] Lloyd's Rep. I.R. 58 reliance on a reasonable care clause in a property policy was abandoned on the basis that the insurers recognised that they had to prove that the assured had been reckless in failing to put right defects in a sprinkler system. See also *Scottish Coal Co Ltd v Royal and Sun Alliance Plc* [2008] Lloyd's Rep. I.R. 718 where a case of recklessness was not pleaded against the assured so that the reasonable care clause was regarded as not having been engaged.

[290] *Bushell v General Accident* [1992] 12 C.L. para.314.

[291] *Hayward v Norwich Union Insurance Ltd* [2000] Lloyd's Rep. I.R. 382, reversed on other grounds [2001] Lloyd's Rep. I.R. 410.

[292] *Glenmuir Ltd v Norwich Union Fire Insurance Society Ltd* Unreported, 1995; *Peabody v Eagle Star Insurance Co* Unreported, 1998.

Fifthly, if the assured does appreciate that there is a risk, and he deliberately runs it, he will have acted recklessly and the reasonable care clause will be effective.[293]

Other types of clause. Contractual obligations to take reasonable care may be more specific. Thus, in the case of goods in transit, the assured will generally be under an obligation not to leave goods unattended. In the case of a building the assured will generally be required to maintain occupancy, and equivalent conditions may be applicable to valuable items of personal property. Thus, in jewellery policies it is a common condition that the subject matter is to be kept in a safe when it is not being worn.[294] Motor policies will also contain additional clauses. It is common to find an exclusion which operates if the vehicle is stolen while the keys are left in or on the vehicle. Further, it has been held that the *Soft* decision does not extend to roadworthiness conditions in motor policies[295] although it does apply to property policies where there is an obligation to maintain hazardous equipment in good condition.[296]

5–051

---

[293] *Devco Holder v Legal and General Insurance Society* [1993] 2 Lloyd's Rep. 567 (keys left in ignition); *Gunns & Gunns v Par Insurance Brokers* [1997] 1 Lloyd's Rep. 173 (failure to take precautions against theft in the knowledge that the premises had been targeted by thieves); *Lambert v Keymood Ltd* [1999] Lloyd's Rep. I.R. 80 (lighting bonfire near to premises despite warnings of the dangers involved); *Frans Maas (UK) Ltd v Sun Alliance & London Insurance Plc* [2004] Lloyd's Rep. I.R. 649 (releasing goods without receiving bills of lading).

[294] See *Stern v Norwich Union Fire Insurance Society* Unreported, 1996 (ring still being worn while temporarily removed but remaining within the assured's sight and reach).

[295] *Amey Properties Ltd v Cornhill Insurance Plc* [1996] L.R.L.R. 259; See also *Roberts v State Insurance General Manager* [1974] 2 N.Z.L.R. 312.

[296] *Paine v Catlins* [2004] EWHC 3054 (TCC). But see *Ecclesiastical Insurance Plc v Axa Insurance Plc* [2006] EWHC 634 (QB), where the condition was stricter and required the assured to take practical measures to cover combustible property. The approach in *Paine* was followed in *Vero Insurance Ltd v Power Technologies Pty Ltd* 2007 NSWCA. 226.

CHAPTER 6

UTMOST GOOD FAITH

1. NON-DISCLOSURE AND MISREPRESENTATION

6–001 **Scope of the duty of utmost good faith.** The governing principle of English contract law is that negotiating parties are under a duty not to mislead each other by positive misrepresentations of fact: in general there is no positive duty upon the parties to make a full and frank disclosure of all material facts.[1] In the case of certain contracts, however, the law demands a higher standard of good faith between the parties, and "there is no class of documents as to which the strictest good faith is more rigidly required in courts of law than policies of assurance".[2] "As the underwriter knows nothing and the man who comes to him to ask him to insure knows everything, it is the duty of the assured, the man who desires to have a policy, to make a full disclosure to the underwriters without being asked of all the material circumstances, because the underwriters know nothing and the assured knows everything. This is expressed by saying that it is a contract of the utmost good faith—uberrima fides".[3] The application of the doctrine of utmost good faith to insurance policies has been established since the eighteenth century. This principle has been codified in s.17 of the Marine Insurance Act 1906:

> "A contract of marine insurance is a contract based on the utmost good faith, and if utmost good faith be not observed by either party, the contract may be avoided by the other party."

Consequently, a party to a contract of insurance[4] is under the ordinary duty to avoid making misrepresentations and under the extended duty to disclose all material facts which are or ought to be known by him and which are material to the formation of the contract. "Material" for these purposes means that the fact would influence the judgment of a prudent insurer in determining whether to accept the risk and in fixing the premium where the risk is accepted: ss.18(2) and 20(2).

---

[1] *Walford v Miles* [1992] 1 All E.R. 453.

[2] *Mackenzie v Coulson* (1869) L.R. 8 Eq. 368 at 375, per James V.C. Uberrima fides has been applied as a doctrine of equity or the common law to differing extents and with differing rules of application most importantly to partnership agreements, company promotion, family settlements and title to land.

[3] *Rozanes v Bowen* (1928) 32 Ll.L.R. 98 at 102, per Scrutton L.J.

[4] The doctrine applies to all kinds of insurance but does not apply to related contracts even if their effect is to leave the insurer exposed to insurance risks, e.g. binding authorities granted by insurers to brokers or contracts for the transfer of insurance or reinsurance portfolios: *Pryke and Excess Insurance v Gibbs Hartley Cooper* [1991] 1 Lloyd's Rep. 602; *GMA v Unistorebrand International Insurance SA* [1995] L.R.L.R. 333. Framework contracts, such as non-obligatory reinsurance treaties, are also not contracts of insurance for these purposes: *HIH Casualty and General v Chase Manhattan Bank* [2000] Lloyd's Rep. I.R. 619, varied [2001] Lloyd's Rep. I.R. 702; [2002] Lloyd's Rep. I.R. 230.

There has long been dispute as to whether the duty of utmost good faith has extra-contractual effect, whether the duty is an implied term in all contracts of insurance[5] or whether it constitutes a tortious duty. In *La Banque Financière de La Cité SA v Westgate Insurance Co Ltd*[6] the Court of Appeal held that the duty is extra-contractual.[7] The House of Lords has confirmed this on two separate subsequent occasions.[8] It is beyond argument that the principles set out in the Marine Insurance Act 1906 apply equally to marine and non-marine insurance.[9]

The duty of disclosure

History and elements. The nature of, and the reasons for, the imposition of a duty of disclosure in the insurance context are apparent from one of the earliest reported decisions on the point, *Carter v Boehm*.[10] This case concerned a policy against the capture of Fort Marlborough on Sumatra by a European enemy, effected on behalf of the governor of the fort. Following the capture of the fort by the French, the assured claimed under the policy, to be met with the plea that the assured had failed to disclose the fact that the forts had not been designed to withstand attack from anyone other than the natives of Sumatra, and that the French were known to have designs on the fort. The Court of Kings Bench held that these facts did not have to be disclosed as the underwriter ought himself to have been aware of them, but the judgment of Lord Mansfield contains the classic statement of the relevant principles[11]:

6–002

> "Insurance is a contract upon speculation. The special facts, upon which the contingent chance is to be computed, lie more commonly in the knowledge of the insured only: the underwriter trusts to his representation, and proceeds upon confidence that he does not keep back any circumstance in his knowledge, to mislead the underwriter into a belief that the circumstance does not exist, and to induce him to estimate the risque as if it did not exist. The keeping back of such a circumstance is a fraud, and therefore the policy is void. Although the suppression should happen through mistake, without fraudulent intention; yet still the underwriter is deceived, and the policy is void; because the risque run is really different from the risque understood and intended to be run at the time of the agreement."

Three features of this judgment have received subsequent judicial modification or amplification. First, what appears to matter in this formulation is the fact that the insurer has been misled, so that fraud is irrelevant. However, later cases have confirmed that the assured need disclose only those facts of which he was aware or to which has turned a blind eye; if the insurer is misled by his being unaware of facts not reasonably discoverable by the assured, the validity of the policy is

---

[5] The balance of old authority has been against the implied term. Contrary dicta may be found, e.g. Parke B. in *Moens v Heyworth* (1842) 10 M. & W. 147 at 157, but these have not been followed. See *Merchants' & Manufacturers' Insurance v Hunt* [1941] 1 K.B. 295 at 313, per Scott L.J.; May J. in *March Cabaret Club and Casino v London Assurance* [1975] 1 Lloyd's Rep. 169 at 175.

[6] *La Banque Financière de la Cité SA v Westgate Insurance Co Ltd* [1989] 2 All E.R. 952, affirmed on different grounds [1990] 2 All E.R. 947.

[7] The main significance of this point is that breach of the duty of utmost good faith cannot give rise to damages: see below.

[8] *Pan Atlantic insurance Co Ltd v Pine Top Insurance Co Ltd* [1994] 3 All E.R. 581; *Manifest Shipping Co Ltd v Uni-Polaris Shipping Co Ltd (The Star Sea)* [2001] Lloyd's Rep. I.R. 247.

[9] *Manifest Shipping Co Ltd v Uni-Polaris insurance Co Ltd (The Star Sea)* [2001] Lloyd's Rep. I.R. 247.

[10] *Carter v Boehm* (1766) 3 Burr. 1905.

[11] *Carter v Boehm* (1766) 3 Burr. 1905 at 1909.

unaffected. Secondly, there is nothing in the judgment to limit the duty of disclosure to the assured, and indeed Lord Mansfield at a later point in his judgment specifically stated that the duty of disclosure applies equally to insurers. Thirdly, Lord Mansfield asserted that a breach of the duty of utmost good faith renders a contract void. However, the case was decided before the distinction between void and voidable had become clearly established in English law, and it is now settled that a policy affected by a failure to disclose is merely voidable at the insurer's option. The effect of non-disclosure on an insurance contract is the same as the effect of misrepresentation: the party aggrieved, when the matter comes to his knowledge, may choose either to carry on with the contract or not.[12] It is voidable at the election of the aggrieved party, as opposed to that class of contract which is void by operation of law.[13]

Lord Mansfield's judgment, with these modifications, has been codified in s.18(1) of the Marine Insurance Act 1906:

"The assured must disclose to the insurer, before the contract is concluded, every material circumstance which is known to the assured, and the assured is deemed to know every circumstance which, in the ordinary course of business, ought to be known by him. If the assured fails to make such disclosure, the insurer may avoid the contract."

The remedy is all or nothing. The courts have no power to apply proportional recovery and to allow the assured to recover that proportion of his loss represented by the premium actually paid; neither may the assured make full recovery by proffering the balance of the premium that would have been charged had full disclosure been made.[14] If the insurer purports to avoid the policy but has no justification for doing so, the insurer's conduct amounts to a repudiation of the contract which the assured can either accept, in which case he may bring proceedings immediately, or reject, in which case the repudiation has no legal effects.[15]

6–003   *The meaning of non-disclosure.* The insurer must demonstrate that, on balance, a full picture of the risk was not presented to him.[16] In *Pan Atlantic Insurance Co v Pine Top Insurance Co Ltd*[17] reinsurers sought to avoid a reinsurance policy on the basis that the assured had failed to disclose the reinsured's full claims experience for the years 1977 to 1979. The evidence demonstrated that full documentary details of all losses had been made available by the reinsured's brokers by means of a long document, but that the brokers had deliberately deflected the reinsurers' attention away from those details and towards the 1980–1981 figures contained in a short document and which were more

---

[12] *Morrison v Universal Marine Insurance Co* (1873) L.R. 8 Ex. 197.

[13] See: *Armstrong v Turquand* (1858) 9 I.C.L.R. 32; *Mackender v Feldia AG* [1967] 2 Q.B. 590.

[14] *Pan Atlantic Insurance Co Ltd v Pine Top Insurance Co Ltd* [1994] 3 All E.R. 581, per Lord Mustill at 598. It had been suggested by Nicholls V.C. in the Court of Appeal in *Pan Atlantic* that the proportionality approach should be considered by Parliament. Proportionality has been adopted by the Insurance Ombudsman.

[15] *Transthene Packaging v Royal Insurance (UK) Ltd* [1996] L.R.L.R. 32.

[16] See *Rendall v Combined Insurance Company of America* [2006] Lloyd's Rep. I.R. 732 (fair presentation made to reinsurers by presentation of an estimate that was clearly stated to he such—it was up to the reinsurers to seek further information).

[17] *Pan Atlantic Insurance Co v Pine Top Insurance Co Ltd* [1992] 1 Lloyd's Rep. 101.

favourable to the reinsured. Waller J. held that in the circumstances there had been sufficient disclosure, although the case was a borderline one, and that[18]:

> "An underwriter knows, as well as anybody, or should know, that the earlier years are the only real guide to assessing a rate. The broker has brought along for the underwriter the history in relation to the earlier years and that history, if the underwriter had bothered to study it, was a perfectly fair presentation of those earlier years. As I see it the negotiation is a commercial one, the broker does not have an obligation to tell the underwriter how to do his job."

This analysis was approved on appeal by the Court of Appeal[19] and a majority of the House of Lords.[20] The position in *Pan Atlantic* should be contrasted with that in which the disclosure made to the insurers is incomplete or misleading. This may well amount to a positive misrepresentation, but even if that is not the case then the insurers can rely upon non-disclosure. Thus in *WISE Underwriting Agency Ltd v Grupo Nacional Provincial SA*[21] it was held that the description of the insured subject matter as including "clocks" did not amount to disclosure of the fact that the goods in question also included Rolex watches.

Knowledge of the existence of facts. Where a false statement is made by the   **6–004** assured, his knowledge of the falsity of the statement is irrelevant to the insurers' right of avoidance: that right exists whether the misrepresentation was fraudulent, negligent or innocent. The position is different as regards non-disclosure, for the assured cannot disclose what he does not know.[22] In some of the early cases on the duty of disclosure, there appears to have been a view that the contract would be voidable by the insurer only where the assured had concealed material facts fraudulently.[23] However, since the passing of the 1906 Act and, for non-marine insurance, since the decision of the Court of Appeal in *Joel v Law Union and Crown Insurance Co*[24] it has been established that the assured is under a duty to disclose material facts that he ought to have known in the ordinary course of business, and that what gives the right to avoid is not just fraud but the very fact that the underwriter has been misled. The questions that arise in every case, therefore, are what the assured actually knew and what information is to be imputed to the assured; in the latter context, s.18(1) states that the assured is deemed to know every material fact that would be known by him in the ordinary course of business. The disclosure obligation is less onerous than at first sight it might appear. The modem authorities draw a distinction between information that the assured ought reasonably to have obtained given the state of his

[18] *Pan Atlantic Insurance Co v Pine Top Insurance Co Ltd* [1992] 1 Lloyd's Rep. 101 at 106.

[19] *Pan Atlantic Insurance Co v Pine Top Insurance Co Ltd* [1993] 1 Lloyd's Rep. 496.

[20] *Pan Atlantic Insurance Co v Pine Top Insurance Co Ltd* [1994] 3 All E.R. 581. Lord Mustill preferred to rest his conclusion on waiver rather than failure to disclose, the alternative ground adopted by Waller J. at first instance.

[21] *WISE Underwriting Agency Ltd v Grupo Nacional Provincial SA* [2004] EWHC 1706 (Comm). There was no appeal on this issue: see [2004] Lloyd's Rep. I.R. 764.

[22] *Hearts of Oak Building Society v Law Union and Rock Insurance Co Ltd* [1936] 2 All E.R. 619 at 625; *Wheelton v Hardisty* (1857) 8 E. & B. 232 at 269; *Joel v Law Union* [1908] 2 K.B. 863; *Whitwell v Autocar Fire and Accident Insurance Co* (1927) 27 Ll. L.R. 418; *Crane v Hannover Ruckversicherungs-Aktiengesellschaft* [2010] Lloyd's Rep. I.R. 93.

[23] *Mayne v Walter* (1787) 3 Dougl. 79.

[24] *Joel v Law Union and Crown Insurance Co* [1908] 2 K.B. 863. See also: *Highland Insurance Co v Continental Insurance Co* [1987] 1 Lloyd's Rep. 109; *Newbury International Ltd v Reliance National Insurance Co (UK) Ltd* [1994] 1 Lloyd's Rep. 83; *Edwards v AA Mutual Insurance Co* (1985) 3 ANZ Insurance Cases 60, 668.

knowledge,[25] and information that a reasonable assured would not have had cause to believe existed.[26] The latter category for the most part involves information in the possession of an agent of the assured, the question in those cases being whether the assured himself ought to have known that information in the ordinary course of its business.[27]

If the assured is a person who is not acting in the ordinary course of business, the extended meaning of knowledge set out in s.18(2) is inapplicable.[28] The sole question thus becomes whether the assured knew of the facts that he had not disclosed. The authorities make it clear that the test of knowledge is satisfied only if the assured had actual knowledge, or at the very least was aware, of facts that would inexorably have led to the relevant knowledge, but the assured deliberately chose to ignore those facts. The key decision is that of the Court of Appeal in *Economides v Commercial Union Assurance Plc*,[29] in which the Court of Appeal held that the only exception to actual knowledge was "Nelsonian blindness", i.e. the situation in which the assured has deliberately shut his eyes to the truth.

6–005 *Knowledge of materiality.* Where the assured conceals something he knows to be material, such concealment is fraud.[30] Deliberate conduct of this sort aside, while it is the case that the assured must either have known, or ought to have been able to discover, the existence of a material fact before he is under any duty to disclose it, his ignorance of the materiality of a fact known to or discoverable by him is not a defence.[31] There are dicta which indicate that the assured's duty extends only to disclosing those facts which a reasonable assured ought to have realised would be material to a prudent insurer,[32] so that the proper test of materiality is some sort of hybrid based on the prudence of both parties, but it may be that what is being said is that a reasonable assured ought to know what is material to a prudent insurer. However, later cases emphasise that the prudence or otherwise of the assured's conduct plays no part.[33] The law is thus settled, but it was

[25] *London General Insurance Co Ltd v General Marine Underwriters Association Ltd* [1921] 1 K.B. 104; *Highland Insurance Co v Continental Insurance Co* [1987] 1 Lloyd's Rep. 109; *Aiken v Stewat Wrightson Members Agency Ltd* [1995] 3 All E.R. 449; *ERC Frankona Reinsurance v American National Insurance Co* [2006] Lloyd's Rep. I.R. 157; *WISE Underwriting Agency Ltd v Grupo Naicional Provincial SA* [2003] EWHC 1707 (Comm). There was no appeal on these issues, [2004] Lloyd's Rep. I.R. 764.

[26] See, e.g. *Decorum Investtnents Ltd v Atkin (The Elena G)* [2002] Lloyd's Rep. I.R. 450 (assured not required to disclose possible criminal infiltration into his business, as he was unaware of it). In *Norwich Union Insurance Ltd v Meisels* [2007] Lloyd's Rep. I.R. 69 the assured was a director of companies controlled by his father but he was unaware of facts leading to their liquidation even though he had signed the documents, so he could not be guilty of non-disclosure. It was also held that the fact that he had signed documents without reading them was not of itself material.

[27] *PCW Syndicates v PCW Insurers* [1996] 1 All E.R. 774; *Group Josi Re v Walbrook Insurance Co Ltd* [1996] 1 All E.R. 791; *Simner v New India Assurance Co Ltd* [1995] L.R.L.R. 240; *Groupama Insurance Co Ltd v Overseas Partners Re Ltd* Unreported, 2003. Cf. *Fowkes v Manchester & London Life Insurance Co* (1862) 3 F. & F. 440.

[28] But contrast *Blackley v National Mutual Life Association of Australasia Ltd* [1970] N.Z.L.R. 919.

[29] *Economides v Commercial Union Assurance Plc* [1997] 3 All E.R. 636. See also *ERC Frankona Reinsurance v American National Insurance Co* [2006] Lloyd's Rep. I.R. 157.

[30] *Dalglish v Jarvie* (1850) 2 Mac. & G. 231 at 243.

[31] *Joel v Law Union and Crown Insurance Co* [1908] 2 K.B. 863.

[32] See in particular *Anglo-African Merchants Ltd v Bayley* [1970] 1 Q.B. 311 at 319.

[33] *Pan Atlantic Insurance Co Ltd v Pine Top Insurance Co Ltd* [1994] 3 All E.R. 581: *James v CGU Insurance Plc* [2002] Lloyd's Rep. I.R. 206; *Mark v West Yorkshire Insurance Co* [1989] 10 C.L. 224; *State Insurance General Manager v McHale* [1992] 2 N.Z.L.R. 399; *Back v National Insurance Co of New Zealand Ltd* [1996] 3 N.Z.L.R. 363.

nevertheless commented by Staughton L.J. in *Kausar v Eagle Star Insurance Co Ltd*[34] that, if the assured has acted innocently, the insurer's right to avoid liability should be confined to "plain" cases, which presumably means cases in which the evidence of materiality is overwhelming.[35]

Disclosure to best of assured's knowledge and belief. A clause on the proposal **6–006** form or other preparatory document which provides that the assured need provide information only to the best of his knowledge and belief, can be read according to its terms where there has been misrepresentation. The only real question is whether the assured knew the truth of what he said.[36] Applying a clause of this type is somewhat trickier where the insurers have alleged non-disclosure, as the law is that the assured is required only to disclose facts which he knew or which he can be assumed to have known. Accordingly, if such a clause is to be given any content, it has to relate not to knowledge of those facts but rather to the assured's knowledge of their materiality.[37]

Misrepresentation

Significance. The parties are also under the general common law duty to avoid **6–007** positive misrepresentation. This is spelt out in s.20(1) of the 1906 Act:

> "Every material misrepresentation made by the assured or his agent to the insurer during the negotiations for the contract, and before the contract is concluded, must be true. If it be untrue, the insurer may avoid the contract."

As a matter of practice, misrepresentation does not play a significant role in many classes of insurance as a result of the operation of warranties given by the assured. Warranties may be created in a variety of ways. Where the insurance is initiated by the completion of a proposal form by or on behalf of the assured, it is common for the assured to warrant, by virtue of a "basis of the contract" clause contained in the form, that his answers are true. The effect of this statement is to convert all the assured's answers on the form into warranties. Conversely, warranties may be created by express provision in policies or in other documents incorporated into policies. The effect of a breach of warranty is to permit the insurer to avoid the policy irrespective of the materiality of the assured's false statement. Consequently, given that proof of materiality is a prerequisite to pleading misrepresentation, breach of warranty is a simpler defence to substantiate.

A policy will be voidable under the principles set out in s.20(1) where the following elements are fulfilled.

Representation. The common law recognises a distinction between a representa- **6–008** tion which is intended to have some impact on the mind of the other party, and a mere puff. In commercial transactions, there is, in principle, little scope for the construction of a statement as mere puff, as it may be assumed that if a statement

[34] *Kausar v Eagle Star Insurance Co Ltd* [2000] Lloyd's Rep. I.R. 154.

[35] In *WISE Underwriting Agency Ltd v Grupo Nacional Provincial SA* [2004] Lloyd's Rep. I.R. 764 Simon J., having noted *Kausar*, made it clear that it was not incumbent upon insurers to prove dishonesty or deliberate withholding of material facts, and that Staughton L.J. was merely expressing a "a broad caution against too readily accepting allegations of material non-disclosure".

[36] *Pedley v Avon Insurance* Unreported, 2004.

[37] *State Insurance v Fry* (1991) 6 ANZ Insurance Cases 77–237; *International Lottery Management Ltd v Dumas* [2002] Lloyd's Rep. I.R. 237.

is not intended to be significant it will not be made. However, the concept is not entirely unknown in the insurance context. In *Allianz Via Assurance v Marchant*[38] it was held that the description of business as "very prestigious" was not a representation but only a "broker's puff". In *Clapham v Cologan*[39] the assured was held not to have represented that his vessel was English simply because it had an English name. It will normally not be the case that the submission of draft wording amounts to the making of representations as to the obligations contained in the draft wording.[40] The underlying point here is that there can be a representation only where there is a specific statement by the assured upon which the insurer can reasonably place reliance. An insurer who has to resort to implicit statements is unlikely to succeed.[41]

In *Limit No.2 Ltd v Axa Versicherung AG*[42] reinsurers were informed in the course of negotiating a facultative obligatory treaty in respect of construction risks that the reinsured "as a matter of principle . . . [maintained high standards]" and "would not normally write construction risks unless the original deductible was at least £500,000 and preferably £1,000,000". It subsequently proved to be the case that most of the risks accepted by the reinsured did not have deductibles of the appropriate level. Jonathan Hirst QC, sitting as a Deputy High Court Judge, was prepared to accept that the phrase "as a matter of principle . . . [maintained high standards]" was not of itself capable of amounting to a representation at all, as it was too vague. However, the phrase "would not normally write construction risks unless the original deductible was at least £500,000 and preferably £1,000,000" was sufficiently specific to amount to a representation: the use of the word "normally" was held not to dilute the specific nature of what had been said.[43] The judge's conclusion that there had been a misrepresentation was reversed, but on other grounds.[44] Looked at another way, a statement which is vague and imprecise is unlikely to be regarded as either material or having had an inducing effect.[45]

6–009   *Statement by assured.* The insurers can avoid the policy only if the false statement had been made by the assured or by a person authorised by the assured to make statements on his behalf.[46] If the assured is requested to obtain an independent legal opinion relating to the risk, the statements made in that opinion are not to be treated as made by the assured.[47]

6–010   *Silence.* Misrepresentation requires a positive statement. However, in some circumstances silence can amount to a representation as opposed to a failure to disclose. This point was made by the House of Lords in *HIH Casualty & General*

---

[38] *Allianz Via Assurance v Marchant* Unreported, 1997.

[39] *Clapham v Cologan* (1813) 3 Camp. 382.

[40] *Kingscroft Insurance Co Ltd and Others v Nissan Fire & Marine Insurance Co Ltd (No.2)* [1999] Lloyd's Rep. I.R. 603.

[41] *Feasey v Sun Life Assurance of Canada* [2002] Lloyd's Rep. I.R. 835 (the point did not arise on appeal, [2003] Lloyd's Rep. I.R. 637); *ERC Frankona Reinsurance v American National Insurance Co* [2006] Lloyd's Rep. I.R. 157; *Crane v Hannover Ruckversicherungs-Aktiengesellschaft* [2010] Lloyd's Rep. I.R. 93.

[42] *Limit No.2 Ltd v Axa Versicherung AG* [2008] Lloyd's Rep. I.R. 330.

[43] Following dicta in *Hill v Citadel Insurance Co Ltd* [1997] Lloyd's Rep. I.R. 167, in which it was said that words such as "approximate" and "around" merely gave additional flexibility but did not detract from the statement to which they related.

[44] *Limit No.2 Ltd v Axa Versicherung AG* [2009] Lloyd's Rep. I.R. 396.

[45] *Crane v Hannover Ruckversicherungs-Aktiengesellschaft* [2010] Lloyd's Rep. I.R. 93.

[46] *Smaill v Buller District Council* [1998] 1 N.Z.L.R. 190.

[47] *International Lottery Management Ltd v Dumas* [2002] Lloyd's Rep. I.R. 237.

Insurance v Chase Manhattan Bank.[48] Silence by the assured in the face of an express question put to him by the insurers is deemed to be an answer in the negative[49] and it is not uncommon for proposals to provide that specifically.[50] Statements made by the assured that are literally true, but which are highly misleading, are also to be regarded as misrepresentations, at least where the question put to the assured was not itself ambiguous.[51]

Correction of earlier statements. Three different situations can here arise. The **6–011** first situation is where the assured has made a false statement that he corrects by the date of the contract. In line with the principle that the duty of utmost good faith has to be judged at the date of contract, as long as the assured has corrected the statement by that date the insurers will have no defence.[52] The second situation is where the assured has made a false statement which he has failed to correct in a manner such that the corrected picture was fairly presented to the insurers: it is not enough for the assured, having made a false statement, to present the insurers with further information from which they could with reasonable care ascertain the true position as there is a need for the assured to act with clarity.[53] Once there has been a valid correction, it can no longer be said that there is either a false statement or inducement. It may be that the statement is not corrected at the time the contract is made but is corrected prior to renewal of the policy. There, the earlier policy will be voidable, but the later policy is unaffected even if the insurers choose to avoid the earlier policy (which may be to their advantage if there are accrued losses prior to renewal). The third situation is where the assured has made a true statement that has become untrue. If the facts have changed before the contract is made, then the assured is required to inform the insurers of that fact, failing which he is guilty of misrepresentation.[54] The same principle applies to renewals: material presented to the insurers when the risk is first taken out carries over to any renewals, so that if any of the statements made in that original material have altered, then the assured is under a duty to correct those statements and is guilty of implied misrepresentation[55] or non-disclosure[56] if he fails to do so.

---

[48] *HIH Casualty & General Insurance v Chase Manhattan Bank* [2003] Lloyd's Rep. I.R. 230. See also *Moore Large & Co Ltd v Hermes Credit & Guarantee Plc* [2003] Lloyd's Rep. I.R. 315.

[49] *Roberts v Avon Insurance* [1956] 2 Lloyd's Rep. 240; *Roberts v Plaisted* [1989] 2 Lloyd's Rep. 341.

[50] *Davies and Co v National Fire and Marine Insurance Co of New Zealand* [1891] A.C. 485.

[51] There are many reported illustrations of this point, see: *Cazenove v British Equitable Assurance Co* (1859) 29 L.J.C.P. 160; *London Assurance v Mansel* (1879) 11 Ch. D. 363; *Condogianis v Guardian Assurance Co Ltd* [1921] 2 A.C. 125; *Harding v Victoria Insurance Co Ltd* [1924] N.Z.L.R. 267; *Norwich Union Fire Insurance Society Ltd v Traynor* [1972] N.Z.L.R. 504.

[52] Cf. *Peekay Intermark Ltd v Australia & New Zealand Banking Group Ltd* [2006] EWCA Civ 386.

[53] *Assicurazioni Generali v SpA v Arab Insurance Group (BSC)* [2003] Lloyd's Rep. I.R. 131. See also *Traill v Baring* (1864) 4 De G.J. & S. 318. Cf. the situation in which a policy induced by a false statement is renewed without any correction to the falsity. In such a case the renewal is itself voidable: *Limit No.2 Ltd v Axa Versicherung AG* [2008] Lloyd's Rep. I.R. 330, affirmed on this point [2009] Lloyd's Rep. I.R. 396.

[54] *With v O'Flanagan* [1936] Ch. 575; *Traill v Baring* (1864) De G. J. & S.M. 318; *Re Marshall and Scottish Employers' Liability Co* (1901) 85 L.T. 757; *Watt v Southern Cross Assurance Co Ltd* [1927] N.Z.L.R. 106.

[55] *Glencore International AG v Alpina Insurance Co Ltd* [2004] 1 Lloyd's Rep. 111; *Back v National Insurance Co of New Zealand Ltd* [1996] 3 N.Z.L.R. 363.

[56] *ERC Frankona Reinsurance v American National Insurance Co* [2006] Lloyd's Rep. I.R. 157.

6–012 *Statement not of law.* False statements of law do not confer rights on either party. This matter is most likely to arise in the insurance context where the assured asserts or is told that he has an insurable interest, or where the insurer or his agent gives incorrect information as to the scope or meaning of the policy: it is established that statements as to insurable interest[57] are of law, although it is unclear whether a statement of cover is law[58] or fact.[59] As a matter of general contract law, the distinction between law and fact has proved to be difficult to draw satisfactorily, and has been abandoned by the House of Lords in relation to restitutionary claims for mistake.[60]

6–013 *Statement not of opinion.* At common law any opinion proffered by the assured is not a statement of fact, subject to the important qualification that if the assured falsely states his opinion he will be regarded as having made a factual misrepresentation as to the state of his mind.[61] The 1906 Act approaches the matter in a rather different way, but reaches the same result: s.20(3) states that representations may be of fact or of belief, but s.20(5) goes on to provide that there is to be no liability for a statement of belief made in good faith.[62] The question in every case is, therefore, whether the assured genuinely held the opinion which he stated.[63]

The main difficulty here is in determining exactly which statements are of fact and which are of opinion. A statement by the captain of a vessel that a rendevous point was "a good and safe anchorage and well sheltered" was held to be an honest opinion and thus not a misrepresentation.[64] A statement by the assured that he is in good health in reference to a proposed life policy will generally be construed to mean in good health to his own knowledge.[65]

By contrast, a view given by the assured as to his temperate habits has been held to be a statement of fact.[66] A statement which is in essence factual, e.g. that there are fire hydrants at the insured premises, cannot be disclaimed simply by expressing it as an opinion.[67] The test was to ask what the words used would have conveyed to a prudent underwriter.[68]

Any answer by the assured to a question which requires him to proffer an opinion[69] will not be construed as a statement of fact by the courts, so that the

---

[57] *Harse v Pearl Life Assurance Co* [1904] 1 K.B. 558.

[58] *Re Hooley Hill Rubber and Chemical Co Ltd and Royal Insurance Co* [1920] 1 K.B. 257.

[59] *Equitable Life Assurance Society of the United States v Bertie* (1890) 8 N.Z.L.R. 579; *Boyd v Colonial Mutual Life Assurance Society* (1910) 29 N.Z.L.R. 41.

[60] *Kleinwort Benson v Lincoln City Council* [1998] 4 All E.R. 513.

[61] *Bisset v Wilkinson* [1927] A.C. 177.

[62] *Wheelton v Hardisty* (1857) 8 E. & B. 232.

[63] *Economides v Commercial Union Assurance Co Plc* [1988] Q.B. 587.

[64] *Anderson v Pacific Fire & Marine Insurance Co* (1872) L.R. 7 C.P. 65.

[65] *Life Association of Scotland v Forster* (1873) 11 M. (Ct of Sess) 351. See also *Delahave v British Empire Mutual Life* (1897) 13 T.L.R. 245.

[66] *Thomson v Weems* (1884) 9 App. Cas. 671. See also: *Merchants & Manufacturers Insurance v Hunt* [1941] 1 K.B. 295; *Zurich v Leven* 1940 S.C. 406.

[67] *Sirius International Insurance Corp v Oriental Assurance Corp* [1999] Lloyd's Rep. I.R. 343.

[68] *Highland Insurance Co v Continental Insurance Co* [1987] 1 Lloyd's Rep. 109; *Crane v Hannover Ruckversicherungs-Aktiengesellschaft* [2010] Lloyd's Rep. I.R. 93.

[69] See *International Lottery Management Ltd v Dumas* [2002] Lloyd's Rep. I.R. 237, where the misrepresentation relied upon by the insurers did not appear in the proposal form but had been contained in documents submitted independently and earlier: H.H. Judge Dean QC ruled that a statement in the proposal form to the effect that the assured had to state facts to the best of his knowledge and belief was inapplicable to answers given by him which were not contained in the proposal form.

fact that the opinion proves not to be justifiable will be immaterial unless the insurer can demonstrate that the stated opinion was not held at the time.[70] The difficulty which may arise here is that the assured's statement, while believed by him, may reflect a view which he could not reasonably have held. In *Economides v Commercial Union Assurance Co Plc*[71] the proposal form required the assured to answer questions to the best of his knowledge and belief, and it was common ground that the primary issue was whether the assured's answer was honest rather than objectively true. The Court of Appeal was unanimously of the view both that the assured had answered the question honestly and that there was an objective basis for his belief, and that he ought to recover. Simon Brown L.J. held that s.20(5) was concerned purely with honesty and not with reasonable care, and that the assured was not required to have any objectively reasonable basis for putting forward his opinion. In particular, there was no duty upon the assured, when putting forward his opinion, to make further inquiries to test the correctness of that opinion, although an assured who in the absence of any knowledge made a "blind guess" would not be acting honestly, he could not be regarded as holding the professed opinion. Peter Gibson L.J. agreed with this analysis, but was prepared to accept that he might be wrong and that some objectivity might be required, the latter being the line taken by Sir Iain Glidewell, who drew a distinction between s.20(5) and the actual question posed to the assured: in his view, the proposal form, as worded, required the assured to give an answer which, as a reasonable man knowing the facts actually in his possession, he honestly believed, a test which he held had been satisfied by the assured. Sir Iain Glidewell declined to rule on the meaning of s.20(5), on the basis that the wording of the proposal form displaced that subsection and made its interpretation irrelevant. The point is of particular significance, as it is the practice of insurers to ask questions which require an answer only to assured's knowledge and belief. In *Sirius International Insurance Corp v Oriental Assurance Corp*[72] Longmore J. regarded *Economides* as deciding that a statement by the reinsured would be false unless there were reasonable grounds for believing its truth, whereas in Cresswell J in *Rendall v Combined Insurance Company of America*[73] appeared to deny the existence of any residual objective test.

The tenor of the judgment of the Privy Council in *Zeller v British Caymanian Insurance Co Ltd*[74] also supports the view that honesty suffices. The assured in this case was asked to answer, to the best of his knowledge and belief, a series of questions about his health: as the assured had answered the questions honestly, the Privy Council, applying *Economides* (although not specifying which of the judgments in that case it was following) held that the assured had not been guilty of misrepresentation because he had exercised his own judgment on what was and was not material.

Where the insurance relates to a specific item such as a work of art or other valuable piece, and the assured proffers an opinion that it is authentic, such opinion constitutes an implied representation of fact that the art world generally accepted the piece as authentic: it is not to be construed as a guarantee of

[70] *Kelsall v Allstate Insurance Co Ltd, The Times*, March 20, 1987.

[71] *Economides v Commercial Union Assurance Co Plc* [1997] 3 All E.R. 635.

[72] *Sirius International Insurance Corp v Oriental Assurance Corp* [1999] Lloyd's Rep. I.R. 343. See also *Eagle Star Insurance Co Ltd v Games Video Co (GVC) SA (The Game Boy)* [2004] Lloyd's Rep. I.R. 867.

[73] *Rendall v Combined Insurance Company of America* [2006] Lloyd's Rep. I.R. 732. See also *Howells v Dominion Insurance Co Ltd* Unreported, 1999, where the court took the view that the sole question was honesty.

[74] *Zeller v British Caymanian Insurance Co Ltd* [2008] Lloyd's Rep. I.R. 545.

authenticity, nor is it to be construed as a mere opinion either of authenticity or of the view of the art market.[75]

6–014   *Statement not of intention or expectation.*   Statements of intention or expectation are not statements of present fact, unless the assured does not hold that intention or expectation when the statement is made, in which case there is a factual misstatement of the assured's state of mind.[76] Section 20(3) of the 1906 Act provides that statements of expectation are representations but under s.20(5), are to be regarded as true unless the intention is not genuinely held. Thus where the assured stated his expectation as to the date of departure of certain vessels, it was held to be an insufficient answer to his claim that the vessels had in fact already departed.[77] Again, where reinsurers alleged that they had been show drawings of the fire precaution systems in a building under construction, it was held that the drawings did not show a built system and did not amount to a representation that the systems were installed and operational at the inception of the risk: the only representation was that as at the date of the presentation the assured intended to install the six systems and that the systems would be those in the drawings.[78]

6–015   *Statement untrue.*   A statement which is literally true might nevertheless amount to a misrepresentation if it carries false implications. Subject to this, a statement is not actionable if it is completely true or, in the case of a statement which is partially untrue, "if it is substantially correct, that is to say, if the difference between what is represented and what is actually correct would not be considered material by a prudent insurer".[79] Thus a statement by the assured that his premises are equipped with a sprinkler system when in fact the system is inoperative because there is no pump attached to it, is not substantially correct as the difference between the statement and the strict truth is a material one.[80] By contrast, a statement by a reinsurer to its retrocessionaires that there had been no losses under the program was held to be true, as the statement related only to the retrocession and not to claims against the reinsured by policy holders and ought to have been so understood by the retrocessionares.[81] Whether a statement is true or false may be a matter of some difficulty.[82]

Any answer given by the assured is to be assessed in the context of the custom and practice of the trade to which it relates.[83] The courts have typically been generous in construing an assured's answers as accurate. Thus it has been held that the description of one room occupied by a lodger as a "dwelling-house" was

[75] *Kamidian v Holt* [2009] Lloyd's Rep. I.R. 242.

[76] *Bowden v Vaughan* (1809) 10 East 415; *Hubbard v Glover* (1812) 3 Camp. 313; *Brine v Featherstone* (1813) 4 Taunt. 869; *Dennistoun v Lillie* (1821) 3 Bli. 202; *Grant v Aetna Insurance Co* (1862) 15 Moo. P.C. 516; *Anderson v Pacific Fire and Marine Insurance Co* (1872) L.R. 7 C.P. 65; *Highland Insurance v Continental Insurance* [1987] 1 Lloyd's Rep. 108.

[77] *Barber v Fletcher* (1779) 1 Doug. K.B. 305.

[78] *Gan Insurance Co Ltd v Tai Ping Insurance Co Ltd (No.2)* [2001] Lloyd's Rep. I.R. 291, reversed on other grounds, [2001] Lloyd's Rep. I.R. 667. See also *Seismik Sekuritik AG v Sphere Drake Insurance Co Plc* [1997] 8 C.L. 351.

[79] Marine Insurance Act 1906 s.20(4). See: *Pawson v Watson* (1778) 2 Cowp. 785; *Nonnen v Kettlewell* (1812) 16 East 176; *Svenska Handelsbanken v Sun Alliance and London Insurance Plc* [1996] 1 Lloyd's Rep. 519; *Avon Insurance Plc v Swire Fraser Ltd* [2000] Lloyd's Rep. I.R. 535.

[80] *Sirius International Insurance Corp v Oriental Assurance Corp* [1999] Lloyd's Rep. I.R. 343.

[81] *Groupama Insurance Co Ltd v Overseas Partners Re Ltd* Unreported, 2003. See also *Crane v Hannover Ruckversicherungs-Aktiengesellschaft* [2010] Lloyd's Rep. I.R. 93.

[82] See the differing views in *Assicurazioni Generali SpA v Arab Insurance Group (BSC)* [2003] Lloyd's Rep. I.R. 131.

[83] *Chaurand v Angerstein* (1791) Peake 43.

accurate,[84] and furniture in lifts in a yard covered by, tarpaulins has been held to be "in store".[85] By contrast a coffee-house has been held not to come under the description of "inn",[86] and a "garage" has been held not to include an unroofed yard.[87]

Innocent, negligent and fraudulent misrepresentations. At common law, any **6–016** false statement which induces a contract entitles the innocent party to avoid the contract. The position is the same in insurance law, assuming objective materiality. It is irrelevant to the remedy of avoidance whether the misrepresentation is fraudulent, negligent or innocent.[88] Thus if the fact misstated by the assured is material, the policy is voidable and it will not avail him that he acted with perfect good faith and honesty of intention. There are a number of dicta[89] and one decision[90] to the effect that life insurance is an exception to the general rule that an innocent misrepresentation may afford grounds for avoiding a policy of life insurance, but there is no modern authority for this view. It may be necessary to distinguish between innocence, negligence and fraud in certain circumstances,[91] but for avoidance purposes the duty to avoid misrepresentation is unitary.

The effect of fraud. A misrepresentation does not give the insurer the right to **6–017** avoid the policy unless it relates to a material fact and has the requisite inducing effect. There is some doubt as to whether these requirements are waived in the case of a fraudulent misrepresentation, so that the insurer is entitled to avoid liability simply because of fraud. There is authority for the proposition that an immaterial fraudulent misrepresentation does give the insurer the right to avoid the policy,[92] although general contract principles indicate that a fraudulent misrepresentation does not give any right of avoidance if it does not operate as an inducement.[93] In *Pan Atlantic Insurance Co Ltd v Pine Top Insurance Co Ltd*[94] Lord Mustill appears indirectly to have overturned the view that an immaterial fraud is enough to allow avoidance by rejecting the argument that the doctrine of utmost good faith has any disciplinary element: his Lordship added that "to enable an underwriter to escape liability when he has suffered no harm would be positively unjust".[95] This comment related to the need to prove inducement rather than to the issue under discussion, but would appear to be relevant to it. The point is, however, far from resolved, and in *Insurance Corporation of Channel Islands Ltd v Royal Hotel (No.2)*[96] Mance J. was of the

[84] *Friedlander v London Assurance* (1832) 1 Moo. & R. 171.
[85] *Wulfson v Switzerland General Insurance Co* (1940) 67 Ll. L.R. 190.
[86] *Doe d. Pitt v Lanning* (1814) 4 Camp. 73.
[87] *Barnett & Block v National Parcels Insurance* (1942) 73 Ll. L.R. 17.
[88] *Dennistoun v Lillie* (1821) 3 Bli. 202; *Hamilton & Co v Eagle Star and British Dominions Insurance Co Ltd* (1924) 19 Ll. L.R. 242; *Graham v Western Australian Insurance* (1931) 40 Ll. L.R. 64 at 66.
[89] *Joel v Law Union and Crown Insurance Co* [1908] 2 K.B. 863; *Anderson v Fitzgerald* (1853) 4 H.L.C. 484 at 504.
[90] *Scottish Provident v Boddam* (1893) 9 T.L.R. 385.
[91] e.g. in respect of return of premium, the availability of damages or where the policy excludes the right of avoidance for innocent or negligent misrepresentation.
[92] *Sibbald v Hill* (1814) 2 Dow 263; *The Bedouin* [1894] P. 1.
[93] *Horsfall v Thomas* (1862) 1 H. & C. 90.
[94] *Pan Atlantic Insurance Co Ltd v Pine Top Insurance Co Ltd* [1994] 3 All E.R. 581.
[95] *Pan Atlantic Insurance Co Ltd v Pine Top Insurance Co Ltd* [1994] 3 All E.R. 581 at 617.
[96] *Insurance Corporation of Channel Islands Ltd v Royal Hotel (No.2)* [1998] Lloyd's Rep. I.R. 151.

view that the mere fact that the assured had been prepared to defraud a third party was of itself a material fact, as it rendered the assured a person with whom the insurers might not want to do business. It thus becomes arguable that a fraudulent statement or omission in the presentation of the risk is, by definition, a material fact under the heading of moral hazard, even though the fact misstated or withheld was not of itself directly material to the risk. The most recent comment on this issue is that of Longmore L.J. in *K/S Merc-Skandia XXXXII v Certain Lloyd's Underwriters*,[97] the Court of Appeal there holding that in the post-contractual situation fraud was entirely neutral in its effect, and the only question was whether the assured's failure to disclose was material to the risk and induced the insurers to act in a different fashion.

Fraud has three possible consequences: the assured may face an action in deceit; if the policy is avoided the assured will lose the right to recover the premium; and any clause which purports to limit or exclude the assured's duty of utmost good faith will not as a matter of public policy extend to fraud, as no person will be permitted to take advantage of his own fraud.[98]

6–018   *Answers to ambiguous questions.* There is misrepresentation where the assured gives a false or misleading answer to a plain question.[99] The many cases which concern ambiguous questions are probably best regarded as confined to their own facts[100] although the question in each of them is whether there is a genuine ambiguity or whether the assured is seeking to rely upon an unjustifiably narrow interpretation of the question, to justify his failure to tell the complete truth. Where the question is ambiguous in that the meaning intended by the insurer would not be readily apparent to a reasonable man,[101] the fact that the assured has misunderstood or misinterpreted the question in giving what he believed to be a truthful answer will in general exonerate him.[102] Thus it is not misrepresentation for an assured to state that he has not been convicted of an offence connected with the driving of a motor vehicle when he has been prosecuted for not possessing a road fund licence or valid insurance: such a question implies that it is concerned with dangerous driving and the like, as opposed to regulatory offences.[103] Where a previous policy had been substituted for the convenience of the insurer, the word "cancelled" in the question "[h]as any proposal for new or renewed insurance, or any policy in which you were interested ever been withdrawn, declined or cancelled?" meant the determination of the contract by

[97] *K/S Merc-Skandia XXXXII v Certain Lloyd's Underwriters* [2001] Lloyd's Rep. I.R. 802.

[98] These propositions flow from the speeches of the House of Lords in *HIH Casualty and General Insurance v Chase Manhattan Bank* [2003] Lloyd's Rep. I.R. 230.

[99] *Galloway v Guardian Royal Exchange (UK) Ltd* [1999] Lloyd's Rep. I.R. 209; *Doheny v New India Assurance Co Ltd* [2005] Lloyd's Rep. I.R. 251.

[100] *Corcos v De Rougemont* (1925) 23 Ll. L.R. 164; *Holt Motors v South East Lancashire Insurance Co Ltd* (1930) 37 Ll. L.R. 1; *Cleland v London General Insurance Co Ltd* (1935) 51 Ll. L.R. 156; *Brentnall v Cornhill Insurance Co Ltd* (1931) 40 Ll. L.R. 166.

[101] There has to be some objective basis for the assured's construction of the question. The test is objective and not subjective: see *R & R Developments Ltd v Axa Insurance Ltd* [2009] EWHC 2429 (Ch), where the court's review of the authorities, including *Joel v Law Union and Crown Insurance Co* [1908] 2 K.B. 863; *Re Etherington and the Lancashire and Yorkshire Accident Insurance Company* [1909] 1 K.B. 591 and *Condogianis v Guardian Assurance* [1921] 2 A.C. 125 showed that the test was objective.

[102] *Yorke v Yorkshire Insurance Co Ltd* [1918] 1 K.B. 662; *Roberts v Plaisted* [1989] 2 Lloyd's Rep. 341; *Royal Insurance Co v Coleman* (1906) 26 N.Z.L.R. 526. This will not be the case if the broker, as the assured's agent, has drafted the proposal: *Pearson Plc v Excess Insurance Co Ltd* Unreported, 1988.

[103] *Taylor v Eagle Star Insurance Co* (1940) 67 Ll. L.R. 136; *Revell v London General Insurance Co* (1934) 51 Ll. L.R. 114.

the unilateral act of the company.[104] A question in a proposal for motor insurance asked for the amount "actually paid" for the vehicle and an ambiguity was found in that "actually paid" could mean "amount actually paid in cash to the vendor" or it could mean the amount actually expended by the purchaser to (in the case of a second hand car) get it on the road.[105] Again, where the assured was asked whether he "ever been the subject of any action of bankruptcy", the question was regarded as ambiguous and was construed as applying only to proceedings which had resulted in bankruptcy rather than to proceedings which had not.[106] Where the assured answered a question as to the cost of her car honestly, the fact that some of the cost was made up by the part-exchange of another car was held not to be material.[107] An assured who is fraudulent will in any event not be permitted to take advantage of an alleged ambiguity to justify misrepresentation.[108]

Difficulty has been encountered where a firm has applied for insurance and has been asked whether the proposer has been a claimant on a fire policy before: in some cases that question has been construed as referring to claims by the firm itself and not by its individual partners,[109] but in others the question has been construed as extending to the individuals who control the firm.[110]

General questions. Where a question is not so much ambiguous as wide, the courts have similarly taken the view that the question is to be confined within reasonable limits. The leading authority is *Connecticut Mutual Life Insurance Co of Hartford v Moore*.[111] In this case the relevant question, in a life policy, was "Have you had any other illness, local disease or personal injury?" The life assured had replied in the negative, although some 12 years previously he had suffered a partial fracture of the skull. The Privy Council expressed the view that[112]:   **6–019**

> "[The insurers] could not reasonably expect a man of mature age to recollect and disclose every illness, however slight, or every personal injury . . . It is manifest that this question must be read with some limitation and qualification to render it reasonable . . . "

The courts have tended to construe general questions ejusdem generis with the preceding specific questions.[113]

Causation. Proof of any connection between the circumstances of the assured's loss and the material fact misrepresented or not disclosed to the insurer is   **6–020**

---

[104] *Willcocks v New Zealand Insurance Co* [1926] N.Z.L.R. 805.

[105] *In re an Arbitration between Barr-Brown and N.I.M.U. Insurance Co* [1942] N.Z.L.R. 444.

[106] *O'Connor v Bullirnore Underwriting Agency Ltd, The Times*, March 10, 2004.

[107] *Brentnall v Cornhill Insurance* (1931) 40 Ll. L.R. 166; cf. *Yorke v Yorkshire Insurance* [1918] I K.B. 662.

[108] *Orakpo v Barclays Insurance Services Ltd* [1995] L.R.L.R. 443.

[109] *Davies v National Fire and Marine Insurance Co of New Zealand* [1891] A.C. 485; *Nicholas v New Zealand Insurance Co* [1930] N.Z.L.R. 699 where the question was quite specific " . . . has proponent either individually or as a member of a partnership or company or his or her wife or husband, . . . ever had property damaged . . . ?"); *Ewer v National Employers' Mutual General Assurance Association Ltd* [1937] 2 All E.R. 193.

[110] *Glicksman v Lancashire and General Assurance Co Ltd* [1927] A.C. 139.

[111] *Connecticut Mutual Life Insurance Co of Hartford v Moore* (1881) L.R. 6 App. Cas. 644.

[112] *Connecticut Mutual Life Insurance Co of Hartford v Moore* (1881) L.R. 6 App. Cas. 644 at 648.

[113] *Roberts v Plaisted* [1989] 2 Lloyd's Rep. 341; *State Insurance v Peake* [1991] 2 N.Z.L.R. 287.

unnecessary[114]; it is enough if the insurer demonstrates that the judgment of a prudent insurer would have been, and that the insurer actually was, influenced by the assured's breach of duty.

2. MATERIALITY AND INDUCEMENT

6–021 **General definition.** Sections 18(2) and 20(2) of the 1906 Act provide: "Every circumstance is material which would influence the judgment of a prudent insurer in fixing the premium, or in determining whether he will take the risk", a test which applies to all forms of insurance.[115] At one time, particularly as regards life insurance, there was a view that the test was that of the prudent assured rather than the prudent underwriter,[116] but that proposition does not represent the law.[117] The sections deal only with the question of materiality and do not touch on the further question of whether it is also necessary for the actual insurer in the case to have been induced to enter into the contract by the assured's failure to disclose or misrepresentation, although this requirement has been implied into the legislation.[118] It is thus necessary for the insurer to satisfy both the materiality and the inducement tests before the contract can be avoided by him for breach of duty by the assured.

Limb 1: the prudent insurer test

6–022 *What is a "prudent insurer"?* The test of materiality is whether a prudent and experienced insurer might be influenced in his judgment if he knew of the fact misstated or withheld.[119] There does not seem to have been any serious attempt to define the term "prudent insurer". However, in *Associated Oil Carriers Ltd v Union Insurance Society of Canton Ltd*,[120] Atkin J. imposed what is in effect a limitation of reasonableness on this concept, and refused to hold that a prudent underwriter would have regarded the German nationality of the charterer of a vessel as a material fact in the absence of war, as to do so would have imposed

---

[114] *Pan Atlantic* [1994] 3 All E.R. 581,

[115] *Joel v Law Union and Crown Insurance Co* [1908] 2 K.B. 863; *March Cabaret Club and Casino v London Assurance* [1975] 1 Lloyd's Rep. 169; *Lambert v Co-operative Insurance Society Ltd* [1975] 2 Lloyd's Rep. 485; *Kelsall v Allstate Insurance Co Ltd, The Times*, March 20, 1987; *Pan Atlantic Insurance Co Ltd v Pine Top Insurance Co Ltd* [1994] 3 All E.R. 581.

[116] *Durrell v Bedereley* (1816) Holt N.P. 283 at 286; *Swete v Fairlie* (1833) 6 Car. & P. 1; *Fowkes v Manchester & London Life Assurance Co* (1862) 3 F. & F. 440; *Joel v Law Union and Crown Insurance Co* [1908] 2 K.B. 853 at 884; Lord President Inglis in *Life Association of Scotland v Forster* (1873) 11 M. (Ct of Sess) 351; *Becker v Marshall* (1922) 12 Ll. L.R. 413 at 414.

[117] *Lindenau v Desborough* (1828) 8 B. & C. 586 at 592–593; *Dalglish v Jarvie* (1850) 2 Mac. & G. 231; *Bates v Hewitt* (1867) L.R. 2 Q.B. 595 at 607–608; *London Assurance v Mansel* (1879) 11 Ch D 363 at 368; *Re Yager and Guardian Assurance Co* (1912) 108 L.T. 38 at 44–45; *Beauchamp v National Mutual Indemnity Insurance Co* [1937] 3 All E.R. 19 at 22; *Browlie v Campbell* (1880) L.R. 5 App. Cas. 295 at 359; *Joel v Law Union and Crown Insurance Co* [1908] 2 K.B. 863 at 878; *Mutual Life Insurance Co of New York v Ontario Metal Products* [1925] A.C. 344; *Zurich General Accident and Liability Insurance Co Ltd v Morrison* [1942] 2 K.B. 53; *Lambert v CIS* [1975] 2 Lloyd's Rep. 485; *CTI v Oceanus Mutual* [1984] 1 Lloyd's Rep. 476.

[118] *Pan Atlantic Insurance Co Ltd v Pine Top Insurance Co Ltd* [1994] 3 All E.R. 581.

[119] *Ionides v Pender* (1874) L.R. 9 Q.B. 531; *Tate & Sons v Hyslop* (1885) 15 Q.B.D. 368 at 379; *Rivaz v Gerussi Bros & Co* (1880) 6 Q.B.D. 222 at 227–229 and 230–231.

[120] *Associated Oil Carriers Ltd v Union Insurance Society of Canton Ltd* [1917] 2 K.B. 184.

upon the assured an unreasonably burdensome duty of disclosure. Atkin J. put the matter thus[121]:

> "I think that [the alleged] standard of prudence indicates an under-writer much too bright and too good for human nature's daily food. There seems no good reason to impute to the insurer a higher degree of knowledge and foresight than that possessed by the more experienced and intelligent insurers carrying on business at that time . . . [If] the standard of prudence is the ideal one contended for . . . there were in July 1914, no prudent insurers in London, or if there were, they were not to be found in the usual places where one would seek for them."

"Fixing the premium or taking the risk". A fact is material only if it would affect **6–023**
the judgment of a prudent insurer in fixing the premium or taking the risk: it is not enough for it to be shown that a prudent insurer would have made further inquiries before accepting the proposal.[122] Not every fact which increases the risk is a material one: there must be a possibility that the insurers might attach some importance to it in assessing the premiums.[123] Thus it has been held to be immaterial that a lorry was garaged in a wooden shed which had been used to store hay, the insurance being a comprehensive motor vehicle policy, and the percentage of the premium allocated to the fire risk being very small, although it might have been held otherwise had the insurance been against fire only.[124] The fact that the insurer would have accepted the risk had disclosure been made does not necessarily mean that the fact was not material,[125] for the test is whether a prudent insurer might have been influenced. Facts have been held not to be material where their disclosure would merely have caused delay pending inquiries.[126] In determining materiality it is necessary to take into account the nature of the policy: thus if the peril insured against is based upon the assured's estimated throughput for the forthcoming year, with the assured bearing the risk of a shortfall so that a higher premium is paid and the insurer bearing the risk that the throughput is greater so that the risk is increased, then historic throughput is immaterial as the insurance has not been written with that consideration in mind.[127]

"Would influence the judgment of a prudent insurer". The 1906 Act is **6–024**
ambiguous in dealing with the question of the degree to which a prudent insurer would have been influenced in his conduct had he been in possession of the relevant facts. There are at least three possible constructions of the phrase, in descending order of generosity to the assured: (a) the "decisive influence" test, under which it is necessary for the insurer to satisfy the court that a prudent insurer would have acted differently had the information withheld or misstated been made available to him; (b) the "increased risk" theory, under which the insurer must demonstrate that the information in question would have been regarded by a prudent insurer as probably increasing the risk, while not

[121] *Associated Oil Carriers Ltd v Union Insurance Society of Canton Ltd* [1917] 2 K.B. 184 at 192.

[122] *Mutual Life Insurance Co of New York v Ontario Metal Products Co Ltd* [1925] A.C. 344, a decision regarded as contrary to the "mere influence" test: *Edwards v AA Mutual Insurance Co* (1985) 3 ANZ Insurance Cases 60–668.

[123] *Dawsons v Bonnin* [1922] 2 A.C. 413 at 420–421.

[124] *Dawsons v Bonnin* [1922] 2 A.C. 413 at 429. The insurers in this case were able to avoid liability on the grounds of breach of warranty, where materiality is not an issue.

[125] Wright J. in *Re Marshall and Scottish Employers' Liability Co* (1901) 85 L.T. 757 at 758.

[126] *Mutual Life Insurance Co of New York v Ontario Metal Products* [1925] A.C. 344.

[127] *Glencore International AG v Alpina Insurance Co Ltd* [2004] 1 Lloyd's Rep. 111.

necessarily leading to a higher premium or a rejection of the assured's proposal; and (c) the "mere influence" test, whereby it is sufficient for the insurer to demonstrate that a prudent insurer would have wanted to know the information in question, and would not necessarily have acted any differently as regards the premium or the risk. Although the concept of the "prudent insurer" dates back to the nineteenth century,[128] the choice between these alternatives was not resolved until 1984, in *Container Transport International Ltd v Oceanus Mutual Underwriting Association*,[129] where the Court of Appeal opted for the "mere influence" test on the basis that the test was whether the fact would have influenced a prudent underwriter in the formation of his opinion. This reasoning was confirmed by a majority of the House of Lords in *Pan Atlantic Insurance Co Ltd v Pine Top Insurance Co Ltd*,[130] it their being laid down that the phrase "influence the judgment of a prudent insurer" meant no more than "an effect on the mind of the insurer in weighing up the risk".[131] The minority's view was that the insurer should not be able to deny liability unless it could be shown that a prudent underwriter would have regarded the information as increasing the risk and would have altered the premium or rejected the risk accordingly.

The majority gave four reasons for adopting a test of apparent generosity to insurers. First, the word "influence" in its ordinary meaning did not mean "change the mind of", so that it could not be right to adopt the "decisive influence" test. Equally, the decisive influence test did not appear in the legislation itself, and the reference to "determining whether" was a plain reference to the prudent insurer's thought processes rather than his final decision. Secondly, the majority regarded the decisive influence test as impractical for a number of reasons: (a) it is for the assured and his broker to assess what must be disclosed, and the adoption of a decisive influence test would make it difficult for this assessment to be made, whereas a wider duty would clarify the position; (b) the decisive influence test could operate only in the exceptional situation in which the underwriters called to give expert evidence were agreed that they would have increased the premium or rejected the risk; (c) the decisive influence test takes as its starting point the assumption that a prudent insurer would have written the risk as disclosed on the terms accepted by the actual underwriter, whereas this is by no means a foregone conclusion; (d) it is meaningless to ask whether any one single piece of information would have had a decisive influence on a prudent underwriter as the consideration of a risk involves balancing all factors. Thirdly, the majority could find no authority for the adoption of a decisive influence test. By contrast, the minority reviewed nineteenth century

---

[128] The origins of the prudent insurer test are obscure. Objectivity was strongly rejected by Lord Mansfield in *Carter v Boehm* (1766) 3 Burr. 1905, on the basis that the evidence of other underwriters was mere hearsay, cf. also *Durrell v Bederley* (1816) Holt N.P. 283; *Campbell v Richards* (1833) 5 B. & Ad. 840. However, the concept was firmly established by the middle of the nineteenth century (*Berthon v Loughman* (1817) 2 Stark. 258; *Richards v Murdoch* (1830) 10 B. & C. 527), based either on a development of the fair dealing theory espoused in *Carter* or, more mundanely, on the rule of evidence—abolished by the Evidence Act 1851—that a party could not give evidence in support of himself. See *Pan Atlantic Insurance Co Ltd v Pine Top Insurance Co Ltd* [1994] 3 All E.R. 581 at 607.

[129] *Container Transport International Ltd v Oceanus Mutual Underwriting Association* [1984] 1 Lloyd's Rep. 476, reversing Lloyd J.'s adoption of the decisive influence test, [1982] 2 Lloyd's Rep. 178.

[130] *Pan Atlantic Insurance Co Ltd v Pine Top Insurance Co Ltd* [1994] 3 All E.R. 581, rejecting the increased risk test propounded by Steyn L.J. in the Court of Appeal, [1993] 1 Lloyd's Rep. 496.

[131] *Pan Atlantic Insurance Co Ltd v Pine Top Insurance Co Ltd* [1994] 3 All E.R. 581 at 587.

decisions[132] and concluded that they pointed to "what underwriters would have done rather than what they wanted to know".[133] Finally, the majority took the view that the "mere influence" test would not operate unfairly on assureds, partly because the rigours of *CTI* had been mitigated by the unanimous *Pan Atlantic* ruling that the insurer has to go on to show actual influence on him (which had been denied in *CTI*),[134] and partly because the "mere influence" test reflected the wording of the statute and the underpinning principle of fair dealing, and that in many cases "the core of material of which good faith demands the disclosure is relatively small and easy to identify".[135]

The majority reasoning in *Pan Atlantic* is primarily negative in rejecting the narrow "decisive influence" test of materiality rather than positive in adopting the broad *CTI* test. This approach left open the argument that the true ratio of *Pan Atlantic* was the denial of decisive influence, and that a choice could still be made between Steyn L.J's "increased risk" theory and the CTI "would be interested" test. That argument was rejected by the Court of Appeal in *St Paul Fire & Marine Co (UK) Ltd v McConnell Dowell Constructors Ltd*,[136] it there being confirmed that the House of Lords' acceptance of the "would be interested" test was to be regarded as part of the ratio of the decision.

Significance of insurer's own underwriting practices. As a matter of strict theory there is a clear division between materiality, which is a purely objective concept, and inducement, which is based on the insurer's own responses to the presentation of the risk. However, in assessing materiality it is necessary to identify as a comparator an insurer who was operating in the market at the same time as the actual insurer and whose underwriting practices were much the same as those of the actual insurer. This point was made by Clarke L.J. in *Drake Insurance Co v Provident Insurance Co.*[137] The insurer in this case operated a mechanical system for underwriting under which points were allocated to particular events, e.g. accidents and convictions, and the premium was fixed on the points accrued by the assured. Clarke L.J. noted that in assessing whether a particular matter caught by the points system was material to a prudent underwriter, it would be necessary to consider one who operated a similar points system.   **6–025**

Truth of facts relied upon. It is uncertain whether a fact can be material if it is not true. A distinction must here be drawn between the materiality of intelligence and the materiality of a presumed fact. Where there is solid intelligence that a material fact may exist then the very existence of that intelligence is a material fact that has to be disclosed to the insurer. Subsequent proof that the intelligence was unfounded does not affect its materiality although it may affect the right of the insurer to rely upon discredited intelligence as a ground for avoiding the policy. By contrast, if the insurer fixes the premium on the basis of an assumed   **6–026**

---

[132] Most importantly, *Ionides v Pender* (1874) L.R. 9 Q.B. 531 and *Tate & Sons v Hyslop* (1885) L.R. 15 Q.B.D. 368.

[133] *Pan Atlantic Insurance Co Ltd v Pine Top Insurance Co Ltd* [1994] 3 All E.R. 581, per Lord Lloyd at 630.

[134] *Pan Atlantic Insurance Co Ltd v Pine Top Insurance Co Ltd* [1994] 3 All E.R. 581, per Lord Goff at 588.

[135] *Pan Atlantic Insurance Co Ltd v Pine Top Insurance Co Ltd* [1994] 3 All E.R. 581, per Lord Mustill at 599.

[136] *St Paul Fire & Marine Co (UK) Ltd v McConnell Dowell Constructors Ltd* [1995] 2 Lloyd's Rep. 116.

[137] *Drake Insurance Co v Provident Insurance Co* [2005] Lloyd's Rep. I.R. 277.

fact, which is subsequently shown not to exist, it has been suggested by Rix and Clarke L.JJ., in *Drake Insurance Co v Provident Insurance Co* that the fact has to be disregarded: on this approach it is objective rather than apparent truth—"state of mind"—that must be taken into account. The insurer bears the risk that the fact relied upon might prove to be untrue. In *Drake* itself the insurer wrongly believed that an accident suffered by the assured's wife had been her fault and relied upon that accident, along with an undisclosed conviction, to justify an avoidance of the policy: Rix and Clarke L.JJ. expressed the provisional view that as the truth of the matter was that the accident was a no-fault accident it was to be disregarded in assessing the materiality of the conviction. Any avoidance based on the two facts taken together would amount to a repudiation of the policy.

Limb 2: Inducement

6–027 *The need for inducement.* Sections 18(2) and 20(2), in defining materiality, make no mention of any requirement that the insurer in question must additionally prove that he was actually induced by the assured's misleading presentation of the risk to enter into the contract on the terms agreed. There is little clear authority on the matter prior to the passing of the 1906 Act, although it appears to have been accepted up to that date that actual inducement had to be proved.[138] The silence of the 1906 Act on the matter did not lead to immediate comment, but there appears to have been a gradual acceptance of the view that the insurer's satisfaction of the "prudent insurer" test in the Act was exhaustive of his obligations.[139]

The rejection of any form of subjective element can be criticised on a number of grounds: insurance law is inconsistent with ordinary contract law; it may be perceptibly unfair for a wholly innocent assured to be deprived of his contract rights simply because a hypothetical insurer would have been affected by his presentation of the risk; and it is a distortion of competition if each underwriter is permitted to assess his premiums on one basis and yet take advantage of the practices of his rivals once a dispute arises. After some uncertainty[140] the House of Lords in *Pan Atlantic Insurance Co Ltd v Pine Top Insurance Co Ltd*[141] unanimously ruled, in the words of Lord Mustill, that "there is to be implied in the 1906 Act a qualification that a material misrepresentation will not entitle the underwriter to avoid the policy unless the misrepresentation induced the making of the contract",[142] a proposition which applied equally to non-disclosure.[143] Their Lordships' main reasons for reaching this conclusion were fairness and the need for insurance law to comply with the general law of misrepresentation. Lord Mustill rejected the argument that an objective test operating in isolation was necessary to impose a disciplinary element on assureds and their brokers, and

---

[138] The dicta were confused. It had been said in a number of cases that the views of the insurers involved in the case were not a relevant consideration, and that the test was wholly objective. Contrast *Rivaz v Gerussi Bros & Co* (1880) L.R. 6 Q.B.D. 222.

[139] *Zurich General Accident and Liability Insurance Co v Morrison* [1942] 2 K.B. 53. See also: *Bates v Hewitt* (1867) L.R. 2 Q.B. 595; *Glasgow Assurance Corp v Williamson Symondson* (1911) 104 L.T. 254 at 257; *Cantiere Meccanico Brindisino v Janson* [1912] 2 K.B. 112.

[140] *Berger and Light Diffusers Pty Ltd v Pollock* [1973] 2 Lloyd's Rep. 442 (in favour of subjectivity); *Container Transport International Ltd v Oceanus Mutual Underwriting Association* [1984] 1 Lloyd's Rep. 476 (rejecting subjectivity).

[141] *Pan Atlantic Insurance Co Ltd v Pine Top Insurance Co Ltd* [1994] 3 All E.R. 581.

[142] *Pan Atlantic Insurance Co Ltd v Pine Top Insurance Co Ltd* [1994] 3 All E.R. 581 at 617.

[143] This point was made with particular force by Lord Lloyd, who pointed out that misrepresentation and non-disclosure commonly appear in tandem in points of claim.

ruled that discipline did not form part of the law, which was concerned only with whether there had been a distortion of the risk. The silence of the 1906 Act was explained by Lord Mustill on the ground that the 1906 Act did not seek to deal with ordinary principles of misrepresentation (which were left intact) but rather with the insurance aspects only, i.e. the definition of materiality. In every case, therefore, the underwriters have to show that but for the assured's presentation of the risk they would have acted differently, either by refusing to write the risk at all or by writing it only on different terms.

Presumption of inducement. While it is clear that an insurer must prove both **6–028** materiality and inducement, it is less clear from the speeches in *Pan Atlantic* how the two requirements are to operate together. One possibility is that the test of materiality is taken as a starting point and that, once the insurer has satisfied the court that a prudent insurer would have been influenced by the fact misrepresented or withheld, it may be assumed that the insurer was in fact so induced. This was the view of Lord Mustill, his Lordship stating that there is "a presumption of inducement", and that "the assured will have an uphill task in persuading the court that the withholding or misstatement of circumstances satisfying the test of materiality has made no difference".[144] The alternative approach is to regard the two limbs as totally distinct, and to take as the starting point the actual inducement of the insurer. Only when actual inducement has been shown does the question of materiality arise. Lord Lloyd expressly supported such an analysis,[145] and specifically stateed that the notion that "inducement can be inferred from proven materiality" is a "heresy long since exploded".[146] The correctness of Lord Mustill's view was confirmed shortly afterwards, in *St Paul Fire and Marine Co (UK) Ltd v McConnell Dowell Constructors Ltd.*[147] The presumption of inducement is available not just to the insurer but also to a broker in third party proceedings.[148]

The presumption of inducement requires the court to whether the insurer would have acted differently had the information been disclosed to him: it has been recognised that this is something of a "loaded" question, as the insurer will have every incentive to state that, with disclosure, his assessment of the risk would have been different, and it is essentially a matter for the court to determine whether, in light of the experience and qualifications of the insurer answering the questions, the evidence is to be given weight.[149] The difficulty faced by an assured in rebutting the presumption of inducement has led to its restriction by the courts to situations in which the underwriter who took the decision to accept the insurance is unable for good reason to give evidence of the state of his mind at the date of the placement.[150] The cases in which the presumption of inducement have been successfully relied upon to date are those involving

[144] *Pan Atlantic Insurance Co Ltd v Pine Top Insurance Co Ltd* [1994] 3 All E.R. 581 at 619. These words were echoed by Moore-Bick J. in *James v CGU Insurance Plc* [2002] Lloyd's Rep. I.R. 206.
[145] *Pan Atlantic Insurance Co Ltd v Pine Top Insurance Co Ltd* [1994] 3 All E.R. 581 at 638.
[146] *Pan Atlantic Insurance Co Ltd v Pine Top Insurance Co Ltd* [1994] 3 All E.R. 581 at 637.
[147] *St Paul Fire and Marine Co (UK) Ltd v McConnell Dowell Constructors Ltd* [1995] 2 Lloyd's Rep. 116.
[148] *Gunns and Gunns v Par Insurance Brokers* [1997] 1 Lloyd's Rep. 173.
[149] *Insurance Corporation of the Channel Islands v Royal Hotel (No.2)* [1998] Lloyd's Rep. I.R. 151. See also *International Lottery Management Ltd v Dumas* [20021 Lloyd's Rep. I.R. 237.
[150] *Marc Rich & Co AG v Portman* [1996] 1 Lloyd's Rep. 430 affirmed [1997] 1 Lloyd's Rep. 225; *Cape Plc v Iron Trades Employers Insurance Association Ltd* [2004] Lloyd's Rep. I.R. 75; See also: *Laker Vent Engineering Ltd v Templeton Insurance Ltd* [2009] Lloyd's Rep. I.R. 704; *Lewis v Norwich Union Healthcare Ltd* [2010] Lloyd's Rep. I.R. 198.

market subscriptions where one of the subscribing underwriters was unable to give evidence of his own state of mind[151] or where the underwriter was not a party to the proceedings at all.[152] These exceptional cases aside, there is no longer any necessary relationship between materiality and inducement. In *Assicurazioni Generali SpA v Arab Insurance Group (BSC)*,[153] Clarke L.J. laid down the following guidelines:

1. In order to be entitled to avoid a contract of insurance or reinsurance, an insurer or reinsurer must prove on the balance of probabilities that he was induced to enter into the contract by a material non-disclosure or by a material misrepresentation.
2. There is no presumption of law that an insurer or reinsurer is induced to enter into the contract by a material non-disclosure or misrepresentation.
3. The facts may, however, be such that it is to be inferred that the particular insurer or reinsurer was so induced even in the absence of evidence from him.
4. In order to prove inducement the insurer or reinsurer must show that the non-disclosure or misrepresentation was an effective cause of his entering into the contract on the terms on which he did. He must therefore show at least that, but for the relevant non-disclosure or misrepresentation, he would not have entered into the contract on those terms. On the other hand, he does not have to show that it was the sole effective cause of his doing so.[154]

Later cases applying the *ARIG* principles have shown that a failure by the insurers to produce evidence from the underwriter who wrote the risk will be a serious impediment to any attempt to prove inducement unless the underwriter is simply unavailable, in which case the insurers must by default produce evidence of their own usual practices.[155] The point is demonstrated with some clarity by the decision of Recorder West-Knights QC in *Lewis v Norwich Union Healthcare Ltd*.[156] Here, insurers sought to avoid a medical policy on the ground that the assured had failed to disclose a visit to his GP, which was a material fact. However, the insurers did not produce evidence from the underwriter who had written the risk, possibly because she had failed to adhere to underwriting guidelines, but instead produced evidence as to the insurers' usual practices from a different underwriter who had not been involved in writing the risk. The court held that that evidence was irrelevant, and that what mattered was whether the underwriter in question had been induced: the court was not satisfied that, with disclosure, she would have acted any differently so that inducement was not made out.

---

[151] *St Paul Fire and Marine Co (UK) Ltd v McConnell Dowell Constructors Ltd* [1995] 2 Lloyd's Rep. 116; *Toomey v Banco Vitalicio de Espana SA de Seguros y Reaseguros* [2004] Lloyd's Rep. I.R. 354, affirmed [2005] Lloyd's Rep. I.R.; *Talbot Underwriting v Nausch Hogan & Murray (The Jascon 5)* [2006] Lloyd's Rep. I.R. 531; *Scottish Coal Co Ltd v Royal and Sun Alliance Plc* [2008] Lloyd's Rep. I.R. 718.

[152] *Gunns and Gunns v Par Insurance Brokers* [1997] 1 Lloyd's Rep. 173.

[153] *Assicurazioni Generali SpA v Arab Insurance Group (BSC)* [2003] Lloyd's Rep. I.R. 131.

[154] *Benjamin v State Insurance Ltd* (1998) 10 ANZ Insurance Cases 74–645.

[155] *Laker Vent Engineering Ltd v Templeton Insurance Ltd* [2009] Lloyd's Rep. I.R. 704; *Lewis v Norwich Union Healthcare Ltd* [2010] Lloyd's Rep. I.R. 198; *Persimmon Homes Ltd v Great Lakes Reinsurance (UK) Plc* [2010] EWHC 1705 (Comm).

[156] *Lewis v Norwich Union Healthcare Ltd* [2010] Lloyd's Rep. I.R. 198.

Thus, while there is a presumption of inducement, it would seem that it has its most important impact where the underwriter is unable to give evidence on his own behalf. If he can give evidence, he must demonstrate a causal link between the presentation of the risk and the acceptance of the risk.

Proof of inducement. The burden of proof is borne by the underwriter to demonstrate that, had the facts not been misstated or withheld, he would not have written the risk at all or on the terms ultimately agreed. This is a matter of fact in every case. Unless the underwriter can show that a different outcome—in terms of the acceptance of the risk or the fixing of the premiums or terms of cover—would have followed had the risk been presented fairly, it cannot be said there has been inducement. Thus if the underwriter has with full disclosure previously accepted a similar risk on the same terms as those offered to an assured who has withheld or misstated material facts, then those facts cannot be regarded as having been an inducement to the underwriter, although evidence of the imposition of different terms or a higher premium in the same circumstances srongly indicates inducement.[157] Equally, an underwriter who placed no significance on or did not understand the disclosures made to him cannot claim to have been induced,[158] as the underwriter must "play his part by listening carefully to what is said to him and cannot hold the insured responsible if by failing to do so he does not grasp the full implications of what he has been told",[159] although evidence of past imprudence in this regard is not admissible, as "the question . . . is whether the underwriter abrogated his functions in relation to these risks not in relation to numerous other risks written on different occasions."[160]

6–029

No inducement if same outcome. Inducement may involve an inquiry as to the full extent of the risk and not simply the matters misstated or withheld. In *Drake Insurance Co v Provident Insurance Co*[161] the assured failed to disclose a speeding conviction. Following a loss, the insurers relied upon the conjunction of the speeding conviction and an accident in which the assured's wife had been

6–030

---

[157] *Aldridge Estates Investments Co v McCarthy* [1996] E.G.C.S. 167. In *Norwich Union Insurance Ltd v Meisels* [2007] Lloyd's Rep. I.R. 69 it was held that if the insurers are willing to issue insurance without asking questions as to the assured's involvement with failed companies, the fact that they have asked specific questions on this point for other cover shows that they regarded the facts as immaterial to the policy in question.

[158] *Marc Rich & Co AG v Portman* [1996] 1 Lloyd's Rep. 430. In *Nam Kwong Medicines & Health Products Co Ltd v China Insurance Co Ltd* [2002] H.K.C.U. 792, there was evidence to the effect that, nothwithstanding the striking absence of adequate information about the vessel to be insured, the insurers were going to issue insurance cover in any event, so that even if the fact that the vessel had been detained in Singapore was material, there was no inducement. Contrast *Persimmon Homes Ltd v Great Lakes Reinsurance (UK) Plc* [2010] EWHC 1705 (Comm), where the underwriter was shown to have been prudent in his writing of the risk.

[159] *Glencore International AG v Alpina Insurance Co Ltd* [2004] 1 Lloyd's Rep. 111.

[160] *Marc Rich & Co AG v Portman* [1996] 1 Lloyd's Rep. 430.

[161] *Drake Insurance Co v Provident Insurance Co* [2004] Lloyd's Rep. I.R. 277. The reasoning in *Drake v Provident* appears to have been overlooked in *Mundi v Lincoln Assurance Co* [2006] Lloyd's Rep. I.R. 353, where it was held that it was necessary to consider only how the underwriter would have reacted had he been told the true facts, and not how events might have unfolded had the true facts been disclosed. *Norwich Union Insurance Ltd v Meisels* [2007] Lloyd's Rep. I.R. 69 appears to be an application of *Drake*, although the judgment was framed in terms of materiality. It was there pointed out that an assured who failed to disclose allegations of criminality against him would be entitled to argue that, had he disclosed them, he would also have disclosed exculpatory evidence showing his innocence of any fraud, thereby negativing any allegation of inducement. Cf. the views of Colman J. in *North Star Shipping Ltd v Sphere Drake Insurance Plc* [2005] EWHC 665 (Comm), where the learned judge pointed out that exculpatory material went to inducement.

involved—which had been disclosed to the insurers as being her fault—as affecting their underwriting criteria. In fact, the accident had not been the fault of the assured's wife and that the speeding conviction taken alone would not have given rise to an increased premium. The assured successfully argued that, if the speeding conviction had been disclosed then the assured would have been informed that his premium was to be raised by reason of the conviction coupled with the accident and the assured would then have been likely to have raised the no-fault basis of the accident, resulting in the accident being discounted and the same premium as that actually paid being fixed. Rix and Clarke L.JJ. ruled that the burden of proving inducement was borne by the insurer, a burden which they had not been able to rebut. Even if that was wrong, the evidence—which was largely gained from the assured's response following the avoidance of the policy by the insurer—showed that on the balance of probabilities the assured would have contested any increase in his premium and the truth about the earlier accident would have come to light. Furthermore, as the policy had been placed through a broker, it would have been the broker's duty to raise the point with the insurer. Pill L.J., dissenting, held that it was not appropriate for a court to speculate on what might have occurred had the relevant fact been disclosed.[162] The *Drake v Provident* approach requires the court to consider a purely hypothetical question, namely how would the insurers have reacted had the true facts been disclosed by the assured. The inquiry will be a difficult one, largely because commercial considerations may come into play, as in *Bonner v Cox Dedicated Corporate Member Ltd*[163] where it was held that the subscribers to a reinsurance slip in the form of a standing offer to insurers would not, for commercial reasons, have withdrawn the slip for future subscription even if they had been informed of a casualty. The inducement principle is, on this approach, clearly one which is of major significance in non-disclosure cases, as the burden is on insurers to show that they would have acted differently had the relevant facts been revealed: the courts in *Drake* and *Bonner* have shown that purely commercial factors may be taken into account to counter an assertion by the insurers that the risk would not have been accepted.

6–031   **Burden of proof.** A number of different matters have to be proved in a non-disclosure or misrepresentation case.

(1) The insurer must prove that there has been a false statement made to him, or that the assured has failed to disclose material facts to him. This burden of proving the fact of the absence or presence of a statement rests squarely on the insurer.[164]

(2) Proof of the absence or falsity of the information provided by the assured rests equally on the insurer.[165]

---

[162] In *Glencore International AG v Alpina Insurance Co Ltd* [2004] 1 Lloyd's Rep. 111, decided shortly before *Drake v Provident*, Moore-Bick J. expressed the view that there might be a distinction between non-disclosure and misrepresentation, in that in the former case it was legitimate to look at the surrounding circumstances whereas in the latter it was necessary to look only at the effect of the false statement on the insurer. It is submitted that this distinction cannot stand after *Drake v Provident*.

[163] *Bonner v Cox Dedicated Corporate Member Ltd* [2005] Lloyd's Rep. I.R. 569, affirmed [2006] Lloyd's Rep. I.R. 385.

[164] *Davies v National Fire & Marine Insurance Co of New Zealand* [1891] A.C. 485; *Joel v Law Union & Crown Insurance Co* [1908] 2 K.B. 863.

[165] *Butcher v Dowlen* [1981] 1 Lloyd's Rep. 310. Cf. *Bond Air Services Ltd v Hill* [1955] 2 All E.R. 476.

(3) The insurer must prove the materiality of the information withheld or misstated. Proof of materiality is generally on the basis of expert evidence, although in appropriate cases the court can make its own decision on materiality even if no expert evidence is adduced.[166] There is a presumption of materiality in respect of express questions put to the assured by the insurer,[167] so that it will be difficult for an assured who has misrepresented the true position to deny the materiality of his answer, even though, in the absence of an express question, disclosure would not have been required.[168] In such a case the parties are considered to have agreed the difficult question as to which facts are material.[169] By contrast, there is no presumption of immateriality in respect of information which is not specifically requested by an insurer.[170] Thus where the assured's answers are literally true, the insurer is nevertheless not prevented from relying on non-disclosure in respect of an answer which is misleading, incomplete or evasive. Proof of materiality is possible only by expert evidence. In some situations such evidence may be given by experts in the field: evidence relating to the assured's state of health may thus be given by doctors.[171] Evidence may also be received from other insurers, from brokers and from the insurer himself acting as a prudent insurer.[172] The admissibility of the evidence of other insurers as to materiality clearly puts the assured under some difficulty, as it will be virtually impossible to rebut unanimous statements from insurers as to the materiality of a given fact.[173] This indeed appears to have been recognised by Lord Mansfield in the root decision on the duty of utmost good faith, *Carter v Boehm*,[174] which the evidence of other underwriters was described by him as: "mere opinion; which is not evidence. It is opinion without the least foundation from any previous precedent or usage".[175] This view has not, however, prevailed.[176] A substantial part of

---

[166] See *AC Ward & Sons Ltd v Catlin (Five) (No.2)* [2009] EWHC 3122 (Comm), applying dicta of the Court of Appeal in *Glicksman v Lancashire and General Assurance Company* [1925] 2 K.B. 593: Flaux J. in *Ward* held that the claimant's expert evidence that a misstatement as to security precautions was not material had been discredited on cross-examination and that the court was able to reach its own conclusion that the fact was material. See also *Babatsikos v Car Owners' Mutual Insurance Co Ltd* (1970) V.R. 297.

[167] Lord Dundas in *Dawsons Ltd v Bonnin* [1922] 2 A.C. 413; *Glicksman v Lancashire and General* [1925] 2 K.B. 593 at 608; [1927] A.C. 139 at 144.

[168] *Herman v Phoenix Assurance Co* (1924) 18 Ll. L.R. 371; *Hamilton & Co v Eagle Star & British Dominions Co Ltd* (1924) 19 Ll. L.R. 242.

[169] *Anderson v Fitzgerald* (1853) 4 H.L. Cas. 484 at 503; *London Assurance v Mansel* (1879) L.R. 11 Ch D 363.

[170] *Schoolman v Hall* [1951] 1 Lloyd's Rep. 139, but contrast Purchas L.J. in *Roberts v Plaisted* [1989] 2 Lloyd's Rep. 341.

[171] *Lindenau v Deshorough* (1828) 8 B. & C. 586. See also Denman C.J. in *Campbell v Richards* (1833) 5 B. & Ad. 840 at 847; *Yorke v Yorkshire Insurance* [1918] 1 K.B. 662 at 669, 671.

[172] *Mundi v Lincoln Assurance Co* [2006] Lloyd's Rep. I.R. 353.

[173] See the comments of Waller L.J. in *North Star Shipping Ltd v Sphere Drake Insurance Plc* [2006] Lloyd's Rep. I.R. 519, noting that it was difficult in practice for the assured to rebut expert evidence presented by underwriters, and that the assured often looked for protection to a robust judge.

[174] *Carter v Boehm* (1766) 3 Burr. 1905.

[175] *Carter* (1766) 3 Burr. 1905 at 1918. See also: *Durrell v Bederley* (1816) Holt N.P. 283; *Richards v Murdoch* (1830) 10 B. & C. 527; *Campbell v Richards* (1833) 5 B. & Ad. 840.

[176] *Girdlestone v North British* (1870) L.R. 11 Eq. 107; *Ionides v Pender* (1874) L.R. 9 Q.B. 531 at 535; *Glasgow Assurance v Symondson* (1911) 104 L.T. 254 at 257; *Yorke v Yorkshire Insurance Co Ltd* [1918] 1 K.B. 662; *Hoff v De Rougemont* (1929) 34 Com. Cas. 291 at 299, 303; *Roselodge v Castle* [1966] 2 Lloyd's Rep. 105 at 129; *Reynolds v Phoenix Assurance Co* [1978] 2 Lloyd's Rep. 440 at 457–459.

the protection for an assured in relation to materiality is, therefore, the commercial sense of the trial judge in assessing the weight to be given to such testimony. There are few cases in which the evidence of other insurers has been rejected or criticised by a court,[177] although Colman J. warned in *Strive Shipping Corp v Hellenic Mutual War Risks Association*[178] that expert evidence would not be uncritically accepted by the courts.

(4) The insurer must prove that he was induced to enter into the contract by the assured's failure to make a fair presentation of the risk.

6–032   **Date of assessment of materiality and inducement.** The materiality of a fact, and its inducing effect on the insurer, are to be determined at the date at which the insurance contract becomes binding. This rule has two consequences. First, if a fact appears to be immaterial prior to the making of a contract, and only proves to be material thereafter, the assured is not in breach of duty for failing to disclose it.[179] Second, if the fact appears to be material prior to the making of the contract, and subsequently proves to be immaterial, it follows that the assured is in breach of duty for failing to disclose it. Thus in the old case of *Seaman v Fonnereau*[180] the assured failed, before the contract had been completed, to disclose to the insurer rumours that the vessel for which insurance was sought had suffered severe damage in a gale. Those rumours proved to be unfounded once the insurer was on risk, but the insurer was nevertheless held to be entitled to avoid the policy.

The principle has, however, been challenged and has not survived unscathed. In *Strive Shipping Corp v Hellenic Mutual War Risks Association*[181] marine insurers relied at the trial on non-disclosure of four previous losses none of which had been satisfactorily explained. The assured was permitted by Colman J. to introduce evidence as to the circumstances of the four earlier losses, and succeeded in demonstrating that nothing untoward had occurred. Colman J. ruled that, while the circumstances of the earlier losses might have been material facts when the policy was obtained, the assured's proof of his innocence prevented the insurers from avoiding their liability in reliance upon those material facts. Colman J. gave two separate grounds for his conclusion. The first was that a purported avoidance for breach of the duty of utmost good faith could be overturned by the court if it was found not to be justified in the light of hindsight. The second was that insurers would be in breach of their own duty of utmost good faith in attempting to rely upon those allegations if it were proved at the trial that the allegations were unfounded. This decision supports the proposition that there is an equitable barrier, preventing an insurer from relying upon facts appearing to be material and true at the policy's inception, but proving not to be true at the trial or by the time the insurer seeks to rely upon them. This is likely to apply only to intelligence received by the assured, criminal charges and suspicions of dishonesty. The point being made was that the facts were material

---

[177] *Roselodge v Castle* [1966] 2 Lloyd's Rep. 113; *Irish National Insurance Co Ltd v Oman Insurance Co* [1983] 2 Lloyd's Rep. 453; *Inversiones Manria SA v Sphere Drake Insurance Co Plc (The Dora)* [1989] 1 Lloyd's Rep. 69.

[178] *Strive Shipping Corp v Hellenic Mutual War Risks Association* [2002] Lloyd's Rep. I.R. 669.

[179] *Seaton v Burnand* [1900] A.C. 135.

[180] *Seaman v Fonnereau* (1734) 2 Str. 1183. See also *Lynch v Hamilton* (1810) 3 Taunt 37.

[181] *Strive Shipping Corp v Hellenic Mutual War Risks Association* [2002] Lloyd's Rep. I.R. 669.

and had to be disclosed a proposition not doubted by Colman J. but that as they had been disproved they could be relied upon to justify avoidance.

Right of a court to overturn a valid avoidance. The suggestion that a court of **6–033** equity can overturn a valid avoidance has been rejected. In *Brotherton v Aseguradora Colseguros SA*[182] the defendants were the fidelity insurers of a Colombian bank and the claimants were London market reinsurers. The reinsurers discovered that there had, before the inception of the cover, been various media reports which cast doubt on the honesty of the bank's president, leading to his suspension from office. The reinsurers avoided the policy, and commenced proceedings seeking a declaration of non-liability. The Court of Appeal held that the reinsured could not introduce evidence to the effect that, whatever the strength and materiality of the reports at the outset, the reports were false. The Court of Appeal held that avoidance is a self-help remedy that requires neither the assistance nor the sanction of the court, so that once the reinsurers avoided the policy their avoidance took effect and could not be overturned by the court.[183] The refusal of the Court of Appeal to countenance intervention where there had been a valid avoidance was justified by Mance L.J. on the ground that were it otherwise it would be necessary to conduct a trial within a trial in order to determine whether the material facts relied upon by the insurers had later been shown to be immaterial.[184] Mance L.J. went on to say that it was by no means obvious which party should pay the costs of that trial within a trial: whilst at first sight it appeared that the reinsurers should make the payment if the reinsured could establish that in hindsight there was no basis for avoidance, the reality of the position would be that insurers would be liable to pay the costs of a mini-trial even though the information in question had not been disclosed at the placement of the risk and was at that time material. The correctness of this reasoning was accepted by a differently constituted Court of Appeal in *Drake Insurance Co v Provident Insurance Co.*[185]

Obligation of insurer to avoid in good faith. The second strand of the reasoning **6–034** in *Strive Shipping* was that an insurer is under a duty of good faith at the date of the avoidance, and is thus required to act in good faith when reaching the decision whether or not to avoid. In *Brotherton*, the Court of Appeal chose to express preliminary views on the proposition that an insurer who is aware at the time of purported avoidance that the material facts had been undermined is precluded by his own continuing duty of utmost good faith from relying upon them. Whilst the point was formally left open, Mance L.J.'s analysis was that the assured's post-contractual duty of utmost good faith had effectively dwindled to nothing[186] and that to introduce a continuing duty on underwriters was inappropriate on the basis that it would create an imbalance between the rights and obligations of the assured and the reinsured. Furthermore, as the only remedy for breach of the duty of utmost good faith is avoidance of the policy *ab initio*, it was difficult to see how this could be appropriate or helpful in the situation under discussion. The dicta of the Court of Appeal in *Brotherton* were rejected by a

---

[182] *Brotherton v Aseguradora Colseguros SA* [2003] Lloyd's Rep. I.R. 758.

[183] Insurers may be liable in damages for an avoidance which was not justified, as this is a repudiation of the policy. This is of course quite different from saying that the court can overturn an avoidance.

[184] As indeed occurred in *Strive* itself.

[185] *Drake Insurance Co v Provident Insurance Co* [2004] Lloyd's Rep. I.R. 277.

[186] See below.

differently constituted Court of Appeal a few months later in *Drake v Provident*, in which insurers purported to avoid a motor policy based on the non-disclosure of a speeding conviction that, when combined with an accident in which the assured had been involved, would have led to a higher premium had both facts been in the possession of the insurers. Rix and Clarke L.JJ. held that the insurers had no right to avoid on the ground that there had been no inducement: had the conviction been disclosed, the insurers would have attempted to charge a higher premium and at that point it would have become apparent that the accident had not been the assured's fault so that ultimately the same premium would have been charged. However, the majority expressed the view that fact of the loss had clearly been a material fact at the date of the later placement with which the court was primarily concerned. The insurers were under a continuing duty of utmost good faith, which bound them not to avoid if at the time of the avoidance they were either actually aware that they were relying upon disproved facts or at least that they turned a blind eye to the possibility that the facts had been disproved. The majority accepted the factual finding of the trial judge that the insurers had not at the time of avoidance possessed either actual or "blind eye" knowledge of the true position relating to the accident and accordingly that they were not in breach of their continuing duty. Pill L.J., dissenting, held that the insurers' continuing duty was not confined to actual or blind eye knowledge, and that good faith extended to making reasonable inquiry of the assured prior to avoidance; had this been done in *Drake v Provident*, then Pill L.J.'s view was that the true position relating to the accident would have come to light and that the avoidance would have been seen to have been unjustified.

The result of *Drake v Provident* is that the proposition that materiality and inducement have to be tested as at the date of the placement remains good, but that the right of the insurers to effect an avoidance at a time they are or ought to be in possession of knowledge that the fact was not material or had not induced them can render their avoidance in breach of their continuing duty of good faith.[187]

3. UTMOST GOOD FAITH AND AGENCY

6–035   Relevance of the knowledge of the assured's agent. A false statement by the assured or a person authorised to act on his behalf may give the insurers the right to avoid the policy if the usual requirements of materiality and inducement are made out. By contrast, in the case of non-disclosure, difficult questions can arise where material facts are in the possession of the assured's agent, but the assured is himself unaware of those facts. It then becomes necessary to know whether the assured is deemed to know those facts. This will depend upon the concept of imputation and attribution of knowledge.

---

[187] In *North Star Shipping Ltd v Sphere Drake Insurance Plc* [2006] Lloyd's Rep. I.R. 519 an argument based on *Drake* was seemingly open to the assured, who had failed to disclose criminal charges which had been dismissed by the date of the loss but which were nevertheless relied upon by underwriters to avoid the policy. The point was only taken on appeal, but the Court of Appeal refused permission to amend the claim as it would have involved the production of fresh evidence at the appellate stage.

The concept of attribution. The principle that the assured need disclose only **6–036**
those facts of which he is, or ought to be, aware in the ordinary course of business
is modified where the broker effecting the policy on behalf of the assured is in
possession of material facts. In such a case, s.19(a) of the 1906 Act states that an
agent to insure must disclose every material circumstance known to himself, or
which he ought to have known, in the ordinary course of business. The legal basis
for this proposition appears to be the decision of the House of Lords in *Blackburn
Low & Co v Vigors,*[188] where their Lordships ruled that facts known to the
assured's producing brokers who had no responsibility for placing the risk but
not to the assured or to the placing brokers did not have to be disclosed to
underwriters. Their Lordships were in agreement that, had the placing broker
been aware of the relevant facts, the insurers would have had a right to avoid for
non-disclosure, although there was a divergence of opinion as to why this would
have been the case. Lord Macnaghten's view was that a placing broker as the
agent of the assured was required to communicate material facts to the
underwriters,[189] whereas other members of the House of Lords, in particular Lord
Halsbury L.C., Lord Watson and Lord Fitzgerald, adopted an attribution of
knowledge analysis[190] under which it was to be assumed that the broker would
communicate facts known to him to the assured and thus that the assured was
under a personal obligation to disclose facts known to his agent by reason of the
imputation of that knowledge to him.

Although it was assumed by Phillips J. at first instance in *DR v Walbrook
Insurance Co*[191] that attribution was the correct basis of *Blackburn Low,* and
accordingly that facts known to the assured's agents are deemed to be known by
the assured, it would seem that Lord Macnaghten's view that the broker's duty
of disclosure is independent is the preferable approach. In the first place the
existence of a separate obligation on the broker to disclose material facts was
confirmed by the House of Lords in *HIH Casualty & General Insurance Ltd v
Chase Manhattan Bank.*[192] Secondly, if attribution is the correct analysis, there is
a blurring of the distinction between ss.18 and 19 of the 1906 Act. Under s.18 the
assured is required to disclose all material facts that are, or ought to be, known
by him in the ordinary course of business, and under s.19 the placing broker is
required to disclose all material facts that are, or ought to be, known to that
broker. If it is the case that legal basis of right of the underwriters to avoid
liability for the broker's failure to disclose material facts is the assured's own
failure to disclose information imputed to him, then s.19 can never operate
independently.[193] Accordingly, the better view of the matter is that information
known to the assured's broker is not imputed to the assured and that there is no

---

[188] *Blackburn Low & Co v Vigors* (1887) 12 App. Cas. 531.
[189] Cf. *Lynch v Dunsford* (1811) 14 East 494.
[190] Based on *Fitzherbert v Mather* (1785) 1 T.R. 12 and *Proudfoot v Montefiore* (1867) L.R. 2 Q.B.
511. In *Simner v New India Assurance* [1995] L.R.L.R. 240 H.H. Judge Diamond QC felt that the
majority approach in *Blackburn Low* was not quite the same thing as attribution, but it is difficult to
see any distinction between the notion of attribution and the notion that the assured is deemed to
know what is known by his agent.
[191] *DR v Walbrook Insurance Co* [1995] 1 Lloyd's Rep. 153.
[192] *HIH Casualty & General Insurance Ltd v Chase Manhattan Bank* [2003] Lloyd's Rep. I.R.
230.
[193] This point was made by Hoffmann L.J. in *El Ajou v Dollar Land Holdings Plc* [1994] 2 All E.R.
685 and again in *Societe Anonyme d'Intermediaires Luxembourgeois v Farex Gie* [1995] L.R.L.R.
116.

personal failure on the part of the assured where the broker withholds material facts from the underwriters.[194]

6–037 *Attribution of knowledge from agent to assured.* It follows that the issue of attribution becomes significant only if the agent who is in possession of material facts is an agent other than the "agent to insure"[195] contemplated by s.19. Whether the knowledge of some other agent is attribution to the assured depends entirely on the relationship between the assured and the agent.[196]

The authorities were analysed by H.H. Judge Diamond QC in *Simner v New India Assurance Co Ltd*,[197] the court holding that information known to the agent is treated as within the knowledge of the assured himself in two situations: (i) where the assured was reliant upon the agent for information, in which case the agent would be an "agent to know" and the assured would be treated as being aware of the information in the ordinary course of his business for the purposes of s.18(2)[198]; (ii) where the agent was in a predominant position in relation to the assured such that the agent's knowledge was that of the assured, in which case the information would fall within s.18(2). If neither of these tests is satisfied, the knowledge of the agent is not treated as the knowledge of the assured, and disclosure is not required.[199]

The leading authority on the point was the decision of the House of Lords in *Blackburn, Low & Co v Vigors*.[200] Here, reinsurance was procured on an overdue vessel through the agency of the assured's London brokers. A member of a Glasgow firm of brokers which had previously acted for the reinsured had been informed that the vessel had been lost, but he did not pass on this information to the reinsured prior to the placing of the insurance by the London brokers. The reinsurers pleaded non-disclosure of this material fact. The House of Lords held that the policy was not voidable and that the knowledge of the Glasgow brokers was not the knowledge of the reinsured. Their Lordships expressly rejected the notion that the knowledge of an agent could be imputed to an assured/reinsured other than in the case where the agent himself effected the policy (the situation

---

[194] In both *PCW Syndicates v PCW Insurers* [1996] 1 Lloyd's Rep. 241 and *Group Josi Re v Walbrook Insurance Ltd* [1996] 1 Lloyd's Rep. 345 (the appeal in *DR v Walbrook*) the Court of Appeal denied that there was any general attribution of knowledge from a broker to the assured, and that s.19 was designed to implement Lord Macnaghten's view of the law (see per Staughton L.J. in *PCW* at 225 and Saville L.J. in *Group Josi* at 367). The same view was expressed by Colman J. and the Court of Appeal in *Kingscroft Insurance Co Ltd v Nissan Fire & Marine Insurance Co Ltd* Unreported, 1996, affirmed [1999] Lloyd's Rep. I.R. 371.

[195] The placing broker: see below.

[196] *Proudfoot v Montefiore* (1867) L.R. 2 Q.B. 511; *Wilson v Salamandra Assurance Co of St Petersburg* (1903) 88 L.T. 96; *St Margaret's Trust Ltd v Navigation & General Insurance Co Ltd* (1949) 82 Ll. L.R. 752; *Australia & New Zealand Bank v Colonial & Eagle Wharves Ltd* [1960] 2 Lloyd's Rep. 241; *Howells v Dominion Insurance Co Ltd* Unreported, 1999; *Simner v New India Assurance Co Ltd* [1995] L.R.L.R. 240.

[197] *Simner v New India Assurance Co Ltd* [1995] L.R.L.R. 240.

[198] Thus the knowledge of an underwriting agent who is under a duty to pass information to the reinsured is deemed to be known by the reinsured in the ordinary course of its business: *ERC Frankona Reinsurance v American National Insurance Co* [2005] EWHC 1381 (Comm).

[199] *Von Lindenau v Desborough* (1828) 8 B. & C. 586; *Daiglish v Jarvie* (1850) 2 Man. & G. 231; *Thomson v Buchanan* (1782) 4 Bro. Parl. Cas. 482; *Société Anonyme d'Intermediaires Luxembourgeois v Farex Gie* [1995] L.R.L.R.116; *Kingscroft Insurance Co Ltd v Nissan Fire & Marine Insurance Co Ltd* [1999] Lloyd's Rep. I.R. 371; *Australia & New Zealand Bank Ltd v Eagle & Colonial Wharves Ltd* [19601 2 Lloyd's Rep. 241; *Simner v New India Assurance Co Ltd* [1995] L.R.L.R. 240; *Group Josi Re v Walbrook Insurance Co Ltd* [1996] 1 All E.R. 791; *ERC Frankona Reinsurance v American National Insurance Co* [2006] Lloyd's Rep. I.R. 157; *Nam Kwong Medicines & Health Products Co Ltd v China Insurance Co Ltd* [2002] H.K.C.U. 792.

[200] *Blackburn, Low & Co v Vigors* (1877) 12 App. Cas. 531.

now dealt with by s.19). The decision may be contrasted with *Blackburn Low & Co v Haslam*[201] which involved a separate policy on the same risk. Here, the Glasgow brokers were instructed to insure, and used London agents to do so on their behalf. In this case, the failure of the reinsured to disclose the non-arrival of the vessel had been the direct responsibility of the Glasgow brokers who had been instructed to insure, and for this reason their default was deemed to be the default of the assured. The decision in the reinsurer's favour did not involve attribution of knowledge, but concerned only the duty of brokers to reinsure and thus to disclose material facts to the reinsurer: the case accordingly formed the basis of s.19.

Attribution within companies. In *Meridian Global Funds Management Asia Ltd v Securities Commission*[202] Lord Hoffmann laid down general principles relating to the imputation of knowledge to a company from its agents. Lord Hoffmann indicated that there was no one rule of attribution appropriate to all cases. In some circumstances there could be no attribution unless there had been unanimous agreement of the shareholders or a resolution of the board of directors, while in other circumstances knowledge or authorisation emanating from a lower level within the company could amount to attribution. The relevant attribution rule was to be fashioned in the context of the substantive rule of law in which the question had arisen. Applying these principles, it has been held that information known to the managing director of a company who procured a composite professional indemnity policy for his fellow directors and the company was not imputed to the company: in such a case the policy was designed to protect innocent co-assureds, so that a rule of attribution which imputed the knowledge of the managing director to the company as a whole would have been inconsistent with the policy.[203]   **6–038**

The fraud exception. English law has long recognised[204] that even if the relationship between the principal and agent is such that the agent's knowledge is that of the principal, there is no attribution of knowledge that the agent has defrauded the assured, as it cannot be expected that the agent will inform the assured of his wrongdoing and accordingly the assured is not aware of such fraud in the ordinary course of business. Thus if an underwriting agent acting for a reinsured is guilty of fraud relating to the reinsured which is material to the risk, the reinsured is not under any duty to disclose that fraud unless he actually knows of it.[205] The principle has also been held by Rix J. in *Arab Bank Plc v Zurich Insurance Co*[206] to cover the case in which the agent's fraud is directed not against the assured himself but rather against the insurers, as the assured is in effect the secondary victim of the agent's fraud in those circumstances.   **6–039**

---

[201] *Blackburn Low & Co v Haslam* (1888) 21 Q.B.D. 144.

[202] *Meridian Global Funds Management Asia Ltd v Securities Commission* [1995] 2 A.C. 500. The attribution issue may arise in other contexts in the insurance field, e.g. whether the assured was aware of breach of condition brought about by an employee: *Bonner-Williams v Peter Lindsay Leisure Ltd* [2001] 1 All E.R. (Comm) 1140. See also: *Re Odyssey (London) Ltd* [2001] Lloyd's Rep. I.R. 1; *HLB Kidsons v Lloyd's Underwriters* [2008] Lloyd's Rep. I.R. 237, reversed in part [2009] Lloyd's Rep. I.R. 178.

[203] *Arab Bank v Zurich Insurance Co* [1999] Lloyd's Rep. I.R. 262.

[204] *Kennedy v Green* (1834) 3 My. & K. 699; *Re Hampshire Land* [1896] 2 Ch. 300; *Société Anonyme d'Intermediaires Luxembourgeois v Farex Gie* [1995] L.R.L.R. 116; *Howells v Dominion Insurance Co Ltd* Unreported, 1999. Contrast Watts, (2001) 117 L.Q.R. 300.

[205] *Group Josi Re v Walbrook Insurance Co Ltd* [1996] 1 All E.R. 791; *PCW Syndicates v PCW Insurers* [1996] 1 All E.R. 774.

[206] *Arab Bank Plc v Zurich Insurance Co* [1999] 1 Lloyd's Rep. 262.

Subsequently, the Court of Appeal ruled in *Moore Stephens v Stone & Rolls Ltd*[207] that the fraud exception does not extend to that situation and that it operates only where the fraud is directed against the assured himself. The Court of Appeal's own decision was upheld on other grounds by the House of Lords,[208] and the point did not there arise, and although Lord Mance, in a dissenting judgment, approved the views of Rix J, that ruling did not form any part of the majority ratio.

The fraud exception does not extend either to mere misconduct or breach of contract by the agent[209] or to fraud which is remote from the agency relationship itself.[210]

Insurance effected by an agent

6–040   *The agent's duty of disclosure.* While the primary responsibility for ensuring that all material facts are disclosed to the insurer rests on the assured, an independent duty is imposed upon a person who is appointed by the assured to insure on his behalf. Section 19 of the 1906 Act provides that an agent must disclose to the insurer:

> "(a) every material circumstance which is known to himself, and an agent to insure is deemed to know every circumstance which in the ordinary course of business ought to have been known by, or to have been communicated to, him[211]; and
> (b) every material circumstance which the assured is bound to disclose, unless it comes to his knowledge too late, to communicate it to the agent."

There are two entirely separate concepts here. Section 19(b) is concerned with the situation in which the assured is aware of information that he has not disclosed to his broker, with the result that the broker is unable to disclose it to the insurers. The cases decided before the passing of the 1906 Act ruled that the assured could not be relieved of his obligation to disclose material facts simply by reason of the fact that he had used a broker, and, accordingly, that facts known to him remained subject to the disclosure obligation even though the broker was unaware of them.[212] The exception to this principle recognised that, if it were impossible for the assured to communicate the relevant information to the broker, then there could be no breach of duty. It is apparent that in an era of instantaneous communication the exception is almost certainly redundant.

The second concept is concerned with the separate obligation of an "agent to insure" to disclose facts known to him, or which ought in the ordinary course of business to have been known to him, independently of any knowledge (or lack of knowledge) on the part of the assured. In *HIH Casualty & General Insurance Ltd v Chase Manhattan Bank*[213] the House of Lords held that the agent's duty of disclosure is independent of the assured's duty, and that the two duties are at any

---

[207] *Moore Stephens v Stone & Rolls Ltd* [2008] EWCA Civ 644.

[208] *Moore Stephens v Stone & Rolls Ltd* [2009] UKHL 39.

[209] *Kingscroft Insurance Co Ltd v Nissan Fire & Marine Insurance Co Ltd* [19991 Lloyd's Rep. I.R. 371.

[210] *ERC Frankona Reinsurance v American National Insurance Co* [2006] Lloyd's Rep. I.R. 157.

[211] See: *Fitzherbert v Mather* (1795) 1 T.R. 12; *Russell v Thornton* (1860) 6 H. & N. 140; *Gladstone v King* (1813) 1 M. & S. 35.

[212] See: *Republic of Bolivia v Indemnity Mutual Assurance Co* [1909] 1 K.B. 785; *Cory v Patton* (1874) L.R. 9 Q.B. 577; *Winter v Irish Life Assurance Plc* [1995] 2 Lloyd's Rep. 274.

[213] *HIH Casualty & General Insurance Ltd v Chase Manhattan Bank* [2003] Lloyd's Rep. I.R. 230.

one time both to be satisfied. In that case the point was of particular significance in considering the scope of a policy term that purported to exclude the assured's duty of disclosure, as their Lordships ruled in *HIH* that such a provision would not exclude the agent's duty unless there is express reference to the agent in it.

Given that the broker's duty is independent of that of the assured, it would seem to follow that even if the law applicable to the policy is not English law, the broker's duty is one which arises under English law and would apply wherever the placement is made in the London market.

Who is an agent to insure? Section 19(a) gives underwriters the right to avoid **6–041** where an agent to insure who is aware of material facts has failed to disclose them. If the agent in question is not an agent to insure then the disclosure obligation is governed by s.18, and the question then becomes whether the information known to the assured's agent is to be regarded as in the possession of the assured by reason of the relationship between the assured and his agent.

The meaning of the phrase "agent to insure" is uncertain. In two cases heard concurrently by the Court of Appeal, *PCW Syndicates v PCW Reinsurers*[214] and *Group Josi Re v Walbrook Insurance Co Ltd*[215] where the issue was whether the fraud of the reinsureds' underwriting agents had to be disclosed to reinsurers under s.19(a), Staughton L.J. decided the case on the basis that the information was not of a quality that was required to be disclosed, as it related to the agent's own fraud. Saville L.J. agreed with the result, but on the narrower basis that an underwriting agent acting on behalf of a Lloyd's syndicate is not an "agent to insure" and so the knowledge of the underwriting agent did not in any event fall to be disclosed. Rose L.J. agreed with both judgments. Two members of the Court of Appeal thus held that the only person who can be an agent to insure is a placing broker. This analysis is not free from doubt, as its effect is that an agent to insure within s.19(a) can only be the last agent in the chain, i.e. the placing broker, so that the knowledge of agents at a lower level in the chain cannot adversely affect the assured insofar as it does not have to be disclosed by the agent himself. This is logical in that, as only the placing broker deals with the insurer, there may not be any opportunity for other agents to make disclosure. However, the reasoning may also mean that, if a broker charged with the duty to insure is aware of detrimental material facts, these can be withheld from the insurer simply by the broker appointing a sub-agent to carry out the placement for him: in some cases this may amount to deliberate concealment by the agent, whereas in others such withholding may occur in the ordinary course of events, as where a foreign or non-Lloyd's producing broker with material information appoints a London placing broker who is not appraised of matters within the producing broker's knowledge. Further, in the root case on s.19(a), *Blackburn, Low & Co v Haslam*[216] the Court of Appeal held that material facts known to the assured's Glasgow producing brokers, but which had not been communicated to London placing brokers, had not been disclosed and thus justified the insurer's avoidance of the contract. Saville L.J.'s conclusion can, therefore, be supported only if s.19(a), is to be regarded as having changed the law in this important respect. It is noteworthy that, in the earlier decision in *GMA v Unistorebrand International Insurance AS*[217] Rix J. assumed that knowledge in the possession

[214] *PCW Syndicates v PCW Reinsurers* [1996] 1 All E.R. 774.
[215] *Group Josi Re v Walbrook Insurance Co Ltd* [1996] 1 All E.R. 791.
[216] *Blackburn, Low & Co v Haslam* (1888) 21 Q.B.D. 144.
[217] *GMA v Unistorebrand International Insurance AS* [1995] L.R.L.R. 333.

of an intermediate agent had to be disclosed.[218] In *ERC Frankona Reinsurance v American National Insurance Co*[219] Andrew Smith J. recognised that there were potentially powerful objections to the reasoning in *PCW*, but regarded himself as bound to follow it given that it had been adopted by a majority of the Court of Appeal in that case.

6–042   *Scope of the agent's duty to disclose.* If it is the case that an agent to insure is not required to disclose his own fraud (at least, against the assured) to the underwriters, the issue becomes whether this is because fraud is a special case or because there is a wider principle that a broker is not required to disclose information that has come to him in some capacity other than that as broker for the assured. The wording of s.19(a) imposes no limitations upon the duty of the "agent to insure" other than that the facts which are to be disclosed are material. This is based upon the formulation of the duty by Lord Macnaghten in *Blackburn Low v Vigors*,[220] who stated that the placing broker was under a personal duty "to communicate to the underwriters all material facts within his knowledge". A problem that has since arisen and which has been discussed in the cases is whether the material facts that have to be disclosed are confined to facts that the broker has acquired in his capacity as agent of the assured, or whether it extends to facts that are (a) known to the broker for reasons entirely unconnected with his functions as a broker or (b) known to the broker by reason of his role as a broker for others but not for the assured in question.

The authorities are not easy to reconcile. Waller J. commented in *PCW Syndicates v PCW Reinsurers*[221] that *Blackburn Low* was not concerned with the extent of the duty of disclosure, but rather only with the person whose knowledge had to be disclosed. On appeal,[222] Staughton L.J.,[223] having ruled that reinsurers were not permitted to avoid the policy for the failure of the underwriting agent to disclose his own fraud, went on to lay down the wider principle that there was nothing in the authorities that provided that "an agent to insure is required by s.19 to disclose information which he has received other than in the character of an agent to insure".[224] By contrast, Hoffmann L.J. in *El Ajou v Dollar Land Holdings Plc*[225] assumed that materiality was the only limit on the broker's duty of disclosure, and that " . . . an insurance policy may be avoided on account of the broker's failure to disclose material facts within his knowledge, even though he did not obtain that knowledge in his capacity as agent for the insured."

The leading authority on this issue is *Société Anonyme d'Intermediaires Luxembourgeois v Farex Gie*,[226] in which brokers appointed by a reinsured to place reinsurance initially obtained retrocession cover and were then able to approach reinsurers with an offer of retrocession protection. The retrocession was

---

[218] In *Baker v Lombard Continental Insurance Plc* Unreported, 1996, Colman J. expressed the view that a majority of the Court of Appeal in *Group Josi* had held that s.19 required an intermediate agent instructing an agent to insure to supply the agent to insure with all material facts actually known to the intermediate agent.

[219] *ERC Frankona Reinsurance v American National Insurance Co* [2006] Lloyd's Rep. I.R. 157.

[220] *Blackburn Low v Vigors* (1877) L.R. 12 App. Cas. 531.

[221] *PCW Syndicates v PCW Reinsurers* [1996] 1 All E.R. 774.

[222] *PCW Syndicates v PCW Reinsurers* [1996] 1 All E.R. 774.

[223] Rose L.J. concurring on the point. See also Staughton L.J.'s judgment in *Group Josi v Walbrook Insurance* [1996] 1 All E.R. 791.

[224] The authorities relied upon Staughton L.J. for this wider view, *Espin v Pemberton* (1859) 3 De. G. & J. 547 and *Cave v Cave* (1880) 15 Ch D 639 are, however, fraud cases.

[225] *El Ajou v Dollar Land Holdings Plc* [1994] 3 All E.R. 685.

[226] *Société Anonyme d'Intermediaires Luxembourgeois v Farex Gie* [1995] L.R.L.R. 116.

subsequently avoided by the retrocessionaires on the basis that their own agent had exceeded his authority, and the reinsurers purported to avoid the reinsurance as against the reinsured on the ground that they had not been informed by the brokers that the retrocession might not be valid. The argument by the reinsurers was rejected on the basis that the brokers had been unaware of the authority issue, but the Court of Appeal held that the result would have been the same even if the brokers had possessed the relevant knowledge, either because the fraud exception would have applied or because the information would not have been material to the reinsurance risk. These points aside, Hoffmann L.J. repeated his earlier view in *El Ajou* that "the insured and his agent are under a duty to disclose every material circumstance of which they have knowledge, irrespective of the way in which it was acquired" and "the agent's duty [was] to disclose material circumstances known to him in any capacity" even though it would be purely coincidental if a broker placing reinsurance had knowledge of material facts relating to retrocession. Saville L.J. felt that the issue did not arise on the facts although commented that "the duty on the agent is not confined to knowledge acquired from the assured but extends to knowledge otherwise acquired".

It may be seen, therefore, that there is some authority for the proposition that s.19(a) is not absolute, and is subject to a gloss relating to the capacity in which a broker has received information: the provision may apply only where the broker is in possession of material facts because he is acting for the assured. Even if this gloss exists, its scope is uncertain. It may well be right to argue that a broker who becomes aware of material facts for reasons entirely separate from his capacity as a broker is not required to disclose them, but the point becomes more difficult where the information has come to the broker not as a private person but rather in the course of other broking activities for different parties. It may be a matter to be resolved by market evidence whether underwriters rely upon a broker's general market expertise rather than information obtained by him from his own client for the purposes of placing the risk.

The fraud exception. The fraud exception also applies to s.19, although in *PCW Syndicates v PCW Reinsurers*[227] the Court of Appeal was not agreed on the correct principles to be applied. The fact alleged by reinsurers to be material was that the reinsured's underwriting agent had defrauded them. Saville L.J. dismissed the claim for avoidance on the ground that an underwriting agent was not an agent to insure within s.19(a). Staughton L.J., by contrast, held that the section did not give an insurer a defence where the assured's agent failed to disclose information which was in the agent's possession other than in his capacity as agent for the assured, and in any event an agent did not act as agent for the assured where he was perpetrating a fraud on the assured.[228] Rose L.J. agreed with both judgments. It could, therefore, be said that at least two members of the Court of Appeal were prepared to recognise a fraud exception. In the parallel decision, *Group Josi v Walbrook Insurance*,[229] Staughton L.J. again stated that s.19(a) had no application to fraud, on the strength of the principle in *Re Hampshire Land*. Saville L.J., whilst preferring to dismiss the claim for avoidance on the principle that s.19 did not require disclosure by an underwriting agent, nevertheless saw some merit in the approach adopted by Staughton L.J., stating that he was unpersuaded by the submission that a fraud being practised upon the assured was a circumstance "known" to the agent. Rose L.J. once again

6–043

---

[227] *PCW Syndicates v PCW Reinsurers* [1996] 1 All E.R. 774.
[228] In accordance with *Re Hampshire Land* [1896] 2 Ch. 743.
[229] *Group Josi v Walbrook Insurance* [1996] 1 All E.R. 791.

agreed with both judgments. *Group Josi* thus appears to provide, with varying degrees of strength, a unanimous decision of the Court of Appeal adopting the fraud exception. The fraud principle as enumerated in these cases involves fraud by the agent to insure on his own client. The exception was extended by Rix J. in *Arab Bank Plc v Zurich Insurance Co*[230] to a senior manager of the assured whose fraud was against both the assured and the insurers in the placing of the risk. In *Moore Stephens v Stone & Rolls Ltd*[231] the Court of Appeal refused to follow *Arab Bank* and held that the fraud exception applied only where the fraud was directed against the assured himself, and not primarily against a third party. The Court of Appeal was of the view that the fraud was directed against the third parties rather than the company itself, and that *Re Hampshire Land* the company had its controller's fraud imputed to it, and was not saved by *Re Hampshire Land* because the two could not be distinguished. The House of Lords[232] by a 3:2 majority upheld the Court of Appeal's decision, but on the rather different basis that *Re Hampshire Land* had no application to a one-man company. Lord Mance, dissenting, alone held that *Re Hampshire Land* could apply where the shareholder in a one-man company was a fraudster, and further held that the principle operated to prevent the imputation of the shareholder's fraud to the company. Lord Scott's dissenting judgment was to similarl effect. There was no indication from the majority as to whether *Re Hampshire Land*, where it did apply, extended to fraud by an agent directed against a third party with the principal being only a secondary victim. Accordingly, the correctness or otherwise of Rix J's decision in *Arab Bank* remains uncertain.

There is one troublesome line of authority that appears to conflict with the fraud principle. It has been held on a number of occasions that, if a broker acting for the assured makes a false statement to the leading underwriter on a market placement, but does not repeat that false statement to the following market, he is nevertheless under a separate duty to disclose that falsity to them.[233] Assuming that the broker has acted fraudulently, as will inevitably be the case, given that a broker is only required to disclose what he actually knows or ought to know, the notion that he is required to disclose his fraud to the following market is inconsistent with the reasoning in *Arab Bank*. As yet this potential conflict has not been considered by the courts.

6–044 *The insurer's remedies for breach of the agent's duties.* The failure of an agent to make full disclosure as required by s.19, confers upon the insurer the right to avoid the policy, just as if the default had been that of the assured himself. Although avoidance is the sole remedy for breach of the duty by the assured himself, breach of the agent's independent duty of utmost good faith may give rise to a claim for damages in circumstances in which the insurer does not have the right possibly by reason of agreement to that effect to avoid the policy, and thus has suffered loss by reason of the broker's breach of duty. The various possibilities were considered by Aikens J., the Court of Appeal and the House of Lords in *HIH Casualty and General Insurance Ltd v Chase Manhattan Bank*.[234]

[230] *Arab Bank Plc v Zurich Insurance Co* [1999] 1 Lloyd's Rep. 262.
[231] *Moore Stephens v Stone & Rolls Ltd* [2008] EWCA Civ 644.
[232] *Moore Stephens v Stone & Rolls Ltd* [2009] UKHL 39.
[233] *Aneco v Johnson & Higgins* [1998] 1 Lloyd's Rep. 565; *International Lottery Management v Dumas* [2002] Lloyd's Rep. I.R. 237; *International Management Group (UK) Ltd v Simmonds* [2004] Lloyd's Rep. I.R. 247; *If P & C Insurance Ltd (Publ) v Silversea Cruises* [2004] Lloyd's Rep. I.R. 217; *Brotherton v Aseguradora Colseguros SA (No.3)* [2003] Lloyd's Rep. I.R. 774.
[234] *HIH Casualty and General Insurance Ltd v Chase Manhattan Bank* [2003] Lloyd's Rep. I.R. 230.

Where an agent has failed to disclose material facts, or has misstated material facts, the relevant principles are as follows.

First, as against the assured, there could not be a claim for damages based on breach of the duty of utmost good faith by the agent, as the law did not recognise the remedy of damages in this context. However, in principle it was possible for there to be, by reason of the assured's vicarious liability,[235] a claim for damages against the assured in the tort of deceit where the agent had been fraudulent, and there might also be a claim in damages against the assured under s.2(1) of the Misrepresentation Act 1967 where there was a positive false statement by the agent (as opposed to a failure to disclose). Moreover, in the case of a declaration policy, e.g. an open cover, which was a contract for insurance not attracting the duty of utmost good faith, there could be damages in deceit, under s.2(1) of the 1967 Act and also for breach of a duty of care by the assured in relation to false statements made by his agent.

Secondly, as against the agent himself, there was no claim for damages for breach of the duty of utmost good faith: while it was the case that the agent had an independent duty of disclosure, that duty arose out of the assured's own duty to make full disclosure to the insurers in furtherance of the duty of utmost good faith. Given that no damages were available against the assured for breach of that duty, there could be no damages against an agent. Moreover, if the insurer had agreed not to exercise a right of avoidance, a right to damages could not arise in its place, as the abandonment of the only remedy recognised by law could not give rise to a remedy not recognised by law. Independently of the duty of utmost good faith, there was no duty on an agent to "speak up" the courts could not fashion a duty of care in tort that ran parallel to the duty of utmost good faith, and the law in general did not recognise a duty of care upon an agent in relation to the third party, as the agent's duties were owed to the principal. There could be a claim for damages in the tort of deceit against the agent in the case of fraud, but there could not be a claim for damages against the agent in respect of negligent misrepresentation under s.2(1) of the 1967 Act as the section is confined to the contracting parties.

Thirdly, any right to damages arising by reason of the assured's vicarious liability for the agent's fraud could, in principle, be excluded by express provision in the contract, either directly or by withdrawing the authority of the agent to present the risk on the assured's behalf, and that the only restriction on the right of exclusion was the principle that an assured could not, as a matter of public policy, exclude liability for his own personal fraudulent misrepresentation. However, this is subject to the qualification that an assured could not exclude liability for the agent's fraud if the assured was in some way implicated in that fraud or if the exclusion was itself part of some fraudulent scheme.

4. MATERIAL FACTS

Classification of material facts. Materiality is defined by the 1906 Act in terms **6–045** of premium sensitivity or risk sensivity. Material facts for the purposes of the duty of utmost good faith normally fall into two classes: those affecting the "physical hazard" and those affecting the "moral hazard". The physical hazard includes any factors which concern the likelihood or degree of a loss; matters such as physical condition, geographical environment and use all fall within this heading. The moral hazard, by contrast, is concerned with the character of the

---

[235] This is absolute liability, and is not based on the fault of the assured.

assured, and in particular whether there is any history of deceit or dishonesty which renders a loss more likely. It has been said that a matter relates to the moral hazard if it affects the desirability of the assured as a person with whom the insurers would want to deal,[236] and that if the evidence presented to the court suggests that a prudent underwriter would have regarded the information as material then it should be treated as such.[237] Moral hazard is relevant to all forms of insurance, including war risks.[238] Both classes of material fact may be the subject of express questions, in which case the materiality of misrepresentations will be presumed, but there is much case law on the materiality of various elements of the physical and moral hazards for the purposes of the duty of disclosure. This is particularly the case for moral hazard involving dishonesty, where in practice insurers are somewhat embarrassed by asking express questions, although the absence of express questions for this reason is not to be construed as waiver of disclosure.[239]

There may be exceptional cases in which a fact is capable of affecting the premium to be charged by the insurer, but does not fall within the ordinary classification of moral and physical hazard. The cases which hold that it may be material that an assured has bargained away rights against third parties and has therefore prejudiced insurers' subrogation rights in the event of a loss, can be explained on this basis.[240] It was held in *Sharp v Sphere Drake Insurance Co Ltd (The Moonacre)*[241] that the fact that the assured had not personally signed the proposal was a material fact, as the proposal amounted to a personal undertaking by the assured: it is difficult to classify this as either physical or moral hazard. A further illustration is *Inversiones Manria SA v Sphere Drake Insurance Co Plc (The Dora)*[242] in which insurance on a yacht was obtained at a lower rate on the basis of a false promise by the assured that cover for at least four other yachts would be placed with the insurers: the misstatement was held to be material. Doubt has been cast on these decisions by that of the Court of Appeal in *North Star Shipping Ltd v Sphere Drake Insurance Plc*,[243] where it was held that the assured's precarious financial position, which could lead to his inability to pay the premium, was a credit risk rather than something which was relevant to the risk insured, and therefore was not a material fact. If this is right, then it would seem that there is an important gloss on the wording of s.18(2) and that materiality is to be confined to facts which affect the risk itself rather than unrelated matters which are simply premium-sensitive.

Moral hazard

6–046   *The identity of the assured.* Given that moral hazard relates not so much to the risk as to the assured's propensity to suffer losses and his character in general,[244]

---

[236] *Locker & Woolf Ltd* v *Western Australian Insurance Co* [1936] 1 K.B. 408; *Insurance Corporation of the Channel Islands v Royal Hotel (No.2)* [1998] Lloyd's Rep. I.R. 151.

[237] *Brotherton v Aseguradora Colseguros (No.2)* [2003] Lloyd's Rep. I.R. 758.

[238] In *North Star Shipping Ltd v Sphere Drake Insurance Plc* [2006] Lloyd's Rep. I.R. 519.

[239] *James v CGU Insurance Plc* [2002] Lloyd's Rep. I.R. 206.

[240] There will be a right to avoid in exceptional circumstances only, where the agreement between the assured and third party was so unusual that the insurers could not have anticipated it. See: *Mercantile Steamship Co v Tyser* (1881) L.R. 7 Q.B.D. 73; *Tate & Sons v Hyslop* (1885) L.R. 15 Q.B.D. 368; *The Bedouin* [1894] P. 1; *Scottish Shire Line v London & Provincial Marine & General Insurance Co* [1912] 3 K.B. 51; *Marc Rich & Co AG v Portman* [1996] 1 Lloyd's Rep. 430.

[241] *Sharp v Sphere Drake Insurance Co Ltd (The Moonacre)* [1992] 2 Lloyd's Rep. 501.

[242] *Inversiones Manria SA v Sphere Drake Insurance Co Plc (The Dora)* [1989] 1 Lloyd's Rep. 69. See also *Sibbald v Hill* (1814) 2 Dow 263 (misstatement as to existence of other insurance).

[243] *North Star Shipping Ltd v Sphere Drake Insurance Plc* [2006] Lloyd's Rep. I.R. 519.

[244] *Lynch v Dalzell* (1729) 4 Bro. P.C. 431.

it would seem obvious that the identity of the assured is the key material fact. Thus any change of name on the part of the assured will be material.[245] The personal nature of insurance was stressed in *The Moonacre*,[246] in which a policy was held to be voidable where brokers had forged the assured's signature on the proposal form as they had been unable to contact him to sign the form personally. The decision was justified by the personal nature of insurance contracts. In the light of these cases it is somewhat surprising to find that English law has endorsed the application of the doctrine of the undisclosed principal—whereby a policy taken out apparently in the name of A but acting for B can be taken over by B—to insurance contracts.[247] However, in *Talbot Underwriting v Nausch Hogan & Murray (The Jascon 5)*[248] Cooke J. expressed strong doubts as to whether the undisclosed principal doctrine could be reconciled with the materiality of the assured's identity. On appeal[249] the Court of Appeal recognised that in many cases the identity of a co-assured might not be material to insurers,[250] but that this was not the case where the co-assured was a person against whom the insurers potentially had subrogation rights.

The nature of the assured's interest. As long as the assured has insurable interest **6–047** in the insured subject matter, the contract will be valid under insurable interest rules and there is in general no need for the assured to disclose the nature of his insurable interest. In *Arlet v Lancashire & General Insurance Co*[251] the assured was held not to be in breach of duty for failing to disclose that his interest in the subject matter was that of hirer under a hire purchase agreement. There are numerous other decisions to the same effect.[252] The decision in *Guardian Assurance Co v Sutherland*[253] nevertheless indicates that the nature of the assured's interest will be material if it is likely to affect the risk. Such a case was *Patel v Windsor Life Assurance Co Ltd*[254] in which the applicant for a life policy named a third party without interest as the beneficiary of the insurance: the court's view was that the absence of any satisfactory explanation for the nomination of that beneficiary—coupled with a series of false statements relating

[245] *Galle Gowns v Licences & General Insurance Co* (1933) 47 Ll. L.R. 186, but see *Britton v Royal Insurance Co* (1866) 4 F. & F. 905 and *Horne v Poland* [1922] 2 K.B. 364 at 365.

[246] *Sharp v Sphere Drake Insurance (The Moonacre)* [1992] 2 Lloyd's Rep. 501; *Galle Gowns v Licences & General Insurance Co* (1933) 47 Ll. L.R. 186 (assured trading under other names); *Goodbarne v Buck* [1940] 1 K.B. 771; in *Norwich Union Insurance Ltd v Meisels* [2007] Lloyd's Rep. I.R. 69 the assured landlord's use of an alias was held not to be material, as the court was satisfied that the purpose of the alias was to maintain as against his tenants, the assured's anonymity.

[247] *Siu v Eastern Insurance Co Ltd* [1994] 1 All E.R. 213; *National Oilwell (UK) Ltd v Davy Offshore Ltd* [1993] 2 Lloyd's Rep. 582.

[248] *Talbot Underwriting v Nausch Hogan & Murray (The Jascon 5)* [2005] EWHC 2359 (Comm).

[249] *The Jascon 5* [2006] Lloyd's Rep. I.R. 531.

[250] It is thus immaterial that an assured is not interested in the subject matter as absolute owner but only as mortgagor or equitable owner: *Foster v Standard Insurance Co of New Zealand Ltd* [1924] N.Z.L.R. 1093; *Ocean Accident and Guarantee Corp v Williams* (1915) 34 N.Z.L.R. 924. Contrast *Gate v Sun Alliance Assurance* Unreported, 1993.

[251] *Arlet v Lancashire & General Insurance Co* (1927) 27 Ll. L.R. 454.

[252] *Carruthers v Sheddon* (1815) 6 Taunt. 14; *Irving v Richardson* (1831) 2 B. & Ad. 193; *Crowley v Cohen* (1932) 3 B. & Ad. 478; *Mackenzie v Whitworth* (1875) L.R. 1 Ex. D. 36; *O'Kane v Jones* [2005] Lloyd's Rep. I.R. 174. The reinsurance cases, in particular *Mackenzie v Whitworth*, can be explained on the basis that the interest of the reinsured is in the insured subject matter rather than its own liability, so that the reinsured need not disclose that it is an insurer rather than a person directly interested in the subject matter: *WASA International Insurance Co Ltd v Lexington Insurance Co* [2009] Lloyd's Rep. I.R. 576.

[253] *Guardian Assurance Co v Sutherland* (1939) 63 Ll. L.R. 220.

[254] *Patel v Windsor Life Assurance Co Ltd* [2008] Lloyd's Rep. I.R. 359.

to the applicant's income, address and reasons for taking out the policy—amounted to a fraudulent breach of the duty of utmost good faith.

6–048   *Criminal convictions.* There will frequently be a specific question concerning criminal convictions, although this may be limited to specific classes of crime (e.g. in relation to a motor policy, the question may be confined to road traffic offences), and there may in addition be a limitation as to time (e.g. all offences of a given type in the last five years). The cases demonstrate that in the absence of an express question the duty to disclose remains. The courts have not sought to establish guidelines as to when a conviction will be material, although it may be deduced from the decided cases that a conviction is more likely to be material when it is of comparatively recent origin, when it is serious,[255] and when it is directly related to the subject matter of the policy.

So far as age of conviction is concerned, the cases have generally adopted an approach highly favourable to insurers, so that convictions of dishonesty occurring many years before have been regarded as material. In *Regina Fur v Bossom*[256] the claimant company insured the furs which were its stock in trade. The managing director of that company had, 12 years previously, been convicted of receiving stolen furs, but this fact was not disclosed. Pearson J. held that the policy was voidable. In *Schoolman v Hall*[257] the claimant jeweller insured his stock in trade against theft in 1948. He omitted to disclose that between 1927 and 1934 he had been convicted of a number of offences of dishonesty. On the basis of this non-disclosure the insurers successfully repudiated liability for a loss which occurred during the currency of the policy. In *Roselodge v Castle*[258] a conviction for diamond smuggling against the sales director of the assured company, involved in the jewellery business, was held to be material, but a conviction for bribing a policeman, obtained against the assured's principal director some 20 years previously, was held to be immaterial. McNair J. was scathing of evidence of materiality of the latter offence given by other insurers.

As far as the relationship between the conviction and the subject matter of the insurance is concerned, there is little doubt that a close connection will lead to the conviction being a material fact. This may be demonstrated by reference to a series of motor insurance cases in which convictions for various motoring offences were held to be material facts.[259] The same point emerges from *March*

[255] *Callaghan and Hedges v Thompson* [2000] Lloyd's Rep. I.R. 125.

[256] *Regina Fur v Bossom* [1957] 2 Lloyd's Rep. 466.

[257] *Schoolman v Hall* [1951] 1 Lloyd's Rep. 139.

[258] *Roselodge v Castle* [1966] 2 Lloyd's Rep. 113. See also the comments in *Norwich Union Insurance Ltd v Meisels* [2007] Lloyd's Rep. I.R. 69, making the point that old convictions were less likely to be material.

[259] *Bond v Commercial Union Assurance Co Ltd* (1930) 36 Ll. L.R. 107 (conviction of assured's son, who was intended to be a driver insured under the policy, for various motoring offences); *Jester-Barnes v Licences and General Insurance Co Ltd* (1934) 49 Ll. L.R. 231 (previous convictions for drunken driving, dangerous driving and driving untaxed all material, as were similar convictions against the assured's chauffeur); *Cleland v London General Insurance Co Ltd* (1935) 51 Ll. L.R. 156 (conviction for theft of motor vehicle held to be material). Contrast: *Mackay v London General Insurance Co Ltd* (1935) 51 Ll. L.R. 201 (motor offences of a very minor nature held not to be material); *Revell v London General Insurance Co Ltd* (1934) 50 Ll. L.R. 114; *Tayor v Eagle Star Insurance Co Ltd* (1940) 67 Ll. L.R. 136 (the latter two cases proceeded on the basis that by giving literally true answers to express ambiguous questions concerning motoring offences, the assured had discharged his duty of utmost good faith; these decisions also indicate that the asking of express limited questions is a waiver of otherwise material facts falling outside the precise scope of the questions. See also: *Dunn v Ocean Accident and Guarantee Corp Ltd* (1933) 47 Ll. L.R. 129; *McCormick v National Motor and Accident Insurance Union* (1934) 40 Com. Cas. 76; *Zurich General Accident and Liability Insurance Co Ltd v Leven* 1940 S.C. 406.

Cabaret Club and Casino Ltd v The London Assurance[260] in which a recent conviction of a director of a trading company for handling stolen property was held to be material, and from *Allden v Raven (The Kylie)*,[261] in which the assured under a marine policy failed to disclose a conviction for handling a stolen dinghy. A more important question, however, is whether an offence unconnected with the insured subject matter but which indicates general dishonesty is to be regarded as within the assured's duty of utmost good faith. At one time there appeared to be a tendency in the courts towards accepting that an offence demonstrating general dishonesty was a material fact. Thus in *Lambert v Co-operative Insurance Society Ltd*[262] two convictions for handling stolen goods against the assured's husband were held to be material to a policy on domestic property, and, in *Woolcott v Sun Alliance and London Insurance Ltd*[263] a single conviction for armed robbery was held to be material to a fire policy. The earlier case of *Cleland v London General Insurance Co Ltd*[264] is even more extreme, as here it was held that the assured under a motor policy should have disclosed earlier convictions for forgery and breaking and entering. This tendency, if it was such, was halted by the decision of Forbes J. in *Reynolds v Phoenix Assurance Co Ltd*,[265] the learned judge there refusing to accept that it was material to a fire policy for the assured to disclose a conviction for receiving stolen goods some 11 years earlier. A similar decision is *Constantinou v Aegon Insurance Co (UK) Ltd*,[266] in which the Court of Appeal held that four convictions for dishonesty were immaterial facts in relation to a fire policy taken out more than 30 years later. By contrast, charges which do not relate to dishonesty and have no real connection with the policy may not be material, Thus in *Norwich Union Insurance Ltd v Meisels*[267] it was held that the facts that the assured had potentially committed a strict liability offence by submitting an incorrect tax return, and that he had been involved in the winding up or striking off of some 20 companies, were not material. The conclusion which may be drawn from the authorities on general dishonesty is that both the seriousness of the offence and the time-gap between the conviction and the policy will serve to reduce the potential materiality of the conviction, but that the possible materiality of general dishonesty cannot be discounted.[268]

Although as a matter of common law previous convictions will be relevant in virtually every form of insurance, notwithstanding that the offences are apparently unrelated to the subject matter of the insurance, the Rehabilitation of Offenders Act 1974 may have a significant bearing on the position in individual cases. The Act is designed to ensure that less serious offences should not continue to be held against an offender after a reasonable lapse of time. Under s.4 a conviction is to be treated as spent once it has been complied with and a further

---

[260] *March Cabaret Club and Casino Ltd v The London Assurance* [1975] 1 Lloyd's Rep. 169, applied in *Howells v Dominion Insurance Co Ltd* Unreported, 1999.

[261] *Allden v Raven (The Kylie)* [1983] 2 Lloyd's Rep. 444. Cf. *Inversiones Manria SA v Sphere Drake Insurance Co Plc (The Dora)* [1989] I Lloyd's Rep. 169, in which Phillips J. held that a series of petty convictions, including smuggling, accumulated by the skipper of a vessel was a material fact pointing towards his unsuitability.

[262] *Lambert v Co-operative Insurance Society Ltd* [1975] 2 Lloyd's Rep. 485.

[263] *Woolcott v Sun Alliance and London Insurance Ltd* [1978] 1 All E.R. 1253.

[264] *Cleland v London General Insurance Co Ltd* (1935) 51 Ll. L.R. 156.

[265] *Reynolds v Phoenix Assurance Co Ltd* [1978] 2 Lloyd's Rep. 440.

[266] *Constantinou v Aegon Insurance Co (UK) Ltd* Unreported, 1996. See also *Alliance Insurance Co of Philadelphia v Laurentian Colonies & Hotels Ltd* [1953] I.L.R. para.1–111.

[267] *Norwich Union Insurance Ltd v Meisels* [2007] Lloyd's Rep. I.R. 69.

[268] *Insurance Corporation of the Channel Islands v Royal Hotel (No.2)* [1998] Lloyd's Rep. I.R. 151.

period of time has elapsed: the rehabilitation period ranges for six months for an absolute discharge to five years to a custodial sentence of more than 10 years, and the benefit of rehabilitation is lost if a further offence is committed under English law (s.6).[269] Where an offender has become rehabilitated, s.4 states that if he is asked questions about previous convictions, offences or proceedings, these are to be construed as not relating to spent convictions, and the rehabilitated person is not to be prejudiced in law by his failure, in answering such questions, to disclose spent convictions. Further, any rule of law imposing an obligation to disclose any matters to another person shall not extend to requiring him to disclose a spent conviction. These provisions clearly cover the obligations imposed by the duty of utmost good faith, the effect being that in completing the proposal form the proposer need not volunteer evidence of spent convictions, and may even decline to disclose them in answer to a specific question without thereby endangering the validity of his insurance cover. A spent conviction may, however, be admitted in evidence in the discretion of the court (s.7(3)) if it goes to the credit of a party to the proceedings.[270]

6–049   *General dishonesty.* In *Reynolds v Phoenix Assurance Co*[271] Forbes J. classified the assured's duty in respect of criminal conduct to disclose both offences which had resulted in conviction and also offences for which the assured had not been charged.[272] The notion that an assured might voluntarily disclose to an insurer criminal conduct which had not come to the attention of the relevant authorities, or in respect of which he had been charged but acquitted, smacks of unreality but is nevertheless established.[273] Whatever the correctness of these comments, what does seem to be beyond argument is that general dishonesty on the part of the assured may be a material fact, on the basis that the moral hazard includes any fact which may merely increase the likelihood of it being made to appear (falsely) that loss or damage has occurred falling within the scope of the policy. In *Insurance Corp of the Channel Islands v Royal Hotel (No.2)* Mance J. held that it was a material fact that the assured had fraudulently prepared documents which it was willing to use to defraud its bankers, even though those documents had no connection as such with the policy itself. The principle that general dishonesty is material was followed in *James v CGU Insurance Plc.*[274] Here, the assured failed to disclose that he was in dispute with the revenue authorities and with Customs and Excise in relation to apparent withholding of national insurance contributions, PAYE income tax and VAT. Insofar as this indicated a trend of general dishonesty on the assured's part, the facts were held to be material, even though taken alone the facts might have been immaterial.[275] Further, the assured—a garage proprietor—had charged customers with insurance premiums to fund vehicle warranties, but had not applied the funds received

---

[269] *Inversiones Manria SA v Sphere Drake Insurance Co Plc (The Dora)* [1989] 1 Lloyd's Rep. 69: offence under Italian law did not affect the rehabilitation period.

[270] *Thomas v Commissioner of the Police of the Metropolis* [1997] 1 All E.R. 747; *Reynolds v Phoenix Assurance Co* [1978] 2 Lloyd's Rep. 440; *Inversiones Manria SA v Sphere Drake Insurance Co Plc (The Dora)* [1989] 1 Lloyd's Rep. 69.

[271] *Reynolds v Phoenix Assurance Co* [1978] 2 Lloyd's Rep. 440.

[272] *Quinby Enterprises Ltd (In Liquidation) v General Accident Fire and Life Assurance Corp Public Ltd Co* [1995] 1 N.Z.L.R. 736.

[273] *March Cabaret Club & Casino v London Assurance* [1975] 1 Lloyd's Rep. 169; *Inversiones Manria SA v Sphere Drake Insurance Co Plc (The Dora)* [1989] 1 Lloyd's Rep. 69; *Insurance Corp of the Channel Islands v Royal Hotel (No.2)* [1998] Lloyd's Rep. I.R. 151.

[274] *James v CGU Insurance Plc* [2002] Lloyd's Rep. I.R. 206.

[275] *Gate v Sun Alliance Insurance Ltd* Unreported, 1994; *Quinby Enterprises Ltd v General Accident Fire and Life Assurance Corporation Public Ltd Co* [1995] 1 N.Z.L.R. 736.

by him for that purpose: once again the assured's dishonesty in this regard was held to be a material fact.

Allegations of dishonesty and outstanding charges. If there are outstanding **6–050** criminal charges against the assured at the date of the application for insurance, those charges must be disclosed whether or not they are well founded. In *March Cabaret Club & Casino v London Assurance*,[276] May J. was of the opinion that material charges must be disclosed to the insurer even if the assured knows that the charges are unfounded. Forbes J. expressly refused to follow this reasoning in *Reynolds v Phoenix Assurance Co*,[277] although Phillips J., in *Inversiones Manria SA v Sphere Drake Insurance Co Plc (The Dora)*,[278] obiter, preferred the views of May J.[279]

The principles to be applied to disclosure of outstanding charges were given detailed consideration by Colman J. in *Strive Shipping Corp v Hellenic Mutual War Risks Association*,[280] the Court of Appeal in *Brotherton v Aseguradora Colseguros (No.2)*[281] and Colman J. and the Court of Appeal again in *North Star Shipping Ltd v Sphere Drake Insurance Plc*.[282] The effects of these decisions are as follows.

First, the assured was under a duty to disclose that he had been charged with and committed to trial for a criminal offence even though the trial had not taken place at the date of his application for insurance. An outstanding charge was a material fact even though the assured knew that he was innocent. Colman J. in *Strive* on this point preferred *March Cabaret* and *The Dora* over *Reynolds*. This analysis was broadly confirmed by the Court of Appeal in *Brotherton*. The Court of Appeal rejected Colman J.'s suggestion that the apparent harshness of this principle could be mitigated by allowing the assured to adduce evidence of his subsequent acquittal at the trial of any claim under the policy. Instead, the Court of Appeal felt that the assured's protection was to be found in making full disclosure of the outstanding charge to the insurers, including his own assertions of innocence and any evidence in his possession which supported that plea of innocence. Mance L.J.'s analysis was considered in *North Star Shipping Ltd v Sphere Drake Insurance Plc*,[283] a case in which persons associated with the assured were at the time of the placement of a war risks cover facing four sets of criminal proceedings in the Greek courts alleging that false statements had been made to induce third parties to invest money, and a fifth set of civil proceedings in Panama in which again dishonesty had been alleged. By the time of the trial, two of the Greek cases had been dismissed and one had not been pursued. The Court of Appeal agreed that it was constrained by the earlier cases to recognise the materiality of outstanding charges,[284] and Waller L.J. saw little protection in the ability of the assured to present exculpatory evidence on placement. The

[276] *March Cabaret Club & Casino v London Assurance* [1975] 1 Lloyd's Rep. 169 at 177.

[277] *Reynolds v Phoenix Assurance Co* [1978] 2 Lloyd's Rep. 440 at 460.

[278] *Inversiones Manria SA v Sphere Drake Insurance Co Plc (The Dora)* [1989] 1 Lloyd's Rep. 69.

[279] The point was left open in *Insurance Corp of the Channel Islands v Royal Hotel (No.2)* [1998] Lloyd's Rep. I.R. 151.

[280] *Strive* [2002] Lloyd's Rep. I.R. 669.

[281] *Brotherton v Aseguradora Colseguros (No.2)* [2003] Lloyd's Rep. I.R. 758.

[282] *North Star Shipping Ltd v Sphere Drake Insurance Plc* [2005] EWHC 665 (Comm), affirmed [2006] Lloyd's Rep. I.R. 519.

[283] *North Star Shipping Ltd v Sphere Drake Insurance Plc* [2005] EWHC 665 (Comm), affirmed [2006] Lloyd's Rep. I.R. 519.

[284] The Court of Appeal encouraged counsel to argue that allegations of dishonesty unrelated to the risk were immaterial, but ultimately rejected the argument in the light of the earlier cases.

subsequent decision of Tugendhat J. in *Norwich Union Insurance Ltd v Meisels*[285] does, however, provide support for the relevance of exculpatory facts in respect of the question of materiality, the court there holding that, in accordance with what had been said by Mance L.J. in *Brotherton*, the facts would be disclosable but along with the exculpatory material, and the two taken together might render the facts immaterial.

Secondly, the assured was under a duty to disclose that prior to placement he had been charged with, but acquitted of, a criminal offence, if he was in fact guilty of that offence. Plainly if the assured had been both charged and convicted prior to the placement of the risk this would be a material fact, although it was open to the assured to produce evidence to the insurers that his conviction was wrongful and that it ought not to be treated as material.

Thirdly, any other specific allegation of dishonesty or misconduct going to moral hazard made against the assured at the time of the inception of the policy amounted to a material fact, and was governed by the same principles as an outstanding charge which had not come to trial at the date of inception. In *Brotherton v Aseguradora Colseguros (No.3)*[286] Morison J. held that media reports to the effect that the president of the insured bank had been guilty of misconduct and had caused the bank to make improper payments to his own company was a material fact for the purposes of a fidelity policy taken out by the bank.

Fourthly, there was no duty of disclosure in relation to circumstances involving the assured or his property or affairs which might objectively raise a suspicion that he had been involved in criminal activity or misconduct going to moral hazard but which the assured knew not to be the case. In those circumstances it was unrealistic for insurers to expect the assured to disclose facts which he knew had no bearing on his honesty or integrity, even though a suspicious third party might have taken a different view.

Fifthly, any circumstances involving the assured or his business or his property which reasonably suggested on objective grounds that the magnitude of the proposed risk might be greater than it would otherwise have been were facts which had to be disclosed, provided that the assured knew of facts which suggested that there were material circumstances in that the assured knew that the suggested circumstances were untrue did not affect his duty of disclosure, as the insurers were entitled to be informed of those circumstances.[287] That said, if the insurers wished to avoid the policy for non-disclosure, the onus was on them to demonstrate the existence of material circumstances.

6–051 *Equality.* The Equality Act 2010 repealed and replaced various pieces of legislation which outlawed discrimination, including the Race Relations Act 1976, the Sex Discrimination Act 1975 and the Disability Discrimination Act 1995. In their place is a unified measure which outlaws discrimination on the grounds of "protected characteristics", namely: age; disability; gender reassignment; marriage and civil partnership; pregnancy and maternity; race; religion or belief; sex; and sexual orientation (s.2). There is direct discrimination where a person (A) discriminates against another (B) if, because of a protected characteristic, A treats B less favourably than A treats or would treat others (s.13). There is indirect discrimination where A discriminates against B if A applies to B a

---

[285] *Norwich Union Insurance Ltd v Meisels* [2007] Lloyd's Rep. I.R. 69.
[286] *Brotherton v Aseguradora Colseguros (No.3)* [2003] Lloyd's Rep. I.R. 774.
[287] *Strive Shipping v Hellenic Mutual War Risks Association* [2002] Lloyd's Rep. I.R. 669.

provision, criterion or practice which is discriminatory in relation to a relevant protected characteristic of B's (s.19).

There is a general prohibition on discrimination in the provision of services (s.29). Such discrimination may take the form of refusing to supply a service, supplying a service on discriminatory terms and not making reasonable adjustments in the supply of a service. Schedule 3 Pt 5 paras 20–32, and Sch.9 Pt 3 para.20 to a significant extent exempts insurance from these principles. The effect of these provisions, which apply to contracts entered into after the 2010 Act comes into force (Sch.3 para.23), is as follows.

First, s.29 does not apply to the provision of insurance in pursuance of arrangements made by an employer for the insurer to provide insurance for the benefit of employees (Sch.3 para.20). If there is discrimination, the complaint is against the employer and not the insurers.

Secondly, in the context of disability, there is no discrimination if the insurers act by reference to information that is both relevant to the assessment of the risk to be insured and from a source on which it is reasonable to rely, and it is reasonable to do so (Sch.3 para.21).

Thirdly, as regards sex, gender reassignment, pregnancy and maternity, it is not unlawful to do anything in relation to an annuity, life insurance policy, accident insurance policy or similar matter involving the assessment of risk if that thing is done by reference to actuarial or other data from a source on which it is reasonable to rely, and it is reasonable to do that thing (Sch.3 para.22(1)). The exception will, however, operate in relation to premiums and benefits only if: the use of sex as a factor in the assessment of risk is based on relevant and accurate actuarial and statistical data; the data are compiled, published (whether in full or in summary form) and regularly updated in accordance with guidance issued by the Treasury; the differences are proportionate having regard to the data; and the differences do not result from costs related to pregnancy or to a woman's having given birth in the period of 26 weeks ending on the day on which the thing in question is done (Sch.3 para.22(3)).

Finally, the Act is not contravened in respect of gender reassignment discrimination, marriage and civil partnership discrimination, pregnancy and maternity discrimination and sex discrimination if there is discrimination by reference to actuarial or other data from a source on which it is reasonable to rely, and it is reasonable to do it (Sch.9 para.20).

There are no relevant exclusions relating to discrimination on the ground of race. There are a number of cases in which it has been held that the nationality or national origins of the assured are material facts. This is undoubtedly the position where the assured is an enemy alien, given the common law prohibition on trading with the enemy, but the materiality of nationality or national origins at common law is apparently wider. Thus a marine insurer has been able to persuade the courts that it is material for the assured to declare his nationality where ships belonging to persons from a given country have an unusually high propensity to suffer casualty.[288] Moreover, in at least one case, *Horne v Poland*,[289] the view has been expressed that persons not born in England but living in England do not share English "values" and are thus more likely to suffer losses. The materiality of nationality and national origins is not, however,

---

[288] *Demetriadis & Co v Northern Assurance Co* (1926) 21 Ll. L.R. 265. See also *Steel v Lacy* (1810) 3 Taunt. 285.

[289] *Horne v Poland* [1922] 2 K.B. 364. See also *Campbell v Innes* (1821) 4 B. & Ald. 423. The point was left open in *Becker v Marshall* (1922) 12 Ll. L.R. 413 and *Lyons v JW Bentley Ltd* (1944) 77 Ll. L.R. 335.

absolute, and there are cases in which the insurer has not been able to show any increase in the moral hazard simply because of these factors.[290]

6–052   *Previous losses and claims.* Almost invariably, the proposal form will ask the proposer to give details of any previous insurance claims which he has made or losses which he has suffered. Even where this is not done, there is of course a duty to disclose previous losses and claims in so far as these are material to the formation of the contract.[291] In general, it may be assumed that the previous claims will be material, since they tend to show that the proposer is more likely to make future claims. Depending upon the circumstances, they may reflect upon the honesty or upon the prudence of the proposer. Where the claim was on the same or similar subject matter, it is clear from the authorities that the claim is a material fact.[292] It is also clear that what is significant is the fact and circumstances of the loss rather than its amount.[293] Thus, in *Marc Rich & Co AG v Portman*[294] previous demurrage liabilities incurred on a specific route was held to be material in relation to later policies obtained against potential demurrage liabilities on the same route. In *James v CGU Insurance Plc*[295] the assured failed to disclose a theft from him by an employee. The employee had been convicted of stealing the sum of £214.75, but the assured's belief (for which there was no evidence before the court) was that the sum stolen was about £130,000. Moore-Bick J. held that the loss for which there had been a conviction was a material fact, and that it was at least arguable (although the point had not been taken) that the assured's belief of the actual size of the theft went to moral hazard although it could not go to the physical hazard. The insurers also asserted that there had been previous break-ins at the premises which were material, although Moore-Bick J. held that any incidents were too trivial to be of interest to a prudent underwriter.

The real difficulties in this area arise where a proposer for one type of insurance has previously suffered losses in connection with other types of insurance. The point arose in *Ewer v National Employers' Mutual General Assurance Association Ltd*,[296] a case of fire insurance. It was contended that the proposer was under a duty to disclose his entire claims history in all kinds of insurance, including specifically the fact that he had once made a claim on a

---

[290] *British and Foreign Marine Insurance Co Ltd v Samuel Sanday & Co* [1916] 1 A.C. 650; *Associated Oil Carriers Ltd v Union Insurance Society of Canton Ltd* [1917] 2 K.B. 184.

[291] *Nuvo Electronics Inc v London Assurance* (2000) 49 O.R. (3d), although there was here held not to have been inducement.

[292] *Krantz v Allen & Faber* (1921) 9 Ll. L.R. 15: *Carlton v R & J Park Ltd* (1922) 10 Ll. L.R. 818; *General Accident Fire and Life Assurance Corp v Campbell* (1925) 21 Ll. L.R. 151; *Dent v Blackmore* (1927) 29 Ll. L.R. 9; *Rozanes v Bowen* (1928) 32 Ll. L.R. 98; *Farra v Hetherington* (1931) 40 Ll. L. Rep. 132: *Condogianis v Guardian Assurance Co Ltd* [1921] 2 A.C. 125 at 131; *Mundy's Trustee v Blackmore* (1928) 32 Ll. L.R. 150; *Lyons v JW Bentley Ltd* (1944) 77 Ll. L.R. 335: *Morser v Eagle Star and British Dominions Insurance Co Ltd* (1931) 40 Ll. L.R. 254; *Simon, Haynes, Barlas & Ireland v Beer* (1946) 78 Ll. L.R. 337; *Arterial Caravans v Yorkshire Insurance Ltd* [1973] 1 Lloyd's Rep. 169; *Stowers v GA Bonus Plc* [2003] Lloyd's Rep. I.R. 402. But contrast *Pedley v Avon Insurance* [2003] EWHC 2007 (QB) where it was held that a question relating to the assured's previous claims history referred to the present business and not to an earlier business.

[293] *Sharp v Sphere Drake Insurance Co Ltd (The Moonacre)* [1992] 2 Lloyd's Rep. 501. In *Noblebright Ltd v Sirius International Corp* [2007] Lloyd's Rep. I.R. 584, it was conceded that three unsuccessful attempts to rob the assured's premises constituted material facts.

[294] *Marc Rich & Co AG v Portman* [1996] I Lloyd's Rep. 430, affirmed on other grounds [1997] I Lloyd's Rep. 225.

[295] *James v CGU Insurance Plc* [2002] Lloyd's Rep. I.R. 206.

[296] *Ewer v National Employers' Mutual General Assurance Association Ltd* [1937] 2 All E.R. 193.

goods in transit policy which he had effected as carrier of the goods.[297] MacKinnon J. held that the duty of disclosure did not extend this far; but the case does not give clear guidance on the extent of the duty. As a general proposition it may be said that previous claims will be relevant where they indicate some want of ordinary prudence on the part of the proposer, or where they show that the proposer's business or life-style are such as render him especially liable to suffer losses of the kind which would be covered by the policy.

Any allegation by the insurer that the assured has been guilty of previous insurance frauds is subject to the same burden of proof as for fraudulent claims: the civil standard, the balance of probabilities applies, but the cogency of the required evidence increases in proportion to the seriousness of what has been alleged.[298]

Previous refusals to insure or to renew. Proposal forms commonly enquire whether the proposer has ever been refused insurance on a previous occasion, or whether any policy of his has not been renewed by the insurer. The cases demonstrate that a previous refusal is a material fact, even where it is related to an entirely different subject matter.[299] The leading authority on this matter is *Locker & Woolf Ltd v Western Australian Insurance Co*,[300] in which a previous refusal on a motor policy was held to be material to a proposal for fire insurance. Despite the protest of MacKinnon J., in *Ewer v National Employers' Mutual General Insurance Association Ltd*[301] that an assured does not have to disclose all previous refusals on all classes of policy,[302] numerous decisions do indeed point towards the materiality of previous refusals, particularly where the policy is of the same type as that previously refused[303] or where the policy is of a different type but an express question has been asked.[304]

6–053

Where an express question as to previous refusals is asked, the assured's duty of utmost good faith is to be determined in accordance with the wording of the question. Delicate questions of construction may arise. In *Holts Motors Ltd v*

[297] This pleading was based on the decision of Salter J. and the Court of Appeal in *Becker v Marshall* (1922) 11 Ll. L.R. 114, which had held a burglary claim to be material to a fire policy. Mackinnon J. distinguished *Becker* on the ground that the case had involved an express question so that the materiality of the previous claim was clear. However, it is settled law that materiality means the same thing whether or not an express question is asked, and *Ewer* must on this basis be confined to its facts.

[298] *Strive Shipping Corp v Hellenic Mutual War Risks Association* [2002] Lloyd's Rep. I.R. 669.

[299] *Glicksman v Lancashire & General Assurance Co Ltd* [1925] 2 K.B. 593 at 608, 611; [1927] A.C. 139; *Holt's Motors v South East Lancashire Insurance Co Ltd* (1930) 35 Com. Cas. 281 at 282–283; *Re Yager and Guardian Assurance Co* (1912) 108 L.T. 38; *Taylor v Yorkshire Insurance* [1913] 2 I.R. 1. Contrast *Re General Provincial Life* (1870) 18 W.R. 396 at 397; *Jones v Environcom Ltd (No.2)* [2010] EWHC 759 (Comm).

[300] *Locker & Woolf Ltd v Western Australian Insurance Co* [1936] 1 K.B. 408.

[301] *Ewer v National Employers' Mutual General Insurance Association Ltd* [1937] 2 All E.R. 193.

[302] *Ewer v National Employers' Mutual General Insurance Association Ltd* [1937] 2 All E.R. 193 at 202.

[303] *Arthrude Press v Eagle Star & British Dominions Insurance Co* (1924) 19 Ll. L.R. 373; *Glicksman v Lancashire and General Insurance Co Ltd* [1927] A.C. 139; *Mundy's Trustee v Blackmore* (1928) 32 Ll. L.R. 150; *Broad & Montague Ltd v South East Lancashire Insurance Co Ltd* (1931) 40 Ll. L.R. 328; *London Assurance v Mansel* (1879) 11 Ch D 363; *Cornhill Insurance Co v Assenheim* (1937) 58 Ll. L.R. 27; *Ascott v Cornhill Insurance Co* (1937) 58 Ll. L.R. 41; *Haase v Evans* (1934) 48 Ll. L.R. 131.

[304] *Locker & Woolf Ltd v Western Australian Insurance Co* (1935) 153 L.T. 334 was a case of this type.

South East Lancashire Insurance Co Ltd[305] it was held by the Court of Appeal
that an assured who was asked whether any insurer had declined to insure him
was required by this wording to disclose not just rejected applications but also an
intimation by an insurer under an earlier policy that the policy would not be
renewed. This, it might be thought, is a somewhat generous interpretation of the
word "declined" in favour of the insurers, and it may be that such information
should be expressly sought[306] or no question being asked at all so that the matter
is left to disclosure.[307]

What is material is the fact that insurance has previously been refused, and not
the reason for that refusal. This is clearly damaging, for it may render particular
assureds either uninsurable or insurable only at a high premium, but for no
apparent objective. This may seem unduly harsh. In many cases, the refusal will
originate from an unsatisfactory claims record or from the past character of the
proposer. In such cases, the relevance of the refusal is of no more than academic
interest, since it is clear that the reasons for it are themselves likely to be material
facts whose non-disclosure will render the insurance voidable. In other cases, the
reason for the refusal may have long since disappeared, and it seems unjust that
facts which have ceased to be material may be regarded as such. In *Mackay v
London General Insurance Co*[308] for example, the assured's failure to disclose
that he had been subjected to an excess on a motor policy at a very young age was
held not to be material. If this decision is of general application, it follows that
an assured who at one time fell into a high-risk category but who has ceased to
do so need not disclose his earlier status: one illustration might be an assured
whose earlier employment involved a good deal of travel, leading to a higher
premium for motor insurance, but who subsequently changes his employment to
one not involving travelling.

Marine insurance has taken a different attitude to this question, the position
being that previous refusals are not material.[309] The rationale of this rule, that
each insurer must assess the risk for himself and not rely upon the judgment of
other insurers, would seem to be logically unassailable. Express questions as to
the nature, scope or refusal of previous cover must, however, be answered
truthfully.[310] The difference between the marine and non-marine insurance rule
appears not to be based on anything inherent in those two classes of insurance,
and indeed historically it may be right to say that the true distinction is not
between marine and non-marine insurance but rather between the subscription
and non-subscription markets. In the subscription market, it would appear to
make little sense for each successive underwriter to have to be told of the attitude
of previous recipients of the broker's slip,[311] and although the nature of
placement in the non-subscription market is somewhat different it might
nevertheless be thought that the same rule should apply in both situations.

---

[305] *Holts Motors Ltd v South East Lancashire Insurance Co Ltd* (1930) 37 Ll. L.R. 1.
[306] In *McGinn v Insurance Corp of Ireland* 73 D.L.R. (4th) 193 (1991) the Alberta Court of Appeal
held that the phrase "declined or refused to renew or issue" was sufficient to impose an obligation
upon the assured to disclose this type of information.
[307] *Re Yager and Guardian Assurance Co* (1912) 108 L.T. 38.
[308] *Mackay v London General Insurance Co* (1935) 51 Ll. L.R. 201.
[309] *Lebon & Co v Straits Insurance Co* (1894) 10 T.L.R. 517; *Glasgow Assurance Corp Ltd v
William Symondson & Co* (1911) 104 L.T. 254; *North British Fishing Boat Insurance Co v Starr*
(1922) 13 Ll. L.R. 206.
[310] *Hamilton & Co v Eagle Star & British Dominions Insurance Co Ltd* (1924) 19 Ll. L.R.
242.
[311] See *Holts Motors Ltd v South East Lancashire Insurance Co Ltd* (1930) 37 Ll. L.R. 1.

Previous breaches of the duty of utmost good faith. At first instance in *CTI v*   **6–054**
Oceanus Mutual[312] Lloyd J. held that such facts were not material and did not
have to be disclosed, on the basis that a breach of the duty of utmost good faith
could be committed innocently and ought thus not to be regarded as impugning
the assured's integrity. The Court of Appeal[313] did not comment upon this part of
the learned judge's decision, although reversed his narrow view of the test for
materiality, and accordingly the point remains open. Some doubt was implicitly
cast upon the first instance ruling by Cresswell J. in *Aneco Reinsurance
Underwriting Ltd v Johnson & Higgins*,[314] the learned judge holding that where
a false statement is made by a broker to the leading underwriter on a Lloyd's slip,
that fact is material and must be disclosed to the following market. This case is
itself not free from doubt, as it appears to sidestep the rule that a false statement
made to the leading underwriter is not deemed to have been made to the
following market if nothing further is said to them.

Whatever the position as regards past breaches of the assured's duty of utmost
good faith, it is clear that Lloyd J.'s comments were based upon the assured
having acted innocently. Where there has been past fraud by the assured, the
fraud is of itself a material fact. Moreover, it appears from *Insurance Corp of the
Channel Islands v Royal Hotel (No.2)*[315] that past fraud is material even if it is
directed against a third party, e.g. the assured's bankers. This reasoning has been
thrown into doubt in an entirely different context, by the decision of Aikens J.
and the Court of Appeal in *K/S Merc-Skandia XXXXII v Certain Lloyd's
Underwriters*,[316] in which underwriters sought to avoid a liability policy for
breach of the continuing duty of utmost good faith in that the assured had
fraudulently informed the insurers that he had not bound himself under an
exclusive jurisdiction agreement to litigate the dispute with the third party in
England. The fraud consisted of the assured manufacturing a letter which sought
to undermine the authority of the assured's representative to enter into that
agreement. Aikens J. ruled that this fraud was immaterial to the claim and,
accordingly, that the insurers had no right to rely upon the duty of utmost good
faith. The Court of Appeal approved the outcome, although adopted the rather
different reasoning that fraud which did not amount to a repudiation of the
assured's contractual obligations did not give rise to a breach of the duty of
utmost good faith. This result can be reconciled with that of Mance J., in
Insurance Corp of the Channel Islands Ltd v Royal Hotel Ltd (No.2) only if it is
assumed that the fraud against the bank was in some way directly material to the
risk: the point is that fraud per se, on the *K/S Merc-Skandia* analysis, is not
material.

---

[312] *CTI v Oceanus Mutual* [1982] 2 Lloyd's Rep. 178. Cf. *Gate v Sun Alliance Insurance Ltd*
Unreported, 1993 HCNZ. In *Norwich Union Insurance Ltd v Meisels* [2007] Lloyd's Rep. I.R. 69 the
assured took out two policies on the same subject matter. One proposal asked for information
concerning his involvement with failed companies, the other did not. It was held that the assured's
misrepresentation on the first proposal form was not a material fact for the purposes of the second
proposal form.

[313] *CTI v Oceanus Mutual* [1984] 1 Lloyd's Rep. 476.

[314] *Aneco Reinsurance Underwriting Ltd v Johnson & Higgins* [1998] 1 Lloyd's Rep. 565,
followed in *International Lottery Management Ltd v Dumas* [2002] Lloyd's Rep. I.R. 237. See also
Forrest & Sons Ltd v CGU Insurance Plc [2006] Lloyd's Rep. I.R. 113, in which a makeweight
ground for the court's decision was that the assured had previously failed to disclose material facts
in relation to an earlier policy, a matter which he was under a duty to disclose on renewal.

[315] *Insurance Corp of the Channel Islands v Royal Hotel (No.2)* [1998] Lloyd's Rep. I.R. 151.

[316] *K/S Merc-Skandia XXXXII v Certain Lloyd's Underwriters* [2000] Lloyd's Rep. IR 694,
affirmed [2001] Lloyd's Rep. I.R. 802.

6–055   *The activities of the assured's agents.* If the assured has appointed an "agent to insure" then, under s.19 of the 1906 Act the agent is required to disclose all material facts known to him other than—in accordance with the principle in *Re Hampshire Land*[317]—his own fraud. A further question that arises here is whether the duty of utmost good faith attaches to the assured himself in respect of the fraud or misconduct of the assured's own agents. As far as disclosure is concerned, irrespective of materiality there can only a duty to if the assured was either actually aware of his agent's misconduct or had turned a blind eye to it, or, in the case of an assured who is acting in the course of business, if the assured ought in the ordinary course of his business to have been aware of the agent's misconduct. By definition, fraud on the part of the agent will generally preclude knowledge of all of these types. The position is slightly different as regards misrepresentation, for if the assured makes a positive statement as to the honesty or otherwise of his broker or other agent, and that statement is objectively false, then it does not matter that the assured is unaware of the falsity: if the statement satisfies the requirement of materiality then the insurers potentially have the right to avoid the policy. The question then becomes, at what point is the fraud or misconduct of an agent a material fact?

The point was considered by Phillips J. in *Deutsche Ruck Akt v Walbrook Insurance Co Ltd.*[318] Here, an underwriting agent acting for the reinsured had misappropriated various commissions due to the reinsured. The reinsurers alleged that such fraud was a material fact that ought to have been disclosed to them, the knowledge of it having been imputed to the reinsured. Phillips J. held that there had been the relevant imputation, a decision that is now inconsistent with the Court of Appeal's subsequent rulings, in *Société Anonyme d'Interme-diaires Luxembourgeois v Farex Gie*[319] and *PCW Syndicates v PCW Insurers*[320] to the effect that there can be no imputation of a broker's knowledge to his assured, and which was reversed by the Court of Appeal in the *Walbrook* appeal itself, *Group Josi Re v Walbrook Insurance Co Ltd,*[321] Phillips J.'s views on when an agent's fraud might be a material fact nevertheless remain valid where the assured has the requisite knowledge or has made a false statement. Phillips J. laid down two principles:

1. If the fraud relates directly to the risk, it is a material fact.
2. If the fraud does not relate directly to the risk, but merely affects the moral hazard, it cannot be a material fact as it would be "an affront to common sense that cover of the insured or reinsured should be at risk because of a failure to disclose a fraud of which the fraudster was aware".

On the facts before him, Phillips J. was satisfied that the fact was not a material one because it did not affect the risk.

The position will nevertheless be different if the fraudster is himself an important part of the assured's enterprise.[322] Furthermore, in an insurance or reinsurance case, if the fraudster plays an important role in the selection of the business to which the placement relates, his fraud may be material. In *Markel*

---

[317] *Re Hampshire Land* [1896] 2 Ch. 743.

[318] *Deutsche Ruck Akt v Walbrook Insurance Co Ltd* [1994] 4 All E.R. 181.

[319] *Société Anonyme d'Intermediaires Luxembourgeois v Farex Gie* [1995] L.R.L.R. 116.

[320] *PCW Syndicates v PCW Insurers* [1996] 1 All E.R. 774.

[321] *Group Josi Re v Walbrook Insurance Co Ltd* [1996] 1 All E.R. 791.

[322] See, e.g. *Regina Fur Co Ltd v Bossom* [1957] 2 Lloyd's Rep. 466; *Australia & New Zealand Bank Ltd v Colonial & Eagle Wharves Ltd* [1966] 2 Lloyd's Rep. 241; *Roselodge v Castle* [1966] 2 Lloyd's Rep. 113; *The Dora* [1989] 1 Lloyd's Rep. 69.

International Insurance Co Ltd v La Republica Compania Argentina de Seguros Generales SA[323] David Steel J. held that this proposition was arguable. In this case the reinsured's placing brokers informed the reinsurers that a key employee of the Argentinian placing brokers had had some minor problems in the London Market. In fact, the employee in question had been required to leave the market following suspicions of fraud in respect of his activities. David Steel J. held that the allegation of material misrepresentation in this regard was not one that should be regarded as unarguable by the reinsurers for the purpose of the grant of permission for service abroad, and that "as a matter of common sense, a dishonest broker, anxious to place a risk and thus earn his commission, may perhaps more readily misrepresent facts or suppress information." In the present case there were separate allegations of fraud against the producing brokers in the placement of the risk, and in that context it was strictly unnecessary to consider the impact of more generalised fraud. Nevertheless, in *ERC Frankona Reinsurance v American National Insurance Co*[324] Andrew Smith J. accepted the proposition that generalised fraud of a person involved in the selection of risks—in this case an underwriting agent—for a reinsured, was a material fact.

Overvaluation of the insured subject matter. It is necessary to draw a distinction **6–056** between valued and unvalued policies. Where the policy is valued, that is, where the value of the subject matter insured has been agreed between the parties (s.27(1)–(2) of the 1906 Act) s.27(3), reproducing the effect of the common law, provides that the valuation is conclusive as between the parties. It had been held, prior to the passing of the Act that the conclusiveness of valuation rule is subject to the duty of utmost good faith, so that it is possible for a valued policy to be avoided where the assured has failed to disclose that an excessive valuation has been submitted to the insurer for its formal acceptance,[325] and it was confirmed in *Inversiones Manria SA v Sphere Drake Insurance Co Plc (The Dora)*[326] that the law has not been altered by the Act.

The guiding principle as to when a valued policy may be avoided for a false statement by the assured as to the value of the insured subject matter is to be found in the judgment of Blackburn J. in *Ionides v Pender.*[327] In that case, a cargo of spirits worth £973 was insured under a valued marine policy for £2,800. The assured argued that the overvaluation was justified in that it took account of the assured's anticipated profits on resale, but the jury found that the overvaluation was excessive and ought to have been disclosed to the insurer. In refusing to order a new trial, Blackburn J. laid down the rule that a duty of disclosure exists where "the overvaluation is so great as to make the risk speculative".[328] As

---

[323] *Markel International Insurance Co Ltd v La Republica Compania Argentina de Seguros Generales SA* [2005] Lloyd's Rep. I.R. 90.

[324] *ERC Frankona Reinsurance v American National Insurance Co* [2006] Lloyd's Rep. I.R. 157.

[325] *Ionides v Pender* (1874) L.R. 9 Q.B. 531; *Hoff v De Rougemont* (1929) 34 Com. Cas. 291; *Haase v Evans* (1934) 48 Ll. L.R. 131; Willes J. in *Britten v Royal Insurance Co* (1866) 4 F. & F. 905.

[326] *Inversiones Manria SA v Sphere Drake Insurance Co Plc (The Dora)* [1989] 1 Lloyd's Rep. 69.

[327] *Ionides v Pender* (1874) L.R. 9 Q.B. 531.

[328] *Ionides v Pender* (1874) L.R. 9 Q.B. 531 at 539. See also: *Herring v Janson* (1895) 1 Com. Cas. 177; *Thames & Mersey Marine Insurance Co Ltd v Gunford Ship Co* [1911] A.C. 529; *Pickersgill v London & Provincial Marine Insurance Co* [1912] 3 K.B. 614; *Gooding v White* (1913) 29 T.L.R. 312; *Visscherij Maatschappij Nieuwe Onderneming v Scottish Metropolitan Assurance Co Ltd* (1922) 27 Com. Cas. 198; *Hoff v Union Insurance of Canton* (1924) 34 Ll. L.R. 81; *Fournier v Valentine* (1930) 38 Ll. L.R. 19; *Piper v Royal Exchange Assurance* (1932) 44 Ll. L.R. 103; *Slattery v Mance* [1962] 1 Lloyd's Rep. 60.

Colman J. noted in *Strive Shipping Corp v Hellenic Mutual War Risks Association*,[329] it was proper for an assured to take account of actual replacement costs even though those costs were in excess of market value, as long as the assured's judgment was honest and based on reasonable commercial grounds: in such a case there was no moral hazard and the insurers could not argue that they had been deprived of the benefit of assessing the discrepancy for themselves, and in any event it was always open to insurers to demand an independent market valuation prior to the inception of the risk. The test applied by Colman J. was whether the difference between the insured value and the market value was consistent with prudent ship management. Extreme overvaluation was found to exist by Simon J. in *Eagle Star Insurance Co Ltd v Games Video Co (GVC) SA (The Game Boy)*[330] where a vessel said to be worth US$1.8 million was worth no more than US$150,000 for scrap. Where, however, the valuation put on the insured subject matter by the claimant is the price actually paid by him for it, any discrepancy between the claimant's figure and the actual market value of the subject matter is not a material fact. This principle was laid down in *Inversiones Manria SA v Sphere Drake Insurance Co Plc (The Dora)*,[331] in which the price paid for the yacht by the assured, and forming the basis of the valuation submitted to the insurer, was $480,000: the market price of the yacht was proved to have been $400,000 but Phillips J. held that the existence of the discrepancy was not a material fact.

The cases on overvaluation under a valued policy are somewhat curious, given that the underwriters themselves can obtain or insist upon a valuation. If they fail to do so, and take premiums based on the agreed value, there is—fraud on the part of the assured aside—an argument based on waiver. This was articulated by Waller L.J. *North Star Shipping Ltd v Sphere Drake Insurance Plc*,[332] where a vessel was insured under a war risks policy for some US$4 million and was found by Colman J. at first instance to have been overinsured by some US$1 million. Colman J.'s view[333] was that the overvaluation had not been consistent with prudent ship management, although he would have permitted a valuation of up to US$3 million. On appeal Waller L.J. doubted that the overvaluation was material, and commented that the discrepancy between market and agreed value should have triggered questions, and that "the underwriter may prefer to take the extra premium rather than investigate whether the good management reasons establish $4 million as opposed to some lesser figure." This is a strong indication of waiver.

In the case of a valued fine art policy the assured may be required to state the provenance of the insured subject matter, as a guide to its value. Any statement by the assured as to provenance is not to be construed as one of fact or, at the other extreme, one of pure opinion, but rather takes effect as a representation of fact that the article is generally accepted by the art world as being authentic. If there are doubts, then in the absence of any express answer the assured is under a duty to disclose those doubts.[334]

---

[329] *Strive Shipping Corp v Hellenic Mutual War Risks Association* [2002] Lloyd's Rep. I.R. 669.

[330] *Eagle Star Insurance Co Ltd v Games Video Co (GVC) SA (The Game Boy)* [2004] Lloyd's Rep. I.R. 867.

[331] *Inversiones Manria SA v Sphere Drake Insurance Co Plc (The Dora)* [1989] 1 Lloyd's Rep. 69.

[332] *North Star Shipping Ltd v Sphere Drake Insurance Plc* [2006] Lloyd's Rep. I.R. 519.

[333] *Strive Shipping Corp v Hellenic Mutual War Risks Association* [2005] 1 Lloyd's Rep. 534.

[334] *Kamidian v Holt* [2009] Lloyd's Rep. I.R. 242.

In the case of an unvalued policy the law is more generous to the assured. This is so because under an unvalued policy the assured must prove the amount of his loss: he will not, therefore, benefit from overvaluation and will indeed have lost in that excessive premiums have been paid by him. [335]

Undervaluation of the insured subject matter. Where the assured has stated that   **6–057** the insured subject matter is worth a given figure which is to provide the ceiling of recovery, and that figure proves to be less than actual value, then at first sight there is no justification for the insurer seeking to avoid liability. The risk is no greater than has been disclosed to the insurer, as the insurer cannot be liable beyond the sum insured. In *Economides v Commercial Union Assurance Co*[336] this view was tentatively expressed, albeit obiter, by Simon Brown L.J. It may be, however, that this is oversimplistic. In the first place, if the value of the subject matter is greater than disclosed, the subject matter may be at greater risk from an insured peril, e.g. theft. Secondly, in underwriting terms, unless the policy is subject to average, the insurer is effectively providing first-layer cover, and this may have some effect on the calculation of the premium.

The existence of other insurance. The fact that the assured has insured the   **6–058** subject matter elsewhere, with the result that it has been in the aggregate overinsured, would prima facie seem to be indistinguishable from overvaluation in terms of materiality, in that in both cases the risk of fraud is enhanced. However, the common law position is seemingly that other policies are not always treated as material facts, possibly because the assured's right to insure his property with as many insurers as he wishes—in order to guard against the insolvency of any of them—was recognised at common law and preserved in s.32 of the 1906 Act. The authorities seem to show that double insurance is material as regards life[337] and accident insurance,[338] as these are not contracts of indemnity and insurers are interested in knowing what other offices have done, whereas the existence of double insurance as regards indemnity insurance is not material.[339] This is so because existence of other insurance will tend to lessen the liability of the insurer by reason of the doctrine of contribution.[340] The existence of other insurances, frequently coupled with a prohibition on future insurances on the same subject matter, is normally dealt with by an express provision of the policy which either prohibit double insurance or at least postpone coverage until other policies have been exhausted.

The assured's financial position. If the assured's financial position is poor, there   **6–059** is always the risk that he may be tempted into fraud against his insurers. Indeed, where there has been an unexplained loss, the courts traditionally regard a weak financial position as one of the key indicia of fraud by the assured. As far as

[335] *Parker & Heard Ltd v Generali Assicurazioni SpA* Unreported, 1988; *Berger and Light Diffusers Pty Ltd v Pollock* [1973] 2 Lloyd's Rep. 442. Cf. *Williams v Atlantic Insurance Co Ltd* [1933] I K.B. 81. Contrast *Haase v Evans* (1934) 48 Ll. L.R. 131.

[336] *Economides v Commercial Union Assurance Co* [1997] 3 All E.R. 635.

[337] *London Assurance Co v Mansel* (1879) L.R. 11 Ch D 363 at 370; *Wainwright v Bland* (1835) I Mood. & R. 481 at 487.

[338] *Re Marshall and Scottish Employers' Liability* (1901) 85 L.T. 757 at 758.

[339] *Sibbald v Hill* (1814) 2 Dow. 263; *Simpson SS Co v Premier Underwriting Association* (1905) 92 L.T. 730; *McDonnell v Beacon Fire* (1857) 7 U.C.C.P. 308; *Thames & Mersey Marine v Gunford Ship Co* (1981) 105 L.T. 312; *Mathie v Argonaut Marine Insurance* (1923) 21 Ll. L.R. 145; *Wilson, Holgate & Co Ltd v Lancashire and Cheshire Insurance Corp Ltd* (1922) 13 Ll. L.R. 486.

[340] *Donaldson v Manchester Insurance* (1836) 14 S. 601.

disclosure is concerned, the materiality of the assured's position was confirmed by Moore-Bick J. in *James v CGU Insurance*.[341] The learned judge here ruled that disputes between the assured and the Customs and the Inland Revenue were material facts as they indicated that the assured did not maintain proper business records and also that the business was in financial difficulty, and that as fraudulent claims for fire damage were often linked to the insured's financial circumstances, it was entirely understandable for property insurers to regard facts bearing on the financial status of the insured as material, forming part of the moral hazard. The assured's financial position may be material for other purposes.

First, if the policy is being taken out by a business, financial failure in the past may indicate that the assured is incompetent: it is thus often an express question on traders' policies as to whether the assured or any person connected with the running of the assured's business has in the past been a bankrupt.[342] A question which asks whether any of the partners or director of the assured have ever been declared bankrupt personally or in connection with any business does not extend to the insolvency or liquidation of any company with which they have may have been involved.[343] In the absence of an express question, it is unclear whether the assured is under any duty to disclose his involvement with dissolved companies: it may be that all depends upon the reason for their dissolution, and that a long history of failed companies may be material whereas the striking off of companies for failure to make timely returns to the registrar of companies may not. In *Norwich Union Insurance Ltd v Meisels*[344] the assured had been involved with four insolvent companies and 16 companies struck off for failure to submit returns. The court was satisfied that the assured's involvement with the insolvent companies had been peripheral, and that the struck off companies had been used as part of his business stratagem. It was also the case that in a parallel policy taken out at the same time the insurers had specifically asked about insolvent companies whereas the proposal for the policy question was silent on the matter, indicating waiver. For all of these reasons the assured was held not to have been in breach of his duty of utmost good faith.

Secondly, the assured may be unable to afford to maintain the insured subject matter in a manner that preserves it from loss. This possibility was referred to in *O'Kane v Jones*.[345]

Thirdly, the fact that the assured is impecunious may lead to the possibility that he will not be able to afford the premiums payable under the policy. This is nothing to do with moral hazard, but nevertheless falls squarely within the definition of "materiality" in s.18(2) of the 1906 Act as the possibility of non-payment is plainly a fact that could influence the judgment of a prudent underwriter in deciding whether or not to take the risk. This point was made by Colman J. in *North Star Shipping Ltd v Sphere Drake Insurance Plc*,[346] the

---

[341] *James v CGU Insurance* [2002] Lloyd's Rep. I.R. 206.

[342] See *Pedley v Avon Insurance* Unreported, 2003, where the assured was found not to have given a false answer as her husband, the bankrupt, was not participating in the business. Contrast *Doheny v New India Assurance Co* [2005] Lloyd's Rep. I.R. 251.

[343] *R & R Developments Ltd v Axa Insurance Ltd* [2009] EWHC 2429 (Ch). The court saw no ambiguity in the question, but would have reached the same result either: (a) by construing the ambiguity against the insurers; or (b) if the question had been ambiguous but construed in the wider sense, by holding that the position of companies with which an assured had been involved had been waived.

[344] *Norwich Union Insurance Ltd v Meisels* [2007] Lloyd's Rep. I.R. 69.

[345] *O'Kane v Jones* [2005] Lloyd's Rep. I.R. 174.

[346] *North Star Shipping Ltd v Sphere Drake Insurance Plc* [2005] EWHC 665 (Comm). The question of general impecuniosity was not considered on appeal, [2006] Lloyd's Rep. I.R. 519.

learned judge commenting that it was irrelevant that—at least in the marine market—the underwriter had the right to seek payment of the premium from the broker under s.53(1) as this could be commercially undesirable, particularly where the amount of premium was large.

A question that arose in both *O'Kane* and *North Star Shipping Ltd* was whether the non-payment of premiums under earlier policies was of itself a material fact. In *O'Kane*, it was held that it was not possible to treat this as a material fact in its own right as there was no automatic link between non-payment and any physical or moral hazard. At first instance in *North Star*, Colman J. accepted that non-payment of earlier premiums did of itself not go to moral hazard other than as part of the assured's general impecuniosity, but felt that the comments in *O'Kane* had gone too far in that they had disregarded the materiality of the possibility that the assured could not afford to pay the premiums under the existing policy. That view was, however, rejected on appeal in *North Star*, Waller L.J. expressing the view that this went to credit risk rather than the insured risk and probably did not qualify as a material fact.[347]

"Premium-skimming" by brokers. The amount of brokerage taken by the brokers **6–060** from the premium may itself be material because non-disclosure or mis-representation of an unusually high brokerage rate may give the impression that the risk is greater than the insurers have been led to believe. If this is correct, then it becomes arguable that the assured's own assessment of the risk is potentially a material fact.[348]

The physical hazard

General definition. Matters which affect the insured subject matter itself, as **6–061** opposed to its owner, clearly vary according to the nature of the subject matter and the scope of the insurance. In general, anything which is likely to increase the insurer's risk or liability is prima facie material: the duty of utmost good faith thus extends to matters as far-reaching as pre-contractual arrangements by the assured which might have the effect of limiting the insurer's rights of subroga-tion. The precise interest of the assured in the subject matter of the policy is not, however, a material fact which requires to be disclosed and any information which the assured has relating to the adequacy or validity of the insurer's reinsurance arrangements is equally immaterial.[349] The physical hazard as it relates to specific classes of insurance is considered at the relevant points in this work.

Threats and rumours. If the assured believes on reasonable grounds that the **6–062** insured subject matter is facing danger, that fact must be disclosed.[350] However, there is no obligation on the assured to disclose threats or rumours which are not

---

[347] *Micro Design Group Ltd v Norwich Union Insurance Ltd* [2006] Lloyd's Rep. I.R. 235 is now, arguably, wrongly decided, although materiality appears to have been conceded and the case turned on inducement.

[348] *Markel International Insurance Co Ltd v La Republica Compania Argentina de Seguros Generales SA* [2005] Lloyd's Rep. I.R. 90.

[349] *Société Anonyme d'Intermédiaires Luxembourgeois v Farex Gie* [1995] L.R.L.R. 116. Contrast *Hill v Citadel Insurance Co* [1997] L.R.L.R. 167, where the reinsurance had been arranged on the reinsurer's behalf.

[350] *De Costa v Scandrett* (1823) 2 Eq. Ca. Ab. 636; *Seaman v Fonereau* (1743) 2 Stra. 1183; *Lynch v Hamilton* (1810) 3 Taunt. 15; *Lynch v Dunsford* (1811) 14 East 494; *Durrell v Bederley* (1816) Holt 283; *Morison v Universal Marine Insurance Co* (1873) L.R. 8 Exch. 197; *Strive Shipping Corp v Hellenic Mutual War Risks Association* [2002] Lloyd's Rep. I.R. 669.

based on evidence.[351] The distinction is between firm intelligence, which has to be disclosed,[352] and loose or idle rumours, which do not.[353]

Orthodox theory indicates that materiality has to be assessed at the date of the inception of the risk, so that a rumour which appears to be based on reasonable evidence has to be disclosed even though by the time of the loss the rumour has been disproved.[354] However, in *Strive Shipping Corp v Hellenic Mutual War Risks Association*[355] Colman J., relying on the notions that the right of an insurer to avoid for non-disclosure is an equitable one, and that the insurer himself owes a continuing duty of utmost good faith, concluded that an insurer would not be permitted to rely upon facts which were apparently material at the outset but which were subsequently proved not to exist. The *Strive* decision was, rejected by Moore-Bick J. in *Drake Insurance Co v Provident Insurance Co*[356] to the extent that Colman J. had suggested that a court could overturn an avoidance by insurers by reference to rebutting evidence that came to light after the avoidance, a point confirmed by the Court of Appeal in *Brotherton (No.2)*. The Court of Appeal did, however, leave open the possibility admittedly with strong doubts that insurers might be precluded from avoiding if by the time of the avoidance they had become aware of the untruth or immateriality of the intelligence which had not been disclosed. A differently constituted Court of Appeal in *Drake Insurance Co v Provident Insurance Co*[357] was nevertheless prepared to accept that the insurers' continuing duty of utmost good faith did indeed preclude an avoidance when the insurers were either actually aware or possessed blind-eye knowledge that the facts relied upon were either unfounded or had not induced the making of the contract.

5. FACTS WHICH NEED NOT BE DISCLOSED

6–063   **Circumstances which diminish the risk.** Section 18(3)(a) states that, in the absence of enquiry, the assured is not required to disclose: "any circumstance which diminishes the risk". The reason for this exception is obvious. It originates in Lord Mansfield's judgement in *Carter v Boehm*,[358] where he said[359]:

> "The underwriter need not be told what lessens the risque agreed and understood to be run by the express terms of the policy . . . If he insures for three years, he need not be told of any circumstance to show it may be over in two; or if he insures a voyage with liberty of deviation, he need not be told what tends to show there will be no deviation."

[351] *Morgan v Pryor* (1823) 2 B. & C. 14; *Cantiere Meccanico Brindisi v Janson* [1912] 3 K.B. 452.

[352] *Brotherton v Aseguradora Colseguros SA (No.2)* [2003] Lloyd's Rep. I.R. 758; *Brotherton v Aseguradora Colseguros SA (No.3)* [2003] Lloyd's Rep. I.R. 774; *International Management Group (UK) Ltd v Simmonds* [2004] Lloyd's Rep. I.R. 774 (where the information was a reliable government leak); *Prifti v Musini Sociedad Anonima de Seguros y Reaseguros* [2004] Lloyd's Rep. I.R. 528.

[353] *Decorum Investments Ltd v Atkin (The Elena G)* [2002] Lloyd's Rep. I.R. 450. In *Howells v Dominion Insurance Co Ltd* Unreported, 1999, rumours as to the possible dishonesty of a company director were held not to have crossed the line into firm intelligence.

[354] *Seaman v Fonnereau* (1734) 2 Str. 1183.

[355] *Strive Shipping Corp v Hellenic Mutual War Risks Association* [2002] Lloyd's Rep. I.R. 669.

[356] *Drake Insurance Co v Provident Insurance Co* [2003] Lloyd's Rep. I.R. 793.

[357] *Drake Insurance Co v Provident Insurance Co* [2004] Lloyd's Rep. I.R. 277.

[358] *Carter v Boehm* (1766) 3 Burr. 1905.

[359] *Carter v Boehm* (1766) 3 Burr. 1905 at 1910.

In *Inversiones Manria SA v Sphere Drake Insurance Co Plc (The Dora)*[360]
Phillips J. noted that the fact that a yacht had been in the builder's yard at the
inception of the policy was a fact which reduced, rather than increased, the risk.
Again, it was held in *Zeus Tradition Marine Ltd v Bell*[361] that the withholding of
a survey report on a vessel was not material as there was nothing unfavourable
in the report. In *Decorum Investments Ltd v Atkin (The Elena G)*[362] the fact that
a yacht was kept in secure moorings was held to be immaterial as the security
precautions diminished the risk.

Circumstances which the insurer knows or is presumed to know. Section 6–064
18(3)(b) states that, in the absence of enquiry, the assured is not required to
disclose "any circumstance which is known[363] or presumed to be known to the
insurer. The insurer is presumed to know matters of common notoriety or
knowledge, and matters which an insurer in the ordinary course of his business,
as such, ought to know".[364]

The insurers' knowledge. Just what constitutes knowledge within an insurer's 6–065
organisation may be a question of some difficulty. It has been held that the
knowledge of one branch is not imputed to an entirely separate branch,[365] and
also—perhaps less credibly—that the knowledge in the possession of the claims
department is not known to the underwriting department.[366] What is beyond
argument, however, is that if an insurer appoints a third party to investigate a
particular aspect of the assured's affairs, e.g. to audit a bank, material facts
obtained by the third party which have nothing to do with the appointment are not
imputed to the insurer.[367] Where there is actual knowledge on the part of the
insurers, there is no duty of disclosure.[368]

Section 18(3) refers to facts in common knowledge and to facts of a
commercial nature, so that the insurer's knowledge is presumed to be both
general and specific. In *Carter v Boehm*[369] Lord Mansfield gave, as examples of
the sort of facts of which the insurer is deemed to be aware: "General topics of
speculation . . . natural perils . . . the difficulty of the voyage . . . the probability
of lightning, hurricanes, earthquakes, etc".[370] There is, however, a fine line
between facts which the insurer ought to know, and facts which could not be
discovered by the insurer other than by making detailed enquiry; it is clear from

---

[360] *Inversiones Manria SA v Sphere Drake Insurance Co Plc (The Dora)* [1989] 1 Lloyd's Rep.
69.
[361] *Zeus Tradition Marine Ltd v Bell* [2000] 2 Lloyd's Rep. 587.
[362] *Decorum Investments Ltd v Atkin (The Elena G)* [2002] Lloyd's Rep. I.R. 450.
[363] See *Willcocks v New Zealand Insurance Co* [1926] N.Z.L.R. 805.
[364] *Foley v Tabor* (1861) 2 F. & F. 663; *Pimm v Lewis* (1862) 2 F. & F. 778; *Bates v Hewitt* (1867)
L.R. 2 Q.B. 595; *Joel v Law Union and Crown Insurance Co* [1908] 2 KB. 863 at 878–879; *Hales
v Reliance Fire Assurance* [1960] 2 Lloyd's Rep. 391.
[365] *Gunns and Gunns v Par Insurance Brokers* [1997] 1 Lloyd's Rep. 173, although in this case a
specific question had been asked of the assured by the second branch, thereby rendering s.18(3)(b)
inapplicable.
[366] *Stone v Reliance Mutual Insurance Association* [1972] I Lloyd's Rep. 469; *Malhi v Abbey Life
Assurance Co Ltd* [1996] L.R.L.R. 237.
[367] *Brotherton v Aseguradora Colseguoros SA (No.3)* [2003] Lloyd's Rep. I.R. 774.
[368] *Friere v Woodhouse* (1817) Holt N.P. 572; *Foley v Tabor* (1861) 2 F. & F 663; *Gandy v Adelaide
Insurance Co* (1871) L.R. 6 Q.B. 746; *Cape Plc v Iron Trades Employers Insurance Association Ltd*
[2004] Lloyd's Rep. I.R. 75; *Kingscroft Insurance Co v Nissan Fire & Marine Insurance Co Ltd
(No.2)* [1999] Lloyd's Rep. I.R. 603.
[369] *Carter v Boehm* (1776) 3 Burr. 1905.
[370] *Carter v Boehm* (1776) 3 Burr. 1905 at 1909. See also: *Planche v Fletcher* (1779) 1 Doug. K.B.
251; *Bates v Hewitt* (1867) L.R. 2 Q.B. 595; *Schloss Brothers v Stevens* [1906] 2 K.B. 665.

the cases that, while the assured is not required to disclose facts which the insurer could have discovered for himself,[371] the insurer is not under an obligation to make enquiries to an extent which would relieve the assured from his own obligation to disclose all material facts.[372] As was commented by Moore-Bick J., in *Kingscroft Insurance Co Ltd and Others v Nissan Fire & Marine Insurance Co Ltd (No.2)*,[373] an underwriter is not presumed to have knowledge of matters simply because he had the means of ascertaining them by appropriate inquiry: the question in every case is whether the assured has made a fair presentation of the risk. Thus an underwriter operating in the London market cannot be assumed to have knowledge of events in Colombia that have not been generally reported in the English media even though the underwriter may have travelled to Colombia on occasion[374] and he cannot be expected to remember details of previous marine casualties.[375]

Matters of common knowledge of which the insurer is deemed to be aware have included the fact that there is war in some part of the world,[376] that war is imminent,[377] that a castle has been used as a prison,[378] that asbestos is dangerous[379] and that certain forms of business may have been infiltrated by organised crime.[380]

The insurer's duty to be aware of matters of a commercial nature was emphasised by Lord Mansfield in *Noble v Kennaway*,[381] in which he stated that "Every underwriter is presumed to be acquainted with the practice of the trade he insures. If he does not know, he ought to inform himself." Thus a marine insurer is deemed to be aware of the mode of loading and unloading cargo used at the ports mentioned in the policy[382] and that stowage on deck may be customary.[383] A particular matter of which the insurer will be deemed to be aware is the rate at which losses are currently being suffered in the class of business for which he provides insurance.[384] In these cases much depends upon the customs

---

[371] Erle C.J. in *Foley v Tabor* (1861) 2 F & F. 663 at 672.

[372] *London General Insurance Co Ltd v General Mutual Marine Underwriters' Association Ltd* [1921] 1 K.B. 104; cf. *Elton v Larkins* (1832) 8 Bing. 198; *Mackintosh v Marshall* (1843) 11 M. & W. 116; *Morrison v Universal Marine Insurance Co* (1872) L.R. 8 Ex. 40; *Bates v Hewitt* (1867) L.R. 2 Q.B. 595.

[373] *Kingscroft Insurance Co Ltd and Others v Nissan Fire & Marine Insurance Co Ltd (No.2)* [1999] Lloyd's Rep. I.R. 603.

[374] *Brotherton v Aseguradora Colseguoros SA (No.3)* [2003] Lloyd's Rep. I.R. 774.

[375] *Strive Shipping Corp v Hellenic Mutual War Risks Association* [2002] Lloyd's Rep. I.R. 669.

[376] *Bolivia Republic v Indemnitv Mutual Marine Assurance Co* [1909] 1 K.B. 785.

[377] *Planche v Fletcher* (1779) 1 Doug. K.B. 251.

[378] *Leen v Hall* (1923) 16 Ll. L.R. 100.

[379] *Canadian Indemnity Co v Canadian Johns-Manville Co* 72 D.L.R. (4th) 478 (1990).

[380] *Decorum Investments Ltd v Atkin (The Elena G)* [2002] Lloyd's Rep. I.R. 450.

[381] *Noble v Kennaway* (1780) 2 Doug KB. 510 at 512 See also: *Salvador v Hopkins* (1765) 3 Burr. 1707; *Harrower v Hutchinson* (1870) L.R. 5 Q.B. 584; *Gandy v Adelaide Insurance Co* (1871) L.R. 6 Q.B. 746; *The Bedouin* [1894] P. 1; *Cantiere Meccanico Brindisino v Janson* [1912] 3 K.B. 452; *Cheshire v Thompson* (1918) 29 Com. Cas. 114; *British and Foreign Marine Insurance Co v Gaunt* [1921] 2 A.C. 41; *George Cohen, Sons & Co v Standard Marine Insurance Co Ltd* (1925) 21 Ll. L.R. 30; *Kingscroft Insurance Co v Nissan Fire and Marine Insurance Co Ltd (No.2)* [1999] Lloyd's Rep. I.R. 603; *Cape Plc v Iron Trades Employers Insurance Association Ltd* [2004] Lloyd's Rep. I.R. 75.

[382] *Tennant v Henderson* (1813) 1 Dow. 324; *Vallance v Dewar* (1808) 1 Camp. 503.

[383] *Da Costa v Edmonds* (1815) 4 Camp. 142.

[384] *North British Fishing Boat Insurance Co Ltd v Starr* (1922) 13 Ll. L.R. 206; *The Moonacre* [1992] 2 Lloyd's Rep. 501.

and usages of the class of insurance in question.[385] It might be added by way of warning that, where the insurer's business consists of insuring a general class, it is likely to be a question of fact whether there is constructive knowledge of particular matters affecting specialised parts of that general class, and if the assured has suffered losses then he must disclose them even though the circumstances which rendered losses likely were known to the insurers.[386] If, by way of contrast, the facts in question affecting the class of business in question are not unusual—in the sense that do not fall outside the contemplation of the reasonable underwriter familiar with the business—then they are presumed to be within the knowledge of the insurers and do not have to be disclosed.[387]

Effect of inquiry by insurers. Section 8(3) is prefaced by the qualification "In the   **6–066** absence of inquiry". Accordingly, if the insurers have made a specific request for information, but that information has not been disclosed, s.18(3)(b) has no application and the assured is unable to argue that the requested information ought to have been known by the insurers.[388]

Dealings between insurers and assured. One question which does not seem to   **6–067** have been the subject of a firm decision in England is whether the assured must disclose to the insurer previous dealings between the assured and the insurer itself. Previous claims were assumed to be material facts by the Court of Appeal in *Stone v Reliance Mutual Insurance Association*[389] but were held to be immaterial by the Supreme Court of Canada in *Coronation Insurance Co v Taku Air Transport Ltd*[390] on the basis that in modern times such information is easy for the insurer to obtain. *Coronation* is in some ways exceptional, as it involved the heavily regulated aviation industry and the policy covered liability for the death of passengers, so that the generous view of the Court is easily explained. It is indeed far from clear that the Court in *Coronation* was seeking to lay down any general principle.

Waiver by the insurer. Section 18(3)(c) states that, in the absence of enquiry   **6–068** the assured is not required to disclose "any circumstance as to which information is waived by the insurer".

Express agreements to waive disleosure. There are at least four different forms   **6–069** of agreement that can be reached between the insurer and the assured under which the duty of utmost good faith is restricted:

  (a) an agreement restricting the duty of utmost good faith itself, possibly by declaring all facts to be immaterial, so that no disclosure is required by the assured or his broker or by restricting materiality to matters so considered by the assured[391];

---

[385] *Vallance v Dewar* (1808) 1 Camp. 503 at 508; *Moxon v Atkins* (1812) 3 Camp. 200; *Stewart v Bell* (1821) 5 B. & Ald. 238; *British and Foreign Marine Insurance Co v Gaunt* [1921] 2 A.C. 41 at 59–62.

[386] *Glencore International AG v Portman* [1997] 1 Lloyd's Rep. 225.

[387] *Glencore International AG v Alpina Insurance Co Ltd* [2004] 1 Lloyd's Rep. 111: it was held that an oil trader did not have to disclose that there were no real methods for verifying the quantities of oil held in storage for the assured as there was nothing unusual in the procedures adopted.

[388] *Brotherton v Aseguradora Colseguoros SA (No.3)* [2003] Lloyd's Rep. I.R. 774.

[389] *Stone v Reliance Mutual Insurance Association* [1972] 1 Lloyd's Rep. 496.

[390] *Coronation Insurance Co v Taku Air Transport Ltd* 85 D.L.R. (4th) 609 (1992).

[391] *State Insurance v Fry* (1991) 6 ANZ Insurance Cases 77–237.

(b) an agreement restricting the duty to disclose specific types of information;

(c) an agreement restricting the authority of an agent or broker to make statements on the part of the assured;

(d) an agreement restricting the insurer's right to avoid the insurance policy in the event of misrepresentation or non disclosure by the assured or his agent.

Type (d) is discussed below in the context of remedies. It may here be noted that there would appear to be at least one critical difference between such waivers and waiver of remedies under clause (d). In *HIH Casualty & General Insurance Ltd v Chase Manhattan Bank*[392] Aikens J. ruled that a clause which excluded the insurer's right to avoid a contract for misrepresentation or non-disclosure could not extend to fraudulent misrepresentation or non-disclosure, as public policy did not allow an assured to exclude the consequences of his own fraud. By contrast, if the clause excludes the duty of utmost good faith entirely, then there is simply no duty to make any disclosure and the fact that information is fraudulently withheld is of no consequence. This point was not the subject of consideration in the House of Lords.

As far as type (c) is concerned, clear wording is required to restrict the authority of a broker to make statements on the part of the assured. In *HIH Casualty & General Insurance Ltd v Chase Manhattan Bank*[393] it was common ground that the wording in a Truth of Statement Clause "[the assured] shall have no liability of any nature to the insurers for any information provided by any other parties and any such information provided by or non disclosure by other parties including, but not limited to [the broker]" did not purport to withdraw from the broker to right to speak on the part of the assured.

As far as types (a) and (b) are concerned, the question will be whether the wording is sufficient to achieve the objective of waiver. Whether a clause operates as an exclusion of the duty of utmost good faith is a matter of its proper construction.[394] In *HIH Casualty & General Insurance Ltd v Chase Manhattan Bank*[395] the clause provided that "[the assured] will not have any duty or obligation to make any representation, warranty or disclosure of any nature, express or implied (such duty and obligation being expressly waived by the insurers) . . . " The House of Lords held that this wording did not relieve the assured from the consequences of non-disclosure of material facts by the assured's broker,[396] but merely relieved the assured of any obligation to make statements. It was ineffective where the assured voluntarily chose to make a statement which was material and false. Furthermore, it was ineffective where the broker failed to disclose a material fact or misstated a material fact. The latter point is of great significance, as their Lordships ruled that any waiver of the

---

[392] *HIH Casualty & General Insurance Ltd v Chase Manhattan Bank* [2001] Lloyd's Rep. I.R. 191. See also: *Property Insurance Co Ltd v National Protector Insurance Co Ltd* (1913) 18 Com. Cas. 19; *Svenska Handelsbanken v Sun Alliance and London Insurance Plc* [1996] 1 Lloyd's Rep. 519; *Sumitomo Bank Ltd v Banque Bruxelles Lambert SA* [1997] 1 Lloyd's Rep. 487.

[393] *HIH Casualty & General Insurance Ltd v Chase Manhattan Bank* [2003] Lloyd's Rep. I.R. 230.

[394] *Svenska Handelsbanken v Sun Alliance & London Insurance Plc* [1996] 1 Lloyd's Rep. 519; *Brotherton v Aseguradora Colseguoros SA (No.3)* [2003] Lloyd's Rep. I.R. 876.

[395] *HIH Casualty & General Insurance Ltd v Chase Manhattan Bank* [2003] Lloyd's Rep. I.R. 230.

[396] It had been held by Aikens J. that the clause was not void as being repugnant to the policy, and this conclusion was not subsequently challenged.

assured's own duty of utmost good faith did not necessarily imply any waiver of the broker's independent duty of disclosure under s.19 of the 1906 Act. Here a distinction was drawn between an absolute waiver of information on the ground that it was simply not material (type (a)) and a waiver of specific information (type (b)). In the former case, if all information is immaterial then it follows that it cannot matter whether the failure to disclose is that of the assured or that of the agent. However, if the waiver was simply confined to specific information, then the waiver clause was to be confined to the assured's personal obligation in relation to such information, as the broker's duty of disclosure was independent. The House of Lords held the purpose of the clause was merely to relieve the assured of its obligation to disclose material facts, and to place the burden of disclosure on the broker. In so deciding, the House of Lords was heavily influenced by the consideration that the risk in question—time variable cover taken out by a bank to protect its investment as a film financier—was a specialised one that had been developed by the brokers and in effect sold to the bank. In those circumstances the bank was unlikely to be in possession of any relevant facts, and accordingly the insurers had by this clause shifted the burden of disclosure onto the broker.

Implied waiver: the principle. The assured is bound not only to give true **6–070** answers to the questions put to him but also spontaneously to disclose any fact exclusively within his knowledge which it is material for the insurer to know.[397] The existence of written questions and answers excuse him from answering oral questions truthfully.[398] While the presumption is that matters dealt with in the proposal form are immaterial, there is no corresponding presumption that matters not so dealt with are not.[399] Thus, in life insurance cases the fact that the assured warrants his answers in the proposal form only to be true does not mean that he is excused the duty to make full disclosure of all facts material to the risk when he is afterwards questioned by the insurer's doctor.[400] Again, where a question was asked in a proposal form as to previous refusals to insure by other companies, it was held that the assured was bound to disclose that his last insurer had failed to invite him to renew a policy.[401] Where the insurer has not asked a specific question, it follows that the assured cannot normally argue that such omission amounts to an implied waiver of disclosure,[402] and at best it may be said that by not asking questions about a matter insurers do run a greater risk of a finding of immateriality.[403]

Nevertheless, there is some authority for the proposition that a failure by insurers to elicit all material facts by express questions may amount to a waiver of such disclosure. In *Laing v Union Marine Insurance Co*[404] Mathew J. stated

---

[397] *Huguenin v Rayley* (1815) 6 Taunt. 186; *Wheelton v Hardisty* (1857) 8 E. & B. 232; *Glicksman v Lancashire & General* [1927] A.C. 139; *Bond v Commercial Assurance* (1930) 35 Com. Cas. 171; *Misirlakis v The New Zealand Insurance Co Ltd* (1985) 3 ANZ Insurance Cases 60–633; *Wayne Wilkinson Insurance Ltd v Kaiaua Downs Ltd* (1995) 8 ANZ Insurance Cases 75–782.

[398] *Wainewright v Bland* (1836) I. M. & W. 32, 35.

[399] *Schoolrnan v Hall* [1951] 1 Lloyd's Rep. 139; *Arterial Caravans v Yorkshire Insurance* [1973] 1 Lloyd's Rep. 169.

[400] Vaughan Williams L.J. in *Joel v Law Union* [1908] 2 K.B. 863 at 876–878.

[401] *Holt's Motors v South-East Lancs Insurance* (1930) 35 Com. Cas. 281.

[402] *Arterial Caravans v Yorkshire Insurance* [1973] 1 Lloyd's Rep. 169. The burden of proving waiver is borne by the assured: *Roberts v Plaisted* [1989] 2 Lloyd's Rep. 341; *Noblebright Ltd v Sirius International Corp* [2007] Lloyd's Rep. I.R. 584.

[403] *Newsholme Bros v Road Transport & General Insurance* [1929] 2 K.B. 356 at 362–363; *McCormick v National Motor & Accident Insurance* (1934) 40 Com. Cas. 76 at 78.

[404] *Laing v Union Marine Insurance Co* (1895) 1 Com. Cas. 11.

that an assured "is not bound to give information which the underwriter waives or as to which the assured may reasonably infer that the underwriter is indifferent".[405] The principle of indifference has led to the rather wider arguments that if the insurer has expressly limited his question, he is to be taken to have waived disclosure of information not requested or outside the scope of the limited question. A more extreme possibility is that an insurer who fails to ask a question on a specific point when he clearly had the opportunity to do so is to be taken as having waived that information. The cases on these matters are not, however, fully consistent, for the simple reason that the notion of waiver in such circumstances cannot easily be reconciled with the principle that spontaneous disclosure is required of the assured.

Insofar as the waiver principle does operate, it applies only to questions asked by the insurers on the placement of the risk: it does not operate where the policy requires limited forms of information to be provided to the insurers during the currency of the policy, as such information is not to be provided for the purposes of assessing the risk but rather for the purposes of the effective administration of the policy. In *Moore Large & Co Ltd v Hermes Credit & Guarantee Plc*[406] the assured was required, under the terms of a credit policy, to provide declarations of turnover to the insurers during the currency of the policy. Colman J. ruled that this obligation did not mean that the insurers had waived the disclosure of material facts relating to the indebtedness of particular customers when the policy was renewed.

6–071   *Limited questions.* The notion that there can be waiver of disclosure where a limited question has been asked is the result of two related concepts. The first is that by limiting the question the insurer is indicating that he has no interest in information which would otherwise be material but which falls outside the scope of that question. The second is that the duty of utmost good faith, consisting of its two strands of misrepresentation and non-disclosure, is nevertheless a unified one, so that the level of disclosure required of the assured is to some extent dictated by the express questions asked by the insurer.

The general rule is that there is no presumption of immateriality in respect of facts not made the subject of express questions, so that the argument that there is a waiver by the asking of a limited question is in conflict with this principle. There are nevertheless cases which have proceeded on the basis that waiver is possible.[407] Particularly noteworthy are two motor insurance cases, *Revell v London General Insurance Co Ltd*[408] and *Taylor v Eagle Star Insurance Co Ltd*,[409] both of which assumed that a question limited to motoring convictions impliedly waived information regarding other convictions. While these cases are

[405] *Laing v Union Marine Insurance Co* (1895) 1 Com. Cas. 11 at 15. See also: *Court v Martineau* (1782) 2 Doug. K.B. 161; *Freeland v Glover* (1806) 7 East 457; *Weir v Aberdeen* (1819) 2 B. & Ald. 320; *Inman SS Co v Bischoff* (1882) 7 App. Cas. 670; *Cantiere Meceanio Bridisino v Janson* [1912] 3 K.B. 452; *Kirkaldy & Sons v Walker* [1999] Lloyd's Rep. I.R. 410.

[406] *Moore Large & Co Ltd v Hermes Credit & Guarantee Plc* [2003] Lloyd's Rep. I.R. 315.

[407] *Joel v Law Union* [1908] 2 K.B. 863 at 878; *State Insurance General Manager v Hanham* (1990) 6 ANZ Insurance Cases 60–990; *State Insurance General Manager v Peake* [1991] 2 N.Z.L.R. 287; *Edwards v AA Mutual Insurance Co* (1985) 3 ANZ Insurance Cases 60 at 668. See also *Norwich Union Insurance Ltd v Meisels* [2007] Lloyd's Rep. I.R. 69, where the assured completed two proposal forms for the same subject matter, one of which contained express questions on his involvement with failed companies and one of which did not. The information was held to be immaterial to the latter policy: the word "waiver" was not mentioned, but the case clearly fits into that pattern.

[408] *Revell v London General Insurance Co Ltd* (1934) 50 Ll. L.R. 114.

[409] *Taylor v Eagle Star Insurance Co Ltd* (1940) 67 Ll. L.R. 136.

explicable on the basis that the convictions were not material, it is nevertheless the case that the possibility of waiver where limited questions only are asked has been taken up by the courts.[410]

It was commented by H.H. Judge Hegarty QC in *Noblebright Ltd v Sirius International Corp*[411] that the cases in which waiver had been found all involved specific and limited information. The authorities were distinguished on that basis in *Noblebright*, a case in which the assured had been asked whether there had been any claims in respect of his business premises in excess of £10,000 at any time, or any smaller claims in the previous five years. The assured had not made any claims, but there had been three incidents in the preceding five or so years of attempted armed robbery. The assured answered these questions in the negative, and asserted that the insurers had by their limited questions waived disclosure. The assured's formulation of what had been waived was circumstances which might have given rise to claims but in respect of which no claim was made or which did not give rise to any loss. The court's view was that this formulation was too general and gave rise to a great deal of uncertainty as to what was and was not waived. Accordingly, the suggestion of waiver was rejected.

Absence of express questions. While it is the case that limited questions may   **6–072**
enable the court to reach a finding of waiver, an absence of questions on a particular point cannot as a matter of principle lead to the same result, as such a proposition is contrary to the very duty of the assured to make full disclosure.[412] More recently, there has been a suggestion that failure to ask specific questions may amount to waiver even where no question of the authority of an agent arises, in that the presentation to the assured of a proposal form seeking only limited information and not warning of any duty of disclosure amounts to a waiver of further disclosure. In *Hair v Prudential Assurance*[413] the assured had procured a fire policy. There was a local authority closing order in force in respect of the insured premises, but no specific question was asked about this possibility and the assured did not disclose it. The assured declared that "all the information entered above is true and nothing materially affecting the risk has been concealed." It was accepted that the existence of the closing order was a material fact, but Woolf J. ruled that its disclosure had been waived. In *Doheny v New India Assurance Co Ltd*[414] it was suggested to the Court of Appeal that *Hair* had been wrongly decided, but the Court of Appeal disagreed and held that the reasoning in *Hair* was correct and that whether or not there was waiver depended upon the terms of the questions actually asked. This analysis is likely to result in many more proposal forms being found to contain an implied waiver of the duty of disclosure.[415] As was said by Simon Brown L.J. in *Economides v Commercial Union Assurance Co Plc*[416]:

---

[410] *O'Kane v Jones* [2005] Lloyd's Rep. I.R. 174; *Cape Plc v Iron Trades Employers Insurance Association Ltd* [2004] Lloyds Rep. I.R. 75; *Doheny v New India Assurance Co* [2005] Lloyd's Rep. I.R. 251; *R & R Developments Ltd v Axa Insurance Ltd* [2009] EWHC 2429 (Ch).

[411] *Noblebright Ltd v Sirius International Corp* [2007] Lloyd's Rep. I.R. 584.

[412] *Arterial Caravans Ltd v Yorkshire Insurance Co Ltd* [1973] 1 Lloyd's Rep. 169.

[413] *Hair v Prudential Assurance* [1983] 2 Lloyd's Rep. 667.

[414] *Doheny v New India Assurance Co Ltd* [2005] Lloyd's Rep. I.R. 251.

[415] *Roberts v Plaisted* [1989] 2 Lloyd's Rep. 341; *GMA v Unistorebrand International Insurance AS* [1995] L.R.L.R. 333; *Johnson v IGI Insurance Co Ltd* [1997] 6 Re. L.R. 283; *International Lottery Management Ltd v Dumas* [2002] Lloyd's Rep. I.R. 237.

[416] *Economides v Commercial Union Assurance Co Plc* [1997] 3 All E.R. 635.

"Where . . . material facts are dealt with by specific questions in the proposal form and no sustainable case of misrepresentation arises, it would be remarkable indeed if the policy could then be avoided on grounds of non-disclosure."

A more extreme situation is that in which a private assured is not requested to complete a proposal form and thus receives no warning of any duty of disclosure. This tends to occur where the insurance procured is ancillary to some other contract, e.g. a mortgage or the purchase of a car, so that the insurance is arranged by an intermediary not directly connected with the insurer. As a matter of general law it might be arguable that an insurer who chooses to allow policies to be initiated in an informal way has waived the usual disclosure rules, although this has yet to be tested and the judicial assumption has been to the contrary.[417] It was thus held by the Court of Appeal in *Johnson v IGI Insurance Co Ltd*[418] that where insurers used, as the basis for the issue of a medical insurance policy, a financing agreement application completed by the assured for the purchase of a taxi, they could not rely upon the assured's failure to disclose material facts as to his health: by failing to issue a proposal form which asked such questions, the insurers were to be taken to have waived disclosure of it.

All of this aside, there is a clear and consistent line of authority for the more traditional proposition that the disclosure of a material fact is not waived by the failure of the insurer to ask specific questions in relation to that effect. Perhaps the strongest statement of principle was by Longmore J. in *Marc Rich & Co AG v Portman*,[419] a view repeated by him in *WISE Underwriting Agency Ltd v Grupo Nacional Provincial SA*,[420] although Rix L.J. expressly reserved his position on the point in *WISE*.

On the assumption that failure by the insurer to ask all relevant questions in full can amount to waiver, this will in any event only be the case if the assured has, by the insurer's request for information, been led to believe that only a limited disclosure is required. In *Orakpo v Barclays Insurance Services Ltd*[421] the proposal form required the assured to tick "yes" or "no" boxes. The assured, faced with a question as to the condition of his house, ticked the box indicating that the house was sound, an answer only partly true as the house was badly affected by dry rot. The assured's defence to a claim of misrepresentation was that the proposal form did not allow a full answer to be given. The Court of Appeal, rejecting this defence, ruled that "an honest man could have overcome that problem". This of course is not universally true: some insurers who have opted for online application, and whose electronic forms leave no room for anything other than answers to specific questions, may well be treated as having waived further information even though the assured as an honest man is desperate to make full disclosure.

Waiver can in any event only relate to the assured's silence: if the assured, faced with a limited question, provides false answers to that question, it is not

[417] *Woolcott v Sun Alliance & London Insurance Co Ltd* [1978] 1 All E.R. 1253; *Orakpo v Barclays Insurance Services Ltd* [1995] L.R.L.R. 443.
[418] *Johnson v IGI Insurance Co Ltd* [1997] 6 Ll. L.R. 283.
[419] *Marc Rich & Co AG v Portman* [1996] 1 Lloyd's Rep. 430, affirmed *sub nom Glencore International AG v Portman* [1997] 1 Lloyd's Rep. 225. See also *James v CGU Insurance Plc* [2002] Lloyd's Rep. I.R. 206.
[420] *WISE Underwriting Agency Ltd v Grupo Nacional Provincial SA* [2004] Lloyd's Rep. I.R. 764.
[421] *Orakpo v Barclays Insurance Services Ltd* [1995] L.R.L.R. 443.

open to the assured to argue that the insurers had waived the information which has been misstated.[422]

Implied waiver: failure to make further enquiries. The general run of English **6–073** cases indicates that an insurer who, having been put on inquiry by what has been said by the assured, proceeds to issue a policy without further investigation, will be deemed to have waived further specific information.[423] A key authority is *Mann, MacNeal & Steeves v Capital & Counties Insurance Co*,[424] where a hull insurer, having been informed that the vessel was carrying a cargo, issued a policy without ascertaining the cargo's nature. The Court of Appeal ruled that the insurer had waived the information, and could not avoid the policy when the cargo proved to be petrol stored in iron drums.[425] A finding of waiver was also made by Waller J. in *Pan Atlantic Insurance Co v Pine Top Insurance Co Ltd*,[426] a case in which the full facts had been presented to reinsurers by the reinsured's brokers, but the brokers had sought success fully to deflect the reinsurers' attention away from information as to poor claims records in earlier years and towards more favourable claims records in more recent years. The learned judge ruled that there was probably full disclosure in the circumstances, but that in any event the reinsurers' failure to read the documentation for themselves constituted waiver of further disclosure. The Court of Appeal and the majority of the House of Lords based their decision on the absence of breach of the duty of disclosure, although Lord Mustill held that the correct analysis was waiver.[427]

This form of waiver is available where the assured has actually volunteered adequate information to put the insurer on notice that further material facts do exist,[428] or where the insurers have themselves learned something which ought to have put them on inquiry.[429] Only where there has been a fair presentation to the insurer can it be argued that the insurer has failed to make its own reasonable inquiries based on what has actually been disclosed.[430] If, for example, the assured leaves a blank in response to a question on a proposal form, his answer is to be taken to be a negative response and does not amount to notice to the insurer that material circumstances may exist.[431] Again, if there has been a positive misstatement by the assured, which has in effect denied the existence of

---

[422] *Moore Large & Co Ltd v Hermes Credit & Guarantee Plc* [2003] Lloyd's Rep. I.R. 315.

[423] *Wheelton v Hardisty* (1857) 8 E. & B. 232 at 269–270, per Lord Campbell; *Scottish Coal Co Ltd v Royal and Sun Alliance Plc* [2008] Lloyd's Rep. I.R. 718.

[424] *Mann, MacNeal & Steeves v Capital & Counties Insurance Co* [1921] 2 K.B. 300.

[425] See, for similar decisions: *Carter v Boehm* (1776) 3 Burr. 1905; *Court v Martineau* (1782) 3 Doug. K.B. 161: *Freeland v Glorer* (1806) 7 East 457; *Perrins v Marine & General* (1859) 2 E. & E. 317; *Asfar & Co v Blundel* [1896] 1 Q.B. 123; *Cantiere Meccanico Brindisino v Janson* [1912] 3 K.B. 452; *Markovitch v Liverpool Victoria Friend/v Society* (1912) 28 T.L.R. 188; *George Cohen v Standard Marine Insurance Co* (1925) 21 Ll. L.R. 30; *Roberts v Plaisted* [1989] 2 Lloyd's Rep. 431; *Rendall v Combined Insurance Co of America* [2006] Lloyd's Rep. I.R. 732.

[426] *Pan Atlantic Insurance Co v Pine Top Insurance Co Ltd* [1992] 1 Lloyd's Rep. 101.

[427] *Pan Atlantic Insurance Co v Pine Top Insurance Co Ltd* [1994] 3 All E.R. 581.

[428] *Ayrey v British Legal & United Provident Assurance Co* [1918] 1 K.B. 136.

[429] *Carter v Boehm* (1766) 3 Burr. 1706; *Becker v Marshall* (1922) 12 Ll. L.R. 413; *Greenhill v Federal Insurance* [1927] 1 K.B. 65 at 85; *Roberts v Plaisted* [1989] 2 Lloyd's Rep. 341.

[430] *St Paul Fire & Marine Insurance Co (UK) Ltd v McConnell Dowell Constructors Ltd* [1993] 2 Lloyd's Rep. 503; *Newbury International Ltd v Reliance National Insurance (UK) Ltd* [1994] 1 Lloyd's Rep. 83; *Marc Rich & Co AG v Portman* [1996] 1 Lloyd's Rep. 430, affirmed sub nom *Glencore Intermational AG v Portman* [1997] 1 Lloyd's Rep. 225: *Aiken v Stewart Wrightson Members Agency Ltd* [1995] 3 All E.R. 449.

[431] *Roberts v Avon Insurance* [1956] 2 Lloyd's Rep. 240; *Forbes v Edinburgh Life* (1830) 10 S. (Ct of Sess) 451.

further material facts, there is no room for waiver.[432] Thus in *Anglo-African Merchants v Bayley*[433] the description of the insured subject matter as "new men's clothes" was held not to be sufficient to alert the insurer to the possibility that the clothes were simply unused, when in fact they were war surplus and some 20 years old. In *New Hampshire Insurance Co v Oil Refineries Ltd*[434] in 1994 brokers placed with underwriters a liability cover on the defendant, an oil-producing company. The brokers disclosed to the underwriters the defendant's claims history for the five years up to the date of the placement, but did not disclose the fact that in the winter of 1988–1989 some 380 greenhouse flower growers had made claims against the defendant which were not settled at the date of the policy. The defendant's argument that the underwriters had waived disclosure on the basis that they had been prepared to accept disclosure based on the previous five years without making further investigation was rejected on the basis that there could not be waiver where underwriters failed to ask for additional information which they had no reason to believe existed, and that limited disclosure by an assured could not put him in a better position than total non-disclosure.

Where the insurer is on notice of the existence of further facts, and seeks further information from the assured, prevarication by the assured in the face of the insurer's further enquiries which prevents the insurer from obtaining the undisclosed facts will preclude any finding of waiver.[435]

The question of exactly when an insurer is, based on what he has been told, deemed to be on notice that there is further information to be elicited, was discussed at length, albeit obiter, by the Court of Appeal in *WISE Underwriting Agency Ltd v Grupo Nacional Provincial SA*.[436] In this case, a policy covered quantities of goods in transit for delivery to a retailer in Cancun, Mexico, a resort known[437] for catering to tourists with expensive tastes. The proposal as presented to reinsurers in London, and translated from Spanish, stated that the goods included "clocks", a mistranslation of a term intended to cover both clocks and watches. In fact a large quantity of valuable Rolex watches were consigned to the assured and the entire consignment was stolen. The reinsurers purported to avoid the reinsurance for the non-disclosure of the inclusion of Rolex watches. Simon J. held at first instance that the fact was material and that there had been inducement of the reinsurers: the materiality point was not appealed and the Court of Appeal upheld the finding on inducement. In the event the Court of Appeal held by a majority that the reinsurers had affirmed the policy after having become aware of a right to avoid it,[438] but chose also to give extended consideration to a further point which in the event proved irrelevant to the outcome, namely whether the reinsurers had waived disclosure of the presence in the cargo of Rolex watches. The argument for the reinsured was that the disclosure which had been made of the inclusion of clocks ought to have put the

---

[432] *Harrower v Hutchinson* (1870) L.R. 5 Q.B. 584; *Greenhill v Federal Insurance* [1927] 1 K.B. 65; *Arterial Caravans Ltd v Yorkshire Insurance Co Ltd* [1973] 1 Lloyd's Rep. 169; *Container Transport International v Oceanus Mutual Underwriting Association* [1984] 1 Lloyd's Rep. 476; *Aiken v Stewart Wrightson Members Agency Ltd* [1995] 3 All E.R. 449; *Stowers v GA Bonus Plc* [2003] Lloyd's Rep. I.R. 402; *Persimmon Homes Ltd v Great Lakes Reinsurance (UK) Plc* [2010] EWHC 1705 (Comm).

[433] *Anglo-African Merchants v Bayley* [1970] 1 Q.B. 311.

[434] *New Hampshire Insurance Co v Oil Refineries Ltd* [2003] Lloyd's Rep. I.R. 386.

[435] *Hill v Citadel Insurance Co Ltd* [1997] L.R.L.R. 167.

[436] *WISE Underwriting Agency Ltd v Grupo Nacional Provincial SA* [2004] Lloyd's Rep. I.R. 764.

[437] At least before the devastating hurricane in November 2005.

[438] The appeal was allowed on this point.

reinsurers on notice of the possibility that watches would also be involved and that the failure of the reinsurers to make further inquiries amounted to waiver. The Court of Appeal by a majority rejected the waiver argument, but the discussion of the point gave rise to an important disagreement of principle. The majority view, that of Longmore and Peter Gibson L.JJ., was that the reinsurers were entitled to rely on what they had been told and that they were not under any duty to go behind the reinsured's presentation of the risk in the absence of a clear indication that further facts existed. Longmore L.J.'s approach was that a two-step investigation was required: (a) was there an unfair presentation of the risk; and (b) if so, were the reinsurers "put on inquiry by the disclosure of facts which would raise in the mind of the reasonable insurer at least the suspicion that there were other circumstances which would or might vitiate the presentation?"[439] What is clear from this approach, therefore, is that it is not enough to establish waiver that a more alert underwriter might have made further inquiries. Peter Gibson L.J. concurred, stating that " . . . the court should not subvert the duty of the assured to make a fair presentation of the risk by finding that the reinsurers were put on inquiry and failed to discover for themselves the material information save in a clear case." On the facts there was held to be nothing in the mention of clocks which would have put a prudent underwriter on notice of the possible shipment of Rolex watches, so that waiver could not be made out, and similarly the mere fact that Cancun was a high-class tourist resort was not of itself enough to cause a prudent underwriter to investigate further.

Rix L.J., dissenting on analysis and on the outcome, emphasised two separate points. First, he held that it was not possible to treat the concepts of fair presentation and waiver separately, and that the question whether there was an unfair presentation of the risk itself encompassed the further question of whether there remained undisclosed facts which were unusual or special and which distorted the presentation of the risk. This analysis was not designed to deprive the doctrine of waiver of independent effect,[440] but merely to emphasise that where there is real unfairness on the part of the assured the doctrine of waiver will not save him. Secondly, Rix L.J. was heavily influenced by the mutual duty of utmost good faith which, in the present context, imposed a duty on the underwriters to act fairly when purporting to avoid. Applying these tests, Rix L.J. was not satisfied that unusual or exceptional facts had been withheld. There was nothing unusual about a person in the assured's position selling valuable watches, and indeed it was to be expected. A single simple question would have resolved the problem, and the reinsurers, having failed to take that step, could not avoid the policy.

The majority view in *WISE* is, therefore, that the assured must make a fair presentation of the risk, and that the insurers are thereafter treated as having waived disclosure of information which is an ordinary incident of the risk. If the facts withheld are not of that nature, there is a right to avoid. The minority view is that the obligation of the assured is to make a fair presentation of the risk, and there is a right to avoid only if the facts withheld are unusual or exceptional. The minority view allows the underwriters to rely upon how what they have been told appears on the face of things, the minority view is that the underwriters will be treated as having waived all further information unless it is unusual or exceptional.

---

[439] The test laid down by Parker L.J. in *Container Transport International Inc v Oceanus Mutual Underwriting Association* [1984] 1 Lloyd's Rep. 476.

[440] The analysis of Hobhouse J. in *Iron Trades Mutual v Compania de Seguros* [1991] 1 Re L.R. 213, following the reasoning of Kerr L.J. in *CTI*.

6–074   **Facts covered by an express warranty.** Section 18(3)(d) states that, in the absence of enquiry the assured is not required to disclose "any circumstance which it is superfluous to disclose by reason of any express or implied warranty." This principle is primarily directed to the implied marine warranties contained in ss.33–41,[441] although it may apply to express warranties. Thus, in *Inversiones Manria SA v Sphere Drake Insurance Co Plc (The Dora)*[442] the policy contained a warranty limiting use of the vessel to pleasure purposes: for this reason the assured's failure to disclose his intention to use the vessel as a demonstration model was held to be immaterial. In *Kirkaldy & Sons Ltd v Walker*[443] an inspection warranty relating to a vessel was held to override the duty of utmost good faith, and in *Gan Insurance Co Ltd v Tai Ping Insurance Co Ltd (No.2)*[444] a warranty relating to fire precautions was held to override any duty of disclosure relating to the condition and operability of the precautions. By contrast, in *O'Kane v Jones*,[445] it was held that disclosure by the assured of his failure to pay premiums under a different policy (assuming this was a material fact, which the court thought was not the case) was not waived by the insurers as the premium payment warranty had been removed and replaced with a quarterly payment obligation.

Section 18(3)(d) is triggered by any clause which has the same effect as a warranty, even though it is not a warranty in the strict sense. Thus, if there is an exclusion in the policy which operates independently of any causative link between the exclusion and the loss, disclosure of information relating to the subject matter of that term is not required.[446]

6. REMEDIES FOR BREACH OF DUTY

The right to avoid[447]

6–075   *Nature of avoidance.* Where the assured has misrepresented, or failed to disclose, a material fact, the insurer's remedy is avoidance of the contract; it is

---

[441] *Heyward v Rodgers* (1804) 4 East 590; *Gandy v Adelaide Insurance Co* (1871) L.R. 6 Q.B. 746.

[442] *Inversiones Manria SA v Sphere Drake Insurance Co Plc (The Dora)* [1989] 1 Lloyd's Rep. 69. See also: *Kirkaldy & Sons Ltd v Walker* [1999] Lloyds Rep. I.R. 410; *International Management Group (UK) Ltd v Simmonds* [2004] Lloyd's Rep. I.R. 247.

[443] *Kirkaldy & Sons Ltd v Walker* [1999] Lloyd's Rep. I.R. 410.

[444] *Gan Insurance Co Ltd v Tai Ping Insurance Co Ltd (No.2)* [2001] Lloyd's Rep. I.R. 291, reversed on other grounds [2001] Lloyds Rep. I.R. 667.

[445] *O'Kane v Jones* [2005] Lloyd's Rep. I.R. 174.

[446] *International Lottery Management Ltd v Dumas* [2002] Lloyd's Rep. I.R. 237. In *Hong Kong Nylon Enterprises Ltd v QBE Insurance (Hong Kong) Ltd* [2003] H.K.E.C. 199 the assured obtained an all risks policy for the transit of a plastic-moulding machine. The insurers alleged that they had not been told that the machine had been exhibited in Shanghai and was not new, and had been damaged during an earlier voyage. It was held that the true facts had been disclosed, but even if that was wrong the policy disclosure was not required because the policy excluded the risk of denting, chipping, cracking and scratching.

[447] Traditionally an insurer is said to have a right of avoidance for breach of the duty of utmost good faith, whereas in the case of misrepresentation the fusion of common law and equity gives the innocent party the right to rescind (*Merchants & Manufacturers Insurance v Hunt* [1941] 1 K.B. 295 at 318). However, the terms rescind and avoid these days tend to be used interchangeably in insurance cases. In *HIH Casualty and General v Chase Manhattan Bank* [2001] Lloyd's Rep. I.R. 702 Rix L.J. commented that the word avoidance in a clause which purported to limit the rights of insurers to set aside the policy for breach of the duty of utmost good faith applied also to rescission at common law for misrepresentation. Whichever word is used would, on this interpretation, appear to be a matter of taste rather than legal significance.

not open to the insurer to affirm the contract but to deny a claim under it.[448] Avoidance takes effect ab initio, so that the contract is treated as never having existed.[449] There is thus a total failure of consideration, and the assured is entitled to a return of his premium,[450] a right confirmed by s.84(1) of the 1906 Act, subject to the qualifications that the policy does not provide otherwise[451] and the assured has not been guilty of fraud. It is unclear whether the fraud eception, set out in s.84 applies to non-marine insurance. It is also the case that the insurer has the right to recover sums paid by him, subject to any defences to the restitutionary claim possessed by the assured. It was stated by Longmore L.J. in *K/S Merc-Skandia XXXXII v Certain Lloyd's Underwriters*[452] that breach of the duty of utmost good faith in an application for a renewal has no effect on the policy current at the time of the breach of duty, as there is no continuing duty of utmost good faith extend ing to the making of an application for renewal. An insurer who wishes to avoid a contract for non-disclosure or misrepresentation may either do so by notice to the assured, or by seeking declaratory relief from the court. Avoidance is an all-or-nothing remedy: English law does not recognise any concept of apportionment of the sum recoverable based upon the proportion of the premium paid against that which would have been demanded with full disclosure.

An avoidance may be unjustified on a number of grounds: there was no misrepresentation or non-disclosure; the fact in question was not material; the assured's presentation of the risk did not induce the contract; the duty of good faith had been waived; the breach of duty had been waived; or the insurers themselves were in breach of their continuing duty of good faith in avoiding the policy. In all of these situations other than the last-mentioned, the insurers are guilty of repudiatory breach of contract[453] and the assured is entitled to recover damages representing any loss suffered as a result of the insurer's conduct. In line with ordinary contractual principles, the assured also has the right to treat the insurance contract as terminated with effect from the date of the insurers' breach (so that the claim itself is not prejudiced) or to affirm the contract and proceed with it as if nothing had happened. If the assured affirms the contract, the insurers are entitled to rely upon any defence open to them after repudiation (e.g. a breach of a claims condition), for an unaccepted repudiation is a "thing writ upon water".[454] An avoidance by the insurer in breach of its duty of utmost good faith does amounts neither to a repudiation of the contract nor does it give rise to an action in damages as the duty of utmost good faith is not one imposed by contract: it is simply the case that the insurer cannot rely upon the avoidance.

Divisibility of policy. It is common in the present market for policies to be sold **6–076** on a combined basis, with cover for different risks being granted by divisible parts of the policy. This has led to the argument that any defences which the insurer has in relation to one part of the cover do not avail him in relation to other

---

[448] *Anderson v Fitzgerald* (1853) 4 H.L. Cas. 484; *Biggar v Rock Life* [1902] 1 K.B. 516.

[449] *Brit Syndicates Ltd v Italaudit SpA* [2008] UKHL 18, which confirms that until avoidance the policy is perfectly valid.

[450] *West v National Motor and Accident Insurance Union* [1955] 1 All E.R. 800. It would appear that that the assured is entitled to gross premium, given that commission is paid by the insurer to the broker: *Intermunicipal Realty & Development Corp v Gore Mutual Insurance Co* [1981] 1 F.C. 151.

[451] *Broad & Montague Ltd v South East Lancashire Insurance Co Ltd* (1931) 40 Ll. L.R. 328.

[452] *K/S Merc-Skandia XXXXII v Certain Lloyd's Underwriters* [2001] Lloyd's Rep. I.R. 802.

[453] *Transthene Packaging v Royal Insurance (UK) Ltd* [1996] L.R.L.R. 32.

[454] *Transthene Packaging v Royal Insurance (UK) Ltd* [1996] L.R.L.R. 32.

parts of the cover. The argument was first successfully put in a warranty case, *Printpak v AGF Insurance Ltd*,[455] and an attempt to use it was made in a non-disclosure case, *James v CGU Insurance Plc*.[456] Here the assured sought to recover for physical loss, asserting that the material facts withheld by him related to other parts of the policy. Moore-Bick J. held that the argument failed on two grounds. First, while the policy was in separate sections, it was clear from its wording that it was a single contract to which a single duty of utmost good faith was applicable. Secondly, even if that was wrong, the facts withheld—which related to the assured's honesty and claims record and thus the moral hazard—would have in any event been material to each section of the policy.

6–077 *Loss of the right to avoid.* Although the duty of utmost good faith is generally regarded as having common law origins, the remedy of avoidance ab initio is plainly rooted in equity as at common law a contract is either void or valid. It is perhaps for this reason that Lord Mansfield's formulation of the duty in *Carter v Boehm*[457] referred to the policy being void, a concept subsequently enshrined in s.17 of the 1906 Act. It is nevertheless now beyond argument that the remedy is the equitable one of avoidance ab initio.[458] The right of avoidance in misrepresentation cases not involving insurance is subject to various restrictions, all of which relate to the notion that the result must be equitable. Accordingly, the right to avoid will be lost by reason of delay or the acquisition of rights by a third party. The loss of a right to avoid by an insurer is, however, a subject which has scarcely been discussed by the English courts, and the cases to date have largely been concerned only with loss of rights by reason of affirmation of the policy.

The possibility that there are other equitable limits on the right of an insurer to avoid for breach of the duty of utmost good faith by the assured was considered by Colman J. in *Strive Shipping Corp v Hellenic Mutual War Risks Association*.[459] The learned judge expressed the view that the right of avoidance had to be exercised in a way that took account of countervailing equitable considerations, of which affirmation was simply an example. More importantly, because the insurer owed a duty of utmost good faith to the assured, the right of avoidance had to be exercised in good faith and could in appropriate circumstances be lost. Colman J. concluded that it would be inequitable for an insurer to purport to avoid a policy on the basis of withheld facts that appeared at the time of the inception of the policy to be material but which by the time of the avoidance or by the time of trial had proved to be immaterial. This might encompass allegations of dishonesty, outstanding criminal charges and rumours, all of which had by the time of avoidance or trial had been demonstrated as unsubstantiated. Colman J.'s analysis was rejected by Moore-Bick J. in *Drake Insurance v Provident Insurance*,[460] a rejection confirmed by the Court of Appeal in *Brotherton v Aseguradora Colseguros SA (No.2)*,[461] the Court of Appeal in that case refusing to admit evidence that would demonstrate the truth or otherwise of those facts once the decision to avoid had been taken by the insurers. However, the Court of Appeal did leave open the possibility that an

---

[455] *Printpak v AGF Insurance Ltd* [1999] Lloyd's Rep. I.R. 542.

[456] *James v CGU Insurance Plc* [2002] Lloyd's Rep. I.R. 206.

[457] *Carter v Boehm* (1766) 3 Burr. 1706.

[458] *Strive Shipping Corp v Hellenic Mutual War Risks Association* [2002] Lloyd's Rep. I.R. 669, para.271.

[459] *Strive Shipping Corp v Hellenic Mutual War Risks Association* [2002] Lloyd's Rep. I.R. 669.

[460] *Drake v Provident Insurance* [2003] Lloyd's Rep. I.R. 793.

[461] *Brotherton v Aseguradora Colseguros SA (No.2)* [2003] Lloyd's Rep. I.R. 758.

insurer might be restrained from avoiding when at the time of the avoidance the insurer was aware that facts which were material when the risk was presented had proved in the light of subsequent events not to be material. That said, the Court of Appeal was doubtful that the continuing duty of utmost good faith which as a matter of principle can only confer a right of avoidance could be of any assistance to the assured in this context.

On appeal in *Drake v Provident*,[462] a differently constituted Court of Appeal rejected the dicta in *Brotherton* and accepted that the insurers' continuing duty of utmost good faith did indeed preclude an avoidance when the insurers were either actually aware, or possessed blind-eye knowledge, that the facts relied upon were either unfounded or had not induced the making of the contract.[463]

Limitation periods. There is no authority on the application of the Limitation Act 1980 to avoidance actions. This is scarcely surprising, given that avoidance is a self-help remedy and the assistance of the courts is not required. Insurers may, therefore, assert the right to avoid and their assertion has immediate effect: if the avoidance is not justified, their conduct is breach of contract and the assured then has under s.5 of the Limitation Act 1980 the usual six years period for actions for breach of contract to commence proceedings against them. In the event that the insurers have not asserted the right to avoid, and seek to invoke the assistance of the court by way of declaratory relief, the outstanding question is the determination of the limitation period to the action. It is settled law that the duty of utmost good faith is not one founded in contract but is imposed by operation of law. Further, there is no tort involved in non-disclosure, although there will be a tort if the assured has deliberately (deceit) or negligently (negligence) made a false statement. There is also some doubt as to whether the duty of utmost good faith is a duty imposed by the common law or in equity, although the balance of modern authority is in favour of the latter. Equitable rights are not subject to any statutory limitation period, although the equitable doctrine of laches has long operated to deprive the claimant of the right to enforce a stale claim, and the statutory limitation periods for common law actions have been applied to equitable rights by analogy. This principle been preserved by s.36 of the Limitation Act 1980, which provides that statutory time limits do not apply to any claim for equitable relief, other than by analogy in the discretion of the court. It might be thought that an action for avoidance is sufficiently analogous to a claim for breach of contract or in tort to justify the application of the ordinary six year limitation period running from the date of placement. In the event of tortuous fraudulent misrepresentation, time runs not from the date of the fraud but from the date on which it could have been discovered, and the equitable doctrine of laches has never applied to fraud so that it will not be open to a fraudulent assured to assert that the right of the insurers to seek avoidance for non-disclosure is time-barred (at least at any time before s.32 of the 1980 Act would by analogy have barred a claim for the tort of deceit).

6–078

Damages

No damages for breach of duty. It is difficult to conceive of a case in which it would be of greater advantage to an insurer to shun its right to avoid the policy and in the alternative to sue for damages. Admittedly an insurer might well have incurred expenditure both in setting up the insurance and in investigating one or

6–079

---

[462] *Drake v Provident* [2004] Lloyd's Rep. I.R. 277.
[463] See below.

more claims, but it will generally be more straightforward for the insurer simply to rescind and, if permitted to do so by the contract, to retain the premium. Accordingly, the question whether damages are available is likely to arise only where the insurers have lost or contracted out of the right of avoidance, or possibly where breach of duty is alleged by the assured. Indeed, it had long been the assumption at common law that the insurer has no right to damages, irrespective of whether the duty of utmost good faith takes effect in the general law—which is now the settled position—or as an implied term. It has in recent years been confirmed by the House of Lords and the Court of Appeal, beginning with the Court of Appeal's judgment in *La Banque Financière de la Cité SA v Westgate Insurance Co Ltd*,[464] that damages are not available for a breach of the duty of utmost good faith. It is not, therefore, arguable that an insurer has the right to seek to recoup lost expenditure by an action for damages following its decision to rescind for breach of duty by the assured. It is apparent that insurers cannot avoid the principle in *La Banque Financière* by seeking damages in the tort of negligence, as it was decided in that case, and also from the subsequent decision of Aikens J. and the Court of Appeal in *HIH Casualty and General Insurance Ltd v Chase Manhattan Bank*, that a contract of insurance cannot be used as a platform for the imposition of a duty of care in the form of a duty to speak. Rix L.J. nevertheless recognised that it would not be sensible to exclude a duty of care in every case, and held that such a duty might arise in exceptional circumstances where, for example, an insurer had undertaken the task of advising the proposer about the suitability of scope of cover.

6–080   *Damages for misrepresentation.* Section 2(1) of the Misrepresentation Act 1967 provides as follows:

> "Where a person has entered into a contract after a misrepresentation has been made to him by another party thereto and as a result thereof he has suffered loss, then, if the person making the misrepresentation would be liable in damages in respect thereof had the misrepresentation been made fraudulently, that person shall be so liable notwith-standing that the representation was not made fraudulently unless he proves that he had reasonable grounds to believe and did believe up to the time the contract was made that the facts represented were true."

The effect of this provision is that, if a false statement is made by one contracting party which induces the other to enter into the contract, that other is entitled to recover damages, measured on the basis of the tort of deceit, unless the person making the statement can demonstrate that he was not negligent in making the statement. The key features are, therefore, the shifting of the burden of proving innocence onto the representor and the measure of damages by means of a fiction of fraud, so that the representee may recover not just damages for foreseeable loss but also damages for loss which flowed naturally and directly from the false statement.[465] It is clear that s.2(1) has no application to non-disclosure, and could potentially afford a remedy only in the event of a positive false statement by the

---

[464] *La Banque Financière de la Cité SA v Westgate Insurance Co Ltd* [1989] 2 All E.R. 952, reversing the first instance decision of Steyn J., sub nom *Banque Keyser Ullman SA v Skandia (UK) Insurance Ltd* [1987] 2 All E.R. 923. The House of Lords was similarly minded, although only Lord Templeman dealt with the point: [1990] 2 All E.R. 947 at 959. See also *Pan Atlantic Insurance Co Ltd v Pine Top Insurance Co Ltd* [1994] 3 All E.R. 581; *HIH Casualty and General Insurance Ltd v Chase Manhattan Bank* [2001] Lloyd's Rep. I.R. 191, varied [2001] Lloyd's Rep. I.R. 702. All doubts were dispelled by the House of Lords in *Manifest Shipping Co Ltd v Uni-Polaris Shipping Co Ltd (The Star Sea)* [2001] Lloyd's Rep. I.R. 247.
[465] The measure laid down in *Doyle v Olby* [1969] 2 Q.B. 158.

assured. However, it is uncertain whether s.2(1) applies to insurance contracts, as its effect would be by a sidewind to undermine the established rule that the only remedy for breach of the duty of utmost good faith is avoidance. The matter has not been discussed in detail by the courts, although it has been assumed that insurance contracts fall within its ambit.[466] Whether or not s.2(1) is applicable to contracts of insurance, there seems to be no reason why it does not extend to contracts for insurance—including declaration policies, open covers and reinsurance treaties—as such contracts do not attract the duty of utmost good faith.[467] The implications could be of some significance. If a declaration policy is issued to an assured on the basis of material false statements made by the assured, and the assured uses the policy to create a series of individual contracts of insurance by declaration to the policy, the insurers seemingly have the right either to avoid the declaration policy itself for misrepresentation, thereby automatically avoiding all of the declarations, or to maintain the contract in existence and seek damages assessed on the basis of fraud in the event that payments had been made under any of the individual declarations. By this means, premiums could be retained in respect of those declarations which have not given rise to losses, whereas damages could be recovered for losses paid (or set-off established against losses payable) under other declarations.

Damages in lieu of rescission. Section 2(2) of the Misrepresentation Act 1967 **6–081** confers upon the court the ability to deny the remedy of avoidance or rescission to a claimant and in its place to substitute an award of damages. There is little authority on the operation of this provision, although it would seem that its purpose is to protect the defendant against the possible disproportionately harsh consequences of avoidance, taking into account the seriousness of the false statement and the potential losses to the innocent party in the event that the contract is to be enforced.[468] The discretion conferred by the section is, therefore, primarily for the benefit of the defendant rather than the claimant. Section 2(2) is of limited application in the insurance context for, as is the case with s.2(1), it offers alternative relief only in the case of positive misrepresentation, as opposed to a failure to disclose. This limitation aside, the use of s.2(2) has attractions, particularly where the insurers seek to avoid the policy for a completely innocent misrepresentation which proves to be totally unconnected to any loss suffered by the assured within the terms of the policy. The effect of the subsection being used in such a case would be to allow recovery by the assured, subject to set-off for any loss suffered by the insurers: it might be thought that in the general run of cases the amount recoverable by insurers would be negligible. On the assumption that the provision is applicable to insurance contracts, the courts have set their face against allowing its use in reinsurance and, presumably, the commercial insurance market, on the basis that the parties to such contracts are fully aware of the consequences of the duty of utmost good faith.[469] Steyn J. expressed the view that, in commercial insurance dealings, the ordinary remedy of avoidance ought not to be denied, even in the case of unintentional misrepresentation, as in

---

[466] *Toomey v Eagle Star Insurance Co (No.2)* [1995] 2 Lloyd's Rep. 88; *HIH Casualty and General Insurance Ltd v Chase Manhattan Bank* [2001] Lloyd's Rep. I.R. 191 (Aikens J.).

[467] *HIH Casualty and General Insurance Ltd v Chase Manhattan Bank* [2001] Lloyd's Rep. I.R. 191 (Aikens J.).

[468] *Sindall (William) Plc v Cambridgeshire County Council* [1994] 3 All E.R. 932.

[469] *Highlands Insurance Co v Continental Insurance Co* [1987] 1 Lloyd's Rep. 109; *Pan Atlantic Insurance Co Ltd v Pine Top Insurance Co Ltd* [1992] 1 Lloyd's Rep. 101; *HIH Casualty and General Insurance Ltd v Chase Manhattan Bank* [2001] Lloyd's Rep. I.R. 702.

those cases the parties are fully aware of their obligations and of the consequences of their breach. Whether the courts would sanction the use of s.2(2) of
the 1967 Act in consumer contracts is less certain.

Contracting out of remedies

6–082 *The permissible ambit of agreements.* The scope of the right of the parties to a
contract of insurance to agree that the right to avoid, or a right to damages under
statute or in tort, is to be waived or restricted, was considered at length in *HIH
Casualty and General Insurance Ltd v Chase Manhattan Bank.*[470] The principles
laid down in that case may be summarised in four propositions.

First, it was permissible, in principle, for the insurers and the assured to agree
that the duty of disclosure on the assured or his agent was to be waived. In the
absence of any duty of disclosure, the issue of remedies became irrelevant, and
it would also be immaterial that the assured or his agent had been guilty of fraud
in withholding information.

Secondly, it was permissible, in principle, for the parties to include a contract
term that purported to limit or exclude the right or the rights of insurers to avoid
a contract of insurance for a breach of the duty of disclosure by the assured or his
agent. Such a clause left the duty unaffected, but simply removed the remedy.
However, there was an important limitation on such a term, in that public policy
would not permit an assured to rely upon such a clause to exonerate him in the
event of fraud on his part in the presentation of the risk.[471] The position was not
clear cut, however, where the fraud was that of the agent. Aikens J. and the Court
of Appeal in *HIH* thought that there was no reason why a suitably worded clause
could not operate to exclude the assured's liability for the consequences of
fraudulent breach of duty by the assured's agent in presenting the risk to the
insurers, as long as the assured was in no way implicated in the agent's fraud.
The House of Lords was divided on this point. Lords Bingham, Steyn and
Hoffmann held that the point should be decided when it arose and refused to
commit themselves, although Lord Hoffmann appeared to be sympathetic to the
suggestion that public policy might preclude a clause of this type. Lord Scott
strongly felt that public policy had no part to play, and that a principal should be
free to exclude liability for the fraud of his agent as long as the principal was not
implicated in the fraud.[472] By contrast, Lord Hobhouse was in favour of the
operation of public policy in this situation. Independently of any public policy
objection, Lord Hobhouse noted that an exclusion clause could be binding only
if the insurers had agreed to it, but if the contract containing the clause had itself
been induced by fraud then it could not be said that there was ever any such
agreement: the assured would be relying upon and seeking to take advantage of
the very fraud that the clause purported to exclude. Lord Hobhouse's view was
that if a party wished to insure against his agent's fraud, he should, independently
of that agent and of the contract entered into through that agent, take out the
appropriate independent fidelity cover rather than be able to rely upon the terms
of the policy itself. It may be that the point is academic, for even if it were

---

[470] *HIH Casualty and General Insurance Ltd v Chase Manhattan Bank* [2003] Lloyd's Rep. I.R.
230.

[471] Followed by David Steel J. in *HIH Casualty and General Insurance Ltd v New Hampshire
Insurance Co* [2001] Lloyd's Rep. I.R. 224. The root cases on the point are *S Pearson & Sons Ltd
v Dublin Corp* [1907] A.C. 351 and *Boyd & Forrest v Glasgow & South Western Ry Co* [1915] S.C.
(H.L.) 20.

[472] If the clause is regarded as one which allocates the responsibility for the fraud of an agent, Lord
Scott's reasoning appears impeccable.

permissible in principle for the parties to agree to exclude the insurers' rights in the event of fraud by the agent, their Lordships were agreed that the clearest possible wording would be required to achieve that effect, and it was indeed pointed out that there was no decided case in which a clause had ever been held to operate in this way.

Thirdly, it was permissible, in principle, for the insurers and the assured to exclude or limit, by agreement, the remedies of the insurers in the event of misrepresentation by the assured or his agents. However, as in the case of non-disclosure, public policy did not allow an assured to exclude or limit remedies for a fraudulent misrepresentation made by the assured personally and which induced the contract in question. Fraud by the assured's agents in the presentation of the risk could be the subject of a clause that restricted the remedies of the insurers, as the assured would not be personally tainted by the fraud of his agents unless he was implicated in the fraud.

Finally, it was permissible, in principle, to include in a contract of insurance a clause limiting the right of the assured's agents to make representations to insurers on the assured's behalf in the placement of the risk. In the event of a misrepresentation by agents, the statement would be treated as unauthorised and so the assured would be free of responsibility, even in the case of fraud.

It is apparent from the various judgments in *HIH*, particularly that of Aikens J at first instance, that exclusionary wording which is designed to have any of these effects has to be clear.

Incontestability clauses. One common method of achieving a waiver of reme- **6–083** dies is for the policy to state that it is incontestable after a given period. This is often used in life insurance.[473] In accordance with *HIH v Chase Manhattan Bank*, this type of clause cannot operate where the assured had been fraudulent in his presentation of the risk. However, a life policy is, in essence, for the benefit of the assured's beneficiaries rather than the assured himself, and there may be an argument that even fraud by the assured ought not to prevent the incontestability clause operating to the advantage of those beneficiaries.[474]

General exclusion of remedies for non-disclosure and misrepresentation. If there **6–084** is a general intention to exclude or restrict the insurers' remedies, the scope of the relevant clause has to be determined on its proper construction. In *Toomey v Eagle Star Insurance Co (No.2)*,[475] a reinsurance contract covering losses at Lloyd's provided that it was "neither cancellable nor voidable by either party". Colman J. held that these words were sufficient to exclude the reinsurers' right to avoid the contract for an innocent breach of the duty of utmost good faith, but were not appropriate to extend to negligent misrepresentations in the absence of clear wording, a principle long settled in exclusion clause cases. That view appears no longer to hold good. The House of Lords in *HIH Casualty and*

---

[473] *Anstey v British National Premium Life Association Ltd* (1908) 24 T.L.R. 871.

[474] The argument becomes stronger in the light of the more relaxed view of privity of contract in the Contracts (Rights of Third Parties) Act 1999. That Act might well, in the case of policies made after May 11, 2000, itself operate to allow the enforcement of the incontestability clause by beneficiaries if the clause can be construed as one which is enforceable by them or is for their benefit.

[475] *Toomey v Eagle Star Insurance Co (No.2)* [1995] 2 Lloyd's Rep. 88. Cf. *HIH v Chase Manhattan Bank* [2001] Lloyd's Rep. I.R. 191 (Aikens J.); *HIH Casualty and General Insurance Ltd v New Hampshire Insurance Co* [2001] Lloyd's Rep. I.R. 224 (David Steel J.); *Pan Atlantic Insurance Co Ltd v Pine Top Insurance Co Ltd* [1993] 1 Lloyd's Rep. 496 (Steyn J.).

General Insurance Ltd v Chase Manhattan Bank[476] held that the true question in every case was the proper construction of the clause, and that it was perfectly proper to construe a clause as extending to negligence even though there was no specific mention of that word. What mattered was whether the clause made commercial sense if it was confined to innocent misrepresentation or non-disclosure.

6–085 *Waiver of avoidance with right of recourse for fraud.* While it is the case that public policy precludes the inclusion of any contract term purporting to waive the insurers' rights in the event of non-disclosure or misrepresentation in the event of fraud by the assured, there would seem to be no reason why a clause of that width should not operate where the insurers have a right of recourse against the individual who was himself responsible for the fraud.[477]

6–086 *Waiver of avoidance other than for fraud.* This type of clause is perhaps the most straightforward and complies with the guidelines laid down in *HIH Casualty and General Insurance Ltd v Chase Manhattan Bank*. In *Rothschild Assurance Ltd v Collyear*[478] the clause provided that the insurers would not avoid the policy for a false statement or for failure to disclose material facts providing that the assureds could establish that they had been "free of any fraudulent intent". The policy went on to exclude the insurers' liability for circumstances known to the assureds prior to inception. Rix J. held that the exclusion was to be read subject to the waiver of remedies, and meant that, if the assured had been fraudulent, the insurers could either avoid the policy or pay for losses falling outside the exclusion.

6–087 *Errors and omissions clauses.* In reinsurance agreements and in declarations policies it is common to find "errors and omissions" clauses, whereby the policyholder's rights are preserved even in the event of any error or omission on his part. However, it has been held that clauses using these words do not amount to a waiver of the underwriters' right to avoid the agreement for misrepresentation or non-disclosure, but rather are merely relevant to errors in documentation.[479] A clause that is confined to mistakes in the details of the risk reported to the underwriters will not excuse a complete failure to declare a risk.[480]

6–088 *Truth of statements clauses.* In *HIH v Chase Manhattan Bank* a policy was effected by brokers for the assured bank. The policy contained a "Truth of Statements" clause under which the bank

> "7 . . . shall have no liability of any nature to the insurers for any information provided by any other parties and any such information provided by or non-disclosure by other parties including, but not limited to [broker] (other than Section I of the Questionnaire)
>
> 8 . . . and any such information provided by or non-disclosure by other parties including, but not limited to [broker] (other than Section 1 of the Questionnaire) shall

---

[476] *HIH Casualty and General Insurance Ltd v Chase Manhattan Bank* [2003] Lloyd's Rep. I.R. 230.

[477] *Kumar v AGF Insurance Ltd* [1998] 4 All E.R. 788.

[478] *Rothschild Assurance Ltd v Collyear* [1999] Lloyd's Rep. I.R. 6.

[479] *Highlands Insurance Co v Continental Insurance Co* [1987] 1 Lloyd's Rep. 109; *Pan Atlantic Insurance Co Ltd v Pine Top Insurance Co Ltd* [1993] 1 Lloyd's Rep. 496.

[480] *Glencore International AG v Alpina Insurance Co Ltd* [2004] 1 Lloyd's Rep. 111.

not be a ground or grounds for avoidance of the insurers' obligations under the Policy or the cancellation thereof."

The preliminary issues posed were whether these words were appropriate to exclude the insurers' rights in relation to misrepresentation and non-disclosure by the assured's brokers. The context emphasised by the House of Lords was that the entire insurance scheme was the work of the brokers, and that it had been sold to the bank as a package. The present case was not, therefore, a typical one in which the brokers acted as the agent of the assured, but rather was one in which the brokers' own involvement meant that they knew far more about the risk than the assured. Given that the brokers were more or less independent of the assured, the commercial purpose of the Truth of Statement Clause was to be regarded as giving generous protection to the assured against the misdeeds of its brokers in presenting the risk. With that point in mind, the principles were as follows.

First, Aikens J. held that the Truth of Statement Clause was concerned with pre-contractual utmost good faith and not post-contractual utmost good faith, as the wording was too elaborate to be regarded as confined to whatever narrow continuing duty might be recognised by the law. This view was not challenged on appeal to the Court of Appeal or in the House of Lords.

Secondly, the words "[the assured] . . . shall have no liability of any nature to the insurers for any information provided by any other parties . . . including, but not limited to, [brokers]" to a large extent excluded the insurers' rights of avoidance. The clause did not, by its terms, limit the authority of the brokers to make representations on the part of the assured[481]; indeed, the wording presupposed that statements were to be made by brokers, as the clause purported to exclude the assured's liability for such statements. However, the clause did impact on the insurers' right to avoid the insurance for misrepresentation by precluding reliance by the insurers on innocent misrepresentation by the brokers and also excluded any liability of the assured for damages under s.2(1) of the 1967 Act for negligent misrepresentation by the brokers and also any right of the insurers to avoid the policy for negligent misrepresentation. The clause on its proper construction also extended to negligence even though that word was not expressly mentioned: the phrase "no liability of any nature . . . " was comprehensive and the possibility of negligence was readily foreseeable. The wording did not, however, protect the bank against any liability for damages or against any risk of avoidance in respect of fraudulent misrepresentation or non-disclosure on the part of the brokers, as it was not sufficiently clear. The majority of their Lordships reserved their position on the conceptual issue of whether such a clause was permitted by the general law. Lord Hobhouse thought that it would be of no effect, whereas Lord Scott, dissenting on the result on this issue, held that public policy did not strike down a clause that purported to exclude liability for the fraud of an agent and that the present clause was sufficiently wide to have that effect.

Thirdly, the words "any such information provided by or non-disclosure by other parties including but not limited to [brokers] . . . shall not be a ground or grounds for avoidance of the insurers' obligations under the Policy or cancellation thereof" were capable of protecting the assured against non-disclosure and misrepresentation on the part of its brokers. The clause did not remove the brokers' duty of disclosure, but simply sought to modify the remedies for its breach in respect of both negligent and non-negligent breaches of duty. The right

---

[481] Contrast the wording in *Overbrooke Estates Ltd v Glencombe Properties Ltd* [1974] 1 W.L.R. 1335.

of avoidance for fraudulent misrepresentation on the part of the brokers was not (Lord Scott dissenting) to be regarded as having been excluded by the general language of the clause. Indeed, as noted above, in the House of Lords only Lord Scott was prepared to hold that public policy allowed a clause to exclude fraud on the part of an agent. In the event of fraudulent non-disclosure on the part of the brokers, the insurers maintained their rights. Half truths were to be treated as misrepresentations, but if there was a pure non-disclosure it was conceptually possible for it to be treated as fraudulent as such and outside the scope of the clause.[482]

6–089   **Loss of right to avoid.** The effect of a breach of the duty of utmost good faith by the assured is to render the contract voidable at the insurer's option. In the usual course of events the fact that the assured is in breach of duty will not be discovered until the claim is under investigation by the insurer, and the question then arises whether any conduct by the insurer in handling the claim amounts to a waiver of its right to avoid the policy, or whether an estoppel has been raised against the insurer. Waiver arises where the insurer, faced with the conflicting choice of avoiding the policy or maintaining it in force, adopts the latter approach: waiver thus consists of an election between contrasting outcomes, and once the election has been made unequivocally the insurer is unable to go back on it. Estoppel arises where the insurer has acted in a manner which makes it unconscionable for the insurer to avoid the policy. Although the two concepts are distinguished by the courts—a point that is of particular significance in relation to breach of warranty and breach of condition precedent, where there is no possibility of waiver by affirmation as the insurer is automatically off risk so that the assured can get home only by relying on estoppel[483]—in practice the requirements for each are similar.

Any assertion of waiver or estoppel must be based upon the conduct of the insurers in relation to the assured. In the case of a liability policy, any statement by the insurers to a person who may have a claim against the assured that they do not intend to waive their rights will not be effective to prevent avoidance of the policy, as a third party has no direct claim against the insurers and thus has no rights under the policy. Even where the assured has become insolvent so that the third party has a contingent claim against the insurers under the Third Parties (Rights against Insurers) Act 2010, the third party cannot prevent an avoidance of the policy by the insurers based on alleged waiver directed at the third party rather than the assured.[484] Similarly, if a reinsurer informs the direct assured that the reinsured will be indemnified, it is not possible for the reinsured to rely upon waiver by reason of the reinsurer's statement. It is arguable that the position may be the same where there is an enforceable cut-through clause under which the reinsurer is obliged to pay the assured in the event of the reinsured's insolvency, because the assured's rights are derived from those of the reinsured but the reinsured itself cannot plead waiver and until there is a judgment the assured's rights are merely contingent. The argument is supported by the consideration that

---

[482] In the Court of Appeal Rix L.J. rejected the notion of fraudulent non-disclosure, on the basis that the duty of disclosure was indivisible and did not depend upon the assured's state of mind. The House of Lords disagreed, and noted that the law did indeed recognise a distinction between fraudulent non-disclosure and other forms of non-disclosure: their Lordships referred to s.84 of the 1906 Act, which prevents an assured from recovering his premium where the policy has been avoided by the insurers on the ground of fraudulent non-disclosure or misrepresentation.

[483] *HIH Casualty & General Insurance v Axa Corporate Solutions* [2002] Lloyd's Rep. I.R. 325.

[484] *Spriggs v Wessingion Court School Ltd* [2005] Lloyd's Rep. I.R. 474.

there may be a number of assureds with cut-through rights, but the policy cannot be good against some assureds and voidable against others.[485] An insurer or reinsurer who exercises rights under the policy to defend the third party's claim against assured or reinsured may, however, arguably be regarded as having waived any right of avoidance,[486] and a similar argument could be made in respect of any alleged act of waiver on the part of the insurers once the third party's rights have crystallised and he has a direct claim against the insurer or reinsurer.

Waiver

Conditions for waiver. The law recognises a general doctrine of waiver of rights, referred to either as waiver by affirmation or waiver by election. What is contemplated here is that the insurers are faced with the choice of whether to affirm the contract or to avoid it for breach of the duty of utmost good faith: if insurers are entitled to such alternative and inconsistent rights, and they have knowledge of the facts which give rise in law to these alternative rights but choose to act in a manner which is consistent only with having chosen to rely on one of those rights, the law holds them to their choice even though they was unaware that waiver would be the legal consequence of their conduct.[487] The conditions which have to be satisfied before it can be said that the insurers have waived their right to avoid the policy and have elected to affirm it have often been restated.[488] The most helpful categorisation is found in the judgment of Simon J. in *WISE Underwriting Agency Ltd v Grupo Nacional Provincial SA*,[489] adopted on appeal by the Court of Appeal:[490]

6–090

(1) The insurer or his authorised agent must have actual knowledge of the facts not disclosed prior to the contract. Constructive knowledge is insufficient.
(2) The insurer must also know that the breach of duty gives rise to the right to avoid.
(3) The insurer has a reasonable time in which to decide what to do.[491]
(4) There must be an unequivocal communication to the assured by words or conduct that the insurer has made an informed choice to affirm the contract and to pay the claim.

---

[485] A key part of the reasoning in *Spriggs*.

[486] *Wood v Perfection Travel* [1996] L.R.L.R. 233, where the point was raised but not fully argued and no ruling was given.

[487] This is adapted from the classic statements of principle in *Kammins Ballrooms Co Ltd v Zenith Investments (Torquay) Ltd* [1971] A.C. 850 and *Motor Oil Hellas (Corinth) Refineries SA v Shipping Corp of India (The Kanchenjunga)* [1990] 1 Lloyd's Rep. 391. See *Kosmar Villa Holidays Plc v Trustees of Syndicate 1243* [2008] Lloyd's Rep. I.R. 489 and *Lexington Insurance Co v Multinacional de Seguros SA* [2009] Lloyd's Rep. I.R. 1.

[488] See, e.g. *Liberian Insurance Agency v Mosse* [1977] 2 Lloyd's Rep. 560; *CTI v Oceanus* [1984] 1 Lloyd's Rep. 476; *Insurance Corporation of the Channel Islands v Royal Hotel (No.2)* [1998] Lloyd's Rep. I.R. 151.

[489] *WISE Underwriting Agency Ltd v Grupo Nacional Provincial SA* [2003] EWHC 1706 (Comm).

[490] *WISE Underwriting Agency Ltd v Grupo Nacional Provincial SA* [2004] Lloyd's Rep. I.R. 764. See also *Persimmon Homes Ltd v Great Lakes Reinsurance (UK) Plc* [2010] EWHC 1705 (Comm).

[491] *Opossum Exports Ltd v Aviation and General (Underwriting Agents) Pty Ltd* (1984) 3 ANZ Insurance Cases 78–829 at 78–837.

(5) Whether such a communication is found depends upon how a reasonable person in the position of the assured would interpret the insurer's words or conduct.

As might be expected, the cases for the most part deal with the possibility of waiver resulting from the insurer's ambiguous post-loss conduct. Any conduct by the insurer which is expressly stated to be "WP" or without prejudice will, in any event, negate an argument based on waiver.[492]

6–091   *Express affirmation of the policy.* An express affirmation by the insurers not to avoid will be binding on them. This is necessarily the case if the insurers enter into a contract to that effect with the assured.[493] The old case of *Wing v Harvey*[494] indicates that where the insurer, in full possession of the relevant facts through an authorised agent, affirms the policy, the right to avoid will be lost. Whether a communication by the insurer to the assured is an affirmation of the policy is a matter of its proper construction and the context in which it is made. Statements by solicitors acting for liability insurers that they believed that the policy covered "most of the relevant period" and that the insurers accepted that they were "on risk" were held in *Spriggs v Wessington Court School Ltd*[495] not to amount to a waiver of a right of avoidance when seen against the background of correspondence in which the insurers were clearly reserving their rights pending further investigations and had not accepted liability.

6–092   *Implied affirmation of the policy.* The question here is whether the insurer's conduct, or failure to act, amounts to an implied waiver. What is required here is an unequivocal communication to the assured by words or conduct that the insurer has made an informed choice to affirm the contract. Leaving aside other issues, and in particular the knowledge of the insurers, the analysis here is concerned with the question as to what sort of acts amount to waiver of the right to avoid. The decided cases illustrate that the following may amount to waiver.

First, actual payment under the policy at a time when the insurers had the requisite knowledge of a breach of duty[496] is an act capable of amount to affirmation.

Secondly, the insurers may affirm by confirming coverage. This may be done by a deliberate decision[497]—as opposed to administrative oversight[498]—to accept future premiums. In *Morrison v Union Marine Insurance Co*[499] the insurer was held not to have affirmed the agreement by the purely ministerial act of issuing

---

[492] *Callaghan & Hedges v Thompson* [2000] Lloyd's Rep. I.R. 125.

[493] As in *Talbot Underwriting v Nausch Hogan & Murray (The Jascon 5)* [2006] Lloyd's Rep. I.R. 531, where the agreement involved an assignment to the insurers of the assured's rights against third parties (in this case, the brokers, who had in contravention of the assured's instructions allegedly been negligent in not seeking an extension of cover to a third party).

[494] *Wing v Harvey* (1854) 5 De G M & G 265.

[495] *Spriggs v Wessington Court School Ltd* [2005] Lloyd's Rep. I.R. 474.

[496] *Barber v Imperio Reinsurance Co (UK) Ltd* Unreported, 1993; *Cape Plc v Iron Trades Employers Insurance Association Ltd* [2004] Lloyd's Rep. I.R. 75.

[497] *Scottish Equitable v Buist* (1877) 4 R. (Ct of Sess) 1076; *Simner v New India Assurance* [1995] L.R.L.R 240; See also *Scottish Coal Co Ltd v Royal and Sun Alliance Plc* [2008] Lloyd's Rep. I.R. 718, where insurers agreed to extend cover despite being aware of non-disclosure as to a change in the assured's method of working.

[498] *Drake Insurance Co v Provident Insurance Co* [2004] Lloyd's Rep. I.R. 277; *Back v National Insurance Co of New Zealand Ltd* [1996] 3 N.Z.L.R. 363.

[499] *Morrison v Union Marine Insurance Co* (1872) L.R. 8 Ex. 197.

a policy following the scratching of a slip, as at the date of the issue the insurer had not had the opportunity to consider whether or not to avoid the agreement for breach of duty.[500]

Thirdly, it is not open to the insurer to seek to reject the claim while not avoiding the entire policy, as the only remedy for breach of the duty of utmost good faith is avoidance; if the insurer does seek to act in this way, its express affirmation of the policy will deprive it of all rights.[501] The assertion of an independent defence which asserts that there was never a contract between the parties will not, however, amount to a waiver of the right to avoid[502]; in *Bolton Metropolitan Borough Council v Municipal Mutual Insurance and Commercial Union Assurance*[503] the Court of Appeal pointed out that waiver requires a choice between inconsistent outcomes and not between alternative means of achieveing the same result.

Fourthly, the insurers may seek to bring an end to the policy in a manner which is inconsistent with the right to avoid the policy ab initio,[504] e.g. by cancellation under a policy term.[505] An agreement between the assured and the insurers to cancel the policy does not, however, amount to a waiver of the insurers' accrued right to avoid should the issue arise at a later stage.[506]

Fifthly, the exercise of a contractual right is inconsistent with an intention to avoid the policy. Thus, reinsurers who had enforced their rights of inspection under a reinsurance agreement were precluded from relying upon an avoidance of the policy, as their two acts were mutually inconsistent.[507] Similarly, a request to the assured to carry out acts which are preparatory to payment by the insurer, e.g. the preservation of rights of recovery from third parties, is capable of giving rise to waiver.[508] However, the position of insurers has to some extent been relieved by the ruling of Colman J. in *Strive Shipping Corp v Hellenic Mutual War Risks Association*,[509] where it was held that insurers did not lose their right to rely upon non-disclosure simply because they put the assured to proof of his loss. While it was the case, in line with earlier authority, that continued performance of the substantive terms of the contract or a request for further performance of such provisions, without reserving entitlement to avoid, would normally be taken as consistent only with an intention to elect to treat the contract as subsisting, that was not the case where the insurers made it clear to the assured that they were doing no more than undertaking further investigation: the requirement for an unequivocal representation to the assured that the insurers did not intend to rely upon their rights was not met in such circumstances. Colman J. also ruled that any contractual entitlement for information or documents was of an ancillary nature, so that the enforcement of that entitlement did not amount

---

[500] Contrast *Sumitomo Marine & Fire Insurance Co Ltd v Cologne Reinsurance Co of America* 552 N.Y.S. 2d 891 (1990) where the issue of documentation was held not to be purely mechanical.

[501] *West v National Motor and Accident Insurance Union* [1955] 1 All E.R. 800; *Moore Large & Co Ltd v Hermes Credit & Guarantee Plc* [2003] Lloyd's Rep. I.R. 315.

[502] *Talbot Underwriting v Nausch Hogan & Murray (The Jascon 5)* [2006] Lloyd's Rep. I.R. 531.

[503] *Bolton Metropolitan Borough Council v Municipal Mutual Insurance and Commercial Union Assurance* [2007] Lloyd's Rep. I.R. 173.

[504] *Mint Security v Blair* [1982] 1 Lloyd's Rep. 188.

[505] *WISE Underwriting Agency Ltd v Grupo Nacional Provincial SA* [2004] Lloyd's Rep. I.R. 764.

[506] *O'Kane v Jones* [2005] Lloyd's Rep. I.R. 174.

[507] *Imperio Reinsurance Co (UK) Ltd v Iron Trades Mutual* [1993] Re. L.R. 213.

[508] *Svenska Handelsbanken v Sun Alliance* [1996] 1 Lloyd's Rep. 519.

[509] *Strive Shipping Corp v Hellenic Mutual War Risks Association* [2002] Lloyd's Rep. I.R. 519.

to a waiver. There would be waiver only where the contractual right relied upon
was substantive, e.g. a claim for premium.

6–093   *Delay.* Perhaps the most difficult cases arise where the insurer has not acted at
all, but has delayed in communicating any form of decision to the assured,
particularly where this is coupled with action which might be construed as
evidencing a willingness to pay. Delay may give rise to waiver by affirmation
where the assured has been given reason for believing that the claim will be
met.[510] In this type of case, unless the insurer takes the obvious step of reserving
his rights,[511] the court may infer an intention to waive, on the principle that "a
businessman knows how to reserve his rights".[512] Nevertheless, it is clear that
not every delay will be construed as waiver, whether or not there is a reservation
of rights. Insurers are entitled to a reasonable time to reach their decision.[513] It
has thus been held that inaction for a period of five days, without prejudice being
caused to the assured, is not an act of implicit waiver.[514]

6–094   *The impact of the insurer's conduct on the assured.* In *Insurance Corp of the
Channel Islands v Royal Hotel (No.2)*[515] Mance J. restated the principles
underlying waiver by affirmation and emphasised that there can be no waiver
unless the assured ought to have appreciated, from the insurer's conduct, or from
that of his authorised agent,[516] that an informed choice to waive had been made.
In this case, insurers had issued separate policies covering business interruption
and material damage in relation to a hotel. Arbitraiton was commenced in respect
of the material damage claim and interim awards were honoured. While the
arbitration was continuing, the insurers commenced judicial proceedings in
which they asserted that the business interruption claim was fraudulent, and
having obtained a judgment to that effect they purported to avoid the material
damage policy for non-disclosure of the fraud. Mance J. held that the material
damage policy had been affirmed. First, the insurers had appreciated at an early
stage that there might be a right to avoid, but they had not acted upon this and
instead had awaited the outcome of the fraud proceedings under the business
interruption policy: delay for tactical reasons was capable of amounting to
affirmation. Secondly, the insurers were to be taken as having affirmed the
material damage policy by failing to object to the continuation of the arbitration
proceedings as they applied to that policy, and in recognising the validity of
interim awards on the material damage policy. Mance J. stated that the accepted
formulation for affirmation the need for an unequivocal communication to the
other party of the making of the choice to affirm involved also some form of
communication that the insurer is aware of the facts and has made an informed
choice: it is necessary, in determining whether there has been an unequivocal

---

[510] *Simon Haynes, Barlas & Ireland v Beer* (1946) 78 Ll. L.R. 357; *Simner v New India Assurance
Co Ltd* [1995] L.R.L.R. 240.

[511] As in *Nicholson v Power* (1869) 20 L.T. 580.

[512] *Barber v Imperio Reinsurance Co (UK) Ltd* Unreported, 1993.

[513] *McCormick v National Motor & Accident Insurance Union* (1934) 40 Com. Cas. 76 at 81–82;
Simon, Haynes Barlas & Ireland v Beer (1946) 78 Ll. L.R. 337; *Orakpo v Barclays Insurance
Services* [1995] L.R.L.R. 443; *Callaghan & Hedges v Thompson* [2000] Lloyd's Rep. I.R. 125.

[514] *McCormick v National Motor & Accident Insurance Union* (1934) 40 Com. Cas. 76.

[515] *Insurance Corp of the Channel Islands v Royal Hotel (No.2)* [1998] 1 Lloyd's Rep. 151.

[516] The broker is the assured's agent, so that a broker who, without the authorisation of the insurer,
informs the assured that the claim will be met, cannot hind the insurer by way of waiver: *Callaghan
& Hedges v Thompson* [2000] Lloyd's Rep. I.R. 125.

communication to the assured, to make an objective assessment of the impact of the communication to a reasonable person in the assured's position.

The result of this analysis is, therefore, that not only must the insurer's statement of intention not to rely on his contract rights be unequivocal and based on knowledge of the assured's breach, but also a reasonable person in the assured's position ought to have realised from the insurer's statement that the insurer had been making an informed choice. Thus, if the assured is aware that the insurer's statement was made without full knowledge of the relevant facts, there can be no waiver.[517] It is unclear, however, whether the test is whether a reasonable assured would in the position of the actual assured appreciate that the insurers were making an informed choice[518] or whether the test is the impact of the insurers' conduct on the actual assured.[519] In *Spriggs v Wessington Court School Ltd*,[520] the court preferred the former view on the ground that it was unusual for subjective intentions or understandings to play any part in determining the existence or termination of a contract.

The principle that the conduct of the insurers must illustrate an informed choice is of particular significance in a case of fraud by the assured, where the essence of the assured's breach of duty is that it has been hidden from the insurer: here, waiver will be almost impossible to make out unless it is clear from the insurer's statement that he was aware of the fraud and did not intend to take any action in relation to it.[521]

The insurer's knowledge. As the general conditions of affirmation set out above demonstrate, there is no possibility of waiver by affirmation until the insurer has become aware of the assured's breach of duty. This is a principle which is of general application in the law of contract.[522]   **6–095**

It is now settled that not only must the insurers be aware of the facts which might give rise to a defence, they must also be aware of the fact that as a matter of law they have the right to avoid the policy, as there cannot be waiver unless the insurers are aware of the rights that they are waiving. The point was expressly left open by Waller J. in *Pan Atlantic Insurance Co v Pine Top Insurance Co Ltd*,[523] but the need for such knowledge was assumed by Mance J. in *Insurance Corp of the Channel Islands v Royal Hotel (No.2)*.[524]

The degree of knowledge necessary to bring waiver into play has not been considered at length in many cases, although it has been held in old cases that knowledge for this purpose means actual knowledge and that it is not sufficient that the insurer is merely put on notice. Thus in the case where, although the assured has suppressed or misrepresented a material fact, he discloses it to the insurance office before they pay a claim, they cannot subsequently recover the money after payment.[525] It is otherwise where the concealment of material facts becomes known to an employee or agent of the insurer who is not under an obligation to communicate in formation to those persons within the insurer's operation with authority to collect premiums, as in such a case continued

---

[517] *Callaghan & Hedges v Thompson* [2000] Lloyd's Rep. I.R. 125.

[518] The holding in *Insurance Corp of the Channel Islands*.

[519] The holding in *Callaghan*.

[520] *Spriggs v Wessington Court School Ltd* [2005] Lloyd's Rep. I.R. 474.

[521] *Baghbadrani v Commercial Union Assurance Co Plc* [2000] Lloyds Rep. I.R. 94.

[522] *Peyman v Lanjani* [1985] 1 Ch. 457.

[523] *Pan Atlantic Insurance Co v Pine Top Insurance Co Ltd* [1992] 1 Lloyd's Rep. 101.

[524] *Insurance Corp of the Channel Islands v Royal Hotel (No.2)* [1998] Lloyd's Rep. I.R. 151. Cf. *Moore Large & Co Ltd v Hermes Credit & Guarantee Plc* [2003] Lloyd's Rep. I.R. 315.

[525] *Bilbie v Lumley* (1802) 2 East 269; *Wing v Harvey* (1854) 5 De G. M. & G. 265.

acceptance of premiums by those persons is to be regarded as taken without knowledge of the concealment.[526] The key analysis is now that of Mance J. in *Insurance Corp of the Channel Islands v Royal Hotel (No.2)*. The learned judge ruled that actual knowledge of the facts is required, but not to the degree of absolute certainty, although constructive knowledge will not suffice.[527] In his words: "For practical purposes, knowledge presupposes the truth of the matters known, and a firm belief in their truth, as well as sufficient justification for that belief in terms of experience, information and/or reasoning." Mance J. held, on the facts before him, that an insurer who for tactical reasons awaits the outcome of proceedings against the assured in which fraud is asserted, in order to use the fraud to avoid a different policy, is to be treated as having sufficient knowledge to give rise to affirmation, as "a person who deliberately and for tactical reasons decides not to acquire definite knowledge of a matter which he believes it likely that he could confirm must be treated as having knowledge of that matter".[528]

Although in most situations the insurer must have actual knowledge of the assured's breach of duty, in some cases a lesser degree of knowledge will suffice. The main modification to the need for actual knowledge arises where the insurer can be taken to have been aware of the breach by reason of information known to it obtained in a different context. It has been held, perhaps somewhat curiously, that knowledge known to the insurers in relation to an earlier policy is not to be treated as within their possession in respect of a later policy,[529] although the better view is that insurers cannot rely upon their own internal organisation to deny knowledge of facts previously disclosed to them.[530]

6–096 *Acquisition of knowledge following waiver.* The knowledge requirement for waiver necessarily means that an insurer who affirms a policy without appreciating that there have been material breaches of the duty of utmost good faith is entitled to resile from the affirmation and avoid the policy. The principle is equally applicable where the insurer, having learned of a non-disclosure, chooses to affirm the policy, and then discovers that there have been other breaches of duty on the part of the assured. Waiver can only operate with regard to the information that the insurer knows: waiver of the right to avoid on a limited matter does not preclude a subsequent decision to avoid on the basis of after-acquired information. This point was made in *Spriggs v Wessington Court School Ltd*,[531] where liability insurers affirmed a policy taken out by a school despite non-disclosure of allegations of abuse against pupils by its headmaster, but were subsequently permitted to avoid the policy on discovering that there were many more undisclosed instances of abuse than had previously been thought.

6–097 *The significance of legal advice.* For the purposes of waiver, the knowledge of the insurers' lawyers is generally to be treated as the knowledge of the insurers themselves. In *Insurance Corp of the Channel Islands v Royal Hotel (No.2)*,[532] in which the insurers' solicitors chose for tactical reasons to await the outcome of an arbitration on a business interruption claim before notifying the assured that they intended to avoid a separate material damage policy. Mance J. held that

---

[526] *Mahli v Abbey Life* [1996] L.R.L.R. 237.
[527] *Laing v Marine Insurance Co Ltd* (1895) 1 T.L.R. 358; *Evans v Bartlett* [1937] A.C. 473.
[528] See also *Callaghan & Hedges v Thompson* [2000] Lloyd's Rep. I.R. 125.
[529] *Mahli v Abbey Life Assurance Co* [1996] L.R.L.R. 237.
[530] *Kingscroft Insurance Co Ltd & Ors v Nissan Fire & Marine Insurance Co Ltd (No.2)* [1999] Lloyd's Rep. I.R. 603.
[531] *Spriggs v Wessington Court School Ltd* [2005] Lloyd's Rep. I.R. 474.
[532] *Insurance Corp of the Channel Islands v Royal Hotel (No.2)* [1998] Lloyd's Rep. I.R. 151.

there was waiver on the part of the insurers, as the knowledge of their solicitors was to be treated as the knowledge of the insurers. The decision was applied by Colman J. in *Moore Large & Co Ltd v Hermes Credit & Guarantee Plc*,[533] in which the insurers' legal advisers, aware of a good faith defence, chose to rely on a coverage defence and sought to introduce good faith by an amendment to their defence in proceedings brought by the assured. Colman J. held that the defence had been waived and that, as the construction point went against them, they were liable on the policy. In so deciding, Colman J. laid down important guidelines on the impact of legal advice:

> "In my judgment, in a case where the party said to have elected has been represented by solicitors and counsel whose conduct is relied upon as amounting to an election, it is normally to be inferred that such conduct has been specifically authorised by the client and has been the subject of legal advice. If, on the evidence before the court it is established that either the legal advisers or the client had knowledge of the facts giving rise to the right said to have been waived at the time when the affirmatory conduct took place, there must be the further inference that the party has been given legal advice as to his rights arising out of those facts. If that inference is to be displaced, there must be evidence of the advice, if any, that was given by solicitors and counsel and of the extent to which the party concerned was aware or was made aware of the right which he appears to have abandoned."

Estoppel. Waiver by estoppel arises where a person conducts himself in such a way that it is inequitable for him to rely upon his contractual rights, normally by reason of the other party's detrimental reliance.[534] As is the case with waiver by affirmation, an unequivocal representation on the part of the allegedly waiving party is required, but waiver by estoppel differs from waiver by affirmation in two respects: waiver by affirmation does not rest upon equitable principles and in particular does not require detrimental reliance; and a finding of waiver by estoppel is not precluded by the absence of knowledge on the part of the representor of his legal rights. Estoppel is, in principle, applicable to insurance, where the insurer has stated that it intends to pay and causes the assured to incur expenditure.[535]

6–098

This form of estoppel has yet to be pleaded successfully in an insurance case, although in *Callaghan & Hedges v Thompson*[536] David Steel J. expressed the view that an insurer would be estopped from denying a claim if the insurer decided not to avoid the policy for breach of the duty of utmost good faith and wrote to the assured in terms that the policy was still alive: such conduct is not waiver as it is a prerequisite of waiver that the insurer has not only indicated to the assured that he intends to pay but also that the manner of such indication makes it clear to the assured that the insurer was aware of the assured's breach of duty and had made an informed choice to pay. The absence of the need to convey informed choice, coupled with the lack of any need for reliance, at first

---

[533] *Moore Large & Co Ltd v Hermes Credit & Guarantee Plc* [2003] Lloyd's Rep. I.R. 315.

[534] *Kammins Ballrooms Co Ltd v Zenith Investments (Torquay) Ltd* [1971] A.C. 850; *Motor Oil Hellas (Corinth) Refineries SA v Shipping Corp of India (The Kanchenjunga)* [1990] 1 Lloyd's Rep. 391; *Kosmar Villa Holidays Plc v Trustees of Syndicate 1243* [2008] Lloyd's Rep. I.R. 489; *Lexington Insurance Co v Multinacional de Seguros SA* [2009] Lloyd's Rep. I.R. 1.

[535] *Orakpo v Barclays Insurance Services Ltd* [1995] L.R.L.R. 443, where there was no unequivocal representation. See also *Insurance Corp of the Channel Islands Ltd v McHugh & Royal Hotel Ltd* [1997] L.R.L.R. 94, where the independent existence of waiver and estoppel was recognised. In that case, there was found not to have been any unequivocal representation by the insurers.

[536] *Callaghan & Hedges v Thompson* [2000] Lloyd's Rep. I.R. 125.

sight appears to render estoppel a serious threat to insurers. However, it is to be borne in mind that the form of estoppel in question, promissory estoppel, based on the insurer's promise as to his future behaviour operates, only in equity. In accordance with the general principle applicable to equitable remedies, promissory estoppel can be relied upon only by an assured who has acted equitably. Accordingly, if the assured has sought to mislead the insurer, and in particular if there has been deliberate fraud in the presentation of the risk, a plea of equitable promissory estoppel against the insurer will not be available to him.[537]

Other forms of estoppel may also be pressed into use. Estoppel by convention may arise where the parties to a contract treat the contract as valid and binding and act accordingly: there is no need for any representation here, and a common mistaken assumption may be enough.[538] A further possibility is issue estoppel, which arises where a point has been disposed of in a set of proceedings, for it then becomes impossible for that point to be reargued in later proceedings. In *Insurance Corp of the Channel Islands v Royal Hotel (No.2)*[539] Mance J. held that the principle was somewhat wider, and extended to the situation in which a point which could have been taken by a party in the first set of legal proceedings is not taken; in such circumstances it is not open to that party to take the point in a later set of proceedings. Applying this approach, Mance J. held that insurers who had not contested the validity of a material damage policy in arbitration proceedings, could not do so in subsequent judicial proceedings.

6–099   **Effect of actual avoidance.** The fact that an insurer has purported to avoid the policy does not preclude a finding of waiver or estoppel against the insurer if its conduct thereafter is equivocal. Thus, if there is correspondence between the assured and the insurer following the avoidance, and it is apparent from the correspondence that the decision is not final, then the insurer may not be able to rely upon the avoidance. Equally, if the insurer takes the decision to continue to collect the assured's premium after avoidance, or otherwise carries out its obligations under the policy, waiver may be found.[540] It must nevertheless be emphasised that the insurer's subjective intentions are irrelevant to a finding of waiver: if the insurer purports to avoid while intending to revisit its decision at some later point but gives no objective indication that the matter is under consideration then there can be no waiver.

On the assumption that there has been a purported avoidance, subsequent equivocal conduct on the part of the insurer which indicates that the decision may be revised, while capable of giving rise to a waiver, will not amount to a reinstatement of the policy. The conditions for reinstatement are far more onerous, and will only be satisfied if the insurer specifically indicates that the policy is to be reinstated.[541]

6–100   **Damages where right to avoid is lost.** Given that the remedy for misrepresentation or non-disclosure is avoidance rather than damages, it becomes possible to argue that, if the right to avoid is not open to insurers, then a fallback remedy in damages might arise. It has never been suggested that this can happen where the

---

[537] *Baghbadrani v Commercial Union Assurance Co Plc* [2000] Lloyd's Rep. I.R. 94; *Persimmon Homes Ltd v Great Lakes Reinsurance (UK) Plc* [2010] EWHC 1705 (Comm).

[538] The elements of estoppel by convention are set out in the judgment of Goff J. in *Amalgamated Investment & Property Co Ltd v Texas Commerce International Bank Ltd* [1982] Q.B. 84.

[539] *Insurance Corp of the Channel Islands v Royal Hotel (No.2)* [1998] Lloyd's Rep. I.R. 151.

[540] Both of these possibilities were found to be operating in *Drake Insurance Co v Provident Insurance Co* [2004] Lloyd's Rep. I.R. 277.

[541] *Drake Insurance Co v Provident Insurance Co* [2004] Lloyd's Rep. I.R. 277.

right to avoid has been lost by operation of law, e.g. where the insurers are, by their conduct, taken to have waived the right of avoidance. Indeed, it is clear from *Pan Atlantic Insurance Co Ltd v Pine Top Insurance Co Ltd*[542] that insurers do not have the right to affirm the contract and refuse to pay a claim: their choice is all or nothing. Nevertheless, there is no objection in principle to a policy term under which insurers agree, in the event of a breach of duty of utmost good faith by the assured, not to avoid the policy but to refuse to pay the claim and to seek damages for any consequential loss. Alternatively, the right to avoid may be waived with an express right of recourse against any individual in the assured's organisation who has been guilty of fraud leading to the loss.[543] The further question is whether an agreement by insurers to exclude their right to avoid impliedly carries with it a right to damages in lieu. This argument was considered and firmly rejected by Aikens J. in *HIH Casualty and General Insurance Ltd v Chase Manhattan Bank.*[544] In that case a "Truth of Statement" clause was held by the learned judge not to operate as a waiver of the insurers' right to avoid, but Aikens J. expressed the view[545] that, had it done so, it would not have given an implicit right to damages in lieu of avoidance. Aikens J. pointed out that if the parties chose to exclude the only remedy recognised by the law, it could not be the case that an alternative remedy, not recognised by the law, could thereby arise. The Court of Appeal reversed Aikens J's construction of the clause,[546] and held that it did to a large extent exclude the right of avoidance, but accepted Aikens J's view that such exclusion did not give rise to a right in damages which would otherwise not have existed.

7. DURATION OF THE DUTY OF UTMOST GOOD FAITH

Duty terminates at date of contract

Effect of making contract. The accepted principle is that the duty of utmost good faith, in so far as it relates to facts material to the underwriting of the risk, comes to an end at the date on which the contract is concluded. This principle is embodied in s.18(1) of the 1906 Act which states that the duty of disclosure continues until the contract is concluded, and in s.20(6) which provides that a representation may be withdrawn or corrected before the contract is concluded.[547] Prior to the date on which the contract is made, the assured remains under a duty to disclose material facts which have come to his attention, or to correct previous statements made to the insurer which to his knowledge have become false, and if he does so the insurers have no right to avoid the policy. Equally, once the contract is made, facts which are subsequently discovered but not disclosed by the assured cannot be material and any false statements made by the assured after the relevant date are necessarily immaterial as they cannot affect

6–101

---

[542] *Pan Atlantic Insurance Co Ltd v Pine Top Insurance Co Ltd* [1994] 3 All E.R. 581.

[543] *Kumar v AGF Insurance Ltd* [1998] 4 All E.R. 788.

[544] *HIH Casualty and General Insurance Ltd v Chase Manhattan Bank* [2001] Lloyd's Rep. I.R. 191.

[545] Relying on the rejection of the availability of damages in *Banque Keyser Uliman SA v Skandia (UK) Insurance Co Ltd* [1990] Q.B. 665.

[546] *HIH Casualty and General Insurance Ltd v Chase Manhattan Bank* [2001] Lloyd's Rep. I.R. 702.

[547] Based on *Edwards v Footner* (1808) 1 Camp. 530. See *Mander v Commercial Union Assurance Co Plc* [1998] Lloyd's Rep. I.R. 93.

the insurer's decision as to whether or not to take the risk and as to the appropriate premium.

6–102 *Correction of statements.* The principles applicable to correction were considered in the judgment of Clarke L.J. in *Assicurazioni Generali SpA v Arab Insurance Group (BSC)*,[548] where it was stated that the assured was up to the date of the making of the contract under a duty to correct any false statements made in the course of his presentation of the risk or to disclose any material facts coming to his attention.[549] Such correction had to be in a manner such that the corrected picture was fairly presented to the insurer, and it was not enough for the assured, having made a false statement, to present the insurer with further information from which the insurer could by acting with reasonable care ascertain the true position, as there was a need for the assured to act with clarity. Once there has been a correction, it can no longer be said that that there is any material misrepresentation or any inducement. There are numerous reported instances of this point. Thus, where the assured accurately states before his proposal has been accepted that no other insurer has refused to issue him with a fire policy, and he is subsequently notified of a refusal to renew by another insurer, his failure to disclose that information amounts to breach of his duty of utmost good faith.[550] Again, where the applicant for a life policy suffers a deterioration in his health between the date of his proposal and the date of the insurer's acceptance of the risk, this must be disclosed to the insurer.[551] Similarly, in the case of a construction policy, any alteration in the intended foundation system for the building which has occurred between proposal and policy must be disclosed to the insurer.[552] The rule applies to statements of intention, and if the assured changes his mind before the contract is complete, he must inform his insurers, though he is not bound to do so if he changes his mind subsequently.[553]

6–103 *Post-contract disclosure or misrepresentation.* Once the risk has been accepted, the fact that the risk has increased ceases to be a material fact and the assured is not required, as a matter of the general law, to disclose any change in circumstances.[554] Equally, if the assured makes a false statement as to the risk following the formation of the insurance contract, that misstatement is not a material fact for the purposes of the duty of utmost good faith. These conclusions flow from the principles that a fact is material only if it is relevant to the fixing of the premium or the taking of the risk[555] and from the related common law rule that the assured is perfectly free to increase the risk under the policy,[556] subject only to express conditions which either prohibit such increase or require the

---

[548] *Assicurazioni Generali SpA v Arab Insurance Group (BSC)* [2003] Lloyd's Rep. I.R. 131.

[549] *Crane v Hannover Ruckversicherungs-Aktiengesellschaft* [2008] EWHC 3165 (Comm).

[550] *Re Yager and Guardian Assurance Co* (1912) 108 L.T. 38.

[551] *British Equitable Insurance v Great Western Ry Co* (1869) 38 L.J. Ch. 314. See also *Morrison v Muspratt* (1827) 4 Bing. 60; *Canning v Farquhar* (1886) L.R. 16 Q.B.D. 727; *Golding v Royal London Auxiliary Insurance* (1914) 30 T.L.R. 350; *Watt v Southern Cross Assurance Co Ltd* [1927] N.Z.L.R. 106.

[552] *St Paul Fire & Marine Insurance Co (UK) Ltd v McConnell Dowell Constructors Ltd* [1993] 2 Lloyd's Rep. 503.

[553] *Benham v United Guarantee and Life Assurance Co* (1852) 7 Ex. 744.

[554] *Crane v Hannover Ruckversicherungs-Aktiengesellschaft* [2008] EWHC 3165 (Comm).

[555] 1906 Act ss.18(2) and 20(2).

[556] *Toulmin v Inglis* (1808) 1 Camp. 421; *Shaw v Robberds* (1837) 6 Ad. & El. 75; *Pim v Reid* (1843) 6 Man. & G. 1; *Thompson v Hopper* (1856) 6 El. & Bl. 172; *Mitchell Conveyor & Transport Co Ltd v Pulbrook* (1933) 45 Ll. L. Rep. 239.

assured to notify the insurer of any such increase,[557] to the overriding rule that a fundamental change to the nature of the risk operates to discharge the insurer from all liability under the policy as the risk being run is not that which was set out in the contract[558] and, in the case of marine voyage policies, to the old rule that the risk terminates automatically if there is deviation, delay or change of voyage.[559]

Thus, an assured who truthfully states that no other insurer has rejected an application for a policy on his life is not in breach of duty if a rejection is notified to him after the policy has been issued to him.[560] If the name of the vessel on which the insured cargo is to be carried is misstated,[561] or if false information as to the installation of a sprinker in the insured building is given to the underwriters, after the risk has incepted, there is no right to avoid.[562]

The date of the contract. The relevant date for the purpose of the duty of utmost **6–104** good faith is the date at which the contract is concluded, i.e. when offer and acceptance coincide.[563] When this occurs will depend upon the formation procedure adopted. Thus, where the policy is initiated by a proposal or other application, the policy will be concluded at the date at which the proposal is accepted by the insurer, and where the insurance is taken out with Lloyd's underwriters, the relevant date is that on which the slip was scratched. If the insurer's offer is in the form of a standing offer, to be accepted by the assured at a later date, then if the assured accepts the offer before becoming aware of material facts, there is no breach of the duty of disclosure even if the risk itself is not to attach until some later date.[564] Nevertheless, it remains possible for the parties to postpone, by express provision, the date at which the duty of disclosure is to come to an end. One common approach is for the commencement of the insurer's liability to be postponed until the first premium has been paid; such a clause was held, in *Looker v Law Union and Rock Insurance Co Ltd*[565] to have the effect of extending the assured's duty of disclosure as to his health until that date. In *Alliss Chalmers v Maryland Fidelity and Deposit Co*[566] the relevant clause, which prevented the insurer from being on risk until the policy had been delivered to the assured, in the same way extended the assured's duty of

---

[557] Such terms are in any event construed narrowly: *Glen v Lewis* (1853) 8 Ex. 607; *Baxendale v Harvey* (1859) 4 H. & N. 445; *Shanley v Allied Traders Insurance Co* (1925) 21 Ll LR. 195; *Mint Securities v Blair* [1982] 1 Lloyd's Rep. 188; *Exchange Theatre Ltd v Iron Trades Mutual Insurance Co Ltd* [1983] 1 Lloyd's Rep. 674; *Kausar v Eagle Star Insurance Co Ltd* [2000] Lloyd's Rep. I.R. 154.

[558] *Hadenfayre Ltd v British National Insurance Ltd* [1984] 2 Lloyd's Rep. 393.

[559] Now enshrined in ss.45 to 49 of the Marine Insurance Act 1906. In these situations the vessel may be "held covered" despite breach.

[560] *Whitwell v Autocar Fire and Accident Insurance Co Ltd* (1927) 27 Ll. L.R. 418.

[561] *Ionides v Pacific Fire and Marine Insurance Co* (1872) L.R. 7 Q.B. 517. See also: *Cory v Patton* (1874) L.R. 9 Q.B. 577; *Lishman v Northern Maritime Insurance Co* (1875) L.R. 30 P. 179; *Niger Co v Guardian Assurance Co* (1922) 13 Ll. L.R. 75; *Iron Trades Mutual Insurance Co Ltd v Companhia De Segums Imperio* [1992] Re L.R. 213; *Bank of Nova Scotia v Hellenic Mutual War Risks Association (Bermuda) Ltd (The Good Luck)* [1988] 1 Lloyd's Rep. 514; *New Hampshire Insurance Co v MGN Ltd* [1997] L.R.L.R. 24.

[562] *Sirius International Insurance Corp v Oriental Assurance Corp* [1999] Lloyd's Rep. I.R. 343.

[563] *Adams v Lindsell* (1818) 1 B. & Ald. 681.

[564] *Bonner v Cox Dedicated Corporate Member Ltd* [2006] Lloyd's Rep. I.R. 385, affirming [2005] Lloyd's Rep. 569.

[565] *Looker v Law Union and Rock Insurance Co Ltd* [1928] 1 K.B. 554. See also *Harrington v Pearl Life Assurance Co Ltd* (1914) 30 T.L.R. 613.

[566] *Alliss Chalmers v Maryland Fidelity and Deposit Co* (1916) 114 L.T. 433.

disclosure until the specified condition had been satisfied. Similarly, if the insurer specifically requires the disclosure of information between the date of the contract and the commencement of the risk, failure to disclose discharges the insurer.

6–105   *Renewals.* The renewal of an insurance policy, other than a life policy, is as a matter of law to be regarded as the creation of a fresh agreement. Consequently, the duty of utmost good faith is reimposed upon the assured at every renewal date, and the assured is, therefore, under a duty to inform the insurer of any material facts which have arisen during the currency of the contract to be renewed[567] or to correct information which has become false.[568] Failure by the assured to adhere to the duty renders the renewal policy voidable, but the original policy is left unaffected and outstanding claims under it must be met in the usual way even though it is the case that the breach of duty has taken place during the currency of the original policy.[569] The difficulty as far as the assured is concerned is that it will be rare for a new proposal to be required by the insurer, so that he will be under a positive duty to disclose material facts without the aid of any real prompt from the insurer other than a notice that the premium is due, possibly accompanied by a bare warning that material facts are to be disclosed.

This principle does not apply to life policies. Insurance on a life is not regarded as a periodically renewable agreement, but is rather a long-term agreement which may be maintained in force by the payment of periodic premiums. Were the position otherwise, the insurer would be at liberty to refuse to renew a policy when the assured had become aged or had developed a serious illness. Personal accident policies are, however, annual agreements.[570] Moreover, it is at least arguable that life policies which are pure indemnities—such as keyman policies and insurances by a creditor on the life of a debtor—are also to be regarded as annual contracts, although there is no authority on this point. The termination of a policy early, followed by its reinstatement, will also amount to a new contract which attracts a fresh duty of disclosure relating to material facts which have arisen prior to the reinstatement.[571]

The termination of a policy early, followed by its reinstatement, will also amount to a new contract which attracts a fresh duty of disclosure relating to material facts which have arisen prior to the reinstatement.[572] By contrast, where a material false representation has been made in year 1, and the policy is renewed in year 2 without the false statement being corrected, the year 2 policy is voidable either because the representation is a continuing one or because the assured is under a duty to disclose the fact of his earlier misrepresentation.[573] It will not normally matter which of these is correct, although if the assured was unaware of the fact that a false statement had been made in year 1 then he cannot be guilty

---

[567] An excellent illustration is provided by *Lambert v Co-operative Insurance Society* [1975] 2 Lloyd's Rep. 485. See also: *Howells v Dominion Insurance Co Ltd* Unreported, 1999; *James v CGU Insurance Plc* [2002] Lloyd's Rep. I.R. 206; *Moore Large & Co Ltd v Hermes Credit and Guarantee Plc* [2003] Lloyd's Rep. I.R. 315.

[568] See *ERC Frankona Reinsurance v American National Insurance Co* [2006] Lloyd's Rep. I.R. 157, where it was assumed that failure to correct a statement which had become untrue by the time of renewal amounted to non-disclosure, and accordingly there was a breach of duty only if the assured was aware that the earlier statement had been made.

[569] *K/S Merc-Skandia XXXXII v Certain Lloyd's Underwriters* [2001] Lloyd's Rep. I.R. 802.

[570] *Re Marshall and Scottish Employers Liability Co* (1901) 85 L.T. 757.

[571] *Mundi v Lincoln Assurance Ltd* [2006] Lloyd's Rep. I.R. 353, a life policy.

[572] *Mundi v Lincoln Assurance Ltd* [2006] Lloyd's Rep. I.R. 353.

[573] *The Moonacre* [1992] 2 Lloyd's Rep. 501; *Hill v Citadel Insurance Co Ltd* [1997] L.R.L.R. 167; *Limit No.2 Ltd v Axa Versicherung AG* [2008] Lloyd's Rep. I.R. 330.

of failing to disclose it in year 2: in that situation the continuing misrepresentation approach would appear to come to the insurers' rescue. The original statement must nevertheless be one that may be regarded as having a continuing effect, and this may not be the case if that statement was merely one of intention. In *Limit No.2 Ltd v Axa Versicherung AG*[574] brokers acting for the reinsured made a representation to reinsurers in negotiations leading to a treaty in 1996 that the reinsured had the intention of normally requiring policyholders to retain for their own account the first £500,000 of any claim. In fact the reinsured had no such intention. The treaty was renewed in 1997, some 19 months later, but this statement was not repeated. The Court of Appeal held that the statement was not a continuing one and the 1997 treaty could not be avoided. Longmore L.J., giving the leading judgment, noted that a representation of intention was not to be treated as lasting indefinitely and related only to the time that it was made. For the same reason, there was no non-disclosure of the lapse of the intention. Longmore L.J. commented as follows:

> "It must also be remembered how powerful the remedy of avoidance is in the hands of an insurer or reinsurer. The entirety of a contract can be avoided for a wholly innocent misrepresentation provided it is material to the risk in the eyes of a prudent underwriter. If the contract is for 12 months (or, as here, 19 months) that is a very stark remedy. I do not, for my part, consider that a court should struggle to hold that everything said at inception is to be impliedly repeated on renewal."

These views were expressed in the context of a representation of intention, and it may be that a stricter test is more appropriate than to a representation of fact. However, Longmore L.J.'s warning makes it clear that blind reliance on a previous presentation is not always appropriate.

Extension of the policy. The duty of utmost good faith will also be relevant after **6–106** the making of the contract where the assured seeks to obtain additional cover, and applies to the insurer for the appropriate extension but fails to disclose material facts relating to the application.[575] Any endorsement to the cover effected in this way is to be treated as a new contract to which the duty of utmost good faith applies. This position is the same in principle even where the insurance itself establishes the mechanism for the extension of cover. London market marine insurance policies contain "held covered" clauses, under which the assured is entitled to obtain an extension of his cover where particular eventualities occur, subject to giving prompt notice to the insurer and paying any additional premium demanded by the insurer. Held covered clauses of this type operate where the assured has misdescribed the insured subject matter or has broken a warranty or, in the case of a voyage policy, has changed voyage.

The cases are clear that a duty of disclosure attaches to the application to the insurer for extended cover[576] and the principle underlying these cases, that the duty of utmost good faith applies to applications for extended coverage, was confirmed in *K/S Merc-Skandia XXXXII v Certain Lloyd's Underwriters*[577] and

---

[574] *Limit No.2 Ltd v Axa Versicherung AG* [2009] Lloyd's Rep. I.R. 396.

[575] *Lishman v Northern Maritime Insurance Co* (1875) L.R. 10 C.P. 179; *Iron Trades Mutual Insurance Co Ltd v Companhia de Seguros Imperio* [1992] Re L.R. 213; *Gaughan v Tony McDonagh & Co* [2005] EWHC 739 (Comm); *Bolton v New Zealand Insurance Co* [1995] 1 N.Z.L.R. 224.

[576] *Liberian Insurance Agency Inc v Mosse* [1977] 2 Lloyd's Rep. 560. Cf. *Overseas Commodities Ltd v Style* [1958] 1 Lloyd's Rep. 546.

[577] *K/S Merc-Skandia XXXXII v Certain Lloyd's Underwriters* [2001] Lloyd's Rep. I.R. 802.

by the House of Lords in *The Star Sea*.[578] In *Fraser Shipping Ltd v Colton*[579] the assured sought an endorsement from the insurers which would have permitted the insured vessel to change its voyage and head for a destination different to that specified in the policy. The insurers agreed to the endorsement, ignorant of the fact that the change of voyage had previously been put into effect. The Court of Appeal held that the fact withheld was material and that the assured was in breach of the duty of disclosure. Potter L.J. stated that the insurers were entitled "to avoid the policy, as varied by the endorsement." The better view of this statement is that the endorsement alone was avoided, and not that the entire policy as amended was avoided either from the date of the endorsement or from the date of the policy's original inception: in *K/S Merc-Skandia* Longmore L.J. stated unequivocally that there had never been a suggestion that in this type of case the assured's breach of duty avoided the entire policy, and that only the extended cover would be voidable even though the breach occurred during the currency of the main original policy.[580] The same approach is to be found in *Limit No.2 Ltd v Axa Versicherung AG*,[581] in which a temporal extension to an earlier treaty, which took effect as an endorsement to the treaty, was regarded as being capable of avoidance separately from the treaty itself if it, but not the treaty, had been induced by misrepresentation or non-disclosure. Again, in *AC Ward & Sons Ltd v Catlin (Five) (No.2)*[582] the assured obtained property insurance cover for two warehouses. The insurers agreed to extend the cover to a third warehouse, but on the basis that they would not be liable for theft outside business hours unless the goods were kept in a secure store. The insurers subsequently agreed to provide such cover on the basis that certain Risk Improvement Requirements (RIR) were complied with and, following a statement by the assured's brokers that the RIR had been satisfied, the insurers amended the endorsement so that out-of-hours cover for theft became an insured risk. The broker's statement was inaccurate, and it was held by Flaux J. that, given that the misrepresentation was both material and had induced the insurers to extend cover, they had the right to avoid the variation to the endorsement so that there was no cover for out-of-hours theft for goods not kept in a secure store. The remainder of the policy was not affected by such avoidance.

A further point to be made here is that if the modification does take effect as an endorsement to the policy, it may—depending upon its nature—be treated as having been merged into the policy. If that is the case, then if the policy itself is capable of being avoided for breach of duty then the endorsement will necessarily be avoided with it. An endorsement which extends the risks covered or in some way modifies the earlier wording must necessarily form a part of the original policy, as it cannot have any independent effect. By contrast, if the endorsement is an extension of the duration of the original policy, then it is at least arguable that it is wholly independent so that avoidance of the original policy does not affect the endorsement in the unlikely event that the matters tainting the original policy have not been corrected at the date of the endorsement. In *Limit No.2 Ltd v Axa Versicherung AG* a reinsurance treaty entered into for a year was extended by endorsement by a further seven months. The Court

---

[578] *The Star Sea* [2001] Lloyd's Rep. I.R. 247.

[579] *Fraser Shipping Ltd v Colton* [1997] 1 Lloyd's Rep. 586.

[580] Applied in *Groupama Insurance Co Ltd v Overseas Partners Re Ltd* Unreported, 2003. See also *O'Kane v Jones* [2005] Lloyd's Rep. I.R. 174.

[581] *Limit No.2 Ltd v Axa Versicherung AG* [2009] Lloyd's Rep. I.R. 396.

[582] *AC Ward & Sons Ltd v Catlin (Five) (No.2)* [2009] EWHC 3122 (Comm). Cf. *Bolton v New Zealand Insurance Co Ltd* [1995] 1 N.Z.L.R. 224 (extension of marine policy to cover ocean cruises imposed a new duty of disclosure in relation to the identity fo the crew).

of Appeal held that the effect of the endorsement was to convert a 12-month treaty into a 19 month treaty, so that avoidance of the former automatically avoided the latter.

If the held covered clause provides for automatic coverage on a pro rata premium—as is the case under a time policy which lapses before the insured vessel has reached its destination and the vessel is missing or in distress—there is arguably no duty of utmost good faith where the assured seeks to invoke that extension, as the premium has been agreed in advance and the insurer can be taken to have agreed to run that additional risk in the event that the assured should require him to do so. As was said by Longmore L.J. in *K/S Merc-Skandia*, any principle that the assured has to make full disclosure on the exercise of rights which he has under the original contract is "somewhat puzzling".

A general continuing duty of good faith?

The Litsion Pride.[583] The idea that the duty of utmost good faith extends beyond the making of the contract and into the relationship between the insurer and assured has its genesis in the decision of Hirst J. in *The Litsion Pride*. The vessel, in this case, had been insured by the defendant underwriters against war risks, the policy providing that in the event of the vessel entering into any one of a number of "additional premium areas", for the most part war zones, notice was to be given to the underwriters "as soon as practicable" and an upward adjustment of the premium was to be made to represent the duration of the vessel's presence in the zone. On August 2, 1982, the vessel entered the Strait of Hormuz, a particularly hazardous zone in the light of the then prevailing Iran–Iraq war and, on August 9, 1982, she was destroyed by a missile fired from an Iraqi helicopter. On August 11, 1982, the owners brokers received a telex from the owners stating that a letter informing the brokers of the imminent entry of the Litsion Pride into a war zone had been written on August 2, 1982 but by oversight not sent: that letter, dated August 2, 1982, was received by the brokers on August 12, 1982 and was in due course submitted to the underwriters. A subsequent claim on the policy by the mortgagees, the assignees of the benefits of the policy, was rejected by the underwriters on the basis of the owners' fraud and breach of duty of utmost good faith in failing to notify an increase of risk in accordance with the terms of the policy, and in attempting to slip the vessel through a war zone without paying the necessary increased premium. Hirst J. concluded that the evidence pointed towards fraud, although also expressed his views on the alternative good faith defence. Hirst J. held that the argument was a sound one, and the principle to be derived from previous authorities was that communications between the assured and the insurer after the making of the contract were subject to a duty of continuing good faith founded on an implied term which required the assured to disclose all material facts and to avoid misrepresentation of material facts. Such breach gave the insurers the right to avoid the policy *ab initio* or, in the alternative, the right to treat themselves as discharged from liability for any claim made without full disclosure.

Hirst J. relied upon three principles to reach this conclusion. First, the learned judge pointed out that s.17 of the 1906 Act provides that: "A contract of marine insurance is a contract based upon the utmost good faith, and if the utmost good faith be not observed by either party, the contract may be avoided by either party". Although there is no specific mention of a continuing duty in the Act, it

6–107

---

[583] *Black King Shipping Corp v Massie (The Litsion Pride)* [1985] 1 Lloyd's Rep. 437.

had previously been suggested[584] that ss.18–20 in a majority of the Court of Appeal expressed the view that ss.18 and 20—dealing with pre-contractual disclosure and misrepresentation—were illustrations of a broader principle. The difficulty here is that the 1906 Act was intended to codify the law and there was no pre-1906 authority to support the proposition.

Secondly, there were various cases in which the courts had, after a loss, ordered a marine assured to provide the insurers with the ships' papers.[585] The power to do so was contained in RSC Ord.72 r.10, a provision which Hirst J. classified as being based on utmost good faith. In fact this appears to have been merely a point of procedure rather than any application of a principle of good faith. In *The Star Sea*[586] Lord Hobhouse commented that the Order was probably based on the need of the common law courts to establish jurisdiction to make an order for discovery.[587] The procedure had, in Lord Hobhouse's experience, been obsolete for many years and was, in any event, of an entirely different character to a post-contractual duty of utmost good faith[588] in relation both to its extent and its enforcement, given that enforcement was in the discretion of the court, required a court order and breach had no consequences on the validity of the contract or the right to claim under the policy.[589]

Thirdly, the held covered cases,[590] in which the assured had been held able to exercise rights under a held covered clause, and to obtain extended coverage on offer under the contract by giving notice to the insurers and paying any additional premium, were regarded as being founded on utmost good faith. However, there is nothing surprising or contrary to principle in the assured being required to disclose information when seeking the benefits of a held covered clause, given that the objective is to obtain additional insurance from the insurer.

It should also be said that the legal basis for the continuing duty—an implied term in the insurance contract—cannot stand, as it has long been clear, and was emphasised by the House of Lords in *Pan Atlantic Insurance Co Ltd v Pine Top*

---

[584] *Container Transport International Inc v Oceanus Mutual Underwriting Association (Bermuda) Ltd* [1984] 1 Lloyd's Rep. 476.

[585] *China Traders Insurance Co v Royal Exchange Assurance Corp* [1898] 2 Q.B. 187; *Boulton v Houlder Brothers & Co* [1904] 1 K.B. 784; *Probatina Shipping Co Ltd v Sun Insurance Office Ltd* [1974] Q.B. 635; *North British Rubber Co v Cheetham* (1938) 61 Ll. L.R. 337; *Keevil and Keevil Ltd v Boag* (1940) 67 Ll. L.R. 263; *Graham Joint Stock Shipping Co Ltd v Motor Union Insurance Co* [1922] 2 K.B. 563; *Leon v Casey* [1932] 2 K.B. 576.

[586] *The Star Sea* [2001] Lloyd's Rep. I.R. 247.

[587] Lord Hobhouse cited, as authority for this proposition: *Goldschmidt v Marryat* (1809) 1 Camp. 559; *Twizell v Allen* (1839) 5 M. & W. 337; *Graham Joint Stock Shipping Co Ltd v Motor Union Insurance Co Ltd* [1922] 1 K.B. 563.

[588] This view of RSC Ord.72 r.10 was rejected by Longmore L.J. in *K/S Merc-Skandia XXXXII v Certain Lloyd's Underwriters* [2001] Lloyd's Rep. I.R. 802. In his words: "There is a certain irony about this conclusion. When Sir Mackenzie Chalmers published the second and last edition of his *Digest of the Law of the Marine Insurance* (1903), on which the Act as ultimately passed was to be based, he included what is now s.17 without any explanation of how (if at all) he envisaged any post-contract requirement of good faith would work in practice. When he published the first edition of his work *The Marine Insurance Act 1906* (1907) he added a note in relation to post-contract good faith, instancing the order of the court for ship's papers as the example of the operation of post-contract good faith. Thus does the whirligig of time exercise its reversals".

[589] This provision, which was in any event available only in the case of marine insurance (*Henderson v Underwriting and Agency Association Ltd* [1891] 1 Q.B. 557, *Village Main Reef Gold Mining Co Ltd v Stearns* (1900) 5 Com. Cas. 246), was initially not re-enacted in the Civil Procedure Rules, which superseded the Rules of the Supreme Court in 1999, although the provision was subsequently reinstated as CPR 58.14.

[590] The authorities relied on were *Overseas Commodities Ltd v Style* [1958] 1 Lloyd's Rep. 546 and *Liberian Insurance Agency Inc v Mosse* [1977] 2 Lloyd's Rep. 560.

Insurance Co Ltd[591] that the duty of utmost good faith is not based on any implied term and arises ex contractu as a matter of law.

Although the principle of continuing utmost good faith espoused in *The Litsion Pride* rested upon very shaky foundations, its existence was accepted in a series of subsequent decisions although in very few of these cases was unequivocal support given to Hirst J.'s analysis. It was thus suggested that the fraudulent grounding of a vessel followed by its total loss in a genuine fire would entitle the insurers to avoid the policy in the event of a claim based on the grounding.[592] Most of the cases involved claims made by the assured in the course of which various facts relating to the loss were not disclosed or were misrepresented, although in a few instances there were allegations of breach of the continuing duty of utmost good faith outside the claims process. Only in the case of claims was there held to be a continuing duty,[593] and even then only if there was a direct link between the claim and the assured's conduct.[594] The authorities for the most part accepted that fraud, or at the very least recklessness, on the part of the assured was required to bring the duty of utmost good faith into play,[595] although others held that Hirst J.'s formulation was correct and that mere culpability, and possibly no more than negligence, would suffice.[596] Doubts were also expressed as to the correctness of Hirst J.'s formulation of the remedies for breach of the continuing duty, and in particular whether *ab initio* avoidance was the correct solution.[597] Shortly before the decision of the House of Lords in *The Star Sea* Aikens J. in *K/S Merc-Skandia XXXXII v Certain Lloyd's Underwriters*[598] undertook a detailed analysis of the authorities decided in the wake of *The Litsion Pride*, and concluded that there was a post-contractual duty of utmost good faith only where the assured sought to extend coverage or where the assured made a

---

[591] *Pan Atlantic Insurance Co Ltd v Pine Top Insurance Co Ltd* [1994] 3 All E.R. 581.

[592] *Continental Illinois National Bank of Chicago v Alliance Assurance Co Ltd (The Captain Panagos)* [1986] 2 Lloyd's Rep. 470. See also *Bank of Nova Scotia v Hellenic Mutual War Risks Association (Bermuda) Ltd (The Good Luck)* [1989] 2 Lloyd's Rep. 238.

[593] *La Banque Financière de la Cité v Westgate Insurance* [1990] 1 All E.R. 947; *New Hampshire Insurance Co v MGN Ltd* [1997] L.R.L.R. 24; *Royal Boskalis Westminster NV v Mountain* [1997] L.R.L.R. 523. See, however, *Hussain v Brown (No.2)* Unreported, 1996, where the view accepted was that any form of contractual obligation to convey information potentially attracted the duty of utmost good faith.

[594] *Total Graphics Ltd v AGF Insurance Ltd* [1997] 1 Lloyd's Rep. 599; *Alfred McAlpine Plc v BAI (Run off) Ltd* [2000] Lloyd's Rep. I.R. 352.

[595] *Bucks Printing Press Ltd v Prudential Assurance Co* [2000] C.L.Y. 880; *Diggens v Sun Alliance & London Insurance Plc* Unreported, 1994; *Trans-Pacific Insurance Co (Australia) Ltd v Grand Union Insurance Co Ltd* (1990) 6 A.N.Z. Insurance Cases 60–949; *Gate v Sun Alliance Insurance Ltd* Unreported, 1993 NZCA; *Parker & Heard Ltd v Generali Assicurazioni SpA* Unreported, 1988; *Orakpo v Barclays Insurance Services Ltd* [1995] L.R.L.R. 443; *Royal Boskalis Westminster NV v Mountain* [1997] L.R.L.R. 523; *Galloway v Guardian Royal Exchange (UK) Ltd* [1999] Lloyd's Rep. I.R. 209; *Baghbadrani v Commercial Union Assurance Co Plc* [2000] Lloyd's Rep. I.R. 94; *Alfred McAlpine Plc v BAI (Run-off) Ltd* [2000] Lloyd's Rep. I.R. 352.

[596] *Hussain v Brown (No.2)* Unreported, 1996; *Transthene Packaging Co Ltd v Royal Insurance (UK) Ltd* [1996] L.R.L.R. 32. For acceptance of *The Litsion Pride* in other jurisdictions, see: *NSW Medical Defence Union Ltd v Transport Industries Insurance Co Ltd* (1984) N.S.W.L.R. 107; *GIO Insurance v Leighton Contractors* Unreported, 1995 (NSW).

[597] *Orakpo v Barclays Insurance Services Ltd* [1995] L.R.L.R. 443, where a variety of views were expressed; *Insurance Corp of the Channel Islands Ltd v Royal Hotel Ltd* [1997] L.R.L.R. 24; *Ford v Bradford & Bingley Building Society* Unreported, 1997; *New Hampshire Insurance Co v MGN Ltd* [1997] L.R.L.R. 24.

[598] *K/S Merc-Skandia XXXXII v Certain Lloyd's Underwriters* [2000] Lloyd's Rep. I.R. 694. His analysis was rejected by the Court of Appeal, [2001] Lloyd's Rep. I.R. 802, decided after *The Star Sea*: see below.

fraudulent claim. That was the state of the authorities when *The Star Sea* came before the House of Lords.

6–108 *The Star Sea.*[599] The vessel, a dry cargo carrier with refrigerated holds, was owned by a one-ship company managed by Kappa Maritime, an English company controlled by the Kollakis family. The vessel was refitted and repaired in 1989. The engine room and cargoholds were protected from fire by a full flood carbon dioxide extinguishing system, consisting of 44 CO_2 cylinders controlled by a single handle. The system depended for effective operation upon the sealing of the area into which gas was discharged. In the case of the engine room that meant, in particular, that as well as doors and skylights, the dampers had also to be closed. Prior to sailing in November 1989 the vessel underwent two inspections, and her fire safety certificate was renewed. She arrived in Zeebrugge in January 1990, and underwent a further inspection which discovered that there were various deficiencies, including a non-operational emergency fire pump. This was not repaired by the master despite instructions to do so. A fire broke out in the engine room of the vessel in May 1990. The master decided, after some delay, to use the CO_2 system to extinguish the fire, but the attempts failed due to defective dampers which would not close, failure to use the system immediately and also failure to discharge all of the gas at the same time. The result was that the Star Sea became a constructive total loss. The underwriters under a hull time policy rejected the owners' claim on the ground that the owners had broken their continuing duty of utmost good faith in making their claim[600] by failing to disclose the reports on the vessel issued in 1989, the second of which had noted that the dampers in the engine room were defective and could not be closed: privilege had been claimed for the reports. The underwriters also pointed to a letter written by the owners' brokers in the course of an attempt to negotiate a settlement, which was alleged to be misleading in relation to lessons learned from an earlier casualty suffered by another vessel, the Kastora, also controlled by the owners.

The House of Lords unanimously held that the owners were entitled to recover on the narrow grounds that: (1) any argument based on the continuing duty in respect of a claim required proof of fraud[601] but on the facts there was no evidence of any fraud; and (2) the continuing duty ceased to operate at the commencement of litigation, in that the disclosure of information after that point was a matter for rules of court and not for underwriters.

Their Lordships did not go as far as abolishing the continuing duty of utmost good faith, but held simply that, in the context of the presentation of claims, fraud was required. Their reluctance to go further was prompted for the most part by the consideration that s.17 was clear in its words and imposed a general duty of utmost good faith during the currency of the contract, a duty which Lord Hobhouse characterised as one of "fair dealing"[602] and which was flexible in that it took on a lesser form post-contract in order to maintain congruity between the rights of assured and insurer[603]:

> "It is not right to reason . . . from the existence of an extensive duty pre-contract positively to disclose all material facts to the conclusion that post-contract there is a

[599] *The Star Sea* [2001] Lloyd's Rep. I.R. 227.
[600] They also relied upon unseaworthiness: see Ch.24, below.
[601] See Lord Hobhouse at para.72 and Lord Scott at para.111.
[602] At para.48.
[603] At para.57.

similarly extensive obligation to disclose all facts which the insurer has an interest in knowing and which might affect his conduct. The courts have consistently set their face against allowing the assured's duty of good faith to be used by the insurer as an instrument for enabling the insurer himself to act in bad faith. An inevitable consequence in the post-contract situation is that the remedy of avoidance of the contract is in practical terms wholly one-sided. It is a remedy of value to the insurer and of disproportionate benefit to him; it enables him to escape, retrospectively the liability to indemnify which he has previously and validly undertaken . . .

[I]t is hard to think of circumstances where an assured will stand to benefit from the avoidance of the policy for something that has occurred after the contract has been entered into; the hypothesis of continuing dealings with each other will normally postulate some claim having been made by the assured under the policy."

A number of points may be derived from the judgments.

First, as to the assured's state of mind, their Lordships did not take the step of saying that only fraud brings the duty into play: that reservation was confined to fraudulent claims in so far as the rules relating to fraudulent claims were derived from the continuing duty of utmost good faith. However, Lord Scott did opine that "unless the assured has acted in bad faith he cannot . . . be in breach of a duty of good faith, utmost or otherwise".[604] Fraud would, therefore, appear to be the touchstone.

Secondly, the House of Lords did not define the matters to which the continuing duty might apply. Lord Hobhouse recognised that the scope of the duty was elusive, and went no further than stating that: (a) the duty did not extend to post-contractual increases of risk, as the cases were clear that the assured was entitled to increase the risk and was not, contract aside, required to disclose any such post-contract increase to insurers, and (b) the ship's papers cases had nothing to do with the continuing duty of utmost good faith.[605] Beyond that he refused to be drawn, although his Lordship would appear to have been of the view that there was relatively little scope for the duty. It would seem, however, that their Lordships did not wish to treat fraudulent claims as an aspect of good faith, and there are comments which indicate a severance of claims from good faith. Lord Hobhouse treated good faith and claims as distinct issues in his speech,[606] specifically stating that the right of the insurer to refuse to pay for a fraudulent claim derived from the rather different principle that a person should not benefit from his own wrong,[607] and Lord Scott similarly recognised that the rule against fraudulent claims might or might not derive from s.17.[608]

Thirdly, the question of remedy was analysed by their Lordships. Lord Hobhouse indicated that, at least as regards fraudulent claims, the appropriate remedy was not avoidance ab initio but rather the loss of the right to derive any benefit from or claim under the policy.[609] It followed from his approach that fraudulent claims were disallowed not by the continuing duty but rather by common law principles. Their Lordships' comments on the consequences of a breach of the continuing duty of utmost good faith under the general provisions of s.17 are less clear. Lord Scott refused to be drawn. There are nevertheless powerful indications in the speech of Lord Hobhouse that the matter should be dealt with purely on the basis of breach of contract. In his words[610]:

[604] At para.111.
[605] At paras 58 to 60.
[606] At para.64.
[607] At para.61.
[608] At para.111.
[609] At para.64.
[610] At para.52.

"A coherent scheme can be achieved by distinguishing a lack of good faith which is limited to the making of the contract itself (or some variation of it) and a lack of good faith during the performance of the contract which may prejudice the other party or cause him loss or destroy the continuing contractual relationship. The former derives from requirements of the law which pre-exist the contract and are not created by it, although they only become material because a contract has been entered into. The remedy is the right to elect to avoid the contract. The latter can derive from express or implied terms of the contract: it would be a contractual obligation arising from the contract and the remedies are the contractual remedies provided by the law of contract."

Finally, as to the duration of the duty, Lord Clyde rejected the argument that the duty of utmost good faith could continue beyond the commencement of litigation[611]: "the idea of a requirement for full disclosure superseding the procedural controls for discovery in litigation is curious and unattractive". Lord Hobhouse agreed: once the parties were in litigation it was the procedural rules which governed the extent of the disclosure in litigation, s.17. His Lordship's reasoning was that the commencement of proceedings crystallised the rights of the parties, and their relationship was from that point governed by the rules of procedure and the orders which the court made on the application of one or other party. Orders for disclosure were discretionary, and there were appropriate sanctions for non-compliance. The need for any other form of disclosure was, thus, removed.[612] Lord Scott inclined to the same view, but reserved his position as he was troubled by the possibility that a claim honestly begun was to be dishonestly continued, in particular where a claim was for the loss of goods which were found or otherwise restored to the owner. It is submitted that Lord Scott's reservation was overcautious. Once the assured has suffered a loss of goods for which he has made a claim, the goods are forfeited to the insurer under the salvage principle and the assured is fully entitled to pursue a claim for the policy moneys and indeed he has a vested right to them: what the assured cannot do, of course, is both retain the goods and make a claim and, if he does so, then plainly the insurers are entitled to take the goods. This, however, is nothing to do with utmost good faith.

As to *The Litsion Pride*,[613] Lord Hobhouse held that its overruling was inevitable. The decision could not be supported as a matter of law, in that the scope given to the duty of utmost good faith by Hirst J. decoupled the duty from what was set out in s.17 and in particular the remedy of avoidance. The issues in *The Litsion Pride* ought to have been dealt with as a matter of contract. As to the facts of the case, Lord Hobhouse's view was that there had not been a fraudulent claim at all, as the actual claim made was a valid claim for a loss which had occurred and had been caused by a peril insured against when the vessel was covered by a held covered clause. The fraud related to an attempt to deprive the insurers of premiums to which they were entitled under the policy. Lord Hobhouse was nevertheless of the view that the result might have been supportable on other grounds, but he did not elaborate. It may be speculated that the correct approach in *The Litsion Pride* was that the assured was not required to disclose the entry of the vessel into a war zone, as the held covered clause gave automatic protection in those circumstances,[614] and that the only claim by the

---

[611] At para.14.

[612] At para.75.

[613] *The Litsion Pride* [1985] 1 Lloyd's Rep. 437.

[614] Had the held covered clause required a further assessment of the risk as a condition of cover, then the duty of utmost good faith would have been attracted by the held covered clause. The clause was, however, automatic.

insurers would have been breach of contract in not paying premiums for the additional premium area. Whether that failure amounts to a repudiation of the contract is extremely doubtful, as time is not generally of the essence in paying a premium unless the contract so provides, and the fact that a breach of contract is fraudulent does not of itself convert a breach which is non-repudiatory by nature into a repudiatory breach. If all of this is right, it follows that the insurers' remedy in *The Litsion Pride* was simply to claim the unpaid premium.[615]

The Mercandian Continent.[616] The reasoning of the House of Lords in *The Star* **6–109** *Sea*[617] was considered by the Court of Appeal in *K/S Merc-Skandia XXXXII v Certain Lloyd's Underwriters (The Mercandian Continent)*, which concerned a document fraudulently manufactured by the assured in the course of negotiations with its liability insurers, the purpose of which was to demonstrate that the assured had not entered into a contract with the claimant third party conferring exclusive jurisdiction on the English courts: such an agreement was at the time thought by the assured to be damaging, in that the measure of damages was (wrongly) believed to be greater in England than in the natural forum for the hearing of the action, Trinidad. The insurers sought to avoid the claim and the policy for breach of the continuing duty of utmost good faith by the assured. The analysis of Longmore L.J. in the Court of Appeal in *K/S Merc Skandia* was at points at variance with that of the House of Lords in *The Star Sea*. It was accepted by Longmore L.J. that a continuing duty did exist, as it was not open to the Court to overturn the express provisions of s.17. Longmore L.J's main proposition was that there was an inextricable link between the continuing duty of utmost good faith and the terms of the policy, for while it was the case as regards pre-contractual breach of duty that the subsequent contract was not a relevant consideration, the assured's post-contract duties were governed primarily by the policy. In Longmore L.J.'s words, "where a contract has been made, it is somewhat perverse to apply to it principles of good faith which are traditionally applicable mainly in pre-contract situations", and the starting point was thus the policy itself.[618] Longmore L.J. then considered the situations in which the continuing duty of utmost good faith had been considered, and ruled that such a duty did exist but that it was limited:[619]

(1) The duty had no application to fraudulent claims, as the right to refuse to make payment following a fraudulent claim rested upon the rule of law that the assured could not profit from his own wrong and, further: "There is no evidence that Sir Mackenzie Chalmers had this line of authority in fire insurance cases in mind when he drafted s.17 of his marine insurance code. The concept, would in any event, be alien in a field, such as marine insurance, where most, if not all, policies, were "valued" policies.

(2) A duty of good faith arose when the assured (or indeed the insurer) sought to vary the contractual risk, in which case the right of avoidance applied only to the variation and not to the original risk itself.

---

[615] But quaere whether it is right. In *K/S Merc-Skandia XXXXII v Certain Lloyd's Underwriters* [2001] Lloyd's Rep. I.R. 802 Longmore L.J. (at para.29) commented that *The Litsion Pride* was a case of making a fraudulent claim and to that extent the decision was good law.

[616] *K/S Merc-Skandia XXXXII v Certain Lloyd's Underwriters* [2001] Lloyd's Rep. I.R. 802.

[617] *K/S Merc-Skandia XXXXII v Certain Lloyd's Underwriters* [2001] Lloyd's Rep. I.R. 247.

[618] At para.9.

[619] At para.22.

(3) A duty of good faith arose on the renewal of a contract. The duty was prospective and did not allow insurers to avoid the earlier policy even though the breach took place during its currency.

(4) A duty of good faith arose in "held covered" cases, although insofar as there was authority for the proposition that there was any such duty where the assured was exercising rights which he had under the original contract, such authority was "puzzling".

(5) Where the insurer had a right to information by virtue of an express or an implied term in the policy—which was of particular significance in liability insurance and reinsurance—there was a duty of good faith in the provision of such information. However, there was no duty of utmost good faith simply because the policy contained a cancellation clause exercisable by the insurers on notice and for any or no reason.[620]

(6) A particular illustration of the continuing duty arose under a liability policy where the insurers exercised their right to take over the assured's defence, as the insurers were required to act in good faith and to take into account the assured's interests in deciding whether to settle with the third party, although the assured's primary remedy in such a case was breach of contract.[621]

Analysing these various possibilities, Longmore L.J. concluded that only the situations in (5) and (6) were true illustrations of the continuing duty of utmost good faith, as situations (2) to (4) were in effect pre-contractual matters and were governed by pre-contractual principles. As far as disclosure by the assured was concerned, therefore, the duty existed only where there was a contractual obligation to disclose (situation (5)), and it remained to consider exactly when there would be a breach of the continuing duty of utmost good faith as well as a breach of contract. In considering this question, Longmore L.J. held that the concepts of breach of contract and breach of the continuing duty of utmost good faith were closely connected. An obligation to provide information was generally to be construed as an innominate term, and insurers would have the right to treat the policy as repudiated only if the assured's breach was such as to show that he regarded himself as no longer bound by the policy.[622] Given that the requirements for treating a policy as having been repudiated were strict, and given also that the consequences of a breach of the duty of utmost good faith were more severe, in that the policy would be avoided ab initio and would thus deprive the assured of all rights under the policy, including accrued rights, it followed that insurers were unable to sidestep the terms of the policy by relying on the continuing duty of

---

[620] Following *New Hampshire Insurance v MGN Ltd* [1997] L.R.L.R. 24.

[621] *Cox v Bankside* [1995] 2 Lloyd's Rep. 437. See, however, the judgment of Mance L.J. in *Gan Insurance Co v Tai Ping Insurance Co (Nos 2 and 3)* [2000] Lloyd's Rep. I.R. 667, where the obligation of an insurer to take into account the interests of the assured in negotiating with third parties was specifically classified as a matter of contract and not a consequence of the continuing duty of utmost good faith.

[622] At the time that *K/S Merc-Skandia* was decided, the accepted view of the breach of a policy condition, based on *Alfred McAlpine Plc v BAI (Run-off) Ltd* [2000] Lloyd's Rep. I.R. 352, was that insurers who had been seriously prejudiced by a breach of a policy term had the right to treat the claim as repudiated, leaving the policy itself untouched. It was unclear whether there could be repudiation of a claim in circumstances where there was no repudiation of the policy itself, and, accordingly, it was also unclear whether the parallel right to avoid applied to repudiation of a claim as well as repudiation of the policy. This is all now academic, as a majority of the Court of Appeal in *Friends Provident Life & Pensions Ltd v Sirius International Insurance Corp* [2006] Lloyd's Rep. I.R. 45 denied the existence of the concept of repudiation of a claim: insurers can refuse to pay a claim only where they are entitled to treat the policy as a whole as having been repudiated.

utmost good faith in circumstances in which they could not have repudiated the policy. In short, there had to be "at least the same quality of conduct as would justify the insurer in accepting the insured's conduct as a repudiation of the contract". On this approach, the disproportionate effects of avoidance *ab initio* were mitigated, as they were confined to the case in which the insurers in any event had a right to terminate the policy as from the date of breach. The words "at least" are also important, as Longmore L.J. does not appear to be saying that every case of repuduiation amounts to a breach of the continuing duty: it remains necessary for insurers to demonstrate that the assured's failure to disclose was material to the issue in that it had some effect on the insurers' ultimate liability and also that the insurers had been induced to alter their behaviour by reason of the assured's presentation of facts. However, it might be thought that, in general, conduct which is repudiatory will fulfil the requirements of materiality and inducement, given that most insurance conditions have to be assessed in relation to their consequences for the insurers, so it is likely that in most cases repudiation and breach of the duty of utmost good faith in the context of failure to disclose will be co-terminous.

The recognition that the continuing duty operates alongside the right of the insurers to treat the policy as repudiated for breach disregards the possibility that the contractual duty amounts to an exhaustive statement of the assured's obligations which overrides the continuing duty of utmost good faith. This was indeed held to be the position in *Hussain v Brown (No.2)*.[623] In that case, it was decided that a contractual obligation on the assured to notify any circumstance which might increase the risk superseded the continuing duty of utmost good faith, so that the insurer's only remedy was breach of contract, and that, as a general principle, an insurer who wished to maintain that duty in existence despite the presence of an express term would have to make clear provision for that in the policy.

Two further points are noteworthy here. First, Longmore L.J. rejected the proposition that fraud per se was enough to trigger a breach of the continuing duty: fraud was a necessary but not a sufficient requirement, and insurers were required to prove that there had been an unfair presentation of information was material which induced their reliance. Secondly, given that there was no obligation on the assured to disclose information in the absence of an express term, then should the insurers ask for information other than under an express term the only duty of the assured was not materially to misrepresent the facts in anything he did say to insurers: there was no duty of disclosure, and in the event of misrepresentation then insurers would have their ordinary common law and statutory remedies for misrepresentation.

The application of this reasoning to the actual facts in *K/S Merc-Skandia* was straightforward. While there had been fraud, that fraud made no difference to the liability of the insurers under the policy and in any event was not directed at them: the worst that had happened was that the insurers' solicitors had maintained their legal proceedings opposing English jurisdiction longer than would otherwise have been the case. The insurers thus had no right to treat the policy as repudiated. It followed that they had no right to rely upon the continuing duty of utmost good faith.

The Aegeon.[624] In *Agapitos v Agnew (The Aegeon)*, the assured's vessel became a total loss. The underwriters denied liability on the basis of various breaches of   **6–110**

[623] *Hussain v Brown (No.2)* Unreported, 1996.
[624] *Agapitos v Agnew (The Aegeon)* [2001] Lloyd's Rep. I.R. 191, affirmed [2002] Lloyd's Rep. I.R. 573.

warranty relating to the date at which "hot works" had been carried out on the vessel, and the assured commenced proceedings. The underwriters in the present application sought to amend their defence by adding an additional defence based on breach of the duty of utmost good faith. The underwriters asserted that the assured's points of claim contained fraudulent misstatements as to the circumstances of the loss, in particular the dates of the hot works, and that those misstatements constituted breaches of the assured's continuing duty of utmost good faith. Picking up on dicta in *The Star Sea* and *K/S Merc-Skandia*, Mance L.J. held that the mere fact that the insurer has a contractual right to cancel does not of itself create any continuing duty of utmost good faith, and that the insurer's decision must be one which relates to a specific disclosure obligation. The Court of Appeal also emphasised that fraudulent claims had nothing to do with the continuing duty of good faith. While there was a continuing duty of utmost good faith—as the court could not overrule s.17—that duty did not encompass fraudulent claims, so that there could be no possibility of avoidance of a policy *ab initio* for a fraudulent claim. As the present case involved an allegation that a fraudulent claim had been made, it was to be determined by the entirely separate principles applicable to fraudulent claims. The Court of Appeal went on to conclude that even if there had been a fraudulent claim, it was not operative in the present case as it had occurred after the commencement of proceedings and, by analogy with the continuing utmost good faith cases—could be disregarded.

6–111 *Summary of the law.* After these three seminal cases, it is possible to summarise the present state of the continuing duty of utmost good faith. However, before the elements of the continuing duty are analysed, it is of interest to note that in *Bonner v Cox Dedicated Corporate Member Ltd*[625] Waller L.J. delivering the judgment of the Court of Appeal simply commented in passing that the duty of utmost good faith was confined to pre-contractual matters and that all else was governed by the express or implied terms of the contract itself. It may be, therefore, that the true function of the continuing duty of good faith is not as a free-standing obligation which gives rise to its own remedies, but rather as a factor which colours the contractual obligations of the assured. In *Goshawk Dedicated Ltd v Tyser & Co Ltd*[626] the Court of Appeal held that there was an implied term in a contract of insurance that the assured would provide to the insurers, post-contractually, documents held by the assured's broker in respect of placing and claims documentation (which the insurers would earlier have seen when writing the risk and paying claims) and accounting information (which the insurers would not have seen). The implied term had its basis in part on the market practice by which brokers retained information whereas insurers did not, but also in part on the assured's duty of utmost good faith.[627] By focusing on the contract, this approach reconciles the need for the assured to act in good faith with the draconian consequences of a breach of the duty of good faith as such.

[625] *Bonner v Cox Dedicated Corporate Member Ltd* [2006] Lloyd's Rep. I.R. 385.
[626] *Goshawk Dedicated Ltd v Tyser & Co Ltd* [2007] Lloyd's Rep. I.R. 224.
[627] Rix L.J. quoted with approval the judgment of Hobhouse J. in *Phoenix General Insurance Co of Greece SA v Halvanon Insurance Co Ltd* [1985] 2 Lloyd's Rep. 599, which recognised good faith as the basis for the implication of terms for the protection of reinsurers into proportional reinsurance contracts. Shortly before *Tyser* a differently constituted Court of Appeal in in *Bonner v Cox* [2006] Lloyd's Rep. I.R. 385 had refused to extend *Phoenix* to proportional reinsurance and cast doubt upon the correctness of the decision. Nevertheless, the use of good faith as a trigger for the implication of terms is not weakened by the *Bonner* decision.

The information to which the duty applies. It is clear from *The Star Sea*[628] that   **6–112**
the continuing duty of utmost good faith is extremely limited in its application.
Lord Hobhouse, having affirmed the view that held covered clauses attracted the
duty, but on the basis that there was fresh insurance on new terms in that
situation, and that the ship's papers cases had nothing to do with utmost good
faith, refused to go beyond stating that the remaining scope of post-contract
disclosure became "more elusive". What, then, can it possibly apply to? It is
clear from the cases prior to *The Star Sea* that the duty does not exist in limbo,
e.g. that it is not a duty triggered on thin air simply because something material
has occurred, and the Court of Appeal in *New Hampshire Insurance Co v MGN
Ltd*[629] held that a cancellation clause conferring on the insurer the right to cancel
at any time did not operate to create a general obligation on the assured to
disclose material facts just in case the insurer might decide to exercise the right
to cancel in the light of information provided by the assured. This significant
limitation on the continuing duty was confirmed by the Court of Appeal in *K/S
Merc-Skandia XXXXII v Certain Lloyd's Underwriters.*[630] Any wider duty would
be inconsistent with two long-established principles: that a misrepresentation or
failure to disclose material facts affecting the risk itself cannot be relied upon by
the insurer once the policy has incepted; and that the assured is free to increase
the risk under the policy at any time providing that there is no contract term to
the contrary. This was accepted even by the expansive approach of Hirst J. in *The
Litsion Pride*[631] where the learned judge stated that the continuing duty arose
"wherever there is a contractual duty for the insured to give the underwriter
information". It is difficult to think of a situation in which failure to comply with
this type of clause could be repudiatory,[632] with the result that the continuing duty
of good faith has almost no practical significance.

It remains to consider exactly what forms of contractual obligation to provide
information are subject to the continuing duty. It was suggested to the court in
Hussain v Brown (No.2)[633] that the continuing duty was confined to "held
covered" clauses, under which there is, of necessity, an obligation to notify
material facts to the insurer to enable the insurer to determine whether to extend
coverage. However, that suggestion was rejected as being inconsistent with the
approach taken by Hirst J. in *The Litsion Pride*, and it is now clear that "held
covered" clauses are not properly regarded as illustrations of the continuing duty.
In *La Banque Financière de la Cité v Westgate Insurance*[634] Lord Jauncey
commented that the continuing duty was "confined to such exceptional cases as
a ship entering a war zone or an insured failing to disclose all facts relevant to
a claim", but this comment would seem to be too limited in the light of the
reasoning in *K/S Merc-Skandia v Certain Lloyd's Underwriters*, in which the
Court of Appeal rejected the view of Aikens J. that the duty was confined to held
covered clauses and to fraudulent claims and applied the continuing duty to an
obligation on the assured to co-operate with insurers.

It would seem from the reasoning in *K/S Merc-Skandia* that, if there is an
obligation on the assured to disclose to the insurer any information which
increases the risk, or to seek the insurer's consent to an increase of risk, the duty

---

[628] *The Star Sea* [2001] Lloyd's Rep. I.R. 247.
[629] *New Hampshire Insurance Co v MGN Ltd* [1997] L.R.L.R. 24.
[630] *K/S Merc-Skandia XXXXII v Certain Lloyd's Underwriters* [2001] Lloyd's Rep. I.R. 802. See
also *Total Graphics Ltd v AGF Insurance Ltd* [1997] 1 Lloyd's Rep. 599.
[631] *The Litsion Pride* [1985] 1 Lloyd's Rep. 437.
[632] See Ch.7, below.
[633] *Hussain (No.2)* Unreported, 1996.
[634] *La Banque Financière de la Cité v Westgate Insurance* [1990] 2 All E.R. 947.

of utmost good faith attaches to that duty. However, the Court of Appeal in *K/S Merc-Skandia* was at pains to stress that a condition precedent to a right to avoid for insurers is proof that they had the right to treat the policy as repudiated for breach. As noted earlier, the Court of Appeal appears to have impliedly rejected the argument that the existence of a contractual duty of disclosure is an exhaustive statement of the assured's obligations and overrides any continuing duty of utmost good faith on the grounds of superfluity.

One further possibility, discussed briefly by the Court of Appeal in *HLB Kidsons v Lloyd's Underwriters*,[635] was whether the assured under a liability policy who was notifying circumstances which may give rise to a claim, thereby triggering the insurers' liability for any claim arising from those circumstances, owed a duty of good faith, owed a duty of good faith in relation to that notification. Toulson L.J. accepted the "proposition that where a policy contains a provision for the insured to notify a circumstance which may give rise to a claim and thereby attach the risk to the policy, it is impliedly incumbent on the insured to see that any such notification is a fair, if summary, presentation of what the insured knows," and Rix L.J. agreed. Both also accepted that there might be an argument for a continuing duty of good faith in these circumstances. The appropriate remedy for a breach of the duty is a holding that the notification is invalid; it is difficult to see why the entire policy should be avoided for a breach of this type.

6–113 *Materiality and inducement.* A fact is material in the pre-contractual sense if it would have influenced a prudent underwriter in his decision whether to accept the risk at all and, if so, on what premium and terms. There also has to be inducement. The pre-contractual test for materiality is plainly inapplicable in the post-contractual context and was accordingly modified by Hirst J. in *The Litsion Pride*.[636] A fact is material, in Hirst J.'s formulation, if "it would influence the judgment of a prudent underwriter in making a decision under the contract for which the information is required". Presumably the decisions which might be relevant here are to increase the premium, to refuse a claim or to cancel the policy. However, as already noted, it was held, in *New Hampshire Insurance Co v MGN Ltd*,[637] *Hussain v Brown (No.2)*[638] and *K/S Merc-Skandia*[639] that the mere fact that the insurers have the right to cancel does not of itself create any continuing duty of good faith.

6–114 *State of mind.* There is need for actual fraud by the assured, in order to distinguish the pre-contractual and post-contractual duties. In cases decided before *The Star Sea* it had been held that actual fraud was required,[640] and this approach was confirmed by the Court of Appeal in *The Star Sea*.[641] The House of Lords in *The Star Sea*, did not deal with the point directly, as it was concerned only with fraudulent claims independently of the duty of utmost good faith. Their Lordships' conclusion was that, where insurers sought to deny liability where

---

[635] *HLB Kidsons v Lloyd's Underwriters* [2009] Lloyd's Rep. I.R. 178.
[636] *The Litsion Pride* [1985] 1 Lloyd's Rep. 437.
[637] *New Hampshire Insurance Co v MGN Ltd* [1997] L.R.L.R.24.
[638] *Hussain v Brown (No.2)* Unreported, 1996.
[639] *K/S Merc-Skandia XXXXII v Certain Lloyd's Underwriters* [2001] Lloyd's Rep. I.R. 802.
[640] *Orakpo v Barclays Insurance Services Ltd* [1995] L.R.L.R. 443; *Royal Boskalis Westminster NV v Mountain* [1997] L.R.L.R. 523, *Alfred McAlpine Plc v BAI (Run-off) Ltd* [2000] Lloyd's Rep. I.R. 352, although contrast *Hussain v Brown (No.2)* Unreported, 1996.
[641] *The Star Sea* [1997] 1 Lloyd's Rep. 360, following *Rego v Connecticut Insurance Placement Facility* (1991) 593 A. 2d 491.

there was non-disclosure in respect of a claim, actual fraud was required, and the assured merely had to act honestly. It is noteworthy that all of the cases in which state of mind has been considered involved fraudulent claims, but that in *The Star Sea* the House of Lords all but divorced fraudulent claims from the continuing duty, an analysis extended by the Court of Appeal in *K/S Merc-Skandia* where Longmore L.J. accepted that the continuing duty of utmost good faith did not extend to fraudulent claims, and the duty was confined to one to disclose all material information where the contract itself imposed an obligation to provide information. The mere fact that the assured had been fraudulent was to be disregarded where that fraud was immaterial to the claim as the object of the duty was to ensure that the insurers received all relevant information[642]; that was the position in *K/S Merc-Skandia* itself, as the fraud related to an ancillary matter, namely, the existence of a jurisdiction clause for the determination of the claim by the third party against the assured. The result is that if an assured who is under a contractual duty to disclose information deliberately fails to disclose facts which are material to the insurers, and the presentation induces the insurers to act or refrain from acting in a particular way, then prima facie the assured is in breach of the continuing duty of utmost good faith as long as the breach would also have amounted to a repudiation of the policy. If the assured makes a false statement to the insurers under a contractual obligation to provide information, then there will be a breach of contract, but not necessarily a breach of the duty of utmost good faith unless fraud is involved and the insurers have been induced to act in a particular way. Any false statement to insurers in response to a request for information which is independent of any contractual obligation, then there cannot be a breach of the continuing duty of utmost good faith, although insurers may have the right to seek damages at common law or under the Misrepresentation Act 1967 if the deceit or negligence can be shown.

Duration. The courts have accepted the view that the duty of utmost good faith **6–115** "continues through the contractual relationship at a level appropriate to the moment".[643] One important consequence of this approach is that the duty dwindles once the parties have entered into a commercial negotiation concerning the loss, and comes to a complete end once legal proceedings have been commenced. The House of Lords, in *The Star Sea*, with only Lord Scott reserving his position, held that once the parties were in litigation, procedural rules governed the extent of the disclosure which should be given in the litigation, not s.17 as such. When a claim form was issued, the rights of the parties were crystallised. The function of the litigation was to ascertain what those rights were and grant the appropriate remedy. The parties' relationship and rights were then governed by the rules of procedure and the orders which the court made on the application of one or other party. The disclosure of documents and facts were provided for with appropriate sanctions; the orders were discretionary within the parameters laid down by the procedural rules. Certain immunities from disclosure were conferred under the rules of privilege. The

---

[642] As had been said by Lord Mustill in *Pan Atlantic Insurance Co Ltd v Pine Top Insurance Co Ltd* [1994] 3 All E.R. 581. The same principle would appear to apply on placement. It might be noted that there is authority for the proposition that an assured who is prepared to he fraudulent is a greater "moral hazard" than an honest assured, so that a predisposition to fraud, even against a third party, is of itself a material fact on placement: this was indeed the essence of the ruling of Mance J. in *Insurance Corp of the Channel Islands Ltd v McHugh and Royal Hotel Ltd (No.1)* [1997] L.R.L.R. 94, where it was decided that it was material for insurers to be told that the assured had contemplated defrauding his bankers. It is not easy to reconcile the approach in these two decisions.

[643] The approach of Professor Malcolm Clarke in his seminal *The Law of Insurance Contracts*.

situation therefore changed significantly. There was no longer the need for the remedy of avoidance under s.17; other more appropriate remedies were available.[644]

Finally, as far as the remedy is concerned, the earlier view[645] was that the insurers had the right to choose between avoiding ab initio or refusing to pay a claim brought in breach of the duty. The Court of Appeal in *The Star Sea* appears to have been of the view that the remedy is avoidance. The Court of Appeal suggested, but refused to decide, that the remedies problem might be overcome by simply regarding as voidable the act performed by the insurer which was induced by the post-contractual breach of duty—thus, if the policy is endorsed by reason of a failure to disclose, the endorsement could be set aside and, if a claim is presented in breach of duty, the claim itself is lost. This approach resolves some, but not all of the problems. On the suggested analysis, if a claim is made in breach of the duty, and the insurer decides to settle, it would follow that only the settlement could be set aside by the insurer, leaving the rest of the policy intact. Again, if the assured's breach of duty relates to the provision of information, e.g. that the risk has increased, and the insurer does not take the steps open to him (e.g. to increase the premium), the analysis would lead to the conclusion that the insurer could not refuse to accept the increased risk, but would merely have the right to reconsider the position in the light of the facts and to increase the premium. The House of Lords, in *The Star Sea*, did not need to deal with this matter. The allegation of a fraudulent claim had been rejected, so that there was no basis for any remedy. Lord Hobhouse was, in essence, of the view that utmost good faith did not apply to fraudulent claims, and that, as far as fraudulent claims were concerned, the appropriate analysis was termination for repudiation and not avoidance ab initio. Lord Scott left open the points (a) whether utmost good faith applied to fraudulent claims, and (b) if it did, whether the appropriate remedy was avoidance ab initio. If it is indeed right that a breach of the continuing duty of utmost good faith renders an insurance contract voidable ab initio, the main consequences are that any claims which are outstanding and which have not been settled at the date of avoidance will lapse, and that sums paid by way of settlement for earlier losses under the same policy will have to be repaid, subject to the rules on mistake and restitution. However, it is almost inconceivable that a court would allow insurers to retake sums paid and repudiate established liabilities simply on the basis of a subsequent fraudulent claim or breach of the continuing duty of utmost good faith by the assured. Whatever the position may be as regards fraudulent claims, the Court of Appeal in *K/S Merc-Skandia XXXXII v Certain Lloyd's Underwriters*[646] accepted that the proper remedy for breach of the continuing duty of utmost good faith is indeed avoidance ab initio. The Court of Appeal accepted that such a remedy would almost always be disproportionate, and thus sought to confine it to the situation in which the assured had repudiated the policy by reason of his failure to disclose under a contractual duty, so that the right to avoid ab initio could

---

[644] As a result it would seem that both *Transthene Packaging Co Ltd v Royal Insurance (UK) Ltd* [1996] L.R.L.R .32 and *Baghbadrani v Commercial Union Assurance Co Plc* [2000] Lloyd's Rep. I.R. 94 are no longer reliable insofar as they suggest to the contrary.

[645] Expressed in *The Litsion Pride* [1985] 1 Lloyd's Rep. 437 and in *The Captain Panagos* [1986] 2 Lloyd's Rep. 470. In the latter case the insured vessel ran aground, and subsequently was destroyed by fire. Evans J. held that both the grounding and the fire were fraudulent, but added that if the grounding alone had been fraudulent, the insurer could either avoid the policy or affirm the policy and reject the claim, and that if it had taken the latter form of action it would have been liable for the genuine fire.

[646] *K/S Merc-Skandia XXXXII v Certain Lloyd's Underwriters* [2001] Lloyd's Rep. I.R. 802.

never be more than an alternative remedy to the insurers' right to terminate of the policy as from the date of breach. Accordingly, reliance upon the continuing duty of utmost good faith, as opposed to the right to terminate as from the date of breach, is significant only where the insurers wish to unwind the entire contract so that previous claims (and indeed settlements) made under the policy may be set aside.

Utmost good faith and insurance created by slip. A particular problem concerning utmost good faith arises in the context of the Lloyd's procedure of the formation of insurance agreements, whereby individual underwriters scratch the slip at different times. It is not difficult to conceive of a situation in which material facts arise between the date at which the slip was scratched by underwriter A and the date at which it has been presented to underwriter B for scratching. The question here is whether the fact that underwriter A has scratched the slip, and has thus become bound, discharges the assured from any duty to disclose further material facts to those underwriters who have yet to scratch the slip.   **6–116**

In strict legal terms, it would appear that the duty of utmost good faith applies individually to each underwriter, so that disclosure would have to be made in these circumstances. However, failure to disclose to underwriter B in the above example would appear not to affect underwriter A's liability. Where disclosure is made to underwriter B, who consequently insists upon a different rate of premium from that agreed to by underwriter A or who inserts policy conditions not demanded by underwriter A, the further problem of underwriters being bound by different terms within the same agreement arises. As a matter of practice, underwriter A would probably receive the benefit of the alterations made by underwriter B, as the broker would, in practice, propose an amendment to the slip for A's benefit, but whether the law follows practice in this respect remains doubtful.[647]

A related issue here is whether a false statement made by the assured to the first, leading underwriter, which is not repeated to subsequent underwriters by the assured, constitutes a breach of duty of utmost good faith by the assured to those subsequent underwriters. Two situations may usefully be distinguished here. First, and as would normally be the case, the leading underwriter does not communicate the assured's false statement to subsequent underwriters. Here, any argument that the assured has broken his duty of utmost good faith to them rests primarily on the notion that subsequent underwriters are likely to rest their rating of the risk to a greater or lesser extent on the skill and judgment of the leading underwriter; if he is misled, then they too are misled. There is indeed early marine insurance authority for this proposition.[648] Such a notion is, however, inconsistent with the marine insurance rule—which admittedly does not extend to non-marine insurance—that each insurer must assess the risk himself and may not rely upon, for example, previous refusals of other insurers to insure the assured.[649] The principle here is that each underwriter may rely only upon what he has been told by the assured, and not upon his guess as to what might have

---

[647] *General Reinsurance Corp v Forsakringsaktiebolaget Fenna Patria* [1982] 1 Lloyd's Rep. 87, reversed [1983] 2 Lloyd's Rep. 287.

[648] *Pawson v Watson* (1778) 2 Cowp. 785; *Barber v Fletcher* (1779) 1 Doug. K.B. 305; *Marsden v Reid* (1803) 3 East 572; *Bell v Carstairs* (1810) 2 Camp. 543. Contrast, however: *Forrester v Pigou* (1813) 1 M. & S. 9; *Robertson v Marjoribanks* (1819) 2 Stark. 573.

[649] *Container Transport International Ltd Inc v Oceanus Mutual Underwriting Association (Bermuda) Ltd* [1984] 1 Lloyd's Rep. 476.

been said to the leading underwriter.[650] This argument is strengthened by the decision in *Pan Atlantic v Pine Top*,[651] where the House of Lords ruled that a contract is voidable for misrepresentation only if there has been inducement of the actual underwriter: in the light of this, following underwriters are likely to demand information in their own right.

An alternative approach to this problem was adopted in *Aneco Reinsurance Underwriting Ltd v Johnson & Higgins*,[652] Cresswell J. ruling that a broker's failure to make a fair presentation to the leading underwriter is itself a material fact which has to be disclosed to the following market, and if it is not disclosed allows them to avoid their participation in the risk. Cresswell J. expressly confined his decision to the Lloyd's market, in respect of which he had heard expert evidence, and made no comment on the companies and overseas markets. It might be thought that the correctness of this decision is open to doubt. The rule that a misrepresentation made to the leading underwriter does not "travel" is based upon the long-established separability of the contracts made between the applicant and each individual syndicate, and it is open to each syndicate to seek a full presentation from the broker. Quite why the courts should discourage this by allowing the following market to avoid simply because a false statement has been made at an earlier stage is difficult to see, particularly following the adoption of the subjective inducement test for utmost good faith by the House of Lords in *Pan Atlantic v Pine Top*. Moreover, *Aneco* appears to run counter to the ruling of Lloyd J. in *CTI v Oceanus Mutual*[653] that previous breaches of the duty of utmost good faith are not material facts, at least in the absence of fraud.[654]

A different approach was taken in *Sirius International Insurance Corp v Oriental Assurance Corp*.[655] Longmore J. held, without reference to *Aneco*, that the following market—unlike the leading undewriter—had no right to avoid the policy as they had not received any misrepresentation, and it was not suggested that the misrepresentation to the leading underwriter constituted a material fact which ought to have been disclosed to them. Longmore J., indeed, stressed the importance of the following market retaining copies of documents shown to them, or at least scratching the documents in the placing broker's file, so that any claim that they have seen a particular document can be substantiated.

The conflict in the authorities was considered by H.H. Judge Dean QC in *International Lottery Management Ltd v Dumas*.[656] The court ruled that the decision in *Aneco* should be followed, as the evidence before the court established that the following market had in fact relied on the leader on the basis that there had been a full and complete presentation of the risk to him, and accordingly that there had to be disclosure to the following market in the event

[650] *Bank Leumi Le Israel BM v British National Insurance Co Ltd* [1988] 1 Lloyd's Rep. 71. Cf. *The Zephyr* [1985] 2 Lloyd's Rep. 529, in which the Court of Appeal held that a signing indication given to the leading underwriter but not communicated to subsequent underwriters could not be relied upon by them, even though they may have been influenced by the leading underwriter's conduct which was consistent with a signing indication having been made to him.

[651] *Pan Atlantic Insurance Co Ltd v Pine Top Insurance Co Ltd* [1994] 3 All E.R. 581.

[652] *Aneco Reinsurance Underwriting Ltd v Johnson & Higgins* [1998]1 Lloyd's Rep. 565. The Court of Appeal varied the outcome on appeal, but on the separate issue of the measure of damages: [2000] Lloyd's Rep. I.R. 12. The Court of Appeal's judgment was upheld by the House of Lords, [2002] Lloyd's Rep. I.R. 91.

[653] *CTI v Oceanus Mutual* [1982] 2 Lloyd's Rep. 178.

[654] *Insurance Corporation of the Channel Islands v Royal Hotel (No.2)* [1998] Lloyd's Rep. I.R. 151.

[655] *Sirius International Insurance Corp v Oriental Assurance Corp* [1999] Lloyd's Rep. I.R. 343.

[656] *International Lottery Management Ltd v Dumas* [2002] Lloyd's Rep. I.R. 237.

that the presentation of the risk to the leading underwriter had been deficient. H.H. Judge Dean QC did not base his decision on custom, but rather on the manner in which business was done in that particular case. Accordingly, the point is not conclusively resolved by this case, as the insurance in question—political risks—was a specialised one and the court was of the view that it was to be expected in the circumstances that the leading underwriter would do most of the work: it may be that the alternative approach would be appropriate in a more standard form of cover. That said, the court noted that the comments of Lloyd J. were not considered in the Court of Appeal in *CTI v Oceanus*,[657] where the decision was reversed on other grounds, and that the issue was not fully argued in *Sirius v Oriental*. Clearly, therefore, H.H. Judge Dean QC may be thought to have been espousing a wider principle.[658] A series of first instance cases decided after *Dumas* have all approved its general approach.[659]

One important limitation on this reasoning that appears to have been overlooked to date is the rule that there can only be a duty to disclose a fact which is known, or which ought to be known, to the assured or to the broker. If the broker has innocently misrepresented a material fact, then there is no obligation on him to disclose his misrepresentation which is the material fact for these purposes to the following market, as he is simply unaware of it. Accordingly, the *Dumas* principle appears to be confined to fraud. However, if this is right then *Dumas* runs into a further obstacle, namely the now accepted rule that a broker is not required to disclose his own fraud to underwriters.[660] It is submitted that, although *Dumas* appears to have received general support, it is incorrect as a matter of law.

Secondly, and perhaps equally problematic, is the situation in which the leading underwriter has expressly communicated to subsequent underwriters the assured's false statement, so that they have all been misled. It might be argued for the assured that, as he has a separate contract with each underwriter, the leading underwriter had not been authorised to pass on to others anything said by the assured and that, on becoming aware that something might have been said, it becomes the duty of each underwriter to ask the assured expressly about the matter. Realistically, however, it might be difficult for a court to resist the conclusion that such communication by the leading underwriter was foreseeable and thus amounts to a breach of the assured's duty of utmost good faith in respect of each of them.

Declaration policies and good faith

The nature of declaration policies. There are various forms of contract available   **6–117**
in the London insurance market which operate as contracts for insurance, as opposed to contracts of insurance. The crucial distinction is that contracts for insurance do not themselves operate as insurance covers, but rather provide a framework under which contracts of insurance can be made by the use of the agreed machinery, consisting of the declaration of individual risks to the framework policy. The general effect of a declaration policy is the modification of the insurers' underwriting discretion where a risk falling within the ambit of

---

[657] *CTI v Oceanus* [1984] 1 Lloyd's Rep. 476.

[658] It should also be said that the ruling is likely to be confined to cases of fraud, for if a broker is unaware that he has made a false statement then he cannot disclose it.

[659] *Brotherton v Aseguradora Colseguoros SA (No.3)* [2003] Lloyd's Rep. I.R. 758; *Toomey v Banco de Espana SA de Serguros y Reaseguros* [2004] Lloyd's Rep. I.R. 354; *International Management Group (UK) Ltd v Simmonds* [2004] Lloyd's Rep. I.R. 247.

[660] See the discussion of s.19 of the 1906 Act, above.

the policy arises and the assured wishes to make it the subject of insurance: by means of a declaration to the contract for insurance, the assured can obtain a contract of insurance. Typically, numerous declarations up to given financial limits may be made by the assured. The right to make declarations may be given either to brokers or to individual assureds. A facility of this type, granted to a broker, is referred to as a binding authority, or "binder". A facility granted to an assured may, for present purposes, be referred to as an open cover, and are of three types:

(1) Obligatory open covers under which the assured is obliged to declare all risks of the agreed type and the insurer is bound to accept them.
(2) Open covers under which the assured is not bound to declare all risks to the open cover but the insurer is obliged to accept those risks which are declared (facultative obligatory covers).
(3) Open covers under which the assured is not obliged to declare all risks, and the insurer is not obliged to accept any risk which is declared (facultative covers)—an agreement of this type is a mere procedural mechanism for the submission of proposals to the insurer.

It may not always be clear into which category an open cover falls. In *Société Anonyme d'Intermediaires Luxembourgeois v Farex Gie*[661] a reinsurance agreement purely facultative form contained held covered provisions under which a declaration made by the reinsured was treated as reinsured for seven days, while renewal declarations were treated as reinsured for 30 days, in which periods the reinsurer was given the opportunity to make a decision. Gatehouse J. held that the held covered provisions did not affect the basic non-obligatory nature of the arrangement. By contrast, in *Glencore International AG v Ryan (The Beursgracht)*[662] H.H. Judge Hallgarten QC and the Court of Appeal construed an open cover, which extended to "all" charterparties entered into by the assured as one which operated automatically to cede risks to the insurers, and was thus obligatory on both sides. The effect of that ruling was that a failure by the assured to complete a monthly bordereau informing the insurers of the acceptance of a new risk did not prevent that risk from attaching to the policy. The significance of this finding is shown by the later decision of Moore-Bick J. in *Glencore International AG v Alpina Insurance Co Ltd*,[663] in which it was held that the risk under a facultative open cover could not attach until the assured had made a declaration because the insurer's risk was triggered by a declaration, and that once a loss had occurred and was known to the assured it was too late for a declaration to be made.

The time that the risk attaches under a declaration policy is relevant not just for disclosure purposes, it also determines which risks the insurers are facing. In the case of an obligatory policy an individual risk attaches automatically as soon as it has been accepted by the assured: that was so held in *The Beursgracht*. In the case of a non-obligatory policy the risk can attach only after it has been declared by the assured and accepted by the insurers. In the case of a facultative obligatory contract the position is more complex. It is less obvious that the reasoning in *The Beursgracht* can apply to a facultative obligatory treaty, because the assured has to make a conscious decision to allocate a risk to the open cover or other facility

---

[661] *Société Anonyme d'Intermediaires Luxembourgeois v Farex Gie* [1995] L.R.L.R. 116.
[662] *Glencore International AG v Ryan (The Beursgracht)* [2002] Lloyd's Rep. I.R. 335, applied in *BC Enterprise SDN BHD v Bank of China Group Insurance Co Ltd* [2003] H.K.E.C. 712.
[663] *Glencore International AG v Alpina Insurance Co Ltd* [2004] 1 Lloyd's Rep. 111.

before the risk can attach, although once the assured has made that decision it is binding on the insurers without more. The question, therefore, is whether the risk attaches in advance of a declaration or its inclusion in a bordereau. It was held in *Baker v Black Sea & Baltic General Insurance Co Ltd*[664] that the risk under a facultative obligatory treaty attached as soon as the reinsured decided to cede the risk and had determined its amount: that intention was carried into effect by coding the slip with a "Y", making an underwriting note and/or making an appropriate entry into the Lloyd's Sceptre system. Notification to the reinsurers was not, therefore, a necessary precondition to the attachment of the risk. This analysis was followed in *Limit No.2 Ltd v Axa Versicherung AG*,[665] the court holding that the risk under a facultative obligatory reinsurance treaty attached automatically where the reinsured so acted, so that the obligation to notify by bordereau was simply an innominate term whose breach did not entitle the reinsurers to deny liability for the risk. In *Glencore International AG v Alpina Insurance Co Ltd* Moore-Bick J. similarly held that risks under a facultative obligatory direct open cover attached in advance of any declaration to the insurers by the assured deciding to accept the risk, and that the declaration was not of itself a trigger for the attachment of the risk. One issue for the court was whether it was possible for a declaration to be made after a loss had occurred. Moore-Bick J. was doubtful whether this was possible, on the basis that the assured would in principle be placing a risk after it had been run.

Disclosure and open covers. The question whether the duty of utmost good faith **6–018** applies to the formation of a declaration policy, as opposed to subsequent declarations under it depends upon the nature of the declaration policy. Where the cover is non-obligatory, in that the insurer is not required to accept individual declarations but retains the right to exercise underwriting judgment in respect of each of them, then it is readily apparent that the open cover itself cannot be a contract of insurance but is a mere contract for insurance and therefore does not attract the duty of utmost good faith. Each declaration is a contract of insurance in its own right, and Gatehouse J. pointed out in *Société Anonyme d'Interme-diaires Luxembourgeois v Farex Gie*[666] that it would be bizarre if an insurer was able to avoid a non-obligatory open cover, and thereby all of the declarations under it, if the assured had withheld material information prior to the making of that contract. The appropriate and proportionate remedy in such a case is to permit the insurer to avoid any individual declaration which is tainted by non-disclosure, but without prejudice to the framework agreement and the other individual declarations. While a contract of this type is close to a contract of insurance, it does not constitute a contract of insurance and the closeness is not enough to import a duty of utmost good faith.[667]

The position of an obligatory declaration policy is more complex. While it is the case that an obligatory open cover does not of itself insure any individual risks, so that it is a contract for insurance rather than a contract of insurance, the critical difference is that the insurer has no discretion to reject risks subsequently

[664] *Baker v Black Sea & Baltic General Insurance Co Ltd* [1995] L.R.L.R. 261.

[665] *Limit No.2 Ltd v Axa Versicherung AG* [2008] Lloyd's Rep. I.R. 330. The point did not arise on appeal, [2008] EWCA Civ 1231.

[666] *Société Anonyme d'Intermediaires Luxembourgeois v Farex Gie* [1995] L.R.L.R. 116. See also *Mander v Commercial Union Assurance Co Plc* [1998] Lloyd's Rep. I.R. 93.

[667] Cf. the analysis of utmost good faith in *L'Alsacienne Premiere Societe Alsacienne et Lorraine D'Assurances Centre L'Incendie Les Accidents et Lea Risques Divers v Unistorehrand International Insurance AS & Kansa Reinsurance Co Ltd* [1995] L.R.L.R. 333.

declared by the assured under this type of contract as long as the declarations fall within the financial, geographical and other risk criteria set out in the open cover. It might be thought, therefore, that such a contract ought itself to attract the duty of utmost good faith, as it may be crucial to the insurer to know exactly how the assured intends to utilise the facility. This was assumed to be the position in *Glasgow Assurance Corp Ltd v Williamson Symondson & Co*,[668] in which reinsurers entered into a binding authority with brokers under which the reinsurers were obliged to accept all risks of a certain class and at a fixed percentage premium. The reinsurers sought to avoid the binder on the basis that they had not been informed that the brokers were not acting as intermediaries but were reinsureds in their own right, and had ceded their own liabilities to the reinsurers under the agreement. Scrutton J. held that the fact withheld was not material to the risk so that there was no basis for avoidance, but that the agreement—while not a contract of reinsurance in its own right—was nevertheless a contract of the utmost good faith. It is unclear whether this proposition represents the law. In *Pryke & Excess Insurance v Gibbs Hartley Cooper*[669] it was held that a binding authority issued to a broker was not a contract of utmost good faith and, subsequently, in *HIH Casualty & General Insurance Ltd v Chase Manhattan Bank*[670] Aikens J. proceeded on the basis agreed between the parties that a line slip arrangement under which individual declarations could be made by the assured was a contract for insurance which did not attract the duty of utmost good faith. No distinction was drawn between obligatory and non-obligatory contracts in this regard, although it appears that the line slip in *HIH* was non-obligatory. The principle that a contract, which is analogous to a contract of insurance but does not quite amount to such a contract, is not subject to the duty of utmost good faith means that a non-obligatory contract is not one of utmost good faith, whereas an obligatory contract for insurance has at least a strong claim to the attraction of a duty of disclosure.[671]

6–119 *Misrepresentation and open covers.* Whether or not a contract for insurance attracts a duty of utmost good faith, it remains a contract and is thus subject to the usual common law rules relating to misrepresentation. Accordingly, a material false statement by the assured which induces the contract for insurance renders the contract voidable and capable of being set aside: if this should occur, then all declarations made under the contract are undermined and are to be treated as never having come into existence. In addition, the insurers have the usual right to claim damages for negligent or fraudulent misrepresentation, and also damages under s.2(1) of the Misrepresentation Act 1967.

---

[668] *Glasgow Assurance Corp Ltd v Williamson Symondson & Co* (1911) 27 T.L.R. 245.

[669] *Pryke & Excess Insurance v Gibbs Hartley Cooper* [1991] 1 Lloyd's Rep. 602.

[670] *HIH Casualty & General Insurance Ltd v Chase Manhattan Bank* [2001] Lloyd's Rep. I.R. 191. The point did not arise on appeal, [2001] Lloyd's Rep. I.R. 702. See also: *Property Insurance Co Ltd v National Protector Insurance Co Ltd* (1913) 18 Com. Cas. 119; *Svenska Handelshanken v Sun Alliance and London Insurance Plc* [1996] 1 Lloyd's Rep. 519; *Sumitomo Bank Ltd v Banque Bruxelles Lambert SA* [1997] 1 Lloyd's Rep. 487; *Tradigrain SA v SIAT SpA* [2002] 2 Lloyd's Rep. I.R. 553.

[671] *L'Alsacienne Premiere Societe Alsacienne et Lorraine D'Assurances Centre L'Incenderie Les Accidents et Lea Risques Divers v Unistorehrand International Insurance AS & Kansa Reinsurance Co Ltd* [1995] L.R.L.R. 333. The decision in *Limit No.2 Ltd v Axa Versicherung AG* [2008] Lloyd's Rep. I.R. 330 proceeded on this assumption. The point did not arise on appeal, [2009] Lloyd's Rep. I.R. 396.

Utmost good faith and declarations to open covers. It is settled law that each **6–120**
declaration under a contract for insurance creates a binding contract of insurance.[672] It is immaterial to this outcome whether the declaration is made under
an obligatory or a non-obligatory declaration policy. The manner in which, and
the persons to whom, risks are to be declared is a matter for the policy itself.
Where there are numerous subscribing underwriters the policy may provide for
notification to the leading underwriter only on behalf of the following market,
although if there is no "leading underwriter" clause to this effect then there has
to be separate notification to each underwriter.[673] Any purported notification
must be viewed objectively to determine whether there was an unconditional
intention on the part of the reinsured to notify a risk.[674]

The further question is whether individual declarations attract the duty of
utmost good faith. Where the open cover is obligatory as far as the insurer is
concerned, so that as soon as a declaration is made a binding contract of
insurance comes into being without the insurer having the opportunity to
consider, rate or reject the subject matter of the declaration, it is difficult to see
how any duty of utmost good faith can be applicable.[675] This is so because the
definition of materiality in ss.18(2) and 20(2) of the Marine Insurance Act
1906—which refers to the fixing of the premium and the taking of the risk by the
insurer—cannot be met in a case where the premium is fixed and the risk
accepted. Thus, although a contract of insurance is created by a declaration, the
declaration does not attract a duty of disclosure: the result is presumably
rationalised by recourse to the doctrine of waiver, i.e. that insurers have agreed
to accept any risk which falls within the ambit of the open cover without regard
to any special circumstances surrounding the risk.

The case of an open cover which is non-obligatory as far as the insurer is
concerned is relatively straightforward. The open cover is no more than a
framework agreement which establishes machinery for the making of individual
contracts. As the insurer has the right to accept or reject any individual
declaration,[676] it follows that the duty of utmost good faith has not been waived
and accordingly that the insurer is entitled to avoid any declaration in the event
of misrepresentation or non-disclosure relating to it[677]; other declarations, and
the declaration policy itself, are necessarily unaffected by the ability of an insurer
to avoid any one declaration.[678]

Extension of the open cover. Different considerations will necessarily apply **6–121**
where the assured attempts to introduce into the open cover a class of business

---

[672] *Citadel Insurance Co v Atlantic Union Insurance Co SA* [1982] 2 Lloyd's Rep. 543; *Sedgwick Tomenson Inc v PT Reasuransi Umum Indonesia* [1990] 2 Lloyd's Rep. 334.

[673] *BP Plc v GE Frankona Reinsurance* [2003] 1 Lloyd's Rep. 537.

[674] *BP Plc v Aon Ltd* [2006] Lloyd's Rep. I.R. 577.

[675] *Law Guarantee Trust and Accident Society Ltd v Munich Reinsurance Co* (1915) 31 T.L.R. 572; *Ionides and Chapeaurouge v Pacific Fire and Marine Insurance Co* (1871) L.R. 6 Q.B. 674.

[676] This appears to be the best explanation of *Berger and Light Diffusers Pty Ltd v Pollock* [1973] 2 Lloyd's Rep. 442; see *CCR Fishing Ltd v Tomenson (The La Pointe)* [1986] 2 Lloyd's Rep. 513, affirmed on other grounds 69 D.L.R. (4th) 112 (1990).

[677] In *Glencore International AG v Alpina Insurance Co Ltd* [2004] 1 Lloyd's Rep. 111 it was suggested by counsel that an assured failing to make a declaration until after the loss had occurred was nevertheless entitled to recover as long as the assured had intended to make the declaration but had by oversight neglected to do so, and that the insurer was protected by the assured's duty of good faith in this regard when the declaration was actually made. Moore-Bick J. rejected the notion that an insurer could be liable under a declaration made after loss, and did not comment on the good faith argument.

[678] *Société Anonyme d'Intermediaires Luxemhourgeois v Farex Gie* [1995] L.R.L.R. 116; *Mander v Commercial Union Assurance Co Plc* [1998] Lloyd's Rep. I.R. 93.

which falls outside its agreed limits. In such a case the declaration is simply not binding on the insurers.[679]

8. THE INSURER'S DUTY OF UTMOST GOOD FAITH

6-122 **Bilateral nature of duty.** It has long been assumed that the duty of utmost good faith is bilateral, and that equivalent duties are owed by the insurer to the assured. Indeed, the original formulation of the duty of utmost good faith in *Carter v Boehm*[680] indicated that this was the case: "Good faith forbids either party by concealing what he knows to draw the other into a bargain from his ignorance of the fact and his belief to the contrary." Moreover, s.17 of the 1906 Act is framed in bilateral terms and isolated cases had come close to recognising the special relationship between insurers and their assureds and the importance of full disclosure by the insurer.[681] However, the first English decision to hold in terms that the insurer owes a duty of utmost good faith to the assured was *Banque Keyser Ullman SA v Skandia (UK) Insurance Co Ltd*,[682] a ruling approved in principle on appeal by the Court of Appeal and the House of Lords in *La Banque Financière de la Cité SA v Westgate Insurance Co Ltd.*[683]

In this case, LBF and two other banks were persuaded by one B to make loans of 26.25 million Swiss francs to his companies, secured by the deposit of gemstones independently valued at 95 million Swiss francs and by a credit insurance policy for 37 million Swiss francs. N, insurance brokers, were instructed by the banks to arrange the credit insurance. L, an employee of N, sought to arrange insurance in three layers: WI was to underwrite the primary layer of 9.25 million Swiss francs, and the remaining layers—giving a total of 37 million Swiss francs—were to be underwritten by insurers. In January 1980 L issued cover notes for the full amount, purportedly with the authority of the insurers; the banks, having taken custody of the gemstones, thereupon advanced the agreed sums to B's companies. L had in fact acted fraudulently, in that the insurance for the two layers above WI's layer had not been arranged when the cover note was issued; by June 1980, however, the full amount of insurance had been obtained by L. By May 1980, D, an employee of WI, became aware of L's fraud, but did not report this to LBF. In the event, that fraud proved to be of no significance as matters were rectified by L in June 1980. Between August 1980 and March 1981 LBF and five other banks made further advances to B's companies, the total amount loaned being 80 million Swiss francs. L was asked to extend the insurance to cover the advances. L extended the existing layers, and sought to arrange a fourth layer; L issued a cover note in respect of a fourth layer when he had not in fact managed to obtain the necessary additional cover. Subsequently B's companies defaulted on repayment of the loans, and it rapidly became clear to the banks that various, apparently independent, frauds had been perpetrated on them: the sums were for all practical purposes irrecoverable from B, the gemstones proved to be virtually worthless, and the fourth layer of

---

[679] *Inversiones Manria SA v Sphere Drake Insurance Co Plc (The Dora)* [1989] 1 Lloyd's Rep. 69; *Seavision Investment SA v Evenett and Clarkson Puckle (The Tiburon)* [1992] 2 Lloyd's Rep. 26.

[680] *Carter v Boehm* (1766) 3 Burr. 1905.

[681] *Horry v Tate & Lyle Refineries Ltd* [1982] 2 Lloyd's Rep. 416, a case involving a settlement contract avoided by the assured for undue influence.

[682] *Banque Keyser Ullman SA v Skandia (UK) Insurance Co Ltd* [1987] 2 All E.R. 923.

[683] *La Banque Financière de la Cité SA v Westgate Insurance Co Ltd* [1989] 2 All E.R. 952; [1990] 2 All E.R. 947.

insurance did not exist. In 1983 LBF and the other banks brought actions against N and L for negligence and fraud respectively. N settled to the extent of their liability insurance. LBF also sought to recover under such insurance as did exist, but were unable to do so as the result of a fraud exclusion in the policies, which stated that the insurers were not liable "for any claim or claims arising directly or indirectly out of or caused directly or indirectly by fraud attempted fraud misdescription or deception by any person firm organisation or company."

The banks, unable to pursue any other line, sought damages against the insurers, representing the advances made after June 1990. Two alternative claims were presented. First, it was argued that the insurers, being aware through D of L's fraud, owed a duty of disclosure to the banks; had there been disclosure, the banks would have gone elsewhere for the additional insurance and would not have used N. Secondly, the banks argued that the insurers owed them a common law duty of care under which the true facts ought to have been disclosed to them. The claims by the banks were upheld at first instance by Steyn J. The Court of Appeal reversed this decision. It dismissed the negligence claim on the grounds of causation. Further, while the Court of Appeal accepted the view adopted by Steyn J. that the duty of utmost good faith is reciprocal, it went on to hold held that it did not give rise to a remedy in damages. The House of Lords affirmed the judgment of the Court of Appeal, but in the House of Lords the case took on a very different appearance, and turned upon the wording of the fraud exception. Consequently, the many interesting issues debated in the courts below proved to be irrelevant and were not pronounced upon with any authority by their Lordships.

Before Steyn J. and the Court of Appeal it was apparently assumed that the fraud exception in the policy covered the fraud not just of B but also of the broker's employee, L. This led to the conclusion that L's fraud had caused WI to reject LBF's claim on the policy, so that L's fraud had been the cause of LBF's loss. In the House of Lords it was argued, and indeed accepted by their Lordships, that a fraud exclusion in an insurance policy does not extend to fraud by the assured's broker in setting up the policy. The only relevant fraud was thus that of B. It followed that any breach of duty by WI in failing to disclose L's fraud to LBF had not caused LBF any loss, and its claim fell away. This short point of construction was in this way determinative of the entire action.

Scope of the insurers' duty. Section 17 of the 1906 Act provides authority for **6–123** the proposition that the duty of utmost good faith is reciprocal, but ss.18 and 20 deal only with the definition of materiality with respect to the assured's duty. The meaning of materiality so far as the insurer is concerned must, therefore, be based on inference from the formulation of the assured's duty. Some guidance may be obtained from certain passages of the judgment of Lord Mansfield in *Carter v Boehm*,[684] which indicate that the definition of materiality in respect of the insurer's duty is the mirror image of that operating for the assured's duty. Lord Mansfield, having stated that the underwriter must be informed of facts which increase the risk but not those which decrease it, continued:

"The policy would be equally void, against the underwriter, if he concealed; as, if he insured a ship on her voyage, which he privately knew to be arrived, and an action would lie to recover the premium."

---

[684] *Carter v Boehm* (1766) 3 Burr. 1905.

Clearly, the arrival of a ship, given as an example of what an insurer has to disclose, is something which decreases rather than increases the risk. It does not follow from this that merely because an insurer has to disclose circumstances which reduce the risk under the policy there are no other classes of fact which may be regarded as material for the purposes of the insurer's duty, although it is logical to suggest that Lord Mansfield's illustration demonstrates the extent of the insurer's duty. After all, information as to circumstances which are likely to increase the possibility of a loss can only serve to influence an insurer not to insure or to increase the premium charged, but the influence exerted by the same information on an assured would be to make him even more anxious to have cover and to pay more for being able to obtain it. It may be concluded, therefore, that as a matter of principle those circumstances which are material and which are to be disclosed by an insurer are circumstances which decrease the risk to the assured.

It is instructive to test the approach suggested above against the facts of, and the conclusions reached in, *La Banque Financière*.[685] The facts alleged to be material were that the leading underwriter had failed to disclose to the banks the earlier fraud of their broker. The question here becomes, does the possible inadequacy of the insurance due to the untrustworthy character of the broker count as a factor which increases the risk? It is suggested that on principle this cannot be the case. In such circumstances, the loss suffered by the assured is the inability to recover under the policy, but this does not arise from the failure of the insurer to disclose circumstances which make the possibility of the occurrence of loss more likely, so much as from the fact that the insurance does not respond to the loss. In *La Banque Financière* the fact alleged to be material related not to the insured risk, which was the likelihood of default by the borrower, but to the circumstances relating to the setting up of the policy itself. It may be concluded, therefore, that the circumstances of *La Banque Financière* did not involve material facts irrespective of the scope of the fraud exception. Steyn J. at first instance[686] reached the opposite conclusion, and held that the failure by the leading underwriters to disclose the fraud of the brokers was actionable non-disclosure. The learned judge's attitude towards materiality was robust and free of technicality: in his view, a fact was material and had to be disclosed by an insurer if failure to disclose would amount to a breach of good faith and fair dealing and would influence the assured in determining whether to conclude the contract of insurance. Applying this broad test, Steyn J. was easily able to decide that the leading underwriters were in breach of duty. Interestingly, the materiality or otherwise of the facts not disclosed was not argued on appeal before the Court of Appeal, and the judgment proceeds on the assumption that materiality had been made out. The approach of the Court of Appeal was nevertheless more guarded than that of Steyn J. It rejected the "good faith and fair dealing" test on the basis that this concept did not form a part of general English commercial law. It also held that an underwriter was not required to disclose all facts which might influence an assured in entering into a contract, as such a duty might require it to disclose, for example, the fact that other insurers offered similar cover but at a lower premium. The Court of Appeal refused to be drawn further than a general statement of principle[687]:

---

[685] *La Banque Financière de la Cité SA v Westgate Insurance Co Ltd* [1990] 2 All E.R. 947.
[686] *La Banque Financière de la Cité SA v Westgate Insurance Co Ltd* [1987] 2 All E.R. 923.
[687] *La Banque Financière de la Cité SA v Westgate Insurance Co Ltd* [1989] 2 All E.R. 952 at 990.

"In our judgment, the duty falling upon the insurer must at least extend to disclosing all facts known to him which are material either to the nature of the risk sought to be covered or the recoverability of a claim under the policy which a prudent insured would take into account in deciding whether or not to place the risk for which he seeks cover with that insurer."

Applying this test, the Court of Appeal held that the leading underwriters were in breach of their duty of disclosure. It may be concluded from this judgment that a fact will be material if it fulfils one of two requirements: (a) it relates to the scope of the peril insured under the policy; or (b) it relates to the recoverability under the policy in respect of risks the coverage of which a prudent assured would have taken into account in determining whether to take out the policy.

Proposition (a) is undoubtedly in conformity with general principle. Proposition (b) is more questionable, at least when measured against the judgment of Lord Mansfield in *Carter v Boehm*, and gives rise to interesting issues of whether the insurer must, for example, disclose the legal meaning of ordinary English words of coverage used in a policy in so far as the assured could not be expected to be aware of the secondary legal meaning.[688] Such issues are unlikely to arise in practice because the assured is not entitled to damages where the policy proves not to cover his loss.[689]

The speeches in the House of Lords in *La Banque Financière*[690] throw little light upon this matter. Lords Templeman, Brandon and Ackner did not comment upon the nature of the insurer's duty of disclosure. Lord Bridge cited the above-quoted passage from the Court of Appeal's judgment and did "not dissent"[691] from the test there propounded. However, Lord Bridge disagreed with the Court of Appeal's conclusion that L's fraud was a material fact within this test. This was so because the fraud exclusion clause did not apply to L's fraud but only to the fraud of B; as L's fraud had thus not contributed to LBF's inability to recover under the policy, it did not affect "the recoverability of a claim" within the Court of Appeal's test of materiality, as the Court of Appeal had wrongly assumed. Had the fraud exception applied to L's fraud, Lord Bridge's speech may be taken to lend tentative support for the conclusion of the Court of Appeal that the fact in question would have been material.

The point arose again in *Norwich Union Life Insurance Society v Qureshi*.[692] Here, the insurers in 1989 issued a life policy to the assured, who was a Name at Lloyd's. The policy formed part of a wider package under which the insurers had guaranteed the assured's possible liabilities to Lloyd's in return for a mortgage on the assured's house; the mortgage was itself supported by an endowment policy on the assured's life. As a result of the crisis at Lloyd's, the insurers were called upon to make payment to Lloyd's under the guarantee, although the losses exceeded the sum guaranteed and the assured failed to

[688] Such an approach in any event conflicts with the rule laid down in *Re Hooley Hill Rubber & Chemical Co Ltd and Royal Insurance Co* [1920] 1 K.B. 257, that a false statement made by the insurer's agent as to the coverage of the policy cannot give rise to remedies.

[689] The impact of the argument in the text, that the Court of Appeal erred in holding that the duty of utmost good faith could extend to matters affecting the policy coverage, is reproduced by the Court of Appeal's decision that damages are not available in this situation. There is, in practical terms, no difference between the absence of a right and the existence of a right which has no remedy.

[690] *La Banque Financière de la Cité SA v Westgate Insurance Co Ltd* [1990] 2 All E.R. 947.

[691] *La Banque Financière de la Cité SA v Westgate Insurance Co Ltd* [1990] 2 All E.R. 947 at 950.

[692] *Norwich Union Life Insurance Society v Qureshi* [1999] Lloyd's Rep. I.R. 263. *Aldrich v Norwich Union Life Insurance Co Ltd* [1999] Lloyd's Rep. I.R. 276 was decided shortly beforehand, and Rimer J. independently came to the same conclusion.

maintain the mortgage payments or the life policy premiums. The assured, seeking to defend a claim by the insurers for reimbursement of the sum paid under the guarantee, argued that the insurers owed him a duty to disclose the potential for losses at Lloyd's which he asserted were known to the insurers. Rix J. held that these facts were not material to the endowment policy, and that the imposition of a duty of disclosure on insurers in relation to an investment to be made by the assured would convert insurers into financial advisers. The Court of Appeal granted leave to appeal against the striking out of the action on this ground,[693] but on the appeal hearing itself, joined cases *Aldrich v Norwich Union Life, Norwich Union Life v Qureshi*,[694] the Court of Appeal dismissed the appeal. Mummery L.J., giving the leading judgment, held that the duty of good faith applied only to matters material to the risk covered by the life policy, i.e. to the recoverability of a claim in respect of the assured's life under the policy. The insured risk was not the risk of losses at Lloyd's, and accordingly the duty of disclosure did not extend to matters relating to Lloyd's itself. Evans L.J., delivering a concurring judgment, noted that if the premiums had been assessed by reference to risks at Lloyd's, the necessary link between the obligation of the insurers and the Lloyd's market would have been forged and a duty of disclosure would have extended to those matters. However, as that was not the case, there was no relevant duty of disclosure. All of this was largely immaterial for, as the Court of Appeal noted, the only remedy for breach of the duty would have been avoidance rather than damages. There is, therefore, acceptance of the proposition that any duty of disclosure owed by insurers relates to recoverability under the policy even though there is no appropriate remedy awardable in the event of breach.

The speech of Lord Jauncey in *La Banque Financière* is perhaps the most instructive in unpicking this conundrum, as it follows closely the narrow *Carter v Boehm* test and confines the insurer's duty of disclosure to insured perils, thus mirroring the scope of the assured's duty. Lord Jauncey held that the insurer's duty of disclosure extended to the safe arrival in port of a vessel which the assured wished to insure, or to the destruction by fire of a house which the insured wished to insure. In short, just as the assured's duty is to disclose facts which would increase the risk of loss, the insurer's duty is to disclose facts which would decrease the risk of loss. Lord Jauncey would thus have found the broker's fraud an immaterial fact even if the fraud exception had applied to it and it had been the reason that L.B.F. had been unable to recover under the policy. On this analysis, premium sensitivity is the test for the insurers' continuing duty. That said, it was suggested in *The Ainikolas*[695] that a claim for premium after the contract is completed, which is not justified by the terms of the contract, is a breach of the insurer's continuing duty, but it was held that such a claim did not equate to a breach of the duty so that the assured could not avoid the contract. Nevertheless, using Lord Jauncey's approach, the second limb of the test propounded by the Court of Appeal in *La Banque Financière* and *Qureshi*—the recoverability of claims—is incorrect.

The present authorities do not, therefore, provide any convincing definition of the scope of the continuing duty and in particular whether the insurer's duty of

---

[693] *Norwich Union Life Insurance Society v Qureshi* [1999] Lloyd's Rep. I.R. 453.
[694] *Aldrich v Norwich Union Life, Norwich Union Life v Qureshi* [2000] Lloyd's Rep. I.R. 1.
[695] *The Ainikolas* (1996) *Lloyd's List*, 5 April.

disclosure extends to the enforceability and meaning of the contract itself.[696] In the absence of any general duty of disclosure on the insurer under the duty of utmost good faith it might nevertheless be thought that there is a stronger case for suggesting that there is a duty to disclose on renewal the implications of any alterations in the coverage of a policy. The practice is for the assured to be sent a renewal slip accompanied by documentation which contains the amended terms of the policy, although it is not always clear from that documentation, first, that a change has been effected and, secondly, that its implications are known to the assured. It may well be the case in certain circumstances, where the fact that incorporation is intended is not made apparent, that no variation has taken place as a matter of law, but even where there has been a contractual variation it would appear at least arguable that there is some room for the application of the doctrine of utmost good faith.

Remedies for breach. The remedy available to an insurer for breach of the **6–124** assured's duty of utmost good faith is avoidance. However, it will be immediately apparent that in cases such as *La Banque Financière*, where the assured does not discover the insurer's breach of duty until a loss has occurred, avoidance is precisely what the assured does not want, as it leaves the assured without a claim under the policy. It was thus argued in *Banque Keyser Uliman SA* that the proper remedy in these circumstances is in damages against the insurer, in that without such a remedy the insurer's duty would be pointless. Steyn J. accepted this argument and held that damages were indeed awardable for breach of the duty of utmost good faith, although the learned judge clearly had severe reservations about the correctness of this ruling. The notion that damages may be awarded for a breach of the duty of utmost good faith was exposed as fallacious by the Court of Appeal in *La Banque Financière*. The Court of Appeal dismissed the arguments that the true basis of the duty of utmost good faith was either an implied term in every contract of insurance or, in the alternative, some previously unrecognised form of tort: had either of these arguments succeeded, it would have been arguable that breach of the duty would have sounded in damages. Instead, the Court of Appeal classified the duty of utmost good faith as an extra-contractual right, equivalent to a non-tortious misrepresentation, breach of which allows the innocent party to avoid the insurance policy subject to making full restitution. The Court of Appeal was influenced by[697] the need to maintain consistency between the duty of utmost good faith and doctrines such as duress, undue influence and innocent misrepresentation, which originated from the same jurisdiction but which did not give rise to damages, the absence of any mention of damages in the 1906 Act; and the application of the duty of utmost good faith to innocent as well as to negligent and fraudulent failures to disclose might lead to damages being awarded for purely innocent conduct. In the House of Lords, Lord Templeman, who alone dealt with the point, found the Court of Appeal's

---

[696] *Lovett v Worldwide (NZ) Ltd* Unreported, October 29, 2004, High Court of New Zealand, Auckland Registry: the principle of uberrimae fidei can never operate as a foundation for a duty owed by an insurer extra contractually to disclose or ensure that an insured party understands terms and conditions already settled between them by agreement.

[697] A further consideration was that at the time it was believed that the test for breach was wholly objective and based on the prudent assured. The subsequent addition of an actual inducement test in *Pan Atlantic v Pine Top* [1994] 3 All E.R. 581 at least removes the problem faced by Steyn J. and the Court of Appeal that damages would be assessed by reference to the assured's notional loss and not his actual loss.

reasoning "cogent".[698] In *The Star Sea*,[699] the House of Lords confirmed that the only remedy for breach of the duty of utmost good faith is avoidance *ab initio*, and the fact that avoidance is, for the most part, of no use to an assured given that the point will tend to arise where there has been a loss, was itself a strong indication that the continuing duty was of limited scope.[700]

The ultimate conclusion of the Court of Appeal in *La Banque Financière*, that damages are not available for the breach by an insurer of its duty of utmost good faith, has the obvious effect as far as the assured is concerned of rendering the insurer's duty almost meaningless. If the assured has not suffered any loss when he discovers the insurer's breach of duty, avoidance of the policy and recovery of the premium are adequate redress for him. Conversely, if he has suffered a loss which is within the policy and the policy coverage is adequate, it will be of little concern to the assured that he has the right to avoid on the basis that his risk of loss was in fact less than he had originally believed. There are at least two situations in which the insurer's duty of utmost good faith may be of some use to the assured, but in each of them the unavailability of damages deprives the duty of any meaning. First, the assured may be undertaking a hazardous endeavour for which insurance is sought, and the insurers may be aware of particular risks which the assured had not appreciated. To date, the courts have ruled this knowledge to be immaterial,[701] but in an exceptional situation where there was materiality, the absence of damages would leave the assured without an effective remedy. Secondly, the assured may have suffered a loss which, contrary to his reasonable belief, is for one or other reason not within the scope of the policy: this was the situation in *La Banque Financière* itself. In these cases, the assured has to be content with reclaiming his premium. However, it might be said that the fact that the assured has suffered a loss which can be compensated only by the award of extra-contractual damages is of itself a strong indication that, as was submitted earlier, the duty of utmost good faith owed by an insurer was never intended to convert the insurer into some form of adviser or to extend to failure by the insurer to disclose the prospects of recovery under the policy.

Where the insurer has avoided a policy for the assured's breach of his duty of utmost good faith, the insurer's only financial loss will take the form of expenses. Where the assured has avoided a policy for the insurer's breach of duty, he has lost his premium and doubtless can recover it for total failure of consideration. Suppose, however, that the assured has suffered a loss under the policy, and discovers that he has paid an excessive premium in that the risk was lower than he had believed in a manner unconnected with the loss. It is submitted that the principle that the premium is not divisible[702] should not be applied to this type of situation, and that the assured should be able to obtain a refund of that part of the premium paid unnecessarily as well as being able to affirm the policy and to claim for his loss. To this limited extent, therefore, it is submitted that damages are recoverable for the insurer's breach of duty.

---

[698] *La Banque Financière de la Cité SA v Westgate Insurance Co Ltd* [1990] 2 All E.R. 947, 959.

[699] *The Star Sea* [2001] Lloyd's Rep. I.R. 247.

[700] See also *Aldrich v Norwich Union Life, Norwich Union Life v Qureshi* [2000] Lloyd's Rep. I.R. 1, where the Court of Appeal held that the continuing duty was of no assitance to an assured who sought damages rather than avoidance.

[701] *Searle v AR Hales & Co Ltd* [1996] L.R.L.R. 68; *Norwich Union Life Insurance Sociely v Qureshi* [1999] Lloyd's Rep. I.R. 263, affirmed 120001 Lloyd's Rep. I.R. 1.

[702] Marine Insurance Act 1906 s.84.

Causation. It is settled law that if the assured withholds a material fact, the **6–125** insurer can avoid liability even if that fact did not cause the assured's loss. It is unclear how this can apply to breach of duty by the assured if the Court of Appeal's test of materiality in *La Banque Financière* is correct. That test deems a fact to be material if, inter alia, it related to the recoverability of a claim. On principle, however, the duty of disclosure operates irrespective of its connection to the loss in question, and it is suggested that the Court of Appeal's test confuses materiality with causation. The true position, as set out by Lord Jauncey in the House of Lords in *La Banque Financière*, is that the insurer's duty of disclosure is limited to facts which reduce the risk of a loss under the policy. The fact that the assured's claim is unrelated to the loss which actually occurs should not prevent him from making a claim and recovering the overpaid amount of premium.

Duration of the duty

Existence of the duty. Welcome as a duty of utmost good faith on the insurer may **6–126** be, it is fraught with difficulties. Perhaps the most intractable are raised by the obiter ruling of the Court of Appeal in *Bank of Nova Scotia v Hellenic War Risks Association (Bermuda) Ltd (The Good Luck).*[703] In this case the owners of the vessel procured war risks insurance, one condition of which was that the vessel was not to enter into an Additional Premium Area (APA) without prompt notice being given to the insurer. The proceeds of the policy were assigned to the claimant bank, as mortgagee of the vessel, under an arrangement to which the insurer itself was a party. The owners caused the vessel to trade in APAs without notification, a fact which became known to the insurer's London agents and ultimately to the insurer itself, but not to the bank. The insurer rejected a claim by the owners following the torpedoing of the vessel in a war zone, so that the bank was deprived of its right to the proceeds. The bank subsequently brought an action against the insurer, asserting that the insurer had owed a continuing duty of good faith to it, which obliged the insurer to disclose that the vessel had been trading in APAs and that the validity of the policy was under threat. The Court of Appeal, breaking new ground, ruled that the insurer indeed owed a continuing duty of utmost good faith, but only to the assured owners and not to the bank; as the bank had been the assignee only of the proceeds of the policy and not of the policy itself, the bank was not the assured. Thus, as the owners were fully aware of their own transgressions, the insurer had nothing to disclose to them, and the bank's claim was dismissed.

If it is correct that a continuing duty of disclosure is imposed on the insurer by the general law, it remains to consider when it will come into effect and to what information it relates. Clearly all accepted definitions of "materiality" are inappropriate here.

Duty to warn assured of right to refuse to pay. The most likely context in which **6–127** the problem may arise is that in which the conduct of the assured known to the insurer jeopardises the validity of the policy or any claim under it; must the insurer warn the assured to desist? Even if there is such a duty, it would seem that any breach of that duty gives rise to avoidance and restitution of premium only. There may be limited cases in which the assured may wish to avoid for some breach of duty by the insurer during the currency of the policy, but in all

---

[703] *Bank of Nova Scotia v Hellenic War Risks Association (Bermuda) Ltd (The Good Luck)* [1989] 2 Lloyd's Rep. 238, reversed on other grounds [1991] 3 All E.R. 1.

probability any such breach will not come to light until after a loss has occurred, and at that stage the right to rescind is cold comfort. Thus, had the bank in *The Good Luck* been an assignee of the policy itself, and thus been owed a duty of utmost good faith by the insurer, it would have recovered nothing by way of damages.

6–128   *Claims handling.* It is accepted that a liability insurer is under a duty to negotiate in good faith on the part of the assured, a duty which takes effect as an implied term.[704] The question is whether this is a general principle. The cases are divided. In *Insurance Corporation of the Channel Islands v McHugh (No.1)*[705] Mance J. held that, even if there was a continuing duty of utmost good faith owed by the insurer, it did not give rise to an implied term obliging the insurer to negotiate, settle and pay a claim in good faith and with reasonable speed. Again, in *Gan Insurance Co Ltd v Tai Ping (Nos 2 and 3)*[706] the Court of Appeal held that a reinsurer was not under any duty to act reasonably in deciding whether to give approval to a settlement reached by the reinsured, and that the reinsurer's only duty was to avoid taking into account irrelevant considerations, i.e. acting irrationally, in reaching any decision on the point. What is clear from these cases is the development in England of a notion that the discretion of insurers at the claims-handling stage is not absolute, although there are indications of the development of such a doctrine. In *K/S Merc-Skandia* Longmore L.J. regarded the obligation of a liability insurer to take into account the interests of the assured in reaching a settlement with the third-party claimant, as one of the few illustrations of the operation of a continuing duty of utmost good faith, but it was recognised that avoidance of the policy would scarcely be an appropriate remedy, and in *Eagle Star Insurance Co Ltd v Cresswell*[707] Rix L.J. expressed the view that the discretion of reinsurers in deciding whether or not to exercise control of a claim against the reinsured, this being a condition precedent to coverage was restricted by one or other of two principles: the continuing duty of utmost good faith, or an implied term in the contract that precluded the reinsurers from taking into account considerations other than the merits of the claim.[708] In appropriate circumstances a failure by insurers to assert their rights may also amount to waiver.[709] Rix L.J. further developed his analysis in *WISE Underwriting Agency*

---

[704] *Groom v Crocker* [1939] 1 K.B. 194; *K/S Merc-Skandia XXXXII v Certain Lloyd Underwriters* [2001] Lloyd's Rep. I.R. 802.

[705] *Insurance Corporation of the Channel Islands v McHugh (No.1)* [1997] L.R.L.R. 94.

[706] *Gan Insurance Co Ltd v Tai Ping (Nos 2 and 3)* [2001] Lloyd's Rep. I.R. 667.

[707] *Eagle Star Insurance Co Ltd v Cresswell* [2004] Lloyd's Rep. I.R. 437.

[708] Echoing Mance L.J.'s comments in *Gan Insurance Co Ltd v Tai Ping Insurance Co Ltd (Nos 2 and 3)* [2001] Lloyds Rep. I.R. 667.

[709] A suggestion made, but not pursued, by Rix L.J. in *Eagle Star v Cresswell*. In *Anders & Kern Ltd v CGU Insurance Plc* [2008] Lloyd's Rep. I.R. 460 it was held that a policy condition under which insurers were permitted to waive by written consent a requirement imposed on the assured as regards leaving his premises unoccupied if its telephone communications had been cut was to be construed as requiring the insurers not to unreasonably withhold their consent and insist that the assured should remain in a situation of potential danger. The court went on to point out that reasonableness here did not mean objective reasonableness, but rather an exercise of discretion in good faith rather than for reasons unconnected with the claim. On the facts want of bad faith was not found. The Court of Appeal on appeal did not find it necessary to go into detail on this aspect of the decision, and agreed with the trial judge that on the facts the condition had been broken. Tuckey L.J. merely commented that there had been no argument before it on the distinction between good faith and reasonableness, and that any duty owed by the insurers in the present case could not have amounted to one under which they agreed to consider whether they should deprive themselves of the benefit of a condition which delimited the very risk which they had accepted.

Ltd v Grupo Nacional Provincial SA,[710] where the issue was whether reinsurers had waived the disclosure of material facts under s.18(2)(c) of the 1906 Act. Rix L.J.'s view, albeit a dissenting one, was that the doctrine of waiver was founded on fairness, and accordingly that it would be a breach of the underwriter's duty of utmost good faith to avoid a policy where the relevant information had been waived. The majority approach was that the reinsurers were entitled to rely upon the information presented to them on its face, although what is of particular interest in Rix L.J.'s analysis is the gradual development of good faith into a general principle governing the underwriter's dealings with the policyholder. In *Diab v Regent Insurance Co Ltd*[711] the Privy Council denied that insurers were under any post-loss duty of good faith to inform the assured of the need to comply with claims conditions, although left open the possibility that a contract term under which insurers had the right to extend time for compliance was subject to an implied term or duty of good faith whereby due consideration to an extension would be given.[712]

Avoidance. The cases support the proposition that the decision to avoid for **6–129**
breach of the duty of utmost good faith is itself one tempered by the insurers' own duty. This was first suggested by Colman J. in *Strive Shipping Corp v Hellenic Mutual War Risks Association*,[713] where it was held that non-disclosure of suspicious circumstances connecting the assured with previous marine casualties, which were proved at the trial to be groundless, were material on inception but that reliance on them once they had been discredited would be a breach of the insurers' own continuing duty of utmost good faith. Colman J.'s decision doubted by the Court of Appeal in *Brotherton v Aseguradora Colseguros SA (No.2)*,[714] but those reservations were swept aside soon afterwards by a differently constituted Court of Appeal, in *Drake Insurance Co v Provident Insurance Co*.[715] Here, insurers had avoided a motor policy by reason of the assured's failure to disclose a speeding conviction: that conviction, coupled with an accident in which the assured's wife had been involved, operated to raise the premium under the insurer's mechanical underwriting criteria. Following an incident involving the assured's wife the insurers avoided the policy. Had they made further investigations, it would have become apparent to them that the earlier accident had not been the fault of the assured's wife and ought to have been left out of account in fixing the premium, thereby rendering the conviction alone incapable of affecting the premium. The Court of Appeal was unanimous that the insurers owed a duty of utmost good faith to the assured in reaching the decision whether or not to avoid the policy, and the remedy for breach of that duty in favour of the assured was to prevent reliance on the avoidance. The Court of Appeal held that the duty of utmost good faith was mutual[716] and that the right

---

[710] *WISE Underwriting Agency Ltd v Grupo Nacional Provincial SA* [2004] Lloyd's Rep. I.R. 764.

[711] *Diab v Regent Insurance Co Ltd* [2006] Lloyd's Rep. I.R. 779.

[712] See also *Quinn Direct Insurance Ltd v The Law Society of England and Wales* [2009] EWHC 2588 (Ch), affirmed [2010] EWCA Civ 647, where it was recognised that insurers cannot make unreasonable demands for documentation in support of a claim.

[713] *Strive Shipping Corp v Hellenic Mutual War Risks Association* [2002] Lloyd's Rep. I.R. 669.

[714] *Brotherton v Aseguradora Colseguros SA (No.2)* [2003] Lloyd's Rep. I.R. 758.

[715] *Drake Insurance Co v Provident Insurance Co* [2004] Lloyd's Rep. I.R. 277.

[716] Relying on *La Banque Financière de la Cité v Westgate Insurance Co Ltd* [1989] 2 All E.R. 952.

to avoid was subject to good faith considerations.[717] Rix L.J. concluded that "the doctrine of good faith should be capable of limiting the insurer's right to avoid in circumstances where that remedy, which has been described in recent years as draconian, would operate unfairly." As to the scope of the duty, Rix and Clarke L.JJ. held that it was confined to the situation in which the insurers were actually aware, or had "blind-eye" knowledge, that the facts upon which they purported to rely were immaterial, had not induced the policy or otherwise with hindsight did not give rise to a right to avoid. On the facts, the majority was satisfied that the avoidance in *Drake* had not been in bad faith as defined by this narrow test. Clarke L.J. expressly noted that there was no authority for the proposition that an insurer had to act reasonably in deciding whether or not to avoid. Pill L.J., dissenting held that the duty of utmost good faith was wider, and that failure by the insurers to make enquiry of the assured before taking the drastic step of avoiding the policy was a breach by the insurer of the duty of good faith; the insurers' knowledge was not relevant, as they owed the assured a duty to tell him what they had in mind and give him an opportunity to update them.

Alternative remedies

6–130 *Duty of care.* At first instance in *Banque Keyser Ullman*[718] Steyn J. awarded damages against the insurer in favour of the assured in the tort of negligence, as an alternative to damages in respect of a breach of the duty of utmost good faith. The Court of Appeal reversed this ruling in *La Banque Financière*,[719] consistently with the emergence of the principle that the relationship between the parties to a commercial contract should be governed by that contract and not by the intervention of tort. In the view of the Court of Appeal, there was no duty of care on the insurers to ensure that material facts of the type in question were disclosed to the banks. The reasoning of the Court of Appeal was that there could only be a duty of care, in the form of a duty to speak, if there had been an assumption of responsibility by the underwriters to the banks, but there was nothing of that sort present on the facts. The House of Lords in *La Banque Financière* did not express a final view on this question, as its finding that the fraud exclusion did not apply to L's fraud led to the conclusion that the insurer's right to reject the claim had nothing to do with L's fraud, so that the necessary causation for a claim in tort was missing. The possible existence of a duty of care in general was left open by Lords Bridge and Jauncey, the latter making the vital point that any duty of care could not in any event go beyond what was required by the insurer's duty of disclosure. The remainder of the House of Lords dealt with the question of duty of care specifically on the issue before it, namely, whether contracting party A owes a duty to contracting party B to disclose to contracting party B the fraud of B's own agent in negotiating the contract. Such a duty was unacceptable to Lord Templeman, with whom Lords Brandon and Ackner agreed. The general question of whether the duty of utmost good faith

---

[717] Lord Lloyd in *Pan Atlantic Insurance Co v Pine Top Insurance Co* [1995] 1 A.C. 501 "Nor is the obligation of good faith limited to one of disclosure. As Lord Mansfield said in *Carter v Boehm*. at 1918, there may be circumstances in which an insurer, by asserting a right to avoid for non-disclosure, would himself be guilty of want of good faith"; Lord Hobhouse in *The Star Sea* [2001] 1 Lloyd's Rep. 389, "The courts have consistently set their face against allowing the assured's duty of good faith to be used by the insurer as an instrument for enabling the insurer himself to act in bad faith".

[718] *Banque Keyser Ullman SA v Skandia (UK) Insurance Co Ltd* [1987] 2 All E.R. 923.

[719] *La Banque Financière de la Cité SA v Westgate Insurance Co Ltd* [1989] 2 All E.R. 952.

gives rise to the necessary relationship for the imposition of a tortious duty of care was thus left open.

A similar, if weaker, argument was put to the Court of Appeal in *The Good Luck*.[720] It was there claimed by the mortgagee bank that a Letter of Undertaking, given by the insurer to the bank in its capacity as assignee of the proceeds of the policy and obliging the insurer to inform the bank in the event of the insurance ceasing, gave rise to a duty on the insurer to disclose any misconduct of the assured. The "duty to speak" was asserted on the ground that the Letter of Undertaking itself constituted a contract of utmost good faith and that whether or not a duty of disclosure existed on that basis a tortious duty to speak arose. The Court of Appeal rejected the first of these alternatives, on the basis that the Letter of Undertaking constituted an ordinary commercial contract and the second on the basis that the relationship between insurer and bank was governed by contract and could not give rise to a duty to speak. The duty to speak argument had little chance of success in respect of a commercial contract given that the same approach had failed in *Banque Keyser Ullman* in respect of a contract of utmost good faith.

While it is clear that the duty of utmost good faith does not carry with it any duty of care, such a duty may exist if the usual requirements for the imposition of that duty are satisfied. Thus, if the insurers undertake additional responsibility towards the assured, it may be appropriate to recognise a duty of care. In the cases decided to date the courts have not been readily persuaded that insurers have gone beyond their ordinary responsibilities under a contract of insurance and have not undertaken any additional duty to warn the assured of the risky nature of the policy.[721] The possibility that insurers have undertaken additional responsibilities capable of triggering a duty of care cannot, however, be dismissed entirely. In *HIH Casualty and General Insurance Co v Chase Manhattan Bank*[722] Rix L.J. left open the possibility that, exceptionally, an insurer may owe a duty of care where he took it upon himself to advise the assured as to the nature of the cover required by him. In *Gorham v British Telecommunications Plc*[723] insurers were held to have assumed responsibility for providing accurate investment advice to the assured in relation to the sale of a personal pension plan, and were held to be liable in damages up to the point at which their advice had been withdrawn and the proper advice had been given.

Statutory remedy. In *Aldrich v Norwich Union Life, Norwich Union Life v Qureshi*,[724] it was argued that breach of s.47 of the Financial Services Act 1986 (now re-enacted as s.397 of the Financial Services and Markets Act 2000) could give rise to an action for damages. Section 47 made it a criminal offence for any person to make a false, misleading, false or deceptive statement, or dishonestly to conceal any material fact. The Court of Appeal held that the section did not give rise to an action for damages. First, the section did not create a duty of disclosure wider than that recognised at common law. Secondly, the section did not expressly give rise to civil rights, whereas the 1986 Act specifically created civil rights in a number of other contexts. The Court of Appeal also rejected the

6–131

---

[720] *Bank of Nova Scotia v Hellenic War Risks Association (Bermuda) Ltd (The Good Luck)* [1989] 2 Lloyd's Rep. 238.

[721] *Searle v AR Hales & Co Ltd* [1996] L.R.L.R. 68.

[722] *HIH Casualty and General Insurance Co v Chase Manhattan Bank* [2001] Lloyd's Rep. I.R. 702.

[723] *Gorham v British Telecommunications Plc* [2001] Lloyd's Rep. I.R. 531.

[724] *Aldrich v Norwich Union Life, Norwich Union Life v Qureshi* [2000] Lloyd's Rep. I.R. 1.

related argument that breach of s.47 prevented the insurers from relying on their rights under the investment scheme and to seek repayment of sums paid by them to Lloyd's under the guarantees, as property rights had accrued to the insurers which could not be affected by any illegality.[725] It is likely that s.397 of the Financial Services and Markets Act 2000 will be construed in the same fashion, as the 2000 Act does not specifically confer civil rights for infringements of the section whereas civil rights are expressly stated to be available for other infringements.[726]

9. REFORM OF THE LAW OF UTMOST GOOD FAITH

6–132 **The Law Commission's 1980 Report.** There has for some years been dissatisfaction with the operation of the doctrine of utmost good faith. The notion of a spontaneous duty of disclosure on the assured, tested by reference to what would be regarded as material by a prudent underwriter, has been regarded as imposing too onerous a duty on the assured. In recent years the courts have mitigated many of the worst features of the existing law, in particular by requiring proof by the insurers of actual inducement. However, prompted by a draft directive on insurance contract law published by the European Commission, the English Law Commission undertook an investigation into the law of utmost good faith and warranties. It published a Consultation Paper in 1979 and a Final Report in 1980, Law Commission Working Paper No.70. The essential elements of the draft bill appended to the Report were the retention of the duty of disclosure and also its modification by the adoption of a prudent assured test for materiality in place of the prudent underwriter test.

6–133 **The Law Commissions' 2007 Proposals.** In January 2006 the English and Scottish Law Commissions launched a second, joint, investigation into the law of insurance. After an initial scoping exercise to determine the views of interested parties as to the areas of investigation, the Law Commissions focused in the initial stage of its inquiry into utmost good faith and breach of warranty. Three Issues Papers were published in 2006 and 2007, and after consultation a consolidated consultation paper Misrepresentation, Non-Disclosure and Breach of Warranty by the Insured, was published in July 2007 (Law Commission Consultation Paper No.182, 2007). This document has made a series of important recommendations for changes to the law. The underlying purposes of the recommendations are: the reaching of a fair balance between the interests of insurers and policyholders, whereby policies meet reasonable expectations of policyholders without imposing undue costs on insurers; and the development of a system of rules which are coherent, clear and readily understandable. After a process which lasted nearly four years, punctuated by frequent consultation documents and position papers, the English and Scottish Law Commissions

---

[725] On the principle in *Tinsley v Milligan* [1994] 1 A.C. 340.

[726] Section 71 of the 2000 Act, which gives a right of private action where a person authorised under the Act allows an unapproved or prohibited person to carry on activities on his behalf.

produced, on December 15, 2009, their first fully formulated draft Bill on reform of insurance law.

The Consumer Insurance (Disclosure and Representations) Bill 2009

Scope and objectives. The Report which accompanies and explains the Bill sets **6–134** out at length the problems identified with the existing law of pre-contractual misrepresentation and disclosure, as enshrined in the Marine Insurance Act 1906 ss.17 to 20. It also notes that the position in the consumer market has been transformed by the Financial Ombudsman Service (FOS) and its industry-established predecessor the Insurance Ombudsman Bureau. The FOS hears virtually all consumer insurance disputes and resolves them by reference to principles of fairness as set out on the Insurance Conduct of Business Rules in the Financial Services Authority Handbook rather than strict rules of law. The Report confirms that "Essentially, the draft Bill codifies what the FOS already does." So, even though the law may change, the practical position may not. Reform may nevertheless be regarded as important, and the Report lists five reasons for this. (1) *"Consumers are only able to obtain justice from the Financial Ombudsman Service, not from the courts"*, and that is in any event only the case where the award is £100,000 or less: sums awarded in excess of that figure are payable only in the discretion of the insurer. The FOS has limited resources and in any event cannot deal with all cases. (2) *"The rules applying to non-disclosure and misrepresentation are unacceptably confusing"* in a number of respects: warnings given by insurers are not always helpful; many consumers are unaware of the existence of the FOS; and even when a case gets to FOS there is little consistency in its decisions. (3) *"Confusion over the law penalises some vulnerable groups"* in that particular groups, such as the aged, may have difficulty in ascertaining their duties, whereas a duty of disclosure removes the possibility of cover from, e.g. persons with criminal convictions or suffering from particular illnesses. (4) *"The present system imposes inappropriate roles on the FOS, the FSA"*, because the FOS has been required to make policy rather than to pronounce on particular disputes. (5) *"Increasingly, differences in law between the UK and its European partners need to be justified"*, particularly because the UK system has become uncertain and confusing in that the FOS may refuse jurisdiction if it believes that the case should be heard by a court (which is required to apply existing strict law) and in that FOS decisions are not readily available nor do they provide reasons.

The Bill applies only to consumer insurances, the term being defined by clause 1 as one entered into by an individual wholly or mainly for purposes unrelated to the individual's trade, business or profession. High-value subject-matter, including yachts and even private jets are not excluded, although if for tax or other reasons a consumer forms a company as nominal owner then the Bill will cease to apply insofar as the company is the assured. There is no attempt to define insurance. The Law Commission's earlier suggested extension of protection to "micro-businesses" has not yet been adopted, although it may reappear in any subsequent bill on commercial insurance. The phrase "wholly or mainly" encompasses a policy which has mixed consumer and business uses, the classic examples being a buildings insurance covering both the private flat above the assured's shop and the shop itself, or on a computer used for mixed purposes. Finding the "main" purpose will inevitably cause problems at the margins.

Abolition of the duty of disclosure. The most important reform is the abolition of **6–135** the duty of disclosure. This is achieved by cll.2(4)–(5) and 11, the latter disapplying ss.18–20 of the Marine Insurance Act 1906 (which set out the rules on pre-contract disclosure and representations) in the context of consumer insurance, and the former modifying the common law and s.17 of the 1906 Act so that these are subject to the Bill. Both the common law and s.17 are in principle capable of extending to post-contractual duties, and the present Bill leaves the law on this matter intact although it will be dealt at a later stage in the reform process. Renewals, endorsements and the like are, however, within the Bill. The right of a motor insurer to avoid a policy, and thereby to relieve itself of the obligation to satisfy a judgment against the assured (see s.152 of the Road Traffic Act 1988), is similarly modified by cl.11(3).

It is not permissible for these rules to be ousted by contract unless the term in question is of benefit to the assured. The prohibition on contracting out includes any term which chooses some other law as the law applicable to the policy if English law would otherwise apply (cl.10).

If the Bill is adopted, cl.12 would postpone its application for a year beginning with the day on which it becomes law, in order to allow insurers an opportunity to adjust to the new regime. The Bill would then apply to contracts made, renewed or varied after that date.

6–136   *The duty not to misrepresent.* These provisions are replaced by a new duty in cl.2(2), the duty on a consumer to take reasonable care not to make a misrepresentation. If reasonable care is taken, the insurers have no remedy. Clause 3(1) defines "reasonable care" in general terms as requiring determination in the light of all relevant circumstances, and cl.3(2) sets out illustrations of such circumstances: (a) the type of consumer insurance policy in question, and its target market; (b) any relevant explanatory material or publicity produced or authorised by the insurer; (c) how clear, and how specific, the insurer's questions were; and (d) whether or not an agent was acting for the consumer. The test of reasonableness is objective, that of a reasonable consumer (cl.3(3)) rather than that of a person with the consumer's characteristics, although such characteristics are to be taken into account under cl.3(5) if the insurer was or ought to have been aware of them. Also, if the assured was by reason of his special knowledge dishonest in making a statement, he will not be saved by the fact that the same answer would have been given by a prudent assured: dishonesty unravels all. The existing test of "prudent underwriter" is thus replaced by "prudent assured". It will be noted that there is nothing to prevent an insurer from asking general question such as, "are there any other matters which may affect the risk?" Unrestricted, this type of question reintroduces disclosure by the back door. In that situation, the criteria in cl.3(2), and in particular the focus on the nature of the insurer's questions, will be relevant in determining whether an assured has acted reasonably in his response.

The effect of these provisions is summarised by the Law Commissions in their report. An assured is to be treated as having acted reasonably if: "(1) the question was general, and a reasonable consumer would not understand that the insurer was asking about the particular information at issue; (2) the consumer had reasonable grounds for believing that what they said was true; (3) a reasonable consumer would not have appreciated that the fact was one which the insurer would want to know about; (4) it was reasonable for the consumer to assume that the insurer would obtain that information for itself; or (5) in particular, if the insurer indicated that it may obtain information from a third party, the consumer might reasonably think the insurer would obtain the information directly from the third party."

The Bill does not attempt to define "misrepresentation", leaving that matter to the common law. The key point is that a positive statement is required, although cl.2(3) modifies that slightly by confirming that a failure by a consumer to comply with the insurer's request to confirm or amend particulars previously given is capable of being a misrepresentation for the purposes of the Bill. This may be particularly important on renewal or where there is a time-lag between the proposal and the insurer's confirmation of willingness to enter into the policy. The common law also recognises the possibility that a positive statement may, by omission, be misleading, and such a statement is also to be recognised as a misrepresentation.

Proof that the assured has not taken reasonable care is not enough to give rise to remedies. Clause 4 preserves the common law rule that the insurer has to prove inducement, in that, but for the misrepresentation, the insurer would not have entered into the policy (or agreed a variation to it) at all or would have done so on different terms. There is no common law presumption of inducement based on the evidence of other underwriters, and this principle is retained by the Bill: the insurer must prove its own inducement.

Remedies for misrepresentation. The insurer cannot avoid a policy where the **6–137** assured has acted reasonably. Remedies are available only where the assured has been guilty of deliberate or reckless conduct, or has been careless (assuming of course that there has also been an inducing effect).

Clause 5(2) of the Bill provides that a misrepresentation is deliberate or reckless if the consumer knew both that: (a) it was untrue or misleading, or did not care whether or not it was untrue or misleading; and (b) the matter to which the misrepresentation related was relevant to the insurer, or did not care whether or not it was relevant to the insurer. For each element the burden of proof is borne by the insurer (cl.5(4)), but there is a presumption that the consumer had the knowledge of a reasonable consumer and that (in relation to requirement (b) that the answer to a specific question was relevant to the insurer. It follows that an assured can act deliberately or recklessly in relation to his knowledge of the truth of the statement itself or in relation to his knowledge of its impact on the insurer, and it may be thought that the Bill does no more than require the assured to answer an express question honestly. For example, if the assured is asked about convictions, a failure to mention something trivial might be justified on the basis that a reasonable consumer would not have thought that trivia might have been relevant to the insurer. If a misrepresentation is deliberate or reckless, then under Sch.1 Pt I para.2, the insurer may avoid the contract and refuse all claims, and need not return any of the premiums paid, except to the extent (if any) that it would be unfair to the consumer to retain them. This reflects the common law, with the slight modification that at common law there is no right to return of premium in the case of fraud (at least in marine insurance, the position elsewhere is uncertain) whereas the Bill contemplates that there might be a full or partial return of premium in some cases: one illustration of such a possibility is a joint policy where only one of the joint assureds was culpable. Earlier suggestions that life policies might become incontestable after five years have not been adopted in the Bill.

Clause 5(3) states that a misrepresentation is careless if it is not deliberate or reckless. The complex consequences of a careless misrepresentation are set out in Sch.1 Pt I paras 3–8. The object is to put the insurers in the position that they would have been in had the truth been told. If they would not have entered into the contract at all, the policy can be avoided but the premium has to be repaid (para.5—this is the same as the common law). If the insurers would have entered into the contract, but on different terms, the insurers are entitled to treat the contract as if it contained those terms (para.6), so that they can rely upon a condition or exclusion that would have been inserted. If the insurers would have entered into the policy on the same terms but on payment of additional premium, the policy is valid but any claim may be reduced proportionately by reference to the proportion of the full premium actually paid by the assured (paras 7–8). These provisions are concerned only with claims. Paragraph 9 deals with the future of the policy itself independently of any claim. In essence, in the absence of a claim: (a) the insurers are entitled to avoid the policy if they would not have entered into the contract at all; (b) if the insurers would have entered into the policy on different terms or with a higher premium, they may at their option either give notice to the assured varying the policy in the relevant respect (an offer which the assured may reject in which case the policy will terminate) or give reasonable notice terminating the policy (subject in the latter case to repaying the unexpired proportion of the premium). It is to be presumed that the insurers have these rights after they have received a claim, but subject to their obligation to deal with the claim in the manner set out in paras 6–8. In the case of life policy, there is no option to terminate but instead the insurers are required to continue cover albeit on amended terms (if acceptable to the assured).

The remedies apply equally to a claim under any variation to a policy which can reasonably be treated separately from the subject matter of the rest of the contract. Thus if the assured obtains an extension of cover for, e.g. a period of unoccupancy, and does so by misstating relevant facts, the insurers can avoid the extension, or reduce their liability for a claim relating to unoccupancy in the usual way, but any other claim has to be met in full. By contrast, if the variation is not separable, then the entire policy is to be regarded as tainted by the false statement (paras 10–12).

The appendices to the Report contain analysis of how the Bill will affect contribution and subrogation claims where the insurer is as a result of the operation of the Bill liable only for a proportion of the claim. These matters are not actually dealt with by the Bill and will have to be worked through by the courts as and when the issues arise. The Law Commissions' view of contribution is that an insurer who is liable to the assured only for a proportion of the sum otherwise payable under the policy should not be any better or worse off where there is a contribution dispute with an insurer who is liable for the full amount payable. As far as subrogation is concerned, the Law Commissions' view (which is not in the Bill) is that if the assured does not receive a full indemnity because recovery is reduced proportionately, any sum recovered from a third party under subrogation rights is not to be regarded as forming part of the uninsured loss and thus to be retained by the assured. Instead, the sum is to be split between the assured and the insurer in the same proportion.

6–138 *The role of intermediaries.* A variety of intermediaries may be involved in placing cover. The assured may negotiate with an agent employed by, or acting on behalf of, the insurers. The assured may approach an independent broker in order to obtain assistance in placing the risk with an appropriate insurer. The assured may use an "aggregator" website which directs him to quotes from one or more insurers. In every case it is necessary to determine on whose behalf the intermediary is acting, as the Bill does not seek to reverse the common law rule that a principal is responsible for the misdeeds of his agent, and indeed the common law is expressly preserved by cl.12(4). Thus, if the assured's agent deliberately makes a false statement to the insurers, the insurers are entitled to treat the statement as one made by the assured himself even though the assured himself had acted perfectly innocently: in such circumstances the assured must look to the agent for relief. Equally, if the assured makes truthful statements to an agent of the insurers, and those statements are altered by the agent in presenting the risk to the insurers, the assured has clearly satisfied his duty under the Bill.

The Bill sets out, in cl.9 and Sch.2, rules for determining the incidence of agency. There are three cases in which the agent is to be treated as the agent of the insurer: (a) when the agent does something in the agent's capacity as the appointed representative of the insurer for the purposes of the Financial Services and Markets Act 2000; (b) when the agent collects information from the consumer, if the insurer had given the agent express authority to do so as the insurer's agent; and (c) (c) when the agent enters into the contract as the insurer's agent, if the insurer had given the agent express authority to do so (para.2). In all other cases (para.3) there is a presumption that the agent is acting on behalf of the consumer, a reversal of the Law Commissions' earlier view that the presumption should be the very opposite. Factors which confirm that presumption are: (a) the agent undertakes to give impartial advice to the consumer; (b) the agent undertakes to conduct a fair analysis of the market; and (c) the assured pays the agent a fee. Factors which may rebut the presumption include: (a) the agent places insurance with only a small proportion of the insurers who provide insurance of the type in question; (b) the insurer provides the relevant insurance through only a limited number of agents; (c) the insurer permits the agent to use the insurer's name in providing the agent's services; (d) the insurance in question is marketed under the name of the agent; and (e) the insurer asks the agent to solicit the consumer's custom.

Basis clauses. The Bill does not attempt to reform the law of warranties in general. Instead, it focuses only on basis clauses, and seeks to remove the potential for the Bill to be undermined by the device of requiring the assured to warrant the correctness of all of his statements by a basis clause: was this device to be retained, insurers would be able to treat themselves as discharged from liability even though a statement was both honest and had no effect on the insurer's judgment. Clause 6 simply provides that a representation leading up to a policy or to a variation in a policy is not capable of being converted into a warranty by means of any policy term or other declaration deeming one or more answers to be the basis of the contract. This leaves it open to the insurers to require particular statements to be warranted, and in that respect the Bill is a retreat from the Law Commissions' earlier proposal to abolish all warranties of present fact. **6–139**

Special cases. Two special cases are dealt with by the Bill. The first is group insurance, defined by cl.7(1) as a contract entered into by party A in order to provide cover to a third party C, in circumstances where C is not a party to the contract, C is a consumer and C has directly or indirectly provided information to the insurer. The most important illustration is that of a policy taken out by an employer for the benefit of employees, with each employee being required to provide information to the employer for transmission to the insurer to determine qualification. Clause 7 disregards the fact that the assured, A, is almost certainly not a consumer, and goes on to treat each beneficiary as an assured in his own right for the purposes of representations. Thus, any breach of the duty to act reasonably by any one beneficiary permits the insurers to obtain the usual relief against him, but leaving the rights of other beneficiaries untouched. Any breach **6–140** by the policyholder himself is, however, outside the scope of the present measure, because the policyholder will almost certainly not be a consumer.

The second special case is a life policy taken out by the assured on the life of another person (L), where L is not himself a party to the policy. Any information provide to the insurer by L is, under cl.8, to be treated as having been provided by the assured himself, but the relevant state of mind for determining remedies is that of L and not the assured. This means that, for example, if a wife takes out a policy on the life of her husband, and the husband deliberately misstates facts about his health, the insurers will have the appropriate remedy against the wife as assured even though she was completely innocent. Independently, the insurers retain their rights under the Bill against the wife in respect of any false statements made by her. In short, any statements made by either person must be honest.

6–141 *Continuing duty.* In March 2010 the Law Commissions published Issues Paper No.6. The Issues Paper is concerned primarily with the assured's ability to recover damages for late payment of policy moneys,[727] but the Law Commissions' provisional recommendation that s.17 of the Marine Insurance Act 1906 should be amended to allow other remedies—and in particular, damages—has clear implications for other breaches of the continuing duty of insurers. A further issues paper on this topic is to be published in 2010.

---

[727] See Ch.10, below.

CHAPTER 7

TERMS OF INSURANCE CONTRACTS

1. TERMINOLOGY

In English law contractual terms are normally divided into three classes: (1) **7–001**
warranties, which are subsidiary or minor terms, the breach of which gives the
innocent party a right to damages only; (2) conditions, which are major terms, the
breach of which confers upon the innocent party, in addition to a right to
damages, the further right to treat the contract as repudiated and to refuse to
proffer or accept future performance; and (3) innominate terms, the significance
of which cannot be assessed at the outset so that the rights of the innocent party
depend upon the seriousness of the consequences of any breach.[1] Determining
whether a contract term is a condition, warranty or an innominate stipulation is
a matter of construing the contract, and the terminology used by the parties is not
conclusive.[2]

The concepts of condition and warranty in insurance law bear a rather different
meaning. An insurance condition is either an obligation on the assured to act in
a particular way, or a contingency—which may be outside the control of the
assured—upon which the validity of the policy or of any claim may depend. As
the nature and types of insurance conditions vary so widely, the consequences of
a breach are not uniform, and may range from the right to terminate the policy
(a bare condition) or to refuse a claim (a condition precedent) down to a mere
right to damages (a minor condition). An insurance warranty is a pre-contractual
promise by the assured that a given fact is true, or that a given fact will remain
true, or that he will behave or refrain from behaving in a particular way. The
effect of a breach of warranty is to bring the risk to an end automatically as from
the date of breach. As is the case with the general law, descriptions are not
necessarily conclusive; this matter is considered below.

2. INSURANCE CONDITIONS

Subject matter of conditions. Insurance policies typically contain conditions **7–002**
relating to the commencement of the risk, including the date at which the
premium must be paid, the conduct of the assured during the currency of the
policy, dealing with matters such as procuring other insurance, increasing the
risk, the duty to exercise reasonable care and the maintenance of accounting or
similar records, and the claims procedure, including duties to present claims
within a specified time and to assist the insurer with the conduct of the claim. The

---

[1] *Hong Kong Fir Shipping Co Ltd v Kawasaki Kisen Kaisha Ltd* [1962] 2 Q.B. 26.
[2] *Schuler AG v Wickman Machine Tool Sales* [1974] A.C. 235.

rights of the insurer on a breach of condition depend upon the terms of the contract and the nature of the condition. It is possible to divide conditions into three classes: conditions precedent to the policy or risk; conditions precedent to liability; and other conditions.

7–003   **Conditions precedent to the validity of the policy or to the attachment of the risk.** It is necessary to draw a distinction between a condition precedent to the contract and a condition precedent to the inception of the risk. The former class of condition must be satisfied before the parties can be treated as having any contract at all. The latter class of condition presupposes a valid contract, but one under which the risk has not attached until the assured has met the requisite conditions. The two types of condition have three common features. The first is that the insurers cannot be liable for any loss occurring before the condition has been satisfied, at least in the absence of express wording which backdates the inception of the risk. The second common feature is that a condition can only be imposed before a binding agreement has been entered into. It is not open to the underwriters, following the making of the contract, to impose conditions on the assured which purport to postpone the date of the contract or the inception of the risk.[3] The third common feature is that a condition precedent cannot operate to remove the assured's accrued rights. Thus, if a policy is issued to a bank covering fidelity losses discovered during the currency of the policy, and the policy imposes a condition precedent that the bank has adopted anti-fraud measures requiring employees to take two weeks' continuous holiday, the fact that those measures had not been complied with before the policy was taken out cannot prevent the bank from reporting discovered losses to the insurers which were incurred before the policy incepted.[4] That said, the distinction may be important for other purposes, in particular the duty of utmost good faith which—unless the policy otherwise provides—comes to an end when the contract is made and not when the risk incepts. Assuming that a valid condition has been imposed and it is never satisfied, the insurers do not ever come on risk and the assured is entitled to a return of his premium for total failure of consideration: the general principle is set out in ss.84(1) and 84(3)(a) of the Marine Insurance Act 1906.

Conditions precedent to the policy or to the inception of the risk may relate to a number of matters, e.g. the provision of further information by the assured,[5] the inspection of the insured subject matter[6] and compliance with any recommendations arising therefrom,[7] the absence of overlapping insurance, the payment of the premium,[8] in the case of a declaration policy a timely declaration of the risk,[9] the implementation of security measures[10] or the satisfactory disclosure of all material facts. In order to create a condition precedent, the insurers must make it

---

[3] *Mulchrone v Swiss Life (UK) Plc* [2006] Lloyd's Rep. I.R. 339; *Bonner v Cox Dedicated Corporate Member Ltd* [2006] Lloyd's Rep. I.R. 385.

[4] *MJ Harrington Syndicate 2000 v Axa Oyak Sigorta AS* [2007] Lloyd's Rep. I.R. 60, where Aikens J. felt that there was some force in this point.

[5] *Mulchrone v Swiss Life (UK) Plc* [2006] Lloyd's Rep. I.R. 339; *Bonner v Cox Dedicated Corporate Member Ltd* [2006] Lloyd's Rep. I.R. 385.

[6] *Zeus Tradition Marine Ltd v Bell (The Zeus V)* [2000] 2 Lloyd's Rep. 587.

[7] *MJ Harrington Syndicate 2000 v Axa Oyak Sigorta AS* [2007] Lloyd's Rep. I.R. 60.

[8] *Aspen Insurance UK Ltd v Pectel Ltd* [2009] Lloyd's Rep. I.R. 440.

[9] *Glencore v Ryan (The Beursgracht)* [2002] Lloyd's Rep. I.R. 135 (not a condition precedent on the facts); *Limit No.2 Ltd v Axa Versicherung AG* [2008] Lloyd's Rep. I.R. 330, reversed in part on other grounds [2009] Lloyd's Rep. I.R. 396.

[10] *MJ Harrington Syndicate 2000 v Axa Oyak Sigorta AS* [2007] Lloyd's Rep. I.R. 60.

clear that the making of the policy or the attachment of the risk is in some way conditional on the condition having been satisfied.

Compliance with a condition precedent may be waived by the underwriters, although given that the breach of such a provision prevents a contract from being made or the risk attaching, as the case may be, waiver by election or affirmation is not an available argument and it is probably necessary for the assured to show that the underwriters are estopped by their conduct from relying on the provision. In *MJ Harrington Syndicate 2000 v Axa Oyak Sigorta AS*[11] a Turkish bank obtained a bankers' blanket bond policy covering, amongst other things, losses caused by the fraud of employees. The policy contained a condition precedent to the insurers' liability that each of the bank's employees was to take an uninterrupted holiday of at least two weeks per year, a standard anti-fraud measure in such policies. The insurers reinsured their liability under a policy which incorporated the holiday clause and which also stated that the reinsurance cover was subject to the bank's compliance with the recommendations of an earlier survey which had recommended implementation of the two-week holiday policy. The reinsurance slips were scratched in August 2003, at a time when the holiday rule had not been implemented. By October 2003 the bank had complied with the provision, and in November 2003 the reinsurers scratched an endorse-ment retroactively extending time for compliance until October 2003. Losses were reported to the reinsurers in November 2003, and it appeared that fraud had been committed by an employee who had not taken the required amount of holiday. The reinsurers refused to authorise payments on account, but in August 2004 they agreed to extend the reinsurance for a further 14 days pending renewal and they also subscribed to a new excess layer reinsurance policy covering the bank. Liability was ultimately denied in November 2004. On these facts Aikens J. held that it was arguable that the reinsurers had waived their rights, by agreeing to an extension of cover, by their inaction in the face of the claim and subsequently (although this point had not been argued) by extending the term of the reinsurance. Subscription to an additional excess of loss layer was thought by Aikens J. to be a less arguable basis for waiver.

Conditions precedent to the insurer's liability. Such conditions are normally, **7–004** but not always, concerned with the claims process. It may, for example, be stipulated that the insurer faces no liability unless the assured has submitted a claim within a fixed or reasonable time of the date of the loss. Conditions precedent may also be imposed in relation to the circumstances of the loss, e.g. that the assured is under a duty to take reasonable steps to avoid or mitigate any damage. Other conditions precedent may be general, e.g. that premium has been paid or that the insurer will not face liability until co-insurers have also accepted liability.

The consequences of a breach of a condition precedent depend upon the wording of the policy and the nature of the condition in question. In general, failure by the assured to comply with a condition precedent simply prevents the assured from making a claim: the assured is not in breach of contract in the sense that he is liable in damages for failing to comply with the condition, and the breach cannot affect the assured's right to pursue a separate claim the conditions relating to which have been complied with. Thus, if the condition precedent requires a claim to be made within a specific period, and the claim is late, that claim is lost but other claims are preserved. The same result follows where the

[11] *MJ Harrington Syndicate 2000 v Axa Oyak Sigorta AS* [2007] Lloyd's Rep. I.R. 60.

condition relates to reasonable care and the assured has failed to meet the required standard. In these types of case it follows that the assured is not in breach of contract for failing to comply with the condition precedent, as the only consequence of that failure is his inability to make a claim: insurers have not, therefore, suffered any loss which can give rise to damages. It follows that the assured may recover for a second loss if he subsequently complies with the condition.[12]

It is also possible to have a condition precedent which does not relate to a specific claim but which is of general application, e.g. an obligation to pay the premium prior to making any claim. In this situation, the effect of any breach is suspensory, i.e. that the assured cannot claim until he has paid the premium, but, pending payment, the assured's right to make a claim remains contingent and cannot crystallise until the premium has been paid. The insurers in such a case may have the right to claim the premium, but their cause of action is not breach of the condition precedent itself but rather the obligation to make payment: thus, insurers do not have to wait for a claim to come in before bringing their own action for the premium. In *Aspen Insurance UK Ltd v Pectel Ltd*[13] there was an attempt to argue that breach of a claims condition operated to prevent any future claim. The clause in question provided that cover was conditional on "the Assured paying in full the premium demanded and observing the terms and conditions of this insurance." Teare J. held that the clause was divisible, and that while payment of the premium may have been a condition precedent to any cover, observing the other terms and conditions (such as notification clauses) was not.

Some policies contain clauses which seek to render any breach of any condition precedent suspensory of the assured's right to make any claim under the policy, even if the breach relates to a specific claim. It is clear from the decision of the Court of Appeal, in *Kazakstan Wool Processors (Europe) Ltd v Nederlandsche Credietverzekering Maatschappij NV*[14] that, wherever possible, a clause of this type will be construed as divisible, allocating any breach to the affected claim rather than other claims. In this case the assured under a credit policy failed, in breach of condition, to submit a monthly trading return and sought to recover losses incurred prior to the breach. The Court of Appeal held that the effect of this condition was to suspend the insurer's liability where the assured was in breach of a policy condition, but only in respect of the claim to which the breach related; other claims were unaffected.[15]

Conditions precedent are likely to be unenforceable as such in consumer insurance contracts to which the Unfair Terms in Consumer Contracts Regulations 1999[16] apply. The Regulations operate to strike down a clause that has not been individually negotiated and which, contrary to the principle of good faith, causes a significant imbalance in the rights of the parties. This may operate to render the clause all but meaningless. In *Bankers Insurance Co Ltd v South*[17] the assured's travel policy contained various conditions precedent in the claims process. These were not adhered to by the assured. Buckley J. held that the

---

[12] *Hood's Trustees v Southern Union General Insurance Co of Australasia* [1928] Ch. 793 at 806.

[13] *Aspen Insurance UK Ltd v Pectel Ltd* [2009] Lloyd's Rep. I.R. 440.

[14] *Kazakstan Wool Processors (Europe) Ltd v Nederlandsche Credietverzekering Maatschappij NV* [2000] Lloyd's Rep. I.R. 371.

[15] The assured failed on the further ground that the insurers were under the policy entitled to give notice of termination, which they had done.

[16] SI 1999/2083.

[17] *Bankers Insurance Co Ltd v South* [2004] Lloyd's Rep. I.R. 1.

Regulations meant that part of the conditions that prevented recovery irrespective of the seriousness of the breach was ineffective, but that the insurers remained entitled to rely upon the conditions as if they were not conditions precedent. As will be seen below, such reliance is likely to be of little use: the condition is almost certainly not to be treated as a term whose breach by its nature gives rise to a repudiation of the policy, but rather will be regarded as an innominate term, the breach of which will leave the policy intact and may at best, but only in exceptional circumstances, give the insurers an action for damages for breach of contract.

Other conditions

Repudiatory and non-repudiatory breaches of contract. These types of condition are, for the most part, concerned with the conduct of the assured during the currency of the policy, and deal with matters such as increase of risk, the taking of reasonable care, double insurance and claims. The insurer may specify in terms the effect of a breach but, if there are no express provisions, the matter is governed by common law principles. In every case the distinction is between repudiation of the policy and a minor breach of the policy. A repudiation is a breach so serious that it amounts to an offer by the assured to bring the policy to an end, which the insurer can accept or reject.[18] Accordingly, if the assured has, by his breach of condition, repudiated the policy as a whole, the insurer has the right to determine the policy as from the date of breach and to claim damages for any loss suffered. Alternatively, the insurer may affirm the contract and confine himself to a claim for damages for proven loss, in which case he will remain liable to meet any claim.[19] By contrast, if the assured has not repudiated the policy by his breach of its terms, the insurer is confined to an action for damages for proven loss. Breach of a policy term can amount to a repudiation in one of two situations: the term is one which is, by its nature, a condition that goes to the root of the contract, breach of which is inevitably repudiatory; or the term is one that cannot at the outset be classified as either fundamental or trivial (i.e. it is innominate) in which case it is necessary to have regard to the consequences of the breach in order to determine whether or not there has been a repudiation.

7–005

Fundamental terms and ancillary terms. The starting point is to determine whether the term broken is by its nature fundamental or ancillary in that the consequences of any breach can be classified from the outset as either serious or minor. In ordinary contractual parlance, a condition is a term that goes to the root of the contract so that its breach is by definition a repudiation, and a warranty is a term that does not go to the root of the contract so that its breach simply gives rise to an action for damages. The word "warranty" has acquired a special meaning in insurance law and accordingly in the present text the distinction is referred to by reference to fundamental[20] and ancillary terms. Upon discovering a breach of a condition that by its nature goes to the root of the contract, the insurer may elect to treat the contract as repudiated; alternatively, he may affirm the policy. If an insurer does choose to affirm the policy notwithstanding repudiation by the assured he will be liable under it in the event of a loss. If the

7–006

---

[18] Sale of Goods Act 1979 s.11. See: *Hain Steamship Co v Tate & Lyle* (1936) 52 T.L.R. 617 at 619; *Heyman v Darwins* [1942] A.C. 356; *Johnson v Agnew* [1980] A.C. 367.

[19] *West v National Motor Insurance* [1955] 1 W.L.R. 343.

[20] The phrases "fundamental breach" and "breach of a fundamental term" have a complex history in English law: the use of the word "fundamental" in the present context is not designed to revert to discredited law but simply reflects the central importance of the term in question.

insurer elects to treat the policy as repudiated, he will have a good answer to any action upon it in respect of losses occurring after the date of the assured's breach, although it may be that a breach which relates to a specific claim—assuming that such a breach can by its nature be repudiatory of the entire policy—is retroactive to the date of the loss giving rise to the claim, thereby preventing the assured from being able to recover for that claim, despite the fact that the insurer has chosen to put an end to the policy.[21]

By contrast, if the term is by its nature relatively minor, its breach cannot be regarded as repudiatory and the policy itself is left intact, although the insurer will have an action for damages for any loss suffered by reason of the breach. The fact that the breach of a minor term has caused prejudice to the insurer is not enough to convert the breach into a repudiation: this was established by Colman J. at first instance in *Alfred McAlpine Plc v BAI (Run-off) Ltd*,[22] a principle not questioned on appeal to the Court of Appeal.[23]

In principle, it would seem that most conditions in an insurance policy are incapable of being classified as fundamental, as it is difficult to think of any particular obligations that may be imposed upon the assured that go to the heart of the contract. One possible candidate is the obligation to pay the premium, but it has been consistently held that a condition requiring payment of the premium is not regarded as a condition, the breach of which entitles the insurer to regard the policy as having been repudiated[24] unless time is or has been made of the essence, or unless the assured is unwilling or, by reason of insolvency, unable to pay.[25] It has also been held[26] that breach of a condition of a reinsurance agreement by the reinsured to maintain a retention and not to reinsure it elsewhere is not repudiatory. Most importantly, it was decided by the Court of Appeal in *Alfred McAlpine* that a notice of loss clause was no more than an ancillary administrative provision, breach of which could not be expected to allow the insurer to determine the policy as a whole. It might be thought that this decision must hold good in respect of all classes of claims provision,[27] given that failing to comply with obligations in respect of a claim can scarcely be regarded as evidencing an intention to offer to terminate the entire contract. This point was made by the majority of the Court of Appeal in *Friends Provident Life &*

---

[21] This point was made by Moore-Bick J. in *Friends Provident Life & Pensions Ltd v Sirius International Insurance Corporation* [2005] Lloyd's Rep. I.R. 135. As the learned judge pointed out, were it otherwise, the assured would be able to argue that his right to claim accrued as soon as the loss occurred, and the failure to give due notice would amount only to a breach of contract on the last date on which notice could have been served, so that the right to claim would be preserved on the accrued-rights principle. On appeal, [2006] Lloyd's Rep. I.R. 45, Mance L.J. referred to the conceptual difficulty raised here but did not seek to resolve the point one way or the other.

[22] *Alfred McAlpine Plc v BAI (Run-off) Ltd* [1998] 2 Lloyd's Rep. 694.

[23] *Alfred McAlpine Plc v BAI (Run-off) Ltd* [2000] Lloyd's Rep. I.R. 352.

[24] *Fenton Insurance Co Ltd v Gothaer Versicherungsbank WaG* [1991] 1 Lloyd's Rep. 172; *Figre Ltd v Mander* [1999] Lloyd's Rep. I.R. 193; *The Beursgracht* [2002] Lloyd's Rep. I.R. 335. A condition in an open cover whereby the policyholder has to make declarations of risks accepted is also not to be treated as a fundamental term even though timely declaration attracts an immediate obligation to pay the premium: *The Beursgracht* [2002] Lloyd's Rep. I.R. 335; *Limit No.2 Ltd v Axa Versicherung AG* [2008] Lloyd's Rep. I.R. 330 (reversed in part on other grounds [2009] Lloyd's Rep. I.R. 396).

[25] *Pacific & General Insurance Co Ltd v Hazell* [1996] L.R.L.R. 65.

[26] *Kingscroft insurance Co Ltd v Nissan Fire & Marine insurance Co Ltd (No.2)* [1999] Lloyd's Rep. I.R. 603.

[27] *Trans-Pacific Insurance Co (Australia) Ltd v Grand Union Insurance Co Ltd* (1990) 6 ANZ Insurance Cases 60–949. The contrary decision of Byrt J. in *Taylor v Builders Accident Insurance Ltd* (1997) M.C.L.C. 247 must be taken to be incorrect.

Pensions Ltd v Sirius International Insurance Corp,[28] although Waller L.J. expressed the view that breach of a claims condition could in exceptional circumstances be repudiatory, e.g. where there were repeated breaches of the same provision. The test in these cases is whether the insurers have been deprived of substantially the entire benefit of the contract, and whether the assured wishes no longer to be bound: indeed, there can be very few conditions breach, of which by the assured can be regarded as amounting to the demonstration by him of an intention no longer to be bound by the agreement, or as amounting to a fundamental denial of the insurer's rights.

It follows that a condition will be classified as setting out a fundamental obligation only in exceptional circumstances. The only reported illustration is in the context of credit insurance, where it was held that failure by the assured to comply with the obligation to apply ordinary lending criteria to the assessment of risks (i.e. to act as if there was credit insurance in place) was a repudiatory breach.[29]

Innominate terms. In practice it is likely that the majority of policy terms cannot   **7–007**
from the outset be stated as either fundamental or ancillary, and such provisions may be regarded as falling into the intermediate "innominate" category recognised by the Court of Appeal in *Hong Kong Fir Shipping Co Ltd v Kawasaki Kisen Kaisha*[30] as representative of the general law of contract. This principle has been applied in the insurance context[31] and, in the case of an innominate condition the seriousness of the consequences of the breach for the insurer determines whether the breach is repudiatory or non-repudiatory. By parity of reasoning with the initial classification of policy terms, it would seem that there are very few breaches which can cause serious prejudice to insurers and which cannot be remedied by an action in damages. This point is borne out by the decided cases. It has thus been held that breach of an innominate term affecting notice of claims against the assured[32] and failure to co-operate with the insurer in the investigation of third-party claims[33] are not repudiatory even though the ability of the insurers to investigate the claims has been hampered, the insurers have been put to additional expense and the assured has deliberately made false statements.[34]

In *Scottish Coal Co Ltd v Royal and Sun Alliance Plc*[35] an inspection clause in the policy provided that:

---

[28] *Friends Provident Life & Pensions Ltd v Sirius International Insurance Corp* [2006] Lloyd's Rep. I.R. 45.

[29] *Svenska Handelsbanken v Sun Alliance & London Insurance Plc* [1996] 1 Lloyd's Rep. 519.

[30] *Hong Kong Fir Shipping Co Ltd v Kawasaki Kisen Kaisha* [1962] 2 Q.B. 26.

[31] The first instance judgment of Hobhouse J. in *Phoenix General Insurance Co v Greece SA v Halvanon Insurance Co Ltd* [1985] 2 Lloyd's Rep. 599, which was concerned with the implication of terms into a facultative-obligatory reinsurance agreement, classified co-operation provisions as innominate by nature. The notion that terms for the protection of reinsurers are to be implied into a non-proportional treaty was rejected by the Court of Appeal in *Bonner v Cox Dedicated Member Ltd* [2006] Lloyd's Rep. I.R. 385, and the Court of Appeal cast strong doubt on the correctness of the decision of *Phoenix v Halvanon* as regards the concept of implying such terms into proportional agreements.

[32] *Alfred McAlpine Plc v BAI (Run-off) Ltd* [2000] Lloyd's Rep. I.R. 352; *Friends Provident Life & Pensions Ltd v Sirius International Insurance Corporation* [2006] Lloyd's Rep. I.R. 45.

[33] *K/S Merc-Skandia XXXXII v Certain Lloyd's Underwriters* [2001] Lloyd's Rep. I.R. 802; *King v Brandywine Reinsurance Co (UK) Ltd* [2004] Lloyd's Rep. I.R. 554, affirmed on other grounds [2005] Lloyd's Rep. I.R. 509.

[34] If there is a fraudulent claim the position is different: see Ch.9 below.

[35] *Scottish Coal Co Ltd v Royal and Sun Alliance Plc* [2008] Lloyd's Rep. I.R. 718.

"The Company's officials shall at all reasonable times have the right to inspect and examine any Property insured hereunder and the Insured shall provide such material with all details and information necessary for the assessment of the risk. Any reports or other material provided to the Company, or to the Insured by the Company, in connection with this Condition shall be regarded as strictly confidential by the parties to this agreement which shall include any agent, broker, re-insurer acting on behalf of the parties to this agreement."

It was held that compliance with this clause was not a condition precedent to the insurers' liability, as that interpretation would effectively have imposed a continuing duty of utmost good faith on the assured. Instead, the condition was innominate and any breaches were minor and did not give the insurers the right to terminate the policy for breach.

7–008 *Non-repudiatory breaches: damages.* Given, therefore, that most conditions are to be regarded either as ancillary or innominate, and that breaches of innominate terms are rarely repudiatory, the question then arises as to the remedy open to the insurer for breach of an ancillary term. In ordinary contract law the remedy for breach of an ancillary term, or for inconsequential breach of an innominate term, is damages. That said, there are no reported cases in which an insurer has been awarded damages for non-repudiatory breach of condition. The reason is simply that it is difficult for the insurers to prove any loss as a result of the assured's breach. This is particularly so where the breach consists of a late claim: the insurers' subrogation rights against third parties may have been prejudiced or, in the case of a liability policy, the ability to defend the claim against the assured may have been hampered. If the loss was the result of the assured's own conduct, then absent fraud or a deliberate intention to cause loss, there is no third party who can be pursued for a subrogation recovery and the insurers' only real prospect of showing loss flowing from breach of a claims or similar provision is that an investigation might have shown that the sums claimed by the insured were inflated: this was the case in *Porter v Zurich Insurance Co*,[36] where the court rejected an assertion by the insurers that a failure to co-operate in investigating a loss entitled them to damages equalling the amount of the claim. In *Friends Provident Life & Pensions Ltd v Sirius International Insurance Corporation* Waller L.J. speaking generally described the prospect of damages for breach of condition as "illusory". Mance L.J. and Sir William Aldous did not go quite so far, recognising that in some cases the measure of damages would be speculative (as where a liability insurer was, by reason of late notification, deprived of the ability to defend a claim against the assured) but that in other cases (e.g. loss of subrogation rights) damages could readily be calculated. That said, the only example of an award of damages is *Hussain v Brown (No.2)*,[37] where insurers were awarded damages worth 50 per cent of the claim for the assured's failure to notify them of an increase of the risk of fire thereby depriving them of the opportunity to insist that additional security be installed.

If the loss under the policy was the result of the assured's own conduct, then absent fraud or a deliberate intention to cause loss, there is no third party who can be pursued for a subrogation recovery and the insurers' only real prospect of showing loss flowing from breach of a claims or similar provision is that an

---

[36] *Porter v Zurich Insurance Co* [2009] EWHC 376 (QB).
[37] *Hussain v Brown (No.2)* Unreported, 1996.

investigation might have shown that the sums claimed by the insured were inflated.[38]

The concept of "repudiation of the claim". If the only possible consequences of **7–009** a breach of condition are the alternatives of termination for repudiation or damages for breach, an insurance condition is worth very little: repudiation is rarely made out, and a claim for damages is equally unlikely to succeed. In recognition of this, Waller L.J. in *Alfred McAlpine*[39]—effectively breaking new ground[40]—suggested held that there was a third possible consequence of the breach of a bare condition, namely, the right of the insurer to reject the claim to which the condition related. Waller L.J. held that the correct approach was to link the condition to the claim itself, and to ask whether the assured had by its non-compliance repudiated the claim. The Court of Appeal was of the view that the clause was to be regarded as innominate, and that whether or not there had been repudiation would depend upon the nature and seriousness of the breach. Thus, there would be repudiation if the assured's conduct showed that there was no intention to make any claim at all or if the lateness of the claim was such as to cause serious prejudice to the insurers. On the facts before them, where a claim had not been made for several months, and only then after the assured had ceased trading, the Court of Appeal held that there had been no repudiation as the insurer had ultimately been given sufficient information to investigate and deal with the claim. The assured was nevertheless in breach of the clause, but as the insurer had abandoned any claim for damages and had rested upon the right not to make payment at all, it followed that the assured was entitled to recover. What was required for a repudiation of a claim to be made out is, in the words of Waller L.J. in *Alfred McAlpine*, "serious consequences and that in reliance on such a breach the claim had been rejected". The serious consequences test will not be made unless the insurer can show that there was liability that would not otherwise have been faced or that the insurers have been put to serious additional expense.

Waller L.J.'s analysis of policy conditions, while obiter, was applied in a series of subsequent cases,[41] although in only one of them—*Bankers Insurance Co v South*[42]—it was held that the claim had been repudiated by reason of the assured's substantial delay in making the claim. However, serious doubt was cast upon the very existence of the concept of repudiation of the claim by a majority of the Court of Appeal in *Friends Provident Life & Pensions Ltd v Sirius International Insurance Corp*,[43] a late claim case. Mance L.J., with whom Sir William Aldous agreed, could find no insurance authority for the suggestion, regarded the doctrine of partial repudiatory breach as a novelty in English law, noted that repudiation of the claim could have disproportionate consequences (as where breach of a claims condition operated to deprive the insurers of a

---

[38] *Porter v Zurich Insurance Co* [2009] EWHC 376 (QB), where the court rejected an assertion by the insurers that a failure to co-operate in investigating a loss entitled them to damages equalling the amount of the claim.

[39] *Alfred McAlpine Plc v BAI (Run-off) Ltd* [2000] Lloyd's Rep. I.R. 352.

[40] In reliance on *Trans-Pacific Insurance Co (Australia) Ltd v Grand Union Insurance Co Ltd* (1990) ANZ Insurance Cases 60–949.

[41] *K/S Merc-Skandia XXXXII v Certain Lloyd's Underwriters* [2001] Lloyd's Rep. I.R. 802; *Glencore International AG v Ryan (The Beursgracht)* [2002] Lloyd's Rep. I.R. 335; *Pilkington United Kingdom Ltd v CGU Insurance Plc* [2004] Lloyd's Rep. I.R. 891; *King v Brandywine Reinsurance Co (UK) Ltd* [2004] Lloyd's Rep. I.R. 554.

[42] *Bankers Insurance Co v South* [2004] Lloyd's Rep. I.R. 1.

[43] *Friends Provident Life & Pensions Ltd v Sirius International Insurance Corp* [2006] Lloyd's Rep. I.R. 45. See also *Limit No.2 Ltd v Axa Versicherung AG* [2008] Lloyd's Rep. I.R. 330, reversed in part on other grounds [2009] Lloyd's Rep. I.R. 396.

subrogation claim worth £50,000 but could be held to deprive the assured of the right to press a claim for a loss of £1 million) and felt that it was always open to insurers to make the provision a condition precedent. Waller L.J., dissenting on the point, reaffirmed his position in *Alfred McAlpine*. In *Ronson International Ltd v Patrick*,[44] decided shortly after Friends Provident, H.H. Judge Richard Seymour QC held that he was bound by the views of Mance L.J. and Sir William Aldous in *Friends Provident* and that it was not open to him to find that insurers were entitled to deny liability for a claim where the term broken was not a condition precedent. Even if it is the case that *Alfred McAlpine* has survived *Friends Provident*,[45] the doctrine of repudiation of the claim can only apply where the condition broken relates directly to a claim, and where the assured's breach was such as to show that there was no intention to make any claim and that serious prejudice had been caused to the insurers.[46]

7–010 **Summary of the present law.** The position may presently be summarised thus:

(a) If the term broken is expressed, or can be construed, as a condition precedent to the liability of the insurers, then breach of that term prevents the assured from bringing a claim for a loss to which the condition relates. The insurers need not prove any prejudice. The policy itself is unaffected, so that past claims remain good and future claims may be made in the usual way.

(b) If the term broken is a condition of the policy in the sense that it goes to the root of the policy, then the breach will be one that entitles the insurers to treat the policy as repudiated and therefore to terminate the policy as of the date of the breach.

(c) If the term broken is a minor one, then the insurers cannot treat the policy as repudiated and must pay the claim despite the breach: their remedy is for damages for breach of contract.

(d) If the term is "innominate", in that it cannot be classified from the outset as either fundamental to the contract or ancillary to the contract, the courts will adopt a wait and see approach, so that the insurers can treat the policy as repudiated only if they have suffered serious prejudice from the breach but are confined to damages if they cannot prove serious prejudice.

(e) The common law does not recognise the concept of "repudiation of a claim", i.e. the notion that if the assured has broken an innominate term the insurers may, if they have suffered serious prejudice or if the assured's breach is a serious one, refuse to pay the claim itself while leaving the policy unaffected.

(f) The only situation in which conduct on the part of the assured may give rise to denial of the claim, even though the policy itself is unaffected is where the claim is fraudulent.

The creation of conditions precedent

7–011 *Significance of classification.* Given the significant variations in the consequences of a breach of each of the above classes of condition, it becomes

---

[44] *Ronson International Ltd v Patrick* [2006] Lloyd's Rep. I.R. 194, affirmed on other grounds [2006] Lloyd's Rep. I.R. 194.

[45] This was assumed in *Evans v Clarke* [2007] Lloyd's Rep. I.R. 16, although no authority was cited and the point appears not to have been in dispute.

[46] In *Ronson v Patrick* H.H. Judge Seymour QC noted that it was unclear whether the intention and prejudice tests were alternative or cumulative.

important to determine into which of those classes any particular condition will fall and in particular whether a condition is to take effect as a condition precedent. A condition precedent may be created in a number of ways: the consequences of a breach of condition may be spelt out; the condition may be described as a "condition precedent"; the policy may contain a general clause which describes all conditions as conditions precedent; or the wording or the significance of the condition is such as to lead to the conclusion that it was intended to be a condition precedent.

The consequences of a breach condition are spelt out. The policy may **7–012** specifically state that if the assured fails to comply with a given condition the insurers have the right to refuse to pay the claim. If this is so, then the condition will be treated as a condition precedent to liability.

The condition is described as a "condition precedent". The policy may simply **7–013** classify particular conditions as conditions precedent to the insurer's risk or to its liability, a formulation that creates a presumption that the parties mean what they say.[47] This presumption is, however, subject to two important modifications.

First, the policy as a whole may indicate that the clause is not to be a condition precedent. Thus if the policy contains a series of conditions all of which are described as conditions precedent but some of which additionally say that in the event of breach no claim is payable, then it is clear that the insurers have drawn a distinction between those and other terms and that the others are not conditions precedent to liability.[48]

Secondly, the term may not be appropriate to operate as a condition precedent. This will be the case where the obligation is unrelated to claims and relates to, e.g. record keeping,[49] or where the obligation is to be performed long after the loss has occurred, e.g. the prosecution of a fraudulent employee[50] or to commence proceedings against a third party.[51]

General clauses. General clauses, declaring all terms to be conditions precedent, **7–014** have long been used in insurance policies. They are not always effective and the authorities are not easily reconciled. Full effect was given to a general clause in *Pilkington United Kingdom Ltd v CGU Insurance Plc.*[52] Here, the provisions of a liability policy required the assured to notify to the insurers in writing of any occurrence which might give rise to a claim as soon as possible; to give immediate notice of any civil proceedings; and to send the insurers immediately every relevant document. These were all conditions precedent by reason of an "Observance of Conditions" clause which provided that "The due observance and fulfilment of the terms and provisions and conditions insofar as they relate to anything to be done or complied with by the Insured and the truth of the statements in the proposal made by him which shall be the basis of this contract

---

[47] *Jones v Provincial Insurance Co* (1929) 35 Ll. L.R. 135; *Shoot v Hill* (1936) 55 Ll. L.R. 29; *Roberts v Eagle Star Insurance Co Ltd* [1960] 1 Lloyd's Rep. 615; *Bennett v Yorkshire Insurance Co Ltd* [1962] 2 Lloyd's Rep. 270; *Gan Insurance v Tai Ping Insurance (No.2)* [2002] Lloyd's Rep. I.R. 612; *Diab v Regent Insurance Co Ltd* [2006] Lloyd's Rep. I.R. 779.

[48] *Stoneman v Ocean Railway and General Accident Insurance Co* (1887) 19 Q.B. 237; *Welch v Royal Exchange Assurance* [1939] 1 K.B. 294; *George Hunt Cranes Ltd v Scottish Boiler and General Insurance Co* [2002] Lloyd's Rep. I.R. 178.

[49] *Re Bradley and Essex and Suffolk Accident Indemnity Society* [1912] 1 K.B. 415.

[50] *London Guarantee v Fearnley* (1886) 5 App.Cas. 911.

[51] *Pioneer Concrete v National Employers Mutual* [1985] 2 All E.R. 395.

[52] *Pilkington United Kingdom Ltd v CGU Insurance Plc* [2004] Lloyd's Rep. I.R. 891.

and held to be incorporated herein shall be conditions precedent to any liability of the Company".[53]

That said, it is not always appropriate to treat a generalised description of terms as conditions precedent as applicable to all of the terms. Some cases have recognised that it may be necessary to protect the assured from ambiguity or obscure wording.[54] Thus, if there is a list of conditions and a general clause stated to apply to them all, the court will examine the list to determine which if any of them are appropriately described as such,[55] and also to ascertain whether the policy ascribes particular weight to certain of the conditions over others by specifying the consequences of their breach.[56] In *Aspen Insurance UK Ltd v Pectel Ltd*[57] a claims condition was held to have been converted into a condition precedent by a general clause, but Teare J. commented that although the clause was by its nature one which was appropriate to be a condition precedent the same did not necessarily apply to other policy provisions which also fell within the ambit of the general clause. Some of the other policy conditions were expressly described as conditions precedent but the claims condition was not. Teare J. nevertheless held that the failure to give that designation to the claims condition did not weaken the operation of the general clause.

If such general wording is regarded as effective, the omission of a particular condition from its ambit does not necessarily mean that that condition is not to be construed as a condition precedent if it would be meaningless other than as a condition precedent. Thus in *British Credit Trust Holdings v UK Insurance Ltd*[58] the clause stated that: "No legal action may be brought under this insurance in respect of any Agreement unless the Insured has complied with all the provisions of the insurance in relation to such Agreement and any such legal action must be commenced within one year after any loss occurs in respect of such Agreement." The wording did not treat the obligation to commence action within one year as a condition precedent, it was nevertheless held that this was a condition precedent as the obligation would be of no effect on any other basis.

7–015　　*Other forms of wording.* Other forms of wording have been held to produce the desired effect of postponing the insurer's liability until the assured has taken the required steps. These include "no claim shall attach to this policy",[59] the assured "shall" comply with certain obligations,[60] the insurers "will not be liable to pay any claim",[61] "no claim under this policy shall be payable unless the terms of

---

[53] See also *Slater v Buckinghamshire County Council* [2004] Lloyd's Rep. I.R. 432; *Shinedean Ltd v Alldown Demolition London Ltd* [2006] Lloyd's Rep. I.R. 846; *Horwood v Land of Leather Ltd* [2010] Lloyd's Rep. I.R. 453 and *Loyaltrend Ltd v Creechurch Dedicated Ltd* [2010] Lloyd's Rep. I.R. 466, in each of which it was held that a claims provision was converted into a condition precedent by such general wording. Cf. *Chan Yiu Sun v Yip Kim Cheung* [1990] 1 H.K.C. 524; *Hussain v GAN Assurance Co* [2007] H.K.E.C. 361.

[54] *Pilkington United Kingdom Ltd v CGU Insurance Plc* [2004] Lloyd's Rep. I.R. 891.

[55] *Re Bradley and Essex and Suffolk Accident Indemnity Society* [1912] 1 K.B. 415, followed in *Bonner Williams v Peter Lindsay Leisure Ltd* [2001] 1 All E.R. (Comm) 1140.

[56] *George Hunt Cranes Ltd v Scottish Boiler and General Insurance Co* [2002] Lloyd's Rep. I.R. 178.

[57] *Aspen Insurance UK Ltd v Pectel Ltd* [2008] EWHC 2804 (Comm).

[58] *British Credit Trust Holdings v UK Insurance Ltd* [2004] 1 All E.R. (Comm) 444.

[59] *Richardson v Roylance* (1933) 47 Ll. L.R. 173.

[60] *Jacobson v Yorkshire Insurance Co* (1933) 45 Ll. L.R. 281.

[61] *Eagle Star v Cresswell* [2004] Lloyd's Rep. I.R. 437.

this condition have been complied with"[62] and the insurer is liable "provided that" conditions are complied with.[63]

Nevertheless, given the severe and often disproportionate consequences that flow from the breach of a condition precedent, the courts have insisted that any ambiguity will be construed against the insurer,[64] and in particular there is a strong presumption that a condition which merely establishes administrative machinery is not to be treated as a condition precedent unless the wording is compelling.[65]

Construction of conditions precedent. Where the courts are constrained to find that a condition is a condition precedent, the obligations imposed by it will be construed narrowly where the clause is capable of operating in a draconian fashion. In *Cornhill Insurance v DE Stamp Felt Roofing*[66] a liability policy issued to the assured subcontractors provided that they "shall have arranged" for fire precautions to be taken. It was held that the condition was not broken once the assured had put the arrangements in place even though the arrangements were disregarded by employees. In *Royal & Sun Alliance Insurance Plc v Dornoch Ltd*[67] the insurers under a liability policy were required to notify reinsurers within 72 hours "upon knowledge of any loss or losses which may give rise to claim under this policy". It was held that the phrase "loss or losses" referred to established losses, so that until judgment had been given against the assured there was no obligation to notify: accordingly there was no breach of the clause by the insurers' failure to inform the reinsurers of claims made against the assured even though that had presumably been the objective of the provision. This decision should be contrasted with the later decision of the Court of Appeal in *AIG Europe (Ireland) Ltd v Faraday Capital Ltd*,[68] which also involved the reinsurance of a Directors and Officers policy, although the decision in that case went against the reinsured on the basis that the announcement by the assured company of a restatement of its accounts, which led to a dramatic fall in the assured's share price, meant that there was a known loss at an early stage and not simply after the settlement, the point at which the loss was notified to the reinsurers.

7–016

Burden of proof. The burden of proving a breach of condition rests upon the insurer: it is not, in the absence of express wording to the contrary, the duty of the assured to prove that he has complied with the conditions of the policy.[69]

7–017

[62] *Welch v Royal Exchange Assurance* [1939] 1 K.B. 294.

[63] *Millichap v Pontrilas Timber & Builders' Merchants Ltd* Unreported, 1992; *Den Dankse Bank A/S v Skipton Building Society* Unreported, 1997; *Colonial Fire & General Insurance Co Ltd v Chung* Unreported, 2002.

[64] *Parklane Floral & Balloons Design v Allianz Insurance (Hong Kong) Ltd* [2006] H.K.E.C. 109.

[65] *Jones & James v Provincial* (1929) 46 T.L.R. 71; *Conn v Westminster Motor Insurance Association* [1966] 1 Lloyd's Rep. 123; *Cox v Bankside* [1995] 2 Lloyd's Rep. 437; *Charter Re v Fagan* [1996] 3 All E.R. 46; *Municipal Mutual Insurance Ltd v Sea Insurance Co Ltd* [1996] L.R.L.R. 265; *Baker v Black Sea* [1995] L.R.L.R. 333; *Taylor v Builders Accident Insurance* [1997] M.C.L.C. 247; *Alfred McAlpine Plc v BAI (Run-off) Ltd* [1998] 2 Lloyd's Rep. 694; *Bonner Williams v Peter Lindsay Leisure Ltd* [2001] 1 All E.R. (Comm) 1140; *King v Brandywine Reinsurance Co (UK) Ltd* [2004] Lloyd's Rep. I.R. 554; *Friends Provident Life & Pensions Ltd v Sirus International Insurance Corporation* [2006] Lloyd's Rep. I.R. 45: *Scottish Coal Co Ltd v Royal and Sun Alliance Plc* [2008] Lloyd's Rep. I.R. 718.

[66] *Cornhill Insurance v DE Stamp Felt Roofing* [2002] Lloyd's Rep. I.R. 648.

[67] *Royal & Sun Alliance Insurance Plc v Dornoch Ltd* [2005] Lloyd's Rep. I.R. 554.

[68] *AIG Europe (Ireland) Ltd v Faraday Capital Ltd* [2008] Lloyd's Rep. I.R. 454.

[69] *Sofi v Prudential Assurance* [1993] 2 Lloyd's Rep. 559.

Waiver of breach of condition

7–018 *Forms of waiver.* English law recognises two main forms of waiver. The first, referred to either as waiver by affirmation or waiver by election, contemplates that insurers are faced with two conflicting courses of action and have by word or deed to the assured unequivocally chosen one course of action over the other. By making that choice, which must be fully informed on the facts and in respect of legal rights, the insurers are taken to have elected it and are unable to change their minds. The second, waiver by estoppel, also rests upon an unequivocal representation by the insurers, and although such a representation need not be supported by the insurers' knowledge of fact or law it requires reliance by the assured in a manner that would render withdrawal of that representation inequitable.[70]

In the leading decision on the operation of waiver in respect of policy conditions *Kosmar Villa Holidays Plc v Trustees of Syndicate 1243*,[71] the Court of Appeal held—in the context of a liability policy—that the principle of waiver by affirmation has no application to policy conditions.[72] Before *Kosmar* there had been a view that a distinction was to be drawn between policy conditions expressed to be conditions precedent and policy conditions not so expressed. In the latter case it was thought that both forms of waiver were applicable (although this is not a significant matter because breach of a condition which is not a condition precedent is most unlikely to give the insurers a defence to a claim, so waiver of the breach is not really a major concern to the assured), whereas in the former case the fact that breach of a condition precedent automatically disentitles the assured from making his claim meant that the insurers were not actually faced with a choice between conflicting courses of action because they were simply not liable. That reasoning, which is reached by analogy with the law relating to waiver of breach of warranty, such a breach automatically terminating the risk[73] and thus not giving rise to any right of election for the insurers,[74] was adopted in *Forrest v CGU Insurance*,[75] leading to the conclusion that only waiver by estoppel could rescue an assured in breach of a condition precedent. At first instance in *Kosmar*[76] the ruling in *Forrest* was rejected by Gross J. on the basis that breach of warranty and breach of condition precedent were quite different in their effects, so that waiver by affirmation remained available to an assured in breach of a condition precedent. However, on appeal in *Kosmar* the Court of Appeal—without specifically drawing a distinction between conditions precedent and bare conditions—held that an assured in breach of condition was entitled to rely upon waiver by estoppel only.

In *Kosmar* itself the assured tour operator was bound by condition precedent to give immediate notice to insurers of any accident for which the assured might be liable. The assured failed to give timely notice of injuries suffered by a client (ironically, between the trial and the decision of the Court of Appeal, it was held in separate proceedings that the assured was not in fact liable for the accident in

---

[70] *Kammins Ballrooms Co Ltd v Zenith Investments (Torquay) Ltd* [1971] A.C. 850; *Motor Oil Hellas (Corinth) Refineries SA v Shipping Corp of India (The Kanchenjunga)* [1990] 1 Lloyd's Rep. 391; *Kosmar Villa Holidays Plc v Trustees of Syndicate 1243* [2008] EWCA Civ 147; *Lexington Insurance Co v Multinacional de Seguros SA* [2009] Lloyd's Rep. I.R. 1.
[71] *Kosmar Villa Holidays Plc v Trustees of Syndicate 1243* [2008] Lloyd's Rep. I.R. 489.
[72] See also *Lexington Insurance Co v Multinacional de Seguros SA* [2009] Lloyd's Rep. I.R. 1.
[73] *Bank of Nova Scotia v Hellenic Mutual Ltd (The Good Luck)* [1992] 1 A.C. 233.
[74] *HIH Casualty and General Insurance v Axa* [2003] Lloyd's Rep. I.R. 1.
[75] *Forrest v CGU Insurance* [2006] Lloyd's Rep. I.R. 113.
[76] *Kosmar Villa Holidays Plc v Trustees of Syndicate 1243* [2008] Lloyd's Rep. I.R. 43.

question) and indeed the insurers were not notified until the client served a claim form on the assured. The insurers did not reserve their rights but sought further information. Just under a month later the insurers determined to reject the assured's claim. Gross J. held that the insurers had waived the breach by election, although there was no estoppel. The Court of Appeal, in finding for the insurers, reversed the trial judge and held that waiver by election was not applicable at all, although it agreed with the trial judge that there had not been any waiver by estoppel. Rix L.J., delivering the only reasoned judgment, held that the doctrine of waiver by affirmation was relevant only where the very existence of the contract was at stake, and that if the issue was simply whether or not a claim was to be paid there was every reason to allow insurers the right to change their minds in the absence of an unequivocal representation which had been relied upon. Rix L.J. having referred to the authorities,[77] noted that they:

" . . . deal with a much more limited field, such as the acceptance of repudiation or the avoidance of contracts or the rejection of goods. They are concerned with contracts in the course of their execution, not with the pathological treatment of claims. While a contract is in operation, it is important to know, in circumstances where it lies in the choice of a party, whether the contract lives or dies (or at least whether purported performance under it, such as a delivery of goods, is accepted or not); and, whether the option is for life or death, acceptance or rejection, the choice is unilateral and irrevocable. But when it is merely a defence to a claim that is in question, there would not seem to be the same necessity to choose timeously and irrevocably between reliance or not on the defence in question. Certainly in the context of litigation, a defence can be utilised at any time subject to the case management discretion of the court, limitation and abuse of process . . .

[A]n insurer who begins to deal with a claim, even if . . . he thereby represents that he views that claim at that time as being, if good, a matter for indemnity under the policy, is not thereby required for all time to maintain his dealing with or conduct of the claim. He can leave it to his insured to conduct a defence, although he may turn out to be liable at the end of the day to indemnify his insured against both liability and the cost of defending liability. Moreover, he may discover matters which lead him to believe that the claim is not within the policy, and it remains open to him to withdraw his support for it. None of this fits happily with the idea that some dealing with a claim is an irrevocable election to accept liability for it under the policy so far as any procedural defect in it is known to the insurer . . .

The doctrine [of waiver by affirmation] is ill-fitting in these circumstances, and unneeded. For there remains the doctrine of estoppel: in circumstances where it can be said that the handling of a claim by an insurer is an unequivocal representation that the insurer accepts liability and/or will not rely on breach of some condition precedent as affording a defence, and there has been such detrimental reliance by the insured as would make it inequitable for the insurer to go back on his representation, the insured will have all the protection that he needs."

The elements of waiver by estoppel. Waiver by estoppel consists of two **7–019** elements: an unequivocal representation by the insurers that they intend to honour their obligations under the policy; and circumstances which make it inequitable for the insurers to withdraw their representation, normally but not exclusively in the form of detrimental reliance by the assured. The point has arisen most commonly in the context of liability insurance, where the assured has

[77] It seems to have been assumed by the Privy Council in *Diab v Regent Insurance* [2006] 1 Lloyd's Rep. I.R. 779 that a condition precedent could be waived by affirmation, although in that case the elements of such waiver had not been made out in any event. A similar assumption was made in *Bolton Metropolitan Borough Council v Municipal Mutual General Insurance Ltd* [2007] Lloyd's Rep. I.R. 173, but again in that case waiver did not form any part of the decision.

been faced with a claim by a third party and the insurers have indicated that they wish to conduct the defence but subsequently change their mind. To give rise to estoppel, the statement must be unequivocal, so that merely commencing to conduct the defence may not suffice,[78] although if insurers make it clear that they wish to conduct the assured's defence and demand the assured's co-operation then their conduct is unequivocal.[79] Delay or silence by insurers is not of itself unequivocal conduct,[80] although it was commented by Rix L.J. in *Kosmar Villa Holidays Plc v Trustees of Syndicate 1243* that:

> "I would certainly not like to give the impression that insurers can equivocate for long while giving the plain impression that they are treating a claim as covered by their policy, especially at a time when a decision might be required, without running at least the risk that they will be treated as having waived some requirement of their contract or their right to avoid it. Moreover, there may well be express options given to insurers under their policy the unguarded exercise of which is simply inconsistent with the right to decline cover."

It follows from the actual decision in *Kosmar* that a failure by insurers to reserve their rights will not of itself estop them from relying upon those rights at a later date.

7–020 *Illustrations of waiver by estoppel.* Acceptance by the insurers of premiums after discovery of the breach of a condition by the assured may amount to a representation on their part to affirm the policy.[81] However conduct on the part of the insurers by which the assured is not prejudiced, and which is not inconsistent with an intention, by the insurers, to repudiate the contract cannot be relied on by the assured.[82] Thus the issue of a policy to replace a slip is not necessarily a representation that the breach has been waived.[83] Similarly, a decision by insurers to rely upon a coverage defence rather than a breach of a notification condition does not amount to a representation by the insurers that they intend to disregard the latter defence.[84] The position may be different once the dispute between the parties has resulted in legal proceedings: the insurers may be treated to have lost the right to rely upon an alternative defence if that defence is not raised until a late stage in the action even though the insurers were aware of it.[85]

Previous failure to rely upon a breach of condition is not of itself waiver of future breaches of condition,[86] unless it is possible to construe the underwriters' previous conduct as a clear statement that future compliance is not required.[87]

---

[78] *McCormick v National Motor and Accident Insurance Union Ltd* (1934) 40 Com. Cas. 76; *Soole v Royal Insurance Ltd* [1971] 2 Lloyd's Rep. 33; *Kosmar Villa Holidays Plc v Trustees of Syndicate 1243* [2008] Lloyd's Rep. I.R. 489.

[79] *Barratt Bros (Taxis) Ltd v Davies* [1966] 2 Lloyd's Rep. 1. See also *Yorkshire Insurance Co Ltd v Craine* [1922] 2 A.C. 541.

[80] *Allen v Robles* [1969] 3 All E.R. 154; *Phillips v Whatley* [2008] Lloyd's Rep. I.R. 111.

[81] *Armstrong v Turquand* (1858) 9 I.C.L.R. 32, 55; *Hemmings v Sceptre Life* [1905] 1 Ch. 365.

[82] *Tioxide Europe Ltd v CGU International Insurance Plc* [2005] Lloyd's Rep. I.R. 114, affirmed on other grounds [2006] Lloyd's Rep. I.R. 131.

[83] *Morrison v Universal Marine* (1873) L.R. 8 Ex. 197.

[84] *Bolton Metropolitan Borough Council v Municipal Mutual Insurance Ltd* [2007] Lloyd's Rep. I.R. 173.

[85] *Moore Large & Co Ltd v Hermes Credit & Guarantee Plc* [2003] Lloyd's Rep. I.R. 315.

[86] *Kosmar Villa Holidays Plc v Trustees of Syndicate 1243* [2008] Lloyd's Rep. I.R. 43 (the point did not arise on appeal, [2008] Lloyd's Rep. I.R. 489). See also *London and Manchester Plate Glass Co Ltd v Heath* [1913] 3 K.B. 411.

[87] *Limit No.2 Ltd v Axa Versicherung AG* [2008] Lloyd's Rep. I.R. 330, reversed in part on other grounds [2009] Lloyd's Rep. I.R. 396.

There can be an estoppel only where the conduct is carried out by insurers or on their behalves by an authorised agent. Thus where agents had accepted life insurance premiums and paid them to the company with knowledge that the assured had broken a condition,[88] and where in a motor insurance case a clerk of the insurers had notice of such a breach and the insurers had subsequently paid a claim under the policy the insurers were held to be estopped from setting up the breach of condition as a defence.[89] Atkin J.'s judgment in *Ayrey v British Legal*[90] is valuable as showing the reasoning behind these decisions: as the agent had no authority to contract on behalf of the insurers he had no authority to waive the breach in the strict sense, but the insurers were nevertheless liable on the policy on the ground of estoppel.

3. INSURANCE WARRANTIES

The nature of a warranty

What may be warranted. A warranty is defined, by s.33(1) of the Marine Insurance Act as "a promissory warranty, that is to say, a warranty by which the assured undertakes that some particular thing shall or shall not be done, or that some condition shall be fulfilled, or whereby he affirms or negatives the existence of a particular state of facts." It is well established by both marine and non-marine authorities that the term "promissory" in this definition simply means that the assured has made a promise, and does not connote any guarantee by the assured that his promise will remain good throughout the currency of the policy; it is thus perfectly possible for a warranty to be restricted to the existence of a given fact at a given time.[91] To avoid confusion the phrase "promissory warranty" should be regarded as a collective expression for all warranties, whilst the terms "present" and "continuing" warranties are best taken as referring respectively to those limited to present facts and those whereby the assured guarantees the continuance of a state of affairs. As seen above, s.33(1) indeed describes all warranties as promissory, and it is clear that the word is here used in a collective sense, seeking to distinguish warranties from excepted perils. So, also in non-marine insurance law, any representation which is warranted to be true is sometimes spoken of as being, for that reason, of a promissory nature.[92] Goddard J. in *Hearts of Oak v Law Union*[93] spoke of those clauses which "have been called in the House of Lords promissory", as if members of that House had used the term to describe warranties as to the future. A perusal of their decisions,[94] however, shows that the adjective "promissory" had been used by their Lordships only to describe those representations which amounted to warranties.

7–021

---

[88] *Wing v Harvey* (1854) 5 De G.M. & G. 265; *Ayrey v British Legal* [1918] 1 K.B. 136; *Brook v Trafalgar Insurance Co Ltd* (1946) 79 Ll. L. Rep. 365; *Webster v General Accident Fire and Life Assurance Corp Ltd* [1953] 1 Q.B. 520.

[89] *Evans v Employers Mutual* [1936] 1 K.B. 505.

[90] *Ayrey v British Legal* [1918] 1 K.B. 136.

[91] In the 1906 Act itself certain of the implied warranties relate only to specified dates.

[92] Lord Wright in *Provincial Insurance v Morgan* [1933] A.C. 340 at 354. In *Sweeney v Kennedy* (1948) 82 Ll. L.R. 294 the Irish courts held that the word "promissory" was effective to create a warranty, but not necessarily a continuing warranty.

[93] *Hearts of Oak v Law Union* [1936] 2 All E.R. 619 at 623.

[94] *Dawsons v Bonnin* [1922] 2 A.C. 413; *Provincial Insurance v Morgan* [1933] A.C. 340.

With this warning in mind, it is possible to list the various contents of warranties as follows:

(1) a promise that a state of affairs does or does not exist;
(2) a promise that a state of affairs will continue to exist, or will not come into being, during the currency of the policy;
(3) a promise that the assured has or has not acted in a stated way;
(4) a promise that the assured will, or will not, act in a stated way during the currency of the policy;
(5) a promise that the assured intends to act or to refrain from acting in a particular fashion during the currency of the policy;
(6) a promise that the assured holds a particular belief.

Warranties (1), (3) and (6) are promises of a present state of affairs, whether fact or opinion, whereas warranties (2), (4) and (5) impose continuing obligations.

The effect of a warranty is that the assured guarantees the truth of his statement, whether or not it is material to the risk. Further, proof of breach is relatively simple. The insurers will have no difficulty in proving that the assured made a misrepresentation if the contract containing the warranty is resolved into writing, for extrinsic evidence will not be admissible to vary it. However, where the insurer relies on answers to questions by the assured strict proof is necessary as to what the assured said at the time, even though the answers were reduced into writing and signed.[95]

7–022 *Significance and characteristics of a warranty.* The following characteristics of a warranty, which are amplified in the following paragraphs demonstrate its significance in insurance law: exact compliance is demanded; the insurer is not required to show that the warranty was in any way material to the risk, or that its breach in any way contributed to the assured's loss; and breach of warranty permits the insurer to disclaim any liabilities accruing after the date of breach.

The existing law relating to warranties was arrived at by means of a number of apparently unsatisfactory[96] decisions. In the early days of insurance, the description of a term as a warranty did not necessarily make it a fundamental term of a contract, and in the early cases where such terms were held to be fundamental it appears that the facts in question were in any event material for the purposes of the duty of utmost good faith, so that the cases could equally well have been decided on that ground.[97] There are numerous other early marine cases in which the matters warranted were clearly material to the risk underwritten by the insurers, e.g., time of sailing and the nature of the voyage,[98] although matters relating to the voyage are now expressly governed by the provisions of ss.42 to 49 of the 1906 Act. Other early illustrations of warranties material to the risk include the obligation on the assured to retain the amount of the deductible under

[95] *Joel v Law Union* [1908] 2 K.B. 863.
[96] Hasson, 24 M.L.R. 29 (1971).
[97] *Bean v Stupart* (1778) 1 Doug. K.B. 11; *De Hahn v Hartley* (1786) 1 T.R. 343; *MacDowell v Fraser* (1779) 1 Doug. 260; *Kenyon v Berthon* (1778) 1 Doug. 12n; *Blackhurst v Cockell* (1789) 3 T.R. 360: *Colby v Hunter* (1827) 3 C. & P. 7.
[98] *Hibbert v Pigou* (1783) 3 Doug. K.B. 224; *Anderson v Pitcher* (1800) 2 Bos. & Pul. 164; *Sanderson v Busher* (1814) 4 Camp. 54n; *Warwick v Scott* (1814) 4 Camp. 62; *Colledge v Harty* (1851) 6 Exch. 205.

the policy for his own account rather than insuring it elsewhere[99] and the exclusion of war risks.[100] The change in the courts' attitude to warranties appears to have started in the nineteenth century in cases in which false statements were held to entitle the insurers to repudiate liability even in the absence of materiality,[101] and this approach became established by a series of decisions of the House of Lords and Privy Council at the end of the nineteenth century and the beginning of the twentieth century,[102] and cannot now be doubted.

Creation of warranties

Express and implied warranties. A marine warranty may be either express or **7–023** implied.[103] Warranties which are implied into contracts of marine insurance as a matter of law are set out in ss.36 to 41 of the 1906 Act; all other warranties in marine policies must be express (s.35), so that there is no possibility of implying a warranty on the basis of commercial convenience or even of commercial necessity.[104] Non-marine warranties may be express only:[105] there is no statute which makes provision for the implication of non-marine warranties, although on occasion the courts have used the analogy of implied marine warranties as an aid to the construction of express non-marine warranties.[106]

Formalities. The formal requirements for the creation of a warranty is expressed **7–024** in s.35(2) of the Marine Insurance Act 1906: "An express warranty must be included in, or written upon, the policy, or must be contained in some document incorporated by reference into the policy." Warranties may be written on its face of the policy or in the margin.[107] As long as there are not probative issues arising, a warranty may be contained in any independent document.[108] Indeed, the most common method of creating warranties is by means of a "basis of the contract" clause in the proposal form. There is no reason why a policy should not be signed subject to an oral condition or warranty that is not even referred to in the

---

[99] *Lishman v Northern Maritime Insurance Co* (1875) L.R. 10 C.P. 179. See also: *Muirhead v Forth & North Sea Steamboat Mutual Insurance Association* [1894] A.C. 72; *Roddick v Indemnity Mutual Marine Insurance Co* [1895] 2 Q.B. 380; *General Insurance Co of Trieste v Cory* [1897] 1 Q.B. 335; *Samuel v Dumas* [1924] A.C. 431; *General Shipping and Forwarding Co v British General Insurance Co Ltd* (1923) 15 Ll. L.R. 175. Cf. *Assicurazioni Generali SpA v Arab Insurance Group* [2002] Lloyd's Rep. I.R. 633.

[100] Under the old wording "warranted free of capture and seizure": *Maydhew v Scott* (1811) 3 Camp. 205; *Dalgleish v Brooke* (1812) 5 East 295.

[101] *Duckett v Williams* (1834) 2 C. & M. 348; *Anderson v Fitzgerald* (1853) 4 H.L. Cas. 484.

[102] *Thomson v Weems* (1884) 9 App.Cas. 671; *Yorkshire Insurance Co v Campbell* [1917] A.C. 218; *Dawsons Ltd v Bonnin* [1922] 2 A.C. 413; *Samuel & Co Ltd v Dumas* [1924] A.C. 431.

[103] Section 33(2) of the 1906 Act.

[104] *Lloyd Instruments Ltd v Northern Star Insurance Co Ltd (The Miss Jay Jay)* [1985] 1 Lloyd's Rep. 264.

[105] *Earo-Diam Ltd v Bathurst* [1988] 2 All E.R. 23.

[106] Thus there has been held to be a limited analogy between the implied "seaworthiness" warranty for voyage policies contained in s.39 and the express "roadworthiness" warranty frequently found in motor policies: the latter has been held not to be a continuing warranty but merely a promise as to the state of affairs existing at the start of a journey, in line with the position of the former under s.39(1)—*Barrett v London General Insurance Co* [1935] 1 K.B. 238. This reasoning was disapproved by the Privy Council in *Trickett v Queensland Insurance Co* [1936] A.C. 159, but the analogy has been pressed subsequently, by the Court of Appeal in *Clarke v National Insurance and Guarantee Corporation* [1964] 1 Q.B. 199, in holding that an overloaded vehicle could be unroadworthy in the same way that an overloaded vessel could be unseaworthy.

[107] *Bean v Stupart* (1778) 1 Doug. K.B. 11 at 14; *Birrell v Dryer* (1884) 9 App.Cas. 345.

[108] *Bensuade v Thames and Mersey Marine Insurance Co* [1897] A.C. 609, doubting on this point *Pawson v Watson* (1778) 1 Doug. K.B. 12n; *Condogianis v Guardian Assurance Co* [1921] 2 A.C. 125.

policy,[109] although a finding to this effect is likely to be exceptional and the general principle remains that a warranty is to be expected to be found on the face of the policy itself.[110] A warranty is binding on the assured even though he is unaware of its existence or contents, as long as it is contained in the policy.[111]

7-025   *Creation of warranty by express statement.* Perhaps the most obvious method of creating a warranty is by use of the word "warranty" in connection with a particular term. If the warranty relates to the risk, then there is a strong presumption that the parties mean what they say. Terminology is not, however, conclusive: if the court is of the view that the provision in question is not by its nature capable of constituting a warranty, it will not be held to be so. Thus in *Marina Offshore Pte Ltd v China Insurance Co (Singapore) Pte Ltd*[112] there was a warranty that the assured would comply with surveyor's recommendations prior to sailing. One of the recommendations related to the route. The Singapore Court of Appeal held that the recommendation could not be a warranty because it could not be complied with before sailing. This should be contrasted with *Royal & Sun Alliance Insurance (Singapore) Ltd v Metico Marine Pte*,[113] where a similar warranty was held to attach to a recommendation not to start the voyage in unfavourable weather. The word "warranty" may be disregarded if it runs counter to what the court perceives to be the true intention of the parties: this proposition is supported by *De Maurier (Jewels) Ltd v Bastion Insurance Co*[114] where a clause under which the assured warranted that his vehicle was fitted with locks and alarms was held to be merely descriptive of the risk.

7-026   *Implication of warranty from other wording.* It is a question of fact whether a particular term of a policy has been given the force of a warranty. It is clear from s.35(1) of the 1906 Act that any form of wording will suffice provided that it evidences an intention to create a warranty, and it is settled that the use of the word "warranty" is not necessary to the creation of a warranty.[115] The modern position is set out in the judgment of Rix L.J. in *HIH Casualty and General Insurance Ltd v New Hampshire Insurance Co.*[116] In this case, the claimant insurers subscribed to two slips for the insurance of banks against the risk that the films which they had funded would not produce sufficient revenue to repay the loans. The slips contained "Interest" clauses which stated, respectively, that "7.23 productions will produce and make six made-for-TV Films" and that "Rojak Films Inc will produce and make 10 made-for-TV films". The required number of films was not made, and the claimants' reinsurers refused to indemnify the claimants on the basis that these terms amounted to warranties the breach of which brought the risk under the direct policies to an end, so that the

[109] *Anglo-Californian Bank v London & Provincial Marine* (1904) 10 Com. Cas. 1.
[110] *ERC Frankona Reinsurance v American National Insurance Co* [2006] Lloyd's Rep. I.R. 157.
[111] *Bennett v Axa Insurance Plc* [2004] Lloyd's Rep. I.R. 615.
[112] *Marina Offshore Pte Ltd v China Insurance Co (Singapore) Pte Ltd* [2007] 1 Lloyd's Rep. 66.
[113] *Royal & Sun Alliance Insurance (Singapore) Ltd v Metico Marine Pte* [2006] 3 S.L.R. 333.
[114] *De Maurier (Jewels) Ltd v Bastion Insurance Co* [1967] 2 Lloyd's Rep. 550. See below for further discussion of the distinction between warranties and suspensory conditions.
[115] *Bean v Stupart* (1778) 1 Doug. K.B. 1; *Sceales v Scanlan* (1843) 6 L.R. Ir. 367 at 371–372; *Thompson v Weems* (1884) 9 App.Cas. 671; *Barnard v Faber* [1893] 1 Q.B. 340; *Union Insurance Society of Canton Ltd v George Wills & Co* [1916] A.C. 281; *Dawsons v Bonnin* [1922] 2 A.C. 413 at 428–429.
[116] *HIH Casualty and General Insurance Ltd v New Hampshire Insurance Co* [2001] Lloyd's Rep. I.R. 596. Cf. *Wheelton v Hardisty* (1858) 8 E. & B. 232 at 302.

claimants could not be under any legal liability to make payment to the assured and, accordingly, the reinsurers could be under no liability to provide an indemnity. The Court of Appeal held that the interest clauses amounted to warranties, and Rix L.J. listed three possible tests for a warranty:

(a) did the term go to the root of the contract;
(b) was it descriptive of the risk or did it bear materially on the risk; and
(c) would damages be an inadequate or unsatisfactory remedy for breach?

All of these tests were held to be satisfied in the present case. It was also held that a term in the reinsurance agreement to the effect the consent of reinsurers had to be obtained for any material increase in risk was a warranty. These criteria are those now generally applied. The following promises have been held to be warranties: a promise by a bank that it would adhere to its usual lending criteria[117]; a promise by a reinsured that it had entered into an indemnity policy when in fact the policy was valued[118]; and a promise by a reinsured that the person responsible for generating the profits of the company invested in by the insured bank would remain in employment.[119]

Statement providing for automatic termination of risk. Perhaps the safest way of creating a warranty is for the insurer to stipulate that in the event of a material or immaterial false statement, or of specific action or inaction by the assured, the risk under the policy is automatically terminated. There are cases which have decided that clauses which provide that if certain things are not done the policy will be void,[120] or of no force, or of no effect, or that all benefits under it will be forfeited, take effect as warranties.[121] The former point is illustrated by *Thomson v Weems*,[122] where the policy itself provided that if anything averred in the declaration "shall be untrue, this policy shall be void" and it was held that these words had the effect of giving the assured's statements in the declaration the force of warranties.   **7–027**

Condition precedent. This term is sometimes, misleadingly, used to denote that a particular term is to be regarded as a warranty.[123] Thus, a clause providing that something shall be a condition precedent to the insurers' liability[124] has been held to have the effect of a warranty. The limitation of this possibility ought, however, to be noted. Conditions precedent themselves may be divided into two different types: those which prevent the risk attaching or which terminate the risk as a whole[125] unless there is compliance; and those which prevent a claim being made unless the assured takes particular steps. A condition precedent of the former type is similar in its effects to a warranty of existing fact, as in either case the risk   **7–028**

---

[117] *Svenska Handelsbanken v Sun Alliance and London Insurance Plc* [1996] 1 Lloyd's Rep. 519;

[118] *Toomey v Banco Viralicio de Espana SA de Seguros v Reaseguros* [2005] Lloyd's Rep. I.R. 423.

[119] *GE Reinsurance Corp v New Hampshire Insurance Co* [2004] Lloyd's Rep. I.R. 404.

[120] *Sceales v Scanlan* (1843) 6 L.R. I.R. 367 at 375: *Glen v Lewis* (1858) 8 Ex. 607.

[121] *Glen v Lewis* (1858) 8 Ex. 607.

[122] *Thomson v Weems* (1884) 9 App.Cas. 671.

[123] *Barnard v Faber* [1893] 1 Q.B. 340 at 343–344, 345; *Ellinger v Mutual Life* [1905] 1 K.B. 31 at 35, 37, 38; *Palatine v Gregory* [1926] A.C. 90 at 93.

[124] *Jones and James v Provincial Insurance* (1929) 46 T.L.R. 71; *Allen v Universal Automobile Insurance* (1933) 45 Ll. L.R. 55 at 57–58.

[125] *US Trading Ltd v Axa Insurance Co Ltd* [2010] Lloyd's Rep. I.R. 505.

will not attach. By contrast, a condition precedent of the latter type is not a warranty. If the assured fails to comply with a claims condition expressed as a condition precedent, he has lost his claim but the policy and the risk itself are otherwise unaffected. By contrast, if the assured fails to comply with a continuing warranty, the risk terminates as of the date of breach and there can be no future liability under the policy.

"Basis of the contract" clauses

7–029 *Nature of clause.* These clauses are probably the most common means of creating warranties. The proposal form will here contain a declaration, to be signed by the proposer, to the effect that all or any of the answers to the questions on the proposal shall form the basis of the subsequent contract of insurance. In this way the assured warrants the truth of his answers, so that the insurer may repudiate the policy should any of those answers—whether or not material to the risk—prove to be untrue. Basis clauses were apparently developed early in the nineteenth century for the purposes of life assurance,[126] and were originally found in proposal forms in conjunction with other clauses permitting the insurer to avoid the policy in the event of any material misstatement or concealment by the assured. The basis clause gradually, however, began to be used in other forms of insurance, e.g. burglary and theft insurance. The use of basis clauses has been condemned, particularly where the assured is under a continuing obligation, as he may not appreciate his obligations if he has not kept a copy of the proposal form.[127] Accordingly, if there is any doubt, the answer to a question in the proposal form will be construed as a representation and not as a warranty,[128] especially where it is not material.[129]

It is possible for insurers to make only some of the assured's answers warranties: in *Anderson v Fitzgerald*[130] only 14 out of 27 answers in the proposal were made the subject of a warranty in the policy. Even where the whole proposal is made the basis of the contract, this will not convert representations not contained in the proposal, such as the answers of the assured to questions put by the medical officer of the company, into warranties.[131] Further, if the basis clause applies to answers on the proposal form and all other information, it is necessary to construe the assured's answer in the light of other information in the insurers' possession.[132]

A basis clause may be qualified in its operation by its own terms. In *MJ Harrington Syndicate 2000 v Axa Oyak Sigorta AS*[133] the claimants were the reinsurers of Turkish insurers who had insured a Turkish bank under a bankers' blanket bond policy against fidelity losses. The proposal form for the renewal of the reinsurance asked whether the bank had complied with a recommendation that every employee was to take two weeks' continuous holiday per year, a

[126] *Duckett v Williams* (1834) 2 C. & M. 348.

[127] See *Beauchamp v National Mutual Insurance* [1937] 3 All E.R. 19. The practice of incorporating the proposal form into the policy by reference has also been criticised by the judges as puzzling to the assured, who may find it difficult to fit the disjointed parts together in such a way as to get a true and complete picture of what his rights and duties are and that acts on his part may involve a forfeiture of the insurance: Lord Wright in *Provincial Insurance v Morgan* [1933] A.C. 240 at 252.

[128] Channell B. in *Wheelton v Hardisty* (1858) 8 E. & B. 232 at 302.

[129] *Dawsons v Bonnin* [1922] 2 A.C. 413 at 429.

[130] *Anderson v Fitzgerald* (1853) 4 H.L.C. 484.

[131] *Joel v Law Union* [1908] 2 K.B. 863.

[132] *MJ Harrington Syndicate 2000 v Axa Oyak Sigorta AS* [2007] Lloyd's Rep. I.R. 60.

[133] *MJ Harrington Syndicate 2000 v Axa Oyak Sigorta AS* [2007] Lloyd's Rep. I.R. 60.

standard form anti-fraud measure imposed upon banks. The proposal form also stated that the reinsureds agreed that "that this proposal, together with any other information supplied by us shall form the basis of any Contract of Insurance effected thereon and shall be incorporated therein . . . ." The recommendation was not complied with by inception in August 2003, and in November 2003 the reinsurers retroactively extended time for compliance until October 2003. Claims were notified in November 2003. The defence of breach of warranty was taken in November 2004. Aikens J. held that it was arguable that the basis clause did not give an automatic defence, in that it referred both to the reinsureds' answers and to "other information supplied by" the reinsureds: if on inception the reinsurers had been told that the holiday provision had not been complied with, then the basis clause applied not just to the proposal form answer but also to that information and the warranty was qualified accordingly.

Materiality. In *Dawsons Ltd v Bonnin*[134] the claimant had taken out insurance on   **7–030** a lorry which he used for the purposes of his business. In answer to a question about where the vehicle would be garaged he stated that it would be kept at an address in central Glasgow, a high-risk area for the purposes of theft. In fact, the lorry was garaged on the outskirts of the city, where the risk of theft was rather less. The proposal form contained the usual basis of the contract clause. A bare majority of the House of Lords held that the insurer was entitled to repudiate the policy for the misstatement as to the garaging of the vehicle, notwithstanding that the risk had been overstated, as there was a breach of warranty. This decision confirmed earlier authorities which had indicated that materiality plays no part where a basis of the contract clause governs a misstatement, and is of particular significance for the reason that the previous cases had either involved facts which clearly had been material[135] or in which the court had striven to find materiality where in reality none existed.[136]

Effect of other policy terms. The effect of a basis clause may be modified by   **7–031** other policy terms.[137] In *Dawsons v Bonnin* the proposal form, as well as containing a basis clause, stated: "Material misstatement or concealment of any circumstance by the insured material to assessing the premium herein, or in connection with any claim, shall render the policy void." Their Lordships were divided on the relationship between the two provisions. Viscounts Haldane and Cave held that the basis clause was not limited by the materiality provision because the two terms covered different, albeit substantially overlapping, ground. By contrast, Lord Dunedin preferred to concentrate on the basis clause itself, in disregard of the materiality provision. This difference of emphasis is potentially of some importance. The former view contemplates that a basis clause may be limited by other policy terms, whereas the latter gives primacy to the basis clause. The Haldane/Cave view has, fortunately, prevailed and there is a series of cases which demonstrate that the effects of a basis clause may be cut back by other terms in the policy. Thus, if the insurer has stated that the policy is incontestable, the basis clause cannot be relied upon,[138] and if it is clear that the

---

[134] *Dawsons Ltd v Bonnin* [1922] 2 A.C. 413.

[135] *Duckett v Williams* (1834) 2 C. & M. 348; *Anderson v Fitzgerald* (1853) 4 H.L. Cas. 483; *Thompson v Weems* (1884) 9 App.Cas. 671.

[136] *Yorkshire Insurance Co v Campbell* [1917] A.C. 218.

[137] Assuming that such other terms have been validly incorporated into the contract: *DSG Retail Ltd v QBE International* [1999] Lloyd's Rep. I.R. 283.

[138] *Collett v Morrision* (1851) 9 Hare 162; *Wood v Dwarris* (1856) 11 Exch. 493. Contrast *Wheelton v Hardisty* (1858) 8 E. & B. 23.

basis clause and the materiality provision are identical in scope, the doctrine of *contra proferentem* almost demands that the basis clause be overridden by the requirement of materiality.[139]

Difficult questions of construction can arise here, and the cases turn upon whether the basis clause and any limiting clause are independent, in which case they have independent effect, or whether they form part of one single obligation, in which case the basis clause may be regarded as restricted. In *Fowkes v Manchester and London Life Assurance Co*[140] the basis clause was qualified by the statement that the assured's answers were to be the basis of the contract "if it shall here after appear that any fraudulent concealment or designedly untrue statement be contained therein". It was held that the word "therein" referred back to the precise ground covered by the basis clause, and accordingly the intention of the clause was to permit reliance on the basis clause only where the assured had acted fraudulently. This decision was followed by Kekewich J. in *Hemmings v Sceptre Life Association*,[141] in which there was a basis clause in usual form, but the policy itself contained a statement entitling the insurer to avoid the policy and retain the premiums in the event of the policy having been obtained by wilful misrepresentation. It was held that the two provisions were cumulative and not alternative, and that the declaration was restricted by the policy itself, so that accidental misrepresentation did not confer any rights on the insurer. *Hemmings* was doubted in the Scottish decision in *Unipac Scotland Ltd v Aegon Insurance Co*,[142] in which the basis clause set out the usual declaration that the assured had answered all questions to the best of his knowledge and belief and "that no material fact has been withheld or suppressed". The insurer was held to be able to avoid liability by proving that false statements had been made but without the need to prove their materiality: the Court of Session's view was that the basis clause contained two separate statements by the assured, one to the effect that answers had been given to the best of his knowledge and belief, and another to the effect that material facts had not been suppressed. As these related to different matters, the first to misrepresentation and the second to non-disclosure, they were independent obligations. The Court of Session was of the view that *Fowkes* was correctly decided but that *Hemmings*—which had relied upon *Fowkes*—was unsupportable as the two provisions were independent and should have been construed as such.

A basis clause will also be regarded as having been overridden by a policy term under which the insurer has undertaken that defences based on mis-representation and non-disclosure will not be taken, a provision which is common in professional indemnity contracts.[143]

Construction and scope of warranties

7–032 *Present and continuing warranties.* Representations can never have continuing effect, even if they relate to the future,[144] unless they can be construed as warranties. Some difficulty has been encountered by the courts in determining whether the assured has warranted merely that a state of affairs exists at the date of the proposal or inception of the risk, or whether he has gone further and

---

[139] See *Condogianis v Guardian Assurance Co* [1921] 2 A.C. 125; *Holmes v Scottish Legal Life Assurance Society* (1932) 48 T.L.R. 306.
[140] *Fowkes v Manchester and London Life Assurance Co* (1862) 3 F. & F. 440.
[141] *Hemmings v Sceptre Life Association* [1905] 1 Ch. 365.
[142] *Unipac Scotland Ltd v Aegon Insurance Co* [1999] Lloyd's Rep. I.R. 502.
[143] *Kumar v AGF Insurance Ltd* [1998] 4 All E.R. 788.
[144] *Shaw v Robberds* (1837) 6 A. & E. 75; *Benham v United Guarantee* (1852) 7 Ex. 744.

warranted that that state of affairs will prevail throughout the currency of the policy. In the absence of clear wording the answer in any given case will be based on a number of factors which may not always point towards the same solution: these will include whether imposing a continuing warranty is appropriate to the peril, whether continuing compliance by the assured is feasible, and whether the insurer requires continuing protection in the form conferred by a continuing warranty particularly in the light of the other terms of the policy. The various decisions on this issue are explicable only by their own individual and peculiar facts, although it may be that there is a presumption in favour of construing the assured's promise as directed towards present facts only; the principle of *contra proferentem* would undoubtedly justify any presumption of this nature, certainly where the assured is a consumer.

A number of cases have construed warranties as imposing continuing obligations. These include: a statement by a trader who stated that the only inflammable material stored was fuel for cigarette lights, when he later stored fireworks[145]; a statement by a builder that he did not use explosives in his work, when he later used explosives for the first time to undertake demolition work[146]; a statement as to the address at which a vehicle would be garaged[147]; a statement that money in transit would be kept in a safe and the key to the safe would not be kept in the building[148]; a statement that a vessel had London Salvage Association approval of location, fire fighting and mooring arrangements, when the approval subsequently lapsed[149]; a statement that Salvage Association recommendations with respect to a vessel would be complied with[150]; and a statement that oily rags were not kept loose in the assured's premises overnight.[151]

These decisions may usefully be contrasted with a series of others in which the warranty has been held to relate to present facts only. Where the assured has been asked to warrant whether it is his intention that an existing state of affairs is not to be altered during the currency of the policy, the courts have refused to treat this wording as amounting to a promise that no change will be made; it is clear that the warranty is, by its very terms a present one, relating to the assured's current state of mind, rather than continuing. This reasoning has been applied to a statement by an assured under a motor policy that no person aged under 25 years would drive the vehicle, other than himself,[152] and to an assured under a fidelity policy who stated the intention of holding fortnightly accounting meetings.[153] Cases in which the assured has warranted a fact are, therefore, the most problematic. It has nevertheless been decided that there is no futurity in: a statement by an employer, for the purposes of a liability policy, that its machinery and plant were properly fenced[154]; a statement that premises would remain occupied[155]; a statement that the assured kept sale and purchase ledgers up to

---

[145] *Hales v Reliance Fire Assurance* [1960] 2 Lloyd's Rep. 391.

[146] *Beauchamp v National Mutual Indemnity Insurance Co* [1937] 3 All E.R. 19.

[147] *Dawsons Ltd v Bonnin* [1922] A.C. 413.

[148] *Vaughan Motors v Scottish General Insurance Co Ltd* [1960] 1 Lloyd's Rep. 479.

[149] *Agapitos v Agnew (No.2)* [2003] Lloyd's Rep. I.R. 54.

[150] *Eagle Star Insurance Co Ltd v Games Video Co (GVC) SA (The Game Boy)* [2004] Lloyd's Rep. I.R. 867.

[151] *Transthene Packaging Co Ltd v Royal Insurance (UK) Ltd* [1996] L.R.L.R. 32.

[152] *Kirkbride v Donner* [1974] 1 Lloyd's Rep. 549.

[153] *Benham v United Guarantee and Life Assurance Co* (1852) 7 Ex. 744.

[154] *Woolfall & Rimmer v Moyle* [1942] 1 K.B. 66.

[155] *Hair v Prudential Assurance Co Ltd* [1983] 2 Lloyd's Rep. 667.

date[156]; a statement that the premises were fitted with a security alarm, the alarm subsequently ceasing to work[157]; information as to the operation of the assured building society's rules and procedures for handling money[158]; a statement by a reinsured as to the existence of other reinsurance of its retention[159]; and a statement as to the future navigation route of a vessel.[160] The Irish and Scottish courts have taken a similar restrictive approach to future warranties.[161]

The general point to be derived from these cases is that if insurers wish to have continuing protection they must expressly stipulate for it, given the draconian consequences of a breach of warranty.[162]

7–033 *Statements of fact and statements of opinion.* An important distinction is that between warranties of fact and warranties of opinion. If it is held that a warranty is of opinion only, it will be complied with so long as the proposer has honestly stated his opinion, whereas there is a breach of a warranty of fact even in the event of an honest mistake by the proposer.[163] The courts are in general reluctant to construe a warranty in a fashion requiring the assured to guarantee facts beyond his knowledge, and will seek to confine the warranty to statements which are true to the best of the assured's knowledge and belief.[164] The proposal form or policy may state specifically that the assured is only required to answer to the best of his knowledge or belief, in which case the main issue is subjective honesty,[165] although there is a residual objectivity requirement so that if the assured could not possibly have held his asserted belief there will be a breach of warranty. Thus, in *Gerling-Konzern General Insurance Co v Polygram Holdings and Metropolitan Entertainment Inc*[166] the assured company warranted that it would ascertain from its employees whether the life assured, a musician (Grateful Dead's Jerry Garcia), was to the best of their knowledge and belief in good health when the policy incepted: the warranty was held to be broken, as the assured had failed to ascertain from its employees their views on this matter, and

---

[156] *Weber & Berger v Employers' Mutual Liability Insurance Corporation* (1926) 24 Ll. L.R. 321.

[157] *Hussain v Brown* [1996] 1 Lloyd's Rep. 627. See also *Victor Melik & Co Ltd v Norwich Union Fire Insurance Society Ltd* [1980] 1 Lloyd's Rep. 523, where a policy condition requiring a burglar alarm to be kept in efficient working order was held not to have been broken when outside telephone lines were cut by a third party (and cf. the later decision in *AC Ward & Sons Ltd v Catlin (Five) (No.2)* [2009] EWHC 3122 (Comm)). *Hussain* and *Victor Melik* were distinguished in *Ansari v New India Assurance Ltd* [2009] Lloyd's Rep. I.R. 562, where the clause caused the risk to terminate if there was a material change to the facts stated by the assured, and it was held that the statement that premises were protected by a sprinkler system was materially changed when the system was disabled by the assured's tenant.

[158] *Hearts of Oak Permanent Building Society v Law Union & Rock Insurance* [1936] 2 All E.R. 619.

[159] *Assicurazioni Generali SpA v Arab Insurance Group* [2002] Lloyd's Rep. I.R. 633.

[160] *Grant v Aetna Insurance* (1862) 15 Moo. P.C. 516.

[161] *Sweeney v Kennedy* (1948) 82 Ll. L.R. 294 (qualifications of drivers); *Kennedy v Smith* 1976 S.L.T. 110 (drinking habits); *Forfar Weavers v MSF Pritchard Syndicate* Unreported, December 2005 (habitual storage of stock).

[162] *Hussain v Brown* [1996] 1 Lloyd's Rep. 627; *Pratt v Aigaion Insurance Co SA* [2009] Lloyd's Rep. I.R. 149; *AC Ward & Sons Ltd v Catlin (Five) Ltd* [2010] Lloyd's Rep. I.R. 30; *AC Ward & Sons Ltd v Catlin (Five) (No.2)* [2009] EWHC 3122 (Comm).

[163] *Arab Bank v Zurich Insurance Ltd* [1999] 1 Lloyd's Rep. 262.

[164] *Groupama Insurance Co Ltd v Overseas Partners Re Ltd* Unreported, 2003, where the reinsured was held not to have warranted the extent of losses suffered by the direct assured.

[165] This wording is now used in consumer cases. Professional indemnity policies also tend to restrict the assured's duties in this way: *Arab Bank Plc v Zurich Insurance Co Ltd* [1999] 1 Lloyd's Rep. 262.

[166] *Gerling-Konzern General Insurance Co v Polygram Holdings and Metropolitan Entertainment Inc* [1998] 2 Lloyd's Rep. 544.

the court added that even if this had been done, the employees could not have believed, in the light of the available evidence, that the life assured was in good health.[167]

If the wording is less than clear, difficult questions of interpretation may arise. The point has frequently arisen in life assurance cases. It used to be the practice to include on the proposal form a question as to the proposer's health, with the result that the courts were often called on to decide whether the proposer's assertion that he was in good health should be treated as a matter of fact or of opinion. In *Thomson v Weems*[168] the proposal form asked the question "Are you now and have you always been strictly temperate?" to which the assured gave a positive answer. Two years later the insured died of liver poisoning, apparently caused by excessive drinking. The insurer's refusal to pay on the policy was upheld in the House of Lords, where it was said that the statement as to temperance in the proposal form was to be construed as a warranty of fact rather than as a warranty of opinion, to be judged on objective grounds. Similarly, where the assured warrants "no known adverse facts", that statement has been held to be objective and not merely subjective.[169] Thus the assured is in breach of warranty if a reasonable man in his position would have been aware of adverse facts even though the assured himself had not been so aware.[170]

Warranties and terms delimiting the risk. Insurance policies on occasion contain **7–034** suspensory provisions which set out the circumstances in which the insurer is not to be on risk. A clause of this nature merely delimits the risk and is not a warranty, for when the specified circumstances come into being the assured is not in breach of contract nor can the insurer terminate the policy; the insurer is simply not to be liable should a loss occur while the circumstances specified in the clause remain in being. The suspension continues only for the duration of those circumstances, so that once the breach is remedied the policy reattaches.

The distinction between a warranty and a clause delimiting the insurer's risk is necessarily fine, for the same wording may be equally appropriate to the creation of either: thus a clause by which an assured householder is required to possess window locks may mean either that the assured is in breach of a continuing warranty for failing to do so, or that the insurer is not to be liable for any loss occurring while window locks are not fitted. It is perhaps not unreasonable to comment that the courts, in most cases, have construed clauses as risk delimitation provisions in order to protect the assured against the frequently harsh consequences of a continuing warranty.[171] It has thus been held

[167] For the meaning of good health, see *Ross v Bradshaw* (1761) 1 Wm. Bl. 312.

[168] *Thomson* (1884) 9 App.Cas. 671. Cf. *Yorke v Yorkshire Insurance Co* [1918] 1 K.B. 662, in which the word "illness" was held to be referring to an objective state of affairs and not to the assureds subjective views as to his own state of affairs. But contrast *Southcombe v Merriman* (1842) Car. & M. 286.

[169] *Kelsall v Allstate Insurance Co Ltd, The Times*, March 20, 1987.

[170] *Re Hooley Hill Rubber* [1920] 1 K.B. 254, 274; *Lake v Simmons* 119271 A.C. 487, 507.

[171] But see *CTN Cash and Carry Ltd v General Accident Fire and Life Assurance Corp* [1989] 1 Lloyd's Rep. 299, where it was held that a term requiring a cash kiosk to be locked while unattended was suspensory and not a warranty, a decision which defeated the assured's claim given that the insurers were apparently unable to rely on breach of warranty by reason of waiver. In order to avoid the strict approach to the construction of warranties adopted by the courts, some insurers have been willing to accept at trial that their "warranties" were merely suspensory clauses, although such concessions have been costless in that in the relevant cases the assured was in breach at the time of loss. The courts have maintained their strict approach to construction even where such concessions have been made: *Pratt v Aigaion Insurance Co SA (The Resolute)* [2004] Lloyd's Rep. I.R. 149; *AC Ward & Sons Ltd v Catlin (Five) Ltd* [2010] Lloyd's Rep. I.R. 30 (the judge at first instance in this case rejected the insurers' concession on this point).

that: a term limiting the use of a vehicle for domestic purposes merely suspended cover while it was being used for commercial purposes[172]; a term stating that a taxi would be driven for only one shift per day relieved the insurers from liability only while it was being driven for a second shift[173]; and a term stating that the vehicle in which the insured jewels were to be carried was fitted with locks and alarms entitled the assured to recover unless at the time of the loss the locks and alarms were disabled.[174] The most important decision is *Provincial Insurance Co v Morgan*,[175] in which a proposal form for the insurance of a lorry contained a "warranty" that the insured lorry was to be used only for carrying coal. It was periodically used to carry timber instead of or as well as coal, and it was involved in an accident shortly after offloading a quantity of timber. The House of Lords held that the user limitation was not a warranty but a description of the circumstances in which the insurer would be on risk, so that, as the lorry had not been carrying timber when damaged, the insurers were liable.[176]

To date, the courts have failed to lay down a convincing, or indeed any, test. It might be thought that a necessary precondition to a finding that a term delimits the risk is that a "breach" of it does not have effects which persist beyond the remedying of that "breach". It was suggested to Morland J. in *Kler Knitwear v Lombard General Insurance Co Ltd*[177] that a once and for all obligation—in the present case, to have a sprinkler inspected within 30 days of the renewal of the policy—was by its nature a warranty rather than a suspensory condition. Instead the court held that the risk was suspended after the expiry of the 30-day period, and reattached once an inspection had actually taken place.

7–035 *Warranties and terminating provisions.* There may similarly be a fine line between a warranty and a term which sets out circumstances in which the policy ceases to have effect. A clear example of the latter provision is a term in a travel policy which provides that cover comes to an end when the journey is completed: the completion of the journey does not put the assured in breach of contract, but merely brings the contract to an end. More difficult is a clause in a motor policy which provides that the policy is to cease to operate if the assured's car is not regularly serviced: such a clause could equally have been phrased as a warranty requiring regular servicing. As a matter of strict law the distinction is of little significance, for in the latter example the insurer is discharged from further liability whether the assured is regarded as being in breach of warranty or whether the policy is regarded as having come to an end, although the point is of importance in consumer and small-business cases governed by the Insurance

---

[172] *Roberts v Anglo-Saxon Insurance Co* (1927) 96 L.J.K.B. 590.

[173] *Farr v Motor Traders Mutual Insurance Society* [1920] 3 K.B. 669.

[174] *De Maurier (Jewels) Ltd v Bastion Insurance* [1967] 2 Lloyd's Rep. 550.

[175] *Provincial Insurance Co v Morgan* [1933] A.C. 240.

[176] The Canadian courts have adopted the same distinction, obligations being construed not as warranties but as suspensory provisions: *Century Insurance Company of Canada v Case Existological Laboratories Ltd, The Bamcell II* [1984] 1 W.W.R. 97 (obligation for watchman to be on board from 22.00 hours to 06.00 hours); *Federal Business Development Bank v Commonwealth Insurance* (1983) 2 C.C.L.I. 200 ("Warranted vessel to be laid up at the north foot of Columbia Street"; *Shearwater Marine Ltd v Guardian Insurance Co* (1997) 29 B.C.L.R. (3d) 13 (warranty requiring daily inspection of vessel and pumped as necessary). Contrast: *Elkhorn Developments Ltd v Sovereign General Insurance Co* [2001] B.C.J. No.630, in which a warranty requiring the assured to obtain the consent of the insurers for movement of the insured barge was a true warranty and not a suspensory provision; *McIntosh v Royal & Sun Alliance* 2007 F.C. 23 (warranty allowing use of boat for pleasure purposes only held to be a true warranty).

[177] *Kler Knitwear v Lombard General Insurance Co Ltd* [2000] Lloyd's Rep. I.R. 47.

Conduct of Business Rules, which preclude reliance on a warranty whose breach is not causative of the loss.

Breach of warranty

Need for actual breach. In order for there to be a breach of warranty, the assured **7–036** has to actually break the term in question and not merely intend to do so without putting the intention into effect,[178] in contrast to the position with a change of voyage under s.45 of the Marine Insurance Act 1906 where the manifestation of the intention is enough to discharge a voyage policy. If a warranty that a particular fact is true is given by the assured, that warranty is normally to be construed as requiring the fact to be true at that point, and there is no leeway to allow the assured a reasonable time for compliance unless this is expressly given. There may, however, be ambiguity on the question whether the warranty must be complied with at the time of the proposal or by the time of the inception of the risk. It is submitted that, clear words aside, the latter date is the correct one, so that non-compliance with the warranty at a time before the risk has incepted has no effect on the attachment of cover.[179]

An obligation on the assured to maintain a system of work is not broken if the assured has put a system of work in place which is not adhered to by employees or contractors.[180]

Construction of the obligations imposed by warranties. Warranties are construed **7–037** in much the same manner as other terms appearing in insurance policies; individual words and phrases are to be given their ordinary or contextual meaning, subject to the overriding requirement that the warranty as a whole must be interpreted in a fashion which gives effect to the commercial objectives of the parties.[181] The question whether or not a warranty has been broken, once the facts have been ascertained, is always simply one of construction of the words constituting the warranty.[182] The question is therefore one of law for the court.[183] Thus a warranty in a property or liability policy must not be given a meaning which in effect puts the assured in breach simply because a loss has occurred[184]; an "occupancy" warranty in relation to a building is not to be construed as requiring that the assured is unable to leave the premises[185]; a marine warranty "no coastal cruising/voyages in coastal waters except during daylight hours" means that the vessel must not undertake coastal cruising at night and does not

[178] *Baines v Holland* (1855) 10 Exch. 802; *Simpson Steamship Co v Premier Underwriting Association* (1905) 10 Com. Cas. 198.

[179] *Agapitos v Agnew (No.2)* [2003] Lloyd's Rep. I.R. 54.

[180] *Cornhill Insurance v DE Stamp Felt Roofing* [2002] Lloyd's Rep. I.R. 648; *US Trading Ltd v Axa Insurance Co Ltd* [2010] Lloyd's Rep. I.R. 505.

[181] *Sumpiles Investments Pte Ltd v Axa Insurance Singapore Pte Ltd* [2006] 3 S.L.R. 12; *AC Ward & Son Ltd v Catlin (Five) Ltd* [2010] Lloyd's Rep. I.R. 30; *AC Ward & Sons Ltd v Catlin (Five) (No.2)* [2009] EWHC 3122 (Comm); *Richfine Development Ltd v Rivington* [2008] H.K.E.C. 1113.

[182] *Thomson v Weems* (1884) 9 App.Cas. 671 at 683, 687; *Condogianis v Guardian* [1921] 2 A.C. 125 at 131. See also: *Simmonds v Cockell* [1920] 1 K.B. 843; *Provincial Insurance v Morgan* [1933] A.C. 240, 247 at 255–256.

[183] *Dunn v Ocean Accident* (1933) 45 Ll. L.R. 276 at 280.

[184] *Hearts of Oak Building Society v Law Union and Rock Insurance Co Ltd* [1936] 2 All E.R. 619; *AC Ward & Sons Ltd v Catlin (Five) Ltd* [2009] EWCA Civ 1098; *AC Ward & Sons Ltd v Catlin (Five) (No.2)* [2009] EWHC 3122 (Comm).

[185] *Winicofsky v Army and Navy General Insurance Co* (1919) 35 T.L.R. 283; *Simmonds v Cockell* [1926] 1 K.B. 843.

extend to sea voyages which takes the vessel close to the coast at night[186] and an assured who gives a warranty as to his health is not in breach if he has failed to disclose matters which a reasonable man would not have disclosed.[187]

The ordinary principles of construction, that attention must be paid to the factual matrix and to the commercial purpose of the warranty, may be illustrated by a series of marine cases concerning "crewing" warranties. In *Brownsville Holdings Ltd v Adamjee Insurance Co Ltd (The Milasan)*[188] a policy on a motor yacht provided, "Warranted professional skippers and crew in charge at all times". The assured did not employ a professional skipper and Aikens J. had little difficulty in holding that the assured was in breach of warranty. In *GE Frankona Reinsurance Ltd v CMM Trust No.1400 (The Newfoundland Explorer)*[189] the warranty in the policy on a yacht provided "Warranted vessel fully crewed at all times". At the time of the fire which destroyed the vessel there were no crew members on board at all. Gross J. held that there was a clear breach of the provision, although the learned judge accepted that the clause could not be construed literally and held that there would not be any breach in the case of emergencies rendering his departure necessary or necessary temporary departures for the purpose of performing his crewing duties or other related activities. These cases were distinguished in *Pratt v Aigaion Insurance Co SA*,[190] where the policy on a fishing vessel provided: "Warranted Owner and/or Owner's experienced skipper on board and in charge at all times and one experienced crew member." The vessel was lost when the vessel was moored and none of the three crew members was on board. The Court of Appeal held that both parties would have known that a vessel of this type would have been tied up from time to time, given restrictions on the number of fishing days under EU law, and even when the vessel was working the skipper would have to go ashore from time to time for both business and leisure purposes. The purpose of the warranty, in the Court of Appeal's view, was to protect the vessel when she was being used, a point emphasised by the concluding words "and one experienced crew member". The words "at all times" could not be given a literal meaning because compliance would have been impossible, and accordingly—given that it was unclear what their meaning should be—the words were ambiguous and were to be construed *contra proferentem* in favour of the assured.

Statements made by the assured must also be construed fairly and reasonably. In *Condogianis v Guardian*[191] the assured was asked if he had made claims before and if so when and on what company. He replied, "Yes. 1917. Ocean", and warranted his answer to be true. He had also made other claims. It was held by the Privy Council that although his answer was literally true in an academic sense, it was nevertheless untrue in the eyes of the law, because on a fair and reasonable construction of the answer it was not true. Similarly, where a proposal in writing for the insurance of a coach against accident was made and signed with a warranty that the statements and particulars contained in it were true, and

[186] *Bolton v New Zealand Insurance Co Ltd* [1995] 1 N.Z.L.R. 224.

[187] *Connecticut Mutual Life Assurance v Moore* (1881) 6 App.Cas. 644; *Yorke v Yorkshire Insurance Co* [1918] 1 K.B. 662; *Kumar v Life Assurance Corporation of India* [1974] 1 Lloyd's Rep. 147.

[188] *Brownsville Holdings Ltd v Adamjee Insurance Co Ltd (The Milasan)* [2000] 2 Lloyd's Rep. 458.

[189] *GE Frankona Reinsurance Ltd v CMM Trust No.1400 (The Newfoundland Explorer)* [2006] 1 Lloyd's Rep. I.R. 704.

[190] *Pratt v Aigaion Insurance Co SA* [2009] Lloyd's Rep. I.R. 149.

[191] *Condogianis v Guardian* [1921] 2 A.C. 125. See also: *Cazenove v British Equitable* (1859) 6 C.B.(N.S.) 437; *Holt's Motors v South-East Lancashire Insurance* (1930) 35 Com. Cas. 281.

reference was made in it to a previous accident in which cattle had been injured, it was held that the assured was in breach of warranty for not disclosing damage to his own vehicle.[192] But where a man was asked whether he had been insured before, it was held that this question referred only to the premises which he was then proposing to insure, and that the answer "No" was therefore true although he had taken out other insurances on other premises.[193] In *Travelers Casualty and Surety Co of Canada v Sun Life Assurance Co of Canada (UK) Ltd (No.2)*[194] a warranty that the assured under a liability policy was not aware of any outstanding "claim . . . within the scope of the proposed coverage" meant a claim which exceeded the retention level under the policy and in ascertaining knowledge the assured was not required to be a prophet of doom but had to consider what was realistically the worst possible scenario.

Strict compliance. The opening words of s.33 of the 1906 Act, which represent **7–038** the law in all classes of insurance, provide that a warranty must be exactly complied with. It makes no difference that the breach is beyond the control[195] or knowledge[196] of the assured, or is someone else's fault,[197] as in *International Management Group (UK) Ltd v Simmonds*,[198] where the organisers of a cricket competition between India and Pakistan warranted for the purposes of a cancellation policy that they would obtain all necessary licences, visas and permits. It was held that the decision of the Indian government to give directions to the Indian Cricket Board to withdraw the team amounted to a breach of warranty on the basis that the consent of the Indian government was in practice necessary to secure the participation of the team.

It is also irrelevant that the risk is not increased by breach.[199] Minor breaches which do not affect the risk, and even temporary breaches which are remedied prior to loss,[200] provide the insurer with a defence. Moreover, where a severable subject matter is insured under an entire policy, breach of warranty in relation to some part of the subject matter will allow the insurer to repudiate the policy.[201] In *Overseas Commodities Ltd v Style*[202] the assured warranted that every tin in the insured cargo of canned pork had been date-stamped by the manufacturer. A number of the tins had not been so marked, and this was held to be sufficient to discharge the insurer from its obligations towards the complete cargo; McNair J. relied in part on the need for strict compliance in reaching this conclusion. The *Style* decision nevertheless indicates that there is a *de minimis* exception to the doctrine of exact compliance, and it is difficult to believe that McNair J. would

[192] *Furey v Eagle Star* [1922] W.C. & Ins.Rep. 149 at 225.
[193] *Golding v Royal London Auxiliary Insurance* (1914) 30 T.L.R. 350. See also: *Perrins v Marine & General Travellers' Insurance* (1859) 2 E. & E. 317; *Simmonds v Cockell* [1926] 1 K.B. 843; *Kumar v Life Assurance Corp of India* [1974] 1 Lloyd's Rep. 147.
[194] *Travelers Casualty and Surety Co of Canada v Sun Life Assurance Co of Canada (UK) Ltd (No.2)* [2007] Lloyd's Rep. I.R. 619.
[195] *Phillips v Baillie* (1784) 3 Doug. K.B. 374.
[196] *Trickett v Queensland Insurance* [1936] A.C. 159 at 165; *Hutchison v National Loan Fund Life* (1845) 7 D. (C of Sess.) 467 at 476.
[197] *Worsley v Wood* (1776) 6 T.R. 710.
[198] *International Management Group (UK) Ltd v Simmonds* [2004] Lloyd's Rep. I.R. 247.
[199] *Newcastle Fire v Macmorran* (1815) 3 Dow. 225; *Bond v Nutt* (1777) 2 Cowp. 601; *Hare v Whitmore* (1778) 2 Cowp. 784; *Earle v Harris* (1780) I Doug. K.B. 357; *De Hahn v Hartley* (1786) 1 T.R. 343; *Sanderson v Rusher* (1814) 4 Camp. 54n; *Hart v Standard Marine Insurance Co* (1889) 22 QBD 499; *Union Insurance Society of Canton v George Wills & Co* [1916] A.C. 281; *Allen v Universal Automobile Insurance Co* (1933) 45 Ll. L.R. 55; *Simons v Gale* [1958] 2 All E.R. 504.
[200] 1906 Act s.34(2).
[201] Contrast the position where the policy is severable. See below.
[202] *Overseas Commodities Ltd v Style* [1958] 1 Lloyd's Rep. 546.

have reached the same conclusion on the warranty issue had only a small proportion of tins not been stamped.

The injustice which may flow from the exact compliance principle has been tempered to some extent by the complementary rule that the assured's duty does not extend beyond exact compliance. This may on occasion produce surprising results. Thus in *Hide v Bruce*[203] a warranty that a vessel had 20 guns was held not to require that there would be sufficient hands available to work those guns. Similarly, in *Mayall v Mitford*,[204] a warranty that a cotton mill would be worked by day only was held not to be broken by the steam engine and other machinery being left running during the night: the working of the part of a mill is not the working of the mill within the meaning of such a warranty. A warranty given by an assured security firm that its procedures, equipment and personnel "shall not be varied to the detriment of the underwriters" is not broken by casual alteration, as single incidents do not amount to a "variation".[205]

If the alleged contravention of a warranty is easily and cheaply remediable, there may be ground for deciding that there is no breach of warranty in the first place.[206]

7–039   *The principle of automatic termination.* Section 33 of the 1906 Act concludes with the words: "If [the warranty] be not exactly complied with, then, subject to any express provision in the policy, the insurer is discharged from liability as from the date of the breach of warranty, but without prejudice to any liability incurred by him to that date." This wording on its face automatically puts an end to the risk as soon as the warranty has been broken, a view confirmed in *Bank of Nova Scotia v Hellenic Mutual War Risks Association (The Good Luck)*,[207] in which insurers were under a contractual undertaking to a mortgagee bank to inform it if the insurers "ceased to insure" the mortgaged vessel but failed to inform the bank of a breach of warranty. The House of Lords held that the risk came to an end automatically on breach of warranty, which meant that the insurance "ceased" at that point and it was irrelevant that the insurers had not given notice to the assured treating themselves as off risk. It has subsequently[208] been held that the same principle applies to non-marine insurance.[209] In that case, which involved pecuniary rather than marine insurance, a clause which purported

---

[203] *Hide v Bruce* (1783) 3 Doug. K.B. 213. Other early marine authorities are to the same effect: *Muller v Thomson* (1811) 2 Camp. 610; *Laing v Glover* (1813) 5 Taunt. 49; *Hart v Standard Marine Insurance Co Ltd* (1889) 22 QBD 499.

[204] *Mayall v Mitford* (1837) 6 Ad. & El. 670. See also: *Dobson v Sotherby* (1827) Moo. & M. 9; *Shaw v Robberds* (1837) 6 Ad. & E. 75; *Whitehead v Price* (1835) 2 Cr. M. & R. 447. Cf. *Hair v Prudential Assurance Co Ltd* [1980] 1 Lloyd's Rep. 52.

[205] *Mint Security Ltd v Blair* [1982] 1 Lloyd's Rep. 188.

[206] *Alum Goolamn Hossen & Co v Union Marine Insurance Co* [1901] A.C. 362.

[207] *Bank of Nova Scotia v Hellenic Mutual War Risks Association (The Good Luck)* [1991] 3 All E.R. 1.

[208] There was earlier non-marine authority for the proposition that a breach of warranty was simply a repudiation of contract which entitled the insurers to terminate for breach or to maintain the policy in existence: *West v National Motor and Accident Insurance Union* [1955] 1 All E.R. 800; *Mint Security Ltd v Blair* [1982] 1 Lloyd's Rep. 188; *CTN Cash and Carry Ltd v General Accident Fire and Life Assurance Corp Ltd* [1989] 1 Lloyd's Rep. 299.

[209] *Kumar v AGF Insurance Ltd* [1988] 4 All E.R. 788, which turned on the fact that wordings prepared before *The Good Luck* was decided were to be construed on the assumption that there was no automatic termination; *Arab Rank Plc v Zurich Insurance Co Ltd* [1999] 1 Lloyd's Rep. 262; *Printpak v AGF Insurance Ltd* [1999] Lloyd's Rep. I.R. 542; *HIH General and Casualty Co v New Hampshire Insurance* [2001] Lloyd's Rep. I.R. 596.

to exclude the rights of the insurer following breach of duty by the assured provided that "the insurer hereby agrees that it will not seek to be entitled to avoid or rescind this policy". The Court of Appeal held that this wording was not appropriate to extend to a warranty: the remedy for breach of warranty was not any action taken by the insurer but rather automatic termination of the risk, as by such breach the assured took himself outside the cover granted by the policy.

Effects of automatic termination of the risk. The effects of a breach of warranty **7–040** depend upon whether the warranty is present or continuing. In the former case, the assured will have made a false statement as to present fact in the proposal form, the effect of which is to prevent the risk from ever attaching.[210] Any premiums paid by the assured are on this basis recoverable by reason of total failure of consideration,[211] and the insurer cannot face any liability for losses. The insurer cannot, therefore, affirm the policy and deny the claim.[212]

By contrast, in the case of a continuing warranty, where the assured is in breach by virtue of his conduct during the currency of the insurance, the risk is treated as having incepted at the outset but automatically coming to an end as of the date of breach. It follows that the insurer is discharged from any future liability, although any liabilities on the insurer which had accrued up to the date of the breach of warranty are unaffected. Thus if the assured has suffered a loss prior to his breach of warranty, the insurer is not discharged from his obligation to make payment.[213] The fact that the risk has incepted but simply come to an end means also that there has not been a total failure of consideration on the part of the insurer, so that insurer is entitled to retain the full amount of the premium even though the insurer may have been on risk for a short period only.[214] On the same basis, if the premium is payable in instalments, and there are unpaid instalments at the date of the breach of warranty, the assured is not discharged from making the remaining payments, on the strength of the rule that the premium is not divisible and is fully earned as soon as the risk incepts: this principle holds good even if the warranty broken by the assured is the obligation to pay instalments of the premium when they fall due[215] and the assured has to continue to make payment even though there is no possibility of making a claim after the breach.[216]

---

[210] *Arab Bank v Zurich Insurance Ltd* [1999] 1 Lloyd's Rep. 262. For this reason, it is not correct to say that the policy has been cancelled or avoided by the insurer. The policy is unaffected; what has terminated, without any action by the insurer, is the risk.

[211] Marine Insurance Act 1906 ss.84(1) and (3)(a).

[212] *West v National Motor and Accident Insurance Union* [1955] 1 All E.R. 800. In *Mint Security Ltd v Blair* [1982] 1 Lloyd's Rep. 188, it was held that a policy term, which made compliance with warranties a condition precedent to the making of a claim, had the effect of conferring upon the insurer the right to terminate the policy or to maintain the policy but reject the claim. After *The Good Luck* [1991] 3 All E.R. 1 it may be that the clause would be construed in the same way, as it appears to amount to a partial waiver of the insurer's right to have the contract treated as automatically terminated.

[213] *Woolmer v Mailman* (1763) 2 Burr. 1419; *Simpson Steamship Co v Premier Underwriting Association Ltd* (1905) 92 L.T. 730; *Brit Syndicates Ltd v Italaudit SpA* [2008] Lloyd's Rep. I.R. 601.

[214] Marine Insurance Act 1906 s.84.

[215] *JA Chapman & Co Ltd v Kadirga Denizcilik Ve Ticaret* [1998] Lloyd's Rep. I.R. 377.

[216] This assumes that the risk is indivisible and does not run from instalment to instalment. It would be highly unusual for a policy to be construed as lasting only for the period covered by each instalment: see *Chapman* itself on this point.

7–041 *Materiality and nexus.* The risk is discharged automatically on breach of warranty whether or not the warranty is material to the risk[217] and whether or not the breach has played a part in any loss which may have occurred.[218] It does not matter that the loss would have happened in any event.[219] Thus where it was warranted under a motor policy that the assured would "take all reasonable steps to maintain the vehicle in an efficient condition", and he removed the foot-brake, leaving only a hand-brake, and an accident occurred, it was held that he was not entitled to recover, although the exact cause of the accident could not be ascertained.[220]

There are numerous authorities for these propositions, ranging from early marine authorities covering fewer than warranted (but nevertheless sufficient for sailing purposes) crew[221] to modern decisions in which the value or cost of insured property has been marginally incorrectly stated,[222] and in which the assured has warranted that all criminal convictions have been disclosed by him when admittedly immaterial convictions have been withheld.[223] In *Yorkshire Insurance Co v Campbell*[224] a horse was insured against marine perils, and was lost along with the vessel. The horse's pedigree was stated on the proposal to be "Soult out of St Paul mare", although this was not accurate. The Privy Council held that the basis clause in the proposal converted the statement into a warranty and that the insurers were never liable.[225] Accordingly, it is clear that where a warranty has been broken, enquiry into its materiality or its role in any subsequent loss is otiose. In *Forsikringsaktieselskapet Vesta v Butcher*,[226] where it was held that the failure of the assured owner of a fish farm to comply with a warranty whereby a 24-hour watch had to be maintained was fatal to his claim for loss from storm damage even though it was conceded that the presence of a watch could not possibly have in any way lessened the likelihood or degree of loss, the absence of a nexus requirement was described by Lord Griffiths as "one of the less attractive features of English insurance law".[227]

Recognition of the draconian effects of a warranty has led to the contractual modification of warranties by requiring a causal link between materiality or breach and loss. Thus in *Bennett v Axa Insurance Plc*[228] a fire policy on a nightclub stated that all trade waste would be swept up and bagged at the end of each day's trading and that non-compliance "with any such warranty in so far as

---

[217] Section 33(3) includes the words "whether it he material to the risk or not". See: *Pawson v Watson* (1778) 2 Cowp. 785 at 788; *Newcastle Fire v Macmorran* (1815) 3 Dow. H.L. 225 at 263; *Anderson v Fitzgerald* (1853) 4 H.L.C. 484 at 503–504; *Glicksmam v Lancashire & General* [1927] A.C. 139 at 143; *Allen v Universal Automobile* (1933) 45 Ll. L.R. 55; *Yorkshire Insurance v Campbell* [1917] A.C. 218.

[218] The effect of a breach of warranty is to bring the risk to an end as from the date of breach, and accordingly it is irrelevant whether or not a loss follows it. The nexus point is worthy of mention (a) because some breaches of warranty are causative of loss, and (b) because breach of warranty is frequently discovered only following a loss.

[219] *Maynard v Rhode* (1824) 1 C. & P. 360; *Glen v Lewis* (1853) 8 Ex. 607; *Foley v Tabor* (1861) 2 F. & F. 663; *Beacon Life v Gibb* (1862) 1 Moo.P.C.C.(N.S.) 73; *Forsikrings Vesta v Butcher* [1989] 1 All E.R. 602.

[220] *Jones and James v Provincial* (1929) 46 T.L.R. 71.

[221] *De Hahn v Hartley* (1786) T.R. 343.

[222] *Allen v Universal Automobile Insurance Co* (1933) 45 Ll. L.R. 55.

[223] *Mackay v London General Insurance Co* (1935) 51 Ll. L.R. 201.

[224] *Yorkshire Insurance Co v Campbell* [1917] A.C. 218. See also: *Woolmer v Mailman* (1763) 1 Wm. Bl. 427; *Rich v Parker* (1798) 7 T.R. 705.

[225] Some attempt, albeit unconvincing, was made to find that pedigree was a material fact.

[226] *Forsikringsaktieselskapet Vesta v Butcher* [1989] 1 All E.R. 402.

[227] *Forsikringsaktieselskapet Vesta v Butcher* [1989] 1 All E.R. 402 at 406.

[228] *Bennett v Axa Insurance Plc* [2004] Lloyd's Rep. I.R. 615.

it increases the risk of loss destruction or damage shall be a bar to any claim in respect of such loss destruction or damage . . . " The assured's claim for a fire loss failed as the evidence showed that the fire was probably caused by trade waste which had not been bagged.

Divisibility of warranties. The automatic termination principle normally applies **7–042** to the entirety of the risk under the policy. However, if the assured can demonstrate that the policy is divisible, and that a particular warranty relates only to a part of the policy, breach of the warranty discharges the insurer only in relation to that part. Thus in *Printpak v AGF Insurance Ltd*[229] insurers were held to be liable to indemnify the assured for loss caused by fire even though the assured was in breach of a burglar alarm warranty contained in a separate section of the policy.[230] However, it is more usual for warranties to be construed as applying to the entirety of a policy and not to its individual sections.[231] Where a policy contains a warranty, in principle the warranty is divisible. The further question which arises is whether a warranty is divisible as between co-assureds, so that breach by one co-assured does not affect the rights of the others. It would seem that all turns upon the proper construction of the warranty, and in particular whether it describes the risk accepted by the insurers or whether it imposes personal obligations on particular co-assureds. In *Arab Bank v Zurich Insurance Co*[232] a professional indemnity policy obtained by the directors of a company contained a warranty that the statements made in the proposal were true to the best of the knowledge and belief of the assureds. Rix J. held that the co-assureds other than the managing director were unaware that the statements were false, and accordingly they were not deprived of cover. The warranty thus applied to each of the co-assureds separately, and only those in breach of it were denied recovery. Rix J. added (a point which did not form a part of the decision itself) that the position would have been different had the warranty simply been that the statements in the proposal were true. Each of the co-assureds would then have been in breach of that warranty if any statement was untrue, whoever made it. But it will be noted that this was a professional indemnity policy written on a claims made basis, so the existence of potential claims against any of the assured was plainly something which was fundamental to the risk being insured: in effect insurers were being asked to provide cover for inevitable claims. The position after *Arab Bank* is, therefore, that a warranty is a promise given by each individual co-assured, but what has been promised is a matter for the proper construction of the warranty. In some situations the promise is one which relates to the very nature of the risk itself, so that if any one co-assured is in breach of it then all are affected by it. In other situations the promise relates to each individual assured and not the risk itself, so that one assured may be in breach of it whereas others may not. There are undoubtedly some warranties which relate to the very risk which is being undertaken by the insurers. Thus if the assured warrants that the vessel is to be used to carry grain on a summer voyage, and it is used to carry explosives on a winter voyage, it is apparent that the insurers are providing cover for a completely different risk to that which they thought was being underwritten and they cannot be liable whoever is at fault for the

---

[229] *Printpak v AGF Insurance Ltd* [1999] Lloyd's Rep. I.R. 542. The principle applies also to good faith: *James v CGU Insurance* [2002] Lloyd's Rep. I.R. 206.

[230] See also: *HTV v JFK Lintner* [1984] 2 Lloyd's Rep. 125; *Den Danske Bank A/S v Skipton Building Society* [1998] 1 E.G.L.R. 155.

[231] *International Management Group (UK) Ltd v Simmonds* [2004] Lloyd's Rep. I.R. 247.

[232] *Arab Bank v Zurich Insurance Co* [1999] 1 Lloyd's Rep. 262.

misstatement. By contrast, if the warranty does not go to the very nature of the risk insured, then there is no reason why an innocent co-assured should lose protection.

7–043 *Remedying a breach of warranty.* If the assured has broken a warranty, but has remedied the breach prior to loss, the insurer's right to treat the risk as terminated remains unimpaired.[233]

7–044 *Burden of proof.* The burden of proving that a warranty has been broken lies upon the insurers.[234] It follows that, if they dispute the assured's right to recover on the policy on the ground that he stated in the proposals that he had not had certain diseases, whereas he in fact had one of them at the time, they will be obliged to give particulars of the symptoms of the disease alleged.[235]

7–045 *The assured's defences.* Leaving aside the possibility of waiver, discussed below, the only defences open to an assured who is in breach of warranty are contained in s.34(1) of the 1906 Act, which provides that "Non-compliance with a warranty is excused when, by reason of a change in circumstances, the warranty ceases to be applicable to the circumstances of the contract, or when compliance with the warranty is rendered unlawful by any subsequent law." The former is based on old decisions.[236] It was unsuccessfully relied upon in *Agapitos v Agnew (No.2)*,[237] where the assured had failed to comply with a warranty requiring London Salvage Association approval of the insured vessel, and asserted that compliance had been rendered unnecessary by reason of the fact that the vessel had subsequently been moved. Moore Bick J. held that the warranty had nothing to do with the location of the vessel.

Waiver of breach

7–046 *Forms of waiver.* Section 34(3) of the 1906 Act states that "a breach of warranty may be waived by the insurer". This provision deals in reality with two distinct situations: (1) cases in which the insurer agrees expressly or impliedly, prior to a breach of warranty, not to take any action against the assured in the event of any breach by him; (2) cases in which the insurer expressly or impliedly agrees, following a breach of warranty, to disregard the breach.

7–047 *Waiver of warranty.* At first sight it appears to be something of a contradiction in terms for an insurer to impose a warranty by a policy and yet in the same policy agree that its breach shall be waived. This position has, however, long prevailed in marine hull and freight insurance by virtue of the "held covered" clause, which operates where the assured and insurers can agree on an appropriate level of additional premium following the breach. This aside, a general waiver of defences by the insurer, in the form of a contract term to that effect, may itself amount to a waiver of the right to rely upon breach of warranty.

---

[233] Marine Insurance Act 1906 s.34(2) specifically so provides. See: *De Hahn v Hartley* (1786) 1 T.R. 343; *Forshaw v Chabert* (1821) 3 Brod. & Bing. 158; *Foley v Tabor* (1861) 2 F & F. 663; *Quebec Marine Insurance Co v Commercial Bank of Canada* (1870) L.R. 3 P.C. 234.

[234] *Stebbing v Liverpool & London & Globe* [1917] 2 K.B. 433 at 438; *Bond Air Services v Hill* [1955] 2 Q.B. 417.

[235] *Marshall v Emperor Life* (1865) L.R. 1 Q.B. 35; *Girdlestone v North British* (1870) L.R. 11 Eq. 197.

[236] *Hore v Whitmore* (1778) 2 Cowp. 784; *Exposito v Bowden* (1857) 7 E. & B. 763.

[237] *Agapitos v Agnew (No.2)* [2003] Lloyd's Rep. I.R. 54.

However, in every case, it is necessary to construe the term to determine whether it is intended to be general or whether it is limited to specific defences, excluding breach of warranty. Where insurers agreed not to avoid or rescind the policy or to reject any claim for non-disclosure or misrepresentation, they were held not to have waived their right to rely upon breach of warranty, given that such breach discharged them automatically and did not involve any avoidance or denial of liability.[238]

In the absence of an express "held covered" provision or other exclusion of this type, an unequivocal representation, whether by act or statement, by the insurer to the effect that a particular breach of warranty will not be relied upon, and in full or partial reliance on which the assured proceeds to break the warranty, may amount to a waiver. In *Samuel & Co Ltd v Dumas*[239] the assured warranted under a hull policy that freight insurance under honour policies in excess of £3,750 would not be procured. Insurance for a greater sum was obtained by means of a slip which the hull insurer had itself scratched. The House of Lords held that the insurer had, by its waiver or acquiescence, demonstrated an intention not to enforce the warranty against the assured. Conversely, in *Sleigh v Tyser*,[240] inspection of the vessel's carrying capabilities by the insurer's agent prior to the voyage was held not to amount to a waiver by the insurer of a warranty that the vessel was to be seaworthy for the purposes of the particular adventure. Previous waivers of breaches of warranty are not to be taken as authorising future disregard of that warranty.[241]

Waiver of breach of warranty. Once a breach of warranty has taken place, and **7-048** the insurer is aware of such breach, the insurer may by statement or act waive the breach, leaving the risk under the policy intact although the assured may remain liable in damages to the insurer for loss caused by the breach of contract.[242]

It remains to consider exactly when a breach of warranty will be taken to have been waived by the insurers. English law recognises two forms of waiver: waiver by affirmation, where insurers choose between their rights to affirm or disaffirm a contract; and waiver by estoppel, which arises where insurers unequivocally represent to the assured that they do not intend to rely upon their rights and that representation is relied upon by the assured. By reason of the principle of automatic termination of risk on breach of warranty, the insurers do not have any choice to make as to whether to affirm or disaffirm the contract, and it follows that waiver by affirmation is not available as a defence to breach of warranty[243]

---

[238] *HIH Casualty and General Insurance Ltd v New Hampshire Insurance Co* [2001] Lloyd's Rep. I.R. 596. No reference was made to a contrary earlier holding on similar words reached by Thomas J. in *Kumar v AGF Insurance* [1994] 4 All E.R. 788, although that case turned on the fact that the wording had been prepared before it had become clear—in *The Good Luck* [1991] 3 All E.R. 1—that breach of warranty had an automatic terminating effect not requiring any action by the insurers.

[239] *Samuel & Co Ltd v Dumas* [1924] A.C. 431. Cf. *Burridge & Son v Hames & Sons Ltd* (1918) 118 L.T. 681.

[240] *Sleigh v Tyser* [1966] 2 Q.B. 333.

[241] *London and Manchester Plate Glass Co v Heath* [1913] 3 K.B. 411. This decision was applied in *Kosmar Villa Holidays Plc v Trustees of Syndicate 1243* [2008] Lloyd's Rep. I.R. 43, where it was said that *Heath* did not give rise to a rule of law that previous conduct could not give rise to an estoppel, but that substantiating a claim of estoppel based on past conduct was difficult. The point did not arise on appeal, [2008] Lloyd's Rep. I.R. 489.

[242] *Motor Oil Hellas (Corinth) Refineries SA v Shipping Corporation of India (The Kanchenjunga)* [1990] 1 Lloyd's Rep. 391; *Kumar v AGF Insurance Ltd* [1998] 4 All E.R. 788.

[243] *Kirkaldy & Sons Ltd v Walker* [1999] Lloyd's Rep. I.R. 410; *Brownsville Holdings Ltd v Adamjee Insurance Co Ltd (The Milasan)* [2000] 2 Lloyd's Rep. 458; *Bhopal v Sphere Drake Insurance* [2002] Lloyd's Rep. I.R. 413; *HIH Casualty and General Insurance Ltd v Axa Corporate Solutions* [2002] Lloyd's Rep. I.R. 325.

It follows that a breach of warranty can be waived by the insurers only if they are estopped from relying on their rights.

In order to establish waiver of breach of warranty by estoppel, it must be shown by the assured that the insurers have made a clear and unequivocal representation that they do not intend to stand on a legal right to treat the risk as discharged and that the assured has relied upon the representation in which it would be inequitable to allow the insurers to resile from the representation. If it simply appears to the assured that the insurers believe that the cover is subsisting and there is no indication that the insurers are aware that they have been discharged, it is not inequitable to permit the insurers to stand on their rights.[244] Thus, where the assured, having broken a warranty, is expressly informed that the insurer intends to honour its obligations, it may not plead breach of warranty.[245] The same conclusion has been reached where the insurer has accepted a premium with knowledge of breach of warranty,[246] has accepted an endorsement to the policy[247] or has indicated its willingness to accept a claim tendered following a breach of warranty of which it was aware.[248]

By contrast, mere inactivity by the insurers once they have become aware of the circumstances constituting the breach will not of itself constitute a waiver.[249]

Reform of the law of warranties

7-049   *The 1980 proposals.* The state of the law outlined in the preceding paragraphs of this chapter has attracted widespread criticism judicial and academic criticism. The possibility of law reform was considered by the Law Commission in its 1980 Report, Law Com. No.104, the recommendations of which may be summarised as follows:

(1) A term of a contract of insurance should not be capable of being a warranty unless it is material to the risk, though a term which would at common law have been a warranty should be presumed material, subject to the assured's right to rebut this presumption by showing that the clause is not in fact material.

(2) If a term is to become a warranty, the insurer must, within a reasonable time of the giving of the warranty, provide the assured with a written

---

[244] See *HIH Casualty and General Insurance Ltd v Axa Corporate Solutions* [2002] Lloyd's Rep. I.R. 325, affirmed [2003] Lloyd's Rep. I.R. 1 and *Kosmar Villa Holidays Plc v Trustees of Syndicate 1243* [2008] Lloyd's Rep. I.R. 489 for these propositions.

[245] *Weir v Aberdein* (1819) 2 B. & Ald. 320.

[246] *Holdsworth v Lancashire and Yorkshire Insurance Co* (1907) 23 T.L.R. 521; *Handler v Mutual Reserve Fund Life Association* (1904) 90 L.T. 192; *Acey v Fernie* (1840) 7 M. & W. 151; *West v National Motor and Accident Insurance Union* [1955] 1 All E.R. 800.

[247] *American International Marine Agency of New York Inc v Dandridge* [2005] EWHC 829 (Comm). Cf. *MJ Harrington Syndicate 2000 v Axa Oyak Sigorta AS* [2007] Lloyd's Rep. I.R. 60.

[248] *Yorkshire Insurance Co v Craine* [1922] 2 A.C. 541; *Evans v Employers' Mutual Insurance Association Ltd* [1936] 1 K.B. 565; *Compagnia Tirrena di Assicurazioni SpA v Grand Union Insurance Co Ltd* [1991] 2 Lloyd's Rep. 143. See, however, *Mint Security Ltd v Blair* [1982] 1 Lloyd's Rep. 188, although this case is based on the notion that insurers had the right to decide whether or not to affirm the contract.

[249] *Allen v Robles* [1969] 3 All E.R. 154; *Melik v Norwich Union Fire Insurance Society Ltd* [1980] 1 Lloyd's Rep. 523; *Brownsville Holdings Ltd v Adamjee Insurance Co Ltd (The Milasan)* [2000] 2 Lloyd's Rep. 458; *Bhopal v Sphere Drake Insurance* [2002] Lloyd's Rep. I.R. 413; *HIH Casualty and General Insurance Ltd v Axa Corporate Solutions* [2003] Lloyd's Rep. I.R. 1; *Phillips & Co v Whatley (Gibraltar)* [2008] Lloyd's Rep. I.R. 111.

copy of the warranty. Failure to comply would preclude the insurer from relying on any breach of the warranty.

(3) The right to repudiate for breach of warranty should remain, but the right to reject liability for a loss which has already occurred should be limited to cases where the warranty was intended to guard against the risk of loss of the type which occurred, and the assured's conduct has made the materialisation of such loss more likely. In other cases the insurer should be entitled to repudiate the policy prospectively.

(4) The right to terminate for breach should take effect only from the date when a written notice of repudiation is served on the assured; it should not be retrospective to the breach itself.

The 2007 proposals. The English and Scottish Law Commissions, in their 2007 Consultation Paper, Consultation Paper No.182, 2007, have echoed the criticisms of the law and have issued recommendations which are more far-reaching than those published in 1980 and in particular which encompass marine warranties. The proposals are as follows.   **7–050**

Warranties of existing fact. The Law Commissions have confirmed that it should no longer be possible for insurers to create blanket warranties of existing fact by the use of basis and equivalent clauses. The recommendation is that such clauses should no longer be of effect. The validity of individual warranties of fact depends upon whether the policy is consumer or business in nature.   **7–051**

In the case of a consumer policy, the recommendation is to go further than the 1980 proposals and to render warranties of fact ineffective. Any representation made by a consumer is to be treated as a representation rather than a warranty, which means that the rights of the insurers are those which apply to mis-representation. Those remedies were discussed earlier in this work in the context of the reform of the law of utmost good faith, but in outline insurers have remedies only against an assured who failed to act honestly and reasonably, and there can be avoidance only against an assured who was dishonest and whose false statement induced the insurers to enter into the contract.

In the case of a business policy, individual warranties of fact are to be permitted. However, unless the policy otherwise provides (as is to be permissible under the proposals) the insurers will have the right to rely upon a breach of warranty only if the breach has some connection with the loss: under this default rule the assured will have the right to recover if the warranty was not material to the risk and the assured can prove that the breach did not cause or contribute to the loss. Any warranty must be set out in writing, although it need not be specifically drawn to the assured's attention in order to be valid. The use of the word "warranty" is sufficient to create a term which gives rise to strict liability and which therefore ousts the default requirements of materiality and causal link.

Future warranties. The Law Commissions have identified three objections to the present law which allows an insurer to treat itself as automatically discharged from liability on breach of warranty: the breach may be immaterial to the risk; the breach may be unconnected with the loss; and the insurer can rely upon a breach even though it has been remedied by the date of the loss.   **7–052**

The basic proposal, which applies to consumer and business policies alike, is that a breach of warranty unconnected with a loss should not give the insurers a defence. A defence is available only if the breach caused or contributed to the loss. The burden is on the assured to prove absence of causation. The Law Commissions have also chosen to adopt the Australian principle that if a breach caused contributed to only a part of the loss, the insurers should be required to pay for loss that was unrelated to the breach. There are nevertheless some differences between consumer and business cases.

In a consumer case, the rules on continuing warranties are mandatory. Further any remedy for breach of warranty is to be available only if the warranty was set out in writing in the policy or some other document supplied to the assured and sets out exactly what is required of the assured in order to comply.

As far as business insurance is concerned, there are two variations. The first is that the default rules can be ousted, so the parties are free to agree that the insurers are to have remedies for breach of warranty even in the absence of any causal link between breach and loss. The safeguard for the assured is that if this principle is set out in the insurers' standard terms and conditions, the clause is operative only if it does not defeat the assured's reasonable expectations. The second is that the assured must be given notice of the warranty in either the policy or an accompanying document but that there is no need for the assured's obligations to be set out in the manner required in a consumer case. "Micro-businesses" (yet to be properly defined) are, under modifications to these proposals introduced in April 2009, to be treated as consumers.

One further important recommendation is the remedy. The concept of automatic termination of risk is an anomaly in English law, and the Law Commissions have recommended its abolition. In its place, a breach of warranty should be regarded in the same way as any other breach of contract: if the breach is sufficiently serious to be repudiatory, the insurers should have the right to treat the policy as terminated as of the date of the breach, whereas if the breach is not repudiatory then they are limited to a claim for damages representing their loss. It will, however, be open to the insurers to include in the policy a cancellation clause which entitles them to terminate even for a minor breach: such a term would be binding in a business case, but subject to the usual controls on the fairness of terms in consumer contracts. The Law Commissions have provisionally proposed that if future liability is terminated, there should be a pro rata return of premium.

7–053   *Other terms.* One of the potential difficulties with a modification to the law of warranties is that it may result in insurers seeking to achieve the same results by the use of different forms of contract provision, e.g. conditions precedent, exclusions and delimitation of risk clauses. The Law Commissions have been timid on this matter. As far as consumer contracts are concerned, no change in the law is recommended, and consumers are to be protected by the Unfair Terms in Consumer Contracts Regulations 1999, although it is not clear that the Law Commissions have fully taken on board the point that those Regulations do not apply to terms which define the risk under an insurance policy. As regards businesses, the control proposed is that a standard policy term (as opposed to a bespoke term) which defines cover in a way that the assured would not reasonably expect (whether it be a warranty, a condition precedent to liability or to cover, an exception or a narrow definition of the risk) would be ineffective insofar as it renders the cover substantially different from what the assured reasonably expected.

7–054   *Marine insurance warranties.* The Law Commissions have provisionally proposed that the causal connection test should also apply to express and implied warranties in marine insurance, although there is a suggestion in the Consultation Paper that the implied marine warranties have outlived their usefulness and could sensibly be abolished.

The Consumer Insurance (Disclosure and Representations) Bill 2009. On **7–055** December 15, 2009 the Law Commissions published the Consumer Insurance (Disclosure and Representations) Bill 2009. It says very little about warranties other than abolishing the use of basis clauses in consumer cases.

CHAPTER 8

THE PREMIUM

1. PAYMENT OF THE PREMIUM

8–001 **Meaning of "premium".** The definition of premium accepted by the courts is "the consideration required of the assured in return for which the insurer undertook his obligation under the contract of insurance."[1] It is a matter of construction whether a policy is issued for a single premium or whether fresh premiums have to be paid in later years.[2] Not all of the sums paid by the assured can be regarded as "premium" in the true sense of the word, and it has been held that ancillary sums representing the cost of claims handling by third parties are not to be treated as premium.[3] However, a premium is in no respect a prerequisite of a contract of insurance: all that is necessary is the undertaking by the insurer for good consideration. Indeed, "after the event" insurance, which provides the assured with an indemnity for his own legal costs and for any costs order made against him in favour of a third party should the assured fail in an action brought against the third party, operates on the basis that the assured does not pay any premium at the outset and is liable for the premium only in the event that his action succeeds and a costs order is made against the third party that encompasses the premium payable under the policy.[4] The policy may be by deed, in which case no premium or other consideration flowing from the assured is necessary to render the insurer bound.

The premium has been defined as "a price paid adequate to the risk",[5] but the adequacy of the premium is purely the insurer's concern. It has been said that the amount of the premium may be of assistance in showing the scope of the policy,[6] for it is measured by the insurer's estimate of the risk formed upon an average of his previous experience of similar risks[7] together with an allowance for office expenses and other charges and profit.[8] However, it has been doubted whether the method by which the premium is calculated is admissible evidence in construing the policy, as it simply demonstrates the insurer's subjective view of what he intended the policy to cover.[9]

---

[1] *Re Claims Direct Test Cases* [2003] Lloyd's Rep. I.R. 677, applying dicta in *Lewis Ltd v Norwich Union Fire Insurance Co* [1916] A.C. 509 and *Swain v The Law Society* [1983] A.C. 598.

[2] *R. v Personal Investment Authority Ombudsman Bureau Ex p. Royal & Sun Alliance Life & Pensions Ltd* [2002] Lloyd's Rep. I.R. 41.

[3] *Re Claims Direct Test Cases* [2003] Lloyd's Rep. I.R. 677.

[4] *Re RSA Pursuit Test Cases* Unreported, May 27, 2005.

[5] Lawrence J. in *Lucena v Craufurd* (1806) 2 Bos. & P.N.R. 269 at 301.

[6] Collins L.J. in *Re George and Goldsmiths' Insurance* [1899] 1 Q.B. 595 at 611.

[7] Cockburn C.J. in *Chapman v Pole* (1870) 22 L.T. 306 at 307; Lord Blackburn in *Thomson v Weems* (1884) 9 App. Cas. 671 at 681.

[8] Lord Cairns in *Re Albert Life* (1871) L.R. 14 Eq. 72n.

[9] *Absalom v TCRU Ltd* [2005] EWCA Civ 1586; *Margate Theatre Royal Trust Ltd v White* [2006] Lloyd's Rep. I.R. 93.

Forms of payment. The form in which payment is required will generally be   **8–002**
provided for in the proposal form, renewal notice or policy itself. The premium
must be paid in money,[10] unless some other mode of payment is substituted by
agreement.[11] Whether or not credit has been extended by the insurers to the
assured or his brokers is a question of fact,[12] but premium is not to be regarded
as having been paid by an agent who is himself the insured person simply by
debiting himself unless it can be shown that he had thereby constituted himself
as a trustee of the sum in question.[13]

Payment may be made by a single premium or by instalments. Where
instalment payments are permitted, it is a matter of construction whether the
policy is a continuing one or whether there is a new contract on the payment of
each instalment. In most cases the contract will remain indivisible, a principle
from which several important consequences will flow. First, in the absence of an
express stipulation in the policy, the rate of premium will not be alterable as
between payment periods. Secondly, the duty to disclose material facts will not
arise at each payment period. Thirdly, as long as all instalments are paid
promptly, the policy will remain in force.

Some policies linked to credit card facilities require payment of the premium
to be by means only of a credit card. If the assured cancels the credit card to
which the premiums have been charged, the card issuer does not have the right
to transfer the liabilities to another card issued by them and held by the
assured.[14]

If the insurers indicate a particular mode of paying the premium, an assured
who complies with that request will not be responsible if the money is lost,
providing he observes any instructions qualifying the request.[15] In the absence of
any instructions or agreement the general rule is that a debtor must seek out and
pay his creditor[16] and, therefore, if the assured chooses, for his own convenience,
to send money, in any form, through the post, he does so at his own risk.[17] A
request to use the post will readily be implied,[18] but mere passive acceptance of
money paid in this way will not amount to a request even if such course of
dealing has been followed for a number of years.[19] When the insurers accept
money from the assured in circumstances from which it can reasonably be
inferred that he intended the money, or some of it, to be applied in the payment
of particular premiums, but the insurers fail to appropriate the money in their
books to the premiums in question, they cannot afterwards complain that the
premiums have not been paid.[20]

Problems may also arise with non-cash payments: a cheque may be dishonoured, or the assured may have inadequate funds in his bank account to meet
a payment due under a standing order or direct debit mandate. So far as a cheque
is concerned, such payment is conditional only, so that the dishonouring of a

[10] *Montreal Assurance v McGillivray* (1859) 13 Moo. P.C.C. 87; *London & Lancashire Life v Fleming* [1897] A.C. 499. The old cases primarily contemplated cash payments. In practice premiums are paid by cheque or automated credits operated by banks. Cf. *Tankexpress v Compagnie Financière* [1949] A.C. 76 at 93, 98, 103.

[11] *Prince of Wales Life v Harding* (1858) E.B. & E. 183.

[12] *Holliday v Western Australian Insurance Co* (1936) 54 Ll. L.R. 373.

[13] *Ingram v Caledonian Insurance Co* (1932) Ll. L.R. 129.

[14] *American Express Services Europe Ltd v Tuvyahu* Unreported, July 12, 2000.

[15] *Robb v Gow Bros* (1905) 8 F. (Ct of Sess) 90 at 107.

[16] Lord Esher in *Norman v Ricketts* (1886) 3 T.L.R. 182.

[17] *Pennington v Crossley & Son* (1897) 77 L.T. 43.

[18] *Mitchell-Henry v Norwich Union* [1918] 2 K.B. 67.

[19] *Mitchell-Henry v Norwich Union* [1918] 2 K.B. 67.

[20] *Kirkpatrick v South Australian Insurance* (1886) 11 App. Cas. 177.

cheque means that payment has not been made[21]; the question whether the insurer must represent the cheque, or whether the assured may offer further payment, will be a matter of contract and in particular of the time limits for payment under the policy. If the cheque is honoured, payment is deemed to have been made at the date on which the cheque was given.

Where a standing order or direct debit payment is not fulfilled due to insufficiency of funds in the assured's account, it is simply the case that there has been a default by the assured in payment. If, by contrast, payment is not made due to an error by the bank, it must be determined whether the bank was acting as the agent of the assured or the insurer in operating the mandate. This may not be an easy question, for while the authority to debit the account is provided by the assured, the entire debiting process will have been prearranged by insurer and bank. A mistake by the insurers is plainly not one which can affect the assured, and it has been held that if the insurers have required or permitted payment of the premium by means of direct debit, and the assured has completed the relevant mandate forms, there is an implied duty on the insurers to forward the forms to the assured's bank and to use their best endeavours to ensure that the direct debit is properly opened and that its effectiveness is not threatened.[22] Further, the view has been expressed that the completion of the mandate is itself deemed to be payment by the assured, at least where the policy requires payment to be by means of direct debit and the assured has duly completed a mandate.[23]

8–003 **Payment to an agent.** If the assured has paid the premium to a duly authorised agent of the insurer it will be prima facie deemed to have been received by the insurer. Difficulties may, however, arise in three contexts. First, the agent to whom the premium was paid may not have been expressly authorised by the insurer to receive it; here, the question will be whether the agent had usual or apparent authority to accept payment.[24] Secondly, the policy may stipulate a particular time and place for payment, but the premium is accepted by the insurer's agent in other circumstances. In this situation, it is difficult for the assured to argue that the agent has usual or apparent authority, as the terms of the insurer's offer or the policy itself will put the assured on notice of the agent's lack of authority. The assured will here succeed only if it can be shown that the insurer had previously acquiesced in the method of payment adopted. Thirdly, the assured may simply have paid the premium to his broker. The ordinary rule here is that the broker is the agent of the assured, so that such payment is in law one by the assured to himself. This position will be varied where it can be shown that the broker had actual or ostensible authority conferred upon him by the insurer in respect of the receipt of the premium, and also in the cases of marine insurance, as here the broker and not the assured is liable for the premium; this matter is discussed below.

[21] Ultimately, whether a cheque is absolute or conditional payment is a question of intention. However, it is extremely improbable that an insurer would intend to abandon the power to forfeit the policy on non-payment in exchange for the mere right to claim personally against the insured in the event of dishonour. This presumption may even survive the giving by the insurer of a formal receipt for the premium in question, *Skey v The Mutual Life Association of Australasia* (1895) 13 N.Z.L.R. 321.

[22] *Weldon v GRE Linked Life Assurance Ltd* Unreported, 2003.

[23] *Weldon v GRE Linked Life Assurance Ltd* Unreported, 2003 per Nelson J.

[24] In *Commercial Union Assurance Co v Gamman* (1908) 10 T.L.R. 672 it was found that even had there been no apparent authority to receive premiums on its behalf (although in this case there was), the insurer ratified its agent's action by issuing policies acknowledging receipt of premiums and suing on the contract the agent had made.

Where the insurer has authorised an agent or broker to accept the premium on its behalf, such payment discharges the assured's obligations towards the insurer. The position as between intermediary and insurer is, however, less certain, as in the absence of an express agency agreement it is by no means clear that the premiums received are held on trust for the insurer. Consequently, if the insurer is to protect the payments, in the event of the intermediary's insolvency, from the claims of the intermediary's general creditors, it will be necessary for the agreement between intermediary and insurer to make it clear that all receipts are held on trust.[25] If a broker placing a non-marine contract[26] is not authorised to receive premium, then the fact that the assured has paid the broker does not relieve the assured from his duty to pay the insurers should the insurers be unable to recover the premium from the broker, e.g., by reason of the broker's insolvency.[27]

Payment and the commencement of the risk. The premium normally becomes **8–004** payable as soon as the risk incepts,[28] but because time is not of the essence then unless the policy itself so provides failure to pay the premium at this stage will not prevent the risk from attaching.[29] In the same way, actual payment of the premium is not, other than by reason of an express term, necessary to the creation of a complete and binding contact of insurance. A stipulation that the insurance shall not attach until the premium is paid will not be implied.[30] It is not uncommon, however, for insurers so to stipulate either in the policy,[31] or by some other means.[32] A provision of this type is binding on the assured[33] unless it has been waived by the insurers.[34] The mere fact that the policy both stipulates prepayment of the premium and, contrary to the truth, acknowledges receipt of it will not necessarily amount to such a waiver.[35] Where, however, such an acknowledgment is contained in the recital of a policy by deed, the company will be estopped from denying that the premium has in fact been paid.[36]

Premium payment stipulations are inherently ambiguous, and may be interpreted in any of three ways:

(1) there is to be no agreement until the premium has been paid;
(2) there is a binding agreement, but the risk runs from the date of payment;

---

[25] *Vehicle and General Insurance Co v Elmbridge Insurances* [1973] 1 Lloyd's Rep. 325.

[26] In the marine context the insurers can look only to the broker for payment: Marine Insurance Act 1906 s.53. See below.

[27] *Con-Stan Industries of Australia Pty Ltd* v *Norwich Winterthur Insurance (Australia) Ltd* (1986) 64 A.L.R. 481, a decision reversed by statute in New Zealand by the Insurance Intermediaries Act 1994.

[28] *Heath Lambert Ltd v Sociedad de Corretaje de Seguros* [2004] Lloyd's Rep. I.R. 905; *Clydesdale Financial Services Ltd v Smailes* [2009] EWHC 3190 (Ch).

[29] *Tapa v Attorney-General* [1977] 2 N.Z.L.R. 35; *Howells v Dominion Insurance Co Ltd* Unreported, 1999.

[30] *Heath Lambert Ltd v Sociedad de Corretaje de Seguros* [2004] Lloyd's Rep. I.R. 905.

[31] *Roberts v Security Co* [1897] 1 Q.B. 111; *Equitable Fire v Ching Wo Hong* [1907] A.C. 96; *Re Yager & Guardian Assurance* (1912) 108 L.T. 38.

[32] *Looker v Law Union* [1928] 1 K.B. 554 (acceptance of assured's proposal).

[33] *Phoenix Life Assurance Co v Sheridan* (1860) 6 H.L. Cas. 745.

[34] *Goit v National Protection* (1844) 25 Barb. (NY) 189; *Supple v Cann* (1858) 9 Ir. C.L. 1; *Bodine v Exchange Fire* (1872) 51 N.Y. App. 117; *Cooper v Pacific Mutual* (1871) 8 Am. Rep. 705: *Hodge v Security Insurance* (1884) 33 Hun. N.Y. 583; *Farnum v Phoenix* (1890) 17 Am. St. Rep. 233.

[35] *Equitable Fire v Ching Wo Hong* [1907] A.C. 96; *Newis v General Accident* (1910) 11 C.L.R. 620.

[36] *Roberts v Security Co* [1897] 1 Q.B. 111.

(3) there is a binding agreement, and the risk runs from the date of the agreement, being backdated from the time of the payment of the premium.

The distinction between possibility (1) on the one hand, and possibilities (2) and (3) has been discussed. Where there is a binding agreement, the distinction between (2) and (3) is significant because should a loss occur after the date of the agreement but prior to the payment of the premium, in case (2) the assured cannot recover but in case (3) he is entitled to recover. The matter is necessarily one of construction, but where the policy states that the risk is to run only from the date at which the premium is paid and accepted, it is clear that the case falls into category (2).[37]

8–005 **Effect of payment on issue of policy.** In non-marine insurance, it does not appear to be the case that the payment of the premium and the issue of the policy are concurrent conditions, and such a condition would in any event be immaterial unless the policy were to state that the risk is not to run until the premium has been paid, for there is no requirement in non-marine insurance that the contract be embodied in a policy before it is admissible in evidence.

The marine position is, however, different. Where there is a binding contract prior to the payment of the premium, then whether or not the insurer is on risk until payment the assured under a marine policy will not be entitled to delivery of the policy until the premium has been paid. Section 52 of the Marine Insurance Act 1906 provides:

> "Unless otherwise agreed, the duty of the assured or his agent to pay the premium, and the duty of the insurer to issue the policy to the assured or his agent, are concurrent conditions, and the insurer is not bound to issue the policy until payment or tender of the Premium."

Section 52 does not operate to prevent a contract between insurer and assured coming into being; indeed s.22 states that a policy may be executed and issued "either at the time when a contract is concluded, or afterwards." Section 52 protects the insurer from liability, as under s.22 a contract of marine insurance is inadmissible unless it is embodied in a marine policy. Consequently, although the insurer may under the terms of the contract be on risk even before the premium has been paid, the assured will be unable to produce any evidence to prove it. However there are decisions to the effect that s.22 does not prevent an action on the contract despite the absence of any policy,[38] so the point may not be of significance.

8–006 **Mutual insurance.** In the case of mutual insurance, premiums as such are not payable. Members of the mutual insurance organisation will generally pay a sum at the beginning of the policy period and will then be required to supplement the initial payment by calls for further funds should the level of losses so require.[39] Section 85 of the Marine Insurance Act 1906 provides as follows:

---

[37] *Ocean Accident and Guarantee Corp v Cole* [1932] 2 K.B. 100.

[38] *Swan v Maritime Insurance Co* [1907] 1 K.B. 116; *Eide UK v Lowndes Lambert Group Ltd (The Sun Tender)* [1998] 1 Lloyd's Rep. 389.

[39] *Lion Insurance Association v Tucker* (1883) 12 QBD 176; *Great Britain 100 A1 Steamship Insurance v Wyllie* (1889) 22 QBD 710; *Standard Steamship Onwers' Protection and Indemnity Association (Bermuda) Ltd v Oceanfast Shipping (The Ainikolas I)* (1996) Lloyd's List, April 5, which makes the point that membership is on the terms of the rules as they may change from time to time, so that members will be liable for calls if made within the rules as they stand at the time.

(1) Where two or more persons mutually agree to insure each other against marine losses there is said to be a mutual insurance.

(2) The provisions of this Act relating to the premium do not apply to mutual insurance, but a guarantee, or such other arrangement as may be agreed upon, may be substituted for the premium.

(3) The provisions of this Act, in so far as they may be modified by the agreement of the parties, may in the case of mutual insurance be modified by the terms of the policies issued by the association, or by the rules and regulations of the association.

(4) Subject to the exceptions mentioned in this section, the provisions of this Act apply to a mutual insurance.

P&I Clubs and other mutual insurers are always incorporated and have separate legal personality, so it is no longer technically correct to say that the members insure eachother. The insurance is provided by the insurer itself.

Role of brokers. As the broker is the assured's agent, it follows that where the assured pays the premium to the broker,[40] the insurer cannot be treated as having received it, so that the insurer should remain free to look for payment from the assured despite his payment to the broker. Similarly, theory would indicate that a broker cannot be personally liable to the insurer for the premium, as the obligation to pay is that of the assured and not that of the broker. There is an exception to the latter principle in the context of marine insurance,[41] where by the custom of the market the premium is paid by the broker,[42] but in non-marine insurance both in the general market[43] and in the Lloyd's market[44] the rule does not apply. **8–007**

2. THE AMOUNT OF THE PREMIUM

The amount of premium payable by the assured is normally determined by standard formulae prior to the inception of the contract. This may not always occur, however. A policy under which the amount of the premium is to be established at a later date by fixed criteria is perfectly valid. Moreover, the Marine Insurance Act 1906 s.31(1) deals with the case in which no premium has been fixed at all: **8–008**

"Where insurance is effected at a premium to be arranged, and no arrangement is made, a reasonable premium is payable."

[40] Where the broker has arranged a number of policies for the assured, there may be difficulty in determining to which policies the payment to the broker relates: *Protopara v Dominion Insurance Co Ltd* [1954] 1 Lloyd's Rep. 402.

[41] And also open covers.

[42] See Ch.24, below.

[43] *Wilson v Avec Audio-Visual Equipment Ltd* [1974] 1 Lloyd's Rep. 81 is inconclusive, but see *Pacific & General Insurance Co v Hazell* [1997] L.R.L.R. 65, where counsel could not find any authority capable of supporting the argument that a non-marine broker was liable for the premium, and Cf. *Goshawk Dedicated Ltd v Tyser & Co Ltd* [2005] Lloyd's Rep. I.R. 379, affirmed on other grounds [2007] Lloyd's Rep. I.R. 224.

[44] In *Julian Praet et Cie SA v H G Poland* [1960] 1 Lloyd's Rep. 416 it was assumed that the practice did apply to Lloyd's, but a report commissioned by Lloyd's and involving senior legal figures, completed in 1994, concluded that there was no binding authority in favour of the proposition that brokers were required to pay premiums in non-marine Lloyd's business.

The principle of the Marine Insurance Act 1906 s.31(1) is equally applicable in non-marine insurance, and indeed represents a general contractual rule. It is nevertheless necessary to add that s.31(1) will not rescue a contract that is void for uncertainty on other grounds. The common law draws a distinction between an agreement that the premium is to be a reasonable one, which is a valid contract because there is an objective mechanism by which the premium can be fixed,[45] and an agreement that the premium is to be agreed, which is an agreement to agree and thus void for uncertainty as there is no basis upon which an objective assessment can be made.[46] Section 31(1) thus confirms the validity of an insurance policy which is made on the basis that the premium is to be a reasonable one, but does not rescue a policy which simply says that the premium is to be agreed.[47]

In most forms of non-marine insurance the premium is fixed from the outset and cannot be varied during the currency of the policy. In marine insurance, by contrast, the policy frequently permits a higher premium to be charged by the insurer in the event of an increase of risk (e.g. the entry of a vessel into a war zone or other Additional Premium Area). Moreover, the Institute clauses contain various provisions whereby the assured is "held covered" in the event of specified breaches of condition or warranty subject to agreement between the insurer and assured as to additional premium. The amount of additional premium may be predetermined. Thus, in the event of a time policy on hull or freight terminating prior to the completion of the voyage when the vessel is in danger, the assured is held covered at a monthly pro rata premium.[48] In other cases, the amount of the additional premium has to be agreed.[49] The latter type of situation is catered for by the Marine Insurance Act 1906 s.31(2):

"Where an insurance is effected on the terms that an additional premium is to be arranged in a given event, and that event happens, but no arrangement is made, then a reasonable additional premium is payable."

The courts have held, in applying this provision, that the amount of additional premium is to be commensurate with the additional degree of risk accepted by the insurer.[50] Failure by the parties to agree a premium for the reinstatement of the risk on a held covered basis will prevent the underwriters from treating the

---

[45] See *RSA Pursuit Test Cases* Unreported, May 2005, an after the event policy was held not to be void simply because the premium was not fixed at the outset, given that there was an agreed mechanism for determining the premium.

[46] This was the distinction drawn by Rix L.J. in *Willis Management (Isle of Man) Ltd v Cable & Wireless Plc* [2005] 2 Lloyd's Rep. 597. Referring to earlier authorities on the analogous provision in s.8 of the Sale of Goods Act 1979. See also: *Foley v Classique Coaches* [1934] 2 K.B. 1; *May & Butcher v R.* [1934] 2 K.B. 17; *Mamidoil-Jetoil Greek Petroleum Co SA v Okta Crude Oil Refinery AD* [2001] 2 Lloyd's Rep. 76.

[47] Longmore L.J. in *Petromec Inc v Petroleo Brasileiro SA Petrobas* [2006] 1 Lloyd's Rep. 121 has noted that the refusal of the common law to recognise agreements to agree, and in particular on obligations to negotiate in good faith, is ripe for reconsideration.

[48] International Hull Clauses 2003 cl.12; Institute Freight Clauses cl.13.

[49] The assured is held covered under the Institute clauses at a premium to be agreed: under a cargo policy, where the contract of carriage is terminated before the delivery of the goods or where the destination is changed by the assured (Institute Cargo Clauses (A), (B) and (C), cll.9 and 10); under a voyage policy on hulls where the vessel is used in loading or discharging operations, and where there is a deviation, change of voyage or breach of warranty (Institute Voyage Clauses Hulls cl.1.2 and 2); under a time policy on freight where the assured is in breach of a warranty (Institute Time Clauses Freight cl.4); and under a voyage policy on freight where there has been a change of voyage, deviation or breach of warranty (Institute Voyage Clauses Freight cl.3).

[50] *Greenock Steamship Co v Maritime Insurance Co Ltd* [1903] 1 K.B. 367; *Hewitt v London General Insurance Co Ltd* (1925) 23 Ll. L.R. 243.

policy as forfeited, as it cannot be said that there was an undisputed sum due and payable.[51]

3. RENEWAL PREMIUMS AND DAYS OF GRACE

Effect of renewal. In cases in which the premium is payable periodically, or the **8–009** policy is renewable by payment of a further premium, it is the custom of insurance companies to send the assured a reminder shortly before a premium falls due. They are, however, under no legal obligation to observe this custom[52] unless they or their agents have, expressly or impliedly, undertaken to do so. Where insurance cover is to be extended beyond the existing insured period into a further period, the policy or renewal notice will contain some stipulation as to the date at which the renewal premium is to be paid. However, policies which give the assured the right to renew by paying a renewal premium nearly always contain a provision "days of grace" enlarging the time for payment. The wording of the relevant term has three consequences: it fixes the date by which the renewal premium must be paid; it determines whether or not the assured is to be covered between the expiry of his existing policy and the payment of the premium for a new policy; and it is relevant to the question whether or not the insurer is entitled to refuse a renewal premium. A provision of this kind does not extend the time allowed to the assured for the doing of other acts or exercising other privileges, so that a clause in a life policy that where it had acquired a surrender value it should remain in force for "twelve calendar months from the date upon which the last premium became due" was held to mean 12 months from the commencement, not from the expiration, of the 30 days' of grace allowed by the policy.[53]

Complex issues of construction may arise where the provision deals expressly only with the date of the payment of the premium: the position of the assured pending payment, and the insurer's ability to refuse tender, must in such cases be implied from the payment provision. The various possibilities are as follows.

(1) The premium is due on or before the date at which the existing policy expires, with no provision for any days of grace in which the assured may pay. Here it is clear that the assured must pay by the specified date, and if he fails to do so he will be uninsured as to the future. It is then a matter for the insurer whether or not a fresh policy is to be issued.

(2) The premium is due on or before the date at which the existing policy expires, but the assured is given a temporary cover note under which he is held covered for a fixed period: payment of the premium in that period operates to backdate any fresh policy to the beginning of it. It would seem that the proper analysis of this situation is that the temporary cover note is an offer which may be accepted by the assured on payment of the premium; if the assured does not pay the premium in that period, or if he otherwise determines not to accept the insurer's offer of fresh insurance, the cover note is of no effect and no insurance exists.[54] The insurer is

---

[51] *Kirby v Cosindit Societa per Azioni* [1969] 1 Lloyd's Rep. 75.
[52] *Windus v Tredegar* (1866) 15 L.T. 108.
[53] *McKenna v City Life* [1919] 2 K.B. 491.
[54] *Taylor v Allon* [1966] 1 Q.B. 304.

presumably free to revoke the cover note by notice to the assured at any time before the premium has been paid.

(3) The premium is due within a fixed period after the end of the existing contract period. If there is a statement to the effect that the assured is not covered in that period, or if the assured fails to pay the premium,[55] it is clear that the insurance has come to an end. Conversely, a statement by the insurer that it is to be liable in the days of grace will be conclusive. In the absence of any express provision, the liability of the insurer will depend upon whether the original policy is to be construed as one which comes to an end but which may be renewed, or one which continues in force until the end of the days of grace, at which point it lapses. If the former construction is adopted, the assured is probably not covered during the days of grace; moreover, the insurer is seemingly entitled to reject any premium tendered to him in the days of grace. It has thus been held that if the insurers have a right to refuse the renewal premium, and elect not to carry on with an insurance which they are not bound to renew, then their liability will cease on the last day of the period for which the insurance was expressed to run, and the tender of the renewal premium by the assured during the days of grace will not alter the position.[56]

(4) The premium is due within a fixed period after the end of the existing contract period, but it is clear from the policy that it is one which is effective until the end of the days of grace period, at which point it lapses. In this situation, the assured remains covered during the days of grace,[57] and it follows that the insurer cannot refuse a renewal premium, as the initial agreement between the parties was that the policy would be perpetual subject to renewal. This is the usual situation in relation to life policies.

The crucial distinction is between cases (3) and (4), i.e. whether the policy is terminated and may be renewed or whether it is continuing subject to renewal. In non-life cases, the position is generally that the contract is not continuing, so that there is no rule compelling the court to find that there is to be coverage in the days of grace and, in the absence of express temporary insurance, situation (3) would appear to cover the case.

As far as life policies are concerned, it is clear that possibility (4) is applicable[58]; a holding that life insurance is an annual contract would reimpose the assured's duty of utmost good faith on each renewal, and would give the insurer the opportunity to reject a further premium where the risk has substantially increased.

8–010   Reinstatement of life policy following lapse. If a life policy has lapsed following the assured's failure to pay a premium, then if accrued benefits are to be carried over it is necessary for the parties to enter into a fresh agreement to revive the policy. The ordinary rules of offer and acceptance are here applicable, so that if the assured under a lapsed life policy has sent the premium to the

---

[55] *McKenna v City Life* [1919] 2 K.B. 491.
[56] *Tarleton v Staniforth* (1794) 5 T.R. 695; *Simpson v Accidental Death* (1857) 2 C.B.N.S. 257.
[57] *Salvin v James* (1805) 6 East 571; *Stuart v Freeman* [1903] 1 K.B. 47.
[58] *Stuart v Freeman* [1903] 1 K.B. 47, disapproving *Pritchard v Merchants' and Tradesmen's Mutual Life Assurance Society* (1858) 3 C.B.N.S. 622.

insurers but they have accepted subject to the assured completing a declaration of good health, there is no cover until the declaration has been made.[59]

4. CONSEQUENCES OF NON-PAYMENT

Possible remedies. Late payment of the premium is not excused by the fact that there have been previous instances of late payment to which the insurer has not objected.[60] Where the assured has not paid the premium on the due date, the insurer may have a choice of remedies: **8–011**

    (a) proceedings for payment may be brought;
    (b) claims may be rejected until the premium has been paid;
    (c) the policy may be forfeited or determined for breach.

Actions for the premium. Where a premium becomes due to the insurers under a contract of insurance they are entitled to bring an action for its payment. The assured cannot escape liability for it on the ground that, as by the terms of the contract the insurers are not liable for any loss which may happen before it is paid, there is no consideration for his promise to pay it:[61] in this situation the original contract of insurance supplies such consideration. Thus, in *Solvency Mutual Guarantee Co v York*,[62] the policy provided that it was to be renewed from year to year unless either party gave notice of cancellation. The assured failed to give notice of cancellation, but did not pay the premium; it was held that the insurer had the right to bring proceedings for the premium.[63] **8–012**

Rejection of claims. If a policy takes effect despite the fact that the premium has not been paid, it is a matter for the contract whether or not the insurer is entitled to reject a claim until the premium has been tendered. In the absence of any specific policy term, the default position is that payment of the premium and the payment of the loss are not concurrent obligations but are independent. However, if the assured has not paid the premium and has submitted a claim, the insurers have a right of set-off and are only required to pay to the assured the amount by which the claim exceeds the premium.[64] **8–013**

Forfeiture or determination for breach. The insurer's rights following late payment of all or any due instalment of a premium are, in the first instance, a matter of contract. A number of provisions may operate. **8–014**

Postponement of the contract or risk. First, the policy may provide that no contract is to come into existence, or that the risk is not to commence, until the premium has been paid: in these situations the insurer is never on risk and no claim may be made by the assured. The policy wording may or may not put the assured in breach of contract by reason of late payment. If there is no breach, and **8–015**

---

[59] *Fontana v Skandia Life Assurance Ltd* Unreported, 2003.
[60] *Laing v Commercial Union Assurance Co Ltd* (1922) 11 Ll. L.R. 54.
[61] *Municipal Mutual Insurance v Pontefract Corp* (1917) 116 L.T. 671.
[62] *Solvency Mutual Guarantee Co v York* (1858) 3 H. & N. 588.
[63] See also *General Accident v Cronk* (1901) 17 T.L.R. 233.
[64] *Lake v Reinsurance Corp Ltd* 1967 (3) S.A. 124 (W), where nothing was payable as the outstanding premiums exceeded the claims.

it is simply the case that the insurer is not on risk, it may be possible to construe the correspondence as a standing offer by the insurer, in which case it, presumably, remains open to the assured to tender the premium at some later date: whether the insurer is obliged to accept the premium would, it might be thought, be determined by asking whether the insurer's offer of insurance has lapsed by effluxion of time, although it is by no means clear how it could be decided whether a reasonable time for acceptance by the assured has elapsed. Any tender of the premium could not in any event confer retroactive cover on the assured in respect of a loss which has occurred prior to tender.

8–016   *Forfeiture clauses: premium warranties.* A second contractual approach is for the policy not to postpone the making of the contract or the running of the risk, but rather to stipulate a time for payment not just of the premium but of each instalment of the premium. If time is made of the essence, late payment will result in forfeiture of the policy unless the insurers are for some reason estopped from enforcing their clause.[65] If the formulation "time is of the essence", or something equally unequivocal, is not used, there is a general presumption that time is not of the essence and the policy will not be regarded as forfeited automatically: whether or not the policy is forfeited by reason of late payment depends upon whether the assured's default can be regarded as repudiatory breach of contract.[66]

Many policies, particularly marine policies, contain a premium warranty by virtue of which the assured warrants that premiums will be paid at given times. In these circumstances, any default by the assured brings the insurer's liability to an automatic end, in accordance with ordinary principles applicable to warranties.[67] However, the obligation of the assured to pay the premium is not brought to an end, as the effect of a breach of warranty affects only the risk and not the policy itself.[68] This result can be avoided only where the court construes the contract as one which is severable so that each instalment of the premium brings about a fresh risk, as in those circumstances there can be no future liability on the assured to pay subsequent premiums. In general it would seem to be correct in principle not to regard a policy as severable, particularly as each instalment falling due would bring about a fresh duty of disclosure on the part of the assured. Where the insurer has a contractual right to treat the policy as having been forfeited for late payment of premiums, the courts will seemingly not exercise their general equitable discretion to grant relief from forfeiture.[69] Accordingly, the right of the insurer to treat its obligations as at an end will be lost only where the insurer has by his conduct waived the late payment or is otherwise estopped from relying upon it, e.g. where the insurer has acknowledged payment by the broker even though no payment has actually been made.[70]

Authority from Australia and New Zealand indicates that, in the case of life insurance at least, a condition providing that cover will be "forfeit" or "null and void" or will lapse for non-payment of premium, is likely to be interpreted to

---

[65] See *Scottish Equitable Life v Buist* (1877) 4 R. (Ct of Sess) 1076; (1878) 5 R. (Ct of Sess) 64; *Wing v Harvey* (1854) 5 De. G.M. & G. 265.

[66] *Figre Ltd v Mander* [1999] Lloyd's Rep. I.R. 193.

[67] *Bank of Nova Scotia v Hellenic Mutual War Risks Association (The Good Luck)* [1992] 1 A.C. 233.

[68] *JA Chapman & Co Ltd v Kadirga Denizcilik Ve Ticaret* [1998] Lloyd's Rep. I.R. 377.

[69] *The Padre Island (No.2)* [1987] 1 Lloyd's Rep. 529.

[70] *Roberts v Security Co* [1897] 1 Q.B. 11 (statement on policy that the premium had been received). Contrast *Equitable Fire and Accident Office v Ching Wo Hong* [1907] A.C. 96.

mean "voidable" only,[71] so that insurers have to take some step to bring the policy to an end. It would also appear to make no difference that the insurer relies not upon a separate provision for forfeiture but upon a provision which makes the passing of the life assured and up to date premiums co-existent conditions of liability.[72]

The International Hull Clauses 2003 provide that the premium, or the relevant instalment, is to be paid in full to the underwriters within 45 days (or such other period as may be agreed) of the inception of the risk. If there is default, the underwriters have the right to cancel the insurance by notifying the assured via the broker, giving 15 days' notice. The assured is free to tender the premium within those 15 days and if he does so the cancellation is automatically revoked, but if he fails to do so the cancellation takes effect. In the event of cancellation, cl.35 does not require the assured to pay the entire premium (as would be the case at common law, given that the risk would have attached for at least 45 days) but only a pro rata premium reflecting time on risk. However, if there has been a loss prior to cancellation, the underwriters are liable for the loss—as would be the case at common law but the full premium is then payable.

Late payment: time not of the essence. If time is not of the essence for the payment of the premium or any instalment of the premium, then late payment does not of itself amount to repudiatory conduct by the assured. Late payment becomes repudiatory in one of two ways. First, it is always open to the insurer to give notice to the assured requiring payment within a reasonable time if the assured's delay is undue.[73] Failure by the assured to pay in these circumstances is regarded as repudiation by him. Secondly, if the insurer has not taken this step to secure payment, the insurer will have to satisfy the court that the assured's delay amounts to a repudiation of contract which has been accepted by the insurer. This involves proving that the assured's intention can only have been repudiatory. If there is delay without more, this may be almost impossible to demonstrate, even if the delay is of some years.[74] Further, by failing to make demands on the reinsured on discovering the arrears, the reinsurers cannot be said to have evidenced an intention to accept any repudiation by the reinsured.[75] In the absence of (a) a term which renders time of the essence, and (b) a demand for payment which is not met, any breach can be that of an innominate term, and the underwriters have the right to treat the contract as repudiated only if it can be shown that the assured acted in a manner denying its future liabilities under the contract, which is not to be assumed simply from late payment[76] although may be assumed if the assured has become insolvent and will never be able to pay.[77] **8–017**

Late payment under marine policies. Marine policies written in the London market may contain a premium warranty by which the assured warrants that each **8–018**

---

[71] *Newbon v City Mutual Life Assurance Society Ltd* (1935) 52 C.L.R. 723; *Smith v Associated Dominions Assurance Society Pty Ltd* (1956) 95 C.L.R. 381; *Boynton v Monarch Life Insurance Company of New Zealand Ltd* [1973] 1 N.Z.L.R. 606; *Spooner-Kenyon v Yorkshire-General Life Assurance Co Ltd* (1982) 2 ANZ Insurance Cases 60–476.

[72] *Turner v Metropolitan Life Assurance Company of New Zealand* (1988) 5 ANZ Insurance Cases 60–861.

[73] *Figre Ltd v Mander* [1998] Lloyd's Rep. I.R. 377.

[74] *Fenton Insurance Co Ltd v Gothaer Versicherungsbank Wag* [1991] 1 Lloyd's Rep. 172.

[75] *Figre Ltd v Mander* [1998] Lloyd's Rep. I.R. 377.

[76] *The Beurgsgracht* [2002] 2 Lloyd's Rep. 608. The point did not arise on appeal: [2002] Lloyd's Rep. I.R. 335. See also *Limit No.2 Ltd v Axa Versicherung AG* [2008] Lloyd's Rep. I.R. 330.

[77] *Pacific and General Insurance Co Ltd v Hazell* [1997] L.R.L.R. 65.

instalment of the premium will be paid by a given day, failing which the assured
is in breach of warranty and the risk automatically comes to an end although the
premium remains payable.[78] The fiction which underlies s.53(1) of the Marine
Insurance Act 1906, that the broker has paid the premium and the underwriters
have loaned it back to the broker so that the broker but not the assured is liable
to make payment, is inconsistent with a premium warranty, in that if there is
deemed payment under the fiction then the warranty can never be broken. In
Heath Lambert Ltd v Sociedad de Corretaje de Seguros,[79] the Court of Appeal
concluded that the basis of the fiction was overridden by the premium warranty
and that, while the underwriters could look only to the broker for payment, there
was no deemed payment. It was recognised that this reasoning put the assured at
the mercy of the broker, in that late payment by the broker would defeat the
assured's rights even if the assured had actually paid the broker, but regarded this
as a consequence of the statutory provision.

5. RETURN OF PREMIUM

8–019   **Return of premium by agreement.** Where the policy provides for return of all
or any part of the premium, it is to be returned in accordance with the
agreement.[80] Such returns may be found in some non-marine policies where, for
example, the policy is cancelled,[81] the risk is reduced,[82] or the subject matter of
the policy is sold.[83] Where the insurer is given discretion as to such partial return
of premium, the courts will not interfere with the insurer's exercise of that
discretion.[84] As far as marine insurance is concerned, cl.25 of the International
Hull Clauses 2003 states that if the insurance is cancelled by agreement, the
underwriters are to pay a pro rata monthly net return of premium for each
uncommenced month, although this obligation does not operate where there has
been a total loss of the vessel (whether or not by insured perils) during the
currency of the insurance. In the event of lay up of the vessel at an approved port
for repair work other than ordinary wear and tear, cl.39 the underwriters—if they
have so agreed—are to repay a proportionate part of the period for each period
of 30 consecutive days. More restricted provision is made for return of premium
by the Institute Time Clauses Freight, cll.15 and 16, which provide that: (a)
where the cover has terminated automatically by reason of either a change in the
class of the vessel or of a change in the ownership or flag of the vessel a pro rata
daily net return of premium is to be made; (b) a pro rata monthly return is to be
made for each uncommenced month of the insurance where it is cancelled by

---

[78] *JA Chapman & Co Ltd v Kadirga Denizcilik Ve Ticaret* [1998] Lloyd's Rep. I.R. 377.

[79] *Heath Lambert Ltd v Sociedad de Corretaje de Seguros* [2004] Lloyd's Rep. I.R. 905 See also
JA Chapman & Co Ltd v Kadirga Denizcilik Ve Ticaret [1998] Lloyd's Rep. I.R. 377, where this
outcome was anticipated. Contrast the decision of Rix J. in *Prentis Donegan & Partners v Leeds &
Leeds Co Inc* [1998] 2 Lloyd's Rep. 126, the learned judge holding that a premium warranty was
ineffective by reason of the operation of s.53.

[80] Marine Insurance Act 1906 s.83.

[81] *Sun Fire v Hart* (1889) 14 App. Cas. 90 at 100; *Re Drake Insurance Co* [2001] Lloyd's Rep. I.R.
643.

[82] *Parr's Bank v Albert Mines* (1900) 5 Com. Cas. 116.

[83] *South East Lancashire Insurance Co Ltd v Croisdale* (1931) 40 Ll. L.R. 22.

[84] It has been suggested that the insurers's discretion has to be exercised reasonably: *Madby v
Gresham Life* (1861) 29 Beav. 439. It might be thought that the modern approach would be not to
attempt to second-guess the insurers' commercial judgment and instead to uphold a decision other
than one which was irrational, e.g. based on considerations extraneous to the policy.

agreement; and (c) an agreed percentage is to be returned for each period of thirty consecutive days during which the vessel is laid up in port.

It was decided by Neuberger J. in *Re Drake Insurance Plc*[85] that a contract term in a motor policy under which the assured was entitled to terminate the policy by giving seven days' notice and then to recover a proportionate part of his premium, led to the implication that the exercise of unrestricted cancellation rights by the insurers equally entitled the assured to proportionate recovery. Such implication was held to be necessary to protect the assured against cancellation immediately after the risk attached, and operated even though the assured had made a claim under the policy.

A policy term which imposes a restricted limitation period for claims against the insurer is, unless the wording is clear, to be confined to claims for loss under the policy and not to claims for return of premium.[86]

Total failure of consideration. The general rule applicable to claims by the **8–020** assured for the return of premium is that if the insurers have never been on risk they have not earned the premium and ought to return it.[87] "Equity," said Lord Mansfield, "implies a condition that the insurer shall not receive the price of running a risk if he runs none".[88] Once, however, the insurer has been at risk under a valid and enforceable policy the premium is in no case recoverable at common law.[89] Thus where the lease of a house expires while an insurance by the lessee is still current,[90] or where the assured sells his interest in a building he has insured,[91] he will not be entitled to a return of premium in whole or in part if the risk has in fact been run for however short a time. Again, where the assured under a life policy commits suicide the policy may by its terms not be enforceable but the insurers will not be liable to return the premiums, for the risk has attached.[92] The principles are neatly illustrated by *Clydesdale Financial Services Ltd v Smailes*,[93] in which solicitors engaged in the activity of pursuing personal injury claims for clients on a contingency fee basis took out bank loans to cover their costs and at the same time obtained financial guarantee insurance which operated to repay a loans in the event that the claim was lost and legal costs were irrecoverable from the defendant. The financial guarantee insurers sought to recover unpaid premiums on 839 policies which had been issued. David Richards J. held that the insurers could not recover premiums on 830 of the policies, because no loans had been made and the risk under them had not attached. Recovery was limited to nine policies in respect of which loans had been made.

In both marine and non-marine insurance the principle is subject to contrary agreement, and it is common for insurers to stipulate that the premium is not to

---

[85] *Re Drake Insurance Plc* [2001] Lloyd's Rep. I.R. 643.

[86] *United India Insurance Co Ltd v Hyundai Engineering Construction Co Ltd* [2005] H.K.E.C. 811.

[87] The premium is to be returned gross and without deduction of the broker's commission, as that sum is paid to the broker by the insurers and not the assured: *Intermunicipal Realty & Development Corporation v Gore Mutual Insurance Company* [1981] 1 F.C. 151.

[88] *Stevenson v Snow* (1761) 3 Burr. 1237 at 1240. See also *Tyrie v Fletcher* (1774) 2 Cowp. 666, codified in s.84(1) of the Marine Insurance Act 1906.

[89] *Swiss Reinsurance Co v United India Insurance Co Ltd* [2005] Lloyd's Rep. I.R. 341. That had also been assumed in *Re Drake Insurance Plc* [2001] Lloyd's Rep. I.R. 643.

[90] *Sadlers Company v Badcock* (1743) 2 Atk. 554.

[91] *Lynch v Dalzell* (1729) 4 Bro. P.C. 431.

[92] Lord Mansfield in *Tyrie v Fletcher* (1777) 3 Cowp. 666 at 668; *Bermon v Woodbridge* (1781) 2 Doug. K.B. 781.

[93] *Clydesdale Financial Services Ltd v Smailes* [2009] EWHC 3190 (Ch).

be returnable in the event of the assured's breach of his duty of utmost good faith.[94]

8–021 **Apportionment.** In *Tyrie v Fletcher*[95] Lord Mansfield held that a premium is not apportionable, so that if any part of the risk has been run by the insurer even if the insurer has been on risk only for one day the insurer is entitled to retain the premium. There may nevertheless be cases in which one policy covers a variety of subject matters, and the premium is apportioned by the parties accordingly.[96] Whether or not the risk under a policy is apportionable is a matter of construction. In *Swiss Reinsurance Co v United India Insurance Co Ltd*[97] insurers issued a construction all risks policy in respect of the building of a power plant, and the risk was reinsured in what appears to have been much the same terms. Section 1 of the policy covered physical loss of or damage to the works under two heads: for 44 months, in respect of the construction period itself; and for a 12 month maintenance period running from the date of the handover of the works. The premium had been calculated by reference to the individual risks, and the global figure reached by totalling the individual elements was then discounted. Work was brought to an end early when the contractors walked off site as they had not been paid, and the reinsured sought a partial return of premium in respect of the premium for the maintenance period. Morison J. dismissed the claim on the basis that the maintenance period had started to run in respect of those sub-contractors whose work had been completed, so that the premium had been fully earned. That point aside, Morison J. ruled that the policy was not apportionable as between building and maintenance risks, and that it was inappropriate to unpick a global premium in order to determine its constituent parts. The premium had plainly been quoted as a global figure and the discount had been applied on a global basis.

8–022 **Fraud and illegality.** Return of premium is, in marine insurance, subject to there having been no "fraud or illegality on the part of the assured or his agents".[98] The most important situations in which the fraud of the assured will lead to a total failure of consideration are where he has been guilty of deliberate concealment or misrepresentation in negotiations leading up to the contract, or where he has wilfully broken a warranty which prevents the risk from attaching. Policies themselves frequently provide for the forfeiture of the premium in the event of a fraudulent breach of the duty of utmost good faith, but such a clause would appear to be unnecessary. The marine rule is based on the principle that, although the risk has never attached, the court will not allow him to set up his own fraud as a basis of a claim.[99] The position in non-marine insurance is not fully resolved,[100] although it is arguable that the court would refuse relief to a

---

[94] Subject to the effect of the Unfair Terms in Consumer Contracts Regulations 1999.

[95] *Tyrie v Fletcher* (1761) 3 Burr. 1237. See also *Stevenson v Snow* (1777) 3 Cowp. 666.

[96] Marine Insurance Act 1906 s.84(2), based on *Gale v Mitchell* (1785) Park on Insurance 797. Contrast *Bermon v Woodbridge* (1781) 2 Doug. 781; *Meyer v Gregson* (1784) 3 Doug. 402; *Annen v Woodman* (1810) 3 Taunt. 299; *Moses v Pratt* (1814) 4 Camp. 297.

[97] *Swiss Reinsurance Co v United India Insurance Co Ltd* [2005] Lloyd's Rep. I.R. 341.

[98] Marine Insurance Act 1906 s.84(1)–(2).

[99] *Chapman v Fraser* (1793) 1 Park (8th ed.) 456. For a discussion of this case and of the origins of the rule, see Stanley Drummond, "Fraudulent misrepresentation or non-disclosure—does the insurer have to return the premium?" (2010) 21 Ins.L.J. 1. See also *Rivaz v Gerussi Brothers & Co* (1880) 6 Q.B.D. 222.

[100] *Andersen v Fitzgerald* (1853) 4 H.L. Cas. 484; *Fowkes v Manchester & London Life Assurance Co* (1862) 3 F. & F. 440.

fraudulent assured who sought restitution of his premiums on the same basis recognised in marine cases, namely that fraud cannot found an action. However, it might be argued that the basis of the action is not recovery of the premiums but the fact that the insurer has avoided the policy. Further, the assured's claim is one for money had and received, which is a common law claim not based on any discretion in the court. Consequently, if the court is to refuse restitution to a fraudulent assured, it must do so on purely public policy grounds. Where, on the other hand, it is the insurer who comes to the court to claim rescission of the policy on the ground of the assured's fraud, a different principle has in the past been applied. Since such rescission is a purely equitable remedy, the court applied the maxim that "he who seeks equity must do equity" and could, therefore, in its discretion, refuse the insurer relief unless he is willing to repay premiums already paid.[101] The premium was in the old cases sometimes ordered in such a case to be applied towards payment of the costs,[102] however gross the fraud of the assured.[103] The modern view, however, is that the insurer has, in the case of fraud, the right to avoid the policy and to retain the premiums, as there appears to be no recent case in which the contrary has been held.[104]

With respect to illegality, ordinary principles of contract law dictate that if a contract is illegal in its inception for any reason and the parties are equally guilty, neither party has any rights under it as the court will not assist either party[105] and sums paid in pursuance of it are thus irrecoverable; *in pan delicto potior est conditio defendentis*. An insurance contract may be unlawful from the outset because it contravenes a statute most importantly, in the case of life insurance, the absence of insurable interest under the Life Assurance Act 1774 or because it is made by the parties with the deliberate intention of achieving an unlawful objective and is thus offensive to the common law. Where the contract is illegal, the ban on restitution of premiums[106] will be relaxed in the following exceptional cases:

(1) Where the assured is under a mistake, whether of fact or law, he may recover his premium. Thus, if the assured is unaware of a state of war which renders illegal the contract made with an enemy alien, the premium may be recovered despite the illegality of the contract.[107]

(2) Where the assured was induced to enter into the contract by the fraud.[108] Thus, where the insurer fraudulently represented that interest was unnecessary under a life policy, an innocent assured was held entitled to recover the premium he had paid[109] but it has been held otherwise where

---

[101] *De Costa v Scandret* (1723) 2 P. Wms. 170; *Barker v Walters* (1844) 8 Beav. 92 at 96; *London Assurance v Mansel* (1879) 11 Ch D 363 at 372.

[102] *Whittingham v Thornburgh* (1690) 2 Vern. 206; *De Costa v Scandret* (1723) 2 P. Wms. 170.

[103] *Prince of Wales Assurance v Palmer* (1858) 25 Beav. 605.

[104] The dicta to the contrary in *London Assurance v Mansel* are of doubtful weight as in that case the insurers voluntarily proffered the premiums.

[105] Lord Mansfield in *Busk v Walsh* (1812) 4 Taunt. 290 at 292.

[106] As to which see: *Lowry v Bourdieu* (1780) 2 Dougl. 468; *Andree v Fletcher* (1789) 3 T.R. 266; *Vandyck v Hewitt* (1800) 1 East 96; *Morck v Abel* (1803) 3 B. & P. 95; *Lubbock v Potts* (1806) 7 East 449; *Palyart v Leckie* (1817) 6 M. & S. 290; *Paterson v Powell* (1832) 9 Bing. 320; *Kelly v Solari* (1841) 9 M. & W. 54; *Howard v Refuge* (1886) 54 L.T. 644.

[107] *Oom v Bruce* (1810) 12 East 225. See also *Hentig v Staniforth* (1816) 5 M. & S. 122 at 123–125.

[108] *Drummond v Deey* (1794) 1 Esp. 151; *Howarth v Pioneer Life* (1912) 107 L.T. 155.

[109] *British Workman's Assurance v Cunliffe* (1902) 18 T.L.R. 502; *Hughes v Liverpool Victoria Friendly Society* [1916] 2 K.B. 482.

the insurer's misrepresentation as to interest was an innocent one.[110] The principle behind this exception is that where the insurer's conduct is fraudulent the parties cannot be said to be equally to blame.

(3) Where the contract remains executory and the assured repents. This curious exception is based upon dicta of Buller J. in *Lowry v Bordieu*[111] and has a subsequent history of confusion.[112] It is uncertain, in particular, whether the assured must subjectively repent or whether it is enough that he seeks to withdraw.[113]

Further, there is no clear authority on the meaning of "executory". In *Lowry v Bordieu* Buller J. appears to have been of the opinion that a marine policy is not executed until the voyage has been completed. This was modified by *Lubbock v Potts*[114] in which it was held that an insurance is executed once a loss has occurred, but in *Howard v Refuge Friendly Society*[115] the court ruled that an insurance policy is fully executed once the risk has started and the premium has been paid. The scope of this exception thus remains open to doubt.

(4) Where the statute is intended to protect assureds[116]; in such a case, depriving the assured of his premium as a result of illegality would be self-defeating.

8–023 **Liability for return of premium.** Where the assured is entitled to a return of all or any part of his premium, it is recoverable by him from the insurers,[117] although if the premium is paid to the agent of the insurers in respect of a contract known, or which ought to be known by the assured, to be outside the scope of the agent's authority it is not recoverable from the insurers.[118] The limitation period for an action to recover the premium depends upon the basis of the action, but in general terms the claim is a contractual one and the period is six years.[119]

As discussed above, under a policy of marine insurance the broker and not the assured is responsible to the insurer for payment of the premium.[120] Where this rule is applicable, the insurer remains liable to the assured for the return of the premium. Thus, if the insurer returns the premium to the broker, and the broker defaults or becomes insolvent, the assured may maintain an action against the insurer for the return of the premium.[121] If the premium is returned to the broker, and the assured is indebted to the broker for commission, the broker is entitled to set-off the sums owing to him before returning the balance to the assured: the fact that the broker is a fiduciary does not render him a mere conduit for the

---

[110] *Harse v Pearl Life Assurance* [1904] 1 K.B. 558; *Phillips v Royal London Mutual* (1911) 105 L.T. 136.

[111] *Lowry v Bordieu* (1780) 2 Doug. 468.

[112] The authorities are reviewed in *Tribe v Tribe* [1996] Ch 107.

[113] In *Palyart v Leckie* (1817) 6 M. & S. 290 it was held that the assured must give express notice of withdrawal; the issue of a claim form is inadequate.

[114] *Lubbock v Potts* (1800) 7 East 449.

[115] *Howard v Refuge Friendly Society* (1886) 54 L.T. 644.

[116] *Re Cavalier Insurance Co* [1989] 2 Lloyd's Rep. 430.

[117] Marine Insurance Act 1906 s.82(a). If the assured has yet to pay the premium, it may be retained by him or his agent: Marine Insurance Act 1906 s.82(b).

[118] *Re Arthur Average, De Winton's Case* (1876) 34 L.T. 942.

[119] A policy term which requires the assured to bring claims within a fixed period of the insurers denying liability does not apply to actions for recovery of premiums: *United India Insurance Co Ltd v Hyundai Engineering Construction Co Ltd* [2005] H.K.E.C. 811.

[120] Marine Insurance Act 1906 s.53(1).

[121] Marine Insurance Act 1906 s.53(1).

return of the premium without deduction.[122] One question that arises commonly in practice is whether insurers who are under an obligation to return the premium to the assured must return the entire premium including brokerage or just the net premium, leaving it to the assured to look to the broker for the return of the amount representing brokerage. This point arises only where the risk has never run, and in particular where the policy has been avoided *ab initio* for breach of the duty of utmost good faith. The rule that broker's commission is fully earned when the risk is placed means that as soon as a valid risk has been placed there can be no return of commission even in the event that some or all of the premium itself is returnable.[123] In the case of an avoidance, by contrast, the risk is treated as never having incepted and the premium plus brokerage is repayable to the assured, the only question being whether the insurers or the broker are responsible for repaying the brokerage. The point is a difficult one. The rule that is generally assumed to be applicable is that the assured pays the gross premium, and that the brokerage is deducted by agreement between insurers and broker. If that rule prevails, it is implicit that the insurers are required to return the gross premium to the assured. However, the decision of the Court of Appeal in *Carvill v Camperdown*[124] indicates that question of who pays the broker is far from resolved. If payment is by the assured, the argument that the insurers must return gross premium would seem to fall away. Furthermore, the Court of Appeal indicated that the correct analysis could be that the gross premium is paid by the assured to the insurers on the understanding that the insurers will pay brokerage to the broker in the amount agreed between the insurers and the broker: if that analysis is right, the insurers are merely a conduit for the payment of brokerage by the assured, and accordingly their obligation on avoidance is simply to return net premium. It may be that there is no single answer to the question, and that all will depend upon the arrangements between insurers, assured and broker for payment of brokerage.

Return of premium in specific cases

No valid contract. If the insurers have issued a policy which does not comply **8–024** with the assured's application, there is no agreement and any premium is returnable.[125] Thus, where the policy did not accord with the terms of a contract of life insurance the court ordered it to be cancelled and the premiums to be refunded as paid under a mistake.[126] But the premium will not be recoverable in such a case where the assured is entitled to rectification of the policy.[127] Under this principle premiums paid under a policy which the company had not the power to issue will be recoverable.[128] Further, premiums paid under a policy which is void, as being made under a mistake are recoverable, as are premiums paid under a non-existent policy which the assured erroneously believed to be in existence.[129] Thus, a house may be insured in the mistaken belief that it is standing, when in fact it has already been burnt down, and a person may be

---

[122] *Velos Group Ltd v Harbour Insurance Services Ltd* [1997] 2 Lloyd's Rep. 461.
[123] *Velos Group Ltd v Harbour Insurance Services Ltd* [1997] 2 Lloyd's Rep. 461.
[124] *Carvill v Camperdown* [2005] Lloyd's Rep. I.R. 55.
[125] *Jackson v Turquand* (1869) L.R. 4 H.L. 305.
[126] *Fowler v Scottish Equitable Life* (1858) 28 L.J. Ch 225.
[127] *General Accident Insurance v Cronk* (1901) 17 T.L.R. 233.
[128] *Re Phoenix Life* (1862) 2 J. & H. 441; *Flood v Irish Provident Assurance* (1912) 46 Ir. L.T. 214.
[129] *Lower Rhine Insurance v Sedgwick* [1899] 1 Q.B. 179.

insured in the belief that he is still alive[130]; in each of these cases the premium must be returned.

8–025 *Avoidance of the contract by the insurer.* Where the misrepresentation is an innocent one, or where the non-disclosure does not amount to a fraudulent concealment, the marine rule is clear: the premium is recoverable on the ground that the risk has never attached.[131] The rule is statutory in marine insurance[132] and, subject to the doubts expressed above as to fraud, this provision is equally applicable in non-marine insurance.[133]

8–026 *Avoidance of the contract by the assured.* Misrepresentation or failure to disclose material facts by the insurer permits the assured to avoid the policy and to recover the premiums[134]; it is immaterial whether the insurer's conduct was fraudulent or innocent for these purposes.[135] Moreover, where the policy is illegal and the assured's entry into the contract was caused by the fraud of the insurer or its agent, the assured may recover the premium.[136]

8–027 *Breach of warranty by the assured.* Where the warranty takes effect from the commencement of the policy, e.g. where the assured warrants that the insured subject matter is in a particular place or in a given condition at the inception of the risk, and the warranty is not complied with, the risk does not begin to run. Consequently, the assured is entitled to restitution of his premium on a consideration that has wholly failed. Thus, where an intemperate assured warrants himself to be temperate in his habits, the risk never attaches, the premiums therefore never become due, and may, if paid, be recovered back as money paid without consideration.[137] The question whether, in non-marine insurance, the position is altered by the assured's fraud is unresolved, although the rule is unlikely to be any different.

By contrast, where the warranty is a continuing one, and is broken after the commencement of the risk, the assured is not entitled to recovery of premiums. The principle here is that the risk terminates automatically on the breach of warranty, leaving the policy intact—including the assured's liability to pay premium instalments on the unexpired term of the policy[138]—but exempting the insurers from all future liability. Because the risk has run, even for a short period, the premium is irrecoverable.[139] This rule is applicable to all cases in which the insurer is entitled to terminate the risk or the contract once the risk has started to

---

[130] See Byles J. in *Pritchard v Merchant's Life* (1858) 3 C.B.N.S. 622 at 645.

[131] *Feise v Parkinson* (1812) 4 Taunt. 640; *Anderson v Thornton* (1853) 8 Ex. 425.

[132] Marine Insurance Act 1906 s.84(3)(a).

[133] *Anderson v Fitzgerald* (1853) 4 H.L.C. 484, 507; *Mulvey v Gore District Mutual Fire* (1866) 25 U.C.Q.B. 424; Wright J. in *Biggar v Rock Life* [1902] 1 K.B. 516 at 526.

[134] *Carter v Boehm* (1766) 3 Burr. 1905; *Duffell v Wilson* (1808) 1 Camp. 40; *Foster v Mutual Life* (1904) 20 T.L.R. 15; *Merino v Mutual Life* (1904) 21 T.L.R. 167; *Molloy v Mutual Life* (1905) 22 T.L.R. 59; *Kettlewell v Refuge Assurance Co Ltd* [1909] A.C. 243; *Hyams v Paragon Insurance Co Ltd* (1927) 27 Ll. L.R. 448.

[135] The view that the premium is recoverable only where the insurer was fraudulent was expressed by Buckley L.J. in *Kettlewell v Refuge Assurance* [1907] 2 K.B. 242, but this approach was not adopted by the House of Lords on appeal at [1909] A.C. 243 and it is scarcely consistent with ordinary contractual principles of misrepresentation.

[136] *Hughes v Liverpool Victoria Friendly Society* [1916] 2 K.B. 482.

[137] Lord Blackburn in *Thomson v Weems* (1884) 9 App. Cas. 671 at 682.

[138] *Chapman & Co Ltd v Kadirga Denizcilik Ve Ticaret AS* [1998] Lloyd's Rep. I.R. 377.

[139] *Annen v Woodman* (1810) 3 Taunt. 299; *Langhorn v Cologan* (1812) 4 Taunt. 330.

run, as a result of the assured's conduct.[140] However, premiums paid after the breach to cover future periods beyond the duration of the original contract will be recoverable: where the life assured has warranted that he will not go abroad but does so, renewal premiums paid by him after the breach of warranty are recoverable.[141]

Insurer in breach of contract. If the insurer is in repudiatory breach of the contract of insurance, the assured is entitled either to affirm the policy (and, if he has suffered any loss as a result of the breach, to sue for damages) or to treat it as terminated and to sue for damages. The general assumption in the latter case is that the assured's loss will be at least the amount of the premiums paid by him under the policy; the premiums are thus recoverable, but by way of damages rather than as part of a restitutionary action as such.   **8–028**

Risk not attaching. In marine insurance there are three governing principles[142]:   **8–029**

(1) Where the risk has never attached, the premium is recoverable in full.[143]

(2) Where the risk has attached to part of the subject matter but not to the remainder, the assured is entitled to a return of the latter proportion of the premium. This rule is illustrated by a number of marine authorities on cargo and freight in which the full cargo insured under the policy has not been shipped.[144] There is, however, no case in which the apportionment rule has been applied to insurances other than marine insurances, and it would seem that non-marine policies cannot be apportioned in this way.

(3) Where the subject matter is insured "lost or not lost" but has arrived safely the insurer may retain the premium unless it was aware at the commencement of the contract that the subject matter was safe.[145] Marine policies alone may insure a subject matter "lost or not lost", an exception which developed in the eighteenth century and which was necessitated by poor communications which made it impossible for an assured to determine whether the vessel, cargo or freight had been lost at any given time. In non-marine insurance, if the subject matter has been lost at the date of the policy, there is a total failure of consideration and the assured may recover the premiums only; whereas in marine insurance the assured can recover the full amount insured under a "lost or not lost" policy if the subject matter has been lost, but he cannot recover the premium should the subject matter arrive safely.

Defeasible interest. Where the assured has a defeasible interest which is terminated during the currency of the risk, the premium is not returnable.[146] This   **8–030**

---

[140] *Hogg v Horner* (1797) 2 Park on Insurance 782; *Tait v Levi* (1811) 14 East 481.

[141] See Bray J. in *Sparenborg v Edinburgh Life* [1912] 1 K.B. 195 at 204.

[142] Marine Insurance Act 1906 s.84(3)(b).

[143] *Martin v Sitwell* (1691) 1 Show 156. See also: *Bankers & General Insurance Co v Brockdorff & Co* (1922) 10 Ll. L.R. 22; *Strickland v Turner* (1852) 7 Ex. 208; *Scott v Coulson* [1903] 2 Ch 249.

[144] *Forbes v Aspinall* (1811) 13 East 323; *Rickman v Carstairs* (1833) 5 B. & Ad. 651; *Tobin v Harford* (1864) 17 C.B.N.S. 528.

[145] This is based on *Bradford v Symondson* (1881) 7 QBD 456.

[146] Marine Insurance Act 1906 s.84(3)(d).

is simply an application of the ordinary principle that, where the risk has commenced, the assured may not recover any part of the premium.

8–031 *Lack of insurable interest.* The position as to return of premium varies as between the different classes of insurance. So far as life insurance is concerned, the Life Assurance Act 1774 applies: if the assured does not have an insurable interest at the outset the policy will be illegal and the premiums will normally be irrecoverable,[147] subject to the rules on illegality discussed above; if the assured loses his insurable interest during the policy he will nevertheless be entitled to claim on the death of the life insured so that no question of return of premium applies. In the case of non-marine indemnity policies, if the assured does not have insurable interest at the outset and never obtains insurable interest then consideration has totally failed and the premium will be recoverable; if the assured has insurable interest but loses it after the risk has commenced he may neither recover under the policy nor, because the risk has run, may he recover his premium.

As far as marine insurance is concerned, a policy not supported by insurable interest is void so that the assured's sole remedy is return of premium, to which he is entitled as long as the policy is not effected by way of gaming or wagering.[148] Three different situations are here contemplated.

(1) The assured did not have insurable interest at the outset, but expected to obtain an interest during the currency of the policy. If no interest was in fact obtained by him this does not convert the policy into one made by way of gaming or wagering, but simply means that there is a valid policy the consideration for which has totally failed so that the premium can be recovered.

(2) The assured did not have insurable interest nor did he have any expectation of acquiring insurable interest, so that the policy was made by way of gaming or wagering contrary. The premium is here irrecoverable.

(3) The assured either had, or held an expectation of acquiring, an insurable interest, so that the policy is not void for gaming or wagering. However, because the policy is in "ppi" form, it is deemed to be made by way of gaming or wagering, so that prima facie restitution is debarred, although the assured has been allowed to recover premiums in this very situation.[149]

8–032 *Double insurance.* Double insurance arises where the assured has taken out two or more policies on the same subject matter, and the aggregate recoverable under those policies exceeds his interest. In the event of double insurance the assured may claim payment from the insurers in such order and in such proportion as he thinks fit, subject to the overriding rule that he cannot recover more than an indemnity.[150] Given that the assured may recover under any policy that he thinks fit, it is necessarily the case that each insurer must be at least partly on risk even though it may be that, following loss, one or more of them is not called upon to pay anything to the assured. The rules of contribution between insurers will,

---

[147] *M'Culloch v Royal Exchange* (1813) 3 Camp. 406.
[148] Marine Insurance Act 1906 s.84(3)(c).
[149] *Re London County Commercial Reinsurance Office* [1922] 2 Ch 67.
[150] Marine Insurance Act 1906 s.32, which applies to non-marine policies.

however, ensure that each insurer pays only its own proportion of the assured's loss.

The effect of these principles on return of premium differs as between non-marine and marine insurance. In non-marine insurance there is no possibility of apportionment of the premium where the risk is only partly run; consequently, as each insurer is to some extent on risk, each may retain the full premium. Marine insurance, by contrast, recognises the concept of a divisible premium where only part of the risk has attached.[151] The marine rule also provides that where the policies are taken out at the same time, so that neither of them bears the entire risk, a proportionate part of the aggregate premium is recoverable. Where, however, one of the policies bears the entire risk for any period, no premium is recoverable in respect of that period.[152]

Overinsurance under an unvalued policy. The non-marine rule here is that the **8–033** premium is not apportionable so that no part of it is returnable even though the assured is overinsured.[153] The marine insurance rule,[154] is to the contrary: where the insured has overinsured under an unvalued policy a proportionate part of the premium is returnable.

Overinsurance under a valued policy. Where the assured and the insurer have **8–034** agreed the value of the subject matter to be insured, the amount of insurance will necessarily be confined that value, so there is no possibility of overinsurance in these circumstances.[155]

---

[151] Marine Insurance Act 1906 s.84(3)(f).

[152] *Fisk v Masterman* (1841) 8 M. & W. 165.

[153] *Wolemberg v Royal Co-operative Collecting Society* (1915) 84 L.J.K.B. 1316.

[154] Marine Insurance Act 1906 s.84(3)(e).

[155] If the assured procures further policies, the matter is determined by s.84(3)(f) of the 1906 Act.

CHAPTER 9

CLAIMS

1. CLAIMS CONDITIONS

9–001 **Electronic claims handling.** The London Market is moving steadily towards electronic claims handling. The Claims Agreement and Settlement Service ("CLASS") is an internet database used by members of the London International Insurance and Reinsurance Market Association (other than Lloyd's Syndicates) for the purpose of exchanging information on matters such as solicitors' reports and bills. Lloyd's Syndicates have developed the Electronic Claims File Scheme ("ECF") which is to contain all brokers' claims files. Both are administered by Xchanging Claims Services ("XCS") a company to which Lloyd's has out-sourced many of its claims-handling processes.

9–002 **Nature of claims conditions.** In the absence of any express policy provision, there is no obligation on the assured to notify a claim to the insurers at any particular time,[1] other than in the specific case of marine insurance where the assured will be required to give a notice of abandonment as soon as possible after a casualty in order to sustain a claim for constructive total loss.[2] In practice, however, all policies set out detailed claims procedures, normally requiring early notification of the occurrence of an insured peril or, in the case of a liability policy or reinsurance agreement, of circumstances which may or are likely to give rise to a claim against the assured at some future point. Notice provisions are generally contained in the policy document itself, although there will be situations in which the assured has been offered temporary cover prior to the issue of the formal wording. There is Court of Appeal authority for the proposition that if the assured's attention is not drawn to the insurers' standard wordings then in the interim period he is not bound by any claims conditions in those terms.[3]

9–003 **Effects of breach of a claims condition.** The consequences of the assured's failure to comply with a claims condition depend upon its wording. The policy may well specify the consequences of a failure to comply with the notice provision, in which case those consequences must follow; in general, such a clause will confer upon insurers the right to reject the claim. However, notification of the loss may simply be expressed as a "condition". Here, it is necessary to classify the condition in order to ascertain the consequences of its breach.[4] The basic distinction is between conditions precedent and other

---

[1] *Vestey Brothers v Motor Union Insurance Co Ltd* (1922) 10 Ll. L.R. 270, although the court here allowed the insurers to deduct the costs incurred by them as a result of the assured's delay.

[2] See Ch.24, below.

[3] *Re Coleman Depositories Ltd and Life & Health Assurance Association* [1907] 1 K.B. 798.

[4] See also the discussion of conditions in Ch.7, above.

conditions. If compliance is expressed to be a condition precedent to the insurers' liability, then any breach by the assured means that the insurers' liability cannot attach[5] and it is immaterial that the insurers have not suffered any prejudice.[6] By contrast, if the condition is not a condition precedent, then it may fall into one of three categories. First, the condition may be of such significance to the contract as a whole that any breach of it is automatically repudiatory and entitles the insurers to determine the insurance contract for breach. There is almost no authority for construing an insurance claims condition in this way,[7] and the Supreme Court of New South Wales in *Trans-Pacific Insurance Co (Australia) Ltd v Grand Union Insurance Co Ltd*[8] denied that a notice clause could have the "quality of essentiality such that any breach thereof entitled [the insurer] to terminate the contract". This sentiment was echoed by Colman J. in *Alfred McAlpine Plc v BAI (Run-off) Ltd*[9] and the majority of the Court of Appeal in *Friends Provident Life & Pensions Ltd v Sirius International Insurance Corp*.[10] Secondly, the condition may be ancillary to the policy, so that a breach could never amount to a repudiation and could only ever sound in damages. The courts have generally refused to classify a term in this manner from the outset. Thirdly, the condition may be incapable of classification on its face, and is to be treated as innominate. The insurers' rights following breach of an innominate term depend upon its effects: if the nature of the assured's breach is repudiatory of the policy as a whole, then the insurers are discharged from all liability under the policy from the date of breach[11]; if, by contrast, the assured's breach is not repudiatory, then the insurers are confined to an action for damages any loss which they have suffered.

[5] *Oldman v Bewicke* (1786) 2 Hy. Bl. 577n; *Worsley v Wood* (1796) 6 T.R. 710: *Ralston v Bignold* (1853) 21 L.T. 106; *Mason v Harvey* (1853) 8 East 819; *Roper v Lendon* (1859) 1. E. & E. 825; *Cawley v National Employers, Accident & General Assurance Association Ltd* (1855) Cab. & El. 597; *Cassel v Lancashire & Yorkshire Accident Insurance Co Ltd* (1885) I T.L.R. 495; *Viner v Bignold* (1887) 20 QBD 172: *Hiddle v National Fire & Marine Insurance Co of New Zealand* [1896] A.C. 372; *Vezey v United General Commercial Insurance Corporation Ltd* (1922) 15 Ll. L.R. 63; *General Motors Ltd v Crowder* (1931) 40 Ll. L.R. 87; *Welch v Royal Exchange Assurance* [1939] 1 K.B. 294; *Allen v Robles* [1969] 3 All E.R. 154; *Pioneer Concrete (UK) Ltd v National Employers' Mutual General Assurance Association* [1985] 2 All E.R. 395; *Millichap v Pontrilas Timber* Unreported, 1991, *Alexander Forbes Europe Ltd v SBJ Ltd* [2003] Lloyd's Rep. I.R. 432; [2003] Lloyd's Rep. I.R. 432; *Gan Insurance Co v Tai Ping insurance Co (No.2)* [2001] Lloyd's Rep. I.R. 667; *Bankers Insurance Co v South* [2004] Lloyd's Rep. I.R. 1; *Eagle Star Insurance Co v Cresswell* [2004] Lloyd's Rep. I.R. 437.

[6] *Pioneer Concrete (UK) Ltd v National Employers' Mutual General Insurance Association Ltd* [1985] 2 All E.R. 395; *Kier Construction v Royal Insurance (UK)* 30 Con. L.R. 45; *Motor & General Insurance Co Ltd v Pavy* [1994] 1 Lloyd's Rep. 607; *Total Graphics Ltd v AGF Insurance Ltd* [1997] 1 Lloyd's Rep. 599; *Diab v Regent Insurance Co Ltd* [2006] Lloyd's Rep. I.R. 779. There have on occasion been suggestions that prejudice is required: *Lickiss v Milestone Motor Policies at Lloyd's* [1966] 2 All E.R. 972; *Farrell v Federated Employers Assurance Association* [1970] 3 All E.R. 632; *CVG Siderurgica del Orinoco SA v London Steamship Owners Mutual General Insurance Association Ltd (The Vainqueur Jose)* [1979] 1 Lloyds Rep. 557.

[7] The exception being the decision of H.H. Judge Byrt QC in *Taylor v Builders Accident Insurance Ltd* [1997] M.C.L.C. 247.

[8] *Trans-Pacific Insurance Co (Australia) Ltd v Grand Union Insurance Co Ltd* (1990) 6 ANZ Insurance Cases 60–949.

[9] *Alfred McAlpine Plc v BAI (Run-off) Ltd* [2000] Lloyd's Rep. I.R. 352.

[10] *Friends Provident Life & Pensions Ltd v Sirius International Insurance Corp* [2006] Lloyd's Rep. I.R. 45. See also, in the context of a time bar clause for the making of claims on a warranty in a share sale agreement, *Forrest v Glasser* [2006] Lloyd's Rep. I.R. 113.

[11] Although this has to be backdated to the loss itself, otherwise the assured would be able to recover for the very loss in respect of which he has repudiated the policy. See the comments of Moore-Bick J. in *Friends Provident Life & Pensions Ltd v Sirius International Insurance Corp* [2005] Lloyd's Rep. I.R. 135.

It is now accepted that claims conditions not expressed to be conditions precedent are to be regarded as innominate terms,[12] so that the rights of the insurers depend upon whether the effect of the assured's conduct has been to repudiate the policy as a whole (by expressing an intention no longer to be bound by it) or whether the breach is minor and sounds only in damages. In principle the notion that a failure to comply with a claims condition amounts to a repudiation of the policy as a whole is all but inconceivable: this follows from the reasoning in *Trans-Pacific* and *Friends Provident*, although Waller L.J. in *Friends Provident* countenanced the possibility of repudiation of the policy as a whole "in extreme circumstances", e.g. "of consistent breach over a number of claims." Even fraud by the assured in his breach of the term does not convert the breach into a repudiatory one.[13] This means that insurers are almost always confined to a claim for damages where a claim is late, although to do so they must prove loss. This, however, may be problematic. Waller L.J. in *Friends Provident* described the possibility of an action for damages as "illusory", although, in the same case, Mance L.J. and Sir William Aldous felt that in many situations damages could be calculated (as where the assured's breach caused the insurers to lose subrogation rights) even though in others (such as late notification to liability insurers of a third party claim which might or might not have been defended successfully) damages would be purely speculative. In *Porter v Zurich Insurance Co*[14] Coulson J. refused to award insurers damages representing 100 per cent of a claim made by the assured for smoke damage to insured goods, in circumstances where the assured had through his agents failed to co-operate with the insurers in breach of a claims co-operation clause not expressed to be a condition precedent. Insurers were unable to examine the premises from which the goods were allegedly stolen, and were also not given explanations of the assured's valuation of allegedly stolen goods when those goods had also appeared as damaged in a separate fire claim. Coulson J.'s view was that it was necessary for the insurers to prove that the breach caused a loss, and that the onus was on them to do so.

The weakness of the insurers' position under a claims provision not expressed to be a condition precedent led to the suggestion by Waller L.J. in *Alfred McAlpine* that there existed the possibility that a serious breach of a claims condition might, while leaving the policy untouched, amount to a repudiation of the claim.[15] That possibility was nevertheless rejected by the majority of the Court of Appeal in *Friends Provident*. The demise of the notion of repudiation of the claim was also recognised in *Limit No.2 Ltd v Axa Versicherung AG*,[16] in which the reinsured under a facultative obligatory treaty had failed to comply with its obligation to submit quarterly risk bordereau to the reinsurers: it was held that the breach was not repudiatory of the treaty as a whole nor did it permit the reinsurers to refuse to pay claims in respect of risks which had been declared late.

---

[12] Cf. *Phoenix General Insurance Co of Greece SA v Halvanon Insurance Co Ltd* [1985] 2 Lloyd's Rep. 599; *Travelers Casualty and Surety Co of Canada v Sun Life Assurance Co of Canada (UK) Ltd (No.2)* [2007] Lloyd's Rep. I.R. 619.

[13] *K/S Merc-Skandia XXXXII v Certain Lloyd's Underwriters* [2000] Lloyd's Rep. I.R. 694; *Axa General Insurance Ltd v Gottlieb* [2005] Lloyd's Rep. I.R. 369.

[14] *Porter v Zurich Insurance Co* [2009] EWHC 376 (QB).

[15] See Ch.7, above.

[16] *Limit No.2 Ltd v Axa Versicherung AG* [2008] Lloyd's Rep. I.R. 330.

A claims condition is not a forfeiture clause. Accordingly, the English courts do not have any equitable jurisdiction to relieve the assured of his obligation to comply with a claims condition.[17]

Classifying the condition. The key distinction is, therefore, between conditions **9–004** precedent, breaches of which enable the insurers to avoid liability without more, and other conditions, breaches of which merely give rise to damages. As noted earlier in this work,[18] it is possible to create a condition precedent by the use of appropriate language, including the description of the term as a condition precedent, an indication of the consequences of any breach, the use of a general clause deeming all provisions to be conditions precedent and otherwise unequivocal wording. However, the courts regard conditions precedent as draconian in their effect and insist upon clear wording. As was said by Colman J. in *Alfred McAlpine*,[19] breach of a notification provision has little impact on the insurers' rights and any problem can be rectified by a relatively modest expenditure: "these considerations point against a mutual intention that insurers should have a complete defence to any claim where there has been any breach of the notification clause however trivial in effect."

The courts will thus seek wherever possible[20]—and on occasion in the face of express terminology[21]—to avoid holding that a notification of loss provision amounts to a condition precedent. The court may conclude that a claims condition makes no sense unless it is construed as a condition precedent even though it is not expressly described as such,[22] although the courts will be slow to imply a condition precedent in this way.[23] If a term contains severable obligations, the contra proferentem rule may be applied to confine the words "condition precedent" only to those parts of the clause to which they unambiguously refer.[24]

The Unfair Terms in Consumer Contracts Regulations prevent automatic reliance on claims conditions by insurers where the assured is a consumer as defined by the Regulations.[25]

Obligations imposed by notification clauses.[26] In practice, the forms of notice **9–005** provisions found in policies fall into three broad classes: (a) those which oblige

[17] *Diab v Regent Insurance Co Ltd* [2006] Lloyd's Rep. I.R. 779.

[18] Ch.7, above.

[19] *Alfred McAlpine Plc v BAI (Run-off) Ltd* [1998] 2 Lloyd's Rep. 694.

[20] Illustrative of the many decisions are: *Stoneham v Ocean, Railway & General Accident Insurance Co* (1887) 9 QBD 237; *Cowell v Yorkshire Provident Life Assurance Co* (1901) 17 T.L.R. 452; *Re Coleman's Depositories* [1907] 2 K.B. 798; *Hadenfayre v British National Insurance Society Ltd* [1984] 2 Lloyd's Rep. 393: *Black King Shipping Co v Massie (The Litsion Pride)* [1985] 1 Lloyd's Rep. 437; *Cox v Bankside Members Agency Ltd* [1995] 2 Lloyd's Rep. 447; *Royal & Sun Alliance Plc v Dornoch Ltd* [2005] Lloyd's Rep. I.R. 544; *Ronson International Ltd v Patrick* [2006] Lloyd's Rep. I.R. 194.

[21] *Re Bradley and Essex & Suffolk Accident Indemnity Society* [1912] 1 K.B. 415.

[22] *British Credit Trust Holdings v UK Insurance Ltd* [2004] 1 All E.R. Comm 444; *Gan Insurance Co v Tai Ping Insurance Co (No.2)* [2001] Lloyd's Rep. I.R. 667; *Banker's Insurance Co v South* [2004] Lloyd's Rep. I.R. 1; *Eagle Star Insurance Co v Cresswell* [2004] Lloyd's Rep. I.R. 437; *Aspen Insurance UK Ltd v Pectel Ltd* [2009] Lloyd's Rep. I.R. 440.

[23] *Friends Provident Life & Pensions Ltd v Sirius International Insurance Corp* [2006] Lloyd's Rep. I.R. 45.

[24] *Insurance Co of Africa v Scor (UK) Reinsurance Co Ltd* [1985] 1 Lloyd's Rep. 312; *Capemel v Roger H Lister* [1989] I.R. 319; *Pioneer Concrete (UK) Ltd v National Employers' Mutual General Insurance Association Ltd* [1985] 2 All E.R. 395.

[25] See *Bankers Insurance Co v South* [2004] Lloyd's Rep. I.R. 1, discussed in Ch.3, above.

[26] The operation of these clauses will be constrained by the obligations of insurers imposed by the Financial Services Authority: see Ch.13, below.

the assured to give "immediate" notice of any loss, or notice "forthwith"; (b) those which oblige the assured to give notice within a specified fixed time from the date of the loss; (c) those which merely require the assured to give notice "as soon as is reasonably practicable". Liability policies are somewhat differently worded: under a claims made policy the assured is required to notify the insurers of any circumstances which may or are likely to give rise to a claim, and thereafter to notify any claim actually made against the assured.[27] Some clauses combine these elements and provide that the assured must notify a claim within a fixed period or as soon as is reasonably practicable. It has been held that such wording does not create an obligation to notify as soon as reasonably practicable, with the specified period operating as no more than a longstop: instead, such a provision means that there is a single obligation to notify within the specified period.[28]

9–006 *"Immediate" notice clauses.* The practice of the courts has been to insist upon strict compliance by the assured with any provision of this nature. The word "immediate" has been said to mean "with all reasonable speed considering the circumstances of the case".[29] It is clear that any delay in notification, whether or not the delay was within the control of the assured, will be a breach of the clause.[30] A particular problem arises where it is not obvious from the outset that a particular event has caused loss. It has been held that an obligation to give immediate notice of any accident causing injury was broken where the assured waited some weeks to ascertain whether the accident had in fact caused injury[31] and where notice was not given due to the supervening insolvency of the assured.[32]

9–007 *Fixed notification periods.* A clause which specifies a time within which a claim is to be presented must be complied with strictly.[33] Again, the most serious problems have arisen in the context of policies under which the assured has been required to give notice within a given period of an event giving or likely to give rise to a loss, the outcome of the event not having become apparent until after the notice period had expired.[34] Policies against fraud also give rise to difficulty where coverage is confined to frauds which are notified to insurers within a fixed period from their occurrence: if the assured does not become aware of the fraud

---

[27] See Ch.21, below.

[28] *AIG Europe (Ireland) Ltd v Faraday Capital Ltd* [2007] Lloyd's Rep. I.R. 267. The point did not arise on appeal and Morision J. was reversed on other grounds, [2008] Lloyd's Rep. I.R. 454.

[29] *Re Coleman's Depositories* [1907] 2 K.B. 798; *Aspen Insurance UK Ltd v Pectel Ltd* [2009] Lloyd's Rep. I.R. 440.

[30] *Loyaltrend Ltd v Creechurch Dedicated Ltd* [2010] Lloyd's Rep. I.R. 466.

[31] *Re Williams and Thomas and Lancashire and Yorkshire Insurance Co* (1902) 19 T.L.R. 82. See also *Hussain v GAN Assurance Co* [2007] H.K.E.C. 361.

[32] *Farrell v Federated Employers Insurance Association Ltd* [1970] 3 All E.R. 632. Cf. *Pioneer Concrete (UK) Ltd v National Employers' Mutual General Insurance Association Ltd* [1985] 2 All E.R. 395.

[33] *Ralston v Bignold* (1853) 21 L.T. 106; *Roper v Lendon* (1859) 1 E. & E. 825. It was suggested in *Diab v Regent Insurance Co Ltd* [2006] Lloyd's Rep. I.R. 779 that the equitable principle that time is not of the essence could mean that the precise time limits laid down in a policy (even in a condition precedent) were not binding on the assured as long as there was compliance within a reasonable time. The point was not developed.

[34] *Cassell v Lancashire and Yorkshire Accident Insurance Co* (1885) 1 T.L.R. 495 (injuries not becoming manifest for some nine months after the event, the policy requiring notice within 14 days); *Cawley v National Employers' Accident and General Insurance Association Ltd* (1885) 1 T.L.R. 255 (onset of peritonitis not diagnosed for 14 days, seven days too late).

within the specified period, notification will be out of time.[35] For this reason fidelity and related policies normally impose a notification period running from the date on which the fraud could have been discovered.[36] Although it is settled law in insurance and reinsurance cases that policy terms specifying time limits are to be strictly enforced, Lord Scott, delivering the opinion of the Privy Council in *Diab v Regent Insurance Co Ltd*[37] cast some doubt on this proposition. Lord Scott noted that in the general law of contract time was not of the essence, and that there was an argument that as long as the assured has given sufficient notice to the insurers there was no basis for holding the assured to strict contractual time limits. This comment was, however, purely *obiter* as the assured was some nine years late in making a claim under a policy which provided for 15 days' notice, and the comment also appears to overlook the significance of making a notification requirement a condition precedent the effect of which may be thought to make time of the essence. Lord Scott also indicated that where a claims provision confers a discretion on insurers to extend time, they may be under an implied obligation (possibly stemming from the continuing duty of good faith) to act reasonably in the face of any request by the assured, although on the facts in *Diab* no such request had been made so the point did not arise. Those points aside, in *Diab* the Privy Council went on to confirm that the equitable doctrine of relief from forfeiture had no application to a late claim under an insurance contract, so that the court did not have any discretion to disapply a claims provision specifying a fixed notice period.

Notification "as soon as is reasonably practicable". This form of wording has **9–008** come before the courts on a number of occasions, and it is clear from the decisions that what is at stake is whether the assured has acted reason ably given all the surrounding circumstances of the loss. The leading authority is *Verelst's Administratrix v Motor Union Insurance Co*,[38] in which the assured's accident policy required notice of any loss to be given to the insurer "as soon as possible" after it had come to the attention of the assured's representative. The assured's death in a motor accident became known to his personal representative soon after its occurrence, but the existence of the policy was not discovered by the representative until a year had elapsed from the assured's death. Roche J. construed the words "as soon as possible" as applying not just to the fact of the assured's death, but also to all the surrounding circumstances of the case, including the ability of the representative to discover the existence of the insurance. On this reasoning, the claim was held not to have been out of time. A reinsurance example of the same point is the first instance decision of Morison J. in *AIG Europe (Ireland) Ltd v Faraday Capital Ltd*[39] in which Morison J. rejected the reinsurers' argument that notification of a loss (April 12, 2004) around three weeks from the reinsured becoming aware of it (March 24, 2004) was out of time. Morison J. noted that the insurers' lawyers had not received the relevant information until March 30, 2004 and that the brokers had refused to

[35] *TH Adamson & Sons v Liverpool and London and Globe Insurance Co Ltd* [1953] 2 Lloyd's Rep. 355.

[36] *Ward v Law Property Assurance and Trust Society* (1856) 27 L.T. 155.

[37] *Diab v Regent Insurance Co Ltd* [2006] Lloyd's Rep. I.R. 779.

[38] *Verelst's Administratrix v Motor Union Insurance Co* [1925] 2 K.B. 137, followed in *Fong Wing Shing Construction Co Ltd v Assurances Generales De France (HK) Ltd* [2003] H.K.E.C. 653.

[39] *AIG Europe (Ireland) Ltd v Faraday Capital Ltd* [2007] Lloyd's Rep. I.R. 267, and see also: *Travelers Casualty and Surety Co of Canada v Sun Life Assurance Co of Canada (UK) Ltd (No.2)* [2007] Lloyd's Rep. I.R. 619; *Fong Wing Shing Construction Co Ltd v Allianz Insurance (Hong Kong) Ltd* [2003] 3 H.K.C. 561.

pass on the information to the reinsurers without further information. Given the intervention of the Easter period shortly afterwards, the insurers had acted as soon as was reasonably practicable. On appeal, *AIG Europe (Ireland) Ltd v Faraday Capital Ltd*,[40] the decision was reversed on the ground that the relevant notifiable loss had occurred at an earlier date so that notification was out of time, but the principle adopted by Morison J., although ultimately inapplicable on the facts, remains good. Delay which is within the control of the assured,[41] or which is excessive in the circumstances,[42] will render his claim time-barred.

Compliance with claims conditions

9–009 *Form of notification.* Unless the policy otherwise provides, there is no particular form in which a claim has to be made against insurers. A claim is no more than a request for payment, and if a notification is not on its face sufficient to amount to a claim then the courts are empowered to take into account any earlier exchanges between the parties relating to the events in question.[43] It was said by Gloster J. in *Merrill Lynch International Bank Ltd v Winterthur Swiss Insurance Co*[44] that a notice was validly given if the recipient was given sufficient information to enable it to meet the claim by preparing and obtaining appropriate evidence, and that there was "no reason why the Insurer should escape liability to indemnify, simply because details which it claims should have been originally provided to it were not." In *HLB Kidsons v Lloyd's Underwriters*[45] Gloster J. again commented that the phrase "notice in writing" required the written communication to be "sufficiently clear and unambiguous that it leaves the reasonable recipient in no reasonable doubt that the assured is by the communication purporting to give notice . . . "[46] This test was, however, disapproved by Rix and Toulson L.JJ. in the Court of Appeal in *HLB Kidsons v Lloyd's Underwriters*,[47] at least in the context of a liability policy where the assured is required to give notice of circumstances of which he was aware which may give rise to a claim. Rix L.J. noted that concepts of awareness and "may" were "open-textured" and it sufficed that a communication could on all objective criteria be treated as a notification: the application of a stricter test requiring the communication to put the matter beyond reasonable doubt was not appropriate in the absence of specific requirements for the form and content of notification. It follows from these comments that exactly what is required will depend upon the wording of the notification clause and exactly how specific the assured is required to be in the circumstances to make the notification meaningful.

9–010 *By whom must notice be given?* Most notification of loss clauses specify that notice must be given by the assured. It is nevertheless arguable that such wording is adopted simply because the assured will normally be the appropriate person to give notice, and that the insurers' intention is not to impose a personal obligation

[40] *AIG Europe (Ireland) Ltd v Faraday Capital Ltd* [2008] Lloyd's Rep. I.R. 454.

[41] *Monksfield v Vehicle & General Insurance* [1971] 1 Lloyd's Rep. 139; *Sharpe v Williamson* [1990] 3 C.L. para.243.

[42] *General Motors Ltd v Crowder* (1931) 47 Ll. L.R. 87; *Alfred McAlpine Plc v BAI (Run-off) Ltd* [2000] Lloyd's Rep. I.R. 352; *Chan Yiu Sun v Yip Kim Cheung* [1990] 2 H.K.C. 524.

[43] *Forrest v Glasser* [2006] Lloyd's Rep. I.R. 113.

[44] *Merrill Lynch International Bank Ltd v Winterthur Swiss Insurance Co* [2007] Lloyd's Rep. I.R. 532.

[45] *HLB Kidsons v Lloyd's Underwriters* [2008] Lloyd's Rep. I.R. 237.

[46] The approach adopted at first instance in *Kidsons* was followed in *Kajima UK Engineering Ltd v Underwriter Insurance Co Ltd* [2008] Lloyd's Rep. I.R. 391.

[47] *HLB Kidsons v Lloyd's Underwriters* [2009] Lloyd's Rep. I.R. 178.

on the assured. It was thus held in *Lickiss v Milestone Motor Policies at Lloyd's*[48] that the assured's obligation under a motor policy to notify the insurer of any accident and of any notice of intended prosecution served on him by the police, had been satisfied where the relevant information had been provided to the insurer by the victim's insurers and the police. In the view of Lord Denning, "law never compels a person to do that which is use less and unnecessary". Salmon L.J., dissenting on this point, preferred the construction that the obligation to notify was personal to the assured. If the majority view in *Lickiss* is good law, it is certainly to be confined to the situation in which the reliability of the notification is beyond doubt. It may also be that if the insurers themselves have actual knowledge of the loss then notification to them is not required.[49]

If the policy is subscribed to by a number of underwriters, it will commonly be the case that the agreement contains a leading underwriter clause under which notification need be made only to the leading underwriter: it is uncertain whether the leading underwriter is an agent for the following market or whether receipt by him is deemed receipt by the following market, but the precise reasoning is irrelevant as far as the assured is concerned. In the absence of a leading underwriter clause, notice has to be given to each subscribing underwriter.[50]

There is a clear distinction between the giving of notice and the exercise of an option under which cover is to be provided. Unless the assured has himself exercised that option it cannot be said to have been exercised. The latter situation arose in *Tioxide Europe Ltd v CGU International Insurance Plc*.[51] Here assured possessed three layers of liability insurance, and was entitled to trigger cover by exercising a loss notification option in respect of accidents occurring during the currency of the policy. The option was duly exercised by notification to the primary layer, but at a later date, once the extent of the loss became apparent, there was a purported exercise of the option in respect of excess layer insurers: this was permitted by the excess-layer policies, as long as notice was given to the excess layer insurers as soon as possible after it appeared that the loss would exceed the primary layer cover. That purported exercise took the form of the sending to the excess layer insurers by the primary layer insurer of a copy of the notice given to the primary layer insurer. The Court of Appeal held that the notification was invalid: the loss notification option was one to be exercised by the assured alone, and notification by a third party could not be said to be a valid exercise of that option. Notification failed for the further reason that it had been given to the assured's own brokers and not, as required by the relevant provisions, the excess layer insurers themselves.

Knowledge of facts underlying claim. The clause may restrict notification to the **9–011** situation in which the assured knows of the loss in question. Plainly, the assured can notify a loss only where he is aware of the matters which have given rise to it. Knowledge here refers to that of the assured and any person within the assured's organisation whose knowledge is to be regarded as having been

[48] *Lickiss v Milestone Motor Policies at Lloyd's* [1966] 2 All E.R. 972.
[49] *Abel v Potts* (1800) 3 Esp. 242. In *Alexander Forbes Europe Ltd v SBJ Ltd* [2003] Lloyd's Rep. I.R. 432 notice was given to underwriters by brokers but under a policy taken out by the assured's group rather than under the assured's own policy. It was not necessary for the court to decide whether the underwriters' knowledge was sufficient to amount to a valid notice as the only question was whether the brokers were in breach of duty by reason of their negligence—a question answered in the affirmative.
[50] *HLB Kidsons v Lloyd's Underwriters* [2008] Lloyd's Rep. I.R. 237.
[51] *Tioxide Europe Ltd v CGU International Insurance Plc* [2006] Lloyd's Rep. I.R. 31.

attributed to the assured under usual attribution rules.[52] In *Kidsons* a liability policy required the assured to give the insurers notice in writing as soon as practicable of circumstances which the assured became aware and which may give rise to a loss. Gloster J. held that the phrase "circumstance . . . which may give rise to a loss or claim" was one which, "objectively evaluated, creates a reasonable and appreciable possibility that it will give rise to a loss or claim against the assured", so that the risk must be real and not imagined but it need not amount to a probability; and the notice must not be premature, so that "if, at the time when the assured purports to give notice in writing or at any other later relevant time, he is not aware of a relevant circumstance, then the notice is ineffective".

Notification creates a particular problem in liability insurance cases, because the assured may be required to notify circumstances likely to give rise to a claim as well as a claim itself. In *Royal & Sun Alliance Insurance Plc v Dornoch Ltd*[53] the reinsured under a directors' and officers' liability cover was required "upon knowledge of any loss or losses which may give rise to claim under this policy, advise the Underwriters thereof by cable within 72 hours". The reinsured became aware of claims against the company and its directors at the end of December 2000, but the reinsurers were not notified of those claims until the middle of January 2001. The Court of Appeal nevertheless held that the notification was not out of time. The reinsured had to have "knowledge" of loss or losses, but until the claimants against the company and its directors had been established and quantified it could not be said that the reinsured had such knowledge: up to that point, the reinsured simply had knowledge of the fact that there were allegations of losses.

The reasoning in *Dornoch* was followed but distinguished by the Court of Appeal in *AIG Europe (Ireland) Ltd v Faraday Capital Ltd*.[54] The assured in this case ran e-learning and other training courses, and obtained a directors' and officers' policy. The insurers obtained reinsurance under a policy which provided, as a condition precedent, that "(a) The Reinsured shall upon knowledge of any loss or losses which may give rise to a claim, advise the Reinsurers thereof as soon as is reasonably practicable and in any event within 30 days . . . " and "(b) The Reinsured shall furnish the Reinsurers with all information available respecting such loss or losses, and shall co-operate with the Reinsurers in the adjustment and settlement thereof." On November 19, 2002 the assured informed the market that it intended to restate its financial statements for the preceding four years and to take into account only actual revenue rather than anticipated revenue. That led to a dramatic fall in the value of the assured's shares, at one point falling by one-third. A number of shareholders who had purchased shares in the period up to November 2002 commenced proceedings, which were notified to AIG in December 2002 and were subsequently consolidated into a class action in March 2003. The reinsured posted a substantial reserve in February 2004. The dispute between the assured and the insurers was referred to mediation, and the insurers were informed on March 25, 2004 that a settlement had been reached. The reinsurers were informed on April 14, 2004, and they pleaded breach of the notification clause. At first instance2 Morison J. held that the case was indistinguishable from *Dornoch*. The relevant losses were

---

[52] See *HLB Kidsons v Lloyd's Underwriters* [2008] Lloyd's Rep. I.R. 237, reversed in part [2009] Lloyd's Rep. I.R. 178, where it was held that the knowledge of the partnership secretary was that of the individual partners within the firm.

[53] *Royal & Sun Alliance Insurance Plc v Dornoch Ltd* [2005] Lloyd's Rep. I.R. 544.

[54] *AIG Europe (Ireland) Ltd v Faraday Capital Ltd* [2008] Lloyd's Rep. I.R. 454.

those of the shareholders: the losses could not be those of the company, as that would render limb (b) of the clause inoperative. The question then became exactly when the insurers became aware that the shareholders had suffered loss, and that could not have been until the outcome of the mediation was known to the insurers: until that point that the assured had restated its financial statements was not of itself proof that it had acted wrongly, and even if there was negligence it could not be said that shareholders had proved that they had suffered any loss at all by purchasing at an inflated price until a settlement had been reached. While the insurers were aware of a "might be" loss far earlier, they could not have had knowledge of an actual loss until March 23, 2004. Morison J. further held that any knowledge possessed by the insurers of legal expenses incurred by the shareholders in proving their claim were outside the claims co-operation clause because they could not have been adjusted by the insurers or the reinsurers, and in any event there had been no proof that expenses had been incurred or that the amount of any such expenses would have exceeded the deductible imposed by the direct policy. Further, Morison J. held the fact that the assured had incurred defence costs was irrelevant, as such costs had never been claimed from the insurers. The learned judge's conclusion on the date of the loss was rejected on appeal by the Court of Appeal. The Court of Appeal held that there was a crucial distinction between the two cases in that in *Faraday* the announcement of November 19, 2002 was a specific event which had led to almost immediate losses, and that to say that there was no coincidence between the announcement and the fall in share prices would have been, in the words of Longmore L.J., "to shut one's eyes to the obvious". As there had been an obvious loss to the shareholders, and as that loss considered at the time was clearly one which might have given rise to a claim (which indeed it did), notification was required within 30 days from AIG becoming aware of that loss. The Court of Appeal was satisfied that AIG knew of the relevant circumstances by late December 2002 when claims against the assured were notified to it, and the 30-day notification period commenced at that stage. The Court of Appeal noted that in *Faraday*, as in *Dornoch*, it was not immediately obvious that the assured faced any liability for the loss and that the insurers faced any liability to the assured, but the notification obligation related to losses which may give rise to claims and not to losses in respect of which liability had been established. In *Dornoch* it was not obvious that shareholders had suffered losses, whereas in *Faraday* it was.

One point which is not fully resolved by these cases is the test for "knowledge". In *Dornoch* Aikens J. held that the test was objective,[55] and it was not necessary on appeal for any view to be expressed. In *Faraday* Longmore L.J. chose not to comment on the point other than in saying that he was not to be taken as disagreeing with Aikens J. and that in any event the subjective and objective approaches would in most cases lead to the same result.

Must the giving of notice be intended? It has been held that the assured may   **9–012** unintentionally give notification of a loss, and that what matters is whether the insurers have received the relevant information. Thus if the assured suffers a loss and discloses the loss in negotiations for renewal of the policy, that amounts to a due notification under a claims condition even though the assured did not intend

---

[55] Cf. *Loyaltrend Ltd v Creechurch Dedicated Ltd* [2010] Lloyd's Rep. I.R. 466.

to so notify. There is no reason why a communication cannot serve two purposes.[56]

9–013 *To whom must notice be given?* Policies commonly specify that notice of loss is to be sent to a specific person or to a specific address, and the general rule is that notice is not valid unless it is so sent. Moreover, it will rarely be successfully arguable by an assured that, where notice to head office is required, it was sufficient for him to give notice of loss to a branch office or local agent: any possible ostensible authority possessed by the branch manager or agent will be negatived by the express policy provision.[57] Consequently, failure to comply with the requirements in the clause may be waived only by the person named in the clause as the recipient of the information: an obligation on the assured to provide written notice of loss to the insurer's head office would, for example, be satisfied where the assured telephones a person authorised to deal with claims at the head office and that person intimates that the call is acceptable as notice.[58] Notice by the assured to his broker will clearly not suffice, unless the insurer has so stipulated; the broker is the agent of the assured, so that notice to him is not deemed to have been received by the insurer if it has not been passed on.[59]

In the case of insurance arranged in layers it is often the case that the terms of the excess layer are the same as those of the primary layer, either expressly or by incorporation. It was held by *Friends Provident Life & Pensions Ltd v Sirius International Insurance Corp* that an obligation in the primary layer policy for the assured to give notice to "the underwriters" is satisfied in respect of all layers by the giving of notice to the primary layer leading underwriter. Some excess layer policies contain express provisions whereby separate notification is required to the excess layers and an additional period is conferred for such notification, running from the date on which the assured became aware that the losses were likely to exceed the extents of the primary layer.[60]

If the policy is subscribed to by a number of underwriters, it will commonly be the case that the agreement contains a leading underwriter clause under which notification need be made only to the leading underwriter: it is uncertain whether the leading underwriter is an agent for the following market or whether receipt by him is deemed receipt by the following market, but the precise reasoning is irrelevant as far as the assured is concerned. In the absence of a leading underwriter clause, notice has to be given to each subscribing underwriter.[61]

---

[56] *Friends Provident Life & Pensions Ltd v Sirius International Insurance Corp* [2006] Lloyd's Rep. I.R. 45; *BP Plc v Aon* [2006] Lloyd's Rep. I.R. 577; *HLB Kidsons v Lloyd's Underwriters* [2009] Lloyd's Rep. I.R. 178, but note the comment of Buxton L.J. (dissenting on the substantive point) although that a document which was subjectively not intended to be a notification could nevertheless objectively amount to a notification, caution was to be exercised in reaching such a conclusion. See also Rix L.J.'s comment "that in certain exceptional circumstances intention may not be irrelevant to a unilateral question such as the giving of a notice."

[57] *Marsden v City & County Assurance Co* (1865) L.R. I C.P. 232: *Re Williams & Thomas and Lancashire & Yorkshire Accident Insurance Co* (1903) 19 T.L.R. 82; *Brook v Trafalgar Insurance Co Ltd* (1946) 79 Ll. L.R. 365.

[58] Cf. *Webster v General Accident Fire & Life Assurance Corp Ltd* [1953] 1 Q.B. 520.

[59] *Roche v Roberts* (1921) 9 Ll. L.R. 59; *Friends Provident Life & Pensions Ltd v Sirius International Insurance Corp* [2006] Lloyd's Rep. I.R. 45; *Toxide Euope Ltd v CGU International Insurance Plc* [2006] Lloyd's Rep. I.R. 31.

[60] *Tioxide Europe Ltd v CGU International Insurance Plc* [2006] Lloyd's Rep. I.R. 31.

[61] *HLB Kidsons v Lloyd's Underwriters* [2008] Lloyd's Rep. I.R. 237, reversed in part on other grounds [2009] Lloyd's Rep. I.R. 178. It was also held at first instance in this case that notification to underwriters' solicitors was inadequate.

Waiver of breach of condition. The issue of waiver is discussed elsewhere in   **9–014**
this work and it suffices here to say that it is always open to an insurer to waive
the requirements of any notice provision, and any express decision to do so by
an authorised person will not give rise to any difficulty.[62] The law recognises two
main forms of waiver: waiver by affirmation, where the insurers choose to
honour the policy rather than to deny liability; and waiver by estoppel, where
they have made an unequivocal representation that they do not intend to rely
upon their rights and the assured has relied upon that statement or has acted to
his detriment.[63] In principle waiver by estoppel is unlikely to be found in the
absence of waiver by affirmation. It was held by the Court of Appeal in *Kosmar
Villa Holidays Plc v Trustees of Syndicate 1243*, adopting the approach in *Forrest
v CGU Insurance*,[64] that the only form of waiver for breach of condition is
waiver by estoppel.

2. CO-OPERATION AND PROOF OF LOSS

Burden of proof. The assured is required to prove that the loss was proximately   **9–015**
caused by an insured peril.[65] Once he has done so, the burden shifts to the
insurers to make out their defence, e.g. that the loss resulted from the assured's
own deliberate act or an excluded peril.[66]

The duties of the assured. A variety of post-notification of loss obligations may   **9–016**
be imposed upon the assured by the policy.[67] These include the duty of an assured
under a burglary policy to inform the police of his loss; the duty of an employer
under a fidelity policy to prosecute the defrauding employee[68]; the duty of an
assured under a life or accident policy to submit to medical examination; and the
duty of the assured under a liability policy either to cede all claims-handling to
the insurers, to seek the insurers' consent to any settlement[69] or at the very least

---

[62] *Webster v General Accident Fire and Life Assurance Corp Ltd* [1953] 1 Q.B. 520; contrast *Brook v Trafalgar Insurance Co Ltd* (1946) 79 Ll. L.R. 365.

[63] *Kammins Ballrooms Co Ltd v Zenith Investments (Torquay) Ltd* [1971] A.C. 850; *Motor Oil Hellas (Corinth) Refineries SA v Shipping Corp of India (The Kanchenjunga)* [1990] 1 Lloyd's Rep. 391; *Kosmar Villa Holidays Plc v Trustees of Syndicate 1243* [2008] Lloyd's Rep. I.R. 489.

[64] *Forrest v CGU Insurance* [2006] Lloyd's Rep. I.R. 113.

[65] *Austin v Drewe* (1816) 6 Taunt. 436; *Everett v London Assurance* (1865) 19 C.B.N.S. 126; *Marsden v City & County Insurance* (1865) L.R. 1 C.P. 232; *London Plate Glass v Heath* [1913] 3 KB. 411; *Century Bank v Young* (1914) 84 L.J.K.B. 385; *Munro, Brice & Co v War Risks Association* [1918] 2 K.B. 78; *Albion Mills Co v Hill* (1922) 12 Ll. L.R. 96; *Watts v Simmons* (1924) 18 Ll. L.R. 177; *Slattery v Mance* [1962] 1 Q.B. 676; *The Alexion Hope* [1988] 1 Lloyd's Rep. 311; *Shakur v Pilot Insurance Co* 73 D.L.R. (4th) 337 (1991). In the case of an all risks policy, that he had suffered a loss: *British & Foreign Marine v Gaunt* [1921] 2 A.C. 41; *Feurst Day Lawson v Orion Insurance* [1980] 1 Lloyd's Rep. 656.

[66] *Greaves v Drusdale* (1935) 53 Ll. L.R. 16;

[67] Some policies do impose obligations on the insurers in the claims procees, e.g. the International Hull Clauses 2003. In the absence of any express obligations, the courts have recognised implied terms based on the duty of utmost good faith. See the authorities discussed in Ch.6, above. The law has hinted that insurers may owe continuing duties of utmost good faith, but at present there is no remedy in damages for breach (a matter which the Law Commissions, in Issues Paper No.6 issued in March 2010, has suggested should be reversed, at least in the context of late payment of claims. See Ch.10, below.

[68] *London Guarantee Co v Fearnley* (1880) 5 App. Cas. 911.

[69] *Horwood v Land of Leather Ltd* [2010] EWHC 546 (Comm), which decides that such a clause applies not just to claims made against the assured but also to claims made by the assured against a third party who is potentially liable to indemnify the assured for claims against the assured.

to co-operate with the insurers in the event of a third party claim as regards the provision of documents and the conduct of negotiations.[70] More generally, policies of all types normally require[71] the assured to submit all necessary proofs concerning his loss and otherwise to co-operate with the insurers.

The time at which a claims obligation requiring notification of loss has to be complied with depends upon its terms, although the obligation is normally to give notice as soon as the assured has become aware of the circumstances. By contrast, in the case of claims co-operation provision the obligation on the assured is to co-operate with the insurers' demands. It is implicit that there has to be compliance within a reasonable time. What constitutes a reasonable time is a matter of fact in every case, and it is not a precondition of breach that the insurers have suffered prejudice by reason of the breach. In *Shinedean Ltd v Alldown Demolition (London) Ltd and Axa Insurance UK Plc*[72] a liability policy required the assured to "give all information and assistance [the insurers] may require" as a condition precedent to recovery. The assured sub-contractor, while carrying out demolition work in April 2002, caused damage to a neighbouring property, and proceedings were commenced against the assured by the head contractor in April 2004, seeking indemnification for sums paid to the owner of the damaged property. A default judgment was obtained shortly thereafter. The assured's liability insurers had been informed of the damage to the wall the day after it occurred, but were not informed of the proceedings for some months after the judgment against the assured had been obtained and in the course of hearings on the assessment of quantum. At first instance H.H. Judge Havery QC held that that there was an implied term in the policy that the assured would co-operate within a reasonable time. However, he went on to rule that prejudice to the insurers was the key determinant of breach of the term, and that in the absence of any prejudice to the insurers—in that they would have been required to indemnify the assured whether or not they had received due co-operation—the assured was not in breach of the term. This decision in effect deprives even a condition precedent of much of its effect, and on appeal the Court of Appeal overturned both the decision and the reasoning. The Court of Appeal agreed that there was an implied term that the assured would co-operate within a reasonable time, but rejected the suggestion that prejudice determined whether or not the term had been broken. The approach to be adopted is a broader one, and what constitutes a reasonable time is, in the words of Sir Anthony Clarke M.R., "essentially a question of fact and depends on all the circumstances of the particular case." On the facts, there had been an unreasonable delay and the term was broken, even though the insurers had not suffered prejudice by reason of the delay.[73]

Submitting proofs of loss

9–017   *Scope of dute*   The time limits specified by the clause must be adhered to in the usual way.[74] If the clause requires immediate notification, or notification within

[70] See *Re T&N Ltd (No.3)* [2006] Lloyd's Rep. I.R. 370 (obligation on reinsured to provide claims information exclusively to reinsurers—clause prevented reinsured from providing information to a third-party broker who had taken over a proportion of the liability).

[71] A term of this type will not be implied, as it is up to the insurers to specify their requirements: *Albany Life Assurance Co v De Montfort Insurance Co Plc* Unreported, 1995.

[72] *Shinedean Ltd v Alldown Demolition (London) Ltd and Axa Insurance UK Plc* [2006] Lloyd's Rep. I.R. 846.

[73] This decision was followed in *Lexington Insurance Co v Multinacional de Seguros SA* [2009] Lloyd's Rep. I.R. 1.

[74] *Roper v Lendon* (1859) 1 E. & E. 825: *Elliott v Royal Exchange Assurance Co* (1867) L.R. 2 Ex. 237; *Northern Suburban Property Ltd v British Law Fire Insurance Co Ltd* (1919) 1 Ll. L.R. 403.

a specified period, no concessions are made to an assured or assignee who is unable, for practical reasons, to provide proofs within the relevant time.[75] It will normally be necessary for the assured to provide details concerning both the circumstances of loss and its amount.[76] In liability policies, the assured's duty is commonly expressed as being one to keep the insurer "fully advised" of the progress of the claim against the assured. If the assured has failed to give complete information, or has given false information, so that there is a breach of the provision, it is open to the assured to make good the deficiency[77] or to correct the error[78] within the time permitted under the policy.[79] In the absence of any time limit for compliance, the assured must comply within a reasonable time, there being no absolute rule that prejudice to the insurers should be included or excluded when determining reasonableness.[80] Unless the condition in question is framed as a condition precedent to the liability of the insurer, any breach of the clause will not permit the insurer to deny liability for the claim unless the assured can be shown to have repudiated the policy itself. This possibility is almost certainly ruled out by the mere fact of failure to comply with a claims condition, and the fact that the assured has acted fraudulently in the course of submitting the relevant documents to the insurers is not of itself enough to put the assured in repudiatory breach of the policy as a whole,[81] although it may in appropriate circumstances amount to a fraudulent claim.[82]

Waiver of breach of duty. In accordance with general principles, insurers or their **9–018** authorised agents and employees may by their conduct be estopped from denying a breach of condition where there is an unequivocal representation to that effect. On that basis, underwriters who give extensions of time for the submission of proofs[83] or who appoint their own surveyors to estimate the extent of the loss[84] may be held to have deprived themselves of the right to rely upon the breach of condition.

Underwriters may deny liability before the assured has had the opportunity to submit a claim, and the question which arises here is whether the denial of liability operates as a waiver of the requirements of the notification clause or creates an estoppel against the underwriters which preclude their reliance on it. There is English authority for the proposition that there is an estoppel in these circumstances,[85] although the balance of authority denies this possibility. In *Trans-Pacific Insurance Co (Australia) Ltd v Grand Union Insurance Co Ltd*[86] it was held that where reinsurers refused to meet any claim by the reinsured in respect of a direct loss, the reinsured remained under an obligation to comply with its claims obligations under the reinsurance policy. This view was also taken

---

[75] *Re Carr and Sun Fire Insurance Co* (1897) 13 T.L.R. 186.

[76] *Atlantic Metal Co v Hepburn* [1960] 2 Lloyd's Rep. 42.

[77] *Mason v Harvey* (1853) 8 Exch. 819.

[78] *Northern Suburban Property Co v British Law Fire Insurance Co* (1919) 1 Ll. L.R. 403.

[79] See *Hiddle v National Fire and Marine Insurance Co of New Zealand* [1896] A.C. 372, in which the policy provided that all particulars in the assured's possession had to he given within 15 days: failure by the assured to give full particulars in that time was held to be fatal to the claim.

[80] *Shinedean Ltd v Alldown Demolition London Ltd* [2006] Lloyd's Rep. I.R. 846.

[81] *K/S Merc-Skandia XXXXII v Certain Lloyd Underwriters* [2001] Lloyd's Rep. I.R. 802.

[82] See below. In *K/S* the assured had not got to the point of making a claim, so there was no fraudulent claim as such.

[83] *Re Carr and Sun Fire Insurance Co* (1897) 13 T.L.R. 186.

[84] *Burridge v Haines* (1918) 87 L.J.K.B. 641.

[85] *Re Coleman's Depositories* [1907] 2 K.B. 798.

[86] *Trans-Pacific Insurance Co (Australia) Ltd v Grand Union Insurance Co Ltd* (1990) 6 ANZ Insurance Cases 60–949.

by the Privy Council in *Diab v Regent Insurance Co Ltd*.[87] Here, the assured under a fire policy, having been informed that the insurers would not meet any claim by reason of fraud, failed to comply with its obligation to make a claim within 15 days from the date of the fire and subsequently commenced proceedings against them. The allegation of fraud was abandoned but the insurers pleaded the notification clause. The Privy Council held that the claims provision remained binding: the insurers had not waived compliance with the clause but had simply sought to dissuade the assured from making a claim; and there was no estoppel because it was not possible to find an unequivocal representation by the insurers that they would not rely on the clause. In so deciding the Privy Council confirmed[88] that the insurers had not repudiated the policy by raising the fraud defence.

These cases were followed by Christopher Clarke J. in *Lexington Insurance Co v Multinacional de Seguros SA*.[89] Here, a reinsurance agreement in respect of a direct liability policy contained a condition precedent to liability that the reinsured would "furnish the reinsurers with all information in respect of such circumstances and shall co-operate with the reinsurers in the adjustment and settlement of the claim." A claim arose against the reinsured in April 1998, and in January 2000 the reinsurers informed the reinsured that they regarded themselves as discharged due to the reinsured's breach of this clause. On April 3, 2002 the reinsured effectively agreed that it would settle with the assured despite the fact that the claim against the assured was potentially time-barred, that letter being held by the court to constitute a breach of the claims co-operation clause. The reinsured nevertheless argued that the reinsurers were not entitled to rely upon the letter of April 3, 2002 because their conduct in January 2000 had relieved them from any further obligations under the claims co-operation clause. The argument was based on: (a) the reinsurers having waived reliance upon the clause by their conduct; and (b) the reinsurers by their own breach of contract had relieved the reinsured from future reliance on the clause. Christopher Clarke J. rejected both the waiver and the construction arguments: the decision of the Court of Appeal in *Kosmar Villa Holidays Plc v Trustees of Syndicate 1243*[90] defeated as a matter of law any suggestion of waiver of breach of condition, the only possibility being estoppel; and irrespective of the question whether the reinsurers had repudiated the contract they had not relieved the reinsured of its future obligation to comply with the clause.

It may be speculated how the law would apply where it was found that insurers had repudiated the policy by their refusal to pay, which will—leaving aside the special cases of liability insurance and reinsurance—normally be the case given that the obligation to pay arises as soon as the loss occurs. As a matter of general contract law the assured has, following a repudiation, the right either to affirm the contract or to treat it as terminated for breach. If the former approach is adopted, then it necessarily remains the case that the claims obligations are binding on the assured as his claim continues under the policy. By contrast, if the assured treats himself as discharged by the breach, then he retains the right to make a claim from the insurers for breach of contract but, arguably, free of his future obligations under the policy including the obligation to claim within a given time. The point did not arise in *Diab*, as no breach of contract was found and in

---

[87] *Diab v Regent Insurance Co Ltd* [2006] Lloyd's Rep. I.R. 779.

[88] In reliance on *Super Chem Products Ltd v American Life and General Insurance Co* [2004] Lloyd's Rep. I.R. 446.

[89] *Lexington Insurance Co v Multinacional de Seguros SA* [2009] Lloyd's Rep. I.R. 1.

[90] *Kosmar Villa Holidays Plc v Trustees of Syndicate 1243* [2008] Lloyd's Rep. I.R. 489.

any event the assured presented his case on the basis that the policy had been affirmed by him. The point was glossed over in *Lexington*. It is at least arguable that if the insurers have repudiated the policy, the assured is fully entitled to treat the policy as terminated as of that date and to press his claim for breach of contract free of any claims conditions.

Submitting proofs and documents to insurers' satisfaction. Where there is a   **9–019**
policy provision requiring the submission to the insurers of documentation satisfactory to them, or where the policy provides that the insurers may demand such proofs as they thinks fit, it is unclear whether or not the insurers' subjective decisions as to what is required override what prudent insurers ought reasonably to require. A number of older authorities suggest that the insurers' own views are paramount and that the relevant clause is not to be subjected to reasonableness limitations. In *Welch v Royal Exchange Assurance*[91] the assured under a fire policy was obliged to submit to the insurer "all such proofs and information as may reasonably be required". Following a loss, the insurers demanded details of various bank accounts; the assured asserted that the accounts were of no materiality to the loss and refused to provide any information. The Court of Appeal, despite acknowledging the immateriality of the information, held that the assured had been in breach of a condition precedent.

It would seem, however, that the balance of authority, particularly more recent authority, denies that the insurer has an absolute right to demand information, and that there are reasonableness limitations. In *Moore v Woolsey*[92] the insurers refused to make payment under a life policy on the basis that satisfactory proof of the claimant's interest under the policy had not been presented. The Court rejected this argument, and held that "all that can be necessary is that proof shall be shown to have been laid before them which reasonable men would be satisfied, and then the inference arises that the proof was to their satisfaction". Tuckey J., in *Napier v UNUM Ltd*[93] felt able to state that "the English cases establish that the insurers' requirements for vouching [what insurers may require as proof of the claim, in the sense of what evidence they can call for to support it] must be reasonable."[94] The point has also arisen in the context of liability insurance, the courts holding that insurers cannot exercise their rights to demand information which is unconnected with claims against the assured.[95] In *Widefree Ltd v Brit Insurance Ltd*,[96] a property insurance case, the assured informed the insurers' loss adjuster that there had been five CCTV cameras in operation at the time of the alleged theft and that the police had advised that only the footage from camera 2 was likely to be of assistance: that had been downloaded and was given to the adjuster. Some weeks later, and after the footage from the other cameras had been wiped, the insurers relied upon breach of the claims co-operation clause in that the assured had failed to provide footage from the other cameras. Peter Leaver QC ruled that, while there might have been an initial

[91] *Welch v Royal Exchange Assurance* [1939] 1 K.B. 294. See also *Wilkinson v Car & General Insurance Co Ltd* (1913) 110 L.T. 468.
[92] *Moore v Woolsey* (1854) 8 E. & B. 243. Cf. *Braunstein v Accidental Death Insurance Co* (1861) 1 B. & S. 782.
[93] *Napier v UNUM Ltd* [1996] 2 Lloyd's Rep. 550.
[94] *Napier v UNUM Ltd* [1996] 2 Lloyd's Rep. 550 at 556. The point was common ground in *Super Chem Products Ltd v American Life and General insurance Co* [2004] Lloyd's Rep. I.R. 446.
[95] *Quinn Direct Insurance Ltd v The Law Society of England and Wales* [2010] EWCA Civ 647. Insurers are also unable to demand privileged information: see *Brown v Guardian Royal Exchange Assurance Plc* Unreported, 1992.
[96] *Widefree Ltd v Brit Insurance Ltd* [2009] EWHC 3671 (QB).

obligation on the assured to retain all footage and other evidence which he reasonably believed might be relevant to the claim, failure by the adjuster to request further footage at the relevant time rendered it unreasonable for the insurers to revert to the point at a later date. It was not the obligation of the assured to attempt to guess what the insurers might want.

In consumer cases, it is now a criminal offence for insurers to require the assured to produce documents which cannot reasonably be relevant for determining whether a claim is valid.[97]

Proof of loss is one matter; the further question is whether it is possible for the assured to challenge the insurers' evaluation of the evidence presented to them. There is old authority for the proposition that all that is required of insurers is to act bona fides in assessing the evidence,[98] although more recently[99] it has been determined that the test was neither reasonableness nor bona fides, but the intermediate position that a decision of insurers in their evaluation of proof of loss could be challenged before a court, and that it was for the court itself to decide whether or not, as a matter of fact, the assured had established his loss.

3. FRAUDULENT CLAIMS

9–020 **Introduction.** A key principle of insurance law is that the assured is under a duty not to submit a fraudulent claim to his insurers. The legal basis of that duty—and therefore of the consequences of a fraudulent claim—has proved to be elusive, for the reason that the early decisions on fraudulent claims, and many of the recent decisions, turned upon the wording of express clauses. A typical fraudulent claim clause provides that in the event of a fraudulent claim the assured is to forfeit all benefit under the policy; it is sometimes further stated that the policy becomes void. While the use of these clauses obviated the need for the courts to develop their own principles of law applicable to fraud, the courts simply assumed that the position at common law was reproduced by them. It was indeed said by Willes J. in *Britton v Royal Insurance Co*[100] that the usual form of wording was "in accordance with legal principle and sound policy". Unfortunately this takes the matter no further, for it does not specify the common law basis on which the assured is to forfeit all benefit under the policy, nor does it make clear what forfeiture of all benefit actually means.

The meaning and duration of a "claim"

9–021 *First party policies.* The word "claim" as generally understood in insurance law is a demand for payment. In the case of a first party policy, the assured makes a claim by demanding payment from the insurers. It may be that the amount of the claim cannot be quantified at the outset, but this does not prevent a claim from

---

[97] Consumer Protection from Unfair Trading Regulations 2008 (SI 2008/1277), implementing European Parliament and Council Directive 2005/29/EC concerning unfair commercial practices. The Directive requires controls to be imposed over "aggressive practices" in financial services contracts, one illustration of which is "a consumer who wishes to claim on an insurance policy to produce documents which could not reasonably be considered relevant as to whether the claim was valid".

[98] *Manby v Gresham Life Assurance Co* (1861) 4 L.T. 347. See also *Teur v London Life Insurance Co* [1936] 1 D.L.R. 161.

[99] *Napier v UNUM Ltd* [1996] 2 Lloyd's Rep. 550.

[100] (1866) 4 F. & F. 905 at 909. See also: *Worsley v Wood* (1796) 6 T.R. 710; *Goulstone v Royal Insurance* (1858) 1 F. & F. 276; *Norton v Royal Insurance* (1885) 1 T.L.R. 460.

coming into existence at the early stage when an initial demand is made. If it is the case that the law prohibits a fraudulent "claim" it is necessary to define the claim itself. If the assured is aware that he has not suffered any loss (or a smaller loss) when the initial demand for payment is made, or if that loss has been deliberately self-inflicted, then it is clear that the initial demand is of itself a fraudulent claim. The difficulty arising here is that there is plenty of scope for the making of false statements to insurers following the initial demand, which will ordinarily be followed by further negotiation, including the submission of receipts, invoices or other proofs of loss. In addition, the assured may act fraudulently if his claim is rejected and legal proceedings are commenced by him against the insurers.

Turning first to the question of subsequent fraud independently of judicial proceedings, it was decided in *Agapitos v Agnew*[101] that a claim can be fraudulent by reason of the assured's post-loss conduct even if the loss itself was perfectly genuine. Here, the assured's vessel was damaged by fire. The defendant underwriters, who had insured the vessel against hull and machinery port risks, failed to make payment and the assured commenced proceedings. The policy contained a warranty that prevented the assured from carrying out "hot work" on the vessel without certain conditions having first been satisfied. The claim, which admittedly fell within the scope of the policy so was to that extent perfectly genuine, was denied on the basis that the fire had been caused by hot works carried out in breach of warranty. The assured maintained, in assertions as to the timings of the hot works, that the hot works had not been carried out in breach of warranty. At first instance Toulson J. ruled that there was no authority to support the proposition that an assured who told lies to support a genuine claim was in the same position as an assured who advanced a fraudulently exaggerated claim. The claim itself was to be regarded as the initial demand for payment, and subsequent false statements did not transmogrify that genuine demand into a fraudulent claim unless those statements were such as to transform the essential basis of his claim, as would be the case where the assured "chooses to invent and put forward to the underwriters a different account of the loss", as such invention "might reasonably be regarded as putting forward a claim of an essentially different and dishonest kind". Toulson J.'s view was that the line had not been crossed in the present case. That analysis was rejected on appeal by the Court of Appeal. Mance L.J. ruled that a genuine claim was nevertheless to be treated as having been made fraudulently if the assured chose to support his initial demand with fraudulent statements designed to improve, and objectively capable of improving, his prospects of effecting recovery. On that basis, if there had been any fraudulent statements made following the initial claim, the underwriters were entitled to raise those statements by way of defence.

If it is the case that post-loss fraud can give rise to a fraudulent claim, it is necessary to determine the point at which fraud ceases to be operative. The cases indicate that this will occur either when the parties settle their dispute, or when legal proceedings are commenced. The former possibility was considered in *Direct Line Insurance Plc v Fox*.[102] Here, the assured's house was damaged by fire. Various sums were paid to the assured, and ultimately the parties entered into a settlement agreement concerning repairs to the assured's kitchen. Under that agreement the assured was to be paid "£46,524.50 in full settlement and discharge of all my Buildings claims under your Policy . . . I understand that my

---

[101] *Agapitos v Agnew* [2002] Lloyd's Rep. I.R. 191, affirmed on other grounds [2002] Lloyd's Rep. I.R. 573.

[102] *Direct Line Insurance Plc v Fox* [2010] Lloyd's Rep. I.R. 324.

Insurers will make an interim payment of £42,412.00, followed by a final payment of £4,112.50, subject to me providing invoices demonstrating my outlay in respect of the VAT element of replacement bespoke kitchen which will be manufactured by Darren Brett Furniture Ltd." The assured duly submitted an invoice from Darren Brett showing that that firm had done the work and that VAT of £4,112.50 had been paid. In fact the document was false, and probably forged. The insurers sought to recover all of the sums paid in respect of the fire. It was nevertheless held by H.H. Judge Seymour QC that the assured had not made a fraudulent claim. The settlement had disposed of the claim, and the submission of an invoice showing VAT was simply a condition precedent to the assured being entitled to recover that amount: by submitting a false receipt the assured had not made a fraudulent claim but had simply failed to comply with the condition precedent. The only consequence was that the assured could not recover that additional sum

The effect of the commencement of legal proceedings was considered in *Agapitos v Agnew*,[103] the basic facts of which were given above. The insurers in addition sought to rely upon allegedly false statements made by the assured about the hot works after the assured had commenced proceedings against the insurers in respect of the claim under the policy. The Court of Appeal, rejecting the fraudulent claim argument, held that the rules relating to fraudulent claims came to an end as soon as proceedings had commenced, as at that point the court's own rules relating to disclosure under the Civil Procedure Rules and to perjury took over, and it was not open to underwriters to rely upon alleged fraud in the judicial proceedings in order to assert contractual or related rights.[104] With regard to post-proceedings fraud, the Court of Appeal sought to bring the law into line with the rules relating to the continuing duty of utmost good faith. Insofar as the assured is under a continuing duty of utmost good faith—and such duty has no part to play in the law relating to fraudulent claims[105]—the House of Lords held in *The Star Sea*[106] that the duty comes to an end as soon as proceedings are commenced and that any post-action failure to disclose is a matter for the rules of court.[107] The Court of Appeal in *Agapitos* felt that it would not be sensible to draw a distinction between fraudulent claims and the continuing duty of utmost good faith in this regard, and that both duties came to an end on the commencement of proceedings.

The position of fraud between the making of the initial demand for payment and the commencement of proceedings is more problematic. In *The Litsion Pride*[108] Hirst J. had ruled that an assured who had acted fraudulently by allowing his vessel to enter a war zone without informing the underwriters at the time, and then by making a declaration after the loss had occurred that purported to date from the time when the vessel entered the war zone, was guilty of a breach of the continuing duty of utmost good faith by reason of a fraudulent claim. In *The Star Sea* Lord Hobhouse overruled *The Litsion Pride* in part on the basis that:

[103] *Agapitos v Agnew* [2002] Lloyd's Rep. I.R. 573.
[104] Presumably the same position attains in arbitration.
[105] So held in *Agapitos* itself.
[106] *The Star Sea* [2001] Lloyd's Rep. I.R. 247.
[107] It had been assumed in earlier cases that fraud by the assured following the commencement of proceedings was a matter that gave a right to avoid the policy, but these cases cannot stand with *The Star Sea*. For the old view, see: *Transthene Packaging v Royal Insurance* [1996] L.R.L.R. 32; *Insurance Corp of the Channel Islands v Royal Hotel and McHugh (No.1)* [1997] L.R.L.R. 94; *Baghbadrani v Commercial Union Assurance Co* [2000] Lloyd's Rep. I.R. 94. See also *The Ainikolas I* (1996) *Lloyd's List*, April 5.
[108] *The Litsion Pride* [1985] 2 Lloyd's Rep. 437.

" ... the actual claim was valid claim for a loss which had occurred and had been caused by peril insured against when the vessel was covered by a held covered clause."

There is no indication in this statement by Lord Hobhouse that he regarded the claim in *The Litsion Pride* as fraudulent, although his Lordship did leave open the possibility that the underwriters may have had other—unspecified—grounds for denying liability. It may indeed be that the apppropriate criticism of *The Litsion Pride* in *The Star Sea*, taken with the ruling in *Agapitos*, relates to the reliance by Hirst J. on the notion that a fraudulent claim formed part of the continuing duty of utmost good faith, and that the result in *The Litsion Pride* holds good on the rather different basis that there had been a fraudulent claim by the submission of false information in support of a genuine claim.

Liability policies. The issues raised by a liability policy are rather different, as the process will generally be initiated by a notification by the assured to the insurers of circumstances likely to give rise to a claim, in due course followed by an actual claim against the assured which is notified to the insurers. Ultimately, there will be a judgment, award or settlement in favour of the third party which the insurers are required to meet. Isolating the "claim" against the insurers from this chain of events is not free from difficulty. It might be thought that there is a claim against them at the very latest when the assured notifies the insurers of the fact that there has been a claim against him, as virtually all liability policies at that stage provide for involvement by the insurers in the negotiations with the third party and liability for defence costs. However, it was held in *K/S Merc Skandia XXXXII v Certain Lloyd's Underwriters*[109] that there cannot be a claim until the assured has suffered a loss, and that this occurs only when the assured's liability has been established and quantified by judgment, award or settlement. The assured in this case entered into an agreement with the third party claimant for the action to be heard in England, but the assured subsequently sought to resile from this agreement when it became apparent that proceedings in Trinidad, the assured's domicile, might result in a lesser damages award. To this end the assured produced a document which purported to negative the jurisdiction agreement, and it was only after the insurers had taken steps to stay the English proceedings that it became clear that the document was false and that the jurisdiction agreement was valid. The Court of Appeal held that the assured had been in breach of the claims co-operation clause, although this was not a defence to his claim for indemnification under the policy as it was not a condition precedent and there had been no repudiation of the policy. The underwriters did not rely upon the fraudulent claims clause, and it was assumed by the Court of Appeal that this was the correct approach given that there had not been any claim made by assured at the relevant time. It may be commented that this reasoning is inconsistent with *Walker v Pennine Insurance Co Ltd*,[110] where it was held that a one-year limitation period running from the rejection of the assured's claim under a liability policy barred an action by the assured even though judgment was not given until much later.

The meaning of fraud

Statutory definition. The word "fraud" was given a statutory definition by the Fraud Act 2006. Three forms of fraud are recognised by the legislation.

9–022

9–023

---

[109] *K/S Merc Skandia XXXXII v Certain Lloyd's Underwriters* [2001] 1 Lloyd's Rep. 802.
[110] *Walker v Pennine Insurance Co Ltd* [1980] 2 Lloyd's Rep. 156.

The first type is fraud by false representation. Under s.2(1) of the 2006 Act there is fraud if a person:

"(a) dishonestly makes a false representation, and
(b) intends, by making the representation—
    (i) to make a gain for himself or another, or
    (ii) to cause loss to another or to expose another to a risk of loss."

A representation is false if it is untrue or misleading and the person making it knows that it is, or might be, untrue or misleading (s.2(2)). A "representation" is any representation as to fact or law, including a representation as to the state of mind of the person making the representation, or of any other person (s.2(3)). A representation may be express or implied (s.2(4)) and it may be made electronically (s.2(5)).

The second type of fraud is by failure to disclose information. Under s.3(1) there is fraud if a person:

"(a) dishonestly fails to disclose to another person information which he is under a legal duty to disclose, and
(b) intends, by failing to disclose the information—
    (i) to make a gain for himself or another, or
    (ii) to cause loss to another or to expose another to a risk of loss."

Thirdly fraud may take place, under s.4, where a person occupies a position in which he is expected to safeguard, or not to act against, the financial interests of another person, and he dishonestly abuses that position.

In each of these situations, the terms "gain" and "loss" mean gain or loss in money or other property (s.5).

9–024 *Definition for insurance purposes.* A claim can only be fraudulent if the assured is dishonest or at the very least culpably reckless.[111] Mere negligence on the part of the assured will not suffice.[112] The fraud must be that of the assured himself[113] and not that of a third party for whom the assured is not responsible. Within an organisation this principle will raise a question of imputation of knowledge. An assured is, however, responsible for the fraud of an agent acting within the scope of his authority.[114]

In *Agapitos v Agnew*[115] Mance L.J. reviewed the authorities and concluded that fraudulent claims fell into the following five categories: (1) the assured had

---

[111] In England the Fraud Act 2006 recognises three forms of fraud, where a person: (1) dishonestly makes a false representation, and intends, by making the representation to make a gain for himself or another, or to cause loss to another or to expose another to a risk of loss (s.2); dishonestly fails to disclose to another person information which he is under a legal duty to disclose, intends, by failing to disclose the information to make a gain for himself or another, or to cause loss to another or to expose another to a risk of loss (s.3); or occupies a position in which he is expected to safeguard, or not to act against, the financial interests of another person, and he dishonestly abuses that position (s.4).

[112] *Royal Boskalis v Mountain* [1997] L.R.L.R. 523; *Alfred McAlpine Plc v BAI (Run-off) Ltd* [2000] Lloyd's Rep. I.R. 352; *The Star Sea* [2001] Lloyd's Rep. I.R. 247; *Tonkin v UK Insurance Ltd* [2007] Lloyd's Rep. I.R. 283; *US Trading Ltd v Axa Insurance Co Ltd* [2010] Lloyd's Rep. I.R. 505. Earlier cases, suggesting a lower standard (based on the now discredited notion that a fraudulent claims fall within the duty of utmost good faith—see below) are no longer of good authority. See: *Bucks Printing Press Ltd v Prudential Assurance Co* [2000] C.L.Y. 880; *Hussain v Brown (No.2)* Unreported, 1996; *Parker & Heard Ltd v Assicurazioni Generali SpA* Unreported, 1998.

[113] *Sumpiles Investments Pte Ltd v Axa Insurance Singapore Pte Ltd* [2006] 3 S.L.R. 12.

[114] *Direct Line Insurance v Khan* [2002] Lloyd's Rep. I.R. 364.

[115] *Agapitos v Agnew* [2002] Lloyd's Rep. I.R. 573.

suffered no loss; (2) the assured's loss was less than had been claimed; (3) the assured believed at the time of his claim that he had suffered a loss, but, having subsequently discovered that he had suffered no loss at all or a loss smaller than that claimed for, failed to correct the loss; (4) the assured had suffered a genuine loss but had suppressed a defence known to him which might be available to insurers; (5) the assured had furthered a genuine claim by the use of fraudulent means or devices.

These categories are considered in detail in the following paragraphs. As a preliminary point, it should be noted that frauds of types (2)–(5) all presuppose that the assured has suffered a genuine loss, but has subsequently committed fraud in relation to that loss. As long as the fraud is substantial, it is clear that, at the very least, the entire claim is lost. Taking these principles together, the types of fraud recognised in *Agapitos* can be relevant only if the subsequent fraud is backdated to the date of the loss itself, and is treated as tainting the entire loss. It follows that, if the assured commits a later fraud following a genuine loss, then: (a) he cannot recover anything at all; (b) he must repay the full amount if he has been paid after the fraud; and (c) he must still repay the full amount if he has been paid on an interim basis before the fraud.[116]

(1) Absence of insured loss. This category encompasses two situations: that in **9–025** which the assured has suffered no loss at all; and that in which the assured has incurred a self-inflicted loss.

The proposition that it is fraud for the assured to assert that he has suffered a loss which has not taken place is an obvious one which is illustrated by numerous authorities.[117]

Deliberate destruction by the assured of the insured subject matter cannot be the basis for a claim by the assured himself on a number of grounds: destruction is an extreme example of wilful misconduct, recovery for which is prohibited by s.55(2)(a) of the Marine Insurance Act 1906; the essence of insurance is contingency, so that recovery for destruction is contrary to the nature of insurance; and any claim submitted following deliberate destruction by the assured is of itself fraudulent. It may matter which of these grounds is relied upon by the insurers, as the remedies for a fraudulent claim may go beyond a simple denial of liability for the claim itself. However, in practice the defences stand and fall together and the only question is whether the insurers can prove that the loss was self-induced, bearing in mind that the civil burden of proof becomes greater along with the seriousness of the misconduct alleged.[118] The courts will be

---

[116] *Axa General Insurance Ltd v Gottlieb* [2005] Lloyd's Rep. I.R. 369.

[117] *Britton v Royal Insurance Co* (1866) 4 F. & F. 905; *Phillips v Chapman* (1921) 7 Ll. L.R. 139; *Harris v Sturge* (1923) 14 Ll. L.R. 20; *Albion Mills Ltd Hill* (1922) 12 Ll. L.R. 96; *Cuppitman v Marshall* (1924) I5 Ll. L.R. 277; *Herman v Phoenix Assurance Co Ltd* (1924) 18 Ll. L.R. 371.

[118] *Piper v Royal Exchange Assurance* (1932) 44 Ll. L.R. 103; *Herbert v Poland* (1932) 44 Ll. L.R. 139; *Shoot v Hill* (1936) 55 Ll. L.R. 29; *Hornal v Neuberger Products* [1957] 1 Q.B. 247; *Grunther Industrial Derelopments Ltd v Federated Employers Insurance Association Ltd* [1976] 2 Lloyd's Rep. 259; *Watkins & Davis Ltd v Legal and General Assurance Co Ltd* [1981] 1 Lloyd's Rep. 674; *Broughton Park Textiles (Services) Ltd v Commercial Union Assurance Co Ltd* [1981] 1 Lloyd's Rep. 94; *S & M Carpets (London) Ltd v Cornhill Insurance Co Ltd* [1981] 1 Lloyd's Rep. 667; *Watkins & Davies Ltd v Legal and General Assurance Co Ltd* [1981] 1 Lloyd's Rep. 674; *Exchange Theatres Ltd v Iron Trades Mutual Insurance Co Ltd* [1983] I Lloyd's Rep. 674; *Polvitte v Commercial Union Assurance* [1987] 1 Lloyd's Rep. 379; *McGregor v Prudential Insurance Co* [1998] 1 Lloyd's Rep. 112: *Davies and Cranton v Royal Insurance Plc* Unreported, 1998; *James v CGU Insurance Plc* [2002] Lloyd's Rep. I.R. 206. See also *Patel v Windsor Life Assurance Co Ltd* [2008] Lloyd's Rep. I.R. 359 (a claim under a life policy where it was not shown that the life assured had actually died); *S-B (Children)* [2009] UKSC 17.

reluctant to reach a finding of fraud by inference: thus, the fact that there is apparent explanation for the casualty which has caused the assured's loss cannot justify a finding of fraud, at least in the absence of evidence that the assured had a strong motive for bringing about the loss.[118a] Failure by the assured to take elementary steps to prevent a minor event escalating into serious damage may itself amount to fraud.[119]

The cases illustrate the types of factors which may give rise to suspicion of deliberate destruction. The majority of cases involve the scuttling of ships, and in that context relevant matters include: (1) the circumstances of the loss, including the sea conditions, the conduct of the crew and the apparent preparedness of the crew, to abandon the vessel with all their belongings neatly packed following a sudden loss; (2) the opportunities for complicity between the master and crew; (3) the financial position of the assured, in particular whether the vessel was important to the assured's continuing business; (4) the age of the vessel and whether it was overinsured; (5) the conduct of the parties following the casualty, for example whether assistance was refused, whether there is consistent evidence of the circumstances of the loss and whether any attempt was made by the assured to investigate the circumstances of the loss; and (6) the reliability or otherwise of navigational aids.[120] Equivalent considerations are applicable in non-marine insurance. In an arson case the court will take into account whether the assured had prepared the ground for a fraudulent claim by reporting to the police threats of arson, the number of seats of fire, the absence of receipts for allegedly lost property and the financial position of the assured immediately before the fire.[121]

9–026   *(2) Exaggerated loss.* The amount of a loss may be inflated by the assured for a number of reasons: the assured may be seeking to make a profit from his loss; he may be presenting a "bargaining" claim in the belief that the ultimate compromise agreement reached with the insurer will approximately represent his

---

[118a] *Yeganeh v Zurich Plc* [2010] EWHC 1185 (QB).

[119] *James v CGU Insurance Plc* [2002] Lloyd's Rep. I.R. 206. There is, however, no general duty on the assured to mitigate a loss: *Yorkshire Water Services v Sun Alliance* [1997] 2 Lloyd's Rep. 21.

[120] *Bowring v Elmslie* (1790) 7 T.R. 216n; *Visscherij Maatschappij Nieuwe Onderneming v Scottish Metropolitan Assurance Co* (1922) 10 Ll. L.R. 579; *Colouras v British General Insurance Co Ltd* (1922) 12 Ll. L.R. 220; *Dorigo y Sanudo v Royal Exchange Assurance Corporation* (1922) 12 Ll. L.R. 126; *Ansolega y Cia v Indemnity Mutual Marine Insurance Co* (1922) 13 Ll. L.R. 231; *De Mario & Gazan v Scottish Metropolitan Assurance Co* (1923) 14 Ll. L.R. 220; *Elfie A Issaias v Marine Insurance Co* (1923) 15 Ll. L.R. 186; *Communidad Naviera Baracaldo v Norwich Union Fire Insurance Society* (1923) 16 Ll. L.R. 45; *Anghelatos v Northern Assurance Co (The Olympia)* (1924) 19 Ll. L.R. 255; *Compania Naviera Martiartu v Royal Exchange Assurance Corporation* (1924) 19 Ll. L.R. 95; *Société d'Avances Commerciales v Merchants Marine Insurance Co* (1924) 20 Ll. L.R. 74; *Domingo Mumbru SA v Laurie* (1924) 20 Ll. L.R. 122; *Banco de Barcelona v Union Marine Insurance Co Ltd* (1925) 22 Ll. L.R. 209; *Empire Steamship Co Inc v Threadneedle Insurance Co* (1925) 22 Ll. L.R. 437; *Lemos v British and Foreign Marine Insurance Co Ltd* (1931) 39 Ll. L.R. 275; *Piper v Royal Exchange Assurance* (1932) 42 Ll. L.R. 103; *Pateras v Royal Exchange Assurance* (1934) 49 Ll. L.R. 400; *Grouds v Dearsley* (1935) 51 Ll. L.R. 203; *Mans v London Assurance* (1935) 52 Ll. L.R. 211; *Compania Naviera Vascongada v British & Foreign Marine Insurance Co Ltd* (1936) 54 Ll. L.R. 35; *Canning v Maritime Insurance Co Ltd* (1936) 56 Ll. L.R. 91; *Bank of Athens v Royal Exchange Assurance* (1937) 59 Ll. L.R. 67; *Compania Naviera Santi SA v Indemnity Marine Insurance Co Ltd* [1960] 2 Lloyd's Rep. 469; *Astrovlanis Compania Naviera v Linard (The Gold Sky)* [1972] 2 Lloyd's Rep. 186; *Piermay Shipping Co SA v Chester (The Michael)* [1979] 2 Lloyd's Rep. 1; *Michalos & Sons v Prudential Assurance Co Ltd* [1984] 2 Lloyd's Rep. 264; *The Captain Panagos DP* [1986] 2 Lloyd's Rep. 470; *The Ikarian Reefer* [1992] 2 Lloyd's Rep. 68; *Brownsville Holdings Ltd v Adanijee Insurance Co Ltd* [2000] 2 Lloyd's Rep. 458.

[121] *McGregor v Prudential Insurance Co Ltd* [1988] 1 Lloyd's Rep. 112; *James v CGU Insurance* [2002] Lloyd's Rep. I.R. 206.

actual loss; or he may genuinely have overestimated the value of his property by, for example, including an element for consequential loss not covered by the policy. It is established that the mere fact that a claim has been inflated is not conclusive evidence of fraud and that bargaining claims and innocent over-valuation will not defeat the assured.[122] In the absence of independent evidence of the assured's state of mind, the decisive dividing factor between fraud and innocence will generally be the degree to which the claim has been inflated, as the greater the inflation the easier it becomes to impute a fraudulent intent to the assured. Thus, a hundredfold exaggeration of the degree of loss will be fraudulent,[123] as will a claim for the purchase price of goods which were at the time of the loss seriously defective[124] or of goods which the assured did not actually lose,[125] whereas a claim for the value of new goods under a policy which provides cover for replacement value only is a bargaining claim and cannot be regarded as fraud.[126] A claim for economic loss will be fraudulent if the loss was never sustained[127] or if the figures provided by the assured in respect of anticipated loss have been exaggerated.[128] There is no fraud where an assured seeks indemnification for lost goods which he has, after the occurrence of the insured peril, replaced at his own cost.[129]

If a claim is partly genuine and partly fraudulent, it is not possible to sever the fraud from the rest of the claim, unless the assured has suffered two entirely separate losses and there is only fraud in relation to one of them.[130] Accordingly, if the fraud is substantial the entire claim will be lost.[131] In determining

---

[122] *London Assurance v Clare* (1937) 57 Ll. L.R. 254; *Nsubuga v Commercial Union Assurance Co Plc* [1998] 2 Lloyd's Rep. 682; *Horne v Norwich Union Insurance Ltd* Unreported, July 2005.

[123] *Central Bank of India v Guardian Assurance Co* (1934) 54 Ll. L.R. 247. See also *Levy v Baillie* (1831) 7 Bing. 349; *Gonlstone v Royal Insurance Co* (1858) 1 F. & F. 276; *Chapman v Pole* (1870) 22 L.T. 306; *Beauchamp v Faber* (1898) 3 Com. Cas. 308; *Harris v Evans* (1924) 19 Ll. L.R. 303; *Herman v Phoenix Assurance* (1924) 8 Ll. L.R. 371; *Shoot v Hill* (1936) 55 Ll. L.R. 29; *Dome Mining Corporation Ltd v Drysdale* (1936) 41 Ll. L.R. 109: *Orakpo v Barclays Insurance Services Ltd* [1995] L.R.L.R. 443; *Hector Hunter Furs v Independent Insurance Ltd* Unreported, 1998; *Danepoint Ltd v Underwriting Insurance Ltd* [2005] EWHC 2318 (TCC).

[124] *Transthene Packaging Co Ltd v Royal Insurance (UK) Ltd* [1996] L.R.L.R. 32.

[125] *Lek v Matthews* (1927) 9 Ll. L.R. 141; *Galloway v Guardian Royal Exchange (UK) Ltd* [1999] L.R.L.R. 209.

[126] *Ewer v National Employers Mutual General Insurance Association* [1937] 2 All E.R. 193; *Norton v Royal life Assurance Co* (1885) 1 T.L.R. 460; *Hodgkins v Wrightson, The Times*, March 24, 1910.

[127] *Direct Line v Khan* [2002] Lloyd's Rep. I.R. 151; *Micro Design Group Ltd v Norwich Union Insurance Ltd* [2005] EWHC 3093 (TCC); *Axa Insurance Ltd v Gottlieb* [2005] Lloyd's Rep. I.R. 369.

[128] *Insurance Corporation of the Channel Islands Ltd v McHugh (No.1)* [1997] L.R.L.R. 94.

[129] *Tonkin v UK Insurance Ltd* [2006] EWHC 1120 (TCC).

[130] *Danepoint Ltd v Underwriting Insurance Ltd* [2006] Lloyd's Rep. I.R. 429, an argument not made out on the facts. It is apparent that the assured cannot take advantage of this principle by an arbitrary subdivision of what is in reality a single claim. In *Yeganeh v Zurich plc* [2010] EWHC 1185 (QB) it was assumed without argument that a claim under a combined property and contents insurance was a single claim, so that although the assured suffered a genuine fire to his house, costing some £270,000 to reinstate, a claim in respect of contents to the value of £12,465, some of which was fraudulent, led to the loss of the claim in its entirety.

[131] *Galloway v Guardian Royal Exchange (UK) Ltd* [1999] L.R.L.R. 209; *Nsubuga v Commercial Union Assurance Co Plc* [1998] 2 Lloyd's Rep. 682; *Baghbadrani v Commercial Union Assurance Co Plc* [2000] Lloyd's Rep. I.R. 94; *Direct Line v Khan* [2002] Lloyd's Rep. I.R. 151; *Micro Design Group Ltd v Norwich Union Insurance Ltd* [2005] EWHC 3093 (TCC); *Axa Insurance Ltd v Gottlieb* [2005] Lloyd's Rep. I.R. 369. Suggestions in *Orakpo v Barclays Insurance Servcies Ltd* [1995] L.R.L.R. 443, followed in *Transthene Packaging Co Ltd v Royal Insurance (UK) Ltd* [1996] L.R.L.R. 32, that a fraudulent claim was apportionable and that the assured was entitled to recover for his actual loss despite exaggeration, were rejected in the later cases on the ground that that rule would not remove any disincentive to dishonesty.

substantiality, it is necessary to "consider the fraudulent claim as if it were the only claim and then to consider whether, taken in isolation, the making of that claim by the insured is sufficiently serious to justify stigmatising it as fraud."[132] The test is not, therefore, whether the proportion of the claim which is fraudulent is sufficiently large, but whether the amount of the fraud is in absolute terms enough to justify a refusal of the entire claim. However, there is some authority for the proposition that fraud which amounts to only a tiny proportion of the genuine loss is to be disregarded, even though the sum itself is a significant one.[133]

9–027   *(3) Subsequent discovery that no loss, or lesser loss, had been suffered.* The principle, that an assured who submits a claim and then discovers that he has suffered no loss (or a smaller loss) is fraud, has to be treated with some caution. The proposition is not obviously correct where the assured has lost property which is restored to or found by him prior to payment by the insurers: in such a case the fraud is not persisting with the insurance claim, but rather in failing to disclose to the insurers that the property has been restored. It is at least arguable that the rights of the parties are fixed at the latest when a claim form is issued, so that the restoration or finding of the lost property leaves the claim unaffected and the assured has the right to continue his claim for the insurance moneys, What constitutes fraud in such a case is not pursuing the insurance claim as such, but failing to disclose to the insurers that the property has been recovered, thereby depriving the insurers of their right of salvage.

9–028   *(4) Suppression of defence.* If the assured deliberately suppresses a defence which he knows to be open to insurers, his claim is fraudulent. In some cases this head of fraud overlaps with those earlier discussed, as where the assured's deliberate act has given rise to the loss but the claim is presented as if the loss had been fortuitous.[134] It might be thought that this head of fraud is superfluous, in that the insurers have their independent defence to fall back on, although the better view is that the insurers should have the right to elect between the fraudulent claim defence and the suppressed defence given that the consequences of the two may be quite different.[135]

9–029   *(5) Use of fraudulent means or devices.* Insurers are entitled to treat a claim as fraudulent if it has been furthered by the use of fraudulent means or devices, even if the loss itself was a genuine one and caused by an insured peril.[136] The phrase "fraudulent means or devices" is derived from the old form of fraudulent claims clause in use in the London market since the nineteenth century. It has been held that a deliberate false statement by the assured as to the cause of his loss amounts to fraudulent claim as it may well induce the insurer to pay out for the occurrence of a peril outside the policy.[137] Again, it has been held that a property insurer may refuse to pay where the assured falsely stated that his burglar alarm was set at the

[132] *Galloway v Guardian Royal Exchange (UK) Ltd* [1999] L.R.L.R. 209.
[133] *Tonkin v UK Insurance Ltd* [2007] Lloyd's Rep. I.R. 283, where a fraudulent claim in the sum of £2000 was held not to be substantial given that it amounted to only 0.3 per cent of the total loss.
[134] *Total Graphics Ltd v AGF Insurance Ltd* [1997] 1 Lloyd's Rep. 599.
[135] *Agapitos v Agnew* [2002] Lloyd's Rep. I.R. 573.
[136] The same result may be achieved by express term: *Cox v Orion Insurance Co Ltd* [1982] R.T.R. 1.
[137] *Thompson v Hopper* (1856) 6 E. & E. 172.

time of the loss[138] or where the assured falsely stated after the loss that he had not attempted to sell the premises before the loss but in fact had attempted to do so.[139] Equally, a goods in transit insurer may refuse to pay where the assured has falsely stated that the goods were properly packed and secured for the purposes of the journey[140] and a marine insurer can refuse payment under a valued policy where the insured subject matter was overvalued and the assured produced a series of forged documents designed to justify the agreed valuation.[141]

It is clear from Mance L.J.'s judgment in *Agapitos v Agnew* that not every false statement made by the assured in support of his claim will taint the entire claim. For there to be fraud, a false statement must be: (i) directly related to the claim; (ii) intended to improve the assured's prospects of obtaining a settlement or winning the case; and (iii) if believed, objectively capable of yielding a not insignificant improvement in the assured's prospects of obtaining a settlement or better settlement. These conditions are perhaps not as onerous as might at first sight appear, in that if the assured makes a false statement as to the circumstances of the loss to insurers not because he wishes to increase his prospects of recovery, but because he does not wish to admit—by reason of embarrassment—the actual reason for the loss, then it is at least arguable that condition (ii) (and possibly also condition (iii)) is not met. The first of the conditions, the need for a causal link between the fraud and the claim, also operates to limit the circumstances in which insurers may deny liability, as where the owners of insured goods forged a certificate of inspection to substantiate their title to the goods.[142] It is irrelevant to a finding of the use of fraudulent means or devices that the assured's lie has unravelled before any settlement or during the course of the trial.[143]

It is unclear whether the use of fraudulent means or devices is confined to the situation in which the assured makes false statements to the insurers, or whether it also imposes some form of disclosure obligation.[144]

Inducement. It is unclear whether a claim is to be regarded as fraudulent only   **9–030**
if it has induced the insurers to enter into a settlement with the agreement. It might be thought that the principle underlying the rule that fraud defeats a claim, that fraud is to be discouraged, is undermined if inducement is a requirement, and there is authority rejecting the need for inducement.[145] However, in *Danepoint Ltd v Underwriting Insurance Ltd*[146] it was held that inducement was required. In this case the assured's block of flats was damaged by fire, and substantially exaggerated claims were submitted for the cost of repairs and also for loss of rental income. H.H. Judge Coulson QC held that the former claim was not fraudulent because the insurers' loss adjusters had inspected the building and had ascertained the building costs for themselves. By contrast, the latter claim was fraudulent because the number of flats which had remained occupied after the fire

---

[138] *Shoot v Hill* (1936) 55 Ll. L.R. 29.

[139] *Stemson v AMP General Insurance (NZ) Ltd* [2006] UKPC 30.

[140] *Bucks Printing Press Ltd v Prudential Assurance Co* [2000] C.L.Y. 880.

[141] *Eagle Star Insurance Co Ltd v Games Video Co (GVC) SA (The Game Boy)* [2004] Lloyd's Rep. I.R. 867.

[142] *Intgerpart Comerciao e Gestaao SA v Lexington Insurance Co* [2004] Lloyd's Rep. I.R. 690.

[143] A statement made by Mance L.J. in *Agapitos* and confirmed by the Privy Council in *Stemson v AMP General Insurance (NZ) Ltd* [2006] Lloyd's Rep. I.R. 852.

[144] See *Marc Rich Agriculture Trading SA v Fortis Corporate Insurance NV* [2005] Lloyd's Rep. I.R. 396, where Cooke J. decided that the defence should not be struck out.

[145] *Interpart Comerciao e Gestao SA v Lexington Insurance Co* [2004] Lloyd's Rep. I.R. 690.

[146] *Danepoint Ltd v Underwriting Insurance Ltd* [2006] Lloyd's Rep. I.R. 429.

was not a matter which could be tested by mere inspection. It is nevertheless submitted that this ruling cannot stand with the earlier authorities, and has also been undermined by the subsequent decision of the Privy Council in *Stemson v AMP General Insurance (NZ) Ltd*.[147] In that case Lord Mance, speaking for the Privy Council on this point, approved his own comments in *Agapitos v Agnew* to the effect that a lie which was detected or which unravelled before a settlement or during a trial was not thereby rendered immaterial. In *Stemson* the assured had initially asserted, following a fire, that before the fire it had never been his intention to sell the premises, a statement corrected a short time afterwards and before the insurers rejected the claim. The assured was held to have submitted a fraudulent claim. It might be possible to draw a distinction between the situation in *Danepoint*, where the lie was such that it was never believed in the first place, and the situation posited in *Stemson* where a lie was given initial credence but was subsequently exposed. If there is a distinction along those lines it gives rise to complex borderline issues where a lie is told initially but is either corrected or the truth is discovered shortly afterwards, and it may be that *Danepoint* is confined to the case in which the lie is so blatant that it is utterly disregarded by the insurers.

9–031 *Retraction of fraud.* In *Agapitos v Agnew*[148] Mance L.J. expressed the view that a lie which unravelled before a settlement or during a trial did not cease to be a lie, so that the claim remained fraudulent. Lord Mance confirmed his own earlier comments in his judgment on behalf of the Privy Council in *Stemson v AMP General (NZ) Ltd*.[149] That principle was applied in *Direct Line Insurance Plc v Fox*,[150] in which the assured, having been paid substantial sums, submitted an additional claim for expenditure which he had not incurred, and then purported to withdraw that additional claim when the insurers discovered its falsity. The court ruled that it was not possible for the assured to withdraw a fraudulent claim as a matter of principle, but even if that was wrong then any withdrawal had to be voluntary and not the result of discovery by the insurers. On the facts the assured was held not to have made a fraudulent claim, because by the time the demand for payment was made the claim had been resolved by binding agreement.

9–032 **Consequences of a fraudulent claim.** In the absence of any express term setting out the consequences of a fraudulent claim, those consequences depend upon the juridical nature of the obligation not to make a fraudulent claim. It was for some time thought that the insurers have the right to avoid the policy from the outset, on the basis that a fraudulent claim is an infringement of the assured's continuing duty of utmost good faith.[151] However, this was denied by Lord Hobhouse in *The Star Sea*,[152] who noted that the rule was designed to protect a

---

[147] *Stemson v AMP General Insurance (NZ) Ltd* [2006] Lloyd's Rep. I.R. 852.

[148] *Agapitos v Agnew* [2002] Lloyd's Rep. I.R. 173.

[149] *Stemson v AMP General Insurance (NZ) Ltd* [2006] Lloyd's Rep. I.R. 852.

[150] *Direct Line Insurance Plc v Fox* [2010] Lloyd's Rep. I.R. 324.

[151] The process started with *The Litsion Pride* [1985] 1 Lloyd's Rep. 437, followed in *Continental Illinois National Bank of Chicago v Alliance Assurance Co Ltd (The Captain Panagos)* [1986] 2 Lloyd's Rep. 470. The point was left open in *Insurance Corporation of the Channel Islands v Royal Hotel (No.1)* [1997] L.R.L.R. 94. In *Orakpo v Barclays Insurance Services Ltd* [1995] L.R.L.R. 433 each member of the Court of Appeal suggested a different remedy, namely avoidance (Sir Roger Parker), termination for breach (Hoffmann L.J.) and an obligation to pay the claim insofar as it was honest (Sir Christopher Staughton).

[152] *The Star Sea* [2001] Lloyd's Rep. I.R. 247.

wrongdoer from making a profit from his wrongdoing and that this was best achieved by a contractual analysis. Lord Hobhouse's views were confirmed by the Court of Appeal in *K/S Merc Skandia XXXXII v Certain Lloyd's Under-writers*[153] and again in *Agapitos v Agnew*[154] those cases making it clear[155] that the duty of utmost good faith and the duty not to make a fraudulent claim are entirely divorced and that a policy cannot be avoided where a claim is fraudulent. In *Axa General Insurance v Gottleib*[156] the Court of Appeal rejected the related argument that a fraudulent claim deprived the assured of all benefit under the policy with effect from the inception of the policy. There is, therefore, no possibility of a fraudulent claim having a retroactive effect earlier than—as was held in *Axa v Gottleib*—the date of the loss which gave rise to the fraudulent claim. This, however, raises the question of what remedy is appropriate where there has been a fraudulent claim.

Two possibilities arise: the claim itself is lost; or the policy is treated as repudiated as of the date of the loss which gave rise to the fraudulent claim. If the only loss suffered by the assured has resulted in a fraudulent claim, then the insurers can satisfy themselves by refusing to pay that claim and it probably matters little to them whether they can also go on and treat the policy as repudiated for breach. The additional right to treat the policy as repudiated will nevertheless be significant if there have been other genuine claims. The following possibilities may arise.

  (i) The assured suffers loss (a) and submits a fraudulent claim in respect of it. He then suffers loss (b) which is unaffected by any fraud.

 (ii) The assured suffers loss (a) and loss (b). He then submits a fraudulent claim in respect of loss (a).

(iii) The assured suffers loss (b), which is unaffected by fraud. He then suffers loss (a) and submits a fraudulent claim in respect of it.

Three general points should be made in considering these situations. The first is that the assured's right to an indemnity for a loss untainted by fraud accrues on the date of the occurrence of the insured peril and not on the date upon which the claim is made. This is important because it is trite law that the termination of a contract for repudiation operates prospectively only and does not affect accrued rights. The second is that whether or not claims have been made or sums have actually been paid in respect of the genuine loss is not conceptually of any relevance to the analysis. Where the assured has been the victim of an insured peril, his rights are to be determined at that point: if the insurers do not at that stage, have any right to determine the policy, the assured has an accrued right to be paid and the fact that no claim or payment has been made will not prevent him from recovering; by contrast, if at the date of the insured peril the insurers have the right to terminate the policy, then the assured does not have an accrued right to claim or to be paid and has neither the right to be paid nor the right to hold on to payments actually made in respect of the loss. The third point, as held in *Axa v Gottlieb*, is that once the policy has reached the end of its natural life, it will be too late for the insurers to treat the policy as repudiated. The right to terminate

---

[153] *K/S Merc Skandia XXXXII v Certain Lloyd's Underwriters* [2001] Lloyd's Rep. I.R. 802.

[154] *Agapitos v Agnew* [2002] Lloyd's Rep. I.R. 573.

[155] It was noted in *Marc Rich Agriculture Trading SA v Fortis Corporate Insurance NV* [2005] Lloyd's Rep. I.R. 396 that the comments in these cases were *obiter* but nevertheless almost certainly right.

[156] *Axa General Insurance v Gottleib* [2005] Lloyd's Rep. I.R. 369.

for breach is thus only significant where the contract is in existence at the point where the insurers seek to exercise that right.

In situation (i), if the insurers have the right to treat the policy as repudiated for fraud, they may refuse to pay loss (a) by reason of the fraudulent claim rule, and may then exercise their additional right to terminate the policy thereby removing their liability for loss (b). It is immaterial whether the insurers' right to terminate arises on the date on which the fraudulent claim is made or whether it is backdated to the date of loss (a), because each of these events predates loss (b). The additional remedy in this situation is thus of some significance.

The difference between situations (i) and (ii) is that in (ii) loss (b) occurs after loss (a) and before the fraud in relation to loss (a). This is what occurred in *Axa v Gottlieb*, which decides that the right of the insurers to refuse to pay loss (a) on the basis of the fraudulent claim rule does not also give them the right to refuse to pay loss (b) in that no retroactivity is involved. Accordingly, the insurers will have to assert the right to treat the policy as repudiated but—as was held in *Axa*—this can only be open to them if the policy has not come to an end by effluxion of time at the date at which they wish to exercise the right. Assuming that the policy remains in existence when the insurers assert their right to treat it as repudiated for fraud, an issue arises as to whether the date on which the policy is to be treated as having been terminated for repudiation is the date of loss (a) or the date of the fraud giving rise to loss (a). In *Axa v Gottlieb* it was decided that the fraudulent claim rule of necessity allows the insurers to backdate the fraud to the date of the loss itself. However, there is no basis for applying that principle where the issue is not the right to refuse to pay a claim but rather the right to treat the policy as repudiated. It is suggested that, in accordance with general contractual principles, any right to treat the contract as repudiated arises only on the date of the fraud, thereby protecting earlier genuine and accrued losses even if claims have not at that point been made in respect of them. This is consistent with the reasoning in *Axa v Gottlieb* itself, refusing to give retroactive effect to fraud where there are other genuine and accrued claims. It may be, therefore, that treating the policy as repudiated is of no assistance to insurers in situation (ii).

In situation (iii) the assured has an accrued right to recover for loss (b) in all circumstances, so that any right to terminate the policy for repudiation by means of fraud cannot affect loss (b) even though a claim is not made until after the fraud.

The point of the above analysis is that the right of the insurer to treat the policy as repudiated for breach is only of significance in situation (i), where a fraudulent claim is made before a genuine loss occurs and the insurers have discovered the fraud before the policy has come to an end. In those limited circumstances, it will be important for the insurers to know whether they do indeed have the additional right to treat the policy as repudiated. There are indications in the judgment of Mance L.J. in *Agapitos v Agnew*[157] that the existence of the additional remedy of prospective termination might depend upon the nature of the fraud, so that if the fraud is serious (as where the assured has caused his own loss or has submitted an exaggerated claim) then the policy can be treated as repudiated, whereas if the fraud is less serious (as where the assured has suffered a genuine loss but has promoted by the use of fraudulent devices) the appropriate remedy may only be denial of the claim.

---

[157] *Agapitos v Agnew* [2002] Lloyd's Rep. I.R. 573.

Express fraudulent claims clauses. Typical wording found in the London **9–033** market, and which has prevailed for the best part of two centuries is that: "If any claim or part of a claim is made fraudulently or falsely, the policy shall become void and all benefit under this policy will be forfeited." Some policies go on to provide that the policy is to be treated as void. Lord Hobhouse in *The Star Sea*[158] took the view that the use of the word "forfeiture" in express wordings, and its treatment in early cases[159] did not imply avoidance of the policy *ab initio*—as demanded by the doctrine of utmost good faith—but rather the loss of the right to claim. It would seem to follow that a statement that the policy becomes void is not intended to have retroactive effect, but simply brings the policy to an end as from the date of the fraudulent claim. Lord Hobhouse's analysis was echoed by Mance L.J. in *Agapitos v Agnew*[160] it being suggested that forfeiture did not mean avoidance *ab initio*. In *Direct Line Insurance Plc v Fox*[161] it was held by H.H. Judge Seymour QC that the standard express fraudulent claims wording did no more than replicate the common law and did not have retroactive effect, the phrase "shall become void" meaning that previous accrued rights were unaffected. That ruling also led the court in *Direct Line* to conclude that the clause was not unreasonable under the Unfair Terms in Consumer Contracts Regulations 1999, because it did not give the insurers greater rights than they possessed in its absence.

Effect of plea of fraud by insurers. In *Jureidini v National British and Irish* **9–034** *Millers Insurance Co Ltd*[162] Viscount Haldane stated that where an insurer repudiated its obligations under a policy of insurance it was not permitted to rely upon the terms of the policy. This led to the suggestion to the Privy Council in *Super Chem Products Ltd v American Life and General Insurance Co*[163] that an insurer who took the defence that the assured had submitted a fraudulent claim was unable at the same time to rely upon defences of failure to adhere to policy conditions regarding notification of losses and limitation periods. In rejecting this argument, the Privy Council ruled that Viscount Haldane's statement did not represent the law:

> "It would be contrary to principle and business common sense, which underpin our commercial law, to require an insurer to choose between alleging fraud, thereby abandoning the right to invoke other conditions of the policy, or to rely on those provisions, thereby giving up the right to allege fraud."

Having rejected Viscount Haldane's views in *Jureidini*, the Privy Council gave three reasons why the insurers' proposition in *Super Chem* could not hold good. First, a defence of fraud was not a repudiation of the contract but rather reliance on a contractual defence. Secondly, even if a repudiation had occurred, it did not bring the contract to an end but merely gave the assured the right to terminate the contract for breach: by pursuing a claim, it was clear that any repudiation had not

---

[158] *The Star Sea* [2001] Lloyd's Rep. I.R. 247.
[159] *Goulstone v Royal Insurance Co* (1859) 1 F. & F. 276; *Britton v Royal Insurance Co* (1866) 4 F. & F. 905.
[160] *Agapitos v Agnew* [2002] Lloyd's Rep. I.R. 573.
[161] *Direct Line Insurance Plc v Fox* [2009] EWHC 386 (QB).
[162] *Jureidini v National British and Irish Millers Insurance Co Ltd* [1915] A.C. 499.
[163] *Super Chem Products Ltd v American Life and General Insurance Co* [2004] Lloyd's Rep. I.R. 446, followed in *Diab v Regent Insurance Co Ltd* [2006] Lloyd's Rep. I.R. 779.

been accepted.[164] Thirdly, the assured's obligations in respect of claims came into existence before the denial of liability for fraud,[165] so that the fraud defence could not affect the insurers' accrued rights. In *Diab v Regent Insurance Co Ltd*[166] the Privy Council rejected the further suggestion that a denial of liability for fraud operated as a waiver of compliance with notification provisions, or at least raised an estoppel against the insurers: such denial did not constitute either an election not to rely upon the notice clause or an unequivocal representation to that effect.

9–035 **Evidence of fraud on appeal.** If the assured brings proceedings against the insurer on the policy, and obtains judgment, the insurers may on appeal, under CPR Pt 52, seek permission from the court to introduce evidence of fraud on the assured's part which was not submitted at the original trial. The court, in reaching its decision, will take into account whether: (1) the insurers could not with reasonable diligence have obtained that evidence at the time of the trial; (2) the evidence is such that it would have an important, although not necessarily decisive, influence on the outcome of the case; and (3) the evidence is credible, without necessarily being incontrovertible.[167]

9–036 **Fraud by a foreign state.** If the assured is a foreign state, and the insurers assert fraud against that state, there is no rule of law which precludes an English court from determining whether or not there had been fraud. The point arose at the reinsurance level in *Korea National Insurance Co v Allianz Global Corporate & Specialty AG*.[168] Here, the claimant reinsured had insured Air Koryo against, amongst other risks, liability. Judgment was given in North Korea against Air Koryo in respect of an accident in which one of its helicopters crashed into a warehouse owned by a relief centre, while on a mercy mission carrying a pregnant woman to hospital. In a subsequent arbitration the reinsured was held liable to indemnify Air Koryo, and the reinsured sought reimbursement from the reinsurers having obtained a judgment against them in North Korea. The present proceedings were an application to the English courts for enforcement of the judgment. The action was contested by the reinsurers on the ground that the entire chain of events constituted an elaborate fraud, in that the alleged accident had never occurred, and that the judicial proceedings in North Korea had been conducted under the control of the Head of State with a view to obtaining foreign currency in the form of a reinsurance payment. The Court of Appeal held that the principle of non-justiciability, whereby the acts of a foreign sovereign within his own territory are not to be reviewed in the English courts, had no application to the present case and that the allegations of fraud could be fully investigated. Waller L.J. held that the cases on non-justiciability:

---

[164] See also *Diab v Regent Insurance Co Ltd* [2006] Lloyd's Rep. I.R. 779. It is not clear whether the assured can put an end to the policy and then pursue an action for breach of contract free of any future obligations under the notice clause. In both *Super Chem* and *Diab* the assured affirmed the contract and pursued a claim under the policy itself, so the point did not arise.

[165] This was not the case in *Diab v Regent Insurance Co Ltd* [2006] Lloyd's Rep. I.R. 779, where the denial of liability for fraud was made before the time limits for compliance with notice clauses had expired.

[166] *Diab v Regent Insurance Co Ltd* [2006] Lloyd's Rep. I.R. 779.

[167] *Zincroft Civil Engineering Ltd v Sphere Drake Insurance Plc* (1996) *Lloyd's List,* December 23; *Prentice v Hereward Housing Association* [2001] EWCA Civ 437. These cases applied the general principles laid down in *Ladd v Marshall* [1954] 3 All E.R. 745.

[168] *Korea National Insurance Co v Allianz Global Corporate & Specialty AG* [2008] EWCA Civ 1355.

"did not support the view that, where in a commercial context allegations are made against the state, not in relation to some sovereign act carried out in its own jurisdiction but in relation to acts which affect the rights of a party under a commercial contract, that the court should exercise restraint to the extent of not being prepared to decide the same, at least without some indication from the executive that a decision will embarrass the diplomatic relations between the United Kingdom and that State. If a foreign state were an insured under an insurance contract the insurers cannot be precluded from alleging a fraudulent claim simply because that might embarrass the foreign state. It cannot be any different if a state entity makes the claim and it is asserted that both the entity and the state owner were involved in the fraud."

Reform of the law on fraudulent claims. In July 2010 the English and Scottish Law Commissions published an Issues Paper on the assured's post-contractual duty of utmost good faith, although the name belies the fact that most of the Issues Paper is concerned with fraudulent claims. The Law Commissions have expressed general satisfaction with the law as it stands, although they note that there are a number of contentious issues which remain unresolved. The Law Commissions have sought views on, inter alia, the following matters: should it be made clear that the remedy for a fraudulent claim is not avoidance of the policy ab initio but rather based on contract; if the remedy is contractual, is it appropriate that the insurers should be entitled to refuse to pay the claim and also have the right to treat the contract as terminated, but without prejudice to any loss incurred prior to termination; is it appropriate to deprive the assured of a genuine claim simply because he has sought to substantiate that claim by the use of fraudulent means or devices; and is it right that an innocent joint assured should be deprived of the right to make a claim by reason of the fraud of another joint assured, thereby unifying the law on joint and composite insurance; and in the case of a group life policy obtained by an employer as assured, should a fraudulent claim by a member of the insured group leave the policy itself unaffected but simply deprive the fraudster of his right to claim?

9–036A

4. LIMITATION OF ACTIONS

The statutory limitation period

Date of accrual of action. By s.5 of the Limitation Act 1980, an action on a contract must be brought within six years from the date of the accrual of the action, although under s.8 the period is 12 years if the contract is by way of deed. The limitation period can be varied by contract. There is a consistent line of authority for the proposition that the date on which the assured's action accrues is the date on which the insured peril occurs and not on the later dates when the loss is manifested,[169] the assured incurs expenditure or the insurers deny liability, the principle being that the insurer has agreed to hold the assured harmless against the occurrence of an insured event so that when the event takes place the insurers are in immediate and automatic breach of contract and are liable for unliquidated damages. Although it has sometimes been indicated that the occurrence of the peril is a breach of contract,[170] the notion that insurers may be

9–037

[169] *Kelly v Norwich Union Fire & Life Insurance Ltd* [1989] 2 All E.R. 888; *Seele Austria GmbH & Co KG v Tokio Marine Europe Insurance Ltd (No.3)* [2010] Lloyd's Rep. I.R. 490.
[170] *Firma C-Trade SA v Newcastle Protection and Indemnity Association (The Fanti) Socony Mobil Oil Co Inc v West of England Ship Owners Mutual Insurance Association (London) Ltd (The Padre Island (No.2))* [1990] 2 All E.R. 705 at 717, per Lord Goff.

in breach of contract several hundred times every day is unattractive[171] and a preferable way of stating the principle is that a contract of insurance is:

"[A]n agreement by the insurer to confer upon the insured a contractual right which, prima facie, comes into existence immediately when loss is suffered by the happening of an event insured against, to be put by the insurer into the same position in which the insured would have been had the event not occurred, but in no better position."[172]

The limitation period is not postponed by reason of the fact that the assured was at the time unaware of the occurrence of the insured peril. Thus, in the case of a fidelity policy which protects the assured against fraud by an employee, the limitation period runs not from the date of the discovery of the fraud but from the date of the fraud itself.[173]

9–038 *Application of the accrual rule.* The rule is that the assured's cause of action accrues on the date of the occurrence of the insured peril. This principle applies to marine policies,[174] property policies,[175] life policies[176] and accident policies.[177] The limitation period for a general average claim under a marine policy is the date of the occurrence of the insured peril and not the date of the adjustment.[178]

9–039 *Liability insurance.* The general rule is that the limitation period under a liability policy[179] commences as soon as the third party has established and quantified the assured's liability by means of a judgment, arbitration award or binding settlement.[180] The limitation period is not postponed to the date on which the assured makes actual payment. One problem raised by the accrual rule is that there is inevitably going to be a considerable time gap between the date on which the assured notifies to the insurers the possibility of a claim against him, and the final date on which the assured's liability is established and quantified. In this period, the insurers might deny liability, or act in a fashion which amounts to a repudiatory breach of contract, e.g. by purporting to avoid the policy for breach

---

[171] *Transthene Packaging Co Ltd v Royal Insurance (UK) Ltd* [1996] L.R.L.R. 33.

[172] *Callaghan v Dominion Insurance Co* [1997] 2 Lloyd's Rep. 541; *City & General (Holborn) Ltd v Royal & Sun Alliance Plc* [2010] EWCA Civ 911.

[173] *Universities Superannuation Scheme Ltd v Royal Insurance (UK) Ltd* [2000] Lloyd's Rep. I.R. 525.

[174] *Boddington v Castelli* (1853) 1 E. & B. 879; *Pellas v Neptune Marine Insurance Co* (1879) 5 C.P.D. 34; *William Pickersgill & Sons Ltd v London and Provincial Marine* [1912] 3 K.B. 614; *Ventouris v Mountain (The Italia Express (No.2))* [1992] 2 Lloyd's Rep. 191; *Bank of America National Trust and Savings Association v Christmas (The Kyriaki)* [1993] 1 Lloyd's Rep. 137.

[175] *Luckie v Bushby* (1853) 13 C.B. 864; *Jabbour v Custodian of Israeli Absentee Property* [1954] 1 W.L.R. 139; *Transthene Packaging Co Ltd v Royal Insurance (UK) Ltd* [1996] L.R.L.R. 32; *Callaghan v Dominion Insurance Co* [1997] 2 Lloyd's Rep. 541; *King v Brandywine Reinsurance Co (UK) Ltd* [2004] Lloyd's Rep. I.R. 554; *Seele Austria GmbH & Co KG v Tokio Marine Europe Insurance Ltd (No.3)* [2010] Lloyd's Rep. I.R. 490.

[176] *Re Haycock's Policy* (1876)1 Ch D 611; *London & Midland Bank v Mitchell* [1899] 2 Ch. 161.

[177] *Mulchrone v Swiss Life (UK) Plc* [2006] Lloyd's Rep. I.R. 339.

[178] *Tate & Lyle Ltd v Hain Steamship Co Ltd* (1934) 151 L.T. 249; *Morrison Steamship Co Ltd v Greystoke Castle* [1947] A.C. 265; *Chandris v Argo Insurance Co Ltd* [1963] 2 Lloyd's Rep. 64; *Castle Insurance Co Ltd v Hong Kong Islands Shipping Co Ltd (The Potoi Chau)* [1983] 2 Lloyd's Rep. 376.

[179] And also a contract of reinsurance: *Halvanon Insurance Co Ltd v Companhia de Seguros do Estado de São Paulo* [1995] L.R.L.R. 303.

[180] *London Steamship Owners Mutual Insurance Association Ltd v Bombay Trading Co Ltd (The Felicie)* [1990] 2 Lloyd's Rep. 21.

by the assured of his duty of utmost good faith. If it is the case that the insurers' conduct is actionable,[181] there may be limitation problems if the assured does not take any action against the insurers at this point and the assured's liability is established and quantified more than six years after the insurer's repudiation. It was held in *Lefevre v White*[182] that although the assured had a cause of action on the date of the repudiation, then as long as the repudiation was not accepted by the assured—thereby bringing the policy to an end—he had a further cause of action on the date on which his liability was established and quantified and did not have to proceed within six years of the repudiation.

Variation of the limitation period

Contract terms varying the limitation period. It is permissible in insurance, as in **9–040** other forms of contract, for the parties to agree that there is to be a shorter or, for that matter, longer limitation period. A policy term in a liability policy which requires the assured to commence proceedings within twelve months from the insurers' denial of liability,[183] failing which the claim is deemed to have been abandoned, is effective to defeat a claim by the assured even though there had been no claim against him by the third party at the time of the expiry of this period.[184] The assured's remedy in such a case is to commence an action for a declaration as to the insurers' liability in the event that a claim is made against the assured.

Fidelity policies, and other types of cover against fraud, often contain restricted limitation periods whereby the assured is required to commence proceedings against the insurers within a given period from the date upon which the fraud was or ought to have been discovered.[185]

Contract terms varying the accrual of the action. The principle that the assured's **9–041** action accrues when the casualty occurs depends for its operation on identifying the casualty in question. A distinction has to be drawn between policy terms which relate to the occurrence of the insured event, and policy terms which either provide the insurer with a defence or merely relate to the assured's ability to prove and quantify a loss which has taken place on the occurrence of the insured event, as quantification of loss is not—other than in the special case of liability insurance—an element of the occurrence of the insured event. The presumption is that a term which restricts recovery does not affect the accrual of the action. It has thus been held that the right of the insurers to reinstate, the calculation of the indemnity by reference to reinstatement value and the right of the reinsurers to pay only after reinstatement, were concerned only with the quantification of loss,[186] and terms governing double insurance and notification of loss were pure defences.[187] In the case of accident insurance the general rule remains that the assured's action accrues on the date of the injury even though no payment is due

[181] So held in *Transthene Packaging Co Ltd v Royal Insurance (UK) Ltd* [1996] L.R.L.R. 32.

[182] *Lefevre v White* [1990] 1 Lloyd's Rep. 569.

[183] See *Kanson Crane Service Co Ltd v Bank of China Group Insurance Co Ltd* [2003] H.K.E.C. 1139: a letter from the insurers reserving their rights amounted to a denial of liability.

[184] *Walker v Pennine Insurance Co* [1980] 2 Lloyds Rep. 156. See also *British Credit Trust Holdings v UK Insurance Ltd* [2004] 1 All E.R. Comm 444. The various hulls clauses also require an action to be commenced within 12 months of the loss.

[185] *Fortisbank SA v Trenwick International Ltd* [2005] Lloyd's Rep. I.R. 464.

[186] *Callaghan v Dominion Insurance Co* [1997] 2 Lloyd's Rep. 541. The contrary ruling, in *Transthene Packaging Co Ltd v Royal Insurance (UK) Ltd* [1996] L.R.L.R. 32, was not referred to.

[187] *Callaghan v Dominion Insurance Co* [1997] 2 Lloyd's Rep. 541.

for a given period after the injury,[188] although the policy may be framed in a manner which defines the insured event as the expiry of a given period following the occurrence of the injury so that the limitation period starts to run only on the expiry of that period.[189]

Some forms of liability cover, and of reinsurance, contain "pay to be paid" clauses, which provide that the policyholder cannot recover until there has been an actual payment to the third party claimant. Such a clause, whatever its effect on the right of the policyholder to recover before making payment,[190] probably does not affect the accrual of the cause of action, which remains the date at which the policyholder' liability to the third party is established and quantified.

9–042 **Loss of right to rely upon limitation period.** The statutory limitation periods applicable to contract actions do not extinguish the claimant's cause of action, but merely provide the defendant with a defence. Accordingly, in an insurance case the insurers can contract out of the right to rely upon a limitation period, either by policy term or by way of "standstill" agreement entered into by the parties following the loss: the latter is common where the parties are involved in negotiation or mediation close to the expiry of the limitation period, as in the absence of such an agreement it will be necessary for the assured to issue a protective claim form and then to serve it within the one-month period permitted by the Civil Procedure Rules.

The right to rely upon a limitation period may also be lost by waiver. This will be made out if four conditions are satisfied[191]:

(1) a clear, unequivocal, unambiguous and unconditional promise by the insurers that they would not raise a limitation defence and that they were giving up that right;

(2) the promise was, construed objectively, not capable of more than one explanation;

(3) the insurers had gone beyond simply negotiating with the bank about the claim; and

(4) there had been reliance on the promise by the bank before the limitation period had expired and in the form of altering its position in such a fashion that it would be inequitable for the insurers to plead their limitation defence.

Mere silence in the course of negotiations does not amount to waiver, as there is nothing capable of being construed as an unequivocal statement.[192]

5. CLAIMS AGAINST INSURERS BY THIRD PARTIES

9–043 **Third party claims in general.** Where a person other than the assured is entitled to claim under the assured's policy, that person is for the most part in

---

[188] *Mulchrone v Swiss Life (UK) Plc* [2006] Lloyd's Rep. I.R. 339.

[189] *Virk v Gan Life Holdings Plc* [2002] Lloyd's Rep. I.R. 159; *Ace Insurance SA-NV v Seechurn* [2002] Lloyd's Rep. I.R. 489.

[190] Such clauses have been held not to require prepayment by a reinsured (*Charter Reiinsurance Co v Fagan* [1997] A.C. 313) but do operate according to their terms in P & I liability covers (*The Fanti and the Padre Island* [1990] 2 All E.R. 705.

[191] *Fortisbank SA v Trenwick International Ltd* [2005] Lloyd's Rep. I.R. 464, per Gloster J.

[192] *Ace Insurance SA-NV v Seechurn* [2002] Lloyd's Rep. I.R. 489; *Fortisbank SA v Trenwick International Ltd* [2005] Lloyd's Rep. I.R. 464; *Super Chem Products Ltd v American Life & General Insurance Co* [2004] Lloyd's Rep. I.R. 446.

precisely the same position as the assured would have been, in so far as a compliance with notice provision is concerned. Thus, an assured's trustee in bankruptcy, personal representative or assignee[193] must comply with the terms of any claims provisions and cannot rely upon the fact that he was not aware of the loss or of the existence of the policy. There is an important modification in respect of a person claiming against liability insurers under the Third Parties (Rights against Insurers) Act 2010 following the insolvency of the assured. Under s.9(1) of the 2010 Act, the third party is in general terms in no better position with the assured, so that if the assured has failed to comply with policy conditions then the insurers retain their ordinary rights as against the third party. There are, however, three modifications the third party is entitled, if he can do so, to satisfy the condition himself even if the personal performance of the assured is required (s.9(2)); any condition which requires the assured to provide information or assistance to the insurers is to be disregarded where the assured cannot comply because it is a dissolved corporation or a deceased individual (s.9(3)); and in the case of any condition requiring the assured to provide information or assistance to the insurers which remains in force insofar as the assured has not died or been dissolved, that condition is ineffective insofar as it requires the assured to notify a claim to the insurer (s.9(4)).[194]

Contracts (Rights of Third Parties) Act 1999

Scope of legislation. There are isolated statutory illustrations of third parties directly or indirectly obtaining rights under another's policy,[195] which until the passing of the 1999 Act took effect as exceptions to the doctrine of privity. That doctrine was abrogated by the 1999 Act. It is now possible for a third party to make a claim against insurers on a contract to which he is not a party if the following conditions are met.

9–044

First, the contract must either (a) provide that the third party can enforce it, or (b) purport to confer a benefit upon him (s.1(1)). In either case, the policy is divisible, so that rights can be given to the third party in respect of some or all of its terms. The 1999 Act can operate in a negative fashion, so that if insurers have promised the assured not to exercise subrogation rights against a third party, the third party can resist any proceedings by the insurers brought by way of subrogation assuming that the requirements of the 1999 Act are otherwise met. What is required by possibility (a) is an express statement to the effect that one or more terms of the policy are enforceable by a third party. Such provisions are relatively rare, although a reinsurance cut-through clause whereby a direct assured is given the right to proceed against reinsurers in the event of the reinsured's insolvency, or a clause which allows a third party mortgagee to bring proceedings against the mortgagor's insurers, would appear to be clear examples of what is covered here. If the contract does not specifically state that one or more of its terms may be enforced by a third party, the third party may acquire

---

[193] *Verelst's Administratrix v Motor Union Insurance Co* [1925] 2 K.B. 137.

[194] The position under the earlier Third Parties (Rights against Insurers) Act 1930 was that a failure by the assured to comply with conditions precedent was fatal to the third party's claim: *Farrell v Federated Employers Insurance Association Ltd* [1970] 3 All E.R. 632; *Pioneer Concrete (UK) Ltd v National Employers Mutual General Insurance Association Ltd* [1985] 2 All E.R. 395: *Alfred McAlpine Plc v BAI (Run-off) Ltd* [2000] Lloyd's Rep. I.R. 352.

[195] Married Women's Property Act 1882; Fires Prevention (Metropolis) Act 1774; Road Traffic Act 1988.

enforcement rights under alternative (b),[196] although this is subject to the qualification in s.1(2) which disapplies (b) "if on a proper construction of the contract it appears that the parties did not intend the term to be enforceable by the third party". The wording creates a presumption in favour of the third party's right to enforce a term which confers benefits upon him. An insurer who wishes to avoid enforcement proceedings by a third party will, therefore, have to demonstrate that the insurance contract—construed in accordance with the ordinary rules of construction applicable to insurance agreements—was not intended to confer enforceable benefits on a third party.

Secondly, under s.1(3), "The third party must be expressly identified in the contract by name, as a member of a class or as answering a particular description but need not be in existence when the contract is entered into." Identification by name is likely to be problematic only where the third party is incorrectly named (in which case the assured although presumably not the third party claiming to be the intended beneficiary could apply for rectification), or when the third party changes name, e.g. following merger. In the latter case, it is likely that the court would regard any successor in title of the named third party as constituting the identified party, although possibly only to the extent of the third party's original business. The possibilities of identification by class or by description emphasise that it is not necessary to be able to name the intended beneficiary at the date of the contract being made. Thus, in the case of a policy taken out by an employer for the benefit of all employees, or of a policy taken out by a head contractor for the benefit of all subcontractors, any person who is an employee or subcontractor at the date of the policy is entitled to benefit from it. Section 1(3) goes further and makes express provision for persons who, at a later date, fall into the relevant class or meet the relevant description, such as employees or subcontractors who are hired, or a company that is acquired, once the policy has commenced: indeed, the fact that the third party is a company which is not formed until after inception is no bar to that company being a beneficiary under the contract. What is less obvious is the position of a person who has ceased to meet the class or description qualifications by the date of the loss, e.g. in the situation in which a policy between an insurer and an employer confers accident benefits on employees, a claim being made by a person who had ceased to be an employee at the date of the accident. It may be thought that the proper way to construe the Act is to require the third party to have been within the class or description at the date of the occurrence of the insured peril: there is no reason why an employee who has ceased to be employed should be regarded as a beneficiary in respect of later accidents, and equally there is no reason to deprive an employee of accrued rights simply because he has left the employment after the occurrence of the insured peril but before any claim has been made.

Thirdly, the beneficiary must be capable of enforcing the policy under ordinary common law rules. The third party must thus be of full capacity. However, the long-standing principle that consideration must be provided by the promise is necessarily rendered inoperative.

The 1999 Act protects non-contracting parties, and leaves unaffected the rules relating to joint or composite insurance: if a person is a party to the insurance in his own right, he does not need to rely on the 1999 Act. There is also a crucial distinction to be drawn between a contract which is intended to confer benefits on a third party, and a contract from which a third party may derive some form

---

[196] See *Laemthong International Lines v Abdullah Mohammd Fahem & Co* [2005] 2 All E.R. (Comm) 167; *Dolphin Maritime & Aviation Services Ltd v Sveriges Angartygs Assurans Forening* [2009] EWHC 716 (Comm); *Crowson v HSBC Insurance Brokers* Unreported, January 26, 2010.

of indirect benefit. On one side of the line is, for example, the situation in which an owner of property insures the property in his own name, but secures the inclusion of a policy term whereby any sums are payable to a third party bank: assuming that the bank is not made a co-assured, this is a typical situation to which the Act was intended to apply. By contrast, on the other side of the line is the ordinary liability policy, under which the insurers agree to indemnify the assured against any successful claim brought by a third party. Plainly, if the insurers adhere to their bargain, there will be a fund of money in the assured's hands which can be used to make payment to the third party. However, it would be a misuse of language to call the third party an intended beneficiary of the policy; at best, he may derive benefit from it. In such a case any attempt by the third party to bring a direct action against the insurers would probably fail for want of the identification of the third party as a beneficiary: membership of the general class of "any person to whom the assured incurs legal liability" is almost certainly too wide to amount to identification. However, even if the identification requirement was met—in the most extreme case, where the insurance protects the assured against claims by a named third party under a specific contract between the assured and the third party—that third party's claim should still, in principle, fall outside the 1999 Act. The fact that the third party is identified in the policy does not make him an intended beneficiary.

Restrictions on third party's right of enforcement. While the 1999 Act confers **9–045** benefits rather than imposes burdens, a distinction has to be drawn between a burden and a conditional benefit. The principle, expressed in s.1(4), is that the Act "does not confer a right on a third party to enforce a contract term otherwise than subject to and in accordance with any other relevant terms of the contract". Accordingly, if a third party is given the right to enforce a contract term, either directly or as its beneficiary, the third party must comply with: (a) any policy conditions which were imposed upon the assured himself, and (b) any policy conditions which relate specifically to the third party's claim. Time limits and other claims conditions, including restricted limitation periods and jurisdiction clauses, imposed upon the assured are thus binding on the third party. One difficulty which arises here is the possibility that a term binding on the assured would not have been binding on the third party had he been a party to the contract itself: this possibility arises where, for example, the assured is a company and thus outside the scope of consumer protection legislation, whereas the third party is an individual who is entitled to be protected against unreasonable terms. The Act provides that it does not affect any independent right or remedy of a third party, and it is possible to construe this provision as meaning that the third party may be entitled to disregard terms which would otherwise have been enforceable against the assured. In the same way, if there is some form of limitation on the insurers' liability, whether financial, temporal or subject-based, it is binding on the third party.

Agreement between assured and insurers to vary or rescind policy. Once the **9–046** third party has been given rights of enforcement or enforceable benefits under a policy, the 1999 Act makes detailed provision to prevent the removal of the third party's rights by means of any subsequent variation of the insurance by agreement between the assured and the insurers. The only situation in which a variation of the agreement is unconditionally binding on the third party is where the insurance contract itself permits the agreement to be varied or rescinded by the agreement of the parties. The policy may, as a lesser alternative, allow the insurers and the assured to vary or rescind the agreement only with the consent of the third party (s.2(3)). The prohibition on variation without the consent of the third party, set out in s.2(1), is triggered if: (a) the third party has communicated his assent to the term to the promisor; (b) the promisor is aware that the third party has relied on the term; or (c) the promisor can reasonably be expected to have foreseen that the third party would rely on the term and the third party has in fact relied upon it. Reliance will be relatively easy to prove in the insurance context: the mere fact that the third party has not insured on his own account when he might otherwise have been expected to have done so is good evidence of reliance, and it is readily within the expectation of insurers that a third party who believes that he is insured will not take steps to seek additional cover.

Where s.2(1) applies, it remains possible for a variation or rescission to be effected providing that the third party has consented to such change. There may be some situations in which the third party is incapable of giving consent, and here s.2(4) authorises a court or arbitral tribunal to dispense with consent where the third party's whereabouts cannot reasonably be ascertained, or where he is mentally incapable of giving his consent. In addition, s.2(5) allows the court or arbitral tribunal to dispense with the consent of the third party on the application of the parties to the contract in the situation in which the insurers can reasonably be expected to have foreseen that the third party would rely on the term but "it cannot reasonably be ascertained whether or not the third party has in fact relied on the term". If an order dispensing with consent is made, s.2(6) permits the court or arbitral tribunal to "impose such conditions as it thinks fit, including a condition requiring the payment of compensation to the third party". By way of example, if insurers have issued a policy to an employer to provide death benefits to the spouses of employees, and the policy is then varied or cancelled by agreement, then any spouse who would have obtained death benefits but for the later agreement might well be entitled to an award of the entire sum that would have been payable under the policy.

9–047 *Defences open to insurers.* The 1999 Act seeks to ensure that the position of the promisor is not prejudiced by reason of having to face a claim by a third party rather than by the promisee. The Act thus allows insurers to rely upon defences that would have been available against the assured himself, and to provide additional defences with respect to claims by any third party if the third party has himself infringed the rights of the insurers. The rather complex provisions of s.3 operate in the following way.

First, under s.3(2), the insurers are entitled to rely on any defence or set off which: "(a) arises from or in connection with the contract and is relevant to the term to be enforced; and (b) would have been available to the insurers by way of defence or set-off if the proceedings had been brought by the assured." This provision allows insurers to rely upon non-disclosure or misrepresentation on the part of the assured or any breach of a condition precedent in the claims process. The insurers are also presumably entitled to claim unpaid premium from the third party. There is, in principle, an important qualification in that the defence must be "relevant to the term to be enforced" by the third party, although in the insurance context the term which the third party will generally want to enforce is payment, so that any defence which goes to the validity of the contract or to the right of the assured to recover under the policy will be "relevant". It is, of course, open to the insurers to agree that they will not rely upon particular defences against the third party which would have been available against the assured, and s.3(5) so provides. The "payee" clause in a property policy, whereby insurers agree to make payment to the mortgagee of the property free of defences that would have been available in any claim by the assured mortgagor is a clear example of such an agreement.

Secondly, if the assured has a right to claim under the policy, but his conduct is such as to deprive him of a remedy against the insurers, on public policy or equitable grounds, s.3(2) appears not to afford the insurers a defence against the third party. It may be, therefore, that the third party continues to have rights against the insurers even though the insurers can defend a claim from the assured himself on the basis that, for example, he is precluded from recovery on public policy grounds.

Thirdly, under s.3(3) the insurers are perfectly free to stipulate that any breach of a policy term, whether or not connected with the claim, and any personal bar which may exist in respect of a claim by the assured, is to provide a defence against the third party.

Fourthly, under s.3(4) any claim by the third party is subject to any defence or set-off that would have been available had the third party been a party to the contract. Thus, if in the application for the insurance the third party has submitted false information, the insurers are entitled to avoid the third party's rights under the policy even though the policy itself is valid as far as the assured is concerned (as would be the case if the third party's misrepresentations were not made with the assured's authority). The insurers can also avail themselves of a counterclaim as against the third party which arose independently of the policy, e.g. under another contract between the insurers and the third party. The insurers cannot, however, as against the third party, avail themselves of a counterclaim which they would have had against the assured under the policy. This is so because the 1999 Act confers benefits but does not impose obligations. Insurers are, under s.3(5), empowered to include in the policy an express clause waiving their right to rely upon defences against the third party.

Enforcement by third party. If the claim is brought by the third party, the **9–048** remedies open to him are, under s.1(5), subject to any contrary provision in the contract, the same as those avail able to the assured himself. The third party can, therefore, seek a declaration as to the insurers' liability. However, this subsection does not confer upon the third party the right to avoid the policy and seek restitution of the premiums, as avoidance is not a remedy for breach of contract. In addition, it would seem that the third party cannot purport to terminate the policy for the insurer's breach, as such a remedy is self-help rather than one available in an action for breach of contract and the effect of any such intervention would be to affect the interests of the assured.

The amount recoverable by the third party is not necessarily the same as that recoverable by the assured. In the case of an indemnity policy, as a matter of common law the third party can only recover the amount of his loss as reflected by his insurable interest at the date of the loss, although in some situations the third party may have a pervasive insurable interest and thus be able to recover the assured's loss as well as his own, the surplus sums being held by the third party for the assured's account. Again, under the Life Assurance Act 1774 s.3, in the case of a life policy the maximum sum recoverable is the amount of the third party's insurable interest.

Effect of settlement between insurers and third party. Where the insurers have, **9–049** in accordance with the terms of the insurance, paid the policy monies to the third party, then plainly the insurers' contractual obligations have been fully discharged and the assured has no separate claim. By contrast, where the third party has entered into an agreement with the insurers under which a sum less than the full amount due under the policy is to be paid to the third party in purported full discharge of the insurers' obligations, it is doubtful whether that agreement is binding on the assured. The point is not dealt with by the Act, although it would seem that a release given to the insurers by the third party would not discharge the insurers' obligation to the assured unless the insurance contract authorised such settlements.

The 1999 Act is also silent on the situation where there are a number of third parties entitled to benefit under the policy. The usual distinction between joint and composite insurance ought to prevail here, so that if promise is for the joint benefit of the parties then its release binds them all, whereas if the benefits are divisible then a release only binds the person whose rights are involved.

9–050   *Enforcement by assured.* The 1999 Act does not strip rights away from the assured: instead, it confers additional rights upon the third party. Thus, s.4 of the 1999 Act provides that the existence of the third party's right of enforcement "does not affect the right of the promisee to enforce any term of the contract". If, therefore, as a matter of common law, the assured had the right to recover his own loss and that of a third party, e.g. by reason of the assured's own pervasive insurable interest, the assured retains the right to bring proceedings against the insurers for the full amount due under the insurance.

9–051   *Separate claims against insurers.* The combined effect of the 1999 Act and common law principles is to remove any risk that the insurers may be called upon to make payments in excess of the total limit of indemnity. The law operates as follows. The following situations may arise.

First, if the third party brings an action against the insurer and recovers the full sum due under the policy, then, while it is the case that s.4 preserves the assured's cause of action, the fact that the third party has been indemnified means that the insurers have fulfilled all of their obligations under the policy.

Secondly, if the insurers have agreed with the assured that payment is to be made to the third party, but the policy monies have not been paid to him and the assured has brought an action under the policy, then, unless the assured has suffered a loss, he will have no entitlement to make a claim: in such circumstances, the third party has a right to make a claim and again the insurers are not at risk of having to make double payment.

Thirdly, if the insurers have agreed with the assured that payment is to be made to the third party, but the policy monies have not been paid to him and the assured has brought an action under the policy, then, if the assured has suffered a loss or has a pervasive insurable interest, he will be entitled to recover some or all of the policy monies. In such a case, the third party's loss remains outstanding, although he has a claim against the assured for the policy monies to the extent that they exceed the assured's own loss. Indeed, it is possible that the insurers have paid the sums to the assured on the basis that he accounts for them to the third party. In each of these cases the third party is required to look to the assured and not to the insurers. This is the effect of s.5, which states that, where sums are payable to the third party, but the promisee (assured) has recovered from the promisor (insurers) a sum representing the third party's loss, then "in any proceedings brought . . . by the third party, the court or arbitral tribunal shall reduce any award to the third party to such extent as it thinks appropriate to take account of the sum recovered by the promisee". The Act says nothing concerning the manner in which the separate claims of the assured and the third party can be made against the insurers. It may be thought that the court would utilise CPR Pt 19, under which a party may be added to the proceedings if it is desirable to do so to allow the court to resolve all the matters in dispute in the proceedings or if there is an issue involving the new party and an existing party which is connected to the matters in dispute in the proceedings, and it is desirable to add the new party so that the court can resolve the issue.

Governing law, limitation and jurisdiction. The 1999 Act will apply if English **9–052** law is the governing law. The limitation rules applicable to claims by the assured are extended to claims by a third party by s.7(3). The usual six-year limitation period for an insurance claim, running from the date of the occurrence of the insured peril (or, in the case of a liability policy, the date on which the assured's liability is established and quantified by a judgment, arbitration award or binding settlement) applies equally to any claim by the third party.

Arbitration clauses are governed by s.8, subs.(1) providing that the third party is to be treated, for the purposes of the 1999 Act, as a party to the arbitration agreement as regards disputes between himself and the promisor relating to the enforcement of the substantive term by the third party. Any claim by the third party must, therefore, be pressed in arbitration if the policy so provides.[197] To this principle there appears to be one exception. An arbitration clause cannot be enforced against a consumer if the sum sought is less than £5,000.[198] Thus, if an arbitration agreement is binding as between, for example, an employer and his insurers, that same agreement may not be binding if the claim is brought by an individual employee who is a beneficiary under the policy.

Exclusive jurisdiction clauses are apparently to be treated in exactly the same way as arbitration clauses, although there is no express legislative provision affecting them. It would seem that an exclusive jurisdiction clause is no more than a condition imposed upon the assured and the third party as the price of making a claim, and is therefore binding on the general principle set out in s.1(4) that the third party is subject to the same conditions as which may affect a claim by the assured.

6. DECLARATORY RELIEF

The right to seek declaratory relief. One or other of the parties to a contract of **9–053** insurance may wish to obtain a declaration of its rights prior to any proceedings in which the scope of those rights might fall to be considered. It may be convenient for either party to seek a declaration as to the meaning of policy terms as the court's ruling may avoid the need for a lengthy trial on factual issues the resolution of which can make no difference to the eventual outcome. The assured under a liability policy who faces potential liability to a third party may wish to establish whether the policy will cover any claim made by the third party. The insurers under any form of insurance who believe that they have a right to avoid the policy, or to rely upon some other defence, may seek a declaration of the validity of their defence—commonly referred to as "negative declaratory relief"—so as to avoid lengthy proceedings against them which are doomed to failure.

[197] *Nisshin Shipping Co Ltd v Cleaves & Co Ltd* [2004] 1 Lloyd's Rep. 38.
[198] Unfair Arbitration Agreements (Specified Amount) Order 1999 (SI 1999/2167), applying the Unfair Terms in Consumer Contracts Regulations 1999 (SI 1999/2083).

The power of the court to grant a declaration as to the rights of the parties is contained in CPR r.40.20, which states that "The court may make a binding declaration whether or not any other remedy is claimed." The issue commonly at stake in the hearing of an application for a declaration is whether it is appropriate for a declaration to be granted, given that the matter upon which a ruling is sought may be either hypothetical or one which is unlikely to give rise to an issue between the parties. In *Arbuthnot Pensions & Investments Ltd v Padden*[199] it was decided that the ability of the court to grant a declaration in any one case is not one restricted by jurisdictional issues but rather involves an exercise of discretion.[200] Under the guidelines set out by May L.J. in *Arbuthnot*, a court will not obtain an academic or theoretical question which has no practical application, but will consider a matter where there is practical utility in doing so. Thus the courts will grant a declaration on the scope of policy coverage where there has been or is likely to be a claim under the policy, although in a liability insurance or reinsurance case the court will have to be convinced that the prospect of a third party claim is not fanciful.[201] Further, the issue must be one between the parties themselves: the court will not hear a claim for a declaration by a liability insurer or reinsurer which asserts that there is no valid third party claim against the policyholder, as that is a matter to be determined between the third party and the policyholder.[202] Nevertheless, liability insurers are entitled to seek a declaration of non-liability under the policy if there is a potential claim, and it has been held that liability insurers who have taken over the defence of the assured in respect of a claim by a third party may go further and seek a declaration that the assured is not liable to the third party: there is no objection in principle to this form of action, subject to the court being satisfied that an early resolution of liability issues is not unfair to the third party by depriving him of the ability to prepare his case properly.[203]

An action by insurers for a declaration in essence pre-empts an action on the policy by the assured, who is clearly the natural claimant. If the assured counterclaims in the proceedings for sums due under the policy, then the action for a declaration ceases to be relevant and the grounds upon which the declaration was sought in effect become the defences open to the insurers even though the insurers remain the notional claimants. It was accordingly held in *Jones v Environcom Ltd*[204] that an assured who counterclaims in proceedings brought by the insurers for a declaration may be required to give security for the costs of the counterclaim under CPR r.25.13. The usual rule that an order for security for costs cannot be made against a defendant has no application in this type of case, where the defendant is in reality the claimant and it was a matter of fortuity that the insurers were first to bring the dispute before the court.

The right of either party to seek a declaration is one that can be ousted by agreement. However, a clause which seeks to impose a contractual time limit on the assured's right to commence proceedings against the insurers in the event that

---

[199] *Arbuthnot Pensions & Investments Ltd v Padden* [2004] EWCA Civ 582.

[200] Disapproving contrary dicta in *Re Clay* [1919] 1 Ch. 66 and *Midland Bank v Laker Airways* [1986] 1 Q.B. 689 and adopting the approach in *Vokins Holdings v Robin Moors Allnutt* [1996] P.N.L.R. 354 and *Financial Services Authority v Rourke* [2002] C.P. Rep. 14.

[201] *Horbury Building Systems Ltd v Hampden Insurance NV* [2007] Lloyd's Rep. I.R. 247; *Tryg Baltica International (UK) Ltd v Boston Compania De Seguros SA* [2005] Lloyd's Rep. I.R. 40.

[202] *Meadows Insurance Co Ltd v Insurance Corp of Ireland* [1989] 2 Lloyd's Rep. 298; *Limit (No.3) Ltd v PDV Insurance Co Ltd* [2005] Lloyd's Rep. I.R. 552.

[203] *Toropdar v D* [2010] Lloyd's Rep. I.R. 358.

[204] *Jones v Environcom Ltd* [2010] Lloyd's Rep. I.R. 140.

a claim is refused will not be construed as an agreement ousting the right to seek declaratory relief prior to that date.[205]

International aspects. Negative declaratory relief is often sought by insurers and reinsurers as a means of securing that the action is heard by the English courts rather than by a foreign court. The ability of the underwriters to obtain English jurisdiction depends upon the domicile of the defendant and the nature of the contract. The points may be summarised as follows.

9–054

First, if the contract is one of insurance and the policyholder is domiciled within the EU or EFTA, special jurisdictional rules for matters relating to insurance are laid down by EC Council Regulation 44/2001 and the Lugano Conventions 1989 and 2009. These provide that a policyholder, whether consumer or commercial, may be sued only in the place of his domicile, and that this right cannot be lost by agreement other than in the case of large commercial risks and certain transport risks.

Secondly, if the contract is one of reinsurance and the reinsured is domiciled within the EU or EFTA, the special insurance jurisdictional rules in Council Regulation 44/2001 and the Lugano Conventions do not apply, and any application for negative declaratory relief by the reinsurers is governed by the ordinary jurisdictional rules contained in these instruments. These rules provide that the reinsured must be sued in the place of his own domicile or, as an alternative in the case of a contract, in the place where the obligation relied upon by the reinsurers was broken by the reinsured. If a court has jurisdiction to hear an action for negative declaratory relief under Regulation 44/2001 or the Lugano Conventions, the court cannot deny jurisdiction on the basis that the action is more conveniently heard elsewhere. All of this is subject to an overriding "first seised" rule, whereby the court first seised of a dispute has exclusive jurisdiction over it. Thus, if the reinsured has first commenced proceedings elsewhere in the EU or EFTA before the reinsurers initiate their action for negative declaratory relief, the second court must decline jurisdiction.

Thirdly, if the defendant is domiciled outside the EEA, then the ability of the English court to hear an action for negative declaratory relief in both insurance and reinsurance cases depends upon two matters. The first is jurisdictional: one of the heads of jurisdiction set out in CPR Practice Direction 6B must be satisfied. One of the most important grounds here are that the contract was made in England, governed by English law or broken in England. CPR Practice Direction 6B also expressly provides that the English court has jurisdiction if a claim is made for a declaration that no contract exists where, if the contract was found to exist, it would: be made within the jurisdiction; be made by or through an agent trading or residing within the jurisdiction; be governed by English law; or contain a term conferring jurisdiction on the English court. The second is discretionary: some useful purpose must be served by the action being heard in England. The position is now established that a claim by underwriters for a declaration is not to be treated any differently to a claim by the policyholder under the contract, and as long as the action for negative declaratory relief is not one designed to frustrate existing or contemplated foreign proceedings by the policyholder the court should hear the action.

---

[205] *British Credit Trust Holdings v UK Insurance Ltd* [2004] 1 All E.R. (Comm) 444.

CHAPTER 10

INDEMNITY

1. MEASURE OF INDEMNITY

The meaning of loss

10–001   *Forms of loss.* Marine insurance recognises three types of loss: total loss, where the subject matter is destroyed, seized without possibility of return or loses its identity[1]; partial loss, where the subject matter is damaged[2]; and constructive total loss, where the subject matter has become an economic loss, in that the cost of repair or retrieval would exceed the repaired value.[3] In the last mentioned case, the assured is entitled to give notice of abandonment to the insurers and thereby to receive an indemnity based on actual total loss rather than partial loss.[4] Non-marine insurance recognises only total and partial loss, and there is no intermediate form of loss. Thus, if the assured's goods are seized and there is some prospect that they will be returned to him, there may be a constructive total loss for marine insurance purposes[5] but there will be no loss at all under a non-marine policy[6] unless they are irrecoverable in all probability[7] or until the goods are finally put beyond the assured's reach.[8] Should the goods be restored to the assured following their seizure and before the insurers have agreed to treat them as lost,[9] then there is plainly no loss at all.[10] If the assured's goods are stolen they are generally to be regarded as lost, if the assured's goods are obtained from him by trick and have passed into the hands of a third party purchaser who has

---

[1] Marine Insurance Act 1906 s.57.

[2] Marine Insurance Act 1906 s.56(1).

[3] Marine Insurance Act 1906 s.60.

[4] Marine Insurance Act 1906 ss.61–62.

[5] *Rodocanachi v Elliott* (1874) L.R. 9 C.P. 518. Contrast *Masefield AG v Amlin Corporate Member Ltd* [2010] EWHC 280 Comm where there was a prospect that goods taken by pirates would be restored following the likely payment of a ransom.

[6] *Moore v Evans* [1918] A.C. 185 (goods deposited in a bank pending the cessation of war); *Holmes v Payne* [1930] 2 K.B. 301. See also: *Molinos de Arroz v Mumford* (1900) 6 T.L.R. 469; *Mitsui v Mumford* [1915] 2 K.B. 27; *Campbell and Phillips v Denman* (1915) 21 Com. Cas. 357; *London and Provincial Leather Processes v Hudson* [1939] 2 K.B. 724

[7] *Moore v Evans* [1917] 1 K.B. 458 at 468–469; *Masefield AG v Amlin Corporate Member Ltd* [2010] EWHC 280 Comm (no loss because the goods would be returned following payment of a ransom).

[8] *Scott v Copenhagen Reinsurance (UK) Ltd* [2003] Lloyd's Rep. I.R. 696 (destruction of aircraft following seizure).

[9] Once there is a binding agreement to indemnify the assured, the assured has a right to enforce the agreement and should the goods be recovered they pass to the insurers by way of salvage: *Holmes v Payne* [1930] 2 K.B. 301.

[10] *Glencore International AG v Alpina Insurance (No.2)* [2004] 1 Lloyd's Rep. 567.

obtained title to them[11] they will also be regarded as lost,[12] and if a trader purchases goods which he is unable to resell because they infringe a third party's intellectual property right they will also be regarded as lost.[13]

Loss of proceeds of sale. A distinction is to be drawn between the loss of the **10–002** insured subject matter and the loss of the proceeds of its sale. In *Eisinger v General Accident Fire and Life Assurance Corp Ltd*[14] the assured agreed to sell his car and received a cheque as payment for it. The cheque was dishonoured, and the assured, having parted with possession of the car, argued that he had suffered a loss of the car. It was held that the assured's loss had been of the proceeds of the sale of the car and not of the car itself. The assured was on these facts in the same position as a person who had agreed to accept credit or even a person who had been paid in cash and who had almost immediately afterwards been robbed of the cash by a third party. However, loss of the proceeds of sale is not necessarily uninsured, as all will depend upon the wording of the policy. In *Dobson v General Accident Fire and Life Assurance Corp*[15] the circumstances of the loss were similar to those in *Eisinger*: the assured accepted a cheque as payment for jewellery, although it subsequently transpired that the cheque had been stolen. The assured's policy covered not just "loss" of the jewellery, but rather "loss by theft". The Court of Appeal held that what had occurred fell squarely within the definition of "theft" in s.1 of the Theft Act 1968, in that property belonging to the assured had been appropriated. It is unlikely that *Eisinger* remains good law on its precise facts, unless it is possible to argue that the word "loss" is narrower than the phrase "loss by theft".

The question to be asked is whether the assured is claiming for the goods or their proceeds. In *Glencore International AG v Alpina Insurance Co Ltd*[16] the assured was held to have lost goods where they were deposited with a buyer pending resale to a third party, and they were misappropriated by the buyer without being resold: in such a case the assured's claim against the buyer was not just for the proceeds of the sale contract but alternatively for the tort of conversion, and on that basis the goods themselves had been lost. By contrast, it may be thought that where the assured buys goods which are later found to have been stolen and which are repossessed by the true owner, the loss is the price paid rather than the goods themselves.

Physical loss. Policies on property, unless they extend to loss of profits or other **10–003** business interruption losses, cover only the physical loss of the insured subject matter. This has four main consequences.

First, mere paper losses are excluded. Accordingly, if the seller of goods misstates the quality or quantity of goods supplied by him, the purchaser's policy will not cover the paper loss suffered by him as it cannot be said that the goods

---

[11] The purchaser of stolen goods will not obtain title to them, so this possibility is for the most part confined to a case where the assured has lost possession under a voidable contract which he has not avoided by the date of the resale. Cf. *National Employers Mutual General Insurance Association v Jones* [1988] 2 All E.R. 385; *Debs v Sibec Developments Ltd, The Times,* May 19, 1988.

[12] *Webster v General Accident Fire and Life Assurance Corporation* [1953] 1 Q.B. 520.

[13] *Grimaldi Ltd v Sullivan* [1997] C.L.C. 64.

[14] *Eisinger v General Accident Fire and Life Assurance Corp Ltd* [1955] 2 All E.R. 897. Cf. *Metal Scrap v Federated Conveyors* [1953] 1 Lloyd's Rep. 221.

[15] *Dobson v General Accident Fire and Life Assurance Corp* [1989] 3 All E.R. 927.

[16] *Glencore International AG v Alpina Insurance Co Ltd* [2004] 1 Lloyd's Rep. I.R. 111.

have been lost at all; they simply never existed.[17] Even in the case of a policy which insures against the loss of an official subsidy on exported cargo, should the export contract not be carried out, the assured is required to show not simply that the contract has failed but rather that it has failed because of the occurrence of an insured peril affecting the cargo.[18]

Secondly, the mere fact that a latent defect becomes patent does not give rise to an insured loss unless additional damage to property is caused.[19] There is no cover for the costs of repairs entailed in putting right the latent defect itself[20] unless the policy actually extends to such costs as well as to the external damage caused.[21]

Thirdly, there is a distinction between actual physical damage and diminution in value due to a fear that physical damage may have occurred. In order to recover the assured must prove either that there has been some physical damage. In *Quorum AS v Schramm (No.1)*[22] a pastel by Degas, *La Danse Grecque*, was stored in a strongroom in a warehouse. A fire broke out at the warehouse, and although the fire did not penetrate the strongroom there was a sudden and severe change in humidity and temperature. This caused "sub-molecular" physical damage to the pastel: the fire had, therefore, shortened of the life of the painting and increased the risk of deterioration. The difficulty was that the damage was not visible, and that the extent of the damage could not be tested without subjecting the pastel to testing which would have caused further damage. Thomas J. emphasised that there was actual physical damage and not merely depreciation in the market value of the pastel, although it was necessary to take into account the market view of the value of the painting in assessing the amount of the loss. The latter possibility is demonstrated by *Jan de Nul (UK) Ltd v Axa Royale Belge SA*.[23] It was there held that the deposition of silt on land amounted to physical damage to that land, and that the amount recoverable was the cost of removing the silt and of investigating whether there was actual damage. The Court of Appeal also noted that property could be regarded as having suffered damage even though it had not been diminished in value, and gave as an example that of a skilful painter who overpainted an earlier work: while it might be the case that the overpainting might fetch a higher price than the earlier work, it would still be the case that the earlier work had been damaged,[24] although the Court of Appeal refused to be drawn on the amount recoverable in such a case.

A fourth consequence, although of a specific nature, arose in *Outokumpu Stainless Ltd v Axa Global Risks (UK) Ltd*,[25] where the subject matter itself, a

---

[17] *Coven Spa v Hong Kong Chinese Insurance Co* [1999] Lloyd's Rep. I.R. 565, where the policy covered "shortage in weight"; *Fuerst Day Lawson Ltd v Orion Insurance Co Ltd* [1980] 1 Lloyd's Rep. 656.

[18] *Agra Trading Ltd v McAuslan (The Frio Chile)* [1995] 1 Lloyd's Rep. 182.

[19] *Promet Engineering v Sturge (The Nukila)* [1997] 2 Lloyd's Rep. 146; *Gerling General Insurance Co Ltd v Canary Wharf Group Plc* [2006] Lloyd's Rep. I.R. 462.

[20] *Shell UK Ltd v CLM Engineering Ltd* [2000] 1 Lloyd's Rep. 612.

[21] *Burts and Harvey v Vulcan & General Insurance Co* [1966] 1 Lloyd's Rep. 161; *Cementation Piling and Foundation Ltd v Commercial Union Insurance Co* [1995] 1 Lloyd's Rep. 97. Note that the International Hull Clauses 2003 allow the assured to recover 50 per cent of the common costs involved in putting right a latent defect which has caused external damage.

[22] *Quorum AS v Schramm (No.1)* [2002] Lloyd's Rep. I.R. 292.

[23] *Jan de Nul (UK) Ltd v Axa Royale Belge SA* [2002] Lloyd's Rep. I.R. 589.

[24] The Court of Appeal also gave the example of a lump of concrete being dropped on a car: property damage would be taken to have been inflicted even if it had been possible to persuade an *avant garde* gallery curator that the resultant object was a work of art worth more than the price paid for the car.

[25] *Outokumpu Stainless Ltd v Axa Global Risks (UK) Ltd* [2008] Lloyd's Rep. I.R. 147.

waste product with no commercial value, became contaminated with radiation and the assured incurred costs in excess of £6 million to dispose of it safely. In the absence of any physical damage, the policy was held not to respond to the asured's claim for recovery of costs.

Effect of payment by a third party. An assured who has a claim against insurers for loss will be deprived of his claim if, prior to payment by the insurers, the loss is made good by a third party who is liable for the loss. This is so because of the indemnity principle: if the assured has suffered no loss, there is nothing in respect of which a claim can be made against the insurers. However, if the assured is obliged by contract with the third party to apply the insurance monies in a particular fashion, e.g. by reinstating the insured property or by accounting to the third party for those monies, the assured will suffer a loss unless he is indemnified by the insurers.[26] **10–004**

Successive losses. The assured is entitled to successive partial losses to the insured property even if those losses in aggregate exceed the limit of indemnity for a total loss, subject to policy provisions which restrict recovery in any one year by reference to the number of losses or to the sum insured. A partial loss which is not repaired merges into a subsequent total loss, so that the assured can recover only for the latter.[27] **10–005**

Valued and unvalued policies. There is an important difference between the measure of indemnity as between valued and unvalued policies: where the policy is valued, the agreed value is the basis for the calculation of the assured's loss, even if the amount recovered is greater than actual loss, but in the absence of valuation the assured's actual loss is the appropriate measure. It is thus necessary initially to distinguish between these two classes of policy. Marine policies are for the most part valued, whereas non-marine policies tend to be unvalued. However, non-marine policies on unique or valuable property, such as land or jewellery, are frequently valued in order to resolve any dispute as to market value in the event of a loss, and life and accident policies are necessarily valued as there is no possibility of calculating the amount of any loss under insurances on persons. Plainly the benefit of a valued policy is the convenience of the removal of post-loss disputes,[28] and the law has been willing to recognise the validity of valued policies on the basis that the sum payable, while not necessarily a perfect indemnity, can be regarded as an indemnity by reference to the terms of the contract.[29] **10–006**

Section 27(2) of the Marine Insurance Act 1906 states that a valued policy is one which specifies the agreed value of the subject matter insured, whereas under s.28 an unvalued policy does not specify the value of the subject matter insured but, subject to maximum sum insured, leaves the amount of the loss to be subsequently ascertained. It is clear from s.28 that the mere fact that the policy contains financial limits does not convert it into a valued policy, as such limits

---

[26] *Lonsdale & Thompson Ltd v Black Arrow Group Plc* [1993] 3 All E.R. 648; *Talbot Underwriting v Nausch Hogan & Murray (The Jascon 5)* [2006] Lloyd's Rep. I.R. 531.

[27] For successive losses in marine insurance, see s.77 of the 1906 Act, discussed in Ch.24, below.

[28] *Barker v Janson* (1868) L.R. 3 C.P. 303; *General Shipping & Forwarding Co v British General Insurance Co* (1923) 15 Ll. L.R. 175. See, however, *Quorum AS v Schramm* [2002] Lloyd's Rep. I.R. 292.

[29] *City Tailors v Evans* (1922) 38 T.L.R. 230 at 234; *Goole Steam Towing Co v Ocean Marine* [1928] 1 K.B. 589 at 594.

merely fix the maximum amount for which the insurer can be liable in respect of any one claim,[30] and whether or not a policy is intended to be a valued policy is mainly a matter of construing the policy itself. There is no need for a policy to be described as a valued policy or "valued at", as long as the intentions of the parties to insure on the basis of a fixed value are otherwise clear from the policy as a whole. There is a consistent line of authority for the proposition that the phrase "sum insured" does not amount to an agreed valuation but merely fixes the maximum sum for which the insurers can be liable,[31] and this has been applied in recent marine[32] and non-marine cases. In *Quorum AS v Schramm*[33] the "sum insured" for a valuable work of art was US\$3 million. The subject matter was damaged by fire, and the parties agreed after the loss that the sum recoverable was the cost of restoration plus depreciation in value, subject to a maximum recovery based on the proportion of loss which the sum insured bore to the market value of the subject matter immediately prior to the loss. Thomas J. held that the policy was unvalued. Prior to the endorsement the "sum insured" referred to the maximum sum recoverable under the policy following proof of loss rather than by reference to any agreed value, so that there was a distinction between "insured value" (valued) and "sum insured" (unvalued). The endorsement did not affect the position, as it referred back to the sum insured and amounted to an average clause.[34]

Measure of indemnity under a valued policy

10–007   *Conclusiveness of valuation.* Where a value of the insured subject matter has been agreed between assured and insurer at the date of the policy, that valuation is deemed to be conclusive between them, and the amount of assured's actual loss is immaterial. This rule applies to both non-marine and marine insurance[35] and is enshrined in s.27(3) of the Marine Insurance Act 1906. The main effect of the rule is to relieve the assured of his normal duty to prove the amount of his loss,[36] although it remains for him to prove that he did have an interest at the date of the loss.[37]

In practice, problems are most likely to arise where the insured property has been overvalued and the insurer is suspicious of fraud. Here the insurer's remedy is not to seek to overturn the valuation, but to avoid the contract itself. Such a remedy may be available on one of four grounds. First, if a fraudulent design at the date of the policy can be demonstrated, the policy is voidable and may be set aside[38]; the greater the overvaluation the easier it becomes to draw an inference

---

[30] *Continental Illinois National Bank & Trust Co of Chicago v Bathurst* [1985] 1 Lloyd's Rep. 625.

[31] *Wilson v Nelson* (1864) 33 L.J.Q.B. 220; *Blascheck v Russell* (1916) 33 T.L.R. 74; *Brunton v Marshall* (1922) 10 Ll. L.R. 689; *Brewster v Blackmore* (1925) 21 Ll. L.R. 258: *British Traders Insurance Co v Monson* (1964) 111 C.L.R. 86; *Re Freesman and Royal Insurance Co of Canada* (1986) 29 D.L.R. (4th) 621.

[32] *Kyzuna Investments Ltd v Ocean Marine Mutual Insurance (Europe) (The Solveig)* [2002] Lloyd's Rep. I.R. 292; *Thor Navigation Inc v Ingosstrak Insurance (The Thor II)* [2005] Lloyd's Rep. I.R. 54.

[33] *Quorum AS v Schramm* [2002] Lloyd's Rep. I.R. 292.

[34] See below.

[35] *Bruce Jones* (1863) 1 H. & C. 769; *Barker v Janson* (1868) L.R. 3 C.P. 303; *Herring v Janson* (1895) 1 Com. Cas. 177; *Muirhead v Forth & North Sea Steamboat Insurance* [1894] 2 A.C. 72.

[36] *Feise v Aquilar* (1811) 3 Taunt. 506.

[37] Marine Insurance Act 1906, s.75(2), codifying *Williams v North China Insurance Co* (1876) 5 C.P.D. 757.

[38] *Haigh v de la Cour* (1812) 3 Camp. 319.

of fraud.[39] Secondly, the assured may have warranted the value of the property as at a certain date; in those circumstances any discrepancy, however slight, between the actual and warranted value will give the insurer the right to avoid the policy, despite its agreement to the valuation.[40] Thirdly, overvaluation by the assured is a material fact of which the insurer has to be informed: the insurer will thus have the right to avoid the policy for non-disclosure where the discrepancy between the agreed and actual values is sufficient to be material. Recent authority has indicated an insurer who has been content to accept a valuation without inquiry, and who has accordingly received a premium based on that valuation, cannot subsequently complain about it.[41] Fourthly, if the overvaluation is gross, it is possible for the policy to be construed as a wagering policy and thus void.[42]

Change in value by reduction of risk. Although the value of the insured subject matter cannot be challenged as between the insurer and the assured, in any case in which the entirety of the insured subject matter is not at risk its total agreed value is clearly inappropriate and the insurer will be liable only for the relevant proportion of the agreed value. This rule is of general application although of most importance in marine insurance in relation to cargo and freight, and s.75(2) of the Marine Insurance Act 1906 states that the insurer is entitled to plead that the whole or part of the subject matter insured was not at risk under the policy at the date of the loss. Thus, where a quantity of goods is insured for a marine voyage, and only a part of that quantity is in fact shipped, the agreed value is reduced proportionately.[43] Similarly, where freight on a given quantity of goods is insured under a valued policy, the shipment of a lesser quantity of goods demands a proportionate reduction in the agreed value of the freight,[44] although in this case it is generally a term of the contract that the insurer is to be liable for the full agreed value of the freight whether or not the vessel is fully loaded at the date of the loss. However, if the only change in the risk between the date of the insurance and the date of the loss is diminution in the actual value of the insured subject matter by loss or otherwise, as opposed to a change in the proportion of the subject matter coming on risk, the agreed value stands and it is not open to an insurer to plead change in circumstances.[45]

10–008

Total loss under a valued policy. In the event of total loss under a valued policy the insurer is liable for the agreed value of the subject matter.[46] If the property has

10–009

---

[39] *Lewis v Rucker* (1761) 2 Burr. 1167 (intention to gamble); *Barker v Janson* (1868) L.R. 3 C.P. 303; *Thames & Mersey Marine Insurance Co v "Gunford" Ship Co* [1911] A.C. 529.

[40] *Allen v Universal Automobile Insurance Co* (1933) 45 Ll. L.R. 55, where the assured had warranted the purchase price of his car.

[41] See Ch.6, above, and in particular *North Star Shipping Ltd and Others v Sphere Drake Insurance Plc* [2006] Lloyd's Rep. I.R. 514.

[42] *Lewis v Rucker* (1761) 2 Burr. 1167; *Irving v Manning* (1847) 1 H.L.C. 287 at 308; *City Tailors v Evans* (1922) 38 T.L.R. 230. See, however, the doubts expressed by Hobhouse J. in *Glafki Shipping v Pinios Shipping (The Maria (No.2))* [1984] 1 Lloyd's Rep. 660, where it was suggested that a policy made on insurable interest could not be a wagering contract even if the sum insured was grossly excessive. Cf. the comments of Lord Eldon in *Lucena v Craufurd* (1806) 2 Bos. & P.N.R. 269 at 322.

[43] *Rickman v Carstairs* (1833) 5 B. & Ad. 651; *Tobin v Harford* (1864) 34 L.J.C.P. 37.

[44] *Forbes v Aspinall* (1811) 13 East 323; *Rickman v Carstairs* (1833) 5 B. & Ad. 651; *Tobin v Harford* (1862) 34 L.J.C.P. 37.

[45] *Woodside v Globe Marine Insurance Co* [1896] 1 Q.B. 105.

[46] Marine Insurance Act 1906 ss.67(1) and 68(1).

been undervalued, the assured is deemed to have received an indemnity.[47] Conversely, if the property has been overvalued, the assured is entitled to recover the full sum insured.[48] The conclusiveness of the agreed value also has important implications for the insurer's rights of salvage and subrogation. As far as salvage is concerned, where the assured has not been fully compensated for his loss by reason of undervaluation under a valued policy, he is apparently estopped from denying the right of the insurer to take over the entire insured subject matter for its own benefit.

10–010 *Partial loss under a valued policy.* In this situation, the insurer is liable only for a proportion of the agreed value represented by the extent of damage to the subject matter. In *Elcock v Thomson*[49] a mansion was insured under a fire policy for an agreed value of £106,850, although its actual worth was only £18,000. The mansion was damaged as the result of a fire, and was thereafter valued at £12,600, a 30 per cent reduction in value. Morris J. held that the assured was entitled to recover 30 per cent of the agreed value, namely, £32,055. In most cases of this type the assured will not be able to recover a sum greatly in excess of actual loss following partial destruction, as the insurer will exercise its usual option under the policy to reinstate. The same principle applies to marine policies on freight[50] and lost goods[51] although special provision is made for partial loss of a vessel (reasonable cost of repairs or depreciation, whichever is greater)[52] and goods delivered damage at their destination (difference between sound and damaged value at destination).[53]

10–011 *Apportionment of valuation.* Where a number of specified items are insured under a single valued policy, without any apportionment of valuation between the items, it would appear to be the case that each item is to be regarded as valued under the policy. Consequently, it will be necessary to establish some form of apportionment for the purposes of the policy. Section 72 of the Marine Insurance Act 1906, which presumably applies equally to non-marine insurance as well, provides that, where different species of property are insured under a single valuation, the valuation must be apportioned over the different species in proportion to their respective insurable[54] values and the assured can recover for each item its proportion of the overall agreed value.

Measure of indemnity under an unvalued policy

10–012 *The principle of indemnity.* The guiding principle is that the assured is entitled to be indemnified for his loss, subject to any excess or other clause limiting recovery, to policy limits and, in the event of underinsurance in certain types of commercial policy where a partial loss has been suffered, to the rules of average. If the policy is unvalued and the assured is underinsured, he cannot recover more

[47] *Steamship Balmoral v Marten* [1902] A.C. 511.
[48] *Barker v Janson* (1868) L.R. 3 C.P. 303; *The Main* [1894] P. 320; *Woodside v Globe Marine Insurance Co* [18961] Q.B. 105; *General Shipping and Forwarding Co v British General Insurance Co Ltd* (1923) 15 Ll. L.R. 175; *Maurice v Goldsbrough Mort & Co Ltd* [1939] A.C. 452.
[49] *Elcock v Thomson* [1949] 2 K.B. 755.
[50] 1906 Act s.70.
[51] 1906 Act s.71(1).
[52] 1906 Act s.69.
[53] 1906 Act s.71(3).
[54] In non-marine insurance, market values; in marine insurance, the insurable value as determined by s.16: see Ch.24, below.

than the sum assured; by contrast, if he is underinsured he will be restricted to his actual loss even though the policy is in a greater sum.

Where the subject matter has merely been damaged, that is, where a partial loss has been suffered, the assured's measure of indemnity is the cost of restoring the property to its condition immediately preceding the loss, although in the case of goods intended for resale the policy may fix the limit of indemnity by reference to the diminution in value rather than the cost of repair. Where the subject matter has been totally destroyed, the assured's loss is the market value of the property immediately preceding the loss. There is an intermediate possibility, namely, where the subject matter has not been destroyed although the cost of restoration exceeds the pre-loss value of the property. This amounts to constructive total loss in marine insurance but in the absence of that possibility in non-marine insurance the loss can be partial only: that said, policy wordings often give the insurer the option to reinstate or to treat the subject matter as totally lost. In consumer cases, particularly where household goods are concerned, cover is provided on a "new for old" basis. This overcomes problems of calculating the amount of loss, but may well lead to the assured receiving a windfall.

Unless the insurers have opted to reinstate the subject matter themselves, they are required to make a money payment to the assured and the assured is entitled to use the moneys as he thinks fit even though he has been indemnified on a reinstatement basis.[55] This principle is to be applied even if the assured's loss proves to be greater or lesser than at the date of the occurrence of the insured event by the time of the trial. In *Dominion Mosaics Co Ltd v Trafalgar Trucking Co*[56] the assured's building was damaged tortiously by the defendant. The Court of Appeal held that the measure of loss was the cost of obtaining a new building, £390,000. Prior to the trial, the claimant had invested around £100,000 in its new building and had resold it for £690,000, producing a paper profit from the fire of £200,000 rather than a loss of £390,000. The Court of Appeal nevertheless held that the claimant was entitled to £390,000, and stressed that a claimant is not obliged to operate a profit and loss account running from the date at which the loss is to be assessed. Similarly, in *Frewin v Poland*,[57] manuscripts were insured up to maximum of £1,000 "in the event of loss resulting in the necessity for the assured to rewrite". Two manuscripts were lost, and it was agreed that the costs of producing the original manuscripts had been about £860 and that rewriting would cost a similar amount. The court rejected the insurers' argument that they were liable only if the books were actually rewritten, although it was held that the policy insured against the loss of the manuscripts and that the cost of rewriting merely fixed the amount that the assured could recover under the policy up to the ceiling of £1,000.

Determining market value. On the basis that the appropriate measure of **10–013** indemnity is diminution in market value, it is necessary for the court to place a market value of the goods both before the occurrence of the insured peril and immediately afterwards. Unless the goods are unique, ordinary market values

---

[55] It was suggested in *Tonkin v UK Insurance Ltd* [2007] Lloyd's Rep. I.R. 283 that an assured who had been paid by the insurers to purchase a kitchen, but who had earlier done so out of his own funds and used the insurance moneys for other purposes, was guilty of fraud. The court rejected that suggestion on the narrow ground that the insurers had on the facts indirectly paid for the kitchen, although it is difficult to see why the assured would have had acted in any way improperly even if the kitchen had not been purchased.

[56] *Dominion Mosaics Co Ltd v Trafalgar Trucking Co* [1990] 2 All E.R. 246.

[57] *Frewin v Poland* [1968] 1 All E.R. 100.

will be readily available. In the case of unique goods which are not insured under
a valued policy the court may have to undertake complex investigations. The
problem is illustrated by *Quorum AS v Schramn*,[58] in which a pastel by Degas,
La Danse Grecque, had been purchased by the assured in 1989 for about US$4.3
million, and was valued the following year at something between US$4 million
and US$5 million. It suffered heat damage in 1991 and, following repairs, was
sold at a price of US$3.275 million. Having received expert evidence, Thomas J.
held that the value of the pastel immediately before the fire was US$3.6 million,
and the value of the pastel immediately after the fire was US$2.2 million, giving
the assured a recovery of US$1.4 million. In fixing these market valuations,
Thomas J. was confronted with the fact that there were two different markets, the
auction market and the private dealers' market, the latter offering higher prices.
Thomas J. held that it was appropriate to assume (in the absence of contrary
evidence) that the assured intended to resell in the higher market, and that resale
value was to be based on that market. Relevant factors to be taken into account
in fixing the value of the painting, given the necessary subjectivity of expert
evidence as to quality and likely price, were held to include sales of comparative
works and provenance.

10–014   *Destruction of or damage to premises.* The assured's loss in the event of damage
to buildings is the cost of reinstatement. The cost is to be ascertained at the date
of the fire[59] and not at some later date, e.g. the date on which the assured receives
tenders for rebuilding,[60] and although the policy may make express provision for
assessment at a later date a policy term which provides that the insurers will pay
for the cost "incurred" in repair does not oust the presumption that the policy is
one of true indemnity based on costs at the time of the insured peril.[61]

Nevertheless, there may be cases in which the cost of reinstatement does not
represent the assured's actual loss, and the cases indicate that the rule may be
ousted where premises bear a value specific to the assured in question. The point
may be illustrated by reference to a particularly ornate building. The value of that
building to the assured may be looked at in at least three different ways,
depending upon the use to which the assured had put the property immediately
prior to the loss.

First, the assured may have wished to use the premises in their actual pre-loss
state, so that his loss is the building in its peculiarly ornate condition. In *Reynolds
v Phoenix Assurance Co Ltd*[62] the claimant purchased an old maltings in 1969 for
a sum under £18,000, and subsequently insured the premises for £628,000. The
maltings were used for the storage of grain. About 70 per cent of the building was
destroyed by fire, and the question to be decided was whether the assured was
entitled to the cost of replacing the maltings in their pre-loss condition—some
£250,000—or the cost of a substitute building which would equally have served
the assured's purposes no more than £50,000. Forbes J. held that the assured's
intention had been to use the maltings in their actual condition prior to the fire,
so that the actual loss was £250,000. This will also be the appropriate measure

---

[58] *Quorum AS v Schramm* [2002] Lloyd's Rep. I.R. 292.
[59] *Re Wilson and Scottish Insurance* [1920] 2 Ch. 28.
[60] *Leppard v Excess Insurance Co Ltd* [1979] 2 Lloyd's L.R. 91; *Sprung v Royal Insurance* [1999]
Lloyd's Rep. I.R. 111.
[61] *Tonkin v UK Insurance Ltd* [2007] Lloyd's Rep. I.R. 283.
[62] *Reynolds v Phoenix Assurance Co Ltd* [1978] 2 Lloyd's Rep. 440. See also *Pleasurama Ltd v
Sun Alliance and London Insurance Ltd* [1979] 1 Lloyd's Rep. 389.

of indemnity where the assured is under an obligation to a third party to reinstate the premises in their previous condition.[63]

Secondly, the assured may have been concerned not with the ornate nature of the premises but with their suitability for his particular purpose: in that situation he is entitled to a modern equivalent building only, and not to full reinstatement cost. In *Exchange Theatre Ltd v Iron Trades Mutual Insurance Co Ltd*[64] a Victorian hall, operated by the assured as a bingo hall, club and discotheque, was damaged by fire. It was held that the assured's actual subjective loss was not the Victorian hall as such, but a modern equivalent building suited to the assured's needs, and awarded a sum representing the cost of such a building.

Thirdly, the assured may have held the building as an investment only, in which case his loss is the amount that the building would have obtained on the open market immediately prior to the occurrence of the insured event. In *Leppard v Excess Insurance Co*[65] the assured's cottage was destroyed by fire. The reinstatement value was £8,000 but the market value of which was £4,500. The evidence showed that the assured's intention prior to the loss had been to sell the cottage; on that basis all that the assured had lost was the market value, as opposed to the reinstatement value, of the cottage, and judgment was given for the lesser amount.

Total loss of domestic goods. The measure of the assured's loss in the event of a total destruction of goods is the market value of the goods immediately before the occurrence of the insured event, as this will generally reflect what the assured has actually lost. A number of features of this rule call for comment. **10–015**

First, the value is to be tested at the place[66] of the loss and at the date of the loss.[67] Consequently, if the goods have appreciated[68] or depreciated[69] since the date of the policy, the assured will be better or worse off, as the case may be.

Secondly, the assured is not permitted to recover for the aesthetic value of the goods.[70]

Thirdly, consequential losses are also excluded, although where fixtures are destroyed, the cost of fixing new ones is necessarily to be allowed as part of the indemnity.[71]

Fourthly, it is generally assumed that the market value is the amount that the goods would have realised had they been sold by the assured, not the (normally) greater amount that the assured would have to expend to replace them. It is not obvious that this presumption is justified. In the law of tort, the measure of damages for a destroyed chattel is its replacement cost rather than its market value[72] where replacement would be reasonable and the amount claimed is objectively fair: these qualifications are an aspect of the duty of the claimant to

---

[63] *Lonsdale & Thompson Ltd v Black Arrow Group Plc* [1993] 3 All E.R. 648.

[64] *Exchange Theatre Ltd v Iron Trades Mutual Insurance Co Ltd* [1983] 1 Lloyd's Rep. 674.

[65] *Leppard v Excess Insurance Co* [1979] 2 All E.R. 668. See also *McClean Enterprises Ltd v Ecclesiastical Insurance Office Plc* [1986] 2 Lloyd's Rep. 416.

[66] *Hercules Insurance v Hunter* (1836) 14 Sh. (Ct of Sess) 1137: *Chapman v Pole* (1870) 22 L.T. 306: *Vance v Forster* (1841) Ir. Circ. Rep. 47: *Re Wilson and Scottish Insurance* [1920] 2 Ch. 28.

[67] *Rice v Baxendale* (1861) 7 H. & N. 96: *Charles Griffin & Co Ltd v De-La-Haye* [1968] 1 Lloyds Rep. 253. Contrast the position under s.16 of the Marine Insurance Act 1906, which requires insurable value to he assessed at the date at which the insurer came on risk.

[68] *Re Wilson and Scottish Insurance* [1920] 2 Ch. 28.

[69] *Edney v De Rougemont* (1927) 28 Ll. L.R. 215.

[70] *Re Egmont's Trusts* [1908] 1 Ch. 821.

[71] *Vance v Forster* (1841) Ir.Circ. Rep. 47.

[72] *Aerospace Publishing Ltd v Thames Water Utilities Ltd* [2005] EWHC 2987 QB.

mitigate his loss, and precludes the claimant from incurring a wholly disproportionate expenditure.[73] That sum is payable even though the claimant has not
replaced the chattel and indeed even if he does not have the intention of doing
so.[74] This indicates that where the measure of indemnity is the market price of the
insured subject matter, the relevant market price should normally be regarded as
the price which the assured would have to pay to replace the subject matter and
not the lower price at which the assured could have sold the subject matter, unless
it can be shown that the assured was prepared to sell at the latter price. In the case
of a written-off car, therefore, a true indemnity would be the cost of replacing the
car with a vehicle of equivalent value. This is the tort measure, and in tort cases
the rule is that the price originally paid by the claimant is not relevant in
determining actual loss, so that if the claimant has had the good fortune to obtain
the subject matter cheaply, he is nevertheless entitled to recover the full cost of
replacement.[75]

If it is correct that the market value test refers to the amount which the assured
would have received in the open market, it is necessary to look at the price from
the point of view of a reasonable purchaser; where the goods have a hidden
defect, the amount payable by a reasonable purchaser may be higher than the
actual value of the goods in their defective state.[76]

10–016 *Total loss of commercial goods.* The rules applicable to the total loss of domestic
goods are equally relevant here. Thus, in *Scottish Coal Co Ltd v Royal and Sun
Alliance Plc*,[77] market price was held to be the general rule. A number of
situations must be distinguished, necessitated by the important principle that a
policy on goods does not cover loss of future profits.

First, if the goods are in the process of being manufactured by the assured and
are destroyed before completion, the assured is entitled to recover their estimated
market value on completion minus the estimated costs of completion. In *Richard
Aubrey Film Productions Ltd v Graham*,[78] the assured film producer claimed for
a stolen film that had nearly been completed. The assured was awarded the
difference between the market value of the completed film and the costs of its
completion, no account being taken of the aesthetic value of the film.

Secondly, where the goods destroyed are themselves used in a process of
manufacture, the assured's loss is the market value of the goods and not the
consequential loss of manufacturing profits flowing from the loss; this follows
from the general rule concerning loss of profits.[79] The price actually paid for the
goods by the assured is irrelevant.[80] An assured who has made a "good buy" is
entitled to benefit from his prudence by claiming full replacement cost.

Thirdly, where the assured is a merchant and loses goods purchased for resale,
there is some debate whether the assured recovers the cost of obtaining new

[73] *Southampton Container Terminals Ltd v Schiffahrtsgesellschaft Hansa Australia mbh & Co (The
Maersk Colombo)* [2001] 2 Lloyd's Rep. 275.
[74] *Ali Reza-Delta Transport Co Ltd v United Arab Shipping Co SAG (No.1)* [2003] 2 All E.R.
(Comm) 269. The question of intention may, however, go to reasonableness: see *Southampton
Container Terminals Ltd v Schiffahrtsgesellschaft Hansa Australia mbh & Co (The Maersk Colombo)*
[2001] 2 Lloyd's Rep. 275. In *Aerospace Publishing Ltd v Thames Water Utilities* [2007] EWCA Civ
3 it was commented that it would be rare to award reinstatement cost to a claimant who did not intend
to reinstate.
[75] *Dominion Mosaics Co v Trafalgar Trucking Co* [1990] 2 All E.R. 246.
[76] *State Insurance Office v Bettany* [1992] 2 N.Z.L.R. 275 (hidden rust).
[77] *Scottish Coal Co Ltd v Royal and Sun Alliance Plc* [2008] Lloyd's Rep. I.R. 718.
[78] *Richard Aubrey Film Productions Ltd v Graham* [1960] 2 Lloyd's Rep. 101.
[79] *Re Wright and Pole* (1834) 1 A. & E. 621.
[80] *Dominion Mosaics Co v Trafalgar Trucking Co* [1990] 2 All E.R. 246.

goods or whether he recovers the price that he would have obtained for them on resale. The latter possibility runs counter to the rule that the assured cannot recover for loss of profits and, moreover, is inconsistent with the marine rule that the assured is entitled to recover only the invoice price of his purchase, irrespective of any sub-sale that he may have arranged or of the fact that the market is rising.[81] However, it may be that the best analogy is with the right of a buyer to damages for non-delivery under s.51 of the Sale of Goods Act 1979, where the rule is that if the buyer is able to go into the market to purchase replacement goods he will be awarded the sum necessary to enable him to do so, with the result that no element for loss of resale profits is available,[82] although where a specific sub-sale has been arranged the buyer may in some circumstances be awarded his loss of profits on that sub-sale.[83] Such a rule would at least reflect the assured's actual loss.

Partial loss of goods. Where the goods are capable of repair, the measure of the **10–017** assured's loss is normally the cost of restoring the goods to their pre-loss condition,[84] although if the goods were intended by the assured for resale then the correct measure is the market value of the goods before and after the loss.[85] If repair is the correct measure of loss, but the cost of repairing the goods is more than the market value of the goods prior to the loss, i.e. the marine constructive total loss, the policy may well confer upon the insurer the right either to pay the assured for a total loss of the goods or to indemnify the assured for the cost of repair. In the absence of such a provision, it would appear that the insurer has no right to exercise this option, and that it must pay the full cost of repairs if the assured so demands; the practice of motor insurers, who are most commonly affected by this matter, is to pay only the market value of the vehicle prior to the loss. The true position would seem to be that the assured is entitled to an indemnity and, by analogy with the buildings cases discussed above, if the assured intends to reinstate then the amount of his loss is reinstatement cost and not market value prior to the loss.

If, by contrast, the cost of repairing the goods is marginally less than their market value prior to the loss the insurer may nevertheless benefit from paying for a total loss rather than paying for repairs. This may arise in the following way. Suppose that a car is worth £1,100 prior to the loss, and that following an accident its unrepaired value is £350 and the cost of repairing it is £1,000. The assured subsequently states his intention of repairing the car. The insurer might fear that if it pays over £1,000 the assured will not reinstate the vehicle but sell it for £350 and thus achieve a net £1,350, more than an indemnity. In principle it would seem that the insurer is liable for the full repairing cost of £1000.

The full repair of a domestic item, and in particular a car, does not necessarily mean that the assured has been fully indemnified, for it is quite clear that if the assured wishes to resell the car it will be worth less than would otherwise have

---

[81] 1906 Act, s.16(3); *Usher v Noble* (1810) 12 East 639.

[82] Sale of Goods Act 1979 s.51(3). See also *Re-Source America International Ltd v Platt Site Services Ltd* [2005] EWHC 2242 (TCC): if there are no available second-hand goods, the assured is entitled to the cost of new replacement goods.

[83] *Re R & H Hall Ltd and William Pim (Junior) & Co Ltd's Arbitration* [1928] All E.R. Rep. 763.

[84] *Westminster Fire v Glasgow Provident* (1883) 13 App.Cas. 669 at 713; *Andrews v Patriotic Assurance (No.2)* (1886) L.R.Ir. 355 at 366; *Scottish Amicable v Northern Assurance* (1883) 11 R (Ct of Sess) 287 at 295.

[85] *Quorum AS v Schramm* [2002] Lloyd's Rep. I.R. 292.

been the case due to the fact that it has been damaged and repaired. This form of accelerated depreciation is treated as loss by the law of tort[86]

10–018 *Loss not capable of measurement.* The rules for determining indemnity are not capable of solving all of the problems of total loss. One often discussed but unresolved question concerns the loss of one of a pair of unique items in the situation in which the market value of the remaining item increases due to the fact that it is now the only one in existence. It might be thought that allowing recovery in such a case would indemnify the assured not for financial loss but rather for loss of aesthetic pleasure, a head of loss which is normally outside the scope of property insurance. It was nevertheless said by Scrutton J. in *City Tailors v Evans*[87] that:

> "if one of two unique china vases is insured and destroyed, it does not avail the underwriter that by the destruction the second vase has become more unique and more valuable."

Again it may be difficult to measure the assured's loss under an insurance against defective title. In *Grimaldi v Sullivan*[88] the assured purchased watches for £57,000. The watches proved to be fakes, with a market price of about £3,500, but they could not be resold without infringing a trade mark. Their scrap value was £750. The Court of Appeal held that the assured could not claim £57,000, as that would have indemnified him for loss of genuine watches, which he had not purchased. The Court of Appeal also rejected the scrap value as the appropriate measure, as this disregarded the fact that fake watches did have some resale value. The proper measure was, therefore, £3,500, the amount which could have been realised for the watches had the trade mark owner not prohibited resale: as it was the defect in title which allowed the trade mark owner to prohibit resale, the loss was the amount which would have been realisable but for that prohibition.

Consequential loss

10–019 *Forms of consequential loss.* Consequential loss can take many forms: in accident insurance it may take the form of future loss of business and general damage to the assured's goodwill while he is recovering[89]; goods may become less saleable in general or a specific lucrative contract of sale may be lost by the assured[90]; buildings may lose their earning capacity while being repaired[91]; the assured may incur disposal costs in respect of waste material which has become contaminated but which of itself has no commercial value[92]; and an assured who insures his potential liability under a commercial transaction will be deprived of the profit that he expected to make under that transaction.[93] Consequential loss

---

[86] *Peyton v Brooks* [1974] 1 Lloyd's Rep. 241.

[87] *City Tailors v Evans* (1921) L.J.K.B. 379, 385. In *Jan De Nul (UK) Ltd v Axa Royale Belge SA* [2002] Lloyd's Rep. I.R. 589, Rix L.J. similarly recognised the possibility that an insured peril which actually increased the value of the subject matter—as where the damage suffered by a car converted it into a work of modern art—could give rise to a claim, although he did not comment on the measure of indemnity in such a case.

[88] *Grimaldi v Sullivan* [1997] C.L.C. 64.

[89] *Theobald v Railway Passengers Assurance Co* (1854) 10 Exch. 45.

[90] *Emmanuel v Hepburn* [1966] 1 Lloyd's Rep. 304.

[91] *Re Wright and Pole* (1834) 1 Ad. & E. 621.

[92] *Outokumpu Stainless Ltd v Axa Global Risks (UK) Ltd* [2008] Lloyd's Rep. I.R. 147.

[93] *Maurice v Goldsborough, Mort & Co Ltd* [1939] A.C. 452.

most commonly takes the form of loss of profit, and in most cases the amount of consequential loss suffered by the assured following the occurrence of an insured peril can only be speculated. However, despite the general principle that speculations are uninsurable for want of insurable interest, it has long been established that loss of profit and other consequential loss is, in the light of its commercial importance, a legitimate subject matter for insurance.[94] The general rule is that insurance covers physical damage resulting from an insured peril, and that consequential loss is not insured unless the policy expressly so provides.

Valued policies. In the case of a valued policy it is permissible for the assured to **10–020** include in his valuation of the subject matter an element for loss of profit, and as long as the insurer has agreed to the valuation that sum is prima facie conclusive of the amount recoverable by the assured in the event of loss. If the same policy covers goods at a valuation and also profits unvalued, the valuation will be taken as the agreed value when the risk begins.[95] Two qualifications to the insurability of profits or other consequential loss should, however, be noted. First, the assured is under a duty—albeit limited by recent authority—to disclose to the insurer any excessive overvaluation of the subject matter by him, so that even where the valuation has been accepted by the insurer there may be some cases in which the policy is voidable on this ground. It will be a question of degree as to whether the overvaluation represented a genuine estimate of the future earning capacity of the subject matter or whether the assured was simply engaging in wild speculation.[96] Second, there is old marine insurance authority for the proposition that, where consequential loss does form an element in the agreed valuation, the assured is required to prove that he would have suffered consequential loss following the occurrence of an insured peril.[97] These cases are, however, scarcely reconcilable with the principle that valuations are conclusive, and indeed detract from the very purpose of the valued policy, which is to remove the need for post-loss valuations to be made, and it is probable that they are no longer authoritative.

Unvalued policies. In the case of an unvalued policy, while it is settled that **10–021** consequential loss is insurable, it is also established that consequential loss will not be recoverable under a policy unless it is expressly included.[98] This is either on causation grounds—because consequential loss is not proximately caused by an insured peril but by the loss of the insured subject matter—or as a matter of construction that consequential loss is different in nature from physical damage. Thus where an inn was burnt down, the policy covered only damage to the fabric

---

[94] *Barclay v Cousins* (1802) 2 East 544; *Lucena v Craufurd* (1806) 2 Bos. & Pul. N.R. 269; *Puller v Staniforth* (1809) 11 East 232; *Puller v Glover* (1810) 12 East 124; *Glengate-KG Properties Ltd v Norwich Union Fire Insurance Society Ltd* [1996] 2 All E.R. 487; *Seele Austria GmbH Co v Tokio Marine Europe Insurance Ltd (No.2)* [2009] EWHC 255 (TCC).

[95] *Smith v Reynolds* (1856) 1 H. & N. 221; *Williams v Atlantic Assurance* [1933] 1 K.B. 81 at 90.

[96] See above.

[97] *Barclay v Cousins* (1802) 2 East 544; *Hodgson v Glover* (1805) 6 East 316.

[98] *Glover v Black* (1763) 3 Burr. 1394; *Eyre v Glover* (1812) 16 East 218; *Re Wright and Pole* (1834) 1 Ad. & E. 621; *Cator v Great Western Insurance Co of New York* (1873) L.R. 8 C.P. 552; *City Tailors v Evans* (1921) 126 L.T. 439; *Lewis Emanuel & Son Ltd v Hepburn* [1960] 1 Lloyd's Rep. 304; *Flying Colours Film Co Ltd v Assicurazioni Generali SpA* [1993] 2 Lloyd's Rep. 184; *Glengate v Norwich Union* [1996] 4 All E.R. 487. See also: *Maurice v Goldsborough, Mort & Co Ltd* [1939] A.C. 452, where there was an express exclusion in a bailee's liability policy for the bailee's own loss of profit; *Emanuel v Hepburn* [1960] 1 Lloyd's Rep. 304 (transit insurance against "physical loss or damage or deterioration" held not to cover loss of market).

of the building and not consequential losses such as rent, the hire of alternative premises and loss of custom while the inn was being rebuilt.[99] Equally, where business premises were burnt down, wages or loss of profits could not be recovered under an ordinary fire policy.[100] So, also, an insurance on goods does not cover the loss in value of uninjured goods due to damage to other goods which are part of the same consignment.[101] Similar principles apply to accident insurance. The assured is ordinarily entitled to the costs of medical attendance and expenses to which he is put by the accident, but not to the loss of business or professional profits.[102]

While it is the case that profits may be insured, they must be described as such.[103] It was held accordingly in *Maurice v Goldsborough Mort*[104] that where consignees insured wool on trust they had to pay over the whole of the insurance moneys to the owners, and that they could retain nothing on account of their loss of commission. Where profits and other consequential losses have been insured, the assured is under a duty to disclose all material facts concerning anticipated profits prior to the inception of the policy, and in order to recover following the occurrence of an insured peril must demonstrate that anticipated profits have been lost.[105]

Damages for late payment

10–022   *The exisxting law.* In addition to any sums payable under the policy, the insurer may render himself liable in damages to the assured for some independent breach of his obligations. It was at one time thought that failure by the insurer to disclose material facts to the assured, in breach of its duty of utmost good faith, gave rise to damages where the assured's cover was less than he had been led to believe. This possibility was, however, denied by the Court of Appeal in *La Banque Financière de la Cité SA v Westgate Insurance Co Ltd*,[106] the views there expressed being approved in the House of Lords by Lord Templeman.[107] The question thus arises whether insurers are under any implied obligation to consider the assured's claim within a reasonable time, to pay the claim within a reasonable time or, in liability insurance cases, to take up the assured's defence in accordance with the terms of the policy. Insofar as any such obligation might be based upon the insurers' post-contractual duty of utmost good faith, a possibility countenanced by Longmore L.J. in *K/S Merc-Skandia v Lloyd's Underwriters*[108] in relation to a liability insurer's obligation to defend, but rejected by Mance L.J. in *Gan Insurance v Tai Ping Insurance (No.2)*,[109] it cannot sound in damages.

---

[99] *Re Wright and Pole* (1834) 1 Ad. & El. 621.

[100] *Menzies v North British* (1847) 9 D (Ct of Sess) 694. See also: *Westminster Fire v Glasgow Provident* (1888) 13 App. Cas. 699; *Theohald v Railway Passengers Assurance* (1854) 10 Ex. 45 at 58.

[101] *Cator v Great Western Insurance of New York* (1873) L.R. 8 C.P. 552.

[102] *Theohald v Railway Passengers Assurance* (1854) 10 Ex. 45.

[103] *Maurice v Goldsborough, Mort & Co Ltd* [1939] A.C. 452, citing *Lucena v Craufurd* (1806) 2 Bos. & P.N.R. 269 and *Mackenzie v Whitworth* (1875) 1 Ex. D. 36 at 43. See also *Stockdale v Dunlop* (1840) 6 M. & W. 224 at 232–233.

[104] *Maurice v Goldsborough Mort* [1939] A.C. 452.

[105] *Stavers v Mountain, The Times*, July 27, 1912 (assured not disclosing that his business was trading at a loss).

[106] *La Banque Financière de la Cité SA v Westgate Insurance Co Ltd* [1988] 2 Lloyd's Rep. 513, reversing the decision of Steyn J. at first instance.

[107] *La Banque Financière de la Cité SA v Westgate Insurance Co Ltd* [1990] 2 All E.R. 947, at 959.

[108] *K/S Merc-Skandia v Lloyd's Underwriters* [2001] Lloyd's Rep. I.R. 802.

[109] *Gan Insurance v Tai Ping Insurance (No.2)* [2001] Lloyd's Rep. I.R. 667.

The Canadian courts have nevertheless taken the view that the insurer's duty of utmost good faith is a fiduciary duty, breach of which gives rise to damages.[110]

Accordingly, an obligation to act timeously can be framed, if at all, as a breach of an implied term in the insurance policy. To date the courts have been reluctant to recognise an implied term. As the insurer's obligation is to hold the assured harmless,[111] the date on which the peril insured against occurs is, subject to some express term to the contrary the date on which damages become payable and on which the limitation period begins to run.[112] Late payment by the insurer cannot, as a matter of principle, amount to a further breach of contract, for it is not possible to be in breach of an obligation to pay damages.[113] In *Sempra Metals Ltd v HM Commissioners of Inland Revenue*[114] the House of Lords refused to follow *The Lips* insofar as the case held that a court could not award interest on a sum due, but Lord Mance described the principle espoused in *The Lips* that "the law knows no such thing as a claim for damages for failing to pay damages" as "straightforward".

The appropriate remedy is, therefore, interest, which will generally be imposed by the court from the date of the loss.[115] Nevertheless, it was suggested by the Court of Appeal in *Sprung v Royal Insurance*[116] that the insurer is under an implied contractual duty to make payment within a reasonable time and that the insurer is liable in damages for failure to do so: such damages might in principle be awardable for loss of business. In *Sprung* the assured's business premises were damaged by vandals. The insurers denied liability. Subsequently, the assured's business collapsed, and he commenced proceedings against the insurers claiming the insurance monies plus further damages representing the loss of his business brought about by the insurers' failure to agree to reinstatement within a reasonable time. The Court of Appeal accepted that there could be no cause of action in damages for late payment of the sums due under a policy, although it was at the very least arguable that insurers owed an implied duty to their assured to accept liability within a reasonable time, a duty which encompassed an early investigation of the loss with a view to determining what their position should be. The Court of Appeal held that, on the present facts, the insurers were arguably in breach of their duty by not inspecting the premises and deciding whether permission should be given for repairs to be effected, but that breach of the duty did not give rise to substantial damages as any loss suffered by the assured was the result of his own decision not to reinstate, whether that decision was voluntary or forced upon him by impecuniosity. Beldam L.J. was prepared to accept that substantial damages might be awardable where the purpose of the policy was to provide for immediate reinstatement of damaged

---

[110] *Plaza Fiberglass Manufacturing Ltd v Cardinal Insurance Co* 68 D.L.R. (4th) 586 (1990). Australian law also allows the assured to recover damages for late payment where such late payment constitutes a breach of the insurers' duty of utmost good faith: see the Law Commissions' Issues Paper 6, *Late Payment*, March 2010.

[111] See, e.g. *Luckie v Bushby* (1853) 13 C.B. 864; *Edmunds v Lloyd's Italico* [1986] 2 All E.R. 249.

[112] *Chandris v Argo Insurance* [1963] 2 Lloyd's Rep. 65; *Castle Insurance v Hong Kong Islands Shipping* [1983] 2 Lloyd's Rep. 276; *Hong Kong Borneo Services v Pilcher* [1992] 2 Lloyd's Rep. 593; *Bank of America v Christmas (The Kyriaki)* [1993] 1 Lloyd's Rep. 137.

[113] *Ventouris v Mountain (The Italia Express)* [1992] 2 Lloyd's Rep. 281; *President of India v Lips Maritime (The Lips)* [1988] A.C. 395.

[114] *Sempra Metals Ltd v HM Commissioners of Inland Revenue* [2007] UKHL 34.

[115] *Burts & Harvey v Vulcan Boiler* [1966] 1 Lloyd's Rep. 354.

[116] [1999] Lloyd's Rep. I.R. 111, followed in *Pride Valley Foods Ltd v Independent Insurance Co Ltd* [1999] Lloyd's Rep. I.R. 120.

buildings or plant and equipment. *Sprung* is supported by earlier dicta to the effect that a refusal by the insurer to make due payment is a distinct repudiation of the policy.[117] Further, it was held in *Charles Griffin & Co Ltd v De-La-Haye*[118] that an assured whose caravan was damaged in a motor accident in November 1966, but whose insurers did not agree to treat the caravan as a write-off until May 1967, had no answer to a claim for damages by the assured representing the cost of hiring a replacement vehicle at £12 per week for that intervening period. If it is the case that damages are available for breach of an implied term, it would appear that damages are limited to pecuniary loss. Damages cannot be obtained for distress, because a contract of insurance is not one which has as its specific objective the assured's peace of mind.[119]

Whenever the question of implied term has come up for specific decision, the implication of a term has been refused. The issue was argued at some length in *Insurance Corporation of the Channel Islands v McHugh (No.1)*.[120] It was there argued that the insurer was under an implied obligation to conduct negotiations, assess the sum due and make payment with reasonable diligence and due expedition. The argument was put in the context of parallel material damage and business interruption policies, the suggestion being that failure to settle the material damage claim increased the business interruption loss. Mance J. rejected the implied term argument on a number of grounds: the implication of a term was not necessary to give business efficacy to the contract the insurers would not have agreed to the term had it been proposed to them in the course of negotiations for issue of the policy and any implied term would have to be mutual, in that the assured would be under an implied duty to make a claim within a reasonable time, a proposition for which there was no authority. Mance J. relied also upon the principle, which proved fatal to the claim in *Sprung*, namely, that the concept of a post-loss duty on the insurer was inconsistent with the rule that the assured's claim accrues when the loss occurs. Similarly, In *England v Guardian Insurance Ltd*[121] H.H.J. Thornton QC held that an assured had no claim against insurers for damages for distress and inconvenience for late payment under an insurance policy. In *Normhurst Ltd v Dornoch Ltd*,[122] a case involving a refusal to make payment under a terrestrial material damage and business interruption policy, H.H.J. Chambers QC followed the *Sprung* principle and ruled that the assured had no cause of action against the insurers for damages for failure to pay the policy proceeds. The court in *Dornoch* accepted that the terms of the policy could alter the common law rule, but further held that the rule was not ousted by provisions in the policy which postponed the date of payment as the policy remained one of indemnity for actual loss. Again, in *Tonkin v UK Insurance Ltd*[123] the ruling in *Sprung* was regarded as precluding any action in damages against a property insurer for late payment based on an implied term in the policy, and that the *Sprung* principle applied even where the insurers had expressly undertaken that they would "always try to be fair and reasonable whenever you

[117] *Lefevre v White* [1990] 1 Lloyd's Rep. 569; *Transthene Packaging v Royal Insurance* [1996] L.R.L.R. 32.

[118] *Charles Griffin & Co Ltd v De-La-Haye* [1968] 2 Lloyd's Rep. 253.

[119] *The Italia Express* [1992] 2 Lloyd's Rep. 281.

[120] *Insurance Corporation of the Channel Islands v McHugh (No.1)* [1997] L.R.L.R. 94.

[121] *England v Guardian Insurance Ltd* [2000] Lloyd's Rep. I.R. 404.

[122] *Normhurst Ltd v Dornoch Ltd* [2005] Lloyd's Rep. I.R. 27.

[123] *Tonkin v UK Insurance Ltd* [2007] Lloyd's Rep. I.R. 283.

have need of the protection of this Policy. We will also act quickly to provide that protection."[124]

One of the possible justifications for the *Sprung* decision at that time was that the proximate cause of the assured's loss was not late payment by the insurers but rather the assured's own impecuniosity. However, that potential barrier to recovery has been removed by the decision of the House of Lords in *Lagden v O'Connor*[125] to depart from the long-established principle laid down in *Owners of Liesbosch Dredger v Owners of SS Edison (The Liesbosch)*[126] to the effect that the victim of a tort has no right of recovery for losses brought about by his own financial inability to replace goods lost or damaged by the tort.

Whatever the position might be in property and other non-marine insurance law, it would seem that there is even less possibility of late payment of a marine claim giving rise to additional damages. In *Ventouris v Mountain (The Italia Express (No.3))*[127] the assured claimed from his insurers additional damages by way of distress and hardship, flowing from the failure of the insurers to make prompt payment. Hirst J. rejected the claim, and held that the insurers' failure to make payment was immaterial as the insurer was in breach of contract and liable for unliquidated damages as from the date of the casualty, and that damages had to be assessed as at that date. That point aside, there was nothing in the 1906 Act which indicated that any further damages could be recovered.

Proposals for reform. In March 2010 the English and Scottish Law Commissions published their Issues Paper No.6, *Late Payement*. The Law Commissions analysed existing law, and expressed the view that the denial of recovery for late payment of insurance proceeds is anomalous, in that in all other areas of law the claimant is entitled to damages for foreseeable or foreseen loss under the ordinary rule for remoteness of damages in *Hadley v Baxendale*.[128] The problem arises from the notion that the insurers' duty is to hold the assured harmless, a concept which has been widely criticised,[129] in turn leading to the idea in *President of India v Lips Maritime Corporation (The Lips)*[130] that damages cannot be awarded for late payment of damages. It may be that in due course the decision of the House of Lords in *Sempra Metals v Inland Revenue Commissioners*[131] will be developed to as to recognise a remedy for late payment, but that step has yet to be taken.

Leaving aside anomaly, the Law Commissions identified a number of other problems with the *Sprung* case. In particular, the law as stated in *Sprung* means that the law is unduly weighted in favour of insurers, in that they the assured has no right to damages if insurers do not pay on time, but the insurers are free to impose whatever obligations they wish upon the assured. Further, the law does not provide an incentive for an inefficient or poorly-run insurer to change its

10–023

---

[124] Contrast, however, *Mandrake Holdings Ltd v Countrywide Assured Group Plc* Unreported, May 2006, in which Rix L.J. in an extempore judgment expressed the hope that the correctness of the *Sprung* principle would in due course be considered by the House of Lords.

[125] *Lagden v O'Connor* [2004] 1 A.C. 1067. See also *Alcoa Minerals of Jamaica Inc v Broderick* [2002] 1 A.C. 371.

[126] *Owners of Liesbosch Dredger v Owners of SS Edison (The Liesbosch)* [1933] A.C. 449.

[127] *Ventouris v Mountain (The Italia Express) (No.3)* [1992] 2 Lloyd's Rep. 281.

[128] *Hadley v Baxendale* (1854) 9 Exch. 341.

[129] See in particular *Transthene Packaging v Royal Insurance* [1996] L.R.L.R. 32, where the court found it very surprising that the law deemed insurers to be in breach of contract simply because a peril had occurred.

[130] *President of India v Lips Maritime Corporation (The Lips)* [1988] A.C. 395.

[131] *Sempra Metals v Inland Revenue Commissioners* [2008] 1 A.C. 561.

ways. Finally, in simple terms, the ability of insurers to use delay as a bargaining tactic, threatening the assured with the loss of his business or other consequential loss if a favourable settlement is not reached, is simply unjust.

The Law Commissions considered two alternative approaches to reform. The first is to give the assured a remedy in either contract (by way of implied term) or tort for late payment. The tort solution was rejected on the ground that the measure of damages is uncertain. The contract solution was similarly rejected, for two different reasons: a contract approach would give rise to strict liability, in that insurers would be liable for damages simply because they did not pay within a reasonable time; but on the other had an implied term would be capable of being excluded. Accordingly, the Law Commissions have provisionally opted for an extension of the rules of utmost good faith, conferring upon the assured a right to damages for breach of that duty on the part of the insurers. That solution has the benefit of imposing a liability in damages only where insurers have acted in bad faith in refusing to pay within a reasonable time.

Interest

10–024   *The power to award interest under statute.* At common law the English courts did not award interest for late payment of sums due in the absence of some contractual provision for interest, and in the same way damages could not be awarded for late payment of a debt: *London, Chatham and Dover Railway Co v South Eastern Railway Co.*[132] The common law rule was gradually reversed by statute, beginning with legislation in 1833 and now culminating in s.35A of the Senior Courts Act 1981. Section 35A(1) provides that:

> "Subject to rules of court, in proceedings (whenever instituted) before the High Court for the recovery of a debt or damages there may be included in any sum for which judgment is given simple interest, at such rate as the court thinks fit or as rules of court may provide, on all or any part of the debt or damages in respect of which judgment is given, or payment is made before judgment, for all or any part of the period between the date when the cause of action arose and:
>
> (a) in the case of any sum paid before judgment, the date of payment; and
> (b) in the case of the sum for which judgment is given, the date of the judgment."

Interest is discretionary and the statute contemplates the award of simple interest only.

Section 35A(6) of the 1981 Act further provides that "Interest . . . may be calculated at different rates in respect of different periods".

Section 35A(1) of the 1981 Act is confined to judgment debts and sums paid before judgment, but the Court of Appeal has additionally held that the High Court may award interest on damages paid in full before the trial where those damages do not include an element for interest.[133]

The amount ordered to be paid by the judgment will also carry interest, from the date of judgment and the date of actual payment. This is the effect of s.17 of the Judgments Act 1838, which provides that a judgment debt is to bear interest at the rate of 4 per cent, a rate that may be altered by statutory instrument under the authority of s.44 of the Administration of Justice Act 1970. The present rate is 8 per cent. These provisions were amended by s.1 of the Private International Law (Miscellaneous Provisions) Act 1995, which inserted s.44A into the

---

[132] *London, Chatham and Dover Railway Co v South Eastern Railway Co* [1893] A.C. 429.
[133] *Edmunds v Lloyd Italicio* [1986] 1 All E.R. 249.

Administration of Justice Act 1970. That section provides that, where a judgment is given for a sum expressed in a currency other than sterling, and s.17 of the 1838 Act applies to it, the court is free to vary the rate of interest on the judgment debt specified in s.17 to such a rate as it considers fit. In the case of arbitration, the Arbitration Act 1996 s.49 empowers the arbitrators to award simple or compound interest at such rate as they consider just, unless the parties have agreed to the contrary. The purpose of these provisions is to allow interest to be awarded on a judgment debt at a rate that reflects the currency in which it has been awarded.

Interest on a judgment or award. The common law dislike of interest has over **10–025** the years been eroded by the courts themselves, a process conducted in parallel with the development of interest under statute. In particular, it was recognised that it is possible in certain circumstances for interest to be awarded in the form of damages for late payment. Initially the judicial view was that late payment could not be assumed to cause any loss (i.e., that interest could not be awarded as a part of general damages), but that if it was possible to establish by proof that the claimant had suffered a loss by reason of late payment then interest could be awarded (i.e., by way of special damages).[134] At this point the law took a curious turn. In *President of India v La Pintada Cia Nav SA*[135] the distinction between general and special damages was confirmed, but Lord Brandon, delivering the leading speech, assumed that general damages constituted loss which would naturally flow from the breach (within the first limb in *Hadley v Baxendale*[136]) whereas special damages constituted loss which was within the contemplation of the parties by reason of their special knowledge (within the second limb of *Hadley v Baxendale*). The anomalous result reached by the House of Lords was, therefore, that loss which naturally flowed from the breach of contract in the form of late payment was irrecoverable even if it is the natural and obvious consequence of breach, whereas it could be recovered only if the parties were actually aware of the possibility of loss flowing from late payment. Their Lordships' failure to recognise the difference between, on the one hand general and special damages, and on the other hand the measure of damages under the two limbs in *Hadley v Baxendale*, was finally corrected by their Lordships in *Sempra Metals Ltd v Inland Revenue Commissioners*.[137] The outcome is that loss caused by late payment of a debt is recoverable if it is pleaded and proved, and that it falls within either of the limbs of *Hadley v Baxendale*, i.e. that it was the natural consequence of the breach or the parties knew that it would be the consequence of the breach.

The emergence of common law liability for interest is of significance in that their Lordships recognised in *Sempra* that it is now all but impossible for money to be borrowed on terms that it bears only simple interest, and that it is to be expected that compound interest is payable. Their Lordships in *Sempra* did not go as far as holding that compound interest may be awarded by way of damages at common law, but the argument is now plainly one that is open to claimants under insurance policies, particularly where the claim is under a contingency policy (i.e., a valued or life policy) given that under such a policy a debt arises immediately on the occurrence of the contingency. By contrast, in the case of

---

[134] *Trans Trust SPRL v Danubian Trading Co Ltd* [1952] 2 Q.B. 297; *Wadsworth v Lydall* [1981] 1 W.L.R. 598.
[135] *President of India v La Pintada Cia Nav SA* [1988] A.C. 395.
[136] *Hadley v Baxendale* (1854) 9 Exch 341.
[137] *Sempra Metals Ltd v Inland Revenue Commissioners* [2007] UKHL 34.

other forms of insurance, although there is an obligation on the insurers to make payment on the occurrence of the event in question, damages are at that point likely to be unliquidated and it cannot be said that there is late payment of a specific sum.

10–026 *Rate of interest.* Assuming that the claim is for interest under statute rather than at common law under *Sempra Metals*, in the Commercial Court the rate of interest will generally be 1 per cent above base rate or the nearest equivalent appropriate index (e.g. the US Prime Rate, for a dollar liability) which is also the appropriate rate for insurance claims. In *Kuwait Airways Corporation v Kuwait Insurance Co SAK (No.3)*[138] Langley J. held that the rate was not to be varied by reference to the ability of the assured to borrow money or to provide security for a loan: such a principle would require an investigation of the assured's financial affairs. Accordingly, in that case the court refused to inquire whether the assured was or was not able to borrow at that rate or whether the assured might even have been able to secure a lower rate of interest from a sympathetic lender. The rate may, however, as discussed below, be varied by reference to the assured's conduct of the proceedings.

It was noted by the Court of Appeal in *Adcock v Co-operative Insurance Society Ltd*[139] that a county court judge dealing with a commercial dispute, such as a claim under an insurance policy, ought to pay attention to the usual practice of the Commercial Court to award interest at 1 per cent above base rate.

10–027 *Date of running of interest.* As to the period of interest, the general rule is that the claimant is entitled to interest from the date on which his cause of action accrued, as the purpose of interest is to ensure that the assured has not suffered any loss: its purpose is not to punish the defendant.[140] Thus, in insurance cases, the starting point for the running of interest is the date on which the insured peril occurred, as that is the deemed date at which the assured's action accrues, and interest terminates at the date of the judgment.[141] However, the court may in appropriate circumstances postpone the running of interest, impose rests or reduce the interest for particular periods. The guiding principles were summarised by Tomlinson J. in *Hellenic Industrial Development Bank v Atkin (The Julia)*[142]:

1. Interest was to be awarded to compensate the claimant for being kept out of the money from the date when it had been established that it was due to him. It was not based on fault or the wrongful withholding of payment by the defendant.
2. The starting date would normally be the date the cause of action arose and therefore in indemnity insurance the date of loss.

[138] *Kuwait Airways Corporation v Kuwait Insurance Co SAK (No.3)* [2000] Lloyd's Rep. I.R. 678.

[139] *Adcock v Co-operative Insurance Society Ltd* [2000] Lloyd's Rep. I.R. 657.

[140] *BP Exploration Co (Libya) Ltd v Hunt (No.2)* [1979] 1 W.L.R. 783.

[141] *Burts & Harvey Ltd v Vulcan Boiler & General Insurance Co* [1966] 1 Lloyd's Rep. 354; *McLean Enterprises v Ecclesiastical Insurance* [1986] 2 Lloyd's Rep. 216; *Insurance Corp of the Channel Islands v McHugh* [1997] Lloyd's Rep. I.R. 94.

[142] *Hellenic Industrial Development Bank v Atkin (The Julia)* [2005] Lloyd's Rep. I.R. 365. See also *Merrill Lynch International Bank Ltd v Winterthur Swiss Insurance Co* [2007] Lloyd's Rep. I.R. 532 (interest to run from the date on which the insurers had been provided with a reasonably comprehensive claim in respect of which a decision could have been made).

3. Generally, the existence of or need to investigate a genuine dispute as to liability was not a material factor in postponing the running of interest and likewise in relation to the investigation of a genuine dispute as to quantum.

4. Those principles might be tempered by asking the question: when would the claimant reasonably and commercially have been expected to be paid? But this had never been applied to extend the starting date beyond the time for completion of reasonable investigation[143] and, even then, the date had only been extended where either:

   (a) the claim was sufficiently unusual as to require special investigation[144]; or

   (b) where there was evidence of a commercial practice of a later date of payment without an interest obligation.

5. Where a claimant has been guilty of excessive delay in making the original claim or in pursuing it, the starting date may be adjusted adversely to him.[145] The rationale for doing so is that it would be wrong to view the claimant as kept out of or deprived of the use of money, payment of which he has delayed in seeking. This is a causation test: has the assured himself caused the late payment by reason of his own dilatory conduct in conducting the proceedings.

Costs. If the assured is required to bring an action against the insurer to recover **10–028** policy moneys, and is successful, the assured will, generally, be entitled to costs, in accordance with ordinary litigation or arbitration principles. The general rule is that the assured will be awarded costs on a standard basis. However, exceptionally, an insurer who mishandles the assured's claim may face liability for costs on an indemnity basis in accordance with the court's discretion under CPR Pt 44[146]:

"Although insurers do not fall into a particular category, so far as litigation is concerned, they do, like others who have public responsibilities, have to approach the decision making properly . . . I hope [to] underline to the insurers the significance of discharging their responsibilities properly, of behaving with responsibility, diligence, prudence, but nevertheless with insight and sympathy in relation to claims that are made."

A successful assured, while generally entitled to his costs, may fail to secure an order for some or indeed all of his costs to the extent that the court takes the view that he has been the author of his own misfortune. Thus the court will not award costs if the assured has refused a payment into court or other offer which is less than the amount awarded by the court, or if the assured has exaggerated his claim beyond the amount which the insurers are willing to pay. A costs penalty may also be imposed if the assured's conduct has resulted in delays in the trial.[147] However, the costs of a successful assured are not to be reduced simply because

---

[143] See *Kuwait Airways Corporation v Kuwait Insurance Co SAK (No.3)* [2000] Lloyd's Rep. I.R. 678.

[144] See *Quorum AS V Schramm (No.2)* [2002] Lloyd's Rep. I.R. 315 (investigation of damage to work of fine art).

[145] See: *Rhesa Shipping Co SA v Edmunds (The Popi M)* [1984] 2 Lloyd's Rep. 555; *Knoller v Evans* (1936) 55 Ll L.R. 40; *Adcock v Co-operative Insurance Society Ltd* [2000] Lloyd's Rep. I.R. 657; *Tonkin v UK Insurance Ltd* [2007] Lloyd's Rep. I.R. 283.

[146] *Wailes v Stapleton Construction and Commercial Services* [1997] 2 Lloyd's Rep. 112, per Newman J.

[147] *Quorum AS v Schramm (No.2)* [2002] Lloyd's Rep. I.R. 315.

the insurers have asserted that the claim is fraudulent and have incurred substantial expenditure in a failed attempt to establish fraud. In such circumstances the assured is entitled to recover under the policy and in the absence of any basis for an allegation of fraud the insurers' expenditure is for their own account.[148]

2. LIMITS ON RECOVERY

10–029   **Average.** The most significant consequence of underinsurance is the application of the principle of average. Where average is applied to a policy, the assured is deemed to be his own insurer for the amount of any underinsurance so that the assured and the insurer are treated as co-insurers and share the loss in proportion to their subscription. Average cannot therefore operate if the assured is fully insured. Further, average has no role to play in the case of a total loss: if the policy is valued, the assured is entitled to the full sum assured whether or not he is underinsured; and if the policy is unvalued, the assured will be entitled to the full amount due under the policy. Average is relevant only to partial loss. Thus, if the insured value of the insured subject matter (valued or unvalued) is £1,000, the sum insured is £500 and the assured suffers a partial loss of £200, the assured can recover only 500/1,000 of £200, an amount representing the proportion by which he is underinsured.[149] Without average, the assured would be able to recover the full £200.

The principle of average is applicable irrespective of the number of insurers involved. Suppose a building valued at £20,000, insured against fire under five policies, each for £2,000, which is damaged to the extent of £5,000. On these figures the assured is 50 per cent underinsured and must, therefore, bear one half of his loss (i.e. £2,500). The remaining loss of £2,500 is to be distributed equally between the insurers, so that each must pay £500. Two qualifications to this general principle may be noted. First, the rights of the insurers between themselves will depend upon the principles of contribution, which may themselves be modified by the terms of the policies held by the assured, and in particular by what is termed the "second condition of average", which seeks to postpone the liability of a general insurer to that of a specific insurer. Second, average may be excluded by the terms of the policies. For example, where insurance is arranged in layers, so that each insurer is responsible for a given amount of loss in excess of a specified financial limit, underinsurance will not limit the assured's ability to seek full recovery at each layer penetrated by the loss.

All marine policies are, unless otherwise agreed, subject to average.[150] Non-marine policies are not for the most part subject to average unless an average condition is incorporated. As a matter of practice fire policies often contain a condition deeming the assured to be his own insurer in respect of the uninsured balance, and it has been suggested that that average clauses in commercial fire policies are sufficiently common to be implied in the absence of any indication

---

[148] *Mehnaz v Sabre Insurance Co Ltd* [2007] EWCA Civ 1525.

[149] In *Bell Taverns (Scotland) Ltd v The National Insurance & Guarantee Corp Ltd* [2009] Scot C.S. C.S.O.H. 70 it was held that an average clause in a property policy applied to the costs of reinstatement, including professional fees and similar expenses.

[150] Marine Insurance Act 1906 s.81.

to the contrary.[151] Moreover, where the words "subject to average" are used in a Lloyd's fire policy, that is sufficient to incorporate by custom into the policy the wording of the Lloyd's standard average clause irrespective of the assured's knowledge or otherwise of that wording.[152] However, earlier authority suggests that unless there is express mention of average no such implication can be made in respect of a fire policy on domestic buildings.[153] There is little authority on the application of average outside marine and fire insurance, the assumption having been made in a number of cases that average has no place outside those categories.[154] Indeed, the issue of whether a policy which covers both marine risks and liability is a marine policy, and thus subject to average, or a liability policy, and thus not subject to average, has exercised the courts on a number of occasions.[155]

Retentions. Most insurance policies contain a provision—variously referred to **10–030** as an excess, deducible or retention—under which the assured has to bear the first part of his own loss: "all sums above the amount of the excess, up to the limits of the policy, are within the scope of the cover." The assured is regarded as his own insurer for that sum, and the position is regarded in law as creating a primary layer of cover consisting of the excess and a second layer of cover consisting of the insurance itself.[156] This point is significant for subrogation purposes, because if there is any sum recovered by the insurers from the third party responsible for the assured's loss, the sums are to be applied to the higher layer of insurance first, so it is likely that the deductible will be recouped.

The retention has two main functions. First, by excluding the most common forms of loss, small losses, the premium can be kept down. Secondly, by requiring the assured to retain a part of the liability, the insurers can impose some incentive on the assured to act prudently and to take steps to avoid suffering loss. At the reinsurance level, there may be an obligation on the reinsured to retain a part of the risk to guarantee to the reinsurers the quality of the business to be ceded. It may be possible for the insurers to be persuaded to remove the retention either by the assured paying a higher premium or by the insurers issuing an extension to the cover (known as "deductible buy-back") and it is also open to the assured to insure the deductible with other insurers unless expressly precluded from doing so.

A franchise clause is a specific form of deductible. This stipulates a minimum figure which triggers the insurer's liability. However, under a franchise, where that figure is exceeded the insurer is liable for the full amount of the loss without deduction.[157] Unless otherwise stated the franchise will apply to each loss individually: consequently, unless the policy permits aggregation, unconnected losses below the level set out in the franchise clause cannot be added together to produce a recoverable loss.[158]

---

[151] *Carreras Ltd v Cunard Steamship Co* [1918] 1 K.B. 118.

[152] *Acme Wood Flooring Co v Marten* (1904) 9 Com. Cas. 157.

[153] *Sillem v Thornton* (1954) 3 E. & B. 868.

[154] *Fifth Liverpool Starr Building Society v Travellers' Accident Insurance Co* (1893) 9 T.L.R. 221 (fidelity insurance); *Anglo Californian Bank v London and Provincial Marine and General Insurance Co Ltd* (1904) 10 Com. Cas. 1 (guarantee insurance).

[155] *Joyce v Kennaway* (1871) L.R. 7 Q.B. 78 (liability policy); *Cunard Steamship Co v Marten* [1903] 2 K.B. 511 (liability policy); *Holman & Sons Ltd v Merchants' Marine Insurance Co Ltd* [1919] 1 K.B. 383 (marine policy).

[156] *Napier & Ettrick v Hunter* [1993] 1 All E.R. 385.

[157] *Paterson v Harris* (1861) 1 B. & S. 336.

[158] *Stewart v Merchants' Marine Insurance Co* (1885) 16 QBD 619.

10–031   **Betterment.** Where the measure of indemnity for damage to property is based upon the cost of repair, reinstatement or replacement, it is almost inevitable that the assured will receive repaired or new property which is more valuable than that which was affected by the insured peril. The principle of betterment requires the assured to account for the profit made by him following the effecting of repairs or replacement by the insurers. It has long been the case in marine insurance that the assured is required to give an allowance, in the form of a one-third customary deduction, where a damaged vessel has been repaired,[159] although in recent times hull damage is now repaired on a new for old basis without deduction.[160]

The position as far as non-marine insurance is concerned is less certain, as there is no fixed standard for betterment in non-marine insurance.[161] Much of the authority on the principle of betterment is to be found in tort law, and it is clear from those cases that deduction for betterment is not a precise science and that the courts will apply a broad brush approach, so that a deduction for betterment may be refused if the claimant has incurred other costs for which no claim has been made.[162] However, a deduction for betterment will normally be made. In *Voaden v Champion (The Baltic Surveyor)*[163] the claimant's pontoon which had a remaining life of eight years was damaged by negligence. A new pontoon cost £60,000 and had a life of 30 years. The appropriate award was £16,000, representing 8/30ths of £60,000.

The same principles are applicable to insurance cases. In *Reynolds v Phoenix Insurance Co*[164] Forbes J. expressed the view that the principle of betterment is too well established to be departed from. It may nevertheless be that the possibility of deduction for betterment is largely confined to recovery for partly damaged buildings, as was indeed the case in *Reynolds*, for many policies on goods are written on a "new for old" basis.

Aggregations and event limits

10–032   *Nature and purpose.* An event limit in an insurance contract, and particularly in a liability policy, has three main functions:

   (a)   it determines the temporal coverage of the policy, e.g. where the event insured against must occur in the policy period or a claim relating to the event must be made within the policy period;

   (b)   it determines how many deductibles the assured has to bear, e.g. where the policy provides that there is a deductible for all losses which flow from an event if the event is an individual loss, then the assured will have to bear the deductible for each individual loss which has arisen and may well recover nothing if losses are small even though there total is significant; and

   (c)   it determines the financial ceiling of the policy, e.g. where there is a maximum sum recoverable under the policy for all losses flowing from a

---

[159] Marine Insurance Act 1906 s.69.
[160] International Hull Clauses 2003 cl.16.
[161] *Vance v Forster* (1841) Ir. Circ. Rep. 47.
[162] *Dominion Mosaics Co Ltd v Trafalgar Trucking Co* [1990] 2 All E.R. 246.
[163] *Voaden v Champion (The Baltic Surveyor)* [2002] 1 Lloyd's Rep. 623.
[164] *Reynolds v Phoenix Insurance Co* [1978] 2 Lloyd's Rep. 440.

single event the event limit here has an aggregating function, restricting the insurer's total liability for losses flowing from the aggregating event and it will be apparent that the potential maximum liability of the insurer is diminished as the aggregating event becomes broader.

There are various terms that can be adopted to determine these issues, including "event", "accident", "happening" and "occurrence". There is now a body of authority on the meaning of these terms, although it should not be assumed that a single word bears a consistent meaning across all policies or even within the same policy as there has been a tendency by those drafting insurance policies to use the different words interchangeably and the same word in different ways.[165] Accordingly, while the authorities now point to the prima facie meaning of words, the courts have emphasised that much will depend upon the context in which they are used.[166] Equally, the same words of aggregation may be construed as bearing different meanings within the same policy if it is apparent that they are being used for different purposes. To avoid dispute, the policyholder may lawfully be given a discretion as to how aggregation to be fixed which is to be binding upon the underwriters[167] and the policy may also incorporate an "aggregate extension clause" under which a large number of unrelated individual losses may be aggregated into a single loss so that a "per loss" deductible does not preclude recovery.[168] In the absence of any express policy provision, individual losses are not to be aggregated for the purpose of determining how many deductibles are to be borne by the assured or whether the limits of recovery under the policy have been exceeded.[169]

Accident. An accident is the individual manifestation of a loss rather than the state of affairs which gave rise to those losses. Thus where a vehicle runs out of control injuring a number of people, there are as many accidents as people so that a "per accident" policy limit applies to each individual claim against the assured.[170] Again, an accident for the purposes of a deductible clause in a product **10–033**

---

[165] *Countrywide Assured Group Plc v Marshall* [2003] Lloyd's Rep. I.R. 195; *Midland Mainline Ltd v Commercial Union Assurance Co Ltd* [2004] Lloyds Rep. I.R. 122.

[166] *Kuwait Airways Corporation v Kuwait Insurance Co SAK* [1996] 1 Lloyd's Rep. 664.

[167] *Brown v Gio Insurance Ltd* [1998] Lloyd's Rep. I.R. 201 (reinsurance).

[168] Such provisions may be found in product liability policies and, more commonly, in excess of loss reinsurance agreements. See *Denby v English and Scottish Maritime Insurance Co Ltd* [1998] 1 Lloyd's Rep. 343.

[169] *Mabey and Johnson Ltd v Ecclesiastical Insurance Office Plc* [2001] Lloyd's Rep. I.R. 369. See also *Wasa International Insurance Co Ltd and AGF Insurance Co Ltd v Lexington Insurance Co* [2009] Lloyd's Rep. I.R. 675, in which a direct policy on property damage and business interruption risks was written on a "per occurrence" basis with respect to deductibles and with respect to the insurers' limit of liability. The maximum sum insured under the reinsurance obtained by the insurers was written on an aggregate of all claims, but as far as the deductible was concerned the reinsurance simply provided "Retention US$1,675,000" without making it clear whether this was per occurrence or per aggregate of occurrences. The House of Lords held that this was a one-off per occurrence deductible, mainly on the basis that it would have been straightforward for the reinsurers to add the words "per occurrence".

[170] *South Staffordshire Tramways Co Ltd v Sickness and Accident Assurance Association Ltd* [1891] 1 Q.B. 402; *Allen v London Guarantee and Accident Co Ltd* (1912) 28 T.L.R. 254. See also *Re Deep Vein Thrombosis and Air Travel Group Litigation* [2005] UKHL 72, where it was held that for the purposes of the Warsaw Convention an accident was a specific incident and not a state of affairs.

liability policy is each instance of individual loss and not negligent manufacture or release onto the market.[171]

10–034 *Occurrence and event.* There are numerous authorities on these interchangeable terms, and it is possible to draw some general conclusions from them.

First, an event or occurrence is a unifying factor that allows a number of individual losses to be aggregated and, therefore, to be treated as having arisen from a single happening.

Secondly, what has occurred must be capable of being described as an event or an occurrence. In *Axa Reinsurance (UK) Plc v Field*[172] Lord Mustill commented that "in ordinary speech, an event is some thing which happens at a particular time, at a particular place and in a particular way", terminology that has now been generally adopted: something specific must have happened. An event is what has happened as opposed to the reason (underlying cause) for what has happened.[173] An event or occurrence is, accordingly, to be distinguished from a general state of affairs, such as a propensity to act negligently or a war, as there is no loss arising from these sources unless and until something specific has happened.

Thirdly, where a number of individual losses have been suffered, it is necessary for those losses to be sufficiently closely connected with each other to be regarded as having resulted from a single event or occurrence. The relevant "unities" are those of time, locality, cause and motive.

Fourthly, there must be sufficient causal connection between the individual losses and the event or occurrence from which they are said to result. The test is not the ordinary rule of proximate cause, although there has to be a sufficient link. The weaker the link, the more difficult it will be to establish the necessary causal connection.

Fifthly, in assessing whether individual losses can be aggregated as a single event or occurrence, the matter must be approached from the perspective of an informed observer and the assessment is to be made both analytically and as a matter of intuition and common sense.

Applying these principles, there is no occurrence simply because a financial institution has collapsed as the result of the negligence of its various officers,[174] tracks in a railway network have been found to be damaged,[175] the assured has a propensity to act negligently[176] or a defective component has been installed into some other product.[177] By contrast, there are occurrences in two situations. First, where there are individual losses, such as: harm being inflicted on a product by

---

[171] *Tioxide Europe Ltd v CGU International Insurance Plc* [2005] Lloyd's Rep. I.R. 114, affirmed on other grounds [2006] Lloyd's Rep. I.R. 31.

[172] *Axa Reinsurance (UK) Plc v Field* [1996] 3 All E.R. 517.

[173] *Countrywide Assurance v Marshall* [2003] Lloyd's Rep. I.R. 195. Earlier cases do not always follow this analysis, and have classified surrounding circumstances rather than individual losses as occurrences, although it may be that the cases can be explained by the context in which the word was used. See: *Allen v London Guarantee and Accident Co Ltd* (1912) 28 T.L.R. 254; *Forney v Dominion Insurance Ltd* [1969] 3 All E.R. 831; *Kelly v Norwich Union Fire and Life Assurance Society* [1989] 2 All E.R. 888.

[174] *American Centennial Insurance Co v INSCO Ltd* [1996] L.R.L.R. 407.

[175] *Midland Mainline Ltd v Commercial Union Assurance Co Ltd* [2004] Lloyd's Rep. I.R. 22.

[176] *Caudle v Sharp* [1995] L.R.L.R. 433.

[177] *Pilkington United Kingdom Ltd v CGU Insurance Plc* [2004] Lloyd's Rep. I.R. 891.

the incorporation of a defective component[178]; each of the losses suffered by a bank by reason of an employee's fraud[179]; each emergency speed restriction affecting a rail network following discovery that the network as a whole had not been properly maintained[180]; and the looting of individual supermarkets in a general atmosphere of dislocation.[181] Secondly, where a particular happening has resulted in a series of losses which are closely related by the unities of time, place, cause and motive, such as: the September 11 attacks on the World Trade Center[182]; the seizure of an airport leading to the loss of the aircraft on the ground at the time[183]; or a decision to install asbestos.[184]

Originating cause. The term "originating cause", by way of contrast to "event"   **10–035** or "occurrence", is concerned with the underlying reason for a series of losses rather than the losses themselves. As was said by Lord Mustill in *Axa Reinsurance (UK) Ltd v Field*,[185]

> "A cause to my mind is something altogether less constricted. It can be a continuing state of affairs; it can be the absence of something happening. Equally, the word "originating" was in my view consciously chosen to open up the widest possible search for a unifying factor in the history of the losses which it is sought to aggregate. To my mind the one expression [originating cause] has a much wider connotation than the other [event]."

An originating cause is thus the propensity of an individual to act in a negligent fashion by reason of a "blind spot",[186] a series of individual acts of pilferage[187]

---

[178] *James Budgett Sugars v Norwich Union Insurance* [2003] Lloyd's Rep. I.R. 114. See also *Seele Austria GmbH & Co KG v Tokio Marine Europe Insurance Ltd* [2008] Lloyd's Rep. I.R. 739, where the assured installed pre-assembled windows into a building being erected in London. The windows were found to be defective and had to be removed: in the course of removal damage was caused to the building itself, and the assured sought to recover from its insurers the cost of making good that damage. The Court of Appeal permitted recovery in principle, but also held that the deductible clause—which required the assured to bear the first £10,000 of the cost of each and every occurrence or series of occurrences arising out of any one event—meant that each defective window was a separate occurrence, and there was no single event (e.g. bad workmanship) which permitted aggregation of the various losses into a single event. In a sequel decision, *Seele Austria GmbH Co v Tokio Marine Europe Insurance Ltd (No.2)* [2009] EWHC 255 (TCC), it was held that the earlier decision had determined that the loss had been caused by bad workmanship rather than bad design, so that the aggregation question could not be reopened.

[179] *Equitable Trust Co of New York v Whittaker* (1923) 17 Ll. L.R. 153; *Philadelphia National Bank v Poole* [1938] 2 All E.R. 199. See also *Pennsylvania Co for Insurance on Lives and Granting Annuities v Mumford* [1920] 2 K.B. 537. In *Dornoch Ltd v Mauritius Union Assurance Co Ltd and Mauritius Commercial Bank Ltd (No.2)* [2007] Lloyd's Rep. I.R. 350 each of a number of acts of infidelity taking place over a period of 11 years was held to be a separate loss.

[180] *Midland Mainline Ltd v Commercial Union Assurance Co Ltd* [2004] Lloyd's Rep. I.R. 22.

[181] *Mann v Lexington Insurance* [2001] Lloyd's Rep. I.R. 179.

[182] *If P & C Insurance Ltd v Silversea Cruises Ltd* [2004] Lloyd's Rep. I.R. 214, affirmed on other grounds [2004] Lloyd's Rep. I.R. 696.

[183] *Kuwait Airways Corporation v Kuwait Insurance Co SAK* [1996] 1 Lloyd's Rep. 664; *Scott v Copenhagen Reinsurance Co (UK) Ltd* [2003] Lloyd's Rep. I.R. 696 (excluding one aircraft belonging to BA which the invading Iraqi forces had not expected to find and which was left untouched by them).

[184] *IRB Brasil Resseguros SA v CX Reinsurance Company Ltd* [2010] EWHC 974 (Comm). The correctness of this decision is open to some doubt, as the so-called "event" more closely resembles a "state of affairs".

[185] *Axa Reinsurance (UK) Ltd v Field* [1996] 3 All E.R. 517.

[186] *Cox v Bankside Members Agency Ltd* [1995] 2 Lloyd's Rep. 43; *American Centennial Insurance Co v INSCO Ltd* [1996] L.R.L.R. 407.

[187] *Municipal Mutual Insurance Ltd v Sea Insurance Ltd* [1998] Lloyd's Rep. I.R. 421.

and a failure by an employer to provide adequate training to its commission agents with the result that they missold financial products to customers.[188]

10–036   *Claim.* The term is important in a number of respects. First, if the policy is written on a claims made basis, there has to be a claim against the assured within the currency of the policy, so that the claim can be notified to the insurers. Secondly, there may be an aggregate limit on the sum insured for all claims or there may be a deductible to be borne for each claim. Thirdly, in determining coverage under the policy, the claim must relate to loss arising from an insured peril as opposed to an uninsured or excluded peril. Policies often define the term "claim" but rarely for each of these purposes, because the term has a different meaning in each of them. Because the word is used to cover a series of different matters, there is sometimes difficulty in ascertaining whether what is being referred to is the claim by or against the assured, as where the assured is required to notify "claims" to the insurers: whose is being referred to?

A claim under a liability policy is a claim made against the assured by a third party.[189] It is often necessary to determine how many claims have been made by the third party. In general a claim is the sum sought in proceedings brought against the assured for breach of duty and not the underlying causes of action constituting those proceedings so that liability per claim means liability for breach of duty flowing from a particular act.[190]

The leading authority is the decision of the House of Lords in *Lloyds TSB General insurance Holdings v Lloyds Bank Insurance Co Ltd,*[191] where the assured accepted liability to a large number of customers for selling private pensions to them in breach of regulatory standards. Liability to each customer was in most cases less than £15,000. The assured's policy laid down a £1 million deductible for each and every third party claim, and continued:

> "If a series of third party claims shall result from any single act or omission (or a related series of acts or omissions) then, irrespective of the total number of claims, all such third party claims shall be considered to be a single third party claim for the purposes of the application of the Deductible."

The House of Lords held that the loss suffered by each customer was a claim, and that it was not possible to aggregate those claims as resulting from "any single act or omission (or a related series of acts or omissions), namely the failure of the assured to provide adequate training to its agents. Their Lordships ruled that a claim was a loss proximately caused by the assured's defaults, but it could not be said that inadequate training was of itself the proximate cause of the customers' losses: what was required was something that proximately caused a loss and accordingly the deductible was applicable to each individual claim made against

---

[188] *Countrywide Assured Group Plc v Marshall* [2003] Lloyd's Rep. I.R. 195.

[189] *West Wake v Ching* [1957] 1 Lloyd's Rep. 45; *Australia and New Zealand Bank Ltd v Colonial and Eagle Wharves Ltd* [1960] 2 Lloyd's Rep. 241; *Thorman v New Hampshire Insurance Co (UK) Ltd* [1988] 1 Lloyd's Rep. 7; *Robert Irving & Burns v Stone* [1998] Lloyd's Rep. I.R. 258. See also *Standard Life Assurance Ltd v Oak Dedicated Ltd* [2008] Lloyd's Rep. I.R. 552: "The word 'claim' is a word frequently used by insurance market professionals but not always to mean precisely the same thing. The word takes its meaning and its colour from its context."

[190] If there are two or more unrelated acts, there are that many claims: *Mabey & Johnson Ltd v Ecclesiastical Insurance Office Plc (No.2)* [2003] Lloyd's Rep. I.R. 724 (an action for breaches of two different contracts held to be two separate claims); *American Centennial Insurance Co v INSCO Ltd* [1996] L.R.L.R. 407.

[191] *Lloyds TSB General Insurance Holdings v Lloyds Bank Insurance Co Ltd* [2003] Lloyd's Rep. I.R. 623.

the assured. Their Lordships were satisfied that, as a matter of the construction of the policy, the intention had been to exclude small losses, and it was for that reason that the deductible level had been set at £1 million. The bracketed phrase was held to add nothing to the clause, as it was plainly designed to be purely subsidiary to the main aggregating phrase "any single act or omission" and was not intended to lay down an entirely separate and wider basis for aggregation.[192]

In *Standard Life Assurance Ltd v Oak Dedicated Ltd*[193] Tomlinson J. considered the meaning of a form of words which was accepted to be unusual (if not unique), namely "each and every claim and/or claimant". The liability policy in this case was taken out by an insurance company which sold mortgage endowment policies to consumers. Misselling led to claims by some 97,000 investors and total liabilities in excess of £100 million, the average payment being less than £10,000. The assured's policy was for £75 million in excess of £25, and there was a deductible "in respect of each and every Claim and/or Loss . . . " The word "claim" was defined in the body of the policy as meaning:

"each Claim or series of claims (whether by one or more than one Claimant) arising from or in connection with or attributable to any one act, error, omission or originating cause . . . and any such series of Claims shall be deemed to be one Claim for all purposes under this Policy."

That wording taken alone would have permitted the assured to aggregate all claims arising out of one originating cause—i.e., failure by the assured to exercise proper controls—so that there would just be one deductible. However, the schedule to the policy contained a definition of the deductible, namely "£25 million each and every claim and/or claimant including costs and expenses." Tomlinson J. held that the definition in the schedule was of equal weight to the policy itself and thus had to be given effect. He then ruled that the phrase "claim and/or claimant" did not give the assured the option of aggregating on the basis of per "claim" (defined as all claims arising from one originating cause) or "and/or claimant", whichever was the most beneficial. Instead, Tomlinson J. held that the words "and/or claimant" were to be given full effect, and meant that the deductible applied to any claim, or any series of claims, by a single claimant. The effect was that nothing was recoverable under the policy. The learned judge recognised that this interpretation deprived the cover of all meaningful effect, and also that the insurers could have achieved that result by a clear exclusion for consumer claims rather than by this indirect method, but that the words meant what they said.

Loss. The word "loss" does not have a fixed meaning, and much will depend **10–037** upon its context. It has been held that the use of a single defective component for 94 articles constituted one loss and not 94 separate losses so that the assured had to bear only one deductible,[194] although it has also been held on different wording that the assured had suffered a series of individual losses by the use of

---

[192] Their Lordships were in any event unable to attribute any obvious meaning to the bracketed words.

[193] *Standard Life Assurance Ltd v Oak Dedicated Ltd* [2008] Lloyd's Rep. I.R. 552.

[194] *Mitsubishi Electric (UK) Ltd v Royal London Insurance (UK) Ltd)* [1994] 2 Lloyd's Rep. 249.

a defective component in the manufacturing process.[195] Individual acts of theft have been held to be separate losses under fidelity[196] and property[197] covers.

Mitigation of loss

10–038   *The duty to mitigate.*   There is little English authority on the question of whether the assured is under a common law duty to mitigate his loss following the occurrence of an event against which insurance has been taken out. The bulk of the authority relates to marine insurance, although in all the marine cases the assured has either been under an express contractual duty to mitigate or at least has had conferred upon him the right to recover for acts of mitigation (thereby implying a duty to mitigate), by virtue of the "sue and labour" clause.[198]

The duty to mitigate arises as a matter of law whenever a claimant has an action for breach of contract, subject only to a limited exception in the case of anticipatory breach. It is settled that a claim under an insurance policy is one for unliquidated damages for breach of contract, it would appear to be arguable that the assured is under a common law duty to mitigate the loss flowing from the occurrence of an insured event, and will be deemed to have caused his own loss in respect of any insured damage which could reasonably have been prevented. However, the courts have rejected the principle that the assured is under any duty to mitigate loss. In *City Tailors v Evans*[199] the assured under a fire policy was held not to be obliged to take on new premises in order to reduce an insured loss of profits, and in *Yorkshire Water v Sun Alliance & London Insurance*[200] the assured under a liability policy was held not to be under any duty to undertake remediation works in order to prevent pollution for which it was responsible from causing damage. There is some justification for refusing to imply a suing and labouring obligation into a liability policy,[201] in that the insurers are not under any obligation to indemnify the assured unless and until liability has been established and quantified, so that any steps taken to avoid a harmful act are not mitigation at all. Further, taking steps to prevent liability arising is plainly more remote than taking steps to prevent property being damaged following the occurrence of an insured peril as the form of loss insured against is quite different from the steps taken by the assured to avoid the loss, a point made by Otton L.J. in *Yorkshire Water.* Stuart Smith L.J. also commented that it was impossible to say just how great the potential liability of the assured might be so that the assessment of the reasonableness of the alleviation measures became problematic.

On the assumption that *Yorkshire Water* is of general application, the decision does not mean that the assured may refuse to react to a peril. Thus if a cigar end thrown into a waste paper bin causes the paper to smoulder, an assured who failed to attend to the matter would not have a claim against his insurers, either because he had acted fraudulently[202] or possibly because he had caused his own loss.

---

[195] *Tioxide Europe Ltd v CGU International Insurance* [2006] Lloyd's Rep. I.R. 31.
[196] *Pennsylvania Co v Mumford* [1920] 2 K.B. 537; *Philadelphia National Bank v Price* (1938) 67 Ll. L.R. 257.
[197] *Glencore International AG v Alpina Insurance Co Ltd* [2004] 1 Lloyd's Rep. 111.
[198] See Ch.24, below.
[199] *City Tailors v Evans* (1921) 7 Ll. L.R. 195.
[200] *Yorkshire Water v Sun Alliance & London Insurance* [1997] 2 Lloyd's Rep. 21, followed in *Bartoline Ltd v Royal & Sun Alliance Insurance Plc* [2007] Lloyd's Rep. I.R. 423.
[201] *MacMillan Bloedel Ltd v Youell* (1993) 95 B.C.L.C. (2d) 130.
[202] This was the suggestion of Moore-Bick J. in *James v CGU Insurance* [2002] Lloyd's Rep. I.R. 206.

Indemnification for the costs of mitigation. Section 78 of the Marine Insurance **10–039**
Act 1906 imposes an obligation on the insurers to indemnify the assured for the
costs of suing and labouring where there is a suing and labouring clauses. Such
clauses rarely appear in non-marine policies,[203] and in the absence of contractual
or statutory authorisation for the recovery of expenses, an assured who has
incurred costs in mitigating a loss may base his claim on two grounds: implied
term, under which the insurer is required to indemnify the assured should the
assured take steps to reduce the amount of any claim against the insurers, or the
general law of restitution under which a person upon whom benefits are
conferred is required to pay for them. The restitutionary argument is weak, as it
is settled law that equity will not assist a volunteer, so that if there is no
obligation on the assured to take mitigating steps there will be no obligation on
the insurers to pay for them. The implied term approach has also been rejected
in the *Yorkshire Water* case[204] where the Court of Appeal held that the policy, by
conferring indemnity for liability flowing from the occurrence of an insured peril,
necessarily excluded costs incurred in preventing the peril, and that there was no
business efficacy basis for implying a term requiring the insurers to indemnify
the assured for mitigation costs, particularly given that the assured was not under
any corresponding duty to take those steps in the first place.[205]

3. REINSTATEMENT

Contractual reinstatement

Purpose. The word "reinstate" in a policy of insurance refers to buildings or **10–040**
chattels which have been damaged, and the word "replace" refers to those which
have been destroyed.[206] "Restoration" is a convenient term to cover both
reinstatement and replacement. It has been common for centuries to find in
policies on property, particularly fire policies on buildings,[207] a clause conferring
upon the insurer the option either to pay to the insured the sum agreed under the
policy or to reinstate or repair the subject matter in question. Reinstatement
clauses have two main objectives. First, if different interests in the same subject
matter have been insured under various policies issued by a number of insurers,
it is possible that the aggregate sum payable under the various policies will
exceed by a significant amount the cost of full reinstatement. The example of a
building is perhaps the simplest in which this might occur. In such a case it is in
the interests of the various insurers to agree amongst themselves to reinstate the
property, sharing the cost proportionately between themselves. Second, a
reinstatement clause is a significant anti-fraud device; an assured who is tempted
to set fire to or otherwise destroy his own property in an attempt to obtain its

---

[203] Although see *King v Brandywine Reinsurance Co (UK) Ltd* [2005] Lloyd's Rep. I.R. 509.
[204] *Yorkshire Water v Sun Alliance & London Insurance* [1997] 2 Lloyd's Rep. 21, albeit obiter, as
the assured was required at its own expense to take steps to prevent or mitigate a loss. Contrast
Emperor Goldmining Co Ltd v Switzerland General Insurance Co Ltd [1964] 1 Lloyd's Rep. 348.
[205] See also *Pilkington United Kingdom Ltd v CGU Insurance Plc* [2004] Lloyd's Rep. I.R. 891 (no
indemnification for costs of preventing cracked glass from falling and causing personal injury);
Gerling General Insurance Co v Canary Wharf Group Plc [2006] Lloyd's Rep. I.R. 462 (no recovery
under a business interruption policy for the costs of changing working methods in order to prevent
losses arising from those methods).
[206] *Anderson v Commercial Union* (1885) 55 LJ.Q.B. 146 at 149.
[207] *Sadlers Co v Badcock* (1743) 2 Atk. 554.

(doubtless inflated) cash value from his insurers will have no incentive to do so if all that he will receive is the same subject matter with repairs.[208]

The obligation of an insurer at common law is to pay to the assured the sum agreed or a sum representing his loss, depending on whether the policy is valued or unvalued. Consequently, it is not open to an insurer to insist upon reinstatement in the absence of a reinstatement clause.[209] The starting point for any analysis is the wording of the reinstatement clause itself; the discussion below proceeds on the basis of the types of reinstatement clause generally found in policies.

10–041 *The benefit of a reinstatement clause.* Where an insurer is given the option to pay or to reinstate, the choice of which route to follow is entirely that of the insurers, even if the liability is expressed as a bare promise to make good. If the insurers have not elected to reinstate but to pay a contractual indemnity based on the market value of the property, the presence of a reinstatement clause does not entitle the assured to claim an indemnity based on the cost of reinstatement.[210]

10–042 *Time for exercise of the option to reinstate.* The policy may stipulate a time within which the insurer is to determine whether to pay or to reinstate; in the absence of any such provision the insurer doubtless has only a reasonable time in which to make up its mind. The rights of the assured on the insurer's failure to reach a decision within the relevant time will depend upon the wording of the policy. If the policy is in terms to the effect that the insurer must pay but may at its option reinstate, it would seem to be the case that failure to act timeously deprives the insurer of the right to reinstate and the assured is entitled to claim the proceeds of the policy but not to insist on reinstatement. The situation may, however, be different when—as is usually the case—the reinstatement clause confers upon the insurer an option to pay or to reinstate, for here the assured does not have a fall-back entitlement under the policy. It is thus arguable that the assured may in these circumstances insist either upon an indemnity under the policy or reinstatement, which in practical terms means payment of the reinstatement value of the subject matter, whichever is more beneficial to him.

10–043 *Exercise of the option.* Once the insurers have determined either to reinstate or to pay, the election is binding on both parties and the insurers cannot change their mind simply because the election has proved to be an unwise one. The selection of one alternative remedy necessarily constitutes an abandonment of the other.[211] However, the insurers' election must be unequivocal to have binding effect. If there is any ambiguity in the insurers' actions, the option may be treated as not having been validly exercised and the insurers are free to change their minds. Thus where the insurers made a cash offer which was rejected by the assured, the right to elect to reinstate was held to remain open to them.[212] By contrast, once the amount of the assured's loss has been referred to arbitration, it is too late for the insurers to insist upon reinstatement.[213]

[208] *Vance v Forster* (1841) Ir. Circ. Rep. 47 at 51.
[209] *Anderson v Commercial Union Assurance Co* (1885) L.J.Q.B. 146.
[210] *Leppard v Excess Insurance Co* [1979] 2 All E.R. 668.
[211] *Times Fire v Hawke* (1858) 1 F. & F 406.
[212] *Sutherland v Sun Fire Office* (1852) 14 D. 775.
[213] *Scottish Amicable Heritage Securities Association v Northern Assurance Co* (1883) 11 R. 287.

Effect of election to reinstate. Once the insurers have elected to reinstate the subject matter, the agreement between the parties is not to be treated as one under which payment is to be made, and instead the case stand as if the policy had been one simply to reinstate in the first place.[214] The election relates back, and the case is the same as if the insurer had originally contracted absolutely to reinstate.[215] The contract of insurance becomes enforceable as a building or repair contract[216] the remedy for breach of which is damages.[217] The fact that the assured may have received a benefit, in that the reinstated property may have a greater value than was previously the case, is immaterial, as an element of betterment is inherent in reinstatement.[218] Following election, the assured becomes obliged to allow the insurers to enter his land to carry out the work, and the court will not grant him an injunction to restrain them.[219] The assured's affirmation of his right to payment amounts to an affirmation of the policy entitling the insurers to enter,[220] and if the assured does not allow the insurers to enter but carries out the work himself he leaves himself without any remedy under the policy.[221]

10–044

The insurers' obligation following an election to reinstate becomes to provide the assured with a fresh or repaired subject matter substantially as good as that which was damaged or lost.[222] This duty may well result in the insurers having to pay out a sum in excess of the maximum liability under the policy for, unless the policy otherwise provides, the obligation on the insurers is to reinstate in full and not merely to reinstate in so far as the policy monies allow.[223] If the insurers replace the lost subject matter with something inferior, the assured is entitled to reject it[224] or to accept it and to claim damages representing the difference between previous worth and repaired or reinstated worth.[225] If the insurers, having determined to reinstate, fail to do so, the assured may not claim specific performance but is entitled to damages.[226] Similarly, if the insurers delay in reinstating the subject matter having elected to do so, they will face liability in damages for any loss of profit or other consequential loss caused to the assured by any delay[227] in failing to reinstate within a reasonable time[228] and the insurers will also face liability to remedy any defects in workmanship in the reinstated subject matter. If the assured has an independent contract with the repairer chosen to carry out the reinstatement work, he may sue the repairer for loss

---

[214] *Brown v Royal Insurance* (1859) 1 El. & El. 853; *Domsalla v Dyason* [2007] EWHC 1174 (TCC).

[215] *Bank of New South Wales v Royal Insurance* (1880) 2 N.Z.L.R. 337.

[216] *Morrell v Irving Fire* (1865) 33 N.Y. 429.

[217] *Home District Mutual Insurance v Thompson* (1847) 1 U.C. Er. & App. 247.

[218] *Brown v Royal Insurance Co* (1859) 1 E. & E. 853.

[219] *Bisset v Royal Exchange Assurance* (1821) 1 Sh. (Ct of Sess) 174.

[220] *Baker v Yorkshire Fire* [1892] 1 Q.B. 144 at 145–146.

[221] *Beals v Home Insurance* (1867) 36 N.Y. 522.

[222] *Lockwood v Moreira* Unreported, 1998, Ontario CA.

[223] *Home Mutual Fire insurance v Garfield* (1871) 14 Am. Rep. 27. The policy may be subject to average, so that the insurers are required only to spend moneys to the extent of the amount that would have been payable had the option to reinstate not been exercised: *Bell Taverns (Scotland) Ltd v The National Insurance & Guarantee Corp Ltd* [2009] Scot C.S. C.S.O.H. 70.

[224] *Braithwaite v Employers' Liability Assurance Corp* [1964] 1 Lloyd's Rep. 94.

[225] *Alchorne v Favill* (1825) L.J. Ch. (O.S.) 47.

[226] *Home District Mutual Insurance Co v Thompson* (1847) 1 E. & A. 247; *Brown v Royal Insurance Co* (1854) 1 El. & El. 854; *Thames Fire Co v Hawks* (1858) 1 F. & F. 406.

[227] *Home Mutual Fire Insurance v Garfield* (1871) 14 Am. Rep. 27; *Davidson v Guardian Royal Exchange Assurance* 11979] 1 Lloyd's Rep. 406. *Ferruzzi France SA v Oceania Maritime Inc (The Palmea)* [1988] 2 Lloyd's Rep. 261 demonstrates that the assured owner of a vessel may face liability towards the charterer if the insurers delay in effecting repairs.

[228] *Insurance of North America v Hope* (1871) 11 Am. Rep. 48 at 49.

caused by delay,[229] although the primary repair contract is between insurers and repairer, so that the assured will not be liable to the repairer for the costs of repair in the event of the insurers' insolvency.[230]

The measure of damages where the insurers have failed totally to carry out their obligation to reinstate is potentially a question of some difficulty. In principle, given that, following an election by the insurers to reinstate, the contract is a building contract, the insurers' liability in damages is the cost of reinstatement. If the reinstatement cost is in excess of the amount that the assured could have recovered under the policy by way of indemnity this rule causes no difficulty, but it might be the case that the reinstatement value of the subject matter is less than the amount that the assured would have been entitled to receive by way of indemnity under the policy. In the latter situation it would appear that the insurers are entitled to elect for reinstatement but then to refuse to reinstate; the assured will thus be held down to the reinstatement cost by way of damages and will lose his right to full indemnity as provided for by the policy.

10–045 *Exclusion clauses.* The extent to which insurers can exclude or limit liability for a defective reinstatement is open to question. The doubt concerns the possible application of the Unfair Contract Terms Act 1977 to a clause in the policy which exempts the insurers from, for example, liability for delay in reinstatement. The 1977 Act does not apply to "any contract of insurance"[231] but it is arguable that the election to reinstate converts the policy into a building contract and that the 1977 Act applies to it.

10–046 *Right of insurers to combine in reinstatement.* When two or more insurers who have granted insurance on the same subject matter elect under their respective policies to reinstate, the assured cannot prevent them from joining to do the work[232] and, when it has been done, their liabilities under the policies will be discharged. This right of insurers may be a valuable one where the policies relate to separate interests, because the cost of reinstatement may then be very much less than the aggregate amount of individual losses.[233]

10–047 *Impossibility of reinstatement: effect on election.* The fact that reinstatement proves to be more difficult or expensive than the insurers originally contemplated does not relieve them from the obligation to reinstate once they have elected to do so. Thus if, after reinstatement has commenced, there is a fire which destroys the building, the insurers must recommence the reinstatement at their own expense.[234]

More difficult is the situation in which reinstatement proves to be physically or legally impossible. Two possibilities arise here. The first is that reinstatement was impossible from the outset, e.g. by reason of planning restrictions, so that the

---

[229] *Charnock v Liverpool Corp* [1968] 2 Lloyd's Rep. 113.

[230] *Godfrey Davis v Culling* [1962] 2 Lloyd's Rep. 349; *Cooter and Green v Tyrell* [1962] 2 Lloyd's Rep. 377; *Brown & Davis v Galbraith* [1972] 2 Lloyd's Rep. 1. In *Bee v Jenson (No.2)* [2008] Lloyd's Rep. I.R. 221 the Court of Appeal noted that the *Charnock* and *Brown & Davis* decisions were not easy to reconcile.

[231] Sch.1 para.1.

[232] *Scottish Amicable Heritage Securities Association v Northern Assurance Co* (1883) 11 R. 287.

[233] *Westminster Fire Office v Glasgow Provident Investment Society* (1888) 13 App.Cas. 699.

[234] *Smith v Colonial Mutual Fire Insurance Co Ltd* (1880) 6 V.L.R. 200. Cf *Waring & Gillow v Doughty, The Times*, February 21, 1922.

insurer did not in reality have any option as to reinstatement to exercise. Here, the election to reinstate is void, and the insurers become liable to pay the sums due under the policy: they cannot, purport to elect to reinstate and then treat themselves as discharged from all liability.[235] The second situation is that reinstatement has become impossible once work on reinstatement has begun, as where the partially reinstated premises are ordered to be demolished by planning authorities. It was held before the development of the doctrine of frustration[236] that impossibility was not a defence to the insurers and that the assured was entitled to claim damages for breach of contract.[237] The proper approach today is that it would first be determined whether impossibility of performance was contemplated by the agreement. If this is not the case, the doctrine of frustration operates to discharge the insurers from their duty to reinstate and they then fall under a duty to make payment under the policy as if they had elected to do so in the first instance. One difficulty arising from this analysis is that the insurers, having spent what may be significant sums on reinstatement, are obliged to meet the assured's claim in full. At common law this is clearly the situation,[238] although there is now the possibility that some apportionment for the lost expenditure is to be made under the terms of the Law Reform (Frustrated Contracts) Act 1943. It is nevertheless suggested that the 1943 Act is unlikely to come to the aid of the insurers, even on the assumption that it can apply to a reinstatement obligation.[239] This is so because the only provision of the Act under which apportionment is available, s.1(3), only applies where the wasted expenditure has conferred a "valuable benefit" on the party from whom apportionment is sought; it can hardly be said that the assured has received a valuable benefit from an abortive reinstatement.

Impossibility of reinstatement: effect on proceeds. Where reinstatement is **10–048** impossible and the proceeds of the policy or damages have become payable by the insurers, nice questions may arise as to the allocation of the money as between the assured and other persons interested in the insured subject matter. There is no real difficulty in the case of a joint policy, as the parties by definition share a common interest in the subject matter and are thus entitled to share the proceeds in proportion to the amount of their respective interests. The problems arise in two other situations, in each of which the assured has taken out the policy on a reinstatement basis in compliance with some contractual obligation to do so, as commonly occurs in landlord and tenant cases: the property may have been insured by the assured in his own name and that of the other party under a composite policy; or the assured may have insured the property in his own name, with the third party's interest being noted on the policy if mentioned at all. If the third party's interest is noted, it becomes arguable that he is a person upon whom the insurance policy is intended to confer a benefit, and that he has a personal claim against the insurers by virtue of the Contracts (Rights of Third Parties) Act 1999, with the noting satisfying the identification requirement in that Act. However, the third party has an action under the 1999 Act only if the insurance purports to confer a benefit upon him and there is nothing in the policy to indicate that a right of direct enforcement was being denied to him. It is submitted that the

---

[235] *Anderson v Commercial Union Assurance* (1885) 55 L.J.Q.B. 146.

[236] In *Taylor v Caldwell* (1863) 3 B. & S. 826.

[237] *Brown v Royal Insurance Co* (1859) 1 E. & E. 853.

[238] *Appleby v Myers* (1867) L.R. 2 C.P. 651.

[239] The Act does not apply to insurance (s.2(5)(b)), although it is arguable that the contract is a building contract and not one of insurance.

mere fact that a tenant's interest is noted on a policy does not of itself make him a beneficiary under it, as noting does not pinpoint any particular term which the tenant is being allowed to enforce. If the tenant's interest is not noted, the 1999 Act cannot in any event apply, as the identification requirement in s.1(3) of the 1999 Act is not satisfied.

Accordingly, the usual question to be determined is whether the assured, as the only person with a claim against the insurers, is solely entitled to the proceeds of the policy or whether he must account for the proceeds—either as trustee or debtor—to other owners of interests in the property. The answer will rest initially upon the proper construction of the contract between the assured and those other parties, although in the event that the point is not expressly provided for, the court must gain what guidance it can from the surrounding terms of the contract. In *Re King*[240] a tenant was obliged under the lease keep the premises insured and to reinstate them in the event of loss or damage by fire using the proceeds of the insurance. A fire occurred and the policy moneys were paid over to the tenant, but they could not be used to reinstate the premises as these had in the meantime been the subject of a local authority compulsory purchase order. The Court of Appeal held by a majority that the proceeds belonged to the tenant absolutely, either because the obligation to reinstate had become frustrated or because the sole beneficiary of the policy was the tenant. However, in *Beacon Carpets Ltd v Kirby*[241] the Court of Appeal distinguished *Re King* on the grounds that the landlord and tenant in *Beacon* had by means of post-loss negotiations entered into an agreement to divide the proceeds and, alternatively, that the policy in *Beacon* contemplated that each of the parties was to benefit from it. The distinctions are not entirely convincing, and it is noteworthy that Slade L.J. in *Beacon* relied heavily for his conclusion on the dissenting judgment of Lord Denning in *Re King*.

10–049   *Duty of assured to reinstate.* At common law an assured who has been paid the proceeds of the policy by the insurer is not under any obligation to apply the proceeds to reinstating the lost or damaged subject matter; he may do as he pleases with any sums received by him.[242] The position may of course be varied by contract between the assured and the insurers: policies on buildings frequently contain a provision whereby the assured agrees to reinstate the subject matter, and it would appear that such a clause cannot be used by the insurer to deny payment to an assured who bona fide holds the intention of reinstating but who cannot afford to reinstate until he has been paid, although it will provide a defence against an assured who has not demonstrated his intention to reinstate on receiving the proceeds of the policy.[243]

The assured may be under an express or implied contractual obligation to a third party to reinstate the premises; such a contract will generally be made with a person interested in the premises, either as co-assured under the policy or as an unnamed assured who directly or indirectly contributes to the insurance premiums. An express obligation to reinstate implies a duty on the assured to make a claim against the insurers and a duty to reinstate in accordance with the needs of the interested party.[244] In the absence of such an obligation, however, the courts have traditionally been reluctant to imply a duty on the assured to reinstate;

---

[240] [1963] Ch. 459.
[241] [1984] 2 All E.R. 726.
[242] *Queen Insurance Co v Vey* (1867) 16 L.T. 239; *Rayner v Preston* (1881) 18 Ch D 1.
[243] *Maclean Enterprises Ltd v Ecclesiastical Insurance Office Plc* [1986] 2 Lloyd's Rep. 416.
[244] *Vural v Security Archives Ltd* (1989) Estates Gazette Legal Supplement 2.

indeed, the general rule is that if a policy is taken out in the name of a single assured, he is entitled to be paid the policy monies and to deal with them as he thinks fit, irrespective of the existence of other interests in the property and of any express obligation to insure.[245]

Reinstatement under statute

Section 83 of the Fires Prevention (Metropolis) Act 1774. This ancient statute provides as follows: **10–050**

"And in order to deter and hinder ill-minded persons from wilfully setting their house or houses or other buildings on fire with a view of gaining to themselves the insurance money, whereby the lives and fortunes of many families may be lost or endangered: Be it further enacted . . . that it shall and may be lawful to and for respective governors or directors of the several insurance offices for insuring houses or other buildings against loss by fire, and they are hereby authorised and required, upon the request of any person or persons interested in or intitled unto any house or houses or other buildings which may hereafter be burnt down, demolished or damaged by fire, or upon any grounds of suspicion that the owner or owners, occupier or occupiers, or other person or persons who shall have insured such house or houses or other buildings have been guilty of fraud, or of wilfully setting their house or houses or other buildings on fire, to cause the insurance money to be laid out and expended as far as the same will go, towards rebuilding, reinstating or repairing such house or houses or other buildings so burnt down, demolished or damaged by fire, unless the party or parties claiming the insurance money shall, within sixty days next after his, her or their claim is adjusted, give a sufficient security to the governors or directors of the insurance office where such house or houses or other buildings are insured, that the said insurance money shall be laid out and expended as aforesaid, or unless the said insurance money shall be in that time settled and disposed of to and amongst all the contending parties, to the satisfaction and approbation of such governors or directors of such insurance office respectively."

The statutory scheme is, therefore, to seek to remove from the assured any incentive to fire his own building in order to realise its value from the insurer. Section 83 has not proved to be of significance in recent times, possibly because of a variety of oddities and uncertainties surrounding its operation.[246]

Operation. The preamble to s.83 of the 1774 Act states that the Act as a whole is to apply to specified districts of London only. However, decisions on s.83 have expanded its operation to the entirety of England and Wales.[247] The section applies only to buildings and fixtures and fittings which would pass by conveyance, but not to trade fixtures removable by the tenant or other fixtures not attached to the freehold.[248] Lloyd's underwriters are excluded.[249] **10–051**

Section 83 may be initiated by the insurers or by any interested third party. It has long been assumed that the effect of s.83 is to confer upon the insurers a discretion to reinstate—as opposed to pay—where fraud by the assured is suspected. If this is so, the section serves no purpose: it is standard practice for policies on buildings to contain reinstatement clauses which confer upon the insurers an absolute discretion whether to reinstate or to pay, irrespective of evidence of fraud; and if there is compelling evidence of fraud the claim will

---

[245] *Leeds v Cheetham* (1827) 1 Sim. 146.

[246] It is likely to be recommended for repeal by the Law Commission under its 2006 investigation of insurance law.

[247] *Ex parte Gorely* (1864) 4 De G. J. & S. 477; *Re Quicke's Trusts* [1908] 1 Ch. 887; *Sinnott v Bowden* [1912] 2 Ch. 414. The Act does not apply to Scotland: *Westminster Fire Office v Glasgow Provident Investment Society* (1888) 13 App.Cas. 699.

[248] *Ex parte Gorely* (1864) 4 De G. J. & S. 477; *Re Quicke's Trusts* [1908] 1 Ch. 887.

[249] *Portavon Cinema Co Ltd v Price* [1939] 4 All E.R. 601.

doubtless be rejected anyway. An alternative interpretation of the section is that insurers are required to reinstate if they suspect but cannot prove fraud, although it may be that this reads too much into the phrase "authorised and required". It has never been suggested that the section overrides ordinary principles relating to fraudulent claims and requires the insurers to reinstate if they have established fraud. It would seem, therefore, that unless the insurers have grounds to suspect fraud, a distinct request from an interested third party is necessary to bring the section into operation.[250]

There is no definition in s.83 of the term "person interested" in the insured building, although the courts have established that the phrase extends to a mortgagee,[251] the parties to a lease,[252] a remainderman claiming under the policy of the tenant for life,[253] and, possibly, a purchaser of a building who is its owner in equity following exchange of contracts but who has yet to become its legal owner by virtue of a conveyance, claiming under the policy of the vendor.[254] The interested party may make a request under s.83 whether or not there is any suspicion of fraud on the part of the assured. The request must be unequivocal and must be made before payment has been made to the assured.[255] The ability of an interested party to exercise his statutory right depends upon the assured having made a valid claim under the policy; s.83 does not give an interested person a right to make a claim against insurers[256] but merely allows such a person to take advantage of any claim which is made by the assured.[257] The position is unaffected by the Contracts (Rights of Third Parties) Act 1999, which only confers rights upon an intended beneficiary and not upon a person who happens to have an interest in the insured subject matter.

The assured himself cannot use s.83 to require the insurers to reinstate the premises,[258] although it may be that a co-assured under a composite policy can

---

[250] *Paris v Gilham* (1813) Coop. G. 56; *Simpson v Scottish Insurance* (1863) 1 H. & M. 615; *Wimbledon Park Golf Club v Imperial Insurance Co* (1902) 18 T.L.R. 815.

[251] *Sinnott v Bowden* [1912] 2 Ch. 414.

[252] *Vernon v Smith* (1821) 5 B. & Ald. 1; *Wimbledon Park Golf Club v Imperial Insurance Co* (1902)18 T.L.R. 815.

[253] *Re Quickes Trusts* [1908] 1 Ch. 877.

[254] *Rayner v Preston* (1881) 18 Ch. D. 1; *Kern Corp Ltd v Walter Reid Trading Pty Ltd* [1987] C.L.R. 164. It is plain that the seller cannot claim against his insurers after completion, as there is no loss (*Ziel Nominees Pty Ltd v Accident Insurance Co* (1975) 7 A.L.R. 667; *Bryant v Primary Industries Insurance Co Ltd* [1990] 2 N.Z.L.R. 142) unless the seller has agreed to reinstate (*Lonsdale & Thompson Ltd v Black Arrow Group Plc* [1993] 3 All E.R. 648). There is Australian authority for the proposition that the Act cannot be used in this situation, on the basis that in the case of a loss occurring after the exchange of contracts the seller's claim against the insurers is provisional only and is extinguished on completion when payment is made by the purchaser. Accordingly, there is no loss. See *Kern Corporation Ltd v Walter Reid Trading Pty Ltd* [1987] C.L.R. 164. It is submitted that the fallacy in this reasoning is the holding that the seller does not have a full claim when the insured peril occurs: the better view is that the assured has an accrued loss and that the insurers are required to make payment, albeit subject to the exercise of subrogation rights against the buyer for the full price.

[255] *Simpson v Scottish Union Insurance Co* (1861) 1 H. & M. 618.

[256] It does not, therefore, amount to an insurance in favour of the third party for the purposes of conditions relating to double insurance: *Portavon Cinema v Price* (1939) 161 L.T. 417.

[257] *Portavon Cinema v Price* (1939) 161 L.T. 417.

[258] *Reynolds v Phoenix Assurance Co* [1978] 2 Lloyd's Rep. 440. But contrast the comments in *Vural v Security Archive Ltd* (1990) 60 P. & C.R. 258 where it was said obiter by Knox J. that the 1774 Act permitted an interested person—there, a tenant—to make a claim in circumstances where the landlord was obliged under the lease to make a claim but did not do so. A similar view may be taken of *Lonsdale & Thompson Ltd v Black Arrow Group Plc* [1993] 3 All E.R. 648, where the landlord of premises which he had contracted to sell to a third party was held to be entitled, following the occurrence of an insured peril, to the policy moneys which were to be accounted for to the tenant, thereby preserving the tenant's rights under s.83.

use s.83. If, for example a policy is issued to a bank and borrower as co-aassureds, then although the borrower himself cannot require the insurers to reinstate his premises, it would be curious if the bank could not do so simply because it has taken the precaution of becoming a party to the policy rather than simply having its interest noted.

Obligations of the insurers. The insurer's obligation or discretion, as the case **10–052** may be, to reinstate under s.83, requires him to do no more than expend the amount recoverable by the assured under the policy. The assured is thus not entitled to a full reinstatement, as is the case where the matter is governed by contract, but will receive reinstatement only to the extent of the policy monies. The sum payable is the amount recoverable by the assured under the policy, even though he has a limited insurable interest.[259] However, the insurers are bound to lay out the money judiciously and bear the burden of showing that they have done so.[260]

There is some conflict in the authorities as to the appropriate remedy available to the third party against insurers who have refused to reinstate and who have stated their intention to pay the policy moneys to the assured. In *Simpson v Scottish Union Insurance Co*[261] it was suggested that a mandatory injunction could be granted, although in *Wimbledon Park Golf Club Ltd v Imperial Insurance Co Ltd*[262] a mandatory injunction was refused on the grounds that the obligation to reinstate was not imperative and that the insurers had no right to enter upon the assured's land to effect a reinstatement: the proper remedy was an injunction against the insurers preventing payment to the assured until the assured had given adequate security for an undertaking that the money would be put towards reinstatement.

If the reinstatement is faulty, or if delays in reinstatement cause loss to the assured, then by analogy with the cases on contractual reinstatement[263] the assured would seem to have a claim in damages against the insurers. The position of an interested person who has requested reinstatement gives rise to greater difficulty, for that person does not have a contract with the insurers and at best might have an action in tort. However, assuming that the courts are prepared to hold that there is the necessary proximity between the insurers and the third party to establish a duty of care, it might well be the case that damages are awardable in respect of physical damage only, and that loss of profits—which is undoubtedly the form of loss to which the third party is most prone—is irrecoverable under the general restriction on the recovery of economic loss in tort in the absence of a specific assumption of responsibility.[264] A further, admittedly weak, possibility is that the assured is permitted to recover damages representing the loss caused to all interested parties, those damages being held on trust by the assured for them.

There are two situations in which the insurers are entitled to pay over the proceeds of the policy to the assured despite the obligation to reinstate: (a) where the assured has, within 60 days of the adjustment of the loss, given security for his undertaking to use the proceeds for reinstatement; and (b) where the

---

[259] *Simpson v Scottish Union Insurance Co* (1863) 1 H. & M. 615.
[260] *Simpson v Scottish Union Insurance Co* (1863) 1 H. & M. 615 at 629.
[261] *Simpson v Scottish Union Insurance Co* (1863) 1 H. & M. 618.
[262] *Wimbledon Park Golf Club Ltd v Imperial Insurance Co Ltd* (1902) 18 T.L.R. 815.
[263] *Alchorne v Favill* (1825) L.J.Ch. (O.S.) 47; *Davidson v Guardian Royal Exchange Assurance* [1979] 1 Lloyd's Rep. 406.
[264] Cf. *Mylius v Royal Insurance Co Ltd* [1928] V.L.R. 126.

destination of the proceeds has been settled between all the contending parties.

4. SETTLEMENTS

10–053 **Interim payments.** CPR 1998, Pt 25, empowers the courts to order an interim payment to be made to the claimant pending final decision if the court is satisfied that the claimant would obtain substantial damages against the defendant should the action proceed to trial and judgment. In principle, this power is exercisable against an insurer, including the Motor Insurers' Bureau where it is to be called upon to meet a possible judgment against an uninsured or untraced driver.[265] An interim payment can be ordered only where the assured is bound to succeed against a particular defendant: if the assured has a claim against insurers, and a fallback claim against brokers, then the court may not make an order for an interim payment until it is established which of the two defendants is legally liable, and it is not enough that one of them will face liability.[266]

10–054 **Ex gratia payments.** Insurers frequently make ex gratia payments in circumstances where, as a matter of strict, the claim under the policy is not maintainable. Thus, irrespective of the possibility of waiver by the insurer of the assured's breach of duty, the insurers may choose to pay where the assured has failed to disclose a material fact or has broken a warranty. Further, there will frequently be cases in which the type of loss suffered by the assured is outside the scope of the policy, but only marginally so; ex gratia payment is common in this situation, although it has been held by the Court of Appeal that an insurer who has always met claims for a particular type of loss outside the policy is not estopped by so doing from denying liability in respect of the same class of loss on any future occasion.[267]

Settlement contracts

10–055 *The binding effect of settlement contracts.* Where a dispute has arisen between two parties, it is the policy of the law to encourage the parties to reach a voluntary settlement and thereafter to enforce it. Consequently, it is not open to a party who has compromised his rights following a genuine dispute as to the existence or quantum of legal liability to seek at a later stage to overturn the settlement if it is subsequently shown that he would have done better by initiating or contesting legal proceedings.[268] The relevant legal principle here is that, by compromising his right to litigate or to defend, either personally or through an authorised agent,[269] each of the parties has provided good consideration to the other. A settlement is binding where the correct legal position between the parties

---

[265] *Sharp v Pereira* [1999] Lloyd's Rep. I.R. 242.

[266] *Ricci Burns Ltd v Toole, The Times*, October 12, 1988.

[267] *London and Manchester Plate Glass Co v Heath* [1913] 2 K.B. 411, followed in *Kosmar Villa Holidays Plc v Trustees of Syndicate 1243* [2008] Lloyd's Rep. I.R. 43, where Gross J. was at pains to point out that the *Heath* decision did not reflect a rule of law but merely demonstrated the difficulties of establishing estoppel on such facts. The point did not arise on appeal, [2008] Lloyd's Rep. I.R. 489.

[268] *Kitchen Design & Advice Ltd v Lea Valley Water Co* [1989] 2 Lloyd's Rep. 221; *Fontana v Skandia Life Assurance Ltd* Unreported, 2001.

[269] *Chandler v Poland* 44 Ll. L.R. 349.

is unclear,[270] and even where one of the parties genuinely believes[271] that he has a valid claim or defence against the other even though that belief has no basis in law.[272] Although settlements are not contracts *uberrimae fidei* so that there is no duty of disclosure as such,[273] a settlement may be avoided if there is a positive misrepresentation,[274] undue influence[275] or other sharp practice.[276] It is not possible to imply into a settlement agreement a term that the settlement sum had been correctly identified as the sum due under the policy.[277]

A settlement contract is a binding agreement in its own right which replaces the policy under which the dispute arose. Accordingly, if the insurers default in making payments under the settlement, the assured has an action under the settlement for the agreed sum and will normally be entitled to summary judgment: the assured does not have the right to treat the settlement as repudiated by the insurers and revert to a claim under the policy[278] unless the settlement itself confers this option. As a matter of law insurers for their part cannot, by refusing to pay sums due under the settlement, argue that they have brought the settlement to an end by repudiation so that the assured is required to bring an action under the policy which requires him to prove his loss. Any term in the settlement which provides that in the event of breach it is to terminate and the parties are to revert to their rights under the policy will be construed as one for the benefit of the assured and not for the benefit of the insurers: were it otherwise, the insurers could simply overturn a settlement which subsequently proved to have been disadvantageous to them by the simply device of refusing to pay and forcing the assured to prove his loss under the policy.[279]

Follow the leader provisions. Many insurances, particularly those on commercial risks, are subscribed to by a number of insurers. Co-insurance is both horizontal and vertical. In its horizontal form, a number of insurers each take a proportion of the risk. Vertical co-insurance is written in excess of loss layers, with numerous insurers subscribing to different layers. In a complex case, there may be numerous insurers from different jurisdictions involved. Where there are a number of subscribing insurers to a policy, it is settled law that each insurer is independently liable to the assured for his own subscription irrespective of the position of the others. It follows that a full and final settlement reached with one **10–056**

---

[270] *Haigh v Brooks* (1839)10 A. & E. 309.

[271] *Wade v Simeon* (1846) 2 C.B. 548.

[272] *Callisher v Bischoffsheim* (1870) L.R. 5 Q.B. 449.

[273] *Bell v Lever Bros* [1932] A.C. 161.

[274] *Saunders v Ford Motor Co* [1970] 1 Lloyd's Rep. 379; *Baghbadrani v Commercial Union Assurance Co Plc* [2000] Lloyd's Rep. I.R. 94; *UCB Corporate Services Ltd v Thomason* [2004] EWHC 1164 Ch. Contrast *Kyle Bay Ltd v Certain Lloyd's Underwriters* [2007] Lloyd's Rep. I.R. 460 (statement of opinion by insurers as to quantum of loss).

[275] *Horry v Tate & Lyle Ltd* [1982] 2 Lloyd's Rep. 416.

[276] *Bank of Credit and Commerce International v Ali* [2001] 1 All E.R. 961. See *Taylor v Walker* [1958] 1 Lloyd's Rep. 490 (payment of secret commission by insurers to assured's loss assessors).

[277] See *Kyle Bay Ltd v Certain Lloyd's Underwriters* [2007] Lloyd's Rep. I.R. 460, where it was held that insurers who give an opinion as to the sum recoverable are simply putting forward their view as to the meaning of the policy rather than representing a fact.

[278] In *Korea Foreign Insurance Company v Omne Re SA* [1999] Lloyd's Rep. I.R. 509, Evans L.J. was seemingly of the opinion that the general law gave the innocent party the right either to enforce the settlement or to treat it as repudiated and to revert to the underlying contract. It is submitted that the better view, as expressed in Foskett's *Law and Practice of Compromise* is that "an agreement or compromise will discharge all original claims and counterclaims unless it expressly provides for their revival in the event of breach", a passage cited with approval by Evans L.J. in *Korea v Omne*.

[279] *Korea Foreign Insurance Company v Omne Re SA* [1999] Lloyd's Rep. I.R. 509.

insurer does not affect the assured's right to claim against other insurers. Equally, if the assured has a number of separate policies covering the same loss, a settlement with any one insurer does not preclude the assured from claiming against other insurers up to the total amount of his loss. The principle is simply that a settlement reached with one defendant does not extinguish as against other defendants any claims arising out of the same events.[280]

To avoid complex litigation in the event of any dispute concerning a claim, a variety of follow the leader provisions may be used by which the authority to settle is conferred upon a leading underwriter whose settlements are then binding on the other insurers. In *Roar Marine Ltd v Bimeh Iran Insurance Co*[281] in which the slip stated that the following market agreed to "follow leading British Underwriters in regard to ... settlements excluding ex gratia and without prejudice settlements". Mance J. held that, provided the settlement did not fall within either of the restrictions contained in the clause, a settlement entered into by the leading underwriter was binding on the following market, and that it was not open to any individual insurer to seek to reopen the settlement by arguing that there was no legal liability to the assured. It was further decided that, in the absence of any express qualification, the settlement was binding on the following market whether or not it was made bona fide and in a businesslike fashion.[282] Where there is a binding follow the settlements clause, it is a condition precedent to the making of any claim by the assured against any of the following insurers that there has been a binding settlement reached with the leading underwriter.[283] An alternative form of wording may require all of the insurers to assent to a settlement before it becomes binding on any of them. The market practice is for the broker negotiating for the assured to submit the proposed settlement to each insurer in the form of an offer, and it is a question of fact whether the proposal has actually been accepted.[284]

10–057 *Settlement contract made under mistake of fact.* A settlement may be affected by a mistake of fact, e.g., as to the circumstances of the loss. Where a contract is entered into on the basis of a fundamental mistake, the contract is void at common law, although for a mistake to have this effect it must be one that undermines the very basis of the contract. If the contract remains capable of performance, albeit in a manner which is disadvantageous to one of the parties, there is no operative mistake at common law,[285] and it was decided by the Court of Appeal in *The Great Peace*[286] that equity does not have any wider jurisdiction to treat a contract as voidable for a mistake which is of a less fundamental nature: earlier decisions asserting the wider jurisdiction[287] are to that extent now to be regarded as wrongly decided. Under the guidelines laid down in *The Great*

---

[280] *Heaton v Axa Equity and Law Assurance Society Plc* [2002] UKHL 15; *Cape and Dalgleish v Fitzgerald* [2002] UKHL 16.

[281] *Roar Marine Ltd v Bimeh Iran Insurance Co* [1998] 1 Lloyd's Rep. 423.

[282] The test for a settlement by an insurer becoming binding on reinsurers under a follow the settlements clause: see Ch.18, below.

[283] Cf. *Hong Kong Borneo Services Ltd v Pilcher* [1992] 2 Lloyd's Rep. 593.

[284] *National Company for Co-operative Insurance v St Paul Reinsurance Co Ltd* Unreported, 1997.

[285] *Bell v Lever Brothers* [1932] A.C. 161; *Great Peace Shipping Ltd v Tsavliris Salvage (International) Ltd (The Great Peace)* [2004] 4 All E.R. 689.

[286] *Great Peace Shipping Ltd v Tsavliris Salvage (International) Ltd (The Great Peace)* [2004] 4 All E.R. 689.

[287] *Solle v Butcher* [1950] 1 K.B. 671; *Grist v Bailey* [1967] Ch. 532; *Magee v Pennine Insurance Co Ltd* [1969] 2 Q.B. 507; *Associated Japanese Bank (International) Ltd v Credit du Nord SA* [1988] 3 All E.R. 902.

Peace, whether a contract is void at common law for mistake is a matter of the construction of the contract, so that it is necessary in the first place to construe the contract terms and then compare the terms with the position in the light of the mistake to see whether the parties have been deprived of substantially the whole benefit of the contract.[288] It was also noted by the Court of Appeal that there can be no mistake if: (a) either party has warranted that the state of affairs in question exists; or (b) the non-existence of a state of affairs is attributable to the fault of either party. As far as settlement contracts are concerned, the narrowness of the mistake doctrine means that a settlement is liable to be attacked on two grounds only.[289]

First, if it can be shown that there never was an insurance agreement in place between the parties, that the subject matter either never existed or had ceased to exist by the date of the inception of the risk[290] or that the assured did not possess insurable interest when the contract was made,[291] then the settlement itself plainly cannot stand. By contrast, if there is a binding insurance policy, but merely one which is capable of being set aside for misrepresentation or non-disclosure, a settlement reached in the absence of the insurers' knowledge of the right to avoid the policy is not sufficient to vitiate the settlement. This was decided by the Court of Appeal in *Magee v Pennine Insurance Co Ltd*,[292] in which the Court of Appeal held that in such a case the settlement was valid at law: the Court of Appeal's further conclusion that the settlement was voidable in equity was overruled in *The Great Peace*.[293]

Secondly, a settlement may be attacked on the basis of the nature of the loss. If it can be demonstrated by the insurers that the loss which had occurred did not fall within the policy at all, then there is a mistake which satisfies the test in *Bell*: while it might be thought that this conclusion is debatable, the point was decided by the House of Lords itself in *Norwich Union Fire Insurance Society Ltd v Price*,[294] shortly after *Bell* and on an application of the principles in *Bell*. By contrast, a settlement cannot be attacked simply because the loss itself was greater or smaller than was appreciated by the parties at the time.[295] Equally, if the insurers cannot show why policy monies have been paid to the assured, and

---

[288] See also: *O'Kane v Jones* [2005] Lloyd's Rep. I.R. 174; *Hurst States & Interiors Ltd v ML Europe Property Ltd* [2004] B.L.R. 249; *Brennan v Bolt Burden* [2005] Q.B. 303; *Champion Investments Ltd v Ahmed* [2005] EWHC 1956 (QB).

[289] It should not matter in principle whether the settlement contract is executed or executory. There is old authority, *Herbert v Champion* (1807) 1 Camp. 134, for the proposition that an executory settlement contract can be overturned irrespective of the quality of the mistake, but it is difficult to see why it should matter whether or not the insurer have honoured the settlement.

[290] *Strickland v Turner* (1852) 7 Ex. 208; *Pritchard v Merchants' and Tradesmen's Mutual Life Assurance Society* (1858) 3 C.B.N.S. 622. In each of these cases, the policyholders successfully recovered premiums paid under life policies where the life assured had died prior to inception. The same principle would presumably apply where the insurer had in error paid the policy proceeds, mistaking the assured's date of death, as the risk would never have attached in the first place.

[291] *Piper v Royal Exchange Assurance* (1932) 44 Ll. L.R. 103.

[292] *Magee v Pennine Insurance Co Ltd* [1969] 2 Q.B. 507.

[293] In *Kyle Bay Ltd v Certain Lloyd's Underwriters* [2006] Lloyd's Rep. I.R. 718 the view was expressed that *Magee* was no longer good law. That comment was not repeated by the Court of Appeal on appeal in this case, [2007] Lloyd's Rep. I.R. 460. See also *Statoil ASA v Louis Dreyfus Energy Services LP* [2008] EWHC 2257 Comm which confirms that the same principle applies to the case in which only one party is mistaken, even if the other is aware of the mistake. In *Statoil* the court refused to imply a term into a settlement contract that there was no mistake.

[294] *Norwich Union Fire Insurance Society Ltd v Price* [1934] A.C. 455.

[295] *Kyle Bay Ltd v Certain Lloyd's Underwriters* [2007] Lloyd's Rep. I.R. 460.

simply assert that there must have been a computer error, the burden of proof required for mistake will not have been satisfied.[296]

10–058 *Settlement contract made under mistake of law.* It was for many years assumed by the common law that there was a distinction between mistake of law and mistake of fact, and that mistakes of law did not give rise to actionable mistake on the basis that every person is assumed to know the law. The same distinction between law and fact was drawn in the context of payments made under a mistake, but the House of Lords in *Kleinwort Benson v Lincoln City Council*[297] abrogated that distinction in the context of restitution, and in *Brennan v Bolt Burden*[298] the Court of Appeal duly confirmed that a settlement contract may be vitiated by mistake of law as well as by mistake of fact. However, it remains the case that the mistake must be fundamental,[299] and it is almost certainly not enough for the insurers to assert the existence of a fundamental mistake when the insurers are fully aware of the facts which may give rise to a defence but has failed to appreciate that the law affords a defence in those circumstances. Accordingly, while a mistake of law is in principle capable of amounting to a fundamental mistake, a misapprehension of established legal principles may not be adequate. The point was forcefully made by Lord Abinger in *Kelly v Solari*,[300] in the context of payments made under mistake of fact: "There may also be cases in which although [the payer] might by investigation learn the state of facts more accurately, he declines to do so, and chooses to pay notwithstanding; in that case there can be no doubt that he is . . . bound." In *Brennan* the Court of Appeal thus accepted that a compromise reached in circumstances where the law was known to be uncertain was normally to be treated as binding and could not be overturned simply because the law was subsequently clarified in a later case.

A more extreme situation is that in which the law has actually been altered after a settlement has been entered into, in a fashion which has a major effect on the settlement. By reason of the declaratory effect of judgments, the law is declared rather than changed, which means that the earlier settlement was based on mistake and that the limitation period for reopening the settlement thus runs from the date of the judgment, the date on which the mistake could have been discovered.[301] Somewhat curiously, the degree of mistake required to overturn a settlement in this situation is less than that required to overturn a settlement based on mistake of fact. This is the consequence of the ruling of the House of Lords in *Bank of Credit and Commerce International v Ali*,[302] in which their Lordships (Lord Hoffmann vigorously dissenting) reopened a settlement of an unfair dismissal claim in the light of a subsequent recognition by the courts in separate litigation that a head of damages which could not have been contemplated by the

---

[296] *Napier v UNUM Ltd* [19961 2 Lloyd's Rep. 550.

[297] *Kleinwort Benson v Lincoln City Council* [1998] 4 All E.R. 513.

[298] *Brennan v Bolt Burden* [2005] Q.B. 303.

[299] See *Home and Colonial Insurance Co Ltd v London Guarantee and Accident Co Ltd* (1928) 32 Ll. L.R. 267, where restitution was denied following payment under a marine policy void for want of stamping under the Stamp Act 1981 s.93, as the error was one of law. The decision would presumably now be in favour of the insurers.

[300] *Kelly v Solari* (1841) 9 M. & W. 54 at 59.

[301] In accordance with the Limitation Act 1980 s.32. See *Kleinwort Benson v Lincoln City Council* [1998] 4 All E.R. 513.

[302] *Bank of Credit and Commerce International v Ali* [2001] 1 All E.R. 961.

parties—stigma damages—was recoverable in employment cases. This unfortunate consequence can be avoided if the settlement refers to all claims "known and unknown".[303]

Conditional settlement. Where the payment has been made under a provisional settlement agreement which expressly stipulates that payment is to be returned or its quantum adjusted in the light of future events, the assured will clearly be unable to deny restitution to the insurers if it is subsequently demonstrated that a lesser (or no) sum was due under the policy.[304] Where insurers agree to make a payment on account following the recommendation of a loss adjuster, such payment is regarded as merely provisional and accordingly may be recovered if it transpires that the insurers did not face liability under the policy.[305] The scope of the condition depends upon its wording; an obligation on the assured to sue to judgment a third party believed to be responsible for the loss has been held to be broken, rendering the policy moneys repayable to the insurers, where the assured simply reached a settlement with the third party.[306]

10–059

Payments in the absence of a settlement contract

Effect of payment. If the insurer has simply paid a sum to the assured without requiring the assured to sign an acceptance form treating the payment as full and final, but merely requiring the assured to sign a receipt, it appears that the validity and amount of the payment may later be challenged by both parties. "The type of mistake necessary to give rise to a right to recover under the restitutionary remedy of money paid under a mistake of fact need not necessarily be of the same fundamental character that makes a contract totally void."[307] Thus, if the assured has accepted a payment, he is not regarded by the law as having agreed to forgo his legal rights simply by paying the cheque into his account and he remains free to go back to the insurers should it prove to be the case that the sum paid was inadequate, e.g. where the loss is shown to be greater than was originally thought or the insurer had misapplied the policy wording in making a smaller payment. Again, insurers are entitled to recover payments made under policy voidable for misrepresentation where they were unaware of the fact that false statements had been made to them on inception.[308]

10–060

The more complex case is where the insurers seeks to recover a sum paid to the assured on the ground that they were mistaken as to their legal liability to pay. The mistake may be one of fact, e.g. that the peril which had been thought to have caused the loss was not operative and the loss was in fact caused by an uninsured peril. Alternatively, since the abrogation of the distinction between law and fact in *Kleinwort Benson v Lincoln City Council*[309] the mistake may be one of law. In so deciding, the House of Lords overruled *Bilbie v Lumley*,[310] in which it had been held that an insurer who was aware that the assured had withheld a fact on presenting the risk but was unaware of his legal rights to refuse payment

---

[303] *Mostcash v Fluour* [2002] B.L.R. 411.

[304] *Sebel Products v Commissioners of Customs and Excise* [1949] 1 Ch. 409; *Boden v Hussey* [1988] 1 Lloyd's Rep. 423.

[305] *Castle Insurance Co v Hong Kong Islands Shipping Co* [1983] 2 Lloyd's Rep. 376; *Attaleia Marine Co Ltd v Iran Insurance Co (The Zeus)* [1993] 2 Lloyd's Rep. 497.

[306] *Euler Hermes UK Plc v Apple Computer BV* [2006] Lloyd's Rep. I.R. 691.

[307] *Midland Bank Plc v Brown Shipley & Co Ltd* [1991] 2 All E.R. 690 at 700.

[308] *Cornhill Insurance Co Ltd v L & B Assenheim* (1937) 58 Ll. L.R. 27.

[309] *Kleinwort Benson v Lincoln City Council* [1998] 4 All E.R. 513.

[310] *Bilbie v Lumley* (1802) 2 East 469.

on the basis of breach of warranty could not recover the payment made to the assured by way of settlement because the mistake was one of law.

The precise circumstances in which a mistaken payment may give rise to restitution for mistake have yet to be fully worked out, although the general view of the courts is that the basic question is of unjust enrichment, namely, has the defendant been unjustly enriched at the claimant's expense? The test as originally formulated in *Kelly v Solari*,[311] an insurance case, was based on the supposed liability of the payer. In *Kelly* itself, the insurers paid the proceeds of a life policy to the assured's executrix, the insurers having failed to appreciate that the policy had lapsed as premiums had not been paid. In allowing restitution, Bramwell B. held that money is recoverable:

> "where money is paid to another under the influence of a mistake, that is, upon the supposition that a specific fact is true, which would entitle the other to the money but which fact is untrue, and the money would not have been paid had it been known to the payer that the fact was untrue."

More recently, it has been emphasised that there has to be a causal connection between the mistake and the payment.[312] It was further held in *Kelly* that negligence on the part of the payer is here immaterial although, if the payer has declined to undertake the necessary factual investigation, he can scarcely complain if he proves to be mistaken.

10–061   *Money payable in any event.* If the insurers intend to make payment whatever their obligations in law may be, then the payment is not recoverable on the ground of mistake. It was thus said in *Kelly v Solari*[313] that restitution will be denied where "the payer intends that the payee shall have the money at all events whether the fact be true or false".[314] On this basis it has been held that an insurer who had paid a building society for losses on loans, in the knowledge that the lender's lending criteria had not been complied with as required by the policy, could not plead recover its payment as no proper investigations had been made.[315]

10–062   *The defence of change of position.* The most important defence to a restitutionary claim is that of change of position. Prior to the recognition of this defence by the House of Lords in *Lipkin Gorman v Karpnale Ltd*,[316] the English courts recognised that a payment made by error might be irrecoverable if the payer had made an unequivocal representation to the payee that the sum was due to him, resulting in an estoppel,[317] although this principle now seems to have been subsumed into the more general flexible of position defence[318] which is

---

[311] *Kelly v Solari* (1841) 9 M. & W. 54.

[312] *Barclays Bank Ltd v WJ Simms Son and Cooke (Southern) Ltd* [1980] Q.B. 677; *Nurdin & Peacock Plc v Ramsden & Co Ltd* [1999] 1 W.L.R. 1249.

[313] *Kelly v Solari* (1841) 9 M. & S. 54.

[314] See also *Barclays Bank Ltd v WJ Simms Son and Cooke (Southern) Ltd* [1980] Q.B. 677; *Nurdin & Peacock v Ramsden & Co Ltd* [1999] 1 W.L.R. 1249; *Woolwich Equitable Building Society v Commissioners of Inland Revenue* [1992] 3 All E.R. 737.

[315] *Den Danske Bank A/S v Skipton Building Society* [1998] 1 E.G.L.R. 155.

[316] *Lipkin Gorman v Karpnale Ltd* [1991] 2 A.C. 548, although for an earlier indication, see *BP (Libya) Ltd v Hunt* [1979] 1 W.L.R. 783.

[317] *Avon County Council v Howlett* [1983] 1 All E.R. 1073.

[318] *Avon* was so regarded in *Scottish Equitable Plc v Derby* [2001] 3 All E.R. 818. See also *Comrnerzbank AG v Price-Jones* [2003] EWCA Civ 1663. Contrast *National Westminster Bank Plc v Somer International (UK) Ltd* [2002] 3 W.L.R. 64.

"available to a person whose position has so changed that it would be inequitable in all the circumstances to require him to make restitution, or alternatively to make restitution in full."[319] In *Niru Battery Manufacturing Co v Milestone Trading Ltd*[320] the Court of Appeal drew together the various authorities on change of position, and laid down the following propositions:

(i) the question was whether it would be unjust to allow restitution or restitution in full;

(ii) it would be unjust to allow restitution where an innocent defendant's position had so changed that the injustice of requiring him to repay outweighed the injustice of denying the claimant restitution;

(iii) the defence of change of position was not available to a defendant who had changed his position in bad faith, a concept which did not necessarily require dishonesty as where the defendant had paid away the money with knowledge of the facts entitling the claimant to restitution; and

(iv) the defence was not available to a wrongdoer.

The cases illustrate that the defence is of limited significance in insurance cases. Thus where an assured was overpaid by his insurers under a pension plan despite his protests that there had been a mistake, and used the money to pay off his mortgage and to make investments, the money was held to be recoverable because the assured could not demonstrate that he would have acted differently without the overpayment: he was allowed to retain only a small sum used to purchase goods and services which he would not otherwise have purchased. The fact that the mistake was due to the negligence of the insurers was held to be irrelevant.[321] Where the assured is aware of the insurers' mistake in making payment but does not draw it to their attention, the defence of position is almost bound to fail.[322]

Where liability insurers have paid a sum to the third party claimant against the assured, and have then discovered a defence to the assured's claim, the insurers would seem to have no right to recover the payment from the third party as long as he was a bona fide recipient of the payment and had no reason to believe that the insurers were acting under a mistake.[323]

Effect of payment to broker. If insurers are able to assert a right to recover a **10–063** payment made by them, that right is exercisable against the assured. It is conceivable, however, that the insurers have paid the money to a broker acting as agent for the assured. In these circumstances a broker who as retained the sum is personally liable to the insurer, in an action for money had and received, to restore the sum paid to him by reason of mistake.[324] However, if the broker has actually paid the money over to the assured, he cannot face personal liability for its return[325] unless he was aware that the insurers had paid under a mistake,[326]

---

[319] *Lipkin Gorman v Karpnale Ltd* [1991] 2 A.C. 548 at 580.

[320] *Niru Battery Manufacturing Co v Milestone Trading Ltd* [2004] 1 Lloyd's Rep. 344.

[321] *Scottish Equitable Plc v Derby* [2001] 3 All E.R. 818.

[322] *Clinton v Windsor Life Assurance Co Ltd* Unreported, 2001.

[323] Cf. *Niru Battery Manufacturing Co v Milestone Trading Ltd* [2002] 2 All E.R. (Comm) 705. In such a case the insurers may have a claim against the assured, for the recovery of sums paid to the benefit of the assured.

[324] *Kleinwort, Sons & Co v Dunlop Rubber Co* (1907) 97 L.T. 263.

[325] *Holland v Russell* (1863) 4 B. & S. 14. Cf. *General Accident, Fire and Life Assurance Corp Ltd v Midland Bank Ltd* [1940] 2 K.B. 388 (payment to co-assured).

[326] *Snowden v Davis* (1808) 1 Taunt. 359; *Oates v Hudson* (1851) 6 Ex. 346.

and repayment by the broker will not be ordered if he has a settled account with the assured and the assured has obtained credit against the sum received by the broker.[327]

10–064 **No loss suffered by assured.** There may be exceptional cases in which an assured, having been paid in full for a loss, discovers that the assumed loss had not taken place. There is little authority on this possibility, but there is a necessary distinction between indemnity and non-indemnity policies. As far as indemnity insurance is concerned, an insurer who has paid for a partial loss is doubtless entitled to a restitutionary remedy on the ground of mistake. Total losses cause more difficulty for, where an insurer pays on the assumption of a total loss, the insurer is entitled to take over the subject matter of the insurance by way of salvage. Consequently, if no loss has in fact occurred, the insured subject matter becomes available for salvage. No less than four solutions may be devised for dealing with this situation.

    (1) The assured might be obliged to repay the insurance moneys and to retain possession of the subject matter, as if no claim had ever been made.

    (2) The insurer might have the right to take possession of the insured subject matter, and the assured the obligation to surrender it to the insurer if the insurer so demands.

    (3) The assured might be able to choose between retaining the policy moneys and surrendering the goods, or retaining the goods and returning the policy moneys.

    (4) The insurer might be able to choose between claiming from the assured either the goods or the policy monies.

In *Holmes v Payne*[328] the assured claimed for the loss of a piece of jewellery, which she later found. In the meantime the insurer had authorised a jeweller to supply to the assured jewellery of the same value, and on the discovery of the original piece sought possession of the replacement goods, on the strength of possibility (4) above. Roche J. held that the action must fail, as the insurer's only right was that of salvage against the insured goods. This indicates that the solution adopted by English law is (2) above, but the ultimate decision is also consistent with possibility (3) and it is interesting to speculate what the outcome would have been had the action been by the assured seeking a declaration that she was entitled to retain the insured subject matter and to surrender the replacement articles. The reasoning of Roche J. suggests that such an action would have failed on the basis that the settlement contract could not be reopened, but it is suggested that *Holmes v Payne* is not conclusive authority for the proposition that possibility (2), rather than possibility (3), represents English law.

Non-indemnity policies raise rather different issues, for there is no possibility of salvage where the insurer had paid under a life or accident policy for an event which has not occurred. It might properly be thought obvious that the insurer is normally entitled to restitution for fundamental mistake, but it is arguable that, as a matter of general principle, this ought not to be the case where the death of the life insured under the policy is a matter of some contention and the insurer has

---

[327] *Buller v Harrison* (1775) 2 Cowp. 565. Contrast *Scottish Metropolitan Assurance Co Ltd v Samuel & Co Ltd* [1923] 1 K.B. 348 (no account in existence).
[328] *Holmes v Payne* [1930] 2 K.B. 301.

paid to avoid litigation by the beneficiary of the policy. The American courts have indeed held that, where an insurer has paid under a life policy on the assumption that the life assured is deceased, it has assumed the risk that the insured event has not occurred and is unable to claim restitution if the person insured under the policy subsequently turns up safe and well.[329]

[329] *New York Life Insurance Co v Chittenden* 112 N.W. 96 (1907).

CHAPTER 11

THE RIGHTS OF INSURERS

1. SUBROGATION

11–001 **General definition and objectives.** The law has long recognised the principle that where A indemnifies B, under some form of agreement between them to that effect, for loss caused by C to B, on providing a full indemnity A is entitled to exercise B's rights against C. Of all the contexts in which subrogation may arise insurance is undoubtedly the most common, and it is apparent that the insurer's right of subrogation has been operating in England since at least the middle of the eighteenth century.[1] While the effect of subrogation is to confer upon the insurer the rights of the assured,[2] it must be borne in mind from the outset that the proper claimant against the third party is the assured; as a result, the subrogation action must be brought in the name of the assured. The significance of this point will emerge at various stages in what follows.[3]

Such judicial explanations of subrogation as are to be found refer primarily to its role in preventing the assured from recovering more than an indemnity. The possibility that the assured may recover more than an indemnity results from the common law principles that a person who is insured and who has recovered his entire loss from an insurer is not prevented from proceeding against the wrongdoer[4] on the principle that insurance recoveries are to be left out of account in determining liability,[5] and that the insurer is required to make payment to the assured despite the fact that the assured has a cause of action against a third party

---

[1] *Randal v Cockran* (1748) 1 Ves. Sen. 98; *Blaaupot v Da Costa* (1758) 1 Eden 130. In *Mason v Sainsbury* (1782) 3 Doug. 61, Lord Mansfield stated at 64 that "every day the insurer is put in the place of the assured". The insurer's right of subrogation has been codified in s.79 of the Marine Insurance Act 1906.

[2] Or at least the right to call for use of the assured's name: *Central Insurance Co Ltd v Seacalf Shipping Corp* [1983] 2 Lloyd's Rep. 25.

[3] The term "subrogation" is traditionally used to cover three situations: (a) the transfer to the insurers of the assured's right of action against a third party; (b) the right of the insurers to recover from the assured sums received from a third party before a claim is made against the insurers; and (c) the right of the insurers to recover from the assured sums received from a third party after the insurers have provided an indemnity. Situation (a) is the only true instance of subrogation: (b) is in essence recovery of a payment made by the insurers under mistake, and (c) is the enforcement by their insurers of their equitable lien over sums received by the assured.

[4] *Mason v Sainsbury* (1782) 3 Doug. 61; *Clark v Blything* (1823) 2 B. & C. 254; *Yates v White* (1838) 4 Bing. N.C. 272; *Bradburn v Great Western Railway* (1874) L.R. 10 Ex. 1; *King v Victoria Insurance* [1896] A.C. 250; *Hobbs v Marlowe* [1978] A.C. 16; *Brown v Albany Construction Co* [1995] N.P.C. 100. Cf. *Bank of Nova Scotia v Hellenic Mutual War Risks Association (Bermuda) Ltd* [1988] 1 Lloyd's Rep. 514, in which Hobhouse J. rejected the argument of a marine insurer to the effect that its alleged breach of duty towards the mortgagee of the vessel had caused no loss simply because the mortgagee had taken out a "mortgagee's interest" policy which covered the events in question.

[5] *Arab Bank Plc v John D Wood Commercial Ltd* [2000] Lloyd's Rep. I.R. 471.

in respect of the loss.[6] To prevent the assured from recovering a double indemnity, the doctrine of subrogation intervenes: where the insurer has paid the assured, any sums recovered by the assured from the third party are to be held in equity for the insurer[7]; and where the insurer is required to pay an assured who has received an indemnity from the third party, the insurer is entitled to set off from his payment the amount received by the assured.[8]

This "negative" role of subrogation was summarised by Brett L.J. in his classic judgment in *Castellain v Preston*[9]:

"The fundamental rule of insurance law [is] that the contract of insurance contained in a marine or fire policy is a contract of indemnity, and of indemnity only, and this contract means that the assured, in the case of a loss against which the policy has been made, shall be fully indemnified, but shall never be more than fully indemnified."

Subrogation, thus understood, rests upon the ground that the insurer's contract is in the nature of a contact of indemnity and that he is therefore entitled upon paying a sum for which others are primarily liable to the assured, to be proportionately subrogated to the right of action of the assured against them.[10] Subrogation by this means prevents the unjust enrichment of the assured.

While the negative side of subrogation is generally emphasised by the courts, subrogation has an equally important "positive" side. The insurers are entitled to take over all of the rights of the assured, whether in contract or tort, legal or equitable, against the person responsible for the loss,[11] and are also entitled to take advantage of any benefit which accrues to the assured which diminishes the loss.[12] The most important consequence of the positive role of subrogation is to permit the insurer to proceed against the assured for taking any action which prejudices the insurer's rights against the third party. Thus, if having recovered from the insurer, the assured enters into a binding agreement with the third party waiving all claims against him, the insurer is entitled to sue the assured for the amount that would have been recoverable from the third party up to the amount of the insurer's own payment.[13] This right may be justified by the argument that, in its absence, the third-party wrongdoer would be unjustly enriched by not having to pay for the loss which he has caused, and in effect is being granted the benefits of an insurance policy to which he is not a party; on this basis it is perhaps misleading to refer to the insurer's right of action against the insured as

---

[6] *Cullen v Butler* (1816) 5 M. & S. 461; *Quebec Fire v Louis* (1851) 7 Moo. P.C. 286; *Dickenson v Jardine* (1868) L.R. 3 C.P. 639 at 644; *North British Insurance v London, Liverpool & Globe Insurance* (1877) 5 Ch D 569 at 575; *Collingridge v Royal Exchange Assurance* (1877) 3 QBD 173 at 176–177.

[7] But only up to the amount paid by the insurer, as the excess over the insurer's payment accrues to the benefit of the assured; see below. For an illustration, see *Falcon Insurance Co (HK) Ltd v Cheshire Cat Restaurant & Pub Co Ltd* [2007] H.K.E.C. 2084.

[8] *Sickness & Accident Assurance Association v General Accident Assurance Corporation Ltd* 1892 R. 277; *Austin v Zurich General Accident* [1945] K.B. 250; *Bovis Construction Ltd v Commercial Union Assurance* [2001] Lloyd's Rep. I.R. 321. If the third party is itself an insurer, the third party can have no subrogation rights against the non-paying insurer (given that the assured himself has no claim by reason of the fact that he has suffered no loss) and the only remedy available to the third party is contribution: see below.

[9] *Castellain v Preston* (1883) 11 QBD 380 at 387.

[10] This paragraph was cited with approval by McCardie J. in *Edwards v Motor Union Insurance* [1922] 2 K.B. 239 at 253.

[11] *Castellain v Preston* (1883) 11 QBD 380 at 388.

[12] *Burnand v Rodocanachi* (1882) 7 App.Cas. 333 at 339.

[13] This point is discussed below. For the original principle, see *Mitchell v Edie* (1787) 1 T.R. 608.

"positive". However, it should be recognised that subrogation is not concerned primarily with preventing the unjust enrichment of the assured under a double indemnity, for where the assured has made it impossible for himself to recover more than an indemnity, by virtue of an agreement with the third party, the rights of the insurer predominate and the assured will be left without payment from any source.

11–002 **Juridical basis.** There is some conflict in the authorities as to whether subrogation is a doctrine stemming from the operation of equity or whether it rests upon an implied term in every contract of insurance permitting the insurer to exercise the assured's rights. The overwhelming weight of early judicial authority accepts the equitable origin of subrogation,[14] although in recent times the implied term theory has been propounded by Lord Diplock,[15] with some support from James L.J.[16] and was accepted uncritically by the Court of Appeal in *Napier and Ettrick (Lord) v Kershaw*.[17] However, the House of Lords in the *Napier and Ettrick case*,[18] after a careful analysis of the authorities, has resolved the dispute in favour of equity,[19] their Lordships pointing out that subrogation in insurance originated in a series of early cases in which subrogation was described as the plainest equity.[20] Their Lordships recognised that the insurer's right of subrogation later came to be expressed on the basis of the contractual relationship between assured and insurer, and in particular by means of four implied obligations (identified by Lord Templeman) on the assured:

(a) to take proceedings against the wrongdoing third party in order to diminish his loss;

(b) to account to the insurer for the proceeds of any such action;

(c) to allow the insurer to use the assured's name in order to proceed against the third party in the event that the assured himself failed to do so;

(d) to act in good faith in proceeding against the third party.

Subrogation as classified by the House of Lords developed, therefore, as an amalgamation of common law and equitable principles. The later fusion of law and equity did not eliminate the equitable origins of the doctrine, and their Lordships emphasised that the doctrine of subrogation continues to confer rights upon the insurer which are recognised solely by equity.[21] The recognition of implied terms in the contract of insurance, regulating the assured's action against the third party, indicates that the assured is potentially liable in damages to the insurer (i) for failing to proceed against the third party, (ii) for refusing to allow the insurer to use his name to sue the third party or (iii) in reaching a settlement

---

[14] The old cases are expertly analysed by Derham, *Subrogation in Insurance Law*, 1985, Ch.1, the author concluding that the equitable theory is the correct one.

[15] In *Yorkshire Insurance Co v Nisbet Shipping Co* [1962] 2 Q.B. 330 and *Hobbs v Marlowe* [1978] A.C. 16. See also *Orakpo v Manson Investments* [1978] A.C. 95.

[16] *Morris v Ford Motor Co Ltd* [1973] Q.B. 792.

[17] *Napier and Ettrick (Lord) v Kershaw* [1993] 1 Lloyd's Rep. 10.

[18] *Napier and Ettrick (Lord) v Kershaw* [1993] 1 All E.R. 385.

[19] See also: *England v Guardian Insurance Ltd* [2000] Lloyd's Rep. I.R. 404; *Arab Bank Plc v John D Wood Commercial Ltd* [2000] Lloyd's Rep. I.R. 471.

[20] *Randal v Cockran* (1748) 1 Ves. Sen. 98; *Blaaupot v Da Costa* (1758) 1 Eden 130; *White v Dobinson* (1844) 14 Sim. 273.

[21] Thus, the insurer has an equitable charge over recoveries made by the assured, and it is arguable that the insurer has an equitable charge over the cause of action against the third party. The latter point was left open by the House of Lords, but was subsequently rejected in *Re Ballast Plc, St Paul Travellers Insurance Co Ltd v Dargan* [2007] Lloyd's Rep. I.R. 742.

with the third party other than a settlement which is a bona fide compromise of the third party's potential liability. After *Napier and Ettrick* it would seem that the only case in which the insurer needs to rely upon an action for damages is (iii). In cases (i) and (ii) the insurer can rely upon equity to compel the assured to allow use of his name by the insurer, particularly if, as Lords Templeman and Goff, Lord Browne-Wilkinson expressing greater doubts, thought might be the case, the insurer has an equitable charge over the assured's action.

Where there is a contractual right of subrogation, the scope of that right will be determined by the contract between the assured and the insurer.[22] Further, it is necessary to bear in mind that subrogation which takes effect under a contract of insurance, whether by means of an express term or by operation of law, is quite separate from subrogation as a general restitutionary defence. An insurer's right of subrogation allows the insurer to recover from the third party the sum paid by the insurer to the assured even though the insurer's own loss may have been less, e.g. by reason of sums received from an entirely separate source.[23]

In the insurance context, it is common for insurers to take an assignment of the assured's claim against the third party. If the insurer takes a legal assignment, the action against the third party is then to be brought in the insurer's own name. This may be done by an express letter of subrogation, or by a policy term, which confers subrogation rights upon the insurer.

Subrogation and related doctrines

Subrogation and abandonment. Where the assured is paid for a total loss, the   **11–003**
remains of the subject matter must be abandoned to the insurer. Abandonment, if accepted by the insurer, confers upon it ownership of the abandoned property, whereas subrogation merely gives the insurer the power to exercise the assured's rights of suit and to claim payments made to the assured in diminution of its loss. Hence the exercise of subrogation rights does not permit the insurer to sue in its own name, nor does it entitle the insurer to claim any profits earned by the insured subject matter. Subrogation and abandonment are nevertheless related doctrines, and probably possess a common origin. Where insurers have not elected to take over the subject matter after payment, and the subject matter has been sold, the insurers cannot seek to recover the proceeds or the residual value of the vessel from the assured: an election not to take over the subject matter relinquishes all interest in it and in its proceeds.[24]

Subrogation and assignment. The principles of maintenance and champerty will   **11–004**
in general prevent the assignment of a bare cause of action. However, it is well established that where the assignee has a genuine and substantial interest in the outcome of the litigation any assignment to him will not be contrary to public policy, even though the assignee stands to profit from the assignment.[25] By reason of this exception, the law allows an insurer to take from its assured an assignment of the assured's rights against a third party in respect of an insured loss.[26] Many policies provide that the assured is to assign his rights if required to do so by the insurer. There are a number of reasons why an insurer might wish to take an assignment rather than to rely upon subrogation rights.

[22] *Banque Financière de la Cité v Parc (Battersea) Ltd* [1998] 1 All E.R. 737 at 745.
[23] *Bee v Jenson (No.2)* [2007] Lloyd's Rep. I.R. 221.
[24] *Dornoch Ltd v Westminster International BV (No.3)* [2009] EWHC 1782 (Admlty).
[25] *Trendtex Trading Corporation v Credit Suisse* [1982] A.C. 679; *Brownton Ltd v Edward Moore Incubon Ltd* [1985] 3 All E.R. 499; *Giles v Thompson* [1994] 1 A.C. 965.
[26] *Compania Colombiana de Seguros v Pacific Steam Navigation Co* [1965] 1 Q.B. 101.

(1) If the insurer takes a legal assignment under s.136 of the Law of Property Act 1925 it may sue the third party in its own name, without the need to join the assured as co-defendant, whereas a subrogated insurer must sue in the assured's name.[27] This means, by way of example, that the judgment is given in the insurer's favour and it has a right to receive the proceeds of the judgment rather than the right to recover them from the assured. Again, if the assured company goes into liquidation and ceases to exist, the insurer's right of action is not lost.

(2) Subrogation rights are, subject to contract, exercisable only where the insurer has made full payment under the policy, and even if the insurer has satisfied its obligations under the policy it has no right to demand control of the action until the assured has received a full indemnity. Thus, if the assured bears an excess or is otherwise underinsured, the insurer cannot prevent the assured entering into a binding compromise agreement with the third party, although there will be recourse to the assured if the agreement is not made bona fide in the interests of both the assured and the insurer.

(3) The insurer is limited under a subrogation recovery to the amount of its own payment to the assured, plus interest.[28] By contrast, where the insurer has taken an assignment of the assured's rights, the benefit of any surplus accrues to the insurer. Thus, if as the result of a favourable movement in currency rates or some other windfall the third party is liable to the assured for an amount greater than the assured's nominal loss, the insurer will receive the benefit of the surplus.[29]

The use of assignment does, however, have some disadvantages. First, the fact that the insurer must sue in its own name may result in unwelcome publicity. This would appear to be the overriding consideration militating against the widespread use of assignment as an alternative to subrogation. Secondly, subrogation operates automatically on payment by the insurer, whereas the insurer may have to take positive steps to obtain an assignment; in practice this problem does not necessarily arise, as policies which provide for assignment may stipulate that assignment is to occur automatically on payment. Thirdly, there is some doubt as to whether the insurer can take an assignment of the assured's rights once the assured has commenced arbitration proceedings against the third party.[30]

The provision of an indemnity

11–005   *Limitation to indemnity policies.* It was decided in the nineteenth century that subrogation is confined to indemnity policies and thus has no place in relation to life[31] and accident[32] insurance. The apparent reason for this is that the impossibility of measuring the value of life means that the assured can never recover a full indemnity for his loss, and it is therefore wrong to deprive him of

---

[27] *Central Insurance Co v Seacalf Shipping Corp* [1983] 2 Lloyd's Rep. 25.

[28] *Yorkshire Insurance Co v Nisbet Shipping Ltd* [1962] 2 Q.B. 330.

[29] See generally *Lucas Ltd v Export Credit Guarantee Department* [1974] 2 All E.R. 889.

[30] Doubts were expressed by Phillips J. in *London Steamship Owners Mutual Insurance Association Ltd v Bombay Trading Co Ltd (The Felicie)* [1990] 2 Lloyd's Rep. 21, but were not shared by Hobhouse J. in *Montedipe SpA v JTP-RO Jugotanker (The Jordan Nicolov)* [1990] 2 Lloyd's Rep. 11 or by the Court of Appeal in *Schiffahrtsgesellschaft Detlev Von Appen GmbH v Voest Alpine Trading GmbH* [1997] 2 Lloyd's Rep. 279.

[31] *Solicitors' and General Life Assurance Society v Lamb* (1864) 1 De G.J. & Sm. 251.

[32] *Theobald v Railway Passengers Assurance Co* (1854) 10 Ex. 45.

any rights he may have against third parties to supplement his insurance recoveries. This reasoning is a little curious, on two grounds. First, there is a strong argument for the proposition that life and accident policies seek to do no more than indemnify the assured or his dependants for loss of earnings and other quantifiable losses. However, it is probably now too late to suggest that life and accident policies are simply sophisticated indemnities.[33] Secondly, the secondary function of subrogation—the conferring of positive rights on the insurer in order to prevent the unjust enrichment of the wrongdoer—takes precedence over the indemnity function of subrogation where the assured puts it beyond his power to take proceedings against the third party. Consequently, if the assured under a life or accident policy enters into a binding discharge with the third party, the fact that the policy in question is not an indemnity does not alter the result that the assured has unjustly enriched the third party by permitting that party to take the benefit of the insurance. This is not, in public policy terms, an attractive argument, for it would lead to the assured being deprived of the benefits of the policy in an action by the insurer for the loss of its subrogation rights.

A shortfall policy, whereby the insurers are to pay the shortfall in sums due to the assured on a given day, is an indemnity policy and the insurers are accordingly entitled to exercise subrogation rights against the defaulting third party.[34]

The requirement of the assured's indemnification. The insurer's rights of **11–006** subrogation come into effect only where the assured has received an indemnity from the insurer.[35] Where the assured is covered for 100 per cent of his loss under the policy, the indemnification requirement simply means that the insurer must pay up fully under the policy before action may be taken by the insurer against the third party.[36] Indemnification need not be by way of actual payment by the insurers: in *Brown v Albany Construction Co,*[37] insurers indemnified the assured by purchasing his newly built house, which had been severely damaged by heave, and were held by the Court of Appeal to be entitled to sue the builder and engineer by way of subrogation for their negligence. An insurer who has not admitted liability, or who seeks to withhold part of the proceeds of the policy, has no subrogation claim.[38]

Where, however, the policy does not cover the entire amount of the assured's loss, the indemnification requirement becomes ambiguous: it may mean that the assured must recover the entire amount of his loss before the insurer can pursue the assured's rights; or it may mean that it is sufficient for subrogation rights to

[33] The decision in *Dalby v India and London Life Assurance Co* (1854) 15 C.B. 365 has long rendered this point unarguable.

[34] *John Meacock v Bryant & Co* (1942) 74 Ll. L.R. 53.

[35] It is partly for this reason that, where there is double insurance and insurer A, having indemnified the assured, calls upon insurer B for contribution, insurer B has no subrogation rights in the use of the name of the assured to sue the wrongdoer: *Speno Rail Maintenance Australia Pty Ltd v Metals & Minerals Insurance Pte Ltd* (2009) 253 A.L.R. 364.

[36] *Edwards v Commercial Union* [1922] 2 K.B. 249; *Page v Scottish Insurance Corp* (1928) L.J.K.B. 308; *Scottish Union and National Insurance Co v Davis* [1970] 1 Lloyd's Rep. 1.

[37] *Brown v Albany Construction Co* [1995] N.P.C. 100.

[38] In *Scottish Union Insurance v Davis* [1970] 1 Lloyd's Rep. 1, insurers claimed by way of subrogation £350 received by the assured from the third party for damage to a motor car, on the grounds that they had paid £409 for repairs. They had no satisfaction note from the assured, and the repairs were useless so that the assured had not been indemnified. The Court of Appeal held that the insurers were entitled to nothing as they had not paid anything as far as the assured was concerned: Russell L.J. stated at 4 that the insurers might as well have thrown the bank notes into the Thames.

be exercised if the insurer has satisfied its own liability under the policy, even if the result is that the assured has not received the entire amount of his loss. The true position where an assured has not recovered his entire loss under the policy because of a policy limit on recovery or the incurring of uninsured losses,[39] is that the insurer may under its rights of subrogation insist that the assured sues the third party once its own liability under the policy has been satisfied. However, until the assured has received a full indemnity for his loss, presumably by a combination of payments from the insurer and the third party, the assured retains the exclusive right to control the proceedings against the third party.[40]

The assured's right of control has two interlinked consequences. First, any recovery made by the assured from the third party is to be appropriated in the first instance to making up the assured's shortfall under the policy; the balance, if any, is held by the assured subject to a charge in the insurer's favour.[41] Secondly, the right to control proceedings carries with it the right to reach a bona fide compromise or settlement with the third party for an amount less than the full extent of the injury caused to the assured. Thus, if the assured's total loss is £1,000, of which £500 is insured and paid to him, a bona fide compromise by the assured with the third party in the sum of £750 is binding on the insurer, who is entitled only to £250 of the sum recovered by the assured.[42]

11–007 *Calculating the amount of the indemnity.* In order to determine whether the assured has recovered a full indemnity from the insurers for his insured loss, it may be necessary to analyse the amount paid by the insurers to see how much of that payment relates to the assured's loss and how much of it relates to payment for other liabilities incurred by the insurers. In *England v Guardian Insurance Ltd*[43] the insurers paid £102,000 to the assured in respect of a property damage claim, and asserted subrogation rights by way of lien for that amount over a subsequent recovery by the assured. The assured argued that part of the sum paid by the insurers represented other claims which the assured had against the insurers, including damages for late payment under the policy: it was held that the law did not recognise an action for damages for late payment, and accordingly that the insurers were entitled to a lien over the recoveries for the full amount of their payment to the assured as the sums paid by the insurers represented only liability under the policy.

---

[39] A policy deductible is seemingly to be disregarded for present purposes: see *Napier and Ettrick v Kershaw* [1993] 1 All E.R. 385.

[40] This was decided in *Commercial Union Assurance Co v Lister* (1874) L.R. 9 Ch. App. 483. Cf. *Farrell Estates Ltd v Canadian Indemnity Co* 69 D.L.R. (4th) 735 (1990).

[41] This is an oversimplification of the position, as the policy may be subject to an excess or to average, in which cases the assured is treated as his own insurer in respect of the uninsured loss; in those circumstances the subrogation recovery is to be apportioned between the insurer and assured according to their respective liabilities. See below for discussion of the allocation of subrogation recoveries. In *Falcon Insurance Co (HK) Ltd v Cheshire Cat Restaurant & Pub Co Ltd* [2007] H.K.E.C. 2084 the assured was unable to prove any loss over and above the policy moneys, so that the insurers were entitled to retain the entirety of the subrogation recovery.

[42] The proposition in the text is supported by dicta in *Commercial Union Assurance Co v Lister* (1874) L.R. 9 Ch. App. 483 at 484, per Sir George Jessel M.R. See also *Horwood v Land of Leather Ltd* [2010] Lloyd's Rep. I.R. 453. Bona fide settlements reached by an insured fully paid by his insurer, but not fully indemnified for his loss, have been upheld by the Canadian courts. See *Globe & Rutgers Fire Insurance Co v Truedell* [1927] 2 D.L.R. 659 and *Willumsen v Royal Insurance Co Ltd* 63 D.L.R. (3d) 112 (1975).

[43] *England v Guardian Insurance Ltd* [2000] Lloyd's Rep. I.R. 404. See also *Stace & Francis v Ashby* [2001] EWCA Civ 1655; *Woolwich Building Society v Daisystar Ltd* Unreported, March 16, 2000.

Rights of insurers prior to provision of indemnity

Pre-indemnity and pre-payment rights. Where the insurer has fully satisfied its **11–008** liability to the assured, but the assured has by reason of underinsurance not recovered his full loss, the insurer may commence subrogation proceedings in the assured's name by insisting that the assured lends his name to the insurer, although the assured retains the right to control those proceedings. Any action by the assured in the conduct of the proceedings which is not bona fide and which prejudices the insurer's rights will confer upon the insurer a cause of action against the assured.

It remains to consider the insurer's rights pending full payment by it to the assured for, as has been seen, the insurer's right to use the assured's name rests upon it meeting its contractual obligations in full and, arguably, by payment obtains a charge on the assured's cause of action. It might be argued that, because the insurer cannot exercise subrogation rights pending payment, those rights do not arise until payment has been made. If this is correct, it follows that any action taken, or indeed any failure to take action, by the assured prior to full payment, the effect of which is to prejudice the insurer's future subrogation rights, cannot be the subject of any action against him by the insurer. The insurer's remedy if the assured is about to perform a prejudicial act, or has failed to perform an act necessary to preserve the action, is to pay to the assured the proceeds of the policy. The contrary argument is that subrogation rights arise as soon as the policy is entered into, but that such rights are contingent and crystallise only on payment. On this view of the matter, the insurer does possess contingent rights against the assured prior to its making full payment under the policy.

A number of cases have proceeded on the assumption that the insurer does, prior to full payment, have the limited right to ensure that its future subrogation rights are not prejudiced by the assured's conduct.[44] What remains unclear is the extent of such rights, but it would seem that they are extremely limited. In *Chan King Wan v Honest Scaffold General Contractor Ltd*[45] insurers asserted that the administratrix of a deceased employee, who was also a former director of the company for which the employee had worked, was required—under the subrogation doctrine—to assist the insurers in defending the claim against the company. Cheung J. held that the doctrine of subrogation had no application in advance of payment by the insurers. The subrogation argument in this case appears to have been misconceived on two grounds: this was not a case in which the insurers were seeking to recover sums from a third party responsible for the assured's loss, and the issue was the extent of any duty to co-operate with a liability insurer imposed on a director of the assured; and in any event co-operation by the administratrix would have created an inevitable conflict of interest. However, the case recognises that subrogation rights do not exist prior to payment.

Preservation of the assured's right of action. There is ample authority for the **11–009** proposition that an assured who compromises his claim against a third party, other than in the form of a bona fide settlement, is liable to an insurer who has

---

[44] See *Boag v Standard Marine Insurance Co Ltd* [1937] 2 K.B. 113, which holds that a primary layer insurer has priority over a subsequent increased value insurer in respect of the proceeds of a claim against a third party, although this reasoning is difficult to reconcile with the subsequent ruling of the House of Lords in *Napier and Ettrick (Lord) v Kershaw* [1993] 1 All E.R. 385 to the effect that subrogation recoveries are allocated on a "recover down" basis: see below.
[45] *Chan King Wan v Honest Scaffold General Contractor Ltd* [1998] 2 H.K.C. 358.

yet to meet the assured's claim but subsequently does so.[46] This type of situation, however, involves positive action by the assured which prejudices his rights against the third party: what has yet to be decided is whether inactivity by the assured has the same effect. One possibility is the problem of limitation. In many cases the insurer will have indemnified, or at least paid, the assured within the limitation period applicable to the assured's action against the third party, and here it is the insurer's responsibility to ensure that the assured's action is brought at the proper time. However, where the assured's action springs from a contract with the third party, or from a relationship governed by international convention, it may be that a short limitation period is provided for. Indeed, there may be a limitation period of as little as one year under contracts of international carriage. The question here is whether an insurer who has yet to pay the assured can obtain a mandatory injunction requiring the assured to commence proceedings within the applicable limitation period in order to preserve the action, or at least whether the insurer can bring an action for damages against the assured for his failure to act timeously. A similar question might arise where the assured has issued his claim form in time but has not taken any steps to serve it within the period permitted by the Civil Procedure Rules. Potentially a more serious problem arises where action by the assured is necessary not to preserve the proceedings as a matter of law or procedure but as a matter of sheer practicality. Thus, if the third-party wrongdoer is known to be taking steps to transfer his assets outside the jurisdiction, proceedings for a freezing order may be essential to ensure that any subsequent judgment against the third party is satisfied. Again, if it is suspected that the third party is about to dispose of evidence vital to the assured's claim, a search and seizure order may be needed to safeguard its existence. It is unclear whether mere inactivity by the assured will entitle the insurer to a mandatory injunction forcing the assured to take the relevant steps, or to damages at a later date. The argument against the insurer having any rights in these circumstances is that it can preserve its position by making payment. The argument in the insurer's favour is that the insurer is entitled to take all necessary steps to preserve its contingent subrogation rights; consequently, it is arguable that there is inherent in the doctrine of subrogation, possibly in the form of an implied contract term, an obligation on the assured prior to payment to take all reasonable steps to preserve the efficacy of his remedy against the third party.[47]

11–010 *The assured's right to sue the third party.* Prior to full indemnification by the insurer, the assured has the right to control any action against the wrongdoing third party; the problems that this principle raises where the assured brings proceedings against the third party to recover only his uninsured loss are discussed below in the context of partial indemnity. A different and more unusual situation in which the insurer wishes to prevent the assured from bringing an action against the third party on the basis that if he does so the third party is less likely to make payment. This arose in *AB Exportkredit v New Hampshire Insurance*,[48] where the Court of Appeal ruled that, in the absence of any express contractual provision,[49] insurers had no right to order the assured not to proceed. Neill L.J., whose judgment was adopted by Woolf L.J., held that the position would have been otherwise had the assured's action been commenced recklessly

---

[46] *Commercial Union Assurance Co v Lister* (1874) L.R. 9 Ch. App. 483.

[47] Such obligations are found in cl.9 of the International Hull Clauses. See also *Moussa H Issa NV v Grand Union Insurance Co Ltd* [1984] H.K.L.R. 137.

[48] *AB Exportkredit v New Hampshire Insurance* Unreported, 1988.

[49] For this purpose a reasonable care clause was held not to suffice.

or in bad faith. The basis for this qualification is unclear, and a number of possibilities suggest themselves:

(1) The law recognises and will protect unaccrued subrogation rights irrespective of the terms of the policy if the assured recklessly or in bad faith diminishes those rights.

(2) The reasonable care clause was in fact applicable to the facts of the case, and imposed an obligation on the assured not to act recklessly in pursuing the third parties.

(3) The rights of the insurer flowed from a general duty of utmost good faith imposed on the assured and operating throughout the currency of the policy.

Possibilities (1) and (3) are doubtful, if only for the reason that there is no mention of them in the judgments. Possibility (2) is equally doubtful, as it is inconsistent with the very ground of the decision, namely that the clause did not apply to the commencement of proceedings.[50] It can only be concluded that, in the absence of an express clause permitting the insurer to debar proceedings by the assured, the scope of the assured's right to commence an action against the third party prior to being indemnified is an open question, and it is also difficult to apply the suggestion, by the House of Lords in *Napier and Ettrick (Lord) v Kershaw*[51] that an equitable lien attaches to the assured's action, to the pre-indemnification position where the insurer has no accrued rights.

The rights of the insurer following the provision of an indemnity

The use of the assured's name. It has long been settled that a subrogation action **11–011** must be brought in the name of the assured and that the insurer is not permitted to bring the action in its own name.[52] The fact that the assured is the nominal claimant is not, however, simply a procedural matter; the substantive effect of the rule is that any legal obstacle applicable to the assured's right of action binds the insurer suing in the assured's name. There are a number of situations in which this becomes relevant.

(1) The insurer's rights against the third party are the same as those of the assured. Thus if the assured has caused his own loss but nevertheless has a claim on the policy the insurer cannot seek any set-off against the assured as wrongdoer. The principle that an assured cannot sue himself was established by *Simpson v Thomson*.[53] Equally, if the contract between the assured and the third party confers immunity upon the third party or entitles the third party to an indemnity from the assured, the insurers are themselves subject to the third party's rights, e.g. any counterclaim.[54]

---

[50] Paradoxically, possibility (2) makes the most sense, as it is plain from the authorities on reasonable care clauses that their only effect is to prevent conduct which is reckless or in bad faith.

[51] *Napier and Ettrick (Lord) v Kershaw* [1993] 1 All E.R. 385.

[52] *London Assurance Co v Sainsbury* (1783) 3 Doug. 245; *Esso Petroleum Co Ltd v Hall Russell & Co Ltd* [1988] 3 W.L.R. 730; *Mercantile and General Reinsurance Co Plc v London Assurance* Unreported, 1989. See also *Insurance Company of Pennsylvania Ltd v IBM UK Ltd* (1989) *Chartered Surveyor Weekly*, October 12, in which the English court noted this rule, but was required to apply New York law which permits a direct action by the insurer in his own name.

[53] *Simpson v Thomson* (1877) 3 App.Cas. 279.

[54] *Moon Fung Hong Co Ltd v Hong Kong International Terminals Ltd* [2007] H.K.E.C. 929.

(2) If the assured has, after the loss, entered into a binding agreement with the wrongdoer third party which relieves that third party from some or all liability, and the agreement is not a bona fide compromise or was made at a time when the assured had lost the right to control the action, the agreement is nevertheless binding on the insurer. Any rights that the insurer may have in these circumstances are against the assured alone, for prejudicing the insurer's rights of subrogation.

(3) If the agreement between the assured and the third party contains a dispute resolution provision, such as an arbitration clause[55] or an exclusive jurisdiction clause, the insurers are bound by that clause and proceedings brought in contravention of it may be stayed. Alternatively, the insurers may be restrained by anti-suit injunction if they seek to bring proceedings in some other jurisdiction in breach of the provision.[56]

(4) The assured's action might be time-barred. Any limitation provision applicable to the assured's action is necessarily operative against an insurer exercising subrogation rights.[57]

(5) If the assured is a company which has been wound up and has ceased to exist, it will be too late for the insurer to seek to use the company's name in subrogation proceedings.[58]

(6) The fact that the insurer is the de facto claimant is to be disregarded.[59] The defendant cannot seek disclosure from the insurer as the insurer is technically not a party to the action.[60] If the assured has funded his claim by entering into conditional fee arrangements with his lawyers, then as long as the sums have been reasonably incurred from the point of view of the assured then they are recoverable from the third party by way of costs even though insurers have insisted that the assured proceeds on that basis.[61] Again, it is irrelevant that the insurers have not incurred the full loss suffered by the assured: if they have indemnified the assured they are entitled to recover the amount of their payment from the wrongdoer even though they have received commission from a supplier of replacement goods to the assured.[62]

(7) The law applicable to the assured's cause of action against the third party similarly governs the subrogation action brought by the assured, irrespective of the law applicable to the contract of insurance.[63] The existence or

---

[55] *Schiffartsgesellschaft Detlef von Appen GmbH v Wiener Allianz. Versicherungs AG* [1997] 2 Lloyd's Rep. 279.

[56] *West Tankers Inc v RAS Riunione Adriatica di Sicurta SpA, The Front Comor* [2005] 2 Lloyd's Rep. 257; *Starlight Shipping Co v Tai Ping Insurance Co* [2008] 1 Lloyd's Rep. 230; *Whitesea Shipping and Trading Corporation v El Paso Rio Clara Ltda (The Marielle Bolten)* [2009] EWHC 2552 (Comm). But note the effect of the decision of the European Court of Justice in Case C-185/07 *Allianz SpA v West Tankers Inc* [2009] 1 All E.R. (Comm) 145, which decides that an anti-suit injunction cannot be granted where the substantive issue is before, or may reach, another EU or EFTA court. On this basis *West Tankers* and *Starlight* would now be decided differently.

[57] *London Assurance Co v Johnson* (1737) Hardw. 269; *RB Policies v Butler* (1949) 65 T.L.R. 436.

[58] *Smith (Plant Hire) Ltd v Mainwaring (t/a Inshore)* [1986] 2 Lloyd's Rep. 244; *Re Ballast Plc, St Paul Travellers Insurance Co Ltd v Dargan* [2007] Lloyd's Rep. I.R. 742.

[59] *Russell v Wilson, The Independent*, June 2, 1989.

[60] *James Nelson v Nelson Line* [1906] 2 K.B. 217.

[61] *Sousa v London Borough of Waltham Forest* [2010] E.W. Misc. 1 (EWCC).

[62] *Bee v Jenson (No.2)* [2008] Lloyd's Rep. I.R. 221.

[63] Rome I Regulation art.15 (contract claims); Rome II Regulation art.19 (tort claims).

otherwise of the right of subrogation itself is, however, a matter for the law governing the contract of insurance.[64]

(8) If the assured's cause of action is lost in any way then the insurers have no right to proceed. It was seen above that the winding up of the assured will preclude an action by the insurers, as will a limitation defence. In *Re Ballast Plc, St Paul Travellers Insurance Co Ltd v Dargan*[65] it was further held that a disclaimer by liquidators of the contract under which the insurers are seeking to exercise subrogation rights will defeat the insurers. In *Ballast* the assured contractor incurred liability under a construction contract and was fully indemnified by its insurers. The assured became insolvent and went into liquidation. Using the assured's name, the insurers sought by exercising subrogation rights to recover some or all of its loss from a sub-contractor employed by the assured to carry out the works. The sub-contractor asserted a counterclaim against the assured. The liquidators took the view that it was on balance beneficial for the sub-contract to be disclaimed as onerous property, and they exercised their statutory powers of disclaimer. Pending the removal of the assured from the register of companies, which would have precluded any subrogation action using the assured's name, the insurers sought an order to the effect that the assured's proprietary interests vested in them. Lawrence Collins J., rejecting dicta of the House of Lords in *Napier and Ettrick (Lord) v Kershaw*,[66] held that a subrogation claim was not a proprietary right—proprietary rights were limited to the proceeds, and did not extend to the cause of action itself—and accordingly that the court had no jurisdiction to make an order vesting the right of action in the insurers.

While it is the case that the assured remains the nominal claimant, it has been held that for limitation purposes it is necessary to look to the reality of the situation and to regard the insurer as the real claimant. Thus, in determining the trigger point for the running of time under the Limitation Act 1980 s.14A in respect of a claim against the third party for latent property damage, namely the date on which "the plaintiff or any person in whom the cause of action was vested before him" (s.14A(5)), became aware of the facts giving rise to the cause of action, the person whose knowledge is relevant is the insurer and not the assured.[67]

Indemnity must be paid in respect of assured's loss. As it is possible to exercise **11–012** subrogation rights only in the name of the assured, it follows that a subrogation claim cannot be made in the name of an assured who has not suffered any loss even though a payment has been made by insurers to a third party.[68]

Control of proceedings following full indemnification of the assured. If the **11–013** assured has received a full indemnity from the insurer, there is nothing to prevent the assured from pursuing his action against the third-party wrongdoer for

[64] Rome I Regulation art.15 (contract claims), and see *West Tankers Inc v RAS Riunione Adriatica di Sicurta SpA (The Front Comor)* [2005] 2 Lloyd's Rep. 257; Rome II Regulation art.19 (tort claims).

[65] *Re Ballast Plc, St Paul Travellers Insurance Co Ltd v Dargan* [2007] Lloyd's Rep. I.R. 742.

[66] *Napier and Ettrick (Lord) v Kershaw* [1978] A.C. 16.

[67] *Graham v Entec Europe Ltd* [2004] Lloyd's Rep. I.R. 660.

[68] *CSE Aviation Ltd v Cardale Doors Ltd* Unreported, 2002; *HSBC Rail (UK) Ltd v Network Rail Infrastructure Ltd* [2006] 1 Lloyd's Rep. 358.

damages; the common law does not allow a defendant to plead that the claimant has been indemnified by insurance,[69] for that would be to confer the benefit of the insurance on the third party. An assured who does not seek to invoke his right to sue the third party will be required by the doctrine of subrogation to lend his name to the insurer's action. If the assured refuses to lend his name to the proceedings, he may be compelled to do so, ultimately by being joined as co-defendant; this device ensures that the assured is a party to the action so that judgment can be given in his favour, subject of course to the imposition of a charge on the proceeds of the action for the benefit of the insurer. Conversely, the assured may, despite having been fully indemnified, commence proceedings in his own name against the third party. As the assured is necessarily a party to the proceedings, the insurer's main concern here is to control those proceedings; if the assured refuses to hand over control to the insurer, he will be ordered by the court to do so.[70] Once the action has vested in insurers, the conduct of the action is a matter for them by virtue of their equitable rights.

The insurer is not bound to take any notice of the assured's wishes as to whether or not subrogation proceedings are to be brought. There are nevertheless a number of situations in which the insurer will not desire to exercise its subrogation rights, as when there are agreements between insurers to the effect that subrogation rights are not to be enforced.[71] This may be illustrated by the case of a motor knock-for-knock agreement in force between insurer A (the negligent driver's insurer) and insurer B (the victim's insurer), under which each insurer bears the loss to its assured. If the victim, having been indemnified by insurer B, sues the negligent driver, insurer A will be called upon to make payment on behalf of its own assured to meet his liability. The victim must, however, hold the sum recovered on trust for insurer B, with the result that the loss has fallen not on insurer B but on insurer A. The knock-for-knock agreement itself will undoubtedly provide that in such circumstances insurer B is to restore insurer A's payment to it, with the overall effect that the knock-for-knock agreement is implemented but at great expense. It is pertinent to enquire, therefore, whether an insurer with subrogation rights is empowered to prevent the assured from bringing an action in his own name against the third party. Knock-for-knock agreements were formally abandoned in the United Kingdom in 1995. Again, insurers who carry on both employers' liability and motor business have agreed that any damage to property caused is to be allocated between them on a three to one ratio, disregarding strict subrogation rights. There is in addition an agreement between insurers and the Government that where an employee causes injury for which his employer is vicariously liable, the employer's liability insurers will not exercise subrogation rights to recoup their payment.[72]

---

[69] *Bradburn v Great Western Ry Co* (1874) I.R 10 Ex. 1; *Hobbs v Marlowe* [1978] A.C. 16; *The Good Luck* [1988] 1 Lloyd's Rep. 514; *Bovis Construction Ltd v Eagle Star Insurance Co Ltd* [2002] Lloyd's Rep. I.R. 321; *Falcon Insurance Co (HK) Ltd v Cheshire Cat Restaurant & Pub Co Ltd* [2007] H.K.E.C. 2084.

[70] *Commercial Union Assurance Co v Lister* (1874) L.R. 9 Ch. App. 483.

[71] See Lewis, (1985) 48 M.L.R. 275.

[72] The right to exercise subrogation rights was established by *Lister v Romford Ice and Cold Storage Co Ltd* [1957] A.C. 555, where the House of Lords held that an employer is not under an implied duty at common law to indemnify an employee for the consequences of his negligence. The agreement does not extend to the case in which liability has been incurred by a person employed by a different employer but for whose acts the insured employer is nevertheless responsible, but in *Morris v Ford Motor Co* [1973] Q.B. 792 the Court of Appeal refused to extend the right of subrogation to this situation.

In these situations, an attempt by the assured to exercise his own right to sue despite receiving a full indemnity will cause either embarrassment or expense to the insurer. The position is not entirely free from doubt. In *Morley v Moore*[73] the assured's insurer instructed him not to institute an action against the tortfeasor in respect of a loss for which a full indemnity had been received from the insurer. The assured proceeded undeterred, and the Court of Appeal held that he had the right to do so. Some doubt was cast upon this conclusion by the House of Lords in *Hobbs v Marlowe*.[74] The point did not actually arise in this case, as the insurer had not instructed the assured to terminate the proceedings, but both Viscount Dilhome and Lord Diplock expressly reserved their position on the issue of whether the insurer would have been able to do this. Since the ruling of the House of Lords in *Napier and Ettrick (Lord) v Kershaw*[75] it has become arguable that the insurer has a lien over the assured's action a view favoured by Lords Templeman, Goff and Browne-Wilkinson and accordingly can use that equitable right to restrain proceedings brought by the assured without reference to the insurer. However, the ruling in *Re Ballast Plc, St Paul Travellers Insurance Co Ltd v Dargan*[76] denying the existence of any form of equitable lien over the cause of action (as opposed to the proceeds of any claim) indicates that *Morley v Moore* remains good law, a point specifically made by Lawrence Collins J. in *Re Ballast Plc*.

Control of proceedings following partial indemnification of the assured. An **11–014** assured who has received a partial but not a full indemnity is free to commence proceedings against the wrongdoer for the full amount of his loss. The assured has, as has been seen, the right to conduct the proceedings even if the insurer has met its full liability under the policy. The assured thus has the right as against the insurer to reach a bona fide compromise with the third party. Any sum recovered will in general be applied to make up the assured's indemnity, the remainder being held by the assured subject to a charge in the insurer's favour.[77] The assured clearly cannot be stopped by the insurer from proceeding against the wrongdoer for his uninsured loss; the doubts concerning the ability of the insurer to prevent the assured from suing for his insured loss were discussed above. Equally, the assured cannot be required by the insurers to commence proceedings until he has been fully indemnified.[78]

Proceedings by the assured for the uninsured sum. Practical problems arise **11–015** where an assured who is underinsured commences proceedings against the third party in his own name but only for the amount of his uninsured loss. If the insurer fails to act in time and the assured obtains judgment for the uninsured sum, the principle that a cause of action may not be litigated twice may operate to bar a subrogation action in the assured's name. In general, a second action by the insurers will be struck out for *res judicata* and abuse of process,[79] although the court has a discretion to set aside the original judgment in exceptional cases if justice so requires, e.g. where an experienced defendant has taken advantage of

---

[73] *Morley v Moore* [1936] 2 K.B. 359.
[74] *Hobbs v Marlowe* [1978] A.C. 16.
[75] *Napier and Ettrick (Lord) v Kershaw* [1993] 1 All E.R. 385.
[76] *Re Ballast Plc, St Paul Travellers Insurance Co Ltd v Dargan* [2007] Lloyd's Rep. I.R. 742.
[77] *Napier and Ettrick (Lord) v Kershaw* [1993] 1 All E.R. 385.
[78] *Andrews v Patriotic Insurance* (1886) 18 L.R. Ir. 355.
[79] *Buckland v Palmer* [1984] 3 All E.R. 554; *Yung Hong Wai v Ng Kam Shing* Unreported, 1994.

an ill-informed claimant.[80] A binding settlement agreement between the assured and the third party in respect of the uninsured loss does not, however, preclude a subrogation action by the insurers for the insured loss.[81]

11–016 *Subrogation following ex gratia payment by the insurer.* There has been some debate whether an insurer who, while not legally obliged to pay the assured under the policy, nevertheless does so, is entitled to exercise subrogation rights. Ex gratia payments are common and arise in a number of contexts: the policy may be voidable for breach of the assured's duty of utmost good faith; the assured may have been in breach of a warranty or condition; the insurer might accept inadequate proofs of loss; or the peril causing the loss might fall outside the scope of cover. If subrogation is regarded as a matter of equity, principle would indicate that subrogation should be permitted in all these cases, for subrogation is simply the right of a consensual indemnifier to take over the rights of the party indemnified. If subrogation is regarded as an implied term in a contract of insurance, matters become more complex. If the insurer waives its right to set the policy aside or to deny a claim, the policy continues in force and the claim may be said to be made in accordance with the policy, so that the implied right of subrogation continues in force. However, if the insurer has made a payment for an uninsured peril, it is difficult to see how it can take advantage of an implied term for subrogation when its payment is not made in accordance with the policy.

There does not appear to have been any discussion of the juridical basis of subrogation in the limited authorities on the availability of subrogation for ex gratia payments. The Privy Council in *King v Victoria Insurance Co*[82] permitted an insurer who had paid the assured despite having a coverage defence to exercise subrogation rights. However, this does not shed any light on the question whether subrogation is available for those forms of ex gratia payments which are inconsistent with the terms of the policy. One solution to the problem is for the assured and the insurers to enter into an agreement under which the insurers make their payment conditional on the assured suing the wrongdoer for the full amount of the loss, and then holding the proceeds on trust for the insurers,[83] the third party being unable to assert that it is the duty of the assured to mitigate its loss by looking to the insurers first.[84] In the absence of any express agreement between assured and insurers that the insurers will pay the loss provided that the assured sues the wrongdoer and holds the proceeds on trust, a trust will generally be implied[85] unless there is some public policy ground for the refusal of a trust, e.g. because the insurance contract is void for want of insurable interest[86] or otherwise unenforceable[87]; in those cases, sums paid by the insurers have to be

---

[80] *Hayler v Chapman, The Times,* November 11, 1988, where no inequitable behaviour was found. Contrast *Burns v Cotton* Unreported, 1988, where the defendant failed to defend a claim by the assured in the knowledge that a larger claim by insurers was pending.

[81] *Taylor v O'Wray & Co Ltd* [1971] 1 Lloyd's Rep. 497.

[82] *King v Victoria Insurance Co* [1896] A.C. 250. See also *Eagle Star and British Dominions Insurance Co v Cayzer Irvine & Co* (1928) 30 Ll. L.R. 19.

[83] *Naumann v Ford* [1985] 2 E.G.L.R. 70. *Quaere* whether an arrangement of this type could nevertheless be attacked on the ground of maintenance: while it is established that an insurer who is legally liable to the assured may take an assignment of the assured's right of action without contravening that principle: see *Compania Colombiana de Seguros v Pacific Steam Navigation Co* [1965] 1 Q.B. 101.

[84] *British Westinghouse Co v Underground Electric Ry of London* [1912] A.C. 673.

[85] *Hunt v Severs* [1994] 2 A.C. 350.

[86] Cf. *John Edwards & Co v Motor Union Insurance Co Ltd* [1922] 2 K.B. 249.

[87] *Dimond v Lovell* [2000] 2 W.L.R. 1121, overruling *McAll v Brooks* [1984] R.T.R. 99.

deducted from the amount recoverable by the assured from the third party so that the insurers' subrogation rights are diminished accordingly.

Certain commercial policies attempt to deal with the volunteer principle where there is a dispute as to which of two policies covers the loss. In the aviation market, for example, hull insurers and war-risks insurers commonly agree that in the event of a dispute as to whether a loss is proximately caused by an ordinary peril or a war-risks peril, each of them will pay 50 per cent of the loss to the assured and the proximate cause question will be referred to arbitration. Without such a provision, payment by either of the insurers gives rise to the risk that a subrogation action brought against the other will fail on the basis that although the other insurer was liable for the loss the payment by the paying insurer was a voluntary one.[88]

Allocation of subrogation recoveries

Principles governing allocation. Where the assured has recovered from the third **11–017** party a sum representing all or part of the damage caused to him by that party, the question arises of how the subrogation recovery is to be distributed between the assured and the insurer. Specific illustrations will be presented in the following paragraphs, but the discussion commences with an explanation of the three guiding principles governing allocation of recoveries as between insurer and assured.

The first principle is that the assured cannot be deprived of an indemnity as the result of the enforcement of subrogation rights by the insurer. It has been noted earlier that if the insurer has met its liability under the policy, but the assured has not been fully compensated, the assured retains the right to control the action against the third party[89] and may deduct the shortfall from the amount of the recovery,[90] the surplus being held by the assured as debtor for the insurer.[91] However, it is important to appreciate that the concept of indemnity refers not to the totality of the assured's loss but rather to that part of the assured's loss which is acknowledged by the policy. Thus, if the assured has agreed to bear a part of his own loss by way of deductible or excess, that part is to be disregarded in ascertaining whether the assured has received an indemnity.[92] The latter rule is not immune from criticism, given that the stated purpose of subrogation is to prevent the assured from being paid twice, whereas the effect of disregarding the deductible is that the assured is deprived of the right to be paid in full at all before the insurer seeks reimbursement.

Secondly, the principle that the assured must receive a full indemnity before the insurer has any right over the proceeds is modified where the policy is subject to average, as under a policy of that nature the insurer and assured are deemed to be co-insurers where the policy does not cover the full amount of the assured's loss. Thus any subrogation recovery is to be apportioned between the parties according to their respective liabilities.[93] A problem might also arise where the

[88] But see *Drake Insuance Co v Provident Insurance Co* [2004] Lloyd's Rep. I.R. 277, where an argument based on the volunteer principle in the context of contribution was rejected by the Court of Appeal.

[89] *Commercial Union Assurance Co v Lister* (1874) L.R. 9 Ch. App. 483.

[90] *Ledingham v Ontario Hospital Services Commission* 46 D.L.R. (3d) 699 (1974). Cf. *Hobbs v Marlowe* [1978] A.C. 16.

[91] *Napier and Ettrick (Lord) v Kershaw* [1993] 1 All E.R. 385.

[92] *Napier and Ettrick (Lord) v Kershaw* [1993] 1 All E.R. 385; *England v Guardian Insurance Ltd* [2000] Lloyd's Rep. I.R. 404.

[93] *The Commonwealth* [1907] P. 216.

policy is a valued one, for the valuation agreed between insurer and assured is conclusive,[94] and it is arguable that indemnity under a valued policy is payment of the agreed value.

The third principle is that the insurer can recover at most the amount that it has paid to the assured. As was said by Lord Atkin in *Glen Line v Attorney-General*,[95] "Subrogation will only give the insurer rights up to 20 shillings in the pound". Consequently, where the sum recovered from the third party exceeds the amount paid by the insurer to the assured, the surplus will accrue to the assured, even if that surplus combined with the insurer's payment gives the assured more than an indemnity. A surplus of this nature is unusual, as it presupposes a greater recovery from the third party than the loss suffered by the assured, but arose in *Yorkshire Insurance Co v Nisbet Shipping Co*[96] as a result of currency fluctuations. The assured, whose loss was £72,000 and who had been fully indemnified for that loss by the insurer, recovered from the Canadian government a sum which, when converted into sterling, realised some £126,000. Diplock J. held that, properly construed, s.79 of the Marine Insurance Act 1906 prevented any recovery by the insurer beyond its own payment to the assured, so that the surplus of £54,000 could be retained by the assured for its own benefit.[97] One exception to this principle concerns interest. If the subrogation recovery is accompanied by an award of interest, it would seem to be the case that the interest is to be apportioned between the assured and insurer in relation to their respective interests in the sum recovered, taking into account the date of any payment by the insurer to the assured. The fact that interest yields to the insurer a greater amount than that paid out by him is immaterial.

11–018 *Specific examples.* There follows a list of illustrations of the interrelationship between the above principles. In all of them it has been assumed that the insurer has met its full liability under the policy, thereby bringing its subrogation rights—but not necessarily the right to control the action—into play.

(1) The assured is insured for his full loss. Any sum recoverable in the assured's name is to be accounted for by the assured to the insurer, although any amount in excess of the actual loss which is recovered may be retained by the assured.[98]

(2) The assured is insured for his full loss, subject to an excess. Any sum recovered from the third party by the assured goes to the insurer up to the extent of the insurer's payment to the assured, the assured's excess being discharged only after the insurer has been reimbursed.[99]

(3) The assured is not fully insured under an unvalued policy. The assured has the right to control the action against the third party, and is entitled to retain such amount of the subrogation recovery necessary to make good the shortfall under the policy before accounting for the balance to the insurer.[100]

(4) The assured under a valued policy not subject to average is insured to the full agreed value of the subject matter (say, £80,000), although its agreed

---

[94] Marine Insurance Act 1906 s.27(3).

[95] *Glen Line v Attorney-General* (1930) 6 Com. Cas. 1 at 14.

[96] *Yorkshire Insurance Co v Nisbet Shipping Co* [1962] 2 Q.B. 330.

[97] Contrary dicta in a number of earlier decisions, notably *North of England Iron Steamship Insurance Association v Armstrong* (1870) L.R. 5 Q.B. 244, were disapproved by Diplock J.

[98] *Yorkshire Insurance Co v Nisbet Shipping Co* [1962] 2 Q.B. 330.

[99] *Napier and Ettrick (Lord) v Kershaw* [1993] 1 All E.R. 385.

[100] *Hobbs v Marlowe* [1978] A.C. 16 proceeds on this assumption.

value is less than its actual value (say, £100,000). If the full £100,000 is recovered from the third party, the assured is entitled to retain £20,000 for his own benefit on the principle that the insurer cannot recover more than it has paid out, here £80,000. Suppose, however, that the sum recovered from the third party is only £90,000. On one view, the assured is entitled to retain £20,000 of that sum to make up his own loss. However, the opposite view might be that the valuation agreed between the parties is conclusive, so that the assured cannot suffer a loss of more than £80,000, and the insurer is entitled to claim up to the amount of its own payment, i.e. £80,000, leaving the balance with the assured[101]; on this view, if the recovery from the third party was only £70,000, the assured would recover nothing. Which of these conflicting views is correct awaits determination.

(5) The assured is insured for £80,000 under a valued policy not subject to average, on a subject matter of an agreed and actual value of £100,000. If the sum of £100,000 is recovered from the third party, no problems arise; the insurer cannot claim more than £80,000 as that is the amount of its payment, so that the assured will receive a full indemnity. Suppose, however, that only £90,000, or for that matter any lesser sum, is recovered from the third party. Here it would seem that the assured may retain £20,000 in order to make up the full indemnity, for it is expressed in the agreement between the parties that the assured is underinsured.

(6) The assured is insured for £80,000 under a valued policy not subject to average, on a subject matter of an agreed value of £100,000 but of an actual value of £120,000. If the reasoning in (5) above is correct, a subrogation recovery of £90,000 would permit the assured to claim £20,000 in order to make up the agreed shortfall in the coverage of the policy. What is not clear is whether he can also claim the additional £20,000 difference between agreed and actual value. This is the same problem arising under (4) above.

(7) The assured is insured for £80,000 under a valued policy subject to average, where the agreed value and the actual value of the insured subject matter are £100,000. The principle of average dictates that the assured is his own insurer for the sum of £20,000, so that any recoveries are to be apportioned between insurer and assured in the proportions in which they share the risk, i.e. 80:20. This was held to be the position in *The Commonwealth*.[102] In this case the insured vessel, the actual and agreed value of which was £1,350, was insured under a valued policy for £1,000. The sum of £1,000 was recovered from the third party, and it was held that this sum was to be apportioned in the proportions 1,000:350, representing the liability of each of the parties.

(8) The assured is insured for £50,000 under a valued policy subject to average; the agreed value of the insured subject matter is £80,000 and its actual value is £100,000. Let it be supposed that the subrogation recovery is £90,000. The average provision requires the assured and insurer to apportion the recovery in the proportions 50:50, as £80,000 is the deemed value of the subject matter. That calculation produces a recovery by the insurer of £56,250 but, as the insurer cannot recover more than its own payment of £50,000, the assured would receive £40,000 of the

---

[101] Cf. *Thames & Mersey Marine Insurance v British & Chilean Steamship Co* [1916] 1 K.B. 30; *Goole & Hull Steam Towing Co v Ocean Marine Insurance* [1928] 1 K.B. 589.

[102] *The Commonwealth* [1907] P. 216.

recovery. If the subrogation recovery had been just £60,000, the insurer and assured, on the basis of the 50:30 proportions demanded by average, would have recovered £37,500 and £22,500 respectively.

11–019   *Insurance in layers.* The illustrations set out above assume a single insurer. Matters may become more complex where the insurance is arranged in layers, so that a number of insurers are competing for limited proceeds. The principle to be applied here is that of "recover down", adopted by the House of Lords in *Napier and Ettrick (Lord) v Kershaw.* Thus if insurer C has insured the first £100,000 of any loss, insurer B has insured £100,000 in excess of £100,000 and insurer A has insured £100,000 in excess of £200,000, a recovery of £250,000 from the third party is applied to pay insurer A, then to insurer B and finally to insurer C, so that insurer C suffers the £50,000 shortfall. This is so, according to Lord Templeman in *Napier*, because insurer A has agreed to pay only if B's and C's policies are insufficient to cover the loss, and similarly B has agreed to pay only if C's policy is insufficient to cover the loss, so that the risk must be borne on a downward basis. It will be appreciated that the House of Lords did not distinguish between insurance in layers and underinsurance by the assured: as commented earlier, if in the above example B was the only insurer, the assured bearing an excess of £100,000 and being uninsured for any loss over £200,000, the recovery is applied first of all to the assured's loss over £200,000, then to B, and then to the assured's excess.

11–020   *Payment of subrogation recoveries.* Any sum recovered by the assured which is to be handed over to the insurer in accordance with the above principles is subject to an equitable charge or lien in the insurer's favour. The assured is not, therefore, either a mere debtor or a full trustee of the sums.[103] Moreover, there is old authority, recently approved by the House of Lords in *Napier and Ettrick (Lord) v Kershaw*, for the proposition that the insurer can seek an injunction preventing the third party from paying over any sums to the assured without first having satisfied the insurer's claims.[104] The result is that the insurer is a secured creditor for its subrogation entitlements in the event of the assured's insolvency before or after the sum due to him has been paid by the third party. If the subrogation recovery finds its way into the hands of the insurer's agent, they are necessarily held on trust by the agent.[105] Where, by contrast, the subrogation recovery is obtained by the assured's agent (normally his broker), there is unlikely to be any trust of the proceeds but the equitable charge principle adopted in *Napier and Ettrick (Lord) v Kershaw* nevertheless serves to confer a security upon the insurer.

11–021   *Recovery of insured property.* Where the assured suffers a total loss of the insured subject matter and receives a full indemnity from insurers, the insurers are entitled to exercise salvage rights over the property and to retain it for their own benefit. By contrast, if there is a partial loss and the insurers pay for a partial loss only, the subject matter remains that of the assured and the insurers have subrogation rights over any damages which the assured can secure from the person responsible for the loss. If various items of property are insured together, and some of them are subsequently recovered, the assured is entitled to an

---

[103] *Re Miller, Gibb & Co* [1957] 2 All E.R. 266; *Napier and Ettrick (Lord) v Kershaw* [1993] 1 All E.R. 385.
[104] *White v Dobinson* (1844) 14 Sim. 273.
[105] *Elgood v Harris* [1896] 2 Q.B. 491.

indemnity up to the full value of the insured subject matter, made up by an aggregate of the sum insured and the actual value of the recovered property: only if there is a surplus do the insurers possess subrogation rights.[106]

Interest on subrogation recoveries. As a matter of strict law interest ought not to **11–022** be awarded to the assured, as nominal claimant in an action against the wrongdoer, for the period after which the assured has received payment from the insurer. This is so because interest simply represents compensation for the claimant being kept out of his money, and if the claimant has received insurance moneys he can hardly allege that he has suffered any loss. That principle was applied by the Court of Appeal in *Harbutt's "Plasticine" Ltd v Wayne Tank and Pump Co*[107] The reality of the matter is, nevertheless, that the insurer is the true claimant, and that a failure to award interest means that it will have suffered loss from the date at which payment was made to the assured; this was recognised by the Court of Appeal in *H Cousins and Co Ltd v D & C Carriers Ltd*[108] soon after its *Harbutt's* decision, and the position now is that interest is awardable in a subrogation action in the usual way, i.e. from the date at which the cause of action arose until the date of payment or judgment.[109]

Where there has been a recovery from the third party, and that recovery includes interest, a further question arises as to the allocation of the interest between the insurer and the assured. It is common for the parties to agree that there is to be an apportionment. Even in the absence of an apportionment clause, the result reached by the general law is that the party kept out of its money is entitled to the interest on it. If, therefore, uninsured sums find their way into the hands of the insurers, the insurers must account to the assured for any interest earned on them as from the date of receipt.[110]

Costs of proceeding against the third party. If the assured has obtained judgment **11–023** against a third party and has recovered some or all of his loss from the third party, the insurers are on ordinary principles liable to pay to the assured only that part of the loss which has not been received from the third party, as the third party's payment reduces the insurers' liability to that extent. However, the insurers' obligation to make good any deficit does not apply to costs which have prior to payment by the insurers been incurred by the assured in pursuing the third party but which have not been recovered from the third party. The basis of this rule is that, prior to payment by the insurers, the assured's only claim against the insurers is under the policy and equity has not at that stage intervened.[111]

By contrast, if the insurers have made payment to the assured, and the assured has subsequently made recoveries from a third party representing both insured and uninsured loss, it was held in *England* that the assured is entitled to recover from the insurers a proportionate share in the costs of pursuing the action against

---

[106] *Kuwait Airways Corporation v Kuwait Insurance Co SAK (No.2)* [2000] Lloyd's Rep. I.R. 439.

[107] *Harbutt's "Plasticine" Ltd v Wayne Tank and Pump Co* [1970] 1 Q.B. 447.

[108] *H Cousins and Co Ltd v D & C Carriers Ltd* [1971] 2 Q.B. 230.

[109] Senior Courts Act 1981 s.35A; *Metal Box Co Ltd v Curry's Ltd* [1988] 1 W.L.R. 175.

[110] *Lonrho Exports Ltd v Export Credits Guarantee Department* [1996] 4 All E.R. 673.

[111] *England v Guardian Insurance Ltd* [2000] Lloyd's Rep. I.R. 404. However, if it is right that insurers have a contingent interest in a claim prior to indemnification, it would seem at least to be arguable that the assured has some form of equity in the costs incurred by him in proceeding against the third party, and the equity takes priority over the insurers' equitable rights of subrogation which attach on payment by them.

the third party. The principles as laid down by H.H. Judge Thornton QC[112] were that: (a) the insurers were liable to contribute to all costs reasonably directed to attempts to reduce the assured's loss; and (b) the ratio in which the costs were borne should be determined by reference to the respective interests of the parties in the recoveries. In *England* itself the assured recovered £126,000 from third parties, against an earlier payment of £102,000 from insurers: it was held that the assured and the insurers were to bear the costs in the ratio 102:126.

Persons immune from subrogation proceedings

11–024　*The assured himself.* The common law principle that a person may not sue himself places a necessary limit on the use of the assured's name by the insurer. In *Simpson v Thomson*[113] the assured was the owner of two vessels which, due to the negligence of the master of one of them, collided and were damaged. The insurers argued that their liability for the vessel not at fault was extinguished by their right to proceed against the assured for the negligence of the master of the vessel at fault. The House of Lords gave judgment for the assured, pointing out that the insurer's use of subrogation rights in these circumstances would amount to the assured suing himself.

Where the assured is an individual, this principle does not give rise to any difficulty. However, it is possible to contemplate cases in which the assured and the wrongdoer are different companies within the same group; it remains to be seen whether the courts are prepared to lift the veil of incorporation and to hold that the companies are in practice the same person.[114]

11–025　*Co-assureds: the issues.* A number of persons may be insured under the same policy, and the issue here is whether, assuming that the insurers are liable to any one assured, subrogation rights can be exercised against another assured for bringing about an insured peril. The question does not arise under a joint policy, i.e. a policy under which the parties insure common identical interests (most commonly, co-ownership) as the rights of the parties stand and fall together. The issue arises solely under a composite policy, where each person is insured in respect of his own respective interests: typically, contractor and sub-contract, bailor and bailee, and landlord and tenant. In the following discussion, let it be supposed that parties A and B are insured under a composite policy and that B has negligently caused loss to A, that loss falling within the scope of the policy. The issue is whether the insurers, having indemnified A, are entitled to exercise subrogation rights against B. Confusingly, composite policies, particularly in the construction industry, are often referred to as "joint names" policies, but that description is convenient shorthand and does not mean that the policy is joint. It will almost inevitably be composite.

Two questions fall to be considered. The first is in determining the scope of the liabilities that B may face to A in the event of breach of duty by B: does the

---

[112] Based on *Duus Brown & Co v Binning* (1906) 11 Com. Cas. 190, *Assicurazioni Generali de Trieste v Empress Assurance Corporation Ltd* [1907] 2 K.B. 814 and *The Italia Express (No.2)* [1992] 2 Lloyd's Rep. 281.

[113] *Simpson v Thomson* (1877) 3 App.Cas. 279. See also *Midland Insurance v Smith* (1881) 6 QBD 561, in which the assured's wife set fire to his house and the insurers paid: they had no right of subrogation against her because under the law as it stood at the time the assured could not sue his wife.

[114] Lord Blackburn in *Simpson v Thomson* thought that the veil of incorporation should not be lifted: see (1877) 3 App.Cas. 279 at 294. It is difficult, on the "benefits and burdens" principle, to disagree with this conclusion.

existence of co-insurance arrangements in any way affect the scope of those liabilities? The second arises where B is liable, the question then becoming whether the insurers, having indemnified A, are entitled to exercise subrogation rights against B.

The liability of B: effect of co-insurance clauses. If B does not face any liability **11–026** to A under the terms of the contract between them, then there cannot be any subrogation action by the insurers against B under any circumstances. Many contracts contain, with varying degrees of complexity, risk allocation and insurance clauses. A matter which has been addressed on a number of occasions by the English courts is whether an obligation on one or other of the parties to the contract to obtain joint names insurance operates to exclude the liability of B to A and instead requires A to look only to the insurers for any loss. If that is the case, then clearly no question of subrogation proceedings can arise. Whether a joint names clause has that effect is a question of the construction of the contract as a whole.

It must first be determined whether there is an intention that the joint names insurance is designed to render the person against whom proceedings have been commenced a co-assured. In *Tyco Fire & Integrated Solutions (UK) Ltd v Rolls-Royce Motor Cars Ltd*[115] the co-insurance clause in a construction contract stated that the employer was to maintain in the joint names of himself, "the Construction Manager and others including, but not limited to, contractors, insurance of existing structures . . . against . . . Specified Perils." This clause was held not to be one under which the employer was required to make the contractor a co-assured, but instead was simply a promise by the employer that there would be cover in place in respect of existing structures so that in the event of the occurrence of a major peril the employer would have sufficient funds in place to reinstate the works so that the construction contract could continue to be performed. The clause did not, therefore, provide any immunity to the contractor in the event that he incurred liability to the employer by negligently bringing about loss from the result of a specified peril.

On the assumption that the joint names insurance covers the interests of both A and B, the next matter to be determined is whether that clause operates to discharge B from liability to A which he would otherwise have faced. That will depend upon the other terms of the policy and whether it is possible to derive from them an intention that losses are to be at A's risk so that the insurance is the only source of recovery. A case in which an insurance clause was held to be intended to remove the liability of co-assured B is *Co-operative Retail Services v Taylor Young Partnership Ltd.*[116] Here, the employer, CRS, appointed W as main contractor for a building project, and W appointed Hall as its domestic sub-contractor. In accordance with the contractual arrangements, W took out a joint names policy covering all three parties in respect of damage by fire to the contract works. Independently, CRS appointed TYP as the architect, and HLP as mechanical and electrical engineers, for the works: TYP and HLP were not within the insurance cover and made their own arrangements. The works were in due course damaged by fire. CRS was indemnified by its insurers, who then commenced subrogation proceedings against TYP and HLP: TYP and HLP in turn sought contribution from W and Hall under the Civil Liability (Contribution) Act 1978 on the basis that they were liable in respect of the same damage. The

[115] *Tyco Fire & Integrated Solutions (UK) Ltd v Rolls-Royce Motor Cars Ltd* [2008] Lloyd's Rep. I.R. 617.
[116] *Co-operative Retail Services v Taylor Young Partnership Ltd* [2001] Lloyd's Rep. I.R. 555.

House of Lords, in dismissing the contribution claim, focused on the arrangements between CRS, W and Hall. Their Lordships were satisfied that the effect of those arrangements was to exclude all liability by way of damages to CRS for fire damage, and that any such damage was to be paid for by the insurance and made good by W and Hall to the extent that there was a policy shortfall. That decision was followed in *Scottish and Newcastle Plc v GD Construction (St Albans) Ltd*,[117] where the Court of Appeal construed a contract which required joint names insurance against specified risks, including fire, as designed to remove the liability of the contractor where the loss was caused by fire even if resulting from the contractor's negligence. In this case the joint names policy had not been taken out at all, and the action was simply by the employer against the contractor. It was nevertheless decided that the existence or otherwise of the policy did not affect the issue, because in the absence of insurance the action would be brought by the contractor in his own name, and if insurance was present then the action would be brought by the insurers in the name of the contractor.[118]

Those cases may be distinguished from a series of others in which the risk allocation provisions of the contract were held to be unaffected by the joint names insurance clause. In *Surrey Heath Borough Council v Lovell Construction Ltd*[119] the contract required the contractor to take out joint names insurance in the name of the employer and contractor against reinstatement of the works in the event of loss. The contractor was also required to provide an indemnity in respect of loss resulting from his negligence. The works were damaged by a fire for which the contractor was responsible, and the employer sought to recover from the contractor professional fees which had been incurred in the course of reinstatement and which were not covered by the joint names policy. The contractor argued that, by agreeing to insure reinstatement liabilities, the employer had agreed to discharge the contractor from all such liabilities, including those falling outside the policy. The Court of Appeal preferred the employer's argument that the obligation on the contractor to provide an indemnity applied whether or not the loss was one which was required to be insured under the joint names policy. Again, in *London Borough of Barking & Dagenham v Stamford Asphalt Co Ltd*,[120] it was held by the Court of Appeal that the employer was entitled to an indemnity for loss caused by the contractor's negligence even though there was a joint names policy covering such loss: the co-insurance provision was construed as requiring the employer to look to the insurers only insofar as the loss was not the result of the contractor's negligence.

These cases raise an interesting hypothetical question. Let it be supposed that A and B agree to take out a joint names policy covering loss for which B would otherwise be liable to A. It is clear that, as long as the policy holds good, the insurers are liable to indemnify A and have no right of recourse by way of subrogation against B. Suppose further, however, that the insurers successfully plead a defence under the policy: does the absence of insurance funds reinstate B's liability to A or is it discharged by the creation of a valid policy? The Court

---

[117] *Scottish and Newcastle Plc v GD Construction (St Albans) Ltd* [2003] Lloyd's Rep. I.R. 821.

[118] See also *London Borough of Barking and Dagenham v Stanford Asphalt Co Ltd* (1997) 82 B.L.R. 25 and *Tyco Fire and Integrated Solutions (UK) Ltd v Rolls-Royce Motor Cars Ltd* [2008] Lloyd's Rep. I.R. 617.

[119] *Surrey Heath Borough Council v Lovell Construction Ltd* (1990) 48 B.L.R. 108.

[120] *London Borough of Barking & Dagenham v Stamford Asphalt Co Ltd* (1997) 82 B.L.R. 25. See also *Dorset County Council v Southern Felt Roofing Co Ltd* (1990) 48 B.L.R. 96.

of Appeal in the *Surrey Heath* case indicated that the answer to that question would depend upon the true construction of the policy:

"It may be the true construction that a provision for insurance is to be taken as satisfying or curtailing a contractual obligation, or it may be the true construction that a contractual obligation is to be backed by insurance with the result that the contractual obligation stands or is enforceable even if for some reason the insurance fails or proves to be inadequate."

The rights of a co-assured. If it is the case that a co-insurance clause removes the   **11–027** liability of B towards A, requiring A to look to the insurers rather than to B to recover any loss, then there is no need for further inquiry. The more difficult scenario is that in which A remains entitled to bring proceedings against B despite the co-insurance clause, and B seeks to rely upon his status as co-assured to fight off the subrogation claim.

The question was first addressed by Lloyd J. in *The Yasin*,[121] in which the learned judge rejected the argument that there was any general principle which prevented insurers from exercising subrogation rights against a co-assured. Lloyd J. held that any subrogation immunity rested on the principle of circuity. To explain this principle, the learned judge drew a distinction between a policy under which the parties had insured their respective interests in property, and a policy in which one party has insured property and the other party has insured against liability for damage to property. The learned judge expressed the view that subrogation is precluded in the latter case by reason of circuity. Suppose that party A is insured against damage to goods, and party B is insured against his liability in respect of those goods: if the insurer indemnifies A for damage negligently caused by B, the insurers plainly cannot exercise subrogation rights in A's name against B because B is himself entitled to claim under the policy, so that the subrogation action would give rise to circuity in claims. By contrast, if parties A and B are both insured against damage to property, and B negligently damaged A's property, B would not be immune from a subrogation action merely because he was a co-assured under the policy, as his interests under the policy would not be the same as those of A. A similar distinction had been drawn in *Simpson v Thompson*.[122] Subsequently, however, in *Petrofina (UK) Ltd v Magnaload Ltd*,[123] Lloyd J. abandoned his distinction between these two types of policy, and, while adhering to his view that the prohibition on subrogation rested upon the principle of circuity, held that circuity was equally applicable where parties A and B had both insured their respective interests under a property policy. Thus, in a case in which A and B have insurable interest in the entire subject matter insured by the policy, and both have insured their full interest, the insurer cannot pay A and then seek to exercise subrogation rights against B because B is himself insured in respect of that loss and could have claimed for it. Applying this principle, Lloyd J. held that the insurers under a contractors' all risks policy covering the employer, the contractor and all subcontractors could not exercise subrogation rights in the employer's name against an allegedly negligent subcontractor, as the subcontractor was himself an assured in respect of the property which had been damaged.

It was subsequently argued in *National Oilwell (UK) Ltd v Davy Offshore Ltd*[124] that Lloyd J.'s view in *The Yasin* was to be preferred to that in *Petrofina*.

[121] *The Yasin* [1979] 2 Lloyd's Rep. 45.
[122] *Simpson v Thompson* (1877) 3 App.Cas. 279.
[123] *Petrofina (UK) Ltd v Magnaload Ltd* [1984] Q.B. 127.
[124] *National Oilwell (UK) Ltd v Davy Offshore Ltd* [1993] 2 Lloyd's Rep. 582.

This was so for the following reason. Suppose that party B negligently damages party A's property, and that the insurers pays A. Irrespective of whether B is himself insured in respect of that property, once A has been paid, the insurers' liability is discharged. This means that B can no longer make a claim against the insurer, so that if the insurer exercises subrogation rights against B there is no possibility of B seeking to claim for a loss against the insurer (given that the policy covers property and not B's liability). Colman J. who had earlier expressed similar views at first instance in *Stone Vickers Ltd v Appledore Ferguson Shipbuilders Ltd*,[125] restated the basis for the immunity of a co-assured in the following terms:

> "For the insurers who had paid the principal assured to assert that they were now free to exercise rights of subrogation and thereby sue the party at fault would be to subject the co-assured to a liability for loss and damage caused by a peril insured for his benefit . . . [I]t is necessary to imply a term into the policy of insurance to avoid this unsatisfactory possibility. The implication of such a term is needed to give effect to what must have been the mutual intention (on this hypothesis) of the principal assured and the insurers, as to the risks covered by the policy. On this basis the purported exercise by insurers of rights of subrogation against the co-assured would be in breach of such a term and would accordingly provide the co-assured with a defence to the subrogated claim."

The basis of a co-assured's immunity was again addressed in *Co-operative Retail Services v Taylor Young Partnership Ltd*.[126] In that case the point did not arise for decision, as the House of Lords was satisfied that any liability of the third party in damages to the assured had been excluded by the agreement between the assured and the third party, so that there was no need to consider whether the insurers were by some wider principle precluded from exercising subrogation rights. However, Lord Hope, following the approach adopted in *Hopewell Project Management Ltd v Ewbank Preece Ltd*,[127] preferred to rest immunity upon a third ground, namely the proper construction of the contract between the parties rather than any implication into the insurance contract itself. That analysis was tentatively adopted by Rix L.J. in *Tyco Fire & Integrated Solutions (UK) Ltd v Rolls-Royce Motor Cars Ltd*.[128] Rix L.J. noted that this analysis was straightforward where the contract between the primary assured and the co-assured by its terms conferred immunity upon the co-assured, because in that case the primary assured—and thus his insurers by way of subrogation—could not have an action against the assured. However, if the contract between the primary assured and the co-assured does not by its terms exclude a possible action for breach of duty on the part of the co-assured, Rix L.J. was of the view that, absent a subrogation waiver clause, the insurers would not be precluded from relying upon that cause of action to bring a subrogated claim even though the co-assured was an insured person under the policy. One possible justification for this approach is that the policy is not one against the co-assured's liability but rather one which covers him for loss of the insured subject matter itself. However, the implied policy term approach leads to the opposite result, in that it precludes recovery for a loss which would have been recoverable by the

---

[125] *Stone Vickers Ltd v Appledore Ferguson Shipbuilders Ltd* [1991] 2 Lloyd's Rep. 288, a judgment reversed by the Court of Appeal on other grounds, [1992] 2 Lloyd's Rep. 578.

[126] *Co-operative Retail Services v Taylor Young Partnership Ltd* [2001] Lloyd's Rep. I.R. 555.

[127] *Hopewell Project Management Ltd v Ewbank Preece Ltd* [1998] 1 Lloyd's Rep. 448.

[128] *Tyco Fire & Integrated Solutions (UK) Ltd v Rolls-Royce Motor Cars Ltd* [2008] Lloyd's Rep. I.R. 617.

co-assured had he been the claimant against the insurers, and it remains to be seen which of the two views ultimately prevails.

Whichever is correct, a number of limitations on the principle that a co-assured may be entitled to immunity from subrogation proceedings should be noted. These all stem from the point that a co-assured is entitled to immunity only if he is entitled to bring an action on the policy in respect of the insured loss: if that is not possible then the co-assured is not an insured person and will not benefit from any subrogation immunity conferred upon him by reason of that status. However, after *Tyco*, an alternative explanation may be that the contract between the primary assured and the co-assured does not give the co-assured immunity from suit in these situations.

Insurable interest. Subrogation is excluded only where the co-assured has **11–028** insurable interest in the damaged subject matter. Suppose, for example, that A and B each own a car, and insure the cars under the same policy: if A negligently causes damage to B's car, there is nothing to prevent B's insurers exercising subrogation rights against A, as A has no insurable interest in B's car even though it is insured under a policy to which A is a party. The essence of the ruling in *Petrofina v Magnaload*[129] was that each of the parties had insurable interest in the entire contract works. Nevertheless, it will not always be possible for the court to conclude that a co-assured has a pervasive insurable interest in the entire subject matter.

In *Appledore Ferguson Shipbuilders Ltd v Stone Vickers Ltd*[130] shipbuilders insured a ship under construction, and made sub-contractors co-assureds in respect of the entire subject matter. The sub-contractors supplied a propeller, but it was alleged by the shipowners that the propeller was defective. The sub-contractors brought an action for the price, but were met by a counterclaim by the shipbuilders in respect of losses due to delays resulting from the defective propeller. These losses had been paid by the insurers, and so the question became whether the insurers could exercise subrogation rights against the sub-contractors as their own assured. Anthony Colman QC, sitting as a Deputy High Court Judge, denied the insurers recovery and held that the sub-contractors possessed insurable interest in the entire contract works and not just in the propeller: this was so because any defect in the propeller would give rise to losses in the works as a whole and would not be confined to the propeller. The Court of Appeal reversed this decision, but only on the basis that the shipbuilders' policy was not intended to extend to the defendant subcontractor.

The principle is, therefore, that subrogation immunity is conferred on a co-assured only if he has an insurable interest in the property in question and if he has insured that interest. The position is further illustrated by *National Oilwell (UK) Ltd v Davy Offshore Ltd*[131] itself, in which works under construction were insured by the contractor and sub-contractors under a joint names policy. All of the parties had an insurable interest in the entire works, so that each could potentially have insured the entire works. The sub-contract between the contractor and the instant sub-contractor obliged the contractor to insure only in respect of losses occurring before goods had been delivered to the contractor by the sub-contractor. Post-delivery losses occurred as the result of the sub-contractor's alleged default, and Colman J. construed the insurance contract as

[129] *Petrofina (UK) Ltd v Magnaload Ltd* [1984] Q.B.127.

[130] *Appledore Ferguson Shipbuilders Ltd v Stone Vickers Ltd* [1991] 2 Lloyd's Rep. 288, reversed [1992] 2 Lloyd's Rep. 578.

[131] *National Oilwell (UK) Ltd v Davy Offshore Ltd* [1993] 2 Lloyd's Rep. 582.

applying to the sub-contractor only for pre-delivery losses. The sub-contractor was, therefore, a co-assured only in respect of such losses, and was held not to be immune from a subrogation action for post-delivery losses.[132] *National Oilwell* was distinguished in *BP Exploration Operating Co Ltd v Kvaerner Oilfield Products Ltd*,[133] where Colman J. held that the obligation on the contractor to insure on behalf of other parties was unrestricted and that, as such, the contractor had been authorised to enter into a co-insurance for the full duration of the cover.

These cases were concerned with the proper construction of the contract between the contractor and the third parties, the purpose being to ascertain the scope of the co-insurance procured by the contractor by reference to the scope of his obligation to insure. If the third party does not have the relevant insurable interest, then irrespective of the terms of the contract with the contractor and of the policy taken out by the contractor, the third party cannot be regarded as a co-assured. This is apparent from *Deepak Fertilisers & Petrochemical Corp v Davy McKee (London) Ltd*,[134] in which the Court of Appeal held that the insurable interest of a sub-contractor came to an end as soon as his work was completed, as his interest rested upon loss which he might suffer by being prevented by an insured peril from completing his contract: thereafter, his interest lapsed, leaving him open to a subrogation action in the event that his earlier work proved to be defective and gave rise to an insured peril.

The nature of the sub-contractor's insurable interest has given rise to some difficulty in the cases. The authorities were reviewed by the Court of Appeal in *Feasey v Sun Life Assurance Co of Canada*,[135] the majority view being that a sub-contractor has an insurable interest in the works by virtue of the fact that he might suffer loss of employment in the event of damage to the works, and also an insurable interest by virtue of his liability for the works: whether the policy covers the latter interest is a matter for its proper construction.

11–029   *Effect of co-assured's wilful misconduct.* This limitation relates to cases in which B has been guilty of wilful misconduct which precludes his own right to recover under the policy. Here, an important distinction has to be drawn between joint and composite policies. Under a joint policy, wilful misconduct by either party provides the insurers with a complete defence against both, so that the question of subrogation never arises. By contrast, where the policy is composite the wilful misconduct of one party precludes recovery by him but will not preclude recovery by other co-assureds[136] unless the resulting loss is not one from an insured peril[137] or the guilty co-assured is acting as agent for the others.[138] Consequently, in the case of a composite policy an innocent co-assured is entitled

---

[132] See also *Matalan Discount Club (Cash & Carry) Ltd v Tokenspire Properties (North Western) Ltd* Unreported, May 18, 2001, where a policy extension in favour of a third party was for limited purposes only, and *John F Hunt Demolition Ltd v ASME Engineering Ltd* [2007] EWHC 1507 (TCC).

[133] *BP Exploration Operating Co Ltd v Kvaerner Oilfield Products Ltd* [2005] 1 Lloyd's Rep. 307.

[134] *Deepak Fertilisers & Petrochemical Corp v Davy McKee (London) Ltd* [1999] 1 Lloyd's Rep. 387, and see also *TWF Printers Ltd v Interserve Project Services Ltd* [2006] EWCA Civ 875.

[135] *Feasey v Sun Life Assurance Co of Canada* [2003] Lloyd's Rep. I.R. 637.

[136] *Lombard Australia Ltd v NRMA Insurance Co Ltd* [1969] 1 Lloyd's Rep. 575; *General Accident Fire and Life Assurance Corp Ltd v Midland Bank Ltd* [1940] 2 K.B. 388; *Woolcott v Sun Alliance and London Assurance Ltd* [1978] 1 Lloyd's Rep. 629.

[137] *Samuel & Co Ltd v Dumas* [1924] A.C. 431, where it was held that deliberate scuttling is not a peril of the seas so that the loss of the insured vessel was not caused by an insured peril.

[138] *Direct Line Insurance v Khan* [2002] Lloyd's Rep. I.R. 364.

to recover. Subrogation will be available against the guilty co-assured in such a case, because he cannot claim to be an insured person in respect of that particular loss. That reasoning was adopted by Colman J. in *National Oilwell (UK) Ltd v Davy Offshore Ltd*, the learned judge holding that, where wilful misconduct can be proved against a co-assured, any damage inflicted by him is uninsured as far as he is concerned and a subrogation action lies against him. That analysis was followed by Rix J. in *State of Netherlands v Youell*.[139] There, a co-insurance policy against building risks in respect of two submarines was taken out by the employer and the contractor. Losses arose, and the insurers asserted that the defects in the submarines were due to the wilful misconduct of the contractor. Rix J. ruled that, if this assertion was to be made out, the contractor would not be an insured person under the policy and could not recover any insurance monies. He further held that the employer could not rely upon its pervasive insurable interest to recover the full amount under the policy and then hand over to the contractor any sums in excess of the employer's own actual insurable interest, as this would amount to indirect enforcement of the policy: any such funds which did find their way into the contractor's hands could, therefore, be recovered from him by the insurers by way of subrogation. However, Rix J. held that on the facts before him, the employer had insurable interest in the entire works and could recover the full sum due under the policy, even though the employer was obliged by contract to allow the sums to be used for the benefit of the contractor in effecting repairs.

Termination of co-assured's cover. If a co-assured ceases to be covered for any reason other than his own wilful misconduct, he again faces subrogation proceedings. In *Matalan Discount Club (Cash & Carry) Ltd v Tokenspire Properties (North Western) Ltd*,[140] the cover granted by a policy had been extended to a third party as co-assured, and had subsequently been cancelled for breach of warranty. It was held by H.H. Judge Seymour QC that if there is a co-insurance agreement, and cover is avoided or terminated in respect of one co-assured, the implied policy term giving immunity from suit from subrogation proceedings no longer operates. The appropriate implied term was thus a limited one, namely that the insurer would not exercise any right of subrogation against a co-assured provided that, and so long as, cover in relation to the particular co-assured had not been avoided. In the same way, if the co-assured is in breach of a policy term or condition which precludes an action by him on the policy, then he ceases to be co-assured and potentially exposes himself to subrogation proceedings.[141]   **11–030**

Persons for whose benefit insurance has been procured. In addition to potential subrogation immunity conferred upon the assured and upon co-assureds, a third possibility is that the policy is designed to be for the benefit of a third party who is not a co-assured under that policy. A good example of this situation is that of landlord and tenant, where the policy is taken out by the landlord but the premiums are indirectly paid by the tenant and the obligation of the landlord is to repair or reinstate the premises in the event of loss, doubtless with the use of the insurance moneys. The cases have developed the principle that the third party   **11–031**

[139] *State of Netherlands v Youell* [1997] 2 Lloyd's Rep. 440.
[140] *Matalan Discount Club (Cash & Carry) Ltd v Tokenspire Properties (North Western) Ltd* Unreported, May 18, 2001.
[141] *Tate Gallery (Trustees) v Duffy Construction Ltd* [2007] Lloyd's Rep. I.R. 758.

may be immune from subrogation proceedings even though he is not a party to the insurance.

The starting point is to ask whether the policy itself is stated to be enforceable by, or for the benefit of, an identifiable third party. If the third party does have rights under the policy, then the nature of those rights will determine whether or not there is subrogation immunity. The third party may be placed in a position akin to that of a co-assured, in that he has the right to claim for the loss. Plainly there can be no subrogation rights against a third party who has the rights of the assured conferred upon him. Alternatively, he may be the beneficiary of an express subrogation waiver or at least a statement in the policy that the assured has no rights against the third party.

In the absence of anything in the policy itself, the subrogation immunity of the third party depends upon the agreement between the assured and the third party. If it can be shown that their agreement intended to exclude a right of recourse by the assured, then the assured has no rights against the third party and it follows that the insurer has no subrogation rights against the third party. No real problem arises where the contract between the assured and the third party specifically states that the third party is to be immune from proceedings brought by the assured, as in such a case it is clear that the insurer has no subrogation rights.[142] The only issue which may here arise is whether the agreement to exclude the third party's liability is valid under, e.g. the Unfair Contract Terms Act 1977: subject to that, the insurers have no subrogation rights and the only recourse which the insurers might possess is the right to avoid the policy for non-disclosure of the fact that the assured had contracted out of his subrogation rights.

As is the case with joint names insurance, an agreement by the assured to look only to the insurers is effective to exclude subrogation rights because there is simply no cause of action vested in the assured. In *Coupar Transport (London) Ltd v Smith's (Alton) Ltd*[143] the parties agreed that the assured alone would insure against particular risks and that the third party was not to do so; this arrangement was held by the court to exempt the third party for losses of those types. In *Canadian Transport Co Ltd v Court Line Ltd*,[144] a case involving a time charterparty, the parties sought to limit the charterer's liability to the owner by providing "owners to give time charterers the benefit of the Protection and Indemnity Club insurances so far as club rules allow". The House of Lords held that the rules of the club with which the owner was insured did not permit the owner to compromise his rights in this way, so that the clause was by its own terms ineffectual. However, it is clear, at least from the judgment of Lord Atkin, that, as a matter of principle, "a man may contract with another on the terms that if he is injured by that other then, if he happens to be insured, he will look to the insurers in relief of the wrongdoers". The point here made is further illustrated by cases involving building contracts, in which the employer has agreed to insure and to have the insured subject matter at his sole risk: in such circumstances, the obvious intention is to remove the liability of any contractor.[145] Whether this principle comes into play depends upon the wording of the agreement between

---

[142] See *Thomas & Co v Brown* (1891) 4 Com. Cas. 186, where the policy additionally acknowledged that the assured was "without recourse to lightermen".

[143] *Coupar Transport (London) Ltd v Smith's (Alton) Ltd* [1959] 1 Lloyd's Rep. 369.

[144] *Canadian Transport Co Ltd v Court Line Ltd* [1940] A.C. 934.

[145] *James Archdale & Co Ltd v Comeservices* [1954] 1 W.L.R. 159; *Scottish Special Housing Association v Wimpey Construction (UK) Ltd* [1986] 2 All E.R. 957; *Norwich City Council v Harvey* [1989] 1 All E.R. 1180.

the parties. Thus if particular forms of loss are excluded from the insurance obligation, the contractor's common law duties towards the employer will remain in place and a subrogation action against the contractor remains available.[146] The mere fact that the employer has agreed to insure is not enough to remove liability for negligence from the contractor if the contract requires the contractor to indemnify the employer for any loss.[147] In such a case, there is an overlap in protection as far as the employer is concerned, and this will enure to the benefit of his insurers.

Implied agreement to benefit third party. Matters may be less straightforward where it is argued by the wrongdoer in subrogation proceedings that it was the intention of the parties that he would have the benefit of the insurance, but there is nothing express in the contract between assured and wrongdoer to this effect. In this type of case, the court must construe the agreement to ascertain the true intention of the parties. The cases are not fully consistent, but it may be said that if there is no mention of insurance in the contract, and the premium is paid by the assured purely for his own benefit, there is no basis for implying a term into the contract exempting the third party from liability for losses covered by insurance. Thus there is no implied term in a contract of employment that an employee who injures a co-worker is immune from proceedings for indemnification by his employer who is vicariously liable,[148] and the owner of premises who takes out employers' liability insurance for his own benefit does not impliedly agree to relieve a negligent contractor from legal proceedings in the event that the contractor's negligence causes losses for which the owner is vicariously liable.[149] There are also landlord and tenant cases in which the courts have construed the lease as not requiring the landlord to insure on behalf of the tenant[150] even if the tenant has contributed to the premium.[151]

11–032

By contrast, if the third party has paid the premium and it is clear that as between the assured and the third party the assured will look to insurers and not to the third party in the event of damage caused by the third party, it will be appropriate to imply a term into the contract which restricts a right of recourse against the third party.[152] Accordingly, where employer A lends an employee to employer B and the employee is injured by an employee of B, it is to be implied in the agreement that A has no recourse to B so that A's insurers have no subrogation rights against B's negligent employee.[153] Again, where a tenant has by his negligence destroyed premises insured by his landlord, and it was the

---

[146] *GE Construction (St Albans) Ltd v Scottish & Newcastle Plc* [2003] Lloyd's Rep. I.R. 821.

[147] *Surrey Heath Borough Council v Lovell Construction* (1990) 48 B.L.R. 108; *National Trust v Haden Young* (1994) 72 B.L.R. 1.

[148] *Lister v Romford Ice and Cold Storage Co Ltd* [1955] A.C. 555. In England the effect of this decision was reversed by an agreement between government and the insurance industry that subrogation rights would not be exercised in these circumstances. In Australia, *Lister* has been reversed by s.66 of the Insurance Contracts Act 1984, which provides that subrogation is available only where the employee has been guilty of "serious or wilful misconduct". See *Boral Resources Ltd v Pyke* (1990) 93 A.L.R. 89.

[149] *Caledonia North Sea Ltd v British Telecommunications Plc* [2002] Lloyd's Rep. I.R. 261.

[150] *Lambert v Keymood Ltd* [1999] Lloyd's Rep. I.R. 80.

[151] *University of Western Ontario v Yanush* 56 D.L.R. (4th) 552 (1988).

[152] Although only in respect of negligence. It is difficult, if not impossible, to imply a term that the assured will look to the insurers and not to the third party where the third party deliberately or recklessly caused the loss: cf. *National Oilwell (UK) Ltd v Davy Offshore Ltd* [1993] 2 Lloyd's Rep. 582; *State of Netherlands v Youell* [1997] 2 Lloyd's Rep. 440.

[153] *Morris v Ford Motor Co* [1973] Q.B. 792, a case which also turned on the exclusion of subrogation on equitable grounds.

obligation of the landlord to obtain insurance on the premises which was indirectly paid for by the tenant, the lease impliedly excludes any obligation on the tenant to indemnify the landlord so that no subrogation action is possible.[154]

11–033 *Mortgage indemnity policies.* One particularly problematic area concerns the use of mortgage indemnity policies. Under this type of insurance, the insurer agrees to indemnify the mortgagee in the event of default by the mortgagor in payment of mortgage instalments. It is often a condition of the mortgage that the mortgagor forwards the premium to the mortgagee for the policy to be taken out by the mortgagee, and the question which here arises is whether the insurer has subrogation rights against the mortgagor. The cases demonstrate that the mere fact that the mortgagor has paid the premium is not enough to protect him from subrogation rights, and the courts have refused to imply a term into the mortgage by which the mortgagee is to look to the insurer and not the mortgagor in the event of default.[155] A related situation arose in *Europe Mortgages Ltd v Halifax Estate Agents*,[156] in which the insurers, having paid the mortgagee, sought to exercise subrogation rights not against the defaulting mortgagor but rather against the valuer whose allegedly negligent overvaluation had caused the mortgagee to advance the loan in the first place. It was here held that the policy was for the benefit of the mortgagee alone, and that the valuer was liable for the full amount of the mortgagee's loss in subrogation proceedings brought by the insurer.

Payments to the assured not affected by subrogation rights

11–034 *Payment must reduce assured's insured loss.* The insurer is as a rule entitled to claim all sums received by, or owing to, the assured in diminution of his loss.[157] The insurer is also entitled to take advantage of any cause of action which the assured has against a third party for a sum in diminution of his loss, provided that the cause of action is not contingent upon the inability of the assured to recover under an insurance policy. Accordingly, if the assured's property has been seized, and payment has been made to him by the person seizing that property, the assured will normally be liable to account for it to his insurer by way of subrogation.[158]

For the purposes of determining whether a sum is due to the assured by a third party the indemnity provided by an insurer is to be regarded as an indemnifier of last resort, so that if the third party is obliged by contract with the assured to provide an indemnity, that indemnity is not to be equated with the indemnity due under the policy. This was decided by the House of Lords in *Caledonia North Sea Ltd v British Telecommunications Plc*.[159] In this case the assured had been indemnified by insurers against liability for injuries caused to persons injured or killed by the disastrous explosion on the Piper Alpha, and the insurers sought to exercise subrogation rights against contractors who were, by contract, obliged to

---

[154] *Mark Rowlands Ltd v Berni Inns Ltd* [1985] 3 All E.R. 473. See also: *Barras v Hamilton, The Times*, June 10, 1994; *Mumford Hotels v Wheeler* [1964] 1 Ch. 117.

[155] *Woolwich Building Society v Brown* [1996] C.L.C. 625.

[156] *Europe Mortgages Ltd v Halifax Estate Agents* Unreported, 1996.

[157] *Randal v Cockran* (1748) 1 Ves. Sen. 98; *Goole and Hull Steam Towing Co v Ocean Marine Insurance Co* [1928] 1 K.B. 589.

[158] See Tucker J. in *Austin v Zurich Insurance* [1944] 2 All E.R. 243 at 246, not disapproved on appeal, [1945] 1 All E.R. 316.

[159] *Caledonia North Sea Ltd v British Telecommunications Plc* [2002] Lloyd's Rep. I.R. 261.

indemnify the assured for any liability incurred by the assured towards any employees of the contractors. The reasoning of the Court of Session,[160] that if the assured has been indemnified by his insurers his loss was diminished to that extent so that no claim could be made against the third party, was rejected on appeal,[161] ultimately the House of Lords. Their Lordships ruled[162] that it had long been settled law that an insurer who had fully indemnified an insured against a loss covered by a contract of insurance could ordinarily enforce any right of recourse available to the insured by use of the assured's name, and that that rule was not ousted where the third party's liability to the assured arose under a contract of indemnity (other than a contract of insurance). For that rule to be ousted it would have to be shown that the third party's contract with the assured restricted the assured to reliance on the assured's own policy, but on the facts there was nothing in that contract which required the assured to possess its own insurance cover and accordingly there was no reason why the third party should be allowed to derive any benefit from the insurance.

Damages for uninsured loss. If the assured's loss includes damage which is not **11–035** covered by the policy, the insurer is not entitled to be subrogated to any payment or liability in respect of the uninsured loss.[163] Thus where a policy indemnified an employer against claims by employees but was subject to a deductible the insurers were not—having satisfied the employer's liabilities to its employees— entitled to exercise subrogation rights against other insurers who had insured the employer against claims falling within the deductible: the sums recoverable from the deductible insurers did not go to reduce the loss insured against by the employers' liability insurers.[164] In particular, insurance policies do not, unless otherwise provided, cover the assured against consequential losses, including, most significantly, loss of profits. The insurer is not, therefore, entitled to damages which the assured may receive from the third party to compensate him for consequential loss.[165] On the same principle, if the assured has a right of action against the third party for an independent form of loss additional to the insured loss, any sum received from the third party in discharge of that liability cannot be claimed by the insurer.[166] The assured bears the burden of proving that he has suffered a loss greater than that recovered from the insurers if he wishes to retain any damages obtained from the third party. In *Falcon Insurance Co*

---

[160] *Elf Enterprise (Caledonia) Ltd v London Bridge Engineering Ltd* [2000] Lloyd's Rep. I.R. 249.

[161] *Caledonia North Sea Ltd v London Bridge Engineering* [2000] Lloyd's Rep. I.R. 249.

[162] Relying on a series of American cases: *Hall & Long v The Railroad Companies* 80 U.S. 367 (1871); *Chicago St Louis & New Orleans Railroad Co v Pullman Southern Car Co* 139 U.S. 79 (1891); *FH Vahlsing Inc v Hartford Fire Insurance Co* 108 S.W. 2d 947 (1937); *Meyer Koulish Co v Cannon* 28 Cal. Rptr. 757 (1963); *Consolidated Freightways Inc v Moore* 229 P. 2d 882 (1951); *North Central Airlines Inc v City of Aberdeen, South Dakota* 370 F. 2d 129 (1966). The absence of English or Scottish authority on the point was regarded by the House of Lords as an indication that the point was an obvious one.

[163] *Law Fire Assurance Co v Oakley* (1888) 4 T.L.R. 309; *Horse, Carriage and General Insurance Co v Petch* (1916) 33 T.L.R. 131.

[164] *T&N Ltd v Royal and Sun Alliance Plc* [2004] Lloyd's Rep. I.R. 134.

[165] *Sea Insurance Co v Hadden* (1884) 13 QBD 706; *Attorney-General v Glen Line* (1930) 37 Ll. L.R. 55. Cf. *Law Fire Assurance v Oakley* (1888) 4 T.L.R. 309; *Horse, Carriage and General Insurance v Petch* (1916) 33 T.L.R. 131.

[166] *Young v Merchants' Marine Insurance Co Ltd* [1932] 2 K.B. 705, but contrast *Assicurazioni Generali de Trieste v Empress Assurance Corporation Ltd* [1907] 2 K.B. 814 where the damages were all attributable to the insured loss.

(HK) Ltd v Cheshire Cat Restaurant & Pub Co Ltd[167] the decorations and furniture in the assured's pub were destroyed by fire, and the assured recovered HK$491,453.00 from its fire insurers. Subsequently the assured recovered HK$760,000.00 from a security company for loss caused by the fire. It was held that the assured was unable to show that it had suffered loss in excess of the sum paid by the insurers, and accordingly they were entitled to recover the full amount paid by them.

A problem will arise in this context where the sum received from the third party does not fully cover both the insured and uninsured losses, for some form of apportionment as between those losses will be necessary. The probable solution is that the payment is to be divided between insurer and assured in proportion to the amount of their losses[168]; it is tempting to apply the rule appropriate in the case of underinsurance, namely that the assured is entitled to a full indemnity before the insurer has a claim to the proceeds, but the proportionality rule must clearly apply, at least where the various subject matters are insured with different insurers.

11–036 *Ex gratia payments.* In a number of cases the assured has received an ex gratia payment in compensation for a loss incurred by him, and the question has arisen whether the insurer is entitled to claim any such payment under its subrogation rights. The usual context of these cases has been that of losses suffered by the assured in the course of war or other governmental action, the ex gratia payment being made by a government directly or indirectly, but not legally, responsible for the loss. Doubts have been expressed by the Court of Appeal as to the ability of an insurer to claim the benefit of a gift to the assured, for the reason that subrogation is confined to "rights" and does not extend to gratuities.[169] But it is clear from authorities directly on the point that there is no automatic exclusion of subrogation for such payments. The proper test concerns the intention with which the ex gratia payment was made: if the intention of the donor was to provide personal compensation to the assured for the losses incurred by him, the insurer has no claim; but if the donor's intention was to make payment in diminution of the assured's loss, the payment may legitimately be regarded as within the scope of subrogation.

The cases appear to demonstrate that, in the absence of a clear indication by the donor that its payment is to be personal compensation, any payment will be presumed to be in diminution of the assured's loss. Thus, in *Stearns v Village Main Reef Gold Mining Co*,[170] compensation granted by the South African government for its requisition of gold belonging to the assured gold mine owner was held by the Court of Appeal to be intended to diminish the assured's loss, as there was no indication that the payment had been made for any other reason. The Court of Appeal in so concluding distinguished *Burnand v Rodocanachi*

---

[167] *Falcon Insurance Co (HK) Ltd v Cheshire Cat Restaurant & Pub Co Ltd* [2007] H.K.E.C. 2084.

[168] Thus if the third party causes damage both to the assured's insured building to the extent of £500, and to the assured's uninsured effects to the extent of £300, but can pay only £400, the recovery is apportioned between insurer and assured in the proportions 500:300; the insurer recovers £250 by way of subrogation and the assured retains £150.

[169] See *Castellain v Preston* (1883) 11 QBD 380.

[170] *Stearns v Village Main Reef Gold Mining Co* (1905) 21 T.L.R. 236. Cf. the earlier decisions in *Randal v Cockran* (1748) 1 Ves. Sen. 98 and *Blaaupot v Da Costa* (1758) 1 Eden 130, in which compensation paid by the British government, in the form of prizes handed over to shipowners who had suffered losses at the hands of the Spanish, was held to be in diminution of loss.

Sons & Co,[171] in which the House of Lords had decided that a payment made by the US government under the authority of an Act of Congress was intended to provide personal compensation only. The Act had been passed in the aftermath of the American Civil War, and expressly stipulated that the funds to be made available were by way of personal compensation to property owners and were not distributable amongst the insurers of such persons. It follows that *Burnand Rodocanachi* represents the exception rather than the rule, and that a payment made by a third party in a commercial context will normally be construed as designed to diminish the insured loss.[172]

The significance of the insurer's conduct. It was argued in *England v Guardian Insurance Ltd*[173] that, as subrogation is an equitable doctrine, the insurer might lose the right to subrogation by reason of inequitable conduct towards the assured in handling the assured's claim. In *England* various allegations were made against the insurer, relating to the time taken to accept liability, but it was held that, even if such complaints had been made out, subrogation rights could not be lost in this way. Although subrogation was an equitable doctrine, its effect was to confer proprietary rights (in the form of a lien) in favour of the insurer over sums received by the assured from third parties, and accordingly those rights were not lost simply because the insurer had acted inequitably in the handling of the assured's claim.

11–037

Loss of subrogation rights: agreements by the insurer

Subrogation waiver agreements. Insurers have entered into a number of legally binding agreements between themselves not to enforce subrogation rights in given circumstances. In addition to these agreements, insurers may on occasion agree with their assureds that subrogation rights will not be enforced against a given third party. One such example is found in a clause of the International Hull Clauses 2003, which states that in the event of the vessel being chartered by an associated, subsidiary or affiliated company of the assured, and in the event of loss of or damage to the vessel by perils insured covered by the policy, the underwriters waive their rights of subrogation against the charterers except to the extent that any charterer has the benefit of liability cover for such loss or damage. If an insurer, in breach of any legally binding agreement not to sue, attempts to do so, it can doubtless be restrained by injunction at the instance of the other party to the agreement, whether insurer or assured.

11–038

At common law a subrogation waiver clause could not be relied upon by the third party for whose benefit it was intended, as a result of the doctrine of privity of contract.[174] That was so even if the third party was a co-assured under the policy in respect of other risks.[175] The narrow common law view of subrogation waiver clauses has not been universally accepted. In Canada, for example, it has been held that a policy provision exempting a third party from liability can be

---

[171] *Burnand v Rodocanachi Sons & Co* (1882) 7 App.Cas. 333. See also *Merrett v Capitol Indemnity Corp* [1991] 1 Lloyd's Rep. 169.

[172] *Colonia Versicherung A.C. v Amoco Oil Co* [1995] 1 Lloyd's Rep. 570; *Talbot Underwriting v Nausch Hogan & Murray (The Jascon 5)* [2006] Lloyd's Rep. I.R. 531.

[173] *England v Guardian Insurance Ltd* [2000] Lloyd's Rep. I.R. 404.

[174] *Tweddle v Atkinson* (1861) 1 B. & S. 395; *Dunlop Pneumatic Tyre Co Ltd v Selfridge & Co Ltd* [1915] A.C. 847.

[175] *National Oilwell (UK) Ltd v Davy Offshore Ltd* [1993] 2 Lloyd's Rep. 582.

relied upon by him,[176] and there is one English case in which it was assumed that an insurer who undertook not to sue a third party was constrained by equitable principles from relying upon the equitable doctrine of subrogation from going back on this undertaking.[177] The outcome in that case has now been confirmed as representing the law by the Contracts (Rights of Third Parties) Act 1999. Under this Act, a person who is not a party to a contract may nevertheless rely upon any term in the contract providing that by the contract either: (a) he has been given a right to enforce that term (s.1(1)(a)); or (b) he is an intended beneficiary of the term (s.1(1)(b)) and the contract on its proper construction does not preclude enforcement by him (s.1(2)). In either case the third party must be identified by name, description or membership of a class (s.1(3)). Reliance on a term by a third party may be positive, in that it gives rise to an action against insurers, or it may be negative, in that it provides a defence against insurers. A subrogation waiver clause falls into the latter category, and accordingly the effect of the 1999 Act is to allow a third party who is given the benefit of a subrogation waiver clause to plead that clause against the insurers who seek to proceed against him in breach of it.

11–039   *Agreements with wrongdoers.* A subrogated insurer may also deprive itself of subrogation rights by entering into an agreement with the third-party wrongdoer limiting the latter's liability to a specific amount. Difficult conceptual questions arise in this type of case, for it is by no means clear that such an agreement prevents the assured—as opposed to the insurer—from proceeding against the third party for a greater sum, in which case the insurer theoretically is entitled to claim that greater sum from the assured and thereby to sidestep its settlement with the third party. The point arose in *Kitchen Design and Advice Ltd v Lea Valley Water Co,*[178] in which the claimant's premises were flooded by the defendant's negligence. The claimant's property insurers entered into a full and final settlement with the defendant's liability insurers, but thereafter the claimant sought additional sums from its property insurers, Blocked by the settlement from recovering the additional sum from the defendant's liability insurers, the claimant's insurers instigated subrogation proceedings in the claimant's name against the defendant, asserting that neither the claimant nor the defendant were bound by the settlement. The court was able to prevent this sidestepping of the settlement by holding that the claimant's policy authorised the insurers to settle all claims and that the settlement was to be construed as an agreement that subrogation rights would not be exercised.

Loss of subrogation rights: agreements by the assured

11–040   *The issues.* Where the assured agrees with a potential third-party wrongdoer that the third party is not to face liability for causing loss of a given description to the assured, and that loss comes within the scope of an insurance policy, two questions fall to be determined. First, is the agreement binding on the insurer, thereby preventing its exercise of rights which the assured would otherwise have had against the third party? Given that the assured is the nominal claimant in subrogation proceedings, and that the insurer cannot have any better rights than

---

[176] *Clark & Sons Ltd v Finnamore* 32 D.L.R. (3d) 236 (1972); *Fraser River Pile & Dredge Ltd v Can-Drive Services Ltd* (1997) 98 B.C.A.C. 138; *Timberwest Forest Corp v Pacific Link Ocean Services Corp* 2008 F.C. 801.

[177] *The Surf City* [1995] 2 Lloyd's Rep. 242.

[178] *Kitchen Design and Advice Ltd v Lea Valley Water Co* [1989] 2 Lloyd's Rep. 221.

those possessed by the assured, the general answer must be that subrogation rights are lost. One possible exception is mentioned below. Second, does the insurer have any cause of action against the assured for prejudicing its rights by entering into such an agreement? The answer to this question depends largely upon when the agreement was entered into, and for the purpose of analysis it is necessary to consider three different situations: agreements prior to the loss; agreements after the loss but before the assured has received a full indemnity; and agreements after full indemnity.

Agreements prior to the loss. The insurer's rights of subrogation depend entirely   **11–041**
on the assured having a right of action against the third party. In the absence of such an action, the insurer has no recourse to the third party. Whether or not the assured does have an action against the third party will depend entirely on their relationship; if it is contractual, it will be necessary for the court to construe the contract to determine whether a cause of action in respect of the loss in question has been preserved. The issues which here arise were discussed earlier in this chapter.

As far as the insurer's rights against the assured are concerned, if the insurer issues a policy to an assured whose legal rights against a third party have previously been defined, it can hardly be said that the insurer's subrogation rights have been prejudiced, for they simply never come into existence. In these circumstances it would seem that the insurer's only remedy is to avoid the policy for the assured's failure to disclose a material fact, namely that there is no recourse to the third party in respect of specific insured losses. Any duty of disclosure is necessarily of limited ambit. In the first place, if the limitation is one customarily or commonly found in the class of contract in question, the insurer is deemed to be aware of it,[179] so that any duty of disclosure must be confined to unusual apportionment of liability clauses. Secondly, facts which diminish the insurer's rights of subrogation and salvage are prima facie immaterial and are required to be disclosed only where the assured is aware that premium-rating depends upon such rights. In *Tate & Sons v Hyslop*,[180] the assured cargo owner entered into an agreement with lightermen under which they were to be liable only for negligence and were not to face the more onerous duties owed by common carriers. The cargo insurer operated a dual premium structure under which a higher premium was charged where lightermen were liable only in negligence, but the assured did not disclose that such an agreement existed and obtained insurance at the lower premium rate. The Court of Appeal held that a material fact had not been disclosed, so that the policy could be avoided. However, the court stressed the exceptional nature of the case and, in particular, that it did not raise the general question whether an agreement which restricted potential subrogation rights amounted to a material fact. If it can be shown that subrogation recoveries do permit premium levels to be kept at a lower level than would otherwise be possible,[181] inability to exercise subrogation rights would appear to fall squarely within the definition of materiality.

There remains the possibility that the assured has entered into an agreement with the third party, exempting the latter from liability, after the inception of the

---

[179] See s.18(3)(b) of the Marine Insurance Act 1906. For a case in which the insurer was either aware of the relevant information, or at least had waived its disclosure, see *The Auditor* (1924) 18 Ll. L.R. 403.

[180] *Tate & Sons v Hyslop* (1885) 15 Q.B.D. 368. See also *Marc Rich & Co AG v Portman* [1996] 1 Lloyd's Rep. 430, a point which did not arise on appeal, [1997] 1 Lloyd's Rep. 225.

[181] There is some doubt as to this: see Hasson (1984) 13 O.J.L.S. 416.

policy but before any loss has occurred. It is clear that, in the absence of any warranty concerning subrogation recoveries, the insurer cannot avoid the policy. It is also clear that the insurer's contingent subrogation rights come into existence as soon as the policy is entered into.[182] Consequently, it is possible that the assured might face liability in damages to the insurer for entering into a pre-loss agreement of this nature, at least if there is no bona fide commercial reason for such an agreement. It is equally arguable, however, that in this situation there is merely an increase in risk which, in line with general principles, the insurer must bear.[183]

It has been held in Australia that there is no implied obligation on an assured to refrain from entering into an agreement after the policy has incepted which exempts or restricts the third party's liability: *State Government Insurance Office (Qld) v Brisbane Stevedoring Pty Ltd.*[184] As was there pointed out, until the contract is made there are no contingent subrogation rights of subrogation available to the insurers so that it cannot be said that the assured has prejudiced those rights.

11–042   *Agreements after the loss but before full indemnity.* Any agreement compromising the third party's liability to the assured is undoubtedly binding on the insurer, and the only question is whether the insurer can bring an action against the assured for compromising its rights. The policy may well prohibit any negotiations between assured and third party or any settlement, in which case the assured will face liability in respect of the loss of subrogation rights suffered by the insurer.[185] Even in the absence of an express provision, the assured may not reach any settlement with the third party which is prejudicial to the insurer's rights of subrogation. This is so because there is an implied term in the insurance contract prohibiting any agreement of this type.[186] Thus, where buildings were destroyed by fire, and the assured agreed to reduce a claim for compensation she had against Plymouth Corporation by the amount she had received from her insurers, the insurers were entitled to recover that amount from her.[187] This principle is subject to the important qualification that, until he has been indemnified in full, the assured retains the right to control the action against the third party, including the right to reach a bona fide settlement with the third party, of the third party's liability. It is thus the case that the assured's liability to the insurer attaches only where the settlement has not been reached bona fide in the interests of both the assured and insurer.[188] On the same principle, where the assured is not insured for the full amount of his loss, and reaches a compromise settlement with the third party, that settlement is presumed to relate only to the uninsured part of the loss in so far as the settlement is not bona fide.[189]

---

[182] *Boag v Standard Marine Insurance Co Ltd* [1937] 2 K.B. 113.

[183] See *SGIO v Brisbane Stevedoring* (1969) 123 C.L.R. 228.

[184] *State Government Insurance Office (Qld) v Brisbane Stevedoring Pty Ltd* (1969) 123 C.L.R. 228.

[185] *Horwood v Land of Leather Ltd* [2010] EWHC 546 (Comm).

[186] See *Napier and Ettrick (Lord) v Kershaw* [1993] 1 All E.R. 385, per Lord Templeman. This was so held in *Horwood v Land of Leather Ltd* [2010] EWHC 546 (Comm).

[187] *Commercial Union Assurance Co v Lister* (1874) L.R. Ch. App. 483.

[188] *Commercial Union Assurance Co v Lister* (1874) L.R. Ch. App. 483; *West of England Fire Insurance Co v Isaacs* [1897] 1 Q.B. 226; *Phoenix Assurance Co v Spooner* [1905] 2 K.B. 753; *Horwood v Land of Leather Ltd* [2010] EWHC 546 (Comm). Cf. *Globe & Rutgers Fire Insurance Co v Truedell* [1927] 2 D.L.R. 659 and *Willumsen v Royal Exchange Insurance Co Ltd* 63 D.L.R. (3d) 112 (1975), where the settlements were bona fide. See also *Pang Wai Chung v Hoi Tat Rubber Factory* [1992] 2 H.K.C. 447.

[189] *Law Fire Assurance Co v Oakley* (1888) 4 T.L.R. 309; *Horse, Carriage and General Insurance Co v Petch* (1916) 33 T.L.R. 131.

However, while it is the case that the assured may not renounce or compromise any rights he has, the insurers have no right to call upon him to exercise a possible option to be released from a contract in circumstances in which no honourable man would exercise it.[190]

Agreements after full indemnity. Once the assured has received a full indemnity **11–043** either from the insurer alone or from a combination of payments by the insurer and the third party, the assured loses the right to control proceedings brought in his name against the third party. Not only is there an implied term to this effect, but it was also suggested by Lords Templeman, Goff and Browne-Wilkinson in *Napier and Ettrick (Lord) v Kershaw* that the insurer has an equitable charge on the cause of action. The latter suggestion has subsequently been rejected, in *Re Ballast Plc, St Paul Travellers Insurance Co Ltd v Dargan*,[191] but even disregarding that point it remains the case that following indemnification the assured has no right as against the insurer to reach any form of settlement with the third party, even one which is bona fide, although in that case the insurer may find it difficult to prove that it has suffered any loss. The outstanding question is the position of the third party under a settlement reached with a fully indemnified assured. As a matter of principle, the settlement between assured and third party would appear to be binding as against the insurer, for the insurer must act in the assured's name and can have no better rights than the assured. There is, however, county court authority for the proposition that a third party who is aware that the assured has lost control of the action may not be able to plead the settlement in defence to a subrogation action by the insurer.[192] The reasoning of the county court judge, that payment by the insurer operates as an equitable assignment of the rights of the assured so that any subsequent conduct by the assured cannot bind the insurer, has its prima facie attractions, but is unsound, for it is settled that subrogation rights arise before payment and in any event do not amount to an equitable assignment but merely to a right conferred upon the insurer to use the assured's name.

2. DOUBLE INSURANCE AND CONTRIBUTION

Double insurance

The rights of the assured. It is perfectly lawful at common law for an assured to **11–044** insure any subject matter in which he has an insurable interest as many times, and under as many policies, as he wishes.[193] The principle was first adopted in early marine insurance cases[194] but is of general application,[195] and doubtless was to a greater or lesser extent based on the absence of any financial controls over

[190] *Sparkes v Marshall* (1836) 2 Bing. N.C. 761; *Inglis v Stock* (1885) 10 App.Cas. 263.
[191] *Re Ballast Plc, St Paul Travellers Insurance Co Ltd v Dargan* [2007] Lloyd's Rep. I.R. 742.
[192] *Haigh v Lawford* (1964) 114 N.L.J. 208.
[193] *Godin v London Assurance Co* (1758) 1 Burr. 489; *Albion Insurance Co Ltd v Government Insurance Office of New South Wales* (1969) 121 C.L.R. 342.
[194] *Newby v Reed* (1763) 1 Wm. Bl. 416; *Rogers v Davis* (1777) 2 Park (8th edn) 601; *Bousfield v.Barnes* (1815) 4 Camp 228; *Morgan v Price* (1849) 4 Exch. 615; *Bruce v Jones* (1863) 1 M. & R. 769.
[195] See North *British Insurance v London, Liverpool & Globe Insurance* (1877) 5 Ch D 569 at 583, per Mellish L.J. and 587, per Baggallay L.J. Continental law makes successive insurers liable in order of date, and American policies generally adopt that rule. However, Canadian law adopted the English approach: *Bank of British North America v Western* (1884) 7 Ont. App. 166.

insurers and the risk that any one of them might not be able to honour his obligations under the policy. Where the assured does take out more than one policy in respect of the same loss, he is said to have taken out double insurance. The meaning of double insurance was worked out in a series of early marine cases, commencing with *Godin v London Assurance Co*, and was codified for marine purposes by the Marine Insurance Act 1906 s.32(1):

> "Where two or more policies are effected by or on behalf of the assured on the same adventure and interest or any part thereof, and the sums exceed the indemnity allowed by this Act, the assured is said to be overinsured by double insurance."

The fact that there is double insurance does not necessarily mean that he can recover separately under each policy, for the common law principle of indemnity provides that an assured can recover in the aggregate at most only an amount representing his actual—or, in the case of a valued policy, his agreed—loss, so that in the case of overinsurance by way of double insurance, part of the total sum insured will not be recoverable. However, there is no restriction in the general law as to the order in which the assured may proceed against individual insurers; he may thus seek to claim his entire loss from one insurer, leaving the others free from liability to him.[196] This rule is obviously essential to the original function of double insurance, the fear of insurer insolvency. Moreover, there is no common law obligation on the assured to disclose that he has earlier taken out a policy covering the same risk, unless the degree of overinsurance is such as to give rise to the prospect of fraud.[197]

The principles governing the relationship between the right of the assured to obtain double insurance and the indemnity principle have also been codified by legislation, in the Marine Insurance Act 1906 s.32(2):

> "Where the assured is overinsured by double insurance:
>   (a) The assured, unless the policy otherwise provides, may claim payment from the insurers in such order as he may think fit, provided that he is not entitled to receive any sum in excess of the indemnity allowed by this Act.
>   (b) Where the policy under which the assured claims is a valued policy, the assured must give credit as against the valuation for any sum received by him under any other policy without regard to the actual value of the subject matter insured.[198]
>   (c) Where the policy under which the assured claims is an unvalued policy he must give credit, as against the full insurable value, for any sum received by him under the policy.
>   (d) Where the assured receives any sum in excess of the indemnity allowed by this Act, he is deemed to hold such sum in trust for the insurers, according to their rights of contribution amongst themselves."

If the assured is insured under both a valued and an unvalued policy, and the subject matter insured has been overvalued so that more is recoverable under the unvalued policy than under the valued policy, the assured does better, in the light of the Marine Insurance Act 1906 s.32(2)(b), to claim under the valued policy first, as he will otherwise be held to the agreed value. Thus if the assured has insured his property for £500 with insurer A under a valued policy, and for £750 with insurer B under an unvalued policy, and a loss of £750 is suffered, the

---

[196] *Newby v Reed* (1763) 1 Wm. Bl. 416; *Bousfield v Barnes* (1815) 4 Camp. 228; *Bruce v Jones* (1863) 1 H. & C. 769.
[197] *Mathie v Argonaut Marine Ins Co* (1925) 21 Ll. L.R. 145.
[198] Based on *Bruce v Jones* (1863) 1 H. & C. 769.

assured cannot claim £250 from B and then £500 from A: the Marine Insurance Act 1906 s.32(2)(b), permits the assured to recover only £250 from A. The assured must in this example look to A first. In *Bruce v Jones*[199] property was valued at £9,000 and insured for £2,000 with one insurer, and valued at £8,000 and insured for £8,000 with another insurer. The assured claimed £2,000 from the first insurer, and it was held that he was entitled to no more than £6,000 from the second insurer, the balance of £8,000. However, if the assured had claimed £8,000 from the second insurer, he would have been entitled to £1,000, the balance of £9,000, from the first insurer. The position is of course reversed if the subject matter has been overvalued under a valued policy.

Return of premium. One question which is of some complexity is whether the assured is entitled to claim a rateable return of his premium from each insurer, in a manner representing the amount by which he is overinsured by double insurance. At common law the guiding principle was and remains that premiums are indivisible, so that once the risk has attached, the assured is not entitled to a return of any part of the premium where the risk subsequently proves to be less than was originally believed to be the case.[200] This rule is now enshrined in the Marine Insurance Act 1906 ss.82 to 84. However, a number of exceptions have been developed to this principle, and early cases on marine insurance established that return of premiums was permissible at common law in the event of double insurance.[201] This exception was taken up by the Marine Insurance Act 1906 s.84(3)(f):   **11–045**

> "Where the assured has overinsured by double insurance, a proportionate part of the several premiums is returnable:
>
>   Provided that, if the policies are effected at different times, and any earlier policy has at any time borne the entire risk, or if a claim has been paid on the policy in respect of the full amount insured thereby, no premium is returnable in respect of that policy, and when double insurance is effected knowingly by the assured no premium is returnable."

What is not clear, however, is whether the limited right of return available in marine insurance extends to property and liability policies. There is no judicial authority on the matter, although in practice, there is no real difficulty because policies frequently state the limited circumstances, if any, in which any part of the premium is to be returnable.

Policy variations on the assured's rights. The above principles have caused some difficulty to insurers. First, the principle that overinsurance is lawful has led to frequent cases of fraud by assureds who overinsure and then destroy the insured subject matter, hoping to recover from a number of insurers independently. Second, the rule that the assured may select the degree of liability to which each insurer is to be subject, while serving to protect the assured against the dangers of the insolvency of one or more of his insurers, has been regarded as unfair by those insurers forced to bear an undue burden of an individual loss. This particular issue is resolved to some extent by the equitable principle of contribution, which permits an insurer who has paid more than his fair share of a loss to recover contributions from other insurers: this is discussed in detail   **11–046**

---

[199] *Bruce v Jones* (1863) 1 H. & C. 769.
[200] *Tyrie v Fletcher* (1772) 2 Cowp. 666.
[201] *Fisk v Masterman* (1841) 8 M. & W. 165.

below. However, the right of contribution does not shift the initial burden on an individual insurer of making disproportionate payment to the assured if he so elects. To overcome these problems insurers have adopted a number of defensive measures. These include: a requirement on the assured to disclose in pre-contractual negotiations the existence of any other insurance covering the same subject matter; an obligation on the assured not to take out any further insurance on the insured subject matter during the currency of the policy, either absolutely, failing which the policy terminates, or in the absence of the insurer's permission; a provision which converts the policy into an excess layer policy in the event that some other insurance is taken out by the assured[202]; and a provision to the effect that in the event of the existence of a number of concurrent insurances, the insurer is to bear only its own proportion of the loss (a rateable proportion clause).

These and similar provisions will only be operative if the assured has actually taken out a second valid policy[203] or has paid the premiums under that policy so that the risk attaches under it.[204] In the same way, effecting a policy which is voidable necessarily constitutes a breach of a clause in an earlier policy banning, or otherwise restricting the assured's right to enter into, any further insurance. However, if the later insurer seeks to avoid his policy, such avoidance is retroactive and will have the effects of eliminating the assured's breach of duty in taking out that policy.[205]

11–047   *Removal or restriction of cover where other cover exists.* A clause of this type relates to the cover provided by the first policy rather than to its existence, and may remove, postpone or limit cover in the event that there is another policy in existence at the date of the loss. This type of clause can operate only if the second policy is valid and subsisting at the date of the loss and, in the case of a voidable policy, has not been retroactively avoided.[206]

Three types of clause are commonly found in English policies. The most extreme is the "escape" clause, under which the insurers are simply not liable in the event that there is any other policy in force. Less extreme but in most cases to similar effect is the "excess" clause, under which the policy becomes an excess cover in the event that there is any other policy in force, so that liability is postponed until all other cover is exhausted. The third mechanism is the rateable proportion clause, under which in the event of other insurance the assured is limited to recovering only a proportionate part of the loss from the insurers.

The difficulty which arises here is that the policies involved may all contain similar provisions, the effect being that each of them purports to cast the loss onto the other. In some cases the problem can be overcome if the wording of one of the policies is not absolute. This was so held in *Evans v Maritime Medical Care*

---

[202] *Chui Man Kwan v Bank of China Group Insurance Co Ltd* [2008] H.K.E.C. 1190. This device is commonly used where a policy is taken out by an international holding company for the benefit of itself and its subsidiaries: the global policy may stipulate that any local policy taken out by a subsidiary is to be a first layer cover, with the global policy operating only as an excess cover which attaches once the limits of indemnity under the local policy have been exceeded.

[203] *Sickness & Accident v General Accident* 1892 19 R. (Ct of Sess) 977; *Woods v Co-operative Insurance* 1924 S.C. 692.

[204] *Equitable Fire and Accident Office Ltd v Ching Wo Hong* [1907] A.C. 96.

[205] *Drake Insurance Co v Provident Insurance Co* [2004] Lloyd's Rep. I.R. 277; *O'Kane v Jones* [2005] Lloyd's Rep. I.R. 174.

[206] *Home Insurance Co of New York v Gavel* (1928) 30 Ll. L.R. 139.

Inc.[207] Here, the claimant, who had been injured in a motor vehicle accident, was covered by two separate policies: a motor liability policy, and a group hospital benefits policy. The motor policy excluded the insurer's liability for any expenses recoverable under a hospital plan. The hospital plan excluded cover if similar benefits were payable under any other contract. The Supreme Court of Nova Scotia held that the hospital plan exclusion was conditional upon payment being available under some other policy, whereas the motor policy's exclusion was absolute. This meant that the hospital plan exclusion could have no effect in the light of the clear wording of the motor policy exclusion, and the hospital plan thus had to meet the assured's claim for hospitalisation expenses. Similarly, a clause which postpones liability under a policy, converting it into an excess cover if there is some other policy in force, is effective if there is no similar provision in that other policy.[208]

Concurrent "escape" clauses. If the wording of an escape clause is absolute, it will cast the loss onto other insurers. It may be, however, that the wording of the clauses in all of the policies is absolute, and the danger is that none of them can respond to the loss. This matter has been the subject of a number of decisions. The first of these was *Gale v Motor Union Insurance Co.*[209] The claimant's car and his road traffic liabilities were insured with Motor Union under a motor policy, one term of which extended its coverage to persons driving the car with his consent. One Loyst, who was himself insured under a motor policy issued by General Accident, caused an accident while driving the claimant's car with his consent, and a dispute arose as to the liability of the respective insurers. Both policies contained clauses the effect of which was to exempt each insurer from liability in the event of the existence of concurrent insurance, and both also contained rateable proportion clauses. Roche J. held that each company was bound to pay one half of the loss, on the ground that the exclusion clauses were modified and explained by the rateable proportion clauses, and had to be read subject to them. The prospect of self-cancelling liabilities was by this means avoided by the learned judge, but there are at least indications in the judgment which point towards the conclusion that exclusion clauses unaccompanied by rateable proportion clauses might well force a court to decide that neither insurer is liable.

Fortunately, this possibility was laid to rest soon afterwards in *Weddell v Road Traffic and General Insurance Co Ltd*,[210] the facts of which were on all fours with those of *Gale* but for the crucial difference that the policy of the assured's brother, who had been driving the assured's car with his consent, did not contain a rateable proportion clause. Rowlatt J. was thus faced squarely with the proposition that where two policies, each casting liability on to the other, have been effected, the policies are self-cancelling. This notion was rejected in clear terms:

"The reasonable construction is to exclude from the category of co existing cover any cover which is expressed to be itself cancelled by such co-existence, and to hold in such cases that both companies are liable ... one would reach the absurd result that whichever policy one looks at it is always the other one which is effective."

11–048

[207] *Evans v Maritime Medical Care Inc* 87 D.L.R. (4th) 173 (1992).
[208] *Chui Man Kwan v Bank of China Group Insurance Co Ltd* [2008] H.K.E.C. 1190.
[209] *Gale v Motor Union Insurance Co* [1928] 1 K.B. 359.
[210] *Weddell v Road Traffic and General Insurance Co Ltd* [1932] 2 K.B. 563.

Weddell was regarded as trite law by Moore-Bick J. in *Structural Polymer Systems Ltd and Structural Polymer Technologies Ltd v Brown*[211] and received the unanimous approval of the Court of Appeal in *National Employers Mutual General Insurance Association Ltd v Haydon*,[212] a decision which is of particular significance to liability insurers. Here, a firm of solicitors had taken out a liability policy which contained a variant of the type of exclusion clause under discussion: the insurer's liability was not eliminated in the event of concurrent insurance, but was merely postponed to that of any other insurance under which the assured could seek indemnity, so that the insurer was responsible only for the amount by which the sums recoverable from other insurers fell short of that necessary to provide the assured with a complete indemnity. The policy had been written on a "claims made", so that the insurer was liable to meet all claims made against the assured during the currency of the policy, although the policy also permitted the assured to notify circumstances likely to give rise to a claim within the policy period and thereby to bring those within the scope of the cover. In accordance with the terms of the insurance, the assured had notified the insurer of an occurrence likely to result in a claim against it, that notice having been given on March 24, 1976, the last day of the currency of the policy. This particular policy was not renewed thereafter, but was replaced by a new liability policy sponsored by the Law Society (the "master policy") which took effect at midnight on March 24, 1976. The master policy was also written on a "claims made" basis, the insurer being responsible for losses arising from claims notified to the assured during the currency of the policy irrespective of the date on which the event giving rise to those losses had occurred. Clause 5 of the master policy limited the insurer's liability in the following way:

" . . . (b) this insurance shall not indemnify the assured in respect of any loss arising out of any claim
(iii) in respect of any circumstance or occurrence which has been notified under any other insurance attaching prior to the inception of this certificate."

The problem for the court was whether the exclusion in the master policy operated to remove liability under that policy. Lloyd J. at first instance approached the problem as one of pure double insurance. In the view of the learned judge, each insurer was on risk in the circumstances which had arisen, and each had sought to avoid liability in the event of some other insurer being on risk. Looked at in this way, the case bore a remarkable resemblance to *Weddell*, the only difficulty being that cl.5(b)(iii) of the master policy was not expressed in traditional *Weddell* form; indeed, the exclusion clauses in the competing policies were in very different forms from each other. However, Lloyd J., looking to the substance rather than to the form of the matter, held that both clauses were nonetheless attempts to exclude liability and that, on the authority of *Weddell*, the clauses were to be construed as not applicable to competing policies; the insurers were thus to bear the assured's loss in proportion to their individual liabilities. This decision was reversed by the Court of Appeal. So far as the Court of Appeal was concerned, cl.5(b)(iii) in the master policy was not an exclusion clause by its nature, but merely defined that insurer's liability: it did not seek to remove a pre-existing liability but rather to prevent any liability from ever arising. By this

[211] *Structural Polymer Systems Ltd and Structural Polymer Technologies Ltd v Brown* Unreported, October 27, 1998. See also *Trenton Cold Storage Ltd v St Paul Fire & Marine Insurance Co* (1999) 11 C.C.L.I. (3d) 127.
[212] *National Employers Mutual General Insurance Association Ltd v Haydon* [1980] 2 Lloyd's Rep. 149, reversing [1979] 2 Lloyd's Rep. 235.

reasoning the Court of Appeal concluded that the facts of the case did not disclose a double insurance at all, as the master policy simply did not extend to losses occurring during its currency but which had been notified under previous claims made liability policies. It might be thought that the distinction between a clause which prevents liability from arising, and a clause which excludes an accrued liability, is too fine to be justified and that the approach taken by Lloyd J. has much to commend it.

There is no authority on the relationship between Policy A containing an "escape" clause and Policy B containing an "excess" clause. There is certainly a plausible argument that the two clauses would not be self-cancelling. There can be no liability under Policy A because Policy B is in existence and provides cover unless there is some other policy in existence which provides cover. However, there is no other policy in existence providing cover, because Policy A is negative by the existence of Policy B.

Concurrent "excess" clauses. Subject to what has been said in the preceding paragraph, an "excess" clause operates in much the same way as an "escape" clause. If each of two policies postpones cover until the liability of the other is exhausted, the only sensible approach is to regard the two clauses as self-cancelling, so that each insurer is liable. This was assumed to be the case in *Austin v Zurich General Accident & Liability Insurance Co Ltd.*[213]   **11–049**

"Rateable proportion" clauses. Rateable proportion clauses differ in their   **11–050** wording, but the broad intention of such clauses is to limit the insurer's liability to the assured to its share of the loss if, at the time of the loss, any other insurance covering the same risk is in effect. The main consequence of such a clause so far as the assured is concerned is to limit his right to proceed against the various insurers in the order of his choice, although his ultimate ability to claim an indemnity is not affected: in the result, then, the contribution takes place at the stage at which the assured has made a claim rather than at the later stage at which one or more insurers have met the loss in full and seek to proceed against other insurers for contribution. The one serious disadvantage of rateable proportion clauses from the assured's point of view is that the risk of the insolvency of any of the insurers in question is removed from the remaining insurers and is imposed upon him. The validity of rateable proportion clauses has been confirmed in numerous decisions, and it is clear that if each of the policies contains a rateable proportion clause, then each insurer can be liable only for its own proportion whereas if only one policy contains such a clause then the other must meet the entire loss. The main issue which arises in respect of rateable proportion clauses is whether an insurer who pays the full amount of the loss despite being required to pay only a proportion of it is thereby precluded, by his voluntary conduct, from exercising contribution rights.

A rateable proportion clause is usually framed so as to limit the insurers' liability where there is other insurance in force at the same time that a claim arises under the policy. This form of wording is obviously satisfied where the two policies are in force for the same period and the loss occurs in that period. However, it poses difficulties where the policies are not concurrent but both nevertheless respond to the same loss. This was the position in *Phillips v Syndicate 992 Gunner.*[214] This case was a sequel to the decision of the House of

[213] *Austin v Zurich General Accident & Liability Insurance Co Ltd* (1944) 77 Ll. L.R. 409.
[214] *Phillips v Syndicate 992 Gunner* [2004] Lloyd's Rep. I.R. 418.

Lords in *Fairchild v Glenhaven Funeral Services Ltd*,[215] in which their Lordships ruled that an employee exposed to asbestos by a succession of employers but unable to prove exactly which exposure led to the development of his mesothelioma could sue any of the employers. Although the point was not decided by *Fairchild*, the assumption was that each of the employers was liable to the employee for the full amount of the employee's loss (subject of course to a subsequent right to seek contribution from other employers). That assumption was subsequently undermined by the House of Lords in *Barker v Corus (UK) Ltd*,[216] their Lordships ruling that an employer was liable only for its proportionate share of the loss, although the method of calculating that proportionate share was left unresolved. However, the assumption underlying *Fairchild* was reinstated by the Compensation Act 1006 s.3, which operates retrospectively to the date of the judgment in *Barker*.[217] *Phillips* itself concerned an employer who was sued by an employee. The defendant insurers had been the employer's liability insurers for the period 1959 to 1968, representing about 72.5 per cent of the employee's period of employment with the employer. The insurance was in losses occurring form, rendering the insurers liable to indemnify the employer for injuries suffered by the employee during the currency of the policy. In light of *Fairchild* it could not be disputed that the employee's injury was suffered on exposure, but it was impossible to ascertain which exposure triggered the disease. The insurers sought to rely upon a rateable proportion clause in the policy, arguing that under the rules of contribution the various insurers on risk during the period of employment would be required to allocate losses between themselves on a time on risk basis. Eady J., without commenting on the correctness of this assumption, held that the rateable proportion clause did not apply to consecutive policies and that the insurers were fully liable to indemnify the employer for the claim against it. The rateable proportion clause applied only where there were two or more policies on risk when the claim arose, but as the claim was the exposure it followed that there could only have been one policy in force on that date even though it was impossible to pinpoint that date. Eady J. also rejected arguments by the insurers for an implied term or a market custom limiting liability to time on risk.

11–051   *"Rateable proportion" clauses and other clauses.* If Policy A contains an escape or excess clause, and Policy B contains a rateable proportion clause, Policy A will not cover the loss by reason of the existence of Policy B, and the rateable proportion clause in Policy B cannot apply because there is no other available cover. In short, a rateable proportion clause is overridden by an escape clause or

---

[215] *Fairchild v Glenhaven Funeral Services Ltd* [2002] 3 W.L.R. 89.

[216] *Barker v Corus (UK) Ltd* [2006] UKHL 20.

[217] Under s.3, an employer or person responsible is liable for the entirety of the employee's claim for mesothelioma if: (a) the person responsible has negligently or in breach of statutory duty caused or permitted the employee to be exposed to asbestos (or has failed to prevent such exposure); (b) the employee has contracted mesothelioma as a result; (c) it is not possible to determine whether that exposure or some other exposure caused the illness; and (d) there is liability in tort (as decided in *Fairchild*). The person responsible does, however, have a contribution claim against other persons who faced similar liability, based on time on risk or any other basis of apportionment that the court thinks appropriate. See *Durham v BAI (Run Off) Ltd* [2009] Lloyd's Rep. I.R. 295 and *Sienkiewicz v Greif (UK) Ltd* [2009] EWCA Civ 1159. The Compensation Act 2006 (Contribution for Mesothelioma Claims) Regulations 2006 (SI 2006/3259) empower the Financial Services Authority to make rules for compensation of mesothelioma victims under the Financial Services Compensation Scheme where employers' liability insurers have become insolvent in respect of claims made before December 1, 2001 (the date on which the FSCS came into effect, replacing the Policyholders' Protection scheme).

excess clause. In *National Farmers Union Mutual Insurance Society Ltd v HSBC Insurance (UK) Ltd*[218] the sellers of a building were insured against damage to it. The sellers' policy also provided cover for the buyers subject to the following clause:

> "We will not pay any claim if any loss, damage or liability covered under this insurance is also covered wholly or in part under any other insurance except in respect of any excess beyond the amount which would have been covered under such other insurance had this insurance not been effected."

The buyers were themselves insured under a policy which provided that "If when you claim there is other insurance covering the same accident, illness, damage or liability, we will only pay our share." The property was damaged by fire between contract and conveyance. The buyers paid the full contract price and were indemnified by their insurers. Those insurers sought contribution from the sellers' insurers, on the basis that the sellers' policy provided cover for the buyers. Gavin Kealey QC, sitting as Deputy High Court Judge, dismissed the buyer's insurers' claim on the short ground that the extension in the sellers' policy did not apply if the buyers had their own insurance, but he further suggested that the excess clause prevailed over the rateable proportion clause, and rejected contrary dicta of Tucker J. in *Austin v Zurich General Accident & Liability Insurance Co Ltd*[219] In that case the claimant's motor policy (Policy A) contained an escape clause and an excess clause. Another policy which also covered the claimant's liability (Policy B) contained an escape clause and a rateable proportion clause. Contribution was held not to be available by reason of a breach of condition in Policy B, but Tucker J. expressed the view that, having cancelled out the two excess clauses, the rateable proportion clause in Policy B meant each insurer was liable for 50 per cent of the loss. That conclusion plainly cannot stand with *National Farmers Union.*

The later English approach has been adopted in other jurisdictions. In *Chui Man Kwan v Bank of China Group Insurance Co Ltd*[220] two liability policies covered injuries to the claimant: one issued by the Bank of China to a subcontractor and one issued by Tugu to his employer. Each policy contained a rateable proportion clause. The Tugu policy also contained a non-contribution clause which rendered the policy an excess policy:

> "if at the time of any claim under this policy there is any other insurance indemnifying any person or insured or insureds who are entitled to be indemnified under this policy, this policy is not to be called upon in contribution and, subject to the policy limits of indemnity, is only to pay any amount if and so far as not recoverable under such other insurance."

The rateable proportion clause was subject to this provision. The Court held that the two rateable proportion clauses did not cancel each other out, and that the position was that Tugu was liable only for any sum uninsured by the Bank of China policy. So where one policy contains a rateable proportion clause and the other contains an excess clause, the excess clause prevails and the rateable

---

[218] *National Farmers Union Mutual Insurance Society Ltd v HSBC Insurance (UK) Ltd* [2010] EWHC 773 (Comm).

[219] *Austin v Zurich General Accident & Liability Insurance Co Ltd* (1944) 77 Ll. L.R. 409, but interestingly Mr Kealey QC did not refer to the fact that the decision of Tucker J. was upheld on appeal by the Court of Appeal, [1945] 2 K.B. 250, and his reasoning was expressly approved.

[220] *Chui Man Kwan v Bank of China Group Insurance Co Ltd* [2008] H.K.E.C. 1190.

proportion clause is overridden. In the present case the Bank of China's policy covered the entire loss and so Tugu was not liable. Similarly, in a New Zealand decision, *State Fire Insurance v Liverpool & London Globe Insurance*,[221] Policy A contained an excess clause and a rateable proportion clause, and Policy B contained a rateable proportion clause only. The court ruled that the rateable proportion clause was to be subordinated to the excess clause, so that Policy A could not respond until Policy B's cover had been exhausted, and Policy B had to pay the whole loss because, until it did, Policy A did not attach.

Contribution: general principles

11–052   *The contribution principle.* If there is double insurance, so that two or more insurers are potentially liable for the same loss, the insurer called upon to make payment may have the right to seek contribution from the other insurers. The right of contribution is an equitable principle of some antiquity which does not rest on contract or statute[222] and which allows one insurer to recover from another by reason of having made payment to the assured in respect of a sum for which the latter was also liable. Contribution should be carefully distinguished from subrogation. Since contribution implies more than one contract of insurance, it is only where there are two or more policies involved that there can be any confusion between the two. Subrogation ensures that the assured receives no more than an indemnity: contribution ensures that the insurers do not suffer injustice amongst themselves because of that rule. Unlike a claim for subrogation, a contribution action must be brought in the insurer's own name.[223] Sometimes both subrogation and contribution are applicable in the same case. Thus, if the owner of premises insures them with two insurers, each of whom pay him in respect of a loss, they will be entitled to contribution between themselves with regard to any subrogation rights against a tenant in respect of repairs. One insurer cannot proceed against the tenant in the assured's name and retain the whole of the proceeds.[224] Contribution, in fact, applies not only to the liabilities, but also to the benefits to which an insurer is entitled, under a policy.

There is a right of contribution only where the following conditions, which are discussed in what follows, are met:

(a) there is double insurance, in that the two policies cover the same assured, the same interest and the same period and are more or less of the same scope;

(b) both policies respond to the loss;

(c) the paying insurer has paid under legal liability and not as a volunteer.

---

[221] *State Fire Insurance v Liverpool & London Globe Insurance* [1952] N.Z.L.R. 5. This case was relied upon in *National Farmers Union*.

[222] In *Bovis Construction Ltd v Commercial Union Insurance Co Ltd* [2001] Lloyd's Rep. I.R. 321 David Steel J. held that the right of contribution is purely equitable, and does not rest on the Civil Liability (Contribution) Act 1978. The equitable principle of contribution was originally one recognised by marine insurance (*Newby v Reed* (1763) 1 Wm. Bl. 416), but was extended to fire (*North British Insurance v London, Liverpool & Globe Insurance* (1877) 5 Ch D 569), liability (*Sickness & Accident Insurance v General Accident Insurance* (1892) 19 R. (Ct of Sess) 977, per Lord Low), fidelity (*American Surety v Wrightson* (1910) 27 T.L.R. 91) and indeed all forms of indemnity insurance. Contribution is an equitable right which rests on the maxim "equality is equity", and equates to the right of contribution between co sureties which exists independent of contract: Hamilton J. in *Amercan Surety Co v Wrightson* (1910) 27 T.L.R. 91 at 93. See also *Legal and General Assurance v Drake Insurance* [1989] 3 All E.R. 923.

[223] *Austin v Zurich Insurance* [1945] 1 K.B. 250.

[224] See Lord Wright in *Boag v Standard Marine Insurance* [1937] 2 K.B. 113 at 123.

Same subject matter. Double insurance arises only where both policies cover the subject matter which has been the subject of the loss. This is essentially a matter of construction of each of the policies. Thus, in *Boag v Economic Insurance Co Ltd*,[225] it was held that a lorry-load of cigarettes insured under an all-risks transit policy did not form part of the assured's stock in trade at a factory at which the load had been temporarily stored, so that the fire insurers of the factory were not liable to contribute towards payments made by the all-risks insurers on the destruction of the factory and the load by fire. **11–053**

Same assured and same interest. The same interest must be covered before there can be double insurance.[226] It commonly occurs that a number of persons each have a different interest in one subject matter, and that each person effects insurance to cover his own interest. Typical illustrations include concurrent interests in land held by landlord and tenant, employer and contractor, or mortgagor and mortgagee, and concurrent interests in goods held by bailor and bailee.[227] There can be no contribution between insurers of these respective parties. **11–054**

There is authority for the proposition that if a mortgagor takes out a policy covering his interest alone, and the mortgagee takes out a policy that covers his own interest only (although the proceeds of which are to be held on trust or account for the mortgagor), there is double insurance and the respective insurers have a right of contribution against each other.[228] That proposition was rejected in *O'Kane v Jones*.[229] Here a hull and machinery policy was taken out by the owner of the vessel and a further hull and machinery policy was taken out by the assured's agent. It was held that there was double insurance on these facts on the basis that the owner's interest was covered under both policies.[230] However, on the hypothesis that the agent's policy covered the agent's interest only, there would not have been double insurance despite the fact that any sums recovered by the agent in excess of his own interest were to be held for the owner.[231]

Whatever the correct position may be as regards the application of contribution to overlapping but not identical policies, it is well established that no right of contribution can arises between the various insurers if the losses relate to different interests. In *North British and Mercantile Insurance Co v London, Liverpool and Globe Insurance Co*,[232] the owners of a quantity of grain entrusted to the custody of wharfingers insured the grain with the claimant company, while the wharfingers insured their liability in respect of the grain with the defendant

[225] *Boag v Economic Insurance Co Ltd* [1954] 2 Lloyd's Rep. 581.
[226] *Andrews v Patriotic Assurance of Ireland* (1886) 18 L.R. Ir. 355.
[227] *Dickson Watch & Jewellery Co Ltd v Mow Tai Insurance & Reinsurance Co Ltd* [1985] 1 H.K.C. 505.
[228] *Nichols v Scottish Union* (1885) 2 T.L.R. 190.
[229] *O'Kane v Jones* [2005] Lloyd's Rep. I.R. 174.
[230] In the situation in which the owner and the agent were insured under the first policy but only the agent was insured under the second policy the court felt that in *O'Kane* it would be immaterial which of the parties made the claim under the first policy: any claim by the owner was to be treated as made on behalf of both himself and the agent, given that the insurers had demanded a signed release from both of them, so that there was double insurance as far as the agent was concerned.
[231] On the principle that an agent is entitled to ensure for the full value of the insured subject matter but may retain as against the assured only that sum representing the agents own insurable interest: this was common ground in *O'Kane*. The court expressed the view, although did not decide the point, that in those circumstances the double recovery by the owner could he resolved by the principle of subrogation.
[232] *North British and Mercantile Insurance Co v London, Liverpool and Globe Insurance Co* (1877) 5 Ch D 569. See also *Darrell v Tibbitts* (1880) 5 QBD 560.

company. Both policies contained a rateable proportion clause whereby, in the event of the existence of other insurances covering the same property, each insurer was to be liable to its assured only for a rateable proportion of the loss. The liability of the insurers fell to be determined following a fire in which the grain was destroyed, and the Court of Appeal concluded that, as the merchants and wharfingers had each insured their own interest, neither policy could be regarded as concurrent insurance on the same property; the rateable proportion clauses thus had no application, nor was there any right of contribution between the insurers, so that each was liable to indemnify its own assured to the full.[233] Thus there is no double insurance between a primary policy and a subsequent excess of loss policy,[234] between a primary policy and an increased value policy[235] or between the insurers of a mortgagor and a mortgagee[236] or a landlord and tenant[237] who have insured their own interests.

The same principle applies where the assured insures different interests in a single subject matter. In a Scottish case, *Westminster Fire Office v Glasgow Provident*,[238] the pursuers, having a hereditable security by bond on certain premises, insured them against fire in the defender's office for £900. Prior securities had been given by the owner upon the same premises to other creditors who had insured in other offices. The premises having been in part destroyed by fire, the prior incumbrancers were paid by their insurers an amount sufficient to reinstate the premises and to pay the rent during the period of reinstatement, but the premises were not in fact reinstated. Before the fire the value of the premises was sufficient to cover the prior bonds and that of the pursuers, but after the fire the value of the premises was so reduced as to be inadequate to meet the balance to the prior creditors, and the pursuers' bond was left entirely uncovered. The House of Lords decided that the pursuers were, notwithstanding the amount paid to the other creditors, entitled to recover their loss.

11–055 *Same period of cover.* As a matter of principle, it is clear that there cannot be double insurance unless there is in existence more than one valid policy attaching to the same interest. There is, for example, no double insurance where one policy is substituted for another.[239] The cases indicate that contribution does not apply to consecutive policies even if they both cover the same loss, a situation which is likely to arise particularly in mesothelioma cases following the passing of the Compensation Act 2006 under which every employer who has negligently exposed an employee to asbestos is liable for 100 per cent of the loss[240]: an employer who has a series of different consecutive liability insurers can seek to recover from any one of them, and the insurer called upon to pay cannot seek to diminish his liability by asserting that a claim could have been made against other insurers.[241]

---

[233] However, the liability of the wharfingers to indemnify the merchants for the loss of the grain would entitle the merchants' insurers to recover in respect of any sums paid by them, by way of subrogation.

[234] *Pacific Employers Insurance Co v Non-Marine Underwriters* 71 D.L.R. (4th) 731 (1990); *Steelclad Ltd v Iron Trades Mutual Insurance Co Ltd* [1984] S.L.T. 304.

[235] *Boag v Standard Marine Insurance* [1937] 2 K.B. 113.

[236] *Scottish Amicable v Northern Assurance* (1883) 11 R. (Ct of Sess) 287.

[237] *Portavon Cinema v Price* (1939) 161 L.T. 417.

[238] *Westminster Fire Office v Glasgow Provident* (1888) 13 App.Cas. 699.

[239] *Union Marine Insurance Co Ltd v Martin* (1866) 35 L.J.C.P. 181.

[240] Reversing *Barker v Corus UK Plc* [2006] UKHL 20.

[241] *Phillips v Syndicate 992 Gunner* [2004] Lloyd's Rep. I.R. 18.

Same scope. The peril which causes the loss must be common to all of the **11–056** policies. Strictly speaking, it would not seem to be material to the existence of double insurance that there is a merely temporary or partial overlap under policies covering entirely different classes of business, so long as the insured subject matter in question happened to fall within each of them, but in practice the English courts have been reluctant to accept this proposition and have been of the opinion that the short-term or coincidental concurrence of policies does not constitute double insurance where rights of contribution are at stake. In *Australian Agricultural Co v Saunders*[242] the assured obtained a fire policy protecting its wool while in transit or warehoused in Sydney prior to shipment, and subsequently effected a marine policy against the loss of the wool during its transportation to London. The fire policy contained a clause preventing any recovery by the assured in the event of the wool being "insured elsewhere" without the insurer's consent and, following a fire at the Sydney warehouse at which the wool had been stored, the fire insurer denied liability on its policy on the basis that loss pending loading was insured by the marine policy. The Court of Exchequer Chamber held that the marine policy did not in fact extend to cover the loss in question, so that the fire insurer had no defence, but there are indications in the judgments to the effect that "insurance elsewhere" was not to be taken to apply to insurances of a different nature which overlapped in part, and that the phrase should be confined to policies covering the same class of business and the same subject matter. It may nevertheless be doubted whether *Saunders* is to be regarded as an authority on double insurance proper, for some emphasis was laid by the court on the fact that the object of the clause in the fire policy was to protect the fire insurer against fraudulent double insurance which increased the peril towards the subject matter insured, a danger which did not arise from accidental overlapping.[243]

The views of Hamilton J. in *American Surety Co of New York v Wrightson*[244] are, however, more difficult to reconcile with the idea that the overlap must be more than incidental. This case concerned a bank which had effected a policy against loss through the dishonesty of its employees, with a limit on recovery of $2,500 per employee, and a further policy for $40,000 against loss caused by any of a number of risks, including theft, fire, dishonesty or negligence of any person, including employees. An individual employee misappropriated the sum of $2,680 and, it having been conceded by both insurers that each policy covered the loss and that a right to contribution arose as a result of the double insurance, it fell to the court to determine exactly how the loss was to be apportioned between them, an aspect of the case discussed further below. In the course of his judgment, Hamilton J. expressed the view, obiter, that the concession relating to double insurance had not been correct, and that the policies were sufficiently different in scope and nature to exclude the contribution requirement. In the light of this, it would seem that the question of whether an incidental overlap in the coverage of two or more policies amounts in law to double insurance remains the subject of some doubt.

The view of this matter taken by the Supreme Court of Ireland is that double insurance does not exist for contribution purposes where the policies incidentally overlap. In *Zurich Insurance Co v Shield Insurance Co*[245] ZI was the motor

---

[242] *Australian Agricultural Co v Saunders* (1875) L.R. 10 C.P. 668.

[243] *Australian Agricultural Co v Saunders* (1875) L.R. 10 C.P. 668 at 678, per Pollock B.

[244] *American Surety Co of New York v Wrightson* (1910) 103 L.T. 663. See also *Boag v Economic Insurance* [1954] 2 Lloyd's Rep. 581.

[245] *Zurich Insurance Co v Shield Insurance Co* [1988] I.R. 174.

insurer of Q and any person driving Q's vehicles with his consent, while SI was Q's employers' liability insurer. S, an employee of Q, was injured by a fellow-employee in a motor accident, with the effect that both of the insurers were potentially liable. Q in fact made a claim against ZI, which paid in full and sought 50 per cent contribution from SI. The Irish Supreme Court held that the policies were different in nature, so that there was no double insurance and thus no right to contribution.

It is not, however, a prerequisite of double insurance for the policies to be identical in scope or in their financial limits, so that the fact that one policy is wider in its scope than the others covering the same property is irrelevant, as is the fact that it is not possible to apportion any specific part of the premium paid under the wider policy to the subject matter in question.

The requirement that the two policies must provide more or less the same cover appears also to have been overlooked in the first instance Scottish decision *Elf Enterprise (Caledonia) Ltd v London Bridge Engineering Ltd*.[246] In this case, the operators of the Piper Alpha oil platform, which exploded with disastrous consequences in 1988, were insured against legal liability. They also had agreements with contractors under which the contractors were to indemnify the operators against any liability which might be incurred by the operators by reason of the contractors' own defaults. The operators were paid substantial sums by the insurers, and the insurers then sought to exercise subrogation rights against the contractors. Lord Caplan held that the insurers and contractors were to be regarded as being in equivalent positions as contractual indemnifiers vis-à-vis the operators, so that the insurers could not exercise subrogation rights against the contractors but merely had a right to seek contribution from them. It is submitted that this reasoning overlooks:

(a) the different nature of the two contracts, which would of itself preclude contribution[247];

(b) the consequence that had the contractors paid first, they could have sought contribution from the insurers even though they were not parties to the insurance contract and had paid no premium for protection under it; and

(c) the long-standing rule applicable to subrogation, namely, that payment by the insurers entitles them to exercise the rights of the assured against any third party who is not an insurer covering the same risk by way of double insurance.

Lord Caplan's decision was subsequently reversed by on appeal, ultimately to the House of Lords, on points (b) and (c).[248] It was held by the House of Lords that, in the case of an indemnity due under a contract of insurance and an indemnity due under any other form of contract, the insurers are indemnifiers of last resort and their liability is subordinate to that of the contractual indemnifiers. The correct remedy for an insurer which has paid in advance of the contractual indemnifier is, therefore, a subrogation action against the third party for the entire sum paid by the insurer rather than a contribution action against the third party for a proportion of the sums paid by the insurer.

---

[246] *Elf Enterprise (Caledonia) Ltd v London Bridge Engineering Ltd* [2000] Lloyd's Rep. I.R. 249.

[247] The parties and their insurable interests were also different: see above.

[248] *Caledonia North Sea Ltd v British Telecommunications Plc* [2002] Lloyd's Rep. I.R. 261.

Financial limits. Contribution applies despite the fact that the policies have **11–057** different financial limits. The method by which contribution is calculated is discussed later in this chapter.

In principle there is no contribution between layers of insurers. However, the situation may arise in which a policy is stated by its terms to become an excess layer policy where some other insurance also responds to the loss. In *Limit (No.3) Ltd v ACE Insurance Ltd*[249] the primary layer insurers denied liability, and the excess insurers, having paid on the basis that they were the only insurers on risk, sought contribution. The Supreme Court of New South Wales ruled that there was no contribution on the facts of the case, because at the date of the loss the excess insurer was not liable—liability arose only after the primary layer had refused to pay. There could be contribution only if both insurers were liable at the date of the loss. Also, there was no contribution because the excess layer was seeking 100 per cent indemnity rather than contribution.[250] However, the court found for the excess layer by applying the equitable concept of recoupment based on unjust enrichment, in that if the primary layer was not bound to indemnify Lloyd's then it would have made a profit from its own wrongdoing.

Defences to contribution claims

Defences available at date of loss. It is apparent that there cannot be a right of **11–058** contribution against an insurer whose policy does not respond to the loss at the time that it occurred.[251] This may be because the cover under the policy is removed under an express policy term where a second policy has been taken out,[252] because the loss falls outside the insuring clause or within the scope of an exception, because the policy has been avoided with retrospective effect for non-disclosure or misrepresentation,[253] because there has been a breach of condition prior to the loss[254] or because there has been a breach of warranty which has had the effect of automatically determining the risk under the policy.

Defences available after loss. There is some conflict in the authorities on the **11–059** availability of a contribution claim where the non-paying insurer has established a defence which takes effect after the loss has occurred. The question which arises is whether the right of contribution attaches as soon as a loss occurs for which both insurers are liable, or whether it attaches only on payment by the paying insurer. It is submitted that the correct analysis is that contribution, as an equitable doctrine, attaches on a contingent basis as soon as the loss occurs and that the right to claim crystallises on payment by the paying insurer. On this reasoning, any defence acquired by the non-paying insurer between the date of the loss and the date on which the claim for payment is made by the paying insurer is to be disregarded. The cases on this cannot be reconciled: there is persuasive authority for the proposition that the relevant date for determining the existence of a contribution claim is the date at which the paying insurer, A, makes

---

[249] *Limit (No.3) Ltd v ACE Insurance Ltd* 2009 N.S.W.S.C. 514.

[250] The most recent English authorities seem to indicate that contribution rights are to be assessed at the date on which payment is made by the paying insurer. The outcome would have been the same by reason of the latter consideration: what was being sought was not contribution but indemnity.

[251] *Sickness & Accident v General Accident* 1892 19 R. (Ct of Sess) 977; *Woods v Co-operative Insurance* 1924 S.C. 692.

[252] *Equitable Fire and Accident Office Ltd v Ching Wo Hong* [1907] A.C. 96; *Home Insurance Co of New York v Gavel* (1928) 30 Ll. L.R. 139.

[253] *Drake Insurance Co v Provident Insurance Co* [2004] Lloyd's Rep. I.R. 277; *O'Kane v Jones* [2005] Lloyd's Rep. I.R. 174.

[254] *Austin v Zurich Insurance* [1945] 1 K.B. 250.

payment, whereas a Court of Appeal decision and subsequent first instance decisions hold that the relevant date is the date at which the assured's loss occurred.

In *Legal and General Insurance Society Ltd v Drake Insurance Co Ltd*[255] the assured had procured two motor policies in broadly similar terms. The assured was involved in an accident in which injuries were suffered by a third party, and made a claim against LG. The police subsequently informed LG of the existence of the policy issued by DI. LG negotiated a settlement of £65,000 with the third party, having kept DI informed of the progress of the claim and having invited DI to participate in the negotiations. DI declined. LG, having settled, sought 50 per cent contribution from DI, which rejected the claim on the basis that the assured's failure to give notice of loss to DI in accordance with the terms of DI's policy invalidated any claim which the assured had against DI: as DI was not liable to the assured, DI argued that it could not be liable to LG to contribute to the claim. The Court of Appeal rejected this defence and held that DI could not rely upon its policy terms to resist a contribution claim. This was a case in which DI's policy had remained valid until the loss had occurred, and, given that the contribution was an equitable right, the contractual restriction on the assured was not to be extended to providing a defence to a contribution claim by LG. In so deciding, the Court of Appeal overruled the contrary first instance decision in *Monksfield v Vehicle and General Insurance Co Ltd*.[256]

The *Legal and General* result might be thought to have much to commend it. The essence of contribution is that the assured may proceed against whichever insurer he thinks fit, but that the paying insurer has a right of contribution against any other insurer who has issued a similar policy. If the assured's failure to proceed against that other insurer involves a breach of the terms of its policy—as will almost inevitably be the case—it is obvious that, if that insurer could rely upon its policy terms in a contribution claim, the very conduct by the assured which gives the paying insurer a contribution claim serves at the same time to defeat the contribution claim. This was the main influence on the Court of Appeal in *Legal and General*, and the Court felt that the other insurer, rather than being able to rely upon its policy terms as a defence to the contribution claim, was protected by the equitable nature of the claim. Thus, if the paying insurer has failed to act reasonably in handling the assured's claim against it, and in particular has failed to keep the other insurer informed of the progress of negotiations, contribution might be disallowed.

Legal and General has nevertheless been disapproved by the Privy Council in *Eagle Star Insurance Co v Provincial Insurance Plc*.[257] In this case ES and PI had both issued policies covering the same motor insurance liability. ES had a right to avoid its policy, but had failed to comply with the formalities laid down by Bahamian legislation equivalent to the Road Traffic Act 1988 and was thus in the position of being bound by statute to meet any third-party liabilities incurred by the assured. The assured, having suffered a loss, made a claim against ES. No claim was made against PI, which meant that PI, under the terms of its policy, had a defence against the assured for breach of the notice of loss provisions: again, under the 1988 Act, that defence could not be relied upon. The question for the Privy Council was whether both insurers were in the same position of facing

---

[255] *Legal and General Insurance Society Ltd v Drake Insurance Co Ltd* [1992] 1 All E.R. 283. See also Goddard J. in *Jenkins v Deane* (1933) 103 L.J.K.B. 250 at 254–255.

[256] *Monksfield v Vehicle and General Insurance Co Ltd* [1971] 1 Lloyd's Rep. 139.

[257] *Eagle Star Insurance Co v Provincial Insurance Plc* [1993] 3 All E.R. 1, on appeal from the Bahamas.

statutory, but not contractual liability, in which case the paying insurer would have a right of contribution against the other. The Privy Council ruled that, for contribution purposes, each insurer was identically placed at the date at which contribution could be called for (i.e. payment by the paying insurer), as each would have a contractual defence, so that contribution was required. The fact that PT's defence arose after the loss occurred was immaterial, as the date at which the right of contribution had to be determined was the date at which it was sought.[258] Translating this decision to the facts of Legal and General, DI would have been able to rely upon its notice of loss clause because, when the claim for contribution was made against it, DI had ceased to be liable under the policy. Privy Council decisions are of course only of persuasive authority, but Eagle Star was decided by a Privy Council consisting of five Lords of Appeal, and *Legal and General* was expressly doubted while *Monksfield* was expressly approved. It would seem, therefore, that *Legal and General* is of doubtful authority.

The injustices that flow from *Eagle Star* were highlighted in *O'Kane v Jones*.[259] In this case a hull and machinery policy was taken out by the assured with the claimant underwriter. However, the premiums were not paid and the broker threatened to invoke the cancellation clause in the policy. Fearful that this had occurred, the assured's agent procured a second policy from the defendant underwriter. The policies were concurrent and gave rise to double insurance. Following a loss, the assured's agent and the defendant agreed that the second policy should be cancelled. The claimant paid the full amount of the loss and sought to recover contribution from the defendant, which relied upon the cancellation. Plainly, if the relevant date for the contribution claim was the date of the loss then the cancellation was ineffective in respect of such a claim, whereas if the relevant date was the date when payment was made by the claimant then the cancellation would preclude contribution. Deputy High Court Judge Richard Siberry QC ruled that the claimant was entitled to contribution from the defendant. The decision was based squarely on the wording of s.80(1) of the Marine Insurance Act 1906, which the court construed as applying to the situation as of the date of the loss rather than at the date of payment. On this reasoning it was unnecessary for the court to choose between the *Legal and General* and *Eagle Star* rulings, although Mr Siberry QC was firmly of the view that non-marine and marine law should be the same and that *Legal and General*—in holding that a right of contribution accrued in equity as soon as the loss occurred—was to be preferred, and that the contrary result in the present case would have been unjust. The same approach was adopted at first instance in *Bolton Metropolitan Borough Council v Municipal Mutual Insurance Ltd*,[260] although on appeal[261] Longmore L.J. speaking for the Court of Appeal preferred the *Eagle Star* analysis. In *Bolton* itself the point did not arise as the non-paying insurers were not on risk at all, but the issue was raised on the assumption that their only defence was late notification, Longmore L.J. saw no reason to deprive

---

[258] This is consistent with the concluding words of the Marine Insurance Act 1906 s.80(1), under which contribution may be claimed from an insurer respect of a sum for "which he is liable under the contract" and not a sum for which he was but has ceased to he liable.

[259] *O'Kane v Jones* [2005] Lloyd's Rep. I.R. 174. See also *Limit (No.3) Ltd v ACE Insurance Ltd* [2009] N.S.W.S.C. 514, which proceeded on the basis that contribution rights had to be assessed at the date of the casualty and not at the date of payment.

[260] *Bolton Metropolitan Borough Council v Municipal Mutual Insurance Ltd* [2006] Lloyd's Rep. I.R. 15.

[261] *Bolton Metropolitan Borough Council v Municipal Mutual Insurance Ltd* [2007] Lloyd's Rep. I.R. 173.

insurers of the benefits of their late notification clause, and indeed suggested that the existence of such a clause prevented double insurance from arising in the first place. *O'Kane* was distinguished on the ground that the facts in that case had involved cancellation of the policy itself after the loss, a scenario quite different from reliance on a contract term which prevented liability from arising. It is nevertheless suggested that, given that a late claim against one insurer is more or less inevitable if there are two insurers on risk, it seems arbitrary to deprive the paying insurer of a contribution claim simply because it happened to be the insurer against whom the claim was first made: this, however, is the effect of *Eagle Star.*

11–060   *Payment as volunteer.* If an insurer makes full payment to the assured despite the presence of a rateable proportion clause under which he is obliged only to pay his rateable share of the loss, the cases indicate that he may well be unable to recover the balance from other insurers by way of contribution. The basis for this principle is that contribution is an equitable principle, but that equity will not assist a volunteer.[262] The most recent authority, however, is dismissive of this notion.

In *Legal & General Assurance Society v Drake Insurance Co Ltd*[263] the assured had taken out two motor policies, each containing a rateable proportion clause. The assured made a claim against LG only: LG, having ascertained that a policy covering the same loss had been issued by DI, nevertheless paid the full amount of the assured's claim and thereafter sought to recover 50 per cent of its payment by way of contribution. The Court of Appeal held that LG was unable to seek contribution.[264] LG's obligation extended only to paying 50 per cent of the loss—the additional 50 per cent was a voluntary payment and could not be recovered from DI under the rules of contribution. The decision is one which takes the volunteer principle to its limits, as it was affected by the compulsory motor insurance provisions of the Road Traffic Act 1988. Under s.148 of the Act, an insurer is not permitted to plead any policy defence (including any rateable proportion clause) to a claim by the third-party victim of the assured, as was the situation here. Consequently, it could not be said that LG's payment of 100 per cent of the loss was "voluntary". However, the Court of Appeal pointed out that under s.151(4) of the Act, LG had a right of recourse against the assured in respect of any sums which it had been obliged to pay to the third party for which it was not liable under the policy. By its failure to exercise the right of recourse, LG had converted its 100 per cent payment into 50 per cent voluntary payment, which it was not able to recover from DI.[265]

---

[262] In *Drake Insurance Co v Provident Insurance Co* [2004] Lloyd's Rep. I.R. 277 the Court of Appeal rejected the suggestion that a rateable proportion clause operated without more as a waiver of the right of contribution in the event that the insurer paid the full amount of the loss despite the presence of the clause. The suggestion to that effect of Ralph Gibson L.J. in *Legal & General Assurance Society v Drake Insurance Co Ltd* [1992] 1 All E.R. 283 was rejected.

[263] *Legal & General Assurance Society v Drake Insurance Co Ltd* [1992] 1 All E.R. 283.

[264] The Court of Appeal did, however, dismiss a further defence by DI based on the fact that the assured had not, in breach of condition in DI's policy, submitted a claim within the stated time; see above.

[265] The Court of Appeal further disallowed a contribution claim in respect of the 50 per cent which LG had paid in accordance with the rateable proportion clause. This holding, it is suggested, must be open to question, although it was followed by David Steel J. in *Bovis Construction Ltd v Commercial Union Insurance Co Ltd* [2001] Lloyd's Rep. I.R. 321.

Legal & General v Drake Insurance was, crucially, distinguished by the Court of Appeal in *Drake Insurance Co v Provident Insurance Co*[266] on facts very similar to those in *Legal & General*. Both insurers faced liability in respect of a motor insurance claim. The defendants purported to avoid the policy for non-disclosure and obtained an arbitration award confirming their entitlement to do so. The claimants ultimately agreed to pay the claim and throughout the process sought to involve the defendants although they were ultimately unsuccessful in doing so. The Court of Appeal, having ruled that the arbitration award was not binding on the claimants and that the claimants had established that the avoidance was invalid so that there was double insurance, held that the claimants were able to recover on the basis that they were not volunteers. This was so for two reasons: the arbitration award itself provided an insuperable difficulty to asserting that the defendants were liable to indemnify the assured; and the claimants' protests to the defendants were inconsistent with any suggestion that their payment had been voluntary. It would be easy to assume that, in light of *Drake v Provident*, little can remain of *Legal & General* as it would appear that the paying insurer can overcome the suggestion that it has paid as a volunteer despite the presence of a rateable proportion clause where the paying insurer has sought—unsuccessfully—to persuade the other insurer to honour its own obligations towards the assured prior to the paying insurer's own payment. It is only where the paying insurer makes payment without ascertaining whether there is concurrent insurance in place, or without attempting to persuade the concurrent insurer itself to make payment, that the paying insurer can be said to be a volunteer. Although the point did not arise for consideration, the Court of Appeal in *Drake v Provident* was extremely critical of the notion adopted in *Legal & General* that a motor insurer who was obliged to make full payment under s.151 of the Road Traffic Act 1988, despite the existence of a rateable proportion clause in the policy was nevertheless to be regarded as a volunteer by failing to exercise the statutory right of recourse against the assured under s.151(7) of the 1988 Act. As the Court of Appeal pointed out, in the vast majority of cases the statutory right of recourse will as a matter of fact prove to be worthless, and it was difficult to see why the paying insurer should be prevented from recovering a contribution from a concurrent insurer by the existence of a theoretical right of recourse.

Determining the amount of contribution. Where it has been established that there is a right of contribution, the remaining question to be answered is how the amount of contribution is to be ascertained. There is no statutory guidance on this matter, as the Marine Insurance Act 1906 s.80, merely states that there is a right of contribution, without going on to say how the amount of such contribution is to be calculated. The determination of the respective liabilities of insurers in relation to one claim is bedevilled by a distinction drawn in practice between policies which provide cover for the same subject matter only (concurrent policies) and those which are different in scope but which happen to cover the particular loss (non-concurrent policies), and by a further distinction drawn as a matter of law between property and liability insurances.[267]   **11–061**

---

[266] *Drake Insurance Co v Provident Insurance Co* [2004] Lloyd's Rep. I.R. 277. The approach taken in this case reflects that in Australia, namely that an insurer who pays more than its rateable share following denial of liability by another insurer is not a volunteer and is entitled to contribution: *GRE Insurance Ltd v QBE Insurance Ltd* [1985] V.R. 83; *Limit (No.3) Ltd v ACE Insurance Ltd* [2009] N.S.W.S.C. 514.

[267] The matter is further complicated by the existence of average clauses, which require the assured to bear his own loss in the proportion by which he is underinsured.

11–062 *Concurrent policies.* If it is assumed that there are two policies, each covering precisely the same subject matter to precisely the same maximum limit, or if the policies are unlimited in amount,[268] it is apparent that each insurer will bear one half of the assured's loss, up to the maximum liability figure of each, whether the assured's claim is under a property or a liability policy. However, matters become more complex where the policy limits of the two policies are different. So far as property insurances are concerned, market practice has evolved three distinct rules. First, where neither policy contains a rateable proportion clause, the respective proportions to be provided by each insurer are determined by the "maximum liability" rule. Under this principle, the maximum possible liabilities of the insurers are added together, and each insurer pays the proportion of the loss which accords with the proportion which its own maximum liability figure bears to the total maximum liability figure. For example, insurer A has issued a property or marine policy under which its maximum liability is to be £50,000, and insurer B has issued a concurrent policy under which its maximum liability is £100,000. Losses would be apportioned in the following ways[269]:

Loss	Insurer A.	Insurer B.
(1) £25,000	$\dfrac{50,000 \times 25,000}{150,000} = £8,333$	$\dfrac{100,000 \times 25,000}{150,000} = £16,667$
(2) £75,000	$\dfrac{50,000 \times 75,000}{150,000} = £25,000$	$\dfrac{100,000 \times 75,000}{150,000} = £50,000$

However, where the insurer who is liable for the greater amount (insurer B) has, or where both insurers have, inserted a rateable proportion clause, the market practice is to apply an "independent liability" test, whereby the liability of each insurer is determined as if it stood alone, and the ratios that those independent liabilities as determined bear to each other fix the proportion of each loss that the insurers have to bear. The examples given above would give rise to the following results under the independent liability principle:

Loss	Insurer A.	Insurer B.
(1) £25,000	Liable for £25,000 thus pays:	Liable for £25,000 thus pays:
	$\dfrac{25,000 \times 25,000}{50,000} = £12,500$	$\dfrac{25,000 \times 25,000}{50,000} = £12,500$
(2) £75,000	Liable for £50,000 thus pays:	Liable for £75,000 thus pays:
	$\dfrac{50,000 \times 75,000}{125,000} = £30,000$	$\dfrac{75,000 \times 75,000}{125,000} = £45,000$

---

[268] *Weddell v Road Transport & General Insurance* [1932] 2 K.B. 563; *Austin v Zurich Insurance* [1945] 1 K.B. 250.
[269] Cf. *Unitarian Congregation of Toronto v Western* (1866) 26 U.C.Q.B. 175.

The third approach, the "common liability" method, is something of a hybrid. Under this method, the parties are equally liable up to the limits of the lower-valued policy, and if there is any surplus then it is to be borne by the higher-valued policy.

The advantage of the independent liability approach is that it disregards maximum liability figures included in policies, such figures generally being arbitrary and bearing no relation to the maximum amount for which the insurer is likely to be called upon to provide indemnity. It is certainly true that the function of a maximum liability figure is not to serve as a basis for the apportioning of losses should double insurance happen to exist, but rather to limit the insurer's liability in respect of any one claim.[270]

While there is no authority on the market practices of insurers as adopted in relation to concurrent property insurances, the question of the choice between these two methods of apportionment in respect of liability insurance came before the Court of Appeal in *Commercial Union Assurance Co Ltd v Hayden*.[271] In this case, Commercial Union had issued a policy covering the public liability of Messrs Cartright up to a maximum limit of £100,000, while Lloyd's underwriters had issued a similar policy with a maximum limit of £10,000. Messrs Cartright then suffered a loss which was settled for £4,425.45, paid in full by Commercial Union, and the question then arose of how the loss was to be apportioned between the insurers. Commercial Union sought contribution on an independent liability basis, while the Lloyd's underwriters argued that the maximum liability basis should be applied. The difference between these two approaches may easily be demonstrated. Under the independent liability principle, each insurer would bear one half of the loss, for each, taken independently, was liable for the full amount of the loss. However, under the maximum liability principle, Commercial Union would be required to bear 100/110ths of the loss, while the Lloyd's underwriters would be responsible only for 10/110ths of it. The Court of Appeal had no doubt but that the independent principle was the correct method of calculation to be applied, a conclusion which the Court believed to be demanded by the fact that the maximum liability figures in the policies had not been inserted in contemplation of the possibility that double insurance might exist, and thus ought not to be used to provide a result which proved to be arbitrary in the event of double insurance. It should be noted, however, that the Court of Appeal went to some lengths to stress that the decision was limited to liability insurances, and it noted that there were at least two grounds upon which liability insurances might be thought to demand separate treatment. First, one important reason for which the maximum liability principle could break down in liability insurance was that some, but not all, liability policies do not provide a financial limit on the insurer's liability: application of the maximum liability principle would be impossible where one policy limited the insurer's liability to a maximum figure and the other was unlimited. The Court of Appeal pointed out, however, that all property and marine policies are subjected to financial limits, so that the maximum liability rule is potentially applicable in every case. Second, even where liability policies do impose maximum financial limits, those limits may refer to different matters. For example, it would be impossible for the maximum

---

[270] In *North British and Maritime Insurance v London, Liverpool and Globe Insurance Co* (1877) 5 QBD 569 the insurers agreed that the independent liability principle was to be applied to concurrent property insurances, although the Court of Appeal made no comment upon this assumption. The case cannot, therefore, be taken as authority for the proposition that the independent liability principle is to be applied as a matter of law.

[271] *Commercial Union Assurance Co Ltd v Hayden* [1977] Q.B. 804.

liability principle to be applied where one liability policy contained an "any one accident" limit while the other imposed a limit on the permissible aggregations of all losses arising from "any one event". Despite these important differences between property and liability policies, the view has been expressed that the English courts would seek to extend the *Hayden* ruling to property policies if faced with the question.[272]

The position as between concurrent marine policies was considered by Deputy High Court Judge Richard Siberry QC in *O'Kane v Jones*.[273] The policies in this case were both on the hull and machinery of a vessel: the first policy was in the sum of US$2.5 million and the second policy was in the sum of US$5 million. A total loss occurred. The application of both the independent liability method and the maximum liability method produced the same result, of a 1:2 ratio between the policies, and the court was thus not required to choose between them and chose not to do so. An alternative possibility—"common liability"—was mooted by the insurers of first policy. The suggestion was that each of the insurers should be liable equally up to the amount for which they were independently liable. Thus the first US$2.5 million would be divided equally between the insurers, and the surplus would be borne by the second insurer, giving a ratio of 1:3. This had been the preferred approach of Lawton L.J. in *Commercial Union v Hayden*. The court's view in *O'Kane* was that wording of s.80(1) of the Marine Insurance Act 1906 required a rateable apportionment of liability and that while that wording was apt to encompass both the maximum and independent liability approaches, it could not apply to common liability as that method did not operate by apportionment.[274]

11–063 *Non-concurrent policies.* It is necessary to distinguish initially between cases in which the entire loss falls within both policies and those in which one of the policies covers a part of the loss only.[275] In the former case, market practice is to apply the maximum liability rule to the apportionment of the loss between the insurers, although this approach has been criticised for failing to take into account the differences in coverage between the policies, and it has been suggested that some notional apportionment of the subject matter concerned should be made under each of the policies, with the maximum liability figure for that subject matter being used as the basis for determining contribution proportions. Whatever the market practice may be, the law has adopted the independent liability principle in these circumstances. It will be remembered that, in *American Surety Co of New York v Wrightson*,[276] the New York company had agreed to indemnify the assured bank for losses caused to it by the dishonesty of its employees, up to a maximum figure of $2,500 (for each employee, and Lloyd's underwriters had issued a more general policy covering burglary, fire and dishonesty by any person, subject to a limit of £40,000. The bank suffered a loss of $2,680 as the result of the fraudulent conduct of one of its employees; the loss was met in full by the Lloyd's underwriters, who then sought contribution from the New York company. The New York company argued that contribution should be ordered on maximum liability lines, which would have required it to

---

[272] [1977] Camb. L.J. 231.

[273] *O'Kane v Jones* [2005] Lloyd's Rep. I.R. 174.

[274] Although in *Tai Ping Insurance Co v Tugu Insurance Co Ltd* [2001] H.K.E.C. 506 the independent liability method was adopted in Hong Kong for marine insurance.

[275] Assuming that contribution is as a matter of law available as between non-concurrent policies. See above.

[276] *American Surety Co of New York v Wrightson* (1910) 103 L.T. 663.

contribute in the ratio 40,000:2,500. The underwriters for their part put forward a variety of alternative formulae, but primarily argued for an independent liability calculation under which the ratio was to be 2,500:2,680, an argument which was accepted by Hamilton J. In reaching this conclusion the learned judge stressed the importance of the fact that the policies were different in nature but nevertheless covered the same loss, and that each policy did bear a maximum liability figure.[277] The judgment may thus be regarded as opting for some form of middle path, and has generally been welcomed as producing the fairest result.

The second situation mentioned above is that in which part of the loss falls within both policy A and policy B, and policy A alone covers the remainder of the loss. Here, different forms of apportionment are made, and the mean of the two is then taken to determine the final contribution ratio. The two forms are as follows:

(1) The greater loss of the two is considered first.
    (a) If the loss covered by policy A is greater than the loss common to both policy A and policy B, the amount of that loss is deducted from the total sum insured by policy A, and the common loss is then aggregated on a maximum liability basis between policy B and the remainder of policy A.
    (b) If the common loss is greater than the loss covered by policy A alone, the common loss is apportioned between the two policies on a maximum liability basis, and the residue of the sum insured under policy A is used to meet the lesser loss.
(2) The lesser loss of the two is considered first, and the procedure laid out under (1) above is then followed.

Contribution based on these principles is hardly satisfactory, as at best they amount to an unscientific compromise position which is difficult to operate where there are more than two policies involved, and which breaks down entirely where the effect is to deprive the assured of the full indemnity to which he is entitled. Nevertheless, the process outlined above appears to be established in practice.

Practical modifications. It was noted above that, in practice, arrangements **11–064** between insurers will often modify contribution rights, the object of such arrangements being to reduce litigation between insurers and therefore to reduce operating costs, in the knowledge that the "swings and roundabouts" principle will ultimately ensure that no one insurer is substantially worse off by agreeing to waive its rights. In practical terms the two most important classes of agreement are those by which losses caused by employees driving motor vehicles are to be settled by employers' liability insurers without contribution from motor insurers, and those by which liability for an accident caused by a driver in control of a vehicle belonging to another who is insured not only on his own behalf but also under an extension to the owner's insurance, is to be indemnified by the owner's insurer without contribution from his own insurer.

The subrogation rights of the contributing insurer. It has been held by the **11–065** Supreme Court of Western Australia, in *Speno Rail Maintenance Australia Pty*

---

[277] For this reason it was held by Hamilton J. to be inappropriate to divide the loss equally between the two insurers, as the New York company's maximum liability figure was exceeded by the loss.

Ltd v Metals & Minerals Insurance Pte Ltd,[278] that a contributing insurer has no subrogation rights against the wrongdoer who caused the assured's loss. In this case Speno, a rail grinding contractor, entered into a contract with Hamersley. Under the agreement Speno was to provide services to Hamersley and to indemnify Hamersley for common law liability for personal injury to any of Speno's employees. Two of Speno's employees were injured by the negligence of Hamersley. Speno and Hamersley were co-insured under a policy obtained by Speno from Zurich, the policy waiving subrogation rights against co-assureds, and Hamersley made a claim against Zurich for the sum of A$1.26 million. Zurich, having made payment, sought contribution from Hamersley's own liability insurers, MMI. MMI in turn commenced a subrogation action against Speno seeking to exercise Hamersley's right of indemnity against Speno. The High Court ruled that MMI, who were merely contributing insurers, had no right of subrogation, because MMI had not met the threshold requirement for subrogation, that of providing an indemnity to the person whose rights it sought to enforce. That indemnity had been provided by Zurich and any subrogation rights against Speno belonged to Zurich alone, rights which had under the policy been waived.[279] Although the facts of this case are somewhat convoluted, the principle is straightforward. If A has policies from U1 and U2, and A suffers a loss at the hands of T which is paid for by U1, only U1 has subrogation rights against T. If U1 chooses not to exercise those subrogation rights, or has waived them, and seeks contribution from U2, then on the basis of *Speno* U2 has no subrogation rights against T.

3. ABANDONMENT AND SALVAGE

11–066   **Abandonment and salvage defined.** It has long been a principle of equity that, where an assured under a marine policy has been paid for a total loss of the subject matter of the policy, the insurer is entitled to claim for its own benefit what remains of the subject matter.[280] The act of the assured in relinquishing the subject matter is referred to as "abandonment", and the insurer's right to take over the subject matter once abandoned is known as "salvage". Abandonment was in its origins linked to the doctrine of subrogation, and shares with subrogation the objective of preventing the assured from obtaining more than an indemnity; today, abandonment is frequently regarded as a sub-rule of the general principle of subrogation.[281] However, abandonment and subrogation differ in a number of significant respects:

[278] *Speno Rail Maintenance Australia Pty Ltd v Metals & Minerals Insurance Pte Ltd* (2009) 253 A.L.R. 364.

[279] The Court ruled also that Zurich had no right of contribution against MMI by reason of a clause in the MMI policy which postponed the liability of MMI to that of any other insurer. An appeal against that ruling was dismissed by the High Court: *Zurich Insurance Co v Metals and Minerals Insurance Pte* (2009) 261 A.L.R. 468.

[280] *Randal v Cockran* (1748) 1 Ves. Sen. 98; *Pringle v Hartley* (1774) 3 Atk. 195; *Milles v Fletcher* (1779) 1 Doug. K.B. 231; *Rankin v Potter* (1873) L.R. 6 H.L. 83. Payment is a precondition, but see *Dream Maker Game Shop v China Merchants Insurance Co Ltd* Unreported, 2003 H.K.D.C. where the right of the insurers to possession of the damaged goods was framed as a condition precedent to payment.

[281] See *Dane v Mortgage Insurance Corp* [1894] 1 Q.B. 54 at 61, in which Lord Esher M.R. uses the word "salvage" as a surrogate for "subrogation".

(1) Subrogation confers the right upon the insurer to pursue the assured's claims against third parties for the loss of the subject matter, whereas abandonment and salvage merely confer rights over the subject matter itself.

(2) Subrogation does not permit the insurer to bring an action in its own name, whereas once an insurer has accepted the abandonment of goods it becomes the owner of those goods.

(3) Any profits earned by abandoned property accrue to the insurer, whereas subrogation does not permit the insurer to recover any more than its own payment to the assured, and even then only by exercising some right of action.[282]

(4) Subrogation operates automatically, by operation of law as a result of the principle of indemnity, to confer rights of action on the insurer, whereas abandoned property apparently need not be accepted by the insurer.

(5) Subrogation is common to all forms of indemnity insurance, whereas abandonment is recognised formally only in the context of marine insurance. This is so because salvage is normally likely to be significant only where the assured has suffered a constructive total loss as opposed to an actual total loss, for in the latter case there will rarely be anything in existence to be abandoned; non-marine insurance does not recognise the concept of a constructive total loss. However, abandonment does operate to a limited extent in non-marine insurance, for example, where subject matter thought to be lost or destroyed turns up safe and well after the insurer has paid out in respect of it.

Abandonment and salvage in non-marine insurance.[283] The principles of salvage and abandonment have been worked out primarily in relation to marine insurance, but they are equally applicable to non-marine insurance. As Brett L.J. said in *Kaltenbach v Mackenzie*[284]: **11–067**

"I concur in what has been said by Lord Blackburn[285] that abandonment is not peculiar to policies of marine insurance abandonment is part of every contract of indemnity. Whenever, therefore, there is a contract of indemnity and a claim under it for an absolute indemnity, there must be an abandonment on the part of the person claiming indemnity of all his right in respect of that for which he receives indemnity."

Abandonment should be distinguished from notice of abandonment, the former conferring upon any insurer a right of salvage while the latter merely being the formal device whereby the assured can convert a marine constructive total loss into an actual total loss for the purpose of calculating his indemnity. As there is no concept of constructive total loss in non-marine insurance, the formalities relating to notice of abandonment are inapplicable in the non-marine context.

In non-marine insurance the measure of the assured's loss is, prima facie, the difference between the value of the insured property before the occurrence of the insured event and its value after that event. Consequently, if property is destroyed in its entirety or otherwise becomes worth nothing, the assured is entitled to a full indemnity up to the policy limits. In addition, as a matter of practice, insurers

---

[282] Hence the reference to "proprietary rights" in s.63(1) of the Marine Insurance Act 1906, which does not appear in s.79(1).

[283] For the position in marine insurance, see Ch.24, below.

[284] *Kaltenbach v Mackenzie* (1878) 3 C.P.D. 467 at 470.

[285] *Rankin v Potter* (1873) L.R. 6 H.L. 83 at 118. See also *Mason v Sainsbury* (1782) 3 Dougl. 61.

frequently pay for a total loss following serious damage which renders repair uneconomic. In any of these cases, assuming that something remains of the subject matter, the insurer is entitled to claim for its own benefit the right of ownership of that subject matter by way of salvage, on general equitable principles,[286] at least where the assured is not underinsured and has received a full indemnity. Once the insurer has agreed to pay for a total loss and to adopt the subject matter by way of salvage, it cannot thereafter seek to change its position and seek recovery of its payment should facts subsequently show that no loss had occurred.[287] It is commonly the case, particularly with cars, that the assured wishes to retain ownership of the property even though it has been classified as a total loss by the insurer. Here, the insurer will normally be willing to sell the property back to the assured for its scrap value. The insurer would not, however, appear to be under any obligation to offer to sell the property back to the assured, and the insurer may treat it as he wishes as soon as he has agreed to pay for a total loss.

11–068   **Abandonment and underinsurance.**[288] In many cases there will be a difference between the value of the insured subject matter and the amount payable, in the event of a total loss, by the insurer. The question which arises here is whether an insurer who has paid up to the policy limits for a total loss, but who has nevertheless failed to compensate the assured fully by reason of underinsurance, is entitled to insist upon an abandonment by the assured.

The following situations must be distinguished:

(1) In the case of a valued policy, whether marine or non-marine, and the sum insured is the full value, then on abandonment the property belongs to insurers and the assured has no legal or equitable interest in it even if it proves to be more valuable than the agree value. This flows from the basic proposition that the valuation is conclusive as between the parties. Insurers may thus potentially profit where the agreed value is less than the actual value.

(2) If the policy is valued, the sum insured is less than the agreed value and if the policy is subject to average (the default rule for marine insurance), the assured is deemed to be his own insurer for the shortfall under the Marine Insurance Act 1906 s.81: to that extent there is co-insurance. That means on abandonment the assured and insurers become co-owners for their respective proportions of the agreed value and they share profits plus the costs of preserving the subject matter.

(3) If the policy is valued, the sum insured is less than the agreed value and the policy is not subject to average (a situation likely to be confined to non-marine cases) then the position is unclear. The parties are not treated as co-insurers in such a case. Accordingly, it could be argued either that the insurers are entitled to the full benefit of the proceeds (possibility (1) above) or that the insurers should not be allowed to profit from the underinsurance and the insurers and assured are to be treated as

---

[286] *Oldfield v Price* (1860) 2 F. & F. 80; *Skipper v Grant* (1861) 10 C.B.N.S. 237; *Rankin v Potter* (1873) L.R. 6 H.L. 83 at 118, per Blackburn J.; *Kaltenbach v Mackenzie* (1873) 3 C.P.D. 467 at 470, per Brett L.J. It is also clear that the insurer in *Moore v Evans* [1917] 1 K.B. 45 would, had it paid for a total loss, have been entitled to claim the jewellery on its return to the assured.

[287] *Da Costa v Firth* (1766) 4 Burr. 1966; *Ruys v Royal Exchange Assurance Co* [1897] 2 Q.B. 135; *Holmes v Payne* [1930] 2 K.B. 301.

[288] See Derham, *Subrogation in Insurance Law*, 1985, at pp.39–41,

co-owners in the abandoned property in proportion to their respective rights and interests (possibility (2) above). It might be thought that the application of the co-ownership principle is more consonant with the general principle which precludes unjust enrichment.

(4) If the policy is unvalued and is subject to average, then the position would seem to be the same as in possibility (2) above: the assured is co-insurer for the uninsured sum, and accordingly is co-owner of the insured subject matter in respect of his proportion of the risk.

(5) If the policy is unvalued and not subject to average, the situation is the same as in possibility (3) above, and the law remains uncertain.

CHAPTER 12

STATUTORY CONTROL OF POLICIES

BY DR JUDITH P. SUMMER

1. THE FINANCIAL OMBUDSMAN SERVICE

History and formation of the Financial Ombudsman Service

12–001   In 1981 the Insurance Ombudsman Bureau (IOB) was founded to resolve complaints against insurers outside of the court system, to be dealt with independently, privately and without charge to the complainant. It was a voluntary, industry, not a government initiative, backed by the National Consumer Council, and decided disputes in accordance with "good insurance practice". Particularly influential were the Statements of Insurance Practice, two voluntary codes for Long-Term (life) and General (non-life) consumer policies issued by the Association of British Insurers originally in 1977[1] and revised in 1986. The IOB, through its published summaries of decided cases, established a substantial jurisprudence of its own which on at least one occasion influenced the development of the law.[2] At that time, there was no regulator for the conduct of investment or insurance business. Other Ombudsman schemes for complaints against other types of institution, including banks and building societies, followed. In 2000, a single financial regulator, the Financial Services Authority was established by the Financial Services and Markets Act 2000, and the earlier voluntary ombudsman schemes merged to become the Financial Ombudsman Service.

At first the FOS followed the rules of the scheme to which the complaint would have related before the FOS existed. From December 1, 2001, when the majority of the 2000 Act came into force, the FOS began dealing with all new complaints under one set of new rules, under the Dispute Resolution: Complaints (DISP) section of the FSA Handbook of Rules and Guidance.[3] DISP 1 also provides rules and guidance for the internal handling of complaints by firms. As far as insurance complaints are treated, the FOS remains similar to the IOB, with its "fair and reasonable" approach in a private and confidential dispute resolution scheme, paid for by firms and free for consumers. However, the jurisdiction of the FOS is wider, as it can consider complaints from small businesses, charities,

---

[1] The price for the exemption of insurance contracts from the Unfair Contract Terms Act 1977.

[2] Reasonable care clauses: see Ch.5, above.

[3] The FSA Handbook of Rules and Guidance can be accessed via the FSA's website at *http://www.fsa.gov.uk* [Accessed June 16, 2010]. The updated rules of DISP 1 came into force on November 1, 2007 (with minor amendments on July 6, 2008) and those of DISP 2 (FOS jurisdiction) and DISP 3 (FOS procedures) came into force on April 6, 2008. Under DISP TP1–1, the version of DISP which applies to any particular case is that which applied at the date on which the complaint was received by the firm.

trustees and residents' associations, and business interruption policies[4] now also come within its remit.

Adjudicators and ombudsmen are recruited from a wide range of backgrounds and tend to have financial services, complaints-handling, compliance or legal experience or qualifications. The FOS is staffed by about 1,500 people.[5]

Aims and values

The FOS was set up by the 2000 Act to help resolve individual disputes between **12–002** consumers and financial firms, "quickly and with minimum formality by an independent person."[6] Under s.228(2) the FOS must make decisions which are "fair and reasonable in all the circumstances of the case." It deals with thousands of disputes every week.[7] As an independent organisation, it is not a regulator, trade body, watchdog or a consumer champion.

In order to be fair and reasonable, the FOS aims to be accessible to everyone,[8] and will try to communicate with people in the format or language they require. It will approach complaints in a practical and businesslike manner and will look at the facts of each complaint, rather than how the case is presented, and give clear reasons for its decisions. It considers that no-one should therefore need legal or other professional help to bring a complaint or understand a decision, and so it will be unusual for the FOS to order reimbursement of any costs incurred in obtaining such advice.

Where a consumer might be disadvantaged by having to wait, for example through financial hardship or for medical reasons, the FOS will consider if it would be fair to prioritise the complaint. However, the identity of the parties and any press involvement will make no difference to the place that the complaint will sit in the queue.

The FOS service is an informal, private and relatively quick[9] and flexible alternative to the courts, and it does not have the set procedures, formal hearings

---

[4] E.g. Case Study 74/08 *Ombudsman News* Jan/Feb 2009.

[5] FOS Annual Review 2009/10 including outsourced staff. The total staff was about 1,000 in 2006/7 (FOS Corporate Plan & 2006/07 Budget).

[6] s.225(1) FSMA.

[7] The FOS Corporate Plan and 2006/7 Budget forecast 13,500 new insurance complaints would be received by adjudicators respectively in 2006/7 and 2007/8 out of a total 105,000 processed complaints in 2006/7 and 87,500 in 2007/8. According to the FOS Annual Review 2008/9, 127,500 new cases were referred to adjudicators in that year, of which 50,000 were insurance related. FOS Annual Review 2009/10 showed 163,000 new cases referred to adjudicators of which nearly 70,000 were insurance-related.

[8] Cf. The Hunt Review dated April 9, 2008 "Opening Up, Reaching Out and Aiming High" which is an independent review of accessibility and transparency of the FOS. Although it praises the work of the FOS and the way it is run and has developed over the years, it suggests wide-ranging and radical reforms to further enhance FOS accessibility and transparency. These include a far reaching advertising campaign and publication of complaints data relating to firms and publication of what Lord Hunt calls FOSBOOK—a handbook which would set out current FOS thinking on all scenarios and issues on which it bases its decisions. From September 2009, complaints data has been published by the FOS bi-annually, about the 150 or so firms which make up 90 per cent of the complaints workload.

[9] According to the FOS Corporate Plan and 2006/7 Budget, most cases, excluding complaints about mortgage endowments, are resolved within six months. The FOS Annual Review April 1, 2004 to March 31, 2005 showed that 64 per cent of all complaints are resolved within six months, and 90 per cent within one year. In 2008/9, 56 per cent of all complaints were resolved within six months and 86 per cent within one year. (FOS Annual Review 2008/9.) In 2009/10 67% were resolved within six months and 80% within one year (FOS Annual Review 2009/10).

or cross-examinations of a court. It is geared to the requirements of ordinary people who have disputes with powerful organisations. All complaints are handled in confidence and will not be discussed in public, other than in a summarised and anonymised form in the FOS publications. The FOS adjudicators will generally try mediation or conciliation, often telephoning the respective parties to speak informally and suggest a way forward. Only if this is unsuccessful and the parties do not accept their views will all the papers be considered further and a formal Ombudsman decision be taken.

Strict law may not be applied

12–003   One of the main differences between the FOS and a court decision is that the FOS does not have to apply strict law and often does not. The FOS decides each case in accordance with what it considers to be fair and reasonable in the circumstances of that particular case.[10] Where the evidence is contradictory, the FOS will decide what it thinks is most likely to have happened, on the balance of probability. Although the FOS aims to be consistent in the way it deals with particular types of complaint, it is not bound by its own decisions.

In determining a matter, the FOS will not ignore the relevant law, which it will consider, but it will also take into account regulations, regulator's rules, guidance and standards, relevant codes of practice and where appropriate, what the FOS considers to be good industry practice at the relevant time.[11] The FOS is guided by the FSA's Insurance: Conduct of Business rule book (ICOB) which took effect on January 14, 2005, superseding the ABI's Statements of Insurance Practice. The ICOB was itself superseded by ICOBS[12] on January 6, 2008.

How the FOS is funded

12–004   The FOS is funded both by a general levy which is calculated each year according to a firm's volume of business[13] and collected from all firms covered by the FSA, and also by individual case fees billed at the end of the month in which the complaint is closed. From April 1, 2004, firms that paid the annual levy were not charged for the first two complaints the FOS received about them in any year, but thereafter a case fee was charged for each complaint against them,[14] whatever the outcome. With effect from April 1, 2008, firms were not charged for the first three complaints in any one year. It is assumed that the case

---

[10] s.228 (2) FSMA, DISP 3.6.1R and 3.6.2G.

[11] DISP 3.6.4R. Good industry practice may also be established through FSA-approved industry guidance—cf. FSA Policy Statement 07/16 published in September 2007.

[12] The ICOBS can be found in the FSA Handbook. It contains the requirements relating to the business processes involved in selling and administering non-investment insurance. This includes marketing, sales, product literature and claims handling. The ICOBS applies to general insurance contracts such as motor or household, and also pure protection contracts such as critical illness and income protection, but not long-term care insurance which is subject to the FSA's investment business rules. Reinsurance contracts are exempt from the ICOBS rules.

[13] In 2003/4, the levy ranged from less than £100 for a small financial adviser to £300,000 for a large insurance company.

[14] This was £360 in 2006/7 for a standard case fee, or £475 for a special case fee. Definitions of standard case fee and special case fee can be found in the Glossary to the FSA Handbook. The special case fee applies in a small minority of cases, mainly where the complaint has been made by a small business. From April 1, 2008 the case fees were £450 for both standard and special cases. From April 1, 2009 they were £500.

fee will be less than the legal and management costs to the firm of a policyholder taking the matter to court instead.[15]

Under the rules, consumers may not pay a fee for using the FOS, and it is not for the complainant to pay the firm's costs.[16] If a firm threatens to penalise a customer for exercising its right to bring its complaint to the FOS, then the FSA has indicated that it will treat the firm as having failed to meet certain of its "Principles for Businesses"[17] which will entitle the FSA to take disciplinary action. The FOS may inform the FSA if it becomes aware of a firm putting pressure on any customer to try to prevent referral of a complaint to the FOS. The FOS has also been known to order an adviser to pay a complainant compensation for distress and inconvenience for trying to persuade her that she would have to pay his costs if she brought a complaint to the FOS which was not upheld.[18]

The government has refused to allow the FOS to make consumers pay towards the scheme, despite s.230(4) of the 2000 Act which allows the scheme operator to provide costs rules with the approval of the FSA for "the making of an award against the complainant in favour of the scheme operator . . . if in the opinion of the ombudsman—(a) the complainant's conduct was improper or unreasonable or (b) the complainant was responsible for an unreasonable delay." Although some consider that payment to the FOS would be a deterrent for persistent or obsessive complainants, former Chief Ombudsman Walter Merricks has commented that he thinks that they would be happy to pay and would demand commensurate service.[19]

The FOS will not charge a case fee where it is readily apparent that: the firm has not yet had a chance to deal with the complaint; the complainant is not an "eligible complainant"; the complaint is out of its jurisdiction; or the complaint should be dismissed without consideration of its merits (for example, because the complainant has not suffered financial loss or material inconvenience or if a complaint is "frivolous and vexatious").[20] A complaint is not automatically frivolous and vexatious just because it has not been upheld, or because the complaint has not been presented in a reasoned and coherent fashion. A fee will be charged if the FOS has to investigate matters before it can establish that any of the reasons above exist for not considering the complaint, and this practice was supported by the Court of Appeal in *FOS v Heather Moor & Edgecomb Ltd.*[21]

---

[15] The FOS Annual Review April 1, 2004 to March 31, 2005 notes that 85 per cent of all firms covered by the FOS had no complaint referred to the FOS during the year, 7 per cent had one complaint and 2.5 per cent had two complaints, which meant that only 5.5 per cent of firms covered by the FOS actually paid a case fee. Also 15 firms alone accounted for half all the case fees in the year 2003/4 (Walter Merricks' Speech October 12 and 28, 2004). In 2008/9 and 2009/10 more than 95% of all firms covered by the FOS had no complaint referred to the FOS, about 1% paid a case fee and 6 and 4 firms respectively accounted for just over half the total number of cases referred (FOS Annual Reviews 2008/9 and 2009/10).

[16] s.230(3) FSMA.

[17] These are Principle 6 (A firm must pay due regard to the interests of its customers and treat them fairly) and Principle 8 (A firm must manage conflicts of interest fairly, both between itself and its customers and between a customer and another client).

[18] Cf. *Ombudsman News* April 2004.

[19] Speech October 12 and 28, 2004.

[20] For details of the circumstances where a complaint may be dismissed without consideration, see DISP 3.3.4R and also below.

[21] *FOS v Heather Moor & Edgecomb Ltd* [2008] EWCA Civ 643.

The insurer's other obligations in relation to the FOS and complaints handling

12–005 DISP 1 of the FSA's Handbook sets out how firms should handle complaints internally. The FOS cannot interpret these rules or issue its own guidance on compliance with them. A firm may display a notice in branches or sales offices showing that it is covered by the FOS[22] and firms may also use the FOS logo on any relevant marketing material or correspondence.[23] Although the FOS has no power to prescribe a form of wording, it suggests: "Complaints we cannot settle may be referred to the Financial Ombudsman Service."[24]

Once a firm has received a complaint, it has eight weeks in which to exhaust its own internal complaints procedure and send the complainant a final response letter or otherwise to write to the complainant explaining why it cannot make a final response, informing the complainant that he may now refer the complaint to the FOS and enclosing a copy of the FOS standard explanatory leaflet.[25] The FOS will not consider a complaint until this time limit is expired[26] or a final response letter has been sent, if sooner. The final response letter should include[27]: a summary of the complaint; a summary of the outcome of the firm's investigation; whether the firm acknowledges any fault on its part; details of any offer the firm has made to settle the complaint; how long any offer to settle the complaint will remain open; and why (if) it thinks the complaint may be outside the FOS jurisdiction. But the firm should explain that jurisdiction is a matter for the FOS, not the firm to decide. The letter must mention the complainant's right to refer the complaint to the FOS within six months of the firm's final response. Firms must send the FOS contact details and a FOS leaflet entitled "Your complaint and the Ombudsman" to customers either when the firm sends its final response letter or if the firm has run out of time and is not yet in a position to send its final response.[28] Sending the leaflet is not sufficient to alert complainants to the six month time limit for bringing a complaint, and this time limit should still be mentioned in the text of the final response letter. If it is not, the FOS will accept cases for consideration outside of the 6 months.[29]

In its "Guide for advice-workers,"[30] the FOS sets out some complaints handling "do's and don't's". This includes a statement saying that the FOS will not treat an apology or expression of regret as an admission of liability, but as recognition of the firm having an unhappy customer. The FOS does not like insurers to cite different reasons for rejecting a claim at different times, rather than all together. It is possible that if firms do not comply with these guidelines, the FOS will penalise them with an award for the complainant for maladministration.

---

[22] DISP 1.2.5G.

[23] DISP 1.2.5G.

[24] Cf. *Ombudsman News* April 2004 and the FOS Technical Note for businesses "Telling Consumers about the Financial Ombudsman Service."

[25] DISP 1.6.2R.

[26] DISP 2.8.1R.

[27] The FSA's full rules on what information should be contained in a final response letter are in the FSA Handbook of Rules and Guidance at the glossary/definitions section. See also the FOS guides, the most up to date of which can be accessed via the FOS website at *http://www.financial-ombudsman.org.uk* [Accessed June 16, 2010].

[28] DISP 1.6.2R.

[29] DISP 2.8.3R, under which the six month time limit will not have started to run if it is not specifically mentioned in the final response letter.

[30] The most up-to-date version can be accessed via the FOS website at *http://www.financial-ombudsman.org.uk* [Accessed June 16, 2010].

Time limits for bringing a complaint

Time limits under the scheme. The rules for time limits for bringing and **12–006**
considering a complaint can be found in detail in the FSA Handbook at DISP 1.6
and 2.8. A complaint must have been referred to the firm for the firm to try to
resolve before the FOS will consider the matter. Firms can resolve most
complaints themselves, generally all but approximately 2–5 per cent of non-
mortgage endowment complaints.[31] Under the FSA's complaint handling rules,
the firm has eight weeks in which to do this from the time it receives a complaint
anywhere within its organisation. DISP 1 of the FSA Handbook sets out a more
detailed timetable of what should be done, and by when, within this eight weeks.
Only after this period, (or after the final response letter if sooner) will the FOS
consider the matter.[32] If the complaint has not been resolved at the end of the
eight-week period, the firm must tell the customer, preferably in a final response
letter, that he has a right to refer the complaint to the FOS within six months. (see
above for details of what else should be included in the final response letter.)

 The consumer has six months in which to bring a complaint to the FOS after
receiving the firm's final response letter.[33] The FOS can consider extending this
period where it considers that there have been exceptional circumstances, such as
where the complainant is incapacitated, or where the firm has not told him about
his right to refer to the FOS or about the six-month time limit. The FOS can also
consider complaints outside the six-month time limit where it is required to do so
by the Ombudsman Transitional Order or where the firm has not objected to the
FOS considering the complaint.[34] This means that the 15-year long stop may not
apply and a firm must still respond to a case as the FOS may not share its view,
even if only to say in its final response letter, which still has to comply with DISP
1.6.2R, but must also say under DISP 1.8.1R that the Ombudsman may waive the
time limits in exceptional circumstances, that it is rejecting the complaint without
considering its merits as a result of the time-bar.

Statutory limitation periods. The FOS cannot consider a complaint made more **12–007**
than six years after the event complained of or (if later) more than three years
from the date on which the complainant became aware (or ought reasonably to
have become aware) that he had cause for complaint, unless[35]: he has referred the
complaint to the firm or the FOS within that period and has a written
acknowledgement or some other record of the complaint having been received;
or in the view of the FOS, the failure to comply with the time limits was as a
result of exceptional circumstances; or the Ombudsman Transitional Order
requires the FOS to review the complaint; or the firm has not objected to the FOS
considering the complaint.[36] The FSA has confirmed that it does not wish to
make any long-stop provision for the FOS to consider complaints under FSMA
and the Consumer Credit Act.[37]

 If a firm wishes to rely on these limitation periods or the six-month limit
above, the FOS will expect it to do so as early as possible in the process, and will

---

[31] Figures from speech by Walter Merricks October 12 and 28, 2004.

[32] DISP 2.8.1R.

[33] DISP 2.8.2R.

[34] DISP 2.8.2R, 2.8.3G and 2.8.4G.

[35] Also see DISP 2.8.5R, 2.8.6G and 2.8.7 regarding exceptions for reviews of past business and
exceptions for certain mortgage endowment complaints.

[36] DISP 2.8.2R (2)–(15).

[37] Cf. FSA Feedback Statement FS08/6 and update dated November 18, 2009 on the FSA website.

give a reminder of the requirement in its initial letter to the firm relating to the complaint.

How complaints are dealt with

12–008 *Making a complaint.* Generally, the FOS settles complaints on the basis of paperwork from the firm and the customer. At any stage in the FOS process, it may ask for further information and it expects this to be provided promptly. The FOS has leaflets which can be downloaded from its website[38] and which describe the process. The FOS has set up specialist teams as they have become necessary (for instance dealing with the huge number of endowment mortgage complaints) and reorganised itself and rapidly grown as a result of a large increase in complaints since it began. There are appropriate support teams. It regularly surveys both firms and complainants for feedback. It has effective systems for applying and sharing knowledge, maintaining quality and achieving consistency.

Consumers can telephone the FOS Customer Contact Division for help and information before the FOS gets formally involved.[39] The FOS will only begin its procedures to deal with complaints unresolved by the firm after the final response letter has been sent, or after eight weeks from the date of the complaint if sooner. The customer contact staff will ask the complainant to complete and sign a concise and comprehensive complaint form. Special ones have recently been designed to streamline the process for the increasing number of payment protection insurance complaints. Because the questions on the form deal with some jurisdiction issues and for instance, whether a firm has had a chance to deal with the complaint internally first, the customer contact staff are able to determine and tell the customer immediately if there is anything obvious which would prevent the FOS from considering the matter at that time or at all. They will also look for opportunities to deal immediately with a straightforward problem, such as where there has been a simple administrative misunderstanding or error.

If the complaint survives this process, the customer contact staff will pass it on to one of the adjudicators and the case becomes "chargeable"[40] whether or not it ultimately succeeds.[41] The firm will be notified of the complaint and asked for its comments and evidence.

12–009 *Adjudicators.* The adjudicators will then try to find a solution to satisfy both parties and will try to conduct an informal mediation or conciliation process,

---

[38] *http://www.financial-ombudsman.org.uk* [Accessed June 16, 2010].

[39] The FOS Annual Review April 1, 2004 to March 31, 2005 says that in 2004/5, the customer contact division dealt with 614,148 front line enquiries, which represented more than 1,500 telephone enquiries and 1,250 written enquiries a day, and which was a 12 per cent increase on the previous year. The FOS Annual Review 2008/9 said that the customer contact division dealt with about 790,000 front line enquiries in that year. There were about 925,000 in 2009/10 (Annual Review 2009/10).

[40] The FOS Annual Review April 1, 2004 to March 31, 2005 states that the customer contact division referred 110,963 new cases to adjudicators in that year, representing a 13 per cent increase on the numbers from the year before. Mortgage endowment complaints accounted for about two thirds of these referrals. 11,484 accounted for insurance related complaints. Mortgage endowment complaints steadily dropped although payment protection insurance replaced them. The FOS Annual Review 2008/9 says that the customer contact division referred 127,500 new cases to adjudicators in that year, of which about 50,000 were insurance claims, of which about 30,000 related to payment protection insurance. The numbers in 2009/10 were, respectively, approximately 163,000, 69,000 and 49,000 (Annual Review 2009/10).

[41] Cf. *FOS v Heather Moor & Edgecomb Ltd* [2008] EWCA Civ 643.

perhaps telephoning the parties to suggest a way forward or to obtain further information. Adjudicators may ask for more documents and information from third parties. Adjudicators will also keep the parties up to date with progress. If the matter is not or cannot be resolved by telephone, or if it is complex, the adjudicator may issue a formal adjudication report. This will set out the details of the dispute, the adjudicator's findings and any redress that is considered appropriate, and will be sent to both parties. Adjudicator and ombudsman decisions are now being given on a newly designed form, rather than a conventional letter, so that key conclusions, whether the firm needs to pay redress and what should be done next is clear at a glance on one page.[42] Both parties may then respond to the adjudicator, asking for clarity where a point has not been understood, and if they do not agree with the adjudicator, setting out why. The adjudicator may modify his view thereafter. In most cases, both sides accept the adjudicator's findings and the complaint is settled. If the adjudicator cannot resolve the complaint, either the firm or the consumer may ask for a review and final decision by an ombudsman.[43]

This is also the stage when any request for a hearing would be considered. The request must be in writing, setting out which issues should be dealt with at a hearing and whether the party thinks it should be held in private.[44] The ombudsman will decide whether the issues are material, whether a hearing should take place and whether it should be held in public or private,[45] and he will have regard to the provisions of the European Convention on Human Rights.[46] Under the updated DISP rules, hearings may also be held by telephone and no hearing can be held after the ombudsman's final determination.[47] Very few hearings take place and in the first ten years of the FOS, there has only been one reported insurance complaint, in Case Study 18/02,[48] where the FOS decided that a hearing would be helpful for each side to put forward their version of events and that it did not need to be a court hearing with cross-examination of witnesses. It was trying to determine whether the insurer had said at inception that the complainant's husband's angina would be covered.[49]

Involvement of ombudsman. Where an ombudsman becomes directly involved, **12–010** he will carry out an independent review of the evidence and then issue a final decision.[50] The ombudsman may ask for further evidence and give directions in relation to evidence, with which the parties are obliged to comply,[51] send both parties a provisional assessment with his reasoning and a time limit for receipt of

---

[42] Cf. *Ombudsman News* April/May 2010.

[43] The FOS Annual Review April 1, 2004 to March 31, 2005 states that about 55 per cent of cases in that year were resolved through an informal guided mediation, and 38 per cent through a more formal adjudication. The remaining 7 per cent (or 1 in 14) were resolved by a review and final determination by an ombudsman. According to the FOS "A Guide for Complaints Handlers" March 31, 2005 edition, a request for a review and final decision by an Ombudsman happens on average only in about 1 in 10 cases. According to the FOS Annual Review 2008/9, in that year, about one in eight cases progressed from adjudicators to ombudsmen. In 2009/10 it was about one in six cases (Annual Review 2009/10).

[44] DISP 3.5.6R.

[45] DISP 3.5.6R (3)–(15).

[46] DISP 3.5.7G.

[47] DISP 3.5.5R.

[48] *Ombudsman News* July 2002.

[49] Cf. also *R. (on the application of Heather Moor & Edgecomb Ltd) v FOS & Simon Lodge* [2008] EWCA Civ 642 and *R. (on the application of Heather Moor & Edgecomb Ltd) v FOS & Ross* [2009] EWHC 2701 (Admin).

[50] DISP 3.5.4R.

[51] DISP 3.5.8R and 3.5.11G.

their comments before issuing a final decision.[52] Before issuing a final decision about jurisdiction, whether the complainant is an "eligible complainant" or whether the case should be dismissed without consideration of its merits under DISP 3.3, the ombudsman must always give the complainant an opportunity to make representations on these points.[53] The ombudsman will set a time limit within which the consumer may accept the decision. If it is accepted, both the consumer and the firm will be bound[54] on awards up to £100,000 plus interest. If it is not accepted or if the complainant stays silent, the firm is not bound and the consumer remains free to bring court proceedings against the firm.[55] Excluding mortgage endowment complaints, between one third and a half of the cases where ombudsmen make formal final decisions are decided wholly or partly in the consumer's favour,[56] although the 2008/9 figures show for the first time a much higher figure of 57 per cent, due in a large part to the flood of payment protection insurance disputes which have an unprecedented uphold rate of more than 90 per cent.[57]

The ombudsman's final decision is the end of the FOS complaints' handling process and neither party can appeal to another ombudsman. The FSA's rules require the firm to comply promptly with an ombudsman decision as well as with any settlement that may have been agreed earlier in the process. If necessary, the consumer can go to court to enforce the ombudsman's decision.[58] An application for judicial review of the ombudsman's determination is also possible. According to *R. (on the application of Heather Moor & Edgecomb Ltd) v FOS & Simon Lodge*,[59] applying *R. (on the application of Thompson) v Law Society*,[60] and *R. (on the application of Heather Moor & Edgecomb Ltd) v FOS & Ross*,[61] it is the ability to apply for a public hearing by way of judicial review which brings the whole FOS procedure within the oral hearing requirements of art.6 of the Convention on Human Rights. Complaints about the FOS handling of a complaint (as opposed to any ombudsman's decisions) can be referred to the FOS Independent Assessor. His Annual Report for the year ending 2009/10 reported that in that year he received 262 referrals, of which he had jurisdiction to investigate 165. He upheld 67 of these wholly or in part, for which an award for distress and inconvenience was made in 60 cases, in the sum of £50–£250 for 40 per cent of them and £250–£500 for 48 per cent of them. An award for distress or inconvenience will take account of any extra interest a firm has had to pay an insured as a result of the FOS's inordinate delay, but an exact calculation will not be made. Of the complaints investigated, only around 5 per cent come from firms, out of which 25–50 per cent are upheld. [62]

---

[52] DISP 3.5.4R.

[53] DISP 3.2.3 R, 3.2.4 R and 3.3.1R.

[54] s.228(5) FSMA; DISP 3.6.6.

[55] s.228(6) FSMA and DISP 3.6.6R.

[56] *Ombudsman News* January 2003. The FOS Annual Review April 1, 2004 to March 31, 2005 shows that only 30–40 per cent of complaints which go before the Ombudsman are upheld.

[57] Speech by Tony Boorman (Principal Ombudsman): PPI complaints and consumer confidence February 24, 2009. For both 2008/9 and 2009/10 this translated into an uphold rate of about 89% of PPI claims but only 40% for other insurance claims (Annual Reviews 2008/9 and 2009/10).

[58] s.229(8) and Sch.17 Pt III s.16 FSMA.

[59] *R. (on the application of Heather Moor & Edgecomb Ltd) v FOS & Simon Lodge* [2008] EWCA Civ 642.

[60] *R. (on the application of Thompson) v Law Society* [2004] EWCA Civ 167.

[61] *R. (on the application of Heather Moor & Edgecomb Ltd) v FOS & Ross* [2009] EWHC 2701 (Admin).

[62] The statistics of complaints referred to the independent assessor have been broadly similar since 2004/5.

Evidence. In conducting its investigations, the FOS can decide whether or not to **12–011** admit evidence, and the decision will not necessarily be the same as a court's.[63] The FOS may instruct its own expert to advise. The FOS will also review an expert's report and possibly also his correspondence with the insurer, and may disagree with his findings.[64] Expert evidence may assist the FOS to decide whether an insured peril was more likely than not the cause of the damage.[65] The FOS may make an award for distress and inconvenience if an insurer wrongly ignores an insured's expert report. £750 was awarded in Case Study 73/08[66] in such circumstances. Under s.231 of the 2000 Act the FOS may require a party to provide information and documents within a reasonable period specified, in such manner or form as specified.[67] Under s.232 if a party fails to comply, the ombudsman may extend time where appropriate,[68] or he may certify the non-compliance in writing to the court and the court will enquire into the failure. If it finds no reasonable excuse, the party will be in contempt. Ultimately, the FOS can proceed to the next stage without the requested information.[69] The FOS will expect a higher standard of record keeping from firms than from consumers, in particular recordings of crucial conversations.[70] It will count against a firm if it cannot produce appropriate records and documents of paperwork specific to the consumer as well as copies of relevant standard documents and marketing material. For instance, in Case Study 13/07,[71] the complaint was upheld because the insurer, who was claiming material non-disclosure on the proposal form, could not produce the signed proposal, so there was no evidence that the insured had been untruthful. However, the FOS is at pains to stress that it is not true that without documentation the firm will automatically lose the case.[72] The FOS will look at whatever evidence is available to see what is most likely to have happened, what advice was given and whether it was appropriate for the customer's circumstances at the time. Information received by the FOS is confidential, although it will usually be passed to the other party and, in order to settle an issue, the FOS may consult and pass on various details to any relevant third party who may be able to shed light on the question. The FOS may also pass information about firms to the FSA or any other regulatory or government bodies.[73]

Dismissal or termination without considering the merits. At DISP 3.3.4R, the **12–012** FSA Handbook sets out seventeen circumstances in which the ombudsman may dismiss a complaint without considering its merits, even though it may be within the FOS jurisdiction. The most important are that: the complainant has not suffered, or is unlikely to suffer, financial loss, material distress or material inconvenience; the complaint is frivolous or vexatious; the complaint clearly does not have any reasonable prospect of success; the firm has already made an

---

[63] DISP 3.5.9R.

[64] Cf. Case Study 65/7, *Ombudsman News* Oct/Nov 2007.

[65] Cf. Case Studies 79/06, 79/08 and 79/09, *Ombudsman News*, Sept/Oct 2009.

[66] *Ombudsman News* Oct/Nov 2008.

[67] Reflected in DISP 3.5.8R and 3.5.13R. *Ombudsman News* April/May 2010 reports on a new 14-day time limit generally being imposed for firms and insureds to respond to FOS requests for information in order to speed up the whole process.

[68] DISP 3.5.13R.

[69] DISP 3.5.15R.

[70] See Case Study 18/01 *Ombudsman News* July 2002, where the assured was given the benefit of the doubt when he asserted that he had disclosed seven previous claims.

[71] *Ombudsman News* January 2002.

[72] *Ombudsman News* July 2006.

[73] DISP 3.8.3R.

offer of compensation which is fair and reasonable in relation to the circum-stances alleged and which is still open for acceptance; the subject matter of the complaint has been the subject of court proceedings where there has been a decision on the merits; it is a complaint about the legitimate exercise of a firm's commercial judgment; or the complaint has already been considered by the FOS, unless material new evidence has subsequently become available. Following *R. (on the application of Cook) v FOS*,[74] a new expert's report may not be material new evidence if it could with reasonable diligence have been obtained and submitted before the Ombudsman's final determination. Under DISP 3.3.5R, the ombudsman may also dismiss a complaint without considering its merits if before it has made a determination, it has received in writing from the firm a statement that the complaint raises an important or novel point of law with significant consequences and an undertaking that the firm will pay the complain-ant's costs if judicial proceedings are commenced within six months.

12–013   *Referral to court.* Few cases where the complainant disagrees with the ombuds-man's decision end up in court.[75] This seems natural for the following reasons. Within the FOS, the complaint will have been reviewed by at least three people all trying to determine what is fair and reasonable in the circumstances, so the ombudsman's decision may feel like a pseudo-appeal in itself. On top of this, it would seem sensible for the claimant to be unwilling to pursue a matter in litigation, at cost and with costs risks, where an independent body, often applying more lenient rules to the consumer than a court would, has already determined that it is a losing case, and where the court would inevitably be shown the ombudsman's reasoned rejection of the complaint. Many complainants will have had enough of the fight. Some cases will be too big for the small claims court, but too small to be commercially viable to bring in the county or high court. And in any case, even if proceedings are commenced, most litigation is settled before trial.

Many consumers will feel satisfied that they have already been heard and that an independent body has looked at the matter impartially. In fact, the FOS customer surveys in 2003/4 showed that 80 per cent of the consumers who replied were satisfied with the FOS, although only 60 per cent had thought the decision had been reasonable. This latter figure may be a reflection of the fact that more complaints are rejected than upheld.[76] The FOS Annual Review 2008/9, shows that 83 per cent of customers who said they felt they had "won" were satisfied with the FOS handling of the matter and 42 per cent of those who said they felt they had "lost". 66 per cent of firms responding thought that the FOS provides a good independent dispute resolution service. The figures in the FOS Annual Review 2009/10 were respectively 87%, 46% and 63%.

Although it was not possible to apply for judicial review of an IOB decision[77] now under the compulsory jurisdiction of the FOS, firms may apply for judicial

---

[74] *R. (on the application of Cook) v FOS* [2009] EWHC 426 (Admin).

[75] See *Margate Theatre Royal Trust Ltd v White* [2006] Lloyd's Rep. I.R. 93, a rare case in which the assured lost before the FOS but won in court, and also *Lewis v Norwich Union Healthcare Ltd* [2009] EW Misc 2 (EWCC).

[76] "Fair and reasonable—An assessment of the Financial Ombudsman Service" by Kempson, Collard and Moore from the Personal Finance Research Centre, University of Bristol, July 2004.

[77] *R. v IOB Ex p. Aegon Life Assurance Ltd* (1994) C.L.C. 88, followed in *R. v Deputy Insurance Ombudsman Ex p. Francis* Unreported, May 20, 1998 and applied in *R. v Panel of the Federation of Communication Services Ltd & Anr Ex p. Kubis* Unreported September 3, 1997, *R. (on the application of Sunspell Ltd (t/a Superlative Travel)) v Association of British Travel Agents* [2001] A.C.D. 16 and *R. v Personal Investment Authority Ombudsman Bureau Ltd Ex p. Johannes Mooyes* [2001] EWCA Admin 247.

review of FOS decisions, although there have only been a few such applications. Presumably this is because of commercial and economic realities and because it would be hard to succeed in an application due to the FOS wide discretion to substitute its own values of fairness and reasonableness in all the circumstances of the case instead of strict law. As long as the ombudsman has considered the strict law and the other matters listed under DISP 3.6.4R, a court will not interfere with an ombudsman's sense of what is fair and reasonable[78] although his decision must still be rational. In *R. (on the application of Garrison Investment Analysis) v FOS*,[79] the ombudsman's redress did not fulfil the aim he set himself, to put the parties into the position they would have been in were it not for the firm's error so was, on its face, irrational. His decision was quashed and remitted back to him to apply the appropriate redress in the light of his earlier conclusions as to the effect of the error made by the financial adviser.

2. Operation of the Ombudsman Scheme

Jurisdiction of the FOS[80]

Compulsory and voluntary jurisdictions. The FOS has compulsory jurisdiction **12–014** over complaints relating to FSA-regulated activities. This includes firms that were covered by one of the predecessor ombudsman schemes for complaints about events before December 1, 2001 and over those which are regulated by the FSA for complaints about events from December 1, 2001. The FOS has voluntary jurisdiction over firms which have chosen to join, in which case they are treated as having submitted to the authority of the FOS as if they fall under the compulsory jurisdiction.[81] These "VJ participants" include: since March 2002, general insurance companies based in Europe and not regulated by the FSA that deal predominantly with customers in the United Kingdom; since April 2003, certain firms regulated by the FSA from December 1, 2001, that wanted to be covered for complaints about events which occurred before that date.

From April 6, 2007, a third type of jurisdiction was created—the Consumer Credit Jurisdiction. Under the Consumer Credit Act 2006, businesses with consumer credit licences issued by the Office of Fair Trading became covered by the FOS even if they are not also regulated by the FSA. From the same date, three additional activities became regulated by the FSA and were put within the remit of the FOS: advice on self-invested personal pensions, the sale and administration of home-reversion plans and the sale and administration of Islamic home-purchase products. From January 14, 2005, insurance intermediaries became regulated by the FSA and so fell within the FOS jurisdiction. This excluded travel agents, loss adjusters and goods' retailers selling extended warranties on their products. From January 1, 2009, travel agents selling insurance as part of a package holiday were added to the FSA and FOS jurisdictions. From November 1, 2009, the FOS also covered money transfer operators.

---

[78] *R. (on the application of IFG Financial Services Ltd) v FOS Ltd and Mr and Mrs Jenkins (interested parties)* [2005] EWHC 1153 (Admin), approved by *R. (on the application of Heather Moor & Edgecomb Ltd v Financial Ombudsman Service and Simon Lodge* [2008] EWCA Civ 642.

[79] *R. (on the application of Garrison Investment Analysis) v FOS* [2006] EWHC 2466 (Admin).

[80] Cf. DISP 2 of the FSA Handbook for fuller details of the FOS jurisdiction.

[81] DISP 4.

The FOS covers activities of a firm carried on from an establishment in the United Kingdom[82] (not the Channel Islands[83]). In some circumstances, the FOS will have jurisdiction over activities carried out from another country within the EEA by a firm which falls under the FOS voluntary jurisdiction.[84] If the FOS does not have territorial jurisdiction over a complaint, there may be a local ombudsman scheme which does. FIN-NET[85] is a network of financial ombudsmen and consumer complaints organisations covering countries of the EEA. The FOS is a member, and any financial dispute resolution body within the EEA can join if it meets certain standards set by the European Commission. All members remain autonomous. Under the scheme, members agree to direct a complainant to the appropriate organisation in the country of the financial organisation (rather than of the complainant), co-operate with each other and exchange practical information (for instance relating to questions of law in the complainant's country).

12–015 *Complaints within the scheme.* The complaint must relate to an action by the insurer (as opposed to the insured event), which was taken after December 1, 2001 when the FOS came into being.[86] However the Ombudsman Transitional Order allows the FOS to deal, with only a few exceptions, with "relevant new complaints", namely those referred to the FOS after December 1, 2001 relating to an event when the firm was subject to a former scheme. Under DISP 2.7.10G, a relevant new complaint must be made by an individual, and must not relate to a business or trade carried on by him. Other transitional arrangements were made for complaints already referred to an Ombudsman scheme, but not resolved before December 1, 2001. The scheme has, since January 14, 2005, applied to complaints about intermediaries. The FOS does not have jurisdiction over claims management providers: the Ministry of Justice is the regulator.[87]

12–016 *Complainants.* DISP 2.2.1G states that the complaint must be brought by or on behalf of an "eligible complainant,"[88] defined until November 2009 by DISP 2.7.3R as a private individual, a business with a group annual turnover of less than £1 million,[89] a charity with an annual income of less than £1 million or a trustee of a trust with net assets worth less than £1 million at the time the complainant refers the complaint to the firm or VJ participant. The ombudsman will determine the eligibility of a commercial complaint by reference to appropriate evidence such as audited accounts or VAT returns.[90] From November 1, 2009, when the Payment Services Directive 2007/64/EC came into effect, the FOS amended DISP 2.7.3R, so that a "private individual" became a "consumer[91]", and a "business with a group annual turnover of less than £1 million"

---

[82] DISP 2.6.1R and 2.6.3R.

[83] Cf. Case Study 32/11 in *Ombudsman News* October 2003, where the complaint was outside the jurisdiction because the firm's activities had been in the Channel Islands, although the complainant's Jersey nationality was not important.

[84] DISP 2.6.4R.

[85] *http://www.fin-net.eu* [Accessed June 16, 2010].

[86] Cf. Case Study 32/9 in *Ombudsman News* October 2003, where the relevant date was not the fire but the date of the matter complained about, which in this case was the date the claim was turned down.

[87] Compensation Act 2006; *Ombudsman News* January/February 2007; *http://www.claimsregula tion.gov.uk* [Accessed June 16, 2010].

[88] Also DISP 2.7R.

[89] i.e. a small business.

[90] DISP 2.7.5G.

[91] See FSA Handbook Glossary of Terms and ICOBS 2.1.1G(3).

became a "micro-enterprise[92]". The new terms have slightly different definitions to the old ones. The definition of small business throughout its jurisdiction was changed to match that of micro-enterprise in the EU legislation; namely a turnover of 2 million Euro with fewer than 10 staff. However, small businesses only account for about 2 per cent of all complaints referred.[93] To be eligible, the complainant must also have been a customer or a potential customer of the firm or VJ participant and the complaint must arise out of a matter relevant to that.[94] Where the complainant lives or his nationality is not important.

Beneficiaries of a group scheme and also tenants whose interest is noted on a block building policy, can bring a complaint to the FOS. However, the FOS will have no jurisdiction to deal with an employee's complaint about a group policy if it is actually for the benefit of the company rather than for the employee, such as if it is a "key man" policy or if the employer is effectively reinsuring its own contractual liability to pay sickness benefits. In such a scenario, the employer may wish to bring the complaint, but will not be able to do so unless it is a micro-enterprise, as defined above.

Principles applicable to claims handling by insurers

A distinction is drawn between a "consumer," defined by ICOBS 2.1.1G(3) as   **12–017**
"any natural person who is acting for purposes which are outside his trade or profession", and a "commercial customer", defined by ICOBS 2.1.1G(4) as "a customer who is not a consumer." ICOBS 8.1.1R requires insurers to handle all claims promptly and fairly, and to provide reasonable guidance to help the assured to make a claim. Consumers are given additional protection against avoidance for non-disclosure or misrepresentation, and in respect of breach of warranty. The key provision is ICOBS 8.1.2R:

> "A rejection of a "consumer policyholder's" claim is unreasonable, except where there is evidence of fraud, if it is for:
> (1) non-disclosure of a fact material to the risk which the policyholder could not reasonably be expected to have disclosed; or
> (2) non-negligent misrepresentation of a fact material to the risk; or
> (3) breach of warranty or condition, unless the circumstances of the claim are connected with the breach and unless (for a pure protection contract):
>> (a) under a 'life of another' contract, the warranty relates to a statement of fact concerning the life to be assured and, if the statement had been made by the life to be assured under an 'own life' contract, the insurer could have rejected the claim under this rule; or
>> (b) the warranty is material to the risk and was drawn to the customer's attention before the conclusion of the contract."

Non-disclosure and misrepresentation

The rights of insurers. The FOS approaches these matters in three stages: (1)   **12–018**
when the customer sought insurance, did the insurer comply with good practice for instance in asking a clear question about the matter which is now under dispute; (2) did the answer to that clear question induce the insurer to enter into the contract at all, or under terms and conditions that it otherwise would not have accepted; (3) if the answers to both questions are "yes", the FOS goes on to

---

[92] See FSA Handbook Glossary of Terms.
[93] *Ombudsman News* Dec 2008/Jan 2009. Ombudsman News April/May 2010 reported 5,000 complaints every year from small businesses.
[94] DISP 2.7.6R.

consider whether the customer's misrepresentation was a dishonest or honest mistake, or something in between—the consequences of the non-disclosure will depend on whether the FOS considers it to be fraudulent or deliberate, innocent, reckless or inadvertent. The Law Commissions have proposed a Consumer Insurance (Disclosure and Representations) Bill 2009[95] which mirrors the FOS approach in relation to non-disclosure and misrepresentations in consumer insurance.[96]

Deliberate non-disclosure involves dishonestly providing information which the discloser knows to be untrue or incomplete, (it will also be fraudulent if the necessary intent is present), and the insurer will be allowed to avoid the policy. An example of a deliberate non-disclosure can be found in Case Study 61/06,[97] where the questions were clear, yet the disparity between the proposer's actual weight (over 21 stone) and height (5ft 9in) and the figures he put on the proposal form (16 stone and 6ft respectively), was so great that, on the balance of probabilities, he could not have believed that his answers were accurate. In Case Study 77/03,[98] the FOS supported insurers' avoidance ab initio of the claim with a return of the premium, where the evidence of the internet sale was that the insured had more likely than not intentionally misled insurers when she said that she had no penalty points on her driving licence. In fact she had nine.

If the disclosure is innocent, the FOS will not allow the insurer to avoid the contract and will require it to pay the claim in full whatever it would have done had it known the true position, subject to policy terms and conditions. The FOS will consider a non-disclosure to be innocent where: (a) the question was unclear or ambiguous, or did not clearly apply to the facts in the case[99]; (b) the relevant information was not something that the proposer should reasonably have known, (nor should the questions relate to matters which the proposer could not possibly have known); or (c) it was reasonable for the proposer to have overlooked the fact. The FOS will take into account any explanation for the discrepancy and will expect the insurer to have asked the policyholder for an explanation so that it can also take it into account.

The FOS will consider a non-disclosure to be reckless where it finds it difficult to believe that the proposer could simply have overlooked the matter, which is typically of significance and well known to the proposer, but the FOS does not find enough evidence to show deliberate non-disclosure. The answers must have been given without a care for truth or accuracy and the proposer must have understood, if only in a limited way, that an answer to the point in question was required, that it was important to the insurer and that there was a consequence to the answer.[100] In such cases, the FOS considers that the firm can decline to meet the claim, can cancel the policy from its start date, recover payments for any previous claims made under that policy and return the premium paid. In other words, the FOS regards a reckless non-disclosure as seriously as a deliberate one.

[95] December 15, 2009.

[96] See Ch.6, above, for further detail.

[97] *Ombudsman News* April/May 2007.

[98] *Ombudsman News* May/June 2009.

[99] E.g. Case Study 79/10, *Ombudsman News* Sept/Oct 2009, where the insured could not reasonably have been expected to know from the wording of the proposal form that the insurer meant that the modifications he had made to his car were of the sort that the insurer required to be disclosed.

[100] Cf. Case Study 61/05 *Ombudsman News* April/May 2007.

Where the non-disclosure is inadvertent,[101] i.e. where the proposer unintentionally misleads the insurer through a one-off, understandable oversight or moment of carelessness, rather than through any deliberate act, the FOS will take into account the circumstances surrounding the information, the clarity of express questions, whether the insurer gave any warning about the consequences of giving false or incomplete information and how clear such a warning was; the degree to which the policyholder should have been aware of the information he was asked to provide and whether the policyholder was likely to have recognised the significance to the firm of this information, especially in the context of the type of insurance applied for; and how recent and significant an event was. If there has been an inadvertent non-disclosure, and the insurer would have declined the insurance had it known the true position, then the FOS may support an avoidance of the policy and no payment of the claim at all. If the insurer would have accepted the risk, but on different terms, the FOS will expect insurers to rewrite the insurance on the terms they would originally have offered if they had been aware of all the information. If the result would have been an increased premium, the FOS may adopt a proportional approach, where it calculates the proportion of the premium that was paid against the higher premium that would have been charged if the true facts were known, and bases the settlement on that proportion.[102] If the result of the disclosure would have been a reduced premium with more exclusions in the policy, the FOS might allow the insurer to add the premium refund to the settlement. If the firm would merely have added an exclusion or amended a term without changing the premium, then the FOS may simply treat the claim as if that amendment or exclusion was in place.

The FOS may award compensation for distress and inconvenience where an insurer wrongly tries to void a policy for non-disclosure, especially in a medical context.

Convictions and previous losses. The FOS considers that if an insurer insists on asking about convictions spent under the Rehabilitation of Offenders Act 1974, it must effectively ignore the answers it receives. Similarly, the FOS will uphold a complaint if a policy is voided for non-disclosure of a licence endorsement relating to a spent conviction. **12–019**

Insurers usually ask questions about previous losses. Where a policyholder fails to mention at inception or renewal, in answer to a question on a proposal form, that he has had a claim, loss or accident within a certain number of years, typically three years, unlike a court, the FOS considers[103] that there will be a cut-off point after which that non-disclosure will no longer be material. So in a typical three-year-period, a 2.5-year-old loss will only be relevant if there is another claim in the first year of cover, but will be too old to be relevant after renewal.

Renewals. Assureds are to be notified in good time when a policy is about to expire.[104] Assureds are required to disclose on renewal any change in circumstances which might be material, but this is only so where an insurer clearly asks **12–020**

---

[101] For examples of inadvertent non-disclosure, see Case Studies 61/01 and 61/03, both *Ombudsman News* April/ May 2007, Case Study 68/10, *Ombudsman News* March/April 2008 and Case Study 79/11, *Ombudsman News* Sept/Oct 2009.

[102] Such as in Case Study 61/03, *Ombudsman News* April/May 2007.

[103] *Ombudsman News* January 2001.

[104] ICOB 5.3.18R suggested at least 21 days before expiry of the policy. However, under ICOBS 6.1.8G, no time is specified.

at renewal for details which the insured can reasonably be expected to possess, as the assured cannot reasonably be expected to remember all information provided at inception, which may be several years previous to the renewal in question. So the FOS will not support an insurer who declines a claim based on non-disclosure of information in response to a general question such as "has anything changed in the information we asked for in your proposal form?", unless the insurer has provided the insured with a copy of the original proposal and asked him to check and re-confirm at renewal all the information originally provided, or unless it asks all the questions afresh.[105] However, there will still be situations where it will be so obvious that new information needs to be disclosed that insurers will be able to rely on the non-disclosure even if the previously disclosed material is not provided: for example the heart murmur not disclosed at renewal of a travel policy in Case Study 64/9.[106]

Insurers are meant to notify an insured of any change of terms on renewal.[107] A problem may arise where employers change the terms or the insurers of a group policy and the terms of the new policy are different. Insurers often expect employers to inform employees about the change of terms, particularly where the changes have been made at the employer's request to reduce the cost of the insurance. But the FOS expects insurers to play an active role in notifying employees of all changes, or requiring the employer to, and insurers may not simply delegate to the employer their responsibility in this respect.[108] Otherwise, the FOS may not support insurers who refuse a claim based on a term which was changed at renewal but not highlighted for the employee.

12–021 *Continuing duty of good faith.* There is generally no continuing duty of disclosure after inception or renewal or claims. However, there may be a duty of disclosure where the risk changes so fundamentally that the subject matter of the insurance is completely different, such as if the customer buys a new car or moves house. Only in such a case, would it be reasonable for the insurer to vary the terms of the policy. If an insurer requires to be notified during the duration of the policy of any other change of circumstances, the FOS may not consider such terms to be fair and reasonable, especially if they were not highlighted when the policy was sold.[109] The most common example is where an insured is required to notify insurers of a change in health between inception of a travel policy and the start of the holiday. The FOS considers that an annual travel policy should be just that. It finds this sort of continuing disclosure obligation to be so inherently unfair that in Case Study 64/86,[110] where the insurer relied on the clause to exclude cover for the cancer condition disclosed, it asked the insurer to reimburse the cost of the alternative policy which the insured had to find at short notice before he went on his holiday, plus £200 for distress and inconvenience. Where a change in health is disclosed at renewal of an annual travel policy and the insurer informs the assured that it cannot provide future cover for the condition disclosed, the FOS considers that it should also give the insured the option of

[105] Cf. Case Study 61/02, *Ombudsman News* April/May 2007.
[106] *Ombudsman News* Sept/Oct 2007.
[107] Cf. ICOBS 6.1.5R and 6.1.6G.
[108] Cf. ICOBS 6.1.12G which says that an insurer should provide appropriate information to the employer and ask it to pass the information on to each employee which is a beneficiary of the group policy.
[109] E.g. Case Study 80/01, *Ombudsman News* Oct/Nov 2009.
[110] *Ombudsman News* Sept/Oct 2007.

cancelling before renewal any holiday already booked and covering the cancellation costs at this time, even though cancellation may not be medically necessary at that stage.

Breach of warranty

Where a commercial entity is more akin to an individual consumer, taking into account the nature and resources of the business, the FOS will treat it like a consumer and will not apply the strict legal position following a breach of warranty. A commercial policyholder is likely to be treated as such if it is a limited company, employs a number of staff, rents substantial business premises, has detailed legal agreements with suppliers and/or could reasonably be expected to have a greater understanding of business issues than a private individual, for instance in view of the director's previous employment, perhaps as a solicitor or insurance broker. So where in Case Study 39/1[111] there was a break in at a small café, the claim for the loss, including that part of it which was not caused by the breach of security warranty was not paid and the complaint was rejected. This was because the café was considered to be a commercial entity, as it employed four full-time staff, it was a limited company and it had access to expert advice in the form of insurance brokers through whom it bought the policy and made the claim. By comparison, in Case Study 74/09,[112] the FOS found that a small graphic design business, with a modest turnover and only two part-time employees should be treated as a consumer. So because the breach of a condition precedent (that the doors should be made of solid wood) was unconnected to the theft (the front door was forced off its hinges, so ingress would have been achieved regardless of the construction of the door), the claim had to be met. The Law Commissions are considering whether micro and small businesses should be treated as consumers,[113] but there are no proposals about this in the Consumer Insurance (Disclosure and Representations) Bill 2009,[114] which in relation to warranties only bans basis of the contract clauses for consumers, which is a practice already adopted by the FOS.

12–022

Particular issues

Construction. Where the meaning of a policy is unclear, the FOS will look first to the common usage of the words and if this does not resolve the question, will interpret them in accordance with the contra proferentem rule in favour of the assured, much as a court might do. Unlike a court, the FOS might also do this where the layout of a policy is confusing, for instance where exclusions are printed on different pages to the paragraphs they modify or where wordings in schedules, policies and marketing material are contradictory.[115]

12–023

A policyholder can be seriously disadvantaged where there is a misleading description of an insurance policy or associated leaflet, especially if it promises the same wide-ranging cover as other policies with a similar title, but contains exclusions which bring the cover far short of the norm. The FOS considers that the customer is entitled to rely, at least to some extent, on the policy headlines. Where cover falls short of the policy description, the FOS will consider whether

---

[111] *Ombudsman News* August 2004.
[112] *Ombudsman News* Dec 08/Jan 09.
[113] Law Commissions Issues Paper 5: Micro-businesses—should micro-businesses be treated like consumers for the purposes of pre-contractual information and unfair terms? April 2009.
[114] See further Ch.7, above.
[115] Case Study 18/15, *Ombudsman News* July 2002.

the customer could have had any reasonable expectation of cover on the wider basis. The FOS will look at what a reasonable person would have concluded about the nature of the cover from the information available to him. The FOS remedy will involve a return of premium as if the contract never happened and an alternative policy is unavailable.[115a] Where better alternative cover is readily available, the FOS is likely to conclude that the insurer should handle the claim as if its unusual or misleading restrictions on cover did not apply.[116]

If the policy includes a special definition which an insured would not generally recognise, or if there is an exclusion or onerous condition which the average insured would not usually expect, the FOS is unlikely to uphold the insurer's interpretation, unless the assured's attention was brought to these points before inception[117] and their significance to the particular policyholder explained.[118] Giving the insured time to read the policy and the option to cancel it is not enough to satisfy this requirement.[119] The key features of a policy must be highlighted in the documentation: see Case Studies 62/5, 62/6 and 62/8[120] for an idea of which features the FOS considers key in a payment protection policy. A term which effectively requires a continuing duty of disclosure will usually be considered onerous.[121]

Sufficient care is not always taken at the point of sale to ensure the suitability of policies or eligibility of prospective policyholders, e.g. Case Studies 71/02, 71/03 and 71/04[121a] and Case Study 86/9[121b] in relation to payment protection policies.[121c] The FOS expects the seller not only to record what the insured discloses, but also to ask questions on relevant matters to determine suitability and eligibility, and to point out the main features and relevant restrictions. The Codes[122] provide more detail of what is expected. If an insurer realises at the claims stage that an unsuitable sale has been made, and if the assured has been prejudiced, the FOS considers that insurers should usually meet the claim.[123] In the interests of fairness, the FOS may also be less strict in its approach when interpreting what situations might fall within a certain condition. For instance, the FOS interpreted "locked accommodation" to include a locked camper van in Case Study 63/8, *Ombudsman News* July/August 2007, where the loss would not have been covered if it had found it to be a vehicle, even though the FOS thought it to be more of a vehicle than an accommodation.

Sometimes, even if a condition is not especially onerous, is perfectly clear and would be applied strictly by a court, the FOS will not apply it strictly if the

[115a] Case Study 86/12, *Ombudsman News* June/July 2010.

[116] Case Study 18/13, *Ombudsman News* July 2002. See also Case Study 62/9, *Ombudsman News* June/July 2007.

[117] Cf. Case Study 65/05, *Ombudsman News* Oct/Nov 2007 and Case Study 86/10, *Ombudsman News*, June/July 2010.

[118] Case Study 85/01, *Ombudsman News* April/May 2010. The remedy for not doing this was the insurer having to pay the claim that by its strict policy terms would have been excluded, on the basis that the policyholder would have sought insurance elsewhere if she had known of the restriction, and in view of the circumstances, another insurer would have covered the risk without such a restriction.

[119] Case Study 07/03, *Ombudsman News* July 2001.

[120] *Ombudsman News* June/July 2007.

[121] E.g. Case Study 80/01, *Ombudsman News* Oct/Nov 2009.

[121a] *Ombudsman News* August 2008.

[121b] *Ombudsman News* June/July 2010.

[121c] Cf. FOS website "Technical Notes—online PPI resource" for further details on the way that the FOS deals with complaints about payment protection policies.

[122] i.e. the old ABI and GISC Codes of Practice, ICOB at s.4.3 and ICOBS 5.1.

[123] Case Study 01/05, *Ombudsman News* January 2001.

circumstances of the case in question would make a strict interpretation unfair.[124]

Causation. The FOS applies the same causation test as is recognised by the general law. However, in the case of concurrent causes where one of the causes is excluded, the FOS will not necessarily adopt the strict view that the exclusion prevails.

12–024

The FOS has commented on this point in relation to personal accident insurance.[125] If the medical evidence shows that the accident caused only 10 per cent of the injury, and the other 90 per cent was due to degenerative change which was excluded, then the FOS would usually ask the insurer to pay 10 per cent of the benefit. This is on the basis of good industry practice, as many insurers voluntarily make a proportionate contribution if the accident is shown to have accelerated pre-existing degenerative changes. The FOS view is that it is neither fair nor reasonable to use the mere presence of degenerative change to exclude genuine personal accident claims to which such policies are clearly designed to respond.

Payment of premium. Usually if the premium has not been paid, there will be no cover. However, in certain circumstances, the FOS might hold that actually there is cover, e.g. where the assured believed that his policy had been renewed automatically and had not noticed that the premium was no longer being taken from his bank.[126] Mistaken cancellation of a direct debit by a bank in one case study, leaving the assured without cover, was found to be 40 per cent the fault of the bank, 40 per cent the fault of the insurer (which should have contacted the assured before cancelling cover) and 20 per cent the fault of the assured for not noticing.[127] There can be the converse problem of overpayment of premium where the insured is over-insured, for example, by reason of automatic re-rating. The FOS will try to remedy this, in one case by requiring the insurer to refund 50 per cent of the premiums paid over the previous five years, plus interest.[128] Where premium is repaid on policy cancellation and the FOS is asked to consider whether a cancellation charge is fair, it will have regard to the Unfair Terms in Consumer Contract Regulations 1999,[129] and the statements on unfair contract terms made by the FSA in its publication "Challenging unfair terms in consumer contracts" available on the FSA website.[130] The FOS does not usually find it unreasonable for the firm to recover the costs necessarily incurred in setting up the policy which will now no longer be spread over the lifetime of the insurance, nor any reasonable additional administrative costs it incurs in cancelling a policy. In Case Study 54/5,[131] £50 for administrative costs was acceptable. The FOS does not generally find unfair a term which says that premiums for an annual contract are not refundable if a claim has been paid. The firm needs to have fair reasons for its approach to premium refunds and to be able to explain this approach clearly to the insured. If a customer decides to cancel the insurance

12–025

---

[124] Case Study 07/10, *Ombudsman News* July 2001 and Case Study 65/3, *Ombudsman News* Oct/Nov 2007.

[125] *Ombudsman News* March 2005.

[126] Case Study 23/14, *Ombudsman News* December 2002.

[127] Case Study 31/1, *Ombudsman News* September 2003.

[128] Case Study 04/17, *Ombudsman News* April 2001.

[129] SI 1999/2083. See Ch.3, above.

[130] *http://www.fsa.gov.uk* [Accessed June 16, 2010].

[131] *Ombudsman News* July 2006.

contract during the applicable regulatory cooling-off period, insurers are not entitled to charge anything.

12–026 *Mitigation.* It would be rare for a policy to cover the costs of taking steps to prevent damage. Yet such action may save the insurer from having to pay out on a large insured risk. If a policyholder acts reasonably to prevent a much larger insured damage, which would have cost significantly more, the FOS considers it reasonable to require the insurer to meet the costs of the damage, even though a court would not adopt this approach.[132]

12–027 *Repair and replacement.* Where the insurer opts for repair, the FOS considers that it must explain to the assured the implications of any choices made about who should be appointed to carry out the repairs and who will control the work. If the insurer chooses or controls the repairer, then it is normally the insurer who will be liable to make good any deficiencies in the repair.[133] Further, the insurer will also be responsible for the cost of an uninsured repair carried out on the advice of the insurer's repairer if it proves to have been unnecessary.[134] If however, the insured insists on a particular repairer, (as opposed to just providing estimates for the insurer to appoint one), the insured will generally be responsible for the quality of the repairs, unless the insurer controls the work such as by requiring the repairer to cut his costs or to use particular materials or parts. The FOS may also impose a reasonableness condition on the insurer's discretion to opt for repair, as it did in Case Study 58/5.[135]

The FOS will only regard replacement as a reasonable option if the object can be replaced, (for example, antique jewellery cannot be replaced by a modern piece), a suitable alternative is found and the insured wishes to purchase a replacement (his personal circumstances may have changed his desire to own the item). Otherwise, the FOS will normally ask the insurer to agree a cash settlement. In such circumstances, the FOS would not regard it as reasonable for the insurer to make a deduction from the cash settlement to represent any discount it would have got if the policyholder had bought a replacement from one of the insurer's nominated suppliers. If there is to be a replacement, the FOS may consider it unreasonable to limit the choice to a particular retailer or for the insurer to offer vouchers to the insured. Insureds should be allowed to choose where they purchase a replacement.

When an insurer opts to reinstate, it is bound to replace as new with no deduction for wear or tear or depreciation. However, the FOS will support those insurers who reduce payment where the total sum insured is inadequate to cover the property at risk, as long as the reduction is not communicated and imposed too late in the process.[136] Even where there is an adequate sum insured on a building, it is possible, although unusual, that this will not be enough to cover reinstatement costs: in these circumstances, the FOS does not believe it reasonable for the insurer to limit its liability to the sum insured.[137]

---

[132] See Ch.10, above. For the FOS approach, see Case Study 10/3, *Ombudsman News*, October 2001. Note FOS comments in *Ombudsman News* January/February 2007 that it will not accept insurers' argument that ground stabilisation work should not be covered as it is preventative rather than restorative work.

[133] E.g. Case Study 83/09, *Ombudsman News* Feb/March 2010.

[134] Case Study 83/08, *Ombudsman News* Feb/March 2010.

[135] *Ombudsman News* December 2006/January 2007.

[136] Case Study 04/18, *Ombudsman News* April 2001.

[137] Case Study 04/20, *Ombudsman News* April 2001.

Proof of loss. The assured must prove the loss. The FOS may be more likely to **12–028** rule in favour of insurers if the insured has disposed of the evidence.[138] In the case of alleged theft, a police report will generally be required,[139] although the requirement will be waived if the assured has done everything which could reasonably be expected to recover the property.[140] If a policyholder fails to resolve discrepancies or to co-operate with insurer's enquiries, insurers may be justified in refusing to meet the claim.[141]

Fraudulent claims. The burden of proving fraud is on the insurer, who will need **12–029** to provide concrete evidence of inconsistent statements or acts of deception and show the appropriate dishonest intent to induce the insurer to pay more than that to which the policyholder is entitled.[142] The insurer cannot just rely on its gut feeling, even in front of the FOS, which, like the court, considers that the burden of proof for fraud is raised to a degree more akin to the criminal standard of beyond reasonable doubt. By the time the case reaches the FOS, it may be too late to uncover any new evidence, so the FOS will expect an insurer to have investigated the matter carefully at an earlier stage. Where a firm suspects fraud, the FOS expects it to make its views known to the policyholder, who can then respond to the allegations. The FOS is unlikely to support an insurer if, instead, it uses a separate and spurious reason to justify rejecting a claim.

An exaggeration will only be fraudulent and entitle the insurer to repudiate the whole claim, when the policyholder has the necessary intent of trying to obtain more than that to which he is entitled. So it would not be fraudulent inaccurately to recall a purchase price or mistakenly give an exaggerated replacement cost. Nor would it be fraudulent for a policyholder to give an exaggerated view of his car's worth, when he would receive the market value from the insurer whatever he said.

The fact that a policyholder has lied in another context, (perhaps in relation to a different claim under another policy), is not sufficient proof of fraud in the current claim, although it may raise doubts about the accuracy of the policy-holder's version of events in the current claim.

Presenting a forged document in support of the claim will not necessarily be fraudulent. For fraud there would have to be evidence showing that the policyholder knew the document's true source and that he intended to obtain more than that to which he was entitled. That would not be the case where, under perhaps unreasonable pressure to provide receipts, a policyholder forged one to substantiate a genuine loss. The FOS calls this an "immaterial fraud." In such a case, the FOS has long considered it harsh for the claim not to be paid or for the policy to be voided or forfeited. The FOS view is that if the insurer's ultimate liability to pay the claim under the terms of the policy is not affected by the fraud, it should, in effect, be disregarded and the claim should be paid.[143] A common example of where a forged document would make no difference to the insurance recovery would be if insurers had asked a policyholder to substantiate the original purchase price in a claim for a written-off vehicle. As the claim will be for the present market value, the original price, whatever it is, will not be

---

[138] Cf. Case Study 58/4, *Ombudsman News* December 2006/January 2007.

[139] Case Study 07/14, *Ombudsman News* July 2001 and Case Study 75/08, *Ombudsman News,* Jan/Feb 2009.

[140] Case Study 13/10, *Ombudsman News* January 2002.

[141] Case Study 13/17, *Ombudsman News* January 2002.

[142] E.g. Case Study 85/04, *Ombudsman News* April/May 2010 and Case Study 86/13, *Ombudsman News* June/July 2010.

[143] *Ombudsman News*, November 2004; *Ombudsman News* December 2004/January 2005.

relevant. So, as long as there is no doubt about ownership and no suggestion of fraud, the FOS would require the insurer to meet such a claim on the basis of the normal market value of the vehicle.[144]

Where there is enough evidence of a sufficiently serious fraud, the firm is only entitled to void the policy and recover payments made in connection with earlier claims if the fraud was at the proposal stage. If the fraud happens at the claims stage, the FOS considers that insurers should only forfeit the policy from the date of the fraud, so that they may refuse to pay that claim (including any non-fraudulent parts) or to provide any future cover, but past claims will remain untouched. Where the evidence of fraud is contradictory, and would be better sorted out in a court, the FOS may decline jurisdiction.[145]

Although in law the insurer can retain the premium after avoidance on the grounds of fraudulent non-disclosure, it is not clear that the FOS will allow this, or whether it makes a distinction in this respect between fraudulent and deliberate non-disclosures. In Case Study 72/02[146] the FOS found that the non-disclosure could not have been accidental or casual, but found no evidence of dishonesty. It said that although the insurer was entitled to refuse the claim, it was wrong to retain the premium, which was to be returned with interest.

Specific policies

12–030   *Extended warranties.* Assureds frequently misunderstand extended warranties, wrongly thinking that they protect from anything and everything which might go wrong with the product. The FOS may uphold complaints if on a common sense approach these thoughts are a result of poor or misleading sales or marketing.[147] In order to be able to claim on an extended warranty, the policyholder may have to follow a complex procedure with strict time limits. Such requirements may represent unfair terms in the eyes of the FOS, especially where little or no effort has been made to draw the customer's attention to this complex "small print."[148]

12–031   *Travel insurance.* Travel insurance is normally sold as an add-on to another product, such as the holiday itself. Customers are often more influenced by price than the terms of the cover, and rarely by the quality of claims administration. Sellers of these products are still obliged to follow the ICOBS code of conduct, which includes explaining key and unusual features including exclusions both at the point of sale and in the explanatory leaflets. The FOS does not consider it sufficient simply to send customers a copy of the policy and expect them to review its terms, without a sufficient explanation at the point of sale. The FOS has decided, inter alia, that: the assured should be entitled to some compensation if he has to curtail his holiday and manages to obtain a return flight at little extra cost; any exclusion for pre-existing medical conditions has to be drawn very clearly to the assured's attention, failing which it cannot be relied upon and it must be reasonable for the insured to disclose the condition before insurers can

---

[144] Case Study 10/10, *Ombudsman News* October 2001.

[145] Case Study 07/13, *Ombudsman News* July 2001; Case Study 48/7, *Ombudsman News* August 2005.

[146] *Ombudsman News* Sept/Oct 2008.

[147] In *Ombudsman News* January 2001, it was commented that the FOS uphold a greater proportion of this type of complaint than average.

[148] Case Study 01/14, *Ombudsman News* January 2001.

rely on its non-disclosure[149]; and any exclusion for hazardous activities must be clear.[150] Insurers must cover during the period of an annual travel policy any condition notified before renewal, and any exclusion for the new medical condition should only apply if the customer travels against medical advice.[151] In Case Study 74/07,[152] the FOS supported insurers' decision to exclude cover for stroke in light of the stroke disclosure at renewal of an annual travel policy, but required the insurer to reimburse the insured for the costs of cancelling the holiday that they had booked before the stroke occurred.

Health insurance. The FOS considers that the marketing of health insurance often does not do enough to highlight significant policy exclusions and their meaning. This may result in assureds believing through the marketing that they have bought cover for every situation of failing health in an environment where they might otherwise be unable to obtain treatment quickly or at all on the NHS. In particular, it is a general feature of private medical expenses insurance that "chronic" (i.e. not curable) conditions are excluded from cover or that cover is limited to "acute" (i.e. treatable) conditions. These are therefore particularly significant terms, so should be explained to assureds before the insurance is purchased, especially as each policy is likely to define "chronic" and "acute" differently. If this is not done, the FOS is unlikely to support insurers rejecting claims that rely heavily on the exclusion.

12–032

Many medical insurance policies exclude unproven or experimental treatment or limit cover to the cost of treatment that has been recommended by specialist doctors. The FOS will consider the evidence of the use of the treatment to determine whether it is a well-established and effective treatment for patients in a similar situation.[153] However, where a condition is covered, but the consultant has advised a newer, untested treatment instead of an established one, the FOS considers it will generally be fair and reasonable for the insurer to indemnify the insured's costs up to the sum for which the insurer would have been liable if the insured had undergone conventional treatment.[154] However, the FOS may not consider a treatment experimental if there is sufficient evidence to show that it could improve or at least stabilise a condition, although the FOS may allow insurers to exclude the cost of any future treatment arising as a consequence of the treatment in question.[155]

Depending on the circumstances, the FOS may also force insurers to cover treatment from doctors or at hospitals which are not on the insurers' approved list, up to the amount that the insurer would have paid for a doctor or at a hospital which was approved.[156]

Most critical illness policies list specified terminal illnesses which will be covered, although there may be limitations on this cover, such as a requirement for survival for 28 days from diagnosis before a lump sum for care until death can

---

[149] E.g. the cough in Case Study 76/10, *Ombudsman News* March/April 2006, was not reasonably discloseable in the circumstances.

[150] Cf. *Quantum Processing Services Co v Axa Insurance UK Plc*, LTL December 15, 2008, [2008] All E.R. (D) 152 (Dec).

[151] *Ombudsman News* Dec 2006/Jan 2007.

[152] *Ombudsman News* Dec/Jan 2009.

[153] Case Study 77/07, *Ombudsman News* May/June 2009.

[154] E.g. Case Study 77/08, *Ombudsman News* May/June 2009.

[155] Case Study 77/07, *Ombudsman News* May/June 2009.

[156] E.g. Case Study 77/06, *Ombudsman News* May/June 2009 and Case Study 85/03, *Ombudsman News* April/May 2010.

be claimed. There may be no cover until the condition is actually diagnosed.[157] The FOS considers that assureds should be made aware of the policy cover, limits and exclusions at the point of sale, otherwise their complaints are likely to be upheld.

As regards exclusions for pre-existing medical conditions, the FOS will consider the intensity of symptoms, the seriousness with which they are regarded, any diagnosis which has been made, any treatment given, the connection between the symptoms at inception and the medical condition which gave rise to the claim, and the assured's knowledge of the condition at inception.[158] Exclusions for illnesses arising from symptoms which were apparent before inception, even if the condition was not diagnosed, are regarded as potentially onerous.

Disability covers which apply only where the assured is unable to carry on "any occupation" are regarded as harsh as they limit protection to comparatively rare cases. Thus if a policy is restricted to "any occupation" or "suited occupation" and there are no further qualifications or definitions, the FOS will interpret this as meaning "any relevant occupation," that is, any occupation for which the insured is suited by reason of his education, training, experience and social standing. Similarly, the words "total disability" or "total incapacity" may be interpreted to mean whether the consumer is totally unable to carry out the essential or substantial duties of their occupation, not whether they are totally unable to carry out all the duties required by their occupation. Total disability in relation to "own occupation" will be interpreted as meaning not being able to carry out the occupation, rather than not being able to carry on with a specific job at the consumer's actual employer, as long as they are not carrying out any other occupation.[159] Much will turn on the individual facts of the case, the medical evidence[160] and to a lesser extent, the evaluation made of the insured's functional capacity. However, the FOS would not usually consider it reasonable to expect an unskilled manual worker to retrain as a skilled professional and vice versa.

Almost all policies exclude disability claims which arise from stress or other forms of mental illness, require the person to be in work when a disability arises and exclude a claim for employment benefit when the person is not actively seeking work. These are significant limitations of cover and should be made clear to the purchaser before the policy sale is completed. When looking at whether someone should receive employment benefit, the FOS will consider whether any illness suffered by the person was so severe that it would have prevented the person from working and the extent of any prejudice to the insurer's position, that is, how likely it is that the insured person would have found work were it not for the illness. The FOS may conclude that the insurer should pay a percentage of the benefits where the redundancy claim would be valid were it not for the disability or the disability claim would be valid were it not for the redundancy. Depending on the circumstances, the FOS may not enforce the terms as strictly as a court might.[161]

12–033 *Motor insurance.* The FOS regards an exclusion for theft if the keys have been left in or near the vehicle as a major restriction on the scope of cover, as its

---

[157] Case Study 80/04, *Ombudsman News* Oct/Nov 2009.

[158] Cf. Case Study 80/03, *Ombudsman News* Oct/Nov 2009 where the insured was paid under the policy because he did not know that his minor, undisclosed, pre-inception symptoms were those of a serious condition.

[159] Cf. FOS Consumer Factsheet on Income Protection Insurance on the FOS website.

[160] E.g. Case Study 80/02, *Ombudsman News* Oct/Nov 2009.

[161] E.g. Case Study 80/05, *Ombudsman News* Oct/Nov 2009, where the insurer had to pay the claim even though the insured did not meet the policy's continuing employment criteria.

experience is that this exclusion is a shock to most assureds even though it will be included in almost every motor insurance policy. Insurers must draw it to the attention of prospective customers at the point of sale. They only have to tell the main policyholder, not other named drivers.[162] Insurers will still be able to refuse to pay the claim if the insured has been reckless and so breached the general condition to take reasonable care of his vehicle, which condition exists independently of the exclusions. It is difficult for insurers to prove recklessness in this sort of scenario, as most people who leave their keys in the car[163] simply fail to recognise the risk, and so do not have the requisite intention for recklessness. If they had been aware of the risk, they would probably not have left the keys in the car or the vehicle unattended in the first place.[164] The FOS might expect the degree of attention required for a high-value car to be greater than for a low-value car.

Where there is an exclusion for theft if the vehicle has been left unattended, the FOS will apply, with some variations, much the same test as that adopted by the courts.[165] The FOS has set out factors which it will consider in reaching its decision and also certain assumptions as follows, some of which a court might not share. These include: (a) whether the driver was in reasonable proximity to the vehicle or had "moved away" from it; (b) whether the driver was able to keep it under observation, (although in some circumstances, a vehicle can still be attended if it is not actually in view); (c) whether the driver would have had a reasonable prospect of intervening; (d) the length of time the driver anticipated the car being unoccupied and unattended; (e) the general attitude to the specific risk—if the complainant's behaviour is likely to be regarded by other drivers as "reasonable", the FOS is unlikely to agree that the claim was validly rejected, and in practice, this may be the factor that tips the balance; (f) the location of the car; (g) any mitigating factors that caused the driver to leave the car; and (h) whether the doors or boot were left open and/or the engine was left running.[166]

The FOS receives many complaints relating to vehicle valuations.[167] If insurers do not assess vehicle valuations in line with good industry practice, the FOS might not only require them to, but also make them liable to compensate the assured for distress and inconvenience. The FOS expects insurers to know the FOS approach to vehicle valuation, which is that the insurance should enable an insured to replace a vehicle that has been stolen or damaged beyond (economic) repair with a similar vehicle. The FOS will expect insurers to make a reasonable assessment of the vehicle's market value and then to pay this amount unless it is an agreed value policy, in which case only the agreed value, not the cost of

---

[162] Case Study 82/12, *Ombudsman News* Dec 09/Jan 2010.

[163] Or in an unattended jacket in a public place as in Case Study 82/09, *Ombudsman News* Dec 09/Jan 2010.

[164] Cf. Case Study 63/7, *Ombudsman News* July/August 2007 where the FOS applied a reasonable care test even to a condition to "take *all* [emphasis added] precautions to reduce or remove the risk of loss of the insured vehicle." It then found that the insured had not been reckless in leaving keys in his van whilst he was moving his tools into a residential garage, because he said that it had not occurred to him that he was taking a risk. However, a court might not have agreed that he had taken *all* precautions.

[165] See Ch.5, above. The FOS found the vehicles unattended in Case Studies 01/11 and 01/12, *Ombudsman News* January 2001 and 82/12, *Ombudsman News* Dec 09/Jan 2010, but attended in Case Studies 01/06, 01/08, 01/09 *Ombudsman News* January 2001 and 82/10, *Ombudsman News* Dec 09/Jan 2010.

[166] See also FOS Technical Note headed "Motor insurance: keys in car" dated October 2009.

[167] See FOS Technical Note headed "Motor insurance: vehicle valuation" dated 15/07/09.

replacement, will be payable.[168] The market value is the likely cost to the customer of buying a vehicle as near as possibly identical to the one that has been stolen or damaged beyond repair. This is not the same as the amount the vehicle was worth when purchased. There can be genuine debate about a vehicle's true market value. The FOS will expect the insurer to consult trade guides and to adjust the price to allow for any unusual features in the vehicle's mileage or condition, e.g. the addition of modifications or accessories. If the value is unclear due to a car's unusual features, the FOS would expect insurers to contact the compilers of a relevant guide and make further enquiries.[169] The insurer should usually be referring to the guide retail price (the price a member of the public might reasonably expect to pay at a dealership), although it may be suitable to use the guide trade value (the price that a motor trader might pay) if the vehicle was not in guide retail condition or where there is evidence that the insured intended to buy a replacement privately. The FOS may also penalise an insurer who does not make a valuation on the basis of these guides or on any reasonable basis, and where this happened in Case Study 66/01,[170] it awarded the insured £150 for distress and inconvenience. The FOS places little weight on forecourt prices advertised in local papers and internet sites, as these are widely understood to be too high and only a starting point for negotiations. A deduction of 10 per cent for left-hand drives, and 20 per cent for a vehicle that the policyholder knew was a repaired write-off might be considered reasonable. Where the insurer has unreasonably delayed settlement of or wrongly declined a claim, or where the insurer has misrepresented the availability of an alternative vehicle, the FOS may award compensation for loss of use of a vehicle over and above what is permitted by the policy terms. If the policyholder has hired a car, this might be the hire cost plus interest. If he has not, this might be the cost of other reasonable transport costs and an inconvenience rate of around £10 per day depending on the circumstances.

In relation to a cloned car, if the insured acted in good faith and took all reasonable steps to ensure the authenticity of the vehicle at the time of the purchase, the FOS will consider that he has a defeasible title to the vehicle and that insurers should pay any claim in accordance with the full market value of a similar vehicle with an unblemished history. Some deduction might be appropriate where the buyer acted in good faith but failed to take reasonable steps at the point of sale which probably would have alerted him to the problem.

12–034   *Householders' policies.* The question may arise as to whether a loss falls under buildings or contents cover. The FOS will normally consider fitted wardrobes, fitted kitchens and built-in appliances to be covered under a buildings policy, whereas furniture, and appliances which are free-standing or easily unscrewed from the wall would probably be considered as contents.[171] The FOS follows the industry convention of treating carpets as contents even though they are often fitted.[172] The FOS views most laminate wooden flooring, where the individual planks are glued together and fixed under a skirting board or beading, as a fixture and fitting, not contents.[173] Unlike a carpet, they are difficult to remove intact and

---

[168] E.g. Case Study 66/04, *Ombudsman News* December 2007/January 2008.

[169] E.g. Case Study 66/02, *Ombudsman News* December 07/January 08 (car with a specialist sports body); Case Study 85/02, *Ombudsman News*, April/May 2010 (horse trailer).

[170] *Ombudsman News* December 07/January 08.

[171] Case Study 30/3, *Ombudsman News* August 2003.

[172] Case Study 30/5, *Ombudsman News* August 2003.

[173] Case Study 30/4, *Ombudsman News* August 2003.

have essentially become part of the building. But re-useable click-together laminate wooden flooring might be contents, as it is more like a fitted carpet. Sometimes an insurer will class items in a non-obvious category. If this leads to an unfair result, the FOS may require the firm to treat it as being within the category under which it thinks it should be classed. For instance, it is common industry practice to class an outside aerial fixed permanently to the roof as contents, even though few would remove it when moving house, and most people would regard it as part of the building. Also, any damage caused to the aerial would most likely be as a result of an insured event such as storm or lightning, which is covered by the buildings insurance.[174] The FOS may have its own approach as to whether damage falls within a wear and tear exclusion, and has developed its own policy in relation to pitch-fibre pipes.[175]

Household insurance cover is often excluded where the premises are unoccupied for a period of time, commonly 30 consecutive days. Policies rarely define "unoccupied". When the meaning is unclear, the FOS is likely to apply the Unfair Terms in Consumer Contracts Regulations[176] and adopt the meaning most favourable to the consumer in light of the particular facts of the case. This may mean that the FOS considers a property to be occupied if it is visited on a reasonably frequent basis, even though it is not being slept in every night.[177] However, even if there has been a breach of the occupation term, the FOS will look at what damage this breach has caused and rule accordingly. So in Case Study 58/2,[178] where the insured were away from the property for more than the 60 days permitted, and the evidence was that the burst pipe had probably occurred within the first 10 days, the FOS found that the breach did not relate to the flood damage. The FOS required insurers to pay for the flood damage, but not for all of the cost of replacing the wooden floor which suffered rot damage as well, the reasoning being that if the insured had not left their home unoccupied for so long, the water damage could have been dealt with more quickly and the floor would probably not have started to rot.

Contents policies do not generally cover personal possessions temporarily away from the home unless an additional premium is paid and such cover is usually limited with lists of included and excluded items. The FOS considers it good practice for insurers to explain this before inception, to prevent assureds thinking that they have more cover than they have paid for and so that they understand what exactly is included in a supposedly "all risks" cover. The FOS acknowledges[179] that it is for an insurer exercising its commercial underwriting decision, not the FOS, to define the nature and scope of the cover. If the scope is unclear, the FOS will apply the *contra proferentem* rule. If the scope is unclear in relation to satellite navigation equipment, the FOS will consider it under a household rather than a car policy if it can be used and has been used outside the car, such as by walkers using it as a global positioning system, unless the insurer can establish a valid reason why this is not appropriate.[180]

Policies usually exclude cover for replacing a whole set where only one part has been damaged and it has not been possible to obtain a replacement which matches the rest. However, the FOS tries to balance the interests of the insured

---

[174] Case Study 30/2, *Ombudsman News* August 2003.

[175] Cf. FOS Technical Briefing Note January 20, 2009.

[176] SI 1999/2083. See Ch.3, above.

[177] Case Study 34/1, *Ombudsman News* January 2004. Contrast Case Study 34/3, *Ombudsman News*, January 2004 (premises left empty and unchecked for more than a year).

[178] *Ombudsman News* December 2006/January 2007.

[179] *Ombudsman News* October/November 2006.

[180] *Ombudsman News* October/November 2006.

who would be left with an unacceptable finish if the wording was applied strictly and who probably did not appreciate its meaning until that point, against the unfairness of distorting the policy wording which may have been clear and may have been sold in line with the appropriate industry codes. The FOS typical award in both buildings and contents insurance is 50 per cent of the cost of replacing the undamaged items.[181] However, this 50 per cent approach will not always be appropriate, for instance, with re-tiling a room when only a few of the tiles have been damaged, and in those circumstances the FOS will assess the claim to see what effect the loss of match has on the remaining items. If there is no substantial loss, then the FOS is unlikely to consider that any compensation should be paid over and above whatever is needed to deal with the damaged item. But where matching is intrinsic to the value of the objects, the FOS will make an award for full replacement.[182]

12–035 *Legal expenses insurance.* Legal expenses policies usually require any legal action for which legal expenses are incurred to have a reasonable prospect of success before the insurer will provide cover. Insurers may use members of their own staff to assess the claim in the first instance, who may or may not be legally qualified. If they consider a claim should be pursued, they usually pass it to solicitors on the insurer's panel to assess. If an insurer has rejected a claim on the basis of no "reasonable prospects of success", the FOS expects it to have acted on professional advice. The FOS will not look at the merits of a complaint about whether a case has reasonable prospects of success, but only whether the firm has given the matter proper consideration, and it will have if it has gone to legal experts and adopted what they have said. Notwithstanding this, if a complainant can show a legal opinion which "trumps" that obtained by insurers, then the FOS may uphold the complaint.[183]

There are circumstances where the FOS may not support insurers' panel appointment at any stage and will expect insurers to agree to the appointment of the insured's preferred solicitors. These include cases: that involve large personal injury claims, that are necessarily complex, (such as those involving allegations of medical negligence), that involve significant boundary or employment disputes (especially if there is a considerable history to investigate and assess), or where the policyholder's own solicitors have had considerable involvement and knowledge of the issue or related matters.

Awards and interest

12–036 *Money awards.* When making an award, the ombudsman's objective is to put the consumer back into the position he would have been in had it not been for the firm's actions. An ombudsman's determination may include a money award[184] to compensate for financial loss[185] or any other loss or damage of a specified kind,[186] if such an award would be fair and reasonable. These include damages for distress or inconvenience, pain and suffering or damage to reputation.[187] The

---

[181] Cf. Case Studies 75/06 and 75/07 in *Ombudsman News* Jan/Feb 2009.
[182] Case Study 10/05, *Ombudsman News* October 2001.
[183] Case Study 47/8, *Ombudsman News* July 2005.
[184] s.229(2)(a) FSMA.
[185] 2000 Act s.229(3)(a).
[186] 2000 Act s.229(3)(b).
[187] DISP 3.7.2R.

current limit on compensation[188] is £100,000 (plus interest[189]), although the ombudsman can recommend that a further payment is made.[190]

Distress or inconvenience: damages for maladministration. The ombudsman **12–037** can make awards for distress or inconvenience even where a court might not, particularly where there has been some maladministration in the handling of an insurance claim.[191] The ombudsman will consider that there has been distress if there has been embarrassment, anxiety, disappointment or loss of expectation, and that there has been inconvenience if there has been expenditure of time and/ or effort by the customer that has resulted from a firm's conduct. The ombudsman will consider whether it is appropriate to make an award for distress or inconvenience in every case, even if the complainant does not request such an award.

The award for distress or inconvenience will only be made if the distress or inconvenience has been caused by the insurer's maladministration or bad handling of a claim, which includes extensive delays, clerical or procedural errors, rudeness, incorrect or inadequate explanations or simply a failure to respond to the customer's requests. Bad handling will also include requiring a customer to take additional and unnecessary steps to pursue a complaint or where a firm refuses to settle a case at an early stage, despite knowing that the FOS had previously upheld similar complaints. Bad handling will not include general distress which is inevitable, for instance, in dealing with a claim after injury or death, or which can be better categorised as a trivial annoyance, such as if a name is spelt incorrectly or the telephone line is sometimes busy.

Where a firm has handled a complaint badly, even if the complaint is not justified and is not upheld, the ombudsman may choose to award compensation for distress and inconvenience. It would not be bad handling if the insurer does everything it should do, but the complainant is still inconvenienced. For instance, in Case Study 01/15,[192] no compensation was payable where a video kept malfunctioning and the insurer kept trying to get it repaired. The complainant was put to considerable inconvenience in the process, but the insurer had provided a satisfactory standard of service because it had done all it could do. Similarly in Case Study 68/09,[193] there was no award for distress and inconvenience for the delay caused when the insurer appointed a firm of engineers to inspect and report on the flood damage. Due to the technically complex nature of the problem, they were entitled to do this, and they had acted promptly both in appointing the engineers and in considering the claim once the report was ready. But it would be bad handling where the insurer refuses to accept that its agents have carried out unsatisfactory repairs and in Case Study 79/07[194] the insured was awarded £200 for the distress and inconvenience of this in addition to the full repairs she had requested.

Most of the ombudsman awards in this category will be modest, usually not more than a few hundred pounds. An example of an exceptional, large award is

---

[188] 2000 Act s.229(5).

[189] DISP 3.7.4R and 3.7.5G.

[190] DISP 3.7.6G. Cf. Case Study 65/12 which related to building repairs totalling at least £750,000 under a contractors' all-risks commercial insurance policy, where the insurer agreed to the FOS recommendation that it should pay the full amount due even if it came to more than the maximum award of £100,000.

[191] FOS Briefing Note November 2001.

[192] *Ombudsman News* January 2001.

[193] *Ombudsman News* March/April 2008.

[194] *Ombudsman News* Sept/Oct 2009.

in Case Study 18/18,[195] where £1,000 was awarded for the distress and inconvenience of living with a cesspit full of water, and the insurer refusing cover meant months of living without proper sanitary conditions. £1,000 was also awarded in Case Study 68/08,[196] for a couple who had to live in alternative accommodation for a further three months (after an initial nine months) whilst snagging was undertaken when insurers were repairing subsidence damage to their flat. This may be a surprising award, especially when compared to the cesspit case above, but it is unlikely to be a sign of increasing awards. It is more likely to be evidence of inconsistency in FOS awards, perhaps subconsciously influenced by the fact that the insured in this case were making a substantial claim for floor repairs which failed when they were given this award instead. More recent examples are the following: an example given in *Ombudsman News* August 2008 of a family awarded less than £300 for having to stay in alternative accommodation for three weeks longer than should have been necessary; £350 for delays in dealing with a boiler repair for an insured and her elderly mother[197]; £250 for delays in a boiler repair over a Christmas period when young children and an elderly relative were staying with the insured, who had to hire temporary heaters and arrange an independent repairer to carry out the work at insurer's cost[198]; £450 for the incompetence and delays of an insurer's repairer which led to a toilet overflowing with sewage and the elderly insured having to move into her neighbour's house for a few days until the problem was sorted out because the smell was so bad[199]; and £150 for the insurer's two-week delay before it confirmed that it would not be repairing a boiler as it was uneconomical to do so.[200] In considering the amount to award, the FOS will look at the severity of the distress or inconvenience caused by the firm's actions, the period of the problem, the nature of the inadequacy, whether any of it was caused by the customer's own actions and delays and, to a limited extent, the customer's own assessment of the distress or inconvenience suffered.

12–038   *Pain and suffering.* The ombudsman considers pain and suffering to be a more extreme form of distress and inconvenience, and it may arise, for example, in cases involving delays in arranging or paying for medical treatment. An award for pain and suffering will be more than one for distress and inconvenience.

12–039   *Damage to reputation.* Damage to reputation may occur if a firm's actions lead to a third party being misinformed, for instance in relation to credit worthiness or if there is improper disclosure of private information such as medical or other confidential records. Any award will be based on how widely available the information had been made, the nature of the information, its impact and the customer's previous reputation. It may be sufficient just for the insurer to correct the third party's records. In Case Study 04/17,[201] one insurer passed on information about the insured's claim to another insurer without authorisation. The insurer offered to pay £100 by way of compensation for distress and inconvenience, and the FOS felt that this was enough, as there was no evidence

---

[195] *Ombudsman News* July 2002.
[196] *Ombudsman News* March/April 2008.
[197] Case Study 83/06, *Ombudsman News* Feb/March 2010.
[198] Case Study 83/07, *Ombudsman News* Feb/March 2010.
[199] Case Study 83/09, *Ombudsman News* Feb/March 2010.
[200] Case Study 83/10, *Ombudsman News* Feb/March 2010.
[201] *Ombudsman News* April 2001.

that the disclosure had caused any loss or influenced the handling of the claim.

The complainant's costs. The ombudsman does not usually award compensation to cover any costs associated with complaining to the firm or to the FOS, such as in writing letters or making telephone calls, although it does have power to.[202] On the rare occasion where an award under this head is made, it is extremely modest, although it could be more for a business complaint. For instance, in Case Study 01/14,[203] the complainant was awarded £25 for her costs in pursuing the complaint against the small print of an extended warranty which promised a return of the premium paid if there was no claim, but only on the condition that the purchaser registered within 21 days of the purchase. Nor will it award the fees of a claims management company or solicitor,[204] because the ethos of the FOS is that the use of this sort of service is not necessary in light of the FOS own user-friendly, informal approach.[205] The FOS tries to review the facts surrounding the complaint, rather than the way the argument has been presented. Indeed, the FOS prefers to hear from consumers in their own words. However, the FOS may order reimbursement of the costs of an expert which the complainant had to instruct in order to prove his point.[206] For instance, in Case Study 28/9,[207] the insured had to consult an independent engineer before the insurance company would accept that the car repairs it had approved were not satisfactory.

12–040

Other awards. The ombudsman can make other awards or directions to suit the circumstances of the particular case, whether or not a court could.[208] For instance, in Case Study 01/16,[209] insurers were asked to make a full apology and a donation to the British Heart Foundation and to set up a system so that the problem could not re-occur. The complainant had made it clear that the complaint was not in order to obtain a financial award. The complaint related to a series of oversights and mistakes which meant that a body was not embalmed abroad, so, to their great distress, the relatives were not allowed to see it because it had decomposed too much by the time it had arrived back in the United Kingdom.

12–041

Interest. Interest may be awarded on a money award,[210] and the FOS now uses a rate of 8 per cent per year simple, in line with the rate used in the county court,[211] visually calculated from when the FOS considers that the firm's actions caused the problem until the date when payment is made.[212]

12–042

---

[202] DISP 3.7.9R.

[203] *Ombudsman News* January 2001.

[204] For instance, in Case Study 13/14 in *Ombudsman News* January 2002, the complainant was not awarded any of the legal fees she claimed, as the FOS determined that she did not need legal advice to be able to answer the insurer's arguments.

[205] DISP 3.7.10G.

[206] For the principles governing the reimbursement of medical costs, see *Ombudsman News*, January 2002.

[207] *Ombudsman News* May 2003.

[208] 2000 Act s.229(2)(b).

[209] *Ombudsman News* January 2001.

[210] 2000 Act s.229(8)(a).

[211] County Courts Act 1984 s.69.

[212] The Bank of England base rate plus 1 per cent per year, compound, is now also used in bad investment advice cases.

12–043   *Enforceability of awards.*   Money awards and interest are enforceable through the
courts.[213] Directions are enforceable by injunction.[214] Firms are required to pay
awards or comply with directions promptly.[215]

---

[213] 2000 Act s.229(8)(b) and Pt III Sch.17 para.16.
[214] 2000 Act s.229(9).
[215] DISP 1.4.4R.

PART II:
THE PARTIES

CHAPTER 13

THE REGULATION OF INSURERS

1. REGULATORY STRUCTURE

Types of insurer. Insurers of various types are able to provide insurance to UK   **13–001**
policyholders. Those writing policies fall into the following categories: (a)
insurance companies authorised to carry on insurance business under the
Financial Services and Markets Act 2000; (b) mutual insurance companies
authorised to carry on insurance business under the 2000 Act; (c) friendly
societies and similar bodies, governed by the Friendly Societies Acts 1982 and
1996 and by the 2000 Act; (d) Lloyd's underwriters, governed by the Lloyd's
legislation, most importantly the Lloyd's Act 1982, as supplemented by the 2000
Act; (e) underwriting agencies, operating in the United Kingdom on behalf of
UK and overseas insurers; (f) insurance companies authorised to carry on
business elsewhere in the EEA, and either carrying on insurance business in the
United Kingdom or selling insurance in the United Kingdom from an establishment elsewhere in the EEA, under EEA "Passport Rights" and being regulated
in their home countries; and (g) offshore insurers, selling directly into the United
Kingdom without carrying on business in the United Kingdom—such insurers
are unregulated by domestic law.

Development of regulation

UK measures. Statutory regulation of insurance companies in the United   **13–002**
Kingdom dates back to the Life Assurance Companies Act 1870, and has as its
major objective the prevention of insurance insolvencies, necessitated by the
expertise required to run an insurance business and the social significance of
leaving policyholders without cover. Historically the UK system (unlike its
Continental counterparts) has not been concerned with "material control" of
policy terms and premium levels but only with solvency, initially in the form of
a system of deposits which was gradually extended from life assurance to other
forms of cover and in the latter part of the twentieth century by the requirement
for insurers to maintain a margin by which assets exceeded liabilities. The law
developed piecemeal, often responding to the spectacular failure of individual
insurance companies, and was consolidated in the Insurance Companies Act
1982. Particularly stringent rules were developed for investment products,
including life insurance, by the Financial Services Act 1986, although the
framework was self-regulatory. The earlier legislation was swept away by the
Financial Services and Markets Act 2000, which came into force on December
1, 2001, which established a consolidated system for the regulation of all forms
of insurance (although more stringent accounting and solvency requirements
apply to life policies[1]) and which substituted central regulation—by the Financial

---

[1] A brief attempt was made to allow self-regulation of non-life insurance, in the form of the
General Insurance Standards Council, but that body's attempts to impose its standards on non-life

Services Authority—for self-regulation. Much of the present law is found in the numerous statutory instruments issued under the 2000 Act and, most significantly, in the FSA's Handbook of Rules and Guidance. The Handbook is a massive document divided into a number of chapters, and contains both regulatory requirements and guidance. It is available online[2] and is updated regularly. The Handbook specifically states in its General Provisions that it is to be given a purposive interpretation.

13–003 *Impact of the European Union.* Much of the present UK regulatory structure is based upon European Union Law. The prime concern of EC law, as it then was, since 1973 has been to create a single market for insurance services, whereby an insurer authorised by the regulatory authorities of its home state is free to establish its branches elsewhere in the EU or to sell insurance on a cross-border basis in any other member state without additional regulation from the host state. In 1973, the European market was characterised by domestic controls, requiring in almost every case authorisation to sell insurance from the relevant national regulator. The rules which now govern the EU Single Insurance Market are derived from twin principles contained in the Treaty of Rome: freedom of establishment, whereby an undertaking with its head office in one Member State is free to operate in any other Member State through an establishment in that Member State, and freedom to provide services, whereby an undertaking may sell directly into another Member State.

These principles have been combined, since July 1, 1994, in the Single European Licence or Passport, under which authorisation granted to an insurer by its home state regulatory authorities operates as an authorisation to become established or to sell insurance in any other EU Member State, with minimal intervention from host state regulatory authorities.

This process, which involved gradual harmonisation of the regulatory rules in all Member States, and which required certain Member States to abandon their long-established "material control" over premium rates, policy terms and conditions in the interests of harmonisation, took some 20 years and three stages to be completed. The First Non-Life Directive[3] and the First Life Directive[4] provided for the authorisation of insurers by their home state authorities and set out their right to become established by means of branches or agencies in other Member States. Insurers were not permitted to offer both life and non-life insurance unless they were doing so at an earlier date. Before the Commission could move to extending the freedoms initiated by these Directives, a series of cases were heard by the European Court of Justice[5] the effect of which was to prevent an immediate move to home state control of EC-wide operations by reaffirming the right of Member States to protect policyholders by the imposition of local control over insurers. The subsequent Second Non-Life Directive[6] was accordingly a transitional measure under which the single European licence

---

brokers fell foul of the Competition Act 1998 and it ceased operations with effect from January 14, 2005.

[2] *http://fsahandbook.info/FSA/html/handbook/* [Accessed June 16, 2010].

[3] Council Directive 73/239/EEC.

[4] Council Directive 79/267.

[5] Case 205/84 *Commission v Germany* [1987] 2 C.M.L.R. 69; Case 220/83 *Commission v France* [1987] 2 C.M.L.R. 113; Case 206/84 *Commission v Ireland* [1987] 2 C.M.L.R. 150; Case 252/83 *Commission v Denmark* [1987] 2 C.M.L.R. 169, all decided under an earlier measure, the Co-Insurance Directive, Council Directive 78/473, which removes national restrictions on co-insurance operations.

[6] Council Directive 88/357/EEC.

principle was extended to insurers of "large" (commercial) risks and the right of member states to regulate other EC insurers was confined to "mass" (consumer) risks. Similarly, the Second Life Directive[7] confined the new freedoms to policyholders who had sought out insurers from elsewhere in the European Union. The adoption of a full single market, abolishing the distinction between mass risks and large risks for most purposes and allowing an insurer to trade anywhere in the EC subject only to home state authorisation, took place in June 1992, by means of the Third Non-Life Insurance Directive[8] and the Third Life Insurance Directive,[9] to be implemented by Member States by July 1, 1994.

As a result of these Directives, the regulatory structure applicable to insurance companies is harmonised across the European Union and it is necessary for an insurer to seek authorisation from the Member State in which its head office is located. That authorisation operates as a licence to become established in any other Member State, and to sell insurance directly to policy holders in any EU Member State from any EU establishment. The regulatory authorities of the insurer's home state have responsibility for regulating the EU-wide operations of the insurer, coupled with the necessary powers to regulate such operations, and the regulatory authorities of host states have only default powers over such insurers. The Single Market has been extended to Switzerland,[10] and to other EFTA countries under the European Economic Area Agreement.[11]

Other EU measures include five Motor Insurance Directives which provide for harmonised protection for the victims of road traffic accidents (consolidated by a single Directive in 2009),[12] two Reinsurance Directives which extend the Life and Non-Life Directives to that sector,[13] the Co-Insurance Directive,[14] the Legal Expenses Directive which protect the assured against any conflict of interest between insurers which provide both legal expenses cover to him and some other form of cover to a different assured,[15] the Reorganisation and Winding Up of Insurers Directive which confers priority over an insolvent insurer's assets on insurance creditors[16] and the Mediation Directive which regulates insurance intermediaries.[17] In July 2010, the European Commission issued a White Paper proposing an EU-wide scheme for policyholder protection in the event of an insurer's insolvency.

The Insurance and Reinsurance Directives, now 13 in number, were repealed and recast by a single Directive, the Solvency II Directive, European Parliament and Council Directive 2009/138/EC "on the taking-up and pursuit of the business of Insurance and Reinsurance", adopted in April 2009 and published in final form in November 2009.[18] This has to be fully implemented by Member States by November 2012. The consolidation and recasting is aimed at eliminating differences in national treatment of insurers and reinsurers, and increasing the level of protection for policyholders in particular by imposing more stringent

---

[7] Council Directive 90/619/EEC.

[8] Council Directive 92/49/EEC.

[9] Council Directive 92/96/EEC. The three Life Directives were repealed and consolidated by European Parliament and Council Directive 2002/83/EC.

[10] Effective October 1989.

[11] Effective January 1994.

[12] See Ch.21, below.

[13] See Ch.17, below.

[14] See above.

[15] See Ch.22, below.

[16] See Ch.16, below.

[17] See Ch.15, below.

[18] [2009] OJ L335/1.

solvency requirements. The key features of the Solvency II Directive are as follows.

(1) New solvency rules replacing the old outdated rules, reflecting the latest developments in prudential supervision, actuarial science and risk management and which allows for updates in the future is necessary. There will be a proportional approach to smaller undertakings.

(2) Increased enforcement powers, with both on-site and off-site supervision: supervisory authorities are to be given the power to conduct on-site inspections at the premises of an insurer or reinsurer.

(3) Introduction of the Supervisory Review Process (SRP), under which supervisory authorities review and evaluate the strategies, processes and reporting procedures established by insurers and reinsurers to comply with the Directive as well as the risks the undertaking faces or may face and its ability to assess those risks. The review also comprises an assessment of the adequacy of the undertakings' methods and practices to identify possible events or future changes in economic conditions that could have unfavourable effects on its overall financial standing. Regulatory authorities are to be given monitoring and remedial powers.

(4) Undertakings will be required to comply with principles rather than rules, an obligation which puts more responsibility on management than is presently the case. This is to be coupled with more robust internal governance systems as identified in the direction, each undertaking being required to have written policies in place which clearly set out how they deal with internal control, internal audit, risk management and, where relevant, outsourcing. All undertakings will be required to have a regular practice of assessing their overall solvency needs with a view to their specific risk profile. This is the own risk and solvency assessment (ORSA).

(5) There is to be enhanced supervisory reporting, including an annual report covering essential and concise information on their solvency and financial condition.

(6) The quantitative requirements of undertakings are to consist of: valuation of assets and liabilities, technical provisions, own funds, Solvency Capital Requirement, Minimum Capital Requirement, and investments. The disclosure is based on "an economic total balance sheet approach", which relies on an appraisal of the whole balance-sheet of insurance and reinsurance undertakings, on an integrated basis, where assets and liabilities are valued consistently. The Solvency Capital Requirement is to reflect "own funds" which can be used to absorb significant losses.

As an interim measure, European Parliament and Council Directive 2007/44/EC amends the third non-life directive and the reinsurance directive so as to increase prudent assessment of the acquisition of an insurance or reinsurance business.[19]

The 2000 Act: regulatory bodies

13–004   *Financial Services Authority.* The FSA is the main regulator under the 2000 Act,[20] with a number of regulatory objectives including: maintaining confidence

---

[19] Other minor amendments to the pre-Solvency II regime were made by European Parliament and Council Directives 2008/19/EC, 2008/36/EC and 2008/37/EC.

[20] For its constitution and functions, see ss.7–11 and Sch.1.

in the financial system; promoting awareness of the benefits and risks involved in investments; securing the appropriate degree of protection for consumers; and reduction of financial crime.[21] The FSA's legislative powers are: making rules; issuing codes; issuing statements; giving directions and issuing general guidance.[22] Contravention of the FSA's rules is actionable at the instance of a private person harmed by such breach, by way of an action for breach of statutory duty,[23] and although contravention is not an offence the FSA has an array of enforcement powers open to it to ensure that its rules are adhered to.

Other bodies. The Treasury has residual functions to make delegated legislation **13–005** and to monitor the operation of the legislation.[24] The Financial Services Compensation Scheme provides compensation to the victims of insolvent regulated firms, and is administered by a scheme manager.[25] The Financial Services Ombudsman Scheme deals with disputes between regulated firms and their customers.[26] Finally, the Financial Services and Markets Tribunal[27] is in effect a judicial body with general power to review the decisions of the FSA under the Act—in particular those relating to authorisation and to the imposition of sanctions—at the instance of persons adversely affected by those decisions.

Principles underlying regulation. The FSA has set out its "Principles for **13–006** Business" in its Handbook. The principles apply to every firm carrying on activities regulated under the 2000 Act, subject to modifications for EEA firms operating in the United Kingdom under EEA passport principles. According to the principles, a firm must: conduct its business with integrity; conduct its business with skill, care and diligence; take reasonable care to organise and control its affairs responsibly and effectively, with adequate risk management systems; maintain adequate financial resources; observe proper standards of market conduct; pay due regard to the interests of its customers and treat them fairly; pay due regard to the information needs of its clients, and communicate information to them in a way which is clear, fair and not misleading; manage conflicts of interest fairly, both between itself and its customers and between a customer and another client; take reasonable care to ensure the suitability of its advice and discretionary decisions for any customer who is entitled to rely upon its judgment; arrange adequate protection for clients' assets when it is responsible for them; and deal with its regulators in an open and co-operative way, and must disclose to the FSA appropriately anything relating to the firm of which the FSA would reasonably expect notice.

Breach of a principle gives rise to enforcement powers, in the form of disciplinary sanctions. The principles are modified in the case of reinsurance and pure protection contracts: the FSA will proceed only in a prudential context, i.e. the FSA would not expect to exercise any of its powers brought into play by the contravention of a principle unless the contravention amounts to a serious or persistent violation which had implications for confidence in the financial

---

[21] ss.2–6.

[22] ss.138–157.

[23] s.150 and the Financial Services and Markets Act 2000 (Rights of Action) Regulations (SI 2001/2256).

[24] ss.15–18, 142, 152, 158 and 404–408.

[25] See Ch.16, below.

[26] See Ch.12, above.

[27] s.132 and Sch.13. See also the Financial Services and Markets Tribunal Rules (SI 2004/2474).

system, for the fitness and propriety of the firm or for the adequacy of the firm's financial resources.

2. INSURANCE BUSINESS REGULATED IN THE UNITED KINGDOM

13–007 **Statutory framework.** Under s.19 of the 2000 Act, no person may carry on a regulated activity in the United Kingdom without the authorisation of the FSA (the "general prohibition") unless he is exempt.[28] A person who carries on a regulated activity without any authorisation at all is guilty of an "authorisation offence", under s.23, and is liable to a fine or imprisonment[29] unless he can demonstrate that he took all reasonable precautions and exercised all due diligence. A regulated activity is one which relates to investment or property, carried on by way of business and specified by secondary legislation made by the Treasury.[30] The definition of investment includes rights under contracts of insurance.[31] The implementing statutory instrument, the Financial Services and Markets Act 2000 (Regulated Activities) Order 2001[32] designates as regulated activities: effecting a contract of insurance; and carrying out a contract of insurance.[33] There are exclusions for: (a) any EEA insurer authorised to carry on insurance business in its home territory who is operating other than through a branch in the United Kingdom and under a co-insurance operation for which it is not the leading insurer[34]; and (b) motor vehicle breakdown insurers.[35] Appointed representatives of authorised persons are not themselves required to be authorised (s.39), although independent insurance intermediaries require authorisation to act in that capacity.[36]

The grant of permission to carry on any one regulated activity does not confer carte blanche in respect of all regulated activity, so that an "authorised person" contravenes the legislation by carrying on any other regulated activity. Such a person is, however, treated more generously than a person who has no authorisation at all: no offence is committed, and contracts are unaffected (s.20(2)), although any private person who suffers loss as a result of the unauthorised activity has the right to claim damages in civil proceedings for breach of statutory duty (s.20(3)).

---

[28] The power of the Treasury to grant exemptions is conferred by s.38: see the Financial Services and Markets Act 2000 (Exemption) Order 2001 (SI 2001/1201), as amended, which excludes trade unions, employers' associations, benevolent societies providing strike benefits and Lloyd's underwriters who ceased membership before December 24, 1996. Designated professional bodies—consisting of law and accountancy societies—are also exempt: see the Financial Services and Markets Act 2000 (Designated Professional Bodies) Order 2001 (SI 2001/1226).

[29] However, a person who is authorised but who carries on a regulated activity which falls outside the scope of the authorisation, is not guilty of a criminal offence: Financial Services and Markets Act 2000 s.20. This is particularly important in the insurance context, as there are numerous classes of insurance business, individual authorisation being required for each, and an insurer may inadvertently carry on business outside the classes for which he is authorised.

[30] Financial Services and Markets Act 2000 s.22.

[31] Financial Services and Markets Act 2000 Sch.2 para.20.

[32] SI 2001/ 544.

[33] art.10. The Order has since been amended to include mediation activities. See Ch.15, below.

[34] art.11.

[35] art.12.

[36] See Ch.15, below.

Insurance business

General definition. The list of contracts which constitute contracts of insurance **13–008**
for the purposes of the legislation, set out in art.2 of the 2001 Order, is not
exhaustive and merely seeks to clarify the position with regard to certain cases
which might not otherwise be regarded as insurance but which are to be subject
to regulation. Some of the matters on the list do not constitute insurance at
common law. Article 2[37] divides insurance contracts into general (non-life) and
long-term (life).

General business. There are 18 classes of general business set out in Pt I of **13–009**
Sch.1 to the 2001 Order. Authorisation is required on a class by class basis, a
principle underlying the various provisions in the Schedule which attempt to
make each class mutually exclusive of the others. The civil and criminal
sanctions against an insurer who is authorised to carry on some classes of
insurance business, but who carries on others without authorisation, are less
severe[38] given that the demarcation lines may not always be clear.

"Accident
1. Contracts of insurance providing fixed pecuniary benefits or benefits in the nature
of indemnity (or a combination of both) against risks of the person insured or, in the
case of a contract made by virtue of section 140, 140A or 140B of the Local
Government Act 1972 (or, in Scotland, section 86(1) of the Local Government
(Scotland) Act 1973), a person for whose benefit the contract is made—

(a) sustaining injury as the result of an accident or of an accident of a specified class;
or
(b) dying as a result of an accident or of an accident of a specified class; or
(c) becoming incapacitated in consequence of disease or of disease of a specified
class,

including contracts relating to industrial injury and occupational disease.

Sickness
2. Contracts of insurance providing fixed pecuniary benefits or benefits in the nature
of indemnity (or a combination of both) against risks of loss to the persons insured
attributable to sickness or infirmity.

Land vehicles
3. Contracts of insurance against loss of or damage to vehicles used on land,
including motor vehicles but excluding railway rolling stock.

Railway rolling stock
4. Contract of insurance against loss of or damage to railway rolling stock.

Aircraft
5. Contracts of insurance upon aircraft or upon the machinery, tackle, furniture or
equipment of aircraft.

Ships
6. Contracts of insurance upon vessels used on the sea or on inland water, or upon
the machinery, tackle, furniture or equipment of such vessels.

Goods in transit
7. Contracts of insurance against loss of or damage to merchandise, baggage and all
other goods in transit, irrespective of the form of transport.

---

[37] The definition of insurance and the classes of insurance business set out in the Order implement
the definitions in the First Non-Life Insurance Directive, Council Directive 73/239/EEC and the First
Life Insurance Directive, Council Directive 79/267/EEC.
[38] Financial Services and Markets Act 2000 s.20.

Fire and natural forces

8. Contracts of insurance against loss of or damage to property (other than property to which paragraphs 3 to 7 relate) due to fire, explosion, storm, natural forces other than storm, nuclear energy or land subsidence.

Damage to property

9. Contracts of insurance against loss of or damage to property (other than property to which paragraphs 3 to 7 relate) due to hail or frost or any other event (such as theft) other than those mentioned in paragraph 8.

Motor vehicle liability

10. Contracts of insurance against damage arising out of or in connection with the use of motor vehicles on land, including third-party risks and carrier's liability.

Aircraft liability

11. Contracts of insurance against damage arising out of or in connection with the use of aircraft, including third-party risks and carrier's liability.

Liability of ships

12. Contracts of insurance against damage arising out of or in connection with the use of vessels on the sea or on inland water, including third party risks and carrier's liability.

General liability

13. Contracts of insurance against risks of the persons insured incurring liabilities to third parties, the risks in question not being risks to which paragraph 10, 11 or 12 relates.

Credit

14. Contracts of insurance against risks of loss to the persons insured arising from the insolvency of debtors of theirs or from the failure (otherwise than through insolvency) of debtors of theirs to pay their debts when due.

Suretyship

15. (1) Contracts of insurance against the risks of loss to the persons insured arising from their having to perform contracts of guarantee[39] entered into by them.

(2) Fidelity bonds, performance bonds, administration bonds, bail bonds or customs bonds or similar contracts of guarantee,[40] where these are—

    (a) effected or carried out by a person not carrying on a banking business;

    (b) not effected merely incidentally to some other business carried on by the person effecting them; and

    (c) effected in return for the payment of one or more premiums.

Miscellaneous financial loss

16. Contracts of insurance against any of the following risks, namely—

    (a) risks of loss to the persons insured attributable to interruptions of the carrying on of business carried on by them or to reduction of the scope of business so carried on;

---

[39] Contracts of guarantee, including surety bonds, are not contracts of insurance: *Trade Indemnity Co v Workington Dock and Harbour Board* [1937] A.C. 1. However, surety contracts entered into by insurers are treated as insurance business for the purposes of the legislation (also been held that insurance protection taken out by insurers who have issued surety bonds is reinsurance for the purposes of the exemption of reinsurance from insurance premium tax: *Travellers Casualty & Surety Co of Europe Ltd v Commissioners of Customs and Excise* [2006] Lloyd's Rep. I.R. 63) so that authorisation of surety business is required.

[40] It is not readily apparent which contracts are caught by this phrase, and it may be that this catch-all provision was included in the legislation by way of safety-net to ensure that forms of suretyship having the same effects as those listed above are caught by the legislation. Ordinary guarantees of indebtedness are not insurance contracts for any other purpose: *The Zuhal K and The Selin* [1987] 1 Lloyd's Rep. 151. Cf. *Travel & General Insurance Co v Barron The Times*, November 25, 1988; *Mercers of the City of London v New Hampshire Insurance Co* [1992] 2 Lloyd's Rep. 365.

(b) risks of loss to the persons insured attributable to their incurring unforeseen expense (other than loss such as is covered by contracts falling within paragraph 18);

(c) risks which do not fall within sub-paragraph (a) or (b) and which are not of a kind such that contracts of insurance against them fall within any other provision of this Schedule.

Legal expenses

17. Contracts of insurance against risks of loss to the persons insured attributable to their incurring legal expenses (including costs of litigation).

Assistance

18. Contracts of insurance providing either or both of the following benefits, namely—

(a) assistance (whether in cash or in kind) for persons who get into difficulties while travelling, while away from home or while away from their permanent residence; or

(b) assistance (whether in cash or in kind) for persons who get into difficulties otherwise than as mentioned in sub-paragraph (a)."

Long-term business. There are nine classes of long-term business set out in Pt II of Sch.1 to the 2001 Order.   **13–010**

"Life and annuity

I. Contracts of insurance on human life or contracts to pay annuities on human life, but excluding (in each case) contracts within paragraph III.

Marriage and birth

II. Contracts of insurance to provide a sum on marriage or on the birth of a child, being contracts expressed to be in effect for a period of more than one year.

Linked long term

III. Contracts of insurance on human life or contracts to pay annuities on human life where the benefits are wholly or partly to be determined by references to the value of, or the income from, property of any description (whether or not specified in the contracts) or by reference to fluctuations in, or in an index of, the value of property of any description (whether or not so specified).

Permanent health

IV. Contracts of insurance providing specified benefits against risks of persons becoming incapacitated in consequence of sustaining injury as a result of an accident or of an accident of a specified class or of sickness or infirmity, being contracts that—

(a) are expressed to be in effect for a period of not less than five years, or until the normal retirement age for the persons concerned, or without limit of time; and

(b) either are not expressed to be terminable by the insurer, or are expressed to be so terminable only in special circumstances mentioned in the contract.

Tontines

V. Tontines.[41]

Capital redemption contracts

VI. Capital redemption contracts, where effected or carried out by a person who does not carry on a banking business, and otherwise carries on a regulated activity of the kind specified by article 10(1) or (2).[42]

---

[41] A tontine is a form of mutual insurance, those participating making contributions at an agreed rate to the common fund. In the simplest version of the tontine all the contributions are paid out to the last surviving participator. In more complex versions payments may begin to be made when the number of survivors falls to a predetermined level.

[42] i.e. carrying on, as principal, the business of effecting and carrying out contracts of insurance.

Pension fund management

VII. (a) Pension fund management contracts, and

(b) pension fund management contracts which are combined with contracts of insurance covering either conservation of capital or payment of a minimum interest,

where effected or carried out by a person who does not carry on a banking business, and otherwise carries on a regulated activity of the kind specified by article 10(1) or (2).[43]

Collective insurance etc.

VIII. Contracts of a kind referred to in article 1(2)(e) of the first life insurance directive.[44]

Social insurance

IX. Contracts of a kind referred to in article 1(3) of the first life insurance directive."[45]

Specific forms of regulated insurance business

13–011   *Mixed contracts.* A contract which contains both insurance and non-insurance elements is an insurance policy provided that the moneys are payable by reference to an uncertain event, and it appears not to matter that the insurance element is not the predominant element.[46] This is clear from the various benevolent societies cases discussed above, and it would seem to be irrelevant that the contract is not framed as a policy of insurance for it to constitute a contract of insurance[47] other than in the special case of marine insurance where the assured must be in possession of a policy before he can enforce the contract evidenced in it.[48] For regulatory purposes under the Financial Services and Markets Act 2000, an insurance contract which contains elements of life and non-life cover is to be treated as a life policy notwithstanding that the fact that it contains related and subsidiary provisions which are non-life, providing that the principal object is to provide life cover.[49] This provision is necessary to take account of the fact that life and non-life businesses are regulated in different ways, and the 2000 Act effects a strict separation between the two.

---

[43] i.e. carrying on, as principal, the business of effecting and carrying out contracts of insurance.

[44] This form of insurance is used in France.

[45] Social insurance is defined as any operation relating to the length of a human life provided for by social insurance legislation which is effected or managed by an insurance undertaking in accordance with the laws of an EC member state: First Life Directive, Council Directive 79/267/EEC art.1(3).This is stated in arts 59 and 60 of the 2001 Order to exclude funeral plan contracts, such a contract being defined as one which is independent of a whole life insurance and under which the provider agrees to provide a funeral for the customer or other person who is living at the date when the contract is made.

[46] *Fuji Finance v Aetna Insurance* [1996] 4 All E.R. 608, but see the comments of Megarry V.-C. in *Medical Defence Union v Department of Trade* [1979] 2 All E.R. 421 at 432, where the application of the legislation to mixed policies was questioned.

[47] *Hampton v Toxteth Co-operative Society* [1915] 1 Ch. 721 and *Hall D'Ath v British Provident Association* (1932) 48 T.L.R. 240 seem to indicate to the contrary, but in those cases the question was the construction of the relevant legislation, the Assurance Companies Act 1909, which regulated a business under which "policies of assurance" were issued. A contract is not necessarily a contract of insurance simply because it is in the form of such a contract: *Fuji Finance v Aetna Insurance* [1994] 4 All E.R. 1015, affirmed [1996] 4 All E.R. 608.

[48] Marine Insurance Act 1906 s.22. But see *Swan v Maritime Insurance Co* [1907] 1 K.B. 116, where it was held that s.22 did not preclude an action by a mortgagee who did not have possession of the policy.

[49] SI 2001/544 art.2.

Breakdown insurance. Class 18 of general business consists of contracts of **13–012** insurance which provide assistance (whether in cash or in kind) for persons who get into difficulties while travelling, while away from home or while away from their permanent residence, or assistance (whether in cash or in kind) for persons who get into difficulties in other ways. This provision prima facie covers breakdown contracts of the kind offered by motoring organisations, and are excluded from the regulatory requirements which attach to insurance if certain conditions are met. The exclusion is set out in art.12 of the Financial Services and Markets Act 2000 (Regulated Activities) Order 2001, and applies where: (a) the person providing the services does not carry on any other form of insurance business; (b) the contract under which the benefits provided are exclusively or primarily benefits in kind in the event of accident to or breakdown of a vehicle; and (c) contains terms to the effect that the assistance is not available outside the United Kingdom and the Republic of Ireland unless an additional premium is paid, and the assistance provided in the United Kingdom and the Republic of Ireland is in most circumstances provided by the provider's servants.

Retailers' and manufacturers' guarantees. It is a common practice for the **13–013** retailers and manufacturers of goods (especially electrical goods) to offer purchasers an arrangement under which the purchase price includes one year's free servicing of the article. On the face of it, this arrangement looks very like a contract of insurance, although the absence of apportionable premium is not a barrier to a finding of insurance and the name which the parties give to the payment cannot be decisive. A distinction may in any event be drawn between cases where the item is guaranteed against defects for a given period and cases where the item is guaranteed against loss from any cause. The regulation of the latter type of arrangement furthers the aims of the Financial Services and Markets Act 2000 much more than does the regulation of the former. It nevertheless remains unclear whether manufacturers' guarantees are contracts of insurance.[50]

Mutual insurance: club benefits. Mutual insurance is in common use in marine **13–014** insurance, but is also adopted by some life offices and for the insurance of professional liability risks. Mutual insurance refers to an arrangement under which two or more persons undertake to insure each other against specified losses. Section 85(2) of the Marine Insurance Act provides that the general rules concerning payment of premium do not apply to mutual insurance: a guarantee, or other similar arrangement, may be substituted for the premium. This conforms to the usual practice, which is for the directors or managers of the administrators of the scheme (in marine insurance, the club) to impose a levy on the members from time to time to provide such sums as they consider necessary to meet the anticipated liabilities and expenses of the club. In marine insurance it is usual to make an initial call at the start of the policy year, each member's share being determined by setting a rate per ton of shipping entered under each member's name. Supplementary calls are then made as necessary during the year. The detailed rules regulating the insurance will depend upon the constitution of the particular club. It is usual to empower the directors to refuse to enter any ship in the club, at their absolute discretion, even where the ship belongs to an existing member of the club, it is also usual to provide a procedure for arbitration in order to resolve disputes between the club and individual members. These proceedings

---

[50] The point was left open in *Re OY Computers* [2004] Lloyd's Rep. I.R. 669.

are binding, and members will be unable to take legal proceedings except by way of appeal from the arbitration in accordance with the Arbitration Act 1996. Mutual insurance is insurance within the Financial Services and Markets Act 2000, and the most common form of benefits available under marine contracts of this type include:

(a) war risks, including the detention or diversion of the vessel, and the consequent prolonging of the voyage;

(b) freight and demurrage risks;

(c) through transit risks;

(d) general risks—these include collision, towage, life salvage, loss of cargo, removal of wrecks; also personal injury, repatriation and crew substitute expenses.

13–015 *Friendly societies.* Friendly societies are associations which exist to provide benefits for their members, usually paid for out of members' contributions. The activities of friendly societies do, therefore, in many ways resemble the activities of an insurance company, and are regulated as such. Up to 1992 friendly societies had been governed by the Friendly Societies Act 1974, which can be traced back directly to the Friendly Societies Act 1875. Under the 1974 Act friendly societies were required to register with the Chief Registrar of Friendly Societies and were thereafter empowered to provide benefits, many of which were insurance benefits, including birth and death benefits and annuities, subject to strict financial limits. This traditional structure was dismantled by the Friendly Societies Act 1992, which extended the powers of friendly societies but imposed upon them a regulatory structure equivalent to that which governs insurance companies proper. Under s.93 of the Friendly Societies Act 1992, no further registrations under the 1974 were to be permitted, and existing and new friendly societies became entitled, under s.5 of the 1992 Act, become registered and incorporated in accordance with the provisions of the 1992 Act, leaving the 1974 Act to wither on the vine. The authorisation provisions of the 1992 Act were repealed by the Financial Services and Markets Act 2000, bringing friendly societies into the same regulatory framework as that applicable to pure insurers.

13–016 *Industrial assurance.* This form of business consists typically of life policies effected for small amounts and paid for by premiums collected on a door-to-door basis. Industrial assurance had for many years prior to the implementation of the Financial Services and Markets Act 2000, occupied an intermediate position in the scheme of regulation of insurance law. Although it had its own regulating statutes, it was not exempted from the authorisation requirement and other regulatory rules of the insurance companies legislation or, where the business was carried on by a friendly society, under the Friendly Societies Act 1992. The governing legislation for industrial assurance business, the Industrial Assurance Act 1923, was repealed by the 2000 Act, and industrial assurance business is regulated on the same basis as any other form of life insurance.

13–017 *Reinsurance.* Reinsurance is, for statutory purposes, treated as insurance business.[51] Further, reinsurance is not regarded as a form of general liability

[51] *Glasgow Assurance Corp v Welsh Insurance Corp* 1914 S.C. 320; *Attorney General v Forsikringsaktieselskabet National of Copenhagen* [1925] A.C. 639; *Re Friends Provident Life Office* [1999] Lloyd's Rep. I.R. 547.

insurance but rather as a further policy on the direct subject matter, with the result that reinsurers have to be authorised on a class by class basis in respect of each class of direct business which they reinsure.[52] Reinsurance is not always, for other purposes, regarded in the same light as insurance.[53]

Carrying on insurance business in the United Kingdom

The meaning of "carries on insurance business". The prohibition in s.19 of the 2000 Act is against carrying on a regulated activity in the United Kingdom without the authorisation of the Financial Services Authority, and s.22 provides that a regulated activity is one specified by secondary legislation and which is "carried on by way of business". "Effecting and carrying out contracts of insurance" is a regulated activity.[54] The phrase "carries on" and "by way of business" are not defined in the 2000 Act, but regulations may be made by the Treasury setting out the circumstances in which these tests are satisfied.[55] The word "business" necessarily imports, other than in the case of mutual insurance, some form of profit motive.[56] Insurance business consists of "effecting" and "carrying out" contracts of insurance. There is a clear prohibition on making insurance contracts, for it has been said that insurance business is carried on where "a company opening business premises for the purpose of carrying on insurance business . . . enter[s] into the very first contract of insurance of a relevant class".[57] However, it would appear that insurance business can be carried on for the purposes of the legislation even though no contracts actually come into existence, and an individual who purports to act on behalf of a non-existent insurance company may face personal criminal liability.[58] The administration of insurance business also constitutes the carrying on of insurance business,[59] and the mere paying of claims constitutes insurance business[60] although, as was pointed out by Lord Goff in *Ackman and Scher v Policyholders Protection Board*,[61] "in the vast majority of circumstances, the same insurance company will both effect the contract of insurance and carry it out (i.e. perform the obligations under it, in particular the obligation to pay claims)". To effect a

13–018

---

[52] A different view was originally taken in *DR Insurance Co v Seguros America Banamex* [1993] 1 Lloyd's Rep. 120, but the reasoning in this case can no longer stand in the light of *Re NRG Victory Reinsurance Ltd* [1995] 1 All E.R. 533.

[53] *Agnew v Lansforsakringsbolagens AB* [2000] Lloyd's Rep. I.R. 317; Case C-412/98 *Group Josi Reinsurance Co SA v Universal General Insurance Co Ltd* [2001] Lloyd's Rep. I.R. 483; *Royal London Mutual Insurance Society Ltd v Barrett (Inspector of Taxes)* Unreported, July 2002.

[54] Financial Services and Markets Act 2000 (Regulated Activities) Order 2001 (SI 2001/544) art.10.

[55] The relevant Order, the Financial Services and Markets Act 2000 (Carrying on Regulated Activities by Way of Business) Order 2001 (SI 2001/1177) does not touch upon the question in relation to insurance contracts. It was argued in *Re T&N Ltd (No.3)* [2006] Lloyd's Rep. I.R. 370 that brokers who took over part of the liability of reinsurers following a settlement between a reinsurer and its reinsured had to be authorised to investigate and pay claims in pursuance of their obligations. David Richards J. expressed no concluded view on this matter, but was plainly doubtful of its validity.

[56] *Hall D'Ath v British Provident Association* (1932) 48 T.L.R. 240.

[57] *Bedford Insurance Co Ltd v Institutio de Resseguros do Brasil* [1985] Q.B. 966 at 982, per Parker J.

[58] *R. v Wilson* [1997] 1 W.L.R. 1247. See also *Re Whiteley Insurance Consultants* [2009] Lloyd's Rep. I.R. 212, where an agent who was issuing policies on behalf of non-existent insurers and exceeding its mandate under binding authorities was held to be carrying on insurance business.

[59] *Re United General Commercial Insurance Corp Ltd* [1927] Ch. 51.

[60] *Bedford Insurance Co Ltd v Institutio de Resseguros do Brasil* [1985] Q.B. 966 at 982, per Parker J.

[61] *Ackman and Scher v Policyholders Protection Board* [1993] 3 All E.R. 384 at 408.

contract of insurance is to enter into new business and to carry out a contract of insurance is to perform obligations under the contract, including the payment of claims.[62] This test was adopted in *Re Whiteley Insurance Consultants*.[63] The business must be carried on "as principal", so that an agent who does not carry on insurance business does not require authorisation, although separate authorisation as an agent is required.

13–019   *Where is insurance business carried on?* One of the most important aspects of the 2000 Act is the restriction of its controls to persons carrying on insurance business in the United Kingdom. Plainly the issue of policies or confirmations of cover from offices in the United Kingdom operated by the insurer is within the concept of carrying on the business of "effecting" insurance business within the United Kingdom even though the risks themselves are situated elsewhere.[64] It is equally the case that an insurer who issues policies on foreign risks, and makes payments outside the United Kingdom, is to be treated as carrying on the business of carrying out insurance contracts within the United Kingdom if the general administration of the business is conducted within this jurisdiction.[65] The activities of offshore insurers may be regulated under the 2000 Act, e.g. where the insurer acts through local agents who carry out activities typical of insurance business.[66] The general test to be applied was laid down by Arden L.J. in *Financial Services Authority v Fradley and Woodward*[67]:

> "FSMA does not require that the entirety of a business activity be carried on in the United Kingdom. If it did, it would be open to obvious abuse . . . [I]t is sufficient if the activities in question which took place in this jurisdiction were a significant part of the business activity."

Section 418 of the 2000 Act deems three situations to amount to carrying on insurance business within the United Kingdom if they would not otherwise fall within the statutory prohibition.[68] The first case is where: (a) the insurer's registered office (or, if he does not have a registered office, his head office) is in the United Kingdom; and (b) he is entitled to exercise rights under a single market directive as a UK firm; and (c) he is carrying on in another EEA state an activity to which that Directive applies. This deals with the situation in which the insurer is authorised in the United Kingdom to carry on insurance business, as such authorisation provides a single passport to carry on insurance business anywhere in the EEA under the EC's single market directives. The effect of the deeming provision is to treat that insurer's business outside the United Kingdom as, for regulatory purposes, UK business. The second case is where: (a) the insurer's registered office (or, if he does not have a registered office, his head office) is in the United Kingdom; and (b) the management of the carrying on of the insurance business is the responsibility of that office or of another establishment maintained by him in the United Kingdom. The third case is where: (a) the

---

[62] *Re AA Mutual Insurance Co Ltd* [2005] 2 B.C.L.C. 8.

[63] *Re Whiteley Insurance Consultants* [2009] Lloyd's Rep. I.R. 212.

[64] *Re United General Commercial Insurance Corp Ltd* [1927] Ch. 51.

[65] *Bedford Insurance Co Ltd v Institutio de Resseguros do Brasil* [1985] Q.B. 966.

[66] *DR Insurance Co v Seguros America Banamex* [1993] 1 Lloyd's Rep. 120; *Re Great Western Insurance Co* [1999] Lloyd's Rep. I.R. 377.

[67] *Financial Services Authority v Fradley and Woodward* [2005] EWCA Civ 1183, where it was held that, in the context of a betting scheme, the maintenance of an accommodation address through which communications with clients and prospective clients took place and also a UK bank account, was sufficient to amount to business being carried on in the United Kingdom.

[68] A fourth case is provided for, but that is confined to collective investment schemes.

insurer's head office is not in the United Kingdom: but (b) the insurance business is carried on from an establishment maintained by him in the United Kingdom. The word "maintained" is not defined, but it would appear to indicate that the establishment must to a large—if not exclusive—extent be funded by the insurer. This would catch a branch or subsidiary, but presumably not an independent agency which the insurer from time to time utilises to a greater or lesser extent.

Contracts made by unauthorised insurers. It is a criminal offence for an   **13–020** insurer to effect an insurance contract as part of UK business without the authorisation of the Financial Services authority for the carrying on of insurance business of that class. The criminality raises the question whether either party to an insurance contract entered into by an unauthorised insurer has any rights under it. It was held under earlier legislation, after some vacillation, that a contract made by an unauthorised insurer was illegal so that neither party had any rights under it: that in turn meant that an unauthorised insurer had no claim against his reinsurers even if the insurer chose to make payment to its policyholders,[69] although if the insurer did not make payment the assured was held to have the right to recover his premium.[70] Section 132 of the Financial Services Act 1986 retrospectively[71] reversed the illegality principle, and rendered a policy entered into by an unauthorised insurer enforceable by the assured at his option, and also enforceable by the insurer if the court was satisfied that the insurer reasonably believed either that it was authorised or that authorisation was unnecessary and if enforcement would be just and equitable.

The position is much the same where the insurer has contravened the 2000 Act. A distinction is drawn between insurers who are authorised under the 2000 Act but who carry on business which is outside the scope of their authorisation, and insurers who are not authorised under the 2000 Act at all. In the former case the sanctions are less severe. Under s.20(2) of the 2000 Act, not only is the insurer immune from criminal sanctions (s.20(2)(a)), but any transaction made in the course of the unauthorised business is not void or unenforceable (s.20(2)(b)). It follows that an unauthorised insurer must pay its policyholders and, by reason of its legal liability to do so and the absence of any public policy stigma, is entitled to recover from its reinsurers in respect of such payments. The assured party to a transaction which forms part of an unauthorised business in general has no cause of action against the insurer for breach of statutory duty (s.20(2)(c)), although, s.20(3) states that in prescribed cases the contravention is actionable as breach of statutory duty, and the Financial Services and Markets Act 2000 (Rights of Action) Regulations 2001[72] permit a claim by a private policyholder. In *Re Whiteley Insurance Consultants*[73] the court was of the view that the policyholders of an insurer which was not authorised to carry on insurance business had not suffered any loss recoverable under the Regulations: they had obtained valid and enforceable policies and, had they been aware of the lack of

---

[69] The illegality approach was adopted in *Bedford Insurance Co v Instituto de Ressaguros do Brasil* [1984] 3 All E.R. 766 but subsequetly denied in *Stewart v Oriental Fire and Marine Insurance Co Ltd* [1984] 3 All E.R. 777. Illegality was reinstated by the Court of Appeal in *Phoenix General Assurance of Greece v ADAS* [1987] 2 All E.R. 152.

[70] *Re Cavalier Insurance Co Ltd* [1989] 2 Lloyd's Rep. 430.

[71] *Group Josi Re v Walbrook Insurance Co Ltd* [1996] 1 All E.R. 791, affirming on this point *Bates v Robert Barrow Ltd* [1995] 1 Lloyd's Rep. 680 and overruling *DR Insurance Co v Seguros America Banamex* [1993] 1 Lloyd's Rep. 120.

[72] SI 2001/2256.

[73] *Re Whiteley Insurance Consultants* [2009] Lloyd's Rep. I.R. 212.

authorisation and insured elsewhere, a similar premium would have been incurred.

Where, by contrast, the insurer is not authorised at all by the Financial Services Authority but has carried on insurance business, then a criminal offence is committed[74] and the agreements made in the course of that business are—in accordance with *Phoenix General Assurance of Greece v ADAS*[75]—void at common law. The saving provisions are set out in ss.26 and 28, the combined effect of which may be summarised as follows.

(1) An agreement made in the course of carrying on insurance business is unenforceable by the insurer against the assured.[76]

(2) The assured has the right to recover any money transferred by him under the agreement, and compensation for any loss suffered by him.[77] The amount of compensation may be agreed or determined by the court.[78] If the assured does so act, he must restore to the insurer any sums received by him under the contract.[79] In *Re Whiteley Insurance Consultants* it was noted that a policyholder who had made claims under a policy would not wish to have the policy treated as unenforceable because he would be required to repay any sums received by him, at least if those claims exceeded the amount of the premium plus compensation. The decision also shows that compensation is unlikely to be significant. Interest is not payable on the amount of the premium paid by the assured, because he would have incurred that expenditure by insuring elsewhere. The court refused to decide whether compensation could include a claim for the profits made by the unauthorised insurers.

(3) The court has a discretion to dispense with the provisions in (1) and (2) and to allow the insurer to enforce the contract and retain sums paid by the assured if satisfied that enforcement is just and equitable in the circumstances. The court must have regard to the question whether the insurer reasonably believed that it was not contravening the prohibition against carrying on unauthorised business.[80] In *Re Whiteley Insurance Consultants* it was held that, in deciding whether the court should allow enforcement by the insurers, the knowledge of the insurers was paramount, so that if they were aware of the contravention then enforcement should be refused. It was irrelevant that the policyholders had benefited from coverage, that liquidation had intervened and that the insurers would incur significant costs in repaying premiums to policyholders.

(4) The agreement is not to be regarded as illegal or unenforceable to any greater extent than that provided by the legislation.[81]

There is no express saving for reinsurance contracts made by unauthorised insurers. Plainly the reinsurers cannot point to an absence of legal liability as between insurer and assured, as such liability is conferred by ss.26 and 28. The only possible defence is that public policy precludes recovery by an unauthorised insurer. However, given that s.26 provides that the insurance agreement is not

---

[74] Financial Services and Markets Act 2000 s.23.
[75] *Phoenix General Assurance of Greece v ADAS* [1987] 2 All E.R. 152.
[76] Financial Services and Markets Act 2000 s.26(1).
[77] Financial Services and Markets Act 2000 s.26(2).
[78] Financial Services and Markets Act 2000 s.28(2).
[79] Financial Services and Markets Act 2000 s.28(7).
[80] Financial Services and Markets Act 2000 s.28(3), (4) and (5).
[81] Financial Services and Markets Act 2000 s.28(9).

illegal but simply unenforceable should the assured choose to treat it as such or should the court order enforcement on the insurer's application, and given also that the commission of an authorisation offence has no greater effect on the validity of the contract than provided for by s.26,[82] there would seem to be little basis for a public policy defence.

The authorisation process. The FSA's Handbook contains a chapter on Authorisation, setting out the procedures involved and the considerations to be taken into account by the FSA. The Act itself lays down requirements as to the form and content of applications and the circumstances and procedures for the grant and revocation of permission.[83] Section 41 provides five threshold conditions[84] which must be met before permission to carry on a regulated activity may be given and which must be satisfied if permission is to be retained. As applied to insurance the conditions are that: the applicant is a body corporate, a registered friendly society or a member of Lloyd's; the head office and registered office is within the United Kingdom; if the insurer has close links with another person—in that it is a parent or subsidiary, or that there is a 20 per cent shareholding by one company in the other—the FSA must be satisfied that those links are not likely to prevent effective supervision of the insurer; the resources of the insurer must be adequate in relation to the regulated activities in question; and the insurer must be a fit and proper person,[85] having regard to his connection with any other person, the nature of the regulated activity and the need to ensure that its affairs are conducted soundly and prudently. There is now a sixth threshold requirement applicable to a motor insurer, namely, that the insurer has an appointed claims representative in each Member State.

13–021

If the insurer has its head office outside the EEA, the insurer must have a representative resident in the United Kingdom with authority to bind its relations with third parties and to represent it before the FSA: asset holding requirements are also imposed.[86]

3. THE SINGLE EEA INSURANCE MARKET

Rights of UK insurers in the EEA

Establishment and services. The general effects of the EU Single Market Directives, as implemented into UK law by 2000 Act are: (1) to permit an insurer established and authorised in the United Kingdom to carry on insurance business in any other EEA state through an establishment in that state, without host state authorisation and subject only to minimal formal requirements; (2) to permit an insurer established and authorised in the United Kingdom to sell insurance into any other EEA state from an establishment anywhere in the EEA without the authorisation of the home state, and subject only to minimal formal requirements;

13–022

---

[82] Financial Services and Markets Act 2000 s.28(9).

[83] See ss.40–54.

[84] There is a sixth for motor insurers, who are required to appoint claims representatives in each EEA state: see Ch.22, below.

[85] Competence requirements are set out in the Training and Competence section of the FSA Handbook.

[86] Financial Services and Markets Act 2000 (Variation of Threshold Conditions) Order 2002 (SI 2002/2702).

(3) to vest regulatory powers in the UK authorities over an insurer's EEA-wide activities, subject to the right of host state authorities to intervene on their own account in exceptional circumstances and of the duty of those authorities to assist the UK regulator where appropriate.

The distinction between becoming established in another Member State, by means of some form of presence in that state, and merely selling insurance into that state, is a fine one, although it remains important as the formalities attaching to each are rather different. Guidance as to the distinction has been given by the European Commission in an Interpretative Communication "Freedom to Provide Services and the General Good in the Insurance Sector" published in May 2000. This states that the provision of services involves temporary presence, while an establishment constitutes a permanent presence, but the distinction is not always clear cut. Thus an insurer who operates in the host Member State through an independent intermediary is to be regarded as established only if the intermediary is under the management or supervision of the insurer, the intermediary is authorised to bind the insurer either in the acceptance of risks or the settlement of losses, the intermediary must be acting under a long-term relationship. A binding authority granted to an agent is not enough to allow the insurer to be treated as established where the agent carries on business. Further, if an insurer has staff in a member state, those staff members do not constitute an establishment unless they engage in insurance activities and do not simply operate as a representative office.

13–023 *Procedural matters.* The requirements which have to be met by a UK established and authorised firm wishing to carry on insurance business in another EEA state through an establishment are set out in the Financial Services and Markets Act 2000 (EEA Passport Rights) Regulations 2001[87] differ slightly from those applicable to a firm wishing to sell insurance elsewhere in the EEA by way of services, although the basic procedure in both cases is that the firm gives a notice of intention to the FSA identifying either the establishment or, in the case of services, the activities which it intends to carry out. The FSA may then issue a "consent notice" to the host state's regulator, and in the absence of any objection or imposition of conditions the insurer may then commence its operations. The European Commission's has said in its February 2000 Interpretative Communication that notification is not required where an insurer merely intends to advertise its products in another EEA Member State.

A UK firm which establishes a branch, or sells insurance in the EEA, without the requisite permission of the FSA, it commits a criminal offence, although it has a defence if it can show that it took all reasonable precautions and acted with due diligence to avoid committing the offence.

13–024 *The "general good".* The Single Insurance Market Directives allow host states minimal control over the selling activities of insurers authorised and established in other Member States. This is, however, subject to the "general good", a concept which is enshrined in the Third Generation of Insurance Directives and which allows a Member State to apply its ordinary consumer protection rules to insurance contracts provided that those rules do not unduly interfere with the single market for insurance and are not disguised restrictions on the provision of services by insurers from elsewhere. A national rule is preserved by the general good if: (a) it relates to an area of economic activity which has not been

---

[87] SI 2001/2511.

harmonised; (b) the rule pursues a legitimate objective, including consumer protection, the protection of the reputation of the financial services sector, the prevention of fraud and the proper administration of justice; (c) it is non-discriminatory; (d) it is objectively necessary to the objective pursued; (e) it is proportionate to the objective pursued, in that the legislation must impose the least restrictive conditions which are necessary to fulfil that objective; and (f) it is a rule to which the insurer is not subject under the domestic law of the Member State in which the insurer is established. Very few rules pass these tests, examples being: the use of local language in policies; professional codes of conduct; maximum technical interest rates for life assurance; the prohibition of cold-calling; and taxation.

Rights of EEA insurers in the United Kingdom. The rights of an EEA insurer **13–025** to carry on insurance business by way of establishment or by the provision of services mirror those open to a UK insurer wishing to conduct business elsewhere in the EEA. An insurer which is authorised and established in any other EEA Member State is exempt from seeking authorisation from the FSA to carry on insurance business in the United Kingdom.[88] The exemption is lost if the EEA firm has had its home state authorisation withdrawn,[89] and where an EEA firm which is qualified for authorisation ceases to carry on regulated activities in the United Kingdom and gives notice of that fact to the FSA, the notice is to be treated as a request for cancellation of the firm's authorisation.

The formal requirements required of an EEA firm vary depending upon whether the firm wishes to become established in the United Kingdom or whether it is merely seeking to sell insurance in the United Kingdom by way of services from another EEA establishment. In either case the requirements are minimal and involve the provision of information rather than any request for permission. The procedure is as described above: the insurer must apply to its own regulator which will issue a "consent notice" to the FSA, and subject to any conditions which may be imposed by the FSA the insurer is entitled to commence its UK activities.

If an EEA firm does not qualify for passport rights but has nevertheless entered into a contract in the United Kingdom, s.26 of the 2000 Act, which renders an agreement made by an unauthorised firm unenforceable at the instance of the firm, but allows the customer to recover any sums paid and to seek damages, is disapplied.[90] The effect is uncertain: one possibility is that the contract is to be treated as unaffected by the 2000 Act, and is thus fully binding on both sides; the alternative is that the agreement is governed by the common law, and that the position established by the cases on unauthorised insurers is that their contracts are illegal and neither party has any rights under them. It might be thought that the former interpretation is the correct one: that was the position under the Insurance Companies Act 1982; and the draconian effects of illegality could scarcely have been intended.

In accordance with the provisions of the Insurance Directives, EEA firms are regulated almost exclusively by their home state regulators, and the role of the FSA in relation to those firms is largely confined to providing information to the home state regulators and to exercising powers on their behalves. Thus, there is no need for an insurer authorised elsewhere in the EEA to maintain a UK margin of solvency, although there is a lesser requirement that the value of the assets of

---

[88] 2000 Act s.31.
[89] s.34.
[90] 2000 Act Sch.3 Pt II para.16.

the UK business does not fall below the amount of its UK liabilities, as valued in accordance with the valuation rules. Further, a non-UK insurer with permission to carry on insurance business in the United Kingdom (other than a Swiss insurer) must: make and maintain a deposit in the United Kingdom; keep in the United Kingdom proper accounts and records in respect of its UK business; and appoint a chief executive and an authorised UK representative authorised to act generally and to accept service of documents—a Swiss general insurer need appoint only a representative. By way of safety-net, there are various provisions in the 2000 Act which permit the FSA to exercise powers in support of EEA regulators. The FSA may provide assistance to an EEA regulator on request (s.47), exercise regulatory functions on behalf of that regulator (section 169) and take action against the insurer for contraventions of the 2000 Act (ss.193–202).

4. CONDUCT OF INSURANCE BUSINESS IN THE UNITED KINGDOM

13–026 **Advertising and promotion.** The FSA's rules relating to advertising and promotion are contained in the 2000 Act, the Conduct of Business Sourcebook (COBS—effective November 1, 2007 and replacing the Conduct of Business Rules) and the Insurance Conduct of Business Sourcebook (ICOBS—effective January 6, 2008 and replacing the Insurance Conduct of Business Rules (ICOB). COBS applies to life and other long-term insurances, and ICOBS apply to general insurance business. COBS and ICOBS extend to insurers and intermediaries. The Rules do not apply directly to appointed representatives, but under the general principle in s.39(3) an insurer is in any event directly liable for their acts and omissions. The statutory rules are as follows.

First, there are under s.397 criminal sanctions in respect of misleading statements and practices. The section does not confer civil rights.[91] An offence is committed by a person who, for the purpose of inducing a contract of insurance in the United Kingdom or influencing the exercise of rights in the United Kingdom under a contract of insurance: (1) makes a statement, promise or forecast which he knows to be misleading, false or deceptive in a material particular; (2) dishonestly conceals any material facts whether in connection with a statement, promise or forecast made by him or otherwise; or (3) recklessly makes (dishonestly or otherwise) a statement, promise or forecast which is misleading, false or deceptive in a material particular.

Secondly, s.21 prohibits any person other than an authorised person from communicating in the course of a business an invitation or inducement to engage in investment activity—including long-term insurance business—unless an authorised person has approved the content of the communication. It is (s.25) a criminal offence for a person to contravene this provision. An agreement resulting from an unlawful communication is unenforceable against the customer, although the customer may at his option either enforce the agreement or seek restitution and compensation, subject to the discretion of the court to allow the agreement to be enforced by the unauthorised person if it is just and equitable to do so, taking into account whether that person reasonably believed that he was

[91] *Norwich Union Life Insurance v Qureshi* [2000] Lloyd's Rep. I.R. 1; *Aldridge v Norwich Union Life Insurance Co Ltd* [1999] Lloyd's Rep. I.R. 276 (decided under the similarly worded superseded s.47 of the Financial Services Act 1986).

authorised. The details of exactly when financial promotions may be communicated by way of exception to the general prohibition on financial promotion by unauthorised persons are set out in the Financial Services and Markets Act 2000 (Financial Promotion) Order 2001.[92]

As far as ICOBS is concerned, an initial distinction is drawn between commercial and consumer customers: a consumer is any natural person who is acting or purposes which are outside his trade or profession (ICOBS 2.1). The requirements of ICOBS are as follows:

(a) The insurer must take reasonable steps to ensure that any communication of information is done in a way that is clear, fair and not misleading (ICOBS 2.2).

(b) The insurer must not seek to exclude or restrict, or rely on any exclusion or restriction of, any duty or liability it may have to a customer unless it is reasonable for it to do so and the duty or liability arises other than under the regulatory system.

(c) An insurer which carries on any distance marketing activity from a UK establishment with consumers must comply with the terms of the Distance Marketing Directive, European Parliament and Council Directive 2002/65/EC (ICOBS 3.1). This requires the provision of information, including all contractual terms and conditions, in a clear and comprehensible manner, prior to the completion of the contract.

(d) Electronic communications must comply with the E-Commerce Directive, European Parliament and Council Directive 2000/31/EC, and in particular their origin and purpose must be clear.

(e) An insurer is to take reasonable steps to ensure that the assured only buys a policy under which he is eligible to claim benefits (ICOBS 5.2).

(f) Before a contract is concluded a customer who is a natural person must be informed of the applicable law and the arrangements for handling complaints. The contract itself must state the address of the insurer, and if the assured is a consumer he must also be provided with information as to his cancellation rights (ICOBS 6.2).

(g) A consumer has a right to cancel, for any or no reason and without penalty, within 14 days. There are exceptions for, *inter alia*, travel policies, and policies which have been fully performed. The cancellation period begins from the date on which the contract is concluded or on which the consumer receives the contractual terms and conditions, whichever is later (ICOBS 7).

The principles in COBS, with respect to life policies, reflect those in ICOBS.

Controls over firms and individuals. In addition to its general powers to issue   **13–027** principles and codes of conduct, and to punish non-compliance, the FSA has a number of different powers to ensure that insurers themselves, persons connected with insurers, and individuals working for insurers, are fit and proper persons.[93] The principle that the affairs of an insurer must be run according to sound and prudent management criteria derives from the EU Directives. There are various aspects to the general principle. Initial permission to carry on a regulated activity will not be given by the FSA unless the firm's controllers are fit and proper

---

[92] SI 2001/1335.
[93] A concept defined in s.61 by reference to honesty and integrity, competence and capability, and financial soundness.

persons, and ss.178 to 192 set out a procedure which enables the FSA to monitor changes in control and to refuse approval for to the new controllers. The FSA may under ss.56 to 58 make prohibition orders against individuals, preventing them from carrying out aspects of an insurer's regulated business.

An authorised person must take reasonable care to ensure that no person performs a "controlled function" unless the FSA has given is approval to the arrangement under which the function is to be performed (ss.59 to 63). Breach of this provision gives a private person affected by the contravention a right to damages. A controlled function is one which enables the person to exercise a significant influence on the firm's affairs, and requires him to deal with customers and their property.[94] The FSA has, under s.64, issued Statements of Principle and Code of Practice for Approved Persons. The Statements of Principle provide that an approved person, must in carrying out his controlled function: act with integrity, due skill, care and diligence; observe proper standards of market conduct; and deal with the FSA and other regulators in an open and co-operative way. If the function is one involving significant influence, he must: take reasonable steps to ensure that the business of the firm for which he is responsible in his controlled function is organised so that it can be controlled effectively; exercise due skill, care and diligence in managing the business of the firm for which he is responsible in his controlled function; and take reasonable steps to ensure that the business of the firm for which he is responsible complies with the relevant requirements and standards of the regulatory system. The Code of Practice identifies defaults as including: misleading a client or giving inappropriate advice; withholding material information from a customer; failing to report promptly to his firm under its procedures (or if none, to FSA direct) information which would be of material significance to FSA; and permitting transactions without a sufficient understanding of the risks involved, expanding business without reasonable assessment of the potential risks, inadequate monitoring of highly profitable or unusual transactions, inappropriate delegation, failure to supervise.

13–028 **The insurance business rules.** The FSA has issued a Prudential Sourcebook for Insurers, INSPRU, which sets out in detail the prudential rules which apply to insurers.[95] INSPRU covers, most importantly: the prohibition on insurers carrying on any other form of business; the obligation on insurers to maintain a margin of solvency using the formulae there laid down; the maintenance of a minimum guarantee fund representing one third of the solvency margin; the separation of long-term and general business in respect of companies permitted to carry on both forms; the maintenance of an equalisation reserve and adherence to matching rules requiring the holding of sufficient of any one currency to cover 80 per cent of liabilities in that currency; and audit rules. Supplementary provision is made for the financial supervision of insurers which form part of a wider financial conglomerate.[96] An insurer carrying on long-term business must also appoint an actuary[97] whose functions are: to identify and monitor risks run by a firm so far as they have a material impact on the firm's ability to meet liabilities to policyholders in respect of long-term contracts; and inform the firm

[94] See the FSA Handbook, chapter on Supervision (SUP).

[95] The provisions here were, before the 2000 Act, enshrined in primary and secondary legislation.

[96] Financial Conglomerates and Other Financial Groups Regulations 2004 (SI 2004/1862), European Parliament and Council Directive 2002/78/EC on supplementary supervision.

[97] 2000 Act ss.340–346.

if he has doubts as to whether the firm is meeting liabilities or is effecting long-term contracts on inadequate terms or does not have assets to meet liabilities as they fall due. He must request information and explanations from the firm. He must pay due regard to generally accepted actuarial best practice. The firm for its part must allow the actuary to perform his duties and must keep him informed of business and other plans and give him sufficient resources to do his job. He is also to be given access to books. The provision of false information to an actuary is a criminal offence.[98]

Enforcement powers

Sources. The 2000 Act confers a variety of supervisory and enforcement powers on the FSA, the manner in which they are exercised being set out in the Supervision (SUP) chapter of the FSA Handbook.   **13–029**

Obtaining information. As far as provision of information is concerned, regulated firms are under a general obligation to notify the FSA of any failure to satisfy threshold conditions, any matter which could have significant impact on firm's reputation, any matter which could affect firm's ability to provide adequate services to customers, or any matter which could have serious financial consequences to the financial system or other firms. There is also an obligation to notify any significant breach of rule, principle, or requirement, the bringing of a prosecution for offence under the Act, civil proceedings under the Act, disciplinary measures imposed by some other regulator, possible fraud by an employee against a customer or the firm itself, or possible insolvency proceedings. More formal matters must also be notified, including any change in name, address, or legal status. SUP provides standard forms for notifications.   **13–030**

The FSA has[99] own initiative powers to require an authorised person to provide information or documents relevant to its regulatory functions, within a reasonable period: that power may also be exercised against persons connected with the regulated person. In addition, the FSA may instigate investigations of the following types: (a) an investigation and report from a person with the appropriate specialised skills into any matter falling within the regulatory functions of the FSA; (b) an investigation by inspectors into the affairs or business (whether or not regulated) of an authorised person, including a person in the same group; (c) an investigation by inspectors into, amongst other things; breach of the asset identification rules; failure to comply with an investigatory requirement; provision of false information to an auditor or actuary; misleading the FSA; failure to obtain authorisation; false claims of authorisation; false or misleading statements; the fit and proper status of any person; breach of a prohibition order made by the FSA; and misconduct by an approved person.

Disciplinary measures against an insurer. The FSA is granted a series of disciplinary powers which may be exercised against insurers who have contravened the requirements of FSMA 2000 or obligations imposed upon them under delegated legislation or by the FSA. These include: (a) withdrawal of authorisation where the insurer no longer meets the threshold conditions for permission[100];   **13–031**

---

[98] For the form of accounts, see Council Directive 91/674/EEC, as amended by European Parliament and Council Directive 2006/46/EC.

[99] 2000 Act ss.165–177.

[100] 2000 Act ss.45–47.

(b) public censure following contravention of a regulatory requirement[101]; (c) the imposition of a financial penalty upon an authorised person who has contravened a regulatory requirement[102]; (d) the right to apply for an injunction where there is a reasonable likelihood that a person will contravene a requirement of the FSMA 2000 or has done so and the infringement is likely to continue—the court order may also include a restitutionary order in favour of any person who has paid over sums to a person who has infringed the 2000 Act,[103] and freezing the defendant's assets[104]; (e) the right to apply to the court for a restitution order where the defendant has contravened a requirement of the 2000 Act, profits have accrued to the defendant as a result of the contravention and one or more persons have suffered loss or have been otherwise adversely affected by reason of the contravention[105]; and (f) in serious cases, the issuing of a prohibition order where it appears to the FSA that an individual is not a fit and proper person to perform functions in relation to a regulated activity carried on by an authorised person.[106]

5. TRANSFERS OF INSURANCE BUSINESS

13–032 **Scope of the controls.** Transfers of long-term business have been regulated since the coming into force of the Insurance Companies Act 1984, and transfers of general business were first controlled by the Insurance Companies Act 1981. Both sets of provisions were consolidated in the Insurance Companies Act 1982 ss.49 to 52, sections themselves replaced by the Insurance Companies Act 1982 Sch.2C added to the legislation in 1994 on the completion of the EU single market for insurance. Under the 1982 Act s.52B and Sch.2E, court sanction was required only for the transfer of long-term business; Treasury approval was required for the transfer of general business. These provisions were repealed and replaced by the Financial Services and Markets Act 2000, which made a number of changes to the earlier rules: significantly, court sanction is now required in all cases. The 2000 Act was amended with effect from December 10, 2007 on the implementation of the Reinsurance Directive, European Parliament and Council Directive 2005/68/EC, which makes provision for the regulation of the transfers of reinsurance business. Implementation was effected by the introduction of amendments to the 2000 Act by statutory instrument: the Reinsurance Directive Regulations 2007,[107] amend the 2000 Act, and the Financial Services and Markets Act 2000 (Reinsurance Directive) Regulations 2007[108] amend the Financial Services and Markets Act 2000 (Control of Business Transfers) (Requirements on Applicants) Regulations 2001.[109] The broad effect of the Reinsurance Directive as implemented is that, as regards the transfer of reinsurance business, approval is to be given by the courts of the transferee rather than the courts of the transferor, and that the transferee must obtain a certificate of solvency as a condition of the transfer. European Parliament and Council

---

[101] 2000 Act ss.205, 207–211.
[102] 2000 Act ss.206–211.
[103] *Financial Services Authority v Martin* [2005] EWCA Civ 1422.
[104] 2000 Act s.380.
[105] 2000 Act s.382.
[106] 2000 Act ss.56–58.
[107] SI 2007/3253.
[108] SI 2007/3255.
[109] SI 2001/3625.

Directive 2007/44/EC modifies the existing law by providing for a prudential assessment of a proposed acquisition of general insurance business. Under the Directive, pre-notification of a proposed acquisition including the acquisition of a significant shareholding is to be given to the relevant regulatory authorities who are them to make an assessment to ensure that the business will be governed in a sound and prudent fashion. All of these measures have now been consolidated into the Solvency II Directive 2009.[110]

A scheme is within the FSMA 2000 controls if the result is that the business transferred will be carried on from an establishment of the transferee within the EEA as long as any one of three conditions is met (2000 Act s.105(1)–(2)): (a) the whole or part of the business to be transferred is carried on in one or more EEA state by a person authorised in the United Kingdom; (b) the whole or part of a reinsurance business to be transferred is carried on in the United Kingdom through a UK establishment by an EEA firm which has passport rights; or (c) the whole or part of the business to be transferred is carried on in the United Kingdom by a person with permission to carry out that business.

The transfer rules apply also to Lloyd's underwriters. In its original form the 2000 Act extended to former underwriting members, defined by s.324 and persons who ceased to be members after December 24, 1996. The Financial Services and Markets Act 2000 (Amendment of Section 323) Regulations 2008 (SI 2008/1469) removed this temporal restriction and the legislation now applies to all former underwriting members of Lloyd's.

The statutory controls do not apply to five Cases set out in FSMA 2000 s.105(4), as modified to take account of the Reinsurance Directive. The Cases to which the statutory controls are inapplicable are as follows:

(1) A friendly society. This situation is governed by the rules set out in the Friendly Societies Act 1992.

(2) The transferor is authorised in the United Kingdom, the transferor is not a reinsurance undertaking, the business to be transferred consists of effecting and carrying out reinsurance in any EEA state other than the United Kingdom and the scheme has been approved by a court in an EEA state other than the United Kingdom. Because the Reinsurance Directive now requires that authorisation for the transfer of reinsurance business by reinsurance undertakings to be given by the home state of the transferee, the exception does not apply to a transfer of reinsurance risks in EEA countries other than the United Kingdom by UK reinsurers.

(3) The transferor is authorised in the United Kingdom, the business to be transferred is carried out outside the EEA and the scheme has been approved by a court or a regulator outside the EEA where the transferee carries on business.

(4) The business to be transferred is the whole of the business of the authorised person concerned, the business consists entirely of reinsurance or all the policyholders are controllers of firms in the same group as the transferee and all of the policyholders affected have given consent.

(5) The business to be transferred is the whole or part of the business of a pure reinsurer, all of the policyholders have consented and a certificate of solvency has been obtained by the transferee's home state regulators—this provision, added in accordance with the Reinsurance Directive, dispenses with the need for the consent of the English court and replaces it with a solvency certificate issued by the transferee's regulators.

[110] European Parliament and Council Directive 2009/138/EC.

The court's sanction

13–033   *Application for sanction.* An application for court sanction has to be made by the transferor or the transferee, or both. An application to the High Court is to be made where either or both the transferor and the transferee have their head offices in England (s.107): time limits and other procedural matters are laid down by statutory instrument.[111] It is necessary for the scheme to be sent to all policyholders and advertised in two UK national newspapers and in any EEA Member State where an insured risk is situated,[112] although a failure to alert all policyholders to the scheme does not deprive the court of jurisdiction to sanction the scheme.[113] The application has to be accompanied by a expert financial report prepared by a person approved by the FSA and in a form required by the FSA[114]; the report is of great significance and can be challenged only if the expert has mistaken his function or has made an error.[115] At the hearing itself, the FSA has a right to be represented, as does any person (including an employee) who alleges that he would be adversely affected by the carrying out of the scheme (s.110).

13–034   *Formalities.* Before a scheme can be sanctioned by the court, three jurisdictional conditions have to be met: the notification and advertising obligations must have been met; the transferee must have the necessary authorisation to carry on the transferred business; and certificates conforming with the requirements in sch.12 to the 2000 Act must be obtained (s.111). The certificates required vary depending upon the nature of the business to be transferred and the EEA regulatory authorities affected by the transfer.

13–035   *Approval.* The court will approve the transfer only if it is shown that the interests of policyholders will not be prejudiced, although adverse effects on some persons or classes is not fatal to the scheme if on balance it is fair as between the different classes affected.[116] The principles were summarised by Evans-Lombe J. in *Re Allied Dunbar Assurance Plc*[117]:

---

[111] Financial Services and Markets (Control of Business Transfers) (Requirements on Applicants) Regulations 2001 (SI 2001/3625), made under s.108. The court has power to waive or modify the publicity requirements under reg.4 of the 2001 Regulations. In *Re Equitas Ltd* [2009] Lloyd's Rep. I.R. 642 the court agreed to a modification with respect to a scheme to transfer the business of Equitas, on the grounds that publicity in the *Financial Times* was more appropriate than one of the daily newspapers, and the requirement to notify all policyholders could not be fulfilled given that Equitas' business dated back some 300 years up to 1992.

[112] *Re Lincoln Assurance Ltd* Unreported, 1996.

[113] *Re Refuge Assurance* Unreported, 2001.

[114] s.109. For the independence requirement, see: *Re Norwich Union* [2004] EWHC 2802 (Ch); *Re Allied Dunbar Assurance Plc* [2005] EWHC 28 (Ch). A report is of great weight and cannot be challenged unless it is shown that the expert has mistaken his functions or has made an error: *Re Axa Equity & Law* [2001] 2 B.C.L.C. 447; *Re Eagle Star Insurance Co Ltd* [2005] EWHC 1850 (Ch). In *Re Equitas Ltd* [2008] EWHC 2960 it was noted that the scheme report was not required at the initial application stage, but rather at some point during the hearing of the proceedings.

[115] *Re Eagle Star Insurance Co Ltd* [2006] EWHC 1850 (Ch).

[116] *Re London Life* Unreported, 1989; *Re Axa Equity & Law Life Assurance Society* [2001] B.C.L.C. 447; *WASA International (UK) Insurance Co Ltd v WASA International Insurance Co Ltd* [2002] EWHC 2698 (Ch); *Re Pearl Assurance (Unit Linked Pensions) Ltd* [2006] EWHC 2291 (Ch); *Re Eagle Star Insurance Co Ltd* [2006] EWHC 1850 (Ch); *Re Pearl Assurance (Unit Linked Pensions) Ltd* [2006] EWHC 2291 (Ch); *Re Alba Life Ltd* [2006] EWHC 3507 (Ch); *Re Equitable Life Assurance Society, Re Canada Life Ltd* Unreported, February 14, 2007; *Re First Alternative Insurance Co Ltd; Re Esure Insurance Ltd,* Unreported, March 2007; *Re Commercial Union Life Assurance Co Ltd* [2009] EWHC 2521 (Ch).

[117] *Re Allied Dunbar Assurance Plc* [2005] EWHC 28 (Ch).

(1) the legislation conferred an absolute discretion on the court whether or not to sanction a scheme, but the discretion was to be exercised by giving due recognition to the commercial judgment entrusted by the company's constitution to its directors;

(2) the court was concerned whether a policyholder, employee or other interested person, or any group of them, would be adversely affected by the scheme;

(3) that was primarily a matter of actuarial judgment involving a comparison between the security and reasonable expectations of policyholders without the scheme and what would be the result if the scheme were implemented—for the purpose of this comparison, the report of the independent expert would be given close attention;

(4) the FSA by reason of its regulatory powers could also be expected to have the necessary material and expertise to express an informed opinion on whether policyholders were likely to be adversely affected, and the court would pay close attention to any views expressed by it;

(5) that individual policyholders or groups of policyholders might be adversely affected did not mean that the scheme had to be rejected by the court—the fundamental question was whether the scheme as a whole was fair as between the interests of the different classes of persons affected;

(6) it was not the function of the court to produce what, in its view, was the best possible scheme—as between different schemes, all of which the court might deem fair, it was the company's directors' choice which to pursue;

(7) under the same principle, the details of the scheme were not a matter for the court provided that the scheme as a whole was found to be fair, so the court would not amend the scheme because it thought that individual provisions could be improved upon.

In *Re Equitas Ltd*[118] the court confirmed a transfer of business to Equitas, established under the 1996 Reconstruction and Renewal Scheme at Lloyd's to act as a reinsurer for Lloyd's Names in respect of business written in 1992 and previous years. Names were, however, left without reinsurance in the event that Equitas became insolvent. Under the scheme, those residual liabilities faced were transferred from the Names to Equitas Insurance, which was able to offer an addition US\$1.3 billion of retrocession cover: Blackburne J. was satisfied that the scheme was fair to all parties concerned.

The court's order. The court's order sanctioning the transfer may deal with the **13–036** following matters in such manner as the court thinks fit (s.112(1)–(7)): the transfer of the undertaking, property or liabilities; the allotment or appropriation of shares, debentures or policies; the continuation by or against the transferee of legal proceedings involving the transferor; and such incidental matters as are necessary to secure that the scheme is fully and effectively carried out. The court may subsequently make an order dissolving the transferor, dealing with the interests of any person objecting to the transfer and reducing the benefits payable under the transferred policies (s.112(8)). The last-mentioned order is designed to ensure that the policyholders of an insurer in financial difficulties do all obtain some benefit from any transfer, even though this may mean reducing the benefits

---

[118] *Re Equitas Ltd* [2010] Lloyd's Rep. I.R. 69.

of one or more particular classes of policy holder entitled to disproportionate benefits, although such an order will not be made before the court has received an independent actuary's report on the request of the FSA.

Under s.112(3)(d) the court may make such provision, if any, as it thinks fit "respect to such incidental, consequential and supplementary matters as are, in its opinion, necessary to secure that the scheme is fully and effectively carried out." It has been held[119] that this subsection authorises the court to approve proposals that were supplementary to the scheme unless they interfered with the contractual rights of policyholders, although there is authority for the narrower proposition that supplementary provisions are authorised only if they were "indeed necessary to secure that the Scheme of Transfer should be fully and effectively carried out".[120] The most recent case has preferred the wider view of the subsection so that the court may sanction supplementary matters even if they achieve things other than a pure transfer.[121]

13–037   *Effects of an order.* Section 114, makes limited provision for the protection of the rights of the policyholders whose agreements are to be transferred under a sanctioned scheme. The section applies to a transferee authorised in the United Kingdom whose policy relates to a risk situated within the EEA. Notice of the court's order must be published, and the policyholders are given the right to cancel the policy, assuming that the law of the EEA state in which the risk insured by the policy is situated so permits. As far as reinsurance business transfers are concerned, under FSMA 2000 s.114A, the court has a discretion to order publication of its sanction.

Where a transfer is effected by an EEA firm, and the business in question consists of policies governed by a law of the part of the United Kingdom, an approval of the transfer elsewhere in the EEA must be published in the United Kingdom and is then automatically binding on UK policyholders (s.116).

It was held in *WASA International (UK) Insurance Co Ltd v WASA International Insurance Co Ltd*[122] that the sanctioning of the transfer of an insurance business carried with it any outwards reinsurance taken out by the reinsured, and that the consent of the reinsurers to such transfer was not required. This decision was codified by the Financial Services and Markets Act 2000 (Control of Business Transfers) (Requirements on Applicants) (Amendment) Regulations 2008[123] and the Financial Services and Markets Act 2000 (Amendments to Part VII) Regulations 2008.[124] The latter provision amended s.112 of the 2000 Act by adding s.112(2A)–(2C) and 112A and thereby authorising the court to order the transfer of reinsurance irrespective of the terms of the reinsurance. SI 2008/1467 amends the Financial Services and Markets Act 2000 (Control of Business Transfers) (Requirements on Applicants) Regulations 2001 (SI 2001/3625), under which notification of an application for a transfer of insurance business is to be given to reinsurers in circumstances where the business to be transferred is subject to contracts of reinsurance.

---

[119] *Re Hill Samuel Life Assurance* Unreported, 1995; *Re Consolidated Life Assurance Co Ltd* Unreported, 1996; *Re Sun Life of Canada Assurance Co* Unreported, 1999.

[120] *Re Lincoln Assurance* Unreported, 1996, per Rattee J.

[121] *Re Norwich Union* [2004] EWHC 2802 (Ch).

[122] *WASA International (UK) Insurance Co Ltd v WASA International Insurance Co Ltd* [2002] EWHC 2698 (Ch).

[123] SI 2008/1467.

[124] SI 2008/1468.

In *Standard Life Assurance Ltd v Oak Dedicated Ltd*[125] (a demutualisation case) it was held that an insurer's own liability policies are transferred to the transferee, so that in the event of a claim against the transferee arising out of the transferor's conduct, the original liability policies continue to operate.

6. LLOYD'S

Origins of Lloyd's. "Lloyd's" was a coffee-shop owned by one Edward Lloyd.   **13–038**
When it first opened is uncertain, but the London Gazette of February 21, 1688 records its existence at that time by an advertisement offering a reward, claimable at Lloyd's Coffee House, for watches stolen from an Edward Bramsby. Lloyd's became established as the centre of marine underwriting, although much marine insurance was underwritten in counting houses belonging to individuals, and also in the Jamaica and Jerusalem coffee houses and at the Coal Exchange. There is no evidence to suggest that Lloyd's was better appointed, more attentively served or had greater brilliance of conversation or debate than the majority of its coffee house contemporaries; it had the advantage, however, of being near the River Thames and thus attracting the patronage of merchants willing to accept insurances on ships and their cargoes. Lloyd's prospered, and the house became recognised as the likely place for persons wanting to find underwriters to write their names beneath the wording of insurance policies, to guarantee commercial ventures on a personal basis. Edward Lloyd prompted the trend towards business by providing his customers with shipping information emanating from the waterfront by runners. In 1696 he published a newsheet, *Lloyd's News*, and although this was discontinued it may be regarded as the forerunner of *Lloyds List and Shipping Gazette*, London's oldest daily newspaper, which first appeared in 1734, 11 years after Lloyd's death. Requirements for more space caused Lloyd's to move to the Royal Exchange in 1774, the move being funded by the Committee of Lloyd's which had been established in 1771. For the next century the private club characteristic of Lloyd's was further moulded by restricting membership, introducing subscriptions, giving the elected committee increased authority, and regulating the basis on which committee members served. Lloyd's moved to Lime Street in 1957.

Lloyd's Acts 1871 to 1982. Lloyd's is a society, and was granted the status of   **13–039**
incorporation under the Lloyd's Act 1871, thereby allowing it to own property and to sue and be sued in its own name and also conferring statutory status on the bye-laws which govern the conduct of business at Lloyd's. The Society of Lloyd's is not, however, an insurer in its own right and does not assume liability for insurance business transacted by its members. Nevertheless, it provides the premises, lays down through a committee strict financial and other regulatory measures regarding membership and the conduct of business, and administers the Society's activities. The Society is immune from suit at the instance of its members,[126] and its decisions are not subject to judicial review as it does not

---

[125] *Standard Life Assurance Ltd v Oak Dedicated Ltd* [2008] Lloyd's Rep. I.R. 552.
[126] Lloyd's Act 1982 s.14. See: *Ashmore v Society of Lloyds (No.2), The Times*, July 17, 1992; *Society of Lloyd's v Clementson* [1995] L.R.L.R. 307. If the issue is not disciplinary but involves an internal investigatory process, the court will not intervene: *R. (On the application of MacMillan and Thompson) v Regulatory Board of Lloyd's of London* [1995] L.R.L.R. 485.

perform public functions.[127] The Lloyd's Act 1871 was amended by the Lloyd's Act 1911, which extended the purposes of Lloyd's,[128] widened the information dissemination role of Lloyd's and conferred upon the Society greater disciplinary powers over members. The 1911 Act established for the first time a guarantee fund intended to ensure that all liabilities under policies would be met. Further amendments took place under the Lloyd's Acts 1925 and 1951, the latter extending Lloyd's borrowing and trustee powers and facilitating its move to larger premises.

The main governing legislation is now the Lloyd's Act 1982, as amended by the Legislative Reform (Lloyd's) Order 2008.[129] Lloyd's is governed by a Council consisting of 16 elected members of Lloyd's, eight of whom are external (Lloyd's Act 1982 s.3). Council members are, since the 2008 amendments, no longer to be approved by the Bank of England. They may be re-elected following the termination of their term of office. The Council may delegate its functions to committees, subcommittees or other bodies (whose members need not be members of the Society) or any person (whether or not a member of the Society). The Council in turn elects a Chairman and Deputy Chairmen. The annual election of the Chairman is to be by special resolution passed Council members (and, since 2008, not just working members). The Chairman or Deputy Chairman need not be a member of Lloyd's, although if he is not a working member then at least one Deputy Chairman must be a working member (Lloyd's Act 1982 s.4). Until 2008 there was a Committee of Lloyd's which had the formal power to issue Codes of Practice (Lloyd's Act 1982 s.5): the Committee was, however, abolished in 2008. Discipline is in the hands of a Disciplinary Committee and an Appeal Tribunal. Since 2008 it ceased to be necessary for a majority of the members of a Disciplinary Committee to be members of Lloyd's; it is enough if one person is a working member, a director of a corporate member or an officer or employee of an underwriting agent or Lloyd's broker where that officer or employee has been approved by the Financial Services Authority, and in the latter two cases, a retired person who immediately before retirement met either description will qualify (Lloyd's Act 1982 s.7).

The members of Lloyd's, known as underwriting members or "Names", are grouped into syndicates and transact business for their own account. Members are personally liable on insurance contracts, may contract only through underwriting agents and membership terminates on bankruptcy (Lloyd's Act 1982 ss.8 and 9). Most of the investment at Lloyd's is these days through corporate capital, permitted since 1994. At one time there was a strict separation of the functions of managing agents and brokers (Lloyd's Act 1982 ss.10–12), but this provision was repealed in 2008.

13–040   Regulation of Lloyd's as a provider of insurance. There are two specific elements of the Financial Services Authority's Handbook which are directly applicable to Lloyd's. First, Pt 8 of the Insurance Prudential Rules (INSPRU) is concerned with the overall management of Lloyd's. It provides, most importantly, that:

[127] *R (On the application of Bridges) v Society of Lloyd's, The Times,* July 30, 1992; *R (On the application of Lorimer) v Corp of Lloyd's* Unreported, 1992; *R. (On the application of Johnson) v Council of Society of Lloyd's* Unreported, 1996; *Doll-Steinberg v Society of Lloyd's* [2002] EWHC 419 (Admin).: *R. (On the application of West) v Lloyd's of London* [2004] EWCA Civ 5; *Society of Lloyd's v Henderson* [2005] EWHC 850 (Comm).
[128] Lloyd's does not owe a duty of care to its members in the pursuit of its objectives under the Lloyd's Act 1911 s.10; *Ashmore v Society of Lloyd's (No.2)* (1992) *The Times,* July 17, 1992.
[129] SI 2008/3001.

(1) A member of Lloyd's may underwrite only through one or more syndicates;

(2) The Society of Lloyd's must establish and maintain systems and controls to enable it appropriately to address the risks to which the Lloyd's market is exposed;

(3) Those systems and controls must include systems and controls to enable the Society to ensure that any assumptions made in calculating a member's capital resources or in determining the individual capital assessment for each member are regularly reviewed and that appropriate action is taken if any assumption is no longer valid;

(4) The Society must take all reasonable steps, including establishing and maintaining adequate systems and controls to enable it to manage the risks to which funds at Lloyd's and central assets are exposed and to ensure that those funds and central assets are adequate to support all balancing amounts;

(5) A syndicate managing agent must establish and maintain adequate systems and controls to manage the risks to which the insurance business carried on through the syndicate is exposed, having particular regard to transactions which may give rise to a conflict of interest and transactions involving the provision of capital, reinsurance or other services;

(6) The Society must take reasonable steps to ensure that systems and controls established and maintained by managing agents are adequate to ensure that risks to which the insurance business carried on through each syndicate is exposed do not have a detrimental effect on funds at Lloyd's or central assets, and in particular the Society must be able to identify any significant overstatement of financial resources resulting from any internal transaction;

(7) The Society must take all reasonable steps to ensure that each member executes the appropriate Lloyd's Trust Deeds and carries to the appropriate Lloyd's Trust Fund all amounts received or receivable by the member in respect of any insurance business (see below).

Secondly, Pt 1 the General Prudential Rules (GENPRU) makes provision for the conduct of managing agents and the Society itself by means of an insurance market direction given under FSMA 2000 s.316. The effect of GENPRU is that:

(1) The members of Lloyd's taken together must at all times maintain overall financial resources, including capital and liquidity resources, that are adequate, both as to amount and quality, to ensure that there is no significant risk that liabilities under or in respect of contracts of insurance written at Lloyd's will not be met as they fall due;

(2) Managing agents must ensure that adequate financial resources are available to support the insurance business carried on through each syndicate that they manage, and the Society must, having regard to the availability and value of the central assets, ensure that the financial resources supporting the insurance business of each member are adequate at all times;

(3) When recognising and valuing assets that are available to meet liabilities arising from a member's insurance business, neither the Society nor managing agents may—subject to limited exceptions—attribute any value to any amounts receivable but not yet received from that member

or another member, although the Society may attribute value to letters of credit and guarantees in prescribed form and to life policies.

Lloyd's is subject to financial reporting rules. It must comply with audit rules (FSMA 2000 s.318) and financial reporting rules set out in the Insurance (Lloyd's) Regulations 1997[130] and in the Insurance Accounts Directive (Lloyd's Syndicate and Aggregate Accounts) Regulations 2008,[131] which implement, in respect of Lloyd's, European Parliament and Council Directive 2003/51/EC on the modernisation of the annual and consolidated accounts of insurance undertakings (the "Modernisation Directive"). Lloyd's underwriters are also subject to Pt VII of the FSMA 2000, which regulates the transfer of insurance business: the governing provision, FSMA 2000 s.323, which permits the Treasury by order to extend some or all of Pt VII to Lloyd's underwriters who wish to transfer some or all of their portfolio, in its original form extended to "former underwriting members", defined by s.324 as any person who ceased to be a member after December 24, 1996. That has now been modified to allow all former underwriting members of Lloyd's to transfer their business.[132]

13–041   **The rights of members of Lloyd's.** As a matter of law, Lloyd's members transact business as individual underwriters, although the complexity of modern commerce and the enormous insured values presently found have produced change. Underwriters are grouped into syndicates which potentially have many hundreds of members, and each syndicate is represented by a managing agent whose duties are to ensure that the syndicate accepts risks at an appropriate level by means of prudent underwriting[133] and that the present and future members of the syndicate are covered by proper reinsurance.[134] Thus, when a syndicate underwriter accepts a risk he can do so for a very much larger amount than if he were acting on his own behalf, as he binds all the members of his syndicate. Apart from the case of domestic motor policies, risks are subscribed to by a number of syndicates, with the result that any single policy constitutes a bundle of contracts between the assured and the various subscribing syndicates.

Membership of a syndicate is arranged by a member's agent, to be appointed by each Name.[135] The role of the member's agent is to ensure that the Name receives advice as to maintaining a properly balanced portfolio, so that, for example, the Name is not allocated exclusively to high-risk syndicates where potential gains are great but where potential losses are also great.[136] Managing

---

[130] SI 1997/686.

[131] SI 2008/1950.

[132] Financial Services and Markets Act 2000 (Amendment of section 323) Regulations 2008 (SI 2008/1469).

[133] *Deeny v Gooda Walker Ltd (No.1)* [1996] L.R.L.R. 183; *Arbuthnott v Fagan* [1996] L.R.L.R. 135; *Wynniatt Hussey v Bromley* [1996] L.R.L.R. 310; *Judd v Merrert* (1996) *Lloyd's List*, June 13; *Arbuthnott v Feltrim* Unreported, 1995; *Arbuthnott v Feltrim (No.2)* Unreported, 1996. In *Deeny v Gooda Walker Ltd (No.2)* [1995] 4 All E.R. 289 Phillips J. assessed damages for past losses but refused to do so for future losses as the level of those losses was at that stage unclear. In *Deeny v Gooda Walker Ltd (No.3)* [1996] L.R.L.R. 176, the House of Lords held that damages awardable to a Name under this head are to be assessed as trading income for the purposes of taxation, and are taxable in the hands of the Names. In *Deeny v Gooda Walker (No.4)* [1996] L.R.L.R. 109, interest was held to be awardable on the damages obtained by Names.

[134] *Aiken v Stewart Wrightson Ltd* [1995] 3 All E.R. 449; *Arbuthnott v Feltrim (No.1)* Unreported, 1995; *Arbuthnott v Feltrim (No.2)* Unreported, 1996.

[135] For the appointment procedure, see *P & B (Run-Off) Ltd v Woolley* [2002] Lloyd's Rep. I.R. 344.

[136] *Sword-Daniels v Pitel* [1994] 4 All E.R. 385; *Brown v KMR Services Ltd* [1995] 4 All E.R. 598.

agents and member's agents are collectively referred to as "underwriting agents", and a strict separation of their business is now required by Lloyd's. Their activities in relation to Names are regulated under the Financial Services and Markets Act 2000.[137]

Under present arrangements, a Name has a contractual relationship both with his member's agent and with his managing agent. It is clear, therefore, that any breach of the above duties sounds in contract. There is a parallel duty of care in tort,[138] so that a Name can take advantage of the more generous limitation period for tort actions. The duties of care in contract and in tort are not identical: a member's agent owes a duty under the express terms of the contract to supervise the activities of managing agents, but in tort the duty of the member's agent in respect of the activities of the managing agent is merely to exercise due diligence in selection and to exercise general vigilance.[139]

A broker who places insurance or reinsurance with a syndicate does not owe any duty of care to persons who become members of the syndicate in the belief that the contracts will be profitable for the syndicate.[140]

The Lloyd's settlement. Severe losses at Lloyd's in the 1980s and 1990s, which **13–042** were allegedly the result of negligent underwriting (particularly in the US liability market) and the operation of the LMX Spiral[141] whereby risks placed in the London market were the subject of a large number of levels of reinsurance and retrocession, led to massive calls on Names for funding. Moreover, many Names who joined the Lloyd's market in this period claimed to have been induced to do so by fraudulent statements made to them on behalf of the Lloyd's market, to the effect that prospects were bright. Many Names were forced into bankruptcy, and litigation was instigated by many affected Names, seeking damages for their losses. The Names organised themselves into action groups. In a series of judgments the courts held that claims in tort were not time barred and that underwriting agents owed the relevant duties of care to Names. A settlement was reached between Lloyd's and the vast majority of Names in October 1996, "Reconstruction and Renewal". Under the settlement, Lloyd's (including brokers) agreed to pay some £3.2 billion, mainly in the form of debt-credits whereby losses were written off. A specialist reinsurance vehicle, Equitas, was established: all Names, including those who had not agreed to the settlement, were required to pay reinsurance premiums to Equitas to cover future losses incurred in the underwriting years to which the settlement related.[142] The possibility that Names might be exposed to such losses in the event of the failure of Equitas was in 2009 removed by the judicial sanctioning of a scheme whereby the Names transferred their outstanding liabilities to an associated company, Equitas Insurance Ltd, bringing into play an additional US$1.3 billion of outwards retrocession cover from a US insurer.[143]

---

[137] Financial Services and Markets Act 2000 (Regulated Activities) Order 2001 (SI 2001/554), regs 56 and 57.

[138] *Henderson v Merrett Syndicates Ltd* [1994] 3 All E.R. 508.

[139] *Aiken v Stewart Wrightson Ltd* [1995] 3 All E.R. 449; *Berriman v Rose Thompson Young* [1996] L.R.L.R. 426.

[140] *Deeny v Stewart Wrightson Ltd* Unreported, 1995.

[141] The LMX Spiral was described by Phillips J. in *Deeny v Gooda Walker Ltd* [1994] C.L.C. 1224 as "rather like a multiple game of pass the parcel." See also *Equitas Ltd v R&Q Reinsurance Company (UK) Ltd* [2009] EWHC 2787 (Comm).

[142] The imposition of compulsory reinsurance was held in *Society of Lloyd's v Lyons, Leighs and Wilkinson* Unreported, 1997, to be valid under the Lloyd's Act 1982. The requirement is not a penalty clause: *Society of Lloyd's v Twinn* Unreported, 2000; *Jones v Society of Lloyd's* Unreported, 2000.

[143] *Re Equitas Ltd* [2010] Lloyd's Rep. I.R. 69.

The consenting Names agreed to abandon all claims.[144] A large number of Names refused to accept the settlement and commenced proceedings alleging that they had been the victims of fraud during their membership. Those Names were held to be liable to pay the Equitas premiums pending the litigation, by reason of a "pay now sue later" provision in their contracts with Lloyd's, and various defences based on errors in the calculation of the premium and the infringement of foreign antitrust laws have been rejected.[145] The substantive allegations of fraud against Lloyd's were subsequently rejected.[146]

Names have also failed in their arguments that the UK government was liable in damages for failing to regulate Lloyd's in accordance with the requirements of the First Non-Life Insurance Directive, Council Directive 73/239/EEC, which came into force on July 27, 1976. Regulation was not extended to Lloyd's until December 1, 2001 under the Financial Services and Markets Act 2000. In *Society of Lloyd's v Levy*[147] it was held that the Directives did not confer rights upon individuals and thus could not found an action for damages against the Government. In *Poole v Her Majesty's Treasury*[148] the Court of Appeal similarly held that the Directive was not intended to confer individual rights, and in any event Names were underwriters in their own right and not policyholders and so were outside the scope of the protection afforded by the Directive.

7. FRIENDLY SOCIETIES AND INDUSTRIAL ASSURANCE

13–043 Friendly societies provide a variety of benefits for their members, including limited forms of insurance on a mutual basis. Legislation dating back to 1793 was consolidated in the Friendly Societies Act 1974 as amended by the Friendly Societies Acts 1984 and 1992. Under this legislation, a friendly society could seek registration, which conferred upon it exemption from the authorisation requirement and regulation under the insurance companies and financial services legislation. The regulatory regime applicable to registered friendly societies under the 1974 Act, as administered by the Friendly Societies Commission, was similar to that which governed insurance companies, but was in many respects more stringent. Registration ceased to be available to new applicants in February 1993, since which date incorporation has been required under the Friendly Societies Act 1992. The regulatory functions of the Commission and the Registrar of Friendly Societies have been transferred to the FSA under ss.334 and

---

[144] For the form of acceptance, see *Manning v Society of Lloyd's* [1998] Lloyd's Rep. I.R. 186.

[145] *Society of Lloyd's v Lyon* Unreported, 1997; *Society of Lloyd's v Fraser* [1999] Lloyd's Rep. I.R. 156; *McAllister v Society of Lloyd's* [1999] Lloyd's Rep. I.R. 489; *Society of Lloyd's White* Unreported, 2000; *Price v Society of Lloyd's* [2000] Lloyd's Rep. I.R. 453; *Society of Lloyd's v Noel* Unreported, 2002; *Society of Lloyd's v Surman* [2004] EWHC 2967 Ch.

[146] *Noel v Poland* [2001] Lloyd's Rep. I.R. 30; *Society of Lloyd's v Jaffray* [2002] EWCA Civ 1101; *Society of Lloyd's v Henderson* [2005] EWHC 850 Comm. The decision in *Henderson* was upheld on appeal, [2008] Lloyd's Rep. I.R. 317. In *Society of Lloyd's v Jaffray* [2002] EWCA Civ 1101, the Court of Appeal refused an application by the claimant to order a retrial on the ground that the evidence presented to Cresswell J. at trial had been fraudulent. In *Harris v Society of Lloyd's* [2009] Lloyd's Rep. I.R. 119, the High Court struck out as an abuse of process an attempt by Names to argue that they had been induced by fraudulent misrepresentation as to the nature of the reinsurance protection provided to them ("reinsurance to close") to become and remain syndicate members.

[147] *Society of Lloyd's v Levy* [2004] 3 C.M.L.R. 1233.

[148] *Poole v Her Majesty's Treasury* [2008] Lloyd's Rep. I.R. 134.

335 of the Financial Services and Markets Act 2000[149] so as to provide a uniform regulatory structure, although there are some variations.[150]

Industrial assurance is in essence life assurance for very small sums, where the premiums are received by means of collectors. Industrial assurance business is long-term insurance business. Prior to the passing of the 2000 Act such business was regulated by the Insurance Companies Act 1982, unless it was carried on by a friendly society, in which case the Friendly Societies legislation was applicable. The business was also regulated by the Financial Services Act 1986. Under s.338 of the 2000 Act, the regulation of this form of business has been transferred to the FSA. The 2000 Act thus repeals the Industrial Assurance Act 1923, which was concerned with matters such as insurable interest, transfers of business, and the resolution of disputes between assureds and industrial assurance companies.

8. Competition Rules Affecting Insurers

UK competition laws. UK competition law is contained in the Competition Act 1998 and the Enterprise Act 2000. It consists of three main elements. First, the Chapter I prohibition in the Competition Act 1998 places a prohibition on agreements which prevent, restrict or distort trade within the United Kingdom.[151] Secondly, the Chapter II prohibition in the Competition Act 1998 outlaws abuse of a dominant position within the United Kingdom.[152] Thirdly, the Enterprise Act 2000 allows the Office of Fair Trading to require the Competition Commission to undertake market investigations (into uncompetitive markets) and into mergers. The Chapter I and Chapter II prohibitions are framed in a fashion almost identical to the equivalent EU prohibitions. Under s.50 of the 1998 Act, UK law is to be construed consistently with EU law. In addition, s.9 of the 1998 Act provides for parallel exemption, so that an agreement which is exempt from EU competition law in that it benefits from an exemption is also afforded immunity under UK law.

13–044

EU competition laws

Sources of EU law. The competition rules are found primarily in the EC Treaty, as amended by the Lisbon Treaty which came into force at the beginning of December 2009. Article 101 prohibits agreements which prevent, restrict or distort trade between Member States, and art.102 prohibits abuse of dominant position within the EU. The Merger Regulation 2004[153] prohibits mergers which adversely affect competition. The Treaty rules on competition have been held to be applicable to insurance in a series of decisions concluding that agreements directly or indirectly fixing premium rates and contract terms, and restricting the persons from whom insurers will accept inward insurance business or to whom

13–045

---

[149] Financial Services and Markets Act 2000 (Mutual Societies) Order 2001 (SI 2001/2617).

[150] e.g. as to controllers: Financial Services and Markets Act 2000 (Controllers)(Exemption) Order 2001 (SI 2001/2638).

[151] See *Qualifying Insurers Subscribing to the Assigned Risks Pool v Ross & Co* [2004] EWHC 1181 (Ch): Solicitors Indemnity Insurance Rules imposing liability cover on a solicitor failing to take out his own held not to contravene the Chapter I Prohibition.

[152] See *Qualifying Insurers Subscribing to the Assigned Risks Pool v Ross & Co* [2004] EWHC 1181 (Ch): no evidence that the insurers used by the Law Society to provide default cover were jointly dominant so as to permit the charging of excessive premiums.

[153] Council Regulation 13/2004/EC.

they will offer outward reinsurance are in contravention of art.101(1),[154] although agreements which do no more than make statistical information available to participating insurers[155] or which permit capacity to be expanded[156] are exempt.

Because arts 101(1) and 102 are directly effective in Member States, where an agreement or practice is found to contravene their terms, persons suffering harm as a result of the breach may bring proceedings in their domestic courts for damages, and there is no absolute rule of EU law prohibiting an award of punitive damages as long as that award complies with the concepts of equivalence (i.e. that such damages are available under domestic law) and effectiveness (i.e. that such damages are necessary to secure compliance with the competition rules).[157] In all cases the EU competition rules are engaged only where the agreement or practice affects trade between Member States, although it has been held that an agreement between insurers in a single jurisdiction may have an adverse impact on interstate trade if it has a significant impact on sales by external insurers within that jurisdiction.[158]

13–046 *Block exemption.* In 1991 the Council of Ministers adopted a Regulation which authorised the European Commission to issue a block exemption under art.101(3) from the prohibition in art.101(1).[159] The Regulation authorised the Commission to extend the Block Exemption to the following matters: (a) the establishment of common risk premium tariffs based on collectively ascertained statistics or the number of claims; (b) the establishment of common standard policy conditions; (c) the common coverage of certain types of risks; (d) the settlement of claims; (e) the testing and acceptance of security devices; and (f) registers of, and information on, aggravated risks, subject to proper protection of confidentiality.

The European Commission took the view that it did not have sufficient market information to grant block exemption for all of these matters, and chose in its initial Block Exemption adopted in 1992[160] and its 2005 replacement[161] to limit protection to four matters: agreements on the joint establishment and distribution of statistics on insurance risks; standard policy terms; common coverage of risks by means of co-insurance pools; and the testing and acceptance of security devices.

The current Block Exemption was adopted in March 2010 and came into effect on April 1, 2010.[162] The European Commission has taken the view that protection should be confined to two matters—data exchanges; and

---

[154] *Inland Waterways Insurers* E.C. Bull. 5, 1969; *Fire Insurance* [1982] OJ L80/76; *Nuovo CEGAM* [1984] 2 C.M.L.R. 484; *P & I Clubs* [1985] OJ L276/2; *Irish Insurance Federation* [1987] OJ C120/5; Case 45/85 *Verband der Sachversicherer eV v Commission* [1998] 4 C.M.L.R. 264; *TEKO* [1990] OJ L13/34; *Halifax Building Society/Standard Life Assurance Co* [1992] OJ C131/2; *Lloyd's Underwriters Association/Institute of London Underwriters* [1993] OJ L4/26.

[155] *Concordato Italiano Incendio* [1990] OJ L15/25; *Assurpol* [1992] OJ L37/16.

[156] *Re P & I Clubs Pooling Agreement* [1999] C.M.L.R. 646.

[157] Cases C-295 to 298/04 *Manfredi v Lloyd Adriatico Assicurazioni SpA* [2007] 1 All E.R. (EC) 27.

[158] Cases C-295 to 298/04 *Manfredi v Lloyd Adriatico Assicurazioni SpA* [2007] 1 All E.R. (EC) 27.

[159] Council Regulation 1534/91/EEC.

[160] Commission Regulation 3932/92/EEC.

[161] Commission Regulation 358/2005/EC.

[162] Commission Regulation 267/2010/EC. The European Commission has published an explanatory communication, OJ [2010] C82/20. Agreements in place and exempted under the 2005 Block Exemption retained protection until September 30, 2010.

co-insurance—and that exemption for agreements relating to standard terms and security devices is no longer justified.

As far as joint compilations, tables and studies are concerned, art.101(1) does not apply to[163]:

"(a) the joint compilation and distribution of information necessary for the following purposes:
    (i) calculation of the average cost of covering a specified risk in the past;
    (ii) construction of mortality tables, and tables showing the frequency of illness, accident and invalidity in connection with insurance involving an element of capitalisation;
(b) the joint carrying-out of studies on the probable impact of general circumstances external to the interested undertakings, either on the frequency or scale of future claims for a given risk or risk category or on the profitability of different types of investment, and the distribution of the results of such studies."

The exemption is subject to a series of exceptions.[164] First, the exemption in (a) is conditional and operates only if the compilations or tables: (a) are based on the assembly of data, spread over a number of risk-years chosen as an observation period, which relate to identical or comparable risks in sufficient numbers to constitute a base which can be handled statistically and which will yield figures on amongst others, the number of claims, the number of risks insured, the total amounts paid and the total amount of capital insured; (b) include as detailed a breakdown of the available statistics as is actuarially adequate; and (c) do not include in any way elements for contingencies, income deriving from reserves, administrative or commercial costs or fiscal or para-fiscal contributions, and take into account neither revenues from investments nor anticipated profits. Secondly, the exemptions in (a) and (b) are to be operated in a way which precludes tacit collusion, so that they operate only if the compilations, tables or study results: (a) do not identify the insurance undertakings concerned or any insured party; (b) when compiled and distributed, include a statement that they are non-binding; (c) do not contain any indication of the level of commercial premiums; (d) are made available on reasonable, affordable and non-discriminatory terms, to any insurance undertaking which requests a copy of them, including insurance undertakings which are not active on the geographic or product market to which those compilations, tables or study results refer; (e) except where non-disclosure is objectively justified on grounds of public security, are made available on reasonable, affordable and non-discriminatory terms, to consumer organisations or customer organisations which request access to them in specific and precise terms for a duly justified reason. Thirdly, the block exemption does not apply where the participating insurers agree not to use compilations or tables that differ from those referred to in art.2(a), or not to depart from the results of the studies referred to in art.2(b).

As far as common coverage of certain types of risks is concerned, the 2010 Block Exemption[165] authorises the use of insurance and reinsurance pools.[166] There are nevertheless restrictions on the use of pools which are designed to

[163] Block Exemption art.2.
[164] Block Exemption art.3.
[165] Block Exemption art.5.
[166] Ordinary subscription policies—"*ad-hoc* co-(re)insurance agreements on the subscription market, whereby a certain part of a given risk is covered by a lead insurer and the remaining part of the risk is covered by fellow insurers who are invited to cover that remainder"—are outside the Block Exemption, but they are almost certainly not caught by art.101(1) of the EC Treaty in the first place.

prevent the reduction or elimination of competition.[167] Block exemption for a pool created in order exclusively to cover new risks lasts for three years only, irrespective of the market share of the participants. In the case of a pool in operation on April 1, 2010, there is block exemption only if the combined market share held by the participating undertakings does not exceed: (a) in the case of co-insurance pools, 20 per cent of any relevant market (if market share rises up to 25 per cent, the exemption continues for two years, and if it rises beyond 25 per cent then it continues for one year); (b) in the case of co-reinsurance pools, 25 per cent of any relevant market (if market share rises up to 30 per cent, the exemption continues for two years, and if it rises beyond 25 per cent then it continues for one year). Market share is assessed by reference to gross premium income. The rules of the pool must also ensure that[168]: (a) each participating undertaking can give a reasonable period of notice to withdraw from the pool, without facing any sanction; (b) members must be free to insure outside the pool, in whole or in part, any risk of the type covered by the pool; (c) the activity of the pool or its participating undertakings is not restricted to the insurance or reinsurance of risks located in any particular geographical part of the EU; (d) output or sales are not limited; (e) markets are not allocated between members; and (f) the participating undertakings of a co-reinsurance pool do not agree on the commercial premiums which they charge for direct insurance.

[167] Block Exemption art.6.
[168] Block Exemption art.7.

CHAPTER 14

THE ASSURED

1. CONTRACTUAL CAPACITY

The principle of capacity. The general rule is that anyone may, as an assured, **14–001**
enter into a contract of insurance provided that he has the requisite insurable
interest. This rule is subject to the limitations on the contractual capacity of
certain classes of persons that apply throughout the law of contract. Enemy aliens
thus have no capacity to contract with UK insurers, and the ordinary rules
affecting persons suffering from drunkenness and mental incapacity at the date of
the contract will apply. Corporations were at one time subject to the doctrine of
ultra vires, but this has been abolished by what is now ss.39 and 40 of the
Companies Act 2006.

Minors. Minors, that is persons under 18 years of age,[1] do not have the full **14–002**
capacity of other persons. This disability is given to them for their own protection
and insurers who grant policies to them will be liable for losses: the only question
to be considered is whether the assured minor is also bound by the obligation that
he has undertaken. Usually, other than in the case of contracts for necessary
goods or services,[2] contracts by a minor are voidable at his election[3] or
unenforceable against him unless he chooses to adopt them.[4] A minor will
generally be bound by a contract of insurance if it is necessary for his benefit.
Thus a minor who joined a mutual society against accident on entering the
service of a railway company was held to be bound by its rules.[5]

The question sometimes arises whether premiums paid by a minor, under a
policy which is not necessary for his benefit and is unenforceable against him
because he has not adopted it, are recoverable. The general rule is that the minor
cannot recover back money paid by him under a contract from which he has had
some advantage, however small, unless the other party can be put back into the
position in which he would have been had the transaction never taken place.[6]
Thus an assured minor cannot recover a premium he has paid once the risk has

---

[1] Family Law Reform Act 1969.
[2] In respect of which the minor must pay a reasonable price: Sale of Goods Act 1979 s.3, which
also applies to persons suffering from drunkenness or mental incapacity.
[3] In that, on reaching his majority, the minor is free to disaffirm them. Various forms of long-term
contracts, such as contracts of partnership, or for interests in land in shares, fall into this category.
[4] All contracts other than contracts for necessaries or which are voidable fall into this category.
Under s.1 of the Minors Contracts Act 1987 a contract of this type is not binding on the minor until
he expressly affirms it on reaching his majority: fresh consideration is not required. This section
repealed the Infants Relief Act 1874, which rendered these contracts absolutely void so that a fresh
contract was required on the minor reaching his majority.
[5] *Clements v London and North-Western Ry* [1894] 2 Q.B. 482.
[6] *Steinberg v Scala (Leeds) Ltd* [1923] Ch. 452.

started to run.[7] Insurances on the property of a minor may be taken out by his guardian.[8]

2. CO-INSURANCE

14–003 **Joint and composite policies.** Where two or more persons are insured under a single policy, it is important to determine whether the policy is joint or composite, in that the former is regarded as a single contract whereas the latter is a bundle of contracts. The distinction is based on the nature of the interests of the assureds. If the assureds share a common interest in the insured subject matter, for example where they are joint owners of property or partners, the policy is joint. By contrast, if the parties have different interests, as in the case of a landlord and tenant or a mortgagor and mortgagee, the policy is composite. It is not clear whether a policy which is by its nature composite, in that it insures different interests, can be converted into a joint policy by express wording; although it has been assumed that this is possible[9] the weight of authority supports the proposition that a policy will not lightly be construed in that fashion given the parties' different insurable interests in the subject matter.[10] Where the parties have the same interest in the insured subject matter, it is theoretically possible for them to insure on either a joint or a composite basis. There can surely be no objection in principle to husband and wife insuring matrimonial property on a composite basis.[11] Again, in the commercial context, if the partners in a partnership insure their liabilities, they can insure jointly on the basis that, as each assured is jointly and severally liable, their liabilities are the same; alternatively, they can insure under a composite policy, given that each assured potentially has a distinct claim against the insurers. Which of these possibilities is the case depends upon the policy wording.[12] It follows that if the parties are co-owners and are referred to jointly, the policy is joint,[13] and if the parties have separate interests and are referred to separately, the policy is composite.

In other jurisdictions, the distinction between joint and composite insurance appears to turn exclusively on policy wording, and there are a number of cases which decide that joint owners of property who co-insure are presumed to be composite rather than joint assureds, with the result that the misconduct of one party does not prejudice the other's right of recovery.[14] If the parties have separate interests in the insured subject matter, it is established that the usual wording of co-insurance, which talks of the parties being insured "for their respective rights and interests", will result in a policy covering different interests being treated as composite only.[15]

---

[7] *Ritchie v Salvation Army Assurance* [1930] I.A.C. Rep. 31. This rule is unaffected by the Minors Contracts Act 1987.

[8] *Worwicker v Bretnall* (1882) 23 Ch D 188.

[9] *New Hampshire Insurance Co v MGN Ltd* [1997] L.R.L.R. 24.

[10] *General Accident Fire and Life Assurance Corp Ltd v Midland Bank Ltd* [1940] 2 K.B. 388 at 405–406; *State of Netherlands v Youell* [1997] 2 Lloyd's Rep. 440; *Ford v Bradford & Bingley Building Society* Unreported, 1997.

[11] The assumption underlying *Direct Line v Khan* [2002] Lloyd's Rep. I.R. 364.

[12] In *HLB Kidsons v Lloyd's Underwriters* [2008] Lloyd's Rep. I.R. 237, reversed in part on other grounds [2009] Lloyd's Rep. I.R. 178 a partnership policy was assumed to be composite.

[13] *Kelly v National Insurance Co of New Zealand* Unreported, 1994.

[14] *Moulder v National Insurance Co of New Zealand* [1993] 2 N.Z.L.R. 351; *Gate v Sun Alliance Insurance Ltd* Unreported, 1995.

[15] *General Accident Fire and Life Assurance Corp v Midland Bank Ltd* [1940] 2 K.B. 88.

The following co-insurances have been held to be composite by their nature: mortgagor and mortgagee,[16] owner of goods and hirer under a hire-purchase agreement,[17] landlord and tenant,[18] contractor and subcontractor under a construction risks policy,[19] the directors of a company,[20] companies in the same group,[21] cohabitees,[22] cruise operators and disponent owners of vessels,[23] members of an association who are insured under a group policy[24] and a husband and wife under a life policy which pays the survivor.[25] In *HLB Kidsons v Lloyd's Underwriters*[26] a partnership policy was assumed to be composite.

Insurable interest and co-insurance. In the case of a joint policy, the insurable   **14–004** interests of the joint assureds are identical, and extend to the entire subject matter insured. This means that either party can recover the full amount insured under the policy. The position under a composite policy is less clear. It might be thought that, as each party is insuring his own interest, the insurable interest of each party is limited to property which he either owns or for which he has possession or responsibility. This would mean in turn that a co-assured could recover from the insurer only a sum representing his own limited interest in the subject matter. The view taken in contractors' insurance cases is, however, that each party has full or "pervasive" insurable interest in the entire subject matter insured despite limited proprietary or possessory rights.[27] The rule gives rise to conceptual difficulties in the context of the distinction between joint and composite insurance, for if it is the case that the parties have the same interest, then it becomes arguable that the policy is joint rather than composite so that the rights of all parties stand or fall by reference to the right of any one of them to claim. This contention was considered and rejected by Rix J. in *State of Netherlands v Youell*.[28] Rix J.'s view was that although each co-assured had the right to make full recovery under the policy, their insurable interests were distinct even though they were co-extensive. A further conceptual problem with this line of authority is the difficulty in holding that a sub-contractor has an insurable interest in property by virtue of his potential liability in respect of that property because the sub-contractor has, at

---

[16] *Samuel & Co Ltd v Dumas* [1924] A.C. 31; *Woolcott v Sun Alliance* [1978] 1 Lloyd's Rep. 629; *Canadian Imperial Bank of Commerce v Dominion of Canada General Insurance Co* 46 D.L.R. (4th) 77 (1987); *Eide UK Ltd v Lowndes Lambert Group Ltd (The Sun Tender)* [1998] 1 Lloyd's Rep. 389; *FNCB Plc v Barnet Devanney (Harrow) Ltd* [1999] Lloyd's Rep. I.R. 459.

[17] *Lombard Australia Ltd v NRMA Insurance Co Ltd* [1969] 1 Lloyd's Rep. 575; *Federation Insurance Ltd v Wasson* (1987) 163 C.L.R. 303.

[18] *General Accident Fire and Life Assurance Corp v Midland Bank Ltd* [1940] 2 K.B. 388.

[19] *Petrofina (UK) Ltd v Magnaload Ltd* [1984] Q.B. 127; *Stone Vickers Ltd Ltd v Appledore Ferguson Shipbuilders Ltd* [1992] 2 Lloyd's Rep. 578; *National Oilwell (UK) Ltd v Davy Offshore Ltd* [1993] 2 Lloyd's Rep. 582; *State of Netherlands v Youell* [1997] 2 Lloyd's Rep. 440; *BP Exploration Operating Co Ltd v Kvaerner Oilfield Products Ltd* [2004] EWHC 999 (Comm); *Tate Gallery (Trustees) v Duffy Construction Ltd* [2007] Lloyd's Rep. I.R. 758.

[20] *Arab Bank plc v Zurich Insurance Co* [1999] 1 Lloyd's Rep. 262.

[21] *New Hampshire Insurance Co v MGN Ltd* [1997] L.R.L.R. 24; *Brit Syndicates Ltd v Italaudit SpA* [2008] Lloyd's Rep. I.R. 601.

[22] *Ford v Bradford & Bingley Building Society* Unreported, 1997.

[23] *Newcastle P & I Association v Ships (USA) Inc* [1996] 2 Lloyd's Rep. 515.

[24] *Swain v The Law Society* [1982] A.C. 598; *Lam v Federation of Small Businesses* [2002] EWCA Civ 1457.

[25] *Murphy v Murphy* [2004] Lloyd's Rep. I.R. 744: the proceeds thus go to the survivor and not equally to the survivor and to the deceased's estate.

[26] *HLB Kidsons v Lloyd's Underwriters* [2008] Lloyd's Rep IR 237.

[27] *Commonwealth Construction Co v Imperial Oil* 69 D.L.R. (3d) 558 (1976); *Petrofina (UK) Ltd v Magnaload Ltd* [1984] Q.B. 127; *National Oilwell (UK) Ltd v Davy Offshore Ltd* [1993] 2 Lloyd's Rep. 582; *Hopewell Project Management Ltd v Ewbank Preece Ltd* [1998] 1 Lloyd's Rep. 448.

[28] *State of Netherlands v Youell* [1997] 2 Lloyd's Rep. 440.

first sight, no legal or equitable interest in the property. At best he has an insurable interest in the pecuniary loss that he might suffer were the property destroyed or damaged by virtue of his loss of employment. The Court of Appeal in *Feasey v Sun Life Assurance Co of Canada*[29] has nevertheless held that the existence of the pecuniary interest provided the necessary link that conferred an insurable interest in the property as regards the sub-contractor's possible liability for damage to the property, and there was no bar to construing a policy expressed to be on the property itself as extending to the sub-contractor's insurable interest in his liability.

Creation of co-insurance

14–005 *Parties insuring together.* The simplest method by which A and B can become co-assureds is for them both to complete a proposal for insurance of their respective interests. The scope of cover for each applicant will then depend upon the proper construction of the policy.

14–006 *One party insuring on behalf of himself and for the benefit of others.* The situation in which parties insure together should be distinguished from that in which one party insures on behalf of himself and other parties, the others being either expressly named in the policy or belonging to a class meeting a description set out in the policy. The mere fact that a policy states that it covers the interests of both the assured and named or identifiable third parties does not of itself give those third parties the right to enforce the contract or to rely upon its terms (e.g. the benefit of a subrogation waiver clause). Third-party rights can arise in one of three ways.

First, as a result of the operation of the rules of agency, the third party may have become a party to the contract in his own right at common law: this was the most important route by which a third party could acquire contractual rights. Secondly, the third party may be the beneficiary of a trust of a promise, whereby the named assured has insured as trustee on behalf of the third party and the third party may enforce the contract in equity. This possibility arises from the decision of the House of Lords in *Les Affreteurs Reunis v Walford*,[30] to the effect that in appropriate circumstances the benefit of a contract may be held on trust for a third party. The concept is an artificial one, designed to circumvent the doctrine of privity of contract, and it is scarcely conceivable that it would be applied today in a pure commercial contract,[31] particularly since the statutory modification of the privity doctrine.[32] Thirdly, a third party, while not a party to the insurance contract may, if the conditions set out in the Contracts (Rights of Third Parties) Act 1999 are satisfied, have a right to enforce the contract on the basis that it was made for his benefit. The doctrinal outcomes of the agency rules and of the application of the 1999 Act are different, in that where there is agency the third party becomes a party to the contract in his own right whereas under the 1999 Act the third party remains a non-party but has rights of enforcement, although their practical effect is likely to be the same.

---

[29] *Feasey v Sun Life Assurance Co of Canada* [2003] Lloyd's Rep. I.R. 637.

[30] *Les Affreteurs Reunis v Walford* [1919] A.C. 801.

[31] *Talbot Underwriting v Nausch Hogan & Murray (The Jascon 5)* [2005] EWHC 2359 (Comm). The point did not arise on appeal, [2006] Lloyd's Rep. I.R. 531.

[32] The existence of a trust is probably also a material fact which has to be disclosed to insurers: see below.

Primary assured authorised to insure. Suppose that assured A is required or   **14–007**
authorised by contract with B to insure a joint or composite risk on behalf of
himself and B. In this situation, any policy taken out by A will cover B's interests
as well as A's if three conditions are satisfied.

The first condition is that A's authority extended to making the contract in
question, which requires consideration of the terms of the authority given by B
to A. Any provision in the contract between them which indicates that B is to be
personally liable for particular losses negates the argument that B has authorised
A to insure in respect of those losses[33] unless there is specific provision for
insurance in the contract to cover such losses.[34] If A's authority to insure is
general, then B will be insured for all risks.[35] By contrast, where A's authority
to insure on behalf of B is limited to particular risks, B can be regarded as
co-assured only in respect of those risks.[36]

The second condition is that A intended, when taking out the policy, to cover
B's interests. It is generally to be assumed that A, when taking out the insurance,
intends to act in accordance with his instructions from B.[37] Indeed, if A's
intention is not to cover B, he is likely to be in breach of contract and may face
an action by B in the event that B finds himself uninsured for a particular loss or
faces a subrogation action brought by A's insurers in A's name for damage
caused by B: in the latter situation B's right of set-off may serve to cancel out
some or all of A's claim. By contrast, if A has no authority to insure on behalf
of B, then it is to be assumed that A has not intended to do so and that the policy
is purely for A's benefit.[38] An intermediate situation is that in which B has
authorised A to insure on his behalf but has not required him to do so, in which
case B must rely—if he can—on the undisclosed principal doctrine.[39]

The third condition is that the policy does not preclude the extension of
coverage to B. The usual situation is that the policy will identify the insured
persons, either by name or description. The initial question is therefore whether
B is covered by the wording. In *O'Kane v Jones (The Martin P)*[40] it was held that
the phrase "Associated and interrelated companies and/or Joint Ventures" in a
marine policy covered both the shipowner and the ship manager even though
they were in different corporate groups, as the relationship between them was
close enough to bring them within the wording. By contrast, in *Talbot
Underwriting v Nausch Hogan & Murray (The Jascon 5)*[41] the phrase in a marine
policy taken out by a shipowner, "and/or Subsidiary, Affiliates, Associated and

---

[33] *Stone Vickers Ltd v Appledore Ferguson Shipbuilders Ltd* [1992] 2 Lloyd's Rep. 578; *Graham
Joint Stock Shipping Co v Merchants Marine Insurance Co* [1924] A.C. 294 at 300; *Dorset County
Council v Southern Felt Roofing Co Ltd* (1989) 48 B.L.R. 96; *National Trust v Haden Young Ltd*
(1994) B.L.R. 1; *Canadian Pacific Ltd v Base Fort Security Services (BC) Ltd* 77 D.L.R. (4th) 178
(1991).

[34] *O'Kane v Jones* [2004] Lloyd's Rep. I.R. 174. It was also held in this case that s.14 of the Marine
Insurance Act 1906, which permits the insurance of a partial interest, did not confer a blanket
authorisation on the holder of a partial interest to insure on behalf of persons with other interests.

[35] *BP Exploration Operating Co Ltd v Kvaerner Oilfield Products Ltd* [2004] EWHC 999
(Comm).

[36] *National Oilwell (UK) Ltd v Davy Offshore Ltd* [1993] 2 Lloyd's Rep. 582; *Deepak Fertilisers
and Petrochemical Corporation v Davy McKee (London) Ltd* [1999] 1 Lloyd's Rep. 387; *LBC
Barking and Dagenham v Samford Asphalt Co Ltd* (1997) 82 B.L.R. 25.

[37] *O'Kane v Jones* [2005] Lloyd's Rep. I.R. 174.

[38] *Colonia Versicherung AG v Amoco Oil Co* [1995] 1 Lloyd's Rep. 570, aff'd [1997] 1 Lloyd's
Rep. 261; *Hopewell Project Management Ltd v Ewbank Preece Ltd* [1998] 1 Lloyd's Rep. 448.

[39] See below.

[40] *O'Kane v Jones (The Marlin P)* [2004] 1 Lloyd's Rep. 389.

[41] *Talbot Underwriting v Nausch Hogan & Murray (The Jascon 5)* [2005] EWHC 2359 (Comm).
The point did not arise on appeal, [2006] Lloyd's Rep. I.R. 531.

Interrelated Companies and/or Joint Ventures" was held not to extend to a person with whom the shipowner had a repairing contract: the repairer was not in the same group of companies, and something more than a repairing contract was required to give rise to a joint venture.[42] It was also held that an additional clause providing "interest of Mortgagees (and Notices of Assignment in respect thereof), Loss Payees, Additional Assureds and Waivers of Subrogation as may be required" did not operate to extend cover to such third parties as the assured might seek to declare to the cover: that meaning could not have been intended given the precise wording of the insuring clause itself; even if it was a declaration clause no declaration had been made.[43] Assuming that there is no express coverage, B can assert coverage only if he can utilise the undisclosed principal doctrine, under which a person, B, who is not identified as a contracting party in a contract between A and X is nevertheless able at a later stage to assert that A was in fact B's agent and that B is the true principal. In *National Oilwell (UK) v Davy Offshore Ltd*[44] Colman J. assumed that the undisclosed principal doctrine applied to insurance contracts, an approach confirmed by the Privy Council in *Siu Yin Kwan v Eastern Insurance Ltd*[45] in which the employers' liability policy taken out by an agent was held to be enforceable by a shipowner, the agent's principal. It was argued in *Siu* that the doctrine of utmost good faith applicable to insurance contracts precluded the application of the undisclosed principal doctrine, as it was inconsistent with the assured's duty to make full disclosure of the nature of the risk to be run by the insurer. The Privy Council rejected that broad proposition, and ruled that the undisclosed principal doctrine could operate in an insurance case if, as in *Siu* itself, the identity of the assured is immaterial and there has otherwise been full disclosure of all material facts. Doubt was cast upon these decisions by Cooke J. in *Talbot Underwriting v Nausch Hogan & Murray (The Jascon 5)*,[46] in which ship repairers asserted that they were entitled to the benefit of a policy taken out by shipowners by reason of the undisclosed principal doctrine. Cooke J. held that the point did not arise because the policy by its terms did not extend to third parties, but the learned judge was doubtful whether the undisclosed principal doctrine in its application to insurance was consistent with the obligation of the assured to disclose all material facts including, importantly, the identity of interested persons. On appeal in *Talbot*[47] the Court of Appeal did not refer to the applicability of the undisclosed principal doctrine to insurance, although it confirmed that this was a case in which the doctrine had been excluded by the wording of the policy and that although in many cases the existence of a co-assured would be a matter of indifference to the insurers for disclosure purposes this would not be the case where, as here, the co-assured was a person against whom the insurers potentially had subrogation rights. It is simple enough to distinguish *Siu* on the basis suggested by Cooke J., as it was clear to the insurers that the named policyholder was the agent for an

---

[42] *Talbot Underwriting v Nausch Hogan & Murray (The Jascon 5)* [2006] Lloyd's Rep. I.R. 531.

[43] See also *Stone Vickers Ltd v Appledore Ferguson Shipbuilders Ltd* [1991] 2 Lloyd's Rep. 288. See also: *Canadian Pacific Ltd v Base Fort Security Services (BC) Ltd* 77 D.L.R. (4th) 178; *Hopewell Project Management Ltd v Ewbank Preece Ltd* [1998] 1 Lloyd's Rep. 448; *Sumitomo Bank Ltd v Banque Bruxelles Lambert SA* [1997] 1 Lloyd's Rep. 487.

[44] *National Oilwell (UK) v Davy Offshore Ltd* [1993] 2 Lloyd's Rep. 582.

[45] *Siu Yin Kwan v Eastern Insurance Ltd* [1994] 1 All E.R. 213.

[46] *Talbot Underwriting v Nausch Hogan & Murray (The Jascon 5)* [2005] EWHC 2359 (Comm).

[47] *Talbot Underwriting v Nausch Hogan & Murray (The Jascon 5)* [2006] Lloyd's Rep. I.R. 531.

unnamed principal and it may be assumed that by failing to inquire further the insurers had waived disclosure of the principal's identity. *National Oilwell* is less easily regarded as an instance of waiver, and it may be that the utmost good faith issue was simply not addressed. The better view would appear to be that in *Talbot Underwriting*, and that even if the undisclosed principal doctrine does apply to insurance then by definition there is a material non-disclosure by the named assured which will—in the absence of waiver where insurers have been alerted to a possible agency situation but have failed to seek further information—render the policy voidable.

Primary assured not authorised to insure. If A is not authorised to insure on behalf of B, B may nevertheless take advantage of the contract by means of ratification. For ratification to be effective, four conditions must be met. **14–008**

First, B must, at the date of the contract, have been of full capacity and legally competent to enter the contract as principal. This is of most importance where B is a company which was not formed at the date of the contract, as it is settled law that a company cannot ratify a contract made on its behalf before the company was formed.[48] One particular aspect of this requirement is the question whether the co-assured must have been capable of identification when the policy was taken out. In the construction insurance context, the situation might arise where a subcontractor who has not been appointed until after the policy has been issued seeks to ratify the policy. There is conflicting authority on the point, although the view most consistent with commercial reality is that ratification is possible: it has thus been held that underwriters could ratify reinsurance agreements made on their behalf by a broker acting as their agent even though the insurance agreements to which the reinsurances related were not made until after the reinsurances had been concluded.[49]

Secondly, the policy must expressly cover B as a co-assured, either by B being named as a co-assured or B falling within a class of persons specified as co-assureds. This excludes the application of the doctrine of the undisclosed principal in ratification cases: the rule is that the principal's identity must be disclosed in cases in which the person purporting to act on his behalf is not authorised to do so.[50] A policy taken out only in the name of A cannot, therefore, be ratified by B as co-assured unless the policy names B or B falls within a class of co-assureds specified in the policy.[51] The requirement will also preclude ratification should the policy so provide, although the mere fact that the assured is identified in the policy does not generally prevent ratification by some other person with an interest in the insured subject matter.[52]

Thirdly, A must, when taking out the policy, have intended to insure on behalf of B. The need for a subjective intention on A's part to insure on behalf of B, will

---

[48] *Natal Land Co v Pauline Syndicate* [1904] A.C. 120.

[49] *General Accident, Fire and Life Assurance Corp v Tauter (The Zephyr)* [1985] 2 Lloyd's Rep. 529, followed in *Tryg Baltica International (UK) Ltd v Boston Campania De Seguros SA* [2005] Lloyd's Rep. I.R. 40. It may be that the correct explanation is that the reinsurers make a unilateral offer which is open to acceptance by an underwriter accepting a direct risk: *Kingscroft Insurance Co and Others v Nissan Fire and Marine Insurance Co Ltd (No.2)* [1999] Lloyd's Rep. I.R. 603; *Bonner v Cox Dedicated Corporate Member Ltd* [2006] Lloyd's Rep. I.R. 385. Contrast *Berger and Light Diffusers Pty Ltd v Pollock* [1973] 2 Lloyd's Rep. 442.

[50] *Keighley, Maxsted & Co v Durant* [1901] A.C. 240.

[51] *Watson v Swann* (1862) 11 C.B. N.S. 756; *Boston Fruit Co v British and Foreign Marine Insurance Co* [1906] A.C. 336; *Graham Joint Stock Shipping Co v Merchants Marine Insurance Co* [1924] A.C. 294; *Canadian Pacific Ltd v Base Fort Security Services (BC) Ltd* 77 D.L.R. (4th) 178 (1991); *Hopewell Project Management Ltd v Ewbank Preece Ltd* [1998] 1 Lloyd's Rep. 448.

[52] *O'Kane v Jones* [2005] Lloyd's Rep. I.R. 174.

generally be fatal to B's claim to be a co-assured where A is not authorised to act on B's behalf. The position adopted by the courts has been that if A is not obliged by contract to insure for B, A cannot be expected to have the intention to do so.[53]

Finally, ratification must have taken place in due time. As far as marine insurance is concerned, s.86 of the Marine Insurance Act 1906 provides that a person on whose behalf a contract of insurance has been made may ratify that contract even after he has become aware of the loss.[54] Non-marine insurance has regarded the marine rule as anomalous, and the traditionally accepted non-marine position is that ratification is not possible once the person seeking to ratify has become aware of the loss. The distinction between marine and non-marine law has nevertheless been criticised by Colman J. in *National Oilwell (UK) Ltd v Davy Offshore Ltd*, the court favouring the general application of the more liberal marine rule.

14–009 *Enforcement as third party under Contracts (Rights of Third Parties) Act 1999.* If the third party is unable to avail himself of agency rules, there remains the possibility of enforcement under the 1999 Act.[55] A third party has a right to enforce contract terms in an insurance contract between the assured and the insurers if two requirements are met. First, the contract must allow for enforcement. This can be achieved in one of two ways: where the contract provides that the third party may enforce one or more of its terms (s.1(1)(a)); and where the term which the third party wishes to enforce "purports to confer a benefit on him" (s.1(2)(b)). The latter possibility is subject to s.1(2), under which the right to enforce a term which purports to confer a benefit "does not apply if on a proper construction of the contract if it appears that the parties did not intend the term to be enforceable by the third party".

Secondly, the third party must be identified by name, or identifiable by description or membership of a class (s.1(3)). How, then, do these requirements apply to the situation in which the assured procures a policy which purports to cover the interests of a third party?

Turning first to the alternative rights of direct enforcement, it is apparent that the mere fact that a third party is named as beneficiary does not bring him within s.1(1)(a), as that provision is satisfied only by an express statement that the third party has a right to enforce a term. Accordingly, it will be necessary for the third party to rely upon s.1(1)(b). It would seem that this provision is readily satisfied in the situation under consideration, as the third party is plainly the recipient of a benefit under the policy, given that his interests are expressly covered, and, in the absence of any term which expressly or impliedly restricts the third party's right of enforcement, the insurers will be unable to rely upon the qualification in s.1(2). A policy which, for example, covers the contractor and all subcontractors plainly identifies the subcontractors by description or by membership of a class.

---

[53] *National Oilwell (UK) Ltd v Davy Offshore Ltd* [1993] 2 Lloyd's Rep. 582. The court distinguished *Reliance Marine Insurance Co v Duder* [1913] 1 K.B. 265 in which it had been held by the Court of Appeal that a reinsured could recover for a loss covered by the policy even though he had not intended to insure against that particular risk. Colman J. held that the *Duder* case was concerned with the construction of a policy rather than the more complex question of who were the parties to the contract.

[54] *Grover v Grover & Matthews* [1910] 2 K.B. 401.

[55] In *Trident General Insurance Co Ltd v McNeice Bros Pty Ltd* (1998) 165 C.L.R. 107 the High Court of Australia anticipated the legislative changes by allowing a contractor to bring direct proceedings against an insurer under a policy procured by a third party, although the reasoning of the members of the court ranged over a variety of concepts.

The fact that the subcontractor was not appointed at the date of the contract would appear not to remove his right to rely on the policy providing that he was appointed at the date of the insured peril. Moreover, as s.1(3) specifically provides that it is immaterial that the third party is not in existence at the date of the policy, a subcontractor who is appointed after the date of the policy is equally entitled to rely upon its terms. In the same way, a policy which covers a parent company and all subsidiaries is effective as regards existing and future subsidiaries, including subsidiaries which were only incorporated after the date of the policy.

Noting. It is common to find that a policy taken out in the name of party A has   **14–010**
the interests of various other persons "noted" on it. Noting is often insisted upon by interested parties and indeed by insurers. The legal protection given by noting is, however, illusory. It is clear that, if the ordinary agency requirements for co-insurance discussed above are not satisfied, the fact that a person's interest has been noted on a policy does not make that person a party to the insurance. This is clear from the decision of Gage J. in *First National Commercial Bank Plc v Barnet Devanney (Harrow) Ltd.*[56] In this case, brokers were sued for negligence for not including in a composite policy issued to a mortgagor and a mortgagee a clause which conferred a right of recovery on the mortgagee in the event of breach of duty by the mortgagor which precluded its own recovery. In support of the argument that such a clause was necessary despite the composite nature of the policy, Gage J. was referred to Canadian authority[57] said to support the proposition that a mortgagee could recover under a composite policy only where such a clause was included in the policy. Gage J. held that the Canadian cases turned on the point that the policies were not composite: the position was that the interests of the mortgagees had been noted, so that they were not parties to the insurance and could recover only on the strength of the mortgagee protection clause. This ruling has even more important implications for English law, which does not recognise any exception to the doctrine of privity which would allow reliance by a third party on a contractual provision inserted for his benefit. Accordingly, noting does not make the named person a party to the insurance, nor does it confer any right to rely upon a policy term for his benefit. Given that noting does not have the main effect often claimed for it, it remains necessary to consider whether noting has any other impact. A number of possibilities may be considered.

First, it might be argued that noting has a negative function, in that it protects the person whose interests have been noted from facing subrogation proceedings by the insurer. It is unlikely that noting per se can achieve this, and noting is probably not necessary to produce subrogation immunity provided that it can be shown that the policy was obtained for the benefit of the third party so as to render him an unnamed beneficiary.[58]

Secondly, at one time, noting was thought to be necessary to preserve the legality of a property policy, as s.2 of the Life Assurance Act 1774 demands that

---

[56] *First National Commercial Bank Plc v Barnet Devanney (Harrow) Ltd* [1999] Lloyd's Rep. I.R. 43. This aspect of the decision was not affected by the reversal by the Court of Appeal on appeal [1999] Lloyd's Rep. I.R. 459.

[57] *Caisse Populaire v Société d'Assurances* 19 D.L.R. (4th) 411 (1984); *Canadian Imperial Bank v Dominion of Canada General Insurance* 46 D.L.R. (4th) 77 (1987).

[58] See the discussion below. In the leading English case, *Mark Rowlands Ltd v Berni Inns Ltd* [1985] 3 All E.R. 473, a tenant was held to be immune from subrogation proceedings brought by the landlord's insurers even though the tenant's interest had not been noted on the policy, as the policy was otherwise for the tenant's benefit.

the names of all interested parties be inserted in a policy regulated by that Act. However, it was decided, in *Siu v Eastern Insurance*[59] that the 1774 Act does not apply to indemnity contracts, so that noting is no longer necessary for the purposes of this statute.

Thirdly, noting may serve a useful function under the Fires Prevention (Metropolis) Act 1774 s.83, which permits a person interested in a fire policy on a dwelling to give notice to the insurer requiring the policy moneys to be used to reinstate the premises rather than to be paid to the assured—the noting of an interest may well remove any dispute as to whether the applicant is entitled to take advantage of the Act.

Fourthly, the giving of notice to an insurer requiring an interest to be noted may have the side effect of conferring priority upon an assignee of the proceeds of the policy whose interest has been noted.[60]

Noting would also appear not to bring the Contracts (Rights of Third Parties) Act 1999 into play and to allow the person whose interest has been noted to bring an action against insurers. For the 1999 Act to apply, the third party must either be given a right of enforcement or the policy must purport to confer benefits upon him. The mere fact that an interest has been noted plainly does not satisfy the first of these alternatives and almost certainly does not satisfy the second; informing the insurers that there are other outstanding interests in the insured subject matter, other than that of the assured himself, appears to be a long way from amounting to a promise by insurers to confer a benefit on the holders of those interests.

14–011 **Rights under joint and composite policies.** Where the policy is joint, the rights of the co-assureds stand or fall together. This is so because the parties, as joint tenants of the insured subject matter, have an undivided interest in it. Under a composite policy, however, each assured is insured in respect of his own interest only and may present an independent claim in respect of that interest. Decisions to date have illustrated the significance of this distinction in four contexts: breach of the duty of utmost good faith by an assured; unlawful conduct by an assured; payment of the proceeds of the policy by the insurer; and termination by one co-assured.

14–012 *Utmost good faith.* In *Woolcott v Sun Alliance and London Insurance Ltd*[61] a dwelling was insured under a building society's block policy which covered the respective interests of the mortgagor and the mortgagee building society. The mortgagor's criminal record had not been disclosed to the insurer and, following damage to the dwelling, the insurer sought to avoid liability. It was here held that, while the insurer was permitted to set the policy aside as regards the mortgagor's interest, the rights of the mortgagee in respect of its own interest were unaffected.[62] The same result would doubtless have been reached had the mortgagor been in breach of warranty. It is clear from the judgment that, had the parties been joint owners of the insured premises and one of them had failed to

---

[59] *Siu Yin Kwan v Eastern Insurance Ltd* [1994] 1 All E.R. 213, confirming *Mark Rowlands Ltd v Berni Inns Ltd* [1985] 3 All E.R. 473.

[60] *Colonial Mutual Insurance v ANZ Banking Group* [1995] 3 All E.R. 987; *Bestquest Ltd v Regency Care Group Ltd* Unreported, 2003.

[61] *Woolcott v Sun Alliance and London Insurance Ltd* [1978] 1 Lloyd's Rep. 629. See also *First National Commercial Bank Plc v Barnet Devanney (Harrow) Ltd* [1999] Lloyd's Rep. I.R. 43, reversed on other grounds [1999] Lloyd's Rep. I.R. 459.

[62] Cf. *Canadian Imperial Bank of Commerce v Dominion of Canada General Insurance Co* 46 D.L.R. (4th) 77 (1987), where the position was confirmed by express wording.

disclose a material fact (even if known only to him), the insurer would have been at liberty to avoid the entire policy.[63]

The underlying assumption, that a composite policy is divisible for utmost good faith purposes, was challenged before Rix J. in *Arab Bank Plc v Zurich Insurance Co.*[64] Here, the managing director of a company, whose business was valuing and surveying, completed a proposal form insuring the company and the directors against professional liability risks. The policy removed the right of the insurers to avoid liability for misrepresentation or non-disclosure which was innocent and free of any attempt to deceive. The managing director had been guilty of mortgage frauds which were not disclosed to the insurers and which gave rise to claims against the company during the currency of the policy. Rix J. held that the policy was composite and insured separately the interests of the company and of each director, and further held that the fraudulent non-disclosure of the managing director defeated his rights but not the rights of the company and the innocent directors. The learned judge, following cases on slightly different issues, *New Hampshire Insurance Co v MGN Ltd*[65] and *Samuel & Co Ltd v Dumas*,[66] held that it was conceptually perfectly possible for an insurer to be able to avoid the contract as against one co-assured but be bound to indemnify the others. The point is, therefore, that there is nothing in principle which distinguishes the defence of utmost good faith from any other defence and that, in all cases, the rights of each assured are divisible.

The divisibility principle was again at stake in *Brit Syndicates v Italaudit SpA*,[67] in which GTI, the umbrella organisation for a group of firms of accountants, took out a composite policy covering itself and each of its members. GTI's own cover applied "in respect of claims made against GTI arising from claims made against a member firm of GTI insured by the terms and conditions of this policy." The insurers purported to avoid the cover of one member, but GTI nevertheless sought to recover in respect of claims made against it arising out of the misconduct of that member. It was common ground that the policy was composite so that avoidance against one member did not without more deprive GTI or other members of cover. The case turned on the proper construction of the policy. The House of Lords, reversing the Court of Appeal, held that the phrase "member firm . . . insured by the terms and conditions of this policy" referred to a firm which had a valid policy at the time the claim was made against it, so that if avoidance took place thereafter then even though avoidance was retroactive such avoidance could not operate to remove from GTI the coverage that was conferred on it as of the date of the claim. On this construction, the key phrase was simply a description of those firms which were as at the date of the claim listed in the policy as being insured members. Lord Mance, delivering the only reasoned judgment in the House of Lords, commented that this interpretation was consistent with the commercial purpose of the policy, which was to protect GTI against the risk of vicarious liability and not to leave it without protection by reason of defects in the cover which were unknown at the time.

Two qualifications should, however, be noted. First, some forms of policy wording may operate to justify avoidance of the entire policy where there has

---

[63] See also *Advance (NSW) Insurance Agencies Pty Ltd v Matthews* (1989) 166 C.L.R. 606. The wording of a joint policy may, however, render interests divisible: *Gill v Insurance Corporation of British Columbia* 50 D.L.R. (4th) 148 (1988).

[64] *Arab Bank Plc v Zurich Insurance Co* [1999] 1 Lloyd's Rep. 262.

[65] *New Hampshire Insurance Co v MGN Ltd* [1997] L.R.L.R. 24 (fraudulent claim).

[66] *Samuel & Co Ltd v Dumas* [1924] A.C. 431 (fraudulent casting away of insured vessel).

[67] *Brit Syndicates v Italaudit SpA* [2008] Lloyd's Rep. I.R. 601.

been breach of duty by any single co-assured. This was the suggested effect of the policy wording in *Arab Bank,* although Rix J. rejected that contention on the basis that the policy simply reserved the insurers rights to avoid for fraud: it would have been necessary for the policy to have gone further and to have stated that the insurers could have avoided in the case of fraud by any assured. The second qualification is that there may, in exceptional circumstances, be an imputation of knowledge as between co-assureds, so that the fraud of one is deemed to be known by the other.

14–013 *Wilful misconduct by an assured.* It is a general principle of insurance law that an assured who has by wilful misconduct brought about the event giving rise to a claim under the policy, or whose actions otherwise offend against public policy, may not mount an action under the policy. In the case of a joint policy, given that the rights of the parties stand or fall together, wilful misconduct by one assured ought in principle to prevent recovery by the co-assured.

A particular problem arises, however, where one jointly assured party commits a wrongful act contrary to the wishes of the other, for example, where an estranged husband deliberately sets fire to jointly owned property. The principle that the rights of the parties stand and fall together is, as indicated above, based upon the notion that the parties are joint tenants of the property and that their interest is single and undivided. However, it is at least arguable that, in the example here postulated, the husband's wrongful act of arson is operative to sever the joint tenancy and to give the parties equal but divided rights in the subject matter under an equitable (or, in the case of personal property, legal) tenancy in common, so that for insurance purposes the policy becomes composite rather than joint. If it is correct that a wrongful act can operate to sever the joint tenancy, it does not necessarily mean that the innocent party will recover under the policy, for it is arguable that the peril insured against—here, fire—had taken place a split second prior to the severance of the joint tenancy. Much may turn on the wording on the policy and on the willingness or otherwise of the courts to apply the *scintilla temporis* principle in this context. As noted earlier, in other jurisdictions this problem has been overcome—particularly in husband and wife cases—by the court construing the policy as composite rather than joint despite the parties' joint ownership of the insured subject matter.[68] It is unclear whether the English courts would be prepared to treat joint owners as parties to a composite policy. In *Direct Line v Khan*[69] the Court of Appeal proceeded on the assumption that the making of a fraudulent claim by a husband defeated the rights of his wife who was jointly insured under the policy, although in that case there was an express finding by the Court of Appeal that the husband had been authorised by the wife to act on her behalf, so that his fraudulent claim was regarded by the Court of Appeal as their joint responsibility.

In the case of a composite policy the wilful misconduct of one assured will be a personal bar to his recovery, but will not prevent a co-assured under the policy from recovering in his own right. Thus, if the mortgagor of a vessel wilfully brings about its loss, the mortgagee nevertheless has a claim under the composite policy in respect of his own interest insured under the policy.[70] Similarly, if two

---

[68] *Moulder v National Insurance Co of New Zealand* [1993] 2 N.Z.L.R. 351; *Gate v Sun Alliance Insurance Ltd* Unreported, 1995.

[69] *Direct Line v Khan* [2002] Lloyd's Rep. I.R. 364.

[70] *Samuel & Co Ltd v Dumas* [1924] A.C. 431. Cf. *Lombard Australia Ltd v NRMA Insurance Co Ltd* [1969] 1 Lloyd's Rep. 575; *Inland Kenworthy Ltd v Insurance Corporation of British Columbia* 66 D.L.R. (4th) 374 (1990); *Maulder v National Insurance Co of New Zealand* [1993] 2 N.Z.L.R. 351; *Gate v Sun Alliance Insurance Ltd* Unreported, 1995.

parties have insured each other's lives under a composite policy, the murder of one party by the other prevents the guilty party from recovering but allows the estate of the innocent party to claim payment.[71] Again, if a group of companies insure against the fraud of corporate officers, each company is to be taken to have suffered a separate loss so that the complicity of one company will not affect the rights of the others.[72] The rights of the innocent party under a composite policy are nevertheless subject to four limitations.

First, the policy may contain an exclusion in respect of loss deliberately caused by any of the named co-assureds.

Secondly, and closely related to the first point, a particular problem arises where the innocent co-assured under a marine policy bases his claim on "perils of the sea"[73]; where a vessel is deliberately scuttled by its mortgagor, the mortgagee's claim under the policy is defeated, not because of the fact that the mortgagor has been fraudulent but because the loss has not been the result of any insured peril.[74] If, by contrast, the mortgagor has destroyed the vessel by arson, the mortgagee is entitled to succeed in respect of his own interest under the composite policy, as fortuity is not an element in the peril "fire".[75] This peculiarity attaching to "perils of the sea" has rendered it essential for mortgagees of vessels to effect independent insurance, payable in the event that the primary insurer is able to deny liability under the composite policy.[76] The fact that a co-assured guilty of wilful misconduct is not insured for a loss caused by his wilful misconduct has effects wider than simply depriving him of recovery. It was held by Colman J. in *National Oilwell (UK) Ltd v Davy Offshore Ltd*[77] that the insurer is entitled to exercise subrogation rights against him so that, having paid the innocent party, the insurer can recover its payment from the guilty party.

Thirdly, the policy may restrict the rights of a co-assured who is aware of the illegality of another but has either encouraged it or done nothing to stop it. Wording found in professional indemnity policies states that the insurers are not liable to a co-assured for any claim "arising from . . . dishonesty . . . committed or condoned" by that co-assured. This wording has been held to mean that if there is a fraudulent course of conduct by one co-assured, and another co-assured is aware of that course of conduct, then the latter cannot seek indemnity for any claim by third parties even though he was unaware of the actual instance of fraud giving rise to that particular claim.[78]

The final limitation flows from the rule that a co-insured with a pervasive insurable interest covering the entire subject matter insured is entitled to recover the full sum due under the policy, but must pay over any surplus above his actual insurable interest to other interested co-assureds. If a co-assured has been guilty of wilful misconduct, it is clear that that co-assured ought not to be able to recover under the policy directly or indirectly, and on this basis it was held by Rix

---

[71] *Davitt v Titcumb* [1989] 3 All E.R. 417, where the insurers did not dispute that they were liable to make payment to someone.

[72] *New Hampshire Insurance Co v MGN Ltd* [1997] L.R.L.R. 24.

[73] Marine Insurance Act 1906 Sch. r.7.

[74] *Samuel & Co Ltd v Dumas* [1924] A.C. 431.

[75] *The Alexion Hope* [1986] 2 F.T.L.R. 655.

[76] This type of insurance is also necessary where the mortgagee takes an assignment of the proceeds of a marine policy rather than becoming co-assured under a composite policy.

[77] *National Oilwell (UK) Ltd v Davy Offshore Ltd* [1993] 2 Lloyd's Rep. 582.

[78] *Zurich Professional Ltd v Karim* [2006] EWHC 3355 (QB); *Goldsmith Williams (A Firm) v Travelers Insurance Company Ltd* [2010] Lloyd's Rep. I.R. 309.

J. in *State of Netherlands v Youell*[79] that an innocent co-assured cannot recover from the insurer a sum which represents the insurable interest of a co-assured guilty of wilful misconduct. In this situation, the innocent co-assured's recovery is limited to his actual insurable interest even though he has insured the entire subject matter by virtue of his pervasive insurable interest. In *Youell* itself, the claimant co-assured had commissioned the building of two submarines, and had obtained a building risks policy covering its own interest and that of the contractor. The insurers asserted that the contractor's wilful misconduct had led to defects in the paintwork of the submarines which were the subject of the claim, and that the claimant ought to be held to recovering its own actual loss under the contract rather than the full sum insured, as it was known that the claimant was obliged by its contract with the contractor to allow policy moneys to be used to pay for repair costs. Various preliminary points of law arose. Rix J. held that, as a matter of principle, the claimant could recover only its own actual loss and could not rely upon its pervasive insurable interest indirectly to benefit the contractor, and that in the event that the claimant was to recover an excess sum which it then paid to the contractor, the insurers would have the right to reclaim it from the contractor by way of subrogation. However, Rix J. found on the facts before him that the claimant's actual insurable interest extended to the entire value of the submarines, and, accordingly, the claimant was entitled to recover the full sum insured: the fact that the claimant intended to pay a part of the insurance moneys to the contractor so that repairs could be effected was not a legitimate concern of the insurer, and such sums could not be recovered by way of subrogation. Rix J. conceded that the position might be different if it could be shown at trial that the claimant was a mere "front" for the contractor.

14–014 *Breach of condition.* Breach of a policy condition by a joint assured will affect the rights of all of the other joint assureds. Thus a claim made by a husband in breach of a fraudulent claims condition will preclude recovery both by him and by his wife.[80] A composite assured will be in a different position unless the insurers can demonstrate that the person making the claim acted as agent for the other composite assureds.[81] Agency issues and express wordings aside, a claim made by one composite assured under a policy does not necessarily amount to a claim on behalf of all of the composite assureds and it may be that each of the composite assureds is required to comply with claims conditions.[82] A composite assured will not be able to recover for a breach of condition by another composite assured if the person in breach was the controlling mind of the organisation to which other composite assured belong and his knowledge is to be regarded as attributed to all of them.[83] In *Tate Gallery (Trustees) v Duffy Construction Ltd*[84] an all risks construction policy covered both the employer and the contractor as co-assureds. The insurers asserted that the contractor had broken a reasonable

---

[79] *State of Netherlands v Youell* [1997] 2 Lloyd's Rep. 440.

[80] *Direct Line Insurance v Khan* [2002] Lloyd's Rep. I.R. 364.

[81] This was the reasoning in *Direct Line Insurance v Khan* [2002] Lloyd's Rep. I.R. 364 in response to the wife's assertion that the policy was composite rather than joint.

[82] *King v Brandywine Reinsurance Co (UK) Ltd* [2004] Lloyd's Rep. I.R. 554, affirmed on other grounds [2005] Lloyd's Rep. I.R. 509.

[83] Contrast *New Hampshire Insurance Co and Others v MGN Ltd* [1997] L.R.L.R. 24 and *Arab Bank Plc v Zurich Insurance Co* [1999] 1 Lloyd's Rep. 262 (knowledge of one composite assured not imputed to the others for disclosure purposes) with *HLB Kidsons v Lloyd's Underwriters* [2008] Lloyd's Rep. I.R. 237 (knowledge of potential claims held by controlling partners within a partnership was imputed to all other partners).

[84] *Tate Gallery (Trustees) v Duffy Construction Ltd* [2007] Lloyd's Rep. I.R. 758.

care clause, and had thereby disentitled itself from claiming under the policy. The court accepted that if the insurers were successful in making out their argument at trial then the contractor would be precluded from recovery and would be subject to a subrogation action. In the event the insurers were unable to prove breach, as their assertions amounted to no more than negligence as opposed to the recklessness required for breach of such a clause.[85]

Payment under the policy Where a loss occurs under a joint policy, the insurer **14–015** meets its obligations by paying the sum due to any of the joint owners; this follows from the ordinary common law principle that a debt owed to joint creditors may be discharged by payment to one of them.[86] The position under a composite policy is more complex, for each assured will have suffered loss to a different type of interest; indeed some of the parties insured may not have suffered any loss at all. The insurer's payment obligation under a composite policy is, in essence, a matter of contract. If the contract provides that the insurer must make payment jointly to all assureds, it must do so and it is for those assureds to allocate the payment between themselves in accordance with losses suffered.[87] Alternatively, the policy may permit each assured to claim against the insurer in respect of his own interest. In the latter case, if the insurer—possibly from a surfeit of caution—insists that payment is made to all persons interested even though only one of them has suffered a loss, payment is deemed to have been received only by the person actually suffering the loss. This principle emerges from the decision of the Court of Appeal in *General Accident Fire and Life Assurance Corp Ltd v Midland Bank Ltd*, the composite policy here covering the respective interests of a tenant, a mortgagee and a landlord in a building and plant. The court construed the policy as authorising each party to claim for his own loss, and for the insurer to be discharged by meeting claims on that basis. Following a fire in which only the tenant suffered loss, the insurers insisted that payment should be made by cheque to each of the three parties, the cheques given to the landlord and mortgagee being indorsed by them in the tenant's favour. The insurers subsequently discovered that the tenant's claim had been fraudulent and sought to recover its payments from the landlord and mortgagee. The Court of Appeal held that this action was misconceived and that, as the only person entitled to receive payment was the tenant, full recovery had to be sought from the tenant alone. Again, in *Murphy v Murphy*[88] it was held that a joint names life policy taken out by a husband and wife was composite in nature so that the proceeds had to be paid in full to the surviving spouse.

The broker's lien over proceeds. In *Eide UK Ltd v Lowndes Lambert Group Ltd* **14–016** *(The Sun Tender)*[89] the Court of Appeal held that s.53(2) of the Marine Insurance Act 1906 confers upon a broker a right of lien over policy proceeds paid to him by the insurer to secure premiums advanced by the broker on behalf of the assured. The Court of Appeal went on to hold that s.53(2) had no application to a composite policy, as any one assured has no right to create a general lien over the interests of another. Accordingly, the principle of independence of rights will prevent any lien arising in the case of a composite policy, and the broker's

[85] *Tate Gallery (Trustees) v Duffy Construction Ltd (No.2)* [2008] Lloyd's Rep. I.R. 159.
[86] *Powell v Broadhurst* [1901] 2 Ch. 160.
[87] *General Accident Fire and Life Assurance Corp Ltd v Midland Bank Ltd* [1940] 2 K.B. 388 at 415, per Sir Wilfrid Greene M.R.
[88] *Murphy v Murphy* [2004] Lloyd's Rep. I.R. 744.
[89] *Eide UK Ltd v Lowndes Lambert Group Ltd (The Sun Tender)* [1998] 1 Lloyd's Rep. 389.

remedy is one of set-off relating to the sums owing to him by way of proceeds against that part of the policy proceeds held by him for an assured who is indebted to him. By contrast, in the case of a joint policy, each assured has a right over the full amount of the proceeds, and it would seem that the lien conferred s.53(2) is available to the broker.

14–017 *Termination.* Where a joint policy is terminated by one of the joint assureds, the principle that the rights of the parties stand or fall together would seem to indicate that—subject, of course, to contrary wording—the entire policy comes to an end. The question is rather more complex in the case of a composite policy, as different interests are there insured. In *Federation Insurance Ltd v Wasson,*[90] Wasson, the lessee under a hire-purchase agreement in respect of a car, procured a composite policy (in accordance with the agreement) covering his own interest and that of the lessor. Wasson unilaterally and without authority from the lessor cancelled the policy, and shortly afterwards the car became a total loss. Wasson brought an action on the policy and argued that his cancellation of it had been ineffective. The policy itself was silent as to the effectiveness of unauthorised termination by one of the co-assureds. It will be appreciated that the court could have reached any one of three results: such termination by one party was ineffective; such termination was fully effective to bring an end to the policy as regards all insured persons; or such termination was effective only as regards the interest of Wasson himself, leaving the lessor's interest unaffected. The Australian court ruled that Wasson's conduct was completely ineffective and that the entire policy remained in existence, so that Wasson could claim. The effect of the decision is to raise a presumption that, in the absence of express wording, unilateral unauthorised termination by one assured under a composite policy is simply inoperative. It is uncertain if this decision represents English law. The divisibility of interests under a composite policy clearly points towards the conclusion that, ostensible authority and express wording apart, one co-assured cannot terminate the cover as regards other interests. It is less certain, however, that the co-assured's own interest should subsist following purported termination by him. The court in *Wasson* nevertheless pointed out that the termination clause in the policy—and indeed the standard form of termination clause found in composite policies—contemplated only termination by all of the interested parties, so that the clause simply did not extend to unilateral acts.

14–018 *The insurer's right of subrogation.* An insurer has the right, once it has indemnified the assured, to step into the shoes of the assured and to enforce any rights which the assured possesses against the person responsible for the loss. Subrogation rights are not, however, available against a co-assured, whether joint or composite, by reason of an implied term in the contract of insurance.[91] Thus, if co-assured B negligently causes loss to co-assured A, co-assured B is immune from a subrogation action brought in A's name on the ground that B himself was insured in respect of that loss.[92] There are, however, various limitations to the principle of immunity in composite insurance cases.

First, if the cover granted by the policy to A and B is not coterminous, and the loss caused by B to A was covered by the policy as far as A was concerned but not as far as B was concerned, B potentially faces a subrogation action. In

[90] *Federation Insurance Ltd v Wasson* (1987) 163 C.L.R. 303.
[91] *Co-operative Retail Services v Taylor Young* [2001] Lloyd's Rep. I.R. 122.
[92] *Petrofina (UK) Ltd v Magnaload Ltd* [1984] Q.B. 127; *BP Exploration Operating Co Ltd v Kvaemer Oilfield Products Ltd* [2004] EWHC 999.

National Oilwell (UK) Ltd v Davy Offshore Ltd[93] the policy covered A in respect of all losses and B in respect only of losses occurring before B had delivered the contract goods to A. It was held that the insurers had subrogated rights against B in respect of B's negligent conduct giving rise to a post-delivery loss suffered by A.

Secondly, if B has by wilful misconduct caused A's loss, B loses the protection of the policy and thus of any subrogation immunity.[94]

Thirdly, the policy may apply at different times to different parties. Thus, in the case of a contractor's all risks policy which insures the interests of the contractor and all subcontractors, while it is the case that each of the insured parties has a full insurable interest in the entire contract works, that of each insured party comes to an end once his work has been performed, as the risk against which he is covered is his own potential loss flowing from his inability to complete the works due to the occurrence of an insured peril. Thus, once an insured party has completed his work, the risk comes to an end and any default by him which becomes apparent at a later date is outside the scope of the policy but rather is covered—if at all—by liability insurance held by that person.[95]

3. UNNAMED CO-ASSUREDS

Direct enforcement against insurer. As will be appreciated from the preceding **14–019** discussion, a policy may cover the interests of the named assured and of other parties, and those other parties may become co-assureds in their own right if the relevant agency relationship exists between them and the assured. In the absence of an agency relationship, a third party may still be able to rely upon the policy even though he is not a party to it, providing that the conditions set out in the Contracts (Rights of Third Parties) Act 1999 are satisfied. The common law rule precluding an action by a third party,[96] as applied in *National Oilwell (UK) Ltd v Davy Offshore Ltd*[97] and *Barras v Hamilton*[98] has been abrogated. The point, therefore, is that, since the 1999 Act came into force, in the majority of cases a person for whose benefit a policy is procured will have some mechanism for enforcing in his own name the rights conferred upon him by the terms of the policy.

Indirect enforcement against insurers. There may, nevertheless, be cases in **14–020** which the third party cannot bring proceedings against the insurers. As discussed above, the fact that the third party's interest has been noted on the policy will generally not be enough to permit enforcement by him under the 1999 Act. Accordingly, some other enforcement mechanism may be required. English law

[93] *National Oilwell (UK) Ltd v Davy Offshore Ltd* [1993] 2 Lloyd's Rep. 582.
[94] *National Oilwell (UK) Ltd v Davy Offshore Ltd* [1993] 2 Lloyd's Rep. 582; *State of Netherlands v Youell* [1997] 2 Lloyd's Rep. 440.
[95] *Deepak Fertilisers and Petrochemical Corp v Davy McKee (London) Ltd* [1999] 1 Lloyd's Rep. 387; *TWF Printers Ltd v Interserve Project Services Ltd* [2006] EWCA Civ 875.The policy on the works may, however, itself be construed as one that extends to the sub-contractor's liability even though it is primarily a property policy: see *Feasey v Sun Life Assurance Co of Canada* [2003] Lloyd's Rep. I.R. 637.
[96] As applied in *National Oilwell (UK) Ltd v Davy Offshore Ltd* [1993] 2 Lloyd's Rep. 582 and *Barras v Hamilton, The Times,* June 10, 1994.
[97] *National Oilwell (UK) Ltd v Davy Offshore Ltd* [1993] 2 Lloyd's Rep. 582.
[98] *Barras v Hamilton, The Times,* June 10, 1994.

does not leave the third party entirely without remedy. Thus, in the case of a tenancy within the Landlord and Tenant Act 1985, the tenant is entitled to initiate a procedure the effect of which is to ensure that the landlord gives notice to the insurer under the policy. Again, if an insured building is damaged by fire, and the assured has made a claim against the insurer, any person interested in the property, whether or not the intended beneficiary of the property, may give notice to the insurer requiring him to secure that the policy moneys are laid out by way of reinstatement rather than as a direct payment to the assured.[99]

It might also be argued that the insurer owes the unnamed co-assured a duty of care in tort which might apply, for example, to claims handling. It has been held in New Zealand that where the assured cancels the policy, the insurer owes no duty to unnamed co-assureds to warn them of that fact, even where their interests have been noted on the policy.[100]

14–021 *Enforcement against named assured.* If the unnamed co-assured is unable to enforce the policy against the insurer, in some cases he may have direct rights against the named assured to ensure that the policy is enforced. A number of possible situations may arise, particularly in the cases of landlord and tenant and bailment.

1. The named assured is under a contractual obligation to make a claim. This will give rise to little difficulty.
2. The named assured and the unnamed assured have contributed towards the premium, and the named assured has covenanted to lay out the policy moneys towards reinstatement. This was the situation in *Vural v Security Archives Ltd*,[101] Knox J. holding that in these circumstances the named assured (landlord) is under an implied obligation to make a claim and to proceed with it within a reasonable time.
3. The named assured has paid the entire premium, and has covenanted to lay out the policy moneys towards reinstatement. This situation differs little from the *Vural* case as a matter of commercial practice, for the underlying relationship between the named and unnamed assureds will doubtless have the effect of the latter paying some or all of the premium (e.g. as an unapportioned part of rent under a lease). It would be unfortunate if the court reached a conclusion different from that in *Vural* on these facts.
4. The named assured has undertaken to insure, without express obligation to claim or to reinstate. The difficulty faced by the unnamed assured in these circumstances is the common law principle that, leaving aside the possibility of an implied obligation on the named assured to reinstate or to account to the unnamed assured for some or all of the policy moneys, those moneys will belong to the named assured only, so that the question of forcing the named assured to sue the insurer will not arise.
5. If the named assured has recovered sums from the insurer, the basic rule is that those sums belong to the assured alone.[102] However, if the amount recovered exceeds the assured's own loss, as will generally be the case

---

[99] Under s.83 of the Fires Prevention (Metropolis) Act 1774.

[100] *Cooper Henderson Finance Ltd v Colonial Mutual General Insurance Co* [1990] 1 N.Z.L.R. 1.

[101] *Vural v Security Archives Ltd* [1989] E.G.L.S. 2. See also *Lonsdale & Thompson Ltd v Black Arrow Group Plc* [1993] 3 All E.R. 648.

[102] *Leeds v Cheetham* (1827) 1 Sim. 146. *Mumford Hotels v Wheeler* [1964] Ch. 117; *Rayner v Preston* (1881) 18 Ch D 1; *Lees v Whiteley* (1866) L.R. 2 Eq. 143.

where, for example, a bailee insures for the full value of goods, the bailee must account to third parties for sums in excess of his own interest, and if the insurance was placed under a contractual duty the bailor has a proprietary claim in respect of the surplus.[103]

4. ASSIGNMENT

Voluntary assignment of subject matter. A policy of insurance is a personal contract,[104] so that the assignment of the subject matter of the policy by the assured to a third party will not—unless the policy itself provides—itself operate as an assignment of the policy to the third party. This is specifically stated in s.15 of the Marine Insurance Act 1906, a principle which applies to all classes of insurance.[105]

14–022

Where the assured voluntarily disposes of his entire interest in the subject matter insured under a policy, whether by sale or gift, the common law indemnity principle means that the assured will be unable to present a claim under the policy on the happening of an insured peril, as he cannot suffer any loss. There is no necessary reason why the policy should lapse automatically on such disposition, particularly in the light of the fact that the assured might retain a limited insurable interest or indeed might regain an insurable interest in the subject matter during its currency, although the cases are clear that if no interest remains then the assignment of the subject matter brings an end to the policy.[106] The sale of a motor vehicle may bring a compulsory motor liability policy to an end if it relates specifically to that vehicle,[107] although a policy which allows the assured to drive any other vehicle continues to protect the assured against third-party liabilities even after the sale of his own vehicle as the assured retains an insurable interest in his liability.[108] A change of partners in a partnership would appear not to affect any policy taken out by the original members of the partnership,[109] although there is some doubt as to whether new partners are covered in the absence of policy wording to that effect[110] and it would seem that any policy on partnership property will not remain in force following the dissolution of the partnership and the transfer of its assets to one or more of the ex-partners.[111]

---

[103] *Re E Dibbens & Sons Ltd* [1990] B.C.L.C. 677.

[104] *Lynch v Dalzell* (1729) 4 Bro. P.C. 431.

[105] *Powles v Innes* (1843) 11 M. & W. 10; *North of England Pure Oil Cake Co v Archangel Marine Insurance Co* (1875) L.R. 10 Q.B. 249.

[106] *Powles v Innes* (1843) 11 M. & W. 10, *North of England Oil Cake Co v Archangel Insurance* (1875) L.R. 10 Q.B. 249 (marine); *Collingridge v Royal Exchange Assurance Corporation* (1877) 3 QBD 173; *Rayner v Preston* (1881) 18 Ch D 1; *Ecclesiastical Commissioners v Royal Exchange* (1895) 11 T.L.R. 476 (property).

[107] *Rogerson v Scottish Automobile Insurance* [1931] 1 All E.R. Rep. 606; *Tattersall v Drysdale* [1935] 2 K.B. 174; *Peters v General Accident Fire and Life Assurance Corp* (1937) 60 Ll. L.R. 311; *Boss v Kingston* [1962] 1 Lloyd's Rep. 431; *Smith v Ralph* [1963] 2 Lloyd's Rep. 439; *Wilkinson v General Accident* [1967] 2 Lloyd's Rep. 182.

[108] *Dodson v Peter H Dodson Insurance Services* [2001] Lloyd's Rep. I.R. 278.

[109] *Jenkins v Deane* (1933) 103 L.J.K.B. 250.

[110] *Jenkins v Deane* (1933) 103 L.J.K.B. 250 at 255; *Maxwell v Price* [1960] 2 Lloyd's Rep. 155.

[111] *McKay v Eagle Star & British Dominions Insurance Co* (1879) 18 M.C.R. (N.Z.) 83.

Assignment of policy

14–023 *Conditions for assignment.* A policy of insurance, being a chose in action, is prima facie freely assignable.[112] However, a valid assignment is subject to the fulfilment of three conditions: the consent of the insurers must be obtained; to avoid problems arising from insurable interest, the assignment of the policy and its underlying subject matter must be contemporaneous; and the assignment must be in proper form. These conditions arise as a matter of law, and are additional to any restrictions which are contained in the agreement between the parties under which the assignment is to be effected. The assignment may, therefore, be postponed until the assignee has paid the agreed price for the policy or until other formalities have been satisfied, so the date on which the policy is regarded as having been assigned will depend upon the terms of the contract: this point may become important where the parties have negotiated an assignment and a loss has occurred prior to the satisfaction of the conditions for assignment. In *CCM Policies Ltd v Amin*[113] it was held that, on the proper construction of a contract of sale of a life policy, the assignees had acquired title to the policy in that the assured had died after the date fixed for completion and the assignee's late payment of the price had been waived by the assignor's agent.

14–024 *Consent of the insurers.* The willingness of equity to permit assignment of choses in action has always been confined to cases "where it can make no difference to the person on whom the obligation lies to which of two parties he shall discharge it".[114] This exception in favour of "personal" contracts has long been regarded as applicable to insurance agreements,[115] for it is clearly of the utmost importance to the insurers to know exactly who the assured is to be. Consequently, irrespective of the terms of the policy itself, an insurance policy—other than a life[116] or a marine policy[117]—is not assignable other than with the consent of the insurer and any purported assignment is void.[118] Consent, where it is given, takes effect as a novation, rather than as a continuation of the old policy substituting the assignee as the assured party. There is thus a new contract, possibly on new terms and at a different premium rate. It is open to insurers to waive the requirement for their consent by including a term in the policy which allows its assignment.

14–025 *Contemporaneous assignment of policy and subject matter.* The need for a contemporaneous assignment stems from the rules of insurable interest. Two situations need to be distinguished. First, the subject matter of the policy is assigned to the third party before the policy itself: here the effect of such assignment is to determine the policy automatically if the assured has no residual insurable interest, although it was noted that such automatic determination is not strictly necessary as the indemnity principle in any event operates to deprive the assured of any right to recover. The third party will not obtain any right to sue under the policy, for by the time of any assignment to him it will have lapsed.

---

[112] The rights of the parties to an assignment, and the assignability of a policy, are governed by the law which governs the policy: Rome Convention art.12; *Raiffeisen Zentralbank Osterreich AG v Five Star General Trading LLC* [2001] Lloyd's Rep. I.R. 460.

[113] *CCM Policies Ltd v Amin* Unreported, March 12, 2001.

[114] *Tolhurst v Associated Portland Cement Manufacturers Ltd* [1902] 1 K.B. 660 at 668.

[115] *Lynch v Dalzell* (1729) 4 Bro. 431; *Sadlers' Co v Badcock* (1743) 2 Atk. 554.

[116] See Ch.18, below.

[117] See Ch.24, below.

[118] *Peters v General Accident Fire and Life Assurance Corp Ltd* [1938] 2 All E.R. 267.

Secondly, the policy is assigned to the third party before the subject matter of the policy. Here, assignment defeats the rights of both the assured and the third-party assignee: the assured cannot recover as he has assigned the policy, while the third party cannot recover as, at the date of the assignment of the policy to him, he did not possess insurable interest.[119]

Form of assignment. The common law rule is that choses in action cannot not be **14–026** assigned to another without the assent of the debtor. Assignments were always valid in equity, however, and courts of equity enabled the assignee even of a legal chose in action to bring an action at law against the debtor in the assignor's name, by restraining the assignor from objecting to his use of it on being given a proper indemnity against costs.[120] The common law rule has been modified by statute. The Policies of Assurance Act 1867, and the Policies of Marine Assurance Act 1868 (subsequently replaced by s.50 of the Marine Insurance Act 1906), made life and marine insurance policies respectively assignable at law, rendering these forms of choses in action exceptions to the general principle of non-assignability at law. In due course s.25(6) of the Judicature Act 1873, subsequently replaced by s.136 of the Law of Property Act, made all debts and other things in action assignable at law, without prejudice to the possibility of assignment in equity and under the specific insurance legislation. The result is that: any policy may be assigned in equity; any policy may be assigned at law under s.136 of the 1925 Act; a marine policy may in the alternative be assigned under s.50 of the 1906 Act[121]; and a life policy may in the alternative be assigned under the Policies of Assurance Act 1867.[122]

A legal assignment under s.136 permits the assignee to sue the insurers in his own name without joining the assured as a party to the proceedings, and confers upon the assignee the right to give a good discharge for the policy monies. Section 136 applies to any absolute[123] assignment by writing under the hand of the assignor (not purporting to be by way of charge only[124]) of any legal chose in action, of which express notice in writing[125] has been given to the debtor, trustee or other person from whom the assignor would have been entitled to claim the chose in action.

The statutes which created the possibility of an assignment at law did nothing to take away the efficacy of equitable assignments.[126] They simply gave the assignee a more convenient remedy, and no alteration in the rights of the parties was contemplated.[127] The main difference between an equitable assignment and a legal assignment is procedural. An equitable assignee, unlike a legal assignee does not acquire the right to sue the insurers in his own name, but must generally join the assignor to the proceedings as defendant if the assignor is not already a

---

[119] *Lloyd v Fleming* (1872) L.R. 7 Q.B. 299.

[120] *Ashley v Ashley* (1829) 3 Sim. 149; *Pearson v Amicable Assurance* (1859) 27 Beav. 229.

[121] See Ch.24, below.

[122] See Ch.18, below.

[123] Residual interests must not be retained: *Raiffeisen Zentralbank Osterreich AG v Five Star General Trading LLC* [2001] Lloyd's Rep. I.R. 476. However, an assignment subject to a trust in favour of the assignor is within s.136: *Burlinson v Hall* (1884) 12 QBD 347.

[124] Although an absolute assignment by way of mortgage subject only to the assignor's equity of redemption can be effected under s.136: *Durham Brothers v Robertson* [1898] 1 Q.B. 765; *Hughes v Pump House Hotel Co* [1902] 2 K.B. 190.

[125] No particular form is required, and may be given after the loss: *Walker v Bradford Old Bank* (1884) 12 QBD 511.

[126] *Brandt's v Dunlop* [1905] A.C. 454 at 461; *Newman v Newman* (1884) 28 Ch D 674; Law of Property Act 1925 s.5.

[127] *Pellas v Neptune Marine* (1879) 5 C.P. 34.

party to the proceedings as claimant in his own right, although the practice of joining the assignor will not be insisted upon if there is no risk of a separate claim by him.[128] It is possible to assign a partial interest in equity,[129] but not under statute.[130] An assignment which does not comply with s.136 for want of writing may take effect in equity provided that there is evidence of an unequivocal intention to assign and may even be effected by way of mouth.[131] Equitable assignments may accordingly be effected in ways not recognised by s.136, including by: the delivery of the policy[132] unless the context shows that the deposit was merely to create a lien[133] or a right of possession[134]; an agreement to assign,[135] if made for valuable consideration[136]; or memorandum in writing.[137] Equity does not demand notice to the insurers as a condition of giving the assignee a good equitable title as against the assignor, although the giving of notice is strongly advisable as notice operates to secure priority in the case of competing assignments.[138] An agreement to assign a future policy is effective to create an equitable charge on the policy in the assignee's favour as soon as the policy comes into existence even though no formal assignment is executed, and a request by the assignee to have his interest noted on the policy operates as notice to the insurer and thereby secures the assignee's priority in the event of competing assignments.[139]

14–027 *Effects of a valid assignment.* Following a valid legal assignment, the assignee steps into the shoes of the assured and the assured drops out of the picture, so that any misconduct on his part will not preclude an action under the policy by the assignee.[140] The general assumption is that assignment creates a perfect substitution of the assignee for the assignor. Thus, the assignee is required to pay the premiums, and any sums payable under the policy will belong to the assignee. A legal assignee has the right to sue the insurers in his own name and to give a good discharge for the policy moneys. Whether he has the right to retain the policy moneys as against the assignor is a matter to be determined by the agreement between them, and the obligation of the insurers to pay the assignee is unaffected. Any assignment of the policy does not transfer to the assignee rights other than those arising under the policy itself. Thus, if the policy is void

---

[128] *Raiffeisen Zentralbank Osterreich AG v Five Star General Trading LLC* [2001] Lloyd's Rep. I.R. 476.

[129] *First National Rank of Chicago v West of England Shipowners Mutual Protection and Indemnity Association (Luxembourg)* [1981] 1 Lloyd's Rep. 54.

[130] *Raiffeisen Zentralbank Osterreich AG v Five Star General Trading LLC* [2001] Lloyd's Rep. I.R. 476.

[131] *Brandt's v Dunlop* [1905] A.C. 454. An equitable assignment of an equitable interest must, however, be in writing and signed by the assignor or his agent: 1925 Act s.53(1)(c).

[132] *Ex p. Kensington* (1813) 2 E. & B. 79; *Row v Dawson* (1749) 1 Ves.Sen. 331; *Dufour v Professional Life* (1855) 25 Beav. 599; *Gurnell v Gardner* (1863) 4 Giff. 626; *Green v Ingham* (1867) L.R. 2 C.P. 525; *Shaw v Foster* (1872) L.R. 5 H.L. 321.

[133] *Chapman v Chapman* (1851) 13 Beav. 599.

[134] *Howes v Prudential* (1883) 49 L.T. 133.

[135] Not simply an intention to assign: *Crossley v City of Glasgow* (1876) 4 Ch D 421.

[136] *Ashley v Ashley* (1829) 3 Sim. 149; *Godsal v Webb* (1838) 2 Keen 99; *Jeston v Key* (1871) L.R. 6 Ch. 610; *Spencer v Clarke* (1878) 9 Ch D 137; *Re Moore* (1878) 8 Ch D 519; *Vavasseur v Vavasseur* (1909) 25 T.L.R. 250.

[137] *Chowne v Baylis* (1862) 31 Beav. 351.

[138] The rule in *Dearle v Hall* (1828) 3 Russ. 1.

[139] *Colonial Mutual General v ANZ Banking Group* [1995] 3 All E.R. 987.

[140] *Davitt v Titcumb* [1989] 3 All E.R. 417.

able due to the negligence of the assignor's broker, the assignment of the policy does not also assign any right of action against the broker.[141]

An insurance policy is not a negotiable instrument, and can only be assigned—whether the assignment is legal or equitable—"subject to equities". This means that while the assignee is permitted, directly or indirectly, to sue the insurer, the insurer retains as against the assignee all rights that it had against the assignor at the date of the assignment. Most significantly, any defence available to the insurers against the assured will also prevail against the assignee. Thus, if the policy is voidable against the assured for breach of the duty of utmost good faith it is also voidable against an assignee even if he is unaware of the assured's breach of duty,[142] and if the assured is an enemy alien so that the policy is void the assignee can have no rights under the policy.[143] So also where a policy is vitiated by the assured's fraud, and the insurers pay his assignee in ignorance of such fraud, they are, on discovering the fraud, entitled to recover the money so paid as money paid under a mistake of fact.[144] A policy may perfectly legitimately provide that, in the event of assignment, the insurers agree to waive as against the third party any defences which they may have against the assured.[145] Thus, if the owner of a vessel or building mortgages the subject matter and assigns the insurance to the mortgagee, the policy may provide that the mortgagee will be paid free of all defences. In such a case the insurers may expressly reserve a right of recourse against the assured in the event that payment is made to the third party in circumstances under which the insurers would have had a defence but for assignment. The rule that the assignment is subject to equities does not extend to equities between the insurers and the assignor existing outside the contract.[146] However, the principle that the assignee takes subject to equities will extend to equities other than those in favour of the insurer. Thus, if the broker has paid the premium on the assignor's behalf and has a lien on the policy, the lien is unaffected by the assignment of the policy.[147]

Priorities of competing assignments. The general rule is that the priority of **14–028** assignments is governed by the order of date in which they were made,[148] but this is subject to the further rule that, where one or more assignees have given notice to the insurers, priority is determined by the date of notice.[149] As notice is nearly always given, the practical effect of the rules is that priorities of competing assignments, whether legal or equitable, will be determined not by the dates of the assignments but by the dates of notice being given to the insurers. The giving of notice to the insurers will not confer priority on an assignee who knew[150] or ought to have known[151] at the date of his own assignment of an earlier assignment. Thus a legal assignee cannot take priority over an equitable assignee

---

[141] *Punjab National Bank v De Boinville* [1992] 1 Lloyd's Rep. 7.

[142] *British Equitable Insurance Co v Great Western Ry* (1869) 38 L.J.Ch. 314; *Pickersgill & Sons Ltd v London and Marine Provincial Insurance Co Ltd* (1912) 107 L.T. 305; *Patel v Windsor Life Assurance Co Ltd* [2008] Lloyd's Rep. I.R. 359.

[143] *Bank of New South Wales v South British Insurance Co Ltd* (1920) 4 Ll. L.R. 266.

[144] *Lefevre v Boyle* (1832) 3 B & Ad 877.

[145] One specific example is the protection of the assignee under a life policy where the life assured has committed suicide.

[146] *Baker v Adam* (1910) 102 L.T. 248.

[147] *Man v Shiffner & Ellis* (1802) 2 East 523.

[148] *Spencer v Clarke* (1878) 9 Ch D 137; *Re Weniger's Policy* [1910] 2 Ch. 291.

[149] *Dearle v Hall* (1828) 3 Russ 1.

[150] *Newman v Newman* (1885) 28 Ch D 674.

[151] *West of England v Batchelor* (1882) 51 L.J.Ch. 199; *Re Weniger's Policy* [1910] 2 Ch. 291.

of whose assignment he had notice, and an equitable assignee cannot take priority over an earlier equitable assignee of whose assignment he had notice. It remains open to an assignee who did not know of other assignments at the date of his own, but who subsequently discovers their existence, to give notice and to obtain priority over them.[152]

Assignability of proceeds of policy

14–029 *The principle of assignability.* The right to recover under a policy of insurance is a chose in action even though it is not regarded as a debt but as a right to unliquidated damages.[153] The right of recovery is freely assignable as a chose in action and may be assigned either at law under the terms of s.136 of Law of Property Act 1925 or in equity. However, a legal assignment under the 1925 Act is possible only where there is an established present claim: the right to make a claim against the insurers in the event that a claim might arise at some future point is not assignable under this legislation.[154] The Policies of Assurance Act 1867 is concerned with the assignment of the policy itself rather than its proceeds and therefore has no application in the present context. Similarly, s.50 of Marine Insurance 1906 is by its terms confined to policy assignments rather than assignments of the right to recover, although if there has been a total loss, or a partial loss which has the effect of exhausting the policy, any assignment of the claim amounts to the assignment of the entire benefit of the policy and thus can be effected under s.50 of the 1906 Act.[155]

In line with principles applicable to the assignment of policies, if the assignment takes effect under statute, the assignee can sue the insurers in his own name. By contrast, if the assignment is purely equitable, then assuming that the necessary intention to effect an assignment can be shown,[156] the assured must be joined to the action as claimant if he consents, or otherwise as defendant, subject to the power of the court to dispense with joinder if the assured does not intend to make any conflicting claim. It is immaterial whether the proceeds of the policy are assigned before or after the loss.

The following differences between an assignment of the policy and an assignment of the proceeds may be noted. First, an assignment of the proceeds does not give rise to a new contract between the insurers and the assignee: the assignor remains the assured.[157] For this reason, the consent of the insurers to assignment is not needed unless the policy expressly so provides. Secondly, a provision against assignment in a life policy will be construed as applying to the policy itself, but not to the proceeds.[158] Thirdly, in line with the principle that assignment takes effect subject to equities, any obligations imposed on the assured under the policy remain to be performed by him even after assignment, so if the assured commits an act which amounts to a breach of a policy term

---

[152] *Mutual Life v Langley* (1886) 32 Ch D 460.
[153] *Jabbour v Custodian of Israeli Absentee Property* [1954] 1 W.L.R. 139; *Edmunds v Lloyd Italico* [1986] 1 All E.R. 249.
[154] *Raiffeisen Zentralbank Osterreich v Five Star General Trading LLC* [2001] Lloyd's Rep. I.R. 460.
[155] *Raiffeisen Zentralbank Osterreich v Five Star General Trading LLC* [2001] Lloyd's Rep. I.R. 460.
[156] *Floods of Queensferry Ltd v Shand Construction Ltd* [2003] Lloyds Rep. I.R. 181.
[157] *Weldon v GRE Linked Life Assurance Ltd* Unreported, 2001.
[158] *Re Turcan* (1880) 40 Ch D 5.

before or after the assignment of the proceeds[159] the insurers are entitled to rely upon that act in the usual way and to refuse to pay: as there are no proceeds payable, the assignee has no rights against the insurers. Equally, if the assured has been indemnified by a third party, he has not suffered any loss and there are no proceeds to assign.[160] By contrast, where the policy itself has been assigned and there is a change of assured, the conduct of the assignor/assured will be immaterial as the insurers' contract is at that stage with the assignee. Fourthly, the assignee need not possess any insurable interest, so that no assignment of the subject matter of the policy is also required. The amount of the assured's recovery is, however, necessarily limited to the amount of the assured's insurable interest measured at the date of loss. Finally, it is possible to assign in equity both a partial interest and an expectancy or future chose in action—e.g. the right to make a claim under a policy if and when such claim arises—whereas neither partial interests nor future claims may be assigned under statute.

There are no public policy restrictions on the assignment of the right to claim under an insurance policy. A claim under an insurance policy[161] may be assigned without infringing the rules against the maintenance of actions, and the assignment is valid even though its purpose is to prevent the insurers as defendants from obtaining an order for security for costs.[162]

Where there has been an assignment of the proceeds, the insurers cannot as against the assignee assert a separate counterclaim which it has against the assured.[163]

Applicable law. There is little English authority on the application of the conflict **14–030** of laws rules to the assignment of a claim under an insurance policy. The matter is now regulated by art.14 of the Rome I Regulation,[164] which provides as follows:

"1. The relationship between assignor and assignee under a voluntary assignment . . . of a claim against another person (the debtor) shall be governed by the law that applies to the contract between the assignor and assignee under this Regulation.

2. The law governing the assigned . . . claim shall determine its assignability, the relationship between the assignee and the debtor, the conditions under which the assignment . . . can be invoked against the debtor and whether the debtor's obligations have been discharged.

3. The concept of assignment in this Article includes outright transfers of claims, transfers of claims by way of security and pledges or other security rights over claims."

The law which governs the assignability of an insurance claim is, under the express terms of art.14.2 of the Rome I Regulation, the law applicable to the claim itself. In insurance cases that will be the law applicable to the policy and

---

[159] *Re Carr and Sun Fire Insurance Co* (1897) 13 T.L.R. 186; *Graham Joint Stock Shipping Co Ltd v Merchants' Marine Insurance Co. Ltd* [1924] A.C. 294; *Bank of Nova Scotia v Hellenic Mutual War Risks Association (The Good Luck)* [1989] 3 All E.R. 1. In *The Litsion Pride* [1985] 1 Lloyd's Rep. 437 Hirst J. rejected the argument that a breach of contract by the assured after the assignment of the proceeds was ineffective to deprive the assignee of his accrued rights.

[160] *Colonia Versicherung AG v Amoco Oil Co* [1997] 1 Lloyd's Rep. 261.

[161] *Giles v Thompson* [1994] 1 A.C. 965.

[162] *Eurocross Sales Ltd v Cornhill Insurance Plc* [1995] 4 All E.R. 950; *Norglen Ltd v Reeds Rains Prudential Ltd* [1998] 1 All E.R. 218.

[163] *Batey v Jewson* [2008] EWCA Civ 18.

[164] Re-enacting art.12 of the Rome Convention.

not the law applicable to the contract of assignment. This reflects the common law. In *Fender v Provincial Bank of Scotland*[165] a married woman domiciled in Scotland sought to assign a policy, on her husband's life and made for her benefit, to a Scottish bank as security for a loan. The policy had been issued by an English insurer, but was governed by Scots law. Such assignment was not possible under Scots law, but was valid under English law, and the Scottish court held that the assignment was invalid on the basis that the policy was governed by Scots law. It follows from the reasoning adopted that the same result would have followed had the assignment been governed by English law and not Scots law. The same conclusion has been reached in the United States. In *Northwestern Mutual Life Insurance Co v Adams*[166] a life policy governed by the law of Wisconsin, which permitted assignments, was assigned under a contract governed by the law of Minnesota, which did not permit assignments: it was nevertheless held that the assignment was valid, in accordance with the law applicable to the insurance agreement.

Secondly, the formal validity of an assignment is governed by the law applicable to the assignment rather than the law of the country in which the debt or the debtor was situated. This was held, by the Court of Appeal in *Raiffeisen Zentralbank Osterreich AC v Five Star General Trading LLC*,[167] to be the correct construction of what is now art.14 of the Rome I Regulation. In that case, an insurance policy governed by English law was assigned in France—the assignment failed to comply with the formal procedural requirements of French law, but took effect in English law as a valid equitable assignment. The Court of Appeal held that the rights assigned were contractual rights rather than proprietary rights, so that the Rome I Regulation was applicable. Given that, it followed from art.14 that the law applicable to the assigned contractual right was the law applicable to the contract, i.e. English law rather than French law. In so deciding, Mance L.J. in the Court of Appeal recognised that applying the *lex situs* of the insurers would give rise to major problems where there was a co-insurance operation involving a number of insurers from different jurisdictions.

Thirdly, the substantive validity of an assignment is governed by the law applicable to the assignment. This is specifically stated to be the case by art.14.1 of the Rome I Regulation. The only common law authority on the matter, *Lee v Abdy*[168] determined that the capacity of an assignor to effect an assignment was governed by the law of the place of the assignor's domicile. However, this decision was reached before the full emergence of the doctrine of the applicable law, and it is thought that—independently of the operation of art.14.1 of the Rome I Regulation—art.12.1 of the Rome Convention—the reasoning adopted no longer has any authority.

Finally, the rules governing the priorities of successive assignments of a claim are provided by the law applicable to the policy, and not by the law of the assignments. It is clearly not possible to apply the governing law of the successive assignments, as each may be governed by a different law. The rule was established by *Le Fevre v Sullivan*,[169] in which an assured, domiciled in Jersey, assigned his policy, which was governed by English law, to an assignee domiciled in England, and subsequently to an assignee domiciled in Jersey. The

---

[165] *Fender v Provincial Bank of Scotland* 1940 S.L.T. 306.
[166] *Northwestern Mutual Life Insurance Co v Adams* 144 N.W. 1108 (1914).
[167] *Raiffeisen Zentralbank Osterreich AC v Five Star General Trading LLC* [2001] Lloyd's Rep. I.R. 460.
[168] *Lee v Abdy* (1886) 17 QBD 309.
[169] *Le Fevre v Sullivan* (1855) 10 Moo. P.C. 1.

Privy Council applied English law to determine the priority of the assignments. The Rome I Regulation does not specifically touch upon this point, but it seems to follow from *Raiffeisen* that if the rights of each assignee and debtor are governed by the law applicable to the policy then the rights of assignees inter se should be governed in the same way.

CHAPTER 15

INSURANCE INTERMEDIARIES

1. GENERAL AGENCY PRINCIPLES

Authority of agents

15–001 *Types of authority.* An agent will bind his principal by any act performed within the scope of the agent's authority. Authority may take one of four forms: (1) actual authority, which stems primarily from express instructions from his principal, although as a matter of law the agent has implied authority to do all acts necessary to carry out matters within his express authority; (2) usual authority, which arises where the agent is, by some hidden limitation, deprived of the authority that an agent of his status would normally possess—unless the principal brings the limitation to the third party's attention[1] by a clear statement,[2] e.g. in the policy,[3] the third party is entitled to assume that no such limitation exists[4]; (3) apparent authority or agency by estoppel,[5] which arises where the agent acts outside his actual or usual authority, so that the power exercised is not one that the agent would normally be expected to have, but has been held out by the principal[6] or by another agent himself clothed with apparent authority,[7] as possessing authority to perform the act in question; and (4) authority gained from a custom or trade usage.[8] Categories (2) and (3) are collectively referred to as "ostensible" authority. Authority, once conferred, may be withdrawn in accordance with the terms of the agency agreement,[9] subject where appropriate to notice being given to persons dealing with the agent.

15–002 *Transfer of agency.* While the authority of an agent may be limited, English law seemingly does not permit the principal, by means of a deeming provision, to

---

[1] A limitation of authority is not an exclusion clause: *Overbrooke Estates v Glencombe Properties* [1974] 3 All E.R. 511.

[2] *HIH Casualty and General Insurance Ltd v Chase Manhattan Bank* [2001] Lloyd's Rep. I.R. 703.

[3] *Horncastle v Equitable Life Assurance Society of the United States* (1906) 22 T.L.R. 735; *Comerford v Britannic Assurance Co Ltd* (1908) 24 T.L.R. 593; *M'Millan v Accident Insurance Co* 1907 S.C. 484.

[4] *Pickering v Buck* (1812) 15 East 38; *Acey v Fernie* (1840) 7 M. & W. 153; *Baines v Ewing* (1866) L.R. 1 Exch. 320; *Mackie v European Assurance* (1869) 21 L.T. 102; *Jenkins v Deane* (1933) 47 Ll. L.R. 342; *Xenos v Wickham* (1867) L.R. 2 H.L. 296; *Zurich General Accident and Liability Insurance Co Ltd v Rowberry* [1954] 2 Lloyd's Rep. 55; *Wilkinson v General Accident Fire and Life Assurance Corp* [1967] 2 Lloyd's Rep. 182.

[5] *Armagas v Mundogas* [198] 1 A.C. 717; *First Energy v Hungarian International Bank* [1993] 2 Lloyd's Rep. 194.

[6] *Willis Faber & Co v Joyce* (1911) 27 T.L.R. 388.

[7] *British Bank of the Middle East v Sun Life Assurance Co of Canada (UK) Ltd* [1983] 2 Lloyd's Rep. 9; *ING Re (UK) Ltd v R&V Versicherung AG* [2006] Lloyd's Rep. I.R. 653.

[8] See Ch.3, above.

[9] *AA Mutual Insurance Co Ltd v Bradstock, Blunt & Crawley* [1996] L.R.L.R. 161.

transfer the agency of his agent to the third party, on the basis that a company "cannot assert that black is white and expect the courts to believe it".[10]

Ratification. Where an act is performed by an agent expressly on behalf of a **15–003**
principal without the authority of the principal, it is open to the principal to ratify the agent's act and thus to become a party to the agreement whether or not the principal has been identified in the policy. The agent must, however, have intended to contract on behalf of the principal at the date the policy was taken out.[11] Ratification requires knowledge of the circumstances surrounding the making of the contract some form of positive act on the part of the principal by which the policy is adopted.[12] The effect of ratification is a retroactive grant of authority to the agent, although because ratification is retrospective to the date at which the contract is purported to be made by the agent the principal must have been of full capacity to enter into the contract at that date.[13] On this basis an insurance company can adopt any acts of its agents by subsequent ratification provided that they are within its own powers,[14] and a policy taken out by the agent of the assured may afterwards be adopted by the assured.[15] An assured without insurable interest cannot ratify a policy taken out on his behalf, although if the premium has been paid by the agent in full or in part from trust funds then the principal has the right to trace the proceeds of the policy into the agent's hands in the proportion that the principal's funds contributed to the premium paid by the agent.[16]

An undisclosed principal cannot ratify a contract which the agent intended to make on his behalf.[17] If the assured is to ratify an insurance contract entered into on his behalf, the identity of the assured, or at least the class of persons into which the assured falls, must have been disclosed to the insurers.[18]

It has been held in marine insurance cases that where a policy has been effected without the assured's authority the assured can ratify the policy even after he has become aware that a loss has occurred.[19] Early authority supports the proposition that this rule is confined to marine insurance so that insurance of premises against fire by an agent without his principal's authority cannot be ratified by the principal after the fire has occurred.[20] More recently, however, it has been said that the distinction between marine and non-marine insurance is illogical and that the marine principle ought to be generally applicable.[21]

---

[10] *Commissioners of Customs and Excise v Pools Finance (1937) Ltd* [1952] 1 All E.R. 775 at 780. See also: *Ayrey v British Legal and United Provident Assurance Co* [1918] 1 K.B. 136; *Stone v Reliance Mutual Insurance Association* [1972] 1 Lloyd's Rep. 469. But contrast *Facer v Vehicle and General Insurance Co Ltd* [1956] 1 Lloyd's Rep. 113, where such a clause was given effect.

[11] *National Oilwell v Davy Offshore* [1993] 2 Lloyd's Rep. 582.

[12] *ING Re (UK) Ltd v R&V Versicherung AG* [2006] Lloyd's Rep. I.R. 653; *Sea Emerald SA v Prominvestbank* [2008] EWHC 1979 (Comm).

[13] *Bird v Brown* (1850) 4 Exch. 786, applied in *Presentaciones Musicales v Secunda* [1994] 2 All E.R. 737 by Dillon and Nolan L.JJ., although Roch L.J. took the wider view that ratification is available unless it would operate to divest property, to create retroactive illegality or to reverse a subsequent act by the agent which purports to deny the original act.

[14] *Re Phoenix Life* (1862) 2 J. & H. 441; *Re Era* (1862) 1 Hem. & M. 672.

[15] *Lucena v Craufurd* (1808) 1 Taunt. 325; *Stirling v Vaughan* (1809) 11 East 619.

[16] *Foskett v McKeown* [2000] Lloyd's Rep. I.R. 627.

[17] *Keighley, Maxsted v Durant* [1901] A.C. 240.

[18] *National Oilwell v Davy Offshore* [1993] 2 Lloyd's Rep. 582.

[19] *Williams v North China Insurance* (1876) I C.P.D. 757, codified by the Marine Insurance Act 1906 s.86; *Hansen v Norske Lloyd Insurance Co* (1919) 1 Ll.L.R. 185.

[20] *Grover and Grover v Matthews* [1910] 2 K.B. 401.

[21] *National Oilwell v Davy Offshore* [1993] 2 Lloyd's Rep. 582.

Where the assured has ratified unauthorised conduct by the broker, such ratification does not operate as an automatic defence to the broker in respect of a claim against him for breach of duty. The questions of ratification and exoneration are distinct, and if this was not the case, "ratification would operate as a shield for professional agents which could be justified neither conceptually nor as a matter of justice".[22] An agent who effects the insurance and pays the premiums takes the risk of losing them, as he is acting outside the scope of his authority, nor can he at any time before the risk ends recover his premiums, as the insurer may answer that the persons beneficially interested are still entitled to adopt the policy.[23]

15–004 *Fraud by the agent.* The fact that the agent has been fraudulent will not affect the question of the scope of his authority.[24] A principal is liable for the fraud, concealment, misrepresentation or wrong[25] of his agent where the agent is acting, or purporting to act, in the course of a business such as he was authorised, or held out as authorised, to transact on behalf of his principal. It does not matter whether the act was intended for his principal's benefit or his own.[26] Thus, the representations of an agent having authority to solicit insurances and receive proposals bind the company,[27] and misrepresentation by the assured's agent is fatal whether made with the assured's knowledge and consent or not.[28] Again, an insurance company will be bound by the contract of their authorised agent even where the assured is under a misapprehension that he is contracting with another company.[29] Where an agent acting for the assured submitted fraudulent evidence to the court in support of the assured's case, it was held that the assured was bound by the agent's conduct and was personally liable to meet the insurer's costs awarded on an indemnity basis to take account of the additional length of the trial caused by the presentation of fraudulent evidence.[30]

The principal will not be bound by fraudulent acts wholly outside the agent's authority.[31] The principal cannot, however, retain the benefit of his agent's fraud, for by keeping the benefit he must be taken to have adopted the act of his agent.[32]

15–005 *Imputation of knowledge from agent to principal.* There is no general doctrine that information known to an agent is imputed to his principal, as all will depend upon the relationship between the agent and the principal. Thus information in the possession of the assured's broker or other agent will not be imputed to the

[22] *National Insurance and Guarantee Corp v Imperio Reinsurance Co UK Ltd* [1999] Lloyd's Rep. I.R. 249; *Suncorp v Milano* [1993] 2 Lloyd's Rep. 225. It was accordingly held in *ING Re (UK) Ltd v R&V Versicherung AG* [2006] Lloyd's Rep. I.R. 653 that the degree of knowledge required by the principal before he can be said to have ratified is less than the degree of knowledge required by the principal before he can be said to have exonerated the agent from breach of duty.

[23] *Hagedorn v Oliverson* (1814) 2 M. & S. 485; *Cory v Patton* (1874) L.R. 9 Q.B. 577.

[24] *Houldsworth v City of Glasgow Bank* (1880) 5 App.Cas. 317.

[25] *Barwick v English Joint Stock Bank* (1867) L.R. 2 Ex. 259.

[26] *Lloyd v Grace Smith* [1912] A.C. 716; *Algemeene Bankvereeniging v Langton* (1935) 40 Com. Cas. 247.

[27] *Splents v Lefevre* (1863) 11 L.T. 114; *Refuge Insurance v Kettlewell* [1909] A.C. 243.

[28] *Fitzherbert v Mather* (1785) 1 T.R. 12.

[29] *Mackie v European* (1869) 21 L.T. 102.

[30] *National Company for Co-operative Reinsurance v St Paul Reinsurance Co Ltd* Unreported, 1998.

[31] *McGowan v Dyer* (1873) L.R. 8 Q.B. 141; *Ruben v Great Fingall Consolidated* [1906] A.C. 439; *Newsholme Brothers v Road Transport and General Insurance* [1929] 2 K.B. 356.

[32] *Refuge Insurance v Kettlewell* [1909] A.C. 243; *Lloyd v Grace Smith* [1912] A.C. 716.

assured so that the assured will not be in breach of duty for failing to disclose that information. In the case of a company information known to an individual within the company's organisation will be regarded as in the possession of the company itself only where that individual is part of the company's controlling mind, although the rule of imputation may vary depending upon the information in question and the role of the individual within the company in relation to that information. Where knowledge would otherwise be imputed, fraud on the part of the agent will prevent any imputation as it is not to be expected that the agent would inform the principal of his own fraud. Where the fraud by the agent is directed against a third party, so that the principal is no more than a secondary victim, it is unclear whether the rule precluding imputation of the agent's fraud to the assured remains applicable. In *Arab Bank v Zurich Insurance Co*[33] Rix J. held that there was no imputation in such circumstances. In *Stone & Rolls Ltd (In Liquidation) v Moore Stephens (A Firm)*[34] the Court of Appeal purported to overrule *Arab Bank* on this point, and although the House of Lords by a majority upheld the Court of Appeal's decision,[35] this point did not fall to be considered.

Undisclosed principal. In the general law, the fact that an agent is contracting as agent rather than principal need not be disclosed to the other party. It is then open to the true principal to identify himself and to take over the contract made on his behalf by the agent. As noted above, the doctrine of undisclosed principal does not extend to ratification: a principal can ratify a contract made on his behalf only where it is clear to the third party that the agent is acting on behalf of a principal. There is some doubt as to whether the doctrine of undisclosed principal can apply to insurance, as there is authority for the proposition that the true identify of the assured is a material fact which has to be disclosed to the insurers as this will be relevant to both the physical and moral hazard.[36] While it has been held, on the application of the undisclosed principal rule, that the benefit of an employer's liability policy taken out by an agent in his own name could be claimed by the principal,[37] and that a policy on building works taken out by a head contractor is capable of extending to sub-contractors whether or not it is stated to do so,[38] it may be that, if the duty of disclosure is taken into account the true rule is that an undisclosed principal can take the benefit of a contract only if the insurers are aware that the person entering into the contract is a mere agent or is likely to be insuring other interests as well as his own, in which case disclosure is to be treated as having been waived.[39]

15–006

Duties of intermediaries. Irrespective of contract, the law imposes certain minimum obligations upon intermediaries. The specific application of these obligations to insurance intermediaries will be discussed elsewhere; here follows an outline of their general scope: (1) the agent must obey his instructions precisely, although he will not necessarily fall foul of this rule if the instructions are ambiguous or cannot be obeyed lawfully; (2) the agent must exercise the degree of care and skill reasonably to be expected of an agent with the

15–007

---

[33] *Arab Bank v Zurich Insurance Co* [1999] 1 Lloyd's Rep. 262.
[34] *Stone & Rolls Ltd (In Liquidation) v Moore Stephens (A Firm)* [2008] EWCA Civ 644.
[35] *Stone & Rolls Ltd (In Liquidation) v Moore Stephens (A Firm)* [2009] UKHL 39.
[36] See Ch.6, above.
[37] *Siu v Eastern Insurance* [1994] 1 All E.R. 213.
[38] *National Oilwell v Davy Offshore* [1993] 2 Lloyd's Rep. 582.
[39] *Talbot Underwriting v Nausch, Hogan & Murray (The Jascon 5)* [2005] EWHC 2359 (Comm). Contrast the more cautious view on appeal, [2006] Lloyd's Rep. I.R. 531.

qualifications which the agent has held himself out as possessing; and (3) as a fiduciary, the agent must not allow his duty to his principal to conflict with any other interest. In particular, he must not make secret profits or accept bribes.[40] The rule is a strict one, and is justified by the considerations that an agent is required to devote his attention to the principal without the temptation of additional profit, and that the problem can easily be resolved simply by disclosure. The strict rule applies also to side contracts made by the agent with the third party, any sums received by the agent being owed to the principal without deduction.[41]

15–008 **Rights of intermediaries.** Subject to contract, an agent has a number of basic rights against his principal: (1) the right to remuneration, which is normally payable in the form of commission—if the agent is paid by commission, he must demonstrate that his conduct has brought about the contract upon which commission was payable,[42] and the right to commission will be lost where the agent is in breach of any of his primary duties or if the policy is avoided[43]; (2) the right to be indemnified in respect of any expenditure reasonably incurred by him on behalf of the principal[44]; and (3) the right to a lien on his principal's property to secure sums owing to him.

15–009 **Liabilities of intermediaries.** Where an agent has a contract with his principal, misconduct is likely to be a breach of contract and the agent may be dismissed and sued for any loss caused to the principal. The agent will also owe a parallel tortious duty to the principal as regards conduct which is fraudulent or negligent.[45]

As a general rule the role of an intermediary is to bring about a contract between his principal and a third party, and he will not face any liability towards that third party. However, there are three situations in which a third party may have a cause of action against the agent. First, the agent may have undertaken personal liability on the contract, as where the agent is acting for an undisclosed principal or where the agent signs the contract in a manner which indicates personal liability.[46] Secondly, the agent may have undertaken responsibility to the third party in a manner which justifies the imposition of a duty of care in tort,[47] although the courts have drawn back from imposing a duty of care where that duty would conflict with the agent's primary duties to his principal.[48] Thirdly, where an agent who is not personally liable on a contract acts without the

---

[40] Receiving a bribe is a criminal offence: Bribery Act 2010 s.2.

[41] *Imageview Management Ltd v Jack* [2009] EWCA Civ 63.

[42] Insurers may reserve to themselves the discretion to refuse to accept proffered business, in which case the agent is not entitled to remuneration: *Sun Alliance Pensions, Life and Investment Services v RJL and Associates* [1991] 2 Lloyd's Rep. 410.

[43] *Eagle Star Life Assurance Co Ltd v Griggs and Miles* [1998] 1 Lloyd's Rep. 256. If the policy is cancelled, the agent may be regarded as having earned that part of the commission which relates to the premium retained by the insurers, although the agency agreement may require full repayment by the agent: *Massmutual Asia Ltd v Leung Kwok Key* [2004] H.K.E.C. 517.

[44] If the agent overinsures the subject matter, he is not entitled to he indemnified for the surplus premium: *Islamic Republic of Iran Shipping Lines v Zannis Compania Naviera SA (The Tzelepi)* [1991] 2 Lloyd's Rep. 265.

[45] *Henderson v Merrett Syndicates* [1994] 3 All E.R. 506.

[46] See the cases on underwriting agents, below. See also *Domsalla v Dyason* [2007] EWHC 1174 (TCC), in which insurers opted to reinstate the assured's premises following a fire and instructed him to enter into a building contract which he signed "as agent" for the insurers: it was held that both the assured and the insurers had contractual relations with the builder.

[47] *White v Jones* [1995] 1 All E.R. 691.

[48] Cf. *Commissioners of Customs and Excise v Barclays Bank* [2006] UKHL 28.

authority of his principal, and the principal chooses not to ratify the agreement, the third party may have an action against the agent for breach of warranty of authority.[49] Liability is incurred by the agent irrespective of his state of mind,[50] and while it is not clear whether the action is grounded in contract or tort, it is settled that the proper measure of damages is contractual.[51]

Regulation of insurance intermediaries

Background. There was no statutory regulation of insurance intermediaries until **15–010** the implementation of the Insurance Brokers (Registration) Act 1977, which established a self-regulatory framework for independent intermediaries. Life intermediaries were subjected to another tier of regulation under the Financial Services Act 1986, which was concerned with the marketing of all investment contracts. Each of these measures was repealed by the Financial Services and Markets Act 2000, which maintained the regulation of the life assurance industry and provided the opportunity for the non-life sector to introduce stricter self-regulatory controls. This led to the establishment of the General Insurance Standards Council ("GISC"), but GISC foundered following a ruling by the competition authorities that its rule designed to ensure that GISC insurance companies could not deal with intermediaries who were not themselves GISC members contravened the Competition Act 1998. GISC abandoned this rule in December 2001, and almost immediately the Government announced that the fallback statutory controls in the 2000 Act would be brought into force. The decision to resort to statutory control was heavily influenced by EU initiatives. By a recommendation issued in 1991, the European Commission indicated that it was contemplating EU legislation on brokers, aimed at harmonising national rules on the regulation of brokers in order to boost the provision of insurance services across EU borders. Wording was finally agreed in 2002, and the Mediation Directive, European Parliament and Council Directive 2002/92/EC, was adopted on December 9, 2002. On January 14, 2005, the 2000 Act was duly extended to non-life intermediaries, with the Directive, being implemented as part of the same process. The changes took effect in statutory instruments[52] and modifications to the FSA Rulebook.[53]

Authorisation. "Assisting in the administration and performance of a contract of **15–011** insurance" is a regulated activity, and any person carrying on this activity in the United Kingdom must be authorised to do so but then has a single European passport entitling that person to become established in any other EEA state or to supply services directly to any other EEA state from an establishment within the EEA without regulation from the host. The equivalent right to establish or provide services in the United Kingdom is granted to persons authorised in any other EEA state. The activities regulated include: (1) arranging insurance contracts, including introducing potential policy holders to insurers or intermediaries, but not merely displaying leaflets; (2) providing specific advice on

---

[49] *Albion Fie v Mills* (1828) 3 Wills & S. 218.
[50] *Collen v Wright* (1857) 8 El. & Bl. 647; *Yonge v Toynbee* [1910] 1 K.B. 215.
[51] *V/O Rasnimport v Guthrie* [1966] 1 Lloyd's Rep. 1.
[52] Insurance Mediation Directive (Miscellaneous Amendments) Regulations 2003 (SI 2003/1473), amending the Financial Services and Markets Act 2000 (EEA Passport Rights) Regulations 2001 (SI 2001/2511); Financial Services and Markets Act 2000 (Regulated Activities) (Amendment No.2) Order 2003 (SI 2003/1476), as amended, amending the Financial Services and Markets Act 2000 (Regulated Activities) Order 2001 (SI 2001/544).
[53] See Ch.13, below.

contracts of insurance; (3) concluding contracts of insurance, including the activities of coverholders; (4) assisting in both the performance and administration of a contract of insurance; and (5) claims handling. The activities must be carried on for remuneration. Authorisation is available only to a firm that: meets the threshold conditions; has its head office in the United Kingdom; possesses adequate resources; and is a fit and proper person assessed by reference to the criteria of honesty, integrity and reputation.

Insurance broking is the main target of these rules, and a number of classes of business are excluded from the authorisation requirement. These consist, most importantly, of: expert appraisal; loss adjusting; managing claims; acting as an intermediary in relation to contracts for large (commercial risks) where the risk is situated outside the EEA; providing information about insurance contracts on an incidental basis by a person whose business is not insurance (e.g. solicitors, accountants); insurance activities carried out in connection with the sale of goods or the supply of services; activities relating to extended warranties on goods (other than motor vehicles) supplied by the person giving the insurance advice; and travel insurance linked to travel booked with the person giving the insurance advice.

Employees and appointed representatives of insurers are not within the 2000 Act and thus do not require personal authorisation. The scheme of the legislation is that the insurer in question has to be authorised and must accept responsibility for its employees and agents. These persons are to be registered on a public record that contains their names and addresses. If a person is removed from the register by the FSA on the ground that he is not a fit and proper person to carry on insurance mediation activities he may no longer be appointed by an insurer as its employee or agent.

15–012   *Conduct of business.* In accordance with the FSA's Handbook, a broker's business has to be conducted with integrity, skill, care and diligence, maintaining adequate financial resources, avoiding conflicts of interest and giving suitable advice. The Prudential Rules ("PRU") demand: all persons in the management structure and staff involved directly in mediation to be of good repute (no relevant convictions or bankruptcy adjudications); capital resource requirements in the form of a basic solvency margin; and liability insurance. The Senior Management Arrangements, Systems and Controls Rules ("SYSC") require an apportionment of responsibilities amongst directors and managers, ensuring that affairs can be adequately monitored and regulatory obligations are complied with. The Supervision Rules ("SUP") requires reporting by intermediaries, in the form of a Retail Mediation Activities Return, twice each year, plus ad hoc reporting of significant matters. There is also a requirement to appoint an auditor. The Training and Competence Rules ("TC") lay down a general obligation to ensure that employees are competent and adequately supervised, and a further obligation to take knowledge and skills into account when recruiting. Appropriate training must be provided and an employee must not be allowed to carry out a task for which he is not competent. The Client Assets Rules ("CASS") apply to client money held in the course or in connection with a mediation activity (other than premiums received by the broker in its capacity as agent for insurers). Client money is to be held on trust and in separate accounts. Also, client documents to be kept safely.

The most important day-to-day aspects of the regulation of insurance intermediary activity are contained in the Insurance Conduct of Business Sourcebook ("ICOBS") for general insurance and in the Conduct of Business Sourcebook ("COBS") for long-term insurance. It is necessary for intermediaries to disclose their status, including links with insurers, to the assured, although if the intermediary's role is limited to effecting introductions (i.e. it is an "introducer") then it need disclose only its name and address and whether it is a member as the same group as the insurers on whose behalf the introduction is being made. The essence of this principle is that the assured must be made aware of whether he is or is not being given advice on the basis of a fair analysis of the market (ICOBS 4.1), and fair analysis advice must be properly given (ICOBS 5.3). The intermediary is required to disclose its fees, but not the amount of any commission (ICOBS 4.3). If an intermediary becomes involved in claims handling, he is required to manage conflicts of interest fairly, in particular through disclosure and consent (ICOBS 8.3).

2. Agents of Insurers

The authority of agents. Insurance companies by virtue of their legal capacity are required to act through agents. Agents employed by insurers who deal with assureds may be classified generally as: employees of the insurer who are concerned with receiving applications, issuing policies and settling claims[54]; selling agents, who are not full employees[55] but are remunerated fully or partly by way of commission and whose function is to obtain proposals for consideration by the insurer; underwriting agents, whose function is to accept risks on behalf of insurers under some form of authority; and loss adjusters who are employed to investigate and settle claims.[56] The insurer will be bound by any acts carried out by the agent acting within the scope of his authority. Further, under s.39 of the Financial Services and Markets Act 2000, the insurer is responsible for the actions and defaults of its appointed representatives, and for that reason minimum training standards will be imposed upon agents.[57]

15–013

Agents of the insurer will be in contact with the assured at every stage in the formation and operation of a policy. The agent may, according to the circumstances, be required either to perform an act on behalf of the insurer or to receive information on behalf of the insurer. The only question in every case is whether the agent has the requisite authority, actual or ostensible, to act or to receive information. Every case will necessarily turn on its facts, in particular the status of the agent and whether any limitations on the agent's authority have been brought to the assured's attention. It is possible to say, by way of broad generalisation, that an agent in a branch office will not normally have the actual authority to take binding decisions in relation to matters connected with the validity or scope of a policy, as these are concerns of the insurer's head office. Similarly, the scope of the actual authority of a mere canvassing or collecting agent is likely to be limited. However, it is common practice for assureds to seek advice from, or to pass on information to, unauthorised agents, and the insurer

---

[54] The administrative aspects of these functions may be outsourced by supplying "back-office" services. Such firms are not insurance agents: *Staatssecretaris van Financien v Arthur Andersen & Co*, (Case C-472/03) [2007] Lloyd's Rep. I.R. 484.

[55] They may be other financial institutions or suppliers of goods or services offering insurance as part of an overall package. The courts have assumed, wrongly it is submitted, that such agents act for the assured and not for insurers: *Woolcott v Sun Alliance & London Insurance Co Ltd* [1978] 1 All E.R. 1253; *Orakpo v Barclays Insurance Services Ltd* [1995] L.R.L.R. 443.

[56] Loss adjusters do not owe duties of care to the assured: *South Pacific Manufacturing v New Zealand Consultants* [1992] 2 N.Z.L.R. 282.

[57] *Eagle Star Life Assurance Co Ltd v Griggs and Miles* [1998] 1 Lloyd's Rep. 256.

may well find itself estopped from denying their authority if it has in the past not taken any objection to this procedure and if there is nothing inconsistent with the appearance of authority in the policy or other contractual documentation.

The assured cannot rely upon ostensible authority where the insurer has brought to his attention any limits on the usual powers of the agent, e.g. by means of provisions in documentation given to the assured, which are inconsistent with the agent's assertion of authority.[58] So where the assured has notice[59] by a condition in a proposal form,[60] receipt[61] or policy[62] he cannot afterwards make the insurer liable.[63]

Illustrations of authority

15–014   *Payment of the premium.* Where an agent is expressly authorised to receive the premium from the assured, or is not authorised but his practice of doing so is acquiesced in by the insurers, any payment made to the agent which is not passed on to the insurers is nevertheless deemed to have been received by them.[64] Similarly, an agent who issues a receipt for a premium which has not been paid by the assured may estop the insurers from denying actual receipt.[65] The position is necessarily different where the assured is aware that the agent is not empowered to accept the premium, or where the policy makes it clear that the procedure adopted by the agent is not authorised.[66] Whether a local agent has authority to receive premiums will depend upon the circumstances of each case.[67] Authority to receive premiums does not necessarily imply authority to give credit or receive premiums overdue.[68]

15–015   *The issue of a policy.* A policy of insurance is normally to be issued from, and its terms settled at, the insurers' head office, so that it will be rare for an agent to be found to possess the authority to bind the insurer to the issue of a policy either at all or on given terms.[69] The agent's want of authority may well be known by the assured.[70] The position may be different where the agent is of some seniority, such as a director of the insurer, but even here any express limitation on his authority known to the assured will prevent a binding contract from coming into being unless ratified by the insurers.[71] The agent's duties are normally limited to receiving and submitting proposals made. Agents may, however, have ostensible authority to give temporary cover pending the insurer's

---

[58] *Acey v Fernie* (1840) 7 M. & W. 153; *Baines v Ewing* (1866) L.R. 1 Exch. 320; *Jenkins v Deane* (1933) 47 Ll.L.R. 342; *Wilkinson v GAFLAC* [1967] 2 Lloyd's Rep. 182.

[59] *Hood v Anchor Line* [1918] A.C. 837.

[60] *Levy v Scottish Employers* (1901) 17 T.L.R. 229.

[61] *Acey v Fernie* (1840) 7 M. & W. 153.

[62] *Biggar v Rock Life* [1902] 1 K.B. 516; *M'Millan v Accident Insurance*, 1907 S.C. 484.

[63] *Horncastle v Equitable Life* (1906) 22 T.L.R. 388; *Comerford v Britannic* (1908) 24 T.L.R. 593; *Baines v Ewing* (1866) L.R. 1 Ex. 320.

[64] *Kelly v London & Staffordshire Fire Insurance Co* (1833) Cab. & El. 47.

[65] *Re Economic Fire Office Ltd* (1896) 12 T.L.R. 142.

[66] *Towle v National Guardian Insurance Society* (1861) 30 L.J. Ch. 900.

[67] *Rossiter v Trafalgar Life* (1879) 27 Beav. 377; *Linford v Provincial Horse & Cattle Insurance* (1864) 34 Beav. 291.

[68] *Acey v Fernie* (1840) 7 M. & W. 153; *London & Lancashire Life v Fleming* [1897] A.C. 499.

[69] *Linford v Provincial Horse and Cattle Insurance Co* (1864) 34 Beav. 291; *Gale v Lewis* (1846) 9 Q.B. 730; *Zurich General Accident and Liability Insurance Co Ltd v Buck* (1939) 64 Ll. L.R. 115.

[70] *Wilkinson v General Accident Fire and Life Assurance Corp* [1967] 2 Lloyd's Rep. 182.

[71] *Baines v Ewing* (1866) L.R. 1 Exch. 320.

decision on a proposal, and this was held to be the case where the agent was in the habit of giving temporary cover with the knowledge and consent of the insurer even though there was no actual authorisation in this respect.[72] It has also been held that where a company supplied its agent with a book of printed forms, the agent had ostensible authority to make contracts on its behalf in accordance with the terms of those forms.[73] The reinstatement of a policy which has lapsed, in the form of the agent accepting a late renewal premium, will again not be binding on the insurers unless there is a holding out by the insurer that the agent is so authorised.[74] An underwriter, by reason of ostensible authority, may be liable on policies made on his behalf by one who had ceased to be his agent where the underwriter has failed to give notice to the assured that the agency has terminated.[75] Local agents have been held not to have ostensible authority to vary the terms of the company's policies.[76]

Waiver of breach of condition or warranty. An agent whose actual authority is limited to the ministerial acts of collecting premiums and issuing receipts cannot bind the insurers as to the issue or reinstatement of a policy, although it was held in *Wing v Harvey*[77] that an agent of this status had been held out as having authority to receive renewal premiums and thereby to waive the assured's breach of a condition relating to the country of his residence.   **15–016**

Receipt of information. An agent may be authorised to receive information on the insurers' behalf, in which case receipt by the agent is deemed to be receipt by the insurers, or he may be authorised to transmit information to the insurers, in which case the insurers are deemed to have received the information at a time when it ought to have been received had it been duly transmitted.[78] Alternatively, there may be situations in which the information passed to the agent is outside his sphere of operation, for example where notice of loss is given to a branch office and, in the absence of a general doctrine of imputation of knowledge from agent to principal or of any principle of constructive knowledge, then whether or not the insurer is deemed to have received the information will turn upon estoppel and the wording of the policy.   **15–017**

Estoppel will be made out where the agent has been allowed in the past to act as the recipient for information, to the knowledge of the assured, and the issue has arisen with regard to a number of items of information, including: notification by the assured of persons within the policy[79]; disclosure by the assured of the true nature of his occupation and the extent of the risk[80]; knowledge of breach of condition[81]; notice of assignment[82]; notice of termination

---

[72] *Murfitt v Royal* (1922) 38 T.L.R. 334.
[73] *Mackie v European* (1869) 21 L.T. 102.
[74] *Acey v Fernie* (1840) 7 M. & W. 151.
[75] *Willis, Faber v Joyce* (1911) 27 T.L.R. 388.
[76] *London and Lancashire Life v Fleming* [1897] A.C. 499; *Comerford v Britannic Assurance* (1908) 24 T.L.R. 593; *Gliksten v State Insurance* (1922) 10 Ll. L.R. 604.
[77] *Wing v Harvey* (1854) De G.M. & G. 265.
[78] *Proudfoot v Montefiore* (1867) L.R. 2 Q.B. 511. Cf. *Malhi v Abbey Life Assurance Co Ltd* [1996] L.R.L.R. 237.
[79] *Jenkins v Deane* (1933) 47 Ll. L.R. 342.
[80] *Ayrey v British Legal and United Providence Assurance Co Ltd* [1918] 1 K.B. 136; *Evans v Employers Mutual* [1936] 1 K.B. 505.
[81] *Wing v Harvey* (1854) De G.M. & G. 265.
[82] *Gale v Lewis* (1846) 9 Q.B. 730; *Jenkins v Deane* (1933) 47 Ll. L.R. 342.

by the assured[83]; notice of loss[84]; and the obtaining of information during the investigation of the circumstances of a loss.[85]

15–018   *Misstatements as to the extent of policy coverage.* An agent who falsely states the scope of a policy to a prospective assured faces criminal liability if his conduct was intentional or reckless.[86] Where the agent is acting in respect of a policy which is within the Financial Services and Markets Act 2000, false statements as to coverage will also impose criminal liability on the insurers (s.39). However, the statutory structure does not assist the assured directly, for there are no civil sanctions under the legislation and he remains the owner of a policy which does not cover the risks intended by him that it should cover. The assured may well have an action against the agent for breach of warranty of authority, although if it is the case that such an action proves to be worthless the question becomes whether he has any action against the insurers whereby the policy is to be regarded as extending to the anticipated risks. Any such action is conditional on it being demonstrated that the agent had authority either to alter the terms of an existing policy or, where the policy has yet to be issued, to bind the insurers as to the scope of that policy. If authority can be shown, the insurers may well be estopped from denying that the coverage is as stated by its agent. If the agent does not have the authority to vary the terms of the contract,[87] as where the policy itself removes from the agent the authority to make statements about coverage,[88] then the assured cannot claim the promised extended coverage.[89]

15–019   *Completion of proposal forms.* It was at one time the practice of insurers to instruct their agents to assist the assured in the completion of any proposal form, frequently by asking the assured appropriate questions and transcribing his oral answers on to the form, which is then presented to the assured for his signature. Difficulties will subsequently arise where the form contains a material mis-representation, or where a material fact which ought to have been disclosed to the insurers does not appear on the form, as it has to be determined whether the insurers are entitled to avoid the contract for the assured's breach of his duty of utmost good faith. Four situations have to be distinguished.

First, the assured has given a false answer to the agent, who has faithfully inserted that answer into the proposal form. Here the assured is guilty of mis-representation.

Secondly, the assured has given a true answer to the agent, but for one or other reason, ranging from fraud to accidental error, the agent has inserted an incorrect answer. The correct question here, it is submitted, is whether the agent's knowledge is imputed to the insurers, which will be the case where the agent is authorised to receive the information or has been held out by the insurers as

---

[83] *Re Solvency Mutual Guarantee Co* (1862) 31 L.J. Ch. 625.

[84] *Marsden v City and Country Assurance Co* (1865) L.R. 1 C.P. 232; *Brook v Trafalgar Insurance Co Ltd* (1946) 79 Ll. L.R. 365.

[85] *Evans v Employers Mutual* [1936] 1 K.B. 505.

[86] Financial Services and Markets Act 2000 s.397.

[87] *Re Hooley Hill Rubber and Chemical Co Ltd* [1920] 1 K.B. 257.

[88] *Horncastle v Equitable Life Assurance Society of the United States* (1906) 22 T.L.R. 735; *Comerford v Britannic Assurance Co Ltd* (1908) 24 T.L.R. 593.

[89] But see *Curtis v Chemical Cleaning and Dyeing Co* [1951] 1 K.B. 805: exclusion clause could not be relied upon following misrepresentation as to its effects.

having the authority to do so.[90] However, there are some decisions which focus not on the authority of the agent to receive information but rather on the authority of the agent to complete the proposal form, and it has been held that in the absence of express authority the agent is to be treated as the amanuensis of the assured in completing the form, that the assured is to blame for signing the document without reading it and that the document constitutes the entire agreement between the parties which cannot be varied by evidence of oral negotiations.[91] The latter view appears to have prevailed.[92]

Thirdly, a material fact which ought to have been disclosed to the insurers (no express question having been contained in the form) does not appear on the form, although the evidence demonstrates that the assured had given the necessary information to the agent but the agent had neglected to add it to the answers on the form. Once again, the question is whether the agent's knowledge can be imputed to the insurers.

Fourthly, a material fact which ought to have been disclosed to the insurers on the form (no express question having been contained in the form) does not appear on the form, and the evidence demonstrates that the assured had not been alerted to his duty to disclose material facts. In this situation it has been held that, as long as the agent has authority to waive information, the insurers cannot rely upon non-disclosure.[93]

3. UNDERWRITING AGENTS

Nature. Underwriting agencies have come to play a significant role in the formation and administration of insurance, reinsurance and retrocession agreements. An underwriting agency operates in much the same manner as might be expected of a branch of an insurance company, by assessing risks, determining the premium to be charged, fixing the terms of the agreement, executing any necessary documentation and arranging reinsurance for the insurers. **15–020**

[90] *Brewster v National Life Insurance Society* (1892) 8 T.L.R. 648; *Bawden v London, Edinburgh and Glasgow Assurance Co* [1892] 2 Q.B. 534; *Cruickshank v Northern Accident Insurance* (1895) 33 S.L.R. 134; *Holdsworth v Lancashire and Yorkshire Insurance Co* (1907) 23 T.L.R. 521; *Thornton-Smith v Motor Union Insurance Co Ltd* (1913) 30 T.L.R. 139; *Golding v Royal London Auxiliary Insurance Co* (1914) 30 T.L.R. 350; *Keeling v Pearl Assurance Co Ltd* (1923) 129 L.T. 573; *Kaufmann v British Surety Insurance Co Ltd* (1929) 45 T.L.R. 399. See also *Keeling v Pearl Assurance Co Ltd* (1923) 129 L.T. 573 (proposal signed in blank).

[91] *Newsholme Brothers v Road Transport and General Insurance Co Ltd* [1929] 2 K.B. 356, a decision predicated by *Biggar v Rock Life Assurance Co* [1902] 1 K.B. 516, *Hough v Guardian Fire and Life Assurance Co Ltd* (1902) 18 T.L.R. 273 and *Paxman v Union Assurance Society Ltd* (1923) 39 T.L.R. 424. See also: *Yule v Life and Health Assurance Association* 1904 6 R. 347; *M'Millan v Accident Insurance Co* 1907 S.C. 484; *Taylor v Yorkshire Insurance Co Ltd* [1913] I.R. 1.

[92] *Dunn v Ocean Accident and Guarantee Corporation Ltd* (1933) 50 T.L.R. 32; *Facer v Vehicle and General Insurance Co Ltd* [1956] 1 Lloyd's Rep. 113. Although in *Stone v Reliance Mutual Insurance Association* [1972] 1 Lloyd's Rep. 469 Lord Denning, obiter, preferred the former approach. The English and Scottish Law Commissions, in their Consultation Paper No.182 issued in July 2007, have recommended the statutory reversal of the *Newsholme* rule. The proposal is that an intermediary who would normally be regarded as acting for the insurer in obtaining pre-contract information should remain the insurer's agent while completing a proposal form, a principle which should apply to both business and consumer policies. It is also provisionally proposed the assured's signature on a proposal form that has been completed incorrectly by a third person should not be regarded as conclusive evidence that the insured knew of or adopted what was written on the form.

[93] *Stone v Reliance Mutual Insurance Association* [1972] 1 Lloyd's Rep. 469. Contrast *Arterial Caravans Ltd v Yorkshire Insurance Co Ltd* [1973] 1 Lloyd's Rep. 169.

An underwriting agency will generally underwrite on behalf of a number of principals, in a "pool".[94] The insurers in the pool will agree the proportions of accepted risks which they will accept. The agency will, particularly where there is a need for the risk to be covered by an insurer authorised to carry on business in the relevant place, accept business on behalf of a single member of the pool (the "fronting" company), and then reinsure the fronting company with the remaining members of the pool by the fronting company so that the agreed proportions agreed between the members are maintained. Typically, the underwriting agency will also arrange a further outwards reinsurance or retrocession to cover the operations of the pool. The underwriting agent will also accept premiums and pay losses on behalf of the members, pending a periodic settlement of account between the parties, and the members will in turn often be under a contractual duty to keep the underwriting agent in funds.[95] The underwriting agency will commonly be required to maintain separate accounts for underwriting receipts.[96] The contract will also, typically, confer upon the pool the right to examine the underwriting agent's books and records,[97] a right which is presumed, subject to express wording to the contrary, to operate even after the underwriting agency agreement has come to an end.[98] Once the pool has ceased to operate, the underwriting agent may be charged with the duties of managing the run-off of the liabilities of individual pool members[99] and dealing with the pool's external reinsurers.[100]

The above processes may, on analysis, be seen to consist of a number of different contractual arrangements: (a) a contract of insurance between the assured and the pool fronting company; (b) a reinsurance agreement between the fronting company and the other pool members; (c) a retrocession agreement

[94] Insurance and reinsurance pools are permitted under UK and EU competition law: see Ch.13, above.

[95] Premiums paid into the pool's account by the underwriting agent pending settlement are the property of the pool, subject to any lien or charge in favour of the underwriting agent: *Kingscroft Insurance Co Ltd v HS Weavers (Underwriting) Agencies Ltd* [1993] 1 Lloyd's Rep. 187.

[96] *D P Mann v Coutts & Co* [2003] EWHC 2138 (Comm).

[97] *New Hampshire Insurance Co v Whiteley* [2003] EWHC 1613 (Comm).

[98] *Yasuda Fire and Marine Insurance Co of Europe Ltd v Orion Marine Insurance Underwriting Agency Ltd* [1995] 1 Lloyd's Rep. 525.

[99] *Sphere Drake Insurance Plc v Basler Versicherungs* [1998] Lloyd's Rep. I.R. 35. In *Europ Assistance Insurance Ltd v Temple Legal Protection Ltd* [2008] Lloyd's Rep. I.R. 216 it was argued by the underwriting agent that the agreement between itself and the underwriters under which the agent was to conduct run-off was irrevocable. Langley J. refused the underwriters' application for a temporary injunction pending trial of the issue as to whether the agreement could be terminated, on the grounds that: the underwriters' alleged causes of action against the agent were "thin"; the agent would be placed in breach of contracts made in its own name with coverholders authorised by it to write business; and the underwriters could protect themselves by exercising inspection rights. *Europ* was an interlocutory action. In *Temple Legal Protection Ltd v QBE Insurance (Europe) Ltd* [2009] Lloyd's Rep. I.R. 544 a majority of the Court of Appeal held that the phrase that, on termination, "unless otherwise agreed in writing by QBE, Temple shall remain liable to perform its obligations in accordance with the terms and conditions of this Agreement in respect of all insurances bound prior to Termination until every such insurance has expired or has otherwise been terminated" did not confer upon Temple as the underwriting agent the right to conduct run-off, but merely required it to do so if QBE as insurers so demanded. Accordingly, QBE was entitled to withdraw the authority of Temple to conduct run-off following the expiry of the underwriting agency agreement. Rix L.J. agreed with the result, but on different ground that the agent was entitled to conduct the run-off but had lost that right by reason of its repudiatory breach of the binder.

[100] *Wurtembergische Akt v Home Insurance Co (No.1)* Unreported, 1994; *Wurtembergische Akt v Home Insurance Co (No.2)* [1997] L.R.L.R. 86.

between the pool members, including the fronting company, and the retro-cessionaires who are reinsuring the activities of the pool; (d) a management agreement between the pool members and the underwriting agency setting out the terms and conditions of the latter's authority to undertake the management of the pool's affairs—the agreement is not contract of insurance but it may impose on the agent a duty of utmost good faith on renewal requiring disclosure of the activities undertaken in previous years[101]; and (e) an implied agreement between the members of the pool that they will each observe their individual agreements with the underwriting agency as pool manager.[102]

Regulation. Section 19 of the Financial Services and Markets Act 2000 prohibits any person from carrying on a regulated activity unless he is authorised under the legislation. The Act in its original form applied only to persons carrying on insurance business in the United Kingdom in the capacity of underwriter, and was not concerned with intermediaries. That meant that an underwriting agent had to be authorised only if it carried on insurance business in its own right, which was held not to be the case.[103] However, as a result of the extension of the legislation in January 2005, persons assisting in the administration and performance of a contract of insurance have to be authorised. Accordingly, underwriting agents have to be authorised and have to seek permission to carry on the regulated activity of intermediary. Accordingly, if the underwriting agent is not an authorised person at all, he commits a criminal offence and if he is an authorised person with respect to activities as an insurance intermediary but has—which is most unlikely[104]—crossed the line into carrying on insurance business without permission then there is no criminality involved.[105] Care should be taken by offshore insurers and reinsurers who operate through an underwriting agent carrying on business as an intermediary in the United Kingdom, as the underwriters themselves may be found to be carrying on insurance business in the United Kingdom by reason of their agent's UK activities.[106]

15–021

Accepting business. The role of the underwriting agent is to procure business for the pool in accordance with the limitations laid down in the management agreement. The question whether pool members are bound by an agreement outside these limits made by the underwriting agent on behalf of the pool depends upon ordinary agency principles. An agent who acts without actual authority may nevertheless bind the pool if he has been held out as possessing the

15–022

---

[101] *Pryke v Gibbs Hartley Cooper* [1991] 2 Lloyd's Rep. 602. Contrast *Mercantile Mutual Holdings Ltd v Territory Insurance Office* [1989] 5 ANZ Cases 60–939.

[102] *North Atlantic Insurance Co Ltd v Nationwide General Insurance Co* [2004] Lloyd's Rep. I.R. 466.

[103] *Re Great Western Insurance Co SA* [1999] Lloyd's Rep. I.R. 377, rejecting dicta in *Re a Company No.007923 of 1994*, Unreported, 1995. But see *Re Whiteley Insurance Consultants* [2009] Lloyd's Rep. I.R. 212, where an underwriting agent who issued policies outside the scope of its mandate, and then paid claims, was held to have been conducting unauthorised insurance business.

[104] *Re Great Western Insurance Co SA* [1999] Lloyd's Rep. I.R. 377.

[105] Under s.21.

[106] *DR Insurance Co v Seguros America Banamex* [1993] 1 Lloyd's Rep. 120, followed in *L'Alsacienne Premiere Societe Alsacienne et Lorraine D'Assurances Centre L'Incendie et Les Risques Divers v Unistorebrand International Insurance AS* [1995] L.R.L.R. 333.

necessary authority[107] or if his conduct has been ratified,[108] although ratification does not exonerate the agent from an action for breach of duty.[109]

An underwriting agent, when accepting business for the pool, owes both duties of care and fiduciary duties to the pool members. There is breach of duty if the agent: (a) puts his own interest in obtaining commission by failing to make a genuine assessment of the business presented to him by brokers; and (b) fails to report all material information concerning the business underwritten.[110] Serious breach of these duties entitles the underwriters to terminate the agency relationship, including other agency contracts between the parties, and to seek damages.[111]

A particular issue of authority relates to fronting. It is crucial to determine whether the actions of the underwriting agent in nominating a pool member to front a risk are binding upon that pool member. If the underwriting agent binds a pool member to fronting arrangements, the fronting company may find that it is bound to make payment to the assured and will have to turn to the underwriting agent for indemnification in the event that the reinsurance provided by the pool is irrecoverable by reason of insolvency.[112] The scope of the authority given to an underwriting agent to use a pool member as a fronting company depends upon the nature of the wording used, although in the absence of actual authority the fronting company may be bound by ostensible authority or if it chooses to ratify the underwriting agent's actions.[113]

Where the broker is authorised to use a pool member as a fronting company it is to be implied into the pool agreement that the remaining members of the pool have agreed to reinsure the fronting company.[114] However, if there is no authority to nominate a fronting company and the underwriting agent does so in breach of his duty, there is no implied obligation on the remaining pool members to act as reinsurers of the fronting company.[115] Equally, if the members of a pool authorise the underwriting agent to write business for a given percentage for each subscriber, and one of the members leaves the pool, the agent does not have the

---

[107] *ING Re (UK) Ltd v R&V Versicherung AG* [2006] Lloyd's Rep. I.R. 653.

[108] *ING Re (UK) Ltd v R&V Versicherung AG* [2006] Lloyd's Rep. I.R. 653.

[109] *Suncorp Insurance and Finance v Milano Assicurazioni SpA* [1993] 2 Lloyd's Rep. 225; *Markel International Insurance Co v Surety Guarantee Consultants Ltd* [2009] Lloyd's Rep. I.R. 77. In the subsequent ruling in *Markel International Insurance Co v Surety Guarantee Consultants Ltd (No.2)* [2008] EWHC 1135 (Comm) the court considered the measure of damages against defaulting individuals. In a second sequel, *Markel International Insurance Co Ltd v Higgins* [2009] EWCA Civ 790 the Court of Appeal rejected an appeal by one of the individual defendants, in which he had asserted that he had not been responsible for his acts by reason of suffering from Alzheimer's Disease.

[110] *Sphere Drake Insurance Ltd v Euro International Underwriting Ltd* [2003] Lloyd's Rep. I.R. 525.

[111] *R+V Versicherung AG v Risk Insurance & Reinsurance Solutions SA* [2006] Lloyd's Rep. I.R. 253. See also *R+V Versicherung AG v Risk Insurance & Reinsurance Solutions SA (No.2)* [2006] EWHC 42 (Comm), where the damages awarded were held to include the costs of investigating the agent's activities.

[112] See the facts of *Companhia de Seguros Irnperio v Heath (REBX) Ltd* [1999] Lloyd's Rep. I.R. 571.

[113] *Suncorp Insurance and Finance v Milano Assicurazioni SpA* [1993] 2 Lloyd's Rep. 225; *Yona International Ltd v La Réunion Franaise SA d'Assurances et de Reassurances* [1996] 2 Lloyd's Rep. 84.

[114] *Deutsche Ruck AG v Zion Insurance Co Ltd* Unreported, 2001; *North Atlantic Insurance Co Ltd v Nationwide General Insurance Co* [2004] Lloyd's Rep. I.R. 466.

[115] *Deutsche Ruckversicherung AG v La Fondaria Assicurazioni SpA* Unreported, 2001.

authority—unless the agreement otherwise provides—to raise the subscription percentages of other members of the pool so as to make good the shortfall.[116]

The pool's outwards reinsurance

Placement. The primary purpose of any reinsurance procured by pool members is to reinsure them against liabilities arising to third parties to whom pool members have issued policies. Unless the wording is clear, an external reinsurance of a pool is a composite policy which covers each pool member for its own rights and liabilities,[117] so that the reinsurance of a pool member covers only its agreed share of the pool's liabilities[118] and not any additional liabilities assumed by the member on the insolvency of other pool members.[119] A policy issued to an underwriting agent on behalf of a pool is to be construed as covering the membership of the pool at the time of the claim, even though the identity of the members has changed from time to time: reinsurance of a pool is to be regarded as a standing offer which is accepted by a new member when it joins the pool.[120]

15–023

The placement of outwards reinsurance is in the hands of the underwriting agent, although in practice the placement will be made by a placing broker. Failure by the placing broker to disclose a material fact which he, the underwriting agent and the pool members did not know or could not reasonably have known in the course of their business will not give the reinsurers the right to avoid the reinsurance, although it is unclear whether a fact known to the underwriting agent but not to pool members has to be disclosed to reinsurers as there is no general doctrine of imputation of knowledge from the agent to the pool[121] and there conflicting decisions on the question whether an intermediate agent (such as an underwriting agent) is an "agent to insure" who owes duties of disclosure under s.19 of the Marine Insurance Act 1906.[122]

The facts material to a reinsurance of pool liability are more or less the same as those material to an ordinary reinsurance agreement. The most important material facts relate to the scope of the direct policies and the pool's loss experience. Internal reinsurance arrangements within the pool are not material.[123] It is undecided whether the fact that the underwriting agent has defrauded the pool is material, as in the cases decided to date that fact was unknown to the pool members and therefore (a) could not be disclosed by them and (b) could not be expected to be disclosed by the agent itself,[124] although there is authority for the

---

[116] *Feasey v Sun Life Assurance Company of Canada* [2003] Lloyd's Rep. I.R. 637.

[117] *Pan Atlantic Insurance Co Ltd v Pine Top Insurance Co Ltd* [1989] 1 Lloyd's Rep. 568; *North Atlantic Insurance Co Ltd v Nationwide General Insurance Co* [2004] Lloyd's Rep. I.R. 466.

[118] Evem though incurred through the negligence of the underwriting agent.

[119] *Wurtembergische Akt v Home Insurance Co (No.3)* [1999] Lloyd's Rep. I.R. 397.

[120] *Kingscroft Insurance Co Ltd v Nissan Fire & Marine Insurance Co Ltd (No.2)* [1999] Lloyd's Rep. I.R. 603.

[121] *Group Josi Re v Walbrook Insurance* [1996] 1 All E.R. 791 and *PCW Syndicates v PCW Insurers* [1996] 1 Lloyd's Rep. 241; *Arab Bank v Zurich Insurance Co* [1999] 1 Lloyd's Rep. 262; *Kingscroft Insurance Co Ltd v Nissan Fire & Marine Insurance Co Ltd* [1999] Lloyd's Rep. I.R. 371.

[122] In *Group Josi Re v Walbrook Insurance* [1996] 1 All E.R. 791 and *PCW Syndicates v PCW Insurers* [1996] 1 Lloyd's Rep. 241 the Court of Appeal was divided on the point; see Ch.6, above.

[123] *Kingscroft Insurance Co Ltd v Nissan Fire & Marine Insurance Co Ltd (No.2)* [1999] Lloyd's Rep. I.R. 603.

[124] *Group Josi Re v Walbrook Insurance* [1996] 1 All E.R. 791 and *PCW Syndicates v PCW Insurers* [1996] 1 Lloyd's Rep. 241; *Arab Bank v Zurich Insurance Co* [1999] 1 Lloyd's Rep. 262; *Kingscroft Insurance Co Ltd v Nissan Fire & Marine Insurance Co Ltd* [1999] Lloyd's Rep. I.R. 371.

proposition that fraud, if known by pool members, would be a material fact.[125]

15–024 *Claiming outwards reinsurance recoveries.* The external reinsurance placed by an underwriting agent on behalf of a pool may identify the reinsured in a number of different ways. Some policies identify the agent itself as the reinsured, whereas others refer to the fronting companies within the pool or the individual members of the pool. It would nevertheless seem that, irrespective of the description used, the underwriting agent itself is empowered to bring an action against the reinsurers.[126] An individual pool member also has the right to sue on the reinsurance, and it has been held that any one member may bring a representative action[127] on behalf of the membership of the pool as a whole, given that the interests of the pool members are common.[128] It is also arguable that a pool member has a pervasive insurable interest which permits an action against the reinsurers for the full sum reinsured, the proceeds thereby recovered being held by the pool member for other members.[129]

15–025 *Allocation of outwards reinsurance recoveries.* The substantive question, following recovery of outwards reinsurance proceeds by the underwriting agent or a pool member, is the manner in which the proceeds are to be allocated amongst the members of the pool. Where all of the members of the pool are solvent no real difficulty arises because the proceeds are simply to be allocated to each member in accordance with its proportionate share on the basis of the notion that the reinsurance is a composite contract that covers each pool member to the extent of its own interest.

The allocation issue becomes acute where one or more members have become insolvent. Suppose that a pool has four members each contributing equally, A, B, C and D, and it is agreed that A is to front a risk for the pool. The internal arrangement is that A is the insurer for 100 per cent of the risk, but will be reinsured by each of B, C and D for 25 per cent of the risk. External reinsurance is then taken out in the name of A for 80 per cent of the exposure. Losses occur and the pool receives the external reinsurance. At this point B becomes insolvent and is unable to pay A its 25 per cent share of the risk. Two possibilities arise in respect of the reinsurance proceeds. The first is that A is the beneficial owner of the external reinsurance proceeds, and so is entitled to retain those proceeds against the administrators or liquidators of B. On this analysis, A is owed 25 per cent of the risk (by B), but is entitled to retain B's 25 per cent share (20 per cent of the overall risk) of the external reinsurance. The second is that B is the beneficial owner of the reinsurance proceeds. In that situation, A is then simply an unsecured creditor as against B for the full 25 per cent of the risk, and can only sit back and watch as B's 25 per cent share of the external reinsurance is allocated by way of dividend between A and other creditors of B. It was held in

[125] *Deutsche Ruck Akt v Walbrook Insurance Co Ltd* [1994] 4 All E.R. 151. Cf. *ERC Frankona Reinsurance v American National Insurance Co* [2006] Lloyd's Rep. I.R. 157.

[126] *Transcontinental Underwriting Agency v Grand Union Insurance Co Ltd* [1987] 2 Lloyd's Rep. 409; *North Atlantic Insurance Co Ltd v Nationwide General Insurance Co* [2004] Lloyd's Rep. I.R. 466. But note the ruling in *Markel Capital Ltd v Gothaer Allgemeine Versicherung AG* [2009] Lloyd's Rep. I.R. 433, where it was found that the underwriting agent was not itself a "reinsured" but merely an agent for the pool members.

[127] Under CPR r.19.6.

[128] *Pan Atlantic Insurance Co Ltd v Pine Top Insurance Co Ltd* [1989] 1 Lloyd's Rep. 568.

[129] *Transcontinental Underwriting Agency v Grand Union Insurance Co Ltd* [1987] 2 Lloyd's Rep. 409; *Pan Atlantic Insurance Co Ltd v Pine Top Insurance Co Ltd* [1989] 1 Lloyd's Rep. 568.

North Atlantic Insurance Co Ltd v Nationwide General Insurance Co[130] that the ownership of the outwards reinsurance proceeds depended upon identifying the parties to the reinsurance agreements, as determined by the proper construction of the reinsurance agreements and the arrangements within the pool. Waller L.J. identified two possible approaches which might have been taken by the parties: the "direct" method under which the proceeds of the reinsurance belonged beneficially to the fronting company; and the "indirect" method under which the proceeds belonged beneficially to the members of the pool, but subject to a contractual obligation—by means of the pool's internal reinsurance arrangements—to pay those proceeds to the fronting company, an obligation which could not be fulfilled in the event of an insolvency. On the facts the Court of Appeal was satisfied that the indirect approach had been taken and that the fronting companies could not assert ownership of the reinsurance proceeds, partly because the fronting arrangements had been made after the reinsurance arrangements had been made and partly because the outwards reinsurances referred to the pool membership as a whole rather than the fronting companies. If it is the case that each pool member has a right to the reinsurance proceeds applicable to its own proportion of pool risk, it was also held in *North Atlantic* that, in the absence of express wording, those proceeds are not held on trust for fronting companies in the event of an insolvency.

4. BROKERS

The role of brokers

Definition. Brokers are independent agents[131] appointed by the assured to carry out various functions, including advice and placement,[132] post-contractual   **15–026**

---

[130] *North Atlantic Insurance Co Ltd v Nationwide General Insurance Co* [2004] Lloyd's Rep. I.R. 466.

[131] *Staatssecretaris van Financien v Arthur Andersen & Co* (C-472/03) [2007] Lloyd's Rep. I.R. 484. In *InsuranceWide.Com Services Ltd v HM Revenue & Customs* [2010] EWCA Civ 422 it was held that the operator of an "aggregator" website which provided price comparisons on premiums was, for the purposes of Value Added Tax legislation, a broker, in that an aggregator was an intermediary between two potential contracting parties whose objective was to facilitate the making of a contract between them.

[132] The assured may have appointed some other agent to place insurance for him, as where one of the parties to a commercial contract agrees to take out insurance covering various of the risks which may arise under the contract: *Jackson v London Motor Sports* (1919) 2 Ll. L.R. 16; *Calafato v Olivier* (1919) 2 Ll.L.R. 648; *Sumitomo Bank Ltd v Banque Bruxelles Lambert SA* [1997] 1 Lloyd's Rep. 487; *Overseas Medical Supplies Ltd v Orient Transport Services Ltd* Unreported, 1999; *Euro Cellular (Distribution) Plc v Danzas Ltd (No.1)* [2003] EWHC 3161 (Comm); *Oxford Aviation Services Ltd v Godolphin Management Co Ltd* [2004] EWHC 232 (QB). An obligation to insure may be implied from the circumstances (*Pozzolonic Lytag v Bryan Hobson Associates* [1999] Lloyd's Rep. P.N. 125) but not in the absence of some form of assumption of responsibility (*Gregoriades v Imperial Ottoman Bank* (1926) 25 Ll. L.R. 68; *Van Oppen v Clerk to Bedford Charity Trustees* [1989] 1 All E.R. 273; *Reid v Rush & Tompkins Group Plc* [1989] 3 All E.R. 228). A gratuitous promise to insure does not of itself give rise to liability: *Argy Trading v Lapid Developments* [1977] 1 Lloyd's Rep. 67. Any person who does assume liability to take out insurance must adhere to the standard of care required of a reasonable man looking after his own interests, and not to the standard of care required of a professional broker: *Smith v Lascelles* (1788) 2 T.R. 187; *Wallace v Telfair* (1788) 2 T.R. 188n; *Wilkinson v Coverdale* (1793) 1 Esp. 75; *Yuill v Scott Robson* [1907] 1 K.B. 685; *Enlayde Ltd v Roberts* [1917] 1 Ch. 109; *British School of Motoring v Simms* [1971] R.T.R. 190; *De Meza v Apple* [1975] 1 Lloyd's Rep. 498; *Frost v James Finlay Bank* [2001] Lloyd's Rep. Bank 302.

assistance and claims handling services.[133] A broker is required to satisfy the standards of a reasonable competent broker in the market at the same time. In determining whether the broker has exercised reasonable care and skill, reference may be made to the provisions of the FSA Handbook.[134]

15–027 *The incidence of agency.* It is generally accepted that a broker, being the appointee of the assured, acts as the agent of the assured in giving advice to the assured and in dealing with the insurer.[135] Consequently, any errors made by the broker while acting on the assured's behalf and within the scope of his actual or ostensible authority bind the assured,[136] any information received by the broker from the assured is not deemed to have been received by the insurers[137] and any information provided by the broker is not to be taken as having been received from the insurers.[138] If in such a case, the assured is unable to take advantage of his full policy rights against the insurer or is otherwise not properly insured, the assured's remedy is against the broker himself. There are isolated decisions which indicate that the broker is the agent of the insurers, but these may be explained by the fact that the agent in question was not a broker at all[139] or that the issue was whether the broker owed duties to a third party other than the assured and the insurers.[140]

15–028 *Dual agency: duties owed to underwriters.* In accordance with the above authorities, the broker is presumed to be the agent of the assured unless that presumption can be rebutted by evidence that the broker is carrying on specific functions on behalf of insurers.[141] There is no objection to a broker performing particular functions on behalf of the insurers as long as the broker, by so acting, does not bring about a conflict of interest[142] or, alternatively, as long as the assured has given his fully informed consent to the broker acting in such a fashion.[143] Nevertheless, the practical operation of the London insurance market, and particularly that of Lloyd's, places brokers in a position whereby they do carry out functions for both parties to the insurance transaction. Hobhouse J. in *General Accident v Tanter (The Zephyr)*[144] thus commented that the broker was "the servant of the market" and Saville L.J. in *SAIL v Farex Gie*[145] said that "a broker carrying out instructions on behalf of an intending assured may have to undertake obligations to others in order to perform his mandate." Each of these

---

[133] Loss assessors may be appointed by the assured for this purpose.

[134] *Dunlop Haywards (DHL) Ltd v Barbon Insurance Group Ltd* [2009] EWHC 2900 (Comm).

[135] *Grimaldi Ltd v Sullivan* Unreported, 1997; *Gerling-Konzern General Insurance Co v Polygram Holdings & Metropolitan Entertainment Inc* [1998] 2 Lloyd's Rep. 544; *Goshawk Dedicated Ltd v Tyser & Co Ltd* [2006] Lloyd's Rep. I.R. 54.

[136] *Rozanes v Bowen* (1928) 32 Ll. L.R. 98; *Zurich General Accident & Liability Co Ltd v Rowberry* [1954] 2 Lloyd's Rep. 55; *Lens v Excess Insurance Co Ltd* (1916) 32 T.L.R. 361.

[137] *Roche v Roberts* (1921) 9 Ll. L.R. 59; *Evans v Ward* (1930) 37 Ll. L.R. 177; *Garthwaite v Rowland* (1948) 81 Ll. L.R. 417; *Friends Provident Life & Pensions Ltd v Sirius International Insurance Corporation* [2006] Lloyd's Rep. I.R. 45; *Tioxide Europe Ltd v CGU International Insurance Plc* [2006] Lloyd's Rep. I.R. 131; *Hazel v Whitlam* [2005] Lloyd's Rep. I.R. 168.

[138] *Enterprise Oil Ltd v Strand Insurance Co Ltd* [2007] Lloyd's Rep. I.R. 186.

[139] *Woolcott v Excess Insurance Co* [1979] 2 Lloyd's Rep. 210.

[140] *Bromley London BC v Ellis* [1971] 1 Lloyd's Rep. 97.

[141] *Winter v Irish Life Assurance Plc* [1995] 2 Lloyd's Rep. 274; *Searle v AR Hales & Co Ltd* [1996] L.R.L.R. 68; *Re Great Western Insurance Co* [1999] Lloyd's Rep. I.R. 377.

[142] *Pryke v Gibbs Hartley Cooper* [1991] 1 Lloyd's Rep. 602.

[143] *Excess Life Assurance Co Ltd v Fireman's Fund Insurance Co of Newark New Jersey* [1982] 2 Lloyd's Rep. 599.

[144] *General Accident v Tanter (The Zephyr)* [1984] 1 Lloyd's Rep. 58.

[145] *SAIL v Farex Gie* [1995] L.R.L.R. 116.

comments was cited with approval by Rix L.J. in *Goshawk Dedicated Ltd v Tyser & Co Ltd*,[146] and there is now some authority for the proposition that in appropriate circumstances a broker acts as a "common agent".[147] In *HIH Casualty and General Insurance Co v JLT Risk Solutions*[148] Auld L.J. noted that the role of a broker was "notoriously anomalous for its inherent scope for engendering conflict of interest in the otherwise relatively tidy legal world of agency". The point here is that a broker is the agent of the assured, but that he may: (a) also perform certain functions as agent of the underwriters, particularly where he acts for them in placing outwards reinsurance; and (b) assume responsibility towards the underwriters for certain matters even though he is not acting as the agent of the underwriters for that purpose. Whether acting as agent for underwriters, or whether simply assuming responsibility towards them in a manner which gives rise to a duty of care, the prospects for a conflict of interest are apparent.

The courts have considered a number of situations in which brokers have seemingly acted for both parties to an insurance transaction. Thus, as discussed in the following paragraphs: (a) it is common in the London market for brokers to devise a new form of policy to meet a commercial need—this will involve seeking the approval of potential insurers and reinsurers in the market before any potential policyholders are ever approached[149]; (b) in the usual course of events in a London market placement it is the responsibility of the broker to prepare the policy wording; (c) the broker owes an independent duty to underwriters to disclose material facts; (d) in marine insurance, s.53(1) of the Marine Insurance Act 1906 has codified the common law principle that the broker rather than the assured is liable for the premium, a point which has led the courts to comment that a broker acting in this way is not simply the agent of the assured but rather a "common agent"[150]; (e) brokers will often perform functions for underwriters following the occurrence of a loss; (f) a broker will be in possession of placing and claims documents which belong to the assured, but he is also under a duty to disclose those documents to underwriters on reasonable request[151]; and (g) the broker is treated by the law as having been paid by the insurers and not by the assured.

These specific points aside, there are two particular situations in which a broker will face a conflict of interest by reason of duties owed to both parties to the transaction. First, a broker may be appointed by underwriters to operate a binding authority. This may be limited to the grant of temporary cover: the power of the broker to bind insurers in this way has been recognised by the Court of Appeal,[152] and this is clearly a situation in which dual agency of the broker operates to the assured's advantage. If, by contrast, the binding authority is a generalised one, dual agency gives rise to more complex issues because it is clear that the broker will be required to act for insurers in matters such as giving advice to them on premium rates and on the acceptability of risks[153] or receiving

---

[146] *Goshawk Dedicated Ltd v Tyser & Co Ltd* [2007] Lloyd's Rep. I.R. 224.

[147] *JA Chapman & Co Ltd v Kadirga Denizcilik Ve Ticaret* [1998] Lloyd's Rep. I.R. 377; *Heath Lambert Ltd v Sociedad de Corretaje de Seguros* [2004] Lloyd's Rep. I.R. 905.

[148] *HIH Casualty and General Insurance Co v JLT Risk Solutions* [2007] Lloyd's Rep. I.R. 742.

[149] *Forsikringsaktieselskapet Vesta v Butcher* [1989] 1 All E.R. 402.

[150] *JA Chapman & Co Ltd v Kadirga Denizcilik Ve Ticaret* [1998] Lloyd's Rep. I.R. 377; *Heath Lambert Ltd v Sociedad de Corretaje de Seguros* [2004] Lloyd's Rep. I.R. 905.

[151] *Goshawk Dedicated Ltd v Tyser & Co Ltd* [2007] Lloyd's Rep. I.R. 224.

[152] *Stockton v Mason* [1978] 2 Lloyd's Rep. 430.

[153] *Re Great Western Insurance* Co [1999] Lloyd's Rep. I.R. 377.

applications for insurance and applying the insurers' underwriting criteria to such applications so that the premium can be fixed.[154] However, the courts have refused to impose a duty of care towards insurers where this would conflict with the broker's primary duty to the assured in matters such as selection of risks.[155]

Secondly, a broker may be instructed by the assured to obtain cover and may take the view that insurance cover will more easily be maintained if reinsurance can be placed in advance. Alternatively, if the broker tries to place insurance he may find that underwriters are prepared to act as reinsurers but not as direct insurers. The broker may, therefore, obtain a promise from reinsurers to reinsure any insurers who subscribe to the direct risk. The promise takes effect as a standing offer which, unless withdrawn, automatically becomes a contract of reinsurance in favour of a subscriber to the direct risk.[156] The broker's status in presenting the risk to the reinsurers is uncertain, although it was held by Hobhouse J. in *The Zephyr*[157] that the brokers were the authorised agents of the insurers, even though the insurers had not been identified until after the reinsurance had been placed, on the principle that:

"[a] broker who approaches an insurer with an offer of reinsurance, is offering to act as the agent of the insurer. If the insurer accepts the reinsurance offered he thereby constitutes the broker his agent to obtain the cover offered."

Despite being the agent of the insurers, the broker was nevertheless held in *The Zephyr* to have entered into an implied contract with the leading reinsurance underwriter to use best endeavours to obtain the promised level of subscription to the reinsurance slip. It is now recognised that a broker who acts an assured in placing insurance, and then for the insurers in placing reinsurance, is inevitably in a position of conflict of interest, particularly where the interests of the assured and reinsured are at variance,[158] although the courts have regarded the problem as one of the broker's own making and have refused to dilute the duties owed to the client at each level of placement.[159]

These situations aside, there may be exceptional circumstances in which the broker is guilty of other forms of breach of duty in his dealings with the insurers. Thus a broker who assists an underwriting agent in defrauding the underwriters for whom the agent is acting may be guilty of knowingly assisting the underwriting agent in breach of fiduciary duty, or possibly even conspiracy,

---

[154] *Drake Insurance Co v Provident Insurance Co* [2004] Lloyd's Rep. I.R. 277.

[155] *Empress Assurance Corporation Ltd v Bowring & Co Ltd* (1905) 11 Com. Cas. 107; *Glasgow Assurance Corporation Ltd v William Symondson & Co* (1911) 16 Com. Cas. 109; *Aneco v Johnson & Higgins* [2002] 1 Lloyd's Rep. 157; *Sphere Drake v European International Underwriting* [2004] Lloyd's Rep. I.R. 525; *Bonner v Cox Dedicated Corporate Member Ltd* [2006] Lloyd's Rep. I.R. 385. But see *Morton Insurance Brokers Ltd v Sidhu* [2008] EWHC 417 (QB) where a motor insurance broker with authority to issue cover notes on the part of the insurers was held to be liable in damages to the insurers where an employee had issued cover notes backdated to before the date of accidents apparently falling within their scope.

[156] *General Accident Fire and Life Assurance Corporation Ltd v Tanter (The Zephyr)* [1984] 1 Lloyd's Rep. 58, reversed in part [1985] 2 Lloyd's Rep. 529.

[157] See also: *Youell v Bland Welch & Co Ltd (No.2)* [1990] 2 Lloyd's Rep. 431; *Societe Anonyme d'Intermediaries Luxembougeois v Farex Gie* [1995] L.R.L.R. 116; *Kingscroft Insurance Co Ltd v Nissan Fire & Marine Insurance Co Ltd (No.2)* [1999] Lloyd's Rep. I.R. 603; *Tryg Baltica International (UK) Ltd v Boston Campania De Seguos SA* [2005] Lloyd's Rep. I.R. 40.

[158] As in *HIH Casualty and General Insurance Ltd v JLT Risk Solutions Ltd* [2007] Lloyd's Rep. I.R. 742: see below.

[159] *Aneco Reinsurance Underwriting Ltd v Johnson & Higgins Ltd* [2002] Lloyd's Rep. I.R. 91.

thereby rendering himself liable to an action by the underwriters.[160] There is no duty on a broker to protect an underwriter from his own foolishness, but the line is crossed where the broker engages in an activity deliberately involving the deceit of the underwriter.

Sub-brokers. In many cases, a broker instructed to obtain insurance or reinsurance (the producing broker) may find it necessary to enlist the services of another broker (the placing broker) to effect the placement. This may be necessary where, for example, the producing broker is not recognised by Lloyd's and has to act through a Lloyd's placing broker to obtain access to the Lloyd's market. Equally, if the producing broker is located overseas, or does not have expertise in the type of cover sought, the use of a local placing broker may be essential. While agency law permits an agent to delegate his authority only where the principal has expressly or impliedly consented, consent may arise from custom or market practice and it may be that the practice of delegation, particularly in the commercial market, may be justified by implied consent. The roles of the producing broker and placing broker may differ from case to case. If both producing broker and placing broker are, to some extent, in breach of duty towards the assured in respect of the same loss, the assured has the right to bring an action against either of them for the full amount of the loss, on the basis of the joint and several liability rule recognised by English law. It is then for the defendants themselves to work out an apportionment. If, by contrast, there is a break in the chain of causation between the breach of duty by one broker and loss caused by the breach of duty of the other broker, only the latter may be sued.

Assured and producing broker. Two possible forms of liability may be faced by the producing broker: personal liability for his own conduct; and vicarious liability for the conduct of the placing broker. Turning to the first, it is apparent from general principles of agency law that an agent who delegates his authority to a sub-contractor is liable for his own negligence. This may arise from the fact that the appointment has been made negligently (e.g. where the placing broker is unqualified) or that the producing broker has failed to monitor the placing broker's activities (e.g. by failing to check that the wording prepared by the placing broker is appropriate[161]). The more difficult question is whether the producing broker is automatically liable for the defaults of the placing broker: there is no direct authority on the point,[162] although such liability is probably to be imposed in line with the ordinary rule of English law that an agent is liable to his principal for the performance of his own duties which have been delegated to a sub-agent.[163] It may nevertheless be thought that the producing broker is responsible for the acts or defaults of the placing broker in circumstances where responsibility for performing the functions delegated to the placing broker were assumed by the producing broker, and this may indeed be confirmed by the contract between the assured and the producing broker.[164]

15–029

15–030

---

[160] *Sphere Drake Insurance Ltd v Euro International Underwriting Ltd* [2003] Lloyd's Rep. I.R. 525.

[161] *Tudor Jones II v Crawley Colosso Ltd* [1996] 2 Lloyd's Rep. 619.

[162] See *Aiken v Stewart Wrightson Members Agency Ltd* [1995] 3 All E.R. 449 (Lloyd's members' agent not vicariously liable for misconduct of Lloyd's managing agent); *Youell v Bland Welch & Co Ltd (No.2)* [1990] 2 Lloyd's Rep. 431 (both placing and producing brokers liable, although they had there acted jointly, and cf. *O'Brien v Hughes-Gibb* [1995] L.R.L.R. 90).

[163] A point made in *Youell v Bland Welch & Co Ltd (No.2)* [1990] 2 Lloyd's Rep. 431.

[164] As in *Dunlop Haywards (DHL) Ltd v Barbon Insurance Group Ltd* [2009] EWHC 2900 (Comm).

15–031 *Assured and placing broker.* In the absence of some express provision, there is no contract between the assured and the placing broker and that any duty owed to the assured by the placing broker can only rise in tort. The absence of a contract means that the placing broker has no action against the assured for indemnification for any premium paid by the placing broker to the underwriters.[165] There may in exceptional circumstances be a finding of privity, but this would require some direct negotiation between the parties. The position is probably unaffected by the Contracts (Rights of Third Parties) Act 1999. While it is at least arguable that a sub-contract under which a producing broker instructs a placing broker to secure insurance for a specific assured is one which is intended to confer benefit upon the assured, it is far from obvious that there is any intention that the assured should be allowed to sue on it.

The further question is whether there is a duty of care in tort. The authorities are consistent in imposing such a duty,[166] and these were confirmed by the decision of Colman J. in *BP Plc v Aon Ltd*,[167] where it was held that a duty could arise in principle but only where the sub-broker assumed responsibility to the assured to perform the functions in question.[168] The necessary assumption of responsibility was found to arise where the arrangements between the assured, producing brokers and placing brokers—contained in a contract between the assured and the producing brokers—operated on the basis that the London placing brokers would declare risks to the London market underwriters: the existence of a contract between the assured and the producing brokers was held not to preclude a duty of care in tort owed by the placing brokers, and that liability was to be imposed where there was:

> "[A]n express or implied representation by or on behalf of the agent by words or conduct not only that it is he who will be responsible in fact for preparing the advice or carrying out the services with proper skill and care, but that he personally will accept legal liability if he fails to do so and if the claimant suffers economic loss by reason of his reliance on such assumption of responsibility."

It may be that the facts of *BP* were exceptional, and involved close contact between the assured and the placing brokers. In the ordinary scenario where a producing broker appoints a placing broker to place a risk, there may be little or no contact between the assured and the placing broker. *BP* decides no more that

---

[165] *Prentis Donegan & Partners Ltd v Leeds & Leeds Co Inc* [1998] 2 Lloyd's Rep. 326, distinguishing *Velos Group Ltd v Harbour Insurance Services Ltd* [1997] 2 Lloyd's Rep. 461; *Heath Lambert Ltd v Sociedad de Corretaje de Seguros* [2004] Lloyd's Rep. I.R. 495. The point did not arise on appeal [2004] Lloyd's Rep. I.R. 905. Contrast *Tryg Baltica International (UK) Ltd v Boston Compania de Seguros SA* [2005] Lloyd's Rep. I.R. 40, where it was assumed that, for the purposes of CPR PD 6B, an English placing broker was the agent of the assured so that service could be effected on the assured outside the jurisdiction.

[166] *Youell v Bland Welch & Co Ltd (No.2)* [1990] 2 Lloyd's Rep. 431; [1995] L.R.L.R. 90; *Tudor Jones II v Crowley Colosso Ltd* [1996] 2 Lloyd's Rep. 619; *Prentis Donegan & Partners Ltd v Leeds & Leeds Co Inc* [1998] 2 Lloyd's Rep. 326. See also *Coolee Ltd v Wing, Heath & Co* (1930) 38 Ll. L.R. 188 and *Mint Security Ltd v Blair* [1982] 1 Lloyd's Rep. 188 for a similar assumption.

[167] *BP Plc v Aon Ltd* [2006] Lloyd's Rep. I.R. 577.

[168] English law recognises three ways in which a duty of care may arise: by way of an assumption of responsibility; by incremental analogy with previous decided cases; and by the threefold test of proximity, foreseeability and whether it is fair, just and reasonable to impose a duty of care. The most recent discussion of the test by the House of Lords *Commissioners of Customs and Excise v Barclays Bank* [2006] UKHL 28, is inconclusive in its approach to the relative significance of these tests in financial loss cases. The cases discussed in the text were decided before *CCE v Barclays* so that the reasoning in them may be open to doubt. In *European International Reinsurance Co Ltd v Curzon Insurance Ltd* [2003] Lloyd's Rep. I.R. 793 the Court of Appeal held that it was arguable that a duty of care was owed by a placing broker even in the absence of an assumption of responsibility.

as a matter of principle a placing broker may assume a duty of care: it does not suggest that this is the usual situation. Indeed, if there is no contact between the assured and the placing broker, and the assured relies solely upon the producing broker, there is little basis for imposing a duty of care on the placing broker.[169]

In *Dunlop Heywards (DHL) Ltd v Erinaceous Insurance Services Ltd*[170] Tomlinson J. regarded it as arguable that there had been assumption of responsibility by the placing broker to the assured in circumstances where the decision as to which placing broker to appoint was made by the assured following a presentation to the producing broker, and where there had been various communications between the placing broker and the assured in the form of the placing broker's fee proposal and in the form of a report on the placement of the risk addressed to the assured and forwarded to the assured by the producing broker.[171]

Producing broker and placing broker. The relationship between the producing broker and the placing broker is based primarily on contract,[172] in the form of a sub-agency agreement. In accordance with general principle, the relationship between producing broker and placing broker also gives rise to a parallel duty of care in tort. There is no contract between the placing broker and the assured. Thus, commission payable to the placing broker is payable by the producing broker and not the assured.[173] Where the policy is one under which the underwriters can look to the broker for the premium,[174] the placing broker remains personally liable to the underwriter for premiums, but the placing broker is entitled to bring an action against the producing broker for reimbursement.[175] Sums received under the policy by placing broker have to be paid to producing broker.[176]

15–032

Insofar as the placing broker has broken his duty and has caused the producing broker to incur liability towards the assured, the placing broker is required to provide an indemnity.[177] The manner in which that indemnity is obtained depends upon the nature of the claim. Where the action is brought by the assured

---

[169] *Pangood Ltd v Barclay Brown & Co Ltd* [1999] Lloyd's Rep. I.R. 405.

[170] *Dunlop Haywards (DHL) Ltd v Erinaceous Insurance Services Ltd* [2008] Lloyd's Rep. I.R. 676. The point did not arise on appeal, [2009] Lloyd's Rep. I.R. 464.

[171] In the event, at the trial the assured pursued only the producing broker. See the subsequent trial, *Dunlop Haywards (DHL) Ltd v Barbon Insurance Group Ltd* [2009] EWHC 2900 (Comm).

[172] Under English conflict of laws rules it is likely that the agreement will be governed by English law (unless there is agreement to the contrary) as the placing broker's obligations are to be performed in England: this was assumed to be the case in *Heath Lambert Ltd v Sociedad de Corretaje de Seguros* [2004] 1 Lloyd's Rep. 495. The point did not arise on appeal, [2004] Lloyd's Rep. I.R. 905.

[173] *Prentis Donegan & Partners Ltd v Leeds & Leeds Co Inc* [1998] 2 Lloyd's Rep. 326. In *Crema v Cenkos Securities* [2010] EWHC 461 Comm it was held, in the context of investment brokers, that a sub-broker was only entitled to commission from the head broker once the head broker had been paid by the principal. The court found no evidence of market practice which pointed to a usage or custom that the sub-broker was to be paid from the head broker's own pocket. The matter is of course subject to contract.

[174] A marine policy (Marine Insurance Act 1906 s.53(1)).

[175] *Harrison & Dixon (Insurance Brokers) Ltd v SF Graham (Run-Off) Ltd* Unreported, 1989; *Heath Lambert Ltd v Sociedad de Corretaje de Seguros* [2004] Lloyd's Rep. I.R. 905.

[176] *Carr & Co v Matthews Wrightson & Co* (1923) 18 Ll. L.R. 170, Cf. *Starr & Co Ltd v Clifford & Sons* (1922) 10 Ll. L.R. 649.

[177] *Dunlop Haywards (DHL) Ltd v Erinaceous Insurance Services Ltd* [2009] Lloyd's Rep. I.R. 464. This case also decides that if the liability of either broker is restricted, e.g. by contract or by the assured's contributory negligence, the right of recovery is restricted to the amount of common liability.

against both the producing broker and the placing broker, and both are found culpable, then the court will apportion responsibility between them in its award of damages. More usually, however, the claim by the assured will be against the producing broker alone based on his responsibility for the acts of the placing broker. If judgment is given against the producing broker, he may proceed against the placing broker either by: (a) an action for breach of contract or in tort, under which the producing broker will recover damages based upon the degree of his own responsibility for the assured's loss; or (b) in the form of a claim for contribution under the Civil Liability (Contribution) Act 1978. In all cases, and leaving aside the possibility of insolvency, the loss will be allocated between the two brokers in accordance with their degree of culpability. However, if the liability of either broker is restricted, e.g. by contract or by the defence of contributory negligence, contribution applies only to the amount of common liability.[178] In some cases the court may be satisfied that one or other of the brokers is entirely responsible for the loss,[179] although this is a question of causation.

The scope of the duty owed by the placing broker to the producing, whether framed in contract or in tort, reflects the duty owed by the producing broker to the assured. The nature of the placing broker's duties was discussed in detail by Hamblen J. in *Dunlop Haywards (DHL) Ltd v Barbon Insurance Group Ltd.*[180] Here, the producing broker was instructed by the assured to obtain £10 million excess layer cover for its activities, but the producing broker erroneously instructed the placing broker to restrict the cover on renewal to the assured's property management activities, a significant reduction in the scope of the existing cover. The placing broker did so, leaving the assured uninsured in respect of valuation claims made by third parties. Hamblen J. held that the placing broker owed duties analogous to those of the producing broker, i.e. to exercise reasonable care and skill in the fulfilment of its instructions and the performance of its professional obligations; carefully to review the terms of any quotations or indications received; to explain the terms of the proposed insurance; and to use reasonable skill and care to draw up a policy, or to ensure that a policy was drawn up, that accurately reflected the terms of the agreement with the underwriters and which was clear and unambiguous so that the insured's rights under the policy were not open to doubt. The learned judge further held that these duties required the placing broker to ensure that the instructions given by the producing broker were clearly understood, and that if they were unclear, illogical or absurd, potentially disadvantageous to the assured or did not appear to meet the assured's requirements, then the instructions had to be queried before being implemented. Again, if the policy is being renewed and the instructions indicate a reduction of cover, the placing broker must draw the attention of the producing broker to that restriction. In *Dunlop Haywards* itself, it was held that the placing broker had been in breach of its duty by failing to query instructions which removed cover for the assured's most risky activity without any apparent reason, and that it was liable to the producing broker, in an action for breach of duty, for that proportion of the producing broker's loss which the placing broker had caused, assessed at 20 per cent on the facts. It is apparent from *Dunlop*

---

[178] *Nationwide Building Society v Dunlop Haywards (DHL) Ltd (t/a Dunlop Heywood Lorenz)* [2009] EWHC 254 (Comm).

[179] As was the case in *Pangood Ltd v Barclay Brown & Co Ltd* [1999] Lloyd's Rep. I.R. 405, where the fault was held to be entirely that of the producing broker.

[180] *Dunlop Haywards (DHL) Ltd v Barbon Insurance Group Ltd* [2009] EWHC 2900 (Comm). See also *Dunlop Hawards (DHL) Ltd (formerly Dunlop Heywood Lorenz Ltd) v Erinaceous Insurance Services Ltd (formerly Hanover Park Commercial Ltd)* [2009] Lloyd's Rep. I.R. 464.

Haywards that if the placing broker has no reason to suspect that the producing broker's instructions do not match the needs of the assured, the placing broker cannot be responsible for any loss: the placing brokers are, after all, entitled to rely upon the professionalism and knowledge of the producing broker.

A similar case is *Tudor Jones II v Crowley Colosso Ltd*.[181] Here, the assured, a US resident, acquired two islands in the Bahamas with a view to developing them. One of the features of the development was a marina. The assured instructed US brokers, MM, to obtain cover for the entire development including the marina, but as MM were unable to obtain insurance in the United States they instructed London brokers, CC, to attempt to find insurance in the London market. CC obtained three policies on the same terms, which contained an exclusion for damage to works following the issue of a certificate of completion in relation to that part of the works. The marina was damaged by Hurricane Andrew, the loss occurring after a certificate of substantial completion had been issued. The assured claimed that the exclusion was not in accordance with his instructions to MM for full "shovel to key" cover. The assured subsequently assigned his rights against CC to MM, doubtless in return for indemnification, and in the present proceedings MM sought to recover the assured's loss from CC. The expert and other evidence demonstrated that MM had not made it clear to CC that cover was required for the entire duration of the building works and was not to come to an end on a gradual basis as and when individual parts of the works were completed, but that a prudent broker in CC's position would have drawn to MM's attention the potential significance of the exclusion. CC was, therefore, negligent on this count and also for failing to present the risk properly to certain of the insurers involved.[182] Langley J. further held that MM had been negligent in not seeking to ascertain the meaning of the exclusion when CC had sent draft wording to MM for its approval. On the question of causation, Langley J. rejected the argument put by CC that the proximate cause of any loss was MM's failure to check that the proposed wording was appropriate and that MM's failure broke the chain of causation from CC's own failure to warn MM of the existence of the exclusion.[183] This meant that both CC and MM had been guilty of negligence which had proximately caused the assured's loss, and Langley J. held that the appropriate apportionment of blame was one-third to MM and two-thirds to CC, representing the two different forms of negligence found in CC's conduct.

There are other illustrations of these principles in the decided cases. Apportionment may be appropriate where the placing broker has himself been negligent by, for example, failing to require the assured to submit a proposal form to underwriters or failing to inform the producing broker of changes to cover on renewal.[184]

---

[181] *Tudor Jones II v Crowley Colosso Ltd* [1996] 2 Lloyd's Rep. 619. A similar issue had arisen in *Youell v Bland Welch & Co (No.2)* [1990] 2 Lloyd's Rep. 431 but Phillips J. was spared from having to determine whether and how an apportionment should be made because, by the time of the trial, the producing broker and the placing broker had merged.

[182] The leading underwriter had been informed that cover was required for the entire works, but the following market had not been told that cover was required despite completion of individual phases of the works.

[183] In *Youell v Bland Welch & Co (No.2)* [1990] 2 Lloyd's Rep. 431, the same point had arisen in that brokers had failed to warn their client reinsureds that the reinsurance cover was limited in duration, and it was held that the reinsureds' failure to appreciate that this was the implication of the wording presented to them for approval did not break the chain of causation flowing from the brokers' negligence.

[184] *Fisk v Brian Thornhill & Son* [2007] Lloyd's Rep. I.R. 699, where the placing broker was required to make 25 per cent contribution to the producing broker on these grounds.

One proviso to the right of contribution, which is independent of the causation principle but which leads to the same result, is that the 1978 Act applies only where the two forms of loss caused by the two defendants are the same and are alternative rather than cumulative, for if this is not the case it is not possible to compare like with like in order to achieve an equitable apportionment.[185] This scenario is, however, unlikely to arise in the context of placing brokers, for the producing broker's own breach will, generally, relate to the appointment or monitoring of the placing broker, and that itself is closely related to the placing broker's own breach of duty.

15-033 **Remuneration.** Any expenditure reasonably incurred by the broker in performing his tasks is recoverable from the assured.[186] In addition, a broker who is the effective cause of the placement of the risk is entitled to commission,[187] which is regarded as fully earned even though the broker may have to perform other duties for the assured during the currency of the contract. One consequence of this rule is that if the policy is cancelled after the risk has incepted, the commission is fully earned and is not returnable to the assured,[188] whereas if the policy is avoided no part of the commission has been earned.

It might be thought that commission is payable by the assured as the broker's principal.[189] However, in practice, brokers simply deduct the commission from the amount of premium before passing it on to the insurers. The amount of commission is typically agreed with the insurers and not with the assured.[190] In the light of this, there is much old authority for the proposition that the broker is paid by the insurers for finding the business, a rule derived either from custom or implied term.[191] This is consistent with the rule that commission is earned as soon as the insurance is effected, but does not sit easily with the incidence of the broker's agency. At first sight the practice of the insurance market in allowing a broker to receive commission from the insurer in the form of a deduction from the premium paid by the broker to the insurer contravenes the equitable principle that an agent cannot make a profit from his office without disclosing the amount of that profit to his principal (the assured). It has indeed been said that the

---

[185] *Birse Construction v Haiste* [1996] 2 All E.R. 1.

[186] *Islamic Republic of Iran Shipping Lines v Zannis Compania Naviera SA (The Tzelepi)* [1991] 2 Lloyd's Rep. 265.

[187] *McNeil v Law Union* (1925) 23 Ll. L.R. 314; *McNeil v Steamship Mutual* (1940) 67 Ll. L.R. 142; *Bright & Co (Insurance) Ltd v Wright* (1946) 79 Ll. L.R. 207; *Velos Group Ltd v Harbour Insurance Services Ltd* [1997] 2 Lloyd's Rep. 461; *Standard Life Assurance Co v Egan Lawson* [2001] 1 E.G.L.R. 27; *Harding Maughan Hambly Ltd v CECAR* [2000] Lloyd's Rep. I.R. 293.

[188] *Velos Group Ltd v Harbour Insurance Services Ltd* [1997] 2 Lloyd's Rep. 461.

[189] *Grace v Leslie & Godwin Financial Services Ltd* [1995] L.R.L.R. 472. See *Wilson v Hurstanger* [2007] EWCA Civ 299, which illustrates the ordinary rule that an intermediary who is paid by the principal but takes commission from the third party in the absence of the principal's approval and informed consent is in breach of duty and indeed the contract between the principal and third party is voidable. In *Wilson* the court felt that avoidance would be disproportionate and contented itself with requiring the intermediary to account for his payment to the principal.

[190] Although in some cases the agreement as to amount is reached between the assured and the broker: *Absalom v TCRU Ltd* [2005] EWCA Civ 1586, which turned on the amount payable.

[191] *Power v Butcher* (1829) 10 B. & C. 329; *Leete v Wallace* (1888) 58 L.T. 577; *Norreys v Hodgson* (1897) 3 T.L.R. 421; *Bancroft v Heath* (1901) 6 Com. Cas. 137; *Workman & Army & Navy Co-operative Supply Ltd v London & Lancashire Fire Insurance Co* (1903) 19 T.L.R. 360; *Gaunt v Gold Star Insurance Co Ltd* [1991] 2 N.Z.L.R. 341; *Searle v AR Hales & Co Ltd* [1996] L.R.L.R. 68. This in turn means that if the premium has to be returned by the insurers to the assured, it is to be returned gross rather than net of brokerage: *Intermunicipal Realty & Development Corp v Gore Mutual Insurance Company* [1981] 1 F.C. 151.

practice is "somewhat anomalous to the equity lawyer".[192] However, the practice has long been recognised by the English courts, subject only to the requirement that the deduction is normal for the type of insurance. Thus, a deduction by the broker which exceeds the usual rate of commission must be disclosed to the assured,[193] and it has also been held that it is arguable that a broker who pays the deducted commission directly to an unconnected third party must disclose that fact to the assured as such conduct is not usual.[194]

The conceptual difficulties in the way of the rule that the broker is paid by the insurers, namely the conflict of interest which arises and also the fact that the broker owes post-contractual duties to the assured for which no consideration has been given, led the trial judge in a reinsurance case, *Carvill America Inc v Camperdown UK Ltd*,[195] to doubt the existence of a custom.[196] On appeal[197] the Court of Appeal gave less weight to the suggestion that the continuing duty owed by a broker gave rise to a consideration problem if the broker was indeed paid by the insurers for placing the risk, and was content to hold that the brokers might have a cause of action against the underwriters for their commission either because: (a) the reinsured had agreed to pay gross premiums to the brokers so that commission could be deducted at source, in accordance with the alleged custom; or (b) the reinsured had agreed to pay gross premiums to the reinsurers who would then pay brokerage to Carvill, thereby imposing a duty on the reinsured not to perform the reinsurance contracts in a manner which deprived the brokers of the opportunity of earning commission.

The broker has a lien over both the policy and on the policy moneys—should they be paid to him—by way of security for any sums due to him by the assured.[198]

Duties of brokers on placement

Obtaining cover. Where a broker is given express instructions to obtain cover, he is required to exercise reasonable care in all the circumstances to adhere to those instructions. Thus where a broker is under a duty to procure a policy on the instructions of the assured, his complete failure to do so will render him liable to the assured.[199] If the required insurance is unobtainable, the broker is prima facie not liable,[200] but will face liability if he fails to warn the assured that he is not covered and the assured acts on the belief that insurance is in place[201] or if the

15–034

---

[192] *Homeserve Membership Ltd v Revenue and Customs* [2009] EWHC 1311 (Ch).

[193] *Turnbull v Garden* (1869) 38 L.J. Ch. 331; *Queen of Spain v Parr* (1869) 39 L.J. Ch. 73: *Great Western Insurance v Cunliffe* (1869) L.R. 9 Ch. App. 525: *Baring v Stanton* (1876) 3 Ch D 502; *Green & Son Ltd v Tunghan & Co* (1913) 30 T.L.R. 64. See also *United Insurance Co of Libya v Aon Ltd* [2008] Lloyd's Rep. I.R. 166, where it unsuccessfully argued that the broker had misrepresented to the reinsured the amount of commission which it was being paid by the reinsurers.

[194] *NV Rotterdamse Assurantiekas v Golding Stewart Wrightson Ltd* Unreported, 1989.

[195] *Carvill America Inc v Camperdown UK Ltd* [2005] Lloyd's Rep. I.R. 55. In *Absalom v TCRU Ltd* [2005] EWCA Civ 1586 Longmore L.J. described the supposed rule as a "curiosity" but did not question its validity.

[196] Or, if it existed, that it did not apply to reinsurance.

[197] *Carvill America Inc v Camperdown UK Ltd* [2006] Lloyd's Rep. I.R. 1.

[198] Marine Insurance Act 1906 s.53(2). See Ch.8, above.

[199] *Tickel v Short* (1750) 2 Ves. Sen. 239; *Glaser v Cowie* (1813) 1 M. & S. 52; *Smith v Price* (1862) 2 F. & F. 748; *Transport and Trading Co v Olivier* (1925) 21 Ll. L.R. 379.

[200] *Smith v Cologan* (1788) 2 T.R. 188n.

[201] *Smith v Lascelles* (1788) 2 T.R. 187; *Callendar v Oelrichs* (1838) 5 Bing. N.C. 58; *Great North Eastern Railway Ltd v Jardine Insurance Services Ltd* [2006] EWHC 1478 (Comm). The broker has a defence if he can demonstrate that he was unable to commnnicate with the assured in good time: *Hurrell v Bullard* (1863) 3 F. & E 445; *Great Western Insurance Co of New York v Cunliffe* (1874) 9 Ch. App. 525; *Gomer v Pitt & Scott* (1922) 12 Ll.L.R. 115.

assured could have taken steps to make the risk insurable, e.g. to dismiss a director with criminal convictions whose presence rendered the risk uninsurable.[202]

All of this is, however, subject to there being a complete agreement between the assured and broker as to the obtaining of cover; if negotiations between the parties are incomplete and fundamental terms have not been agreed, the assured clearly has no action against the broker for failure to insure unless the broker has had previous dealings with the assured and ought to be aware of the nature of the insurance required.[203] Instructions which are sent by e-mail and which are not in any way conditional are to be acted on by the broker, and there is no duty on the assured to confirm the instructions or to check that they have been duly received.[204]

The broker must procure insurance within a reasonable time. What is reasonable will necessarily be a matter of fact, taking into account both the needs of the assured and the fact that the risk may be unusual and insurance for it difficult to obtain speedily.[205] It is for the assured to prove that his instructions were communicated to the broker in time for insurance to be effected in accordance with those instructions.[206]

Where the broker is given express instructions to insure particular risks, and the policy obtained by him is in some way deficient, he will be in breach of duty if he does not inform the assured of this fact. Liability has thus been imposed upon brokers for obtaining policies which did not cover the stated persons,[207] property,[208] liability[209] or geographical area,[210] and for obtaining policies inadequate either in duration[211] or amount.[212] The same position prevails where the broker is required to obtain cover against all risks but fails to do so.[213] In the absence of express instructions as to the scope of cover, the broker must rely upon previous dealings with the assured or upon his knowledge of the risks likely

---

[202] O & R Jewellers Ltd v Terry [1999] Lloyd's Rep. I.R. 436.

[203] Turpin v Bilton (1843) 5 Man. & G. 455; Hurrell v Bullard (1863) 3 F. & F. 445.

[204] BP Plc v Aon Ltd [2006] EWHC 424 (Comm).

[205] Cock, Russell v Bray, Gibb (1920) 3 Ll. L.R. 71.

[206] Icarom Plc v Peek Puckle International Ltd [1992] 2 Lloyd's Rep. 600.

[207] Ackbar v Green [1975] Q.B. 582; Bromley LBC v Ellis [1971] 1 Lloyd's Rep. 97.

[208] Dickson v Devitt (1916) 21 Com. Cas. 291 (cargo coverage limited to named vessel); National Insurance and Guarantee Corp Plc v Imperio Reinsurance Co UK and Russell Tudor-Price & Co [1999] Lloyd's Rep. I.R. 249 (policy endorsement not covering loss of interest on the reinsured's own funds); Ramco Ltd v Weller Russell & Laws Insurance Brokers [2009] Lloyd's Rep. I.R. 29 (policy not extending to property in possession of bailee but for which there was no liability).

[209] Forsakringsaktieselskapet Vesta v Butcher [1986] 2 Lloyd's Rep. 179 (liability of reinsurer narrower than the liability of the reinsured); Dunlop Haywards (DHL) Ltd v Barbon Insurance Group Ltd [2009] EWHC 2900 (Comm) (no cover for surveying claims).

[210] Zurich General Accident and Liability Insurance Co Ltd v Rowberry [1954] 2 Lloyd's Rep. 55 (travel insurance limited in its operation to Paris).

[211] Youell v Bland Welch & Co Ltd (No.2) [1990] 2 Lloyd's Rep. 431 (breach of duty towards a reinsured for arranging indefinite insurance while reinsurance was limited to 48 months); Tudor Jones II v Crawley Colosso Ltd [1996] 2 Lloyd's Rep. 619 (failure by brokers to insure entire building works for the full duration of the works).

[212] Arbory Group Ltd v West Craven Insurance Services [2007] Lloyd's Rep. I.R. 491, in which a business interruption policy was written "subject to average"; Standard Life Assurance Ltd v Oak Dedicated Ltd [2008] Lloyd's Rep. I.R. 552 where, the brokers procured a professional indemnity policy designed to protect the assured against small claims but failed to appreciate that there was a deductible of £25 million for each claimant against the assured. Contrast William Jackson & Sons Ltd v Oughtred & Harrison (Insurance) Ltd [2002] Lloyd's Rep. I.R. 230, where it was held that the broker was not under an obligation to go behind expert valuations obtained by the assured's own architects.

[213] Yuill & Co v Robson [1908] 1 K.B. 270; Fines Flowers v General Accident Insurance 81 D.L.R. (3d) 139 (1978).

to be faced by the assured as a matter of practice or custom.[214] It follows from this that a broker who does not understand the nature of the business for which he is seeking insurance,[215] or who fails to appreciate that standard forms of policy may not deal adequately with the assured's requirements,[216] will face liability. Similarly, a broker will be liable for placing insurance with an insurer who does not insure a class of persons of which the assured forms a part.[217]

The early English cases were not fully clear as to the extent to which the duty of a broker extended beyond the passive requirement of obeying instructions and to the positive act of seeking to ascertain from the assured whether his instructions actually reflect his needs. Those cases indicate that if the broker is given specific instructions, it is not his duty to alert the assured to the fact that he may be underinsured; it is enough if he obeys those instructions even if they are ambiguous.[218] Those cases indeed go further and hold that the assured is deemed to know his own business, so that the broker is not required to bring the assured's attention to the deficiencies in his instructions.[219] It would seem, however, that the law has caught up with the standards that brokers undoubtedly set for themselves, and more recent authority supports the proposition that it is the duty of a broker carefully to ascertain the client's insurance needs and to use reasonable skill and care to obtain insurance that met those needs.[220] Thus the broker is required to ask sufficient questions of the assured to satisfy himself that the assured falls within the classes of persons whom the insurers will cover,[221] that the use to which the assured's property is to be put is within the scope of the policy,[222] that the risks faced by the subject matter are insured[223] and that the policy extends to the required interests.[224] In so doing the broker must comply with the standards expected of a prudent broker in the market at the relevant time. These cases do not make the broker a guarantor that the assured's every need will be covered by the policy whether or not a specific request for cover has been made. Instead, the principle is that a broker is under a duty to undertake a reasonable inquiry as to the assured's likely needs: if the broker has not been alerted to the assured's specific needs and there is nothing in the arrangements to alert the broker to the possibility that additional protection is required, there is no breach of duty.[225]

The policy obtained by the broker must be reasonably suited to the assured's needs. It need not necessarily be the cheapest of its type on the market in respect of the risks covered,[226] although the insurers must be financially stable.[227]

---

[214] *Mallough v Barber* (1815) 4 Cowp. 150; *Strong & Pearl v Allison* (1926) 25 Ll. L.R. 584.

[215] *Commonwealth Insurance Co of Vancouver v Groupe Sprinks* [1983] 1 Lloyd's Rep. 67.

[216] *Forsikringsaktieselskapel Vesta v Butcher* [19861 2 Lloyd's Rep. 179.

[217] *Seavision Investment SA v Evenett and Clarkson Puckle Ltd* [1992] 2 Lloyd's Rep. 26.

[218] *Comber v Anderson* (1808) 1 Camp. 523; *Fomin v Oswell* (1813) 3 Camp. 357; *Vale v Van Oppen* (1921) 6 Ll. L.R. 167.

[219] *Waterkyn v Price Forbes & Co* (1920) 5 Ll. L.R. 42; *United Mills Ltd v Bray* [1952] 1 All E.R. 225.

[220] *Dunlop Haywards (DHL) Ltd v Barbon Insurance Group Ltd* [2009] EWHC 2900 (Comm); *1013799 Ontario Ltd v Kent Line International Ltd* (2000) 22 C.C.L.I. (3d) 312 (Ont SC).

[221] *McNealy v Pennine Insurance Co Ltd* [1978] 2 Lloyd's Rep. 18.

[222] *The Moonacre* [1992] 2 Lloyd's Rep. 501.

[223] *O'Brien v Hughes-Gibb* [1995] L.R.L.R. 90.

[224] *FNCB Ltd v Barnet Devanney (Harrow) Ltd* [1999] Lloyd's Rep. I.R. 43.

[225] *National Insurance and Guarantee Corp Plc v Imperio Reinsurance Co UK Ltd* [1999] Lloyd's Rep. I.R. 249; *William Jackson & Sons Ltd v Oughtred and Harrison (Insurance) Ltd* [2002] Lloyd's Rep. I.R. 230.

[226] *Moore v Mourgue* (1776) 2 Cowp. 479; *Dixon v Hovill* (1828) 4 Bing. 665.

[227] *Osman v Moss* [1970] 1 Lloyd's Rep. 313; *Bell v Lothiansure, The Times*, February 2, 1990; *Bates v Robert Barrow Ltd* [1995] 1 Lloyd's Rep. 680.

A broker who negligently advises his client that insurance of a particular risk is not available will be liable for the assured's loss if it is subsequently found that insurance could have been obtained.[228]

15–035 *Preparing the policy wording.* In certain types of commercial insurance the broker will be responsible for drafting the policy wording, and the course of business at Lloyd's requires the broker to prepare wording, following his obtaining adequate subscription to the slip, for presentation to the assured and to the leading underwriter for their respective approval. It is the broker's duty to provide intelligible wording.[229] In many cases the broker may be required to respond to quotations or subjectivities insisted upon by underwriters, and the broker is under a duty carefully to review the terms of the policy and of any quotations or indications received, and to explain them fully to the assured.[230]

The issue of the policy is not always immediate, and indeed in exceptional circumstances it may never occur at all[231]; in the facultative reinsurance market, for example, the parties are normally content to rely upon the slip as a slip policy. A problem may nevertheless arise where the underwriters seek to rely upon standard policy wording which has not been communicated to the assured in the form of a policy, and the issue will arise as to whether the broker was under any duty to procure the issue of a policy. It has been held[232] that the broker is under a duty to communicate the terms of the policy in good time to the assured, so that the assured is made aware of any warranties or other obligations which may be imposed on him under the policy.

Once the broker has received the policy wording, then he is required to check it to ensure that it corresponds to the assured's requirements and does not contain any exclusions which remove the cover desired by the assured.[233] The broker is required to exercise reasonable care in responding to any questions by the assured as to the meaning of warranties and conditions precedent in the policy,[234] although proof by the broker that the assured would have disregarded the warranty even if it had been brought to his attention will on causation grounds relieve the broker from any liability.[235]

The broker acts here as agent of the assured, so that if the wording is ambiguous it has to be construed *contra proferentem* in favour of the insurers,[236] although if the ambiguity relates to an exclusion clause the distinct rule of construction that such clauses are to be construed narrowly will operate to cancel out the *contra proferentem* rule.[237] If the policy wording is inaccurate, it may be

[228] *Sarginson v Moulton* (1942) 73 Ll. L.R. 104.

[229] *Charman v Gordian Run-Off Ltd* [2003] Lloyd's Rep. I.R. 337.

[230] *Dunlop Haywards (DHL) Ltd v Barbon Insurance Group Ltd* [2009] EWHC 2900 (Comm).

[231] Since the adoption of the London Market Principles 2001, followed by the Market Reform Contract, policy wordings are now to be issued.

[232] *Pangood Ltd v Barclay Brown & Co Ltd* [1999] Lloyd's Rep. I.R. 405.

[233] *King v Chambers & Newman* [1963] 2 Lloyd's Rep. 130; *Dickson v Devitt* (1916) 21 Com. Cas. 291.

[234] *Strong & Pearl v Allison & Co* (1926) 25 Ll. L.R. 504; *Sarginson v Moulton* (1942) 73 Ll. L.R. 104; *King v Chambers & Newman* [1963] 2 Lloyd's Rep. 130; *Victor Melik & Co Ltd v Norwich Union Fire Insurance Society Ltd* [1980] 1 Lloyd's Rep. 523; *Pangood Ltd v Barclay Brown & Co Ltd* [1999] Lloyd's Rep. I.R. 405; *Bollom & Co Ltd v Byas Moseley & Co Ltd* [2000] Lloyd's Rep. I.R. 136.

[235] *Bhopal v Sphere Drake Insurance Plc* [2002] Lloyd's Rep. I.R. 413.

[236] *Abrahams v Mediterranean Insurance and Reinsurance Ltd* [1991] 1 Lloyd's Rep. 216; *Pearson Plc v Excess Insurance Co Ltd* Unreported, 1988 (broker drafting proposal form).

[237] *Youell v Bland Welch & Co Ltd (No.1)* [1992] 2 Lloyd's Rep. 127.

that there can be rectification. If for whatever reason rectification is not possible, the broker, as the agent of the assured, owes no duty of care to the underwriters for errors in the wording.[238]

It should be borne in mind that in preparing the policy wording it is the duty of the broker towards the assured not just to secure the required coverage, but also to use wording that puts the coverage beyond reasonable doubt. If the wording is opaque and the outcome is litigation between the assured and the insurers as to its meaning, then the brokers are in breach of duty even though the outcome is ultimately favourable to the assured.[239]

Assisting in the application process. One important feature of the duties of a **15-036** broker is the obtaining of all material facts from the assured. If facts are withheld from the broker, or false answers are given to him, the assured clearly has no complaint if the policy is subsequently avoided by the insurers.[240] The difficulty arises where the relevant information is given to the broker and not passed on, or is not given to the broker at all, in circumstances in which the broker has acted in breach of his duty; in submitting an application for insurance the broker acts as the agent of the assured, so that information received by the broker but not passed on cannot be imputed to the insurers.[241] Accordingly it is the broker's duty to the assured to pass to the insurers' material facts disclosed to him by the assured on the basis that a reasonable broker ought to be aware of which facts are, and which facts are not, material.[242] If the court takes the view that a reasonable broker would have disclosed the material in question then, even though it is subsequently established in the court proceedings that the broker was correct as a matter of law not to have disclosed that material, the court could still find the broker liable for breach of duty by exposing his client to unnecessary litigation.[243]

On the same principle, if the broker chooses not to ask the assured questions which appear on the proposal form and which are thus presumed to be material, the broker is liable if the policy is subsequently avoided.[244] However, if the assured is given an opportunity to examine the application completed by the

---

[238] *Stanton & Stanton v Starr* (1920) 3 Ll. L.R. 259.

[239] *FNCB v Barnet Devanney* [1999] Lloyd's Rep. I.R. 459; *Charman v Gordian Run-Off Ltd* [2003] Lloyd's Rep. I.R. 337, reversed in part [2004] Lloyd's Rep. I.R. 373; *Talbot Underwriting v Nausch Hogan & Murray* [2006] 2 Lloyd's Rep. 195; *Standard Life Assurance Ltd v Oak Dedicated Ltd* [2008] Lloyd's Rep. I.R. 552; *Ramco Ltd v Weller Russell & Laws Insurance Brokers Ltd* [2009] Lloyd's Rep. I.R. 27; *Dunlop Haywards (DHL) Ltd v Barbon Insurance Group Ltd* [2009] EWHC 2900 (Comm).

[240] *Stowers v GA Bonus Plc* [2003] Lloyd's Rep. I.R. 402. In *Malik v Moneywise Investments Plc* [2009] Lloyd's Rep. I.R. 141, the court was satisfied that the broker had not been given the information to pass on to insurers.

[241] *Roche v Roberts* (1921) 9 Ll. L.R. 59; *Lyons v Bentley* (1944) 77 Ll. L.R. 335; *O & R Jewellers Ltd v Terry* [1999] Lloyd's Rep. I.R. 436; *Winter v Irish Life* [1995] 2 Lloyd's Rep. 274; *Hazel v Whitlam* [2005] Lloyd's Rep. I.R. 168; *Lewis v Norwich Union Healthcare Ltd* [2010] Lloyd's Rep. I.R. 198.

[242] *Seller v Work* (1801) 1 Marshall on Insurance 305; *Maydew v Forrester* (1815) Holt 80; *Campbell v Richards* (1833) 5 B. & A. 840; *Cheshire v Vaughan* [1920] 3 K.B. 240; *Rozanes v Bowen* (1928) 32 Ll. L.R. 98; *Total Graphics Ltd v AGF Insurance Ltd* [1997] 1 Lloyd's Rep. 599; *Aneco Reinsurance Underwriting Ltd v Johnson & Higgins* [1999] Lloyd's Rep. I.R. 565; *Limit No 2 Ltd v Axa Versicherung AG* [2009] Lloyd's Rep. I.R. 396.

[243] See below.

[244] *Warren v Sutton* [1976] 2 Lloyd's Rep. 276.

broker, and fails to notice any errors[245] that failure by the assured will break the chain of causation and accordingly there is no remedy against the broker.[246]

The broker is under a duty of care to the assured to warn the assured of the duty of disclosure,[247]so that it will not be enough for the broker to confine his advice to questions which actually appear on the proposal form. It is not enough for the broker to draw the assured's attention to the duty in general terms, e.g. in the broker's terms of engagement or on premium invoices:

> "The broker must satisfy himself that the position is in fact understood by his client and this will usually require a specific oral or written exchange on the topic, both at the time of the original placement and at renewal".[248]

The broker is also under a duty to ascertain material facts for itself, and that duty is more strictly applied where the broker has failed to give proper warning to the assured of the duty of disclosure.[249]

Although the broker acts as agent for the assured in placing cover,[250] s.19 of the Marine Insurance Act 1906 imposes an independent duty on the broker towards the insurers to disclose to them all material facts known to him.[251] Breach of the independent duty will give the insurers the right to avoid the policy as against the assured, so in general its existence may not be significant. However, if the insurers have agreed that they will not avoid the policy in the event of any breach of the duty by assured or broker or the contract removes from the broker the authority to make statements on the part of the assured, they will have no right to avoid in the case of non-disclosure or misrepresentation by the broker. Where insurers have no right to avoid for these reasons, they may maintain an action against the broker for negligent[252] or fraudulent[253] misrepresentation, although it is settled law that damages are unavailable for pure non-disclosure[254] and that a broker does not owe any duty of care to the insurers.[255]

---

[245] It is unclear whether the same rule applies to omissions: *Commonwealth Insurance v Groupe Sprinks* [1983] 2 Lloyd's Rep. 67.

[246] *O'Connor v Kirby* [1972] 1 Q.B. 90; *Kapur v JW Francis & Co* [2000] Lloyd's Rep. I.R. 361 (which rejected the alternative suggestion in *O'Connor* that the assured owed the broker a duty of care to ensure that the answers were correct). *Kapur* and *O'Connor* were distinguished in *Arbory Group Ltd v West Craven Insurance Services* [2007] Lloyd's Rep. I.R. 491, in which the assured signed a proposal form for business interruption insurance which understated the amount of gross profit earned by the assured: the figure provided the basis for calculating the amount of cover. That error was the result of a negligent explanation by the broker, and it was held that the assured had not caused his own loss or been guilty of contributory negligence by signing the form and by failing to appreciate the explanation of the calculation of profit set out in the detailed notes accompanying the form.

[247] Dicta in *Warren v Sutton* [1976] 2 Q.B. 276 appear to deny any such duty, but its existence was confirmed in *Gunns and Gunns v Par Insurance Brokers* [2000] Lloyd's Rep. I.R. 361 and *Jones v Environcom Ltd (No.2)* [2010] EWHC 759 (Comm).

[248] *Jones v Environcom Ltd (No.2)* [2010] EWHC 759 (Comm), per David Steel J.

[249] *Jones v Environcom Ltd (No.2)* [2010] EWHC 759 (Comm).

[250] *Roberts v Plaisted* [1989] 2 Lloyd's Rep. 341.

[251] *SAIL v Farex Gie* [1995] L.R.L.R. 116; *PCW Syndicates v PCW Insurers* [1996] 1 Lloyd's Rep. 241; *HIH Casualty and General Insurance Ltd v Chase Manhattan Bank* [2003] Lloyd's Rep. I.R. 230.

[252] Under s.2(1) of the Misrepresentation Act 1967.

[253] In the tort of deceit.

[254] *Banque Keyser Ullman SA v Skandia (UK) Insurance Co Ltd* [1990] Q.B. 665.

[255] *Gran Gelato Ltd v Richcliff (Group) Ltd* [1992] Ch. 560; *Williams v Natural Life Health Foods Ltd* [1998] 1 W.L.R. 830.

Assistance during the currency of the policy

Duties on amendment and renewal. Just as a broker is required to act in a **15–037**
prudent fashion in attempting to obey instructions given to him by the assured as
to the scope of the original policy, the broker is required also to exercise
reasonable care—if necessary, by taking legal advice—to ensure that any
indorsement to the policy obtained by him on the request of the assured meets the
assured's requirements.[256] As an indorsement takes effect as a new contract, the
broker's duty to disclose all material facts to the insurers is revived.[257]

The broker may be under an express or implied duty to renew cover. A broker
who is expressly required to renew a policy but who fails to do so and neglects
to inform the assured of his omission, will be liable to the assured,[258] and in the
same way a broker who was at the outset instructed to obtain long-term cover but
who has obtained a policy of lesser duration is required to renew the policy on
its expiry.[259] In the case of failure to renew, the broker may not plead as a defence
that a renewal notice was not sent to him by the insurers.[260] It is also the broker's
duty to ensure that all material facts are disclosed to the insurers on
renewal.[261]

The same duties in relation to securing satisfactory cover apply on renewal in
the same way as on original application. In *Frost v James Finlay Bank Ltd*[262] it
was held that an insurance broker would be in breach of a duty of care by
advising the assured to renew with a different insurer where there might be some
dispute as to whether any losses fell under the original or renewed insurance.
Again, in *Dunlop Haywards (DHL) Ltd v Barbon Insurance Group Ltd*,[263] the
instructions given to the broker were to renew the assured's cover on no worse
terms than the expiring insurance. The earlier policy covered all of the assured's
liabilities, but the broker arranged a cover—which took effect three months
before the existing policy had been due to expire and had been brought forward
by a change in the assured's ownership—was limited by the broker to the
assured's property management activities. The broker was held to have been in
breach of duty by failing to secure cover for other activities (including the
assured's most risky activity, valuation, which had in fact given rise to claims),
Hamblen J. commenting that the broker's obligation was in particular to explain
any changes to the terms of the expiring policy necessitated by the state of the
professional indemnity insurance market or the changes to the assured's
structure, which it had failed to do. Equally, once the policy has been renewed,
the broker is under a duty to advise the assured of any changes to the cover or
to his obligations under the policy.[264]

---

[256] *National Insurance and Guarantee Corp Plc v Imperio Reinsurance Co UK Ltd* [1999] Lloyd's
Rep. I.R. 249. See, however, *Yechiel v Kerry London Ltd* [2010] Lloyd's Rep. I.R. 295, where the
assured was unable to establish that he had ever requested the broker to seek an indorsement.

[257] *Gaughan v Tony McDonagh & Co* [2005] EWHC 739 (Comm).

[258] *United Marketing Co v Hasham Kara* [1963] 2 All E.R. 553.

[259] *Youell v Bland Welch & Co Ltd (No.2)* [1990] 2 Lloyd's Rep. 431.

[260] *Fraser v Furman* [1967] 3 All E.R. 57.

[261] *Coolee v Wing Heath & Co* (1930) 47 T.L.R. 78; *Dunbar v A & B Painters Ltd* [1986] 2 Lloyds
Rep. 38.

[262] *Frost v James Finlay Bank Ltd* [2002] Lloyd's Rep. I.R. 503.

[263] *Dunlop Haywards (DHL) Ltd v Barbon Insurance Group Ltd* [2009] EWHC 2900 (Comm). See
also *Percy v West Bay Boat Builders and Shipyards Ltd* Unreported, 1997 BCCA.

[264] *Mint Securities Ltd v Blair* [1982] 1 Lloyd's Rep. 188; *Harvest Trucking Ltd v Davis* [1991] 2
Lloyd's Rep. 638. Earlier authority indicates that there is no duty of this type—*Michaels v Valentine*
(1923) 16 Ll. L.R. 244; *Avondale Blouse Ltd v Williamson* (1948) 81 Ll. L.R. 492—but these cases
are probably now unreliable.

A broker is not under an automatic duty to effect a renewal, as that duty is only imposed if the broker has a continuing relationship with the assured. If the broker has terminated its relationship with the assured before the renewal date then the broker is under no liability with respect to any renewal. In *United Insurance Co of Libya v Aon Ltd*[265] the broker had acted for the claimant insurer, UIC, in placing reinsurance cover in respect of a major direct risk. The broker decided that it would work with another insurer and secured reinsurance cover for that insurer, leading to the transfer of the direct business to it. Langley J. held, in an action by UIC for an account of the broker's profits, that the broker had not committed itself to working with UIC and had informed UIC accordingly. Langley J. also rejected the suggestion that there was any rule of law to the effect that a broker who agreed to execute an agency but without agreement on remuneration was bound to the client: the question in every case was whether there had been consensus, which on the facts there was not.

15–038 *Advising the assured as to coverage issues.* If the broker becomes aware of circumstances which may threaten the ability of the assured to recover under the policy in the event of a loss, the broker may be under a duty to draw the attention of the assured of those circumstances so that the relevant remedial action can be taken. The point is illustrated by *HIH Casualty and General Insurance Ltd v JLT Risk Solutions Ltd*,[266] in which brokers acting for the reinsured[267] were held to be under a duty to the reinsured to draw its attention to breaches of warranty by the assured which removed the liability of the reinsured to pay any claims and thus which operated to prevent any recovery by the reinsured from its reinsurers in the even that claims were paid.[268] The brokers were in a somewhat special position in this case, having developed the insurance and reinsurance products in question and having accepted some responsibility for the administration of the policy, and it was held to be their duty not simply to forward to the reinsured general reports from which information as to breaches could be gleaned but rather to highlight that information. Langley J. specifically rejected the argument that the brokers were a mere postbox whose duties were reactive as opposed to proactive, and that the brokers owed a duty to speak up even though they had no specific instructions to that effect from the claimant. Langley J.'s more general proposition was that brokers owed a duty to alert their client to any information which comes into their possession and which was material to the cover. In the usual course of events, brokers who have placed cover will not be under any continuing duty to monitor the assured's business to see whether any change in circumstances might require an extension of cover.

The Court of Appeal, affirming the judgment of Langley J.,[269] held that the brokers owed a duty of care and were in breach of it. The brokers had assumed responsibility for setting up the insurance and reinsurance arrangements in what was more or less a joint venture arrangement with the investors, and owed a duty of care to the claimant to ensure that the claimant was kept aware of potential coverage issues likely to affect the reinsurance. There were two main arguments against the imposition of a duty of care, each of which was swept aside by the

---

[265] *United Insurance Co of Libya v Aon Ltd* [2008] Lloyd's Rep. I.R. 166.

[266] *HIH Casualty and General Insurance Ltd v JLT Risk Solutions Ltd* [2007] Lloyd's Rep. I.R. 742.

[267] They were also acting for the assured, a situation which gave rise to a potential conflict of interest: the point was not explored.

[268] No liability was imposed on causation grounds, as the reinsured was found to have made payment despite actually knowing of the problems.

[269] *Ballast Plc, Re* [2007] Lloyd's Rep. I.R. 742.

Court of Appeal. The first was that the brokers' responsibility had been confined to passing on information which came to their attention: the Court of Appeal, adopting Langley J.'s reasoning on the point, held that the brokers had assumed responsibilities beyond those of merely acting as a "postbox". As was said by Auld L.J., a broker may:

"effectively devise, structure and establish a scheme, acting together with the insurer and reinsurers in which the insurer is little more than a 'front' for the reinsurers who shoulder the bulk of the risk . . . Where a broker has been at the centre of devising and structuring a risky scheme of that sort for insurers and reinsurers . . . it is plainly a strong candidate for post-placement monitoring obligations of the sort alleged here."

The second was that the brokers faced a conflict of interest, in that they were also the agents of the assured investors. By informing the claimant of information which was likely to affect coverage under the reinsurance and which would induce the claimant not to make payment, the brokers were automatically prejudicing the rights of the assured under the direct policy in breach of their duty to promote the assured's interests. The Court of Appeal refused to accept that the conflict of interest engendered where a broker acts for the various placing parties along a chain of insurance and reinsurance in any way precluded the imposition of a duty of care at each stage. Longmore L.J. specifically rejected, as "both unnecessary and unprincipled" the brokers' suggestion that there could be a duty of care to the reinsured only where the information in question related to the reinsurance but not to the insurance. Auld L.J. commented that the fact that the insurance and reinsurance were back to back did not dilute the prospects of a duty of care:

"[S]ince a potential risk to the reinsurance cover would necessarily reflect a corresponding risk to the insurance cover, which [the reinsured] in its own interests, might want to do something about".

Longmore L.J. expressed the principle as follows:

"I agree with the judge and my Lords that an insurance broker who, after placing the risk, becomes aware of information which has a material and potentially deleterious effect on the insurance cover which he has placed is under an obligation to act in his client's best interest by drawing it to the attention of his client and obtain his instructions in relation to it . . . Indeed, as between a lay client unversed in insurance matters and his insurance broker, I would think that the existence of such a duty should be comparatively uncontroversial . . . [I]n the case of reinsurance the broker acts for a professional client rather than a lay client, [but] the duty owed to each client should, in principle, be the same. If there is information which may potentially put cover at risk, both clients will want to know about it and, in normal circumstances, both clients should be informed."

Longmore L.J. recognised that there might be exceptional circumstances in which it might not be in the interests of the assured for information to be passed to the reinsured, but the duty of care was nevertheless unaffected:

"[T]he prudent broker may be well advised to discuss the matter first with his lay client and obtain his instructions before sending the information to the insurer in his capacity as reinsurance broker. But such a situation would be rare . . . The fact, however, that it is possible to envisage a rare case of difficulty does not mean that the precise scope of a broker's duty should be artificially restricted to cater for that rare case. The fact is that he has assumed duties to two principals and must properly carry out his duties to both those principals until a conflict arises; if it does arise, he would then have to consider his position. Of course, the likelihood is that if the lay client is given information that might put his cover at risk, he will instruct his brokers to discuss the matter with his insurers so that an accommodation can be reached before any question of loss arises. That is the way in which the market usually works."

It followed that on the facts of the case the brokers owed a duty of care to the claimant to bring to its attention the potential breaches of warranty. The brokers were in the present case in breach of their duty. Two points may be derived from this case. The first is that a potential conflict of interest does not preclude the imposition of a duty of care. The second is that a broker may in appropriate circumstances assume responsibility to his client to keep him informed of matters which may affect the right of recovery under the policy. As to the latter point, at first instance Langley J. admitted that the decision on a duty of care was not on the facts before him an easy one, and it may be that the case represents the outer limits of a continuing duty of care. The *HIH* case turned on the specific facts of the case, and in particular the central role of the brokers in establishing the entire funding scheme backed by insurance and reinsurance and thereafter in administering the scheme. Plainly it cannot be the case, for example, that a broker who is employed to place a particular cover is under a duty to monitor the interests and activities of the assured so that unrequested advice can be given as to whether the policy remains adequate for the assured's needs. Equally, it must be doubtful whether, in the absence of an agreement or other exceptional circumstances, a broker is under any duty to give continuing advice to the assured on coverage issues unless he is requested to do so and assumes responsibility for giving accurate answers. In *Great North Eastern Railway Ltd v JLT Corporate Risks Ltd*[270] Cresswell J. refused to strike out a claim by the assured that the broker's duty to ensure that his placement instructions had been obeyed was a continuing one running from the date of placement up to date of loss, although this appears to run counter to the settled rule that the limitation period against a broker who places a deficient policy runs from the date of the placement and not from any later date unless there is a further act of negligence.

15–039 *Duties under a declaration policy.* A policy in declaration form requires declarations to be made to the underwriters. A broker administering such a policy will have the responsibility for making declarations on receipt of information from the policyholder. The nature of the notification obligation will depend upon the form of the policy. If the policy is obligatory for both parties, the risk will attach as soon as it is accepted by the policyholder, and any notification provision is for information only: this may take the form of informing the underwriters at agreed intervals of the new risks accepted by the assured or reinsured and declared to the policy. If the policy is non-obligatory from the point of view of the assured, then the making of a declaration is essential to secure the attachment of the risk. If the policy is non-obligatory from the point of view of both parties, then the submission of a notification is an offer to the underwriters to accept the declared risk. Failure to make a notification will be fatal to coverage in the second and third of these cases, and may be fatal in the first case if the information provision is a condition precedent to the attachment of liability. In *BP Plc v Aon Ltd*[271] the assured obtained an open cover for offshore projects, the risk under the open cover attaching to a project only if there was a valid declaration by the assured within the currency of the policy. Colman J. held that

[270] *Great North Eastern Railway Ltd v JLT Corporate Risks Ltd* [2007] Lloyd's Rep. I.R. 38.
[271] *BP Plc v Aon Ltd* [2006] Lloyd's Rep. I.R. 577.

the broker had assumed responsibility for the making of valid declarations within the currency of the policy, and was in breach of that duty by notifying only the leading underwriters where the coverage provided by the following market required notification to them as well.

Termination and cancellation. The cancellation of a policy by a broker is **15–040** binding upon the assured only where such cancellation is within the actual or ostensible authority of the broker.[272] It might be thought that cancellation would not generally be within the scope of a broker's authority, and is thus unlikely to be effective unless there has been some direct communication between the assured and the insurers. Thus, if the broker fraudulently cancels a life policy and by this means procures payment to himself of the surrender value of the policy, the insurers may well be bound to reinstate the policy on the basis that the broker's fraudulent unauthorised act is a nullity. If brokers are instructed to cancel a policy but inform the assured that they have not done so, so that the assured believes that the remains covered, the brokers are under a duty to inform the assured once the cancellation takes effect so that he can place alternative insurance.[273]

Duties following loss. The duties of brokers in respect of claims made by the **15–041** assured are found in the common law and also in the general principles laid down by the ICOBS Rules in the Financial Services Authority's Handbook. ICOBS 8.3 provides that the broker must: act with due care, skill and diligence; avoid conflicts of interest in the absence of full and informed consent by the assured; and disclose to the assured any relationship with the insurers.

It is generally assumed that a broker is under some form of obligation to the assured to provide assistance with a claim. There is little authority to support this proposition, which runs counter to the notion that the broker's remuneration is fully earned as soon as the risk is placed. However, it was held by Clarke J. in *Grace v Leslie & Godwin Financial Services Ltd*[274] that brokers at Lloyd's were under a duty to retain placing documentation so that, in the event of a claim by the reinsured, it is possible to identify the reinsurers who have subscribed to the cover. Clarke J. held that: (1) the commission received by the broker included an element for collecting claims,[275] and market practice did not establish any custom that the broker was to receive additional commission for collecting claims, so there was an implied contractual obligation on the broker to collect claims on the reinsured's behalf; and (2) a broker was under an implied contractual duty to retain sufficient information to enable a claim to be made, particularly where the broker is aware that the reinsured did not himself possess that information or that the reinsured could not reasonably be expected to retain such information by reason of his reliance on the broker to do so. It is to be noted that *Grace* was concerned only with the Lloyd's market, and turned specifically on the evidence presented to the judge of what was to be expected of a Lloyd's broker. Further, *Grace* concerned a broker remunerated by commission. Accordingly, it is uncertain if the principles set out in *Grace* apply outside the Lloyd's market and to brokers remunerated by a fixed sum agreed with the assured: in the latter situation the scope of the broker's obligations would have to be determined

---

[272] *Xenos v Wickham* (1866) L.R. 2 H.L. 296.
[273] *Cherry Ltd v Allied Insurance Brokers Ltd* [1978] 1 Lloyd's Rep. 274.
[274] *Grace v Leslie & Godwin Financial Services Ltd* [1995] L.R.L.R. 472.
[275] Clarke J. did not review the earlier cases denying this. See above.

by the proper construction of any agreement of this type, as demonstrated by expert evidence as to the practice of the London market.

Where the broker is required to provide assistance to the assured in the claims process, the broker must exercise reasonable care in doing so. It is the duty of the broker to ensure that the assured's claim form is complete and submitted in due time[276] and that any claim handed to the broker is transmitted to the proper insurers or under the appropriate policy.[277] Although it appears long to have been the practice of Lloyd's brokers to perform certain functions for Lloyd's underwriters in the resolution of claims by the assured, the conflict of interest thereby created has been condemned by the courts on a number of occasions.[278] The position is, despite market practice, that the broker is not the agent of the underwriters in handling claims, so that notice of loss given to brokers rather than to underwriters is not deemed to have been received by the underwriters[279] unless the policy so specifies or the underwriter has otherwise agreed that notice to the broker is adequate,[280] and a promise by the broker that the underwriters will accept liability is not binding on them.[281] It is frequently the case that the broker is authorised by the assured to negotiate with the insurers and to reach a settlement, in which case the broker must act without negligence and only in the interests of the assured.[282]

Insurers are required to pay any claim directly to the assured, although if payment is made to a broker authorised[283] to receive the policy moneys the insurers are discharged from liability on making such payment. Where the policy proceeds are received by the broker, they may not be paid to any third party without the assured's consent.[284] Lloyd's brokers commonly operate net accounting arrangements with underwriters, under which the broker receives the premiums from, and pays losses to, the assured, settling any balances with the underwriter at the end of the agreed accounting period.[285] Payment of losses is generally made "subject to collection", so that if the broker, having made payment to the assured, does not receive reimbursement from the underwriter within an agreed time, the broker has the right to recover his payment from the assured. In such a case, the assured must pursue the underwriter directly. Should the broker pay the loss without reserving any rights, the payment is to be treated as a voluntary payment which does not diminish the assured's loss and thus

---

[276] *Comber v Anderson* (1808) 1 Camp. 523.

[277] *Alexander Forbes Europe Ltd v SBJ Ltd* [2003] Lloyd's Rep. I.R. 428.

[278] *North & South Trust Co v Berkeley* [1971] 1 All E.R. 980; *Anglo-African Merchants Ltd v Bayley* [1970] 1 Q.B. 311; *Eagle Star Insurance Co v Spratt* [1971] 2 Lloyd's Rep. 116.

[279] *Roche v Roberts* (1921) 9 Ll. L.R. 59.

[280] See, e.g. *Friends Provident Life & Pensions Ltd v Sirius International Insurance Corp* [2006] Lloyd's Rep. I.R. 45; *Tioxide Europe Ltd v CGU International Insurance Plc* [2006] Lloyd's Rep. I.R. 31.

[281] *Callaghan & Hedges v Thompson* [2000] Lloyd's Rep. I.R. 125.

[282] *Bousfield v Cresswell* (1810) 2 Camp. 545. But see *Re Great Western Insurance Co* [1999] Lloyd's Rep. I.R. 377.

[283] *Hine Bros v Steamship Insurance Syndicate Ltd* (1895) 72 L.T. 79.

[284] *Poullorizos & Co v Capel-Cure & Co* (1926) 26 Ll. L.R. 19; *Wolf & Korkhaus v Tyser & Co* (1921) 8 Ll. L.R. 340.

[285] The assured is not party to this arrangement, and remains able to sue the insurers for the loss: *Scott v Irving* (1830) 1 B. & Ad. 605; *Stewart v Aberdein* (1834) 4 M. & W. 211; *Sweeting v Pearce* (1859) 9 C.B.N.S. 534; *Legge v Byas, Mosely & Co* (1901) 7 Com. Cas. 16; *Matvieff v Crossfield* (1903) 8 Com. Cas. 120; *Pollard, Ashby & Co v Franco-British Marine Insurance Co* (1920) 5 Ll. L.R. 286; *McGowin Lumber & Export Co v Pacific Marine Insurance Co Ltd* (1922) 12 Ll. L.R. 496; *McCarthy v Dixon & Co (London) Ltd* (1924) 19 Ll. L.R. 29; *Provincial Assurance v Crowder* (1927) 27 Ll. L.R. 28; *Stolos Compania SA v Ajax Insurance Co Ltd (The Admiral C)* [1981] 1 Lloyd's Rep. 9.

which leaves the assured with the right to recover the policy moneys from the insurers without any obligation to repay the broker.[286]

Documents in the broker's possession

The right of insurers to obtain documents. The general principle that the broker **15–042** is the agent of the assured at first sight indicates that underwriters have no rights over documents generated in pursuit of that relationship and subsequently held by the broker. The common law position was discussed by the Court of Appeal in *Goshawk Dedicated Ltd v Tyser & Co Ltd*,[287] in which a syndicate claimed as against brokers the right to see claims files and placing files (which the syndicate had previously seen but not kept copies), and accounting information relating to premiums paid (which the syndicate had not previously seen). The brokers resisted disclosure on the ground that the documents belonged to the assureds and disclosure of them might put the brokers in breach of duty to the assured if they contained anything adverse to the assured's interests. The Court of Appeal held that the brokers were under a duty to disclose all three classes of documents to the syndicate. There was an implied term in the contract of insurance whereby the assured was required to authorise the broker to disclose their claims and placing files,[288] such implication being necessary: to reflect the market practice that documentation was held by brokers and not underwriters; to recognise that, without subsequent disclosure, the insurance contract itself could not effectively or safely be operated. Disclosure of the placing file was a part of the assured's duty of good faith, given that the documents were originally presented to the syndicate in furtherance of the duty of good faith; disclosure of the claims file was necessary to allow the syndicate to deal properly with later claims; disclosure of the accounting documents was benign as those documents contained information for the benefit of both the syndicate and the assureds. The Court of Appeal went on to hold that, in order to give effect to the implied term, it was necessary to imply a contract between brokers and underwriters under which the brokers would make disclosure without reference to the assured.[289] There are three important limitations on the implied term in the insurance contract: it does not extend to the meeting of disclosure requests which are unnecessary or unreasonably wide; the duty is one to hand over documents which

---

[286] *Merrett v Capitol Indemnity Corporation* [1991] 1 Lloyd's Rep. 169, where the problem was overcome by an express agreement to hand over the proceeds to the broker.

[287] *Goshawk Dedicated Ltd v Tyser & Co Ltd* [2007] Lloyd's Rep. I.R. 224, reversing [2005] Lloyd's Rep. I.R. 379.

[288] Rix L.J. expressed the view that there was support for the implication of the term on business efficacy grounds in the doctrine of utmost good faith. Failure to disclose was not of itself a breach of that duty, but rather that "the duty informs the content of the contractual obligation at the time of contract", a point of particular significance in relation to the placing information which was of itself subject to a duty of good faith when originally used to present the risk. Rix L.J. also felt that good faith underlay the implication of underwriting and claims terms into proportional reinsurance treaties, as so decided in by Hobhouse J. in *Phoenix General Insurance Co of Greece SA v Halvanon Insurance Co Ltd* [1985] 2 Lloyd's Rep. 599, and thus strengthened the argument in support of disclosure of claims and accounting information. However, very shortly before the decision in *Goshawk*, a differently constituted Court of Appeal had in *Bonner v Cox* [2006] Lloyd's Rep. I.R. 385 rejected the suggestion that there were any such implied terms in non-proportional treaties and doubted whether *Phoenix* itself was good law in the context of proportional reinsurance. This development does not, however, undermine Rix L.J.'s reasoning in *Goshawk*, which is rooted in the need for claims and accounting information to be disclosed to make the contract workable.

[289] The argument for such an agreement based on market custom had been rejected by Christopher Clarke J. at first instance and was not revived on appeal: in the Court of Appeal the basis of the alleged agreement was commercial necessity.

are in the brokers' possession; and there is no obligation to provide underwriters with what they already have.

With effect from December 20, 2001 the Lloyd's market introduced a standard Terms of Business Agreement (TOBA) compliance with which is now compulsory for those operating within Lloyd's. TOBA was revised in January 2005, but without material change. TOBA relates to the relationship between broker and syndicate managing agent. TOBA deals expressly with Access to Records. Clause 8 provides that the broker agrees to allow the syndicate on reasonable notice to inspect accounting information and documents previously presented to the syndicate, although this is subject to cl.2 which gives priority to the broker's duty to place the interests of its client before all other considerations.

As seen in the preceding paragraphs, the Court of Appeal held that even before TOBA brokers were obliged to disclose documents of all three types to underwriters under an implied term in the insurance and under an implied contract between brokers and underwriters. The introduction of TOBA formalised the disclosure obligations of brokers, and there was no possible conflict between cl.8.1 and cl.2.2, because the implied term in the contract of insurance meant that "the brokers' clients and principals have themselves agreed that such documents in the possession of their brokers should be disclosed by their brokers to their underwriters." That meant that there was no need to consider the relationship between the two clauses in other contexts.[290]

15–043 *The right of the assured to obtain documents.* Because the broker is the agent of the assured, any documents generated or obtained by the broker in the course of fulfilling his duties towards the assured belong to the assured and he is entitled at the very least to sight of them, if not—where appropriate—possession of them. Thus any reports on the loss obtained by the broker are the property of the assured even though the insurers may have commissioned the broker to obtain those reports.[291] The most important documents likely to be in the possession of the brokers relate to premium payments and receipts from insurers, and it is clear that the broker is required not just to hand over the relevant documents but to keep accounts in a fashion which allows the relevant information to be given to the assured. In *Equitas Ltd v Horace Holman & Co*[292] the claimant was the successor in title of Lloyd's Syndicates which had reinsured their losses under policies for the years up to and including 1992. The defendant brokers had placed the reinsurances and continued to administer them. The claimant sought information from the brokers as to the sums due under the outward reinsurances placed by the brokers, a request which was initially refused but which ultimately resulted in the production of a composite account from which it was not possible to identify individual transactions. The case was for the most part concerned with the allocation of the costs of the legal proceedings launched by the claimant to obtain the information, but in the course of his judgment Andrew Smith J. held (and indeed it was common ground) that the brokers owed:

"a duty to take reasonable care to maintain proper and adequate records which would allow the Syndicates at any stage to ascertain the true state of the account with them and

[290] Although Rix L.J. did express the view that "it may after all be easier to give clause 2.2 a full and proper content while at the same time giving effect to clause 8.1, than vice versa."
[291] *Anglo-African Merchants Ltd v Bayley* [1969] 1 Lloyd's Rep. 268; *North and South Trust v Berkeley* [1970] 2 Lloyd's Rep. 467; *Pryke v Gibbs Hartley Cooper* [1991] 1 Lloyd's Rep. 602.
[292] *Equitas Ltd v Horace Holman & Co* [2007] Lloyd's Rep. I.R. 567.

to ascertain what sums were owed to the Syndicates and Equitas by their reinsurers."

As a part of that duty, and based on the expert evidence presented to the court, the brokers were held to be obliged to disclose or provide copies of internal documents, in the form of ledgers and cash books in so far as those documents recorded transactions carried out by the brokers for their clients. The fact that the brokers did not keep records in a form which enabled them to provide information on individual transactions did not excuse them from their duty of providing appropriate records when the claimant called for them.

Remedies for breach of duty

Basis of liability. There is undoubtedly a contractual relationship between the **15–044** assured and his broker, so that negligence on the broker's part will render him liable in an action for breach of contract. The existence of a contract between a professional adviser and his client was at one time regarded by the English courts as excluding the possibility of a tortious duty of care, but it is now the case that contractual and tortious duties may exist side by side. Consequently, in the event of negligence, the assured may choose whether to sue in contract or in tort,[293] and the decided cases on brokers' liabilities are almost equally divided as to the cause of action. It will rarely matter whether the assured's action is contractual or tortious, for the broker's duty in contract or tort is to maintain the standards reasonably to be expected of a competent broker, the measure of damages will be the same, and the defence of contributory negligence is available to the broker in both situations. These may, however, be some advantage in suing in tort where time is a factor, as tortious limitation periods are potentially more generous. A further potential advantage of tort over contract is that in the event that the contract fails for uncertainty or on some other ground, the assured may still be able to establish a tortious duty of care. Moreover, establishing a duty independent of contract allows the assured to proceed in tort directly against an employee of the broker.[294] A final point is that different choice of law rules apply to contract claims and to tort claims.

Basic measure of damages. It was at one time believed that a broker acted as a **15–045** fall-back insurer, guaranteeing payment if as the result of his neglect, no cover existed,[295] but it was eventually established by *Charles v Altin*[296] that breach of duty merely demands payment of damages by the broker in contract or tort representing the loss suffered by the assured. The amount recoverable by the assured depends upon the nature of the broker's breach of duty and the loss that has been caused to the assured. The most common situation is that the assured has been left without a claim for any one of a number of reasons: a policy has not been procured or does not cover the loss; the policy has been avoided by the insurer for breach of the duty of utmost good faith or terminated for breach of warranty; or a claim has not been submitted in good time. In these and similar cases the assured's loss is measured by the sum that he would have been able to claim under the policy, coupled with any costs that he may have incurred in pursuing unsuccessfully the insurer.[297]

---

[293] *Henderson v Merrett Syndicates Ltd* [1994] 3 All E.R. 506.
[294] *Punjab National Bank v De Boinville* [1992] 1 Lloyd's Rep. 7.
[295] *Tickel v Short* (1750) 2 Ves. Sen. 239; *Smith v Price* (1862) 2 F. & F. 748.
[296] *Charles v Altin* (1854) 15 C.B. 46.
[297] *Ramco Ltd v Weller Russell & Laws Insurance Brokers Ltd* [2009] Lloyd's Rep. I.R. 27.

If there have been no losses which would have been insured by the policy had it been placed properly, or only small losses, the assured has the option of claiming from the broker by way of damages the amount of premium paid by the assured, on the ground that the policy did not meet his requirements and that it was of no use to him.[298] If as a result of the broker's negligence a policy is avoided ab initio, and the assured is required to repay sums to the insurer which were paid to the assured prior to the avoidance of the policy, the broker's liability to the assured is not reduced by the fact that the assured has become insolvent and is unable to make payment to the insurer.[299]

Some deduction may have to be made from damages awarded against a broker to give credit for any increased premium which the assured would have had to pay had proper cover been secured by the broker[300] and also the increased fees which the assured would have had to pay to any assessor appointed by him to negotiate the claim with insurers, although a claim is not to be discounted to take account of the speculative possibility that, had there been full insurance, the assured might have negotiated a lesser sum from the insurers.[301]

15–046   **Wasted costs.** In many cases, the assured has alternative causes of action against the insurers and the brokers, on the basis that if the claim against the insurers fails then an alternative claim against the brokers will succeed. Frequently, the brokers will concede that they are liable in the event that the claim against the insurers should fail, and assist the assured in his primary action against the insurers. Where brokers do face liability in such circumstances, it is also clear that the costs incurred by the assured in pursuing the insurers unsuccessfully are recoverable from the brokers. The manner in which those costs are recoverable depends upon whether the brokers are proceeded against in joined proceedings or in separate proceedings.

(1) If the brokers are parties to the original action against the insurers, the assured's costs in the action against the underwriters are recoverable from the brokers as costs proper rather than as damages.[302] The sum awarded is, therefore, within the discretion of the trial judge, against whose exercise of discretion there is no appeal unless the judge gives permission: Supreme Court Act 1981 s.18(1)(j). It will normally be appropriate for the judge to award costs against the brokers on a standard (i.e. reasonable cost) rather than an indemnity (i.e. actual cost) basis.[303]

(2) If the brokers have not been joined to the action against the underwriters, but are proceeded against separately, the lost costs in the first action are recoverable from the brokers by way of damages rather than by way of a discretionary award of costs. This means that there may be an appeal against the sum awarded under this head without the leave of the trial judge. Once again, the damages should reflect the assured's costs in the

---

[298] *Transport and Trading Co Ltd v Olivier & Co Ltd* (1925) 21 Ll. L.R. 379.

[299] *Aneco Reinsurance Underwriting Ltd v Johnson & Higgins* [1998] 1 Lloyd's Rep. 565, a point which did not arise on appeal.

[300] *Banque Paribas (Suisse) SA v Stolidi Shipping Co Ltd* Unreported, 1995.

[301] *Bollom & Co Ltd v Byas Moseley & Co Ltd* [2000] Lloyd's Rep. I.R. 136.

[302] *Seavision Investment SA v Evenett and Clarkson Puckle Ltd (The Tiburon)* [1992] 2 Lloyd's Rep. 26.

[303] *Seavision Investment SA v Evenett and Clarkson Puckle Ltd (The Tiburon)* [1992] 2 Lloyd's Rep. 26.

action against the insurers on a standard rather than indemnity basis.[304]

In *Ramco Ltd v Weller Russell & Laws Insurance Brokers Ltd*[305] the court allowed the assured to recover in a claim against its brokers: (a) the difference between the costs awarded to it in its (partially) successful action against the insurers and the actual amount which the assured paid by way of costs; and (b) the costs incurred by it in unsuccessfully petitioning the House of Lords for permission to appeal against the ruling of the Court of Appeal, on the basis that the sum was small and that a failure to petition could have given the brokers an argument that the assured had not mitigated its loss.

Consequential loss. An assured who is left without insurance cover, or whose insurance cover is inadequate, has an action against, the broker responsible, for the shortfall in the sum which would have been recovered under the policy. The further question is whether the broker can be liable for additional loss suffered by the assured. To take a typical example, the assured may have instructed his broker to obtain property insurance for a small business: if the broker fails to do so and the premises are destroyed, and the assured does not have the financial resources to fund the rebuilding of the premises in the absence of any insurance proceeds, the assured may lose the entire business. Is the broker liable for such loss? The impecuniosity of the assured is no longer to be regarded as the proximate cause of the loss in such a situation: the authority for that earlier proposition, *Liesbosch Dredger v Edison (The Liesbosch)*,[306] was overruled by the House of Lords in *Lagden v O'Connor*.[307] However, that does not automatically mean that the assured is entitled to recover consequential loss. The test for recovery is that laid down by the House of Lords in *South Australia Asset Management Corporation Respondents v York Montague Ltd (SAAMCO)*,[308] namely, whether the loss claimed was that in respect of which the broker's duty of care was owed. Accordingly, as long as this test is satisfied, the broker may in principle be liable for a sum greater than that which was insured under the policy even though the insurers themselves could not have been liable for an additional sum.[309]

In *Arbory Group Ltd v West Craven Insurance Services*, brokers through their admitted negligence failed to place adequate business interruption cover for the assured's business. The assured's premises were damaged by fire, but the assured was, in the absence of insurance proceeds, unable to reinstate the premises from his own resources so that significant financial loss was sustained. H.H. Judge

15–047

---

[304] *Seavision Investment SA v Evenett and Clarkson Puckle Ltd (The Tiburon)* [1992] 2 Lloyd's Rep. 26.

[305] *Ramco Ltd v Weller Russell & Laws Insurance Brokers Ltd* [2009] Lloyd's Rep. I.R. 27.

[306] *Liesbosch Dredger v Edison (The Liesbosch)* [1933] A.C. 449.

[307] *Lagden v O'Connor* [2004] Lloyd's Rep. I.R. 315. In both *Ramwade v WJ Emson & Co* [1987] R.T.R. 72 and *Verderame v Commercial Union Assurance Co Plc* [1992] B.C.L.C. 793 consequential loss was held to be precluded on the ground that it had been caused by the assured's own parlous financial position, but those cases clearly cannot survive *Lagden v O'Connor*: see *Arbory Group Ltd v West Craven Insurance Services* [2007] Lloyd's Rep. I.R. 491.

[308] *South Australia Asset Management Corporation Respondents v York Montague Ltd* [1997] A.C. 191.

[309] In accordance with *Sprung v Royal Insurance* [1999] Lloyd's Rep. I.R. 111 had they been liable but refused to pay in a timely fashion. See: *Aneco Reinsurance Underwriting Ltd v Johnson & Higgins* [2002] Lloyd's Rep. I.R. 91; *Arbory Group Ltd v West Craven Insurance Services* [2007] Lloyd's Rep. I.R. 491. The contrary had been suggested by Parker L.J. in *Ramwade v WJ Emson & Co* [1987] R.T.R. 72.

Grenfell QC, applying *SAAMCO*, held that the duty of care accepted by the brokers was to preserve the assured from the type of loss that he had actually suffered, namely business interruption loss, and that the broker was liable not just for the uninsured sum but also for the consequential loss suffered by the assured. Therefore, the assured was entitled to recover not just the proceeds of the policy but also consequential loss which fell within the scope of the duty adopted by the broker. The court was not called upon to decide, and did not comment on, the question of whether the broker could have been liable for consequential loss flowing from loss of business if the policy sought had been purely against physical damage. There is certainly a powerful argument, based on *SAAMCO*, that the broker's duty in such a case would be restricted to finding business interruption cover, and indeed in *Arbory* the judge emphasised the fact that the policy was business interruption and that the loss was precisely that which the policy was designed to prevent.

The principle applies also in reinsurance cases. The reinsured may never have agreed to acting as insurer without the security of reinsurance cover. If that cover is not in place, the reinsured may seek by way of damages not just the amount of lost security but also the full amount of its exposure under the direct policy. Clearly the amount of lost security is recoverable by way of damages. In *Youell v Bland Welch & Co (No.2)*[310] brokers had failed to secure reinsurance cover of the proper duration. The market evidence was that appropriate cover was not available at the relevant time. Phillips J. ruled that the correct measure of damages for the reinsured against the brokers was the difference between the sum that the reinsured had paid the assured, and the sum that the reinsured would have paid on the basis that they would have limited their participation in the insurance had they known that reinsurance was unavailable. It will be noted that the damages were based on the assumption that the reinsured would not have entered into the underlying transaction to that extent in the absence of reinsurance. Again, in *Aneco Reinsurance Underwriting Ltd v Johnson & Higgins*,[311] a retrocession agreement covering two reinsurance treaties was avoided by retrocessionaires on the strength of a false statement by the retrocedant's brokers as to the nature of the reinsurance treaties. The retrocedant sought to recover all sums for which it was liable under the treaties, on the basis that it would not have entered into them had the brokers not been apparently successful in obtaining retrocession cover. At first instance Cresswell J. held that this measure overstated the retrocedant's loss flowing from the brokers' breach of duty, as it covered loss which would not have been recoverable from the retrocessionaires if there had been valid retrocession in place which was too remote. The proper measure, in the view of Cresswell J. was the amount which the retrocedant had not been able to recover under the actual retrocession contracts placed by the brokers rather than all underwriting losses suffered by the retrocedant. Had the retrocedant been able to establish that, in the absence of negligence by the brokers, it would not have been possible for the brokers to have placed cover elsewhere in the market the higher measure would have been appropriate. When the case went on appeal to the Court of Appeal,[312] it was regarded as one in which the retrocedants would not have subscribed to any part of the risk had it not been for the presentation by the brokers: in other words, this was a case in which the brokers had acted not simply as agents to secure retrocession but rather were instrumental in obtaining the retrocedant's entire subscription. In so deciding, the Court of Appeal gave its

[310] *Youell v Bland Welch & Co (No.2)* [1990] 2 Lloyd's Rep. 431.
[311] *Aneco Reinsurance Underwriting Ltd v Johnson & Higgins* [1998] 1 Lloyd's Rep. 565.
[312] *Aneco Reinsurance Underwriting Ltd v Johnson & Higgins* [2000] Lloyd's Rep. I.R. 12.

express approval to the ruling of Phillips J. in *Youell v Bland Welch & Co (No.2)*, which was regarded as being on all fours with Aneco as regards the effect of the broker's extended role. Aneco was subsequently appealed to the House of Lords,[313] which, by a 4:1 majority, approved the reasoning of the Court of Appeal. It follows from *Aneco* that there is no general rule that the broker cannot be liable for a sum greater than the amount of the lost cover, and that the sole question is whether the broker's duty extends solely to placing insurance cover of the type sought or whether the broker has also assumed duties akin to those of an investment adviser, the position found in *Aneco*.

Damages for exceeding authority. A broker who acts outside his actual, usual and apparent authority will not bind the assured by his conduct, and is thus unlikely to cause the assured any loss. The remedy of the insurers in such a case is against the broker, for breach of warranty of authority, and not against the assured. The broker will, however, be capable of inflicting loss on the assured where he acts within his usual or ostensible authority contrary to the assured's wishes, and the question then becomes whether the broker is liable to the assured in damages; a good illustration of the problem may be where the broker wrongfully cancels a policy, or makes a false statement to the insurers on the assured's behalf. It would seem that a distinction must be drawn between usual and apparent authority. In the case of usual authority, where the broker has simply exceeded his powers, there is no reason why the assured should not have a remedy. In the case of apparent authority, that is, authority by estoppel, the position is somewhat different, for the broker's authority exists only because the assured has represented to the third party that that is the case. Given that the assured is estopped as against the insurers from denying the broker's authority, it would seem to follow that the assured is similarly estopped against the broker from denying the broker's right to act as he did.[314]

15–048

Interim payments. Under CPR Pt 25, the court may award an interim payment to a claimant who would succeed against the defendant should the action proceed to final judgment. This power is, in principle, exercisable against a defendant broker in an action for breach of duty brought by the assured but, as a matter of practice, only where the insurer has established that it is not liable under the policy. Thus, if the assured brings an action against the insurers on the policy, and in the alternative against the broker in the event that the insurers is found not liable, it cannot be said at the outset which of the defendants will be found liable and no interim payment is possible against either of them.[315]

15–049

Defences open to brokers

Mitigation of loss. Where the broker has failed to obtain any cover at all, or has failed to obtain appropriate cover, and the problem comes to light before any loss has occurred, the assured will be under a duty to mitigate his loss. Thus if the assured faced with this situation takes no steps to obtain alternative cover, it may be open to the broker to argue that the assured's loss is not the sum which would have been recovered had proper insurance been in place, but rather the amount that it would have taken to have purchased the correct level of cover. However,

15–050

[313] *Aneco Reinsurance Underwriting Ltd v Johnson & Higgins* [2002] Lloyd's Rep. I.R. 91.
[314] *Great Atlantic Insurance Co v Home Insurance Co* [1981] 2 Lloyd's Rep. 219.
[315] *Ricci Burns Ltd v Toole* [1989] 3 All E.R. 478.

this argument will succeed in exceptional cases only. In *BP Plc v Aon Ltd*[316] the broker made declarations under an open cover only to the leading underwriters, and not to the following market. The problem came to light after the open cover had expired but before any losses had arisen. The brokers unsuccessfully argued that they were liable only for the cost of purchasing a further policy to cover the loss. Colman J. held that the assured could be deprived of the full amount of his damages only if his conduct amounted to "a complete departure from the conduct that could reasonably be expected from an [assured] in that position knowing the information which it had". In *BP* itself, Colman J. found that this was not the case: the assured remained in negotiation with the following market; premium rates had dramatically increased; and the brokers themselves had not recommended any such course of action. It might be thought that the last-mentioned point will be fatal in this type of situation.

15–051 *Contributory negligence.* At common law, a defendant in a negligence suit who was able to demonstrate that the claimant had himself been guilty of negligence which contributed to the loss, had an absolute defence. This principle was modified by the Law Reform (Contributory Negligence) Act 1945, which introduced the possibility of apportionment. Section 1(1) provides that:

> "Where any person suffers damage as the result partly of his own fault and partly of the fault of any other person or persons, a claim in respect of that damage shall not be defeated by reason of the fault of the person suffering the damage, but the damages recoverable in respect thereof shall be reduced to such extent as the court thinks just and equitable having regard to the claimant's share in the responsibility for that damage."

The word "fault" is defined in s.4 as meaning: "negligence, breach of statutory duty or other act or omission which gives rise to a liability in tort". The Act thus specifically applies to actions in tort but does not cover actions for breach of contract. A claim against a broker for negligence may be framed either in contract or in tort, and it has been held[317] that the 1945 Act permits apportionment where the defendant's liability in contract is the same as his liability in the tort of negligence independently of the existence of any contract. Accordingly the courts are free to apportion liability where a claim is made against a broker either in contract or in tort.[318]

A number of cases decided before the passing of the 1945 Act, when contributory negligence was an absolute defence to the claimant's action, show an understandable reluctance to admit that a negligent broker could ever defeat the claimant by demonstrating that the claimant was partly responsible for his own loss.[319] Since apportionment has become possible, it is established that there is a two-step test. The initial question is whether the assured has been negligent

---

[316] *BP Plc v Aon Ltd* [2006] Lloyd's Rep. I.R. 577.

[317] *Forsikringsaktielskapet Vesta v Butcher* [1988] 1 All E.R. 19: the point did not arise in the House of Lords. See also: *Youell v Bland Welch & Co Ltd (No.2)* [1990] 2 Lloyd's Rep. 431; *Barclays Bank Plc v Fairclough Building Ltd* [1995] 1 All E.R. 289.

[318] Apportionment is not possible where the defendant's liability arises from some contractual provision which does not depend on negligence on the part of the defendant or where the defendant's liability arises from a contractual obligation which is expressed in terms of taking care but does not correspond to a common law duty to take care which would exist in the given case independently of contract.

[319] *Dickson v Devitt* (1916) 21 Com. Cas. 291; *British Citizens Assurance Co v Woolland & Co* (1921) 8 Ll. L.R. 89; *General Accident Fire and Life Assurance Corp Ltd v Minet & Co Ltd* (1942) 74 Ll. L.R. 1.

in the sense that the assured has failed to act prudently in respect of its own interests.[320] In *Dunlop Haywards (DHL) Ltd v Barbon Insurance Group Ltd*[321] for example, the broker was instructed to renew the assured's professional indemnity cover on no worse terms than the expiring insurance. The broker obtained quotations and then a policy which restricted cover to the assured's property management activities, leaving uninsured the far riskier activity of valuation, which ultimately gave rise to claims. The draft wording had been sent by the broker to the assured along with various other documents, but the assured's attention was not drawn to the offending limitation. Hamblen J. held that the assured had not been at fault in not reading the documents, in that the assured had required an executive summary to save him from trawling through the documents and had paid the broker to obtain cover in accordance with instructions. By contrast, in *HIH Casualty and General Insurance Ltd v JLT Risk Solutions Ltd*[322] the reinsured was held by the Court of Appeal (affirming the judgment of Langley J. on the point) to have caused its own loss by making payment to the assured knowing that reinsurers would be unlikely to provide an indemnity, so that the broker's breach of duty in failing to warn the assured of the existence of a defence open to the reinsures was to be disregarded. In so holding the Court of Appeal rejected the need for the trial judge's alternative ruling that there should be a 70 per cent deduction for contributory negligence, but expressed the view that 100 per cent deduction for contributory negligence was its favoured approach in such a case.

If the assured has been negligent and has contributed to his own loss, the second question is how the blame is to be apportioned between the assured and the broker. The authorities indicate that the benchmark figure for deduction where an assured or reinsured fails to check the wording obtained by the broker for conformity with the policyholder's instructions is normally 20 per cent,[323] although this figure may be increased if the broker's error was an obvious one[324] or reduced—potentially to zero[325]—where the assured is a consumer or has relied completely on the broker's performance of his obligations.

The courts may also refuse deduction in commercial cases. *Standard Life Assurance Ltd v Oak Dedicated Ltd*[326] involved a professional insurer relying on the advice of a broker and once again the court refused to make any deduction on the basis of contributory negligence. In this case the broker procured a professional indemnity policy aimed at protecting the assured—an insurance

---

[320] *Youell v Bland Welch (No.2)* [1990] 2 Lloyd's Rep. 431; *Dunlop Haywards (DHL) Ltd v Barbon Insurance Group Ltd* [2009] EWHC 2900 (Comm).

[321] *Dunlop Haywards (DHL) Ltd v Barbon Insurance Group Ltd* [2009] EWHC 2900 (Comm).

[322] *HIH Casualty and General Insurance Ltd v JLT Risk Solutions Ltd* [2007] Lloyd's Rep. I.R. 742.

[323] *Youell v Bland Welch & Co Ltd (No.2)* [1990] 2 Lloyd's Rep. 431. Cf. *Forsikringsaktielskapet Vesta v Butcher* [1988] 1 All E.R. 19.

[324] 30 per cent in *National Insurance and Guarantee Corp Plc v Imperio Reinsurance Co UK Ltd* [1999] Lloyd's Rep. I.R. 249 where the reinsured confirmed that the broker had properly obtained an indorsement contained in a single sentence.

[325] *The Moonacre* [1992] 2 Lloyd's Rep. 501 (consumer assured not under duty to read policy); *Tudor Jones II v Crawley Colosso Ltd* [1996] 2 Lloyd's Rep. 619 (no duty on assured to read policy); *GE Reinsurance Corporation v New Hampshire Insurance Co* [2004] Lloyd's Rep. I.R. 404 (no duty on reinsured to read wording specifically developed by brokers for a novel risk where it was clear that the brokers were driving the transaction); *Grace v Leslie & Godwin Financial Services Ltd* [1995] L.R.L.R. 472 (no duty on reinsured to retain its own records of reinsurance placements by broker); *O'Brien v Hughes-Gibb* [1995] L.R.L.R. 90 (no duty on assured to give comprehensive instructions to broker); *Dunlop Haywards (DHL) Ltd v Barbon Insurance Group Ltd* [2009] EWHC 2900 (Comm) (no duty to read policy when assured given an executive summary by broker).

[326] *Standard Life Assurance Ltd v Oak Dedicated Ltd* [2008] Lloyd's Rep. I.R. 552.

company—against pensions misselling liabilities towards consumers. The per claimant deductible of £25 million included in the policy by the brokers was effective to preclude any possible recovery by the assured. Tomlinson J. held that the assured company was not an expert in professional indemnity insurance and had relied on the brokers to procure cover which met with its instructions. In those circumstances, there could be no deduction for contributory negligence even though the assured had seen the cover note and had been asked by the brokers to check that the policy provided the required coverage. Deduction was also denied in *Arbory Group Ltd v West Craven Insurance Services*,[327] where the broker gave an erroneous explanation as to how the assured was to calculate his gross profit for the purpose of calculating the amount of cover under a business interruption policy. The incorrect figure was inserted on the proposal form by the broker, and the form was signed by the assured after having read the notes provided by the insurers and also the form itself. It was held that the assured had genuinely failed to understand the notes, and that the inadequacy of cover was entirely the fault of the brokers.

15–052 *Waiver and estoppel.* The assured may be treated as having waived a broker's breach of duty but has acted in a fashion which makes it clear that the breach is not to be relied upon. However, an assured is not to be treated as having waived the broker's failure to obtain proper cover simply by reading the documents provided to him and confirming that are in conformity with his instructions. Further, the assured is not estopped from bringing an action for breach of duty by this means, either by promissory estoppel or estoppel by convention.

> "It is extremely difficult to envisage any factual situation arising out of a negligent breach of duty by a placing broker to his principal insured which it would be unconscionable for a representor or promisor insured to rely on his legal right to claim in respect of a breach of professional duty and where the insured has been at fault in representing his satisfaction with the cover which the broker has obtained."[328]

15–053 *Ratification.* The fact that the assured has ratified a defective policy obtained by the broker does not relieve the broker of liability for breach of duty. While it is the case that the assured is bound by the policy, he retains his right to seek damages from the broker for any loss suffered.[329]

15–054 *Absence of causation.* If there is no causal link between the broker's breach of duty and the assured's loss, the assured plainly has no action against the broker as the elements of liability have not been established. Accordingly if the broker can show that its advice would have been ignored had it been properly given,[330] the chain of causation between the broker's breach of duty and the loss suffered by the assured is to be regarded as having been broken. Again, there is no liability if the broker can show that full disclosure would have led to insurers imposing

---

[327] *Arbory Group Ltd v West Craven Insurance Services* [2007] Lloyd's Rep. I.R. 491.

[328] *National Insurance and Guarantee Corporation Plc v Imperio Reinsurance Co UK Ltd* [1999] Lloyd's Rep. I.R. 249, per Colman J.

[329] *Suncorp Insurance and Finance v Milano Assicurazione SpA* [1993] 2 Lloyd's Rep. 225; *National Insurance and Guarantee Corporation Plc v Imperio Reinsurance Co UK Ltd* [1999] Lloyd's Rep. I.R. 249.

[330] *PWS Holdings Plc v Edmondson* Unreported, 1996; *Bhopal v Sphere Drake Insurance Plc* [2002] Lloyd's Rep. I.R. 413; *Stowers v GA Bonus Plc and Helm Insurance Brokers Ltd* [2003] Lloyd's Rep. I.R. 402; *HIH Casualty and General Insurance Ltd v JLT Risk Solutions Ltd* [2007] Lloyd's Rep. I.R. 742; *McIntosh v Royal & Sun Alliance* 2007 F.C. 23.

conditions which, if fulfilled, would have meant that no loss would have occurred.[331]

Existence of fallback insurance as a defence. An assured who is unable to recover under one form of policy, by reason of a defence open to the insurers caused by the default of the brokers, may have some form of fallback insurance in place which provides an indemnity where the primary policy fails to respond. It has been held that such insurance does not provide a defence to the brokers, as there is no obligation on the assured to make a claim under other policies[332] and even if a claim is made against the fallback insurers the alleged defence would interfere with the subrogation rights otherwise open to the fallback insurers against the brokers.[333]

15–055

Independent ground for denial of liability. Difficult issues arise where the insurer is entitled to reject the assured's claim both on the ground of the broker's breach of duty and on some ground wholly independent of the broker's misconduct and stemming from the assured's own misconduct. If the assured sues the broker in respect of the broker's breach of duty, the broker may justifiably argue by way of defence that his misconduct was immaterial as the insurer would, had it been aware of the assured's wrongful actions, have refused to pay on that ground. In this type of case, therefore, the court must seek to ascertain exactly how the insurer would have reacted to the assured's claim if faced only with the assured's misconduct.[334] The courts have not sought evidence from the relevant insurer on this point, but have exercised their own commercial judgment as to the likely outcome. The test to be applied is, "what were the prospects that a reputable insurer would in circumstances such as the present have relied on the breach of policy?"[335] In *Fraser v BN Furman (Productions) Ltd*[336] the broker neglected to renew the assured's employer's liability policy and, in defence to the assured's action for breach of duty, pleaded that the assured had failed to take reasonable precautions for the safety of its employees, in breach of a condition in the policy which would have entitled the insurer to repudiate liability. The Court of Appeal held that the assured had not contravened the condition, and thus rejected the defence on its merits, but nevertheless added that the insurer would not have been likely to have pleaded a defence of that nature, so that the assured's inability to recover from the insurer was entirely the fault of the broker.

15–056

A similar point arose in *Everett v Hogg, Robinson and Gardner Mountain (Insurance) Ltd*,[337] a case involving reinsurance, in which both the reinsured and the broker had been guilty of breaches of the reinsured's duty of utmost good faith. In the course of his judgment, Kerr J. drew a distinction between cases in which the assured's own breach rendered the policy totally void and cases in which the assured's error conferred upon the insurer a discretion as to whether or

---

[331] *Jones v Environcom Ltd (No.2)* [2010] EWHC 759 (Comm) (use of plasma guns would have been prohibited had such use been disclosed; but for that use no fire would have occurred).

[332] *Alexander Forbes Europe Ltd v SBJ Ltd* [2003] Lloyd's Rep. I.R. 428.

[333] *FNCB Ltd v Barnet Devanney (Harrow) Ltd* [1999] Lloyd's Rep. I.R. 459.

[334] *Seavision Investment SA v Evenett and Clarkson Puckle Ltd (The Tiburon)* [1992] 2 Lloyd's Rep. 26.

[335] *Phillips & Co v Whatley (Gibraltar)* [2008] Lloyd's Rep. I.R. 111.

[336] *Fraser v BN Furman (Productions) Ltd* [1967] 3 All E.R. 57. See also *Carlton v Park* (1922) 12 Ll. L.R. 246; *Dunbar v A & B Painters Ltd* [1986] 2 Lloyd's Rep. 38 and *Kennecott Utah Copper Corp v Minet Ltd* [2003] Lloyd's Rep. I.R. 563.

[337] *Everett v Hogg, Robinson and Gardner Mountain (Insurance) Ltd* [1973] 2 Lloyd's Rep. 217.

not to avoid the policy or to pay: in the former case, the assured bore the burden of proving that the insurer would nevertheless have honoured the policy; while in the latter case, the burden of proving that the insurer would not have honoured a valid policy shifted to the broker. On the facts before him, Kerr J. concluded that, taking into account the friendly relationship between reinsurer and rein- sured, the amount of business conducted between them and the relevant personalities involved, the likely outcome (based on "intelligent guesswork") of the reinsured's failure to disclose material facts taken in isolation would have been a two-thirds' settlement between the parties. Kerr J. thus ruled that the brokers were liable for two-thirds of the policy moneys. By contrast, in *Jones v Environcom Ltd (No.2)*,[338] the court was satisfied that insurers who, by reason of the fault of brokers, avoided the policy for non-disclosure of fires at the assured's premises, would have avoided the policy for an independent failure by the assured to disclose that it was operating in breach of its Waste Management Licence had the alternative ground for avoidance not existed.

In some situations there may be clear evidence of the insurers' likely attitude to the alternative defence pleaded by the brokers, as where the dispute relates to the amount of cover. In *Arbory Group Ltd v West Craven Insurance Service*[339] the assured company instructed a broker to obtain business interruption insurance. The broker did not explain to the assured the method of calculation of the anticipated profits to be insured, with the consequence that the policy was obtained for an inadequate amount. The insurers paid the sum due under the policy, leaving the assured with a shortfall and also with a consequential loss of business. In response to an action against the broker for damages, the broker's response was that the insurers had a valid insurable interest defence in that the policy was taken out in the name of the assured company which was simply the parent company in the group and which had not itself suffered any loss. The court noted that the insurers had not sought to rely upon this defence, and indeed had paid the claim insofar as it was covered under the policy, so that the broker's defence ought not to succeed. It may also be commented that the insurable interest issue was itself the fault of the broker, in that the court found that it had been understood by the broker that it was the entire business of the group which was to be insured, so that the defence had no merit in any event.

15–057 *Risk uninsurable.* A broker who places a risk by misstating or withholding material information does not have an automatic defence to breach of duty by arguing that, had the facts been properly stated, the insurers would have refused the risk or that it would have been uninsurable by reason of want of insurable interest. The proper approach to such cases is to ask whether the assured could have taken steps to make the risk insurable.[340] In many cases there will be at least a prospect of finding insurance, so that damages can be awarded for loss of opportunity. In *O & R Jewellers Ltd v Terry*[341] brokers had failed to advise the assured company to disclose to the insurers the criminal convictions of one of the company's controllers, and also had not passed on to the insurers information which had been given to the brokers by the assured relating to the security

---

[338] *Jones v Environcom Ltd (No.2)* [2010] EWHC 759 (Comm).

[339] *Arbory Group Ltd v West Craven Insurance Service* [2007] Lloyd's Rep. I.R. 491.

[340] *Cee Bee Marine v Lombard Insurance Co* [1990] 2 N.Z.L.R. 1; *Stowers v GA Bonus Plc* [2003] Lloyd's Rep. I.R. 402. Contrast *Gunns and Gunns v Par Insurance Brokers* [1997] 1 Lloyd's Rep. 173 where non-disclosure of facts which made the risk uninsurable was thought to be an absolute defence.

[341] *O & R Jewellers Ltd v Terry* [1999] Lloyd's Rep. I.R. 436.

procedures operating in the assured's building. The assured suffered a loss of £850,000. The brokers asserted that they were not liable on the basis that, even if their breaches of duty had not occurred, the assured would not have been able to recover under the policy. This was so because: it would have been impossible to obtain cover for the assured, given the criminal record of the director; and the assured had been in breach of various conditions of the policy. The court held that the correct approach was to assess the assured's recovery prospects in the absence of any breach of duty. He ruled that: had the assured been informed of the significance of the controller's convictions, steps might have been taken to get rid of him; and there had been at least one breach of a security condition which the insurers would have taken. The prospects of successful recovery against the insurers were judged to be about 30 per cent and, accordingly, the sum of £255,000 was awarded against the brokers. The defence that a risk was uninsurable was rejected on its facts in *Standard Life Assurance Ltd v Oak Dedicated Ltd*,[342] where brokers unsuccessfully asserted that a policy without a large deductible was unobtainable. By contrast, in *Jones v Environcom Ltd (No.2)*,[343] David Steel J. was satisfied that the assured's record of fires would, if disclosed, have prevented any offer of insurance either from renewing insurers or other insurers, and that even if an offer had been forthcoming it would have been on terms and premium unacceptable to the assured.

Failure by broker to obey unlawful orders. If the broker is requested to obtain a policy which would for some reason be unlawful, it would appear that the broker cannot be liable in damages. This follows from the ordinary contractual principle that an agreement facilitating the performance of an unlawful act is itself unlawful.[344] Thus a broker cannot be liable in damages for failing to obtain a policy which would be void for want of insurable interest.[345]   **15–058**

Liability following the assured's settlement with insurers. The basic measure of damages against a broker who has failed to place valid or appropriate cover is the difference between the amount for which insurance should have been placed, and the amount recovered by the assured from the insurers. That sum will in many cases have been the result of a settlement between the assured and the insurers, and the question that arises is whether the broker is automatically liable for the difference between the insured sum and the amount of the settlement or whether the broker is entitled to challenge the settlement, arguing that the assured should have either sued for the full amount or at least for a larger sum. It would seem that the issue is one of mitigation of loss. If the settlement reached by the assured was a reasonable one in the circumstances, then the assured has mitigated his loss and the broker will be required to pay the balance. The broker does not have an automatic defence by showing that the insurers were as a matter of law liable, as it is a part of the broker's duty not to expose the assured to unnecessary litigation,[346] and in determining whether the quantum of the settlement was   **15–059**

---

[342] *Standard Life Assurance Ltd v Oak Dedicated Ltd* [2008] Lloyd's Rep. I.R. 552.

[343] *Jones v Environcom Ltd (No.2)* [2010] EWHC 759 (Comm).

[344] *Thomas Cheshire & Co v Vaughan Bros & Co* [1920] 3 K.B. 240; *Fraser v Furman* [1967] 3 All E.R. 57.

[345] *Newbury Internarional Ltd v Reliance National Insurance Co (UK) Ltd* [1994] 1 Lloyd's Rep. 83.

[346] *Aiken v Stewart Wrightson* [1996] 2 Lloyd's Rep. 577; *FNCB v Barnet Devanney* [1999] Lloyd's Rep. I.R. 459; *Frost v James Finlay* [2002] Lloyd Rep. I.R. 503; *Talbot Underwriting v Nausch Hogan & Murray (The Jascon 5)* [2006] Lloyd's Rep. I.R. 531; *Standard Life Assurance Ltd v Oak Dedicated Ltd* [2008] Lloyd's Rep. I.R. 552.

reasonable the court will attempt to assess what would have occurred had the settlement not been reached.[347] The fact that the settlement was based on a view of the law which ultimately proves to be erroneous is not, therefore, a barrier to recovery, so that if the assured settles for a sum less than that to which he was in law entitled the full amount of the loss may be recoverable as long as the settlement was reasonable.[348] The principle has been expressed by the High Court of Australia, *CGU Insurance Ltd v AMP Financial Planning Pty Ltd*[349] as follows:

"Where one party to a contract is in breach and the breach forces the innocent contracting party into litigation with a third party, the innocent party may properly conclude that its best interest is to settle the third party's claim. The contract breaker will then be liable in law for the settlement where (1) it is in breach of its legal obligations and (2) the settlement is reasonable when judged objectively, by reference to all of the circumstances prevailing at the time the settlement was reached."

In *Alexander Forbes Europe Ltd v SBJ Ltd*[350] brokers suggested that the failure of the assured to sue the underwriters in an attempt to recover from them was the proximate cause of the assured's loss and that, had an action been brought, the assured would have recovered a substantial part of the claim. The court's view was that there was no invariable rule that the assured had to sue the insurers first, although if he does not do so it is open to the brokers to show that they were not negligent or that, had the claim been brought against the insurers, they would have been liable on the policy.

15–060 *Contribution from third parties.* As a result of the decision of the House of Lords in *Royal Brompton Hospital NHS Trust v Hammond*,[351] a broker who has failed to put in place an insurance policy in accordance with the assured's instructions cannot seek contribution from the third party who was responsible for the assured suffering a loss which would have been covered by the policy. The basis for any contribution claim is s.1(1) of the Civil Liability (Contribution) Act 1978, which provides that:

"[A]ny person liable in respect of any damage suffered by another person may recover a contribution from any other person liable in respect of the same damage (whether jointly with him or otherwise)."

The House of Lords decided that the words "same damage" required a single loss which was caused by two or more defendants, and not two different forms of loss. In so deciding the House of Lords overruled *Hurstwood Developments Ltd v Motor & General & Andersley & Co Insurance Services*[352] in which brokers who had failed to procure a buildings policy were held to be entitled to

---

[347] *Mander v Commercial Union Assurance Plc* [1998] Lloyd's Rep. I.R. 93.

[348] *Biggin & Co Ltd v Permanite Ltd* [1951] 2 K.B. 314; *Comyn Ching & Co Ltd Oriental Tube Co Ltd* (1979) 17 B.L.R. 47; *The Sargasso* [1994] 1 Lloyd's Rep. 412; *General Feeds Inc Panama v Slobodna Plovidba Yugoslavia* [1999] 1 Lloyd's Rep. 688; *P & O Developments Ltd v Guys and Thomas' National Health Service Trust* [1999] B.L.R. 3; *John F Hunt Demolition Ltd v ASME Engineering Ltd* [2007] EWHC 1507 (TCC); *Supershield Ltd v Siemens Building Technologies FE Ltd* [2010] EWCA Civ 7.

[349] *CGU Insurance Ltd v AMP Financial Planning Pty Ltd* [2007] H.C.A. 36, citing *Unity Insurance Brokers Pty Ltd v Rocco Pezzano Pty Ltd* (1998) 192 C.L.R. 603.

[350] *Alexander Forbes Europe Ltd v SBJ Ltd* [2003] Lloyd's Rep. I.R. 428.

[351] *Royal Brompton Hospital NHS Trust v Hammond* [2002] 2 All E.R. 801.

[352] *Hurstwood Developments Ltd v Motor & General & Andersley & Co Insurance Services* [2002] Lloyd's Rep. I.R. 185.

contribution from the third party who had carried out defective work. In this type of case, the broker must bear the full amount of the loss if proceedings are brought against him.[353]

Limitation of actions. Under s.5 of the Limitation Act 1980 an action for breach **15–061** of contract must be brought, by the issue of a claim form, within six years of the date on which the breach occurred. In the case of an action against a broker, therefore, the action must be brought against him within six years of the date of his breach of duty. This requirement may cause some difficulty where the date of the breach and the date at which it becomes apparent are far apart, as is possible where, for example, the broker errs in passing on information to the insurer or exceeds his authority and the error does not come to light until a claim is made some years later: in such a case, it is possible for the action against the broker to become time-barred before the assured is aware that the action even exists.[354] In most cases, the date of the broker's breach of contract will be traceable to a single event and readily ascertainable. Where, however, the breach has occurred within a certain period, but the precise date is unascertainable and it is unclear whether the breach occurred within or outside the limitation period, the action would appear to be doomed to fail although this problem may be overcome by a finding that the broker's duty was a continuing one.[355]

An action in tort must be brought within six years of the date on which the action accrued; s.2 of the Limitation Act 1980. An action accrues when the claimant suffers damage, and not when the damage becomes apparent; consequently, if the claimant does not become aware that he has suffered damage until after six years from its occurrence, he will be time-barred.[356] The question of when damage occurs in cases involving professional advice has given rise to some difficulty, although it is now settled law[357] that the damage occurs when the advice is acted upon and not at the later date at which the claimant's loss becomes apparent. Applied to actions against brokers in respect of the placement of inadequate or voidable insurance, the assured's cause of action accrues when the policy was placed and not when the insurers deny liability.[358]

The unsatisfactory position under the Limitation Act 1980 has to some extent been mitigated by the Latent Damage Act 1986, which made a number of significant changes to the 1980 Act, including the insertion into the 1980 Act of s.14A. This provision introduces a "discoverability" test in negligence cases: the claimant has, as an alternative to the usual six-year period running from the date of damage, a three-year period in which to issue a writ running from the date at which the damage, and the defendant's responsibility for it, became apparent.

---

[353] Equally, if the assured sues the third party, there is no contribution claim against the broker.

[354] *Companhia de Seguros Imperio v Heath (REBX) Ltd* [1999] Lloyds Rep. I.R. 571.

[355] *Grace v Leslie & Godwin Financial Services* [1995] L.R.L.R. 472 (duty to retain documents); *Gaughan v Tony McDonagh & Co* [2006] Lloyd's Rep. I.R. 230 (duty to provide further information to insurers). The limitation period for breach of duty during the currency of the policy commences from the date of the breach of duty rather than from the inception of the policy. In *Great North Eastern Ry Ltd v JLT Corporate Risks Ltd* [2007] Lloyd's Rep. I.R. 38 it was held to be arguable that a broker's duty was not simply to place the risk but to ensure up to the date of the loss that the policy was suitable for the assured's needs, so that the limitation period ran up to the date of the placement.

[356] *Pirelli General Cable Works v Oscar Faber and Partners* [1983] 2 A.C. 1.

[357] *Law Society v Sephton & Co* [2006] UKHL 22.

[358] *Iron Trades Mutual Insurance Co Ltd v Buckenham Ltd* [1989] 2 Lloyd's Rep. 85; *Islander Trucking Ltd v Hogg Robinson & Gardner Mountain (Marine) Ltd* [1990] 1 All E.R. 808; *Knapp v Ecclesiastical Insurance Group* [1998] Lloyd's Rep. I.R. 390. This line of authority was approved by the House of Lords in *Law Society v Sephton & Co* [2006] UKHL 22.

Section 14A has been held not to apply to actions for breach of contract even where the breach was allegedly negligent,[359] but it does apply to actions framed in tort and is likely to be useful in actions against insurance brokers where the effects of negligence are not felt for some years after it occurs, as is commonly the case where the negligence relates to the formation of the contract of insurance.[360]

Brokers, as agents, owe fiduciary duties to their principals in a number of contexts, perhaps most importantly in respect of their holding and managing funds belonging to their client, normally the assured but possibly the insurer where the broker has undertaken specific duties. The Limitation Act 1980 does not set out a limitation period for breach of fiduciary duty, but instead provides, in s.36, that the court may apply contract and tort time limits, by analogy, to a claim for breach of fiduciary duty. Many claims for breach of fiduciary duty are simply the equitable counterpart of common law actions: for example, absconding with funds may be classified as the tort of conversion or breach of fiduciary duty, and the ordinary six-year period will be applied by analogy in the case of a claim against a broker for breach of fiduciary duty.[361]

Under s.32 of the Limitation Act 1980, where there has been fraud, mistake or deliberate concealment on the part of the defendant, time does not begin to run until the claimant actually discovered, or could with reasonable diligence have discovered, the facts giving rise to his cause of action. Fraud, mistake or deliberate concealment after the limitation period has commenced have the same effect.[362] Once the assured has, or ought with due diligence to have, become aware of the facts giving rise to a cause of action, the limitation period will, at that point, start to run even though the assured did not, until a later stage, appreciate that there had been a fraud against him. Thus if an insurer appreciates that his underwriting agent has wrongfully been using him as a fronting company for other members of an insurance pool, but only acquires knowledge that this was done fraudulently at a later stage, the limitation period runs from the date of the earlier knowledge and not that the later knowledge.[363]

15–062   **Liabilities to third parties.** Although a broker's duties are owed primarily to the assured, it was seen above that the broker may in limited situations owe duties to underwriters. It is also possible for a broker to owe a duty of care to a third party if the broker has assumed responsibility to act on behalf of the third party.[364] A duty of care may arise where the broker has undertaken to obtain a policy which he knows is to be assigned to the third party[365] or the third party is the intended beneficiary of the policy.[366] A broker whose contract is with a company does not owe any duty of care to the shareholders or directors of that company[367] unless the directors are intended co-assureds or otherwise the

---

[359] *Iron Trades Mutual Insurance Co Ltd v Buckenham Ltd* [1989] 2 Lloyd's Rep. 85; *Scor v ERAS (International) Ltd* [1992] 2 All E.R. 82.

[360] See *Iron Trades Mutual Insurance Co Ltd v Buckenham Ltd* [1989] 2 Lloyd's Rep. 85 (date of discoverability left for trial). For the meaning of s.14A, see *Haward v Fawcetts* [2006] UKHL 9.

[361] *Companhia de Seguros Imperio v Heath (REBX) Ltd* [1999] Lloyds Rep. I.R. 571.

[362] *Sheldon v RHM Outhwaite (Underwriting Agencies) Ltd* [1995] 2 All E.R. 558.

[363] The alleged facts in *Companhia de Seguros Imperio v Heath (REBX) Ltd* [1999] Lloyds Rep. I.R. 571.

[364] See generally *Customs and Excise Commissioners v Barclays Bank* [2006] UKHL 28.

[365] *Bromley LBC v Ellis* [1971] 1 Lloyd's Rep. 97; *Punjab National Bank v De Boinville* [1992] 3 All E.R. 104.

[366] *Banque Paribas (Suisse) SA v Stolidi Shipping Co Ltd* Unreported, 1995.

[367] *Verderame v Commercial Union Assurance Co Plc* [1992] B.C.L.C. 793 (directors).

beneficiaries of the policy.[368] Where the broker has by contract agreed to take out a policy for the benefit of another, that other may have a claim against the broker under the Contracts (Rights of Third Parties) Act 1999[369] to the extent that the third party is identified by name or class and the contract with the broker does not exclude third party rights.

There will not, however, be a duty of care towards a person who subsequently becomes the assignee of the policy but whose identity was not known to the broker at the outset,[370] or in the case of a liability policy, to a person who subsequently has a claim against the assured but is unable to enforce that claim under the Third Parties (Rights against Insurers) Act 1930 by reason of the absence of valid insurance.[371]

---

[368] *Crowson v HSBC Insurance Brokers* Unreported, January 26, 2010 (where the broker was instructed by a company to obtain a directors' and officers' policy covering the liability of directors).

[369] *Crowson v HSBC Insurance Brokers* Unreported, January 26, 2010.

[370] E.g. under a policy taken out by the seller of goods under a CIF contract. See: *Den Danske Bank A/S v Skipton Building Society* [1998] 1 E.G.L.R. 155.

[371] *Federation General Insurance Co v Knott Becker Scott* [1990] 1 Lloyd's Rep. 98.

CHAPTER 16

THE INSOLVENCY OF INSURANCE COMPANIES

1. INSOLVENCY PROCEEDINGS INVOLVING INSURERS

16–001 **Background.** The insolvency procedures applicable to all companies are relevant also to insurance companies. The Financial Services and Markets Act 2000 allows the usual procedures to operate, but with significant modifications to ensure adequate protection of policyholders. The Financial Services Authority has the right to be informed of the initiation of insolvency proceedings relating to a regulated insurer, and has powers of intervention where the proceedings relate to a regulated insurer other than an exempt person or a friendly society.[1]

The Insurers (Reorganisation and Winding Up) Regulations 2004[2] implemented into UK law European Parliament and Council Directive 2001/17/EC[3] on the reorganisation and winding-up of insurance undertakings. The Regulations are, in part, concerned with cross-border insolvencies, and provide for insolvency procedures to be opened in the EEA country in which the insurer has its head office for regulatory purposes.[4] To this end, the 2004 Regulations prohibit the opening of insolvency procedures in the United Kingdom against an insurer regulated in some other EEA state. That point aside, the English courts may wind up a foreign insurer if: there is sufficient connection with England; there is reasonable prospect of benefit accruing to the applicant for winding up; and one or more persons interested in the assets are subject to the jurisdiction of the English court.[5] Once insolvency procedures have been opened in any one EEA state, they have to be recognised in all other EEA states. There is at present no harmonisation of insolvency procedures within the EEA, and claims in insolvency available in other EEA states are to be recognised in UK insolvency procedures.

Independently of the EEA rules, the English courts possess jurisdiction to give support to foreign liquidations on the request of a competent foreign court.[6]

---

[1] Financial Services and Markets Act 2000 (Insolvency) (Definition of "Insurer") Order 2001 (SI 2001/2634).

[2] SI 2004/353.

[3] This Directive has now been repealed and its provisions re-enacted in the Solvency II Directive, European Parliament and Council Directive 2009/138/EC, discussed in Ch.13, above.

[4] The rule is different for pure reinsurers: insolvency procedures have to be opened in the EEA State from which the reinsurer carries on its main activities.

[5] *Stocznia Gdanska SA v Latreefers Inc (No.2)* [2001] 2 B.C.L.C. 116.

[6] The power arises under s.426 of the Insolvency Act 1986 and there is also an inherent power. In *McGrath v Riddell* [2008] Lloyd's Rep. I.R. 756 the House of Lords held that the UK assets of an Australian insurance company in liquidation in Australia—HIH—were to be remitted to the Australian liquidators of HIH even though HIH was in liquidation in England as an oversea company. The House of Lords found that there was no risk of any prejudice to UK policyholders from the application of Australian insurance insolvency rules (those rules giving priority to policyholders over ordinary creditors). Lords Phillips, Scott and Neuberger rested their decision on s.426 whereas Lords Hoffmann and Walker relied upon inherent jurisdiction.

Liquidation

Nature. The liquidation of a company involves its winding up with a view to the **16–002** orderly distribution of its assets by the liquidator.[7] There are two main disadvantages of liquidation as regards insurance. First, claims against the company have to be valued at the date of the insolvency and, where necessary, converted into sterling at that date, a process that is inflexible. Secondly, the liquidation process will generally conclude by a voluntary scheme under which dividends are to be paid to creditors. However, if the insurers' business is long-tail, then claims may arise for many years after the liquidation has commenced and these will have to be admitted by the liquidator: reserves will have to be maintained to meet such claims, and for this reason there will be delay in paying out to creditors the full amount of their ultimate entitlement to dividend.

Voluntary winding up. A company may go into voluntary liquidation by **16–003** resolving by special resolution that it be wound up or by resolving by extraordinary resolution that by reason of its liabilities it can no longer carry on business. If the directors have made a statutory declaration of solvency within a five-week period immediately prior to the passing of the resolution, the winding up takes effect as a members' voluntary winding up: if there is no such declaration, the winding up takes effect as a creditors' voluntary winding up. In either case, the purpose of the liquidation is to ensure that the assets of the company are to be distributed to preferred creditors, unsecured creditors and then to members. In the case of a members' voluntary winding up, the company in a general meeting is required to appoint a liquidator, who must report to the company at the end of each year as to the progress of the liquidation. As soon as the company's affairs are fully wound up, the liquidator must prepare an account of what has occurred and lay it before a final general meeting of shareholders. As long as the company has been able to pay its debts, the winding up takes full effect. If, however, the liquidator is of the view that the company is insolvent, he must summon a meeting of creditors, and the liquidation then proceeds as a creditors' voluntary winding up. A creditors' voluntary winding up arises where the directors have been unable to issue a statutory declaration of solvency or where the liquidator of a members' voluntary winding up has established that the company is insolvent.

The Financial Services and Markets Act 2000 makes significant modifications in the case of insurance. An insurer carrying on long-term business may be voluntarily wound up only with the consent of the FSA, and the intention of a company to pass a resolution for voluntary, winding up must be notified to the FSA, failing which a criminal offence is committed. In addition, a copy of the resolution forwarded to the registrar in accordance with the requirements of the Companies Act 2006 must be accompanied by a certificate of the FSA's approval, failing which the resolution is of no effect.[8] As far as insurance companies carrying on general business are concerned, there may be voluntary winding up but s.365 of the Financial Services and Markets Act 2000 requires the FSA to be sent all documents sent to creditors, and the FSA is then allowed to attend creditors' meeting and to be represented at any court hearing which takes place in the course of the winding up. The FSA is also entitled to refer any question to the court and if during the course of the liquidation a compromise between the company and its creditors is proposed, the FSA may apply to the

---

[7] Insolvency Act 1986 ss.73–251; Insolvency Rules 1986 (SI 1986/1925).
[8] Financial Services and Markets Act 2000 s.366.

court so that the issue may be put to a meeting of creditors. If the liquidator finds that the company has been carrying on a regulated activity without permission, this matter must be reported to the FSA. The FSA Handbook provides that the FSA may exercise its power to apply to the court for a compulsory winding up order under s.367 of the Financial Services and Markets Act 2000, thereby converting the winding up from a voluntary one, if it regards the intervention of the court as necessary to protect customers.

16–004   *Compulsory winding up.* Application to the court for a winding-up order may be made by the company itself, by its directors, by any creditor or by any shareholder who has held his shares for at least six months during the 18 months prior to the presentation of the petition. The most important ground on which the court may make a winding-up order is that the company is unable to pay its debts,[9] a concept defined[10] as meaning that: (a) a creditor to whom the company is indebted for a sum exceeding £750 which is due, has served on the company a statutory demand for payment which has not been met within three weeks; (b) execution or other process issued following a court order, judgment or decree is unsatisfied in whole or in part; (c) the company cannot pay its debts as they fall due; or (d) the value of the company's assets is less than the amount of its liabilities, taking into account any contingent and prospective liabilities. The courts will not permit the use of winding up as a device to intimidate an insurer who contests liability under a policy,[11] and if the insurer is solvent, the presentation of a winding up petition will be regarded as abuse of process.[12]

These rules are modified in respect of insurance companies. The FSA may itself present a petition for the winding up of an insurance company if it is unable to pay its debts or if it is just and equitable[13] that the company is wound up.[14] A copy of any winding-up petition which is presented to the court by any other person must be served on the FSA.[15] A copy of an application to the court for the appointment of a provisional liquidator must also be served on the FSA.[16] The FSA is entitled to be heard by the court at the hearing of the petition and at any other hearing which may take place during the course of the liquidation; the FSA must receive copies of documents or notices required to be sent to any creditor; and a representative of the FSA is entitled to attend any meeting of the creditors or the liquidation committee and to make representations.[17] The FSA may also apply to the court for the sanctioning of any compromise or arrangement between the company and its creditors. If the liquidator finds that the company has been carrying on a regulated activity without permission, this matter must be reported

---

[9] Insolvency Act 1986 s.122.

[10] Insolvency Act 1986 s.123.

[11] *Re A Company Ex p. Pritchard, Financial Times*, November 22, 1991; *Re A Company, No.0013734 of 1991 Financial Times*, June 3, 1992.

[12] *Re A Company, No.0012209 of 1991* [1992] 2 All E.R. 797.

[13] The FSA Handbook notes that a petition for just and equitable winding up has nothing to do with solvency and is a last resort measure to protect creditors, particularly of an insurer who is carrying on unauthorised business.

[14] Financial Services and Markets Act 2000 s.368. The Secretary of State may also present a winding up petition if it is expedient in the public interest for the company to be wound up. See *Re Equity and Provident Ltd* [2002] EWHC 186 (Ch) (insurer misleading public as to nature of its contracts).

[15] Financial Services and Markets Act 2000 s.369(1).

[16] Financial Services and Markets Act 2000 s.369(2).

[17] Financial Services and Markets Act 2000 s.371.

to the FSA.[18] Equivalent rights of participation are conferred on the scheme manager of the Financial Services Compensation Scheme.[19]

Schemes of arrangement. A winding up petition rarely proceeds to a winding-up order. The practice is for an insolvent insurer to be put into provisional liquidation and for a scheme of arrangement under ss.895 to 901 of the Companies Act 2006 to be prepared.[20] Any scheme must then be approved by the court. Approval of a scheme of arrangement takes place in a number of stages.[21]   **16–005**

First, under s.896(1), there must be an application to the court for an order that meetings of creditors are to be summoned. At this point, the various classes of creditors are to be determined, and meetings summoned for each class. The court is not concerned with the merits of the scheme at this stage.[22] In accordance with a Practice Statement issued in April 2002,[23] it is the responsibility of the company to draw to the court's attention any issue that might arise as to the constitution of the meetings of creditors. The court is to decide into which classes the creditors fall. There may be difficulties in determining classes of creditors, and the test to be applied is:

"[A]re the rights of those who are to be affected by the scheme proposed such that the scheme can be seen as a single arrangement; or ought it to be regarded, on a true analysis, as a number of linked arrangements".[24]

It has been held that, in the case of an insolvent insurer,[25] non-insurance creditors, insurance creditors with unsettled paid claims, insurance creditors with outstanding losses and insurance creditors who had suffered losses not reported to the company (IBNR—"incurred but not reported") all formed part of a single class of creditors as they had a common interest in the funds of the insolvent company and the only difference between them was in the valuation of their losses.[26]

The second stage is for the meetings to be held in accordance with the court's order, and the scheme must at those meetings be approved by majority in number representing three quarters in value of the creditors present and voting.

---

[18] Financial Services and Markets Act 2000 s.370.

[19] See below.

[20] Schemes of arrangement may also be entered into by solvent companies. However, the courts have set their faces against solvent schemes of arrangement for insurers, on the basis that the sole effect is to deprive policyholders of any benefit of long-tail claims. As was said in *Re British Aviation Insurance Co Ltd* [2006] B.C.C. 14, "where the company is solvent it is unnecessary for the body of creditors or class of creditors as a whole that there should be any scheme, still less a scheme forced upon unwilling participants." The position in Scotland is unresolved: *Re Scottish Lion Insurance Co Ltd* [2010] CSIH 6.

[21] *Re Hawk Insurance Co* [2001] 2 B.C.L.C. 480; *Re British Aviation Insurance Co Ltd* [2005] EWHC 1621 (Comm).

[22] *Re Telewest Communications Ltd* [2004] B.C.C. 342.

[23] Published at [2002] 1 W.L.R. 1345.

[24] *Sovereign Life Assurance Co v Dodd* [1892] 2 Q.B. 573; *Re Osiris Insurance Ltd* [1999] 1 B.C.L.C. 182; *Re Hawk Insurance Co Ltd* [2001] 2 B.C.L.C. 480.

[25] Schemes of arrangement may also be used for solvent insurers with long-tail business, although creditors with accrued claims and creditors claiming for IBNR are generally in different classes for the purposes of class meetings: *Re British Aviation Insurance Co Ltd* [2005] EWHC 1621 (Ch); *Re NRG Victory Reinsurance Ltd* Unreported, March 2006; *Re Sovereign Marine & General Insurance Co Ltd* [2006] EWHC 1335 (Ch).

[26] *Re Hawk Insurance Co* [2001] 2 B.C.L.C. 480.

At the third stage there is to be an application to the court under s.896(2) of the Companies Act 2006 for the court's sanction. The court may refuse to sanction the scheme even if it has been approved by the meetings of creditors. Indeed the court has no jurisdiction to sanction the scheme if the meetings were not properly constituted. The court may also, as a matter of discretion, refuse its sanction if there are procedural irregularities arising in the summoning of the meetings[27] or at the meetings themselves. Subject to jurisdictional bars, the court's discretion has in practice been exercised in favour of the scheme,[28] although the court will be wary to ensure that the voting at the meeting was not unrepresentative and was not swayed by those with particular interests at variance with the interest of other creditors.[29] The test is whether:

"[T]he arrangement is such as an intelligent and honest man, a member of the class concerned and acting in respect of his interest, might reasonably approve . . . the test is not whether the opposing creditors have reasonable objections to the scheme".[30]

Schemes of arrangement are unaffected by the EU's rules on jurisdiction over insolvencies, and the English courts have the power to approve a scheme of arrangement in respect of an insurer regulated elsewhere in the EU[31] or subject to foreign insolvency proceedings.[32]

There are various forms of arrangement which can be entered into between an insurance company and its creditors. Reserving schemes allow creditors to make claims, with reserves being set aside to meet claims in accordance with the statutory rules on allocation of assets. This procedure is potentially a lengthy one as full payment cannot be made until all out standing claims have been identified. Valuation schemes involve the company and its creditors agreeing the value of claims, which are then paid. The creditors may also agree to a contingent scheme, which may be entered into before insolvency with a view to the possibility of insolvency and the need for a smooth transition to that state: this type of scheme may provide for reduced payments, and thereby allows some payments to be made rather than all payments suddenly ceasing once an insolvency procedure has been put in place.

16–006   *Reduction of contracts.* The court has a general discretion, following the presentation of a winding-up petition, to refuse the application or to wind the company up. Where an insurance company is insolvent, s.377 of the Financial Services and Markets Act 2000 confers upon the court an intermediate, possibility. The court may reduce the value of one or more of the contracts of the company on such terms and subject to such conditions as the court thinks fit. This provision has a substantial pedigree, having been in existence in one form or another since 1870, the older cases establishing that winding up is appropriate where the insurer has been operating a disastrous scheme.[33] The leading decision, *Re Capital Annuities Ltd*,[34] establishes that: (1) the initial requirement of proof

---

[27] *Re British Aviation Insurance Co Ltd* [2005] EWHC 1621 (Ch).

[28] *Re BTR Plc* [2000] 1 B.C.L.C. 740.

[29] In *Re British Aviation Insurance Co Ltd* [2005] EWHC 1521 (Ch) counsel were unable to identify any case in which a sanction had been refused once jurisdiction had been established.

[30] *Re British Aviation Insurance Co Ltd* [2005] EWHC 1521 (Ch) (undue preference given to holders of accrued claims as against IBNR creditors, although the case turned on want of jurisdiction).

[31] *Re Sovereign Marine & General Insurance Co Ltd* [2006] EWHC 1335 (Ch).

[32] *Re Home Insurance Co* [2005] EWHC 2485 (Ch).

[33] *Re Nelson & Co* [1905] 1 Ch. 551.

[34] *Re Capital Annuities Ltd* [1978] 3 All E.R. 704.

that the company cannot pay its debts is not satisfied as easily as might be the case where a creditor petitions for the winding up; (2) what may be reduced is "the value of the contracts of the company" and not other debts or liabilities; (3) reduction is permissible only in the case of future liabilities and not liabilities in respect of claims which have accrued at the date of the winding up petition[35]; (4) there is no need for a pari passu reduction in contracts, all that is required being broad equity[36]; and (5) the court is not under a duty to consult policyholders when determining whether to wind up the insurer or to order a reduction in its contracts, although it will normally summon meetings of policyholders to ascertain their views on the matter if that would be useful.

Continuation of long-term business of an insurer in liquidation. The general **16–007** scheme of insurance regulation, carried over into liquidation, is the strict separation of the long-term and general business. One specific illustration is s.376 of the Financial Services and Markets Act 2000, supplemented by the Insurers (Winding-Up) Rules 2001,[37] which provide for the continuation of the long-term business of a company which has gone into liquidation. The liquidator is, subject to a "stop order" by the court,[38] under a statutory duty to carry on its long-term business with a view to transferring that business to another authorised company (whether existing or created for the purpose) as a going concern; the liquidator is empowered to agree to the variation of any contracts in existence when the winding-up order was made, but he cannot enter into any new insurance contracts on behalf of the company.[39] Specific powers are conferred to ensure that the insurer is permitted to carry on with its long- term business despite being in liquidation. Specifically: (a) the Secretary of State may require that the whole or a specified proportion of the assets representing the fund maintained by the company in respect of its long-term business are to be held by an approved trustee; (b) the liquidator must, with a view to the long-term business of the company being transferred to another insurer, maintain such accounting, valuation and other records as will enable such other insurer upon the transfer being effected[40]; (c) the liquidator must continue the contracts of long-term insurance although the Secretary of State may require him not to make investments of a specified class or description, or to realise the whole or a specified proportion of specified investments[41]; (d) the liquidator must supply the Secretary of State with such accounts as may be required[42]; (e) the court may allow a dividend to be declared and paid on debts which fell due before the liquidation date and on claims which have fallen due for payment after the liquidation date[43]; and (f) the liquidator is entitled to receive remuneration for his services.[44]

The liquidator may apply to the court for the reduction of the amount of the contracts of the company made in the course of carrying on its long-term

---

[35] *Re Great Britain Mutual Life Assurance Society* (1882) 20 Ch.D. 351; *Re Briton Medical and General Life Assurance Co Ltd* (1887) 3 T.L.R. 670; *Re Fidelity Life Assurance Co Ltd* Unreported, 1976.

[36] See *Re Nelson & Co* [1905] 1 Ch. 551.

[37] SI 2001/3635.

[38] 2001 Rules r.2.

[39] Financial Services and Markets Act 2000 s.376(2)–(3).

[40] 2001 Rules r.16.

[41] 2001 Rules r.17.

[42] 2001 Rules r.18.

[43] 2001 Rules r.23.

[44] 2001 Rules r.25.

business.[45] The liquidator may also apply to the court for the appointment of a special manager to conduct the business if he is satisfied that the interests of the policyholders so demand; any special manager appointed by the court may be given such powers as the court thinks fit.[46] The liquidator, the special manager or the FSA may appoint an independent actuary to investigate the long-term business of the company in order to determine whether it is advisable for it to be carried on and whether the amount of any contracts should be reduced[47]; application may presumably be made to the court by any of the above for the grant of a "stop order" if the actuary is of the view that the business ought not to be continued.

The liquidator may[48] also grant relief to a policyholder who has failed to pay the premiums on the due date under the policy, by accepting the premium or issuing a paid up policy.

16–008   *Effect of winding up on assets.*   A voluntary winding up is deemed to commence at the time of the passing of the resolution for winding up, and the company is to cease trading from that date except in so far as may be required for its beneficial winding up. A compulsory winding up is deemed to commence at the date of the presentation of the petition for winding up, although where the company has voluntarily been wound up by resolution and a winding-up petition has subsequently been presented to the court the winding up is deemed to have commenced at the date of the resolution and the validity of action taken after that date and before the presentation of the petition is, in the absence of fraud or mistake, preserved. Once a compulsory winding up has commenced, any disposition of the company's property is, subject to a contrary order of the court, void, the court may stay any legal proceedings against the company, any attachment, sequestration, distress or execution against the company's assets is void, and no action may be proceeded with or commenced against the company or its assets except by leave of the court.

It is the liquidator's duty to gather in and realise the assets of the company for the benefit of its creditors. The liquidator must, to this end, take into his custody or control all property to which the company is entitled, and the court may order that all or any part of that property is to vest in the liquidator. The liquidator may also bring in his official name any action which relates to the company's property for the purposes of winding up the company and recovering its property. In the insurance context a major concern of the liquidator will be to gather in any unpaid premiums. The common law rule is that the insurer is entitled to the full premium once the risk has attached.[49] Consequently, the liquidator is entitled to retain, or to sue for, the full amount of any premium, in relation to a risk which had attached prior to the commencement of the winding up. However, this principle is now subject to the Insurers (Winding Up) Rules 2001, which in certain situations permit the assured to recover a proportion of his premium from an insurer in compulsory or voluntary[50] liquidation.

16–009   *Proof of debts.*   The submission of proofs of debts by creditors in the liquidation of any company, including an insurance company, is governed by the Insolvency

---

[45] 2000 Act s.376(8)–(9).

[46] 2000 Act s.376(4)–(7).

[47] Financial Services and Markets Act 2000 s.376(10)–(11).

[48] 2001 Rules r.21, subject to actuarial advice (r.12).

[49] *Tyrie v Fletcher* (1774) 2 Cowp. 666.

[50] *Re Continental Assurance Co Plc, Hughes & Buchler v Hogg Insurance Brokers*, Unreported, 1998.

Rules 1986, which provide that claims must be submitted to the liquidator in writing and must contain the name and address of the claimant, the amount of the debt and particulars of how the debt was incurred. If the alleged debt is for a fixed sum, proof must be entered for that sum; if the sum owing does not bear a certain value for any reason, the liquidator must estimate its value. Proof may be entered for debts payable at some future date. If an insurer carries on both long-term and general business, the liquidator may fix different days for creditors of long-term and general business to prove their debts.[51]

Where the creditors of a company include persons to whom debts in a foreign currency are owed, it is necessary to fix a common date for converting the debts into sterling in order to prevent currency fluctuations from providing a windfall or working an injustice in respect of each such creditor. The common law rule was that the date of conversion was that of the commencement of the winding up, in line with the general principle that all debts are to be valued at that date.[52] This rule has been codified by the Insolvency Rules 1986 r.4.91.

Distribution of assets by the liquidator. Fundamental changes to the rules on **16–010** distribution of assets of insurers in liquidation were made by the Insurers (Reorganisation and Winding Up) Regulations 2004,[53] which give effect to the EU's Regulation on the Winding Up of Insurance Undertakings.[54] These are to be read with other important alterations made by the Enterprise Act 2002. Under the earlier law, the assets of an insurance company were to be applied in the first instance to discharge the debts owing to secured creditors, then to the debts owed to preferential creditors (the Inland Revenue, the Customs and Excise authorities and employees' wages for four months), then to the costs of the liquidation and, finally, to unsecured creditors. In the case of an insurance company, the main losers would be policy- holders, who formed the bulk of unsecured creditors, and the burden of compensating them was cast onto the Financial Services Compensation Scheme. The 2004 Regulations and the Enterprise Act 2002 have significantly improved the rights of policyholders.

The preferential status of debts owing to the Inland Revenue and to Customs and Excise was abolished by s.251 of the Enterprise Act 2002, so that now the only preferential creditors are employees. The position of floating chargees as secured creditors with priority over unsecured creditors has also been modified, by s.252[55] under which a proportion of the company's net property to be specified by statutory instrument is to be made available for unsecured creditors. These rules, which apply to all companies, mean that there will inevitably be additional sums available for distribution to unsecured creditors.

As far as companies in general are concerned the basic rule is that any sum available for unsecured creditors after the secured and preferred creditors have been satisfied is to be divided between the unsecured creditors in equal proportions.[56] This principle is disapplied by the 2004 Regulations in the case of companies carrying on insurance business: in that situation, insurance debts— sums due to policyholders—are to be paid off in advance of all other debts. If

---

[51] 2001 Rules r.20.

[52] *Re Dynamics Corp of America* [1976] 2 All E.R. 669.

[53] SI 2004/353. The principles also apply to Lloyd's: Insurers (Reorganisation and Winding Up) (Lloyd's) Regulations 2005 (SI 2005/1998).

[54] European Parliament and Council Regulation 2001/17/EC.

[55] Taking effect as s.176A of the Insolvency Act 1986.

[56] Insolvency Rules 1986 r.4.181.

there is a shortfall, then insurance debts rank equally and are to be paid proportionately.

As far as insurers carrying on reinsurance business are concerned, sums due to direct policyholders are given priority over sums due to a cedant that has reinsured with the insurer in liquidation. Reinsureds thus rank as unsecured creditors for priority purposes. The effect of this on reinsurance is obvious: reinsureds cease to have the same right as all other unsecured creditors in the insolvency of their reinsurers, and instead are subordinated to direct policyholders. Reinsurance recoveries are thus at greater risk than was previously the case. Pure reinsurers are unaffected by the 2004 Regulations.

16–011 *Valuing an insurance policy.* The proper value to be placed upon an insurance policy in the liquidation of an insurer has proved to be a matter of some difficulty. Where the assured has suffered a loss before the date at which his interest is to be valued, that interest will include at least the amount for which the insurer is liable and the amount of the loss may be proved in the insurer's liquidation in the usual way.[57] However, where there is no outstanding claim at the relevant date, measuring the value of the policy becomes more speculative. Two questions thus fall to be considered: at what date is the value of the assured's policy to be measured; and on what principles is the valuation to be made if there has been no loss at that date. These issues are now dealt with by the Insurers (Winding Up) Rules 2001,[58] which replace principles originally developed by the courts of equity. The 2001 Rules apply also to an unauthorised insurer which has gone into liquidation.[59]

The basic rule under the 2001 Regulations is valuation at the date of the winding up order.[60] The 2001 Regulations divide policies into three classes.

(1) General business policies (i.e. all non-life policies): the date of valuation is the date of the winding up order, so that a claim which has fallen due before the date of the winding-up order may be proved for in the liquidation.[61] If the policy provides for periodic payments, and these arise from an event occurring before the winding-up order but fall due after the winding-up order, the value to be ascribed to those payments is to be determined on such actuarial principles and assumptions as the court may determine.[62]

(2) Long-term policies where no stop order has been made so that the liquidator is permitted to carry on the company's business with the aim

---

[57] *Transit Casualty Co v Policyholders Protection Board* [1992] 2 Lloyd's Rep. 358n; *Re Whiteley Insurance Consultants* [2009] Lloyd's Rep. I.R. 212.

[58] Replacing the Insurance Companies (Winding Up) Rules 1985.

[59] *Re Whiteley Insurance Consultants* [2009] Lloyd's Rep. I.R. 212,

[60] The equitable rule was that the amount of the assured's loss had to be measured not at the date of the presentation of the winding-up petition or the date of the winding-up order, but at the later date at which the liquidator had completed his valuation of the assets and liabilities of the company: *Re Craig's Executor* (1870) L.R. 9 Eq. 706; *Re Northern Counties of England Fire Insurance Co, MacFarlane 's Claim* (1880) 17 Ch.D. 337. The equitable rule was reversed in respect of life policies by the Life Assurance Companies Act 1870, which fixed the relevant date for valuing life policies as the date of the winding-up order, a principle subsequently extended to most other forms of policy by the Insurance Companies Act 1958 Sch.3, but not to policies on goods, merchandises, property on board aircraft and vessels, and various other transit risks, which remained governed by the old equitable rule. The law was overhauled in 1985.

[61] 2001 Rules r.6.

[62] 2001 Rules Sch.1 para.1. See also *Re Whiteley Insurance Consultants* [2009] Lloyd's Rep. I.R. 212.

of transferring it as a going concern the date for valuing the policy is the date of the winding-up order, so that a claim under a policy which has fallen due for payment before the date of the winding-up order is to be admitted without proof for the amount.[63]

(3) Long-term policies where a stop order has been made preventing the liquidator from carrying on business: the date for valuing the policy is the date of the stop order, so that a claim under the policy which has fallen due after the date of the winding-up order but before the date of the stop order is to be admitted without proof for the amount.[64]

The 2001 Rules provide an exhaustive[65] code for valuation of a policy where there has been no loss at the date of the winding up order.[66] In all cases the assured's claim is entitled to be admitted without proof for the amount of the value of the policy, although actuarial advice must be taken by the liquidator before the valuation of a policy is carried out.[67] The code is as follows:

(1) General business (i.e. non-life) policies.[68] If the policy provides for a repayment of the premium on early termination, or is expressed to run from one definite date to another,[69] or may be terminated by either party with effect from a definite date, the value of the policy is the greater of either the agreed sum repayable or a sum representing the unexpired portion of the policy. In any other case, including that in which the policy does not run from one definite date to another,[70] a just estimate is to be made of the value of the policy. Where a liability policy is involved, loss of cover in respect of future occurrences is valued in the former fashion, whereas loss of cover in respect of past occurrences or claims made is valued on the latter basis.[71]

(2) Long-term policies where no stop order has been made.[72] Different methods of valuation are provided for in relation to non-linked life policies,[73] linked life policies[74] and all other forms of long-term policies.[75]

(3) Long-term policies where a stop order has been made.[76] The rules governing the various classes of long-term policies under (2) apply, with the modification that the relevant date for calculation is that of the stop order and not that of the winding-up order.

[63] 2001 Rules r.7.
[64] 2001 Rules r.8.
[65] *Transit Casualty Co v Policyholders Protection Board* [1992] 2 Lloyd's Rep. 358.
[66] The equitable rule was that a loss occurring after the making of the winding up order but before valuation was to be taken into account (*Re Northern Counties of England Fire Insurance Co* (1885) 1 T.L.R. 629) a rule reversed in relation to some classes of insurance by the Assurance Companies Act 1909 so that the only recovery was of the premium representing the unexpired term (see *Re Law, Car and General Insurance Corp* [1913] 2 Ch. 103).
[67] 2001 Rules r.12.
[68] 2001 Rules r.6 and Sch.1.
[69] E.g. a motor policy: *Re Drake Insurance Plc* [2001] Lloyd's Rep. I.R. 643.
[70] *Re Continental Insurance Co Plc, Hughes and Buchler v Hogg Insurance Brokers*, Unreported, 1998.
[71] *Transit Casualty Co v Policyholders Protection Board* [1992] 2 Lloyd's Rep. 358n; *Ackman and Scher v Policyholders Protection Board* [1992] 2 Lloyd's Rep. 321.
[72] 2001 Rules r.7.
[73] 2001 Rules Sch.2.
[74] 2001 Rules Sch.3.
[75] 2001 Rules Sch.4.
[76] 2001 Rules r.8 and Sch.5.

16–012   *Meeting insurance liabilities: separation of long-term and general business.* The obligation on an insurer to maintain separate accounts for long-term and general business and to apply the assets of long-term business only for is carried over into liquidation by s.378 of the Financial Services and Markets Act 2000, which is implemented by the Insurers (Winding Up) Rules 2001 and also by the Financial Services and Markets Act 2000 (Treatment of Assets of Insurers on Winding Up) Regulations 2001.[77] The effect of the latter provision is that: (a) the assets representing the fund or funds maintained by the company in respect of its long-term business shall be available only for meeting the liabilities of the company attributable to that business; and (b) the other assets of the company shall be available only for meeting the liabilities of the company attributable to its other business.[78] This rule is modified where there is an excess of assets over liabilities in one category, the excess being applicable to the liabilities incurred in the other category, in which case permission may be sought from the court for utilisation of surplus assets for the other business.[79] Actuarial advice must be taken for the purposes of identifying long-term liabilities and assets, and for determining the amount of the excess of long-term business assets.[80] Where the liquidator intends to transfer the long-term business of the company as a going concern to another company, the expenses likely to be incurred in so doing are to be treated as an element in the company's long-term liabilities for determining the amount of any excess,[81] and in the event of a transfer, the excess of assets over liabilities relating to the company's long-term business allocated to its general business are not to be transferred to the new company.[82] Separate creditors' meetings must be summoned in respect of each and any recoveries from directors and other officers in respect of their wrongful use of assets are to be applied as between long-term and general business depending upon the category of business to which the assets belonged.[83] The costs of the liquidation are also to be apportioned as between long-term and general business.[84]

The Insurers (Winding Up) Rules 2001 confirm that the assets and liabilities of an insurance company in liquidation which are attributable to its long-term business, are to be treated as if they were the assets and liabilities of a separate company, and provide for the situation in which a strict accounting separation has not been maintained by the company: here the liquidator is to make a determination into which category the assets fall with the objective of reducing any deficit in either of the broad categories of business. If there happens to be a deficit in both categories, the attribution of assets is to be in the ratio that the deficits bear to each other, until the deficits are eliminated. Once both deficits are eliminated, the surplus attribution is to be in the ratio that the general and long-term business liabilities bear to each other.[85]

16–013   **Administration.** Part II of the Insolvency Act 1986 created the process of administration whereby, following an application to the court, an administrator is appointed either to formulate a method of restructuring the company's business so as to maintain the company as a going concern, or to allow the disposal of the

[77] SI 2001/2968.
[78] SI 2001/2968 reg.3.
[79] 2001 Rules r.13.
[80] 2001 Rules r.12.
[81] 2001 Rules r.11.
[82] 2001 Rules r.13.
[83] 2001 Rules r.24; SI 2001/2968 reg.4.
[84] 2001 Rules r.26.
[85] 2001 Rules rr.5, 9 and 10.

company's assets without the need for a winding-up order.[86] The Enterprise Act 2000, which inserted Sch.2B into the 1986 Act, modified the nature of administration by treating it as part of a "rescue culture" under which the main objective is to preserve the business of the company as a going concern and thereby to achieve a better result than in winding up.

Until the passing of the Financial Services and Markets Act 2000 it was not possible to put an insurance company into administration,[87] but s.360 contained an enabling power for the repeal of that prohibition and the repeal duly took effect on May 31, 2002.[88] Administration has in practice become the most important mechanism for dealing with insolvent insurance companies, and liquidation has all but fallen into disuse. Administration is far more flexible and most of the powers conferred upon a liquidator are also conferred upon an administrator: the one exception is the power of a liquidator to initiate proceedings against the directors for wrongful trading under s.214 of the Insolvency Act 1986, which involves trading by the directors in the knowledge that insolvency is inevitable. Administration may be more expensive than liquidation at the outset, because a scheme has to be established and agreed to by the creditors, but thereafter the process is less rigid and can be brought to an early end.

Since the passing of the Enterprise Act 2000 it has become possible for an administrator to be appointed by the company or its creditors as an alternative to court appointment. However, the EU's Insurance Insolvency Directive[89] precludes an insolvency process not conducted by a court, and accordingly the Insurers (Reorganisation and Winding Up) Regulations 2004, which implement the Directive, remove the possibility of an administrator being appointed other than by a court. An administrator may be appointed by the court only if it is "likely" (i.e. more probable than not) that the company cannot pay its debts and that it is "reasonably likely" (i.e. that there is a real prospect) that one or more of the stated objectives of administration will be achieved.[90] The Financial Services and Markets Act 2000 (Administration Orders Relating to Insurers) Order 2002[91] allows the FSA either to initiate the process if the insurer cannot pay debts due under its insurance policies,[92] or at least to be heard at an application made by some other person. Once the process has started, the FSA has a right to receive all documents sent to creditors, to attend creditors' meetings and to apply to the court if the activities of the administrator are thought to be unfairly prejudicial to creditors.[93]

Administration is possible even though the company is in liquidation or receivership and in such cases administration becomes the governing procedure. An administration order prevents a winding up order being made (other than on public interest grounds by the FSA) and otherwise suspends all legal processes

---

[86] Insolvency Act 1986 ss.8 to 27.

[87] Insolvency Act 1986 s.8(4).

[88] Financial Services and Markets Act 2000 (Administration Orders Relating to Insurers) Order 2002 (SI 2002/1242).

[89] European Parliament and Council Directive 2001/17/EC.

[90] See *Re AA Mutual International Insurance Co Ltd* [2004] EWHC 2430 (Ch), which also confirms that administration may be used by in respect of a reinsurer.

[91] As amended by the Financial Services and Markets Act 2000 (Administration Orders Relating to Insurers) (Amendment) Order 2003 (SI 2003/2134).

[92] Enterprise Act 2000 s.359.

[93] Enterprise Act 2000 ss.361–362A, as amended. Equivalent rights are conferred on the scheme manager of the Financial Services Compensation Scheme: Financial Services and Markets Act 2000 s.215, as amended.

against the company. The administrator is then free to continue the company's business for the duration of the order, which is 30 months in the case of an insurer. The administrator has the power to make payments to any creditor, including any policyholder. However, the sums paid must not exceed the amount that administrator reasonably considers that the creditor would be entitled to receive in the event of a winding up, and payments may be prevented by a three-quarters majority at a meeting of creditors.

The 2002 Order addresses the problem that debts assigned after an application for an administration order may be taken into account in any set off between the company and its creditors, leading to the possibility in insurance cases that a policyholder with an accrued claim could assign that claim to a debtor of the insurer, thereby allowing the debtor to set off the debt against the assigned claim. Article 5 of the 2002 Order, as substituted by the 2003 Amendment Order, thus states that if the insurer subsequently goes into liquidation, debts assigned after the application or onset of administration are to be disregarded for the purposes of set off.

16–014 **Company voluntary arrangement.** Under a voluntary arrangement the company's creditors can—subject to various judicial safeguards—agree on the best method to deal with company's assets.[94] The directors of a company may, therefore, at any time—including a time during which the company is in liquidation or subject to administration proceedings—put a proposal to the company and to its creditors for a composition in satisfaction of its debts. They may also apply to the court for a moratorium following their presentation of proposals for a voluntary arrangement, in order in particular to preclude a creditor from frustrating the proposals by presenting a winding-up petition, but also to prevent legal proceedings or the enforcement of a security. If the creditors and the company reach agreement the voluntary arrangement comes into effect and binds every person who was entitled to vote at the meetings whether or not he did so, and the court may then stay any winding-up proceedings and discharge any administration order. If there is no agreement application may be made to the court to resolve the matter.

The voluntary arrangement procedure applies to insurance companies as well as other companies, but a number of modifications are made: (a) the ability of the directors to apply to the court for a moratorium following their presentation of proposals for a voluntary arrangement has no application to insurance companies[95]; (b) the FSA has the right to be heard on any application to the court to resolve differences between the meeting of the company and the meeting of the creditors[96]; and the FSA may intervene where a voluntary arrangement has been effected in relation to an authorised insurance company, in order to challenge its content or operation.[97]

16–015 **Receivership.** The use of receivership, which involves the appointment of an administrative receiver by the holders of chargees of the company's assets,[98] has ceased to be of real significance since the Enterprise Act 2002 amended the Insolvency Act 1986[99] by removing from the holder of a floating charge other

---

[94] Insolvency Act 1986 ss.1–7, as amended by the Insolvency Act 2002 Sch.2.
[95] InsolvencyAct 2000 Sch.1 para.2.
[96] Insolvency Act 2000 s.4(5).
[97] Financial Services and Markets Act 2000 s.356.
[98] Insolvency Act 1986 ss.28–49.
[99] By inserting s.72A into that Act.

than in exceptional cases the power to appoint an administrative receiver. Instead primacy is given to the administration procedure, and the holder of a floating charge may instead appoint an administrator or seek an order from the court. Where an administrative receiver has been appointed, he has full control over the company's assets and may sell or grant security over them, bring and defend legal proceedings in the company's name, transfer the company's business and do all other acts in the name of the company. He may also dispose of property subject to a security if the court is satisfied that the disposal is likely to result in a more advantageous disposition of the property than would otherwise be the case.

The receivership provisions of the 1986 Act are also applicable to insurance companies, although in a modified form.[100] In brief: (a) a receiver of a company which has carried on insurance business must inform the FSA of his appointment; (b) the FSA is entitled to be heard on an application to the court for directions by a receiver; (c) the FSA may apply to the court for an order requiring the receiver to make the financial returns required of him; (d) any report issued by a receiver must be sent to the FSA; and (e) a person appointed by the FSA is entitled to attend any meeting of the creditors' committee established in the receivership. The FSA Handbook notes that the FSA will not normally intervene in a receivership unless the company is or is likely to become insolvent and intervention will benefit consumers. The FSA may as a last resort present a petition for a winding up order[101]; whether it does so will depend upon a number of factors, particularly benefit to consumers and the long term prospects of the insurer.

2. THE PROTECTION OF POLICYHOLDERS

Background. Insurance companies legislation in the United Kingdom has from 16–016 its inception in 1870 been confined to securing the solvency of insurers. However, until 1975 there was no statutory scheme to protect the policyholders of an insurer which had become insolvent. The Policyholders Protection Act 1975 filled this gap, by establishing the Policyholders Protection Board to administer a fund—established by levies on authorised insurance companies—from which losses suffered by the policyholders of insolvent insurance companies could be fully or partially indemnified. The fund also protected third parties whose claims against policyholders could not be met by reason of the insolvency of liability insurers. The 1975 Act was extended to insolvent friendly societies by the Friendly Societies Act 1986 and sweeping changes were made to the legislation by the Policyholders Protection Act 1997 removing its application to policyholders outside the EEA although these were never brought into effect. The Financial Services Compensation Scheme, established under Financial Services and Markets Act 2000, replaced the policyholders protection legislation with effect from December 1, 2001, and in its application is based on the scheme which would have operated had the 1997 amendments ever been implemented.

---

[100] Set out in ss.363–364 of the Financial Services and Markets Act 2000.
[101] Financial Services and Markets Act 2000 s.367.

The Financial Services Compensation Scheme

16–017 *Date of application.* The FSCS, rules are made by the FSA under s.213 of the Financial Services and Markets Act 2000[102] and are contained in the FSA Handbook chapter "Compensation (COMP)". They apply to any insurance insolvency[103] which takes place after December 1, 2001, if either: (a) the policy was a "United Kingdom policy at the beginning of the liquidation", for the purposes of the 1975 Act; or (b) the policy was one of compulsory employers' liability insurance entered into before January 1, 1972, the claim was agreed after the insurer's liquidation and the risk was situated in the United Kingdom. Where the insurer has gone into liquidation before December 1, 2001, then, subject to an exception in relation to compulsory liability insurance, the payment of compensation is governed by the earlier schemes, as modified by rules made by the FSA, and in the case of compensation payable under the 1975 Act, the scheme manager under the FSCS assumes the liabilities of the PPB.[104] Where compensation is sought in respect of an insurer who had issued a compulsory liability policy the FSCS applies in full if the extent of the insurer's liability had not been determined by December 1, 2001.

16–018 *Scheme manager.*[105] The scheme manager of the FSCS is established as a company by the FSA under s.212 of the Financial Services and Markets Act 2000. The scheme manager is independent of the FSA and has immunity from liability in damages for any act or omission in the performance or purported performance of its functions unless the act or omission was in bad faith (s.222). The functions of the scheme manager are to assess and pay compensation under the FSCS and to impose levies on authorised persons for the purposes of establishing the scheme, meeting compensation claims and meeting the expenses of the scheme manager (s.213(3)–(6), although management expenses are capped under s.223). It is the intention of the legislation that, where an insurance company goes into liquidation or administration, the FSCS should be involved in the insolvency proceedings from the outset, given that the FSCS bears the risk of the insurer's assets not meeting all claims against it. The FSCS scheme manager thus has the right to be represented at the presentation of a petition for the winding up or the administration of an insurer (s.215(3)–(4)). In exercising its functions, the FSCS scheme manager may require the disclosure of information or documents by the authorised person or its appointed representatives insofar as this is required for the fair determination of claims (s.219). The FSCS scheme manager also has the right to receive relevant information from the insurer's liquidator, administrative receiver or administrator (s.220). If in either situation the FSCS scheme manager cannot obtain the information or documents required, the court may enquire into the case and, if appropriate, treat the defaulter as if he were in contempt of court (s.221). The scheme manager has a separate power to inspect documents held by the official receiver (s.224).

---

[102] s.214 sets out the matters with which the rules may provide for, s.215 allows the rules to confer subrogation rights upon the scheme manager where payment has been made to the policyholder of an insolvent insurer, and s.216 allows rules to be made for the continuation of long-term policies.

[103] Lloyd's has its own scheme.

[104] See Financial Services and Markets Act 2000 (Transitional Provisions, Repeals and Savings) (Financial Services Compensation Scheme) Order 2001 (SI 2001/2967), amended by the Financial Services and Markets Act 2000 (Transitional Provisions, Repeals and Savings) (Financial Services Compensation Scheme) (Amendment) Order 2004 (SI 2004/952).

[105] COMP 2.

The FSCS scheme manager must make an annual report to the FSA on the discharge of its functions, setting out the value of the funds maintained by it. The report is to be published (s.218).

The scheme is funded by a levy on insurers (s.223). The amount of the levy is set out in the FSA Handbook, FEES 6.

Eligible claimants.[106] The claimant must be a "policyholder", a word defined   **16–019**
as:

"[T]he person who for the time being is the legal holder of the policy, and includes any person to whom, under the policy, a sum is due, a periodic payment is payable or any other benefit is to be provided or to whom such a sum, payment or benefit is contingently due, payable or to be provided".[107]

COMP identifies four classes of eligible claimant[108]:

(1) The claimant is an individual.

(2) The claim is respect of a general contract of insurance and the claimant is a small business operated as a partnership, so that relevant exclusions are: supranational institutions and governments; local authorities; directors and managers of the defaulting insurer; close relatives of directors and managers of the defaulting insurer; bodies corporate in the same group as the insurer in default; 5 per cent shareholders of the defaulting insurer or any company in the same group; auditors of the defaulting insurer or of any body corporate in the same group, and the appointed actuary of a defaulting insurer; persons who have contributed to the default; large companies and large mutual associations; large partnerships; and any person whose claim arises from a convicted offence of money laundering.

(3) The claim is in respect of a long-term policy, the relevant exclusions being: directors and managers of the defaulting insurer; close relatives of directors and managers of the defaulting insurer; bodies corporate in the same group as the insurer in default; 5 per cent shareholders of the defaulting insurer or any company in the same group; auditors of the defaulting insurer or of any body corporate in the same group, and the appointed actuary of a defaulting insurer; persons who have contributed to the default; and any person whose claim arises from a convicted offence of money laundering.

(4) The claimant is a person with rights under the Third Parties (Rights against Insurers) Act 2010 (even if he would have otherwise have been excluded under any of the exclusions set out in (1) above) as long as any one of three conditions is satisfied: (a) the person insured would have been an eligible claimant at the time that his rights against the insurer vested in the third party—a third party with a contingent claim against the assured which has not been resolved by judgment, award or settlement at the date of the liquidation is protected as long as the assured

---

[106] COMP 4.

[107] Financial Services and Markets Act 2000 (Meaning of "Policy" and "Policyholder") Order 2001 (SI 2001/2361) art.3.

[108] The 1975 Act applied to "private policyholders", a term held to include a member of an American "professional corporation" acting in a private capacity but not the corporation itself: *Ackman and Scher v Policyholders Protection Board (No.2)* [1993] 3 All E.R. 384.

was eligible at the date of the insolvency[109]; or (b) the liability of the person insured was a liability an employers' liability policy which would have been compulsory had the contract been entered into after January 1, 1972; or (c) the liability of the assured had been established and quantified or agreed by the insurer in writing before the date of the insurer's default, in which case it is does not matter whether the assured was himself eligible at the date of the insolvency.

16–020   *"Protected claim"*.[110] A "protected claim" is a claim under a protected contract of insurance. The term "protected contract of insurance" is a long-term or general policy[111] issued on or after December 1, 2001 which satisfies two conditions: it must have been issued through an establishment in the United Kingdom, another EEA state, the Channel Islands or the Isle of Man; and it must relate to a protected risk or commitment, of which there are three classes:

(1) in the case of a contract of insurance issued by a UK establishment, the risk must be situated in an EEA state, the Channel Islands or the Isle of Man;

(2) in the case of a contract of insurance issued by an establishment in an EEA state other than the United Kingdom, the risk must be situated in the United Kingdom;

(3) in the case of a contract of insurance issued from an establishment in the Channel Island or the Isle of Man, the risk must be situated in the United Kingdom, the Channel Islands or the Isle of Man.

The situation of a risk is defined by COMP 5.4 as follows[112]: (a) if the insurance relates to a building or a building and its contents (insofar as the building and contents are covered by the same contract), the risk is situated where the building is situated; (b) if the insurance relating to vehicles of any type, the risk is situated where the vehicle is registered; (c) if the insurance lasts four months or less and covers travel or holiday risks, the risk is situated where the policyholder took out the contract of insurance; and (d) in all other cases (i) where the policyholder is an individual, the risk or commitment is situated where he has his habitual residence at the date when the contract of insurance commenced, or (ii) where the policyholder is not an individual, the risk or commitment is situated where the establishment to which the risk or commitment relates is situated at the date when the contract of insurance commenced. The policy must thus relate to a risk situated in the United Kingdom, reversing the position under the 1975 Act where a risk was covered irrespective of its location if it arose under a policy issued in the course of insurance business carried on in the United Kingdom.[113]

---

[109] This is the effect of the definition of "policyholder", which reverses *Ackman and Scher v Policyholders Protection Board (No.2)* [1993] 3 All E.R. 384 where it was held that a contingent claimant was not a "policyholder" as defined in the 1975 Act.

[110] COMP 5.

[111] The term "policy" is defined by the Financial Services and Markets Act 2000 (Meaning of "Policy" and "Policyholder") Order 2001 (SI 2001/2361) art.2, as meaning "(a) a contract of insurance, including one under which an existing liability has already accrued, or (b) any instrument evidencing such a contract". If no policy has been issued, but the FSA is satisfied that there is nevertheless a binding contract of insurance, COMP 5 states that FSCS nevertheless applies.

[112] The definition is the same as for the situation of a risk for the purposes of choice of law rules: see Ch.2, above.

[113] *Ackman and Scher v Policyholders Protection Board (No.1)* [1993] 3 All E.R. 408.

There are two situations in which a claim is not a protected claim even though it relates to a protected contract of insurance. These arise where other remedies, discussed below, are open to the scheme operator under FSCS as regards transferring long-term business or the provision of financial assistance.

Claims against relevant persons.[114] The claim must be against a "relevant person", i.e. an authorised firm or an appointed representative of an authorised firm. Insurance companies authorised and established else where in the EEA and exercising passport rights in the United Kingdom through EEA establishments are covered by the scheme.[115] An insurer which does not have its head office within the EEA and which is not authorised in the United Kingdom but is selling insurance in the United Kingdom by way of services is required to draw the attention of policyholders, by notice, that they are not protected by FSCS in the event of the insurer's insolvency.[116] The policyholders of unauthorised insurers are not protected, irrespective of where the insurer is carrying on insurance business.

16–021

Relevant person in default.[117] An insurance company is in default if: (a) the FSA has determined it to be in default, in that it is unable to satisfy protected claims or is likely to be unable to satisfy protected claims; or (b) in advance of such determination, a judicial authority has made a ruling that had the effect of suspending the ability of eligible claimants to bring claims. For claims arising in connection with protected contracts of insurance, the FSCS must treat any term in an insurance undertaking's constitution or in its contracts, limiting the undertaking's liabilities under a long-term insurance contract to the amount of its assets, as limiting the undertaking's liabilities to any claimant to an amount which is not less than the gross assets of the undertaking.

16–022

Duties and liabilities of FSCS on the insolvency of an insurer

Extent of liability. The amount of compensation payable to a policyholder is "the amount of his overall net claim against the relevant person at the quantification date".[118] The overall net claim is the liability of the insurer after taking into account any set off (e.g. unpaid premiums) against the assured. FSCS must also take into account any payments to the policyholder made by the insurer or by any other person, if that payment is connected with the relevant person's liability to the claimant.

16–023

The quantification date, by reference to which the liability of FSCS to the policyholder is to be determined, depends upon whether the claim is for the proceeds of the policy (where a loss has occurred at the date of the insurer's liquidation), for the premium paid under a general policy (where no loss has occurred at the date of the insurer's liquidation) or for the value of a long-term policy (where the insured event has not occurred at the date of the insurer's liquidation). In the event of a loss under the policy or a valuation under a long-term policy, the quantification date is the specific date fixed by the FSCS. In the event of a claim for return of premium under a general policy, the quantification date is the date on which the policy was terminated or cancelled.

---

[114] COMP 6.
[115] COMP 14.
[116] Conduct of Business Rules COB, 7.
[117] COMP 6.
[118] COMP 12.

COMP 11 lays down the payment rules. Payment to be made to policyholder himself by the FSCS, although in the case of a long-term insurer in provisional liquidation or liquidation in respect of whose policies FSCS is seeking continuity of insurance, payment may be made by the provisional liquidator or liquidator, subject to indemnification by FSCS.[119] It is also within the power of FSCS to make interim payments and interest may be paid in such circumstances as FSCS considers appropriate: if interest is paid, it is to be disregarded in the calculation of the maximum sums payable.

16–024   *Liability insurance policies.*[120] Where the policy is one which is compulsory, most importantly under the Road Traffic Act 1988 or the Employers Liability (Compulsory Insurance) Act 1969, FSCS must pay a sum equal to 100 per cent of any liability of an insolvent insurer to the policyholder as soon as reasonably practicable after it has determined that the insurer is insolvent, although if the claim arises under a policy compulsory under the 1969 Act entered into on or after January 1, 1972, and the insurer became insolvent before December 1, 2001, FSCS's liability is for 90 per cent of the claim plus the costs awarded against the assured and also the first party defence costs incurred by the assured.[121]

If the claim is not in respect of non-compulsory insurance, the question of what amounts to the "liability" of the insurer becomes more complex. In cases decided under earlier legislation,[122] which hold good under the FSCS, it was decided that four situations have to be distinguished:

(1) Overdue claims, i.e. claims which have accrued and fallen due for payment by the date of the insurer's liquidation. Here, the policyholder and the third party are both persons to whom the sums are due, so that FSCS is applicable.

(2) Mature claims, i.e. claims against the policyholder which have been established and quantified but in respect of which no payment obligation has crystallised, e.g. because policy conditions have not been complied with. Once again, the insurer faces liability for such claims.

(3) Contingent claims, i.e. claims yet to be established and quantified but which are based on events for which the insurer is potentially liable. In such a case the policyholder is a person to whom sums are contingently due.

(4) Unexpired period claims, i.e. claims for loss of protection for the unexpired duration of the policy. Here, no sums are due to the policyholder under the policy, so that FSCS cannot face liability other than for return of premiums.

16–025   *General first party policies.* FSCS must calculate the liability of the insurer to the policyholder in accordance with the terms of the policy and must pay to the policyholder the first £2000 of the loss and 90 per cent of the remaining loss,[123]

---

[119] See *Policyholders Protection Board v Official Receiver* [1976] 2 All E.R. 58.

[120] COMP 10.

[121] *R. (on the application of Geologistics Ltd) v Financial Services Compensation Scheme* [2004] Lloyd's Rep. I.R. 336. The Scottish courts have reached the opposite conclusion in respect of first party costs: *Aitken v Financial Services Compenation Scheme Ltd*, 2003 S.L.T. 878.

[122] *Ackrnan and Scher v Policyholders Protection Board (No.2)* [1993] 3 All E.R. 384 (the point did not arise on appeal); *Transit Casualty v Policyholders Protection Board* [1992] 2 Lloyd's Rep. 358.

[123] COMP 10 and 12.

as soon as is reasonably practicable. If the loss has occurred by the date of the liquidation, FSCS is liable for the loss; if there is no loss, FSCS is liable merely for the unexpired amount of the premium. FSCS does not make express provision for a policy which provides for mixed first party risks and compulsory third party risks, of which a fully comprehensive motor policy is perhaps the best example. The position is doubtless the same as under the 1975 Act, namely that the FCS is liable for 100 per cent of the former and 90 per cent of the latter.

Long-term policies. The amount payable by FSCS depends upon whether FSCS **16–026** has put in place arrangements to continue the long-term policy, or whether no such arrangements have been possible.

Section 216 of the Financial Services and Markets Act 2000 authorises the FSCS to include provisions in the scheme allowing for the continuation of long-term policies. The relevant provisions are contained in COMP 3 which requires the scheme manager to make arrangements to secure the continuity of a long-term insurance policy where the insurer is the subject of insolvency proceedings and it is reasonably practicable to make such arrangements. As anticipated by s.216, the arrangements include: the transfer of the long-term insurance business, or any part of it to another insurer; or procuring the issue of equivalent policies by another insurer by way of substitution for the existing policies. FSCS must, when securing continuity of cover, seek insurance which has terms corresponding to those in the original policy, so far as appears to FSCS to be reasonable, and if lesser benefits are secured then future premiums are to be reduced accordingly. In the period during which FSCS is seeking to secure continuity of cover for a policyholder, it must ensure that the policyholder is paid compensation to represent loss suffered by him for that period. FSCS must pay in respect of future benefits, in full the first £2000 of any loss, and 90 per cent of any additional loss. Payment must be made as soon as reasonably practicable after the time when the benefit would have fallen due under the policy, subject to the terms of the policy. A bonus is to be disregarded unless declared before the beginning of the liquidation.

If FSCS cannot make arrangements to secure the continuation of a long-term policy, it must pay compensation. FSCS must calculate the liability of the insurer to the policyholder in accordance with the terms of the contract as valued in the liquidation in accordance to such valuation techniques as FSCS considers appropriate, and pay that amount in full to the policyholder as soon as is reasonably practicable. There are a number of specific limitations on the obligation to pay 100 per cent of the value of the policy: (1) any bonus is to be excluded from the claim unless it was declared prior to the commencement of the liquidation; (2) if FSCS considers that the benefits or future benefits are excessive, and this has been confirmed by an independent actuary, payment may be reduced; (3) FSCS must treat any term in the insurer's constitution or policies which limits its liabilities to the amount of its assets, as limiting liability to any policyholder to an amount not less than the insurer's gross assets.

Payment procedures.[124] Application has to be made to FSCS for compensation. **16–027** FSCS may reject an application for compensation which contains any material inaccuracy, and it will also reject a claim which, had it been made against the insurer, would have been time-barred under the Limitation Act 1980. An offer of compensation may be withdrawn if it is not accepted within 90 days, although if

---

[124] COMP 8 and 11.

the offer is disputed then FSCS may withdraw the offer but must consider making an interim offer. Compensation wrongly paid by FSCS may be recovered by it.

The duty of FSCS is to make payment in all cases as soon as reasonably practicable following the date of the winding up order in the case of a compulsory liquidation, or the date of the resolution in the case of a voluntary liquidation. The concept of "reasonably practicable" is amplified by COMP 9, which states that a claim must be paid by FSCS as soon as reasonably possible after: (1) it is satisfied that the qualifying conditions have been met; and (2) it has calculated the compensation due to the claimant, and in any event within three months of the latter date unless the FSA has granted an extension. In the case of insurance, COMP 9 further provides that FSCS may delay payment if it considers that "the liability to which the claim relates or any part of that liability is covered by another contract of insurance with a solvent insurance undertaking, or where it appears that a person, other than the liquidator, may make payments or take such action to secure the continuity of cover as the FSCS would undertake".

16–028 **Insurers in financial difficulties.** Section 217 of the Financial Services and Markets Act 2000 allows special rules to be made whereby the FSCS scheme manager can take measures for safeguarding policyholders of an insurer which is in financial difficulties. The section is implemented by COMP 3. An insurer is deemed to be in financial difficulties if: (1) the insurer is in provisional liquidation; (2) it has been proved, in any proceedings on a petition for the insurer's winding up, or in the course of a voluntary winding up, that the insurer is unable to pay its debts; (3) an application has been made to the court under s.896 of the Companies Act 2006 to sanction a scheme of arrangement between the insurer and its creditors, under which benefits under policies may be reduced or deferred; or (4) the FSA has determined that the insurer is likely not to be able to satisfy protected claims against it. In any of these cases, the FSCS must take such measures for the purpose of protecting eligible claimants as it considers appropriate, if in the FSCS's opinion the cost of taking those measures is likely to be less than the cost of paying compensation. The relevant date for making the assessment is the time at which FSCS proposes to take the measures, so that if its judgment subsequently proves to be incorrect it must nevertheless maintain the measures rather than pay compensation.

The assistance measures contemplated by COMP 3 are: transferring the insurance business to another insurer; or providing financial assistance to the insurer in financial difficulties to enable it to carry out its contracts. In practice, where the powers are exercised, a scheme of arrangement will be entered into, subject to the approval of the court under s.896 of the Companies Act 2006. The terms on which these measures are taken are a matter for the FSCS, and they may include reducing or deferring policy benefits. In the case of a long-term policy, the FSCS is in any event required to reduce the claimant's interest to 90 per cent of the amount payable under the policy, subject to an equivalent reduction in premiums which have not yet fallen due.

16–029 **Reducing and limiting the FSCS's liability.** The FSCS ensures that the policyholder receives 90 per cent or, in the case of compulsory insurance, 100 per cent of the amount which his contract with the insurer provides that he should receive. It is not intended that the policyholder is to profit from his insurer's insolvency. Consequently, the scheme goes to some lengths to ensure that the policyholder does not recover the value of his policy both from the FSCS and from some other source. Section 215 of the 2000 Act allows the rules of FSCS to make provision for conferring a right of recovery by the FSCS following a payment by it, although its recovery is limited to the amount which it has paid to the policyholder.

First, under COMP 7, if FSCS makes payment to a policyholder, it may do so conditionally on the policyholder assigning his rights against the insurer to FSCS, so that FSCS can prove in the insurer's liquidation for the amount of the value of the policy. FSCS is then under a duty to make such recoveries as it can in the liquidation. Where there has been an assignment and recoveries are made by FSCS, then FSCS can retain the recoveries but only to the extent of their own payment to the policyholder: any surplus is to be paid to the policyholder. This is important, given that that FSCS is obliged to pay only 90 per cent of general insurance claims, so that in the unlikely event that the insurer's liquidation realises a recovery of more than 90 per cent, that surplus goes to the policyholder. However, the principle that the policyholder bears the residual loss in such a case is modified where the policyholder has been prejudiced by the fact that he has accepted the FSCS's offer of compensation promptly rather than delaying to await the outcome of the liquidation.

Secondly, irrespective of any assignment of rights, FSCS—having indemnified the policyholder—has subrogation rights against the insolvent insurer. These rights may be inferior to rights conferred by an assignment, in that there has to be actual payment before subrogation rights attach, and that any claim must be brought in the name of the policyholder rather than in the name of FSCS. It is unlikely that FSCS will seek to rely upon subrogation, as it may insist upon assignment as a condition of making payment in the first place. Further, given that FSCS is only liable for 90 per cent of a general business claim, the policyholder would on general principles in any event retain the right to control the proceedings in the absence of a full indemnity from FSCS.

Thirdly, COMP 12 states that FSCS must also take into account any payments to the policyholder made by the insurer or by any other person, if that payment is connected with the relevant person's liability to the claimant. Any sums obtained from the insurer itself are plainly to be deducted. Any sums actually paid by another insurer are also to be deducted. Voluntary payments paid by a broker on an interim basis are apparently also to be taken into account, so there is no obvious reason why a broker should choose to make such a payment.

PART III:
SPECIAL TYPES OF INSURANCE CONTRACT

CHAPTER 17

REINSURANCE

1. DEFINITION OF REINSURANCE

Basic forms. Reinsurance has been defined as the insurance of insurers.[1] It is in **17–001** essence a contract of insurance[2] under which the insurer takes out cover on its own risk. Reinsurance is of two broad types. The first type is facultative, which consists of the reinsurance of a single risk reinsured on a proportional basis, in that the reinsured retains an agreed proportion of the risk and passes some or all of the remainder to the reinsurers. This form of reinsurance is commonly used to bring to the London market risks which cannot be insured directly, by reason of local regulatory requirements. The reinsured will act as a "front" by under-writing the risk and reinsuring most or all of it with reinsurers.[3]

The second type of reinsurance is by treaty, which is a mechanism for insuring a large number of risks, either by class or by way of whole account. Treaties may be proportional—the most common types being surplus and quota share—in that the reinsured cedes to the reinsurers an agreed proportion of all risks accepted. Alternatively, treaties may be non-proportional, the most common forms being excess of loss, under which the reinsurers become liable when the reinsured's aggregate losses reach a stated sum[4] net of fixed expenses and subrogation recoveries,[5] and stop loss, which is similar in nature and which is designed to

---

[1] *Travellers Casualty & Surety Co of Europe Ltd v Commissioners of Customs and Excise* [2006] Lloyd's Rep. I.R. 63. It has also been defined as "insurance between consenting adults": *Reinsurance Practice and the Law*, edited by Barlow Lyde & Gilbert, looseleaf. Other works are *Butler and Merkin's Reinsurance Law* looseleaf; Edelman, *The Law of Reinsurance* 2005; O'Neill and Woloneski, *The Law of Reinsurance* 2nd edn (London: Sweet & Maxwell, 2005). In *Gater Assets Ltd v Nak Naftogaz Ukrainy* [2008] EWHC 237 (Comm) a contract described as "reinsurance" was found not to involve any element of transfer of risk whatsoever but merely operated as a device for overcoming a prohibition on a transfer of rights under a contract between the "assured" and a third party. The only question was whether there had been a deliberate attempt to withhold the true nature of the transaction from arbitrators, an allegation which was dismissed on the facts.

[2] *Delver v Barnes* (1807) 1 Taunt. 48; *China Traders Insurance v Royal Exchange* [1898] 2 Q.B. 187; *Australian Widows Fund v National Mutual Life* [1914] A.C. 634; *Re London County Commercial Reinsurance Office* [1922] Ch. 67.

[3] See *Sirius International Insurance Co (Publ) v FAI General Insurance Ltd* [2005] Lloyd's Rep. I.R. 294. The reinsured will generally receive an additional proportion of the premium by way of reward for acting in that capacity: see *Wasa International Insurance Co Ltd v Lexington Insurance Co* [2008] Lloyd's Rep. I.R. 510. The word "facultative" is derived from the Latin, "facultas" which is "a one off, a happening or chance of one thing happening": see Longmore L.J. in *Wasa International Insurance Co Ltd v Lexington Insurance Co* [2008] Lloyd's Rep. I.R. 510. These points did not arise on appeal, [2009] Lloyd's Rep. I.R. 675.

[4] Whether an excess limit has been reached is a matter of fact, to be proved by the reinsured by the best available evidence: *Equitas Ltd v R&Q Reinsurance Company (UK) Ltd* [2009] EWHC 2787 (Comm).

[5] The ultimate net loss clause, used in excess of loss reinsurance.

protect the reinsured against insolvency.[6] A treaty is in essence a framework facility under which risks falling within its scope may be ceded to the reinsurers. The most usual type of treaty is obligatory, so that risks accepted by the reinsured are automatically ceded to the treaty with neither party having any discretion in the matter: there may be an obligation on the reinsured to keep the reinsurers informed of risks as and when they are accepted,[7] but unless the treaty otherwise provides a failure in this regard by the assured will not prevent the risk from attaching and the only remedy open to the reinsurers is to seek damages in the unlikely event that loss can be proved.[8] Alternatively, the treaty may be facultative, in that the reinsured has the discretion to declare individual risks and the reinsurers have the right to refuse them: the treaty in this situation is little more than a mechanism for the submission of offers. An intermediate possibility is a facultative obligatory treaty, under which the reinsured has the discretion whether or not to make a declaration but the reinsurers are required to accept anything which is ceded. This type of arrangement is relatively uncommon, given that the reinsurers run the risk of receiving only those risks which are likely to be unprofitable, although it is not unknown.[9] Subject to any contrary wording in the policy, a declaration may be made at any time before the reinsured has become aware that a loss in respect of it has occurred.[10]

17–002 **The parties.** Reinsurance is a contract distinct from the underlying policy, and there is no privity of contract between reinsurers and assured, a point which may be important if the reinsured has become insolvent. This is the case even in proportional reinsurance, where the relationship is close to partnership or agency[11] or in a fronting arrangement where the reinsured's functions are strictly limited, so that in the event of the reinsured's insolvency its policyholders have no claim against the reinsurers.[12] In the event of a loss, the reinsurance agreement may require the reinsured to hand over to the reinsurers all negotiations with the assured, although the fact that there is direct contact between the assured and reinsurers is not of itself enough to create a contract between them under which the assured may sue the reinsurers directly.[13] Reinsurers who exercise contractual

---

[6] See *Society of Lloyd's v Morris* [1993] 2 Re. L.R. 217. An analogous form of reinsurance is reinsurance to close, whereby a Lloyd's Syndicate reinsures its members' future liabilities into the next accounting year. There is extended discussion of reinsurance to close in *Harris v The Society of Lloyd's* [2009] Lloyd's Rep. I.R. 119, in which Lloyd's Names asserted that they had been induced to become and remain members of Lloyd's by misrepresentations as to the nature of reinsurance to close. David Steel J. rejected the suggestion that there had been any false statements made, although he confirmed that reinsurance to close does not take effect as a novation or assignment of liability but is simply reinsurance of the members of the closed syndicate, so that those members still face primary liability to policyholders. The reasoning was followed in *Re Equitas Ltd* [2010] Lloyd's Rep. I.R. 69.

[7] Generally by means of periodic bordereaux.

[8] *Glencore International AG v Ryan (The Beursgracht)* [2002] 1 Lloyd's Rep. 574.

[9] *Allianz Via Assurance v Marchant*, Unreported, 1996. In *Aneco Reinsurance Underwriting Ltd v Johnson & Higgins* [1998] 1 Lloyd's Rep. 565 the difference between obligatory non-obligatory agreements was held to be material in relation to a retrocession agreement procured by the reinsurers.

[10] *Glencore International AG v Alpina Insurance Co* [2004] 1 Lloyd's Rep. 111.

[11] *Re Norwich Equitable Fire* (1887) 57 L.T. 241; *Motor Union v Mannheimer* [1933] 1 K.B. 812; *Glasgow Assurance v Welsh Insurance*, 1914 S.C. 320; *English Insurance v National Benefit Insurance* [1929] A.C. 114.

[12] *Re Law Guarantee Trust* [1915] 1 Ch. 340; *Re Harrington Motor Co* [1928] Ch. 105. The Third Parties (Rights against Insurers) Act 2010 does not apply to reinsurance (see s.15), so there is no direct action under that statute. For the rights of the policyholder of an insolvent insurer, see Ch.16, above.

[13] *Grecoair v Tilling* [2005] Lloyd's Rep. I.R. 151.

rights against the reinsured to preclude settlement of a claim by the reinsured cannot face liability to the assured, as in such circumstances there is no basis for the imposition of any duty on the reinsurers towards the assured. Equally, the assured is unlikely to be able to assert successfully that the reinsurers have committed the tort of interfering with the contractual relations between the assured and the reinsured, as it would have to be shown that the reinsurers intended to interfere with the contract rather than pursue their own interests in a manner which subsequently affected the rights of the assured.[14]

Some reinsurance agreements contain cut-through clauses. A provision of this type gives the assured a direct claim against the reinsurers, normally in the event of the reinsured's insolvency. Since the passing of the Contracts (Rights of Third Parties) Act 1999[15] there is no privity of contract objection to the enforcement of a cut-through clause, although it is arguable that a cut-through clause constitutes a charge on the insurer's assets which is registrable under s.860 of the Companies Act 2006,[16] and, more importantly, that the clause might be unenforceable in that it gives the assured a prioritised claim over the reinsured's assets (the sum due from reinsurers) and accordingly contravenes the pari passu rule which applies as between unsecured creditors.[17] An agreement whereby assureds agreed to assign to reinsurers their claims against the reinsured in return for direct payment of those claims by the reinsurers is effective as a matter of contract in that it relieves the reinsurers from their own obligation to make payment to the reinsured, but may also contravene insolvency principles affecting the reinsured's assets.[18]

Regulation. Reinsurance in all of its forms is regarded for regulatory purposes **17–003** as insurance and the class of business reinsured also determines the class of reinsurance. Reinsurers are therefore subject to the regulatory regime established under the Financial Services and Markets Act 2000, albeit modified in some respects, and must be authorised to carry on business in the United Kingdom.[19]

Reinsurance regulation, under European Parliament and Council Directive 2005/68/EU, was adopted on November 16, 2005,[20] and was due to be in place for all EU Member States by December 10, 2007. Prior to the adoption of this measure member states had been required to abolish any rules which provided for discriminatory treatment of reinsurers on the ground of nationality or residence,[21] and insurers who carried on reinsurance business were regulated under the ordinary rules applicable to insurers under the Insurance Directives.[22] The Reinsurance Directive 2005 applies to pure reinsurers, and overcomes the inconsistencies in regulation found within member states, ranging from no

---

[14] *Equitas Ltd v Wave City Shipping Co Ltd* [2006] Lloyd's Rep. I.R. 646.

[15] See Ch.15, above, for discussion of this Act.

[16] Cf. *General Insurance of Trieste v Miller* (1896) 12 T.L.R. 395; *Leo Steamship v Corderoy* (1896) 1 Com. Cas. 300.

[17] As laid down in *British Eagle International Airlines Ltd v Compagnie Nationale Air France* [1975] 2 Lloyd's Rep. 43.

[18] *McMahon v AGF Holdings (UK) Ltd* [1997] L.R.L.R. 159.

[19] *Forsakringsaktieselskapet National of Copenhagen v Attorney General* [1925] A.C. 639; *DR Insurance Co v Seguros America Banamex* [1993] 1 Lloyd's Rep. 120; *Re NRG Victory Reinsruance Ltd* [1995] 1 W.L.R. 239; *Re NRG Victory Insurance* [1995] 1 All E.R. 533; *Re Friend's Provident Life* [1999] Lloyd's Rep. I.R. 547; *WASA International (UK) Insurance Co Ltd v WASA International* Unreported, 2003.

[20] [2005] O.J. L323/1. The Directive has been replaced by the Solvency II Directive, European Parliament and Council Directive 2009/138/EC. See Ch.13, above.

[21] Council Directive 64/225/EEC of February 25, 1964.

[22] See Ch.14, above.

regulation to UK-style full regulation. The Reinsurance Directive extends the principles in the Insurance Directives to pure reinsurers.[23] It provides for authorisation by the regulator for the EU state in which the reinsurer has its head office, authorisation operating as a single European licence to establish, or to sell reinsurance, anywhere in the EU, authorisation to be based not on the direct insurance classes but rather on the general headings of life, non-life, or both. Strict conditions are laid down for authorisation, i.e. (a) the reinsurer must limit its objects to the business of reinsurance and related operations; (b) the reinsurer must submit a scheme of operations; (c) the reinsurer must possess the minimum guarantee fund provided for in the draft directive; and (d) the reinsurer must be effectively run by persons of good repute with appropriate professional qualifications or experience. Authorisation may be withdrawn if the reinsurer: has not made use of its authorisation within 12 months; no longer meets the conditions required for authorisation; has infringed accounting and solvency rules and has failed to implement a financial plan to correct the infringements; and in general has failed seriously in its obligations under the regulations to which it is subject. Once authorised, the reinsurer is regulated exclusively by its home state regulator, which may act either on its own initiative or following a complaint by any host state in which the reinsurer is carrying on its operations. Supervisory controls over the business of a reinsurer following authorisation include: regulation of the persons who control or own substantial shareholdings or voting rights in the reinsurer; and the maintenance of technical provisions, a solvency margin and a guarantee fund.

The Reinsurance Directive was implemented in the United Kingdom at the end of 2006, by changes to the FSA Handbook. Three points are worthy of note. The first is the introduction of a "principles based" approach (the "Prudent Person" approach) for the determination of assets constituting the reinsurers' technical provisions under which technical provisions are to be covered by assets in such a way as to secure sufficient liquidity, security, equality, profitability and matching of its investments, while leaving the detailed choice of assets with the reinsurer itself. The rules apply to pure reinsurers and also to companies carrying on both insurance and reinsurance business (mixed companies). The second is the modification of solvency requirements for reinsurance of life and pensions business. The Insurance Directives impose more stringent solvency requirements on life insurers as opposed to non-life insurers. The Reinsurance Directive, by contrast, adopts the non-life solvency test for both non-life and life reinsurance, and allows Member States either to apply the non-life solvency test to life reinsurance or to confine the non-life solvency test to protection business and to extend life solvency requirements to life reinsurance. The Handbook applies the rules in the Insurance Directives for life insurance to investment contracts but not to protection contracts. Finally, as noted above, the Directive requires Member States which permit special purpose vehicles ("SPVs") to authorise and supervise them, as regards both insurance and reinsurance business. At one time the United Kingdom adopted this approach, but the amended Handbook no longer requires full authorisation for SPVs as if they were insurers or reinsurers and has adopted a more restricted form of regulation: less extensive information is required on an application for authorisation, although a business plan does

---

[23] The measure is an interim one: all of the insurance and reinsurance provisions are to be replaced in due course under the EU's Solvency 2 Project.

have to be submitted and there has to be certification by legal advisers that reinsurance creditors have priority over other creditors. Most importantly, reinsurance liabilities must not exceed available assets. In accordance with the Directive, sums owing from SPVs count towards technical provisions for the purposes of solvency margin.

There has been much regulatory concern over transactions, described as "reinsurance", which may have purposes other than the protection of the reinsured's capacity and solvency, in particular "finite reinsurance" and special purpose vehicles. Finite reinsurance operates to spread losses over the period of reinsurance, and in many cases the only risk transferred to the reinsurer is the time value of money rather than any underwriting risk. Special purpose vehicles are used by insurers and reinsurers as methods of funding losses other than by conventional underwriting, in particular through the use of securitisation. These devices have been recognised by the FSA as having both legitimate and illegitimate uses, in that they may either emphasise or obscure the true nature of the parties' financial positions. The Reinsurance Directive does not impose a common EU-wide scheme for the regulation of these matters, but seeks to ensure that where such arrangements are permitted by Member States minimum regulatory standards are imposed. As far as financial reinsurance is concerned, member states may require disclosure of financial reinsurance contracts (the approach adopted by the FSA in the United Kingdom) and they may also require measures to protect the solvency of insurers using financial reinsurance. As far as special purpose vehicles are concerned, if they are permitted by a Member State they must be authorised and generally treated in much the same way as insurance companies.

The Reinsurance Directive was implemented in the United Kingdom at the end of 2006, by changes to the FSA Handbook. Three points are worthy of note. The first is the introduction of a "principles based" approach (the "Prudent Person" approach) for the determination of assets constituting the reinsurers' technical provisions under which technical provisions are to be covered by assets in such a way as to secure sufficient liquidity, security, equality, profitability and matching of its investments, while leaving the detailed choice of assets with the reinsurer itself. The rules apply to pure reinsurers and also to companies carrying on both insurance and reinsurance business (mixed companies). The second is the modification of solvency requirements for reinsurance of life and pensions business. The Insurance Directives impose more stringent solvency requirements on life insurers as opposed to non-life insurers. The Reinsurance Directive, by contrast, adopts the non-life solvency test for both non-life and life reinsurance, and allows Member States either to apply the non-life solvency test to life reinsurance or to confine the non-life solvency test to protection business and to extend life solvency requirements to life reinsurance. The Handbook applies the rules in the Insurance Directives for life insurance to investment contracts but not to protection contracts. Finally, as noted above, the Directive requires Member States which permit special purpose vehicles ("SPVs") to authorise and supervise them, as regards both insurance and reinsurance business. At one time the United Kingdom adopted this approach, but the amended Handbook no longer requires full authorisation for SPVs as if they were insurers or reinsurers and has adopted a more restricted form of regulation: less extensive information is required on an application for authorisation, although a business plan does have to be submitted and there has to be certification by legal advisers that reinsurance creditors have priority over other creditors. Most importantly, reinsurance liabilities must not exceed available assets. In accordance with the

Directive, sums owing from SPVs count towards technical provisions for the purposes of solvency margin.

17–004 **Insurable interest in reinsurance.** There was, at least until the decision of the House of Lords in *Wasa International Insurance Co Ltd v Lexington Insurance Co*,[24] some debate as to the nature of the reinsrued's insurable interest. One view is that the reinsured's insurable interest is in its liability, which renders a reinsurance agreement something akin to a liability policy.[25] The alternative view is that reinsurance is "the insurance of an insurable interest in the subject matter of an original insurance".[26] The point has been left open in a number of cases.[27] In *Wasa International Insurance Co Ltd v Lexington Insurance Co*,[28] insurers, who had issued environmental liability cover to a US corporation for a three-year period, were held by the US courts to be liable for losses which had occurred both before and after the inception of that policy. Reinsurance had been taken out for 36 months on the same terms and conditions as the original, and the reinsurers raised a series of arguments as to why the reinsurance cover was not coterminous with that of the direct insurance. Part of the reinsurers' case was that the reinsurers were not simply liable to indemnify the insurers but that the reinsurers were entitled to rely upon the specific wording of their own cover, and that the reinsurance was to be regarded as a separate policy on the direct risk as defined in the reinsurance. In the Court of Appeal Longmore L.J. held that this argument was irrelevant to the outcome, and that the only question to be determined was whether the reinsurers had on the proper construction of their wording assumed the same risk as the insurers, which was held to be the case. Pill L.J. again did not comment. Sedley L.J., by contrast, was clear in the view that reinsurance is by its nature a form of liability cover and not a further policy on the direct risk, and that the fiction that reinsurance was not an independent contract but rather one on the original risk had arise simply because marine reinsurance was illegal from 1745 to 1864. Accordingly, the need for that fiction was:

"[T]hus long spent. The practice and vocabulary of reinsurance law have for a long time now reflected the reality that what is reinsured is the insurer's own liability."

On appeal to the House of Lords, Lord Phillips referred to this comment and expressed the view that it was not well-founded. Their Lordships preferred the view that reinsurance was not liability insurance at all but constituted a further insurance on the original subject matter, although it was accepted that there was

[24] *Wasa International Insurance Co Ltd v Lexington Insurance Co* [2009] Lloyd's Rep. I.R. 675, reversing [2008] Lloyd's Rep. I.R. 510.

[25] *DR Insurance v Seguros America Banamex* [1993] 1 Lloyd's Rep. 120. Cf. *Agnew v Lansforsakringsbolagens AB* [2003] Lloyd's Rep. I.R. 637.

[26] *Delver v Barnes* (1807) 1 Taunt. 48; *Mackenzie v Whitworth* (1875) 1 Ex. D. 36; *Uzielli v Boston Marine* (1884) 15 Q.B.D. 11; *British Dominions General v Duder* [1925] A.C. 639; *Forsikringsaktieselskapet National v Attorney General* [1925] A.C. 639; *Toomey v Eagle Star* [1994] 1 Lloyd's Rep. 516; *CNA International Reinsurance Co Ltd v Companhia de Seguros Tranquilidade SA* [1999] Lloyd's Rep. I.R. 289; *CGU International Insurance Plc v AstraZenica Insurance Co Ltd* [2006] Lloyd's Rep. I.R. 409. This is also the approach adopted in the cases on regulation, cited above.

[27] *Charter Reinsurance Co Ltd v Fagan* [1996] 3 All E.R. 46; *Enterprise Oil Ltd v Strand Insurance Co Ltd* [2007] Lloyd's Rep. I.R. 186. Section 9(1) of the Marine Insurance Act simply refers to the reinsured reinsuring the risk.

[28] *Wasa International Insurance Co Ltd v Lexington Insurance Co* [2008] Lloyd's Rep. I.R. 510, reversed [2009] Lloyd's Rep. I.R. 675.

much to be said for the liability insurance argument and that it was open to the parties to frame their contact as one on liability.

It may be that the position depends upon the manner in which the reinsurance agreement is drafted, a proposition supported by *Feasey v Sun Life of Canada*[29] in which the Court of Appeal saw no objection to a reinsurance treaty indemnifying the reinsured against liability claims by shipowners being redrafted as a contract under which the reinsurers' obligation to pay was linked not to the reinsured's own liability but rather to the fact that an accident had occurred which might have led to a claim against a shipowner and then against the reinsured. The majority ruled that the subject matter of the policy was the wellbeing of the life or lives of shipowners' employees; that the reinsured had an insurable interest in its liability for those employees; and that the policy should be construed as extending to the reinsured's liability interest even though it was framed as a life policy.

The reinsurers are only obliged to indemnify a reinsured which itself faces liability to the assured. Accordingly, where the assured's has no insurable interest but the reinsured chooses to pay the claim, the reinsurers do not face any liability to indemnify the reinsured.[30]

2. FORMATION OF REINSURANCE CONTRACTS

Reinsurance in advance of insurance. Reinsurance is frequently formed in advance of insurance. A broker instructed to place insurance may decide that the risk is easier to place if reinsurance can be arranged for those insurers willing to subscribe to the direct risk, and the broker may arrange for reinsurers to issue a standing offer for reinsurance under which an insurer who subscribes to the direct risk is automatically covered by the reinsurance. This type of arrangement is a unilateral contract, which can be withdrawn at any time other than against insurers who have subscribed to the direct risk.[31] This type of arrangement raises as yet unresolved questions as to the agency of the broker, as he plainly cannot be the agent of the assured, as the assured has not employed the broker to place reinsurance[32] nor can he be the agent of non-existent insurers, and it may be that the broker is best regarded as acting as an independent intermediary. That approach is consistent with *General Accident Fire and Life Assurance Corp v Tanter (The Zephyr)*,[33] in which personal contractual liability towards reinsures was imposed upon a broker who had failed to use best endeavours to obtain the level of oversubscription promised when the reinsurance slip was placed.

17–005

---

[29] *Feasey v Sun Life of Canada* [2003] Lloyd's Rep. I.R. 637. Cf. *Re London County Commercial Reinsurance Office* [1922] 2 Ch. 67.

[30] *Re Overseas Marine Insurance Co Ltd* (1930) 36 Ll. L.R. 183. Contrast *Hewitt v London General Insurance Co Ltd* (1925) 23 Ll. L.R. 243, where the relevant interest existed.

[31] *General Accident Fire and Life Assurance Corp v Tanter (The Zephyr)* [1985] 2 Lloyd's Rep. 529; *Youell v Bland Welch (No.2)* [1990] 2 Lloyd's Rep. 431; *Kingscroft v Nissan (No.2)* [1999] Lloyd's Rep. I.R. 603; *Tryg Baltica International (UK) Ltd v Boston Compania De Seguros SA* [2005] Lloyd's Rep. I.R. 40; *Bonner v Cox Corporate Member* [2006] Lloyd's Rep. I.R. 385.

[32] *SAIL v Farex Gie* [1995] L.R.L.R. 116.

[33] *General Accident Fire and Life Assurance Corp v Tanter (The Zephyr)* [1985] 2 Lloyd's Rep. 529.

Utmost good faith

17–006 *Nature of the duty.* In the case of a facultative contract, the reinsurers will normally be shown the proposal made to the reinsured by the assured and they will also receive any further information known to the reinsured. If false statements made to the reinsured are passed on the reinsurers, then the reinsurers will have the right to avoid the reinsurance[34] whether or not the reinsured has chosen (or, under local law, is required) to affirm the contract.[35] The correctness of information passed to the reinsurers by the reinsured may be warranted, so that if false statements have been made—material or otherwise—the reinsurers will never be on risk. The warranty may, however, extend not to just to information provided by the reinsured but may also extend to information known to the reinsurers, so that facts actually known to the reinsurers are to be taken into account in deciding whether the reinsured's own statements are actually false.[36]

The nature of the duty of disclosure under a treaty depends upon its nature.[37] A treaty which is obligatory, in that risks ceded must be accepted by the reinsurers, is a contract *of* reinsurance in its own right and it is arguable that a duty of disclosure exists at that time,[38] although there cannot be a separate duty of disclosure in respect of each individual declaration given that the premium has been fixed in advance and the reinsurers cannot refuse to accept any declaration. By contrast, if the treaty is facultative so that the reinsurers have the right to refuse proffered declarations, it is to be regarded as a contract *for* insurance which does not of itself attract a duty of utmost good faith, although each declaration is a contract of reinsurance in its own right and disclosure is required. In the event that an individual declaration under a facultative treaty can be set aside for breach of the duty of utmost good faith, the treaty itself and other declarations are unaffected.[39]

17–007 *Material facts.* A number of facts may be material for reinsurance purposes. Anything material to the direct risk is itself material for reinsurance purposes, e.g. the fact that the president of a bank insured under a fidelity policy is under investigation for fraud,[40] that footballer insured under an accident policy has a previous injury[41] or that the insured subject matter is not clocks but valuable

---

[34] *Foster v Mentor Life* (1854) 3 E. & B. 48; *Equitable Life Assurance v General Accident Insurance*, 1904 12 S.L.T. 348; *Australian Widows Fund v National Mutual Life* [1914] A.C. 634; *Highlands Insurance v Continental Insurance* [1987] 1 Lloyd's Rep. 109.

[35] *Sirius v Oriental* [1999] Lloyd's Rep. I.R. 343.

[36] *MJ Harrington Syndicate 2000 v Axa Oyak Sigorta AS* [2007] Lloyd's Rep. I.R. 60. In *Limit No.2 Ltd v Axa Versicherung AG* [2008] Lloyd's Rep. I.R. 330 a facultative obligatory treaty was held to be subject to the duty of utmost good faith, so that misrepresentation by the reinsured as to the underlying risks accepted gave the reinsurers an entitlement to avoid the treaty.

[37] See Ch.6, above.

[38] *HIH Casualty and General Insurance v Chase Manhattan* [2001] Lloyd's Rep. I.R. 191. Thus the fact that the reinsured has declared risks to the treaty which are not within its scope will be material on renewal: *Reliance Marine v Duder* [1913] 1 K.B. 265; *Mander v Commercial Union Assurance Co Plc* [1998] Lloyd's Rep. I.R. 93; *Abrahams v Mediterranean Insurance and Reinsurance Co* [1991] 1 Lloyd's Rep. 216. In *Limit No.2 Ltd v Axa Versicherung AG* [2008] Lloyd's Rep. I.R. 330, reversed in part on other grounds [2009] Lloyd's Rep. I.R. 396, a facultative obligatory treaty was held to be subject to the duty of utmost good faith, so that misrepresentation by the reinsured as to the underlying risks accepted gave the reinsurers an entitlement to avoid the treaty.

[39] *SA d'Intermediaries Luxembourgeios v Farex Gie* [1995] L.R.L.R. 116.

[40] *Brotherton v Aseguradora Colseguros SA (No.3)* [2003] Lloyd's Rep. I.R. 774.

[41] *Prifti v Musini Sociedad Anonima de Seguros y Reaseguros* [2004] Lloyd's Rep. I.R. 528.

Rolex watches.[42] There will in addition be matters specific to reinsurance which the reinsurers will want to know. Underwriting practices are plainly material.[43] In proportional covers the premium paid to the reinsurers is based on that paid to the reinsured[44] so that the amount of the premium may be material.[45] The nature of the cover provided by the reinsured is also material, in that unusual terms have to be disclosed,[46] e.g. that the reinsured's liabilities are based on facultative obligatory contract issued to the reinsured's policyholder[47] or that the reinsured has issued a valued policy rather than a policy under which the assured must prove its loss.[48] A key material fact is claims experience,[49] and it has been held that the reinsured's assessment of its anticipated losses—IBNR (losses incurred but not reported)—must be disclosed,[50] although only if the amount of anticipated losses is likely to penetrate the reinsurers' level of cover.[51] In the same way, the reinsured's reserving policy is material if it varies from what the reinsurers might reasonably have anticipated,[52] as would be the case where the reinsured did not recognise a loss for reserving purposes until every "i" was dotted and every "t" was crossed. Previous fraudulent conduct on behalf of the reinsured's brokers may also be material,[53] at least if it relates directly to the risk to be reinsured.[54]

The amount of the reinsured's retention which has actually been retained and not reinsured elsewhere is not material unless the reinsurers have asked an express question about it.[55] The reinsured's retention is primarily regarded as a restriction of the reinsurers' liability rather than a guarantee of the quality of the reinsured's underwriting, so that a requirement that the reinsured is to bear a

---

[42] *WISE Underwriting Agency Ltd v Grupo Nacional Provincial SA* [2004] Lloyd's Rep. I.R. 764. See also *Limit No.2 Ltd v Axa Versicherung AG* [2008] Lloyd's Rep. I.R. 330, reversed in part on other grounds [2009] Lloyd's Rep. I.R. 396, where it was held that a false statement by the reinsured as to the retention demanded of policyholders was a material fact.

[43] *Feasey v Sun Life of Canada* [2002] Lloyd's Rep. I.R. 835.

[44] Minus sums for expenses and commission.

[45] *Allianz Via Assurance v Marchant* 1996; *Mander v Commercial Union Assurance Co Plc* [1998] Lloyd's Rep. I.R. 93. Cf. *Markel International Insurance Company Ltd and Another v La Republica Compania Argentina de Seguros Generales SA* [2005] Lloyd's Rep. I.R. 90, where the fact that assureds were willing to pay higher premiums than had been disclosed, was a material fact.

[46] *Charlesworth v Faber* (1900) 5 Com. Cas. 408; *Property Insurance v National Protector Insurance* (1913) 108 L.T. 104; *Mander v Commercial Union Assurance Co Plc* [1998] Lloyd's Rep. I.R. 93.

[47] *Aneco Reinsurance Underwriting Ltd v Johnson & Higgins* [2002] Lloyd's Rep. I.R. 91.

[48] *Toomey v Banco Vitalico de Espana de Seguros y Reaseguros* [2005] Lloyd's Rep. I.R. 423.

[49] *General Fire and Life Assurance Corp v Campbell* (1925) 21 Ll. L.R. 151; *Aiken v Stewart Wrightson Members Agency Ltd* [1995] 2 Lloyd's Rep. 618. In *Limit No.2 Ltd v Axa Versicherung AG* [2008] Lloyd's Rep. I.R. 330, reversed in part on other grounds [2009] Lloyd's Rep. I.R. 396, a reinsurance case, it was held that, on the facts, developments in the claims position between the date of the original treaty and its renewal, were material as the potential losses were significant. By contrast, it was also held that an increase of reported incidents did not have to be disclosed because the number of new incidents was unremarkable and evidence from the market showed that incidents which did not lead to reserving by the reinsured were not material as regards reinsurers.

[50] *Aiken v Stewart Wrightson* [1995] 3 All E.R. 449.

[51] *Groupama Insurance Co Ltd v Overseas Partners Re Ltd* Unreported, 2003.

[52] *Assicurazioni Generali SpA v Arab Insurance Group* [2002] Lloyd's Rep. I.R. 131 (not made out on the facts).

[53] *Markel International Insurance Company Ltd and Another v La Republica Compania Argentina de Seguros Generales SA* [2005] Lloyd's Rep. I.R. 90.

[54] *Deutsche Ruck v Walbrook* [1995] 1 Lloyd's Rep. 153.

[55] *SA d'Intermediaries Luxembourgeios v Farex Gie* [1995] L.R.L.R. 116, explaining *Traill v Baring* (1864) De G.J. & S.M. 318; *New Hampshire Insurance Co v Grand Union Insurance Co Ltd* [1995] 2 H.K.C. 1. See also *Halvanon Insurance v Central Reinsurance* [1984] 2 Lloyd's Rep. 420.

retention "net for its own account" does not preclude the reinsured from ceding the retention elsewhere.[56] There is plainly no implied term that a retention cannot be insured elsewhere.[57]

It is often the case that reinsurers agree to act in that capacity only on condition that retrocession cover has been put in place for them, normally by the brokers acting for the reinsured. Any information which the reinsured has about the security of that cover is not a material fact, as it is for the reinsurers to determine this matter for themselves and the information possessed by the reinsured will be purely coincidental.[58] The position may be different if the contracts are interlinked and the reinsurers' subscription to the reinsurance agreement is conditional on the existence of valid retrocession,[59] and the brokers will face liability to the reinsurers if they have not placed retrocession in accordance with their instructions.[60]

17–008 *Immaterial facts.* As is the case with direct insurance,[61] reinsurers cannot rely upon the non-disclosure of facts of which they are or ought to be aware in the ordinary course of their business of reinsurers[62] although the mere fact that the information could have been discovered on inquiry by the reinsurers[63] will not suffice to relieve the reinsured of its duty to disclose. Disclosure may also be waived by reinsurers who, having been altered to the existence of material facts, choose not to ask further questions.[64] The fact that the contract is one of reinsurance rather than insurance is not, however, a material fact[65]: this is so because reinsurance is not a form of liability insurance but rather a further policy on the original subject matter.[66]

17–009 *Waiver of breach of duty.* Breach of the duty of utmost good faith can be waived in reinsurance in the same way as in insurance, although there is the additional

---

[56] *Great Atlantic Insurance v Home Insurance* [1981] 2 Lloyd's Rep. 219. See also: *GE Reinsurance Corp v New Hampshire Insurance Co* [2004] Lloyd's Rep. I.R. 404; *Kingscroft v Nissan (No.2)* [1999] Lloyd's Rep. I.R. 603.

[57] *Phoenix General Insurance of Greece v Halvanon Insurance* [1985] 2 Lloyd's Rep. 599.

[58] *Societe Anonyme d'Intermediares Luxembourgeois v Farex Gie* [1995] L.R.L.R. 116.

[59] *Hill v Citadel Insurance Co Ltd* [1997] L.R.L.R. 167.

[60] *Aneco Reinsurance Underwriting Ltd v Johnson & Higgins* [2002] Lloyd's Rep. I.R. 91, which decides that the brokers' liability may extend not just to the amount of the retrocession but to the full amount of the reinsurers' subscription if it can be shown that the reinsurers would not have agreed to reinsure at all without retrocession cover and the brokers assumed responsibility for finding that cover.

[61] See s.18 of the Marine Insurance Act 1906.

[62] *British and Foreign Marine Insurance Co Ltd v Sturge* (1897) 2 Com. Cas. 24; *North British Fishing Boat Insurance Co Ltd v Starr* (1922) 12 Ll. L.R. 206; *Kingscroft Insurance Co v Nissan Fire & Marine Insurance Co Ltd (No.2)* [1999] Lloyd's Rep. I.R. 603.

[63] *London General Insurance Co Ltd v General Marine Underwriters Association Ltd* [1921] 1 K.B. 104; *Brotherton v Aseguradora Colseguros (No.3)* [2003] Lloyd's Rep. I.R. 774.

[64] *Pan Atlantic Insurance Co v Pine Top Insurance Co* [1994] 2 Lloyd's Rep. 527. Contrast *WISE Underwriting Agency Ltd v Grupo Nacional Provincial SA* [2004] Lloyd's Rep. I.R. 764, where the majority view was that the reinsurers had not been alerted to the existence of possible material information.

[65] *Crowley v Cohen* (1832) 3 B. & Ad. 478; *Mackenzie v Whitworth* (1875) 1 Ex. D. 36; *Imperial Marine v Fire Insurance Corp* (1879) 4 C.P.D. 166; *Re London County Commercial Reinsurance Office* [1922] 2 Ch. 67.

[66] *Wasa International Insurance Co Ltd v Lexington Insurance Co* [2009] Lloyd's Rep. I.R. 675.

trap that reinsurance treaties generally provide for inspection of the reinsured's books: once inspection has taken place, and there is no reservation of rights, the reinsurers may be taken to have waived any breach of duty provided that the reinsurers ought to have realised prior to the inspection that there might be a right to avoid.[67] Again, a failure to disaffirm without a reservation of rights might amount to waiver in the usual way.[68]

Renewal. Reinsurance treaties often run for a period of years, subject to annual review provisions. Where reinsurers have reserved the right to increase the premium at the anniversary date following any adverse developments in underlying claims, the reinsurance does not terminate automatically at the anniversary date but continues unless and until the review provision has been invoked by them. Should the clause be invoked, the policy will come to an end on the anniversary date if the parties have not been able to agree upon a new premium.[69]   **17–010**

3. TERMS OF REINSURANCE CONTRACTS

Express terms. The principles here are identical to those applicable to direct policies.[70] If the term broken by the reinsured is a condition precedent then the reinsurers are not liable for the loss whether or not they have suffered prejudice. Breach of a term which is not a condition precedent will rarely give the reinsurers a defence, as the reinsurers have to show that the reinsured has repudiated the reinsurance agreement in its entirety. This is plainly inconceivable if the breach relates to a specific provision, e.g. a claims or inspection clause, and it has even been held that late payment of the premium does not have a repudiatory effect[71] unless reinsurers have made time for payment of the essence, or have demanded payment or it is clear that the reinsured will never make payment.[72]   **17–011**

Incorporation from insurance contract. In addition to any express terms which may have been agreed between the parties, it has long been the tradition for facultative covers to state "warranted terms and conditions as per original" or its equivalent,[73] the apparent purpose of which is to incorporate the terms of the direct cover into the reinsurance. The general assumption is that the phrase does have an incorporating effect, although the point is far from certain and there   **17–012**

---

[67] *Iron Trades Mutual v Imperio* [1992] Re. L.R. 213, although note *Strive Shipping v Hellenic Mutual War Risks Association* [2002] Lloyd's Rep. I.R. 669 which indicates that an insistence on adherence to claims conditions is not waiver of the right to avoid. An inspection clause is not, however, a claims provision as it may be exercised at any time.

[68] *Hill v Citadel Insurance* [1995] L.R.L.R. 218.

[69] *Charman v New Cap Reinsurance Corp Ltd* [2004] Lloyd's Rep. I.R. 373.

[70] See Ch.7, above.

[71] *Fenton Insurance Co Ltd v Gothaer Versicherungsbank VVag* [1991] 1 Lloyd's Rep. 172; *Figre Ltd v Mander* [1999] Lloyd's Rep. I.R. 193; *Glencore AG v Ryan (The Beursgracht)* [2002] Lloyd's Rep. I.R. 335.

[72] *Pacific and General Insurance Co Ltd v Hazell* [1997] L.R.L.R. 65 (insolvency).

[73] The first part of the "full reinsurance" clause. It continues "and to follow settlements": see below.

is some authority for the proposition that the phrase creates a warranty in the reinsurance agreement that the terms of the direct policy are those which have been disclosed to the reinsurers.[74]

On the basis that incorporation is potentially effected by the clause, the nature and scope of such incorporation is not always clear. In *HIH Casualty and General Insurance v New Hampshire Insurance*[75] the question was whether a waiver of disclosure provision contained in the direct policy had been incorporated into the reinsurance. The Court of Appeal distinguished between the fact of incorporation and the effect of the term as incorporated. As to the fact of incorporation, it was held that incorporation of a term by general words could be achieved only if: (i) the term was germane to the reinsurance; (ii) the term made sense, subject to permissible "manipulation", in the context of the reinsurance; (iii) the term was consistent with the express terms of the reinsurance; and (iv) the term was apposite for inclusion in the reinsurance (which will generally be the case if the insurance is in essence a "front"). As regards the effect of incorporation, the Court of Appeal held that it was not always appropriate to "manipulate" the words of the term to make it fit into the reinsurance context if to do so would change its meaning. In the present case, the clause was held to have been incorporated in fact, but that it had been incorporated in an unmanipulated form which meant that it did not amount to a waiver of reinsurers' rights of avoidance for independent breaches of duty by the reinsured. Instead, it operated only to: (a) allow the reinsured to recover from reinsurers in circumstances where the reinsured's own right of avoidance against the assured had been lost by reason of the clause (i.e. it was a form of follow the settlements clause); and (b) allow the reinsured to recover where there had been a common presentation of the risk to the reinsured and reinsurers, so that both parties had agreed to waive their rights and the result was back to back cover. This was a case in which converting, by manipulation, the clause into one which operated at the reinsurance level would have led to a surrender by the reinsurers of their right to have the risk fairly presented to them.

In general, the "as original" wording will be effective to incorporate provisions which relate directly to the risk,[76] including warranties,[77] although

---

[74] *Joyce v Realm Marine Insurance Co Ltd* (1872) L.R. 7 Q.B. 580; *Barnard v Faber* [1893] 1 Q.B. 340; *Walker & Sons v Uzielli* (1896) 1 Com. Cas. 492; *Bancroft v Heath* (1901) 17 T.L.R. 425 Lord Griffiths in *Forsikrings Vesta v Butcher* [1989] 1 All E.R. 402, warned that incorporation was a most unsatisfactory method of doing business, and preferred the view that the phase amounted to a warranty that the terms of the direct policy had been accurately communicated to the reinsurers. In *Toomey v Banco Vitalico de Espana de Seguros y Reaseguros* [2005] Lloyd's Rep. I.R. 423 Thomas L.J. noted that the effect of the clause had yet to be finally determined. Cf. *Prifti v Musini Sociedad Anonima De Seguros Y Reaseguros* [2004] Lloyd's Rep. I.R. 528. The point was also raised in argument before the House of Lords in *Wasa International Insurance Co Ltd v Lexington Insurance Co* [2009] Lloyd's Rep. I.R. 675, but was not resolved.

[75] *HIH Casualty and General Insurance v New Hampshire Insurance* [2001] Lloyd's Rep. I.R. 596.

[76] *Joyce v Realm Marine Insurance Co Ltd* (1872) L.R. 7 Q.B. 580; *Barnard v Faber* [1893] 1 Q.B. 340; *Sulphite Pulp v Faber* (1895) 111 T.L.R. 547; *Walker v Uzielli* (1896) 1 Com. Cas. 452; *General Insurance Co of Trieste Ltd v Corp of the Royal Exchange* (1897) 2 Com. Case. 144; *Marten v Nippon Sea and Land Insurance Co Ltd* (1898) 3 Com. Cas. 164; *Beauchamp v Faber* (1898) 3 Com. Cas. 308; *Charlesworth v Faber* (1900) 5 Com. Cas. 408; *Bancroft v Heath* (1901) 17 T.L.R. 425; *Mountain v Whittle* [1921] A.C. 615; *Wasa International Insurance Co Ltd v Lexington Insurance Co* [2009] Lloyd's Rep. I.R. 675.

[77] *Duckett v Williams* (1834) 2 Cr. & M. 348; *Life Association of Scotland v Forster* (1973) 11 M. 351; *Walker v Uzielli* (1896) 1 Com. Cas. 452.

reinsurers are not bound by wording which is unusual[78] or which has been added to the direct policy after the inception of the reinsurance,[79] and reinsurers are in any event not liable to indemnify the reinsured for losses arising from changes to the risk accepted by the reinsured during the currency of the policy.[80] The wording will not operate to incorporate ancillary clauses, such as notice provisions, insofar as those provisions are inconsistent with the express terms of the reinsurance or otherwise cannot be given full effect in the reinsurance context.[81] Dispute resolution provisions, such as arbitration,[82] jurisdiction[83] and choice of law[84] clauses will not be incorporated by "as original" wording, specific reference in the reinsurance to such provisions being required to effect an incorporation.

Incorporation of terms from the direct policy should be distinguished from incorporation of terms from other sources, e.g. by reference to identified market wordings. In that situation there is no objection to incorporation, although unless care is taken there is a risk that the incorporated terms may conflict with terms which have expressly agreed by the parties, in which case the court will be required to resolve the conflict.[85]

Implied terms. Terms may be implied into reinsurance agreements on business efficacy grounds, as long as there is no inconsistency between the alleged implied term and the express terms of the agreement.[86] In *Phoenix General Insurance of Greece v Halvanon Insurance*,[87] which involved a facultative-obligatory proportional treaty, Hobhouse J. stated obiter, in a ruling that was thought to extend to

17–013

---

[78] *Joyce v Realm Marine Insurance* (1872) L.R. 7 Q.B. 580; *Marten v Nippon Sea and Land Insurance* (1898) 3 Com. Cas. 164; *Charlesworth v Faber* (1900) 5 Com. Cas. 408; *Maritime Insurance Co v Stearns* [1901] 2 K.B. 912. See also *Allianz Insurance Co of Egypt v Aigaion Insurance* [2009] Lloyd's Rep. I.R. 69 (premium payment clause).

[79] *Lower Rhine and Wurttemburg Insurance Association v Sedgwick* [1899] 1 Q.B. 179; *Norwich Union Fire Insurance Society Ltd v Colonial Mutual Fire Insurance Co Ltd* [1922] 2 K.B. 461; *Excess Insurance Co Ltd v Mander* [1995] L.R.L.R. 359; *Cigna Life Insurance Co of Europe SA-NV & Others v Intercaser SA de Seguros y Reaseguros* [2001] Lloyd's Rep. I.R. 821; *American International Speciality Lines Insurance Co v Abbott Laboratories* [2004] Lloyd's Rep. I.R. 815.

[80] *Lower Rhine Insurance v Sedgwick* [1899] 1 Q.B. 179; *Scottish National v Poole* (1912) 107 L.T. 687; *Emmanuel v Weir* (1914) 30 T.L.R. 518; *Norwich Union v Colonial Mutual Fire* [1922] 2 K.B. 461; *Swiss Reinsurance Co v United India Insurance Co Ltd* [2005] Lloyd's Rep. I.R. 341; *American International Marine Agency of New York Inc v Dandridge* [2005] Lloyd's Rep. I.R. 643 (no incorporation of leading underwriter clause whereby any decision of the direct leading underwriter to vary the risk was binding on the following market).

[81] *Home Insurance of New York v Victoria-Montreal Fire* [1907] A.C. 59; *CNA International Reinsurance v Companhia de Seguros Tranquilidade* [1999] Lloyd's Rep. I.R. 289; *Municipal Mutual Insurance Ltd v Sea Insurance Co Ltd* [1996] L.R.L.R. 265, reversed in part on other grounds [1998] Lloyd's Rep. I.R. 421.

[82] *Pine Top Insurance Co Ltd v Unione Italiana Anglo Saxon Reinsurance Co Ltd* [1987] 1 Lloyd's Rep. 476; *Excess Insurance Co v Mander* [1995] L.R.L.R. 358;) *Tryg Hansa v Equitas* [1998] 2 Lloyd's Rep. 439; *Cigna Life Insurance Co of Europe SA-NV v Intercaser SA de Seguros y Reaseguros* [2001] Lloyd's Rep. I.R. 821; *American International Speciality Lines Insurance Co v Abbott Laboratories* [2004] Lloyd's Rep. I.R. 815.

[83] *Arig Insurance Company Ltd v Sasa Assicurazione Riassicurazione SpA*, Unreported, 1998; *AIG Europe (UK) Ltd v The Ethniki* [2000] Lloyd's Rep. I.R. 343; *AIG Europe SA v QBE International Insurance Ltd* [2002] Lloyd's Rep. I.R. 22; *Prifti v Musini Sociedad Anonima de Seguros y Reaseguros* [2004] Lloyd's Rep. I.R. 528.

[84] *Gan Insurance Co Ltd v Tai Ping Insurance Co Ltd* [1999] Lloyd's Rep. I.R. 472.

[85] As in *Axa Re v Ace Global Markets Ltd* [2006] Lloyd's Rep. I.R. 683—arbitration clause and exclusive jurisdiction/choice of law clauses incorporated side by side: the court gave priority to the former.

[86] *GE Reinsurance Corp v New Hampshire Insurance Co* [2004] Lloyd's Rep. I.R. 404.

[87] *Phoenix General Insurance of Greece v Halvanon Insurance* [1985] 2 Lloyd's Rep. 599. Cf. *Baker v Black Sea* [1995] L.R.L.R. 287 (implied inspection clause); *Economic v Le Assicurazioni*

all obligatory and factultative obligatory covers, that a number of terms are to be implied for the protection of reinsurers.[88] These are:

(a) keeping proper records and accounts of risks accepted, premiums received and claims made or notified;
(b) investigating all claims and confirm that there is liability before liability is accepted;
(c) acting prudently in the acceptance of risks;
(d) keeping full and accurate accounts showing sums owing and owed;
(e) ensuring that all amounts owing are collected promptly, and that all amounts payable are paid promptly;
(f) making all documents reasonably available to reinsurers.

Implied term (3) was discussed by the Court of Appeal in *Bonner v Cox Dedicated Corporate Member Ltd*,[89] where it was alleged by reinsurers that the reinsured under a non-proportional obligatory treaty had engaged in "writing against" the reinsurance by accepting risks which were not profitable and which ought not to have been accepted by a prudent insurer. The Court of Appeal denied the existence of any such implied term in a non-proportional treaty, noting that it was inconsistent with the accepted notion that negligence on the part of the assured short of recklessness does not preclude a claim, although left open (with obvious reservations) the correctness of *Halvanon* in the context of proportional treaties. As long as the reinsured does not engage in arbitrage, in the form of dishonestly writing loss-making business,[90] there is nothing to restrict the reinsured from writing business purely to expand its own capacity or to protect itself against insolvency.

This analysis throws doubt on the other implied terms identified in *Phoenix*, and it may be thought that there is little justification for such implication given that there are various market wordings governing claims handling and that reinsurers have no right to assume that the courts will protect them if their contract is silent.

17–014 **Presumption of back to back cover.** In proportional contracts, particularly facultative agreements, independently of any incorporation of the insuring clause into the reinsurance, there is rule of construction—generally referred to as the presumption of back to back cover—which assumes that the cover afforded by the insurance and the reinsurance are consistent. The point was first made in *Forsakrings Vesta v Butcher*,[91] in which a fish farm in Norway was insured under a contract governed by Norwegian law, and was reinsured on identical terms in London under a policy governed by English law. The assured was guilty of breach of a warranty which required a 24-hour watch to be maintained over the fish farm, but the assured was nevertheless able to recover for storm damage because Norwegian law provided a defence in warranty cases only where there was a causal link between the breach and the loss. English law does not require any causal link between breach of warranty and loss to provide a defence to

d'Italia Unreported, 1996 (duty of care owed in underwriting). Contrast *New Hampshire Insurance Co v Grand Union Insurance Co Ltd* [1995] 2 H.K.C. 1.

[88] These were held in *Baker v Black Sea* [1995] L.R.L.R. 287 not to be conditions precedent to liability.

[89] *Bonner v Cox Dedicated Corporate Member Ltd* [2006] Lloyd's Rep. I.R. 385.

[90] See the facts of *Sphere Drake Insurance Ltd v Euro International Underwriting Ltd* [2003] Lloyd's Rep. I.R. 535.

[91] *Forsakrings Vesta v Butcher* [1989] 1 All E.R. 402.

underwriters,[92] and the reinsurers relied upon the reinsurance warranty. The House of Lords held that they were not entitled to do so: while the reinsurance contract was governed by English law, the presumption of back to back cover required the English court to construe the reinsurance agreement consistently with the construction that the direct policy would receive in Norway, and on that basis the English warranty was to be treated as effective only if there was a causal relationship between breach and loss.[93] The *Vesta* principle has been applied in a number of other cases in order to ensure that the coverage,[94] the financial limits[95] and the duration[96] of the two agreements are consistent. It has even been extended so as to allow an express warranty contained in a reinsurance agreement governed by English law to be overridden by an equivalent warranty incorporated from the direct policy governed by Venezuelan law.[97] The presumption of back to back cover cannot apply where the reinsurance contains a warranty which has no counterpart in the direct policy: it is not possible to deprive a reinsurance term of its effect in order to achieve back to back cover.[98] Further, the presumption will not apply where it is shown that the two agreements have been separately negotiated.[99]

It was nevertheless held by the House of Lords in *Wasa International Insurance Co v Lexington Insurance Co*[100] that the approach to construction adopted in *Vesta* does not necessarily apply to all coverage provisions set out in the reinsurance. In this case a direct policy on property and business interruption risks was stated to run from July 1, 1977 to July 1, 1980. The reinsurance was written on a facultative basis, the premium was based on that received under the direct policy and the terms were stated to be "as original". There was also a follow settlements clause. The duration clause stated "36 months 1.7.77 L/U &/or pro rata to expiry of original". The assured faced claims for contamination clean-up costs incurred for damage arising over a period of some 50 years, and

---

[92] See Ch.7, above.

[93] This ruling renders *St Paul Insurance v Morice* (1906) 22 T.L.R. 449 of doubtful authority: it was there held that the word "mortality" bore different meanings in the insurance agreement (governed by New York law) and the reinsurance agreement (governed by English law). The decision in *St Paul Fire* cannot now stand with *Wasa International Insurance Co Ltd v Lexington Insurance Co* [2009] Lloyd's Rep. I.R. 675.

[94] *AIG v The Ethniki* [2000] Lloyd's Rep. I.R. 343; *Mann v Lexington Insurance Co* [2001] Lloyd's Rep. I.R. 179; *Ace Insurance SA-NV v Zurich Insurance Co* [2001] Lloyd's Rep. I.R. 504; *HIH Casualty and General v New Hampshire* [2001] Lloyd's Rep. I.R. 596. Contrast *St Paul Fire & Marine Insurance Co v Morice* (1906) 22 T.L.R. 449, which is out of line with the modern approach. The decision in *St Paul Fire* was held to be unsupportable by Lord Collins in *Wasa International Insurance Co Ltd v Lexington Insurance Co* [2009] Lloyd's Rep. I.R. 675.

[95] *Phillips v Dorintal Insurance* [1987] 1 Lloyd's Rep. 482; *Insurance Co of Pennsylvania v Grand Union Insurance* [1990] 1 Lloyd's Rep. 208; *Goshawk Syndicate Management Ltd and Others v XL Speciality Insurance Co* [2004] Lloyd's Rep. I.R. 683. Cf. *Allianz Marine Aviation (France) v GE Frankona Reinsurance Ltd London* [2005] Lloyd's Rep. I.R. 437.

[96] *Commercial Union Assurance v Sun Alliance* [1992] 1 Lloyd's Rep. 475, although contrast *Youell v Bland Welch (No.1)* [1992] 2 Lloyd's Rep. 127 where the reinsurance cover on a construction risk was specifically limited to 48 months although there was no such restriction in the direct policy.

[97] *Groupama Navigation et Transports v Catatumbo CA Seguros* [2001] Lloyd's Rep. I.R. 141. The Court of Appeal unconvincingly disposed of the reinsurance warranty by suggesting that it was provisional, and had been inserted only to protect the reinsurers in the event that no such warranty had been included in the direct policy.

[98] *GE Reinsurance Corp v New Hampshire Insurance Co* [2004] Lloyd's Rep. I.R. 404.

[99] *GE Reinsurance Corp v New Hampshire Insurance Co* [2004] Lloyd's Rep. I.R. 404; *Youell v Bland Welch & Co (No.1)* [1992] 2 Lloyd's Rep. 127; *Gan Insurance Co Ltd v Tai Ping Insurance Co Ltd* [1999] Lloyd's Rep. I.R. 472

[100] *Wasa International Insurance Co v Lexington Insurance Co* [2009] Lloyd's Rep. I.R. 675.

in proceedings between the assured and its insurers heard in Supreme Court of Washington the court decided that the insurers on risk in that period faced joint and several liability to the assured. The effect of the ruling was that the present insurers faced liability for losses going back many years, and they settled with the assured on that basis. The reinsurers refused indemnification, arguing that the duration clause in the reinsurance confined their liability to losses occurring in the years of coverage. The House of Lords, reversing the decision of the Court of Appeal,[101] and reinstating the first instance decision of Simon J.,[102] agreed with this analysis. In their Lordships' view the words of the duration clause in the reinsurance were clear and were not to be distorted by the different meaning of the direct policy. In so holding the House of Lords regarded clauses in a reinsurance agreement dealing with temporal restrictions as being subject to stricter rules of construction than, for example, warranties, and that the principle of back to back cover did not apply to duration clauses.[103]

The difficulty which is posed by *Wasa* is distinguishing those reinsurance terms which are to be afforded back to back cover and those which are not. Lord Collins, whose judgment was approved by all members of the House of Lords, laid down the following principle:

"The reinsurer takes a proportional share of the premium and bears the risk of the same share of any losses. Consequently, the starting point is that normally reinsurance of that kind is back-to-back with the insurance, and that the reinsurer and the original insurer enter into a bargain that if the insurer is liable under the insurance contract, the reinsurer will be liable to pay the proportion which it has agreed to reinsure. In the usual case, any loss within the coverage of the insurance will be within the coverage of the reinsurance . . . [I]t would almost invariably be the case that losses for which the insurer has indemnified the original insured would be within the reinsurance even if the losses are payable under a foreign law or a foreign judicial decision which takes a view different from English law of what losses are recoverable."

All members of the House of Lords nevertheless emphasised that there was no inflexible rule of law that the coverage of insurance and reinsurance always matched. Rather, there is a presumption of matching cover which may be ousted by the express wording of the reinsurance or by other relevant circumstances. A duration clause is to be regarded as exceptional, but it is not clear whether other coverage clauses fall into the same category. Lord Mance was at pains to stress the technical nature of warranties, thereby indicating that in his view at least the back to back presumption is somewhat narrower than regarded by Lord Collins. It was also held in *Wasa* that the reinsurers were entitled to an English law construction of the duration clause because it had been unclear when the risks were written in 1977 which law would govern any claim against the reinsured under the direct policy. That policy contained a "Service of Suit" clause under which the assured had the right to sue in any US court of competent jurisdiction and the relevant court was to apply its own law. In the event proceedings were

---

[101] *Wasa International Insurance Co v Lexington Insurance Co* [2008] Lloyd's Rep. I.R. 510.
[102] *Wasa International Insurance Co v Lexington Insurance Co* [2007] Lloyd's Rep. I.R. 604.
[103] *Municipal Mutual Insurance Ltd v Sea Insurance Ltd* [1998] Lloyd's Rep. I.R. 421 was cited in support of this proposition. But contrast *Stronghold Insurance Co Ltd v Bulstrad Insurance and Reinsurance Plc*, Unreported, November 2006, (not referred to in *Wasa*) in which a contract of retrocession was entered into on the basis that "all clauses terms and conditions as original insofar as applicable." Long-tail asbestos claims which fell within the scope of the reinsurance were also held to be within the scope of the retrocession. H.H. Judge Mackie QC rejected reliance by the retrocessionires holding that *MMI* was not relevant and that the parties were to be taken to have intended to contract for matching cover.

brought in Washington and the Washington court, applying its conflict of laws rules, held that the policy was governed by the law of Pennsylvania. The absence of an identifiable applicable law in the direct policy meant that a reinsurance term as fundamental as a duration clause had to be governed by English law. Their Lordships rejected the further argument, which had been accepted at first instance, that duration clause had to be construed in accordance with English law because the law in Pennsylvania was uncertain in 1977 and had been transformed in a way that could not have been predicted by a series of cases beginning in 1983. It was here pointed out by Lord Collins that "It is elementary that an insurer under the original insurance takes the risk of changes in the law. The insurer cannot escape liability by saying that the liability of the insured has been increased by judicial decisions extending the scope of the insured's duty. Nor, correspondingly, can the reinsurer be heard to say that it rated the risk by reference to the then current scope of the original insured's duty, or by the scope of the insurer's duty to indemnify the original insured, provided that the risk is within the reinsurance."

Independently of the *Wasa* ruling, there is no back to back cover if the wording of the two contracts is quite different. In *Aegis Electrical and Gas International Services Co Ltd v Continental Casualty Co*[104] the reinsurance incorporated additional definitions which made it clear that the scope of coverage of the reinsurance was narrower than that of the direct insurance.

The presumption of back to back cover does not extend to non-proportional reinsurances. The terms of the direct policies and excess of loss covers are quite different, and premiums are assessed on different bases. It has thus been held that aggregation provisions contained in a reinsurance agreement are not to be assumed to have the same meaning as direct policy aggregation provisions when different words with established different wordings are used in each of the contracts.[105]

Inspection clauses. Reinsurance treaties generally contain inspection clauses whereby the reinsurer is entitled to examine the reinsured's books and records in so far as they contain details of the business written by the reinsured within the scope of the reinsurance. The clause may also extend to the provision of information for the purpose of settling claims made by the direct assured against the reinsured, although there will generally be a separate claims co-operation or claims control provision dealing with that matter. Inspection clauses tend to be framed in general terms, so that the reinsurers can exercise the right of inspection at any time during the currency of the reinsurance agreement. Although inspections can be conducted at any time, they tend to become of particular significance when there have been heavy losses or when the reinsured has actually presented a claim. The effect of a breach of an inspection clause depends upon the manner in which it is drafted. If the clause is a condition precedent to the reinsurers' liability then, subject to any waiver by the reinsurers, no claim may be made by the reinsured until the obligations in the clause have been complied with. Inspection clauses are not really appropriately drafted as conditions precedent to liability to meet a claim, given that—in theory at least—they may be called into use whether or not there has been a loss. **17–015**

---

[104] *Aegis Electrical and Gas International Services Co Ltd v Continental Casualty Co* [2008] Lloyd's Rep. I.R. 17.

[105] *Axa Reinsurance v Field* [1996] 3 All E.R. 517 ("event" not the same as "originating cause"—see Ch.10, above. Cf. *Municipal Mutual Insurance Ltd v Sea Insurance Co Ltd* [1996] L.R.L.R. 265.

Accordingly, many inspection clauses are not framed as conditions precedent. If an inspection clause which is not a condition precedent is broken by the reinsured, the reinsurers are unlikely to have any appropriate remedy, as breach of the clause is unlikely to be regarded by the courts as a repudiation of the treaty by the reinsured[106] and the reinsurers are unlikely to be able to prove any loss sufficient to justify a claim for damages. The reinsurer's right to inspect has in the past been regarded by the courts as sufficiently important to give rise to an implied term,[107] albeit not a condition precedent.[108] However, it is uncertain whether such implication can survive the decision of the Court of Appeal in *Bonner v Cox*,[109] discussed above.

A right of inspection can normally be exercised on reasonable notice, and reinsurers do not have to possess or to provide a reason for such exercise.[110] Assuming that the right of inspection has been exercised, there is a general rule of insurance law that any demand by the insurer for co-operation by the assured under the terms of the policy is subject to a reasonableness requirement,[111] and it has been said that an inspection is not to be conducted in an excessive fashion or in bad faith[112] so that it constitutes a fishing expedition conducted merely in the hope that something might turn up.[113]

3. REINSURANCE LOSSES AND CLAIMS

17–016 **Use of "honourable engagement" arbitration clauses.** It was at one time common for reinsurance agreements to provide in their arbitration clauses that the agreement was an honourable engagement and that the arbitrators were discharged from their duty of applying strict rules of law to resolve any dispute and were to apply principles of equity. It was unclear to what extent such clauses were valid at common law, as they risked rendering the arbitration clause, if not the entire reinsurance agreement void for uncertainty, and it would seem that the parties could go no further than agreeing that the arbitrators were to adopt market rather than strict interpretations of the words used in an agreement.[114] Section 46 of the Arbitration Act 1996, which came into force with respect to contracts made after January 1997, now validates such clauses, as the parties are free to agree to have their dispute determined under any system of law or by reference to such other principles as they may specify. In the absence of such agreement, the arbitrators are required to resolve the dispute by the law applicable to the agreement. Ironically, honourable engagement clauses have, since the 1996 Act, fallen into disuse.

17–017 **"Loss".** A loss is incurred under a reinsurance agreement, as is the case with a liability policy, when the reinsured's liability has been established and quantified

[106] *Baker v Black Sea and Baltic Insurance* [1995] L.R.L.R. 261.
[107] *Phoenix General Insurance Co of Greece SA v Halvanon Insurance Co Ltd* [1985] 2 Lloyd's Rep. 599.
[108] *Baker v Black Sea and Baltic Insurance* [1995] L.R.L.R. 261.
[109] *Bonner v Cox* [2006] Lloyd's Rep. I.R. 385.
[110] *Re A Company No.008725 of 1991 Ex p. Pritchard* [1992] B.C.L.C. 633.
[111] *Welch v Royal Exchange Assurance* [1939] 1 K.B. 294; *Napier v UNUM Ltd* [1996] 2 Lloyd's Rep. 550.
[112] *Re A Company No.008725 of 1991 Ex p. Pritchard* [1992] B.C.L.C. 633.
[113] *SAIL v Farex Gie* [1995] L.R.L.R. 116.
[114] *Home Insurance Co v Mentor Insurance* [1989] 3 All E.R. 74.

by judgment, arbitration award or binding settlement, and not at the (later) date when actual payment is made by the reinsured.[115] The position is not the same in all jurisdictions.[116] It is open to the parties to agree that the date of the reinsurers' liability is to be postponed to actual payment, although unambiguous wording is required to achieve this result: were it otherwise, the reinsurers would be given a windfall exemption from liability in the event that the reinsured became insolvent and unable to pay its policyholders. The point has been considered in the context of the wording of the "ultimate net loss" clause in excess of loss treaties, which provides that the reinsured "shall actually have paid". Despite the apparent clarity of this phrase, it has been held in England[117] that payment by the reinsured is not required. The basis of these cases is that the contract as a whole is expressed as one which is triggered by the establishment and quantification of liability, and that the ultimate net loss clause is potentially ambiguous in that it can refer either to the amount of payment or to the time at which it is made.

The obligation to indemnify. In the absence of any contrary provision,[118] the reinsured must satisfy two conditions before the reinsurers' become liable to provide an indemnity: the reinsured must establish that as a matter of law it faced liability to the assured; and the reinsured must show that the reinsurers were liable under the terms of the reinsurance agreement.[119] The second condition is a matter of construction, although in the case of a facultative agreement it is likely that the insuring and reinsuring provisions are to the same effect. The first condition may be satisfied in one of three ways: the reinsured may have been sued to judgment; the reinsured may have been subject to an adverse arbitration award; or the reinsured may have entered into a binding settlement with the assured.

    17–018

A judgment, whether of an English court or of a foreign court, is to be given recognition in English law as a conclusive disposition of the issues which it decides. In principle such a judgment is binding only between the parties, i.e. the assured and the reinsured. It was said in *Commercial Union Assurance Co v NRG Victory Reinsurance Ltd*[120] that a judgment was nevertheless binding on the reinsurers, and conclusively established the liability of the reinsured, so that if the reinsured has been sued to judgment by the assured, the reinsured's loss is established as a matter of law. The Court of Appeal recognised that there may be exceptional circumstances in which a foreign judgment may not be binding, e.g. where the court was not of competent jurisdiction or had not acted in contravention of an exclusive jurisdiction or arbitration clause, where there was a manifest error of law, where the judgment was perverse or where the reinsured had failed to defend itself properly, but these remote possibilities aside a

---

[115] *Re Eddystone Marine* [1892] 2 Ch. 423; *Re Law Guarantee* [1914] 2 Ch. 617. The contrary view, expressed in *Fireman's Fund v Western Australian Insurance* (1927) 138 L.T. 108 at 110, is no longer supportable. The policy may require actual payment: *Nepean v Marten* (1895) 11 T.L.R. 256.

[116] *Cleaver and Bodden v Delta American Reinsurance Co* [2002] Lloyd's Rep. I.R. 167, a case decided under New York law, proceeds on the basis that the reinsurers' liability arises on actual payment by the reinsured.

[117] *Home Insurance Co v Mentor Insurance* [1989] 3 All E.R. 74; *Re A Company No 0013734 of 1991* [1992] 2 Lloyd's Rep. 413; *Charter Re v Fagan* [1996] 3 All E.R. 46.

[118] i.e. a follow the settlements or follow the fortunes clause: see below.

[119] *Hill v Mercantile and General* [1996] L.R.L.R. 341.

[120] *Commercial Union Assurance Co v NRG Victory Reinsurance Ltd* [1998] Lloyd's Rep. I.R. 439.

judgment is conclusive. However, in *Wasa International Insurance Co v Lexington Insurance Co*[121] Lord Mance expressed the view that the Court of Appeal's analysis in *Commercial Union* was *obiter* and that a foreign judgment was not necessarily binding in the absence of a follow the settlements clause (see below).

Arbitral awards give rise to the same issues. Although an arbitration award is only binding as between the parties to the arbitration, and indeed is confidential to them, it has been held that reinsurers are under an implied obligation to indemnify the reinsured in the event of an arbitration award in favour of the assured,[122] although in the light of Lord Mance's comments in *Wasa* this may be true only where the reinsurers have agreed to follow the reinsured's settlements.

A settlement between the assured and the reinsured is not, however, automatically binding on the reinsurers. A settlement is merely the first stage in establishing the reinsurers' liability, and the reinsured must go on to establish that, had it been sued to judgment by the assured, there would have been a finding of liability under the law applicable to the insurance contract[123] of at least the amount provided for in the settlement. It is not enough for the reinsured to prove that the settlement was a reasonable one or that it was made in the face of foreign legal proceedings and removed the risk of punitive damages being awarded against the reinsured. The position is illustrated by *Commercial Union Assurance Co v NRG Victory Reinsurance Ltd.*[124] The reinsured was the insurer of the *Exxon Valdez*, which ran aground in 1989. The assured incurred substantial losses, including clean-up costs, and sought to recover those costs from the reinsured under a policy which covered first and third party liability for losses caused by the cleaning up of "debris". Proceedings were commenced against the reinsured in Texas, which the reinsured settled on favourable terms when faced with legal advice that the Texas jury would be likely to find in favour of the assured. The Court of Appeal rejected the reinsured's claim for summary judgment against the reinsurers, and held that the reinsured had not proved its loss simply by relying on the advice of local lawyers: it was necessary for the reinsured to go further and to demonstrate that there was legal liability as a matter of law. In subsequent proceedings the reinsured sought a declaration that it had faced liability to the assured, but failed on the ground that under New York law—the law governing the insurance contract—the word "debris" did not include an oil spill, so that there had never been any liability under the policy.[125]

"Follow the settlements"

17–019 *Meaning of "follow the settlements"*. The difficult position in which a reinsured may find itself in establishing liability at law to the assured after[126] a

---

[121] *Wasa International Insurance Co v Lexington Insurance Co* [2009] Lloyd's Rep. I.R. 675.

[122] *Sun Life Assurance Co of Canada v Lincoln National Life Insurance Co* [2005] 1 Lloyd's Rep. 606.

[123] *Enterprise Oil Ltd v Strand Insurance Co Ltd* [2007] Lloyd's Rep. I.R. 186.

[124] *Commercial Union Assurance Co v NRG Victory Reinsurance Ltd* [1998] Lloyd's Rep. I.R. 421.

[125] *King v Brandywine Reinsurance Co (UK) Ltd* [2005] Lloyd's Rep. I.R. 509.

[126] The reinsured and the reinsurers may agree on a liability figure under the reinsurance agreement in advance of any settlement between the reinsured and the assured, in which case the reinsurance settlement is binding and the problems discussed in this paragraph do not arise. See *National Company for Co-operative Insurance v St Paul Reinsurance Co*, Unreported, 1996.

settlement[127] has been reached with the assured is ordinarily mitigated by the use of "follow the settlements" and "follow the fortunes"[128] clauses. These clauses originally appeared in facultative agreements in the 1930s, in order to extend the reinsurers' liability to bona fide settlements,[129] preventing the reinsurers from questioning the basis on which the settlement had been made, and now appear as the second part of the full reinsurance clause which provides "as original[130] and follow the settlements". In *Insurance Co of Africa v Scor (UK) Reinsurance*[131] the Court of Appeal held, *obiter*,[132] that the reinsured is to be taken to have established its own liability under a settlement unless the reinsurers can establish[133] that the settlement was not entered into in a "bona fide and businesslike fashion". For this purpose the reinsurers are entitled to put the reinsured to proof of its loss by receiving information from the reinsured as to how the settlement was reached.[134] Once these conditions have been satisfied, the reinsurers are liable to indemnify the reinsured even though it subsequently proves that the reinsured was not as a matter of strict law liable to the assured, e.g. by reason of fraud on the part of the assured having subsequently been established[135] or that the claim was otherwise bad.[136]

There are two aspects to a bona fide and businesslike settlement.[137] First, the reinsured must determine whether there is, on reasonable interpretation of the direct policy, a serious possibility that the policy covers the assured's claim and that there are no available defences to it[138]; if the policy covers a foreign risk, this

---

[127] It was held by Colman J. in *Lumberman's Mutual Casualty Co v Bovis Lend Lease Ltd* [2005] Lloyd's Rep. I.R. 74 that an agreement under which various liabilities were settled for a global sum without any attempt to specific parts of the that sum to individual claims did not qualify as a "settlement" at all. That view was rejected by Aikens J. in *Enterprise Oil Ltd v Strand Insurance Co Ltd* [2007] Lloyd's Rep. I.R. 186, although the position of reinsurance in this regard remains uncertain.

[128] The authorities are all concerned with follow the settlements. There is no decided English case on "follow the fortunes", although it was common ground in *CGU International Insurance Plc v AstraZenica Insurance Co Ltd* [2006] Lloyd's Rep. I.R. 489 that these words were narrower than "follow the settlements" and did not have the effect of binding reinsurers to the reinsured's bona fide and businesslike settlements.

[129] Replacing the earlier "pay as may be paid thereon" wording. The phrase was held to mean that the reinsurers were liable to indemnify the reinsured only on proof of legal liability (*Chippendale v Holt* (1895) 65 L.J.Q.B. 104; *Merchants' Marine Insurance Co Ltd v Liverpool Marine and General Insurance Co Ltd* (1928) 31 Ll. L.R. 45; *Excess Insurance v Matthews* (1925) 21 Com. Cas. 43; *Traders and General Insurance v Bankers & General Insurance* (1921) 38 T.L.R. 94) although there was a view that once liability had been established reinsurers were bound by the settlement quantum figure (*Western Assurance Co of Toronto v Poole* [1903] 1 K.B. 376, a view doubted in *Gurney v Grimmer* (1932) 44 Ll. L.R. 189 but subsequently approved in *Hong Kong Borneo Services Ltd v Pilcher* [1992] 2 Lloyd's Rep. 593).

[130] See above for the effect of these and similar words.

[131] *Insurance Co of Africa v Scor (UK) Reinsurance* [1985] 1 Lloyd's Rep. 312. Cf. *Excess Liability Insurance Co Ltd v Mathews* (1925) 31 Com. Cas. 43.

[132] In that case the reinsured had been sued to judgment, so the point did not arise.

[133] *Insurance Company of the State of Pennsylvania v Grand Union Insurance Co* [1990] 1 Lloyd's Rep. 208.

[134] *Charman v Guardian Royal Exchange Assurance* [1992] 2 Lloyd's Rep. 607; *Württembergische Aktiengesellschaft Versicherungs-Beteili Gungsesellschaft v Home Insurance Co (No.1)* Unreported, 1994; *Hill v Mercantile and General Reinsurance Co Plc* [1996] 3 All E.R. 865.

[135] *Insurance Co of Africa v Scor (UK) Reinsurance* [1985] 1 Lloyd's Rep. 312.

[136] *Assicurazioni Generali SpA v CGU General Insurance Plc* [2004] Lloyd's Rep. I.R. 457.

[137] Although the reinsured's conduct may be dictated by a claims clause: see below.

[138] *Municipal Mutual Insurance Ltd v Sea Insurance Co Ltd* [1996] L.R.L.R. 265. See also *English and American Insurance Co Ltd v Axa Re SA* [2007] Lloyd's Rep. I.R. 359, where it was held that there was no evidence that the reinsured had acted other than in a bona fide and businesslike fashion by entering into a settlement based on US court judgments which represented the at least the reinsured's potential actual liability.

may involve taking advice from local lawyers. Secondly, the reinsured must ascertain the facts to ascertain whether the claim is a good one and the amount sought is justified, and if necessary the advice of loss adjusters and other experts is to be obtained and given due regard.[139] The views of co-insurers may be an indication of whether the reinsured has acted in a bona fide and businesslike fashion.[140] It follows that a pure ex gratia payment will not suffice, and the settlement must also be final and binding and not simply "without prejudice".[141]

17–020   *Other wordings.* It is in theory possible for reinsurers to undertake absolute liability to the reinsured following a settlement, by waiving their right to insist that the settlement was bona fide and businesslike. To date, however, the courts have tended to construe other wordings as replicating the ordinary meaning of follow the settlements. Thus the addition of the words "whether liable or not liable",[142] "in every respect unconditionally binding"[143] and "without question" has been held not to alter the meaning of the clause.[144]

Equally, the reinsurers may qualify a follow the settlements clause so as to replicate the effect of the common law, so that the reinsured is required to prove its loss as a matter of law. In *Aegis Electrical and Gas International Services Co Ltd v Continental Casualty Co*[145] the addition of the words "so far as applicable" to the follow the settlements clause were held to mean that reinsurers were not liable unless the reinsured had proved its loss. Again, a clause which requires the reinsured to prove that the loss is "within the terms and conditions of the original policies" and "within the terms and conditions of this reinsurance" does not permit the reinsured to recover simply by putting forward a settlement reached in a bona fide and businesslike fashion.[146] *Equitas Ltd v R&Q Reinsurance Company (UK) Ltd*[147] was a case involving an excess of loss reinsurance treaty which used a follow the settlements clause of this type. Losses had been presented and paid in the LMX Spiral[148] on two major claims: the *Exxon Valdez* grounding and the loss of aircraft following the invasion of Kuwait. The *Exxon Valdez* ran aground in March 1989, leading to major claims in Texas by the owners Exxon under a Global Corporate Excess Policy governed by English law. The proceedings were settled on the advice of local lawyers, but it was subsequently demonstrated in English proceedings at the reinsurance level that an important element of the claim, relating to pollution damage and amounting to about 6 per cent of the claim, fell outside the scope of cover.[149] The Kuwaiti claim was paid on the basis that the loss of 15 Kuwait Airways Corporation aircraft and one BA aircraft constituted a single event, but it was later decided by the Court of Appeal that there were two separate events so that additional

---

[139] *Charman v Guardian Royal Exchange Assurance Plc* [1992] 2 Lloyd's Rep. 607.

[140] *Gan Insurance Co Ltd v Tai Ping Insurance Co Ltd (No.3)* [2002] Lloyd's Rep. I.R. 612.

[141] *Faraday Capital Ltd v Copenhagen Reinsurance Co Ltd* [2007] Lloyd's Rep. I.R. 23.

[142] *Charman v Guardian Royal Exchange Assurance Plc* [1992] 2 Lloyd's Rep. 607.

[143] *Hiscox v Outhwaite (No.3)* [1991] 2 Lloyd's Rep. 524.

[144] *Assicurazioni Generali SpA v CGU General Insurance Plc* [2004] Lloyd's Rep. I.R. 457.

[145] *Aegis Electrical and Gas International Services Co Ltd v Continental Casualty Co* [2008] Lloyd's Rep. I.R. 17.

[146] *Hill v Mercantile & General* [1996] L.R.L.R. 160.

[147] *Equitas Ltd v R&Q Reinsurance Company (UK) Ltd* [2009] EWHC 2787 (Comm).

[148] A system involving successive layers of excess of loss reinsurance.

[149] Summary judgment in favour of the reinsured had been denied in *Commercial Union v NRG Victory* [1998] 2 Lloyd's Rep. 600, and the reinsured's claim was ultimately dismissed in *King v Brandywine Reinsurance Co* [2005] 1 Lloyd's Rep. 655.

deductibles had to be borne in respect of the claims for the BA aircraft.[150] The BA aircraft loss amounted to about 12.5 per cent of the total claim. It was common ground that the clause required the reinsured to prove that the loss fell within the scope of both the insurance and the reinsurance. The dispute between the parties was what the clause actually required. Gross J. held that the mere fact that wrongly paid claims had entered the LMX spiral was not of itself enough to preclude any recovery from the reinsurers: the clause demanded that loss had to be proved, but it did not follow that the presence of wrongly paid claims defeated any action. Gross J. drew a distinction between: the requirement for the reinsured to prove *as a matter of law* that there were losses falling within both the insurance and the reinsurance, which was clearly the case on the facts; and the requirement for the reinsured to establish the amount of correctly paid losses *as a matter of fact*, in order to show that excess attachment points had been reached. Given that there were reinsured losses, Gross J. held that the reinsured had on the balance of probabilities proved its loss by relying upon an actuarial model which, although incapable of replicating the LMX Spiral exactly, was sufficiently close to the operation of the LMX Spiral to satisfy the reinsured's burden of proof. It is to be noted that, had a pure *Scor* clause been used, the reinsured would have been able to recover simply on the basis that the losses had been settled in a bona fide and businesslike fashion and that the losses as recognised fell within the scope of the reinsurance: subsequent proof of error would not have affected that outcome.

   It will be appreciated that the decision in *Equitas* comes close to holding that the *Hill* restricted follow the settlements clause has more or less the same effect as an ordinary follow the settlements clause. While it is the case that the restricted wording requires the reinsured to prove its loss as a matter of law, whereas the ordinary follow the settlements clause merely that the reinsured has settled in a bona fide and businesslike fashion, the reinsured is entitled to prove its loss by relying on the best available evidence. In *Equitas* the reinsured did so by relying on an actuarial model, and had the contract in *Equitas* contained an unrestricted follow the settlements clause the outcome would have been exactly the same, in that reliance on the actuarial model would have constituted bona fide and businesslike behaviour. The point is made even more clearly by *IRB Brasil Resseguros SA v CX Reinsurance Company Ltd*,[151] in which the reinsured under a worldwide excess of loss casualty and liability cover settled a series of product liability claims against the assured. Those claims were class actions, and inevitably some members of the class might not have had valid claims against the assured or under the settlement might have been overcompensated. Nevertheless, Burton J. was satisfied that the reinsured had proved its loss on the balance of probabilities, doubtless on the "swings and roundabouts" principle. Had the contract contained a follow the settlements clause, the outcome would have been the same, albeit on the different basis that the reinsured's settlement would have been regarded as bona fide and businesslike.

Right of reinsurers to insist upon liability under reinsurance. The follow the   **17–021** settlements clause is concerned only with the ability of the reinsured to establish its own liability, and it remains necessary for the reinsured to demonstrate that its own claim falls within the terms of the reinsurance agreement.[152] Some difficulty is here raised by the full reinsurance clause—"as original and follow the

---

[150] *Scott v Copenhagen Re Co (UK) Ltd* [2003] Lloyd's Rep. I.R. 696.
[151] *IRB Brasil Resseguros SA v CX Reinsurance Company Ltd* [2010] EWHC 974 (Comm).
[152] *Hill v Mercantile & General* [1996] L.R.L.R. 160.

settlements" or equivalent wording—which provides in its first part that the cover of the direct policy and the reinsurance are to match, and in its second part that the reinsurers are bound by bona fide and businesslike settlements. If it is the case that the insurance and reinsurance provide the same coverage, and if it is also the case that the reinsured has validly settled its own liability based on the common wording, then any right of the reinsurers to require the reinsured to prove that there is liability as a matter of law under the reinsurance agreement may in some cases undermine the efficacy of the full reinsurance clause. It has been held that the reinsured can satisfy the separate obligation to demonstrate coverage under the reinsurance by showing that, in the formulation of Robert Goff L.J. in *Insurance Co of Africa v Scor (UK) Reinsurance*,[153] the claim so recognised by the reinsured under the direct policy falls within the risks covered by the policy of reinsurance as a matter of law. In *Assicurazioni Generali Spa v CGU International Insurance Plc*[154] this was held to mean that the basis on which the claim was accepted by the reinsured had to be one which fell, or at least arguably fell, within the scope of the direct policy and the reinsurance. This approach prevents the reinsurers from challenging both the facts as found by the reinsured and the reinsured's conclusions as to the coverage of the direct policy: all that they can do is to put the reinsured to proof of the basis upon which the claim had been admitted to ensure that the facts and the wording had not been disregarded. In *Aegis Electrical and Gas International Services Co Ltd v Continental Casualty Co*[155] reinsurers were held to be entitled to deny liability on the ground that the reinsured had simply accepted liability and had therefore not recognised the claim as one which fell within the scope of the direct policy.

17–022 *Commutations.* A commutation is an agreement between reinsured and reinsurers under which all outstanding liabilities are incorporated into a full and final settlement. If direct liabilities prove to be greater than the commuted sum, the settlement cannot be reopened.[156] Where reinsurers fail to honour the commutation, the reinsured may seek summary judgment on it: he does not, in the absence of any express provision to that effect, have the right to treat the settlement as repudiated for breach and seeking indemnity under the reinsurance agreement itself.[157]

17–023 *Allocation of losses.* Where an insurer has been on risk for a number of years, and has different reinsurance cover (either with different reinsurers, or with the same reinsurers on different terms or with fixed limits of indemnity) over those years, it will be necessary for the reinsured to be able to allocate losses to individual years of reinsurance cover. The difficulty here is that it may not be possible to say for certain into which year the losses occurred. In a property case, and other things being equal, there is an inference that the losses have occurred on a regular and linear basis. Thus in *Municipal Mutual Inusrance Ltd v Sea Insurance Ltd*[158] losses by way of pilferage occurred over a period of 24 months,

[153] *Insurance Co of Africa v Scor (UK) Reinsurance* [1985] 1 Lloyd's Rep. 312. Cf: *Hiscox v Outhwaite (No.3)* [1991] 2 Lloyd's Rep. 524; *Baker v Black Sea and Baltic General Insurance Co* [1995] L.R.L.R. 261.

[154] *Assicurazioni Generali SpA v CGU International Insurance Plc* [2004] Lloyd's Rep. I.R. 457.

[155] *Aegis Electrical and Gas International Services Co Ltd v Continental Casualty Co* [2008] Lloyd's Rep. I.R. 17.

[156] In line with the general principles relating to settlements: see Ch.10, above.

[157] *Korea Foreign Insurance Company v Omne Re SA* [1999] Lloyd's Rep. I.R. 509.

[158] *Municipal Mutual Inusrance Ltd v Sea Insurance Ltd* [1998] Lloyd's Rep. I.R. 421.

straddling three years of reinsurance cover. The Court of Appeal allocated the losses between the years of cover on a proportional basis. In *IRB Brasil Resseguros SA v CX Reinsurance Company Ltd*[159] a similar issue arose under a excess of loss cover which protected the reinsured's worldwide liability book of business, although the matter was complicated by the fact that the losses under the direct policies were not themselves based on a purely proportional calculation. The reinsured was on risk for about 64 per cent of a period during which the assured exposed employees and others to asbestos. Burton J., rejecting an appeal against the ruling of arbitrators, held that the reinsured had proved that 70 per cent of the loss fell within the reinsurance protection: that was because the US courts operated the "triple trigger" theory of liability, under which an insurer on risk in a period of exposure retains liability until the period in which the injury becomes manifest, even if the policy has terminated by that time. On the facts there was a risk that the reinsured could face 100 per cent liability, so that it had plainly proved its loss of 70 per cent of that liability.

The reinsured's costs. In *Baker v Black Sea and Baltic General Insurance Co Ltd*[160] the House of Lords held that, in the absence of an express term or a term implied by market usage,[161] reinsurers are not required to indemnify the reinsured for the variable costs incurred by the reinsured in defending any claim by a direct policyholder, even if the reinsurers refuse to accept liability unless and until the reinsured has been sued to judgment.[162] *Baker* involved a surplus treaty which contained a "follow the settlements" clause, the House of Lords holding that business efficacy did not justify the implication of a costs indemnification term.[163]   **17–024**

"Claims co-operation" or "Claims control" clauses. A claims co-operation   **17–025**
clause typically requires the reinsured to notify the reinsures of the occurrence of circumstances likely to give rise to a claim,[164] to investigate the circumstances of the loss[165] in order to satisfy themselves that an insured peril has occurred and that sums are due under the policy, and to provide information to reinsurers.[166] It will normally give the reinsurers the right to refuse to agree to any settlement

---

[159] *IRB Brasil Resseguros SA v CX Reinsurance Company Ltd* [2010] EWHC 974 (Comm).

[160] *Baker v Black Sea and Baltic General Insurance Co Ltd* [1998] Lloyd's Rep. I.R. 327.

[161] Of which no market evidence had been produced. It remains open for a market usage argument to be substantiated in a later case, although it is thought that there is a remote prospect of the requirements for the establishment of such a usage being met.

[162] *Insurance Company of Africa v Scor (UK) Reinsurance Ltd* [1985] 1 Lloyd's Rep. 312.

[163] Following *Scottish Metropolitan Assurance v Groom* (1925) 20 Ll. L.R. 44, and cf. *British General Insurance v Mountain* (1919) 1 Ll. L.R. 605. The contrary decision in *British Dominions General Insurance v Duder* [1915] 2 K.B. 394 was dismissed by the House of Lords as a case in which either the point was conceded or the costs held to be recoverable were those of the direct policyholder and not the reinsured.

[164] A clause which requires the reinsured to give notification of a loss is inappropriate, as there cannot be a loss until the reinsured's liability has been established and quantified: *Royal and Sun Alliance Insurance Plc v Dornoch Ltd* [2005] Lloyd's Rep. I.R. 554; *Faraday Capital Ltd v Copenhagen Reinsurance Co Ltd* [2008] Lloyd's Rep. I.R. 454.

[165] Such wording does not of itself require the reinsured to investigate whether it has a defence based on utmost good faith: *Gan Insurance Co v Tai Ping Insurance Co (No.3)* [2002] Lloyd's Rep. I.R. 612.

[166] There is no implicit prohibition on providing information to third parties, e.g. brokers: *Re T&N Ltd (No.3)* [2006] Lloyd's Rep. I.R. 370. If there is no date for the provision of information, there is no breach of the clause if the information is not provided until proceedings have been brought against the reinsured: cf. *Shinedean Ltd v Alldown Demolition (London) Ltd and Axa Insurance UK Plc* [2006] Lloyd's Rep. I.R. 846.

by the reinsured. Admission of liability to the assured is also generally precluded, and the phrase "no settlement and/or compromise shall be made and liability admitted without the prior approval of reinsurers" has been held to impose cumulative and not alternative obligations on the assured despite the use of the word "and", so that a compromise made without an admission of liability is a breach of the clause.[167]

A claims control clause wider in its effect. It takes the settlement out of the reinsured's hands and confers upon reinsurers the right to negotiate with the assured. Claims control clauses are most commonly found where the reinsured has acted as a front for the reinsurers and has reinsured the vast bulk or all of the risk.

There is an obvious conflict between these clauses and a follow the settlement provision, and was held in *Insurance Company of Africa v Scor (UK) Reinsurance Ltd*[168] that the follow the settlements clause is emasculated by the claims provision. The burden of proving non-compliance with the claims provision is borne by the reinsurers, but if this is established and clause is to be construed as a condition precedent to the reinsurers' liability, the reinsured cannot recover from the reinsurers even though the reinsured is able to prove its liability as a matter of law or has been sued to judgment by the assured.[169] By contrast, if the claims provision is not a condition precedent, then in line with ordinary principles governing insurance contract terms,[170] breach of the term does not permit the reinsurers to deny liability and their sole remedy is damages. It was accordingly said in *Scor* that the reinsured is able to recover as long as the reinsured can prove its loss. Thus, if the reinsured fails to comply with a claims condition and has been sued to judgment, the reinsurers are under an obligation to indemnify the reinsured.[171] It is less certain whether breach of a claims condition automatically deprives the reinsured of the right to rely on a follow the settlements clause, although there is no obvious reason why this should be the case and it is submitted that a reinsured who is in breach of a claims provision is entitled to recover from reinsurers where there has been a bona fide and businesslike settlement with the reinsured.

Whether the claims provision is a condition precedent is a matter of its proper construction. A clause which provides that it is a condition precedent to the reinsurers' liability that claims obligations are followed will be construed according to its terms,[172] although if it is not apparent from the wording that the claims aspect of the clause is subject to a condition precedent then it will be construed against the reinsurers.[173] It was held in *Eagle Star Insurance Co Ltd v Cresswell*[174] that the words "The Underwriters hereon shall control the negotiations and settlements of any claims under this Policy. In this event the Underwriters hereon will not be liable to pay any claim not controlled as set out above" meant that the reinsurers had the option whether or not to control negotiations, and it was only where they did exercise control that they potentially faced liability. Any discretion conferred upon reinsurers under a condition

---

[167] *Gan Insurance Co Ltd v Tai Ping Insurance Co Ltd (Nos 2 and 3)* [2001] Lloyd's Rep. I.R. 667.

[168] *Insurance Company of Africa v Scor (UK) Reinsurance Ltd* [1985] 1 Lloyd's Rep. 312.

[169] *Gan Insurance Co v Tai Ping Insurance Co (No.3)* [2002] Lloyd's Rep. I.R. 612. But see below for a possible qualification.

[170] See Ch.7, above.

[171] *Insurance Company of Africa v Scor (UK) Reinsurance Ltd* [1985] 1 Lloyd's Rep. 312.

[172] *Gan Insurance Co v Tai Ping Insurance Co (No.3)* [2002] Lloyd's Rep. I.R. 612.

[173] *Insurance Company of Africa v Scor (UK) Reinsurance Ltd* [1985] 1 Lloyd's Rep. 312.

[174] *Eagle Star Insurance Co Ltd v Cresswell* [2004] Lloyd's Rep. I.R. 437.

precedent in a manner which precludes recovery by the assured, e.g. in refusing to agree to a settlement or in refusing to take over negotiations with the assured under a claims control clause, cannot be challenged on the ground that the reinsurers have acted unreasonably, as this would require the court to second-guess the reinsurers' commercial judgment,[175] although the reinsurers owe a duty—based either on implied term[176] or good faith[177]—to act rationally in the sense that the considerations taken into account by them must relate to the claim and not to any extraneous matter.

Reinsurers are not to be treated as having waived their right to rely upon the terms of a claims provision simply because they have informed the reinsured that they will not meet a claim when it is finally made.[178]

Inspection provisions. As previously noted, where the reinsurance agreement **17–026** contains a provision requiring the reinsured to allow an inspection by the reinsurers, the right of inspection may be exercised at any time whether or not there has been a loss, so that compliance to such a provision will not generally be a condition precedent to the liability of the reinsurers to meet a claim. Some treaties do contain specific additional clauses which require the reinsured to open its books and records to the reinsurers following a claim and compliance with any request for inspection may be expressed as a condition precedent.[179] The right to insist upon inspection may not, however, be used by reinsurers as a device to delay payment. Where the reinsured has suffered losses and has commenced proceedings against the reinsurers to recover those losses, the success of any application by the reinsurers to obtain a stay of the action so that an inspection clause may be invoked will depend upon three considerations[180]; had the reinsurers sought to exercise the right of inspection at an earlier date, only to be met by a refusal by the reinsured; had the reinsurers sought to rely upon a right of inspection at the door of the court in order to stave off summary judgment; and was there in existence some good reason for inspection to be granted? Thus proceedings will be stayed pending inspection in the absence of sharp practice by the reinsurers,[181] although a stay will be refused if the reinsurers have delayed in making their request and have sought to invoke the clause only on the basis that something might turn up.[182] Reinsurers faced with a claim to which they believe they have a defence, and who insist upon inspection without any reservation of rights, run the risk of being held to have waived the right to rely upon the defence.[183]

---

[175] *Gan Insurance Co Ltd v Tai Ping Insurance Co Ltd (Nos 2 and 3)* [2001] Lloyd's Rep. I.R. 667.

[176] *Gan Insurance Co Ltd v Tai Ping Insurance Co Ltd (Nos 2 and 3)* [2002] Lloyd's Rep. I.R. 667.

[177] *K/S Merc-Skandia XXXXII v Lloyd's Underwriters* [2001] Lloyd's Rep. I.R. 802; *Eagle Star Insurance Co Ltd v Cresswell* [2004] Lloyd's Rep. I.R. 437.

[178] *Lexington Insurance Co v Multinacional de Seguros SA* [2009] Lloyd's Rep. I.R. 1.

[179] *Re A Company No.008725 of 1991 Ex p. Pritchard* [1992] B.C.L.C. 633; *Pacific and General Insurance Co Ltd v Baltica Insurance Co (UK) Ltd* [1996] L.R.L.R. 8.

[180] *Pacific and General Insurance Co Ltd v Baltica Insurance Co (UK) Ltd* [1996] L.R.L.R. 8.

[181] *Pacific and General Insurance Co Ltd v Baltica Insurance Co (UK) Ltd* [1996] L.R.L.R. 8.

[182] *Trinity Insurance Co Ltd v Overseas Union Insurance Ltd* [1996] L.R.L.R. 156; *Aetna Reinsurance Co (UK) Ltd v Central Reinsurance Corp* [1996] L.R.L.R. 165.

[183] *Iron Trades Mutual Insurance Co Ltd v Companhia de Seguros Imperio* [1992] Re. L.R. 213, which would seem not to be affected by the holding in *Strive Shipping v Hellenic Mutual War Risks Association (The Grecia Express)* [2002] Lloyd's Rep. I.R. 669 that reliance on a claims condition cannot amount to waiver, because an inspection clause is not a claims condition as such.

17–027   **Limitation of actions.** The reinsured has, under s.5 of the Limitation Act 1980, six years from the date on which its action against the reinsurers has accrued to issue a claim form against the insurers. The date on which an action against reinsurers accrues is the date on which the reinsured's liability towards the assured is established and quantified by a judgment, arbitration award or binding settlement.[184] In reinsurance contracts there are often contractual provisions which operate to defer the reinsurers' liabilities, and such provisions may operate also to defer the running of the limitation period. It would seem, by analogy with cases on direct insurance, that the general rule continues to apply even where the reinsured is required to make payment under the policy as a condition of recovering from the reinsurers[185] or that an account has to be rendered.[186]

---

[184] *Baker v Black Sea & Baltic General Insurance Co Ltd* [1995] L.R.L.R. 261; *Halvanon Insurance Co Ltd v Companhia de Seguros do Estado de Sao Paulo* [1995] L.R.L.R. 303; *North Atlantic Insurance Co Ltd v Bishopsgate Insurance Ltd* [1998] 1 Lloyd's Rep. 459; *Sphere Drake Insurance Plc v Basler Versicherungs-Gesellschaft* [1998] Lloyd's Rep. I.R. 35.

[185] *Callaghan v Dominion Insurance Co* [1997] 2 Lloyd's Rep. 541.

[186] *Sphere Drake Insurance Plc v Basler Versicherungs-Gesellschaft* [1998] Lloyd's Rep. I.R. 35.

CHAPTER 18

LIFE AND ACCIDENT INSURANCE

1. NATURE OF LIFE AND ACCIDENT POLICIES

Life insurance. Life policies may be of various types, but in general can be 　**18–001**
subdivided into four classes:

(a) endowment policies, whereby the primary liability of the insurers is to pay
 a fixed sum at the end of a fixed period or on the death of the life assured,
 whichever first occurs;
(b) whole life policies, where the sum insured is payable on death only, and
 not on the expiry of any fixed period;
(c) accidental death policies, which insure death by accident only;
(d) investment contracts in the form of life policies, whereby the assured pays
 premiums which are used to purchase investments capable of being
 realised on the assured's death or by the policyholder's voluntary
 surrender of the policy.

There are a number of statutes containing different definitions of life insurance
for different purposes.[1] A life policy is, as a general rule, not a contract of
indemnity.[2] Rather it is a contract to pay a specified sum or a sum realisable from
a fixed level of investment upon the happening of an event which is uncertain in
time, e.g. death or a given date if death has not first occurred. Where an
indemnity is payable on the death of a third party, for example under an
employer's liability policy in respect of the death of an employee, it is not a case
of life insurance at all.[3] Further, not all contracts under which liability is
dependent on the happening of a contingency related to human life are contracts
of life insurance. Thus a contract whereby two or more people purchase property
as joint tenants with the object of the survivor getting the benefit of survivorship
would clearly not be a contract of insurance.[4]

A contract which gives the policyholder equivalent benefits on the assured's
death or on voluntary surrender, while not one on an uncertain event, nevertheless constitutes life insurance as the death of the life insured forms the basis
of the policy.[5] As was made clear in *Gould v Curtis*,[6] the assured may recover
under a life policy without proof of loss; it is only necessary to prove that the
insured event, i.e. the death of the life assured, has occurred. This general rule

---

[1] Policies of Life Assurance Act 1867, Life Assurance Companies (Payment into Court) Act 1896,
Life Assurance Act 1774 Financial Services and Markets Act 2000.
[2] *Prudential Assurance v IRC* [1904] 1 K.B. 558.
[3] See Bruce J. in *Lancashire Insurance v Inland Revenue Commissioners* [1899] 1 Q.B. 353 at
359.
[4] Channel J. in *Prudential v Inland Revenue Commissioners* [1904] 2 K.B. 658 at 664.
[5] *Fuji Finance v Aetna insurance Co Ltd* [1996] 4 All E.R. 608.
[6] *Gould v Curtis* [1913] 3 K.B. 84.

does not apply outside those areas of family relationships where the law deems a person to have an unlimited interest in the life of another. Thus, if an employee under a fixed-term contract seeks to insure the life of his employer, his recovery will in strict theory be limited to the value of his outstanding salary under his contract of employment.[7] The same rules apply to personal accident policies.[8] All other forms of insurance operate by reference to the occurrence of one or more specified events. In the case of a life policy, that event must be connected to the life or death of the assured. At one time it was thought that the event had to be adverse to the assured,[9] but it was subsequently established that a contract is none the less a life policy even though the event is not adverse to the assured.[10] Thus, contracts under which a sum is payable to the assured on death or when he reaches a given age, or on the expiry of a fixed period if the assured has survived to the end of that period, are life policies.

The life or death of the assured need not be the event which triggers payment, provided that there is sufficient connection between the assured's life or death and the availability of benefits. It was held in *Fuji Finance Inc v Aetna Life Insurance Ltd*[11] that a policy taken out for a single premium and whose proceeds were payable on death or early surrender by the assured was one of life insurance within the 1774 Act and that a broad approach was called for in order to recognise the changing nature of life insurance. In the present case, there were two links to the life and death of the assured: the policy came to an end on the assured's death and the right to surrender could be exercised only while the assured was alive. These links were sufficient to render the policy closely related to life or death. In so deciding, the Court of Appeal approved earlier decisions holding that contracts providing benefits on survival to a given date,[12] to a given event (e.g. retirement)[13] and on the exercise of an option were contracts of life insurance.

18–002 Accident insurance. Accident insurance, as generally understood, is a branch of insurance closely allied to life insurance, by which persons are enabled to provide against loss to themselves or their families in case they are injured or disabled for a time or permanently, or killed, by some cause operating on them from without.

Accident policies, like marine policies, may be divided into time and voyage policies. Railway and aviation insurance against accident are common instances of the latter type. Most accident policies are, however, for a fixed period.

A distinction is drawn, for regulatory purposes, between accident insurance and sickness insurance under the Financial Services and Markets Act 2000. Accident insurance provides benefits in the event of the person assured:

   (a) sustaining injury as the result of an accident or of an accident of a specified class; or
   (b) dying as the result of an accident or of an accident of a specified class; or

---

[7] *Hebdon v West* (1863) 3 B. & S. 579.
[8] *Theobald v Railway Passengers' Assurance Co* (1854) 10 Ex. 45.
[9] *Prudential Assurance v Inland Revenue Commissioners* [1904] 2 K.B. 658.
[10] *Joseph v Law Integrity* [1912] 2 Ch. 581; *Gould v Curtis* [1913] 3 K.B. 84.
[11] *Fuji Finance Inc v Aetna Life Insurance Ltd* [1996] 4 All E.R. 608.
[12] *Joseph v Law Integrity* [1912] 2 Ch. 581.
[13] *NM Superannuation Pty Ltd v Young* [1993] 113 A.L.R. 39.

(c) becoming incapacitated in consequence of disease or of disease of a specified class.

Sickness insurance, by contrast, insures against risks of loss to the persons insured attributable to sickness or infirmity. Both classes constitute general business rather than long-term business, and are mutually exclusive. A policy of insurance against accidents, as usually drawn, is not a contract of indemnity. It is a contract to pay a certain fixed sum per week in case of injury, and a certain other fixed sum in case of death. But accident policies need not necessarily be drawn in this way. Thus in *Theobald v Railway Passengers' Assurance*[14] there were two distinct contracts contained in the policy: (a) to pay £1,000 to the assured's executors if he was killed by accident, and (b) to compensate him to any amount, not exceeding £1,000, for the expense and pain and loss caused to him by accident. The second, though not the first, of these contracts was a contract of indemnity. So a policy insuring against personal accident to a third person was held to be a contract of indemnity in a case in which the employer of a lecturer insured her performances for £100 each against her absence owing to accident or illness.[15]

Whether a policy taken out against accidents to a third party is construed as a contract of indemnity or not, the person taking it out must have an interest at the time of taking it out in the health or life of the assured, as the Life Assurance Act 1774 applies to accident policies[16] except to those taken out by a local authority against accidents to members under s.140 of the Local Government Act 1972.

The fact that an injured person's loss is covered by an accident policy is no bar to his right to sue a tortfeasor who has injured him for damages,[17] nor can a tortfeasor, who has caused an accident, plead an insurance against accident in mitigation of damages.[18] This principle is common to all policies, but applied to accident policies which are not policies of indemnity it may have the result that the assured makes a considerable profit out of an accident, as the doctrine of subrogation is not applicable. There used to be one exception to this principle in the case of accidents resulting in death, for the right of the deceased's dependents to sue the tortfeasor under s.2 of the Fatal Accidents Act 1846 was restricted to the actual pecuniary loss suffered by them, and this was held to mean that insurance moneys were to be deducted from the damages awardable under the Act.[19] However, it is now provided by s.4 of the Fatal Accidents Act 1976, replacing the earlier legislation, that in assessing damages "there shall not be taken into account any insurance money, benefit, pension or gratuity which has been or will or may be paid as a result of the death". These words clearly apply to moneys paid on the death of the husband under a policy taken out by his employer in which the deceased had no legal or equitable interest, if it was envisaged that they would be applied for his benefit.[20]

It is the practice to insert a condition in accident policies requiring notice of other insurances against the same risk.[21] Such notice is of special importance in the case of accident policies, since the principle of indemnity does not apply and the insurers are deprived of the benefit of the principle of contribution.

[14] *Theobald v Railway Passengers' Assurance* (1854) 10 Ex. 45.
[15] *Blascheck v Bussell* (1916) 33 T.L.R. 74.
[16] *Shilling v Accidental Death* (1857) 2 H. & N. 42.
[17] *Port Glasgow & Newark Sailcloth Co v Caledonian Ry* (1892) 29 S.L.R. 577.
[18] *Bradburn v Great Western Railway* (1874) L.R. 10 Ex. 1.
[19] *Hicks v Newport, Abergavenny & Hereford Railway* (1857) 4 B. & S. 403.
[20] *Green v Russell* [1959] 3 W.L.R. 17.
[21] See, e.g. *Marshall and Scottish Employers' Liability* (1901) 85 L.T. 757.

18–003   Renewal of life and accident policies. Life policies are continuous, so that a renewal does not bring the policy to an end and create a new policy: were that the case, insurers would have a right to demand full disclosure on renewal, and might refuse to renew at all or other than at a substantially increased premium. In the event that a life policy is prematurely terminated, a situation most likely because the assured has failed to pay premiums, and is then reinstated by the insurers, the reinstatement takes effect as a new contract and accordingly a fresh duty of disclosure applies to it.[22]

Accident policies, by way of contrast to life policies, are annual and there is no obligation on the insurers to renew,[23] so that each renewal takes effect as a new policy[24] attracting a fresh duty of disclosure. However, there is usually no obligation on the insurer to continue an accident policy, as there is in the case of a life policy,[25] and where a policy against accident is for one year, renewable from time to time by consent, each renewal is a new contract, and not a continuation of the original contract.[26]

2. INSURABLE INTEREST

18–004   Existence and timing of insurable interest. The Life Assurance Act 1774 s.l provides as follows:

> "From and after the passing of this Act no insurance shall be made by any person or persons, bodies politick or corporate, on the life or lives of any person or persons, or on any event or events whatsoever, wherein the person or persons for whose use, benefit, or on whose account such policy or policies shall be made, shall have no interest, or by way of gaming or wagering; and that every insurance made contrary to the true intention and meaning hereof shall be null and void to all intents and purposes whatsoever."

The section does not specify whether insurable interest is required by the assured: (a) at the inception of the policy only; (b) at the date of death only; or (c) at both the inception of the policy and the date of death. The phrase "no insurance shall be made" without insurable interest indicates that interest is required from the outset. Moreover, s.3 states that an assured cannot recover more than the amount of his interest, strongly implying that insurable interest is required on death as well. Early cases on the 1774 Act indicated that (c) was indeed the correct approach, so that a creditor who had been paid prior to the assured's death, was unable to show any loss for the purposes of a claim.[27] These decisions were inconvenient to the development of the life assurance market, for they classified life policies as contracts of indemnity and thus prevented their marketability, and the practice developed whereby insurers paid up on policies which had been supported by insurable interest at their inception but not at the date of the death of the life assured.[28]

---

[22] *Mundi v Lincoln Assurance Ltd* [2006] Lloyd's Rep. I.R. 353.

[23] *Simpson v Accidental Insurance Co* (1857) L.J.C.P. 280.

[24] *Stockell v Heywood* [1897] 1 Ch. 459. Contrast *Mulchrone v Swiss Life (UK) Plc* [2006] Lloyd's Rep. I.R. 339, in which an accident policy was held to have been made for an initial 22-month period, rather than for ten months renewable for 12 months.

[25] *Simpson v Accidental Death Ins Co* (1857) 26 L.J.C.P. 289.

[26] *Stokell v Heywood* [1897] 1 Ch. 459.

[27] *Godsall v Boldero* (1807) 9 East 72; *Henson v Blackwell* (1845) 4 Hare 434.

[28] *Barber v Morris* (1831) 1 Mood. & R. 62.

Matters were, in the eyes of the insurance industry at least, eventually put right by the decision in *Dalby v India & London Life Assurance Co*.[29] This was seemingly a reinsurance case in which Anchor Life had insured one Wright under four policies on the life of the Duke of Cambridge. Anchor thereafter reinsured its liability under those policies with the defendants. Wright subsequently surrendered his policies, but Anchor Life maintained the reinsurance, and on the death of the Duke claimed under it. The defendants argued that the policy, being one of indemnity, required proof of loss on death, which on the facts Anchor Life clearly could not do. However, judgment was given in favour of Anchor Life, on two grounds. First, the premium paid had been calculated at the outset, so that it would be "contrary to justice, and fair dealing, and common honesty"[30] to hold that the policy lapsed on loss of interest, as that would have deprived Anchor Life of the benefit of the premium paid by it. Secondly, life policies are not contracts of indemnity, but are agreements under which a fixed sum is payable on death, so that loss of interest is immaterial.

The effect of *Dalby* is that a person may not insure a life if he has no insurable interest at the outset, and if the interest of the policy holder in the life assured is already covered to its full extent by a policy any subsequent policy taken out by him will be struck down by s.1 of the 1774 Act on the ground that he has no insurable interest left to support it.[31] However, subsequent dealings with a policy taken out on interest are permissible. While the *Dalby* decision paved the way for the growth of life assurance as a commercial commodity, in law at least its results are somewhat curious. In the first place, it is difficult to reconcile the notion that life policies are not indemnity contracts with the provision in s.3 of the Life Assurance Act 1774 that the assured cannot recover any more than the amount of his interest. Secondly, *Dalby* itself involved reinsurance; this class of cover is indemnity and not life. Thirdly, the decision is open to various forms of abuse which sidestep the notions fundamental to insurable interest, namely that the assured must not gamble or be put into a position whereby it is in his interests to destroy the insured subject matter for the insurance moneys. Thus, assignment or auctioning of policies is permissible,[32] as is the maintenance of insurance once insurable interest has ceased: the latter may occur in the case of divorced spouses, a key-man policy on a departed employee and a policy by a creditor on a debtor who has paid off his debt[33] or the debt has become statute barred before the death of the life assured.[34]

It was suggested by Langley J. at first instance in *Feasey v Sun Life Assurance Corp of Canada*[35] that the effect of s.1 of the 1774 Act was merely to outlaw life policies that were expressed to be payable with or without interest, given that at the time the Act was passed it was believed that life policies were contracts of indemnity and accordingly that the common law itself imposed an insurable interest requirement in the form of the prohibition of wagering agreements.[36] Accordingly, unless the parties were wagering (in which case the policy would be void at law) or a claim was payable on a "policy proof of interest" basis (in

[29] *Dalby v India & London Life Assurance Co* (1854) 15 C.B. 365.

[30] (1854) 15 C.B. 365 at 391 per Parke B.

[31] *Simcock v Scottish Imperial Insurance Co* (1902) 10 S.L.T. 286. See also *Hebdon v West* (1863) 3 B. & S. 579.

[32] See below.

[33] See (1980) 4 *Anglo-American Law Review* 331 at 345 to 352.

[34] *Garner v Moore* (1855) 3 Drew. 277.

[35] *Feasey v Sun Life Assurance Corp of Canada* [2002] Lloyd's Rep. I.R. 835.

[36] This suggestion is not, however, wholly borne out by the early authorities, some of which were prepared to enforce wagers.

which case the policy was rendered void by s.1), the policy was unaffected by the Act. The Court of Appeal rejected this analysis,[37] and held that the absence of an intention to wager was not of itself enough to validate a policy under the 1774 Act.

18–005 **Assignment of policy to person without interest.** Assignment of life policies is permitted by virtue of the rule that insurable interest is required by s.1 of the Life Assurance Act 1774 only at the inception of the policy and not at any later date. There is a fine factual line between the case in which an assured, having taken out a life policy, determines to assign it to a third person without insurable interest,[38] and the case in which the assured procures an own-life policy with the intention of acting for the benefit of a third person who has no insurable interest. The latter situation, but not the former, is a contravention of s.1. Pollock C.B. put the matter thus in *M'Farlane v Royal London Friendly Society*[39]:

> "There is nothing to prevent any person from insuring his own life a hundred times . . . provided it is bona fide an insurance on his own life, and at the time, for his benefit, and . . . there is nothing to prevent him from dealing with such policies by assigning them to some-one else . . . even though at the time he effected the policies he had the intention of so dealing with them . . .
> But if *ab initio* the policy effected in the name of A is really and substantially intended for the benefit of B and B only . . . that is within the evil and mischief of [the 1774 Act]."

What is being said here is that it is legitimate to take out a policy with the general intent of assigning it, but it is unlawful to take out a policy with the intention of assigning it to a specified person who does not have insurable interest. All will turn upon the intention of the assured, which may in practice be almost impossible to ascertain on either an objective or subjective basis.[40] The test is whether the insurance was effected by the party nominally insured at the instance of, and for the benefit of, another without interest who was to pay the premiums, in pursuance of an arrangement between them under which that other was immediately to secure the sole benefit of it, by assignment, bequest or otherwise.[41] Thus, where the assured sold for £5 a policy on his own life for £500, which he had not then taken out, the policy was held to be illegal under the Life Assurance Act 1774.[42] But it has been held on the other hand that an insurance company lending money may validly agree with the borrower that he

---

[37] *Feasey v Sun Life Assurance Corp of Canada* [2003] Lloyd's Rep. I.R. 637.

[38] For a description of commercial purchasing of life policies see the facts of *Goshawk Dedicated Ltd v Tyser & Co Ltd* [2007] Lloyd's Rep. I.R. 224, in which the purchasers of life policies themselves insured against the risk that the outstanding premiums payable by them would be greater than the sums recoverable under the policies.

[39] *M'Farlane v Royal London Friendly Society* (1886) 2 T.L.R. 755 at 756.

[40] See the facts of *M'Farlane* itself, and cf. *Brewster v National Life Insurance Society* (1892) 8 T.L.R. 648. In both cases the assured was held not to have intended at the outset to take out an own-life policy for the specific benefit of a third person.

[41] *Shilling v Accidental Death* (1858) 1 F. & F. 116. See *Patel v Windsor Life Assurance Co Ltd* [2008] Lloyd's Rep. I.R. 359, in which the claimant took assignments of policies on the life of one B before they were even issued, and even though there was no evidence of any insurable interest possessed by the claimant. No question of insurable interest was raised by the insurers, although the policy was avoided for fraudulent misrepresentation and also for doubts as to whether B had actually died before a claim had been made.

[42] *Macdonald v National Mutual Life of Australasia* (1906) 14 S.L.T. 173.

shall insure his life to a greater amount than the debt, and assign the policy to the company as security.[43]

Payment of premiums by a third party without interest. There may on **18–006** occasion be some difficulty in ascertaining exactly who is interested in a policy where the policy purports to be an own-life policy but the premiums have been paid by a third party. In *Wainwright v Bland*[44] a policy was taken out by one Miss Abercrombey, and on her death her personal representative claimed the insurance money. The insurers pleaded that this was in truth an insurance by the claimant for his own benefit, evidenced by the fact that there was some doubt as to whether Miss Abercrombey could herself have afforded the premiums. The jury was directed that Miss Abercrombey's impecuniosity was not of itself con-clusive, as the claimant might have loaned her the money; the policy might thus properly have been regarded as one by Miss Abercrombey on her own life. It will thus be a question of fact as to whether the premiums have been loaned or given to the assured or whether they have been paid by the third party for his own purposes. Where the payer is the parent or spouse of the life assured, the law assumes that the payment is a gift,[45] but in other cases matters may not be so straightforward.

Insertion of names of interested persons. The Life Assurance Act 1774 s.2 **18–007** provides as follows:

"It shall not be lawful to make any policy or policies on the life or lives of any person or persons, or other event or events, without inserting in such policy or policies the person or persons' name or names interested therein, or on whose account such policy is so made or underwrote."

This provision is designed to prevent evasion of s.1 of the 1774 Act by the device of making of what appear to be own-life policies but which are in fact for the benefit of some other person without insurable interest; s.2 requires the name of that other person to be inserted. It is probable that s.2 adds nothing to s.1 in this regard, for in the situation outlined above the policy would in any event fall foul of s.1. Thus, the leading authorities on s.2 all involve circumstances in which s.1 itself had been infringed.[46] Where s.2 does have some independent impact is the case in which the true assured under the policy does have an insurable interest in the life in question, so that s.1 has not been infringed, but for some reason the name of the true assured has not been inserted into the policy.[47]

Most of the problems surrounding the operation of s.2 have in recent times been eliminated. First, the problem that it was impossible for an employer to organise a group life scheme providing insurance for present and future employees, as the requirement that the names of all persons within the scheme had to be inserted into the master policy could not be complied with was overcome by the Insurance Companies Amendment Act 1973 s.50, which

---

[43] *Downs v Green* (1844) 12 M. & W. 481.

[44] *Wainwright v Bland* (1835) 1 Mood. & R. 481.

[45] *Crabb v Crabb* (1834) 1 My. & K. 511; *Moate v Moate* [1948] 2 All E.R. 486; *Shepherd v Cartwright* [1955] A.C. 481; *Pettitt v Pettitt* [1970] A.C. 777.

[46] *Wainwright v Bland* (1835) 1 Mood. & R. 481; *Shilling v Accidental Death* (1858) 1 F. & F. 116; *Downs v Green* (1844) 12 M. & W. 481.

[47] *Evans v Bignold* (1859) L.R. 4 Q.B. 622; *Forgan v Pearl Life Assurance Co* (1907) 51 S.J. 230.

provides that s.2 of the 1774 Act is deemed to have been complied with if the beneficiaries fall:

> "within a specified class or description ... stated in the policy with sufficient particularity to make it possible to establish the identity of all persons who at any given time are entitled to benefit under the policy."[48]

Secondly, as a result of the Contracts (Rights of Third Parties) Act 1999, if the intended beneficiary has the necessary insurable interest and his or her name is inserted in the policy, that person has a direct action against the insurers for the sums payable under the policy. The requirements of the 1999 Act are also satisfied if the intended beneficiaries can be identified either by description or by membership of a class, so that in the case of, for example, a group life policy for employees, any employee meeting the relevant description is entitled to benefit directly from the policy. Thirdly, s.2 caused difficulties in respect of policies on property, but the decision in *Mark Rowlands Ltd v Berni Inns Ltd*[49] has now confirmed that the Act does not extend in its impact beyond non-indemnity insurance.[50]

18–008   **The amount recoverable.** Section 3 of the Life Assurance Act 1774 provides as follows:

> "And ... in all cases where the insured hath interest in such life or lives ... no greater sum shall be recovered or received from the insurer or insurers than the amount of value of the interest of the insured in such life or lives."

This provision does not stand easily alongside the principles that life insurance is not indemnity insurance and that the assured need not prove loss at the date of the death of the life assured, the agreed sum being payable on the occurrence of the contingent event. Reconciliation of these rules would appear to give rise to the following results:

1. Where there is an unlimited insurable interest, as in the cases of own-life insurance and of insurance by one spouse on the life of the other, s.3 has no application and the sum insured may be recovered.
2. Where the assured has a limited insurable interest in the life assured, as in the cases of financial dependence within families and of "key-man" insurance by an employer on the life of an employee, the assured may not recover more than the amount of his interest measured at the inception of the policy. Where, therefore, a policy was taken out to the full value of the assured's insurable interest, a subsequent policy was void.[51] As life

---

[48] In *Feasey v Sun Life Assurance Corporation of Canada* [2003] Lloyd's Rep. I.R. 637 it was noted that the amendment to s.2 would have been pointless had s.1 independently outlawed a policy under which the persons insured were not identified.

[49] *Mark Rowlands Ltd v Berni Inns Ltd* [1985] 3 All E.R. 473.

[50] The difficulties in relation to land concerned the inability of the assured to insure his own interest and that of another person without inserting the name of that other person. The 1774 Act has never applied to goods and merchandises, which are expressly excluded by s.4. This exemption has been used by the courts to uphold motor policies providing liability cover for persons driving with the assured's permission. Identification of such drivers from the outset clearly being impossible (such policies have been classified as goods rather than liability policies) and to uphold a group policy insuring personal effects of a number of a group of trade union members, cash having been regarded as "goods" for its purposes: see *Prudential Staff Union v Hall* [1947] 1 K.B. 685.

[51] *Hebdon v West* (1863) 3 B. & S. 379, as explained by the Court of Appeal in *Feasey*.

policies are always in the form of an agreement by the insurer to pay a stated sum on the death of the life assured, and are thus quasi-valued policies, the sum agreed between the parties is conclusive of the value of the assured's initial interest unless there is some fraud on the assured's part or the sum insured is so grossly excessive as to amount to a wager, contrary to s.1. It cannot be the proper test of indemnity to measure interest at the date of death, for that would introduce an indemnity element into life insurance, the existence of which was denied in the *Dalby* decision.

3. Where the interest consists of a debt owing to the assured that debt need not be made up in full at the time the insurance is taken out, so that where A was obliged to maintain B and entitled to be repaid the maintenance money, it was held that his insurable interest extended to each sum of money as it was successively expended[52] and not merely to sums already expended at the time the policy was taken out.

If the claimant is a third party who is not an assured under the policy but who has a right to make a direct claim under the Contracts (Rights of Third Parties) Act 1999, then at first sight the claimant can recover only a sum representing the amount of his own insurable interest. This proposition flows from s.3(4) of the 1999 Act, which states that insurers have, as against the third party, any defences which could have been raised against him had he been a party to the contract. It may be, therefore, that in a case in which the beneficiary had no insurable interest or a limited insurable interest at the inception of the risk, only the estate of the assured can recover the full sums due under the policy. This would be a curious result but, if correct, means that the 1999 Act has left unaffected the rights of third-party beneficiaries.

Consequences of lack of insurable interest

The general rule; illegality of contracts. Section 1 of the Life Assurance Act **18–009** 1774 does not stipulate the legal consequences of a contract falling within its terms being made without interest, other than in providing that "no insurance shall be made" and that any contravening policy is to be "null and void". This is to be contrasted with s.2 of the 1774 Act, which expressly states that a policy made without the insertion of the names of all interested parties is illegal. Prima facie it might be thought that failure to refer to illegality in s.1 implies that the contract is merely void. The difference between a contract of insurance which is simply void and one which is illegal concerns not its enforcement, but the availability of restitution of premiums: under a void contract premiums are recoverable for a total failure of consideration,[53] but under an illegal contract the maxim in *pari delicto potior est conditio defendentis* prevents a restitutionary action on the basis that the claimant cannot mount his action without pleading his own illegality.[54] In *Harse v Pearl Life Assurance Co*[55] the assured, having paid premiums under a policy on the life of his mother suggested to him by the

---

[52] *Barnes v London, Edinburgh & Glasgow Life Assurance Co* [1892] 1 Q.B. 864 at 867, per A.L. Smith J.

[53] Marine Insurance Act 1906 s.84(1), although recovery is denied where the policy was made by way of gaming or wagering: s.84(3)(c).

[54] Cases decided under the Marine Insurance Act 1745, which provided for illegality in respect of want of interest, demonstrate the point: *Andree v Fletcher* (1789) 3 T.R. 266: *Morck v Abel* (1802) 3 Bos. & P. 35; *Lubbock v Potts* (1806) 7 East 449; *Allkins v Jupe* (1875) L.R. 2 C.P.D. 375.

[55] *Harse v Pearl Life Assurance Co* [1904] 1 K.B. 558.

insurer's agent, was held on her death not to be able to recover either the sum insured or the premiums. In the view of the Court of Appeal, the wording of s.1 was sufficiently indicative of an intention to impose the illegality sanction to life insurances without interest. This remains the general rule as a matter of law, although the courts have fashioned a number of exceptions to this principle under which the premium will be recoverable despite the illegality.

18–010 *Inequality of guilt.* The *in pari delicto* principle operates only where the parties are equally guilty. Thus, if one party bears a greater degree of responsibility than the other for the formation of an illegal contract, restitution by the innocent party will be permitted. The difficult question, however, is: what constitutes equality of guilt? In *Harse v Pearl Life Assurance Co*[56] itself the Court of Appeal was unimpressed by the assured's argument that the policy had been induced by the insurer's agent, for it went on to hold that in the absence of some form of fraud by the agent, he was not to be expected to have any better knowledge of the law than the assured, so that the parties remained equally guilty. A contrasting decision is that of the Court of Appeal in *Hughes v Liverpool Victoria Friendly Society*,[57] in which the assured was persuaded by an agent of the insurer to reinstate life policies which had previously been validly held by a third person but which had lapsed. The court here found that the agent had acted fraudulently, in the knowledge that the policies would be illegal, and restitution was permitted.

In practice fraud has proved to be hard to establish,[58] although the modern trend in the cases is to be more generous to a person who has been induced to enter into an illegal contract[59] and it may be more difficult today for an insurer to argue that it should retain the benefits of an illegal contract entered into by an improperly trained agent. It may also be noted that the Financial Services and Markets Act 2000 s.397, makes it a criminal offence for any person knowingly or recklessly to make a false statement, or knowingly to fail to disclose material facts, in order to induce another person to enter into a contract of insurance.

18–011 *Repentance.* Where an illegal contract is executory, a party is permitted by the law to repent of the unlawful purpose and to claim restitution of any property transferred by him to the other. This rule appears to derive from the judgment of Buller J. in *Lowry v Bordieu*,[60] a marine insurance decision, and while the principle is clearly established, the scope of the rule is not: doubts still remain in particular as to whether the claimant must genuinely have had a change of heart or whether the fact that he wishes to withdraw—whether for moral or commercial reasons—is enough,[61] and exactly when a contract is regarded as "executory" for the purposes of the rule. In the only life insurance case in which Buller J.'s exception has been considered, *Howard v Refuge Friendly Society*,[62] the argument that the contract remained executory until the death of the life assured

---

[56] *Harse v Pearl Life Assurance Co* [1904] 1 K.B. 558.

[57] *Hughes v Liverpool Victoria Friendly Society* [1916] 2 K.B. 482.

[58] See *Phillips v Royal London Mutual* (1911) 105 L.T. 136; *Elson v Crooks* (1912) 106 L.T. 462; *Howarth v Pioneer Life* (1912) 107 L.T. 155; *Goldstein v Salvation Army Assurance Society* [1917] 2 K.B. 291.

[59] *Kiriri Cotton v Dewani* [1960] A.C. 192; *Re Cavalier Insurance Co* [1989] 2 Lloyd's Rep. 541.

[60] *Lowry v Bordieu* (1780) 2 Doug. K.B. 468.

[61] In *Tribe v Tribe* [1995] 4 All E.R. 236 the Court of Appeal adopted the genuine repentance test.

[62] *Howard v Refuge Friendly Society* (1886) 54 L.T. 644.

was rejected by the court, which appears to have decided that repentance is not possible once the premium has been paid. However, the judgment demonstrates some confusion between the Life Assurance Act 1774 and the Gaming Act 1845, and it is suggested that the availability of the exception remains arguable.

Mistake. It has long been settled that where a party to an unlawful contract is under a mistake of fact which, if it had been correct, would have led to the contract being lawful, restitution is possible.[63] The policy was unlawful as it involved the insurance of subject matter belonging to an enemy alien, but the court nevertheless permitted recovery of the premiums on the ground that the assured had been unaware at the date of the policy that war had been declared. In *Kleinwort Benson v Lincoln City Council*[64] the House of Lords removed the old distinction between mistake of fact and mistake of law, and held that restitution is possible in both situations. The result of *Kleinwort Benson* is that if by error of law a payment which is not due is made, it is recoverable. It is unclear whether *Kleinwort Benson* applies to payments under illegal—as opposed to merely void—contracts, and although there is nothing in the speeches in *Kleinwort Benson* which indicates that the rules relating to illegal contracts have been affected by the removal of the distinction it may be thought that this is likely to be the case and that premiums are now recoverable for any type of mistake. **18–012**

Examples of insurable interest in lives: personal and family relationships

Own life. The assured is conclusively presumed to have an unlimited insurable interest is his or her own life,[65] and this is the case even if the insurance is for a portion only of his life.[66] The nature of that interest is a matter of some controversy and becomes important to determine where the assured has for some reason been deprived of the benefit of the policy.[67] In *McLellan v Fletcher*[68] the assured's interest was classified as pecuniary. In that case the claimant's solicitors had negligently failed to procure a life policy, and on the claimant's death his personal representatives brought an action against the solicitors seeking to recover from them the amount which would have been payable under the policy, minus the premiums which would have been payable. Lincoln J. allowed the action, on the basis that the assured had lost his contingent pecuniary interest in the policy. A different view was taken by Phillips J., on similar facts, in *Lynne v Gordon, Doctors & Walton*,[69] the court ruling that an assured's interest in his own life could not be classified as pecuniary so that it could not be said that depriving him of the benefit of a life policy caused him a pecuniary loss. Phillips J. also rejected an alternative argument that, had the claimant successfully procured a life policy during his lifetime, it would have increased in value, so that a loss would have been suffered during the claimant's lifetime. **18–013**

---

[63] *Oom v Bruce* (1810) 10 East. 225. See also *Hentig v Staniforth* (1816) M. & S. 122. This principle seems to underlie *British Workman's Assurance Society v Cunliffe* (1902) 18 T.L.R. 425, affirmed (1902) 18 T.L.R. 502. See also *Phillips v Royal London Mutual* (1911) 105 L.T. 136.
[64] *Kleinwort Benson v Lincoln City Council* [1998] 4 All E.R. 513.
[65] *Wainwright v Bland* (1835) 1 Mood. & R. 481.
[66] *Wainwright v Bland* (1835) 1 Mood. & R. 481.
[67] Where the unexpired term of a life policy is lost through the insolvency of the insurer, statutory valuation principles apply.
[68] *McLellan v Fletcher* (1987) 3 P.N. 202.
[69] *Lynne v Gordon, Doctors & Walton, The Times*, June 17, 1991.

18–014   *Spouses.* A husband is presumed to have an unlimited insurable interest in his wife's life,[70] and a wife is presumed to have an unlimited insurable interest in her husband's life.[71] The reciprocal rights and duties created by the marriage tie are alone sufficient to support both interests,[72] irrespective of their pecuniary relationship.[73] In both cases the presumption is conclusive. Thus evidence to show that either husband or wife stands to gain by the death of the other is inadmissible in rebuttal of this presumption.

Parties to a civil partnership are, under s.253 of the Civil Partnerships Act 2004, to be treated in the same way as spouses, and each party is presumed to have an unlimited insurable interest in the life of the other partner. A civil partnership, as defined in s.1 of the 2004 Act, is "a relationship between two people of the same sex", although it only gives rise to rights where the parties are registered as civil partners of the other. The position of other cohabiting couples is unclear, although it would seem that there is a presumption of insurable interest and that there is no need to demonstrate a financial interest to support a policy.

The above rules are supplemented by the Married Women's Property Act 1882 s.11, which was passed to reverse the common law rule that a woman had no capacity to contract in her own right.[74] The section, as amended, reads as follows:

> "A married woman may effect a policy upon her own life or the life of her husband for her own benefit; and the same and all benefit thereof shall enure accordingly.
>
> A policy of assurance effected by any man on his own life, and expressed to be for the benefit of his wife, or of his children, or of his wife and children, or any of them, or by any woman on her own life, and expressed to be for the benefit of her husband, or of her children, or of her husband and children, or any of them, shall create a trust in favour of the objects therein named, and the moneys payable under any such policy shall not, so long as any object of the trust remains unperformed, form part of the estate of the insured, or be subject to his or her debts: Provided, that if it shall be proved that the policy was effected and the premiums paid with intent to defraud the creditors of the insured, they shall be entitled to receive, out of the moneys payable under the policy, a sum equal to the premiums so paid. The insured may by the policy, or by any memorandum under his or her hand, appoint a trustee or trustees of the moneys payable under the policy, and from time to time appoint a new trustee or trustees thereof, and may make provision for the appointment of a new trustee or trustees thereof, and for the investment of the moneys payable under any such policy. In default of any such appointment of a trustee, such policy, immediately on its being effected, shall vest in the insured and his or her legal personal representatives, in trust for the purposes aforesaid.
>
> The receipt of a trustee or trustees duly appointed, or in default of any such appointment, or in default of notice to the insurance office, the receipt of the legal personal representative of the insured shall be a discharge to the office for the sum secured by the policy, or for the value thereof, in whole or in part."

The effects of this section are, first, that a married woman has the right to effect a policy upon her own life or the life of her husband for her own benefit and,

---

[70] *Griffiths v Fleming* [1909] 1 K.B. 805, although only Vaughan Williams L.J. was prepared to so hold. The husband's insurable interest was not questioned in *Murphy v Murphy* [2004] Lloyd's Rep. I.R. 744.

[71] *Reed v Royal Exchange Assurance Co* (1975) Peake Add. Cas. 70; *Murphy v Murphy* [2004] Lloyd's Rep. I.R. 744.

[72] Manning J. in *Rombach v Piedmont Life* (1883) 48 Am.Rep. 239.

[73] Kennedy L.J. in *Griffiths v Fleming* [1909] 1 K.B. 805 at 820–823.

[74] *Cahill v Cahill* (1883) L.R. 8 App.Cas. 420.

secondly, that a policy taken out by a husband for the benefit of his wife or children, or by a wife for the benefit of her husband or children, creates a statutory trust of the policy in the hands of his or her executors, free of debts. The significance of s.11 is that a trust is created even though the ordinary requirements for the making of an express trust are not satisfied: providing that the policy is "expressed to be for the benefit of" a spouse or child, there is no need for a formal declaration of trust. The section does not apply to joint names policies,[75] nor does it confer rights upon divorced spouses,[76] although it does extend to all forms of life and accident insurance[77] and the children of existing and previous marriages may benefit from the trust.[78] It is immaterial that other beneficiaries are named,[79] and that the benefits provided under the trust are contingent.[80] Where a statutory trust operates, the beneficiaries acquire an immediate vested interest in the proceeds of the policy as soon as it is taken out, so that on the death of any beneficiary that interest passes to his or her estate rather than reverting to the assured's own estate.[81]

The provisions of the 1882 Act have been extended to registered same-sex civil partnerships by the Civil Partnerships Act 2004: under s.70 of the 2004 Act a life policy effected by a civil partner on his or her own life, and which is expressed to be for the benefit of that person's civil partner, or the children of either of them, will be treated in the same way as a life policy taken out by a spouse.

The statutory trust may fail on one of two grounds. First, the trust is overridden where it can be shown that its object was to defraud creditors: this is specifically stated in the proviso to s.11 of the 1882 Act. Secondly, if one spouse is guilty of murdering the other, the statutory trust is ousted as the murderer is unable, by virtue of s.1 of the Forfeiture Act 1982 to obtain any benefit from the crime. In such a case, there is a resulting trust of the proceeds of the policy for the deceased's estate.[82] However, if there is unlawful killing not amounting to murder, the court has a discretion under s.2 of the 1982 Act to modify the forfeiture rule. In *Re S (Deceased)*[83] the discretion was exercised so as to declare the deceased's husband to be a trustee of the policy proceeds for the benefit of the son of the marriage.

Section 11 of the 1882 Act is not satisfactory in all respects. The Law Revision Committee, reporting in 1937, recommended that the provision be extended to all life, endowment and education policies where there was a named beneficiary. The provision was reconsidered by the Law Commission in its 1996 Report on Privity of Contract. The Law Commission concluded that there was no need to extend the statutory trust in the light of proposals to give all third parties the right to enforce contracts for their benefit. The Law Commission's proposals on privity were implemented by the Contracts (Rights of Third Parties) Act 1999, which—in line with the Law Commission's proposal—made no changes to the 1882 Act. One important consequence of the 1999 Act is that, once a trust has

---

[75] And not a joint names policy: *Griffiths v Fleming* [1909] 1 K.B. 805.

[76] *Re Browne* [1903] 1 Ch. 188.

[77] *Re Gladitz* [1937] Ch. 588.

[78] *Re Davies* [1892] 1 Ch. 90; *Re Griffiths* [1903] 1 Ch. 739. Illegitimate children also benefit: Family Law Reform Act 1969 s.19.

[79] *Re Clay* [1937] 2 All E.R. 548.

[80] *Equitable Life Assurance of the United States v Mitchell* (1911) 27 T.L.R. 213; *Re Iokanides* [1925] 1 Ch. 403; *Re Fleetwood* [1926] Ch. 48.

[81] *Cousins v Sun Life Assurance Co* [1933] Ch. 126.

[82] *Cleaver v Mutual Reserve Fund Life Association* [1892] 1 Q.B. 147.

[83] *Re S (Deceased)* [1996] 1 W.L.R. 235.

been established for named or identifiable beneficiaries, the policy cannot be varied or rescinded without the consent of those beneficiaries.

18–015 *Parents and children.* In the absence of proof of interest it has been held that a parent cannot insure his child,[84] however much he may have expended on his education,[85] unless he has a pecuniary interest.[86] The mother of an illegitimate child has the same interest in the life of her child as would have been the case had the child been born in wedlock.[87] By s.9 of the Children Act 1958, a person undertaking for reward the nursing and maintenance of a child under the age of nine apart from its parents or having no parents is expressly deemed to have no interest in the life of the child for the purposes of the Life Assurance Act 1774, and by the same section insurance by such a person on the life of such child is a criminal offence. In *Barnes v London, Edinburgh and Glasgow Life Assurance Co*[88] the claimant had taken out a life policy on a child. This child was her stepsister and she had promised its mother to maintain it. It was held that she had an insurable interest in the life of the child "so far as to secure the repayment of the expenses incurred by her."[89] In so far as this case implies that a mere moral obligation to repay one's benefactor can support an insurance it has been criticised,[90] and would not on principle appear correctly to represent the law.[91] The true rule appears to be that support given to a dependant does not give an insurable interest in his life[92] unless it can be shown that he was liable to repay the money expended on him.[93]

Further, a child cannot insure his parent. Thus an adult son was held to have no insurable interest in the life of his pauper father whom he supported,[94] and a son was held to have no interest in the life of his mother, whom he supported, even though she in fact performed the duties of house-keeper for him.[95] But an infant child entitled to be supported by his parents[96] would no doubt have an insurable interest in the life of both of them. An illegitimate child has no greater interest in the life of its mother than one born in wedlock.[97]

By Sch.8 para.11A of the Children Act 1989, a person who fosters a child privately and for reward is deemed for the purposes of the Life Assurance Act

---

[84] *Halford v Kymer* (1830) 10 B. & C. 724; *Attorney General v Murray* [1904] 1 K.B. 165. See, however, s.99 of the Friendly Societies Act 1992, which allows up to £800 to be recovered under a friendly society policy by a parent on a child where there is no insurable interest.

[85] *Worthington v Curtis* (1876) L.R. 1 Ch D 419 at 423, per Mellish L.J.

[86] *Law v London Indisputable Life Insurance Policy Co* (1855) 1 K. & J. 223. There is no common law obligation of mainentance.

[87] *Morris v Britannic* [1931] 2 K.B. 125.

[88] *Barnes v London, Edinburgh and Glasgow Life Assurance Co* [1892] L.R. 1 Q.B. 864.

[89] *Barnes v London, Edinburgh and Glasgow Life Assurance Co* [1892] L.R. 1 Q.B. 864, per Coleridge C.J. at 865, 866.

[90] See per Lord Alverstone C.J. in *Harse v Pearl Life Assurance Co* [1903] 2 K.B. 92 at 96; per Kennedy L.J. in *Griffiths v Fleming* [1909] 1 K.B. 805 at 819.

[91] See, for instance, Lord Eldon in *Lucena v Craufurd* (1806) 2 Bos. & P.N.R. 269.

[92] *Halford v Kymer* (1830) 10 B. & C. 724.

[93] See *Anctil v Manufacturers' Life* [1899] A.C. 604; *Goldstein v Salvation Army* [1917] 2 K.B 291 at 295, per Rowlatt J.; *Barnes v London, Edinburgh & Glasgow Life Assurance Co* [1892] 1 Q.B. 864.

[94] *Shilling v Accidental Death* (1858) 1 F. & F. 116. See also *Howard v Refuge Friendly Society* (1886) 54 L.T. 644 at 646; *Elson v Crookes* (1911) 106 L.T. 462; *Shilling v Accidental Death* (1858) 1 F. & F. 116.

[95] *Harse v Pearl Life Assurance Co* [1903] 2 K.B. 92. See also *Goldstein v Salvation Army* [1917] 2 K.B. 291.

[96] See A.L. Smith J. in *Barnes v London, Edinburgh & Glasgow Life Assurance Co* [1892] 1 Q.B. 864 at 866.

[97] *Re Swainbank and Co-operative Insurance* [1953] 1 A.C. 29.

1774 to have no interest in the life of the child, and the same principle is extended to adopted children by s.37 of the Adoption Act 1976.

Funeral expenses. It has been debated how far one has an insurable interest on the life of another on account of the expenses of burying him. Since every house-holder in whose house a dead body lies is bound by common law to inter the body decently according to Christian rites,[98] it would seem to follow that he has an insurable interest in the lives of those living with him.[99] Industrial societies had for many years been in the practice of insuring parents against the funeral expenses of their children before the practice was, prior to its abolition, recognised by statute.[100] Under s.99 of the Friendly Societies Act 1992 it has once again become permissible for the lives of children to be insured by friendly societies, although if the child dies before the age of 10 the amount recoverable is limited to £800 unless some independent insurable interest exists. **18–016**

Other family relationships. In all other cases involving family relationships there is no presumption of any insurable interest, and some sort of financial reliance must be shown. The general rule relating to relatives is that where one relative, who effects an insurance on the life of another, is so related to that other as to have against him a claim for support enforceable by law, the relationship gives an insurable interest. But natural love and affection arising out of kinship, however close, does not by itself do so and unless there is some pecuniary interest enforceable by law, one relative cannot validly insure the life of another. Thus a family relationship such as brother or sister, does not give rise to insurable interest.[101] **18–017**

Insurable interest in lives: business relationships

Partners. Partners have an insurable interest in each other's lives up to the amount of loss which might potentially be caused following withdrawal of capital in the event of the death or retirement of a partner.[102] **18–018**

Employer and employee. An employee may insure the life of his employer, but his insurable interest is limited to a sum representing his contractual rights against the employer, namely the minimum notice period or the amount of the unexpired term of a fixed-term contract.[103] Insurance for any greater sum is on an expectation and is thus wagering. Conversely, an employer has an insurable interest in the life of his employees. It would seem as a matter of strict law that any such interest is limited to the duration of the notice period or unexpired part **18–019**

[98] *R v Stewart* (1840) 12 Ad. & El. 773.
[99] Phillimore L.J. in *Tofts v Pearl* [1915] 1 K.B. 189 at 194.
[100] Shearman J. in *Hatley v Liverpool Victoria Friendly Society* (1918) 88 L.J.K.B. 237 at 239 at 240. The payment of funeral expenses of the husband, wife or child of a member was recognised by s.1 of the Friendly Societies Act 1896 as one of the purposes of a friendly society, and s.3 of the Industrial Assurance Act 1923 authorised policies issued by collecting societies and industrial assurance companies to cover the funeral expenses of a parent, child, grandparent, grandchild, brother or sister. Insurance of funeral expenses under the above provisions was prohibited by s.1 of the Industrial Assurance and Friendly Societies Act 1948, and insurance under the Act of the life of a child under 10 was also prohibited: s.6(1).
[101] *British Workman's Assurance v Cunliffe* (1902) 18 T.L.R. 502. See generally: *Howard v Refuge Friendly Society* (1886) 54 L.T. 644; *Elson v Crooks* (1912) 106 L.T. 462; *Evanson v Crooks* (1912) 106 L.T. 264.
[102] *Griffiths v Fleming* [1909] 1 K.B. 805.
[103] *Hebdon v West* (1863) 3 B. & S. 579.

of a fixed-term agreement, as anything beyond that is a mere expectation.[104] This is, however, a clearly unrealistic approach to measuring the value of an employee as it omits a variety of factors, the most important of which is the cost of training a new employee to the same levels of skill and competence. Consequently, it has become the practice for insurers to issue keyman policies on senior employees; these are in effect valued policies, the insurer agreeing to pay the agreed sum on the death or retirement of the employee. Such policies have never been challenged as unlawful under the Life Assurance Act 1774 and it has been held that it is legitimate to insure a senior employee for the full value of his actual worth to the employer.[105]

18–020   *Creditor and debtor.* A creditor may insure the life of his debtor for the amount of the debt,[106] although he may not insure the general assets of the debtor over which he holds no security.[107] The creditor must have some right against the thing itself, such as a right in rein against a vessel,[108] in order to support an insurance of it. There is nothing, however, to prevent the creditor insuring against the insolvency of the debtor caused by the loss of the debtor's assets,[109] or against default in payment.

A mere expectation that a creditor will not call in a debt during the creditor's lifetime does not give the debtor an insurable interest in the creditor's life.[110]

A creditor has an insurable interest in the life of any other person whose death will or may take away from the creditor some security which, but for the death, would have been available to satisfy the debt.[111] So also a surety has an insurable interest in the life of his co-surety to the extent of the co-surety's proportion of the debt,[112] and also in the life of the principal debtor,[113] and a joint debtor has an insurable interest in the life of the other joint debtor.[114] A creditor has an insurable interest in any property of his debtor over which he has a lien[115] or similar interest[116] or which has been mortgaged to him to secure payment of the debt, and it makes no difference whether or not the debtor has insured such property.[117]

18–021   *Liability to indemnify third party for death or personal injury.* It is an obvious proposition that a liability insurer has insurable interest in his liability to the assured, so as to support a reinsurance. In *Feasey v Sun Life Assurance Co of*

---

[104] *Simcock v Scottish Imperial Insurance Co* (1902) 10 S.L.T. 286; *Tumbull & Co v Scottish Provident Institution* (1896) 34 S.L.R. 146.

[105] *Fuji Finance Ltd v Aetna Insurance Co Ltd* [1996] 4 All E.R. 608.

[106] *Anderson v Edie* (1795) 2 Park 14; *Lindenau v Desborough* (1828) 8 B. & C. 586; *Law v London Indisputable Life* (1855) 1 Kay & J. 223; *Branfoot v Saunders* (1877) 25 W.R. 650 (co-debtors).

[107] Buller J. in *Wolff v Homcastle* (1798) 1 Bos. & P. 316; *Stainbank v Penning* (1851) 11 C.B. 51; *Macaura v Northern Assurance* [1925] A.C. 619.

[108] Walton J. in *Moran, Galloway & Co v Uzielli* (1905) 2 K.B. 555.

[109] *Waterkeyn v Eagle Star* (1920) 5 Ll. L.R. 42 at 43, per Greer J.

[110] *Hebdon v West* (1863) 3 B. & S. 579. See also *Lea v Hinton* (1854) 5 De G.M. & G. 82 (surety in life of debtor).

[111] *Henson v Blackwell* (1845) 4 Hare 434.

[112] *Branfoot v Sounders* (1877) 25 W.R. 650.

[113] *Lea v Hinton* (1854) 4 De G.M. & G. 823.

[114] *Davitt v Titcumb* [19891 3 All E.R. 417; *Dunbar v Plant* [1997] 4 All E.R. 289.

[115] Buller J. in *Wolff v Horncastle* (1798) 1 Bos. & P. 316 at 323; Walton J. in *Moran, Galloway & Co v Uzielli* (1905) 2 K.B. 555 at 562–563.

[116] *Briggs v Merchant Traders' Association* (1849) L.R. 13 Q.B. 167.

[117] Lord Halsbury L.C. in *Westminster Fire v Glasgow Provident* (1888) L.R. 13 App.Cas. 699 at 709.

Canada[118] the insurer's insurable interest was expressed by the policy to be in the lives of employees and other persons injured who might make claims against the assured. The Court of Appeal by a majority held that there was no objection to the insurer's insurable interest being classified as a contingent one on the lives of the assured's employees rather than as a simple liability cover. The majority approach was that the policy was not simply a life policy under which the P&I club was to receive a fixed sum in the event of the death or injury of an employee, but rather was designed as a policy that covered the Club for losses that it would suffer as an insurer of its members' liabilities over a three-year period. In those circumstances the Club had a clear insurable interest capable of pecuniary evaluation, and the policy itself was capable of being construed as covering that interest. Ward L.J.'s dissent was based on the argument that the policy was a life policy and could not extend to cover the Club's own insurable interest, which was confined to its own liability.

3. ASSIGNMENT OF LIFE POLICIES

Assignability. Life policies are to be considered something more than contracts. They are choses in action[119] and are treated as securities for money[120] payable at an uncertain but future date which is bound to occur. Apart from the operation of an excepted peril, the insurers will be bound to pay the sum insured at some date, and the original contract is therefore to be considered as the purchase of a reversionary sum in consideration of the payment of an annuity.[121] Even the present "surrender" value of the policy is computable actuarially. Insurance offices will usually accept surrender for such a consideration, and banks will therefore lend money on it to this amount. If a life policy is in the possession of a third party on the death of the assured, his personal representatives can maintain an action against the third party to recover possession of it.[122] If the insurance is upon the assured's own life, the right to the policy moneys will devolve on his personal representatives on his death, who will be bound to treat it as money owing to him and forming part of his estate.[123]

18–022

Life policies are freely assignable whether they are expressed to be payable to the assigns of the assured[124] or not.[125] The assignment may take the form of sale, mortgage, settlement or gift. An assignment passes a right to the insurance moneys whether or not the assignor[126] or the assignee[127] has an insurable interest in the life assured, provided that the assurance was valid in the first place. The free assignability of a life policy thus means that the assignee is able to recover under it following the death of the life assured or the occurrence of the event

---

[118] *Feasey v Sun Life Assurance Co of Canada* [2003] Lloyd's Rep. I.R. 637.

[119] *Re Moore* (1878) 8 Ch D 519.

[120] *Stokoe v Cowan* (1861) 4 L.T. 675 at 685.

[121] *Fryer v Morland* (1876) 3 Ch D 675 at 685; *Re Harrison and Ingram Ex p. Whinney* [1900] 2 Q.B. 710 at 718.

[122] *Rummens v Hare* (1876) 1 Ex. D. 169.

[123] *Petty v Wilson* (1869) L.R. 4 Ch. 574.

[124] *Williams v Thorp* (1828) 2 Sim. 257.

[125] *Haas v Atlas Insurance* [1913] 2 K.B. 209.

[126] *Dalby v India & London Life* (1854) 15 C.B. 365; *Law v London Indisputable Life* (1855) 1 K. & J. 223.

[127] *Ashley v Ashley* (1829) 3 Sim. 149.

specified in the policy merely on proof that he is the assignee.[128] The general law imposes only one limitation on the assignability of life policies, which is that assignment may not be used as a method of overcoming the rule in s.1 of the Life Assurance Act 1774. To this end the courts have established the rule that a policy is void if it is taken out by a person having insurable interest with the immediate intention of assigning the policy to a specific person without insurable interest. By contrast, the policy is valid if the assured simply has a general intention to assign in the future, or if the intention to assign to a specified person is formed at some later date.[129]

The right of the assured to deal with the policy as he chooses is subject to any condition in the policy to the contrary. Thus a condition forbidding assignment has been held to make a policy non-assignable at law.[130] A court would be slow, however, to construe such a condition in such a way as to prevent an assignee's interest from being enforceable in equity, nor will it affect the interest of a beneficiary under a declaration of trust. In the same way, a restriction on the assured's ability to assign his "rights, powers or obligations" under a policy cannot preclude him from agreeing with a third party how the recoveries under the policy will be applied.[131] Further the assignment of a claim on a policy after loss is not a breach of a condition against alienation of the property insured.[132] A life policy which is not assignable is not in fact the full property of the assured at all, but comprises the type of insurance in which he has only a limited power of appointment of funds standing to his credit.

18–023   **Policies of Assurance Act 1867.** The purpose of the 1867 Act was to provide a method for the assignment at law of life policies at a time when choses in action in general were assignable only in equity. The availability of legal assignment of choses in action, first introduced by the Judicature Act 1873 and re-enacted as s.136 of the Law of Property Act 1925,[133] rendered the 1867 Act of less significance, and the two provisions today provide alternative methods of achieving the same end. Both statutes have the same effect, in that they give the assignee the legal right to sue the insurers in his own name without joining the assignee, and that they give the insurers the power to discharge their liability by paying the assignee. However, assignment under the 1867 Act is available only where the assignee is entitled in equity to the proceeds of the policy, a condition which does not apply to s.136 and which makes the latter the more attractive and widely used form of legal assignment. The 1867 Act applies only to life policies and extends to mortgages of life policies[134] as well as other types of assignment: the ability to assign partial interests is one which is not available under s.136 of the 1925 Act. Where its requirements are fulfilled, the assignee obtains a legal assignment and may sue the insurers in his own name. The form of assignment

---

[128] See *NM Rothschild & Sons (CI) Ltd v Equitable Life Assurance Society* [2003] Lloyd's Rep. I.R. 371, where the insurers wrongly refused to accept assignments as evidence of the assignee's title and caused loss to the assignee who was unable to surrender the policies at the most favourable time.

[129] *M'Farlane v Royal London Friendly Society* (1886) 2 T.L.R. 755; *Brewster v National Life Insurance Society* (1892) 8 T.L.R. 648.

[130] *Re Turcan* (1888) 40 Ch D 5; *Floods of Queensferry Ltd v Shand Construction Ltd* [2003] Lloyds Rep. I.R. 181.

[131] Cf. *Freakley v Centre Reinsurance International Co* [2005] Lloyd's Rep. I.R. 284 (liability insurance).

[132] *Garden v Ingram* (1852) 23 L.J. Ch. 478; *Randall v Lithgow* (1884) 12 Q.B.D. 525.

[133] See Ch.4, above.

[134] *Re Haycock's Policy* (1876) 1 Ch D 611.

is set out in s.5 of and the Schedule to the 1867 Act, which set out a simple form of words, consisting of the names of the parties, the consideration provided by the assignee and a statement that the policy is attached. Under s.3 of the 1867 Act, notice to the insurer is required to perfect the assignment, and the section also states that the order of giving notice to the insurers regulates priorities as between competing assignees and that if the assignee fails to give such notice a payment made by the insurers in good faith will be valid against him. Section 4 of the Act requires all insurers to specify on life policies their principal place of business: this is necessary to enable the assured to give proper notice under s.3. Under s.6 they must give a written receipt of any notice of assignment if requested to do so by the assignee.

Payment of proceeds. It is common in the case of insurances on the assured's **18–024** own life, for the assured to nominate a beneficiary at the time of taking out a policy. At common law the person nominated, by reason of his status as a stranger to the contract, had no remedy at law against the insurers. Further, such a nomination did not by itself constitute the assured a trustee of the proceeds.[135] The weakness of the nominee's position has, however, been reversed by the Contracts (Rights of Third Parties) Act 1999, although if the Act is for some reason inapplicable, or if it has been expressly excluded, the property in the policy will pass to the personal representatives of the assured on his death and the nominee has no rights whatsoever,[136] unless: (a) the nomination amounts to a declaration of trust[137]; (b) the person taking out the policy is merely the agent of the nominee[138]; (c) the nomination is made under s.11 of the Married Women's Property Act 1882[139]; or (d) the nomination creates a binding contract between insurer A and B to pay C on an event or contingency, so that B can use the equitable remedy of specific performance against A to obtain an order against him to pay what may be due to C.[140]

If there is a dispute as to whom the proceeds of a policy are to be paid, the Life Assurance Companies (Payment into Court) Act 1896 allows life insurance companies[141] to pay into court "moneys payable by them under a life policy in respect of which, in the opinion of their board of directors, no sufficient discharge can otherwise be obtained" (s.3, as amended). By this means the rival claimants are left to apply for payment out, and the receipt of the proper officer of the court for the money paid in discharges the insurance company (s.5). Apart from rival claims the company may pay the money into court under this provision where the policy has been lost.[142] Provided the opinion of the directors that no sufficient discharge can otherwise be obtained is an honest one, payment into court gives them an absolute discharge, but where their opinion although honest is unreasonable, they may be made liable for the costs of payment out. They will usually have to bear the costs of payment in.

---

[135] *Re Engelbach's Estate* [1924] 2 Ch. 348 (wrongly decided: *Beswick v Beswick* [1968] A.C. 58); *Re Burgess's Policy* (1915) 85 L.J. Ch. 273; *Re Schebsman* [1944] Ch. 83. Cf. *Green v Russell* [1959] 2 Q.B. 226; *Bowskill v Dawson (No.2)* [1955] 1 Q.B. 13.

[136] *Re Sinclair's Policy* [1938] Ch. 799; *Re Clay's Policy* [1937] 2 All E.R. 548.

[137] *Johnson v Ball* (1851) 5 De G. & Sm. 85; *Pedder v Mosley* (1862) 31 Beav. 159; *Re Keen's Estate* [1937] 1 Ch. 236; *Re Gordon* [1940] Ch. 851; *Re Webb* [1941] Ch. 225; *Re Foster's Policy* [1966] 1 W.L.R. 222. Cf. *Re Independent Air Travel Ltd* [1961] 1 Lloyd's Rep. 604.

[138] *Re Scottish Equitable Life Policy 6402* [1902] 1 Ch. 282.

[139] See above.

[140] *Beswick v Beswick* [1968] A.C. 58.

[141] Not being friendly societies: s.2.

[142] *Harrison v Alliance Assurance* [1903] 1 K.B. 194.

4. Utmost Good Faith

18–025 **Materiality.** The following facts have been found to be material for the purposes of pre-contract disclosure. In considering the decided cases, it is necessary to bear in mind the requirements of the Equality Act 2010, discussed in Ch.6, above, which preclude unjustified discrimination on the grounds of age; disability; gender reassignment; marriage and civil partnership; pregnancy and maternity; race; religion or belief; sex; and sexual orientation.

18–026 **Age.** The proposer's age is material since it affects his life expectancy, and in the case of an endowment policy, it may affect the date on which the policy is to mature.[143]

18–027 **Residence and domicile.** In the absence of a warranty the failure by the assured to disclose his domicile[144] is not normally fatal, though such omissions might be so were the occupation of the assured a particularly dangerous one, or had he been for a long period in an unhealthy climate. The term "residence" in a proposal for insurance means the place where the proposer is living or residing at the time of making the proposal, and not where he has been residing before or where he is going to reside afterwards. It is a matter of fact whether the assured's imprisonment is material and therefore to be disclosed.[145]

18–028 **Health.** Life insurance is peculiar in that the assured is often ignorant as to the fact most material in assessing the premium, the state of his own health. Though he may have a general idea as to his own physical well-being, he may well be unaware of an incipient but deadly disease within his system that a doctor might have diagnosed. A man might not even know, it has been held, that he has gout.[146] And if an assured may be ignorant as to his own health, one who takes out a policy on the life of another is even less in a position to inform the insurers accurately as to the state of that other's health. The rule is, warranties apart, that the insurers may avoid the policy if the assured knowingly misrepresents his state of health, or that of the life insured. Similarly he is bound to disclose no more than he actually knows,[147] though he is bound to disclose a serious disease of which he is aware.[148] Insurance companies therefore put upon applicants for life insurance the responsibility of disclosing the true state of their health or that of the life assured by asking them questions in the proposal on this matter, and by giving the assured's answers to them the force of warranties by means of a declaration in the proposal and a reference to it in the policy. By the employment of such a scheme the assured is made responsible for the absolute truth of his answers,[149] irrespective of their materiality[150] if they are not true, they will afford

---

[143] *Keeling v Pearl Assurance Co* (1923) 129 L.T. 573; *Hemmings v Sceptre Life Association Ltd* (1905) 92 L.T. 221.

[144] *Grogan v London and Manchester Industrial Assurance* (1855) 2 T.L.R. 75.

[145] *Huguenin v Rayley* (1815) 6 Taunt. 186.

[146] *Fowkes v Manchester and London Life* (1863) 3 B. & S. 917.

[147] *Swete v Fairlie* (1833) 6 Car. & P. 1; Lord Campbell in *Wheelton v Hardisty* (1857) 8 El. & Bl. 232 at 269–273; *Joel v Law Union and Crown Insurance Co* [1908] 2 K.B. 863.

[148] *British Equitable Insurance Co v Musgrave* (1887) 3 T.L.R. 630. See also *Godfrey v Britannic Assurance Co* [1963] 2 Lloyd's Rep. 515; *Winter v Irish Life Assurance Plc* [1995] 2 Lloyd's Rep. 274.

[149] Blackburn J. in *Macdonald v Law Union* (1874) L.R. 9 Q.B. 328 at 332–333; *Hutton v Waterloo Life* (1859) 1 F. & F. 735.

[150] *Pawson v Watson* (1778) 2 Cowp. 785.

the insurers a ground for repudiating liability on the policy, even though he gave them innocently, although the ABI's 1986 Statement of Long Term Insurance Practice requires that insurers seek information only to the best of the assured's knowledge and belief.

Independently of this development, courts the world over have been slow to construe such answers as stating anything more than the belief of the assured,[151] but unless the questions are so framed as to require him to answer as to his own knowledge only, he is advised to qualify his answers in this respect.[152] Where the assured warrants his answers to questions to be put to him in the future by the company's medical examiner to be true, this binds him to do no more than tell the truth to the best of his knowledge, and will be construed accordingly.[153] In fact it may be said in general that, unless the insurers put the matter beyond all doubt by using the clearest language in their policies, it is the accuracy of the assured's knowedge and not the truth of his answers that the assured warrants in life insurance.[154]

Medical history. Information as to past illnesses and medical attendance is **18–029** plainly material, as it may impact on life expectancy.[155] However, express questions on this matter are in a different position from questions as to present state of health, since from their nature the insurers can expect the answers to be true in fact, and not mere matters of belief.[156] But even such questions have been construed to have a limited meaning.[157] Thus a question as to how long it was since the assured had been "attended" by a doctor has been construed not to include attendance for mere minor ailments[158] and the question, "What medical men have you consulted?" has been construed not to extend to consultations during early childhood.[159] Similarly, questions as to the medical history of the assured's relatives will be given a reasonable and limited meaning.[160] The principle upon which such decisions rest was clearly enunciated by the Privy Council in *Condogianis v Guardian*[161]:

---

[151] Burton J. in *Sceales v Scanlan* (1843) 6 Ir. L. R. 367 at 401; Cockburn C.J. in *Fowkes v Manchester and London Life* (1863) 3 B. & S. 917 at 925–926; *Life Association of Scotland v Foster* (1873) 11 M. 351; *Thomson v Weems* (1884) L.R. 9 App.Cas. 671. But see *National Mutual of Australasia v Smallfield* [1922] N.Z.L.R. 1074.

[152] *Wheelton v Hardisty* (1857) 8 El. & Bl. 232 at 271–273.

[153] *Delahaye v British Empire Mutual Life* (1897) 13 T.L.R. 245.

[154] Fletcher Moulton L.J. in *Joel v Law Union and Crown Insurance Co* [1908] 2 K.B. 863 at 884.

[155] *Ashby v Bates* (1846) 15 M. & W. 589; *Wheelton v Hardisty* (1858) 8 El. & Bl. 232; *Fowkes v Manchester and London Life* (1863) 3 B. & S. 917; *Winter v Irish Life Assurance Plc* [1995] 2 Lloyd's Rep. 274.

[156] *Huckman v Fernie* (1838) 3 M. & W. 505; *Metropolitan Life v Madden* (1941) 117 Fed. Rep. 446.

[157] In *Kumar v Life Assurance Co of India* [1974] 1 Lloyd's Rep. 147 the deceased had had a Caesarian operation, consulted a doctor and was prescribed an oral contraceptive. She had taken out a life policy, declaring that she had not consulted a medical practitioner and had not had an operation. Kerr J. held, in an action on the policy, that it could be avoided. Quaere, whether a Caesarian is usually thought of as an operation, or seeking a prescription for a contraceptive as "consulting" a medical practitioner.

[158] *Connecticut Mutual v Moore* (1881) L.R. 6 App.Cas. 644. See also *Mundi v Lincoln Assurance Co* [2006] Lloyd's Rep. I.R. 353: failure to disclose consulting a doctor in advance of a trip to India, and subsequent consultation in respect of digestive infection contracted in India, not material facts. Contrast *Lewis v Norwich Union Healthcare Ltd* [2010] Lloyd's Rep. I.R. 198, where a visit to the assured's GP was held to be a material fact.

[159] *Joel v Law Union and Crown Insurance Co* [1908] 2 K.B. 863.

[160] *Joel v Law Union and Crown Insurance Co* [1908] 2 K.B. 863 at 891.

[161] *Condogianis v Guardian* [1921] 2 A.C. 125 at 130.

"In a contract of insurance it is a weighty fact that the questions are framed by the insurer, and that if an answer is obtained to such a question which is upon a fair construction a true answer, it is not open to the insuring company to maintain that the question was put in a sense different from or more comprehensive than the proponents' answer covered. Where an ambiguity exists, the contract must stand if an answer has been made to the question on a fair and reasonable construction of that question. Otherwise the ambiguity would be a trap against which the insured would be protected by courts of law."

Not every trivial illness which will call for disclosure, even in answer to specific questions about medical history.[162] It has been held that questions as to past illnesses include diseases of the mind,[163] but not minor ailments.[164] "Afflictions of the liver" do not include every disorder of that organ,[165] and "afflicted with fits" does not include a fit caused by an accident.[166] But the question "Have you ever had fits?" has a wider significance.[167] "Spitting of blood" means the disorder so called, but one act of spitting blood should be stated to the insurers.[168] A disorder is not one "tending to shorten life" simply from the circumstance that the assured dies from it.[169] Good health means reasonably good health.[170] A warranty of good health can "never mean that a man has not in him the seeds of some disorder. We are all born with the seeds of mortality in us".[171] But where a man suffering from tuberculosis, of which his mother, brother and sister had died, stated that he was in good health, the policy was held voidable,[172] and more generally the health of the assured's close relatives is also potentially material.[173] "Paralysis" has been held to mean the shock of paralysis, and not local paralysis resulting in lameness caused by a fall.[174] Near-sightedness has been held not to be a bodily infirmity.[175] The assured's "usual" medical attendant is not

[162] Life Association of Scotland v Foster (1873) 11 M. 351; Chattock v Shawe (1835) 1 Mood. & R. 498. In Lam Charn Yung v AXA China Region Insurance Co (Bermuda) Ltd [2007] 1 H.K.L.R.D. 770 the assured had complained of an occasional pain in her right breast, and she was advised by a doctor in 1996 to have her breast rechecked. In 1997 the assured submitted a proposal for life insurance, and at a medical examination by the insurers answered "no" to the question "Have you ever had any disorder of the breast, uterus, ovaries, or tubes?" A lump was detected in March 1998, and the insurers rejected her claim for major illness and purported to avoid the policy for misrepresentation. The assured's answer was held to be misrepresentation. Where the assured has suffered various unexplained symptoms, nice questions as to materiality may arise, the issue being whether the assured ought to have realised from his symptoms that material facts might be involved. See Morrison v Muspratt (1827) 6 Bing. 60; Lindenau v Desborough (1828) 8 B. & C. 586; Joel v Law Union and Crown Insurance Co [1908] 2 K.B. 863; Godfrey v Britannic Assurance [1963] 2 Lloyd's Rep. 515; British Equitable Insurance Ltd v Great Western Railway Co (1869) 20 L.T. 422; Lee v British Law Insurance Co [1972] 2 Lloyd's Rep. 49.

[163] Connecticut Mutual v Akens 150 U.S. 468 (1893).

[164] Connecticut Mutual v Moore (1881) L.R. 6 App.Cas. 644, 648.

[165] Connecticut Mutual v Union Trust Co 112 U.S. 250 (1884).

[166] Chattock v Shawe (1835) 1 Mood. & R. 498; Shilling v Accidental Death (1858) 1 F. & F. 116.

[167] Aetna Life v France 94 U.S. 561 (1876).

[168] Geach v Ingall (1845) 14 M. & W. 95.

[169] Watson v Mainwaring (1813) 4 Taunt. 763.

[170] See Yorke v Yorkshire Insurance [1918] 1 K.B. 662 at 668–669 and National Mutual v Smallfield [1922] N.Z.L.R. 1074.

[171] Per Lord Mansfield in Willis v Poole (1780) 2 Park on Insurance 935.

[172] Davian v Canadian Order of Foresters (1923) 61 C.S. 492.

[173] Duff v Gant (1852) 20 L.T.O.S. 71; Holmes v Scottish Legal Life Assurance Society (1932) 48 T.L.R. 306.

[174] Cruikshank v Northern Accident (1895) 23 R. 147.

[175] Cotten v Fidelity & Casualty Co (1890) 41 Fed. Rep. 506.

necessarily his last one,[176] but if he denies that he has a doctor, though one has attended him recently, he is precluded from recovering on his policy.[177]

In order to ascertain the health of a proposer, the insurer may well seek a medical report, in which case the provisions of the Access to Medical Reports Act 1988 allow the proposer to obtain access to any medical report on him and to refuse permission for the report to be forwarded to insurers either at all or without amendment.

If an insurer refuses to accept a proposal for a motor policy on the grounds of the assured's health, the insurer must give full details of its refusal to the Treasury.[178]

Intemperate habits and other risks. In some of the older cases[179] this was the **18–030** subject of an express question or warranty. Even in the absence of such a question, it would appear to be material that the proposer is in the habit of drinking more than is good for him, since the harmful effects of excessive consumption of strong drink are well known.[180] Once again, though, the difficulty will lie in determining how much (and how regularly) the proposer may drink before the fact needs to be disclosed to the insurers. Dicta suggest[181] there is no simple test, not least since the ability to withstand alcohol differs so much from one person to another. No satisfactory judicial definition of "intemperance" has been given, but it has been held not to be limited to such intemperance as would impair the general health of the assured.[182] It is essentially a matter of degree as to what constitutes intemperance.[183] In an insurance policy it means habitual, immoderate indulgence in alcohol, or addiction to it, not immoderate consumption on an isolated occasion.[184] The exemption of death of or injury to the assured while "under the influence of liquor" sometimes to be found in accident policies raises a similar problem: to fall within it "the balance of a man's mind or the intelligent exercise of his faculties"[185] must be disturbed. The taking of drugs on regular occasions is equally capable of being a material fact.[186] In Canada it has been held that the fact that the assured smokes tobacco is material,[187] although the modern practice is to ask a specific question on this matter and to load the premium accordingly.

---

[176] *Huckman v Fernie* (1838) 3 M. & W. 505; *Maynard v Rhode* (1824) 1 Car. & P. 360; *Scanlan v Sceales* (1849) 13 Ir. L.R. 71, but see *Everett v Desborough* (1829) 5 Bing. 503.

[177] *Palmer v Hawes* (1841) Ellis, Ins. 131. See also: *Connecticut Mutual Life Insurance Co of Hartford v Moore* (1881) L.R. 6 App.Cas. 644; *British Equitable Ins Co v Musgrave* (1887) 3 T.L.R. 630.

[178] Road Traffic Act 1988 s.95.

[179] *Pole v Rogers* (1840) 2 Mood. & R. 287; *Craig v Penn* (1841) Car. & M. 43; *Thomson v Weems* (1884) L.R. 9 App.Cas. 671; *Southcombe v Merriman* (1842) Car. & M. 286; *Hutton v Waterloo Life* (1859) 1 F. & F. 735.

[180] *Mundi v Lincoln Assurance Co* [2005] EWHC 2678 (Ch).

[181] *Thomson v Weems* (1884) L.R. 9 App.Cas. 671 at 697–698; *Southcombe v Merriman* (1842) Car. & M. 286 at 287.

[182] Coleridge J. in *Southcombe v Merriman* (1842) Car. & M. 286 at 287.

[183] *Scottish Widows Fund v Buist* (1876) 3 R. 1078; *Scottish Equitable v Buist* (1877) 4 R. 1076 at 1078; *Thomson v Weems* (1884) L.R. 9 App.Cas. 671.

[184] *Ridley v Bradford Insurance* [1971] R.T.R. 61. Thus, for the purpose of an exclusion clause in a private motor car insurance policy, in a case where there was 145 mg. of alcohol in 100 ml. of blood in a man of moderate drinking habits who died in a road accident, this could not be described as "intemperance".

[185] *Mair v Railway Passengers' Assurance* (1877) 37 L.T. 356, applied in *Louden v British Merchants' Insurance Co Ltd* [1961] 1 W.L.R. 798.

[186] *Yorke v Yorkshire Insurance Co* [1918] 1 K.B. 662.

[187] *Hammill v Gerling Global Life Insurance Co* 71 D.L.R. (4th) 566 (1990).

Modern life policies expressly ask whether the assured belongs to a group which is high-risk in respect of AIDS, e.g. intravenous drug users or homosexuals.

18–031 **Occupation and hobbies.** The proposer's occupation will affect the hazards to which he is exposed. In the absence of an express question, occupation will not be a material fact unless that occupation has some direct link to the physical hazard.[188] In practice life assurance companies operate according to a number of different classes of occupation, and all that is material is to disclose accurately the class into which the proposer falls. Thus, in *Biggar v Rock Life Assurance Co*[189] the assured was described on the proposal form as a tea-traveller. It was held that he should have disclosed that he was also a publican, this being an occupation attracting significantly higher premiums. By contrast, in *Perrins v Marine & General Travellers' Insurance Society*[190] an esquire omitted to state that he was also an ironmonger. The court held that the fact omitted was not material, after hearing evidence that the rate of premium was the same for either class of person.

Similarly with hobbies, the proposal form commonly enquires whether the proposer engages in any dangerous leisure activity, such as rock-climbing or hang-gliding. Even without a specific question, it is obvious that such a fact would be material to the assessment of the risk run. In practice, personal insurances will in any event exclude loss resulting from dangerous activities, although whether this removes the duty of disclosure is unclear.

5. Coverage of Life Policies

18–032 **Scope of policies.** The cover afforded by policies of life insurance, unlike that of other policies, is not restricted to loss by accident: they cover also the death of the assured from disease or other natural causes. The exception of inherent vice, which might be compared with disease, and that of wear and tear, which might be compared with senile decay of the life insured, apply to insurance policies generally, but do not apply in the case of life insurance.

Suicide

18–033 *Common law principles.* Prior to the Suicide Act 1961, suicide (otherwise than while of unsound mind) was a crime in English law. In *Beresford v Royal Assurance*,[191] the policy expressly included sane suicides as one of the insured perils. The House of Lords held that there could be no recovery under the policy where the life assured committed suicide while of sound mind.[192] The *Beresford* decision was based upon both the fact that in committing suicide the life assured had committed a crime, so that it was contrary to public policy for his estate to benefit by that crime, and upon the further consideration that the assured, by his wilful act, had brought about the insured event. The reasoning in the decision in *Beresford* has been undermined by the Suicide Act 1961 as suicide is no longer

---

[188] *Lindenau v Desborough* (1828) B & C. 586 at 592. Contrast *McNealy v Pennine Insurance Co Ltd* [1978] 2 Lloyd's Rep. 18.

[189] *Biggar v Rock Life Assurance Co* [1902] 1 K.B. 516.

[190] *Perrins v Marine & General Travellers' Insurance Society* (1859) 2 El. & El. 317.

[191] *Beresford v Royal Assurance* [1938] A.C. 586.

[192] See also Erskine J. in *Borradaile v Hunter* (1843) 5 M. & G. 639 at 658.

a crime and, although there is no reported authority on the point subsequent to the Suicide Act 1961, the general understanding is that a policy which covers the risk of sane suicide by the life assured is fully enforceable, a wilful act being expressly within the scope of the cover. However, as the implied term that the assured is not entitled to recover where the loss is caused by his wilful misconduct is still applicable to life policies, where an own-life policy is silent on recoverability following suicide, sane suicide by the assured precludes recovery by his personal representatives.

By contrast, insane suicide is absent an express exclusion an insured risk as there is no wilful act involved.[193] Suicide is insane if the balance of the assured's mind was affected so that his actions cannot be regarded as intentional if he was killed after deliberately performing an act which he believed could not hurt him (e.g. jumping from a high building).

Express terms. There is now nothing to prevent the insurers from expressing the   **18–034**
policy to cover even sane suicide by the assured, on the one hand, or from excepting all suicide, sane or insane, from the risk on the other,[194] provided they use apt words to do so. In the former case innocent assignees of the assured before his death will be entitled to recover,[195] and also assignees or others deriving title through him after his death. But no one can recover who assisted in the suicide, or otherwise committed the serious crime introduced by s.2 of the Act of 1961 (that of assisting suicide by providing lethal drugs), who would be making a profit from his own crime.

Generally no suicide exception clause is inserted in life policies. If it does appear it is as a result of investigation revealing that the life assured's family has a history of suicide, or the life assured himself seems otherwise likely to take his own life. If an investigation is unfavourable to the assured on this point, he is usually given an option: he can either accept the policy with the exception clause, or pay a higher premium and have the clause excluded. When a suicide exception clause is inserted, there is a tendency for it to be limited so as to apply only for one or two years from the date of the policy. If the suicide clause does operate and the life assured take his own life whilst insane, the insurers might make an ex gratia return of premiums.

Exceptions for "suicide", or of death by the assured's "own hands" have been construed, in effect, to cover all cases of intentional self-destruction,[196] where the assured knew the nature of his act and the natural consequence of what he was doing.[197] Thus, like the implied exception of sane suicide, "suicide" so expressed does not cover cases in which the assured did not know what he was doing, for in such cases his act cannot be said to have been intentional, and his representatives will be entitled to recover. But, unlike the implied exception, such words will cover circumstances such as those in *Borradaile v Hunter*[198] where the assured voluntarily threw himself into the Thames, knowing that he would destroy his life, but without being able at the time to judge between right and

[193] *Horn v Anglo-Australian Life* (1861) 30 L.J. Ch. 511.

[194] *Horn v Anglo-Australian Life* (1861) 30 L.J. Ch. 511; *White v British Empire Mutual Life* (1868) L.R. 7 Eq. 394; *Ellinger v Mutual Life of New York* [1905] K.B. 31.

[195] *Beresford v Royal* [1938] A.C. 586.

[196] *Borradaile v Hunter* (1843) 5 Man. & G. 639; *Clift v Schwabe* (1846) 3 C.B. 437; *Dufaur v Professional Life* (1858) 25 Beav. 599; *Rowett, Leakey & Co v Scottish Provident* [1927] 1 Ch. 55.

[197] Maule J. in *Borradaile v Hunter* (1843) 5 Man. & G. 639 at 654; Patteson J. in *Clift v Schwabe* (1846) 3 C.B. 437 at 465; *Stormont v Waterloo Life* (1858) 1 F. & F. 22.

[198] *Borradaile v Hunter* (1843) 5 Man. & G. 639.

wrong. His act was held to amount to death by his own hands, within the meaning of the policy, although it did not amount to the crime of suicide owing to his temporary moral insanity.

Policies sometimes provide that in cases of suicide during insanity the policy shall not be paid in full, but treated as surrendered, and that its surrender value shall be paid to the deceased's representatives. By this means substantial justice is done, since the insurer avoids having his risk increased by the acceleration of death by suicide and the representatives of the assured are not deprived of the benefit of the policy so far as it has already been earned by the payment of premiums.

18–035   *Death caused by wilful misconduct.* A life policy does not cover death caused by the wilful misconduct of the assured himself unless the policy otherwise provides. Such misconduct is an implied exception to the risk, as in the case of insurance generally. The misconduct must be the proximate cause of the death[199] and not merely the occasion of it, to exclude the death from the risk covered by the policy: the latter was found to be the case where the assured was killed in a motor accident while driving while intoxicated and at excessive speeds.[200]

Where the person whose life is insured is murdered by the person who took out the policy neither he nor anyone claiming through him will be entitled to recover, by reason of an implied term in the policy excepting loss caused by his wilful misconduct from the risk, quite irrespective of any questions of public policy.[201] Public policy will in any event prevent a murderer from obtaining any financial benefit from his crime.[202] This principle has been given statutory force by the Forfeiture Act 1982. Section 1(1) defines the forfeiture rule as the rule of public policy which precludes a person who has unlawfully killed another from acquiring a benefit in consequence of the killing. Illustrations of unlawful killing, set out in s.1(2), include aiding, abetting, counselling or procuring the death of another. The court is, other than in a case of murder, which is excluded by s.5 of the Forfeiture Act 1982, given a discretion by s.2(1) to modify the forfeiture rule by allowing a person convicted of an offence involving unlawful killing to acquire an interest in property under the victim's will, or as the deceased's nominee or as the beneficiary under a trust (s.2(4)). The power of modification may be exercised where the court is satisfied that the justice of the case so demands, having regard to the conduct of the offender and of the deceased and to such other circumstances as appear to the court to be material (s.2(2)). In the case of a life policy, these provisions operate to deprive a murderer of any interest under the victim's life policy, although if there is an offence of unlawful killing short of murder the court does have the discretion to allow the wrongdoer to recover as the victim's nominee under the policy, or as testamentary benefici-ary[203] or, in the case of an own life policy by a married person, by the spouse or children as statutory beneficiaries under s.11 of the Married Women's Property Act 1882.[204] It follows from these principles that a murderer who is the beneficiary of the deceased's life policy can never himself recover any sums under the policy. The bar on recovery by the murderer himself extends also to any

---

[199] A claim on a policy on the life of a murderer who was hanged was thus held not to be valid: *Amicable Insurance v Bolland* (1830) 4 Bligh (N.S.) 194.

[200] *Marcel Beller v Hayden* [1978] Q.B. 694.

[201] See Lord Atkin in *Beresford v Royal* [1938] A.C. 586 at 595.

[202] *Cleaver v Mutual Reserve Fund Life Association* [1892] 1 Q.B. 147.

[203] See *Dunbar v Plant* [1997] 4 All E.R. 289 (failed suicide pact); *Re H* [1991] 1 F.L.R. 441.

[204] *Re S (Deceased)* [1996] 1 W.L.R. 235.

assignee of the murderer's rights under the policy, as the murderer has no entitlement to the proceeds and therefore has nothing to assign. By contrast, if the murderer has assigned the policy itself, the assignee's rights are not derived from those of the murderer and a claim may be made by the assignee.[205]

The forfeiture principle does not apply where the misconduct is by a stranger to the original contract of insurance, even where such stranger is the beneficiary under the policy by reason of a trust in his favour.[206] An ordinary policy covers the risk of the assured being murdered by third parties just as it covers the risk of death by accident or disease, and there is no reason in such a case why the innocent assured, or his representatives, should not enforce the policy.[207] Thus where a policy was taken out on the joint lives of A and B, and was assigned to a building society, the building society was able to recover under the policy where A murdered B.[208] Had the assignment been merely of the right to recover under the policy, A would have remained the assured and no claim under the policy could have been presented by him.

Provisions as to age. Life policies may be expressed as providing cover only if the assured is "not over" a specified age. Thus in *Lloyds Bank Ltd v Eagle Star Insurance Ltd*[209] the insurers were to be liable only if the assured were not over the age of 65 years. At the material time he was 65 years and seven months, and it was held that he had exceeded the age limit, so that the insurers were not liable.   **18–036**

Territorial limitations and restrictions on occupation. A condition that once commonly appeared in life policies limited the territory in which the assured might reside,[210] allowing him to go outside the specified geographical limits only on payment of an increased premium. Similarly restrictions may be made in the policy against the assured engaging in military service[211] or other such dangerous occupations unless he pays an increased premium. But there has long been a general tendency on the part of insurers to remove local restrictions and grant "whole-world" policies so as to avoid the obvious inconveniences of this old system. By questioning the assured as to his occupation and intentions they are able fairly to estimate the probable risk of his travelling to unhealthy localities, and can fix the premium accordingly. The answers to such questions amount to no more than an expression of intention and, if they are made in good faith, the policy will continue to be valid even if the assured changes his mind.[212] An insurer who wishes to restrict the assured's future conduct must obtain an express continuing warranty to this effect.   **18–037**

As regards hazardous occupations, a motor racing driver insured his life under a policy excluding the recovery of full profits accruing under it if he were killed whilst engaging in "motor racing, motor speed hill climbs, motor trials or

---

[205] *Davitt v Titcumb* [1983] 3 All E.R. 417.
[206] *Cleaver v Mutual Reserve* [1892] 1 Q.B. 147, but the person guilty of the misconduct will not be able to benefit and the proceeds will be held on resulting trust for the estate of the life assured.
[207] Lord Abinger in *Wainewright v Bland* (1835) 1 Moo. & Rob. 481 at 486.
[208] *Davitt v Titcumb* [1989] 3 All E.R. 417. The building society used the funds to discharge the mortgage debt owing to it. When the mortgaged property was subsequently sold, it was held that the proceeds belonged entirely to B's estate. This result prevented A from deriving any benefit as the result of his wrongful act.
[209] *Lloyds Bank Ltd v Eagle Star Insurance Ltd* [1951] 1 All E.R. 914.
[210] *Wing v Harvey* (1854) 5 De G.M. & G. 265.
[211] *Duckworth v Scottish Widows Fund* (1917) 33 T.L.R. 430.
[212] *Grant v Aetna Assurance* (1862) 15 Moo. P.C.C. 516.

rallies". He died as the result of an accident in a sprint event. While "motor racing" covered sprint events as a matter of ordinary English, it was held, "motor racing" had a restricted meaning, known to the insurers, which did not cover sprint events, and they were liable in full on the policy.[213]

18–038 Indisputable life policies. Life insurance companies often advertise in their prospectus, and some times insert a statement in their policies, that they are "indisputable". If such a statement is included in a policy, or the assured can prove that he effected a policy on the faith of such a statement in a prospectus,[214] the company is precluded from relying on a breach of a warranty by him that his statements were true,[215] and the fact that he made a mistake in filling in the proposal offers them no defence. But it does not preclude the company from relying on their common law right to avoid the policy for fraudulent mis-representation.[216] The words "except in the case of fraud" are sometimes added to the statement to make this position clear to the assured. Nor does such a statement preclude the company from alleging that the policy is void on the ground of no interest.[217]

18–039 Effect of war on a life policy. A contract of life insurance with an enemy, unlike an insurance of property, is not abrogated by the outbreak of war, at any rate, where the policy is expressed as an entire contract for life.[218] A contract of life insurance with an enemy made during a war is, by contrast, illegal and void as it amounts to trading with the enemy.

6. COVERAGE OF PERSONAL ACCIDENT POLICIES

"Accident"

18–040 *General definition of "accident".* Personal accident policies always include a requirement that the injury suffered be caused "accidentally" or "by accident" or some similar phrase. Many questions arise concerning the true meaning of this word, and it is difficult to define the word so as to include the innumerable mishaps which occur in the daily course of human life. It is equally difficult to decide whether a mishap comes within the risk taken, or the exceptions made, by the terms of a particular policy: this is in essence a matter of causation. In general terms, the courts have been generous to assureds and have held that the assured may claim when an accidental event gives rise to illness or when illness gives rise to an accidental event, as in both cases the loss is the result of "accident" rather than sickness. Appropriate wording may, however, restrict the causation principle and may allow the assured to recover only where accident was the sole or independent cause of the loss.

One of the most litigated issues in this area has been the meaning of the word "accident". The Workmen's Compensation Acts, which were repealed in 1947, conferred upon employees a cause of action in respect of "injury by accident" arising in the course of employment. Such actions were to be determined by

---

[213] Mocatta J. in *Scragg v UK Temperance* [1976] 2 Lloyd's Rep. 227.
[214] *Wood v Dwarris* (1856) 11 Ex. 493; *Wheelton v Hardisty* (1858) 8 E. & B. 232.
[215] *Anstey v British Natural Premium Life* (1908) 99 L.T. 765.
[216] *Re General Provincial Ex p. Daintree* (1870) 18 W.R. 396.
[217] *Anctil v Manufacturers Life* [1899] A.C. 604.
[218] *Seligman v Eagle Insurance* [1917] Ch. 519.

arbitration, and were intended to afford a cheap and speedy method of compensating employees for industrial injuries. The term "accident" was considered in a series of cases brought under the Act, and was defined by the House of Lords in *Fenton v Thorley*[219] as "denoting an unlooked-for mishap or an untoward event which is not expected or designed" and "any unexpected personal injury. . . from any unlooked-for mishap or occurrence".[220] It was thus held in *Brintons v Turvey*[221] that a workman who was employed to sort wool and who became infected by anthrax by a bacillus passing from the wool to his eye, had died from an "injury by accident". However, it has now been decided by the Court of Appeal in *De Souza v Home and Overseas Co Ltd*[222] that little weight should be given to the decisions under the Workmen's Compensation Acts, for two reasons: decisions under those Acts were intended to further the objectives of the Acts and were thus unreliable in relation to the meaning of words in private contracts; and the legislation covered industrial diseases as well as injuries, whereas accident policies generally exclude diseases, so that authorities which treated as "accidents" exposures to disease ought to be disregarded.

Mustill L.J. in *De Souza* laid down the general definition of "accident" for insurance purposes[223]:

"The word 'accident' involves the idea of something fortuitous and unexpected, as opposed to something proceeding from natural causes and injury caused by accident is to be regarded as the antithesis to bodily infirmity by disease in the ordinary course of events."

The requirement of fortuity. The requirement of fortuity may be satisfied either **18–041** by the nature of the cause of the injury or by the nature of the result. In *De Souza*, the Court of Appeal adopted verbatim the analysis in *Welford on Accident Insurance* on the question of fortuity, and held that there is an injury by accident in four situations:

(1) "Where the injury is the natural result of a fortuitous and unexpected cause, as, for instance, where the assured is run over by a train,[224] or thrown from his horse while hunting,[225] or injured by a fall, whether through slipping on a step[226] or otherwise[227] or where the assured drinks poison by mistake,[228] or is suffocated by the smoke of a house on fire[229] or by an escape of gas,[230] or is drowned while bathing.[231] In this case the

---

[219] *Fenton v Thorley* [1903] A.C. 433.

[220] *Fenton v Thorley* [1903] A.C. 433 at 448 (Lord Macnaghten), 451 (Lord Shand).

[221] *Brintons v Turvey* [1905] A.C. 230.

[222] *De Souza v Home and Overseas Co Ltd* [1995] L.R.L.R. 453.

[223] *De Souza v Home and Overseas Co Ltd* [1995] L.R.L.R. 453 at 458.

[224] *Lawrence v Accidental Insurance* (1881) 7 QBD 216; *Cornish v Accident Insurance Co* (1889) 23 QBD 453.

[225] *Re Etherington and Lancashire and Yorkshire Accident Insurance* [1909] 1 K.B. 591.

[226] *Theobold v Railway Passengers Assurance Co* (1854) 10 Exch. 45.

[227] *Fitton v Accidental Death Co* (1864) 17 C.B.N.S. 122; *Isitt v Railway Passengers Association* (1889) 22 QBD 504. If a man walks and stumbles, thus spraining his ankle, the injury is accidental for while he intends to walk he does not intend to stumble: *Re Scarr and General Accident* [1905] 1 K.B. 387 at 394, per Bray J.

[228] *Cole v Accident Insurance Co Ltd* (1889) 61 L.T. 227, although here the policy excluded death by poison.

[229] *Trew v Railway Passengers Assurance Co* (1861) 6 H. & N. 839 at 844, per Cockburn C.J.

[230] *Re United London and Scottish Insurance Co* [1915] 2 Ch. 167.

[231] *Trew v Railway Passengers Assurance Co* (1861) 6 H. & N. 839; *Reynolds v Accidental Insurance* (1870) 22 L.T. 820.

element of accident manifests itself in the cause of the injury." To this list may be added, reacting adversely to medical treatment,[232] or choking on aspirated food while drunk.[233]

(2) "Where the injury is the fortuitous or unexpected result of a natural cause, as, for instance, where a person lifts a heavy burden in the ordinary course of business and injures his spine,[234] or stoops down to pick up a marble and breaks a ligament in his knee,[235] or scratches his leg with a nail while putting on a stocking,[236] or ruptures himself whilst playing golf. In this case the element of accident manifests itself, not in the cause, but in the result."

(3) Where the injury is the result of the intervention of a third person, the accident being the act of that person.

(4) Where the injury is the result of the assured's own activities, provided that the injury is not the natural and direct cause of an act deliberately done by the assured as in such a case the assured must he taken to intend the natural consequences of his activities.

Category (2) may be illustrated by *Hamlyn v Crown Accidental Insurance Co*,[237] where the assured bent down to pick up a marble which had been dropped on the floor. In the process he dislocated his cartilage. The Court of Appeal held that there had been an accident within the meaning of the policy, since the event was unexpected and unforeseen, and was not such as might be considered the natural consequence of the act of bending down. This decision was followed in *Voison v Royal Insurance Co of Canada*,[238] in which the assured suffered spinal injuries as the result of moving while lying in an unusual position: the injury was accidental as it was unforeseen, unintended and unusual. By contrast, in *Sinclair v Maritime Passengers' Assurance Co*[239] the assured, the master of a vessel, was insured against personal injury or death resulting from any "accident". He died of sunstroke incurred while commanding the vessel on a river in India. It was held that his personal representatives could not recover on the policy.[240] Cockburn C.J., speaking of the distinction between accidental death and death from natural causes, said[241]:

"If, from the effects of ordinary exposure to the elements, such as is common in the course of navigation, a mariner should catch cold and die, such death would not be accidental; although if, being obliged by shipwreck or other disasters to quit the ship and take to the sea in an open boat, he remained exposed to wet and cold for some time, and death ensued therefrom, the death might properly be held to be the result of accident."

---

[232] *Groves v AMP Fire & General Insurance Co (NZ) Ltd* [1990] 2 N.Z.L.R. 408.

[233] *Tracy-Gould v Maritime Life Assurance Co* 89 D.L.R. (4th) 726 (1992). If the drunkenness was self-induced, recovery might be denied on that ground: see the discussion below of *Dhak v Insurance Co of North America (UK) Ltd* [1996] 1 Lloyd's Rep. 632.

[234] *Martin v Trarellers' Insurance Co* (1859) 1 F & F 505.

[235] *Hamlyn v Crown Accident Insurance Co* [1893] 1 Q.B. 750: the Court of Appeal held that the injury was accidental as the assured did not intend to get into such a position that he might wrench his knee.

[236] *Mardorf v Accident Insurance Co Ltd* [1903] 1 K.B. 584.

[237] *Hamlyn v Crown Accidental Insurance Co* (1893) 68 L.T. 701.

[238] *Voison v Royal Insurance Co of Canada* 53 D.L.R. (4th) 299 (1989).

[239] *Sinclair v Maritime Passengers' Assurance Co* (1861) 3 E. & E. 478.

[240] See also *De Souza v Home and Overseas Insurance Co Ltd* [1995] L.R.L.R. 453.

[241] *Sinclair* (1861) 3 E. & E. 478 at 485.

This decision was followed by the Court of Appeal in *De Souza v Home and Overseas Insurance Co Ltd*.[242] Here, a travel policy was obtained to cover Mr and Mrs De Souza for a holiday in Torremelinos. The policy was applicable "if the insured person shall sustain accidental bodily injury caused solely by outward violent and visible means". On death, the sum of £15,000 was payable. Mr De Souza died during the course of the holiday, his death being attributed to heatstroke, in that he had dehydrated as a result of excessive exposure to the sun and had suffered cardio-respiratory arrest. The insurers argued that Mr De Souza's death was not accidental. The Court, relying in particular on *Sinclair*, held that the circumstances of Mr De Souza's death could not be regarded as accidental. The Court of Appeal further held that Mr De Souza had not suffered any "injury", as it was simply the case that he had become ill and had died. It would seem to follow from this that, unless the assured can point to an event which has caused him injury, he cannot recover under an accident policy.

Accident excludes disease. It follows from the above principles that a disease cannot be classified as an accident. Although disease proximately caused by an accident will be covered by a personal accident policy, it is well established that the word "accident" does not include disease and other natural causes, and implies that intervention of some cause which is brought into operation by chance and which can be described as fortuitous. The matter was put thus by Mustill L.J. in *De Souza v Home & Overseas*[243]:   **18–042**

"An injury is not caused by an accident when it is the natural result of a natural cause as, for instance, where a person is exposed in the ordinary course of his business to the heat of a tropical sun and in consequence suffers from heatstroke,[244] or where a person with a weak heart injures it by running to catch a train,[245] or by some other intentional act involving violent physical exertion.[246] In this case the element of accident is broadly speaking absent, since the cause is one which comes into operation in the ordinary course of events, and is calculated, within the ordinary experience of mankind, to produce the result which it has in fact produced. In considering whether an injury is caused by accident, it is necessary to take into consideration the circumstances in which the injury is received."

Thus, there is no accident where the injury results from natural cause without the intervention of any fortuitous event, and where the injury results from a latent disease. In *Weyerhauser v Evans*[247] it was held that an assured who suffered septicaemia following the accidental piercing of a pimple had not died as the result of any accident, as the pimple itself was not an accident and there was no evidence that the pimple had been pierced by accident.

Accident limited to particular activities and purposes. An accident policy may provide cover for the assured only where the assured was, at the time of the accident, engaged in an activity specified by the policy or for a particular purpose   **18–043**

---

[242] *De Souza v Home and Overseas Insurance Co Ltd* [1995] L.R.L.R. 453.

[243] *De Souza v Home and Overseas Insurance Co Ltd* [1995] L.R.L.R. 453. See also *Re Deep Vein Thrombosis Litigation* [2006] 1 Lloyd's Rep. 231.

[244] *Sinclair v Maritime Passengers Assurance* (1861) 3 E. & E. 478.

[245] See *Appel v Aetna Life* 86 App. Div. Rep. S.C.N.Y. 83 (1903), approved by Bray J. in *Re Scarr & General Accident* [1905] 1 K.B. 387.

[246] *Re Scarr & General Accident* [1905] 1 K.B. 387. Here there was held to be nothing accidental in the assured pushing and pulling a drunken man from his premises, even though unknown to the assured his heart was in a weak condition, and he died from the exertion.

[247] *Weyerhauser v Evans* (1932) 43 Ll. L.R. 62.

specified by the policy. If the assured's intention is mixed, the question for the court is to isolate the predominant purpose: if the predominant purpose is insured, the assured may recover,[248] although if a predominant purpose cannot be found then the assured will be unable to recover if any one of the purposes was an excluded peril.[249]

In *Theobald v Railway Passengers' Assurance*[250] the cover was limited to railway accidents. Cover may also be restricted to injuries sustained by the assured in the discharge of his duty. This will not be confined to his ordinary everyday duties. Thus a signalman, so insured, was held to be covered when he was injured trying to stop a train, one of the carriages of which was broken.[251]

18–044   **Pre-existing disability.** Accident policies often contain an exclusion of liability where the death of or injury to the life assured is caused by a pre-existing disability.[252] In any event, the policy is likely to be voidable if such disability has not been disclosed in the proposal form. However, the ambit of utmost good faith is, as regards consumer contracts, in practice limited to facts which the assured ought to have known and answers given to the best of the assured's knowledge and belief, so that misrepresentation or failure to disclose relating to a pre-existing disease which had not given obvious symptoms will not constitute a breach of duty.

Where there is an express exclusion, on its proper construction it may not be absolute and may apply only to any disease or condition in respect of which the assured had received treatment prior to the inception of the policy. This was the terminology used in *Cook v Financial Insurance Co Ltd*,[253] in which the assured collapsed while on a training run in September 1992. He was diagnosed as suffering from a mild infection. In October 1992, the assured completed a proposal form for disability insurance, and paid the premium on the same day. The policy excluded: "any sickness, disease, condition or injury for which an insured person received advice, treatment or counselling from any registered medical practitioner during the 12 months preceding the commencement date." The following day, the assured was examined by a cardiologist who diagnosed angina. The House of Lords, by a four-to-one majority, held that the exclusion was inapplicable. The assured had not received advice, treatment or counselling for angina before October 15, 1992 as the disease had not, at that point, been diagnosed. Lord Lloyd, speaking for the majority, ruled that a disease could not be said to have been treated until it had been diagnosed and, in any event, the inhaler and the antibiotic were inappropriate treatments for angina. The House of Lords further held that the policy exclusion did not apply to treatment or advice which related to symptoms which had not been diagnosed. The policy required

---

[248] *Caple v Sewell* [2002] Lloyd's Rep. I.R. 627.

[249] *Passmore v Vulcan Boiler & General Insurance Co Ltd* (1936) 54 Ll. L.R. 92; *Killick v Rendal* [2000] Lloyd's Rep. I.R. 581. By contrast, if none of the purposes is actually excluded, but simply uninsured, then the assured can recover as long as one of the purposes was an insured purpose. This follows from the ordinary rules relating to losses proximately arising from two or more causes.

[250] *Theobald v Railway Passengers' Assurance* (1854) 10 Exch. 45 at 57, 58.

[251] *Pugh v LB & SC Railway* [1896] 2 Q.R. 248. See also *Wilkinson v Downton* [1897] 2 Q.B. 57.

[252] As in *Southampton Leisure Holdings Plc v Avon Insurance Plc* [2004] EWHC 571 (QB), where a policy taken out in respect of a professional footballer confined coverage to accidental bodily injury occurring solely and independently of any other cause. The player was unable to recover for an injury which ended his career, as the injury was found to be partly the result of an earlier injury.

[253] *Cook v Financial Insurance Co Ltd* [1999] Lloyd's Rep. I.R. 1.

advice, treatment or counselling for a "condition", and this was something more than symptoms which might indicate any one of a number of diseases or indeed no disease at all.

An exclusion in respect of pre-existing disabilities may, if appropriate wording is used, be construed as applying to pre-existing disabilities that would normally be expected of a person in the assured's position. Thus where a policy on a footballer excluded "Permanent Total Disablement attributable either directly or indirectly to arthritic or other degenerative conditions in joints, bones, muscles, tendons or ligaments", and the assured suffered a training ground injury, it was held that a degenerative condition of the lower spine that affected some 75 per cent of the population in general and was a particular problem for top-class footballers would nevertheless operate to exclude the liability of the insurers if it was a contributory cause of the footballer's career coming to an end.[254]

Violent, external and visible means

General meaning. The usual form of wording of a personal accident policy provides cover in the event of injury caused by "violent, accidental, external and visible means". Despite the comment of Cozens-Hardy M.R. in 1915[255] that "It seems to me seriously open to doubt whether that does not exempt the company upon every occasion which it is likely to occur" the phrase has remained in widespread use. In recent years it has been given a restricted meaning. In *De Souza v Home and Overseas Insurance Co Ltd*,[256] the policy covered the assured where he sustained "accidental bodily injury caused solely and directly by outward violent and visible means". The assured died of sunstroke. The Court of Appeal held that the insuring clause had to be read as a whole so that, while the existence of accidental bodily injury was a condition precedent to any claim, the remaining words were purely explanatory and did not impose a further requirement. Thus the words "by violent, external and visible means" add little, if anything, to an accident policy and were accordingly criticised by the Court of Appeal in *De Souza*.

18–045

"Violent". The notion of violence in the context of personal accident policies is a very wide one. It is not limited to the situation where another person does violence to the assured, and it has been said that the word is used simply as the antithesis of "without any violence at all".[257] "Violent means" include any external, impersonal cause, such as drowning,[258] or the inhalation of gas.[259] Thus "violent" does not necessarily imply actual violence, as where the assured is bitten by a dog.[260] The heat of the sun is not, therefore, "violent".[261] As is illustrated by cases such as *Hamlyn v Crown Accidental Insurance Co*[262] and *Re*

18–046

---

[254] *Blackburn Rovers Football & Athletic Club Plc v Avon Insurance Plc* [2005] Lloyd's Rep. I.R. 447 (preliminary issue); *Blackburn Rovers Football and Athletic Club Plc v Avon Insurance Plc* [2007] Lloyd's Rep. I.R. 1 (the trial, where Dobbs J. found that a cause of the injury had been the degenerative condition and that the assured could not recover).

[255] *Re United London and Scottish Insurance Co* [1915] 2 Ch. 167 at 170.

[256] *De Souza v Home and Overseas Insurance Co Ltd* [1995] L.R.L.R. 453.

[257] *Sinclair v Maritime Passengers' Assurance Co* (1861) 3 E. & E. 478.

[258] *Trew v Railway Passengers' Assurance* (1861) 6 H. & N. 839; *Reynolds v Accidental Insurance* (1870) 22 L.T. 820.

[259] *Re United London & Scottish Insurance, Brown's Claim* [1915] 2 Ch. 167.

[260] See Wright J. in *Mardorf v Accident Insurance* [1903] 1 K.B. 584 at 588.

[261] *De Souza v Home and Overseas Insurance Co Ltd* [1995] L.R.L.R. 453.

[262] *Hamlyn v Crown Accidental Insurance Co* [1893] 1 Q.B. 750.

Scott and General Accident Insurance Corp,[263] there will be violence for these purposes where the injury arises from any extra or unusual exertion on the part of the assured. The element of violence will obviously be present where the injury is inflicted by a third party or by some natural phenomenon,[264] since there could otherwise be no effect upon the body of the assured.

18–047   *"External"*. It is the means of causing the injury which must be external, rather than the injury itself. Thus, a rupture or other internal injury is quite capable of falling within the ambit of a personal accident policy.[265] Given this distinction, it appears that the word "external" in these policies merely serves to reiterate the general principle that the injury must not be attributable to natural causes.[266] It will therefore be obvious that a given type of injury may fall within or without the policy according to the event which caused it, and it is this cause which must always be examined.

18–048   *"Visible"*. It is probable that this word adds nothing to the policy coverage, since every external cause must also be visible. It appears to be included merely for purposes of emphasis.

Relevance of the assured's conduct

18–049   *Scope of "accident"*. An injury brought about by the conduct of the assured may still be considered to have been an "accident" within the meaning of a personal accident policy. It is here that the distinction between an accidental result and an accidental means must be most clearly borne in mind. Save in the wholly exceptional case where the assured inflicts injury upon himself for the purpose of making a claim, the result of the assured's behaviour will hardly ever be intended; but the means by which the injury is arrived at may well have been deliberate. Thus, it is likely that an assured who wilfully exposes himself to the risk of serious injury will be held not to have been injured "by accident".[267] It appears, though, that the notion of wilful exposure may be given a somewhat restricted construction. In *Marcel Beller Ltd v Hayden*,[268] the claimant company insured the life of a key employee. He attempted to drive home one night after consuming so much alcohol that, according to the medical evidence, he would have been unable to steer a car with any degree of certainty. He was killed after losing control of the car and crashing through some railings. It was nevertheless held that his death was an "accident" for the purposes of the policy, though it may be observed that the learned judge was still able to find for the insurers as there was in the policy an exception applying where the death was caused by the assured's own criminal act.

The dicta in *Marcel Beller* should, however, be regarded with some care in the light of more recent authority. In *De Souza v Home and Overseas Insurance Co*

---

[263] *Re Scott and General Accident Insurance Corp* [1905] 1 K.B. 387.

[264] E.g. exposure to light: *Aguilar v London Life Insurance Co* 70 D.L.R. (4th) 510 (1990). But contrast *De Souza*, where it was held that the Mediterranean sun could not be described as per se "violent".

[265] As in *Aguilar v London Life Insurance Co* 70 D.L.R. (4th) 510 (1990).

[266] As in *De Souza*, where the sun, while doubtless an "outward" event, had not given rise to accidental injury. See also *Hamlyn v Crown Accidental Insurance* [1893] 1 Q.B. 750 at 754, per Lopes L.J.

[267] *Shaw v Robberds* (1837) 6 Ad. & El. 75; *Re Scarr and General Accident Insurance Corp* [1905] 1 K.B. 387.

[268] *Marcel Beller Ltd v Hayden* [1978] 1 Lloyd's Rep. 472.

Ltd,[269] the Court of Appeal indicated that a deliberate act of the assured directly caused death or injury as the act's natural consequence could not be regarded as an accident. In the words of Mustill L.J.:

"A man must be taken to intend the ordinary consequences of his acts, and the fact that he did not foresee the particular consequence or expect the particular injury does not make the injury accidental if, in the circumstances, it was the natural and direct consequence of what he did, without the intervention of any fortuitous cause."

This comment was amplified by the Court of Appeal in *Dhak v Insurance Company of North America (UK) Ltd.*[270] Here, the deceased was the assured under a personal accident policy under which benefits were payable in respect of "bodily injury resulting in death or injury within 12 months of the accident occurring during the period of insurance and caused directly or indirectly by the accident". The deceased, a hospital ward sister, had suffered a severe back injury as the result of lifting a patient, and found alcohol to be a means of controlling the pain. The deceased died from asphyxiation due to vomiting while under the influence of alcohol. The Court held that four matters had to be considered:

(1) Did the assured intend to inflict some bodily injury upon herself?
(2) Did the assured take a calculated risk that she might sustain bodily injury if she continued with the course of conduct in question?
(3) Was the bodily injury the direct and natural cause of the assured's actions?
(4) Did some fortuitous cause intervene?

In the instant case, the deceased had plainly not intended to inflict the injuries upon herself, but the Court was of the view that she had taken a calculated risk of bodily injury, a conclusion reinforced given her medical knowledge, and also that her drunkenness directly resulted in death. In the absence of some fortuity, the injuries could not be regarded as accidental and the claim had to fail. It might be thought that this decision is unduly harsh, particularly as the Court of Appeal recognised that other jurisdictions permitted recovery in these circumstances. However, it may be that in many other situations a deliberate course of conduct will lead to an intervening fortuitous event which may of itself be regarded as the accident. In *Morley v United Friendly Insurance Plc*,[271] a claim was upheld under an accident policy where the assured jumped onto the bumper of a moving car and fell off: the accident appears to have been regarded as the falling off, thereby breaking the chain of causation from the jump itself, even though injury was a natural consequence of the conduct. Indeed, the only question which the Court regarded as being of any difficulty was whether the policy's exclusion of "wilful exposure to needless risks" precluded recovery, a question answered in the negative.

An exception to this general principle is found where the act is done for the purpose of avoiding some imminent danger, such as jumping from the window of a burning house,[272] or, possibly, where it is done in an effort to rescue another person from imminent danger.[273] Cases of this latter kind are perhaps best

---

[269] *De Souza v Home and Overseas Insurance Co Ltd* [1995] L.R.L.R. 453.
[270] *Dhak v Insurance Company of North America (UK) Ltd* [1996] 1 Lloyd's Rep. 632. Cf. *Tracey-Gould v Maritime Life Assurance Co* 89 D.L.R. (4th) 726 (1992).
[271] *Morley v United Friendly Insurance Plc* [1993] 1 Lloyd's Rep. 490.
[272] *McLennan v Segar* [1917] 2 K.B. 325.
[273] *Pugh v London, Brighton and South Coast Ry* [1896] 2 Q.B. 248.

explained as resting on a notion of public policy that such behaviour is to be encouraged,[274] or even as an attempt at mitigation. This exception may underlie the otherwise difficult decision of the Court of Session in *Connelly v New Hampshire Insurance Co*[275] This was a claim brought by a fireman, who had suffered post-traumatic stress disorder following his attendance at two fires where he had witnessed particularly gruelling scenes. The Court of Session, distinguishing *De Souza* and *Dhak*, held that while the assured had deliberately attended the fires, it was not his intention to suffer injury nor was injury the natural and probable consequence of his loss, and, accordingly, it could be said that his injury was accidental. The Court of Session's findings on the assured's intentions and on the limited natural or probable consequences of his attendance at the fire were enough to distinguish the English authorities, although it is noteworthy that counsel for the assured was prepared to ask the Court to refuse to follow those cases; the Court ultimately decided that this drastic step was not necessary to justify the result.

18–050 *Wilful exposure to risk.* Accident policies frequently contain express conditions against wilful or voluntary exposure to risk. These words add little to the common law. In *Sangster v General Accident*,[276] the Court of Session ruled that an assured who drowned while bathing alone in a loch on a cold spring evening had not wilfully exposed himself to risk, as what was required was an act by the assured "so grossly imprudent as to infer utter recklessness of his own safety". Equally, the exception does not apply merely because one travels[277] in a vehicle along the road,[278] or crosses the street. By contrast, in *Cornish v Accident Insurance*[279] the assured had crossed a main line and waited for one train to pass, and was re-crossing when a second train killed him. There was no crossing at the place and nothing to obstruct his view. The assured's death was held to fall within an exception of "exposure of the insured to obvious risk of injury". The exception will also apply to an assured who takes a short cut along a railway line,[280] or goes too near the edge of a cliff whilst gathering flowers and falls over.[281]

18–051 *Negligence.* The assured is not disqualified from recovering on the ground that he has himself caused the injury where his act is merely negligent rather than a wilful exposure to danger. In fact, one of the commonest causes of accidents is negligence, and an accident policy applies, excepted perils apart, whether the injury is caused by the negligent act of the assured himself or of a third party.[282] An injury to the assured otherwise falling within an exception to the policy will do so even though it is caused by his negligence or mistake, unless the express words of the exception clearly read otherwise. In *Cole v Accident Insurance*

---

[274] Compare cases such as *Baker v TE Hopkins* [1958] 1 W.L.R. 31, where rescuers have been held entitled to recover in tort from those who have created the dangerous situation.

[275] *Connelly v New Hampshire Insurance Co* 1997 S.L.T. 1341.

[276] *Sangster v General Accident* (1896) 24 R. 56. See also *Morley v United Friendly Insurance Plc* [1993] 1 Lloyd's Rep. 490.

[277] But it would appear to be negligent to travel as a passenger in a car knowing that the driver is unfit to drive owing to the consumption of intoxicating liquor: *Owens v Brimmel* [1976] 3 All E.R. 765.

[278] *Re United London & Scottish Insurance* [1915] 2 Ch. 167.

[279] *Cornish v Accident Insurance* (1889) 23 QBD 453.

[280] *Lovell v Accident Insurance* (1875) 39 J.P.J. 293.

[281] *Walker v Railway Passengers' Assurance* (1910) 129 L.T. 64.

[282] Lord M'Laren in *Cildero v Scottish Accident* (1892) 19 R. (Ct of Sess) 355 at 363.

Co^{283} the assured drank poison from a bottle under the impression that it was medicine, and died. The policy excepted "poison or intentional self-injury" and it was held that his representatives could not recover under the policy. Again, where in the policy there was a clause excepting liability where the injury was caused by "anything . . . inhaled", and the assured accidentally inhaled coal gas, it was held that the injury was within the exception, which could not be read as being limited to "anything voluntarily inhaled".[284]

Act or omission of a third party. There is no difficulty where the assured suffers **18–052** injury through the negligence or inadvertence of a third party. In such a case there is, by any possible standard, an "accident" and it is clear that the assured will be able to recover. It is irrelevant to this whether or not the conduct of the third party amounts to a civil wrong or even to criminal negligence. The difficult cases in this area occur where the third party deliberately inflicts the injury on the assured. In these cases there is, from the point of view of the third party, no "accident", but it is submitted that this is irrelevant as between insurer and assured. So far as the assured is concerned, the chain of events is accidental, and this is sufficient to satisfy the terms of the policy.[285]

Influence of liquor. Another common exception excludes injuries while the **18–053** assured is under the influence of liquor. It does not matter whether or not the assured's drunkenness caused the accident: it is enough for the insurers, relying on this exception, to show that the assured was under the influence of liquor when he received the injury.[286] The expression "under the influence of liquor" in accident policies has been held to refer to circumstances where "a man's conduct is banefully influenced by the liquor he has drunk"[287] or where he is "under such influence of intoxicating liquor as disturbs the balance of a man's mind or the intelligent exercise of his faculties".[288]

Disablement

Meaning of "disablement". Accident policies are commonly expressed to **18–054** provide cover in the event of the "death or disablement" of the assured. The meaning of the term "disablement" has sometimes given rise to difficulty although in most cases it will not be necessary to make a once-and-for-all determination of this question as the insurer can normally insist upon periodic health checks.

Some policies respond only where the assured is unable to carry on any occupation whatsoever or to undertake gainful employment, whereas others are more widely drafted and allow the assured to recover if he is unable to carry on his own previous occupation. The usual tendency of the courts is to construe the former type of wording in a narrow fashion and to hold that unless the wording is clear the assured is entitled to recover where he is no longer able to carry on his own previous occupation.[289] If a clause is construed as applying to the

[283] *Cole v Accident Insurance Co* (1889) 61 L.T. 227. See also *Cornish v Accident Insurance Co* (1889) 23 QBD 453.
[284] *Re United London & Scottish Insurance* [1915] 2 Ch. 167.
[285] *Trim v Kelly* [1914] A.C. 667. Cf. *Hawley v Luminar Leisure Plc* [2006] EWCA Civ 18.
[286] *Mair v Railway Passengers' Assurance* (1877) 37 L.T. 356: *Louden v British Merchants Inc* [1961] 1 W.L.R. 798.
[287] *MacRobbie v Accident Assurance* (1886) 23 S.L.R. 391.
[288] *Mair v Railway Passengers' Assurance* (1877) 37 L.T. 356.
[289] *Sargent v GRE (UK) Ltd* [2000] Lloyd's Rep. I.R. 77.

assured's own previous occupation, it is necessary to determine what constitutes carrying on that occupation. In *Johnson v IGI Insurance Co Ltd*[290] the clause restricted recovery to the case in which the assured was unable to undertake "similar gainful employment": it was there held that a taxi driver who was injured in an accident and thereby rendered unable to drive was not capable of similar gainful employment simply because he remained able to derive an income from renting his taxis to other drivers. In *Hooper v Accidental Death Insurance Co*[291] a policy which granted recovery where the assured was unable to "follow usual business or occupation" was read as meaning that the assured was entitled to be paid if he was preventing from following a substantial part of his occupation: the policy was not to be read as applying only where the assured was entirely unable to perform any part of his business or occupation since, if the policy was to be so restricted, it should expressly say so. By contrast, in *Howells v IGI Insurance*[292] a professional footballer who was forced by injury to drop from the Premier League to a lower division and reserve football was held not to have been permanently disabled from carrying on his "occupation" as a footballer.

Where the policy applies only in the situation in which the assured is unable to carry on any occupation or paid employment whatsoever, it is necessary to define exactly what constitutes an occupation or paid employment. In *Pocock v Century Insurance Co Ltd*[293] the policy stated that cover attached where the assured suffered an "inability to attend to business of any kind". The assured, a travelling buyer, was injured in an accident and was no longer able to drive but remained able to carry out different functions for his employer on a part-time basis: the court ruled that, if an assured is restricted to a minor contribution, he no longer has the ability to attend to his business. In *Walton v Airtours Plc*[294] it was held that a pilot was unable to carry on any occupation even though he could undertake temporary employment: the term "occupation" was held to imply full-time employment with an element of continuity rather than sporadic part-time work, or work that could not be carried out without structured support. It is not sufficient, however, for the assured to show that he was incapable of carrying out some forms of work but not others. In *McGeown v Direct Travel Insurance*[295] the assured's travel policy provided cover against "permanent physical disability which prevents you from doing any paid work (if you are not in paid work we will provide the same cover for any permanent disability which prevents you from doing all your usual activities)—£50,000." The assured was injured in a road accident in Turkey and suffered severe injuries that prevented her from carrying on one of her usual activities: horse-riding. The Court of Appeal held that the wording was not ambiguous and was to be construed as meaning that cover was granted only where the assured was unable to carry on any substantial activity: this followed from a reading of the policy as a whole (which applied only to catastrophic events) and from reading the insuring clause as a whole (which referred back to "any" paid work). Accordingly, the clause was not satisfied by picking out one activity to see whether the assured was able to carry it out, and that it was necessary to refer back to the trial judge the question whether the assured's condition met the test laid down by the clause. The Court

---

[290] *Johnson v IGI Insurance Co Ltd* [1997] 6 C.L. 358.
[291] *Hooper v Accidental Death Insurance Co* (1860) 3 H. & N. 546.
[292] *Howells v IGI Insurance* [2003] Lloyd's Rep. I.R. 803.
[293] *Pocock v Century Insurance Co Ltd* [1960] 2 Lloyd's Rep. 150.
[294] *Walton v Airtours Plc* [2004] Lloyds Rep. I.R. 97.
[295] *McGeown v Direct Travel Insurance* [2004] Lloyd's Rep. I.R. 599.

of Appeal did comment, however, that whether the claimant was unable to carry on all of her usual activities was a matter of degree, and that if the assured was unable to carry on the normal incidents of living, including "reasonable mobility, coping with domestic chores and personal care" then there would be a strong indication that the assured could no longer pursue all of her usual activities.

Causation. The mere fact that there has been an accident and the assured has thereafter become unfit for work does not automatically mean that there is a causal link between the accident and the assured's inability to work. The assured's inability to work must be based on objective medical evidence[296] and not the assured's own perception of the nature of his incapacity.[297]   **18–055**

Loss of sight. Complete loss of sight is another particular peril sometimes specifically insured against. This may occur where a one-eyed man loses his remaining eye in an accident.[298] In a Canadian case it was held that the assured had "irrevocably lost" the "entire sight of one eye" so as to recover for it under a policy when he had lost all useful sight of the eye, although still able to distinguish light from darkness and to "see a shadow" if an object was placed close to his injured eye.[299]   **18–056**

Mitigation of loss: medical treatment. Even where the assured can demonstrate that he is disabled,[300] a further question arises as to whether the assured can be obliged to mitigate his loss. In *Porter v NEL*[301] the Scottish courts ruled that the assured is entitled to recover for total and permanent disability rendering him unfit to carry on his trade or profession despite the facts that: (a) he has refused to undergo an operation which might relieve the problem; or (b) he is fit for other forms of work. The court held as to (a) that an assured cannot be required to undergo medical treatment in respect of which success is not guaranteed and that if this is required by the insurer the policy must so specify, and as to (b) that a general allegation that the assured is fit for some (unspecified) work cannot be a defence unless it can be shown that there is an alternative occupation open to the assured in which he has reasonable prospects of employment.   **18–057**

Return of policy benefits. In *Alder v Moore*[302] a group personal accident policy for professional football players provided that no claim for permanent total disablement should be paid unless the claimant signed a declaration that he would not play professionally in the future "and that in the event of infringement of this condition he will be subject to a penalty of the amount paid . . . " The Court of Appeal (Devlin L.J. dissenting) held that such repayment was to be regarded as a payment by way of damages and not a penalty, and was therefore enforceable.   **18–058**

Bodily injury. It is usual for the policy to require an accident to manifest itself as "bodily injury" to the assured. The most obvious form of bodily injury is   **18–059**

---

[296] *Cathay Pacific Airways Ltd v National Life & General Assurance Co Ltd* [1966] 2 Lloyd's Rep. 179.
[297] *Haghiran v Allied Dunbar Insurance* [2001] 1 All E.R. (Comm) 97.
[298] *Bawden v London, Edinburgh & Glasgow Insurance* [1892] 2 Q.B. 534.
[299] *Shaw v Globe Indemnity* [1921] 1 W.W.R. 332 British Columbia CA.
[300] Particular sympathy has been shown by the courts in personal accident cases: see *Napier v UNUM Ltd* [1996] 2 Lloyd's Rep. 550.
[301] *Porter v NEL* Unreported, 1992.
[302] *Alder v Moore* [1960] 2 Lloyd's Rep. 325.

external trauma causing physical injury, but the phrase is not limited to injury to the exterior of the body: the term "bodily injury", when used in a personal accident policy, is not limited to lesions, abrasions or broken bones.[303] Nor is it essential that there should be an external mark of injury on the assured's body.[304] Thus the introduction of some foreign agent into the assured's body which causes injury or death remains a bodily injury. On this basis bodily injury has been held to include asphyxia following the ingestion of alcohol,[305] food [306] or drugs,[307] and drowning.[308] On the other hand, a disease developed in the body by natural causes is not "bodily injury"[309] for these purposes, although a disease which is capable of occurring naturally may still be "bodily injury" if it is in fact caused by accident.[310] Exposure to a potentially harmful substance is not of itself injury; there is only injury at some later stage where the assured develops a disease caused by the exposure.[311]

More difficulty may be caused by the effects of mental grief or nervous shock, although in recent years the distinction between physical and mental injury has become increasingly blurred. In *McLoughlin v O'Brien*[312] the House of Lords paved the way for this development, by holding that the witness to an accident or its aftermath may, in certain circumstances, be entitled to proceed against the wrongdoer in tort, and subsequently in *Page v Smith*,[313] the House of Lords ruled that, whether the claim is for physical injury or nervous shock, the test for liability is foreseeability. This principle was applied by the Court of Session in *Connelly v New Hampshire Insurance Co*,[314] in which it was decided that the term "bodily injury" encompassed both physical and psychological injury, in that case post-traumatic stress disorder suffered by a fireman following his attendance at two harrowing incidents. It is unclear whether this ruling represents English law, in the light of the ruling of the House of Lords in *Rothwell v Chemical and Insulating Co Ltd*[315] that exposure to a harmful substance does not amount to bodily injury unless and until the organs of the body are affected, and the mere fear of such injury following exposure is not of itself injury.

18–060   **Causation.** The issues of causation which may arise in the context of personal accident policies are rather different from those commonly found in insurance law. In personal accident policies there are two issues. First, is the assured's death

---

[303] *Trew v Railway Passengers' Assurance Co* (1861) 6 H. & N. 839: *Re United London and Scottish Insurance Co* [1915] 2 Ch. 167.

[304] *Fitton v Accidental Death Insurance* (1864) 17 C.B.N.S. 122; *Hooper v Accidental Death Insurance* (1860) 5 H. & N. 546.

[305] *Dhak v Insurance Co of North America (UK) Ltd* [1996] 2 All E.R. 609.

[306] *Dhak v Insurance Co of North America (UK) Ltd* [1996] 2 All E.R. 609 at 616–617, where Neill L.J. gave the example of a peanut becoming lodged in the assured's windpipe.

[307] *Life and Casualty Insurance Co of Tennessee v Brown* 95 Ga. App. 354 (1957); *Johnson v Mutual of Omaha Insurance Co* 139 D.L.R. (3rd) 358 (1982).

[308] *Trew v Railway Passengers Assurance Co* (1861) 6 H. & N. 839.

[309] *De Souza v Home and Overseas Insurance Co Ltd* [1995] L.R.L.R. 453.

[310] See, e.g. *Mardorf v Accident Insurance Co* [1903] 1 K.B. 584; *Fitton v Accidental Death Insurance* (1864) 17 C.B.N.S. 122; *Isitt v Railway Passengers' Assurance Co* (1889) 22 QBD 504.

[311] *Dhak v Insurance Co of North America (UK) Ltd* [1996] 1 W.L.R. 936; *Bolton Metropolitan Borough Council v Municipal Mutual Insurance Ltd* [2007] Lloyd's Rep. I.R. 173; *Rothwell v Chemical and Insulating Co Ltd* [2008] 1 A.C. 28; *Durham v BAI (Run Off) Ltd* [2009] Lloyd's Rep. I.R. 295.

[312] *McLoughlin v O'Brien* [1982] 2 All E.R. 298.

[313] *Page v Smith* [1996] 1 A.C. 155.

[314] *Connelly v New Hampshire Insurance Co* 1997 S.L.T. 1341.

[315] *Rothwell v Chemical and Insulating Co Ltd* [2008] 1 A.C. 28.

or disablement the result of bodily injury? Secondly, is that injury proximately caused by an accident? It is only when both questions can be answered in the affirmative that the assured is entitled to recover on the policy. As appears above, it may also be necessary to consider the circumstances of the accident, since an accident brought about by the wrongful act of the assured may well not be covered.

Many of the problems in this area have arisen under accident policies which contained clauses excluding the insurer's liability if the injury arose from "natural disease or weakness", or some similar phrase.[316] Thus, in *Winspear v Accident Insurance Co*,[317] the assured suffered an epileptic fit while fording a stream. He fell into the water and drowned. The policy contained a clause of the kind under discussion, and the insurers relied upon it as a defence to the claim. However, the court held that the true cause of the death was the drowning, and, since this was clearly accidental, it followed that the insurers were liable. Similarly, in *Lawrence v Accident Insurance Co Ltd*,[318] the assured suffered a fit while standing on a railway platform. He fell on to the track, where he was run over by a train, and suffered injuries from which he died. Again the insurer's defence was rejected, the court holding, by analogy with *Winspear's* case, that the true cause of the death was being run over by the train rather than the fit. Of course, it might be said that decisions such as these are authorities only on their own particular facts, but they do illustrate the tendency of the courts in such cases to look only at the immediate cause and to refuse to look any further back in the chain of causation. However, it is instructive to compare with these cases the observations of Cockburn C.J. in *Sinclair v Maritime Passengers' Assurance Co*.[319] There it was assumed that a supervening event could be sufficient to change the true cause of the death from natural causes to accident. It is submitted that any apparent contradiction between these two approaches can be reconciled if it is remembered that in *Sinclair* the issue was whether the assured had brought himself within the policy coverage, whereas in the other two cases it was whether the insurers had brought themselves within the terms of an exception contained in the policy. In all three cases the answer to the relevant question was in the negative, but this produced different results according to the form of the question.

Effect of the assured's insolvency. In the event of the assured's insolvency, the   **18–061**
proceeds of a permanent disability policy accrue to the assured's trustee in bankrupcty and not to the assured personally. In *Cork v Rawlins*[320] it was held that an assured who became permanently disabled after his bankruptcy was not entitled to treat the proceeds of his life and permanent disability policies as his own, and that they vested in his trustee in bankruptcy. Such policies were to be regarded as assets forming part of his estate, and the proceed became payable because the assured was no longer able to work. The Court of Appeal noted that the common law did not treat personal damages for pain and suffering as forming part of a bankrupt's estate, but that the policy was not based on pain and suffering.

---

[316] This type of clause applies even if the assured was unaware of his earlier illness: *Cook v Financial Insurance Co* [1999] Lloyd's Rep. I.R. 1 (angina).

[317] *Winspear v Accident Insurance Co* (1880) 43 L.T. 459.

[318] *Lawrence v Accident Insurance Co Ltd* (1881) 45 L.T. 29.

[319] *Sinclair v Maritime Passengers' Assurance Co* (1861) 3 E. & E. 478 at 485.

[320] *Cork v Rawlins* [2001] Lloyd's Rep. I.R. 587.

CHAPTER 19

PROPERTY INSURANCE

1. INSURABLE INTEREST IN PROPERTY

The insurable interest requirement

19–001   *Goods.* There is no statute which requires that a policy on goods is to be supported by insurable interest in the assured, other than on goods involved in a marine adventure, which are governed by the Marine Insurance Act 1906. "Goods" and "merchandises" are indeed expressly excluded from the ambit of the Life Assurance Act 1774 by s.4. Before its repeal by the Gambling Act 2005 s.18 of the Gaming Act 1845 operated to ban insurance contracts under which the assured neither had an insurable interest, nor an expectation of acquiring such an interest, at the date of the inception of the policy. However, the effect of the replacement of this provision by s.335 of the 2005 Act is to remove the need for the assured to prove insurable interest at inception. The assured nevertheless remains under an obligation to prove his loss following the occurrence of the insured peril. If the assured cannot prove his loss, the common law principle of indemnity prevents recovery.

19–002   *Land and buildings.* Fundamental to any discussion of insurable interest in land and buildings is the determination of the question of whether the Life Assurance Act 1774 is applicable to policies on these classes of property. The significance of this question is threefold: (a) if the 1774 Act does apply, the assured must demonstrate insurable interest at the inception of the policy in accordance with s.1 in addition to showing some interest at the date of the loss in order to satisfy the common law indemnity principle; (b) s.3 of the 1774 Act restricts the assured's recovery to the amount of his interest, so that if the Act governs policies on land and buildings it follows that it is impossible for the assured to insure both his own full interest and the interest of any other person, as any recovery by the assured under the policy will be limited to an amount representing his own interest; and (c) s.2 requires the insertion into the policy of the names of all the persons interested in the insurance—there is no equivalent provision governing policies falling outside the 1774 Act which is capable of applying to land and buildings.[1]

At first sight it would seem that the Act ought to apply to such policies. In the first place, s.1 provides that it extends to insurance "on the life or lives of any person or persons, *or on any other event or events whatsoever*": it is difficult to see what meaning is to be given to the highlighted words if the Act does not extend beyond life and accident policies. Secondly, s.4 specifically excludes "ships, goods and merchandises", thereby indicating that the Act does extend to

---

[1] The Marine Insurance Act 1788 requires this formality to be complied with in the case of a policy on goods, but that Act is for the most part an irrelevance in practice.

non-life policies other than those mentioned. Support for the proposition that the Act does govern real property insurances is to be found in the decision of the Court of Appeal in *Re King*.[2] Nevertheless, the Court of Appeal in *Mark Rowlands Ltd v Berni Inns Ltd*,[3] a landlord and tenant case, boldly stated that the 1774 Act had no application to indemnity policies so that s.2 did not operate to require the name of the tenant to be inserted into the landlord's policy. This holding was not supported by any sort of analysis, and indeed counsel for all the parties appear not to have been willing to argue to the contrary. The *Berni Inns* decision is doubtless convenient, and it was confirmed by the Privy Council in *Siu v Eastern Insurance Co Ltd*[4] that the 1774 Act is confined to non-indemnity insurance.

It would seem, therefore, that policies on land and buildings are governed by the same rules as those relating to policies on goods. The only doubt concerns a sole authority of some antiquity, *Sadlers Co v Badcock*,[5] which indicates that a policy on land has to be supported by insurable interest at the date of its inception, but there is no modern repetition of this point.

The amount of recovery. Given that policies on property are by implication of law contracts of indemnity, it is necessarily the case that the assured cannot recover more than his actual loss. However, it should be appreciated that the indemnity rule takes effect as an implied term, and that it is possible to contract out of it. Three illustrations of the possibility of an assured contracting for more than an indemnity may be given. **19–003**

1. Valued policies. Where the insurer and assured fix a valuation on the insured subject matter, and agree that the valuation is to be the basis of what is payable in the event of a loss, the valuation is conclusive as between the parties in determining the amount payable following a loss. It is, therefore, perfectly possible for the assured to make a profit under a valued policy, the most important control on that ability being the insurer's initial agreement to the valuation at the date of the policy.
2. Insurance of more than one interest. Where the assured insures both his interest and that of some other person in a single policy, he is entitled to recover the full sum insured. The excess over the assured's own interest is, however, to be held for the other person, so that ultimately the assured will not receive more than an indemnity.[6]
3. Where the assured is entitled to recover under the policy for property belonging to him at the outset, but which by the time of loss belongs to another. In *Thomas v National Farmers' Union Mutual Insurance Society Ltd*[7] the assured's policy, on farm produce, provided that the insurance ceased to be in force as to any property passing from the assured to any other person "otherwise than by will or operation of law". Diplock J. held that these words permitted the assured to recover for a quantity of hay and straw which had become the property of his father by the operation of the Agricultural Holdings Act 1948. Diplock J. was called upon to decide only the rights of the assured as against the insurer; the learned judge did

---

[2] *Re King* [1963] Ch. 459.
[3] *Mark Rowlands Ltd v Berni Inns Ltd* [1985] 3 All E.R. 473.
[4] *Siu v Eastern Insurance Co Ltd* [1994] 1 All E.R. 213.
[5] *Sadlers Co v Badcock* (1743) 2 Atk. 554.
[6] See below.
[7] *Thomas v National Farmers' Union Mutual Insurance Society Ltd* [1961] 1 All E.R. 363.

not, therefore, consider whether the policy proceeds were held by the assured on trust for his father, although it is suggested that this would have been the case.

19–004 **Consequences of lack of insurable interest.** Lack of interest at the date of the loss means that the ordinary application of the indemnity principle will prevent an action by the assured. The consequences of lack of interest at the inception of a policy on property are less certain. As far as goods policies are concerned, if the assured has failed, contrary to his expectations, to obtain an interest, he cannot recover on the happening of an insured peril by reason of the indemnity principle, but will be entitled to a return of premiums for total failure of consideration, the insurer never having been at risk; this is the position in marine insurance under s.84(1) and (3)(a) of the Marine Insurance Act 1906.

19–005 **Insurance of two or more interests under a single policy.** It is open to two or more persons to insure their respective interests under a single policy as co-assureds: if their interests are in an undivided whole (as in the case of joint owners) the policy is said to be joint, whereas if their interests are different or divisible (as in the case of, for example, mortgagor and mortgagee) the policy is said to be composite. The significance of the distinction between joint and composite policies is considered elsewhere in this work,[8] and it is sufficient to note for present purposes that each owner of an interest is party to the policy and may claim under it in his own right and in respect of his own interest. The position under a joint or composite policy is to be distinguished from that under a policy whereby the assured. A, insures both his interest and that of another person, B, under a single policy. In this type of case A is the only assured, with the result that B has no right to claim under the policy unless it can be shown that A had been acting as the agent of B in effecting it. This form of policy is common, but its efficacy is limited to some extent by the rules of insurable interest.

Where the policy is on goods little difficulty arises, for it is settled that a person in A's position who has a limited interest in goods coupled with an interest in their preservation as in the case of a bailee, mortgagor, hirer or other person liable for the goods or required by contract to insure them may insure the goods to their full value. Any sum recovered by A in excess of his own interest is to be held for B,[9] so that it cannot be said that A is wagering by insuring in excess of his own interest. The fact that the 1774 Act does not apply to policies on goods means that there is no need for B's name to be inserted in the policy as a person interested (as otherwise required by s.2[10]) and that A's recovery is not limited to the amount of his own interest (as otherwise required by s.3). Where the policy is on land and buildings, the decision in *Mark Rowlands Ltd v Berni Inns Ltd*[11] means that the position is identical to that prevailing for goods.

19–006 **The destination and transfer of policy benefits.** As a general rule, subject to contract and to the exceptions outlined below, where A procures a policy on his own interest and for his own benefit, no other person with an interest in the

---

[8] Ch.15, above.

[9] *Tomlinson (Hauliers) v Hepburn* [1966] A.C. 451. The sum is held in trust if there is a contractual duty to insure, but not otherwise: *Re E Dibbens & Sons Ltd* [1990] B.C.L.C. 677.

[10] Marine Insurance Act 1788, which requires the names of persons interested in a policy on goods to be inserted, is satisfied by the insertion of the name of an agent.

[11] *Mark Rowlands Ltd v Berni Inns Ltd* [1985] 3 All E.R. 473.

subject matter insured has any claim on the proceeds or any right to dictate to the assured how those proceeds are to be applied.[12] This was settled in *Rayner v Preston*,[13] which concerned real property insured by its vendor and damaged between the time of the contract of sale and the conveyance of the land to the buyer. In line with the general principle that on contract the risk in land passes to the purchaser,[14] the full purchase price was paid to the vendor, who was also able to recover on his insurance policy. The purchaser's argument, that the insurance moneys were held on trust for him or were otherwise to be applied by the vendor in reducing the purchaser's liability, was rejected by the Court of Appeal, which held that the insurance moneys belonged to the vendor alone. In a sequel to this case, the decision of the Court of Appeal in *Castellain v Preston*,[15] it was held that the vendor's insurers were entitled, by way of subrogation, to the sum paid to the vendor by the purchaser. The effect of these decisions is to hold the vendor to a single recovery in respect of the loss but, as the purchaser is liable to pay the vendor yet cannot claim the benefit of the vendor's policy, to require the purchaser himself to take out insurance. Given that a prudent vendor will himself wish to be insured, for in the event that the property is damaged after contract and before conveyance it is simpler to look to an insurer than to an understandably reluctant purchaser, the *Rayner* and *Castellain* decisions operate to insist upon two policies on a single risk.

There are, nevertheless, a number of situations in which the proceeds of a policy are to be applied in accordance with the wishes of a person not party to the policy. These are as follows:

1. The Fires Prevention (Metropolis) Act 1774 s.83, requires the insurer to apply the policy moneys towards reinstatement if requested to do so by an interested person and before payment to the assured has been made.[16]
2. The Law of Property Act 1925 s.47, contains an attempt to reverse the rule in *Rayner v Preston* by effecting a statutory transfer of the proceeds of a policy from an insured vendor to a purchaser who bears the risk.
3. The assured may be under a statutory duty to reinstate or to hold the proceeds on behalf of another person interested in the insured subject matter. A bailee of goods thus holds the proceeds of the policy, insofar as they exceed his own interest, for the bailor.[17]
4. The proceeds of the policy may have been assigned to another person.
5. The policy may have been made for the benefit of a third party, or may state that the sums are to be paid to a third party, in which case the insurer may be required to make such payment in accordance with the Contracts (Rights of Third Parties) Act 1999.

---

[12] *DG Finance Ltd v Scott* [1999] Lloyd's Rep. I.R. 387 (owner of vehicle had no claim against hirer's insurers).

[13] *Rayner v Preston* (1881) L.R. 18 Ch D 1. See also the landlord and tenant cases discussed below.

[14] Although this rule is ousted by contract under the Law Society's Standard Conditions of Sale.

[15] *Castellain v Preston* (1883) L.R. 11 QBD 380.

[16] The purchaser in *Rayner v Preston* (1881) L.R. 18 Ch D 1 failed to obtain reinstatement under the Fires Prevention (Metropolis) Act 1774 s.83, as the assured vendor had been paid before the demand for reinstatement had been made.

[17] See below. Contrast *Simon Container Machinery Ltd v Emba Machinery AB* [1998] 2 Lloyd's Rep. 429 where the claimant had no insurable interest of his own.

19–007   **Buyer and seller of goods.** Goods may be insured by a buyer or seller who:

    (a) is the owner of them (or, in the language of the Sale of Goods Act 1979, the person in whom the property in the goods is vested);

    (b) carries the risk of the goods being lost or destroyed; or

    (c) has neither property nor risk but is in possession of the goods by way of security for the price or as bailee.

The buyer will be unable to benefit from an insurance by the seller unless it is taken out for his benefit.[18] It will be appreciated that matters may become complex where there is some time-lag between the making of the contract, the delivery of the goods or documents of title, and payment. The relevant general presumptions of English sales law are that, in the case of ascertained goods property passes on contract irrespective of payment and delivery[19] and that the risk passes with property.[20] However, these rules are subject to contract[21] and, in particular, are rarely applicable in international sales. The following possibilities may be countenanced.

First, neither property nor risk passes on contract. This will be the position where the goods are future goods, purely generic, or where the contract is in some way conditional.[22] Property will not pass in an unascertained part of a bulk unless the buyer has paid the price, in which case he becomes the owner of the relevant proportion of the undivided bulk and owner in common of the whole bulk.[23] The seller clearly has insurable interest by virtue of ownership and risk. The buyer will also be able to insure whether or not he has paid for the goods, as by virtue of his expectation he cannot be classed as a gambler. He may, therefore, take out a floating policy[24] to cover all the goods in his warehouse or otherwise ascertainable at the time of loss, up to a named amount, or a "declaration" policy covering goods declared from time to time.[25] In some trades it is the practice to take out an open policy against all risks by sea and land, and to provide that the assured may declare thereon so soon as he learns that property at his risk of the class insured is in transit to him and whether such property is at the time lost or not. Firms which have to transmit valuable property or securities through the post insure them thus and even when they are simultaneously advised of transmission and loss, they can still declare their loss under such a policy, provided only that they observe good faith in the transaction[26]; certificates for assignment to a buyer are sometimes issued by insurers under a floating policy already taken out by the seller covering the goods sold. Such certificates themselves usually constitute contracts of insurance, and the terms of

---

[18] *Martineau v Kitching* (1862) L.R. 7 Q.B. 436; *Dalgleish v Buchanan* (1854) 16 D. 332.

[19] Sale of Goods Act 1979 s.18 r.1; *Rugg v Minett* (1809) 11 East 210; Lord Blackburn in *Anderson v Morice* (1875) L.R. 10 C.P. 609 at 619.

[20] Sale of Goods Act 1979 s.20.

[21] Blackburn J. in *Martineau v Kitching* (1872) L.R. 7 Q.B. 436 at 454. See *Inglis v Stock* (1885) L.R. 10 App.Cas. 263.

[22] Sale of Goods Act 1979 s.18 rr.2–5. Cf. *Piper v Royal Exchange Assurance* (1932) 44 Ll. LR. 103. See also *Kamidian v Holt* [2009] Lloyd's Rep. I.R. 242, where the court was satisfied that the alleged "buyer" of property had never obtained title in his own right.

[23] Sale of Goods Act 1979 ss.20A and 20B, inserted by the Sale of Goods (Amendment) Act 1995.

[24] *Crowley v Cohen* (1832) 3 B. & Ad. 478; *Joyce v Kennard* (1871) L.R. 7 Q.B. 78; *Ewing v Sicklemore* (1918) 35 T.L.R. 55.

[25] *Rivaz v Gerussi Bros & Co* (1880) L.R. 6 QBD 222.

[26] For the application of good faith to declaration policies, see Ch.6, above.

the floating policy are generally incorporated in them.[27] However, if the goods are lost before the buyer has obtained property, risk or possession, he cannot be said to have suffered any loss and thus will be unable to recover for them under any loss of anticipated profits.[28]

Secondly, property but not risk has passed to the buyer. This situation is rare, but where it occurs both parties may insure and recover the full value of the goods subject to the existence of any subrogation rights.[29]

Thirdly, risk, but not property, has passed to the buyer. This will occur most commonly under export contracts under which risk passes to the buyer on shipment but property passes only where the buyer has paid for the goods on receiving the shipping documents, although here the usual arrangement is that insurance is arranged by the seller and assigned to the buyer. This situation is not however, confined to CIF contracts, and it is possible for risk to pass in part of a bulk prior to the passing of property.[30] The buyer will indeed be able to insure in any case in which the passing of the risk precedes the passing of property, for he is bound to pay for the goods even if they are destroyed before property was due to pass to him.[31] Once the risk has passed to the buyer the seller, although he may retain a legal title sufficient to support a claim against his insurers, has to cede to his insurers by way of subrogation his rights against the seller in respect of a loss. The seller has an insurable interest by virtue of his ownership, and is advised to maintain insurance (irrespective of whether he is required to do so by contract with the buyer) in case of failure by the buyer to meet his payment obligation. As was seen earlier in this chapter, the buyer cannot rely upon the seller's insurance unless he can pray in aid s.47 of the Law of Property Act 1925.

Fourthly, where both property and risk pass to the buyer, even where the seller remains in possession, the seller, his lien apart, no longer has any interest in the goods though his possession entitles him to make an insurance covering the buyer's interest if he so intends and provided there is nothing in the policy to preclude him from doing so.[32]

There will in addition be a number of situations in which insurable interest exists irrespective of the normal rules governing the passing of property and risk:

1. The buyer has an insurable interest even though he had a right to reject the goods for breach of condition.[33] The buyer's interest in the goods ceases if he exercises his right to reject them, provided, by redelivering them to the seller, he is no longer responsible for their safety.[34]

[27] *Macleod Ross v Compagnie d'Assurances* [1952] 1 T.L.R. 314; *Phoenix Insurance v De Monchy* (1929) 35 Com. Cas. 67.
[28] *M'Swiney v Royal Exchange Assurance Co* (1849) L.R. 14 Q.B.D. 634; *Halhead v Young* (1856) 6 El. & Bl. 312; *Andersen v Morice* (1875) 1 App.Cas. 713.
[29] *Sparkes v Marshall* (1836) 2 Bing. N.C. 761; *Wunsche International v Tai Ping Insurance Co* [1998] 2 Lloyd's Rep. 8.
[30] *Inglis v Stock* (1885) L.R. 10 App.Cas. 263; *Wunsche International v Tai Ping Insurance Co* [1998] 2 Lloyd's Rep. 8.
[31] *Joyce v Swann* (1864) 17 C.B.N.S. 84 at 103 at 104 per Willes J.; *Inglis v Stock* (1885) L.R. 10 App.Cas. 263; *Colonial Insurance Co of New Zealand v Adelaide Marine Insurance Co* (1886) L.R. 12 App.Cas. 128; *Ambler v Graves-Togo* (1930) 36 Ll. L. Rep. 145; *Re National Benefit Assurance Co Ltd* (1933) 45 Ll. L. Rep. 147.
[32] *North British Insurance Co v Moffatt* (1871) L.R. 7 C.P. 25 at 30, 31.
[33] Marine Insurance Act 1906 s.7(2).
[34] *Colonial Insurance Co of New Zealand v Adelaide Marine Insurance* (1886) L.R. 12 App.Cas. 128.

2. If the risk has not passed to the buyer, but the buyer delays in fulfilling his contractual obligation to take delivery, the seller may treat the risk as having passed to the buyer, so that the buyer has an insurable interest.[35]
3. If the risk has passed to the buyer, but the seller delays in fulfilling his contractual obligation to deliver the goods, the buyer may treat the risk as having revested in the seller, who may insure on that basis.[36]
4. If either party is in possession of the goods without property or risk, he is deemed to owe the duties of a bailee[37] and may insure as such.
5. If the seller has not been paid and has the ability to exercise real rights over the goods, culminating ultimately in resale,[38] he has an insurable interest. The seller may thus insure and recover under the policy:
    (a) by virtue of his lien if he retains possession[39]; and
    (b) by virtue of the right of stoppage in transit where the buyer has become insolvent while the goods remain in the course of transit,[40] although if the right of stoppage is not exercised the seller will not possess an insurable interest. Where there is stoppage in transit, the purchaser has no insurable interest.[41]

    In both of these cases, the seller's acts do not rescind the contract of sale, although the buyer's insurable interest will terminate on any resale to a third party by the seller.[42] But the fact that the seller retains a lien in no way affects an insurance by the buyer, if the risk has passed to him,[43] nor do the seller's lien or his right to stop in transit entitle him to benefit under policies by the buyer.[44]

One unresolved question is whether a buyer has insurable interest where the seller has fraudulently shipped goods of a description entirely different from those specified in the contract of sale. It was held in *Anderson v Morice*,[45] a pre-Act authority, that in such a case the buyer's loss is not the goods themselves but loss of profit flowing from the seller's breach of contract; consequently, the buyer could recover only if his policy covered loss of profits. It is not clear whether the distinction between insurable interest in goods and in loss of profits has survived the MIA 1906: in *Fuerst Day Lawson Ltd v Orion Insurance Co Ltd*,[46] Mustill J. left the point open, although that distinction was confirmed, albeit in a different context, in *Glengate-KG Properties Ltd v Norwich Union Fire*.[47]

Vendor and purchaser of land

19–008   *Insurable interest.* A purchaser of land has an insurable interest in the premises purchased from the signing of the contract and before completion, since: (a) he has the equitable interest in it, being generally entitled to specific performance of the contract; and (b) the property is at his risk and if it is burnt down he must still

[35] Sale of Goods Act 1979 s.20(2).
[36] Sale of Goods Act 1979 s.20(2).
[37] Sale of Goods Act 1979 s.20(3).
[38] Sale of Goods Act 1979 s.47.
[39] Sale of Goods Act 1979 s.41.
[40] Sale of Goods Act 1979 s.48(1).
[41] *Clay v Harrison* (1829) 10 B. & C. 99.
[42] Sale of Goods Act 1979 s.48(2).
[43] Blackburn J. in *Anderson v Morice* (1875) L.R. 10 C.P. 609 at 619.
[44] *Berndtson v Strong* (1868) L.R. 3 Ch. App. 588, per Cairns L.C. at 591.
[45] *Anderson v Morice* (1876) L.R. 1 App.Cas. 713.
[46] *Fuerst Day Lawson Ltd v Orion Insurance Co Ltd* [1996] 2 All E.R. 487.
[47] *Glengate-KG Properties Ltd v Norwich Union Fire* [1980] 1 Lloyd's Rep. 656.

pay for it.[48] After completion, of course, he has an insurable interest as legal owner of the land. An unpaid vendor of land who is still in possession has an insurable interest in it and can recover to the full extent of its value under a policy of fire insurance for until he is paid he cannot tell for certain whether he will ultimately receive the purchase money. If it were otherwise he would have to rely entirely on the solvency of the purchaser if the property were destroyed by fire.[49] But once the transfer is complete he will be unable to recover on a policy insuring his own interest alone.[50]

Proceeds of the policy. The position at common law where the vendor alone **19–009** insured was that if a loss occurred after the contract for sale was executed the insurers would eventually escape all responsibility for it, unless the buyer was insolvent or the vendor's title proved defective. For while the vendor, as legal owner, could, in the first place, recover from his insurers the entire amount of the purchase money,[51] the insurers would become subrogated to his right to the purchase money as against the purchase.[52] The purchaser had no right to benefit under the vendor's policy,[53] for the benefit of such policies does not run with the land.[54] The vendor might assign the policy to the purchaser, on executing the contract of sale, but such an assignment would require the assent of the insurers in order to confer on the purchaser the right to benefit under it. Should that assent be refused, the policy would become virtually worthless, and the purchaser's only remedy would be to effect an insurance of his own. Not even a condition in the contract of sale that the purchaser was to have the benefit of the vendor's policy could take away from the insurers their right of subrogation.[55] Nor could the exercise by the purchaser of his rights under s.83 of the Fires Prevention (Metropolis) Act 1774, materially assist him[56]; though he might require the insurers to lay out the money in reinstatement of the property under that Act, there would be no reason why they should not thereupon be subrogated to the vendor's right to payment against him.[57] Moreover, if the purchaser has actually paid the purchase price, the vendor suffers no loss and are thus in any event discharged. These principles applied in the case of compulsory purchase of land under a statute: once the transfer is complete neither party can recover under a policy taken out by the original owner.[58]

This unsatisfactory state of the law was remedied a little by s.47(1) of the Law of Property Act 1925, whereby insurance money that becomes payable to the vendor after the date of the contract for sale or exchange of any property, under a policy maintained by him against damage to or destruction of that property, shall, "on completion of the contract, be held or receivable by the vendor on

---

[48] *Paine v Meller* (1801) 6 Ves. 349; *Sutherland v Pratt* (1843) 11 M. & W. 296.

[49] *Collingridge v Royal Exchange Insurance Co* (1877) 3 Q.B.D. 173 at 177.

[50] *Ecclesiastical Commissioners v Royal Exchange Assurance Corporation* (1895) 11 T.L.R. 476; Lush J. in *Collingridge v Royal Exchange Insurance Co* (1877) L.R. 3 Q.B.D. 173 at 177.

[51] *Collingridge v Royal Exchange Insurance Co* (1877) L.R. 3 Q.B.D. 173.

[52] *Castellain v Preston* (1883) L.R. 11 Q.B.D. 380.

[53] *Poole v Adams* (1864) 10 L.T. 287.

[54] *Rayner v Preston* (1881) L.R. 18 Ch. D. 1. Further, many modern householders' comprehensive policies do not cover against risks where a house is left unfurnished, and an additional premium is usually required to cover them.

[55] *Phoenix Assurance v Spooner* [1905] 2 K.B. 753.

[56] See Younger L.J. in *Matthey v Curling* [1922] 2 A.C. 180 at 219.

[57] See Cotton L.J. in *Rayner v Preston* (1881) L.R. 18 Ch. D. 1 at 7; Bowen L.J. in *Castellain v Preston* (1883) L.R. 11 Q.B.D. 380 at 400.

[58] *Ecclesiastical Commissioners v Royal Exchange Assurance Corporation* (1895) 11 T.L.R. 476.

behalf of the purchaser and paid by the vendor to the purchaser on completion of the sale or exchange, or so soon thereafter as the same shall be received by the vendor." Thus, this subsection reverses the decision in *Rayner v Preston*, but since by s.47(2) it has effect subject to:

(a) any stipulation to the contrary contained in the contract,
(b) any requisite consents of the insurers,
(c) the payment by the purchaser of the proportionate part of the premium from the date of the contract,

it merely saves introducing a condition into the contract that the purchaser is to have the benefit of the vendor's policy, and the consent of the insurers is always necessary in order to give the purchaser any rights under it, unless there is a condition in the policy giving the benefit of it to any purchaser, or unless it was taken out with that intent.[59] The section applies to sales or exchange by an order of the court.[60] In practice s.47 is rarely relied upon, for its operation is defeated by the doctrine of subrogation: if the purchaser pays the purchase price the insurer is discharged from liability to the vendor as the vendor has suffered no loss, so that there are no proceeds to which s.47 can attach. By contrast, if the purchaser does not pay, any benefit he receives under s.47 will be lost if the insurer exercises the vendor's subrogation rights in respect of the price. The solution adopted in practice—under the Law Society's Standard Conditions of Sale (operative since 2003)—is to vest the risk of damage pending completion in the vendor, so that only the vendor need insure. A prudent purchaser will nevertheless continue to insure to overcome the vendor's refusal or inability to make good any loss.

Bailor and bailee

19–010 *The bailee's insurable interest.* The insurable interest of a bailee in the goods of which he is custodian may be one of three types.

First, the bailee has an insurable interest in any liability of his to the bailor in the event of the goods coming to harm.[61] Such a policy is a liability cover rather than a property cover, which indemnifies the bailee in the event that a claim is made against him by the bailor. In this type of case, the measure of indemnity is based not on the value of the goods, but on the amount of the bailor's liability, which may be less than the value of the goods where, e.g. the bailee does not owe any duty of care in respect of them, or has in some way limited his liability to the bailor.

Secondly, the bailee may insure his own contractual entitlement to earned profits or commission for the performance of his services. The bailee's insurable interest here exists only in respect of accrued charges so that he cannot recover prospective profits and charges under the policy unless he has expressly insured against loss of profits.[62] On this principle, a bailee may recover under a fire policy covering his own interest only where he has a lien on goods for accrued

---

[59] See Bowen L.J. in *Castellain v Preston* (1883) L.R. 11 Q.B.D. 380 at 406.
[60] Law of Property Act 1925 s.47(3).
[61] *Coggs v Bernard* (1703) 1 Smith's Leading Cases 13th edn 175; *North British v London, Liverpool & Globe* (1877) 5 Ch D 569; *Sidaways v Todd* (1818) 2 Stark. 400; *Engel v Lancashire and General Assurance* (1925) 41 T.L.R. 408.
[62] *Maurice v Goldsborough Mort & Co* [1939] A.C. 452.

charges—in which case those charges alone are recoverable where the bailee has incurred no liability for the loss of the goods by fire.[63]

Thirdly, in addition to insuring in respect of his own direct interests, the law also recognises that a bailee has a pervasive insurable interest under which he is entitled to insure for the full value of the goods in his possession. This is a somewhat anomalous principle because the bailee plainly has no proprietary or equitable interest in the goods, but insurance to that extent is permitted apparently to lessen the risk to the bailor, thus making the services of a bailee a more attractive proposition.[64] This form of insurance is a property insurance rather than a liability cover and the sums recoverable are measured by the value of the goods in the bailee's possession. The proceeds of a policy that covers both those taken out by reference to the bailee's pervasive insurable interest cannot, however, be retained by him, and he must account to the bailor for any sums in excess of his own interest.[65] This type of policy does not, however, mean that the assured can recover the full value of all of the goods in his possession: it is necessary to construe the policy to ascertain exactly which goods in the assured's possession are within its terms.

In any individual cases, two questions fall to be determined: the first is the identification of the goods covered by the policy. The second is whether the bailee's measure of indemnity is the full value of the goods, or the amount for which the bailee is liable to the bailor in respect of loss of or damage to the goods.

Scope of policy. The initial question is determining the scope of the policy, by defining the goods to which the policy applies. Certain forms of wording have been given authoritative interpretation by the courts. In *Waters v Monarch Fire and Life Assurance Co*[66] the bailees were warehousemen who had taken out two policies, insuring respectively "goods in trust or on commission therein" and "property of the assured or held by them in trust or on commission". The policies were construed as covering all third-party property and not simply third-party property in respect of which the bailees owed duties of care to the bailors. The phrase "in trust" was held not to bear its strict technical meaning, but rather referred to goods which had been "entrusted" to the bailees. The policy in *London & North-Western Ry v Glyn*[67]—an insurance of goods by carriers—contained a clause: "goods in trust are to be insured as such, otherwise the policy will not extend to cover such property".[68] The subject matter was described as "goods their own and in trust as carrier". It was held that that policy covered the owner's interest as well as that of the carriers, and that carriers were not limited in their claim against the insurers to goods in respect of which they owed duties of care to the owners, the words of the policy not being sufficient to limit the insurers' liability in that way.

19–011

---

[63] *Crowley v Cohen* (1832) 3 B. & Ad. 478.

[64] The root decision is *Waters v Monarch Fire and Life Assurance Co* (1856) 5 E. & B. 870. See also the discussion by Lloyd J. in *Petrofina (UK) Ltd v Magnaload Ltd* [1984] Q.B. 127.

[65] *Maurice v Goldsborough Mort & Co* [1939] A.C. 452.

[66] *Waters v Monarch Fire and Life Assurance Co* (1856) 5 E. & B. 870.

[67] *London & North-Western Ry v Glyn* (1859) 1 E. & E. 652.

[68] Such a provision does not mean that the assured cannot recover at all where he holds goods on trust, but simply that he cannot recover more than his own interest in them. The effect of the clause is to cut down the common law right of a bailee with possession to insure the owner's interest if he intends to do so by requiring that such intention must be expressed in the policy. See also *South Australian Central Insurance v Randell* (1869) LR 3 P.C. 101–112.

By contrast, if the policy covers goods in the bailee's trust "for which he is responsible" a bailee who bears no responsibility for the goods—e.g. because he is a seller of the goods and both property and risk have passed to the buyer—is to be taken as having insured only those goods for which he faces liability.[69] The effect of this type of wording was confirmed in *North British and Mercantile Insurance Co v Moffatt*.[70] Here, insurance was taken out by sellers who remained in possession of certain chests of tea after both risk and property in the subject matter had passed to the buyers.[71] The policy covered goods "the assured's own, in trust or commission, for which they are responsible". It was held that, as mere bailees without any interest in the chests of tea, the sellers were no longer responsible for them and the words were insufficient to cover the goods in question. It is apparent from the judgment in this case that the critical distinguishing feature between this case and the earlier authorities—*Waters* and *Glyn*—was the addition of the word "responsible" in *Moffatt*. The use of the word "responsible", as in *Moffatt*, will therefore preclude the assured from obtaining a sum in respect of the goods greater than his own liability for those goods.

In *Engel v Lancashire & General Assurance Co Ltd*[72] the bailee, a furrier, took out a burglary policy covering his own stock in trade and goods belonging to third parties held by him in trust or on commission for which he was responsible. Goods were stolen from the bailee's premises without any fault on his behalf so that he bore no liability to the owners of those goods. The bailee nevertheless argued that the goods were covered by the policy, but it was held by Roche J. that the word "responsible" limited recovery to goods lost in circumstances under which the bailee was liable to the third party. In *Ramco (UK) Ltd v International Insurance Co of Hannover Ltd*[73] the earlier authorities were approved. Andrew Smith J. followed those cases and ruled that the phrase "property of the Insured or held by the Insured in trust for which the Insured is responsible" meant that the bailee could recover only in respect of those goods for which he was legally liable to the bailor.[74] The Court of Appeal on appeal in *Ramco*[75] reluctantly agreed with this conclusion. As far as the word "responsible" was concerned. Waller L.J.—delivering the judgment of the Court of Appeal—was of the view that the natural meaning of the word "responsible" in this context was not a narrow concept of legal liability, but a rather broader concept. As such, Waller L.J. saw no good reason why the addition of the word "responsible" should operate as a limiting factor on the scope of the cover. However, the Court of Appeal felt that it would be wrong, for two reasons, to overrule the decisions in *Moffatt* and *Engel*. First, the meaning of this form of wording had been established and it would be inappropriate to overturn the expectation of the

---

[69] *North British Insurance Co v Moffatt* (1871) L.R. 7 C.P. 25. Cf. *Engel v Lancashire and General Insurance Co* (1925) 21 Ll. L.R. 327.

[70] *North British and Mercantile Insurance Co v Moffatt* (1871) L.R. 7 C.P. 25.

[71] The sellers were, therefore, in the position of bailees despite having no remaining interest of their own in the goods.

[72] *Engel v Lancashire & General Assurance Co Ltd* (1925) 21 Ll. L.R. 327.

[73] *Ramco (UK) Ltd v International Insurance Co of Hannover Ltd* [2004] Lloyd's Rep. I.R. 606.

[74] The obiter comment of Lloyd J. in *Petrofina (UK) Ltd v Magnaload Ltd* [1984] Q.B. 127 to the effect that the word "responsible" in the phrase "belonging to the insured or for which they are responsible" referred to a general as opposed to legal responsibility was not followed in *Ramco*. The Court of Appeal in *Ramco* [2004] Lloyd's Rep. I.R. 606 noted that the comment had been made *per incuriam* as the relevant authorities on the word "responsible" had not been cited to him.

[75] *Ramco* [2004] Lloyd's Rep. I.R. 606. See also the sequel claim against the brokers, *Ramco Ltd v Weller Russell & Laws Insurance Brokers Ltd* [2009] Lloyd's Rep. I.R. 27.

parties that the words used did not bear the anticipated meaning. Secondly, the rule in *Waters*, which allowed a bailee to recover for goods which did not belong to him and for which he bore no liability, was anomalous and constituted an exception to the common law privity of contracts rule. While the privity rule had been abolished by the Contracts (Rights of Third Parties) Act 1999, Waller L.J. was of the view that:

> "enabling a party to a contract to recover for a loss he has not suffered or enabling a goods-owner to recover pursuant to a contract to which he is not a party is still the exception rather than the rule; the 'exception' established in *Waters* should not itself be extended beyond its proper limits without good reason."

Nature of policy: property or liability. Once the goods falling within the scope of the policy have been ascertained, the further question is whether the amount recoverable by the bailee is the full value of the goods or the amount of liability which the bailee bears in relation to those goods, i.e. whether the policy is one on the property itself or against liability. There is an initial presumption that a policy taken out by a bailee is a property policy based on the value of the goods, rather than a liability policy protecting the bailee's personal interests.[76] This point is important both because the amount of liability and earned charges is likely to be less than the full value of the goods given the use of clauses limiting the liability of bailees, and because the bailee is liable only for losses caused by his own default or negligence so that loss by causes beyond the bailee's control will be outside a liability policy, but within a goods policy.[77] Thus, although in the absence of clear wording, it will be a matter of construction whether the policy covers the interest of the bailee only or additionally the interest of the owner of the goods, the courts will lean in favour of an insurance on property rather than liability. In *Tomlinson (Hauliers) v Hepburn*[78] carriers insured cigarettes, the property of a third party. The cigarettes were stolen. The carriers had insured not as agents, but on their own behalf. It was held by the House of Lords that, on its true construction, the policy was not a personal liability policy, but a goods policy, and that, accordingly, the carriers were entitled to recover in full from the insurer irrespective of whether they were personally liable to the third party. Thereafter the law required the carriers to account to the owner of the goods who had suffered the loss.

There are numerous authorities supporting the proposition that a policy taken out by a bailee is generally to be construed as a property rather than as a liability policy.[79] The cases were considered by Andrew Smith J. in *Ramco (UK) Ltd v International Insurance Co of Hannover Ltd.*[80] In this case the insured—the

19–012

---

[76] *London & North-Western Ry v Glyn* (1859) 1 E. & E. 652. Erle J. said, at 663, that insurers had to "employ precise words" to create liability cover, and cf. Hill J. at 665. The presumption in favour of property insurance was confirmed by the House of Lords in *Tomlinson (Hauliers) v Hepburn* [1966] A.C. 451 and see also *Ramco (UK) Ltd v International Insurance Co of Hannover Ltd* [2004] Lloyd's Rep. I.R. 606.

[77] *Crowley v Cohen* (1832) 3 B. & Ad. 478.

[78] *Tomlinson (Hauliers) v Hepburn* [1966] A.C. 451. See also *GRE Assurance of New Zealand Ltd v Roberts* [1991] 2 N.Z.L.R. 106.

[79] *Waters v Monarch Fire and Life Assurance Co* (1856) 5 E. & B. 870; *London and North Western Railway Co v Glyn* (1859) 1 E. & E. 652; *North British and Mercantile Insurance Co v Moffatt* (1871) L.R. 7 C.P. 25; *Petrofina (UK) Ltd v Magnaload Ltd* [1984] Q.B. 127; *Ramco (UK) Ltd v International Insurance Co of Hannover Ltd* [2003] EWHC 2360 (Comm).

[80] *Ramco (UK) Ltd v International Insurance Co of Hannover Ltd* [2003] EWHC 2360 (Comm). The distinction between property and liability policies did not fall for consideration on appeal in *Ramco* [2004] Lloyd's Rep. I.R. 606.

occupiers of industrial premises—had taken out "All Risks" insurance in respect of the "property of the Insured or held by the Insured in trust for which the Insured is responsible". Goods belonging to the insured and to third parties were damaged in the fire, and the initial issue for the court was whether the policy was one on the goods themselves, or one which covered the liability of the insured for the goods. Andrew Smith J. held that the policy was a property policy rather than a liability cover, and that the terms of the policy were consistent with the former rather than the latter. In particular: the obligation of the insurers was expressed in terms of paying the value of the property at the date of the insured peril, the insurers had a right to reinstate damaged property and the policy was subject to average, each of those provisions being inappropriate to liability cover; the policy covered the insured's own goods as well as third-party goods, and construing this cover as composite, covering first-party property and third-party liability, created a degree of complexity which could not have been intended; and none of the terms typically found in a liability policy were present. In *North British and Mercantile Insurance Co v London, Liverpool & Globe Insurance Co*,[81] where the question was whether there was double insurance, Jessel M.R. expressed the view, obiter, that the phrase "goods . . . in the assured's own, in trust, or on commission, for which they are responsible" meant that the policy was one on the assured's liability rather than on property.[82] However, there was no support for this analysis in the Court of Appeal in *North British*, and the approach adopted by Andrew Smith J. in *Ramco (UK) Ltd v International Insurance Co of Hannover Ltd*[83] was that the word "responsible" does not convert the policy into a liability policy, but simply confines the bailee to recovering the full value of the property for which he was legally liable in the circumstances of the loss. This point did not arise for consideration in the Court of Appeal in *Ramco*[84] although the Court of Appeal did comment that it was a curious result if the policy restricted cover to goods for which the bailee was legally responsible, but nevertheless allowed the bailee to recover the full value of those goods.[85]

19–013 *Allocation of policy proceeds.* Where the insurance does cover the value of goods and not just the liability or other interest of the bailee, it takes effect as one of the different interests of the bailor and bailee: it is well established that, as such an insurance covers both their own interest, e.g. the bailee's lien for warehouse rent and the interest of the owners of such goods, the bailees are entitled as against the insurers to recover the entire value of the goods whether the owners have assented to the insurance or not.[86] The policy is not joint or composite, and is not necessarily for the benefit of the bailor so that the bailor cannot sue under it in his own right unless he is given express rights to do so in accordance with the Contracts (Rights of Third Parties) Act 1999; his only cause of action is against the bailee for the surplus amount.

---

[81] *North British and Mercantile Insurance Co v London, Liverpool & Globe Insurance Co* (1876) 5 Ch D 569.

[82] This was also seemingly the minority view of Lord Pearce in *Tomlinson v Hepburn* [1966] A.C. 451.

[83] *Ramco (UK) Ltd v International Insurance Co of Hannover Ltd* [2003] EWHC 2360 (Comm).

[84] *Ramco* [2004] Lloyd's Rep. I.R. 606.

[85] See also *Ramco Ltd v Weller Russell & Laws Insurance Brokers Ltd* [2009] Lloyd's Rep. I.R. 27.

[86] *Donaldson v Manchester Insurance* (1836) 14 Sh. (Ct of Sess) 601; *Waters v Monarch Fire & Life* (1856) 5 E. & B. 870; *Cochran v Leckie's Trustee* (1906) 8 F. (Ct of Sess) 975.

However, the bailee is entitled to retain only those sums representing his own interest in the goods and must hold the balance for the bailor.[87] Provided that the assured has of his own free will and at his own expense included the interests of others, other interested parties can only lay claim to what remains after the assured's own loss has been indemnified. Thus, in the case of sellers of goods who retained possession of such goods—the risk having passed to the buyers— included "goods on the premises, sold and paid for but not removed" under floating policies covering also their own goods, it was held that they were entitled to appropriate to their own losses the whole of a sum received from their insurers under these policies, the insurance moneys being insufficient to cover their losses alone. It would of course have been held otherwise had they been under any obligation to the buyers to make the insurance.[88] It will be necessary for this purpose to determine the extent of the assured's insurable interest and the scope of the policy.

For many years, it had been uncertain whether the bailee holds the surplus in a fiduciary capacity or whether he is merely susceptible to a common law action by the bailor for money had and received, a point of crucial importance in the event of the bailee's insolvency. The general assumption had been that the bailee held the surplus sums as a trustee, on the basis of dicta in the early cases that the goods themselves were held by the bailee "on trust".[89] This assumption was demonstrated to be fallacious by Harman J. in *Re E Dibbens & Sons Ltd*.[90] This case involved a policy procured by a warehouseman of furniture and domestic property, describing the goods as being held "on trust". On the warehouseman's insolvency, the question arose whether the insurance proceeds in excess of the warehouseman's own interest were held in a fiduciary capacity for the bailors. Harman J. held that those customers who had contracted with the warehouseman on the basis that their goods would be insured by him were owed fiduciary duties in relation to the insurance premiums paid to them by the warehouseman and were thus able to make proprietary claims against the surplus policy proceeds.[91] By contrast, those bailors who had not required insurance to be taken out had no fiduciary relationship with the warehouseman, and remained mere unsecured creditors in any claim for the proceeds of the policy.

Other persons in possession of goods or land. Not all forms of possession   **19–014**
amount to bailment, although there is no agreement as to the precise scope of bailment: the positions of the finder, the thief and the person involuntarily in possession are particularly problematic.[92] If the assured is not a bailee, he cannot insure for the full value of the goods or land but only for the amount of his own interest. Exactly what interest a person in possession has is of some legal complexity; as a matter of strict theory, a person in possession may always insure for something, for possession is a defeasible, second-best interest which is capable of being overridden only by the person with immediate right to pos-

---

[87] *Sidaways v Todd* (1818) 2 Stark. 400; *Armitage v Winterbottom* (1840) 1 Man. & G. 130.
[88] *Dalgleish v Buchanan* (1854) 16 Ct. of Sess. (2nd Series) 322; *Martineau v Kitching* (1862) L.R. 7 Q.B. 436; *Ferguson v Aberdeen* 1916 S.C. 715.
[89] *Waters v Monarch Fire and Life Assurance Co* (1856) 5 E. & B. 870; *London and North Western Railway Co v Glyn* (1859) 1 E. & E. 652. Similar comments are found in the judgments in *Tomlinson (Hauliers) v Hepburn* [1966] A.C. 451.
[90] *Re E Dibbens & Sons Ltd* [1990] B.C.L.C. 677. See also *DG Finance Ltd v Scott* [1999] Lloyd's Rep. I.R. 387.
[91] See also *Cochran v Leckie's Trustee* (1906) 8 F. (Ct of Sess) 975.
[92] See Palmer, *Bailment*, 11–36.

session.[93] There is little insurance authority on the insurable interest of a person in possession, although three propositions can be put forward on the strength of the existing cases.

1. Possession coupled with a right to enjoy property gives rise to an insurable interest in the property for its full value. This was held to be the case in *Goulstone v Royal Insurance Co*[94] in relation to a husband's use of certain of his wife's goods for he is by law entitled to share her enjoyment in such goods,[95] and the principle undoubtedly extends to hire purchase, conditional sale and similar arrangements.[96] A right to enjoy, conferred by an express power of attorney, also suffices to create an insurable interest.[97] The application of this principle to goods which have been gratuitously loaned is unclear. However, if the policy also covers the bailee's liability, then he may have a claim in the event that the goods are damaged by his failure to live up to the required standard of care and is sued by the owner.

2. An assured who is the owner of goods liable to be seized by the customs authorities, by virtue of their having been smuggled, retains full insurable interest in them, although he is prevented by public policy from recovering under the policy in the event of their theft.[98] The defeasible interest of the assured in this case might be equated by analogy with the arguable defeasible insurable interest of a thief: however, no English court has held that a thief does have insurable interest,[99] and the public policy principle would doubtless in any event prevent recovery.

3. Where goods are on the land of the assured but they belong to a third party and the assured has no right to enjoy or use them, he cannot insure them against loss. This was the notorious ruling in *Macaura v Northern Assurance Co*,[100] in which the assured, who had sold a large quantity of trees planted on his land to a company of which he was the sole effective shareholder, and who had insured the trees in his own name, was held to be unable to recover, for want of insurable interest. The House of Lords classified the assured's only interest as being in the solvency of his company, as its creditor, and not in any specific assets of the company.[101] It does not appear to have been argued that the assured was the bailee of the trees and was thus able to insure to their full value on that basis. The decision denies recovery on the technicality that the insurance had been taken out in the name of the assured rather than that of the company, and doubtless the technical defence would not have been taken in the absence of strong circumstantial evidence of fraudulent destruction by the assured. The principle of *Macaura* was nevertheless confirmed by Deputy Judge Colman QC in *The Moonacre*,[102] a case in which a yacht was purchased

---

[93] See the masterly analysis in Goode, *Commercial Law*, 4th edn (2009), Chs 1 and 2.
[94] *Goulstone v Royal Insurance Co* (1858) 1 F. & F. 276.
[95] *Goulstone v Royal Insurance Co* (1858) 1 F. & F. 276.
[96] IOB Annual Report for 1991, para.2.25. See also *Linelevel Ltd v Powszechny Zaklad Ubezpieczen SA (The Nore Challenger)* [2005] EWHC 421 Comm (bareboat charterer of vessel).
[97] *Sharp v Sphere Drake Insurance Co Ltd (The Moonacre)* [1992] 2 Lloyd's Rep. 501.
[98] *Geismar v Sun Alliance & London Insurance* [1978] Q.B. 383.
[99] But a captor of a vessel has been held to have an insurable interest in it: *Boehm v Bell* (1799) 8 T.R. 154.
[100] *Macaura v Northern Assurance Co* [1925] A.C. 619.
[101] Cf. on this point *Moran, Galloway & Co v Uzielli* [1905] 2 K.B. 555.
[102] *Sharp v Sphere Drake Insurance Co Ltd (The Moonacre)* [1992] 2 Lloyd's Rep. 501.

in the name of a one-man company for the benefit of the shareholder, and was insured in the shareholder's name. The court ruled that the company could not recover under the policy as it was not the assured, and that prima facie the shareholder had no insurable interest in the yacht merely by having been left in possession of it. However, the court was able to distinguish *Macaura* on the basis that the shareholder had been granted powers of attorney by the company permitting him to use and enjoy the yacht, and it was that additional precaution which served to confer the necessary insurable interest on the shareholder.[103]

Landlord and tenant. Premises may be insured by the landlord on his own behalf, by the tenant on his own behalf, and by either party on behalf of himself and the other. This will be determined by the terms of the lease. The last-mentioned arrangement is increasingly common: the insuring party will often be the landlord, particularly where the lease is long term, although the tenant will contribute to the insurance premium by an additional element in his rent or by way of service charges. It is important for insurance to be settled by the lease, for if the landlord voluntarily procures a policy but does not maintain it, the tenant will have no action against him.[104] Where the landlord insures on behalf of himself and the tenant (or vice versa), with the tenant's authority or with subsequent ratification by the tenant then whether or not the tenant is named in the policy as an assured, the policy is a composite one, and each party—as an independent assured—has independent rights against the insurer.[105]   **19–015**

Landlord's insurable interest. The landlord has an insurable interest in his reversion. Moreover, he may have agreed to keep the premises in repair,[106] in which case he has insurable interest in the costs of repair. In the latter case he can recover in full under an insurance for his own benefit only, and his claim will not be limited by the principle of indemnity to the value of the reversion. But where the tenant is responsible for repairs, although the landlord may, by virtue of his legal estate, recover the whole value of the premises under his own insurance,[107] the insurers will be subrogated to his claim for repairs as against the tenant.[108]   **19–016**

Application of insurance moneys under landlord's insurance. A tenant can recover nothing under an insurance by the landlord alone even if he is not bound to repair and the tenant's liability for rent continues.[109] He has no equity otherwise to compel the landlord to use the insurance moneys to repair the damage and the landlord can apply those moneys as he thinks fit,[110] although in the case of a single name policy by the landlord or the tenant where there is no contractual obligation by the assured to reinstate, the other party may give notice   **19–017**

---

[103] See also *O'Kane v Jones* [2005] Lloyd's Rep. I.R. 174: the ship's managers had insurable interest in vessel by virtue of possession coupled with obligations to equip and otherwise maintain the vessel.

[104] *Argy Trading v Lapid Developments* [1977] 1 W.L.R. 444.

[105] See the principles set out in *National Oilwell (UK) Ltd v Davy Offshore Ltd* [1993] 2 Lloyd's Rep. 582.

[106] *Tredway v Machin* (1904) 91 L.T. 310.

[107] *Collingridge v Royal Exchange Insurance Corporation* (1877) L.R. 3 QBD 173.

[108] *Darrell v Tibbitts* (1880) L.R. 5 QBD 560.

[109] *Belfour v Weston* (1786) 1 T.R. 310; *Hare v Groves* (1796) 3 Anstr. 687.

[110] Leach M.R. in *Leeds v Cheetham* (1827) 1 Sim. 146 at 150; *Lofft v Dennis* (1859) 28 L.J. Q.B. 168; *Edwards v West* (1878) L.R. 7 Ch D 858. See also *Andrews v Patriotic (No.2)* (1886) 18 L.R. Ir. 355.

to the insurer, before the insurance moneys have been paid to the assured, requiring the insurer to use the policy moneys to reinstate the premises.[111] But where the tenant covenants to insure both their interests, and the landlord also takes out an insurance, and thus reduces the amount to which the tenant is entitled on a loss, due to an apportionment by the insurers between the two policies, the landlord must account to the tenant for the difference.[112] He is not entitled both to the retention of this amount and to the repair of the premises. Where the tenant covenants to insure in the landlord's name he is not entitled to receive the policy moneys in case of a fire, or to reinstate and then demand the policy moneys,[113] as he is a mere agent. His remedy is to serve a notice to reinstate upon the insurer under the Fires Prevention (Metropolis) Act 1774.

The position is different where the tenant is intended to benefit from the insurance and has paid the premiums directly or indirectly, as he may well have rights under the policy, and for these purposes the noting of the interest of an unnamed party, while common, is legally not necessary, provided that it was the common intention of the parties that the policy should ensure to the tenant's benefit.[114]

In the first place, at the very least he will be regarded as having sufficient interest in the policy, by virtue of having contributed to the premiums, to avoid a subrogation action by the insurer in the landlord's name if the loss is due to the tenant's negligence.[115]

Secondly, the tenant may be able to insist upon reinstatement. In *Mumford Hotels v Wheeler*[116] the lease was held, inter alia, to enure for the benefit of both because the tenant had covenanted to pay "a yearly insurance rent equal to the premium", the result being that the landlord was obliged under the lease to use the insurance money towards reinstatement of the property, even in the absence of a covenant in the lease to reinstate. Difficulties may be encountered where the policy moneys are to be applied for the purposes of reinstatement[117] either by contract or under statute but where reinstatement is impossible as a matter of practice or law. It here falls to be decided how the policy moneys are to be allocated between the parties. In *Re King*[118] the tenant insured the premises under a policy in the joint names of himself and the landlord. The insuring covenant in the lease required the tenant to lay out the policy sums towards reinstatement in the event of a loss. Following a fire the premises became subject to a compulsory purchase order, and the Court of Appeal, Lord Denning dissenting, held that the tenant was entitled to retain the policy moneys. However, in *Beacon Carpets v Kirby*[119] a case in which the landlord insured in the joint names of himself and the tenant, with the tenant contributing to the premium, the Court of Appeal held in similar circumstances that the policy moneys received by the landlord were to be apportioned between him and the tenant in accordance with their respective interests in the property. In the light of this, it is doubtful whether *Re King* can any longer safely be relied on.

---

[111] Under the Fires Prevention (Metropolis) Act 1774.

[112] *Reynard v Arnold* (1875) L.R. 10 Ch D 386.

[113] Lord St. Leonards in *Garden v Ingram* (1852) 23 L.J. Ch. 478 at 479.

[114] *Lambert v Keymood Ltd* [1999] Lloyd's Rep. I.R. 80.

[115] *Mark Rowlands Ltd v Bemi Inns Ltd* [1985] 3 W.L.R. 964.

[116] *Mumford Hotels v Wheeler* [1964] Ch. 117.

[117] If the landlord is obliged to reinstate, the building provided must be reasonably suitable for the tenant: *Vural v Security Archives Ltd* [1989] E.G.L.S. 2.

[118] *Re King* [1963] Ch. 459.

[119] *Beacon Carpets v Kirby* [1984] 2 All E.R. 726.

Thirdly, the tenant may be able to bring an action against the insurers in his own name where the Contracts (Rights of Third Parties) Act 1999 is applicable. The 1999 Act allows a third party to bring an action against insurers on a policy which states that he may sue them or which purports to confer benefits upon him. In principle, therefore, the 1999 Act gives the tenant a direct action against the insurers on the policy, so that the tenant can recover the amount of his own loss from the insurers. Two points should here be made. First, under s.1(2) of the 1999 Act the right of a beneficiary of an insurance contract to make a direct claim against the insurers is ousted if the insurers can demonstrate that, on a proper construction of the contract, it appears that the insurers and the landlord did not intend the term to be enforceable by the tenant. Any provision that the policy moneys are to be paid to the landlord would presumably be sufficient to oust the tenant's right of direct enforcement. Secondly, there is a potential overlap of the rights of recovery of the landlord and the tenant: the landlord will be able to recover the full sum insured, by virtue of his insurable interest in the entire premises; whereas the tenant will be able to recover an amount representing his own insurable interest in the demised premises. However, there is no prospect that the insurers can face having to pay more than the amount due under the policy: while there is no priority as between competing claimants, any payment to the landlord or the tenant necessarily discharges the insurers' liability to the other, to the extent of that payment. If the landlord has received the policy moneys, the tenant's claim—if any—is against the landlord alone, as was the case prior to the 1999 Act.

The Copyhold and Leasehold Reform Act 2002 s.164, confers various rights upon a tenant under a long lease (21 years or more) who is under an obligation to insure the premises with an insurer nominated or approved by the landlord. Under this section, the tenant is not required to effect insurance with the landlord's insurer, but may insure with some other insurer if the following conditions are met:

(a) the house is insured under a policy of insurance issued by an authorised insurer;
(b) the policy covers the interests of both the landlord and the tenant;
(c) the policy covers all the risks that the lease requires be covered by insurance provided by the landlord's insurer;
(d) the amount of the cover is not less than that which the lease requires to be provided by such insurance; and
(e) the tenant has given notice of cover in the form prescribed by regulations[120] within 14 days of it taking effect, specifying the name of the insurer, the risks covered by the policy, the amount and period of the cover, the address of the house insured under the policy, the registered office of the insurer, the number of the policy, the frequency with which premiums are payable, the amount and nature of any policy deductible. The notice must include a statement that the tenant is satisfied that the policy covers his interests and has no reason to believe that it does not cover the interests of the landlord.

Breach of landlord's covenant to insure. Unless the lease relates to a dwelling, **19–018** in which case the Landlord and Tenant Act 1985 applies, the tenant cannot

---

[120] The relevant regulations are the Leasehold Houses (Notice of Insurance Cover) (England) Regulations 2004 (SI 2004/3097), as amended by the Leasehold Houses (Notice of Insurance Cover) (England) (Amendment) Regulations 2005 (SI 2005/177).

challenge the landlord's choice of insurer or policy even if this means that a high premium is payable,[121] unless the lease lays down qualifications or the tenant is required to give approval.[122] This rule is reversed in the case of a tenancy of a dwelling, under the Landlord and Tenant Act 1985.

If the landlord, in breach of an insuring covenant, fails to insure at all or for the agreed risks,[123] he is liable in damages to the tenant, although in the absence of any damage to the property which would otherwise have been covered by the insurance it follows that damages will not be substantial.[124] However, if the property is damaged by an insurable peril, the measure of damages will be the cost of reinstatement, assuming that the obligation of the landlord was to insure on a reinstatement basis.[125] In *Naumann v Ford*[126] the landlord failed to renew a policy, in breach of covenant, but the insurer reached an agreement with the tenant whereby the tenant was to be paid the cost of repairs in consideration for his bringing an action for breach of covenant against the landlord and holding the proceeds on trust for the insurers. It was held that the landlord could not resist the tenant's action by pleading that the tenant had received an indemnity from the insurers.

19–019   *Other rights of the tenant*   The common law rights of a tenant of a dwelling who indirectly pays insurance premiums to a landlord who has effected insurance in his, the landlord's, own name have to some extent been improved by the Landlord and Tenant Act 1987, inserting Sch.1 in the Landlord and Tenant Act 1985 (as subsequently amended by the Commonhold and Leasehold Reform Act 2002), although the changes are procedural rather than substantive. The rights of the tenant are as follows:

1. To receive, within 21 days following written notice to the landlord, a summary of the insurance. This must include the name of the insurer, the sum insured, and the main perils insured against (but not, apparently, the main exceptions). The landlord may, in the alternative, supply the tenant with a copy of the policy.[127] Where the insurance has been effected by a superior landlord, so that the landlord himself is not in possession of the policy or the relevant details, the landlord is required to obtain the information from the superior landlord.[128] The assignment of the tenancy does not affect the validity of the tenant's request.[129] It is an offence for the landlord and superior landlord not to comply with these provisions.[130]

2. Where the tenant has sought and obtained particulars of the policy from the landlord, to be afforded following notice reasonable facilities for

---

[121] *Bandar Property Holdings Ltd v Darwen* [1968] 2 All E.R. 305.

[122] *Chaplin v Reid* (1858) 1 F. & F. 315, where the insurer was identified in the covenant; *Enlayde Ltd v Roberts* [1917] 1 Ch. 109, where the insurer was thought to be reputable. In some cases the other party may be required to approve the insurer, in which case there is authority for the proposition that consent can be withheld for any reason, rational or otherwise: *Tredegar v Harwood* [1929] A.C. 72.

[123] Other than war risks, as such risks are not insurable: Landlord and Tenant (War Damage) Act 1941 s.11.

[124] *Hey v Wyche* (1842) 12 L.J.Q.B. 83.

[125] *Burt v British Transport Commission* (1955) 166 E.G. 4.

[126] *Naumann v Ford* [1985] 2 E.G.L.R. 70.

[127] Landlord and Tenant Act 1985 Sch.1 para.2.

[128] Landlord and Tenant Act 1985 Sch.1 para.4.

[129] Landlord and Tenant Act 1985 Sch.1 para.5.

[130] Landlord and Tenant Act 1985 Sch.1 para.6

inspecting the policy itself and proofs that the premiums have been paid, and for taking copies or extracts.[131] If these documents are in the possession of a superior landlord, the landlord must in turn give notice in writing to him, and he must comply within a reasonable time.[132] Once again, assignment of the tenancy does not affect the validity of the tenant's request, and the landlord and superior landlord commit an offence by not meeting their respective obligations.[133]

3. If it appears that the premises have suffered damage for which a claim could be made by the landlord, and if the policy contains a provision requiring notification to the insurer within a given period, the tenant may within that period serve a notice on the insurer, the effect of which is to extend the notification period to a period of six months. This provision does not confer upon the tenant the right to claim under the policy, but preserves the landlord's right to claim while giving the tenant the opportunity to proceed against the landlord to require a claim to be made.[134] The tenant may, ultimately, appoint a receiver in order to ensure that the landlord's policy is enforced.

4. Where the lease requires the tenant to procure insurance, and confers upon the landlord the right to nominate or approve an insurer, the tenant may apply to the court for a ruling that the insurer is unsatisfactory or that the premiums required are excessive. The court may order the landlord to nominate or approve another insurer.[135]

Independently of these statutory rights, the courts have held that where a landlord insures in his own name but is required under the lease to apply the policy moneys towards reinstatement, the landlord is under an implied obligation to make a claim under the policy and to prosecute it with all reasonable despatch.[136]

Tenant's insurable interest. The tenant has an insurable interest, by virtue of his possession, in the premises leased, and he may insure them for his own benefit and for the benefit of his landlord to the full extent of their value. But if he insures for his own benefit only, by the principle of indemnity he will be able to recover no more than he has personally lost, and unless either by virtue of his liability by obligation of law, or by a covenant to repair, on his part, in the lease, he is liable to his landlord in respect of the whole value of the loss, he will be unable to recover it.[137] Nor will the right to claim reinstatement under the Fire Prevention (Metropolis) Act 1774 s.83, aid either the landlord or the tenant in such a case, since this only requires the insurers to lay out "the insurance money . . . as far as the same will go" and does not authorise the assured to claim more than an indemnity.[138] A tenant who is liable to his landlord in the event of the destruction of the premises leased, under a covenant to repair for instance,

19–020

---

[131] Landlord and Tenant Act 1985 Sch.1 para.3.
[132] Landlord and Tenant Act 1985 Sch.1 para.4.
[133] Landlord and Tenant Act 1985 Sch.1 paras 5 and 6 respectively.
[134] Landlord and Tenant Act 1987 Sch.3 para.7.
[135] Landlord and Tenant Act 1987 Sch.3 para.8. See *Berrycroft Management Co Ltd v Sinclair Gardens Investments (Kensington) Ltd* (1997) 29 H.L.R. 444. The Court of Appeal rejected an alternative argument that terms relating to the reasonableness of the premium should be implied into the lease.
[136] *Vural v Security Archives Ltd* [1989] E.G.L.S. 2.
[137] Bowen L.J. in *Castellain v Preston* (1883) L.R. 11 QBD 380 at 400, 401.
[138] Younger L.J. in *Matthey v Curling* [1922] 2 A.C. 180 at 219.

and insures them, will not be limited in a claim against his insurers to the marketable value of his lease,[139] even if he only insures his own interest.

In any event a tenant has usually an insurable interest in the premises commensurate with his liability for rent. In the absence of an express stipulation on the matter this liability continues even after the total destruction of the premises, however it may occur.[140] Even a covenant excluding the liability to repair in case of casualties by fire will not remove this liability for rent, whether or not the landlord has insured the premises,[141] and even though the landlord has covenanted to repair the part burnt down the tenant must pay the rent meanwhile.[142]

19–021 *Tenant's covenant to insure.* Since covenants to repair afford no security to the landlord in the event of the insolvency of the tenant, the lease may require the tenant to insure the premises. Apart from such a covenant, tenants for years are not at common law obliged to do so. Frequently, moreover, the case of loss or damage by fire is excluded from the covenant to repair, and a covenant by the tenant to insure the landlord's interest is then necessary to protect the landlord from such loss or damage.[143] The covenant to repair, in effect, makes the tenant an insurer to the full value of the premises, even if he also covenants to insure for a fixed sum. The latter covenant is a collateral security to the landlord. It supplies a fund out of which the tenant may, in whole or in part, recoup himself in respect of liability under a covenant to repair but in no way limits his liability under that covenant.[144] Thus if he does not insure for the full amount, or if the loss is due to an excepted peril, he will have to pay the balance, or the whole, of the loss himself.

Covenants to insure, unless expressed to be personal, run with the land, and an assignee of the landlord is entitled to enforce them.[145] Even though the landlord has assented to a breach of such covenant by the lessee, this will not protect the lessee against an assignee of the landlord,[146] and he should always, therefore, strictly comply with its terms. Such a covenant is, however, to be construed reasonably.[147]

But while such covenants are enforceable by the landlord's assignee, as a cause of forfeiture, for instance, he will not be able to benefit or control the policy moneys under an insurance made for the benefit of the original landlord and tenant only, unless either he exercises his statutory right of requiring reinstatement, or there is a provision in the lease that such moneys are to be laid out in restoring premises.[148] While a covenant to insure may run with the land, the benefit of insurance does not normally do so.[149] Thus, covenants apart, the

---

[139] *Simpson v Scottish Union Insurance Co* (1863) 1 Hem. & M. 618 at 628, and Bowen L.J. in *Castellain v Preston* (1883) L.R. 11 QBD 380 at 400.

[140] *Paradine v Jane* (1647) Aleyn 26; *Matthey v Curling* [1922] 2 A.C. 180; *Cricklewood Property v Leighton* [1945] A.C. 221; *National Carriers v Panalpina* [1981] A.C. 675.

[141] *Belfour v Weston* (1786) 1 T.R. 310, and *Pindar v Ainsley* (1767) therein cited, at 312.

[142] *Leeds v Cheetham* (1827) 1 Sim. 146.

[143] See *Weigall v Waters* (1795) 6 T.R. 488; *Darrell v Tibbitts* (1880) L.R. 5 QBD 560.

[144] *Digby v Atkinson* (1815) 4 Camp. 275 at 278, per Lord Ellenborough C.J.

[145] *Bullock v Domitt* (1796) 6 T.R. 650; *Vemon v Smith* (1821) 5 B. & Ald. 1. See now Landlord and Tenant (Covenants) Act 1995.

[146] *Doe d. Muston v Gladwin* (1845) L.R. 6 Q.B. 953.

[147] *Doe d. Pittman v Sutton* (1841) 9 Car. & P. 706.

[148] *Garden v Ingram* (1852) 23 L.J. Ch. 478; *Rayner v Preston* (1881) L.R. 18 Ch. D. 1 at 7, 8 per Cotton L.J.

[149] *Rayner v Preston* (1881) L.R. 18 Ch D 1.

landlord's assignee could not benefit under a policy taken out by the tenant and covering the landlord's interest.

The landlord is not entitled to benefit under an insurance made by the tenant alone,[150] either voluntarily[151] or in pursuance of a simple covenant to insure, unless it was made for his benefit, or he exercises his statutory right to reinstatement,[152] or unless he can make use of the Contracts (Rights of Third Parties) Act 1999.

Content of tenant's covenant to insure. The covenant to insure may stipulate a **19–022** named insurer,[153] and the risk to be insured against. If not, an insurance with a company which normally accepts the agreed risks will satisfy it,[154] but the covenanter must choose an office which will give him full protection, not, for example, an office which excludes losses due to enemy action,[155] unless the covenant expressly stipulates offices approved by the lessor and he has approved the office in question.[156] Where the covenant is to insure in a named office, or in some other responsible office to be approved by the lessor, the primary obligation on the tenant is to insure in the named office and the landlord has an absolute right to withhold his approval of an alternative office, without giving any reason. Neither the fact that a covenant to insure omits the words "against fire" nor the name of any office makes it void for uncertainty.[157]

The covenant to insure generally stipulates in whose name the tenant is bound to insure. Where he covenants to insure jointly in the names of himself and his landlord he is entitled to insure in the name of his landlord only.[158] But he is not entitled, on the other hand, to insure in the joint names of himself, his landlord and another, for such other would be entitled to give the insurers a good discharge for the insurance moneys and would have a control over them.[159] Thus, if he mortgages his lease, and binds himself to insure in the mortgagee's name, he will be bound to make a separate insurance. The difficulty may be avoided by his assigning to the mortgagee his interest in the policy which he has promised his landlord to take out, provided the mortgagee assents to this arrangement in place of an insurance in his name.

Insurance must normally be made immediately on the commencement of the term,[160] and failure to pay a renewal premium is a breach of the covenant to keep insured, once the days of grace have run out and any extension granted by the insurers has expired. Payment afterwards will not mend the breach,[161] nor does the fact that the insurers antedate the receipt affect the position.[162]

Where the covenant fixes the amount of the insurance it will not be affected by a change in the value of the premises. Thus, where the covenant was to insure for

[150] *Lees v Whiteley* (1866) L.R. 2 Eq. 143.

[151] *Leeds v Cheetham* (1827) 1 Sim. 146.

[152] Under the Fires Prevention (Metropolis) Act 1774. See *Reynard v Arnold* (1875) L.R. 10 Ch. 386; *Andrews v Patriotic Assurance (No.2)* (1886) 18 L.R. Ir. 355.

[153] *Tredegar v Harwood* [1929] A.C. 72.

[154] *Doe d. Pitt v Shewin* (1811) 3 Camp. 134; *Berrycroft Management v Sinclair Gardens Investments (Kensington) Ltd* (1997) 29 H.L.R. 444.

[155] *Enlayde v Roberts* [1917] 1 Ch. 109.

[156] *Upjohn v Hitchins* [1918] 2 K.B. 48.

[157] *Doe d. Pitt v Shewin* (1811) 3 Camp. 134.

[158] *Havens v Middleton* (1853) 10 Hare 641.

[159] *Penniall v Harborne* (1848) 11 Q.B. 368.

[160] *Doe d. Darlington v Ulph* (1849) 18 L.J.Q.B. 106, but see *Doe d. Pittman v Sutton* (1841) 9 Car. & P. 706.

[161] *Wilson v Wilson* (1854) 14 C.B. 616.

[162] *Howell v Kightley* (1856) 21 Beav. 331.

£2,000, and the lease excluded part of the premises after six years, it was held that the tenant was nevertheless obliged to keep the remainder insured for £2,000.[163] Conversely an increase in the market value of the subject-matter will not oblige the covenanter to insure for more than the named sum.[164]

An obligation on the tenant to insure for the "full cost of reinstatement" means the cost of reinstatement at the time when it is to take place, and not the cost of reinstatement at the date of the casualty.[165]

19–023 *Landlord's remedies for breach of covenant to insure.* In the event of a breach by the tenant of his covenant to insure, the landlord may have two remedies: (a) an action for damages and (b) if there is a provision in the lease reserving him a right of re-entry in the event of breach of covenant, forfeiture of the lease. A landlord has no right of forfeiture in the absence of such a stipulation; in such a case his only remedy for a breach of the covenant is an action for damages.

19–024 *Tenant's liability for increase of risk.* In the absence of any covenant by the tenant to insure, a landlord who wishes so to be protected must bear the cost of insurance himself. At common law, even if the tenant did something to increase the premium, as by storing matches on premises, he could not be called upon to breach the additional premium unless he was in breach of the lease in so doing,[166] or the lease expressly provided that he should do so.[167] But now, where the landlord has undertaken to pay the premiums on a fire policy on the premises, the tenant is liable to him for any increase in the rate of premium due to any improvements executed by him on the premises.[168]

Mortgagor and mortgagee

19–025 *Insurable interest.* Both parties have an insurable interest. A mortgagor has an insurable interest in property mortgaged[169] to its full value, even though he parts with the legal title,[170] because: (a) an equitable interest, the equity of redemption, that is to say the right to regain his whole interest in the property on repayment of the debt, is still vested in him[171]; and (b) even if the property is destroyed, he is still liable to pay the debt.[172] It follows, therefore, that if the owner of property, after insuring it, charges it by way of mortgage, the liability of the insurers will not be diminished.[173] The mortgagor's interest ceases on sale or foreclosure by the mortgagee. The mortgagee also has an insurable interest in the property mortgaged, for the security upon which he relies will be diminished by its loss,[174] but if he insures for his own benefit only the amount of the mortgage debt owing

---

[163] *Heckman v Isaac* (1862) 6 L.T. 383.

[164] See *Carreras v Cunard Steamship Co* [1918] 1 K.B. 118, an agreement to insure goods.

[165] *Glennifer Finance Corporation Ltd v Bamar Wood & Products Ltd* [1978] 2 Lloyd's Rep. 49.

[166] *Heckman v Isaac* (1861) 4 L.T. 825 (1862) 6 L.T. 383.

[167] *Duke of Hamilton's Trustees v Fleming* (1870) 9 M. 329.

[168] Landlord and Tenant Act 1927 s.16.

[169] *Smith v Lascelles* (1788) 2 T.R. 187.

[170] *Alston v Campbell* (1779) 4 Bro. P.C. 476; *Hutchinson v Wright* (1858) 25 Beav. 444.

[171] *Glover v Black* (1763) 1 Wm. Bl. 396; *Lees v Whiteley* (1866) L.R. 2 Eq. 143.

[172] *Provincial Insurance Co of Canada v Leduc* (1874) L.R. 6 P.C. 224 at 244.

[173] Lord St. Leonards in *Garden v Ingram* (1852) 23 L.J. Ch. 478.

[174] Lord Mansfield in *Glover v Black* (1763) 1 Wm. Bl. 396; Bovill C.J. in *Ebsworth v Alliance Marine Insurance Co* (1873) L.R. 8 C.P. 596 at 608; *Westminster Fire v Glasgow Provident Society* (1888) L.R. 13 App.Cas. 699; *Samuel & Co Ltd v Dumas* [1924] A.C. 431.

to him at the time of the loss is all he can recover.[175] Moreover the insurers will be entitled to be subrogated to the mortgagee's right to be repaid the mortgage debt, to the full extent of moneys paid by them.[176] Where the mortgagor reinstates the premises the mortgagee can recover nothing since his security has not been impaired.[177]

It follows from these principles that both mortgagor and mortgagee can take out separate insurances on the same property. Unless one of them reinstates the premises, both can recover in full from their insurers, subject to the right of the mortgagee's insurers to subrogation. In such a case the insurers are not entitled to contribution between themselves, provided the policies cover only the limit of the interests of each assured. But it is otherwise where one of the two policies covers the interest of both.[178] Successive mortgagees can insure their respective interests to their full value, and it will be no defence to their insurers that claims made by them together amount to more than the value of the property destroyed.[179]

Where the policy is composite, taken out in the names of mortgagor and mortgagee, either of them can give the insurers a good discharge for the insurance money,[180] but the court will not allow him to apply it in disregard of the rights of the other.[181] As under a composite policy of this type each party is insured for his own rights and interests, the ability of each party to make a claim is independent. Thus if the mortgagor has failed to disclose a material fact to the insurer, the mortgagee's claim is not affected.[182]

Payment of the proceeds. The mortgagee's main concern is to ensure that, where the mortgagor has insured in his own name, the policy proceeds are used either to reinstate the premises or to pay off the mortgage debt, although the common law is clear that, in the absence of agreement between mortgagor and mortgagee, the mortgagor can apply the proceeds for any purposes,[183] leaving the mortgagee as an unsecured creditor. This is the result of the rule in *Lees v Whiteley*, in which it was decided that the assignee under a bill of sale of certain chattels had no claim to the benefit of a policy against fire effected by the mortgagor, even though the bill of sale contained a covenant by him to insure. The principle is clear that apart from special contract or statutory provisions a mortgagee has no rights under a policy taken out by the mortgagor for his own benefit.[184] The mortgagor is in no sense a trustee of the insurance moneys for the mortgagee.[185] However, the mortgagee will be an interested person for the purposes of the Fires

19–026

---

[175] *Ebsworth v Alliance Marine* (1873) L.R. 8 C.P. 596; *Castellain v Preston* (1883) L.R. 11 QBD 380 at 398 per Bowen L.J.

[176] See Bowen L.J. in *Castellain v Preston* (1883) L.R. 11 QBD 380 at 405; Jessel M.R. in *Commercial Union Assurance Co v Lister* (1874) L. R. 9 Ch. App. 483 at 484; Mellish L.J. in *North British and Mercantile Insurance Co v London, Liverpool & Globe* (1877) L.R. 5 Ch D 569 at 583.

[177] *Darrell v Tibbitts* (1880) L.R. 5 QBD 560.

[178] *Nichols v Scottish Union and National Insurance Co* (1885) 2 T.L.R. 190.

[179] *Westminster Fire v Glasgow Provident* (1888) L.R. 13 App. Cas. 699.

[180] *Penniall v Harbourne* (1848) 11 Q.B. 368; *General Accident Fire and Life Assurance Corporation v Midland Bank Ltd* [1940] 2 K.B. 388.

[181] *Rogers v Grazebrooke* (1842) 12 Sim. 557.

[182] One exception arises where the assured under a marine policy deliberately scuttles the insured vessel, for here there is no insured peril (wilful misconduct not constituting "perils of the seas") and the mortgagee has no claim: *Samuel & Co v Dumas* [1924] A.C. 431. For this reason the mortgagees of vessels will generally take out a fall-back policy in the form of a mortgagees' interest policy.

[183] *Lees v Whiteley* (1866) L.R. 2 Eq. 143; *Mumford Hotels v Wheeler* [1964] Ch. 117.

[184] Parker J. in *Sinnott v Bowden* [1912] 2 Ch. 414 at 419.

[185] Wright J. in *Halifax Building Society v Keighley* [1931] 2 K.B. 248 at 255.

Prevention (Metropolis) Act 1774[186] and may require the insurer to use the proceeds to reinstate fire-damaged premises, assuming that the mortgagor has made a claim under the policy and has not at the time of the mortgagee's request been paid by the insurer.[187] Moreover, where the policy has been effected by the mortgagor in compliance with an obligation in the mortgage deed, or by the mortgagee under the statutory power,[188] the mortgagee may require the proceeds of the policy to be used to reinstate the premises or to pay off the mortgage debt.[189]

19–027 *The mortgagee's statutory power to insure.* In practice the mortgage instrument will require the mortgagor to procure insurance covering the mortgaged property, with the proceeds being either payable or assigned to the mortgagee. The obligation is a strict one, and if the mortgagor expressly covenants to insure, not even the impossibility of effecting such insurance will excuse him for failure to effect it.[190] However, since, where property is mortgaged, a mortgagee has no inherent right to effect any insurances upon it at the borrower's expense,[191] nor will he necessarily be able to take advantage of insurances taken out by the mortgagor unless the mortgage insurance or policy so provides, it is important that he should ensure that his interests in this respect are safe-guarded in the mortgage instrument in the event that the mortgagor has not complied with the mortgage instrument either in failing to insure in the names of both parties, or in failing to insure in his own name for the benefit of his own and the mortgagee's interests. The mortgagee has thus been given a statutory right, under s.101(1)(ii) of the Law of Property Act 1925.

19–028 *The proceeds of policies.* Where the mortgagee has effected a policy in accordance with the provisions of s.101(1) of the Law of Property Act 1925, or where the mortgagor is required by the mortgage deed to maintain insurance, the mortgagee may require the proceeds of the policy to be applied by way of reinstatement[192] or, in the alternative, to discharge the mortgage debt.[193]

19–029 **Creditor insuring property of debtor.** A creditor who has taken a security over his debtor's specified or general assets may insure them up to a maximum sum equalling the full amount of the debt secured by them. However, if the creditor is not secured, the courts have determined that he does not have insurable interest in any of the debtor's assets[194]; his interest is not in the assets as such, but in the general solvency of the debtor. No great problem is caused by this rule, for a creditor is permitted to insure the life of his debtor for the full amount of the debt, and the creditor may in any event take out insurance against the debtor's insolvency.

19–030 **Trustee and beneficiary.** The beneficiary under a trust has insurable interest to the full extent of his equitable interest. A trustee has legal title and may thus

---

[186] *Sinnott v Bowden* [1912] 2 Ch. 414.
[187] *Simpson v Scottish Union Insurance Co* (1863) 32 L.J. Ch. 329.
[188] Law of Property Act 1925 s.101(1)(ii).
[189] Law of Property Act 1925 s.108(3)–(4).
[190] *Re Moorgate Estates* [1942] Ch. 321.
[191] *Bellamy v Brickenden* (1861) 2 John. & H. 137; *Dobson v Land* (1850) 8 Hare 216.
[192] Law of Property Act 1925 s.108(3).
[193] Law of Property Act 1925 s.108(4).
[194] *Moran, Galloway & Co v Uzielli* [1905] 2 K.B. 555; *Macaura v Northern Assurance Co* [1925] A.C. 619; *The Moonacre* [1992] 2 Lloyd's Rep. 501.

insure the subject matter of the trust to its full value.[195] Trustees are empowered, but not directed, by statute to insure against fire to the extent of three-fourths of the full value of buildings or chattels.[196] The premiums on insurances thus taken out or renewed are payable out of the income arising from the whole of the funds comprised in the same trust: thus where the trust comprises heirlooms and other property bearing income the trustees are entitled, without the consent of all or any of the beneficiaries, to insure the heirlooms out of this income.[197] Money recovered for losses occurring under such policies will be capital money for the benefit of all those entitled under the trust,[198] and will not belong to the person at present entitled to the income out of which the premiums have been paid.

A party to a contract can constitute himself a trustee for a third party of rights under a contract and thus confer rights on the third party,[199] although an unequivocal declaration of trust will generally be required.[200] Where more than one person has an interest in the same subject matter and one of them insures to the extent of the whole value, constituting himself a trustee to the extent of the others' interest of any benefit he may receive under the policy,[201] he cannot actually benefit to more than the extent of his own interest, and the principle of indemnity will not be offended. Thus, Bowen L.J. said in *Castellain v Preston*:[202] "A person with a limited interest may insure either for himself and to cover his own interest only, or he may insure so as to cover . . . the interest of all others who are interested in the property". Thus, a person without any interest at all can insure, provided he holds himself trustee for interested parties and provided interest in such insurance is not required by statute. So a trade union may insure against its members' losses of goods, provided it regards itself as their trustee in respect of any moneys it may receive under the policy.[203] Such an insurance is not a wager and illustrates the general principle that lack of interest is not fatal to the assured at common law.

Personal representatives. The personal representatives of a deceased person, be they executors or administrators, have, like trustees, an insurable interest in property comprised in his estate.[204] They may take out new insurances, or renew old ones.[205] They have also a sufficient interest to insure in their own name the life of a person who has granted an annuity to the deceased, and which the deceased has bequeathed to persons not parties to the insurance.[206] Personal representatives, while they may not allow existing insurances to expire, cannot be

19–031

[195] Ashhurst J. in *Smith v Lascelles* (1788) 2 T.R. 187; *Camden v Andersen* (1794) 5 T.R. 709; Lord Eldon in *Ex. p.Yallop* (1808) 15 Ves. 60 at 67, 68; *Ex. p. Houghton* (1810) 17 Ves. 251.

[196] Settled Land Act 1925 s.102; Trustee Act 1925 s.19.

[197] Trustee Act 1925 s.19; *Re Egmont's Trusts* [1908] 1 Ch. 821.

[198] Trustee Act 1925 s.20. See also Settled Land Act 1925 s.102 and *Re Bladon* [1911] 2 Ch. 350 at 354.

[199] *Vandepitte v Preferred Accident Insurance Corporation of New York* [1933] A.C. 70 at 79 per Lord Wright. See also *Lloyd's v Harper* (1880) 16 Ch D 290; *Beswick v Beswick* [1968] A.C. 58, doubting *Re Engelbach's Estate* [1924] 2 Ch. 348. As to how such rights are to be enforced, see *Harmer v Armstrong* [1934] 1 Ch. 65.

[200] *D.G. Finance v Scott* [1999] Lloyd's Rep. I.R. 387.

[201] *Sidaways v Todd* (1818) 2 Stark. 400; Lord Campbell C.J. in *Waters v Monarch Fire & Life Assurance Co* (1856) 5 El. & Bl. 870 at 881; *London & North West Railway Co v Glyn* (1859) 1 El. & El. 652.

[202] *Castellain v Preston* (1883) L.R. 11 Q.B.D. 380 at 398.

[203] *Prudential Staff Union v Hall* [1947] K.B. 685.

[204] *Tidswell v Ankerstein* (1792) Peake 204; *Stirling v Vaughan* (1809) 11 East 619; *Bailey v Could* (1840) 4 Y. & C. 221; *Re Betty* [1899] 1 Ch. 821.

[205] *Parry v Ashley* (1829) 3 Sim. 97.

[206] *Tidswell v Ankerstein* (1792) Peake 204.

called to account for failing to insure against fire property not insured by the deceased.[207] Where the deceased lessee was bound to insure, but allowed the insurance to expire, his executors were held not liable for failing to renew it.[208] So also where the deceased left a business partner who failed to renew the insurance on the business premises it was held that the deceased's executors were not chargeable as for wilful default for not having done so.[209] But while they may be under no legal obligation to insure they ought normally to do so at the expense and for the benefit of the estate,[210] and they will be entitled to recover the premiums from that part of the estate which is protected by the insurance.[211] Moreover, an obligation to insure may be expressly laid upon them by the terms of the deceased's will. And once an executor takes out a policy, a life policy for instance to secure a debt owing to the estate, he may be called to account if he drops it without good reason.[212]

Money paid under a policy effected or renewed by an executor is payable to the parties interested in the property insured: it does not form part of the testator's general personal estate.[213]

19–032 **Contractor.** It is common practice in the building industry for the head contractor on a site to insure, in his name and on behalf of subcontractors, the entire contract works against all risks. This form of insurance is commercially convenient, as there may be a diversity of property on a site, with a multitude of different owners, and requiring separate insurance would in a large operation inevitably give rise to overlapping policies as well as to great uncertainty in respect of who exactly was the owner of which piece of property at any given time. The validity of insurance on the entire works by the head contractor was challenged in *Petrofina (UK) Ltd v Magnaload Ltd*,[214] which involved a policy on a major oil refinery, the insured sum being £92 million. The main issue in the case was whether the head contractor's name, as assured, could be used in subrogation proceedings against an allegedly negligent subcontractor who had caused the loss on which the insurance claim was based. This defence ultimately failed on the unavailability of subrogation in the circumstances, a point discussed below, but the immediate interest of the case is the argument as to the scope of the insurance cover. The insurers argued that the proper construction of the policy was that it was an insurance on goods actually belonging to the head contractor, but that in relation to all other property it was simply a policy on the liability of the head contractor as bailee of that property. The counter-argument was that the policy was one on goods simpliciter and that, by analogy with the rule applying to bailments, the head contractor had insured the entire contract works as bailee and could recover the full sum insured, although any cash surplus over his own interest was to be held on trust for the subcontractors and other persons whose interests were covered. Lloyd J. held that, for the sake of commercial convenience, the latter construction ought to be adopted. Consequently, a policy in the standard form considered in *Petrofina (UK) Ltd v Magnaload Ltd* may be construed as one on the entire contract works. The decision is, therefore, an

---

[207] *Croft v Lyndsey* (1676) Freeman Ch. 1; *Fry v Fry* (1859) 27 Beav. 144; *Re McEacham* (1911) 103 L.T. 900.

[208] *Tidswell v Ankerstein* (1792) Peake 204.

[209] *Bailey v Gould* (1840) 4 Y. & C. 221.

[210] North J. in *Re Betty* [1899] 1 Ch. 821 at 829.

[211] *Re Smith's Estate* [1937] Ch. 636.

[212] *Garner v Moore* (1855) 3 Drew. 277.

[213] *Parry v Ashley* (1829) 3 Sim. 97.

[214] *Petrofina (UK) Ltd v Magnaload Ltd* [1984] Q.B. 127.

application of the decisions in *Waters v Monarch Fire and Life Assurance Co*[215] and *Tomlinson (Hauliers) Ltd v Hepburn*.[216]

The *Petrofina* decision was followed by Colman J. in *National Oilwell (UK) Ltd v Davy Offshore Ltd*.[217] The learned judge accepted that a contractors' all risks policy which covers the head contractor and all sub-contractors is a property policy, and that every party to the policy has an insurable interest in the entire subject matter insured under the policy. A subcontractor responsible for only a small part of the works possessed a clear insurable interest in the property which he either owned or possessed, and his insurable interest in the remainder of the works arose from the sub-contractor's proximate physical relationship to those works and the risk that damage to the works could result in the loss of his contract. While this analysis at first sight appears to blur the line between property and liability insurance, Colman J. justified his approach by the fact that commercial considerations demanded it, and also by the fact that the market offered contractors' all risks insurance only on a property rather than a liability basis. The proposition accepted in *Petrofina* was, before the ruling in *National Oilwell*, adopted by the Court of Appeal in *Stone Vickers Ltd v Appledore Ferguson Shipbuilders Ltd*[218] an approval confirmed in *Deepak Fertilisers and Petrochemical Corporation v Davy McKee (London) Ltd*.[219] It was said in *Deepak* that subcontractors possessed:

> "an insurable interest in the plant under construction and on which they were working because they might lose the opportunity to do the work and to be remunerated for it if the property or structure were damaged or destroyed by any of the 'all risks' such as fire or flood".

An important qualification was, however, established in *Deepak*, namely that, once the subcontractor has finished working on the property, any insurable interest comes to an end, so that if there is a fault in the subcontractor's work which becomes manifest at a later date, the policy does not provide cover for the subcontractor: this would operate to convert the policy from a property policy into a liability policy. As was noted by Stuart-Smith L.J.:

> "[The subcontractors] would only suffer disadvantage if the damage to or destruction of the property or structure was the result of their breach of contract or duty of care. In order to protect the contractor and subcontractors against the risk of disadvantage by reason of damage or destruction of the property or structure resulting from their breach of contract or duty, they would, in accordance with normal practice, take out liability insurance or... professional indemnity insurance."

The correctness of the contractors' decisions, and of the reasoning in *Deepak*, was analysed by the Court of Appeal in *Feasey v Sun Life Assurance Corporation of Canada*.[220] Waller L.J., with whose judgment Dyson L.J. agreed, held that a sub-contractor had an insurable interest in the plant on which he was working by reason of the possibility of his loss of work in the event of loss or

---

[215] *Waters v Monarch Fire and Life Assurance Co* (1856) 5 El. & Bl. 870.

[216] *Tomlinson (Hauliers) Ltd v Hepburn* [1966] A.C. 451.

[217] *National Oilwell (UK) Ltd v Davy Offshore Ltd* [1993] 2 Lloyd's Rep. 582.

[218] *Stone Vickers Ltd v Appledore Ferguson Shipbuilders Ltd* [1991] 2 Lloyd's Rep. 288.

[219] *Deepak Fertilisers and Petrochemical Corporation v Davy McKee (London) Ltd* [1999] 1 Lloyd's Rep. 387. See also *Hopewell Project Management Ltd v Ewbank Preece Ltd* [1998] 1 Lloyd's Rep. 448.

[220] *Feasey v Sun Life Assurance Corporation of Canada* [2003] Lloyd's Rep. I.R. 637.

destruction, and a separate insurable interest in his liability for the plant in the event that it was damaged by his negligence. The risk of liability was arguably not of itself enough to create an insurable interest, but the existence of a further legal link—actual interest in the plant itself—was sufficient to create an insurable interest in the plant by reason of liability for it. The only question then became whether the policy, which was typically expressed as one on the plant, was appropriately worded to cover the sub-contractor's insurable interest in his own liability for the plant. During the period of construction there was no reason why the policy should not be construed as extending to both insurable interests. The outcome is, therefore, that a policy under which a sub-contractor is co-insured, whilst primarily a property policy, is capable of extending to liability. Ward L.J., dissenting, held that the only insurable interest possessed by a sub-contractor in the plant is his own pecuniary loss in the event of damage to the plant, and that his liability for the loss of the plant could not support a property policy as there was no legal or equitable relationship between the sub-contractor and the insured subject matter itself.

2. Utmost Good Faith

19–033   **Material facts.** The materiality of facts will depend upon the type of property insured, e.g. whether it is movable or immovable. It is also important to bear in mind the risks which are being covered by the policy: it is unlikely, for example, that a fire hazard is material to a burglary policy. In very general terms, for all types of property material facts will include: the location of the property[221]; the uses to which the property is put and by whom[222]; the age of the property[223]; the controls exercised by the assured over the insured subject matter[224], security measures[225]; and any particular features which render the property peculiarly susceptible to loss.[226] Use of property in breach of an operating licence is also a material fact.[227]

3. Coverage

19–034   **Types of cover.** Property policies may generally be divided into policies on buildings and policies on goods. As far as goods are concerned, in the case of

---

[221] *Dawsons v Bonnin* [1922] 2 A.C. 413. See also *Bansalou v Royal Insurance* 15 Lt. Cam. Rep. 1 (wooden building behind an insured warehouse used as a kitchen).

[222] *Anderson v Commercial Union Assurance Co* (1885) 55 L.J. Q.B. 146: *Bond v Commercial Union Assurance Co Ltd* (1930) 36 Ll. L.R. 107; *Broad v Waland* (1942) 73 Ll. L.R. 263.

[223] *Santer v Poland* (1924) 19 Ll. L.R. 29.

[224] *Brotherton v Aseguradora Colseguros SA (No.3)* [2003] Lloyd's Rep. I.R. 774.

[225] *AC Ward & Sons Ltd v Catlin (Five) (No.2)* [2009] EWHC 3122 (Comm).

[226] *Bufe v Turner* (1815) 6 Taunt. 338 (neighbouring fire); *Dunn v Campbell* (1920) 4 Ll. L.R. 36 (aircraft to be flown before tested for safety); *Hales v Reliance Fire Assurance* [1960] 2 Lloyd's Rep. 391 (storage of flammable material); *Dawsons Bank v Vulcan Insurance Co* (1927) 30 Ll. L.R. 129 (timber building described as brick); *James v CGU Insurance Plc* [2002] Lloyd's Rep. I.R. 206 (hazardous business run from premises); *WISE Underwriting Agency v Grupo Nacional Provincial SA* [2004] Lloyd's Rep. I.R. 764 (insured property—Rolex watches—of particular value and attractiveness to thieves); *Forrest & Sons Ltd v CGU Insurance Plc* [2006] Lloyd's Rep. I.R. 113 (use of hazardous equipment).

[227] *Jones v Environcom Ltd (No.2)* [2010] EWHC 759 (Comm).

domestic goods cover will generally apply to household contents, although specific extensions are available for goods belonging to the assured which are lost or damaged away from the assured's premises. Where property is insured against damage under a policy, most wordings will exclude losses to defective property which has itself caused loss to other property. Thus if the policy insures property damaged by the escape of molten metal from equipment, any part of the equipment itself which is damaged by the molten metal will be outside the scope of the insurance.[228]

It is common to find property policies which are described as "all risks", especially in the case of insurances of jewellery, goods in transit and household goods generally. Marine cargo is generally ignored on this basis. Although described as "all risks", in fact, such policies are invariably subject to a number of exceptions as may be specified[229] and, as a matter of general principle, will not cover loss caused by wear and tear, inherent vice or the fault of the assured. The real effect of the term "all risks" is simply that the assured is required to prove only that there has been a loss and that the loss was fortuitous.[230] The burden of proof then shifts to the insurer to show that the loss was caused by one of the excepted perils. If he cannot do so, the assured is entitled to recover on the policy.[231] Under an "all risks" transit policy it is prima facie sufficient, to establish a claim, to prove that the goods were undamaged before transit and arrived damaged,[232] and it has been held that seizure of goods by an administrator in bankruptcy, or a wrongful conversion of them amounting to theft, are losses falling within such a policy.[233] It is not always easy to ascertain whether a policy is "all risks". A policy is not all risks where it refers to specific risks and requires loss to be caused by one or more of those risks.[234] There is no magic in using the term "all risks", as the words may be used to refer to the quantum of loss, in which case they do not cover all casualties but merely mean that the loss will be payable in full whatever its actual amount.[235]

Property policies often include clauses which purport to prevent the assured from increasing or altering the risk. Some policies include clauses which seek to protect the owner against unauthorised conduct by any third party. In *Ansari v New India Assurance Ltd*[236] the policy provided that:

---

[228] *Algoma Steel Corporation v Allendale Mutual Insurance Co* 68 D.L.R. (4th) 404 (1990).

[229] Thus the Institute cargo clauses contain exclusion for, e.g. war risks. Equally, contractors' all risks policies may exclude liability for "defects in design" (no negligence required *Queensland Government Railways v Manufacturers Mutual Insurance* [1969] 1 Lloyd's Rep. 214) or "defective design" (negligence required *Hitchins v Prudential Assurance* [1991] 2 Lloyd's Rep. 580).

[230] *CA Blackwell (Contracts) Ltd v Gerling General Insurance Co* [2007] Lloyd's Rep. I.R. 511; the point did not arise on appeal, [2008] Lloyd's Rep. I.R. 529; *Bevan v Gartside Marine Engines Ltd* [2000] B.C.J. No.528.

[231] *British & Foreign Marine Insurance Co v Gaunt* [1921] 2 A.C. 41; *Fuerst Day Lawson v Orion Insurance* [1980] 1 Lloyd's Rep. 656. In *Tektrol Ltd v International Insurance Co of Hanover Ltd* [2006] Lloyd's Rep. I.R. 38 Carnwath L.J. was highly critical of an all-risks policy in which "one has to search long and hard, through a bewildering and apparently comprehensive list of exclusions, to discover the extent to which any risks are in fact covered." The Court of Appeal went on to construe the exceptions narrowly and to hold that the assured was afforded cover.

[232] *Electro Motion v Maritime Insurance* [1956] 1 Lloyd's Rep. 420, but contrast *Theodorou v Chester* [1951] 1 Lloyd's Rep. 204, and see *Gee & Garnham v Whittall* [1955] 2 Lloyd's Rep. 562 where inherent vice was alleged.

[233] *London Leather Processes v Hudson* [1939] 2 K.B. 724.

[234] *Brownsville Holdings v Adamjee Insurance (The Milasan)* [2002] 2 Lloyd's Rep. 458. See also *Cory & Sons v Friedlander* (1922) 10 Ll. L.R. 40.

[235] Per Hamilton J. in *Vincentelli v John Rowlett & Co* (1911) 10 S L.T. 411 at 414.

[236] *Ansari v New India Assurance Ltd* [2009] Lloyd's Rep. I.R. 562.

"The interest of the freeholder lessor or mortgagee in this insurance shall not be prejudiced by any act or neglect whereby the risk of destruction or damage is increased without the authority or knowledge of the freeholder lessor or mortgagee provided they shall immediately on becoming aware thereof give notice in writing to the insurer and on demand pay such reasonable additional premium as the insurer may require."

The freeholder in that case was held to have been aware of conduct by his lessor—change of use, and failure to ensure that a sprinkler system was operative—which contravened the terms of the policy and accordingly was unable to rely upon the "non-invalidation" clause set out above.

Insured perils

19–035   *Storm.* The Oxford English Dictionary offers the following as the principal definition of "storm":

"A violent disturbance of the atmosphere, manifested by high winds, often accompanied by heavy falls of rain or snow, by thunder and lightning, and (at sea) by turbulence of the waves. Hence sometimes applied to a heavy fall of rain, hail or snow, or to a violent outbreak of thunder and lightning, unaccompanied by strong wind."

The reported cases give some support to this definition. It has been held that "storm" means "something more prolonged and widespread than a gust of wind",[237] and that heavy rain by itself does not amount to a storm.[238] In *Young v Sun Alliance*[239] Shaw L.J. said that "storm" implied rain accompanied by high wind. These dicta render of doubtful authority the decision of the Outer House of the Court of Session in *Glasgow Training Group (Motor Trade) Ltd v Lombard Continental Plc*.[240] There had here been a heavy fall of snow unaccompanied by high winds. Snow had accumulated on the roof of the claimant's premises, and eventually its sheer weight caused the roof to collapse. The Scottish court held that the damage fell within the word "storm" in the insuring clause: in the view of the court, while a "storm" indicated turbulence and an event of extreme or unusual intensity, it was not essential for a finding of storm for there to have been high winds. It remains to be seen, therefore, whether the English courts will treat heavy rain and heavy snowfall differently, as this decision indicates might be the case.

19–036   *Tempest.* There appears to be no reported case turning directly upon the definition of "tempest", but in *Young v Sun Alliance*[241] Shaw L.J. expressed the view that a "tempest" is simply a more violent form of storm.[242] Support for this view may be found in the Oxford English Dictionary, which offers as the principal definition of "tempest" the following: "A violent storm of wind, usually accompanied by a downfall of rain, hail or snow, or by thunder."

---

[237] *S & M Hotels v Legal and General Assurance* [1972] 1 Lloyd's Rep. 157.

[238] *Anderson v Norwich Union* [1977] 1 Lloyd's Rep. 253.

[239] *Young v Sun Alliance* [1976] 2 Lloyd's Rep. 189 at 191. See also *Oddy v Phoenix Assurance Co Ltd* [1966] 1 Lloyd's Rep. 134.

[240] *Glasgow Training Group (Motor Trade) Ltd v Lombard Continental Plc*, *The Times*, November 21, 1988.

[241] *Young v Sun Alliance* [1976] 2 Lloyd's Rep. 189.

[242] *Young v Sun Alliance* at 192. See also *Oddy v Phoenix Assurance Co Ltd* [1966] 1 Lloyd's Rep. 134.

Flood. In *Young v Sun Alliance*[243] the assured's house was built on a meadow. **19–037**
Water seeped in to a depth of three inches. The Court of Appeal held that a policy
covering "storm, tempest, flood" did not respond because "flood" was to read in
the context of the clause as a whole, and what was required was an inundation
of water brought about by severe weather conditions. This decision rests largely
upon the presence in the insuring clause of the additional words "storm, tempest"
and it may be suggested that a different result could be reached in a case where
these words were not present, so that even a seepage of water such as occurred
in *Young v Sun Alliance* could amount to a "flood" within the meaning of such
a clause. Nevertheless, *Young* is not as restrictive as it at first sight appears, as
was confirmed by the subsequent decision of the Court of Appeal in *Rohan
Investments Ltd v Cunningham.*[244] Here the assured's flat was damaged by an
ingress of water resulting from heavy rainfall lasting over a period of some days.
The Court of Appeal held that there had been a flood: there was sufficient
evidence that the amount of rainfall was "abnormal"; and the volume of water
involved had to be assessed by reference to the amount which entered the
premises rather than any absolute amount. It is not easy to reconcile *Young* with
Rohan, as in *Young* the emphasis of the Court of Appeal was on the reason for
the ingress of water, whereas in *Rohan* the Court of Appeal was more concerned
with impact of the ingress on the householder.

Rohan also casts doubt upon another decision of the Court of Appeal, in
Computer & Systems Engineering Plc v John Lelliott (Ilford) Ltd.[245] It was in that
case ruled that a flood has to be the result of a natural occurrence, so that water
damage caused to property when a metal purlin was negligently dropped on to a
sprinkler system causing a pipe to fracture and to release water under pressure,
was not insured. No adverse comment was made on this case as such in *Rohan*,
although Auld L.J. commented that there was no reason to confine the term
"flood" to an ingress of water originating from a natural phenomenon, as that
approach was "to confuse the insurable event with preconditions".

Some attempt was made by Jackson J. in *Tate Gallery (Trustees) v Duffy
Construction Ltd*[246] to reconcile the authorities. In this case a part of the Tate
Gallery under reconstruction became submerged to a depth of about 1.4 metres
following the decoupling of a pipe from a water main. Jackson J. held that this
was a flood, and adopted the following test:

> "In determining whether the unwelcome arrival of water upon property constitutes a
> 'flood', it is relevant to consider (a) whether the source of the water was natural; (b)
> whether the source of the water was external or internal; (c) the quantity of water; (d)
> the manner of its arrival; (e) the area and character of the property upon which the water
> was deposited; (f) whether the arrival of that water was an abnormal event. Ultimately,
> it is a question of degree whether any given accumulation of water constitutes a
> flood."

The learned judge regarded both *Young* and *Lelliott* as "fairly unusual", and
rejected the argument that there was an absolute rule which required the property
to be affected by a large volume of water accumulating rapidly. In the present
case there was a significantly greater volume of water than in *Young* in a larger

---

[243] *Young v Sun Alliance* [1976] 2 Lloyd's Rep. 189.

[244] *Rohan Investments Ltd v Cunningham* [1999] Lloyd's Rep. I.R. 90.

[245] *Computer & Systems Engineering Plc v John Lelliott (Ilford) Ltd* (1990) 54 B.L.R. 1.

[246] *Tate Gallery (Trustees) v Duffy Construction Ltd* [2007] Lloyd's Rep. I.R. 758, followed in *Tyco
Fire & Integrated Solutions (UK) Ltd v Rolls-Royce Motor Cars Ltd* [2007] EWHC 137 (TCC) (the
point did not arise on appeal in *Tyco* [2008] Lloyd's Rep. I.R. 617).

area, the water had come from a source outside the insured premises and its arrival had been abnormal: it was irrelevant that the event causing the flood had not been natural. Although this is only a first instance decision, it appears to confirm that *Young* should be limited to its specific facts in which there had been a gradual ingress by seepage of a small amount of water which was not the result of some form of external event.

19–038   *Subsidence.* In ordinary usage the term "subsidence" appears to be limited to collapse or sinking of property in a vertical direction. However, in *David Allen & Sons Billposting Ltd v Drysdale*[247] it was held that a policy providing cover against "subsidence and/or collapse" extended also to the risk of settlement, i.e. the building structure moving in a horizontal direction. It is improbable that the word "subsidence" covers "heave", i.e. a bulging in soil, commonly caused by a chemical reaction; "heave" may well have the same symptoms as subsidence proper, in that it will cause cracking in the walls of buildings, but it would seem to be a misuse of language to include "heave" within the term subsidence. It is noteworthy that the NHBC scheme, which provides quasi-insurance cover for the first 10 years of the life of a new dwelling, mentions both subsidence and heave.

Assuming that subsidence can be demonstrated, two further difficulties arise in practice. First is the problem of causation, for where there has been subsidence this will frequently have resulted from poor workmanship on the part of the architect, builder or structural engineer: the question then becomes whether the assured's loss is due to subsidence or to negligence. On closer analysis the problem disappears, for it is clear that the event insured against is subsidence and it is immaterial how the subsidence came about.

The second issue relates to the fact that subsidence may cause damage prior to the damage becoming manifest: the usual symptom of subsidence is the appearance of cracks in the walls of a building, although structural damage to the foundations may have occurred some time previously. Questions arise here of which, if any, insurers face liability. Let it be supposed that damage occurs to the foundations of a building when it is owned by assured A and insured by insurer X; the building is sold to assured B and is insured by insurer Y, the damage subsequently becoming manifest.[248] As a matter of strict law, if there is any liability at all it must be borne entirely by insurer Y, for only B has suffered a loss; A has not suffered any loss because he has presumably obtained full market price for the building, so that insurer X cannot be called upon to contribute to any expenditure for which insurer Y is liable. The effect is that insurer Y may be responsible for a large sum even though it had been on risk only for a short time, whereas insurer X escapes liability even though it may have been on risk at the time when the actual damage occurred.[249] It is not, however, certain that insurer Y will be liable to pay B at all, for it might argue that the loss had occurred prior to its coming on risk, which has been held to be the case where the policy insures

---

[247] *David Allen & Sons Billposting Ltd v Drysdale* [1939] 4 All E.R. 113.

[248] The example in the text assumes that A has not been fraudulent by disguising serious cracking through decoration in such a case, B may well have a remedy against A.

[249] Insurer Y's position is improved to some extent by the Latent Damage Act 1986 s.3. Prior to that Act the purchaser of property which was subject to damage which had not become manifest had no right to sue the builder or other person responsible. The action belonged to the seller alone, but as he had not suffered damage (by obtaining the full market price) he could not sue the wrongdoer: see *Perry v Tendring District Council* (1985) 3 Con. L.R. 74; *Audsley v Leeds City Council, The Times*, June 2, 1988. Section 3 now confers a remedy upon the purchaser, which will be exercisable by his insurer by way of subrogation.

against "events",[250] and that the provision of funds to B would put him in a better position than he was when he acquired the property. B's loss is not, therefore, caused by subsidence, but by the fact that he paid too much for the property. Identical difficulties are apparent where A remains the owner of the property but simply changes insurers: insurer Y may not be liable because the damage existed when it came on risk, while insurer X may not be liable because it may be too late under the terms of the contract for A to claim against it.

Fire. Property policies usually provide insurance against loss caused by fire. **19–039**
There has been some uncertainty as to the scope of this term, largely because damage may result not only from flames but also from scorching or smoke. The following propositions may be ascertained from the cases.

(1) There must be an ignition of some material before there can be a fire.[251] Thus if the insured property has merely been scorched but no ignition of material has taken place, the damage is not covered by the fire clause.[252] Smoke damage would appear to be covered as long as the smoke resulted from a fire, and in the same way it might be thought that burns to furniture caused by cigarettes or by it being left too close to an open fire are covered. Burns caused by electrical equipment rather than open fires are probably not "fire" damage as a matter of strict law.

(2) The insurer will be liable even though the fire does not leave the fireplace. Thus in *Harris v Poland*[253] the assured had hidden certain valuables in the grate of her fireplace for safekeeping but, having forgotten about this, she lit a fire and the property was destroyed. Atkinson J. ruled that there was loss by fire even though the fire was in its proper place.

(3) There is no reason in principle why the insurer should not be liable for fire damage to property which was intended to be subjected to a fire but which has been destroyed due to the fire going out of control. The best examples of this are boilers and fireplaces. There has long been a belief that the insurer is not liable for fire damage to such property unless the entire premises in which it was housed have been destroyed by fire, but that there is no legal basis for it. The notion is based on *Austin v Drewe*,[254] in which it had been held that the claimant was unable to recover for sugar damaged by excessive heat when furnace dampers were not properly opened; the basis of that decision was, however, that the loss did not fall within the wording of the policy and had in any event been occasioned by negligence. Consequently, property subject to fire may be within the policy if it is damaged by fire, although progressive damage will be excluded as this is classed as wear and tear.

(4) There is a fire within the meaning of a policy whether or not the fire is fortuitous. Consequently, there is no onus upon the assured to prove that the fire was not started deliberately. However, if the insurer can

---

[250] *Kelly v Norwich Union Fire & Life Insurance Ltd* [1898] 2 All E.R. 888. Contrast *Annlar & Co v Attenborough* (1940) 68 Ll. L.R. 147 (policy covering manifestation of loss).

[251] *Fleming v Hislop* (1886) 11 App.Cas. 686; *Duncanson v Continental Insurance Co* 69 D.L.R. (4th) 198 (1990).

[252] *Tempus Shipping Co v Louis Dreyfus & Co* [1930] 1 K.B. 699.

[253] *Harris v Poland* [1941] 1 K.B. 462.

[254] *Austin v Drewe* (1816) 6 Taunt. 436.

demonstrate that the fire was deliberately started by the assured, he will be unable to recover for it on the ground of his own misconduct.[255]

Policies on buildings, particularly on commercial properties, may require the assured to take steps to prevent fire. In *LEC (Liverpool) Ltd v Glover*[256] the assured's policy contained a condition precedent on the use of oxyacetylene cutting equipment, requiring the occupier of the building to provide at least one workman to be present to see that there was no outbreak of fire. The Court of Appeal held that the clause required the occupier to provide a workman who was not himself involved in the operation of the cutting equipment so that he could act as a fire watcher. In *Bonner Williams v Peter Lindsay Leisure Ltd*[257] the assured's policy provided cover for loss caused by fire resulting from the use of blow lamps and similar appliances only where appropriate precautions were first taken. It was held that the clause had been broken.

Policies on premises where the preparation of food is to be carried out normally contain provisions that require constant cleaning of food preparation areas. *Paine v Catlins*[258] considered a clause that is found in many policies issued to hotels and restaurants under which it is a condition precedent that: "All flues exhausts and extraction ducting are cleaned in accordance with the manufacturers' instructions and at least annually and all grease traps extraction hoods canopies sumps and filters are inspected regularly cleaned as necessary and at least once a month." The dispute in *Paine* concerned the "canopy plenium/ extract duct"—a small horizontal area between the grease filters above the kitchen cooking range and at the bottom of the ducting system—in which residues of fat had accumulated and had dripped back onto the range causing a serious fire. H.H. Judge Coulson QC held, having heard detailed technical evidence that the duct formed a part of the flue and not of the filter so that the cleaning obligation was annual rather than monthly, and that even if it was monthly the assured was not in breach of the condition because the duct was as clean as could reasonably be expected given its inaccessibility.

Fire policies commonly contain conditions preventing the introduction of stipulated dangerous things such as steam engines and stoves.[259] Such a condition applies even to a temporary introduction of the prohibited thing, and the fact that it does not cause the loss is immaterial.[260] The clause also precludes decisions such as *Stokes v Cox*,[261] in which the jury found that the introduction of a steam engine did not constitute a breach of a condition prohibiting an increase in the risk.

Such conditions, unlike conditions against variation of the risk, are strictly construed. Thus, in *McEwan v Guthridge*,[262] the Privy Council held that the assured could not recover where he kept more than 56lb of gun powder on the

---

[255] *Busk v Royal Exchange Assurance* (1818) 2 B. & Ald. 73: *Shaw v Robberds* (1837) 6 Ad. & E. 75; *Harris v Poland* [1941] 1 K.B. 462; *The Alexion Hope* [1988] 1 Lloyd's Rep. 311; *Kiriacoulis Lines SA v Compagnie D'Assurance Maritime Aériennes et Terrestres (The Demetra K)* [2002] Lloyd's Rep. I.R. 823; *Scottish & Newcastle Plc v GD Construction (St Albans) Ltd* [2003] Lloyd's Rep. I.R. 809.

[256] *LEC (Liverpool) Ltd v Glover* [2001] Lloyd's Rep. I.R. 315.

[257] *Bonner Williams v Peter Lindsay Leisure Ltd* [2001] 1 All E.R. (Comm) 1140.

[258] *Paine v Catlins* [2005] Lloyd's Rep. I.R. 665.

[259] Parke B. in *Glen v Lewis* (1853) 8 Ex. 607 at 619.

[260] *Glen v Lewis* (1853) 8 Ex. 607 at 619.

[261] *Stokes v Cox* (1856) 1 H. & N. 533.

[262] *McEwan v Guthridge* (1860) 13 Moo. P.C.C. 304. See also *Beacon Life & Fire v Gibb* (1862) 1 Moo. P.C.C. (NS) 73.

insured premises, contrary to a condition in the policy. Again, in *Transthene Packaging Co v Royal Insurance*,[263] it was held that a clause requiring the assured to keep the premises clear of oily rags at night was a continuing warranty, so that any transgression would have had the effect of bringing the risk to an end, although on the facts no breach could be demonstrated.

Lightning. A policy which does not expressly include lightning as one of the insured perils will not cover damage by lightning unless that lightning also causes a fire which can properly be regarded as the immediate cause of the damage.[264]   **19–040**

Explosion. In the absence of any express policy provision a fire policy will cover loss from an explosion caused by a fire,[265] or from a fire following an explosion.[266] It will not cover loss arising independently of fire.[267] The determination of the true cause of the loss depends upon the principles of causation. In practice, explosion is commonly expressly included as one of the insured perils. In *Commonwealth Smelting Ltd v Guardian Royal Exchange Assurance*[268] it was held that "explosion" for these purposes meant an event which was violent, noisy and caused by rapid chemical or nuclear reaction or the bursting out of gas or vapour under pressure. In that case a compressed air blower had been insured against fire, lightning and explosion, and the question was whether the loss to the blower had been caused by explosion when a piece of the blower broke off and was forced outwards by the centrifugal force of compressed air inside the blower, rupturing and shattering its outer casing. Staughton J. held that the word "explosion" implied some violent or noisy event caused by rapid chemical or nuclear reaction, or the bursting out of gas or vapour under pressure. On this test, there was no explosion. In so deciding Staughton J. relied on the context of violent events in which the word appeared, and pointed out that it was necessary to look at the cause of a destructive event rather than its possible appearance to bystanders. The judgment was affirmed by the Court of Appeal.[269]   **19–041**

Commonwealth Smelting was followed by Andrew Smith J. in *Aegis Electrical and Gas International Services Co Ltd v Continental Casualty Co*.[270] A reactor unit (the "DIAR") in an oil refinery suffered damage following a power cut in the refinery and an attempt to repressurise the DIAR. Due to excessive heat being generated within the DIAR, a part of the outside of the DIAR bulged and cracked, and there was also found to be a four inch rupture in the outside plating. The rupture was tiny compared to the overall size of the DIAR, which had an overall surface area of 3,240 square feet. Andrew Smith J.'s assessment of the evidence was that the puncture had occurred after the bulging and cracking, and

[263] *Transthene Packaging Co v Royal Insurance* [1996] L.R.L.R. 32. See also *Bennett v Axa Insurance Plc* [2004] Lloyd's Rep. I.R. 615, where the warranty was by its terms triggered only where its breach caused the fire.

[264] *Gordon v Rimmington* (1807) 1 Camp. 123.

[265] *Stanley v Western Insurance Co* (1868) L.R. 3 Ex. 71.

[266] *Everett v London Assurance* (1865) 19 C.B.N.S. 126.

[267] *Re Hooley Hill Rubber and Chemical Co Ltd and Royal Insurance Co Ltd* [1920] 1 K.B. 257.

[268] *Commonwealth Smelting Ltd v Guardian Royal Exchange Assurance* [1984] 2 Lloyd's Rep. 608.

[269] *Commonwealth Smelting Ltd v Guardian Royal Exchange Assurance* [1986] 1 Lloyd's Rep. 121.

[270] *Aegis Electrical and Gas International Services Co Ltd v Continental Casualty Co* [2008] Lloyd's Rep. I.R. 17.

that it had produced some noise but not at a level which could be described as dramatic. The learned judge held that there was no "explosion", as what was required was "violence and manifest violence . . . [and] a shattering destruction": on the facts neither of these requirements had been satisfied. Referring to *Commonwealth Smelting*, Andrew Smith J. further held that the need for an event which was violent, noisy and caused by "a very rapid chemical or nuclear reaction, or the bursting out of gas or vapour under pressure" had not been met: there was nothing noisy or violent. The learned judge was also of the view that the damage to the DIAR had not been proximately caused by explosion, as the evidence showed that the bulging and cracking had taken place before the rupture. For the reinsurers to establish that the proximate cause of the loss was explosion, it would have been necessary for them to show that the bulging, cracking and rupture were a single event, but the rupture was a minor part of the damage and did not characterise the damage as a whole. By contrast, in *Martini Investments v McGinn*,[271] the eruption of a volcano was held to satisfy the requirements of "explosion".

19–042 *Escape of liquid.* The escape of oil or water from a fixed installation is a peril commonly covered by householders' policies. There is no judicial authority on the meaning of these words, although it would seem on general principle that the loss against which indemnity is available is damage to property affected by the escape and not damage to the installation itself or of the liquid. A related widely used phrase is "bursting or overflowing of water tanks, apparatus or pipes". This peril comes into operation only where some internal force in the container or pipe has caused the bursting or overflowing. This was decided in *Computer & Systems Engineering Plc v John Lelliott (Ilford) Ltd*,[272] where it was held that the dropping of an object onto a pipe, causing water under pressure to escape from the pipe and to damage property, was not within a "bursting or overflowing" provision. It has also been held in Scotland that this phrase does not apply to the expulsion of a bung from a pipe under pressure by steam, which causes an escape of steam subsequently condensing into water.[273] These cases were both considered by Jackson J. in *Tate Gallery (Trustees) v Duffy Construction Ltd*,[274] where the coupling of a pipe to a water main failed by reason of the water pressure inside the main, causing an escape of water. The learned judge ruled that there was cover. The case was held to be unlike *Lelliott*, in that the cause of the escape was internal pressure rather than some form of external event. It was also held that the earlier authorities did not lead to the conclusion that a "burst" necessarily had to be a sudden and violent event, nor did they require a fracture which was incapable of being mended. It was enough, therefore, that a coupling ceased to operate even though neither the pipe nor the main had been damaged in the process. In his words:

"In determining whether a pipe or apparatus 'burst', it is relevant to consider (a) whether the incident occurred because of internal pressure rather than external intervention; (b) whether the integrity of the pipe or apparatus was broken; (c) whether the incident was sudden and violent."

---

[271] *Martini Investments v McGinn* [2001] Lloyd's Rep. I.R. 374.

[272] *Computer & Systems Engineering Plc v John Lelliott (Ilford) Ltd* (1990) 54 B.L.R. 1.

[273] *MW Wilson (Lace) Ltd v Eagle Star Insurance Co Ltd* 1993 S.L.T. 938.

[274] *Tate Gallery (Trustees) v Duffy Construction Ltd* [2007] Lloyd's Rep. I.R. 758, followed on this point by *Tyco Fire & Integrated Solutions (UK) Ltd v Rolls-Royce Motor Cars Ltd* [2007] EWHC 137 (TCC); the point did not arise on appeal in *Tyco* [2008] Lloyd's Rep. I.R. 617.

The connection between the main and the pipe was held not to constitute "apparatus", so there had to be a bursting of the pipe itself. This was held to have been the case.

Impact damage. One of the commonest problems arising in buildings insurance   **19–043**
in practice is loss by impact damage. The usual form of wording refers to "impact with the building by any vehicle, train, animal or aircraft", and this plainly requires some form of collision. Other forms of damage arising from these sources, such as loss of fragile goods following shock waves from aircraft and damage to furniture by animals chewing at it, are thus outside the meaning of the phrase.

Situation of insured subject matter. Where goods, the subject-matter of an   **19–044**
insurance, are named in the policy by reference to a named place, it is a question of construction which of the following classes of goods is covered.

   (1) All goods in that place when a loss happens. Such insurances have been made on goods in canal boats[275] and in lighters.[276] Such a policy would obviously cease to apply to goods removed. It will not, on the other hand, become exhausted when goods to the amount named in it have been carried, but only when losses to that amount have been paid.

   (2) Named goods in that place when the policy is taken out, but only so long as they are not removed. A policy of fire insurance on two ricks of hay in a haggard was held to fall into this category in an Irish case; it did not therefore include hay that had been removed and replaced since the insurance was effected.[277] The condition against removal may make express provision for removal with the assent of the insurer.[278] Where furniture was insured "whilst in store at the Pall Mall Depositories", and owing to lack of covered space, it was left in two lift vans placed in an enclosed yard and covered with tarpaulins, it was held that the furniture was "in store" within the meaning of the policy.[279]

   (3) Goods merely identified by the place in which they are when the policy is effected. In this case the removal of the goods will not affect the assured's right to recover.[280]

In the first two cases the risk is limited by the place, in the third case the place merely identifies the subject-matter of the insurance. A policy covering the third

---

[275] *Crowley v Cohen* (1832) 3 B. & Ad. 478.

[276] *Joyce v Kennard* (1871) L.R. 7 Q.B. 78. See also *Crozier v Phoenix* (1870) 13 New.Br. (2 Han.) 200; *London and Lancaster v Graves* (1883) 43 Am.Rep. 35; *British American v Joseph* (1857) 9 Lr.Can.Rep. 448; *Butler v Standard Fire* (1879) 4 Ont.App. 391; *Lyons v Providence* (1881) 43 Am.Rep. 32 at 33.

[277] *Gorman v Hand-in-Hand* (1877) Ir.R. 11 C.L. 224. See also *Harrison v Ellis* (1857) 7 E. & 8. 465 (marine policy on goods).

[278] *McClure v Lancashire Insurance* (1860) 13 Ir.Jur. 63. Or for a limited right of removal: *Pearson v Commercial Union* (1876) 1 App.Cas. 498 at 505.

[279] *Wulfson v Switzerland General* (1940) 56 T.L.R. 701. But "warehouse" has been held not to include a loaded lorry in a locked open compound: *Leo Rapp v McClure* [1955] 1 Lloyd's Rep. 292. In *Boag v Economic Insurance* [1954] 2 Lloyd's Rep. 581 goods in a lorry at factory B of the assured in transit from his factory A to docks were held not to be "stock-in-trade" of factory B for the purpose of a floating policy.

[280] Many such cases appear in American reports. See *McClure v Girard Fire* (1876) 22 Am. Rep. 249; *London & Lancaster v Graves* (1883) 43 Am. Rep. 35; *Noyes v North-Western* (1885) 54 Am.Rep. 641.

class would not generally be appropriate where goods are insured against fire, because fire risk is essentially local.[281]

Where there was an exclusion in an all risks policy on furs of those in the "shop portion of L. Ltd" it was held that this meant only those premises at the time of the contract, and not premises subsequently acquired by L. Ltd. It was a reference to premises not persons. [282] Policies may also be restricted to particular forms of use, e.g. commercial or business use. The location of the insured subject matter is not conclusive as to its use. Thus in *Willsden Borough Council v Municipal Mutual Insurance*[283] it was held that a boiler used to heat commercial premises was in domestic use and covered by the policy.

19–045 Burglary and theft policies. Burglary, theft and related phrases are terms of art in the criminal law, in the Theft Act 1968, and must be construed in accordance with the meaning which they have in the criminal law, though it should be remembered that the policy itself may define, for its own purposes, any of the expressions which it uses. Financial loss caused by the infidelity of an employee is not regarded as property losses for the purposes of a policy against the physical loss of property, and such risks are typically insured against under separate fidelity cover.[284]

19–046 *Violent and forcible entry.* Burglary policies are often expressed to cover the risk of loss from theft "following upon actual forcible and violent entry upon the premises".[285] In *Re George and Goldsmith and General Burglary Insurance Association Ltd*[286] a loss occurred after a thief obtained entry to the premises through a door which was closed but not locked or bolted, the proprietor being temporarily absent. Once in the premises, the thief broke open a locked show case and stole the contents. The Court of Appeal held that the insurers were not liable, since entry to the premises had been gained without force or violence. This case should be contrasted with *Re Calf and Sun Insurance Office*,[287] in which a thief entered the insured premises by day and without force, and hid in the basement. After the premises had been locked up for the night he went to the ground and first floors, gaining access to them by force, and stole various items covered by the policy. The Court of Appeal held that there had been forcible entry upon the premises. The case may be distinguished from *Re George and Goldsmith* on the basis that there was forcible entry to some part of the premises, although the original entry to the premises themselves was not forcible. In *Re George and Goldsmith* the forcible entry was not to the premises, but to something stored upon them.

The words "violent" and "forcible" in the usual form of clause are used in a cumulative sense and bear different meanings. In *Nash v Prudential Assurance Co Ltd*[288] the assured suffered a burglary when the keys to his premises were stolen from his car and were used to effect entry. It appears to have been common

---

[281] *Pearson v Commercial Union* (1876) 1 App.Cas. 498 at 505.

[282] *Simon Brooks v Hepburn* [1961] 2 Lloyd's Rep. 43.

[283] *Willsden Borough Council v Municipal Mutual Insurance* (1946) 78 Ll. L.R. 256.

[284] *Dornoch Ltd v Mauritius Union Assurance Co Ltd and Mauritius Commercial Bank Ltd (No.2)* [2007] Lloyd's Rep. I.R. 350.

[285] For the meaning of "premises", see *Pike (Butchers) Ltd v Independent Insurance Co Ltd* [1998] Lloyd's Rep. I.R. 410 (yard part of premises).

[286] *Re George and Goldsmith and General Burglary Insurance Association Ltd* [1899] 1 Q.B. 595.

[287] *Re Calf and Sun Insurance Office* [1926] 2 K.B. 366.

[288] *Nash v Prudential Assurance Co Ltd* [1989] 1 Lloyd's Rep. 379.

ground that the theft of the keys from his car and their subsequent use amounted to "forcible" entry: this was so because the use of even a minimal amount of force fell within the meaning of the term. The claim failed, however, on the basis that entry had not been "violent": although the entry onto the premises had been unlawful, that fact did not of itself make such entry "violent". It thus remains the case that the term "violent" is satisfied only where some aggression has been displayed towards, or damage inflicted upon, persons or property.[289]

Some policies provide as alternative heads of cover theft following entry into premises by violent and forcible means, and theft following threats of violence to individuals. In many cases it will not matter which of these heads of cover is triggered, although different conditions may apply to each so that the distinction becomes crucial. In *Anders & Kern Ltd v CGU Insurance Plc*[290] the policy covered "(a) theft or attempted theft involving entry into or exit from The Premises by forcible and violent means" at a time when alarms were operative and "(b) theft involving violence or threat of violence to You, Your partners, directors or Employees." The assured's alarm was disabled at night, and although the assured initially attended the premises he took the view that it might be safe to stay alone, so he left. A theft followed. The Court of Appeal held that what had occurred was not a "threat" within ground (b) of the theft insuring clause, as what had occurred was not a threat of physical violence but merely a reasonably anticipated fear of physical violence. The policy distinguished between theft from unoccupied premises (ground (a)) and theft from occupied premises (ground (b)). Had the word "threat" been construed so as to allow the loss to fall within ground (b), the distinction between occupied and unoccupied premises drawn by the clause would have been undermined as would the requirement for alarms to be operative when the premises were unoccupied. It was also argued in this case that the coverage clause was subject to an implied term of the assured's safety. The Court of Appeal's response was that such implication would operate to transfer to the insurers the risk of premises being both unoccupied and not protected by an alarm.

Occupation. Occupancy may be significant in two respects. First, policies in **19–047** respect of the contents of a domestic dwelling often contain a term providing that cover shall cease if the premises are unoccupied for a specified period, commonly 30 days. In this context attention is drawn to *Marzouca v Atlantic and British Commercial Insurance*[291] where the Privy Council held that premises were not occupied merely because of the attendance of a night watchman who never entered them. Lord Hodson noted that "occupation to be effectual must, however, be actual not constructive. It must at least involve the regular daily presence of some one in the building."[292]

Thus "occupation" means actual use as a dwelling-house: mere use for storage is not enough.[293] *Clements v National General Insurance Co*[294] goes even further, since there it was held that premises were unoccupied for the purposes of such a clause where there was a caretaker who looked after them by day, but no one slept there. However, as long as there is a regular occupant, temporary

---

[289] *Fabriques de Pmduites Chiminiques v Large* [1923] 1 K.B. 203.

[290] *Anders & Kern Ltd v CGU Insurance Plc* [2007] Lloyd's Rep. I.R. 555, affirmed [2008] Lloyd's Rep. I.R. 460.

[291] *Marzouca v Atlantic and British Commercial Insurance* [1971] 1 Lloyd's Rep. 449.

[292] *Marzouca v Atlantic and British Commercial Insurance* [1971] 1 Lloyd's Rep. 449 at 453.

[293] *Ashworth v Builders' Mutual* (1873) 17 Am. Rep. 117; *Hussain v Brown (No.2)* Unreported, 1996.

[294] *Clements v National General Insurance Co, The Times*, June 11, 1910.

unoccupancy is not breach of the obligation. Thus a condition that premises shall remain "occupied" was not broken where the assured sought refuge in a shelter during an air-raid,[295] or in case of temporary absence on business or for family convenience,[296] and absence for as much as three days was held not to constitute a breach of such condition in a Canadian case.[297]

Domestic householders' policies often contain, as an ancillary or alternative provision to the occupancy requirement, an exclusion which operates where the property "is left insufficiently furnished for full habitation for thirty consecutive days or more". Even in the absence of such a clause, failure to occupy a building may fall foul of an express increase of risk provision. It is a question of fact in each case whether leaving a building unoccupied amounts to an increase in the risk[298]:

> "A house may be so situated that to leave it vacant for any length of time would expose it to be fired by some malicious or wantonly wicked person. On the other hand, it may be so situated that its want of occupancy may be to reduce the danger."[299]

19–048   *Conditions as to burglar alarms.* Burglary policies (particular those for commercial premises) commonly include a requirement that the insured premises shall be fitted with a suitable burglar alarm, and that this shall be set to operate whenever the premises are unoccupied. Compliance with this term is likely to be made a condition precedent to liability, or even a matter of warranty, so that the risk will come to an end in the event of any breach of the term.[300] In *Victor Melik & Co Ltd v Norwich Union Fire Insurance Society Ltd*[301] it was held that a term which required an alarm to be "kept" in working order is not broken where the alarm becomes defective unless the assured has failed to repair it after the defects have come to his attention. The case turns on specific wording of the policy, and although it has been distinguished on quite different wording[302] the generous attitude of Woolf J. to this type of clause has been confirmed. In *AC Ward & Sons Ltd v Catlin (Five) (No.2)*[303] the policy contained a Protection Maintenance Warranty and a Burglar Alarm Maintenance Warranty. The PMW was in the following terms:

> "It is warranted that . . . the whole of the protections provided for the safety of the insured property shall be maintained in good order throughout the currency of this insurance and that they shall be in full and effective operation at all times when the Insured's premises are closed for business and at all other appropriate times, including when the said premises are left unattended, and that such protections shall not be withdrawn or varied to the detriment of the Interest of Insurers without their consent."

---

[295] *Winicofsky v Army & Navy General Assurance* (1919) 88 L.J.K.B. 1111.

[296] *Shackleton v Sun Fire* (1884) 54 Am. Rep. 379.

[297] *Canada Landed Credit Co v Canada Agricultural Insurance* (1870) 17 Grant (U.C.) 418.

[298] *Cooper v Toronto Casualty Insurance* [1928] 2 D.L.R. 1007.

[299] Harrison C.J. in *Abrahams v Agricultural Mutual* (1876) 40 U.C.Q.B. 175 at 182.

[300] See, e.g. *Roberts v Eagle Star Insurance* [1960] 1 Lloyd's Rep. 615. See also *Shoot v Hill* (1936) 55 Ll.L.R. 29.

[301] *Victor Melik & Co Ltd v Norwich Union Fire Insurance Society Ltd* [1980] 1 Lloyd's Rep. 523.

[302] *Ansari v New India Assurance Ltd* [2009] Lloyd's Rep. I.R. 562 where that analysis was held not to apply to a clause under which the risk was discharged if there was a material alteration in the facts stated in the proposal form. A statement that the premises were "protected" by a sprinkler system was held to mean that the sprinkler system was operative and not that it was merely installed.

[303] *AC Ward & Sons Ltd v Catlin (Five) (No.2)* [2009] EWHC 3122 (Comm).

The BAMW provided that:

"It is warranted that—

(a) the premises containing the Insured property are fitted with the burglar alarm system stated in the Schedule, which has been approved by the Insurers and that no withdrawal, alteration or variation of the system, or any structural alteration which might affect the system shall be made without the consent of the Insurers,

(b) the burglar alarm system shall have been put into full and effective operation at all times when the Insured's premises are closed for business, and at all other appropriate times, including when the said premises are left unattended."

In each case, "All defects occurring in any protections must be promptly remedied." Goods were stolen from the assured's premises, but the burglar alarm failed to operate and the CCTV system was not at the time working. The clauses were held in preliminary proceedings to be warranties,[304] but it was held by Flaux J. in the main trial that neither, on their proper construction, had been broken. The words in the PMW "the protections provided for the safety of the insured property" referred to those protections in place when the risk incepted so that the warranty did apply to the burglar alarm, and the BAMW similarly applied to the burglar alarm in place on inception even though there was no alarm "stated in the Schedule". However, the learned judge held that the words "All defects occurring in any protections must be promptly remedied" meant that the warranties were confined to defects of which the assured was aware but which had not been remedied. As the assured was not aware of the defects, there was no breach of either warranty. Although the *Melik* case had turned on the use of the word "kept" as indicating that the assured had in some way to be at fault, the qualifying words in *Ward*, plus the description of the warranties as "maintenance" provisions, led to the same conclusion.

Theft. The word bears the meaning ascribed to it by the s.1 of the Theft Act **19–049** 1968.[305] A person is thus guilty of theft "if he dishonestly appropriates property belonging to another with the intention of permanently depriving the other of it." The dependence of insurance law upon the intricacies of the criminal law may on occasion have surprising results. In *Dobson v General Accident Fire and Life Assurance Corp*,[306] the assured parted with possession of certain items of jewellery in exchange for what proved to have been a stolen cheque. The jewellery was irrecoverable, and the assured claimed that he had suffered a "loss by theft" within the meaning of the policy. The Court of Appeal agreed, but in so doing was required to deal with two complex defences. The insurers argued, first, that by the time of payment the property in the jewellery had passed to the "rogue" by the earlier agreement to sell, so that at the time at which the jewellery was appropriated by the rogue he had become the owner of it: in short, there had been no appropriation of property "belonging to another". The Court of Appeal was able to dispose of this argument by finding that the true intention of the parties was that property would pass only on payment[307] by the rogue. The second argument by the insurers was that there had been no "appropriation" by

---

[304] *AC Ward & Sons Ltd v Catlin (Five) Ltd* [2010] Lloyd's Rep. I.R. 30.

[305] *Lim Trading Company v Haydon* [1968] 1 Lloyd's Rep. 154; *Grundy (Teddington) Ltd v Fulton* [1983] 1 Lloyd's Rep. 16; *Dobson v General Accident Fire and Life Assurance Corp* [1990] 1 Q.B. 274; *Peabody v Eagle Star Insurance Co* Unreported, December 1, 1998, Worksop County Court.

[306] *Dobson v General Accident Fire and Life Assurance Corp* [1990] 1 Q.B. 274.

[307] Or here, conditional payment in the form of a cheque.

the rogue as the assured had voluntarily (albeit misguidedly) parted with possession. The Court of Appeal, having considered conflicting decisions of the House of Lords on this point,[308] ruled that "appropriation" meant interference with or usurpation of rights of ownership irrespective of apparent consent. The *Dobson* interpretation of the "appropriation" requirement was subsequently approved by the House of Lords in *R. v Gomez*.[309]

One of the difficulties with the term "theft" as construed in these cases is that it is a wide one, and may overlap with other offences in the Theft Act 1968. As long as the offences are themselves insured perils or at least are not excluded perils, the overlap is of no significance, although it may be problematic if there is an express exclusion. In *Peabody v Eagle Star Insurance Co Ltd*[310] the claimant's policy covered "theft" but excluded "deception". The assured lost two watches in circumstances which amounted to theft within the wider sense approved in Dobson, but also involved some deception by the thief. The court was not satisfied that what had occurred amounted to the crime of deception, but was of the view that even if both offences had been committed the principle of *contra proferentem* saw the claimant home.

Some policies may restrict the general meaning of theft by imposing additional conditions for the establishment of liability. In marine policies, for example, the theft must be violent. A further illustration is *Deutsche Genossenschaftsbank v Burnhope*,[311] where the policy covered theft "committed by persons present on the premises of the assured". It was held that all the elements of theft— appropriation and dishonesty—had to coincide on the assured's premises before cover attached. Consequently, where an innocent agent collected securities from the assured's premises, and handed them to his principal who had intended from the outset to abscond with them, the insurers were held to be not liable for the loss as the agent's appropriation on the assured's premises had not been dishonest.

19–050   *Joy riding.* The definition of "theft" in s.1 of the Theft Act 1968 requires that there be an intention permanently to deprive the owner of the property. Such intention frequently cannot be proved where motor cars are taken for the purpose of a "joy-ride".[312] To deal with this problem, s.12 of the Theft Act 1968 lays down the offence of "taking a conveyance", which does not require proof of such intention. Section 12(1) provides that "a person shall be guilty of an offence if, without having the consent of the owner or other lawful authority, he takes any conveyance for his own or another's use or, knowing that any conveyance has been taken without such authority, drives it or allows himself to be carried in or on it", subject to the defence in s.12(6) that "A person does not commit an offence under this section by anything done in the belief that he has lawful authority to do it or that he would have the owner's consent if the owner knew of his doing it and the circumstances of it." The section covers not just unauthorised taking, but also unauthorised use of a motor vehicle where permission for use for some other purpose has been given[313] and unauthorised

---

[308] *Lawrence v Commissioner of Police for the Metropolis* [1972] A.C. 16 (lack of consent irrelevant); *R. v Morris* [1984] A.C. 320 (lack of consent essential).

[309] *R. v Gomez* [1993] 1 All E.R. 1, disapproving contrary indications in *R. v Morris* [1984] A.C. 320.

[310] *Peabody v Eagle Star Insurance Co Ltd* Unreported, December 1, 1998, Worksop County Court.

[311] *Deutsche Genossenschaftsbank v Burnhope* [1993] 2 Lloyd's Rep. 518.

[312] *Greenleaf Monksfield* [1972] R.T.R. 451.

[313] *R. v Phipps* (1970) 54 Cr. App. R. 300; *McNight v Davies* [1974] R.T.R. 4.

lending by an authorised driver.[314] Where a motor policy provides cover against "theft" without reference to a taking under s.12, it is submitted that, as a matter of strict law, the insurer will not be liable if the car is damaged in the course of a joy-ride falling within s.12.

Burglary. Under s.9 of the Theft Act 1968, a person is guilty of burglary if: **19–051**

"(a) he enters any building or part of a building as a trespasser and with intent to commit any of the offences of stealing anything in the building or part of a building in question, of inflicting on any person therein any grievous bodily harm, and of doing unlawful damage to the building or anything therein; or

(b) having entered any building or part of a building as a trespasser he steals or attempts to steal anything in the building or that part of it or inflicts or attempts to inflict on any person therein any grievous bodily harm."

It is increasingly common to exclude loss of computer coding and software from burglary policies. In *Tektrol Ltd v International Insurance Co of Hanover Ltd*[315] two computers containing computer source code, and a paper print out of the code, were stolen from the assured's premises. The policy was an all risks policy so that burglary was an insured peril. The policy excluded, amongst other things, "other erasure loss distortion or corruption of information on computer systems or other records programmes or software." The Court of Appeal, by a majority, held that "loss" had to be construed in its context, and the context pointed to loss of software rather than loss of the equipment on which the software was stored.

Robbery. Under s.8 of the Theft Act 1968, a person is guilty of robbery if: **19–052**

"he steals, and immediately before or at the time of doing so, and in order to do so, he uses force on any person or puts or seeks to put any person in fear of being then and there subjected to force."

In *Canelhas Comercio Importacao e Exportacao Ltd v Wooldridge*[316] a jeweller's policy excluded cover where property was lost by robbery at a time when the premises were open for business or when any of the assured's employees were present. The family of the assured's proprietor were kidnapped and the proprietor was ordered to go to the premises and remove all of the emeralds there, which would be exchanged for his family. The proprietor did so while the premises were open for business, having instructed his staff to fill bags with emeralds. The Court of Appeal held that the exclusion was inapplicable because there had not been a robbery: the clause was designed to exclude the liability of the insurers for violent theft while the premises were open or occupied, but in the present case there had been no threat of violence against anyone responsible for removing the emeralds from the premises.

Valuable items. Many policies against burglary and theft require the assured to   **19–053** make a separate declaration of articles which are of special value or whose value exceeds a stated sum. The former type of wording may well give rise to dispute as to whether a particular article was or was not of particular value. A generous

---

[314] *McMinn v McMinn* [2006] EWHC 827 (QB).

[315] *Tektrol Ltd v International Insurance Co of Hanover Ltd* [2006] Lloyd's Rep. I.R. 38.

[316] *Canelhas Comercio Importacao e Exportacao Ltd v Wooldridge* [2004] Lloyd's Rep. I.R. 915.

interpretation of the phrase "specially valuable articles" was given in *King v Travellers' Insurance Association*.[317] In this case the court ruled that a fur coat did not fall within this description and did not require separate declaration: fur coats were regarded as forming part of the wardrobe of every woman of means and were thus commonplace, and the fact that some were very expensive did make them of special value.

19–054 **Defects in title.** Both real property and personal property can be insured by a prospective buyer against defects in the seller's title. The amount recoverable under a title insurance policy is, in the absence of any express provision in the policy, the amount representing the loss caused to the assured by the defect in title. Thus, if the seller has no right to sell, e.g. because the seller is a thief, the assured's loss will be the amount which he has paid for the property: loss of profits will, in accordance with general principles, be recoverable only if the policy so provides. If, by contrast, the seller's defect in title arises from the fact that the goods sold have been manufactured in breach of an intellectual property right belonging to a third party, the amount paid for the goods by the assured is not lost to him by reason of a defect in title but rather by a defect in the description or quality of the goods.[318]

Exclusions from property cover

19–055 *Wear and tear.* A common source of difficulty in property policies concerns the effects of wear and tear. Insurance, by its nature, is intended to provide protection against the risk of fortuitous happenings. The purpose of a policy is to secure an indemnity against accidents which may happen, not against events which must happen.[319] Wear and tear is not a fortuitous happening, but part of the processes of nature, and is therefore not covered by any policy of insurance.[320] There must be some abnormal circumstance, accident or casualty even when the insurance is expressed to be against "all risks".[321] Thus, damage to a ship by rats is not covered by a marine policy,[322] although the sudden splitting of a tube leading to corrosion is a fortuitous event and not wear and tear.[323] The main issue here is causation. It is possible for damage to flow from the gradual occurrence of an insured peril, for example where a leak in a pipe causes the ground which supports it to give way and to cause physical damage to the pipe, where heavy rainfall penetrates a roof and causes damage to house contents, or where tree roots slowly undermine a building.[324] In these cases, the damage is accidental and thus within the coverage of a policy, even though occurring gradually, whereas had the damage been regarded as the result of wear and tear the insurers would not have been liable. By contrast, in *Midland Mainline Ltd v Commercial Union Assurance Co Ltd*[325] the assured train operators suffered substantial losses following the imposition of emergency speed restrictions on the railway network in the aftermath of the Hatfield rail crash in October 2000. The restrictions were

---

[317] *King v Travellers' Insurance Association* 41 Ll. L.R. 13.
[318] *Grimaldi Ltd v Sullivan* Unreported, 1997.
[319] Lord Herschell in *The Xantho* (1887) 12 App.Cas. 503 at 509.
[320] Marine Insurance Act 1906 s.55(2)(c).
[321] Lord Birkenhead in *British Marine v Gaunt* [1921] 2 A.C. 41 at 46–47.
[322] *Hunter v Potts* (1815) 4 Camp. 203. But see *Hamilton v Pandorf* (1887) 12 App.Cas. 518, as explained by *Leyland Shipping v Norwich Union* [1918] A.C. 350.
[323] *Burts & Harvey Ltd v Vulcan Boiler and General Insurance Co* [1966] 1 Lloyd's Rep. 161.
[324] *Mills v Smith* [1964] 1 Q.B. 30.
[325] *Midland Mainline Ltd v Commercial Union Assurance Co Ltd* [2004] Lloyd's Rep. I.R. 239.

imposed on those parts of the network where rails were known to be weak or cracked. The business interruption policy obtained by the operators excluded loss caused by "wear and tear" and the insurers sought to rely upon rolling contact fatigue, which they maintained was the cause of the rails' weakening and cracking. The Court of Appeal upheld this defence, deciding that wear and tear constituted more than the background to the loss and was a proximate cause of the loss in its own right. In line with the principle that an express exclusion prevails over the insuring clause, the Court of Appeal ruled that the assured was not entitled to recover.

Inherent vice.[326] Risks insured against do not, without clear words include the inherent vice of the subject-matter insured, i.e. its natural behaviour, being what it is, in the circumstances under which it is. The meaning of this phrase has for the most part been worked out in the context of marine insurance, and is considered in that context.[327]   **19–056**

Risks that it is not lawful to cover. Certain risks, such as the capture of an enemy ship by a British vessel, cannot be lawfully insured, and such risks are therefore impliedly excepted from any policy.[328]   **19–057**

Mysterious disappearance exclusions. "Mysterious disappearance" clauses, which appear in many forms of property insurance and also in some liability policies, exempt the insurers from liability in the event that the insured subject matter is the subject of "mysterious" or "unexplainable" disappearance. It is unlikely that this type of wording has very much effect. If the policy is one against specific perils, the assured bears the burden of proving that the loss was proximately caused by an insured peril. An assured who is able to do so will by definition defeat the mysterious disappearance exclusion, because the disappearance has been shown not to be unexplained. Conversely, an assured who is unable to identify which insured peril has caused the loss will not be able to recover anyway, so the mysterious disappearance clause adds nothing to the insurers' rights. The clause is potentially of more significance in an all risks policy. Under that type of policy the assured is not required to prove that his loss has any specific cause, and it suffices that he is able to show that he has suffered a loss. A mysterious disappearance exclusion in an all risks policy, by contrast, largely undermines the basic cover of the policy itself, and it may be that the effect of the clause is to require the assured to prove his loss. This is the implication of the decision in *Widefree Ltd v Brit Insurance Ltd*,[329] in which the assured jewellery retailer obtained an all risks policy which excluded loss of "Property Insured found to be missing at stockholding where the Insured is unable to prove the date and circumstances of any loss." The assured's premises were visited on October 9, 2008 by two women, who left without making any purchase. On October 22, 2008 the assured, while looking for a valuable ring for a customer, discovered that the ring was missing. The insurers relied upon mysterious disappearance clause. The trial judge, Peter Leaver QC, was satisfied that the assured had established, by reference to CCTV footage, that the ring had been stolen by the women on October 9, 2008, so that the mysterious disappearance clause could have no application. The court further held that the   **19–058**

---

[326] Marine Insurance Act 1906 s.55(2)(c).
[327] See Ch.24, below.
[328] *Brandon v Curling* (1803) 4 East 410. Cf. *Janson v Driefontein Mines* [1902] A.C. 484.
[329] *Widefree Ltd v Brit Insurance Ltd* [2009] EWHC 3671 (QB).

discovery of the loss had not occurred in the course of "stocktaking" so that the clause was in any event inapplicable. The wider point, however, is that the effect of the mysterious disappearance clause on the facts of the case was to put the assured to proof of loss, which the assured was able to do.

19–059   **Defective design.**   Where there is an exclusion for loss of or damage to property due to defective design, it is necessary to determine whether that exclusion is confined to the property subject to the defect or whether it extends to other property which is damaged by the defective property. The scope of the exclusion depends upon its wording. *CA Blackwell (Contracts) Ltd v Gerling General Insurance Co*[330] discussed the meaning of an exclusion commonly used in English policies, which runs as follows:

> "This Policy excludes loss of or Damage to and the cost necessary to replace repair or rectify.
> (a)   Property insured which is in a defective condition due to a defect in design plan specification materials or workmanship of such Property Insured or any part thereof
> (b)   Property insured lost or damaged to enable the replacement repair or rectification of Property insured excluded by a) above.
> Exclusion a) above shall not apply to other Property insured which is free of the defective condition but is damaged in consequence thereof.
>   For the purpose of the Policy and not merely this Exclusion the Property insured shall not be regarded as lost or damaged solely by virtue of the existence of any defect in design plan specification materials or workmanship in the Property insured or any part thereof . . . ."

It will be seen that the purpose of this wording is to exclude property which is defective and which suffers damage as a result, but brings back into cover other property itself free from defects which is itself damaged. In *Blackwell* itself delay to the construction of capping to a road was caused by inadequate temporary drainage used in the building process. The court's interpretation of the wording was that only defective property was excluded, but that on the facts the defect did not relate to the capping of the road at all but rather affected the drainage process which was quite separate from the road. It followed that the capping of the road was not itself defective and that the exclusion did not operate.

In *Seele Austria GmbH & Co KG v Tokio Marine Europe Insurance Ltd*[331] the policy wording was complex and contradictory, but was construed by a majority of the Court of Appeal as providing cover for loss of or damage to the insured property which was deliberately caused in an attempt to rectify a defect in another party or the insured property. The assured designed and installed pre-assembled "punched windows" in the second and fourth floors of a building under development. Following their installation the windows were sealed with a waterproof membrane, and cladding was then added to the building. The windows leaked, and their replacement necessitated the stripping away of the cladding and the opening up of internal walls and ceilings. The assured's policy gave cover for accidental loss of or damage to the works. In the event of defective design: condition 18(1) excluded the cost necessary to replace repair or rectify accidental loss to insured property which was defective, and loss or

---

[330] *CA Blackwell (Contracts) Ltd v Gerling General Insurance Co* [2008] Lloyd's Rep. I.R. 529.
[331] *Seele Austria GmbH & Co KG v Tokio Marine Europe Insurance Ltd* [2008] Lloyd's Rep. I.R. 739.

damage to the insured property caused to enable replacement repair or rectification of the defective insured property; condition 18(2) excluded the cost necessary to replace, repair or rectify insured property which was in a defective condition due to a defect in design plan, specification, materials or workmanship, and also insured property lost or damaged to enable the replacement or repair or rectification of defective property; and condition 18(3) went on to provide an indemnity in respect of intentional damage necessarily caused to the Insured Property to enable the replacement repair or rectification of insured property in a defective condition. The Court of Appeal by a majority held that the assured could recover: condition 18(1) operated to exclude the cost of making good any defect in the works and the cost of access damage in making good the defect; condition 18(2) allowed recovery in the event of accidental damage consequent on a defect but excluded cover for a defect which was not likely to give rise to other damage; and condition 18(3), which was free-standing and did not require proof of accidental damage, allowed recovery for access damage necessarily and deliberately caused to the works to enable a defect to be made good.

CHAPTER 20

LIABILITY INSURANCE

1. PRINCIPLES GOVERNING LIABILITY POLICIES

Compulsory and voluntary liability insurance

20–001 *Compulsory insurance in English law.* Where a person of limited financial resources becomes liable for a substantial amount of damages to a third party, that liability is likely to be met only if that person carries liability insurance. Consequently, liability insurance is carried voluntarily by prudent persons whose everyday activities might result in them facing legal action for losses caused.[1] At this point the law has stepped in and has imposed a requirement that liability insurance be carried in respect of particular perils: the most important of these relate to road traffic liabilities (under the Road Traffic Act 1988) and employers' liability (under the Employers' Liability (Compulsory Insurance) Act 1969). In each of these cases, elaborate steps have been taken to ensure that the misconduct or insolvency of the assured does not prejudice the third-party victim's ability to recover the moneys earmarked for him under the insurance.[2] There are other illustrations of compulsory insurance in English law.

20–002 *Nuclear installations.* Under the Nuclear Installations Act 1965 those engaged in the management of nuclear installations are required to have insurance against certain of the risks associated with the running of such installations.

20–003 *The professions.* As far as the professions are concerned, members may be required to effect insurance against the risks of legal liability arising from the negligent exercise of their profession. At present this requirement is imposed by statute on solicitors,[3] estate agents[4] and osteopaths.[5] Other professions are required by their rules of membership to insure against liability risks. Insurance

---

[1] The common law seems not to recognise any obligation to insure. In *Lister v Romford Ice and Cold Storage Co Ltd* [1957] A.C. 555, the House of Lords held that an employer is not under an implied obligation to insure for the benefit of its employees in respect of their potential liabilities. Again, in *Van Oppen v Trustees of the Bedford Charity* [1989] 1 All E.R. 273, Boreham J. held that a school was not obliged at common law to take out insurance for the benefit of its pupils covering injury to them for which the school was not legally liable. Moreover, Boreham J. rejected the argument that, by failing to warn parents that insurance was not in place, the school could be in breach of a duty of care. Similarly, an employer is not required to insure its employees against personal injuries incurred abroad: *Reid v Rush & Tompkins* [1989] 3 All E.R. 228.

[2] For motor insurance, see Ch.22, below. Employers' liability insurance is discussed in this chapter, below.

[3] Solicitors Act 1974 s.37.

[4] Estate Agents Act 1979 s.16.

[5] Osteopaths Act 1993, implemented by the General Osteopathic Council (Professional Indemnity Insurance Rules) Order in Council 1998 (SI 1998/1329).

brokers are required to insure under the rules of the Financial Services Authority.

Oil and other pollution. The International Convention on Civil Liability for Oil **20–004** Pollution Damage 1992 (the CLC Convention) and the International Convention on Civil Liability for Bunker Oil Pollution Damage 2001 (the Bunkers Convention), both implemented in the United Kingdom by the Merchant Shipping Act 1995 (as amended) both impose compulsory insurance obligations in respect of liability by reason of the escape or discharge of oil. The CLC Convention applies to any vessel carrying in bulk a cargo of more than 2,000 of persistent oil, in respect of that cargo, and the Bunkers Convention applies to any vessel having a gross tonnage greater than 1,000 tons in respect of bunker oil. Any claim may be brought directly against the insurers. The 1995 Act was amended by the Merchant Shipping and Maritime Security Act 1997, which inserted s.192A into the 1995 Act. Under that section, the Secretary of State may make regulations requiring that a ship in UK waters must be insured against risks, other than pollution risks, to be specified in regulations. Two other Conventions imposing an insurance requirement have been adopted, but are not yet in force, namely the Civil Liability for Oil Pollution Damage resulting from Exploration for and Exploitation of Seabed Mineral Resources Convention 1977 and the International Convention on Liability and Compensation in Connection with the Carriage of Hazardous and Noxious Substances by Sea 1996, the latter conferring a direct action against insurers.

Other shipping measures. Two EU measures have imposed compulsory insur- **20–005** ance obligations upon shipowners. First, European Parliament and Council Directive 2009/20/EC on the insurance of shipowners for maritime risks requires each Member State to require ships of 300 gross tonnage or more flying its flag (other than warships, auxiliary warships or other State owned or operated ships used for a non-commercial public service) to be insured against liability for maritime claims. As regards ships flying the flags of other countries, each Member State is to require insurance to be in place before any such ship enters a port under that Member State's jurisdiction. The measure is to be implemented before January 1, 2012.

Secondly, European Parliament and Council Regulation 392/2009/EC of April 23, 2009 on the liability of carriers of passengers by sea in the event of accidents implements (and indeed extends to domestic carriage) the Athens Convention relating to the Carriage of Passengers and their Luggage by Sea, 1974, as amended by the Protocol of 2002. The Regulation applies to any international carriage and to carriage by sea within a single Member State where: the ship is flying the flag of or is registered in a Member State; the contract of carriage has been made in a Member State; or the place of departure or destination, according to the contract of carriage, is in a Member State. The Regulation only applies to classes A and B passenger vessels (see the requirements in Council Directive 98/18/EC on safety rules and standards for passenger ships). It operates where: the ship is flying the flag of or is registered in a Member State; the contract of carriage has been made in a Member State; or the place of departure or destination, according to the contract of carriage, is in a Member State. However, Member States may apply the Regulation to all domestic sea-going voyages. Insurance against liabilities under the Athens Convention is compulsory.

Compulsory insurance for the removal of wrecks will also be required when the Nairobi International Convention on the Removal of Wrecks, 2007 comes into force.

Scope of coverage

20–006 *Forms of liability insurance.* Liability insurance provides cover against the risk of the assured incurring liability to third parties, rather than against the risk of damage to property as such, and is a contract of indemnity.[6] It is nevertheless common for policies to provide both first-party property or personal-injury cover and third party liability cover[7]; motor and householder's policies are generally in this combined form. Similarly, there may be some difficulty in ascertaining whether a policy procured by a bailee is an insurance on the goods or an insurance on the bailee's liability for the goods, as the bailee is entitled to insure in respect of both matters.[8]

Liability policies may cover liability arising from the use of goods or the provision of services. Under a liability policy it is generally the case that the conduct which gives rise to liability will occur some time before the assured actually incurs liability for that conduct. It may also be the case that different policies are in force at the times of the former and latter events. It is important to determine, therefore, whether the policy covers liability flowing from the assured's conduct within the policy period, or whether it covers the establishment of the assured's liability within the policy period, as both are possibilities.

Liability policies may be written in a number of different ways. Professional indemnity covers, including directors' and officers' insurance, are these days written on a "claims made" basis. Under a claims made policy the insurers face liability for any claims made by a third party against the assured during the currency of the policy, even though those claims do not result in the assured's liability actually being established and quantified (the trigger for the insurers' liability under a liability policy) for some years to come and possibly at a time when the insurers in question are no longer providing cover for the assured. Claims made policies typically provide an extension, in the form of the right or obligation on the assured to notify to the insurers any circumstances which have occurred during the currency of the policy and which "may" or "are likely" to give rise to a claim at some point in the future: notification by the assured during the currency of the policy is then deemed to be treated as a claim made against the assured during the currency of the policy should a claim actually be made at some later date. A further typical form of extension is found in the form of an Extended Period of Discovery, which is triggered where the policy is not renewed: the policy will provide that in the event of non-renewal, any claims made against the assured within 12 months following expiry are to be treated as covered. This type of extension is normally by its terms removed if any other insurance covering the loss is in force. A claims-made policy will exclude claims made against the assured during some earlier policy, and in some cases the exclusion will extend to claims arising out of circumstances which could have been notified under an earlier policy.

---

[6] Fletcher Moulton L.J. in *British Cash & Parcel Conveyors v Lamson Store Service* [1908] 1 K.B. 1006 at 1014. See also *Goddard & Smith v Frew* [1939] 4 All E.R. 358.

[7] The two types of insurance found in a single policy are sometimes not properly distinguished. See *Williams v Baltic Insurance* [1924] 2 K.B. 282, where it was held that the liability cover provided by a motor policy was in fact insurance on goods. The purpose of this holding was, however, to overcome the argument that the Life Assurance Act 1774 applied to the policy. See also *Prudential Staff Union v Hall* [1947] K.B. 685.

[8] The presumption operated by the courts is that the policy is on the goods; the bailee thus holds the sum in excess of his own insurable interest for the assured: *Tomlinson (Hauliers) v Hepburn* [1966] A.C. 451. See Ch.19, above.

Policies covering liability for personal injury or damage to property may be **20–007** written on a claims made basis, but are more commonly written on a losses occurring or events basis. There are two separate concepts here. A "losses occurring" policy is one that responds to injuries inflicted upon the third party during the currency of the policy even though the assured's liability for those injuries is not established until a later date. An "events" policy provides indemnity for events that occur during the currency of the policy, even though those events do not give rise to injury until a later date and so to liability at an even later date. The distinction between losses occurring and events policies will often be unimportant, because the assured's act of negligence and the loss to the third party which flows from that act will be simultaneous, as in the case of a road accident. However, the distinction becomes significant in exposure cases, where the third party is exposed to a harmful substance by the assured during the currency of the policy but the substance does not cause physical injury to the third party for some time afterwards. The provision of an indemnity "in respect of all sums which [the assured] shall become legally liable to pay as compensation arising out of . . . accidental bodily injury or illness . . . to any person . . . which occurs during the currency of the policy" was held in *Bolton Metropolitan Borough Council v Municipal Mutual Insurance & Commercial Union Assurance*[9] to provide losses occurring cover and not exposure cover, on the basis that exposure is not of itself an injury and that the phrase "accidental bodily injury" did not require the accident giving rise to the injury to be in the same policy year as the injury, as the word accidental referred to the initial exposure.

The *Bolton* case concerned a public liability policy. In *Bolton* the judgments were careful to confine the ruling to that context. Different considerations clearly apply to a policy which covers the liability of an employer for injury caused to an employee. If the reasoning in *Bolton* is extended to that context, there is a powerful possibility that the operation of that form of insurance will be undermined. Suppose that an employee is negligently exposed to asbestos in year one and suffers significant injury in year 15. If the policy in year one is written on a losses occurring basis, that policy will not apply because mere exposure to asbestos is not injury.[10] Accordingly, there is no insurance cover in year one, the year in which insurance is required, and the employee will be protected by his employer's insurance only if, fortuitously, he is still employed in year 15 and the employer has a losses occurring policy in force at that date, or—even more fortuitously—if the employer happens to have a claims made employers' liability policy in force at the date that the employee makes a claim. All of this was recognised by Burton J. in *Durham v BAI (Run Off) Ltd*,[11] which was a hearing of a group of test cases involving employers' liability policy wording which had in common the requirement that the injury was "sustained" during the period of coverage. Burton J., having held that the mere inhalation of asbestos was not of itself an injury, but felt able to conclude, by reference to the "factual matrix" in which the policies had been written that the word "sustained" was appropriate to refer to exposure: the wording was ambiguous; the practice had been for payment to be made on an exposure basis (although there was no custom or usage to that effect); there were significant difficulties in fixing the date on which injury actually occurred, and in every case speculative medical evidence would be

---

[9] *Bolton Metropolitan Borough Council v Municipal Mutual Insurance & Commercial Union Assurance* [2007] Lloyd's Rep. I.R. 173.
[10] *Rothwell v Chemical and Insulating Co Ltd* [2008] 1 A.C. 28; *Durham v BAI (Run Off) Ltd* [2009] Lloyd's Rep. I.R. 295.
[11] *Durham v BAI (Run Off) Ltd* [2009] Lloyd's Rep. I.R. 295.

involved if the relevant trigger date was the date of injury; and the notion of compulsory insurance to protect employees would be undermined by a finding that the policies were losses occurring, particularly as regards persons who were no longer employed at the date that injury was sustained. This might be thought to be a generous interpretation of the wording, as the notion of injury being "sustained" would normally imply an injury having been suffered as opposed to an injury having been caused. However, it plainly makes sense to construe policy wording so as to meet statutory requirements in exposure cases. The case nevertheless sits uneasily with *Bolton*.

There is some dispute as to when injury actually occurs following exposure to asbestos. In *Vero Insurance Ltd v Power Technologies Pty Ltd*[12] the New South Wales Court of Appeal held that the phrase "shall become legally liable to pay for compensation in respect of . . . bodily injury (which expression includes death and illness) . . . occurring during the Period of Insurance as a result of an accident and happening in connection with The Business . . . " clearly referred to the date of injury, but that the relevant date was the date on which fibres penetrated the lung (i.e. inhalation) and not the later date of the onset of actual disease. It might be thought that this decision blurs the distinction between events occurring and losses occurring.[13]

20–008   *The claimant under a liability policy.* Although the true beneficiary of a liability policy is frequently the third party who has suffered loss at the hands of the assured, particularly where the level of damages awarded against the assured is such that the assured cannot afford to make payment, the third party has no direct cause of action against the insurers in most cases.[14] The Third Parties (Rights against Insurers) Act 2010 provides the victim with a direct claim against the assured's liability insurers, by way of statutory assignment or subrogation where the victim has established and quantified the assured's liability but the assured has become insolvent: the operation of the 2010 Act is discussed in Ch.21, below. It is to be emphasised that the 2010 Act applies only to the case of insolvency. If the assured has not become insolvent, then the victim is most unlikely to have a direct claim against the insurers. Such an action is precluded by the doctrine of privity of contract, and although the doctrine has been substantially modified by the Contracts (Rights of Third Parties) Act 1999 and allows a third party to sue on a contract made for his benefit, the 1999 Act is unlikely to apply to victims, for three reasons:

    (1) Under s.1(2) of the 1999 Act, a third party can bring an action on a contract only: (a) if the contract says that he may; or (b) if the contract confers a benefit on him. Liability policies rarely provide that third

---

[12] *Vero Insurance Ltd v Power Technologies Pty Ltd* 2007 N.S.W.C.A. 226.

[13] Contrast *Orica Ltd v CGU Insurance Ltd* [2003] N.S.W.C.A. 331, in which the same court had earlier held that a liability policy which covered "a disease which is contracted by the worker in the course of his employment" was referring to the onset of injury rather than to mere inhalation. See now *Rothwell v Chemical and Insulating Co Ltd* [2008] 1 A.C. 28 and *Durham v BAI (Run Off) Ltd* [2009] Lloyd's Rep. I.R. 295, both of which confirm that where a victim has developed, not full mesothelioma, but rather pleural plaques, i.e. symptomless fibrous thickening of the pleural membrane, there is no physical injury because that symptom did not of itself increase susceptibility to asbestos-related diseases or shorten life. At worst it gave rise to a risk that some other disease might develop, but that was not injury. Nor was there injury because the victim became anxious about the risk of future disease. In *Durham* it was noted that speculative medical evidence is necessary in every case.

[14] There is an important exception in the case of motor insurance: see Ch.22, below.

parties may sue, and most are framed in terms of indemnifying the assured against his own legal liability rather than making payment to a third party. Accordingly, neither of these alternative tests will be met in the normal course of events.

(2) Under s.1(3) of the 1999 Act, a third party who satisfies one or other of the conditions in s.1(2) can only use the Act if he is identified by name, class or description. Most liability policies contemplate potential liability to the world at large, so that again an essential prerequisite will not be met.

(3) The operation of the 1999 Act may be excluded by agreement, and this is generally the case.

As the 1999 Act is virtually untested, and there is a good deal of uncertainty as to how it might operate, a number of liability policies have taken the precaution of excluding the 1999 Act. Liability insurers may, independently of the 1999 and 2010 Acts, become directly liable to the third-party claimant where they enter into some form of contract with the third party under which they agree to pay the losses directly to him.[15] It is also possible that the insurers may be treated as having waived their rights under the policy, or are estopped from enforcing them, by reason of their conduct towards the third party.[16]

Liabilities covered by a liability policy. Although policy wordings may differ,   **20–009** liability policies are commonly expressed in terms of covering "liability at law" or some similar phrase. Consequently, ex gratia payments made by the assured will not be recoverable under a liability policy irrespective of their commercial prudence. The insurers' liability is triggered by liability against the assured being established or quantified by judgment, arbitration award or binding settlement.

The term "liability at law" will apply most often to negligence or strict liability in tort,[17] and although it has also been held to apply to liability under contract for breach of the implied terms of the Sale of Goods Act 1979[18] that ruling is contrary to Canadian authority[19] as well as to English marine cases construing the phrase "legally liable by way of damages".[20] The true position would seem to be that a liability policy covers contractual liabilities if they have a tortious parallel, and that a liability policy will not—in the absence of clear wording—extend to pure contractual liability. The two forms of liability are indeed quite different: that in tort is concerned primarily with compensating for physical loss, whereas that in contract compensates for loss of expectation of profit. It is admittedly the case that most liability policies do specifically exclude liability for contractual claims with no tortious counterpart, by adopting an exclusion for liability voluntarily incurred, although it may be that this form of

---

[15] Such an agreement will not, however, be implied simply because there are negotiations between the insurers and the third party: cf. *Grecoair Inc v Tilling* [2005] Lloyd's Rep. I.R. 151, where the same issue arose as between reinsurers and assured.

[16] An argument to this effect was raised but rejected on the facts, in *Spriggs v Wessington Court School* [2005] Lloyd's Rep. I.R. 474.

[17] *Davies v Hosken* [1937] 3 All E.R. 192; *Goddard & Smith v Frew* [1939] 4 All E.R. 358; *West Wake Price & Co v Ching Wo Hong* [1957] 1 W.L.R. 45. Defamation is an insurable risk: see s.11 of the Defamation Act 1952.

[18] *M/S Aswan Engineering Establishment Co v Iron Trades Mutual Insurance Co Ltd* [1989] 1 Lloyd's Rep. 289.

[19] *Canadian Indemnity v Andrews & George* [1952] 4 D.L.R. 690; *Dominion Bridge v Toronto General Insurance* [1964] 1 Lloyd's Rep. 194.

[20] *Furness, Withy & Co v Duder* [1936] 2 K.B. 461; *Hall Brothers SS Co Ltd v Young* (1939) 63 Ll. L.R. 143.

exclusion would generally be implicit and if there is to be cover for contract claims this would normally be spelt out. In *Enterprise Oil Ltd v Strand Insurance Co Ltd*[21] there was express cover for all sums which the assured "may be obligated to pay by reason of liability imposed . . . by law or assumed under Contract or Agreement . . . or otherwise, on account of . . . the infringement of contract rights". It was held that the phrase "assumed under Contract" referred to a contract entered into by the assured under which the assured had incurred liability, and not to a settlement contract reached by the assured in respect of alleged tortious liability.

The distinction between contractual and tortious liability is apparent from *Tesco Stores Ltd v Constable*.[22] In *Constable* the assured wished to construct a supermarket, part of the works involving the construction of a tunnel over a railway cutting. The assured agreed to provide an indemnity to the operator of trains on the line. Following a collapse of a section of the tunnel the assured honoured its indemnity to the operator and sought to recover from its liability insurers under a policy which provided insurance in respect of "all sums for which [the assured] shall be liable at law for damages in respect of a) death of or bodily injury to or illness or disease of any person b) loss or damage to material property . . . c) obstruction, loss of amenities, trespass, nuisance or any like cause . . . " The basic cover was supplemented by a Contractual Liability Extension which provided indemnity in respect of "liability assumed by [Tesco] under contract or agreement and which would not have attached in the absence of such contract or agreement". The insurers were found not to be liable under either the insuring clause or the Extension. As far as the former was concerned, Field J. and the Court of Appeal held that a "public liability" policy was one which, unless otherwise framed, covered general liability to the public and not "private liability" assumed under a contract. The Extension was held not to affect the position, as this was held merely to extend cover to the assured where it faced liability in contract for a tort falling within the insuring clause, its function being to permit the parties to a construction contract to transfer tortious liabilities between themselves without impairing the assured's public liability cover.

Certain forms of professional policies cover "E & O" liability, a collective term for phrases such as "any error, omission or negligent act". The use of the disjunctive "or" in this phrase has been held to mean that the insurer is liable to indemnify the assured for his errors or omissions whether or not they were negligent.[23] It is settled law that fraud or an act deliberately intended to cause loss falls outside the scope of a liability policy.[24]

20–010 *Statutory liability.* The term "liability at law by way of damages" and equivalent wording has been held not to encompass compensation payable under a statutory obligation which imposes liability irrespective of the fault of the assured.[25] In

[21] *Enterprise Oil Ltd v Strand Insurance Co Ltd* [2007] Lloyd's Rep. I.R. 186.
[22] *Tesco Stores Ltd v Constable* [2008] Lloyd's Rep. I.R. 636, and cf. *Encia Remediation Ltd v Canopius Managing Agents Ltd* [2008] Lloyd's Rep. I.R. 79.
[23] *Wimpey Construction v Poole* [1984] 2 Lloyd's Rep. 499.
[24] *Total Graphics Ltd v AGF Insurance Ltd* [1997] 1 Lloyd's Rep. 599.
[25] *The North Britain* [1894] P. 77 (statutory liability under Belgian law for the cost of removing a wreck). See also *Tatham, Bromage & Co v Burr (The Engineer)* [1898] A.C. 382 (cost of removing a wreck under English law); *Hall Brothers Steamship Co Ltd v Young* [1939] 1 K.B. 748 (compensation payable under French law for damage to a vessel in a collision which was not the fault of the assured).

Bartoline Ltd v Royal & Sun Alliance Insurance Plc[26] H.H. Judge Hegarty QC held that liability incurred by the assured to the Environment Agency under the Water Resources Act 1991 for clean-up costs following pollution by the assured was held to be a liability imposed by statute and not a liability imposed by tort and thus not within the insuring words "legal liability for damages in respect of . . . accidental loss". The court was satisfied that liability under the 1991 Act was not dependent upon proof of negligence and the cause of action was not breach of statutory duty in tort but rather one imposed directly by the legislation.[27] This ruling and the other earlier authorities were distinguished by the court of Appeal in *Bedfordshire Police Authority v Constable*,[28] which was a claim by a police authority under a liability policy covering sums which it was "legally liable to pay as damages". Recovery was sought for sums payable by the authority under the Riot (Damages) Act 1886, which imposes strict liability upon a police authority to pay for property damage resulting from a riot within its territory.[29] It was held that the policy responded, in that liability under the 1886 Act was either tortious or akin to tort and it was irrelevant that liability was strict or that the Act referred to "compensation" rather than damages because the word "compensation" encompassed "damages".[30] *Bartoline* and the earlier cases were regarded by the Court of Appeal in *Bedfordshire* as illustrations of liability being imposed on the assured in the absence of any duty owed to third parties by the assured.

Contribution claims. Contribution claims are within the scope of a liability **20–011** policy which encompasses "liability at law for damages".[31] However, where the assured has a contractual relationship with a member of some other profession whereby they jointly provide services to third parties, the policy may well exclude the insurer's liability in respect of any claim brought against the assured by the other party to the agreement. The scope of the insurer's liability is necessarily dependent upon the words used, but it is clear that such exclusion may well extend to liability other than contractual liability.[32]

Payments made to avoid liability. Not every situation in which the assured **20–012** becomes obliged to pay money to a third party will give rise to a claim under a liability policy. Thus, if the payment is made in order to permit the assured to carry on an activity which a third party could restrict by means of legal action (e.g. a nuisance),[33] or if other commercial pressure has been applied,[34] the assured has not incurred "liability" for the purposes of a liability policy.

---

[26] *Bartoline Ltd v Royal & Sun Alliance Insurance Plc* [2007] Lloyd's Rep. I.R. 423.

[27] There is also a need for the assured to prove that the sums which he has incurred arose out of liability and not out of an attempt to mitigate liability: *Yorkshire Water Services Ltd v Sun Alliance and London Insurance Plc* [1997] 2 Lloyd's Rep. 21; *Bartoline Ltd v Royal & Sun Alliance Insurance Plc* [2007] Lloyd's Rep. I.R. 423.

[28] *Bedfordshire Police Authority v Constable* [2009] Lloyd's Rep. I.R. 607.

[29] In *Yarl's Wood Immigration Ltd v Bedfordshire Police Authority* [2009] EWCA Civ 1110 the Court of Appeal held that the police faced liability under the 1886 Act in the circumstances of the case.

[30] It may be commented that in *Charterhouse Development (France) Ltd v Sharp* [1998] Lloyd's Rep. I.R. 266 it was held that the phrases "compensation" and "compensatory damages" were indistinguishable.

[31] *Matalan Discount Club (Cash & Carry) Ltd v Tokenspire Properties (North Western Ltd)* Unreported, 2001.

[32] *Cooke & Arkwright v Haydon* [1987] 2 Lloyd's Rep. 579.

[33] *Corbin v Payne*, The Times, October 11, 1990.

[34] *Smit Tak Offshore Services Ltd v Youell (The Mare)* [1992] 1 Lloyd's Rep. 154.

However, it has been held that a liability which becomes effective only through a waiver of diplomatic immunity is within a liability policy.[35]

2–013 *Costs incurred in averting liability.* In *Yorkshire Water v Sun Alliance*[36] the assured incurred expenditure in preventing the flooding of neighbouring properties, and sought to recover those costs from liability insurers who had provided coverage against liability caused by an event or occurrence. The policy required the assured, "at his own expense" to take reasonable precautions to prevent a loss. The Court of Appeal held that this clause precluded the implication into the policy of a term requiring the insurer to indemnify the assured for such expenditure. The Court further held that, in the absence of express provision: (a) the assured is not under a duty to take reasonable steps to avoid or mitigate a loss and (b) if the assured incurs expenditure in taking steps to avoid or mitigate a loss, the insurer is not liable to indemnify the assured for that expenditure.

20–014 *Costs of investigating liability.* The insurers may face liability in respect of a claim against the assured for costs incurred by the third party in investigating whether the assured's conduct has caused damage to property.[37]

20–015 *Punitive damages.* In English law there is little scope for an award of punitive or exemplary damages against a defendant. In contract cases, damages are based primarily on the claimant's loss[38] or, in exceptional cases, a profit made by the defendant due to a wilful breach of contract,[39] while in tort cases punitive damages may be awarded in two situations only: (a) where there has been oppressive or arbitrary conduct by government or public officials; or (b) where the defendant's conduct is designed to produce a profit for himself in excess of the claimant's loss.[40] As cases of punitive damages are comparatively rare, the courts have had little opportunity to consider whether liability policies indemnify assureds against awards of punitive damages against them. In *Lancashire County Council v Municipal Mutual Insurance Ltd*,[41] the assured local authority's policy covered it in respect of "all sums which the [assured] shall become legally liable to pay as compensation". An award of punitive damages was made against it on the basis of its vicarious liability for police officers who had been guilty of oppressive conduct. The Court of Appeal held that the policy covered punitive damages: (1) the word "compensation" was capable of covering both forms of damages, and on the basis of *contra proferentem* should be held to do so; (2) in practice it was difficult to determine from a global liability judgment the amount awarded by way of exemplary damage; and (3) by means of an endorsement to the policy there was a specific exclusion for exemplary damages in the limited context of pollution liability, thereby indicating that exemplary damages were otherwise covered. The Court of Appeal saw no public policy grounds objection to insurance coverage given that liability was vicarious, but as regards personal liability Staughton L.J. was of the view that public policy would operate where the assured had been guilty of conduct akin to "deliberate, intentional and unlawful violence or threats of violence" whereas Simon Brown L.J. thought that

---

[35] *Dickinson v Del Solar* [1930] 1 K.B. 376.
[36] *Yorkshire Water v Sun Alliance* [1997] 2 Lloyd's Rep. 21.
[37] *Jan de Nul (UK) Ltd v Axa Royal Belge* [2002] Lloyd's Rep. I.R. 589.
[38] *Surrey County Council v Bredero Homes Ltd* [1993] 3 All E.R. 705.
[39] *Attorney-General v Blake* [2000] 4 All E.R. 365.
[40] *Rookes v Barnard* [1964] A.C. 1129; *AB v South West Water Services Ltd* [1993] 1 All E.R. 605.
[41] *Lancashire County Council v Municipal Mutual Insurance Ltd* [1996] 3 All E.R. 545.

a person could not insure himself against the consequences of any criminality although in the absence of criminality public policy required the insurer to indemnify the assured for exemplary damages on the grounds that insurance contracts should be honoured, that refusal to pay could not be shown to be an effective deterrent against future misconduct, and that the real effect of denying recovery is to deprive the victim of the assured's wrongdoing of any effective remedy.[42]

Liability for death and personal injury: NHS charges and social security benefits

Outline. Part 3 of the Health and Social Care (Community Health and Standards)   **20–016** Act 2003 (HSCA 2003), which came into force with effect from January 29, 2007,[43] establishes a statutory scheme under which a person who has inflicted an injury on any other person is liable to meet National Health Service or ambulance service charges incurred as a result of the injury. In practice most of the charges will be met by the liability insurers of the wrongdoer. The 2003 Act extends to the NHS and ambulance service a scheme originally developed in respect of social security payments, under the Social Security (Recovery of Benefits) Act 1997 (SSA 1997). The 1997 Act established the Compensation Recovery Unit of the Department for Work and Pensions (CRU), the purpose of which was to ensure that a person liable to compensate a person suffering personal injury was also liable to indemnify the Government for any social security benefits payable to the victim which were generated by the injury. The principle established in the 1997 Act was extended to NHS charges in respect of motor vehicle accidents, under the Road Traffic (NHS Charges) Act 1999: compulsory motor insurance legislation has from its origins required the user of a motor vehicle to insure against liability for the costs of medical treatment in both NHS and private hospitals, but the 1999 Act for the first time sought to impose liability for the full costs of NHS treatment. The 1999 Act is repealed by s.169 of the 2003 Act and the principle of NHS recovery has been extended from personal injuries incurred on the road to personal injuries incurred in all situations by a unified scheme. Under transitional arrangements the 1999 Act continues to apply to injuries caused by motor accidents occurring on or before January 28, 2007 and the 2003 Act applies to all accidents occurring on or after January 29, 2007. The SSA 1997 and the HSCA 2003 operate more or less identically, and the following paragraphs discuss the provisions of the HSCA 2003 and conclude with a brief mention of any variations under the SSA 1997. HSCA 2003 is implemented by three sets of statutory instruments: the Personal Injuries (NHS Charges) (General) and Road Traffic (NHS Charges) (Amendment) Regulations 2006[44] (the General Regulations 2006); the Personal Injuries (NHS Charges) (Reviews and Appeals) and Road Traffic (NHS Charges) (Reviews and Appeals) (Amendment) Regulations 2006[45] (the Reviews and Appeals Regulations 2006); and the

---

[42] See also *Charterhouse Development (France) Ltd v Sharp* [1998] Lloyd's Rep. I.R. 266, where there was an express exclusion.

[43] Health and Social Care (Community Health and Standards) Act 2003 (Commencement) (No.11) Order 2006 (SI 2006/3397).

[44] SI 2006/3388, as amended by the Personal Injuries (NHS Charges) Amendment Regulations 2009 (SI 2009/316) and as corrected by the Personal Injuries (NHS Charges) (Amendment No.2) Regulations 2009 (SI 2009/834).

[45] SI 2006/3398.

Personal Injuries (NHS Charges) (Amounts) Regulations 2007[46] (the Charges Regulations).

20–017 *Circumstances in which the 2003 Act applies.* The 2003 Act applies where a person (the injured person) suffers any injury, whether physical or psychological but not a disease unless one attributable to an injury (s.150(5)–(6)) for which he has received NHS treatment (including any examination: s.150(7)) at a health service hospital (the power in s.165 to extend the scheme to non-NHS hospitals has not yet been exercised) or has been provided with NHS ambulance services for the purpose of taking him to a hospital for NHS treatment (s.150(1)). Hospitals outside the NHS are excluded from the 2003 Act, although it should be noted that non-NHS hospitals and any doctor who provides emergency treatment remain entitled to recover for treatment afforded to the victims of road traffic accidents, under ss.157 and 158 of the Road Traffic Act 1988.

If another person has made a compensation payment to the injured person either voluntarily, in pursuance of a court order, by agreement or otherwise (s.150(4)) and whether or not with an admission of liability (s.150(14)), the paying party is liable to pay NHS charges in respect of the treatment and the provision of the ambulance service (s.150(2)). In the case of a structured settlement providing for periodic payments to the victim, the person liable to make the payment is to be taken to have made a single compensation on the date of the agreement or court order (General Regulations 2006 reg.7), and in the case of a payment into court there is payment only if it has been accepted (General Regulations 2006 reg.9). A compensation payment is one made: (a) by or on behalf of a person who is, or who is alleged to be, liable to any extent in respect of the injury; or (b) in pursuance of a compensation scheme for motor accidents (s.150(3)). Excluded payments are set out in Sch.10 to the 2003 Act, supplemented by the General Regulations 2006 reg.10, and consist of, most importantly compensation orders against convicted persons, and payments made under the Criminal Injuries Compensation Act 1995 or the Vaccine Damage Payments Act 1979. In addition, any payment made to the injured person by his own accident or personal injury insurers is exempted from the legislation (Sch.10 para.4).

As far as liability insurance is concerned, point (a) includes in particular the liability insurers of the paying party, and s.164(1) of the 2003 Act provides that a liability policy which covers the liability of the paying party to make a compensation payment is extended to cover liability under the 2003 Act. The provision is retroactive in that it applies to policies whenever issued (s.164(4)). Such liability cannot be excluded or restricted by any policy term (s.164(2)), and the prohibition extends to any provision which makes the liability or its enforcement subject to restrictive or onerous conditions, which subjects any person to any prejudice in consequence of his pursuing any such right or remedy or which excludes or restricts the rules of evidence or procedure (s.164(3)). In the event that the policy has a maximum sum insured (which is not permitted in respect of personal injury suffered in a motor accident, under s.145 of the Road Traffic Act 1988) and as a result a proportion of the compensation would not be covered by the policy, the insurers' liability under the 2003 Act is reduced by the same proportion (General Regulations 2006 reg.10). This makes it clear that the statutory liability imposed on insurers by the 2004 Act is in addition to, and not

---

[46] 2007, SI 2007/115, as amended by the Personal Injuries (NHS Charges) (Amounts) Amendment Regulations 2008 (SI 2008/252) and the Personal Injuries (NHS Charges) Amendment Regulations 2009 (SI 2009/316), as corrected by the Personal Injuries (NHS Charges) (Amendment No.2) Regulations 2009 (SI 2009/834).

a part of, the maximum liability of insurers under the policy. The reference in point (b) to "a compensation scheme for motor accidents" is defined as referring to payments by the Motor Insurers Bureau under the Uninsured Drivers Agreement and the Untraced Drivers Agreement (s.150(11)).

Certification. In all cases a person facing liability under the 2003 Act must apply **20–018** to the Secretary of State for a certificate in the prescribed manner (s.151(9)). The General Regulations 2006 reg.2(1), provide that an application is to be made to the CRU and is to include: (a) the full name and address of the injured person; (b) the date of birth, and where known, the national insurance number of that person; (c) the date on which the injury occurred; (d) the nature of the injury; (e) the name and address of any hospital at which the injured person received NHS treatment in respect of his injury; (f) where the applicant has made a compensation payment in respect of the injury, the date on which that payment was made; and (g) if there is an application for a reduction in respect of contributory negligence, a statement of the proportion by which the damages payable in respect of the claim are to be reduced and a copy of the order, judgment, minute or document which provides for that reduction.

A certificate must specify the amount, if any, for which the person to whom it is issued is liable, as determined in accordance with regulations issued under the 2003 Act (s.153(1)–(2), (4)). The Charges Regulations 2007 regs 3 and 3A and set out the relevant figures. They are: (a) £171 for each occasion on which, as a result of his injury, the injured person was provided with NHS ambulance services for the purpose of taking him to a hospital for NHS treatment; (b) where the injured person received NHS treatment at a hospital in respect of his injury, either, if he was not admitted to hospital, the sum of £566, or if he was admitted to hospital, the sum of £695 for each day or part day of admission. The aggregate maximum is £41,545. There is no charge in respect of overseas visitors. The certificate must only take into account sums incurred before the date on which the certificate is issued (Charges Regulations 2007 reg.4). The applicant is also entitled to particulars of the name of the ambulance service or hospital providing the services, the date on which they were provided and the duration of any treatment (s.153(11)–(12) and the General Regulations 2006 reg.4). The amount payable is to be reduced in proportion to any reduction from the compensation payment itself based on contributory negligence of the injured person as reflected in any judgment (s.153(3)). Where the claim has been resolved by a settlement which takes account of contributory negligence, the settlement is binding for the purposes of the 2003 Act if the applicant for the certificate sends to the CRU a report which contains a statement as to how the agreement was reached and if it appears to the Secretary of State from the report that the agreement was reached in a fair manner (s.154(9)–(10) and the General Regulations 2006 reg.3).

The application for a certificate may be made before a compensation payment is made (s.151(1), in which case a certificate must be issued as soon as is reasonably practicable (s.151(2)). A certificate may provide that it is to remain in force until a specified date, until the occurrence of a specified event, or indefinitely (s.151(3)), and if the certificate expires a fresh application may be made although a renewed certificate may be issued without further application (s.151(4)–(6)). If the certificate is issued before the date on which the compensation payment is made (the "settlement date"), the payment under the 2003 Act must be made within 14 days of the settlement date (s.154(1)). If, by contrast, the certificate is issued after the settlement date, payment under the 2003 Act must be made within 14 days of the date of the certificate (s.154(2)). In the event that full payment has not been made within the time allowed, a demand for immediate payment may be made by the Secretary of State (s.155(1)–(2)) and this is enforceable as if it were a court order (s.155(7)).

If a compensation payment has been made before there has been an application for a certificate, or if the certificate has expired at the time, and no application for a certificate had been made in the 28-day period immediately preceding the payment, the paying person must apply to the Secretary of State for a certificate (s.151(7)–(8); General Regulations 2006 reg.2(3)) within 14 days (s.151(9); General Regulations 2006 reg.2(2)), and a certificate must be issued as soon as is reasonably practicable (s.151(10)). Failure by the paying person to apply for a certificate may lead to a demand for immediate payment by the Secretary of State (s.155(1)–(2)), which is enforceable as a court order (s.155(7)).

Sums received by the Secretary of State must be paid to the relevant health service hospital or ambulance trust (s.162; Charges Regulations 2007 reg.6) no more than 40 days after receipt (General Regulations 2006 reg.6).

20–019 *Review and appeal.* The general provisions applicable to appeals, including waiver of formalities and of time limits, are in the Reviews and Appeal Regulations 2006 regs 6–8. The mechanics of repaying overpayments are set out in the Charges Regulations regs 7–10.

A certificate issued by the Secretary of State must be reviewed by him if, after issue, a court has ordered a reduction in damages by reason of contributory negligence (s.156(1)). The review may be on the Secretary of State's own initiative or on written application by the paying party on a form approved by the Secretary of State (s.156(4)): the judgment or document reducing the award must be sent to the CRU along with particulars of the proportionate reduction, and the review must be completed within three months (Review and Appeals Regulations 2006 reg.2). On review, the Secretary of State may confirm, vary (by reduction only, unless the paying party had supplied the Secretary of State with incorrect or insufficient information: s.156(7)) or revoke the certificate (s.156(5)).

It is also possible for an appeal to be made against a certificate, on the grounds that: an amount specified in the certificate is incorrect; an amount takes into account treatment or ambulance services not provided by the NHS; two compensators face liability and there has been an incorrect apportionment between them (Charges Regulations 2007 reg.5); and any payment made to the injured person was not a compensation payment (s.157(1)). The possible grounds of appeal and details of the manner in which an appeal may be made must be issued to the paying party at the same time as the certificate (Reviews and Appeals Regulations 2006 reg.3). In outline, an appeal must be sent to the CRU within three months of the date of the certificate or the date on which the compensation payment was made, if later, setting out the ground of appeal and a summary of the arguments (Reviews and Appeals Regulations 2006 reg.5). An appeal may not be made until two conditions have been satisfied. The first is that the claim which gave rise to the compensation payment has been finally disposed of. For this purpose, an order for provisional damages is to be treated as one disposing of the claim (s.157(3)), although if the court subsequently orders that the full amount of the damages is to be repaid then the Secretary of State must repay the sums paid to him (General Regulations 2006 reg.8. If the sums have been paid to a hospital or ambulance service, they are to be deducted from future payments). The second condition is that payment of the amount specified in the certificate has been made to the Secretary of State (s.157(2)). However, the pre-payment condition may be waived by the Secretary of State if it appears to him that payment of the amount in the certificate would cause exceptional financial hardship (s.157(4)–(5)). A waiver application setting out must be sent to the CRU within three months of the date of the certificate, setting out the grounds of exceptional financial hardship and the Secretary of State then has a month to issue a decision which is to be reasoned if the application is refused (Reviews and Appeals Regulations 2006 reg.4). An appeal may be made against a refusal to grant a waiver within a month (s.157(6) and the Reviews and Appeals Regulations 2006 reg.4).

Any appeal against a certificate or against refusal of waiver of payment must be referred to a Social Security Appeal Tribunal (s.158(1)). On an appeal against a certificate the tribunal may confirm the amount specified in the certificate, specify any variations or declare that the certificate is to be revoked (s.158(3)), and the Secretary of State must then—in accordance with the decision—confirm the certificate, issue a fresh certificate or revoke the certificate (s.158(4)). On an appeal against refusal of waiver of payment, the tribunal may confirm the decision or waive the requirement in question (s.158(6)).

There is a further appeal to a Social Security Commissioner from a decision of a tribunal, but only on the ground that the tribunal's decision was wrong in law (s.159(1)). An appeal may be made either by the Secretary of State or by the person to whom the certificate was issued (s.159(2)). Appeals take effect as if made under the Social Security Act 1998 (s.159(3)).

Provision of information. Where compensation is sought by an injured person, **20–020** the CRU is, on the request of the Secretary of State, to be provided with prescribed information in respect of the claim by the person against whom the claim is made, the injured person, and the relevant NHS hospital or ambulance trust (s.160(1)). The information must be provided in the form and time prescribed (s.160(2)). The General Regulations 2006 reg.5, require information to be provided within 14 days of the date of any request by the Secretary of State, and it must (so far as it is known) consist of: the full name and address of the injured person; the full name and address of the person against whom the claim is made and anyone acting for him; the date of birth or national insurance number of that person; the date on which the injury occurred; the nature of the injury; in respect of NHS treatment received at a hospital in respect of the injury, the name and address of the hospital and the date of admission and discharge; in respect of NHS ambulance services provided to the injured person as a result of his injury, the name and address of the ambulance trust which provided those services and the date on which the services were provided. Hospitals are themselves required to provide information on the duration and nature of any treatment, and ambulance trusts must provide details of services provided by them.

Any information received by the Secretary of State is to be used only for the purposes of Pt 3 of the 2003 Act or for the purposes of the SSA 1997 (s.161).

The Social Security (Recovery of Benefits) Act 1997. As commented earlier, the **20–021** Social Security (Recovery of Benefits) Act 1997 was the model for the Health and Social Care (Community Health and Standards) Act 2003 and the two pieces of legislation operate almost identically. The 1997 Act came into force on September 3, 1997[47] and it applies where a compensation payment has been made by any person—including his insurers and the Motor Insurers Bureau—in respect of personal injury or disease suffered by another, but excluding first party insurance proceeds (1997 Act s.1 and Sch.1). The paying party is also liable to

---

[47] Supplemented by the Social Security (Recovery of Benefits) Regulations 1997 (SI 1997/2205) and the Social Security (Recovery of Benefits) (Appeals) Regulations 1997 (SI 1997/2237), as amended.

indemnify the Secretary of State for relevant social security benefits payable to
the victim, including incapacity benefit, income support, invalidity allowance,
disablement benefit, sickness benefit, statutory sick pay, unemployment benefit,
attendance allowance and mobility allowance (1997 Act s.6 and Sch.2) insofar as
the compensation payment does not encompass losses which would otherwise be
reflected in the benefits (1997 Act ss.8–9). An application is to be made to the
Secretary of State for certification of the amount of recoverable benefits (1997
Act ss.4–5), failing which he can be issued with a demand for payment (1997 Act
s.7). The Secretary of State is required to review a certificate if it is based on a
mistake (1997 Act, s.10, as amended), and there is an elaborate appeals structure
involving reference to a medical appeal tribunal and then, on a point of law, to
a Social Security Commissioner (1997 Act ss.11–14, as amended). As far as
liability insurers are concerned, any liability of the paying party covered by a
policy is deemed to include liability under the 1997 Act, and that statutory
liability cannot be excluded or restricted by restrictive or onerous conditions, or
by policy terms which subject any person to any prejudice in consequence of his
pursuing any such right or remedy or which exclude or restrict the rules of
evidence or procedure (s.22).

Disclosure

20–022   *Utmost good faith.* Whether the policy is in the form of losses occurring or
claims made, detailed pre-contract disclosure will be required by the insurers. In
the case of a losses occurring policy, the insurers may face liability for injuries
suffered by the third party during the currency of the policy, even if they arise out
of acts of negligence that occurred prior to inception. Accordingly, the insurers
will wish to be informed of circumstances occurring in earlier years that may
potentially manifest themselves as injuries during the coming policy year. Under
a claims made policy there is an equal need for disclosure. Such a policy is
concerned with claims actually made against the assured during the policy
period, and these will typically be the result of acts of negligence committed by
the assured and occurring in earlier years. In each situation, the common law duty
of disclosure is generally supplemented by an express term requiring the assured
to inform the insurers of any circumstances known to the assured that may or are
likely to give rise to a claim during the currency of the new policy. Material facts
include the assured's claims history and events which may give rise to future
claims.[48] The insurer will also wish to be informed of the assured's risk
assessment mechanisms[49] and of any arrangements which mean that the
assured's liability will be greater than that contemplated by the insurers.[50]

20–023   *Waiver of the duty.* In claims-made policies issued to professions, the duty of
disclosure is often waived in order to comply with professional requirements
(e.g. those of the Law Society and in respect of accountants) that policies are to
cover all claims made against the assured. In some cases the duty to disclose is

---

[48] *New Hampshire Insurance Co v Oil Refineries Ltd* [2003] Lloyds Rep. I.R. 386.
[49] The point is illustrated by reinsurance cases: *Assicurazioni Generali SpA v Arab Insurance
Group (BSC)* [2002] Lloyd's Rep. I.R. 131; *Feasey v Sun Life Assurance Co of Canada* [2002]
Lloyd's Rep. I.R. 637; *ERC Frankona Reinsurance v American National Insurance Co* [2006]
Lloyd's Rep. I.R. 157.
[50] See *Toomey v Banco Viialicio de Espana SA de Seguros y Reasseguros* [2005] Lloyd's Rep. LR.
423 (reinsurers able to avoid facultative reinsurance where reinsured stated that direct policy was
unvalued when in fact it was valued).

waived entirely. [51] In others the duty to disclose is waived if the assured can show that the failure to make a fair presentation of the risk was not fraudulent.[52]

Exclusion of liability for earlier events. In addition to relying upon disclosure of earlier events, many policies exclude liability for claims arising out of circumstances known to the assured at the inception of the policy[53] or for claims arising from circumstances which could have been notified under any earlier policy.[54] The exclusion of known claims and known circumstances may in some cases be extended to circumstances which a reasonable person in the assured's person would have thought might result in a claim covered by the policy. This wording has been held by the High Court of Australia to refer to a reasonable person in the same professional position of the assured, disregarding the assured's personal idiosyncracies.[55]

20–024

Classifying the assured's liability. Many professional indemnity policies are limited to claims against the assured which are based on "negligence" or "errors and omissions". The problem raised by this form of wording is that the claim made against the assured may be framed in terms which take it outside the policy, although the actual substance of the claim is nevertheless insured. The key question is not how the claim is framed, but rather its actual substance. It was thus held in *West Wake Price & Co v Ching*[56] that a policy which covered only negligence did not extend to a "mixed claim", based partly upon negligence and partly upon fraud. Where, however, a claim against the assured may be classified in a number of ways, there is coverage if any one of those classifications is insured.[57] In determining the nature of the claim made against the assured, it is necessary to consider the substance of the action rather than the manner in which it has been framed. Thus in *Citibank v Excess Insurance*[58] it was held that an action for damages following a fire was the relevant claim, rather than the acts and omissions which constituted the underlying causes of the fire. Again, if the third party makes a claim against the assured which is plainly based on allegations of fraud, but in respect of which damages for negligence are sought, the court is entitled to consider the underlying nature of the claim and to hold it to be outside the scope of the policy if fraud is regarded as the key issue. Similarly, if the claim against an assured company is based on negligent failure to supervise employees, but the factual basis for the claim is that those controlling the assured have been guilty of wilful misconduct, the assured is unable to recover.[59] That said, where there has been an administrative or judicial decision fixing the assured's liability on a particular basis, the finding will be conclusive for the purposes of ascertaining the cause of the assured's liability for insurance purposes.[60]

20–025

---

[51] *Kumar v AGF Insurance Ltd* [1998] 4 All E.R. 788.
[52] *Rothschild Assurance Ltd v Collyear* [1999] Lloyd's Rep. I.R. 6.
[53] *Tilley v Dominion Insurance* (1987) 2 E.G.L.R. 34.
[54] *Rothschild Assurance Ltd v Collyear* [1999] Lloyd's Rep. I.R. 6; *Kumar v AGF Insurance Ltd* [1998] 4 All E.R. 788.
[55] *CGU Insurance Ltd v Porthouse* [2008] H.C.A. 30.
[56] *West Wake Price & Co v Ching* [1957] 1 W.L.R. 45.
[57] *Capel-Cure Myers Capital Management Ltd v McCarthy* [1995] L.R.L.R. 498.
[58] *Citibank v Excess Insurance* [1999] Lloyd's Rep. I.R. 122.
[59] *KR v Royal & Sun Alliance Plc* [2007] Lloyd's Rep. I.R. 368.
[60] *Redbridge LBC v Municipal Mutual Insurance Ltd* [2001] Lloyd's Rep. I.R. 545; *Charterhouse Development (France) Ltd v Sharp* [1999] Lloyd's Rep. I.R. 266.

There is no reason why the parties should not contract out of the basic proximate cause rule, and allow the assured to recover on the basis of the specific allegations made by the third party rather than the underlying nature of the claim. However, there is general judicial reluctance to hold that a policy responds to the allegations made against the assured rather than the real substance of the claim. Thus a policy which covered allegations of breach of contract was held not to respond to a claim the true nature of which was fraud.[61]

Coverage based on the assured's activities

20–026 *Express and implied restrictions.* The coverage under a liability policy will generally cover liabilities arising out of specified activities of the assured, and it may be that cover extends also to liabilities incurred in connection with those activities.[62]

20–027 *Restrictions based on purpose of activities.* Where a policy limits the right to recover to cases in which property is being used for a specific purpose, difficulties may arise if the assured at the time had mixed motives. The test to be applied in such a case is that of the predominant purpose looked at from the assured's point of view.[63] If the two purposes are concurrent, one of which is insured and the other excluded, the exclusion takes priority.[64]

20–028 *Restrictions based on capacity.* Householders' liabilities policies commonly limit the insurer's responsibility to loss arising from the assured's activities "as occupier".[65] Occupancy may be purely temporary and transitory.[66] Some policies may draw a distinction between ownership and occupation, and provide cover only for the latter, although it has been held that liability for nuisance attaches to an occupier and not to an owner so that such a policy provides coverage for a nuisance claim.[67] The phrase "legally liable as owner" in a composite policy covering the interests of both the owner and charterer of a vessel extends to liability incurred by either of them, and that the phrase refers to the form of liability rather than the identity of the person who incurred that liability: any other interpretation would negative the charterer's coverage.[68] The phrase liability arising "by reason of interest" has been held to extend coverage to a user of property under a lease,[69] a decision which is at first sight difficult to reconcile with the earlier capacity cases but which has been explained as turning on the specific wording used.[70]

The coverage of a liability policy may also be restricted by reference to the business carried on by the assured. The policy is likely to contain a description,

---

[61] *MDIS Ltd v Swinbank* [1999] Lloyd's Rep. I.R. 516. See also: *Thornton Springer v NEM Insurance Co Ltd* [2000] Lloyd's Rep. I.R. 590; *Enterprise Oil Ltd v Strand Insurance Co Ltd* [2007] Lloyd's Rep. I.R. 186.

[62] The point was left open in *Smit Tak Offshore Services Ltd v Youell (The Mare)* [1992] 1 Lloyd's Rep. 154.

[63] *Seddons v Binions* [1978] 1 Lloyd's Rep. 381; *Caple v Sewell* [2002] Lloyd's Rep. I.R. 627.

[64] *Passmore v Vulcan Boiler General Insurance Co Ltd* (1936) 54 Ll. L.R. 92.

[65] *Sturge v Hackett* [1962] 1 W.L.R. 1257.

[66] *Oei v Foster* [1982] 2 Lloyd's Rep. 170.

[67] *Rigby v Sun Alliance* [1980] 1 Lloyd's Rep. 359, followed in *Pan-United Shipyard Pte Ltd v India* [2000] 4 S.L.R. 303.

[68] *Christmas v Taylor Woodrow Civil Engineering* [1997] 1 Lloyd's Rep. 407, where the policy did not respond because the liability arose out of contract rather than ownership.

[69] *Turner v Manx Line Ltd* [1990] 1 Lloyd's Rep. 137.

[70] *Christmas v Taylor Woodrow Civil Engineering* [1997] 1 Lloyd's Rep. 407.

often in the schedule, of the assured's business and then to restrict cover to liabilities arising out of that business. If liability arises from an activity of the assured which is partly inside and partly outside his business, it is a matter of construction whether the policy responds where the losses relate to the insured business or whether the insurers are discharged completely. The former construction might be thought to be more attractive, as otherwise the exclusion for non-business liabilities would operate as some form of suspensory condition which precludes recovery while uninsured activities were being carried on even though the liability itself would otherwise be covered. The point arose in *Encia Remediation Ltd v Canopius Managing Agents Ltd*,[71] in which a liability policy covered any liabilities incurred by the assured arising out of its business of supplying professional services in respect of civil and commercial engineering, but excluded loss arising from any contract under which the assured supplied or installed materials. The assured entered into a contract under which it both provided professional services and also installed piling foundations for a housing development. Cracks developed in the houses, and Cresswell J. held as a preliminary point of construction that the assured would be entitled to an indemnity in respect of liability for negligence in the supply of professional services but not in respect of negligence in the manufacture or construction of the piling. This decision is consistent with decisions from Australia and Canada which have held that liability for the supply of professional services does not include liability for defects in products supplied with those services.[72]

Common policy provisions

Event limits and aggregations. Liability policies frequently limit the insurer's liability in one or both of two ways: by requiring the assured to bear the first £X arising from any claim, or by limiting the insurer's liability to a maximum £Y from any one claim. Wording differs as between policies: the limitation may be expressed in terms, most commonly, of any one "claim", "loss", "occurrence", "accident" or "event". The issue here is in determining whether these words are referring to the single event which gives rise to losses, or to the individual losses flowing from a single event.[73]   **20–029**

Reinstatement. Liability policies commonly provide for automatic reinstatement, so that if losses reach the maximum sum insured, coverage under the policy is reinstated automatically and the assured can claim as if the cover had not been exhausted. Reinstatement provisions are, however, generally subject to event limit provisions, so that if loss from a single event exceeds the event limit, the reinstatement clause cannot be used to impose additional liability upon the insurer. Thus, if a policy with an event limit of £1,000,000 per cause covers loss up to £1,000,000, and provides for reinstatement for a further £1,000,000, the reinstatement clause cannot be used to impose liability upon the insurer for a loss   **20–030**

---

[71] *Encia Remediation Ltd v Canopius Managing Agents Ltd* [2008] Lloyd's Rep. I.R. 79.
[72] *Fitzpatrick v Robert Norman Job and Wendy Barbara Job t/as Jobs Engineering & Ors* [2007] W.A.S.C.A. 63; *Vero Insurance Ltd v Power Technologies Pty Ltd* 2007 N.S.W.C.A. 226; *Chemetics International Ltd v Commercial Union Assurance Co of Canada* (1984) 11 D.L.R. (4th) 754. Contrast *Bedfordshire Police Authority v Constable* [2009] Lloyd's Rep. I.R. 607, where it was held that the business of a police authority included the obligations under statute (the Riot (Damages) Act 1884) to prevent riots occurring and causing damage, so that liability arising under that Act to property owners was incurred in the courts of its business.
[73] See Ch.10, above.

in excess of £1,000,000 arising from a single cause.[74] In *Cox v Deeny*[75] losses of £500,000 from originating cause A were incurred, and losses of £500,000 from originating cause B were then incurred. It was held by H.H. Judge Diamond QC that the discovery of additional losses of £500,000 arising from originating cause A did not prevent the operation of the reinstatement clause, as long as the assured did not recover more than £1,000,000 from originating cause A. An event limit is therefore, to be taken against both the original and the reinstated cover.[76]

20–031   *Reasonable care and misconduct.* As the main purpose of a liability policy is to permit the assured to recover for negligence, the policy presumes that there will have been some misconduct on the assured's part. Consequently, in the absence of any express provision restricting the insurer's liability, the assured will be able to recover unless his liability is attributable to an intentional criminal act on his part.[77] However, the mere fact of criminality is not sufficient to prevent recovery: the courts have recognised that the true beneficiary of a liability policy is the third-party victim, and have, with notable exceptions,[78] allowed the assured to recover despite the criminal nature of his conduct. The assured will thus be precluded from recovering where he has deliberately brought about his own loss[79] or where a deliberate criminal act is the cause of his loss.[80] In the case of manslaughter, the law does not generally permit recovery by the assured if he was in any way responsible for his acts.[81]

While it is contrary to public policy for the assured to insure against liability for his own criminal conduct, a policy may be effective to cover the criminal acts of the assured's employee.[82] However, a policy merely providing cover in respect of a clerk's "neglect, omission or error" will not extend to loss occasioned by his fraud or criminal acts.[83]

Express clauses may limit the insurer's obligations in the event of the assured's misconduct. It is common for the consequences of criminality to be excluded, although the courts have generally confined such an exclusion to

[74] *Cox v Bankside Members Agency* [1995] 2 Lloyd's Rep. 437.

[75] *Cox v Deeny* [1996] L.R.L.R. 288, a sequel to *Cox v Bankside*. The figures given in the text are notional, for illustrative purposes only.

[76] A further issue arose, as a consequence of the fact that there were additional layers of cover which took effect when the limits of indemnity under the first layer cover had been reached. It was held that the second layer took effect only when the reinstated sum under the first layer had been reached. Where insurance is arranged in layers, and reinstatements do not apply until all layers have been exhausted, the process is known as "round the clock reinstatement".

[77] *Haseldine v Hosken* [1933] 1 K.B. 822.

[78] *Gray v Barr* [1971] 2 Q.B. 554.

[79] A deliberate decision to terminate a commercial contract, which subsequently gives rise to claims in tort for interfering with contractual rights, is not to be regarded as barred by a policy which confers cover for "liability . . . on account of the infringement of contract rights", as such liability can only be incurred where the interference is deliberate and wilful: *Enterprise Oil Ltd v Strand Insurance Co Ltd* [2007] Lloyd's Rep. I.R. 186.

[80] *Charlton v Fisher* [2001] Lloyd's Rep. I.R. 387.

[81] *Gray v Barr* [1971] 2 Q.B. 554; *Dunbar v Plant* [1997] 4 All E.R. 289. Contrast the motor manslaughter cases, in particular *Tinline v White Cross Insurance* [1921] 3 K.B. 327 and *James v British General Insurance* [1927] 2 K.B. 311, which appear to be based on special considerations.

[82] *Hawley v Luminar Leisure* [2006] Lloyd's Rep. I.R. 307. However, if the employee is the controlling mind of the assured, so that his acts can be imputed to the assured, there can be no recovery: *KR v Royal & Sun Alliance Plc* [2007] Lloyd's Rep. I.R. 368.

[83] *Davies v Hosken* (1937) 53 T.L.R. 798. See also: *Goddard and Smith v Frew* [1939] 4 All E.R. 358; *West Wake Price v Ching* [1957] 1 W.L.R. 45; *Warrender v Swain* [I960] 2 Lloyd's Rep. 111.

deliberate criminal misconduct.[84] Similarly, where a policy requires the assured to take "reasonable precautions" against the incurring of liability, it has been held consistently that nothing short of recklessness will bring the exception into play, as any other interpretation would defeat the entire purpose of the policy from the assured's point of view.[85]

Professional indemnity policies seek by express term to protect the insurer against losses resulting from the conduct of unqualified or inexperienced persons in the assured's employ. This is commonly achieved by requiring the assured to maintain adequate supervision over the activities of such employees.[86]

Drop-down cover and excess layers. Professional indemnity insurance is typi- **20–032** cally arranged in layers. In cases where the assured is a parent company with numerous subsidiaries, there may be an arrangement whereby the parent company takes out a master policy covering all subsidiaries, and each subsidiary procures a local policy which is to provide primary layer cover. The master policy thus operates as an excess layer policy. In *Flexsys America LP v XL Insurance Company Ltd*[87] the local policy provided cover for the annual aggregate sum of US$1 million, and the Master Policy provided cover for US$25 million in excess of US$1 million. The master policy contained a "drop-down" clause which stated that "In the event of total exhaustion of a local policy this Policy will continue in force as the underlying insurance subject to the terms Exceptions and Conditions of the particular local Policy." It was held that the purpose of the clause was to reinstate cover of US$1 million where the policy limits under the local cover had been exhausted by earlier claims, in which case the Master Policy dropped down to provide the coverage that would have been available under the local policy. The clause had no application to the case in which a single claim exceeded the limits of the local policy but fell outside the insuring provisions of the Master Policy.

No admission of liability or settlement of claims. Liability policies often make it **20–033** a condition precedent to coverage that the assured has not admitted liability to a potential third-party claimant. A plea of guilty to a criminal prosecution relating to the events which have given rise to a claim is not to be regarded as an admission of liability for this purpose.[88]

In *Horwood v Land of Leather Ltd*[89] a clause which prohibited the assured from settling any claim without the consent of the insurers was held to extend to a claim *by* the assured as well as to a claim *against* the assured. The effect of the settlement in *Horwood* was to remove any possibility of the assured retailer seeking damages from a supplier beyond the amount agreed between them for the

---

[84] *Marcel Beller v Hayden* [1978] Q.B. 694; *Linden Alimak v British Engine Insurance* [1984] 1 Lloyd's Rep. 416.

[85] *Fraser v Furman* [1967] 3 All E.R. 57; *Woolfall & Rimmer v Moyle* [1942] 1 K.B. 66; *Linden Alimak v British Engine Insurance* [1984] 1 Lloyd's Rep. 416; *M/S Aswan Engineering v Iron Trade's Mutual Insurance* [1989] 1 Lloyd's Rep. 289; *Jan de Nul (UK) Ltd v NV Royal Belge* [2001] Lloyd's Rep. I.R. 327.

[86] *Summers v Congreve Horner, The Times*, August 24, 1992.

[87] *Flexsys America LP v XL Insurance Company Ltd* [2010] Lloyd's Rep. I.R. 132.

[88] *Harbourfield Engineering Co Ltd v Falcon Insurance Co (Hong Kong) Ltd* [2003] H.K.E.C. 959.

[89] *Horwood v Land of Leather Ltd* [2010] Lloyd's Rep. I.R. 453.

settlement of all claims by the retailer against the supplier. The effect of the agreement was to prejudice the subrogation rights of the retailer's liability insurers when faced with claims against the retailer by customers.

Claims under liability policies

20–034 *Liability to be established and quantified.* The assured's right to indemnification under a liability policy will, in the absence of express wording to the contrary, be regarded as arising once the assured's liability to the third party has been ascertained, i.e. established and quantified.[90] This can happen in one of three ways: the assured has been sued to judgment; there is a binding arbitration award against the assured; and the assured has entered into a settlement with the third party.

Judgments and awards are automatically binding on insurers, as there is an implied obligation on insurers in the insurance contract that they will recognise them.[91] It was suggested in *Commercial Union Insurance v NRG Victory Reinsurance*[92] that a judgment would not be binding on insurers if it was perverse or if the assured had not put in a proper defence, and doubtless the same principle applies also to arbitration awards. Settlements raise entirely separate issues and are considered below.

20–035 *No need for actual payment.* There is no need for the assured to show that he has actually made payment to the third party. Wording ousting this principle is rarely found in non-marine or marine policies, although the rules of P&I Clubs offering liability cover frequently contain "pay to be paid" clauses under which the Club is not liable to the member until the member has made full payment to the third party. These clauses are relied upon primarily in relation to cargo claims against carriers and are not used where the claim against the member is for damages in respect of death or personal injury. Pay to be paid clauses are undoubtedly effective as between the Club and its member, and they are also effective against a person seeking to proceed directly against the Club of an insolvent member under the Third Parties (Rights against Insurers) Act 2010 insofar as the claim does not relate to death or personal injury.[93] Some reinsurance agreements contain similar pay to be paid provisions, although these have been construed as requiring payment by the reinsurers once the reinsured has established and quantified its liability to the assured.[94] The effect of the decisions is to remove a possible windfall from reinsurers on the insolvency of the reinsured, although the

---

[90] *Johnston v Salvage Association* (1897) 19 QBD 458; *Lancashire Insurance v IRC* [1899] 1 Q.B. 353; *West Wake Price & Co v Ching* [1957] 1 W.L.R. 45; *Post Office v Norwich Union Fire Insurance Society Ltd* [1967] 2 Q.B. 363; *Bradley v Eagle Star Insurance Co Ltd* [1989] A.C. 957; *Durham v BAI (Run Off) Ltd* [2009] Lloyd's Rep. I.R. 295.

[91] *Lumbermen's Mutual Casualty Co v Bovis Lend Lease Ltd* [2005] Lloyd's Rep. I.R. 74; *Sun Life Assurance Co of Canada v Lincoln National Life Insurance Co* [2005] 1 Lloyd's Rep. 606.

[92] *Commercial Union Insurance v NRG Victory Reinsurance* [1998] Lloyd's Rep. I.R. 439.

[93] 2010 Act s.9(5)–(6). It had been held by the House of Lords that the Third Parties (Rights against Insurers) Act 1930 that a pay to be paid clause precluded a claim against a P&I Club whose assured member had become insolvent: *The Fanti and the Padre Island* [1990] 2 All E.R. 705. That principle is confined to cargo, other property and financial loss claims by the 2010 Act.

[94] *Re Eddystone Marine* [1892] 2 Ch. 423; *Home & Overseas Insurance Co Ltd v Mentor Insurance Co (UK) Ltd* [1989] 2 Lloyd's Rep. 473; *Re A Company (No.0013734 of 1991)* [1992] 2 Lloyd's Rep. 415; *Charter Reinsurance Co Ltd v Fagan* [1996] 3 All E.R. 46.

distinction between the P&I wordings and those of reinsurance agreements is at first sight somewhat difficult to ascertain.[95]

Interim awards. For the purposes of determining whether liability has been **20–036** established and quantified in respect of a claim under a liability policy, an interim award of damages against the assured under CPR Pt 25 will be treated as "damages".[96]

Notification obligations

Types of obligations. Notification obligations vary as between the classes of **20–037** liability insurance. The consequences of a breach of these provisions is a matter for the wording of the clause: in the usual way, a condition precedent will preclude recovery unless there has been compliance, whereas a bare condition is to be regarded as innominate and its breach will only give the insurers the right to seek damages for any loss suffered by them from late notification. Whether or not a claims provision is a condition precedent is a matter of its proper construction.

The assured under a losses occurring policy will be under a duty to provide a speedy notification of any loss as soon as the assured becomes aware of it.[97] Liability policies in claims made form are more complex. A claims made policy responds to claims made against the assured during the currency of the policy, so the making of a claim against the assured is the trigger to the insurers' liability: some policies define what is meant by a "claim", in terms of a claim form, letter before action, or a written demand for compensation, although others leave the word "claim" undefined. On the basis that a claim has been made against the assured within the policy year, there will still be a duty on the assured to notify the assured of the claim. English policies are not generally written on a claims made and notified basis, so it is not a requirement of coverage that the assured notifies the claim within the policy period. This is often made clear by an extension clause. Wording of this type was considered in *HLB Kidsons v Lloyd's Underwriters*,[98] where the policy required claims to be notified as soon as practicable but the extension clause provided that:

> "Any claim first notified to the Assured prior to the expiry date of this policy will be deemed to fall to be dealt with under this policy provided it is properly notified to Underwriters within 15 calendar days of the expiry day."

At first instance Gloster J. held that this wording had the purely negative effect of providing a cut-off point for the notification of claims. In the Court of Appeal, this analysis was rejected, although Rix and Toulson L.JJ. each gave a different explanation of the clause. Rix L.J. (with whom Buxton L.J. agreed) held that the

---

[95] The reasoning of the House of Lords in *Charter Re v Fagan* turns largely on the overall context of the excess of loss contract there under consideration, which their Lordships regarded as for the most part pointing towards payment on establishment and quantification of liability rather than on actual payment, so that the pay to be paid clause itself was incongruous. However, there are clear indications that not all of their Lordships were fully convinced by the argument in favour of the reinsured's liquidators, and wider policy considerations may well have motivated the ultimate conclusion.

[96] *Cox v Bankside Members Agency Ltd* [1995] 2 Lloyd's Rep. 437: *P&O Steam Navigation Co v Youell* [1997] 2 Lloyd's Rep. 136.

[97] See, e.g. *Fong Wing Shing Construction Co Ltd v Allianz Insurance (Hong Kong) Ltd* [2003] 3 H.K.C. 561; *Hussain v GAN Assurance Co* [2007] H.K.E.C. 361.

[98] *HLB Kidsons v Lloyd's Underwriters* [2009] Lloyd's Rep. I.R. 178.

clause had a positive effect and allowed the assured to notify a claim within 15 days of the expiry of the policy, as long as the claim was made against the assured during the currency of the policy. The obligation to notify a claim as soon as practicable did not restrict the extension, and indeed operated to confer an additional benefit on the assured in that a claim made against the assured but not notified within the 15-day period following the expiry of the policy would nevertheless be within the scope of cover as long as it was notified as soon as reasonably practicable. Toulson L.J., by contrast, held that the extension was designed purely to deal with the situation in which a claim was made against the assured at the end of the policy year, and permitted the assured an extended period to notify such claims.

Once the assured has notified a claim, he will then be under a further duty to provide information relating to the circumstances of the claim and to forward all communications to the insurers. In some circumstances the initial notification may be enough to comply with this additional obligation.[99] The continuing obligation to co-operate is, however, tied to the claim made against the assured and thus does not authorise any demands by the insurers which relate to matters unrelated to the claim. In *Quinn Direct Insurance Ltd v The Law Society of England and Wales*[100] a solicitors' professional indemnity policy required notification of claims and circumstances, and then required the assured to "give all such information and assistance as [the insurers] may require". The insurers, in reliance on this clause, demanded disclosure[101] of a variety of documents relating to the solicitors' business. Peter Smith J., whose judgment on this point was affirmed by the Court of Appeal, ruled[102] that the clause was not freestanding, and was concerned only with information which could assist the insurers in defending claims already made against the assured. The clause could not be used to justify a fishing expedition to determine whether, for example, there had been breach of policy terms by the solicitors.

Claims made covers are almost always extended so as to allow the assured to notify to the insurers circumstances known to the assured that are likely to give rise to a claim: if notification of circumstances is made during the currency of the policy, then the third-party claim itself—even though it actually comes in at a later date—is deemed to have been made during the currency of the policy. Notification of circumstances is normally to be given as soon as practicable or within a fixed time from the assured becoming aware of the relevant circumstances. The ability of the assured to notify circumstances in this way is an extension to cover which is triggered by the exercise of a notification option by the assured, and is entirely unrelated to the primary pure claims made cover provided by the policy; the extension operates by deeming claims arising from circumstances notified during the currency of the policy themselves to have been made during the currency of the policy. It follows that if the assured fails to give a timely notification of circumstances which become known to him during the currency of the policy, and a claim is then made against the assured during the currency of the policy, then he is entitled to coverage under the policy in respect of the actual claim (assuming of course that he has complied with any reporting

---

[99] *Hamptons Residential Ltd v Field* [1998] 2 Lloyd's Rep. 248.

[100] *Quinn Direct Insurance Ltd v The Law Society of England and Wales* [2009] EWHC 2588 (Ch), affirmed [2010] EWCA Civ 647.

[101] From the Law Society, which had taken over the operation of the firm. It was held that the clause could not in any event override the Law Society's duty of confidentiality.

[102] Following dicta of Mance L.J. in *Gan Insurance Co Ltd v Tai Ping Insurance Co Ltd (No.3)* [2002] Lloyd's Rep. I.R. 612.

obligations) even though the obligation to notify circumstances is expressed to be a "condition precedent" to liability.[103]

The notification of circumstances provision, although providing an extension of cover, is nevertheless difficult to operate in practice. The assured is entitled to notify only those circumstances of which he is aware and which may give rise to a later claim. If the assured notifies too little, then the policy will only respond to those circumstances actually notified and others will fall into another policy year, although the assured will generally be under a duty when a new policy is taken out to disclose circumstances which may give rise to a claim: if the assured does not notify, and for the same reason does not disclose the circumstances on renewal, the renewed agreement will be voidable. By contrast, if the assured notifies too much, then the policy under which the circumstances are notified will only respond to those validly notified whereas later policies may exclude all circumstances notified under an earlier policy: a notification which is too wide will, therefore, be excluded from both years.

Notification of claims against the assured. As noted above, the primary form of **20–038** cover under a claims made policy is in respect of claims made against the assured. In the absence of any definition it will be necessary to define the term "claim". Clearly the service of a claim form on the assured, or the receipt of a letter before action, is a claim, although a demand for payment will also suffice. In *Robert Irving & Burns v Stone*[104] Staughton L.J. defined a claim as "a communication by [a third party] to the [assured] of some discontent which will, or may, result in a remedy expected from the [assured]".[105] A mere communication to the assured notifying him of the possibility that a claim may at some future stage may be made against him is not, however, a claim,[106] so that a later policy which excluded claims against the assured under earlier policies had to respond to the claim when it was finally made.

Assuming that claims have been made by the third party, or circumstances have arisen, and that there has been due notification to the insurers, the fact the claims or circumstances subsequently develop in an unpredicted way from the circumstances or claims originally notified does not relieve the insurers from liability as long as it is apparent that the final claims are based on the original notification. In *Thorman v New Hampshire Insurance Co Ltd*[107] a claim form[108] was issued against the assured, a firm of architects, in June 1992, alleging that brickwork for which the assured was responsible was faulty, although the specific claims were not identified. The claim form was served in December 1993, and the defects were particularised in January 1994. The assured's claims made policy expired in October 1993, by which time the assured had been informed that proceedings were to be commenced and this information had been passed to the insurers. The insurers argued that they bore no liability under the policy other than in respect of the brickwork, as that was the only claim which had been particularised before October 1993. The Court of Appeal rejected this argument, and held that a claim form in general terms is to be taken as including all specific claims subsequently particularised under it.

---

[103] *HLB Kidsons v Lloyd's Underwriters* [2009] Lloyd's Rep. I.R. 178.

[104] *Robert Irving & Burns v Stone* [1998] Lloyd's Rep. I.R. 258.

[105] See also: *West Wake Price & Co v Ching* [1956] 2 Lloyd's Rep. 618; *Rothschild Assurance Ltd v Collyear* [1999] Lloyd's Rep. I.R. 6.

[106] *Immerzeel v Santam Ltd,* December 2005 Unreported Supreme Court of Appeal of South Africa.

[107] *Thorman v New Hampshire Insurance Co Ltd* [1998] 1 Lloyd's Rep. 7.

[108] At the time the RSC were in force, so the document was a generally indorsed writ.

Given that a claim against the assured has to be the assertion of some form of discontent for which a remedy is required, a further question that arises at this point is whether the claim has to be initiated by the third party or whether it can originate from the assured himself. This issue arose in an acute form in *Rothschild Assurance Ltd v Collyear*.[109] The assured in this case, having become aware that their appointed representatives may have been guilty of pensions mis-selling, and having been prompted to take steps to investigate and remedy any problems by the financial services regulators, sent questionnaires to investors. An analysis of the responses indicated that numerous investors had not received proper advice, and the claimants indemnified or agreed to indemnify them. This raised the fundamental question of whether the events which had led to the claimants' acceptance of liability were "claims" against them. Rix J. held that the policy was applicable. He rejected the argument that the claimants had not received any claims and had merely, on a voluntary basis, investigated the circumstances of its investors and had agreed to make payments to them. Rix J. preferred the view that it had been made clear to investors that if they completed the questionnaires and were found to have been given incorrect advice that they would be compensated, and their participation in that process amounted to the making of claims by them. Rix J. was influenced by the fact that the insurers had issued a claims made policy in the context of the regulatory regime relating to the financial services industry, and could not sensibly complain that the liability which had been imposed upon them was beyond what might have been contemplated when the policy was issued.

If the third party has not actually made a claim against the assured within the currency of the policy, and the assured is unaware that a claim by a third party is pending so that notice of circumstances likely to give rise to a claim cannot be given to the insurers, the inevitable conclusion is that the policy does not attach. In *Robert Irving & Burns* itself, the assured's policy was in force from July 1994 to July 1995. Third parties had issued a claim form against the assured in April 1995, but had not sent a letter before action and did not serve the claim form until after July 1995. Accordingly, the assured was unaware that he was to be sued until after the policy had expired. The Court of Appeal held[110] that there had not been a claim against the assured until the claim form had been served on it, and that the issue of a claim form without prior notification to the assured—admittedly a rare sequence of events—was not a "claim" against the assured within the terms of the policy. This case was decided under the RSC, under which proceedings were not to be treated as having been commenced until they were served. By contrast, under CPR r.7.2 "proceedings are started when the court issues a claim form". Accordingly, it could be argued that the claim is now to be regarded as made on the issue of the claim form rather than when it is served. If the assured is unaware of the issue of the claim form, then plainly they will not fall foul of a notification clause which requires notification of claims of which the assured is aware, but it may be different if the policy is triggered by the making of a claim whether or not the assured is aware of it. Had the third parties in *Robert Irving & Burns* given notice to the assured either of an intention to sue or of the issue of the claim form, the assured would have then been in possession of either a claim or at the very least the knowledge that there were circumstances

[109] *Rothschild Assurance Ltd v Collyear* [1999] Lloyd's Rep. I.R. 6. See also: *Forrest v Glasser* [2006] EWCA Civ 1086; *CGU Insurance Ltd v AMP Financial Planning Pty Ltd* [2007] H.C.A. 36.

[110] Following *St Paul Fire & Marine Insurance Co v Guardian Insurance Co of Canada* [1983] 1 D.L.R. 342.

which were likely to give rise to a claim, and notice could then have been given to the insurers: as noted earlier, the giving of notice within the policy period has the effect of bringing all claims flowing from the notice within the temporal scope of the policy. This would appear to be the distinction between *Robert Irving & Burns* and *Thorman v New Hampshire Insurance Co Ltd*.[111] In the latter case, as noted above, a claim form had been issued against the assured, although it had not been served until after the policy had expired. However, the assured had been aware of the issue of the claim form and had received a letter before action. The Court of Appeal held that the combination of these circumstances meant that a claim had been made against the assured. In *Robert Irving & Burns*, Staughton L.J. expressly stated that *Thorman* was not authority for the proposition that the mere fact that a claim form has been issued against the assured is enough to give rise to a claim against the assured, and that the case had turned upon the fact that the assured had been given notice that a claim was to be made against him.

Notification of circumstances. As previously discussed, virtually all professional indemnity and other claims made policies confer upon the assured an extension to cover where no claim is made against him during the currency of the policy but circumstances arise during the currency of the policy which could potentially lead to a claim. The assured is entitled to notify those circumstances to the insurers, and thereby brings any later claim back into the policy year. Notification of circumstances is an option which, if not exercised, does not affect any right of indemnity in respect of an actual claim made against the assured during the currency of the policy.[112] That said, notification of circumstances not only confers a benefit on the assured, but is advantageous to the insurers because they receive early warning of what may well crystallise into a claim at some future date. Notification is not generally expressed to be a condition precedent to the right of the assured to this extension of cover, but it is inherent in the clause that the option can only be triggered by notification in accordance with its provisions. Accordingly, a failure to comply with the requirements of the notification clause will preclude the assured from recovery. The clause used in *HLB Kidsons v Lloyd's Underwriters* is typical of its type:

20–039

> "The Assured shall give to the Underwriters notice in writing as soon as practicable of any circumstance of which they shall become aware during the period specified in the Schedule which may give rise to a loss or claim against them. Such notice having been given any loss or claim to which that circumstance has given rise which is subsequently made after the expiration of the period specified in the Schedule shall be deemed for the purpose of this Insurance to have been made during the subsistence hereof."

In *Kidsons* the Court of Appeal held that this wording created a condition precedent, so that failure to adhere to any of its requirements meant that the optional extension of cover to circumstances was not brought into play. As Gloster J. pointed out at first instance, were it otherwise, it would be possible for the assured to produce a "laundry list" of circumstances at one time and notify them, thereby converting the policy into an occurrence-based cover under which notification of circumstances whenever occurring would give rise to cover. The clause contains a number of distinct elements.

---

[111] *Thorman v New Hampshire Insurance Co Ltd* [1998] 1 Lloyd's Rep. 7.
[112] *HLB Kidsons v Lloyd's Underwriters* [2009] Lloyd's Rep. I.R. 178.

First, notice in writing must be given either to the subscribing underwriters individually (unless the policy otherwise provides) or to their authorised agents: in *Kidsons* at first instance it was held that solicitors retained by the underwriters were not their agents for the purpose of receiving notifications. As long as writing is used, there is no specific form for notification of occurrences or circumstances which may or are likely to give rise to a claim, and it is enough that the insurers are made aware of the possibility that a claim will be made against the assured. The test is how, on an objective appraisal, a reasonable recipient with knowledge of the terms of the policy and the overall context, would have understood the communication that was actually made. What is required is identification of some act or omission, and of a potential claimant or class of claimants. In *Kidsons* a letter to the underwriters from the secretary of the assured's partnership setting out the concerns of an employee was held by a majority of the Court of Appeal, reversing Gloster J., to be a notification of circumstances even though the letter was unsatisfactory. The Court of Appeal accepted that the matter was to be looked at objectively and the question to be asked was, "what did the presentation reasonably convey to recipients?" and not whether the presentation left the underwriters in no doubt. Rix L.J. emphasised the "open-textured" nature of the notification obligation. Accordingly, a communication which does not specify that circumstances are being notified but which objectively contains enough information to achieve that purpose will suffice. It is to be noted that Rix L.J. felt that in exceptional circumstances the assured's intentions might not be completely irrelevant. Nevertheless, the point is that the communication must on its face justify an objective finding that it amounted to a notification. It is immaterial that the communication by the assured to the insurers was not intended to be a notification of circumstances likely to give rise to a claim. In *Friends Provident Life & Pensions Ltd v Sirius International Insurance Corporation*[113] the assured, in the course of negotiating a renewal of the policy, informed the insurers of potential claims by third parties: Moore-Bick J. held that this was sufficient to amount to notification under the policy, and that the communication by the assured was perfectly capable of fulfilling a dual purpose. This point is now well established.[114] It was further held by Moore-Bick J. in *Friends Provident* that the proper construction of the policy, which was an excess layer, was that notification to the primary layer underwriters amounted to notification to all layers, although if that was wrong then there had been no notification to the excess layer as the broker to whom notification had ultimately been given was the agent of the assured. The Court of Appeal accepted this analysis.

20–040   Secondly, the notification must be made as soon as practicable after the assured has become aware of the relevant circumstances. There are four aspects to this point:

(a) The assured must be aware of the circumstances themselves. This is a significant point, because it means that the assured cannot simply notify a vague possibility and then expect to treat all subsequent claims—some of which may have no more than a tenuous link to the notification—to be brought within its

---

[113] *Friends Provident Life & Pensions Ltd v Sirius International Insurance Corporation* [2005] Lloyd's Rep. I.R. 135, affirmed [2006] Lloyd's Rep. I.R. 45.

[114] *BP Plc v Aon* [2006] Lloyd's Rep. I.R. 577. But note that in *Kidsons* Buxton L.J., dissenting on the substantive point, noted that although it was possible that a document which was subjectively not intended to be a notification could nevertheless objectively amount to a notification, caution was to be exercised in reaching such a conclusion. Rix L.J. also stated "that in certain exceptional circumstances intention may not be irrelevant to a unilateral question such as the giving of a notice."

scope. The mere fact that the assured has been prosecuted with respect to an accident does not of itself mean that there is a notifiable circumstance.[115]

(b) The assured must have the requisite degree of knowledge of the possibility that the circumstances may give rise to a claim. This was a live issue in *Kidsons*, because at the date of one of the notifications—the second—the assured was aware of its employee's concerns but, acting on legal advice, believed them to be groundless. The Court of Appeal did not give a clear answer to the question whether there could be a valid notification if the assured has no genuine belief that a claim may be made. Rix and Buxton L.JJ. were of the view that there could be an awareness of an allegation even though there was no belief in its truth. In Rix L.J.'s words, "We must surely be aware of allegations about many things in which we have no genuine belief." On this analysis, knowledge of an allegation is enough, whether or not the assured believes that the allegation is or is not good. By contrast, Toulson L.J. thought that a circumstance could be notified only if it could reasonably be regarded in itself as a matter which may give rise to a claim, thereby excluding wide notifications. His Lordship put the matter as follows:

> "In my judgment the right general approach to a policy clause which entitles an insured to give notification of a circumstance which may give rise to a claim, and thereby cause the risk to attach to that policy, is to treat the right as subject to an implicit requirement that the circumstance may reasonably be regarded in itself as a matter which may give rise to a claim. The right general approach to a policy clause which goes further and imposes a duty on the insured to give such a notification is to treat it as implicitly limited, not only by the requirement that the circumstance may reasonably be regarded as a matter which may give rise to a claim, but to a circumstance which either the insured notifies or which any reasonable person in his position would recognise as a matter which may give rise to a claim and therefore requiring notification to the insurer."

On Toulson L.J.'s approach, if there is genuine room for disagreement as to whether or not a claim may be made from a circumstance, notification would be valid but a failure to notify could not be regarded as precluding notification under a later policy. In *Aspen Insurance UK Ltd v Pectel Ltd*[116] Teare J. drew from *Kidsons* the proposition that there had to be "a real as opposed to a fanciful risk of the underwriters having to indemnify the assured and that in determining whether there was such a risk the court applied an objective test, taking into account the knowledge that the assured possessed in order to determine the extent to which the assured was aware of, and hence capable of notifying, occurrences which may give rise to an indemnity". The word used in the insuring clause in this case was "occurrence" rather than "circumstance". It was held that a fire caused by the assured was plainly an occurrence which may give rise to a claim, and that it ought to have been notified immediately and not delayed (as was the case). In *Laker Vent Engineering Ltd v Templeton Insurance Ltd*[117] the Court of Appeal could see no real difference in practical terms between the judgments in *Kidsons*, and that the test was an objective one.[118]

(c) For the purposes of knowledge, ordinary principles of imputation are relevant, so that it is necessary to consider who, within an organisation, is to be

---

[115] *Harbourfield Engineering Co Ltd v Falcon Insurance Co (Hong Kong) Ltd* [2003] H.K.E.C. 959.

[116] *Aspen Insurance UK Ltd v Pectel Ltd* [2009] Lloyd's Rep. I.R. 440.

[117] *Laker Vent Engineering Ltd v Templeton Insurance Ltd* [2009] Lloyd's Rep. I.R. 704.

[118] This test has also been adopted in Australia: *CGU Insurance Ltd v Corrections Corporation of Australia Staff Superannuation Pty Ltd* [2008] F.C.A.F.C. 173.

regarded as acting on its behalf for the purposes of the receipt of the relevant information. This may, within a partnership, be the partnership secretary but it is unlikely to be any one individual partner or employee. This was so held by Gloster J. on the facts of *Kidsons*, and within a company it will be the controlling mind of the company but not an individual director.[119] The test of knowledge of circumstances is objective: *Kidsons*.

(d) Notification must be given to the insurers as soon as practicable after the assured has obtained the relevant knowledge. In *Kidsons* a presentation to underwriters was given some four months after a presentation to other under-writers, and consisted of the same information. For that reason the Court of Appeal was satisfied that the later notification was invalid by reason of lapse of time. It would also seem to be the case that, absent any express provision to the contrary in the policy, the assured may notify circumstances after the policy has expired, as long as the notification was as soon as reasonably practicable after his becoming aware of circumstances during the currency of the policy. That was the view of Rix and Buxton L.JJ. in *Kidsons*, Rix L.J. stating that the suggestion was "an impossible one". Toulson L.J., by contrast, was attracted by the argument that notification had to be within the currency of the policy, and in particular he regarded as "hopeless" the suggestion by the assured that if the assured became aware during the policy year of a circumstance which might give rise to a claim he could validly notify it at any time, subject only to the underwriters being able to refuse to pay on the grounds of prejudice.

20–041   Thirdly, the notification must relate to "circumstances". A circumstance is a matter which may give rise to a loss or claim against the assured and is one which, objectively evaluated, creates a reasonable and appreciable possibility that it will give rise to a loss or claim against the assured. The term "circumstances" is a broad one. In *Rothschild Assurance Ltd v Collyear*[120] the claimants issued opt-out pensions to numerous investors, to replace their occupational pension schemes. By the beginning of 1993, it had become apparent that there had been a generalised problem of pensions mis-selling, whereby investors had not been properly advised by appointed agents operating through-out the industry. The claimants' liability policy incepted in February 1993 and in January 1994—once it had become clear that investors would at some point have to be compensated for purchasing inappropriate contracts—the claimants notified their insurers that liability might arise in the future. It was not, at the time of the letter, possible for the claimants to identify the precise contracts that could give rise to liabilities, and the claimants simply stated that they were reviewing some 2,500 contracts. Rix J. held that this letter was enough to amount to a notification of circumstances which could give rise to a claim. The purpose of the notification clause was to alert the insurers to the possibility of action against their assured, so that they could take steps to mitigate or prevent a future loss, and the notification had been adequate for that purpose. Rix J. rejected the further argument that the purpose of notification had been to make it easier for the claimants to obtain fresh insurance, given that the policy under which the notification had been made was about to lapse. Even if that had been the case, it would not appear to have invalidated the notification. Rix J. further held that it was permissible for him to consider later events, and it had indeed proved to be the case that the claimants had become liable to indemnify investors as had been indicated in the notice. The circumstances notified in *Kidsons* were the concerns

---

[119] *Meridian Global Funds Management Asia Ltd v Securities Commission* [1995] 2 A.C. 500.
[120] *Rothschild Assurance Ltd v Collyear* [1999] Lloyd's Rep. I.R. 6.

of an employee, and it was assumed for the purposes of the proceedings that such concerns were indeed notifiable "circumstances". Rix L.J. in *Kidsons* nevertheless expressed doubts on this point. Accordingly it may legitimately be queried whether an assured who informs his insurers that an employee has expressed doubts as to whether a course of conduct on the part of the assured is problematic is to be treated as having notified "circumstances" at all.

Finally, there has to be a causal link between the circumstances and the possibility of a claim. Two main forms of wording are used in respect of English policies: notification of circumstances which "may" give rise to a claim, and it is this formulation which is most commonly used in the modern professional indemnity market; and notification of circumstances which "are likely" to give rise to a claim. The latter phrase means that notice need be given only if a claim is more likely than not, i.e. if there is more than a 50 per cent chance that a claim will be made.[121] Thus, the fact that a third party has been injured on the assured's premises does not have to be notified to insurers if the assured has no reason to believe that a claim would be made against him as the injury at the time appeared to be a pure accident.[122] By contrast, the duty may be more onerous if the policy merely requires notification of circumstances which may give rise to a claim. Insurers prefer to use the "may" formulation: while this has the effect of exposing them to a larger number of claims during the policy year, it also allows them to take early control of the matter, so that they can investigate whether the assured has been at fault or whether there is a third party against whom contribution proceedings can be brought.

A matter which featured large in the arguments in *Kidsons*, but which ultimately played no role in the final outcome, was whether the assured owed a duty of good faith when making a notification. Toulson L.J. was prepared to accept the "proposition that where a policy contains a provision for the insured to notify a circumstance which may give rise to a claim and thereby attach the risk to the policy, it is impliedly incumbent on the insured to see that any such notification is a fair, if summary, presentation of what the insured knows," and Rix L.J. was of a similar view. Neither Toulson L.J. nor Rix L.J. took the further step of holding that notification was subject to the duty of utmost good faith, so that if the assured chose to be deliberately misleading or economical with the truth the notification would be invalid, but it was clear that both Rix and Toulson L.J. saw some force in that possibility.

Circumstances falling within the notification. It was previously commented that **20–042** great care has to be taken with the notification of circumstances. If the assured is aware of a specific problem with a project he has to decide whether to notify that problem alone or whether to notify the project as a whole so as to catch other as yet unidentified problems. The dilemma here is that a general notification will be excluded because the assured has to be aware of possible future claims, whereas a narrow notification will confine the insurers' liability to the circumstances notified and other claims arising out of the same project may be the subject of an express exclusion by later insurers. There is no easy answer to exactly what should be notified.

The courts have been faced on a number of occasions with the problem of interpreting a notification of circumstances to ascertain its scope. The matter was

---

[121] *Sinclair Harder O'Malley Ltd v National Insurance Co of New Zealand* [1992] 2 N.Z.L.R 706: *Layher Ltd v Lowe* [2000] Lloyd's Rep. I.R. 510; *Laker Vent Engineering Ltd v Templeton Insurance Ltd* [2009] Lloyd's Rep. I.R. 704 (a legal expenses case, but the issues are much the same).
[122] *Jacobs v Coster* [2000] Lloyd's Rep. I.R. 506.

addressed this way by Gloster J. at first instance in *Kidsons*, a passage approved by Akenhead J. in *Kajima UK Engineering Ltd v Underwriter Insurance Co Ltd*[123]:

> "At the end of the day, it is in my view largely a question of interpretation and analysis of the document setting out the notification, in the context of the facts known to the assured, as to what precise circumstance or set of circumstances has in fact been notified to insurers. I am not therefore convinced that semantic cavilling over the precise formulation of the test assists the ultimate resolution of the problem. There may well be uncertainty at the time of notification as to what the precise problems or potential problems are; there well may be, whether known, or unknown, to the assured a 'hornets' nest which may give rise to numerous types of claims of presently unknown quantum and character at the date of the notification. Whilst in principle, there is no reason why such a state of affairs should not be notified as a circumstance if the assured is aware of it, in each case the extent and ambit of the notification and the claims that are covered by such notification will depend on the particular facts and terms of the notification."

In *Kajima* Akenhead J. noted that, although it was possible for specific or general circumstances (including a "hornets' nest" or "can of worms" type of circumstance) to be notified, there had to be a causal rather than coincidental link between the notified circumstances and the later claim, so that a later claim arising from other circumstances which were discovered after notification will not be within the scope of the notification. These points may be illustrated by the decided cases.

In *Hamptons Residential Ltd v Field*[124] the assured, a firm of surveyors, in October 1989 gave notice to its insurers under a claims made policy that an employee had been guilty of a mortgage fraud by overvaluing property that was to be purchased on the security of a mortgage. At that stage the mortgagee had not made a formal claim, but the assured nevertheless notified the insurers on the basis that a claim might arise by reason of the employee's fraud. This notice secured the coverage of the policy for any claim subsequently to be made against it by the mortgagee. The assured later discovered that the employee had been guilty of mortgage fraud against a different mortgagee, and sought to relate back that fraud to the notification given to the insurers in October 1989. The Court of Appeal held that such relation back was permissible. The policy itself simply required that the insurers be told of "the discovery or reasonable cause for suspicion of dishonesty or fraud", and this term did not demand the identification of the victims or of the form that the fraud had taken.

A similar decision, albeit in a rather different context, is that of Colman J. in *King v Brandywine Reinsurance Co (UK) Ltd*.[125] Following the grounding of the Exxon Valdez in 1989 and a catastrophic oil spill, the insurers were notified of circumstances likely to give rise to a loss in excess of policy deductibles by Exxon as the owners of the oil on board the vessel. At a later date it fell to be decided whether the shipowner, a subsidiary company, was precluded from claiming by reason of its failure to notify a loss. Colman J. held that it had been

---

[123] *Kajima UK Engineering Ltd v Underwriter Insurance Co Ltd* [2008] Lloyd's Rep. I.R. 391.
[124] *Hamptons Residential Ltd v Field* [1998] 2 Lloyd's Rep. 248.
[125] *King v Brandywine Reinsurance Co (UK) Ltd* [2004] Lloyd's Rep. I.R. 554, affirmed on other grounds [2005] Lloyd's Rep. I.R. 509.

sufficient for a general notification to be given by Exxon itself and that the notification encompassed all subsequent claims by associated companies.[126]

These decisions may be contrasted with *Kajima UK Engineering Ltd v Underwriter Insurance Co Ltd*. The assured's liability policy in this case required written notice to be given to the underwriters "as soon as possible after becoming aware of circumstances which might reasonably be expected to produce a claim or on receiving information of a claim for which there may be liability under this insurance." The assured erected a five-storey block of flats consisting of pre-constructed pods. In February 2001 the assured notified to insurers of the fact that the pods were "settling and moving excessively causing adjoining roofing and balconies and walkways to distort under differential settlement". Thereafter it became apparent that there were serious structural problem with the building as a whole, and by the end of 2005 it had become clear that the entire building had become unstable: ultimately the assured was forced to purchase the building. Akenhead J. held that the later problems fell outside the scope of the initial notification. The learned judge held that the notification was effective only in respect of the specific notified circumstances and did not extend to damage unless such damage was causally linked to the notified circumstances. The assured was accordingly under an obligation to make further notifications as and when further problems were identified.

Again, in *Kidsons* itself, the assured firm tax advisers had a subsidiary which marketed various tax avoidance products. Following concerns expressed by an employee, the assured wrote to the insurers informing them that the employee had "expressed the view that the Inland Revenue, if minded, could be critical of some procedures followed in certain cases" but that no claims were anticipated. It was common ground that this letter did not of itself amount to a valid notification. Subsequently, the insurers were sent a copy of the original letter coupled with other documents in a claims file, an accompanying bordereaux and a further letter setting out details of five particular cases. A majority of the Court of Appeal, overturning the judgment of Gloster J., held that there had been a valid notification but it was confined only to one scheme and to procedures which might attract the criticism of the Revenue: it did not extend to other views expressed by the employee nor to other products supplied by the assured. A third presentation by the assured, which amplified the information in the second presentation was, however, held to be a valid notification of all circumstances relating to the assured's various schemes. There was a fourth notification, some weeks later, to underwriters excluded from the third notification. This was held to be too late, in that it had not taken place as soon as reasonably practicable.

Defending the claim against the assured

Conducting the defence. There is no unlawful maintenance involved where a liability insurer undertakes the defence of an action against its assured.[127] Since the insurers cannot make use of their ordinary rights of subrogation to contest the assured's liability as against a third party unless they first pay the assured the full amount of his estimated loss, the policy usually specifically reserves their right to conduct all negotiations with third-party claimants against the assured, to

20–043

---

[126] See also *Alexander Forbes Europe Ltd v SBJ Ltd* [2003] Lloyd's Rep. I.R. 432 notification of an individual claim was made by brokers under the policy taken out by the assured's group rather than under the assured's own policy. A number of other claims subsequently arose. The court, without deciding whether the notification was sufficient to amount a notification so as to trigger the assured's own policy, held that the brokers had failed to comply with their duty of care.

[127] *Giles v Thompson* [1994] 1 A.C. 965.

defend any proceedings which may be brought and to approve any settlement with the third party on the assured's behalf.

The insurers' rights and duties in respect of defending the assured depend entirely upon the wording of the policy. One possibility is that the insurers are under a duty to defend. Alternatively, the insurers may retain a discretion to defend where the claim against the assured is capable of giving rise to a loss within the terms of the policy. If it is clear from the outset that the claim is for an uninsured risk then, special wording apart, any obligation to defend will not be applicable.[128] That said, it is not always apparent from the outset whether any judgment against the assured will ultimately fall within the policy, e.g. where the claim brought by the third party asserts two matters, one of which constitutes an insured peril and the other amounts to an uninsured peril. In this type of case, the policy any obligation to defend is applicable, but there may be implications for the assured as regards the recovery of defence costs incurred by him in defending the proceedings, as it may be necessary for an apportionment to be effected. This point is considered below. The obligation to indemnify the assured is dependent upon the assured entering a proper defence.[129]

Where the insurers have a discretion to take over the assured's defence, and determine not to do so, the insurers will be obliged meet any judgment against the assured or any settlement entered into by the assured and based on legal liability.[130] If the insurers deny liability under the policy, the assured will be free to accept their repudiation and defend or settle a third-party claim despite any condition which allows them to take over the defence, reserving his right to proceed against the insurers.[131] A refusal to take over the assured's defence following the appointment by the insurers of solicitors to conduct the defence may give rise to the question of whether documents passing between the assured and the solicitors prior to the termination of their mandate by the insurers are privileged. In *Brown v Guardian Royal Exchange Assurance Plc*[132] it was held that the appointment of solicitors involves two separate retainers, between the assured and the solicitors and between the insurers and the solicitors, and that unless the policy otherwise provides documents passing between the assured and the solicitors are privileged as against the insurers. That privilege will not, however, operate if there is a joint retainer or if insurers have opted to take over the defence.

20–044   Although the insurer may be obliged or may choose to defend the assured, as far as the third party is concerned the insurer plays no formal part in the proceedings, as the defence has to be conducted in the assured's name.[133] The only real exception to this principle is the possibility of an award of costs against the insurer itself, under s.35 of the Senior Courts Act 1981,[134] the circumstances in which this might arise are considered below. The fact that the defence is conducted in the assured's name is critical, for if there is a dispute between two liability insurers as to which of them is liable to meet any claim—as where it is unclear in which year the events giving rise to liability occurred—the insurers

---

[128] *Nichols v American Home Assurance Co* 68 D.L.R. (4th) 321 (1990) (fraud exception in policy—assured accused of fraud).

[129] *Liberian Insurance Agency Inc v Mosse* [1977] 2 Lloyd's Rep. 560.

[130] See below for the binding effect of settlements.

[131] *General Omnibus Co v London General Insurance* (1932) 66 Ir. L.T. 96.

[132] *Brown v Guardian Royal Exchange Assurance Plc* Unreported, 1992.

[133] *Murfin v Ashbridge* [1941] 1 All E.R. 231.

[134] See below.

will not be permitted to raise competing defences against the claimant: the claimant's concern is only to establish the assured's liability.[135]

Where the insurers wish to dispute liability under a policy they should be cautious in doing so: if they continue the conduct of the proceedings after having acquired knowledge of facts which show that they are not liable under the policy, they may be estopped from denying liability. It may be, however, that a distinction is to be drawn between, on the one hand, the situation in which the insurers have the right to avoid the policy or to terminate it for breach, and on the other hand the situations in which the insurers have a defence based on breach of condition or are able to rely upon a coverage defence. In the former case, if the insurers, aware of their right to bring the policy to an end, have taken up the assured's defence, they may be taken to have waived their rights and are liable to meet any judgment against the assured.[136] In the case of a coverage defence, it was held in *Soole v Royal Insurance*[137] that the insurers are not precluded from relying on their defence because, by conducting the assured's defence, the insurers cannot be said to have caused the assured to suffer any detriment through not having the opportunity to conduct his own defence. The reasoning in *Soole* was approved by the Court of Appeal in *Kosmar Villa Holidays Plc v Trustees of Syndicate 1243*,[138] where it was pointed out that estoppel rather than affirmation is the applicable principle in coverage cases, and in *Kosmar* the Court of Appeal went on to hold that only estoppel and not affirmation was available where the question was whether the insurers had waived their right to rely upon breach of condition despite having started to conduct the assured's defence.[139]

In practice, where there is some doubt on the part of the insurers whether they are liable to indemnify the assured for a potential loss reported by the assured, the insurers may not deny all liability but instead they may continue to process the claim but under an express reservation of rights. Such reservation prevents the reinsurers from being treated as having waived coverage provisions or any breach of duty on the part of the assured. In some situations, insurers may go further and refuse to participate in the settlement process at all, simply directing the assured to act as a "prudent uninsured". This direction is commonly given in both liability insurance and also in reinsurance cases, although there is no direct authority on its meaning in English law. Some guidance may be obtained from the decision of the majority of the High Court of Australia in *CGU Insurance Ltd v AMP Financial Planning Pty Ltd*,[140] in which the assured under a liability policy was told by its insurers, pending a decision on coverage, to act as a prudent uninsured in dealing with third-party claims. The Court ruled that the insurers could not rely upon their rights to be consulted and other procedural obligations imposed upon the assured in making the claim, but that they retained the ultimate right to dispute liability and quantum where the assured had entered into a settlement. However, in the absence of a direction of this type which can

---

[135] *Myers v Dortex International* [2000] Lloyd's Rep. I.R. 529, in which the Court of Appeal refused to join a second set of liability insurers to an action the defence in which was being conducted by a first set of liability insurers, as the applicant insurers intended to raise a competing defence.

[136] *Hansen v Marco Engineering* 1948 V.L.R. 198; *Etchells v Eagle Star* (1928) 72 S.J. 242; *Evans v Employers Mutual* [1936] 1 K.B. 505.

[137] *Soole v Royal Insurance* [1971] 2 Lloyd's Rep. 332.

[138] *Kosmar Villa Holidays Plc v Trustees of Syndicate 1243* [2008] Lloyd's Rep. I.R. 489.

[139] See also *McCormick v National Motor and Accident Insurance Union Ltd* (1934) 40 Com. Cas. 76 and *Lexington Insurance Co v Multinacional de Seguros SA* [2009] Lloyd's Rep. I.R. 1. The point had earlier been left open in *Wood v Perfection Travel Ltd* [1996] L.R.L.R. 233.

[140] *CGU Insurance Ltd v AMP Financial Planning Pty Ltd* [2007] H.C.A. 36.

be construed as removing any future obligation to comply with claims conditions, a decision by reinsurers to deny liability does not deprive the assured of its obligation to comply with claims conditions.[141]

20–045 *The insurers' duties towards the assured in conducting the defence.* If the insurer is required or decides to defend the assured, and enters into settlement negotiations with the third-party claimant, then as long as the claim is comfortably within the limits of indemnity under the policy the assured has (at least as far as the financial implications of the claim itself are concerned) no real interest in the outcome, as the assured cannot face any personal liability. In particular, if the insurer fails to agree to a settlement, and the case proceeds to judgment with interest being awarded against the assured, such interest will constitute "damages" within the scope of the insuring clause and the insurer will be liable for it, although not in addition to the overall financial limits imposed by the policy.[142]

The danger for the assured arises where the claim exceeds policy limits. If the third party is willing to settle the claim close to or at the insurer's limit of indemnity, the insurer has little or nothing to lose by declining to settle and leaving the matter to be litigated. From the insurer's point of view, if the claim fails then it will incur no liability at all, whereas if the claim succeeds then it simply pays up to policy limits[143] and the excess liability is for the assured to bear. The assured thus has a strong desire to see the claim settled in a manner which removes his potential personal exposure to possible liability in excess of policy limits. English law has recognised that insurers do owe various responsibilities to their assured in conducting the defence of the assured's claim. Insurers owe a duty of care to the assured to conduct any negotiations with the third party with the interests of the assured in mind.[144] Thus, if they make a settlement in good faith instead of contesting a claim the assured cannot complain[145] but it is otherwise if they unreasonably accept liability.[146] Solicitors appointed by insurers to defend the claim by the third party owe a separate duty to the assured to keep his interests in mind and must advise him if they are giving priority to the insurers' interests in handling a third-party claim.[147]

Subsequently, in *K/S Merc-Skandia XXXXII v Certain Lloyd's Underwriters (The Mercandian Continent)*[148] Longmore L.J. classified the obligation on the insurers to take into account the assured's interests in their decisions as to settlements with third parties as part of the continuing duty of utmost good faith imposed upon insurers. The difficulty with this analysis is that as the only remedy for breach of the duty of utmost good faith is avoidance *ab initio*: the obligation classified in terms of utmost good faith is of no help whatsoever to the assured.

---

[141] *Lexington Insurance Co v Multinacional de Seguros SA* [2009] Lloyd's Rep. I.R. 1.

[142] *Cox v Bankside Members Agency Ltd* [1995] 2 Lloyd's Rep. 437.

[143] Although there may of course be additional defence costs, if these do not form a part of the overall limit of indemnity.

[144] *Groom v Crocker* [1939] 1 K.B. 194; *Patteson v Northern Accident* [1901] 2 Ir. R. 262.

[145] *Beacon Insurance v Langdaie* (1939) 65 Ll. L.R. 57.

[146] As in *Groom v Crocker* [1939] 1 K.B. 194.

[147] *Groom v Crocker* [1939] 1 K.B. 194; *TSB Bank Plc v Robert Inling and Burns* [1999] Lloyd's Rep. I.R. 528.

[148] *K/S Merc-Skandia XXXXII v Certain Lloyd's Underwriters (The Mercandian Continent)* [2001] Lloyd's Rep. I.R. 802.

It may be, therefore, that the correct analysis is implied term,[149] so that the assured at least has a source of damages in the event that his interests are not taken into account and he is exposed to excess liability.

The QC clause. Professional indemnity policies normally include a clause **20–046** requiring the insurers to pay any claim made against the assured unless the opinion of leading counsel is obtained to the effect that on balance of probabilities the claim will fail. This provision, usually referred to as the "QC clause", is inserted to avoid the need for the assured to defend claims, thereby avoiding undesirable publicity. In some policies there is a further provision that the insurer will pay the claim despite the opinion of leading counsel if the assured reasonably objects to contesting the claim. The clause effectively imposes three possible obligations on the underwriters. They must pay the costs of any claim; they must pay the claim itself unless Queen's Counsel advises that it can probably be resisted; and they must pay claims which can probably be resisted if the assured reasonably objects to contesting them. The question whether the policy responds to any claim which may be made against the assured is not usually within the terms of the clause, and it is open to the underwriters to see a judicial determination of coverage on assumed facts, as if there is coverage the QC clause can then be applied to the question of whether the assured was or was not liable.[150]

Defence costs

Nature of defence costs clauses. A liability policy will generally impose an **20–047** obligation on the insurers to meet the costs of defending any claim against the assured or of reaching a settlement in respect of any such claim.[151] Insurers will provide or, in the alternative, fund, the assured's defence where the claim against the assured falls within the coverage of the policy.[152] The insurers typically agree either to conduct the defence or, if not, to indemnify the assured against costs which may be or have been incurred in respect of the defence of claims against him. Some policies specify that a claim includes one made in civil, criminal and administrative proceedings , although if the policy is silent on the point the word "claim" is likely to be construed as covering all of these matters.[153] Policies typically cover the following matters:

(a) defence costs—reasonable fees, costs and expenses incurred for the principal purpose of representing the assured
(b) investigation costs
(c) extradition costs
(d) bail bond and civil bond premiums
(e) prosecution costs, and asset and liberty expenses, i.e. disqualification and confiscation proceedings

---

[149] Cf. *Gan Insurance v Tai Ping Insurance (Nos 2 and 3)* [2001] Lloyd's Rep. I.R. 667, where the existence of any limits on the right of the reinsurers to approve settlements was specifically stated by Mance L.J. to rest upon an implied term and not upon the continuing duty of utmost good faith. In *Eagle Star Insurance Co v Cresswell* [2004] Lloyd's Rep. I.R. 437 Rix L.J. regarded the implied term and continuing utmost good faith principles as alternatives leading to much the same result, preventing reinsurers from acting irrationally or in bad faith in making decisions concerning the claims process.

[150] *West Wake Price & Co v Ching* [1957] 1 W.L.R. 45.

[151] See Lord Birkenhead in *British General v Mountain* (1919) 36 T.L.R. 171.

[152] *A & D Douglas Pty Ltd v Lawyers Private Mortgages Pty Ltd* 2006 F.C.A. 691.

[153] Conceded in *Porter v GIO* 2002 N.S.W.S.C.

(f) public relations expenses

(g) travel costs.

The assured's overheads, such as staff time and resources, are invariably expressed to be irrecoverable.

Such costs may form a part of the overall limit of indemnity[154] or they may have their own limit of indemnity above and beyond the substantive cover. Normally, however, the insurers' maximum liability under the policy is fixed by an aggregate of the sum awarded against the assured plus defence costs. Where defence costs are treated separately in the policy, deductibles which apply to the policy itself will not extend to defence costs unless otherwise stated.[155] Equally, the coverage of the policy may be irrelevant to the costs provisions. Separate causes of action against the insurers are vested in the assured in relation to the insuring clause and in relation to defence costs.[156]

Contractual provisions for the payment of defence costs vary. Some state that insurers are not under any obligation to fund defence costs, and that the assured is entitled to a reimbursement of defence costs only if the assured is ultimately found to be liable on grounds which fall within the scope of the policy, in particular that the assured was not dishonest.[157] At one time it was common for policies to provide that the insurers would indemnify the assured after the termination of the proceedings against him, thereby requiring the assured to fund costs out of his own pocket up to that date, but the modern practice is for insurers to agree to fund, or to pay, costs as and when they are incurred. In this type of case, if the claim against the assured is ultimately shown not to have been covered by the policy, the policy will generally provide that the insurers' expenditure—to the extent that there is no coverage[158]—is to be returned to them, an obligation which is more often than not in practice unenforceable. If there is to be funding on this basis, the costs clause may impose a duty to fund or there may be merely a discretion to fund: in the latter case, insurers are under an obligation of good faith in reaching a decision on whether or not to provide ongoing funding.[159] The distinction between an obligation and a discretion may not always be obvious from the policy wording, although the English courts at least will construe any ambiguity in favour of compulsory cover.[160] Alternatively, insurers may be under a duty to pay defence costs only if they require the assured to defend the claim.[161]

---

[154] See *Helfand v National Union Fire Insurance Co* 13 Cal. Rptr. 2d 295 (Cal CA, 1992); *Safeway v National Union Fire Insurance Co* 1992, N.D. Cal.; *American Casualty Co v Rahn* 854 F. Supp. 494 (WD Mich, 1994).

[155] *Kansa Insurance Co v Elbow Skiing Ltd* (1991) 6 C.C.L.I. (2d) 299; *Agra Foundations Ltd v Commonwealth Insurance Co* (2001) 214 Sask. R. 255

[156] *CGU Insurance Ltd v Watson* 2007 N.S.W.C.A. 301. This must be the proper explanation of the Court of Appeal's otherwise curious assertion in *K/S Merc-Skandia XXXXII v Lloyd's Underwriters* [2001] Lloyd's Rep. I.R. 802 that the assured under a liability policy does not have a claim against insurers unless and until the assured's liability to the third party is established and quantified by judgment, award or settlement.

[157] See *Kenai Corporation v National Union Fire Insurance Co* 136 B.R. 59 (S.D.N.Y., 1992); *Harristown Development Corporation v International Insurance Co* 1988 M.D. Pa.

[158] Allocation issues are discussed below.

[159] See below.

[160] *Glencore International AG v Ryan (The Beursgracht)* [2001] 2 Lloyd's Rep. 608.

[161] As in *Enterprise Oil Ltd v Strand Insurance Co Ltd* [2007] Lloyd's Rep. I.R. 186.

The nature of the obligation undertaken is a matter for the proper construction of the policy. In *The Beursgracht*[162] the costs provision in a marine liability policy was as follows:

"(1) Costs incurred by the Assured shall be payable by . . . Underwriters only if leading Underwriter hereon gives written consent to the incurring of such costs in respect of any particular claim, suit or proceedings and if such costs are not covered by underlying insurance . . .

. . .

(3) All costs incurred for claims where the total claim settlements by the Assured are in excess of the deductible, shall be for the account of the . . . Underwriters."

H.H. Judge Hallgarten QC ruled that the correct interpretation of these admittedly inconsistent words[163] was that para.(1) was concerned with the costs incurred by the assured as claimants, whereas para.(3) was dealing with costs incurred by the assured as defendants: on that interpretation, the consent of the insurers was not required in respect of defence costs.[164]

If the policy is silent, or if the assured has not met the requirements of the clause,[165] defence costs are not payable, although defence costs may be encompassed by a general statement that the insurers will provide an indemnity in respect of all sums incurred "in respect of claims".[166] Insurers who insist upon defending the assured without consulting him are liable to indemnify him for the costs incurred by them.[167]

In general terms, a defence costs clause is triggered by the making of a claim against the assured within the policy period: insurers are not liable for costs incurred by the assured in anticipation of a claim[168] unless the assured has notified circumstances which may give rise to a claim and the wording permits such notification to be the trigger for costs coverage.

Insurers who are liable for defence costs are entitled, by way of subrogation, to recover any payments from the unsuccessful third party.[169]

The assured is entitled to any costs reasonably incurred by him in resisting a claim from a third party where insurers who are obliged to pay defence costs wrongfully repudiate liability under the policy.[170] The insurers will in any event face liability for costs incurred by the assured in forcing the insurers to admit liability under the policy.[171]

Scope of defence costs provisions. Unless otherwise stated, defence costs are not payable in respect of claims which are outside the scope of the policy.[172] Thus if **20–048**

[162] *The Beursgracht* [2001] 2 Lloyd's Rep. 608. The case was upheld on appeal, although this point was not a live one: [2002] Lloyd's Rep. I.R. 335.
[163] He initially held that the term had been incorporated into the renewed policy.
[164] The court did not explain why it was thought necessary to include in a liability policy a clause, cl.(1), which was in essence "before the event" legal expenses insurance protecting the assured as claimants.
[165] As in *Enterprise Oil Lid v Strand Insurance Co Ltd* [2007] Lloyd's Rep. I.R. 186, where the assured had not been required by the insurers to defend the claim: a refusal by insurers to defend the claim themselves was not regarded as imposing an obligation on the assured to do so for itself.
[166] *Pictorial Machinery Ltd v Nicholls* (1940) 67 Ll. L.R. 524: *Forney v Dominion Insurance Co Ltd* [1969] 1 Lloyd's Rep. 502.
[167] *Allen v London Guarantee* (1912) 28 T.L.R. 254.
[168] *MWH International Inc v Lumbermens Mutual Casualty Co* [2007] B.C.J. No.559.
[169] *Cornish v Lynch* (1910) 3 B.W.C.C. 343.
[170] *Pictorial Machinery Ltd v Nicholls* (1910) 67 Ll. L.R. 524. It may be that defence costs are payable even if the insurers are not liable under the policy itself.
[171] *Capel-Cure Myers v Capital Management Ltd* [1995] L.R.L.R. 498.
[172] *John Wyeth v Cigna* [2001] Lloyd's Rep. I.R. 420.

insurers have the right to rely on a defence to the substantive claim, they will also have the right to refuse to indemnify the assured for defence costs, or if the policy limits have been reached, there is no duty to defend further claims.[173] This has been held to be the position in two Australian cases, *Silbermann v CGU Insurance Ltd*[174] and *Wilkie v Gordian Run Off Ltd*,[175] both involving dishonesty which operated as a defence to substantive cover.

There may nevertheless be exceptions if the wording so provides. In *Poole Harbour Yacht Club Marina Ltd v Excess Insurance Co*[176] the policy was construed as providing separate cover for sums payable by the assured to a third party by reason of legal liability, and for all costs and expenses of litigation incurred by the assured with the written consent of the insurers. Thomas J. held that if the costs of litigation resulted from the activities of the assured as described by the policy (repairing boats), the insurers were liable to indemnify the assured even if the claim was outside the scope of the cover: this was not an uncommercial result as the insurers had to give their consent for costs to be incurred.

Where the general rule is applicable, the trigger for payment of defence costs is not necessarily the same as the trigger for payment of liability claims. Assuming that the claim made is insured under the policy, then defence costs are presumed to be payable whether or not the claim against the assured is made out:

> "while the duty to indemnify only extends to claims which are actually covered by the policy, the duty to defend is much broader. It even applies to claims which are groundless, fraudulent or false."[177]

It is possible to draft wording which confines recovery of defence costs to cases in which the assured is actually liable to the third party so that there is a substantive claim against the insurers, although that type of wording is relatively rare in liability insurance. In *Thornton Springer v NEM Insurance Co. Ltd*,[178] a special condition in the policy allowed the assured to recover defence costs whether or not liability to the third party had been established, although the court noted the general rule that, in the absence of express provision, there is no room for the implication of a term to the effect that insurers are liable to meet defence costs where the assured has been found not to be liable to the third party in respect of a claim which, if substantiated, would have triggered an obligation to pay defence costs.

20–049 *Advance funding of the defence.* Let it be assumed that the policy imposes an obligation on the insurers to defend or pay defence costs, either because they are required to do so or because they have exercised an option to pay, but there is then a dispute as to whether the claim made against the assured, if substantiated, would fall wholly or partly within the scope of the substantive cover, or whether the insurers have some form of defence. Are insurers required to fund the defence

---

[173] *Boreal Insurance Inc v Lafarge Canada Inc* (2004) 70 O.R. (3d) 502, which holds that the costs of defending such claims are for excess layer insurers.

[174] *Silbermann v CGU Insurance Ltd* [2003] N.S.W.C.A. 203.

[175] *Wilkie v Gordian Run Off Ltd* [2003] N.S.W.S.C. 109.

[176] *Poole Harbour Yacht Club Marina Ltd v Excess Insurance Co*, 1996, [2001] Lloyd's Rep. I.R. 580.

[177] *Cooper v Farmers' Mutual Insurance Society* [2001] O.T.C. 652. Cf. *Harbourfield Engineering Co Ltd v Falcon Insurance Co (Hong Kong) Ltd* [2006] H.K.E.C. 315.

[178] *Thornton Springer v NEM Insurance Co Ltd* [2000] Lloyd's Rep. I.R. 590.

and to seek repayment of some or all of their outlay after the trial, or are insurers entitled to raise coverage and defence issues immediately? The practice in England is not to insist upon "pay to be paid", but that is practice rather than adherence to policy wording. The matter has been litigated in a number of jurisdictions, perhaps most extensively in Canada where liability policies are drafted on the basis of an obligation to defend or in the alternative to pay defence costs if a defence is refused. English authorities are consistent with the Canadian approach. The cases make it clear that the duty to fund a defence and the obligation to provide indemnification against substantive liability are separate issues. The duty to defend is determined prospectively, and depends on the claim made against the insured. There are tens of cases on the point, but the root decision is *Nichols v American Home Assurance Co*,[179] from which, taken with later authorities, the following principles can be derived.[180]

First, the duty to defend arises where there is a "mere possibility" that the claim advanced against the insured is covered by the policy.[181] It was accordingly held in *John Wyeth v Cigna Insurance Co of Europe SA/NV*[182] that the obligation of an insurer to indemnify the assured against defence costs incurred by him arises where there are claims made against the assured which potentially fall within the terms of the primary cover provided by insurance. The Court of Appeal noted that it was open to the parties to agree that defence costs are recoverable only where the claims definitely fall within the scope of the substantive cover, or to suspend recovery of defence costs until liability under the policy has been established. However, where, as on the facts before the Court of Appeal, the obligations to meet claims and to indemnify for defence costs were distinct, insurers were liable to meet defence costs for claims potentially within the scope of the cover up to the point at which it was shown that the claims against the assured were not covered by the policy.

Secondly, if the pleadings in the third party's claim against the assured allege facts which, if true, could require the insurer to indemnify the assured for the claim, then the insurer is obliged to provide a defence.[183] This remains so even though the actual facts may differ from the allegations pleaded.[184] It is also settled law that "the widest latitude should be given to the allegations and the pleadings in the underlying actions, in determining whether they raise a claim within the policy".[185] The pleadings are to be read in a realistic way, so that it is not the labels used by the pleader, but the true nature of the claim that matters.

---

[179] *Nichols v American Home Assurance Co* [1990] 1 S.C.R. 801.

[180] See the statements of principle in *Fermes Dionne ltée/Dionne Farms Ltd v Fermes Gervais ltée* (2002) 255 N.B.R. (2d) 6 and *Conservation Council of New Brunswick Inc v Encon Group Inc* [2006] N.B.J. No.190.

[181] *Kerr v Lawyers' Professional Indemnity Co* (1995) 25 O.R. (3d) 804; *Alie v Bertrand & Frere Construction Co* [2002] OJ No.4697; *Trafalgar Insurance Co of Canada v Imperial Oil Ltd* (2001) 57 O.R. (3d) 425); *Co-operator's Insurance Co v Ross* [2003] 65 O.R. (3d) 135; *Rotating Equipment Services Inc v Continental Insurance Co* [2004] A.J. No.1340; *Scott v Optimum Frontier Insurance Ltd* [2006] OJ No.4204; *S v Gross* (2002) 100 Alta. L.R. (3d) 310; *Conservation Council of New Brunswick Inc v Encon Group Inc* 2006 N.B.C.A. 51; *Portage La Prairie Mutual Insurance Co v Commission du District d'aménagement du Madawaska* [2006] N.B.J. No.454.

[182] *John Wyeth v Cigna Insurance Co of Europe SA/NV* [2001] Lloyd's Rep. I.R. 420.

[183] *Bacon v McBride* (1984) 5 C.C.L.I. 146; *Comeau v Roy* (1999) 217 N.B.R. (2d) 242; *Russel Metals Inc v Ball Construction Inc* [2007] OJ No.4673.

[184] *Palmieri v Misir* [2003] OJ No.3518; *Wi-Lan v St Paul Guarantee Insurance Co* [2005] A.J. No.1416; *Monenco Ltd v Commonwealth Insurance Company* [2001] S.C.J. No.50.

[185] *Hironaka v Co-operators' General Insurance Co* [2005] A.J. No.1313; *Nash v R* (1995) 27 O.R. (3d) 1; *Hope v Dominion of Canada General Insurance Co* [2000] O.T.C. 426.

The courts are to be aware of "manipulative pleading" which asserts claims that cannot be supported on the facts, e.g. that there is negligence when the true allegation is fraud or deliberate conduct.[186] The term "pleadings" means allegations in the pleadings filed against the assured, and the court is not to look at anything other than the claim made against the assured. Extrinsic evidence explicitly referred to within the pleadings may be considered only for the purpose of determining the substance and true nature of the allegations made in the statement of claim and to appreciate the nature and scope of the insurer's duty to defend.[187] This approach has been adopted in England. In *Thornton Springer v NEM Insurance Co Ltd*[188] a special condition, as construed by Colman J., provided that the assured was entitled to recover defence costs as long as the third party's claim was in substance capable of falling within the insuring clause and as long as the insurers had given their consent to costs being incurred, which on the facts was found to have been given. Colman J. recognised that the third party's pleadings could not be conclusive and that "it may be necessary to investigate what the basis of the claim really amounts to, as distinct from the manner in which it is expressed in the claimant's pleadings."[189]

20–050　　Thirdly, once this rather low threshold is met, then other things being equal the assured is entitled to defence costs coverage. If prima facie coverage is established, it becomes incumbent upon the insurer to establish that the third party's claim actually falls outside the coverage provided by the policy or that the assured is in breach of a policy condition which precludes recovery.[190] Where it is clear that the allegations in the pleadings against the assured fall outside the insuring agreement or are excluded by an applicable exclusion, the duty to defend does not arise.[191] Importantly, if the insurers assert that they are not liable under the policy so that they are not liable for defence costs, and they lose at the hearing on defence costs, they are not estopped from relying on their substantive defence to liability under the policy at a later stage.[192] It would seem that there is nothing to prevent the insurers from seeking at this stage a final order that it is not under any obligation to indemnify the assured, by reason of a coverage or other defence to the substantive claim: this was so held in *Silbermann v CGU*

---

[186] *Non-Marine Underwriters, Lloyd's of London v Scalera* [2000] 1 S.C.R. 551; *Godonoaga v Khatambakhsh* (2000) 132 O.A.C. 391; *Randhawa v Da Rosa* [2000] O.T.C. 738; *Joachin v Abel* [2001] O.T.C. 299; *Unrau v Canadian Northern Shield Insurance Co* [2004] B.C.J. No.33; *Morrison v Co-operators' General Insurance Co* [2004] N.B.J. No.290; *O'Leary v AXA Pacific Insurance Co* 95 O.R. (3d) 315 (2009).

[187] *Aiken v Harris* (1999) 45 O.R. (3d) 266; *Hamel Construction Inc v Lombard Canada Ltd* 2005 N.S.C.A. 65.

[188] *Thornton Springer v NEM Insurance Co Ltd* [2000] Lloyd's Rep. I.R. 590.

[189] Certain US jurisdictions adopt the same approach. In Texas, the principle is known as the "eight corners" rule, under which "the duty to defend does not depend upon the truth or falsity of the allegations . . . a plaintiff's factual allegations that potentially support a covered claim is all that is needed to invoke the insurer's duty to defend": *Nautilus Insurance Co v Country Oaks Apartments Ltd* 566 F. 3d 452 at 454 (5th Cir 2009), applied in *Century Surety Co v Dewey Bellows Operating Co Ltd* 2009 B.L. 187750 (SD Tex Sept 2, 2009).

[190] *Laughlin v Sharon High Voltage Inc* (1993) 12 O.R. (3d) 101.

[191] *Slough Estates Canada Ltd v Federal Pioneer Ltd* (1994) 20 O.R. (3d) 329; *Picken v Guardian Assurance Co of Canada* (1993) 66 O.A.C. 39; *Ross v American Home Assurance Co* 1999 O.T.C. 360; *Non-Marine Underwriters, Lloyd's of London v Scalera* [2000] 1 S.C.R. 551; *Mailet v Halifax Insurance ING Canada* [2003] N.B.J. No.5; *Hanis v University of Western Ontario* (2003) 67 O.R. (3d) 539; *Westridge Construction Ltd v Zurich Insurance Co* [2004] S.J. No.43; *James v Lawyers' Professional Indemnity Co* [2006] OJ No.46.

[192] *R. v Kansa General Insurance Co* (1991) 2 O.R. (2d) 269.

Insurance Ltd.[193] English law would similarly entertain declaratory proceedings in such circumstances.

Fourthly, if some of the allegations in the pleadings appear to be insured, and a dispute arises in respect of others, there is a duty to defend in full. The court is then to allocate the costs after the trial and not beforehand.[194] This is the case even where there are both insured and uninsured parties.[195] However, if it is clear that certain claims are not covered, in that the facts alleged in relation to the insured and uninsured claims are quite different, then there is no duty to defend the uninsured claim: the test is whether the two claims arise from the same actions and have caused the same harm so that the uninsured claim can be said to be derivative.[196]

Fifthly, if there are two policies which respond to the loss, the court may order the insurers to share the defence costs equally, subject to a subsequent apportionment based on actual liability after the trial,[197] and this remains the case even though one insurer asserts that it can be liable only for a small proportion of the loss.[198] This, however, is subject to express clauses, e.g. rateable proportion provisions.[199] Equally, if an insurer is on risk for only a limited period during which the losses occurred, the insurer only has to provide defence costs in the relevant proportion.[200] The same apportionment principle applies as between primary and excess layer insurers.[201]

A discretion to defend. Most policies do not impose on the insurers an absolute **20–051** obligation to fund the assured's defence. If a discretion exists, there is no obligation to pay defence costs where the insurers have denied substantive cover at the outset, and funding will cease (and repayment of costs will be sought) during the course of the proceedings or thereafter if there proves to be no coverage. Policies often state that an allegation of fraud does not justify a refusal of defence costs unless and until the exclusion is established. In the absence of a denial of coverage, the insurers will advance defence costs promptly on receipt of invoices, providing that the costs have been incurred with their consent (such consent not to be unreasonably withheld). To that extent, therefore, there is a

---

[193] *Silbermann v CGU Insurance Ltd* [2003] N.S.W.C.A. 203. There was no appeal against this ruling: see [2005] H.C.A. 16, where an appeal against the lower court's ruling that the insurers were entitled to refuse coverage on the ground of dishonesty, on the basis that the claim against the assured should be determined before dishonesty could be adjudicated, was held to be hypothetical given the assured's acceptance of the right of the court to make such a ruling.

[194] *St Paul Fire & Marine Insurance Co v Durabla Canada Ltd* (1996) 29 O.R. (3d) 737; *Daher v Economical Mutual Insurance Co* (1996) 31 O.R. (3d) 472; *Great West Development Marine Corp v Canadian Surety Co* [2000] B.C.T.C. 339; *Conservation Council of New Brunswick Inc v Encon Group Inc* [2005] N.B.J. No.109; *Agresso Corp v Temple Insurance Co* [2007] B.C.J. No.21; *ING Insurance Co v SREIT (Park West Centre) Ltd* [2009] N.S.J. No.158.

[195] *Continental Insurance Company v Dia Met Minerals Ltd* (1996) 20 B.C.L.R. (3d) 331.

[196] *JAS v Gross* (1998) 231 A.R. 228; *Continental Insurance Co v Dia Met Minerals Ltd* (1996) 20 BCLR (3d) 331; *Sommerfield v Lombard Insurance Group* (2005) 74 O.R. (3d) 571.

[197] *Prudential Life Insurance Co Ltd v Manitoba Public Insurance Corp* (1976) 67 D.L.R. (3d) 521; *General Accident Insurance Co of Canada v Ontario Provincial Police Force* (1988) 30 C.C.L.I. 178; *Royal Insurance Company v Coronation Insurance* (1993) 17 C.C.L.I. (2d) 13; *Skyline Gold Corporation v American Home Insurance* [1997] B.C.T.C. G22; *Incerto v Landry* (2000) 47 O.R. (2d) 622.

[198] *Axa Pacific Insurance Co v Guildford Marquis Towers Ltd* [2000] B.C.T.C. 37.

[199] *Family Insurance Corp v Lombard Canada Ltd* (2000) B.C.T.C. 273.

[200] *Royal and Sun Alliance Insurance Co of Canada v Fiberglass Canada Inc* (1999) 99 O.T.C. 196.

[201] *Broadhurst & Ball v American Home Insurance* (1990) 40 O.A.C. 261; *American Assurance Co v Temple Insurance Co* 94 O.R. (3d) 534 (2007); *St Mary's Cement Company Inc v ACE INA Insurance* [2008] OJ No.2622.

discretion whether or not to fund defence costs. A "consent not to be unreasonably withheld" provision was considered in *Hulton & Co v Mountain*,[202] where the assured had obtained a libel policy for £7,000 with a £200 deductible. The policy provided, by way of condition precedent, that in event of claim likely to exceed the deductible, no costs were to be incurred without the consent of underwriters which was not to be unreasonably withheld. The assured faced a claim, but the underwriters refused to give their consent to the incurring of defence costs as they asserted that the claim should be settled for less than £200. The Court of Appeal held that the underwriters had acted unreasonably in the circumstances.[203]

If the discretion has been exercised in favour of funding, then the wording of the costs clause may permit the insurers to withdraw funding once fraud is alleged or it becomes apparent that there is no substantive coverage under the policy. In *Silbermann v CGU Insurance Ltd*[204] the Australian High Court held that the insurers were entitled to refuse their consent to defence costs being incurred, by means of the insurers themselves establishing that the assured had been dishonest: the wording of the policy was such that the discretion was an overriding one, even in respect of allegations of fraud. The wording may, however, be to the contrary. In *Wilkie v Gordian Run Off Ltd*,[205] the same Court ruled, on the policy terms before it, that fraud could not be relied upon as a defence until fraud had been established "in fact" in proceedings against the assured, so the insurers were under an obligation to fund the defence once they had given their consent to defence costs being incurred.

By contrast, if the discretion has not been exercised in favour of funding and there has been no ruling on substantive coverage, a question arises as to whether the insurers' exercise of discretion can be challenged, particularly where the effect of refusal is to cut out any realistic possibility of the assured mounting a defence. In *Thornton Springer v NEM Insurance Co Ltd*[206] Colman J., in construing a condition requiring the insurers' consent to be given to costs being incurred, indicated that the condition was to be read subject to an implied term that the insurers' consent could not unreasonably be withheld. Earlier, in *Poole Harbour Yacht Club Marina Ltd v Excess Insurance Co*[207] Thomas J. had expressed much the same point of view, that insurers did not have an unfettered discretion, and that they could not unreasonably withhold their consent. Again, in *The Beursgracht*,[208] H.H. Judge Hallgarten QC stated that if he had been of the view that the policy required the consent of the insurers for costs to be incurred, that consent could not unreasonably have been withheld. These *dicta* have not been specifically challenged, but it is noteworthy that in *Gan Insurance Co Ltd v Tai Ping Insurance Co. Ltd (Nos 2 and 3)*,[209] the Court of Appeal firmly rejected the argument that a discretion vested in reinsurers to approve a

[202] *Hulton & Co v Mountain* (1929) 8 Ll. L.R. 249.

[203] The Court of Appeal also held that the underwriters had on the facts waived their rights by impliedly giving consent to the assured.

[204] *Silbermann v CGU Insurance Ltd* [2003] N.S.W.C.A. 203. This point did not arise on appeal, which was dismissed unanimously on procedural grounds, but by a 3:2 majority the High Court agreed with the lower court's analysis.

[205] *Wilkie v Gordian Run Off Ltd* 2005 H.C.A. 17.

[206] *Thornton Springer v NEM Insurance Co Ltd* [2000] Lloyd's Rep. I.R. 590.

[207] *Poole Harbour Yacht Club Marina Ltd v Excess Insurance Co* [2001] Lloyd's Rep. I.R. 580.

[208] *Glencore International AG v Ryan (The Beursgracht)* [2001] 2 Lloyd's Rep. 608. The point did not arise on appeal.

[209] *Gan Insurance Co Ltd v Tai Ping Insurance Co Ltd (Nos 2 and 3)* [2001] Lloyd's Rep. I.R. 667. See also *Eagle Star v Cresswell* [2004] Lloyd's Rep. I.R. 537.

settlement reached by its reinsured with the direct policy holder was subject to an implied reasonableness requirement. Reasonableness was in that case abandoned in favour of a "rationality" test, i.e. that used for judicial review: the question is not whether the insurers had acted unreasonably in denying funding, but rather whether they had reached their conclusion by taking into account considerations which were extraneous to the dispute itself (e.g. for the purpose of asserting leverage in an entirely unrelated dispute). The test has been laid down, but there is no case in England in which insurers have been found to have acted irrationally in their exercise of discretion. It may be, therefore, that there is some scope to challenge the implied restrictions imposed by the courts on costs clauses.

Allocation between insured and uninsured claims. The situation may arise in which the claim made by the third party is partly in respect of insured liabilities and partly in respect of uninsured liabilities. Three separate issues arise here. **20–052**

The first is where some of the claims made against the assured are covered by the policy and some are not. In directors and officers insurance, for example, typically the director will be accused of both negligent and fraudulent conduct, the former being covered by the policy but the latter not. In such a case there is an obligation to defend, but the assured may not be entitled to recover the full amount of his costs. As seen above, if the question is upfront funding, the authorities suggest that the insurers are required to fund the entire defence and worry about the problem afterwards. However, once there has been a judgment finding that some parts of the claim are insured and some are not, the issue becomes whether costs are to be allocated between the two so that repayment is required. In *Structural Polymer Systems Ltd and Structural Polymer Technologies Ltd v Brown*[210] it was assumed by both parties that costs are generally apportionable as between insured and uninsured losses, so that the insurer is liable for only that proportion of the costs represented by the proportion of loss which was insured. Thus, in the absence of express wording, there has to be an allocation, however difficult that may be,[211] although allocation is not required if the assured can show that the overall costs were not increased by the need to defend the fraud element of the claim.[212] In *John Wyeth & Brothers Ltd v Cigna Insurance Co of Europe SA/NV*,[213] product liability insurance had been procured by the assured, and losses were incurred over a number of years. Not all of the claims were within the time periods covered by the insurance. The policy provided that the insurers were to pay "all costs and expenses of litigation" incurred with their written consent. The Court of Appeal ruled that the insurers were liable for the full amount of the defence costs even though the amount expended might have incidentally assisted the assured in fighting claims which were uninsured. The insurers' remedy in such a case was to seek contribution from other insurers who were on risk during the uninsured periods. In *McCarthy v St Paul International Insurance Co Ltd*[214] a number of claims were made against the assured, some in respect of fraud and some in respect of insured perils. The insurers asserted that the cause of defence costs being incurred was both insured and excluded perils, and in line with the general rule that an

---

[210] *Structural Polymer Systems Ltd and Structural Polymer Technologies Ltd v Brown* [2000] Lloyd's Rep. I.R. 64.

[211] *Structural Polymer Systems Ltd v Brown* [2000] Lloyd's Rep. I.R. 64; *Hanis v Teevan* 92 O.R. (3d) 594 (2008).

[212] *John Wyeth v Cigna* [2001] Lloyd's Rep. I.R. 420.

[213] *John Wyeth & Brothers Ltd v Cigna Insurance Co of Europe SA/NV* [2001] Lloyd's Rep. I.R. 420.

[214] *McCarthy v St Paul International Insurance Co Ltd* 2007 F.C.A.F.C. 28.

exception always trumps an insuring clause if there are concurrent proximate causes, there was no liability for defence costs. The court's response was that the claims were separable so that defence costs were payable in respect of the insured claims and, further, that to the extent that there were common costs the insurers were liable for them. The court noted that it might be possible to devise wording which produced a different result, e.g. if the policy covered $X defence costs in any one year, excluding defence costs caused directly or indirectly by fraud: such wording might have the effect of preventing recovery of any defence costs even if the claims in question were not referable to fraud. Such language is not found in practice. Further, the right to apportion may be lost by agreement. In *Knight v Hosken*[215] the assured's insurers were under an obligation to indemnify him up to the sum of £2,000 and in addition to pay defence costs if they insisted upon conducting his defence. A claim was made against the assured in the sum of £3,700, and the assured agreed to pay 17/37 of the costs, representing the uninsured proportion. The Court of Appeal held that the insurers were unable to rely upon this promise as there was no consideration for it and in any event they had not relied upon it in their conduct of the defence.

The second issue arises where there are both insured and uninsured defendants. There are various theories propounded in the United States as to how this matter should be judged, but that which has been accepted in England is the "reasonably related" test. The effect of this is that if the assured would have incurred the same costs without the addition of an uninsured party, the insurers are to pay the entire amount of the costs and they are not entitled to contribution from the uninsured party. In *New Zealand Forest Products Ltd v New Zealand Insurance Co Ltd*[216] the assured company had procured directors' and officers' liability cover. The assured and one of its directors were successfully sued in California in respect of the breach of a joint venture agreement which had been entered into by the director on behalf of the assured. There were a number of co-defendants in the Californian proceedings, who were associated to the assured but were not parties to the insurance cover. The same lawyers were used by all of the defendants, and the Privy Council was asked to determine whether the policy required the costs to be notionally allocated between the defendants with the insurer being liable only for its share. The Privy Council held that, in the absence of clear wording, the policy was to be construed as covering all of the costs incurred in the defence of the claim, even though this might benefit the other defendants, provided only that the costs were reasonably related to the assured's director's own liability. The decision was based on the wording before the court, which referred to "costs, charges and expenses . . . incurred in the defence of legal actions", and the Privy Council's interpretation was that in the absence of clear wording severability was not intended. It follows that there is to be apportionment of costs only if uninsured claims or claims against third parties are separable from those relating to insured claims: this was, as noted above, the assumption in *Structural Polymer Systems v Brown*. The same approach has been adopted in Australia, in *Vero Insurance Ltd v Baycorp Advantage Ltd*,[217] where the defence costs were incurred on behalf of the insured directors and the

[215] *Knight v Hosken* (1943) 75 Ll. L.R. 74.

[216] *New Zealand Forest Products Ltd v New Zealand Insurance Co Ltd* [1996] 2 N.Z.L.R. 20. See also *Thornton Springer v NEM Insurance Co Ltd* [2000] Lloyd's Rep. I.R. 590; *Coronation Insurance Co v Clearly Canadian Beverage Corp* (1999) 117 B.C.A.C. 22.

[217] *Vero Insurance Ltd v Baycorp Advantage Ltd* [2004] N.S.W.C.A. 390 affirming the principles set out by Einstein J. at first instance, *Baycorp Advantage Ltd v Royal and Sun Alliance Insurance Australia Ltd* 2003 NSWSC 941.

uninsured company. *New Zealand Forest Products* was applied in *Thornton Springer v NEM Insurance Ltd*.[218] In that case defence costs were payable in respect of claims for insured perils whether or not the claims against the assured were successful. Claims were brought against two defendants, but the policy covered only the claims against one of them. The claims were ultimately dismissed. Colman J. held that the insurers were liable to meet the defence costs, and that it was not possible for insurers to reclaim any part the defence costs on the ground that the costs had been incurred for the mutual benefit of both defendants: if costs were incurred for a dual purpose, one of which was an insured purpose, the indemnity extended to the dual purpose work and was not to be apportioned. The trend in the US cases on this matter has been to adopt the "larger settlement" rule, under which there is to be no allocation of defence costs between insured and uninsured defendants unless the settlement is larger as a result of the presence of the uninsured defendants, so that if liability is concurrent there is no apportionment.[219]

The third is where there are two or more insurers, each with a duty to defend. Ordinary contribution principles apply here. If one insurer has paid the full defence costs, that insurer is entitled to an appropriate contribution from the other representing its share of liability.[220]

Allocation may be governed by express provision. However, there is a risk that an allocation clause might be void for uncertainty if it does no more than say that the parties are to agree on an equitable allocation: such a clause was struck down by the trial judge in *Vero Insurance Ltd v Baycorp Advantage Ltd*, his reasoning being approved on appeal.[221]

Failure to insist upon repayment. A problem which has arisen in England, but which has not yet been litigated (although it has been arbitrated), becomes apparent where there is an aggregate limit of cover for defence costs and the sums available have been eroded. Included in the sums paid are sums forwarded to directors who, by reason of findings of fraud against them, are required to repay those sums to the insurers. If those sums are repaid, then the amount available to fund other defences is reinstated to that extent. But what is the situation if insurers fail to seek repayment, or are unsuccessful in obtaining repayment so that the policy limits are not eroded? Absent contrary policy wording (and it may certainly be possible to construe some policies as imposing an obligation on insurers to pay directors up to the policy limit, disregarding sums which have been but should not have been paid), it is most unlikely that a court would conclude that there is some form of implied obligation on the insurers to pursue recovery to the full so that policy limits can be reinstated in respect of defence costs incurred by other directors. If there are recoveries, it would seem that they have to be allocated to reinstate the limit of indemnity (possibly net of recovery costs). **20–053**

---

[218] *New Zealand Forest Products* was applied in *Thornton Springer v NEM Insurance Ltd* [2000] Lloyd's Rep. I.R. 590.
[219] *Caterpillar Inc v Great American Insurance* 62 F. 3d 1995 (7th circuit, 1995); *Norstrom Inc v Chubb & Sons* 54 F. 3d (9th circuit, 1995); *Safeway Stores Inc v National Union Fire Insurance Co* 64 F. 2d 1282 (9th circuit, 1995).
[220] As in *Ing Insurance Co of Canada v Federated Insurance Co of Canada* 75 O.R. (3d) 457 (2005), where the dispute was between primary and excess layer insurers.
[221] *Vero Insurance v Baycorp Advantage Ltd* [2004] N.S.W.C.A. 390.

20–054 *Excess liability cover for defence costs.* The decision in *John Wyeth & Brothers Ltd v Cigna Insurance Co of Europe SA/NV*[222] concerned the correct interpretation of an excess layer cover for defence costs, and in particular the triggers for the attachment of the policy and the obligation of the assured to maintain the primary layer policy in force. The primary layer policy in this case contained a buy-out clause, under which the primary layer insurers could cap their liability by making payment of the maximum sums due under the policy for claims, at which point they would be discharged from liability. This option was exercised. The Court of Appeal (applying the governing New York law) held that: (a) the excess layer insurers were liable for costs subsequently incurred by the assured, as their liability was triggered once the primary layer insurers' maximum liability had been reached, whether or not that was the result of a contractual cap rather than the payment of actual claims; and (b) a maintenance clause in the excess layer insurance, under which the assured was required to maintain in force primary layer insurance, had no application to the capping of primary layer cover, as it could not be said that exhaustion of primary layer cover (by whatever means) amounted to a failure to maintain that cover.

Liability for the claimant's costs

20–055 *Grounds for making an order against an insurer.* The fact that the insurer's total liability is expressed in terms of sum insured plus costs means that if the third party is successful in his action against the assured, and obtains a judgment with costs for a sum in excess of total policy limits, the insurer's liability is fixed at the policy limits and the third party will have to look to the assured's own assets. A possible mechanism whereby the third party can look to the insurer directly for the third party's costs in successfully pursuing the assured arises under s.51 of the Senior Courts Act 1981, which confers an absolute discretion on the court[223] as to the award of costs, and it has been held by the House of Lords[224] that, in exceptional circumstances, costs can be awarded against a person who is not party to legal proceedings although he is closely related to them. The jurisdiction is important as far as the third party is concerned, for it is settled that the exercise by the insurers of their power to conduct litigation on the assured's behalf cannot give the third party any rights against them except in respect of costs,[225] nor will they be liable to him for the tort of maintenance.[226]

A series of cases has established that, subject to important limits, s.51 can be used to make an award of costs against an insurer who is not formally a party to legal proceedings but who has conducted the assured's defence to those proceedings. In the leading authority, *TGA Chapman Ltd v Christopher*,[227] the Court of Appeal held that a costs order could be made if five conditions were satisfied.

---

[222] *John Wyeth & Brothers Ltd v Cigna Insurance Co of Europe SA/NV* [2001] Lloyd's Rep. I.R. 420.

[223] Plainly this provision can have no application to arbitrations, as the arbitrators may award costs only against the nominal parties to the arbitration.

[224] *Aiden Shipping Co Ltd v Interbulk Ltd (The Vimeira)* [1986] A.C. 965. See also *Hamilton v Al Fayed* [2002] 3 All E.R. 641.

[225] *Nairn v South-East Lancashire Insurance* 1930 S.C. 606; *Vandepitte v Preferred Accident Assurance* [1933] A.C. 70.

[226] Fletcher Moulton L.J. in *British Cash & Parcel Conveyors v Lamson Store Service* [1908] 1 K.B. 1006 at 1015.

[227] *TGA Chapman Ltd v Christopher* [1998] 2 All E.R. 873, applied in *Pendennis Shipyard Ltd v Magrathea (Pendennis) Ltd* [1998] 1 Lloyd's Rep. 315.

(1) The insurers had taken the decision to defend the claim.
(2) The defence of the claim had been funded by the insurers.
(3) The insurers had conducted the litigation.
(4) The insurers had fought the claim exclusively to defend their own interests.
(5) The defence had failed in its entirety.

The Court of Appeal held that on the facts all five conditions had been satisfied and, accordingly, that it was appropriate for a costs order to be made against the insurers. It was pointed out that, had the defence succeeded, the insurers' would have recovered their costs from the third party, so that reciprocity was appropriate. The Court of Appeal was for this reason unperturbed by the argument that an order for costs against the insurers exposed them to an aggregate level of liability greater than that specified in the policy. The argument that the power under s.51 is to be exercised in exceptional circumstances only was similarly not regarded as a barrier, given that it was exceptional in ordinary litigation—although possibly not in cases involving a liability insurer—for a person to fund litigation to which he was not a nominal party entirely for his own interests.

It is clear from subsequent cases that the conditions are not lightly satisfied and that a costs order against insurers will be exceptional. It has to be shown that the assured had no interest in the outcome, that the insurers were purely self-interested and that their intervention has caused the third party to incur costs which would not otherwise have been incurred.[228] If the assured remains in business and its reputation is at stake,[229] or if the assured is required to share the defence costs,[230] it cannot be said that the defence is purely for the insurers' own interests (condition (4)) and if the assured has expressed the desire to contest liability then condition (1) is not satisfied.[231] The provision of assistance by the assured to the insurers in the conduct of the defence is not, however, enough to prevent the operation of condition (3): a distinction is to be drawn between taking tactical decisions as to how a claim should be defended (control) and providing information which allows the defence to be conducted properly (assistance).[232] Insurers who withdraw from the proceedings at a late stage, leaving the assured without cover for any potential costs order, do not by reason of that fact alone expose themselves to a costs order in favour of the third party unless there has been some statement by them to the third party that coverage will not be withdrawn.[233]

While it is the case that a third party costs order is exceptional, and while the courts appear to have added a sixth requirement, namely that, but for the intervention of the insurers, the claim would not have been defended, the most recent cases seem to indicate that it is somewhat easier to justify a costs order against liability insurers than in other contexts. In *Plymouth & South West Co-operative Society Ltd v Architecture, Structure & Management Ltd*[234] the assured architects ceased trading in 2001 with assets valued at less than

---

[228] *Monkton Court Ltd v Perry Prowse (Insurance Services) Ltd* [2002] Lloyd's Rep. I.R. 408.
[229] *Gloucester Health Authority v Torpy* [1999] Lloyd's Rep. I.R. 203; *Citibank NA v Excess Insurance Co Ltd* [1999] Lloyd's Rep. I.R. 122.
[230] *Cormack and Cormack v Excess Insurance Co Ltd* [2002] Lloyd's Rep. I.R. 398.
[231] *Citibank NA v Excess Insurance Co Ltd* [1999] Lloyd's Rep. I.R. 122.
[232] *Citibank NA v Excess Insurance Co Ltd* [1999] Lloyd's Rep. I.R. 122.
[233] *Bristol and West Plc v Bhadresa and Mascarenhas* [1999] Lloyd's Rep. I.R. 138.
[234] *Plymouth & South West Co-operative Society Ltd v Architecture, Structure & Management Ltd* [2007] Lloyd's Rep. I.R. 596.

£100,000, and proceedings were commenced against the assured in 2002. The assured's liability policy was subscribed to by five insurers in equal proportions, and had an upper limit of £2 million. In 2006 judgment was given against the assured for the sum of £2,076,332, exclusive of costs which were likely to exceed £1 million. The insurers satisfied the judgment, leaving a shortfall of £76,332, and were then faced with a claim for costs under the Senior Courts Act 1981 s.51. H.H. Judge Thornton QC duly made the order and required each of the insurers to contribute equally. As to the criteria, the court ruled that: the decision to instruct solicitors was taken by the insurers at a time when the assured had ceased to trade; the insurers funded the entirety of the defence; the defence had been conducted by the insurers and the assured had simply co-operated with the insurers' requests to the extent that any instructions had emanated from the assured; the claim had been defended purely in the insurers' interests, in that the assured had no assets and had remained on the register of companies purely so that the claim could be defended; and the defence had failed in its entirety even though the sum recovered was only about two-thirds of that originally sought. As regards causation, the court was satisfied that, but for the intervention of the insurers, the claim would not have been defended. An order was made on much the same basis in *Palmer v Palmer*,[235] where the assured under a liability policy—a manufacturer of safety devices for child car seats—was in a parlous financial state with no ongoing business to protect, and the claim against it had been defended by the insurers in their own interests.

20–056   *Procedural aspects.* An order may be made against an insurer under s.51 of the Senior Courts Act 1981 without the insurer being joined to the main proceedings.[236] Express provision is made for such service by CPR PD 6B para.18 which states that the English court may give permission for service abroad where "a claim is made by a party to proceedings for an order that the court exercise its power under s.51 of the Senior Courts Act 1981 to make a costs order in favour of or against a person who is not a party to those proceedings". An application for a costs order against an insurer will be allowed to proceed only in the clearest cases when the matter can be resolved in hours rather than days, and discovery and interrogatories are inappropriate. Expensive satellite litigation is thus to be avoided, and the very fact that the application gives rise to complex questions which may require, e.g. waiver of privilege, is of itself a reason for refusing the application.[237]

Where the third party against whom a costs order is sought is outside the jurisdiction, it is necessary to seek permission to serve him outside the jurisdiction in order to join him to the proceedings. This remains the case even if the defendant is domiciled in a contracting state which is party to Council Regulation 44/2001 or the Lugano Convention: those Conventions have no application to this situation, as the third party is not being "sued".[238]

Liability of insurers to follow the assured's settlements

20–057   *Proof of loss under a settlement with a third party.* The assured must, in order to recover from his insurers, demonstrate that he has incurred an actual liability

[235] *Palmer v Palmer* [2008] Lloyd's Rep. I.R. 535.

[236] *Citibank NA v Excess Insurance Co Ltd* [1999] Lloyd's Rep. I.R. 122; *Bristol and West Plc v Bhadresa and Mascarenhas* [1999] Lloyd's Rep. I.R. 138.

[237] These principles were laid down by Lightman J. in *Bristol and West Plc v Bhadresa and Mascarenhas.*

[238] *National Justice Compania Naviera SA v Prudential Assurance Co Ltd (The Ikarian Reefer) (No.2)* [2000] Lloyd's Rep. I.R. 230.

within the scope of the policy, in that his liability has been established and quantified by a judgment, arbitration award or a binding settlement. Proof of actual liability may cause various problems for the assured, as the safest method requires him to allow himself to be sued to judgment.[239] However it may be eminently sensible for the assured to settle despite the fact that as a matter of law, there is a dispute as to liability, given that if the matter is allowed to proceed to judicial resolution there is a strong possibility that there will be a substantial judgment against the assured. In practice, insurers are commonly given the right to take over negotiations between the assured and the third party, and the rights of the assured depend upon his compliance with the provision. Further, insurers may have the right to approve any settlements. However, in the absence of terms of this type and the assured proceeds to reach a settlement with the third party, the law is clear that the assured can recover from his insurers only if he can demonstrate that he was liable to the third party as a matter of law. This was the position in *Commercial Union Insurance v NRG Victory Reinsurance*,[240] a reinsurance case in which the insurance agreement was governed by English law and provided what appeared to be a good defence to the assured's claim. However, the proceedings against the reinsured were to be conducted in the United States before a judge not experienced in insurance matters, and a jury, and it was apparent to all concerned that the wording of the policy was unlikely to provide any defence in that forum. The Court of Appeal, nevertheless, held that the reinsured had to prove its loss and that any settlement reached with the assured would be binding on the reinsurers only insofar as it was based on actual legal liability: the fact that the settlement was probably beneficial both to the reinsured and to the reinsurers was not regarded as a relevant factor.[241] The decision is consistent with the general rule that, other than in marine insurance, an assured or reinsured is not required to take any steps to mitigate loss, and cannot recover for any costs incurred in doing so.[242]

The liability of the reinsured in *Commercial Union v NRG Victory* arose under a policy governed by English law, and it was relatively straightforward for the Court of Appeal to apply strict rules of English law to the question whether such liability had in fact been established for the purposes of a claim under the reinsurance. The Court of Appeal rejected an approach to the determination of liability whereby what should be considered was not strict rules of English law but rather the possible application of English law in the foreign court in which the issue was to be determined. In *Enterprise Oil Ltd v Strand Insurance Co Ltd*[243] Aikens J. held that if liability fell to be determined under a foreign law it was in the same way appropriate to consider the strict rules of that foreign law rather than any possibility that the foreign court might have applied its own law in a more flexible way. In *Enterprise Oil* the assured settled a claim brought against it in respect of alleged torts committed in Texas and subject to the law of Texas. Aikens J. ruled that on a strict application of Texas law there was no liability in tort so that the assured had not proved its loss for the purpose of a claim against its liability insurers. The learned judge rejected the argument that the assured

---

[239] Although even this is not foolproof. In *WASA International Insurance Co Ltd v Lexington Insurance Co* [2009] Lloyd's Rep. I.R. 675 Lord Mance expressed doubts as to the binding effect of a foreign judgment.

[240] *Commercial Union Insurance v NRG Victory Reinsurance* [1998] Lloyd's Rep. I.R. 439.

[241] See also *Lark v Outhwaite* [1991] 2 Lloyd's Rep. 132, which makes it clear that the mere fact that a settlement by the reinsured is beneficial is not enough to carry the reinsurers.

[242] *Yorkshire Water Services Ltd v Sun Alliance & London Insurance Plc* [1997] 2 Lloyd's Rep. 21.

[243] *Enterprise Oil Ltd v Strand Insurance Co Ltd* [2007] Lloyd's Rep. I.R. 186.

established its liability by showing that the Texas court—consisting of a fact-finding jury as well as a judge—might reasonably have concluded that there was such liability irrespective of the precise rules of Texas law.

A "settlement" for the purposes of a liability policy requires a binding contract between the assured and the third-party claimants, whether or not it is expressed in a formal document. An arrangement which is provisional or which is otherwise subject to being reopened is not a settlement at all and thus cannot be relied upon to justify a claim against the insurers.[244]

20–058 *Follow the settlements.* Most reinsurance agreements contain "follow the settlements" clauses under which the reinsurers are required to provide indemnity as long as the settlement was reached on a bona fide and businesslike fashion.[245] Other reinsurances contain narrower provisions which require the reinsured to prove its liability to the assured and also to prove that the loss falls within the scope of the reinsurance: such clauses do little more than replicate the common law in that the reinsured is required to prove its loss as a matter of law.[246] In practice, follow the settlements clauses are cut back by claims co-operation and claims control provisions, the effect of which will be to remove the right of recovery unless reinsurers have been given the right to approve the settlement.[247] Follow the settlements provisions in liability policies are less common, but it is presumably the case that the same interpretation would be applicable. The meaning of the word "settlement" for these purposes was tested in *Rothschild Assurance Ltd v Collyear*,[248] in which the claimants had compensated purchasers of investment products which had been sold by appointed (agents who had not given proper advice to the purchasers). The claimants spent large sums in investigating the circumstances of each of the purchasers and paid compensation to a large number of them. Rix J. held that the process could properly be described as "settlement" and not, as the insurers had contended, concession, and that it fell within the terms of a costs clause which obliged the insurers to indemnify the claimants. Rix J. did accept that the costs had not been incurred by way of defence, although this was immaterial, given that the clause covered both settlement and defence.

[244] *Faraday Capital Ltd v Copenhagen Reinsurance Co Ltd* [2007] Lloyd's Rep. I.R. 23. For the evidence required to support an allegation that a settlement has been entered into, see *Korea National Insurance Corporation v Allianz Global Corporate & Speciality AG* [2008] Lloyd's Rep. I.R. 413, where it was pointed out that the absence of writing is all but fatal to an assertion that a commercial settlement has been reached.

[245] *Insurance Co of Africa v Scor (UK) Reinsurance Co Ltd* [1985] 1 Lloyd's Rep. 312; *Hill v Mercantile & General Reinsurance Co Plc* [1996] L.R.L.R. 381; *Assicurazioni Generali SpA v CGU International Insurance Plc* [2004] Lloyd's Rep. I.R. 457; *Eagle Star Insurance Co Ltd v Cresswell* [2004] Lloyd's Rep. I.R. 437; *English and American Insurance Co Ltd v Axa Re SA* [2007] Lloyd's Rep. I.R. 359; *Aegis Electrical and Gas International Services Co Ltd v Continental Casualty Co* [2008] Lloyd's Rep. I.R. 17.

[246] *Hill v Mercantile & General Reinsurance Co Plc* [1996] L.R.L.R. 381. However, in proving that loss the reinsured is entitled to rely upon evidence of what that loss may have been even though there is no absolute proof. Accordingly, where there have been global settlements of a series of claims, the reinsured can rely upon actuarial models (*Equitas Ltd v R&Q Reinsurance Company (UK) Ltd* [2009] EWHC 2787 (Comm)) and upon the reasonableness of the settlement in the circumstances (*IRB Brasil Resseguros SA v CX Reinsurance Company Ltd* [2010] EWHC 974 (Comm)) as a basis for proving the loss on the balance of probabilities.

[247] *Gan Insurance Co v Tai Ping Insurance Co Ltd (No.2)* [2001] Lloyd's Rep. I.R. 667; *Eagle Star v Cresswell* [2004] Lloyd's Rep. I.R. 437.

[248] *Rothschild Assurance Ltd v Collyear* [1999] Lloyd's Rep. I.R. 6.

Multiple losses. As the law requires the assured to prove each separate loss, the **20–059** assured will only be able to recover for those losses in respect of which he was clearly liable. This requirement was met in *P & O Steam Navigation Co v Youell*,[249] where the assured shipping company was able to satisfy the court, in proceedings for summary judgment against the insurer, that it had incurred liability to a large number of passengers on board three vessels each of which had been unable to complete its voyage, and that the exclusion clauses in the assured's contracts with the passengers were unenforceable in English law under the Unfair Contract Terms Act 1977. However, where the settlement encompasses both insured and uninsured losses, as long as the total amount settlement reached by the assured is no greater than the total amount of its actual liability at law to the claimants, there is no basis for the insurers going behind the settlement.

Allocation issues. The settlement figure agreed between the assured and the third **20–060** party is often a global one, encompassing all of the claims by the third party against the assured and any claims that the assured may have against the third party by way of counterclaim. The question which this scenario may give rise to is whether the insurers are entitled to insist upon some form of allocation of the settlement figure to the various losses and counterclaims. In *Lumbermen's Mutual Casualty Co v Bovis Lend Lease Ltd*[250] Colman J. decided that if there are both insured and uninsured losses in a settlement the insurers are only liable if the settlement agreement contains a money allocation of each of the claims and any counterclaims. Colman J. envisaged a two-stage process: (a) establishment and quantification of the assured's liability by judgment, arbitration award or settlement; and (b) proof of the insurers' liability, which was automatic in the case of a judgment or award but required evidence of liability at law in the case of a settlement. In the present case Colman J.'s view was that the assured failed at step (a) because a settlement which did not specify the amount of the assured's liability by allocation between claims was not one which could be said to establish or quantify liability. Accordingly, it was simply not open to the assured to proceed to step (b) and to show that there was as a matter of law liability to the employer in any given amount.

It might be thought that this approach is both uncommercial and technical. Where there are various insured and uninsured claims, and counterclaims between the parties, it is usual for a global settlement to be reached without any admission of liability on either side and without any attempt to allocate sums to the various claims which been compromised. Requiring an assured to identify in the settlement the amounts for which liability has been accepted is likely to militate against a settlement being reached in the first place and is contrary to commercial practice. Furthermore, it seems strange that the assured's failure to take the technical step of seeking to have sums written into the settlement should have the draconian consequence of preventing the assured from even attempting to prove its loss as a matter of law. Any figure would have to be justified as a matter of law, so it is difficult to see why the absence of such a figure should have any major significance. Furthermore, the need to allocate will almost inevitably put the assured in breach of the usual contractual obligation not to admit liability

---

[249] *P & O Steam Navigation Co v Youell* [1997] 2 Lloyd's Rep. 136. See also *Structural Polymer Systems Ltd and Structural Polymer Technologies Ltd v Brown* [2000] Lloyd's Rep. I.R. 64. These decisions are clearly correct despite the contrary ruling in *Lumberman's Mutual Casualty Co v Bovis Lend Lease Ltd* [2005] Lloyd's Rep. I.R. 74, which is no longer authoritative.

[250] *Lumbermen's Mutual Casualty Co v Bovis Lend Lease Ltd* [2005] 1 Lloyd's Rep. 494.

for any one claim. The reasoning in *Lumbermen's* was subsequently rejected by Aikens J. in *Enterprise Oil Ltd v Strand Insurance Co Ltd*,[251] in which the parties had made no attempt to allocate parts of the settlement to individual claims. The assured failed to recover an indemnity on the basis that all of the claims were uninsured, but Aikens J. ruled that if the assured had been able to show legal liability for some but not all of the claims, the better view was that an assured who had entered into a global settlement encompassing insured and uninsured losses should be able to recover to the extent that he could prove his loss, and there was no precondition requiring the settlement itself to allocate settled sums to specific claims. This was so for two reasons. First, given that insurers were entitled to put the assured to proof of liability and quantum, there was no need for the assured to show as a precondition that the amount to be claimed under the settlement had been the subject of specific ascertainment. The settlement was not concerned with a claim under the policy, but simply resolved the respective liabilities of the parties to the settlement as between themselves. The making of a settlement was a precondition of a claim against the insurers, but there was no need for the settlement to allocate sums as between claims. Secondly, an allocation requirement was uncommercial and would lead to artificial statements in settlements, a state of affairs which the law ought to strive to avoid. Aikens J. was also of the view that the *Lumbermen's* principle applied also to judgments and arbitration awards, so that a judgment or award which did not allocate losses in the manner required by Colman J. could not found a claim against liability insurers.[252] This reasoning is, it is submitted, impeccable. *Enterprise Oil* was favoured over *Lumbermen's* by Morison J. in *AIG Europe (Ireland) Ltd v Faraday Capital Ltd*,[253] although the point did not arise on the facts of the case.[254]

20–061 *Approval of the assured's settlements.* The insurers' approval for the assured's settlements may be required by the policy. Consent may relate to the liability of the insurers to follow the assured's settlements, and it may instead relate to the liability of the insurers to meet the assured's defence costs in reaching settlements. It was noted earlier that, in the absence of any express terms affecting settlements, the assured can recover only if he can prove his loss: this was so held in *Commercial Union Insurance v NRG Victory Reinsurance*.[255] The extent to which there is any implied limitation on the discretion of insurers to withhold consent for a settlement reached by the assured has not been considered in detail at the direct insurance level, but there is reinsurance authority on the point for the proposition that, although there is no implied obligation on reinsurers to act reasonably, they are required not to act irrationally, i.e. not to take into account considerations which were arbitrary or were other than those which related directly to the claim itself.[256] A desire to drive the reinsured out of business for competition reasons, or to create pressure in relation to other claims, might fall into the prohibited category. On the assumption that this reasoning

---

[251] *Enterprise Oil Ltd v Strand Insurance Co Ltd* [2007] Lloyd's Rep. I.R. 186.

[252] Aikens J. commented that it was unclear whether his approach applied also to reinsurance, given the ongoing dispute as to whether reinsurance is or is not a form of liability insurance.

[253] *AIG Europe (Ireland) Ltd v Faraday Capital Ltd* [2007] Lloyd's Rep. I.R. 267. The decision of Morison J. was subsequently reversed by the Court of Appeal, *AIG Europe (Ireland) Ltd v Faraday Capital Ltd* [2008] Lloyd's Rep. I.R. 454, but purely on the question of the date on which the relevant loss had occurred: no comment on *Enterprise Oil* was made.

[254] See also *Equitas Ltd v R&Q Reinsurance Company (UK) Ltd* [2009] EWHC 2787 (Comm).

[255] *Commercial Union Insurance v NRG Victory Reinsurance* [1998] Lloyd's Rep. I.R. 439.

[256] *Gan Insurance v Tai Ping (Nos 2 and 3)* [2001] Lloyd's Rep. I.R. 667.

applies also to direct insurance, it would seem that only in exceptional circumstances can an assured seek to overturn a decision by insurers not to approve a settlement reached by him.

2. Insurable Interest in Liability Insurance

The insurable interest requirement. It had long been assumed that liability   **20–062** policies fell within the words "other events" contained in the Life Assurance Act 1774 s.1, and were thus regulated by the insurable interest requirements of that Act. On this basis, insurable interest was required at the outset of the insurance (s.1) and the names of all interested parties had to be inserted in the policy (s.2). However, it was held by the Court of Appeal in *Mark Rowlands Ltd v Berni Inns Ltd*[257] and by the Privy Council in *Siu v Eastern Insurance Co Ltd*[258] that 1774 Act does not apply to any form of indemnity insurance. It may be possible to frame what is in essence a liability policy as a life policy. If this occurs, then the 1774 Act is applicable to that policy. This was the situation in *Feasey v Sun Life Assurance Co of Canada*,[259] in which a P & I club was under its direct covers liable to indemnify its shipowner members for any liabilities incurred by them to employees or other persons injured on board members' vessels. For regulatory reasons the club's insurable interest for reinsurance purposes was expressed to be in the lives of injured persons rather than in its liability to members. Langley J. held that the policy, while subject to the 1774 Act was nevertheless valid: there was no intention to wager, so that s.1 was satisfied; and the amounts payable in the event of death or personal injury did not in the aggregate exceed the club's interest, so that s.3 was satisfied. The Court of Appeal affirmed this result by a majority and made the point that a policy expressed to be on a specific subject matter, e.g. lives or property, was capable of being construed as extending to the assured's liability in respect of those lives or property. In the present case, the reinsurance properly construed covered the Club's liabilities to its members even though the policy was expressed as one confined to life.

A liability policy is a policy by which the insurer undertakes to indemnify the assured in the event of his incurring particular forms of liability to third parties. Policies covering property may thus have a first-party element, insuring the property itself, and a third-party element, insuring any liability which might arise from the use of that property. The distinction between goods insurance and liability insurance was of some significance prior to the *Berni Inns*[260] decision, for it was then assumed that the 1774 Act applied to liability policies but not to goods policies. This caused a particular difficulty in respect of motor policies which, in addition to insuring the vehicle itself and the liability of the assured, gave cover to any person driving with the assured's permission. The problem here arose from s.2, which requires the names of all persons interested in the policy to be inserted into it; a strict application of s.2 would have required the assured to add to the policy the names of all persons who he could anticipate as being likely to drive with his permission, so that a failure to do this, or to do so accurately, would result in the policy being illegal. This manifest absurdity was

---

[257] *Mark Rowlands Ltd v Berni Inns Ltd* [1985] 3 All E.R. 473.
[258] *Siu v Eastern Insurance Co Ltd* [1994] 1 All E.R. 213.
[259] *Feasey v Sun Life Assurance Co of Canada* [2003] Lloyd's Rep. I.R. 637, affirming [2002] Lloyd's Rep. I.R. 835.
[260] *Mark Rowlands Ltd v Berni Inns Ltd* [1985] 3 All E.R. 473.

ingeniously overcome by the courts, which held that the policy looked at as a whole was on the car as goods, and was not liability insurance, so that s.2 did not apply to it.[261] The problem of s.2 in the context of motor insurance was solved rather differently by Parliament in what is now s.148(7) of the Road Traffic Act 1988[262] which provides that the insurer is liable to indemnify unidentified persons insured under the policy "notwithstanding anything in any enactment".[263]

Any person who by contract is liable to pay any money in case of the loss of anything has an insurable interest in that thing.[264] On this ground, a shipper may insure his freight,[265] or a consignee his commission.[266] A distinction has nevertheless to be drawn between genuine liability policies and policies disguised as covering liability but in reality amounting to wagering. In *Newbury International Ltd v Reliance National Insurance Co (UK) Ltd*[267] the assured was the sponsor of a series of motor cycle races, and faced liability to pay an associated company £425,000 in the event that a named driver, X, was to finish in the top three in races to be held in New Zealand. Under the agreement between the assured and the associated company, the insurance moneys recovered by the assured were to be paid to the associated company and were to be used by way of investment in a motor racing team run by yet another company in the same group, but there was to be no liability unless insurance moneys were received. Hobhouse J. held that the entire arrangement was a wager, constructed to allow the assured to bet on the ability of X. The assured was not under any genuine liability to make payments to its associated company, but was merely recycling insurance moneys received from the insurer in the event of X's success. The policy was, therefore, void for want of insurable interest. This decision should not be taken to mean that the sponsors of sporting events do not have insurable interest in the outcome of those events where they face a genuine liability to a third party: one illustration given by Hobhouse J. was the promoter of a golf tournament facing liability, by way of a prize, to a competitor who obtained a hole-in-one. That point aside, the abolition by the Gambling Act 2005 of the prohibition on the enforceability of wagering contracts means that the policy would no longer have been void for want of insurable interest, although it might still be argued that the assured had not suffered a loss within the terms of the policy and thus would be precluded from recovering under the common law indemnity principle.

3. EMPLOYER'S LIABILITY INSURANCE

20–063 **Obligation to insure.** An employer faces a variety of common law and statutory liabilities to employees. At common law, an employer is required to provide a

---

[261] *Williams v Baltic Insurance Association of London Ltd* [1924] 2 K.B. 282.

[262] Originally Road Traffic Act 1930 s.30(4), subsequently re-enacted in various forms.

[263] For the use of this provision, see *McCormick v National Motor and Accident Insurance Union* (1934) 49 Ll. LR. 361; *Jones v Birch Brothers Ltd* [1933] 2 K.B. 597 and *Tattersall v Drysdale* [1935] 2 K.B. 174.

[264] Parke J. in *Miller v Warre* (1824) 1 Car. & P. 237 at 239 (1825) 4 B. & C. 538; *Stock v Inglis* (1884) 12 Q.B.D. 564; *Andersen v Morice* (1876) L.R. 1 App.Cas. 713.

[265] *Thompson v Taylor* (1795) 6 T.R. 478: *Flint v Flemyng* (1830) I B. & Ad. 45; *De Vaux v J'Anson* (1839) 7 Scott 507.

[266] *King v Glover* (1806) 2 Bos. & P.N.R. 206; *Knox v Wood* (1808) 1 Camp. 543.

[267] *Newbury International Ltd v Reliance National Insurance Co (UK) Ltd* [1994] 1 Lloyd's Rep. 83.

safe system of work and must also accept vicarious liability for the negligence of any fellow-employee whose negligence has caused injury to his workmate. Under statute, the Factories Act 1961 creates a number of torts, particularly in relation to the fencing of machinery, and the Employers' Liability (Defective Equipment) Act 1969 imposes liability on an employer for injuries caused to an employee by equipment supplied by the employer, even if the manufacturer of that equipment was a third party. The Employers' Liability (Compulsory Insurance) Act 1969 requires every employer to take out liability insurance for the benefit of its employees in order to remove the risk of the employer's insolvency defeating the common law and statutory right of its employees to damages for breach of its duty of care. The basic obligation to insure is contained in s.1(1):

> "Except as otherwise provided by this Act, every employer carrying on any business in Great Britain shall insure, and maintain, insurance, under one or more approved policies with an authorised insurer or insurers against liability for bodily injury or diseases sustained by his employees, and arising out of and in the course of their employment in Great Britain in that business, but except in so far as regulations otherwise provide not including injury or disease suffered or contracted outside Great Britain."

The 1969 Act is supplemented by the Employers' Liability (Compulsory Insurance) Regulations 1998, which came into effect in at various times in 1999, replacing earlier sets of regulations dating back to 1971. The Act applies to employees employed on offshore installations,[268] although the legislation is modified in a number of respects with regard to such employees.[269] A policy must, to comply with the legislation, be issued by an insurer authorised by the Treasury to carry on insurance business in the United Kingdom, in accordance with the Financial Services and Markets Act 2000,[270] or by an insurer authorised elsewhere in the EC selling direct into the United Kingdom.

Employers within the legislation. Section 1(1) restricts compulsory insurance **20–064** to every employer "carrying on any business in Great Britain". The word "business" includes a trade or profession and any activity carried on by a body of persons whether incorporated or unincorporated,[271] and an employer who does not have a place of business in Great Britain is deemed not to carry on business in Great Britain.[272] The latter restriction has been modified by the Offshore Installations and Pipeline Works (Management and Administration) Regulations 1995 reg.21, which provide that insurance is compulsory in respect of employees on oil rigs and similar structures outside territorial waters.

Exempted employers. Section 3 of the 1969 Act, supplemented by reg.9 of and **20–065** Sch.2 to the 1998 Regulations, list the employers exempted from the compulsory insurance requirement. Those exempted by s.3 are:

(1) a health service body, as defined in s.60(7) of the National Health Service and Community Care Act 1990, and a National Health Service trust

---

[268] Defined by the Offshore Installations and Pipeline Works (Management and Administration) Regulations 1995 (SI 1995/738) reg.3, as a structure standing in water for the exploitation or transport of mineral resources.

[269] The modifications are set out in the Offshore Installations and Pipeline works (Management and Administration) Regulations 1995 (SI 1995/743), revoking earlier provisions.

[270] 1969 Act s.1(3)(b) (as amended) and s.1(3A).

[271] 1969 Act s.(3)(c).

[272] 1969 Act s.1(3)(d).

established under s.25 of the National Health Service Act 2006, s.18 of the National Health Service (Wales) Act 2006 or the National Health Service (Scotland) Act 1978, an NHS foundation trust and a Primary Care Trust established under s.18 of the National Health Service Act 2006;

(2) the Common Council of the City of London, the Council of a London Borough, the council of a county or county borough in Wales, the Broads Authority, a council constituted under s.2 of the Local Government etc. (Scotland) Act 1994 in England and Wales or joint committee in Scotland which is so constituted as to include among its members representatives of any such council, the Strathclyde Passenger Transport Authority, any joint authority established by Pt IV of the Local Government Act 1985, the London Fire and Emergency Planning Authority and any police authority;

(3) the Commission for Equality and Human Rights;

(4) any body corporate established by or under any enactment for the carrying on of any industry or part of an industry, or of any undertaking, under national ownership or control.

The list in the Regulations for the most part consists of governmental or quasi-governmental bodies, including government departments, foreign governments, inter-governmental organisations, and transport, judicial and educational bodies. A further exception was added by the Employers' Liability (Compulsory Insurance) (Amendment) Regulations 2004, namely:

"Any employer which is a company that has only one employee and that employee also owns fifty per cent or more of the issued share capital in that company."

This exception is designed to remove from the compulsory insurance require-ment sole traders who have adopted the corporate form for trading. Unin-corporated sole traders are not within the legislation, and the amendment created a "level playing field between the self-employed who have no employees and companies that employ only their owner".

20–066   Employees within the legislation. The employer is required to insure, in respect of an individual who has entered into or works under a contract of service or apprenticeship, whether the work is manual or clerical and whether the contract is express or implied, oral or written.[273] Independent contractors used by the employer, and other visitors to the employer's premises, are outside the scope of the 1969 Act. Also excluded are near relations of the employer. Under s.2(2)(a) insurance is not required in respect of: an employee of whom the employer is the husband, wife, civil partner, father, mother, grandfather, grandmother, step-father, step-mother, son, daughter, grandson, granddaughter, step-son, step-daughter, brother, sister, half-brother or half-sister;

There is no obligation to insure any employee not ordinarily resident in Great Britain.[274] That exclusion has been modified by reg.1 of the 1998 Regulations, which requires cover to be extended to "relevant employees", defined as any employee who is ordinarily resident in the United Kingdom, and any employee

---

[273] 1969 Act s.2(1).

[274] 1969 Act s.2(2)(b). Such an employee has no action against the employer if the employer has not insured against injuries suffered abroad, and has not warned of the absence of insurance: *Reid v Rush & Tompkins Group Plc* [1989] 3 All E.R. 228.

who is not ordinary resident in Great Britain but who has been employed on an offshore installation for a continuous period of not less than seven days[275] or an employee not ordinarily resident in Great Britain but who has been present in Great Britain for a continuous period of not less than fourteen days in the course of his employment.

Scope of the duty to insure. The insurance requirement is imposed only in respect of bodily injury or diseases.[276] The employer's liability for any property belonging to employees which is lost or damaged by the employer's negligence may or may not be insured, at the employer's option. The insurance need cover only the liability of an employer to his employees arising out of the course of employment. Thus an employee who has an action against his employer for reasons unconnected with his work on behalf of his employer is not required to be covered by the employer's insurance.

20–067

The amount of insurance required under a policy effected on or after January 1, 2000 or falling for renewal during 1999 is £5 million in respect of claims relating to any one or more of his employees arising out of any one occurrence, although this sum includes costs and expenses incurred by the employer in respect of any claim.[277] The word "occurrence" has given rise to some difficulty in insurance law, as it may be taken, with equal plausibility, to mean either the event giving rise to injuries, or the injuries themselves, although the generally accepted view is that the former is correct. It may be assumed that the deliberate use of the word "occurrence" is intended to achieve that interpretation, and indeed reg.3(1)(a) specifically refers to "a claim relating to one or more of the employees". This has the potential for unfortunate consequences, for it is easy to con template an occurrence which causes multiple injuries exceeding the obligatory figure, and it might have been better to stipulate a minimum figure in respect of each individual employee or claim.

A parent company may insure to this extent on behalf of itself and all of its subsidiaries.[278]

Approved policies. A policy is "approved" for the purposes of s.1(1) if it does not contain exemptions which are prohibited by the 1998 Regulations. Regulation 2 states that there is prohibited in any contract any condition which provides (in whatever terms) that no liability (either generally or in respect of a particular claim) shall arise under the policy, or that any such liability so arising shall cease if[279]:

20–068

(a) "Some specified thing is done or omitted to be done after the happening of the event giving rise to a claim under the policy".[280]
(b) "The policyholder does not take reasonable care to protect his employees against the risk of bodily injury or disease in the course of their

---

[275] See also the Offshore Installations and Pipeline Works (Management and Administration) Regulations 1995 reg.21(3).

[276] Including claims by dependants under the Fatal Accidents Act 1976: *Re T&N Ltd (No.4)* [2006] Lloyd's Rep. I.R. 817.

[277] 1998 Regulations reg.3(1).

[278] 1998 Regulations reg.3(2).

[279] The 1969 Act is far less generous to employee victims than is the Road Traffic Act 1988 to the victims of negligent motorists, the 1988 Act containing a comprehensive list of unenforceable policy restrictions. See Ch.22, below.

[280] 1969 Act s.2(1)(a).

employment".[281] This largely reflects the common law rule that a reasonable care provision excludes a claim only if the assured intends to cause harm or is carried out with reckless disregard for the consequences.

(c) "The policyholder fails to comply with the requirements of any enactment for the protection of employees against the risk of bodily injury or disease in the course of their employment".[282]

(d) "The policyholder does not keep specified records or provides the insurer with or makes available to it information from such records".[283] At common law this type of obligation is effective to discharge the insurers only where it is construed as a condition precedent.[284]

It will be noted that the legislation does nothing to prevent the insurer's reliance on the assured's misrepresentation of, or failure to disclose, a material fact, and on the assured's breach of warranty.

The Regulations also prohibit any condition which requires either the employee or the employer to pay the first amount of any claim or any aggregation of claims.[285] The effect of this is to prohibit the use of deductibles, although this may be overcome in practice by imposing upon the assured employer an obligation to repay a given sum to the insurers in the event of claims (either generally or of a given type) under the policy: by this means, the insurance moneys are made available in full to the assured, and the risk of his insolvency is borne by the insurers rather than by injured claimant employees. If the sum which has to be repaid is substantial, the assured may take out separate insurance against liability for having to repay that sum.[286]

The insurer is, despite these prohibitions, entitled to include in a policy a condition which confers a right of recourse against the employer in respect of the satisfaction of any claim paid by the insurer. The effect of this is that, while the insurer cannot avoid liability to pay claims made by reason of the injuries to an employee, the insurer may in specified circumstances—most importantly, with regard to the circumstances which would otherwise have fallen within any of the conditions prohibited by the 1998 Regulations—seek to recover some or all of its payment from the employer. The point here is that the risk of the employer's insolvency is borne by the insurer and not by the injured employee.

20–069   Form and duration of cover. There is nothing in the 1969 Act or the Regulations made under it which dictates the type of policy to be obtained by the employer. As discussed above, liability policies may be in any one of three forms: claims made, which respond to claims made against the assured during the currency of the policy; losses occurring, which respond to injuries suffered by an employee during the currency of the policy; and events, which respond to incidents occurring during the currency of the policy. Traditionally employers' liability policies are written on an events basis, which means that the insurer on risk in the year when the employer's negligence occurs is the insurer facing liability. A losses occurring policy, by contrast, will not catch an incident

---

[281] 1969 Act s.2(1)(b).

[282] 1969 Act s.2(1)(c).

[283] 1969 Act s.2(1)(d).

[284] *Re Bradley and Essex and Suffolk Accident Indemnity Society* [1912] 1 K.B. 415.

[285] 1998 Regulations reg.2(2).

[286] These arrangements had been adopted by T&N in respect of their liability to employees for asbestos injuries. See *T&N v Sun Alliance* [2004] Lloyd's Rep. I.R. 102; *T&N v Sun Alliance (No.2)* [2004] Lloyds Rep. I.R. 106.

occurring during the currency of the policy which gives rise to injury in a later year, typically the pattern with asbestos exposures. This means, for example, that if an employee is exposed to asbestos in a year where there is losses occurring cover in force, and suffers injury as a result of that exposure in a later year when a claim is made then unless the employer happens to have losses occurring or claims made cover for that year then there is no insurance in place to cover the loss. For this reason it might be thought that only events-based coverage can comply with the legislation. In practice, however, there are some instances in which claims made insurance has been taken out with respect to employers' liability risks, and such policies will plainly not cover incidents occurring during their currency unless a claim is made against the employer in the course of the policy year. It is thus doubtful whether losses occurring and claims made policies comply with the legislation. In *Durham v BAI (Run Off) Ltd*[287] Burton J. held that employers' liability insurance written on an "injury sustained" basis was ambiguous and referred to the date of exposure rather than to the date of injury. By virtue of this reasoning an employee who is negligently exposed to asbestos or some other harmful agent (at least after the commencement date of the 1969 legislation) will, armed with a judgment against his employer, be able to enforce that judgment against the insurers on risk in the year of exposure (or the Financial Services Compensation Scheme if the insurers are no longer in business).

However, in *Re T&N Ltd (No.4)*[288] it was held that there was nothing in the Act which, following the termination of the policy for a given policy year, prevented the assured and insurers from entering into a commutation agreement which puts a financial cap on the amount of all claims against the insurers in that year. This reasoning was based on interpreting the Act as requiring no more than that liability insurance has to be in place at any one time: once the policy has lapsed (and has been replaced) it can be commuted even though this may have the effect of reducing (or extinguishing) the sums available to compensate employees may subsequently make claims based on exposure or injury, as the case may be. This reasoning is open to severe doubt to the extent that it undermines the efficacy of the 1969 Act, but it does indicate that losses occurring and claims made covers are valid, the only requirement being that there is insurance in force at any one time even though it may not be possible for claims to be made under it.

Failure to insure. An employer who fails to conform with the requirements of **20–070** s.1(1) is guilty of a criminal offence.[289] In the case of an offshore installation, the duty to insure, and criminal liability for the failure to do so, is imposed upon the owner of the installation.[290] The courts have held under the Road Traffic Act 1988 that a person using or causing or permitting the use of a vehicle without insurance commits the tort of breach of statutory duty. However, in *Richardson v Pitt-Stanley*,[291] the Court of Appeal held that the 1969 Act does not give rise to civil liability, so that neither the employer company nor its defaulting directors could be sued for damages. The decision is of little impact as regards the company itself, which is in any event liable to the employee for the act which caused his injuries. The real effect is to prevent the employee from seeking

---

[287] *Durham v BAI (Run Off) Ltd* [2009] Lloyd's Rep. I.R. 295.
[288] *Re T&N Ltd (No.4)* [2006] Lloyd's Rep. I.R. 817.
[289] 1969 Act s.5.
[290] 1969 Act s.5A, inserted for the purpose by the Offshore Installations and Pipeline Works (Management and Administration) Works Regulations 1995 reg.2. The consent of the Secretary of State is required for any prosecution: s.5B. as inserted by the 1995 Regulations.
[291] *Richardson v Pitt-Stanley* [1995] 1 All E.R. 460.

damages from directors who, while not personally responsible for any injuries inflicted, are party to the company's failure to insure. There is a further important difference between the road traffic and employers' liability schemes. Under the former, the Motor Insurers Bureau provides a fall-back compensation scheme so that the third-party victim is protected where the user of the vehicle has failed to insure. By contrast, the employers' liability scheme is not supported by any fall-back funding of this nature. This lacuna is potentially a serious one, as injuries caused to an employee by an uninsured and insolvent employer may go uncompensated, at least in terms of common law damages. In February 2010 the Department of Work and Pensions issued a Consultation Paper in which the establishment of such a body was proposed, but its activities are to be confined to cases where the employer's insurers cannot be traced; it will not benefit the employees of uninsured employees. It has yet to be determined whether, if this body is established, it will deal with all claims, or only long-tail claims, or possibly only mesothelioma claims: it is indeed only in the latter two situations that the body is likely to be needed.

20–071   **Enforcement.** The Act is enforced by disclosure, and the disclosure requirements are themselves backed by criminal sanctions.[292] The insurer must give to the employer a certificate of insurance in statutory form under s.4(1), and this is then to be displayed and otherwise made available to inspection in accordance with s.4(2). The certificate must be issued within thirty days of the insurance commencing or being renewed,[293] and must state the name of the policy holder, the date of the commencement of the insurance policy, the date of the expiry of the insurance policy and that the minimum cover provided by the insurance is £5 million, although if the greater figure is insured that figure must itself be stated.[294] If the insurance relates to the subsidiaries of a parent company, the certificate must also state in a prominent place that subsidiaries are also covered.[295]

Display requirements are set out in reg.5. The employer must display one or more copies of the certificate at each place of business at which a relevant employee is employed. Each copy displayed must be in such position and of such size and legibility that it may easily be seen and read by relevant employees, and must be reasonably protected from being defaced or damaged.[296] Each copy is to be kept on display until the policy itself has expired or been terminated. The display rules do not apply in relation to offshore installations: the employer's duty in such cases is to make a copy of the certificate available to any employee who requests it, within ten days of such request. Display is no longer mandatory; reg.5 was amended by the Employers' Liability (Compulsory Insurance) (Amendment) Regulations 2008,[297] which permit electronic record keeping as an alternative to display.

---

[292] 1969 Act s.4(3).

[293] 1998 Regulations reg.4(2).

[294] 1998 Regulations Sch.1. The form of the certificate has been changed from that existing under the earlier Regulations. Where a policy is current on January 1, 1999, the 1971 Regulations apply to the certificate until the policy expires or until January 1, 2000, whichever is sooner. A policy renewed between January 1, 1999 and April 1, 1999 may be in 1971 form, provided that it is replaced no later than April 1, 2000: reg.1.

[295] 1998 Regulations Sch.1.

[296] 1998 Regulations reg.5(2). Under the earlier regulations the certificate had only to be protected against the weather.

[297] SI 2008/1765.

Certificates are subject to two forms of administrative supervision. First, an inspector authorised by the Secretary of State may issue a written notice to an employer requiring him to produce or send the certificate or a copy of the certificate to the inspector[298]; the requirement may extend to any certificate which the employer is required to retain after the expiry of the policy under the forty year rule introduced the 1998 Regulations, discussed below. Secondly, an inspector appointed by the Secretary of State who is visiting premises may demand the production of the certificate of insurance,[299] although the inspector must himself show his authorisation to the employer on request.[300]

The employer's insolvency. If the employer should become insolvent at a time when it is liable to an employee, that employee is entitled to stand in the shoes of the employer in relation to its liability policy under the general provisions of the Third Parties (Rights against Insurers) Act 2010. The employer is required to adhere to the conditions of the policy in much the same way as the employer, a rule which greatly limits the efficacy of the 2010 Act in insolvency cases. A major difficulty which has arisen in relation to the operation of the 2010 Act is that, in a case in which the employee does not appreciate for some years after his employment has terminated that he has suffered injury or disease which is work-related—typically a disease caused by exposure to a dangerous substance but symptoms do not emerge for some years—and the employer has ceased to trade, the employee may find some difficulty in tracing his employer's insurers who were on risk in the year in which the event causing the injury occurred. This matter has been addressed by reg.4(4). Under this provision, the employer is required to retain in any eye-readable form[301] the certificate issued to him for a period of 40 years beginning on the date on which the insurance to which it relates is commenced or renewed. The obligation to retain the certificate applies only to insurance policies in force immediately before January 1, 1999,[302] so that the obligation to retain is not retroactive. The statutory scheme is supplemented, since November 1999, by the Code of Practice agreed between the Government, the Association of British Insurers and the Lloyd's Market Association for tracing employers' liability insurance policies (ELCOP). Proposals published in 2010 would replace that body by a new organisation, the Employers' Liability Tracing Office (ELTO) which would operate an electronic database of policies and would operate the existing tracing service.

20–072

Transfer of the employer's business. Under the Transfer of Undertakings (Protection of Employment) Regulations 2006,[303] which implement the EC's 1977 Acquired Rights Directive,[304] any transfer of an undertaking from one employer to another is not to prejudice the rights of the transferor's employees. The effect of the Regulations is that the transfer does not terminate the employment contract, and that the transferor's obligations and liabilities towards the employee are transferred to the transferee. In each of the joined cases *Martin v Lancashire County Council* and *Bernadone v Pall Mall Services*,[305] an

20–073

---

[298] 1998 Regulations reg.6.
[299] 1998 Regulations reg.7.
[300] 1998 Regulations reg.8.
[301] 1998 Regulations reg.4(5).
[302] 1998 Regulations reg.10.
[303] SI 2006/246.
[304] Council Directive 77/187/EEC (a consolidated version of which was adopted in 2001).
[305] *Martin v Lancashire County Council* and *Bernadone v Pall Mall Services* [2000] Lloyd's Rep. I.R. 665.

employee was injured due to the negligence of the transferor employer, and subsequently the undertaking was transferred to a fresh employer. The Court of Appeal held that the Regulations operated to transfer the assured's personal injury claim, so that it had to be brought against the transferee. The problem posed by that ruling was that the transferor's liability policy would have covered a claim against the transferor, whereas it was almost certain that the transferee's liability policy would not respond to a claim by a transferred employee. The Court of Appeal overcame this difficulty by holding that the Regulations were to be taken as transferring to the transferee the transferor's claim against its liability insurers. This was so because prior to the transfer the transferor had a contingent right of claim against its liability insurers, and the Regulations were effective to transfer all rights, duties and obligations to the transferee, including the transferor's contingent insurance claim. The fact that the right was under a separate insurance contract and not the contract of employment was immaterial, as the right arose in connection with the employment contract.

4. PRODUCT LIABILITY POLICIES

20–074 **Period of cover.** A typical product liability cover will be taken out on a claims made basis, with the insurance applying to all claims made against the assured by a third party during the currency of the policy. However, some policies may specify, as the trigger of cover, that the loss must occur within the period of the policy. This was held, in *AS Screenprint Ltd v British Reserve Insurance Co Ltd*,[306] to be the proper construction of a policy which provided cover against loss or damage "happening . . . during the period of insurance".

20–075 **Risks covered.** The insurance is generally against all sums which the assured becomes liable to pay in respect of death, personal injury or property damage caused by goods supplied by the assured.

The words "in respect of" presuppose a causative link between the event or occurrence and the physical consequences of the damage. This principle was restated in *Tesco Stores Ltd v Constable*.[307] Accordingly, pure financial loss is excluded. Thus, there is no indemnity for liability flowing from the loss of goodwill suffered by the purchaser of the products[308] or for loss of potential future custom where premises have to be closed by reason of a defect in products supplied in the construction of the premises.[309]

20–076 **Loss must be external to products supplied.** The law of tort does not impose liability upon a contractor to a purchaser or occupier of land in respect of defects which reduce its value but which do not cause physical damage to other property or personal injury.[310] In the same way, a products liability policy is concerned with damage caused to persons and other property by a defective product

---

[306] *AS Screenprint Ltd v British Reserve Insurance Co Ltd* [1999] Lloyd's Rep. I.R. 430.

[307] *Tesco Stores Ltd v Constable* [2008] Lloyd's Rep. I.R. 636.

[308] *AS Screenprint Ltd v British Reserve Insurance Co Ltd* [1999] Lloyd's Rep. I.R. 430; *Rodan International Ltd v Commercial Union* [1999] Lloyd's Rep. I.R. 495; *Jan de Nul (UK) Ltd v NV Royal Belge* [2001] Lloyd's Rep. I.R. 327; *James Budgett Sugars Ltd v Norwich Union Insurance* [2003] Lloyd's Rep. I.R. 114.

[309] *Horbury Building Systems Ltd v Hampden Insurance* [2007] Lloyd's Rep. I.R. 247.

[310] *D and F Estates Ltd v Church Commissioners* [1989] A.C. 177; *Murphy v Brentwood District Council* [1991] 1 A.C. 398.

supplied by the assured: it is not concerned with a claim against the assured for breach of contract on the basis that the product supplied does not work or is damaged. There must, therefore, be some form of external loss.[311] In *Horbury Building Systems Ltd v Hampden Insurance*[312] Keene L.J. commented that a product liability policy which is aimed at covering liabilities in tort should be construed consistently with tort law. It follows, therefore, that a product liability policy designed to cover tortious liabilities (as opposed to general contractual liabilities) will not cover claims for pure economic loss, and that what is required is that the product supplied has caused external physical damage.[313]

The principle may give rise to borderline difficulties where the product supplied by the assured is to be installed in some larger item for use or resale by the customer. The distinction to be drawn here is between physical damage being caused to the larger item and the devaluing of the larger item without it suffering any damage as such, the test being whether there has been any physical change to the larger item by reason of the incorporation of the defective product into it. It is clear, therefore, that if a contaminated raw material is supplied to a food manufacturer, and is incorporated into the food which thereby undergoes a physical change and becomes contaminated, the insurers are liable for any claim against the assured in respect of the larger item itself but not for the defective nature of the product itself. It was thus held in *Tioxide Europe Ltd v CGU International Insurance Plc*[314] that a whitening pigment is used in the manufacture of PVC replacement doors and windows, but which caused the PVC to "pink" under certain conditions, had caused physical damage to the PVC. It was similarly held in *Pilkington United Kingdom Ltd v CGU Insurance Plc*[315] that the costs of repairing 13 defective glass panels installed in a roof consisting of some 3,000 glass panels was not covered by a product liability policy as the policy responded only to external physical damage to some other item, and that the installation of a defective product into a larger item did not amount to such damage.

A typical exclusion codifying this principle would be in respect of liability for injuries suffered by third parties:

> "[R]esulting from the failure of the named Insured's products . . . to perform the function or serve the purpose intended by the named insured, if such failure is due to a mistake or deficiency in any design, formula, plan, specification, advertising material or printed instructions prepared or developed by any insured".

In *John Wyeth & Brothers Ltd v Cigna Insurance Co. of Europe SA/NV*[316] the Court of Appeal held the assured's liability for supplying a drug which achieved

---

[311] *Rodan International Ltd v Commercial Union* [1999] Lloyd's Rep. I.R. 495. See *Tesco Stores Ltd v Constable* [2008] Lloyd's Rep. I.R. 636, which confirms that pure contractual liability is excluded even though external damage is caused.

[312] *Horbury Building Systems Ltd v Hampden Insurance* [2007] Lloyd's Rep. I.R. 247.

[313] *Bovis Construction Ltd v Commercial Union Assurance* [2001] Lloyd's Rep. I.R. 321. See also *Reilly v National Insurance & Guarantee Corporation Ltd* [2008] Lloyd's Rep. I.R. 695, where an exclusion clause applying to "the failure of any fire or intruder alarm switch gear control panel or machinery to perform its intended function" was construed as meaning that a failure of any of the listed elements removed the insurers' liability whether or not it related to a fire or intruder alarm, part of the reasoning being that the policy by its nature did not cover the failure of the subject matter to fulfil its function.

[314] *Tioxide Europe Ltd v CGU International Insurance Plc* [2005] Lloyd's Rep. I.R. 114, affirmed on other grounds [2006] Lloyd's Rep. I.R. 31. See also *James Budgett Sugars Ltd v Norwich Union Insurance* [2003] Lloyd's Rep. I.R. 114.

[315] *Pilkington United Kingdom Ltd v CGU Insurance Plc* [2004] Lloyd's Rep. I.R. 891.

[316] *John Wyeth & Brothers Ltd v Cigna Insurance Co of Europe SA/NV* [2001] Lloyd's Rep. I.R. 420.

its purpose but which had severe side-effects not drawn to the attention of users was not excluded under this provision, as it applied only where the drug failed to work at all: any injuries caused were, therefore, within the scope of the cover. This ruling is consistent with the general principle that a product liability policy covers extraneous damage, and not devaluation of the product itself.

In the same way, product liability policies may also exclude liability in respect of recalling and repairing goods which are found to be defective.

20–077   *Strict liability and contractual liability.*   Product liability policies typically cover negligence claims against the manufacturer, although cover will often also be extended to cover strict liability torts, and also to contractual claims against the manufacturer which have a tortious counterpart. The consideration underlying the latter point is that a typical products liability policy is not designed to protect the assured against claims for loss of profits by a customer but only against claims for physical injury to persons and damage to other goods. Some policies may, however, extend cover to claims for strict liability torts and to breach of contract. The insuring clause in *Lumbermen's Mutual Casualty Co v Bovis Lend Lease Ltd*[317] applied to:

> "1.   any neglect error or omission or breach of warranty of authority in the conduct of the Insured or of any party presently or previously employed or engaged by the Insured or for whom the Insured is responsible
> 2.   breach of warranty or guarantee of the fitness or suitability for purpose or the reasonable fitness or suitability of any work or materials which are the subject of a contract (including any deed of collateral warranty or duty of care agreement) entered into by the Insured, or by any party on behalf of the Insured".

Colman J. construed para.1 of this wording as covering tort claims, including strict liability torts: there was no need for the assured to show negligence-based liability. This was apparent from the reference to breach of warranty of authority, which could be both negligent and innocent. Paragraph 2 was held to apply to contract-based claims, although those contract claims falling outside para.2 were potentially covered by para.1 if there was a relevant neglect or error giving rise to an action in tort.

5. Directors' and Officers' Liability Insurance

20–078   **The need for insurance.**   The potential liabilities faced by company directors have been developed over many years by the courts, and consist of a combination of common law duties of care and fiduciary duties. Those duties have now been codified in the Companies Act 2006 and replace the pre-existing law although the legislation is to be interpreted and applied consistently with the old law: Companies Act 2006 s.170(3)–(4). There remain other common law duties to third parties. The duties are now as follows. In all cases the civil remedy for breach of duty is the same as would apply at common law or in equity: Companies Act 2006 s.178.

> (1)   A director of a company must act in accordance with the company's constitution and must exercise his powers only for the purpose for which

---

[317] *Lumbermen's Mutual Casualty Co v Bovis Lend Lease Ltd* [2005] Lloyd's Rep. I.R. 74.

they were conferred: Companies Act 2006 s.171. It is unlikely that breach of this duty would give rise to damages against the director, although he may face an action for injunctive relief.

(2) A director of a company must act in the way he considers, in good faith, would be most likely to promote the success of the company for the benefit of the members as a whole, having regard to the likely consequences of any decision, the interests of the company's employees, the need to foster business relationships, the impact of the company's operations on the community and the environment, the desirability for maintaining a reputation for high standards of business conduct and the need to act fairly as between members of the company: Companies Act 2006 s.172. This is largely an aspirational duty which almost certainly cannot found a cause of action against him.

(3) A director of a company must exercise independent judgment: Companies Act 2006 s.173. Similarly, this is an aspirational duty.

(4) A director of a company must exercise reasonable care skill and diligence to the standard to be expect of a reasonably diligent person with both the general knowledge, skill and experience to be expected of a person expected to be carrying out the director's functions and the general knowledge, skill and experience of the director himself: Companies Act 2006 s.174. Breach of this duty may well give rise to an action in damages.

(5) A director of a company must avoid conflicts of interest, and in particular must not exploit any property or opportunity whether or not the company could itself have done so: Companies Act 2006 s.175. This is a codification of equitable principles. If a director does make a profit from his office, he is required to disgorge his profit to the company. This is not a liability in damages as such, because the company may not have suffered any loss, and in any event the profit made by the director is not one which he was permitted to make. Accordingly, any liability to account for secret profits is almost certainly not covered by a liability policy.

(6) A director of a company must not accept benefits from a third party by reason of his capacity as director or by reason of his doing or not doing any act: Companies Act 2006 s.176. This is similar in nature to the secret profits rule in (5) above.

(7) A director of a company must declare the nature and extent of his interest in any proposed or actual transaction with the company: Companies Act 2006 s.177. This type of conduct is most unlikely to give rise to damages.

(8) Other statutory duties set out in the Companies Act 2006. These are numerous and for the most part technical, and involve matters such as the holding of meetings and the issue of shares. Only rarely do these duties give rise to civil liability.

(9) Duties may be owed to persons dealing with the company. Personal liability may be incurred by a director who acts without authority or who gives misleading advice to a potential investor in, or a client of, his company, although the House of Lords held in *Williams v Natural Life Health Products*[318] that such liability can arise in exceptional circumstances only involving a special assumption of personal responsibility

[318] *Williams v Natural Life Health Products* [1998] 2 All E.R. 577.

and not in the ordinary case where the director has purported to act on behalf of the company.

(10) In appropriate circumstances a director may be found to be a joint tortfeasor with his company, but this requires conduct on the part of the director which actively induces the company to incur tortious liability.[319]

As will be seen, therefore, many of the duties owed by a company director are unlikely to give rise to civil liability at all, or if they do then of a type which is not insurable. Much of the value of a directors' and officers' policy is in the coverage that it provides for defence costs.

20–079 **The right to insure.** Under the Companies Act 2006 s.232(1) any provision in any contract or in the articles (Companies Act 2006 s.232(3)) which purports to exempt (to any extent) a company director from any liability for negligence, default, breach of duty or breach of trust in relation to the company, is void. Further, any provision by which a company directly or indirectly provides (to any extent) an indemnity for a director of the company or an associated company is also void (Companies Act 2006 s.232(2)). The latter principle is subject to three important exceptions.

First, the company is, by the Companies Act 2006 ss.232(2)(b) and 234(1), permitted to grant an indemnity to a director under a "qualifying third party indemnity provision" in the circumstances specified by s.234 of the Act. Protection is extended on much the same terms by the Companies Act 2006 s.235 to a qualifying pension scheme indemnity provision. A third-party indemnity provision is a provision which gives indemnity against liability incurred by the director to a person other than the company or an associated company (Companies Act 2006 s.234(2)). Such a provision is a qualifying provision if it satisfies two conditions:

(1) It does not provide any indemnity against any liability incurred by the director to pay either a fine imposed in criminal proceedings or a sum payable to a regulatory authority by way of a penalty in respect of non-compliance with any requirement of a regulatory nature (however arising) (Companies Act 2006 s.234(3)).

(2) The provision does not provide any indemnity against any liability incurred by the director:

(a) in defending any criminal proceedings in which he is convicted; or

(b) in defending any civil proceedings brought by the company, or an associated company, in which judgment is given against him; or

(c) in connection with any unsuccessful application by the director for relief in respect of honest acquisition of shares by the director as nominee (Companies Act 2006 s.661) or for general relief from liability in the case of honest and reasonable conduct (Companies Act 2006 s.1157): see Companies Act 2006 s.234(6).

---

[319] *MCA Records Inc v Charly Records Ltd* [2003] 1 B.C.L.C. 93; *Societa Explosivi Industriali SpA v Ordnance Technologies (UK) Ltd* [2007] EWHC 2875 (Comm).

In each of these cases the judgment must have become final, in that time has expired for the making of an appeal or the final appeal has been disposed of by the courts (Companies Act 2006 s.234(4)–(5)).

A qualifying third-party indemnity provision must be included in the directors' annual financial report to the company (Companies Act 2006 s.236) and a copy must otherwise be available for inspection: Companies Act 2006 ss.237 and 238.

Secondly, s.205 of the Companies Act 2006 permit the company to make a loan to a director: (a) to fund his director's defence costs in defending any civil or criminal proceedings; and (b) to fund the costs of a director applying for relief from liability (under the Companies Act 2006 ss.661 and 1157). However, in the event that a director is unsuccessful in the proceedings brought against or by him, as the case may be, the company must be reimbursed by the director at the completion of the proceedings. Under s.206 of the Companies Act 2006 the company may fund the costs of a director defending himself before a regulatory authority, and here there is no provision for repayment.

Thirdly, ss.232(2)(c) and 233 of the Companies Act 2006 authorise a company to purchase and maintain for a director of the company or an associated company insurance against any liability for negligence, default, breach of duty or breach of trust. The power of the company to take out liability insurance cover was in doubt until the passing of the Companies Act 1989 s.137, which introduced the power to insure. A company which wishes to take out insurance for the benefit of directors must disclose any payments by way of premium in the company's accounts.

Nature of the policy

Risks covered. A D&O policy may potentially cover three categories of claims.   **20–080**

First, under *Side A Cover*, the insurers agree to pay any loss suffered by a director where the director has not been indemnified by the company. Some clauses go on to exclude liability if the company is permitted to indemnify the director. The latter exclusion is of some significance, because if the company is permitted to grant an indemnity then there is no insurance and is of no assistance to the director for him to argue that the company has refused to indemnify him or does not have the funds to do so. The proviso does not say that Side A cover attaches if the company has not provided an indemnity, or that it is unable to provide an indemnity, only that it is not *permitted* to provide an indemnity. If the company is not permitted by law to indemnify the director, there are relatively few other cases in which the Side A can respond either as a matter of general law or according to the terms of the policy.

Secondly, under *Side B Cover*, the policy covers any sums paid by the company to the director by way of indemnification for the director's own liability. A director may not himself sue under Side B cover: the only insured person in respect of that cover is the company.[320] The company is not insured by Side B against any personal liability faced by the company itself. Thus if a claim is made against the company, and the directors are not named as co-defendants, Side B does not respond.[321] It was similarly held in Victoria in *Intergraph Best*

[320] *Porter v GIO* 2002 N.S.W.S.C.
[321] *Medical Mutual Insurance Co of Maine v Indian Harbor Insurance Co* 2009 B.L. 219379 (1st Cir, October 8, 2009).

(Vic) Pty Ltd v QBE Insurance Ltd[322] that if a company takes upon itself the liability for meeting the legal costs incurred by directors in proceedings covered by the policy, as opposed to indemnifying the directors for costs incurred by them in those proceedings, the policy does not respond to a claim by the company. In such a case the company is seeking to recover its own legal costs, not those of the directors. The distinction is a technical one, in that the policy would have responded had the company required the directors to incur the costs for themselves and then indemnified the directors. That, however, did not happen. Care thus has to be taken in drafting a settlement where the potential liability of the directors is at stake. In *Vero Insurance v Baycorp Advantage*[323] a claim was made against a company and its directors, and the company entered into a settlement "on behalf of itself and each of the" directors for a sum which exceeded the amount claimed from the directors themselves. The New South Wales Court of Appeal held that the company, by entering into that settlement, had not thereby rendered the directors personally liable for the agreed amount.

Thirdly, under *Side C Cover*, the company insures against its own personal liability. This may be found in many D&O policies, and there is stand-alone Side C Cover now on offer. There is an increasing trend in shareholder actions against the company itself. That trend was given a significant boost by the ruling of the House of Lords in *Soden v British and Commonwealth Holdings Plc*,[324] holding that a claim by shareholders against the company may in some cases rank equally with a claim by other unsecured creditors, so that a major claim against the company will erode whatever personal cover is open to directors under Side A.[325] For that reason, Side C cover has been removed from some policies and may instead be purchased as a stand-alone product.

In addition, directors may seek their own private insurance cover if they fear that Side A cover may not be adequate for their needs. This may be the case in particular where the policy provides for A, B and C cover, and the limits of indemnity are eroded by B and C claims.

20–081 *The assured.* The policyholder under a D&O policy will be the company itself, although the directors will be named as assured parties. The company acts as agent for the directors in making the placement, and accordingly they will have contractual rights against the insurers. Independently of agency, the directors will (subject to exclusion) be allowed to enforce its terms under the Contracts (Rights of Third Parties) Act 1999. For the same reasons, where a broker is instructed to obtain D&O cover for its directors, but fails to do so, the directors can bring proceedings against the broker either on the basis that the broker owes them a duty of care or on the basis that they are beneficiaries of the contract with the broker and can enforce its terms in accordance with the 1999 Act.[326]

---

[322] *Intergraph Best (Vic) Pty Ltd v QBE Insurance Ltd* 2005 V.S.C.A. 180. The decision contains copious citation of US authority on the distinction between a company which indemnifies its directors and a company which assumes direct liability for them.

[323] *Vero Insurance v Baycorp Advantage* [2004] N.S.W.C.A. 390.

[324] *Soden v British and Commonwealth Holdings Plc* [1998] A.C. 298. The Australian High Court has followed suit: *Sons of Gwalia Ltd v Margaretic* [2007] H.C.A. 1.

[325] It is understood that some policies now contain order of payment clauses which require directors to be paid first. However, these can work only if claims against directors are simultaneous, otherwise the common law "first past the post" principle will apply to insurance recoveries. Attempts are being made to draft clauses which give director indemnity claims priority.

[326] *Crowson v HSBC Insurance Brokers* Unreported, January 2010.

If the company is a parent company the policy will generally be expressed as extending to all subsidiaries under the ownership or control of the insured parent.

The result is a composite policy which covers the respective rights and interests of the directors of each company separately[327] as well as—if Side C cover is included—the companies themselves. The creation of composite insurance at one time gave rise to some difficulty, as it had to be shown that the parent company acted as agent for the subsidiaries for the necessary privity of contract to be created as between the insurer and the subsidiaries, in accordance with the principles laid down in *National Oilwell (UK) Ltd v Davy Offshore Ltd*.[328] In practice no problem arose in relation to existing subsidiary companies, as the parent company would plainly be regarded as the agent for its subsidiaries and as possessing the necessary authority from its subsidiaries to act on their behalf by virtue of its ownership or control of them. However, subsidiaries which were formed or acquired by the parent company after the policy had incepted were necessarily excluded from the cover as named assureds, and that was likely to have been the case even if the policy simply stated that "all subsidiaries" were to be insured, as English agency law appeared not to allow ratification in these circumstances.[329] For that reason, it was necessary for policies to be in declaration form allowing such additions to be made merely by notification to the insurer: some declaration policies provided that if the company merges, or acquires or creates any subsidiary, the policy covered only those directors and officers who were serving as directors and officers may be covered at the discretion of the insurer. If the policy was not in declaration form, it would then be necessary for the parent to seek an endorsement to the policy adding the names of newly acquired subsidiaries.

The use of declaration policies continues, but is of less significance following the passing of the Contracts (Rights of Third Parties) Act 1999. Unless the Act is excluded by the policy, the effect of a policy which covers the parent company and all subsidiaries will be to extend the benefit of the policy not just to present subsidiaries but also to subsidiaries who join the group at some later date.

The consequences of the composite nature of the policy are significant. The directors are parties to the insurance in their own right, as co-assureds, even though the insurance is in the name of the company.[330] Policies are composite, in that each individual director is an assured in his own right. The conduct of any one director which takes him outside the protection of the policy does not necessarily affect the rights of others: this was held in *Arab Bank v Zurich Insurance Co*.[331] The point is often specified in the policy, e.g.:

> "This policy covers each Insured for its own individual interest. No statements made by or on behalf of an Insured or breach of any term of this policy, or any information or knowledge possessed by an Insured, shall be imputed to any Insured for the purpose of determining whether any individual Insured is covered under this policy."[332]

Directors and officers. The coverage will extend to "directors and officers" of the company. Some policies define these terms as referring to past, present and   **20–082**

---

[327] *New Hampshire Insurance Co v MGN Ltd* [1997] L.R.L.R. 24.

[328] *National Oilwell (UK) Ltd v Davy Offshore Ltd* [1993] 2 Lloyd's Rep. 582.

[329] This follows from the analysis in *National Oilwell v Davy Offshore*.

[330] *Carden v CE Heath Casualty and General Insurance Ltd*; *CE Heath Casualty and General Insurance v Grey* 1993 NSW LEXIS 8082.

[331] *Arab Bank v Zurich Insurance Co* [1999] 1 Lloyd's Rep. 262.

[332] AIG wording.

future directors and officers, including their assignees and heirs. In most cases, it is relatively easy to determine whether a person is a director or officer of the company, as there will be a formal appointment as such. However, it may be unclear whether a particular person employed by the company is a director or officer or simply an employee or some form of independent contractor, as D&O policies generally exclude employees from their coverage.[333] There is no exhaustive statutory definition of "officer" which can be relied upon to provide an answer to this question: the Companies Act 2006 s.1173(1) simply states that the term includes a director, manager or secretary, and it may be that the proper test is whether the person in question is involved in managing the affairs of the company or whether the role is more limited. It was held in *Mutual Reinsurance Co v Peat Marwick Mitchell & Co*[334] that an auditor is an "officer" for the purposes of this form of cover.

A further area of difficulty concerns persons who have not been formally appointed by the company but who have acted on its behalf, possibly for many years. The companies legislation treats such persons as de facto directors and officers (the Companies Act 2006 s.250), although it has yet to be decided whether unappointed persons are within the scope of liability cover as a de facto director may be a director for some statutory purposes but not others.[335] A particular issue may arise with "shadow directors" (a concept set out in the Companies Act 2006 s.251), who are persons not formally appointed by the company but whose instructions are generally followed by the directors. It is unclear whether the statutory treatment of such persons as shadow directors is enough to bring them within the scope of the cover: in particular, it might be difficult to argue that a lending bank, which may qualify as a shadow director, is covered by a company's insurance. Policies often make express provision for this matter by extending coverage to any person who acts as director or who has performed the functions of a director.

20–083   *Capacity.* D&O policies apply to any director or person who incurs liability in his capacity as a director, often whether or not appointed to that post. Some policies restrict cover to a director solely whilst acting in that capacity, and others exclude liability arising from professional services (the territory of an ordinary public liability policy). The major problem posed by the limitation of cover to a person acting, solely or otherwise, in his capacity as director, is that the present state of the common law does not recognise that a director can incur personal liability to a third party while he is acting in his capacity as director and that what is required is a personal assumption of responsibility.[336] Absent special words of extension, in the exceptional circumstances where liability is incurred by a director to a third party, the director will potentially not be protected by D&O cover. There is a counter-argument to the effect that the suggestion made above equates a personal assumption of responsibility with acting in a personal capacity. The counter-argument runs that a director who entices a third party to invest in, or to enter into contractual arrangements, with his company, is acting in his capacity as a director even though assuming personal responsibility: the

---

[333] However, policies may well waive subrogation rights against employees who have been guilty of the conduct for which the directors and officers may face ultimate liability.

[334] *Mutual Reinsurance Co v Peat Marwick Mitchell & Co* [1997] 1 Lloyd's Rep. 253.

[335] See, e.g. *Re Lo Line Electric Motors Ltd* [1988] B.C.L.C. 698.

[336] *Williams v Natural Life Health Foods Ltd* [1998] 2 All E.R. 577.

purpose of the personal capacity limitation is to distinguish the acts of a director from the acts of a private citizen.[337]

Liability incurred by a director in his capacity as an employee of the company rather than by reason of his capacity as director is not covered by a D&O policy.[338] In *Tosich v Tasman Investment Management Ltd*[339] it was held that typical coverage wording "relates to those duties or liabilities imposed upon a director or senior officer as such, rather than all conduct in the course of employment" does not extend to employment duties.[340] This means, for example, that if a policy expressly provides coverage for, say, discrimination or health and safety claims, and liability is incurred by a director, such liability will not fall within the terms of the policy by reason of the overriding requirement for that liability to have been incurred by the director in his capacity as such. However, it has been held in Canada that a shareholder/director who allegedly oppressed minority shareholders does so in his capacity as director and not shareholder.[341] It might be thought that the capacity argument is unduly technical. The difficulty here is that capacity has proved a stumbling block to recovery in other contexts. Thus if a policy protects the assured against liabilities arising from his activities as occupier of premises, an owner-occupier may not be covered if he inflicts loss in his capacity as owner.[342] Equally, a distinction has been drawn between the insured supply of professional services and the uninsured supply of products.[343]

Form of cover. All D&O policies, in line with the position relating to **20–084** professional indemnity insurance in general, are written on a claims made basis. Here, the insurer is liable for any claims made against the directors within the currency of the policy even though their liability is not established until some later date, often after the policy has ceased to operate. D&O policies otherwise share the ordinary characteristics of other professional indemnity insurances. There will be a per claim deductible, and a maximum level of indemnity which may be calculated on the basis of either (or both) per loss or claim or per aggregate of all losses in the insurance period. Where there is a per loss or claim ceiling, it is necessary to define the terms "loss" and "claim". Cases on liability covers generally indicate that the courts regard a series of related incidents as a single claim,[344] and similarly regard a number of different forms of breach of duty giving rise to a loss as a single claim.[345] D&O policies tend to state that all losses based on a single wrongful act are to be treated as a single loss or claim,

[337] The London market has thus seen claims paid in respect of actions brought by shareholders against directors for securities mis-selling. But it is far from obvious that such a claim against a director has any basis in law in any event

[338] *Ross v American Home Assurance Co* 1999 O.T.C. 360.

[339] *Tosich v Tasman Investment Management Ltd* 2008 F.C.A. 377.

[340] On that basis it might be thought that where a director discriminates on the ground of race, sex, religion or disability against an employee, any personal claim against him is not covered by a D&O policy because of the capacity issue. However, London market insurers have provided indemnity in such situations. That of course does not mean that they were legally obliged to do so.

[341] *Alofs v Temple Insurance Co* [2005] OJ No.4372.

[342] *Sturge v Hackett* [1962] 1 W.L.R. 1257; *Rigby v Sun Alliance* [1980] 1 Lloyd's Rep. 359; *Oei v Foster* [1982] 2 Lloyd's Rep. 170; *Turner v Manx Line Ltd* [1990] 1 Lloyd's Rep. 137; *Christmas v Taylor Woodrow Civil Engineering* [1997] 1 Lloyd's Rep. 407.

[343] *Encia Remediation Ltd v Canopius Managing Agents Ltd* [2008] Lloyd's Rep. I.R. 79; *Fitzpatrick v Robert Norman Job and Wendy Barbara Job t/as Jobs Engineering & Others* [2007] W.A.S.C.A. 63; *Vero Insurance Ltd v Power Technologies Pty Ltd* 2007 N.S.W.C.A. 226; *Chemetics International Ltd v Commercial Union Assurance Co of Canada* (1984) 11 D.L.R. (4th) 754.

[344] *Haydon v Lo & Lo* [1997] 1 Lloyd's Rep. 336.

[345] *West Wake Price v Ching Wo Hong* [1957] 1 W.L.R. 45.

so that any per loss or claim cap will apply to the aggregate of losses. This form of aggregation may also assist the assured, in that only one deductible has to be borne for a series of losses or claims flowing from one wrongful act.

Insured and excluded perils

20–085   *Insured perils.* Wordings vary, but a D&O policy covers sums for which a director becomes legally liable to pay by way of damages resulting from liability at law. The insuring clause almost invariably provides that the indemnity becomes available where a claim has been brought in respect of a "wrongful act". This term is defined widely, encompassing, inter alia, any breach of duty, breach of trust, error, misstatement, misleading statement, breach of warranty of authority or other act done or wrongfully attempted. This type of wording will cover acts done by the directors in the course of their duties, and also acts done on behalf of the company but without its authorisation. There has to be a causal link between the wrongful act and the loss for which a claim is made: by way of example, if an investment company lends money to a property developer and then sells participation interests in the loan to banks, the failure of a director of the investment company to ensure that the borrower complies with conditions relating to the loan does not trigger cover under his D&O policy in response to a claim against him by the banks, as the cause of their loss is the insolvency of the borrower and not the director's breach of duty.[346]

Liability may be established by a judgment, arbitration award or settlement, at which point the obligation to pay is triggered, although the insurers always retain their right to challenge any settlement reached by the assured on the ground that it does not fall within the terms of the insuring provisions.[347]

Cover is aimed primarily at tort claims: contract claims are regarded as excluded[348] unless the policy otherwise provides or unless the claim is one which could have been brought in either contract or tort. Employee claims are also often excluded. Separate cover is available for Securities Claims, namely, claims alleging a violation of any law or regulation regulating the purchase or sale or offer or solicitation of an offer to purchase or sell securities. But just how valuable is all of this cover?

20–086   *Perils excluded by operation of law.* The ordinary law precludes recovery in three situations.

The first is that a director cannot make a claim where his own deliberate or reckless conduct has caused the loss: just as an arsonist cannot recover when he has chosen to burn down his premises, a director cannot recover if he acts in a way designed to cause loss to the company.

Secondly, there can be no recovery where the director makes profits to which he is not entitled. If, therefore, a director takes advantage of a corporate opportunity, or corporate information, to make secret profits, and a restitutionary action is brought against him by the company for the profit to be disgorged, D&O insurance cannot respond. In many cases the company will not have suffered any loss, but breach of fiduciary duty does not rest upon the beneficiary proving loss

---

[346] *Southwest Georgia Financial Corp v Colonial American Casualty & Surety Co* 2009 B.L. 201259 (MD Ga, 21 September 2009).

[347] *CGU Insurance Ltd v AMP Financial Planning Pty Ltd* [2007] H.C.A. 36; *Commercial Union Assurance Co v NRG Victory Reinsurance Ltd* [1998] Lloyd's Rep. I.R. 439.

[348] On the basis that they give rise to "private" liability and not "public" liability: *Tesco Stores Ltd v Constable* [2008] Lloyd's Rep. I.R. 636.

but rather on the fiduciary making a profit.[349] That point aside, as was said by Lord Phillips in *Stone & Rolls Ltd v Moore Stephens*,[350] "If a person starts with nothing and never legitimately acquires anything he cannot realistically be said to have suffered any loss."

The third, and perhaps the most complex, is that if the director has infringed the law, then he may be unable to recover. The scope of the public policy rule *ex turpi causa non oritur action* is a matter of some contention, and the most recent discussions of the point, by the House of Lords in *Tinsley v Milligan*,[351] *Gray v Thames Trains*[352] and *Stone & Rolls* itself are inconclusive. The stated principles are that an assured cannot recover if he has to rely upon his own illegality or if he is seeking to make a profit from his own illegality. Taken to their extreme, these principles mean that if a claim against a director has arisen following an infringement of the Insolvency Act 1986, the Companies Act 2006 or the Financial Services and Markets Act 2000 which gives rise to criminal liability, the policy—whatever it might say—cannot respond.[353] However, it may be that the *ex turpi causa* defence to recovery is more limited, and applies only where there is some degree of moral turpitude involved in the assured's criminality.[354] Accordingly, the insurability of liabilities imposed liability under any of the provisions of these pieces of legislation may depend upon the nature of the offence or regulatory infringement and the degree to which the assured's conduct involved moral turpitude. Therefore, in principle, there may be a possibility of cover in respect damages are awarded in circumstances of pure negligence and no criminal sanction is involved,[355] and even in some cases where criminality is involved.

Careful analysis of the situations in which a director may face liability to the company show that most involve conduct on his part which is uninsurable as a matter of law. One important exception may be statutory liability for negligent wrongful trading.[356] However, many policies have adopted insolvency clauses of various types, the effect of which is to exclude liability under the policy if the claim arises out of or relates to the inability of the company to pay its debts.

Contractual exclusions. Fines for criminal conduct, punitive or exemplary **20–087** damages and multiple damages are generally excluded. Punitive damages are rarely available under English law, and multiple damages are not available at all. However, in the United States, punitive damages are commonly awarded, and multiple damages—generally treble damages, particularly in antitrust suits—are also possible. It is by no means clear that such damages are recoverable from an insurer even in the absence of an express exclusion, although in *Lancashire County Council v Municipal Mutual Insurance*[357] the Court of Appeal was of the tentative view that punitive damages awarded in a civil case might be recovered provided that the policy so states. It is almost certainly the law that a fine

---

[349] *Boardman v Phipps* [1967] 2 A.C. 46, although the position is different if the company has authorised the profit—*Queensland Mines Ltd v Hudson* [1978] 2 A.J.L.R. 379.

[350] *Stone & Rolls Ltd v Moore Stephens* [2009] UKHL 39, para.5.

[351] *Tinsley v Milligan* [1993] 3 All E.R. 65.

[352] *Gray v Thames Trains* [2009] UKHL 33.

[353] See, e.g. *KR v Royal & Sun Alliance Plc* [2007] Lloyd's Rep. I.R. 268.

[354] *Nayar v Denton Wilde Sapte* [2009] EWHC 3218 QB; *Griffin v UHY Hacker Young & Partners* [2010] EWHC 146 (Ch); *Safeway Stores Ltd v Twigger* [2010] EWHC 11 (Comm).

[355] If a crime has been committed, but no prosecution has been brought, the *ex turpi causa* principle would not cease to operate and indemnity would still be unavailable as a matter of law.

[356] Insolvency Act 1986 s.214.

[357] *Lancashire County Council v Municipal Mutual Insurance* [1996] 3 All E.R. 545.

imposed by state authorities for infringement of regulatory provisions is irrecoverable under a liability policy, as this would largely defeat the purpose of the fine.

D&O policies also typically exclude civil liability arising from infringement of legislative provisions and from any deliberately dishonest or deliberately fraudulent act. In either case, these matters have to be established by final adjudication of a judicial or arbitral tribunal[358] or by any formal written admission by the assured. It will be seen that these exclusions are in most cases little more than confirmatory: the law does not permit recovery in either of these circumstances unless no fraud is involved. The concluding words of the exclusion become significant where a dispute arises in relation to defence costs: insurers cannot refuse to defend or pay defence costs simply because fraud has been alleged, they only have the right to withdraw coverage once fraud is proved, points established in Australia in *Wilkie v Gordian Run Off Ltd*[359] and *Silbermann v CGU Insurance Ltd.*[360]

A further common exclusion is that for "Insured v Insured" claims. This provides that there is no cover for claims by directors, or by the company against a director where the director is himself a shareholder and thus would benefit from the claim.[361] To that extent the "Insured v Insured" exclusion protects the insurers against collusive claims. Some policies limit this exclusion to US claims, a jurisdiction in which derivative and stockholder class actions are common fare. Another version of this exclusion confines it to "consensual claims" so that its scope is limited to collusion. Once the company has gone into liquidation and proceedings are brought by the liquidator, it would seem that the clause no longer applies, and the insurers are liable to provide an indemnity to the directors in proceedings brought by the liquidator,[362] although this possibility is often specifically excluded independently. Further, the clause does not apply where the director is sued in his capacity as employee of the company.[363] It may be that the clause is unnecessary: in *Moore Stephens v Stone & Rolls* Lord Brown was firmly of the view that a director/shareholder could never benefit from a derivative claim brought by the company against him in his capacity as director.

Within the policy limits, the sums for which the insurer takes responsibility are those which the directors and officers are legally liable to pay to third parties. As is the case with other forms of liability insurance, legal liability excludes ex gratia payments and other payments which the company may have thought expedient in a business sense to pay to a third party, but which are not based on legal liability as such. Thus, if the directors are threatened with legal proceedings to prevent them from acting in a particular fashion, and they pay a sum to a third party to allow their intended conduct to go ahead, such payment is not based on legal liability but rather is in the form of a business interruption loss, which is not insured by liability cover.[364] However, if the payment forms part of a bona fide

---

[358] See *Herley Industries Inc v Federal Insurance Co Inc* 2009 B.L. 179695 (ED Pa, Aug 21, 2009).

[359] *Wilkie v Gordian Run Off Ltd* 2005 H.C.A. 17.

[360] *Silbermann v CGU Insurance Ltd* [2003] N.S.W.C.A. 203.

[361] See *Kohanski v St Paul Guarantee Insurance Co* 78 O.R. (3d) 684 (2006).

[362] *Re People's Department Stores Ltd (1992) Inc* (1998) 23 C.B.R. (4th) 200; *Markham General Insurance Co v Bennett* 81 O.R. (3d) 389 (2006); *Cigna Insurance Co v Gulf United States Corp* 1997 W.L. 1878757 (D Idaho 1997); *Township of Center v First Mercury Syndicate Inc* 117 F. 3d 115 (3rd Cir 1997).

[363] *Conklin Co Inc v National Union Fire Insurance Co* 1987 W.L. 108957 (D. Minn. 1987).

[364] See *Corbin v Payne*, *The Times*, October 11, 1990.

settlement of a doubtful claim, it may be recoverable: this depends upon whether the insurer has the right under the policy to negotiate with third parties or whether that power is delegated to the company.

Other exclusions commonly found are as follows.

(a) pollution liability and clean-up costs—the potential scope of pollution liability is massive, particularly in the United States where there is strict liability for clean-up costs, and insurers have taken the view that this form of protection is unavailable at a standard premium;

(b) liability for the escape of nuclear material;

(c) liability for death and personal injury, and for damage to property, including product liability;

(d) liability for defamation or the infringement of intellectual property rights;

(e) liability incurred by directors and officers with respect to the restitution to the company of secret profits or remuneration to which they were not entitled—as noted above, there is no loss in such a situation in any event.

D&O policies may also restrict the insurer's liability to the situation in which there is no other available insurance. It is often the case that two or more policies covering the same loss each seek to cast the burden onto another insurer, and here the courts have regarded the restrictions as self-cancelling, so that each insurer remains liable for the full amount of the loss in the usual way, subject to the right of the paying insurer to seek contribution from the others.

Other policy terms. Conditions in D&O policies are much the same as are found in other professional liability policies. There will be a condition that premiums are paid, and in most cases the company is required to guarantee the payment of premiums due directly from the directors and officers. There may also be a reasonable care clause, whereby the assured is able to recover only where reasonable care has been exercised to avoid or mitigate a loss, although this type of clause is largely meaningless.   **20–088**

Claims. D&O polices contain claims provisions which are generally found in other forms of professional indemnity insurance written on a claims made basis. There are three triggers of cover.   **20–089**

The primary trigger for cover under a claims made policy is that a claim by a third party against the assured is first made during the currency of the policy. The assured will be under a duty to notify the claim to the insurers as soon as practicable and some policies require this to occur during the policy period. Some policies define "claim". A typical definition is: "a civil proceeding commencing by the service of a complaint, summons, statement of claim or similar pleading . . . against an Insured Person alleging facts or circumstances that constitute a Wrongful Act". There may be a notification problem if the claim is made towards the end of the policy year, and for that reason there is generally a short post-policy period—30 to 60 days after the date of the claim—for notification. That period can be extended on payment of an additional premium. It should be noted that full use of the extended period is not an entitlement, but rather it is a maximum period, because the controlling obligation is to notify as soon as practicable.[365] In the absence of any express policy provision, the date of the wrongful act in respect of which the claim has been made is irrelevant, as all that matters is that the claim in respect of the wrongful act is made against the assured within the policy period. Policies often make provision for the date of the wrongful act: in some cases there is no limit; in some cases there is a retroactive date in the policy, so that claims arising from any wrongful act earlier than that date are excluded; and in some cases the wrongful act, the claim and the notification of the claim to the insurers must all have occurred in the policy period.[366]

The secondary trigger for cover arises where the policy is not renewed or replaced. Policies tend to offer a Discovery Period, running for 30/60/90 days (it varies from policy to policy) from the termination of the policy. If a claim is first made against the director during the discovery period in respect of a wrongful act taking place before the commencement of the discovery period, there is cover subject to notification of the claim to the insurers as soon as practicable or within 30/60 days of the termination of the Discovery Period. In the case of a retired director, the Discovery Period is often much longer: policies range from 84 months to no limit.

The third trigger for cover, and in practice perhaps the most significant, is that the assured is given the right during the policy period (or, if appropriate, Discovery Period) to notify the insurers of any circumstances which may/is likely to/may reasonably be expected to, give rise to a claim. Any contractual notification of circumstances is normally required to include the reasons for anticipating a claim, and full relevant particulars with respect to dates, the nature of the wrongful act and the identity of the potential claimant. If circumstances are notified, any later claim is deemed to have been made during the period of insurance, so that the claim is dragged back into the policy year of notification by way of "deeming". Some policies are framed as imposing an obligation on the assured to notify circumstances which may give rise to a claim, but it is clear from the leading authority, *HLB Kidsons v Lloyd's Underwriters*,[367] that the notification of circumstances and the making of claims are entirely distinct heads of cover, so that a failure to notify circumstances does not preclude a subsequent notification of a claim against the assured arising from those circumstances later in the policy year. In short, the notification of circumstances is an option which may be exercised by the assured.

---

[365] The opposite conclusion was reached by Morison J. in *AIG Europe (Ireland) Ltd v Faraday Capital Ltd* [2007] Lloyd's Rep. I.R. 267, holding that the assured was entitled to notify within the specified period. The point did not arise on appeal and Morison J. was reversed on other grounds, [2008] Lloyd's Rep. I.R. 454. A majority of the Court of Appeal in *HLB Kidsons v Lloyd's Underwriters* [2009] Lloyd's Rep. I.R. 178 held that an obligation to notify as soon as practicable and within 15 days of the expiry of the policy conferred a right to notify up to the expiry of that period rather than merely imposing a long-stop.

[366] This type of policy is unlawful in some jurisdictions. See *Sparks v St Paul Insurance Co* 100 N.J. 325 (1985), in which the New Jersey Supreme Court, in striking down such a policy, stated that it "combine[d] the worst features of 'occurrence' and 'claims made' policies and the best of neither."

[367] *HLB Kidsons v Lloyd's Underwriters* [2009] Lloyd's Rep. I.R. 178.

CHAPTER 21

THIRD PARTY RIGHTS UNDER LIABILITY POLICIES

1. BACKGROUND

The common law. At common law, where an assured under a liability policy   **21–001**
became liable to a third party in damages, but had become bankrupt or had gone
into liquidation before having received the insurance monies from the insurer for
transmission to the third party, any payment by the insurer to the trustee in
bankruptcy or liquidator was deemed to form part of the assured's general assets
for distribution to creditors.[1] Consequently, the third party for whom the money
had in reality been earmarked was confined to proving as an unsecured creditor
in the bankruptcy or liquidation for his loss, and inevitably would recover at best
only a small dividend.

The 1930 Act. This position was widely regarded as unjust, and indeed debased   **21–002**
the very concept of the protection of third parties under compulsory liability
insurance, and as soon as the common law on the point had become clear it was
reversed by Parliament in the form of the Third Parties (Rights against Insurers)
Act 1930, a measure at the time intended to supplement the compulsory motor
insurance regime introduced by the Road Traffic Act 1930. The broad effect of
the Act is to effect a statutory subrogation, by virtue of which the third-party is
entitled to exercise the rights of the assured as against the insurer; in this way the
insurance moneys will not become part of the insolvent assured's assets.

Within a very short period after the passing of the 1930 Act, the Road Traffic
Act 1934 laid down a discrete mechanism whereby the victim of a negligent
driver could enforce his judgment against the driver's insurers whether or not the
driver had become insolvent. That mechanism is retained by the Road Traffic Act
1988 s.151, and has been supplemented by a parallel mechanism, set out in the
European Communities (Rights against Insurers) Regulations 2002,[2] which
permit a direct action against motor liability insurers without the need for the
victim to obtain a judgment against the driver.[3] The 1930 Act is, therefore, no
longer needed in motor cases, but since 1934 the Act has been used in a variety
of different contexts, in particular in respect of employers' liability and
professional negligence claims.

It is to be emphasised that the 1930 Act operates only where the assured has
become insolvent. In the absence of an insolvency, the assured's victim has no
direct claim against the assured's liability insurers, and that position is, in the vast
majority of cases, unaffected by abolition of the doctrine of privity of contract by
the Contracts (Rights of Third Parties) Act 1999. While the 1999 Act does permit

---

[1] *Hood's Trustees v Southern Union General Insurance Co of Australasia* [1928] Ch. 793; *Re Harrington Motor Co* [1928] Ch. 105.
[2] SI 2002/26.
[3] These provisions are discussed in Ch.22, below.

a direct action against the promisor by an identified or identifiable third-party beneficiary under a contract, a person who subsequently acquires a claim against the holder of a liability policy is most unlikely to be a beneficiary under the policy even if there is sufficient identification. There is a distinction between a person who is the intended beneficiary of a policy and a person who may at some stage eventually benefit from a policy: a liability cover would appear to fall into the latter category. Independently of this consideration, the 1999 Act requires the third party to be identified by name or class, and an ordinary liability policy which protects the assured against claims from, at least potentially, any person will not satisfy this test: the fact that potential claimants can be identified does not overcome the first objection above.[4]

21–003   **The 2010 Act.** The 1930 Act has proved to be bedevilled with limitations and infelicities of drafting which greatly hamper its efficacy. Widespread dissatisfaction with the operation of the 1930 Act emerged during the Law Commission's consultations on the general law relating to privity of contract, which ultimately led to the implementation of the Contracts (Rights of Third Parties) Act 1999. The English and Scottish Law Commissions undertook a separate investigation into the 1930 Act, and in 1998 published a consultation paper on the operation of the 1930 Act. This was followed by the publication by the Law Commissions, in July 2001, of a final Report and draft Bill.[5] Following the publication of the draft Bill, a series of judicial decisions removed many of the apparent shortcomings of the 1930 Act, so the need for reform became less pressing. The draft Bill lay dormant for nine years, and but was presented to Parliament in November 2009 to test a new expedited procedure for the adoption of non-contentious Law Commission Bills. The Law Commissions' Bill passed both Houses of Parliament without amendment, and became the Third Parties (Rights against Insurers) Act 2010.

The 2010 Act will come into force on a day to be appointed by statutory instrument. As from the appointed day the 2010 Act will apply to all cases other than those in which: (a) the assured both became insolvent and incurred liability to the third party before the appointed day; or (b) the assured died before the appointed day.[6] Accordingly, for some time to come it will be necessary for reliance to be placed upon the 1930 Act. This chapter thus discusses the regime under the 1930 Act and then the regime under the 2010 Act.

2. THIRD PARTIES (RIGHTS AGAINST INSURERS) ACT 1930

Events triggering the operation of the 1930 Act

21–004   *Automatic events.* The third party acquires rights against the assured's insurer if the assured has become liable to the third party before or after the happening of any of the following events, listed in s.1(1) (as amended):

(1) the assured becoming bankrupt[7];

---

[4] One exceptional situation in which the benefit of a liability policy may accrue to a third party is in the context of employers' liability insurance where there has been a transfer of the employer's undertaking.

[5] Law Commission No.272; Scottish Law Commission No.184.

[6] 2010 Act s.21 and Sch.3.

[7] The matter is not affected by the death of the bankrupt: s.1(2).

(2) the assured making a composition with his creditors;
(3) where the assured is a company
   (a) the making of a winding-up order,
   (b) the passing of a resolution for voluntary winding up, other than merely for the purpose of reconstruction or amalgamation with another company,[8]
   (c) the company entering administration,
   (d) the appointment of a receiver or manager,
   (e) possession of property comprised in a floating charge being taken by or on behalf of debenture holders,
   (f) the approval of a voluntary arrangement under Pt I of the Insolvency Act 1986.

The Act was extended to limited partnerships by the Limited Liability Partnership Regulations 2000,[9] made under the Limited Liability Partnerships Act 2000. The Regulations inserted a new s.3A, into the 1930 Act, which provides simply that the Act applies to limited liability partnerships as it applies to companies, and that references to a resolution for a voluntary winding-up being passed are to be treated, for a limited liability partnership, as references to a determination for a voluntary winding-up being passed. The 1930 Act does not, however, make express reference to other partnerships[10] and, moreover, was not—on their introduction—extended to individual voluntary arrangements under the Insolvency Act 1986, but only to those entered into by companies. The latter omission has given rise to difficulties, discussed below.   **21–005**

Action by the third party: seeking a winding-up order. If none of these events has occurred, and the third party has obtained a judgment against the assured which has not been satisfied, there is nothing preventing him from petitioning the court for a winding-up order so that the Act can be brought into play. This is relatively straightforward in the case of a company registered in England and thus subject to the jurisdiction of the English courts. If the company is not registered in England, it may be wound up in England if three conditions are met: (1) there must be a sufficient connection with England and Wales which may, but does not necessarily have to, consist of assets within the jurisdiction; (2) there must be a reasonable possibility, if a winding up order is made, of benefit to those applying for the winding-up order; and (3) one or more persons interested in the distribution of assets of the company must be persons over whom the court can exercise a jurisdiction.[11] Accordingly, if a creditor has obtained a judgment against a company registered abroad, he may seek its winding up in England so as to trigger the 1930 Act even if the company's only asset in England is a possible claim against liability insurers.[12]   **21–006**

---

[8] 1930 Act s.1(6).

[9] SI 2000/3316.

[10] Although an insolvency order against an individual partner triggers the operation of the 1930 Act against the partnership as a whole, on the principle of joint and several liability: see *Re Greenfield. Jackson v Greenfield* [1998] B.P.I.R. 699, where it was assumed that the insolvency of two partners would have operated to transfer their rights to the third party had the third party established their liability towards him.

[11] Insolvency Act 1986 s.221; *Stocznia Gdanska v Latreefers (No.2)* [2001] 2 B.C.L.C. 116, 137.

[12] *Re Compañia Merabello San Nicholas SA* [1973] Ch. 75; *Re Allobrogia Steamship Corporation* [1978] 3 All E.R. 423; *Re Eloc Electro-Optieck and Communicatie BV* [1982] Ch. 43; *Re A Company (No.00359 of 1987)* [1987] 3 W.L.R. 339; *Irish Shipping Ltd v Commercial Union Assurance Co Plc (The Irish Rowan)* [1989] 2 Lloyd's Rep. 144.

Contracts within 1930 Act

21–007   *Liability insurance.* Section 1(1) refers to "any contract of insurance", a term which has been held to cover mutual insurance.[13] Despite the generality of the wording, it was at one time thought that the legislation extended only to policies covering tort liabilities and not to any policy covering voluntarily undertaken liabilities. In *Tarbuck v Avon Insurance*[14] it was decided that the 1930 Act did not apply to a legal expenses policy, so that solicitors who had acted for the assured in defending proceedings were unable to recover their fees from the assured's legal expenses insurers following the assured's insolvency. The basis of the decision was that the liability was one for a voluntarily incurred debt rather than for liability as such. The ruling in *Tarbuck* was followed by Lawrence Collins J. in *T&N Ltd v Royal and Sun Alliance Plc*,[15] where it was held that the 1930 Act did not apply to a claim for damages for breach of contract. However, in *Re OT Computers* the Court of Appeal[16] overruled *T&N* and disapproved the ruling in *Tarbuck*. This case concerned the insurance of liabilities to purchasers of computers under extended warranties, the insurers arguing that the liabilities insured arose under contract and thus were outside the 1930 Act. The Court of Appeal, rejecting this defence, held that the opening words of s.1(1) of the 1930 Act—"Where under any contract of insurance a person is insured against liabilities to third parties which he may incur"—drew no distinction between tortious and contractual liabilities, and there was nothing in the Act which justified that distinction. This reasoning meant that *T&N* had been wrongly decided. *Tarbuck* was regarded by Longmore L.J. as distinguishable as the case related to debt rather than damages. However, Longmore L.J. was of the view that it was inappropriate to draw a distinction between a sum owing by reason of a breach of contract and a sum owing by reason of a contractual obligation to pay that sum, and for this reason *Tarbuck* ought not be followed. In reaching these conclusions the Court of Appeal recognised that it was perfectly possible for a liability policy to exclude claims for breach of contract or for sums due under a contract, and indeed it is common in many forms of liability insurance for the policy to exclude claims which have arisen purely as a result of the agreement between the parties. Nevertheless, if the policy is not so limited, the 1930 Act will, as a result of the appeal in *Re OT Computers*, be fully applicable.

21–008   *Reinsurance.* Section 1(5) provides that the legislation does not apply to a claim involving a person acting "in the capacity of insurer under some other contract of insurance". The purpose of this subsection is to remove reinsurance from the 1930 Act so that if an insurer becomes insolvent its policyholders cannot proceed against the reinsurers. In *Re OT Computers* it was contended that the customer warranties were themselves contracts of insurance and accordingly that the policy taken out by the supplier was in reality a contract of reinsurance, although the point was not resolved.

---

[13] *Wooding v Monmouthshire and South Wales Mutual Indemnity Society Ltd* [1939] 4 All E.R. 570: *Firma C-Trade SA v Newcastle Protection and Indemnity Association (The Fanti)* [1987] 2 Lloyd's Rep. 299: *Socony Mobil Oil Co Inc v West of England Shipowners Mutual Insurance Association Ltd (The Padre Island) (No.1)* [1984] 2 Lloyd's Rep. 408; *Socony Mobil Oil Co Inc v West of England Shipowners Mutual insurance Association Ltd (The Padre Island) (No.2)* [1987] 2 Lloyd's Rep. 529.

[14] *Tarbuck v Avon Insurance* [2002] Lloyd's Rep. I.R. 393.

[15] *T&N Ltd v Royal and Sun Alliance Plc* [2004] Lloyd's Rep. I.R. 106.

[16] *Re OT Computers* [2004] Lloyd's Rep. I.R. 669.

Extraterritorial effect. The 1930 Act is silent on the extent to which it has   **21–009**
extraterritorial effect, and it is undecided whether the Act applies by virtue of the
fact that the insolvency procedure is conducted in England or by virtue of the fact
that the law applicable to the insurance contract is English law.[17] In the event that
insolvency proceedings are in effect against the assured in some other jurisdiction, the English court is required to recognise those proceedings,[18] although the
power of the English court to stay English proceedings against the debtor[19] may
not affect any transfer of rights to the third party under the 1930 Act and any
claim brought against the insurers under the 1930 Act.[20]

Establishing and quantifying the liability of the assured to the third party

The principle. The 1930 Act comes into play when, in accordance with s.1(1),   **21–010**
the assured's liability has been incurred before or after any of the events listed
above which trigger the operation of the Act. Once an insolvency event has
occurred, the rights of the assured are transferred to the third party. It is not
enough, however, that the third party has a claim against the assured. In order for
the third party to recover from the insurers, it is necessary that the third party has
established and quantified that liability, in that he has obtained a judgment or an
arbitration award against the assured, or at least a compromise settlement
(assuming that the assured is not in breach of condition by compromising or
admitting liability, as will often be the case). This was held to be the position by
the Court of Appeal in *Post Office v Norwich Union Fire Insurance Society*,[21] in
which an action was brought against the assured's insurers under the 1930 Act
even though the assured had at that time not admitted liability to the third party.
The Court of Appeal ruled that the action against the insurers was premature and
had to be postponed until the liability of the assured had been established and
quantified. This does not mean, however, that the third party has no rights at all
under the 1930 Act before establishing and quantifying the assured's liability:
later cases have made it clear that the third party has contingent rights which, in
particular, permit him to obtain information from the assured and the insurers.[22]

The *Post Office* rule is an important limitation on the effectiveness of the 1930
Act, as the third party may well find, having incurred the cost of obtaining a
judgment against the assured, that the insurers have policy defences which were
effective against the assured and thus which preclude the third party from making
a successful claim under the 1930 Act. One possible solution to this problem—an
action by the third party for a declaration as to the insurers' liability to the
assured, in advance of the substantive proceedings against the assured—has been
held not to be available to the third party.[23] These decisions must nevertheless be
open to doubt, in light of the recognition of the principle that the third party has
a contingent claim against the insurers as soon as the assured has become

---

[17] *Irish Shipping Ltd v Commercial Union Assurance Co Plc (The Irish Rowan)* [1989] 2 Lloyd's
Rep. 144.
[18] Under the Cross-Border Insolvency Regulations 2006 (SI 2006/1030), which incorporate into
English law the UNCITRAL Model Law on Cross-Border Insolvency.
[19] Model Law arts 19–21.
[20] Model Law art.1.5.
[21] *Post Office v Norwich Union Fire Insurance Society* [1967] 1 All E.R. 577.
[22] *Cox v Bankside Members Agency Ltd* [1995] 2 Lloyd's Rep. 437; *Centre Reinsurance
International Co v Freakley* [2005] Lloyd's Rep. I.R. 284; *Re OT Computers Ltd* [2004] Lloyd's Rep.
I.R. 669.
[23] *Nigel Upchurch Associates v Aldridge Estates Investment Co Ltd* [1993] 1 Lloyd's Rep. 535;
Burns v Shuttlehurst [1999] 1 W.L.R. 1449.

insolvent, even though the liability of the assured has not been established and quantified at that stage. Once it is recognised that a contingent claim exists, then the possibility of a crystallised claim vesting in the third party against the insurers cannot be regarded as purely hypothetical or academic, and there is no reason why the court should not exercise its discretion[24] to issue a declaration as to the coverage of the policy. The courts will, after all, readily grant declaratory relief to an assured under a liability who is facing a claim by a third party, and who wishes to know whether the policy will respond.[25]

21–011 *Manner in which assured's liability may be established and quantified.* The liability of the assured to the third party may be established and quantified by a judgment, an arbitration award or a binding settlement.

The effect of an adjudication award made under s.108 of the Housing Grants Construction and Regeneration Act 1996 was considered in *Galliford v Markel Capital Ltd.*[26] The scheme of the legislation is to provide a rapid method of resolving disputes under construction and related contracts, allowing work to proceed while the dispute is being resolved. A dispute may thus be referred to adjudication and the adjudicator's award is binding unless and until it is overturned by a ruling in arbitration or by the courts. In *Galliford* an adjudication award was not satisfied and the claimant took steps to enforce the award against the defendant's liability insurers under the 1930 Act. It was held that the claim under the 1930 Act was premature: an adjudication award, while binding, was enforceable only by an application to the court for summary judgment at which point the jurisdiction of the adjudicator and the validity of the award could be raised, and until summary judgment had been obtained it could not be said that the liability of the assured had been established and quantified.

21–012 *Effect of insurers defending liability proceedings.* In practice, where the third party brings an action against the assured, the insurers will be involved in the proceedings. Most liability policies confer upon the insurers the right to take over the assured's defence, so that the true defendant in respect of the third party's liability claim will be the insurers. Even if the insurers choose not to defend the action, possibly because they have denied liability under the policy or purported to avoid it, they may be joined to the proceedings by the assured as co-defendants so that a claim under the policy may be pressed. It will be appreciated, therefore, that there are two quite different issues to be resolved in cases of this type: is the assured liable to the third party; and, if so, are the insurers liable to the assured under the policy. In the absence of joinder, separate proceedings will be involved as separate parties are involved.

If the assured has become insolvent at an early stage, the assured may have no interest in defending the liability proceedings. Accordingly, unless the insurers defend the proceedings by the exercise of their contractual rights of defence or subrogation rights, there is a danger that the third party will obtain a default judgment against the assured: it was held in *Rees v Mabco (102) Ltd*[27] that insurers faced with a default judgment have no right to seek to overturn it, and they are confined to contesting liability based upon the binding effect or terms of

---

[24] Under CPR r.40.20. See *Arbuthnot Pensions & Investments Ltd v Padden* [2004] EWCA Civ 582, where it was confirmed that there are no jurisdictional barriers to the grant of a declaration, and that each case turns on discretionary issues.

[25] See, e.g. *Pilkington United Kingdom Ltd CGU Insurance Plc* [2004] Lloyd's Rep. I.R. 891.

[26] *Galliford v Markel Capital Ltd* [2003] EWHC 1216 (QB).

[27] *Rees v Mabco (102) Ltd* Unreported, 1998.

the policy itself. Alternatively, if insurers do opt to conduct the defence on the part of the assured, there is some, albeit weak, authority for the proposition that any judgment against the assured estops the insurers from relying upon policy defences. Insurers can avoid this danger by seeking permission to be joined to the proceedings in their own name, despite for all practical purposes being represented albeit by using the assured's name, and then pleading the policy terms in those proceedings.[28]

Individual voluntary arrangements. Voluntary arrangements consist of individual voluntary arrangements (IVAs) entered into by individuals, and company voluntary arrangements (CVAs) entered into by companies. The effect of a voluntary arrangement is to relieve the debtor from the full amount of his debts as long as he pays the agreed proportion in instalments: any creditor who is bound by the arrangement—that is, one who is party to it or who was entitled to vote at the meeting whether or not he did so—is precluded from enforcing his claim against the debtor. An alternative voluntary arrangement open to companies is the arrangement under s.896 of the Companies Act 2006, which is similar in its effects to a CVA and is binding on all creditors of a given class once three-quarters of those voting at a creditors' class meeting have approved the arrangement.   **21–013**

The particular problem here is the fact that the 1930 Act has no application to individual voluntary arrangements entered into under the Insolvency Act 1986, although it does apply to CVAs. That means that where an assured has entered into an IVA before the third party has obtained a judgment or arbitration award against the assured, the third party's action may be halted in its tracks as the general effect of an IVA under the Insolvency Act 1986 is to suspend outstanding legal proceedings against the assured unless the court gives its consent to their continuation. However, it was held, in *Sea Voyager Inc v Bielecki*,[29] that where an assured has entered into an IVA under the Insolvency Act 1986, a third party who has a claim against the assured which is potentially covered by insurance under the 1930 Act is potentially unfairly prejudiced by the moratorium on legal proceedings implied into an IVA and may apply to have the IVA set aside under s.262 of the Insolvency Act 1986. Thus the ultimate outcome may be satisfactory, but the procedure is expensive and cumbersome.

The IVA gives rise to further problems. First, even where the third party has successfully sued the assured, while it is the case that the 1930 Act operates to transfer the assured's rights against the insurers to the assured as soon as the IVA has been entered into and approved by the creditors' meeting, it is possible that the assured's liability to the third party, and therefore the value of the insurance claim, will be reduced by virtue of the IVA. It was denied in *Bielecki* that this would of itself be a ground for having the IVA set aside, although the point is undecided. Secondly, it was held in *Re Greenfield, Jackson v Greenfield*[30] that a third party who has not obtained a judgment cannot block a settlement reached between the assured (or at least the supervisor acting for him) and the insurers as at that stage he has no rights under the 1930 Act given that the Act is not triggered by the assured entering into an IVA.

Dissolved companies. The *Post Office v Norwich Union* principle has proved to be a particular hurdle in the case of a corporate assured which had been   **21–014**

---

[28] *Wood v Perfection Travel Ltd* [1996] L.R.L.R. 233.
[29] *Sea Voyager Inc v Bielecki* [1999] Lloyd's Rep. I.R. 356.
[30] *Re Greenfield, Jackson v Greenfield* [1998] B.P.I.R. 699.

dissolved. In *Bradley v Eagle Star Insurance Co*[31] B had been employed by a company which had been put into liquidation and had subsequently been removed from the register of companies; the latter act of dissolution meant that, as from the date of removal from the register, the company had ceased to exist. A later attempt to commence proceedings against the company was rejected by a majority of the House of Lords on the ground that a dissolved company has no legal existence, so that it is impossible to prove its liability by legal action: in the absence of any ruling on liability, the 1930 Act could not be engaged. The unfortunate effect of this decision was to confirm that in many personal injury cases—particularly those involving industrial diseases (typically, those arising from asbestos) where the symptoms do not develop for a long period after the alleged negligence—the liquidation and dissolution of the defendant deprived the third party of any possible remedy. The *Bradley* case also had the curious effect of drawing a distinction between bankrupt individuals, who can be sued after, and dissolved companies, which cannot. Parliament acted quickly to reverse *Bradley*. Some limited relief had at the time of *Bradley* been available in s.651 of the Companies Act 1985, which permitted the court to resurrect a company within two years of its dissolution in order for its liability to be established. That provision was, however, of no assistance on the facts of *Bradley* itself, as the period for resuscitation had long passed by the time proceedings were initiated. Section 141 of the Companies Act 1989 made significant retroactive amendments to s.651 of the 1985 Act, since re-enacted with some changes as ss.1029–1031 of the Companies Act 2006. Where a third party seeks to establish the liability of a dissolved company for death or personal injury, in order to found an action under the 1930 Act against its liability insurer, s.1030(1) permits the court to resurrect a dissolved company at any time. The period for resurrection thus remains in force only for other forms of action against the company (notably, property damage claims), that period being six years (Companies Act 2006 s.1030(4)).[32]

Section 1030 of the Companies Act 2006 is not, however, free from difficulty. First, two actions are required: one to resurrect the company; and a further one to prove its liability. Secondly, s.1030(2) requires the court to be satisfied, in resurrection proceedings, that the applicant's action would not be time-barred. This may be a costly process, for in personal injuries actions the court has, under s.33 of the Limitation Act 1980, an absolute discretion to override time limit.[33] It was held in *Re Workvale*[34] that an application under what is now s.1030 was not the appropriate place for the court to consider whether permission was or was not likely to be given for extension of time under s.33 of the Limitation Act 1980, that the company should be restored as long as there is shown to be an arguable case for the use of s.33 and that the question should be determined at the trial of the substantive action.

Section 1031(3) of the Companies Act 2006 provides that the court may, on making an order restoring a company to the register, further order that "the period between the dissolution of the company and the making of the order" is to be discounted in the subsequent proceedings in which the application of the Limitation Act 1980 is considered. This provision operates to preserve the

---

[31] *Bradley v Eagle Star Insurance Co* [1989] 2 W.L.R. 568.

[32] Raised from the two years allowed by the 1985 Act.

[33] Other than in respect of actions brought under the Consumer Protection Act 1987 (injuries inflicted by dangerous products), as these are subject to a maximum 10-year period from the date on which the product was first marketed.

[34] *Re Workvale* [1992] All E.R. 627. See also *Re Philip Powis Ltd*, *The Times*, March 6, 1998.

limitation position of the applicant where the company has been dissolved within the limitation period. In *Re Workvale* the Court of Appeal held that, as long as the insurers are parties to the application for restoration and the relevant evidence is before the court, an order under ss.1031(3) should be made as a matter of course, thereby avoiding the need for a subsequent application under s.33 of the Limitation Act 1980. By contrast, if the limitation period has expired before the application for restoration is made, there is no basis for an order under s.1031(3).[35] In *Smith v White Knight Laundry Ltd*[36] the Court of Appeal refused to make a restoration order coupled with an order under s.1031(3) discounting for limitation purposes the period between the dissolution of the company and its restoration to the register. The action was under the Fatal Accidents Act 1976, and it was strongly arguable that the claimant was time-barred under s.12 of the Limitation Act 1980. The effect of the Court of Appeal's decision was that the company was restored to the register, but the limitation issue was left over to be dealt with as a preliminary issue rather than as part of the restoration order itself.

Bankrupt assureds. The bankruptcy of the assured is one of the trigger events **21–015** which brings the 1930 Act into play. In most cases the judgment against the assured will bring about the assured's bankruptcy, but the position is more complex if the assured has become bankrupt before the third party has obtained judgment. In that scenario it will be necessary for the third party to prove the debt in the bankruptcy proceedings. In *Law Society of England and Wales v Shah*[37] Floyd J. held, relying on dicta in *Financial Services Compensation Scheme Ltd v Larnell*,[38] that the third party is able to establish his claim against the assured so as to enable use of the 1930 Act as long as the trustee in bankruptcy has admitted the debt: there is no need for a judgment, award or settlement. Floyd J. commented that:

> "[W]hat is required to establish an indemnifiable loss under the policy is that the third party's claim is raised to the status where it is established, in the sense that it no longer merely a disputed claim. The effect of its admission in bankruptcy is . . . to give it that elevated status . . . It matters not that there is no money in the estate, any more than it would matter if any other insured was unable to pay. It matters not that the loss to the bankrupt can be said to have been caused by the vesting of the estate in the trustee in bankruptcy: that will always be the case where liability is established after insolvency . . . "

The point here is that the bankrupt's estate is entirely unaffected by the third party's claim, because without that claim the insurance proceeds could not in any event form a part of the estate.

The precise difficulty which arose in *Shah* was that the assured had been discharged from bankruptcy before claims had been accepted by the trustee in bankruptcy. It was argued by the insurers that once the assured had been discharged from bankruptcy his previous debts were wiped out and it ceased to

---

[35] Although, in any later application under s.33 of the Limitation Act 1980, the delays caused by the need for the applicant to have obtained a restoration order will plainly not count against him in the overall discretion of the court.

[36] *Smith v White Knight Laundry Ltd* [2001] EWCA Civ 660. See also *Laroche v Spirit of Adventure (UK) Ltd* [2008] EWHC 788 (QB), which emphasises that the court cannot exercise this power once the limitation period has expired.

[37] *Law Society of England and Wales v Shah* [2008] Lloyd's Rep. I.R. 442.

[38] *Financial Services Compensation Scheme Ltd v Larnell* [2006] Lloyd's Rep. I.R. 448.

be possible for the third party to establish his claim. That argument was rejected by Floyd J., who noted that the effect of the discharge of a bankrupt was not to extinguish the cause of action against him but rather to prevent the enforcement of any claim against the bankrupt, so the claim remained a live one and, if admitted in the bankruptcy, could be enforced against the bankrupt's liability insurers. There is a potential further problem here, in that even though the debt is admitted in bankruptcy, so that it is established, the law requires both establishment and quantification of the claim. Floyd J.'s response to the latter requirement was that the admission of the debt in the bankruptcy was sufficient, and that the amount of the debt need not be quantified according to strict rules of law at that stage. However, such quantification will of course be necessary before any claim can be presented to the insurers.

21–016 *Interim payments.* Under CPR, Pt 23, the High Court may order a defendant to pay an interim sum to the claimant where there is no doubt as to the defendant's eventual liability and the only issue is quantum. In *Cox v Bankside Members Agency Ltd*[39] the court had made an interim award in the claimant's favour against the defendant assured, and the claimant sought to recover that sum from the defendant's liability insurers under the 1930 Act. Phillips J. held that an interim award presupposes that the assured's liability has been established, and that the amount of the interim award satisfies the requirement that the amount of the assured's liability has been quantified. Consequently, an interim award is in principle recoverable under the 1930 Act. This will not be the case where the policy itself excludes liability for an interim award, although in *Cox* the standard liability insurance wording, which covers the assured for all sums which he has become "legally liable to pay by way of damages", was held to extend to interim payments. Phillips J. regarded an interim award as "damages" within the indemnification clause, and not merely as a loan or other payment on account.

21–017 *The effect of the assured's insolvency on limitation periods.* The third party's claim against the assured is governed by the ordinary principles set out in the Limitation Act 1980, so that a claim which is time-barred by the date on which the proceedings against the assured are commenced will be lost. The position is nevertheless complicated by the assured's insolvency, as the general effect of an insolvency is to prevent the running of an unexpired limitation period for claims against the insolvent person.[40] Any outstanding claim is replaced by a right to prove in the insolvency proceedings, to which the Limitation Act 1980 is inapplicable. In *Financial Services Compensation Scheme Ltd v Larnell*[41] the Court of Appeal held that the general insolvency rule applies equally to claims which may ultimately be satisfied by insurers under the 1930 Act, so that if the assured becomes insolvent before the expiry of the limitation period for the third party's claim, time stops running and the third party has the right to prove in the assured's insolvency irrespective of provisions of the Limitation Act 1980. The doubt concerning this point arose from the principle that the Limitation Act 1980 is disapplied only as regards claims which affect the assured's assets in general, and that a claim against the insolvent person which is to be satisfied from a trust fund or secured assets remains subject to statutory limitation periods on the basis that those funds do not form a part of the insolvent person's assets available for distribution to unsecured creditors. In *Larnell* the Court of Appeal held that the

[39] *Cox v Bankside Members Agency Ltd* [1995] 2 Lloyd's Rep. 437.
[40] *Re General Rolling Stock Co Ltd* (1872) L.R. 7 Ch. App. 646.
[41] *Financial Services Compensation Scheme Ltd v Larnell* [2006] Lloyd's Rep. I.R. 448.

fact that a claim against an insolvent assured was to be satisfied by insurers under the 1930 Act did not alter the nature of the claim itself, which was and remained a claim against the assured and not against specific assets: only if the assured's claim was upheld did the question of the source of the funds to satisfy the judgment become relevant. In so deciding the Court of Appeal noted that, were it otherwise, the anomalous situation might arise that those parts of the third party's claim covered insurance would be time-barred whereas those parts which were not within the insurance—under a deductive or by reason of exhaustion of policy limits—would not be time-barred. It might be added that the third party would never know whether or not his claim against the assured was time-barred until policy coverage issues had been resolved.

Obtaining payment from the insurers

Nature of the third party's claim. Section 1(1) of the 1930 Act provides that the **21–018** rights of the assured against his insurers are to vest in the third party.[42] A claim under the 1930 Act is, therefore, a claim against insurers based on the assured's rights: it is not a claim for personal injury or property damage or for whatever other form of injury the assured has inflicted on the third party, even though the sum recoverable is assessed by reference to the third party's loss up to the limits of the policy.[43]

The rights transferred are those under which the assured has a claim against the insurers under the policy. Other rights possessed by the assured outside the scope of the policy are not transferred. Thus, if under a liability policy the assured has the right to control claims until insolvency—at which point the right of control is transferred to the insurers—such a right is plainly outside s.1(1). Were it otherwise, the right of the assured to control claims would be transferred to the third-party claimant—plainly an absurd result.[44]

The wording of the legislation has been held to mean that the third party cannot be in any better position against the insurers than the assured himself had been. There is, in effect, a perfect substitution, and the third party cannot, to quote Harman L.J. in *Post Office v Norwich Union Fire Insurance Society*,[45] "pick out the plums and leave the duff behind". This principle is perhaps the greatest limitation on the operation of the 1930 Act, and has proved to be significant in a number of contexts. The financial limits of the policy are, on this principle, applicable to the third party just as much as they were to the assured.[46]

Acquiring rights under the 1930 Act. It is a precondition to the exercise of the **21–019** third party's rights against the insurers under the 1930 Act that the third party has established and quantified the liability of the assured by means of judgment, arbitration award or settlement. This does not mean, however, that the third party

---

[42] It was held in *Cavaliere v Legal Services Commission* [2003] EWHC 323 (QB), that where the third-party claimant is legally aided in bringing his successful claim against the assured a statutory trust in favour of the Legal Services Commission representing the sums paid by way of legal aid immediately attaches to the judgment. Accordingly, when the claimant seeks to enforce the judgment against the assured's insurers, the proceeds of that action are themselves subject to the statutory trust and the assured cannot retain that sum for his own benefit.

[43] *Burns v Shuttlehurst* [1999] 1 W.L.R. 1449.

[44] *Centre Reinsurance International Co v Freakley* [2005] Lloyd's Rep. I.R. 284.

[45] *Post Office v Norwich Union Fire Insurance Society* [1967] 1 All E.R. 577 at 581.

[46] See *Avandero (UK) Ltd v National Transit Insurance Co Ltd* [1984] 2 Lloyd's Rep. 613: specified goods clause limited cover to £1,500 and derogated from general cover for CMR liability, with the result that the third party was limited to a £1,500 claim against the carrier's insurers.

is devoid of rights against the insurers pending the establishment and quantification of the assured's liability. The settled position is that, as soon as the assured
has become insolvent, the third party has contingent rights against the insurers,
and those rights crystallise with the establishment and quantification of the
assured's liability to the third party.[47] The significance of the contingent claim
analysis is that the scope of the rights of the third party against the assured are
to be assessed at the date of the assured's insolvency, even though the third party
cannot at that stage make a claim against the insurers. In *Centre Reinsurance
International Co v Freakley*[48] the policy taken out by the assured was subject to
a deductible. The insurers argued that, until the deductible figure was reached, the
insurers bore no liability to the third party and it was therefore open to them up
to the point at which the deductible level was reached to rely upon policy terms
that varied the rights of the assured on insolvency which would be unenforceable
against the third party after judgment. Blackburne J., whose decision was
affirmed by the Court of Appeal, held that this was not the case and that, as soon
as the assured became insolvent while facing claims from the third party, the
1930 Act became contingently applicable. This meant that the insurers could not
vary the rights of the assured even though the deductible levels had not been
exceeded.

The contingent rights principle has important procedural implications. The
third party is entitled to take advantage of the right to obtain insurance
information from the assured and from the insurers as soon as the assured has
become insolvent: this matter is discussed in detail below. The view was also
expressed above that the contingent claim means that a third party ought to be
permitted to apply to the court for a declaration as to the coverage of the policy
in advance of any judgment, award or settlement in respect of the assured's
liability. It was further held, in *Chubb Insurance Co of Europe SA v Davies*,[49] that
the third party has a right to be joined to proceedings brought by the insurers
against the assured to avoid the policy or otherwise to deny liability under it even
though the third party has not at that stage established and quantified the
assured's liability. As Langley J. noted, the true beneficiary of the policy is the
third party, and it is appropriate to allow him to be represented.

21–020   *Policy providing discretionary benefits.* It has been held that an agreement under
which the insurer is not legally obliged to pay the assured, but is merely under
a duty to consider any claim that the assured may present, is not a contract of
insurance.[50] Consequently, such an arrangement would appear to fall outside the
1930 Act as a matter of principle. However, if there is a contract of insurance an
element of which consists of the discretion to pay certain forms of loss, so that
the 1930 Act does apply, the third party is in no better position than the assured
in respect of that discretion.[51]

21–021   *Right to terminate risk or avoid policy.* If the assured has been guilty of a breach
of warranty or of his duty of utmost good faith, thus rendering the risk terminated

---

[47] *Cox v Bankside Menbers Agency Ltd* [1995] 2 Lloyd's Rep. 437; *Spriggs v Wessington Court
School Ltd* [2005] Lloyd's Rep. I.R. 474; *Re T&N Ltd (No.4)* [2006] Lloyd's Rep. I.R. 817.

[48] *Centre Reinsurance International Co v Freakley* [2005] Lloyd's Rep. I.R. 284, affirming [2005]
Lloyd's Rep. I.R. 22.

[49] *Chubb Insurance Co of Europe SA v Davies* [2005] Lloyd's Rep. I.R. 1.

[50] *Medical Defence Union v Department of Trade* [1979] 2 All E.R. 421.

[51] *CVG Siderugicia del Orinoco SA v London Steamship Owners' Mutual Insurance Association
(The Vainqueur Jose)* [1979] 1 Lloyd's Rep. 557.

or giving the insurer the right to avoid the policy as against the assured, as the case may be, the third party is equally affected.[52]

Illegality by the assured. If the assured has committed an illegal act, the effect   **21–022**
of which is to prevent him recovering under the policy, the rule that the third party can obtain no better rights against the insurer than were possessed by the assured himself prima facie operates to prevent recovery under the 1930 Act. However, in a number of cases decided under the road traffic legislation—*Hardy v Motor Insurers' Bureau*,[53] *Gardner v Moore*[54] and *Charlton v Fisher*[55] it was held that public policy merely operates as a personal bar on the assured which prevented him from recovering an indemnity under his own policy, and that it did not preclude an action by the assured's victim against the Motor Insurers' Bureau on the basis that injury deliberately inflicted by the assured was nevertheless a risk against which insurance was required. This approach has been applied to the 1930 Act, by Mance J. in *Total Graphics Ltd v AGF Insurance Ltd*.[56] It was there held that the fraud of an insurance intermediary, which precluded any recovery by him under his policy, did not preclude an action by the intermediary's victim. In many cases, however, the type of conduct which attracts a public policy defence will be excluded from the coverage of the policy, and if this is the case, the victim cannot recover, for the effect of the policy wording is not merely to impose a personal bar against the assured but rather to prevent a claim being made.

Notice provisions and other conditions. It is frequently a condition precedent to   **21–023**
the liability of an insurer that a claim is presented by the assured within a stated time of the event giving rise or likely to give rise to the assured's liability and that the assured must thereafter co-operate with the insurers in the provision of information. It has been held on a number of occasions that the third party must himself comply with that condition to the extent that the assured has not done so.[57] A condition of this nature may, however, be almost impossible for the third party to comply with, for if the assured himself has not presented a claim to the insurer, it may be too late for the third party to do so by the time the assured's insolvency has come to light.[58] Moreover, the assured may have committed some other serious breach of the policy, e.g. by submitting false information to the

---

[52] *McCormick v National Motor & Accident Insurance Union Ltd* (1934) 40 Com. Cas. 76; *Cleland v London General Insurance Co* (1935) 51 Ll. L.R. 156.

[53] *Hardy v Motor Insurers' Bureau* [1964] 2 Q.B. 745.

[54] *Gardner v Moore* [1984] A.C. 548.

[55] *Charlton v Fisher* [2001] Lloyd's Rep. I.R. 387.

[56] *Total Graphics Ltd v AGF Insurance Ltd* [1997] 1 Lloyd's Rep. 599.

[57] *Hassett v Legal and General Assurance Society Ltd* (1939) 63 Ll. L.R. 278; *Farrell v Federated Employers Insurance Association Ltd* [1970] 3 All E.R. 632; *Monksfield v Vehicle and General Insurance* [1971] 1 Lloyd's Rep. 139; *Edwards v Minster insurance Co Ltd* Unreported, 1994; *Pioneer Concrete (UK) Ltd v National Employers Mutual General Insurance Association Ltd* [1985] 2 All E.R. 395; *Cox v Bankside Members Agency Ltd* [1985] 2 Lloyd's Rep. 437; *Total Graphics Ltd v AGF Insurance Ltd* [1997] 1 Lloyd's Rep. 599; *Alfred McAlpine v BAI (Run-off) Ltd* [2000] Lloyd's Rep. I.R. 352; *K/S Merc-Skandia v Certain Lloyd's Underwriters* [2001] Lloyd's Rep. I.R. 802.

[58] *Berliner Motor Corp v Sun Alliance and London Insurance Ltd* [1983] 1 Lloyd's Rep. 320. See, however, the discussion below of s.2 of the 1930 Act which requires certain information to be given to the third party. Where the policy is compulsory under the Road Traffic Act 1988 or the Employers' Liability (Compulsory Insurance) Act 1969, such a provision is of no effect with respect to the claim.

insurers with regard to the nature of the loss,[59] settling with another person who may be liable to indemnify the assured for any claims against it[60] or failing to comply with obligations relating to the operation of the insured business.[61] The problem of pre-transfer breach has proved to be serious where the third party has been unaware of the assured's insolvency or even of the existence of a policy, but the rule is incapable of mitigation even in those cases. The courts have applied the same principle to other conditions in the policy, such as provisions by which the assured is prevented from admitting liability to the third party but nevertheless does so.[62] A rateable proportion clause which limits the liability of the insurer to its own proportion of the loss in the event of concurrent insurance is also binding on the third party.[63]

21–024   *The requirement of prepayment.* P&I club rules commonly contain provisions whereby the club is not to be liable to its member under a liability insurance agreement until the member has itself satisfied its liability towards the third party. Such provisions do not generally appear in other contracts of liability insurance, but there is nothing in principle to stop them from doing so. The question which has been raised, however, is the effect of a prepayment obligation attaching to the assured on the rights of a third party under the 1930 Act; this produced a sharp disagreement in two cases at first instance, although the matter was subsequently resolved by the House of Lords in a combined appeal. Both cases involved cargo claims. In the first case on this point, *The Fanti*,[64] the rules of the P&I club provided that a member could seek indemnification only where he "shall become liable to pay and shall in fact have paid".[65] The member in this case had become insolvent before having met its liability to the third party, and the third party brought proceedings under the 1930 Act. Staughton J. held that the effect of s.1(1) was to transfer to the third party on the assured's winding up the contingent contractual right of the member to be paid following its own payment; the fact that the contractual right to be paid had not accrued was immaterial to its transfer. Moreover, as it would be futile to order the third party to pay itself, that requirement would be disregarded and the third party was thus entitled to claim the insurance monies from the club. However, shortly afterwards, in *The Padre Island (No.2)*[66] Saville J. reached a different conclusion on similar facts involving an identically worded clause. In the view of the learned judge, the

---

[59] This is not a fraudulent claim as such, as there is authority for the proposition that under a liability policy there is no "claim" until the assured's liability to the third party has been established and quantified: accordingly, conduct of this type may well amount to a breach of a claims co-operation clause or the continuing duty of utmost good faith, but only when the consequences for the insurers are serious. It has been held that fraud per se is not sufficient to allow the insurers to treat the policy as repudiated or voidable: *Alfred McAlpine v BAI (Run-off) Ltd* [2000] Lloyd's Rep. I.R. 352; *K/S Merc-Skandia v Certain Lloyd's Underwriters* [2001] Lloyd's Rep. I.R. 802.

[60] *Horwood v Land of Leather Ltd* [2010] Lloyd's Rep. I.R. 453.

[61] *George Hunt Cranes Ltd v Scottish Boiler and General Insurance Co Ltd* [2002 Lloyd's Rep. I.R. 178.

[62] *Post Office v Norwich Union Fire Insurance Society* [1967] 1 All E.R. 577; *Total Graphics v AGF Insurance* [1997] 1 Lloyd's Rep. 599. But note that an employee claiming under the 1930 Act has the benefit of the principle in the Employers' Liability (Compulsory Insurance) Act 1969 which prevents the insurer from pleading post-loss breaches of condition.

[63] *Phillips v Syndicate 992 Gunner* [2004] Lloyd's Rep. I.R. 418.

[64] *The Fanti* [1987] 2 Lloyd's Rep. 299.

[65] The wording was held to be effective to impose a prepayment obligation. Such wording may, however, be modified in its effect by the context in which it is found. See *Charter Reinsurance Co Ltd v Fagan* [1996] 3 All E.R. 46 where the phrase "shall actually have paid" was held not to require prepayment by the reinsured.

[66] *The Padre Island (No.2)* [1987] 2 Lloyd's Rep. 529.

member had no contractual claim until it had made payment; consequently, there was nothing to transfer to the third party until such payment had been made. The effect of the rule was, therefore, to deprive the third party of the benefit of the Act. These cases were subsequently joined in an appeal to the Court of Appeal,[67] which accepted the views of Staughton J. and rejected those of Saville J. A subsequent appeal to the House of Lords, however, produced the reinstatement of the views of Saville J.[68] Their Lordships held that the approach adopted by Staughton J. and the Court of Appeal would confer upon the third party better rights than the assured himself possessed against the insurer, contrary to the intentions of the 1930 Act: the correct view was that if the assured could not—for want of payment—mount an action against the insurers, it was not possible for the third party to do so. The House of Lords also rejected an alternative argument to the effect that equity intervened to override the assured's obligation to pay before receiving payment. This decision, while undoubtedly correct upon the wording of s.1(1), gives rise to the illogicalities highlighted by the Court of Appeal.

Premium. There may be cases in which the assured has not paid all or some part 　21–025
of the premium under the policy. This raises the question whether a third party claiming under the 1930 Act is required to tender the unpaid premium as a precondition to bringing his action against the insurer. The answer would appear to depend upon the wording of the policy. If the payment of the premium is a condition precedent to the presentation of a claim, it would seem that the third party must comply, given his status as the statutory assignee of the assured. Conversely, if there is no condition precedent to that effect, payment of the premium is not a condition affecting the insurer's liability and it would thus seem not to be an obligation which is transferred to the assured.[69] However, in *Cox v Bankside Members Agency Ltd*,[70] Phillips J. rejected the subtleties of this distinction and held that if there was unpaid premium the insurers had a right of set-off against the third party when the policy moneys fell due. The result is that the insurers will always be entitled to receive the premium, either in advance of any claim if there is a condition precedent to liability, or by way of set off thereafter in the absence of a condition precedent to liability.

Interest awarded against the assured. If interest is awarded by the court in 　21–026
favour of the third party against the assured, the third party will be able to claim the interest from the insurer if the policy covers the assured's liability for interest. In *Cox v Bankside Members Agency Ltd*[71] interest was awarded in favour of the third party for the period prior to the judgment against the assured. Such interest could not be awarded at common law, and is permissible by virtue of s.35A of the Senior Courts Act 1981. The policy in *Cox* provided an indemnity for "compensatory damages". Phillips J. held that this phrase included pre-judgment interest, particularly in the light of the consideration that the policy conferred upon the insurer the right to refuse to settle, thereby implying an obligation to pay interest in the event that the matter had to be decided by a court. However,

---

[67] *The Padre Island (No.2)* [1989] 1 Lloyd's Rep. 239.
[68] *The Fanti* [1990] 2 All E.R. 705. This approach was followed by the Supreme Court of South Africa, on differently worded legislation, in *Canadian Superior Oil Ltd v Concord insurance Co Ltd* Unreported, 1990.
[69] *Murray v Legal and General Assurance Society Ltd* [1970] 2 Q.B. 495.
[70] *Cox v Bankside Members Agency Ltd* [1995] 2 Lloyd's Rep. 437 at 451.
[71] *Cox v Bankside Members Agency Ltd* [1995] 2 Lloyd's Rep. 435.

it was further decided in *Cox* that such interest is generally not to be regarded as a liability additional to the insurer's maximum financial liability under the policy, but merely forms a part of that liability: an intention by the insurer to accept additional liability for interest is unlikely to be found where the policy makes any provision at all for the allocation of interest as between the parties.

21–027   *Interest awarded against insurer.* In *Aluminium Wire and Cable Co Ltd v Allstate Insurance Ltd*[72] it was held that a court may award interest in a claim between third party and insurer irrespective of what the position would have been as between insurer and assured. This decision was based on the premise that the right to interest is conferred by statute rather than by contract, so that the third party's right does not depend upon any right of the assured.

21–028   *Costs.* If the assured is under the policy required to indemnify the insurer for the costs of defending the action brought against the assured by the third party, either unconditionally or in specific circumstances (e.g. where the costs have been incurred without the insurer's consent), the insurer has the right to deduct the costs from the policy monies. This right is also enforceable against claimants under the 1930 Act, on the basis that third-party claimants can be in no better position than the assured in the claim against the insurers.[73] In the same way, if the costs of settling a claim form a part of the sum insured, the amount of those costs is to be deducted from the total amount available under the policy to compensate third parties.[74]

21–029   *Arbitration clauses.* Where the policy contains an arbitration clause by virtue of which the assured has no rights against the insurer unless an arbitration award has been made in his favour, the third party cannot claim against the insurer until he has himself obtained an arbitration award against the insurer.[75] It now seems to be too late to argue that the obligation to arbitrate is personal and is not capable of assignment.[76] If the assured becomes insolvent before he has commenced arbitration against the insurer, the third party must himself initiate arbitration proceedings and he must adhere to the contractual time limits for commencing the proceedings set out in the contract.

There is, however, some doubt as to the position where the assured has commenced arbitration proceedings against the insurer before the assured's insolvency. In *The Felicie*[77] Phillips J. held that, once the assured has become

---

[72] *Aluminium Wire and Cable Co Ltd v Allstate Insurance Ltd* [1985] 2 Lloyd's Rep. 280.

[73] *Cox v Bankside Members Agency Ltd* [1995] 2 Lloyd's Rep. 437.

[74] *Centre Reinsurance International Co v Freakley* [2005] Lloyd's Rep. I.R. 284. On appeal, in *Freakley v Centre Reinsurance International Ltd* [2007] Lloyd's Rep. I.R. 32, the House of Lords held that claims-handling expenses incurred by the assured's administrators were not costs of administration and accordingly were not given priority in the administration under the Insolvency Act 1986 s.19(5).

[75] *Freshwater v Western Australia Assurance Co Ltd* [1933] 1 K.B. 515: *Dennehy v Bellamy* [1938] 2 All E.R. 262: *Smith v Pearl Assurance Co* [1939] 1 All E.R. 95; *The Padre Island (No.1)* [1984] 2 Lloyd's Rep. 408; *Ryoden Engineering Co Ltd v New India Assurance Co Ltd* [2008] H.K.E.C. 135.

[76] *Montedipe SpA v JTP-RO Jugotanker (The Jordan Nicolov)* [1990] 2 Lloyd's Rep. 11. But see the residual doubts of Phillips J. in *London Steamship Owners' Mutual Insurance Association Ltd v Bombay Trading Co Ltd (The Felicie)* [1990] 2 Lloyd's Rep. 21 based on the decision of Wright J. in *Cottage Club Estates Ltd v Woodside Estates Co (Amersham) Ltd* [1928] 2 K.B. 463.

[77] *The Felicie* [1990] 2 Lloyds Rep. 21 (decided in 1987).

insolvent, fresh arbitration proceedings against the insurers were required because the 1930 Act did not allow the third party to be substituted for the assured in arbitration proceedings commenced by the assured, although this was thought not to give rise to a problem in that the limitation period for a claim under the 1930 Act started to run on the date of the assured's winding up, so that fresh proceedings could be issued immediately. However, in *Lefevre v White*[78] Popplewell J., without being referred to *The Felicie*, held that time begins to run under the 1930 Act not from the date of the assured's insolvency but rather from the date at which the assured's claim against the insurer first accrued. On that principle, the third party in *The Felicie* would have been deprived both of the right to take over existing arbitrations and of the right to commence fresh proceedings, an outcome which Phillips J. in *The Felicie* refused to countenance. It follows that either *The Felicie* is wrongly decided on the assignment of the arbitration proceedings, or that *Lefevre v White* is wrongly decided as to the date of the accrual of the third party's action against the insurer.[79]

The question as to the assignability of arbitration proceedings was subsequently discussed by Hobhouse J. in *The Jordan Nicolov*,[80] a case not involving the 1930 Act. The learned judge saw no reason why a third party who took an assignment of the rights of the claimant in arbitration proceedings could not continue the proceedings subject only to the formalities that notice was given to the respondents in the arbitration and to the arbitrators. *The Felicie* was held to be good law only on the basis that it was confined to 1930 Act cases and did not extend to consensual assignment. However, it is clear that the reasoning in *The Felicie* was disapproved, and the only issue in *The Felicie* which can be regarded as surviving *The Jordan Nicolov* is the purely procedural point that a transfer of rights under the 1930 Act can take effect without the insurer being given formal notice. If this is indeed the only objection to the assignment of arbitration proceedings under the 1930 Act, it is hardly convincing. Nevertheless, it must be concluded that the effect of the assured's winding up upon existing arbitration proceedings remains uncertain.

Limitation of actions. Section 5 of the Limitation Act 1980 provides that an **21–030** action must be brought for breach of contract within six years from the date of the breach. A claim under an insurance policy is regarded by the law as an action for breach of contract, so that the assured has, subject to contractual restrictions, a period of at least six years to commence proceedings against the insurer from the date at which his liability to the third party has been established and quantified by judgment, award or binding settlement. The 1930 Act does not make it clear exactly how the Limitation Act is applicable to third-party claims, and in particular whether the third party's rights are derived from, or independent of, the assured's claim against the insurers. If the third party has an independent right to pursue the insurer, that right presumably accrues at the date on which the assured has become insolvent within the terms of the 1930 Act, as only at that point does the legislation operate to transfer rights to the third party. By contrast, if the third party's right is derivative, it begins to run as soon as the assured's

---

[78] *Lefevre v White* [1990] 1 Lloyd's Rep. 569.
[79] See below for discussion of limitation periods.
[80] *The Jordan Nicolov* [1990] 2 Lloyd's Rep. 11. See also *Ryoden Engineering Co Ltd v New India Assurance Co Ltd* [2008] H.K.E.C. 135.

liability to him has been established and quantified: however, as the third party cannot sue in his own name until the assured has become insolvent, the third party can do nothing until an insolvency has occurred. It follows that the third party must ensure that an insolvency event has occurred within six years from the date on which the third party established and quantified the assured's liability to him, which he can do by making the assured bankrupt or presenting a winding up petition: he can then sue the insurers in his own name.

On the assumption that the third party's rights are derivative and not independent, a potential problem arises if the third party has not taken steps to put the assured into insolvency and assured has commenced his own proceedings against the insurers within six years of his liability to the assured having been established and quantified. In the absence of an insolvency, the third party has no cause of action against the insurers. If the assured becomes insolvent during the course of the proceedings, and within the six-year limitation period, all is well as the third party can issue fresh proceedings in his own name. However, the difficult case arises where the assured's insolvency occurs after the expiry of the limitation period for his action against the insurers.

The point first arose in *The Felicie*,[81] where Phillips J. assumed that the limitation period for a third party's claim under the 1930 Act did not commence until the date of the assured's winding up. This analysis was rejected in *Lefevre v White*,[82] a case in which the third party obtained judgment against the assured and the assured then commenced proceedings against the insurers but became insolvent in the course of those proceedings more than six years after the judgment in favour of the third party. Popplewell J. held that the 1930 Act transferred only contractual rights and not the benefit of the action, so that it was necessary for the third party to commence a fresh action against the insurers. However, the court also ruled that the 1930 Act did not put the third party in any better position than the assured, which meant that the third party's cause of action against the insurers accrued at the same time as the assured's cause of action, i.e. on the establishment and quantification of the assured's liability to the third party. The third party was accordingly time-barred from commencing a fresh action. The wording of the 1930 Act plainly supports the first of the strands in Popplewell J.'s ruling, as s.1(1) transfers only "rights under the contract". However, there is no necessary justification in the 1930 Act for the second ground of judgment, as the point is simply not dealt with by the legislation. It may be commented that *The Felicie* was not brought to the attention of Popplewell J. in *Lefevre v White*, Phillips J having there commented that a decision which imposed a time bar on the third party to which the assured was not himself subject would be both "diametrically opposed to the purposes of the Act" and "suspect". The approach in *Lefevre* has nevertheless been confirmed by the Privy Council.[83]

The solution to the limitation problem, at least where the third party has failed to instigate bankruptcy proceedings, is a procedural one. Under CPR, Pt 19, the court has a general power to substitute a party to proceedings. That power can be exercised, under CPR 19.1, if either (a) it is desirable to substitute the new party so that the court can resolve all the matters in dispute in the proceedings, or (b)

[81] *The Felicie* [1990] 2 Lloyd's Rep. 21.
[82] *Lefevre v White* [1990] 1 Lloyd's Rep. 569.
[83] *Matadeen v Caribbean Insurance Co* [2002] UKPC 69.

there is an issue involving the new party and an existing party which is connected to the matters in dispute in the proceedings and it is desirable to substitute the new party so that the court can resolve that issue. It would seem that the addition of the third party following the assured's bankruptcy during the course of proceedings duly commenced within the limitation period by the assured falls within the latter of these grounds. Special provision is made in CPR 19.4 for the very situation encountered in *Lefevre v White*, where the application to join the new party is made after the expiry of the limitation period for the original action. There are two additional conditions imposed here[84]: (a) the relevant limitation period must have been current when the proceedings were commenced; and (b) the substitution of a party is necessary. Necessity is exhaustively defined in CPR 19.4(3), and the grounds relevant to the present situation are: that the claim cannot properly be carried on by or against the original party unless the new party is substituted as claimant; or the original party has had a bankruptcy order made against him and his interest has passed to the new party. The former ground is a catch-all and would seem to encompass the situation under discussion: individual bankruptcy of the assured is specifically caught by the latter provision.

Prioritising competing claims. Consistently with the rule that the third party obtains, as against the insurer, the same rights as had been possessed by the assured against the insurer, the financial limits of the policy apply equally to claims under the 1930 Act. If, therefore, the sums owed by the assured to the third party exceed the sums insured, the third party will have to bear the shortfall, and must prove in the assured's bankruptcy or liquidation for the balance.[85] The possibility that losses may exceed the financial limits of the policy gives rise to particular difficulty where there are a number of competing claimants, and the question in such a case is how to prioritise the various claims. In *Cox v Bankside Members Agency Ltd*[86] a Lloyd's members agency was insured against errors and omissions liability under a series of layered policies subject to a deductible. The agency was faced with a large number of negligence claims by Lloyd's names and, despite the fact that the litigation was being conducted under a management plan, judgments in particular actions were being given at different times. The question for Phillips J. was whether the sum insured should be frozen, and distributed proportionately to all ultimately successful claimants, or whether each successful claimant could claim as soon as the agency's liability to him had been established and quantified, so that the insured sums would be applied on a purely chronological or "first past the post" basis. Phillips J. accepted that "first past the post" operated in an arbitrary fashion, as the date of any individual judgment was as much due to factors outside the claimant's control as to design, but the learned judge ruled that "first past the post" was the legally correct solution. This particular solution was found to accord with the position which would have existed had the agency not been insolvent: the liability insurers would have been required to meet the agency's claims under the policies in the order in which the agency's liabilities were established and quantified by third parties. Phillips J. commented that a pro rata approach as an alternative to "first past the post" could not be operated as a matter of practice, as it would require postponement of any payments until all contingent liabilities had been determined, an approach which was all but impossible given the number of present and potential future claimants

21–031

---

[84] CPR 19.4(2).

[85] 1930 Act s.1(4))(b); *Avandero (UK) Ltd v National Transit Insurance Co Ltd* [1984] 2 Lloyd's Rep. 613.

[86] *Cox v Bankside Members Agency Ltd* [1995] 2 Lloyd's Rep. 437.

in the Lloyd's litigation. In *Cox* itself, the claimant names argued that the basic rule accepted by Phillips J. should not be applied, on the ground that the Lloyd's litigation implied some form of pro rata agreement as between the names. Phillips J. could find no justification for any such implication.

21–032 **Waiver of rights by insurers.** On the strength of the principle that the third party's rights are the same as those of the assured, the third party is plainly able to take advantage of any waiver or estoppel in favour of the assured which precludes the insurers from avoiding the policy or otherwise pleading policy defences. A more complex question is whether the third party can obtain his own rights by waiver or estoppel against the insurers by reference to statements made to the third party, but not to the assured, by the insurers. A number of situations must here be distinguished.

The simplest case is that in which the third party has obtained a judgment against an insolvent assured and the insurers have then conducted themselves in a fashion that amounts to a waiver of any defences. Here, the third party is in the same position as the assured and has accrued rights against the insurers so that any waiver at that stage can be relied upon by the third party.

A second possibility is that the third party has made a claim against a solvent assured, and the third party's liability insurers have intimated to the third party that the policy covers the claim. It is difficult to see how there can be any waiver in this situation because the third party has no rights at all against the insurers at this stage.[87]

The intermediate situation is that in which the assured has become insolvent and the third party is then informed by the insurers that policy defences will not be relied upon in respect of his claim. It is settled that the insolvency of the assured confers upon the third party contingent rights under the policy, although these rights do not crystallise until the third party has established and quantified the assured's liability. The question then becomes whether a third party with contingent rights can rely upon waiver by the insurers.[88] In *Spriggs v Wessington Court School Ltd*[89] the assured had become insolvent in 1984, and third parties relied upon correspondence written by the assured's liability insurers in 2002 as evidencing an intention to waive a non-disclosure defence under the policy. Stanley Burnton J. ruled that the correspondence did not amount to waiver, but held that if that was wrong a third party with mere contingent rights against insurers could not rely upon waiver. This was because an election to affirm or disaffirm was effective only if notified to the other contracting party and not to some third party[90] and because in the case of a general defence such as avoidance for breach of the duty of utmost good faith, or breach of warranty it would be curious if waiver could be relied upon by those third parties who had been in communication with the insurers, but not by third parties who had not received

---

[87] This was the view of Stanley Burnton J. in *Spriggs v Wessington Court School Ltd* [2005] Lloyd's Rep. I.R. 474.

[88] The point was left open in *Wood v Perfection Travel* [1996] L.R.L.R. 233.

[89] *Spriggs v Wessington Court School Ltd* [2005] Lloyd's Rep. I.R. 474.

[90] The only exception being where the other party cannot be contacted and the electing party has taken all possible steps to communicate the election. This exception was fashioned by the Court of Appeal in *Car and Universal Finance v Caldwell* [1965] Q.B. 525, where the seller of a motor vehicle induced by fraud to sell to a rogue was held to be able to avoid the contract (and thus to prevent the acquisition of rights by a bona fide purchaser for value without notice) by informing the police of what had occurred.

any notification from them capable of amounting to waiver.[91] This reasoning is not, it is submitted, beyond criticism or fatal to third parties. As to the first point, once the assured has become insolvent, the only persons with any real interest in the policy are third parties, and the fact that their rights are at that stage contingent rather than crystallised does not mean that those rights should not be afforded protection. As to the second point, a third party who has relied upon a waiver to bring proceedings, and who has thereby assumed the usual risks of litigation, is arguably in a different position to a third party who has not been given any indication that claims will be met. It may be that the matter is better classified as one of equitable estoppel, to make the point that the conduct relied upon is personal to the third-party claimant rather than conduct which relates to the policy as a whole.

Surpluses and deficits. If the liability of the insurer to the assured exceeds the liability of the assured to the third party (as may be the case where the insurer is liable for defence costs), the assured's rights against the insurer in respect of the surplus are left unaffected.[92] The surplus will, therefore, become available to the assured's general creditors. The possibility of a shortfall is governed by the s.1(4), which states that: **21–033**

"... if the liability of the insurer to the insured is less than the liability of the insured to the third party, nothing in this Act shall affect the rights of the third party against the insured in respect of the balance."

The apparent purpose of this provision is to preserve the right of the third party to proceed against the assured in the event of a shortfall. In practice, such an action will rarely be worthwhile unless the insurers themselves have become insolvent, although even here there is a possibility of recourse against the Financial Services Compensation Scheme. In *Centre Reinsurance International Co v Freakley*[93] it was suggested by Chadwick L.J. that s.1(4) had the further effect of removing from the third party any claim against the assured until the insurance moneys had been exhausted, failing which, there was a risk of double recovery by the third party. Arden L.J. was doubtful of the correctness of this proposition for a number of reasons: it reduced the rights of the third party where the insurers were themselves insolvent or their assets were untraceable; the purpose of the 1930 Act was to give the third party additional rights and not to remove them; and there was no risk of double recovery because if the third party chose to sue the assured then the assured himself—and not the third party—would have a claim against the insurers. Latham L.J. reserved his position. It is suggested that the doubts expressed by Arden L.J. are strongly persuasive.[94]

Contracting out

Section 1(3) of the 1930 Act. Section 1(3) provides as follows: **21–034**

"In so far as any contract of insurance made after the commencement of this Act in respect of any liability of the insured to third parties purports, whether directly or

---

[91] This problem does not arise if the defence is in relation to a specific claim, e.g. breach of a notification provision. Estoppel was not in fact argued in *Spriggs* as there had been no reliance. Stanley Burnton J. did accept, however, that in appropriate circumstances the insurers could be estopped as against a third party if they represented that they intended to make payment, assuming that the necessary reliance could be found.

[92] 1930 Act s.1(4)(a).

[93] *Centre Reinsurance International Co v Freakley* [2005] Lloyd's Rep. I.R. 284.

[94] The point was left open in *Re T&N Ltd (No.4)* [2006] Lloyd's Rep. I.R. 817.

indirectly, to avoid the contract or to alter the rights of the parties thereunder upon the happening to the insured of any of the [insolvency events set out above], the contract shall be of no effect."

The general intention of this provision is to negate any attempt in the contract of insurance to cause the assured's rights to abate upon insolvency, thereby preventing the third party from taking advantage of the 1930 Act. Thus, a provision in the rules of a P&I club whereby a member loses membership automatically upon becoming bankrupt is clearly contrary to s.1(3) and is struck down by that subsection.[95]

Section 1(3) by its terms applies to every policy provision that purports to avoid the contract or alter the rights of the assured on the occurrence of a statutory insolvency event. In *Centre Reinsurance International Co v Freakley*[96] the Court of Appeal held that section applied only to a term that sought to oust or limit the rights of the third party and not to one that either left the rights of the third party unaffected, or that improved the rights of the third party.[97] In *Centre Reinsurance* the employers' liability policy in question contained a claims control clause under which, in the event of the assured's insolvency, the insurers were to have "the full, exclusive and absolute authority, discretion and control of the administration, defence and disposition (including but not limited to settlement) of all Asbestos Claims". The Court of Appeal held that this clause did not operate to reduce the rights of the parties: the right of the third party to claim was unaffected; all that had changed was the identity of the person with the right to control those claims. In the words of Blackburne J. at first instance,[98] s.1(3) applies only to those terms which constitute "an alteration in the enjoyment by the third party of his rights against the insurers by prejudicing or reducing those rights in some material way".

21–035 *Date at which section 1(3) applies.* The principle that the assured has a contingent claim against the insurers under the 1930 Act as soon as the assured has become insolvent, even though the third party has not at that stage obtained a judgment against the assured, means that the third party is protected by s.1(3) as from the date of the assured's insolvency, and not simply from the date upon which the assured is found to be liable to the third party. In *Centre Reinsurance International Co v Freakley* the policy cover was not triggered until the assured's aggregate losses reached the figure of £690 million. The issue here raised was whether any terms in the policy that purported to vary the rights of the assured on insolvency, and that fell foul of the 1930 Act nevertheless remained valid until the deductible level had been exceeded, because until that point had been reached the assured (and accordingly the third party) could have no claim against the insurers. The Court of Appeal, affirming the first instance judgment of Black-burne J., held that the 1930 Act attached to the policy as soon as the assured became insolvent, which in turn meant that the prohibition in s.1(3) on variations in the rights of the assured was applicable from the outset and did not begin to operate only after the deductibles under the policy had been exhausted. As

---

[95] *The Fanti and the Padre Island* [1989] 1 Lloyd's Rep. 329.

[96] *Centre Reinsurance International Co v Freakley* [2005] Lloyd's Rep. I.R. 284.

[97] In *Centre Reinsurance* the policy contained a pay to be paid" clause, although—under the term of the policy—this ceased to operate on the insolvency of the assured, so that the third party had a direct claim. Latham L.J. noted that the pay to be paid clause was unaffected by s.1(3) as it was for the benefit of the third party.

[98] *Centre Reinsurance International Co v Freakley* [2005] Lloyd's Rep. I.R. 22.

Blackburne J. pointed out, were it otherwise, a policy could legitimately state that the deductible level was to double on the insolvency of the assured.

Trigger for the application of section 1(3). As previously noted, the 1930 Act is   **21–036** contingently applicable to any claim against the assured where any of the insolvency events listed in s.1(1) of the 1930 Act occurs. Those events are statutory insolvency procedures. The list does not extend to contractual events that may be the immediate precursor of a statutory insolvency procedure. This lacuna gives rise to the possibility of a policy providing that the rights of the assured are to be varied at some point before the occurrence of a statutory insolvency event. Thus, when the statutory event subsequently occurs, the rights of the assured have already been varied and there is no variation upon which s.1(3) is able to bite. The point was discussed in *Centre Reinsurance International Co v Freakley*, where the right to take over defence of proceedings against the assured was under the policy to be transferred on the assured's administration. The assured went into administration on October 1, 2001, but the application to the court required to regularise the position—the statutory insolvency event—was not presented until later in the day. The argument that s.1(3) was inapplicable because the variation had taken effect before the statutory insolvency event had occurred was rejected on the ground that the administration order had been made on the basis of an undertaking for the presentation of a petition and it was thus possible to treat the presentation of the petition (the contractual insolvency event) and the making of the administration order (the statutory insolvent event) as having occurred concurrently. The Court of Appeal refused to consider how s.1(3) would have been affected had it not been possible to reach this conclusion, although at first instance Blackburne J. had suggested that it would be unsatisfactory if s.1(3) could be sidestepped by a contractual provision that could operate to alter rights under the policy in advance of a statutory insolvency procedure. Blackburne J.'s solution was that s.1(3) is not triggered solely by the statutory insolvency procedures listed in s.1(1) and that, if there was a "sufficient connection" between the contractual variation trigger and the statutory insolvency event, the former was caught by s.1(3). Thus, the administration of the assured immediately prior to the presentation of the petition for administration would have brought s.1(3) into play because the "two events could scarcely have been more closely connected." Blackburne J. did accept, however, that a contractual variation clause that was triggered by an event entirely divorced from statutory insolvency procedures and having no statutory equivalent would be outside s.1(3).

Pay to be paid clauses. A key issue which has arisen is whether the prepayment   **21–037** provision contained in the rules of P&I clubs, discussed above, is avoided by s.1(3). In *The Fanti*[99] Staughton J. ruled that the 1930 Act passed to the third party all the rights and liabilities of the assured under the policy, including the contingent right to claim subject to payment. Staughton J. went on to hold, in the event that that was wrong, that the imposition of an obligation to pay necessarily altered the rights of an insolvent assured, as its practical effect was that a solvent assured would be able to seek an indemnity under the rules while an insolvent assured would be deprived of an indemnity. On this basis, Staughton J. decided that the prepayment requirement was struck down by s.1(3). Saville J. disagreed

---

[99] *The Fanti* [1987] 2 Lloyd's Rep. 299.

with this reasoning in *The Padre Island (No.2)*.[100] In his view the prepayment clause did not alter the assured's legal rights in the event of insolvency, as the right was the same in all cases; an indemnity could be claimed by an assured only when he had paid the third party. In other words, in the view of Saville J., what altered the assured's rights was not the contract but the fact of his insolvency. It may be seen that the learned judges in these cases were taking a different view of the meaning of the word "alter": in *The Padre Island (No.2)* that word was taken as referring to the legal rights of the assured following insolvency, whereas in *The Fanti* it was taken as referring to the practical rights of the assured following insolvency. Saville J. went on to hold in *The Padre Island (No.2)* that the pre-payment provision could not be attacked as a penalty clause, as it did not impose any obligation on the assured to pay any money in the event of its contravention, nor was relief from forfeiture available on equitable grounds, for that doctrine has no part to play in commercial transactions.

The conflict between Staughton J. and Saville J. was resolved by the Court of Appeal and subsequently the House of Lords in a joint appeal, in *The Fanti and the Padre Island*.[101] The Court of Appeal preferred the views of Saville J.: while an insolvent member would not in practice be able to make a claim against his club because of the pre-payment obligation, it could not be said that his legal rights had been modified by reason of his insolvency. This part of the decision was obiter as the Court of Appeal had independently of this point concluded that the pre-payment clause did not constitute a barrier to the third party's right to make a claim. The House of Lords overturned the Court of Appeal's reasoning on the latter, point, but as to the former confirmed its view that there was a distinction between a practical and a legal variation in the rights of the third party, and that a pay to be paid clause left the third party in exactly the same legal position whether or not the assured was insolvent.

21–038   Settlement contracts. At common law any agreement reached between the assured and his liability insurers in respect of a claim by a third party cannot be challenged by the third party even if the result is to leave the assured with insufficient funds to meet the third party's claim.[102] By contrast s.3 of the 1930 Act prohibits settlement agreements between the insurer and assured which are made after an event triggering the operation of the Act has taken place. Clearly, given that the third party obtains the rights of the assured, any such agreement will inevitably be intended to limit the recovery possible by the third party. Section 3 is in the following terms:

> "Where the insured has become bankrupt or where in the case of the assured being a company, a winding-up order or an administration order has been made or a resolution for a voluntary winding-up order has been passed, with respect to the company, no agreement made between the insurer and the insured after liability has been incurred to the third party and after the commencement of the bankruptcy or winding up or the day of the making of the administration order, as the case may be, nor waiver, assignment, or other disposition made by, or payment made to the insured after the commencement or day aforesaid shall be effective to defeat or affect those rights transferred to the third party under this Act, but those rights shall be the same as if no such agreement, waiver, assignment, disposition or payment had been made."

---

[100] *The Padre Island (No.2)* [1987] 2 Lloyd's Rep. 529.
[101] *The Fanti and the Padre Island* [1989] 1 Lloyd's Rep. 329; [1990] 2 All E.R. 705.
[102] *Rowe v Kenway & United Friendly Insurance Co* (1921) 8 Ll. L.R. 225, where the third party failed in his assertion that the assured and insurer had unlawfully conspired against him.

Section 3 does not apply to settlements between the assured and third party claimants.[103] The section is confined to post-insolvency settlements between the assured and the insurers, and does not cover any other pre-insolvency agreement between them. Thus if the assured and the insurers enter into a pre-insolvency agreement to compromise potential claims against the assured, that agreement is not caught by s.3, and creates a limitation on the insurers' liability which is binding on a third party with a claim against the assured at the date of the insolvency[104] once the assured has become insolvent and a claim is made by the third party.[105]

Provision of information

Obtaining information under the 1930 Act. Section 2 is designed to assist a third   **21–039**
party who would not otherwise be aware of the existence of insurance, by requiring disclosure of the relevant information to him. The persons under a duty to supply the relevant information on the request of the third party are listed in ss.2(1)–(1A) as:

> "[T]he bankrupt debtor, personal representative of the deceased debtor or company, and, as the case may be, the trustee in bankruptcy, trustee, the supervisor of a voluntary arrangement approved under Part I or Part VIII of the Insolvency Act 1986, liquidator, administrator, receiver, or manager, or a person in possession of the property".

The information to be provided is, under s.2(1), "such information as may reasonably be required by [third party] for the purpose of enforcing [rights under the 1930 Act]". The duty also requires the third party to be permitted to inspect and take copies of all contracts of insurance, receipts for premiums and other relevant documents in the possession or power of the person upon whom the duty is imposed (s.2(3)). Where the third party has obtained sufficient information to give him reasonable ground for supposing that rights have been transferred to him under the Act the insurers in question are under the same duty to provide information as attaches to the persons set out above (s.2(2)).

Until recently the most important apparent weakness in the operation of the section was that it could not be utilised by the third party until the assured's liability had been established. It had been held that the third party's rights to information did not arise until he had obtained a judgment, award or settlement which established and quantified the assured's liability to him,[106] the effect being to require the third party to proceed to judgment against the assured in the hope that liability insurance was in place. This result was criticised by the Law Commissions in the 2001 Report, which proposed changing the law to allow information to be sought when the claim against the assured was brought. Mance J., speaking extra-judicially,[107] also felt that the position could not be justified. The earlier authorities were overruled by the Court of Appeal in *Re OT Computers*,[108] the Court of Appeal holding that the third party obtained contingent rights on the assured's insolvency and that the section made sense

[103] *Re T&N Ltd (No.4)* [2006] Lloyd's Rep. I.R. 817.
[104] If the third party does not have a claim at this point because he has not suffered any loss, then he is in any event not protected by s.3: *Re T&N Ltd (No.4)* [2006] Lloyd's Rep. I.R. 817.
[105] *Normid Housing Association Ltd v Ralphs* [1989] 1 Lloyd's Rep. 265.
[106] *Nigel Upchurch Associates v Aldridge Estates Investment Co Ltd* [1993] I Lloyd's Rep. 535; *Woolwich Building Society v Taylor* [1995] 1 B.C.L.C. 132. The cases proceeded on different reasoning.
[107] [1995] L.M.C.L.Q. 34.
[108] *Re OT Computers* [2004] Lloyd's Rep. I.R. 669.

only if it could be utilised in advance of legal proceedings against the assured. As a result of *Re OT Computers*, once the assured has become insolvent a third party with a claim against the assured has contingent rights under the 1930 Act and is thus entitled to obtain the relevant information from the assured (under s.2(1)) and from the insurers (under s.2(2)). By this means the third party can determine whether the policy is likely to cover the loss, whether the policy has lapsed by non-payment of premiums and whether the insurers have purported to deny liability.

21–040 *Information from other sources.* In *Burns v Shuttlehurst*[109] the Court of Appeal held that s.2 provides the only significant mechanism for the provision of information to the third party. In that case the third party had obtained a judgment on liability but not quantum against the insolvent assured. The third party's attempt to use the pre-action disclosure rules in what is now CPR 31.16 for his proposed action against the insurers was dismissed on the ground that third party was not, until he obtained a judgment on quantum against the assured, a "likely" party to any action.[110]

There may be other ways of obtaining information. Under s.155 of the Insolvency Act 1986, a third party may apply for permission to inspect the books or records of a company in the course of winding-up: this provision is not directed to insurance, and in their 2001 Report the Law Commissions were unable to identify a case in which this procedure had been adopted to supplement an action under the 1930 Act.

It would also seem that a third party cannot utilise CPR 31.17, which is concerned with third-party disclosure, against insurers. This provides, so far as relevant, as follows:

> "(1) This rule applies where an application is made to the court under any Act for disclosure by a person who is not a party to the proceedings.
> (2) The application must be supported by evidence.
> (3) The court may make an order under this rule only where—
>> (a) the documents of which disclosure is sought are likely to support the case of the applicant or adversely affect the case of one of the other parties to the proceedings; and
>> (b) disclosure is necessary in order to dispose fairly of the claim or to save costs."

CPR 31.17(3) contemplates that the documents sought are likely to support the case of the applicant or adversely affect the case of one or other of the parties to the proceedings. However, insurance documents have no relevance to the third party's case against the assured, and the insurers themselves are not parties to the action until the assured has obtained judgment on quantum and liability. The provision thus appears to be inapplicable.

A further possibility for the early disclosure of insurance information is CPR 18.1, which is in the following terms:

> "(1) The court may at any time order a party to—
>> (a) clarify any matter which is in dispute in the proceedings; or

---

[109] *Burns v Shuttlehurst* [1999] 1 W.L.R. 1449.
[110] The Court of Appeal also held that it had no jurisdiction to grant a disclosure order under the parent provision, s.33 of the Senior Courts Act, as at the time the provision confined pre-action disclosure to personal injury cases. That limitation was removed by the Access to Justice Act 1999.

(b) give additional information in relation to any such matter, whether or not the matter is contained or referred to in a statement of case."

It was held by Irwin J. in *Harcourt v FEF Griffin*[111] that CPR 18.1(1)(b) confers upon the court the jurisdiction to order the assured to disclose its insurance position to the claimant even though the validity or scope of the insurance was not of itself the subject matter of the dispute between the parties. However, that conclusion was rejected by David Steel J. in *West London Pipeline and Storage Ltd v Total UK Ltd*,[112] the learned judge holding—with undisguised reluctance—that it could not be said that insurance information could clarify any matter in dispute in the proceedings within the meaning of CPR18.1(1)(b), and that the most that could be said was that it would be advantageous for the claimant to know whether the defendant was able to pay.

Information provisions are also contained in reg.4(4) of the Employers' Liability (Compulsory Insurance) Regulations 1998.[113] Under this provision, an employer is required to retain for a period of 40 years any certificate of insurance issued to him in compliance with the compulsory insurance rules in the Employers' Liability (Compulsory Insurance) Act 1969. By this means, an injured employee ought to be able to establish which insurer was on risk when he was injured, assuming that the employee can pinpoint a particular year during which the act or exposure giving rise to his injuries occurred.[114] The duty to retain the certificate applies only to policies in force immediately before January 1, 1999, so that the 1998 Regulations are not retroactive in this respect. Some 96 per cent of employers' liability insurers have proved to be traceable, and in 1999 the Association of British Insurers and the Lloyd's Market Association in 1999 adopted a voluntary Code of Practice for tracing the remaining employers' liability insurance policies (ELCOP). It appears from a Department of Work and Pensions Consultation Paper published in February 2010 that something over half of the outstanding policies have been traced by the use of ELCOP.[115] The Consultation Paper has proposed the creation of an Employers' Liability Tracing Office (ELTO) which would operate an electronic database of policies and would operate the existing tracing service. ELTO as proposed is eventually to provide a complete record of all new employers' liability policies issued.[116]

3. Third Parties (Rights Against Insurers) Act 2010

General features. The 2010 Act retains the basic notion of the 1930 Act that a third party should be entitled to recover from the assured's liability insurers in the event of the assured's insolvency, but a number of important changes are made in order to remove some of the procedural obstacles thrown up by the 1930 Act. In outline: **21–041**

---

[111] *Harcourt v FEF Griffin* [2008] Lloyd's Rep. I.R. 386.
[112] *West London Pipeline and Storage Ltd v Total UK Ltd* [2008] Lloyd's Rep. I.R. 688.
[113] SI 1998/2573.
[114] This may be problematic in an exposure case where there has been a change of insurer.
[115] For an illustration of the problem, see *Hall v Newall Heating Ltd and AGF Insurance Ltd* Unreported, April 14, 2010, where there was simply no record of who had acted as the employer's liability insurers in the relevant period.
[116] There is a supplementary proposal for the establishment of an Employers' Insurers Bureau, akin to the Motor Insurers Bureau, which will pay claims in the event that it is not possible to trace the insurers.

(a) The 2010 Act applies to a wider range of situations, including individual voluntary arrangements.

(b) There is a single stage whereby, if the assured has become insolvent, the third party can bring a single action against the assured and his liability insurers, rather than bringing an action against the assured and then seeking to enforce it in separate proceedings against the insurers. This removes the need for a struck off company to be revived so that it can be sued, and allows the court to resolve coverage questions as preliminary issues so that, if there is no coverage, an expensive trial on the assured's liability can be avoided.

(c) The third party has a right to obtain information about the insurance from the assured, the insurers or any third parties in possession of that information.

(d) The court is empowered to grant declaratory relief on either policy coverage or liability issues.

(e) Jurisdiction is based squarely on the place of the insolvency.

Other features of the 1930 Act have been retained. Thus: the "first past the post" principle, which applies to allocate limited funds amongst a large number of third parties, has not been reversed; and genuine pre-insolvency settlements between the assured and the insurers are left untouched.

As is the case with the 1930 Act, the 2010 Act is concerned with two situations. The first is the right of a third party who wishes to pursue an insolvent assured, to turn to the assured's insurers once a judgment has been obtained. The second is the ability of the third party to use the 1930 Act as a method of enforcing a judgment against a solvent assured. The third party can bring an action against the assured, obtain a judgment and, if it is not satisfied, then insolvency proceedings can be initiated against the assured, thereby giving the third party direct access to the assured's liability insurers.

21–042   Events triggering the operation of the 2010 Act. The statutory transfer of rights from the assured to the third party arises where the assured becomes a "relevant person". That phrase is defined by ss.4–7, and seeks to encompass all of the situations in which there is a statutory insolvency. The statutory insolvency procedures for the most part post-dated the 1930 Act, so it was necessary for the 2010 Act to pick them all up. The 2010 Act also extends to the case of a struck-off company, whether or not it was struck off when insolvent. The major lacuna in the 1930 Act, that of individual voluntary arrangements, has been remedied.

21–043   *Individuals.* Under s.6(1),[117] an individual is a "relevant person" if any of the following is in force in respect of him in England and Wales:

(a) a deed of arrangement registered in accordance with the Deeds of Arrangement Act 1914,

(b) an administration order made under Part 6 of the County Courts Act 1984,

(c) an enforcement restriction order made under Part 6A of that Act,

(d) a debt relief order made under Part 7A of the Insolvency Act 1986,

---

[117] Section 4(2) sets out an equivalent list for Scotland, and s.4(3) applies to insolvency procedures in Northern Ireland.

(e) a voluntary arrangement approved in accordance with Part 8 of the Insolvency Act 1986,

(f) a bankruptcy order made under Part 9 of the Insolvency Act 1986.

An individual who dies insolvent, i.e. an individual whose estate falls to be administered in accordance with an order under s.421 of the Insolvency Act 1986, is treated as a "relevant person" under para.(b) above (s.5(1)–(2)), so that the Act applies to his estate (s.5(3)).

The Act does not deal with a discharged bankrupt, and is limited to the situation in which a bankruptcy order is "in force". However, the position of a discharged bankrupt was dealt with by the Court of Appeal in *Law Society v Shah*,[118] it there being held that if a bankrupt has been discharged then the claim against him is not extinguished but simply becomes unenforceable against him, so that it remains open to a third party to establish and quantify the liability of a discharged bankrupt for the purpose of obtaining judgment against the bankrupt's insurers.

Legal persons. Under s.6(1)–(2) of the 2010 Act[119] a body corporate or an unincorporated body is a relevant person if—   **21–044**

(a) a compromise or arrangement between the body and its creditors (or a class of them) is in force, having been sanctioned in accordance with s.899 of the Companies Act 2006[120];

(b) the body has been dissolved under s.1000, 1001 or 1003 of the Companies Act 2006 and the body has not been restored to the register or ordered to be restored to the register[121];

(c) a voluntary arrangement approved in accordance with Pt 1 of the Insolvency Act 1986 is in force in respect of it;

(d) an administration order made under Pt 2 of the Insolvency Act 1986 is in force in respect of it;

(e) there is a person appointed in accordance with Pt 3 of the Insolvency Act 1986[122] who is acting as receiver or manager of the body's property (or there would be such a person so acting but for a temporary vacancy);

(f) the body is, or is being, wound up voluntarily in accordance with Ch.2 of Pt 4 of the Insolvency Act 1986;

(g) there is a person appointed under s.135 of the Insolvency Act 1986 who is acting as provisional liquidator in respect of the body (or there would be such a person so acting but for a temporary vacancy);

(h) the body is, or is being, wound up by the court following the making of a winding-up order under Ch.6 of Pt 4 of the Insolvency Act 1986 or Pt 5 of that Act.

---

[118] *Law Society v Shah* [2008] Lloyd's Rep. I.R. 442.

[119] Scottish procedures are set out in ss.6(3) and 7, and those for Northern Ireland are set out in s.6(4).

[120] A transfer of rights under the 2010 Act applies only to a third party who is bound by the scheme of arrangement: s.6(6).

[121] The effect of this provision is that proceedings can be initiated against a dissolved company's insurer in order to establish its liability without the need to apply to the court for the restoration of the company to the register, as is required under the 1930 Act.

[122] Including a receiver appointed under s.101 of the Law of Property Act 1925: 2010 Act s.6(9).

The 2010 Act does not cover contractual insolvencies, as where a receiver is appointed under a floating charge following the occurrence of an event which causes the floating charge to crystallise: neither the third party nor the insurers are likely to be aware of this situation, and a statutory insolvency event is very likely to follow closely on behind.

21-045 **Contracts within the 2010 Act.** The 2010 applies only to rights under a contract of insurance (s.1(5)). This term is not defined, but it may be assumed that it encompasses P&I Club rules which technically do not qualify as contracts of insurance to the extent that the Club does not undertake any legal liability to pay but rather merely has a discretion to do so.

By s.16, the Act applies to a liability whether or not voluntarily incurred. The purpose is to catch liability only in contract as well as liability in tort. Most liability policies do not extend to liabilities voluntarily incurred, unless there is a parallel tortious action, but the Act brings such claims within its scope where the policy covers them. The provision codifies the decision of the Court of Appeal in *Re OT Computers*,[123] which extended the 1930 Act to legal expenses incurred under contract. It may be noted that at the time of the Law Commissions' Reports the 1930 Act was thought not to cover voluntarily incurred liabilities,[124] a decision which the Law Commissions thought should be reversed. The Court of Appeal in *Re OT Computers* did just that, anticipating the 2010 Act.

The 2010 Act, continuing the policy of the 1930 Act, does not apply to reinsurance (s.15). This may give rise to problems in a very small number of cases, as it is not always clear whether an insurer's liability has arisen under a contract of insurance or under some other form of arrangement, e.g. a captive insurer, a bond or an extended consumer warranty.[125] These issues are quite properly left to be resolved as and when they arise.

21-046 **Extraterritorial effect.** As discussed above, it was uncertain how the 1930 Act applied to a case with a foreign element, and in particular whether the policy had to be governed by English law or whether some other link was required.[126] Section 18 of the 2010 Act lays down a straightforward rule, which is that if the insolvency procedure is one conducted under the law of one of the constituent parts of the United Kingdom, then the Act will apply irrespective of the place in which liability was incurred, the domicile of the parties, the law applicable to the policy and the place where payment has to be made.

Assuming that there is an insolvency procedure, jurisdiction and applicable law rules are laid down in Council Regulation 44/2001 (the Brussels Regulation), the Civil Procedure Rules and the Rome I Regulation.

21-047 *Jurisdiction.* Turning first to jurisdiction, if the insurer is domiciled in the EU then, under art.9 of the Brussels Regulation, the insurers can be sued in the country of its domicile or in the country of the assured's domicile. Article 11, which deals with liability insurance, lays down the rule (art.11.2) that if a direct action is permitted, art.9 applies. This has been held by the European Court of Justice in the *Odenbreit*[127] case to mean that the action can be brought against the

---

[123] *Re OT Computers* [2004] Lloyd's Rep. I.R. 669.
[124] *Tarbuck v Avon Insurance* [2002] Lloyd's Rep. I.R. 393.
[125] The latter was discussed inconclusively in *Re OT Computers* [2004] Lloyd's Rep. I.R. 669.
[126] *Irish Shipping v Commercial Union* [1989] 2 Lloyd's Rep. 144.
[127] Case C-463/06 *FBTO Shadverzekerigen NV v Odenbreit* [2008] Lloyd's Rep. I.R. 354.

insurers in the country where the injured party is domiciled, the law allows a direct action. The *Odenbreit* case, however, does not decide which law has to permit the direct action. This matter was discussed in *Thwaites v Aviva Assurances*,[128] where it was held that the relevant law is the law applicable to the policy and not—as had often been assumed—the law of the forum. The effect of this on a claim under the 2010 Act is that a third party domiciled in England can bring an action in England against an insurer domiciled elsewhere in the EC or EFTA as long as the policy is governed by a law which permits such a direct action. If the policy is governed by English law, all is well. However, if the policy is governed by the law of another EC or EFTA Member State which does not recognise a direct action, the English court will simply not possess jurisdiction to hear the third party's claim.

As regards intra-UK jurisdiction, s.13 of the 2010 Act states that a third party domiciled in one part of the United Kingdom may bring an action against an insurer domiciled in another part of the United Kingdom in the domicile of either, any contractual provision on jurisdiction being overridden.

Where the insurers are not domiciled in the European Union, the ability of the third party to bring proceedings against the insurer depends upon the jurisdiction rules in CPR PD 6B. The claim brought by the third party is as transferee of the assured's contractual rights, so that the claim is presumably to be classified as contractual.[129] It follows that the third party may find some difficulty in establishing the jurisdiction of the English courts over the insurers if the policy is not made in England, governed by English law or to be performed by the insurers in England.[130] If, however, the third party has a claim against the assured which is subject to the jurisdiction of the English courts, it may be that the insurers can be joined to the proceedings on the basis that they are necessary and proper parties to such proceedings.[131] A jurisdiction agreement is presumably binding on the assured, although the English court has an overriding jurisdiction to allow a claim to proceed in England if the interests of justice demand the overriding of a jurisdiction clause.

Applicable law. Under the Rome I Regulation the English courts are required to determine the law applicable to the insurance policy and then to apply that law to the policy. It would not appear to matter that the applicable law—if it is not English law—does not permit a transfer of rights. That law is relevant only to determine whether there is or there is not liability under the policy. If the third party has established and quantified the assured's liability, he can—subject to jurisdictional issues—seek judgment in England under the policy irrespective of its applicable law.   **21–048**

Transfer of rights

Conditions for transfer. Under s.1(1) of the 2010 Act there is a transfer of rights if "a relevant person" (i.e. a person who has become subject to a statutory insolvency or equivalent procedure): (a) incurs liability against which there is insurance; or (b) an insured person having incurred liability becomes a relevant person. The effect of s.1(2) is that if the assured is insolvent and has incurred   **21–049**

---

[128] *Thwaites v Aviva Assurances* Unreported, February 2010, Mayors and City of London Court.

[129] Contrast a direct claim against motor insurers, which does not depend upon any form of assignment and thus is to be classified as tortious: *Maher v Groupama Grand Est* [2009] EWCA Civ 1191.

[130] Under CPR PD 6 para.3.1(6).

[131] Under CPR PD 6 para.3.1(3).

liability, or has incurred liability and then becomes insolvent (probably because he has been made the subject of insolvency proceedings by the third party), there is a transfer of the assured's rights to the third party and a direct action can be brought against the relevant person's insurers.

Under s.1(3), the third party can bring proceedings in respect of transferred rights against the insurers without having established and quantified the insolvent assured's liability, but the third party cannot enforce those rights without having established and quantified that liability. The third party can establish and quantify the assured's liability under s.1(4) by: obtaining a judgment against the assured; obtaining an arbitration award against the assured; entering into a settlement with the assured (although a settlement can ultimately be challenged by the insurers on the ground that it is not in full or in part made on the basis of legal liability); or obtaining a declaration to that effect under s.2. The position is in clear contrast to the earlier law. Under the 1930 Act, the third party has to establish and quantify the assured's liability, and then show that the assured is insolvent, as a precondition to bringing an action against the insurers under the policy; an immediate action against the insurer pending the determination of the assured's liability is not possible.[132] Under the 2010 Act, once there is insolvency, the third party can turn his attention to the insurers in order to establish their liability under the policy, but he cannot actually enforce the assured's rights until he has established and quantified the assured's own liability. The third party may do this by separate proceedings against the assured, or, more likely, by seeking a declaration as to the assured's liability in the same proceedings as have been brought to establish the insurers' liability under the policy. In practice, therefore, once the assured has become insolvent, the third party will seek to establish and quantify the assured's liability to him as a matter of law, and to establish liability under the policy, in a single set of proceedings.

It has been held under the 1930 Act that a third party who obtains a judgment on liability against the assured, with damages to be assessed, can obtain an interim award from the insurers under CPR Pt 23. It is not clear whether this remains possible under the 2010 Act.

21–050   *The amount transferred.* Section 8 of the 2010 Act is concerned with the case in which the assured's liability to the third party is less than the amount of the liability of the insurers to the assured. This may be the case because, for example, the policy defence costs. Section 8 thus provides that the transfer of rights to the third party is only for the former amount.

Declaratory relief

21–051   *Scope of declaratory relief.*[133] A third party who claims that rights have been transferred to him under a contract of insurance by reason of the assured's insolvency, but who has not yet established and quantified the assured's liability, has the right to seek declaratory relief: this is the effect of s.2(1), (6) and (8).[134]

---

[132] *Post Office v Norwich Union* [1967] 1 All E.R. 577.

[133] What follows relates to England. For the position in Scotland, see s.3 of the 2010 Act.

[134] The section refers to an "insured" rather than to a "relevant person", to distinguish between an assured who has become insolvent and one who has not, thereby making the point that s.2 is triggered by a mere claim that the assured has become insolvent. In the same way, s.2 refers to a "person" rather than to a third party, because a third party under the Act is a person who has established that rights have been transferred to him.

The third party is entitled to seek a declaration in respect of: (a) the liability of the assured to him; or (b) the insurers' potential liability to the third party (s.2(2)). Section 2(2)(a) is concerned with the validity of the third party's claim against the assured, and s.2(2)(b) is concerned with whether the assured has become insolvent (failing which there cannot be a transfer) and whether there is liability under the policy (see s.2(11)). The effect is that the liability of the assured, and the liability of the insurers, can be resolved in a single set of proceedings. Section 2(6) allows the court to give an "appropriate judgment" in conjunction with a declaration, which will generally mean a money judgment. All of this means that, if the assured is a struck off company, the third party does not need to initiate separate preliminary proceedings to resurrect the company in order to attempt to establish and quantify its liability so that the claim can be pressed against the company's insurers and can lead to judgment.

The right to a declaration (the court has no power to refuse) is, under cl.2(3), subject to any defence on which the insurer may rely. In relation to (a) the defence will be in respect of the substantive claim or its quantum, and in relation to (b) it will be the absence of the assured's insolvency or a defence under the policy. These points are amplified later in the clause. If declarations under both heads are sought, the insurer may be faced by the possibility of being forced to run conflicting defences. An example may be a product liability matter, where the defence to the claim by P against the assured is that the product was not defective, and the defence to the claim by the assured under the policy is that the defect in question is excluded by the policy wording. In such a case the insurer is perfectly entitled to run alternative defences.

Defences: limitation. If a declaration is sought against the insurers in respect of   **21–052** the assured's liability to third party under s.2(2)(a), then s.2(4) states that the insurers can rely upon any defence that would have been open to them in proceedings brought against the assured. There is one important exception here in relation to limitation periods. Where the third party has commenced proceedings against the assured within the limitation period applicable to the claim (the statutory limitation period for a claim in contract or tort, as the case may be) and the claim has not been resolved but the limitation period has expired in the course of those proceedings, then the effect of s.12 of the 2010 Act[135] is to prevent the insurers from relying upon the expiry of the limitation period should the third party seek a declaration as to the liability of the assured to him in declaration proceedings against the insurers.

Joinder of assured. Section 2(9) provides that the assured can be made a   **21–053** defendant to the declaration proceedings, which may have procedural advantages in respect of evidence and documents. Further, if the assured is not a party to the proceedings then any judgment obtained by the third party against the insurers will not be binding on the assured, but if he is joined then he is bound (s.2(10)). This may be useful to the third party where the declaration relates to the assured's liability to the third party but there is loss outwith the policy.

If the assured is a company which has been dissolved and not restored to the register, there is no need for the third party to apply to have the company restored to the register so that it can be joined to the proceedings. The action against the insurers can simply go ahead (by way of contrast to the position under the 1930 Act).

---

[135] To which s.2 is subject: s.2(5).

It is possible to contemplate the situation in which the third party's claim against the assured arises under a contract containing an arbitration clause, or is a claim in tort which is nevertheless subject to arbitration, or which has become the subject of an ad hoc submission to arbitration once the dispute has arisen. If a direct claim is brought against the insurers for a declaration that the assured is liable to the third party, the arbitration clause is irrelevant because the insurers are not parties to the arbitration clause. However, if the third party has a residual claim against the assured, or for procedural reasons wishes to join the assured, the arbitration clause presents a potential bar to such joinder. The 2010 Act does not prevent the assured from relying on the arbitration clause to contest joinder.

If a declaration is sought in respect of the insurers' liability under the policy, in accordance with s.2(2)(b), the third party will have to commence proceedings within the limitation period applicable to a claim under the policy, namely, six years from the date on which the assured's liability has been established and quantified. The Act does not permit the assured to be joined to the proceedings if s.2(2)(b) is the sole ground of application, although the CPR are likely to be amended to allow for this possibility.

21–054   *Declaration where policy subject to arbitration.* If the policy contains an arbitration clause, the position under the 1930 Act and also the 2010 Act is that the third party is also bound by it.[136] By s.2(7), which is not a model of clarity, at the same time as the third party seeks a declaration from the arbitrators as to the scope of the policy, he may also seek a declaration as to the assured's liability to the third party. The effect of this is to extend the jurisdiction of the arbitrators from policy disputes to matters relating to the assured's underlying liability to the third party. The assured, through his insurers, may find himself defending an arbitration in the absence of any arbitration agreement, particularly if—and this is not clear—s.2(9) permits the assured to be joined the proceedings where the arbitrator is asked to deal with s.2(2)(a) liability issues. This may have unfortunate consequences. There may be aspects of the arbitration agreement which are inappropriate to a hearing on liability, e.g. an agreement to exclude judicial review for error of law under s.69 of the Arbitration Act 1996. Further, an arbitration clause is unenforceable in a consumer contract, but the third party may be a consumer who could not as a matter of law be required to pursue his dispute in arbitration but under the 2010 Act is required to do so.

21–055   *Declaration sought by insurers.* The 2010 Act does not deal with the situation in which the insurers take pre-emptive action in advance of any judgment in favour of the third party against the assured, and seek a declaration that they are not under any liability for any claim which may be made by the third party against the assured. *Chubb Insurance v Davies*[137] recognises the right of the third party to be joined to such proceedings, in order to prevent a default judgment where the assured has no interest in defending them. Presumably this right is retained where the assured has, or where the third party asserts that the assured has, become insolvent.

21–056   **Effect of transfer on claim against assured.** Under the 1930 Act it is unclear whether the third party is entitled to pursue his claim against the assured

---

[136] *Freshwater v Western Australia Insurance* [1933] 1 K.B. 515.
[137] *Chubb Insurance v Davies* [2005] Lloyd's Rep. I.R. 1.

notwithstanding a statutory transfer of rights. The 2010 Act makes it clear that the third party is confined to his claim against the insurers. Where the assured's rights have been transferred to the third party, s.14(1) of the 2010 Act prevents the third party from enforcing his claim against the assured itself insofar as the claim is covered by insurance. The claim has to be brought against the insurers for the insured sum, and a claim against the assured remains only in respect of uninsured sums. Thus the third party can proceed against the assured only for the amount of any deductible under the policy and also in respect of the amount by which liability exceeds the amount of the insurers' liability (s.14(6)(b)). If there is some arrangement with creditors, then s.14(2)–(3) take the insured sums outside those arrangements and confer upon the third party a prior claim on the policy moneys.

If the insurers have insufficient funds to meet a claim, the third party may also proceed against the assured for the relevant sum (s.14(6)(a)) but under s.14(7) only to the extent that the third party's claim is not protected by the Financial Services Compensation Scheme (which applies when an insurer becomes unable to pay claims).

The consequences of transfer: effect on insurers' rights. The general effect of the 2010 Act is to leave the insurers' rights unaffected. Accordingly, if the insurers have a defence against the assured, whether it be a right of avoidance for breach of the duty of utmost good faith, or breach of a policy provision—warranties, fraudulent claims, compliance with statutory obligations and the like—the insurers may plead that defence against the third party. This replicates the position under the 1930 Act.[138] Equally, under a P&I Club or other mutual policy, the only right of the assured is to have a claim fairly and properly considered, so that the third party has the same right and not an absolute right to be paid.[139] However, the 2010 Act makes a number of inroads into this general principle.   **21–057**

Information conditions. A major problem with the 1930 Act has proved to be the assured's non-compliance with claims conditions. There are numerous cases in which the assured has failed to give required information to the insurers in respect of a third party claim, often because the assured has become insolvent and has no interest in whether or not the claim is defended, and the insurers have been able to rely upon a breach of the claims condition. The only weapon open to the courts in this situation is to construe the claims condition as one which does not make compliance a condition precedent to liability, so that breach does not give a defence to a claim. Section 9 is concerned in general with conditions imposed upon the assured's own rights under the policy. The basic rule is that the third party has no better rights than the assured, but there are three modifications to this principle in respect of claims information.   **21–058**

The first is that if the third party satisfies the condition, then it cannot be relied upon by insurers (s.9(2)). Some conditions require personal performance, so this provision is needed.

The second is that any condition which requires the assured to provide information or assistance to the insurers is to be disregarded where the assured cannot comply because it is a dissolved corporation or a deceased individual (s.9(3)). This would typically be the case under an occurrence or events policy

---

[138] *Cleland v London General* (1935) 51 Ll. L.R. 156.
[139] *CVG Siderugicia v London Steamship Owners' Mutual* [1979] 1 Lloyd's Rep. 557.

which relates to an exposure or injury affecting the third party occurring years in the past, and in respect of which a claim is made by the third party at a much later date (s.9(3)).

The third is that, although any condition requiring the assured to provide information or assistance to the insurers remains in force insofar as the assured has not died or been dissolved, that condition is ineffective insofar as it requires the assured to notify a claim to the insurer (s.9(4)).

The effect of all of this is as follows.

Take, first, a claims made liability policy. This will typically state that coverage for a policy year is triggered if either: (a) the assured notified to the insurer within the currency of the policy (and as soon as is reasonably practicable) any circumstances which may give rise to a claim—any later claim is then deemed to have been made in the policy year; or (b) a claim is actually made against the assured in the policy year. Nothing in the Act prevents the insurers from denying liability for circumstances arising in the currency of the policy if those circumstances have not been notified. This will not matter if a claim arising out of those circumstances is subsequently made against the assured in the policy year, because the assured can rely upon (b) and cover is provided by reason of the claim and there is authority for the proposition that (a) and (b) are distinct heads of cover so that a breach of (a) does not prevent recovery under (b). However, it will matter if the claim against the assured is not made until a later year, because a later year's policy may exclude claims arising out of circumstances that could have been notified under an earlier policy. So, where notifiable circumstances have not been notified under an earlier year, a later policy may not respond to the actual claim made against the assured and there is nothing that the third party can do about it. A claims made cover is, therefore, likely to be preserved only in the absence of circumstances notifiable under a previous policy year. Once a claim has been notified, the assured will be under a duty to co-operate with the insurers in defending the claim, by providing information and documents. The Act allows the insurers to rely upon a condition precedent to recovery in the case of breach, although the Act operates on the assumption that the third party will, having exercised rights to obtain insurance information, be aware of the problem and will itself co-operate so as to bring itself within s.9(2).

Alternatively, the policy may be in exposure or injury form, thereby imposing long-tail cover on the insurers. The issues are slightly different, in that the insurer's obligation to indemnify does not rest upon a claim being made but upon an exposure or injury having taken place. Nevertheless, there will be a notification clause, and it is only notification of the claim itself that is protected, by s.9(4). Thereafter, the third party has to obtain the necessary insurance information as soon as possible and then to act so as to bring itself within s.9(2). Section 9 is thus of limited effect.

In some situations, the relevant information is provided by the asssured to a broker, and the broker fails to communicate the information to the insurers. Plainly the assured has a claim against the broker in such a case, but it is far from obvious that the broker owes a duty of care to the third party, and it is only rights under the policy—as opposed to claims against others—that are transferred under the 2010. This issue is indeed outside the scope of the Act.

21–059	*Pay to be paid.* P&I Club rules are written on a "pay to be paid" basis, so that the assured cannot recover from the insurer unless and until it has paid the third party. Such clauses have been upheld under the 1930 Act,[140] with the effect that the third party can rely upon a direct claim against the insurers only in the case where such a claim is not needed, ie, where the third party has been paid. Section 9(5) reverses that position generally, but s.9(6) lays down an exception in the case of a marine policy where the claim is one for death or personal injury: in such a case pre-payment is not an enforceable requirement. Pay to be paid provisions are rarely (and possibly never) found outside P&I Club rules, so removing the pay to be paid exception generally is unlikely to have much effect in practice. A distinction is nevertheless drawn between personal injury claims and other claims, e.g. cargo losses, collision liabilities, pollution liabilities and other risks covered by P&I Clubs. In the marine context the Act rescues only personal injury claims.

Set-off. Section 10 is concerned with unpaid premiums or other sums due to the   **21–060**
insurers under the policy. Section 10 provides that if the insurers possess a right of set-off, then that can be enforced against the third party. This codifies the position under the 1930 Act.[141] It is to be noted that s.10 does not permit the insurers to exercise anything other than contractual set-off in respect of the "policy": that means that there is no set-off of sums payable by the assured under separate contracts, or indeed under earlier years of cover in respect of which the premium remains outstanding. It is also to be noted that the Act does not rescue the third party if the payment of premiums is not simply a debt obligation but rather is a condition precedent to the inception or continuation of cover (or even, in marine cases, a warranty). It is only where non-payment has no impact on cover but merely creates a debt that s.10 is of assistance.

The right of set-off may in some cases operate to negative the third party's rights. That will occur where the sums owing by way of premium are significant but the amount of the assured's claim is relatively small.

Public policy. One unresolved issue under the 1930 Act is whether a public   **21–061**
policy defence open to the insurers against the assured can be pressed against the third party. It has been suggested that if the insurers' defence is based upon, e.g. the criminality of the assured's act which gave rise to liability, that criminality is merely a personal bar which does not prevent a valid claim from being transferred.[142] It may be thought that the Act does not affect this reasoning: if the policy is construed as providing a defence only against the assured personally, then there are valid rights to be transferred if the claim is brought by the third party.

Limitation periods for direct claims. The limitation period applicable to a   **21–062**
claim by the assured against his liability insurers starts to run from the date on which the assured's liability has been established and quantified by judgment, award or settlement. So the assured has six years from that date to bring his claim. If the third party has established and quantified the assured's liability, and commences direct proceedings against the insurers under the 2010 Act, the limitation period for the third party's claim is not to be any different. So the claim has to be brought against the insurers within the assured's limitation period.

This gives rise to a problem where the assured has himself commenced proceedings against the insurers within the limitation period and then—in the

---

[140] *The Fanti and the Padre Island* [1990] 2 All E.R. 705.
[141] *Cox v Bankside* [1995] 2 Lloyd's Rep. 435.
[142] *Total Graphics v AGF* [1997] 1 Lloyd's Rep. 559.

course of the proceedings and after the expiry of the limitation period—has become insolvent. Prior to the assured becoming insolvent, the third party has no rights under the Act, so there is no possibility of a direct action until insolvency occurs. However, following the assured's insolvency, the third party cannot commence a fresh action because he is time-barred. So he can keep within the limitation period only if the Act transfers to him the right to take over the assured's proceedings against the insurers. However, the Act does not achieve that: it merely transfers rights "under the contract" (s.1(2)). It would seem therefore that the third party must take steps to enforce his judgment, award or settlement against the assured within six years, so that if the assured defaults an insolvency procedure can be initiated and a direct claim can be brought by the third party against the insurers.

There is a procedural solution under CPR 19.4, which permits one party to be substituted for another even after the expiry of the limitation period, so in effect the proceedings may be transferred from the assured to the third party and the limitation position is preserved. But the CPR does not apply to arbitration. So the rights of the third party could be defeated if the insurance contains an arbitration clause. There is complex case law on this point, and it remains unresolved. *The Felicie*[143] holds that fresh arbitration proceedings have to be commenced (so that any limitation period has to be satisfied), although it has since been assumed in cases not involving the 1930 Act[144] that existing arbitration proceedings can be assigned.

21–063   Contracting out. Section 17 negatives any policy term which directly or indirectly avoids or terminates a policy, or alters the rights of the assured, in the event that the assured becomes insolvent or an individual dies insolvent. This reflects the 1930 Act. It was held in *The Fanti and the Padre Island*[145] that a "pay to be paid" clause was unaffected because it did not alter the assured's legal (as opposed to practical) rights on insolvency: the assured's rights were always the same, solvent or insolvent, namely to pay in order to be paid. Where pay to be paid remains permissible, i.e. in marine cases other than claims for death and personal injury, this provision is to be construed in the same fashion.

The Act does not cover the issue of changes in the assured's rights prior to his insolvency. This point may arise in two ways. First, the policy may provide for a variation of the assured's rights in given circumstances which do not amount to a statutory insolvency covered by s.4 of the Act: this possibility was left open in *Centre Reinsurance v Freakley*.[146] The second is that the insurer and the assured may enter into a settlement contract in respect of the claim before the assured has become insolvent. The 1930 Act does not preclude any such settlement,[147] at least in the absence of proof of conspiracy.[148] This may give rise to a problem where an insured employer enters into a commutation agreement in respect of all future claims arising out of, e.g. asbestos exposures (where the policy covers year of exposure), injuries (where the policy covers year of injury) or claim (if the policy is claims made). Future claimants may find that there is only a limited sum available to pay all claims.[149]

---

[143] *The Felicie* [1990] 2 Lloyd's Rep. 21.
[144] Notably *Baytur v Finagro* [1991] 4 All E.R. 129.
[145] *The Fanti and the Padre Island* [1990] 2 All E.R. 705.
[146] *Centre Reinsurance v Freakley* [2007] Lloyd's Rep. I.R. 32.
[147] *Normid Housing v Ralphs* [1989] 1 Lloyd's Rep. 265.
[148] Alleged but not proved in *Rowe v Kenway* (1921) 8 Ll. L.R. 225.
[149] As in *Re T&N Ltd (No.4)* [2006] Lloyd's Rep. I.R. 817.

Exhaustion of funds. Where there are competing claims to a limited fund, the **21–064** insurance moneys can be allocated pro rata or they can be allocated on a "first past the post" basis. The 1930 Act operates on the latter basis,[150] and the 2010 Act does not deal with the matter. It would thus seem that "first past the post" remains good law.

Obtaining information

The significance of information. A major weakness with the 1930 Act is its **21–065** failure to make proper provision for a third party to obtain insurance information before launching a claim against the assured: if insurance is not in place, of limited value or for one or other reason unenforceable, then an action is simply a waste of time and money. The cases on the 1930 Act initially deprived a third party of any right to information, and although that lacuna was remedied by the Court of Appeal in *Re OT Computers*,[151] the actual method for obtaining information has remained unresolved. Section 11 of, and Sch.1 to, the 2010 Act, deal with this matter in some detail, although they do not deal with all of the issues. In particular, the rules are effective where the assured has become insolvent at the date of the proceedings, but provide no assistance to a third party who wishes to bring proceedings but is unsure as to the insurance status of the potential defendant.

A contract of insurance is of no effect in so far as it purports, whether directly or indirectly: (a) to avoid or terminate the contract or alter the rights of the parties under it in the event of a person providing information, or giving required disclosure; or (b) otherwise to prohibit, prevent or restrict a person from providing such information or giving such disclosure (Sch.1 para.5).

Where there is an alternative right to information under the Civil Procedure Rules or from any other source, the statutory right to information does not preclude reliance upon it (Sch.1 para.6).

Obtaining information from the assured. The right to obtain insurance informa- **21–066** tion arises where a person (A) reasonably believes that another (B) has incurred liability to A and also reasonably believes that B is a relevant person (i.e. has become insolvent). In that case, under Sch.1 para.1(1), A may give notice to B[152] requesting insurance information set out in Sch.1 para.1(3). That information is:

> "(a) whether there is a contract of insurance that covers the supposed liability or might reasonably be regarded as covering it;
> (b) if there is such a contract—
>   (i) who the insurer is;
>   (ii) what the terms of the contract are;
>   (iii) whether the assured has been informed that the insurer has claimed not to be liable under the contract in respect of the supposed liability;
>   (iv) whether there are or have been any proceedings between the insurer and the assured in respect of the supposed liability and, if so, relevant details of those proceedings;[153]

---

[150] *Cox v Bankside* [1995] 2 Lloyd's Rep. 437.

[151] *Re OT Computers* [2004] Lloyd's Rep. I.R. 669.

[152] Which must include particulars of the facts relied upon by A as entitlement to give the notice: Sch.1 para.1(6).

[153] Under Sch.1 para.1(4), relevant details of proceedings are: (a) in the case of court proceedings the name of the court, the case number, the contents of all documents served in the proceedings in accordance with rules of court or orders made in the proceedings, and the contents of any such orders; and (b) in the case of arbitral proceedings, the name of the arbitrator and information corresponding to that in para.1(4)(a).

(v) in a case where the contract sets a limit on the fund available to meet claims in respect of the supposed liability and other liabilities, how much of it (if any) has been paid out in respect of other liabilities;

(vi) whether there is a fixed charge to which any sums paid out under the contract in respect of the supposed liability would be subject."

That information will allow A to determine whether there is a policy in force and, if so, what and how much it covers. There are two potential weaknesses with this provision. The first is that the assured may refuse disclosure and is then able to satisfy the court that there is no insolvency procedure in place: Sch.1 para.2(3) does not say that the court must make an order, so even if absence of an insolvency procedure is not a jurisdictional barrier to disclosure, at best the assured is reliant upon the court exercising its discretion to order disclosure. The second is that there is no insolvency procedure in place, and the third party is close to certain that the assured will be unable to satisfy any judgment. However, the Act does not in that situation permit the third party to seek information, and CPR 18.1 does not appear to allow the third party to obtain that information.[154] The only solution is for the third party to commence proceedings against the assured and to attempt to obtain disclosure of insurance information under the disclosure rules in CPR 31, but such disclosure will not reveal whether the insurer has a potential defence under the policy. So, the position as it stands is that proceedings against the assured will have to be initiated and taken to the point of disclosure, but that will secure only limited information.

21–067 *Information from third parties.* An alternative right to obtain information arises under Sch.1 para.1(2), where A reasonably believes that B has incurred liability to A, that B is insured, that rights have been transferred to A (i.e. that B is insolvent) and that there is another party, C, (who may be, for example, an insurer or broker) possesses the relevant information. In that situation the information may by notice[155] be requested from C. The difficulty is that A may have no idea about B's insurance position, and so is unable to trigger the procedure. In any event, the provision applies only where B is insolvent, and so cannot be used if A merely suspects that B may not be able to satisfy a judgment (even if A knows exactly who the insurers are). If a request for disclosure is validly made, the information to be disclosed is that set out in Sch.1 para.1(3), set out above. Under para.2 the information must be disclosed within 28 days, failing which a court order may be obtained. Special provision is made for documents not under the control of C, and for privileged documents.

In the case of a direct action against insurers involving the liability of a defunct company which has not been restored to the register, that information may be obtained from an ex-officer or insolvency practitioner (Sch.1 para.3). Disclosure and inspection then follow (Sch.1 para.4).

21–068 *Obligations following notice.* Where a valid notice has been received, the recipient must within the period of 28 days beginning with the day of receipt of the notice provide to the person who gave the notice any information specified in it that the recipient is able to provide and, in relation to any such information that the recipient is not able to provide, state why he cannot provide it (Sch.1

---

[154] See the discussion of *Harcourt v Griffin* [2008] Lloyd's Rep. I.R. 386 and *West London Pipeline v Total UK* [2008] Lloyd's Rep. I.R. 688, above.

[155] Which must include particulars of the facts relied upon by A as entitlement to give the notice: Sch.1 para.1(6).

para.2(1)). If the recipient is unable to provide information because it is in a document no longer in his control, and he knows or believes that it is in someone else's control, the recipient is under a duty within 28 days from receipt to identify that other person (Sch.1 para.2(2)). In the event of failure by the recipient to comply with these obligations, an application may be made to the court for an order requiring compliance (Sch.1 para.2(3)).

A person is able to provide information only if he can obtain it without undue difficulty from a document in his control (i.e. if he has possession of it or a right to inspect or take copies of it) or, if he is an individual, within his knowledge (Sch.1 para.7). There is no duty on the recipient to provide information which is protected by legal professional privilege (Sch.1 para.2(4)).

Struck off companies. Special provision is made in Sch.1 para.3, for the situation **21–069** in which the third party wishes to obtain insurance information in respect of a struck off company where that company has not been restored to the register. In this situation, notice requiring disclosure of documents may be served on any person who was, immediately before its striking off, an officer or employee or an insolvency practitioner acting in respect of the company. A person liable to provide information must do so in accordance with the rules for standard disclosure under CPR 31.6 (Sch.1 para.4).

CHAPTER 22

MOTOR VEHICLE INSURANCE

1. COMPULSORY MOTOR INSURANCE

22–001 **Legal framework.** The scheme for compulsory motor insurance is contained in Pt VI of the Road Traffic Act 1988. This has its origins in a statutory scheme dating back to the Road Traffic Acts 1930 and 1934, many of the principles of which remain in force. Most recently, a number of important extensions have been made to the legislation to implement a series of five EU Motor Insurance Directives,[1] consolidated by European Parliament and Council Directive 2009/103/EC of September 16, 2009 "relating to insurance against civil liability in respect of the use of motor vehicles, and the enforcement of the obligation to insure against such liability". The Directives established a harmonised system of compulsory insurance throughout the European Union, although they did not attempt to harmonise the grounds upon which a road user may incur liability to third parties: the sole objective of the Directives is to ensure that, if there is liability under the relevant law, such liability is covered by insurance.[2]

The broad effect of the 1988 Act is to require drivers to carry insurance against possible liability to passengers and other road users in respect of death, personal injury and property damage.[3] First party risks are not the subject of compulsory insurance, so that the law does not require the policy to cover, for example, damage to the assured's own vehicle or personal injuries to the assured while driving his vehicle.[4] As will be seen, the 1988 Act limits the exceptions which may be contained in motor policies, safeguards the rights of the third party in the

---

[1] The 1988 Act consolidates the Road Traffic Act 1972. as amended, most importantly, by (a) the Motor Vehicles (Compulsory Insurance) (No.2) Regulations 1973 (SI 1973/2143), which implement the First Motor Insurance Directive, Council Directive 72/166/EC (as amended by Council Directive 72/430/EC) concerning insurance in respect of motor vehicles and trailers; (b) with effect from December 31, 1987, the Motor Vehicles (Compulsory Insurance) Regulations 1987 (SI 1987/2171), which implement the Second Motor Insurance Directive, Council Directive 84/5/EC; (c) the Motor Vehicles (Compulsory Insurance) Regulations 1992 (SI 1992/3036), which implement the Third Motor Insurance Directive, Council Directive 90/232/EC; (d) the Insurance Companies (Amendment) Regulations 1992 (SI 992/2890) which extend Council Directive 88/357/EC (the Second Non-Life Directive) to motor policies. The Fourth Motor Insurance Directive, European Parliament and Council Directive 2000/26/EC, has been implemented in the UK, by the European Communities (Rights against Insurers) Regulations 2002 (SI 2002/3061) and by the Motor Vehicles (Compulsory Insurance) (Information Centre and Compensation Body) Regulations 2003 (SI 2003/37). The Fifth Motor Insurance Directive, European Parliament and Council Directive 2005/l4/EC, was adopted in June 2005 after a gestation period of some three years from the initial publication of the draft. The implementation of the Fifth Directive in the UK was completed by the Financial Services and Markets Act 2000 (Motor Insurance) Regulations 2007 (SI 2007/2403).

[2] *Ferreira v Companhia de Seguros Mundial Conficanca* Unreported, 2000.

[3] Discussion of third-party claims is outside the scope of this work. Such claims are, since April 30, 2010, governed by the RTA Protocol set out in CPR Pts 36 and 45, and Practice Direction 8B.

[4] The scope of non-compulsory cover is discussed below.

event that the assured has broken either his duty of utmost good faith towards the insurer or some term in the policy, preserves the rights of the third party in the event of the assured's insolvency, and protects third parties where the vehicle is driven by a person not covered by the assured's policy.

The compulsory insurance structure possesses two inherent weaknesses. First, there is the problem of the driver who, in contravention of the law, fails to insure; some means must be found of providing the third-party victim with a source of compensation in the absence of the availability of insurance proper. Secondly, the victim may have been injured by an untraced driver, so that even if insurance exists it will not benefit that victim. Both these problems are for the most part dealt with by a non-statutory scheme administered by the Motor Insurers' Bureau, a body consisting of all motor insurers in the United Kingdom. Under a series of agreements with government, the MIB has undertaken to provide indemnity to the victims of uninsured and untraced drivers where it can be shown that the liability incurred would have been the subject of compulsory insurance under the 1988 Act. The MIB also plays an important role under EU law. It is thus apparent that the MIB scheme, although technically voluntary, is an important supplementary part of the overall regulatory structure, and this will be considered below.

The obligation to insure

Offences. Section s.143(1) of the 1988 Act is in the following terms: **22–002**

"(a) a person must not use a motor vehicle on a road or other public place unless there is in force in relation to the use of the vehicle by that person such a policy of insurance or such security in respect of third party risks as complies with the requirements of this Act, and

(b) a person must not cause or permit any other person to use a motor vehicle on a road or other public place unless there is in force in relation to the use of the vehicle by that other person such a policy of insurance or such a security in respect of third party risks as complies with the requirements of this part of this Act."

Contravention of either provision is, by s.143(2), a criminal offence.[5] The offences are strict liability, although the accused has a defence under s.143(3) if he can demonstrate that the vehicle did not belong to him and was not in his possession under any contract of hiring or loan, that he was using the vehicle in the course of his employment, and that he neither knew nor had reason to believe that he was not insured while using the vehicle.[6] Where a prosecution is brought, the burden of proving use of the vehicle on the road is borne by the prosecutor, and the burden of showing that the use was covered by insurance switches to the defendant.[7]

The Act does not require that the person using the vehicle is the holder of a policy; it is permissible, and indeed often the case, for the owner of a vehicle to effect a policy under which the insurance is to be operative while the vehicle is being driven by named persons or indeed by any persons acting with the

---

[5] Prosecutions in respect of uninsured driving are generally brought by the police, although it was held in *Middlesbrough Borough Council v Safeer* [2001] 4 All E.R. 630 that a local authority has power to prosecute under its general powers in s.222 of Local Government Act 1972.

[6] See below.

[7] *Williams v Russell* (1933) 149 L.T. 190; *R. v Oliver* [1944] K.B. 68; *Bracegirdle v Apter* (1951) 49 L.G.R. 790; *Leathler v Drummond* [1972] R.T.R. 293; *Davey v Towle* [1973] R.T.R. 328; *DPP v Kavaz* [1999] R.T.R. 40.

assured's permission. Consequently, the statutory offences are frequently committed by perfectly innocent persons under the mistaken belief that the owner's policy covers the use of the vehicle by another.[8]

22–003 *Exclusions.* A compulsory policy is not, under s.144(1), required where the vehicle is owned by a person who has deposited and keeps deposited with the Accountant General of the Supreme Court the sum of £500,000,[9] at a time when the vehicle is being driven under the owner's control.[10] The formalities relating to deposits are set out in the Motor Vehicles (Third-Party Risk Deposit) Regulations 1992,[11] which regulates the permitted securities which must be deposited, the manner in which interest on the sum deposited is to be allocated and the documentation necessary to accompany a deposit: a person making a deposit must do so by means of statutory certificate which fulfils all of the functions of the certificate of insurance which has to be issued with a compulsory policy.

In addition to this exception, under s.144(2) insurance is not required in the following cases[12]:

"(a) Any vehicle owned:
   (i) by the council of a county or county district in England and Wales, the Broads Authority, the Common Council of the City of London, the council of a London Borough, a National Park authority, the Inner London Education Authority, the London Fire and Emergency Planning Authority, or a joint authority (other than a police authority) established by Part IV of the Local Government Act 1985;
   (ii) by a county, town or district council constituted under s.2 of the Local Government etc (Scotland) Act 1994;
   (iii) by a joint board or joint committee in England or Wales, or a joint committee in Scotland, which is so constituted as to include among its members representatives of any such council,
   in all cases at a time when the vehicle is being driven under the owner's control.
(b) Any vehicle owned a police authority, at a time when it is being driven under the owner's control, or to a vehicle at a time when it is being driven for police purposes by or under the direction of a constable, or by a person employed by a police authority. In *Jones v Chief Constable of Bedfordshire*[13] it was held that the exception extended to the case in which a police officer used his own car in the course of police business, and that it would also cover the situation in which a police officer commandeered a vehicle in an emergency or drove the car of an incapacitated driver.
(ba) A vehicle owned by the Service Authority for the National Criminal Intelligence Service or the Service Authority for the National Crime Squad, at a time when it is being driven under the owner's control, or to a vehicle at a time when it is being driven for the purposes of the body maintained by such an Authority by or under the Direction of a constable, or by a person employed by such an Authority.
(c) A vehicle which is being driven on a journey to or from any place undertaken for salvage purposes pursuant to Part IX of the Merchant Shipping Act 1995.

---

[8] *Davey v Towle* [1973] R.T.R. 328.
[9] The amount may be varied by statutory instrument: s.144(1A)–(1B).
[10] 1988 Act s.144.
[11] SI 1992/1284.
[12] These derogations are permitted by art.5(1) of the Consolidated Motor Insurance Directive 2009.
[13] *Jones v Chief Constable of Bedfordshire* [1987] R.T.R. 332.

(d) A vehicle used for the purpose of its being provided in pursuance of a direction under s.166(2)(b) of the Army Act 1955 or under the corresponding provision of the Air Force Act 1955.

(da) A vehicle owned by a health service body, as defined in s.60(7) of the National Health Service and Community Care Act 1990 by a Primary Care Trust established under s.16A of the National Health Service Act 1977, by a Local Health Board established under s.16BA of that Act or by the Commission for Health Improvement, at a time when the vehicle is being driven under the owner's control.

(db) Any ambulance owned by a National Health Service trust established under Part I of the National Health Service and Community Care Act 1990 or the National Health Service (Scotland) Act 1978, at a time when a vehicle is being driven under the owner's control.

(dc) An ambulance owned by an NHS foundation trust, at a time when the vehicle is being driven under the owner's control.

(e) A vehicle which is made available by the Secretary of State to any person, body or local authority in pursuance of ss.23 or 26 of the National Health Service Act 1977 at a time when it is being used in accordance with the terms on which it is so made available.

(f) A vehicle which is made available by the Secretary of State to any local authority, education authority or voluntary organisation in Scotland in pursuance of s.15 or 16 of the National Health Service (Scotland) Act 1978 at a time when it is being used in accordance with the terms on which it is so made available.

(g) A vehicle owned by the Commission for Social Care Inspection, at a time when the vehicle is being driven under the owner's control."

In addition to these express exclusions, a vehicle in Crown use is outside the 1988 Act, on the usual basis that an Act does not bind the Crown unless it is specifically stated to do so.

Security as an alternative to insurance. As an alternative to taking out a **22–004** compulsory policy, a person may obtain a security in respect of third-party risks. The security must comply with s.146 and with the Motor Vehicles (Third-Party Risk Deposit) Regulations 1992.[14] As is the case with an insurance policy, the person providing the security must be either an authorised insurer or a body carrying on in the United Kingdom the business of giving securities. Again, as is the case with insurance coverage, the person providing the security must issue a certificate of security which fulfils the same functions as a certificate of insurance. The certificate must comply with the requirements of the Motor Vehicles (Third Party Risks) Regulations 1972,[15] and must be produced on the demand of a police constable or in judicial proceedings in the same manner as a certificate of insurance.

Change of insurer. Where the assured wishes to change his insurers the existing **22–005** insurers are required to provide him on request with his claims history going back for a maximum of five years so that this can be presented to new insurers.[16]

---

[14] SI 1992/1284.

[15] SI 1972/1217.

[16] Consolidated Motor Directive 2009 art.16, re-enacting amendments made to the Second Motor Directive 1984 by the Fifth Motor Directive 2005.

Elements of the statutory requirement

22–006   *"Motor vehicle"*. A "motor vehicle" is defined as "a mechanically propelled[17] vehicle intended or adapted for use on roads."[18] It is not enough that a vehicle can be used on a road; it must be "intended or adapted" for such use.[19] The basic test of whether a motor vehicle is intended for use on roads is objective, and is whether a reasonable person looking at the vehicle would say that one of its users would be a road user.[20] In *DPP v Saddington*[21] it was held that a "Go-ped"—a motorised scooter—was a motor vehicle within the statutory definition, even though the manufacturers had specifically indicated that it was not suitable for use on roads: the court, applying the objective test, held that the instructions would in practice be ignored. Vehicles which have been held to be motor vehicles include farm tractors[22] and miniature motor cycles.[23] Vehicles falling outside the statutory definition include go-karts,[24] diesel dumpers used for constructing roads[25] and vehicles specifically adapted for use in sporting events.[26]

     The meaning of term "adapted" is uncertain. It has been held to mean either "altered" on a semi-permanent basis for use on a road"[27] or, alternatively, "fit and apt"[28] for such use. As noted above, mere use is not enough. Thus two dumpers, used in the ordinary way for the construction of works, were held, although mechanically propelled vehicles, not to be "motor vehicles" only because they happened to be propelled on a road.[29] Equally, vehicles specifically adapted for use in sporting events are not motor vehicles for this purpose.[30]

     A motor car remains a "mechanically propelled vehicle" even though it is not in use at the time. A parked vehicle is thus a motor vehicle which must be insured.[31] A vehicle which is inoperative is also within the statutory definition. It has thus been held that a car with its engine has been temporarily removed[32] (by theft or otherwise) is a motor vehicle, as indeed is a vehicle which is for any

---

[17] Irrespective of the form of power used to effect the propulsion: The phrase "mechanically propelled" appears to extend to any form of propulsion. See *Eleison v Parker* (1917) 81 J.P. 265 (electricity); *Waters v Eddison Steam Rolling Co* (1914) 78 J.P. 327 (steam).

[18] s.185(1), excluding invalid carriages (s.143(4)).

[19] *Martin v Redshaw* 65 D.L.R. (4th) 476 (1990)—"snowmobile" not a "vehicle".

[20] *Daley v Hargreaves* [1961] 1 W.L.R. 487; *Burns v Currell* [1963] 2 Q.B. 433; *Chief Constable of Avon and Somerset v Fleming* [1987] 1 All E.R. 318; *Percy v Smith* [1986] R.T.R. 252.

[21] *DPP v Saddington* Unreported, 2000.

[22] *Woodward v James Young (Contractors) Ltd* 1958 S.L.T. 289.

[23] *O'Brien v Anderton* [1979] R.T.R. 388.

[24] *Burns v Currell* [1963] 2 Q.B. 433. Contrast *Carstairs v Hamilton* Unreported, 1998.

[25] *MacDonald v Carmichael* 1941 S.C. (J.) 27. See also: *Daley v Hargreaves* [1961] 1 W.L.R. 487; *Maclean v McCabe* 1964 S.L.T. 39; *Chalgray v Apsley* (1965) 109 Sol. J. 437. Contrast *Childs v Coghlan* (1968) 112 S.J. 175, where an earth scraper was held to be a motor vehicle in the light of the evidence that it could travel at 45 miles per hour and was too large to be transported on a road other than by being driven.

[26] *Brown v Abbott* (1965) 109 Sol. Jo. 437; *Chief Constable of Avon v Fleming* [1987] 1 All E.R. 318. Contrast *Nichol v Leach* [1972] R.T.R. 476.

[27] *Westacott v Centaur Overland Travel* [1981] R.T.R. 182; *Taylor v Mead* [1961] 1 All E.R. 626.

[28] *Burns v Currell* [19631 2 Q.B. 435 (the Go-Kart case); *O'Brien v Anderton* [1979] R.T.R. 388.

[29] *Daley v Hargreaves* [1961] 1 W.L.R. 487; *Chalgray v Apsley* (1965) 109 S.J. 437.

[30] *Burns v Currell* [1963] 2 Q.B. 435; *Brown v Abbott* (1965) 109 Sol. Jo. 437; *Chief Constable of Avon v Fleming* [1987] 1 All E.R. 318. Contrast the requirement of art.1 of the Consolidated Motor Insurance Directive 2009 for compulsory insurance to be in place for "any motor vehicle intended for travel on land".

[31] *Law v Thomas* (1964) 62 L.G.R. 195; *Pumbien v Vines* [1996] R.T.R. 37.

[32] *Newberry v Simmonds* [1961] 2 Q.B. 345.

reason not capable of being driven under its own power at the relevant time,[33] unless there is no reasonable prospect of it ever being made mobile again.[34]

A vehicle which is capable of being propelled either mechanically or manually is a motor vehicle. An auto-pedal cycle with vital parts of its auxiliary motor removed was held not to be a "motor vehicle" within the legislation,[35] but such a motor assisted pedal cycle has been held to be "mechanically propelled" even though the engine had been turned off at the material time.[36] A vehicle which cannot safely be used by pedal-power alone is a motor vehicle.[37]

The following are excluded from the definition of "motor vehicle" by s.189:

(a) A mechanically propelled vehicle being an implement for cutting grass which is controlled by a pedestrian and is not capable of being used or adapted for any other purpose.

(b) Any other mechanically propelled vehicle controlled by a pedestrian which may be specified by regulations.[38]

(c) An electrically assisted pedal cycle of such a class as may be prescribed by regulations.

Section 189(2) defines the phrase "controlled by a pedestrian" for the purposes of the first two exceptions as meaning that the vehicle either is (a) constructed or adapted for use only under such control, or (b) constructed or adapted for use either under such control or under the control of a person carried on it, but is not for the time being in use under, or proceeding under, the control of a person carried on it.

"Road or other public place" The 1988 Act in its original form was concerned **22–007** only with liabilities incurred on roads, a term defined by s.192(1) as "any highway and any other road to which the public has access, and includes a bridge." At one time it was thought that the only real limitation on the word "road" was to exclude private land from its ambit. There are thus numerous authorities which hold that purely private land cannot be a road, as the public do not have access to such land.[39] That said, private land may nevertheless qualify as a road if members of the public do in fact regularly use the land as a thoroughfare: the leading authority on the point is *Harrison v Hill*,[40] in which a farm road which ran between a farm and the public highway was held to be a road in the light of regular public use. The test laid down by Lord Sands was as follows:

---

[33] *Newberry v Simmonds* [1961] 2 Q.B. 345; *Law v Thomas* (1964) 62 L.G.R. 195; *Cobb v Wharton* [1971] R.T.R. 392; *Nichol v Leach* [1972] R.T.R. 476.

[34] *Lawrence v Howlett* [1952] 2 All E.R. 74; *Law v Thomas* (1964) 62 L.G.R. 195; *Smart v Allan* [1963] 1 Q.B. 291; *Binks v Department of the Environment* [1975] R.T.R. 318; *Reader v Bunyard* [1987] R.T.R. 406.

[35] *Lawrence v Howlett* [1952] 2 All E.R. 74.

[36] *Floyd v Bush* [1953] 1 W.L.R. 242. See also *McEachran v Hurst* [1978] R.T.R. 462.

[37] *Winter v DPP* [2003] R.T.R. 14.

[38] Electrically Assisted Pedal Cycle Regulations 1983, which exclude from the legislation bicycles and tricycles fitted with pedals by means of which it is capable of being propelled but which also have electric motors as long as the motor is unable to propel the vehicle at a speed exceeding 15 miles per hour.

[39] As in *Lister v Romford Ice & Cold Storage Co Ltd* [1957] A.C. 555 (factory courtyard).

[40] *Harrison v Hill* 1932 J.C. 13.

"In my view, any road may be regarded as a road to which the public have access upon which members of the public are to be found who have not obtained access either by overcoming a physical obstruction or in defiance of prohibition express or implied."

On the application of this principle, private land may be a road if: (a) in practice the public are allowed free access[41] with the express or tacit consent of the owner,[42] unless there is some form of screening process operated by the owner based on criteria personal to potential users[43]; and (b) the public in practice exercise their right of free access.[44] The use of effective barriers will prevent land from constituting a road,[45] although warning notices which are in practice not enforced by the owner and widely ignored by the public will not have that effect.[46]

However, in two joined cases in the House of Lords, *Cutter v Eagle Star Insurance Co* and *Clarke v Kato*,[47] it was ruled that the mere fact that the public have unrestricted access to land is not enough to make that land a "road", and that the word implies a number of other criteria. In each of these cases, a victim was injured in a car park by an uninsured driver, and the victim sought to claim against the Motor Insurers' Bureau under the Uninsured Drivers Agreement. That Agreement, however, applies only where insurance should have been in force under the 1988 Act, and the MIB was found not to be liable on the basis that a car park is not a road so that insurance was not required in respect of the use of a motor vehicle in a car park. In *Cutter*, the victim was injured while sitting in the passenger seat of a car parked in a designated parking bay in a multi-storey car park: the injury occurred when he lit a cigarette, thereby igniting a leaking can of lighter fuel stored in the car. In *Clarke*, the victim was injured by a passing car while sitting on the wall of a car park; the car park here was an open area with two access points. The House of Lords held that whether a piece of land was a

---

[41] See: *Bugge v Taylor* [1941] 1 K.B. 198; *O'Brien v Trafalgar Insurance Co Ltd* (1945) 78 Ll. L.R. 223; *Buchanan v Motor Insurers Bureau* [1954] 2 Lloyd's Rep. 519; *Walton v Newcastle upon Tyne Corp* [1957] 1 Lloyd's Rep. 412; *Chapman v Parlby* (1964) 62 L.G.R. 150; *Cox v White* [1976] R.T.R. 248; *May v DPP* [2005] EWHC 1280 (Admin); *Evans v Clarke* [2007] Lloyd's Rep. I.R. 16.

[42] E.g. hotel or shop car park. See: *Thomas v Dando* [1951] 2 K.B. 620; *Griffin v Squires* [1958] 1 W.L.R. 180; *Severn Trent Water v Williams* [1995] 10 C.L. 638; *Charlton v Fisher* [2001] Lloyd's Rep. I.R. 387.

[43] *Thomas v Dando* [1951] 2 K.B. 620; *Griffin v Squires* [1958] 1 W.L.R. 180; *DPP v Vivier* [1991] 4 All E.R. 18; *Severn Trent Water v Williams* [1995] 10 C.L. 638; *Charlton v Fisher* [2001] Lloyd's Rep. I.R. 387.

[44] Limited public use prevented land from being a road in the following cases: *O'Brien v Trafalgar Insurance* (1945) 109 J.P. 107; *Knaggs v Elson* (1965) 109 S.J. 596; *Hogg v Nicholson* 1968 S.L.T. 265; *Deacon v A* [1976] R.T.R. 244; *Lock v Leatherdale* [1979] R.T.R. 201; *Kreet v Rawcliffe* Unreported, 1984. Contrast the following cases in which there was sufficient public use to amount to public access: *Newcastle Corp v Walton* [1957] Crim. L.R. 479; *Harrison v Co-operative Insurance Co Ltd* (1968) 118 N.L.J. 910; *R. v Shaw* [1974] R.T.R. 225; *Adams v Commissioner of Metropolitan Police* [1980] R.T.R. 289.

[45] *O'Brien v Trafalgar Insurance Co Ltd* 78 Ll. L.R. 223; *Cox v White* [1976] R.T.R. 248.

[46] *Bugge v Taylor* (1940) 104 J.P. 467; *Chapman v Parlby* (1964) 62 L.G.R. 150; *Houghton v Schofield* [1973] R.T.R. 239; *Adams v Commissioner of the Metropolitan Police* [1980] R.T.R. 289.

[47] *Cutter v Eagle Star Insurance Co* and *Clarke v Kato* [1998] 4 All E.R. 417. Car and caravan parks which are not designed to provide through access for vehicles are not roads, even though pedestrians do in practice use them as through routes: *Director of Public Prosecutions v Vivier* [1991] 4 All E.R. 18; *Brewer v Director of Public Prosecutions* [2004] EWHC 355 (Admin); *Dunmill v Director of Public Prosecution* [2004] EWHC 1700 (Admin); *Barrett v Director of Public Prosecutions* [2009] EWHC 423 (Admin).

road depended upon its physical character and its function. The relevant criteria were held to be the following:

(1) A road is required to have definable physical limits, so that it must have sides. In so deciding, their Lordships implicitly approved *McGurk & Dale v Coster*,[48] in which it was decided that Southport beach could not be a road even though it led to a car park as the beach had no definable boundaries.

(2) A road must bear a physical resemblance to a thoroughfare, so that it must have a prepared surface or at the very least a surface which has been fashioned by continuous use.

(3) A road is a means of access between two or more points, and must not be a destination in its own right[49]—on this basis, a car park is excluded from the definition of road.[50] The House of Lords was doubtful of the possibility that a route through a car park could itself be a road, but did not rule out the point entirely. Their Lordships also noted that there may in later cases prove to be fine distinctions between the access to a place and the place itself.

(4) A road may be continuous or it may terminate, and it may have branches leading to defined places, but it must be intended to go somewhere. It would seem from *Clarke* and *Cutter* that all parts of a road are themselves the road itself, including hard shoulders and lay-bys, although this point was again left open for further consideration.

(5) The purpose of a road is to allow traffic to flow—any place, such as a car park, whose purpose is to allow cars to be parked, cannot for this reason alone constitute a road.

The House of Lords was also satisfied that the narrow definition of road was **22–008** compatible with the United Kingdom's obligations under the EU's Motor Insurance Directives. The First Motor Insurance Directive, Directive 72/166/EEC, was construed as conferring upon Member States the ability to vary the scope of cover required so as to comply with domestic civil law. The Third Motor Insurance Directive, Directive 90/232/EEC art.2[51]—which provides that Member States are to ensure that any motor policy covers "on the basis of a single premium . . . the entire territory of the Community"—did not mean that every piece of land within the European Union was subject to compulsory insurance, but rather that a policy issued in any one Member State had to meet the requirements of the law in all other Member States.[52]

The effect of the House of Lords' interpretation was reversed by legislative amendment. The Motor Vehicles (Compulsory Insurance) Regulations 2000[53] inserted the words "or any public place" into s.143, thereby requiring the use of a motor vehicle to be insured against liability incurred in any "public place" as well as on any road. The phrase "public place" is not defined, but there are numerous decisions on other parts of the Act where the phrase has been considered. Those authorities make it clear that the test for a public place is the

[48] *McGurk & Dale v Coster* [1995] 10 C.L. 521.
[49] *Oxford v Austin* [1981] R.T.R. 416.
[50] Although see *O'Connor v Royal Insurance* [1996] C.L.Y. 5142, where it was held that a pub car park constituted a road, as it had defined entrances and exists. This decision probably cannot stand in the light of *Cutter* and *Clarke*.
[51] Now re-enacted as art.14(1) of the Consolidated Motor Directive 2009.
[52] Achieved in the UK by s.145(3): see below.
[53] SI 2000/726.

same as the test for a place to which the public have access, as contained in the definition of road.[54] Thus land will constitute a public place if members of the public are expressly or tacitly permitted to use it[55] and if in practice there is widespread[56] rather than limited public use[57]; effective[58] physical barriers or other enforcement mechanisms are required if land is not to be regarded as a public place.[59]

Whether a vehicle is on[60] a road when the accident occurs is a matter of fact in every case. In *Randall v Motor Insurers Bureau*,[61] the claimant was knocked down by a lorry which was emerging from private land onto a public road, and had its front wheels on the road. Megaw J. held that, as the greater part of the vehicle was on the road, the liability was one for which compulsory insurance was required even though the victim was, at the time of the accident, on private land. It will be noted that a vehicle need not be on a public road at the time of any accident for the compulsory insurance requirement to attach. If a vehicle which is being driven on a public road leaves the road due to the driver's negligence and causes damage to a building or injury to a pedestrian, the loss is nevertheless one which arises out of the use of the vehicle on the road.

22–009   *"Use" of vehicle.* It is the user of the vehicle, and not the driver or owner, who must be insured.[62] It is immaterial whether the user is insured as owner of the vehicle, by way of extension under the owner's policy[63] or by way of extension under a policy which the user has taken out on his own vehicle. An employee who uses a vehicle without being covered personally for insurance does not commit an offence if his employer has a policy which covers his vicarious liability for the employee, as the employee's use is thereby insured.[64]

The test of use is control of the vehicle. For most purposes the only person who can be regarded as using a car is its driver. The restricted meaning of use was established in *Brown v Roberts*,[65] where the passenger in a van negligently opened its door and injured a pedestrian. Megaw J. held that the compulsory insurance requirement did not apply to that particular risk. There are nevertheless situations in which a passenger may be regarded as a "user" for statutory

---

[54] *DPP v Vivier* [1991] 4 All E.R. 18.
[55] *DPP v Neville* Unreported, 1996.
[56] *Elkins v Cartlidge* [1947] 1 All E.R. 829; *Clift v Long* (1961) C.L.R. 121; *Pugh v Knipe* [1972] R.T.R. 286; *Oake v Cowley* Unreported, 1988.
[57] *Bowman v DPP* [1991] R.T.R. 263; *Taussik v DPP* Unreported, 2001; *Planton v DPP* [2001] EWHC 450 (Admin).
[58] *R. v Murray* [1984] R.T.R. 203; *Adams v Commissioner of the Metropolitan Police* [1980] R.T.R. 289.
[59] *Taussik v DPP* Unreported, 2001; *Planton v DPP* [2001] EWHC 450 (Admin).
[60] A vehicle can be "on" a road even though it is not physically touching the road but is on some other conveyance.
[61] *Randall v Motor Insurers Bureau* [1969] 1 All E.R. 21.
[62] *Ellis v Hinds* [1947] K.B. 475.
[63] In which case the user is treated as an insured person: s.148(7). The European Court of Justice, in Case C-518/06, *Commission of the European Communities v Italy* [2009] EUECJ, upheld Italian legislation under which any motor insurer operating in Italy is required to offer motor insurance to all-comers. There is no equivalent rule in England, where the market prevails.
[64] *Marsh v Moores* (1949) 65 T.L.R. 318; *Langman v Valentine* [1952] 2 T.L.R. 713.
[65] *Brown v Roberts* [1965] 1 Q.B. 1. See also *Windle v Dunning* [1968] 2 All E.R. 46; *Carmichael v Cottle* [1971] R.T.R. 11; *Bennett v Richardson* [1980] R.T.R. 358; *West Yorkshire Trading Standards Service v Lex Vehicle Leasing* [1996] R.T.R. 70.

purposes.[66] Guidelines for distinguishing between a passive passenger and a user were laid down by Simon Brown L.J. in *O'Mahoney v Jolliffe*,[67] as follows:

(1) A user is, by definition, someone required to provide third party cover and, if he fails to do so, is potentially liable both criminally and civilly. User must therefore be given a restricted meaning.

(2) Plainly not all passengers are users even when they know that the vehicle is being driven without insurance.

(3) There must be present in the putative user some element of controlling, managing or operating the vehicle.

(4) That element may exist as a result of a joint venture to use the vehicle for a particular purpose or where the passenger procures the making of the journey.

(5) Not every such joint venture or procurement, however, will involve the element of control or management necessary to constitute the passenger a user.

(6) Whether in any given case there is a sufficient element of control or management to constitute the passenger a user is a question of fact and degree for the trial judge.

The need for some form of joint enterprise has been applied in a series of cases. It has thus been held that a passenger was a user: where the passenger was himself the owner and had allowed another person to drive the vehicle[68]; where the passenger was knowingly being driven in a car which he had helped to misappropriate[69]; where the passenger was assisting a drunken driver to drive the car,[70] as opposed to being merely passive in the operation of the controls[71]; and where the passenger had encouraged the driver to drive the vehicle for the purposes of a mutually beneficial enterprise.[72] It has also been suggested that an enterprise which involves "flagrant criminality" is enough to justify a passenger being treated as a user.[73] If there is evidence that the passenger had at some point driven the vehicle, he is to be regarded as a user even though he was not driving at the time of the accident.[74] If the owner of the car is a passenger, then he is to be taken as using it.[75]

The control test has been applied in employment cases to mean that the person using a vehicle being driven by an employee is the driver's employer,[76] and it is immaterial that the employee himself is uninsured.[77] An employer remains the

---

[66] The point arose also under cl.6 of the MIB Uninsured Drivers Agreement 1972, under which a passenger who is also a user is precluded from recovering from the MIB if he knew or ought to have known that the vehicle was stolen or uninsured. The "user" requirement was deleted from the revised version of the MIB Uninsured Drivers Agreement 1987 which took effect in 1988 and is similarly omitted from the 1999 revision: see below.

[67] *O'Mahoney v Jolliffe* [1999] Lloyd's Rep. I.R. 321.

[68] *Cobb v Williams* [1973] R.T.R. 113. Cf. *Pratt v Patrick* [1924] 1 K.B. 488.

[69] *Leathley v Tatton* [1980] R.T.R. 358. Contrast *B v Knight* [1981] R.T.R. 136, in which the passenger had not been aware that the vehicle had been stolen.

[70] *Stinton v Stinton* [1995] R.T.R. 157.

[71] *Hatton v Hall* [1997] R.T.R. 167.

[72] *O'Mahoney v Jolliffe* [1999] Lloyd's Rep. I.R. 321.

[73] Per Simon Brown L.J. in *O'Mahoney v Jolliffe* [1999] Lloyd's Rep. I.R. 321.

[74] *O'Mahoney v Jolliffe* [1999] Lloyd's Rep. I.R. 321.

[75] *Cobb v Williams* [1973] R.T.R. 113; *Bretton v Hancock* [2005] EWCA Civ 404, where the point was conceded.

[76] *Lees v Motor Insurers Bureau* [1952] 2 T.L.R. 356; *Windle v Dunning & Son Ltd* [1968] 2 All E.R. 46; *West Yorkshire Trading Standards Service v Lex Vehicle Leasing* [1996] R.T.R. 70.

[77] *John T Ellis Ltd v Hinds* [1947] K.B. 475.

user of the vehicle even if the employee is acting in contravention of his instructions, as long as the employee's acts remain within the course of his employment.[78] If the owner is a partnership, then each of the individual owners is to be treated as the user of the vehicle while it is being driven by an employee of the partnership.[79] However, a vehicle being driven by a partner in a partnership is not deemed to be in the use of each of the other partners,[80] and the control principle does not apply where the driver is an independent contractor working on the instructions of an employer[81]; a full employment relationship is required before the employer is to be treated as the user.[82]

A vehicle may be in "use" even though it is not being driven at the time,[83] even where it has broken down,[84] become immobilised[85] or been abandoned.[86] The point here is that the word "use" means "having the use of" as opposed to "in actual use".[87]

A statutory defence is given to the charge of using a vehicle without insurance. The "employment" defence, conferred by s.143(3), is available if the user can prove[88] that:

(a) the vehicle did not belong to him and was not in his possession under a contract of hiring or loan;
(b) he was using the vehicle in the course of his employment; and
(c) he neither knew nor had reason to believe that there was not in force a policy of insurance as required by s.143(1).

22–010 *"Causing or permitting" use of vehicle.* Causing or permitting another person to use a vehicle without insurance is of itself a criminal offence. There are two separate concepts here.

"Causing" use involves "some degree of dominance or control, or some express or positive mandate . . . in or by the person alleged to have caused the prohibited act",[89] as where an employer directs his employee to drive a motor vehicle.[90]

"Permitting" use is a looser concept which involves the express or implied grant of permission for the use of a vehicle.[91] There can be permission only where the user of the vehicle has been given the unconditional right to use the vehicle independently of the existence of insurance, or at least where the person

---

[78] *James & Son Ltd v Smee* [1955] 1 Q.B. 78; *Richardson v Baker* [1976] R.T.R. 56.

[79] *Passmoor v Gibbons* [1979] R.T.R. 53.

[80] *Garrett v Hooper* [1973] R.T.R. 1; *Bennett v Richardson* [1981] R.T.R. 358.

[81] *Howard v GT Jones & Co Ltd* [1975] R.T.R. 150.

[82] *Jones v Director of Public Prosecutions* [1999] R.T.R. 1. Cf.: *Windle v Dunning & Son Ltd* [1968] 2 All E.R. 46; *Crawford v Haughton* [1972] R.T.R. 125.

[83] *Andrews v Kershaw* [1951] 2 All E.R. 764; *DPP v Heritage* Unreported, 2002.

[84] *Elliott v Gray* [1960] 1 Q.B. 367; *Eden v Mitchell* [1975] R.T.R. 425; *Gosling v Howard* [1975] R.T.R. 429. The contrary decision in *Thomas v Hooper* [1986] R.T.R. 1 was doubted in *Pumbien v Vines* [1996] R.T.R. 37.

[85] *Hewer v Cutler* [1974] R.T.R. 155 to the contrary is probably not good authority for the position in the context of insurance: see *Pumbien v Vines* [1996] R.T.R. 37.

[86] *Williams v Jones* [1975] R.T.R. 433.

[87] *Elliott v Gray* [1960] 1 Q.B. 367, per Lord Parker C.J.; *Williams v Jones* [1975] R.T.R. 433.

[88] *R v Carr-Briant* [1943] 2 All E.R. 156.

[89] *Shane v Rosner* [1954] 2 Q.B. 113, approved in *Shulton (Great Britain) Ltd v Slough Borough Council* [1967] 2 Q.B. 471.

[90] *Biddle v Johnston* [1965] 2 Lloyd's Rep. 121.

[91] Per Lord Wright in *McLeod v Buchanan* [1940] 2 All E.R. 179.

in control of the vehicle has not attempted to prevent use by another.[92] If the person giving permission has imposed some form of limit on use, including that the user is fully insured, then that person does not commit a criminal offence if the vehicle is used in a manner which goes beyond the conditions imposed and without insurance.[93] Thus where a vehicle is insured for use in the course of a business and is loaned for such use, then use of the vehicle by the borrower for private purposes cannot be said to have been permitted by the owner.[94] Failure by the owner to impose an insurance condition on the borrower[95] will amount to permission to use the car, and if the user is not in fact insured then the owner commits a criminal offence.[96] By contrast, if the owner of the vehicle has expressly restricted the use of his vehicle to a person who is properly insured, there is no offence on his part if the user is shown not to have been insured. This was so held in *Newbury v Davis*,[97] a case in which the owner of a vehicle gave permission to a friend to use the vehicle on condition that the friend effected the requisite insurance, although in *Director of Public Prosecutions v Fisher*[98] it was said that *Newbury v Davis* had to be treated with "extreme caution".

In order for there to be liability on the grounds of causing or permitting uninsured use, it must be shown that the defendant had some element of control over the vehicle. In *Thompson v Lodwick*,[99] the defendant had acted as supervisor to a learner driver who was not covered by the necessary insurance: it was here held that he was not guilty of permitting the learner to use the vehicle, since it would have been possible for the learner to have done so in the defendant's absence. In the same way, a trader or auctioneer who sells a car to an uninsured purchaser does not commit any offence as by the sale he relinquishes control over the vehicle[100] and a motor insurer who treats the policy as repudiated for breach of condition does not thereby cause or permit the ex-assured to use it.[101] Again, a person who assists another to obtain a motor policy which is voidable for misrepresentation is not guilty of causing or permitting that other to drive without insurance.[102] It is nevertheless too restrictive to say that the only person who has the necessary control over the vehicle is its owner[103]: accordingly, the borrower

---

[92] *Churchill v Norris* (1938) 138 L.T. 255; *Browning v Watson, Rochester, Ltd* [1953] 2 All E.R. 775; *Evans v Dell* [1937] 1 All E.R. 349; *Reynolds v GH Austin & Sons Ltd* [1951] 2 K.B. 135.

[93] *Monk v Warbey* [1935] 1 K.B. 75; *Daniels v Vaux* [1938] 2 K.B. 203; *Mumford v Hardy* [1956] 1 Lloyd's Rep. 173.

[94] *McLeod v Buchanan* [1940] 2 All E.R. 179.

[95] Or to restrict further lending by the borrower: *Director of Public Prosecutions v Fisher* [1992] R.T.R. 93.

[96] *Lyons v May* [1948] 2 All E.R. 1062; *Lloyd v Singleton* [1953] 1 Q.B. 357; *Ferrymaster v Adams* [1980] R.T.R. 139; *Baugh v Crago* [1975] R.T.R. 453; *Lloyd-Wolper v Moore* [2004] Lloyd's Rep. I.R. 730.

[97] *Newbury v Davis* [1974] R.T.R. 367. Cf. *McLeod v Buchanan* [1940] 2 All E.R. 179; *Sheldon Deliveries Ltd v Willis* [1972] R.T.R. 217; *Sands v O'Connell* [1981] R.T.R. 42; *Macdonald v Howdle* 1995 S.L.T. 779.

[98] *Director of Public Prosecutions v Fisher* [1992] R.T.R. 93.

[99] *Thompson v Lodwick* [1983] R.T.R. 76.

[100] *Peters v General Accident Fire and Life Assurance Corp* [1938] 2 All E.R. 267; *Watkins v O'Shaughnessy* [1939] 1 All E.R. 385; *Smith v Ralph* [1963] 2 Lloyd's Rep. 439.

[101] *Richards v Port of Manchester Insurance* (1934) 152 L.T. 413.

[102] *Goodbarne v Buck* [1940] 1 All E.R. 613.

[103] The suggestion that only the owner has the necessary control was made by MacKinnon L.J. in *Goodbarne v Buck* [1940] 1 All E.R. 613, but his comments were doubted by Lord Goddard C.J. in *Lloyd v Singleton* [1953] 1 Q.B. 357 Lord Goddard C.J. held that this formulation was too narrow. Cf. *Williamson v O'Keefe* [1947] 1 All E.R. 307; *Napthen v Place* [1970] R.T.R. 248.

of a vehicle who himself lends it to a third party may be guilty of the statutory offence.[104]

The person who has control of the vehicle will be in breach of his duty if, the vehicle being insured for a limited purpose only, he gives another permission to use it for purposes which are not so limited.[105] However, there is no breach of the legislation if the personal liability of the driver is not covered, as long as the vicarious liability of the person giving permission is insured.[106]

The state of the defendant's mind is of limited significance where he is charged with causing or permitting uninsured use. If he has given unconditional permission for the use of a vehicle, then it is irrelevant that he was unaware that the user had no insurance[107] or that he believed that insurance was not required.[108] This is demonstrated by *Ferrymaster v Adams*,[109] in which the defendant failed to check whether its employee drivers renewed their licences when necessary. It was subsequently found that one of the drivers did not have a current licence, a fact which invalidated the defendant's policy, and the Divisional Court held that the defendant had been properly convicted of permitting use while uninsured. The fact that the assured genuinely believed that the permitted user was covered by insurance, and had been induced into that belief by a misrepresentation by the user, is immaterial in the absence of the imposition of any condition by the assured that the user is validly insured. In *Lloyd-Wolper v Moore*[110] the evidence put to the court was that the assured believed that the person using the vehicle—the assured's son—was 17, when he was in fact 16, and thus not allowed to drive by law or under the policy. The belief was allegedly based on misrepresentation by the son to the assured as to his age, and this had been communicated to the insurers so that the policy named the son as an authorised driver. The Court of Appeal held that the failure by the assured to place a condition on the son was fatal to the assured's argument that he had not permitted use of the vehicle.[111] The position is different where the policy provides cover unless the assured is unaware that the user does not fulfil the conditions of the policy. In *John T Ellis Ltd v Hinds*[112] the policy indemnified the owner and any other person driving with his consent unless that other person was "to the knowledge of" the assured, not licensed to drive a vehicle: it was held that the assured's lack of knowledge that one of his employees did not possess a driving licence meant that the policy continued to apply, and thus there was no liability for permitting uninsured use.

22–011 *Policy must be "in force".* A defendant clearly cannot be convicted if he is using, or causing or permitting the use of, a vehicle while a valid policy exists in relation to such use. It is thus important to draw a distinction between policies

---

[104] *Lloyd v Singleton* [1953] 1 Q.B. 357. As indeed may the original owner: *DPP v Fisher* [1992] R.T.R. 93.

[105] *McLeod v Buchanan* [1940] 2 All E.R. 179.

[106] *Ellis v Hinds* [1947] K.B. 475; *Marsh v Moores* (1949) 65 T.L.R. 318; *Langman v Valentine* [1952] 2 T.L.R. 713.

[107] *Rushton v Martin* [1952] W.N. 258. In the case of a company, the knowledge must have been that of the relevant directing mind: *Ross Hillman Ltd v Bond* [1974] R.T.R. 279.

[108] *James & Son Ltd v Smee* [1955] 1 Q.B. 78.

[109] *Ferrymaster v Adams* [1980] R.T.R. 139. See also *Baugh v Crago* [1975] R.T.R. 453.

[110] *Lloyd-Wolper v Moore* [2004] Lloyd's Rep. I.R. 730.

[111] The policy also restricted coverage to the son while driving a vehicle of 1600cc or less. In fact he was driving a vehicle of 1760cc capacity. The Court of Appeal ruled by a majority that this was an independent ground for holding that the use was uninsured, and again no condition had been imposed in relation to this matter.

[112] *John T Ellis Ltd v Hinds* [1947] K.B. 475.

voidable for fraud, misrepresentation, non-disclosure and the like which have not been set aside by the insurer at the date of use, and policies which are void *ab initio* or which have been avoided. In the former case the defendant is entitled to be acquitted,[113] even though it is the case that the policy is subsequently avoided: the fact that the avoidance takes effect *ab initio* does not operate to render criminal conduct which was at the time perfectly lawful.[114] By contrast, in the latter case, there never was any cover and accordingly the defendant is guilty of an offence.[115] Even where the policy is valid, the defendant will be guilty of an offence if there is an exception in the policy in respect of the particular use to which the vehicle has been put.[116] As will be seen below, however, certain exceptions commonly found in motor policies are inoperative in respect of compulsory third-party risks.[117] Under the modern law, an insurer may be required to make payment to a third party in circumstances where, as between the assured and the insurer, the policy is for some reason ineffective or does not cover the loss: for the purposes of the statutory offence, the assured is treated as uninsured despite the statutory obligation on the insurer to make payment.

If the insurers have indicated that, irrespective of the operation of a policy exception or some other defence available to them they intend to make an ex gratia payment, the user is nevertheless to be treated as driving without insurance even if payment has actually been made.[118] However, if insurers determine to make payment on the basis that the policy wording is ambiguous, the assured has met the statutory requirements.[119]

Civil consequences of failing to insure

Action for breach of statutory duty. Section 143(1) by its terms merely creates **22–012** criminal offences. However, it has been established by the courts that any breach will also give rise to a civil action in damages for breach of statutory duty. Thus, where the user of a vehicle is uninsured, both that person and the owner of the vehicle who caused or permitted use of it will be liable in damages to the claimant victim: this was first held to be the case in *Monk v Warbey*.[120] The original purpose of such an action was to provide a claimant with some prospect of obtaining recompense for his injuries in the absence of insurance, although such actions are now rare for the reason that the Motor Insurers' Bureau now accepts liability for the victims of uninsured drivers, and s.151 obliges the insurer under a motor policy to meet the liabilities of a person not covered by the policy but driving the assured's vehicle. However, a victim who has a claim against the MIB is not prevented from pursuing his action for breach of statutory duty

---

[113] *Goodbarne v Buck* [1940] 1 K.B. 771; *Durrant v McLauren* [1956] 2 Lloyd's Rep. 70; *Evans v Lewis* [1964] 1 Lloyd's Rep. 258; *Adams v Dunne* [1978] R.T.R. 281.

[114] *Goodbarne v Buck* [1940] 1 K.B. 771.

[115] *Evans v Lewis* [1964] 1 Lloyd's Rep. 258.

[116] *Kerridge v Rush* [1952] 2 Lloyd's Rep. 305; *Mumford v Hardy* [1956] 1 Lloyd's Rep. 173; *JRM Plant v Hodgson* [1960] 1 Lloyd's Rep. 538; *Telford and Wrekin District Council v Ahmed* [2006] EWHC 1748 Admin. See also the series of cases dealing with the meaning of "social, domestic and pleasure purposes", "hire or reward" and related phrases, discussed below.

[117] 1988 Act s.148(1)–(5).

[118] *Egan v Bower* (1939) 63 Ll. L.R. 226; *John T Ellis Ltd v Hinds* [1947] K.B. 475; *Mumford v Hardy* [1956] 1 Lloyd's Rep. 173.

[119] *Carnill v Rowland* [1953] 1 Lloyd's Rep. 99.

[120] *Monk v Warbey* [1935] 1 K.B. 75. See also *Richards v Port of Manchester Insurance Co Ltd* (1933) 152 L.T. 413; *Daniels v Vaux* [1939] 2 K.B. 203; *Corfield v Groves* [1950] 1 All E.R. 488; *McLeod v Buchanan* [1940] 2 All E.R. 179; *Lees v Motor Insurers Bureau* [1952] 2 All E.R. 511; *Martin v Dean* [1971] 2 Q.B. 208.

against a person who caused or permitted the vehicle to be driven without insurance: this was so held in *Corfield v Groves*,[121] a principle confirmed more recently by H.H. Judge Kershaw QC in *Norman v Aziz*[122] where it was decided that changes to motor insurance law since the decision in *Corfield v Groves*— including revised legislation,[123] new MIB agreements[124] and harmonisation under EC law[125]—had not been designed to remove the right of a victim to sue for breach of statutory duty. The existence of the civil action means that the MIB, having indemnified the victim, has subrogation rights against the driver or the person who caused or permitted uninsured driving,[126] and the MIB is entitled to enforce any express subrogation clause in a policy obtained by the defendant.[127] In any event the MIB has reserved for itself, in cl.15 of the Uninsured Drivers Agreement 1999, the right to demand from the victim an assignment of the unsatisfied judgment obtained against the uninsured driver. Where an action for breach of statutory duty for causing or permitting uninsured use does in principle lie, the claimant must demonstrate that the fact that the user was uninsured caused the loss; if, for example, the claimant's loss is the result of his own delay in commencing proceedings against the uninsured user, no action will lie.[128] In principle, therefore, the amount recoverable in an action against the person causing or permitting uninsured use will be the amount that would not have been recoverable from the uninsured user of the vehicle had proceedings been brought against him.[129]

The *Monk v Warbey* statutory tort is concerned only with compensating the third party for losses that ought to have been covered by insurance, i.e. death, personal injury or property damage. Any consequential or economic loss suffered by the third party by reason of the absence of insurance falls outside the tort. This was so held by the Court of Appeal in *Bretton v Hancock*,[130] where the loss suffered by the third party was the inability to recover contribution from the

---

[121] *Corfield v Groves* [1950] 1 All E.R. 488.

[122] *Norman v Aziz* [2001] Lloyd's Rep. I.R. 52.

[123] The legislation under which *Corfield v Groves* was decided, the Road Traffic Act 1930, provided that "it shall not be lawful for any person to use, or to cause or permit any other person to use, a motor vehicle on a road unless there is in force in relation to the user of the vehicle by that person . . . a policy of insurance . . . ". Section 143(1)(b) of the 1988 Act is worded "A person must not cause or permit any other person to use a motor vehicle on a road unless there is in force in relation to the use of that vehicle by that other person . . . a policy of insurance . . . ". In *Norman v Aziz*, the court's view was that the change in wording was not intended to effect any change in the law. This was so because: it was not to be assumed that Parliament had intended to change the law by a "slender" variation in drafting; and the purpose of the legislation was to strengthen the rights of injured victims, not to weaken them.

[124] The survival of the statutory tort despite the introduction of the MIB Agreements was first confirmed in *Corfield v Groves*. Judge Kershaw, in *Norman v Aziz*, pointed out that the loss suffered by the victim of an uninsured driver, caused by the person who caused or permitted uninsured driving, was the inability to recover from the driver himself through insurers: that remained loss even though the MIB was prepared to provide an indemnity. Judge Kershaw also noted that the MIB was not under any contractual duty to the victim and that any payment by the MIB was subject to various conditions, and it would be wrong to remove a civil action under the 1988 Act on the basis of a claim against the MIB which might prove to be less beneficial.

[125] Judge Kershaw's view was that the EU Directives were not to be construed as removing domestic civil rights, but rather were intended to provide a guaranteed source of indemnity for the victim.

[126] If it is assumed either that subrogation is available as regards ex gratia payments or that the MIB does not pay ex gratia as it has agreed with the government to do so.

[127] Cl.20.

[128] *Daniels v Vaux* [1938] 2 K.B. 203.

[129] *Martin v Dean* [1971] 3 All E.R. 279.

[130] *Bretton v Hancock* [2005] Lloyd's Rep. I.R. 454.

uninsured driver of the vehicle. The claimant was injured in an accident involving a collision between her car—at the time being driven without insurance by her fiancé—and the third party's car. The claimant's fiancé was killed in the collision, and his estate was impecunious. The claimant obtained judgment against the third party, although the trial judge found that the claimant's fiancé had been 25 per cent to blame. The third party was unable to recover anything by way of contribution and counterclaimed against the claimant for a sum equal to 25 per cent of the damages awarded to the claimant. The third party's argument was that the claimant was, as the owner of the vehicle and a passenger in it, a user of the vehicle, and accordingly she was liable under *Monk v Warbey* for allowing the vehicle to be used without insurance. The Court of Appeal rejected this argument and held that the statutory duty imposed by s.143 was to insure against those liabilities referred to in the legislation; namely death, personal injury or property damage. Rix L.J. noted that all of the earlier cases in which *Monk v Warbey* had been invoked involved personal injury suffered by the third party, and felt that the consequences—if the third party's argument was correct—were contrary to the spirit of the legislation:

> "[I]t would be undesirable if a wife who could in some sense be said to be the user of the household car could lose 90 per cent of her recovery because her husband, who told her he was insured, was not insured and was found 90 per cent responsible for a collision involving another driver and tortfeasor."

Limitation period for statutory tort. Identifying the limitation period for an action based on *Monk v Warbey* is a matter of some difficulty. The date on which such an action accrues was addressed indirectly by Greer L.J. in *Monk v Warbey* itself,[131] in the comment that it was not necessary for the claimant to obtain judgment against the uninsured user, as quantification of loss was not a precondition of the action: it sufficed that the claimant could show that the defendant had caused or permitted his vehicle to be driven without insurance and that the user would not be able to satisfy any judgment against him. In *Norman v Aziz*[132] H.H. Judge Kershaw QC ruled that the action accrued as soon as it became apparent that the user would not be able to satisfy any judgment, so that the date of the accrual of the action would vary from case to case depending upon the user's financial position: if it was obvious from the outset that the user was impecunious, then the action against the defendant would accrue immediately, whereas if the user became insolvent at some later date, e.g. after the claimant has obtained judgment against him, then the action against the defendant would accrue at that point. However, in *Norman v Ali*[133] Otton L.J. was of the view that the better view was that the action against the user and the person causing or permitting use arose at the same time, when the accident occurred, with the result that they were joint tortfeasors.

22–013

The limitation period applicable to a claim for breach of statutory duty is the three-year period applicable to personal injury claims under s.11 of the Limitation Act 1980, as it is a claim "in respect of personal injuries", rather than the usual six-year period applicable to general tort claims. The point was of importance in *Norman v Ali*,[134] in which the claimant was instructed by the Motor Insurers Bureau, as a condition of recovery from it, to commence

---

[131] A view repeated by Hilberry J. in *Corfield v Groves* [1950] 1 All E.R. 488.

[132] *Norman v Aziz* [2000] Lloyd's Rep. I.R. 52.

[133] *Norman v Ali* [2000] Lloyd's Rep. I.R. 395.

[134] *Norman v Ali* [2000] Lloyd's Rep. I.R. 395.

proceedings against the owner of the vehicle as well as against the user. The claimant was held to be unable to do so, as the accident giving rise to her injuries had occurred in October 1992 but the action against the owner of the vehicle had not been commenced until June 1996, by which time it was statute-barred.

Formal requirements

22–014 *Policy of insurance.* Section 145, sets out the requirements for a valid policy complying with the legislation. There must be in existence a binding contract of insurance. There is no need for insurers to issue a formal policy document, as it is sufficient that the agreement is contained in the form of a covering note,[135] although the legislation refers to the "policy".

22–015 *Certificate of insurance.* The certificate of insurance is an important enforcement mechanism for the compulsory insurance requirement, and fulfils five functions:

(1) A police constable may demand the production of a certificate of insurance[136] or a duplicate thereof from the user of a vehicle to produce his certificate of insurance or a duplicate copy thereof.[137] The certificate may be examined, details taken and further information demanded.[138] Failure to comply with a demand made by a police officer either at the time or within seven days is a criminal offence.[139]

(2) In the event of an accident which causes third party injury, the assured must produce his certificate of insurance to a police constable at the time of the accident or otherwise report the accident to a police constable as soon as is reasonably practicable and at the latest within 24 hours.[140] The victim has a right to demand insurance information from the user,[141] but this does not include the right to see the certificate.

(3) The assured must produce his certificate of insurance or a copy of it[142] in order to obtain a vehicle excise licence under the Vehicles Excise and Registration Act 1994.[143]

(4) Production of the certificate in judicial proceedings is evidence that the user was duly insured,[144] and failure to produce the certificate is evidence that the user was uninsured.[145] The court may in appropriate circumstances demand further proof of insurance beyond the certificate itself.[146]

---

[135] 1988 Act s.161(1).

[136] 1988 Act s.165(1)–(2). If the vehicle is normally based outside the UK but in the territory of an EEA country and specified Eastern European countries, and there is no certificate of insurance issued by the insurer, the insurer is required to issue an equivalent document identifying the insurer, the policy and the period of cover: Motor Vehicles (Third Party Risks) Regulations 1972 (SI 1972/1217), reg.7.

[137] Motor Vehicles (Third Party Risks) Regulations 1972 (SI 1972/1217) reg.7.

[138] 1988 Act s.171; *Tremelling v Martin* [1971] R.T.R. 196.

[139] 1988 Act s.165(3)–(4).

[140] 1988 Act s.170(1)–(6).

[141] 1988 Act s.154.

[142] Motor Vehicles (Third Party Risks) Regulations 1972 (SI 1972/1217) reg.9(1)(a). This may include a printed version of an electronic copy.

[143] 1988 Act s.156.

[144] *Borders v Swift* [1957] Crim. L.R. 194; *Re MaClay* Unreported, 1991.

[145] *London and Scottish Corporation v Ridd* 65 Ll. L.R. 46.

[146] *Leathley v Drummond* [1972] R.T.R. 293.

(5) Delivery of the certificate to the assured fixes the point at which the assured is permitted to use his vehicle in compliance with the 1988 Act. For as long as the assured is in possession of the certificate, he is deemed to be insured even though the policy itself has otherwise been brought to an end: for this reason elaborate provision is made in the 1988 Act for the enforced surrender of the certificate once the policy has come to an end. The issue of a certificate does not estop the insurers from subsequently pleading, as against the assured or third parties, that the policy was obtained by fraud,[147] although the insurer must follow the statutory procedures for the recovery of the certificate, failing which liability under the policy will remain in place.[148]

It is a criminal offence under s.173 for any person with intent to deceive to forge or alter a certificate of insurance, and under s.174 it is a criminal offence for a person to produce a forged certificate of insurance when required to produce his certificate. A person who makes a false statement or withholds material information for the purposes of obtaining the issue of a certificate is guilty of a criminal offence,[149] and an insurer who knowingly issues a certificate which is false in a material particular itself commits an offence.[150]

A certificate is not a policy of insurance in its own right, and to the extent that it does not reflect the terms of the policy the latter will prevail. Thus in *Biddle v Johnston*[151] the terms of the certificate did not agree with those of the policy, and it was held that the contract of insurance was constituted by and contained in the policy alone.

The most important formality required for compliance with the legislation is contained in s.147, which requires a certificate of insurance to be delivered to the assured by the insurer. The form of certificates and ancillary matters are governed by the Motor Vehicles (Third Party Risks) Regulations 1972,[152] and insurers are required to keep their own records of policies and certificates.[153] It is the duty of the insurer to deliver a certificate to the assured or his authorised agent[154] within four days of the date on which the policy itself was issued.[155] Under the Motor Vehicles (Electronic Communication of Certificates of Insurance) Order 2010, amending s.147, it is possible for a certificate to be delivered electronically with the consent of the assured: this may be done either by a direct electronic communication to the assured's electronic addresss (s.147(1A)–(1B)) or by making the certificate available on a website, s.147(1A) and (1C)–(1E)). In the

---

[147] *McCormick v National Motor Insurance Co* (1934) 40 Com. Cas. 76.

[148] 1988 Act s.152: see below.

[149] 1988 Act s.174(5).

[150] See *Ocean Accident and Guarantee Corp v Cole* [1932] 2 K.B. 100.

[151] *Biddle v Johnston* [1965] 2 Lloyd's Rep. 121.

[152] SI 1972/1217, as amended by the Motor Vehicles (Third Party Risks) (Amendment) Regulations 1999 (SI 1999/2392), the Motor Vehicles (Third Party Risks) (Amendment) Regulations 2010 (SI 2010/1115) and the Motor Vehicles (Electronic Communication of Certificates of Insurance) Order 2010 (SI 2010/1117).

[153] Motor Vehicles (Third Party Risks) Regulations 1972 (SI 1972/1283), as amended by the Motor Vehicles (Third Party Risks) (Amendent) Regulations 2001 (SI 2001/2266). Under the Regulations as amended, the insurer must, for seven years, retain the following information: the number of the policy; the name and address of the person to whom the policy was issued; the names or descriptions of persons covered by the policy; the registration numbers or descriptions of vehicles insured; the date on which the policy came into force; and the conditions on which indemnity is available.

[154] See *Starkey v Hall* [1936] 2 All E.R. 18, where the certificate was delivered to the owner of the vehicle rather than to the insured hirer.

[155] Motor Vehicles (Third Party Risks) Regulations 1972 (SI 1972/1217) reg.6.

latter case the certificate must remain continuously accessible. In the event that
the certificate is lost or destroyed a duplicate must be issued on request.[156]

Some difficulty may arise where the insurer has entered into a binding contract
of insurance with the assured, but has failed to deliver a certificate to him. Prima
facie, the 1988 Act cannot apply to the policy, as s.147(1) provides as follows:

"A policy of insurance shall be of no effect for the purposes of this Part of this Act
unless and until there is delivered by the insurer to the assured a . . . certificate of
insurance in the prescribed form."

It is scarcely conceivable, however, that the courts would allow the failure of the
insurer to issue a certificate to nullify the operation of the 1988 Act, particularly
since the failure of insurer to issue a certificate does not prevent the policy from
taking effect as between the insurer and the assured. Support for this suggested
approach may be found in the opinion of the Privy Council in *Motor & General
Insurance Co Ltd v Cox*.[157] In this case the assured obtained cover in October
1979, but did not receive a certificate until February 1980. Between these dates
an authorised driver employed by the assured incurred liability to a third party,
in respect of which the third party brought a direct action against the insurer
under the equivalent of s.151. That section provides that a direct action is
possible "after a certificate of insurance has been delivered under s.147 of this
Act [to the assured]". The Privy Council held that the requirements of s.151 had
been satisfied, in that a certificate had been delivered to the assured before the
date of the judgment against the insurer, and it would therefore be wrong to allow
the formal requirements of s.147(1) to defeat the third party's claim.

Where a certificate of insurance has been delivered to the assured, and the
policy to which it relates has been cancelled by mutual consent or by virtue of the
express terms of the policy, the assured must within seven days surrender the
certificate to the insurer,[158] and this may be done by means of an electronic
communication to an electronic address specified by the insurer in the form a
statement confirming that the policy to which the certificate relates has ceased to
have effect.[159] If the certificate has been lost or destroyed, the assured may either
make a statutory declaration to that effect and deliver it to the insurer forthwith[160]
or transmit to the insurer, by means of an electronic communication to an
electronic address specified by the insurer, a statement confirming that the
certificate has been lost or (as applicable) destroyed.[161] In the event that the
certificate has been delivered to the assured in electronic rather than physical
form, and the policy has been cancelled, the assured must, within seven days
from the taking effect of the cancellation, either transmit to the insurer, by means
of an electronic communication to an electronic address specified by the insurer,
a statement confirming that the policy to which the certificate relates has ceased
to have effect, or deliver to the insurer a legible printed copy of the certificate

---

[156] Motor Vehicles (Third Party Risks) Regulations 1972 (SI 1972/1217) reg.13. A defaced
certificate must be returned to the insurer before a fresh one may be issued.

[157] *Motor & General Insurance Co Ltd v Cox* [1990] 1 W.L.R. 1443. This was an appeal to the
Privy Council from Barbados under identically worded Barbadian legislation.

[158] 1988 Act s.147(4)(a); Road Traffic (Third Party Risks) Regulations 1972 (SI 1972/1217)
reg.12(3).

[159] 1988 Act s.147(4A).

[160] 1988 Act s.147(4)(b).

[161] 1988 Act s.147(4B).

endorsed with a statement made and signed by him to that effect.[162] It is a criminal offence for the assured to fail to comply with these requirements.[163] If the policy has for any other reason been suspended or has ceased to be effective, the certificate must be returned to the insurer within seven days and no new policy is to be issued by the insurer until the certificate has been returned to the insurer or it is otherwise satisfied that the certificate has been lost or destroyed.[164] If the policy is to be transferred to some other person, the assured must surrender the certificate and the insurers must then issue a fresh certificate.[165]

The insurer. The policy must be issued by an insurer authorised under the **22–016** Financial Services and Markets Act 2000 to carry on the business of motor insurance.[166] The insurer must also be, and remain, a member of the MIB.[167] In accordance with the EU's Fourth Motor Insurance Directive,[168] any insurer authorised in the United Kingdom must appoint a claims representative in every EEA state, with authority to represent the insurer with respect to claims and in legal proceedings.[169] The position is modified[170] in the case of an EU insurer, that is, an insurer which is incorporated and has its head office in another member state of the European Union, and is authorised to carry on motor insurance business by the authorities of that state. An EU insurer may sell motor insurance in the United Kingdom either through a UK branch or directly from an establishment elsewhere in the European Union: in either case no UK authorisation is required. An EU insurer must, however, meet the following conditions:

(1) It must join the United Kingdom's MIB.
(2) It must appoint a claims representative based in the United Kingdom, empowered by the insurer to represent the insurer in any claim or proceedings, but not empowered by the insurer to decide whether or not to pay in any individual case or to carry on insurance business generally.
(3) It must comply with the general requirements laid down for EU companies selling through UK branches or directly into the EU from other Member States as regards the provision of information to the Secretary of State.
(4) It must comply with the general requirements laid down for EU companies selling through UK branches or directly into the EU from other Member States as regards the provision of information to policyholders.

---

[162] 1988 Act s.147(4D).

[163] 1988 Act s.147(5).

[164] Road Traffic (Third Party Risks) Regulations 1972 (SI 1972/1217) reg.12(2). This does not apply to electronic certificates.

[165] Road Traffic (Third Party Risks) Regulations 1972 (SI 1972/1217) reg.12(1). This does not apply to electronic certificates.

[166] 1988 Act s.145(2).

[167] 1988 Act s.145(5)–(6).

[168] Now re-enacted as art.21 of the Consolidated Motor Insurance Directive 2009.

[169] Financial Services and Markets Act 2000 (Variation of Threshold Conditions) Order 2002 (SI 2002/2702), amending Sch.6 to the Financial Services and Markets Act 2000.

[170] By the implementation of the Third Non-Life Directive, Directive 1992 by the Insurance Companies (Third Insurance Directives) Regulations 1994 (SI 1994/1696), with effect from July 1, 1994.

These conditions are mirrored in respect of a UK company which wishes to sell motor insurance in an EU Member State.[171]

Liabilities to be insured under policy

22-017 *Death and personal injury in Great Britain.* Under s.145(3)(a) the policy:

> "must insure such person, persons or classes of persons as may be specified in the policy in respect of any liability which may be incurred by him or them in respect of the death of or bodily injury to any person ... caused by, or arising out of, the use of the vehicle on a road or public place in Great Britain." [172]

The phrase "liability to any person" clearly covers third-party victims of the user's negligence, and also any passengers in the vehicle[173] including the assured owner if he is a passenger at the time.[174] The sum insured must be unlimited.[175] Insurance is not required for contractual liability.[176]

The section does not refer to the driver himself, and it is clear from the scheme of the legislation that a compulsory policy does not cover the driver's own injuries.[177] The main outstanding question is whether a person permitted to use the vehicle by its owner is covered by compulsory insurance. This point arose in *Cooper v MIB*,[178] where the owner of a motorcycle lent it to the claimant for road-testing. The brakes were defective, and the claimant was, as a result, seriously injured; the owner was not insured for this peril, so the claimant brought proceedings against the MIB on the ground that the risk was one which ought to have been covered by insurance under the legislation. The Court of Appeal dismissed this argument and held that a permitted driver is not "any person" for the purposes of s.43. This result is unfortunate in policy terms, and was not inevitable, for it is perfectly plausible to argue that, so far as the owner of a vehicle is concerned, a permitted driver is in the position of a third party.

Section 145(4)(a) removes the insurance requirement for the death or personal injury of an employee arising out of and in the course of his employment. The exclusion of liability for employees dates back to the Road Traffic Act 1930, s.36(1)(b). However, s.36(1)(b)(ii) of that Act provided an exception in the case

---

[171] The requirements are summarised in ch.7.6 of the Insurance Conduct of Business Rules contained in the Financial Services Authority's Handbook. In essence, a UK insurer must appoint at least one claims representative for every EAA state other than the UK. The claims representative must be resident or established in the relevant EEA state, capable of examining claims in that language, and authorised to handle and settle claims.

[172] Under the Consolidated Motor Insurance Directive 2009 art.12(3), the insurance must cover personal injury to and property damage suffered by pedestrians, cyclists and other non-motorised users. This is a watered-down version of one of the most controversial proposals in the original draft of the Fifth Motor Insurance Directive 2005, namely that there was to be a strict liability regime in respect of injuries to pedestrians and cyclists, subject only to the driver proving that the accident was wholly or partly the fault of the victim.

[173] *Barnet Group Hospital Management Committee v Eagle Star Insurance Co Ltd* [1960] 1 Q.B. 107. As to passengers, see s.149 discussed below.

[174] *Limbrick v French and Farley* [1990] 11 C.L. para.329: the House of Lords had reached this conclusion in relation to express policy wording in *Digby v General Accident* [1943] A.C. 121.

[175] Article 9 of the Consolidated Motor Insurance Directive 2009 permits Member States to cap liability at €1,000,000 per victim, or in the alternative at €500,000 for all personal injury irrespective of the number of claims and victims. This derogation has not been taken up, and the amount of cover for personal injury has been unlimited since the origins of the legislation in 1930.

[176] 1988 Act s.145(4)(f).

[177] *R v Secretary of State for Transport Ex p. National Insurance Guarantee Corporation Plc*, *The Times*, June 3, 1996.

[178] *Cooper v MIB* [1985] 1 All E.R. 449.

of liability towards an employee who was injured while being carried on in or upon or entering or getting on to or alighting from the vehicle at the time of the event giving rise to injury, as long as the carriage was by reason of or in pursuance of a contract of employment. The exception was narrowly construed, and compulsory insurance was held to be required only where the injured person was shown to be an employee[179] who by reason of the employment relationship was contemplated as a person who would be carried.[180] The proviso was removed by s.203(4) of the Road Traffic Act 1960, leaving the position that there was no requirement for any liability towards an employee arising out of a road traffic incident to be covered by a motor policy. This position has been maintained by the 1988 Act.[181] Liability to employees has instead to be covered by compulsory insurance under the Employers Liability (Compulsory Insurance) Act 1969. As discussed in Ch.21 of this work, the requirements of that legislation are less rigid that those of the 1988 Act and there are numerous situations in which an employee injured in a motor vehicle accident will be worse off in insurance terms than any other person so injured. The position has nevertheless been modified by the implementation of the provisions of art.1 of the Third EC Motor Insurance Directive 1990.[182] The Directive required there to be in place compulsory liability cover "for personal injury to all passengers other than the driver arising out of the use of the vehicle". In the absence of any specific exclusion of employees, the 1988 Act was amended[183] so as to extend compulsory motor insurance to employees being carried as passengers. Section 145(4A) now reads:

"In the case of a person—
  (a) carried in or upon a vehicle, or
  (b) entering or getting on to, or alighting from, a vehicle,
the provisions of paragraph (a) of subsection (4) of this section do not apply unless cover in respect of the liability referred to in that paragraph is in fact provided pursuant to a requirement of the Employers' Liability (Compulsory Insurance) Act 1969."

The effect of the legislation is that the liability of an employer towards **22–018** employees[184] who are injured as passengers in or on a motor vehicle has to be covered by compulsory motor insurance under the 1988 Act even where the injuries arise while the employee was being carried in pursuance of an employment obligation, whereas all other forms of liability towards an employee injured in a motor vehicle accident (e.g. by being run down by a fellow employee) are to be covered by insurance in accordance with the Employers' Liability (Compulsory Insurance) Act 1969. The word "passenger" is not actually used in the legislation which, refers only to persons being carried in or upon a vehicle, entering in or getting on to or alighting from a vehicle. The statutory formulation is, however, synonymous with "passenger".[185] The phrase

---

[179] *Weldrick v Essex & Suffolk Equitable Insurance Society Ltd* 83 Ll. L.R. 91.

[180] *Baker v Provident Accident & White Cross Insurance Co* 64 Ll. L.R. 14; *Izzett v Universal Insurance Co* [1937] A.C. 773; *Tan Ken Hong v New India Assurance Co Ltd* [1978] 1 Lloyd's Rep. 233; *Nottingham v Aldridge* [1971] 2 All E.R. 751.

[181] See *Lees v Motor Insurers Bureau* [1952] 2 Lloyd's Rep. 210.

[182] Now re-enacted as art.12(1) of the Consolidated Motor Insurance Directive 2009.

[183] By the Motor Vehicles (Compulsory Insurance) Regulations 1992 (SI 1992/3036).

[184] A police constable, as an office holder, is not an employee—*Miller v Hales* [2007] Lloyd's Rep. I.R. 54.

[185] *R. v Secretary of State for Transport Ex p. National Insurance Guarantee Corporation Plc* Unreported, 1996; *Axa Insurance UK Plc v Norwich Union Insurance Ltd* [2008] Lloyd's Rep. I.R. 122.

"carried in or upon a vehicle" does not cover every situation in which an employee other than the driver is injured by his employer's vehicle. In *Miller v Hales*[186] the phrase was held not to encompass an employee who was dragged along by a vehicle which he had attempted to stop from being stolen, because he was not being carried as a passenger. In *Axa Insurance UK Plc v Norwich Union Insurance Ltd*[187] an employee working on a hoist on his employer's vehicle was similarly held not to have been "carried in or upon" the vehicle, which was stationary at the time: Andrew Smith J. held that the s.145(4A)(a) implied that the employee was at the time being transported or moved from one place to another and not that he was using the vehicle for other purposes. The learned judge noted that the subsection might be satisfied even though the vehicle is not in motion at the time, as where it had stopped temporarily or was waiting to start: in each of those cases the employee would be in or upon the vehicle for the purpose of being carried. The phrase "entering in or getting on to or alighting from, a vehicle" in s.145(4A)(b), unlike s.145(4A)(a), clearly covers the situation in which the employee is not being transported at the time, and indeed appears to cover a case in which the employee is entering or leaving the vehicle for other purposes: whether s.145(4A)(b) is so wide, or whether it applies only where the employee is entering or leaving the vehicle for purposes connected with transportation, was left open in *Axa Insurance v Norwich Union*, although Jack J. in *Miller v Hales* felt that the subsection applied only to a person who attempted to enter (or leave) a vehicle for the purpose of being carried as a passenger, a ruling which precluded the application of the subsection to an employee who jumped in or on a vehicle to prevent its theft. These cases do mean that the demarcation line between employers' liability insurance and motor insurance is not always obvious and may give rise to curious results, but it was commented by Andrew Smith J. that this did not require that s.145(4A) was to be construed as covering all employees, because even if that was the case there could be anomalies in the application of the two regimes. It was also argued in *Axa Insurance v Norwich Union Insurance* that the requirement in art.2 the Third Motor Insurance Directive,[188] that a policyholder was to receive motor liability cover throughout the European Union for a single premium, was not necessarily contravened by the United Kingdom's decision to draw a line between employers' liability risks and other risks, given that the apparent purpose of art.2 was to ensure that a driver could use his vehicle in any EU member state without discrimination as to jurisdictions on the part of the insurers.

The concluding words of s.145(4A) appear to contemplate that the 1988 Act does not apply to a passenger employee if there is insurance in place "pursuant to a requirement" of the 1969 Act. However, as the 1969 Act specifically excludes from the compulsory employers liability insurance requirement any employee who is injured while being "carried in or upon a vehicle, or entering or getting on to, or alighting from a vehicle . . . where that bodily injury is caused by or arises out of the use by the employer of a vehicle on a road",[189] it is difficult to see that the concluding words can ever be operative. Accordingly, every passenger employee is to be covered by insurance under the 1988 Act rather than under the 1969 Act.

---

[186] *Miller v Hales* [2007] Lloyd's Rep. I.R. 54.
[187] *Axa Insurance UK Plc v Norwich Union Insurance Ltd* [2008] Lloyd's Rep. I.R. 122.
[188] Now re-enacted as art.16 of the Consolidated Motor Insurance Directive 2009.
[189] Employers' Liability (Compulsory Insurance) Regulations 1998 (SI 1998/2573) Sch.2 para.14.

An employee who is himself the user of the vehicle is not protected by the 1988 Act,[190] which is concerned only with liability. There is, nevertheless, some difficulty with the position of an employee who is injured by reason of his employer's negligence while driving the vehicle, e.g. where the vehicle has not been properly maintained. The Third Motor Insurance Directive[191] specifically states that the driver is not covered, as the compulsory insurance requirement applies only to "personal injury to all passengers, other than the driver, arising out of the use of the vehicle". However, the 1988 Act does not specifically exclude the driver, and instead s.145(4A) provides that an employee who is being carried on a vehicle—a phrase which can apply equally to the driver as well as to his passengers—is protected by the road traffic legislation. The point was tested before Popplewell J. in *R. v Secretary of State for Transport Ex p. National Insurance Guarantee Corp Plc*.[192] The learned judge held that the Directive had been properly implemented, and that an employed driver was excluded from the protection of the 1988 Act. While some of the reasoning is directed towards the situation in which the driver's injuries are the result of his own negligence, where it is clear that the 1988 Act cannot apply as no third-party liability is involved, Popplewell J.'s interpretation of s.145(4A) was that the driver was not covered in any circumstances, so that in the case of a driver being injured by the negligence of his employer the 1969 Act rather than the 1988 Act regulates the compulsory cover. Popplewell J. was of the view that the wording was clear enough, but that in the event of any ambiguity it was appropriate to adopt an interpretation consistent with the Directives.[193]

Property damage. Under s.145(3)(a) the policy: **22–019**

"must insure such person, persons or classes of person as may be specified in the policy in respect of any liability which may be incurred by him or them in respect of . . . damage to property caused by, or arising out of, the use of the vehicle on a road or public place in Great Britain."

The 1988 Act does not require insurance in respect of property damage falling within any of the following classes:

(1) Liability under an employers' motor policy in respect of damage to the property of an employee arising out of and in the course of his employment (s.145(4)(a)).

(2) Damage in excess of £1,000,000[194] in respect of all such liabilities as may be incurred in respect of damage to property caused by, or arising out of, any one accident involving the vehicle (s.145(4)(b)). The term "any one accident" includes two or more causally related accidents (see

---

[190] *Lees v Motor Insurers Bureau* [1952] 2 Lloyd's Rep. 210; *Cooper v Motor Insurers Bureau* [1985] 1 All E.R. 449.

[191] Now re-enacted as art.12(1) of the Consolidated Motor Insurance Directive 2009.

[192] *R. v Secretary of State for Transport Ex p. National Insurance Guarantee Corp Plc* Unreported, 1996.

[193] The judgment does not touch upon the situation in which a vehicle has co-drivers. It remains to be determined whether a co-driver not actually driving at the time of an accident caused by the negligent driving of his colleague is covered by 1988 Act or the 1969 Act.

[194] The figure was raised from £250,000 to £1,000,000 with effect from June 11, 2007, by the Motor Vehicles (Compulsory Insurance) Regulations 2007 (SI 2007/1426). These Regulations implemented the Fifth Motor Insurance Directive, now reproduced as art.9 of the Consolidated Motor Insurance Directive 2009, under which the minimum amount of cover for property damage has been raised from €100,000 per claim to €1 million per claim.

s.161(3)). Thus, the figure of £1,000,000 operates as an aggregate ceiling for all property damage flowing from an occurrence such as, for example, a multiple collision. Without the definition of "any one accident" it would be open to the courts to hold that the property damage sustained by each individual could constitute an accident in its own right.

(3) Liability for damage to the vehicle itself (s.145(4)(c)). The assured must insure the vehicle separately if he wishes for such cover.

(4) Liability in respect of damage to goods carried for hire or reward in or on the vehicle or on any trailer (whether or not coupled) drawn by the vehicle (s.145(4)(d)). Such liability is to be dealt with by contract.

(5) Liability to property under the custody or control of the person covered by the policy (s.145(4)(e)). Once again, it is up to the parties to allocate responsibility by contract or disclaimer.

(6) Contractual liability,[195] in so far as it is not within (4) and (5) above (s.145(4)(f)).

22–020   *Vehicle normally based elsewhere in EU.* Under s.145(3)(aa), the policy:

> "must in the case of a vehicle normally based in the territory of another member State, insure him or them in respect of any civil liability which may be incurred by him or them as a result of an event related to the use of the vehicle in Great Britain if,—
>
> (i) according to the law of that territory, the user would be required to be insured in respect of any civil liability which would arise under that law as a result of that event if the place where the vehicle was used when the event occurred were in that territory, and
>
> (ii) the cover required by that law would be higher than that required by [s.145(3)(a)]."

The Consolidated Motor Insurance Directive 2009 requires each Member State to demand compulsory insurance for all vehicles "normally based" in its territory.[196] However, as the 2009 Directive does not harmonise the scope and forms of liability within Member States, the rights of a victim to seek compensation vary depending upon where an injury takes place. This problem was initially addressed by art.2 of the Third Motor Insurance Directive 1990, now re-enacted as art.14 of the Consolidated Motor Insurance Directive 2009, which states that the insurance cover required of a vehicle must be the greater of that demanded by the law of the Member State in which the accident occurred, or that demanded by the law of the Member State in which the vehicle was normally based. The effect is to require each Member State to provide by its domestic law that any compulsory policy against civil liability arising out of the use of a vehicle covered, on the basis of a single premium, the entire territory of the European Union, and to ensure that the scope of cover provided was either that of the Member State in which the vehicle was normally based, or that of the Member State in which it was used, whichever was greater. This principle has been implemented by s.145(3)(aa) of the 1988 Act.

The place where a vehicle is "normally based" is defined in art.1(4) of the Consolidated Motor Insurance Directive 2009, which states that a vehicle is normally based in:

(a) the territory of the State of which the vehicle bears a registration plate, irrespective of whether the plate is permanent or temporary; or

---

[195] 1988 Act s.145(4)(f).
[196] art.3(1), re-enacting art.3 of the First Motor Insurance Directive 1972.

(b) in cases where no registration is required for a type of vehicle but the vehicle bears an insurance plate, or a distinguishing sign analogous to the registration plate, the territory of the State in which the insurance plate or the sign is issued; or

(c) in cases where neither a registration plate nor an insurance plate nor a distinguishing sign is required for certain types of vehicle, the territory of the State in which the person who has custody of the vehicle is permanently resident; or

(d) in cases where the vehicle does not bear any registration plate or bears a registration plate which does not correspond or no longer corresponds to the vehicle and has been involved in an accident, the territory of the State in which the accident took place, for the purpose of settling the claim.

This definition is a re-enactment of art.1 of the First Motor Insurance Directive 1972, as amended by the Fifth Motor Insurance Directive 2005. The 2005 amendments had three purposes. First, in order to facilitate the cross-border purchase of motor vehicles, a vehicle is permitted to bear a temporary plate, and where a vehicle is to be exported from one Member State to another then for 30 days running from the date of acceptance for delivery it is to be regarded as at risk in the destination Member State even though it has not at that time been registered there.[197] Accordingly, the MIB of the destination Member State will be responsible for any accident in that interim period. Secondly, false plates no longer determine the place of registration, and in the event of any accident the MIB situated in the place of the accident is liable to compensate the victim. Thirdly, any policy term which seeks to restrict cover where a vehicle is removed from the Member State of its registration for any period of time, so that the place of registration rather than the place in which the vehicle is actually kept determines the insurance cover. The amended definition in the Fifth Motor Insurance Directive 2005 was implemented in the United Kingdom by the Financial Services and Markets Act 2000 (Motor Insurance) Regulations 2007.[198] The Regulations provide that if the vehicle is exported within 30 days, the place of the situation of the risk is the place to which the vehicle has been exported, so the applicable law is based upon that law and not the law of the state of origin.

Use of vehicle elsewhere in the EU. Under s.145(3)(b)[199] the policy: **22–021**

"must, in the case of a vehicle normally based in Great Britain, insure him or them in respect of any liability which may be incurred by him or them in respect of the use of the vehicle and of any trailer, whether or not coupled, in the territory other than Great Britain and Gibraltar of each of the member States of the Communities according to

(i) the law on compulsory insurance against civil liability in respect of the use of vehicles of the State in whose territory the event giving rise to the liability occurred; or

(ii) if it would give higher cover, the law which would be applicable under this Part of this Act if the place where the vehicle was used when that event occurred were in Great Britain."

This is the mirror image of s.145(3)(aa) of the Act, discussed in the preceding paragraph.

[197] Consolidated Motor Insurance Directive 2009 art.15.
[198] SI 2007/2403.
[199] Implementing art.3 of the Consolidated Motor Insurance Directive 2009.

22–022 *Emergency treatment.* Under s.145(3)(c), the policy:

> "must also insure him or them in respect of any liability which may be incurred under the provisions of [the Road Traffic Act 1988] relating to payment for emergency treatment."

The relevant provisions governing the calculation and payment of the costs of medical treatment are contained in ss.157 to 161. Until April 1999, the sums available were relatively small. However, government policy changed early in 1997, when it was announced that, for the purposes of boosting the funding of the NHS, the full cost of NHS medical treatment for the victims of road traffic accidents would be recoverable from the insurers of those responsible for such accidents. The changes were effected by the Road Traffic (NHS Charges) Act 1999, which was brought into force on April 5, 1999,[200] although it is retroactive in that it applies to all accidents whenever occurring, and is supplemented by two statutory instruments, the Road Traffic (NHS Charges) Regulations 1999[201] and the Road Traffic (NHS Charges) (Reviews and Appeals) Regulations 1999.[202] The 1999 Act is based on the Social Security (Recovery of Benefits) Act 1997, under which social security benefits can be recouped from persons who become liable to compensate the victims of personal injuries, most importantly motor insurers and the MIB,[203] and the same recoupment machinery—the Compensation Recovery Unit of the Department of Social Security (CRU)—is employed under both pieces of legislation. The 1999 Act amends ss.157 to 161 of the Road Traffic Act by confining their operation to private hospitals, with NHS hospitals having a separate regime for recovery under the 1999 Act itself.

The 1999 legislation only applies to accidents occurring on or before January 28, 2007. The position after that date is governed by Pt 3 of the Health and Social Care (Community Health and Standards) Act 2003, which was brought into effect on January 29, 2007 by the Health and Social Care (Community Health and Standards) Act 2003 (Commencement) (No.11) Order 2006.[204] The 2003 Act as supplemented by statutory instrument,[205] has extended the principle of NHS recovery from motor liability policies to all liability policies covering death or personal injury. The 2003 Act replicates the position under the 1999 legislation.

As far as private hospitals are concerned, s.157 of the 1988 Act is confined to any "hospital", a word defined by s.161[206] as meaning any institution which provides in-patient medical or surgical treatment other than an NHS hospital or a military hospital.[207] A hospital so defined is entitled to claim, from an insurer liable for a personal injuries claim under the 1988 Act, the expenses reasonably incurred by the hospital in affording treatment, after deductions for any moneys actually received by the hospital (e.g. from private health insurers). The amount recoverable from motor insurers is capped at £2865.00 for each in-patient and

---

[200] By the Road Traffic (NHS Charges) (Commencement No.1) Order 1999 (SI 1999/1075).

[201] SI 1999/785 (the "Charges Regulations").

[202] SI 1999/786 (the "Reviews and Appeals Regulations").

[203] The MIB is, however, only affected by the 1999 Act with regard to accidents occurring after April 5, 1999: SI 1999/1075.

[204] SI 2006/3397.

[205] Personal Injuries (NHS Charges) (General) and Road Traffic (NHS Charges) (Amendment) Regulations 2006 (SI 2006/3388); Personal Injuries (NHS Charges) (Reviews and Appeals) and Road Traffic (NHS Charges) (Reviews and Appeals) (Amendment) Regulations 2006 (SI 2006/3398).

[206] As amended by s.18 of the 1999 Act.

[207] Regulations are to be made under s.15 of the 1999 Act in relation to military hospitals. As yet such regulations have not been made.

£286.00 for each out-patient.[208] Insurers have to be informed of the fact that hospital treatment has been given,[209] and payment must be made directly to the hospital.[210]

Other forms of loss. Section 145 of the 1988 Act only applies to damages for **22–023** death, personal injuries and property damage set out above, so that the owner of a vehicle is not required to be insured against other forms of loss which may be caused to a third party. Such losses might include, for example, the loss by the third party of the unexpired part of his own motor insurance premium or loss of his no claims bonus: these sums are recoverable from the assured by way of damages, but the assured will be able to recover an indemnity from his insurers in respect of them only if the policy so provides.[211] It has been held in Australia, however, that if the third party is injured by the malicious act of the assured, the insurer is liable under the compulsory part of the policy for the aggravated damages awarded against the insured.[212]

Where a vehicle is stolen, and is then recovered and stored, the persons storing the vehicle are entitled to an appropriate fee for storage under s.101 of the Road Traffic Regulation Act 1984, and this is enforceable by a possessory lien. There is no exemption from payment of the fee in favour of innocent owners of stolen vehicles.[213] It is unclear whether such fee is recoverable by the assured from his insurers, although if the insurers have accepted an abandonment of the vehicle and seek to recover it from storage the insurers are themselves liable for the fee.[214] There is no statutory scheme for the costs incurred in recovering vehicles which are burnt out and which cause a hazard to the public, although there is a scheme approved by the Association of British Insurers whereby the police will instruct a person providing recovery services to recover the vehicle, the insurer then accepting liability for recovery and storage pending disposal following instructions by the insurer. In *Eagle Recovery Services v Parr*[215] the insurers, who were not members of the ABI, refused to pay the claimant recovery firm for recovery and storage. The county court ruled that the police had acted as agent for the assured in instructing the plaintiff to remove the vehicle and that the insurers were accordingly liable for removal and storage charges. Damages were, however, reduced by the court as the claimant had retained the vehicle for longer than necessary.

Liability for cost of replacement vehicles. One particular problem which has **22–024** arisen is the issue of liability of insurers to indemnify the assured for damages in respect of the victim's cost of hiring a replacement vehicle. Such cover is often included, but it is unclear whether the cost of hiring a replacement vehicle forms a part of the compulsory insurance requirement under the Consolidated Motor Insurance Directive 2009. In *McCall v Poulton*[216] a reference was made to the

---

[208] The figures were substituted by the Road Traffic Accidents (Payment for Treatment) Order 1993 (SI 1993/2474).

[209] *Barnett Group Hospital Management Committee v Eagle Star Insurance Co Ltd* [1960] 1 Q.B. 107.

[210] Road Traffic 1988 s.159(1).

[211] See *Patel v London Transport Executive* [1981] R.T.R. 29; *Ironfield v Eastern Gas Board* [1964] 1 W.L.R. 1125n; *Baker v Courage* [1989] 9 C.L. 297.

[212] *Lamb v Cotogno* (1988) 164 C.L.R. 1.

[213] *Service Motor Policies at Lloyd's v City Recovery Ltd* [1997] 10 C.L. 423.

[214] *Service Motor Policies at Lloyd's v City Recovery Ltd* [1997] 10 C.L. 423.

[215] *Eagle Recovery Services v Parr* [1998] C.L. 405.

[216] *McCall v Poulton* [2008] EWCA Civ 1263.

European Court of Justice for a preliminary ruling on whether the MIB's Uninsured Drivers Agreement is to be read subject to the Directive or whether the MIB is an emanation of the state so that the Directive is directly effective against it.[217] In *McAll v Brooks*[218] the Court of Appeal assumed that such damages were awardable against the assured, although the case turned on the different question of whether insurers had a right of subrogation despite the fact that they could not enforce the insurance agreement. In *Giles v Thompson*[219] the victim entered into an agreement with a third party under which the third party provided the victim with a replacement motor vehicle in return for an assignment of the victim's right to recover the hire charges from the wrongdoer's insurers. The House of Lords held that this form of arrangement did not amount to unlawful maintenance or champerty, and that, in principle, the third party was entitled to proceed against the wrongdoer's insurers. Their Lordships did not, however, rule on the question whether the victim's damages against the wrongdoer actually included the costs of hiring a replacement vehicle. That point has, however, been considered by the House of Lords in *Dimond v Lovell*.[220]

In *Dimond*, a vehicle belonging to the nominal claimant, D, was damaged as a result of the negligence of L. The vehicle remained usable. D's brokers recommended that she enter into an agreement with a third party, IAL, under which IAL would supply a replacement motor vehicle for eight days at a cost of £346.63 while repairs were effected, and D in turn passed control of her claim for repair costs and hiring charges against L (or, in reality, L's liability insurers) to IAL. L's insurers paid the repair costs but disputed L's liability for hiring charges. Various technical questions relating to the formation of the agreement between D and IAL arose under the Consumer Credit Act 1974, and the House of Lords concluded that the agreement amounted to one for consumer credit under s.8 of the 1974 Act[221] and that IAL's failure to provide relevant information as to credit rendered the agreement improperly executed and unenforceable.[222] This meant that IAL had provided the vehicle to D gratuitously, and that D had suffered no loss in respect of it: accordingly, no action for damages lay against L.[223] However, the House of Lords went on to consider whether the costs incurred by D would have been recoverable had this objection not arisen. Their Lordships, while unanimous on the point that costs were in principle recoverable, were divided on the issue of quantum. The majority view

---

[217] If there is a favourable ruling in either respect, the further issue in *McCall v Poulton* will be whether the MIB has to pay damages representing hiring costs.

[218] *McAll v Brooks* [1984] R.T.R. 99. See also *Mattocks v Mann, The Times*, June 19, 1992.

[219] *Giles v Thompson* [1994] A.C. 965.

[220] *Dimond v Lovell* [2000] 2 All E.R. 897.

[221] Thereby confirming that a consumer hire agreement, falling within the definition of s.15 of the 1974 Act but excluded from the operation of that section by virtue of its duration, can also amount to a consumer credit agreement within s.8 of the 1974 Act and thereby attract the full regulatory structure of the 1974 Act.

[222] Under the Consumer Credit Act 1974 ss.65 and 127, and the Consumer Credit (Agreements) Regulations 1983 (SI 1983/1553).

[223] The House of Lords on this point held that *McAll v Brooks*—in which subrogation proceedings brought by the victim's insurers against the wrongdoer for the costs of hiring a replacement vehicle were permitted, even though the insurance contract with the victim was void by reason of the insurers' breach of regulatory legislation—could no longer stand in the light of *Hunt v Severs* [1994] 2 A.C. 350. In *Hunt*, the House of Lords decided that services provided to a victim in principle did not go to reduce the victim's loss and that damages would be held in trust for the service provider, unless for some reason a trust could not be implied. A trust was denied in *Hunt* on the basis that the wrongdoer had himself provided the services. The House of Lords in *Dimond* was of the view that no trust could have been implied in favour of the victim's indemnifiers, given that they had infringed regulatory legislation.

was that D was entitled to recover only the "spot rate", i.e. the hiring rate quoted by car hire firms local to D, and not the higher rate charged by IAL, given that IAL's rate included a number of benefits—mainly the claims recovery service— other than simply the provision of a replacement vehicle. Lord Nicholls, dissenting, felt that D had been fully justified in enlisting the services of IAL to assist with recovery of the claim: Lord Nicholls relied to some extent on the practical consideration that IAL's services served to bridge the gap between the victims and the insurers of negligent drivers.[224]

The point arose again in *Everson v Flurry*,[225] a decision of Slough county court **22-025** the main question in which was whether a contract, under which an insurer agreed to pay hire charges in the event that the assured's car was damaged by a third person, was a contract of insurance and thus a contract which gave rise to subrogation rights in favour of the insurer against the wrongdoer who caused the damage to the assured's vehicle. The court held that the contract was one of insurance, and accordingly that subrogation rights existed. It was not necessary for the court to decide whether, on the facts, the hire charges incurred by the assured were recoverable, but the court confirmed that a reasonableness test had to be applied before such charges could qualify as recoverable damages. In *Clark v Ardington Electrical Services*[226] the reasonableness of hire charges fell to be decided, as the credit hire agreement in that case were exempt from the Consumer Credit Act 1974.[227] The Court of Appeal ruled that the victim was entitled to recover the actual cost of hiring a replacement vehicle and was not, as had been held at first instance, held to the cost of local spot rates for car hire. However, as the victim was under a duty to mitigate his loss, evidence of local spot rates was relevant to determine whether the victim had acted reasonably. The Court of Appeal further accepted that if the victim had, by reason of impecuniosity, not been able to obtain a replacement car other than by entering into a credit hire agreement, the full cost of that agreement would have been recoverable from the negligent driver's insurers assuming that such hiring was the cheapest method for the victim to remedy his loss. The Court of Appeal also noted that the victim could recover hire charges for a period longer than was reasonable for repairs to his own vehicle to be effected, and that in such a case it was open to the insurers to seek contribution or indemnity from the repairers reflecting the unjustified length of repairs. The victim is, however, only entitled to recover the costs of hiring a vehicle equivalent to his own, although if he

---

[224] In the Court of Appeal in *Dimond v Lovell* [1999] 3 All E.R. 1, the majority opinion had been in favour of the more generous approach subsequently adopted by Lord Nicholls. Scott V.-C. and Thorpe L.J. held that the question was whether D had acted reasonably in seeking to mitigate her loss by hiring a replacement vehicle from IAL, and that on the facts she had done so: D had relied upon the advice of her broker; the agreement with IAL removed from D the need to worry about recovery from L; and even if IAL's charges had exceeded the market norm—which was not the case—that of itself was not enough to suggest that D had acted unreasonably. Judge L.J., by contrast, was less than satisfied that the reasonableness test had been met, although ultimately he was not prepared to dissent. Judge L.J.'s approach required the court to take into account, in addition to the considerations recommended by the majority, the extent of damage to the car, and in particular whether the car was usable while D conducted a proper investigation of the costs of hiring a replacement. The absence of urgency in D's case, and the fact that she had not sought other quotations, pointed towards unreasonable conduct.

[225] *Everson v Flurry* [1999] 8 C.L. 406.

[226] *Clark v Ardington Electrical Services* [2002] Lloyd's Rep. I.R. 524, varying the decision of Oxford County Court, reported at [2002] Lloyd's Rep. I.R. 138.

[227] The Court of Appeal held that this was so because: (a) the agreements were not consumer credit agreements at all; (b) and the agreements benefited from the Consumer Credit (Exempt Agreements) Order 1989 as the total payments required did not exceed four and the period of hire did not exceed 12 weeks.

chooses to hire an inferior vehicle the insurers cannot be liable beyond the costs of the actual hiring.

The obligation on the victim to mitigate his loss merely means that he has to act reasonably in the circumstances, Thus in *Brain v Yorkshire Rider Ltd*[228] the court allowed the full cost of hiring a replacement vehicle, whereas in *Evans v TNT Logistics Ltd*[229] the costs were in part disallowed where the vehicle hired was unnecessarily expensive. In *Brain* it was held that the decision of the Court of Appeal in *Watson Norie Ltd v Shaw and Nelson*[230] did not support the general proposition that the full cost of hire of a prestige vehicle should not be allowed so long as a car provided by the defendant is adequate for the claimant's needs.[231] The victim is entitled to a replacement vehicle more or less equivalent to that he has lost, even if the vehicle is an expensive one.[232]

The fact that the victim is insured against such loss is irrelevant to the reasonableness of the assured's conduct—the reasonableness of mitigation has to be looked at from the point of view of the victim himself and not from the point of view of his insurers. Thus in *Bee v Jenson (No.1)*[233] it was held that the fact that the victim's insurers might have entered into more favourable arrangements with the third party who supplied the vehicle to the victim was irrelevant to the victim as he had no such opportunity himself, and in *Bee v Jenson (No.2)*[234] it was further ruled that the fact that the victim's insurers had received some financial benefit from entering into arrangements with a particular supplier was to be left out of account as no benefit had accrued to the victim himself. It was also held in *Bee v Jenson (No.2)* that the victim was entitled to obtain a credit hire agreement which, for an additional fee, gave the victim a full indemnity despite the fact that his policy required him to bear the first £100 of any loss by way of deductible: had it not been for the assured's negligence, the victim would not have suffered any loss at all and it was reasonable for him to maintain himself in that position.

22–026   The victim is not required to take advantage of any arrangements put in place by the defendant's insurers to supply a replacement vehicle. This was decided by the Court of Appeal in the joined cases *Copley v Lane; Maden v Haller*.[235] In *Copley* the claimant agreed to hire a replacement car but was, within the cancellation period for that contract, contacted by the defendant's insurers who offered her a free car. The offer was declined. The defendant's insurers subsequently asserted that the claimant had failed to mitigate her loss by not accepting their offer. In *Madden* the defendant insurers' offer came within 24 hours of the accident and before the claimant had entered into third-party

---

[228] *Brain v Yorkshire Rider Ltd* [2007] Lloyd's Rep. I.R. 564.

[229] *Evans v TNT Logistics Ltd* [2007] Lloyd's Rep. I.R. 708.

[230] *Watson Norie Ltd v Shaw and Nelson* [1967] Lloyd's Rep. 515.

[231] See also *Heap-Hammond v TNT UK* Unreported, June 15, 2007 Yeovil County Court, where the damages awarded to the assured were reduced to reflect the fact that the assured had hired a vehicle at a cost significantly in excess of the spot rate: the court in this case rejected the defendant's suggestion that a part of the loss had been the result of delays by the assured's insurers and repairers in authorising and effecting the necessary repairs to the assured's own vehicle. In *Kelly v Mackle* [2009] N.I.Q.B. 39 the court held that it was not reasonable for the victim, a taxi-driver, to hire a replacement taxi at a daily rate of £227.00 + VAT when the daily cost greatly exceeded the likely revenue that the taxi would have generated in the same period: the victim was held to the cost of hiring a replacement vehicle based on spot hire rate of £55 per day.

[232] *Bent v Highways & Utilities Construction Ltd* [2010] EWCA Civ 292.

[233] *Bee v Jenson (No.1)* [2007] Lloyd's Rep. I.R. 541.

[234] *Bee v Jenson (No.2)* [2008] Lloyd's Rep. I.R. 221.

[235] *Copley v Lane; Maden v Haller* [2009] EWCA Civ 580. See also *Salt v Helley* [2009] N.I.Q.B. 69.

arrangements: again the offer was declined and the claimant hired his own replacement vehicle. The Court of Appeal[236] held that each of the claimants had not failed to mitigate their losses. Looked at from a claimant's point of view, a free car was being supplied, so it could not be said that preferring one source over another was a failure to mitigate loss unless it was clear to the claimant from the insurers' communication that it would have been more expensive to hire a car from another source, but a mere offer of a free car did not operate in that fashion. Longmore L.J. further indicated that if the claimant was seeking to recover no more than the spot rate, any argument that further mitigation was required would be met with some scepticism.

The problem of the impecunious claimant was subsequently the subject of an appeal to the House of Lords in *Lagden v O'Connor*,[237] which was heard by the Court of Appeal concurrently with *Clark v Ardington*, and the House of Lords by a 3:2 majority, Lords Nicholls, Slynn and Hope confirmed the Court of Appeal's approach that such a claimant was entitled to take advantage of the services offered by credit hire companies and to recover the additional costs of those services by way of damages from the defendant. In *Lagden* the claimant's car was damaged by the negligence of the defendant. The claimant was unemployed, in poor health and impecunious and was able to fund the hiring of a replacement car only by entering into a credit hire agreement. Lord Nicholls expressed the sentiments of the majority when faced with a claimant who had no choice other than to use credit hire, by stating that:

"The law does not assess damages payable to an innocent plaintiff on the basis that he is expected to perform the impossible . . Credit hire companies provide a reasonable means whereby innocent motorists may obtain use of a replacement vehicle when otherwise they would be unable to do so. Unless the recoverable damages in such a case include the reasonable costs of a credit hire company the negligent driver's insurers will be able to shuffle away from their insured's responsibility to pay the cost of providing a replacement car. A financially well placed plaintiff will be able to hire a replacement car, and in the fullness of time obtain reimbursement from the negligent driver's insurers, but an impecunious plaintiff will not. This can not be an acceptable result."

The fact that the claimant had obtained additional benefits—in the form of credit—as well as the use of the hire car itself, provided no ground for a deduction from damages if there was no way of avoiding those additional benefits. The majority of their Lordships distinguished *Dimond v Lovell*, and confirmed that a motorist who had the financial ability to hire a replacement vehicle without using credit hire would be able to recover by way of damages only the spot rate for such a vehicle and not the credit hire price. The majority view was based primarily on the notion of mitigation of loss, in that the claimant was entitled to damages for the costs of obtaining a replacement vehicle and the question was whether it was appropriate to deduct the credit hire cost from those damages for failure by the claimant to mitigate his loss. The minority approach,

---

[236] Approving the views expressed in *Evans v TNT Logistics Ltd* [2007] Lloyd's Rep. I.R. 708 that there is no obligation on the claimant to accept an offer of a free vehicle from the defendant's insurers.

[237] *Lagden v O'Connor* [2004] Lloyd's Rep. I.R. 315. See also *Gilheaney v McGovern* [2009] N.I.Q.B. 38 where the claimant asserted that he was entitled to credit hire rate rather than the spot rate because he was impecunious: the court was satisfied that the claimant was impecunious (a student) and was therefore entitled to use credit hire. The fact that there were cheaper credit hire rates than the company he used did not lead to a reduction in damages, because there was no evidence that alternative sources could have been discovered without undue effort and at a time when the claimant was doing his A levels and had little time to search the market.

that of Lords Scott and Walker, was that the issue was not one of mitigation of loss at all but rather the measure of damages and if it was the case that credit hire as a head of damages was not available to a claimant who could afford to hire a replacement car then the same result had to follow where the claimant was unable to afford a replacement vehicle. A major obstacle to the majority conclusion was the long-established principle laid down by the House of Lords itself in *Liesbosch Dredger (Owners of) v Owners of SS Edison (The Liesbosch)*,[238] to the effect that following a wrongful act by the defendant additional damage suffered by a claimant by reason of his own impecuniosity is irrecoverable. Their Lordships in *Lagden*—unanimously on this point—having analysed the gradual erosion of that principle, held that the time had now come to depart from it and accordingly that the decision did not preclude damages of the type sought in *Lagden*.[239]

An assured who has no need to hire a replacement vehicle, e.g. because he is a trader who has a stock of other vehicles from which a replacement can be drawn pending repairs to the damaged vehicle, is not automatically debarred from recovering damages for loss of use, although he will have to prove that loss has been suffered. In *Beechwood Birmingham Ltd v Hoyer Group UK Ltd*[239a] the Court of Appeal held that in such a case, the measure of damages is based on the interest and capital employed and any depreciation sustained over the period of repairs, allowed in respect of the vehicle of the type damaged in the accident. The claimant may be precluded from recovering credit hire costs by way of damages by ordinary principles of tort law. Thus, if it is shown that the claimant had been using the damaged vehicle without insurance, and that he would have continued to do so but for the accident which was the fault of the claimant, public policy—in the form of the maxim *ex turpi causa non oritur actio*—will preclude any action for damages in that the claimant would thereby be deriving benefit from his own wrongdoing.[240]

Scope of compulsory policy

22–027   *Persons insured under the policy.* Section 145(3) of the 1988 Act provides that the policy must insure "Such person, persons or classes of person as may be specified in the policy". The insurer's liability is thus not just to indemnify the assured, but to indemnify any person who is stated by the policy to be covered by it. At common law other named or authorised drivers are not parties to the contract as such and probably cannot sue under it.[241] The right of other users

---

[238] *Liesbosch Dredger (Owners of) v Owners of SS Edison (The Liesbosch)* [1933] A.C. 449.

[239] The litigation on the credit hire problem has to a large extent been resolved by an agreement between insurers and credit hire companies regulating the amounts payable by motor insurers for replacement vehicles. The agreement was exempted from the Chapter 1 prohibition in the Competition Act 1998 by the Office of Fair Trading by a decision dated April 22, 2004.

[239a] [2010] EWCA Civ 647.

[240] *Agheampong v Allied Manufacturing (London) Ltd* [2009] Lloyd's Rep. I.R. 379.

[241] *Vandepitte v Preferred Accident Insurance Corp of New York* [1933] A.C. 70. There were indeed doubts as to whether such policies were lawful, in the light of the requirement that liability policies were at one time thought to fall within LAA 1774 s.2 which required the insertion into the policy of the names of all persons interested in it, a requirement which could by definition not be fulfilled. The problem of LAA 1774 s.2 was neatly sidestepped in *Williams v Baltic Insurance Association of London* [1924] 2 K.B. 282, which decided that a policy of this nature was on goods rather than on liability, the former category being excluded from LAA 1774. See now *Mark Rowlands Ltd v Berni Inns Ltd* [1985] 3 All E.R. 473 and *Siu v Eastern Insurance Co* [1994] 1 All E.R. 213, which make it clear that LAA 1774 is confined to non-indemnity policies.

covered by a policy to sue under it where there is compulsory insurance is conferred by s.148(7).[242] This provides:

"Notwithstanding anything in any enactment, a person issuing a policy or insurance under s.145 of this Act shall be liable to indemnify the persons or classes of persons specified in the policy in respect of any liability which the policy purports to cover in the case of those persons or classes of persons."

Section 148(7) does not, therefore, demand that motor policies contain named or authorised user extensions, but states merely that if such an extension is present the insurer is liable to adhere to it at the instance of the persons stated to be covered.[243] The right of action conferred upon the person to whom cover has been extended is not dependent upon the owner insuring as trustee or agent for that person,[244] as the provision operates to create a contract between the insurers and the authorised user.[245] Section 148(7) does not put the claimant under the policy in any better position than the assured himself. Consequently, if the insurer has a right as against the assured to avoid the policy, or to insist upon arbitration, such rights are also available as against other persons covered.[246] Such a person is bound by the conditions of the policy: he must take it as he finds it,[247] subject, of course, to the general provisions of the 1988 Act which limit the rights of the insurers. Typical extension clauses will extend the coverage of the policy to: (a) the assured while driving other cars; and (b) other persons while driving the assured's car. Nothing in s.148(7) gives a direct right of action against the insurers to the injured victim: there was a faint argument to that effect in *Charlton v Fisher*,[248] but this was decisively rejected.

Motor policies frequently provide cover in respect of a person who is driving the vehicle with the consent of the assured, although the policy may also place limits on who is permitted to drive the vehicle, e.g. by reference to age or occupation.[249] A clause extending coverage to other persons is of limited impact as against a third party, given that the insurer is bound to indemnify the third party for loss caused by most classes of unauthorised driver, a point discussed below. However, the point may in some situations—notably, first-party claims—remain of significance. One problem which has arisen in this context is whether a person who obtains possession with the assured's consent but uses the vehicle for an unauthorised purpose, in the course of which an accident occurs, can nevertheless be said to be driving with the assured's consent. The answer may well depend upon the application of technical rules of construction to an informal statement of the assured. In *Singh v Rathour*[250] R borrowed a minibus from X, ostensibly on the basis that it would be used for X's purposes; it was in fact used

[242] The subsection at one time took effect as a statutory exception to the privity doctrine. The abolition of privity by the Contracts (Rights of Third Parties) Act 1999 has now probably theoretically rendered s.148(7) redundant, but in practice it is likely to be continued to be relied upon. The 1999 Act appears to have no different effect.

[243] *Tattersall v Drysdale* [1935] 2 K.B. 174; *Digby v General Accident Fire and Life Assurance Corp* [1943] A.C. 121.

[244] *Tattersall v Drysdale* [1935] 2 K.B. 174; *Austin v Zurich Insurance* [1945] 1 K.B. 250.

[245] *Sutch v Burns* (1943) 60 T.L.R. 1.

[246] *Austin v Zurich General Accident and Liability Insurance Co* [1945] K.B. 250; *Freshwater v Western Australian Assurance Co* [1933] 1 K.B. 515; *Jones v Birch Brothers Ltd* [1933] 2 K.B. 597; *Guardian Assurance Co v Sutherland* [1939] 2 All E.R. 246.

[247] *Freshwater v Western Australian Insurance Co* [1993] 1 K.B. 515

[248] *Charlton v Fisher* [2001] Lloyd's Rep. I.R. 387.

[249] See below.

[250] *Singh v Rathour* [1988] 1 W.L.R. 422.

to drive a group of people to a wedding. On the journey the minibus was involved in an accident resulting from R's negligence, and S's husband was killed and S herself injured. The question for the Court of Appeal was whether R was a person driving the vehicle "with the consent of the owner". It was held that, while R had obtained possession with X's consent, that consent was conditional on its use for X's purposes—a fact known to R—so that X's consent had been nullified and R was not entitled to an indemnity under X's policy. It should be stressed that in this case R was aware that X's consent had been given for a limited purpose, and the Court of Appeal expressly left open the question of whether its decision would have been the same had R not been aware of the limited nature of X's consent.

A further question which has arisen is the effect of the assured's death upon any permission given by him to another person to drive the vehicle. In *Kelly v Cornhill Insurance Co Ltd*[251] the assured gave permission to his son to drive the insured vehicle. During the currency of the policy the assured died, but his son continued to drive the vehicle and was involved in an accident in which he incurred liability to a third party. The House of Lords held by a 4:1 majority that the son was nevertheless driving with "permission" within the terms of the policy. In the view of the majority of their Lordships, "permission" was not revoked by death, by the son receiving notice of death or even by the lapse of a reasonable period following death.

If the cover under the policy is defined by reference to a specified vehicle owned by the assured, the policy will remain effective while he retains an interest in that vehicle.[252] Where the policy contains an extension under which the assured's liability is insured, the insured car or any other vehicle, or contemplates that the assured may replace the vehicle, then its sale does not bring the policy to an end. There is a series of cases in which the courts adopted a presumption that a policy was directed only towards the specified car, so that sale would bring the policy to an end. However, in *Dodson v Peter H Dodson Insurance Services*[253] the Court of Appeal concluded that the cases depended upon express terms[254] and that, insofar as they favoured a presumption that the policy would come to an end[255] that presumption no longer held good. The effect of *Dodson* is, therefore, that a motor policy will be construed as remaining in force as regards third-party liability aspects despite the assured's sale of his own vehicle unless there is express wording which brings the policy to an end where there is such a sale.

22–028   *Deliberate running down.* The obligation under s.145(3) is for the insurance to cover "any liability which may be incurred" by assured or other person covered by the insurance under the terms of the policy. Most motor accident cases involve liability for negligence, and no problems arise from this. The difficult issues are, however: (1) whether a policy is required to cover injury or damage deliberately inflicted by the assured or permitted driver; (2) if so, whether public policy in any way precludes recovery; and (3) if for any reason the user is unable to sue the insurers, whether the victim has any alternative rights of recovery.

---

[251] *Kelly v Cornhill Insurance Co Ltd* [1964] 1 All E.R. 321.

[252] *Peters v General Accident Fire and Life Assurance Corp* (1937) 60 Ll. L.R. 311; *Wilkinson v General Accident* [1967] 2 Lloyd's Rep. 182.

[253] *Dodson v Peter H Dodson Insurance Services* [2001] Lloyd's Rep. I.R. 278.

[254] *Rogerson v Scottish Automobile General Insurance Co Ltd* (1932) 38 Ll. L.R. 142; *Tattersall v Drysdale* [1935] 2 K.B. 174.

[255] *Boss and Hansford v Kingston* [1962] 1 Lloyd's Rep. 431.

As to the first question, it is clear that s.145(3) requires the policy to cover liability for personal injuries which are inflicted in a manner which renders the defendant liable to the victim. If the injuries are inflicted by deliberate running down or in the course of some other criminal activity, the policy is required to cover the loss. This was held to be the case in *Hardy v Motor Insurers Bureau*,[256] a running down case. Lord Denning there emphasised that that liability arising from deliberate misconduct has to be insured in exactly the same way as negligence liability as far as the legislation is concerned.

The second question is whether the assured can recover from his insurers under a compulsory cover. The rules of public policy do not automatically preclude recovery by the assured simply because he has committed a criminal act, and the relevant distinction is whether the damage was inflicted intentionally or recklessly, or unintentionally. Thus in *Tinline v White Cross Insurance Association Ltd*[257] and *James v British General Insurance Co Ltd*,[258] two early first instance judgments on motor insurance, it was held that the fact that the assured had been convicted of motor manslaughter, in that death had been caused by driving while intoxicated, did not preclude recovery by an assured under a policy insuring against motor liability. The effect of these decisions is that a compulsory policy must cover loss inflicted by an intoxicated driver. However, where the injuries or damage are caused by an intentional act of the assured, then while the assured faces liability to the victim public policy will prevent any recovery by him under the policy. In *Hardy v Motor Insurers Bureau*[259] the claimant, a security guard, sought to stop a stolen car and in consequence was injured by its uninsured driver. One of the questions was whether the driver was entitled to recover under the policy in his own right, a question which the Court of Appeal answered in the negative. The same conclusion was reached in *Charlton v Fisher*.[260] Here, the victim was in a car deliberately rammed by the assured, and suffered personal injuries. Although the evidence demonstrated that the assured had not been aware of the victim's presence, his act was a deliberate one and accordingly he was precluded from recovering an indemnity under his policy. The effect of these decisions is that the perpetrator of a deliberate running down cannot recover from his insurers and accordingly that the victim will be unlikely to recover damages from the driver himself.

The third question is, therefore, whether the victim of deliberate running down **22–029** may seek compensation by other means. Two possibilities arise: a direct claim against the insurers; and a claim against the Motor Insurers Bureau.

The victim may have a direct action against the insurers under s.151, which confers upon the victim of a driver who has not satisfied a judgment against him the right to proceed against the driver's insurers where the liability was incurred from a risk required to be insured under the 1988 Act. The early authorities proceeded on the basis that the victim has a direct action as he is not subject to the personal bar to recovery which is imposed upon the user himself. In *Hardy v Motor Insurers Bureau*[261] Lord Denning MR indeed distinguished between a personal bar to recovery, which affected the assured and any person who was his successor as a matter of law (including his personal representative or trustee in bankruptcy), and any other person in whom the right arising out of the contract

---

[256] *Hardy v Motor Insurers Bureau* [1964] 2 Q.B. 745.
[257] *Tinline v White Cross Insurance Association Ltd* [1921] 3 K.B. 327.
[258] *James v British General Insurance Co Ltd* [1927] 2 K.B. 311.
[259] *Hardy v Motor Insurers Bureau* [1964] 2 Q.B. 745.
[260] *Charlton v Fisher* [2001] Lloyd's Rep. I.R. 387.
[261] *Hardy v Motor Insurers Bureau* [1964] 2 Q.B. 745.

was vested (including an injured third party). Lord Denning's analysis was approved by the House of Lords in *Gardner v Moore*.[262] Lord Hailsham L.C., giving the only reasoned speech, held that the personal bar imposed on the assured was "no impediment in the way of a suit by those who claim with clean hands themselves and as assigns of the innocent assured". Neither of these cases was concerned with the effects of s.151, and the point fell to be considered by the Court of Appeal in *Charlton v Fisher*.[263] In this case the majority of the Court of Appeal, Kennedy and Laws L.JJ., held that this meant that the assured was required to insure against deliberate running down: the fact that the assured was for public policy reasons unable to recover where there was a deliberate running down did not weaken the fact that the law required insurance in that situation. Given the requirement for insurance, the victim was held by Kennedy and Laws L.JJ. in principle[264] to be able to bring a direct action against the insurers under s.151. Rix L.J. disagreed with this conclusion, and ruled that the 1988 Act did not require an insurer to insure against deliberate running down, and the question was whether the policy by its terms provided the necessary coverage. Rix L.J. saw no basis for the distinction drawn by Lord Denning in *Hardy* between the assured's legal successors and his third party victim. If the majority view in *Charlton* is right, it follows that the insurers themselves will be liable to indemnify the victim where a direct action is brought against them under s.151.

Assuming that s.151 permits a direct action against insurers, the remaining question is whether the policy itself can exclude that possibility. The question has arisen in the context of the question whether a policy limited to "accidents" can give rise to a direct claim by the victim in a running down action. The issue was sidestepped in the early decisions: in *Tinline v White Cross Insurance Association Ltd*[265] it was decided that causing death by driving at excessive speed was an accident for the purposes of a motor policy, and again in *James v British General Insurance Co Ltd*,[266] the inflicting of personal injury by a drunken driver was held to be accidental for the purposes of a motor policy. However, such sidestepping is not always possible in the light of the Court of Appeal's ruling in *Gray v Barr*,[267] which was not a motor case: it was there held that the term "accident" reflected the public policy rule that an accident could not be a loss which was brought about either deliberately or with reckless disregard for the consequences. The point was addressed indirectly by Lord Hailsham in *Gardner v Moore*.[268] The case was decided on the basis that the policy terms were irrelevant to the existence of a direct action. The case provides authority for the proposition that the victim has a direct action against the insurers in a running down case even though the policy is limited to accidents. In *Charlton v Fisher*[269] the Court of Appeal by a majority held that the victim had a direct action where the policy was confined to "accidents" even in a deliberate running down case. Kennedy and Laws L.JJ., in reaching this conclusion preferred the construction approach: in their view, it was appropriate to construe the word "accident"

---

[262] *Gardner v Moore* [1984] 1 All E.R. 1100.

[263] *Charlton v Fisher* [2001] Lloyd's Rep. I.R. 487.

[264] But not on the facts of the case, as the incident occurred off a "road" and thus was in any event outside the scope of the 1988 Act. The facts of *Charlton v Fisher* arose before the amendment of s.143, extending the legislation to "any public place".

[265] *Tinline v White Cross Insurance Association Ltd* [1921] 3 K.B. 327.

[266] *James v British General Insurance Co Ltd* [1927] 2 K.B. 311.

[267] *Gray v Barr* [1971] 2 Q.B. 554.

[268] *Gardner v Moore* [1984] 1 All E.R. 1100 at 1107.

[269] *Charlton v Fisher* [2001] Lloyd's Rep. I.R. 387.

consistently with the purposes of the 1988 Act, and the word should not be given the meaning that it might bear in other liability cases. Both Kennedy and Laws L.JJ. relied on the comments of Lord Hailsham L.C. in *Gardner v Moore*,[270] although for the narrower proposition that the policy should be construed generously rather than entirely disregarded. Rix L.J. dissenting on this point in *Charlton* rejected the analysis adopted in the earlier cases, and preferred the view that it was open to insurers to restrict cover to particular forms of use. In Rix L.J.'s view, the obligation on the user of a motor vehicle to insure against liability arising from all of its uses, under s.145, did not impose a corresponding obligation on an insurer to issue a policy which covered all uses: thus if a policy was restricted in some respect even though insurance was required, the assured might be in contravention of the legislation but the insurers would be acting perfectly legitimately. It might be thought that Rix L.J.'s view is the correct one, as s.148 sets out an exhaustive list of terms and restrictions which are unenforceable in third-party claims cases, and the use of the term "accident" is not one of them. That said, however, in *Bernaldez*[271] the European Court of Justice appeared to hold that, for the purposes of the EU's Motor Insurance Directives, an insurer is indeed an unconditional guarantor irrespective of the actual terms of the policy, so that Rix L.J.'s conclusion may ultimately prove to be inconsistent with EU law and that of Lord Hailsham affirmed.[272]

There is an alternative route by which the victim can obtain compensation, i.e. by means of an action against the Motor Insurers Bureau. Under the MIB Uninsured Drivers Agreement, the most recent version of which came into force in 1999, the MIB has undertaken to indemnify the victim of an uninsured driver where the injury or damage was inflicted from a risk which is required to be covered by insurance. It was decided by the Court of Appeal in *Hardy v MIB* that in a deliberate running down case, while the rules of public policy prevent the driver from recovering under a policy of his own in respect of his own injuries, it was not appropriate to apply those rules to what was in effect a claim by a third party. On that basis, the victim's claim was one based on liability against which the Road Traffic legislation demanded insurance, and the MIB was bound to meet the claim. It is readily apparent that the Hardy decision is one based purely on public policy, and it was given the blessing of the House of Lords on that understanding in *Gardner v Moore*.[273] The Court of Appeal was unanimous in *Charlton v Fisher* that, if it was the case that the victim did not have a direct action against the driver's insurers in a running down case, the MIB was in principle liable to indemnify the victim under the Uninsured Drivers Agreement.[274]

Liability "arising out of the use of". Compulsory insurance applies to liability "arising out of the use of" a motor vehicle on a road, a concept which is clearly intended to be wider than liability "caused by" such use. The difference is illustrated by the decision of the High Court of Australia in *Dickinson v Motor*   **22–030**

---

[270] *Gardner v Moore* [1984] 1 All E.R. 1100 at 1107. See also *Keeley v Pashen* [2005] Lloyd's Rep. I.R. 289, where it was assumed that an action under s.151 lay in a deliberate running down case.

[271] *Bernaldez* [1996] All E.R. (EC) 741.

[272] See the discussion of *Bernaldez*, below.

[273] *Gardner v Moore* [1984] 1 All E.R. 1100.

[274] However, there was no liability in the present case as the accident had not occurred on a road and thus the liability was not one which was required to be insured against under the 1988 Act.

Vehicle Insurance Trust.[275] In this case, the assured left his two children, aged four and two, alone in his car while he went shopping. In his absence, the older child, while playing with a box of matches, set fire to the car and caused his younger sister severe burn injuries. The injured child brought an action against her father, alleging that her injuries arose out of the use of the car. The Court, denying that the law of causation had any part to play in this matter, held that the father—and therefore his liability insurers—was liable to the child under the compulsory insurance provisions.

The scope of this phrase in the 1988 Act was considered by the Court of Appeal in *Dunthorne v Bentley.*[276] Here, the assured's car ran out of petrol and the assured pulled into the side of the road. Some minutes later, the assured saw a colleague driving by on the opposite side of the road: she ran out of her car and across the road in an attempt to attract her colleague's attention, but unfortunately she ran in front of a car being driven by the claimant and was killed. The claimant sought to recover his own losses from the assured's insurers, and claimed that the policy was required to cover the situation as in the circumstances the events were arising out of the use of a motor vehicle. The Court of Appeal upheld this argument, and accepted that an accident could arise out of the use of a vehicle even when the vehicle was not at the time being driven by the assured. The Court was at pains to stress that each case turned upon its own facts, and that the result in *Dunthorne* could not necessarily predict the result in any other case. Nevertheless, it is possible to draw some general conclusions. One obvious example where cover would be required is where the assured's vehicle is parked dangerously and results in an accident. Beyond that, matters become more difficult. It would seem that an accident does not arise out of the use of a vehicle when it is no longer being used or when it is about to be used, so that had the facts of *Dunthorne* involved an assured who had just parked her vehicle or was crossing the road to get to her vehicle, compulsory cover would not be required. However, it might be noted that in *Cutter v Eagle Star Insurance Co Ltd*[277] the House of Lords assumed that the 1988 Act applied to an accident occurring to a passenger while the vehicle was parked with the engine switched off. By contrast, if the assured is in the course of using the vehicle but temporarily stops for purposes connected with its use—e.g. to purchase petrol—it is arguable that any incident flowing from this is arising out of the use of the vehicle.

The limits of *Dunthorne* are illustrated by *Slater v Buckinghamshire County Council.*[278] In this case the assured was the operator of a minibus service that transported disabled persons to and from a day centre run by a local authority. The minibus was staffed by a driver and by an escort. The claimant, who suffered from Down's syndrome, disregarded instructions from the escort and ran across a busy road to board the minibus: he was hit by an oncoming vehicle and seriously injured. The assured was cleared of any negligence, so insurance issues did not arise, but Morland J.[279] held that the claimant's accident was neither caused by nor arising out of the use of the minibus as the accident was too remote from the use of the vehicle. Morland J. emphasised that every case turned on its own special facts.

---

[275] *Dickinson v Motor Vehicle Insurance Trust* (1987) 163 C.L.R. 500. The legislation there considered is, for present purposes, identical to the 1988 Act.
[276] *Dunthorne v Bentley* [1999] Lloyd's Rep. I.R. 560.
[277] *Cutter v Eagle Star Insurance Co Ltd* [1998] 4 All E.R. 417.
[278] *Slater v Buckinghamshire County Council* [2004] Lloyd's Rep. I.R. 432.
[279] Following a Canadian decision on similar facts, *Law Union & Rock Insurance Co Ltd v Moore's Taxi Ltd* 22 D.L.R. (2d) 254 (1959).

It was decided by the House of Lords in *Lister v Romford Ice and Cold Storage Co Ltd*[280] that an accident occurring on a private road soon after the vehicle had left a public road did not "arise out of the use of" the vehicle on a public road.

The protection of passengers

Background. In the earliest road traffic legislation there was no obligation to **22–031** insure against injuries to passengers,[281] although policies were by means of voluntary extension often imposed liability upon insurers to meet claims by injured passengers.[282] There was an exception in favour of "passengers carried for hire or reward, leaving the outcome that a passenger carried for hire or reward was to be covered by the driver's motor policy, but that any other passenger was not covered. The apparent purpose of this distinction was to protect passengers on public service vehicles who were regarded as having little choice as to whether or not they travelled, and passengers in private vehicles who were regarded as having made a conscious decision to be carried. The meaning of the phrase "hire or reward" was extensively litigated, and the cases culminated in the ruling of the House of Lords in *Albert v Motor Insurers Bureau*.[283] Regrettably, their Lordships were divided on the key issues. In that case A was killed in a motor accident while travelling as a passenger in a car driven by Q, and the judgment obtained by A's estate was not satisfied. Proceedings were thus brought against the MIB, which contested liability on the basis that Q had regularly carried fellow employees to work, and that this was a regular arrangement in respect of which Q on occasion received payment in cash or kind. Their Lordships ruled that this was carriage for hire or reward. Lords Donovan, Dilhorne, Pearson and Diplock, Lord Cross dissenting, ruled that there was no need for a binding contract,[284] held that there could be hire or reward in the absence of a binding contract. Given the absence of any need for a contract, Lords Donovan, Pearson and Diplock went on to adopt a "business" test, expressed by Lord Donovan as: "has there been a systematic carrying of passengers for reward which goes beyond the bonds of mere social kindness".[285] On this analysis, the focus was on the nature of the vehicle used to carry passengers, rather than the fact that passengers happened to be carried in a vehicle: accordingly, carriage for hire or reward related primarily to public service vehicles. Viscount Dilhorne and Lord Cross dissented, holding that every use of a vehicle had to be considered in isolation to determine whether it was for hire or reward.[286]

The distinction between passengers carried for hire or reward and other passengers was heavily criticised by the courts, and was abandoned by the Motor Vehicle (Passenger Insurance) Act 1971. This statute extended compulsory cover

---

[280] *Lister v Romford Ice and Cold Storage Co Ltd* [1957] A.C. 555.

[281] Road Traffic Act 1930 s.36(1)(b), re-enacted as Road Traffic Act 1960 s.203(4)(a).

[282] Cf. *Barnet Group Hospital Management Committee v Eagle Star Insurance Co Ltd* [1959] 2 Lloyd's Rep. 335: liability to "any person" extended to passengers.

[283] *Albert v Motor Insurers Bureau* [1971] 2 Lloyd's Rep. 229.

[284] The view taken by Lord Denning in *Connell v Motor Insurers Bureau* [1969] 2 Lloyd's Rep. 1; the contrary view in *Coward v Motor Insurers Bureau* [1963] 1 Q.B. 259 was rejected. In an earlier decision, *Bonham v Zurich General Accident and Liability Insurance Co Ltd* [1945] 2 K.B. 292, the Court of Appeal had been divided on the point.

[285] See also *Wyatt v Guildhall Insurance Co Ltd* [1937] 1 K.B. 653; *Connell v Motor Insurers Bureau* [1969] 2 Lloyd's Rep. 1.

[286] The business test was applied in *Motor Insurers Bureau v Meanen* [1971] 2 Lloyd's Rep. 251, heard concurrently with *Albert*.

to all passengers. The position has been maintained by s.145 of the 1988 Act, which requires the user of a vehicle to be insured against liability to all persons, with no specific mention being made of passengers who are to be treated in the same way as other persons injured by the user of the vehicle. Even in the absence of the change of the law in 1971, an extension to passengers would have been required by art.1 of the Third Motor Insurance Directive 1990, now re-enacted as art.12(1) of the Consolidated Motor Insurance Directive 2009, which provides that compulsory insurance "shall cover liability for personal injury to all passengers, other than the driver, arising out of the use of the vehicle".

The meaning of the word "passenger" has been left to individual member states in their implementation of the Directive. As far as the United Kingdom is concerned, the point does not arise because there is compulsory cover for all persons. In those jurisdictions in which coverage is confined to passengers, a person who is not a "passenger" within the definition set out in the domestic legislation but who is nevertheless being carried in or on a motor vehicle will fall outside the scope of cover, although such a person will have an action against the Member State in question for failing to implement the Directive properly.[287]

22–032 *Owner of vehicle as passenger.* As compulsory policy extends only to third-party liabilities, a user who is injured by his own negligence plainly cannot claim against his liability insurers as he cannot sue himself. In such a case, the user may recover only if the policy by voluntary extension covers first-party losses. Nevertheless, if the passenger is himself the owner of the vehicle who is injured by the negligent use of the vehicle by another, the owner must as passenger be covered by the user's cover. In *Digby v General Accident Fire and Life Assurance Corp*[288] the actress Merle Oberon had taken out a motor policy which provided an indemnity to any person driving the vehicle on her order or with her permission in respect of injuries to "any person". Her chauffeur, who was clearly an authorised driver, was involved in a collision in which Miss Oberon suffered personal injuries. The chauffeur was held to be 100 per cent responsible for her injuries and she obtained judgment for £5,000 plus costs. The House of Lords held that she was entitled to be indemnified by her insurers, as the phrase "any person" meant anyone other than the person driving, including the policy holder while being driven as a passenger. That case was decided before the insurance of passengers became compulsory, and was concerned purely with the proper construction of the policy in question. However, in *Limbrick v French and Farley*[289] it was held that the legislation has the same effect. In this case the claimant insured her liability under a motor policy issued by the second defendant. She gave permission for the vehicle to be driven by the defendant, and was injured when the vehicle in which she was a passenger was involved in an accident. The vehicle was uninsured, as the policy extended cover only to the claimant and her mother, and accordingly the claimant—having obtained a judgment against the first defendant—sought to enforce the judgment against the Motor Insurers Bureau.[290] Simon Brown J. held that the words "any person" in

---

[287] Case C-356/05 *Farrell v Whitty and Motor Insurers Bureau of Ireland* [2007] Lloyd's Rep. I.R. 525 (victim being carried in the back of a van which had no seating for passengers). See also Case C-158/01 *Withers* [2002] E.C.R. I-8301, where the European Court of Justice commented that persons being carried in a vehicle were passengers irrespective of the design of the vehicle.

[288] *Digby v General Accident Fire and Life Assurance Corp* [1943] A.C. 121.

[289] *Limbrick v French and Farley* [1990] C.L.Y. 2710.

[290] Which had nominated the second defendant to act on its behalf in respect of the claim.

what is now s.145(3) of the Road Traffic Act 1988 extended to any passenger, including the claimant herself.[291]

Volenti non fit injuria. The position of passengers is a matter of common law **22–033** weaker than that of other persons injured by a negligent driver, in that the driver was entitled to absolve himself from liability towards a passenger by contract or by a disclaimer of tortious liability. There was even a possibility that a passenger in a vehicle might have been regarded by the common law as voluntarily assuming the risk of negligence by its driver. Consequently, while the road traffic legislation required that insurance of the driver's liability would exist for the benefit of passengers, the common law operated in many cases to prevent the driver's liability towards the passenger from arising.[292] These possibilities were removed by s.149 of the Road Traffic Act 1988, which is in the following terms:

"(1) This section applies where a person uses a motor vehicle in circumstances such that under s.143 of this Act there is required to be in force in relation to his use of it such a policy of insurance or such a security in respect of third party risks as complies with this part of the Act.

(2) If any other person is carried in or upon the vehicle while the user is so using it, any antecedent agreement or understanding between them (whether intended to be legally binding or not) shall be of no effect so far as it purports or might be held—

(a) to negative or restrict any such liability of the user in respect of persons carried in or upon the vehicle as is required by s.145 of this Act to be covered by a policy of insurance, or

(b) to impose any conditions with respect to the enforcement of any such liability of the user.

(3) The fact that a person so carried has willingly accepted as his the risk of negligence on the part of the user shall not be treated as negativing any such liability of the user.

(4) For the purposes of this section—

(a) references to a person being carried in or upon a vehicle include references to a person entering or getting on to, or alighting from, the vehicle, and

(b) the reference to an antecedent agreement is to one made at any time before liability arose."

The main effect of s.149 is to remove the possibility of any defence against the injured passenger based on *volenti non fit injuria.* The scope of this was tested in *Pitts v Hunt.*[293] The events, in this case, arose following a drinking spree at a discotheque by P (then aged 18) and H (aged 16). They left for home on a motorbike driven uninsured by H. Witnesses saw the motorbike speeding and

[291] *Limbrick* reflects the position demanded by the Consolidated Motor Insurance Directive 2009 art.12(1), that the owner of the vehicle who is a passenger at the time of the accident is entitled to the same protection as any other passenger: Case C-537103 *Candolin v Vahinkovakuutusosakeyhtio Pohjola* [2006] Lloyd's Rep. I.R. 209. In *Churchill Insurance Company Ltd v Wilkinson*; *Evans v Equity Claims Ltd* [2010] EWCA Civ 556 the Court of Appeal confirmed that if the victim passenger is the policyholder, then he is "with one possible qualification" entitled to be treated to the fullest extent as a passenger and is entitled to the rights conferred by the Directive on a passenger. The one qualification is the right of recourse conferred upon an insurer against a policyholder under s.151(8) of the Road Traffic Act 1988 where the insurer has been required to provide an indemnity to third party for loss caused by an uninsured person driving with the policyholder's consent. The Court of Appeal has referred to the European Court of Justice the question whether and to what extent a right of recourse is exercisable by the insurer against the policyholder himself.

[292] See generally: *Dann v Hamilton* [1939] 1 K.B. 509; *Nettleship v Weston* [1971] 2 Q.B. 691; *Owens v Brimmell* [1977] Q.B. 859.

[293] *Pitts v Hunt* [1990] 3 All E.R. 344.

swerving from side to side in an apparent attempt to frighten oncoming traffic: both P and H were shouting in apparent enjoyment. Ultimately the motorbike was involved in a collision with a car driven by J. H was killed and P was partially but permanently paralysed. P initiated proceedings against H's estate and against J for negligence, although the action against J proved to have no basis. One of the questions was whether H's estate had a defence against P based on *volenti non fit injuria*. The Court of Appeal, following the decision of the Court of Session in *Winnick v Dick*,[294] held that s.149(3) prevented reliance on this defence, and the degree of the passenger's recklessness was immaterial to the operation of the section.[295]

The subsection does not affect the validity of any agreement between user and passenger after the accident has occurred, as there is no public policy objection to the victim entering into a settlement contract with the user, or waiving any rights against the user.[296]

22–034   *Public policy.* The 1988 Act makes no mention of the common law principle that the victim of a negligent driver may be precluded from bringing an action against the driver by reason of the public policy rule *ex turpi causa*. A claimant will lose his action only where his conduct is such that the court regards it as inappropriate to award a remedy. In the case of a passenger in a motor vehicle, what is generally required is some participation in a common illegal enterprise with the driver rather than mere knowledge of some criminality on the part of the driver. This is, in essence, the same test for the question whether a passenger is "using" the vehicle on his own account, in which case compulsory insurance has to attach to his actions and he will be precluded, by virtue of his capacity as user, from recovering from the Motor Insurers' Bureau where the actual driver is uninsured.

A clear example of participation in a common illegal enterprise is *Ashton v Turner*,[297] in which the Court of Appeal refused to allow an action by the passenger of a negligent driver who caused injury to the passenger while driving the vehicle away from the scene of a crime in which they had both participated. More difficult are the cases of drunken drivers. In *Pitts v Hunt*,[298] the facts of which were given above, the Court of Appeal relied on the distinction between passive and active passengers. In the present case, the claimant's conduct had not simply been passively to accept a lift from a driver who was intoxicated and driving in a dangerous fashion: the claimant had actively participated in the defendant's conduct by encouraging the defendant to drive in that manner.[299] It is possible to object to this reasoning on the basis that, given that a driver who drives in a criminally reckless manner is entitled to an indemnity from his insurers for any injuries caused to a third party,[300] a passenger who participates in such conduct ought himself to be able to take advantage of the fact that

---

[294] *Winnick v Dick* 1984 S.L.T. 185.

[295] The Court of Appeal was also influenced by the undesirability of English law not conforming to Scots law on this matter: rights were not to depend upon which side of the border the vehicle happened to be when the accident occurred.

[296] Road Traffic Act 1988 s.149(4)(b).

[297] *Ashton v Turner* [1981] Q.B. 137.

[298] *Pitts v Hunt* [1990] 3 All E.R. 344.

[299] See, by way of contrast, *Weir v Wyper*, *The Times*, May 4, 1992, in which a passenger who accepted a lift from a learner driver was held not to be debarred on public policy from bringing an action against the driver.

[300] *Tinline v White Cross Insurance Association* [1921] 3 K.B. 327; *James v British General Insurance Co* [1927] 2 K.B. 311. Both of these cases involved drunken drivers.

insurance is in place and would otherwise be available. Again, the MIB is liable to the victim of a driver who had been engaged in an unlawful activity.[301]

Whether the public policy defence remains intact is an issue yet to be considered by the European Court of Justice, although it may in passing be noted that a passenger in a stolen vehicle who knew or ought to have known that the vehicle had been stolen is precluded, by s.151, from bringing proceedings against the driver's insurers even if the passenger does obtain a judgment against the driver in circumstances in which rules of public policy are inapplicable: this restriction on the rights of a passenger, which is specifically provided in EU law, is discussed below. The argument in favour of regarding public policy as having been removed as a defence to a passenger is the very fact that EU law makes specific provision for passengers in stolen vehicles.[302]

Contributory negligence. The Law Reform (Contributory Negligence) Act 1945 permits the court to reduce a defendant's damages by such proportion as represents the defendant's own contribution to his loss. There are numerous cases in which the courts have reduced the damages awardable to a passenger by anything up to 30 per cent for failure by the passenger to wear a safety belt or crash helmet.[303] It was held by the Court of Appeal, in *Pitts v Hunt*,[304] that the 1945 Act does not authorise deductions of 100 per cent and thus zero awards, and that in every case a proper apportionment is to be made.[305] It may be, however, that the English practice of deducting up to 30 per cent in safety belt and crash helmet cases will have to be reappraised in the light of the decision of the EFTA Court in *Storebrand Skadforsikring AS v Finanger*.[306] The claimant in this case was seriously injured in a road traffic accident caused by the driving of a driver who had, at the time of the accident, been intoxicated. The claimant had been aware of that fact when she accepted the lift. Under the Norwegian Automobile Liability Act 1961 s.7, it was provided that an injured passenger cannot obtain compensation if he or she knew or must have known that the driver of the vehicle was under the influence of alcohol. The EFTA Court's advisory opinion was that this provision was inconsistent with EC law. The Court pointed out that the overall purpose of the Directives was to facilitate the free movement of goods and persons, and to safeguard the interests of persons who might be the victims of accidents—including passengers—by setting a high level of protection. The EFTA Court also rejected the argument that the Directives were concerned only with the scope of insurance policies rather than the underlying civil liability in respect of which insurance claims might be generated, as such a limitation would jeopardise the operation of the Directives and could distort competition between motor insurers in different contracting states. This reasoning was enough to

22–035

---

[301] *Hardy v MIB* [1964] 2 Q.B. 745; *Gardner v Moore* [1984] A.C. 548; *Charlton v Fisher* [2001] Lloyd's Rep. I.R. 387.

[302] Consolidated Motor Insurance Directive 2009 art.13(1).

[303] See, e.g. *Froom v Butcher* [1976] Q.B. 786. In *Gawler v Raettig* [2007] EWHC 373 (QB) it was confirmed that there is a standard 25 per cent deduction to be made for a passenger who is not wearing a seatbelt, and that this figure is to be departed from in rare and exceptional cases only. But see *Stanton v Collinson* [2010] EWCA Civ 81 where the Court of Appeal affirmed the decision of Cox J. that the negligent driver had not shown that the injuries would have been "to a considerable extent" (the test laid down in *Froom*) less severe had the claimant been wearing a seatbelt.

[304] *Pitts v Hunt* [1990] 3 All E.R. 344.

[305] The trial judge had made a deduction of 100 per cent, a decision overturned on appeal. The Court of Appeal did not need to decide what the appropriate deduction might have been on the facts in *Pitts v Hunt*, given its ruling that, on public policy ground, the claimant had no cause of action.

[306] *Storebrand Skadforsikring AS v Finanger* [1999] 3 C.M.L.R. 863.

justify a finding that the Norwegian law could not stand, although the EFTA Court made some interesting comments on the role of contributory negligence. In its view, contributory negligence could be a permitted defence "in exceptional circumstances", although only on the basis that compensation was to be reduced in a way proportionate to the contribution to the injury suffered by the passenger.[307]

As far as English law is concerned, the acceptance of a lift with a drunken driver is potentially contributory negligence, a point left open in *Pitts v Hunt*, but the EFTA Court's ruling makes it clear that the amount of any deduction has to be proportionate to the cause of the loss: if the driver's negligence is the entire reason for the accident, it is arguable that there should be no deduction at all. It is uncertain how *Finanger* affects the English practice of making contributory negligence deductions in respect of seat belts and crash helmets: the proportionality test is probably satisfied by the test for apportionment under the 1945 Act, but it remains to be decided whether the "exceptional circumstances" requirement is satisfied.[308]

Control of policy terms

22–036   *Perils which cannot be excluded.* Section 148(1)–(4) sets out a list of perils, liability for which cannot be excluded by the insurer.[309] In each of these cases, however, the prohibition extends only to compulsory insurance; if the policy relates to risks which do not fall within the 1988 Act—such as first-party risks—liability for loss arising from all or any of the listed matters may be excluded by the insurer. The list, which is exhaustive,[310] is as follows:

(1) The age or physical or mental condition of persons driving the vehicle. This does not extend to a condition requiring the assured to exercise reasonable care and to employ only steady and sober drivers,[311] but conditions prohibiting driving by persons under the influence of drugs or alcohol are outlawed.[312]

---

[307] See also the subsequent decision of the European Court of Justice in Case C-537103 *Candolin v Vahinkovakuutusosakeyhtio Pohjola* [2006] Lloyd's Rep. I.R. 209, a case involving a passenger accepting a lift with an intoxicated driver, holding that deduction from the compensation payable to a passenger is permissible only to the extent that that the deduction is proportionate to the passenger's contribution to his own loss.

[308] Under art.13(3) of the Consolidated Motor Insurance Directive 2009, a policy may not exclude liability to the passenger of an intoxicated driver to the extent that the passenger has a civil action: it remains open to Member States to retain the contributory negligence rule so that deductions can be made from damages to the extent that the passenger has caused his own loss.

[309] This section has its origins in the Road Traffic Act 1934. It was commented by Goddard J. in *Zurich General Accident and Liability Insurance Co Ltd v Morrison* [1942] 2 K.B. 53 that the statutory requirement for compulsory insurance in the Road Traffic Act 1930 was of little value if it was open to insurers to freely to exclude liability for common risks.

[310] *Gray v Blackmore* [1934] 1 K.B. 95.

[311] *National Farmers' Union Mutual Insurance Society Ltd v Dawson* [1941] 2 K.B. 424.

[312] See *Louden v British Merchants' Insurance Co Ltd* [1961] 1 Lloyd's Rep. 154 for the construction of such a clause. In *Bernaldez* [1996] All E.R. (E.C.) 791 the European Court of Justice ruled that a compulsory cover could not exclude liability for drunken drivers, although the law could permit the insurer to seek indemnity from the driver in the event of a successful claim by a third party. On the latter point, see s.148(4). In *Storebrand Skadforsikring AS v Finanger* [2000] Lloyd's Rep. I.R. 462 the EFTA Court ruled that it is not permissible for domestic law to exclude from coverage injury or damage caused by an intoxicated driver.

(2) The condition of the vehicle. Such restrictions are common outside the context of compulsory insurance and exclude the insurer's liability, inter alia, if the vehicle is unroadworthy.[313]

(3) The number of persons that the vehicle carries. This provision does not cover the case in which a policy imposes a weight, as opposed to a numerical, limit on passengers. Interestingly enough, in *Houghton v Trafalgar Insurance Co Ltd*,[314] the Court of Appeal held that the phrase 'any load in excess of that for which the vehicle is constructed' did not apply to the case in which the car carried a number of passengers greater than that for which the car was designed. A *Houghton* clause is thus permitted by the 1988 Act in so far as it applies to persons, but not in so far as it applies to goods; see (4) below.

(4) The weight or physical characteristics of the goods that the vehicle carries. This provision does not outlaw a condition against the use of a vehicle for social or domestic purposes only, so that it will not provide relief to an assured who carries business goods in contravention of such a condition.[315]

(5) The times at which or the areas in which the vehicle is used.[316]

(6) The horsepower or cylinder capacity or value of the vehicle.

(7) The carrying on the vehicle of any particular apparatus.

(8) The carrying on the vehicle of any particular means of identification other than any means of identification required to be carried by or under the Vehicles Excise and Registration Act 1994.

If an insurer is liable on any of these grounds, it has a right of recourse against the insured person in respect of the payment to the third party: s.148(4).[317]

The 1988 Act does not seek to prevent the operation as against a third party of one of the most common restrictions in motor policies, that of use of the vehicle for social, domestic or pleasure purposes only. Section 150, does, however, modify the meaning of this and similar phrases for the purposes of compulsory insurance. The statutory modification applies to a vehicle which is not adapted to carry more than eight passengers, which on the journey in question does not

---

[313] Where those words are used, the assured is in breach only where the vehicle is unroadworthy at the start of the journey during which the accident occurred: *Barrett v London General Insurance Co Ltd* [1935] 1 K.B. 238. The reasoning in this case, in so far as it was based on an analogy with the marine implied seaworthiness warranty contained in the Marine Insurance Act 1906 s.39(1), was rejected by the Privy Council in *Trickett v Queensland Insurance Co Ltd* [1936] A.C. 159. However, in *Clarke v National Insurance and Guarantee Corp Ltd* [1964] 1 Q.B. 199, the Court of Appeal, in effect, reinstated the analogy and held that a vehicle which was overloaded was unroadworthy. See the discussion below. Other forms of wording may be used, e.g. an obligation on the assured to maintain the vehicle in efficient condition: *Taylor v National Insurance and Guarantee Corp* [1989] 6 C.L. 248. In *Lefevre v White* [1990] 1 Lloyd's Rep. 569, the assured's obligation to "take every reasonable precaution" to maintain the vehicle in a safe condition was held not to require him to have the brakes tested on the vehicle which he had just purchased, but did oblige him to change tyres which he knew to be in a worn condition. The test for breach of a roadworthiness clause is whether the assured has acted reasonably: *Amey Properties Ltd v Cornhill Insurance Plc* [1996] L.R.L.R. 259; *Conn v Westminster Motor Insurance* [1966] 1 Lloyd's Rep. 407.

[314] *Houghton v Trafalgar Insurance Co Ltd* [1954] 1 Q.B. 247.

[315] *Piddington v Co-operative Insurance Society Ltd* [1934] 2 K.B. 236.

[316] See *Palmer v Cornhill Insurance Co Ltd* (1935) 52 Ll. L.R. 78 for an example of such a clause.

[317] See *Liverpool Corp v Roberts* [1964] 2 Lloyd's Rep. 219. If that right is not exercised, the insurer's payment is to be treated as *ex gratia*, thereby precluding contribution proceedings from any other insurer on risk: *Legal and General Insurance Society Ltd v Drake Insurance Co Ltd* [1992] 1 All E.R. 238.

realise fares in excess of its running costs (which include an element for depreciation) and in respect of which arrangement for the payment of fares were made before the journey commenced. If the vehicle falls within this definition, then for the purposes of a journey on which one or more passengers are carried at separate fares, the vehicle is to be regarded as having been used for social, domestic or pleasure purposes, or non-business purposes, or other than for hire or reward. The effect, then, is to treat car-sharing arrangements—even as between fellow-employees for journeys to work—as social, domestic or pleasure uses of the vehicle.

It is apparent from the drafting of s.148 that UK law contemplates that certain forms of exclusion clause in a motor policy are valid even in respect of third-party claims. It has been held that the list is exhaustive.[318] Rix L.J. in his dissenting comments in *Charlton v Fisher*[319] assumed much the same, as his view was that a policy could legitimately restrict cover to "accidents".[320] This approach would appear to put the law into conflict with the Consolidated Motor Insurance Directive 2009 art.13, which precludes the use of exclusion clauses in policies. In *Bernaldez*,[321] the European Court of Justice ruled that a Spanish law which required motor insurers to exclude liability for claims in the event of drunken driving was contrary to the then operative provisions of the First Motor Insurance Directive 1972 in so far as it related to third-party risks, and the language of the Court indicates that all exclusion clauses are void, as the purpose of the compulsory policy is to ensure that the third party receives compensation for his losses. It may be, therefore, that, irrespective of the limits in the 1988 Act, a motor policy has to provide absolute coverage in respect of third-party risks, and the insurer's only remedy is to seek recourse against the assured for driving the vehicle in breach of the policy's conditions.[322] *Bernaldez* does not, however, affect the right of an insurer to avoid a policy for non-disclosure or misrepresentation (as to which, see below): it provides only that, where the policy is valid, it must cover the third party's losses assuming that the civil law imposes liability on the assured in those circumstances.

22–037   *Breach of condition by the assured.* By virtue of s.148(5)–(6), if the assured breaks a condition of the policy after the happening of the insured event giving rise to a claim, and the effect of the breach of condition would otherwise have been to prevent the insurer's liability from arising or to have put an end to its liability under the policy, the breach is to be regarded as having no effect for the purposes of compulsory insurance. However, if the insurer is required to meet a claim under this provision, it may seek an indemnity from the assured if the

---

[318] In addition to the "social, domestic and pleasure" purposes condition, other conditions outside s.148 include conditions relating to: the mode of carrying passengers (*Bright v Ashfold* [1932] 2 K.B. 153); and restrictions on particular forms of use (*Samuelson v National Insurance and Guarantee Corp* [1985] 2 Lloyd's Rep. 541).

[319] *Charlton v Fisher* [2001] Lloyd's Rep. I.R. 287.

[320] The majority view was that the word "accident" was to be construed against the statutory background, and should be construed as meaning any loss suffered by the victim at the hands of the assured.

[321] *Bernaldez* [1996] All E.R. (E.C.) 791.

[322] See also the comments in *Axa Insurance UK Plc v Norwich Union Insurance Ltd* [2008] Lloyd's Rep. I.R. 122. Even if it is the case that the policy must cover all third-party risks, this is so because any exclusion in the policy is not binding on a third-party claimant. If there is an exclusion, and the assured uses his vehicle in breach of that exclusion, he is still to be treated as driving without insurance for the purposes of the criminal law even though the insurers would be required to meet any third-party claim: *Singh v Solihull Metropolitan BC* [2007] EWHC 552 (Admin).

policy so provides.[323] The object here is clearly to counteract the effect of late claims, failure by the assured to provide the necessary proofs and assistance to the insurer, and the assured's admission of liability to the third party in contravention of the terms of his policy.[324] It should be stressed that s.148(5)–(6) is confined in its operation to post-loss breaches of condition: if the assured has broken a condition of the policy prior to the loss, e.g. in the case of a motorcycle, carrying passengers other than in a sidecar,[325] or using a car for the purposes of the motor trade contrary to the provisions of the policy,[326] s.148(5)–(6), will not prevent the insurer from denying liability.

One outstanding doubt concerns the effect of s.148(5)–(6), on an arbitration clause in the *Scott v Avery* form, i.e. one which prevents the insurer from incurring any liability under the policy until an arbitration award has been made against it. The wording of the legislation, would appear to be appropriate to negate the effect of an arbitration clause, although in *Jones v Birch Brothers Ltd*[327] the Court of Appeal expressed differing provisional views on the matter: Greer and Romer L.JJ. were of the opinion that the statutory provision overrode the arbitration clause, whereas Scrutton L.J. expressed the view that the arbitration clause was left unaffected.

2. ACTIONS FOR THE PROCEEDS OF COMPULSORY MOTOR POLICIES

Forms of proceedings. Sections 151 and 152 of the 1988 Act confer upon the victim of a negligent driver a mechanism to enforce any judgment which the victim may obtain against the driver. The essence of the procedure is that, once the judgment has been obtained, the victim may bring proceedings against the insurers for payment of the amount in the judgment insofar as the liability is one which was required to be covered by insurance. As discussed earlier in this chapter, the insurers cannot rely upon breach of policy conditions by the assured, and there are also restrictions imposed upon the right of insurers to rely upon the defences of misrepresentation and non-disclosure.   **22–038**

Since January 19, 2003 an alternative course of action is open to the victim of an insured driver. The victim may, in accordance with the European Communities (Rights against Insurers) Regulations 2002,[328] bring a direct action against the insurers without first having to obtain a judgment against the user which can then be enforced against the user's insurers. An action under the 2002 Regulations is not available in all cases in which an enforcement action under s.151 is available: this matter is discussed below.

It was argued in *Charlton v Fisher*[329] that s.148(7) of the 1988 Act, under which the insurers are liable "to indemnify the persons or classes of persons specified in the policy in respect of any liability which the policy purports to cover in the case of those persons or classes of persons", had the effect of

---

[323] Section 148(6), which provides that such a clause is valid. See, for an illustration, *Royal & Sun Alliance Plc v Hume* [2009] C.S.I.H. 24. Compare the position where liability arises under a specified risk, where the right of recourse is statutory rather than contractual.

[324] *Revell v London General Insurance* (1935) 152 L.T. 258; *Bright v Ashfold* [1932] 2 K.B. 153; *Croxford v Universal Insurance* [1936] 2 K.B. 253.

[325] *Bright v Ashfold* [1932] 2 K.B. 153.

[326] *Gray v Blackmore* [1934] 1 K.B. 95.

[327] *Jones v Birch Brothers Ltd* [1933] 2 K.B. 597.

[328] SI 2002/3061.

[329] *Charlton v Fisher* [2001] Lloyd's Rep. I.R. 387.

allowing the victim of an insured user to bring a direct action against the user's insurers. The Court of Appeal held that the section was concerned with allowing a user whose liability was covered by means of policy extension to recover from the insurers, and said nothing about the rights of a victim.

These provisions operate irrespective of the assured's financial position. The Third Parties (Rights against Insurers) Act 1930 (subsequently repealed and replaced in 2010), reversing the common law, confers upon the third-party victim of the assured's wrongful conduct a right to proceed directly against the assured's liability insurers in the event of the assured's insolvency. This is a general measure which applies to all forms of liability insurance, although in its origins it was devised to accompany the Road Traffic Act 1930 and to provide a means whereby the victim had direct access to the driver's insurers if a judgment was obtained against the driver which was not satisfied by him. The significance of the Third Parties (Rights against Insurers) Act 1930 to motor insurance claims was all but removed by Road Traffic 1934, which contained the provisions now enacted as s.151 of the 1988 Act, allowing the victim to bring an action against the driver's insurers if a judgment was unsatisfied whether or not the driver had become insolvent. Consequently, s.153, updated to take account of the 2010 Act, simply provides that the 1988 Act has no effect on the direct enforcement action under the 2010 Act. The implementation of the additional right of direct action against insurers without first having to obtain judgment against the assured, by the European Communities (Rights against Insurers) Regulations 2002, is also a straight alternative to the use of the 2010 Act, with the added benefit for the victim that there is no need for him to obtain a judgment against the driver before suing the insurers.

The right to proceed against the user's insurers

22–039   *Conditions for direct action.* For an enforcement action to be brought under s.151, four conditions must be satisfied.

First, the victim must have obtained a judgment against the assured. Section 151(1) is an enforcement mechanism only, allowing the victim to bring a direct action against the insurers to satisfy a judgment left unsatisfied by the user.

Secondly, the insurers must have delivered a certificate of insurance to the assured. It was held by the Privy Council, on appeal from Barbados, in *Motor & General Insurance Co Ltd v Cox*[330] that this requirement is satisfied in a case in which the certificate is delivered to the assured between the date at which the assured's liability arises and the date of the judgment against him, notwithstanding that s.147(1) of the Act provides that the policy does not fall within the 1988 Act until the certificate has been delivered. If the certificate has not been delivered to the assured, it would seem that he has the right to demand such delivery from the insurer, on the basis that the contract with the insurer was for a policy complying with the 1988 Act. If *Cox* is followed in England, the effect of the demand is to preserve the rights of the claimant third party against the insurer.

Thirdly, the liability incurred by the assured must be one in respect of which insurance was required by the Road Traffic Act 1988. If any of the conditions for compulsory cover are not met—i.e. if the claim does not arise out of the use of a motor vehicle on a road or public place—then no direct action is possible.

Finally, the policy must have covered the use in question. This condition is modified by s.148, discussed above, which prevents insurers from relying upon

---

[330] *Motor & General Insurance Co Ltd v Cox* [1990] 1 W.L.R. 1443.

various forms of policy limitation or exception. Further, under s.151(3),[331] so much of the policy which purports to restrict the use of the vehicle by a person not holding a driving licence has no effect on the right of the victim of an unlicensed driver to bring a direct action against the insurers: where the insurer becomes liable to indemnify an unlicensed driver, there is a right of recourse against the driver.[332] It was held by a majority of the Court of Appeal in *Charlton v Fisher*[333] that a deliberate running down is a use which must be covered by compulsory insurance. This means that the victim of a deliberate running down has a direct action against insurers under s.151.

Liability of insurers to meet judgments against insured users. Under s.151(2)(a), **22–040** the insurers are required to satisfy any judgment which "is obtained against any person who is insured by the policy". Policies frequently provide that any person may drive the assured's vehicle with his consent, so that such persons are within the scope of s.151; as noted earlier, if the person to whom consent is given does not have a relevant driving licence, that person is nevertheless deemed to be within s.151.[334] The effect of the section is to require the insurer to pay the proceeds of the policy to any third party entitled to the benefit of a judgment against the assured or any person covered under the policy "notwithstanding that the insurer may be entitled to avoid or cancel, or may have avoided or cancelled, the policy".[335]

A majority of the Court of Appeal in *Charlton v Fisher*[336] concluded that, in the case of a direct action by the victim against the assured's insurers, any public policy bar which prevents the assured recovering under his policy does not extend to a direct claim by the third party against the insurers under s.151. Here, the assured had deliberately rammed his vehicle into a stationary vehicle in which the victim had been sitting. The Court of Appeal was unanimous that the assured was himself unable to recover from his insurers, as his claim was precluded by the public policy rule that insurers are not liable for the natural consequences of deliberate acts by the assured. However, the majority view was that the public policy bar was personal to the assured, and did not operate to prevent the victim from bringing a direct claim against the insurers under s.151. This ruling was obiter, as the injuries had not been inflicted on a road and thus were outside the compulsory insurance provisions of the legislation were inapplicable. Rix L.J., dissenting on the public policy point, preferred the view that s.151 operated only where the claim was one within the policy itself.

Liability of insurers to meet judgments against uninsured users. A major change **22–041** incorporated into the 1988 Act with effect from the beginning of 1989,[337] implementing the Second Motor Insurance Directive 1984, now re-enacted as art.13(1) of the Consolidated Motor Insurance Directive 2009, is an obligation on the insurer to meet a judgment debt in favour of a third party against a person driving the assured's vehicle but not covered by the assured's policy: the effect is to deem the policy to cover all persons.[338] The Second Motor Insurance

---

[331] Enacting what is now art.13(1) of the Consolidated Motor Insurance Directive 2009.

[332] 1988 Act s.151(7)(a).

[333] *Charlton v Fisher* [2001] Lloyd's Rep. I.R. 387.

[334] 1988 Act s.151(3).

[335] 1988 Act s.151(5).

[336] *Charlton v Fisher* [2001] Lloyd's Rep. I.R. 387.

[337] Under the earlier law, the insurer was only liable where the driver was the assured under the policy or the policy by its terms extended to him: *Haworth v Dawson* (1946) 80 Ll. L.R. 19.

[338] 1988 Act s.151(2)(b).

Directive was originally implemented in 1987 by modifying the then Road Traffic Act 1972, and the changes were codified in s.151 of the Road Traffic Act 1988. Accordingly, a motor insurer will now be liable to meet judgments against both insured and uninsured users of the vehicle who have inflicted personal injury or property damage on third parties.[339] Unlicensed drivers who would otherwise be covered by the policy are, it will be recalled, treated as insured drivers,[340] so that this particular extension of the insurer's liability is not required to extend to them.

There is one situation in which the third party's judgment is not required to be met by the insurer, referred to by s.151(4) as a case of "excluded liability". This term means:

" . . . a liability in respect of the death of, or bodily injury to, or damage to the property of any person who, at the time of the use which gave rise to liability, was allowing himself to be carried in or upon the vehicle and knew or had reason to believe that the vehicle had been stolen or unlawfully taken, not being a person who—
  (a) did not know and had no reason to believe that the vehicle had been stolen or unlawfully taken until after the commencement of his journey, and
  (b) could not reasonably have been expected to have alighted from the vehicle."

In *McMinn v McMinn*[341] it was decided that the phrases "theft" and "unlawful taking" were to be given the meaning conferred on them by the Theft Act 1968, so that there could be an "unlawful taking" where a person authorised to use a vehicle for a limited purpose changed the nature of his use.[342] The effect of the subsection is that:

  (1) The victim of a thief or other unauthorised driver may recover from the assured's insurer as long as the victim is not in or on the vehicle at the time of his loss. If the victim is a party to the unauthorised taking, it would seem that he can recover as long as he was not in or on the vehicle at the time of the event causing the loss.
  (2) If the victim is in or on the vehicle at the time of his loss, and he was aware from the outset that it had been taken in an unauthorised fashion, he cannot recover for his loss.
  (3) If the victim is in or on the vehicle at the time of his loss, and he had only become aware that it had been taken in an unauthorised fashion after the start of the journey, he can recover as long as he has not had a reasonable opportunity to alight.

Section 151(4) implements art.2 of the Second Motor Insurance Directive 1984, now re-enacted as art.13(1) of the Consolidated Motor Insurance Directive 2009, and provides that policy terms restricting coverage:

"may be invoked against persons who voluntarily entered the vehicle which caused the damage or injury, when the insurer can prove that they knew the vehicle was stolen."

---

[339] See *Miller v Hales* [2007] Lloyd's Rep. I.R. 54 (insurers liable to meet claim by a person injured in seeking to prevent a car from being stolen). The Consolidated Motor Insurance Directive 2009 art.13(2)–(3), re-enacting the Second Motor Insurance Directive contains two derogations which the UK has not adopted: where the victim is indemnified by a social security body; and where compensation is paid by the national MIB in respect of loss inflicted by a stolen vehicle.

[340] Under s.151(3).

[341] *McMinn v McMinn* [2006] Lloyd's Rep. I.R. 802.

[342] See: *R. v Phipps* (1970) 54 Cr. App. R.; *McNight v Davies* [1974] R.T.R. 4.

This restriction operates only in relation to a passenger who, knowing of the theft or unlawful taking, allowed himself to be carried on the vehicle, and it may be that the United Kingdom's wider formation "had reason to believe" is in the light of the Directive to be construed as meaning little more than "blind eye" knowledge. It is noteworthy that, in the context of the equivalent exclusion from the MIB Uninsured Drivers Agreement relating to uninsured drivers, the House of Lords in *White v White*[343] construed the phrase "knew or ought to have known" as requiring actual or blind eye knowledge rather than constructive knowledge. This point appears to have been overlooked in *McMinn v McMinn*, Keith J. holding that the phrase "or ought to have known" was partly subjective (in that the passenger had to be aware of the essential facts) and partly objective (in that he ought to have appreciated from them that the vehicle had been stolen or unlawfully taken). On the facts the test was satisfied, as the victim was the brother of the driver, the latter being only 17, unlicensed and driving a vehicle belonging to a company which had given use of it to an employee who was a friend of the victim. It may be that the facts would have justified a finding of blind-eye knowledge, but it may be thought that the application of a lesser test was unsound.

Extent of insurers' liability under section 151. The insurer's liability under s.151   **22–042**
in all cases extends to the costs of the third party,[344] and otherwise depends upon whether the third party is claiming for personal injuries or property damage. In the case of death or personal injury, the sum payable by the insurer is any sum payable under the judgment in respect of the liability, together with any interest awarded by the court[345]; it will be appreciated that the Act does not provide for any minimum amount of compulsory insurance for death and personal injury, so that the insurer must meet the entire judgment.[346] In the case of property damage, the Act imposes a minimum figure of £1,000,000[347] for compulsory insurance, so that it is possible for property damage in excess of that figure not to be covered by the policy. For this reason, the amount of a judgment in so far as it relates to property damage is in effect limited to £1,000,000.[348]

The precise way in which this is achieved is as follows:

(1) If the amount payable under the judgment, plus interest but excluding costs, does not exceed £1,000,000, the insurer is liable for the full amount[349];

(2) if the total, excluding costs, exceeds £1,000,000, the insurer is liable for the lesser of two amounts[350]:

(a) such proportion of any sum payable under the judgment as £1,000,000 bears to the total (a figure which will always be £1,000,000), together with a similar proportion in respect of interest payments; or

[343] *White v White* [2001] Lloyd's Rep. I.R. 493.
[344] 1988 Act s.151(5)(c).
[345] 1988 Act s.151(5)(a).
[346] The insurer cannot rely upon any policy deductible: Consolidated Motor Insurance Directive 2009 art.17.
[347] The figure of £250,000 was raised to £1,000,000 with effect from June 11, 2007, by the Motor Vehicles (Compulsory Insurance) Regulations 2007 (SI 2007/1426).
[348] 1988 Act s.151(5)(b).
[349] 1988 Act s.151(6)(a).
[350] 1988 Act s.151(6)(b).

(b) the difference between the amount actually paid under the policy and
£1,000,000, together with the relevant proportion in interest appropriate to that sum.

22–043 *Right of recourse.* The 1988 Act attempts to shift the insurer's statutory liability
to a third party back on to the assured. Where the insurer is required to make
payment to a third party under a policy which was voidable or cancellable as
against the assured, the insurer is given a right of recourse against the assured to
recover from him the amount of its payment to the third party.[351] Similarly, if the
insurer becomes liable under the policy as a result of its statutory obligation to
meet a judgment given against a person who had driven the vehicle without an
appropriate driving licence but who would otherwise have been covered by the
assured's policy,[352] the insurer has a right of recourse against that person and not
against the assured.[353] Finally, if the assured has caused or permitted an
uninsured person to drive the vehicle, the insurers have a right of recourse against
the assured who has cause or permitted such uninsured use[354] in respect of
liability incurred by the driver for which the insurers are liable.[355]

It is uncertain whether s.151(8) can operate where the claimant has permitted
an uninsured person to drive the vehicle, and there is an accident caused by the
uninsured driver's negligence in which the claimant is injured. In those
circumstances the obligation of the insurers under s.151(5) to satisfy the
judgment obtained by the claimant would for all practical purposes be negatived
if the insurers could then recover their payment from the claimant under s.151(8).
In *Churchill Insurance Company Ltd v Wilkinson*[356] the claimant was a named
driver of the vehicle under a policy of insurance. The claimant, who had been
drinking, allowed himself to be carried as a passenger while the vehicle was
being driven by a friend who was not insured. An accident occurred and the
claimant sought to recover damages in reliance on the Road Traffic Act 1988
s.151(5), which imposes liability on an insurer to meet any judgment against an
uninsured person driving the vehicle. The insurers refused indemnity, arguing
that they were entitled to a right of recourse against the claimant under s.151(8),
so that their liability was negatived. At first instance Blair J. disagreed. The
learned judge ruled that it was not permissible under the Motor Insurance
Directives to create a class of claimants who were not entitled to recover from
insurers following an accident caused by an uninsured driver. The Road Traffic
Act 1988 s.151(8) was accordingly to be read as removing the right of recourse
from a person entitled to the benefit of a judgment under the Road Traffic Act

---

[351] 1988 Act s.151(7)(b).

[352] 1988 Act s.151(3).

[353] 1988 Act s.151(7)(a).

[354] The meaning of the phrase "caused or permitted" is the same here as in s.143, discussed above.
Thus if the assured has allowed another to use the vehicle without insurance, the assured will escape
liability under s.151 only if he has imposed a condition on the user as to insurance coverage which
the user has disregarded: *Lloyd-Wolper v Moore* [2004] Lloyd's Rep. I.R. 730. It was further held in
Lloyd-Wolper that if the user has misrepresented his insurance position to the assured, and the assured
on the strength of that misrepresentation allows the vehicle to be used without imposing any condition
on the user, then the insurers' right of recourse under s.151(8) is maintained. Liability can be averted
only if a condition has been imposed on the user.

[355] 1988 Act s.151(8). In *Pearl Assurance Plc v Kavanagh* [2001] C.L.Y. 3832 a policy term that
sought to impose liability on the assured to indemnify the insurers whether or not the assured had
caused or permitted use by the driver was struck down under the Unfair Terms in Consumer Contracts
Regulations 1994 (SI 1994/3159) (since re-enacted with modifications in 1999).

[356] [2010] EWCA Civ 556, an appeal heard jointly with *Evans v Equity Claims Ltd*, varying the
decision of Blair J., [2010] Lloyd's Rep. I.R. 278.

1988 s.151. Blair J. focused upon the policy of the Directives in ensuring that passengers were always fully compensated, although his reasoning is not confined to passengers. Thus, if the claimant had been run over by the defendant rather than injured as a passenger, it would seem that the same result would have followed. The Court of Appeal on appeal disagreed with the learned judge and held that s.151(8) was not to be construed as creating an exception to coverage under s.151(5), because the two provisions were entirely distinct, so that the statute on an ordinary reading did not exclude a right of recourse. That did not mean, however, that s.151(8) was compatible with the requirement in art.12(1) of the Consolidated Life Directive demanding the same protection for a passenger as for any other third-party victim. The Court of Appeal felt it necessary to refer to the European Court of Justice questions as to whether it was permissible for English law to allow a right of recourse against a passenger who was himself the assured and, if so, whether the right ought to rest on the knowledge of the assured that the driver was uninsured.

If an insurer has a right of recourse against the assured, and fails to exercise it, his payment to the third party is to be regarded as voluntary and the insurer will be unable to exercise contribution rights against any other insurer in respect of the payment.[357]

Defences of insurers to an enforcement action. Section 152 gives an insurer immunity from liability under a direct enforcement action brought under s.151, if any of the following defences are made out: **22–044**

(1) The insurer has not been given due notice of the proceedings against the assured (s.152(1)(a)).
(2) Enforcement of the judgment obtained by the victim has been stayed (s.152(1)(b)).
(3) The certificate of insurance has been surrendered (s.152(1)(c)).
(4) The insurer has obtained a declaration of its right to avoid the policy for breach of the duty of utmost good faith by the assured (s.152(2)).

A further limitation on the third party's wide rights under s.151 is the insurer's ability to apply for an order setting aside a judgment obtained by the third party against the assured where it was obtained in default of appearance.[358] It must be questioned, however, whether the statutory defence open to the insurer as regards avoidance of the policy is consistent with the requirements of EC Law.[359]

Notice of proceedings. Section 152(1)(a) provides: **22–045**

"No sum shall be payable by an insurer . . . in respect of any judgment, unless before or within seven days after the commencement of proceedings in which the judgment was given, the insurer had notice of the bringing of the proceedings."

Proceedings commence when the claim form is issued rather than when it is served.[360] However, where the insurer's liability arises under a counterclaim, the

---

[357] *Legal and General Insurance Society Ltd v Drake Insurance Co Ltd* [1992] 1 All E.R. 283. That proposition was, however, doubted by the Court of Appeal in *Drake Insurance v Provident Insurance Co* [2004] Lloyd's Rep. I.R. 277.
[358] *Windsor v Chalcraft* [1939] 1 K.B. 279.
[359] See the discussion of *Bernaldez* Case C-129/94 [1996] All E.R. (E.C.) 741, below.
[360] CPR, r.7.2(1): "Proceedings are started when the court issues a claim form at the request of the claimant".

relevant date is the date of the counterclaim.[361] In principle, while there is a seven-day cut-off point for the service of notice, there is no equivalent anterior restriction and notice may be given at any time between the accident giving rise to liability and the statutory cut-off. Thus in *Robson v Marriott*[362] the Court of Appeal raised no objection to notice of proceedings being given in February 1993 even though the claim form was not issued until June 1994. In *Stinton v Stinton*[363] the Court of Appeal indicated that the greater the gap between the notification and the commencement of proceedings the easier it will be for the court to find that the notification did not fulfil the requirements for statutory notice.

There have been a number of decisions on the meaning of "notice". The Court of Appeal in *Wylie v Wake* recognised that the cases were not fully consistent, and laid down the following guidelines based upon the decided cases

(a) *To show that the insurers had notice of the proceedings there had to be more than evidence of a casual comment to someone who at times acted as an agent for the insurers.* In *Herbert v Railway Passengers Assurance Co*[364] the victim mentioned in a casual conversation with the insurer's agent that he was bringing an action against the insurers, and this was held not to be sufficient notice. However, in *Wylie v Wake*[365] the Court of Appeal doubted the result in *Herbert* as what had been said was specific and enough to constitute notice. Notice may be given by the assured or by an authorised agent, e.g. his solicitors,[366] and it may be that if the insurers receive notice from any reliable source then the statutory requirements are satisfied.[367] It was said by the Court of Appeal that a notice to the insurers which was sufficiently specific could come from any source. It was accepted by the Court of Appeal in that notice to the insurers' solicitors satisfied statutory requirements, and in *Nawaz and Hussain v Crow Insurance Group*[368] it was held that notice to the secretary of the solicitor acting for the insurers was sufficient as it could be assumed that an experienced legal secretary would pass the information to the solicitor. It should be said, however, that notice to the assured's brokers will not suffice, as the brokers are not to be regarded as the agents of the insurers unless the insurers have authorised the brokers to act for them in the handling of the claim.

(b) *Any notification relied upon could not be subject to a condition which might or might not be fulfilled, e.g. where notification simply states that the victim has been advised to commence proceedings, but if the only condition was one which required action from the recipients which they chose not to take then by making that choice they rendered the notice unconditional and thus effective.* In *Ceylon Motor Insurance Association Ltd v Thambugala*[369] the insurers were advised by the victim's solicitors that unless the claim was settled by a given date proceedings would be

[361] *Cross v British Oak Insurance Co Ltd* [1938] 2 K.B. 167.
[362] *Robson v Marriott* Unreported, 1997.
[363] *Stinton v Stinton* [1999] Lloyd's Rep. I.R. 305.
[364] *Herbert v Railway Passengers Assurance Co* [1938] 1 All E.R. 650.
[365] *Wylie v Wake* Unreported, 2000.
[366] *Robson v Marriott* Unreported, 1997.
[367] This was the view of the Court of Appeal in *Harrington v Link Motor Policies at Lloyd's* [1989] 2 Lloyd's Rep. 310.
[368] *Nawaz and Hussain v Crow Insurance Group* [2003] Lloyd's Rep. I.R. 471.
[369] *Ceylon Motor Insurance Association Ltd v Thambugala* [1953] A.C. 584.

commenced: this was held to be enough to amount to notice. By contrast, in *Harrington v Link Motor Policies at Lloyd's*,[370] the solicitors merely informed the insurers that unless the claim was settled they would be advising their client to commence proceedings, and the Court of Appeal held that the letter failed to amount to a statutory notice as it did not specifically state that proceedings were to be commenced. The distinction between these authorities is technical rather than substantive, and in *Robson v Marriott*[371] the Court of Appeal held that a solicitor's letter stating that if the claim was not settled it would be necessary for proceedings to be commenced was held to be indistinguishable from *Thambugala*.

(c) *The notice could be oral and it need not have emanated from the claimant himself—it could be given before the proceedings had commenced, and it did not have to be specific as to the nature of the proceedings.* In *Ceylon Motor Insurance Association Ltd v Thambugala* the Privy Council regarded it as immaterial that the notice did not indicate the name of the court or the number of the action. This reasoning was doubted by the Court of Session in *McBlain v Dolan*,[372] in reliance on the apparent unhappiness of Lord Woolf with *Thambugala* in *Harrington v Link Motor Policies at Lloyd's*.[373] In *Harrington* the Court of Appeal indeed held that a vague notification would not suffice, and in *Robson v Marriott*[374] the Court of Appeal emphasised that even if omission of these details was not a prerequisite the information should be given if available.

(d) *Whether in any given case it was shown that the insurer had notice of the bringing of proceedings (as opposed merely to making a claim) was a matter of fact and degree.* This distinction was drawn by Lawton J. in *McGoona v Motor Insurers' Bureau*.[375] In *Desouza v Waterlow*[376] the victim wrote two separate letters to the insurers stating that he intended to sue the assured, and subsequently telephoned them with the same information. This was held to be notice of proceedings rather than a claim. As long as the notice conveys the appropriate message it is immaterial that the notice was given unintentionally; in *Nawaz and Hussain v Crow Insurance Group*[377] the insurers' solicitors were contacted by a trainee solicitor acting for the claimant. The purpose of the call was to obtain the address of the driver so that service could be effected upon him. The Court of Appeal held that it was clear from what the trainee had said that proceedings were to be issued and the fact that the trainee had been unaware of the requirements of s.152 did not prevent what had been said from amounting to a notice under the section. By contrast, in *Wylie v Wake*[378] itself, the commencement of proceedings had been preceded only by the assertion of a claim, and for that reason it was held that the statutory notice had not been given.

(e) *The essential purpose of the requirement of notice was to ensure that the insurer was not suddenly faced with a judgment which he had to satisfy*

[370] *Harrington v Link Motor Policies at Lloyd's* [1989] 2 Lloyd's Rep. 310.
[371] *Robson v Marriott* Unreported, 1997.
[372] *McBlain v Dolan* [2001] Lloyd's Rep. I.R. 309.
[373] *Harrington v Link Motor Policies at Lloyd's* [1989] 2 Lloyd's Rep. 310.
[374] *Robson v Marriott* Unreported, 1997.
[375] *McGoona v Motor Insurers' Bureau* [1969] 2 Lloyd's Rep. 34.
[376] *Desouza v Waterlow* [1999] R.T.R. 71.
[377] *Nawaz and Hussain v Crow Insurance Group* [2003] Lloyd's Rep. I.R. 471.
[378] *Wylie v Wake* Unreported, 1999.

without having had any opportunity to take part in the proceedings in which the judgment was obtained. This point is illustrated by *Weldrick v Essex & Suffolk Equitable Insurance Society*,[379] in which the victim contacted the insurers only to seek confirmation that they did not intend to make payment: plainly this did not give them the ability to participate in the proceedings. In *Stinton v Stinton*[380] the insurers were told by the victim's solicitors that the victim had obtained legal aid and that medical evidence was to be obtained: once again, this was held not to amount to notification of proceedings.

Insurers can in appropriate circumstances be taken to have waived their right to rely upon the absence of proper notice. In principle there may be waiver or estoppel in either of two ways: conduct by the insurers prior to the commencement of proceedings which indicates that they have waived notification; and post-claim conduct which indicates that they do not wish to rely upon a failure to notify in good time.

The former situation was considered in a Scottish decision, *McBlain v Dolan*.[381] Here, the victim of a motor accident gave notice to the insurers two months after proceedings had been commenced, in contravention of the seven-day requirement in s.152(1)(a). The insurers had nevertheless been aware of the likelihood of proceedings for some ten months, in that the victim had to the insurers' knowledge applied for legal aid. The insurers applied for a declaration that, due to the victim's failure to give timely notice, they were not liable under the Act. The Court of Session held that the insurers were not entitled to the relief sought, and that it was appropriate to allow to go to trial the issue whether the insurers, having been aware of the proceedings but not having received the proper statutory notice, were able to rely upon the absence of notice, by reason of a personal bar.[382]

Post-claim conduct was considered by the Court of Appeal in *Wylie v Wake*.[383] In this case a letter of claim had been written to the assured's insurers, and their solicitors had subsequently requested medical evidence of the claimant's injuries, which was duly provided. Proceedings were commenced some months later. No formal notice of the commencement of proceedings had been, and insurers were finally informed of the proceedings some nine weeks after the issue of the claim form, in February 1997. This was clearly out of time, but no objection was taken until May 1999, while preparations were being made for the trial: this was so because of an oversight on the part of the insurers' then legal advisers. The Court of Appeal rejected that the insurers' conduct prevented them from relying upon s.152(1)(a), on the factual basis that the insurers had not been aware of their rights at the relevant time and thus could not be taken to have waived them. The Court of Appeal went somewhat further, and doubted whether it was possible to treat insurers as having waived their statutory entitlement under s.152(1)(a) by choosing not to rely upon the point until the very last minute: the section was not so much a statutory defence but rather a condition precedent to the insurers' liability which had to be met by the claimant, and—at least in the absence of a statement to the contrary which could give rise to an equitable estoppel—the insurers were entitled to defend the action on behalf of the first defendant right

---

[379] *Weldrick v Essex & Suffolk Equitable Insurance Society* (1949) 83 Ll. L.R. 91.
[380] *Stinton v Stinton* [1999] Lloyd's Rep. I.R. 305.
[381] *McBlain v Dolan* [2001] Lloyd's Rep. I.R. 309.
[382] Waiver or estoppel.
[383] *Wylie v Wake* Unreported, 2000.

up to judgment and then for the first time raise the s.152(1)(a) notice point. This reasoning implicitly casts some doubt upon the approach in *McBlain*.

Stay of execution. Section 152(1)(b) provides: **22–046**

> "No sum shall be payable by an insurer... in respect of any judgment, so long as execution thereon is stayed pending an appeal."

Surrender of certificate. The certificate of insurance plays a central role in the   **22–047**
operation of the 1988 Act. The rules relating to the surrender of a certificate are of great significance to the potential liability of insurers to meet unsatisfied judgments incurred by users of vehicles. If there has been a claim against the assured, and the assured is in possession of a certificate of insurance, the insurers are liable to indemnify the victim in a direct enforcement action under s.151 even though the policy has been cancelled by mutual consent or by reason of its terms. It is thus essential for the insurers to secure the surrender of the certificate following the cancellation of the policy. Section 152(1)(c) sets out the situations in which the insurer can escape liability under a direct enforcement action where the policy has been cancelled:

  (i) before the happening of that event the certificate was surrendered to the insurer, or the person to whom the certificate was delivered made a statutory declaration stating that the certificate had been lost or destroyed, or
 (ii) after the happening of that event, but before the expiration of a period of fourteen days from the taking effect of the cancellation of the policy or security, the certificate was surrendered to the insurer, or the person to whom it was delivered made a statutory declaration stating that the certificate had been lost or destroyed, or
(iii) either before or after the happening of that event, but within that period of fourteen days, the insurer has commenced proceedings under this Act in respect of the failure to surrender the certificate.

The effect of these provisions is that if the policy has been cancelled but the assured is in possession of the certificate at the date of the insured peril, and is allowed to retain it beyond a period of 14 days from that date, then the insurers are treated as being on risk in respect of the third-party claim even though the policy is otherwise to be regarded as having terminated on the expiry of the notice of cancellation. Possibility (3) deals with the case in which the assured has failed to surrender the certificate, as it is then in the hands of the insurers to avoid their liability by commencing proceedings for recovery of the certificate within the time limits allowed. In *Re Drake Insurance Plc*[384] the assured was given notice of cancellation following the insolvency of the insurers. Neuberger J. held that the assured was entitled to restitution of his premium for the unexpired period of the policy, that period running from the date on which the notice of cancellation expired rather than the date on which the assured actually surrendered his certificate: Neuberger J.'s choice of this date was based on the fact that it was open to the insurers—by bringing proceedings to recover the certificate—to ensure that their liability came to an end on the expiry of the notice of cancellation, and if they failed to do so and the assured wrongfully retained the certificate the continued operation of the policy was a problem of

---

[384] *Re Drake Insurance Plc* [2001] Lloyd's Rep. I.R. 643.

their own making and ought not to prevent restitution of the premium from the date on which the certificate could have been rendered ineffective.

22–048 *Declaration as to entitlement to avoid policy.* Section 152(2)–(4) sets out a procedure whereby the insurer is permitted to seek a declaration as to its entitlement to avoid the policy. The procedure has been described as a "fair compromise"[385] between the interests of the victim and the rights of the insurers. A number of elements are involved in this procedure:

(1) The insurer must obtain a declaration[386] from the court of its entitlement to avoid the policy or, where the policy has previously been avoided, the insurer must obtain from the court a declaration that it was entitled to do so.[387]

(2) The reason for the avoidance must be a material misrepresentation or failure to disclose a material fact on behalf of the assured. "Material" in this context bears its ordinary meaning of a fact of such a nature as to influence the judgment of a prudent insurer in determining whether it will take the risk and, if so, at what premium and on what conditions.[388]

(3) The policy must have been "obtained" by a material misrepresentation or a material failure to disclose. This wording has been taken to mean that it is not enough for the insurer to show that a prudent insurer might have been influenced in its judgment; the insurer in question must go on to demonstrate that it was actually influenced by the assured's breach of duty.[389] After decades of uncertainty, the House of Lords confirmed in *Pan Atlantic Insurance Co Ltd v Pine Top Insurance Co Ltd*[390] that the two-limb test of materiality and inducement represents the general law.

(4) The declaration must be obtained by the insurer either before or within three months of the commencement of the action in which judgment for the third party was given.[391]

(5) Even if the insurer has obtained a declaration, it may not rely upon it unless it has given to the claimant in the liability proceedings, before or within seven days of the commencement of the proceedings, notice of its intention to rely upon it: s.152(3). Whether notice has actually been served on the third party is a question of fact, although the burden of proof is on the insurers.[392] The notice given by the insurer under s.152(3)

---

[385] *Merchants and Manufacturers Insurance Co Ltd v Hunt* (1941) 68 Ll. L.R. 117, per Scott LJ at 120.

[386] *National Farmers' Mutual v Tully* 1935 S.L.T. 547.

[387] It was held in *Guardian Assurance v Sutherland* [1939] 2 All E.R. 246 that a declaration may be made in the absence of the assured.

[388] 1988 Act s.151(1)(a)–(b). See *General Accident Fire and Life Assurance Corporation v Shuttleworth* 60 Ll. L.R. 301; *Guardian Assurance Co Ltd v Sutherland* [1939] 2 All E.R. 246; *Wing Lung Insurance Co Ltd v Kong Yau Choi* [2008] H.K.E.C. 1363; *Wing Lung Insurance Co Ltd v Lo Wai Fai* [2008] H.K.E.C. 305.

[389] *Zurich General Accident and Liability Insurance Co Ltd v Morrison* [1942] 2 K.B. 53; *Merchants' and Manufacturers' Insurance Co v Davies and Owen* [1938] 1 K.B. 196.

[390] *Pan Atlantic Insurance Co Ltd v Pine Top Insurance Co Ltd* [1994] 3 All E.R. 581.

[391] *Croxford v Universal Insurance* [1936] 2 K.B. 253. If the person driving the vehicle at the time of the accident was not the assured person, the Road Traffic Act 1988 s.152(3) does not require the driver to be joined to the avoidance proceedings: *Colonial Fire and General Insurance Co Ltd v Harry* [2008] Lloyd's Rep. I.R. 382.

[392] See *Colonial Fire and General Insurance Co Ltd v Harry* [2008] Lloyd's Rep. I.R. 382, where the Privy Council reinstated the finding of the trial judge that notice had been served, and rejected the decision of the Court of Appeal to overturn the trial judge's factual findings which had been reached in the absence of any contradictory evidence by the third party.

should specify every instance of non-disclosure or misrepresentation on which the insurer proposes to rely, as he will not be able to rely upon further instances not so specified as against the third party,[393] but only against the assured. The claimant in the liability proceedings is entitled to be made a party to the declaration proceedings if his own action was commenced beforehand: s.152(4). The admissions of the assured are not evidence as against the third party in an action by the insurer for such a declaration.[394]

Since the right to avoid for non-disclosure or misrepresentation of a material fact does not arise out of the policy itself, the better view appears to be that a clause to the effect that nothing in the policy is to affect third-party rights under the legislation does not affect the insurer's right to a declaration.[395]

Primary direct actions against insurers

EU law background. The rule that the victim has to bring an action against the driver which is then enforceable against the driver's insurers, rather than bringing a direct action against the insurers themselves, has been modified under EU law. The regime for compulsory insurance established in EU Member States under the three implemented Motor Insurance Directives was amended by the Fourth Motor Insurance Directive 2000, and the relevant provisions are now found in the Consolidated Motor Insurance Directive 2009. The Directive is concerned to protect visitors, and sets out a procedure whereby a victim of a motor accident in a Member State other than that of his residence can in the first instance in the Member State of his domicile seek indemnification from the insurers, failing which he recovers compensation from his local Motor Insurers Bureau, which will then have a right of recourse against the Motor Insurers Bureau of the Member State in which the accident occurred. The original proposal in the drafts of the Fourth Directive had been simply to allow the victim to sue insurers directly in all cases, although the eventual outcome was a restricted provision protecting visiting victims. The EU's Fifth Motor Insurance Directive went further, and conferred a direct action against insurers on all victims, the relevant provision now being art.8 of the Consolidated Motor Insurance Directive 2009. The United Kingdom's implementation of the regime for the protection of visiting victims is considered below.

22–049

Accidents occurring in the United Kingdom: the direct action. The United Kingdom, by means of the European Communities (Rights against Insurers) Regulations 2002,[396] moved directly to the adoption of a direct cause of action against insurers in all cases involving accidents occurring in the United Kingdom, in anticipation of what was at the time the Draft Fifth Motor Insurance Directive, rather than confining direct rights to visiting victims under the limited provisions of the Fourth Motor Insurance Directive. The Regulations came into force on January 19, 2003, and apply to all actions on or after that date

22–050

---

[393] *Contingency Insurance Co v Lyons* (1939) 65 Ll. L.R. 53; *Zurich v Morrison* [1942] 1 All E.R. 529.

[394] *Merchants and Manufacturers Insurance Co Ltd v Hunt* [1941] 1 K.B. 295.

[395] Atkinson J. in *Zurich v Morrison* [1942] 1 All E.R. 529 at 535; *Merchants' Assurance v Hunt* [1941] 1 K.B. 295. It is unlikely that the Contracts (Rights of Third Parties) Act 1999 affects this situation, as the third party would not have been capable of identification by name or description at the outset.

[396] SI 2002/3061.

irrespective of when the accident giving rise to the claim occurred. In general terms, the victim of a driver may, as an alternative to obtaining a judgment against the driver and then seeking to enforce that judgment against the insurers under s.151, instead proceed directly against the driver's insurers. In such proceedings the victim steps into the shoes of the driver, in accordance with reg.2(3):

> "the entitled party may, without prejudice to his right to issue proceedings against the insured person, issue proceedings against the insurer which issued the policy of insurance relating to the insured vehicle, and that insurer shall be directly liable to the entitled party to the extent that he is liable to the insured person."

The insurers faced with such an action have the right to defend the proceedings on the basis that the driver was not liable to the victim, and also on the basis that, for whatever reason, the policy did not respond to the claim. In the latter context it should be borne in mind that section precludes the insurers from relying upon the policy limitations and policy conditions specified in that section.

22–051 *Availability of direct action.* A direct action may be brought by the victim of the driver if the following conditions are met[397]:

    (1) the victim is *an entitled party*;
    (2) the entitled party has a cause of action against *an insured person* in tort;
    (3) the cause of action arises out of an *accident*; and
    (4) the accident was caused by or arose out of the use of a *vehicle* on a road or other public place in the United Kingdom.

22–052 *Entitled party.* An entitled party, as defined by reg.2(1) is

    (a) a resident of a Member State; or
    (b) a resident of any other State which is a Contracting Party to the Agreement on the European Economic Area.

The direct action is thus available to any EC or EEA national, as well as a British national, and is not confined to an EEA national who happens to be injured in the United Kingdom while visiting the United Kingdom.

22–053 *An insured person.* The entitled party must have a cause of action against the "insured person". That term is defined by reg.2(1) of the 2002 Regulations as a person insured under a policy of insurance (including a covering note) which is in force in relation to the use of that vehicle on a road or other public place in the United Kingdom by the insured person and which fulfils the requirements of s.145 of the Road Traffic Act 1988.[398]

22–054 *Accident.* The term "accident" is defined by reg.2(1) as meaning:

> "an accident on a road or other public place in the United Kingdom caused by, or arising out of, the use of any insured vehicle".

---

[397] SI 2002/3061 reg.3(1).
[398] SI 2002/3061 reg.2(3).

The conditions are the same as for the attachment of a compulsory policy under the 1988 Act, with the additional requirement that the liability must have arisen from an "accident". The word "accident" is an ambiguous one, a point demonstrated by the decision of the Court of Appeal in *Charlton v Fisher*.[399] In that case the Court of Appeal was divided on the question whether a deliberate running down was an accident within the meaning of a motor policy: the majority view was that the injuries inflicted were accidental from the point of view of the victim, but Rix L.J. dissenting held that an accident had to be looked at from the point of view of the perpetrator and did not extend to injuries resulting from deliberate or reckless conduct. Which of these interpretations of the word "accident" in the 2002 Regulations is probably of no significance, for an action under the Regulations puts the victim in exactly the same position as the assured, and if the assured is precluded from recovering on public policy grounds it would seem that the same barrier affects the victim.

Vehicle. A vehicle as defined by reg.2(1) means: 22–055

> "any motor vehicle intended for travel on land and propelled by mechanical power, but not running on rails, and any trailer whether or not coupled, which is normally based in the United Kingdom."

The definition is taken from what is now art.1(1) of the Consolidated Motor Insurance Directive 2009, and is somewhat different to the definition of motor vehicle which determines the scope of the compulsory insurance obligation in s.185 of the 1988 Act. The latter provision defines a motor vehicle as "a mechanically propelled vehicle intended or adapted for use on roads." In addition, the vehicle must be "normally based" in the United Kingdom.[400]

Limitations of the direct action. There are a number of situations in which the   22–056
direct action under the 2002 Regulations is unavailable, and in which the victim will have to adopt the traditional approach of obtaining judgment against the driver which can then be enforced against the insurers under s.151.

(1) Any defence which the insurers have against the driver will prevail against the victim. The position is much the same in the case of an action under s.151, the only difference being the view of the majority of the Court of Appeal in *Charlton v Fisher*[401] that an action under s.151 is not precluded in a deliberate running down case: the wording of reg.2(3)— that the insurers are liable to the victim "to the same extent" that they would have been liable to the assured—appears to extend the assured's personal bar to the victim.

(2) Section 151 allows an action to be brought against insurers in respect of the uninsured use of the vehicle. The 2002 Regulations do not extend to such a case, as they simply transfer to the victim the assured's claim on the policy. Accordingly, it will remain necessary to use s.151 where the driver was a thief or some other person not covered by the policy.

(3) If the policy has been cancelled but the assured has retained possession of the certificate of insurance, insurers remain liable to an enforcement action under s.151 unless they take the statutory steps in s.152 to recover

[399] *Charlton v Fisher* [2001] Lloyd's Rep. I.R. 287.
[400] See above for the definition of "normally based".
[401] *Charlton v Fisher* [2001] Lloyd's Rep. I.R. 287.

the certificate. The 2002 Regulations, by contrast, do not depend upon the assured's possession of a certificate of insurance for their operation. Thus, if the policy had been cancelled at the date of the accident then, whether or not the certificate has been surrendered, the insurers cannot face a direct action by the third party under the 2002 Regulations.

3. Uninsured and Untraced Drivers: The Motor Insurers Bureau

The MIB and the Agreements

22–057   *The current Agreements.* The MIB was originally set up in 1946 to deal with the problems created by accidents involving drivers who should have been insured but were not. All insurers authorised to carry on motor insurance in the United Kingdom, or who provide motor insurance by way of services from elsewhere in the EU, are required to be members of the MIB. There are two agreements between the MIB and the Secretary of State, one dealing with uninsured drivers and one dealing with untraced drivers.[402] The Uninsured Drivers Agreement, dated August 13, 1999, replaces earlier agreements made in 1946, 1972 and 1988, and is concerned with accidents occurring on or after October 1, 1999: the 1988 Agreement continues to apply to accidents occurring between December 31, 1988 and September 30, 1999. The Uninsured Drivers Agreement is concerned with cases in which the driver responsible for causing a motor vehicle accident is identified but is not insured against the risks for which insurance is required under the Road Traffic Act 1988. This may be because he has no insurance at all, he has a policy under which the insurers have a defence, or his insurers are insolvent and cannot satisfy any liability which he has incurred. The Untraced Drivers Agreement, dated February 7, 2003, replacing earlier agreements reached in 1969, 1972 (supplemented by a further agreement in 1977) and 1996, applies to accidents occurring on or after February 14, 2003 and is concerned with cases where the identity of the driver, or any one of the persons, responsible cannot be ascertained. This may be because the accident is "hit and run", or because the driver has given false particulars to the victim following the accident. In respect of accidents caused by untraced drivers on or after July 1, 1996 and February 2003, the 1996 Agreement remains in force. The following text considers both the 1996 and 2003 Agreements as the former will have practical effect for some years to come.

A claim is to be made against the Motor Insurers' Bureau only where there is no insurer with responsibility for the victim's loss. If the MIB is involved by a victim where there is an identifiable insurer who has accepted liability, the court may order that the Bureau's costs be borne by the victim or his solicitors.[403]

22–058   *Enforcement of the Agreements.* As the only parties to the agreements are the MIB and the Secretary of State, it follows that, as a matter of strict law, an injured claimant has no right to sue on them. In practice, though, the MIB has never sought to take this point, since to do so would defeat the whole purpose of making the agreements. The courts have, generally, turned a blind eye to this

---

[402] The two Agreements are mutually exclusive in their coverage: *Gurtner v Circuit* [1968] 2 Q.B. 587; *Clarke v Vedel* [1974] R.T.R. 26.
[403] *Severn Trent Water v Williams* [1995] C.L.Y. 3724; *Mills v Toner* [1995] C.L.Y. 3726; *Mastin v Blanchard* [1995] C.L.Y. 3727; *Granada UK Rental & Retail v Fareway* [1995] C.L.Y. 3238.

clear breach of the then principles of privity of contract. Exceptionally, in *Gurtner v Circuit*,[404] Diplock L.J. expressed the view that in cases involving the MIB the court was[405]:

> "entitled to proceed on the assumption that the Bureau has, before action is brought, contracted for good consideration with the plaintiff to perform the obligations specified in the contract with the minister or has by its conduct raised an estoppel which would bar it from relying on absence of privity of contract."

The logic of the argument is plainly unconvincing, but the result is undeniably convenient, and it is to be expected that the courts will continue to promote this fiction. Some validity is given to the judicial approach by the enactment of the Contracts (Third Parties) Act 1999, under which the doctrine of privity is abolished with respect to contracts made after May 2000. The Uninsured Drivers Agreement 1999 is unaffected by this legislation because it was made before the 1999 Act came into force and also because the 1999 Act requires the third parties intended to benefit from a contract to be identifiable at the outset by name or class—a condition clearly not met as a victim could be anybody. The Untraced Drivers Agreement 2003 is nevertheless drafted on the assumption that the 1999 Act does apply to it and cl.31 does indeed make provision for the application of the Agreement in a modified form. The clause states that the Agreement "is intended to confer a benefit on an applicant but on no other person . . . subject to the terms and conditions set out herein", and goes on to provide that the Agreement can be varied or terminated without the consent of any beneficiary and that the MIB retains its right to rely upon defences to it which are available under the Agreement. It is unlikely that cl.31 has much effect as the identification problem remains and cl.31 is simply an attempt to give formal recognition to the practical position as it has existed since the MIB was established. It has long been settled that the courts will not allow a victim better rights than are available under the agreements. Thus, in *Evans v Motor Insurers' Bureau*[406] it was held that an estoppel by convention, whereby the Secretary of State was bound by an understanding that interest was not awardable under the Untraced Drivers Agreement 1972 applied equally to a claimant against the MIB.

An alternative approach to the problem of privity of contract is to join the MIB to the action as an additional defendant by means of a claim for a declaration that the MIB is liable (to the Secretary of State) to indemnify the claimant. However, the practice of joining an insurer as second defendant was disapproved as long ago as 1939 in *Carpenter v Ebblewhite*,[407] where it was said that the proper practice was to obtain judgment against the tortfeasor and then wait to see whether he could satisfy it before proceeding against the insurer. The principle of this case is equally applicable to cases involving the MIB. It follows that, in cases dealt with under the Uninsured Drivers Agreement, the MIB should not normally be brought into the case until judgment has been obtained against the tortfeasor. Indeed, cl.6 of the Uninsured Drivers Agreement stipulates that the MIB's liability does not arise unless and until such judgment has been obtained and has remained unsatisfied for at least seven days. It is nevertheless appropriate to join the MIB as defendant in a case under the Uninsured Drivers Agreement where

---

[404] *Gurtner v Circuit* [1968] 2 Q.B. 587.

[405] *Gurtner v Circuit* [1968] 2 Q.B. 587 at 598.

[406] *Evans v Motor Insurers' Bureau* Unreported, 1997. On appeal, [1999] Lloyd's Rep. IR 30, there was found to be no estoppel on the facts.

[407] *Carpenter v Ebblewhite* [1939] 1 K.B. 347.

the tortfeasor cannot be contacted, as happened in *Gurtner v Circuit*[408] where the defendant had emigrated to Canada after the accident.

22–059   *Impact of EU law.* Under the Consolidated Motor Insurance Directive 2009, re-enacting the earlier EU Motor Insurance Directives, Member States are required to establish national bodies which provide compensation to the victims of uninsured and untraced drivers. The United Kingdom, prior to the EU measures, had the MIB structure in place on a voluntary basis, and chose not to put the MIB on a statutory basis. The question which has inevitably arisen is whether the MIB can be sued on the terms of the Directive independently of the wording of the Agreements, a possibility which arises under the "direct effects" doctrine against an "emanation of the state". Alternatively, if the MIB is not subject to the direct effects doctrine, the alternative question is whether the MIB's Agreements are to be construed so that they accord with the requirements of the Directive, or whether the words used in the Agreements are to be construed in the same way as any other commercial contract. Adopting the former approach would entail a purposive interpretation, possibly amounting to artificiality in some cases. Adopting the latter approach would, in the event that the agreements did not conform to the Directive and could not be construed as doing so, place the UK government in breach of its obligation under EU law to implement the Directive and in principle could expose the government to a *Francovich*[409] action for damages where non-implementation had caused loss to an individual. Such an action may succeed if three conditions are satisfied: (a) the directive must confer individual rights; (b) there must be a "manifest and grave" failure on behalf of the government in its failure to implement the directive; and (c) there is a causal link between that failure and the loss.

    The courts have accepted that, while it is the case that the MIB has a purely contractual relationship with the government, the MIB nevertheless has a quasi-governmental function insofar as it is the mechanism chosen by the UK government to secure compliance with the United Kingdom's obligations under the Motor Insurance Directives, namely, to ensure that compensation is paid to the victims of untraced and uninsured drivers. The status of the MIB was raised in a series of joined cases before the Court of Appeal, *Mighell v Reading*,[410] *Evans v Motor Insurers Bureau* and *White v White*,[411] in which it was asserted that the MIB Agreements failed in a number of respects to confer upon the victims of uninsured or untraced drivers the protection required by the Directives. The Court of Appeal was prepared to assume in these cases that there was non-compliance, but held that the Directives did not override the terms of the MIB Agreements in order to allow the victim of an untraced or uninsured driver to bring an action against the MIB as if the Directives had been properly implemented. The Court of Appeal based its decision upon the principle that the Directives required the UK government to comply with their terms by the use of whatever machinery was thought to be appropriate, and the fact that the United Kingdom had chosen to use the MIB did not give the victim any cause of action against the MIB by means of the doctrine of direct effect.[412] This reasoning made

---

[408] *Gurtner v Circuit* [1968] 2 Q.B. 587.

[409] See *Francovich v Italian Republic* [1991] E.C.R. I-5337.

[410] *Mighell v Reading* [1999] Lloyd's Rep. I.R. 30.

[411] *White v White* [1999] Lloyd's Rep. I.R. 30. See also *Norman v Aziz* [2000] Lloyd's Rep. I.R. 52.

[412] The majority relied upon the European Court of Justice's decision in *Francovich v Italian Republic* [1991] E.C.R. I-5337 as authority for the proposition that if a directive does not identify a body to be used to secure compliance, the directive cannot be relied upon in proceedings against the body nominated by the implementing member state.

it unnecessary for the Court of Appeal to decide whether the MIB was an emanation of the state, rendering it susceptible to the direct effects doctrine, although Hobhouse L.J. was of the view that the MIB was a private law contractor only.[413] Accordingly, a victim who is unable to recover from the MIB in circumstances in which recovery is required by the Directives, will have to resort to an action in damages against the UK government for failing in its duties to implement the Directives properly.

In *Evans v Motor Insurers Bureau (No.2)*[414] an attempt was made to bring a *Francovich* action for damages following the ruling in the first *Evans* case. The specific allegation was that the MIB's Untraced Drivers Agreement made no provision for the award of interest and costs, contrary to the then provisions of the Second Motor Insurance Directive, now art.10 of the Consolidated Motor Insurance Directive 2009. The Court of Appeal refused to decide the point itself, and referred to the European Court of Justice for a preliminary ruling under art.234 of the EC Treaty a series of questions concerning whether the Directive did require interest and costs to be awarded and, more fundamentally, whether the United Kingdom had infringed EU law by designating the MIB as the relevant body for handling compensation applications by the victims of unin- sured and untraced drivers.[415] The European Court of Justice's subsequent ruling, in *Evans v Secretary of State for the Environment, Transport and the Regions*,[416] confirmed that the United Kingdom was in breach of EU Rules by adopting a non-statutory approach to the provision of compensation for the victims of untraced drivers although made adverse comments on various aspects of the Untraced Drivers Agreement 1972 as regards procedure, interest and costs. Those matters were addressed in the 2003 Agreement shortly before the Court delivered its judgment.

A *Francovich* action was also attempted in *Byrne v Motor Insurers Bureau*,[417] in which it was alleged that the UK Government was in breach of the Second Motor Insurance Directive (now art.10 of the Consolidated Motor Insurance Directive 2009) by failing to ensure that a claimant against the MIB under the Untraced Drivers Agreement 1996 (the relevant provisions being reproduced in the 2003 Agreement) had the benefit of the statutory limitation periods under the Limitation Act 1980; the Agreement made no provision for postponing the running of time where the victim was minor at the date of his injury (a matter corrected with respect to accidents occurring in respect of accidents occurring after midnight on February 1, 2009 by amendments to the Untraced Drivers Agreement). Flaux J. at first instance held that the Second Motor Insurance Directive gave rise to individual rights: in so deciding the learned judge ruled that dicta to the contrary in *Mighell v Reading*[418] had been superseded by subsequent decisions of the European Court of Justice: it is to be noted that the question of individual rights was considered both in *Mighell* and in *Byrne* not for the purposes of a *Francovich* action but for the purposes of the requirements of an

---

[413] For similar views, see: *Norman v Aziz* [2000] Lloyd's Rep. I.R. 52; *White v White* [2001] Lloyd's Rep. I.R. 493; *Byrne v Motor Insurers Bureau* [2008] Lloyd's Rep. I.R. 61, affirmed, without reference to this issue, [2008] Lloyd's Rep. I.R. 705.

[414] *Evans v Motor Insurers Bureau (No.2)* [2002] Lloyd's Rep. I.R. 1.

[415] The Court of Appeal made the reference with some reluctance, as the sums in question were relatively small.

[416] *Evans v Secretary of State for the Environment, Transport and the Regions* Case C-63/01, [2004] Lloyd's Rep. I.R. 391.

[417] *Byrne v Motor Insurers Bureau* [2008] Lloyd's Rep. I.R. 61, affirmed [2008] Lloyd's Rep. I.R. 705.

[418] *Mighell v Reading* [1999] Lloyd's Rep. I.R. 30.

action on the basis that the MIB was an emanation of the state, although it is clearly strongly arguable that the individual requirement test is the same for both purposes. Flaux J. left over for trial the questions of whether what he regarded as the United Kingdom's "inexcusable lack of thoroughness" in reaching the 1996 Agreement amounted to a "manifest and grave failure" of the type required by *Francovich*, and whether there was a causal link between that failure and the loss suffered by the claimant by having his claim time-barred. The Court of Appeal agreed, albeit for different reasons, that the United Kingdom's breach of the requirement to implement the Directive was sufficiently serious to justify a finding of liability in principle. It will be seen that these cases are inconclusive on the questions whether the MIB Agreements are subject to the "purposive" construction principle and, if not, whether the MIB is an emanation of the state so that the Directive is directly effective against the MIB and override the Agreements in the event of inconsistency. Each of these matters was referred to the European Court of Justice for a preliminary ruling by the Court of Appeal in *McCall v Poulton*.[419] The issues in this case arose under the Uninsured Drivers Agreement, the specific issue being whether the victim of an untraced driver could recover from the MIB the credit hire costs incurred by him in hiring a replacement vehicle for the duration of the repair period in respect of his own vehicle.

22–060   *The scope of the MIB's liability.* The Uninsured Drivers Agreement is available where the identity of the defendant is known, even if the claimant is unable to contact him.[420] The Untraced Drivers Agreement is appropriate only where the identity, as distinct from the whereabouts, of the defendant, is unknown.[421] If all attempts to establish the whereabouts of the defendant fail, service of process on the MIB may be ordered.[422]

It is to be emphasised that the MIB's liability is restricted to the range of the risks which are the subject of compulsory insurance under the 1988 Act.[423] Further, the liability of the MIB depends upon an actual or notional finding of negligence against the driver whose liability the MIB is asked to accept, and there can be no liability on the MIB in a case covered by one of the exemptions from the insurance requirement provided by s.144. It is no defence for the MIB to show that the injury results from the tortfeasor's deliberate wrongdoing, so that the tortfeasor, would on public policy grounds have been precluded from claiming indemnity from his own insurer.[424] However, the claimant's participation in the defendant's illegal conduct may debar him from suing the defendant[425] and thus from access to the MIB, and it should also be noted that deliberate running down is excluded from the Untraced Drivers Agreement.

22–061   **The Uninsured Drivers Agreement 1999.** The 1988 version of the Uninsured Drivers Agreement was modified, with respect to accidents occurring on or after

---

[419] *McCall v Poulton* [2009] Lloyd's Rep. I.R. 454.
[420] *Gurtner v Circuit* [1968] 2 Q.B. 587.
[421] *Clarke v Vedel* [1979] R.T.R. 26.
[422] *Gurtner v Circuit* [1968] 2 Q.B. 587.
[423] See the numerous authorities cited in the preceding paragraphs as to the scope of s.143, many of which have involved the MIB. The MIB has thus sought to defend itself, inter alia, on the basis that the accident did not occur on a road (*Randall v MIB* [1969] 1 All E.R. 21). Cf. *Severn Trent Water v Williams* [1995] 10 C.L. 638 where the MIB was held to be entitled, as against the claimant, to its costs where it was joined to an action occurring on private land.
[424] *Hardy v MIB* [1964] 2 Q.B. 745, approved in *Gardner v Moore* [1984] A.C. 548, and followed in *Charlton v Fisher* [2001] Lloyd's Rep. I.R. 387.
[425] *Pitts v Hunt* [1990] 3 All E.R. 344.

October 1, 1999, by the 1999 Agreement (cl.4 of the 1999 Agreement). The 1988 Agreement had been drafted to take account of the extension of the 1988 Act to liability for damage to property, and the 1999 Agreement makes a number of both substantial and minor changes to take account of developments since 1988, in particular the new terminology adopted by the Civil Procedure Rules 1988 in replacing the Rules of the Supreme Court 1965 with effect from April 1999.

Scope of liability. Clause 5 of the 1999 Agreement sets out the circumstances in which the MIB faces liability: where a claimant has obtained in the courts of Great Britain a judgment which is not satisfied, the MIB will pay the relevant sum to the claimant or, at least, cause that sum to be paid.[426] The liability arises whether or not the person against whom the judgment has been obtained is in fact covered by a contract of insurance, and irrespective of the reason for the defendant's default. The MIB is under an obligation to indemnify the victim if the judgment has not been satisfied within seven days after the date on which the judgment became enforceable (cl.1), which is also the position under the 1988 Agreement. The term "relevant sum" is defined by cl.6 of the 1999 Agreement as referring not just to the amount of the judgment, but also to any interest on that sum and also the costs awarded in favour of the victim: the 1988 Agreement is to the same effect.

22–062

The MIB's liability in respect of personal injury is unlimited in amount. Liability in respect of property damage is, by contrast, limited. Under cl.16, the MIB is not liable for any loss below the figure of £300, the "specified excess"[427] and in respect of any one accident is not liable for any property damage greater than £250,000 consistently with the property damage limits in the 1988 Act and with the position under the 1988 Agreement. Accordingly, the MIB's maximum possible liability for property damage arising out of any one accident is £250,000 minus the specified excess. These figures have been varied by a Supplementary Agreement between the Government and the MIB, dated November 7, 2008. The Supplementary Agreement applies to accidents occurring after midnight on October 7, 2008, and its effects are: (a) to remove the excess, so that the victim is entitled to make a full recovery from the MIB for the first £300 of any loss; and (b) to increase the MIB's liability for property damage arising out of one accident to £1,000,000 from £250,000.

It is uncertain whether the Agreement is required to cover the costs incurred by the victim in hiring a replacement vehicle: *McCall v Poulton*.[428] The point did not arise directly because the issue referred to the European Court of Justice by the Court of Appeal was whether the MIB Agreements were to be read subject to the EU Directive in this regard, although it was not decided what the Directive requires insurance for liability for hiring costs.

The MIB is liable to make payments in respect of medical treatment administered by private hospitals and in respect of emergency medical treatment administered by qualified medical practitioners, under ss.157 to 159 of the Road Traffic Act, and it is also liable to make payments to the NHS under the Road

---

[426] In practice, an insurer will be nominated by the MIB to deal with the claim. The matter is governed by art.75 of the MIB's Regulations, which requires any insurer who had issued a relevant policy to cover the claim as an art.75 insurer on behalf of the MIB even though the policy is voidable or its terms do not cover the loss.

[427] This sum may be varied from time to time by agreement between the MIB and the Secretary of State. The figure was £175 under the 1988 Agreement. In *Mastin v Blanchard* [1995] 9 C.L. 355 a claim for a lesser sum was made on behalf of the victim by his solicitors: the solicitors were held to be personally liable for the MIBs costs in respect of the application.

[428] *McCall v Poulton* [2009] Lloyd's Rep. I.R. 454.

Traffic (National Health Service Charges) Act 1999 in respect of accidents occurring on or after April 5, 1999. The MIB's liability under the Road Traffic (National Health Service Charges) Act 1999 is only in respect of accidents occurring between April 5, 1999 to January 28, 1999 inclusive. As far as accidents occurring on or after January 29, 2007, the MIB's liability is under the Health and Social Care (Community Health and Standards) Act 2003.

By virtue of cl.17 of the 1999 Agreement, where a victim has received compensation from any other source, including payment under the Financial Services Compensation Scheme or payment under any other insurance policy, the MIB is entitled to deduct that sum from the amount payable by it in respect of the losses suffered by the victim. These deductions are in addition to those for property damage set out in cl.16. There is an important change here from the position under the 1988 Agreement: the earlier provision permitted the MIB to deduct recoveries from other sources only for property damage, whereas the 1999 Agreement authorises deductions in respect of compensation from other sources for death and personal injuries. The MIB is entitled, under cl.15, to require the victim to undertake to hand over such sums as a condition precedent to payment by the MIB.

22–063   *Interim payments.*   Under r.25.7(1) of the Civil Procedure Rules 1998, the court may make an order for an interim payment of damages, before the claimant has obtained a judgment against the defendant, where the defendant has admitted liability to pay damages or where the court is satisfied that, if the case went to trial, the defendant would be to obtain judgment for a substantial amount. The position of the MIB is governed by CPR r.25.7(2). This provides as follows:

> "[In] a claim for personal injuries, the court may make an order for an interim payment of damages only if:
>   (a) the defendant is insured in respect of the claim;
>   (b) the defendant's liability will be met by
>   (i) an insurer under s.151 of the Road Traffic Act 1988; or
>   (ii) an insurer acting under the Motor Insurers Bureau Agreement; or
>   (c) the defendant is a public body."

This provision has a chequered history. Interim damages were originally governed by RSC Ord.29 rr.9 to 11, and the power of the court to make an interim award applied only where the defendant was "a person insured in respect of the plaintiff's claim" (now CPR 1988 r.25.7(1)(a)). It was held, in *Powney v Coxage*,[429] that the MIB was not an insurer as such, so that an uninsured defendant fell outside the rule. The result was that even if the MIB had accepted liability for a claim, no interim payment could be ordered pending the final determination of quantum. This unsatisfactory position was addressed by an amendment to RSC Ord.29 r.11 made in 1996, and it then became possible for the court to award interim damages against "a person insured in respect of the plaintiff's claim or whose liability will be met by an insurer under s.151 of the Road Traffic Act 1988 or by an insurer concerned under the Motor Insurers Bureau Agreement". The amended wording put beyond doubt the potential liability of the MIB for an interim payment in the situation in which the defendant was uninsured by reason of the fact that his insurers had a defence under the policy. However, doubts remained about the liability of the MIB in respect of a driver who had never been insured at all. The reason for these doubts

---

[429] *Powney v Coxage, The Times*, March 8, 1988.

was that the MIB's own internal rules, prior to 1988, had drawn a distinction between the situation in which there was a policy under which a defence existed and the situation in which there was no policy at all: in the former case, the MIB would require the insurer in question to meet the victim's claim as "the insurer concerned"; in the latter case, the claim would be met from the MIB's own funds through an insurer nominated by the MIB to handle the claim. The Domestic Regulations Agreement, entered into in 1988, discontinued the use of the phrase "insurer concerned" and replaced it with "domestic regulations insurer". However, it remained possible to argue that the phrase "insurer concerned" in the amended version of RSC Ord.29 r.11, referred only to what is now a "domestic regulations insurer", so that if the driver had no policy and the claim was to be met from MIB funds there was no "insurer concerned" and thus no potential liability for an interim payment. This narrow interpretation of RSC Ord.29 r.11 was rejected by Deputy Judge Smith QC in *Crisp v Marshall*,[430] a decision approved by the Court of Appeal in *Sharp v Pereira*.[431] In the latter case, the Court of Appeal held that:

(1) the phrase "insurer concerned" was not to be regarded as having been used as term of art in RSC Ord.29 r.11, given the earlier abandonment of that phrase;

(2) the MIB's internal rules could not affect the proper construction of RSC Ord.29 r.11; and

(3) even if RSC Ord.29 r.11 applied only to a domestic regulations insurer, it remained applicable to payments out of MIB general funds given that even a domestic regulations insurer could become liable only once the MIB was itself liable.

Grounds (1) and (2) were adopted by Lord Woolf M.R. and Pill L.J.; Millett L.J. preferred ground (3). All of these issues have been removed by the wording of CPR 1998 r.25.7(2), which refers to an insurer "acting" under the MIB Agreement, a word which encompasses both a domestic regulations insurer and an insurer nominated by the MIB to deal with the claim on behalf of the MIB where there never was any policy in place.

Sharp v Pereira does remain good authority on one matter relating to the wording of the MIB Agreement. The 1999 Agreement, like its 1988 predecessor, refers to the liability of the MIB for a "judgment". The Court of Appeal, in *Sharp*, held that the use of this word did not preclude an award of interim damages against the MIB even though such an award was not a judgment: for the purposes of RSC Ord.29 r.11—and presumably now for the purposes of CPR 1988 r.25.7(2)—an award of interim judgment was to be regarded as a judgment.

General exceptions to the 1999 Agreement. The MIB is under no liability in respect of a claim of any of the following descriptions (cl.6(1)):   **22–064**

"(a) A claim arising out of liability incurred by the user of a vehicle owned by or in the possession of the Crown (including a vehicle which has been unlawfully removed from the possession of the Crown), unless—

(i) responsibility for the existence of a contract of insurance under Part VI of the 1988 Act in relation to that vehicle had been undertaken by some other

[430] *Crisp v Marshall* [1997] C.L.Y. 1761.
[431] *Sharp v Pereira* [1999] Lloyd's Rep. I.R. 242.

person (whether or not the person liable was in fact covered by a contract of insurance), or,

(ii) the liability was in fact covered by a contract of insurance.

(b) A claim arising out of the use of a vehicle which is not required to be covered by a contract of insurance by virtue of s.144 of the 1988 Act, unless the use is in fact covered by such a contract.

(c) A claim by, or for the benefit of, a person ('the beneficiary') other than the person suffering death, injury or damage which is made either—

(i) in respect of a cause of action or a judgment which has been assigned to the beneficiary, or

(ii) pursuant to a right of subrogation or contractual or other right belonging to the beneficiary."[432]

These exceptions mirror those in the 1988 Agreement, other than exception (c)(i), which is new.

22–065   *Motor vehicle damage exception based on the knowledge of the victim.* Clause 6(1)(d) of the 1999 Agreement, reproducing an equivalent provision in the 1988 Agreement, excludes the MIB's liability for:

"a claim in respect of damage to a motor vehicle or losses arising therefrom where, at the time when the damage to it was sustained—

(i) there was not in force in relation to the use of that vehicle such a contract of insurance as is required by Part VI of the 1988 Act, and

(ii) the claimant either knew or ought to have known that that was the case."

This is a narrowly drawn exception, applying where the owner of a vehicle has allowed it to be used on a road when he knew, or ought to have known, that there was no insurance—be it under his own policy or under that of the user—in respect of such use.

22–066   *Exception based on criminal conduct.* Clause 6(1)(e) contains three important exceptions to the MIB's liability. It operates to exclude a claim which is made in respect of the liability of the owner (including a hirer under a hire-purchase or hiring agreement) or user of a vehicle for injury or loss suffered by the victim while he was voluntarily allowing himself to be carried in (or, in the case of a motorbike, on) the vehicle and could not reasonably have been expected to have alighted from it. The exceptions apply if the victim knew or ought to have known any of the following:

"(i)   that the vehicle had been stolen or unlawfully taken;

(ii)   [second numbered exception relates to the absence of insurance—see below];

(iii) that the vehicle was being used in furtherance of a crime; or

(iv) that the vehicle was being used as a means of escape from, or avoidance of, lawful apprehension."

Exceptions (iii) and (iv) are new to the 1999 Agreement, although their effect is probably no more than a confirmation of the common law principle that a passenger has no claim in tort when he is injured in a motor accident while

---

[432] One of the underlying questions in *McCall v Poulton* [2009] Lloyd's Rep. I.R. 454, referred to the European Court of Justice is whether an insurer who has paid hire costs is subrogated to the victim's rights to recover those costs from the MIB where the defendant was uninsured, despite art.6(1)(c).

participating in criminal activity. The 1999 Agreement contains detailed provision concerning the burden of proof, all of which are also new. The burden of proving that the victim knew or ought to have known any of these things is borne by the MIB (cl.6(3)), so that, in the absence of any evidence, the victim will be able to recover. However, under cl.6(4), the fact that the victim was, at the relevant time, incapacitated by the self-induced influence of drugs or drink is irrelevant: the victim's knowledge is to be assessed by reference to matters of which he could reasonably be expected to have been aware in the absence of such intoxication. Thus, where the intoxication is self-induced, the court is required to disregard the intoxication entirely and not to ask the factual question whether the degree of intoxication prevented the formation of the relevant knowledge. In *White v White*,[433] decided under the 1988 Agreement, the Court of Appeal held that the drunken state of the passenger had not prevented him from possessing the relevant knowledge: that issue did not arise in the appeal to the House of Lords in *White v White*.[434]

Exception based on knowledge of absence of insurance. Clause 6(1)(e)(ii) **22–067** contains what is perhaps the most important exception to the MIB's liability. The MIB is not liable for a claim which is made in respect of the liability of the owner (including a hirer under a hire-purchase or hiring agreement) or user of a vehicle for injury or loss suffered by the victim while he was voluntarily allowing himself to be carried in (or, in the case of a motorbike, on) the vehicle and could not reasonably have been expected to have alighted from it, where the victim knew, or ought to have known, that the vehicle was being used without there being in force in relation to its use such a contract of insurance as would comply with Pt VI of the 1988 Act.[435] A mere passenger[436] who meets these conditions has no claim against the MIB. As with the other exceptions referred to earlier, the burden of proof is borne by the MIB (cl. 6(3)), and cl.6(4) also applies, so the fact that the victim was, at the relevant time, incapacitated by the self-induced influence of drugs or drink is irrelevant: the victim's knowledge is to be assessed by reference to matters of which he could reasonably be expected to have been aware in the absence of such intoxication. However, in the absence of evidence to the contrary, the MIB is able to establish the relevant degree of knowledge in relation to cl.6(1)(e)(ii) by showing any of the following:

(a) that the victim was the owner or registered keeper of the vehicle or had caused or permitted its use;

---

[433] *White v White* [1999] Lloyd's Rep. I.R. 30.

[434] *White v White* [2001] Lloyd's Rep. I.R. 493.

[435] A person claiming under the Fatal Accidents Act 1976 in respect of the death of a passenger who had the requisite knowledge has a personal cause of action which is not defeated by cl.6(1)(e)(ii): *Phillips v Rafiq* [2007] Lloyd's Rep. I.R. 413.

[436] Pre-1988 versions of this provision excluded the MIB's liability only in respect of a person himself "using" the vehicle, a word which excluded a passenger who was not participating in the driving of the vehicle. In *Stinton v Stinton* [1999] Lloyd's Rep. I.R. 305, it was held that a passenger could "use" a vehicle by participating in its driving where the driver was inebriated. This decision was distinguished in *Hatton v Hall* [1999] Lloyd's Rep. I.R. 313, where a pillion passenger was held not to have been using the vehicle despite the fact that the driver was in a state of inebriation. See also *O'Mahoney v Joliffe* [1999] Lloyd's Rep. I.R. 321. EU law does not permit a national Motor Insurers Bureau to exclude liability for a passenger in an uninsured vehicle where the injuries were caused by the driver of another uninsured vehicle: Case C-211/07 *Commission of the European Communities v Republic of Ireland* [2008] Lloyd's Rep. I.R. 526.

(b) that the victim knew that the vehicle was being used by a person who was below the minimum age at which he could be granted a licence authorising the driving of a vehicle of that class;

(c) that the victim knew that the person driving the vehicle was disqualified from holding or obtaining a driving licence;

(d) that the victim knew that the user of the vehicle was neither its owner nor registered keeper nor an employee of the owner or registered keeper of any other vehicle.

The exception in respect of a lack of insurance is permitted by what is now art.10(2) of the Consolidated Motor Insurance Directive 2009,[437] which provides that:

"Member States may, however, exclude the payment of compensation by [the MIB] in respect of persons who voluntarily entered the vehicle which caused the damage or injury when the [MIB] can prove that they knew it was uninsured."

This wording, on its face, does not appear to authorise the exclusion of the MIB's liability on the basis of the lesser test of presumed knowledge, and seems to demand actual knowledge. Moreover, the present wording may well be more restrictive to the rights of the victim than the pre-1988 formulation, which excluded recovery only if the victim "had reason to believe" that the vehicle was uninsured, so that an assertion by the driver that there was insurance in place was sufficient to allow the victim to recover under the MIB Agreement in the absence of clear contradictory evidence.[438] The Court of Appeal was prepared to assume, in the joined cases *Mighell v Reading* and *White v White*,[439] decided under the 1988 Agreement, that that Agreement was in conflict with the provision of the Directive, but went on to hold that, even if this was correct, the victim could not rely upon the Directive as against the MIB and the MIB Agreement was not rendered illegal or unenforceable to the extent that it conflicted with the Directive. Moreover, it was not possible to construe the MIB Agreement as complying with the Directive; its wording was clear and it was not possible to impute to the MIB an intention to extend its liability to that required by the Directive where the UK government had mistakenly accepted the terms of the Agreement as fulfilling the United Kingdom's obligations under the Directive.

Given that the wording of the 1988 Agreement was confirmed by the 1999 Agreement, those responsible for the 1999 Agreement plainly believe that it meets the requirements of EU law. This is only right if the words "knew or ought to have known" are, as a matter of English law, no wider than the word "knew" as used in the Directive. The matter was given detailed consideration by the House of Lords in *White v White*.[440] Here, the injured passenger, who was the negligent driver's brother, did not actually know that his brother was uninsured,[441] although there were numerous indications which strongly pointed to that conclusion: in particular the passenger knew that his brother had in the past driven without a licence. The trial judge found that the passenger did not actually know that the driver was uninsured, but that he ought to have done so, and accordingly he was excluded from the MIB Agreement. However, the trial judge

[437] Re-enacting art.1(4) of the Second Motor Insurance Directive 1984.
[438] *Porter v MIB* [1978] 2 Lloyd's Rep. 463.
[439] *Mighell v Reading* and *White v White* [1999] Lloyd's Rep. I.R. 30.
[440] *White v White* [2001] Lloyd's Rep. I.R. 493.
[441] Even though he was unlicensed and had never passed a driving test.

went on to decide that the Directive overrode the MIB Agreement, and that only actual knowledge could defeat the passenger's rights against the MIB. The Court of Appeal reversed this ruling. It accepted, albeit with severe reservations, the judge's finding that the passenger did not actually know that his brother was uninsured and agreed that the passenger ought to have known that fact, but rejected the suggestion that the MIB Agreement was to be read subject to the Directive, as it was not directly effective given that it imposed obligations on Member States rather than conferred individual rights.[442] The House of Lords, by a four to one majority reinstated the trial judge's finding that the passenger was able to recover from the MIB, but on the quite different reasoning that the phrase "knew or ought to have known" was confined to actual and blind eye knowledge. Lord Nicholls, speaking for the majority, accepted that knowledge could consist of anything between actual knowledge, wilfully shutting one's eyes to the obvious (blind eye knowledge) and mere negligence. Lord Nicholls held that the Second Directive required a narrow interpretation of the word "knew", as it constituted an exception to the principle of the availability of compensation and accordingly a high degree of knowledge was required. Accordingly, if the passenger had been told by the driver that he was uninsured or that he had not passed a driving test, the knowledge requirement would be met, and the position would be the same if the passenger deliberately refrained from making inquiries after he had been alerted to the possibility of the absence of insurance. Negligence was not enough, as what was required was collusion between the driver and the passenger. The problem for the majority was the phrase "or ought to have known". Lord Nicholls here concluded that this phrase had no fixed meaning and that it had to be construed in accordance with its context: the context here was the Second Directive, which used only the word "knew". The result was, therefore, that the words "ought to have known" were to be construed as adding nothing to "knew", and that—as was the case with the Directive—the passenger was entitled to recover as, on the trial judge's findings of fact, he did not actually know, and had not deliberately shut his eyes to, the fact that his brother was uninsured. Lord Scott delivered a powerful dissenting judgment, holding that English law generally recognised the phrase "ought to have known" as referring to negligence, and there was no reason to depart from that settled principle.

The decision in *White v White*[443] now means that the only question in cases of this type is whether the passenger had actual or blind eye knowledge of the absence of insurance.[444] The issue of actual knowledge was also considered by

22–068

---

[442] *White v White* [1999] Lloyd's Rep. I.R. 30.

[443] *White v White* [2001] Lloyd's Rep. I.R. 493.

[444] Earlier authorities on the meaning of constructive knowledge are no longer of authority. The scope of constructive knowledge, within the meaning of the phrase "ought to have known" has been considered in two cases. See *Hadfield v Knowles* Unreported, 1993, in which the victim had been injured while riding as a passenger on a motorbike driven by X who, to the victim's knowledge, had been disqualified from driving. The victim had not, due to a lack of comprehension on her part, appreciated that X could not have been insured in the circumstances. The court ruled that the proper question to be asked was whether a reasonable person possessing the victim's actual knowledge ought to have known that there was no insurance in place: on the facts this was held to be the case, and the victim's claim against the MIB was dismissed. That reasoning can no longer stand in the light of *White v White*, and it is unlikely that cl.6(3)(c) of the 1999 Agreement, which lays down a presumption of knowledge of lack of insurance where the victim knows that the driver is disqualified, would be of any assistance to the MIB in the light of *White v White*.

the Court of Appeal in *Mighell v Reading*.[445] The claimant in this case, the front seat passenger in his own motor vehicle, had been injured in an accident while the vehicle was being driven negligently by the defendant. It was established at the trial that the claimant had become aware that the defendant was unemployed and had no significant income, so that the defendant was not himself insured. It was further established that the claimant knew that the defendant was not permitted to drive under the claimant's own policy. The Court of Appeal held that the trial judge had been entitled to conclude on these facts that the MIB had discharged its burden of proof and had demonstrated that the claimant had known that the defendant was uninsured.

As noted earlier, as a result of cl.6(4) of the 1999 Agreement, self-induced intoxication is no excuse for a passenger who, prior to his intoxication, knew that the driver was uninsured but subsequently accepted a lift with him. However, it is unclear from the wording of the 1999 Agreement whether self-induced intoxication can give rise to the possibility that the claimant was not voluntarily being carried in the vehicle. Clause 6(4) does not say that intoxication is to be disregarded for all purposes, but only for the purpose of ascertaining whether the claimant knew or ought to have known that the driver was uninsured: accordingly, it appears to remain arguable that self-induced intoxication remains relevant to the question whether the passenger was being carried voluntarily.

Assuming that the requisite knowledge exists, a further question is whether a passenger who at first agreed voluntarily to be carried can revoke that consent during the course of the journey, thereby obtaining the benefit of cover under the MIB Agreement in the event of a later accident. It will be recalled that the wording of cl.6(1)(e)(ii) removes protection "in a case where . . . at the time of the use which gave rise to the liability the person suffering death or bodily injury or damage to property was allowing himself to be carried in or upon the vehicle"—wording that indicates that the time at which the existence of consent has to be judged is the time immediately before the accident occurs, and not the start of the journey. In *Pickett v Motor Insurers Bureau*[446] the Court of Appeal was unanimous that consent could be revoked, but there was disagreement as to how that could be achieved. In *Pickett* the claimant cohabited with the defendant and they purchased a car that they could not afford to insure. They decided to "go for a drive and have some fun". They took the car to a remote path, and the defendant began to carry out handbrake turns by driving at a high speed and stopping the car by spinning it using the handbrake. The claimant shouted at the defendant to stop—"For God's sake stop the car"—as she feared for her own safety and for that of their dog on the back seat. The defendant slowed down: the claimant, assuming that he was stopping, undid her safety belt and prepared to alight. However, at that point the defendant speeded up and performed another handbrake turn. Unfortunately, he lost control of the car, which left the path, and both the claimant and the defendant were seriously injured. The Court of Appeal by a majority held that the claimant had no action against the MIB. The majority view of Chadwick and May L.JJ. was that the claimant had not done enough to revoke her consent to being carried. There had been a common venture to "have some fun". What was required was, in Chadwick L.J.'s words, an unequivocal repudiation of the common venture by the passenger. May L.J. expressed the same point by saying that the passenger must have made it clear that the venture was over so that the continuation of the journey by the driver was akin to the

[445] *Mighell v Reading* [1999] Lloyd's Rep. I.R. 30. See also *Akers v Motor Insurers Bureau* [2003] Lloyd's Rep. 427.
[446] *Pickett v Motor Insurers Bureau* [2004] Lloyd's Rep. I.R. 513.

passenger's false imprisonment. Applying these tests to the facts, Chadwick and May L.JJ. held that the passenger had not withdrawn her consent to being carried as passenger simply by objecting to the driver's method of driving. Pill L.J. rejected the tests proposed by the majority. In his view the claimant had made clear her objections to the specific use of the vehicle to perform handbrake turns: the risk to which the vehicle was being put was greater than the one to which she had consented, namely the risk of injury through normal driving. Her exhortation "For God's sake stop the car", coupled with an attempt to get out of the car, readily satisfied the requirement for a withdrawal of consent. Pill L.J. rejected the suggestion by Chadwick L.J. that there had to be a repudiation of a common venture, defined as "going for a drive to have some fun" as that test did not focus sufficiently on the exact position immediately before the loss. Further, Pill L.J. regarded May L.J.'s false imprisonment analogy as unhelpful. It was enough that consent to further driving had actually been withdrawn.

Notice to the MIB. The MIB's liability under the 1999 Agreement is subject to **22–069** a series of conditions precedent which must be complied with by the victim. These have both been expanded and clarified by comparison with the 1988 Agreement. In outline, the procedure is as follows:

(1) The claimant or a solicitor acting for the claimant[447] must make an application in such form, containing such information and accompanied by such documents, as the MIB may reasonably require (cl.7(1), reproducing in modified form the 1988 Agreement).

(2) The application is to be made within 14 days of the commencement by the claimant of proceedings against any person liable to him in respect of his loss, i.e. the user of the vehicle or any person causing or permitting use, and is to be made in the form of "proper notice" to the insurers of the vehicle if their identity can be ascertained or, in any other case, the MIB itself (cl.9(1), reproducing in modified form the 1988 Agreement under which seven days were allowed from the commencement of proceedings).

(3) "Proper notice" under cl.9(2)–(3) requires[448]

(a) notice in writing that proceedings have been commenced;

(b) a copy of the claim form;

(c) a copy or details of any insurance policy under which the claimant is entitled to benefit in respect of his loss;

(d) copies of all correspondence relevant to the claimant's loss and the defendant's insurance;

(e) a copy of the particulars of claim, whether or not they have been indorsed on the claim form or served on the defendant, although as far as England and Wales are concerned it is sufficient if the particulars of claim are served on the MIB within seven days of having been served on the defendant;

---

[447] If the application is made by any other person, the MIB may refuse to accept it until the relationship between the claimant and the applicant is established: cl.7(2) (not in the earlier Agreement).

[448] Under the County Court Rules in existence before the CPR 1998, difficulties had been encountered in relation to the date of commencement of proceedings and also proceedings commenced by default summons. The courts proved to be unwilling to allow the complexities of these technicalities to excuse the MIB's liabilities under the 1988 Agreement. See, e.g. *Silverton v Goodall* [1997] P.I.Q.R. P451; *Cambridge v Callaghan, The Times*, March 21, 1997.

> (f) a copy of any documents which are required to be served on the defendant; and
>
> (g) such other information about the proceedings as the MIB may reasonably specify.
>
> (4) In relation to proceedings in England and Wales only, the claimant must give notice in writing to the identified insurers or the MIB (as the case may be) within seven days of his receiving notification from the court or the defendant that the claim form has been served, or within seven days of effecting personal service (cl.10, new to the 1999 Agreement).
>
> (5) Once proceedings have been commenced, the claimant must, within seven days, give notice to the insurers or MIB of the filing of any defence, any amendment to the particulars of claim and any communication by the court as to the date of trial. The applicant must also provide such further information as is reasonably required by the MIB (cl.11, new to the 1999 Agreement).
>
> (6) If the claimant intends to apply for judgment, he must, not less than thirty five days before doing so, give notice to the insurers or MIB of his intention to do so (cl.12, new to the 1999 Agreement).
>
> (7) Any notice or documents required to be supplied to the MIB must be sent by fax or by registered post (cl.8, new to the 1999 Agreement).

It is also a condition precedent to the MIB's liability under cl.13 (a modified version of the requirement in the 1988 Agreement) that the claimant has, as soon as is reasonably practicable, sought from the defendant the details of his insurance: the defendant is under a duty to provide that information under s.154 of the 1988 Act.

22–070   *The proceedings against the defendant.* Under cl.14, which is a modified form of the requirement in the 1988 Agreement, the MIB is entitled, as a condition precedent of its liability to the claimant, to require the claimant to take all reasonable steps to obtain judgment against any person who may be liable in respect of the loss suffered by the claimant. This will include the driver, any person who caused or permitted the vehicle to be driven without insurance, and any person facing vicarious liability. The claimant must also permit the MIB to be joined to the proceedings. In return, the MIB is required to give the claimant a full indemnity as to costs. The MIB is also under no obligation to the claimant unless the claimant has: (a) assigned to the MIB or its nominee the unsatisfied judgment in so far as that judgment relates to compulsory insurance falling within the 1988 Act; and (b) undertaken to pay to the MIB any sum paid to him by the MIB in the event that the judgment is set aside, and also any sum paid to him by any other person by way of compensation for his loss (see cl.15, reproduced in a different form from the requirement in the 1988 Agreement). The MIB is entitled to take such sums into account in assessing the amount of its payment (cl.17).

The scope of the obligation on the assured to proceed against the third party was considered by the Court of Appeal in *Norman v Ali*.[449] Here, N was injured by X, who had been driving a vehicle belonging to Y without insurance. N commenced proceedings against X within the three-year limitation period allowed for personal injury claims. Subsequently the MIB exercised its powers under the 1988 Agreement and demanded that Y be brought into the action as

[449] *Norman v Ali* [2000] Lloyd's Rep. I.R. 395.

co-defendant. It had earlier been established by H.H. Judge Kershaw QC in *Norman v Aziz*[450] that changes to the 1988 Act brought about by the implementation of the Motor Insurance Directives had not affected the right of a victim to bring a civil action against a person who had caused or permitted a vehicle to be used without insurance, so that N had an action against Y for breach of statutory duty[451] and that the MIB was entitled to require Y to be sued. N did in fact seek to join Y to the proceedings, but this was not validly done until more than three years had expired from the date of the injury. In *Norman v Aziz* the Court of Appeal held that the limitation period for the claim against Y was three years, as the claim was one for personal injury, and accordingly that N's claim was time-barred and had failed to comply with the condition precedent imposed by the demand made under the MIB Agreement. The Court of Appeal further held that the MIB was entitled to make a demand under the Agreement, and there was no requirement that its demand be a reasonable one. The only limit is the victim's right of challenge under the appeals procedure in cl.19, discussed below.

Appeals procedure. Any claimant to the MIB has, under cl.19, the right to apply to the Secretary of State for a determination as to the reasonableness of any requirement imposed upon the claimant by the MIB. The Secretary of State's decision is final. An equivalent provision appeared in the 1988 Agreement. **22–071**

Claims handling. Claims-handling under the Uninsured Drivers Agreement is regulated by art.75 of the MIB's Memorandum and Articles of Association 2009, replacing the Domestic Regulations which operated until May 31, 2001. The general effect of art.75 is to require an insurer who, but for defences open to him, would have been liable to meet claims under the Road Traffic Act 1988 s.151. Such an insurer is designated the "Article 75 Insurer", and is to meet claims on behalf of the MIB even though the insurance has been obtained by fraud, misrepresentation, there has been non-disclosure of material facts, or mistake, the cover has been back dated, or the use of the vehicle was other than that permitted under the policy. **22–072**

If a Road Traffic Act Judgment is obtained, the Article 75 Insurer must satisfy the original judgment creditor if and to the extent that the judgment has not within seven days of the execution date been satisfied by the judgment debtor.[452] The MIB may, if appropriate, pay the claim itself and then seek reimbursement from the Article 75 Insurer. The Article 75 Insurer is not entitled to any reimbursement from the MIB, although contribution rights between Members are unaffected.

An insurer's status as an Article 75 Insurer ceases in the following cases:

(1) if a renewal notice is issued, incorporating a temporary cover note extending cover, conditionally or otherwise, beyond the date of expiry of the policy, as of the expiry date of that extension of cover;

(2) from the expiry date specified in the policy if, by provision in the policy or by notice in writing by either party to the policy, the policy is not intended to be renewed;

---

[450] *Norman v Aziz* [2000] Lloyd's Rep. I.R. 52.

[451] On the principle in *Monk v Warbey* [1935] 1 K.B. 75.

[452] Such arrangements are required by art.11 of the Consolidated Motor Insurance Directive 2009, which demand that compensation is to be paid to the victim without delay irrespective of any dispute between an insurer and a compensation body.

(3) from the expiry date of a short period insurance (being any insurance proposed for a term of less than twelve months, where there is no intention on the part of the Member to renew, nor any renewal documents issued), save where a new insurance for the same vehicle and policy-holder begins within a period of fifteen days of the expiry date;

(4) when the insurance has been cancelled and the certificate of insurance has been recovered before the date on which the Road Traffic Act Liability was incurred, by specific request of the insured, or strictly in accordance with the power of cancellation contained in the Member's contract for the Risk, notwithstanding that such contract may not have been issued (provided that where an intermediary cancels the policy and the certificate of insurance has been recovered by the intermediary, either as agent for the Member or under the terms of any separate agreement between the intermediary and the insured, cancellation of the policy must be exercised strictly in accordance with the Member's standard form of contract for the risk and there must be clear evidence that the intermediary is empowered to do so by the policy wording);

(5) when, before the date on which the Road Traffic Act Liability was incurred, the Member has obtained a declaration from a court of competent jurisdiction that the insurance is void or unenforceable;

(6) when the insurance has ceased to operate by reason of a transfer of interest in the vehicle involved in the accident, which the insurance purports to cover, and which transfer is proved by evidence;

(7) when the theft of the certificate of insurance was reported to the police (provided that the report was made within 30 days of the date of discovery of the theft); or

(8) if the certificate of insurance has been forged by someone other than the Member or an intermediary acting on behalf of the Member or an officer, employee or agent of the Member or of an intermediary acting on behalf of the Member.

A member asserting that it is not an Article 75 Insurer bears the burden of so proving. If there is more than one Article 75 Insurer in respect of a particular vehicle—as where the accident is caused by two or more people or there are two or more insurers in respect of the same vehicle—then the handling of any claims will be by agreement between them or resolved by the MIB's Technical Committee, and indeed all disputes relating to the interpretation of art.75 are to be dealt with by the Technical Committee, subject to a right of appeal.

The Untraced Drivers Agreements

22–073　*Background to the 2003 Agreement.* The original Motor Insurers' Bureau Agreement of 1946 was limited to uninsured drivers, and specifically excluded untraced "hit and run" drivers. This exclusion was highlighted by Sachs J. in *Adams v Andrews*,[453] who described it as lamentable and demanding of action. This decision resulted in an agreement reached in 1969, replaced in 1972 and again in 1996.[454] The 1996 Agreement applied only to death and personal injury and did not extend to property damage, a derogation then open under the Second Motor Insurance Directive, and relied upon by the United Kingdom. Necessarily

---

[453] *Adams v Andrews* [1964] 2 Q.B. 347.

[454] The obligation to establish a compensation body for the payment of damages caused by untraced vehicles is set out in art.10 of the Consolidated Motor Insurance Directive 2009.

there was no identifiable tortfeasor, and accordingly the MIB was to be treated as a surrogate defendant. The victim was required to make a claim in writing against the MIB within three years of the accident, and the MIB would produce a report on the incident under which payment would be made if the untraced driver would on the balance of probabilities have faced liability. Interest was not payable under the Agreement, a point challenged in *Evans v Motor Insurers Bureau*.[455] At first instance Thomas J. held that the Agreement on its proper construction applied only to damages, and that the Second Motor Insurance Directive 1984 did not itself provide for interest. On appeal the Court of Appeal felt that the Directive did require the payment of interest but that it did not have direct effect in English law and could not be relied upon by a victim. There was also no provision for the recovery of legal costs by the victim. Any dispute between the MIB and the victim in respect of the sum awarded was to be referred to a sole arbitrator, against whose decision it would be almost impossible to appeal.[456] There was no direct recourse to the courts as an alternative.[457]

In July 2000 the Department of Transport published a Consultative Document setting out possible changes to the Untraced Drivers Agreement. At much the same time the Court of Appeal in *Evans v Secretary of State for the Environment, Transport and the Regions*[458] the Court of Appeal upheld the decision of Buckley J. to refer to the European Court of Justice for a preliminary ruling various questions as to the compatibility of the Untraced Drivers Agreement with the Motor Insurance Directives. The outcome of these developments was a new Untraced Drivers Agreement signed on February 7, 2003. The Agreement applies to claims arising out of accidents occurring on or after February 14, 2003 and extends to victims a number of substantive and procedural benefits unavailable under the 1996 Agreement.

On December 4, 2003 the European Court of Justice delivered its judgment in *Evans v Secretary of State for the Environment, Transport and the Regions*.[459] Many of the issues considered by the Court have been expressly dealt with by the 2003 Agreement and in general the 2003 Agreement appears to comply with the *Evans* ruling. However, there are a number of points in *Evans* not provided for in the 1972 and 1996 Agreements—in particular in relation to interest and costs—and insofar as awards under those Agreements fall short of what is demanded by *Evans* there is arguably a *Francovich* damages action against the UK government by the victim for failure to implement the Directives properly. The European Court of Justice did not decide whether the *Francovich* conditions for an award of damages had been satisfied but referred this matter back to the English courts for their determination.

The European Court of Justice in *Evans* made a number of rulings of principle and referred back to the English courts the question of whether the rulings were satisfied by the 1972 and 1996 Agreements. The issues related to interest, costs, the arbitral procedure and the non-statutory basis of the MIB. The Court ruled as follows:

(1) Compensation to the victim of an untraced driver required by the Second Directive had to include an element for interest. This was to be done by

---

[455] *Evans v Motor Insurers Bureau* Unreported, 1997, varied [1999] Lloyd's Rep. I.R. 30.
[456] Under the terms of the Arbitration Act 1996.
[457] *Persson v London County Buses* [1974] 1 All E.R. 1251.
[458] *Evans v Secretary of State for the Environment, Transport and the Regions* [2001] Lloyd's Rep. I.R. 1.
[459] Case C-63/01, *Evans v Secretary of State for the Environment, Transport and the Regions* [2004] Lloyd's Rep. I.R. 391.

"awarding interest or paying compensation in the form of aggregate sums which take account of the effluxion of time."

(2) Some payment of the claimants' costs was also required: "compensation awarded for damage or injury caused by an unidentified or insufficiently insured vehicle, paid by the body authorised for that purpose, is not required to include reimbursement of the costs incurred by victims in connection with the processing of their application for compensation except to the extent to which such reimbursement is necessary to safeguard the rights derived by victims from the Second Directive in conformity with the principles of equivalence and effectiveness."

(3) The arbitration procedure for appeals from MIB awards was broadly fair. What was required was that "the procedural arrangements laid down by the national law in question do not render it practically impossible or excessively difficult to exercise the right to compensation conferred on victims of damage or injury caused by unidentified or insufficiently insured vehicles by the Second Directive and thus comply with the principle of effectiveness". This was, however, subject to the consideration that "the procedure established must guarantee that, both in dealings with the MIB and before the arbitrator, victims are made aware of any matter that might be used against them and have an opportunity to submit their comments thereon." In *Evans* itself the victim had asserted that an allegation of fraud had been made against him in the arbitral proceedings and had not been given the opportunity to rebut it. The Court held that whether the procedure had been defective in this regard was for the national court.

(4) The implementation of the Directive by use of the MIB Agreements rather than by a statutory mechanism was valid. The ruling on this point was that "the fact that the source of the obligation of the body in question lies in an agreement concluded between it and a public authority is immaterial, provided that that agreement is interpreted and applied as obliging that body to provide victims with the compensation guaranteed to them by the Second Directive and as enabling victims to address themselves directly to the body responsible for providing such compensation."

Subsequently, a *Francovich* action was brought in England, in *Evans v Secretary of State for the Environment, Transport and the Regions (No.3)*,[460] seeking damages for, most importantly: (a) the wasted costs of appealing against the award; (b) the deduction and the costs order, in that had the procedure been fair neither finding would have been made by the arbitrator; and (c) legal costs and interest incurred in the claim against the MIB the MIB action. H.H. Judge Mackie QC struck out claim (a) on remoteness grounds and claim (b) on the basis that it was hopeless on its merits. Claim (c) was held to be arguable but was struck out as being a waste of time and money given that the maximum sum recoverable—£13,000—had been outweighed by an offer made to the claimant.

In *Moore v Secretary of State for Transport*[461] a series of breaches of the Second Directive were alleged, including a failure to provide interest, costs and a fair procedure for the resolution of disputes. It was held that the limitation

---

[460] *Evans v Secretary of State for the Environment, Transport and the Regions* Unreported, February 16, 2006.

[461] *Moore v Secretary of State for Transport* [2007] Lloyd's Rep. I.R. 469.

period for a *Francovich* action based on non-implementation of the Directives was the date of the accident, as that was the date on which the victim was entitled to receive compensation, so that the claim was time-barred.

Scope of the Untraced Drivers Agreement 2003. The 2003 Agreement, like the **22–074** 1996 Agreement, applies to claims for death or personal injury. The 2003 Agreement goes on to make limited provision for property damage caused by an untraced driver. To counter the fear of deliberate damage by the owner of the vehicle and a fraudulent claim against the MIB, the 2003 Agreement imposes an important restriction on property damage claims: it is necessary for the victim to identify the vehicle that actually caused the damage (cll.4(1), 5(1) and 5(3)). This means that: (a) compensation for death or personal injury is recoverable where the loss was inflicted by an untraced driver whether or not the vehicle can be traced; and (b) compensation for damage to property is recoverable where it is caused by an untraced driver as long as the victim is able to take the number of the vehicle or otherwise identify it. It is uncertain whether this complies with the Consolidated Motor Insurance Directive 2009 art.10(3),[462] which allows Member States to exclude property damage caused by an unidentified vehicle, but removes that derogation where there are "significant personal injuries" as well as property damage in the same accident.

The 2003 Agreement applies where the following conditions are satisfied:

(a) The claim arose from the use of a motor vehicle on a road or public place in Great Britain on or after February 14, 2003 (cl.4(1)(a)–(c)).
(b) The driver of the vehicle or any other person potentially liable—including the employer of the driver—cannot be traced (cl.4(1)(d)).
(c) Had the driver been traced he would on the balance of probabilities have been liable to the victim in tort (cl.4(1)(c)). In appropriate circumstances there may be a presumption of liability.[463] Deliberate running down was excluded from the 1996 Agreement, but there is no corresponding exclusion in the 2003 Agreement other than in cases of terrorism (cl.5(1)(d)).
(d) Where the property damaged is a vehicle the MIB is not liable for that damage if the vehicle was uninsured against liability at the relevant time (cl.5(1)(f)).

Amount of the MIB's liability. The basic measure of the compensation to be paid **22–075** to the victim of an untraced driver under the 2003 Agreement, echoing the 1996 Agreement, is the amount that would have been awarded by a court had the driver been traceable and had an action been brought against him (cl.8(1)). With regard to personal injury the MIB is not liable for loss of earnings unless there is no other source of compensation—state or private insurance—open to the victim (cl.8(2)). As far as property damage is concerned—which is recoverable under the 2003 Agreement for the first time—there is a "specified excess" per applicant presently fixed at £300 and the maximum sum for recoverable is capped at £250,000 for all property damage arising out of one event (cl.8(3)).

The 2003 Agreement for the first time states that interest is payable on claims "in an appropriate case" (cl.9(1)) and interest may be awarded from the date of the accident although the MIB is not required to pay interest for the period of one

---

[462] Re-enacting the Fifth Motor Insurance Directive 2005.
[463] *Elizabeth v MIB* [1981] R.T.R. 405.

month leading up to the MIB's receipt of a police report on the incident (cl.9(2)). Interest is thus discretionary, although it may be thought that it will be awarded in the majority of cases. The 2003 Agreement also for the first time requires the MIB to pay a sum representing the victim's legal costs incurred in the application to the MIB and in any appeals process. The sum payable by way of costs takes effect as a contribution to the costs actually incurred by the victim and is calculated by reference to the amount of the award: if the award does not exceed £15,000 then the MIB must pay 15 per cent of that sum, capped at £3,000; if the award is more the costs are fixed at 2 per cent of the award (Sch.1). The MIB is also liable to make payments for medical treatment under the Health and Social Care (Community Health and Standards) Act 2003, replacing the Road Traffic (NHS Charges) Act 1999.

In all cases the MIB is insurer of the last resort so that if compensation is available under any other insurance policy (other than a life policy), or from an identified person liable for the loss, then the MIB's liability is reduced accordingly (cl.6, which has no counterpart in the 1996 Agreement). The MIB is also entitled to an assignment of the victim's rights against any third party (cl.11(4)).

22–076   *Limits on the MIB's liability.* There are a number of provisions in the 2003 Agreement that restrict the liability of the MIB to a victim. These are unchanged from the 1996 Agreement unless otherwise stated.

First, if two or more persons are responsible to the victim for death or bodily injury, and any one of them can be traced, then the 2003 Agreement empowers the MIB to require the victim to commence proceedings against the identified person or his insurers, in which case the sum actually recovered from the identified person goes to reduce the MIB's liability under the Untraced Drivers Agreement (cll.12–15). The MIB may, however, not impose this obligation and may simply make payment although the award may be reduced by reference to the contribution of the identified person to the loss. As was the case under the 1996 Agreement the MIB cannot be joined to any proceedings by the victim against an identified person.[464]

Secondly, the MIB is not liable if the application arises out of the use of a vehicle owned by or in the possession of the Crown. The 2003 Agreement, unlike the 1996 Agreement, removes this exception in the case of a vehicle stolen from the Crown (cl.5(1)(b)).

Thirdly, a new exception removes the MIB's liability for death, bodily injury or damage to property caused by or in the course of an act of terrorism (cl.5(1)(d)). The 1996 Agreement excluded deliberate running down: the exclusion in the 2003 Agreement is far narrower.

Fourthly, the exclusions in respect of a passenger being carried in a stolen or uninsured vehicle which appeared in the earlier Agreements have been retained by the 2003 Agreement, but in a modified form. Clause 5(1)(c) of the 2003 Agreement states that the MIB is not liable to a person in respect of death, personal injury or property damage where, at the time of the accident carried[465] in the responsible vehicle[466] and before the commencement of his journey in the

---

[464] *White v London Transport Executive* [1971] 2 Lloyd's Rep. 256.

[465] References to a person being carried in a vehicle include references to his being carried in or upon, or entering or getting on to or alighting from the vehicle: cl.5(4)(a).

[466] The "responsible vehicle" means the vehicle the use of which caused (or through the use of which there arose) the death, bodily injury or damage to property which is the subject of the application: cl.5(4)(e).

vehicle (or after such commencement if he could reasonably be expected to have alighted from the vehicle) he knew or ought to have known that the vehicle:

(i) had been stolen or unlawfully taken; or
(ii) was being used without there being in force in relation to its use a contract of insurance or security which complied with the 1988 Act; or
(iii) was being used in the course or furtherance of crime[467]; or
(iv) was being used as a means of escape from or avoidance of lawful apprehension.

Points (3) and (4) are new to the 2003 Agreement. It should be noted that the requisite knowledge of the passenger for the purposes of the 2003 Agreement is expressed in the formulation "knew or ought to have known", replacing the 1996 version "knew or had reason to believe". The change reflects the ruling of the House of Lords in *White v White*[468] that EU law permits only actual knowledge or blind-eye knowledge. The burden of proving knowledge is borne by the MIB and self-induced intoxication is to be disregarded in ascertaining whether the passenger had the appropriate knowledge. However, in the case of the passenger of an uninsured driver, the MIB will satisfy its burden of proof if it can show any of the following (cl.6(3)):

(a) that the applicant was the owner or registered keeper of the vehicle or had caused or permitted its use;
(b) that the applicant knew the vehicle was being used by a person who was below the minimum age at which he could be granted a licence authorising the driving of a vehicle of that class;
(c) that the applicant knew that the person driving the vehicle was disqualified from holding or obtaining a driving licence;
(d) that the applicant knew that the user of the vehicle was neither its owner nor registered keeper nor an employee of the owner or registered keeper nor the owner or registered keeper of any other vehicle.

Claims. Any claim against the MIB under the 2003 Agreement must be made in **22–077** writing and in such form as the MIB may require (cll.4(1)(e) and 11(1)(a)). Separate applications are permissible but not mandatory for personal injury and property damage claims. An application for death or personal injury must be made within the statutory limitation period of three years from the date of the event (cl.1(1)(f), adopting s.11 of the Limitation Act 1980), extendable for a maximum of 15 years where the victim did not know and could not reasonably have been expected to be aware of the injuries (cl.4(3)(b)(i)). A claim for property damage must be brought within nine months from the date of the event, with a maximum extension up to the end of two years from the date of the event if the victim did not know and could not reasonably have become aware of the loss after the date of the event that is the subject of the application (cl.4(3)(b)(ii)).[469] The accident itself must have been reported to the police within

---

[467] Under cl.5(4)(c), "crime" does not include the commission of an offence under the Road Traffic Regulation Act 1984, the Road Traffic Act 1988 and the Road Traffic Offenders Act 1988, other than the offence of using a motor vehicle without insurance contrary to the Road Traffic Act 1988. The mere act of speeding or dangerous driving is not, therefore, enough to preclude recovery by the applicant passenger.

[468] *White v White* [2001] Lloyd's Rep. I.R. 493.

[469] These time limits are less generous than those in the Limitation Act 1980, which gives the victim a three-year limitation period with a fifteen-year long-stop.

14 days under cl.4(3)(c)(i) (death or personal injury) or five days under cl.4(3)(c)(ii) (property damage), in either case with an indefinite extension until notification was reasonably possible. The 2003 Agreement for the first time requires the victim to produce satisfactory evidence of notification of the accident to the police (cl.4(3)(d)). Each of these requirements is a condition precedent to the MIB's liability. Thereafter, the victim is required to co-operate with the MIB in its investigation of the claim (cl.11).

The limitation periods contained in the 2003 Agreement make no provision for the situation dealt with in s.28 of the Limitation Act 1980, whereby time does not run against a minor until he has reached his 18th birthday, so that in a personal injury case the limitation period does not expire until the victim has reached the age of 21. In *Byrne v Motor Insurers Bureau*,[470] decided under the equivalent provisions of the 1996 Agreement, it was held by the Court of Appeal that the principle of equivalence in EU law, which applied to what was then the Second Motor Insurance Directive (now the Consolidated Motor Insurance Directive 2009), required victims of traced and untraced drivers to be treated in the same way, and given that the victim of an identified driver was entitled to the benefit of s.28 of the Limitation Act 1980 it followed that the Untraced Drivers Agreement—which was to be construed according to its terms—failed to comply with the requirements of the Directive. In the light of the principle that the MIB was not an "emanation of the state" so that the Directive was not binding in any proceedings against the MIB, it followed that any remedy that the victim might have would be against the UK government under the *Francovich* principle assuming that the elements of such an action could be made out.

The effect of the *Byrne* decision has been reversed by a Supplementary Agreement entered into between the Government and the Motor Insurers Bureau, dated December 30, 2008. Under the Supplementary Agreement cl.4 has been amended, but only with respect to accidents occurring after midnight on February 1, 2009. Revised cl.4(3)(a) provides that an application for a personal injury claim (whether or not there is property damage as well) must be made within the time limits provided for by the Limitation Act 1980 for tort claims (cl.4(3)(a)(i)), and if the damage is purely to property then the claim must be brought within nine months of the event (cl.4(3)(a)(ii)). Clause 4(3)b) is redundant and is thus omitted. In the event that a claim is referred to an arbitrator, the arbitrator has the power to determine whether time for a personal injury claim should be extended in accordance with the court's statutory discretion under s.33 of the Limitation Act 1980 (new cl.23(1)(f)).

22–078   *Report and award.* Once a valid claim has been received the MIB must undertake at is own cost a preliminary investigation to determine whether it falls within the 2003 Agreement. If jurisdiction is established the MIB must then conduct a full investigation and must as soon as is reasonably practicable make a report (cl.11(1)(b)). In light of the report the MIB must proceed to a decision on liability and quantum (cl.11(2)). The 2003 Agreement for the first time permits the MIB to make an interim report, a power likely to be utilised where the extent of the victim's injuries are not apparent at the outset (cl.11(4)), and this may be followed by an interim award (cl.11(5)).

In every case the MIB must notify its decision and its award to the victim and must give reasons (cl.16)). The MIB must then, where it is bound to do so, to make payment to the victim (cl.17). The 2003 Agreement, unlike the 1996

[470] *Byrne v Motor Insurers Bureau* [2008] Lloyd's Rep. I.R. 705.

Agreement, countenances the making of interim awards, provisional awards (where the victim believes that he may develop a medical condition or that his condition may deteriorate), and payment by instalments in the form of structured settlements.

The 2003 Agreement retains the accelerated settlement procedure originally introduced in 1977 as a modification to the 1972 Agreement. Under this procedure, set out in cll.26 and 27, the MIB may in lieu of an investigation and report make an offer of compensation, interest and costs. This must then be accepted or rejected within six months.

If MIB fail to pay compensation in accordance with the provisions of the Agreement the victim is entitled to enforce payment through the courts (cl.32, a new provision).

Appeals. The victim may appeal to an arbitrator against any decision against the MIB within six weeks of the decision (cll.18 and 19). Once a decision to appeal has been notified to the MIB it must within seven days either apply to the Secretary of State for the appointment of a QC as arbitrator, or undertake a further investigation based upon the additional evidence presented by the victim. If the appeal is limited to quantum the MIB may itself raise the question of liability and quantum before the arbitrator so that if the appeal proceeds the victim may lose his compensation or have it reduced. The 2003 Agreement for the first time requires the arbitrator to reach a preliminary decision that is to be notified to the parties (cl.22(3)). The parties may agree to accept this in which case the matter is at an end. Either party may, however, reject the preliminary decision and make further observations: if the victim does make further observations the MIB may itself consider them. The parties are entitled to request an oral hearing and the arbitrator must grant such a request (cl.22(7)): there was no oral hearing procedure in the 2003 Agreement. Thereafter the arbitrator must issue a final award on the matters referred to him (cl.23). The 2003 Agreement confers upon the arbitrator the power to order the payment of costs and interest.

22–079

4. Compulsory Insurance: The International Dimension

The EU scheme

Legal structure. The Consolidated Motor Insurance Directive 2009, re-enacting the Fourth Motor Insurance Directive 2000, seeks to protect a person injured in a Member State other than that of his residence, by allowing him to recover compensation without having to bring an action against the wrongdoer in the Member State where the accident occurred. An accident is within the Directive if the victim is a resident of an EU Member State; the accident has occurred in a Member State other than that in which the victim was resident; the vehicle is to be insured by an insurer established in a Member State other than that in which the victim was resident; and the vehicle is registered in a Member State other than that in which the victim was resident. If these conditions are satisfied, the victim may recover compensation without first having to obtain judgment against the negligent driver. This means that a UK resident injured elsewhere in the European Union can utilise the terms of the Directive to claim compensation in the United Kingdom and equally an EU resident injured in the United Kingdom

22–080

can seek compensation in the Member State of his residence without having to sue the driver in the relevant part of the United Kingdom.

The essence of the scheme is that the victim may in the first instance approach in the Member State of his residence the claims representative appointed by the insurers. To this end the Consolidated Motor Insurance Directive art.21 requires an insurer authorised anywhere in the EEA to appoint a claims representative for each Member State. The claims representative may be a branch of the insurer and may carry on insurance business, and must have the authority to negotiate and settle motor accident claims, whether or not the insurer sets insurance in that state.[471] If the claims representative and the insurers fail to compensate the victim, he may proceed directly against the Motor Insurers Bureau of the Member State of his residence, and the Motor Insurers Bureau may then seek recourse from the Motor Insurers Bureau the Member State in which the accident occurred.

To assist in the tracing of the insurers of an identifiable vehicle, the Consolidated Motor Insurance Directive 2009 art.23 requires every Member State to establish within its territory an information centre responsible for maintaining a register of all vehicles registered in that state the register is also to contain the names and addresses of the policyholder and the insurer.

22–081 *UK implementation.* The Motor Vehicles (Compulsory Insurance) (Information Centre and Compensation Body) Regulations 2003[472] came into force on January 19, 2003. They implement the requirements of the Consolidated Motor Directive 2009 art.22,[473] by allowing a person resident in the United Kingdom who has been injured in an accident elsewhere in the EEA to obtain indemnification from either the driver's insurers or from the Motor Insurers Bureau,[474] which is designated as the relevant compensation body for the purposes of the Regulations.[475]

The 2003 Regulations are triggered by an accident falling within their ambit. The following conditions must be met[476]:

(1) the victim is a UK resident;
(2) the victim must have sustained loss or injury in a motor accident occurring outside the United Kingdom but within the EEA;
(3) the loss or injury must have been caused by or arise out of the use of a vehicle normally based in an EEA State other than the United Kingdom;
(4) the vehicle must have been insured through an establishment in an EEA State other than in the United Kingdom.

---

[471] This was implemented as regards UK authorised insurers by the Financial Services and Markets Act 2000 (Variation of Threshold Conditions) Order 2002 (SI 2002/2707).

[472] SI 2003/37. This measure was amended by the Motor Vehicles (Compulsory Insurance) (Information Centre and Compensation Body) (Amendment) Regulations 2007 (SI 2007/2982), deleting the superfluous definition of "guarantee fund".

[473] The Regulations also apply to countries outside the EEA which have subscribed to the Green Card scheme.

[474] The insurance information in the database maintained by the Motor Insurers' Information Centre under the 2003 Regulations is also to be made available to the Police Information Technology Organisation in order to allow police officers to ascertain whether particular vehicles are or are not properly insured: see the Disclosure of Vehicle Information Regulations 2005 (SI 2005/2833).

[475] SI 2003/37 reg.10.

[476] SI 2003/37 reg.11.

The victim must in the first instance apply for compensation from the insurer's UK claims representative. The manner in which a claim is to be handled is set out in Ch.8.2 of the Insurance Conduct of Business Rules contained in the Financial Services Authority's Handbook. Once a claim has been received, the claims representative must within three months either make a reasoned offer of settlement if liability has been admitted and damages have been quantified or, if liability is denied or damages have not been quantified, provide a reasoned reply. If the victim's claim for damages is not fully quantified when first presented but liability has not been denied, then a reasoned offer must be made within three months of the date of proof of quantum. If there is a failure by the claims representative to comply with these provisions, then simple interest must be paid on any sums for which the insurer is ultimately liable. If the victim has not received a reasoned reply within three months, or the insurer has not appointed a UK claims representative, the victim may make a claim against the MIB as long as he has not commenced legal proceedings against the insurer. On receiving a claim, the MIB must under reg.12 immediately notify: the insurer of the vehicle or its claims representative; the local MIB in the EEA state in which the insurer's establishment is situated; and the driver (if known). The MIB must respond to a claim within two months, and must provide an indemnity to the claimant once it is satisfied that the user was liable to the claimant and that the amount of loss and damage (including interest) claimed by the claimant is recoverable under the law applying to that part of the United Kingdom in which the claimant was resident at the date of the accident. The MIB's obligations come to an end as soon as the insurer or claims representative has made a reasoned response to the claim, or the claimant has commenced legal proceedings against the insurer. If the MIB does make payment, it is entitled to be indemnified by the compensation body of the Member State in which the accident occurred.

If the vehicle which has caused the victim's loss or injury cannot be identified, reg.13 of the 2003 Regulations allow the victim to proceed directly against the MIB. The conditions which must be satisfied are the following:

(1) the victim is resident in the United Kingdom;
(2) the victim must have sustained loss or injury in a motor accident occurring outside the United Kingdom but within the EEA;
(3) the accident was caused by or arose out of the use of a vehicle normally based in an EEA State;
(4) the victim has made a request for information as to the identity of the insurer but it has proved impossible either to identify the vehicle responsible for the accident or—within two months from the date of the request—to identify the insurers of the vehicle.

In such a case, the victim may make a claim for compensation from the MIB, and reg.13(2)(b) then provides that the MIB "shall compensate the injured party . . . as if it were . . . [the insurer] and the accident had occurred in Great Britain." In *Jacobs v Motor Insurers Bureau*[477] it was held that although this provision seems to state that compensation is to be awarded on the basis of English law, it is not a free-standing rule and is subject to EU rules on tort claims set out in the Rome II Regulation,[478] which provides that damages are to be assessed in accordance with the law applicable to the tort, that law under art.4(1) of the Rome II

---

[477] *Jacobs v Motor Insurers Bureau* [2010] Lloyd's Rep. I.R. 244.
[478] European Parliament and Council Regulation 864/2007/EC on the Law Applicable to Non-Contractual Obligations.

Regulation being the law of the place where the tort occurred. Thus, in *Jacobs* itself, the victim was entitled to recover damages assessed under Spanish law rather than English law in circumstances where the English claimant was injured in Spain by an uninsured driver domiciled in Spain.[479]

Matching the ability of the MIB to seek indemnification from a compensation body in another EEA Member State where it has indemnified a UK resident victim in an accident occurring outside the United Kingdom, the MIB is required to indemnify foreign compensation bodies. Two situations are distinguished by the 2003 Regulations: identified insurers and unidentified insurers.

First, in the case of an identified insurer, under reg.14 of the 2003 Regulations the MIB's obligation to indemnify a foreign compensation body arises if a number of conditions are met:

(1) the victim is resident in an EEA state other than the United Kingdom;
(2) the victim has been compensated by the compensation body of the State of his residence;
(3) the accident was caused by or arose out of an accident in the United Kingdom;
(4) the vehicle involved is insured under a UK insurance policy[480] by an insurer established in the United Kingdom;
(5) the vehicle is normally based in an EEA state other than the state in which the victim resides.

The MIB, having indemnified the foreign compensation body, is—up to the extent of its payment—subrogated to the rights of the victim against the person responsible for the accident.

Secondly, if the insurer is unidentified, reg.15 of the 2003 Regulations states that the MIB's obligation to indemnify the foreign compensation body arises if the following conditions are met:

(1) the victim is resident in an EEA state other than the United Kingdom;
(2) the victim has been compensated by the compensation body of the state of his residence;
(3) the accident took place in the United Kingdom and was caused by or arose out of the use of either an unidentified vehicle, an identified vehicle normally based in a territory outside the EEA;
   or a vehicle normally based in the United Kingdom whose insurers cannot be identified within two months from the date when the request for compensation was lodged with the foreign compensation body.

22–082 *Information centres.* A key aspect of the Consolidated Motor Insurance Directive 2009 is the establishment of national information centres within Member States,[481] so that the insurers of motor vehicles responsible for accidents may be identified. The information centre for the United Kingdom is, under reg.3, the

---

[479] Article 4(3) of the Rome II Regulation permits the court to disapply the law of the place of the tort in favour of the law of a country with which the tort is manifestly more closely connected. The court ruled that the tort was not manifestly more closely connected with England even though the claim was against the MIB, because the claim was based on what had occurred in Spain.

[480] One issued in compliance with the 1988 Act.

[481] Under art.26 of the Directive every Member State is additionally to establish a central office charged with responsibility for collating information on motor accidents so that information can be obtained by insurers more rapidly than is presently the case.

Motor Insurers' Information Centre.[482] Its most important functions relate to "specified information" which is defined by reg.4 as meaning:

"(a) a list of all vehicles normally based in the United Kingdom the names and addresses of their registered keepers and the registration marks assigned to them by the Secretary of State;

(b) the following information in relation to every UK insurance policy under which the use of any such vehicle is insured—

    (i) the number of the policy,

    (ii) the name of the policyholder,

    (iii) the name and address of the insurer,

    (iv) the names and addresses of that insurer's claims representatives, and

    (v) the period during which the use of the vehicle is insured under that contract;

(c) a list of all vehicles which may lawfully be used without insurance in accordance with s.144 of the 1988 Act and the registration marks assigned to them;

(d) the name and address of the person or body designated as responsible for compensating an injured party."

The MMIC has a number of functions. First, it must establish a means of access to the specified information in a manner whereby it can co-ordinate and disseminate that information. That information must be retained for a period of not less than seven years commencing, in respect of items (a), (c) and (d), on the date when the vehicle ceased to be registered under the Vehicle Excise and Registration Act 1994 and, in the case of item (b), from the day immediately following the date of expiry of the policy of insurance to which that information relates.

Secondly, the MMIC must respond to requests for information from: a victim injured or suffering loss from a motor accident occurring in the United Kingdom involving a vehicle normally based in an EEA state; the victim of an accident occurring elsewhere in the EEA involving a vehicle normally based in the United Kingdom; the victim of an accident occurring in an EEA state other than the United Kingdom involving a vehicle normally based in an EEA state where the victim is resident in the United Kingdom. The MMIC's obligation to respond applies where the request is made in writing and not later than seven years after the date of the accident, and the information which must be provided consists of:

(a) the name and address of any insurer who has issued a UK insurance policy or European insurance policy[483] covering the use of that vehicle at the time the accident occurred;

(b) the number of that policy;

(c) the name and address of that insurer's claims representative in the state of residence of the injured party; and

(d) where the MMIC is satisfied that the injured party has a legitimate interest in obtaining that information, the name and address of the registered keeper of the vehicle or, where the territory in which the vehicle is normally based is an EEA State other than the United Kingdom, the person having custody of the vehicle.

---

[482] A limited company, formed in 1998.

[483] A policy issued in an EEA state and meeting the compulsory insurance requirements of the EEA state in which the vehicle is normally based.

A fee of no more than £10.00 may be charged by the MMIC. Insofar as the information requested does not form part of the "specified information" as defined by the Regulations, in particular because it relates to vehicles normally based outside the United Kingdom, the MMIC must obtain that information from its correspondent foreign compensation bodies. In the same way, the MMIC must liaise with foreign compensation bodies in supplying information concerning vehicles normally based in the United Kingdom.

To ensure that the MMIC can itself obtain the specified information, insurers are themselves under a duty to maintain records which must be supplied to the MMIC on request. The records must include[484]:

(a) the number of the policy,
(b) the name of the policyholder,
(c) the registration mark of every vehicle the use of which is covered by the policy, and
(d) the period during which the use of each of those vehicles is (or has been) covered under the policy.

In the case of open covers where vehicles are declared rather than insured separately for 15 days or fewer, the information to be retained by the insurer is much the same, although under reg.6 of the 2003 Regulations[485] the policy holder is also required to maintain the corresponding information.

22–083   **The Green Card Scheme.** In 1968 the United Kingdom adopted the United Nations' Green Card Scheme under which a person insured in one contracting state is to be treated as insured in any other contracting state on production of a Green Card. The scheme was implemented in the United Kingdom by the Motor Vehicles (International Motor Insurance Card) Regulations 1971,[486] under which a Green Card issued to a visitor to the United Kingdom operates as a valid certificate of insurance. Since 1973 border checks on the possession of Green Cards by drivers from other EU Member States have been abolished.[487] The international agreement underlying the 1971 and 1973 Regulations is the Multilateral Guarantee Agreement Between National Insurers Bureaux entered into on May 31, 1996 in Casablanca and applying to accidents occurring on or after July 1, 1997. The member countries are at present: Austria, Albania, Andorra, Belgium, Bulgaria, Bosnia-Herzegovina, Croatia, Cyprus, the Czech Republic, Denmark, Estonia, France, Finland, Germany, Greece, Hungary, Iceland, Iran, Ireland, Israel, Italy, Latvia, Luxembourg, Macedonia, Malta, Morocco, Moldova, the Netherlands, Norway, Poland, Portugal, Romania, Slovakia, Spain, Sweden, Switzerland, Tunisia, Turkey, the United Kingdom and Uruguay.

The Motor Vehicles (Compulsory Insurance) (Information Centre and Compensation Body) Regulations 2003, discussed above, extend to the Green Card Scheme.

---

[484] Reg.5 of, and Pt I of the schedule to, the 2003 Regulations.
[485] Supplemented by Pt II of the schedule to the 2003 Regulations.
[486] SI 1971/792.
[487] Under the First Motor Insurance Directive 1972, implemented in the United Kingdom by the Motor Vehicles (Compulsory Insurance) (No.2) Regulations 1973 (SI 1973/2143). The Fifth Motor Insurance Directive 2005 permitted random and non-discriminatory insurance checks. These measures are now found in the Consolidated Motor Insurance Directive 2009 art.4.

Operation of EU and Green Card Schemes. The relationship between the   **22–084**
European Union[488] and Green Card Schemes is complex. The various situations
in which they may operate may be summarised as follows.

First, a motorist from outside the European Union visiting the United
Kingdom causes an accident in the United Kingdom. The motorist must be
insured for the use of his vehicle in the United Kingdom in accordance with the
requirements of the Road Traffic Act 1988.[489] He may either insure with a UK
insurer or he may seek to have his own insurance cover extended to cover driving
within the United Kingdom: in the latter case, if he is a national of a country that
has signed up to the Green Card Scheme, he may take advantage of that scheme
so that in the event of an accident any claim will be met by the United Kingdom's
Motor Insurers Bureau as agents for the foreign insurers as represented by the
foreign Motor Insurers Bureau.

Secondly, a motorist from within the European Union visiting the United
Kingdom causes an accident in the United Kingdom. The effect of the
Consolidated Motor Insurance Directive 2009 art.3, is that the motorist's local
policy must cover all liabilities incurred anywhere in the EEA so that the Green
Card Scheme is inapplicable. The mechanism is nevertheless much the same as
under the Green Card Scheme: in its place is a the Multilateral Guarantee
Agreement 2003 between European Motor Insurers Bureaux, under which the
United Kingdom's Motor Insurers Bureau is under an obligation to meet the
claim subject to a right of indemnification from the relevant European Motor
Insurers Bureau. However, if the victim is resident in a Member State other than
the United Kingdom, he may in circumstances be able to take advantage of art.22
of the Consolidated Motor Insurance Directive 2009 and to seek indemnification
from the insurers' claims representative or—in the case of default, the Motor
Insurers Bureau—of the Member State in which he is resident.

Thirdly, a UK resident using his vehicle outside the European Union causes an
accident outside the European Union. The motorist will either have to be insured
locally in accordance with the relevant local law or, if the country is a party to
the Green Card Scheme, he may extend his UK insurance so that he can use his
vehicle in that country. In the event of any accident the claim will be met by the
local Motor Insurers Bureau acting as agent for the UK Motor Insurers Bureau
and the motorist's insurers.

Fourthly, a UK resident using his vehicle within the European Union causes an
accident within the European Union. The motorist's policy must by virtue of the
Consolidated Motor Insurance Directive 2009 extend to all liabilities incurred
anywhere in the EEA. If loss is inflicted by the motorist, the claim will—under
the Multilateral Guarantee Agreement 2003—be met by the local Motor Insurers
Bureau and indemnification will be sought from the United Kingdom's Motor
Insurers Bureau or the insurers.

Fifthly, a UK resident is injured in a motor accident outside the European   **22–085**
Union. If the accident occurs in a non-EU State or in a country not party to the
Green Card scheme neither domestic nor EU law has any role to play. The victim
must bring an action in accordance with local law and his ability to recover will
be determined by reference to local insurance requirements. However, if the
accident takes place in a country that has subscribed to the Green Card system
there is in force a Protection of Visitors Agreement between Motor Insurers
Bureaux under which the victim may seek assistance in obtaining the insurance

---

[488] Iceland, Norway and Switzerland have signed reciprocal agreements with the EU and are
subject to EU rules.
[489] This is demanded by the Consolidated Motor Insurance Directive 2009 arts 7 and 8.

and other details of the alleged wrongdoer, although there is no right to seek compensation from any Motor Insurers Bureau in this situation. In the relatively unlikely event that the accident occurs within a Green Card country and is the result of the use of a motor vehicle normally kept in an EEA State other than the United Kingdom, the victim's position is far more favourable as he has the benefit of what was the Fourth Motor Insurance Directive 2000, now the Consolidated Motor Insurance Directive 2009, implemented in the United Kingdom by the Motor Vehicles (Compulsory Insurance) (Information Centre and Compensation Body) Regulations 2003 and may seek compensation in the United Kingdom from the insurers' claims representative or, in the event of default, the United Kingdom's Motor Insurers Bureau.

Sixthly, a UK resident is injured in a motor accident within the European Union. Assuming that the accident was the result of the use of a motor vehicle normally kept in an EU state other than the United Kingdom, elaborate provision has been made by the Consolidated Motor Insurance Directive 2009, previously the Fourth Motor Insurance Directive 2000, as implemented in the United Kingdom by the Motor Vehicles (Compulsory Insurance) (Information Centre and Compensation Body) Regulations 2003, for the protection of a visiting victim, discussed in detail above. Most importantly the victim is not required to bring legal proceedings in the Member State in which his injuries were inflicted. The insurers are required to have a claims representative in every Member State so the victim may in the first instance request compensation from the insurers' claims representative in the victim's own Member State of residence. If compensation is not forthcoming, the Motor Insurers Bureau established in the Member State of the victim's residence is required to make good the loss subject to a right of indemnification from the Motor Insurers Bureau of the Member State in which the injuries were suffered. The right of the victim of a negligent driver domiciled in the European Union to bring a direct action against the driver's insurers, under art.18 of the Consolidated Motor Insurance Directive 2009, as anticipated in the United Kingdom by the European Communities (Rights against Insurers) Regulations 2002, is not itself subject to any jurisdiction rules of its own. The mechanisms set out in the Directive operate on the assumption that a victim injured outside his own Member State will pursue the MIB. However, the decision of the European Court of Justice in *FBTO Shadverzekerigen NV v Odenbreit*[490] gives the victim another option. Under art.9(1)(b) of Council Regulation 44/2001, the assured is entitled to sue his insurers in the place of his own domicile, and art.11(2) of the Regulation states that art.9(1)(b) also applies to an action brought by the injured party directly against a liability insurer, where such direct actions are permitted (which is necessarily the case in the motor context throughout the European Union by virtue of the Consolidated Motor Insurance Directive). This was construed by the ECJ as meaning that the victim can bring an action against the insurers in the courts of the victim's own domicile. In the context of motor insurance this will mean that if the victim is injured elsewhere in the European Union by a driver domiciled in the European Union then although he may only sue the driver in the place of the driver's domicile (and join the insurers to the action under art.11(1) if the law of that jurisdiction so permits), he may in the alternative sue the insurers directly in the courts of his own domicile: that was indeed the very situation in *Odenbreit*, where a German national injured in The Netherlands by a local driver insured with local insurers was held to be entitled to bring a direct action against those

---

[490] Case C-463/06, *FBTO Shadverzekerigen NV v Odenbreit* [2008] Lloyd's Rep. I.R. 354,

insurers in Germany. The point has been confirmed in England in *Maher v Groupama Grand EST*,[491] where English claimants were injured in France by a French driver who was insured by French insurers. The Court of Appeal held, applying *FBTO*, that the claimants were entitled to sue the insurers in England under art.11(2). The action was classified as one in tort, as it was derived from the claimants' action against the driver, although it was noted that any issues as to coverage or as to the policy itself would arise in contract as the claimants would in essence be standing in the shoes of the assured in seeking to establish liability under the policy. As noted above, the English court has no jurisdiction to hear a claim against the driver himself where the driver is not domiciled in England and the accident took place outside England, although in *Maher* Moore-Bick L.J. was of the view that it might be possible to join the driver to the direct action brought against the insurers.[492]

Finally, an EU resident is injured in a motor accident within the United Kingdom. This is the mirror image of the sixth situation, above and the same principles are applicable. The victim need not proceed in the United Kingdom, but may in the first instance seek indemnification from the insurers' claims representative in his home Member State. If the claim is not satisfied he may turn to his local Motor Insurers Bureau to make good the default. Alternatively he may take advantage of the direct action conferred by English law in respect of EEA nationals injured in a motor accident in the United Kingdom. The Insurance Conduct of Business Sourcebook, 8.2, requires any UK authorised motor insurer to have a claims representative in every EEA member state, authorised for handling and settling claims in accordance with the requirements of the Consolidated Motor Insurance Directive 2009.

5. NON-COMPULSORY COVER UNDER MOTOR POLICIES

First party cover. In addition to providing indemnity against liability, motor policies may protect the assured against first-party injury, whether to the driver or to the vehicle itself. Such cover may be minimal, and confined to fire and theft, or it may be "fully comprehensive" and extending to all first-party losses. Fully comprehensive policies may contain clauses restricting cover to specified circumstances, such as where a lorry is used to carry coal: such restrictions should be distinguished from conditions precedent to liability, such as that a lorry should be used for no other purpose.[493] If the vehicle is used in circumstances that the policy does not cover, the policy remains effective under circumstances covered by it, although the insurer will not be liable for any loss occurring while the condition was not complied with by the assured. By contrast, if the condition is not a condition precedent, the insurer may be able to treat the policy as terminated in the unlikely event that the assured's breach can be construed as repudiatory, but in the overwhelming majority of cases the assured's breach will be minor and the insurer will continue to face liability.

A few examples of how the more common extensions of cover and restrictions to cover have been construed by the courts are considered in the following

22–086

---

[491] *Maher v Groupama Grand EST* [2010] R.T.R. 10, and see also *Knight v Axa Assurance* [2009] Lloyd's Rep. I.R. 667.

[492] Under art.11(3) of the Brussels Regulation, which permits joinder of the tortfeasor if the law applicable to the direct action so permits.

[493] *Provincial Insurance v Morgan* [1933] A.C. 240. Contrast *Dawsons v Bonnin* [1922] 2 A.C. 413. See also *Farr v Motor Mutual* [1920] 3 K.B. 669: *Roberts v Anglo-Saxon Insurance* (1927) 137 L.T. 243.

paragraphs. It should be remembered that conditions restricting cover are binding as between the insurers and the assured in relation to first-party cover, although s.148(2) of the Road Traffic Act 1988 prohibits the use of certain conditions by way of defence where the claim by the assured is in respect of his liability to a third party, namely: (a) the age or physical or mental condition of persons driving the vehicle; (b) the condition of the vehicle; (c) the number of persons that the vehicle carries; (d) the weight or physical characteristics of the goods that the vehicle carries; (e) the times at which or the areas in which the vehicle is used; (f) the horsepower or cylinder capacity or value of the vehicle; (g) the carrying on the vehicle of any particular apparatus; and (h) the carrying on the vehicle of any particular means of identification other than any means of identification required to be carried by or under the Vehicles Excise and Registration Act 1994.

It may be that in respect of third-party claims all conditions are outlawed as a result of EU law, although the view accepted by the English courts is that s.148 is unaffected and that provisions not caught by its express terms may be relied upon even in respect of third-party claims[494] although policy terms of this type are to be construed as narrowly as rules of interpretation permit.[495]

22–087   **Utmost good faith.** Material facts which have to be disclosed or not misstated on formation include as the age of the vehicle,[496] where it is to be kept[497] and its condition.[498] The identity of the driver is particularly important, as this will point to the degree of risk faced by the insurer. Relevant matters will include: the driver's occupation,[499] age and experience,[500] driving record,[501] previous losses and claims[502] and previous refusals to insure either at all or other than on special terms.[503]

Users of the vehicle

22–088   *Named and permitted users.* A policy will cover the named assured only, in which case any other person driving the vehicle will not be covered.[504] It may

---

[494] *Charlton v Fisher* [2001] Lloyd's Rep. I.R. 387.

[495] *Keeley v Pashen* [2005] Lloyd's Rep. I.R. 289.

[496] *Santer v Poland* (1924) 19 Ll. L.R. Rep. 29.

[497] *Dawsons v Bonnin* [1922] 2 A.C. 413.

[498] *Bramhill v Edwards* [2004] EWCA Civ 403: the Court of Appeal, seemingly with some reluctance, refused to overturn the trial judge's acceptance of expert evidence that the fact that the vehicle could not, by virtue of its width, be lawfully used on a road in the UK was not material.

[499] *Holmes v Cornhill Insurance* (1949) 82 Ll. L.R. 575; *McNealy v Pennine Insurance Co Ltd* [1978] 2 Lloyd's Rep. 18; *Hazel v Whitlam* [2005] Lloyd's Rep. I.R. 168.

[500] *Corcos v De Rougemont* (1925) 23 Ll. L.R. 164; *Bond v Commercial Union Assurance Co Ltd* (1930) 36 Ll. L.R. 107; *Zurich General Accident and Liability Insurance Co Ltd v Morrison* (1942) 72 Ll. L.R. 167; *Broad v Waland* (1942) 73 Ll. L.R. 263.

[501] *Jester-Barnes v Licences and General Insurance* (1934) 49 Ll. L.R. 231; *Cleland v London General insurance Co Ltd* (1935) 51 Ll. L.R. 156; *Mackay v London General Insurance Co Ltd* (1935) 51 Ll. L.R. 201; *Taylor v Eagle Star Insurance Co* (1940) 67 Ll. L.R. 136.

[502] *Dent v Blackmore* (1927) 29 Ll. L.R. 9; *Mundy's Trustee v Blackmore* (1928) 32 Ll. L.R. 150; *Farra v Hetherington* (1931) 40 Ll. L.R. 132.

[503] *Dent v Blackmore* (1927) 29 Ll. L.R. 9; *Holts Motors v South East Lancashire Insurance* (1930) 37 Ll. L.R. 1; *Norman v Gresham Fire* (1935) 22 Ll. L.R. 292; *Locker & Woolf Ltd v Western Australian Insurance Co* (1936) 54 Ll. L.R. 211. Contrast *Mackay v London General Insurance Co Ltd* (1935) 51 Ll. L.R. 201, where a higher excess charged to a minor was held to be immaterial thereafter.

[504] *Herbert v Railway Passengers Assurance Co* (1938) 60 Ll. L.R. 143; *Lester Brothers v Avon Insurance Co Ltd* 72 Ll. L.R. 109. If the assured is a company, then persons driving on its behalf will be covered: *Briggs v Gibson's Bakery* [1948] N.I. 165. Contrast: *Biddle v Johnston* [1965] 2 Lloyd's Rep. 121.

also extend to other named persons, such as members of the assured's family,[505] or to any person driving the vehicle with the consent of the assured. The numerous authorities on the meaning of "consent" show that: consent must be express, so that leaving a vehicle in the possession of a third party does not amount to consent to drive it[506]; consent given by an agent of the assured will suffice[507]; consent given to a specific person to drive the vehicle does not extend to a third party[508]; consent given for limited purposes is to be regarded as confined to those purposes[509]; the death of the assured does not automatically withdraw consent given to a third party to drive the vehicle[510]; an assured selling a vehicle to a third party does not consent to the third party's driving of the vehicle for the purposes of the seller's policy[511]; and once the assured has sold his vehicle he cannot give consent to a third party to drive it.[512] The hiring of the vehicle is normally governed by express policy terms,[513] although hiring is generally excluded by domestic policies.

A policy taken out by an employer will normally extend coverage to any employee driving the vehicle in the course of his employment. The concept of "course of employment" is a wide one, and will encompass the situation in which the employee is disobeying his employers' instructions as long as he is furthering the employers' business[514] rather than off on a frolic of his own. There may be restrictions on the categories of employees permitted to drive, e.g. unlicensed or inexperienced employees may be excluded.[515] An employee for these purposes is a person acting under a contract of employment,[516] although wider terminology can give rise to extended cover, e.g. any person "in his employ" will encompass the assured's agent.[517] The phrase "or his paid driver" has been held to include a driver in the pay of a third party but borrowed by the assured.[518]

Where a third party is given the right to drive the vehicle by the policy, that person has, in respect of a claim by a third party against him only, the right under s.148(7) of the Road Traffic Act 1988 to enforce the policy against the insurers despite the absence of any contract between them.[519] It is also to be borne in mind that liability incurred to a third party by a person not permitted by the

---

[505] GFP Units v Monksfield [1972] 2 Lloyd's Rep. 79 (spouse).

[506] Greenleaf v Monksfield [1972] R.T.R. 451. Contrast Tattersall v Drysdale [1935] 2 K.B. 174, where consent was regarded as implicit.

[507] Pailor v Co-Operative Insurance Society (1930) 38 Ll. L.R. 237.

[508] Paget v Poland (1947) 80 Ll. L.R. 283.

[509] Browning v Phoenix Assurance Co Ltd [1960] 2 Lloyd's Rep. 360; Singh v Rathour [1988] 1 W.L.R. 422.

[510] Kelly v Cornhill Insurance Co Ltd [1964] 1 All E.R. 321.

[511] Peters v General Accident Fire & Life Assurance Corporation (1942) 73 Ll. L.R. 175.

[512] Guardian Assurance Co Ltd v Sutherland (1939) 63 Ll. L.R. 220.

[513] Bonney v Cornhill Insurance Co Ltd 40 Ll. L.R. 39; Allen v Johns [1955] 1 Lloyd's Rep. 27.

[514] Marsh v Moores [1949] 2 All E.R. 27.

[515] Robertson v London Guarantee [1915] 1 S.L.T. 195; John T Ellis Ltd v Hinds [1947] K.B. 475; Lester Brothers v Avon Insurance Co Ltd 72 Ll. L.R. 109.

[516] Lyons v May [1948] 2 All E.R. 1062.

[517] Burton v Road Transport & General Insurance Co (1939) 63 Ll. L.R. 253; Ballance v Brown [1955] Crim LR 384.

[518] Bryan v Forrow [1950] 1 All E.R. 294.

[519] 1988 Act s.148(7), which purported to codify the common law position reached in Williams v Baltic Insurance Association of London Ltd [1924] 2 K.B. 282 and to overcome the problems of privity subsequently raised by the Privy Council in Vandepitte v Preferred Accident Insurance Co of New York [1933] A.C. 70. See Tattersall v Drysdale [1935] 2 K.B. 174; Austin v Zurich General Accident & Liability Insurance Co [1945] K.B. 250.

policy to drive the vehicle is to be covered by the insurers under s.151(2), subject to a right of recourse against the driver and also against the assured if he caused or permitted such use. It is at least arguable that an extension clause, at least one in favour of an identifiable third party, is enforceable by him against the insurers under the Contracts (Rights against Third Parties) Act 1999 even in respect of non-compulsory cover.

22–089   *Competence of driver.* Policy terms may restrict the use of the vehicle to drivers of between a minimum and maximum age,[520] to drivers not under the influence of any intoxicating substance,[521] to drivers who are in possession of a valid driving licence[522] (provisional licences count as valid for this purpose[523] unless there is express wording to the contrary in which case a provisional licence holder is covered only if he is supervised by an experienced driver[524]), to drivers who have not been disqualified,[525] and to drivers with clean licences.[526] The exclusion may be less restrictive and may be confined to the situation in which the assured has given permission to drive the vehicle to a third party known by the assured to be unlicensed or disqualified.[527]

22–090   *First party personal injury* Liability imposed upon the assured for injury to passengers in a vehicle must be covered by a motor policy. However, there is no obligation upon the driver to insure in respect of injuries which may be suffered by him or in respect of injuries to passengers caused without the fault of the driver. Such extensions are available, and where such an extension is obtained then in practice policies pay fixed amounts for specific forms of injury.[528] There must be a causal link between the injury and the use of the vehicle; a motor policy will cover an assured who is injured in a road accident and who suffers further injury in the aftermath of the accident, but it will not extend to an accident which is the result of a pre-existing medical complaint[529] or to injuries which are the result of a pre-existing medical condition.[530] The driver himself will be excluded from coverage if his injuries are the desired or inevitable result of his own deliberate or reckless conduct[531] or if criminality is involved and there is an express exclusion to that effect.[532]

---

[520] *Lloyds Bank Ltd v Eagle Star Insurance Co Ltd* [1951] 1 Lloyds Rep. 385; *Sweeney v Kennedy* (1948) 82 Ll. L.R. 294; *Kirkbride v Donner* [1974] 1 Lloyd's Rep. 549.

[521] *Mair v Railway Passengers Association* (1877) 37 L.T. 356; *Louden v British Merchants Insurance Co Ltd* [1961] 1 Lloyd's Rep. 154; *Kennedy v Smith* 1976 S.L.T. 10.

[522] *Lester Bros (Coal Merchants) v Avon Insurance Co Ltd* (1942) 72 Ll. L.R. 109; *Kinsey v Herts County Council* [1972] R.T.R. 498.

[523] *Rendlesham v Dunne* [1964] 1 Lloyd's Rep. 192.

[524] *Langman v Valentine* [1952] 2 All E.R. 803; *Tyler v Whatmore* [1976] R.T.R. 83.

[525] *Mumford v Hardy* [1956] 1 W.L.R. 163; *Edwards v Griffiths* [1953] 1 W.L.R. 1199.

[526] *Spraggon v Dominion Insurance Co* (1941) 69 Ll. L.R. 1; *Haworth v Dawson* (1946) 80 Ll. L.R. 19. Contrast *Evans v Walkden* [1956] 3 All E.R. 64 where there was no supervision.

[527] *John T Ellis Ltd v Hinds* [1947] K.B. 475.

[528] *Lloyd's Bank Ltd v Eagle Star Insurance Co Ltd* [1951] 1 Lloyd's Rep. 385.

[529] But see *Winspear v Accident Insurance Co* (1880) 6 QBD 42; *Lawrence v Accidental Insurance Co* (1881) 7 QBD 216.

[530] *Re Scarr and General Accident Assurance Corporation* [1905] 1 K.B. 307; *Fidelity and Casualty Co of New York v Mitchell* [1917] A.C. 592; *Jason v Batten (1930) Ltd* [1969] 1 Lloyd's Rep. 281. Contrast *Blackburn Rovers Football and Athletic Club Plc v Avon Insurance Plc* [2005] Lloyd's Rep. I.R. 447.

[531] *Morley v United Friendly Insurance Plc* [1993] 1 Lloyd's Rep. 490.

[532] *Marcel Beller Ltd v Hayden* [1978] 1 Lloyd's Rep. 472.

Vehicles covered by the policy. The vehicle covered by the insurance will be   **22–091**
identified by the certificate of insurance, although in the case of fleet covers the
certificate may refer more generically to vehicles from time to time owned[533] by
the assured. In respect of first-party losses, the cover relates to all constituent
parts of the vehicle[534] even if they are unattached at the time: the test is whether
the item in question is clearly a part of the vehicle (e.g. the engine)[535] or whether
it is a mere accessory: in the latter situation, specific cover is required.[536] Typical
exclusions from motor policies include: wear and tear, depreciation, worn tyres
and damage to tyres, mechanical and electrical breakdown and war risks.

It is common for the policy to extend coverage to the assured while driving
other vehicles with the consent of the owner.[537] The classes of vehicle may be
defined narrowly, e.g. "any farm implement or machine"[538] or any vehicle whose
use is logged in a register prior to the journey,[539] but in the absence of any such
limitation cover will extend to any vehicle within the definition in the Act[540]
although presumably not one for which a special licence is required.

The condition of the vehicle

Roadworthiness. In *Barrett v London General*,[541] Goddard J. held that a   **22–092**
provision restricting the cover to accidents while the car is in a safe and
roadworthy condition means roadworthy at the commencement of its journey, not
at the time of the accident, on the analogy of the implied warranty of
seaworthiness in marine policies.[542] This reasoning was, however, disapproved
by the Privy Council in *Trickett v Queensland Insurance*,[543] on the ground that
such an analogy is unsound. The principle that may be deduced from these two
cases is that where the unroadworthiness, e.g. the failure of a footbrake, occurs
only at the moment of the accident, the policy is effective, but that it is not so
where the unroadworthiness, e.g. failure of lights, occurs some time before the
accident. Knowledge by the assured of the unroadworthiness is irrelevant. In
some factual situations, however, the law of seaworthiness is of assistance in
determining whether or not a vehicle is roadworthy. Thus in *Clarke v National
Insurance*,[544] the Court of Appeal held that a car overloaded with passengers was
"unroadworthy" by analogy to the rule that overloading or bad stowage can
render a ship unseaworthy, although the court rejected the *Barrett* approach that
unroadworthiness had to be assessed at the outset. Faulty loading, or defects in
a tow rope, do not render a vehicle unroadworthy.[545]

---

[533] Including vehicles to be purchased on conditional sale or hire-purchase: *De Maurier (Jewels)
v Bastion Insurance Co* [1967] 2 Lloyd's Rep. 550.
[534] *Brown v Zurich General Accident and Liability Insurance Co Ltd* [1954] 2 Lloyd's Rep.
243.
[535] *Seaton v London General Insurance Co* (1932) 43 Ll. L.R. 398.
[536] *Rowan v Universal Insurance Co Ltd* (1939) 64 Ll. L.R. 288.
[537] *Police v Bishop* [1956] Crim. L.R. 569; *Bullock v Bellamy* (1941) 67 Ll. L.R. 392.
[538] *JRM Plant v Hodgson* [1960] 1 Lloyd's Rep. 538 (cement mixer excluded).
[539] *Laycock v Road Transport and General Insurance Co Ltd* (1940) 67 Ll. L.R. 250.
[540] *Laurence v Davis* [1972] 2 Lloyd's Rep. 231.
[541] *Barrett v London General* [1935] 1 K.B. 238.
[542] MIA 1906 s 39.
[543] *Trickett v Queensland Insurance* [1936] A.C. 159.
[544] *Clarke v National Insurance* [1964] 1 Q.B. 199.
[545] *Salmon Contractors Ltd v Monksfield* [1970] 1 Lloyd's Rep. 387; *Jenkins v Deane* [1933] 3 All
E.R. 699.

22–093 *"In efficient condition".* A condition that the assured should maintain the vehicle in "an efficient condition"[546] or other such words requires the assured to exercise reasonable care to eliminate obvious or easily discoverable defects. The phrase is generally regarded as interchangeable with roadworthiness.[547] Thus in *Conn v Westminster Motor Insurance Association*[548] it was held, in the context of the policy, that the insurers were not liable for an accident where the vehicle's tyres were visibly inefficient. "In efficient condition", it was held, meant "in roadworthy condition." On the other hand, the fact that the brakes were defective was held not to be a breach of condition, since their state could only be discerned by dismantling them. In *Liverpool Corp v Roberts*[549] the policy provided that the assured "shall take due and reasonable precautions to safeguard the property insured, and to keep it in a good state of repair". It was held that these words merely imposed a personal obligation on the assured to take due and reasonable precautions: if only a casual negligence or failure on the part of an employee to carry out his duty had been proved against the assured, there would have been no breach of this provision. In *New India Assurance v Yeo Beng Chow*[550] a comprehensive policy contained a condition that the assured should "take all reasonable steps to safeguard the motor vehicle from loss or damage and to maintain it" in "efficient condition". Section I of the policy form provided cover against loss or damage, and Section II against "Liability to Third Parties". Section I was deleted, and the question was whether the condition to maintain remained as affecting Section II. The Judicial Committee of the Privy Council held that although these parts of the condition which related to loss or damage might have been inserted in the policy bearing in mind that it was drafted to provide comprehensive cover, it did not follow that it was to be implied from the deletion of Section I that the condition was altered the condition could and did survive the deletion, in their Lordships' opinion.

In *Amey Properties v Cornhill Insurance*[551] the assured was required to maintain the vehicle in an "efficient and roadworthy condition". It was held that this wording was intended to exclude the insurer's liability where the assured had been negligent, as in the present case, where the vehicle had a defective clutch and handbrake. It follows from this case that the general rule applicable to reasonable care clauses—that the insurer must demonstrate recklessness—does not apply to this type of clause in a motor policy.

Protecting the vehicle

22–094 *Precautions against theft.* It is common, particularly in the case of cars regularly visiting the metropolis, for insurers to require an alarm system or special locks to be fitted to the relevant vehicle. In the case of a jeweller's all risk insurance against loss of jewellery it was held that: (i) "fitted with locks and alarm systems

---

[546] See *Brown v Zurich* [1954] 2 Lloyd's Rep. 243.

[547] *Brown v Zurich General Accident and Liability Insurance Co Ltd* [1954] 2 Lloyd's Rep. 243; *Conn v Westminster Motor Insurance Association* [1966] 1 Lloyd's Rep. 407; *Jones v Provincial Insurance* (1929) 35 Ll. L.R. 135.

[548] *Conn* [1966] 1 Lloyd's Rep. 407. See also: *Crossley v Road Transport and General Insurance Co* (1925) 27 Ll. L.R. 219; *Jones v Provincial Insurance* (1929) 35 Ll. L.R. 135; *Brown v Zurich* [1954] 2 Lloyd's Rep. 243; *McInnes v National Motor and Accident Insurance Union* [1963] 2 Lloyd's Rep. 415; *Lefevre v White* [1990] 1 Lloyd's Rep. 569.

[549] *Liverpool Corp v Roberts* [1965] 2 Lloyd's Rep. 219.

[550] *New India Assurance v Yeo Beng Chow* [1972] 1 W.L.R. 786.

[551] *Amey Properties v Cornhill Insurance* [1996] L.R.L.R. 259. See also: *Roberts v State Insurance General Manager* [1974] 2 N.Z.L.R. 312; *Lee On Realty v Kwok Lai Cheong* [1985] 2 H.K.C. 592.

approved by underwriters and in operation" meant "approved" not by the insurers, but by underwriters generally; (ii) "locks" meant, in the context, locks of a greater security value than those supplied by car manufacturers; and (iii) the alarm system was "in operation" notwithstanding that two switches were faulty.[552]

Motor policies often contain "reasonable care" clauses which require the assured to take reasonable care or steps to avoid loss or damage to the vehicle. It is established that such clauses mean no more than that the assured must avoid reckless behaviour in relation to his car.[553] Goods in transit policies generally contain terms requiring the assured not to leave the vehicle unattended. It is also common to find an exclusion in motor policies to the effect that the assured cannot recover if, at the time of the loss, the assured had "left" the keys in or on the vehicle. The meaning of this form of wording was considered in *Hayward v Norwich Union Ltd*.[554] Here, the assured's Porsche was stolen from a service station while the keys were in the ignition and the assured was paying for his petrol. The assured had believed that the car was safe, as it was fitted with an immobiliser and alarm. However, the thief had employed an electronic device which overrode the immobiliser, and the assured was unable to prevent him from driving the car away. The Court of Appeal, reversing the trial judge,[555] held that the keys had been left in the car, and that the test was whether the driver had (deliberately or otherwise) allowed the keys to remain in the car and had moved away from the car. The Court of Appeal did not regard the exclusion as unduly wide, as in its view it would not have excluded liability in the event of a hijacking, as in such a case it could not be said that the assured would have voluntarily "left" the keys in the car.

Precautions against loss or damage to vehicle. A general obligation to safeguard **22–095** the vehicle against loss or damage is concerned with the manner in which the vehicle is parked or secured.[556] Unless clearly worded, this type of clause does not apply to the manner in which the vehicle is being driven and in particular the qualifications of persons permitted to drive.[557]

Uses to which the vehicle is put

Social, domestic and pleasure purposes. This phrase has been used since the **22–096** earliest days of motor insurance and remains an important limitation on the coverage provided by a policy. The phrase is not prohibited by s.148 of the 1988 Act, and accordingly will be effective both as regards first-party losses and against third-party liability claims. It is rare for the phrase "social, domestic and pleasure" to be used in isolation, and it is standard practice for cover to be extended to use of the vehicle in respect of travel to and from the assured's place of employment or business,[558] and also in respect of the assured's business.

[552] *De Maurier (Jewels) v Bastion Insurance Co* [1967] 2 Lloyd's Rep. 550.

[553] *Sofi v Prudential Assurance* [1993] 2 Lloyd's Rep. 559; *Devco Holder v Legal and General Insurance Society* [1993] 2 Lloyd's Rep. 567; *Glenmuir Ltd v Norwich Union Fire Insurance Society Ltd* 1995; *Hayward v Norwich Union Ltd* [2001] Lloyd's Rep. I.R. 410.

[554] *Hayward v Norwich Union Ltd* [2001] Lloyd's Rep. I.R. 410, reversing [2000] Lloyd's Rep. I.R. 382.

[555] Whose view had been that the keys could not be said to be "left" in the car unless the car itself had been left unattended.

[556] See *Martin v Stanborough* (1924) 41 T.L.R. 1 (vehicle parked on slope supported only by a block of wood).

[557] *Rendlesham v Dunne* [1964] 1 Lloyd's Rep. 192.

[558] *Orr v Trafalgar Insurance* (1948) 82 Ll. L.R. 1.

Where cover is restricted to social, domestic and pleasure use only, loss arising from any form of business use will not be insured. Insured purposes will include the use of the vehicle for carrying tools or timber for use in a garden[559] or furniture for a third party but without charge,[560] but not for carrying cattle feed[561] or passengers.[562] The distinction between social and business purposes is not always clear: it has been held that a local authority has both social and business roles, so that the use of a car to collect a visiting dignitary on a social visit is covered by the social, domestic and pleasure formulation.[563]

If the assured's business is covered as well, then the use of the vehicle for any other person's business will not be insured, as where the vehicle is used for business purposes by the assured's brother[564] or friend[565] even if those persons are permitted to drive the vehicle for other purposes. Again, if the assured forms a company for business purposes, the doctrine of corporate personality will prevent the policy from applying for the use of the vehicle on the company's business.[566]

The assured's business use may be limited to a particular trade or profession, e.g. "agricultural or forestry purposes".[567] Alternatively, business use may be covered but there may be specific exclusions for use in the course of a particular trade or profession, given that some are known to be higher risk than others.[568] One common exclusion is in respect of use of a vehicle in the motor trade.[569] Quare whether use for agricultural purposes includes taking a show pony to a show.[570]

22–097   *Hire or reward.* Use of the vehicle by the assured for the purpose of "hire or reward" is also generally[571] excluded from cover. At one time this phrase was of particular significance in relation to passengers, as insurance of passengers was, in successive pieces of legislation after 1930, required only "in respect of a vehicle in which passengers were being carried for hire or reward". The apparent intention was to ensure that passengers in public service vehicles were protected by liability insurance in their favour. The position has been since 1972 that all passengers, whether or not carried for hire or reward, are required to be covered by the driver's insurance. The statutory phrase did not require consideration of whether passengers were being carried for hire or reward, but rather whether the vehicle was one in which passengers were being carried for hire or reward. The question was, therefore, whether the vehicle was one whose habitual or normal

---

[559] *Piddington v Co-operative Insurance Society Ltd* [1934] 2 K.B. 236.

[560] *Lee v Poole* [1954] Crim. L.R. 942.

[561] *Whitehead v Unwins (York) Ltd* [1962] Crim. L.R. 323.

[562] *Keeley v Pashen* [2005] Lloyd's Rep. I.R. 289.

[563] *Moody (Chemists) v Iron Trades Mutual Insurance Co* [1971] R.T.R. 120; *Willesden Corp v Municipal Mutual Insurance* (1945) 172 L.T. 245.

[564] *Jones v Welsh Insurance Co Ltd* (1939) 57 Ll. L.R. 13.

[565] *Pailor v Co-Operative Insurance Society* (1930) 38 Ll. L.R. 237.

[566] *Levinger v Licences and General Insurance Co Ltd* (1936) 54 Ll. L.R. 68.

[567] *Agnew v Robertson* 1956 S.L.T. 90. See also *Stone v Licenses and General Insurance Co Ltd* (1942) 71 Ll. L.R. 256.

[568] See the cases on non-disclosure discussed in Ch.6, above, which make it clear that failure by the assured to state correctly or to disclose his trade or profession may be a material fact.

[569] *Gray v Blackmore* [1934] 1 K.B. 95 (towing another vehicle); *Browning v Phoenix Assurance Co Ltd* [1960] 2 Lloyd's Rep. 360 (test drive of vehicle by garage following servicing). Contrast *Samuelson v National Insurance and Guarantee Corp* [1985] 2 Lloyd's Rep. 541 (use of vehicle by repairer to collect spare parts in order to effect repairs covered as a result of express insuring provisions for vehicle under repair).

[570] *Henderson v Robson* (1949) 113 J.P. 313.

[571] But not always: *Kaufmann v British Surety Insurance Co Ltd* (1929) 33 Ll. L.R. 315.

use was for the carriage of passengers for hire or reward. The scope of the phrase was considered on a number of occasions by the courts, culminating in the decision of the House of Lords in *Albert v Motor Insurers Bureau*,[572] a case in which a worker gave regular lifts to his workmates in return for payment. This was held not to be the use of a vehicle for carriage for hire or reward. Their Lordships held by a 4:1 majority that there could be hire or reward in the absence of a legally binding contract[573] as long as payment was made[574] and, by a 3:2 majority that the test was "has there been a systematic carrying of passengers for reward which goes beyond the bonds of mere social kindness"[575] so that an isolated instance of carriage for hire or reward did not meet the statutory test.[576]

These cases aside, there are some authorities on the meaning of "hire or reward" outside the statutory context. The phrase means carriage under a business relationship under which payment is to be made either under an express agreement[577] or by necessary implication from the circumstances.[578] If the vehicle is not being used in the course of a business relationship, it cannot be said that it is being used for hire or reward.[579]

Use of vehicle for concurrent purposes. If a vehicle is used for two purposes, one **22–098** of which is insured and the other is excluded, the general principle is that the exclusion takes priority and the assured has no cover. For this situation to occur, the two purposes must be of equal weight: if the insured purposes is the primary or predominant purpose, the assured is entitled to coverage. In *Wood v General Accident*[580] the cover only extended to the user of a motor car for social, domestic and pleasure purposes. It was held that a Daimler car was not being so used was being driven in it with the object of making a business contract at the end of his journey, although it was a pleasurable way of making the journey. The leading authority on concurrent purposes is *Seddons v Binions*,[581] in which the assured loaned his car to his father for business purposes. The assured's father was in need of emergency dental treatment during the course of the day, and when the accident occurred the vehicle was being driven by the assured's father to a dentist, his intention being to return to work thereafter. The Court of Appeal

---

[572] *Albert v Motor Insurers Bureau* [1971] 2 Lloyd's Rep. 229.

[573] Upholding on this point the majority view in *Bonham v Zurich General Accident and Liability Insurance Co Ltd* [1945] 2 K.B. 292 and the decision in *Connell v Motor Insurers Bureau* [1969] 2 Lloyd's Rep. 1 and rejecting the contrary holding in *Coward v Motor Insurers Bureau* [1963] 1 Q.B. 259.

[574] See *McGoona v Motor Insurers Bureau* [1969] 2 Lloyd's Rep. 34, where payment was made by a third party, the employer, to an employee who gave lifts to his fellow employees. Cf. *Motor Insurers Bureau v Meanen* [1971] 2 Lloyd's Rep. 251, where there was no payment at all.

[575] The "business" test adopted by Lord Donavan. Cf. *Wyatt v Guildhall Insurance Co Ltd* [1937] 1 K.B. 653.

[576] Thereby undermining *East Midland Area Traffic Commissioners v Tyler* [1938] 3 All E.R. 39.

[577] *Wyatt v Guildhall Insurance Co Ltd* [1937] 1 K.B. 653; *Keeley v Pashen* [2005] Lloyd's Rep. I.R. 289.

[578] *Orr v Trafalgar Insurance* 82 Ll. L.R. 1; In *Murray v Scottish Automobile and General Insurance Co* 1929 S.C. 49,

[579] *McCarthy v British Oak Insurance Co Ltd* [1938] 3 All E.R. 1.

[580] *Wood v General Accident* (1948) 65 T.L.R. 53. See also *Passmore v Vulcan Boiler and General Insurance Co Ltd* (1936) 54 Ll. L.R. 92; *Browning v Phoenix Assurance Co Ltd* [1960] 2 Lloyd's Rep. 360; *McGoona v Motor Insurers Bureau* [1969] 2 Lloyd's Rep. 34.

[581] *Seddons v Binions* [1978] 1 Lloyd's Rep. 381, applied and distinguished in a marine context in *Caple v Sewell* [2002] Lloyd's Rep. I.R. 627.

held that at the time of the accident the vehicle was being used for concurrent domestic and business purposes and that the insurers were not liable.

By contrast, if at the time of the accident the prohibited purpose has come to an end, the assured is entitled to recover. In *Keeley v Pashen*[582] the defendant's motor policy covered "use only for social, domestic and pleasure purposes including travel to and from permanent place of business", and excluded "use for hire or reward". The defendant used his vehicle in his capacity as a mini-cab driver, and he deliberately drove at K who he had just dropped off and who P claimed had attacked him. K was killed. The issue was whether the defendant's insurers were liable under s.151 of the Road Traffic Act 1988 to meet the judgment against him. The Court of Appeal held that at the time of the accident the defendant was driving his car for social, domestic or pleasure purposes, and was not driving his car for hire or reward, because the defendant had by that time dropped off his last passenger and the purpose of the journey was to go home within the terms of the insuring clause: the fact that he unwisely deviated in order to frighten K did not change the nature of that journey.

22–099   **Loads carried by the vehicle.** A clause excluding liability "whilst the car is conveying any load in excess of that for which it was constructed" has been held not to apply where more passengers were carried than a motor car was designed to carry[583]: it covered only cases where there was a specific weight which must not be exceeded, as in the case of lorries or vans. Clauses prohibiting excessive loads do not extend to the carrying of unsafe loads.[584] The policy may also impose restrictions on towing,[585] although a general prohibition on the carrying of loads does not apply to towing.[586]

22–100   **Place and time of use of vehicle.** The policy may limit the geographical areas in which the vehicle may be used[587] and, in the case of a commercial policy, the amount of time for which a vehicle can be used in any given period.[588]

---

[582] *Keeley v Pashen* [2005] Lloyd's Rep. I.R. 289.

[583] *Houghton v Trafalgar Insurance* [1954] 1 Q.B. 247. Contrast *Clarke v National Insurance* [1964] 1 Lloyd's Rep. 199 (express restriction on number of passengers).

[584] *Jenkins v Deane* (1933) 47 Ll. L.R. 342; *Salmon Contractors Ltd v Monksfield* [1970] 1 Lloyd's Rep. 387.

[585] *Kerridge v Rush* [1952] 2 Lloyd's Rep. 305; *JRM Plant Ltd v Hodgson* [1960] 1 Lloyd's Rep. 538.

[586] *Jenkins v Deane* (1935) 47 Ll. L.R. 342.

[587] *Palmer v Cornhill Insurance Co Ltd* (1935) 52 Ll. L.R. 78.

[588] *Farr v Motor Traders Mutual Insurance Society Ltd* [1920] 3 K.B. 669.

CHAPTER 23

FINANCIAL INSURANCE

1. Mortgagees' Interest Insurance

Significance. The situation commonly arises whereby the purchase of the **23–001** insured subject matter is financed by a bank or similar institution. If the subject matter is the assured purchaser's main asset—as will be the case with a one-ship company or a house-buyer—the lender's security over that subject matter (generally in the form of a mortgage) is meaningful only if some form of insurance exists in the lender's favour. The lender may seek to utilise the assured's own insurance in one of two ways. First, the lender may require insurance to be taken out by the purchaser in the joint names of purchaser and lender. This arrangement produces a "composite" policy under which the parties are insured for their respective interests, and has the legal merit, as far as the lender is concerned, that misconduct by the purchaser which debars an action by him under the policy will not affect the lender's right to recover.[1] This form of insurance is commonly used by mortgagees of land: the lending building society or bank will procure a block policy and simply add the mortgagor's name to it. The courts have indeed held that under an arrangement of this nature, arson by the assured will prevent recovery by him but does not debar the building society.[2] There is, however, a major drawback to the composite insurance approach in marine insurance: if the assured connives in the scuttling of his own vessel by causing an ingress of water there is simply no loss under the policy, for the reasons that "perils of the sea" require an element of fortuity and also that the proximate cause of the loss is not the ordinary action of the wind and the waves as required by the definition of "perils of the sea".[3] Interestingly enough, if the assured under a marine policy destroys the vessel in some other way, for example by fire, the loss will have been caused by an insured peril and the mortgagee under a composite policy would be entitled to recover.[4] It will nevertheless be appreciated that the mortgagee of a vessel is less likely to be able to recover under a composite hulls policy than is the mortgagee of terrestrial subject matter.

An alternative step available to the lender is to take an assignment of the insurance from the assured. What is actually involved here is an assignment of the proceeds of the policy rather than the policy itself, as there is no question of the lender becoming the substituted assured under the policy. Consequently, the lender's rights are dependent upon those of the assured and the cases have demonstrated that the lender will have no action for the proceeds if the assured

---

[1] *Samuel & Co Ltd v Dumas* [1924] A.C. 431; *Lombard Australia Ltd v NRMA Insurance Co Ltd* [1969] 1 Lloyd's Rep. 575.

[2] *Reynolds v Phoenix Assurance* [1978] 2 Lloyd's Rep. 440.

[3] *Samuel & Co Ltd v Dumas* [1924] A.C. 431.

[4] *The Alexion Hope* [1988] 1 Lloyd's Rep. 311.

has been guilty of wilful misconduct in relation to the subject matter,[5] has been in breach of his duty of utmost good faith,[6] has submitted a fraudulent claim[7] or has been guilty of breach of warranty.[8]

Some protection may commonly be afforded to the lender by separate arrangements involving insurer and lender. The policy may nominate the lender as the loss payee: such a provision may be enforced by the lender under the Contracts (Rights of Third Parties) Act 1999, although it will only be of real use if the insurers agree also to make payment irrespective of any defences that they might have had against a claim by the assured. There may also be a Letter of Undertaking issued by the insurer: such a document will typically guarantee that payment will be made directly to the lender and that the lender is to be informed by the insurer if the insurance should "cease". It is clear, from *Bank of Nova Scotia v Hellenic Mutual War Risks Association (The Good Luck)*,[9] that the insurer's liability "ceases" from the date of breach of warranty and that no further action by the insurer is necessary. Breach of warranty is, however, exceptional in this regard. By contrast, breach of a notice provision or a wilful casting away do not cause a policy to cease but merely provide the insurer with a defence to a particular claim. Similarly, if the assured has failed to disclose a material fact the policy will only cease when the insurer chooses to avoid. Those rules mean in effect that sums advanced to the assured by the lender before or after the assured's misconduct but before the insurer terminates the policy are at risk of being unsecured and an attempt in *The Good Luck*, to persuade the Court of Appeal[10] that a Letter of Undertaking obliged the insurer to disclose to the lender any misconduct on the part of the assured which could threaten a valid claim under the policy, failed. The Court of Appeal held that a Letter of Undertaking is not a contract of utmost good faith in its own right, so that disclosure is not required and, further, that it would be improper to impose a tortious "duty to speak" in a commercial context of this nature.

The weakness of the lender's position under the assured's policy, as either co-assured or assignee, has prompted the development of mortgagees' interest insurance for the protection of lending banks. In essence, such insurance provides a fall-back or guarantee policy for the bank: in the event that the assured's insurer fails to pay the bank, the mortgagees' interest insurer will incur liability. Since 1986, such insurance has been written on the London marine market in the terms of the Institute of London Underwriters' Clauses, the Institute Mortgagees Interest Clauses Hulls, as revised in 1997.

The Institute Mortgagees' Interest Insurance Clauses

23-002 *Risks covered and excluded.* Clause 1 provides that the policy insures the interest of the assured, as the mortgagee, in a vessel or vessels which are set out in the

---

[5] *Samuel & Co Ltd v Dumas* [1924] A.C. 431.

[6] *Black King Shipping Corporation v Massie (The Litsion Pride)* [1985] 1 Lloyd's Rep. 437. The breach of duty in this case was post-contractual. The analysis of Hirst J. of the continuing duty of utmost good faith was rejected by the House of Lords in *The Star Sea* [2001] Lloyd's Rep. I.R. 247, but the proposition in the text that a breach of duty defeats the rights of a mortgagee holds good.

[7] *The Litsion Pride.* In *The Star Sea*, the House of Lords ruled that there had not been a fraudulent claim on the facts of *The Litsion Pride* although, once again, the proposition in the text remains good where fraud is established.

[8] *Bank of Nova Scotia v Hellenic Mutual War Risks Association (The Good Luck)* [1991] 3 All E.R. 1.

[9] *Bank of Nova Scotia v Hellenic Mutual War Risks Association (The Good Luck)* [1991] 3 All E.R. 1.

[10] [1989] 1 Lloyd's Rep. 514: the point did not arise in the House of Lords.

schedule to the policy. Other vessels may be added by way of endorsement. Clause 4 emphasises the nature of the policy, by providing a series of clauses under which the assured warrants that hull and machinery policies in standard form are effected and maintained by the owner of the vessel, with the interest of the assured bank as first mortgagee endorsed on the hulls policy. The primary obligation of the insurer under the policy is, in accordance with cl.1.1, to indemnify the assured bank for loss resulting from the loss of a vessel which is prima facie covered by hull and machinery insurance but in respect of which full payment is not made due to any of the causes listed in cl.2.1.1 of the wording. The insured perils include: breach of any warranty or condition; failure by the assured to exercise due diligence where required (as under the Hulls Clauses' Inchmaree clause); deliberate fraud or casting away by the owner; avoidance of the policy by reason of the breach of the duty of utmost good faith; the operation of a limitation period under the main policy; and, in the case of a total loss, failure to prove that the loss was proximately caused by an insured peril, providing that the loss fell outside any of the specific exclusions under the policy.

A number of exclusions are provided for by cl.3. These include financial defaults such as non-payment of premium by the owner, the insolvency of the owner, any fluctuation in exchange rates and the operation of any franchise, deductible or provision for self-insurance, and loss caused by nuclear and radiation risks.

Duration of cover. The normal period of insurance for the policy is 12 months. **23–003** The policy will determine automatically on the change of ownership, management or control of the vessel of which the assured bank has knowledge, unless the bank gives prompt notice of such change and is willing to pay any additional premium demanded by the insurer (clause 5). There are also provisions for termination automatically or by notice in the event of certain war risks (cl.10).

Nature of policy and measure of indemnity. In *The Captain Panagos*[11] Mustill J. **23–004** held that a mortgagee's interest policy which insured against non-payment following loss or damage to the vessel, was a marine policy and not a financial guarantee policy. This principle has been retained by cl.1 of which specifically states that the policy insures the mortgagee's interest in the vessel as opposed to his interest in his liability. However, the most important consequence flowing from the classification of a policy as a marine policy—the calculation of the measure of indemnity—has been altered. In *The Captain Panagos* the policy covered "loss of or damage to . . . the vessel" and provided that the insurer would pay "the lesser amount of such damage or liability and the total indebtedness". Mustill J. ruled that the words "such damage or liability" in the indemnity clause referred back to the words "loss or damage to . . . the vessel", so that the measure of indemnity was not financial loss as such but loss determined by the insurable value of the vessel. As the policy was not a valued policy, Mustill J. was thrown back on to s.68 of the Marine Insurance Act 1906, which provides that, subject to any contrary express provision of the policy, the insurable value of a vessel is to be determined in accordance with s.16; this in turn states that the insurable value of a vessel is its value at the commencement of the voyage. Mustill J. nevertheless felt that this measure would not be appropriate to a policy of this nature and thus held that there was sufficient in the policy to exclude the normal rule in s.68: the learned judge thus concluded that

[11] *The Captain Panagos* [1985] 1 Lloyds Rep. 625.

the amount recoverable was the market value of the vessel at the time and place of its loss.

This decision was greeted with some dismay by mortgagee banks. As it is the practice to insure vessels under valued policies, and as it is common to overvalue a vessel, it may be seen that the amount which the bank would have loaned—and would thus have stood to lose by the failure of the hull insurer to pay—would generally exceed the market value of the vessel at the time of its loss. The Clauses seek to overcome this problem by providing that the indemnity is not linked to the value of the vessel. Under cl.1.2, the amount payable is the lesser of:

> "1.2.1 the amount of the Assured's Net Loss and any amounts recoverable under Clause 6 herein [the suing and labouring clause], collectively not exceeding the Sum Insured on the Mortgaged Vessel, or
> 1.2.2 the amount of any unrecoverable claim or part thereof under any of the Owners' Policies and Club Entries."

If, however, the assured is underinsured, in that the maximum amount insured per vessel (in accordance with clause 9) is less than the potential loss, the principle of average applies. Thus, in the event of a partial loss, the bank can recover under its policy only that proportion of a total loss for which it was insured. The bank cannot recover any additional sums insured, e.g. for loss of profit or business interruption.[12]

23–005 *The right to payment.* Given that a mortgagee's interest policy is aimed at protecting the assured against non-payment by the hull insurer, detailed provision is required to determine at exactly what point the hull insurer has refused to pay. This is determined by cl.7. Under this clause, the mortgagee is able to prove a claim under the policy by demonstrating to the satisfaction of the insurers that, by reason of an insured peril, there is no reasonable prospect of the claim being made under owners' policy or that there is an arbitration award denying liability under the owners' policy. Once a failure to pay has been established and a formal claim under the mortgagees' interest policy has been presented, the insurer has a period of three months to make payment.

23–006 *The insurer's right of subrogation.* Clause 8 confers an express subrogation right upon the mortgagees' interest insurer. The subrogated rights, which are not elaborated, are twofold. First, there is the assured's right—as the assignee of the owner—to proceed against the hull insurer, although this may in practice be of limited value given that the mortgagees' interest policy will often only come into play where the hull insurer has a good defence under the hull policy. Secondly, the mortgagees' interest insurer arguably has the right to proceed against the owner of the vessel as the assured's debtor, for ultimately the policy protects the assured against the debtor's default. On this basis, cl.8.2, provides that the proceeds of the policy are not to be applied in the discharge of the owner's indebtedness. It is far from clear, however, that subrogation does extend this far, for the specific event against which the bank is insured is the failure of the hull underwriter to pay and not the inability of the owner of the vessel to meet its loan obligations, although the latter event will in most cases be a direct consequence of the former.

---

[12] Cf. *Canadian Imperial Bank of Commerce v Insurance Company of Ireland* 75 D.L.R. (4th) 482 (1991).

Suing and labouring. The insured bank is, under cl.6.1, obliged to keep the **23–007** insurer informed of any event which might give rise to a claim. Further, cl.6 imposes a suing and labouring duty upon the assured: it is the duty of the assured, his servants and his agents to take such measures as may be reasonable for the purpose of averting or minimising a loss which would otherwise be recoverable under the policy. The remainder of cl.6 provides for indemnification of the assured in respect of costs properly incurred in pursuance of this duty; the amount recoverable is in addition to the policy moneys, although if the assured is underinsured on the policy itself then the principle of average is to be applied to the suing and labouring indemnity.

2. LEGAL EXPENSES INSURANCE

Nature of legal expenses insurance, Legal expenses insurance, which is of **23–008** comparatively recent origin at least in England, enables the assured to protect himself to some extent against the risk of becoming involved in litigation, by insuring against the costs of such litigation. The growth in the number of these policies has corresponded to the decline in the availability of legal aid. A typical policy will provide that expenses are payable only if the assured has a reasonable prospect of success in bringing or defending the proceedings, and that in the event of a dispute the opinion of counsel may be sought. The meaning of the phrase "reasonable prospects of success" has yet to be considered by the courts.[13] Where an assured litigant is refused assistance by the insurers, or assistance is granted but is subsequently withdrawn because the insurer has taken the view that the assured has unreasonably failed to settle, and the assured proceeds to court and obtains judgment, a typical policy will allow the assured to recover his reasonable costs from the insurer insofar as they have not been recovered from the other party. In the event that the insurer has accepted liability under the policy, the assured will have the right to nominate a solicitor to act on his behalf, although the policy will generally provide for liaison between the insurer and the assured's solicitor, in the form of provision of documents.

Regulation

Purpose of regulation. Legal expenses insurance give rise to possible conflicts of **23–009** interest where the liability insurer of party A to a dispute is also the legal expenses insurer of party B to the same dispute: the temptation for the insurer to frustrate party B's action against party A is a potential danger. For this reason, the European Communities adopted in 1987 the Legal Expenses Insurance Directive,[14] which was designed to minimise this danger. The Directive was implemented into English law by the Insurance Companies (Legal Expenses Insurance) Regulations 1990[15] and the Insurance Companies (Legal Expenses Insurance) (Application for Authorisation) Regulations 1990,[16] the latter being

---

[13] The Insurance Ombudsman has suggested that the proper approach is objective and should be based upon the Legal Aid Board's merits test for the provision of legal aid, namely, whether, in the light of the strength of the evidence and the legal position there is a case which should be put before a court. See IOB Annual Report for 1993, paras 6.61 to 6.65.

[14] Council Directive 87/344/EEC.

[15] SI 1990/1159.

[16] SI 1990/1160.

replaced first by the Insurance Companies Regulations 1994[17] and then by the
Financial Services and Markets Act 2000. The rules discussed below came into
force on July 1, 1990 and apply to legal expenses insurance as defined for the
purposes of the Financial Services and Markets Act 2000. Class 17 of the classes
of General Insurance Business defines legal expenses insurance business as
"effecting and carrying out contracts of insurance against risks of loss the
persons insured attributable to their incurring legal expenses (including costs of
litigation)". Breach of the regulations (other than those relating to authorisation,
is to be treated as failure to satisfy an obligation under the Financial Services and
Markets Act 2000, with all the regulatory consequences of such a breach.

The Regulations do not apply to: (a) legal expenses insurance concerning
disputes or risks arising out of, or in connection with, the use of seagoing vessels;
(b) anything done by a person providing civil liability cover for the purpose of
defending or representing the assured in an inquiry or proceedings which is at the
same time done in the insurer's own interest under such cover; and (c) legal
expenses cover provided under a contract the principal object of which is the
provision of assistance to persons who fall into difficulties while travelling, while
away from home or while away from their permanent residence and where the
costs are incurred outside the state in which the assured normally resides—in
such a case the policy must state that the legal expenses cover is so
restricted.[18]

23–010 *Authorisation.* Prior to July 1, 1990 an insurer authorised to carry on any class
of general business did not require separate authorisation to offer legal expenses
insurance as a subsidiary and related part of the same policy. Separate
authorisation for legal expenses insurance is now required in all cases unless: (a)
the principal object of the contract is the provision of assistance for persons who
get into difficulties while travelling, while away from home or while away from
their permanent residence; or (b) those subsidiary provisions concern disputes or
risks arising out of, or in connection with, the use of sea-going vessels.

23–011 *Requirement for separate policy.* Legal expenses insurance must be contained
either in a separate policy or, where the insurance is contained in another policy
offering general business cover, in a separate section of the policy relating to
legal expenses insurance only. In the latter case, the legal expenses section of the
policy must specify the nature of the cover provided.[19]

23–012 *Avoiding conflicts of interest.* An insurer who carries on legal expenses insurance
and other forms of insurance must adopt internal arrangements which avoid
conflicts of interest. In furtherance of this obligation, it must adopt at least one
of three alternative arrangements:[20]

(1) The company must ensure that no member of staff who is concerned with
management of claims under legal expenses policies, or with legal advice
in respect of such policies, carries on at the same time any similar activity
in relation to another class of general business carried on by the company
or by any other company which has financial, commercial or administrative links with his company.

---

[17] SI 1994/1516.
[18] 1990 Regulations reg.3.
[19] 1990 Regulations reg.4.
[20] 1990 Regulations reg.5.

(2) The company must entrust the management of legal expenses insurance claims to a body with separate legal personality. If, however, the legal expenses insurance company has financial, commercial or administrative links with the parent insurer, members of staff may not process claims or give legal advice in both companies at the same time.

(3) The insurer must, in the policy, afford the assured from the moment the claim against the insurer arises the right to entrust the defence of his interests to a lawyer of his choice.

Irrespective of which of these options is adopted by the insurer, once proceedings have been initiated the assured is entitled to choose his own lawyer to represent his interests. A similar obligation is imposed on the insurer wherever a conflict of interests arises.[21] These rights do not operate, however, in one situation, namely where[22]: (a) the policy covers only legal assistance in respect of an accident involving, or the breakdown of, a motor vehicle in the United Kingdom; and (b) neither the legal expenses insurer nor the assistance insurer carries on any class of liability business; and (c) arrangements exist whereby, if the parties to a dispute are insured by the same insurer, each is provided with completely independent legal advice.

Where, following the institution of legal proceedings, the assured does have the right to choose his own lawyer, that right is not affected by the fact that the claim brought by the assured is one of many of the same type and that numerous different lawyers may be involved. In *Eschig v UNIQA Sachversicherung*[23] the assured, along with several thousand others, suffered substantial losses on the failure of two investment companies. He wished to commence proceedings against the directors and also against the Austrian Government (on the basis of its regulatory failures), but his legal expenses insurers—having been asked to fund a significant number of cases arising out of the same facts—asserted a right to appoint legal representatives so that test cases could be brought. The European Court of Justice ruled that the right of the assured to appoint his own lawyer was restricted only by the express derogation relating to motor insurance and that even in the case of group claims every member of the group was entitled to insist upon separate legal representation. The Court commented that group actions were not unknown when the Directive had been adopted, so it could not be said that the issue had not been contemplated.

Dispute resolution. A legal expenses insurance policy must give the assured the right to go to arbitration to resolve any dispute between the parties to it.[24] In the event of a dispute arising, the insurer must give written notice to the assured informing him of his right to independent legal advice and of his right to go to arbitration.[25]

23–013

Disclosure of material facts. A legal expenses policy will generally cover the costs of any action commenced during the currency of the policy, and thus the insurers will generally ask an express question of the assured concerning any possible causes of action by the assured outstanding at the time of the application. Whether or not this is the case, if the assured is aware of a possible

23–014

[21] 1990 Regulations reg.6
[22] 1990 Regulations reg.7.
[23] *Eschig v UNIQA Sachversicherung* [2009] EUECJ Case C-199/08.
[24] 1990 Regulations reg.8.
[25] 1990 Regulations reg.9.

claim against a third party, this is clearly a material fact to be disclosed even though the facts upon which the claim against the third party are to be based have yet to be fully established. Whether or not there is a disclosable risk is a matter of fact in every case, and will depend upon the context and the precise relationship between the parties. In *Laker Vent Engineering Ltd v Templeton Insurance Ltd*[26] the assured, a firm specialising in the installation of pipework, agreed to act as sub-contractor on a major engineering project. A variety of disputes arose, with allegations of delay in the works and unpaid invoices being exchanged by the parties. The trial judge summarised the position by saying that "Despite the delays to the works and the differences of opinions between the parties, the relationship . . . remained fairly amicable at least up until [the date of the renewal of the policy]; and there was no obvious indication, prior to that date, that the differences between them would or might lead to any form of process of adjudication, arbitration or litigation." The trial judge, whose ruling was upheld by the Court of Appeal, was satisfied by expert evidence that construction contracts always gave rise to disputes and that in a legal expenses case a fact was material only if it showed a real risk of escalation to the point at which formal dispute resolution procedures might be initiated.

23–015   **Coverage.** Legal expenses policies are designed for both businesses and consumers. Business policies provide funding for the assured to participate in legal proceedings, either as claimant or defendant, in matters such as employment disputes, contractual disputes and investigations by the Inland Revenue and Customs. Consumer policies cover neighbour disputes, personal injury claims and proceedings against suppliers. In cases where the assured is the claimant, coverage will generally be restricted to cases where there is a better than evens chance of success.

Where cover is tied to a particular activity, there has to be the appropriate causal connection between the head of coverage and the legal proceedings. The decision of Simon J. in *Wickham Van Eyck v Norwich Union Insurance Ltd*[27] demonstrates a generous approach to interpretation. The relevant head of coverage in this case was for contract disputes, and the policy provided that there was cover "in a contractual dispute arising from [an] agreement or that alleged agreement . . . for the . . . provision of goods and services." A claim was made by the assured for a share of profits in a joint venture, the defendant in those proceedings asserted that the arrangement between the parties was not a joint venture but merely one for the provision of services by the assured. The insurers denied liability on the basis that the claim made by the assured was not in respect of the provision of services, or if it was then the provision of services was not the main element of the claim. Simon J., ruling for the assured on the point, held that the availability of cover did not depend upon the precise way in which the claim against the defendant was formulated, and even if that was wrong there was no predominant purpose test so that as long as there was a dispute as to the provision of services then the policy would respond.

23–016   **Third party costs.** The insurer's liability under the policy will have financial limits per claim or series of claims arising out of one event or originating cause, and there may also be an aggregate limit on sums payable. As far as the assured is concerned, the contractual limit imposed by the insurer is fixed.

---

[26] *Laker Vent Engineering Ltd v Templeton Insurance Ltd* [2009] Lloyd's Rep. I.R. 704.
[27] *Wickham Van Eyck v Norwich Union Insurance Ltd* [2009] EWHC 2625 (Comm).

The other party to the proceedings may, however, have an additional claim for costs against the insurer on the basis that the action is in reality supported by the insurer. In *Murphy v Young & Co's Brewery*[28] M possessed legal expenses insurance up to the sum of £25,000 per claim arising out of one event. M brought proceedings for wrongful dismissal against YC, but the action was dismissed and costs of £42,806.93 were awarded in favour of YC. M's own costs amounted to £17,000. The insurers paid M's costs, and a further £8,000 in respect of YC's costs, but made no further payment on the ground that the limits of its indemnity had been reached. The present action was an application by YC that the insurers should pay the balance of YC's costs, the basis being s.51 of the Supreme Court Act 1981, which provides that a court has a discretion to determine by whom and to what extent costs shall be paid. YC's argument was that s.51 allowed the court to order costs against a third party, and that this was a case in which that discretion should be exercised as, without SA's intervention, M's action against YC would not have been brought.[29] The Court of Appeal refused the order, holding that a costs order may be made against a legal expenses order in exceptional circumstances only. The mere fact that the provision of funding by the insurer had enabled the claimant to bring the proceedings was not of itself enough to justify a costs order, as a legal expenses insurer had no interest in the outcome of the dispute and was in any event under a general obligation to fund litigation. Subsequently, in *Chapman Ltd v Christopher*,[30] a case in which the question was whether the court should exercise its powers under s.51 against a liability insurer who had conducted the defence of its assured, clear principles for the order of costs against insurers were set out. An order may be made if five conditions[31] are satisfied:

(a) the decision to bring the proceedings had been taken by the insurers;
(b) the action had been funded by the insurers;
(c) the insurers had conducted the claim;
(d) the insurers had acted purely in their own interests; and
(e) the action failed in its entirety.

It will be apparent that these criteria will rarely be met in the ordinary case of legal expenses insurance where the insurers are simply fulfilling their legal obligation to fund proceedings brought by the assured. Even if they are met, it remains necessary to defendants to demonstrate that there was something exceptional about the case, and also that, but for the insurers' intervention, the defendants would not have incurred costs at all or to the extent to which they were actually incurred, i.e. a causative link.[32]

Direct action against insurers by third party. Legal expenses insurance is by its nature a first-party cover rather than a third-party liability cover. However, its purpose is to enable the assured to fund payments to third parties, in particular the assured's own legal advisers and also the defendants in respect of their own

23–017

---

[28] *Murphy v Young & Co's Brewery* [1997] 1 All E.R. 518.

[29] The action sought to cast the burden of M's insolvency onto M's legal expenses insurers rather than onto YC: had YC succeeded in this action, the insurers would (for what it was worth) clearly have had a right of recourse against M for restitution of sums paid out by them to satisfy M's liability.

[30] *Chapman Ltd v Christopher* [1998] Lloyd's Rep. I.R. 1.

[31] The principles have been adapted from the liability insurance cases, where the insurer funds the defendant: in legal expenses insurance cases, the insurer funds the claimant.

[32] *Worsley v Tambrands Ltd and Syndicate 582 at Lloyd's* [2002] Lloyd' Rep. I.R. 382.

legal costs. In *Tarbuck v Avon Insurance Plc*[33] the issue was whether a third party had a direct claim against the insurers under the policy. The assured brought proceedings against the third party, but the action was dismissed and costs were awarded against her. The assured was in due course adjudged bankrupt when she defaulted on the order to pay the third party's costs. The assured's own solicitors then sought to recover their costs from her, but she was unable to make payment and refused to authorise her legal expenses insurers to make payment. The solicitors thus commenced proceedings against the insurers under the Third Parties (Rights against Insurers) Act 1930 (now 2010), arguing that they had a direct claim following the assured's insolvency. Toulson J. rejected the claim, ruling that the 1930 Act applied only to liability policies, and did not extend to cases where the assured had voluntarily incurred a contractual liability to her solicitors. The Law Commission, in its August 2001 Report on the Third Parties (Rights against Insurers) Act 1930 and its draft bill, recommended the extension of the 1930 Act to obligations voluntarily incurred under contract. Taking this into account, the *Tarbuck* decision was subsequently strongly doubted by the Court of Appeal in *Re OT Computers Ltd*.[34] The Court of Appeal rejected the argument that the 1930 Act did not apply to claims for damages for breach of contract, and although it was not called upon to determine the applicability of the 1930 Act to claims for debt—the issue in *Tarbuck*—the Court of Appeal could see no difference in principle between claims for damages and claims in debt. Accordingly *Tarbuck* must now be taken not to be good law as far as the 1930 Act is concerned.

The Third Parties (Rights against Insurers) Act 2010, which implements the Law Commission's proposals, makes express provision for this matter. Section 16 of the Act states that applies to any liability, whether or not voluntarily incurred.

3. GUARANTEE INSURANCE

23–018 **Insurance business and guarantees.** Insurance companies and Lloyd's underwriters engage in a considerable amount of guarantee business. This includes guarantees against employees' dishonesty, guarantees for the payment of debts, performance bonds issued to customers guaranteeing either on demand payment or payment where breach of contract by the supplier is demonstrated, and other forms of fidelity bonds relating to matters such as the insolvency of tour operators and payment of VAT. There are two distinct legal arrangements by which guarantees of potential liabilities may be effected:

1. the insurers may stand surety for the employee's fidelity, for the completion of the contract, or for the payment of the debt, or
2. the insurers may insure their client against loss arising from specified dishonesty, non-completion of a contract, or non-payment of a debt.

The former arrangement is not a contract of insurance,[35] whilst the latter is a contract of insurance. It is worth noting, however, that credit insurance, miscellaneous financial loss insurance and suretyship—including the issuing of

[33] *Tarbuck v Avon Insurance Plc* [2001] 2 All E.R. 503.
[34] *Re OT Computers Ltd* [2004] Lloyd's Rep. I.R. 669.
[35] *Trade Indemnity Co Ltd v Workington Harbour and Dock Board (No.1)* [1937] A.C. 1.

fidelity bonds, performance bonds, administration bonds, bail bonds and "similar contracts of guarantee"—are all forms of general insurance business for the purposes of the Financial Services and Markets Act 2000. The distinction between insurance and guarantee is thus insignificant for regulatory purposes, and it has been held that financial cover against claims provided to an insurer who issues a fidelity bond constitutes "reinsurance", as the definition of reinsurance is satisfied where the cover relates to a contracts which are not strictly contracts of insurance but are made by an insurer as part of its statutory insurance business.[36] However, the distinction is important for contractual reasons; further, contracts of guarantee must be evidenced in writing,[37] whereas there is no such formal requirement for insurance contracts.

Guarantee insurance and guarantee distinguished. Guarantee insurance and **23–019** suretyship share some common features, but there are clear distinctions between the two. A surety promises a creditor that he will be paid; an insurer promises to indemnify him if he is not. In neither case does the surety or insurer come under any obligation to pay unless or until the debtor is in default. But while payment by a surety discharges the principal debt, payment by an insurer does not affect it. In the former case the surety has a direct right in equity against the debtor, in the latter case the insurer is only subrogated to the rights of the assured against him. The rules of guarantee insurance are a part of the law of contract and were developed in the courts of common law. Suretyship does not necessarily depend upon a contract, and its rules were developed in courts of equity. While these two branches of the law have developed on similar lines, and it is often immaterial to which of the two classes a contract belongs,[38] their principles sometimes differ in their effect. Thus the doctrine of subrogation has been carried further in suretyship cases.

It is often a difficult question whether a given contract is one of guarantee or of insurance. In *Seaton v Heath*[39] Romer L.J. stated that the distinction does not depend on the mere use of the words "insurance" or "guarantee",[40] but they can generally be distinguished by the way in which they are effected:

"Contracts of insurance are generally matters of speculation, where the person desiring to be insured has means of knowledge as to the risk, and the insurer has not the means or not the same means. The insured generally puts the risk before the insurer as a business transaction, and the insurer on the risk stated fixes a proper price to remunerate him for the risk to be undertaken and the insurer engages to pay the loss incurred by the

---

[36] *Travellers Casualty & Surety Co of Europe Ltd v Commissioners of Customs & Excise* [2006] Lloyd's Rep. I.R. 63, in which it was held by the VAT Tribunal that cover provided to insurance companies which had issued fidelity bonds was "reinsurance" and thus exempt from insurance premium tax.

[37] Statute of Frauds 1677 s.4. See: *Eastwood v Kenyon* (1840) 11 Ad. & E. 438; *Hargreaves v Parsons* (1844) 13 M. & W. 561 at 570. The legislation remains in force in respect of "any special promise to answer for the debt, default or miscarriage of another person" despite repeal of other parts of the section by the Law Reform (Enforcement of Contracts) Act 1954 and the Law of Property (Miscellaneous Provisions) Act 1989.

[38] Kay J. in *Dane v Mortgage Insurance* [1894] 1 Q.B. 54, 62; Kennedy J. in *Re Law Guarantee Trust* [1914] 2 Ch. 617 at 636; Lord Robertson in *Seaton v Burnand* [1900] A.C. 35 at 148; Warrington J. in *Shaw v Royce Ltd* [1911] 1 Ch. 138 at 147.

[39] *Seaton v Heath* [1899] 1 Q.B. 782, reversed [1900] A.C. 135 on other grounds. Romer L.J.'s judgment was approved in the Court of Appeal in *Re Denton's Estate* [1904] 2 Ch. 178 at 188, per Vaughan Williams L.J.

[40] See *Re Denton's Estate* [1904] 2 Ch. 178, where a contract expressed to be of insurance in fact operated as a contract of guarantee. Contrast *Dane v Mortgage Insurance* [1894] 1 Q.B. 54, and *Finlay v Mexican Investment* [1897] 1 Q.B. 517.

insured in the event of certain specified contingencies occurring. On the other hand . . . [where contracts of guarantee are concerned] the creditor does not himself go to the surety, or represent, or explain the surety, the risk to be run. The surety often takes the position from motives of friendship, and generally not as the result of any direct bargaining between him and the creditor, or in consideration of any remuneration passing to him from the creditor."

The lack of premium rating by the "insurer", and of consideration passing from the "assured" to the "insurer" are clearly important factors, and were recognised as such by Sheen J. in *The Zuhal K and The Selin*.[41] In that case a further factor found to be relevant was the existence of a term whereby the issuer of a bond was entitled to a counter-indemnity from the beneficiary of the bond; in the view of Sheen J. the presence of a counter-indemnity was wholly inconsistent with the notion of insurance. The question must, therefore, ultimately depend upon the expressed intention of the parties in each case.[42] Where the intention is that the surety should on the default of the debtor pay the original debt, the contract is one of guarantee; where the intention is that a new debt should arise on default, the contract is one of insurance.[43]

23–020 Non-disclosure. The rule requiring full disclosure of material facts applies to guarantee insurance as to contracts of insurance generally. As regards what is material, it has been held that the assured's suspicions of earlier fraud by an employee must be disclosed.[44] Where the subject-matter of the insurance was the repayment of a loan it was held that the rate of interest was not material, even though it was exceptionally high.[45] The financial position of the debtor, on the other hand, is always material, though the assured need not disclose it where the insurer is already acquainted with it.[46]

4. Fidelity Insurance

23–021 Nature. Fidelity policies are the most common type of guarantee insurance. They are usually intended to protect an employer against breaches of confidence on the part of his employee, and have displaced the arrangement by which relatives of employees stood surety for their honesty. Fidelity policies should be distinguished from policies against liability incurred through a servant's negligence. Thus a policy against "all losses . . . by reason of any act, neglect . . . or error" of the assured's employees has been held to be a liability policy only, and not to extend to a loss due to embezzlement by an employee.[47] Liability policies are normally restricted to liability incurred through negligence.[48] Fidelity policies are essentially aimed at losses due to criminal misappropriation of money or

[41] *The Zuhal K and The Selin* [1987] 1 Lloyd's Rep. 151. See also *Travel & General Insurance v Barron, The Times*, November 25, 1988; *Mercers of the City of London v New Hampshire Insurance* [1992] 2 Lloyd's Rep. 365.
[42] Lord Esher in *Dane v Mortgage Insurance* [1894] 1 Q.B. 54 at 60.
[43] *Re Law Guarantee* [1914] 2 Ch. 617; *Albany Life Assurance Co v De Montfort Insurance Co Plc* Unreported, 1995; *Arab Bank Plc v John D Wood Commercial Ltd* [2000] Lloyd's Rep. I.R. 471.
[44] *Alliss-Chalmers Co v Maryland Fidelity & Deposit* (1916) 32 T.L.R. 263.
[45] *Seaton v Burnand* [1900] A.C. 135.
[46] *Anglo-Californian Bank v London & Provincial Marine* (1904) 20 T.L.R. 665.
[47] *Goddard & Smith v Frew* [1939] 4 All E.R. 358.
[48] See *Davies v Hosken* (1937) 53 T.L.R. 798.

securities[49] by an employee.[50] The same policy may, however, cover both these types of loss.[51] And banks frequently insure against loss by reason of securities turning out to be invalid, where the fraud, if any, is that of a stranger.[52]

The distinction between fidelity losses and third-party liability may be a fine one, in that an employee's fraud may result in the assured facing liability to a third party, but the courts have resisted any attempt to extend coverage of a fidelity policy to liabilities. The point is illustrated by *New Hampshire Insurance Co v Philips Electronics North America Corp*,[53] in which a senior employee of the assured had been accused of knowingly supplying defective goods to customers in order to earn commission on sales, and the assured had incurred substantial losses in replacing the defective goods. Clarke J. held that there had been no loss within the terms of the policy: no goods had been appropriated by the employee; and the costs of replacing the defective goods were incurred by the assured by way of legal liability to customers for breach of contract rather than as a loss of the assured's own property.

Losses covered. A fidelity policy covers the assured against theft or embezzle-   **23–022**
ment by his employees. The key, therefore, is dishonesty. In determining whether there has been dishonesty by an employee, the civil standard of proof is applied.[54] It is often provided that the employee's "manifest intent" has to be to deprive the assured of property or to make a profit at the assured's expense. There is no clear authority on the meaning of this phrase: various possibilities were suggested to Clarke J. in *New Hampshire Insurance Co v Philips Electronics North America Corp*,[55] and the learned judge held that it was not necessary to go any further than to state that what was required was a "clear, obvious or apparent" intent where a particular result was substantially certain to follow from the employee's conduct.

Typically, a fidelity policy will cover the assured against the theft or misappropriation of "money, securities and other property", wording commonly used for the US market. The terms "money" and "securities" are normally defined respectively as "currency, coin, banknotes and bullion", and "all negotiable and non-negotiable instruments representing money". Given that the definitions refer to tangible property, doubts have been raised as to whether the sweeping-up phrase "other property" is itself confined to tangible property or whether it can extend to misappropriation of choses in action. The wider view has prevailed to date. In *Proudfoot Plc v Federal Insurance Co*[56] Rix J. commented, obiter, that there was no objection in principle to intangible property falling within the cover: the term "property" is defined in the Theft Act 1968 as including intangible property, and the ruling of the House of Lords in *R. v Preddy*[57] to the effect that the obtaining of an unauthorised payment by means of

[49] Jessel MR in *Re Norwich Provident* (1878) 8 Ch. D. 334 at 341.

[50] See *Walker v British Guarantee Association* (1852) 21 L.J.Q.B. 257. They appear to be a form of property insurance for the purposes of the Financial Services and Markets Act 2000.

[51] *Wasserman v Blackburn* (1926) 43 T.L.R. 95; *Lazard Bros v Brooks* (1932) 38 Com. Cas. 46.

[52] *Equitable Trust Co of New York v Henderson* (1930) 47 L.T. 90; *Philadelphia National Bank v Price* (1938) 43 Com. Cas. 238; *Lazard Bros v Brooks* (1932) 38 Com. Cas. 46.

[53] *New Hampshire Insurance Co v Philips Electronics North America Corp* [1999] Lloyd's Rep. I.R. 66.

[54] *Abbey National Plc v Solicitors Indemnity Fund Ltd* [1997] P.N.L.R. 306.

[55] *New Hampshire Insurance Co v Philips Electronics North America Corp* [1999] Lloyd's Rep. I.R. 66.

[56] *Proudfoot Plc v Federal Insurance Co* [1997] L.R.L.R. 659.

[57] *R. v Preddy* [1996] 3 W.L.R. 225.

electronic transfer did not constitute theft, was based on the separate principle that a transfer of funds created a new chose in action with no previous owner, so that there had not been an appropriation of property belonging to another. In *New Hampshire Insurance Co v Philips Electronics North America Corp*[58] Clarke J. independently came to a similar conclusion. Here, a senior employee fraudulently caused a series of fictional sales to appear in the assured's books, in order to earn bonuses on the sales. The assured had not lost any tangible property as such, but it had plainly been defrauded of sums of money which had been credited to the employee to represent the bonuses apparently earned. Clarke J. held that it could not have been intended by the parties that a distinction was to be drawn between actual notes and coins and choses in action, and accordingly the policy responded to the bonus fraud.

There are numerous illustrations of the scope of fidelity policies. A policy covering a bank against losses by reason of currency being taken out of their possession by fraudulent means does not include the case where the bank is induced by fraud to give credit and afterwards pay out the money[59] and a policy covering "making away with" securities does not include fraud by an employee where no security is physically made away with.[60] Some policies cover any form of dishonesty.[61] By a Lloyd's policy of insurance, the claimant was insured against "loss or deprivation of bonds, debentures, stocks, scrip, shares, transfers, certificates, coupons, warrants or other securities, cash, cheques, bank notes, bills of exchange, promissory notes, or any documents of value", by robbery, theft, fire, explosion, embezzlement, burglary or abstraction, whether with or without violence, or any other loss whatsoever through theft or any other dishonesty. The claimant was induced by false representations to discount bills of exchange which were afterwards dishonoured. It was held that the claimant's loss was caused by dishonesty within the meaning of the policy and that he was entitled to recover.[62]

23–023   **Exclusions.** Generally excluded from cover are losses suffered by the assured representing salary, commission, bonuses and "other benefits earned in the normal course of employment". The concluding words "earned in the normal course of employment" were construed in *New Hampshire v Philips* as applying to all of the matters listed in the exclusion and not just "other benefits". The case is also authority for the proposition that a bonus or benefit can be "earned" only if the employee was entitled to it, so that a bonus obtained by defrauding the employer falls outside the scope of the exclusion and is recoverable under the policy. Clarke J. was of the view that the phrase, "normal course of employment" ought in the present context to be construed as excluding fraud, even though for other purposes fraud is disregarded in determining whether an act carried out by an agent was in the ordinary course of his authority.[63]

---

[58] *New Hampshire Insurance Co v Philips Electronics North America Corp* [1999] Lloyd's Rep. I.R. 66.
[59] *Century Bank v Young* (1914) 84 L.J.K.B. 385.
[60] *Liberty National Bank v Bolton* (1925) 21 Ll. L.R. 3.
[61] *Ravenscroft v Provident Clerks' Assurance* (1885) 5 T.L.R. 3; *American Surety Co v Wrightson* (1910) 103 L.T. 663.
[62] *Wasserman v Blackburn* (1926) 43 T.L.R. 95. Cf. also *European Assurance Society v Bank of Toronto* (1875) 7 Rev. Leg. 57 — fraudulent grant of overdraft to a customer known to be insolvent. For a policy of insurance against loss incurred through acting on any document which might prove "to have been forged", see *Equitable Trust Co of New York v Henderson* (1930) 47 T.L.R. 90.
[63] *Lloyd v Grace Smith & Co* [1912] A.C. 716.

Persons covered. Fidelity policies are commonly worded to cover any **23–024** employee, director or trustee of the assured while performing acts coming within the scope of the usual duties of an employee. This wording has been construed as providing cover where: (a) the acts in question fall within the usual duties of an employee, director or trustee, as the case may be and (b) the acts fall within the usual duties of an employee even though they are performed by a director or trustee. Thus where a company engages an independent contractor to administer the payroll, and that company misappropriates funds, the policy attaches on the basis that the company is a trustee of the funds and that it is performing the usual duties of a trustee or an employee. This was so held by Rix J. in *Proudfoot v Federal Insurance Co*,[64] although in that case the claim failed as there was an express exclusion in respect of independent contractors.

Since the risk of loss under a fidelity policy depends on the opportunity to be dishonest afforded by an employee's employment, the risk covered is generally restricted to losses occurring while he is employed in a specified capacity in which case the policy will not extend to misappropriation by him after the scope of his duties has been enlarged,[65] or where he is employed in a different capacity.[66]

Term of policy. Fidelity policies are usually made for a term of one or more **23–025** years. It is sometimes stipulated that unless notice to terminate be given, the policy shall be treated as a renewal contract of like nature and conditions.[67] The effect of this is merely to continue the contract for a second term. At the end of that term, if no notice to continue is given, or other arrangement made, the policy drops. Where one of the conditions indorsed was that all guarantees, whatever might be the original term, should from the expiration of such original term be treated as a renewal contract of the like nature and conditions, unless either the member interested therein or the board of directors should give two calendar months' notice of an intention not to renew the same, it was held that the renewed contract was not itself to be deemed to contain this particular condition as to renewal, and that therefore, even in the absence of notice, the contract did not extend beyond one renewal.[68] "A" renewal is one renewed contract. The fact that the rules of the company, on the faith of which the assured took the guarantee,[69] are altered, will not have the effect of determining such a renewed contract if no notice to terminate has been given by either party,[70] and the insurers will be entitled to the renewal premium.

The liability of the insurers was at one time written on the basis of coverage where there was a default of the employee within the period for which the guarantee is given, whether found out within the period or after its expiration, unless limited by apt words to a default committed and discovered within the period.[71] However, modern fidelity policies are generally expressed to cover losses by fraud, as long as the fraud itself is discovered during the currency of the policy: it is irrelevant when the loss itself occurred. Some policies may provide

---

[64] *Proudfoot v Federal Insurance Co* [1997] L.R.L.R. 659. See also: *Wembley Urban District Council v Poor Law Mutual* (1901) 17 T.L.R. 516: *Cosford Union v Poor Law Mutual* (1910) 103 L.T. 463.

[65] *Wembley UDC v Poor Law Mutual* (1901) 17 T.L.R. 516.

[66] See *Cosford Union v Poor Law Mutual* (1910) 103 L.T. 463.

[67] *Solvency Mutual Guarantee Co v Froane* (1861) 7 H. & N. 5.

[68] *Solvency Mutual Guarantee Co v Froane* (1861) 7 H. & N. 5.

[69] *Solvency Mutual Guarantee Co v Freeman* (1861) 7 H. & N. 17.

[70] *Solvency Mutual Guarantee Co v York* (1858) 3 H. & N. 588.

[71] *Fanning v London Guarantee & Accident Co* (1884) 10 Vict. L.R. 8.

these possibilities as alternatives, so that there is coverage if the fraud either takes place or is discovered during the currency of the policy. Fraud discovered at any time prior to inception, or events notified to earlier insurers, are normally excluded from coverage. The meaning of "discovered" was considered in *La Positiva Seguros y Reaseguros SA v Jessel*.[72] In this case the policy incepted on February 28, 1992. On January 29, 1992 the assured bank's internal auditors discovered that a large sum of money had been taken from a safe by four employees some days earlier. One of the employees gave an explanation which was false, but the auditor was satisfied that there had been no fraud involved but simply an unauthorised loan to another bank. In June 1992 an earlier event of the same type was discovered by the bank, at which point it became apparent that there had been fraud. H.H. Judge Jack QC held that the insurers were liable, as the assured had not discovered any fraud prior to inception. The word "discovered" required actual knowledge on the part of the assured as opposed to suspicion: mere constructive knowledge, arising from facts known to the assured and on which a reasonable person would have taken the view that there was fraud did not suffice. Had the insurers intended constructive knowledge to be sufficient, they could have expressly stated that to be the position.

Where the policy responds to fraud occurring during the currency of the policy, it may, by means of an "hours" clause, impose some temporal limitation on the period between the fraud and its discovery. Such a clause was considered by David Steel J. in *Dornoch Ltd v Mauritius Union Assurance Co Ltd and Mauritius Commercial Bank Ltd (No.2)*,[73] a reinsurance dispute in which the reinsurance obtained by the insurers of the defendant bank covered employee infidelity which occurred or was discovered during the currency of the policy but which confined recovery to losses discovered within 72 hours of their occurrence. The bank suffered a series of individual frauds over a period of some eleven years and notice was given to insurers in respect of each of these losses when they were ultimately discovered. The reinsurers successfully argued that the 72 hours clause was not merely a notice clause under which cover was provided for any loss provided that notice was given to insurers within 72 hours of discovery, but rather was a clause which removed indemnity for any loss not discovered within 72 hours of its occurrence. David Steel J. described the purpose of the clause as follows:

> "The purpose of the 72 Hour Condition is . . . to focus the insured's attention on their security procedures by ensuring that cover is not provided in respect of cumulative losses caused by the failure of an insured's controls to identify a deceitful employee stealing property or assisting in its theft over a long period of time. Indeed, the purpose of the 72 Hour Condition is precisely to exclude cover in respect of any systemic infidelity involving a series of losses which go undiscovered for a lengthy period, such as those which form the basis of the Mauritian Proceedings and the Mauritius Fraud Claim."

Other provisions as to duration may also be found. In *Universities Superannuation Scheme Ltd v Royal Insurance (UK) Ltd*[74] a fidelity policy covered (a)

---

[72] *La Positiva Seguros y Reaseguros SA v Jessel* Unreported, 2002. See also *Fortisbank SA v Trenwick International Ltd* [2005] Lloyd's Rep. I.R. 464 (Comm), where the assured was clearly aware of the fraud but failed to commence proceedings within the two-year contractual limitation period running from the date on which the assured was or ought to have been aware of the fraud.

[73] *Dornoch Ltd v Mauritius Union Assurance Co Ltd and Mauritius Commercial Bank Ltd (No.2)* [2007] Lloyd's Rep. I.R. 350.

[74] *Universities Superannuation Scheme Ltd v Royal Insurance (UK) Ltd* [2000] Lloyd's Rep. I.R. 525.

fraudulent acts committed during the currency of the policy and discovered within 24 months of the termination of the policy, and (b) fraudulent acts committed prior to inception and discovered within 24 months of the termination of the policy. It was held that, for the purposes of the six-year limitation period, the trigger for the running of time was the occurrence of a loss and not its discovery, so (a) the limitation period for acts of fraud causing loss committed during the currency of the policy was the date of the fraud, and (b) the limitation period for losses prior to the inception of the risk ran from the date of the policy, as that was the date on which the assured could first bring an action against the insurers.

Conditions. The duty of utmost good faith applies to fidelity policies, so that the assured must disclose his suspicions as to the earlier fraud of an employee.[75] It is in practice usual in fidelity insurance, particularly where the questions relate to earlier fraud and to accounting procedures, to give the assured's answers in the proposal form the force of warranties,[76] but a mere declaration of the course intended by the assured to be pursued in checking the accounts of an employee only relates to his present intention, and a warranty based on it will not therefore be broken simply because this course is not subsequently pursued.[77] A major change in the assured's financial procedures which amounts to a complete change in the nature of the risk will, independently of any express term, discharge the insurer.[78]

 23–026

 Prosecution of an employee who has been guilty of a criminal offence such as embezzlement is not a condition precedent to recovery under a fidelity policy unless such policy expresses it to be so.[79]

 Notice of loss may be made a condition precedent to liability under the policy,[80] but the employer is not usually under any duty to notify the insurer of mere suspicion that a servant has been dishonest until he has satisfied himself that his suspicions are justified.[81]

 A condition cannot be a condition precedent to payment if it relates only to matters to be done after payment, such as a condition that the employer shall give assistance to enable the company to obtain reimbursement from the employee.[82]

Calculation of indemnity. Fidelity policies generally contain a deductible clause whereby the insurer's liability in respect of every "loss" or "occurrence" arises only where the loss exceeds a stated sum. In addition, there may be a cap on losses arising from a single "occurrence". The definition of these terms is, therefore, a matter of some importance, as it will be necessary to determine whether the fraud consists of a number of single "occurrences" so that the insurer can apply the deductible or cap to each claim, or whether the fraud is part of a single course of conduct, so that the assured bears only one deductible but

 23–027

[75] *Alliss Chalmers Co v Maryland Fidelity & Deposit* (1916) 32 T.L.R. 263.

[76] *Towle v National Guardian* (1861) 30 L.J. Ch. 900; *Haworth v Sickness & Accident Assurance* (1891) 28 S.L.R. 394.

[77] *Bedham v United Guarantee Co* (1852) 7 Ex 744; *Hearts of Oak Building Society v Law Union* [1936] 2 All E.R. 619. Contrast *Haworth v Sickness & Accident Assurance* (1891) 28 S.L.R. 394.

[78] *Wembley UDC v Poor Law Mutual* (1901) 17 T.L.R. 516.

[79] *London Guarantee Co v Fearnley* (1880) 5 App. Cas. 911.

[80] *Clydebank Water Trustees v Fidelity Co of Maryland* (1915) S.C. 362.

[81] See *Ward v Lace Property* (1856) 4 W.R. 605.

[82] *London Guarantee v Fearnley* (1880) 5 App.Cas. 911. See also Humphreys J. in *Pictorial Machinery v Nichols* (1940) 45 Com. Cas. 334.

is subject to an aggregated cap. In *Philadelphia National Bank v Poole*[83] it was held that each individual fraud constituted a "loss or occurrence" for the purposes of the policy in the result the assured was unable to recover any of its loss of £300,000, as each individual "loss or occurrence" was within the per-loss deductible of £25,000. This decision followed that of Greer J. in *Equitable Trust of New York v Whittaker*,[84] where it was held that the deductible of £2,500 carried in respect of "each and every loss" applied to each of the seven individual occurrences of fraud taking place under one master agreement.

23–028   **Subrogation.** The insurer is entitled to the benefit of the assured's rights against the wrongdoer. Thus, under an employers' fidelity policy, the insurer is usually entitled to deduct any money which would have been payable to the employee but for the misappropriation. However, where the loss exceeds the sum insured, he is only entitled to so much of such money, if any, as exceeds the difference, after payment of the sum insured.[85]

Under a fidelity guarantee the surety is entitled on payment to any stolen property recovered after deducting the costs of recovery.[86] It would seem on principle[87] that an insurer would be similarly subrogated to the assured's rights against his employee.[88]

5. INSURANCE OF DEBTS

23–029   **Principles applicable.** Wherever a debt exists, or is contemplated,[89] the creditor may insure its due payment. The assignee of book debts may also insure against the fraud of the assignor.[90] Policies insuring against the non-payment of a debt are contracts of indemnity, and if the debt is not paid on the date when it falls due the insurers will, on payment, be subrogated to the assured's rights against the debtor.[91] It is also possible for the policy to cover not just the debtor's actual

[83] *Philadelphia National Bank v Poole* [1938] 2 All E.R. 199. See also *Dornoch Ltd v Mauritius Union Assurance Co Ltd and Mauritius Commercial Bank Ltd (No.2)* [2007] Lloyd's Rep. I.R. 350.

[84] *Equitable Trust of New York v Whittaker* (1923) 17 Ll. L.R. 153, following *Pennsylvania Co v Mumford* [1920] 2 K.B. 537.

[85] *Liverpool Starr-Bowkett Building Society v Travellers' Accident Insurance* (1893) 9 T.L.R. 221.

[86] *Hatch, Mansfield & Co v Weingott* (1906) 22 T.L.R. 366.

[87] The employer's right to proceed against the employee was established in *Lister v Romford Ice* [1957] A.C. 555.

[88] See, however, Scott L.J.'s language in *Goddard & Smith v Frew* [1939] 4 All E.R. 358, contrasting fidelity policies with contracts of indemnity.

[89] *Seaton v Burnand* [1900] A.C. 135 at 141; *Anglo-Californian Bank v London & Provincial Marine* (1904) 10 Com. Cas. 1.

[90] As in *Fortisbank SA v Trenwick International Ltd* [2005] Lloyd's Rep. I.R. 464. This type of policy is akin to a fidelity policy as opposed to a credit policy as such, because the cover is not against the default of the debtor, but rather against the risk that the debt never existed in the first place.

[91] *Meacock v Bryant & Co* (1942) 59 T.L.R. 51; *Parr's Bank v Albert Mines* (1900) 5 Com. Cas. 116. Prior to payment by the insurer, however, the assured cannot in the absence of some express policy term be prevented from taking such action to recover the debt as he thinks reasonable: see *AB Exportkredit v New Hampshire Insurance* Unreported, March 1989. The Court of Appeal further held that a "reasonable care" clause does not alter this general principle. *Meacock v Bryant & Co* (1942) 59 T.L.R. 51; *Parr's Bank v Albert Mines* (1900) 5 Comm. Cas. 116. Prior to payment by the insurer, however, the assured cannot in the absence of some express policy term be prevented from taking such action to recover the debt as he thinks reasonable: see *AB Exportkredit v New Hampshire Insurance* Unreported, March 1989. The Court of Appeal further held that a "reasonable care" clause does not alter this general principle.

default but also the commencement of insolvency proceedings by or against the debtor: see *Merrill Lynch International Bank Ltd v Winterthur Swiss Insurance Co*,[92] where the issue was whether French insolvency proceedings akin to English administration triggered payment under the policy (which was held to be the case).

Such policies sometimes cover non-payment from specified causes only,[93] but where the insurance is simply against non-payment of a debt on a specified date it is immaterial to consider the cause of the default.[94] It has even been held that a policy which provides indemnity to the lender when its loan is irrecoverable "for any reason" applies even to a loan which is not enforceable, e.g. by reason of infringement of regulatory legislation. *Bank of Scotland v Euclidian (No.1) Ltd*[95] was a case involving bank loans to enable claimants to purchase "after the event" litigation insurance which was then assigned to the bank and which gave an indemnity for the amount of the loans in the event that the sums were irrecoverable by way of costs from defendants. The loans infringed the Consumer Credit Act 1974, but the insurers were nevertheless required to repay the loans under insuring wording whereby the insurers were to indemnify the bank for the amount of any outstanding loans.

The policy moneys become payable immediately on such default; the assured is not bound to sue the debtor or enforce his securities first,[96] unless it is the deficiency only after he has done so that is insured.[97] In *British Credit Trust Holdings v UK Insurance Ltd*[98] the assured provided credit on vehicles in the form of hire-purchase contracts with borrowers. The insurance was designed to protect the assured against default by any borrower which had not been made good within 90 days of the termination of the contract. The policy thus distinguished three separate situations: (a) where a vehicle was repossessed by the assured and sold within 90 days, the insurers were liable for the difference between the sum received and the hire-purchase price; (b) where the vehicle was repossessed by the assured, but not sold within 90 days, the insurers were liable for the difference between the Glass's Guide price and the hire-purchase price; and (c) if the vehicle could not be repossessed within 90 days then the insurers were liable for the outstanding balance of the hire-purchase agreement. It was held by Morison J. that the assured's cause of action accrued in situation (a) on the date of the resale, and the cause of action accrued in situations (b) and (c) on the ninety-first day following termination.

The fact that the assured has assented to a scheme of arrangement with the debtor will not avail the insurers.[99] Such arrangement is a form of non-payment, not an alteration of the risk vitiating the policy.[100] In such a case they will be subrogated on payment to the creditor's rights under the scheme.[101] The same **23–030**

---

[92] *Merrill Lynch International Bank Ltd v Winterthur Swiss Insurance Co* [2007] Lloyd's Rep. I.R. 532.
[93] *Hambro v Burnand* [1904] 2 K.B. 10 at 19. per Collins M.R; *Waterkeyn v Eagle Star* (1920) 5 Ll. L.R. 42.
[94] Hawkins J. in *Mortgage Insurance v Inland Revenue Commissioners* (1887) 57 L.J.Q.B, 174 at 181; Lord Maclaren in *Laird v Securities Insurance* (1895) 22 R. (Ct of Sess) 452.
[95] *Bank of Scotland v Euclidian (No.1) Ltd* [2008] Lloyd's Rep. I.R. 182.
[96] Lord Esher in *Dane v Mortgage Insurance* [1894] 1 Q.B. 54 at 61.
[97] *Murdock v Heath* (1899) 80 L.T. 50; *Re Law Guarantee Trust* [1914] 2 Ch. 617.
[98] *British Credit Trust Holdings v UK Insurance Ltd* [2004] 1 All E.R. (Comm) 444.
[99] *Dane v Mortgage Insurance* [1894] 1 Q.B. 54; *Laird v Securities Insurance* (1895) 22 R. 452.
[100] See *Law Guarantee v Munich Reinsurance* [1912] 1 Ch. 138.
[101] *Dane v Mortgage Insurance* [1894] 1 Q.B. 54; *Laird v Securities Insurance* (1895) 22 R. 452.

principle applies where the holder of a debenture insures payment thereunder, and by a special resolution of debenture-holders such payment is postponed,[102] or where a bank whose debts a creditor has insured becomes insolvent and forms a realisation company.[103] *Shaw v Royce*[104] must be contrasted with these decisions. In that case the assured, a debenture-holder, was held to be bound, as against the insurers of the debentures, by a scheme of arrangement to which the insurers were a party substituting new uninsured debentures for those whose payment they had insured. This case may be distinguished from those above on the ground that the original contract of insurance was a tripartite one between the insurers, the company and the debenture-holders providing for such a scheme.

The policy will normally extend to all debts owed or the assured rather than to individual debts. In the former case, it is normally a condition of the policy that the insurer is kept informed of any defaults. In *Kazakstan Wool Processors (Europe) Ltd v Nederlandsche Credietverzekering Maatschappij NV*,[105] the assured was required to provide monthly trading returns, and the premium was calculated on the basis of the last trading return. The assured ceased trading and failed to submit a nil trading return. The insurers sought to rely upon a policy condition which provided that due performance of all conditions was a condition precedent to liability, to deny payment of losses which had arisen prior to the assured's breach. The Court of Appeal held that the policy was to be construed as applying only to claims tainted by the breach, and that earlier claims were not to be lost by reason of it. A policy which protects the assured against bad debts will generally require the assured to comply with its own underwriting criteria in extending credit. This type of condition is clearly fundamental to the risk run by the insurers, so that failure to comply with its terms will preclude the application of the policy to the debts affected by the breach.[106]

In the case of a policy that covers individual debtors,[107] there will generally be an aggregate credit limit applicable to the debtor. The relationship between the credit limit and the measure of indemnity was discussed by Colman J. in *Moore Large & Co Ltd v Hermes Credit & Guarantee Plc*.[108] The policy in this case covered the assured, a supplier of cycles and cycle accessories, against default by named individual customers, including Motorworld. The insured loss was defined by the policy as the amount of "Qualifying Debt" not exceeding the "Credit Limit" on the "Due Date", i.e. the date upon which the invoice fell due for payment. The initial aggregate credit limit was £600,000, which was subsequently raised to £2,500,000 for the period of trading covering Christmas 2000. Motorworld went into administration in October 2000, leaving total debts to the assured of £1,152,077.93. The insurers argued that the definitions in the policy meant that the policy attached to a particular debt only if both at the time the invoice was issued and the time the debt fell due the aggregate of the sums owing the assured did not exceed the credit limit. Colman J. held that this was a wholly uncommercial interpretation of the policy, and that the matter was to be looked at only at the date upon which the debt fell due: if that result had been

[102] *Finlay v Mexican Investment Co* [1897] 1 Q.B. 517.

[103] *Murdock v Heath* (1899) 80 L.T. 50.

[104] *Shaw v Royce* [1911] 1 Ch. 138.

[105] *Kazakstan Wool Processors (Europe) Ltd v Nederlandsche Credietverzekering Maatschappij NV* [2000] Lloyd's Rep. I.R. 371.

[106] *Svenska Handelsbanken v Sun Alliance & London Insurance Plc* [1996] 1 Lloyd's Rep. 519.

[107] The policy may be written on a declaration basis, so that individual debtors have to be declared to the insurers before cover incepts, and the provision of cover rests upon the credit-rating of the debtor in question: *Close Invoice Finance Ltd v Watts* [2009] EWCA Civ 1182.

[108] *Moore Large & Co Ltd v Hermes Credit & Guarantee Plc* [2003] Lloyd's Rep. I.R. 315.

intended, far clearer wording would have been required. Had the insurers been right, it would have been necessary to attempt to work out the outstanding aggregate debt of Motorworld to the assured at every date on which a further invoice was issued, whereas focusing on the aggregate indebtedness on the date of Motorworld's insolvency and measuring it against the credit limit at that point was a comparatively simple exercise. Colman J. also held that the duty of utmost good faith attached to the assured when seeking an increase in credit limit, and that while the assured had been in breach of duty by not disclosing the amount of Motorworld's indebtedness when seeking the increase the insurers had waived the breach of duty by relying upon a coverage defence only and not taking the utmost good faith point until shortly before the trial: the utmost good faith issues of this case are discussed in Ch.6 of this work.

The cover offered by the insurance in relation to an individual debtor may also depend upon the assured adhering to the underwriting criteria laid down by the policy and not lending an amount in excess of a specific sum. In *College Credit Ltd v The National Guarantee Corp Ltd*[109] the assured arranged the financing of motor vehicles to "sub-prime" (impaired credit rating) customers. The advance by the assured in any one case was not to exceed "110% Glass's Guide Trade Value" for the vehicle, and the insurers agreed to indemnify the assured in the event of default by a customer for the shortfall between the hire-purchase price and the amount recovered by the assured. The assured advanced to customers not just the purchase price of the vehicle, but also sums for "accidental death benefit" and "guaranteed asset protection" insurance policies. The credit insurers argued that these sums were to be included in the advance made by the assured so that the underwriting criteria had been broken in a large number of cases. Toulson J. held in favour of the assured and ruled that the commercial purpose of the policy was to protect the assured against losses on hire-purchase contracts and not losses from ancillary debts. The learned judge concluded that it was "improbable that the parties intended to agree that compliance with the "Maximum Advance" criterion should hinge on "Uninsured add-ons".[110]

Insurance of completion of contract. Due completion of a contract may similarly be insured.[111] Where A employed B to do a job and A insured with C against loss arising out of failure duly to complete, and by a condition of the policy A was required to notify C in writing of any non-performance or non-observance on the part of B of the terms of the contract between A and B which might involve a loss for which C would be responsible under the contract of insurance, and where it was a term of the contract between A and B that the work should be done at a definite rate, and it was not, but the failure so to do on the part of B was not notified by A to C, and then B went bankrupt and A had to complete at a loss, it was held that C was not liable.[112]

23–031

The modern practice in relation to specific forms of contracts, notably large-scale building works (frequently to be carried out in other countries), is for the contractor rather than the employer to procure "insurance" against the contractor's default, by the means of a performance bond. Such bonds are issued by

[109] *College Credit Ltd v The National Guarantee Corp Ltd* [2005] Lloyd's Rep. I.R. 5.
[110] It might be thought that the greater the debt owed by a customer, the greater the risk of default: accordingly, additional loans by the assured could in principle prejudice the possibility of repayment under the hire-purchase agreement and thus increase the insurers' risk. As against that, the insurers were to some extent protected by their subrogation rights, which were secured by the assured's proprietary interest in the vehicles themselves.
[111] See *Trade Indemnity v Workington Harbour Board* [1937] A.C. 1.
[112] *Clydebank Water Trustees v Fidelity & Deposit Co of Maryland* 1915 S.C. 362.

insurers, banks and surety companies. Where the construction contract calls for a bond, it will be the contractor's obligation to procure a bond from an issuer, payable to the employer. The bond will normally be payable on demand, and will not require the employer to prove that the contractor is in breach of contract: consequently, it is possible for the contractor to find that the issuer has been called upon by the employer to honour the bond even though there was no objective justification for the employer's demand, and the contractor is unable in English law to prevent the issuer from making payment.[113] Contractors are, therefore, reluctant to agree to an obligation to procure a bond, although it may be that such an obligation is the price of obtaining a potentially lucrative contract: to overcome the possibility of fraud or abuse by the employer, some insurers have developed for the benefit of contractors "unfair calling" insurance policies.

23–032   **Export credit insurance.** Under the Export and Investment Guarantees Act 1991, replacing the Export Guarantee and Overseas Investment Act 1978, the Secretary of State is empowered to make arrangements which facilitate the export of goods or services from the United Kingdom. These powers are exercised through the Export Credit Guarantees Department. One of the most important functions carried out by the ECGD is the provision of guarantee insurance for exporters against the risk of loss arising from the non-performance of contracts by overseas purchasers. The guarantees given by the ECGD are treated as ordinary insurance contracts by the courts.[114]

In May 1998 the European Commission published a Directive on the harmonisation of the law relating to the provision of export credit insurance by member states,[115] the objective being to ensure that each member state offers export credits on the same terms and that no one Member State confers unfair advantages upon its own exporters by providing either subsidised export credit insurance or unduly generous cover. The Directive establishes criteria for the assessment of risks, and for the definition of the risks against which insurance may be granted. Premiums are to be calculated by reference to an assessment of the risk from the country in which the supply contract is to be performed, the credit-worthiness of the debtor, and the duration of the period over which the contract is to be performed. The premium must cover the insurer's long-term operating costs. The insurable risks are: insolvency of the debtor, default of the debtor, arbitrary cancellation by the debtor state, the imposition of restrictions on the making of payment and force majeure. The state insurer is not to be liable where the loss is directly or indirectly attributable to: any act or omission on the part of the assured which renders the supply contract unenforceable, any provision in the supply contract restricting the assured's rights, any agreement after the conclusion of the supply contract which prevents or delays payment by the debtor and failure by sub-contractors or third parties to fulfil their obligations other than by reason of an insured peril.

Under the Directive, losses are payable if the default continues for a waiting period of six months, following which there is to be indemnification within a

---

[113] See, as illustrative of the many cases on the point, *Edward Owen Engineering Ltd v Barclays Bank* [1978] 1 All E.R. 976.

[114] See *Lucas (L) v Export Credit Guarantees Department* [1974] 1 W.L.R. 909 and *Lonrho Exports v Export Credit Guarantees Department* [1996] 4 All E.R. 673, both of which involved subrogation.

[115] Directive 98/29, [1998] OJ L148/22.

further month provided that the assured has not broken any policy terms or that there is no dispute as to quantum or liability.

Time variable cover. This relatively modern form of insurance was developed **23–033** in the early 1990s to protect investors in films and television productions.[116] The essence of the cover is that the investors who are to be repaid from the revenues earned from the films insure against the possibility of non-payment out of those revenues. In *Screen Partners London Ltd v VIF Film Production GmbH*[117] the claimants arranged for the defendants a policy of this type referred to as shortfall contingency insurance.[118] The policy insured the defendants for their "ascertained net loss" up to a maximum sum insured. The ascertained net loss was defined as meaning the whole or any part of the sum insured which was outstanding and unpaid from revenues as at a fixed date, the claim date. The sum insured was the difference between budgeted production costs and actual production costs. The agreement contained an exclusivity provision under which the defendants were not permitted to obtain "TVC, shortfall or gap insurance" from any other source. The defendants did in fact obtain a further policy from a third party. That policy, described as a "Pecuniary Loss Indemnity Policy" insured against the difference between the sums insured under the policy and the revenues available to make payment on that day. The issue was whether the second policy constituted "TVC, shortfall or gap insurance" within the terms of the exclusivity clause. The Court of Appeal, reversing the trial judge, held that there was a serious question to go to trial on this point. While the TVC policy was concerned with the difference between budgeted and actual costs, and the second policy was concerned with a revenue gap, the Court of Appeal felt that there was a strong argument for treating both policies as forms of gap or shortfall insurance, or at the very least the new policy met that description.

6. AFTER THE EVENT INSURANCE

Nature of ATE insurance. This form of insurance is new to the United **23–034** Kingdom, and has developed since the abolition of legal aid. In essence, state funding is no longer available for most civil actions, and instead the claimant can fund his action by a combination of legal expenses insurance, contingency fee arrangements with lawyers,[119] and "after the event" insurance. Legal expenses insurance is "before the event" insurance, as it is general and applies to future claims which the assured may seek to bring. By contrast, ATE insurance is taken out by the potential claimant to fund a specific claim, and the insurers will assess the likelihood of success before agreeing to issue cover.

---

[116] TVC policies were in issue in *HIH Transit and Casualty Insurance v Chase Manhattan Bank* [2001] Lloyd's Rep. I.R. 703 and the various sequel decisions involving claims against reinsurers and brokers.

[117] *Screen Partners London Ltd v VIF Film Production GmbH* [2002] Lloyd's Rep. I.R. 283.

[118] See also *John Meacock v Bryant & Co* (1942) 74 Ll. L.R. 53.

[119] At one time contingency fee arrangements were void at common law for champerty or maintenance. The common law on these points has more or less been superseded by the new statutory arrangements for funding civil actions, and little remains of the stigma of champerty and maintenance: *R. (on the application of Factortame) v Secretary of State for Transport* [2002] EWCA Civ 932; *RSA Pursuit Test Cases* Unreported, May 2005.

A typical ATE policy will work in the following way. The claimant's case will be assessed[120] to determine whether it stands at least a 50 per cent chance of success. The insurers will also insist upon a likelihood that a specified minimum sum is recoverable. If these conditions are met,[121] a policy will be issued[121a] and the claimant will be granted credit for the amount of the premium, so that no premium is actually paid at the time. In the event that the claimant's case succeeds, the amount of the ATE premium will form a part of the claimant's costs and recovery will be sought from the defendant. If the claim fails, the insurers pay the defendant's costs as well as the premium and the claimant's costs. The effect, therefore, is that the claimant does not at any point actually pay the premium. Solicitors involved in such claims may themselves obtain funding, by way of bank loan, for their ongoing costs: if the claim succeeds the costs awarded against the defendant will be used to discharge the loan, and if the claim fails then the loan will be repaid by separate financial guarantee insurance obtained by solicitors for their own benefit and which is issued when a loan is obtained.[122]

If the solicitors acting for the assured claimant provide their own guarantee to the claimant that his costs will be paid by the ATE insurers, and the ATE insurers default so that the solicitors have to honour their guarantee and pay the claimant's costs, the solicitors may have an action for breach of contract against the insurers on the basis that there is an implied term in the arrangements that the insurers will honour the policy. In the alternative the solicitors may have a valid claim for contribution under the Civil Liability (Contribution) Act 1978.[123]

Recovery of premium by way of costs

23–035 *Guidelines.* The main issue which has to date arisen in relation to ATE insurance is whether the premium paid by the assured for his cover is recoverable from the defendant in the proceedings (or, in many cases, the defendant's liability insurers) as an element in his costs. The test cases, *Callery v Gray (No.1)*[124] and *Callery v Gray (No.2)*[125] both concerned small personal injury claims in motor vehicle accident cases, and in these cases the Court of Appeal laid down basic guidelines on the recoverability of costs. The cases were appealed to the House of Lords, and the House of Lords by a 4_1 majority approved the Court of Appeal's guidelines on the narrow basis that the responsibility for monitoring and controlling the developing practice in a field such as ATE insurance lay with the Court of Appeal and not the House of Lords, as the House could not respond to changes in practice with the speed and sensitivity of the Court of Appeal,

---

[120] There are frequently a number of stages to this process. For the operation of privilege in respect of documents generated in the assessment process, see *Winterthur Swiss Insurance Co v AG (Manchester) Ltd, The TAG Group Litigation* [2006] EWHC 839 (Comm).

[121] For the role of solicitors in the assessment process, and for the running of time where they allegedly perform their role negligently, see *Axa Insurance Ltd v Akther & Darby Solicitors* [2009] EWCA Civ 1166.

[121a] A misrepresentation or non-disclosure by the assured in respect of the genuine nature of the claim being funded by the policy may constitute a material fact for the purposes of the duty of utmost good faith: *Persimmon Homes Ltd v Great Lakes Reinsurance (UK) Plc* [2010] EWHC 1705 (Comm).

[122] See the description of the process in *Clydesdale Financial Services Ltd v Smailes* [2009] EWHC 3190 (Ch), in which the issue was whether premiums were payable by the solicitors before loans had been made to them, a question answered in the negative by the court on the basis that no risk had attached until a loan was made.

[123] *Greene Wood & McLean v Templeton Insurance Ltd* [2009] EWCA Civ 65.

[124] *Callery v Gray (No.1)* [2001] 3 All E.R. 835. See also *Home Office v Lownds* [2002] EWCA Civ 365.

[125] *Callery v Gray (No.2)* [2001] 4 All E.R. 1.

before which a number of cases were likely over time to come. Thus, although the House of Lords had serious misgivings over some aspects of the Court of Appeal's guidelines, and even as to the outcome of the case itself, the Court of Appeal's judgments were allowed to stand.

In *Callery*, the sum recovered by way of settlement was £1,500 plus costs. The Court of Appeal ruled that the ATE premium of £350 plus £7.50 insurance premium tax was recoverable from the defendant. In so deciding the Court of Appeal held that there was jurisdiction to award an ATE premium by way of costs in a costs-only hearing conducted under CPR r.44.12A. As to the recoverability the premium itself, the Court of Appeal noted that, in accordance with the express terms of s.29 of the Access to Justice Act 1999, an ATE premium was recoverable by way of costs if it was reasonable in the circumstances of the case. Reasonableness involves two considerations: the taking out of the policy; and the amount of the premium.

Reasonableness of procuring ATE insurance. In *Callery v Gray (No.1)* the Court **23–036** of Appeal, having heard evidence as to the operation of the ATE market, held that it was reasonable for a claimant to take out an ATE policy at the outset, even before the defendant had indicated whether or not liability would be contested. The Court of Appeal's primary concern was with the viability of the ATE market, for if ATE premiums could be justified only where liability was to be contested and where the prospects of success were in doubt there could be an adverse effect on the market as a whole. Put rather differently, the Court of Appeal was fearful that disallowing ATE premiums might cause the entire market to wither. The House of Lords on appeal,[126] while plainly unhappy with this analysis, chose not to overturn it. Lord Scott, dissenting vigorously, held that the question of the award of costs was not one to be determined by the market for ATE insurance but rather for the facts of any given case, and if it was unreasonable for the victim to procure ATE insurance by reason of the fact that the defendant was almost certain to be able to contest liability, or had not been given the opportunity to state his position in relation to the claim, then the ATE premium ought to be disallowed. In *Re Claims Direct Test Cases*,[127] Chief Master Hurst, having considered the analysis of the House of Lords, ruled that in the case of an incident causing minor injuries in respect of which the defendant had from the outset admitted liability, it would generally be disproportionate and unreasonable to take out an ATE policy unless there were live issues as to matters such as causation.

The converse argument put in *Ashworth v Peterborough United Football Club*[128] was that the policy had been taken out too late. This was a dismissal claim. The claimant procured an ATE policy at a late stage in the proceedings against his employers. In a costs application, Master Wright held that in principle the premium was recoverable: it had not been appropriate to secure a policy at an earlier stage, given that the duration of the proceedings had not then been apparent, and in any event even if cover had been available at an earlier stage[129] it would almost certainly have been more expensive.

---

[126] *Callery v Gray (No.1)* [2003] Lloyd's Rep. I.R. 203.

[127] *Re Claims Direct Test Cases* [2003] Lloyd's Rep. I.R. 73, affirmed [2003] Lloyd's Rep. I.R. 677.

[128] *Ashworth v Peterborough United Football Club* Unreported, 2002.

[129] This was far from clear, as an earlier proposal by the claimant had indeed been rejected by insurers.

In *Sarwar v Alam*,[130] which was also a small personal injuries claim arising out of a motor vehicle accident, the defendant challenged the reasonableness of the claimant's ATE premium on the basis that it was inappropriate in the circumstances of the case for any policy to have been taken out at all as alternative insurance had been available to the claimant. In that case the claimant had been a passenger in the defendant's vehicle, and the defendant's motor vehicle liability policy conferred upon any passenger the right to recover his legal costs in the event that he brought proceedings against the driver. The defendant's argument was that the claimant should have relied upon the legal expenses cover rather than seeking separate ATE cover. The Court of Appeal accepted that in principle it would be wrong for a claimant who had the benefit of before the event insurance to seek ATE insurance covering the selfsame risk, but held that on the facts the claimant had acted reasonably. The claimant had not been aware that he was covered for legal expenses under the defendant's policy, and it would have been unreasonable for him to seek to find out whether such cover did in fact exist. The Court of Appeal set out guidelines for the procedure to be followed by the claimant's solicitors in considering whether to advise the client to procure ATE insurance. Solicitors should first require the claimant to produce his own before the event policies, to determine whether any of them offered the appropriate cover, but the claimant could not be obliged to procure copies of the policy held by the defendant in the proceedings. It is perhaps to be stressed that the amount of the claim was very small, and the Court of Appeal accepted that in the case of larger claims, where the ATE premium might be extremely large, it might be reasonable to require the claimant to call for the defendant's policy.

23–037 *Reasonableness of amount of premium.* In every case it is necessary for the ATE premium to be proportionate to the claim. This is not, however, a question of measuring the amount of the premium against the amount of the claim. The test for proportionality is whether the premium has been necessarily incurred, which in turn depends upon whether the claimant would have been able to bring the claim without procuring ATE insurance: accordingly, an ATE premium which is large when compared to the claim itself is not necessarily disproportionate.[131] There is no objection in principle to an ATE premium which, rather than taking the form of a lump sum assessed at the outset, is determined in stages so that there is an initial sum payable when the case is taken up, a further sum payable when the proceedings are issued and a final sum payable shortly before the trial. The staged approach has the advantage of allowing insurers to assess the actual risks at each relevant point of the claim.

In *Callery (No.2)*[132] the Court of Appeal, in laying down guidelines for determining the reasonableness of an ATE premium,[133] held that a premium would generally be regarded as reasonable if it was calculated by the insurers on the individual assessment of the risk and not by any form of block rating method. The premium could include sums based on the possibility that the case would be lost so that the premium might prove to be irrecoverable, the cost of reinsuring the risk, administrative costs, and commission. On appeal to the House of Lords[134] it became apparent that in fact the premium in this case had been fixed

---

[130] *Sarwar v Alam* [2001] 4 All E.R. 541.

[131] *Rogers v Merthyr Tydfil County Borough Council* [2006] Lloyd's Rep. I.R. 759.

[132] *Callery v Gray (No.2)* [2001] 4 All E.R. 1.

[133] The guidelines were based, with modifications, on a report from Master O'Hare commissioned by the Court of Appeal for the purposes of the case.

[134] *Callery v Gray (No.2)* [2003] Lloyd's Rep. I.R. 73, affirmed [2003] Lloyd's Rep. I.R. 677.

on a block-rating basis which laid down a standard premium for every case with a greater than 50 per cent likelihood of success, rather on an individual assessment of the risk. Lord Scott of Foscote, in a powerful dissenting speech, made much of this point and noted that it was wholly inappropriate for the defendant to have to pay by way of costs awarded against him an ATE premium representing a 50 per cent chance of success when in fact the likelihood of success in the instant case had been in excess of 90 per cent. The majority chose not to overturn the Court of Appeal's judgment despite the apparent mis-understanding.

The recoverability of ATE premiums payable on a block-rating basis was confirmed by Chief Master Hurst in *Re Claims Direct Test Cases*.[135] In his view it was reasonable for a claimant to take out insurance costed on a block-rated basis, as there could be no criticism of a scheme which was designed to be easily accessible and understandable rather than one which was sophisticated and accurately costed. However, this conclusion was to some extent tempered by the findings that the novelty of ATE insurance and the absence of statistical evidence made it all but impossible for underwriters to assess premiums on any other basis for the time being, and that it was unlikely that the premium would have been much different even if an accurate costings exercise had been undertaken.

The content of premium. Under s.29 of the Access to Justice Act 1999 it is **23–038** possible for the court to award by way of costs the amount of an insurance premium incurred by the claimant to secure the costs of the action. The section provides as follows:

> "Where in any proceedings a costs order is made in favour of any party who has taken out an insurance policy against the risk of incurring liability in these proceedings, the costs payable to him may, subject in the case of court proceedings to Rules of Court, include costs in respect of the premium of the policy."

The Rules of Court here referred to, CPR r.43.2(1)(m), defines "insurance premium" as meaning "a sum of money paid or payable[136] for insurance against the risk of incurring a costs liability in the proceedings, taken out after the event that is the subject matter of the claim." The principles governing the reasonable-ness of a premium are set out in the CPR Cost Direction, which requires the court to have regard to: the level and extent of the cover provided; the availability of any pre-existing insurance cover; whether any part of the premium is to be rebated in the event of early settlement; and the amount of commission payable to the claimant and his legal representatives or other agents.[137] The key question here is the scope of the word "premium", as costs which may be incurred and included in the charge for insurance may have little or nothing to do with the insurance coverage itself but may be related to litigation support. The problem of disentangling the component parts of a "premium" was addressed by Chief Master Hurst and the Court of Appeal in *Re Claims Direct Test Cases*.[138] The cases involved claimants who had taken out ATE insurance in respect of personal

[135] *Re Claims Direct Test Cases* Unreported, 2004.

[136] See *RSA Pursuit Test Cases* Unreported, May 2005, in which Master Hurst held that the fact that the assured has not paid any premium, and indeed that no premium is payable unless the assured succeeds in his action and is awarded the notional amount of the premium by way of costs, was an arrangement which nevertheless fell within the definition of "premium" in s.29.

[137] CPR Costs Direction s.11, para.10.

[138] *Re Claims Direct Test Cases* [2003] Lloyd's Rep. I.R. 73, affirmed [2003] Lloyd's Rep. I.R. 677. See also *Sharratt v London Central Bus Co* [2004] EWCA Civ 57.

injury claims. The actions were successful but the amount of the ATE premium to be included in the costs order was challenged by the defendants. The insurance scheme adopted[139] was a complex one, involving the use of a number of companies which provided various services. In outline, the total premium payable was £1,312.50 which was broken down as: £1,000 payable to a separate company for claims handling services, including initial risk assessment and claims monitoring; £110 commission payable to Claims Direct as the operator of the system; £140 to Lloyd's brokers and underwriters; and £62.50 by way of insurance premium tax. In light of claims experience the scheme was subsequently adjusted so that an additional £311.55 per policy was paid retrospectively to underwriters. Chief Master Hurst, whose decision was upheld by the Court of Appeal, held that on £621.13 of the total sum paid of £1,312.50 qualified as premium, the test for which was "the consideration required of the assured in return for which the insurer undertook his obligation under the contract of insurance." The reasoning was as follows:

(1) The £140 paid to the underwriters and the brokers was clearly premium and thus allowable. The additional sums of £311.55 paid to underwriters following the adjustment of the scheme[140] were also premium.

(2) Claims Direct's commission of £110,[141] which was high, was nevertheless not unreasonable and constituted premium.

(3) Only those parts of the £1000 claims handling payments were premium. A distinction was to be drawn between sums actually paid for insurance services and sums paid for claims handling and ancillary services. Allowable as part of the premium were the costs of arranging for completion of the Claims Direct application form, arranging for the client to complete a credit agreement application form, obtaining further information, monitoring the conduct of the case and maintaining relevant financial information. Sums not forming part of the premium were those representing the costs of obtaining further information for a solicitor contemplating taking on the claim, the costs of obtaining witness statements from clients, witnesses and experts, and the costs of arranging medical examinations of the claimant. Of the sum of £1000 paid for these services, only £395 represented insurance services. However, as that was payable to the solicitor nominated by Claims Direct by way of disbursement it was irrecoverable, and the only sum which could be treated as premium was £30 paid directly from Claims Direct's funds to the supplier of the services.

(4) An additional premium of £245 paid by the claimant, representing the risk that the damages recovered might not be enough to cover the insurance premium, was irrecoverable, as this was a discrete add-on which fell outside s.29 of the Access to Justice Act 1999.[142]

(5) Insurance premium tax was recoverable only to the extent that it related to actual allowable premium rather than to the cost of ancillary services.

---

[139] Which had been discontinued by the time of the action.

[140] Chief Master Hurst ruled that even though the amount had been paid in a block sum in arrears, it was to be allocated between existing policies rather than applied to future policies.

[141] This was used to advertise in order to generate new business.

[142] Cf. *Ashworth v Peterborough United Football Club* Unreported, 2002, where a similar principle was accepted, although on the facts of that case no additional premium had been paid for this form of cover.

Further issues relating to the amount of the premium arose in *Ashworth v Peterborough United Football Club*.[143] In this case the claimant, at a late stage in the proceedings, had procured an ATE policy with a limit of indemnity of £125,000, a figure which had been reached by a full assessment of the past and likely future costs of the action. The premium was approximately one-third of the limit of indemnity. Master Wright held that the premium was recoverable, and laid down the following principles:

(1) There was no obligation on the claimant to disclose to the defendant the size of the premium that he intended to pay for ATE cover.

(2) The proportion of the premium to limit of indemnity was not unreasonable given the complexity of the case and the state of the market. Further, it was not rendered disproportionate even though the amount of the premium was some two-thirds of the anticipated damages recovery (£75,000).[144]

(3) It was permissible for the premium to cover costs incurred in the period before the inception of the risk.

As noted earlier, an ATE is normally not paid by the claimant as such. The premium in practice only becomes payable if the claimant wins the case and recovers costs sufficient to cover the premium. If the case is lost, the premium is not paid at all. The mechanism by which this is achieved is to include in an ATE premium an amount which represents the risk that the case is lost, which in effect insures the claimant against any potential liability to pay the premium. This device has been held to be perfectly legitimate and a recoverable part of the premium in any costs order.[145]

Reasonableness of premium in non-standard cases. The *Callery* and related **23–039** litigation considered the reasonableness of a premium charged for a mass-market policy involving a relatively small personal injury claim with at least a 50 per cent prospect of success. There will be many situations in which the claim is non-standard in that the prospects of success are less than 50 per cent, or in that the claim is one in respect of which there is no mass-market rate. In *RSA Pursuit Test Cases*[146] Master Hurst considered the reasonableness of ATE premiums in five test cases under a scheme where premiums were individually assessed and were calculated by reference to three variables: the percentage prospects of success; an estimate of the assured's solicitors' own costs to the end of trial; and an estimate of the amount of any adverse costs order. The assured was not required to pay the premium unless and until he obtained judgment against the defendant in the proceedings and obtained a costs order, and in that event there was no mechanism for reducing the originally assessed premium even if the assured's own costs were reduced by assessment or agreement. Master Hurst laid down a series of principles in relation to the reasonableness of the premium.

(a) The amount of the premium had to be reasonable, and was to be based on factors such as the risk of a costs award and the size of the claim.

---

[143] *Ashworth v Peterborough United Football Club* Unreported, 2002.

[144] In the event, £66,000 was awarded by way of damages.

[145] *Callery v Gray (No.2)* [2001] Lloyd's Rep. I.R. 765; *Rogers v Merthyr Tydfil County Borough Council* [2006] Lloyd's Rep. I.R. 759.

[146] *RSA Pursuit Test Cases* Unreported, May 2005.

(b) If the sum insured proved to be too great, so that the premium was excessive in relation to the sums which the insurers could have been called upon to pay had the claimant lost the action, the claimant could not avoid a reduction of the costs award by arguing that he had relied on legal advice. A claimant could not expect the defendant to indemnify him against bad legal advice from the claimant's own solicitors. As Master Hurst noted, "There is a difference between reasonableness and negligence as between solicitor and client and the question of reasonableness as between claimant and defendant".

(c) The stipulation in the policies that the amount of the premium was not to be affected by a subsequent reduction of the claimant's legal costs by assessment or agreement was unreasonable and disproportionate: the proper approach was to allow the premium rate to be based on estimated costs but to determine the actual premium in the light of actual costs when known. This had the advantages of avoiding hindsight in calculating the rate of the premium and reverting to reality for the actual premium.

(d) The use of estimates for the assessment of the premium rendered the assessment seriously flawed. It was not enough that the claimant acted reasonably, because the point was that the defendant was liable only to pay reasonable and proportionate costs. The problems with the method of calculation of the premium were that: it assumed a constant relationship between costs at risk and own costs, which was unlikely to be the case—the claimant's costs would mount up first, followed by those of the defendant; it was based on unreliable estimates of the parties' costs; it was based on an estimate of success; and it was calculated on the claimant's costs even if they were found to be disproportionate and unreasonable.

23–040   **Disclosure of ATE policy.** CPR Practice Direction 44 para.19.4, requires a party to include in the funding information provided to the court under CPR 44.15 whether he has obtained an ATE policy and to give basic information about the policy. The provision does, however, allow a defendant to obtain detailed information on the amount of cover in advance of the proceedings. It will plainly be important for a defendant, faced with a claim by an assured who is protected by an ATE policy, to obtain early disclosure of the policy so that its coverage and financial limits can be determined. If the policy covers costs only to a low limit, a defendant who successfully defends proceedings brought by the claimant may find that he is in practice unable to recover a part of the costs awarded to him by the court. In general terms a party's insurance arrangements are not disclosable until proceedings are under way and formal disclosure orders have been made,[147] and CPR 18.1, which empowers the court to order disclosure of documents in advance of trial, appears not to apply to liability insurance[148] because such a policy does not clarify any of the issues in dispute, as required by CPR 18.1, but at best is relevant only to the enforceability of an ultimate judgment. By analogy it would seem that an ATE policy is to be treated in the same way. However, it would seem from *Barr v Biffa Waste Services Ltd*[149] that pre-trial disclosure may be ordered under CPR 31.14, which states that a party may inspect a document which is mentioned in a statement of case, a witness statement, a witness

---

[147] A claimant has no right to know about the defendant's liability insurance cover: *Bekhor v Bilton* [1991] Q.B. 923; *Cox v Bankside Members Agency* [1995] C.L.Y. 4122.

[148] *West London Pipe Line Storage Ltd v Total UK Ltd* [2008] Lloyd's Rep. I.R. 688, doubting *Harcourt v FEF Griffin* [2008] Lloyd's Rep. I.R. 386.

[149] *Barr v Biffa Waste Services Ltd* [2009] EWHC 1033 (TCC).

summary or an affidavit. In *Barr* the existence of an ATE policy had been referred to in correspondence relating to an application by the claimants' solicitor for a Group Litigation Order in respect of a large number of small claims. Coulson J. made the disclosure order. As far as jurisdiction was concerned, Coulson J. held that the word "mentioned" in CPR 31.14 was to be construed widely, and encompassed a case in which there had been an express reference to the policy to support an application for a Group Litigation Order. Further, there was no applicable litigation privilege attaching to the ATE policy. As far as discretion was concerned, Coulson J. felt that disclosure should be ordered as long as the ATE policy bore some relevance to the proceedings. It is to be noted that the learned judge's conclusions were based on the application for the Group Litigation Order, the court finding the necessary relevance in that the ATE policy underlay the application for the Group Litigation Order and there would not have been any proceedings without the Group Litigation Order given that each of the individual claims to be consolidated was relatively small. It may be that the facts of the case do not make it a convincing authority in other circumstances, although it is to be noted that Coulson J. held in the alternative that the court's general case management powers under the CPR permitted the making of a disclosure order going beyond what was required by CPR 44.15, and that this should be done in the interests of creating a level-playing field: the defendant's accounts were a matter of public record, so its ability to pay costs could easily be discovered, and it was thus appropriate to allow the defendants to ascertain the claimants' financial position. It would seem from the latter finding that there is no impediment to the making of disclosure orders at the outset of proceedings.

ATE policy as substitute for security for costs. The court is empowered by **23–041** CPR 25.13 to order the claimant to provide security for the defendant's costs where there is reason to believe that the claimant will not be able to meet a costs order in the event that the claim is unsuccessful. If the claimant has obtained an ATE policy which covers any costs order made against him and in favour of the defendant, the court may take that policy into account in deciding whether or not it is appropriate to order security. The effect of the authorities was summarised by Akenhead J. in *Michael Phillips Architects Ltd v Riklin*[150]:

   (a) There is no reason in principle why an ATE insurance policy which covers the claimant's liability to pay the defendant's costs, subject to its terms, could not provide some or some element of security for the defendant's costs. It can provide sufficient protection.

   (b) It will be a rare case where the ATE insurance policy can provide as good security as a payment into court or a bank bond or guarantee. That will be, amongst other reasons, because insurance policies are voidable by the insurers and subject to cancellation for many reasons, none of which are within the control or responsibility of the defendant, and because the promise to pay under the policy will be to the claimant.

   (c) It is necessary where reliance is placed by a claimant on an ATE insurance policy to resist or limit a security for costs application for it to be demonstrated that it actually does provide some security. Put another way,

[150] *Michael Phillips Architects Ltd v Riklin* [2010] EWHC 834 (TCC). The principles were derived from *Nasser v United Bank of Kuwait* [2001] EWCA 556; *Al-Koronky and another v Time-Life Entertainment Group Ltd* [2006] EWCA Civ 1123; and *Belco Trading Co v Kondo* [2008] EWCA Civ 205.

there must not be terms pursuant to which or circumstances in which the insurers can readily but legitimately and contractually avoid liability to pay out for the defendant's costs.

(d) There is no reason in principle why the amount fixed by a security for costs order could not be somewhat reduced to take into account any realistic probability that the ATE insurance would cover the costs of the defendant.

In *Riklin*, the claimant issued proceedings against the defendants for unpaid fees, and the defendants counterclaimed for breach of contract and sought security for the costs of the counterclaim. Akenhead J. held the policy provided little security and that an order should be made. That was so because: the policy was ambiguous as to whether it would cover costs awarded in respect of the counterclaim submitted by the defendants; the sum insured could be eroded by first-party costs; the policy applied only where there was a reasonable prospect of success, so the insurers could withdraw cover once it had seen the witness statements from the defendants; the policy would not respond if any of its conditions were broken; the insurers were off risk in the event of a fraudulent claim; and there were various rights to cancel.

7. BUSINESS INTERRUPTION INSURANCE

23–042 This form of policy is intended to protect the assured against financial loss consequent upon the occurrence of some other form of peril in the form of material damage, for example, strike, fire, flood or subsidence.[151] Business interruption insurance[152] is generally written on a "gross profits" basis. An assessment of gross profits in the coming year is made at the outset, and a premium is paid on that figure. If the sum proves less than actual gross profit, then the principle of average is applied to shortfall so that the assured is treated as his own insurer in respect of the uninsured proportion of any loss. An alternative, although less common, form of business interruption insurance is "declaration linked" basis. Here, the assured estimates gross profits for the coming year and pays an interim premium: at the end of the year, the premium is adjusted to take account of actual gross profits and the full amount of any loss is recoverable, although it is usual to cap the adjusted uplift so that the assured can never recover more than, say, 133 per cent, of the original estimated gross profits.

Under a typical business interruption policy the assured will be entitled to recover for defined financial losses which he has suffered in the "indemnity period", which is a fixed period, often 12 months, running from the date on which the peril insured against has occurred. There is very little English authority on this type of insurance, although it is commonly assumed that the indemnity period is to be treated in isolation so the fact that the assured is able to make good his losses following the expiry of the indemnity period does not give the insurers any right to reclaim their payment. This is in any event a relatively unusual scenario as the assured will normally have suffered opportunity cost losses in making good insured losses so that it cannot be said that the assured has received

---

[151] *Loyaltrend Ltd v Creechurch Dedicated Ltd* [2010] EWHC 425 (Comm).

[152] The following paragraph is based on the evidence given to the court in *Kyle Bay Ltd v Certain Lloyd's Underwriters* [2006] EWHC 607 (Comm), affirmed [2008] Lloyd's Rep. I.R. 460.

more than an indemnity. The principle is, therefore, that if losses are made good in the indemnity period, then the insurers are entitled to bring those gains into account, but the insurers may not do so if the losses are made good outside the indemnity period. The assured's action under a business interruption policy accrues when the insured peril occurs: the end of the indemnity period is simply the point at which the assured's loss can be quantified.[153] The business losses which are recoverable within the indemnity period are those defined by the policy: in *Coromin Ltd v AXA Re*[154] the policy referred to losses in respect of "all operations and activities of the Insured", and it was held that this wording extended to businesses which were not in operation at the date of the insured peril but which were brought on stream during the indemnity period.

The calculation of the amount of loss within the indemnity period is generally based on the period leading up to the insured peril. By way of example, if a fire occurs on January 1, 2010, and the indemnity period runs for one year, terminating on January 1, 2011, the amount of loss in that period will generally be assessed by reference to the assured's profits in the year starting January 1, 2009. This is a crude measure, and is often tempered by a "trends" clause, a typical wording being the following[154a]:

"adjustments shall be made as may be necessary to provide for the trend of the Business and for variations in or special circumstances affecting the Business either before or after the Damage or which would have affected the Business had the Damage not occurred so that the figures thus adjusted shall represent as nearly as may be reasonably practicable the results which but for the Damage would have been obtained during the relative period after the Damage."

The assessment thus takes into account special circumstances affecting the business in the year leading up to the fire, e.g. that the market was artificially depressed by temporary external factors and that the base figure of revenue in that year should be higher. The trends clause also takes into account the possibility that the year following the fire would have seen an increase in revenue, e.g. because additional investment had been made which was expected to produce enhanced results in that year. The trends clause may of course work against the assured, where the insurers can show that revenue in the year before the fire was artificially inflated or that revenue in the indemnity period would have declined from that in the year before the fire independently of the occurrence of the insured peril. As to the latter point, the insured peril may itself be a relevant factor in determining whether adjustments should be made for trends in the indemnity period. In *Orient-Express Hotels Ltd v Assicurazioni General SpA* the assured's luxury hotel in New Orleans was damaged by Hurricane Katrina in 2005. The damage resulted in the closure of the hotel for some weeks, and it also led the authorities to close the city for a short period, with the result that potential custom was lost. The assured argued that the closure of New Orleans was a factor which had to be left out of account in determining

---

[153] *Normhurst Ltd v Dornoch Ltd* [2005] Lloyd's Rep. I.R. 27. See also *If P & C Insurance Ltd (Publ) v Silversea Cruises Ltd* [2004] Lloyd's Rep. I.R. 696, where it was held that the phrase "subject to a maximum period per event of 6 months from date" in a business interruption policy taken out by a cruise operator meant that the operator could recover for all actual and anticipated losses of business in that period and was not confined to recovering for cruises scheduled to commence in that period.

[154] *Coromin Ltd v AXA Re* [2008] Lloyd's Rep. I.R. 467.

[154a] Taken from *Orient-Express Hotels Ltd v Assicurazioni General SpA* [2010] EWHC 1186 (Comm), but the wording is much in use.

whether there were special circumstances other than the damage to the hotel which would have diminished revenue in the indemnity period. Hamblen J. ruled that the fact that, but for the damage to the hotel, revenue in the indemnity period would in any event have been reduced by reason of the effect of Hurricane Katrina on the tourist trade, was to be taken into account.

As noted above, the trigger for loss is the occurrence of an insured peril giving rise to material damage, and it thus becomes crucial for the assured to prove that the business interruption loss was the result of material damage[155] rather than the assured's own commercial decision. In *If P & C Insurance Ltd v Silversea Cruises Ltd*[156] the assured provided luxury cruises for the North American market and insured against business interruption losses resulting from government action in response to war and terrorism risks "which interfere with the scheduled itinerary of the vessel". In the wake of the attack on the World Trade Center many customers cancelled their bookings, in addition, the number of anticipated bookings did not materialise, resulting in the assured laying up one of its vessels and diverting others. Tomlinson J. held that these losses were not covered. The insured peril was the occurrence of an external event that interfered with schedules rather than the assured's own decision to rearrange sailings. This reasoning was upheld on appeal with Rix L.J. stressing that the relevant part of the policy was concerned with the immediate consequence of insured perils upon the operation of the assured's vessels and not with commercial decisions taken by the assured following the occurrence of those perils. Again, in *International Management Group (UK) Ltd v Simmonds*,[157] the policy was against the cancellation of a cricket tournament between India and Pakistan. The Indian government withdrew its consent for the participation of its team following the outbreak of hostilities in Kashmir: the cause of the loss was held to be the actions of the Indian government rather than the outbreak of hostilities.

It is also necessary for the assured to prove that the loss was proximately caused by the material damage rather than by some other external cause. If there are concurrent causes, one insured and one uninsured, the general rule is that the assured is entitled to recover. However, if one cause is insured and one excluded, the exclusion takes priority. The former rule may be varied by express wording, so that if the policy requires the business interruption loss to be solely or directly by material damage, then the interposition of any other cause will preclude recovery. This was the ruling in *Orient-Express Hotels Ltd v Assicurazioni General SpA*, the facts of which were given above, in which the policy provided business interruption cover as a result of "direct physical loss destruction or damage". It was held that the loss suffered by the hotel had to be assessed by reference only to such losses that would not have arisen had the damage to the hotel not occurred. Any loss resulting from the closure of New Orleans thus had to be left out of account even though, on other wording, it might have been regarded as a concurrent uninsured peril.

In *Omega Inn Ltd v Continental Insurance Co*[158] the assured procured a single property and business interruption policy. The period of cover for business interruption was limited to "such length of time as would be required with the

---

[155] And indeed whether it has occurred during the currency of the policy. See *Loyaltrend Ltd v Creechurch Dedicated Ltd* [2010] EWHC 425 (Comm), where the policy required material damage to be sustained during the currency of the policy.

[156] *If P & C Insurance Ltd v Silversea Cruises Ltd* [2004] Lloyd's Rep. I.R. 696. See also *Scottish Coal Co Ltd v Royal and Sun Alliance Plc* [2008] Lloyd's Rep. I.R. 718, where it was held that the insured peril rather than business decision was the proximate cause of the loss.

[157] *International Management Group (UK) Ltd v Simmonds* [2004] Lloyds Rep. I.R. 247.

[158] *Omega Inn Ltd v Continental Insurance Co* 55 D.L.R. (4th) 766 (1988).

exercise of due diligence and dispatch to rebuild". Following a fire, the insurer took some six months to accept liability, and rebuilding took a further four months. The assured claimed business interruption for the entirety of this ten-month period. This claim was rejected by the British Columbia Court of Appeal. In its view the period for rebuilding ran from the date of the fire, and this was so even though the insurer's failure to admit liability delayed the rebuilding work. The court ruled that the assured ought to have commenced the rebuilding work from the date of the fire without waiting for the insurer to admit liability, and the fact that the assured had been unable to afford reinstatement until payment was immaterial. In effect, then, the Court took the view that the assured's impecuniosity, rather than the insurer's delay, had caused the loss. This decision is somewhat surprising, given that both forms of loss were insured under a single policy; it would have made more sense had the business interruption insurer been a wholly independent company unconnected to the property insurer.

CHAPTER 24

MARINE INSURANCE

1. THE COVERAGE OF MARINE POLICIES

Hulls and freight clauses

24–001 *Modern wordings.* The modern form of the hull and machinery clauses goes back to 1982, and those clauses remain in widespread use. The Hull clauses were revised in a number of significant respects in 1995, although the reforms were themselves found to be unsatisfactory, with the result that the clauses were not used as widely as had been hoped. Accordingly, those clauses were replaced with effect from November 1, 2003 by the International Hull Clauses, those clauses themselves replacing an earlier version adopted in November 2002. The International Hull Clauses are at the time of writing used in a relatively small number of transactions. The International Hull Clauses provide cover under four main heads: (1) marine perils for which liability is accepted irrespective of whether the assured, owners or managers of the vessel have acted with due diligence; (2) marine perils for which liability is dependent upon the exercise of due diligence by the assured, owners or managers of the vessel; (3) pollution hazards; (4) collision liabilities. The clauses are not "all risks" so that the assured has to prove which peril has caused the loss.[1] Crew negligence is irrelevant in determining whether there has been loss by an insured peril.[2] The International Hull Clauses cover hull and machinery owned by the assured and also leased equipment (cl.3) and parts taken off the vessel (cl.4). The Institute Freight Clauses, Time (cl.7) and Voyage (cl.5) are in much the same form as the International Hull Clauses.

24–002 *Marine perils covered irrespective of due diligence.*[3] The perils are:

> "[P]erils of the seas, rivers, lakes or other navigable waters[4]; fire, explosion[5]; violent theft by persons from outside the vessel[6]; jettison[7]; piracy[8]; contact with land conveyance, dock or harbour equipment or installation; earthquake, volcanic eruption

---

[1] *Brownsville Holdings v Adamjee Insurance (The Milasan)* [2000] 2 Lloyd's Rep. 458.

[2] 1906 Act s.55(2)(a).

[3] Clause 2.1.

[4] See r.7 of the Schedule to the 1906 Act.

[5] See Ch.20, above.

[6] See r.9 of the Schedule to the 1906 Act.

[7] Most of the cases involving jettison have involved throwing cargo overboard to protect it from loss by another peril, e.g. fire. However, as both perils are insured, it matters little whether fire or jettison is regarded as the proximate cause. See: *Butler v Wildman* (1820) 3 B. & Ald. 398; *Symington v Union Insurance Society of Canton Ltd* (1928) 44 T.L.R. 635; *Taylor v Dunbar* (1869) L.R. 4 C.P. 206.

[8] See r.8 of the Schedule to the 1906 Act.

or lightning; accidents in loading, discharging or shifting cargo, fuel, stores or parts[9]; and contact with satellites, aircraft, helicopters or similar objects, or objects falling therefrom."

Marine perils covered subject to due diligence.[10] The perils are: **24–003**

"[B]ursting of boilers or breakage of shafts but does not cover any of the costs of repairing or replacing the boiler which bursts or the shaft which breaks; any latent defect in the machinery or hull, but only to the extent that the cost of repairing the loss or damage caused thereby exceeds the cost that would have been incurred to correct the latent defect; negligence of Master, Officers, Crew or Pilots; negligence of repairers or charterers provided such repairers or charterers are not an Assured under this insurance; barratry of Master, Officers or Crew.[11]"

There is little in the way of English authority on the meaning of the phrase "due diligence", although it would appear that the assured cannot be held responsible for crew errors of a basic and fundamental nature,[12] assuming that the crew had been selected with reasonable care. The assured bears the burden of proving fortuity but thereafter the insurers bear the burden of proving a want of due diligence.[13]

Coverage for bursting of boilers and breakage of shafts was incorporated into the Institute clauses following the decision in *Thames & Mersey Marine Insurance Co Ltd v Hamilton, Fraser & Co (The Inchmaree)*,[14] in which it was held that damage to a donkey-pump resulting from the clogging of a valve with salt was not a peril of the sea nor was it within the general provision of "all other perils". The risk covered is loss caused by the bursting of boilers or breakage of shafts, while damage to the boiler or to the shaft itself[15] are excluded. The purpose of the exclusion is to prevent a court finding that the cost of repairing damage external to the boiler or shaft themselves which can be repaired only where the boiler or shaft is itself repaired is also covered. Without an express exclusion, the apparent position would be that common costs would be covered by way of analogy with the causation rule that if there are two causes, one of which is covered and one of which is uninsured but not excluded, the insurers remain liable. However, the 2003 Clauses produce a compromise in that under cl.2.3 the insurance is stated to cover "one half of the costs common to the repair of the burst boiler or the broken shaft and to the repair of the loss or damage caused thereby." Further, the assured may for an additional premium insure against damage to the boiler or shaft.[16]

Coverage for loss or damage caused by latent defect in the machinery or hull, raises two questions. The first is the meaning of the phrase "latent defect". It was held by Robert Goff J. in *Prudent Tankers Ltd SA v Dominion Insurance Co (The*

---

[9] See *Stott (Baltic) Steamers Ltd v Marten* [1916] 1 A.C. 304.

[10] Clause 2.2. This is the modern version of the Inchmaree Clause.

[11] See r.11 of the Schedule to the 1906 Act.

[12] *Rhesa Shipping Co SA v Edmonds (The Popi M)* [1983] 2 Lloyd's Rep. 19; *Martin Maritime Ltd v Provident Capital Indemnity Fund Ltd (The Lydia Flag)* [1998] 2 Lloyd's Rep. 652. Contrast *Coast Ferries Ltd v Century Insurance Co of Canada* [1974] 2 N.R. 436.

[13] *Global Process Systems Inc v Syarikat Takful Malaysia Berhad (The Cendor Mopu)* [2009] EWHC 637 Comm; *PT Karumin Granite v Insurance Company of North America* [1993] 1 S.L.R. 650; *Sumpiles Investments Pte Ltd v Axa Insurance Singapore Pte Ltd* [2006] 3 S.L.R. 12; *Secunda Marine Services Ltd. v Liberty Mutual Insurance Co* 2006 N.S.C.A. 82.

[14] *Thames & Mersey Marine Insurance Co Ltd v Hamilton, Fraser & Co (The Inchmaree)* (1887) 12 App.Cas. 484.

[15] *Scindia SS (London) Ltd v London Assurance* (1936) 56 Ll. L.R. 136.

[16] Clause 41.1.1.

Caribbean Sea)[17] that a latent defect was one not capable of discovery during reasonable inspection by a skilled man. It was further held that clause covered both a defect in the design or manufacture of the hull and a defect in the materials used in its construction.[18] The second question is, what may be recovered as a result of a latent defect. Under an earlier version of the Hull Clauses, it had been held by the Court of Appeal in *Promet Engineering (Singapore) Pte Ltd v Sturge (The Nukila)*[19] that the costs of putting a latent defect which became patent and which did not cause any additional damage were irrecoverable, but that if the latent defect caused any additional damage then the costs of putting right that damage were recoverable even if this entailed expenditure to correct the latent defect. The decision in *The Nukila* has been reversed in part by the 2003 wording. Clause 2.2.2 now provides that the insurers remain liable for additional loss caused by latent defects, but "only to the extent that the cost of repairing the loss or damage caused by the latent defect exceeds the cost that would have been incurred to correct the latent defect." The costs of repairing the latent defect itself thus operate as a deductible. This position is nevertheless modified in two respects. First, cl.2.4, echoing the compromise position applicable to the bursting of boilers and the breaking of shafts, provides, by way of compromise, that the assured "can recover one half of the costs common to the correction of the latent defect and to the repair of the loss or damage caused thereby". Secondly, it is possible to insure for an additional premium the costs of repairing a latent defect.[20]

Coverage for crew and repairer negligence at first sight seems otiose, given that at common law as long as the loss is caused by an insured peril it is irrelevant that it occurred through negligence.[21] It may be that the Clause simply codifies the common law, although there is also authority for the proposition that any negligence by the crew or repairers which causes loss confers cover even though the manner of the loss would not otherwise have been an insured peril.[22]

24–004   *Pollution hazards.*[23] Cover is provided for loss of or damage to the vessel caused by any governmental authority acting under the powers vested in it to prevent or

---

[17] *Prudent Tankers Ltd SA v Dominion Insurance Co (The Caribbean Sea)* [1980] 1 Lloyd's Rep. 338.

[18] In so deciding, the court distinguished *Jackson v Mumford* (1902) 8 Com. Cas. 61 on the basis that in that case there was no defect in the hull at all, but simply an attempt to use the vessel for a purpose for which it had not been designed.

[19] *Promet Engineering (Singapore) Pte Ltd v Sturge (The Nukila)* [1997] 2 Lloyd's Rep. 146. See also: *Oceanic SS Co v Faber* (1907) 13 Com. Cas. 28; *Hutchins Bros v Royal Exchange Corporation* [1911] 2 K.B. 398; *MacColl & Pollock Ltd v Indemnity Mutual Marine Assurance Co* (1930) 38 Ll. L.R. 79, all of which involved latent defects becoming patent and not causing any additional loss. Contrast *Wills & Sons v World Marine Insurance Ltd* [1980] 1 Lloyd's Rep. 350n.

[20] Clause 41.1.2.

[21] See s.55(2)(a), below.

[22] This may have been the position at common law, as in *Bell v Carstairs* (1811) 14 East 374 and *Tanner v Bennett* (1825) Ry. & M. 182, although in *State of Netherlands v Youell* [1998] 1 Lloyd's Rep. 236 Phillips L.J. was of the view that negligence by its nature could not be an insured peril. For the operation of the clause itself, see: *Cohen, Sons & Co v National Benefit Assurance Co Ltd* (1924) 18 Ll. L.R. 199; *Lind v Mitchell* (1928) 45 T.L.R. 54; *Mountain v Whittle* [1921] 1 A.C. 615; *Baxendale v Fane (The Lapwing)* [1940] P 112; *Martin Maritime Ltd v Provident Capital Indemnity Fund Ltd (The Lydia Flag)* [1998] 2 Lloyd's Rep. 652; *HIH Casualty & General Insurance Co Ltd v Waterwell Shipping Inc* Unreported, 1998, NSWCA. In *Sumpiles Investments Pte Ltd v Axa Insurance Singapore Pte Ltd* [2006] 3 S.L.R. 12 it was alleged that the proximate cause of the loss was crew negligence, but the court was satisfied that wear and tear was the relevant proximate cause.

[23] Clause 5.

mitigate a pollution hazard or damage to the environment or threat thereof, subject to the assured having exercised due diligence.

Collision liabilities.[24] The assured is provided with a 75 per cent indemnity[25] in respect of legal liability by way of damages[26] arising out of collisions[27] with other vessels.[28] First-party losses are perils of the seas and are recoverable under the insuring clause. If both vessels are to blame then the sum recoverable is calculated by reference to cross-liabilities.

24–005

Cargo clauses. The Institute Cargo Clauses fall into three classes, (A), (B) and (C). The Clauses found in most modern contracts date from 1982, but were revised with effect from January 1, 2009 and are now widely used. The Institute Cargo Clauses (A) provide all-risks cover,[29] subject to specific exclusions. The Institute Cargo Clauses (B) and (C) are narrower and are limited to coverage of defined risks, subject again to specific exclusions.[30] The (B) Clauses cover: fire or explosion; vessel or craft being stranded, grounded, sunk or capsized; overturning or derailment of land conveyance; collision or contact of vessel, craft or conveyance with any external object other than water; discharge of cargo at a port of distress; earthquake, volcanic eruption or lightning; general average sacrifice; jettison or washing overboard; and entry of sea, lake or river water into vessel, craft, hold, conveyance, container, liftvan or place of storage. The (C) clauses exclude washing overboard, entry of water and losses on loading and unloading. Piracy is covered under the 2009 (A) Clauses, in the absence of any express exclusion from all risks cover, but is not a named peril under the (B) and (C) clauses. Clause 2 of all three classes of clauses permits the recovery of general average and salvage charges. Clause 3, which is also common to all three classes, provides the assured with an indemnity against any liability that he is under to the carrier in respect of a "both-to-blame" collision clause. War and strikes losses are excluded by cll.6 and 7 of the Institute Cargo Clauses (A), (B) and (C), although are insurable under the Institute Cargo War and Strikes

24–006

---

[24] Clause 6.

[25] The missing 25 per cent can be insured with a P&I Club or, under the 2003 Clauses, from the underwriters themselves on payment of an additional premium: cl.38.

[26] This covers tortious liability only, and not liability in contract: *Furness, Withy & Co Ltd v Duder* [1936] 2 K.B. 461; *Hall Brothers SS Co Ltd v Young* (1939) 63 Ll. L.R. 143.

[27] Coming into contact with a fishing net is not a collision: *Bennett SS v Hull Mutual SS Protecting Society Ltd* [1914] 3 K.B. 57.

[28] A vessel for this purpose is part of a vessel which is essential to its structure (*Re Margetts and Ocean Accident and Guarantee Corporation* (1901) 2 K.B. 792), and must be something which has the characteristics of a ship (*Merchants Marine Insurance Co Ltd v North of England Protection and Indemnity Association* (1926) 26 Ll. L.R. 201 crane; *Polpen Shipping Co Ltd v Commercial Union Assurance Co Ltd* [1943] K.B. 161—seaplane). A barge used on inland waters is a vessel even though not capable of self-propulsion: *The Mac* (1882) 7 P. 126. There are cases on the meaning of "ship" both for tax purposes and for the purposes of the Merchant Shipping legislation and its predecessors. The test applied in those cases is similarly whether the subject matter was constructed to be navigated or for the carriage of cargo or passengers, so that a "light ship" is not a "ship" (*The Gas Float Whitton* [1897] A.C. 337) although a jack-up drilling rig is a ship because it is designed to be navigated from one place to another in order to fulfil its functions (*Parks v Clark* [2001] 2 Lloyd's Rep. 431). Clause 37 allows the assured to obtain additional cover for collision with other floating objects

[29] See *British and Foreign Marine Insurance Co v Gaunt* [1921] 2 A.C. 41, which decides that under an all risks policy proof of loss by reason of fortuity is all that is required of the assured, and the burden then switches to the insurers to establish the operation of an excluded peril. If the assured cannot establish fortuity, he will not make out his claim: *Bevan v Gartside Marine Engines Ltd* [2000] B.C.J. No 528.

[30] See s.55, below.

Clauses. Loss arising from the unseaworthiness of the vessel is excluded by cl.5.

24–007 **Mutual insurance.** Mutual insurance is in common use in marine insurance, through P&I Clubs. Mutual insurance developed as a result of the Bubble Act 1719, which conferred a monopoly on two insurance companies, the Royal Exchange and the London, and prevented other companies from offering insurance. To overcome the prohibition, shipowners formed mutual associations—later to become known as P&I Clubs—the purpose of which was to share losses at a lower premium. Mutual insurance became of increasing importance in the nineteenth century for a number of reasons: the courts ruled that liability for collision damage was excluded from the standard marine policy[31] and insurers were prepared to offer only three-quarters cover; the Fatal Accidents Act 1846 provided that an action could be brought by the dependants of a deceased victim of negligence, which imposed significant liabilities upon shipowners whose negligence resulted in the death of passengers[32]; the Harbours, Docks and Piers Clauses Act 1847 imposed strict liability on shipowners for damage to port installations; and in *The Westenhope*[33] it was established that shipowners were liable for loss of or damage to cargo.

It was necessary, to comply with the Bubble Act, for each member to accept personal liability for losses,[34] although that no longer remained strictly necessary after the repeal of the Bubble Act in 1824. Following the passing of the Companies Act 1862, associations consisting of 20 or more persons had to be incorporated and registered[35] so that an unregistered mutual association with more than the statutory number of members was to be treated as an unlawful association.[36] The position today is that mutual associations are registered as companies limited by guarantee. Mutual insurance is defined by s.85(1) as an arrangement under which two or more persons undertake to insure each other against specified losses, although this is not an accurate statement of the position given that mutual insurers are today incorporated bodies with separate legal personality.

Section 85(2) of the 1906 Act provides that the general rules concerning payment of premium do not apply to mutual insurance: a guarantee, or other similar arrangement, may be substituted for the premium. This conforms to the usual practice, which is for the association to impose a levy on the members from time to time to provide such sums as they consider necessary to meet the anticipated liabilities and expenses of the club. In marine insurance, it is usual to make an initial call at the start of the policy year, each member's share being determined by setting a rate per ton of shipping entered under each member's name. Supplementary calls are then made as necessary during the year.

---

[31] *De Vaux v Salvador* (1836) 4 & E. 420.

[32] However, the Merchant Shipping Act 1854 allowed shipowners to limit their liability to some extent.

[33] *The Westenhope* Unreported, 1870.

[34] *Strong v Harvey* (1825) 3 Bing. 304; *Re London Marine Insurance Association* (1869) L.R. 8 Eq. 176.

[35] See *Lion Mutual Marine Insurance Association v Tucker* (1883) 12 QBD 176; *Re Bangor & North Wales Mutual, etc., Association, Baird's Case* [1899] 2 Ch. 593; and *Corfield v Buchanan* (1913) 29 T.L.R. 258, as to the effect of a limitation by guarantee in the event of the winding-up of an association. Nowadays, the majority of the Clubs are incorporated in countries overseas, principally for fiscal reasons.

[36] *Re Arthur Average Association* (1875) L.R. 10 Ch. 542; *Re Padstow Total Loss Association* (1882) 20 Ch D 137.

Membership of a mutual association is effected by a proposal which may be accepted or rejected. In the case of marine insurance, if the proposal is accepted, a binding contract comes into force at the point of acceptance,[37] although the shipowner is generally issued with a certificate of entry at a later date. The certificate of entry generally incorporates the other terms of the contract, which include the Club's articles of association and its rules, although the certificate is conclusive evidence of the matters stated in it, including the date of entry.[38] The power to take decisions on behalf of a P&I Club, on matters such as admission to entry, claims handling and reinsurance, are vested in the directors under the articles of association, but the management of each Club is in practice delegated to managers.[39] Many of the powers vested in the directors and by delegation the managers are discretionary in their nature, including in some cases the payment of claims,[40] and there is certainly an argument that such a discretion prevents the contract from being one of insurance at all,[41] although in practice Club agreements are regarded as giving rise to insurance contracts.[42] Club rules generally contain arbitration provisions, so that any challenge may be made by way of arbitration only.

Mutual insurance is insurance within the Financial Services and Markets Act 2000, and the most common form of benefits available under marine contracts of this type include:

(a) war risks, including the detention or diversion of the vessel, and the consequent prolonging of the voyage;
(b) freight and demurrage risks;
(c) through transit risks; and
(d) general risks—these include collision, towage, life salvage, loss of cargo, removal of wrecks; also personal injury, repatriation and crew substitute expenses.

2. TEXT OF THE MARINE INSURANCE ACT 1906

The following paragraphs set out the text of the 1906 Act. Sections which set out **24–008** general principles applicable to all forms of insurance are discussed at the appropriate places elsewhere in this work. Only those sections which are specific to marine insurance are considered below.

Marine insurance defined

"**1.** A contract of marine insurance is a contract whereby the insurer undertakes to **24–009** indemnify the assured, in manner and to the extent thereby agreed, against marine losses, that is to say, the losses incident to marine adventure."

---

[37] *Container Transport International v Oceanus Mutual* [1984] 1 Lloyd's Rep. 476.
[38] *Compania Maritima San Brasilio SA v Oceanus Mutual Underwriting Association (Bermuda) Ltd (The Eurysthenes)* [1976] 2 Lloyd's Rep. 171.
[39] *Gregory Maritime Ltd v Thomas R Miller & Son Ltd* [1966] 1 Lloyd's Rep. 296.
[40] *Compania Maritima San Basilio SA v Oceanus Mutual Underwriting Assn. (Bermuda) Ltd (The Eurysthenes)* [1976] 2 Lloyd's Rep. 171; *C.V.G. Siderurgicia del Orinoco SA v London SS. Owners' Mutual Ins Assn Ltd (The Vainqueur José)* [1979] 1 Lloyd's Rep. 190.
[41] *Medical Defence Union v Department of Trade* [1979] 2 W.L.R. 686.
[42] *Wooding v Monmouthshire & South Wales Mutual Indemnity Society Ltd* [1939] 4 All E.R. 570; *Compania Maritima San Basilio SA v Oceanus Mutual Underwriting Association (Bermuda) Ltd (The Eurysthenes)* [1976] 2 Lloyd's Rep. 171; *Re Allobrogia Steamship Corp* [1979] 1 Lloyd's Rep. 190.

While the definition talks of "marine losses", it also refers to incidental losses. The possibility of insuring cargo for mixed land and sea risks under a marine policy has long been accepted, and is formally recognised in s.2(1). Equally, construction risks can be insured under marine policies. It is also the practice to insure maritime structures, e.g. oil rigs, under marine policies.[43] Whether a policy is marine or non-marine is a matter of degree, depending upon the primary coverage conferred by the policy.[44] A policy in marine form is only a marine policy if the subject matter is appropriate to a marine policy.[45]

Mixed sea and land risks

24–010   "**2.**—(1) A contract of marine insurance may, by its express terms, or by usage of trade, be extended so as to protect the assured against losses on inland waters or on any land risk which may be incidental to any sea voyage.

(2) Where a ship in course of building, or the launch of a ship, or any adventure analogous to a marine adventure, is covered by a policy in the form of a marine policy, the provisions of this Act, in so far as applicable, shall apply thereto; but, except as by this section provided, nothing in this Act shall alter or affect any rule of law applicable to any contract of insurance other than a contract of marine insurance as by this Act defined."

Marine adventure and maritime perils defined

24–011   "**3.**—(1) Subject to the provisions of this Act, every lawful marine adventure may be the subject of a contract of marine insurance.

(2) In particular there is a marine adventure where—

(a) Any ship goods or other moveables are exposed to maritime perils. Such property is in this Act referred to as 'insurable property';

(b) The earning or acquisition of any freight, passage money, commission, profit, or other pecuniary benefit, or the security for any advances, loan, or disbursements, is endangered by the exposure of insurable property to maritime perils;

(c) Any liability to a third party may be incurred by the owner of, or other person interested in or responsible for, insurable property, by reason of maritime perils.

'Maritime perils' means the perils consequent on, or incidental to, the navigation of the sea, that is to say, perils of the seas, fire, war perils, pirates, rovers, thieves, captures, seisures, restraints, and detainments of princes and peoples, jettisons, barratry, and any other perils, either of the like kind or which may be designated by the policy."

The list of maritime perils set out in the 1906 Act has been held not to be exhaustive, although the concluding words "or which may be designated by the policy" do not permit the insurance of non-marine risks as marine risks simply by designating them to be marine risks. It was held in *Continental Illinois National Bank & Trust Co of Chicago v Bathurst (The Captain Panagos DP)*[46]

---

[43] *National Oilwell v Davy Offshore* [1993] 2 Lloyd's Rep. 582; *Heesens Yacht Builders BV v Cox Syndicate Management Ltd (The Red Sapphire)* [2006] Lloyd's Rep. I.R. 476.

[44] *Rodanachi v Elliott* (1874) L.R. 9 CP 518; *Simon Israel & Co v Sedgwick* [1893] 1 Q.B. 303; *Hyderbad (Deccan) Co v Willoughby* [1899] 2 Q.B. 530; *Ide and Christie v Chalmers and White* (1900) 5 Com. Cas. 212; *Schloss Bros v Stevens* [1906] 2 K.B. 665; *Allagar Rubber Estates Ltd v National Benefit Insurance Co* (1922) 10 Ll. L.R. 564; *Leon v Casey* [1932] 2 K.B. 756; *Cousins v D & C Carriers Ltd* [1971] 2 Lloyd's Rep. 230; *Fuerst Day Lawson Ltd v Orion Insurance Co Ltd* [1980] 1 Lloyd's Rep. 656; *Hibernia Foods v McAuslin (The Joint Frost)* [1998] 1 Lloyd's Rep. 310; *Wunsche International v Tai Ping Insurance Co* [1998] 2 Lloyd's Rep. 8.

[45] *Re London County Commercial Reinsurance* [1922] 2 Ch. 67; *Re Argonaut Marine Insurance Co* [1932] 2 Ch. 34.

[46] *Continental Illinois National Bank & Trust Co of Chicago v Bathurst (The Captain Panagos DP)* [1985] 1 Lloyd's Rep. 625.

that: (a) the phrase "incidental to the navigation of the seas" is wider than the key marine insuring phrase "perils of the seas", and is appropriate to include perils which arise simply because a voyage has been undertaken, e.g. the bursting of a boiler; (b) the words "that is to say" in s.3(2) indicate that the list of "marine perils" provided is inclusive and not exhaustive; and (c) the concluding words of s.3(2) of the 1906 Act, "or which may be designated by the policy", cannot mean that any policy in which risks are designated as marine risks becomes a policy of marine insurance, and no sensible meaning could be attributed to those words.

3. INSURABLE INTEREST

Avoidance of gaming or wagering contracts   24–012

> "**4.**—(1) Every contract of marine insurance by way of gaming or wagering is void
> (2) A contract is deemed to be a gaming or wagering contract—
> (a) where the assured has not an insurable interest as defined by this Act, and the
> contract is entered into with no expectation of acquiring such an interest; or
> (b) where the policy is made 'interest or no interest', or 'without further proof of
> interest than the policy itself, or without benefit of salvage to the insurer', or
> subject to any like term:
> Provided that, where there is no possibility of salvage, a policy may be effected without
> benefit of salvage to the insurer."

Section 4(1) of the Act adopts the principles originally set out in the Marine Insurance Act 1745. It is unclear whether the provisions of s.4 have survived the implementation of the Gambling Act 2005 s.335. Whether or not that is the case there remains an insurable interest requirement laid down by the indemnity principle, namely that on the occurrence of the insured peril the assured must prove his loss.

The origins of s.4(2), and in particular the purpose of s.4(2)(b), were discussed in Ch.4. It is here necessary to comment upon the meaning of certain of the phrases to be found in it.

By way of gaming or wagering. The assured must intend to enter into a wagering 24–013
contract for this provision to be offended.[47] It was held by Hobhouse J. in *Glafki Shipping Co SA v Pinios Shipping Co (The Maria (No.2))*[48] that this phrase is directed only against the case in which an insurance is taken out by someone without interest, as opposed to the case in which a person with an interest has grossly overvalued that interest.

Expectation of acquiring such interest. Section 6 provides that it is sufficient if 24–014
the assured has an insurable interest at the time of loss. Consequently, the absence of insurable interest at the inception of the policy is fatal only where the assured does not have any expectation of acquiring such interest during the currency of the policy.[49]

---

[47] *Kent v Bird* (1777) 2 Cowp. 583; *Gedge v Royal Exchange Assurance Corporation* [1900] 2 Q.B. 214; *Coker v Bolton* [1912] 3 K.B. 315.
[48] *Glafki Shipping Co SA v Pinios Shipping Co (The Maria (No.2))* [1984] 1 Lloyd's Rep. 660.
[49] For old illustrations based on the equivalent provisions of the Marine Insurance Act 1745, see *Kent v Bird* (1777) 2 Cowp. 583 (wager on the arrival of a ship); *Lowry v Bordieu* (1780) 2 Doug. K.B. 468 (wager on the repayment of a debt).

24–015 *Interest or no interest.* The object here is to avoid "ppi" and similarly worded policies, which were intended to permit the assured to recover for a pure wager in marine insurance form in the eighteenth and nineteenth centuries. The term "without benefit of salvage" served a similar purpose. The significance of the use of this particular phrase was that it removed the usual right of a marine insurer to take over an insured subject matter which had become a total loss, thereby indicating that the assured had no right to abandon the subject matter to the insurer. The proviso to s.4(2)(b) thus makes it clear that if there is no possibility of salvage the policy is not avoided merely because that fact is expressly stated, although salvage is generally available, even in respect of policies for loss of profits.[50] The prohibition on using the phrase "ppi" and similar terms is absolute; a policy which is made on interest but which contains any such provision is nevertheless void under s.4(2)(b).[51]

24–016 *Criminal sanctions.* The prohibition on wagering policies contained in s.4 is supplemented by the criminal sanctions contained in the Marine Insurance (Gambling Policies) Act 1909. The basic provision is contained in the Marine Insurance (Gambling Policies) Act 1909 s.1(1) which makes it an offence where:

(a) any person effects a contract of marine insurance without having any bona fide interest, direct or indirect, either in the safe arrival of the ship in relation to which the contract is made or in the safety or preservation of the subject matter insured, or a bona fide expectation of acquiring such an interest; or

(b) any person in the employment of the owners of a ship, not being a part owner of the ship, effects a contract of marine insurance in relation to the ship, and the contract is made "interest or no interest"; or "without further proof of interest than the policy itself"; or "without benefit of salvage to the insurer", or subject to any like term.

By s.1(2) of the 1909 Act, a broker who arranges a policy which contravenes s.1(1), and in the knowledge that it does so, commits a similar offence himself. These provisions are similar to, and obviously derived from, the rules in s.4 of the 1906 Act. It should be understood, however, that there can be situations in which the policy is void under s.4 but no criminal offence is committed under the Marine Insurance (Gambling Policies) Act 1909. Thus the offence under s.1(1)(a) of the 1909 Act can be committed by any person, whereas the offence under s.1(1)(b) of the 1909 Act is restricted to a person in the employment of the owner of the vessel; if a person with insurable interest enters into a "ppi" policy, the policy is void under s.4 of the 1906 Act but no offence will be committed under the 1909 Act unless the assured is an employee.

Insurable interest defined

24–017 "5—(1) Subject to the provisions of this Act, every person has an insurable interest who is interested in a marine adventure.

---

[50] *De Mattos v North* (1868) L.R. 3 C.P. 185.

[51] *Thomas Cheshire & Co v Vaughan Bros & Co* [1920] 3 K.B. 240; *Re Overseas Marine Insurance Co Ltd* (1930) 36 Ll. L.R. 183; *Re London County Commercial Reinsurance Office* [1922] 2 Ch 67 (which also decides that, if the policy is illegal but made on interest, the assured can at least recover his premium by way of exception to the usual *in pari delicto* rule that denies restitution under illegal contracts): *Re Overseas Marine Insurance Co Ltd* (1930) 36 Ll. L.R. 183.

(2) In particular a person is interested in a marine adventure where he stands in any legal or equitable relation to the adventure or to any insurable property at risk therein, in consequence of which he may benefit by the safety or due arrival of insurable property, or may be prejudiced by its loss, or by damage thereto, or by the detention thereof, or may incur liability in respect thereof."

The general definition of insurable interest is based upon the judgment of Lawrence J. in *Lucena v Craufurd*.[52] Section 5(1) defines insurable interest in terms of interest in a "marine adventure", a term itself defined by s.5(2). The words "in particular" in s.5(2) make it clear that the interests identified are not exhaustive of the possibilities of insurable interest,[53] and that what is required in more general terms is a legal or equitable interest in the subject matter. Thus a mere expectation on the part of the assured that he may benefit from a marine adventure does not confer insurable interest upon him.[54] An unsecured creditor of, (including a shareholder in) the company which owns the insured subject matter, has no insurable interest,[55] unless he has a contractual or other right to possess or enjoy the subject matter.[56]

Liability gives rise to insurable interest. Thus managers of a vessel have insurable interest in it by virtue of their obligations to the owner for maintenance, equipping, repair, survey, classification, crewing, provisioning, operation and navigation of the vessel. Possession, coupled with these obligations, is sufficient[57] even in the absence of ownership. Again, the bareboat charterer of a vessel has insurable interest in it under a hull and machinery policy, such interest arising from the duty of the charterer to make good any loss suffered by the vessel.[58]

When interest must attach

"**6.**—(1) The assured must be interested in the subject-matter at the time of the loss   **24–018**
though he need not be interested when the insurance is effected:
Provided that where the subject matter is insured "lost or not lost" the assured may recover although he may not have acquired his interest until after the loss, unless at the time of effecting the contract of insurance the assured was aware of the loss, and the insurer was not.
(2) Where the assured has no interest at the time of the loss, he cannot acquire interest by any act or election after he is aware of the loss."

General principles as to timing. The basic rule in s.6(1) of the 1906 Act is that   **24–019**
the assured need not have an interest at the inception of the policy although unless he has an expectation of obtaining an interest the policy will be void as a wager under s.4. The principle that a marine policy is a contract of indemnity means that the assured must possess an insurable interest at the date of the loss.

---

[52] *Lucena v Craufurd* (1806) 1 Taunt. 325.
[53] *O'Kane v Jones* [2005] Lloyd's Rep. I.R. 174.
[54] *Devaux v Steele* (1840) 6 Bing. N.C. 358; *Buchanan & Co v Faber* (1899) 4 Com. Cas. 223; *Price v Maritime Insurance Co* [1901] 2 K.B. 412.
[55] *Manfield v Maitland* (1821) 4 B. & Ald. 582: *Moran, Galloway & Co v Uzielli* [1905] 2 K.B. 555.
[56] *Sharp v Sphere Drake Insurance (The Moonacre)* [1992] 2 Lloyd's Rep. 501.
[57] *O'Kane v Jones* [2005] Lloyd's Rep. IR 174.
[58] *Linelevel Ltd v Powszechny Zaklad Ubezpieczen SA (The Nore Challenger)* [2005] EWHC 421 (Comm).

Thus, if insurable interest is lost by the date of the occurrence of the insured peril, the assured has no claim.[59]

24–020 *"Lost or not lost" cover.* Difficulties of communication between distant geographical locations frequently meant that the assured would be seeking to insure a vessel or cargo in which he had just obtained an interest but which might by the time of his acquiring his interest have in fact been lost or damaged. For this reason, marine insurers were prepared to offer "lost or not lost" cover, permitting the assured to make a claim even if the subject matter had been the subject of a casualty prior to the agreement. This is recognised by the proviso to s.6(1) of the 1906 Act.[60] The Institute Cargo Clauses themselves provide that:

> "The assured shall be entitled to recover for insured loss occurring during the period of this insurance, notwithstanding that the loss occurred before the contract of insurance was concluded, unless the assured were aware of the loss and the underwriters were not."

The cover under a policy which insures cargo on a "lost or not lost" basis is backdated to the date of loading, so that if the loss occurs after that date but before the date of the policy then the assured can recover.[61]

Section 6(2) codifies the principle that an assured who is aware of a loss before he obtains his insurable interest cannot recover.[62]

Defeasible of contingent interest

24–021 "**7.**—(1) A defeasible interest is insurable, as also is a contingent interest.

(2) In particular, where the buyer of goods has insured them, he has an insurable interest notwithstanding that he might, at his election, have rejected the goods, or have treated them at the seller's risk, by reason of the latter's delay in making delivery or otherwise."

An interest which may be defeated by subsequent events is insurable. Thus the captor of a vessel in time of war has an insurable interest in the vessel.[63]

Partial interest

24–022 "**8.**—A partial interest of any nature is insurable."

Partial interests are insurable. The most important illustration of a partial interest concerns the purchaser of an unascertained part of a bulk, who may insure if the risk has passed to him. His insurable interest is derived from the fact that he must pay for the goods whether or not the goods comprising the bulk are ultimately delivered to him.[64]

---

[59] *Cepheus Shipping Corp v Guardian Royal Exchange Assurance Plc (The Capricorn)* [1995] 1 Lloyd's Rep. 622. For the consequences of the absence or loss of interest on the recovery of the premium see the discussion of s.84, below.

[60] Based on: *Mead v Davidson* (1835) 3 Ad. & El. 303; *Sutherland v Pratt* (1843) 11 M. & W. 296; *Gibson v Small* (1843) 4 H.L. Cas. 353: *Gledstanes v Royal Exchange Assurance Corp* (1864) 34 L.J.Q.B. 30; *Brtadford v Symondson* (1881) L.R. 7 Q.B. 456.

[61] *Marine Insurance Co Ltd v Grimmer* [1944] 2 All E.R. 197. See also *New South Wales Leather Co Pty Ltd v Vanguard Insurance Co Ltd* (1991) 25 N.S.W.L.R. 699.

[62] *Andersen v Morice* (1876) L.R. 1 App.Cas. 713.

[63] The right of a captor to insure was confirmed by *Lucena v Craufurd* (1806) 2 Bos. & P.N.R. 269.

[64] *Inglis v Stock* (1885) L.R. 10 App.Cas. 263.

The specific case of mortgages is governed by s.14, below. Any person who has a lien over the insured subject matter may insure for the amount owing to him.[65] This may apply to the pawnee of a bill of lading[66] and to a salvor who has a claim for his expenses.[67] However, the holder of a lien may not assert a claim against his debtor's insurance moneys unless it can be shown that the debtor had constituted himself a trustee of those moneys.[68]

Reinsurance

"**9.**—(1) The insurer under a contract of marine insurance has an insurable interest in his risk, and may re-insure in respect of it.

    (2) Unless the policy otherwise provides, the original assured has no right or interest in respect of such re-insurance."[69]

24–023

Bottomry

"**10.** The lender of money on bottomry or respondentia has an insurable interest in respect of the loan.

24–024

At common law the master of a vessel was empowered, by means of bottomry and respondentia, to raise money by way of security on the vessel and the cargo. The lender could insure the subject matter for the amount of his loan accordingly.[70] These forms of security have long been obsolete.

Master and seamen's wages

"**11.** The master and any member of the crew of a ship has an insurable interest in respect of his wages."

24–025

The common law rule that wages were payable only on receipt of freight was abolished by s.183 of the Merchant Shipping Act 1854, but it remained the case at common law that wages were not payable after the loss of the vessel. Section 11 provides that loss of wages consequent on the loss of the vessel is insurable.

Advanced freight

"**12.** In the case of advance freight, the person advancing the freight has an insurable interest, in so far as such freight is not repayable in case of loss."

24–026

Freight may fall into one of three broad classes: chartered freight, which is the hire payable to the owner of a vessel by the charterer under a charterparty; ordinary freight, which is the amount to be earned by an owner or charterer in carrying cargo belonging to another; and trading freight, which is the sum notionally earned by an owner or charterer in the carriage of his own cargo.[71] An assured is not gambling by taking out insurance on freight which he expects to earn from a given transaction or voyage. However, as far as presenting a claim

---

[65] *Wolff v Horncastle* (1798) 1 Bos. & P. 316.
[66] *Sutherland v Pratt* (1843) 11 M. & W. 296.
[67] *Briggs v Merchant Traders' Association* (1849) L.R.13 Q.B.D. 167.
[68] *Ellerman Lines Ltd v Lancaster Maritime Co Ltd* [1980] 2 Lloyd's Rep. 497.
[69] See Ch.25, below.
[70] *Simonds v Hodgson* (1832) 3 B. & Ad. 50; *Stainhank v Fenning* (1851) 11 C.B. 59; *Stainhank v Shepard* (1853) 13 C.B. 418; *The James W Elwell* (1921) P. 351.
[71] See also the definition of "freight" in Sch.1 r.16.

is concerned, in each of these three cases the basic question will be whether the assured had entered into a contract under which freight is or is to be payable, as in the absence of such a contract the assured cannot demonstrate a loss for which a claim can be made. The matter, then, will rest upon the contract under which the freight is payable and in particular upon who bears the risk of loss of freight in the event that the voyage on which freight is to be earned is not completed. It is possible to deduce a number of principles from the decided cases.

1. Insurable interest in ordinary freight commences as soon as there is a binding contract under which freight is payable.[72] If, as is common, freight is not due until the cargo owner's goods have been delivered at their port of destination,[73] the carrier may insure against the loss of freight in the event that the voyage is determined by an insured peril.[74] Where, however, freight is payable by the cargo owner irrespective of the safe arrival of his goods, the cargo owner may insure for loss of freight as an element in the overall loss suffered by him by the failure of his goods to arrive undamaged and in full at their agreed destination.[75]

2. Where freight has been paid in advance, the person bearing the risk of its loss has an insurable interest in it. Thus if the freight is not repayable in the event of the cargo failing to arrive, the cargo owner has an insurable interest; conversely, if the freight is repayable in the event of a loss, the carrier may insure.[76] There is, however, a crucial distinction between advance freight and a payment of some other description, for example by way of loan, as in the latter case the sum is repayable irrespective of the outcome of the voyage, so that neither party may insure it.[77]

3. Where freight is payable, but has not been paid, in advance, the position would appear to be as in (2) above.

4. In the case of trading freight, there is clearly no possible equivalent of a binding contract for freight in order to determine insurable interest. Old authorities on this matter indicate that there is an insurable interest in this type of freight only when the vessel is ready and able to carry a cargo, and the cargo is capable of being shipped.[78]

If the vessel is off-hire, the assured will have no insurable interest in freight.[79]

---

[72] There are many old authorities on the question of the point at which insurable interest in freight arises; these are analysed in Arnould's *Law of Marine Insurance and Average* 17th edn (2008), paras 11–73 et seq.

[73] *Weir & Co v Girvin & Co* [1899] 1 Q.B. 193 at 196.

[74] *Patrick v Eames* (1813) 3 Camp. 441; *Miller v Warre* (1824) 1 Car. & P. 237; *Flint v Flemyng* (1830) 1 B. & Ad. 45; *Dakin v Oxley* (1864) 15 C.B. N.S. 646; *Barber v Fleming* (1869) L.R. 5 Q.B. 59; *Scottish Shire Line Ltd v London and Provincial Marine and General Insurance Co Ltd* [1912] 3 K.B. 51.

[75] *Oriental Steamship Co v Tylor* [1893] 2 Q.B. 518.

[76] Section 12 itself deals only with the case in which advance freight is not repayable. See *Allison v Bristol Marine Insurance Co* (1876) L.R. 1 App.Cas. 209.

[77] *Manfield v Maitland* (1821) 4 B. & Ald. 582; *Wilson v Martin* (1856) 1) Ex. 684; *Hicks v Shield* (1857) 7 El. & Bl. 633; *The Varnak* (1869) L.R. 2 P.C. 505; *Allison v Bristol Marine Insurance Co* (1876) L.R. 1 App.Cas. 209; *The Red Sea* [1896] P. 20.

[78] *Flint v Flemyng* (1830) 1 B. & Ad. 45; *De Vaux v J'Anson* (1839) 5 Bing. N.C. 519.

[79] *Cepheus Shipping Corp v Guardian Royal Exchange Assurance Plc* [1995] 1 Lloyd's Rep. 622.

Charges of insurance

"**13.** The assured has an insurable interest in the charges of any insurance which he may effect."[80] **24–027**

Quantum of interest

"**14.**—(1) Where the subject matter insured is mortgaged, the mortgagor has an insurable interest in respect of the full value thereof, and the mortgagee has an insurable interest in respect of any sum due or to become due under the mortgage. **24–028**

(2) A mortgagee, consignee, or other person having an interest in the subject-matter may insure on behalf of and for the benefit of other persons interested as well as for his own benefit.

(3) The owner of insurable property has an insurable interest in the full value thereof, notwithstanding that some third person may have agreed, or be liable, to indemnify him in case of loss."

Mortgage. The mortgagor of a vessel—who will generally be its owner—may insure for its full value, but the mortgagee may insure only for the amount of the mortgage debt: s.14(1).[81] If the mortgagee or other interested person does insure the vessel for more than the amount secured on it, he will not be able to recover the latter sum unless he can show that the policy was in addition intended to cover the interest of the mortgagor.[82] In such a case the surplus over the value of the mortgagee's interest is, in accordance with the principles set out in *Tomlinson (Hauliers) Ltd v Hepburn*[83] to be held on trust for the mortgagor. If the debt is paid off, the mortgagee's insurable interest comes to an end.[84] **24–029**

Insurance on behalf of others. An agent generally has no insurable interest in goods or documents of title which might pass through his possession, as he does not incur personal liability in respect of them.[85] However, an agent may insure: **24–030**

(a) as agent on behalf of a person with insurable interest[86];

(b) as a bailee, if he is left in possession of the goods[87];

(c) if he has advanced any money in respect of the goods and has taken possession of them, in respect of his lien;

---

[80] See: *Usher v Noble* (1810) 12 East 639; *United States Shipping Co v Empress Assurance Co* [1907] 1 K.B. 259.

[81] Based on *Alston v Campbell* (1779) 4 Bro. P.C. 476; *Irving v Richardson* (1831) 2 B. & Ad. 193; *Hutchinson v Wright* (1858) 25 Beav 444; *Ward v Beck* (1863) 13 C.B. N.S. 668.

[82] Section 14(2) recognises that a person with a limited interest may insure on behalf of himself and others: *Irving v Richardson* (1831) 2 B. & Ad. 193; *Ladbroke v Lee* (1850) 4 De G. & Sm. 106; *Scott v Globe Marine Insurance Co Ltd* (1896) 1 Com. Cas. 370.

[83] *Tomlinson (Hauliers) Ltd v Hepburn* [1966] A.C. 451. See: *Robertson v Hamilton* (1811) 14 East 522; *Irving v Richardson* (1831) 2 B. & Ad. 193; *Crowley v Cohen* (1832) 3 B. & Ad. 478; *Joyce v Kennard* (1871) L.R. 7 Q.B. 78; *Stephens v Australasian Insurance Co* (1872) L.R. 8 C.P. 18; *Ebsworth v Alliance Marine Co* (1873) L.R. 8 C.P. 596; *Williams v Atlantic Insurance Co Ltd* [1933] 1 K.B. 81.

[84] *Levy & Co v Merchants Marine Insurance Co* (1885) Cab. & Ell. 474; *Chartered Trust & Executor Co v London Scottish Assurance Corporation Ltd* (1923) 39 T.L.R. 608.

[85] *Wolff v Horncastle* (1798) 1 Bos & P. 316; *Seagrave v Union Marine Insurance Co* (1866) L.R. 1 C.P. 305.

[86] *Provincial Insurance Co of Canada v Leduc* (1874) L.R. 6 P.C. 224; *Transcontinental Underwriting Agency v Grand Union Insurance Co Ltd* [1987] 2 Lloyd's Rep. 409; *Pan Atlantic Insurance v Pine Top Insurance* [1994] 3 All E.R. 581; *O'Kane v Jones* [2004] Lloyd's Rep. I.R. 174.

[87] *North British Insurance Co v Moffatt* (1871) L.R. 7 C.P. 25.

(d) for anticipated profits or commission.[88]

24–031 *Ownership.* The owner[89] of a vessel or its cargo, including any joint owner,[90] is entitled to insure it for its full value. In the case of a vessel, this is even if the vessel has been chartered to a third party on terms which allow the owner to recover its full value from the charterer in the event of loss; in such a case the doctrine of subrogation would give the assured's insurers a right to proceed against the charterer or his insurers, thereby preventing the assured from recovering a double indemnity. The right of the owner to insure in these circumstances was established prior to the passing of the 1906 Act,[91] and is confirmed by s.14(3).

The most difficult questions here concern the respective insurable interests of the buyer and seller of a vessel or the cargo, for ownership is simply one interest in goods: if goods are at the risk of the assured or if he has agreed to buy them he has an insurable interest in them.[92] Marine and non-marine principles do not differ.

Assignment of interest

24–032 "**15.** Where the assured assigns or otherwise parts with his interest in the subject-matter insured, he does not thereby transfer to the assignee his rights under the contract of insurance unless there be an express or implied agreement with the assignee to that effect.

  But the provisions of this section do not affect a transmission of interest by operation of law."

A marine policy, unlike a non-marine property policy, is assignable unless assignment is restricted by contract: see s.50, below: other policies can be assigned only with the consent of the insurers. However, s.15—which applies to all forms of insurance—prevents a mere sale of the insured subject matter from transferring the policy[93]

4. INSURABLE VALUE

Measure of insurable value

24–033 "**16.** Subject to any express provision or valuation in the policy, the insurable value of the subject-matter insured must be ascertained as follows—

  (1) In insurance on ship,[94] the insurable value is the value, at the commencement of the risk, of the ship, including her outfit, provisions and stores for the officers and crew, money advanced for seamen's wages, and other disbursements (if any) incurred to make the ship fit for the voyage or adventure contemplated by the policy, plus the charges of insurance upon the whole:

---

[88] *Carruthers v Sheddon* (1815) 6 Taunt. 14; *Ebsworth v Alliance Marine Insurance Co* (1873) L.R. 8 C.P. 596. *O'Kane v Jones* [2005] Lloyd's Rep. I.R. 174.

[89] See *Piper v Royal Exchange Assurance* (1932) 44 Ll. L.R. 103, where property had not passed to the purchaser.

[90] *Page v Fry* (1800) 2 Bos. & P. 240; *Robertson v Hamilton* (1811) 154 East 522; *Griffiths v Bramley-Moore* (1878) L.R. 4 QBD 70.

[91] *Herbert v Carter* (1787) 1 T.R. 745; *Hobbs v Hannam* (1811) 3 Camp. 93; *Provincial Insurance Co of Canada v Leduc* (1874) L.R. 6 P.C. 224.

[92] *Stephens v Australasian Insurance Co* (1872) L.R. 8 C.P. 18; *Allison v Bristol Marine Insurance Co* (1876) L.R. 1 App.Cas. 209; *Inglis v Stock* (1885) L.R. 10 App.Cas. 263; *Wunsche International v Tai Ping Insurance Co* [1998] 2 Lloyd's Rep. 8.

[93] *North of England Pure Oil Cake Co v Archangel Maritime* (1875) L.R. 10 Q.B. 249.

[94] As defined in Sch. r.15.

The insurable value, in the case of a steamship, includes also the machinery, boilers, and coals and engine stores if owned by the assured, and, in the case of a ship engaged in a special trade, the ordinary fittings requisite for that trade:

(2) In insurance on freight, whether paid in advance or otherwise, the insurable value is the gross amount of the freight at the risk of the assured, plus the charges of insurance:

(3) In insurance on goods or merchandise, the insurable value is the prime cost of the property insured, plus the expenses of and incidental to shipping and the charges of insurance upon the whole:

(4) In insurance on any other subject-matter, the insurable value is the amount at the risk of the assured when the policy attaches, plus the charges of insurance."

Where the policy is unvalued, the starting point for the calculation of the amount recoverable by the assured is the insurable value of the insured subject matter. The relevant definitions of insurable value in s.16 distinguish between ships, freight, goods and all other subject matters. The common principle is that the insurable value is to be assessed at the commencement of the risk rather than immediately prior to the loss. The insurers therefore bear the risk of any depreciation of the insured subject matter between the inception of the risk and the date of the loss. This is a curious principle, and one that has, to a large extent, been eroded both by standard policy wordings and by the attitude of the courts, it having been held that a marine policy expressed as one which provides an indemnity ousts the principle in s.16 and instead the assured is entitled to recover only for his actual loss, the difference between the value of the subject matter immediately before and immediately after the occurrence of the insured peril.[95]

5. DISCLOSURE AND REPRESENTATIONS[96]

Insurance is uberrimae fidei

"**17.** A contract of marine insurance is a contract based upon the utmost good faith, and, if the utmost good faith be not observed by either party, the contract may be avoided by the other party."

24–034

Disclosure by assured

"**18.**—(1) Subject to the provisions of this section, the assured must disclose to the insurer, before the contract is concluded, every material circumstance which is known to the assured, and the assured is deemed to know every circumstance which, in the ordinary course of business, ought to be known by him. If the assured fails to make such disclosure, the insurer may avoid the contract.

(2) Every circumstance is material which would influence the judgment of a prudent insurer in fixing the premium, or determining whether he will take the risk.

(3) In the absence of inquiry the following circumstances need not be disclosed namely—

(a) Any circumstance which diminishes the risk;

(b) Any circumstance which is known or presumed to be known to the insurer.
The insurer is presumed to know matters of common notoriety or knowledge, and matters which an insurer in the ordinary course of his business, as such, ought to know;

24–035

---

[95] *The Captain Panagos* [1985] 1 Lloyd's Rep. 625; *Thor Navigation Inc v Ingosstrak Insurance (The Thor II)* [2005] 1 Lloyd's Rep. 547.

[96] See Ch.6, above.

(c) Any circumstance as to which information is waived by the insurer;

(d) Any circumstance which it is superfluous to disclose by reason of any express or implied warranty.

(4) Whether any particular circumstance, which is not disclosed, be material or not is, in each case, a question of fact.

(5) The term 'circumstance' includes any communication made to, or information received by, the assured."

The general principles relating to utmost good faith are discussed in Ch.6, above. There is a large body of case law, both before and after the 1906 Act, dealing with the materiality of particular facts relating to the vessel and its cargo. The general principle is that anything which makes the voyage more hazardous is material.[97] The following headings are illustrative of the general position.

24–036   *Loss of or damage to vessel prior to inception of policy.* Material facts here will include the loss[98] or grounding[99] of the vessel, whether it is in danger or missing[100] and whether the assured believes that the vessel has been captured.[101]

24–037   *Situation of vessel at commencement of the risk.* It will normally be material for the insurer to know whether the vessel is ready to sail[102] or has already sailed.[103] Again, the date of sailing may be material.[104] The characteristics of the port, including whether the port is particularly subject to delay, will also be material facts.[105] These facts are important in assessing the weather conditions and, therefore, the risk of loss. The fact that the vessel is to remain in its builder's yard is not, however, material, as it reduces the risk of loss.[106]

---

[97] See: *De Costa v Scandret* (1723) 2 P. Wms. 170: *Seaman v Fonnereau* (1743) 2 Str. 1183; *Beckwaite v Nalgrove* (1810) 3 Taunt. 41; *Lynch v Dunsford* (1811) 14 East 494; *Kirby v Smith* (1818) 1 B. & Ald. 672; *Westbury v Aberdein* (1837) 2 M. & W. 267; *Russell v Thornton* (1860) 6 H. & N. 140; *Bates v Hewitt* (1867) L.R. 2 Q.B. 595; *Ionides v Pacific Fire & Marine Insurance Co* (1872) L.R. 7 Q.B. 517; *Bird's Cigarette Manufacturing Co Ltd v Rouse* (1924) 19 Ll. L.R. 301; *Berger & Light Diffusers Pty Ltd v Pollock* [1973] 2 Lloyd's Rep. 442; *Liberian Insurance Agency v Mosse* [1977] 2 Lloyd's Rep. 560.

[98] *Fitzherbert v Mather* (1785) 1 T.R. 12.

[99] *Russell v Thornton* (1860) 6 H. & N. 140.

[100] *Lynch v Dunsford* (1811) 14 East 494; *Kirby v Smith* (1818) 1 B. & Ad. 672; *Westbury v Aberdein* (1837) 2 M. & W. 267; *Stribley v Imperial Marine insurance Co* (1876) 1 QBD 507; *Bridges v Hunter* (1813) 1 M. & S. 15.

[101] *De Costa v Scandret* (1723) 2 P. Wms. 170.

[102] *McAndrew v Bell* (1795) I Esp. 373; *Elton v Larkins* (1832) 8 Bing. 198.

[103] *Uzielli v Commercial Union Insurance Co* (1865) 12 L.T. 399; *Harper v Mackechnie* (1925) 22 Ll. L.R. 514.

[104] The older cases treated the date of sailing as inevitably material. See: *Fillis v Bruton* (1782) 1 Park's Marine Insurances 414; *Macdowall v Fraser* (1779) 1 Doug. KB. 260; *Shirley v Wilkinson* (1781) 3 Doug. 41; *Bridges v Hunter* (1813) 1 M. & S. 15; *McAndrew v Bell* (1795) 1 Esp. 373; *Willis v Glover* (1804) 1 Bos. & P. 14; *Fort v Lee* (1811) 3 Taunt. 381; *Foley v Moline* (1814) 5 Taunt. 430. However, later authorities emphasise that this is a question of fact for every case: *Stribley v Imperial Marine Insurance* (1876) 1 QBD 507; *Scottish Shire Line v London & Provincial Marine and General Insurance Co Ltd* (1912) 107 L.T. 46; *Harper v Mackechnie* (1925) 22 Ll. L.R. 514.

[105] *Marc Rich & Co AG v Portman* [1996] 1 Lloyd's Rep. 430, affirmed [1997] I Lloyd's Rep. 225, which casts doubt upon older cases, indicating that the insurer is deemed to be aware of such facts: *Kingston v Knibbs* (1808) 1 Camp. 508; *Stewart v Bell* (1820) 5 B. & Ald. 238. It would seem, however, that in *Marc Rich* the facts in question were specific to the assured's own business. See also *Fraser Shipping Ltd v Colton* [1997] I Lloyd's Rep. 586.

[106] *Inversiones Manria SA v Sphere Drake Insurance Co Plc (The Dora)* [1989] 1 Lloyd's Rep. 69.

The nature of the vessel. The name of the vessel will be material, as the insurer **24–038**
may possess some knowledge of the vessel which is itself material,[107] as is the
history of the vessel where its background may render it particularly liable to
loss.[108]

Its place of manufacture, and the fact that it is a prototype and to be used for
tests and demonstrations, may well be material facts.[109] In the London market, it
is standard practice for the insurers to require the vessel to be inspected prior to
the inception of the risk, as a pre-condition to the commencement of cover[110] or
by means of a warranty,[111] although compliance with such a condition does not
remove the assured's duty of disclosure in relation to material facts relating to the
condition of the vessel[112] in so far as they cover additional matters.[113] Threats to
the vessel will be material only insofar as they are based on hard evidence, as
opposed to mere speculation.[114]

Facts affecting the voyage. Anything which affects the viability of, or the risk **24–039**
inherent in, a marine adventure, is prima facie material.[115] This will include the
fact that the master has a record of incompetence,[116] that a vessel is sailing
without a convoy in wartime,[117] that the vessel is to follow a route to its
destination which is unusual,[118] the estimated date of arrival at port,[119] the fact
that the port of destination has inadequate facilities for unloading[120] and the fact
that the cargo is to be carried as deck cargo[121] or is otherwise likely to be an
increased hazard.[122]

---

[107] *Lynch v Hamilton* (1810) 3 Taunt. 37.

[108] *Bates v Hewitt* (1867) L.R. 2 Q.B. 595; cf. *British Citizens Assurance Co v Woolland & Co* (1921) 8 Ll. L.R. 89; *Neue Fischmehl v Yorkshire Insurance Co* (1934) 50 Ll. L.R. 151.

[109] *Inversiones Manria SA v Sphere Drake Insurance Co Plc (The Dora)* [1989] 1 Lloyd's Rep. 69, where no false statements had been made.

[110] *Zeus Tradition Marine Ltd v Bell* [2000] 2 Lloyd's Rep. 587; *Kirkaldy & Sons Ltd v Walker* [1999] Lloyd's Rep. I.R. 410.

[111] *Kirkaldy & Sons Ltd v Walker* [1999] Lloyd's Rep. I.R. 410.

[112] *Zeus Tradition Marine Ltd v Bell* [1999] 2 Lloyd's Rep. 703.

[113] *Kirkaldy & Sons Ltd v Walker* [1999] Lloyd's Rep. I.R. 410.

[114] *Decorum Investments Ltd v Atkin (The Elena G)* [2002] Lloyd's Rep. I.R. 450.

[115] *Middlewood v Blakes* (1797) 7 T.R. 162; *Edwards v Footner* (1808) 1 Camp. 530; *Feise v Parkinson* (1812) 4 Taunt. 640; *Westbury v Aberdein* (1837) 2 M .& W. 267; *Anderson v Thornton* (1853) 8 Exch. 425; *Harrower v Hutchinson* (1870) L.R. 5 Q.B. 584; *Leigh v Adams* (1871) 25 L.T. 566; *Ionides v Pacific Fire and Marine Insurance Co.* (1871) L.R. 6 Q.B. 674; *Laing v Commercial Marine Insurance Co Ltd* (1895) 1 Com. Cas. 1.

[116] See *Anon* (1699) 12 Mod. Rep. 325. In *Thames & Mersey Marine Insurance v Gunford Ship Co* [1911] A.C. 529 it was held to be immaterial that the master had not been to sea for some 20 years and that his last vessel had been lost. The decision does not, however, provide authority for the general proposition that the master's history is always immaterial.

[117] *Sawtell v London* (1814) 5 Taunt. 359.

[118] *Middlewood v Blakes* (1797) 7 T.R. 162. Where the vessel changes its voyage, or deviates, the insurer is in any event discharged. Non-disclosure nevertheless remains an independent defence where the assured seeks to obtain permission from the insurer for a deviation or change of voyage without disclosing that it has already occurred: *Fraser Shipping Ltd v Colton* [1997] 1 Lloyd's Rep. 586.

[119] *Scottish Shire Line v London & Provincial Marine and General Insurance Co Ltd* (1912) 107 1.1. 47. This is particularly important in a policy on freight where the contract of carnage provides that freight is payable only where the vessel arrives by a given date.

[120] *Harrower v Hutchinson* (1869) L.R. 4 Q.B. 523.

[121] *Alluvials Mining Machinery Co v Stone* (1922) 10 Ll. L.R. 96. Cf. *Greenhill v Federal Insurance Co* [1927] 1 K.B. 65; *Clarkson v Young* (1870) 22 L.T. 41; *Hood v West End Motor Car Packing Co* [1917] 2 K.B. 38.

[122] *Blackett v Royal Exchange Assurance Co* (1832) 2 Cr. & J. 244.

24–040 *Scuttling and allegations of scuttling.* Specific allegations of earlier scuttling by the assured, as opposed to mere unsubstantiated rumours, are material facts.[123]

Disclosure by agent effecting insurance

24–041 "**19.** Subject to the provisions of the preceding section as to circumstances which need not be disclosed, where an insurance is effected for the assured by an agent, the agent must disclose to the insurer—

    (a) Every material circumstance which is known to himself, and an agent to insure is deemed to know every circumstance which in the ordinary course of business ought to be known by, or to have been communicated to, him; and

    (b) Every material circumstance which the assured is bound to disclose, unless it come to his knowledge too late to communicate it to the agent."

Representations pending negotiation of contract

24–042 "**20.**—(1) Every material representation made by the assured or his agent to the insurer during the negotiations for the contract, and before the contract is concluded, must be true. If it be untrue the insurer may avoid the contract.

(2) A representation is material which would influence the judgment of a prudent insurer in fixing the premium, or determining whether he will take the risk.

(3) A representation may be either a representation as to a matter of fact, or as to a matter of expectation or belief.

(4) A representation as to matter of fact is true, if it be substantially correct, that is to say, if the difference between what is represented and what is actually correct would not be considered material by a prudent insurer.

(5) A representation as to a matter of expectation or belief is true if it be made in good faith.

(6) A representation may be withdrawn or corrected before the contract is concluded.

(7) Whether a particular representation be material or not is, in each case, a question of fact."

When contract is deemed to be concluded

24–043 "**21.** A contract of marine insurance is deemed to be concluded when the proposal of the assured is accepted by the insurer, whether the policy be then issued or not; and, for the purpose of showing when the proposal was accepted, reference may be made to the slip or covering note or other customary memorandum of the contract . . . "

Section 23 was amended by the Finance Act 1959 Sch.8.

6. The Policy

Contract must be embodied in policy

24–044 "**22.** Subject to the provisions of any statute, a contract of marine insurance is inadmissible in evidence unless it is embodied in a marine policy in accordance with this Act. The policy may be executed and issued either at the time when the contract is concluded, or afterwards."

---

[123] *Strive Shipping Corp v Hellenic Mutual War Risks Association* [2002] Lloyd's Rep. I.R. 669.

Section 22 does not, as a matter of law, preclude an action in the absence of a policy.[124]

What policy must specify

"**23.** A marine policy must specify—
(1) The name of the assured,[125] or of some person who effects the insurance on his behalf:[126]
. . . "

24–45

The Finance Act 1959 repealed those provisions of the Marine Insurance Act 1906 which required the insertion of details as to the insured subject matter, the sum insured and the duration of the risk.

Signature of insurer

"**24.**—(1) A marine policy must be signed by or on behalf of the insurer, provided that in the case of a corporation the corporate seal may be sufficient, but nothing in this section shall be construed as requiring the subscription of a corporation to be under seal.
(2) Where a policy is subscribed by or on behalf of two or more insurers, each subscription, unless the contrary be expressed, constitutes a distinct contract with the assured."

24–046

Voyage and time policies[127]

"**25.**—(1) Where the contract is to insure the subject-matter 'at and from', or from one place to another or others, the policy is called a 'voyage policy', and where the contract is to insure the subject-matter for a definite period of time the policy is called a 'time policy'. A contract for both voyage and time may be included in the same policy.
(2) . . . "

24–047

The word "definite" in s.25(1) does not require that the time be fixed irretrievably. Thus a policy is a time policy even though it is terminable by earlier notice or capable of being extended either automatically or by the assured.[128] The distinction between time and voyage policies is of particular significance in that it determines the effect of the unseaworthiness of the vessel. A vessel insured under a voyage policy is warranted seaworthy at the start of its voyage, whereas a vessel under a time policy is not warranted seaworthy at any stage although the assured may not recover for a loss resulting from unseaworthiness when the

---

[124] *Swan v Maritime Insurance Co* [1907] 1 K.B. 136; *Eide UK Ltd v Lowndes Lambert (The Sun Tender)* [1998] 1 Lloyd's Rep. 389. Earlier authority to the contrary is now unreliable. See: *Fisher v Liverpool Marine Insurance Co* (1874) L.R. 9 Q.B. 418; *Genforsikrings & Co v Da Costa* [1911] 1 K.B. 137; *Re National Benefit Assurance Co Ltd* [1931] 1 Ch. 46. The section does not in any event apply to war risks covers within ss.1 and 2 of the Marine and Aviation (War Risks) Insurance Act: see s.7 of that Act.

[125] The mere fact that the names of persons interested in the insured subject matter are inserted into the policy does not of itself make them parties to the policy, as if it was effected by a broker or agent it is necessary to show that he possessed the necessary authority to make a contract on their behalves: *Sutherland v Pratt* (1843) 12 M. & W. 16; *Boston Fruit Co v British and Foreign Marine Insurance Co* [1905] 1 K.B. 637; *National Oilwell (UK) Ltd v Davy Offshore Ltd* [1993] 2 Lloyd's Rep. 582.

[126] The requirement here is minimal, as if the policy is effected by a broker it is sufficient if the broker is identified: *Bell v Gibson* (1798) 1 Bos. & P. 345.

[127] Section 25 was amended by the Finance Act 1959 Sch.8.

[128] *Compania Maritima San Basilio SA v Oceanus Mutual Underwriting Association (Bermuda) Ltd (The Eurysthenes)* [1977] Q.B. 49.

vessel had, with his privity, put to sea in an unseaworthy state.[129] Voyage policies are appropriate for all forms of marine subject matter. Time policies, by contrast, are most commonly used in respect of hulls and freight, it being more usual to insure cargo under voyage policies. A policy which is for a specified time, but which allows a particular voyage outside the general scope of the policy, is to be construed as a time policy with an extension to trading limits rather than as a mixed policy.[130]

The concluding words of s.25 provide that a contract for both voyage and time may be included in the same policy. A policy of this nature is generally referred to as a "mixed" policy and will insure, e.g. a journey from A to B for a period of X months. Under a mixed policy the vessel must comply with the requirements imposed by voyage and time policies. Thus a vessel which sets out from the incorrect destination, and to which the risk does not attach by virtue of s.43, is uninsured even though the temporal risk under the policy has attached.[131] Under cl.12 of the International Hulls Clauses 2003, a time policy provides "held covered" protection if the vessel is on a voyage which has not been completed at the date of the expiry of the agreed term and if the vessel is in distress or missing: such a policy takes effect as a mixed policy consisting of a time policy followed by a voyage policy, so that the rules as to deviation do not apply once the policy has been converted from a time policy to a voyage policy.[132]

The International Hulls Clauses 2003, cl.13 and the Institute Time Clauses (Freight), cl.5, provide for automatic termination of the risk on the happening of a one or more of a number of specified events relating to classification unless the insurers have agreed in writing to the contrary.[133] This is subject to two provisos: (1) if the vessel is at sea at that date, automatic termination is deferred until arrival at her next port; and (2) in a case where loss of classification is the result of an insured peril, automatic termination operates only if the vessel sails from her next port without the prior approval of the Classification Society. Where automatic termination takes effect, a pro rata daily net return of premium is to be made by the insurers as long as there has not been a total loss of the vessel during the currency of the policy. Automatic termination is also provided for in the event of changes in the management of the vessel, by cl.14 of the 2003 International Hulls Clauses.

Designation of subject-matter

24–048   "**26.**—(1) The subject-matter insured must be designated in a marine policy with reasonable certainty.

(2) The nature and extent of the interest of the assured in the subject-matter insured need not be specified in the policy.

(3) Where the policy designates the subject-matter insured in general terms, it shall be construed to apply to the interest intended by the assured to be covered.

(4) In the application of this section regard shall be had to any usage regulating the designation of the subject-matter insured."

---

[129] Marine Insurance Act 1906 s.39: see below.

[130] *Lombard Insurance Co v Kin Yuen Co Pte Ltd* (1995) *Lloyd's List*, July 25.

[131] *Way v Modigliani* (1787) 2 T.R. 30.

[132] *Gambles v Ocean Insurance Co* (1876) 1 Ex. D. 141; *Maritime Insurance Co v Alianza Insurance Co of Santander* (1907) 13 Com. Cas. 46; *Royal Exchange Assurance Corp v Sjoforsakrings Aktibolaget Vega* [1902] 2 K.B. 384.

[133] These provisions apply to a post-inception change of class, and not to a change of class prior to the commencement of the risk, although there may be separate warranties in respect of that matter: *Sun Alliance & London Insurance Plc v PT Asuransri Dayan Mitra TBK (The No.1 Dae Bu)* [2006] Lloyd's Rep. I.R. 860.

Section 26(2) does not require the assured to disclose to the insurer the precise nature of his interest in the subject matter. Thus a policy is not invalidated by the fact that the assured has insured his liability in respect of cargo rather than the cargo itself,[134] that the assured is a mortgagee,[135] that the assured has an interest in the subject matter other than purely as owner,[136] or that the policyholder is a reinsured as opposed to an owner.[137]

The precise meaning of s.26(3) is not fully clear, but the provision would appear to mean that in the case in which a variety of interests are insured under one policy the assured can recover only in respect of the interest intended by him to be covered.[138] There is, nevertheless, potentially contradictory Court of Appeal authority for the proposition that where a particular event clearly falls within the wording of a policy, the fact that the assured had a subjective and uncommunicated intention not to cover that particular event will not bring s.26(3) into play and to prevent him from recovering.[139] This does not, however, prevent the introduction of evidence other than of uncommunicated intention demonstrating the meaning of the words used by the parties.[140] In particular, the subjective intention of a contracting party remains important for the purpose of determining whether that party intended the policy to cover the interests of some other person as well as his own[141] and if that is not the case then the assured can recover only in respect of his own interest.[142]

Valued policy[143]

"**27.**—(1) A policy may be either valued or unvalued.   24–049

(2) A valued policy is a policy which specifies the agreed value of the subject-matter insured.

(3) Subject to the provisions of this Act, and in the absence of fraud, the value fixed by the policy is, as between the insurer and assured, conclusive of the insurable value of the subject intended to be insured, whether the loss be total or partial.

(4) Unless the policy otherwise provides, the value fixed by the policy is not conclusive for the purpose of determining whether there has been a constructive total loss."

Unvalued policy

"**28.** An unvalued policy is a policy which does not specify the value of the subject-   24–050
matter insured, but, subject to the limit of the sum insured, leaves the insurable value to be subsequently ascertained, in the manner herein-before specified."

Floating policy by ship or ships

"**29.**—(1) A floating policy is a policy which describes the insurance in general terms,   24–051
and leaves the name of the ship or ships and other particulars to be defined by subsequent declaration.

---

[134] *Crowley v Cohen* (1832) 3 B. & Ald. 478.
[135] *Irving v Richardson* (1831) 1 Mo. & R. 153.
[136] *Carruthers v Sheddon* (1815) 6 Taunt. 14.
[137] *Mackenzie v Whitworth* (1875) L.R. 1 Ex. D. 36.
[138] *Dunlop Brothers & Co v Townend* [1919] 2 K.B. 127.
[139] *Reliance Marine Insurance Co v Duder* [1913] 1 K.B. 165.
[140] *Janson v Poole* (1912) 18 Com. Cas. 9.
[141] *National Oilwell (UK) Ltd v Davy Offshore Ltd* [1993] 2 Lloyd's Rep. 582.
[142] *Stephens v Australasian Insurance Co* (1872) L.R. 8 C.P. 18; *Scott v Globe Marine Insurance Co* (1896) 1 Com. Cas. 370; *Dunlop Brothers v Townend* [1919] 2 K.B. 127.
[143] See Ch.10, above.

(2) The subsequent declaration or declarations may be made by indorsement on the policy, or in other customary manner.

(3) Unless the policy otherwise provides, the declarations must be made in the order of dispatch or shipment.[144] They must, in the case of goods, comprise all consignments within the terms of the policy,[145] and the value of the goods or other property must be honestly stated, but an omission or erroneous declaration may be rectified[146] even after loss or arrival, provided the omission or declaration was made in good faith.

(4) Unless the policy otherwise provides, where a declaration of value is not made until after notice of loss or arrival, the policy must be treated as an unvalued policy as regards the subject-matter of that declaration."

A floating policy resembles, and fulfils a similar function to, an open cover,[147] although the use of such policies has all but fallen into disuse in the modern market. A floating policy in essence an agreement by the insurer to provide cover for all subject matter of a given class and description for which the assured from time to time requires insurance. The main differences between a floating policy and an open cover are, first, that the facility granted under a floating policy is for a fixed sum rather than for a specified period, so that a floating policy will become exhausted by declarations, and, secondly, that the premium under a floating policy is payable in advance rather than as and when declarations are made. In past marine insurance practice it was common for the assured to procure an initial floating policy up to a specified amount, and to supplement that with an open cover so that insurance could be arranged immediately the limit of the floating policy is exceeded. Floating policies appear to have developed in the marine context, merchants insuring a cargo to be shipped at a future date in unspecified quantities and on unspecified vessels.

The nature of a floating policy requires post-contractual declarations to be made to the insurer, relating to the cargo, its value and the name of the vessel.[148] The rules on declarations are codified in s.29(3). At common law it was not necessary for a declaration to be made before the loss had occurred,[149] although s.29(4) provides that where a declaration of value has not been made before the loss has occurred, the policy is to be treated as an unvalued policy as regards the subject matter of that particular declaration.[150] Moreover, it is open to the insurer to specify, by way of promissory warranty, that any declaration is to be made as soon as is practicable, so that any failure to declare in compliance will allow the insurer to reject a claim for the subject matter of the declaration.[151]

---

[144] *Henchman v Offley* (1782) 3 Doug. K.B. 135; *Kewley v Ryan* (1794) 2 H. Bl. 343; *Gledstanes v Royal Exchange Assurance Corp* (1864) 5 B. & S. 797; *Stephens v Australasian Insurance Co* (1872) L.R. 8 C.P. 18; *Imperial Marine Insurance Co v Fire Insurance Corp Ltd* (1879) 4 C.P.D. 166; *Dunlop Bros & Co v Townend* [1919] 2 K.B. 127.

[145] *Dunlop Bros & Co v Townend* [1919] 2 K.B. 127

[146] *Robinson v Touray* (1811) 3 Camp. 158; *Stephens v Australasian Insurance Co* (1872) L.R. 8 C.P. 18; *Imperial Marine Insurance Co v Fire Insurance Corp Ltd* (1879) 4 C.P.D. 166.

[147] See Ch.6, above.

[148] In the absence of any declaration, no loss is recoverable: *Union Insurance Society of Canton Lid v George Wills & Co* [1916] 1 A.C. 281. A declaration will, unless the policy otherwise states, be operative for as long as the risk is borne by the assured, and will not be subject to time limits: *Glencore International AG v Alpina Insurance Co (No.2)* [2004] 1 Lloyd's Rep. 567.

[149] *Harman v Kingston* (1811) 3 Camp. 150.

[150] *Harman v Kingston* (1811) 3 Camp. 150; *Gledstanes v Royal Exchange Assurance Corp* (1864) 34 L.J.Q.B. 30; *Union Insurance Society of Canton Ltd v George Wills & Co* [1916] 1 A.C. 281. This is significant in respect of the assured's measure of indemnity, which differs between valued and unvalued policies: see below.

[151] *Union Insurance Society of Canton Ltd v George Wills & Co* [1916] 1 A.C. 281.

As may be seen from s.29(3), the common law had developed specific rules relating to the correctness of declarations. The assured is under a duty to make honest declarations, but an omission or erroneous declaration may be rectified at any time—even after loss—as long as the original declaration had been made in good faith. Consequently, unless the assured has been fraudulent in his declarations,[152] it would appear that non-disclosure or misrepresentation does not afford a ground for the insurer to avoid the policy. Thus in *Robinson v Touray*[153] and *Ionides v Pacific Fire and Marine Insurance Co*[154] the assured was able to recover despite the fact that there had been an error in notifying to the insurer the name of the vessel.[155]

Construction of terms in policy

"**30.**—(1) A policy may be in the form in the First Schedule to this Act.   **24–052**
(2) Subject to the provisions of this Act, and unless the context of the policy otherwise requires, the terms and expressions mentioned in the First Schedule to this Act shall be construed as having the scope and meaning in that schedule assigned to them."

Premium to be arranged

"**31.**—(1) Where an insurance is effected at a premium to be arranged, and no   **24–053**
arrangement is made, a reasonable premium is payable.
(2) Where an insurance is effected on the terms that an additional premium is to be arranged in a given event, and that event happens but no arrangement is made, then a reasonable additional premium is payable."

Section 31(2) is primarily concerned with "held covered" clauses. In essence, such a clause will come into effect where the policy has terminated prior to the completion of the voyage, and the insurer has agreed to extend the duration of the cover. There are two constituent elements of the "held covered" clause: ascertaining the amount of additional premium to be paid; and determining exactly what constitutes due notice by the assured.

The first of these matters is governed by s.31(2) itself. The approach adopted by the courts in determining a reasonable premium is to assess the premium that would have been agreed between the parties had the event in question occurred.[156] This calculation assumes the existence of a market rate of premium for an event of the type in question, but there may be cases in which the parties cannot agree upon a reasonable additional premium and the insurer can demonstrate that the market would not have accepted the risk at any premium in those circumstances.[157] The second aspect of the held covered clause is the obligation of the assured to give "due notice" of the event in question. This phrase has been interpreted by the courts in a liberal fashion in the assured's favour. The general principle emerging from the decisions is that notice by the assured is in time if the insurer is not adversely affected by any delay.[158] Where

---

[152] *Rivaz v Gerussi Bros & Co* (1880) L.R. 6 QBD 222.
[153] *Robinson v Touray* (1811) 3 Camp. 158.
[154] *Ionides v Pacific Fire and Marine Insurance Co* (1871) L.R. 6 Q.B. 674.
[155] See also *Gledstanes v Royal Exchange Assurance Co* (1864) 5 B. & S. 797.
[156] *Greenock Steamship Co v Maritime Insurance Co Ltd* [1903] 1 K.B. 367; *Mentz, Decker & Co v Maritime Insurance Co Ltd* [1910] 1 K.B. 132; *Hewitt v London General Insurance Co Ltd* (1925) 23 Ll. L.R. 243.
[157] *Liberian Insurance Agency v Mosse* [1977] 2 Lloyd's Rep. 560.
[158] *Mentz Decker & Co v Maritime Insurance Co* [1910] 1 K.B. 32; *Hewitt v London General Insurance Co Ltd* (1925) 23 Ll. L.R. 243.

a loss has occurred, the fact that the insurer cannot itself arrange reinsurance to cover the additional period provided for by the held covered clause in the original policy, is immaterial and will not render a notice out of time. It should be noted, however, that these cases are of no assistance where "prompt notice" is required; ordinary English usage indicates that the word "prompt" or notice "as soon as possible"[159] does not imply any requirement of prejudice to the insurer. Similarly, the use of the term "immediate notice" in certain of the Institute Clauses appears to overcome the common law rule. Exactly what constitutes "immediate notice" has yet to be determined by the courts, although, in *Fraser Shipping Ltd v Colton*,[160] it was conceded that a delay in giving notice of change of voyage of just under a month failed the immediacy test. The notice requirement may be waived by the insurers. Waiver will, potentially, operate where the insurers are aware of the assured's failure to give due notice but act in a manner which is inconsistent with any intention to deny liability.

7. Double Insurance[161]

Double insurance

24–054   "32.—(1) Where two or more policies are effected by or on behalf of the assured on the same adventure and interest or any part thereof, and the sums insured exceed the indemnity allowed by this Act, the assured is said to be over-insured by double insurance.
(2) Where the assured is over-insured by double insurance—
(a) The assured, unless the policy otherwise provides, may claim payment from the insurers in such order as he may think fit, provided that he is not entitled to receive any sum in excess of the indemnity allowed by this Act;
(b) Where the policy under which the assured claims is a valued policy, the assured must give credit as against the valuation for any sum received by him under any other policy without regard to the actual value of the subject-matter insured;
(c) Where the policy under which the assured claims is an unvalued policy he must give credit, as against the full insurable value, for any sum received by him under any other policy;
(d) Where the assured receives any sum in excess of the indemnity allowed by this Act, he is deemed to hold such sum in trust for the insurers, according to their right of contribution among themselves."

8. Warranties, Etc[162]

Nature of warranty

24–055   "33.—(1) A warranty, in the following sections relating to warranties, means a promissory warranty, that is to say, a warranty by which the assured undertakes that some particular thing shall or shall not be done, or that some condition shall be fulfilled, or whereby he affirms or negatives the existence of a particular state of facts.
(2) A warranty may be express or implied.

---

[159] The latter formulation is used by cl.12 of the International Hull Clauses 2003.
[160] *Fraser Shipping Ltd v Colton* [1997] 1 Lloyd's Rep. 586.
[161] See Ch.11, above.
[162] See also Ch.7, above.

(3) A warranty, as above defined, is a condition which must be exactly complied with, whether it be material to the risk or not. If it be not so complied with, then, subject to any express provision in the policy, the insurer is discharged from liability as from the date of the breach of warranty, but without prejudice to any liability incurred by him before that date."

When breach of warranty excused

"**34.**—(1) Non-compliance with a warranty is excused when, by reason of a change of circumstances, the warranty ceases to be applicable to the circumstances of the contract, or when compliance with the warranty is rendered unlawful by any subsequent law.

(2) Where a warranty is broken, the assured cannot avail himself of the defence that the breach has been remedied, and the warranty complied with, before loss.

(3) A breach of warranty may be waived by the insurer."

24–056

Express warranties

"**35.**—(1) An express warranty may be in any form of words from which the intention to warrant is to be inferred.

(2) An express warranty must be included in, or written upon, the policy, or must be contained in some document incorporated by reference into the policy.

(3) An express warranty does not exclude an implied warranty, unless it be inconsistent therewith."

24–057

Warranty of neutrality

"**36.**—(1) Where insurable property, whether ship or goods, is expressly warranted neutral, there is an implied condition that the property shall have a neutral character at the commencement of the risk, and that, so far as the assured can control the matter, its neutral character shall be preserved during the risk.

(2) Where a ship is expressly warranted "neutral" there is also an implied condition that, so far as the assured can control the matter, she shall be properly documented, that is to say, that she shall carry the necessary papers to establish her neutrality, and that she shall not falsify or suppress her papers, or use simulated papers. If any loss occurs through breach of this condition, the insurer may avoid the contract."

24–058

In the eighteenth and nineteenth centuries it was common for vessels to be declared neutral in order to avoid capture in time of war. The law did not imply a warranty of neutrality, and s.36(1) merely replicates this position.[163] Subject to express stipulation, any warranty of neutrality must be complied with when the risk incepts[164] but is not, in its absolute form, to be construed as continuing, as the assured will not be in breach of warranty if neutrality is lost after the commencement of the risk for reasons beyond his control.[165]

A neutral vessel which does not carry the necessary documentation to prove its neutrality runs the risk of being treated as an enemy and thus liable to sinking or seizure: this is the basis for s.36(2),[166] which applies to vessels and not cargo.[167]

---

[163] *Tyson v Gurney* (1789) 3 T.R. 477: *Baring v Claggett* (1802) 3 B. & P. 201; *Lothian v Henderson* (1803) 3 B. & P. 499; *Baring v Christie* (1804) 5 East 395; *Bolton v Gladstone* (1809) 2 Taunt. 85.

[164] *Tabbs v Bendelack* (1801) 3 Bos. & P. 207n; *Baring v Christie* (1804) 5 East 398.

[165] *Eden v Parkinson* (1781) 2 Doug. 732, although contrast *Garrels v Kensington* (1799) 8 T.R. 230.

[166] *Barzillai v Lewis* (1782) 3 Doug. K.B. 126; *Rich v Parker* (1798) 7 T.R. 705; *Steel v Lacy* (1810) 3 Taunt. 285; *Oswell v Vigne* (1812) 15 East 70.

[167] *Dawson v Atty* (1806) 7 East 367; *Bell v Carstairs* (1811) 14 East 374; *Carruthers v Gray* (1811) 3 Camp. 142.

This is not a warranty proper, for two reasons: the term is broken only where the assured is able to control the matter; and there is a nexus test in that the breach must cause the loss before the insurer has a defence.[168]

No implied warranty of nationality

24–059   "**37.** There is no implied warranty as to the nationality of a ship, or that her nationality shall not be changed during the risk."[169]

Where there is an express warranty of nationality, it is to be presumed not to be continuing warranty, so that it is confined in its operation to the commencement of the risk,[170] and it relates to legal rather than beneficial ownership.[171]

Warranty of good safety

24–060   "**38.** Where the subject-matter insured is warranted "well" or "in good safety" on a particular day, it is sufficient if it be safe at any time during that day."[172]

Warranty of seaworthiness of ship

24–061   "**39.**—(1) In a voyage policy there is an implied warranty that at the commencement of the voyage the ship shall be seaworthy for the purpose of the particular adventure insured.

    (2) Where the policy attaches while the ship is in port, there is also an implied warranty that she shall, at the commencement of the risk, be reasonably fit to encounter the ordinary perils of the port.

    (3) Where the policy relates to a voyage which is performed in different stages, during which the ship requires different kinds of or further preparation or equipment, there is an implied warranty that at the commencement of each stage the ship is seaworthy in respect of such preparation or equipment for the purposes of that stage.

    (4) A ship is deemed to be seaworthy when she is reasonably fit in all respects to encounter the ordinary perils of the seas of the adventure insured.

    (5) In a time policy there is no implied warranty that the ship shall be seaworthy at any stage of the adventure, but where, with the privity of the assured, the ship is sent to sea in an unseaworthy state, the insurer is not liable for any loss attributable to unseaworthiness."

A distinction is drawn between voyage and time policies. Under a voyage policy[173] there is an implied warranty of seaworthiness[174] under s.39(1) and a further implied warranty for port perils under s.39(2).[175] The warranties do not apply to cargo (s.40(1)) although there is an implied warranty that, at the commencement of the voyage, the vessel is reasonably fit to carry the goods to the destination contemplated by the policy (s.40(2)). Where the warranties are applicable, the assured's knowledge or otherwise of the unseaworthiness of the

---

[168] *Le Cheminant v Pearson* (1812) 4 Taunt. 367.

[169] *Eden v Parkinson* (1781) 2 Doug. K.B. 732; *Tyson v Gurney* (1789) 3 T.R. 477; *Clapham v Cologan* (1813) 3 Camp. 382; *Dent v Smith* (1869) L.R. 4 Q.B. 414.

[170] *Dent v Smith* (1869) L.R. 4 Q.B. 414.

[171] *Seavision Investment SA v Evenett and Clarkson Puckle (The Tiburon)* [1990] 2 Lloyd's Rep. 418.

[172] *Blackhurst v Cockell* (1789) 3 T.R. 360.

[173] Excluding lighters carrying cargo to and from the ship: *Lane v Nixon* (1866) L.R. 1 C.P. 412.

[174] Based on *Christie v Secretan* (1799) 8 T.R. 192.

[175] *Parmeter v Cousins* (1809) 2 Camp. 235; *Annen v Woodman* (1810) 3 Taunt. 299; *Gibson v Small* (1853) 4 H.L. Cas. 353; *Buchanan & Co v Faber* (1899) 4 Com. Cas. 223.

vessel is not a relevant consideration in determining whether the warranty has been broken.[176]

The warranties are stated to apply only at the commencement of the risk: the warranties are thus not continuing, but are relevant only at the inception of the risk.[177] This principle gives rise to evidential problems where a vessel goes down, without apparent explanation, during its voyage. Much may in these circumstances depend upon the burden of proof, and it would seem that the following principles are applicable: (a) the initial burden of proof rests upon the assured to demonstrate that the loss was proximately caused by an insured peril, so that if the assured is unable to identify any possible cause for the loss, he will be unable to recover and the implied warranty of seaworthiness has no part to play[178]; (b) where the assured can demonstrate the occurrence of an insured peril, the burden of proof shifts to the insurer to demonstrate that the vessel had been unseaworthy at the outset[179]; (c) it may in appropriate circumstances be presumed that the vessel was unseaworthy from the commencement of the risk[180]; and (d) if the assured can demonstrate that the loss was proximately caused by an insured peril, while the insurer can simultaneously demonstrate that the vessel was unseaworthy at the commencement of the risk, the breach of warranty is effective whether or not it is causative of the loss will operate to defeat the assured's claim.

The principle that the warranty of seaworthiness attaches at the outset only is modified by s.39(3) where the voyage is in stages,[181] e.g. where the vessel has to negotiate both inland waterways and the open sea. As different risks may be faced, the vessel must be properly equipped to face the changed circumstances.[182]

The implied warranty of seaworthiness in a voyage policy is subject to **24–062** contrary agreement. However, the courts have been reluctant to hold that the warranty has been ousted in the absence of unambiguous words to that effect: in this way, an express warranty of seaworthiness which overlaps with the implied warranty has been held not to override the latter.[183] For this reason, it is necessary to use wording such as "seaworthiness admitted" to achieve an effective ouster.[184] The Institute Cargo Clauses 1982 set out an express waiver of the seaworthiness warranty, as follows:

> "5.2   The Underwriters waive any breach of the implied warranties of seaworthiness of the ship and fitness of the ship to carry the subject matter insured to destination

---

[176] *Lee v Beach* (1762) Park on Insurance 468; *Douglas v Scougall* (1816) 4 Dow. 269.

[177] *Bermon v Woodbridge* (1781) 2 Doug. 781; *Holdsworth v Wise* (1828) 7 B & C 794; *Hollingsworth v Brodrick* (1837) 7 Ad. & E. 40; *Dixon v Sadler* (1841) 8 M. & W. 895; *Gibson v Small* (1853) 4 H.L. Cas. 353; *Biccard v Shepherd* (1861) 4 Moo. P.C.C. 471.

[178] *The Popi M* [1985] 2 All E.R. 712.

[179] *Watson v Clark* (1813) 1 Dow. 336; *Parker v Potts* (1815) 3 Dow. *23; Pickup v Thames and Mersey Marine Insurance Co Ltd* (1878) 3 K.B. 594: *Alum Goolan Hossen & Co. v Union Marine Insurance Co* [1911] A.C. 362.

[180] *Parker v Potts* (1815) 3 Dow. 23; *Douglas v Scougall* (1816) 4 Dow. 276; *Pickup v Thames and Mersey Marine Insurance Co* (1878) 3 QBD 594.

[181] *Dixon v Sadler* (1839) 5 M. & W. 405.

[182] *Bouillon v Lupton* (1863) 5 C.B.N.S. 113; *Quebec Marine Insurance Co v Commercial Bank of Canada* (1870) L.R. 3 P.C. 234; *Buchanan & Co v Faber* (1899) 4 Com. Cas. 223; *Greenock Steamship Co v Maritime Insurance Co* [1903] 2 K.B. 657; *The Vortigern* [1899] P. 140.

[183] *Quebec Marine Insurance Co v Commercial Bank of Canada* (1870) L.R. 3 P.C. 234; *Sleigh v Tyser* [1900] 2 Q.B. 333.

[184] *Phillips v Nairne* (1847) 4 C.B. 343; *Cantiere Meccanico Brindisio v Janson* [1912] 3 K.B. 452; *Parfitt v Thompson* (1844) 13 M. & W. 392.

unless the Assured or their servants are privy to such unseaworthiness or unfitness."

The 2009 revision of the Institute Cargo Clauses contain a rather broader waiver: "The Insurers waive any breach of the implied warranties of seaworthiness of the ship and fitness of the ship to carry the subject-matter insured to destination".

There is no implied seaworthiness warranty in a time policy.[185] There is, in substitution, a somewhat lesser provision in s.39(5)[186] which requires that the loss is attributable to unseaworthiness and that the vessel was sent to sea in an unseaworthy condition "with the privity of the assured". The phrase has been held to mean that: (a) the assured must be aware that the vessel was unseaworthy[187] and indeed must be aware of the precise unseaworthiness which gave rise to the loss[188]; (b) in the case of a company, the relevant knowledge must be that of its controller[189]; and (c) the degree of knowledge is actual or blind-eye knowledge.[190] The cover for negligence of the master and crew in the Hulls Clauses has been held to qualify the seaworthiness warranty, so that if the reason for the unseaworthiness of the vessel is negligence the warranty is not to be regarded as broken.[191]

The concept of seaworthiness, which is relevant to time and voyage policies, has been considered in a numerous cases. The principles are as follows:

(1) Seaworthiness is not an absolute standard but relates the purposes of the particular adventure insured.[192]

(2) Seaworthiness is a flexible concept, as a vessel is seaworthy "when she is reasonably fit in all respects to encounter the ordinary perils of the seas of the adventure insured". Thus, if the assured has made the vessel as seaworthy as is possible in the circumstances, the section will have been complied with.[193] The test is whether "a prudent owner would have made the defect good before sailing out of concern about the safety of the vessel, her crew and cargo (and not, for example, out of prudent regard for his economic or commercial interests because repairs, if delayed, might be more expensive)",[194] although the Court of Appeal has stressed that seaworthiness is concerned with the state of the vessel and the use of the prudent owner test is based on the response of a prudent owner who was aware of the defect.[195]

---

[185] *Biccard v Shepherd* (1861) 14 Moo. P.C. 471.

[186] *Gibson v Small* (1853) 4 H.L. Cas. 353; *Thompson v Hopper* (1858) E.B. & E. 1038; *Fawcus v Sarsfield* (1856) 6 E. & B. 192; *Dudgeon v Pembroke* (1877) 2 App.Cas. 284.

[187] *Cohen & Sons v Standard Marine Insurance Co* (1925) 21 Ll. L.R. 30; *Wilmott v General Accident Fire and Life Assurance Corporation Ltd* (1935) 53 Ll. L.R. 156.

[188] *Thomas v Tyne and Wear Steamship Freight Insurance Association* (1917) 117 L.T. 55.

[189] *Manifest Shipping Co Ltd v Uni-Polaris Co Ltd (The Star Sea)* [2001] Lloyd's Rep. I.R. 247.

[190] *Compania Maritima San Basilio SA v Oceanus Mutual Underwriting Association (Bermuda) Ltd (The Eurysthenes)* [1976] 2 Lloyd's Rep. 171; *The Star Sea* [2001] Lloyd's Rep. I.R. 247; *Laing v Boreal Pacific* [2000] F.C.J. No. 1665.

[191] *Martin Maritime Ltd v Provident Capital Indemnity Fund Ltd (The Lydia Flag)* [1998] 2 Lloyd's Rep. 652.

[192] *Steel v State Line Steamship Co* (1877) 3 App.Cas. 72; *The Fjord Wind* [2000] 2 Lloyd's Rep. 191; *Papera Traders Co Ltd v Hyundai Merchant Marine Co Ltd (The Eurasian Dream)* [2002] EWHC 118 (Comm).

[193] *Hibbert v Martin* (1808) Park on Marine Insurance 473; *Burgess v Wickham* (1863) 3 B. & S. 669; *Clapham v Langton* (1864) 10 L.T. 875; *Turnbull v Janson* (1877) 36 L.T. 635: *Steel v State Line Steamship Co* (1877) 3 App.Cas. 72.

[194] *Project Asia Line Inc of Delaware v Shone* [2002] 1 Lloyd's Rep. 659, at para.27.

[195] *Eritanie SpA v Oetker (The Fjord Wind)* [2000] 2 Lloyd's Rep. 191.

(3) Trivial defects which can easily be put right in the course of the voyage do not render a vessel unseaworthy,[196] but there is a presumption of unseaworthiness "if there is something about it which endangers the safety of the vessel or its cargo or which might cause significant damage to its cargo".[197]

(4) A vessel may be unseaworthy for any of the following reasons:[198] (a) the condition of the vessel,[199] including failure to comply with classification requirements,[200] and inadequate supplies and documentation,[201] fittings,[202] fuel[203] and fire-fighting facilities[204]; (b) incompetent or insufficient master and crew,[205] although there is a distinction between a single act of incompetence[206] and a disabling lack of knowledge[207]—incompetence may be the result of an inherent lack of ability, a lack of adequate training, a lack of knowledge about the vessel,[208] a disinclination to perform the job properly or physical or mental incapacity[209]; and (c) overloading.[210]

The Institute Cargo Clauses 1982 set out an express waiver of the seaworthiness warranty, as follows:

> "5.2 The Underwriters waive any breach of the implied warranties of seaworthiness of the ship and fitness of the ship to carry the subject matter insured to destination unless the Assured or their servants are privy to such unseaworthiness or unfitness."

The 2009 revision of the Institute Cargo Clauses contain a rather broader waiver: "The Insurers waive any breach of the implied warranties of seaworthiness of the ship and fitness of the ship to carry the subject-matter insured to destination".

---

[196] *Hong Kong Fir Shipping Co v Kawasaki Kisen Kaisha* [1962] 2 Q.B. 26.

[197] *Athenian Tankers Management SA v Pyrena Shipping Inc (The Arianna)* [1987] 2 Lloyd's Rep. 376.

[198] See the judgment of Cresswell J. in *Papera Traders Co Ltd v Hyundai Merchant Marine Co Ltd (The Eurasian Dream)* [2002] EWHC 118 (Comm).

[199] *Turnbull v Janson* (1877) 3 L.T. 635; *Hoffman & Co v British General Insurance Co* (1922) 10 Ll. L.R. 434; *Neue Fischmel Vertriebs-Gesellschaft mbH v Yorkshire Insurance Co Ltd* (1934) 50 Ll. L.R. 151; *Silcock & Sons Ltd v Maritime Lighterage Co Ltd* (1937) 57 Ll. L.R. 78.

[200] *Stewart v Wilson* (1843) 2 M. & W. 11.

[201] *Woolf v Claggett* (1800) 3 Esp. 257.

[202] *Wilkie v Geddes* (1815) 3 Dow. 57; *Wedderburn v Bell* (1807) I Camp. 1; *Quebec Marine Insurance Co v Commercial Bank of Canada* (1870) L.R. 3 P.C. 234.

[203] *Greenock Steamship Co v Maritime Insurance Co* [1903] 2 K.B. 657; *The Vortigern* [1899] P. 40; *Cohen Sons & Co v Standard Marine Insurance Co Ltd* (1925) 21 Ll. L.R. 30; *Harocopus v Mountain* (1934) 49 Ll. L.R. 267.

[204] *Manifest Shipping v Uni-Polaris Shipping Co Ltd (The Star Sea)* [2001] Lloyds Rep. I.R. 247.

[205] *Annen v Woodman* (1810) 3 Taunt. 299; *Tait v Levi* (1811) 14 East 481; *Busk v Royal Exchange Assurance Co* (1818) 2 B. & Ald. 73; *Forshaw v Chabert* (1821) 3 Brod. & B. 158; *Clifford v Hunter* (1827) 3 C. & P. 16; *Holdsworth v Wise* (1828) 7 B. & C. 794; *Phillips v Headlam* (1831) 2 B. & Ad. 383; *Thomas v Tyne & Wear Insurance Association* [1917] 1 KB. 938; *Thomas & Son Shipping Co Ltd v London & Provincial Marine & General Insurance Co Ltd* (1914) 30 T.L.R. 595; *Russell v Provincial Insurance Co Ltd* [1959] 2 Lloyd's Rep. 275.

[206] *Manifest Shipping v Uni-Polaris Shipping Co Ltd (The Star Sea)* [2001] Lloyds Rep. I.R. 247.

[207] *Standard Oil v Clan Line Steamers* [1924] A.C. 100; *The Makedonia* [1962] 1 Lloyd's Rep. 316.

[208] *The Farrandoc* [1967] 2 Lloyd's Rep. 276.

[209] *Moore v Lunn* (1923) 15 Ll. L.R. 155; *Rio Tinto v Seed Shipping* (1926) 24 Ll. L.R. 316.

[210] *Weir v Aberdeen* (1819) 2 B. & Ald. 320; *Foley v Tabor* (1861) 2 F. & F. 663; *Biscard v Shepherd* (1861) 14 Moo. P.C.C. 471; *Daniels v Harris* (1874) L.R. 10 C.P. 1.

No implied warranty that goods are seaworthy

24–063   "**40.**—(1) In a policy on goods or other moveables there is no implied warranty that the goods or moveables are seaworthy.[211]

(2) In a voyage policy on goods or other moveables there is an implied warranty that at the commencement of the voyage the ship is not only seaworthy as a ship, but also that she is reasonably fit to carry the goods or other moveables to the destination contemplated by the policy."[212]

The adventure must be illegal under English law and not under some foreign law.[213] The warranty is both present and continuing, in that it avoids the insurer's liability if the adventure is unlawful at the outset or if it becomes unlawful at some later point. Post-inception breaches are, however, treated differently, in that the assured loses the benefit of the policy only if he could not control the matter, e.g. where he was induced by duress to act in an unlawful fashion.[214] The illegality must form part of the adventure: it was thus held in *Royal Boskalis v Mountain* that if the assured makes an unlawful payment to secure the release of the insured subject matter from detention, that does not form any part of the marine adventure itself.[215] Even where there has been an act of illegality in the adventure, it is unlikely that it will have the effect of amounting to a breach of warranty only where it relates to the "core" of the adventure. This is the general principle which applies to illegality at common law.

Warranty of legality

24–064   "**41.** There is an implied warranty that the adventure insured is a lawful one, and that, so far as the assured can control the matter, the adventure shall be carried out in a lawful manner."

The implied warranty of legality, which has no counterpart in non-marine insurance,[216] is based on a series of cases in which it had been held that unlawful conduct on the part of the assured precluded recovery. The cases covered matters such as sailing without a convoy,[217] sailing without the requisite licence,[218] transporting prohibited cargo,[219] undertaking a voyage in breach of the navigation laws,[220] and hiring an incompetent master.[221] It was clear from these cases that as long as the assured was aware of the background facts, [222] knowledge as

---

[211] *Koebel v Saunders* (1864) 33 L.J.C.P. 310.

[212] *Daniels v Harris* (1874) L.R. 10 C.P. 1; *The Moon King* [1895] 2 Q.B. 550; *Sleigh v Tyser* [1900] 2 Q.B. 333; *Blackett v National Benefit Insurance Co* (1921) 8 Ll. L.R. 293.

[213] *Royal Boskalis Westminster NV v Mountain* [1997] 2 All E.R. 929.

[214] *Royal Boskalis Westminster NV v Mountain* [1997] 2 All E.R. 929.

[215] It would seem, however, that a ransom is not to be classified as an illegal payment: *Masefield AG v Amlin Corporate Member Ltd* [2010] EWHC 280 (Comm).

[216] *Euro Diam Ltd v Bathurst* [1988] 2 All E.R. 23.

[217] *Ingham v Agnew* (1812) 15 East 517.

[218] *Johnston v Sutton* (1779) 1 Doug. 254: *Cowie v Barber* (1814) 4 Cowp. 100.

[219] *Lubbock v Potts* (1806) 7 East 449; *Gray v Lloyd* (1811) 4 Taunt. 136; *Gibson v Service* (1814) 5 Taunt. 433.

[220] *Chalmers v Bell* (1804) 3 B. & P. 604.

[221] *Farmer v Legg* (1797) 7 T.R. 186.

[222] *Carstairs v Allnutt* (1813) 3 Camp. 497, which decided that the assured was able to recover under a policy of insurance, despite the fact that the ship was without a convoy as demanded by statute, as the result of the activity of his agent of which he was unaware. See also: *Wilson v Rankin* (1865) L.R. 1 Q.B. 162; *Dudgeon v Pembroke* (1874) L.R. 9 Q.B. 581.

to the legality or otherwise of his conduct played no part.[223] The cases were based on the concept of an "adventure", and in effect required the assured to refrain from breaking the law in the course of the adventure in so far as he can control the matter. This principle was codified by s.41. Lawfulness here relates only to English law,[224] and it is unlikely that pure incidental illegality could amount to a breach of the warranty[225]—it would seem that the entire adventure must be tainted,[226] and illegality which does not form part of the adventure does not break the warranty.[227] If the loss occurs at a time when the voyage is being conducted lawfully, the warranty does not apply.[228] It would seem that the warranty is in principle capable of waiver by the insurer in accordance with s.34(3), and may otherwise be excluded by contrary agreement, in so far as it has effects beyond those of the general law.

9. THE VOYAGE

Implied condition as to commencement of risk

24–065

"**42.**—(1) Where the subject-matter is insured by a voyage policy 'at and from' or 'from' a particular place, it is not necessary that the ship should be at that place when the contract is concluded, but there is an implied condition that the adventure shall be commenced within a reasonable time, and that if the adventure be not so commenced the insurer may avoid the contract.

(2) The implied condition may be negatived by showing that the delay was caused by circumstances known to the insurer before the contract was concluded, or by showing that he waived the condition."

The main purpose of this rule is to prevent a summer risk from being converted into a winter risk or adverse conditions otherwise becoming more likely.[229] The risk will, however, attach where the insurer was aware that a delay might take place or where the insurer has waived the delay by his subsequent conduct.[230] What is reasonable time is a question of fact.[231]

There is little in the 1906 Act which is concerned with the termination of the voyage.

---

[223] *Cunard v Hyde (No.2)* (1859) 2 E. & E. 1. See also: *Marryat v Wilson* (1799) 1 Bos. & P. 430; *Parkin v Dick* (1809) 11 East 502; *Gray v Lloyd* (1812) 4 Taunt. 136; *Camelo v Britten* (1820) 4 B. & Ald. 184; *Redmond v Smith* (1844) 7 Man. & G. 457; *Cunard v Hyde (No.1)* (1858) E.B. & E. 670; *Australian Insurance Co v Jackson* (1875) 33 L.T. 286.

[224] *Planche v Fletcher* (1779) 1 Doug. 251; *Royal Boskalis Westminster NV s Mountain* [1997] 2 All E.R. 929.

[225] *Atkinson v Abbott* (1809) 11 East 135; *Waugh v Morris* (1873) L.R. 8 Q.B. 202; *Dudgeon v Pembroke* (1874) L.R. 9 Q.B. 581; *Royal Boskalis v Mountain* [1997] 2 All E.R. 929; *Elaz International Co v Hong Kong & Shanghai Insurance Co Ltd* [2006] H.K.E.C. 825.

[226] *Pipon v Cope* (1808) 1 Camp. 434; *Cunard v Hyde* (1859) 29 L.J.Q.B. 6; *James Yachts Ltd v Thames and Mersey Marine Insurance Co Ltd* [1977] 1 Lloyd's Rep. 206.

[227] *Royal Boskalis v Mountain* [1997] 2 All E.R. 929.

[228] *Ocean Masters Inc v Allianz AGF MAT Ltd* 2007 N.L.C.A. 35.

[229] *Chitty v Selwyn & Martyn* (1742) 2 Atk. 359; *Grant v King* (1802) 4 Esp. 175; *Hull v Cooper* (1811) 4 East 479; *Mount v Larkins* (1831) 8 Bing. 108; *Palmer v Marshall* (1832) 8 Bing. 317; *Palmer v Fenning* (1833) 9 Bing. 460; *De Wolf v Archangel Insurance Co* (1874) L.R. 9 Q.B. 451; *Maritime Insurance Co v Stearns* [1901] 2 K.B. 912; *Bah Lias Tobacco and Rubber Estates v Volga Insurance Co* (1920) 3 Ll. L.R. 155.

[230] *Bah Lias Tobacco and Rubber Estates Ltd v Volga Insurance Co Ltd* (1920) 3 Ll. L.R. 155.

[231] 1906 Act s.89. See: *Moxon v Atkins* (1812) 3 Camp. 200; *Smith v Surridge* (1801) 4 Esp. 25.

A voyage policy on a vessel will come to an end in accordance with the definition of the voyage in the contract. The terminating event which has traditionally been used appears in Sch.1: the vessel is under this provision covered "until she hath moored at anchor twenty-four hours in good safety". This phrase has the effect of determining both when the risk attaches where a vessel is insured "at and from" a particular place, and when the voyage terminates, and is thus of some significance. The decided cases indicate that the question of good safety is one of degree: a vessel is not in good safety when she is incapable of floating independently[232] but she may be in good safety despite having sustained some damage.[233] Similarly, where the vessel is liable to seizure or other external control, fine factual distinctions may have to be made: a vessel which has actually been seized or is under the control of another is not in good safety,[234] whereas a vessel which is merely liable to seizure may be in good safety, even if she is in fact subsequently seized.[235] There is frequently a further extension to this period; in the reported cases the extension has been for 30 days. It is established that where such an extension exists it is additional to the 24 hours provided for by the policy[236] and commences from the exact time at which the original policy would have expired.[237] If the policy is stated to determine at the "final port", this refers to the final port of discharge and not at a port where refitting is carried out after final discharge.[238]

The risk under a freight policy necessarily determines when the freight has been paid. Where there has not been prepayment, the risk will terminate at the time stated in the policy, which will often be when the vessel has been at anchor 24 hours and in good safety.

24–066   Policies on cargo are normally voyage policies. The 1982 Cargo Clauses cl.8, provides for cover on a "warehouse to warehouse" basis, set out in standard transit clause. The risk attaches when the cargo leaves the warehouse of origin, and there are three potential terminating events, the first of which to occur brings the risk to an end: (a) delivery to the final warehouse or place of storage; (b) delivery to warehouse or place of storage other than in the course of transit; or (c) 60 days after completion of discharge at the final port of discharge. The 2009 version of the transit clause is differently worded. The risk commences when the goods are first moved in the warehouse of origin (so that the risk of damage within the warehouse is covered), and the risk terminates on the happening of the first of four events: (a) completion of unloading from the carrying vehicle or other conveyance in or at the final warehouse or place of storage at the destination named in the contract of insurance; (b) completion of unloading from the carrying vehicle or other conveyance in or at any other warehouse or place of storage, whether prior to or at the destination named in the contract of insurance, which the Assured or their employees elect to use either for storage other than in the ordinary course of transit or for allocation or distribution; (c) when the Assured or their employees elect to use any carrying vehicle or other conveyance or any container for storage other than in the ordinary course of transit; or (d) the expiry of 60 days after completion of discharge overside of the subject-matter insured from the oversea vessel at the final port of discharge. The

---

[232] *Shawe v Felton* (1801) 2 East 109; *Parmenter v Cousins* (1809) 2 Camp. 235.
[233] *Lidgett v Secretan* (1870) L.R. 5 C.P. 190.
[234] *Waples v Eames* (1746) 2 Str. 1243; *Minett v Anderson* 1(794) Peake 277; *Horneyer v Lushington* (1812) 15 East 46.
[235] *Lockyer v Offley* (1786) 1 T.R. 252; *Bell v Bell* (1810) 2 Camp. 475.
[236] *Mercantile Marine Insurance Co v Titherington* (1864) 5 H. & S. 765.
[237] *Cornfoot v Royal Exchange Assurance* [1904] 1 K.B. 40.
[238] *Martin v Vestey Bros* [1920] A.C. 307.

insurance is not terminated by reason of delay beyond the control of the assured or any deviation arising from the exercise of a liberty granted to the ship-owners.[239] There is much authority on previous versions of the transit clause, which used phrases such as "arrival"[240] at a "port"[241] of "final discharge or destination"[242] and "safely deposited" or "safely landed"[243]: these points do not arise under the present wording. There is an overriding obligation on the assured in the Cargo Clauses to act without delay, so that if there is delay the risk may terminate independently of the happening of a terminating event.[244]

As regards point (a) of the 2009 Clauses, the phrase "final warehouse or place of storage" does not extend to transit sheds and other temporary housing, given the obvious intention of the assured to transfer the goods elsewhere.[245] Thus if goods are deposited in such places the policy will not terminate until the expiry of 60 days from delivery or unless the goods are delivered to a warehouse other than in the course of transit[246] or the assured has elected to treat that warehouse as the final destination.[247] Further, if goods are in transit at a port and are stored temporarily awaiting trans-shipment, they remain covered by the transit clause.[248] As regards point (b), the risk does not determine if the goods have been unloaded but are transported to a warehouse without the consent of the assured.[249]

There has to be physical loss of the cargo between the warehouses. If, therefore, the amount of cargo is overstated on the shipping documents, the insurance does not cover the shortfall as it cannot be said that the cargo has been lost during the currency of the cover.[250] Once the cover has come to an end by reason of the occurrence of any of the events agreed upon, any subsequent losses are obviously uninsured, although in some situations the policy may cover loss of profits separately from the cargo itself and may specify an extended duration for pure economic loss.[251]

[239] Clause 8.3. See *Hong Kong Nylon Enterprises Ltd v QBE Insurance (Hong Kong) Ltd* [2003] H.K.E.C. 199.

[240] Which was held to refer to arrival at the part of the port where discharge was to be effected: *Lindsay v Jamson* (1859) 4 H. & N. 699; *Samuel v Royal Exchange Assurance* (1828) 8 B. & C. 19; *Stone v Marine insurance Co of Gothenburg* (1876) 81.

[241] Which had to be a friendly port: *Browne v Vigne* (1810) 12 East 283.

[242] *Renton & Co Ltd v Black Sea and Baltic General insurance Co Ltd* [1941] 1 K.B. 206 (final destination reached when goods discharged and left on quayside). See also *Marten v Vestey Brothers* [1920] A.C. 307; *Crocker v Sturge* [1897] 1 Q.B. 330; *Crocker v General Insurance Co Ltd* (1897) 3 Com. Cas. 22; *Kynance SS Co v Young* (1911) 16 Com. Cas. 123.

[243] *Sadafi v Western Assurance Co* (1933) 46 Ll. L.R. 140; *Allagar Rubber Estates Ltd v National Benefit Assurance Co* (1922) 10 Ll. L.R. 564; *Lindsay Blee Depots Ltd v Motor Union Insurance* (1930) 37 Ll. L.R. 220.

[244] *Wiggins Teape Australia Pty Ltd v Baltica Insurance Co Ltd* [1970] 2 N.S.W.R. 77; *Verna Trading Pty Ltd v New India Assurance Co Ltd* [1991] 1 V.R. 129.

[245] *Bayview Motors Ltd v Mitsui Marine and Fire Insurance Co* [2003] Lloyd's Rep. I.R. 121; *Eurodale Manufacturing Ltd v Ecclesiastical Insurance Office Plc* [2003] Lloyd's Rep. I.R. 440; *Garfield Container Transport Inc v Chubb Insurance Co of Canada* (2002) 114 A.C.W.S. (3d) 1100; *Miruvaor Ltd v National Insurance Co Ltd* [2003] H.K.E.C. 237.

[246] *Westminster Fire Office v Reliance Mutual Insurance Co* (1903) 19 T.L.R. 668; *John Martin Ltd v Russell* [1960] 1 Lloyd's Rep. 554; *Bayview Motors Ltd v Mitsui Marine and Fire Insurance Co* [2003] Lloyd's Rep. I.R. 121

[247] *Leaders Shoes (Aust) Pty Ltd v Liverpool & London & Globe Insurance Co Ltd.* [1968] 1 N.S.W.R. 279.

[248] *Portvale Steamship Co v Royal Exchange Assurance Corp* 43 Ll. L.R. 161; *Elaz International Co v Hong Kong & Shanghai Insurance Co Ltd* [2006] H.K.E.C. 825.

[249] *Anbest Electronic Ltd v CGU International Insurance Plc* [2008] H.K.E.C. 562.

[250] *Coven Spa v Hong Kong Chinese Insurance Co* [1999] Lloyd's Rep. I.R. 565.

[251] *Hibernia Foods Plc v McAuslin (The Joint Frost)* [1998] 1 Lloyd's Rep. 310.

Clause 9 of the Institute Cargo Clauses provides for automatic termination where, owing to circumstances beyond the control of the assured, either the contract of carriage is terminated at a port or place other than the named destination, or the transit is otherwise terminated prior to the delivery of the goods. However, if the assured gives prompt notice to the insurers, and is willing to pay any additional premium required by the insurers, the policy may be extended either:

> "until the goods are sold and delivered at such port or place, or, unless otherwise specifically agreed, until the expiry of 60 days after arrival of the goods hereby insured at such port or place, whichever shall first occur, or if the goods are forwarded within the said period of 60 days (or any agreed extension thereof) to the destination named herein or to any other destination, until terminated in accordance with [the transit clause]."

Alteration of port of departure

24–067   **"43.** Where the place of departure is specified by the policy, and the ship instead of sailing from that place sails from any other place, the risk does not attach."[252]

Sailing for different destination

24–068   **"44.** Where the destination is specified in the policy, and the ship, instead of sailing for that destination, sails for any other destination, the risk does not attach."

In this type of case, the voyage which the insurer has agreed to insure has simply not commenced.[253] There must be an actual change, and not merely an intention to do so which is not put into effect.[254] There is some difficulty in reconciling s.44 with the terms of the warehouse to warehouse clause. This commences with the words: "This insurance attaches from the time the goods leave the warehouse or place of storage at the place named herein for the commencement of the transit . . ." The problem raised here arises where the goods leave the warehouse, so that the risk has attached under cl.8, but are then loaded on board a vessel which sails for a destination other than that specified in the policy, as then s.44 prevents the risk from attaching. In *Nima SARL v Deves Insurance Plc*[255] the Court of Appeal held that the words of the statute took priority. *Nima* involved a so-called "phantom vessel". The insured cargo was removed from the warehouse and loaded onto the vessel, but the vessel failed to arrive at its destination, and the Court of Appeal was satisfied that the intention of the crew had from the outset been to sail for an entirely different destination and to sell the cargo in fraud of the assured. The Court of Appeal held that in such a case the risk attached as soon as the cargo left the warehouse, but as the insured adventure had never commenced, the correct analysis was that the cover was cancelled retroactively. The significance of this reasoning is that, for the short period between the goods leaving the warehouse and loading on board the vessel, there is insurance in place

---

[252] See *Way v Modigliani* (1787) 2 T.R. 30, a case involving a mixed policy. Cf. *Driscol v Passmore* (1798) 1 B. & P. 200.

[253] For illustrations of the principle at common law, see *Woolridge v Boydell* (1788) 1 Doug. 16; *Sellar v McVicar* (1804) 1 B. & P. 23; *Simon, Israel & Co v Sedgwick* [1893] 1 Q.B. 303.

[254] *Hare v Travis* (1827) 7 B. & C. 14; *Simon, Israel & Co v Sedgwick* [1893] 1 Q.B. 303; *Hewitt v General Insurance Co Ltd* (1925) 23 Ll. L.R. 243; *George Kallis (Manufacturers) Ltd v Success Insurance Ltd* [2002] Lloyd's Rep. I.R. 752.

[255] *Nima SARL v Deves Insurance Plc* [2002] Lloyd's Rep. I.R. 752.

and any loss then occurring is recoverable.[256] The decision has been restricted in effect by cl.10.2 the 2009 Institute Cargo Clauses, which provides that:

"Where the subject-matter insured commences the transit contemplated by this insurance, but, without the knowledge of the Assured or their employees the ship sails for another destination, this insurance will nevertheless be deemed to have attached at the commencement of such transit."

In some of the old cases the insurers imposed warranties which required the vessel to have sailed or departed by a given date.[257] The general effect of those cases was that a vessel was treated as having sailed once she had left port with an intention on the part of the master to commence the voyage,[258] but not in the absence of any such intention[259] or if the vessel was not fully equipped to sail.[260]

Change of voyage

"**45.**—(1) Where, after the commencement of the risk, the destination of the ship is voluntarily changed from the destination contemplated by the policy, there is said to be a change of voyage.
(2) Unless the policy otherwise provides,[261] where there is a change of voyage, the insurer is discharged from liability as from the time of change, that is to say, as from the time when the determination to change it is manifested; and it is immaterial that the ship may not in fact have left the course of voyage contemplated by the policy when the loss occurs."

24–069

If there is a change of voyage, which is subsequently remedied, the risk does not reattach.[262]

Two main issues arise under s.45: when a change of voyage is voluntary; and what amounts to a manifestation of a determination to change the voyage.

The leading authority on voluntary change of voyage is *Rickards v Forestal Land, Timber and Railways Co Ltd*,[263] in which the House of Lords ruled that the vessel had been navigated in accordance with instructions from government, so that the alteration of destination had not been voluntary, as required by s.45. A similar question arises under s.46 in relation to deviation, for deviation is excused

---

[256] This is the case because under s.44, there has to be an actual failure to commence the voyage rather than a mere intention on the part of the carrier that this should be the case. Contrast the rules on change of voyage in s.45, which simply require a manifested intention to attain a new destination.

[257] Breach of warranty for any reason prevented the risk from attaching: *Hore v Whitmore* (1778) 2 Cowp. 784; *Moir v Royal Exchange Assurance Co* (1815) 3 M. & S. 461; *Nelson v Salvador* (1829) Mood & M. 309; *Graham v Barras* (1834) 5 B. & Ad. 1011.

[258] Even if the voyage was for external reasons unable to be commenced: *Earle v Harris* (1780) 1 Doug. K.B. 357; *Lang v Anderton* (1824) 3 B. & C. 495; *Cockrane v Fisher* (1835) 1 C. M. & R. 809.

[259] *Sea Insurance v Blogg* [1898] 2 Q.B. 398.

[260] *Ridsdale v Newnham* (1815) 3 M. & S. 456; *Pittegrew v Pringle* (1832) 3 B. & Ad. 514; *Graham v Barras* (1834) 5 B. & Ad. 1011; *Thompson v Gillespy* (1855) 5 E. & B. 209; *Hudson v Bilton* (1856) 2 Jur. N.S. 784; *Bouillon v Lupton* (1863) 15 C.B.N.S. 113; *Price v Livingstone* (1882) 9 QBD 679.

[261] A clause which permits change of voyage is not sufficient to protect the assured in the event of the risk not having attached on the basis that a new destination had been selected before the voyage had commenced under s.44: *Simon, Israel & Co v Sedgwick* [1893] 1 Q.B. 303.

[262] *Way v Modigliani* (1787) 2 T.R. 30.

[263] *Rickards v Forestal Land, Timber and Railways Co Ltd* [1942] A.C. 50. See also *British and Foreign Marine Insurance Co v Samuel Sanday & Co* [1916] 1 AC. 650.

where the alteration of route resulted from circumstances beyond the control of the master or the assured,[264] and it is clear from cases on that point that a command which can lawfully and physically be resisted is not a circumstance beyond the control of the master or assured[265]; it is probable that obedience to such a command would be voluntary for the purposes of s.45. As to what constitutes a change of voyage, it was held in *Tasker v Cunningham*[266] that there can be a change of voyage which discharges the insurer before the vessel has physically departed from the route to its agreed or anticipated destination. In that case the vessel was lost while en route for the destination stated in the policy, but after the assured had determined that the vessel was to alter its destination. Proof of that determination was to be found in a series of messages between the owners and the master, and the court ruled that this was sufficient to discharge the insurers. This principle is now codified in the plain wording of s.45(2). In many cases, of course, evidence of an intention to change voyage will not always be available prior to the vessel actually having changed its voyage, and it is clear from *Tasker v Cunningham* that a mere contemplation by the assured that the vessel might be instructed by him to change its voyage is not enough; what is needed is, in the words of s.45(2), some manifestation of a determination to change voyage. Where the assured has plainly intended to abandon the insured voyage, for example by undue delay in proceeding with the voyage, the insurer will similarly be discharged, presumably from the date at which such an intention became manifest from the delay.[267]

Deviation

24–070   "**46.**—(1) Where a ship, without lawful excuse, deviates from the voyage contemplated by the policy, the insurer is discharged from liability as from the time of deviation,[268] and it is immaterial that the ship may have regained her route before any loss occurs.

(2) There is a deviation from the voyage contemplated by the policy—
   (a) Where the course of the voyage is specifically designated by the policy, and that course is departed from; or
   (b) Where the course of the voyage is not specifically designated by the policy, but the usual and customary course is departed from.

(3) The intention to deviate is immaterial; there must be a deviation in fact to discharge the insurer from his liability under the contract."

A number of elements in the concept of deviation may be isolated from the section:

(1) The term "without lawful excuse" refers to a list of "excuses" for deviation set out in s.49. This list, which is to all intents and purposes exhaustive, is discussed below.
(2) Unlike change of voyage, there must be an actual deviation in route before the insurer is discharged.[269] Thus, if the master of the vessel has

---

[264] 1906 Act s.49(1)(b).
[265] *Phelps v Auldjo* (1809) 2 Camp. 350.
[266] *Tasker v Cunningham* (1819) 1 Bligh. 87. See also *Bottomley v Bovill* (1826) 5 B. & C. 210.
[267] *Thames and Mersey Marine Insurance Co v Van Laun* [1917] 2 K.B. 48n.
[268] Previous accrued losses must be met: *Green v Young* (1702) 2 Ld. Raym. 840; *Hare v Travis* (1827) 7 B. & C. 14.
[269] *Foster v Wilmer* (1746) 2 Str. 1249; *Woolridge v Boydell* (1778) 1 Doug K.B. 16; *Thellusson v Ferguson* (1780) I Doug. K.B. 360; *Kewley v Ryan* (1794) 2 H. B.I. 343; *Heselton v Allnutt* (1813) 1 M. & S. 46; *Hewitt v London General Insurance Co Ltd* (1925) 23 Ll. L.R. 243.

the intention of deviating, but before that intention is put into effect the vessel is forced to deviate by the operation of circumstances amounting to a lawful excuse, for example bad weather, there is no deviation.[270] These principles are now enshrined in s.46(3).

(3) If, following a deviation, the vessel regains its route, the risk does not recommence. The principle is quite simply that a deviation discharges the insurer from all future liability when such deviation takes place.[271]

(4) There is no requirement for any connection between a deviation and a subsequent loss. Thus, as is the case with breach of warranty, if a loss has occurred following deviation, the insurer is discharged by the deviation and it is no defence for the assured to argue that the loss occurred independently of the deviation.[272] It is immaterial that the risk has not been increased by reason of the deviation.[273]

(5) The insurer's right to treat itself as discharged following a deviation is not dependent upon the insurer demonstrating any increase in risk, although this was undoubtedly the problem which the rule was originally developed by the common law courts to counter. It would appear to be enough for the insurer to demonstrate that a deviation has taken place, for the insurer has agreed only to insure a specified route and not some other route.

(6) Section 46(1) talks in terms of an automatic discharge of liability following deviation. It is perhaps better to interpret this as meaning that the insurer has a right to determine its liability, rather than that its liability determines by operation of law: the former approach gives rise to the possibility of post-deviation waiver irrespective of anything in the policy excusing deviation.

Deviation is departure from the route: it is immaterial that the destination is unchanged.[274] Deviation may arise: (a) where the voyage is specifically designated by the policy, and that course is departed from (s.46(2)(a))[275]—if there is a customary route for a particular voyage, which is at variance with the route specified in the policy, adherence to the customary route is nonetheless deviation as the policy takes priority[276]; (b) deviation from usual and customary route—the question that has arisen in most of the cases is whether it is usual or customary to stop off at intermediate ports, and there is much eighteenth- and early nineteenth-century learning on the customs affecting major imperial trading routes.[277] The dearth of cases in recent times is explained by the adoption of

---

[270] *Kingston v Phelps* (1793) 1 Peake 299; *Hewitt v London General Insurance Co Ltd* (1925) 23 Ll. L.R. 243.

[271] *Way v Modigliani* (1787) 2 T.R. 30.

[272] *Elliott v Wilson* (1776) 4 Bro. P.C. 470; *Davis v Garrett* (1830) 6 Bing 716; *Thompson v Hopper* (1856) 6 E. & B. 172.

[273] *Hartley v Buggin* (1781) 3 Doug. K.B. 39.

[274] *Thames & Mersey Marine Insurance Co v Van Laun & Co* [1917] 1 K.B. 48n.

[275] See: *Phyn v Royal Exchange Assurance Co* (1798) 7 T.R. 505; *Tait v Levi* (1811)14 East 481 (in which the court held that the employment of a master who is incompetent and deviates as a result is breach of an implied warranty on behalf of the assured); *Brown v Tayleur* (1835) 4 A. & E. 241; *Wingate v Foster* (1878) 3 QBD 582; *Diffori v Adams* (1884) 53 L.J.Q.B. 437.

[276] *Elliott v Wilson* (1776) 4 Bro. P.C. 470.

[277] See: *Salvador v Hopkins* (1765) 3 Burr. 1707; *Gregory v Christie* (1784) 3 Doug. 419; *Middlewood v Blakes* (1797) 7 T.R. 165; *Ougier v Jennings* (1800) 1 Camp. 505n; *Vallance v Dewar* (1808) 1 Camp. 503; *Cormack v Gladstone* (1809) 11 East 347; *Frenkel v MacAndrews & Co* [1929] A.C. 545; *Reardon Smith Line v Black Sea and Baltic General Insurance Co* [1938] 2 K.B. 730. Contra: *Davis v Garrett* (1830) 6 Bing. 716; *Thompson v Hopper* (1858) E.B. & E. 1038; *Frenkel v MacAndrews & Co Ltd* [1929] A.C. 545.

deviation waivers in the Institute clauses, the most important historically being
the grant to the assured of "liberty to touch and stay" at intermediate ports.

Independently of the statutory rules, the policy itself, while not necessarily
contemplating any particular voyage, will set out the limits of navigation. Thus
the risk may be suspended or terminated if the vessel enters particular waters[278]
at certain times of the year or, in the case of war zones, at all. The navigation
clauses contained in the International Hull Clauses 2003 set out the permissible
navigation limits (cl.32) and state that any breach suspends the cover unless
anterior agreement has been reached (cl.33) or notice has been given to the
underwriters after the breach has occurred and new terms have been agreed
(cl.11). The vessel may sail or navigate with or without pilots, go on trial trips
and assist and tow vessels or craft in distress, but is precluded from being towed
or undertaking towage or salvage services under contract (cl.10).

Several ports of discharge

24–071   "47.—(1) Where several ports of discharge are specified by the policy, the ship may[279]
proceed to all or any of them,[280] but, in the absence of any usage or sufficient cause to
the contrary, she must proceed to them, or such of them as she goes to, in the order
designated by the policy. If she does not there is a deviation.[281]

(2) Where the policy is to "ports of discharge", within a given area, which are not
named, the ship must, in the absence of any usage or sufficient cause to the contrary,
proceed to them, or such of them as she goes to, in their geographical order. If she does
not there is a deviation."[282]

Delay in voyage

24–072   "48. In the case of a voyage policy, the adventure insured must be prosecuted
throughout its course with reasonable dispatch, and, if without lawful excuse it is not
so prosecuted, the insurer is discharged from liability as from the time when the delay
became unreasonable."

The 1906 Act limits in three respects the right of the assured to recover following
delay. First, s.55(2)(b) states that the insurer is not liable for any loss proximately
caused by delay, even though the delay is the result of an insured peril. Secondly,
delay may prevent the risk attaching under s.42, where the subject matter is
insured "at and from" a particular place but the vessel fails to arrive there within
a reasonable time. Thirdly, delay is effectively afforded the same status as
deviation by s.48. A number of points may be made on the scope of this section:

(1) The words "without lawful excuse" refer to the list of "excuses" for
deviation and delay, in s.49.

---

[278] *Birrell v Dryer* (1884) 9 App.Cas. 345; *Simpson SS Co Ltd v Premier Underwriting Association
Ltd* (1905) 10 Com. Cas. 198. The vessel may also be confined to port: *Pearson v Commercial Union
Assurance Co* (1876) 1 App.Cas. 498; *Mountain v Whittle* [1921] 1 A.C. 615.
[279] It need not do so: *Marsden v Reid* (1803) 3 East 572.
[280] If only one port is specified, the vessel is permitted to proceed to different parts of it: *Warre v
Miller* (1825) 4 B. & C. 538.
[281] See: *Beatson v Haworth* (1796) 6 T.R. 531; *Marsden v Reid* (1803) 3 East 572; *Metcalfe v Perry*
(1814) 4 Camp. 123; *Kynance Sailing Ship Co Ltd v Young* (1911) 16 Com. Cas. 123.
[282] See: *Gairdner Stenhouse* (1810) 3 Taunt. 16; *The Dunbeth* [1897] P. 133; *Marten v Vestey
Brothers* [1920] A.C. 307.

(2) What is reasonable is a matter of fact,[283] and it is plain from the cases that all the surrounding circumstances must be gone into to determine whether or not a delay has been reasonable, so that it is not possible to lay down a test purely in terms of time. Thus the courts have determined that the voyage has been pursued with reasonable despatch where it has been delayed due to war perils,[284] bad weather,[285] lack of cargo,[286] lack of crew,[287] the need for repairs,[288] and the need for permission from port authorities to unload.[289] Even where the assured has some justification for delay, failure to resume the voyage with reasonable despatch once the cause of delay has ceased to operate will amount to a "delay" within the meaning of the section. Any amount of delay, however brief, will discharge the insurer where it has resulted from causes totally unconnected with the purpose of the voyage.[290]

(3) The delay may be operative to discharge the insurer at any stage of the voyage. Thus a delay in unloading may be fatal to the assured.[291]

(4) In appropriate circumstances undue delay may amount to evidence of an intention by the assured to abandon the voyage entirely, in which case there is a change of voyage which operates to discharge the insurer.[292]

Excuses for deviation or delay

"**49.**—(1) Deviation or delay in prosecuting the voyage contemplated by the policy is excused—   **24-073**

(a) Where authorised by any special term in the policy; or

(b) Where caused by circumstances beyond the control of the master and his employer; or

(c) Where reasonably necessary in order to comply with an express or implied warranty; or

(d) Where reasonably necessary for the safety of the ship or subject-matter insured; or

(e) For the purpose of saving human life, or aiding a ship in distress where human life may be in danger; or

(f) Where reasonably necessary for the purpose of obtaining medical or surgical aid for any person on board the ship; or

(g) Where caused by the barratrous conduct of the master or crew, if barratry be one of the perils insured against.

(2) When the cause excusing the deviation or delay ceases to operate, the ship must resume her course, and prosecute her voyage, with reasonable dispatch."[293]

---

[283] 1906 Act s.88. See *Langhorn v Allnutt* (1812) 4 Taunt. 511.

[284] *British American Tobacco Co v Poland* (1921) 7 Ll. L.R. 108; *Niger Co Ltd v Guardian Assurance Co Ltd* (1922) 13 Ll. L.R. 75.

[285] *Samuel v Royal Exchange Assurance Co* (1828) 8 B. & C. 119.

[286] *Schroder v Thompson* (1817) 7 Taunt. 462.

[287] *Grant v King* (1802) 4 Esp. 175.

[288] *Smith v Surridge* (1801) 4 Esp. 25.

[289] *Bain v Case* (1829) 3 C. & P.496.

[290] *Mount v Larkins* (1831) 8 Bing 108; *Doyle v Powell* (1832) 4 B. & Ad. 267; *Hamilton v Sheddon* (1837) 3 M. & W. 49; *Company of African Merchants v British Insurance Co* (1873) L.R. 8 Ex. 154; *Pearson v Commercial Union Assurance Co* (1876) 1 App.Cas. 498; *Phillips v Irving* (1884) 7 Man. & G. 325; *Hyderebad (Deccan) Co v Willoughby* [1899] 2 Q.B. 530.

[291] *Samuel v Royal Exchange Assurance Co* (1828) 8 B. & C. 119.

[292] *Thames and Mersey Marine Insurance Co v Van Laun* [1917] 2 K.B. 48n.

[293] See *Harrington v Halkeld* (1778) 2 Park on Insurance 639; *Delany v Stoddart* (1785) 1 T.R. 22; *Lavabre v Wilson* (1779) 1 Doug. 284.

Ground (a). Waiver clauses are now standard in marine policies. Prior to the adoption of the Institute clauses in 1983, it had long been the practice of marine insurers to waive their common law right to determine policies for various forms of increase of risk during the currency of the voyage. The relevant clause gave the assured liberty to touch and stay at any port or place whatsoever, a provision which for the most part excused deviation and delay. Indeed, most of the cases concerning deviation concerned the right of the assured to call at intermediate ports. It was held on numerous occasions, however, that the clause did not permit a change of voyage, nor did it justify the assured in calling at ports which were off the agreed route.[294] Further, where an insured vessel visited a port in the course of its voyage for reasons unconnected with the voyage, the clause did not provide protection.[295] Clause 8.3 of the Institute Cargo Clauses (A), (B) and (C) sets out the contractual saving for cargo policies: "This insurance shall remain in force . . . during delay beyond the control of the assured, any deviation, forced discharge, reshipment or transhipment[296] and during any variation of the adventure arising from the exercise of a liberty granted to shipowners or charterers under the contract of affreightment." Deviation is thus covered as long as the assured is acting within the terms of the contract of affreightment, and delay is covered where resulting from causes beyond the assured's control. In the context of delay, it should be noted that cl.18 of the Institute Cargo Clauses makes it a condition of the insurance that the assured acts with reasonable despatch in all circumstances within his control. The delay waiver does not, therefore, go much beyond what is provided for by way of excuse in s.49(1). Change of voyage is dealt with under the Cargo Clauses by a "held covered" provision. This is contained in cl.10: "Where, after attachment of this insurance, the destination is changed by the assured, held covered at a premium and on conditions to be arranged subject to prompt notice being given to the underwriters." In *Nima SARL v Deves Insurance Plc*[297] Andrew Smith J. at first instance (the point did not arise on appeal) expressed the view that clause 10 was concerned only with change of voyage under s.45 and did not amount to a waiver of the provisions of s.44 in relation to the attachment of the risk in the first place. The Institute Voyage Clauses Freight cl.3, is a "held covered" provision covering deviation and delay and change of voyage:

> "Held covered in case of deviation or change of voyage . . . provided notice be given to the underwriters immediately after receipt of advices and any amended terms of cover and any additional premium required by them be agreed."

Ground (b). This is a general ground, and overlaps with a number of more specific grounds. Superior orders may bring this ground into play,[298] although orders to a vessel which are neither based on legal authority nor supported by threats of enforcement do not justify an obedient deviation.[299] Other possible justifications of deviation or delay under this head are belligerent action,[300] bad

---

[294] These decisions were given statutory effect by r.6 in the Schedule to the 1906 Act.

[295] *Hammond v Reid* (1820) 4 B. & Ald. 72.

[296] Under s.59 the effect of transhipment is to maintain the liability of the insurer.

[297] *Nima SARL v Deves Insurance Plc* [2002] Lloyd's Rep. I.R. 752.

[298] *Rickards v Forestal Land, Timber and Railways Co* [1942] A.C. 50; *Scott v Thompson* (1805) 1 B. & P. 181.

[299] *Phelps v Auldjo* (1809) 2 Camp. 350.

[300] *Blackenhagen v London Assurance Co* (1808) 1 Camp. 454; *Schroder v Thompson* (1817) 7 Taunt. 462.

weather[301] and action taken by the crew.[302] The negligence of the master of the vessel is not, however, a good excuse.[303]

Ground (c). This general ground is based upon the narrow decision in *Bouillon v Lupton*,[304] in which it was held that a delay, the object of which was to ensure that a vessel which had completed the inland stage of its voyage was equipped for the sea voyage, was justified; this precaution was necessary to comply with the implied warranty of seaworthiness attaching at the beginning of each stage of a voyage, now contained in s.39(3). It may be that this ground is confined to that situation.

Ground (d).[305] There is a clear overlap between ground (b) above and this ground, and in *Rickards v Forestal Land, Timber and Railways Co* deviation in time of war was held to be justified on this ground. Deviation or delay to repair a dangerous vessel, or to remedy overloading, is also permissible.[306] One limitation on the generality of this provision is the phrase "subject matter insured", which implies that a deviation to preserve cargo on the vessel which is not within the policy in question, or indeed for the purposes of any other uninsured risk,[307] is not permitted. For the same reason, a deviation to undertake salvage services in respect of another vessel will discharge the insurer.[308]

Ground (e).[309] It would appear that this does not extend to the saving of property.[310]

Ground (g).[311] This provision must be read with s.55(2)(a), which establishes that, in the absence of any agreement to the contrary, the insurer is liable for the misconduct of the master or crew: s.49(2)(g) simply provides that, where the misconduct results in deviation or delay, the insurer is nevertheless liable.[312] If the insurer is not liable for loss resulting from barratry, s.49(2))(g) is of no assistance to the assured. Barratry requires fraud on the part of the master or crew: negligence does not suffice.[313]

A number of points concerning the general interpretation of s.49 remain unresolved. First, it is uncertain whether it is exhaustive of the grounds of "lawful excuse" for deviation and delay. The main lacunae would seem to be in respect of deviation and delay flowing from measures taken to assist another vessel where no life is in danger and from measures taken to preserve uninsured subject matter. This point must await resolution. Secondly, there is some conflict in the authorities on the question whether a deviation or delay is justifiable to

---

[301] *Harrington v Halkeld* (1778) 2 Park's Marine Insurance 639; *Delany v Stoddart* (1785) 1 T.R. 22; *Kingston v Phelps* (1795) 7 T.R. 165n; *Samuel v Royal Exchange Assurance Co* (1828) 8 B. & C. 119.

[302] *Elton v Brogden* (1747) 2 Str. 1264; *Driscoll v Bovil* (1798) 1 Bos. & P. 313.

[303] *Phyn v Royal Exchange Assurance Co* (1798) 7 T.R. 505; *Tait v Levi* (1811) 14 East 481.

[304] *Bouillon v Lupton* (1863) 33 L.J.C.P. 37. See also *Motteux v London Assurance* (1739) 1 Atk. 545.

[305] See: *Clason v Simmons* (1741) 6 T.R. 533n; *Smith v Surridge* (1801) 4 Esp. 25; *Weir v Aberdeen* (1819) 2 B. & Ald. 320; *Raine v Bell* (1808) 9 East 195.

[306] *Guibert v Readshaw* (1781) 2 Park on Insurance 637; *Weir v Aberdein* (1819) 2 B. & Ald. 320.

[307] *Scott v Thompson* (1805) 1 Bos. & P.N.R. 181.

[308] *Company of African Merchants v British Insurance Co* (1873) L.R. 8 Ex. 154.

[309] *Lawrence v Sydebotham* (1805) 6 East 45.

[310] *Company of African Merchants v British Insurance Co* (1873) L.R. 8 Ex. 154; *Scaramanga v Stamp* (1880) 5 C.P.D. 295.

[311] This is based on *Ross v Hunter* (1790) 4 T.R. 33.

[312] See *Mentz, Decker & Co v Maritime Insurance Co* [1910] 1 K.B. 132.

[313] *Tait v Levi* (1811) 14 East 481; *Mentz, Decker & Co v Maritime Insurance Co* [1910] 1 K.B. 132.

prevent potential loss threatened by an uninsured peril. *Scott v Thompson*,[314] which concerned deviation to avoid loss by uninsured war risks, decided that the insurer is not discharged in these circumstances, but *O'Reilly v Gonne*[315] is authority to the contrary. It is probable that the former decision accurately reflects the law. This view is justified by the wording of s.49(1)(d), which excuses deviation or delay in order to preserve the insured subject matter; a subject matter remains "insured", in that it is covered by the policy, even though it happens not to be protected against a given peril.

10. Assignment of Policy

When and how policy is assignable

24–074   "50.—(1) A marine policy is assignable unless it contains terms expressly prohibiting assignment. It may be assigned either before or after loss.

(2) Where a marine policy has been assigned so as to pass the beneficial interest in such policy, the assignee of the policy is entitled to sue thereon in his own name; and the defendant is entitled to make any defence arising out of the contract which he would have been entitled to make if the action had been brought in the name of the person by or on behalf of whom the policy was effected.

(3) A marine policy may be assigned by indorsement thereon or in other customary manner."

International contracts of sale have long been transacted on the basis that the seller will insure the goods in his own name and will transfer to the buyer the documents of title (i.e. ownership) relating to the goods on payment; this is the nature of the classic c.i.f. contract. This form of business depends upon the seller's policy being assignable to the buyer, and the recognition by the nineteenth-century courts of this necessity is confirmed by s.50(1). The final sentence reflects the fact that under a c.i.f. contract the risk will have passed to the buyer when the goods crossed the ship's rail, so that he is bound to pay for them on receipt of the shipping documents even if they have been damaged or destroyed in the meantime; it is thus made clear that the right to assign—and, therefore, the efficacy of the policy—is preserved. The recognition of assignment in marine insurance was purely for the benefit of facilitating international sales of goods; the same rule was not intended to be applicable to vessels themselves or to freight. The section thus permits the insurer to prohibit assignment. In practice the right to assign both the policy and its proceeds is not excluded.

The words "so as to pass the entire beneficial interest in such policy" in s.50(2) have been held to mean that the right of the assignee to sue in his own name is available only where the entire sum[316] due under the policy has been assigned to him or where an absolute right to receive payment has been assigned to him.[317] A distinction has to be drawn between pre-loss and post-loss assignments, In the former case, the assignor cannot be said to have parted with the entire beneficial interest in the policy unless the entire insurable interest has been transferred to the assignee: if the assignor retains any insurable interest

[314] *Scott v Thompson* (1805) 1 B. & P. 181.
[315] *O'Reilly v Gonne* (1815) 4 Camp. 249.
[316] *Williams v Atlantic Insurance Co Ltd* [1933] 1 K.B. 81.
[317] *First National Bank of Chicago v West of England P&I Association* [1981] 1 Lloyd's Rep. 54.

covered by the policy the entire beneficial interest cannot have been transferred, even if the entire right to recover the proceeds has been assigned to the assignee. In the case of a post-loss assignment, at least in a case of a total loss, or a partial loss which has exhausted the policy, the only property covered by the policy is the claim under it, so that an assignment of the claim operates as an assignment of the entire beneficial interest in the policy and can be effected under s.50(3). Thus, if there is a partial loss and the property remains in existence, an assignment of the right to make a claim in respect of the partial loss cannot be effected under s.50(3).[318]

The customary manner of assigning a marine policy relating to cargo is delivery of a policy endorsed in blank.[319]

Assured who has no interest cannot assign

"**51.** Where the assured has parted with or lost his interest in the subject-matter insured, **24–075** and has not, before or at the time of so doing, expressly or impliedly agreed to assign the policy, any subsequent assignment of the policy is inoperative:

Provided that nothing in this section affects the assignment of a policy after loss."

11. THE PREMIUM[320]

When premium payable

"**52.** Unless otherwise agreed, the duty of the assured or his agent to pay the premium, **24–076** and the duty of the insurer to issue the policy to the assured or his agent, are concurrent conditions, and the insurer is not bound to issue the policy until payment or tender of the premium."

Policy effected through broker

"**53.**—(1) Unless otherwise agreed, where a marine policy is effected on behalf of the **24–077** assured by a broker, the broker is directly responsible to the insurer for the premium, and the insurer is directly responsible to the assured for the amount which may be payable in respect of losses, or in respect of returnable premium.

(2) Unless otherwise agreed, the broker has, as against the assured, a lien upon the policy for the amount of the premium and his charges in respect of effecting the policy; and, where he has dealt with the person who employs him as a principal, he has also a lien on the policy in respect of any balance on any insurance account which may be due to him from such person, unless when the debt was incurred he had reason to believe that such person was only an agent."

Usage in the London marine market[321] operates contrary to strict legal theory, by rendering the broker alone responsible to the insurer for the premium, whether or

---

[318] *Raiffeisen Zentralbank Osterreich AG v Five Star General Trading* [2001] Lloyd's Rep. I.R. 460.

[319] *Aron & Co v Miall* (1928) 31 Ll. L.R. 242. Contrast: *Baker v Adam* (1910) 102 L.T. 248; *Sadafi v Western Insurance Co* (1933) 46 Ll. L.R. 140.

[320] See Ch.8, above.

[321] The fact that the law applicable to the insurance contract or to the contract between the assured and the broker (or between the producing and placing broker) is not English law would appear not to be relevant to the operation of the custom, which arises out of the market relationship between the broker and the underwriters and not out of the surrounding contracts. In *Heath Lambert Ltd v Sociedad de Corretaje de Seguros* [2004] 1 Lloyd's Rep. 495 the court disposed of the argument that s.53(1) was inapplicable to a reinsurance contract with a Venezuelan reinsured by holding that the law applicable to the policy was English law—which will generally be the case in a London market placement—so that the operation of s.53(1) was unaffected. The point did not arise on appeal, [2004] Lloyd's Rep. I.R. 905.

not the assured has made payment to the broker.[322] The juridical basis of the custom is not entirely clear, it having been said in *Power v Butcher*[323] either that the broker is the principal to receive money from the assured and to pay it to the underwriters, or that the underwriters are deemed to have received the premium but have loaned it back to the broker, rendering him personally liable. The fiction of lending has received most support in the later cases, although both approaches have in common the crucial point that the broker does not become the agent of the insurer in receiving the premium; the insurer's remedy against the broker or his assigns is, therefore, in simple debt and does not entitle the insurer to claim a proprietary remedy.[324] The custom has been justified on the grounds that the broker will generally be known to the insurer, whereas the assured may not be, and that the existing account between underwriter and broker is a convenient way of dealing with the payment of new premiums.[325]

The obligation of the broker under the usage is to pay the premium when it falls due under the policy. In the absence of contrary agreement, this will be when the risk incepts. This may, however, be extended by the terms of the policy, although a distinction is to be drawn between the provision of credit for late payment[326] and a later due date.[327]

A broker who has become liable to pay the premium on behalf of the assured is entitled to be indemnified by the assured for the amount of the payment. The obligation of the assured to provide an indemnity arises as soon as the premium falls due under the policy, whether or not the broker has made payment at that date: this follows from the fiction that the broker has actually made payment and the amount of the premium has been loaned back to him by the insurer. If the policy is silent as to the time of payment, then the premium is payable on inception and it is that date on which the broker becomes liable to pay the premium to the insurer. Accordingly, the obligation on the assured to indemnify the broker arises on the same date even if the broker has not actually paid the premium because, e.g. the broker has been granted days of grace by the insurer to make payment.[328] By contrast, if under the policy the premium is not due on the inception of the risk but within a credit period granted by the insurer, the obligation on the assured to indemnify the broker arises on the date on which the credit period expires.[329]

24–078   The fiction of a loan from insurer to broker operates on the basis that the broker has paid the premium to the insurer and that it has been loaned back to the broker so that the insurer has an action against the broker for repayment of the loan as of the date on which the premium falls due to be paid. It has been held that the fiction is subject to the express terms of the policy, so that the broker is not to be treated, as against the insurers, to have made payment in accordance with a premium warranty when this is not in fact the case.[330]

The broker's ability to recover the premium advanced by him is protected by two forms of security. First, the broker has a lien over the policy and also over

---

[322] *Universo Insurance Co of Milan v Merchants Marine Insurance Co* [1897] 2 Q.B. 93; *Bankers & General Insurance Co v Brockdorff & Co* (1922) 10 Ll. L.R. 22.

[323] *Power v Butcher* (1829) 10 B. & C. 329.

[324] Which probably explains why the reinsurers in the *Milan* case chose to go against the reinsureds rather than the brokers' trustee in bankruptcy.

[325] *Universo Insurance Co of Milan v Merchants Marine Insurance Co* [1897] 2 Q.B. 93.

[326] *JA Chapman & Co Ltd v Kadirga Denizcilik Ve Ticaret* [1998] Lloyd's Rep. I.R. 377.

[327] *Heath Lambert Ltd v Sociedad de Corretaje de Seguros* [2004] Lloyd's Rep. I.R. 905.

[328] *JA Chapman & Co Ltd v Kadirga Denizcilik Ve Ticaret* [1998] Lloyd's Rep. I.R. 377.

[329] *Heath Lambert Ltd v Sociedad de Corretaje de Seguros* [2004] Lloyd's Rep. I.R. 905.

[330] *Heath Lambert Ltd v Sociedad de Corretaje de Seguros* [2004] Lloyd's Rep. I.R. 905; *Allianz Insurance Co of Egypt v Aigaion Insurance* [2009] Lloyd's Rep. I.R. 69.

any policy moneys received by him from the insurers.[331] The lien allows the broker to retain the actual policy until he is paid: once he parts with the possession of the policy his lien is lost, and he has no rights at law against the policy moneys if and when they become payable. If the policy moneys are paid to the broker, he has a lien on them in respect of premium advanced by him,[332] and for this purpose it does not matter whether the broker's duty to account for the proceeds is owed to the assured directly or to an intermediate producing broker,[333] although there is no lien if the policy is a composite one covering the interests of two or more policyholders and only one of the policyholders is indebted to the broker: the principle here is that the rights of each policyholder are entirely separate, and that the broker cannot exercise his security against a person who is not indebted to him.[334] The lien operates even though the broker is a placing broker who is entitled to be indemnified by the producing broker and not the assured.[335] Secondly, it is common in the marine market for the policy to contain a brokers' cancellation clause under which the broker is given the right to cancel the policy if he has not been reimbursed, with the insurer undertaking to repay that proportion of the premium which represents the unexpired term of cover. The right of the placing broker to exercise the right to cancel should in principle depend on the law applicable to the policy.[336] The broker may not, however, arrest the vessel under s.20(2)(p) of the Senior Courts Act 1981, as he is not a maritime agent for this purpose neither are premiums "disbursements . . . on account of a ship".[337]

In the event the risk originates with a producing broker, who in turn instructs a placing broker to negotiate with underwriters, the placing broker rather than the producing broker is liable for the premiums under s.53(1). As there is no contractual relationship between the placing broker and the assured,[338] the placing broker being only the sub-agent of the producing broker,[339] the placing broker can only look to the producing broker and not to the assured for indemnification[340] and the producing broker can then seek indemnification from the assured.[341]

---

[331] Marine Insurance Act 1906 s.53(2). See: *Godin v London Assurance Co* (1758) 1 Burr. 489; *Mildred, Goveneche & Co v Maspons* (1883) 8 App.Cas. 874; *Fairfield Shipbuilding & Engineering Co Ltd v Gardner Mountain & Co Ltd* (1912) 104 L.T. 288.

[332] *Eide UK Ltd v Lowndes Lambert Group Ltd (The Sun Tender)* [1998] 1 Lloyd's Rep. 389.

[333] *Heath Lambert Ltd v Sociedad de Corretaje de Seguros (No.2)* [2006] Lloyd's Rep. I.R. 797 (Comm).

[334] *Eide UK Ltd v Lowndes Lambert Group Ltd (The Sun Tender)* [1998] 1 Lloyd's Rep. 389.

[335] *Mann v Forester* (1814) 4 Camp. 60; *Westwood v Bell* (1815) 4 Camp. 349; *Fishter v Smith* (1878) 4 App.Cas. 1.

[336] In *Ruby Steamship Corporation v Commercial Union Assurance Co* (1934) 46 Ll. L.R. 265 it was held that the law applicable to the right to cancel was that of the contract between the producing and placing broker, but this case is almost certainly wrongly decided.

[337] *Bain Clarkson Ltd v Owners of Sea Friends* [1991] 2 Lloyd's Rep. 322; *Gatoil International Inc v Arkwright-Boston Manufacturers Mutual Insurance Co* [1985] 1 All E.R. 129.

[338] *Velos Group Ltd v Harbour Insurance Services* [1997] 2 Lloyd's Rep. 461 appears to hold otherwise, but was a case turning on its own special facts. It was distinguished on this basis by Rix J. in *Prentis Donegan & Partners Ltd v Leeds & Leeds Co Inc* [1998] 2 Lloyd's Rep. 326.

[339] See *De Bussche v Alt* (1878) 8 Ch D 286, holding that the principal does not have any contract with a sub-agent.

[340] *Prentis Donegan & Partners Ltd v Leeds & Leeds Co Inc* [1998] 2 Lloyd's Rep. 326; *Heath Lambert Ltd v Sociedad de Corretaje de Seguros* [2004] 1 Lloyd's Rep. 495. The point did not arise on appeal, [2004] Lloyd's Rep. I.R. 905.

[341] *Harris & Dixon (Insurance Brokers) Ltd v SF Graham (Run-Off) Ltd* Unreported, 1989, a case in which the assured had become insolvent so that the producing broker himself was unable to recover the sums for which it was liable.

The rule in s.53(1) of the Marine Insurance Act 1906 that the broker is personally liable to the insurers for the premium applies "unless otherwise agreed". In *JA Chapman & Co Ltd v Kadirga Denizcilik Ve Ticaret*[342] the Court of Appeal held that the operation of s.53(1) was not to be regarded as ousted in the absence of clear and express agreement to the contrary. It was thus held that a premium warranty clause, whereby each instalment was warranted payable on a given due date, did not oust s.53(1) in that the obligation to pay the premiums was with the brokers alone, and that if the premiums were not paid on time by them the premium warranty would be broken. This meant that the shipowners remained liable to indemnify the brokers for premium.[343] Although the premium warranty clause was not easily reconciled with s.53(1), it was not to be regarded as overturning established practice, a conclusion reinforced by the presence of a brokers' cancellation clause under which the brokers were empowered to give notice to the insurers cancelling the insurance in the event that the assured did not pay the premium to the brokers: this made it clear that the brokers were liable to the insurers for the premium. A further clause relied upon in *Chapman* was a premium clause, under which the brokers were "specifically authorised until further notice to receive payment on behalf of the underwriters", and that in the event of late payment the policy would come to an end. The Court of Appeal held that this clause did not have the effect of requiring the brokers to be regarded as agents for the underwriters with regard to receipt of premium and that the premiums were to be paid by the assured to the underwriters through the brokers. The clause was regarded as a standard provision which had been added to the policy without full regard for its consequences, and that it could not have been the intention of the parties to oust almost by accident the established relationships set out in s.53(1). This type of wording used without qualification in other parts of the policy may, however, operate to oust s.53(1) and confer a duty on the assured to pay underwriters directly.[344]

24–078A   In July 2010 the English and Scottish Law Commissions published an Issues Paper on the operation of s.53. The Law Commissions' provisional conclusion was that s.53(1) is anomalous, unclear and has produced conflicting and unprincipled case law. Their solution is the abolition of the rule that a marine broker is required to fund the premium, and in its place to provide that the primary obligation is upon the assured to pay, so that the credit risk is transferred from the broker to the underwriters. Payment to the broker would not discharge the assured's liability to the underwriters, so that in the event of the broker's default or insolvency the assured would be required to pay again: however, that was thought not to give rise to a major problem given that under existing regulatory rules a broker is required to keep client funds in a separate account which is immune from claims by other creditors. In the event that the parties agree that the premium is to be paid by the broker, the Law Commissions have suggested that the insurers should not be permitted to cancel the policy for default by the broker unless the assured has been given reasonable notice. The lien provisions in s.53(2) were regarded by the Law Commissions as operating satisfactorily.

---

[342] *JA Chapman & Co Ltd v Kadirga Denizcilik Ve Ticaret* [1997] L.R.L.R. 65. See also *Prentis Donegan & Partners v Leeds & Leeds Co Inc* [1998] 2 Lloyd's Rep. 326 and *Greater Britain Insurance Corporation v Bowring & Co* (1925) 24 Ll. L.R. 7.

[343] For this reason the statement in the International Hulls Clauses 2003 that "The Assured undertakes that the premium shall be paid" does not oust the operation of s.53(1).

[344] *Black King Shipping v Massie (The Litsion Pride)* [1985] 1 Lloyd's Rep. 437, overruled on other grounds by *The Star Sea* [2001] Lloyd's Rep. I.R. 247.

Effect of receipt on policy

"**54.** Where a marine policy effected on behalf of the assured by a broker acknowledges **24–079** the receipt of the premium, such acknowledgment is, in the absence of fraud, conclusive as between the insurer and the assured, but not as between the insurer and broker."

The English and Scottish Law Commissions in their July 2010 Issues Paper could **24–079A** find no modern use of s.54.

12. LOSS AND ABANDONMENT

Included and excluded losses

"**55.**—(1) Subject to the provisions of this Act, and unless the policy otherwise **24–080** provides, the insurer is liable for any loss proximately caused by a peril insured against, but, subject as aforesaid, he is not liable for any loss which is not proximately caused by a peril insured against.

(2) In particular—

(a) The insurer is not liable for any loss attributable to the wilful misconduct of the assured, but, unless the policy otherwise provides, he is liable for any loss proximately caused by a peril insured against, even though the loss would not have happened but for the misconduct or negligence of the master or crew;

(b) Unless the policy otherwise provides, the insurer on ship or goods is not liable for any loss proximately caused by delay, although the delay be caused by a peril insured against;

(c) Unless the policy otherwise provides, the insurer is not liable for ordinary wear and tear, ordinary leakage and breakage, inherent vice or nature of the subject-matter insured, or for any loss proximately caused by rats or vermin, or for any injury to machinery not proximately caused by maritime perils."

Wilful misconduct is a deliberate act by the assured which was intended to cause the loss or which was reckless as to whether or not a loss resulted and which was intended to, or did in fact, lead to a claim.[345] Mere negligence on the part of the assured will not suffice.[346] Crew negligence is not an excluded peril.[347]

Loss of a hull[348] or cargo[349] proximately caused by delay is not an insured peril. By contrast, loss of freight as the result of a delay consequent upon the operation of a peril of the sea was in principle recoverable under a freight policy

---

[345] *National Oilwell (UK) Ltd v Davy Offshore Ltd* [1993] 2 Lloyd's Rep. 582.

[346] *Papademitriou v Henderson* [1939] 3 All E.R. 908; *Russell v Canadian General Insurance Co* (1999) 11 C.C.L.I. (3d) 284.

[347] For negligence, see *Busk v Royal Exchange Assurance Co* (1818) 2 B. & Ald. 73; *Walker v Maitland* (1821) 5 B. & Ald. 171; *Kahn v Corbett* (1824) 2 Bing. 205; *Bishop v Pentland* (1827) 7 B. & C. 219; *Shore v Bentall* (1828) 7 B. & C. 798n; *Dixon v Sadler* (1839) 5 M. & W. 405; *Redman v Wilson* (1845) 14 M. & W. 476; *Thompson v Hopper* (1856) 6 E. & B. 172; *Trinder Anderson Co v Thames & Mersey Marine Insurance Co* [1898] 2 Q.B. 114; *Blackburn v Liverpool, Brazil & River Plate Steam Navigation Co* [1902] 1 K.B. 290; *Cohen, Sons & Co v National Benefit Assurance Co Ltd* (1924) 18 Ll. L.R. 199; *Lind v Mitchell* [1928] All E.R. 447.

[348] *St Margaret's Trust Ltd v Navigators & General Insurance Co Ltd* (1949) 82 Ll. L.R. 752. Contrast *Talbot Underwriting v Nausch Hogan & Murray (The Jascon 5)* [2005] EWHC 2359 (Comm) where delay was held not to be the proximate cause of the loss.

[349] *Gregson v Gilbert* (1783) 3 Doug. 232; *Tatham v Hodgson* (1796) 6 T.R. 656; *Taylor v Dunbar* (1869) L.R. 4 CR 206; *Pink v Fleming* (1890) 25 QBD 396.

in the old Lloyd's SG form,[350] and this is recognised by s.55(2)(b) which does not refer to freight. The decisions imposing liability on freight insurers for delay produced an immediate reaction, by the adoption of the "time charter" clause. The wording of the clause has not altered since its inception in the 1890s, and it is currently to be found as cl.14 of the Institute Time Clauses Freight and cl.12 of the Institute Voyage Clauses Freight: "This insurance does not cover any claim consequent on the loss of time whether arising from a peril of the sea or otherwise." The clause does not refer to any proximity test, and was held in *Naviera de Canarias SA v National Hispanica Aseguradora SA*[351] to contemplate the situation in which there had been a chain of events, namely: an insured peril; delay consequent on the occurrence of that peril; and subsequent loss of freight by the assured. The clause was thus effective to prevent recovery both where delay was the proximate cause of the loss of freight and where the delay was simply the intermediate consequence of the occurrence of a peril itself the proximate cause of the loss of freight.

Risks insured against do not include the inherent vice of the subject-matter insured. There is no statutory definition of "inherent vice", and it is now accepted that:

"inherent vice ... refers to a peril by which a loss is proximately caused; it is not descriptive of the loss itself. It means the risk of deterioration of the goods shipped as a result of their natural behaviour in the ordinary course of the contemplated voyage without the intervention of any fortuitous external accident or casualty."[352]

In *Global Process Systems Inc v Syarikat Takaful Malaysia Berhad*[353] the Court of Appeal held that insurers have a defence only where inherent vice is the proximate cause of the loss. The test is not whether the subject matter was lost by reason of its natural behaviour in the conditions to which it had been subjected or whether the loss was foreseeable,[354] but rather whether the subject matter was unable to withstand the ordinary incidents of the voyage, i.e. the wind and waves which were bound to occur on the voyage being undertaken. Although inherent vice need not be the sole cause of the loss, it will operate only if no other external cause amounts to an insured peril. In *Global Process Systems* the legs of an oil rig cracked and fell off when the vessel was hit by a wave towards the end of a lengthy sea voyage. The Court of Appeal held that, where a loss is the result of a combination of inherent vice and sea conditions, the ordinary rule—that a loss proximately caused by one insured and one excepted peril is not covered—is displaced, so that the assured is able to recover unless the sea conditions were no more than the ordinary motion of the wind and waves not amounting to a proximate cause of the loss resulting from the operation of a peril of the sea. Applied to the facts of the case, the Court of Appeal held that the loss was the result of a combination of perils of the sea and metal fatigue: a leg-breaking wave was not bound to occur, even though it was highly probable, and the insurance was against that probability. *Global Process Systems* confirms that the burden of

---

[350] *Inman Steamship Co Ltd v Bischoff* (1881) 7 App.Cas. 670; *Mercantile SS Co v Tyser* (1881) 7 QBD 73; *Manchester Liners Ltd v British and Foreign Marine Insurance Co* (1901) 7 Com. Cas. 26.

[351] *Naviera de Canarias SA v National Hispanica Aseguradora SA* [1978] A.C. 853.

[352] *Soya GmbH v White* [1983] 1 Lloyd's Rep. 122 at 125, per Lord Diplock..

[353] *Global Process Systems Inc v Syarikat Takaful Malaysia Berhad* [2010] Lloyd's Rep. I.R. 221.

[354] This approach, in *Mayban General Insurance v Alston Power Plants* [2004] 2 Lloyd's Rep. 609, was rejected.

proving inherent vice is borne by the insurers, and that the burden cannot be satisfied simply by proving that the actions of the sea on the voyage were no more than would reasonably be contemplated on that particular voyage.

Inherent vice gives a defence where the loss has arisen from the very nature of the insured subject matter. Ordinary leakage and breakage may be regarded as inherent vice, because damage arising from them occurs not from any marine peril but from the nature of the cargo or the manner in which it has been shipped.[355] Thus, damage to cargo which is the result of inadequate packing or loading,[356] natural sweating,[357] mildew[358] or spontaneous combustion[359] is the result of inherent vice and is not covered by the ordinary form of policy. The mere fact that goods shipped in a similar condition in the past have survived the voyage does not preclude a finding of inherent vice in respect of goods which have not survived in similar circumstances.[360] By contrast, damage which cannot be explained by the very nature of the cargo, such as unusual leakage of palm oil not attributable to the barrels in which it was stored,[361] fungus damage to paper not naturally susceptible to mould,[362] mildew damage to tobacco which ought not to have occurred in the ordinary course of events,[363] denting, rusting and pilferage of tins,[364] and damage caused to cigarettes by sea water,[365] is not attributable to inherent vice. Again, if a cargo which is thought to be capable of surviving a sea voyage is damaged as a result of adverse wind or waves, the loss is not one by inherent vice even though the weather encountered was foreseeable.[366] A vessel is also capable of being lost by inherent vice, where the loss is the inevitable product of a quality inherent in the vessel. The mere fact that inadequate repairs to a vessel have been effected would appear not to constitute inherent vice.[367]

Most cases of inherent vice are those arising from some physical change to the insured subject matter caused by the nature of the subject matter or the way in which it has been packed. Loss arising from factors external to the assured subject matter cannot be regarded as inherent vice, although if the cargo contains moisture which in the course of voyage is given off as steam and then condenses and drips onto the cargo, the loss is not to be regarded as having been caused by an external element.[368]   **24–081**

---

[355] See *De Monchy v Phoenix Insurance Co of Hartford* (1929) 34 Ll. L.R. 201; *Blower v Great Western Railway Co* (1872) L.R. 7 C.P. 655; *Biddle, Sawyer & Co Ltd v Peters* [1957] 2 Lloyd's Rep. 339.

[356] *Crofts v Marshall* (1836) 7 C. & P. 597; *Gee and Garnham Ltd v Whittall* [1955] 2 Lloyd's Rep. 562; *E W Berk & Co Ltd v Style* [1955] 2 Lloyd's Rep. 382; *Rainbow Technicoloured Wood Veneer Ltd v The Canmar Conquest* [2000] F.C.J. No.1032.

[357] *Bowring & Co Ltd v Amsterdam London Insurance Co Ltd* (1930) 36 Ll. L.R. 309. Cf. *Nelson Marketing International Inc v Royal & Sun Alliance Insurance Company of Canada* 2006 B.C.C.A. 327.

[358] *Bird's Cigarette Manufacturing Co Ltd v Rouse* (1924) 19 Ll. L.R. 301.

[359] *Boyd v Dubois* (1811) 3 Camp. 133.

[360] *Noten BV v Harding* [1990] 2 Lloyd's Rep. 283.

[361] *Wilson, Holgate & Co Ltd v Lancashire and Cheshire Insurance Corporation Ltd* (1922) 13 Ll. L.R. 486. Contrast *De Monchy v Phoenix Insurance Co of Hartford* 29 Ll. L.R. 179.

[362] *Whiting v New Zealand Insurance Co Ltd* (1932) 44 Ll. L.R. 179.

[363] *Sassoon & Co Ltd v Yorkshire Insurance Co* (1923) 16 Ll. L.R. 129.

[364] *Wunsche International v Tai Ping Insurance Co* [1998] 2 Lloyd's Rep. 8.

[365] *Bird's Cigarette Manufacturing Co Ltd v Rouse* (1924) 19 Ll. L.R. 301.

[366] *Global Process Systems Inc v Syarikat Takaful Malaysia Berhad* [2010] Lloyd's Rep. I.R. 221. *Mayban General Insurance v Alston Power Plants* [2004] 2 Lloyd's Rep. 609, to the contrary, is to be regarded as wrongly decided insofar as the test applied was the foreseeability of the adverse weather conditions.

[367] *CCR Fishing Ltd v Tomenson (The La Pointe)* 69 D.L.R. (4th) 112 (1990).

[368] *Noten BV v Harding* [1990] 2 Lloyd's Rep. 283 (leather gloves).

It is unclear whether inherent vice can be insured against. Where loss is inevitable and that is known to the parties, then the risk is uninsurable on the simple ground that insurance is against contingencies and not certainties. Insurance is nevertheless possible where the loss is not inevitable, and loss from inherent vice is not necessarily inevitable[369] so there is nothing to prevent the assured from insuring against damage caused by inherent vice under a marine policy,[370] and it may be that even inevitable loss can constitute an insurable risk if that inevitability was unknown to the parties when the risk incepted.[371]

Ordinary wear and tear is a specific example of inherent vice, and the problem raised by this exception is ultimately one of evidence; was the loss caused by the advanced age of the subject matter or by some independent insured peril?[372] In many cases it will not be necessary to consider whether ordinary wear and tear is the proximate cause of the loss, for if the assured cannot point to the occurrence of an insured event he will fail on the basis that he has not proved his loss.[373]

It has been held in Australia[374] that the perils listed in s.55(2)(a) are not exclusions but simply situations in which the insurers are not liable, so if the policy itself does not obtain a corresponding exclusion then the assured is entitled to recover if the loss is proximately caused by one of the listed perils and also an insured peril.

Partial and total loss

24–082   "**56.**—(1) A loss may be either total or partial. Any loss other than a total loss, as hereinafter defined, is a partial loss.

(2) A total loss may be either an actual total loss, or a constructive total loss.

(3) Unless a different intention appears from the terms of the policy, an insurance against total loss includes a constructive, as well as an actual, total loss.

(4) Where the assured brings an action for a total loss and the evidence proves only a partial loss, he may, unless the policy otherwise provides, recover for a partial loss.

(5) Where goods reach their destination in specie, but by reason of obliteration of marks, or otherwise, they are incapable of identification, the loss, if any, is partial, and not total."

---

[369] It was nevertheless implicitly recognised in *Global Process Systems Inc v Syarikat Takaful Malaysia Berhad* [2010] Lloyd's Rep. I.R. 221 that the definition of inherent vice adopted in that case brought the test closer to inevitability than was previously thought to be the case.

[370] *Maignen & Co v National Benefit Insurance Co* (1922) 10 Ll. L.R. 30; *Traders & General Insurance Association v Bankers & General Insurance Co* (1921) 9 Ll. L.R. 223.

[371] *Soya v White* [1983] 1 Lloyd's Rep. 122 makes it clear that inherent vice is insurable if it is not inevitable, but their Lordships left open the question of whether inherent vice is an insurable peril if the loss is, unknown to the assured, inevitable. A similar reservation was adopted by Blair J. in *Global Process Systems Inc v Syarikal Takaful Malaysia Berhad* [2010] Lloyd's Rep. I.R. 221. The point did not arise on appeal, [2009] EWCA 637 (Comm). Ambiguous wording will be construed against coverage for inherent vice: *Berk v Style* [1956] 1 Q.B. 181; *Overseas Commodities v Style* [1958] 1 Lloyd's Rep. 546. Cf. *Maignen v National Benefit* (1922) 10 Ll. L.R. 30; *Traders & General v Bankers & General* (1921) 9 Ll. L.R. 223; *Dodswell v British Dominion* [1955] 2 Lloyd's Rep. 391.

[372] *Russell v Canadian General Insurance Co* (1999) 11 C.C.L.I. (3d) 284.

[373] *Wadsworth Lighterage and Coaling Co Ltd v Sea Insurance Co Ltd* [1958] 1 Lloyd's Rep. 546.

[374] *HIH Casualty & General Insurance Co Ltd v Waterwell Shipping Inc* Unreported, 1998, NSWCA.

Actual total loss

"**57.**—(1) Where the subject-matter insured is destroyed, or so damaged as to cease to **24–083** be a thing of the kind insured, or where the assured is irretrievably deprived thereof, there is an actual total loss.

(2) In the case of an actual total loss no notice of abandonment need be given."

The section encompasses three forms of actual total loss destruction; damage which means that the subject matter ceases to meet its description, and irretrievable deprivation. It was said in *Masefield AG v Amlin Corporate Member Ltd*[375] that "an assured is not irretrievably deprived of property if it is legally and physically possible to recover it (and even if such recovery can only be achieved by disproportionate effort and expense)."[376] Capture may be an actual total loss where it is clear from the outset that the subject matter is unlikely to be restored to the assured.[377] In *Masefield* seizure by pirates was held not to be an actual total loss, because it was anticipated from the outset that a ransom would be paid and that the subject matter would be restored.

Missing ship

"**58.** Where the ship concerned in the adventure is missing, and after the lapse of a **24–084** reasonable time no news of her has been received, an actual total loss may be presumed."

Effect of transhipment, etc

"**59.** Where, by a peril insured against, the voyage is interrupted at an intermediate port **24–085** or place, under such circumstances as, apart from any special stipulation in the contract of affreightment, to justify the master in landing and re-shipping the goods or other moveables, or in transhipping them, and sending them on to their destination, the liability of the insurer continues, notwithstanding the landing or transhipment."

Constructive total loss defined

"**60.**—(1) Subject to any express provision in the policy, there is a constructive total **24–086** loss where the subject-matter insured is reasonably abandoned on account of its actual total loss appearing to be unavoidable, or because it could not be preserved from actual total loss without an expenditure which would exceed its value when the expenditure had been incurred.

(2) In particular, there is a constructive total loss—
(i) Where the assured is deprived of the possession of his ship or goods by a peril insured against, and (a) it is unlikely that he can recover the ship or goods, as the case may be, or (b) the cost of recovering the ship or goods, as the case may be, would exceed their value when recovered; or
(ii) In the case of damage to a ship, where she is so damaged by a peril insured against that the cost of repairing the damage would exceed the value of the ship when repaired.

In estimating the cost of repairs, no deduction is to be made in respect of general average contributions to those repairs payable by other interests, but account is to be taken of the expense of future salvage operations and of any

[375] *Masefield AG v Amlin Corporate Member Ltd* [2010] EWHC 280 (Comm).
[376] See also *Marstrand Fishing Co v Beer* [1937] 1 All E.R. 158; *George Cohen, Sons & Co v Standard Marine Insurance Co* (1925) 21 Ll. L.R. 30; *Panamanian Oriental Steamship Corp v Wright* [1970] 2 Lloyd's Rep. 365; *Fraser Shipping Ltd v Colton* [1997] 1 Lloyd's Rep. 586.
[377] As in *Stringer v English and Scottish Marine Insurance Co* (1868–69) L.R. 4 Q.B. 676.

future general average contributions to which the ship would be liable if
repaired; or

(iii) In the case of damage to goods, where the cost of repairing the damage and
forwarding the goods to their destination would exceed their value on arrival."

The section provides for six forms of constructive total loss:

(a) Where the subject matter insured is reasonably abandoned[378] on account
of its actual total loss appearing to be unavoidable.[379] The tests for
"reasonable" abandonment and apparent unavoidable actual total loss are
objective, although the requirements can be judged only on the facts
known to the assured at the time.[380]

(b) Where the subject matter insured could not be preserved from actual total
loss without an expenditure which would exceed its value when the
expenditure had been incurred". Actual or estimated repair and refloating
costs at the place of the casualty are to be included,[381] but no account is
to be taken of any sums payable by third parties in respect of the loss, of
the value of the unrepaired wreck,[382] or of the fact that the vessel was of
an advanced age and therefore required greater expenditure on repairs
following the casualty than would otherwise have been the case.[383] The
post-repair value of the insured subject matter is its market value, as the
agreed value is not conclusive (see s.27(4)). Under cl.21 of the International
Hulls Clauses 2003, in ascertaining whether a vessel is a
constructive total loss, 80 per cent of the insured value of the vessel is to
be taken as the repaired value, disregarding the damaged or break-up value
of what is left of the vessel.

(c) Where the assured is deprived of the possession of his ship or goods by a
peril insured against and it is unlikely that he can recover the ship or
goods, as the case may be. The test is unlikelihood and not uncertainty,[384]
although in the case of a vessel the assured need not demonstrate that
deprivation is likely to be permanent as the cases indicate that there is a
constructive total loss if the assured is unlikely to recover his property

---

[378] The phrase "reasonably abandoned" in s.60(1) is to be contrasted with the concept of
"abandonment" in s.62. The latter refers to the assured exercising an option to treat the vessel as
totally lost for the purpose of his claim; the former refers to decision by the assured to leave the
subject matter to its fate and to give up any hope of recovery: *Masefield AG v Amlin Corporate
Member Ltd* [2010] EWHC 280 Comm, where the assured was aware that the payment of a ransom
would secure the release of goods seized by pirates so that it could not be said that the assured had
"abandoned" them within the meaning of s.60(1).

[379] See: *Dean v Hornby* (1854) 3 El. & Bl. 180; *George Cohen Sons & Co v Standard Marine
Insurance Co* (1925) 21 Ll. L.R. 30; *Fraser Shipping v Colton* [1997] 1 Lloyd's Rep. 586.

[380] *Lind v Mitchell* (1928) 32 Ll. L.R. 70.

[381] *Thompson v Calvin* (1830) Ll. & Wels. I. 40; *Young v Turing* (1841) 2 M. & G. 593.

[382] *Hall v Hayman* [1912] 2 K.B. 5. This was the position at common law at the date of the passing
of the 1906 Act (*Angel v Merchants' Marine Insurance Co Ltd* [1903] 2 K.B. 811) although the
House of Lords overturned that ruling in *Macbeth & Co Ltd v Marine Insurance Co* [1908] A.C. 144,
a case decided after the Act had come into force but on a policy entered into before that date. Bray
J. in *Hall v Hayman* held that the words of the Act were consistent with pre-Act authority, and that
Macbeth was to be disregarded.

[383] *Phillips v Nairne* (1847) 4 C.B. 343.

[384] See, for illustrative cases involving vessels, *Marstrand Fishing Co Ltd v Beer* (1936) 56 Ll.
L.R. 163, *Rickards v Forestal Land, Timber & Railway Co Ltd* [1942] A.C. 50, *Panamanian Oriental
Steamship Co v Wright* [1971] 1 Lloyd's Rep. 487; for cargo, see *Bayview Motors Ltd v Mitsui
Marine and Fire Insurance Co* [2003] Lloyd's Rep. I.R. 121.

within a reasonable time,[385] treated as 12 months by the War Risks Clauses.

(d) Where the assured is deprived of possession of his ship or goods by a peril insured against and the cost of recovering the ship or goods, as the case may be, would exceed their value when recovered.

(e) In the case of damage to a ship, where she is so damaged by a peril insured against that the cost of repairing the damage would exceed the value of the ship when repaired.

(f) In the case of damage to goods, where the cost of repairing the damage and forwarding the goods to their destination would exceed their value on arrival.

With one exception this list is exhaustive: the exception relates to loss of voyage, where the assured is entitled to claim for a constructive total loss where goods have failed to arrive at their destination,[386] although in practice this form of loss is excluded from the War Risks clauses and thus is of little significance.

The time at which the existence of a constructive total loss is to be ascertained is the date on which proceedings against the insurers are commenced,[387] although in practice it is accepted by underwriters that the refusal of a notice of abandonment is deemed to be the date of the commencement of proceedings for this purpose.[388]

Effect of constructive total loss

24–087

"**61.** Where there is a constructive total loss the assured may either treat the loss as a partial loss, or abandon the subject-matter insured to the insurer and treat the loss as if it were an actual total loss."

Notice of abandonment

24–088

"**62.**—(1) Subject to the provisions of this section, where the assured elects to abandon the subject-matter insured to the insurer, he must give notice of abandonment. If he fails to do so the loss can only be treated as a partial loss.

(2) Notice of abandonment may be given in writing, or by word of mouth, or partly in writing and partly by word of mouth, and may be given in terms which indicate the intention of the assured to abandon his insured interest in the subject-matter insured unconditionally[389] to the insurer.

(3) Notice of abandonment must be given with reasonable diligence after the receipt of reliable information of the loss, but where the information is of a doubtful character the assured is entitled to a reasonable time to make inquiry.

(4) Where notice of abandonment is properly given, the rights of the assured are not prejudiced by the fact that the insurer refuses to accept the abandonment.

(5) The acceptance of an abandonment may be either express or implied from the conduct of the insurer.[390] The mere silence of the insurer after notice is not an acceptance.

---

[385] *Pollurian Steamship Co v Young* [1915] 1 K.B. 922; *Irvine v Hine* [1949] 2 All E.R. 1089; *The Bamburi* [1982] 1 Lloyd's Rep. 312.

[386] *British and Foreign Marine Insurance Co v Samuel Sanday* [1916] A.C. 650.

[387] *Hamilton v Mendes* (1761) 2 Burr. 1199; *Sailing Ship "Blaimore" Co v Macredie* [1898] A.C. 593.

[388] *The Bamburi* [1982] 1 Lloyd's Rep. 312; *Masefield AG v Amlin Corporate Member Ltd* [2010] EWHC 280 (Comm).

[389] See *Panamanian Oriental Steamship Corporation v Wright* [1970] 2 Lloyd's Rep. 365.

[390] See, e.g. *Provincial Insurance Co of Canada v Leduc* (1874) L.R. 6 P.C. 224; *Captain JA Cates Tug and Wharfage Co Ltd v Franklin Insurance* [1927] A.C. 698.

(6) Where notice of abandonment is accepted the abandonment is irrevocable. The acceptance of the notice conclusively[391] admits liability for the loss and the sufficiency of the notice.

(7) Notice of abandonment is unnecessary where, at the time when the assured receives information of the loss, there would be no possibility of benefit to the insurer if notice were given to him.[392]

(8) Notice of abandonment may be waived by the insurer.

(9) Where an insurer has re-insured his risk, no notice of abandonment need be given by him."

The effect of giving a notice of abandonment is an election between two remedies, payment for a partial loss or payment for a total loss[393]; a constructive total loss does not lose its identity merely because a notice of abandonment has not been served, so that the assured can recover under a total loss only policy.[394] The election must be made with reasonable diligence, and if the assured has sold the subject matter then he plainly cannot give notice of abandonment[395] although the assignee may be able to do so. In the absence of an express notification of acceptance, the insurer will be taken to have accepted an abandonment only where its conduct is not consistent with any other conclusion. Thus an underwriter who repairs and sells the insured subject matter[396] or who forbids the assured to deal with the subject matter[397] will be taken to have accepted the abandonment, but the contrary conclusion will be reached where the underwriter does not assert any claim over the damaged property[398] or enters into negotiations with salvors following salvage operations.[399] Paying salvage expenses does not operate as an election to take over the vessel under s.63(1): *Dornoch Ltd v Westminster International BV (No.2)*.[400]

It will be seen from the wording of s.62(5) that the insurer is not estopped by silence from denying its acceptance of an abandonment, so that it may do nothing following the receipt of a notice of abandonment. However, in practice, an express rejection will be given whether or not the insurer is minded to refuse the claim. The express rejection of a notice of abandonment by an insurer has one important practical effect. If the assured is to pursue a successful claim for a constructive total loss, he must show that facts known both at the date of the casualty and at the date at which proceedings against the insurer were commenced justified a finding of constructive total loss. However, marine underwriters have established the practice of permitting the assured to treat any notification of a rejection of a notice of abandonment as the equivalent of the commencement of proceedings; any facts discovered after that date which indicate that a constructive total loss had not occurred are, therefore, irrelevant in fixing the rights of the parties.

---

[391] Unless there is a fundamental mistake which renders the acceptance a nullity: *Norwich Union Fire Insurance Society Ltd v William Price Ltd* [1934] A.C. 455.

[392] See: *Rankin v Potter* (1873) L.R. 6 H.L. 83; *Bayview Motors Ltd v Mitsui Marine and Fire Insurance Co* [2003] Lloyd's Rep. I.R. 121; *Kastor Navigation Co Ltd v Axa Global Risks (UK) Ltd* [2004] Lloyd's Rep. I.R. 481.

[393] *Kastor Navigation Co Ltd v Axa Global Risks (UK) Ltd* [2004] Lloyd's Rep. I.R. 481.

[394] *Bank of America v Christmas (The Kyriaki)* [1993] 1 Lloyd's Rep. 137; *Dornoch Ltd v Westminster International BV (No.2)* [2009] Lloyd's Rep. I.R. 573 (Admlty).

[395] *Ngo Chew Hong Edible Oil Pte v Knight* [1988] 1 S.L.R. 414.

[396] *Provincial Insurance Co of Canada v Leduc* (1874) L.R. 6 P.C. 224, a particularly strong case as the insurer had the right to avoid the entire policy for a breach of warranty.

[397] *Hudson v Harrison* (1821) 3 B. & B. 97.

[398] *Thellusson v Flelcher* (1793) 1 Esp. N.P. 72.

[399] *Captain JA Cates Tug and Wharfage Co Ltd v Franklin Insurance Co* [1927] A.C. 698.

[400] *Dornoch Ltd v Westminster International BV (No.2)* [2009] Lloyd's Rep. I.R. 573.

Until a notice of abandonment is accepted by the insurers, it has no real effect. A notice of abandonment is effectively an offer by the assured to the insurer to abandon the subject matter. Accordingly, if a notice of abandonment is not accepted, it may be withdrawn by the assured and once it has been withdrawn it cannot be accepted.[401] As is the case with ordinary offers, a notice of abandonment can be withdrawn by conduct as well as by express words, e.g. when the assured, having sought to abandon a vessel to the insurers on the ground of seizure, recovers the vessel and continues to use it.[402] Similarly, if the assured resells the wreck of the vessel before acceptance he thereby withdraws his notice of abandonment and thereafter can recover only for a partial loss.[403] The principle is that where a notice of abandonment has been given but not accepted, the assured must continue to be prepared to abandon the subject matter to the insurers, and once he does an act inconsistent with the possibility of abandonment then the right to claim for a constructive total loss is lost.[404] Presumably, however, unless the act is irrevocable—as in the case of a sale—then a further notice can be tendered.

Section 62(4) states that the fact that the insurers have refused to accept a notice of abandonment is not to prejudice the rights of the assured. It follows that the assured is entitled at any subsequent trial to assert that there was a constructive total loss.

Failure of insurers to accept a notice of abandonment is, as noted earlier, **24–089** commonly the case, as there remains a possibility that such acceptance amounts also to the exercise of the option under s.63(1), to take over the vessel or other subject matter. Accordingly, the vessel remains the property of the assured and he may deal with it as he thinks fit, although such dealing may operate as a withdrawal of the notice of abandonment. The safest course for insurers who are concerned about opting to take over the subject matter is, therefore, to refuse to accept a notice of abandonment—thereby keeping open the option to take over the subject matter or to decline to do so—but nevertheless to make a payment on the basis that there has been a constructive total loss. The legal consequences of this course of action were considered by Tomlinson J. in *Dornoch Ltd v Westminster International BV (No.2)*,[405] the learned judge holding that rejection of a notice of abandonment did not amount to an irrevocable election not to exercise a future right to take over the subject matter under s.63(1) (although such rejection meant that the insurers lost the benefit of the equitable lien over the subject matter which is conferred by the acceptance of a notice of abandonment), and if there was a subsequent payment for constructive total loss without any acceptance of the notice of abandonment then the insurers retained their right to opt to exercise proprietary rights over the subject matter under s.79(1).

There remains an issue of the status of the subject matter in the period between payment of the claim for a constructive total loss and the exercise of the option under ss.63(1) and 79(1). In *Dornoch* itself the insurers had rejected the notice of abandonment but paid for a constructive total loss, and thereafter some had elected to take over the vessel while others had not. The vessel was sold, and at that point the remaining insurers purported to exercise their right to take over the vessel. Tomlinson J. ruled that those insurers who had exercised their statutory

---

[401] *Pesqueras y Secaderos de Bacalao de Espana SA v Beer (1946)* 79 Ll. L.R. 417, 433, per Atkinson J.; *Royal Boskalis v Mountain* [1997] L.R.L.R. 523.

[402] *Royal Boskalis Westminster NV v Mountain* [1997] L.R.L.R. 523.

[403] *Dornoch Ltd v Westminster International BV (No.2)* [2009] Lloyd's Rep. I.R. 573.

[404] *Dornoch Ltd v Westminster International BV (No.2)* [2009] Lloyd's Rep. I.R. 573.

[405] *Dornoch Ltd v Westminster International BV (No.2)* [2009] Lloyd's Rep. I.R. 573.

rights were individually entitled to a share in a vessel represented by their proportion of the paid loss and were not bound by the sale because at the time of the sale the assured had no title to pass to the purchaser. By contrast, those insurers who had not exercised their rights to take over the vessel at the time of the sale had neither a legal nor an equitable interest in the vessel so that the purchaser acquired rights in the vessel which could not be displaced by the subsequent sale. The learned judge felt that it was not appropriate to impose an equitable lien on the vessel in favour of the insurers in the period between payment and exercise of the option to take over the vessel, as there was nothing in the Marine Insurance Act which conferred security where a notice of abandonment had been rejected, and as a matter of principle there was no justification for equity to protect insurers who remained undecided: equity was in favour of the assured, who was entitled to deal with the vessel in the absence of an election by the insurers to take it over.

If an abandonment has been accepted, the insurer is entitled to elect to take over the insured subject matter and all rights attaching thereto, in accordance with s.63, and the insurer thereby obtains an equitable lien over the subject matter. Once payment is made, the insurer obtains full legal title under s.79(1).[406] Section 62(6) states that acceptance is irrevocable. Accordingly, the assured is entitled to recover a sum representing the full insured value of the subject matter. The assured's right to withdraw a notice of abandonment and to seek recovery for a partial loss only thus terminates on acceptance of abandonment by the insurer. There are nevertheless two outstanding questions on the effect of acceptance on a notice of abandonment.

The first is whether such acceptance by the insurers operates automatically as an exercise by them of their right under s.63(1) to take over the vessel. If that is the case, then the consequences are that they immediately require an equitable lien over the vessel, and that lien becomes perfected into legal title under s.79(1) when payment is actually made. By contrast, if that is not the case and there is no automatic exercise of the election, then insurers do not acquire any equitable interest in the subject matter but retain their right to refuse to take over the insured subject matter, and when they actually make payment then they have the right to take over the subject matter under s.79(1) but they do not acquire any equitable interest in the subject matter pending any decision to exercise that right. In *Dornoch Ltd v Westminster International BV (No.2)*[407] Tomlinson J. noted that the point remained open, although it did not arise in that case because the insurers had paid for a constructive total loss and had thereby acquired the right to take over the vessel under s.79(1), a right exercised by some of them but not by others.

The second is the extent to which the notion of irrevocable acceptance is limited by the ordinary common law rules relating to fundamental mistake. Leaving aside for one moment s.62(6) itself, it would appear that, as a matter of ordinary law, the acceptance of a notice of abandonment amounts to a contract to pay for a constructive total loss, and that such a contract is to be treated as void only where it was made on the basis of a fundamental mistake common to the parties when the agreement was entered into. This was certainly the view taken at common law. Thus, in *Smith v Robertson*[408] it was held by Lord Eldon that a seized vessel remained a constructive total loss under an accepted notice of abandonment despite the fact that it was recaptured soon afterwards. Non-marine

---

[406] *Dornoch Ltd v Westminster International BV (No.2)* [2009] Lloyd's Rep. I.R. 573.
[407] *Dornoch Ltd v Westminster International BV (No.2)* [2009] Lloyd's Rep. I.R. 573.
[408] *Smith v Robertson* (1814) 2 Dow. 474.

authority relating to settlement contracts is in accordance with this decision.[409] If it is correct that marine and non-marine insurance are at one on the issue of mistake, it follows that, irrespective of s.62(6), the insurer would have no right to withdraw its acceptance for non-fundamental matters such as the extent of the loss, but would be entitled to withdraw on the ground of a fundamental mistake as to the very existence of the loss at the time the agreement was entered into (although if the insurer is aware of any fact which permits it to deny liability on the policy, but nevertheless accepts a notice of abandonment, it will be deemed to have waived its rights.[410] It would appear that s.62(6) adds nothing to the common law position as far as the rights of the assured are concerned. The only situation in which it is potentially applicable is that of fundamental mistake as to the existence of a loss, as in all other situations the contract relating to abandonment is unassailable as a matter of general law, although the Privy Council in *Norwich Union Fire Insurance Society Ltd v William Price Ltd*[411] expressed the view obiter that in the event of a fundamental mistake the notice of abandonment is itself a nullity and is thus not capable of acceptance under s.62. Here the insurer's error related to the cause of the loss of a cargo of lemons, which was assumed to be an insured peril but which in fact proved to be an uninsured peril. The decision turned on whether or not a settlement for an actual total loss could be overridden by the discovery of the mistake, but the Privy Council appeared to be of the view that permitting a distinction to be drawn between actual total and constructive total losses would be illogical.

Effect of abandonment

"**63.**—(1) Where there is a valid abandonment the insurer is entitled to take over the interest of the assured in whatever may remain of the subject-matter insured, and all proprietary rights incidental thereto.   **24–090**

(2) Upon the abandonment of a ship, the insurer thereof is entitled to any freight in course of being earned, and which is earned by her subsequent to the casualty causing the loss, less the expenses of earning it incurred after the casualty; and, where the ship is carrying the owner's goods, the insurer is entitled to a reasonable remuneration for the carriage of them subsequent to the casualty causing the loss."

The concept of abandonment. There is much marine authority prior to MIA 1906   **24–091** which indicates that, following payment of a total loss, the assured must abandon the property to the insurer, and the insurer may thereupon take it up for its own account.[412] This principle is now contained in s.63(1).

The requirements for valid abandonment. The assured's right or duty to abandon   **24–092** depends upon the occurrence of a total, as opposed to a partial, loss. If the loss is an actual total loss, that is, where the insured subject matter is destroyed or ceases to exist as such, or where the assured is irretrievably deprived of the subject matter (s.57(1)) abandonment is automatic on the occurrence of the casualty, and in particular the assured is not required to serve a notice of abandonment on the insurer (s.60(1)). Conversely, where there is a constructive total loss as defined by s.61 as including the situations in which an actual total loss appears to be inevitable or where the subject matter could not be prevented

[409] *Holmes v Payne* [1930] 2 K.B. 301.

[410] *Provincial Insurance Co of Canada v Leduc* (1874) L.R. 6 P.C. 224.

[411] *Norwich Union Fire Insurance Society Ltd v William Price Ltd* [1934] A.C. 555.

[412] *Randal v Cockran* (1748) 1 Ves. Sen. 98; *Houstman v Thornton* (1816) Holt N.P. 242; *Rankin v Potter* (1873) L.R. 6 H.L. 83; *Kaltenbach v Mackenzie* (1878) 3 C.P.D. 467.

from suffering an actual total loss without an expenditure which would exceed its reinstated value, the assured has the option of treating the loss as a total loss or as a partial loss (s.61). If the assured wishes to claim for a total loss, notice of abandonment must be served on the insurer (s.62(1)), failing which the assured is deemed to have suffered a partial loss only and there is no possibility of abandonment. In essence, then, abandonment will be valid where the assured has suffered a total loss which must be treated as such by the insurer.

It is important to distinguish abandonment from notice of abandonment. Abandonment is the transfer of the insured subject matter from the assured to the insurers, which takes place (if at all) on payment of the loss by the insurers. Notice of abandonment, by contrast, is the formal means by which the assured elects to treat a constructive total loss as an actual total loss as opposed to a partial loss. Whether the loss is an actual total loss in its own right, or a constructive total loss which the assured has elected to treat as an actual total loss, there is a right to be paid for a total loss only where the assured is willing to hand over—abandon—what, if anything remains, of the insured subject matter to the insurers. There is no independent obligation on the assured to notify the insurers that the subject matter has been abandoned.[413] If the assured has suffered a partial loss, any profits which are made by the assured from the subject matter of the insurance necessarily remain the property of the assured.[414]

In determining the effect of a total loss on the insured subject matter, three situations have to be distinguished. The first is where there has been an actual total loss. In that situation, as soon as the insurers have paid for a total loss they are entitled to the insured subject matter. The right is conferred by s.79(1). The second is where there has been a constructive total loss of the insured subject matter and the assured has served a notice of abandonment which has been accepted by the insurers. Such acceptance confers a right upon the insurers to take over the subject matter, in accordance with s.63(1). In this situation the acceptance of the notice of abandonment confers at least a right—and arguably an obligation—on the insurers to take over the insured subject matter. If the right has been exercised (or the obligation has taken effect) the insurers are given an immediate equitable lien over the subject matter,[415] and this crystallises into a proprietary right under s.79(1) once payment has actually been made. The third is where there has been a constructive total loss of the insured subject matter and the insurers have refused to accept a notice of abandonment but have subsequently paid for a total loss. In that situation s.63(1) is not engaged and the insurers have no equitable rights over the insured subject matter, although once payment has been made then they have the right to take over the subject matter in accordance with s.79(1).

24–093   *Taking over the subject matter.* As noted above, the insurers may opt to obtain rights over the abandoned subject-matter in two stages. At the first stage they may accept a notice of abandonment under s.62(6), in which case s.63(1) is triggered and they obtain an equitable lien over the subject matter. The issue here is whether s.62(6) operates automatically as an exercise of the option to take over the subject matter or whether a further election is required. In other words, can insurers accept a notice of abandonment without at the same time exercising the right to take over the subject matter? The legal uncertainty over this question has

---

[413] See *Kastor Navigation Co Ltd v Axa Global Risks (UK) Ltd* [2004] Lloyd's Rep. I.R. 481.
[414] *Tunno v Edwards* (1810) 12 East 488: *Goldmid v Gillies* (1813) 4 Taunt. 803: *Brooks v McDonnnell* (1836) 1 Y. & C. Ex. 502.
[415] *Dornoch Ltd v Westminster International BV (No.2)* [2009] Lloyd's Rep. I.R. 573.

led to the practice that insurers typically refuse to accept a notice of abandonment for fear of triggering s.63(1), but the point has nevertheless been discussed by the courts, in particular in *Dornoch Ltd v Westminster International BV (No.2)*,[416] where Tomlinson J. refused to come to a conclusion on the point. At the second stage, if insurers have opted to take over the subject matter under s.63(1), they obtain an automatic equitable lien in the subject matter. Once payment is made, s.79(1) provides that the insurers are entitled to take over the subject matter. It is uncertain whether this means that the election made under s.63(1) has to be confirmed by a further election, or whether payment transfers legal title to the insurers without more. Happily, this is likely to remain an academic question, in that insurers in practice refuse to accept a notice of abandonment so that the provision is not triggered. If they have rejected the notice of abandonment then on payment for a total loss the insurers have an election to take over the subject matter under s.79(1). The insurers do not, by paying a salvage or wreck removal claim, exercise their rights to take over the subject matter under either ss.63(1) or 79(1).[417]

A variety of different scenarios may arise in applying these principles to the situation in which the assured has sold or purported to sell the insured subject matter to a third party. The most important are as follows (the analysis follows from the judgment of Tomlinson J. in *Dornoch Ltd v Westminster International BV (No.2)*).[418]

First, the insurers have accepted a notice of abandonment under s.62(2). It is not clear whether by so doing they have exercised their option to take over the subject matter under s.63 or whether that has to be done separately. But, if the insurers have exercised their right to take over the subject matter under s.62 either automatically by accepting a notice of abandonment under s.62(6), or by election, the insurers do not have actual proprietary rights unless and until they have paid under s.79, it also being unclear whether a separate affirmation of ownership is required or whether this is automatic. Once the right under s.79 has been triggered, legal ownership passes to the insurers and any purported sale by the assured to a third party cannot pass title to the third party: the assured has no title and cannot confer title on the purchaser, a principle expressed by the Latin maxim *nemo dat quod non habet*.

Secondly, the situation is the same as above, in that the insurers have exercised their right to take over the subject matter under s.63, but the subject matter has been sold by the assured before full payment by the insurers so that the right of the insurers under s.79(1) to obtain ownership has not been exercised. In this situation the insurers have an equitable lien over the subject matter in the period between the exercise of the s.63 option and payment under s.79(1). If, therefore, the assured purports to sell the subject matter in that intervening period, the rights of the purchaser depend upon the interaction of the rules of law and equity. A bona fide purchaser of the legal estate for value and without notice of the insurers' equity, whereas a purchaser who does not meet one or more of these requirements will obtain a title which subject to that equity and which can be overridden once the insurers have made full payment under s.79.

Thirdly, the assured has tendered a notice of abandonment which has been **24–094** declined. Should the assured at that point sell the subject matter to a third party,

[416] *Dornoch Ltd v Westminster International BV (No.2)* [2009] Lloyd's Rep. I.R. 573.
[417] *Dornoch Ltd v Westminster International BV (No.2)* [2009] Lloyd's Rep. I.R. 573.
[418] *Dornoch Ltd v Westminster International BV (No.2)* [2009] Lloyd's Rep. I.R. 573.

he thereby withdraws his notice of abandonment and title passes to the third party, who can then press make a fresh claim against the insurers.

Fourthly, the insurers have refused to accept a notice of abandonment but have nevertheless paid for a constructive total loss. The insurers are thereby entitled to exercise an option to take over the subject matter under s.63(1): failure to accept a notice of abandonment is irrelevant to the exercise of rights under s.79(1). If they do exercise that option, then the assured has no legal title to pass to the third party so that any purported sale at that stage will be ineffective under the *nemo dat* principle.

Fifthly, the insurers have refused to accept a notice of abandonment and have nevertheless paid for a constructive total loss, but they have not reached a decision as to whether they will exercise their right under s.79(1) to take over the subject matter. This was the situation in *Dornoch Ltd v Westminster International BV (No.2)* Tomlinson J. holding that the insurers have no equitable interest merely by having paid without first accepting a notice of abandonment, and that the assured retains both legal and equitable title in the subject matter. A sale of the subject matter in that situation will pass good title to the purchaser, whether or not the third party was bona fide and without notice of the payment.

Sixthly, the insurers have refused to accept a notice of abandonment and have paid for a constructive total loss but have elected not to exercise their right under s.79(1) to take over the subject matter. In that situation the insurers are to be taken to have renounced all rights in the subject matter, and they cannot subsequently by way of subrogation claim the proceeds of any sale of the subject matter by the assured.[419]

If there are two or more insurers, it is trite law that each insurer who subscribes to a contract of insurance has his own distinct rights. It follows that insurers may exercise the options under ss.63(1) and 79(1) independently or collectively, and that any insurer who does exercise an option obtains a proportionate share in whatever equitable or legal rights exist in the subject matter.[420]

24–095   *The consequences of abandonment.* Section 63(1) transfers to the insurer the remnants of the insured subject matter and all incidental proprietary rights. Pre-Act authorities had established that abandonment takes effect at the date of the loss, so that the insurer's rights over the subject matter following its acceptance of the abandoned property are backdated to the time of the loss; in particular, the insurer's rights are not retroactive to the inception of the policy nor are they postponed until its acceptance of the abandoned property. This principle is now embodied in s.63(2), which regulates the most significant proprietary right attaching to a vessel, the right to freight. The first part of s.63(2) confirms the rule in *Case v Davidson*,[421] in which it was held that freight earned after the occurrence of the insured casualty passes to hull underwriters by way of salvage, as opposed to freight underwriters by way of subrogation.[422] The insurer's inability to claim freight previously earned under an apportionable agreement, or advance freight, stems from the common law principle that abandonment is retroactive to the date of the casualty but not to the date of the commencement

[419] *Dornoch Ltd v Westminster International BV (No.3)* [2009] EWHC 1782 (Admlty).
[420] *Dornoch Ltd v Westminster International BV (No.2)* [2009] Lloyd's Rep. I.R. 573.
[421] *Case v Davidson* (1816) 5 M. & S. 79.
[422] This result was approved by the House of Lords in *Stewart v Greenock Marine Insurance Co* (1848) 2 H.L. Cas. 159.

of the risk.[423] The right of the assured to deduct expenses incurred by him in earning the freight subsequently accruing to the insurer was also recognised by the common law, the cases on the point demonstrating that only those expenses incurred for the sole benefit of the insurer are deductible from the freight earned.[424]

The final part of s.63(2) deals with the situation in which the vessel is lost while carrying the assured's own goods. In this situation there is no loss of freight to the assured in respect of his own goods, but the statute awards "reasonable remuneration" to the insurer where the vessel is, following abandonment, able to complete its voyage carrying goods belonging to the assured. What is reasonable will doubtless depend upon current market rates, as was the position at common law.[425]

Section 63(2) is not an exhaustive statement of the common law, and at least three matters remain governed by common law principles. First, if the assured, following abandonment, trans-ships the goods on another vessel and thereby earns freight in his own right, the insurer has no claim on such freight where the abandoned vessel completes its voyage, as that vessel did not earn the freight.[426] However, freight earned by any goods remaining on board the abandoned vessel is the property of the insurer in the usual way.[427] Second, the freight to which the insurer is entitled does not extend to that to be earned under future voyages.[428] Third, where the hull insurer is entitled to claim freight under s.63(2), the assured cannot seek to recover that sum from freight underwriters. This is so for two reasons: there has been no loss of freight, as all that has happened is that the right to recover freight has been transferred from the assured to the hull insurer; and in the case of a constructive total loss the assured has, by voluntarily abandoning the vessel, caused his own inability to recover freight.[429] In practice this rule is normally reversed, as cl.15.1 of the Institute Time Clauses Freight and cl.13.1 of the Institute Voyage Clauses Freight grant to the assured payment "in full" for loss of freight, wording which has been taken to confer upon the assured a right to claim against freight underwriters where the hull insurer has exercised its rights under s.63(2).[430]

The principles contained in s.63(2) may be excluded by contrary agreement. It is standard practice for English marine policies on vessels to incorporate a waiver of freight.[431] Any freight earned by the vessel following its abandonment will, therefore, accrue to the assured (generally for the benefit of freight insurers by way of subrogation).

---

[423] *Luke v Lyde* (1759) 2 Burr. 882; *Barclay v Stirling* (1816) 5 M. & S. 56; *The Red Sea* [1896] P. 20.

[424] *The Red Sea* [1896] P. 20, affirming the principles in *Leathem v Terry* (1803) 3 B. & P. 479; *Thompson v Rowcroft* (1803) 4 East 34; *Sharp v Gladstone* (1806) 7 East 24; *Barclay v Stirling* (1816) 5 M. & S. 56.

[425] *Miller v Woodfall* (1857) 8 E. & B. 493.

[426] *Hickie and Borman v Rodocanachi* (1859) 4 H. & N. 455.

[427] *Miller v Woodfall* (1857) 8 E. & B. 493 (notional freight for the assured's own goods).

[428] *Sea Insurance Co v Hadden* (1884) 13 QBD 706; *Glen Line v Attorney General* (1930) 36 Com. Cas. 1.

[429] *M'Carthy v Abel* (1804) 5 East 388; *Scottish Marine Insurance Co v Turner* (1853) 1 Macq. H.L. Cas. 334.

[430] *United Kingdom Mutual Steamship Assurance Association v Boulton* (1898) 3 Com. Cas. 330; *Coker v Bolton* [1912] 3 K.B. 315.

[431] International Hull Clauses cl.22: "If a total or constructive total loss of the vessel has been admitted by the Underwriters, they shall make no claim for freight whether notice of abandonment have been given or not."

24–096   *The effects of abandonment on the abandoned property.* Where the assured has suffered a total loss and has abandoned the insured subject matter, then, by virtue of s.63(1) the insurer may take it up. Difficulties may nevertheless arise where the assured has abandoned but the insurer has refused to take up the subject matter by way of salvage; such conduct is possible where the obligations attaching to the subject matter are too onerous to render salvage an economic proposition.

What is clear is that, by the act of abandonment, which is both a right and a duty following a total loss, the assured divests himself of all liabilities affecting the subject matter following abandonment,[432] in particular with regard to disposal of the wreck.[433]

If the insurers have taken up the abandoned property either by accepting a notice of abandonment under s.63(1) and paying for a total loss and exercising their right of salvage under s.79(1), or by rejecting the notice of abandonment and then paying for a total loss accompanied by an exercise of rights under s.79(1), then they become owners of that property and also become subject to the rights and liabilities of ownership. The assured himself ceases to be liable for the subject matter. Actions against the assured for, e.g. negligent conduct arising out of his use of the subject matter before abandonment are not, of course, extinguished by abandonment.[434] In *Barraclough v Brown*[435] the assured was held, following abandonment and payment of a total loss, not to be the "owner" of the vessel, and thus not liable to a river authority for the costs of the vessel's recovery and destruction. Although the point did not arise, it was clear that any claim had to be brought against the underwriters. By contrast, if insurers have refused to exercise their right to take up the subject-matter by rejecting the notice of abandonment and subsequently by refusing to exercise their proprietary rights under MIA 1906 s.79(1),[436] but they have nevertheless paid for a total loss, the status of the subject matter is uncertain. It was held in *Boston Corp v France Fenwick & Co Ltd*[437] that a harbour authority could not recover from the assured sums due under statute from the "owner" of a vessel for its recovery, the assured having abandoned the vessel but not having been paid by the insurers. However, the insurers themselves cannot be held to be owners, because they have not exercised any option to assume ownership.[438] The modern view is that expressed in *Royal Boskalis v Mountain*[439] by Rix J.[440]:

---

[432] Actions against the assured for, e.g. negligent conduct arising out of his use of the subject matter before abandonment are not, of course, extinguished by abandonment: *Dee Conservancy Board v McConnell* [1928] 2 K.B. 159; *The Ella* [1915] P. 111.

[433] *Barraclough v Brown* [1897] A.C. 615; *Boston Corporation v France Fenwick & Co Ltd* (1923) 15 Ll. L.R. 85.

[434] *Dee Conservancy Board v McConnell* [1928] 2 K.B. 159; *The Ella* [1915] P. 111.

[435] *Barraclough v Brown* [1897] A.C. 615.

[436] In *Dornoch Ltd v Westminster International BV (No.3)* [2009] EWHC 1782 (Admlty) Tomlinson J. held that an endorsement on the loss settlement, "Net open market residual value of vessel to be accounted to insurers" did not amount to an election by the insurers not to take over the vessel, but merely recognised that the assured would either assist in facilitating the sale of the vessel to a third party or, if they wished to retain the vessel, to account for the residual value to under-writers.

[437] *Boston Corp v France Fenwick & Co Ltd* (1923) 15 Ll. L.R. 85.

[438] *Allgemeine Versicherungs-Gesellschaft Helvetia v Administrator of German Property* (1931) 14 L.T. 705, although see the conflicting views in *Allgemeine Versicherungs-Gesellschaft Helvetia v Administrator of German Property* (1934) 50 Ll. L.R. 1; *Royal Boskalis v Mountain* Unreported, 1995; *Kastor Navigation Co Ltd v AGF MAT* [2003] Lloyd's Rep. I.R. 262; *Dornoch Ltd v Westminster International BV (No.2)* [2009] Lloyd's Rep. I.R. 573.

[439] *Royal Boskalis v Mountain* Unreported, 1995.

[440] See also *Kastor Navigation Co Ltd v AGF MAT* [2004] Lloyd's Rep. I.R. 481.

"An underwriter may pay the claim without accepting the abandonment: he is not obliged to take over a wreck, which may be a *damnosa hereditas*—see *Allgemeine Versicherungs-Gesellschaft Helvetia v Administrator of German Property* [1931] 1 K.B. 672 at 687/88 per Scrutton L.J. If, however, he wishes, he is 'entitled' to take over the assured's interest in the property (s.63(1)). That is in any event the right of any underwriter who pays for a total loss, whether or not there is abandonment."

Contracting out of the right of salvage. In the eighteenth century, when marine **24–097** policies were commonly used as a cover for wagering, it was the practice to deem such policies to be "without benefit of salvage to the insurer", which made it clear that neither the "assured" nor the "insurer" had any real interest in the subject matter of the policy other than in whether or not the voyage was completed successfully. The practice of wagering by marine policy was outlawed by the Marine Insurance Act 1745, which is substantially re-enacted by s.4 of the 1906 Act. Section 4(2) deems a contract of marine insurance to be made by way of gaming or wagering, and thus void, if it is stated to be, inter alia, "without benefit of salvage to the insurer" or is subject to any stipulation with the like effect.[441] While s.4 does not permit a policy to be without benefit of salvage, it is nevertheless clear that an insurer may forgo particular salvage rights. For this reason a hull underwriter may agree not to take advantage of its right to claim freight in accordance with s.63(2). As mentioned above, this is indeed the position under the Hull Clauses.

The proviso to s.4(2) of the 1906 Act validates a policy made "without benefit of salvage to the insurer" if there is no possibility of salvage under the policy. The proviso is not of wide effect, but operates in at least one context. Where the assured takes out a valued marine policy on cargo, such insurance may be supplemented by increased value insurance, which pays the difference between the insured value of the cargo under the primary policy and the actual loss suffered by the assured. If the cargo suffers a total loss in these circumstances, and both insurers pay, any sums recoverable from third parties in respect of the loss accrued by way of subrogation to the original cargo insurer and not to the increased value insurer.[442] There is, therefore, no realistic possibility of salvage accruing to the latter, and an increased value policy made "without benefit of salvage" would on this basis appear to be validated by the proviso.

13. Partial Losses

Particular average loss

"**64.**—(1) A particular average loss is a partial loss of the subject-matter insured, caused **24–098** by a peril insured against, and which is not a general average loss.

(2) Expenses incurred by or on behalf of the assured for the safety or preservation of the subject-matter insured, other than general average and salvage charges, are called particular charges. Particular charges are not included in particular average."

---

[441] Under cl.6 of the Institute Time Clauses Freight, the insurer of freight agrees to pay the assured "in full" for a total loss of freight. In *Coker v Bolton* [1912] 3 K.B. 315 it was suggested to the court that such an undertaking amounted to a promise by the insurer to pay without benefit of salvage. Hamilton J. held that no such implication could be read into these words, and that their true effect was to reverse the common law rule in *M'Carthy v Abel* (1804) 5 East 388 and to permit the assured to treat as a policy loss freight denied to him by the operation of s.63(2).

[442] *Boag v Standard Marine Insurance Co Ltd* [1937] 2 K.B. 113.

Salvage charges

24–099   "**65.**—(1) Subject to any express provision in the policy, salvage charges incurred in preventing a loss by perils insured against may be recovered as a loss by those perils.

(2) 'Salvage charges' means the charges recoverable under maritime law by a salvor independently of contract. They do not include the expenses of services in the nature of salvage rendered by the assured or his agents, or any person employed for hire by them, for the purpose of averting a peril insured against. Such expenses, where properly incurred, may be recovered as particular charges or as a general average loss, according to the circumstances under which they were incurred."

Salvage charges as here defined are those payable by the assured to a maritime salvor acting in the absence of a contract.[443] Such charges are recoverable as part of particular average where they are incurred in consequence of an insured peril. The result is that partial losses, including maritime salvage, are recoverable under the policy as particular average. Particular charges, consisting of salvage effected under contract, are excluded from the policy but are recoverable under the separate undertaking in the suing and labouring clause: see s.78(2).

General average loss[444]

24–100   "**66.**—(1) A general average loss is a loss caused by or directly consequential on a general average act. It includes a general average expenditure as well as a general average sacrifice.

(2) There is a general average act where any extraordinary sacrifice or expenditure is voluntarily and reasonably made or incurred in time of peril for the purpose of preserving the property imperilled in the common adventure.

(3) Where there is a general average loss, the party on whom it falls is entitled, subject to the conditions imposed by maritime law, to a rateable contribution from the other parties interested, and such contribution is called a general average contribution.

(4) Subject to any express provision in the policy, where the assured has incurred a general average expenditure, he may recover from the insurer in respect of the proportion of the loss which falls upon him; and, in the case of a general average sacrifice, he may recover from the insurer in respect of the whole loss without having enforced his right of contribution from the other parties liable to contribute.

(5) Subject to any express provision in the policy, where the assured has paid, or is liable to pay, a general average contribution in respect of the subject insured, he may recover therefor from the insurer.

(6) In the absence of express stipulation, the insurer is not liable for any general average loss or contribution where the loss was not incurred for the purpose of avoiding, or in connexion with the avoidance of, a peril insured against.

(7) Where ship, freight, and cargo, or any two of those interests, are owned by the same assured, the liability of the insurer in respect of general average losses or contributions is to be determined as if those subjects were owned by different persons."

---

[443] *Kidston v Empire Marine Insurance* (1867) L.R. 2 C.P. 357.
[444] As a matter of practice average adjustments are governed by the York Antwerp Rules 1974, revised in 1994 and again in 2004. Detailed consideration of these rules and of general average is outside the scope of this work. The reader is referred to Arnould, Ch.26, and Carver, *Carriage by Sea*, Ch.14.

14. MEASURE OF INDEMNITY

Extent of liability of insurer for loss

"**67.**—(1) The sum which the assured can recover in respect of a loss on a policy by **24–101** which he is insured, in the case of an unvalued policy to the full extent of the insurable value, or, in the case of a valued policy to the full extent of the value fixed by the policy, is called the measure of indemnity.

(2) Where there is a loss recoverable under the policy, the insurer, or each insurer if there be more than one, is liable for such proportion of the measure of indemnity as the amount of his subscription bears to the value fixed by the policy in the case of a valued policy, or to the insurable value in the case of an unvalued policy."

In the case of a valued policy the sum recoverable is based on the agreed value. In the case of an unvalued policy, the sum recoverable is based on the insurable value as defined by s.16. Once that value has been ascertained, s.67(1) goes on to state that the assured is permitted to recover up to the extent of the insurable value, subject to any deductible and, in the case of underinsurance, the principle of average as set out in ss.67(2) and 81 so that the assured is his own insurer to the extent of the uninsured balance. The principle of average does not have any impact on valued policies, as the assured recovers a proportion of the valuation, nor is it relevant to cases of total loss, for in such cases the insurer is liable up to the limits of the policy: it applies only where the assured has suffered a partial loss under an unvalued policy which does not cover the entire insurable value of the subject matter.

Total loss

"**68.** Subject to the provisions of this Act and to any express provision in the policy, **24–102** where there is a total loss of the subject-matter insured,—
  (1) If the policy be a valued policy, the measure of indemnity is the sum fixed by the policy:
  (2) If the policy be an unvalued policy, the measure of indemnity is the insurable value of the subject-matter insured."

Partial loss of ship

"**69.** Where a ship is damaged, but is not totally lost, the measure of indemnity, subject **24–103** to any express provision in the policy, is as follows:—
  (1) Where the ship has been repaired, the assured is entitled to the reasonable cost of the repairs, less the customary deductions, but not exceeding the sum insured in respect of any one casualty:
  (2) Where the ship has been only partially repaired, the assured is entitled to the reasonable cost of such repairs, computed as above, and also to be indemnified for the reasonable depreciation, if any, arising from the unrepaired damage, provided that the aggregate amount shall not exceed the cost of repairing the whole damage, computed as above:
  (3) Where the ship has not been repaired, and has not been sold in her damaged state during the risk, the assured is entitled to be indemnified for the reasonable depreciation arising from the unrepaired damage, but not exceeding the reasonable cost of repairing such damage, computed as above."

This section prevents the assured from recovering more than an indemnity where a ship has been damaged but not totally lost. Where the vessel has been repaired, the assured is entitled to the reasonable cost of repairs minus customary deductions. The customary deductions are fixed at one-third by the common law, although under the International Hulls Clauses 2003 the assured can recover on a new for old basis without deduction. Where the ship has been partially repaired, the assured can recover the reasonable cost of repairs or the reasonable depreciation, capped at the cost of reasonable repairs. In the case of a valued policy, reasonable depreciation is calculated by reference to the agreed value,[445] although under the International Hulls Clauses 2003 reasonable depreciation refers to the depreciation in the market value of the vessel at the determination of the risk capped at the reasonable cost of repairs.

The section does not deal with the situation in which the vessel has been sold unrepaired. In this situation the agreed value has no part to play in the amount recoverable by the assured: he is entitled to recover market value immediately prior to the loss minus the actual proceeds of sale as the measure of depreciation, assuming that this sum is smaller than the reasonable cost of repairs.[446]

Partial loss of freight

24–104   "**70.** Subject to any express provision in the policy, where there is a partial loss of freight, the measure of indemnity is such proportion of the sum fixed by the policy in the case of a valued policy, or of the insurable value in the case of an unvalued policy, as the proportion of freight lost by the assured bears to the whole freight at the risk of the assured under the policy."

Partial loss of goods, merchandise, etc

24–105   "**71.** Where there is a partial loss of goods, merchandise, or other moveables, the measure of indemnity, subject to any express provision in the policy, is as follows:—

(1) Where part of the goods, merchandise or other moveables insured by a valued policy is totally lost, the measure of indemnity is such proportion of the sum fixed by the policy as the insurable value of the part lost bears to the insurable value of the whole, ascertained as in the case of an unvalued policy:

(2) Where part of the goods, merchandise, or other moveables insured by an unvalued policy is totally lost, the measure of indemnity is the insurable value of the part lost, ascertained as in case of total loss:

(3) Where the whole or any part of the goods or merchandise insured has been delivered damaged at its destination, the measure of indemnity is such proportion of the sum fixed by the policy in the case of a valued policy, or of the insurable value in the case of an unvalued policy, as the difference between the gross sound and damaged values at the place of arrival bears to the gross sound value:

(4) 'Gross value' means the wholesale price, or, if there be no such price, the estimated value, with, in either case, freight, landing charges, and duty paid beforehand; provided that, in the case of goods or merchandise customarily sold in bond, the bonded price is deemed to be the gross value. 'Gross proceeds' means the actual price obtained at a sale where all charges on sale are paid by the sellers."

Apportionment of valuation

24–106   "**72.**—(1) Where different species of property are insured under a single valuation, the valuation must be apportioned over the different species in proportion to their respective insurable values, as in the case of an unvalued policy. The insured value of any part of a species is such proportion of the total insured value of the same as the

---

[445] *Kusel v Atkin (The Catariba)* [1997] 2 Lloyd's Rep. 749. Cf. *Irvin v Hine* [1950] 1 K.B. 555.

[446] *Pitman v Universal Marine Insurance Co* (1882) 9 Q.B. 192.

insurable value of the part bears to the insurable value of the whole, ascertained in both cases as provided by this Act.

(2) Where a valuation has to be apportioned, and particulars of the prime cost of each separate species, quality, or description of goods cannot be ascertained, the division of the valuation may be made over the net arrived sound values of the different species, qualities, or descriptions of goods."

General average contributions and salvage charges

"**73.**—(1) Subject to any express provision in the policy, where the assured has paid, or is liable for, any general average contribution, the measure of indemnity is the full amount of such contribution, if the subject-matter liable to contribution is insured for its full contributory value; but, if such subject-matter be not insured for its full contributory value, or if only part of it be insured, the indemnity payable by the insurer must be reduced in proportion to the under insurance, and where there has been a particular average loss which constitutes a deduction from the contributory value, and for which the insurer is liable, that amount must be deducted from the insured value in order to ascertain what the insurer is liable to contribute.

(2) Where the insurer is liable for salvage charges the extent of his liability must be determined on the like principle."

24–107

Liabilities to third parties

"**74.** Where the assured has effected an insurance in express terms against any liability to a third party, the measure of indemnity, subject to any express provision in the policy, is the amount paid or payable by him to such third party in respect of such liability."

24–108

General provisions as to measure of indemnity

"**75.**—(1) Where there has been a loss in respect of any subject-matter not expressly provided for in the foregoing provisions of this Act, the measure of indemnity shall be ascertained, as nearly as may be, in accordance with those provisions, in so far as applicable to the particular case.

(2) Nothing in the provisions of this Act relating to the measure of indemnity shall affect the rules relating to double insurance, or prohibit the insurer from disproving interest wholly or in part, or from showing that at the time of the loss the whole or any part of the subject-matter insured was not at risk under the policy."

24–109

Particular average warranties

"**76.**—(1) Where the subject-matter insured is warranted free from particular average, the assured cannot recover for a loss of part, other than a loss incurred by a general average sacrifice unless the contract contained in the policy be apportionable; but, if the contract be apportionable, the assured may recover for a total loss of any apportionable part.

(2) Where the subject-matter insured is warranted free from particular average, either wholly or under a certain percentage, the insurer is nevertheless liable for salvage charges, and for particular charges and other expenses properly incurred pursuant to the provisions of the suing and labouring clause in order to avert a loss incurred against.

(3) Unless the policy otherwise provides, where the subject-matter insured is warranted free from particular average under a specified percentage, a general average loss cannot be added to a particular average loss to make up the specified percentage.

(4) For the purpose of ascertaining whether the specified percentage has been reached, regard shall be had only to the actual loss suffered by the subject-matter insured. Particular charges and the expenses of and incidental to ascertaining and proving the loss must be excluded."

24–110

Successive losses

24–111   "77.—(1) Unless the policy otherwise provides, and subject to the provisions of this
Act, the insurer is liable for successive losses, even though the total amount of such
losses may exceed the sum insured.
    (2) Where, under the same policy, a partial loss, which has not been repaired or
otherwise made good, is followed by a total loss, the assured can only recover in respect
of the total loss:
Provided that nothing in this section shall affect the liability of the insurer under the
suing and labouring clause."

The effect of this section, coupled with general common law principles, is as
follows:

(a) Where a partial loss is followed by a further partial loss, under s.77(1) the
insurer is liable for each of those losses as they occur, whether or not the
total sum which the insurer is required to pay out in the period of the
policy exceeds the maximum amount for which the insurer can be liable
in respect of any single claim.[447] This is subject to contract, so that the
insurers may limit their aggregate liability for all losses to the sum insured
in respect of a total loss. Section 77(1) only applies to repaired losses, so
that if the assured suffers a partial loss which is not repaired, and then
suffers a further partial loss, then he is entitled to recover only the
reasonable cost of actual repairs or depreciation at the date the policy
terminates and not the notional cost of each of the repairs.[448]

(b) Where a partial loss is made good, and is then followed by an insured total
loss, the assured is entitled to recover for both,[449] although if the partial
loss is not repaired before the total loss occurs then under the doctrine of
merger set out in s.77(2) the partial loss merges into the total loss and the
assured can recover only for the latter.

(c) Where a partial loss is followed by a total loss not falling within the policy,
once again the doctrine of merger operates and the assured does not have
any claim for the notional cost of depreciation or repairs flowing from the
partial loss.[450]

(d) Where a partial loss occurring during the currency of the policy is
followed by a total loss after the termination of the policy, the doctrine of
merger does not apply and the assured's loss must be assessed as of the
date of termination given that his rights crystallise at that point. Accordingly the partial loss is insured.[451] The same principle applies where a
constructive total loss which the assured elects to treat as a partial loss by
not serving a notice of abandonment is followed by an actual or
constructive total loss: the former merges into the latter.[452]

(e) Where a constructive total loss is followed by an actual total loss, the
assured may claim for either of them, so that if the latter is uninsured the
assured will have a valid claim for the former. This principle was

[447] *Lidgett v Secretan* (1871) L.R. 6 C.P. 616; *The Dora Foster* [1900] P. 241.
[448] *Kusel v Atkin (The Catariba)* [1997] 2 Lloyd's Rep. 749.
[449] *Le Cheminant v Pearson* (1812) 4 Taunt. 367.
[450] *Livie v Janson* (1810) 12 East 648; *Rankin v Potter* (1873) L.R. 6 H.L. 83; *British & Foreign
Marine Insurance Co v Wilson Shipping Co Ltd* [1921] 1 A.C. 188.
[451] *Lidgett v Secretan* (1871) L.R. 6 C.P. 616.
[452] *Woodside v Globe Marine Insurance Co Ltd* [1896] 1 Q.B. 105; *Fooks v Smith* [1924] 2 K.B.
508.

confirmed in *Kastor Navigation Co Ltd v Axa Global Risks (UK) Ltd,*[453] where the vessel became a constructive total loss by fire and almost immediately afterwards sank for reasons which were unexplained so that the sinking was not covered by the policy. The Court of Appeal held that the fire was a constructive total loss in its own right and that the assured could recover for the fire.[454]

Suing and labouring clause

"**78.**—(1) Where the policy contains a suing and labouring clause, the engagement thereby entered into is deemed to be supplementary to the contract of insurance, and the assured may recover from the insurer any expenses properly incurred pursuant to the clause, notwithstanding that the insurer may have paid for a total loss, or that the subject-matter may have been warranted free from particular average, either wholly or under a certain percentage.

(2) General average losses and contributions and salvage charges, as defined by this Act, are not recoverable under the suing and labouring clause.[455]

(3) Expenses incurred for the purpose of averting or diminishing any loss not covered by the policy are not recoverable under the suing and labouring clause.[456]

(4) It is the duty of the assured and his agents, in all cases, to take such measures as may be reasonable for the purpose of averting or minimising a loss."

24–112

The duty of the assured in s.78(4) is independent of any suing and labouring clause, although in practice such clauses are all but universal in marine insurance. The word "duty" is perhaps misconceived,[457] as the cases upon which s.78(4) is based appear to have turned on causation principles, in that the assured had by his inaction caused the loss.[458] There is, moreover, some difficulty in reconciling the "duty" with the ordinary principle set out in s.55(2)(a) that the assured is entitled to recover "even though the loss would not have happened but for the misconduct or negligence of the master or crew." It was suggested in *Astrovianis Compania Naviera SA v Linard (The Gold Sky)*[459] that s.78(4) was a drafting error, although it could be reconciled with s.55(2)(a) (and thereby deprived of much of its effect) by confining the duty to the assured personally and to his direct agents other than the master or crew. That view has been rejected,[460] and it now clear that s.78(4) states a rule of causation so that the assured is precluded

[453] *Kastor Navigation Co Ltd v Axa Global Risks (UK) Ltd* [2004] Lloyd's Rep. I.R. 481, confirming *Hahn v Corbett* (1824) 2 Bing. 206 and *Pesquerias v Beer* (1946) 79 Ll. L.R. 417.

[454] It had not been possible to serve a notice of abandonment, given the proximity of the two perils, but service was held to have been excused by s.62(7): see above.

[455] Contractual salvage is, however, recoverable. See *Aitchison v Lohre* (1879) 4 App.Cas. 755 and the note to s.65, above. Use of the Lloyd's Open Form, a standard document in salvage cases, renders the salvage contractual: *China Pacific SA v Food Corp of India* [1982] A.C. 939; *The Choko Star* [1989] 2 Lloyd's Rep. 42; *Seashore Marine SA v Phoenix Assurance Plc* [2002] Lloyd's Rep. I.R. 51.

[456] See, e.g. *Meyer v Ralli* (1876) 1 C.P.D. 358; *Ballantyne v Mackinnon* [1896] 2 Q.B. 455; *Field SS Co v Burr* [1899] 1 Q.B. 579; *Weissberg v Lamb* (1950) 84 Ll. L.R. 509; *FW Berk & Co v Style* [1958] 2 Lloyd's Rep. 382; *Nishna Trading Co Ltd v Chiyoda Fire and Marine Insurance Co* [1968] 3 All E.R. 712; *Ikerigi Compania Naviera SA v Palmer (The Wondrous)* [1992] 2 Lloyd's Rep. 566.

[457] *British & Foreign Marine Insurance Co v Gaunt* [1921] 2 A.C. 41 at 65; *Lind v Mitchell* (1928) 32 Ll. L.R. 70 at 75.

[458] *Kidston v Empire Marine Insurance Co* (1866) L.R. 1 C.P. 535; *Currie v Bombay Native Insurance Co* (1869) L.R. 3 C.P. 72; *Benson v Chapman* (1849) 2 H.L.C. 496; *Notara v Henderson* (1872) L.R. 7 Q.B. 225.

[459] *Astrovianis Compania Naviera SA v Linard (The Gold Sky)* [1972] 2 Lloyd's Rep. 187.

[460] *National Oilwell (UK) Ltd v Davy Offshore Ltd* [1993] 2 Lloyd's Rep. 582; *State of Netherlands v Youell* [1998] 1 Lloyd's Rep. 236.

from recovering in those rare cases where his conduct has been the proximate cause of the loss[461]; damages as such are not payable by the assured. The test is whether the relevant steps would have been taken by a reasonable person to protect his own property, i.e. a prudent uninsured.[462] The "duty" by its terms, applies only to "averting or minimising" a loss, so that any action or inaction after the loss which does not affect the degree of the loss, e.g. failing to obtain a dry dock survey of the damage[463] and failing to obtain a freezing order against the person who caused the damage,[464] is not a breach of the statutory duty. The scope of the duty is a matter for the construction of the clause. It may, for example, extend to requiring the assured to commence proceedings against a third party responsible for the loss within the statutory limitation period.[465]

The right of the assured to recover suing and labouring expenses[466] under s.78(1) is confined to the case in which there is a suing and labouring clause, although even in the absence of such a clause the weight of authority supports the proposition that an obligation to indemnify the assured for costs incurred under s.78(4) will be implied.[467] Suing and labouring expenses are not recoverable under a reinsurance agreement.[468] The expenditure must have been "properly incurred", i.e. reasonable in the circumstances. There are numerous decisions on this matter. In a policy on a vessel it is reasonable to incur expenses in towing the vessel to a place of safety,[469] and in securing her release.[470] In a policy on cargo it is reasonable to unload the goods and to repair any damage in order to avoid a total loss,[471] or to seek to recover them from an insolvent bailee,[472] but not to warehouse the goods without attempting to tranship them at a favourable rate of freight.[473] In a policy on freight the costs of storing and trans-shipping cargo so that the full amount of freight can be earned are recoverable,[474] although there cannot be recovery beyond transshipment costs if the assured has decided to retain the cargo pending repairs to his vessel.[475] Again, under a policy on an oil

[461] *National Oilwell (UK) Ltd v Davy Offshore Ltd* [1993] 2 Lloyd's Rep. 582; *State of Netherlands v Youell* [1998] 1 Lloyd's Rep. 236; *Strive Shipping Corp v Hellenic Mutual War Risks Association* [2002] Lloyd's Rep. I.R. 669; *Bayview v Mitsui Motor Corp* [2002] Lloyd's Rep. I.R. 121; *Linelevel Ltd v Powszechny Zaklad Ubezpieczen SA (The Nore Challenger)* [2005] EWHC 421 (Comm).

[462] *Integrated Container Service Inc v British Traders Insurance Co Ltd* [1984] 1 Lloyd's Rep. 154; *Stephen v Scottish Boatowners Mutual Insurance Association* [1989] 1 Lloyd's Rep. 535; *The Vasso* [1993] 2 Lloyd's Rep. 309; *Strive Shipping Corp v Hellenic Mutual War Risks Association* [2002] Lloyd's Rep. I.R. 669; *Marc Rich Agriculture Trading Ltd v Fortis Corporate Insurance NV* [2005] Lloyd's Rep. I.R. 396.

[463] *Irvine v Hine* [1950] 1 K.B. 555.

[464] *Noble Resources Ltd v Greenwood (The Vasso)* [1993] 2 Lloyd's Rep. 309.

[465] *Sitra Wood Products Pte Ltd v Royal & Sun Alliance (Singapore) Pte Ltd* [2001] 4 S.L.R. 121.

[466] Including the foregoing of sums due to the assured: *Royal Boskalis NV v Mountain* [1997] 2 All E.R. 929.

[467] *Emperor Goldmining Co v Switzerland General Insurance Co* [1964] 1 Lloyd's Rep. 348; *Netherlands Insurance Co (Est 1845) Ltd v Karl Ljungberg & Co AB* [1986] 2 Lloyd's Rep. 19. Contrast the view of Neill J. at first instance in *Integrated Container Service Inc v British Traders Insurance Co* [1981] 2 Lloyd's Rep. 460.

[468] *Uzielli v Boston Marine Insurance Co* (1884) 15 QBD 11.

[469] *St Margaret Trust Ltd v Navigators and General Insurance Co Ltd* (1949) 82 Ll. L.R. 752.

[470] *Royal Boskalis Westminster NV v Mountain* [1997] 2 All E.R. 929; *Masefield AG v Amlin Corporate Member Ltd* [2010] EWHC 280 (Comm).

[471] *Meyer v Ralli* (1876) 1 C.P.D. 358; *The Pomeranian* [895] P. 349.

[472] *Integrated Container Service Inc v British Traders Insurance Co Ltd* [1984] 1 Lloyd's Rep. 154.

[473] *Meyer v Ralli* (1876) 1 C.P.D. 358; *Wilson Bros Bobbin Co Ltd v Green* [1917] 1 K.B. 860.

[474] *Kidson v Empire Marine Insurance Co* (1866) L.R. 1 C.P. 535.

[475] *Lee v Southern Insurance Co* (1870) L.R. 5 C.P. 397.

platform, the costs of preventing the platform's collapse were recoverable, but not the costs of towing the platform to port for repairs and thereafter restoring it to its place of operations because the policy did not require the vessel to be kept in any particular places, thus rendering those costs uninsured.[476]

Expenditure flowing from a loss but not forming a direct part of mitigation costs is, therefore, outside the ambit of the clause. The following are examples of what is not covered:

(a) general average and salvage costs;
(b) the costs of successfully defending a collision action, the benefit of the proceedings being for the insurer, as such proceedings are not an insured peril[477];
(c) the costs of defending a claim by salvors[478];
(d) expenditure relating to the assured's liability, as opposed to the normal subject matter of a marine policy[479];
(e) the costs of formulating a claim against the insurers[480];
(f) in the context of a reinsurance policy, the costs incurred by a reinsured in successfully defending proceedings against its original assured (the assured not being in a position to meet the costs by reason of insolvency)[481];
(g) measures taken in anticipation of an insured peril.[482]

In addition to these specific exclusions there is a reasonableness limitation on the amount recoverable, as in a number of the decisions the courts have refused to allow expenditure beyond the amount necessary to avert or mitigate the loss. Thus, if the assured has expended large sums on mitigation, the court will determine what steps were reasonable and allow recovery based upon the cost of those steps. [483]

15. RIGHTS OF INSURER ON PAYMENT[484]

Right of subrogation

"**79.**—(1) Where the insurer pays for a total loss, either of the whole, or in the case of   **24–113**
goods of any apportionable part, of the subject-matter insured, he thereupon becomes entitled to take over the interest of the assured in whatever may remain of the subject-matter so paid for, and he is thereby subrogated to all the rights and remedies of the

---

[476] *The Nukila* [1996] 1 Lloyd's Rep. 85, reversed on other grounds [1997] 2 Lloyd's Rep. 146.
[477] *Xenos v Fox* (1868) L.R. 4 C.P. 665.
[478] *Dixon v Whitworth* (1879) 4 C.P.D. 371.
[479] *Cunard SS Co v Marten* [1903] 2 K.B. 511. This case also holds that if there are suing and labouring costs incurred in respect of both insured and insured property, there is to be an apportionment. That analysis has been rejected in Canada: *North Coast Sea Products Ltd v ING Insurance Company of Canada* 2004 B.C.C.A. 95.
[480] *Irvine v Hine* [1950] 1 K.B. 555.
[481] *Scottish Metropolitan Assurance Co Ltd v Groom* (1924) 20 Ll. L.R. 44.
[482] See *Integrated Container Service Inc v British Traders Insurance Co Ltd* [1984] 1 Lloyd's Rep. 154, which appears to contradict this proposition, although in that case it would seem that the peril had actually occurred prior to the assured's action.
[483] *Lee v Southern Insurance Co* (1870) L.R. 5 C.P. 397; *Meyer v Ralli* (1876) 1 C.P.D. 358; *Wilson Bros Bobbin Co Ltd v Green* [1917] 1 K.B. 860.
[484] See Ch.11, above.

assured in and in respect of that subject-matter as from the time of the casualty causing the loss.

(2) Subject to the foregoing provisions, where the insurer pays for a partial loss, he acquires no title to the subject-matter insured, or such part of it as may remain, but he is thereupon subrogated to all rights and remedies of the assured in and in respect of the subject-matter insured as from the time of the casualty causing the loss, in so far as the assured has been indemnified, according to this Act, by such payment for the loss."

Right of contribution

24–114   "**80.**—(1) Where the assured is over-insured by double insurance, each insurer is bound, as between himself and the other insurers, to contribute rateably to the loss in proportion to the amount for which he is liable under his contract.

(2) If any insurer pays more than his proportion of the loss, he is entitled to maintain an action for contribution against the other insurers, and is entitled to the like remedies as a surety who has paid more than his proportion of the debt."

Effect of under insurance

24–115   "**81.** Where the assured is insured for an amount less than the insurable value or, in the case of a valued policy, for an amount less than the policy valuation, he is deemed to be his own insurer in respect of the uninsured balance."

16. RETURN OF PREMIUM[485]

Enforcement of return

24–116   "**82.** Where the premium or a proportionate part thereof is, by this Act, declared to be returnable,—
        (a) If already paid, it may be recovered by the assured from the insurer; and
        (b) If unpaid, it may be retained by the assured or his agent."

Return by agreement

24–117   "**83.** Where the policy contains a stipulation for the return of the premium, or a proportionate part thereof, on the happening of a certain event, and that event happens, the premium, or, as the case may be, the proportionate part thereof, is thereupon returnable to the assured."

Return for failure of consideration

24–118   "**84.**—(1) Where the consideration for the payment of the premium totally fails, and there has been no fraud or illegality on the part of the assured or his agents, the premium is thereupon returnable to the assured.

(2) Where the consideration for the payment of the premium is apportionable and there is a total failure of any apportionable part of the consideration, a proportionate part of the premium is, under the like conditions, thereupon returnable to the assured.

(3) In particular—
        (a) Where the policy is void, or is avoided by the insurer as from the commencement of the risk, the premium is returnable, provided that there has been no fraud or illegality on the part of the assured; but if the risk is not apportionable, and has once attached, the premium is not returnable;

[485] See Ch.8, above.

(b) Where the subject-matter insured, or part thereof, has never been imperilled, the premium, or, as the case may be, a proportionate part thereof, is returnable: Provided that where the subject-matter has been insured 'lost or not lost' and has arrived in safety at the time when the contract is concluded, the premium is not returnable unless, at such time, the insurer knew of the safe arrival.

(c) Where the assured has no insurable interest throughout the currency of the risk, the premium is returnable, provided that this rule does not apply to a policy effected by way of gaming or wagering;

(d) Where the assured has a defeasible interest which is terminated during the currency of the risk, the premium is not returnable;

(e) Where the assured has over-insured under an unvalued policy, a proportionate part of the premium is returnable;

(f) Subject to the foregoing provisions, where the assured has over-insured by double insurance, a proportionate part of the several premiums is returnable: Provided that, if the policies are effected at different times, and any earlier policy has at any time borne the entire risk, or if a claim has been paid on the policy in respect of the full sum insured thereby, no premium is returnable in respect of that policy, and when the double insurance is effected knowingly by the assured no premium is returnable."

17. MUTUAL INSURANCE

Modification of Act in case of mutual insurance

"**85.**—(1) Where two or more persons mutually agree to insure each other against **24–119** marine losses there is said to be a mutual insurance.

(2) The provisions of this Act relating to the premium do not apply to mutual insurance, but a guarantee, or such other arrangement as may be agreed upon, may be substituted for the premium.

(3) The provisions of this Act, is so far as they may be modified by the agreement of the parties, may in the case of mutual insurance be modified by the terms of the policies issued by the association, or by the rules and regulations of the association.

(4) Subject to the exceptions mentioned in this section, the provisions of this Act apply to a mutual insurance."

18. SUPPLEMENTAL

Ratification by assured

"**86.** Where a contract of marine insurance is in good faith effected by one person on **24–120** behalf of another, the person on whose behalf it is effected may ratify the contract even after he is aware of a loss."

Implied obligations varied by agreement or usage

"**87.**—(1) Where any right, duty, or liability would arise under a contract of marine **24–121** insurance by implication of law, it may be negatived or varied by express agreement, or by usage, if the usage be such as to bind both parties to the contract.

(2) The provisions of this section extend to any right, duty, or liability declared by this Act which may be lawfully modified by agreement."

Reasonable time, etc, a question of fact

"**88.** Where by this Act any reference is made to reasonable time, reasonable premium, **24–122** or reasonable diligence, the question what is reasonable is a question of fact."

Slip as evidence

24–123 "**89.** Where there is a duly stamped policy, reference may be made, as heretofore, to the slip or covering note, in any legal proceeding."

Interpretation of terms

24–124 "**90.** In this Act, unless the context or subject-matter otherwise requires—
'Action' includes counter-claim and set off:
'Freight' includes the profit derivable by a shipowner from the employment of his ship to carry his own goods or moveables, as well as freight payable by a third party, but does not include passage money:
'Moveables' means any moveable tangible property, other than the ship, and includes money, valuable securities, and other documents:
'Policy' means a marine policy."

Savings

24–125 "**91.**—(1) Nothing in this Act, or in any repeal effected thereby, shall affect—
(a) The provisions of the Stamp Act 1891, or any enactment for the time being in force relating to the revenue;
(b) The provisions of the Companies Act 1862, or any enactment amending or substituted for the same;
(c) The provisions of any statute not expressly repealed by this Act.
(2) The rules of the common law including the law merchant, save in so far as they are inconsistent with the express provisions of this Act, shall continue to apply to contracts of marine insurance."

Sections 92 and 93 were repealed by the Statute Law Revision Act 1927.

Short title

24–126 "**94.** This Act may be cited as the Marine Insurance Act 1906."

19. FORM OF POLICY

24–127 "BE IT KNOWN THAT   as well in   own name as for and in the name and names of all and every other person or persons to whom the same doth, may, or shall appertain, in part or in all doth make assurance and cause   and them, and every of them, to be insured lost or not lost, at and from
Upon any kind of goods and merchandises, and also upon the body, tackle, apparel, ordnance, munition, artillery, boat, and other furniture, of and in the good ship or vessel called the   whereof is master under God, for this present voyage,   or whosoever else shall go for master in the said ship, or by whatsoever other name or names the said ship, or the master thereof, is or shall be named or called; beginning the adventure upon the said goods and merchandises from the loading thereof aboard the said ship.
upon the said ship, etc
and so shall continue and endure, during her abode there, upon the said ship, etc
And further, until the said ship, with all her ordnance, tackle, apparel, etc, and goods and merchandises whatsoever shall be arrived at upon the said ship, etc, until she hath moored at anchor twenty-four hours in good safety; and upon the goods and merchandises, until the same be there discharged and safely landed. And it shall be lawful for the said ship, etc, in this voyage, to proceed and sail to and touch and stay at any ports or places whatsoever without prejudice to this insurance. The said ship, etc, goods and merchandises, etc, for so much as concerns the assured by agreement between the assured and assurers in this policy, are and shall be valued at

Touching the adventures and perils which we the assurers are contented to bear and do take upon us in this voyage: they are of the seas, men of war, fire, enemies, pirates, rovers, thieves, jettisons, letters of mart and counterpart, surprisals, takings at sea, arrests, restraints, and detainments of all kings, princes, and people, of what nation, condition, or quality soever, barratry of the master and mariners, and of all other perils, losses, and misfortunes, that have or shall come to the hurt, detriment, or damage of the said goods and merchandises, and ship, etc, or any part thereof. And in case of any loss or misfortune it shall be lawful to the assured, their factors, servants and assigns, to sue, labour, and travel for, in and about the defence, safeguards, and recovery of the said goods and merchandises, and ship, etc, or any part thereof, without prejudice to this insurance; to the charges whereof we, the assurers, will contribute each one according to the rate and quantity of his sum herein assured. And it is especially declared and agreed that no acts of the insurer or insured in recovering, saving, or preserving the property insured shall be considered as a waiver, or acceptance of abandonment. And it is agreed by us, the insurers, that this writing or policy of assurance shall be of as much force and effect as the surest writing or policy of assurance heretofore made in Lombard Street, or in the Royal Exchange, or elsewhere in London. And so we, the assurers, are contented, and do hereby promise and bind ourselves, each one for his own part, our heirs, executors, and goods to the assured, their executors, administrators, and assigns, for the true performance of the premises, confessing ourselves paid the consideration due unto us for this assurance by the assured, at and after the rate of

IN WITNESS whereof we, the assurers, have subscribed our names and sums assured in London.

N.B.—Corn, fish, salt, fruit, flour, and seed are warranted free from average, unless general, or the ship be stranded—sugar, tobacco, hemp, flax, hides and skins are warranted free from average, under five pounds per cent, and all other goods, also the ship and freight, are warranted free from average, under three pounds per cent unless general, or the ship be stranded."

Schedule 1 to the Marine Insurance Act 1906 contains the standard form of marine policy which had been perfected in the eighteenth century. This was adopted formally in 1779. The Institute of London Underwriters, formed in 1884, established standard terms for different classes of marine insurance agreements and to be appended to them. Most important of these clauses was the exclusion of the war risks set out in the Lloyd's SG Policy, although war risks were separately insurable under the standard Institute War Clauses. The Institute clauses have on a number of occasions sought to reverse the effect of rulings made by the courts as to the meaning of the Lloyd's SG Policy. The pattern until the early 1980s was, therefore, that the Lloyd's SG Policy was adopted in conjunction with the relevant Institute clauses for the class of policy in question, the latter modifying the former in many material respects. The Lloyd's SG Policy was in 1983 replaced by simpler[486] common forms, one for Lloyd's policies and one for use by insurance companies. The modern forms are, leaving aside differences necessitated by the varying nature of the organisations concerned, identical, and simply specify that the underwriter or company (as the case may be) agrees, in consideration of the payment of the specified premium, "to insure against loss damage liability or expense" as set out in the policy. The relevant terms are contained in the appropriate Institute clauses, which will be appended to the policy.

---

[486] The old wording was criticised by judges from the time of its adoption (*Brough v Whitmore* (1791) 4 T.R. 208—"absurd and incoherent") to the date of its demise (*Amin Rasheed v Kuwait Insurance*—[1983] 2 All E.R. 84 (1—"obsolete language").

20. Rules for Construction of Policy

Lost or not lost

24–128   "**1.** Where the subject-matter is insured "lost or not lost," and the loss has occurred before the contract is concluded, the risk attaches unless, at such time the assured was aware of the loss, and the insurer was not."

From

24–129   "**2.** Where the subject-matter is insured 'from' a particular place, the risk does not attach until the ship starts on the voyage insured."

Under a marine voyage policy the risk will commence at a geographical location, whether specific or general, rather than at a particular time. Two forms of words have traditionally been used to fix the commencement of the risk: "from" a given place, or "at and from" a given place, although the policy may also be stated to attach only after the vessel has left port. The phrases "from" and "at and from" as defined by rr.2 and 3 in the Schedule to the Marine Insurance Act 1906 2 and 3 differ in that the former covers only perils encountered after the commencement of the voyage,[487] while the latter covers port risks pending the commencement of the voyage. A voyage is treated as having commenced when the vessel left her moorings in a state of readiness to undertake the voyage.[488]

At and from

24–130   "**3.**—(a) Where a ship is insured 'at and from' a particular place, and she is at that place, in good safety when the contract is concluded, the risk attaches immediately.

(b) If she be not at that place when the contract is concluded, the risk attaches as soon as she arrives there in good safety, and, unless the policy otherwise provides, it is immaterial that she is covered by another policy for a specified time after arrival.

(c) Where chartered freight is insured 'at and from' a particular place, and the ship is at that place in good safety when the contract is concluded the risk attaches immediately. If she be not there when the contract is concluded, the risk attaches as soon as she arrives there in good safety.[489]

(d) Where freight, other than chartered freight, is payable without special conditions and is insured 'at and from' a particular place, the risk attaches pro rata as the goods or merchandise are shipped; provided that if there be cargo in readiness which belongs to the shipowner, or which some other person has contracted with him to ship, the risk attaches as soon as the ship is ready to receive such cargo.[490]"

---

[487] *Sun Alliance & London Insurance Plc v PT Asuransri Dayan Mitra TBK (The No.1 Dae Bu)* [2006] Lloyd's Rep. I.R. 860.

[488] *Pittigrew v Pringle* (1832) 3 B. & Ald. 514. See also: *Hunting & Son v Boulton* (1895) 1 Com. Cas. 120; *Sea Insurance Co v Blogg* [1898] 2 Q.B. 398.

[489] See *Foley v United Fire & Marine Insurance Co of Sydney* (1870) L.R. 5 C.P. 155 (if the vessel has arrived in good safety, but is lost in port, the assured may recover under an "at and from" policy on freight).

[490] The possibility of the risk attaching pro rata, or even in advance of shipment, is only applicable to "at and from" policies. In particular, where the risk is stated to attach "from loading", actual loading of the entire cargo is required before the risk will attach (*Beckett v West of England Marine Insurance Co* (1871) 25 L.T. 739; *Jones v Neptune Marine Insurance Co* (1872) L.R. 7 Q.B. 702), unless it can be shown that the insurer was aware that the cargo on which the freight was to be earned was not to be loaded at the first-named port and that the policy contemplated the attachment of the risk from that port (*Hydarnes Steamship Co v Indemnity Mutual Marine Assurance Co* [1895] 1 Q.B. 500).

From the loading thereof

"**4.** Where goods or other moveables are insured 'from the loading thereof,' the risk   **24–131**
does not attach until such goods or moveables are actually on board, and the insurer is
not liable for them while in transit from the shore to ship."

Safely landed

"**5.** Where the risk on goods or other moveables continues until they are 'safely landed,'   **24–132**
they must be landed in the customary manner and within a reasonable time after arrival
at the port of discharge, and if they are not so landed the risk ceases."

Touch and stay

"**6.** In the absence of any further license or usage, the liberty to touch and stay 'at any   **24–133**
port or place whatsoever' does not authorise the ship to depart from the course of her
voyage from the port of departure to the port of destination."

Perils of the seas

"**7.** The term 'perils of the seas' refers only to fortuitous accidents or casualties of the   **24–134**
seas. It does not include the ordinary action of the winds and waves."

The expression "perils of the sea" has long been used to express the basic risk
accepted by a marine insurer, and is retained by the Hull Clauses as the starting
point for the insurer's liability. There is a significant body of case law, dating
back to the middle of the eighteenth century, on the meaning of this phrase,
although a large number of those cases have ceased to be of importance in the
light of the current Institute Clauses, many of which were indeed a reaction to
individual decisions of the courts.

A loss as a result of perils of the sea must be fortuitous and unexpected,[491] or
"accidental, unintended and not inevitable."[492] This follows from the very nature
of insurance, which is concerned with contingencies and possibilities as opposed
to certainties and inevitabilities.[493]

Loss caused by the ordinary action of the wind and waves is not a peril of the
sea.[494] Thus the chemical action of sea water on a cable is not a sea peril,[495] nor
is leakage from casks unfit to undertake any sea voyage.[496] Ordinary wear and
tear on a vessel and inherent vice are not perils of the sea.[497] The word
"ordinary" in the phrase "ordinary action of the winds and waves" refers to
"action" so that what is "ordinary" may vary from place to place.[498] This does
not mean, however, that insurers are liable only if the weather conditions are in
some way exceptional. It has long been settled that there can be peril of the sea

[491] *Neter v Licenses & General Insurance Co* (1944) 77 Ll. L.R. 202.
[492] *Seashore Marine SA v Phoenix Assurance plc* [2002] Lloyd's Rep. I.R. 51, per Aikens J.
[493] *Wilson, Sons & Co v Xantho (The Xantho)* (1887) 12 App.Cas. 503 at 509, per Lord Herschell.
[494] *Hagedorn v Whitmore* (1816) 1 Stark. 157; *Fletcher v Inglis* (1819) 2 B. & Ald. 315; *Lawrence
v Aberdein* (1821) 5 B. & Ald. 107; *Gabay v Lloyd* (1825) 3 B. & C. 793; *Montoya v London
Assurance Co* (1851) 6 Ex. 451; *Magnus v Buttemer* (1852) 11 C.B. 876; *Paterson v Harris* (1861)
1 B. & S. 336; *Mountain v Whittle* [1921] 1 AC. 615 *Lind v Mitchell* (1928) 32 Ll. L.R. 70; *Baxendale
v Fane (The Lapwing)* (1940) 66 Ll. L.R. 174.
[495] *Paterson v Harris* (1861) 1 B. & S. 336.
[496] *Crofts v Marshall* (1836) 7 C. & P. 597.
[497] *Samuel v Dumas* [1924] A.C. 431.
[498] *JJ Lloyd Instruments v Northern Star Insurance Co (The Miss Jay Jay)* [1985] 1 Lloyd's Rep.
264, affirming [1987] 1 Lloyd's Rep. 32.

even though the weather conditions faced by the assured were reasonably anticipated[499] and even though those conditions were not abnormal.[500] In *The Miss Jay Jay*[501] Mustill J. distinguished three classes of weather: "abnormally bad weather", which lay outside the range of conditions which the assured could reasonably have foreseen that the vessel might encounter on the voyage in question; "adverse weather", being weather which lay within the range of what could be foreseen, but at the unfavourable end of that range; and "favourable weather", namely, weather which was foreseeable but was not bad enough to be classed as adverse.

Fortuity is to be found in the unexpected consequences of the action of the wind and the waves. Thus, in *Global Process Systems Inc v Syarikat Takaful Malaysia Berhad*,[502] it was held that damage to the legs of an oil rig resulting from its unsuitability to undertake a sea voyage was not inevitable damage even though it was very likely. The definition of "perils of the sea" is concerned to remove from cover any loss which could be expected to occur from ordinary wear and tear of the insured subject matter as a result of the ordinary action of the wind and waves, so that if there was a loss in perfect conditions then there would be no cover because the action of the wind and waves was ordinary and it could not be said that there was a fortuity: there would also be a strong inference that the loss was caused by inherent vice.[503]

The negligence of the crew is immaterial,[504] and although deliberate scuttling is not a peril of the sea[505] the assured will be able to recover for barratry if the misconduct was of the crew in which the assured played no part.

The concept of a peril "of the sea" was at one time to be distinguished from a peril "on the sea", which meant that collisions with rocks and other vessels were not insured perils. The distinction between perils on the sea and perils of the sea was, however, laid to rest by the House of Lords in *The Xantho*.[506] Thus a vessel which is damaged by hitting rocks is clearly affected by a peril of the sea even if the waters are perfectly calm at the time.

---

[499] *Neter v Licenses & General Insurance Co* (1944) 77 Ll. L.R. 202.

[500] *Wilson, Sons & Co v Xantho (The Xantho)* (1887) 12 App.Cas. 503; *Thames & Mersey Marine Insurance Co v Hamilton, Fraser & Co* (1887) 12 App.Cas. 484; *Hamilton, Fraser & Co v Pandorf & Co* (1887) 12 App.Cas. 518; *Canada Rice Mills Ltd v Union Marine & General Insurance Co Ltd* [1941] A.C. 55; *Global Process Systems Inc v Syarikat Takaful Malaysia Berhad* [2010] Lloyd's Rep. I.R. 221; *Marina Offshore Pte Ltd v China Insurance Co (Singpore) Pte Ltd* [2007] 1 Lloyd's Rep. 66.

[501] *The Miss Jay Jay* [1985] 1 Lloyd's Rep. 264.

[502] *Global Process Systems Inc v Syarikat Takaful Malaysia Berhad* [2009] EWHC 637 (Comm), a point which did not arise in the Court of Appeal, [2010] Lloyd's Rep. I.R. 221. Blair J. at first instance left open the question—as had the House of Lords in *Soya GmbH Mainz KG v White* [1982] 1 Lloyd's Rep. 136—whether an inevitable loss was insurable where the assured was unaware of the inevitability.

[503] *Global Process Systems Inc v Syarikat Takaful Malaysia Berhad* [2010] Lloyd's Rep. I.R. 221.

[504] *Trinder, Anderson & Co v Thames & Mersey Marine* [1892] 2 Q.B. 114; *Mountain v Whittle* [1921] 1 A.C. 615; *Blackburn v Liverpool, Brazil and River Plate Steam Navigation Co* [1902] 1 K.B. 290; *Cohen, Sons & Co v National Benefit Assurance Co Ltd* (1924) 18 Ll. L.R. 199.

[505] *Samuel & Co v Dumas* [1924] AC 431. The position is different if the proximate cause of the loss is a peril of the seas and the conduct of the crew is designed to mitigate loss or to prevent the vessel from becoming a hazard to shipping: *Lind v Mitchell* (1928) 32 Ll. L.R. 70. Cf. *Canada Rice Mills Ltd v Union Marine & General Insurance Co Ltd* [1941] A.C. 65; *Redman v Wilson* (1845) 14 M. & W. 476.

[506] *Wilson, Sons & Co v Xantho (The Xantho)* (1887) 12 App.Cas. 503.

Damage to a vessel which is not at sea cannot be recovered under a perils of the seas clause unless the policy also covers port risks. By way of example, a vessel which is damaged by the tide while being cleaned on the beach is not to be regarded as having been subject to a sea peril.[507] Stranding is, however, a peril of the seas.[508] Failure of mechanical equipment on board is not a peril of the seas,[509] although losses caused by mechanical failure are recoverable under the Hull Clauses. The assured can recover for loss caused by perils of the seas even if the vessel was in a poor condition,[510] assuming no breach of any seaworthiness warranty[511] and that unseaworthiness was not of itself the proximate cause of the loss.[512]

The mere ingress of water is not enough to establish a loss by perils of the sea: the assured has to show that the ingress was the result of the operation of a peril of the sea.[513] The assured must demonstrate that: (a) there has been a peril of the sea, and it is not enough simply to show that the vessel has suffered unexplained loss[514]; (b) the loss was fortuitous[515]; and (c) a peril of the seas was the proximate cause of the loss.

---

[507] *Thompson v Whitmore* (1810) 3 Taunt. 227. See also *Rowcroft v Dunmore* Unreported, 1801, cited in *Thompson v Whitmore*; *Carruthers v Sydebotham* (1815) 4 M. & 5. 77: *Fletcher v Inglis* (1819) 2 B. & Ald. 315; *Phillips v Barber* (1821) 5 B. & Ald. 161; *De Vaux v J'Anson* (1839) 5 Bing. N.C. 519; *Magnus v Buttemer* (1852) ii C.B. 876.

[508] *Fletcher v Inglis* (1819) 2 B. & Ald. 315.

[509] *Thames & Mersey Marine Insurance Co Ltd v Hamilton, Fraser & Co (The Inchmaree)* (1887) 12 App.Cas. 484; *Stott (Baltic) Steamers v Marten* [1916] 1 A.C. 304.

[510] *Dudgeon v Pembroke* (1877) 2 App.Cas. 284: *Ballantyne v Mackinnnon* [1896] 2 Q.B. 455; *Marmion v Johnston* (1928) 31 Ll. L.R. 78; *Frangos v Sun Insurance Office* (1934) 49 Ll. L.R. 354; *Lloyd Instruments Ltd v Northern Star Insurance Co Ltd (The Miss Jay Jay)* [1987] 1 Lloyd's Rep. 32; *Marine Offshore Pte Ltd v China Insurance Co (Singapore) Pte Ltd* [2006] S.G.C.A. 28.

[511] See s.39, above.

[512] *Fawcus v Sarsfield* (1856) 6 E. & B. 192; *Grant, Smith & Co v Seattle Construction & Dry Dock Co* [1920] A.C. 162; *Sassoon & Co Ltd v Western Assurance Co* [1921] A.C. 561.

[513] *Cobb & Jenkins v Volga Insurance Co Ltd of Petrograd* (1920) 4 Ll. L.R. 130; *Miceli v Union Marine and General Insurance Co Ltd* (1938) 60 Ll. L.R. 275; *Brownsville Holdings v Adamjee Insurance (The Milasan)* [2000] 2 Lloyd's Rep. 458; *Lamb Head Shipping Co Ltd v Jennings (The Marel)* [1994] 1 Lloyd's Rep. 624; *Seashore Marine SA v Phoenix Assurance Plc* [2002] Lloyd's Rep. I.R. 51; *Kastor Navigation Co Ltd v Axa Global Risks (UK) Ltd* [2003] Lloyd's Rep. I.R. 266. See *566935 BC Ltd (t/a West Coast Resorts) v Allianz Insurance Co of Canada* [2006] B.C.C.A. 469, where an aged vessel which leaked badly could be kept afloat while at its moorings only by the operation of an electrical pump. The vessel sank. The British Columbia Court of Appeal found no evidence for pump failure and instead concluded that the most likely cause of the loss was a further widening of the holes in the vessel which permitted an ingress of water with which the pump could not cope: that was not a fortuitous event.

[514] *Rhesa Shipping Co v Edmunds (The Popi M)* [1985] 2 All E.R. 712; *Miceli v Union Marine and General Insurance Co Ltd* (1938) 60 Ll. L.R. 275; *Houghton and Mancon Ltd v Sunderland Marine Mutual insurance Co (The Ny-Easteyr)* [1988] 1 Lloyd's Rep. 60; *Mayban General Assurance BHD v Alstom Power Plants Ltd* [2005] Lloyd's Rep. I.R. 18; *CA Blackwell (Contracts) Ltd v Gerling General Insurance Co* [2008] Lloyd's Rep. I.R. 529; *Datec Electronic Holdings Ltd v United Parcels Service Ltd* [2008] UKHL 23; *Ide v ATB Sales Ltd* [2008] EWCA Civ 424; *Fosse Motor Engineers Ltd & Ors v Conde Nast and National Magazine Distributors Ltd* [2008] EWHC 2037 (TCC): "what is not acceptable . . . is to identify that there are, say, (as here) five possible causes, rank them each in percentage terms as possibilities and then select the possibility with the highest percentage as the probable cause. The only circumstances in which it would be legitimate would be if the highest ranked cause was the one which on all the evidence the judge was satisfied was the probable cause of the incident or loss in question." See also *Yeganeh v Zurich plc* [2010] EWHC 1185 (QB).

[515] *The Alexion Hope* [1988] 1 Lloyd's Rep. 311; *National Justice Compania Naviera SA v Prudential Assurance Co (The Ikarian Reefer)* [1995] 1 Lloyd's Rep. 455. Proof of fortuity is a "low hurdle": *Global Process Systems Inc v Syarikat Takaful Malaysia Berhad* [2009] EWHC 637 (Comm): the point did not arise on appeal.

Pirates

24–135   "**8.** The term 'pirates' includes passengers who mutiny and rioters[516] who attack the ship from the shore."

A pirate is not only a person who operates from a vessel on the high seas, as passengers who mutiny[517] and rioters who attack from the shore[518] are covered by the definition. Piracy can be committed by the crew,[519] although in practice acts of the crew are today classified as barratry. Piracy need not be successful; an attempted robbery which fails is nonetheless piracy.[520] Piracy can occur other than on the high seas, and may also take place at a port and in territorial waters,[521] but not on inland waterways.[522] Violence is a necessary element of piracy,[523] although it must relate to the theft itself rather than any attempts to escape the vessel following the theft.[524] The theft must also be for personal gain and not for political motives.[525] There is no loss by piracy if the seized subject matter is likely to be recovered on the payment of a ransom.[526]

The 2009 version of the Institute Cargo Clauses B and C do not include piracy in the list of insured marine perils.

Thieves

24–136   "**9.** The term 'thieves' does not cover clandestine theft or a theft committed by any one of the ship's company, whether crew or passengers."

The Hulls Clauses cover "violent theft by persons outside the vessel", words which are more or less equivalent to those in r.9.[527] Theft by crew members is barratry, which is also an insured peril. The word "violent" in the Hulls Clauses refers only to the manner of the theft, and it is not necessary that any individual has been harmed or threatened with harm.[528] The insured perils of piracy and violent theft from persons outside the vessel potentially cover the same ground,[529] and although theft requires an intention permanently to deprive the owner of his property piracy conducted with an intention to return property on the payment of a ransom will amount to theft still.[530]

---

[516] See Ch.25, below.

[517] *Palmer v Naylor* (1854) 10 Exch. 382; *Kleinwort v Shepherd* (1859) 1 E. & E. 447.

[518] *Nesbitt v Lushington* (1792) 4 T.R. 783.

[519] *Brown v Smith* (1813) 1 Dow. 349.

[520] *Re Piracy Jure Gentium* [1934] A.C. 586.

[521] *The Magellan Pirates* (1853) 1 Ecc. & Ad. 81 at 84; *United Africa Co v NV Tolten* [1946] P. 135n, 151; *Athens Maritime Enterprises Corp v Hellenic Mutual War Risks Association (Bermuda) Ltd (The Andreas Lemos)* [1983] 1 All E.R. 591.

[522] *Republic of Bolivia v Indemnity Mutual Marine Assurance Co Ltd* [1909] 1 K.B. 785.

[523] *Shell International Petroleum Co Ltd v Gibbs (The Salem)* [1982] Q.B. 946, 986.

[524] *The Andreas Lemos* [1983] 1 All E.R. 591.

[525] *Republic of Bolivia v Indemnity Mutual Marine Assurance Co Ltd* [1909] 1 K.B. 785; *Monetaca v Motor Union Insurance Co Ltd* (1923) 14 Ll. L.R. 48.

[526] *Masefield AG v Amlin Corporate Member Ltd* [2010] EWHC 280 (Comm). Contrast *Dean v Hornby* (1854) 3 El. & Bl. 180.

[527] For the origins of the statutory definition, see: *Harford v Maynard* (1785) 1 Park on Marine Insurance 36; *Taylor v Liverpool and Great Western Steam Co* (1874) L.R. 9 Q.B. 546. See also *Nishna Trading Co Ltd v Chiyoda Fire & Marine Insurance Co Ltd* [1969] 2 Q.B. 449.

[528] *Fabriques de Produits Chimiques v Large* [1923] 1 K.B. 203.

[529] *Bayswater Carriers Pte Ltd v QBE Insurance (International) Pte Ltd* [2005] 1 S.L.R. 69.

[530] *Masefield AG v Amlin Corporate Member Ltd* [2010] EWHC 280 (Comm) states to the contrary, but this comment disregards s.6 of the Theft Act 1968, as construed in *R. v Raphael* [2008] EWCA (Crim) 1014 (Comm).

Restraint of princes

"**10.** The term 'arrests, etc, of kings, princes, and people' refers to political or executive acts, and does not include a loss caused by riot[531] or by ordinary judicial process."   **24–137**

Barratry

"**11.** The term 'barratry' includes every wrongful act wilfully committed by the master or crew to the prejudice of the owner, or, as the case may be, the charterer."   **24–138**

A potentially important source of loss to the assured is the misconduct of the master or crew of the vessel to which the policy relates, and from the earliest times it would seem that insurers were willing to provide cover for this risk in the face of the danger of concealed conspiracy between the assured and the vessel's master. The Institute Clauses require due diligence on the part of the assured, to overcome this problem. The landmark decision was *Earle v Rowcroft*[532] which decided that barratry consisted of a fraud on the assured, even if the object was to benefit the assured.[533] Barratry is an act of fraud[534] committed by the crew against an owner or charterer by demise[535] who is not implicated in the crew's actions[536] and has no knowledge of them.[537] The insurers bear the burden of proving the assured's complicity.[538]

There are numerous cases illustrating the scope of barratry. The following broad heads of barratry would appear to be the most important: scuttling[539] or appropriation[540] of the vessel, often to disguise the fact that the crew have sold the cargo[541]; illegal trading,[542] including failure to pay port dues,[543] breaking an embargo or a blockade,[544] trading in contravention of English domestic law,[545]

---

[531] See Ch.25, below.

[532] *Earle v Rowcroft* (1806) 8 East 126.

[533] The Act appears to be in error in its drafting on this point.

[534] And not merely negligence or a failure to understand the assured's intentions: *Phyn v Royal Exchange Assurance Co* (1798) 7 T.R. 505; *Hibbert v Marten* (1808) 1 Camp. 538; *Todd v Ritchie* (1816) 1 Stark. 240. *Bottomley v Bovill* (1826) 5 B. & C. 210.

[535] *Shell International Petroleum Co Ltd v Gibbs (The Salem)* [1981] 2 Lloyds Rep. 316. If the owner is aware of the fraud but the charterer is not, the conduct remains barratrous as far as the charterer is concerned: *Vallejo v Wheeler* (1774) 1 Cowp. 143; *Soares v Thornton* (1817) 7 Taunt. 627; *Ionides v Pender* (1872) 27 L.T. 244; *Shell International Petroleum Co v Gibbs (The Salem)* [1982] 1 Lloyd's Rep. 369

[536] *Visscherij Maatschapp Nieuw Onderneming v Scottish Metropolitan Assurance Co Ltd* (1922) Ll. L.R. 579.

[537] *Stamma v Brown* (1743) 2 Str. 1173; *Pipon v Cope* (1808) 1 Camp. 434.

[538] *Continental Illinois National Bank of Chicago v Alliance Assurance Co Ltd* [1986] 2 Lloyd's Rep. 47.

[539] *Heyman v Parrish* (1809) 2 Camp. 149; *Soares v Thornton* (1817) 7 Taunt. 627; *Small v UK Marine Insurance Association* [1897] 2 Q.B. 311; *Elfie A. Issaias v Marine Insurance Co Ltd* (1923) 15 Ll. L.R 186; *Piermay Shipping Co SA v Chester (The Michael)* [1979] 2 Lloyd's Rep. 1.

[540] *Falkner v Ritchie* (1814) 2 M. & S. 290; *Brown v Smith* (1813) 1 Dow. 349; *Dixon v Reid* (1822) 5 B. & Ald. 597; *Marstrand Fishing Co v Beer (The Girl Pat)* (1936) 56 Ll. L.R. 163.

[541] *Pole v Fitzgerald* (1754) Amb. 214; *Toulmin v Anderson* (1808) 1 Taunt. 227; *Heyman v Parrish* (1809) 2 Camp. 149; *Brown v Smith* (1813) 1 Dow. 349; *Falkner v Ritchie* (1814) 2 M. & S. 290; *Hucks v Thornton* (1815) Holt N.P. 30; *Soares v Thornton* (1817) 7 Taunt. 627; *Dixon v Reid* (1822) 5 B. & Ald. 597; *Ionides v Pender* (1872) 27 L.T. 244; *Small v UK Marine Insurance Association* [1897] 2 Q.B. 311; *Compania Naviera Bachi v Henry Hosegood & Co Ltd* [1938] 2 All E.R. 189; *The Girl Pat* (1937) 56 Ll. L.R. 163.

[542] *Stamma v Brown* (1742) 2 Str. 1173; *Lockyer v Offley* (1786) 1 T.R. 252; *Havelock v Hancill* (1789) 3 T.R. 277

[543] *Knight v Cambridge* (1724) 1 Str. 581.

[544] *Robertson v Ewer* (1786) 1 T.R. 127; *Goldschmidt v Whitmore* (1811) 3 Taunt. 508.

[545] *Earle v Rowcroft* (1806) 18 East 126; *Australian Insurance Co v Jackson* (1875) 33 L.T. 286.

and smuggling[546]; and deliberate deviation by the crew.[547] It has been noted that all reported cases of barratry involve the master and not the crew alone.[548]

All other perils

24–139   "**12.** The term "all other perils" includes only perils similar in kind to the perils specifically mentioned in the policy."[549]

Average unless general

24–140   "**13.** The term 'average unless general' means a partial loss of the subject-matter insured other than a general average loss, and does not include 'particular charges'."

Stranded

24–141   "**14.** Where the ship has stranded, the insurer is liable for the excepted losses, although the loss is not attributable to the stranding, provided that when the stranding takes place the risk has attached and, if the policy be on goods, that the damaged goods are on board."

Ship

24–142   "**15.** The term 'ship' includes the hull, materials and outfit, stores and provisions for the officers and crew, and, in the case of vessels engaged in a special trade, the ordinary fittings requisite for the trade, and also, in the case of a steamship, the machinery, boilers, and coals and engine stores, if owned by the assured."

Freight

24–143   "**16.** The term 'freight' includes the profit derivable by a shipowner from the employment of his ship to carry his own goods or moveables, as well as freight payable by a third party, but does not include passage money."

Goods

24–144   "**17.** The term 'goods' means goods in the nature of merchandise, and does not include personal effects or provisions and stores for use on board.
    In the absence of any usage to the contrary, deck cargo and living animals must be insured specifically, and not under the general denomination of goods."

---

[546] *Havelock v Hancill* (1789) 3 T.R. 277; *Pipon v Cope* (1808) 1 Camp. 434.

[547] *Ross v Hunter* (1790) 4 T.R. 33; *Moss v Byrom* (1795) 6 T.R. 379; *Vallejo v Wheeler* (1774) 1 Cowp. 143; *Roscow v Corson* (1819) 1 Taunt. 684; *Mentz, Decker & Co v Maritime Insurance Co Ltd* [1910] 1 K.B. 132.

[548] *Wong Wing Fai Co SA v Netherlands Insurance Co* (1945) [1980–1981] 1 S.L.R. 242.

[549] Codifying a number of earlier cases, including: *Thompson v Whitmore* (1810) 3 Taunt. 227; *Cullen v Butler* (1816) 5 M. & S. 461; *Butler v Wildman* (1821)) 3 B. & Ald. 395; *Phillips v Barber* [1821] 5 B. & Ald. 161; *Thames & Mersey Marine Insurance Co Ltd v Hamilton, Fraser & Co (The Inchmaree)* (1887) 12 App.Cas. 484.

CHAPTER 25

WAR RISKS

1. THE INSURABILITY OF WAR AND RELATED RISKS

Private insurance. Insurers are in general reluctant to provide insurance against   **25–001**
the occurrence of war perils, particularly in time of war. This attitude is readily
understandable, for the destructiveness of war both nullifies the statistical basis
of insurance and may lead to civil disorder which itself has the effect of
increasing losses dramatically. Policies on property commonly exclude damage
resulting from war, civil commotion, nuclear explosion and the like, although
cover may be obtained on payment of a suitable premium, and insurance is in any
event commonly available for lesser forms of violence or disruption, such as riot
and strikes.

Vessels are, due to their mobility, necessarily a lesser risk in time of war, and
insurance has long been available against war and related perils as they affect
marine adventures. Aviation insurance is these days conducted on much the same
basis. The Lloyd's standard form of policy, dating back to the eighteenth century
and embodied in Sch.1 to the Marine Insurance Act 1906 covered a range of war
risks, namely "men of war, fire, enemies, pirates, rovers, thieves, takings at sea,
arrests, restraints, and detainments of all kings, princes, and people, of what
nation . . . soever." However, much of this coverage was removed from the
standard policy by the "fcs" clause, itself of some antiquity, whereby the subject
matter was warranted "free of capture and seizure". This clause has undergone
many changes over the years, the version adopted in 1983 and still in widespread
use providing:

> "Warranted free of capture, seizure, arrest, restraint or detainment, and the conse-
> quences thereof or any attempt thereat; also from the consequences of hostilities or
> warlike operations, whether there be a declaration of war or not; but this warranty shall
> not exclude collision, contact with any fixed or floating object (other than a mine or
> torpedo), stranding, heavy weather or fire unless caused indirectly (and independently
> of the nature of the voyage or service which the vessel concerned or, in the case of a
> collision, any other vessel involved therein is performing) by a hostile act by or against
> a belligerent power; and for the purposes of this warranty 'power' includes any
> authority maintaining naval, military or air forces in association with a power.
>
> Further warranted free from the consequences of civil war, revolution, rebellion,
> insurrection, or civil strife arising therefrom, or piracy."

Further exclusions relate to strikes, riots, civil commotions and the detonation of
weapons of war. The clause was revised in the International Hulls Clauses 2003,
and its provisions now exclude war, strikes, malicious acts and nuclear
explosions from standard marine cover, although certain of these risks are
capable of protection under war risks cover.

State provision for insurance of war risks. The virtual uninsurability of war   **25–002**
risks in time of war, coupled with the necessity that insurance is available to

allow commercial activity to be carried on as far as possible, has led to legislation providing for state support for insurance in time of war. Two schemes exist for this purpose. The first is contained in the Marine and Aviation Insurance (War Risks) Act 1952, which authorises the government to enter into insurance and reinsurance agreements for vessels and aircraft in time of war. The second is contained in the Reinsurance (Acts of Terrorism) Act 1993, which was passed following a terrorist bombing campaign in London which resulted in the withdrawal of terrorism cover for commercial buildings. The Act provides that any insurer who does offer terrorism cover is entitled to reinsurance by a reinsurance company, Pool Re, established for the purpose. The terms of the insurance, reinsurance and retrocession agreements are laid down in documents formulated under the scheme. Insurers adhere to the Underwriting Manual and Pool Re operates on the terms of the Reinsurance Underwriting Manual. The retrocession agreement is drafted in commercial terms, and contains the usual reinsurance provisions relating to the inspection of books, claims co-operation and the exclusion of liability for ex gratia payments by Pool Re.

2. Specific War Risks

25–003 **Causation issues.** Many of the terms discussed in the following paragraphs— for example war, civil war, civil commotion and insurrection—are not physical risks as such, but are abstract states of affairs from which loss might result following specific acts. Thus it cannot properly be said that the sinking of a merchant vessel by an enemy torpedo is proximately caused by war, although the loss is undoubtedly the result of the existence of war as a state of affairs. It has nevertheless been accepted by the courts, doubtless to make sense of policies which include or exclude (as the case may be) losses caused by war and related circumstances, that a loss arising from an act of war or carried out in furtherance of a war is proximately caused by it[1] whereas a loss which is purely ancillary—such as the hijacking of an aircraft in support of a war elsewhere—is not proximately caused by war.[2] Equally, a loss which is incurred by a premature anticipation of war, as where an exhibition is cancelled and a claim is made against business interruption insurers, is not proximately caused by war.[3] Some policies seek to modify the causation rules in war cases, and provide that any loss which is directly or indirectly caused by war is excluded.[4]

25–004 **War.** Four classes of event may constitute war within the meaning of an insurance policy. The first is war between nations. Where there has been a formal declaration of war, the existence of a war is beyond dispute. However, the English courts may recognise as war an outbreak of hostilities which is not accompanied by a declaration of war, which is not formally recognised as war by the British government, and the parties to which have maintained diplomatic relations.[5]

---

[1] *Curtis & Sons v Matthews* [1918] 2 K.B. 852 (loss of building by fire during fighting caused by war).

[2] *Pan American World Airways Inc v Aetna Casualty & Surety Co* [1975] 1 Lloyd's Rep. 77.

[3] *Office Appliance Trades Association of Great Britain v Roylance* (1940) 67 Ll. L.R. 86.

[4] *American Tobacco Co v Guardian Assurance Co* (1925) 22 Ll. L.R. 37.

[5] *Kawasaki Kisen Kabushiki Kaisha of Kobe v Banham Steamship Co Ltd* [1939] 2 K.B. 544.

Secondly, civil war is treated as war,[6] even though usually civil war is identified as a separate peril or exclusion in its own right. The leading authority on the meaning of civil war in English law is *Spinney's (1948) Ltd v Royal Insurance Co Ltd*,[7] which concerned property damage arising from the situation in Lebanon in the 1970s where there were a number of religious factions struggling for power. Mustill J., in concluding that there was no civil war, held that it was not proper to seek to ascertain the views of the British government as its view was not conclusive, and that there were three questions to be asked: (1) could it be said that the conflict was between opposing "sides"—the existence of factional disputes between the constituent elements on each side, fighting between groups which did not form the government and a struggle between a number of opposing organisations did not preclude a finding of civil war, although ultimately there had to be some polarisation of warring factions; (2) what were the objectives of the "sides"—there had to be a dispute, not necessarily over land but possibly in respect of political concessions, although there had to be something more than a "tumultuous internal upheaval" without coherence and community of purpose and which did not threaten the institutions of state; and (3) what was the was the scale of the conflict, and its effect on public order and the lives of inhabitants—there was no need for each of the parties to possess land,[8] but relevant factors included:

". . . the number of combatants; the number of casualties, military and civilian; the amount and nature of the armaments employed; the relative sizes of the territory occupied by the opposing sides; the extent to which it is possible to delineate the territories so occupied; the degree to which the population as a whole is involved in the conflict; the duration and degree of continuity of the conflict; the extent to which public order and the administration of justice have been impaired; the degree of interruption to public services and private life; the question whether there have been movements of population as a result of the conflict; the extent to which each faction purports to exercise executive, legislative, administrative and judicial powers over which it controls."

Thirdly, it has been held in the United States that guerrilla war constitutes war, although it is necessary for the guerrillas to be acting on behalf of a sovereign or quasi-sovereign government; evidence that the guerrillas are well organised will not suffice.[9]

Finally, it is an open question whether terrorist activity can be a war.[10] In *If P & C Insurance Ltd (Publ) v Silversea Cruises Ltd*[11] the Court of Appeal considered briefly whether the attacks on September 11 on the World Trade Center and the Pentagon could be regarded as "acts of war" or "armed conflict". Ward L.J. thought not, as the attacks were random, albeit part of a wider series of attacks, and the response of the US Government—the "war on terrorism"— was simply rhetorical because there was no opposing "side" against which a war could be waged. Rix L.J. was less sure, emphasising that the issue was not the meaning of these terms in a general sense, but rather their meaning in a

---

[6] *Curtis & Sons v Matthews* [1919] 1 K.B. 425 (Irish Easter uprising); *Pesqueras y Secaderos de Bacaiao de Espania SA v Beer* [1949] 1 All E.R. 845 (Spanish Civil War).

[7] *Spinney's (1948) Ltd v Royal Insurance Co Ltd* [1980] 1 Lloyd's Rep. 406.

[8] *Curtis & Sons v Matthews* [1919] 1 K.B. 425.

[9] *Pan American World Airways Inc v Aetna Casualty & Surety Co* [1975] 1 Lloyd's Rep. 77.

[10] This was assumed not to be the case in *Pan American World Airways Inc v Aetna Casualty & Surety Co* [1975] 1 Lloyd's Rep. 77.

[11] *If P & C Insurance Ltd (Publ) v Silversea Cruises Ltd* [2004] Lloyd's Rep. I.R. 696.

commercial setting. Rix L.J. also expressed the view that the mere fact that an act could be classified as one of terrorism did not prevent it from also being classified as an act of war.

The fact that a war of any of the above types exists does not mean automatically that all losses occurring as a consequence of it will be caused by it. There has to be a close link between the loss and the fact of war, and damage arising from dislocation which has been facilitated by the war will be too remote to be regarded as having been caused by war.[12] A loss which has occurred after the suspension of hostilities cannot be said to have been proximately caused by war.[13]

25–005 **Hostile acts.** The original fcs warranty excluded loss arising from "all the consequences of hostilities and warlike operations", such risks being undertaken by war risks insurers. The phrase was taken to mean that a loss was within its terms whether it was a direct or indirect consequence of a hostile or warlike operation, so that, for example, the loss of a fuel vessel in unusual tide conditions was held to be a war risk.[14] This and similar decisions proved to be unacceptable to the war risks market, as they had the general effect of casting the burden of loss by marine perils onto war risks underwriters where a vessel was engaged in, or collided with a vessel engaged in,[15] hostile or warlike operations. For this reason the wording of the clause was altered to apply only to losses "caused directly by a hostile act by or against a belligerent power". Since 1983 the relevant cover is now for losses directly caused by "hostile acts", which presumably endorses the cases on "hostilities" (meaning belligerent acts)[16] but

---

[12] *Welts v Mutual Life Insurance Co* 48 N.Y. 34 (1871) (murder of civilian by soldiers not a war loss). See also: *France. Fenwick & Co v North of England Protection and Indemnity Association* [1917] 2 K.B. 522: *Moor Line v R.* (1920) 4 Ll. L.R. 208; *Green v British India Steam Navigation Co (The Matiana)* [1921] 1 A.C. 99; *Harrison v Shipping Controller, The Inkonka* [1921] 1 K.B. 122: *Adelaide Steamship Co v R. (The Warilda)* (1923) 14 Ll. L.R. 41; *Mazarakis Brothers v Furness (Withy & Co)* (1924) 17 Ll. L.R. 113: *Clan Line Steamers v Board of Trade (The Clan Matheson)* [1929] A.C. 514: *Hain Steamship Co v Board of Trade* [1929] A.C. 534.

[13] *Schneiderman v Metropolitan Casualty Co* 220 N.Y.S. 947 (1961); *Pan American World Airways Inc v Aetna Casualty & Surety Co* [1975] 1 Lloyd's Rep. 77.

[14] *Yorkshire Dale Steamship Co v Minister of War Transport (The Coxwold)* [1942] A.C. 691. For similar decisions, see *The Caroline* (1921) 7 Ll. L.R. 56; *Hindustan SS Co v Admiralty Commissioners* (1921) 8 Ll. L.R. 230; *Ocean Steamship Co Ltd v Liverpool & London War Risks Onsurance Association (The Priam)* [1948] A.C. 243. The mere existence of a war situation was not enough to bring a loss by marine perils within the clause: *Moor Line v R.* (1920) 4 Ll. L.R. 208; *Green v British India Steam Navigation Co (The Matiana)* [1921] 1 A.C. 99; *Harrison v Shipping Controller (The Inkonka)* [1921] 1 K.B. 122.

[15] *Atlantic Transport Co v R. (The Maryland and The Pacuare)* (1921) 9 Ll. L.R. 208; *Charente SS Co v Director of Transport* (1922) 10 Ll. L.R. 514; *Liverpool & London War Risks Insurance Association v Marine Underwriters of SS Richard de Larringa* [1921] 2 A.C. 144; *Ard Coasters v Attorney General* [19211 2 A.C. 141; *Peninsular and Oriental Branch Service v Commonwealth Shipping Representative (The Geelong)* [1922] 1 K.B. 76; *R. (on the application of Fogg) v Secretary of State for Defence* [2005] EWHC 2888 (Admin). The position was different if the collision took place with a vessel not engaged in a hostility or warlike operation at the time of the collision; *Larchgrove (Owners) v R.* (1919) 1 Ll. L.R. 408; *Britain SS Co v R. (The Petersham)* [1921] 1 A.C. 99; *Admiralty Commissioners v Brynawel SS Co* (1923) 17 Ll. L.R. 89; *Marshall Bros v Furness (Withy & Co)* (1924) 18 Ll. L.R. 514; *Wynnstay SS Co v Board of Trade* (1925) 23 Ll. L.R. 278; *Wharton (Shipping) v Mortelman* [1941] 2 K.B. 283. The chain of causation was also broken if the collision was entirely the fault of the assured in failing to keep watch and nothing to do with the fact that the other vessel was engaged in a warlike operation, a distinction which was far from easy to draw; *Adelaide SS Co v R. (The Warilda)* (1923) 14 Ll. L.R. 41; *Mazarakis Bros v Furness, Withy & Co* (1924) 17 Ll. L.R. 113; *Clan Line Steamers Ltd v Board of Trade (The Clan Matheson)* [1929] A.C. 514; *Hain SS Co v Board of Trade* [1929] A.C. 534.

[16] *Britain Steamship Co v R.* [1921] A.C. 99.

excludes other matters which were previously regarded as warlike operations (such as evacuation,[17] treating casualties,[18] transporting troops[19] or refuelling or resupplying war vessels[20]). The most likely construction of the present wording is that the loss of a merchant vessel in time of war cannot be said to have been caused by a hostile act unless the vessel has been attacked by the enemy[21] or has been lost while attacking the enemy.[22] Vessels lost as the result of perils of the sea while being used for war functions ancillary to combat—hospitalisation, refuelling, supplies and the like—are now protected by marine risks cover rather than war risks cover.

Military or usurped power. This phrase formed a significant part of the old fcs warranty, but was removed in the latest revision of the Institute clauses. However, it continues to appear in other forms of policy. The phrase appears to have its origins in fire policies issued in the first quarter of the eighteenth century, and was seemingly aimed at losses resulting from treasonable acts of violence,[23] so that nothing short of armed rebellion which sought to establish a change in sovereignty would suffice.[24] Riots which did not challenge authority were thus held not to fall within this term.[25] However, more recently it has been said that[26]:

25–006

"[It is] . . . enough to show a mob in posture of war, acting with a common intent and some degree of leadership, in pursuance of aims which properly lie within the prerogative of the sovereign. [is not necessary] that events should amount to a rebellion or insurrection."

"Usurped power" does not extend to the activities of external enemies, such as bombing raids, although the term "military power" is clearly applicable to that situation.[27] Once an internal force has overthrown the government and established itself as the new regime, it is possible that property will be expropriated or otherwise lost as the result of the actions of the new government. If the court is satisfied that there has been an effective change of government, expropriation by the new government cannot amount to the exercise of "military or usurped power".[28]

---

[17] *The Geelong* [1922] 1 K.B. 766.

[18] *Adelaide SS Co v R. (No.1)* [1923] A.C. 292.

[19] *Charente Steamship Co v Director of Transport* (1922) 10 Ll. L.R. 514.

[20] *Harrison's Ltd v Shipping Controller* [1920] 1 K.B. 122; *The Maryland* (1921) 9 Ll. L.R. 208; *Eagle Oil Transport Co v Board of Trade* (1925) 23 Ll. L.R. 301; *Clan Line Steamers Ltd v Liverpool & London War Risks Insurance Association Ltd* [1943] K.B. 209; *Willis Steamship Co Ltd v United Kingdom Mutual War Risks Association Ltd (The Harborough)* (1947) 80 Ll. L.R. 398; *Athel Line Ltd v Liverpool and London War Risks Association Ltd (The Atheltemplar)* [1946] K.B. 117; *The Priam* [1948] A.C. 243.

[21] *United Scottish Insurance Co Ltd v Scottish Fishing Vessels Mutual War Risks Association Ltd (The Braconbush)* (1944) 78 Ll. L.R. 70.

[22] *Henry & M'Gregor Ltd v Martin* (1918) 34 T.L.R. 504, in which a merchant vessel damaged while ramming what its master erroneously believed to be an enemy submarine was held to have been lost in a warlike operation. This would seem also to be encompassed by the term "hostile act".

[23] See generally the judgment of Mustill J. in *Spinney's (1948) Ltd v Royal Insurance Co Ltd* [1980] 1 Lloyd's Rep. 406 at 432–433.

[24] *Drinkwater v The Corp of London Assurance* (1767) 2 Wils. K.B. 363; *Curtis & Sons v Matthews* [1919] 1 K.B. 425.

[25] *Langdale v Mason* (1780) 2 Park on Insurance 965. For a discussion as to what amounts to treason or constructive treason, see *R. v Gordon* (1781) St Tr 485.

[26] *Spinney's (1948) Ltd v Royal Insurance Co Ltd* [1980] 1 Lloyd's Rep. 406 at 435.

[27] *Rogers v Whittaker* [1917] 1 K.B. 942.

[28] *White, Child & Beney v Simmons* (1922) 11 Ll. L.R. 71.

25–007   Revolution and rebellion. The word "revolution" appears not to have been defined in the context of insurance. In *Spinney's (1948) Ltd v Royal Insurance Co Ltd*[29] Mustill J., adopting as a starting point the definition of "rebellion" in the Oxford English Dictionary, namely "organised resistance to the ruler or government of one's country; insurrection, revolt", and added to it the further requirement that the object of the rebels must be "to supplant the existing rulers or at least to deprive them of authority over part of their territory". This was found not to be the case in *Spinney's*.

25–008   Insurrection. The word "insurrection" implies an event or series of events forming part of a purely internal conflict, and it has indeed been held that action by an external enemy is not insurrection.[30] Insurrection, then, fits into the pattern of events ranging between riot and civil war. In *Spinney's*, Mustill J. expressed the opinion that an insurrection was, in the context of a war risks clause, a limited or incipient rebellion, and that a greater degree of organisation was necessary for a rebellion than for an insurrection. However, Mustill J. went on to hold that both rebellion and insurrection implied action against the existing government with a view to supplanting that government, and that, as the events in Lebanon did not demonstrate an intention by any of the various factions involved in the fighting to overthrow the government, there was no insurrection. By contrast, in *National Oil Company of Zimbabwe (Private) Ltd v Sturge*,[31] in which the policy excluded liability for insurrection, Saville J. was able to find that the intention of the Mozambique opposition party, Renamo, was to overthrow by violent means the governing party, Frelimo. Saville J. was able to rely upon Renamo's own published propaganda, all of which proclaimed this aim. It is unclear whether intentions need to be supported by objective evidence that those intentions were capable of being achieved, although it has been held in the United States that there is an insurrection where there is an intention to overthrow the government, no matter how fanciful that intention is.[32]

25–009   Civil commotion. In *Levy v Assicurazioni Generali*,[33] Luxmoore L.J., delivering the judgment of the Privy Council, defined civil commotion as follows:

> "The phrase is used to indicate a stage between a riot and a civil war.[34] It has been defined to mean an insurrection of the people for general purposes,[35] though not amounting to rebellion; but it is probably not capable of any precise definition. The element of turbulence or tumult is essential;[36] an organised conspiracy to commit civil acts, where there is no tumult or disturbance until after the acts, does not amount to civil

---

[29] *Spinney's (1948) Ltd v Royal Insurance Co Ltd* [1980] 1 Lloyd's Rep. 406 at 430.

[30] *Rogers v Whittaker* [1917] 1 K.B. 942.

[31] *National Oil Company of Zimbabwe (Private) Ltd v Sturge* [1991] 2 Lloyd's Rep. 281. See also *Tappoo Holdings Ltd v Stuchbery* [2006] F.J.S.C. 1, in which the Supreme Court of Fiji held that looting following an attempted coup in Fiji was the result of an insurrection.

[32] *Pan American World Airways Inc v Aetna Casualty & Surety Co* [1975] I Lloyd's Rep. 77 at 96.

[33] *Levy v Assicurazioni Generali* [1940] A.C. 791.

[34] Based on *Republic of Bolivia v Indemnity Mutual Marine Assurance Co Ltd* [1909] 1 K.B. 785.

[35] *Langdale v Mason* (1780) 2 Park on Insurance 965. It has subsequently been doubted whether there is any need for a general uprising: *Lindsay & Pirie v General Accident Fire and Life Assurance Corp Ltd* (1914) S.A.R. (App. D.) 574; *Spinney's (1948) Ltd v Royal Insurance Co Ltd* [1980] 1 Lloyd's Rep. 406.

[36] See *London and Manchester Plate Glass Co v Heath* [1913] 3 K.B. 411 (isolated, albeit co-ordinated, acts of vandalism not sufficient).

commotion. It is not, however, necessary to show the existence of any outside organisation at whose instigation the acts were done."

The cases demonstrate that internal and violent struggles falling short of full civil war are civil commotions: leading authorities on this matter are those in the Irish troubles at the beginning of the twentieth century,[37] and the *Spinney's* decision.[38] Consistent with these authorities is the *Republic of Bolivia*[39] case, in which Farwell L.J. expressed the view that the events in the area contested by Bolivia and by its inhabitants, who wished to set up a free republic, amounted to a civil commotion. However, the term is confined to internal conflicts.[40] In all cases, however, there has to be a causal connection between the civil commotion and the loss suffered by the assured: this requirement has been interpreted widely, and it has been held that the theft of a car for later use in a political struggle is a loss caused by civil commotion.[41]

Riot. Section 1 of the Public Order Act 1986 abolished the common law offence of riot and replaced it with a statutory offence:　　　　　　　　　　　　　　**25–010**

"(1) Where twelve[42] or more persons who are present together use or threaten unlawful violence for a common purpose and the conduct of them (taken together) is such as would cause a person of reasonable firmness present at the scene to fear for his personal safety, each of the persons using unlawful violence for the common purpose is guilty of riot.
(2) It is immaterial whether or not the twelve or more use or threaten unlawful violence simultaneously.
(3) The common purpose may be inferred from conduct.
(4) No person of reasonable firmness need actually be, or be likely to be, present at the scene.
(5) Riot may be committed in private as well as in public places."

The definition is stated by s.10 to be applicable to marine insurance cases unless the parties otherwise provide, and it is to be assumed that the definition operates also in respect of non-marine policies. Apart from the requirement for twelve or more persons, which removes the possibility that a small-scale armed robbery can constitute a riot as well as a theft,[43] the statutory definition more or less reproduces the effects of the common law. The earlier cases established that: riot refers to internal strife only, and not enemy action[44]; co-ordinated violent acts committed by individuals in different places cannot be aggregated and treated as

---

[37] *Crozier v Thompson* (1922) 12 Ll. L.R. 291; *Cooper v General Accident Fire and Life Assurance Corp Ltd* (1922) 13 Ll. L.R. 219; *Boggan v Motor Union Insurance Co* (1923) 16 Ll. L.R. 64; *Johnson & Perrott Ltd v Holmes* (1925) 21 Ll. L.R. 330.

[38] *Spinney's (1948) Ltd v Royal Insurance Co Ltd* [1980] 1 Lloyd's Rep. 406.

[39] *Republic of Bolivia v Indemnity Mutual Marine Assurance Co Ltd* [1909] 1 K.B. 785.

[40] *Rogers v Whittaker* [1917] 1 K.B. 942.

[41] *Boggan v Motor Union Insurance Co* (1923) 16 Ll. L.R. 64; *Johnson & Perrott Ltd v Holmes* (1925) 21 Ll. L.R. 330; *Cooper v General Accident Fire and Life Assurance Corporation* (1922) 13 Ll. L.R. 219. See also *Crozier v Thompson* (1922) 12 Ll. L.R. 291 (insured vehicle lost by falling into trench intended to trap government vehicles). Cf. *Grell-Taurel Ltd v Caribbean Home Insurance Co Ltd* [2002] Lloyd's Rep. I.R. 655.

[42] At common law the minimum number of persons required was three: *Field v Receiver of Metropolitan Police* [1907] 2 K.B. 853.

[43] *London and Lancashire Fire Insurance Co v Bolands* [1924] A.C. 836, the assured being unable to recover for the theft on the principle that an excluded peril takes priority over an insured peril.

[44] *Rogers v Whittaker* [1917] 1 K.B. 942.

one riot, as there is a need for an actual gathering[45]; violence which is used only to allow a group to effect their escape is not a riot[46]; and there can be a riot even if there is no noise.[47] It remains necessary for the riot to have been the proximate cause of the loss, so that there has to be some physical proximity between the riot and the loss.[48]

The Riot (Damages) Act 1886 confers a statutory right of compensation upon a person whose house, shop or building has been damaged, or any property therein has been injured, stolen or destroyed, "by any persons riotously and tumultuously assembled together". Compensation is payable by the local police authority under a procedure set out in regulations made under s.4.[49] The main significance of this Act in respect of insurance is that it confers upon an insurer who pays losses falling within the Act a right of subrogation under s.2(2) whereby an action can be brought by it against the police authority for the amount for which the latter is liable. The Act protects a body exercising public functions.[50]

The liability of a police authority under the 1886 Act is covered by a liability policy which covers sums which the authority is "legally liable to pay as damages".[51]

25–011   **Invasion.** There is no English authority on the meaning of invasion for the purposes of insurance law.[52]

25–012   **Seizure.** In *Cory v Burr*,[53] "seizure" was defined by Lord Fitzgerald as a term larger than capture, and could "reasonably be interpreted to embrace every act of taking forcible possession either by a lawful authority or by overpowering force". "Capture", by contrast, was to be regarded as confined to belligerent taking. In *Cory v Burr*, the argument that "seizure" did not extend to a non-belligerent taking was rejected, and it was held that the arrest of a vessel by revenue officers amounted to a seizure.[54] This left open the question whether a belligerent taking was itself a "seizure", given that belligerent takings were covered by the term "capture". The House of Lords, in *Kuwait Airways Corp SAK v Kuwait Insurance Co SA*,[55] answered this question in the affirmative, their Lordships ruling that the taking of aircraft on the ground in Kuwait by invading Iraqi forces amounted to a "seizure", and that both belligerent and non-belligerent acts fell within the scope of this term. Seizure is confined to a taking by or on behalf of state authorities,[56] and also requires an act which can be

---

[45] *London and Manchester Plate Glass Co v Heath* [1913] 3 K.B. 411.

[46] *Athens Maritime Enterprises Corp v Hellenic Mutual War Risks Association (Bermuda) Ltd (The Andreas Lemos)* [1983] 1 All E.R. 591.

[47] *Boggan v Motor Union Insurance Co* (1923) 16 Ll. L.R. 64.

[48] *Gliksten and Son Ltd v State Assurance Co* (1922) 10 Ll. L.R. 604.

[49] SI 1986/74.

[50] *Yard's Wood Immigration Centre Ltd v Bedfordshire Police Authority* [2000] EWCA Civ 1110.

[51] *Bedfordshire Police Authority v Constable* [2009] EWCA Civ 64.

[52] See *Spinney's* [1980] 1 Lloyd's Rep. 406, where the issue—which ultimately did not need to be resolved—was whether a foreign peace-keeping force could be regarded as invaders.

[53] *Cory v Burr* (1883) 8 App.Cas. 393.

[54] See also *Kleinwort v Shepherd* (1859) 1 E. & E. 447; *Miller v Law Accident Insurance Co* [1903] 1 K.B. 712.

[55] *Kuwait Airways Corp SAK v Kuwait Insurance Co SA* [1999] 1 Lloyd's Rep. 803.

[56] *Robinson Gold Mining v Alliance Assurance* [1906] A.C. 359; *Lozano v Janson* (1859) 2 E. & E. 160; *Powell v Hyde* (1855) 2 E. & E. 160.

described as seizure[57] which involves some form of threat,[58] so where customs authorities, acting in an unauthorised fashion, expropriated goods which they had stored in a customs compound, there was no seizure for both of these reasons.[59]

Infringement of customs or trading regulations. The phrase "customs regulations" is a narrow one, and is confined to seizure under regulations which are concerned purely with customs matters—import or export duties or licences, and the import or export of controlled drugs and other prohibited goods, substances or materials—rather than trading generally.[60] The phrase "trading regulations" is concerned with trade and not with ecological or environmental concerns, so that seizure of a vessel for unlawful fishing is not caught by the phrase.[61]

25–013

Terrorists and persons acting from a political motive. There is no insurance authority on the phrase "persons acting from a political motive".

25–014

There are various definitions of "terrorism" in English legislation. Section 1 of the Reinsurance (Acts of Terrorism) Act 1993 defines terrorism as:

"Acts of persons acting on behalf of, or in connection with, any organisation which carries out activities directing towards the over throwing or influencing, by force or violence, of Her Majesty's Government in the United Kingdom or any other government de jure or defacto."

The definition is a narrow one, and was designed to cover the threat to commercial buildings by the IRA. A more general definition is set out in s.1 of the Terrorism Act 2000. Under the latter provision,[62] the use or threat of action is terrorism if:

(1) it is designed to influence the government or to intimidate the public;
(2) it is done for the purpose of advancing a political, religious or ideological cause; and
(3) it involves any of: serious violence against a person, serious damage to property, endangering life, creating a serious risk to the health or safety of the public, or is designed to disrupt an electronic system.

This definition applies only if there is some ascertained motive for an act which inflicts loss or damage. If there is a violent act for which no responsibility has been claimed, it may be difficult to classify the act as one of terrorism, although in most cases some form of motive could doubt less be imputed to the perpetrators. In *If P & C Insurance Ltd (Publ) v Silversea Cruises Ltd*[63] the Court of Appeal was firmly of the view that the September 11 attacks in the United States were acts of terrorism. Ward L.J. thought that they could not also amount to acts of war, although Rix L.J. was more cautious on this point.

---

[57] *The Salem* [1983] 2 A.C. 375.
[58] *Kleinwort v Shepherd* (1859) 1 E. & E. 441; *Johnson v Hogg* (1883) 10 QBD 432; *Cory v Burr* (1883) 8 App.Cas. 393; *Kuwait Airways v Kuwait Insurance* [1999] 1 Lloyd's Rep. 803.
[59] *Bayview Motors Ltd v Mitsui Marine and Fire Insurance Co* [2003] Lloyd's Rep. I.R. 117.
[60] *Sunport Shipping Ltd v Atkin (The Kelovoulos of Rhodes)* [2003] Lloyd's Rep. I.R. 349 (seizure of vessel by customs authorities for drug-smuggling held to be loss arising from infringement of customs regulations).
[61] *Svenska Handelsbanken AB v Dandridge (The Alicia Glacial)* [2003] Lloyd's Rep. I.R. 10.
[62] Which applies also to subsequent legislation, the Terrorism Act 2005.
[63] *If P & C Insurance Ltd (Publ) v Silversea Cruises Ltd* [2004] Lloyd's Rep. I.R. 696.

In December 2004 the Treasury published guidance on the meaning of "acts of terrorism". The Treasury's document reads as follows:

"In applying the definition of '*acts of terrorism*' in s.2(2) of the 1993 Act in the context of the Pool Re scheme, HM Treasury would expect to be guided by the following general principles of interpretation. In view of the fact that the definition has not been the subject of a judicial decision, these principles cannot be taken as a definitive legal interpretation. Nor are they offered as legal advice to parties who might be affected by the scheme, or as any legally binding undertaking by HM Treasury to any person.

The essence of the definition is the relationship between the act in question and an '*organisation*'.

'*Organisation*'
The scope of the term '*organisation*' is not expressly limited, and includes '*any association or combination of persons*' (s.2(3)). Diffused, decentralised structures would not be excluded.

There is no defined upper or lower limit on the numbers of persons required to constitute an 'organisation', and no express minimum duration for its existence as such. However, it is clear that there would need to be a significant element of continuity before an 'organisation' could be said to exist: persons acting spontaneously in concert (without more) would be unlikely to constitute an 'organisation', although their actions might still be carried out 'on behalf of', or 'in connection with' an organisation (see further below).

'*Overthrowing or influencing a government by force or violence*'.
The activities relied on to characterise the organisation need not of themselves be forceful or violent, provided they are directed towards overthrowing or influencing a Government by such means (e.g. an organisation whose activities were limited to funding or otherwise supporting the forceful or violent acts of others would not be excluded). The Government in question may be anywhere in the world and may or may not be recognised.

'Multi-purpose' organisations are not excluded. An organisation is not excluded merely because it carries on a diverse range of activities, provided that at least some of them are directed towards the overthrow or influencing of a Government by force or violence.

The precise motive, or subject on which influence is sought to be brought to bear makes no difference: it could be political, ethnic, religious, cultural, or anything else.

The '*force or violence*' envisaged does not have to be carried out by the organisation itself, nor does it need to be successful in its aims. The fact that the organisation's activities are directed towards the end of exerting influence over a Government by force or violence would be sufficient.

The fact that an organisation's activities are not aimed at specific government targets would not be decisive: the organisation might seek to influence a Government by attacking private property, and would not fall outside the definition for this reason.

Acts '*on behalf of*' or '*in connection with*' an organisation
The act in question needs to be related to the organisation. However, the act would not need to be carried out by a member of, or person authorised by, the organisation. The fact that it was carried out by a sympathiser, or 'cell' acting independently of the organisation's hierarchy would not exclude it from the definition.

In the case of a sympathiser acting alone, the mere fact of sharing an organisation's objectives is unlikely to be sufficient. There would probably have to be something additional to connect the act to a specific organisation. However, there would be a variety of circumstances that could potentially establish a connection of the required kind."

Persons acting maliciously. Section 58 of the Malicious Damage Act 1861   **25–015**
provides that where the term "malice" falls to be construed it covers "malice
conceived against the owner of the property in respect of which it shall be
committed or otherwise", wording which has been held[64] to mean that malice can
be aimed against the property itself, or against its owner, and extends also to
random vandalism so that it is not necessary for it to be shown that the persons
causing the damage cared about, or even knew, the identity of the assured.
However, the meaning of the term "malice" can be varied by its context, and in
the phrase "persons taking part in labour disturbances or civil commotion or
malicious persons" it has been held to refer only to malicious conduct targeted
against the assured personally, as that was the tenor of the other conduct covered
by the phrase, so that a virus contained in an e-mail sent to a large number of
persons including the assured was not the act of a malicious person within the
meaning of the clause.[65]

Strikes, lock-outs and labour disturbances. These terms are commonly found   **25–016**
in insurance policies, but are rarely defined by them. The courts might well look
for guidance to the statutory definitions of "strike" and "lock-out" which appear
in s.235 of the Employment Rights Act 1996. These are laid down primarily for
the purpose of computing the continuity of an employee's employment and thus
not necessarily of general application, but they might nevertheless be persuasive
in insurance cases. The term "lock-out" means:

(a) the closing of a place of employment; or
(b) the suspension of work; or
(c) the refusal by an employer to continue to employ any number of persons
    employed by him in consequence of a dispute, done with a view to
    compelling those persons, or to aid another employer in compelling
    persons employed by him to accept terms or conditions of or affecting
    employment.

The term "strike" means:

(a) the cessation of work by a body of persons employed acting in combina-
    tion; or
(b) a concerted refusal or a refusal under a common understanding of any
    number of persons employed to continue to work for an employer in
    consequence of a dispute, done as a means of compelling their employer
    or any person or body of persons employed, or to aid other employees, in
    compelling their employer or any employed person or body of employed
    per sons, to accept or not to accept terms or conditions of or affecting
    employment.

Strikes cover generally insures against physical loss and delay. Unless the policy
specifically so provides, claims for loss of market consequent upon delay are
excluded from cover, in line with the general principle that consequential losses
are excluded.[66]

---

[64] *Strive Shipping Corp v Hellenic Mutual War Risks Association (Bermuda) Ltd* [2002] Lloyd's
Rep. I.R. 669.
[65] *Tektrol Ltd v International Insurance Co of Hanover Ltd* [2006] Lloyd's Rep. I.R. 38.
[66] *Lewis Emanuel & Son Ltd v Hepburn* [1960] 1 Lloyd's Rep. 304.

INDEX

"Abandonment"
abandoned property, 24–096
acceptance, 24–088, 24–089, 24–093, 24–096
concept, 24–091
consequences, 24–095
definition, 11–066
effect, 24–090, 24–096
equitable lien, 24–089
freight clauses, 24–095
fundamental mistake, 24–089
insurers
    multiple insurers, 24–094
    rights, 24–093—24–095
irrevocable, 24–088
loss
    actual total loss, 24–092
    constructive total loss, 11–067, 24–088, 24–089, 24–092, 24–094
    measure of loss, 11–067
    partial loss, 24–088
    total loss, 11–066, 11–067, 24–088
negligence, 24–096
non-marine insurance, 11–067
notice of abandonment, 9–002, 10–001, 11–067, 24–088, 24–089, 24–092—24–094, 24–096
proprietary rights, 24–095
remuneration, 24–095
requirements, 24–092
salvage
    contracting out, 24–097
    expenses, 24–088
scrap value, 11–067
subrogation, distinguished, 11–066
transhipment, 24–095
underinsurance, 11–068

Acceptance
see also **Formation of contract**
counter offers, 1–024
insured persons, 1–026
insurers, 1–024, 1–025
marine insurance, 24–043
notification, 1–025
reasonable period, 1–029
silence as acceptance, 1–025

Accident insurance
see also **Accidents**
benefits, 18–002
bodily injury, 18–059
causation, 18–049, 18–040, 18–042, 18–060
contingency insurance, 1–009
disability, 18–002
disablement
    benefits, 18–058
    causation, 18–055

Accident insurance—*cont.*
disablement—*cont.*
    health checks, 18–054
    loss of sight, 18–056
    meaning, 18–054
    medical treatment, 18–057
    mitigation, 18–054
    occupational provisions, 18–054
disclosure, 18–003
discrimination, 6–051
double insurance, 6–058
fixed period, 18–002
fixed sum payments, 18–002, 18–004
general business, 18–002
injury, 18–002
insurance policies
    express exclusions, 18–044
    predominant purpose, 18–043
    pre-existing disability, 18–044
    specified activities, 18–043
    specified purposes, 18–043
    utmost good faith, 18–044
insured person's conduct
    accidental means, 18–049
    accidental result, 18–049
    calculated risk, 18–049
    causation, 1–049
    fortuitous cause, 18–049
    imminent danger, 18–049
    insolvency, 18–061
    intoxication, 18–053
    negligence, 18–051
    risk of serious injury, 18–049
    self-inflicted injury, 18–049
    third party act or omission, 18–052
    wilful exposure to risk, 18–050
mental injury, 18–059
nervous shock, 18–059
notice requirements, 18–002
renewal, 18–003
risk, 5–030, 5–031
sickness insurance, distinguished, 18–002
third party accidents, 18–002
time policies, 18–002
tortfeasors, 18–002
violent, external and visible means
    external, 18–047
    meaning, 18–045
    violent, 18–046
    visible, 18–048
voyage policies, 18–002

Accidents
causation, 18–040, 18–042
definition, 18–040
diseases excluded, 18–042
fortuity, 18–041, 18–042

Accidents—*cont.*
Green card system, 22–084
health and safety at work, 18–040
indemnities, 5–042
individual loss, 10–033
intended consequences, 5–042
limitations, 10–033
meaning, 5–042, 10–033
motor insurance 22–084
natural causes, 18–042
negligence, 5–048
personal injury, 18–040
recklessness, 5–042
Administration
see also **Liquidation**
administration orders, 16–013
administrators, 16–013
applications, 16–013
assets, 16–013
assignment of debts, 16–013
company rescue, 16–013
EU law, 16–013
legislation, 16–013
restructuring, 16–013
set-off, 16–013
"After the event insurance"
claims procedure, 23–034
costs, 23–035, 23–036
disclosure, 23–039
insurance premiums, 23–034, 23–035,
23–038, 23–039
non-standard cases, 23–039
reasonableness, 23–036—23–039
security for costs, 23–041
specific claims, 23–034
Agency
see also **Agents**
agreements, 15–001
attribution of knowledge
agent to insure, 6–037
companies, 6–038
concept, 6–036
fraud, 6–039
breach of contract, 15–009
disclosure
agent to insure, 6–037, 6–040—6–042,
6–055
breaches, 6–044
damages, 6–044
fraud, 6–043, 6–055
imputation of knowledge, 6–036
misrepresentation, 6–055
non-disclosure, 6–035
renewal, 6–055
scope, 6–040, 6–042, 6–055
goods, 4–021
estoppel, 15–001
false statements, 6–035
fraud, 6–039, 6–043, 6–044, 6–055, 15–004
illegality, 5–046
inducement, 6–035
insurable interests, 4–019

Agency—*cont.*
insurance brokers
agent of assured, 15–027, 15–035,
15–036, 15–042, 15–043
breach of duty, 15–028
conflicts of interest, 15–028, 15–033
disclosure, 15–028
dual agency, 15–028
duties to underwriters, 15–028
reinsurance, 15–028
insurance premiums, 8–003, 15–014
life insurance, 4–021
marine insurance, 4–021
materiality, 6–035, 6–036, 6–037, 6–040,
6–041, 6–055
ratification, 4–022, 4–023
property insurance, 4–021
protected interests, 4–020
ratification
effect, 15–003
knowledge of circumstances, 15–003
liability, 15–009
marine insurance, 15–003
unauthorised conduct, 15–003
undisclosed principal, 15–003
regulation
authorisation, 15–011
background, 15–010
conduct of business, 15–012
EU law, 15–010
insurance brokers, 15–011
legislation, 15–010
regulated activities, 15–011
third party rights, 15–009
transfer of agency, 15–002
undisclosed principal, 4–021, 15–006,
15–009
vicarious liability, 5–046, 6–044
Agents
see also **Insurance agents**
authority
actual authority, 15–001, 15–013, 15–016
apparent authority, 15–001
breach of condition, 15–016
breach of warranty, 15–018
estoppel, 15–014, 15–017, 15–018
generally, 15–013
insurance premiums, 15–014
insurer's liability, 15–013
issue of policy, 15–015
ostensible authority, 15–001, 15–013
proposal forms, 15–019
receipt of information, 15–017
renewal, 15–016
trade usage, 15–001
unauthorised conduct, 15–003
usual authority, 15–001
waiver, 15–016
withdrawal, 15–001
breach of contract, 15–009
duties, 15–007
duty of care, 15–009
fraud, 6–039, 6–043, 6–044, 6–055, 15–004
imputation of knowledge, 15–005

Agents—*cont.*
 insurance premiums, 8–003
 liabilities, 4–024, 15–009
 rights, 4–024, 15–008
Aggravated vehicle-taking
 property insurance, 19–050
Applicable law
 absence of express/implied choice of law
  characteristic performance, 2–041—2–043
  centre of gravity test, 2–040, 2–044
  common law, 2–040
  country of closest connection, 2–041,
   2–042, 2–043
  differing applicable laws, 2–044
  Giuliano and Lagarde Report, 2–041
  habitual residence, 2–042
  hybrid policies, 2–044
  intention, 2–040, 2–050
  life insurance, 2–040
  Lloyds, 2–043
  marine insurance, 2–040
  multiple insurers, 2–043
  place of business, 2–040, 2–041, 2–043
  presumptive rules, 2–042
  reinsurance, 2–040, 2–041, 2–042
  Rome I Regulation, 2–042, 2–043
  Rome Convention, 2–041, 2–042, 2–043
  supply of services, 2–041, 2–042
 acts committed abroad, 2–061, 2–062
 arbitration clauses, 2–034, 2–052, 2–053
 assignment, 2–060
 cause of action, 2–062
 choice of law agreements
  choice of law clauses, 2–027,
   2–029—2–031, 20–033—2–035
  co-insurers, 2–031
  express agreements, 2–028–02–030
  floating choice of law, 2–032, 2–033
  incorporation of foreign law, 2–035
  party autonomy, 2–028
  restrictions, 2–030
  Rome I Regulation, 2–028—2–030, 2–033
  Rome Convention, 2–028—2–030
  service of suit clauses, 2–033
  validity, 2–029
 common law, 2–016
 consumer insurance, 2–024
 consumer risks
  choice of law, 2–045
  consumer protection, 2–045
  habitual residence, 2–045
  Rome I Regulation, 2–045
  Rome Convention, 2–045
  supply of services, 2–045
 contribution, 2–060
 determination, 2–027
 duress, 2–055
 employment claims, 2–061
 EU law, 2–017, 2–018, 2–022
 formation of contract
  arbitration clauses, 2–052, 2–053
  choice of law clauses, 2–052
  consumer contracts, 2–054
  differing applicable laws, 2–052

Applicable law—*cont.*
 formation of contract—*cont.*
  express provisions, 2–052
  formalities, 2–054
  habitual residence, 2–053, 2–054
  illegality, 2–057
  jurisdiction clauses, 2–052
  putative applicable law, 2–051—2–053
  reinsurance, 2–051, 2–052
  Rome I Regulation, 2–051—2–054
  validity, 2–052, 2–054
 illegality
  formation of contract, 2–057
  law of forum, 2–057, 2–058
  lex loci contractus, 2–057
  lex loci solutionis, 2–057
  performance, 2–058
  place of performance, 2–057, 2–058
  public policy, 2–057
 implied choice of law
  arbitration clauses, 2–038
  common law, 2–036
  follow London clauses, 2–039
  freedom of choice, 2–036
  general principles, 2–036
  Giuliano and Lagarde Report, 2–036
  jurisdiction clauses, 2–037
  reinsurance, 2–036
  Rome I Regulation, 2–036, 2–037
  Rome Convention, 2–036, 2–037
 insurance risks, 2–021—2–024, 2–027
 interest, 2–059
 interpretation, 2–050
 lex loci delicti, 2–061, 2–062
 limitation periods, 2–056
 non-contractual claims, 2–061—2–065
 non-large risks
  compulsory insurance, 2–047
  country of closest connection, 2–048
  EU law, 2–046, 2–048
  express choice of law, 2–047
  life insurance, 2–048
  Rome I Regulation, 2–046—2–048
  situation of risk, 2–047
  state of commitment, 2–048
 performance
  defective, 2–050
  manner of performance, 2–050
  place of performance, 2–050
 place of business, 2–022
 procedural matters, 2–050
 product liability, 2–065
 reinsurance, 2–021, 2–050
 renvoi, 2–049
 restitution, 2–061
 Rome II Regulation, 2–061, 2–065
 Scots law, 2–050
 set-off, 2–060
 subrogation, 2–060, 2–061, 2–065
 substantive matters, 2–050
 tort
  extent of liability, 2–065
  general rule, 2–061, 2–062, 2–064
  misrepresentation, 2–063

Applicable law—*cont.*
tort—*cont.*
negligence, 2–063
personal injury, 2–063
property damage, 2–063
variation, 2–033
Arbitration
arbitration clauses, 2–001, 2–034, 2–038,
3–015, 17–016, 17–018, 21–053,
21–054
International Chamber of Commerce rules,
2–034
jurisdiction, 2–001
UNCITRAL rules, 2–034
Assignment
applicable law, 2–060, 14–030
insurance policies
assignment subject to equities, 14–027,
14–029
competing assignments, 14–028
conditions, 14–023
consent, 14–023, 14–024, 14–029
contemporaneous assignment, 14–023,
14–025
defences, 14–027
effects of assignment, 14–027
equitable assignments, 14–026, 14–029
form of assignment, 14–023, 14–026
future interests, 14–029
legal assignments, 14–026, 14–027
legislation, 14–026
marine insurance, 24–074, 24–075
partial interests, 14–029
postponement, 14–023
public policy restrictions, 14–029
life insurance
conditions, 18–022
effect, 18–022
form, 18–023
gift, 18–022
insurable interests, 18–005
legislation, 18–023
limitations, 18–022
method, 18–023
mortgage, 18–022
notice requirements, 18–023
payment of proceeds, 18–024
place of business, 18–023
sale, 18–022
settlement, 18–022
third parties, 18–005
marine insurance
beneficial interest, 24–074
generally, 24–074
indorsement, 24–074
lack of insurable interest, 24–075
method, 24–074
partial loss, 24–074
post-loss assignment, 24–074
pre-loss assignment, 24–074
timing, 24–074
proceeds
counterclaims, 14–029
general principle, 14–029

Assignment—*cont.*
proceeds—*cont.*
public policy, 14–029
voluntary assignment, 14–022
"Assured"
see **Insured persons**
Authority
see also **Agency**
actual authority, 15–001, 15–013, 15–016
apparent authority, 15–001
breach of condition, 15–016
breach of warranty, 15–018
estoppel, 15–014, 15–017, 15–018
generally, 15–013
insurance premiums, 15–014
insurer's liability, 15–013
issue of policy, 15–015
ostensible authority, 15–001, 15–013
proposal forms, 15–019
receipt of information, 15–017
renewal, 15–016
trade usage, 15–001
unauthorised conduct, 15–003
usual authority, 15–001
waiver, 15–016
withdrawal, 15–001
Average
see **General average**
Avoidance
avoidance ab initio, 6–075, 6–077
declaratory relief, 6–075
divisibility of policy, 6–076
effect, 6–075
good faith, 6–077
inducement, 6–033, 6–034
limitation periods, 6–078
loss of right, 6–077, 6–087
materiality, 6–033, 6–034
misrepresentation, 6–075
non-disclosure, 6–075
return of premium, 8–023, 8–025, 8–026
settlement, 10–055
unjustified, 6–075
Bailment
duty of care, 19–011
goods, 19–007
insurable interests, 19–010
insurance policies
goods, 19–011, 19–012
liability insurance, 19–012
nature of policy, 19–012
proceeds, 19–013
recovery, 19–012, 19–013
liability insurance, 20–006
Barratry
meaning, 24–138
Beneficiaries
insurable interests, 19–030
Betterment
damage to property, 10–031
deductions, 10–031
marine insurance, 10–031
reinstatement, 10–044
tort principles, 10–031

Bottomry
insurable interests, 24–024
Brokers
see **Insurance brokers**
Brussels Regulation
see also **Jurisdiction**
generally, 2–001
insurance rules, 2–009, 2–015
insured persons' claims, 2–011
insurers' claims, 2–010
jurisdictional rules, 2–008
liability insurance, 2–013, 2–014
property insurance, 2–012
third party claims, 2–014
Burglary
burglar alarms, 19–048
CCTV systems, 19–048, 19–058
definition, 19–051
electronic information, 19–051
forcible and violent entry, 19–046
occupancy requirement, 19–047
valuable items, 19–053
Business interruption insurance
external events, 23–042
financial loss, 23–042
gross profits basis, 23–042
indemnity period, 23–041
limitations, 23–042
purpose, 23–042
Choice of law
see also **Applicable law**
choice of law clauses, 2–027,
2–029—2–031, 20–033—2–035
co-insurers, 2–031
express agreements, 2–028–02–030
floating choice of law, 2–032, 2–033
incorporation of foreign law, 2–035
party autonomy, 2–028
restrictions, 2–030
Rome I Regulation, 2–028—2–030, 2–033
Rome Convention, 2–028—2–030
service of suit clauses, 2–033
validity, 2–029
Claims
see **Insurance claims**
Claims handling
see also **Financial Ombudsman Service**
breach of warranty, 12–017, 12–022
causation test, 12–024
change of risk, 12–021
change of terms, 12–020
commercial customers, 12–017
compensation, 12–018
consumers, 12–017
continuing good faith, 12–021
convictions, 12–019
disclosure, 12–021
electronic claims handling, 9–001
forgery, 12–029
fraudulent claims, 12–029
insurer's rights, 12–018
non-disclosure, 12–017—12–020
previous losses, 12–019
principles, 12–017

Claims handling—*cont.*
renewal, 12–020
uninsured drivers, 22–072
utmost good faith, 6–129
"Claims Agreement and Settlement Service"
electronic claims handling, 9–001
Co-insurance
breach of condition, 14–011, 14–014
composite policies, 14–003, 14–004, 14–011
creation
authorisation, 14–007, 14–008
parties insuring on behalf of himself/
others, 14–006
parties insuring together, 14–005
differing interests, 14–003
enforcement, 14–019—14–021
identical interests, 14–003
insurable interests, 14–004
insurance broker's lien, 14–016
joint and several liability, 14–003
joint policies, 14–003, 14–004, 14–011
noting
function, 14–020
legal protection, 14–010
partnerships, 14–003
payment under policy, 14–011, 14–015
subrogation, 14–018
termination, 14–011, 14–017
third party enforcement, 14–009, 14–010
unnamed co-assured
direct enforcement, 14–019
indirect enforcement, 14–020
third parties, 14–019, 14–020
utmost good faith, 14–011, 14–012
wilful misconduct, 14–011, 14–013
Companies
accounting requirements, 1–005
financial probity, 1–005
insolvency, 1–010
profit motive, 1–005
transfer of risk, 1–010
Company voluntary arrangements
composition, 16–014
effect, 16–014
moratorium, 16–014
Competition law
abuse of dominant position, 13–044
block exemptions, 13–046
distortion of competition, 13–044
EU law, 13–045, 13–046
legislation, 13–044
market investigations, 13–044
mergers, 13–045
Complaints
see also **Claims handling**
adjudicators, 12–008, 12–009
complainants, 12–016
complaints handling, 12–066
consumers, 12–006
contradictory evidence, 12–003
dismissal, 12–012
eligibility, 12–015
evidence, 12–011
insurance complaints, 12–001

Complaints—*cont.*
internal complaints procedure, 12–001, 12–005
judicial proceedings, 12–012
judicial review, 12–013
limitation periods, 12–007
ombudsman's involvement, 12–010
procedure, 12–008
referrals, 12–013
termination, 12–012
time limits, 12–006
Compulsory insurance
carriage by sea, 20–005
EU law, 20–005
legislation, 20–001, 20–004
nuclear installations, 20–002
oil pollution, 20–004
professional indemnity insurance, 20–003, 20–006
shipowners, 20–005
Concurrent causes
concurrent proximate causes, 5–034
excluded perils, 5–034
insured perils, 5–033, 5–034
meaning, 5–032
proximity rule, 5–033
uninsured perils, 5–033
Conditions
see also **Conditions precedent**; **Warranties**
ancillary terms, 7–006, 7–008
assignment, 14–023
breach of condition
agency, 15–016
co-insurance, 14–011, 14–014
conditions precedent, 7–004, 7–012, 7–018
motor insurance, 22–037
waiver, 7–018—7–020, 15–016
fidelity insurance, 23–026
fundamental conditions, 7–006
insurance premiums, 7–006
inception of risk, 7–003
liability insurance, 20–037, 20–039
repudiation, 7–005, 7–006, 7–008
subject matter, 7–002
Conditions precedent
application, 7–004
attachment of risk, 7–003, 7–028
breach of condition, 7–004, 7–012, 7–018
claims conditions, 9–003, 9–004
compliance, 7–003
consumer insurance, 7–004
creation, 7–011—7–015, 9–004
enforcement, 7–004
general clauses, 7–014
insurer's liability, 7–004
interpretation, 7–016
liability insurance, 20–037, 20–039
unfair contract terms, 7–004
validity of policy, 7–003, 7–028
waiver, 7–003
warranties, 7–028
Conduct of business
see also **Insurance contracts**

Conduct of business—*cont.*
advertising, 13–026
agency, 15–012
authorisation
authorisation offences, 13–007
process, 13–021
cancellation rights, 13–026
commercial customers, 13–026
complaints handling, 13–026
consumers, 13–026
control over individuals, 13–027
criminal sanctions, 13–026
disciplinary measures, 13–031
electronic communications, 13–026
enforcement powers, 13–029
EU law, 13–019
Financial Services Authority, 13–028
foreign risks, 13–019
general business. 13–009
head office, 13–019
Insurance Prudential Rules, 13–028
legislation, 13–007
long-term business, 13–010
management controls, 13–027, 13–028
meaning, 13–018
misleading advice, 13–027
misleading information, 13–026
offshore insurers, 13–019
provision of information, 13–030
registered office, 13–019
reporting requirements, 13–027
UK-based business, 13–019
unauthorised insurers, 13–020
withholding information, 13–027
Conflict of laws
see **Applicable law**; **Jurisdiction**
Consequential loss
forms, 10–019
insurance brokers, 15–047
unvalued policies, 10–021
valued policies, 10–020
"Consumer insurance"
see also **Consumer Insurance (Disclosure and Representatives) Bill 2009**
applicable law, 2–024
contracts of insurance, 1–018
obligations, 1–022
Consumer Insurance (Disclosure and Representatives) Bill 2009
agency, 6–139
basis clauses, 6–140
contribution principle, 6–138
duty of disclosure, 6–136
intermediaries, 6–139
misrepresentation, 6–137, 6–138
recklessness, 6–138
special cases, 6–141
subrogation, 6–138
warranties, 6–134
Contingency insurance
ascertained net loss, 23–033
exclusivity provision, 23–033
revenue gap, 23–033

Contingency insurance—*cont.*
shortfall contingency insurance, 23–033
Contra proferentem
see also **Interpretation**
ambiguity, 3–010
applications for insurance, 3–010
exclusion clauses, 3–010
insured risk, 3–010, 5–004
obligations on insured persons, 3–010
unfair contract terms, 3–018
Contract terms
see also **Conditions**; **Formation of contract**
breach
ancillary terms, 7–006, 7–008
bare conditions, 7–009
basic conditions, 7–009
burden of proof, 7–017
damages, 7–008, 7–009
late claims, 7–008
legal position, 7–010
repudiation, 7–008, 7–009
subrogation rights, 7–008
waiver, 7–018—07–020
breach of condition
agency, 15–016
co-insurance, 14–011, 14–014
conditions precedent, 7–004, 7–012,
7–018
motor insurance, 22–037
waiver, 7–018—7–020, 15–016
cancellation rights, 13–026
fundamental terms, 7–006
innominate terms, 7–001, 7–007, 7–008
interpretation, 7–001
reinsurance
advance of insurance, 17–005
arbitration clauses, 17–016, 17–018
agency, 17–005
back to back cover, 17–014
claims control clauses, 17–025
claims cooperation clauses, 17–025
conditions precedent, 17–025
dispute resolution, 17–016
duration clauses, 17–014
express terms, 17–011
honourable engagement clauses, 17–016
implied terms, 17–013
incorporation, 17–012
inspection clauses, 17–015, 17–026
insurance brokers, 17–005
interpretation, 17–014
loss, 17–017
ultimate net loss clause, 17–017
unilateral contracts, 17–005
utmost good faith, 17–006—17–010
void for uncertainty, 17–016
waiver, 17–008, 17–009
warranties, 17–014
unfair contract terms, 3–018, 7–004
warranties
development, 7–029
generally, 7–001
interpretation, 7–031
materiality, 7–030

Contract terms—*cont.*
warranties—*cont.*
misrepresentation, 7–031
modification, 7–031
nature of clause, 7–029
qualification, 7–029
subject of warranty, 7–029
Contractors
insurable interests, 19–032
insurance policies
all risks policies, 19–032
co-insurance, 19–032
entire works, 19–032
sub-contractors, 19–032
subrogation, 19–032
Contribution
amount of contribution
calculation, 11–061
common liability method, 11–062
concurrent policies, 11–061, 11–062
independent liability test, 11–062
marine insurance, 11–062
maximum liability rule, 11–062
non-concurrent policies, 11–061, 11–063
applicable law, 2–060
contribution principle, 11–052
defences
date of loss, 11–058
post-loss, 11–059
voluntary payments, 11–060
double insurance, 11–046, 11–052
financial limits, 11–057
liability insurance, 20–011
modifications, 11–064
mortgage indemnity policies, 19–025
overlapping policies, 11–054, 11–056
similar elements
insurable interests, 11–054
insured persons, 11–054
period of cover, 11–055
same scope, 11–056
subject matter, 11–053, 11–054, 11–061
subrogation
distinguished, 11–052
subrogation rights, 11–065
Convictions
age of conviction, 6–048
duty of disclosure, 6–048
materiality, 6–048
previous convictions, 6–048
Costs
Civil Procedure Rules, 20–056
claimant's costs, 20–055, 20–056
contribution, 20–052
costs orders, 20–055
defence costs, 20–044, 20–047
entitlement, 10–028
indemnity basis, 10–028
insured claims, 20–052
liability insurance
advance funding, 20–049
apportionment, 20–050, 20–052
averting liability, 20–013
co-defendants, 20–052

Costs—*cont.*
  liability insurance—*cont.*
    defendants, 20–052
    discretion to defend, 20–051
    duty to defend, 20–049, 20–050
    entitlement, 20–047, 20–050
    excesses, 20–054
    investigating liability, 20–014
    limitations, 20–048
    manipulative pleading, 20–049
    option to pay, 20–049
    repayment, 20–049, 20–053
    separate causes of action, 20–047
    uninsured claims, 20–052
  limit of indemnity, 20–047
  marine insurance, 20–047
  penalties, 10–028
  standard basis, 10–028
  subrogation, 20–047
  third party claims, 20–049, 20–050, 20–052, 20–055
  wasted costs, 15–046
Creditors
  indemnities, 23–030
  insurable interests, 19–029
  sureties, 23–019
  third party claims, 21–001
Criminal conduct
  culpability, 5–046
  mens rea, 5–046
  misconduct, 5–043, 5–046
Damages
  entitlement, 6–079
  exemplary damages, 20–015
  in lieu of avoidance, 6–098
  in lieu of rescission, 6–081
  liability insurance, 20–015
  misrepresentation, 6–080
  motor insurance, 22–012
  negligence, 6–079
  third party claims, 21–001
"Declaration policies"
  attachment of risk, 6–117
  binders, 6–117
  directors and officers liability insurance, 20–081
  effect, 6–117
  insurance brokers, 6–117
  insured persons, 6–117
  non-obligatory cover, 6–118
  obligatory cover, 6–118
  open cover, 6–117—6–121
  utmost good faith, 6–120
Declaratory orders
  availability, 9–053
  Civil Procedure Rules, 9–053, 9–054
  counter claims, 9–053
  effect, 9–053
  international aspects, 9–054
  jurisdiction, 9–054
  negative declaratory relief, 9–054
Defective title
  property insurance, 19–054

Directors
  conflicts of interest, 20–078
  declaration of interests, 20–078
  exercise of powers, 20–078
  good faith, 20–078
  independent judgment, 20–078
  liability, 20–078
  reasonable care, skill, judgment, 20–078
  statutory duties, 20–078
Directors' and officers' liability insurance
  breach of duty, 20–078
  claims, 20–089
  company loans, 20–079
  defence costs, 20–078, 20–079
  duty of care, 20–078
  fiduciary duties, 20–078
  indemnities, 20–079
  insurance policies
    capacity, 20–083
    claims made policies, 20–084
    composite policies, 20–081
    conditions, 20–088
    declaration policies, 20–081
    directors and officers 20–082
    excluded perils, 20–086
    exclusions, 20–080, 20–087
    indemnities, 20–080
    insured perils, 20–085
    losses, 20–084
    maximum level of indemnity, 20–084
    per claim deductible, 20–084
    personal liability, 20–080
    policyholders, 20–081
    privity of contract, 20–081
    risk, 20–080
  legislation, 20–078
  reimbursement, 20–079
  right to insure, 20–079
  statutory duties, 20–078
  third party indemnity provision, 20–079
Disclosure
  see also **Utmost good faith**; **Valuation**
  accident insurance, 1–003
  acquittals, 6–050
  agency
    agent to insure, 6–037, 6–040—6–042, 6–055
    breaches, 6–044
    damages, 6–044
    fraud, 6–043, 6–055
    imputation of knowledge, 6–036
    misrepresentation, 6–055
    non–0disclosure, 6–035
    scope, 6–040, 6–042, 6–055
  burden of proof, 6–031
  convictions, 6–048
  criminal charges, 6–050
  degree of risk, 6–050
  dishonesty, 6–050
  double insurance, 6–058
  false statements, 6–004, 6–114
  financial status, 6–059
  generally, 6–001, 6–002

Disclosure—*cont.*
insurance brokers, 6–060, 15–028, 15–036, 15–042
insurer's duty, 6–0123
knowledge
best knowledge and belief, 6–006, 6–013
knowledge of facts, 6–004
knowledge of materiality, 6–005
legal expenses insurance, 23–014
liability insurance, 20–022, 20–023, 20–027
marine insurance
agents, 24–041
details of voyage, 24–039
insured persons, 24–035
nature of vessel, 24–038
port details, 24–037
prior loss, 24–036
sailing date, 24–037
situation of vessel, 24–037
materiality, 6–001, 6–002, 6–004, 6–114
misconduct, 6–050
motor insurance, 22–087
non-disclosure
common knowledge, 6–065
contract void, 6–002
diminution of risk, 6–063
express warranties, 6–074
implied warranties, 6–074
inquiry by insurers, 6–066
insurer's knowledge, 6–065
meaning, 6–003
misrepresentation, 6–003
presumed circumstances, 6–064, 6–065
previous dealings, 6–067
repudiation, 6–002
open cover, 6–118
reinstatement, 6–105
reinsurance, 17–006, 17–008
renewal, 6–103
scope, 6–002
slips, 6–116
underwriters, 15–020
waiver, 6–068, 6–069, 6–071, 6–072
warranties, 6–074
Discrimination
accident insurance, 6–051
age discrimination, 6–051
civil partnerships, 6–051
direct discrimination, 6–051
disability discrimination, 6–051
gender reassignment, 6–051
indirect discrimination, 6–051
insurance premiums, 6–051
legislation, 6–051
life insurance, 6–051
maternity, 6–051
pregnancy, 6–051
provision of services, 6–051
race discrimination, 6–051
religious discrimination, 6–051
sex discrimination, 6–051
Double insurance
accident insurance, 6–058
common law, 11–044

Double insurance—*cont.*
concurrent clauses, 11–048, 11–049
contribution, 11–046, 11–052
disclosure provisions, 11–046
escape clauses, 11–047, 11–048
excesses, 11–047, 11–049
fire, 6–058
indemnities, 6–058
indemnity principle, 11–044
insurance premiums, 11–045
insured person's rights, 11–044
legislation, 11–044
liability, 11–046
life insurance, 6–058
marine insurance, 11–044, 11–045, 24–054
meaning, 11–044
over-insurance, 11–044—11–046
policy variations, 11–046
rateable proportion clauses, 11–046, 11–047, 11–050, 11–051, 11–060
removal of cover, 11–047
restriction of cover, 11–047
retroactive avoidance, 11–046
return of premium, 8–032
separate recovery, 11–044
unvalued policies, 11–044
valued policies, 11–044
Duress
applicable law, 2–055
Duty of disclosure
see **Disclosure**
Employers' liability insurance
amount of insurance, 20–067
breach of statutory duty, 20–070
common law, 20–063
compulsory insurance, 20–064
criminal liability, 20–070
duty to insure, 20–067, 20–070
enforcement, 20–071
exempted employers, 20–065
failure to insure, 20–070
generally, 20–063
information provisions, 21–040
insolvency, 20–072
insurance policies
approved policies, 20–068
claims made policies, 20–069
conditions, 20–068
contingent insurance, 20–069
losses occurring policies, 20–069
termination, 20–069
relevant employees, 20–066
relevant employers, 20–064
statutory liability, 20–063
transfer of undertakings, 20–073
Escape
property insurance, 19–042
Estoppel
agency, 15–001, 15–014, 15–017, 15–018
estoppel by convention, 6–098
issue estoppel, 6–098
promissory estoppel, 6–098
waiver by estoppel, 6–098, 7–018—7–020

European Economic Area
establishment provisions, 13–022, 13–023, 13–025
general good provision, 13–025
insurer's rights, 13–025
jurisdiction 2–008, 2–009
services, 13–022, 13–023
EU law
agency, 15–010
block exemptions, 13–046
competition law, 13–045, 13–046
EU Directives, 13–003, 13–019, 13–022, 13–024, 13–025
export credits, 23–032
freedom of establishment, 13–003
harmonisation, 13–003
insolvency, 16–001, 16–005, 16–013
legal expenses insurance, 23–009
liability insurance, 20–005
mergers, 13–045
motor insurance
claims procedure, 22–081
claims representatives, 22–080, 22–081
compensation claims, 22–080, 22–081
compulsory insurance 22–001, 22–036, 22–041
direct actions, 22–049, 22–050
foreign compensation bodies, 22–081
identity of vehicle, 22–080, 22–081
implementation, 22–081
indemnification, 22–081
information centres, 22–082
insurance policies, 22–036, 22–041
liabilities, 22–017, 22–018, 22–020
Member State residence, 22–080
passengers, 22–031, 22–035
specified information, 22–082
subrogation, 22–081
unidentified insurers, 22–081
reinsurance, 17–003
single market, 13–003, 13–022
solvency requirements, 13–003
untraced drivers
compensation, 22–059
direct effect, 22–059
fair trial, 22–073
implementation, 22–059, 22–073
Motor Insurers' Bureau, 22–059
preliminary rulings, 22–059, 22–073
"Event"
limitations, 10–034
uncertain events, 1–008
Ex gratia payments
settlement, 10–054
subrogation, 11–016, 11–036
Excesses
double insurance, 11–047, 11–049
franchise clauses, 10–030
functions, 10–030
insured person's liability, 10–030
subrogation, 10–030
Explosions
marine cargo insurance, 24–006
property insurance, 19–041

Export credits
EU law, 23–032
Export Credit Guarantees Department, 23–032
legislation, 23–032
risks, 23–032
Fidelity insurance
breach of confidence, 23–021
conditions, 23–026
criminal misappropriation, 23–021, 23–022, 23–026
deductibles, 23–027
exclusions, 23–023
guarantees, 23–021
indemnities, 23–027
insurance period, 23–025
insured persons, 23–024
loss, 23–022
purpose, 23–021
subrogation, 23–028
third party liability, distinguished, 23–021
utmost good faith, 23–026
Financial Ombudsman Service
see also **Complaints**
access, 12–002
awards
bad handling, 12–037
charitable donations, 12–041
compensation, 12–018, 12–037, 12–040
complainant's costs, 12–040
damage to reputation, 12–039
damages, 12–036, 12–037
distress, 12–037
enforcement, 12–043
inconvenience, 12–037
interest, 12–042
maladministration, 12–037
monetary awards, 12–036
pain and suffering, 12–038
background, 12–001
claims handling
breach of warranty, 12–017, 12–022
causation test, 12–024
change of risk, 12–021
change of terms, 12–020
commercial customers, 12–017
compensation, 12–018
consumers, 12–017
continuing good faith, 12–021
convictions, 12–019
disclosure, 12–021
forgery, 12–029
fraudulent claims, 12–029
insurer's rights, 12–018
non-disclosure, 12–017—12–020
previous losses, 12–019
principles, 12–017
renewal, 12–020
creation, 12–001
dispute resolution, 12–001, 12–002
fair and reasonable decisions, 12–001—12–003, 12–013
fees, 12–004
FIN-NET, 12–014

Financial Ombudsman Service—*cont.*
  funding, 12–004
  insurance policies
    eligibility, 12–023
    extended warranties, 12–030
    fraudulent claims, 12–029
    health insurance, 12–032
    household insurance, 12–034
    insurance premiums, 12–025
    interpretation, 12–023
    legal expenses insurance, 12–035
    misleading descriptions, 12–023
    mitigation, 12–026
    motor insurance, 12–033
    onerous conditions, 12–023
    proof of loss, 12–028
    reinstatement, 12–027
    repairs, 12–027
    replacement, 12–027
    special definitions, 12–023
    travel insurance, 12–031
  jurisdiction, 12–001, 12–014
  role, 6–135, 13–005
  structure, 12–001
Financial Services and Markets Tribunal
  function, 13–005
Financial Services Authority
  conduct of business, 13–028
  disciplinary measures, 13–031
  Handbook of Rules and Guidance, 13–002
  insolvency
    company voluntary arrangements, 16–014
    compulsory winding up, 16–004
    receivership, 16–015
    voluntary winding up, 16–003
  investigations, 13–030
  powers, 13–004, 13–006, 13–026, 13–027,
    13–029, 13–030
  provision of information, 13–030
  role, 1–001, 13–004
Financial Services Compensation Scheme
  claimants, 16–019
  claims, 16–021, 16–022
  compensation, 16–023, 16–027
  date of application, 16–017
  financial difficulties assistance
    insurers, 16–028
    measures, 16–028
    transfer of business, 16–028
  first party insurance, 16–025
  function, 13–005
  liability, 16–023, 16–029
  liability insurance, 16–024
  long-term policies, 16–026
  payment procedures, 16–027
  protected claims, 16–020
  scheme managers, 16–018, 16–028
Fire
  double insurance, 6–058
  general average, 10–029
  increase of risk, 5–017—5–020, 5–022
  marine cargo insurance, 24–006
  negligence, 5–048
  property insurance, 19–039, 19–040

Fire—*cont.*
  reinstatement, 1–011, 10–050, 10–051
Floods
  property insurance, 19–037
Formation of contract
  see also **Applicable law**
  acceptance
    counter offers, 1–024
    insured persons, 1–026
    insurers, 1–024, 1–025
    marine insurance, 24–043
    notification, 1–025
    reasonable period, 1–029
    silence as acceptance, 1–025
  arbitration clauses, 2–052, 2–053
  certainty, 1–021
  choice of law clauses, 2–052
  conditions, 1–027
  consideration, 1–021
  consumer contracts, 2–054
  differing applicable laws, 2–052
  express terms, 1–022, 2–052
  general principles, 1–012
  formalities, 2–054
  fundamental mistake, 1–021
  habitual residence, 2–053, 2–054
  illegality, 2–057
  incorporation, 1–022, 24–044
  intention to create legal relations, 1–021
  jurisdiction clauses, 2–052
  marine insurance
    acceptance, 24–043
    incorporation, 24–044
    slips, 24–043
    waiver clauses, 24–073
  offer
    express terms, 1–022
    incorporation, 1–022
    insured persons, 1–022, 1–024
    insurers, 1–023
    lapsed offers, 1–029
  putative applicable law, 2–051—2–053
  reinsurance, 2–051, 2–052
  Rome I Regulation, 2–051—2–054
  slips
    binding contracts, 1–018, 1–033, 1–034
    formation, 1–034
  utmost good faith, 1–028
  validity, 2–052, 2–054
  warranties
    development, 7–029
    generally, 7–001
    interpretation, 7–031
    materiality, 7–030
    misrepresentation, 7–031
    modification, 7–031
    nature of clause, 7–029
    qualification, 7–029
    subject of warranty, 7–029
Fraud
  see also **Misrepresentation**
  agency, 6–039, 6–043, 6–044, 6–055,
    15–004
  definition, 9–023

Fraud—*cont.*
deliberate destruction, 9–025
dishonesty, 9–024
effect, 6–017
evidence, 9–035
false statements, 9–029
foreign states, 9–036
fraudulent means or devices, 9–024, 9–029
imputation of knowledge, 9–024
loss
    absence of loss, 9–024
    exaggerated loss, 9–024, 9–026
    subsequent discovery, 9–024, 9–027
partly fraudulent claims, 9–026
recklessness, 9–024
reinstatement, 10–051
retraction, 9–031
subsequent fraud, 9–024
substantial fraud, 9–024, 9–026
suppression of defence, 9–024, 9–028
Fraudulent claims
see also **Fraud**
avoidance, 9–032, 9–033
commencement of proceedings, 9–021
consequences, 9–020, 9–032—9–034
definition, 9–021
duration, 9–021
express clauses, 9–033
false statements, 9–029
indemnities, 9–032
inducement, 9–030
initial demand, 9–021
insured person's duty, 9–020
insurer's plea, 9–034
first party policies, 9–021
liability insurance, 9–022
partly fraudulent claims, 9–026
post-loss fraud, 9–021
repudiation, 9–032, 9–034
retroactive effect, 9–032
termination, 9–032
utmost good faith, 9–032, 9–033
"Freight clauses"
see also **Hull clauses; Marine cargo insurance**
abandonment, 24–095
advanced freight, 24–026
chartered freight, 24–026
ordinary freight, 24–026
trading freight, 24–026
time policies, 24–047
Friendly societies
registration, 13–043
regulation, 1–005, 13–015, 13–016, 13–043
role, 13–043
Gambling
see also **Wagering contracts**
absence of intent, 4–015
betting, 4–008
indemnity principle, 4–009
insurable interests, 4–008—4–010, 4–015
Law Commission reforms, 4–025, 4–027
legislation, 4–007—4–009
lotteries, 4–008

Gambling—*cont.*
marine insurance, 24–012
public policy, 4–009
General average
contribution, 1–011
fire, 10–029
marine insurance, 10–029, 24–101, 24–107
multiple policies, 10–029
partial loss, 10–029
total loss, 10–029
under-insurance, 10–029
unvalued policies, 10–029
valued policies, 10–029
Goods
agency, 4–021
bailment, 19–007
buyers, 19–007
contracts of insurance, 1–016
enjoyment, 19–014
floating policies, 19–007
fraudulent shipments, 19–007
insurable interests, 4–010, 19–001
liability insurance, 20–006
marine insurance, 24–063
ownership, 19–007
possession, 19–007, 19–014
risk, 19–007
seizure, 10–001
sellers, 19–007
smuggled goods, 19–014
theft, 10–001
third party ownership, 19–014
Goods in transit insurance
bailment, 5–009
carriage of goods, 5–009
floating time policies, 5–009
goods held in trust, 5–010
legislation, 5–010
marine insurance, 5–013
misappropriated goods, 5–012
negligence, 5–051
owner of goods, 5–009
possession of goods, 5–010
risk
    commencement of cover, 5–003
    deviation from agreed risk, 5–013
    duration, 5–009
security measures, 5–012
transhipment, 5–014
transit
    commencement, 5–010
    meaning, 5–011
    normal course, 5–011
    termination, 5–014
unattended goods, 5–012
Green card system
see also **Motor insurance (compulsory insurance)**
accidents
    EU visitors, 22–084
    inside EU, 22–084
    non-EU visitors, 22–084
    outside EU, 22–084
    within UK, 22–084

Green card system—*cont.*
accidents—*cont.*
UK residents, 22–084
border checks, 22–083
implementation, 22–083
insurance certificate, 22–083
Guarantees
see also **Sureties; Suretyship**
disclosure, 23–020
employee dishonesty, 23–018
fidelity bonds, 23–018
fidelity insurance, 23–021
insurance contracts, 23–018, 23–019
materiality, 23–020
payment of debts, 23–018
performance bonds, 23–018
Health care
accidents, 20–016, 20–017
appeals, 20–019
certification, 20–018, 20–019
contributory negligence, 20–018, 20–019
legislation, 20–016, 20–017, 20–021
medical treatment, 20–016
NHS charges, 20–016
NHS treatment, 20–016, 20–017
information requirements, 20–020
personal injury, 20–016
reviews, 20–019
social security benefits, 20–021
structured settlements, 20–017
waiver, 20–019
Health insurance
disability, 12–032
exclusions, 12–032
experimental treatment, 12–032
marketing, 12–032
pre-existing medical conditions, 12–032
terminal illnesses, 12–032
Household insurance
buildings insurance, 12–034
contents insurance, 12–034
exclusions, 12–034
interpretation, 12–034
personal possessions, 12–034
satellite navigation equipment, 12–034
unoccupied premises, 12–034
"Hull clauses"
see also **"Freight clauses"; Marine cargo insurance**
collision liability, 24–001, 24–005
latent defects, 24–003
marine perils
dependent on due diligence, 24–001, 24–003
irrespective of due diligence, 24–001, 24–002
negligence, 24–003, 24–062
pollution hazards, 24–001, 24–004
proof of loss, 24–001
time policies, 24–047
Illegality
see also **Misconduct**
accidents, 5–042
agency, 5–046

Illegality—*cont.*
criminal conduct, 5–043
effect, 5–035
marine insurance, 5–036—5–039
motor insurance, 5–036, 5–037, 5–039
post-contract illegality, 5–039
public policy
culpability, 5–046
deterrence, 5–044, 5–046
negligence, 5–046
proximity, 5–045, 5–046
punishment, 5–044
recklessness, 5–046
scope, 5–044
strict liability, 5–046
third party conduct, 5–047
vicarious liability, 5–046
statutory prohibitions, 5–036
subject matter
deliberate destruction, 5–041
tainted, 5–038, 5–045
unlawful conduct, 5–037, 5–038, 5–043
Immunity from suit
co-insurance, 11–025—011–030
composite policies, 11–025—11–027
insurable interests, 11–028
insured persons, 11–024
Lloyds, 13–039
mortgage indemnity policies, 11–033
termination of cover, 11–030
third parties, 11–031, 11–032
wilful misconduct, 11–029
Incorporation
arbitration clauses, 3–015
commercial context, 3–015
effects, 3–014, 3–016
excess layer policy, 3–015
express reference, 3–015
generally, 3–014
implied reference, 3–015
judicial criteria, 3–015
manipulation, 3–016
primary layer policy, 3–015
reinsurance, 3–016
"Increase of risk"
see also **Warranties**
alteration of risk, 5–016, 5–019, 5–022
alteration of subject matter, 5–016, 5–024
change of risk
alteration of subject matter, 5–016, 5–024—5–028
common law, 5–024
continuing warranties, 5–026, 5–027
express warranties, 5–024
failure to meet description, 5–024—5–026
interpretation of policy, 5–024, 5–026, 5–027
material changes, 5–019, 5–027
notification requirements, 5–027
suspension of risk, 5–028
change of use, 5–022
common law, 5–016, 5–017
concurrent causes
concurrent proximate causes, 5–034

"Increase of risk"—*cont.*
concurrent causes—*cont.*
excluded perils, 5–034
insured perils, 5–033, 5–034
meaning, 5–032
proximity rule, 5–033
uninsured perils, 5–033
contractual provisions, 5–018
fire, 5–017—5–020, 5–022
good faith, 5–017, 5–019
life insurance, 5–018
marine insurance, 5–017, 5–018
material changes, 5–019, 5–027
meaning, 5–019
notification clauses, 5–023
notification requirements, 5–018, 5–019
permission, 5–018, 5–019
property insurance, 19–034
reinsurance, 5–017
restrictions, 5–016
successive causes
accident insurance, 5–030, 5–031
chain of causation, 5–030
causation test, 5–029
exclusions, 5–031
inevitability cases, 5–030
intention, 5–029
marine insurance, 5–030
property insurance, 5–030
proximity rule, 5–029, 5–030
series of events, 5–029
state of affairs cases, 5–030
weakening cases, 5–030
suspension of cover, 5–018
temporary increases, 5–022
termination of risk, 5–021
variation of risk, 5–017, 5–018
Indemnities
see also **Valuation**
contingency insurance
ascertained net loss, 23–033
exclusivity provision, 23–033
revenue gap, 23–033
shortfall contingency insurance, 23–033
debts
individual debtors, 23–030
payment, 23–029, 23–030
double insurance, 6–058
generally, 1–001
insurance contracts
completion, 23–031
creditors, 23–030
debts, 23–029, 23–030
export credits, 23–032
measure of indemnity, 23–030
payment of policy moneys, 23–029
repossessions, 23–030
schemes of arrangement, 23–030
specified causes, 23–029
subrogation, 23–030
underwriting criteria, 23–030
insured persons, 1–009
loss, 1–009, 10–001—10–004
over-insurance, 1–009

Indemnities—*cont.*
sum insured, 1–009
under-insurance, 1–009
unvalued policies
calculation of loss, 10–006
cost of repair, 10–012, 10–017
damage to property, 10–014
diminution in value, 10–012, 10–013
indemnity principle, 10–012
market value, 10–013—10–018
partial loss, 10–012, 10–017
reinstatement, 10–012, 10–014
total loss, 10–015, 10–016
unique goods, 10–018
unmeasurable loss, 10–018
valued policies
agreed value, 10–006
calculation of loss, 10–006
change in value, 10–008
generally, 1–009
marine insurance, 10–006
partial loss, 10–009
overvaluation, 10–007
reduction in risk, 10–008
total loss, 10–009
Indemnity principle
basis, 4–004
double insurance, 11–044
exceptions, 4–004
implied term, 4–005
insurable interests, distinguished, 4–005
Law Commission reforms, 4–027
life insurance, 4–004, 4–005
quantification of loss, 4–005
third parties, 4–006
valued policies, 4–004, 4–005
Inducement
actual inducement, 6–028
agency, 6–035
assessment date, 6–032
avoidance, 6–033, 6–034
fraudulent claims, 9–030
full extent of risk, 6–030
misrepresentation, 6–021
non-disclosure, 6–021, 6–030
presumption, 6–028
proof, 6–027—6–031
requirement, 6–027
underwriters, 6–025
Industrial assurance
long-term business, 13–043
regulation, 13–016, 13–043
Insolvency
see also **Administration**; **Liquidation**
bankruptcy, 21–015
company voluntary arrangements
composition, 16–014
effect, 16–014
moratorium, 16–014
third party rights, 21–013
individual voluntary arrangements, 21–013,
21–041, 21–042

Insolvency—*cont.*
  Financial Services Compensation Scheme
    see **Financial Services Compensation**
      Scheme
  Policyholders Protection Board, 16–016
  proceedings
    EU law, 16–001
    generally, 16–001
    legislation, 16–001
  receivership, 16–015
  reinsurance, 17–002
Insurable interests
  see also **Gambling**; **Wagering contracts**
  agency, 4–019
  bailment, 19–010
  beneficiaries, 19–030
  buildings, 19–002
  co-insurance, 14–004
  common law, 4–010
  contractors, 19–032
  contribution, 11–054
  creditors, 19–029
  definition, 4–013
  destruction of subject matter, 4–001
  effect of payment, 4–011
  future interests, 4–017
  goods, 4–010, 19–001, 19–005, 19–007,
    19–014
  historical background, 4–002
  immunity from suit, 11–028
  indemnity principle, 4–004—4–006, 4–027
  insurance policies
    interest or no interest, 4–002, 4–003,
      4–011
    policy proof of interest, 4–002, 4–003,
      24–015
  land, 19–002
  landlord and tenant, 19–015—19–017,
    19–020
  Law Commission reforms, 4–025—4–027
  legal or equitable interests, 4–016
  legal or equitable relations, 4–013
  legislation, 4–003
  liability insurance, 4–010
  life insurance, 4–009, 4–010, 4–015
  limited interests
    contingent interests, 4–016, 4–017
    defeasible interests, 4–016
    partial interests, 4–016
  marine insurance, 1–011, 4–001, 4–003,
    4–009, 4–010, 4–015, 4–027
  moral obligations, 4–018
  mortgage indemnity policies, 19–025
  motor insurance, 20–062
  pecuniary interests, 4–014, 4–026
  personal representatives, 19–031
  property insurance, 4–010
  purchasers, 19–008
  reinsurance, 17–004, 20–062
  requirement, 4–001
  sellers, 19–008
  statements of interest, 4–012
  third parties, 4–006
  trustees, 4–019, 19–030

Insurable interests—*cont.*
  valued policies, 4–014
  wagering contracts, 20–062
Insurance
  see also **Conduct of business**; **Insurance**
    contracts
  contingency insurance, 1–009
  definition, 1–001, 1–002, 13–008, 13–018
  endowment insurance, 1–008
  general business, 13–009
  indemnities, 1–009
  legal development, 1–011
  long-term business, 13–010
  transfer of risk, 1–010
Insurance agents
  see also **Agency**; **Agents**
  classification, 15–013
  civil proceedings, 15–018
  criminal liability, 15–018
  misstatements, 15–018
Insurance brokers
  see also **Agency**
  accounting for proceeds, 4–024
  breach of duty
    agency principles, 15–028
    basis of liability, 15–044
    consequential loss, 15–047
    damages, 15–045, 15–048
    exceeding authority, 15–048
    interim payments, 15–049
    negligence, 15–044, 15–047
    placement, 15–036
    reinsurance, 15–047
    tortious liability, 15–044
    wasted costs, 15–046
  conflicts of interest, 15–028, 15–033,
    15–038, 15–041
  contribution, 15–032, 15–060
  declaration policies, 6–117
  defences
    contributory negligence, 15–051
    denial of liability, 15–056
    estoppel, 15–052
    fallback insurance, 15–055
    lack of causation, 15–054
    mitigation, 15–050, 15–059
    ratification, 15–053
    risk uninsurable, 15–057
    waiver, 15–052
  definition, 15–026
  disclosure, 6–060, 15–028, 15–036
  documents
    access, 15–042
    claim files, 15–042
    duty of disclosure, 15–042
    insurance premiums, 15–043
    insured person's rights, 15–043
    insurer's rights, 15–042
    ownership, 15–043
    placing files, 15–042
    receipts, 15–043
  duties during currency of policy
    accounting arrangements, 15–041
    amendments, 15–037

Insurance brokers—*cont.*
  duties during currency of policy—*cont.*
    breach of duty, 15–037
    breach of warranty, 15–038
    cancellation, 15–040
    claims assistance, 15–041
    conflicts of interest, 15–038, 15–041
    coverage issues, 15–038
    declaration policies, 15–039
    duty of care, 15–038
    indorsements, 15–037
    legal advice, 15–037
    payment of losses, 15–041
    receipt of policy money, 15–041
    reinsurance, 15–038
    remedial action, 15–038
    renewal, 15–037
    termination, 15–040
  duties on placement
    application process, 15–036
    breach of duty, 15–036
    drafting insurance policy, 15–035
    duty of disclosure, 15–036
    express instructions, 15–034
    insured person's needs, 15–034
    misrepresentation, 15–036
    obtaining cover, 15–034, 15–036
    previous dealings, 15–034
    proposal forms, 15–036
    slips, 15–035
  duty of care, 15–031, 15–036, 15–062
  failure to obey orders, 15–058
  Firm Order Notification Sheets, 1–034
  insurance premiums, 8–007
  liability
    damages, 15–058, 15–059
    generally, 15–030—15–032
    post-settlement, 15–059
    third parties, 15–062
  lien, 14–016
  misrepresentation, 6–060
  negligence, 15–030, 15–032
  placing brokers, 15–029—15–032
  producing brokers, 15–029—15–032
  recovery of loss, 4–024
  regulation, 15–011
  reinsurance, 15–028, 15–038, 15–047,
    17–005
  remuneration, 15–033, 15–041
  role, 1–032, 15–026
  settlement, 10–063
  signing indications, 1–038
  sub-agency agreements, 15–032
  sub-brokers, 15–029—15–032
  temporary cover, 1–032
  third parties, 15–060, 15–062
Insurance claims
  see also **Fraudulent claims; Third party
    rights**
  conditions
    ancillary nature, 9–003
    breach of condition, 9–003, 9–004, 9–014,
      9–018, 14–011, 14–014
    classification, 9–003, 9–004

Insurance claims—*cont.*
  conditions—*cont.*
    compliance, 9–003, 9–009—9–013
    conditions precedent, 9–003, 9–004
    essential nature, 9–003
    innominate terms, 9–003
    repudiation, 9–003
    unfair contract terms, 9–004
    waiver, 9–014
  electronic claims handling, 9–001
  limitations
    aggregate limit, 10–036
    different meanings, 10–036
    notification, 10–036
    third party rights, 10–036
  notification of loss clauses
    breach of condition, 9–004
    condition precedent, 9–004
    exercise of options, 9–010
    fixed notification periods, 9–005, 9–007
    form of notice, 9–009
    knowledge of loss, 9–011
    immediate notice clauses, 9–005, 9–006
    liability insurance, 9–011
    notice of abandonment, 9–002
    obligations, 9–005, 9–016, 9–017
    primary layer policy, 9–013
    recipients of notice, 9–013
    requirement, 9–002
    responsibility for notice, 9–010
    timely notification, 9–005, 9–008
    underwriters, 9–013
    unintentional notification, 9–012
  proof of loss
    breach of condition, 9–018
    burden of proof, 9–015
    CCTV footage, 9–019
    circumstances of loss, 9–017
    co-operation provisions, 9–016
    details of loss, 9–017
    documentation, 9–019
    insurer's satisfaction, 9–019
    liability insurance, 9–017
    obligations, 9–016
    time limits, 9–017
    waiver, 9–018
Insurance contracts
  see also **Applicable law; Contract terms;
    Formation of contract; Renewal**
  acceptance
    counter offers, 1–024
    insured persons, 1–026
    insurers, 1–024, 1–025
    notification, 1–025
    reasonable period, 1–029
    silence as acceptance, 1–025
  avoidance, 6–033, 6–034
  consideration, 1–006
  documentation, 1–004
  exclusion clauses, 1–001
  formalities
    common law, 1–012
    "consumer insurance", 1–018
    generally, 1–012

Insurance contracts—*cont.*
  formalities—*cont.*
    goods, 1–016
    legislation, 1–013—1–016
    liability insurance, 1–015
    life insurance, 1–013
    oral agreements, 1–012
    property insurance, 1–014
    written agreements, 1–017
  friendly societies, 13–015, 13–016
  general business, 13–009
  generally, 1–001, 1–002
  guarantees, 13–013
  illegality, 5–035, 5–036
  indemnities, 1–009
  industrial insurance, 13–016
  insurers' liabilities
    absence of agreement, 1–029
    commencement of risk, 1–030
    earlier loss, 1–029
    open cover, 1–031
    prior to issue of policy, 1–031
    provisional cover, 1–031
    reinsurance, 1–031
    voyage policies, 1–031
  insurer's obligations, 1–007
  long-term business, 13–010
  loss, 1–009
  mixed contracts, 13–011
  mutual societies, 13–014
  offer
    express terms, 1–022
    incorporation, 1–022
    insured persons, 1–022, 1–024
    insurers, 1–023
    lapsed offers, 1–029
  reasonable care clauses, 5–049, 5–050
  reinsurance, 13–017
  statutory prohibitions, 5–036
  surrender value, 1–008
  third parties, 1–001
  tontines, 13–010
  uncertain events, 1–008
  unfair contract terms, 3–018
  unlawful conduct, 5–037, 5–043
  utmost good faith, 6–001
Insurance policies
  see also **Contract terms; Insurance
    contracts; Insurance premiums;
    Renewal**
  assignment, 14–023—14–029
  consideration, 1–006
  documentation, 1–004
  duration of cover
    automatic extension, 5–008
    automatic renewal, 5–008
    notice of cancellation at anniversary date
      (NCAD), 5–008
  Financial Ombudsman Service
    fraudulent claims, 12–029
    health insurance, 12–032
    household insurance, 12–034
    insurance premiums, 12–025
    interpretation, 12–023

Insurance policies—*cont.*
  Financial Ombudsman Service—*cont.*
    legal expenses insurance, 12–035
    motor insurance, 12–033
    proof of loss, 12–028
    reinstatement, 12–027
    repairs, 12–027
    replacement, 12–027
    special definitions, 12–023
    travel insurance, 12–031
  interest or no interest, 4–002, 4–003, 4–011
  policy proof of interest, 4–002, 4–003,
      24–015
  rectification, 1–018
  standard form, 1–018
  termination, 5–028
Insurance premiums
  see also **Renewal**
  adequacy, 8–001
  amount
    additional premium, 8–008
    agreement, 8–008
    calculation, 8–008
    contract terms, 8–001
    fixed amount, 8–008
    variation, 8–008
  definition, 8–001
  discrimination, 6–051
  double insurance, 11–045
  late payment
    effect, 8–011, 8–014, 8–017
    marine insurance, 8–018
    repudiation, 8–017
    time not of the essence, 8–017
  marine insurance, 1–011, 8–005, 8–008,
      24–076—24–079
  non-payment
    actions for payment, 8–011, 8–012
    cancellation, 8–016
    forfeiture, 8–011, 8–014, 8–016
    liability, 8–012
    life insurance, 8–016
    postponement of contract, 8–015
    premium warranties, 8–016, 8–018
    repudiation, 8–017
    rejection of claims, 8–011, 8–013
    termination of policy, 8–011, 8–014,
      8–015
  notional premiums, 1–019
  payment
    agency, 8–003, 15–014
    apportionment, 1–003
    binding agreement, 8–004
    cheques, 8–002
    commencement of risk, 8–004
    credit arrangements, 1–003
    credit cards, 8–002
    direct debits, 8–002
    forms of payment, 8–002
    instalments, 8–002
    insurance brokers, 8–007
    insured persons, 1–001
    issue of policy, 8–005

Insurance premiums—*cont.*
  payment—*cont.*
    late payment, 8–011, 8–014, 8–017,
      8–018
    marine insurance, 8–005
    mutual societies, 8–006
    non-cash payments, 8–002
    periodical payments, 1–003
    rate of premium, 8–002
    single premium, 8–002
    standing orders, 8–002
    stipulations, 8–004
  reinstatement, 8–010
  return of premiums
    agreement, 8–019
    apportionment, 8–021, 8–032
    attachment of risk, 8–029
    avoidance, 8–023, 8–025, 8–026
    defeasible interests, 8–030
    double insurance, 8–032
    executory contracts, 8–022
    failure of consideration, 8–020
    fraud, 8–022, 8–025
    illegality, 8–022
    insurable interests, 8–031
    liability, 8–023
    life insurance, 8–020, 8–024, 8–031
    marine insurance, 8–019, 8–022, 8–023,
      8–025, 8–031, 8–032
    misrepresentation, 8–025, 8–026
    mistake, 8–022, 8–024
    motor insurance, 8–019
    no valid contract, 8–024
    over-insurance, 8–033, 8–034
    rectification, 8–024
    repudiation, 8–028
    warranties, 8–027
  risk assessment, 1–003
  unfair contract terms, 3–018
Insured persons
  see also **Co-insurance**; **Insurable interests**
  capacity, 14–001, 14–002
  financial status, 6–059
  indemnities, 1–009
  insurance premiums, 1–001, 1–003
  minors, 14–002
  transfer of risk, 1–010
Insurers' liabilities
  absence of agreement, 1–029
  commencement of risk, 1–030
  earlier loss, 1–029
  open cover, 1–031
  prior to issue of policy, 1–031
  provisional cover, 1–031
  reinsurance, 1–031
  voyage policies, 1–031
Interest
  applicable law, 2–059
  common law, 10–024, 10–025
  compound interest, 10–025
  damages, 10–024, 10–025
  discretionary nature, 10–024
  interest period, 10–027
  late payments, 10–022, 10–024

Interest—*cont.*
  rate of interest, 10–026
  recovery of debt, 10–024, 10–025
  simple interest, 10–024, 10–024
  statutory powers, 10–024—10–026
Interim payments
  Civil Procedure Rules, 10–053
  insurance brokers, 15–049
  settlement, 10–053
Interpretation
  see also **Contra proferentem**;
    Incorporation
  admissible evidence, 3–013
  ambiguity, 3–009, 3–010
  conflicting clauses, 3–011
  context, 3–001, 3–006
  contradictory clauses, 3–001
  custom, 3–013
  deletions, 3–017
  development, 3–001
  disputed meanings, 3–001, 3–003
  effective legal document, 3–009
  ejusdem generic effect, 3–006
  factual matrix, 3–005, 7–037
  general words, 3–006
  insurance policy
    considered as a whole, 3–011
    underlying purpose, 3–006
  intention
    commercial approach, 3–005
    expert evidence, 3–005
    negotiations, 3–005
    objectivity principle, 3–004
    reasonable man test, 3–004, 3–005
    specialist knowledge, 3–004
    state of knowledge, 3–005
  interpretative rules, 3–002
  judicial decisions, 3–002, 3–003
  natural meaning, 3–005, 3–007
  obvious meaning, 3–011
  ordinary meaning, 3–005, 3–007
  plain meaning, 3–011
  precedent, 3–003
  reasonable construction, 3–009, 3–011,
    3–013
  redundant clauses, 3–011
  subsequent conduct, 3–012
  technical terms, 3–008
  uncertainty, 3–009
  unfair contract terms, 3–018
  unreasonable result, 3–009
  US authorities, 3–003
  warranties, 5–020, 5–021, 7–032, 7–033,
    7–037
Jurisdiction
  see also **Brussels Regulation**
  anti-suit injunctions, 2–004, 2–006
  arbitration, 2–001, 2–005, 2–008
  Brussels Convention, 2–001
  certainty principle, 2–008
  Civil Procedure Rules, 2–001, 2–004
  claim forms
    service, 2–002—2–004
    service out of jurisdiction, 2–004

Jurisdiction—*cont.*
contractual claims, 2–004
court first seised, 2–008
discretion, 2–005
domicile
EFTA domicile, 2–001
EU domicile, 2–001, 2–011
European Economic Area, 2–008, 2–009
forum non conveniens, 2–005
forum shopping, 2–007
generally, 2–001
governing law, 2–005
insurance rules, 2–009, 2–015
insured persons' claims, 2–011
insurer's claims, 2–010
jurisdiction agreements, 2–015
jurisdiction clauses, 2–003, 2–005, 2–008,
2–037
liability insurance, 2–013
lis alibis pendens, 2–005
Lugano Conventions, 2–001
negative declaratory relief, 2–007
overlapping jurisdiction, 2–005
place of performance, 2–008
property insurance, 2–012
reinsurance, 2–008
third parties, 2–008
tort claims, 2–004
Landlords
see also **Tenants**
breach of insuring covenant, 19–018,
19–023
damages, 19–018, 19–023
forfeiture, 19–023
increased risk, 19–024
indemnity principle, 19–016
insurable interests, 19–015—19–017, 19–020
landlord's insurance, 19–017, 19–018
long leases, 19–017
reinstatement, 19–017, 19–021
recovery, 19–017
repairs, 19–016, 19–018, 19–021
third party claims, 19–017, 19–021
Late payments
damages, 10–022—10–025
implied terms, 10–022
insurance premiums
effect, 8–011, 8–014, 8–017
marine insurance, 8–018
repudiation, 8–017
time not of the essence, 8–017
insurer's obligations, 10–022
interest, 10–022, 10–024
Law Commission reforms, 10–023
utmost good faith, 10–022
Legal expenses insurance
after the event insurance
see **"After the event insurance"**
assessment procedure, 12–035
"before the event" insurance, 23–034
direct actions, 23–017
duty of disclosure, 23–014
future claims, 23–034
generally, 23–008

Legal expenses insurance—*cont.*
insurance policies
business policies, 23–015
consumer policies, 23–015
particular activities, 23–015
legal aid, 23–008, 23–034
litigation
costs, 23–008
risk, 23–008
materiality, 23–014
outstanding causes of action, 23–014
reasonable prospects of success, 12–035,
23–008
refusal, 23–008
regulation
authorisation, 23–010
conflicts of interest, 23–009, 23–012
dispute resolution, 23–013
EU law, 23–009
exemptions, 23–009
legislation, 23–009
separate policies, 23–011
third parties
actions, 23–017
costs, 23–016
Liability insurance
see also **Employers' liability insurance;**
Health care; Product liability;
Professional indemnity
insurance
claims
binding awards, 20–034
establishment of liability, 20–034, 20–057,
20–060
interim awards, 20–036
marine cargo claims, 20–035
"pay to be paid" clauses, 20–035
payment requirement, 20–035
quantification of liability, 20–034, 20–057,
20–060
compulsory insurance
carriage by sea, 20–005
EU law, 20–005
legislation, 20–001, 20–004
nuclear installations, 20–002
oil pollution, 20–004
professional indemnity insurance, 20–003,
20–006
shipowners, 20–005
contracts of insurance, 1–015
costs
advance funding, 20–049
apportionment, 20–050, 20–052
averting liability, 20–013
Civil Procedure Rules, 20–056
claimant's costs, 20–055, 20–056
co-defendants, 20–052
contribution, 20–052
costs orders, 20–055
defence costs, 20–044, 20–047
defendants, 20–052
discretion to defend, 20–051
duty to defend, 20–049, 20–050
entitlement, 20–047, 20–050

Liability insurance—*cont.*
  costs—*cont.*
    excesses, 20–054
    insured claims, 20–052
    investigating liability, 20–014
    limit of indemnity, 20–047
    limitations, 20–048
    manipulative pleading, 20–049
    marine insurance, 20–047
    option to pay, 20–049
    repayment, 20–049, 20–053
    separate causes of action, 20–047
    subrogation, 20–047
    third party claims, 20–049, 20–050,
      20–052, 20–055
    uninsured claims, 20–052
  defence of claims
    avoidance, 20–044
    breach of condition, 20–044
    claims exceeding policy limits, 20–045
    competing defences, 20–044
    conduct of defence, 20–043—20–045
    discretion to defend, 20–043, 20–051
    duty to defend, 20–043
    insurer's rights and duties, 20–043,
      20–045
    leading counsel's opinion, 20–046
    reservation of rights, 20–044
    termination of policy, 20–044
    third party claims, 20–045
    waiver, 20–044
  disclosure
    earlier events, 20–027
    professional requirements, 20–023
    utmost good faith, 20–022
    waiver, 20–023
  fraudulent claims, 9–022
  insurable interests
    generally, 4–010
    motor insurance, 20–062
    payment for loss, 20–062
    reinsurance, 20–062
    requirement, 20–062
    sporting events, 20–062
    wagering contracts, 20–062
  insurance policies
    asbestos-related claims, 20–007
    bailment, 20–006
    claimants, 20–008
    contingency insurance, 20–007, 20–009,
      20–025
    contractual liability, 20–009
    contribution, 20–011
    costs, 20–013, 20–014
    damage to property, 20–007
    drafting, 20–006
    errors and omissions, 20–009, 20–025
    exemplary damages, 20–015
    goods, 20–006
    indemnities, 20–006, 20–062
    losses occurring, 20–007
    liability at law, 20–009
    limitations, 20–026—20–029
    no admission of liability, 20–033

Liability insurance—*cont.*
  insurance policies—*cont.*
    no admission of settlement, 20–033
    payments to avoid liability, 20–012
    personal injury, 20–007
    professional indemnity insurance, 20–006,
      20–009, 20–032
    reasonable care, 20–031
    reinstatement, 20–030
    services, 20–006
    statutory liability, 20–010
    third party claims, 20–008
    third party liability, 20–006
    tortious liability, 20–009
  insured persons' liability
    claims, 2–013
    classification, 20–025
    criminal conduct, 20–031
    errors and omissions, 20–025
    establishment, 20–037
    fraud, 20–025
    misconduct, 20–031
    negligence, 20–025, 20–031
    proximate cause, 20–025
    reasonable care, 20–031
    recklessness, 20–031
    wilful misconduct, 20–025
  jurisdiction, 2–013
  limitation periods, 9–039
  limitations
    capacity, 20–028
    conduct of business, 20–028
    express limitations, 20–026, 20–031
    implied limitations, 20–026
    limit of liability, 20–029
    purpose of activities, 20–027
  notification of loss clauses
    assertion of discontent, 20–038
    bare conditions, 20–037
    claims made policies, 20–037, 20–038
    conditions precedent, 20–037, 20–039
    demands for payment, 20–038
    disclosure, 20–037
    extension clauses, 20–037
    generally, 9–011, 20–037
    losses occurring policies, 20–037
    notification of circumstances,
      20–037—20–042
    obligations, 20–037
    prompt notification, 20–040
    relevant circumstances, 20–042
    relevant knowledge, 20–038—20–040
    service of claim form, 20–038
    third party claims, 20–038
    written notice, 20–039
  regulation, 13–009
  settlement
    admissions of liability, 20–060
    allocation, 20–060
    approval, 20–057, 20–061
    binding agreement, 20–057
    counterclaims, 20–060
    determination of liability, 20–057
    follow the settlement clauses, 20–058

Liability insurance—*cont.*
　settlement—*cont.*
　　insured losses, 20–060
　　multiple losses, 20–059
　　proof of loss, 20–057, 20–060
　　third parties, 20–057, 20–060
　　uninsured losses, 20–060
　third party claims, 2–013
　time of loss, 5–015
　voluntary insurance, 20–001
Life insurance
　see also **Suicide**
　accidental death, 18–001
　age provisions, 18–036
　agency, 4–021
　assignment
　　conditions, 18–022
　　effect, 18–022
　　form, 18–023
　　gift, 18–022
　　insurable interests, 18–005
　　legislation, 18–023
　　limitations, 18–022
　　method, 18–023
　　mortgage, 18–022
　　notice requirements, 18–023
　　payment of proceeds, 18–024
　　place of business, 18–023
　　sale, 18–022
　　settlement, 18–022
　　third parties, 18–005
　benefits, 18–001
　choice of law, 2–040
　contingency insurance, 1–009
　continuous nature, 18–003
　contracts of insurance, 1–013
　definition, 18–001
　discrimination, 6–051, 18–029
　double insurance, 6–058
　endowment policies, 18–001
　illegal contracts, 18–008—18–012
　increase of risk, 5–018
　indemnity principle, 4–004, 4–005
　indisputable policies, 18–038
　insurable interests
　　assignment, 18–005
　　beneficiaries, 18–007
　　business relationships, 18–018, 18–019
　　civil partnerships, 18–014
　　creditors, 18–020
　　debtors, 18–020
　　funeral expenses, 18–016
　　insertion of interests parties, 18–007
　　requirement, 4–009, 4–010, 4–015,
　　　18–004, 18–005
　　lack of insurable interests, 18–009,
　　　18–012
　　married women's property, 18–014
　　own life, 18–013
　　parents and children, 18–015
　　payment of premiums, 18–006
　　pecuniary interest, 18–013, 18–015
　　policy proof of interest, 18–004
　　proof of loss, 18–004, 18–008

Life insurance—*cont.*
　insurable interests—*cont.*
　　spouses, 18–014
　　statutory trusts, 18–014
　　subsequent policies, 18–004
　　third parties, 18–005, 18–006, 18–008,
　　　18–021
　　timing, 18–004
　insurance premium
　　non-payment, 8–016
　　renewal, 8–009
　　return, 8–020, 8–024, 8–031
　insured event, 18–001
　investment contracts, 18–001
　Law Commission reforms, 4–025, 4–026
　materiality
　　age, 18–026
　　alcohol abuse, 18–030
　　domicile, 18–027
　　generally, 6–021
　　health, 18–028
　　HIV/AIDS, 18–030
　　hobbies, 18–031
　　occupation, 18–031
　　residence, 18–027
　medical history, 18–029
　medical reports, 18–029
　occupational restrictions, 18–031, 18–037
　regulation, 13–010
　reinstatement, 8–010
　renewal, 1–048, 6–103, 8–009
　risk, 5–005
　territorial limitations, 18–037
　wartime provisions, 18–039
　warranties, 7–033
　whole life policies, 18–001
Limitation periods
　applicable law, 2–056
　contracting out
　　contract terms, 9–042
　　standstill agreements, 9–042
　　waiver, 9–042
　motor insurance, 22–013
　statutory periods
　　accrual of action, 9–037
　　liability insurance, 9–039
　third party claims, 9–052, 21–017, 21–030,
　　21–052
　untraced drivers, 22–059, 22–073, 22–077
　variation, 9–037, 9–040, 9–041
Limitations
　accidents, 10–033
　aggregation of loss, 10–032, 10–034,
　　10–036
　causal connection, 10–034
　deductibles, 10–032, 10–036
　event, 10–034
　insurance claims, 10–036
　interpretation, 10–032
　loss, 10–033, 10–034, 10–037
　maximum sum recoverable, 10–032
　occurrence, 10–034
　originating cause, 10–035
　temporal coverage, 10–032

Liquidation
see also **Schemes of arrangement**
application refused, 16–006
assets, 16–002, 16–008, 16–010
claims
  future claims, 16–002
  value, 16–002
compulsory winding up, 16–004, 16–008
debts
  preferential debts, 16–010
  proof of debts, 16–009
Financial Services Authority, 16–003,
  16–004
independent actuaries, 16–007
liabilities
  actuarial advice, 16–012
  general business, 16–012
  insurance liabilities, 16–012
  long-term business, 16–007, 16–012
  transfer of business, 16–012
policy valuations, 16–011
reduction of contracts, 16–006, 16–007
special managers, 16–007
winding up petitions, 16–004—16–006
voluntary winding up
  effect, 16–008
  members, 16–003

Lloyds
see also **Slips**; **Underwriters**
applicable law, 2–043
Contract Certainty Code of Practice, 1–043,
  1–044
contracts of insurance, 1–032, 1–034
disciplinary powers, 13–039
electronic claims handling, 9–001
immunity from suit, 13–039
insurance brokers, 1–032
In-sure, 1–032
insurance policies
  assignment, 1–011
  endorsements, 1–039
  joint and several liability, 1–032
  marine insurance, 1–011
  war risks, 25–001
legislation, 13–039
Lloyds Settlement, 13–042
managing agents, 13–041, 15–042
members
  duty of care, 13–041
  names, 1–032, 13–039, 13–041, 13–042
  personal liability, 13–039
  rights, 13–041
  syndicates, 13–039, 13–041
  underwriters, 13–039, 13–041
organisation, 13–039, 13–041
origins, 13–038
placement arrangements
  contract certainty, 1–043, 1–044
  leading underwriter clauses, 1–040
  line slips, 1–041
  principles, 1–043
regulation
  General Prudential Rules, 13–040

Lloyds—*cont.*
regulation—*cont.*
  Insurance Prudential Rules, 13–028,
    13–040
  reinsurance, 1–032, 1–034
  status, 13–039
  subscription procedure
    modifications, 1–037
    oversubscription, 1–038
    slips, 1–032—1–034, 1–036
London market
see **Lloyds**
Loss
see also **Notification of loss clauses**
abandonment
  actual total loss, 24–092
  constructive total loss, 11–067, 24–088,
    24–089, 24–092, 24–094
  measure of loss, 11–067
  partial loss, 24–088
  total loss, 11–066, 11–067, 24–088
aggregation, 10–032, 10–034, 10–036
consequential loss
  forms, 10–019
  insurance brokers, 15–047
  unvalued policies, 10–021
  valued policies, 10–020
constructive total loss
  abandonment, 11–067, 24–088, 24–089,
    24–092, 24–094
  effect, 24–082, 24–086—24–089
  generally, 1–011
  indemnities, 10–001, 24–111
contamination, 10–003
diminution in value, 10–003
indemnities, 1–009
indemnity principle, 10–004
insurance brokers, 4–024
insured subject matter, 10–002
latent defects, 10–003
limitations, 10–033, 10–034, 10–037
marine insurance
  actual total loss, 24–082, 24–083, 24–092
  delays, 24–080
  external accident, 24–080
  freight, 24–080
  good in specie, 24–082
  hull, 24–080
  inherent vice, 24–080, 24–081
  injury to machinery, 24–080
  insurer's liability, 24–080
  leakage and breakage, 24–080
  marine cargo, 24–080
  missing vessel, 24–084
  negligence, 24–080
  proximate cause, 24–080
  total loss, 10–001, 10–009, 10–029,
    11–066, 11–067
  transhipment, 24–085
  vermin, 24–080
  war risk claims, 24–085
  wear and tear, 24–080, 24–081
  wilful misconduct, 24–080

Loss—*cont.*
partial loss
abandonment, 24–088
assignment, 24–074
general average loss, 24–100
generally, 10–001, 24–082
indemnities, 24–101, 24–103, 24–104, 24–111
particular average loss, 24–098
salvage charges, 24–099
valued policies, 10–009
physical loss, 10–003
proceeds of sale, 10–002
proof of loss
breach of condition, 9–018
burden of proof, 9–015
CCTV footage, 9–019
circumstances of loss, 9–017
co-operation provisions, 9–016
details of loss, 9–017
documentation, 9–019
insurer's satisfaction, 9–019
liability insurance, 9–017
obligations, 9–016
time limits, 9–017
waiver, 9–018
property insurance, 10–003
proximate cause, 5–048
quantification, 4–005
seizure, 10–001
successive losses, 10–005
theft, 10–001
time of loss, 5–015
Marine cargo insurance
see also **"Freight clauses"**; **"Hulls clauses"**
commencement of risk, 24–066
explosions, 24–006
fire, 24–006
insurance contracts
all risks, 24–006
defined risks, 24–006
exclusions, 24–006
insurance policies
generally, 19–034
voyage policies, 24–047
termination, 24–066
Marine insurance
see also **General average; Voyage**
agency, 4–021, 15–003
assignment
beneficial interest, 24–074
generally, 24–074
indorsement, 24–074
lack of insurable interest, 24–075
method, 24–074
partial loss, 24–074
post-loss assignment, 24–074
pre-loss assignment, 24–074
timing, 24–074
betterment, 10–031
choice of law, 2–040
collisions
damage, 24–007

Marine insurance—*cont.*
collisions—*cont.*
liability, 24–001, 24–005
constructive total loss
abandonment, 11–067, 24–088, 24–089, 24–092, 24–094
effect, 24–082, 24–086—24–089
generally, 1–011
indemnities, 10–001, 24–111
contribution, 11–062
defence costs, 20–047
destruction of subject matter, 4–001, 4–003
development, 1–011
disclosure
agents, 24–041
details of voyage, 24–039
insured persons, 24–035
nature of vessel, 24–038
port details, 24–037
prior loss, 24–036
sailing date, 24–037
situation of vessel, 24–037
double insurance, 11–044, 11–045, 24–054
enforcement, 1–011
general principles, 24–008
goods in transit, 5–013
held covered clauses, 5–008
illegality, 5–036—5–039, 24–063
indemnities
constructive total loss, 24–111
extent of liability, 24–101
general average, 24–101, 24–107
measure of indemnity, 24–109
partial loss, 24–101, 24–103, 24–104, 24–111
particular average warranties, 24–110
salvage charges, 24–107
successive losses, 24–111
suing and labouring clauses, 24–112
third party liabilities, 24–108
total loss, 24–102
unvalued policies, 24–101
valuation, 24–106
valued policies, 24–101
insurable interests
advanced freight, 24–026
agency, 24–030
assignment, 24–032
bottomry, 24–024
contingent interests, 24–021
criminal sanctions, 24–016
defeasible interests, 24–021
definition, 24–017
expectation of interest, 24–014
lack of insurable interest, 24–075
lost or not lost cover, 24–020
master's wages, 24–025
mortgages, 24–029
ordinary freight, 24–026
ownership, 24–031
partial interest, 24–022
policy proof of interest, 24–015
quantum of interest, 24–028—24–031
reinsurance, 24–023

Marine insurance—*cont.*
  insurable interests—*cont.*
    seaman's wages, 24–025
    time of loss, 24–014, 24–018
    timing, 24–019
    trading freight, 24–026
    wagering contracts, 24–012, 24–013,
      24–015
  insurable value
    undervaluation, 24–033
    valuation, 24–033
  insurance charges, 24–027
  insurance contracts
    acceptance, 24–043
    incorporation, 24–044
    slips, 24–043
    waiver clauses, 24–073
  insurance policies
    details, 24–045
    floating policies, 24–051
    form of policy, 24–127
    held covered clauses, 24–053
    incorporation, 24–044
    interpretation, 24–052
    notice provisions, 24–053
    signature, 24–046
    subject matter, 24–048, 24–065
    time policies, 24–047
    unvalued policies, 24–050
    valued policies, 24–049
    voyage policies, 24–047
  insurance premiums
    assessment, 24–053
    failure of consideration, 24–118
    fraud, 24–118
    generally, 1–011
    illegality, 24–118
    insurance brokers, 24–077—24–079
    market rate, 24–053
    payment, 8–005, 24–007, 24–076
    premium to be arranged, 24–053
    receipt, 24–079, 24–079
    return, 8–019, 8–022, 8–023, 8–025,
      8–031, 8–032, 24–116—24–118
  insurable interests, 1–011, 4–001, 4–003,
    4–009, 4–010, 4–015
  insurers' rights
    contribution, 24–114
    subrogation, 24–113
    underinsurance, 24–115
  interpretation
    all other perils, 24–139
    at and from, 24–130
    average unless general, 24–140
    barratry, 24–138
    freight, 24–143
    from, 24–129
    from the loading thereof, 24–131
    goods, 24–144
    lost or not lost, 24–128
    maritime perils, 24–137
    perils of the sea, 24–134
    pirates, 24–135
    safely landed, 24–132

Marine insurance—*cont.*
  interpretation—*cont.*
    ship, 24–142
    scuttling, 24–138
    stranded, 24–141
    thieves, 24–137
    touch and stay, 24–133
  Law Commission reforms, 4–027
  legislation, 1–011
  liability, 24–001, 24–005, 24–007
  loss
    actual total loss, 24–082, 24–083, 24–092
    delays, 24–080
    external accident, 24–080
    freight, 24–080
    good in specie, 24–082
    hulls, 24–080
    inherent vice, 24–080, 24–081
    injury to machinery, 24–080
    insurer's liability, 24–080
    leakage and breakage, 24–080
    marine cargo, 24–080
    missing vessel, 24–084
    negligence, 24–080
    proximate cause, 24–080
    total loss, 10–001, 10–009, 10–029,
      11–066, 11–067
    transhipment, 24–085
    vermin, 24–080
    war risk claims, 24–085
    wear and tear, 24–080, 24–081
    wilful misconduct, 24–080
  Marine Insurance Act 1906
    marine adventure, 24–011
    marine insurance, 24–009
    maritime perils, 24–011
    mixed sea and land risks, 24–010
    savings, 24–125
    short title, 24–126
  materiality, 24–036, 24–037
  mitigation, 1–011, 10–038
  negligence, 5–048, 24–007
  non-marine insurance, distinguished, 1–011
  partial loss
    abandonment, 24–088
    assignment, 24–074
    general average loss, 24–100
    generally, 10–001, 24–082
    indemnities, 24–101, 24–103, 24–104,
      24–111
    particular average loss, 24–098
    salvage charges, 24–099
    valued policies, 10–009
  P&I clubs
    function, 24–007
    members, 24–007
    rules, 24–007
  ratification, 1–011, 24–120
  reasonable time provisions, 24–122
  renewal, 6–053
  representations
    material representations, 24–042
    representations of expectations, 24–042
    representations of fact, 24–042

Marine insurance—*cont.*
 representations—*cont.*
  withdrawal, 24–042
 risk
  commencement of cover, 5–003
  deviation from agreed risk, 5–013
  generally, 1–011
  increase of risk, 5–017, 5–018
  successive causes, 5–030
 seaworthiness, 24–061, 24–062
 scuttling, 24–040, 24–138
 slips, 24–123
 sources, 1–011
 subject to average, 1–011
 theft, 19–049
 time policies, 24–047
  see also **Time policies**
 transhipment, 5–014
 utmost good faith, 24–034
 variation, 24–121
 voyage policies, 24–047
  see also **Voyage policies**
 warranties
  breach of warranty, 24–056
  change of circumstances, 24–056
  commencement of risk, 24–061
  compliance, 24–055
  express, 7–023, 24–055, 24–057
  good safety, 24–060, 24–065
  implied, 7–023, 24–055, 24–059,
   24–061—24–064
  law reform, 7–054
  legality, 1–011, 24–064
  meaning, 24–055
  nationality, 24–059
  neutrality, 24–058
  promissory, 24–055
  proximate cause, 24–061
  seaworthiness, 24–061, 24–062
  waiver, 24–056
"Marine perils"
 dependent on due diligence, 24–001, 24–003
 irrespective of due diligence, 24–001,
  24–002
 maritime perils, 24–137
 perils of the sea, 24–134
Market Reform Contract
 contents, 1–045
Materiality
 see also **Moral hazard**; **"Prudent insurer
  test"**; **Valuation**
 agency, 6–035
 assessment date, 6–032
 avoidance, 6–033, 6–034
 convictions, 6–048
 definition, 6–021, 6–045
 disclosure, 6–001, 6–002, 6–004, 6–005,
  6–114
 discrimination, 6–051
 dishonesty, 6–049, 6–050
 double insurance, 6–058
 express questions, 6–045
 life insurance, 6–021
 marine insurance, 24–036, 24–037

Materiality—*cont.*
 materiality of intelligence, 6–026
 misconduct, 6–050
 motor insurance, 22–087
 physical hazard, 6–045, 6–061, 6–062
 premium-sensitive factors, 6–045
 presumed fact, 6–026
 previous loss, 6–052
 proof of materiality, 6–007
 refusals to insure
  agency, 6–055
  interpretation, 6–053
  marine insurance, 6–053
  motor insurance, 6–053
  utmost good faith, 6–053
 reinstatement, 6–103
 renewal, 6–103
 warranties, 7–041
Misconduct
 co-insurance, 14–011, 14–013
 criminal conduct, 5–043, 5–046
 deliberate destruction, 5–041
 effect, 5–035, 5–040
 immunity from suit, 11–029
 materiality, 6–050
 moral hazard, 6–050
 recklessness, 5–042, 5–043, 5–046
 wilful misconduct, 5–041, 5–043, 5–047,
  14–011, 14–013
Misrepresentation
 best knowledge and belief, 6–013
 burden of proof, 6–031
 causation, 6–020
 common law, 6–007
 correction of earlier statements, 6–011
 damages, 6–080
 false answers, 6–018
 fraud, 6–017
 fraudulent misrepresentation, 6–016, 6–017
 inducement, 6–021
 innocent misrepresentation, 6–016
 insurance brokers, 6–060
 materiality, 6–007
 misleading answers, 6–018
 negligence, 6–016
 open cover, 6–119
 questions
  ambiguity, 6–018
  general questions, 6–019
 representation, 6–008
 return of premium, 8–025, 8–026
 silence, 6–010
 statements
  expectation, 6–014
  fact, 6–012—6–014
  false statements, 6–009, 6–012, 6–013
  intention, 6–014
  opinion, 6–013
  untrue statements, 6–015
 utmost good faith, 6–001, 6–004
 warranties, 6–007
Mitigation
 breach of contract, 10–038
 costs, 10–039

Mitigation—*cont.*
  damage prevention, 10–038
  common law duty, 10–038
  marine insurance, 1–011, 10–038
  motor insurance, 22–025, 22–026
Moral hazard
  convictions, 6–048
  dishonesty, 6–045, 6–050
  insurable interests, 6–047
  insured persons, 6–046
  meaning, 6–045
  misconduct, 6–050
Mortgage indemnity policies
  contribution, 19–025
  foreclosure, 19–025
  immunity from suit, 11–033
  insurable interests, 19–025
  mortgagees
    interest insurance, 19–025
    power to insure, 19–027
  mortgagor's interest insurance, 19–025
  proceeds, 19–026, 19–028
  reinstatement, 19–025, 19–026, 19–028
  sale, 19–025
  subrogation, 19–025
Mortgagees' interest insurance
  assignment, 23–001
  bank finance, 23–001
  breach of warranty, 23–001
  building societies, 23–001
  composite policies, 23–001
  fraudulent claims, 23–001
  generally, 19–025, 23–001
  indemnities, 23–004
  insurable value, 23–004
  interest insurance clauses
    exclusions, 23–002
    insurance period, 23–003
    insurance policy, 23–003
    risks, 23–002
  lender security, 23–001
  marine insurance, 23–001
  payment, 23–005
  protection, 23–001
  subrogation, 23–006
  suing and labouring clauses, 23–007
  utmost good faith, 23–001
Motor insurance
  see also **Motor insurance (compulsory
    insurance)**; **Motor Insurers' Bureau**;
    Motor vehicles
  breakdown insurance, 13–012
  cloned cars, 12–033
  disclosure, 22–087
  exclusions, 12–033
  first party cover
    conditions precedent, 22–086
    extensions, 22–086
    fully comprehensive, 22–086
    generally, 22–001
    minimal cover, 22–086
    repudiation, 22–086
    limitations, 22–086
    third party claims, 22–086

Motor insurance—*cont.*
  illegality, 5–036, 5–037, 5–039
  insurance certificates
    fleet vehicles, 22–091
    identity of vehicle, 22–091
  insurable interests, 20–062
  insurance policies
    exclusions, 22–091, 22–097, 22–098,
      22–099
    extensions, 22–091
    first party loss, 22–091
    vehicles covered, 22–091
  insurance premiums
    return, 8–019
  materiality, 22–087
  misstatement, 22–087
  negligence, 5–050, 5–051
  regulation, 13–009
  renewal, 6–053
  temporary cover, 1–050
  theft, 12–033
  third party claims, 21–002
  utmost good faith, 22–087
  valuation, 12–033
Motor insurance (compulsory insurance)
  see also **Green card system**; **Passengers**;
    Uninsured drivers; **Untraced drivers**
  causing or permitting uninsured use, 22–010
  change of insurer, 22–005
  Crown use, 22–003
  defences, 22–002, 22–009
  enforcement actions
    avoidance declarations, 22–048
    breach of condition, 22–038
    defences, 22–044
    delivery of insurance certificate, 22–039
    form of proceedings, 22–038
    notice of proceedings, 22–045
    policy limitations, 22–039
    post-claim conduct, 22–045
    prior judgments, 22–038, 22–039
    right of recourse, 22–043
    stay of execution, 22–046
    surrender of insurance certificate, 22–047
    user's insurers, 22–039
  EU law
    claims procedure, 22–081
    claims representatives, 22–080, 22–081
    compensation claims, 22–080, 22–081
    compulsory insurance 22–001, 22–036,
      22–041
    direct actions, 22–049, 22–050
    foreign compensation bodies, 22–081
    identity of vehicle, 22–080, 22–081
    implementation, 22–081
    indemnification, 22–081
    information centres, 22–082
    Member State residence, 22–080
    passengers, 22–031, 22–035
    specified information, 22–082
    subrogation, 22–081
    unidentified insurers, 22–081
  exclusions, 22–003

Motor insurance (compulsory insurance)—*cont.*
failure to insure
breach of statutory duty, 22–012, 22–013
civil action, 22–012
criminal offence, 22–012
damages, 22–012
limitation periods, 22–013
Motor Insurer's Bureau, 22–012
subrogation, 22–012
tort, 22–012, 22–013
third party losses, 22–012
insurance certificates
delivery, 22–015, 22–039
destruction, 22–015
duplicates, 22–015
electronic communication, 22–015
failure to issue, 22–015
forgery, 22–015
formalities, 22–015
functions, 22–015
loss, 22–015
policy cancellation, 22–015
production, 22–015
return to insurer, 22–015
surrender, 22–047
insurance policies
breach of condition, 22–037
condition of vehicle, 22–036
criminal conduct, 22–028
driver's condition, 22–036
driving with permission, 22–027, 22–028
engine capacity, 22–036
EU law, 22–036, 22–041
exclusion clauses, 22–036, 22–041
extension clauses, 22–027
formalities, 22–014
goods carried, 22–036
insured persons, 22–027
intentional damage, 22–028
intoxication, 22–028
limitations, 22–039
misconduct, 22–028
negligence, 22–028
non-business purposes, 22–036
passenger restrictions, 22–036
running-down cases, 22–028, 22–029, 22–039
social and domestic use, 22–036
specified vehicles, 22–027
use in question, 22–039
use of vehicle, 22–036
user extensions, 22–027
value of vehicle, 22–036
vehicle identification, 22–036
insurers
authorisation, 22–016
EU-based insurers, 22–016
legislation, 22–001
liabilities
aggravated damages, 22–023
arising out of use, 22–030
damage to property, 22–019
death, 22–017

Motor insurance (compulsory insurance)—*cont.*
liabilities—*cont.*
driver's injuries, 22–017
emergency medical treatment, 22–022
employees, 2–017, 22–018
EU-based vehicles, 22–020
EU law, 22–017, 22–018, 22–020
EU use of vehicle, 22–021
exclusions, 22–036, 22–041
extent, 22–042
health care, 22–022
hire charges, 22–024—22–026
insured drivers, 22–040
legislation, 22–017, 22–018
loss of no claims bonus, 22–023
loss of unexpired premium, 22–023
mitigation, 22–025, 22–026
negligence, 11–017, 22–024
passengers, 22–017, 22–018
personal injury, 22–017
private health insurance, 22–022
replacement vehicles, 22–024, 22–026
statutory liability, 22–040—22–042
storage of vehicles, 22–023
sum insured, 22–017
uninsured drivers, 22–041, 22–043
unlicensed drivers, 22–041
motor vehicles, 22–006
named drivers, 22–002
offences, 22–002
policy in force, 22–011
policyholders, 22–002
roads or other public places, 22–007, 22–008
right of direct action
accidents, 22–050, 22–054
conditions, 22–039
entitlement, 22–038, 22–051, 22–052
EU law, 22–049, 22–050
insured persons, 22–053
limitations, 22–056
public policy, 22–040
strict liability, 22–002
third party claims, 22–001
third party risks, 22–004
use of vehicle, 22–009, 22–010
Motor Insurers' Bureau
see also **Uninsured drivers**; **Untraced drivers**
claims, 22–057
EU law, 22–001
failure to insure, 22–012
jurisdiction, 22–078
liability
generally, 22–060
uninsured drivers, 22–062, 22–069
untraced drivers, 22–075, 22–076
members, 22–057
reasoned decisions, 22–078
role, 22–001, 22–057
running-down cases, 22–029
subrogation, 22–012

Motor Insurers' Information Centre
see also **Motor Insurers' Bureau**
information, 22–082
fees, 22–082
function, 22–082
records, 22–082
Motor vehicles
adapted vehicles, 22–006
control, 22–009, 22–010
damage, 22–095
efficient condition, 22–093
hire or reward, 22–097
identity, 22–080, 22–081, 22–091
loads, 22–099
loss, 22–095
meaning, 22–006, 22–055
mechanically propelled vehicles, 22–006
roadworthiness, 22–092
theft, 22–094
use
business use, 22–096
competence of driver, 22–089
concurrent use, 22–098
consent, 22–088
course of employment, 22–088
first party personal injury, 22–090
generally, 22–006, 22–009, 22–010
named users, 22–088
permitted users, 22–088
place of use, 22–010
social or domestic use, 22–096
third party claims, 22–088
time of use, 22–100
Mutual societies
insurance premiums, 8–006
marine insurance, 24–007, 24–119
P&I clubs
function, 24–007
members, 24–007
rules, 24–007
regulation, 13–014
Negligence
accidents, 5–048
common law, 5–048
damages, 6–079
fire, 5–048
goods in transit insurance, 5–051
liability, 5–048
marine insurance, 5–048
motor insurance, 5–050, 5–051
proximate cause of loss, 5–048
reasonable care clauses, 5–049, 5–050
recklessness, 5–050
Non-payment
actions for payment, 8–011, 8–012
cancellation, 8–016
forfeiture, 8–011, 8–014, 8–016
liability, 8–012
life insurance, 8–016
postponement of contract, 8–015
premium warranties, 8–016, 8–018
repudiation, 8–017
rejection of claims, 8–011, 8–013
termination of policy, 8–011, 8–014, 8–015

Notification of loss clauses
assertion of discontent, 20–038
bare conditions, 20–037
breach of condition, 9–004
claims made policies, 20–037, 20–038
conditions precedent, 9–004, 20–037,
20–039
demands for payment, 20–038
disclosure, 20–037
exercise of options, 9–010
extension clauses, 20–037
fixed notification periods, 9–005, 9–007
form of notice, 9–009
generally, 9–011, 20–037
knowledge of loss, 9–011
immediate notice clauses, 9–005, 9–006
liability insurance, 9–011
losses occurring policies, 20–037
notice of abandonment, 9–002
notification of circumstances,
20–037—20–042
obligations, 9–005, 9–016, 9–017, 20–037
primary layer policy, 9–013
prompt notification, 20–040
recipients of notice, 9–013
relevant circumstances, 20–042
relevant knowledge, 20–038—20–040
requirement, 9–002
responsibility for notice, 9–010
service of claim form, 20–038
third party claims, 20–038
timely notification, 9–005, 9–008
underwriters, 9–013
unintentional notification, 9–012
written notice, 20–039
"Occurrence"
limitations, 10–034
Offer
see also **Formation of contract**
express terms, 1–022
incorporation, 1–022
insured persons, 1–022, 1–024
insurers, 1–023
lapsed offers, 1–029
Open cover
duty of disclosure, 6–118
facultative cover, 1–031, 6–117
facultative obligatory cover, 6–117
insurer's liability, 1–031
obligatory, 1–031, 6–117, 6–118, 6–120
risk, 1–031
"Originating cause"
limitations, 10–035
Passengers
see also **Motor insurance (compulsory
insurance)**
carried for hire or reward, 22–031
common illegal enterprise, 22–034
contributory negligence, 22–035
crash helmets, 22–035
drunk drivers, 22–034, 22–035
EU law, 22–031, 22–035
injuries, 22–031
insurance requirements, 22–031

Passengers—*cont.*
meaning, 22–031
owners. as, 22–032
private vehicles, 22–031
public policy, 22–034
public service vehicles, 22–031
restrictions, 22–036
seat belts, 22–035
users, as, 22–009
volenti non fit injuria
acceptance of risk, 22–033
negligent drivers, 22–033
recklessness, 22–033
Payments
agency, 8–003, 15–014
apportionment, 1–003
binding agreement, 8–004
cheques, 8–002
commencement of risk, 8–004
credit arrangements, 1–003
credit cards, 8–002
direct debits, 8–002
forms of payment, 8–002
instalments, 8–002
insurance brokers, 8–007
insured persons, 1–001
issue of policy, 8–005
late payment
effect, 8–011, 8–014, 8–017
marine insurance, 8–018
repudiation, 8–017
time not of the essence, 8–017
marine insurance, 8–005
mutual societies, 8–006
non-cash payments, 8–002
non-payment
actions for payment, 8–011, 8–012
cancellation, 8–016
forfeiture, 8–011, 8–014, 8–016
liability, 8–012
life insurance, 8–016
postponement of contract, 8–015
premium warranties, 8–016, 8–018
repudiation, 8–017
rejection of claims, 8–011, 8–013
termination of policy, 8–011, 8–014,
8–015
periodical payments, 1–003
rate of premium, 8–002
single premium, 8–002
standing orders, 8–002
stipulations, 8–004
Personal representatives
insurable interests, 19–031
Pirates
meaning, 24–135
Policies
see **Insurance policies**
Premiums
see **Insurance premiums**
Product liability
applicable law, 2–065
contractual liability, 20–077
damage to persons, 20–076

Product liability—*cont.*
damage to property, 20–076
defective products, 20–076
economic loss, 20–076
exclusions, 20–076
installation of product, 20–076
insurance policies
period of cover, 20–074
risk, 20–075
negligence, 20–077
resale, 20–076
strict liability, 20–077
tortious liability, 20–076, 20–077
Professional indemnity insurance
compulsory insurance, 20–003, 20–006
drop down clauses, 20–032
excess layer policy, 20–032
leading counsel's opinion, 20–046
liability insurance, 20–006, 20–009, 20–032
master policy, 20–032
primary layer policy, 20–032
unqualified persons, 20–031
Proof
breach of condition, 9–018
burden of proof, 9–015
CCTV footage, 9–019
circumstances of loss, 9–017
co-operation provisions, 9–016
details of loss, 9–017
documentation, 9–019
insurer's satisfaction, 9–019
liability insurance, 9–017
obligations, 9–016
time limits, 9–017
waiver, 9–018
Property insurance
see also **Burglary**; **Goods**; **Landlords**;
Tenants
agency, 4–021
bailment
duty of care, 19–011
insurable interests, 19–010
insurance policies, 19–012, 19–013
contracts of insurance, 1–014
defective title, 19–054
exclusions
defective design, 19–059
inherent vice, 19–056
mysterious disappearance clauses, 19–058
unlawful risks, 19–057
wear and tear, 19–055
indemnity principle
amount of recovery, 19–003
contracting out, 19–003
indemnities, 19–003
lack of insurable interest, 19–004
return of insurance premiums, 19–004
insurable interests
amount of recovery, 19–003
bailment, 19–010
beneficiaries, 19–030
buildings, 19–002
co-insurance, 19–005
composite policies, 19–005

Property insurance—*cont.*
  insurable interests—*cont.*
    contractors, 19–032
    creditors, 19–029
    destination of benefits, 19–006
    generally, 4–010
    goods, 19–001, 19–004, 19–005, 19–007,
      19–014
    joint policies, 19–005
    lack of insurable interests, 19–004
    land, 19–002
    landlords, 19–015—19–017, 19–020
    personal representatives, 19–031
    possession of goods, 19–007, 19–014
    purchasers, 19–008
    sellers, 19–008
    tenants, 19–015—19–017, 19–020
    transfer of benefits, 19–006
    trustees, 4–019, 19–030
  insurance policies
    aggravated vehicle-taking, 19–050
    all risks policies, 19–034
    buildings, 19–034, 19–043
    defective property, 19–034
    escape, 19–042
    explosions, 19–041
    fire, 19–039, 19–040
    floods, 19–037
    goods, 19–034
    impact damage, 19–043
    increase of risk, 19–034
    location of subject matter, 19–044
    marine cargo insurance, 19–034
    storm, 19–035
    subsidence, 19–038
    tempest, 19–036
  jurisdiction, 2–012
  materiality
    immoveable property, 19–033
    moveable property, 19–033
  purchasers
    assignment, 19–009
    insurable interests, 19–008
    proceeds of policy, 19–009
    subrogation, 19–009
  robbery, 19–052
  sellers
    assignment, 19–009
    insurable interests, 19–008
    proceeds of policy, 19–009
    subrogation, 19–009
  theft, 19–045, 19–046, 19–049, 19–050
  time of loss, 5–015
"Prudent insurer test"
  assumed facts, 6–026
  degree of knowledge, 6–022
  decisive influence test, 6–024
  inducement, 6–113
  insurance premiums, 6–023
  materiality, 6–026, 6–113
  mere influence, 6–024
  nature of policy, 6–023
  risk
    increased risk, 6–024

"Prudent insurer test"—*cont.*
  risk—*cont.*
    risk assessment, 6–023
  standard of prudence, 6–022
  underwriters, 6–025
Purchasers
  assignment, 19–009
  insurable interests, 19–008
  proceeds of policy, 19–009
  subrogation, 19–009
Receivership
  administrative receivers, 16–015
  floating charges, 16–015
  legislation, 16–015
  procedure, 16–015
Rectification
  common intention, 1–018, 1–019
  entitlement, 1–019, 1–020
  insurance premiums, 8–024
  refusal, 1–020
  requirements, 1–018
Regulation
  see also **Conduct of business**; **Financial**
    Services Authority; **Transfer of going**
    concern
  disciplinary sanctions, 13–006
  enforcement powers, 13–004, 13–006
  EU law, 13–003, 13–019, 13–022, 13–024,
    13–025
  European Economic Area, 13–022—13–025
  General Prudential Rules, 13–040
  Insurance Prudential Rules, 13–028, 13–040
  legislation, 13–002
  Lloyds, 13–040
  general principles, 13–006
  types of insurer, 13–001
  underwriters, 15–021
Reinstatement
  contractual reinstatement
    betterment, 10–044
    combination of insurers, 10–046
    damaged buildings, 10–040
    damaged chattels, 10–040
    damages, 10–044
    delay, 10–044
    duty to reinstate, 10–049
    election to reinstate. 10–044, 10–046,
      10–047
    exclusion clauses, 10–045
    frustration, 10–047
    impossibility of reinstatement, 10–047,
      10–048
    option to reinstate, 10–042, 10–043
    purpose, 10–040
    reinstatement clauses, 10–040, 10–041
  disclosure, 6–105
  fire, 1–011, 10–050, 10–051
  life insurance, 8–010
  materiality, 6–105
  mortgage indemnity policies, 19–025
  new agreements, 6–105
  statutory reinstatement
    composite policies, 10–051
    damages, 10–052

Reinstatement—*cont.*
  statutory reinstatement—*cont.*
    delays, 10–052
    discretion to reinstate, 10–051, 10–052
    faulty reinstatement, 10–052
    fraud, 10–051
    injunctions, 10–052
    insurer's obligations, 10–052
    interests parties, 10–051
    proceeds of policy, 10–052
    refusal to reinstate, 10–052
    third parties, 10–052
Reinsurance
  applicable law, 2–021, 2–036, 2–040, 2–041, 2–043, 2–050
  assets, 17–003
  authorisation
    minimum guarantee fund, 17–003
    professional qualifications, 17–003
    scheme of operations, 17–003
  contract terms
    advance of insurance, 17–005
    arbitration clauses, 17–016, 17–018
    agency, 17–005
    back to back cover, 17–014
    claims control clauses, 17–025
    claims cooperation clauses, 17–025
    conditions precedent, 17–025
    dispute resolution, 17–016
    duration clauses, 17–014
    express terms, 17–011
    honourable engagement clauses, 17–016
    implied terms, 17–013
    incorporation, 17–012
    inspection clauses, 17–015, 17–026
    insurance brokers, 17–005
    interpretation, 17–014
    loss, 17–017
    ultimate net loss clause, 17–017
    unilateral contracts, 17–005
    utmost good faith, 17–006—17–010
    void for uncertainty, 17–016
    waiver, 17–008, 17–009
    warranties, 17–014
  cut-through clauses, 17–002
  definition, 17–001
  EU law, 17–003
  facultative, 17–001, 17–006, 17–014, 17–018
  finite reinsurance, 17–003
  follow the settlements
    allocation of loss, 17–023
    bona fide settlements, 17–019, 17–020
    clauses, 17–019, 17–020, 17–024
    commutations, 17–022
    costs, 17–024
    facultative agreements, 17–019
    liability, 17–019—17–021
    meaning, 17–019
    proof of loss, 17–019, 17–020
    rights, 17–021
  incorporation, 1–022
  increase of risk, 5–017
  insolvency, 17–002

Reinsurance—*cont.*
  insurable interests, 17–004, 20–062
  insurance brokers, 15–038
  jurisdiction, 2–008
  legislation, 17–003
  liability, 17–018
  limitations, 17–027
  outwards reinsurance
    generally, 15–020
    placement, 15–023
    recoveries, 15–024, 15–025
  parties, 17–002
  privity of contract, 17–002
  regulation, 13–017, 17–003
  renewal, 1–047, 17–010
  retrospective effect, 1–031
  settlement, 17–018
  solvency requirements, 17–003
  special purpose vehicles, 17–003
  treaties
    excess of loss, 17–001
    facultative obligatory treaty, 17–001, 17–007
    framework facility, 17–001
    non-proportional reinsurance, 17–001
    obligatory, 17–001
    proportional reinsurance, 17–001, 17–002, 17–007, 17–014
    quota share, 17–001
    stop loss, 17–001
    surplus, 17–001
  utmost good faith
    disclosure, 17–006, 17–008
    duty, 17–006
    excesses, 17–007
    false statements, 17–006
    immaterial factors, 17–007
    materiality, 17–007
    retrocession cover, 17–007
    underwriting practices, 17–007
    waiver, 17–008, 17–009
    warranties, 17–006
Renewal
  accident insurance, 18–003
  agency, 15–016
  agreement, 1–047
  annual re-signing, 1–047
  automatic renewal, 5–008
  continuation of policy, 8–009
  days of grace, 8–009
  disclosure, 6–105
  effect, 1–046, 8–009
  false representations, 6–105
  interpretation, 8–009
  life insurance, 1–048, 6–105, 8–009
  materiality, 6–105
  new agreements, 6–105
  notice of cancellation at anniversary date (NCAD), 1–047, 5–008
  payment, 8–009
  refusal to tender, 8–009
  reinsurance, 1–047, 17–010
  self-renewal, 1–047
  temporary cover, 8–009

Renewal—*cont.*
  termination of policy, 8–009
  terms, 1–049
  utmost good faith, 6–105
Renvoi
  exclusion, 2–062, 2–065
  meaning, 2–049
  non-recognition, 2–049
Repudiation
  breach of contract terms, 7–008, 7–009,
    8–028
  conditions, 7–005, 7–006, 7–008, 9–003
  fraudulent claims, 9–032, 9–034
  insurance premium
    late payment, 8–017
    non-payment, 8–017
    return of premium, 8–028
  non-disclosure, 6–002
Retentions
  see **Excesses**
Return of premiums
  agreement, 8–019
  apportionment, 8–021, 8–032
  attachment of risk, 8–029
  avoidance, 8–023, 8–025, 8–026
  defeasible interests, 8–030
  double insurance, 8–032
  executory contracts, 8–022
  failure of consideration, 8–020
  fraud, 8–022, 8–025
  illegality, 8–022
  insurable interests, 8–031
  liability, 8–023
  life insurance, 8–020, 8–024, 8–031
  marine insurance, 8–019, 8–022, 8–023,
    8–025, 8–031, 8–032
  misrepresentation, 8–025, 8–026
  mistake, 8–022, 8–024
  motor insurance, 8–019
  no valid contract, 8–024
  over-insurance, 8–033, 8–034
  rectification, 8–024
  repudiation, 8–028
  warranties, 8–027
Right of direct action
  accidents, 22–050, 22–054
  conditions, 22–039
  entitlement, 22–038, 22–051, 22–052
  EU law, 22–049, 22–050
  insured persons, 22–053
  limitations, 22–056
  public policy, 22–040
Riot
  compensation, 25–010
  definition, 25–010
  marine insurance, 25–010
  police authorities, 25–010
  statutory offence, 25–010
Risk
  see also **"Increase of risk"; Notification of
    loss clauses**
  change of risk
    alteration of subject matter, 5–016,
      5–024—5–028

Risk—*cont.*
  change of risk—*cont.*
    common law, 5–024
    continuing warranties, 5–026, 5–027
    express warranties, 5–024
    failure to meet description, 5–024—5–026
    interpretation of policy, 5–024, 5–026,
      5–027
    material changes, 5–019, 5–027
    notification requirements, 5–027
    suspension of risk, 5–028
  commencement of cover
    attachment of risk, 5–001, 5–002
    contract date, 5–001
    liability backdated, 5–001
    postponement of risk, 5–001
  contra proferentem, 5–004
  duration of cover, 5–008
  duration of risk, 5–005
  early termination clauses, 5–007
  goods in transit insurance, 5–003,
    5–009—5–011
  marine insurance, 5–003
  notification of loss clauses
    breaches, 5–023
    limitations, 5–023
  open cover, 1–031
  termination, 5–005, 5–006—5–008
  time of loss, 5–015
  time policies, 5–003, 5–004
  transfer of risk, 1–010
  voyage policies, 5–003
Risk clauses
  see also **Notification of loss clauses**
  contractual provisions, 5–015
  good faith, 5–017, 5–018
  notification clauses, 5–023
  notification requirements, 5–018, 5–019
  variation of risk, 5–017, 5–018
Robbery
  definition, 19–052
  property insurance, 19–052
Rome I Regulation
  choice of law, 2–028—2–030, 2–033, 2–036,
    2–037, 2–042, 2–043
  consumer risks, 2–045
  contracts of insurance, 2–019,
    2–021—2–023, 2–027, 2–028
  formation of contract, 2–051—2–054
  non-large risks, 2–046—2–048
Rome Convention
  choice of law, 2–028—2–030, 2–036, 2–037,
    2–041, 2–042, 2–043
  consumer risks, 2–045
  contracts of insurance, 2–018—2–022,
    2–027
Salvage
  see also **"Abandonment"**
  contracting out, 24–097
  expenses, 24–088, 24–099
  partial loss, 24–099
  subrogation, 11–021
Schemes of arrangement
  see also **Liquidation**

Schemes of arrangement—*cont.*
approval, 16–005
contingent schemes, 16–005
creditors' meetings, 16–005
EU law, 16–005
reserving schemes, 16–005
valuation schemes, 16–005
Seaworthiness
concept, 24–062
goods, 24–063
negligence, 24–062
presumption of unseaworthiness, 24–062
privity of assured, 24–062
state of vessel, 24–062
time policies, 24–061, 24–062
trivial defects, 24–062
voyage policies, 24–061, 24–062
warranties
burden of proof, 24–061
implied, 1–011, 24–061
Seizure
goods, 10–001
war risks, 25–012
Sellers
assignment, 19–009
insurable interests, 19–008
proceeds of policy, 19–009
subrogation, 19–009
Set-off
applicable law, 2–060
insolvency, 16–013
third party claims, 9–047
Settlement
avoidance, 10–055
binding agreement, 10–055
co-insurance, 10–056
conditional settlement, 10–059
enforcement, 10–055
ex gratia payments, 10–054
following market, 10–056
interim payments, 10–053
liability insurance, 20–057—20–061
misrepresentation, 10–057
mistake
degree of mistake, 10–058
fundamental mistake, 10–057, 10–058
mistake of fact, 10–057, 10–058
mistake of law, 10–058
nature of loss, 10–057
no loss suffered
indemnities, 10–064
non-indemnity policies, 10–064
partial loss payments, 10–064
total loss payments, 10–064
non-disclosure, 10–057
prior payment
acceptance, 10–060
change of position, 10–062
effect, 10–060
insurance brokers, 10–063
mistake of fact, 10–060
mistake of law, 10–060
money payable in any event, 10–061
recovery, 10–060

Settlement—*cont.*
prior payment—*cont.*
restitution, 10–060, 10–062
subsequent challenges, 10–060
third parties, 10–062
separate policies, 10–056
voluntary settlement, 10–055
Slips
amendment slips, 1–039, 1–040
amount of liability, 1–032
contracts of insurance
binding contracts, 1–018, 1–033, 1–034
formation, 1–034
duty of disclosure, 6–116
false statements, 6–116
following market, 1–032
fronting arrangements, 1–042
insurance brokers, 1–032
insurance policies
interpretation, 1–033
issue, 1–033
status, 1–033
line slips, 1–041
marine insurance, 24–043
materiality, 6–116
misrepresentation, 6–116
modification, 1–037
oversubscription, 1–038
scratching, 1–032—1–035, 1–037, 1–039,
6–116
slip policy, 1–032
subscription procedure, 1–032—1–034,
1–036
underwriters, 1–032, 1–033, 1–035
utmost good faith, 1–033
"Storm"
insurance policies, 19–035
Subrogation
see also **Immunity from suit**
applicable law, 2–060, 2–061, 2–065
co-insurance, 14–018
contractual right, 11–002
contribution, 11–052, 11–065
definition, 11–001
effect, 11–001
equitable origins, 11–002, 11–037
fidelity insurance, 23–028
implied terms, 11–002
indemnities
calculation of amount, 11–007
contract of indemnity, 11–001, 11–005,
23–030
receipt of indemnity, 11–006
requirement, 11–006
insurer's conduct, 11–037
insurer's rights (post-indemnity)
abuse of process, 11–015
control of proceedings, 11–013, 1–014,
11–017, 11–018
ex gratia payments, 11–016
full indemnification, 11–013
insured person's loss, 11–012
insured person's name, 11–011
partial indemnification, 11–014

Subrogation—*cont.*
  insurer's rights (post-indemnity)—*cont.*
    res judicata, 11–015
    uninsured losses, 11–015
    volunteer principle, 11–016
  insurer's rights (pre-indemnity)
    insured person's claims, 11–009
    pre-indemnity rights, 11–008
    pre-payment rights, 11–008
    third party claims, 11–010
  juridical basis, 11–002
  loss of rights (agreements)
    after full indemnity, 11–043
    after loss, 11–042
    before full indemnity, 11–042
    insured persons, 11–040—11–043
    insurers, 11–038, 11–039
    prior to loss, 11–041
    subrogation waiver, 11–038
  mortgage indemnity policies, 19–025
  negative role, 11–001
  objectives, 11–001
  payments to insured persons
    damages for uninsured loss, 11–035
    diminution of loss, 11–034
    ex gratia payments, 11–036
    third party indemnity, 11–034
  positive aspects, 11–001
  proper claimants, 11–001
  recoveries
    allocation, 11–017
    costs, 11–023
    interest, 11–022
    layered insurance, 11–019
    payment, 11–020
    salvage rights, 11–021
    specific examples, 11–018
    surpluses, 11–017, 11–021
    third parties, 11–022
  related doctrines
    abandonment, 11–003
    assignment, 11–004
  restitution, 11–002
  third party claims, 11–002, 21–002
  unjust enrichment, 11–001
Subsidence
  property insurance, 19–038
Successive causes
  accident insurance, 5–030, 5–031
  chain of causation, 5–030
  causation test, 5–029
  exclusions, 5–031
  inevitability cases, 5–030
  intention, 5–029
  marine insurance, 5–030
  property insurance, 5–030
  proximity rule, 5–029, 5–030
  series of events, 5–029
  state of affairs cases, 5–030
  weakening cases, 5–030
Suicide
  assisted suicide, 18–033, 18–034
  common law, 18–033
  criminal nature, 18–033, 18–034

Suicide—*cont.*
  life insurance policies
    exceptions, 18–034
    express terms, 18–034
    forfeiture principle, 18–035
    insane suicide, 18–033, 18–034
    wilful misconduct, 18–033, 18–035
  murder, 18–035
  sound mind, 18–033, 18–034
"Suing and labouring clauses"
  amount recoverable, 24–112
  averting and minimising loss, 24–112
  exclusions, 24–112
  expenses, 24–112
  mitigation costs, 24–112
Sureties
  discharge of debt, 23–019
  employee fidelity, 23–018
  payment of creditors, 23–019
Suretyship
  guarantees, distinguished, 23–019
  equitable basis, 23–019
  general insurance business, 23–018
"Tempest"
  property insurance, 19–036
Temporary cover
  cover notes, 1–050
  creation, 1–051
  documentation, 1–050
  duration, 1–052
  issue, 1–054
  motor insurance, 1–050
  oral agreements, 1–050
  terms, 1–055
  third party interests, 1–054
  utmost good faith, 1–053
Tenants
  see also **Landlords**
  covenant to insure, 19–021, 19–022
  insurable interests, 19–020
  tenant's insurance, 19–017, 19–019, 19–021
  rights, 19–019
Terrorism
  definition, 25–014
  force or violence, 25–014
  organisation, 25–014
  overthrow of governments, 25–014
  political motive, 25–014
  terrorist acts, 25–004, 25–014
Theft
  see also **Property insurance**
  appropriation, 19–049
  marine insurance, 19–049
  meaning, 19–046, 19–049, 19–050
  motor vehicles, 22–094
  overlapping offences, 19–049
  thieves, 24–137
  valuable items, 19–053
Third Parties (Rights against Insurers) Act 1930
  alteration of rights, 21–034
  arbitration clauses, 21–029
  automatic events, 21–005
  avoidance, 21–021, 21–034

Third Parties (Rights against Insurers) Act 1930—*cont.*
background, 21–002
bankruptcy, 21–015
company dissolution, 21–014
company voluntary arrangements, 21–013
competing claims, 21–031
conditions precedent, 21–023
contingent claims, 21–035, 21–036
contracting out, 21–034—21–037
costs, 21–028
damages, 21–026
default judgments, 21–012
defences, 21–012
deficits, 21–033
disclosure, 21–040
establishing liability, 21–010, 21–011, 21–019
extraterritorial effect, 21–009
false information, 21–023
illegality, 21–022
individual voluntary arrangements, 21–013
information provisions, 21–039, 21–040
insurance premiums, 21–025
interest, 21–026, 21–027
interim payments, 21–016
liability insurance, 21–007
limitation periods, 21–017, 21–030
notice provisions, 21–023
partnerships, 21–005
pay to be paid clauses, 21–037
payment from insurers, 21–018, 21–019, 21–021—21–030, 21–032
pre-payment, 21–024, 21–037
pre-transfer breaches, 21–023
quantifying liability, 21–010, 21–011, 21–019
reinsurance, 21–008
risk, 21–021
settlement, 21–039
subrogation, 21–012
surpluses, 21–033
third party actions, 21–006
third party rights, 21–005, 21–039, 21–040
utmost good faith, 21–021
winding up orders, 21–006

Third Parties (Rights against Insurers) Act 2010
applicable law, 21–046, 21–048
application, 21–041, 21–045
arbitration clauses, 21–053, 21–054
background, 21–003
claim conditions, 21–058
claims against insured persons, 21–056
contracting out, 21–063
declaratory relief, 21–041, 21–051—21–055
defences, 21–051
disclosure, 21–065
exhaustion of funds, 21–064
extraterritorial effect, 21–046
individual voluntary arrangements, 21–041, 21–042
individuals, 21–043

Third Parties (Rights against Insurers) Act 2010—*cont.*
information provisions, 21–041, 21–058, 21–065—21–069
insolvency, 21–042
insurance contracts, 21–045
insurers' rights, 21–057
jurisdiction, 21–041, 21–046, 21–047
legal persons, 21–044
liability voluntary incurred, 21–045
limitation periods, 21–052, 21–062
marine insurance, 21–059
notification, 21–058, 21–068
pay to be paid clauses, 21–059
public policy, 21–061
set-off, 21–060
single actions, 21–041
third party actions, 21–041
third party rights, 21–041, 21–051
transfer of rights, 21–042, 21–049, 21–050, 21–058, 21–059

Third party rights
arbitration clauses, 9–052
beneficiaries, 21–002
capacity, 9–044
common law, 21–001
Contract (Rights of Third Parties) Act 1999
enforcement, 9–044—9–046, 9–048
identification of third party, 9–044
non-contracting parties, 9–044
rescission, 9–046
restrictions, 9–045
set-off, 9–047
subrogation rights, 9–044
variation of policy conditions, 9–045
creditors, 21–001
damages, 21–001
enforcement, 9–044—9–046, 9–048, 9–050
generally, 9–043
governing law, 9–052
identification of third party, 21–002
information provisions, 21–039, 21–040
insolvency, 21–001, 21–002, 21–012, 21–015, 21–017, 21–023
jurisdiction clauses, 9–052
law reform, 21–003
legislation, 21–002, 21–003
limitation periods, 9–052, 21–017
limitations, 10–036
motor insurance, 21–002, 22–001, 22–086, 22–088
privity of contract, 9–044, 21–002
separate claims, 9–051
settlement, 9–049
subrogation, 11–002, 21–002
surpluses, 21–033
Third Parties (Rights against Insurers) Act 1930
alteration of rights, 21–034
arbitration clauses, 21–029
automatic events, 21–005
avoidance, 21–021, 21–034
background, 21–002
bankruptcy, 21–015

Third party rights—*cont.*
Third Parties (Rights against Insurers) Act
1930—*cont.*
company dissolution, 21–014
company voluntary arrangements, 21–013
competing claims, 21–031
conditions precedent, 21–023
contingent claims, 21–035, 21–036, 21–03
contracting out, 21–034—21–037
costs, 21–028
damages, 21–026
default judgments, 21–012
defences, 21–012
deficits, 21–033
disclosure, 21–040
establishing liability, 21–010, 21–011,
21–019
extraterritorial effect, 21–009
false information, 21–023
illegality, 21–022
individual voluntary arrangements,
21–013
information provisions, 21–039, 21–040
insurance premiums, 21–025
interest, 21–026, 21–027
interim payments, 21–016
liability insurance, 21–007
limitation periods, 21–017, 21–030
notice provisions, 21–023
partnerships, 21–005
pay to be paid clauses, 21–037
payment from insurers, 21–018, 21–019,
21–021—21–030, 21–032
pre-payment, 21–024, 21–037
pre-transfer breaches, 21–023
quantifying liability, 21–010, 21–011,
21–019
reinsurance, 21–008
risk, 21–021
settlement, 21–039
subrogation, 21–012
surpluses, 21–033
third party actions, 21–006
third party rights, 21–005, 21–039,
21–040
utmost good faith, 21–021
winding up orders, 21–006
Third Parties (Rights against Insurers) Act
2010
applicable law, 21–046, 21–048
application, 21–041, 21–045
arbitration clauses, 21–053, 21–054
background, 21–003
claim conditions, 21–058
claims against insured persons, 21–056
contracting out, 21–063
declaratory relief, 21–041,
21–051—21–055
defences, 21–051
disclosure, 21–065
exhaustion of funds, 21–064
extraterritorial effect, 21–046
individual voluntary arrangements,
21–041, 21–042

Third party rights—*cont.*
Third Parties (Rights against Insurers) Act
2010—*cont.*
individuals, 21–043
information provisions, 21–041, 21–058,
21–065—21–069
insolvency, 21–042
insurance contracts, 21–045
insurers' rights, 21–057
jurisdiction, 21–041, 21–046, 21–047
legal persons, 21–044
liability voluntary incurred, 21–045
limitation periods, 21–052, 21–062
marine insurance, 21–059
notification, 21–058, 21–068
pay to be paid clauses, 21–059
public policy, 21–061
set-off, 21–060
single actions, 21–041
third party actions, 21–041
third party rights, 21–041, 21–051
transfer of rights, 21–042, 21–049,
21–050, 21–058, 21–059
waiver, 21–032
Time policies
accident insurance, 18–002
duration, 5–004
freight clauses, 24–047
hulls clauses, 24–047
interpretation, 5–004
meaning, 24–047
mixed policies, 24–047
risk, 5–003, 5–004
termination, 24–047
voyage policies, distinguished, 24–047
Transfer of going concern
EU law, 13–032
exempted transfers, 13–032
general business, 13–032
judicial sanction
application, 13–033
approval, 13–035
court orders, 13–036, 13–037
formalities, 13–034
legislation, 13–032
Lloyds, 13–032
long-term business, 13–032
Trustees
insurable interests, 4–019, 19–030
Underwriters
acceptance of business, 15–022
actual authority, 15–022
breach of duty, 15–022, 15–028
criminal offences, 15–021
disclosure, 15–020
duty of care, 15–022
fiduciary duties, 15–022
following market, 1–032, 1–040
fronting arrangements, 15–020, 15–022
function, 1–032, 1–033, 1–035, 15–020
inducement, 6–025
insurance pools, 15–020
leading underwriter clauses, 1–040
liability, 1–036, 1–037

Underwriters—*cont.*
management agreements, 15–020, 15–022
notice provisions, 9–013
offshore insurers, 15–021
outwards reinsurance
    generally, 15–020
    placement, 15–023
    recoveries, 15–024, 15–025
regulation, 15–021
reinsurance pools, 15–020, 15–023
retrocession agreements, 15–020
rights and obligations, 1–035, 1–040
separate accounts, 15–020
utmost good faith, 15–020
Unfair contract terms
claims conditions, 9–004
common law, 3–018
conditions precedent, 7–004
contra proferentem, 3–018
contracts of insurance, 3–018
core provisions, 3–018
examples, 3–018
fairness, 3–018
generally, 1–001
good faith, 3–018
individual negotiation, 3–018
insurance premiums, 3–018
nature of goods, 3–018
nature of services, 3–018
notice of terms, 3–018
reasonableness, 3–018
significant imbalance, 3–018
warranties, 7–053
Uninsured drivers
appeals, 22–071
claims handling, 22–072
common ventures, 22–068
conditions precedent, 22–069
criminal conduct, 22–066
damage to property, 22–062
deductions, 22–062
exceptions, 22–064—22–067
interim payments, 22–063
intoxication, 22–067
knowledge of victim, 22–065, 22–068
lack of insurance, 22–067
liability, 22–060—22–062
medical treatment, 22–062
payment of relevant sums, 22–062
personal injury, 22–062
presumed knowledge, 22–067
replacement vehicles, 22–062
Untraced drivers
agreements
    enforcement, 22–058
    joinder, 22–058
    privity of contract, 22–058
arbitration, 22–073
claims
    accident reports, 22–077
    accidents after midnight, 22–077
    appeals, 22–079
    appropriate knowledge, 22–076
    awards, 22–078

Untraced drivers—*cont.*
claims—*cont.*
    compensation, 22–075
    conditions, 22–074
    costs, 22–075
    damage to property, 22–074, 22–075,
        22–077, 22–076
    death, 22–074, 22–076
    deliberate damage, 22–074
    exclusions, 22–076
    interest, 22–075
    interim awards, 2–078
    intoxication, 22–076
    liability, 22–075, 22–076
    limitation periods, 22–077
    loss of earnings, 22–075
    minors, 22–077
    personal injury, 22–074, 22–075, 22–077
    preliminary investigation, 22–078
    separate applications, 22–077
    written claims, 22–077
costs, 22–059, 22–073
EU law
    compensation, 22–059
    direct effect, 22–059
    fair trial, 22–073
    implementation, 22–059, 22–073
    Motor Insurers' Bureau, 22–059
    preliminary rulings, 22–059, 22–073
false particulars, 22–057
hit and run accidents, 22–057, 22–073
injuries, 22–001
interest, 22–059, 22–073
liability, 22–060, 22–073
limitation periods, 22–059, 22–073
Utmost good faith
see also **Agency; Duty of disclosure;
    Materiality**
avoidance, 6–033, 6–034, 6–124, 6–130
bilateral duty, 6–122
breaches, 6–002, 6–032, 6–044, 6–054,
    6–124, 6–132, 10–022
causation, 6–126
claims handling, 6–129
co-insurance, 14–011, 14–012
consumer insurance, 6–135
    see also **Consumer Insurance
        (Disclosure and Representatives)
        Bill 2009**
continuing duty, 6–107—6–112, 6–115,
    6–123, 6–125, 6–127, 6–129, 6–130,
    6–142
contracts of insurance, 6–001
correction of statements, 6–102
damages, 6–124, 6–125, 6–128, 6–131,
    10–022
declaration policies, 6–0120
disciplinary element, 6–017
duration, 1–028, 6–101, 6–104
duty of care, 6–131
duty to warn insured person, 6–128
extra-contractual right, 6–001, 6–124
false representations, 6–105
fidelity insurance, 23–026

Utmost good faith—*cont.*
financial loss, 6–125
fraud, 6–114, 6–122
generally, 1–001, 1–011, 6–001
implied term, 6–124
insurer's duty, 6–122, 6–123, 6–127
Law Commissions' reforms, 6–133, 6–134
marine insurance, 6–001, 24–034
misrepresentation, 6–001, 6–004, 6–138
motor insurance, 22–087
negligence, 6–131
open cover, 6–120
policy extensions, 6–106
post-contract disclosures, 6–103
post-contract misrepresentation, 6–103
previous presentations, 6–105
renewal, 6–053, 6–105
reinstatement, 6–105
reinsurance, 17–006—17–010
state of mind, 6–114
tortious duty, 6–001
underwriters, 15–020
waiver, 6–068, 6–069, 6–071
Valuation
apportionment, 10–011
change in value, 10–008
conclusive nature, 10–007
diminution in value, 10–003, 10–012,
10–013
false statements, 6–056
indemnity principle, 4–004, 4–005
market value, 10–013—10–018
motor insurance, 12–033
overvaluation, 4–004, 6–056, 10–007
undervaluation, 6–057
unvalued policies, 6–056
valued policies, 6–056
Volenti non fit injuria
acceptance of risk, 22–033
negligent drivers, 22–033
recklessness, 22–033
Voyage
see also **Marine insurance**
change of voyage, 24–069
commencement of risk, 24–065, 24–066,
24–069
delay, 24–072, 24–073
deviation, 24–070, 24–073
different destination, 24–068
freight clauses, 24–065
good safety, 24–065
marine cargo insurance, 24–066
misconduct, 24–073
port
departure, 24–067
discharge, 24–071
superior orders, 24–073
termination, 24–065
transit clauses, 24–066
Voyage policies
accident insurance, 18–002
insurer's liability, 1–031
marine cargo insurance, 24–047, 24–066
meaning, 24–047

Voyage policies—*cont.*
mixed policies, 24–047
retrospective effect, 1–031
risk, 5–003
seaworthiness, 24–061, 24–062
termination, 24–065
time policies, distinguished, 24–047
Wagering contracts
common law, 4–002
enforcement, 4–002, 4–008
insurable interests, 4–008, 4–009, 20–062
legislation, 4–001, 4–003, 4–007
liberalisation, 4–001
marine insurance, 24–012, 24–013, 24–015
opposition, 4–001, 4–002
third party interests, 4–002
Waiver
affirmation, 7–018, 7–048, 9–014
agency, 6–082, 15–016
attachment of risk, 6–070
avoidance, 6–082—6–087, 6–092, 6–099,
6–070
breach of condition, 7–018—7–020, 15–016
conditions, 6–090, 9–014
delays, 6–091
disclosure
convictions, 6–071
express agreements, 6–069
express questions, 6–071, 6–072
failure to make enquiries, 6–073
implied waiver, 6–070, 6–071
limited questions, 6–071, 6–072
non-disclosure, 6–084, 6–086
utmost good faith, 6–068, 6–069, 6–071
election, 7–018
errors and omissions clauses, 6–087
estoppel, 6–098, 7–018—7–020, 7–048,
9–014
express affirmation, 6–091, 6–094, 6–098
fraud, 6–082, 6–083, 6–092
implied affirmation, 6–092
implied waiver, 6–092
incontestability clauses, 6–083
insurer's conduct, 6–094
insurer's knowledge, 6–095, 6–096
interpretation, 6–084
legal advice, 6–097
misrepresentation, 6–082, 6–084, 6–086
reinsurance, 17–008, 17–009
subsequent knowledge, 6–096
truth of statement clauses, 6–088, 6–099
warranties, 7–046—7–048
War risks
see also **Terrorism**
marine insurance, 24–085
private insurance
aviation insurance, 25–001
exclusions, 25–001
free of capture and seizure, 25–001
Lloyds, 25–001
marine adventures, 25–001
property insurance, 25–001
specific risks
causation, 25–003

War risks—*cont.*
specific risks—*cont.*
civil commotion, 25–009
customs regulations, 25–013
hostile acts, 25–005
insurrection, 25–008
invasion, 25–011
lock outs, 25–016
malicious damage, 25–015
military power, 25–006
rebellion, 25–007
revolution, 25–007
riot, 25–010
seizure, 25–012
strikes, 25–016
terrorism, 25–014
trading regulations, 25–013
usurped power, 25–006
vandalism, 25–015
war, 25–004
state provision
aircraft, 25–002
legislation, 25–002
reinsurance, 25–002
terrorism cover, 25–002
vessels, 25–002
war
civil wars, 25–004
declarations of war, 25–004
guerrilla wars, 25–004
terrorist acts, 25–004
war between nations, 25–004
Warranties
see also **"Increase of risk"**
breaches
actual breach, 7–036
agency, 15–018
increase of risk, 5–022
insurance brokers, 15–038
misrepresentation, 6–007
waiver, 7–046—7–048
burden of proof, 7–044
causation, 7–052
characteristics, 7–022
compliance, 7–022, 7–038
conditions precedent, 7–028
consumer insurance, 7–051—7–053, 7–055
continuing warranties, 5–020, 7–032, 7–034,
7–040, 7–052
contents, 7–021
contract terms
development, 7–029
generally, 7–001
interpretation, 7–031
materiality, 7–030

Warranties—*cont.*
contract terms—*cont.*
misrepresentation, 7–031
modification, 7–031
nature of clause, 7–029
qualification, 7–029
subject of warranty, 7–029
creation
contract terms, 7–029
express statements, 7–025
express warranties, 7–023
formalities, 7–024
implied warranties, 7–023
intention, 7–026
defences, 7–045
definition, 7–021
degree of risk, 7–038
delimitation of risk, distinguished, 5–021
disclosure, 6–074
divisibility, 7–042
existing facts, 7–051
fundamental nature, 7–022
future warranties, 7–052
general warranties, 5–018
generally, 1–001
insured persons, 1–029, 1–030
interest clauses, 7–026
interpretation, 5–020, 5–021, 7–032, 7–033,
7–037
Law Commissions' reforms, 7–049, 7–050
life insurance, 7–033
marine insurance, 7–023, 7–054,
24–055—24–064
materiality, 7–041
misrepresentation, 6–007
present warranties, 5–020, 7–032, 7–040
promissory nature, 7–021
reinsurance, 17–014
remedy prior to loss, 7–043
risk
automatic termination, 7–027, 7–052
delimitation, 7–034
statements of fact, 7–033
statements of opinion, 7–033
termination, 7–035, 7–039—7–042, 7–048
unfair contract terms, 7–053
waiver, 7–046—7–048
Winding up
compulsory winding up, 16–004, 16–008
Financial Services Authority, 16–003,
16–004
winding up petitions, 16–004—16–006
voluntary winding up
effect, 16–008
members, 16–003